PRENTICE HALL

UNITED STATES
HISTORY

Emma J. Lapsansky-Werner
Peter B. Levy
Randy Roberts
Alan Taylor
Grant Wiggins

PEARSON

Upper Saddle River, New Jersey   Boston, Massachusetts   Chandler, Arizona   Glenview, Illinois

Cover Images: Bkgd, Corbis Royalty-Free; BM, NASA/Johnson Space Center; M, Getty Images; BL, Barry Rosenthal/Getty Images; BFL, Bettmann/CORBIS; TR, Bettmann/CORBIS; BR, George K.Warren/Corbis; TL, Illustration by Michael J. Deas; B, Getty Images; **Title page:** Bkgrnd, © Darwin Wiggett; BL, © Digital Vision Ltd./SuperStock; BM, Dave King © Dorling Kindersley; BR, © Tunyaluck Phuttal/istockphoto.com; **Spine:** Corbis Royalty-Free; **Back cover:** Corbis Royalty-Free; **NY 33:** Niagara Falls, David Ball/Stone/Getty Images; **NY 34–NY35:** Long Island harbor, Dorling Kindersley Media Library; **NY 43:** Grand Rush for Indian Territory poster, Brown Brothers; **NY 47:** Police dog attacking civil rights demonstrator in Birmingham, AL; AP/Wide World Photos; Civil rights sit-in demonstration, Bettmann/CORBIS; **NY 48:** Elizabeth Eckford, AP/Wide World Photos.

Text Credits: SH32: Source: The History of New York State Book II. Chapter II, Part II. Edited by Dr. James Sullivan. Lewis Historical Publishing Company, 1927; **94:** Source: The Founders' Constitution, Volume 1, Chapter 8, Document 39 Edited by Philip B. Kurland and Ralph Lerner. Copyright © 1987 University of Chicago Press; **432:** Source: Vanderbilt Mansion National Historic Site, New York National Park Service; **1136:** Text from The Catskill Mountains Historical Marker. Reprinted courtesy of the New York State Museum, Albany, NY; Text from James Gordon Historical Marker in Saratoga County. Reprinted courtesy of the New York State Museum, Albany, NY

Acknowledgments appear on page 1258, which constitutes an extension of this copyright page.

PEARSON

ISBN-13: 978-0-13-368657-9
ISBN-10:   0-13-368657-4

1 2 3 4 5 6 7 8 9 10   13 12 11 10 09

Emma J. Lapsansky-Werner

Emma J. Lapsansky-Werner is Professor of History and Curator of the Quaker Collection at Haverford College. After receiving her doctorate from the University of Pennsylvania, she taught at Temple University for almost two decades.

Dr. Lapsansky-Werner's recent publications include *Quaker Aesthetics,* coauthored with Ann Verplanck, and *Back to Africa: Benjamin Coates and the Colonization Movement in America, 1848–1880,* coedited with Margaret Hope Bacon.

Peter B. Levy

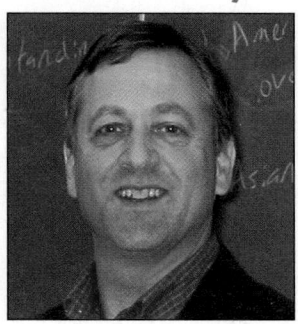

Peter B. Levy is a Full Professor in the Department of History at York College of Pennsylvania, where he teaches a wide variety of courses in American history. He received his B.A. from the University of California, Berkeley, and his Ph.D. from Columbia University. Dr. Levy is the author of eight books and many articles, including *The New Left and Labor in the 1960s; Civil War on Race Street: The Civil Rights Movement in Cambridge, Maryland;* and *100 Key Documents in American Democracy.* He lives in Towson, Maryland, with his wife, two children, and a yellow Labrador.

Randy Roberts

Randy Roberts, Professor of History at Purdue University, specializes in twentieth-century American history and the history of popular culture. He has written, cowritten, or edited more than 20 books, including biographies of John Wayne, Jack Johnson, and Oscar Robertson.

Dr. Roberts has also written histories of American sports and of the Vietnam War. His books have been nominated for and won a number of national prizes. At Purdue University, he has won the University Teacher of the Year award. Dr. Roberts has also appeared frequently on the History Channel and in documentaries for HBO, NBC, ESPN, and PBS.

Alan Taylor

Alan Taylor, Professor of History at the University of California, Davis, earned his Ph.D. in history from Brandeis University and did a postdoctoral fellowship at the Institute of Early American History and Culture in Williamsburg, Virginia. He teaches courses in early American history and the history of the American West. Dr. Taylor is the author of five books, including *American Colonies* and *William Cooper's Town,* which won the Bancroft and Beveridge prizes, as well as the 1996 Pulitzer Prize for American history. He is a contributing editor for *The New Republic.*

Senior Consultants

John R. Chavez is Professor of History at Southern Methodist University, Clements Department of History. He earned his Ph.D. from the University of Michigan, with a specialty in Mexican American history. Dr. Chavez's publications include *Eastside Landmark: A History of the East Los Angeles Community Union, The Lost Land: The Chicano Image of the Southwest,* and *Teaching Mexican American History,* co-authored with Neil Foley.

Herman Viola specializes in the history of the American West, the American Indian, and the Civil War and has published such books on these subjects as *After Columbus* and *Little Bighorn Remembered: The Untold Indian Story of Custer's Last Stand.* He earned his Ph.D. from Indiana University. Dr. Viola currently serves as curator emeritus at the Smithsonian's National Museum of Natural History.

Senior Reading Consultants

Kate Kinsella, Ed.D., is a faculty member in the Department of Secondary Education at San Francisco State University. A specialist in second-language and adolescent literacy, she teaches coursework addressing language and literacy development across the secondary curricula. Dr. Kinsella earned her M.A. in TESOL from San Francisco State University, and her Ed.D. in Second Language Acquisition from the University of San Francisco.

Kevin Feldman, Ed.D., is the Director of Reading and Early Intervention with the Sonoma County Office of Education (SCOE) and an independent educational consultant. At the SCOE, he develops, organizes, and monitors programs related to K–12 literacy. Dr. Feldman has an M.A. from the University of California, Riverside, in Special Education, Learning Disabilities and Instructional Design. He earned his Ed.D. in Curriculum and Instruction from the University of San Francisco.

Differentiated Instruction Consultants

Don Deshler

Don Deshler, Ph.D., is the director of the Center for Research on Learning (CRL) at the University of Kansas. Dr. Deshler's expertise centers on adolescent literacy, learning strategic instruction, and instructional strategies for teaching content areas classes to academically diverse classes. He is the author of *Teaching Content to All: Evidence-Based Inclusive Practices in Middle and Secondary Schools,* a text which presents the instructional practices that have been tested and validated through his research at CRL.

Anthony S. Bashir
Director, Academic and Disability Services
Emerson College
Boston, Massachusetts

Dr. Cathy Collins Block
Professor of Curriculum and Instruction
Texas Christian University
Fort Worth, Texas

Anna Uhl Chamot
Professor of Secondary Education (ESL)
The George Washington University
Washington, D.C.

John Guthrie
Professor of Human Development
University of Maryland
College Park, Maryland

Susan P. Miller
Professor of Special Education
University of Nevada, Las Vegas
Las Vegas, Nevada

Jennifer Platt
Executive Associate Dean for Academic Affairs College of Education
University of Central Florida
Orlando, Florida

Reviewers

Academic Reviewers

William Childs
Professor of History
The Ohio State University
Columbus, Ohio

Michael Jay Friedman, Ph.D.
Bureau of International Information Programs
U.S. Department of State
Washington, D.C.

Jennifer Giglielmo
Assistant Professor of History and American Studies
Smith College
Northampton, Massachusetts

Huping Ling, Ph.D.
Professor of History
Truman State University
Kirksville, Missouri

Judith Ridner
Department of History
Muhlenberg College
Allentown, Pennsylvania

Carol Schneider
Rock Point Community School
Rock Point, Arizona

Contributing Editor

Richard Snow
former Editor in Chief
American Heritage Magazine
New York, New York

Accuracy Panel

Esther Ratner, M.L.S.
Greyherne Information Services

Barbara Whitney Petruzzelli, M.L.S.

Amy Raff, M.L.S.

Bernard Rosen, Ph.D.

Wilma Schmidt, M.L.S.

Teacher Reviewers

Janet Chandler
Hamilton Southeastern High School
Fishers, Indiana

Joyce Cooper
Dallas Independent School District
Dallas, Texas

Peter DiNardo
Mt. Lebanon High School
Pittsburgh, Pennsylvania

Robert Hasty
Lawrence Central High School
Indianapolis, Indiana

Dee Ann Holt
Mann Magnet School
Little Rock, Arkansas

Bruce Lesh
Franklin High School
Reisterstown, Maryland

Seth Massey
Station Camp High School
Gallatin, Tennessee

Dr. Robert McAdams
East Burke High School
Connelly Springs, North Carolina

Cynthia Mostoller
Alice Deal Middle School
Washington, D.C.

Dr. Brent Muirhead
University of Phoenix
Atlanta, Georgia

Deborah W. Powers
Westlake High School
Atlanta, Georgia

Jeanne Salvado
Montgomery County Public Schools
Rockville, Maryland

Dr. Francis N. Sheboy
Assistant Principal
Cornwall Central High School
New Windsor, New York

Jim Thovson
Rapid City Central High School
Rapid City, South Dakota

Social Studies Master Teacher Board

Peggy Altoff
K-12 Social Studies Facilitator
District 11 Colorado Springs
Colorado Springs, Colorado

David Burns
Foothill High School
Sacramento, California

Katherine A. Deforge
Marcellus Central School
Marcellus, New York

Teacher's Edition Consultants

Diane Hart
Social Studies Author and Assessment
    Consultant
Menlo Park, California

Sam Intrator
Professor of Education
    and Child Studies
Smith College
Northampton, Massachusetts

John Poggio
Professor, Department of Educational
    Psychology and Research
University of Kansas
Lawrence, Kansas

Program Adviser

Michal Howden
Social Studies Consultant
Zionsville, Indiana

 # New York Program Advisers

Nelson Acevedo
NYC Alternative Schools and Programs
The Ohio State University
New York, New York

Anthony Barbetta
Thomas Edison Voc/Tech High School
New York, New York

Jonathan Barnett
John Adams High School
Ozone Park, New York

Daryl Blank
Fashion Industries High School
New York, New York

Dorene A. Lorenzoni-Pericic
Grover Cleveland High School
Ridgewood, New York

Thomas Gray
De Ruyter Central School
De Ruyter, New York

Sheila Hanley
James Madison High School
Brooklyn, New York

Geraldine L. Hayes
Louis D. Brandeis High School
New York, New York

Howard P. Krug
John Marshall High School
Rochester, New York

Eric Lincoln
The Laboratory School of Finance and
    Technology
Bronx, New York

Suzette Sherry Lippa
Susan E. Wagner High School
Staten Island, New York

Matteo Mannino
New Beginnings High School
New York, New York

William Neer
Le Moyne College
Syracuse, New York

Catherine Piszko
Staten Island Technical High School
Staten Island, New York

Wade Tam
Bronx Academy High School
Bronx, New York

Mark Tarantino
John Bowne High School
Flushing, New York

Andrew M. L. Turay
Peace and Diversity Academy
Bronx, New York

NY Core Curriculum

1.I.A.2c	2.I.A.1
1.I.A.2d	2.I.A.1b
1.I.A.3d	2.I.A.2
1.I.A.3e	2.I.A.2a
1.I.A.3g	2.I.A.2b
1.I.A.4	2.I.A.2c
1.I.B.1	2.I.A.3
1.I.B.3	2.I.A.3a
1.I.B.4	2.I.A.3c
1.I.D.1	2.II.B.1a
1.I.D.1c	2.II.B.2c
1.I.D.1d	2.II.C.3
1.I.D.4b	2.II.C.6
1.I.D.4c	
1.I.D.2	

(NY) **Core Curriculum**

2.I.A.2a	2.I.B.4
2.I.A.3a	2.I.B.4b
2.I.A.4	2.I.E.1
2.I.A.4a	2.I.E.10
2.I.A.4b	2.I.F.1
2.I.A.4c	2.I.F.3b
2.I.A.5d	2.I.F.4b
2.I.A.6	2.I.F.4c
2.I.A.7	2.I.F.4d
2.I.B.1	2.II.A.3
2.I.B.1a	2.II.C.1
2.I.B.1b	
2.I.B.2	
2.I.B.2a	

NY Core Curriculum

1.I.D.1d	2.II.C.2
1.I.D.1e	2.II.C.3
2.I.A.2c	2.II.C.4
2.I.A.5c	2.II.C.5
2.I.F.3	2.II.C.6
2.I.F.4e	2.II.D.1
2.II.A.1	3.II.B.1
2.II.A.2	3.II.B.4
2.II.A.3	3.III.A.2c
2.II.B	3.III.A.3
2.II.B.1a	3.III.D.2
2.II.B.1d	3.III.D.3
2.II.B.2	4.I.B.2b
2.II.B.2b	4.I.C.4e
2.II.B.2d	

NY Core Curriculum

2.I.A.5d	3.I.C.2a
2.II.B.2	3.I.C.2b
2.II.B.3	3.I.C.3
2.II.C.4	3.I.C.4
2.II.D.1a	3.I.C.5
2.II.D.1b	3.I.D.1
2.II.D.2	3.I.D.3
2.II.D.2a	3.I.E.1
2.II.D.2b	3.I.E.2
2.II.D.2c	3.I.E.3
2.II.D.2d	3.I.E.4
3.I.A.1	3.I.E.5
3.I.A.2	
3.I.B.1	
3.I.C.1	

INDUSTRIALIZATION OF THE UNITED STATES   1865–1914

Core Curriculum

1.I.D.2	3.II.F.1a
2.II.C.6	3.II.F.1b
3.I.B.3	3.II.F.1c
3.I.C.1	3.III.A
3.I.C.2a	3.III.A.1
3.I.C.2b	3.III.A.2b
3.I.C.3	3.III.A.3
3.I.D.3	3.III.A.4
3.II.B	3.III.A.5
3.II.C	3.III.B.1
3.II.C.1	3.III.B.4
3.II.C.3	3.III.C.1
3.II.D.3	3.III.C.2
3.II.E.1	3.III.D.1a
3.II.E.1c	3.III.D.1c
3.II.E.1d	3.III.D.3
3.II.E.2d	4.I.B.2c

NY Core Curriculum

1.I.A.4	4.II.A.2b
4.I.A.1	4.II.A.2c
4.I.A.4	4.II.A.3
4.I.B.1a	4.II.A.3a
4.I.B.1b	4.II.A.3b
4.I.B.2a	4.II.A.4b
4.I.B.2b	4.II.A.4c
4.I.B.2c	4.II.B.1a
4.I.B.2e	4.II.B.1b
4.I.C.1	4.II.B.1c
4.I.C.2	4.II.C.1
4.I.C.3a	4.II.C.2
4.I.C.3c	4.II.C.4
4.I.C.4a	4.II.D.1
4.I.C.4c	4.II.D.2
4.I.C.4d	4.II.D.3
4.I.C.5	4.II.D.4
4.II.A.1	5.I.A.1
4.II.A.1a	5.I.A.3
4.II.A.1b	5.I.B.4
4.II.A.2a	

NY Core Curriculum

4.II.D.6	5.II.A.3b
5.I.A.3	5.II.A.4
5.I.B.2	5.II.B.1a
5.I.B.3	5.II.B.1b
5.I.B.5	5.II.B.1c
5.I.C.1a	5.II.B.3c
5.I.C.1b	5.II.B.3d
5.I.C.2a	5.II.B.4
5.I.C.2b	5.II.B.5a
5.I.C.2c	5.II.B.6b
5.I.C.1d	5.II.B.6d
5.I.C.3b	5.II.B.6e
5.I.C.3c(2)	5.II.B.6f
5.II.A.1a	5.II.B.7a
5.II.A.1b	5.II.B.7b
5.II.A.2	5.II.B.7c
5.II.A.3a	

WORLD WAR II AND POSTWAR AMERICA
1931–1960

Core Curriculum

3.II.C.6	6.II.A.1
4.II.D	6.II.A.2a
5.I.B.1	6.II.B.1
6.I.A.1	6.II.B.3a
6.I.A.3	6.II.B.3b
6.I.A.4	6.II.B.3d
6.I.B.1	6.II.C.2
6.I.B.2	6.II.C.3
6.I.B.3	6.II.C.4a
6.I.B.4	6.II.C.4b
6.I.C.1	6.II.C.4c
6.I.C.2a	6.II.D.1
6.I.C.2b	6.II.D.2
6.I.C.2c	6.II.D.3
6.I.C.2d	6.II.D.4
6.I.C.2e	7.I.A.4
6.I.C.2f	7.I.A.5
6.I.C.3b	7.II.B.2
6.I.C.3c	7.II.B.5
6.I.C.4a	7.II.B.6
6.I.C.4b	7.II.B.7
6.I.C.4d	7.II.B.8
6.I.C.5a	7.II.C.1b
6.I.C.5c	7.II.C.1c
6.I.C.5d	7.II.C.2c
6.I.C.6a	7.II.D.1
6.I.C.6b	7.II.D.1a
6.I.C.6c	7.II.D.1b
6.I.C.6e	7.II.D.1c
6.I.C.6f	7.II.D.2
6.I.C.6g	7.II.D.2a

(NY) Core Curriculum

3.III.A.3	7.IV.A
5.I.C.3	7.IV.A.1
6.II.D.4	7.IV.A.2
7.II.C.1d	7.IV.A.3
7.II.C.2a	7.IV.A.4
7.II.C.2b	7.IV.A.4b
7.II.C.2c	7.IV.A.5
7.II.D.1c	7.IV.A.5c
7.III.A.1	7.IV.A.6
7.III.A.1a	7.IV.A.6d
7.III.A.2	7.V.A
7.III.A.2a	7.V.A.1
7.III.A.2c	7.V.A.1a
7.III.A.2f	7.V.A.1c
7.III.A.2g	7.V.A.1d
7.III.A.3	7.V.A.2a
7.III.A.4	7.V.A.2a(1)
7.III.B.1	7.V.A.3b
7.III.B.3a	7.V.A.3c
7.III.B.3b	7.V.A.3d
7.III.B.3c	7.V.B
7.III.B.3c(1)	7.V.B.2a
7.III.B.4	7.V.B.2b
7.III.B.4a	7.V.B.2c(1)
7.III.B.4b	7.V.B.3
7.III.B.5	7.V.B.3c
7.III.B.6	7.V.B.3e

NY Core Curriculum

1.I.D.1	7.V.E.1
1.I.D.2	7.V.E.2
2.I.E.1	7.V.F.1
2.I.E.4	7.V.F.2
2.I.E.6	7.V.G
2.I.E.9	7.VI.A
7.I.A	7.VI.A.3
7.I.A.3	7.VI.A.3a
7.I.A.4	7.VI.A.3b
7.I.A.5	7.VI.A.3d
7.V.A.3	7.VI.B
7.V.A.3d	7.VI.B.1a
7.V.B.3	7.VI.B.1c(2)
7.V.C	7.VI.B.1d
7.V.C.1	7.VI.B.2
7.V.C.2	7.VI.B.2a
7.V.C.5	7.VI.B.2b
7.V.D.3	7.VI.B.2c

SPECIAL FEATURES AND MULTIMEDIA

Witness History: The Latest Fad

As baby boomers went to school, new fads came and went with amazing speed. One such fad revolved around a popular television show about the American folk hero Davy Crockett. Steven Spielberg, who later would become one of Hollywood's most successful movie directors, recalled the craze.

"I was in third grade at the time. Suddenly, the next day, everybody in my class but me was Davy Crockett. And because I didn't have my coonskin cap and my powder horn, or Old Betsy, my rifle, and my chaps, I was deemed the Mexican leader, Santa Anna. And they chased me home from school until I got my parents to buy me a coonskin cap."

—Steven Spielberg, recalling the Davy Crockett craze of 1955

WITNESS HISTORY 🔊 AUDIO

Primary source audio accounts throughout the text bring the voices and sounds of history to life.

WITNESS HISTORY DVD

Witness History Discovery School™ Videos bring the events you read about in the text to life.

Events That Changed America

See how certain events changed the course of our nation's history.

History *Interactive*

Audio, video, and animation-filled features help you explore major turning points in history.

Primary Source

Full-page excerpts allow you to relive history through eyewitness accounts and documents.

American Humanities

Experience great American literature and art.

In-Text Primary Source

Gain insights as you read by reading the words of people who were there.

Comparing Viewpoints

Explore issues by analyzing two opposing viewpoints.

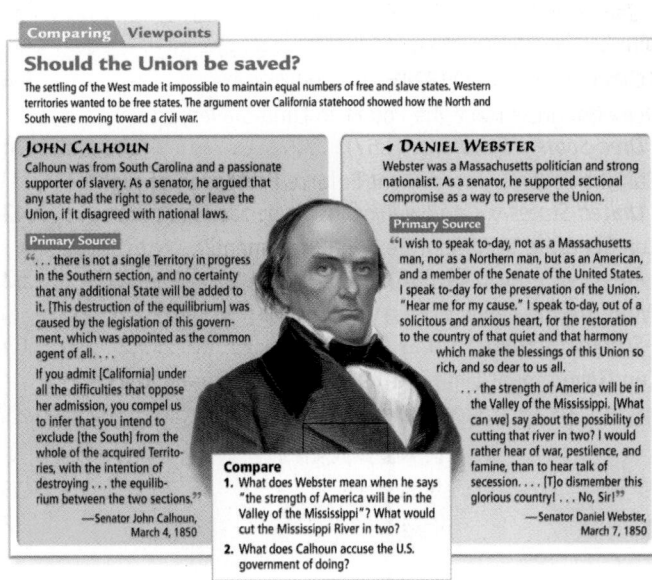

Comparing Viewpoints

Should the Union be saved?

The settling of the West made it impossible to maintain equal numbers of free and slave states. Western territories wanted to be free states. The argument over California statehood showed how the North and South were moving toward a civil war.

JOHN CALHOUN

Calhoun was from South Carolina and a passionate supporter of slavery. As a senator, he argued that any state had the right to secede, or leave the Union, if it disagreed with national laws.

Primary Source

"... there is not a single Territory in progress in the Southern section, and no certainty that any additional State will be added to it. [This destruction of the equilibrium] was caused by the legislation of this government, which was appointed as the common agent of all. . . .

If you admit [California] under all the difficulties that oppose her admission, you compel us to infer that you intend to exclude [the South] from the whole of the acquired Territories, with the intention of destroying . . . the equilibrium between the two sections."
—Senator John Calhoun, March 4, 1850

◄ **DANIEL WEBSTER**

Webster was a Massachusetts politician and strong nationalist. As a senator, he supported sectional compromise as a way to preserve the Union.

Primary Source

"I wish to speak to-day, not as a Massachusetts man, nor as a Northern man, but as an American, and a member of the Senate of the United States. I speak to-day for the preservation of the Union. "Hear me for my cause." I speak to-day, out of a solicitous and anxious heart, for the restoration to the country of that quiet and that harmony which make the blessings of this Union so rich, and so dear to us all.

. . . the strength of America will be in the Valley of the Mississippi. [What can we] say about the possibility of cutting that river in two? I would rather hear of war, pestilence, and famine, than to hear talk of secession. . . . [T]o dismember this glorious country! . . . No, Sir!"
—Senator Daniel Webster, March 7, 1850

Compare
1. What does Webster mean when he says "the strength of America will be in the Valley of the Mississippi"? What would cut the Mississippi River in two?

2. What does Calhoun accuse the U.S. government of doing?

Decision Point

Consider how you would have decided key questions in American history.

Cause and Effect

**Diagrams help you see the short- and long-term causes
and effects of history's most important events.**

Landmark Decisions of the Supreme Court

Explore key Supreme Court cases and link the decisions to today.

HISTORY MAKERS

Meet many fascinating people.

HISTORY MAKERS

Helen Hunt Jackson
(1830–1885)
Helen Hunt Jackson grew up in Massachusetts. In the late 1870s, she heard some Native Americans speak about their peoples' plight. Deeply moved, she was determined to publicize their cause. In *A Century of Dishonor*, she sharply criticized the U.S. government's history of shattered treaties. She elaborated on the situation in a report on Indian policy written for the government and in the highly popular novel *Ramona*. Jackson's work helped build sympathy for the plight of Native Americans.

American Issues
•—•—•— Connector

Examine key issues that have endured throughout American history.

✓ Quick Study Timeline

Illustrated timelines with a Web code help you review and explore key events.

INFOGRAPHIC

Photographs, maps, charts, illustrations, and text help you understand the significance of important historical events and developments.

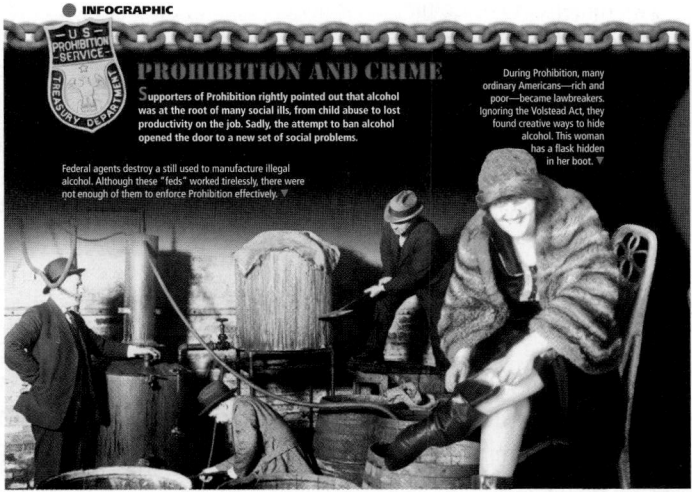

Document-Based Assessment

Practice the art and science of a historian by analyzing an event through multiple historical documents, data, and images.

Focus On Geography

See how geography has affected events in American history.

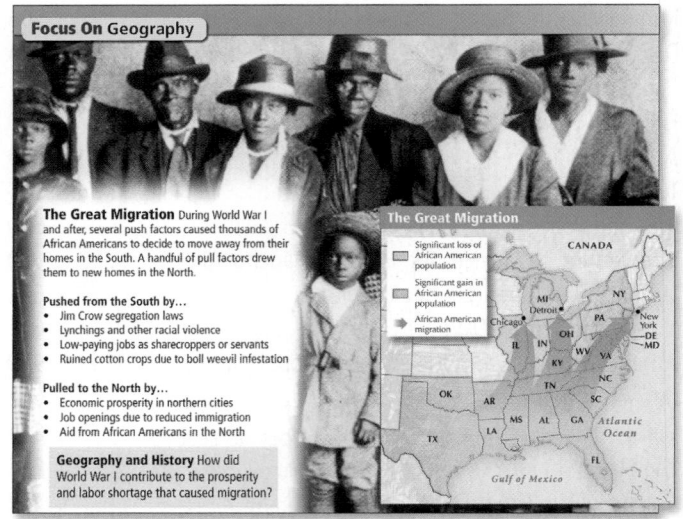

Focus On Geography

The Great Migration During World War I and after, several push factors caused thousands of African Americans to decide to move away from their homes in the South. A handful of pull factors drew them to new homes in the North.

Pushed from the South by...
- Jim Crow segregation laws
- Lynchings and other racial violence
- Low-paying jobs as sharecroppers or servants
- Ruined cotton crops due to boll weevil infestation

Pulled to the North by...
- Economic prosperity in northern cities
- Job openings due to reduced immigration
- Aid from African Americans in the North

Geography and History How did World War I contribute to the prosperity and labor shortage that caused migration?

The Great Migration
- Significant loss of African American population
- Significant gain in African American population
- African American migration

Charts and Graphs

Diagrams and data help you understand history through visuals.

Maps Geography *Interactive*

Interactive maps with a Web code help you understand where history happened.

Political Cartoons

Examine how artts have expressed their points of view about events of their day.

Discover
the enduring issues of our nation's history

The **American Issues Connector** explores the enduring questions that frame our American past, present, and future.

Here's how it works:

1 **Highlight issues as you learn**
Review issues in every chapter using the American Issues Connector Cumulative Review.

2 **Study Issues in depth**
The American Issues Connector feature focuses on a modern debate about an enduring issue.

3 **Track Issues over time**
Take notes in the Study Guide to prepare for thematic essays on enduring issues.

Here's an example:

What is the proper balance between national security and civil liberties?

Patrick Henry addressing Congress

American Issues
Connector

By connecting prior knowledge with what you have learned in this chapter, you can gradually build your understanding of enduring questions that still affect America today. Answer the questions below. Then, use your American Issues Connector study guide (or go online: www.PHSchool.com **Web Code:** neh-8503).

Issues You Learned About

● **Civil Liberties and National Security** From the beginning of the American republic, Americans have debated to what extent individual freedom should be limited when the safety of the nation is at stake.

1. How does the Bill of Rights guarantee the rights of people accused of crimes?

2. During the Civil War, what action did President Lincoln take that limited these guaranteed rights? Why?

3. During the Cold War, what effect did the actions of HUAC and McCarthy have on individual rights?

● **America Goes to** debate whether U.S. en

7. What were argumen against North Korea

8. What were argumen

Connect to You

America and the Wo when dealing with thre

NY32

American Issues
Connector — Civil Liberties and National Security

TRACK THE ISSUE

What is the proper balance between national security and civil liberties?

The Constitution guarantees rights and freedoms to all American citizens. But during war and other crises, government leaders have limited such civil liberties in order to protect citizens' lives. Should they? Use the timeline below to explore this enduring issue.

1790s Undeclared War With France
Alien Act allows President to imprison or deport resident aliens. Sedition Act limits freedoms of speech and press.

1860s Civil War
Lincoln suspends the right of habeas corpus.

1940s World War II
Government sends more than 100,000 Japanese Americans into internment camps.

A traveler has his baggage searched at an airport security checkpoint.

DEBATE THE ISSUE

Terrorism and the Patriot Act After the devastating terrorist attacks of September 11, 2001, the United States declared a "War on Terrorism." Congress passed the Patriot Act to help law enforcement agencies prevent future terrorist attacks. The Act was to expire in 2005. In spite of controversy regarding it, Congress voted to extend the provisions of the Patriot Act to 2009.

"I have a lot of problems with the Patriot Act. . . . It gives the govern-

"Right after 9-11, the President turned to the Attorney General and

American Issues Journal

Ci**berties and National Security**

Question: What is the proper balance between national and civil liberties?

1780	1860s Civil War Habeas Corpus suspended	1940s World War II Internment of Japanese Americans		

1790s **tion Acts**

1950s Cold War Red Scare

the U.S. government has faced moments when the safety of the portant than preserving all the rights and liberties of its citizens. shows when this issue surfaced in U.S. history. nal security and civil liberties surface in American lives. But how n safety and liberty surface in your life?

the term "safe?" **1. (b)** How do you define the term "freedom?"

ents assemble to learn, discuss, and acquire essential Schools are also organizations with rules and regulations

you think **2. (b)** What three freedoms do you think

Your Guide to the Core Curriculum and Regents Exam

Reading Your Core Curriculum Codes

In each section of this book, you will see special codes that identify content from the **New York Core Curriculum for United States History and Government**. Below is an example.

2.I.A.4a

Unit of Study	Content Strand	Topic	Subtopic(s)
Constitutional Foundations for the United States Democratic Republic	The Constitution: The Foundation of American Society	Historical Foundations	4. The Revolutionary War a. Causes of the American Revolution

2.1.A.4a Causes of the American Revolution

A Word About the Regents

The **Regents Examination in U.S. History and Government** is an achievement test designed to measure your understanding of the standards and core curriculum for United States history and government. It is a timed test, and you will be given three hours to complete your work. You must answer all of the questions on the test.

What to Expect on the Exam

You will have to answer three types of questions on the U.S. History and Government Regents Examination:

Part I: Multiple-Choice Questions

There are 50 multiple-choice questions on Part I of the test. Each is followed by four answer choices, numbered one through four. You will mark your answers on a separate answer sheet.

Test Tips

- Read the question carefully. Make sure you understand the question.
- Read all four answer choices. Reread the question and all the answer choices to make sure you have not missed a key word in the question or answer.
- Use process of elimination to find the answer. Begin by rejecting any answer choice you know is wrong.
- Eliminate answer statements that do not relate to the question.

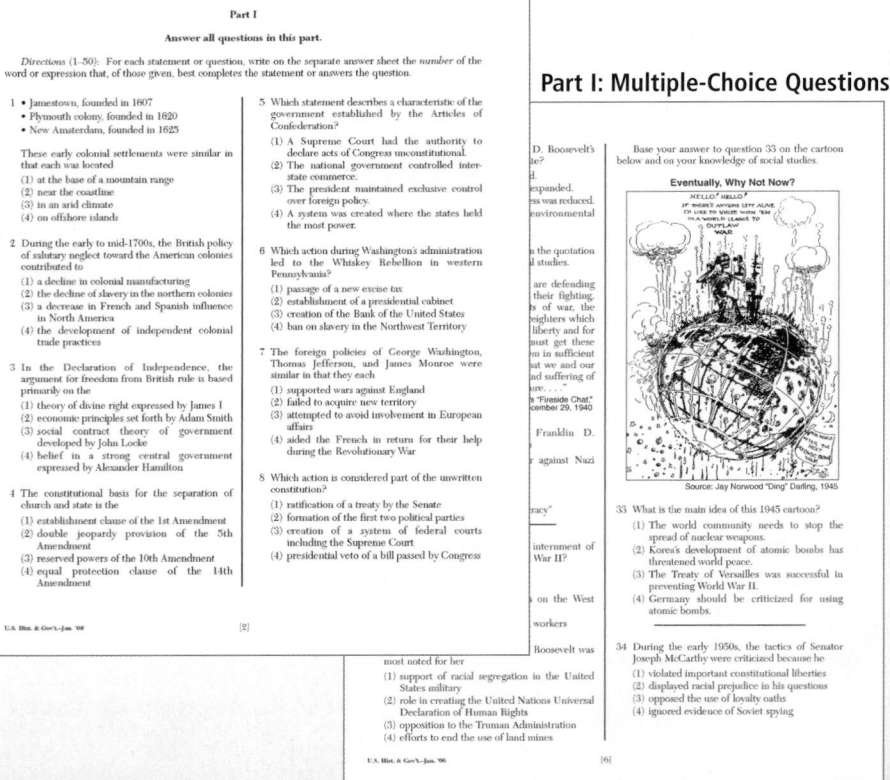

Part I: Multiple-Choice Questions

A Long Island harbor

Part II: Thematic Essay Question

Part II of the exam contains one **thematic essay question**. Thematic essay questions focus on broad themes, such as political systems, civil rights, cooperation or conflict.

Tips for Thematic Essay Questions

- Carefully read the theme and task directions.
- Write down any ideas you have. Consider the suggestions provided.
- Decide on a clear thesis statement and make a brief outline.
- Analyze and evaluate the ideas in your outline.
- Support your ideas with specific examples that address each task.
- Create a strong introduction and conclusion.

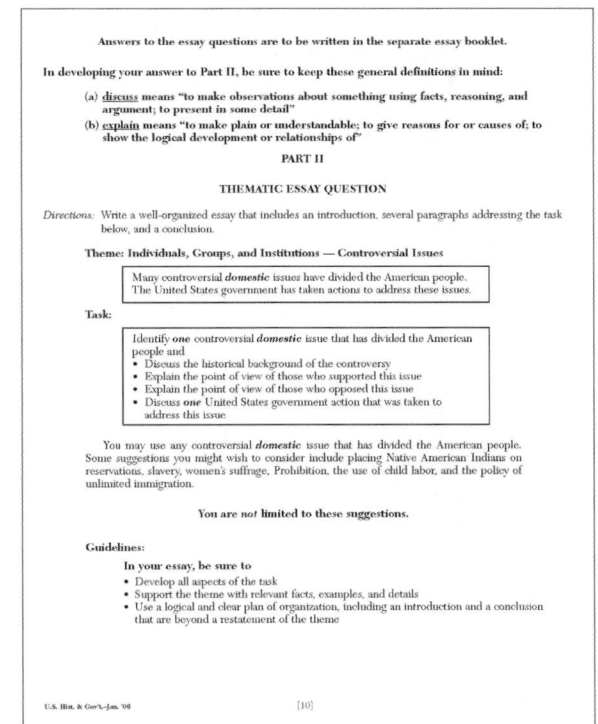

Part II: Thematic Essay Question

Part III: Document-Based Question

Part III of the exam is designed to test your ability to work with historical documents. There are two parts to this section:

Part A contains the documents. Analyze each document and answer the questions that follow.

Part B contains one essay question based on the documents. You should use your answers to the Part A questions to help you develop your response. You will write your answer to this question in a separate essay booklet.

Part III: Document-Based Question

How to Approach Document-Based Questions

Step 1: Read the essay question several times to make sure you fully understand it.

Part A: Document-Based Questions

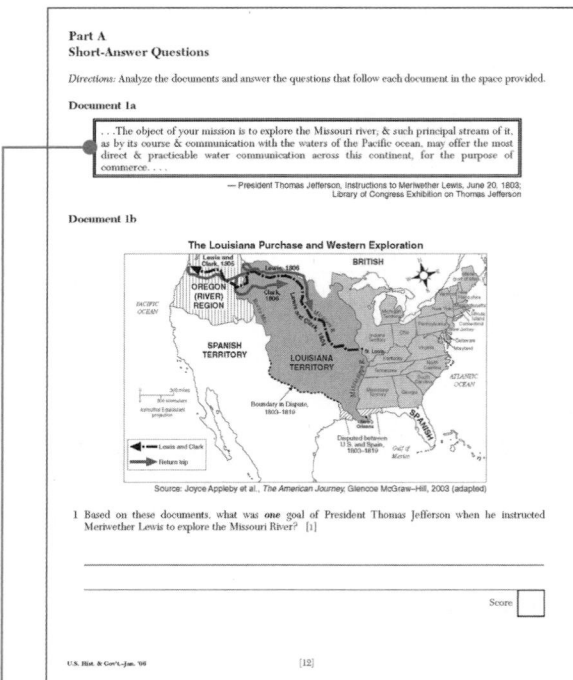

Part A
Short-Answer Questions

Directions: Analyze the documents and answer the questions that follow each document in the space provided.

Document 1a

. . .The object of your mission is to explore the Missouri river, & such principal stream of it, as by its course & communication with the waters of the Pacific ocean, may offer the most direct & practicable water communication across this continent, for the purpose of commerce. . . .

— President Thomas Jefferson, Instructions to Meriwether Lewis, June 20, 1803;
Library of Congress Exhibition on Thomas Jefferson

Document 1b

The Louisiana Purchase and Western Exploration

Source: Joyce Appleby et al., *The American Journey,* Glencoe McGraw-Hill, 2003 (adapted)

1 Based on these documents, what was **one** goal of President Thomas Jefferson when he instructed Meriwether Lewis to explore the Missouri River? [1]

Score ☐

U.S. Hist. & Gov't.—Jan. '06   [12]

Part B: Document-Based Questions

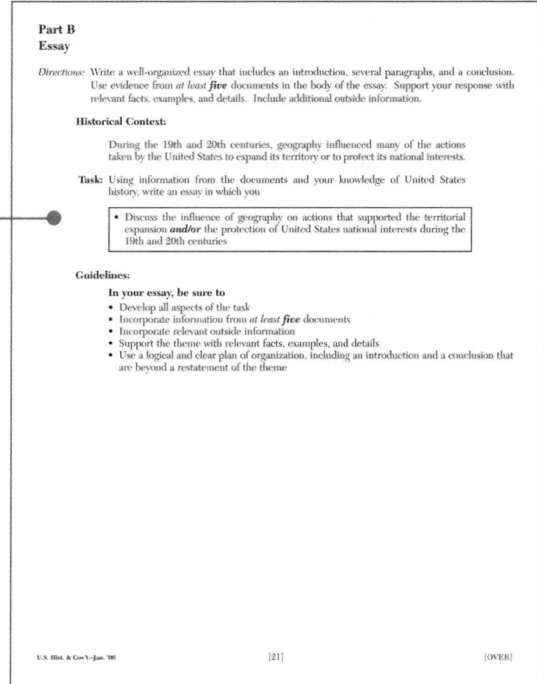

Part B
Essay

Directions: Write a well-organized essay that includes an introduction, several paragraphs, and a conclusion. Use evidence from *at least five* documents in the body of the essay. Support your response with relevant facts, examples, and details. Include additional outside information.

Historical Context:

During the 19th and 20th centuries, geography influenced many of the actions taken by the United States to expand its territory or to protect its national interests.

Task: Using information from the documents and your knowledge of United States history, write an essay in which you

- Discuss the influence of geography on actions that supported the territorial expansion **and/or** the protection of United States national interests during the 19th and 20th centuries

Guidelines:

In your essay, be sure to
- Develop all aspects of the task
- Incorporate information from *at least five* documents
- Incorporate relevant outside information
- Support the theme with relevant facts, examples, and details
- Use a logical and clear plan of organization, including an introduction and a conclusion that are beyond a restatement of the theme

U.S. Hist. & Gov't.—Jan. '06   [21]   [OVER]

Step 2: Read or study each document. First, make sure that you understand what the document says or shows. Then, decide whether the document is a **primary** or a **secondary** source. See the box below.

Step 3: Highlight, circle, or number the area of the document or image that helps you answer the question.

Step 4: Answer all parts of the questions that follow the document.

Step 5: After you have read the documents, read the essay question again. Outline your essay. Think about how to use each document to support your idea.

Step 6: Write your essay. It should have an introduction that states your answer to the question, a body that develops your answer, and a conclusion that restates your answer.

Step 7: Edit your essay. Make your sentences clear and effective. Correct errors in spelling and punctuation.

Primary sources are original works or documents that provide first-hand information about something. Photographs, drawings, letters, posters, songs, or speeches are all primary sources.

Secondary sources provide the background necessary to understand the primary sources. Some types of secondary sources are textbooks, journal articles, histories, criticisms, commentaries, and encyclopedia articles.

The rubric below will be used to score your DBQ essay.

Document-Based Essay Question Rubric

Score of 5:
- Thoroughly develops all aspects of the task evenly and in depth
- Is more analytical than descriptive (analyzes, evaluates, and/or creates information)
- Incorporates relevant information from most or all of the documents
- Incorporates substantial relevant outside information
- Richly supports the theme with many relevant facts, examples, and details
- Demonstrates a logical and clear plan of organization; includes an introduction and a conclusion that are beyond a restatement of the theme

Score of 4:
- Develops all aspects of the task but may do so somewhat unevenly
- Is both descriptive and analytical (applies, analyzes, evaluates, and/or creates information)
- Incorporates relevant information from many of the documents
- Incorporates relevant outside information
- Supports the theme with relevant facts, examples, and details
- Demonstrates a logical and clear plan of organization; includes an introduction and a conclusion that are beyond a restatement of the theme

Score of 3:
- Develops all aspects of the task with little depth or develops most aspects of the task in some depth
- Is more descriptive than analytical (applies, may analyze, and/or evaluate information)
- Incorporates some relevant information from some of the documents
- Incorporates limited relevant outside information
- Includes some relevant facts, examples, and details; may include some minor inaccuracies
- Demonstrates a satisfactory plan of organization; includes an introduction and a conclusion that may be a restatement of the theme

Score of 2:
- Minimally develops all aspects of the task or develops some aspects of the task in some depth
- Is primarily descriptive; may include faulty, weak, or isolated application or analysis
- Incorporates limited relevant information from the documents or consists primarily of relevant information copied from the documents
- Presents little or no relevant outside information
- Includes few relevant facts, examples, and details; may include some inaccuracies
- Demonstrates a general plan of organization; may lack focus; may contain digressions; may not clearly identify which aspect of the task is being addressed; may lack an introduction and/or a conclusion

Score of 1:
- Minimally develops some aspects of the task
- Is descriptive; may lack understanding, application, or analysis
- Makes vague, unclear references to the documents or consists primarily of relevant and irrelevant information copied from the documents
- Presents no relevant outside information
- Includes few relevant facts, examples, or details; may include inaccuracies
- May demonstrate a weakness in organization; may lack focus; may contain digressions; may not clearly identify which aspect of the task is being addressed; may lack an introduction and/or a conclusion

Score of 0:
- Fails to develop the task or may only refer to theme in a general way; OR includes no relevant facts, examples, or details; OR includes only the historical context and/or task as copied from the test booklet; OR includes only entire documents copied from the test booklet; OR is illegible; OR is a blank paper

*This rubric (without reference to documents) will also be used to score your thematic essay response.

Sample DBQ Essay

Here is an abbreviated example of a DBQ, followed by a sample student response. The essay shows how the student completed the task. Note her teacher's comments and how her essay was scored, based on the rubric on page NY 37.

Before you begin the exercise below, review Chapter 10, **The Union in Crisis**.

Part III: Document-Based Question

Historical Context

The question whether to expand slavery deeply divided Americans for decades before the Civil War began. Over the years, Congress adopted a series of compromises aimed at diffusing escalating sectional tensions over the issue. One-by-one, however, these measures failed and in 1861 the American Civil War began.

Task

Using information from the documents and your knowledge of United States history answer the questions that follow each document. Your answers will help you write an essay in which you will be asked to:

- Describe at least *two* of the compromises adopted by Congress between 1820 and 1850 *and* evaluate why they failed

- Explain how President Abraham Lincoln's stance on the slavery issue precipitated the American Civil War

Document 1

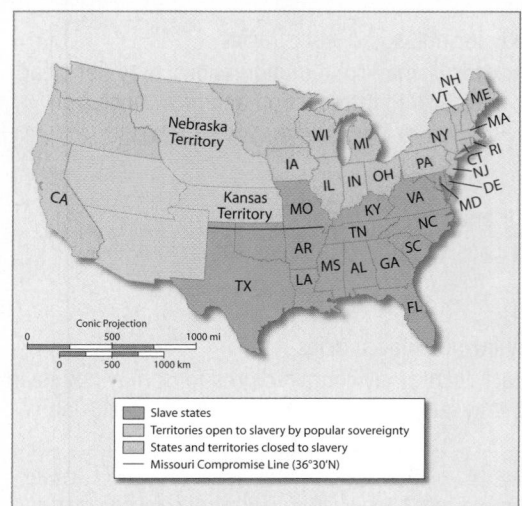

1 According to the map, what was the effect of the Kansas-Nebraska Act?

Document 2

" A house divided against itself cannot stand. I believe this government cannot endure permanently half slave and half free. I do not expect the Union to be dissolved—I do not expect the house to fall—but I do expect it will cease to be divided. It will become all one thing, or all the other."

Abraham Lincoln
June 16, 1858

2 According to this excerpt, how does Lincoln predict the national crisis will end?

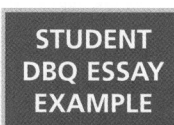
Name: Sophia Muñoz   Period 5

The compromises enacted by Congress before the Civil War failed to resolve the issue of slavery's expansion and actually deepened the sectional crisis. When President Lincoln took office in 1861, he ruled out any compromise with the South over the expansion of slavery, yet also declared his intention to preserve the Union at any cost. The crisis had reached a turning point.

The Missouri Compromise of 1820 maintained a balance between slave and free states by making slavery illegal above the 36th parallel, except in Missouri. But the nation's continued expansion westward, and acquisition of new territories from Mexico, threatened to tip that balance. To ward off conflict, Congress passed the Compromise of 1850. California would be allowed to enter the Union as a free state, but popular sovereignty would decide the question of slavery in the Mexico territory, and a new, stronger Fugitive Slave Act would be strictly enforced.

Then, in 1854 Congress passed the Kansas-Nebraska Act. This measure also relied on popular sovereignty to settle the slavery question. Yet, by allowing the possibility of slavery in the Nebraska and Kansas territories, areas that were free before, the Act effectively reversed the Missouri Compromise, angering antislavery supporters. In 1856, the Kansas territory erupted into violence as antislavery and proslavery factions battled one another over how to admit Kansas into the Union.

Into this national crisis stepped Abraham Lincoln. Lincoln condemned slavery as morally wrong and staunchly opposed its expansion. Yet, Lincoln believed the crisis could not be resolved through compromise. The United States would be either all free or all slave, but it would remain a Union.

By rejecting compromise as the solution to solving the nation's sectional differences, Lincoln precipitated the Civil War, but in so doing, he also paved the way for a final resolution to the slavery issue and preserved the Union.

Teacher's Comment: Your introduction is strong and carefully articulated, going beyond a restatement of the theme to demonstrate a clear understanding of the context and reasons for the war. Nicely done.

Teacher's Comment: What were the effects of the Compromise of 1850? You neglect to explain why it failed to alleviate growing sectional differences. More detail and examples, please.

Teacher's Comment: You need to describe in more detail the provisions of the Kansas-Nebraska Act, its effects, and why it too failed to resolve the slavery issue.

Teacher's Comment: You conclude nicely with an accurate and thorough explanation of Lincoln's beliefs and how he became a catalyst for the war. Good job.

Rubric Score: 3 Develops all aspects of the task with some depth; is more descriptive than analytical; incorporates some relevant information from some of the documents; incorporates limited relevant outside information; includes some relevant facts, examples, and details; may contain some minor inaccuracies; demonstrates a satisfactory plan of organization; includes an introduction and conclusion that might be a restatement of the theme

Regents Exam Practice

Before you begin the exercises below, review chapters 4–6 in your textbook.

Exam Practice 1

Part I: Multiple-Choice Questions

Read the question and choose the best answer.

1 In 1803 the Supreme Court decision in *Marbury v. Madison*

 (1) declared the Alien and Sedition acts unconstitutional.

 (2) established the power of judicial review.

 (3) led to the end of the National Bank.

 (4) created the supremacy of states' rights.

2 What effect did the Louisiana Purchase have on the United States?

 (1) It doubled the size of the nation.

 (2) It brought Texas into the Union.

 (3) It created an alliance between the United States and France.

 (4) It improved relations with the British.

Part II: Thematic Essay Question

Directions: Write a well-organized essay that includes an introduction, several paragraphs addressing the task below, and a conclusion.

Theme: Civil Unrest

> From the earliest days, civil unrest has played an important part in shaping the course of United States history. During the colonial period, early settlers used a variety of methods to resist the Acts of Parliament passed by British authorities. Their acts of resistance eventually led to the American Revolution and the formation of the nation.

Task

Identify *two* tactics American colonists used to resist the Acts passed by British Parliament and for *each*:

> • Discuss the circumstances surrounding the use of the tactic
>
> • Describe the extent to which the tactic achieved the colonists' original goal
>
> • Discuss the short-term and long-term effects of the tactic on United States history

You may use any examples from your study of United States history. Some suggestions you might wish to consider include the Stamp Act Congress, the Sons of Liberty, the Boston Massacre, and the Boston Tea Party.

Exam Practice 1

Part III: Document-Based Question

Historical Context

> The leaders of the American Revolution were greatly influenced by the 18th century historical intellectual movement known as The Enlightenment. The democratic principles espoused by Enlightenment philosophers are embodied in the historical documents of the United States and form the basis for the American republican representative government we know today.

Task

Using information from **Documents 1** and **2** and your knowledge of United States history, answer the questions that follow each document. Your answers will help you write an essay in which you will be asked to:

- Describe the principles expressed in these documents

- Discuss the influence of these principles on United States history and the structure and function of the United States federal government

Document 1

> "The reason why men enter into society, is the preservation of their property; and the end while they chuse [choose] and authorize a legislative, is, that there may be laws made, and rules set, as guards and fences to the properties of all the members society . . ."
>
> Excerpt from John Locke:
> *Two Treatises on Government*

1 According to this document, what is Locke's view of the main purpose and function of society?

Document 2

> "Congress shall make no law respecting an establishment of religion, or pro-hibiting the free exercise thereof; or abridging the freedom of speech, or of the press; or the right of the people peacefully to assemble, and to petition the government for a redress of griev-ances."
>
> Excerpt from
> *First Amendment to the United States Constitution, 1791*

2a Based on this document, state **two** rights that are protected by the First Amendment.

2b Based on this document, how does the First Amendment limit the power of Congress?

Regents Exam Practice

Before you begin the exercises below, review chapters 13–16 in your textbook.

Exam Practice 2

Part I: Multiple-Choice Questions

Read the question and choose the best answer.

1 Which of the following led to the American industrial growth of the late 1800s?

(1) the household economy
(2) technological advances
(3) government regulations
(4) the development of labor unions

2 Which famous black leader of the late 19th century argued that African Americans should accommodate segregation?

(1) W.E.B. Du Bois
(2) Ida B. Wells
(3) Booker T. Washington
(4) Frederick Douglass

Part II: Thematic Essay Question

Directions: Write a well-organized essay that includes an introduction, several paragraphs addressing the task below, and a conclusion.

Theme: Immigration

> Throughout United States history, people from different countries and cultures have migrated to America seeking economic opportunity and religious freedom. In the late 1800s, a sharp rise in immigration to the United States doubled the nation's foreign-born population, and transformed American society and culture.

Task

> • Explain the different factors that led immigrants to the United States in the late nineteenth century
> • Discuss the immediate and long-term effects of this massive wave of immigration

You may use any examples from your study of United States history. Some suggestions you might wish to consider include the Homestead Act, and the wars and political revolutions in China and Eastern Europe.

Part III: Document-Based Question

Historical Context

Many Americans in the nineteenth century believed in Manifest Destiny, the idea that the United States was a divinely favored nation destined to expand its greatness westward across North America. Yet, the nation's expansion into western territories had disastrous consequences for Native Indians already inhabiting this region.

Task

Using information from **Documents 1** and **2** and your knowledge of United States history, answer the questions that follow each document. Your answers will help you write an essay in which you will be asked to:

- Discuss the reasons why white settlers migrated west

- Explain how the U.S. federal government's Indian policies affected Native Americans

Document 1

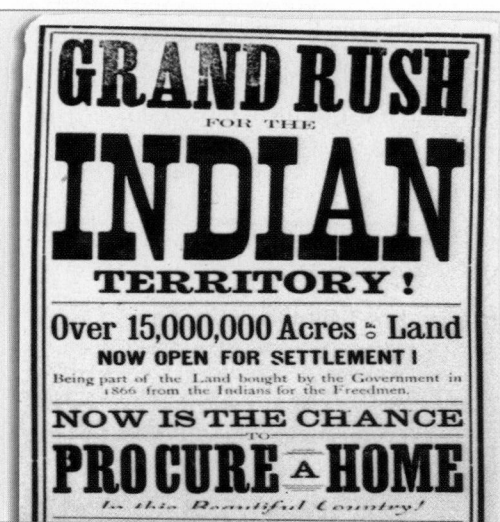

1a According to the poster, what might entice settlers to move west?

1b Based on the poster, how did proponents of westward expansion view Native Americans' rights?

Document 2

"In order to become sole masters of our land they relegated us to small reservations as big as my hand and make us long promises, as long as my arm; but the next year the promises were shorter and got shorter every year until now they are the length of my finger, and they keep only half of that."

— Chief Piapot, 1895

2a According to the passage, how does Chief Piapot view the federal government's treatment of Native Americans?

2b Based on the passage, what is Piapot referring to when he says promises are getting "shorter?"

Regents Exam Practice

Before you begin the exercises below, review chapters 20–22 in your textbook.

Exam Practice 3

Part I: Multiple-Choice Questions

Read the question and choose the best answer.

1 A major factor in the success of Henry Ford's Model T was

   (1) scientific advancements in rubber
   (2) the low wages earned by Ford factory workers
   (3) the car's ability to go faster than any other automobile
   (4) improved mass-production techniques

2 The 1919 Volstead Act officially

   (1) enforced the Eighteenth Amendment
   (2) repealed Prohibition laws
   (3) established a quota system for immigration
   (4) superseded the nineteenth amendment

Part II: Thematic Essay Question

Directions: Write a well-organized essay that includes an introduction, several paragraphs addressing the task below, and a conclusion.

Theme: Economics and Depression

> The booming economy Americans enjoyed during the Roaring Twenties collapsed in October 1929 with the crash of Wall Street. The worldwide Great Depression that followed lasted through most of the 1930s and is remembered today as the nation's worst economic crisis. There were several factors that contributed to the Depression.

Task

Identify *two* events or problems that preceded or followed the stock market crash of 1929 and for *each*:

> • Explain how the event or problem led to the collapse of the American economy
>
> • Describe *one* factor that contributed to the event or problem

You may use any examples from your study of United States history. Some suggestions you might wish to consider include investor overspeculation and the Dust Bowl.

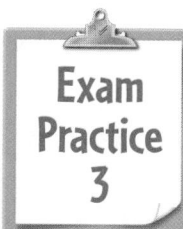

Part III: Document-Based Question

Historical Context

In his first inaugural address to Americans at the depth of the Depression in March 1933, President Franklin Delano Roosevelt boldly asserted the nation's ability to confront and overcome its worst economic crisis. Roosevelt pledged a "New Deal," creating a series of government programs to end the Depression. These programs marked the beginning of the federal government's role in reforming the nation's economy.

Task

Using information from **Documents 1** and **2** and your knowledge of United States history, answer the questions that follow each document. Your answers will help you write an essay in which you will be asked to:

- Discuss the ways New Deal projects benefited Americans and the economy
- Analyze the chief complaint against the New Deal

Document 1

1 Based on this map, how did the Tennessee Valley Authority benefit the region it served?

Document 2

"Something has taken place in this country—there is a certain kind of foreign "ism" crawling over [it]....There can be only one Capitol, Washington or Moscow! There can be only one atmosphere of government, [the] clear, pure, fresh air of free America, or the foul breath of Communistic Russia."

— Alfred E. Smith

2 According to the excerpt, why does Alfred E. Smith oppose the New Deal?

Regents Exam Practice

Before you begin the exercises below, review chapters 27–31 in your textbook.

Exam
Practice
4

Part I: Multiple-Choice Questions

Read the question and choose the best answer.

1 Kennedy's "flexible response" defense policy

(1) emphasized construction of nuclear weapons

(2) increased funding for the Army and Navy

(3) promoted peace through the Peace Corps

(4) cultivated good relations with Fidel Castro

2 Which of the following was a major part of Johnson's Great Society?

(1) a tax increase

(2) aid to foreign countries

(3) healthcare legislation

(4) reductions in antipoverty programs

Part II: Thematic Essay Question

Directions: Write a well-organized essay that includes an introduction, several paragraphs addressing the task below, and a conclusion.

Theme: Foreign Policy and War

> Beginning in the 1950s, the country of Vietnam became the focal point of the United States' Cold War efforts to prevent the spread of communism. America's involvement in the Vietnam War lasted for decades, cost hundreds of thousands of American lives and casualties, sparked massive protests at home, and ended in the withdrawal of U.S. troops without success.

Task

> • Analyze how the United States began its involvement in Vietnam
> • Assess the nature of the war in Vietnam and the difficulties faced by both sides

You may use any examples from your study of United States history. Some suggestions you might wish to consider include Ho Chi Minh, the Geneva Accords, Dien Bien Phu, and the Gulf of Tonkin Resolution.

Part III: Document-Based Question

Historical Context

> The Civil Rights Movement compelled the nation to live up to the ideals of equality espoused in its own founding documents. Broad and diverse, the movement demonstrated that ordinary men and women could perform extraordinary acts of courage and sacrifice to attain racial equality, a lesson that continues to inspire people around the world.

Task

Using information from **Documents 1, 2 (below), 3** and **4 (page NY 48)**, and your knowledge of United States history, answer the questions that follow each document. Your answers will help you write an essay in which you will be asked to:

- Discuss the role **and** effects of nonviolent protests during the Civil Rights Movement

- Explain the importance of *Brown v. Board of Education*

Document 1

1 Based on this photograph, what measures did police use to break up civil rights marches?

Document 2

2 Based on this photograph, what kind of demonstration is taking place and what effect is it having?

"In these days, it is doubtful that any child may reasonably be expected to succeed in life if he is denied the opportunity of an education. Such an opportunity, where the state has undertaken to provide it, is a right which must be made available to all on equal terms . . . To separate them [children in grade and high schools] from others of similar age and qualifications solely because of their race generates a feeling of inferiority as to their status in the community that may affect their hearts and minds in a way unlikely to ever be undone."

—Excerpt from Earl Warren decision in *Brown v. Board of Education*

3a Based on the passage, what is Chief Justice Warren's opinion of education?

3b According to the passage, how are children affected by segregation?

Document 4

4 Based on this photograph, state **one** effect of the *Brown* decision.

Contents

A series of handbooks provides skills instruction to help you read, learn, and demonstrate your knowledge of American history.

Reading Informational Texts

Writing Handbook

Critical Thinking About Visuals and Text Sources

Speaking and Listening

Reading Informational Texts

Reading a newspaper, a magazine, an Internet page, or a textbook differs from reading a novel. You read nonfiction texts to acquire new information. Researchers have shown that the reading strategies presented below will help you maximize your understanding of such informational texts.

Strategies to Use Before You Read

Before you read informational text, it's important to take the time to do some prereading. These strategies will help.

Set a Purpose for Reading

Try to focus on a goal when you're reading the text. Preview a section by reading the objectives and looking at the illustrations. Then, write a purpose for your reading, such as:

- "I'll learn about the development of the North and South and find ways to compare these regions."
- "I'll find out about the growth of railroads."

Ask Questions

Before you read a section, consider what you'd like to know about a topic. Then, ask questions that will yield relevant information. Scan the section headings and illustrations and write a few questions in a chart like the one below. As you read, try to answer each of your questions. Use phrases and words to fill in the chart.

Question	Answer
Why did immigrants come to the United States in the late 1800s?	To find religious freedom, to escape poverty, to flee persecution
What was life like for immigrants when they arrived?	It was hard at first, but opportunities opened up; sometimes they faced hostility and prejudice

Predict

Engage in the reading process by making predictions about what you are preparing to learn. Scan the section headings and the visuals. Then, write a prediction, such as:

• "I will find out what caused the United States to fight Spain in 1898."

Keep your predictions in mind as you read—do they turn out to be accurate or do you need to revise them?

Use Prior Knowledge

Research shows that if you connect the new information in your reading to your prior knowledge, you'll be more likely to remember the new information. You'll also see the value of studying history if you see how it connects to the present. After previewing a section, create a chart like this one. Complete the chart as you read the section.

What I Know	What I Want to Know	What I Learned
Older Americans are worried about Social Security and whether it will provide for them when they retire.	When did Social Security start?	Social Security was a program that started during the Great Depression of the 1930s to help provide for older Americans when they retire.

Strategies to Use As You Read

It's important to be an active reader. Use these strategies as you read informational text.

Reread or Read Ahead

If you do not understand a certain passage, reread it to look for connections among the words and sentences. For example, look for cause-and-effect words that link ideas or sequence words that show when events took place. Or, try reading ahead to see if the ideas are clarified later on. Once you find new clarifying information, return to the confusing text and read it again with the new information in mind.

Paraphrase/Summarize

To paraphrase is to restate information in your own words. Summarizing—a version of paraphrasing—can also help you confirm your understanding of the text. Summarizing focuses on restating the main ideas of a passage, as you can see in the example below. Include a few important details, such as the time period, to orient yourself or other readers to the text.

Original Paragraph	Summary
During the 1920s, the National Women's Party took a more militant position, demanding complete economic, social, and political equality with men. Their primary goal was the passage of the Equal Rights Amendment. Most women, however, believed that a new constitutional amendment was premature.	In the 1920s, the National Womens Party demanded complete equality with men, working for passage of the Equal Rights Amendment. Most women thought it was too soon for such an amendment.

Identify Main Ideas and Details

A main idea is the most important point in a paragraph or section of text. Some main ideas are stated directly, but others are implied. You must determine these yourself by reading carefully. Pause occasionally to make sure you can identify the main idea.

Main ideas are supported by details. Record main ideas and details in an outline format like the one shown here.

Changes in the South and West, 1880–1900

Main Idea → I. The South changed economically
Details → A. Industry developed
   B. Train and road transportation grew
   C. Cities attracted workers

Analyze the Text's Structure

Just as you might organize a story about your weekend to highlight the most important parts, authors will organize their writing to stress their key ideas. Analyzing text structure can help you tap into this organization. In a social studies textbook, the author frequently uses one of the structures listed in the chart at right to organize information. Learn to identify structures in texts and you'll remember text information more effectively.

Structures for Organizing Information

Compare and Contrast Here, an author highlights similarities and differences between two or more ideas, cultures, processes, people, etc. Look for clue words such as *on the other hand* or *similarly*.

Sequence Here, an author recounts the order in which events occurred or steps were taken. History is often told in chronological sequence but can also involve flashbacks from later times to earlier times. Look for sequence words such as *initially*, *later*, and *ultimately*.

Cause and Effect Here, an author highlights the impact of one event on another or the effects of key events. Cause and effect is critical to understanding history because events in one time often strongly influence those in later times. Look for clue words such as *because*, *so*, or *as a result*.

Analyze the Author's Purpose

Different reading materials are written with different goals, or purposes. For example, this textbook is written to teach you about American history. The technical manual that accompanies a cellphone is written to explain how to use the product.

An author's purpose influences not only how the material is presented but also how you read it. Thus you must identify the purpose, whether it is stated directly or merely suggested. If it is not directly stated, use clues in the text—such as opinion words in an editorial—to identify the author's purpose.

Vocabulary

Here are several strategies to help you understand the meaning of a word you do not recognize.

Use Context Clues   You can often define an unfamiliar word with clues from the surrounding text. For example, in the sentence "One campaign of the Progressives had the goal of improving sanitation in cities," the words *campaign* and *improve* are clues that Progressives were reformers. Context clues can be in the same sentence as the unfamiliar word or in nearby sentences or paragraphs.

Analyze Word Parts   Use your knowledge of word parts to help you define unfamiliar words. Break the word into its parts—root, prefix, suffix. What do you know about these parts? For example, the prefix *inter* means "between" and the suffix *ism* means "belief in." The word *international* means "between nations" and *internationalism* means "belief in relations between nations."

Recognize Word Origins   Another way to figure out the meaning of an unfamiliar word is to understand the word's origins. Use your experience with Greek or Latin roots, for example, to build meaning. The word *bilingual* contains the Latin root *lingua,* which means "tongue." *Bilingual* means "two tongues" or "two languages."

Distinguish Between Facts and Opinions/Recognize Bias

It's important to read actively, especially when reading informational texts. Decide whether information is factual—which means it can be proven—or if it includes opinions or bias—that is, people's views or evaluations.

Anytime you read material that conveys opinions, such as an editorial, keep an eye out for author bias. This bias might be revealed in the use of emotionally charged words or faulty logic. For example, the newspaper editorial below includes factual statements (in blue) and opinion statements (in red). The emotionally charged words (underlined) will get a rise out of people. Faulty logic may include circular reasoning that returns to its beginning and either/or arguments that ignore other possibilities.

Editorial
Some day, Dwight Eisenhower will be remembered as the best President of the 20th century. He kept government small; he left the states alone to tend to their affairs; and the economy hummed. Any American with any sense will agree that these things contributed to the overall well-being of the nation.

Identify Evidence

Read critically. Do not accept an author's conclusion automatically. Identify and evaluate the author's evidence. Does it justify the conclusion in quantity and content? An author may present facts to support a claim, but there may be more to the story than facts. For example, what evidence does the writer of the editorial above present to support the claim that Eisenhower was a great President? Perhaps Americans who didn't prosper in the 1950s would disagree with the assertion.

Evaluate Credibility

After you evaluate evidence, check an author's credentials. Consider his or her level of experience and expertise about the topic. Is he or she likely to be knowledgeable *and* objective about the topic? Evaluating credibility is especially important with Web sites you may visit on the Internet. Ask the following questions to determine if a Web site and its author are reliable.

- Who sponsors the Web site? Is it a respected organization, a discussion group of individuals, or a single person?
- What is the source of the Web site's information? Does the site list sources for facts and statements?
- Does the Web site creator include his or her name and credentials?
- Is the information on the Web site balanced and objective or biased to reflect only one point of view?
- Can you verify the Web site's information using two other sources, such as an encyclopedia or news agency?
- Is the information current? Is there a date on the Web site to show when it was created or last updated?

Strategies to Use After You Read

Evaluate Understanding

Evaluate how well you understand what you've read.
- Go back to the questions you asked yourself before reading. Try to answer each of them.
- Check the predictions you made and revise them if appropriate.
- Draw a conclusion about the author's evidence and credibility.
- Check meanings of unfamiliar words in the dictionary to confirm your definitions.

Recall Information

Before moving on to new material, you should be able to answer the following questions fully:
- What was the text about?
- What was the purpose of the text?
- How was the text structured?

You should also be able to place the information you have just read in the context of your prior knowledge of the topic.

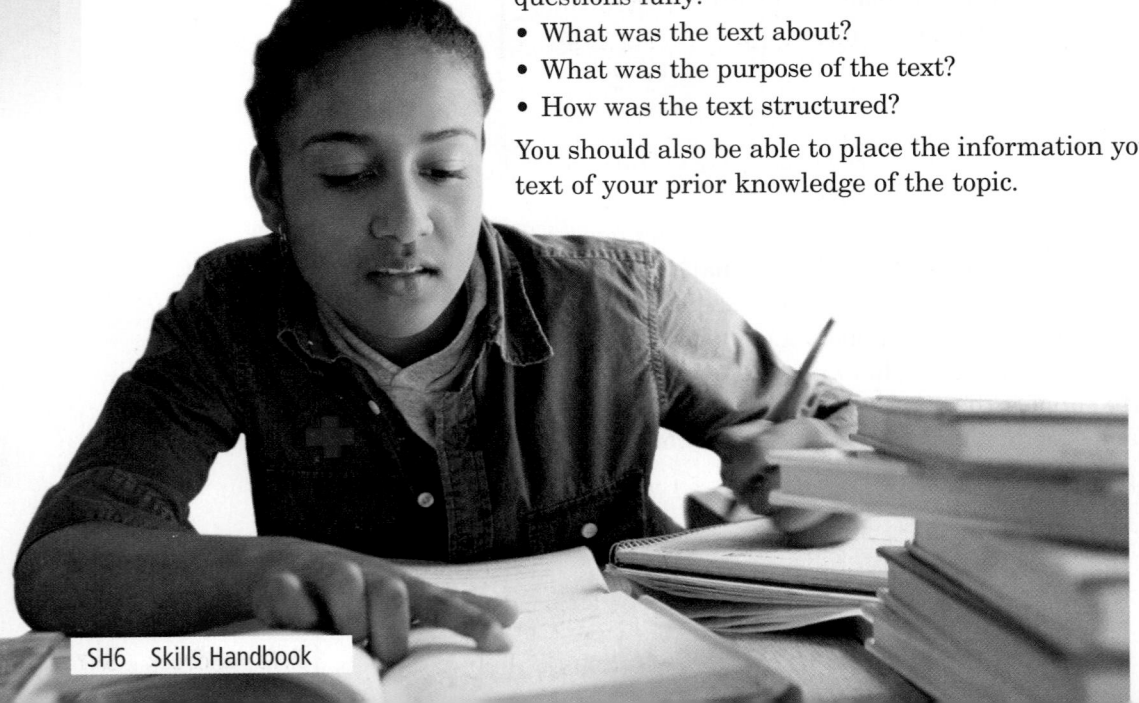

Writing Handbook

Writing is one of the most powerful communication tools you will use for the rest of your life. Research shows that writing about what you read actually helps you learn new information and ideas. A systematic approach to writing—including prewriting, drafting, revising, and proofreading—can always help you write better.

Narrative Essay

Narrative writing tells a story about a personal experience or a historical event. This story might also recount a person's life or tell about an important accomplishment.

1 Prewriting

Choose a topic. The focus of your essay will often be about a historical event from a particular point of view. Use these ideas as a guide.

- **Review the details of the event** you will be writing about.
- **Choose a person,** actual or fictional, who would have experienced the event.
- **List words** describing why the person caused the event or how he or she might have reacted to it.
- **Brainstorm** about the story you will write. Jot down ideas like the ones below.

> Teenager in the 1920s responds to hearing jazz music for the first time.
> • Circumstances: standing in the street outside an apartment building, overhearing a musician practicing
> • Reactions: startled at first because the music is different; intrigued; spellbound; wants to dance to the music; goes home and tries to play jazz

Consider audience and purpose.

- Keep your **audience's** knowledge and experience level in mind. Make sure you provide any necessary background information.
- Choose a **purpose** as well. If you want to entertain, include humorous details. You might also include more serious insights.

Gather details.

- Collect the facts and details you need to tell your story.
- Research any background about the historical event that readers might need to know about.

2 Drafting

Identify the climax, or most interesting part of your story. Then, logically organize your story into a beginning, middle, and end. Narratives are often told in chronological order.

Open strongly with an engaging sentence, such as the one below, that will catch your reader's attention.

Use sensory details, such as sights, sounds, or smells, to make the story vivid for readers. Describe people's actions and gestures. Pinpoint and use detail to describe locations.

Write a conclusion that sums up the significance of the event or situation you are writing about.

Strong opening engages the reader.

Sensory details help the reader envision the experience.

Insight or significance tells the reader what this event means to the person in the narrative or to history.

> I never could have imagined how a simple stroll down the street would change my life. I was walking down the street yesterday, whistling to myself, when the most strange and enticing harmonies drifted toward me from an open third-floor window. Now, I'm pretty cool, but I've never heard such music before. It set me tingling; it set me to swaying. It made me want to dance right there on the spot. I emerged from the trance as the saxophonist let the last full note drift into the air. Then, I rushed home to see if I could replicate the smooth new sound on my clarinet. I know this chance encounter has changed my life forever.

3 Revising

Add dialogue or description. Dialogue, or conveying a person's thoughts or feelings in his or her own words, can make a narrative more effective. Look for places where the emotions are especially intense. In the model, this might be when the writer began to "feel" the music.

First Draft	Revised Original
The music made me feel very involved. It made me want to dance.	It set me tingling; it set me to swaying. It made me want to dance right there on the spot.

Revise word choice. Replace general words with more specific, colorful ones. Choose vivid action verbs, precise adjectives, and specific nouns to convey your meaning. Look at the example above. Notice how much more effective the revised version is at conveying the experience.

Read your draft aloud. Listen for grammatical errors and statements that are unclear. Revise your sentences as necessary.

4 Publishing and Presenting

Share by reading aloud. Highlight text you want to emphasize and then read your essay aloud to the class. Invite and respond to questions.

Expository Writing

Expository writing explains ideas or information in detail. The strategies on these pages examine each of several types of expository writing.

1 Prewriting

Choose a topic. In social studies, the focus of your writing might be comparing and contrasting economic trends, explaining causes and effects of current events, or exploring problems the nation has faced and the solutions it has sought. These ideas are a guide.

- **Create a compare/contrast grab bag.** With a small group, write on separate slips of paper examples from each category: ideas, events, or time periods. Mix the slips in a bag and choose two. Compare and contrast the two ideas, events, or time periods.
- **Interview** someone who made a major change in lifestyle, such as moving from one part of the country to another. Find out how and why the person did this. Understanding why is the basis of any cause-and-effect essay.
- **Take a mental walk.** Study a map and envision taking a tour of the region. Think about problems each area you visit might face, such as economic challenges or natural disasters. Choose a problem and suggest solutions for it.

Consider audience and purpose. Consider how much your readers know about the problem, comparison, or event you will address. Suit your writing to your audience's knowledge or plan to give explanations of unfamiliar terms and concepts.

Gather details. Collect the facts and details you need to write your essay.

Research the topic. Use books, the Internet, or interviews of local experts. List facts, details, and other evidence related to your topic. Also consider your personal experience. For example, you might know about a problem from your own experience or have witnessed the effects of a historic legal decision.

Create a graphic organizer. For cause-and-effect or problem-solution essays, use a two-column chart. Process writing can be listed as a bulleted list of steps. A Venn diagram can help you compare and contrast.

World War I
- New weapons used: machine guns, poison gas, submarines
- 8.5 million military deaths

- Fought by two powerful alliances
- Began in Europe, then spread

World War II
- New weapon used: atomic bomb
- 20 million military deaths

Identify causes and effects. List possible explanations for events. Remember that many events result from multiple causes. Identify effects both large and small. Note that some events may have effects that in turn cause other events. Look for causes and effects in all your expository essays. But be aware that sometimes there are limitations on determining cause and effect.

2 Drafting

Match structure to purpose. Typically, cause-and-effect essays are written in sequence order. Problem-solution essays benefit from block organization, which presents the entire problem and proposes a solution. For compare/contrast essays, you can organize by subject or by point.

> By subject: Discuss the events and outcomes of World War I, and then compare and contrast these with those of World War II.
>
> By point: Introduce a category, such as use of new weapons. Relate both wars to this category, comparing or contrasting them along the way.

Give background. To discuss events from history, first orient the reader to time and place. Choose the important facts but don't overwhelm the reader with detail. If you need to, return to prewriting to narrow your topic further.

Elaborate for interest and emphasis. Give details about each point in your essay. For example, add facts that make the link between events so that a cause-and-effect relationship is clear. Also, readers will support proposed solutions more if your details clearly show how these solutions will solve the stated problem. Use facts and human experiences to make your essay vivid.

Connect to today. Even when you write about historical events, you may find links to today. Explore these links in your essay.

Identify the topic to orient readers.

The United States population underwent tremendous change in the first half of the twentieth century. In the early part of the century, Americans moved from rural to urban areas. Later, people moved out of cities into suburbs in increasing numbers. These changes resulted from many causes.

Chronological order walks readers through the cause-and-effect sequence.

Lured by jobs in the cities' factories, rural Americans and growing numbers of immigrants settled in cities during the late nineteenth and early twentieth centuries. By 1920, urban population had surpassed rural population.

Elaboration supports the relationship you are highlighting.

Thirty years later, Americans were again on the move. Cities had become overcrowded, and Americans longed to own homes and live in more space. The explosion of highways also made it easier to commute from the suburbs to the cities for work.

Connection to today tells readers why this matters to them.

Americans continue to be on the move today. Now they are moving to the Sunbelt or "exurbs" in a continuing effort to improve their lives.

3 Revising

Add transition words. Make cause-and-effect relationships clear with words such as *because, as a result,* and so on. To compare or contrast ideas, use linking words, such as *similarly, both,* and *equally* or *in contrast, instead,* and *yet.* Use words such as *first, second, next,* and *finally* to help readers follow steps in a sequence or chain of causes. Look at the following examples. In the revised version, a reader knows the correct order in which to perform the steps.

First Draft	Revised
Historians form an educated guess called a hypothesis. They test that hypothesis with further research.	<u>Next</u>, historians form an educated guess called a hypothesis. <u>Then</u>, they test that hypothesis with further research.

Remember purpose. Shape your draft so that it answers the question or thesis you began with. For a problem-solution essay—in which your purpose is to sell your solution—that means anticipating opposing arguments and responding to them. For a cause-and-effect essay, you want to stress the way one event leads to the next. Always tell readers why they should care about your topic.

Review organization. Confirm that your ideas flow in a logical order. Write main points on index cards. Reorganize these until you are satisfied that the order best strengthens your essay.

Add details. Make sure you have not left out any steps in your essay, and do not assume readers will make the connections. For example, you might forget to state explicitly that your narrative represents a particular point of view. Add more background if necessary for clarity.

Revise sentences and words. Look at your sentence length. Vary it to include both short and long sentences. Then, scan for vague words, such as *good.* Replace them with specific and vibrant words, such as *effective.* Use technical terms only when necessary, and then define them.

Peer review. Ask a peer to read your draft. Is it clear? Can he or she follow your ideas? Revise areas of confusion.

4 Publishing and Presenting

Contribute to a class manual. Include your comparison essay in a class History Journal.

Submit to a library. Find a specialized library, such as a presidential library. Mail your essay to the library's publications or public relations department.

Seek publication. If your historical events or issues are local, seek publication in a local historical magazine or contact a historical society. You might speak to their members.

Mail to an advocacy group. Find a local, national, or international organization that is concerned with your topic. Send them your essay and ask for comments on its ideas. Make sure to include a self-addressed stamped envelope and a note explaining your essay and offering thanks for its review.

Research Writing

1 Prewriting

Choose a topic. Often, a teacher will assign your research topic. You may have flexibility in choosing your focus or you may have the opportunity to completely define your topic. These ideas are a guide.

- **Catalog scan.** Using a card or electronic catalog in a library, or Internet search engine, search for topics that interest you. When a title looks promising, find the book on the shelves. Or follow up on your Internet search results by reviewing the linked Web sites. You can use what you find to decide on your final topic.

- **Notes review.** Review your social studies notes from the last month or so. Jot down topics that you found interesting. Then, repeat the process with your other classes. For example, you might find a starting point for research into an environmental issue from a biology experiment.

- **Social studies categories game.** With a group, brainstorm categories in social studies. For example, you might list key American leaders or important wars. Within each category, take turns adding subtopics. The chart below shows different topics related to agriculture.

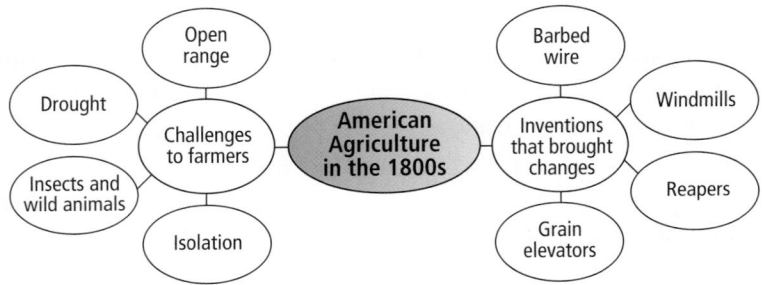

You can use sources such as newspapers to get ideas.

Analyze the audience. Your research and your paper should be strongly influenced by the audience. How much will readers know about this topic and how much will you have to teach them?

Gather details. Collect the facts and details you need to write your paper. Use resources beyond the typical history books. Look at nonfiction books such as memoirs or collections of letters. Also look at magazine and newspaper articles. Consider news magazines, as well as those focused on topics such as history or travel. Search the Internet, starting with online encyclopedias, news organizations, and history Web sites. Remember to check Web sites for reliability.

Organize evidence and ideas. Use note cards to record information and to help you organize your thoughts. Start with a general thesis statement in mind. Then, begin reading and taking notes. Write a heading at the top of each note card to group it under a subtopic. Note a number or title to identify the information source. In the examples below, the number 3 is used. Use the same number for an additional source card containing the bibliographic information you will need.

Information source I.D. number

Heading

3   Background about barbed wire
p. 16
Invented in 1874

Bibliographic information for source 3

3
Razac, Oliver. *Barbed Wire: A Political History.* Cahners Business Information, Inc., 2002

Valley Regional High School Library

② Drafting

Fine-tune your thesis. Review your notes to find relationships between ideas. Shape a thesis that is supported by the majority of your information, then check that it is narrow enough to address thoroughly in the allotted time and space. Remember, you can fine-tune your thesis further as you draft or even when you revise.

Organize to fit your purpose. Do you want to persuade readers of a particular position about your topic, compare and contrast aspects of the topic, or show a cause-and-effect relationship? Organize appropriately.

Make an outline. Create an outline in which you identify each topic and subtopic in a single phrase. You can then turn these phrases into sentences and later into the topic sentences of your draft paragraphs. Study the example at the top of the next page to see how to do this well.

Write by paragraph. Write an introduction, at least three body paragraphs, and a conclusion. Address a subtopic of your main topic in each body paragraph. Support all your statements with the facts and details you gathered.

An outline helps you structure your information.

Each body paragraph looks at a part of the whole topic.

The introduction puts the topic in a context of time and place. The entire paragraph conveys the thesis: dividing up the Plains with barbed wire had lasting effects for the region.

The conclusion recaps key points and leaves readers with a final statement to remember.

The Importance of Barbed Wire

Outline

I. Introduction
II. Why barbed wire was invented
III. How barbed wire was used
IV. Effects of the use of barbed wire
    A. End of open grazing lands for cattle
    B. End of cowboys' way of life
    C. Increased importance of farming on the Plains
V. Conclusion

Introduction

No invention was more important to the development of the American Plains than barbed wire. Until its widespread use in the late 1800s, cattle herds roamed the Plains region and farmers worried about their crops getting trampled. With the advent of barbed wire, all of this changed.

Conclusion

By the end of the nineteenth century, the Plains had been sectioned off through the use of barbed wire. The earlier life on the Plains had been changed forever.

---

3 Revising

Add detail. Mark points where more details would strengthen your statements. Look at the following examples. Notice the added details in the revised version. When adding facts, make certain that they are accurate.

Make the connection for readers. Help readers find their way through your ideas. First, check that your body paragraphs and the information within them flow in a logical sequence. If they do not, revise to correct this. Then, add transition words to link ideas and paragraphs.

Give credit. Check that you have used your own words or given proper credit for borrowed words. You can give credit easily with parenthetical notes. These include the author's last name and the relevant page number from the source. For example, you could cite the note card on the previous page as "(Razac, 16)."

First Draft	Revised
Cowboys would ride the range with huge herds of cattle. Their goal was to bring the herd to Kansas for shipping to markets in Chicago and the East.	Cowboys worked long hours on the dusty Plains, keeping constant vigilance on their herd of hundreds of cattle. They always kept the goal in sight: reaching Kansas, a key shipping center, then taking a well-deserved rest.

4 Publishing and Presenting

Plan a conference. Gather a group of classmates and present your research projects. You may each wish to create visual materials to accompany your presentations. After you share your papers, hold a question-and-answer session.

Persuasive Essay

Persuasive writing supports an opinion or position. In social studies, persuasive essays often argue for or against positions on historical or current issues.

1 Prewriting

Choose a topic. Choose a topic that provokes an argument and has at least two sides. Use these ideas as a guide.

- **Round-table discussion.** Talk with classmates about issues you have studied recently. Outline pro-and-con positions about these issues.
- **Textbook flip.** Scan the table of contents or flip through the pages of your textbook. Focus on historical issues that engage your feelings.
- **Make connections.** Relate current events to history. Develop a position for or against a situation of importance today using historical evidence.

Narrow your topic.

- **Cover part of the topic** if you find too many pros and cons for a clear argument of the whole topic.
- **Use looping.** Write for five minutes on the general topic. Circle the most important idea. Then write for five minutes on that idea. Continue looping until the topic is manageable.

Consider your audience. Choose arguments that will appeal to the audience for your writing and that are likely to persuade them to agree with your views.

Gather evidence. Collect the evidence to support your position convincingly.

- **Identify pros and cons.** Use a graphic organizer like the one below to list points on both sides of the issue.

The United States should increase its efforts to send astronauts to Mars.	
Pro ⟵————————————————⟶ **Con**	
• Space travel increases human knowledge about Earth and inspires young people to learn about science. • Space travel leads to technologies that can be used to improve life on Earth. • The United States has a history of exploration beyond its borders; this would be just one more step.	• Space travel is too expensive. • Space travel is a luxury; the nation should concentrate on needs at home. • There is no need to send humans to Mars when we can learn as much from robots traveling there.

- **Interview** adults who remember the first moon landing. What do they think about sending astronauts to Mars? Ask them for reasons to support their views.
- **Research** to get your facts straight. Read articles or books about the space program.

2 Drafting

State your thesis. Clearly state your position, as in this example:

> The United States should strongly promote the space program by sending people to Mars. We have so much to learn from the challenge of space travel that can help us at home.

Use your introduction to provide a context for the issue. Tell your readers when and why the issue arose, and identify the important people involved.

Sequence your arguments. Open or close with your strongest argument. If you close with the strongest argument, open with the second-best argument.

Acknowledge opposition. State, and then refute, opposing arguments.

Use facts and details. Include quotations, statistics, or comparisons to build your case. Include personal experiences or reactions to the topic, such as those a family member might have shared when interviewed.

Write a conclusion that restates your thesis and closes with a strong, compelling argument.

Background orients readers.

Thesis identifies your main argument.

Supporting argument clarifies your thesis.

Opposing argument, noted and refuted, adds to your position.

> For a long time, the United States led the world in space exploration. But recently, the space program has become more limited. This situation should change. The United States should strongly promote the space program by sending people to Mars. We have so much to learn from meeting the challenge of space travel that can help us here at home.
>
> Sending people into space has already yielded great rewards in the development of technology and other advances. Improved computers, medicines, and GPS systems are all positive by-products of space exploration. Some people might argue that space exploration is too expensive and that we have problems to tackle right here at home. However, the benefits of space exploration will help us at home today and in the future. The benefits outweigh the costs....

3 Revising

Add information. Extra details can generate interest in your topic. For example, in the essay on space travel add a quotation from a news article that assesses the importance of space exploration to solving problems on Earth.

Review arguments. Make sure your arguments are logically sound and clearly developed. Avoid faulty logic such as circular reasoning (arguing a point by merely restating it differently). Evidence is the best way to support your points. Look at the following examples. Notice how much more effectively the revised version supports the argument.

First Draft	Revised
Space exploration will help our nation in many ways.	Space exploration will provide jobs, new technologies, and inspiration to young scientists.

Use transition words to guide readers through your ideas.
- **To show contrast:** *however, although, despite*
- **To point out a reason:** *since, because, if*
- **To signal conclusion:** *therefore, consequently, so, then*

4 Publishing and Presenting

Persuasive Speech. Many persuasive essays are delivered orally. Prepare your essay as a speech, highlighting words for emphasis and adding changes in tone, volume, or speed.

Writing for Assessment

Assessment writing differs from all other writing that you do. You have many fewer choices as a writer, and you almost always face a time limit. In social studies, you'll need to write both short answers and extended responses for tests. While these contrast in some ways, they share many requirements.

① Prewriting

Choose a topic. Short-answer questions seldom offer a topic choice. For extended-response questions, however, you may have a choice of more than one question. Use the following strategies to help you navigate that choice.

- **Examine the question.** To choose a question you can answer effectively, analyze what each question is asking. Use key words such as those listed below to help you choose topics and respond to short-answer questions in which the topic is given.

Key Words	What You Need in an Answer
Explain	Give a clear, complete account of how something works or why something happened.
Compare/Contrast	Show how two or more things are alike and different.
Define	Give examples to explain meaning.
Argue, Convince, Support, Persuade	Take a position on an issue and present strong reasons to support your side of the issue.
Summarize	Provide the most important elements of a subject.
Evaluate/Judge	Assign a value or explain an opinion.
Interpret	Support a thesis with examples from the text.

Notice in the examples below that the key words are underlined:

> **Short answer:** <u>Describe</u> one way that Chief Joseph showed his <u>military expertise</u>.
> **Extended response:** According to the author of this article, Chief Joseph was both a <u>peace chief</u> and a <u>military genius</u>. Use information from the article to <u>support this conclusion</u>.

- **Plot your answer.** After choosing a question, quickly plot the answer in your mind. Do you have the information to answer this question? If the answer is no, try another question.

Measure your time. Your goal is to show the instructor that you've mastered the material. To stay focused on this goal, divide your time: one-quarter on prewriting; half on drafting; one-quarter on revising. For short-answer questions, determine how much of the overall test time you can spend on each question. Don't spend more than that.

Gather details. Organize the facts and details you need to write your answer. For short-answer questions, this usually involves identifying exactly what information is required.

Use a graphic organizer. For extended-response questions, divide your topic into subtopics that fit the type of question. Jot down facts and details for each. For the question on Chief Joseph, the following organizer would be effective:

Chief Joseph of the Nez Percés
Peace Chief
• traded peacefully with white settlers (1)
• reluctantly went to war (2)
• famous speech, "I will fight no more forever." (3)
Military Genius
• won battles with fewer warriors than opposing troops had (a)
• avoided capture for many months (b)
• led his people more than 1,000 miles (c)
• knew when to surrender for the good of his people (d)

❷ Drafting

Choose an organization that fits the question. With a short-answer question, write one to three complete sentences. With extended responses, you'll need more elaborate organization. For the question on Chief Joseph, organize your points by importance within each subtopic. For a summary or explanation, use chronological order. For compare/contrast, present similarities first, then differences.

Open and close strongly. Start your answer by restating the question or using its language to state your position. This helps you focus and shows the instructor that you understand the question. Finish with a strong conclusion that restates your position. For short answers, include some language from the question in your response.

> One way that Chief Joseph showed his military expertise was by defeating U.S. Army troops despite having fewer warriors than they had.

Support your ideas. Each paragraph should directly or indirectly support your main idea. Choose facts that build a cohesive argument. The numbered sentences in the draft below show how this writer organized support.

The opening restates the question and presents the writer's main idea.

The writer uses information from the graphic organizer, in order of importance.

The writer supports the second subtopic in a separate paragraph.

The conclusion recaps the main idea and again references the question's language.

> Chief Joseph was both a peace chief and a military genius. He was a peace chief because he traded peacefully with white settlers for many years. (1) He went to war reluctantly after the government ordered his people to move to a reservation. (2) When he finally surrendered, he said in a famous speech, "I will fight no more forever." (3)
> Chief Joseph was also a military genius. He fought off U.S. Army forces with fewer warriors than they had, (a) and he avoided capture for many months. (b) He led his people more than 1,000 miles (c) before he made the decision to surrender. (d) Chief Joseph will long be remembered for his dual roles as peace chief and military genius.

3 Revising

Examine word choice. Replace general words with specific words. Add transitions where these improve clarity. Read the following examples. The revised version shows the relative importance of the writer's supporting evidence.

First Draft	Revised
Chief Joseph was both a peace chief and a military genius. He was a peace chief because he traded peacefully with whites for many years. He went to war reluctantly....	Chief Joseph was both a peace chief and a military genius. He was a peace chief for several reasons. First, he traded peacefully with whites for many years. Second, he went to war reluctantly....

Check organization. Make sure your introduction includes a main idea and defines subtopics. Review each paragraph for a single main idea. Check that your conclusion summarizes the information you've presented.

4 Publishing and Presenting

Edit and proof. Check spelling, grammar, and mechanics. Make sure that tenses match, that subjects agree with verbs, and that sentences are not too long. Finally, confirm that you have responded to all the questions you were asked to answer.

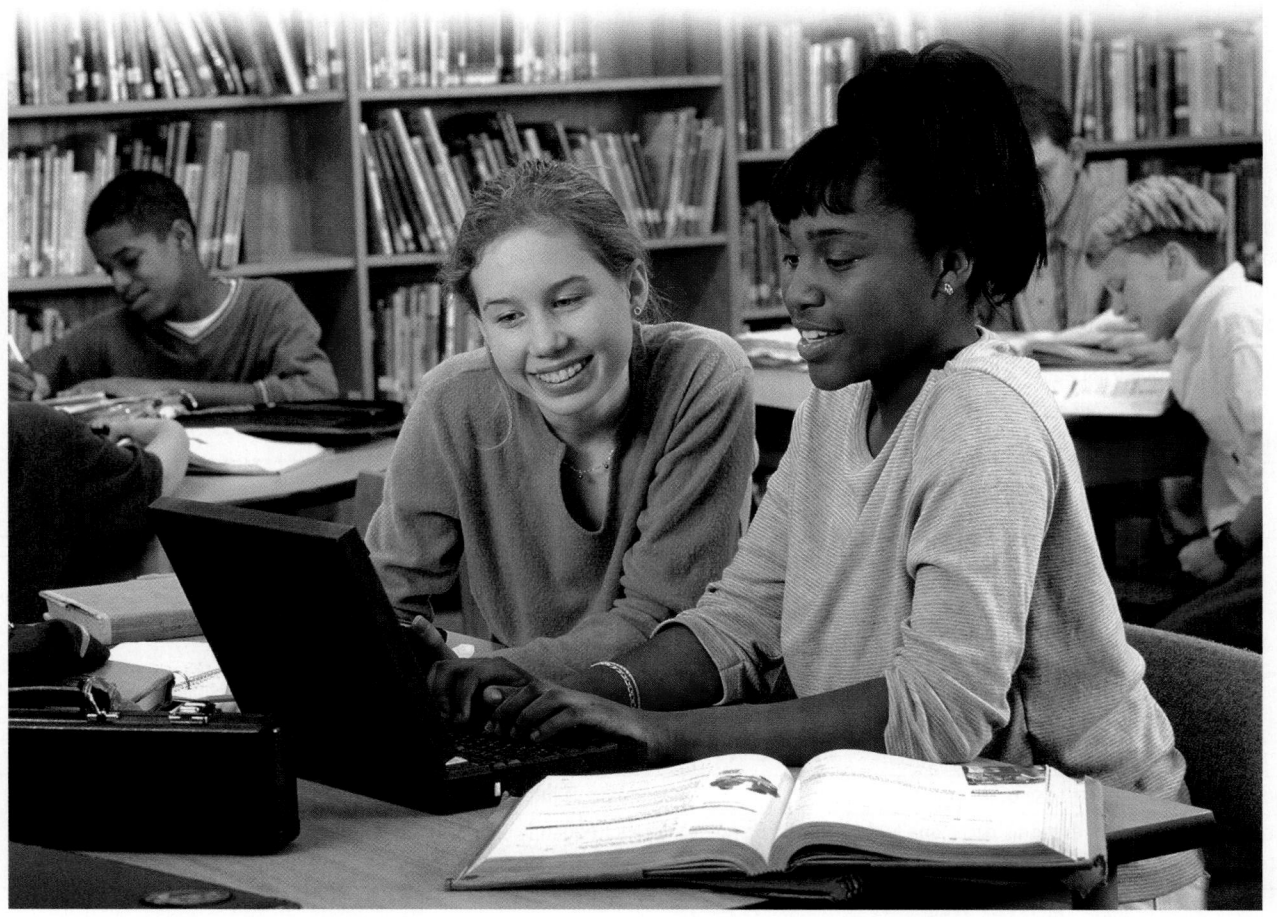

Writing Rubrics

Use these charts, or rubrics, to evaluate your writing.

SAT® PREP ACT

SAT

SCORE OF 6

An essay in this category is **outstanding**, demonstrating **clear and consistent mastery**, although it may have a few minor errors. A typical essay

- effectively and insightfully develops a point of view on the issue and demonstrates outstanding critical thinking, using clearly appropriate examples, reasons, and other evidence to support its position.
- is well organized and clearly focused, demonstrating clear coherence and smooth progression of ideas.
- exhibits skillful use of language, using a varied, accurate, and apt vocabulary.
- demonstrates meaningful variety in sentence structure.
- is free of most errors in grammar, usage, and mechanics.

SCORE OF 5

An essay in this category is **effective**, demonstrating **reasonably consistent mastery**, although it will have occasional errors or lapses in quality. A typical essay

- effectively develops a point of view on the issue and demonstrates strong critical thinking, generally using appropriate examples, reasons, and other evidence to support its position.
- is well organized and focused, demonstrating coherence and progression of ideas.
- exhibits facility in the use of language, using appropriate vocabulary.
- demonstrates variety in sentence structure.
- is generally free of most errors in grammar, usage, and mechanics.

SCORE OF 4

An essay in this category is **competent**, demonstrating **adequate mastery**, although it will have lapses in quality. A typical essay

- develops a point of view on the issue and demonstrates competent critical thinking, using adequate examples, reasons, and other evidence to support its position.
- is generally organized and focused, demonstrating some coherence and progression of ideas.
- exhibits adequate but inconsistent facility in the use of language, using generally appropriate vocabulary.
- demonstrates some variety in sentence structure.
- has some errors in grammar, usage, and mechanics.

SCORE OF 3

An essay in this category is **inadequate**, but demonstrates **developing mastery**, and is marked by **one or more** of the following weaknesses:

- develops a point of view on the issue, demonstrating some critical thinking, but may do so inconsistently or use inadequate examples, reasons, or other evidence to support its position
- is limited in its organization or focus, but may demonstrate some lapses in coherence or progression of ideas
- displays developing facility in the use of language, but sometimes uses weak vocabulary or inappropriate word choice
- lacks variety or demonstrates problems in sentence structure
- contains an accumulation of errors in grammar, usage, and mechanics

SCORE OF 2

An essay in this category is **seriously limited**, demonstrating **little mastery**, and is flawed by **one or more** of the following weaknesses:

- develops a point of view on the issue that is vague or seriously limited, demonstrating weak critical thinking, providing inappropriate or insufficient examples, reasons, or other evidence to support its position
- is poorly organized and/or focused, or demonstrates serious problems with coherence or progression of ideas
- displays very little facility in the use of language, using very limited vocabulary or incorrect word choice
- demonstrates frequent problems in sentence structure
- contains errors in grammar, usage, and mechanics so serious that meaning is somewhat obscured

SCORE OF 1

An essay in this category is **fundamentally lacking**, demonstrating **very little** or **no mastery**, and is severely flawed by **one or more** of the following weaknesses:

- develops no viable point of view on the issue, or provides little or no evidence to support its position
- is disorganized or unfocused, resulting in a disjointed or incoherent essay
- displays fundamental errors in vocabulary
- demonstrates severe flaws in sentence structure
- contains pervasive errors in grammar, usage, or mechanics that persistently interfere with meaning

SCORE OF 0

Essays not written on the essay assignment will receive a score of zero.

ACT	Scores of 4–6	Scores of 1–3
Purpose	shows a clear understanding of the essay's purpose by articulating a perspective and developing ideas	does not clearly articulate a perspective
Support	most generalizations developed with specific examples to support the perspective	demonstrates some development of ideas but may be overly general or repetitious
Focus	clear focus maintained throughout	focus maintained on general prompt topic but is not sufficiently specific
Language	shows competent use of language	language is mostly understandable, organization is clear but simple
Mechanics	minimal errors that only occasionally distract and do not interfere with meaning	errors frequently distract and interfere with meaning

Critical Thinking About Visuals and Text Sources

Analyze Graphic Data

The study of history requires that you think critically about the text you're reading as well as any visuals or media sources. This section will allow you to practice and apply some important skills for critical thinking.

Graphs show numerical facts in picture form. Bar graphs and line graphs compare things at different times or places, such as changes in school enrollment. Circle graphs show how a whole is divided into parts. To interpret a graph, look closely at its features. Use the graphs below and the steps that follow to practice analyzing graphic data.

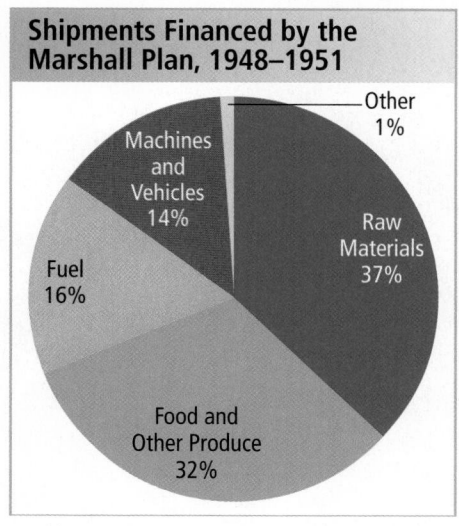

Shipments Financed by the Marshall Plan, 1948–1951

Other 1%
Machines and Vehicles 14%
Raw Materials 37%
Fuel 16%
Food and Other Produce 32%

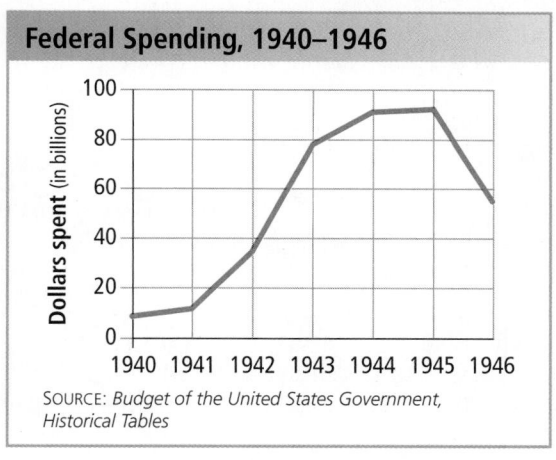

Federal Spending, 1940–1946

Dollars spent (in billions)

SOURCE: *Budget of the United States Government, Historical Tables*

Read the title to learn the main topic of the graph.

Use labels and the key to read the data given in the graph. The line graph is labeled in years, with single-year intervals. The different colors on the circle graph represent the different shipments.

Interpret the graph. Look for interesting patterns in the data. Look at changes over time or compare information for different categories.

Practice and Apply the Skill

Use the graphs above to answer the following questions:

1. What is the title of the line graph? What is its topic?
2. In which year did federal spending increase at the fastest rate? State two generalizations that are supported by the graph.
3. The Marshall Plan was a program under which the United States helped European countries devastated by World War II. According to the circle graph, what proportion of shipments contained fuel? What proportion of shipments contained items that could help factories run?
4. Could the information in the circle graph be shown as a line graph? Explain.

Analyze Maps

Maps can show many different types of information. A physical map represents what a region looks like by showing its major physical features, such as mountains and plains. A political map focuses on elements related to government, such as nations, borders, and cities.

A special-purpose map provides information on a specific subject—for example, land use, population distribution, natural resources, or trade routes. Road maps are special-purpose maps, as are weather maps. These maps often use a variety of colors and symbols to show different pieces of information, so the key is very important. Use the map below and the steps that follow to practice analyzing a special-purpose map.

Louisiana Purchase

Study the title, locator globe, scale bar, and compass rose. Together, these features tell you the map's context—what part of the world it shows and why.

Read the key. Use the key to learn the specific details shown on the map.

Apply the key and labels to the map. Locate the symbols, lines, or colors from the key on the map. Also read any labels on the map. Then, use the information given in the key and labels to understand what the map shows.

Practice and Apply the Skill

Use the map above to answer the following questions:

1. What is the purpose of this map? What part of the world does it show?
2. What does the red dotted line on the map represent?
3. Where did Zebulon Pike's expedition end?
4. Through which region did Lewis and Clark travel on their way to Oregon Country?
5. Does the map provide information about the effects of the Louisiana Purchase? Explain.

Analyze Images

Television, film, the Internet, and print media all carry images that seek to convey information or influence attitudes. To respond, you must develop the ability to understand and interpret visuals. Use the photograph below and the steps that follow to practice analyzing images.

In the 1950s, people everywhere worried about nuclear attacks. This 1952 image shows schoolchildren and their teacher ducking under desks during a nuclear air raid drill.

Identify the content. Look at all parts of the image and determine which are most important.

Note emotions. Study facial expressions and body positions. Consider the emotions they may suggest.

Read captions/credits. Gather information about the image, such as when it was produced.

Study purpose. Consider who might have created this image. Decide if the purpose was to entertain, inform, or persuade.

Consider context. Determine the context in which the image was created—in this case, the Cold War between the United States and the Soviet Union.

Respond. Decide if a visual's impact achieves its purpose—to inform, to entertain, or to persuade.

Practice and Apply the Skill

Use the photograph above to answer the following questions:

1. What is the focus of this photograph?

2. What feelings are conveyed by the children's facial expressions?

3. What do you think the photograph's purpose is?

4. When was this image produced? How did historical context influence its production?

Analyze Primary Sources

Primary sources include official documents and firsthand accounts of events or visual evidence such as photographs, paintings, and political cartoons. Such sources provide valuable information about the past. Use the excerpt below and the steps that follow to learn to analyze primary sources.

In 1914, a great war broke out in Europe. Americans debated whether the United States should take sides in the war. In this excerpt, President Wilson expresses his views:

> **Primary Source** 66The people of the United States are drawn from many nations, and chiefly from the nations now at war. It is natural and inevitable that there should be the utmost variety of sympathy and desire among them. . . . Some will wish one nation, others another, to succeed in the momentous struggle. . . . The people of the United States, whose love of their country and whose loyalty to its government should unite them as Americans all, . . . may be divided in camps of hostile opinion. . . .
>
> Such divisions amongst us would be fatal to our peace of mind and might seriously stand in the way of the proper performance of our duty as the one great nation at peace.99
>
> —speech by Woodrow Wilson, August 19, 1914

Read the headnote, caption, or attribution line. Determine the source's historical context—who wrote it, when, and why.

Read the primary source. Identify and define unfamiliar words. Then, look for the writer's main point.

Identify facts and opinions. Facts can be proven. Opinions reflect a person's views or feelings. Use clues to help identify opinion words: exaggeration, phrases such as *I think*, or descriptive words such as *gorgeous*.

Identify bias and evaluate credibility. Consider whether the author's opinions suggest bias. Evaluate other factors that might lead to author bias, such as his or her previous experiences. Decide if the author knows enough to be credible and was objective enough to be reliable. Determine whether the source might be propaganda, that is, material published to promote a policy, an idea, or a cause.

Practice and Apply the Skill

Political cartoons reflect an artist's observations about events of the time. They often use symbols to represent things or exaggeration to make a point. Use the cartoon at left to answer the following questions.

1. What was happening in Europe when this cartoon was published?
2. What does the kneeling woman represent? the man?
3. What is exaggerated in this cartoon?
4. What opinion is the cartoonist expressing?

The Only Way We Can Save Her

Compare Viewpoints

A person's viewpoint is shaped by subjective influences such as feelings, prejudices, and past experiences. For example, two politicians may recommend two different policies to address the same problem. Likewise, historians often have different interpretations of past events, based on their research and review of other historians' work. Comparing such viewpoints will help you understand issues and develop your own interpretations. The excerpts below offer two different views on why the founders wrote a new U.S. Constitution in 1787. Use the excerpts and the steps that follow to learn about comparing viewpoints.

Comparing Viewpoints

> "[People who favored the Constitution] believed the slogans of 1776 were outmoded; . . . that certain political processes such as war, foreign affairs, and commerce, were national by nature; that the right to tax was essential to any government; and that powers wrested from king and parliament should not be divided among thirteen states, if the American government was to have any influence in the world."
>
> —Samuel E. Morison and Henry S. Commager, *The Growth of the American Republic.* New York: Oxford University Press, 1962.

> "The 55 delegates [to the Constitutional Convention] had much in common. All were white, male, and well educated, and many already knew one another. . . . Not surprisingly, all seemed to agree that the contagion of liberty had spread too far. . . . Most delegates hoped to replace the existing Confederation structure with a national government capable of controlling finances and creating [lender]-friendly [economic] policies. . . ."
>
> —Jacqueline Jones, Peter W. Wood, Elaine Tyler May, Thomas Borstelmann, and Vicki L. Ruiz, *Created Equal: A Social and Political History of the United States.* Boston: Pearson Education, 2003.

Identify the authors. Determine when the historians studied or wrote.

Examine the viewpoints. Identify each author's main idea and evaluate his or her supporting arguments. Determine whether the arguments are logical and the evidence is sufficient to support the main idea. Confirm that the evidence is valid by doing research if necessary.

Determine the author's frame of reference. Consider how the author's background and historical specialty might affect his or her viewpoint.

Recognize facts and opinions. Identify which statements are opinions and which are facts. Opinions represent the author's viewpoint.

Evaluate each viewpoint's validity. Decide whether the viewpoints are based on facts and/or reasonable arguments. Consider whether or not you agree with the viewpoints.

Practice and Apply the Skill

Use the excerpts above to answer the following questions.

1. Who are the authors of these two excerpts? When was each excerpt written?
2. What is each historian's main argument about the U.S. Constitution? What evidence or supporting arguments does each provide?
3. How might each historian's frame of reference affect the viewpoint?
4. Are these two viewpoints based on reasonable arguments? Explain.

Synthesize Information

Just as you might ask several friends about a movie before deciding to see it, you can combine information from different sources to develop a fuller understanding of any topic. This process, called synthesizing, will help you become better informed. Study the documents below about developments during the Great Depression in the 1930s. Then, use the steps that follow to learn to synthesize information.

Document A

Rural poverty during the Great Depression of the 1930s.

Document B

Unemployment, 1928–1933

3% of workforce

25% of workforce

SOURCE: *Historical Statistics of the United States*

Document C

> **Primary Source** ❝ This great nation will endure as it has endured, will revive and will prosper. So, first of all, let me assert my firm belief that the only thing we have to fear is fear itself—nameless, unreasoning, unjustified terror which paralyzes needed efforts to convert retreat into advance. ❞
>
> —President Franklin Roosevelt, First Inaugural Address, 1933

Identify thesis statements. Before you can synthesize, you must understand the thesis, or main idea, of each source. Analyze how the information and ideas in the sources are the same or different. When several sources agree, the information is more reliable and thus more significant.

Draw conclusions and generalize. Look at all the information. Use it to draw conclusions that form a single picture of the topic. Make a generalization, or statement that applies to all the sources.

Construct and test hypotheses. As you learn new information about history, you can begin to form hypotheses, or educated guesses, about events and trends. You might form a hypothesis about why something happened or about the connection between two events. Then, as you learn more, you should test your hypothesis against new information. You should continue to refine your hypothesis based on the new information.

Practice and Apply the Skill

Use the documents above to answer the following questions.

1. What is the main idea of each source?
2. Which sources support the idea that the depression affected people throughout the United States?
3. Form a hypothesis about the Great Depression, based on the information presented.

Analyze Cause and Effect

One of a historian's main tasks is to understand the causes and effects of the event he or she is studying. Study the facts below, which are listed in random order. Then, use the steps that follow to learn how to analyze cause and effect.

The United States, with other nations, fought a war in North and South Korea in the 1950s. This list shows key trends and events related to that war.

- South Korea and its allies fight a 3-year war against North Korea and its allies.
- At the end of World War II, Korea was divided into North Korea, a communist nation, and South Korea, a noncommunist nation, divided at the 38th parallel.
- President Truman worried about the spread of communism in Europe and Asia.
- Communists gained control of mainland China.
- By the end of the Korean War, the border between North Korea and South Korea stood at about the 38th parallel, where it still is today.
- North Korea invaded South Korea.
- As a result of the north's invasion, the south and its allies pushed back.
- The United States continues to station troops along the border dividing North Korea from South Korea.
- Thousands of Americans were killed in the Korean War.
- The United States stations thousands of troops in West Germany.

Identify the central event. Determine to what event or issue all the facts listed relate.

Locate clue words. Use words such as *because, so,* and *due to* to spot causes and effects.

Identify causes and effects. Causes precede the central event and contribute to its occurrence. Effects come after the central event. They occur or emerge as a result of it.

Consider timeframe. Decide if causes have existed for a long period of time or if they emerged just prior to the central event. Short-term causes are usually single or narrowly defined events. Long-term causes usually arise from conditions that are ongoing.

Notice relationships that are not causal. Sometimes events are related, but the earlier event did not cause the later event. For example, although there are parallels, the Russian Revolution was not caused by the American Revolution.

Practice and Apply the Skill

Use the list above to answer the following questions:

1. Which item on the list describes the central event whose causes and effects can be determined?
2. Name two facts that are long-term effects.
3. Name two facts that are probably causes of the central event.
4. Name one fact that is not a cause or effect of the central event, though it is related.

Problem Solving and Decision Making

When you have a problem to solve or decision to make, you can find solutions if you think in a logical way. Study the situation outlined below. Then, use the steps that follow to learn the skills of problem solving and decision making.

Ending the Woes of the Great Depression

In 1929, the United States entered a period of extreme economic difficulties, known as the Great Depression. Thousands of businesses closed, millions of people lost their jobs, and many people had to leave their homes because they couldn't afford the rent or other costs. When the Depression began, Herbert Hoover was President. Later, Franklin Roosevelt was elected to replace Hoover. Both Presidents tried strategies to solve the problems brought on by the Depression.

Options for Presidents Hoover and Roosevelt

Option	Advantages	Disadvantages
1. Allow the economy to correct itself.	• The economy works better when left alone. • The government does not have the right to intervene in local economic affairs.	• This could take a long time, while people continue to suffer. •
2. Let the federal government do whatever is necessary to relieve the effects of the Depression.	• •	• •
3. Take certain federal actions, but rely mainly on the states and on private economic activities.	• •	• •

The Decisions
• President Hoover decided to follow Option 3.
• President Roosevelt decided to follow Option 2.

Effects of the Decisions
• Hoover's actions did not relieve the problems of the Depression quickly enough and he lost his bid for reelection in 1932.
• Roosevelt's actions put some people back to work and relieved some hunger, but did not end the Depression.

Identify the problem. You cannot solve a problem until you examine it and understand it.

Gather information and identify options. Most problems have many solutions. Identify as many solution options as possible.

Consider advantages and disadvantages. Analyze each option by predicting benefits and drawbacks.

Decide on and implement the solution. Pick the option with the most desirable benefits and least important drawbacks.

Evaluate the decision. After awhile, reexamine your solution. If necessary, make a new decision.

Practice and Apply the Skill

Use information from the box above to answer the following questions:

1. What problems did Presidents Hoover and Roosevelt face?
2. Identify at least one advantage and one disadvantage of Options 2 and 3.
3. Why do you think that neither President was able to end the Depression?

Draw Inferences and Conclusions

Text and artwork may not contain all the facts and ideas you need to understand a topic. You may need to draw inferences, that is, to add information from your own experience or knowledge, or use information that is implied but not directly stated in the text or artwork. Study the biography below. Then, use the steps that follow to learn how to draw inferences and conclusions.

HISTORY MAKERS

Ida B. Wells (1862–1931)
Wells had gained fame for her campaign against the lynching of African Americans. But she was also a tireless worker for women's suffrage and joined in the famous 1913 march for universal suffrage that took place in Washington, D.C. Not able to tolerate injustice of any kind, Ida B. Wells, along with Jane Addams, successfully blocked the establishment of segregated schools in Chicago. In 1930, she ran for the Illinois State legislature, which made her one of the first black women to run for public office in the United States.

Study the facts. Determine what facts and information the text states.

Summarize information. Confirm your understanding of the text by briefly summarizing it.

Ask questions. Use who, what, when, where, why, and how questions to analyze the text and learn more. For example, you might compare and contrast, or look for causes or effects.

Add your own knowledge. Consider what you know about the topic. Use this knowledge to evaluate the information.

Draw inferences and conclusions. Use what you learned from the text and your own knowledge to draw inferences and conclusions about the topic.

Practice and Apply the Skill
Use the biography above to answer these questions.
1. Who is discussed in the biography? When did she live?
2. Briefly summarize the text.
3. How might Wells's activities have been unusual for her time?
4. What inferences can you draw about Wells's character from the information in the biography?

Speaking and Listening

Speaking and listening are forms of communication you use every day. In certain situations, however, specific skills and strategies can increase the effectiveness of your communication. The strategies offered in this section will help you improve both your speaking and listening skills.

Participate in Group Discussions

A group discussion is an informal meeting of people that is used to openly discuss ideas and topics. You can express your views and hear those of others.

Identify Issues

Before you speak, identify the issues and main points you want to address. Incorporate what you already know about these issues into your views. Then, find the best words to convey your ideas effectively.

Interact With the Group

As with persuasive writing, in a discussion it helps to accept the validity of opposing views, then argue your position. Always acknowledge the views of others respectfully, but ask questions that challenge the accuracy, logic, or relevance of those views.

Debating

A debate is a formal argument about a specific issue. Explicit rules govern the procedure of a debate, with each debater or team given an allotted time to make arguments and respond to opposing positions. You may also find yourself arguing a position you do not personally hold.

Prepare Your Arguments

If you support a position, use your existing knowledge of it to direct your research. If you personally oppose an assigned position, use that knowledge to identify likely opposing arguments. Generate an outline and then number note cards to highlight key information for each of your main points.

Avoid Common Pitfalls

Stay focused on your arguments. Be aware of words that may reveal bias, such as *unpatriotic*. Speak assertively, but avoid getting overly emotional. Vary the pitch and tone of your voice to keep listeners engaged. Try to speak actively, rather than just reading aloud, and use eye contact and gestures to emphasize your message.

Give an Oral or Multimedia Presentation

An oral or multimedia presentation provides an audience with information through a variety of media.

Choose Media

If you are limited to speaking only, focus your time on developing a presentation that engages listeners. If you can include other media, consider what kind of information each form of media conveys most effectively.

Maps	Graphs/Charts	Pictures	Diagrams	Audio/Video
Clarify historical or geographical information	Show complicated information in an accessible format	Illustrate objects, scenes, or other details	Show links between parts and a whole or a process	Bring the subject to life and engage audiences

Prepare Your Presentation

Gather information using library and online sources. Develop your most important ideas in the body of your presentation. Back up assertions with solid facts and use multimedia examples to illustrate key points.

Present With Authority

Practice your presentation to gain comfort with the ideas and the presentation sequence. Experiment with the timing of how to include multimedia elements. Make sure you have the necessary equipment and know how to use it.

Active Listening

Active listening is a key component of the communication process. Like all communication, it requires your engaged participation.

Focus Your Attention on Ideas

Look at and listen to the speaker. Think about what you hear and see. Which ideas are emphasized or repeated? What gestures or expressions suggest strong feelings? Can you connect the speaker's ideas to your own experiences?

Listen to Fit the Situation

Active listening involves matching your listening to the situation. Listen critically to a speech given by a candidate for office. Listen empathetically to the feelings of a friend. Listen appreciatively to a musical performance.

Ask Questions

Try to think of questions while you're listening. Look at these examples:

Open-ended	Closed	Fact
Why do you think it is so important for young people to vote?	Do you support the current voting age of 18?	How many people between the ages of 18 and 25 voted in the most recent election?

NY Connect to New York

Early Immigrants: The Walloons

Although it is widely known that Dutch immigrants settled in New York, 30 Belgian families (of Walloon background) also traveled on the *Nieu Nederlandt*, the ship chartered by the merchant-owned Dutch West India Company in March 1624. The Walloons were not emigrating for religious freedom, like the English Pilgrims, but simply to gain employment.

The Walloons were French Protestants who had avoided persecution in France by settling in the southern Netherlands. Under the direction of Jesse de Forest, they originally sought permission in 1621 to settle in the Virginia Colony controlled by England and were denied. However, the Walloons had better luck with the Dutch West India Company. Like the Virginia Company you will read about, the Dutch West India Company offered incentives such as free land, free travel, and inexpensive livestock for people to settle in the Americas. The Walloons were attracted by the company's encouragement to find "mines of gold, silver, copper or any other metals, as well as of precious stone, such as diamonds, rubies and the like, together with pearl fisheries."

After arriving in the Manhattan area, some of the families went toward the Delaware River in present-day New Jersey, while others traveled close to the Connecticut River. Yet the majority of Walloon families made their homes in the Dutch colony of New Netherland near the Hudson River, a popular fur trade route. Many of the Walloons worked as fur trappers or traders to pay off their passage to the continent.

Today, visitors can see the Walloon Settlers Monument in Battery Park in lower Manhattan. The approximately 10-foot-tall granite sculpture that commemorates the seventeenth-century immigrants was dedicated on May 20, 1924—the 300th anniversary of the settlers' arrival. In addition, Liberty Island, the location of the Statue of Liberty, was previously called Bedloe's Island after an early Walloon settler named Isaac Bedloe, who owned the island property.

As you will read in the following chapters, the hopes and dreams that drew and continue to draw immigrants to the country helped to transform the United States from sparsely settled territories into a thriving, highly industrialized nation.

ORIGINS OF A
NEW NATION

CONTENTS

**Christopher Columbus
lands in the Caribbean.** ▶

1 Many Cultures Meet
Prehistory–1550

The Discovery

Since departing from Spain, Christopher Columbus and his crew of 90 men had traveled westward across the Atlantic Ocean for more than 3,000 miles. After more than a month at sea, they finally sighted land on October 12, 1492.

The Europeans had hoped to find Asian lands. They had no idea that the islands upon which they landed were not near Asia but near two other continents about which they knew nothing. Columbus's accidental discovery began a chain of events that would bring death and devastation to some and wealth and success to others. In 1776, economist Adam Smith described the effects of European exploration:

66The discovery of America, and . . . a passage to the East Indies by the Cape of Good Hope, are the . . . most important events recorded in the history of mankind. By uniting, in some measure, the most distant parts of the world, by enabling them to relieve one another's wants, to increase one another's enjoyments, and to encourage one another's industry, their general tendency would seem to be beneficial.99
—Adam Smith, *The Wealth of Nations,* 1776

◄ Columbus approaches an island near North America in 1492

 Core Curriculum Preview

Chapter Focus Question: How did the interaction of many cultures after 1492 affect the Americas?

Section 1
The American Indians 1.I.A.2d, 1.I.A.3g, 1.I.A.4, 1.I.B.1

Section 2
The Europeans 1.I.A.3d, 1.I.A.3e, 1.I.A.4, 1.I.D.1c, 1.I.D.1d

Section 3
The West Africans 1.I.D.1, 1.I.D.1c, 1.I.D.1d, 1.I.D.4b, 1.I.D.4c, 2.I.A.2b

Section 4
First Encounters 1.I.B.1, 2.II.B.2c, 2.II.C.3, 2.II.C.6

Use the ☑ **Quick Study Timeline** at the end of this chapter to preview chapter events.

An ivory saltcellar from West Africa

Beaded leather moccasins from the Iroquois

Hohokam plates made from buffalo skin and decorated with red designs

Note Taking Study Guide *Online*
For: Note Taking and American Issues Connector
Web Code: nce-6101

▲ Portrait of a Blackfoot woman by artist George Catlin

The First People

Scholars have studied where the first people of the Americas came from. Many American Indian groups have their own stories about how they came into being. This story comes from the Blackfoot people:

❝One day Old Man decided that he would make a woman and a child. So he formed them both of clay. . . . After he had made the clay into human shapes, he said to it, "You must be people." And then he covered it up and went away. The next morning he went to the place and took off all the covering, but the clay had changed little. The fourth morning, he went to the place . . . and said "Get up and walk. They did so. . . . And that is how we came to be people. It was he who made us.❞

—Story of the origin of the Blackfoot people

The American Indians

 Core Curriculum Objectives

- **1.I.A.2d** Natural resources.
- **1.I.A.3g** Abundance of natural resources.
- **1.I.A.4** Barriers to expansion/development.
- **1.I.B.1** Influences on early Native American Indians.

Terms and People

ice age
migrate
Mayas

Aztecs
adobe
Iroquois League

NoteTaking

Reading Skill: Identify Main Ideas As you read this section, complete an outline like the one below with the main ideas.

> I. The First People of the Americas
>   A. Paleo-Indians
>   1.
>   2.

Why It Matters The people who first inhabited North and South America found a land rich in resources and varied in geographic features. As they spread out across the land, they developed distinctive ways of living and surviving. Their cultures represent a central part of our heritage and history. **Section Focus Question: How did the spread of civilization begin in the Americas?**

The First People of the Americas

Scholars refer to the first humans to live in the Americas as Paleo-Indians. They think these people came from Siberia, a region in Asia that lies just across the narrow Bering Strait from Alaska. Scholars disagree, however, about when and how the Paleo-Indians arrived.

People Migrate to the Americas Until recently, most scholars insisted that the first Americans were hunters who arrived about 15,000 years ago. At that time, the world was experiencing an **ice age,** a time lasting thousands of years during which the Earth was covered by ice and glaciers. Much of the planet's seawater was frozen in polar ice caps. Therefore, the sea level fell as much as 360 feet below today's level. The lower sea levels exposed a land bridge between Siberia and Alaska. Scholars believe Paleo-Indian hunters crossed this land bridge in pursuit of their favored prey—immense mammals such as mammoths, mastodons, and giant bison.

However, some scholars today theorize that the first Americans **migrated,** or traveled, from Asia as many as 40,000 years ago. These were coastal peoples who gathered wild plants and hunted seals and small whales. According to this view, the first people to arrive in the Americas arrived in small boats, eventually working their way down the west coasts of North and South America.

Paleo-Indians Adapt to Climate Change Scholars do agree that about 12,000 to 10,000 years ago, the climate warmed. As temperatures rose, the polar ice melted and the oceans rose close to present-day levels. Together, the warming climate and the spread of skilled Paleo-Indian hunters killed off the mammoths and other large mammals. Meanwhile, the environment became more <u>diverse</u>. The northern grasslands shrank while forests expanded northward.

Paleo-Indians adapted by relying less on hunting large mammals and more on fishing and on gathering nuts, berries, and roots. They also developed tracking techniques needed for hunting small, mobile animals such as deer, antelope, moose, elk, and caribou. The broader array of new food sources led to population growth. As the population grew, it expanded throughout the North and South American continents.

Diverse Cultures Emerge The Indians became culturally diverse as they adapted to their varying local climates and environments. Overtime, their languages, rituals, mythic stories, and kinship systems became more complex and varied. By 1492, the American Indians spoke at least 375 distinct languages, including Athapaskan, Algonquian, Caddoan, Siouan, Shoshonean, and Iroquoian. Each language group divided into many ethnic groups later called tribes or nations. In turn, these subdivided into many smaller groups that identified with a particular village or hunting territory. Each group was headed by a chief, who was usually advised by a council of elders.

The Beginnings of Agriculture Some of these peoples learned how to domesticate wild plants, so that they could be planted and grown for food. About 3,500 years ago in central Mexico, American Indians developed three important crops: maize (corn), squashes, and beans. The expanded food supply promoted population growth, which led to larger, permanent villages. In Mexico, some villages grew into great cities ruled by powerful chiefs. Residents built large pyramids topped with temples. By carefully studying the sun, moon, and stars, the Mexican peoples developed precise calendars of the seasons and the days. Along the Gulf of Mexico and the Caribbean coast, the leading peoples were the Olmecs and later the **Mayas.** In the highlands of central Mexico, the **Aztecs** became the most powerful people.

From Mexico, the methods of learning how to plant, cultivate, and harvest crops slowly spread northward. By about A.D. 1200, crop cultivation was common in the American Southwest, Midwest, Southeast, and parts of the Northeast.

In some places, people clung to a traditional mix of hunting, gathering, and fishing. Some lived in regions that were too cold or dry for farming, such as

Vocabulary Builder
<u>diverse</u>–(duh VERS) *adj.* varied

Geography *Interactive*
For: Interactive map
Web Code: ncp-0102

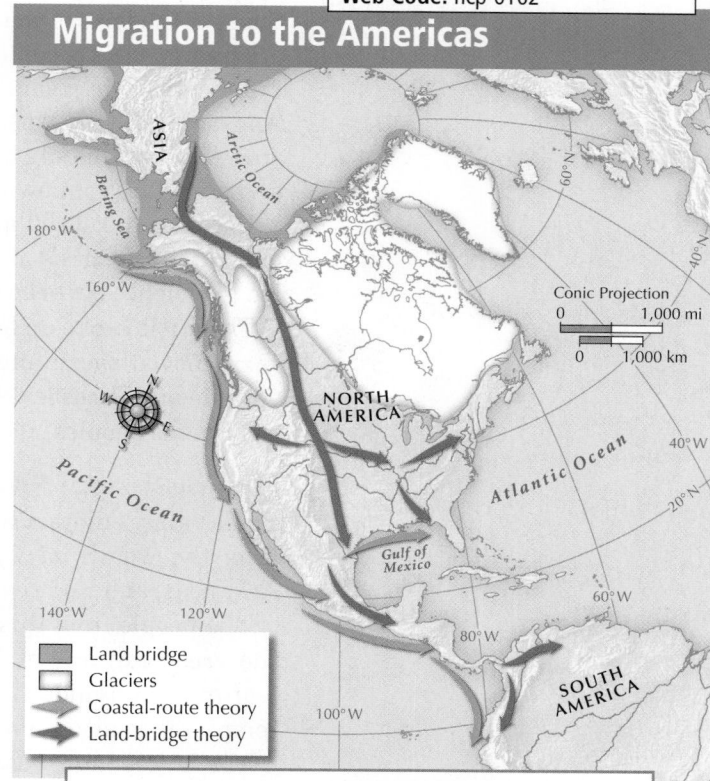

Migration to the Americas

Map Skills The first people to come to the Americas spread slowly across the continents.
1. **Regions** What part of North America was filled with glaciers?
2. **Analyze Information** What geographical features may have caused people to keep moving south?

the frigid subarctic regions of Alaska, the Sierra Nevada, the Rocky Mountains, and the arid western Great Plains and Great Basin. In addition, coastal peoples of present-day California and the Pacific Northwest did not need to farm because their fishing—usually for salmon—and their gathering of nuts, seeds, and berries was so productive.

✓ **Checkpoint** How did the ice age lead to the migration of people to the Americas?

Early American Indian Cultures

As you just read, early people grew in numbers and developed permanent villages in areas where farming was practiced. A little more than 2,000 years ago, such villages began to appear in what would later become the United States.

The Southwest The first farming villages north of present-day Mexico emerged in the arid Southwest. There, the cultivation of crops required building ponds, dams, and ditches in order to irrigate, or bring water to, the fields. Building such complex systems required leadership by a group of priests and chiefs.

The Hohokams lived in the Gila and Salt river valleys of present-day southern Arizona. Over the course of their history, they built more than 500 miles of irrigation canals. The Hohokam irrigation canals were so elaborate that later peoples referred to the Hohokams as Canal Builders. In their largest village, about 1,000 people inhabited row houses built of **adobe**, a type of sun-dried brick. Some of the houses were three stories tall.

The Anasazis occupied the upland canyons in the Four Corners region at the intersection of Arizona, New Mexico, Utah, and Colorado. At Chaco Canyon, the Anasazis built an especially complex village that required 30,000 tons of sandstone blocks. This site became the center of the Anasazi world. Some of the multistory dwellings, known as pueblos, rose five stories and had about 600 rooms.

Between A.D. 1100 and 1300, both the Hohokams and the Anasazis experienced a severe crisis as a prolonged drought reduced crops. The resulting famine led to violence between rival villages that were competing for scarce resources.

The crisis broke up both the Hohokam and Anasazi villages. Most of the Anasazis moved south and east in search of water. They resettled along the Rio Grande and Pecos River, in present-day New Mexico. Today, they are known as the Pueblo peoples.

The Mississippi River Valley Unlike the arid Southwest, the Mississippi River valley enjoys a humid and temperate climate. The Mississippi River collects the waters of wide-ranging tributaries, including the Ohio, Missouri, Arkansas, and Red rivers.

The people from this area, known as the Mississippians, were influenced by the great cultures of Mexico. They built large towns around central plazas, featuring pyramids made of earth. At the top of the pyramids, they built wooden temples that also served as the residences of chiefs.

The largest and wealthiest city of the Mississippian culture was at Cahokia, in present-day southwestern Illinois. Cahokia benefited from being located near the junctures of the Missouri, Tennessee, Ohio, and Mississippi rivers. That site provided fertile soil and excellent trade connections with distant groups. At its peak in the year 1100, Cahokia had a population of at least 10,000 people and perhaps as many as 40,000.

During the twelfth century, Cahokia's residents abandoned the city. As in the Southwest, evidence suggests that an environmental crisis led to social conflict. The growing population had depleted the soil and deer. Hunger led to disease

ANCIENT CLIFF DWELLERS

The word *Anasazi* has come to mean "ancient people." However, the term is not a Pueblo word but a Navajo word meaning "enemy ancestors." Today, Pueblo Indians refer to their ancestors as Ancestral Puebloans.

Before the ancient Pueblo people moved into cliff dwellings, they lived on the flat tops of mountains. As the population increased, residences built from hand-cut stone blocks rose along the sides of canyon walls. Shown here is Cliff Palace, built nearly 900 years ago. It is located in Mesa Verde National Park in Colorado. Embedded in the mountainside, the building gained heat from the sun in winter, while overhanging rock protected the structure from rain and snow.

▲ Ancestral Puebloan rock art

A black-on-white ceramic jar ▲ shows a typical design used by the Ancestral Puebloans.

The people living here inhabited nearly 220 rooms. The circular chambers are entryways into kivas, which were large underground rooms used for religious ceremonies and political meetings. Kiva walls were painted with geometric designs and scenes from daily life. As illustrated here, the men and women had specific daily chores to accomplish. ▼

Thinking Critically

1. **Draw Conclusions** How did the cliff dwellings protect inhabitants from enemy attack?

2. **Analyze Information** Why do you think water-control features such as canals were important?

Conic Projection
0   250   500 mi
0   250   500 km

Locations of Native American Culture Groups

Culture Region	Culture Groups
Arctic	Aleuts, Inuits, Kutchins
Subarctic	Beavers, Crees, Tlingits
Northwest Coast	Bella Coolas, Chinooks, Coos, Nootkas, Tlingits, Yakimas
California/Great Basin/Plateau	Pomos, Shoshones, Nez Percés
Southwest	Apaches, Hohokams, Navajos, Pimas, Pueblos, Hopis, Zunis
Great Plains	Arapahos, Blackfeet, Cheyennes, Comanches, Crees, Crows, Kiowas, Omahas, Pawnees, Sioux, Wichitas
Southeast	Chickasaws, Choctaws, Creeks, Delawares, Cherokees, Tuscaroras, Mississippians, Natchez, Seminoles
Northeast	Algonquins, Hopewells, Iroquois, Leni-Lenapes, Winnebagos

Map Skills Many Native American cultures emerged in the Americas centuries before the arrival of Columbus.

1. **Locate:** In which region did Native Americans live mainly by hunting?

2. **Draw Inferences** What factors may have contributed to the rapid population growth in the Northeast?

and to fighting among villages. Although Cahokia disappeared, Mississippian culture still thrived to the south at Moundville in Alabama, Etowah in Georgia, and Spiro in Oklahoma.

The Great Plains Between the Rocky Mountains and the Mississippi River, the Great Plains is an immense, windy, and arid grassland in the heart of North America. The Great Plains receive only between 12 and 20 inches of rain a year. Only a few major rivers flow year-round. Instead of trees, drought-resistant grasses cover the land. Thus, the Great Plains favor grazing animals, especially the bison, or buffalo. When Europeans first arrived, the Great Plains probably supported more than 20 million bison.

During the ninth century, some Mississippians moved westward up the major river valleys onto the Great Plains. They built villages and planted crops beside the rivers. In the hotter southern valleys, people lived in well-ventilated beehive-shaped houses made from wooden frames covered with grass thatch. In colder northern valleys, villagers built log lodges well insulated with earth. In the summer, villagers ventured on foot onto the plains to hunt bison. While on the hunt, they lived in mobile camps. Their shelters were called tepees—cone-shaped tents of tanned bison hides stretched over a frame of cottonwood poles.

Great Plains villagers sometimes clashed with nomads who came from the Rocky Mountains to the west. Devoted to hunting, the nomads did not cultivate crops. By the fifteenth century, most of these nomads were Athapaskan speakers. Their enemies called them Apaches.

Some nomad bands established economic ties with the villagers of the valleys. The nomads traded buffalo meat and hides for maize, beans, squash, turquoise, pottery, and cotton blankets. The villagers would <u>forgo</u> this trade, however, when they lacked surplus food. Angered, the nomads raided the villages.

Eastern Woodlands The eastern region featured a vast forest atop rolling hills and a low range of mountains, the Appalachians. Many streams, rivers, and lakes drained this wooded land.

Stretching from eastern Texas to the Atlantic Ocean, the Southeast has mild winters and warm summers with plenty of rainfall. The Cherokees were the largest group in the Southeast. They lived in present-day western North Carolina and eastern Tennessee. Other people in the Southeast included Choctaws, Chickasaws, Natchez, and Creeks. Because of the long growing season, the Choctaws, the Creeks, and other southeastern groups were primarily farmers, but they also depended on hunting and fishing. They knew what plants to use to make rope, medicine, and clothing. Their main crops were corn, beans, squashes, and pumpkins.

Northeastern people developed into two major language groups: the Algonquians and the Iroquoians. The Algonquins occupied the Atlantic seaboard from present-day Virginia north to the mouth of the St. Lawrence River. The Iroquois lived around Lake Ontario and Lake Erie and along the upper St. Lawrence River.

A chief difference between the two cultures lay in their housing. Algonquins lived in wigwams: oval frames between 10 and 16 feet in diameter that are made of saplings covered with bark sheets or woven mats. Using similar materials, the Iroquois built larger multifamily longhouses, some more than 200 feet in length.

Five Iroquois peoples—the Mohawks, Oneidas, Onondagas, Cayugas, and Senecas—united to form a loose confederation, known as the **Iroquois League**. The Iroquois League was not a European-style nation. Lacking central authority, it was mainly a ritual forum for promoting peaceful cooperation among the member nations.

Vocabulary Builder
<u>forgo</u>—(for GOH) *v.* to decide not to do something

▼ Painting of an Algonquin village

The Iroquois League's guiding law was a constitution, which was passed down orally. One version of this constitution includes the following:

> **Primary Source** "The Lords of the Confederacy of the Five nations shall be mentors of the people for all time. . . . Their hearts shall be full of peace and good will and their minds filled with a yearning for the welfare of the people of the Confederacy."
> —The Iroquois Constitution

 Checkpoint What building style did the Mississippian culture take from Mexican culture?

Common Cultural Features

Despite their cultural diversity, most Native American groups shared several cultural features. For example, most American Indians did not have centralized nations like those in Europe. Instead, political power was spread among many local chiefs with limited authority.

American Indians believed that spirits could be found in every plant, animal, rock, cloud, and body of water. If properly flattered, the spirits could help people catch or grow what they needed. If offended, spirits might hide the animals or fish or destroy the corn crop. The spiritual leaders of the tribe, known as shamans, mediated between their people and the spirit beings. They conducted rituals to promote the hunt, secure the crops, and protect warriors.

American Indians owned little private property. Some families owned garden plots and hunting territories, but they could not sell them. Most local land was considered a common ground for every resident to use.

There was a respectful equality among the various groups of Indians. Usually, socioeconomic division ran along gender lines. Men assumed more dangerous tasks, such as hunting and warfare. Women, meanwhile, cared for the young children, wove baskets and made pottery, prepared meals, and gathered food. If their people cultivated crops, that work also usually fell to women.

 Checkpoint What were three common cultural characteristics shared by most Native Americans?

Progress Monitoring *Online*
For: Self-test with vocabulary practice
Web Code: nca-0104

Comprehension

1. **Terms and People** Explain how each of the following terms is significant in understanding American Indian culture in North America.
   - ice age
   - migrate
   - Mayas
   - Aztecs
   - adobe
   - Iroquois League

2. **NoteTaking Reading Skill: Identify Main Ideas** Use your outline to answer the Section Focus Question: How did the spread of civilization begin in the Americas?

Writing About History

3. **Quick Write: Gather Details** Narrative essays tell a story and challenge you to use your imagination. List the details you will use to write a narrative essay about how life changed when your group shifted from nomad ways to farming.

Critical Thinking

4. **Identify Points of View** What two leading theories explain how the first humans came to the Americas?

5. **Summarize** What sequence of events led to the expansion of people throughout the continents of North America and South America?

6. **Analyze Information** Why do you think more advanced cultures would develop among farming societies rather than among hunting-and-gathering societies?

◀ Prince Henry

WITNESS HISTORY AUDIO

Prince Henry the Navigator

For some time, Europeans dreamed of finding a shorter and easier route to Asia. Portugal led the way. Prince Henry the Navigator established a school where his sailors learned about navigation, mapmaking, and ship design. His sailors breached the unknown, taking voyages to islands off the coast of Africa. Duarte Pacheco Pereira, a Portuguese sea captain and explorer, explained the significance of the explorations in his navigation manual:

❝The benefits conferred on Portugal by the virtuous Prince Henry are such that its kings and people are greatly indebted to him, for a great part of the Portuguese people now earn their livelihood in the lands which he discovered, and the kings of Portugal derive great profit from this commerce.❞

—from *Esmeraldo de situ orbis,* by Duarte Pacheco Pereira, 1505–1508

▲ Portuguese sailors traveled in caravels, a new kind of sailing ship.

The Europeans

NY Core Curriculum Objectives

- **1.I.A.3d** Atlantic/Pacific oceans
- **1.I.A.3e** Coastlines
- **1.I.A.4** Barriers to expansion/development
- **1.I.D.1c** Ethnicity
- **1.I.D.1d** Religion

Terms and People

Middle Ages
Renaissance
reconquista

Prince Henry
  the Navigator

NoteTaking

Reading Skill: Summarize As you read this section, fill in a chart like the one below to describe Europe before and after the 1400s.

```
            Europe in the 1400s
    ┌───────────┬──────────┬──────────┐
  Economy      Society     Politics
• Agriculture     •            •
    •             •            •
```

Why It Matters Europe in the 1400s experienced enormous cultural, economic, and technological changes. As new ideas swept the continent, some Europeans began to look beyond their shores to satisfy their growing ambitions. They were about to enter an age of discovery and exploration that would change not only Europe but much of the world as well. **Section Focus Question: How did Europeans begin to explore more of the world?**

Life in Europe in the 1400s

As the 1400s dawned, Europe concentrated on developing its political and cultural institutions. The earlier years of the **Middle Ages,** which began with the collapse of the Roman Empire, were marked by the absence of an effective central government and the constant threat of famine, disease, and foreign invasion. However, as new institutions and ideas slowly took hold, a new civilization emerged in Europe.

An Economy Based on Agriculture Hand tools and draft animals sustained an economy that was overwhelmingly agricultural. The population was recovering from the drastic effects of bubonic plague, known as the Black Death. During the 1340s, that epidemic had killed about a third of the Europeans. The great majority of the people lived in the countryside. Cities, however, were growing, especially in northern Italy and in the Netherlands. There, the small-scale manufacturing of cloth, tools, weapons, and ceramics came

Trade Towns

As trade increased during the Middle Ages, towns located near rivers prospered. Large trade fairs were set up in some cities, where the townspeople and merchants bought and sold goods. *How might location near a river or ocean lead to the economic growth of a town?*

Vocabulary Builder

adhere–(ad HEER) *v.* to stay firm in supporting or approving

from many workshops of artisans rather than from mechanized factories. The cities also served as bases for the merchants.

A Society of Unequal Classes Extremes of wealth and poverty characterized European society. A ruling elite of less than 5 percent of the population controlled almost all of the land. The most prestigious men were aristocrats—people who had inherited social rank and title and, generally, landed estates worked by peasants. Less honored, but often wealthier, were the great merchants who shipped cargoes between cities for profit. The elite also included leaders of the Roman Catholic Church. A monarch—usually a king but sometimes a queen—sat on top of the social pyramid in each kingdom.

Under the domination of this small elite class were the commoners. About three fifths of western Europeans were working poor. In good years, they subsisted by farming on land rented from an aristocrat or by selling their labor. In hard times, many fell into the ranks of the beggars. The most prosperous commoners were middle-class families. They owned enough property to employ themselves as farmers, artisans, and shopkeepers. Such people, however, accounted for only a fifth of the population.

Warring Kingdoms Western Europe was divided into a number of warring kingdoms. The most important were Castile, Portugal, France, and England. Each was ruled by a monarch who, in turn, depended on the elite class to do much of the governing. By waging war to conquer new territories, monarchs hoped to build their own power and to distract their often unruly aristocrats.

 Checkpoint What was the structure of European society during the 1400s?

Europe Looks Beyond Its Borders

During the Middle Ages, the Church strictly controlled intellectual life. Church leaders sought to ensure that all thought <u>adhered</u> to their understanding of the world. Church leaders felt that everything worth knowing had been discovered by the Greeks and Romans and recorded in the Bible. Those who pursued scientific discoveries that went against Church teachings risked prosecution for heresy by Church courts.

Europe in the 1400s was in an era of rapid change. Though old ways of thinking persisted, many factors, especially rapidly widening trade, were broadening people's views of the world.

The Crusades and the Expansion of Trade In the latter half of the Middle Ages, European Christians and Southwest Asian Muslims fought one another in a series of religious wars known as the Crusades. The goal was to capture and hold Jerusalem and all of the Holy Land where Jesus had lived and died. In the end, the Muslims defeated the Christian Crusaders.

However there were other lasting effects of the Crusades that benefited the people of Europe. Europeans became aware of distant lands and different ways of life. Trade was encouraged. Crusaders returned home with goods and raw materials from the East, including silks, gems, and spices. Increasing demand for these products caused European traders to expand their businesses to Asia.

Trade Routes in Europe, 1000–1300

Geography *Interactive*
For: Interactive map
Web Code: ncp-0105

○ Major centers of trade
— Major trade routes

Conic Projection
0 200 400 mi
0 200 400 km

The Renaissance and New Ideas By the mid-1400s, a new era had begun in Europe. Known as the **Renaissance,** it featured renewed interest in learning and the advancement of the arts and sciences. During the Renaissance, trade with and awareness of the world beyond Europe expanded. This, in turn, produced wealth for the increasingly powerful nations of Europe. This wealth and power would fuel more explorations. The effect for the people of Europe—and for the rest of the world—would be profound.

Popular literature reinforced the European longing for access to the fabled riches of India and China. During the fifteenth century, the development of the printing press lowered the cost and increased the volume of publishing. Books became available to more than the wealthy and leisured elite. The spread of literature helped promote the daring new Renaissance ideas of individualism and experimentation.

Readers especially delighted in vivid reports of the wealth and power of India and China. The most famous travel account came from Marco Polo, a thirteenth-century Italian merchant who had traveled across Asia to visit the emperor of China. Inspired by such accounts, Europeans longed to enlist Asian peoples and Asian wealth for a renewed crusade against Islam.

Europeans Seek New Trade Routes The Europeans, who were Christian, felt hemmed in by the superior wealth, power, and technology of their rivals and neighbors, the Muslims. Muslims subscribed to the religion of Islam. Dominated by the Ottoman Turks, the vast Muslim realm stretched across North Africa and around the southern and eastern Mediterranean Sea to embrace parts of Eastern Europe and Southwest Asia. It also continued east through Central

Map Skills As trade increased after the Middle Ages in Europe, major trade routes were established across the Mediterranean.

1. **Region** What major trade cities were located in Africa and Asia?

2. **Synthesize Information:** How do you think the lives of people living in the trade cities were affected?

Renaissance Changes Europe ☑ Quick Study

- Increased trade and exploration bring knowledge of other lands.
- Printing press spreads literature and new ideas throughout Europe.
- Prince Henry the Navigator improves navigation and shipbuilding techniques.
- Competing monarchs sponsor voyages to gain wealth and territory.
- Portuguese shipbuilders develop the caravel, designed to travel long distances.
- New navigation tools such as the compass, the astrolabe, and more accurate maps allow longer voyages.

The Astrolabe
Navigators could determine a ship's latitude, as well as local time, with an astrolabe.

and Southeast Asia. The long and usually secure trade routes of the Muslim world extended from Morocco to the East Indies and from Mongolia to West Africa. The Ottoman Turks even invaded southeastern Europe, capturing the strategic city of Constantinople in 1453.

✔ **Checkpoint** How did the Crusades help to expand Europe's horizons?

The Portuguese Begin to Explore

European expansionists found hope on the Iberian Peninsula of southwestern Europe. There, the kingdoms of Aragon, Castile, and Portugal were waging the *reconquista* (reconquest) to drive out the Muslim Moors who had ruled Iberia for centuries. In 1469, the marriage of Prince Ferdinand and Queen Isabella united Aragon and Castile to create "Spain." In 1492, Ferdinand and Isabella completed the *reconquista* by seizing Granada, the last Muslim stronghold in Iberia. Long and violent, the *reconquista* promoted a zealous crusading spirit for spreading the Christian faith.

Facing the Atlantic Ocean and close to Africa, Spain and Portugal were well situated to seek new trade routes and to expand European influence. The Portuguese took the early lead in venturing out into the Atlantic. They relied on several new devices: the compass, the astrolabe, and the quadrant. These innovations helped sailors determine their location and direction when beyond sight of land. Shipbuilders were producing sturdier ships capable of sailing hundreds of miles. The caravel had a stern rudder, three masts, and a combination of square and triangular *lateen* sails.

Starting in 1419, **Prince Henry the Navigator** directed Portuguese efforts to sail into the Atlantic, spread Christianity, and outflank Muslim domination of trade. Henry founded a school of navigation and sponsored several expeditions down the coast of West Africa. By sailing southward, the Portuguese hoped to reach the sources of the gold, ivory, and slaves that Muslim merchants transported across the great Sahara.

✔ **Checkpoint** Why were the Portuguese venturing into the Atlantic Ocean?

SECTION 2 Assessment

Progress Monitoring *Online*
For: Self-test with vocabulary practice
Web Code: nca-0106

Comprehension

1. **Terms and People** Explain how each of the following terms describes Europe in the fifteenth century.
   - Middle Ages
   - Renaissance
   - *reconquista*

2. **NoteTaking** **Reading Skill: Summarizing** Use your chart to answer the Section Focus Question: How did Europeans begin to explore more of the world?

Writing About History

3. **Quick Write: Use Sensory Details** You are a traveler entering a trade city. Use the image of the trade town to describe the sights and sounds that you encounter.

Critical Thinking

4. **Draw Inferences** Why do you think European technology became more advanced after the 1500s?

5. **Analyze Information** How did the Renaissance affect Europeans in the fifteenth century?

6. **Synthesize Information** Why do you think the *reconquista* sparked Spain's interest in exploration?

SECTION 3

▲ Mansa Musa, ruler of Mali

WITNESS HISTORY 🔊 AUDIO

Timbuktu

The city of Timbuktu first flourished as a trade center in the kingdom of Mali before becoming the intellectual center of West Africa. In the early 1500s, Leo Africanus, a Muslim of Spanish birth who had traveled widely in Africa, published his description of the great West African city of Timbuktu. It tells of the learned populace—and of a practice that would have a deep impact on West Africa's future.

❝The people of Timbuktu are of a peaceful nature. They have a custom of almost continuously walking about the city in the evening (except for those that sell gold), between 10 P.M. and 1 A.M., playing musical instruments and dancing. The citizens have at their service many slaves, both men and women.❞

—Leo Africanus, *The Description of Africa*, 1526

The West Africans

NY Core Curriculum Objectives

- **1.I.D.1** Characteristics
- **1.I.D.1c** Ethnicity
- **1.I.D.1d** Religion
- **1.I.D.4b** Distribution
- **1.I.D.4c** Density
- **2.I.A.2b** Slave trade

Terms and People

Ghana   Mansa Musa
Mali   Songhai

NoteTaking

Reading Skill: Identify Details As you read, complete a concept web like the one below with details about major West African kingdoms.

Why It Matters While American Indian cultures developed in the Americas and Europeans experienced the Renaissance, rich and varied cultures emerged in West Africa. The interaction between European and West African cultures in the 1400s helped set the stage for the transatlantic system of slavery. **Section Focus Question: What was life like in West Africa before the age of European exploration?**

West African Kingdoms

Throughout the 1400s, Portuguese sailors explored farther and farther south along the West African coast. By 1470, they had passed the equator to reach the Gulf of Guinea. Initially, the mariners acted as pirates, seizing gold, pepper, and slaves. But African resistance soon forced the Portuguese to shift to trade. The West Africans possessed civilizations that compelled grudging respect from the European mariners.

Geography Encourages Trade Western Africa is a varied land. An enormous desert—the Sahara—dominates the northern part. To the south of the Sahara lies a broad grassland, or savanna. South of this savanna is a lush region that is well watered by several major rivers, including the Niger and the Senegal. The West African landscape abounds with valuable natural resources—in particular, salt, found in the Sahara, and gold, located in the valleys along the Atlantic coast.

West African Trade Routes, A.D. 800–A.D. 1600

Map Skills Trade routes across West Africa were well established by 1600.

1. **Locate:** (a) Ghana, (b) Mali, (c) Songhai

2. **Synthesize Information** Besides keeping European rivals away, why do you think African rulers allowed only Portuguese trading posts along the coast?

Geography *Interactive*

For: Interactive map
Web Code: ncp-0107

Vocabulary Builder

<u>domain</u>–(doh MAYN) *n.* an area of land owned or controlled by one person, group, or government

Hundreds of years ago, these resources provided for a thriving trade network among the people of West Africa. This trade revolved around certain trading towns, which grew into great and powerful empires. The trading empires of West Africa commanded trading routes that linked the region with North Africa, the Mediterranean, and Asia. Trade promoted rich and thriving cultures.

Ghana Between A.D. 300 and 1500, three kingdoms rose and fell in West Africa. The earliest kingdom, **Ghana,** would expand from the Sahara to the Gulf of Guinea and from the Atlantic Ocean to the Niger River. Ghana rose to prominence around A.D. 800.

A thriving caravan trade with African peoples across the Sahara to Morocco resulted in extensive Muslim influence in North Africa. By the eleventh century, Ghana supplied much of the gold for the Mediterranean region.

The ancient kingdom had large towns, beautifully designed buildings, a system of commerce, and a complex political structure. A Spanish Muslim writer from the eleventh century recorded this account of the lavish lifestyle of Ghana's king:

Primary Source "The King adorns himself . . . wearing necklaces around his neck and bracelets on his forearms, and he puts on a high cap decorated with gold and wrapped in a turban of fine cotton. He sits in audience to hear grievances against officials in a domed pavilion around which stand ten horses covered with gold-embroidered materials."

—Al-Bakri, *The Book of Routes and Realms*

Mali Attacks from outsiders eventually weakened Ghana's control of West African trade. The kingdom's power faded until, finally, Ghana was supplanted around A.D. 1200 by a new kingdom known as **Mali.** The most famous ruler of Mali was a king named **Mansa Musa.** During his reign in the early 1300s, he expanded Mali's <u>domain</u> westward to the Atlantic coast and increased the role of Islam, a religious faith that spread slowly through North Africa in the early 700s, when the region was under Muslim conquest. His promotion of Islamic scholarship helped lead to the founding of the famous university at Timbuktu. This great center of learning and culture was known throughout the Islamic world. The kingdom of Mali weakened after the death of Mansa Musa in 1332.

Songhai By the 1400s, another empire emerged: **Songhai.** Under the rule of Askia Muhammad, Songhai sustained an Islamic system of education based at the capital of Timbuktu. Like Ghana and Mali, Songhai grew rich from trade. In 1468, Songhai's armies conquered Mali and its capital. As a result, Songhai became the most powerful and largest kingdom in West Africa.

Other Kingdoms In addition to the great empires of Ghana, Mali, and Songhai, West Africa also hosted smaller kingdoms. For example, to the south of

TRADE FLOURISHES IN
ANCIENT GHANA

Gold and salt dominated the trans-Sahara trade in ancient Africa. Caravans carried salt from mines in the Sahara to trading areas along the Niger River in present-day Mali. Traders from these caravans hoped to exchange salt for gold that was mined in forests near the source of the Niger River. This trade established the wealth of ancient Ghana because salt traders, after crossing the Sahara, passed through the capital of Ghana, where they paid a tax on goods brought into Ghana.

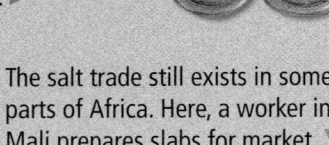

Ghana markets ▲ offered a variety of food products, including dates.

Standard weights, such as the one shown, were used to weigh gold. ▶

The salt trade still exists in some parts of Africa. Here, a worker in Mali prepares slabs for market. ▼

Thinking Critically

1. **Draw Inferences** Why do you think the ruler of Ghana guarded the location of the gold mines?

2. **Analyze Information** The king of Ghana built a special city to receive Muslim merchants, traders, and foreigners. Why do you think the king felt this was needed?

History *Interactive* ✳

For: To discover more about Ancient Ghana
Web Code: ncp-0113

The route taken by most traders to Ghana would have started in North Africa and ended in Kumbi Saleh, the capital of ancient Ghana. Built on the edge of the Sahara, the city became an important trade center. After traveling many months through the desert in large camel caravans (sometimes taking as long as three months), prosperous Muslim merchants, as illustrated below, arrived to trade and sell goods.

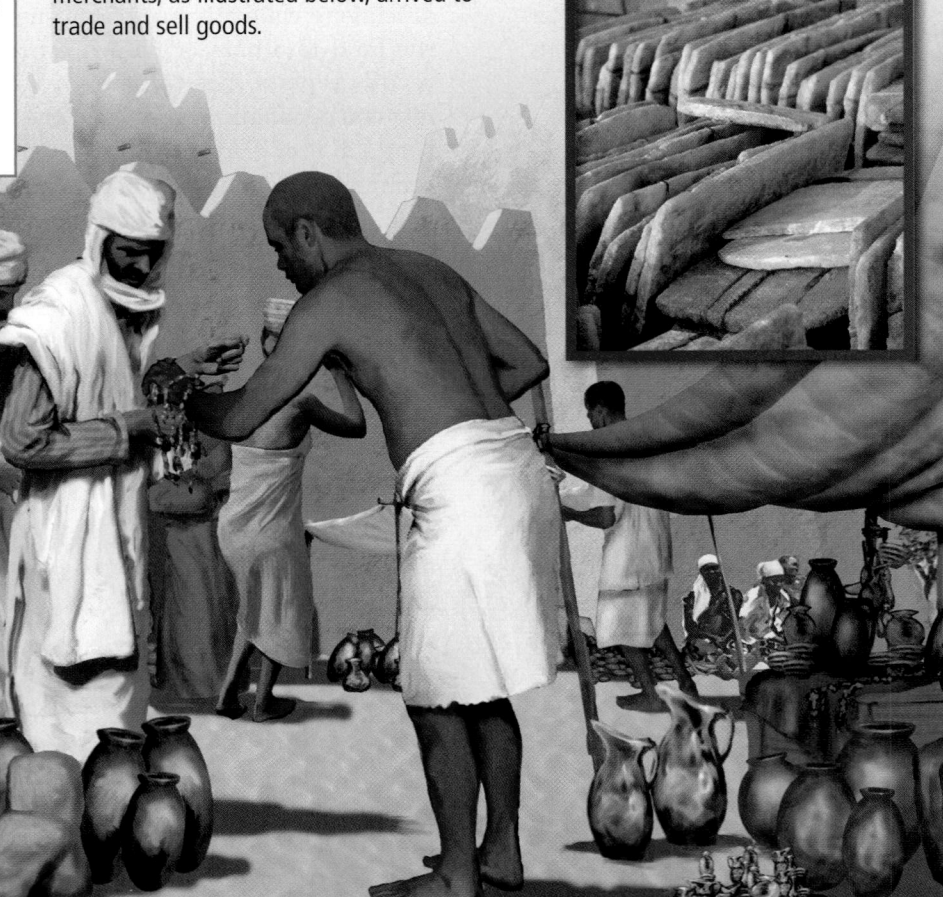

Songhai, the kingdom of Benin occupied the tropical forest along the Gulf of Guinea. Known as "obas," the kings of Benin promoted art, especially sculptures in bronze or ivory. The Hausa people built seven cities in present-day Nigeria and Niger. Both became well known for producing beautiful cloth and for establishing extensive trade.

 Checkpoint Why did West Africa become an important trade center?

West African Life

The peoples of West Africa, like the peoples of the Americas, were a diverse group with highly developed civilizations. Religious beliefs and family bonds were among the ways of life that reinforced a sense of community.

Religious Beliefs West African spiritual beliefs varied. Caravans brought Islam across the Sahara to the people of the savanna. In many places, such as along the coast of the Gulf of Guinea, Africans held traditional beliefs. These involved a supreme creator supplemented by many spirit beings who inhabited every object and creature of the natural world. The people of West Africa believed, just as the Amerian Indians did, that spirits lived in rain, trees, rocks, and animal life. Furthermore, these spirit beings could also intervene in human affairs. Therefore, the spirits were specially honored. Ancestors, too, became spirits of enduring influence in the extended families that formed the major support system of African society.

Economy and Society Land did not belong to individuals as private property. Instead, land belonged to extended kinship networks derived from an ancient ancestor. Powerful kings could assign particular territories to favored officials to collect tribute from the peasants. But these favorites could not sell the land to others or pass it on to their heirs. Furthermore, the kings could readily replace these officials, reassigning that particular land to a new favorite. The peasants who worked the land could not be removed from it, nor could they sell it or rent it to others. Often the people of a village worked the land in common and divided the harvest according to the number of people in each household. Owning slaves (or wives), rather than property, determined one's wealth.

 Checkpoint What role did landownership hold in West African culture?

Slavery in Africa

Slavery was common in West Africa. In fact, human beings were frequently used as items of trade, along with gold, salt, ivory, and other valuable resources found in the region.

African Rulers and Arab Traders West African rulers sold about 1,000 slaves annually to Arab traders, who carried them in caravans across the Sahara to the Mediterranean. Thus, the slave trade was an important part of West Africa's economy.

Slavery was a common fate for people who were conquered or captured during warfare. People who committed crimes or were otherwise found undesirable to the community might also be enslaved.

African slavery was certainly brutal in many ways. Individual slaves were often mistreated, and some even died. In general, however, African slavery differed from the system that would eventually develop in the Americas. In Africa, slaves were usually adopted by the families into which they were sold. They could also marry and, as a rule, their children did not inherit the status of

slaves. They could even become important officials and soldiers. Powerful kings relied on slave armies and slave officials to control local nobles. Although dependent upon the king, successful slave commanders and officials could become wealthy from the rewards of their positions. Most importantly, slavery was not based on the notion of racial superiority or inferiority.

The Portuguese Exploit the Slave Trade When the Portuguese first sailed along the coast of Africa, they were largely interested in gold. As they began to extend their influence, Portuguese explorers established a profitable trade with the people of West Africa. They exported a variety of goods, including peppers, ivory, copper, and African slaves. In this way, Europeans in the mid-1400s first became involved in the long-standing slave trade of Africa.

To conduct their African trade, the Portuguese mariners needed the assent of the powerful West African kings. Commercial treaties permitted the Portuguese to construct fortified trading posts at key harbors along the coast. The forts served to keep away rival European vessels. Indeed, the Portuguese treated rivals brutally, confiscating their vessels and casting their crews into the ocean to drown.

The Portuguese did not invent the slave trade, but they did greatly expand it. The first major European trading fort was established in 1482. It became a major trading center for slaves. By 1500, Europeans purchased about 1,800 African slaves a year. This nearly doubled the previous trade of some 1,000 slaves between Arab traders and the West African rulers. Some slaves were shipped to Europe. Most, however, worked on sugar plantations located on the Madeira, Canary, and Azore islands. These were islands in the East Atlantic claimed in the 1400s by Iberian explorers. Growing numbers went across the Atlantic to new plantations in the Americas. Thus began the brutal exploitation of West Africans enslaved by Europeans—a fate that would befall millions more African men and women in the centuries ahead.

✔ **Checkpoint** How did the Portuguese come into contact with West Africans?

Slave Trade
Local African rulers allowed Europeans to build slaveholding compounds. Captured Africans were marched to these compounds.

Progress Monitoring *Online*
For: Self-test with vocabulary practice
Web Code: nca-0108

Comprehension

1. **Terms and People** Explain how each term or person below describes West African culture between 1400 and 1600.
   - Ghana
   - Mali
   - Mansa Musa
   - Songhai

2. **NoteTaking Reading Skill: Identify Details** Use your concept web to answer the Section Focus Question: What was life like in West Africa before the age of European exploration?

Writing About History

3. **Quick Write: Research Details** Mansa Musa has invited several well-known scholars to teach at a university in Timbuktu. Research a description of the city. Then, write an account of the scholars' visit to the city.

Critical Thinking

4. **Understanding Cause and Effect** How did the presence of resources such as gold and salt help lead to the development of great kingdoms in West Africa?

5. **Compare and Contrast** How did slavery as practiced in West Africa differ from that later practiced in the Americas?

6. **Summarize** How did the Portuguese benefit from the slave trade?

▲ In this painting, Native Americans and newly arriving Europeans greet one another.

WITNESS HISTORY AUDIO

The First Meeting

The arrival of Europeans in the Americas dramatically affected the native peoples who had lived there for centuries. The consequences included the rapid spread of devastating diseases among the Indian population. These not only claimed lives but also demoralized the survivors. One eyewitness described an epidemic of smallpox in Mexico:

❝[The victims] could no longer walk about, but lay in their dwellings and sleeping places. . . . The pustules [fluid-filled sores] that covered people cause great desolation; very many people died of them, and many just starved to death; starvation reigned, and no one took care of the others any longer.❞

—Bernardino de Sahagún, *General History of the Things of New Spain,* c. 1575–1580

First Encounters

 Core Curriculum Objectives

- **1.I.B.1** Influences on early Native American Indians
- **2.II.B.2c** Native Americans
- **2.II.C.3** The Spanish, Mexican, and Native American West
- **2.II.C.6** Impact of western expansion upon Mexicans and Native Americans

Terms and People

Bartolomeu Dias	Ferdinand Magellan
Vasco da Gama	Hernán Cortés
Christopher Columbus	Moctezuma
John Cabot	conquistador
Pedro Alvarez Cabral	Columbian exchange
Amerigo Vespucci	

NoteTaking

Reading Skill: Understand Effects As you read, complete the chart below with the effects of the arrival of the Europeans in the Americas.

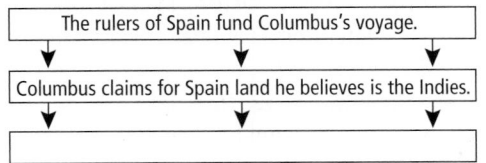

The rulers of Spain fund Columbus's voyage.
↓
Columbus claims for Spain land he believes is the Indies.
↓

Why It Matters With financial backing from Spain's monarchs, Isabella and Ferdinand, Christopher Columbus found the Americas. He then returned to conquer the land, exploit its wealth, and convert its people to Christianity. That process changed the Americas, Europe, and Africa. **Section Focus Question: How did European exploration affect the Americas?**

Spain Looks to the West

Throughout the 1400s, the Portuguese continued to sail farther and farther from home. They sought a route around Africa's southern tip into the Indian Ocean. Then, their ships could continue east in search of India, the East Indies, and eventually China. In 1487, the Portuguese mariner **Bartolomeu Dias** learned how to use the counterclockwise winds of the South Atlantic to get around southern Africa. In 1498, **Vasco da Gama** exploited that discovery to reach India, opening an immensely profitable trade. The Portuguese dominated the trade routes south and east around Africa.

By default, in the late 1400s the Spanish looked westward into the open Atlantic. They took inspiration from the profitable discovery and exploitation earlier in the century of islands in the Atlantic—the Azores, Madeiras, and Canaries. Perhaps, they thought, similar islands could be found farther to the west. Furthermore, by leaping from one set of islands to another, perhaps mariners could one day reach the coveted coast of China.

Columbus's Voyages, 1492–1504

Geography *Interactive*
For: Interactive map
Web Code: ncp-0108

Map Skills After his first voyage to the Americas in 1492, Columbus crossed the Atlantic three more times.

1. Locate: (a) Spain, (b) Hispaniola, (c) Caribbean Sea, (d) Canary Islands, (e) Portugal

2. Analyze Information Around which island did Columbus navigate in 1498?

3. Identify Point of View Based on the map of Columbus's voyages and what you have read, do you think the Portuguese explorers were better navigators than Columbus? Explain.

Contrary to popular belief, fifteenth-century Europeans did not think that the world was flat. They did, however, worry that China lay too far away and that ships could not complete a voyage west over what they believed was a vast, open ocean.

✔ **Checkpoint** Why was Spain eager to find a new route across the Atlantic?

The Voyages of Christopher Columbus

To pursue the western dream, Spain relied on an Italian mariner from the city of Genoa named **Christopher Columbus.** He sought a route to China as a means of reviving the Christian struggle against Islam. By converting the Chinese to Christianity, he hoped to recruit their people and use their wealth to assist Europeans in a new crusade.

Columbus dared the westward trip because he underestimated the size of Earth. He believed the planet was 18,000 miles around—almost 7,000 miles smaller than it actually is.

Columbus Investigates Viking Stories An experienced Atlantic mariner, as a young man, Columbus had investigated stories about mysterious lands to the west. He may have sailed to Iceland. If so, he probably heard about the western discoveries by the Vikings from Scandinavia. During the ninth and tenth centuries, Viking mariners had probed the North Atlantic to discover and colonize Iceland and then Greenland. From Greenland, some mariners reached the northeastern coast of North America. About the year 1000, they founded a little

Christopher Columbus (1451–1506)
Born in the seaport city of Genoa, Columbus began his seafaring life at 14. Eventually, he went to Portugal for navigator's training.

At first, Columbus approached Alphonso V, the King of Portugal, with his plan to sail to the Indies. But Alphonso, in an unprincipled move, gave the command to another seaman who was instructed to follow Columbus's planned route. The expedition failed, and the crew returned to Portugal. Disgusted by Alphonso's deceit, Columbus set out for Spain, hopeful of achieving success for his petition.

settlement on the northern tip of Newfoundland. But they soon abandoned it because of the isolation and because of resistance by American Indians.

Columbus Sets Sail In 1492, Queen Isabella and King Ferdinand of Spain provided 3 ships, 90 men, and most of the funding for Columbus's voyage west in search of China. After 33 days at sea, he reached what we now call the Bahamas. Turning south, Columbus found another set of islands. He supposed that these belonged to the East Indies, which lay near the mainland of Asia. Based on his mistaken notion, he referred to the people living on the islands as Indians, a name that has endured to this day.

The presence of native people did not stop Columbus from claiming the land for Spain. As the representative of a Christian nation, Columbus believed that he had the right and duty to dominate the people he found. In his journal, he recorded:

Primary Source "They should be good servants and intelligent, for I observed that they quickly took in what was said to them, and I believe that they would easily be made Christians, as it appeared to me that they had no religion. I, our Lord being pleased, will take hence, at the time of my departure six natives. . . ."
—Journal of Christopher Columbus, October 1492

Reaction to Columbus's Voyage Columbus continued to explore the islands of the Caribbean. He established a settlement on the island he called Hispaniola. Then, in early 1493, leaving a number of his crew behind, he returned to Spain.

Later that year, Columbus returned to the Caribbean to colonize Hispaniola. The new colony was supposed to produce profits by shipping gold, sugar, and Indian slaves to Spain. The Spanish planned to dominate the natives and forge an empire based in Europe.

Upon his return to Hispaniola, Columbus discovered that the natives had killed the colonists he had left behind. Columbus turned to force. Employing the military advantages of horses, gunpowder, and steel, Columbus killed and captured hundreds of Indians on Hispaniola and the <u>adjacent</u> islands.

Unfortunately for Columbus, his bullying angered the European colonists, who persuaded the king and queen to recall him in 1500. Columbus returned to Spain and died in 1506. The Spanish colonization of the Americas, however, continued.

Columbus had not reached Asia, but he had found a source of riches that enabled European Christendom to grow more powerful and wealthy than the Muslim world. During the next three centuries, the mineral and plantation wealth of the Americas—produced by the labor of African slaves—helped finance the expansion of European commerce. In turn, that commerce promoted the development of new technologies and the growth of military power.

Spain and Portugal Divide the Americas With the assistance of the pope, the Spanish and the Portuguese negotiated the 1494 Treaty of Tordesillas. They agreed to split the world of new discoveries by drawing a north-south boundary line through the mid-Atlantic west of the Azores. The Portuguese secured a monopoly to exploit the coast of Africa and the Indian Ocean. In return, the Spanish claimed Columbus's western lands. Further exploration later determined that South America bulged eastward beyond the treaty line, placing Brazil in the Portuguese sphere.

Vocabulary Builder
<u>adjacent</u>–(uh JAY suhnt) *adj.*
near or close

In dividing the world, no one bothered to consult the Native Americans. The Iberians and the pope considered them pagan savages without any rights. The other European kings refused to honor the treaty, for they claimed an equal right to explore and exploit the new lands. But no European leaders thought that the Native Americans could, or should, be left alone in their former isolation and native beliefs.

✓ **Checkpoint** What was Columbus's purpose in sailing west across the Atlantic?

The Spanish Expand Their American Empire

Until his last breath, Columbus insisted that his discoveries lay close to the coast of China. Other explorers, however, demonstrated that he had reached the margins of two previously unknown continents. In 1497, **John Cabot,** a Genoese mariner employed by the English, sailed to Newfoundland. In tropical waters far to the south, a Portuguese fleet commanded by **Pedro Alvarez Cabral** discovered the coast of Brazil in 1500. A year later, **Amerigo Vespucci,** another Genoese mariner, explored enough of South America's coast to deem it a new continent. European mapmakers began to call the new continents by a variant of Vespucci's first name—America. Between 1519 and 1522, a voyage begun by **Ferdinand Magellan** succeeded in encircling the entire globe, filling in even more of the increasingly detailed picture of Earth.

Cortés Conquers the Aztecs At the start of the 1500s, the Spanish learned of a spectacular Indian empire in central Mexico. Those soldiers who explored central Mexico and defeated the Indian civilizations there were called **conquistadors.** In 1519, the brilliant and ruthless **Hernán Cortés** led a group of about 600 volunteers from Cuba to the coast of Mexico. Born in 1485, Cortés had university training as a lawyer. An ambitious man, he left Spain in 1504 to try his luck in Cuba, where he became rich by acquiring plantations and gold mines. But he hungered for more.

Marching inland, Cortés reached the great central valley, home of the Aztec Empire. The approach of Cortés's army alarmed the Aztec ruler, **Moctezuma.** Hoping to intimidate them with his own power, Moctezuma invited the Spanish into his great city.

The largest and richest city in the Americas, Tenochtitlán occupied a cluster of islands in a large lake. The population of about 200,000 dwarfed Spain's largest city, Seville, which had about 70,000 inhabitants. The Aztec city's central plaza of tall stone pyramid-temples dazzled with a combination of red, blue, and ochre stucco. Bernal Diaz, a soldier, recalled, "These great towns and pyramids and buildings arising from the water, all made of stone seemed like an enchanted vision. . . . Indeed, some of our soldiers asked whether it was not all a dream."

The city's gold and silver inflamed the Spanish desire to conquer and plunder. By seizing and killing Moctezuma, the Spanish provoked violent street fighting that initially drove them from the city. Returning with reinforcements, including many revenge-seeking local Indians who had themselves been brutalized by the Aztecs, Cortés captured Tenochtitlán. The cost, however, was high. Four months of fighting had reduced the city to a bloody rubble.

The Conquistadors
Eager for wealth and fame, the men known as conquistadors established a Spanish empire in the Americas. *What factors allowed a small force of conquistadors to overwhelm larger numbers of Indians?*

WITNESS HISTORY DVD

Watch *Conquest: Spain and the Aztecs* on the **United States Witness History DVD** to explore the conflict between the Spanish and the Aztecs in the Americas.

The victors put thousands of captive Indians to work raising a Spanish capital, Mexico City, on the ruins of Tenochtitlán. The slaves reworked stones from the great pyramids into a Christian cathedral. They transformed the shell of Moctezuma's palace into a residence for Cortés. Grateful for the stunning conquest and a share in the immense plunder, the Spanish king appointed Cortés to govern Mexico.

The Conquistadors March On The Spanish extended their empire deep into North and South America. During the 1530s, Francisco Pizarro conquered the powerful Incas of Peru with just 180 soldiers.

Aside from wealth, conquistadors were motivated by their religious faith and by loyalty to their monarch. They reasoned that riches were wasted on the non-Christian Indians. Those riches should belong to Christians who served the Spanish Crown—and who were willing to help convert the native people. These notions had been deeply ingrained in Spanish culture as a result of the centuries-long *reconquista.*

The conquistadors benefited from their superior weapons. These included steel-edged swords, pikes, and crossbows. Such weapons were far more durable and deadly than the stone-edged swords, axes, and arrows of the Indians. Because sixteenth-century guns were so heavy, inaccurate, and slow to reload, only a few conquistadors carried them. Yet their few guns gave the Spanish a psychological advantage. Belching fire and smoke, they produced a thunderous roar that was terrifying.

Although most conquistadors fought on foot, the few with horses proved especially dreadful. The Indians had never experienced the shocking power and speed of mounted men. "The most essential thing in new lands is horses," observed a conquistador. "They instill the greatest fear in the enemy and make the Indians respect the leaders of the army." But the greatest advantage came from something the conquistadors did not even know they carried—disease.

The Devastation of Disease Brutal exploitation and disease combined to destroy the natives of Hispaniola. From about 300,000 in 1492, the island's population declined to a mere 500 by 1548. The Spanish forced the natives, known as the Tainos, to labor in mines and on ranches and plantations. Those who resisted suffered deadly raids on their villages by colonial soldiers. Overworked and underfed, the native population was especially vulnerable to disease.

The ravages of these diseases were not confined to Hispaniola. In the century after the arrival of the Europeans in the Americas, experts believe that successive epidemics reduced the native population to about one fifth of its pre-1492 numbers.

The great European killers included smallpox, typhus, diphtheria, bubonic plague, and cholera. These were diseases that had existed in Europe for centuries. As a result, the European population over the generations had developed some natural defenses against them. That is, among the population there was a percentage of people whose bodies were able to fight off the diseases before they became fatal. The native populations of the Americas had not built up such natural defenses. The European diseases hit with devastating effect. In some cases, entire villages simply disappeared.

For the Spanish, the reduction of the Indian population complicated their colonization plans. They had depended on Indians to provide the labor for their new enterprises. Left with large tracts of fertile but depopulated lands, the colonists needed a new source of workers. They turned to importing Africans as slaves to work the new sugar plantations on the tropical coasts.

✔ **Checkpoint** What role did disease play in the defeat of the native populations of the Americas?

The Columbian Exchange

In 1972, Alfred W. Crosby, a social historian, used the term Columbian Exchange to describe the exchange of plants, animals, and diseases between Europe and the Americas. The term held. The exchange also included the continents of Africa and Asia. As people, products, animals, and ideas flowed, their impact was greater than anyone could have imagined. The images below represent some results of the global exchange.

▼ Aztecs fell victim to European diseases, such as smallpox.

From the Americas to Europe, Africa, and Asia
- beans
- maize
- potatoes
- sweet potatoes
- pumpkins
- squash
- tomatoes
- peppers
- peanuts
- avocados
- cocoa
- tobacco
- turkeys

▲ Potatoes from Peru, cultivated by the farmers in this drawing, became an important staple of the European diet.

Quinine Ga

Quinine, native to South ▲ America, provided a cure for people in Africa suffering from malaria.

From Europe, Africa, and Asia to the Americas
- wheat
- bananas
- rice
- coffee
- grapes
- sugar
- barley
- chickens
- cattle
- pigs
- horses
- typhus, smallpox, measles

◄ Silver and gold for coins like these came from the Americas.

◄ The Spanish brought horses to the Americas by ship.

The Transatlantic Exchange

The Europeans who began arriving in the Americas in the late 1400s brought more than weapons, diseases, and a thirst for wealth and power. The colonizers also brought plants and animals that were new to the Americas. Indeed, the European arrival brought about an ecological revolution. Never before in human history had so many of the world's plants, animals, and microorganisms been so thoroughly and so abruptly mixed and <u>dispersed</u>. We call this phenomenon the **Columbian Exchange.**

Thinking Critically
1. **Draw Inferences** How do you think the Columbian Exchange affected the environment in the Americas?
2. **Analyze Information** Is there still a global exchange among the continents? Explain.

Vocabulary Builder
<u>disperse</u>—(dih SPERS) *v.* to spread about; distribute widely

Exchange of Plants and Animals Determined to farm the American land in a European manner, the colonists introduced their domesticated livestock: pigs, horses, mules, sheep, and cattle. They also brought seeds for their domesticated plants. These included wheat, barley, rye, oats, grasses, and grapes.

In a land where large mammals such as cattle and horses did not live, the new plants and animals brought drastic changes to the environment. Ranging cattle and pigs consumed the wild plants and the shellfish that the Indians needed for their own diet. The livestock also invaded the Indians' fields to consume their maize, beans, and squashes.

The Indians proved remarkably resilient as they adapted to the new plants and animals. In time, the Indians learned to raise and consume European cattle. On the Great Plains, the Indians acquired runaway horses. Once mounted, the Indians could more easily hunt bison and could more forcefully resist efforts to colonize their land.

While exporting domesticated plants and livestock to the Americas, the Europeans imported productive plants cultivated by the Indians. Maize and potatoes from the Americas produced more food per acre than traditional European crops such as wheat. European farmers enjoyed larger harvests by adding, or switching to, the American plants. Europeans also adopted tomatoes, beans, peppers, and peanuts.

Population Shifts The Columbian Exchange helped trigger enormous population shifts around the world. Larger harvests aided by new American crops fueled European population growth. From about 80 million in 1492, Europe's population grew to 180 million by 1800. That growth nearly doubled Europe's share of the world's population from about 11 percent in 1492 to 20 percent in 1800. Meanwhile, the Native American proportion of the global population collapsed from about 7 percent in 1492 to less than 1 percent in 1800.

The European surplus population flowed westward across the Atlantic to replace the Indians in the Americas. Those colonizers brought along millions of Africans as slaves. Never before had so many people moved so far with such a powerful impact. As a result, maritime trade and migration integrated four great continents: Europe, Africa, South America, and North America.

✓ **Checkpoint** What was the Columbian Exchange?

Progress Monitoring *Online*
For: Self-test with vocabulary practice
Web Code: nea-0109

Comprehension

1. **Terms and People** Explain the role of the people listed below in the European exploration of the Americas.
   - Christopher Columbus
   - John Cabot
   - Pedro Alvarez Cabral
   - Amerigo Vespucci
   - Ferdinand Magellan
   - Hernán Cortés

2. **NoteTaking** **Reading Skill: Understand Effects** Use your chart to answer the Section Focus Question: How did European exploration affect the Americas?

Writing About History

3. **Quick Write: Write a Monologue** Stories about the Aztec ruler Moctezuma claim that he feared newcomers. Write a monologue—a long speech by one person—by Moctezuma upon his learning about the arrival of the Spaniards in his empire.

Critical Thinking

4. **Understanding Cause and Effect** How did the success of Portugal's exploration of Africa affect Spain?

5. **Analyze Information** How did the conquistadors justify their conquest of the Aztec and Inca empires?

6. **Make Generalizations** How did the Columbian Exchange affect population size and movement?

TRACK THE ISSUE

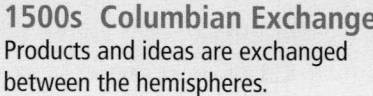

Is global interdependence good for the American economy?

Like many nations, the United States depends on trade and commerce with other countries to support its economy. Employment is a part of the global economy, as a growing number of U.S. companies outsource jobs overseas. Use the timeline below to explore this enduring issue.

1500s Columbian Exchange
Products and ideas are exchanged between the hemispheres.

1812 War of 1812
United States goes to war in part to protect its trade rights.

1944 World Bank
The World Bank and International Monetary Fund are established at Bretton Woods Conference.

1990s World Trade Increases
NAFTA joins the United States, Mexico, and Canada in a free-trade pact, and the World Trade Organization is founded.

2000s Globalization Debated
Critics and advocates debate benefits of globalization.

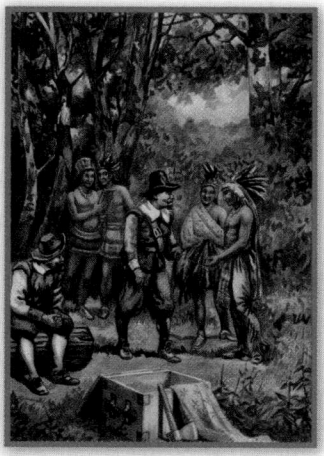

Europeans trade goods with Native Americans.

1.I.D.1e

U.S. firms outsource work to such nations as India and Nigeria.

DEBATE THE ISSUE

Outsourcing Jobs Many American companies send work overseas where wages are lower. This is called outsourcing. In the past, most of the jobs lost through outsourcing were factory jobs. Now, office work and computer jobs are being sent abroad, too. How does outsourcing affect America?

"Sending jobs overseas is part of corporate America's quest for short-term profits at the expense of the well-being of our workers. In effect, forcing the middle class to compete with the cheapest foreign labor can only result in a decline in our nation's standard of living and a diminished quality of life."
—Lou Dobbs, News Anchor, CNN

"Will [the outsourcing of services] lead to jobs going overseas? You bet, but that is not a disaster. For a start, America runs a large and growing surplus in services with the rest of the world. The jobs lost will be low-paying ones. . . . By contrast, jobs will be created that demand skills to handle the deeper incorporation of information technology, and the pay for these jobs will be high."
—*The Economist* magazine

TRANSFER Activities

1. **Compare** How do these two views on outsourcing differ?

2. **Analyze** Do you think either Lou Dobbs or the writer in *The Economist* would have considered the Columbian Exchange a danger to European or Native American economies? Explain.

3. **Transfer** Use the following Web site to see a video, try a WebQuest, and write in your journal. **Web Code:** neh-6102

Quick Study Guide

Progress Monitoring *Online*
For: Self-test with vocabulary practice
Web Code: nca-0110

■ Native American Cultures

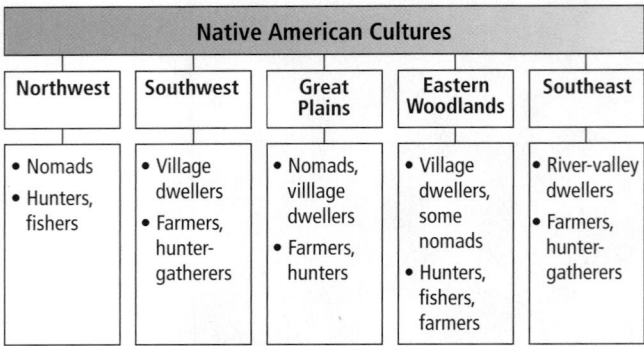

Native American Cultures				
Northwest	Southwest	Great Plains	Eastern Woodlands	Southeast
• Nomads • Hunters, fishers	• Village dwellers • Farmers, hunter-gatherers	• Nomads, villlage dwellers • Farmers, hunters	• Village dwellers, some nomads • Hunters, fishers, farmers	• River-valley dwellers • Farmers, hunter-gatherers

■ West African Kingdoms, A.D. 800–A.D. 1600

- ☐ Ghana, A.D. 800–A.D. 1050
- ☐ Mali, A.D. 1200–A.D. 1450
- ☐ Songhai, A.D. 1460–A.D. 1600

■ Europe, 1400s

Renaissance

New technology

Europe, 1400s

Growth of commerce

Rise of nations

Population increase

■ European Exploration

Causes	Events	Effects
• Europeans search for route to Asia and Africa. • Countries desire to accumulate wealth through trade. • Navigation technology is improved.	• Portuguese make voyages to Africa and India. • Columbus reaches the West Indies. • Columbus makes other voyages to the Americas. • After Columbus, other European explorers set sail for the Americas.	• Portugal establishes gold and slave trade in Africa. • Spain establishes colonies in the Americas. • Europeans enter the West African slave trade. • European diseases devastate Native Americans. • The Columbian Exchange begins.

☑ Quick Study Timeline

1200s
Anasazi culture declines

1300s
Mansa Musa rules the kingdom of Mali

Around the World

Prehistory	1200	1300

30,000–10,000 years ago
First people arrive in the Americas

Late 1300s
Renaissance begins in Europe

American Issues
●—●—● Connector

2.I.A.2a

By connecting prior knowledge with what you have learned in this chapter, you can gradually build your understanding of enduring questions that still affect America today. Answer the questions below. Then, use your American Issues Connector study guide (or go online: www.PHSchool.com **Web Code:** nch-6103).

Issues You Learned About

● **Global Interdependence** As Europeans explored the Americas, these regions became linked by culture and economics.

1. Write a short essay explaining why Europeans began to set sail for new lands and what effects their journeys had on the people of the Americas and on the Europeans. Consider:
   • the religious wars in Europe
   • the importance of trade
   • settlements in the Americas
   • American Indian empires
   • the Columbian Exchange

● **Technology and Society** Throughout history, people have developed new technologies that changed culture, economics, and international relations.

2. How did technology help some Native Americans develop agricultural societies?

3. How did technology benefit the Spanish conquistadors?

● **Interaction With the Environment** American Indians adapted to their environment and modified their environment.

4. How did Paleo-Indians adapt to the changes brought by the end of the ice age?

5. In some areas of North America, people did not turn to farming. Why not?

6. Give at least one example of the way that some American Indian groups modified their environment.

Connect to Your World | New York

Migration and Urbanization In addition to Columbus and Cabot, Giovanni da Verrazano was another early Italian explorer of America. Verrazano was hired by the French to conduct a voyage to discover a western route to Asia, and in 1524 he arrived along the eastern coast of North America. During the voyage, Verrazano made several discoveries, including the present-day site of New York Harbor. Verrazano anchored his boat near Staten Island, and was greeted by members of the Lenape Native American group traveling in small boats. Conduct research to list the Native American groups living in New York State at the time of Verrazano's voyage. Create a map that uses shading to illustrate the location of each group.

History *Interactive*
For: Interactive timeline
Web Code: nep-0112

Mid–1400s
Europe's first books are printed on a printing press

1591
Songhai Empire falls to invaders from Morocco

1400   1500   1600

1492
Columbus reaches America

Chapter Assessment

Terms and People

1. Define **adobe**. Which American Indian group used adobe, and what did they use it for?

2. What was the **Iroquois League**? What were its key characteristics?

3. What were the **Middle Ages** and the **Renaissance**? In what way were these two eras different?

4. Who was **Mansa Musa**? How did Mansa Musa increase the influence of Islam?

5. Who was **Hernán Cortés**? What role did he play in Spanish Mexico?

Focus Questions

The focus question for this chapter is **How did the interaction of many cultures after 1492 affect the Americas?** Build an answer to this big question by answering the focus questions for Sections 1 through 4 and the Critical Thinking questions that follow.

Section 1
6. How did the spread of civilization begin in the Americas?

Section 2
7. How did Europeans begin to explore more of the world?

Section 3
8. What was life like in West Africa before the age of European exploration?

Section 4
9. How did European exploration affect the Americas?

Critical Thinking

10. **Analyze Information** How did the environment influence the American Indian's way of life?

11. **Draw Inferences** What effect do you think the printing press had on European exploration?

12. **Make Generalizations** How would you describe the social class and ruling system in western Europe in the fifteenth century?

13. **Compare Points of View** How were the views of American Indians and West Africans about land similar? How were these views different?

14. **Synthesize Information** How did the Columbian Exchange impact the food traditions of Europe and the Americas?

15. **Analyze Visuals** The map below, drawn in the 1400s, shows only an accurate location for Europe. How and why would the rendering of this map change by the 1500s?

Writing About History

Write a Narrative Essay Research the life of Dekanawidah, who, according to Iroquois tradition, helped found the Iroquois League. Write an account of how he worked to persuade Native American nations to unite. Use dialogue and details to make the narrative more vivid.

Prewriting
• Research any background information you need to tell your story.
• List details.
• Consider your audience.

Drafting
• Open strongly with an engaging sentence.
• Use sensory details to make the story more interesting for the readers.
• Add dialogue or descriptions.

Revising
• Use the guidelines on page SH14 of the Writing Handbook to revise your report.

Regents DBQ Practice

Government in Pre-Columbian America

By the time of European contact, the Americas were home to millions of people. Hundreds of different cultures had developed and adapted to the various environments of their particular regions. Were the governments as varied as the cultures? Use your knowledge of the history of American Indian cultures and Documents 1, 2, and 3 to answer questions 1 through 4.

Document 1

"For most Native North Americans . . . there existed no institutionalized forms of social or political power—no state, no bureaucracy, and no army. Native American societies, as a rule, were egalitarian, without the kind of centralized authority and social hierarchy typical of modern societies. Custom and tradition rather than law and coercion regulated social life. While there were leaders, their influence was generally based on personal status and not any formal or permanent status. As an early French missionary, Father LeJeune, observed in 1634 of the Montagnais-Naskapis of Labrador, Indians would not "endure in the least those who seem desirous of assuming superiority over others." Authority within a group derived from the ability to make useful suggestions and knowledge of tribal tradition and lore. Among the Eskimos, for example, a person of importance was called *Isumatag,* 'he who thinks.'"

—*Carl Waldham,* Atlas of the North American Indian

Document 2

"All the business of the Five Nations Confederate Council shall be conducted by the two combined bodies of Confederate Lords. First the question shall be passed upon by the Mohawk and Seneca Lords, then it shall be discussed and passed by the Oneida and Cayuga Lords. Their decisions shall then be referred to the Onondaga Lords (Fire Keepers), for final judgment. . . .

"In all cases the procedure must be as follows: when the Mohawk and Seneca Lords have unanimously agreed upon a question, they shall report their decision to the Cayuga and Oneida Lords who shall deliberate upon the question and report a unanimous decision to the Mohawk Lords. The Mohawk Lords will then report the standing of the case to the Fire Keepers, who shall render a decision as they see fit in case of a disagreement by the two bodies, or confirm the decisions of the two bodies if they are identical. The Fire keepers shall then report their decision to the Mohawk Lords who shall announce it to the open council."

—*the Iroquois Constitution*

Document 3

"Inca society and government were hierarchal and pyramidal in form. The Sapa Inca, or emperor, was believed to be a descendant of the sun god and stood at the apex of the pyramid as the absolute ruler of Inca lands. His senior councilors and provincial governors, each of whom was responsible for 10,000 people, were chosen from the aristocracy which consisted principally of his relatives. Beneath them came lesser bureaucrats and military officers, some drawn from the leaders of assimilated conquered peoples, who in turn controlled smaller numbers of imperial citizens. The system continued downward to the smallest unit, the nuclear family, with each official responsible to the Sapa Inca through the administrator who was ranked directly above him."

—*Margaret Oliphant,* The Atlas of the Ancient World

---

1. Which term best describes the majority of government systems in pre-Columbian America?
   (1) hierarchical
   (2) bureaucratic
   (3) constitutional
   (4) egalitarian

2. What can you conclude from Document 2?
   (1) that the Iroquois valued consensus
   (2) that the Iroquois created a dictatorship
   (3) that the Iroquois rejected hierarchy
   (4) that the Iroquois encouraged conflict

3. In comparing Document 1 and Document 3, a reader should conclude that Inca government was
   (1) a typical pre-Columbian American government.
   (2) an early stage of pre-Columbian American government.
   (3) the most advanced pre-Columbian American government.
   (4) an unusual form of pre-Columbian American government.

4. **Writing Task** What categories, or types of government existed in pre-Columbian America? What are some examples of Native American people who developed each type of government? Use your knowledge of American history and evidence from the sources above to explain your answer.

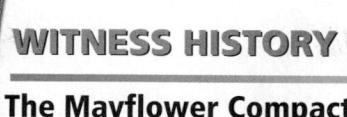

The Mayflower Compact

On September 16, 1620, the *Mayflower* set sail from England to North America. Some of the passengers were religious dissenters called Puritans, who hoped to establish a colony of their own.

After a journey of about two months, the colonists sighted land. Before landing, the men aboard signed an agreement establishing a government—one that derived from the consent of the governed:

“. . . [we] hereof to enact, constitute, and frame, such just and equal Laws, Ordinances, Acts, Constitutions and Offices, from time to time, as shall be thought most meet and convenient for the General good of the Colony; unto which we promise all due Submission and Obedience.”

—The Mayflower Compact, November 11, 1620

◄ Colonists aboard the *Mayflower* sign the Mayflower Compact.

Spanish coin, called a doubloon

Beaver hat

(NY) Core Curriculum Preview

Chapter Focus Question: In what ways were the colonial societies established by the Spanish, French, and English similar? In what ways were they different?

Section 1
Spain's Empire in the Americas 2.I.A.2a, 2.I.A.2b, 2.I.A.2c

Section 2
The French Empire 1.I.B.1, 2.I.A.2a

Section 3
England's Southern Colonies 2.I.A.2a, 2.I.A.3a, 2.I.A.3c

Section 4
The New England Colonies 2.I.A.2a, 2.I.A.2c, 2.I.A.3a

Section 5
The Middle Colonies 1.I.D.1d, 2.I.A.2, 2.I.A.3

Powhatan's deerskin cloak

Use the ☑ **Quick Study Timeline** at the end of this chapter to preview chapter events.

Note Taking Study Guide *Online*
For: Note Taking and American Issues Connector
Web Code: nce-6201

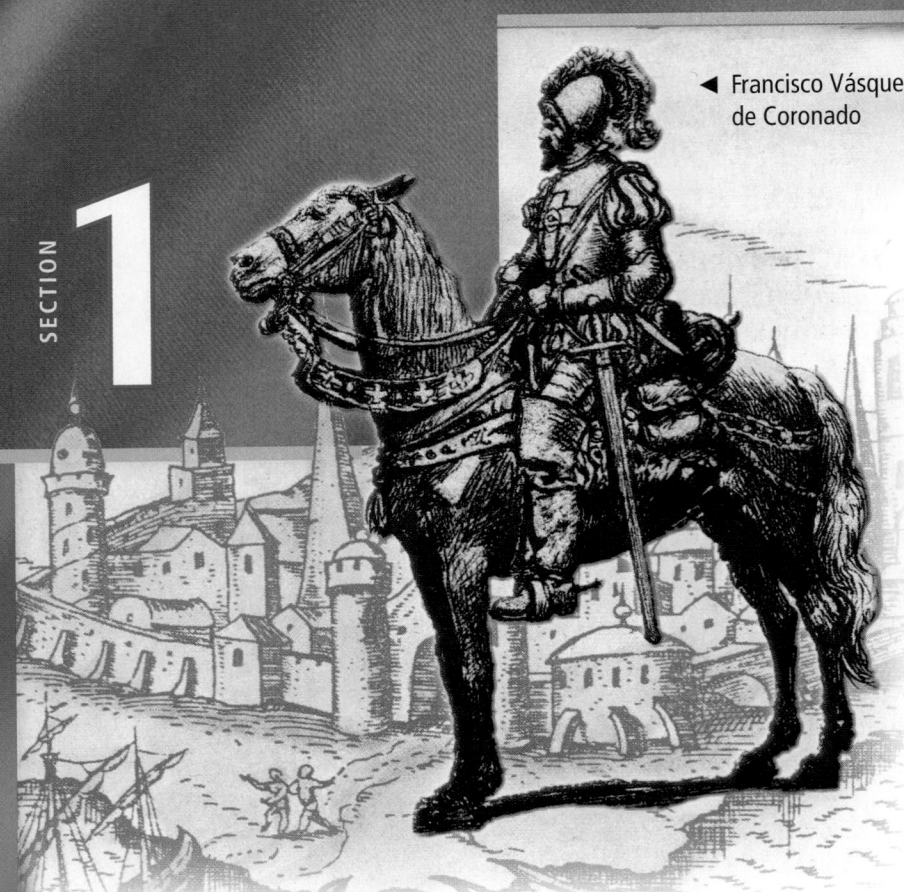

◀ Francisco Vásquez
de Coronado

Cities of Gold

In 1540, the Spanish explorer Francisco Vásquez de Coronado, along with 300 soldiers, set out to find Cibola, one of the fabled Seven Cities of Gold. Hoping to discover riches that equaled those found in Mexico, the expedition journeyed into the lands north of Mexico (the present-day U.S. Southwest). Instead of Cibola, the group found:

❝ . . . a little, crowded village, looking as if it had been crumpled all up together. There are ranch houses in New Spain which make a better appearance at a distance. It is a village of about 200 warriors. . . .❞

—Pedro de Casteneda,
The Journey of Coronado, 1596

Disappointment turned to rage as Coronado's men searched the village for gold. When they found none, they attacked the village, defeating it in about an hour.

Spain's Empire in the Americas

 Core Curriculum Objectives

- **2.I.A.2a** The peoples of the American colonies: Native American Indians
- **2.I.A.2b** The peoples of the American colonies: Slave trade
- **2.I.A.2c** The peoples of the American colonies: Immigrant motivation, ethnicities, and experiences

Terms and People

missionary   mestizo
presidio   mission
viceroy

NoteTaking

Reading Skill: Summarize Complete a concept web to summarize how each item strengthened the Spanish American Empire.

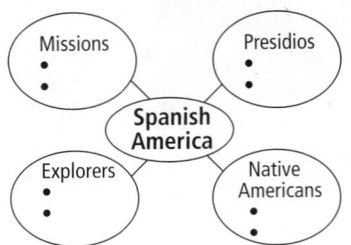

Why It Matters During the sixteenth century, the Spanish created a great empire by conquering and colonizing the lands in the Caribbean as well as large portions of North and South America. This American empire was more than ten times larger than Spain and rich in gold and silver. The potential for great wealth motivated other European nations to join the quest for colonies in the Americas. Soon rivalries emerged in the Americas as European empires vied for territory. **Section Focus Question: How did Spain strengthen its colonies in the Americas?**

Religious Divisions Cause Conflict

Enriched by conquests in the Americas, Spain financed an aggressive military policy in Europe. This aggression alarmed the Dutch, French, and English, who sought their own share of the riches in the Americas. These nations probed the coast of North America, seeking places where they might establish their own colonies. They also encouraged pirates to rob Spanish treasure ships.

Religious divisions added to the conflict among nations in Europe. In 1517, a movement called the Protestant Reformation began in Germany when a monk named Martin Luther challenged the authority of the Catholic Church. Luther and other dissenters became known as Protestants because they protested against the power of the pope and against the Church, which they viewed as corrupt and materialistic.

Protestants favored the individual's right to seek God by reading the Bible and by heeding ministers who delivered evangelical sermons. Without the unifying power of the pope, Protestants soon divided into many different denominations, including Lutherans, Calvinists, Baptists, Anglicans, and Quakers.

The Protestant movement spread throughout northern Europe, including the Netherlands and England. The French divided into hostile Protestant and Catholic camps, but the Spanish remained Catholic. Indeed, Spanish monarchs led the Catholic effort to suppress Protestantism. Rival nations carried the conflict across the Atlantic to their new colonies in the Americas.

 Checkpoint What issues divided the nations of Europe during the 1500s?

Spain Organizes Its American Empire

Although the conquistadors were successful at conquering territory and establishing colonies for Spain, they were not effective at running the colonies. Under Spanish rule, Indians were enslaved and forced to labor on encomiendas, large Spanish-owned plantations. They were also forced to mine for silver and gold. They suffered harsh treatment and were often beaten or worked to death.

The Spanish king worried that the conquistadors killed too many Indians, who might otherwise have become tax-paying subjects. Eager to stabilize the new conquests, the king heeded priests such as Bartolomé de Las Casas, who urged the royal government to adopt laws protecting Indians. Catholic friars served as **missionaries**—people who work to convert others to their religion. The friars aimed to convert Indians to Christianity and to persuade them to adopt Spanish culture.

Although less brutal than the conquistadors, the friars demanded that the Indians surrender their traditions in favor of Christian beliefs and Spanish ways. The friars destroyed Indian temples and sacred images. Then, missionaries ordered the Indians to build new churches and adopt the rituals of the Catholic faith. The missionaries also forced Indians to work for them. The friars relied on Spanish soldiers who set up **presidios,** or forts, near the missions.

New Spain and Peru Established During the 1530s and 1540s, the Spanish Crown divided the American empire into two immense regions, known as viceroyalties, each ruled by a **viceroy** appointed by the king. The viceroyalty of New Spain consisted of Mexico, Central America, and the Caribbean islands. The viceroyalty of Peru included all of South America except Portuguese Brazil. To control the viceroys, the Spanish Crown forced them to share power with a Crown-appointed council and an archbishop. The Spanish did not permit elected assemblies in their colonies.

Society in Spain's American Colonies During the sixteenth century, about 250,000 Spanish people, mostly men, immigrated across the Atlantic to the American empire. The male colonists generally took Indian wives. Children of mixed Spanish and Indian ancestry became known as **mestizos.** As the Native American population declined from diseases, the mestizos became the largest segment of Spain's colonial population by the eighteenth century. Next in proportion were enslaved Africans, especially in the Caribbean region.

To maintain their authority, colonial officials developed a complex system of racial hierarchy known as the *castas.* At the bottom lay the pure Africans and Indians, while

Missionaries and Indians

Soon after the Spanish conquest of a region, missionaries arrived to convert Indians to Christianity and to persuade them to adopt Spanish culture. In this painting, friars and conquistadors watch in approval as an Indian is baptized.

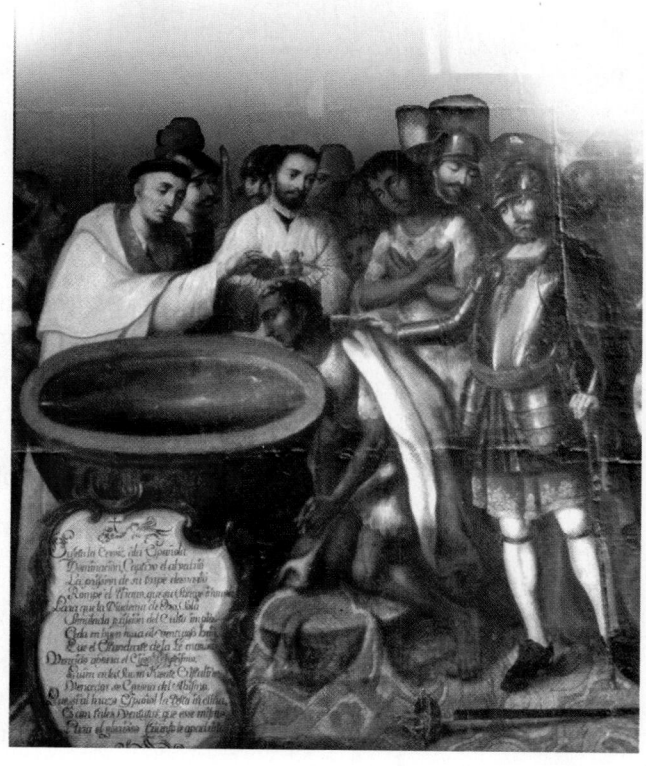

Europeans Explore the Americas, 1497–1682

Map Skills After Columbus's voyages, other European explorers sailed on behalf of any power that would sponsor them. For example, Verrazano was Italian but sailed for France.

1. Locate: (a) Mississippi River, (b) St. Lawrence River, (c) Gulf of Mexico

2. Movement Describe the journey of Jolliet and Marquette.

3. Predict Consequences Based on this map, what regions do you think France will control in North America?

Vocabulary Builder
urban–(UHR buhn) *adj.* relating or belonging to a city

Spaniards were at the pinnacle. The higher *castas* enjoyed superior status and greater legal privileges at the expense of those of lower status.

In both New Spain and Peru, the Spanish developed an <u>urban</u> and cosmopolitan culture. Carefully planned towns possessed a spacious grid of streets, with the town hall and a church arranged around a central plaza. The wealthiest families dwelled near the central plaza. The common people lived in the outer districts of the towns.

✓ **Checkpoint** How did Spain maintain control over its American colonies?

Spanish Explorers Push North

Cortés's success in conquering and plundering Mexico inspired later conquistadors. Seeking their own golden empires, Hernando de Soto and Francisco Vásquez de Coronado led expeditions into the lands north of Mexico.

De Soto Explores Florida In 1539, de Soto's conquistadors crossed present-day Florida, Georgia, South Carolina, North Carolina, Tennessee, Alabama, Mississippi, and Arkansas. Frustrated in their search for riches, the conquistadors massacred Indian villages, ravaged fields, emptied storehouses, and burned towns. After de Soto died of disease in 1542, his men gave up and fled to Mexico in boats. They left behind deadly new diseases, which continued to spread among the Indians of the Southeast.

Coronado Searches for Golden Cities Coronado marched north from Mexico into the Rio Grande valley in 1540. Unable to defeat the Spanish, the Pueblo Indians in the region tried to get rid of them by appealing to their greed. The Pueblos told alluring stories of a golden kingdom named Quivira to the northeast, on the far side of a great, grassy plain. In pursuit of Quivira, Coronado and his men crossed the Great Plains to what is now Kansas. They found only villages of grass-thatched lodges inhabited by Wichita Indians, who possessed neither gold nor silver. Returning to the Rio Grande in a rage, the Spanish took a bloody revenge on the Pueblos before retreating to Mexico in 1542.

Spain Colonizes Florida After the expensive failures of de Soto and Coronado, the Spanish Crown lost interest in the northern lands. Lacking <u>tangible</u> wealth, the northern frontier did not seem worth the effort to conquer and colonize. But attacks by French, Dutch, and English pirates began to change Spanish minds during the 1560s. By occupying Florida and the Rio Grande valley, the Spanish hoped to create a defensive zone, to keep hostile European rivals far from the precious mines and towns of Mexico. This plan became urgent when the Spanish learned that the French had built a small base on the Atlantic coast of Florida. Worse still, these French colonists were Protestants, whom the Spanish hated as heretics.

In 1565, Pedro Menendez de Avilés attacked and destroyed the French base, slaughtering the captured Protestants. He then founded the fortified town of St. Augustine, which became the first enduring colonial town within what would later become the United States. However, Florida failed to attract a large number of Spanish colonists, who numbered a mere 1,000 by the end of the century. Friars tried to convert Indians to Christianity by building **missions** in the native villages. By 1675, the friars had gathered 20,000 native converts in 36 mission churches spread across northern Florida. (See the infographic on the next page.)

Spain Colonizes New Mexico During the 1590s, a Spanish expedition led by Juan de Oñate returned to the lands explored by Coronado in the Rio Grande valley. There, Spain established the colony of New Mexico, with Santa Fe as the capital (after 1607). The colony's isolation from Mexico, however, reduced the colonists' income and drove up the cost of their imported goods. Because few Spanish settlers wished to join such an isolated and poor colony, New Mexico's colonial population stagnated. In 1638, the 2,000 colonists were greatly outnumbered by the 40,000 Pueblo Indians. A soldier described New Mexico as "at the ends of the earth . . . remote beyond compare."

As in Florida, only the friars thrived in New Mexico. By 1628, they had founded 50 missions. The progress was remarkable because the friars demanded so much from their converts. Christian churches replaced the circular *kivas,* the sacred structures for religious dances and ceremonies. The priests smashed or burned the *katsina* figures held sacred by the Indians. (*Katsinas* are wooden figures that represent ancestral spirits.) The friars also expected the Indians to dress, cook, eat, and speak like Spaniards.

For a couple of generations, the Pueblos did their best to adapt to the friars. In part, the Indians acted from fear of the Spanish soldiers, who backed up the

tangible–(TAN juh buhl) *adj.* solid; capable of being touched or understood

Pueblo Indians create *katsinas,* images that represent ancestral spirits.

MISSIONS AND FORTS

As Spanish conquistadors explored and conquered territory in the Americas, Spanish missionaries worked to convert American Indians to Christianity. During the 1500s and 1600s, Spanish soldiers and missionaries established a number of settlements in New Mexico and Florida. Missions, or religious settlements run by friars or priests, included a church, a friary, houses, and often a fort to protect settlements from attacks by European rivals or Indian adversaries. The illustrations and pictures here depict the Spanish settlement at San Luis de Apalachee in Florida, established in 1656. San Luis was the western capital of Spanish Florida, while St. Augustine was its eastern capital. Today, archaeologists and historians are re-creating the site.

▼ Silver crucifix and rosary beads belonging to Christian Indians

Wooden Palisade
Firing Platform
Blockhouse
Bastion
Main Gate
Dry Moat

▲ A drawing shows the plan of the fort at San Luis de Apalachee.

▼ This illustration shows the construction of the fort at San Luis de Apalachee. Spaniards direct Apalachee Indians to complete the walls of the fort.

Thinking Critically

1. **Recognize Effects** How did Spanish missionaries affect Indian culture?

2. **Draw Conclusions** Why do you think the Spanish built forts as well as missions in many of the places they settled?

▲ A reconstruction of the church at San Luis

friars with firearms and horses. The Pueblos were also interested in the domesticated animals and metal tools provided by the missions.

But the Pueblos would not give up all of their traditional beliefs. Instead, they considered Christianity a supplement to their own sacred practices. To please the priests, the Indians became public Christians, but they privately mixed Christianity with traditional ways, keeping in secret their *kivas* and *katsinas*. When the missionaries discovered these secrets, they felt the fury of betrayal. The harsh punishments inflicted by the friars angered the Pueblos.

✓ **Checkpoint** Why did the Spanish explore and colonize New Mexico and Florida in the 1600s?

The Pueblos Revolt Against the Spanish

Conditions worsened during the 1660s and 1670s. A prolonged drought undercut the harvests, reducing many Pueblos to starvation. Disease, famine, and violence cut their population from 40,000 in 1638 to 17,000 by 1680. The losses made it harder for the Pueblos to pay tribute in labor and produce to the missionaries and colonists.

Fed up, in 1680 the Pueblos revolted under the leadership of a shaman named Popé. Encouraging resistance to Spanish ways, Popé urged a return to the traditional Pueblo culture and religion. The rebels also drew support from the Apaches, who had their own scores to settle with the Hispanic slave raiders. The Indians destroyed and plundered missions, farms, and ranches. Abandoning Santa Fe, the colonial survivors and Christian Indians fled to El Paso, which at the time was on the southern margin of New Mexico. The Pueblo Revolt was the greatest setback that the Indians ever inflicted on colonial expansion.

After victory deprived them of a common enemy, the Pueblos resumed feuding with one another and with the Apaches. The renewed violence discredited Popé, who had promised that the rebellion would bring peace and prosperity. Losing influence, he died sometime before 1690. During the following three years, the Spanish reclaimed New Mexico.

The bloody revolt taught the Pueblos and the Spanish to compromise. The Pueblos accepted Spanish authority, while the Spanish colonists practiced greater restraint. The Pueblos once again became public Catholics while quietly maintaining traditional ceremonies in their *kivas*. The Spanish and the Pueblos increasingly needed one another for mutual protection against the Apaches of the surrounding plains and mountains.

✔ **Checkpoint** How did Popé manage to defeat the Spanish settlers?

HISTORY MAKERS

Popé (1630?–1690?)
In 1675, the Spanish governor of New Mexico ordered more than 40 Pueblo shamans publicly whipped for following traditional religious practices. One of those punished that day was Popé. That mistreatment spurred him to plan the Pueblo Revolt of 1680. He even convinced the Apaches, traditionally the Pueblos' enemies, to join the fight to rid the region of the Spanish. The Spanish fled and did not return for 12 years. During that time, Popé worked to restore Pueblo ways of life and religion. When and where he died is not certain, but it likely happened before the Spanish return in 1692.

Progress Monitoring *Online*
For: Self-test with vocabulary practice
Web Code: nca-0203

Comprehension

1. **Terms and People** For each item below, write a sentence explaining its relationship to Spain's American colonies.
   - missionary
   - presidio
   - viceroy
   - mestizo
   - mission

2. **NoteTaking** **Reading Skill: Summarize** Use your concept web to answer the Section Focus Question: How did Spain strengthen its colonies in the Americas?

Writing About History

3. **Quick Write: Identify Effects** Write a paragraph describing the effects of the Spanish in the Americas from a Native American point of view. Your paragraph should state a main idea and contain supporting details.

Critical Thinking

4. **Recognize Ideologies** How did Spanish friars view Native American religions? Explain.

5. **Analyze Information** What was the *casta* system, and why was it created?

6. **Recognize Cause and Effect** What were the causes and effects of the Pueblo Revolt?

A beaver ▶

▲ French fur trader

A Profitable Fur Trade

While the Spanish grew rich mining silver and gold in South America, the French profited from the fur trade in Canada. But the trade relied on good relations with the Indians, who hunted and traded valuable beaver pelts with the French. At times, conflicts with the Iroquois halted the trade. As one missionary reported, New France faced ruin:

❝At no time in the past were the beavers more plentiful in our lakes and rivers and more scarce in the country's stores. . . . The war against the Iroquois has exhausted all the sources. . . . The Montréal store has not purchased a single beaver from the Natives in the past year. At Trois-Rivières, the few Natives that came were employed to defend the place where the enemy is expected. The store in Québec is the image of poverty.❞

—François Joseph Le Mercier,
Relations des Jésuites, 1653

The French Empire

Core Curriculum Objectives

- **1.I.B.1** Influences on early Native American Indians
- **2.I.A.2a** Relations between colonists and Native American Indians

Terms and People

Northwest Passage	*coureurs de bois*
Quebec	*metis*
Samuel de Champlain	

NoteTaking

Reading Skill: Compare and Contrast Fill in a Venn diagram like the one below comparing Spanish America and French America.

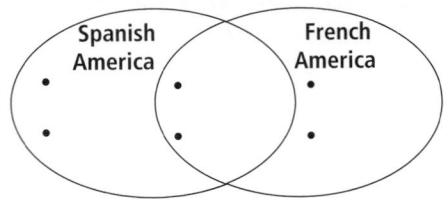

Why It Matters Spain's success with its American colonies encouraged other European nations to establish colonies. French explorers led expeditions along the North American Atlantic seaboard during the 1500s. These explorers established a number of French settlements along the St. Lawrence River and began trading fish and animal furs with Native Americans in the region. In time, these small settlements grew and became the nucleus of present-day Canada. **Section Focus Question: How did France's American colonies differ from Spain's American colonies?**

The French Establish a Fur Trade

During the early 1500s, explorers who sailed for France, including Giovanni da Verrazano and Jacques Cartier, were less interested in establishing colonies and more interested in finding a **Northwest Passage**—a water route to Asia through the cold waters of present-day Canada. They probed the eastern coastline of North America, from present-day North Carolina to Newfoundland. During the 1530s and 1540s, Cartier investigated the St. Lawrence River.

France Establishes New France The French king claimed the region that Cartier explored as New France. At the mouth of the St. Lawrence River, French mariners fished for cod and hunted for whales and seals. The mariners met Indian hunters, who offered furs in trade. Rendered scarce in Europe by excessive hunting, furs, especially beaver fur, commanded high prices.

Indians eagerly traded fur for metal arrowheads, hoes, axes, knives, and hatchets, all useful both as tools and weapons, and for iron or brass kettles, which made it easier to boil their meals. A Montagnais Indian explained, "The Beaver does everything perfectly well, it makes kettles, hatchets, swords, knives, bread; in short, it makes everything." Increasingly, the Indians hunted for a foreign market rather than just for their own subsistence.

Killing the beaver faster than the animals could reproduce, the coastal Indians sought new stocks by invading the hunting territories of their neighbors. This provoked wars between Indian groups. Those without metal weapons lost these wars, which also gave them a powerful incentive to trade with the French. Every American Indian nation tried to attract European traders and keep them away from their Indian enemies.

Quebec
Founded in 1608, Quebec was the first permanent European settlement in Canada. *How did Quebec's location contribute to its defense and economic prosperity?*

Just as the Indians fought one another over trade, the traders plundered and killed one another in their competition for furs. To repel rivals, a French company built a fortified trading post at Quebec on the St. Lawrence River in 1608. **Quebec** was the first permanent European settlement in Canada.

French–Indian Relations Unlike the Spanish in Mexico, the Canadian French could not afford to intimidate, dispossess, or enslave the Indians. The French needed them as hunters and suppliers of furs—roles that the Indians eagerly performed. Few in number, the French took little land, coming into little conflict with Canada's Native Americans.

Samuel de Champlain, Quebec's founder, traded with the Montagnais, Algonquin, and Huron Indians. In return, they expected Champlain to help them against their foes: the Iroquois, who lived to the south in what is now New York. In 1609, Champlain and nine French soldiers helped their allies attack an Iroquois camp beside the lake later named after Champlain. Expecting a traditional Indian battle, rich in display and light in casualties, the Iroquois formed up in a mass. They counted on their wooden shields, helmets, and body armor for protection from arrows. They were shocked when Champlain and his soldiers fired their guns, instantly killing Iroquois chiefs and warriors. Bewildered, the Iroquois warriors ran away.

Champlain won the battle at a high long-term cost. He made enemies of the powerful Iroquois, who for decades thereafter raided the French settlements. The battle also revolutionized Indian warfare. The Iroquois abandoned wooden armor, and they avoided massed formations. Instead, they relied on trees for cover and shifted their tactics to hit-and-run raids. They also demanded their own guns as the price of trade. Obtaining guns from Dutch traders on the Hudson River, the Iroquois became better armed than their Algonquin, Montagnais, and Huron enemies.

Exploring the Mississippi
French explorers Louis Joliet and Father Jacques Marquette traveled together from the Great Lakes to the Mississippi River in 1673.

Jesuit Missionaries Like the Spanish, the French dispatched Catholic priests as missionaries to convert the Indians. Belonging to the Jesuit order, the French missionaries enjoyed their greatest success among the Hurons, who lived beside Lake Huron, one of the Great Lakes. But that success attracted Iroquois warriors, who destroyed the Huron villages between 1648 and 1649. Killing hundreds, including most of the priests, the raiders carried away thousands of Huron captives for forced adoption by the Iroquois. The Jesuit missions survived only in the St. Lawrence Valley, between the major towns of Montreal and Quebec.

✓ **Checkpoint** How did the battle at Lake Champlain change the methods used by the Iroquois to fight the French?

Life in New France

New France's government resembled that of New Spain. Both were strictly controlled by the powerful monarchs of the homeland. The French king appointed a military governor-general, a civil administrator known as the *intendant,* and a Catholic bishop. Like the Spanish, the French king did not permit an elected assembly in Canada.

New France Grows Slowly Attracting few immigrants, New France grew slowly. By 1700, the colony still had only 15,000 colonists. Potential colonists balked at the hard work of clearing dense forests to plant new farms. The long Canadian winter shocked newcomers from temperate France. Worst of all, immigrants dreaded the Iroquois raids.

Most French colonists were farmers who settled in the St. Lawrence Valley. To the west, Indians <u>dominated</u> the vast hinterland of forests and lakes, where the colonists were few and scattered. In the Great Lakes and Illinois countries, the French established a handful of small settlements, including Detroit. They lived by a mix of farming and trade.

Vocabulary Builder
<u>dominate</u>—(DAHM uh nayt) *v.* to have control, power, or authority over somebody or something

Alliances With Indians Bring Benefits To survive and prosper in an Indian world, the French had to adopt some of the Indians' ways. Known as ***coureurs de bois*** (koo rer duh BWAH), many fur traders married Indian women. The children of these marriages became known as the ***metis.***

With the help of the *coureurs de bois* and the *metis,* the French allied with the Great Lakes Indians, who primarily spoke an Algonquian language. The allies defeated the Iroquois during the 1680s and 1690s, compelling them to make peace in 1701. At last, the fur traders of the Great Lakes and the grain farmers of the St. Lawrence Valley could work in safety from Iroquois raids.

Louisiana and New Orleans In 1682, the French explorer Robert de LaSalle was hoping to find a Northwest Passage. Guided by Native Americans, he made his way south on the Mississippi River toward what he hoped was an opening to the Pacific Ocean. Instead, he found the Gulf of Mexico. La Salle claimed the territory around the Mississippi River basin for France, naming it Louisiana, in honor of King Louis XIV. In 1718, near the river's mouth, the French founded New Orleans, which became the colony's largest town and leading seaport.

Like Canada, Louisiana struggled to attract colonists. The economy provided few opportunities beyond trading with the Indians for deerskins or raising tobacco of poor quality. The hot climate and swampy landscape also promoted deadly diseases, especially dysentery and malaria. Only a third of the immigrants remained alive in Louisiana in 1731, when the colony had just 2,000 whites and 4,000 enslaved Africans.

The French primarily valued Louisiana as a military base to keep the English from grabbing the immense Mississippi watershed. As in the Great Lakes country, the French sought Indian allies to help them confine the English colonies that were growing to the east along the Atlantic coast.

New Orleans
Despite a hot, humid climate and the danger of coastal storms, the French built a settlement at New Orleans. *Why was control of New Orleans important to the French?*

✔ **Checkpoint** Why did New France attract few colonists?

SECTION 2 Assessment

Progress Monitoring *Online*
For: Self-test with vocabulary practice
Web Code: nca-0204

Comprehension

1. **Terms and People** For each item below, write a sentence that tells how it contributed to the development of New France.
   • Northwest Passage
   • Quebec
   • Samuel de Champlain
   • *coureurs de bois*
   • *metis*

2. **NoteTaking Reading Skill: Compare and Contrast** Use your Venn diagram to answer the Section Focus Question: How did France's American colonies differ from Spain's American colonies?

Writing About History

3. **Quick Write: Identify Effects** Make a list of one or two effects of each of the following events: the search for the Northwest Passage, the fur trade, and Champlain's attack on the Iroquois in 1609.

Critical Thinking

4. **Analyze Information** Why did the economy of the French colonies in the Americas depend on a good relationship with Native Americans?

5. **Recognize Cause and Effect** How did trade and warfare with France affect the Iroquois and other Native American nations?

6. **Support Generalizations** What evidence supports the following generalization: Conflicts among the nations of Europe emerged as they competed for territory in the Americas.

▲ Pocahontas in European clothing

WITNESS HISTORY AUDIO

Pocahontas

The earliest English settlers at Jamestown would have perished without assistance from Native Americans. A young Indian girl named Pocahontas was especially helpful. A daughter of Chief Powhatan, Pocahontas visited the Jamestown settlement and carried messages between the settlers and her father.

Despite Pocahontas's help, conflict arose between the Native Americans and the Jamestown colonists. During a period of warfare, Pocahontas was held captive in Jamestown. During this captivity, she and settler John Rolfe became engaged and later married. Both the Indians and the English settlers viewed the marriage between Rolfe and Pocahontas as a chance to end the war.

England's Southern Colonies

 Core Curriculum Objectives

- **2.I.A.2a** Relations between colonists and Native American Indians
- **2.I.A.3a** Colonial charters and self-government: House of Burgesses
- **2.I.A.3c** Colonial slavery

Terms and People

charter	royal colony
joint-stock company	proprietary colony
Powhatan	Bacon's Rebellion
John Smith	Lord Baltimore
House of Burgesses	James Oglethorpe

NoteTaking

Reading Skill: Sequence As you read this section, use a flowchart to list the important events in the founding of the Southern Colonies. Add boxes as you need them.

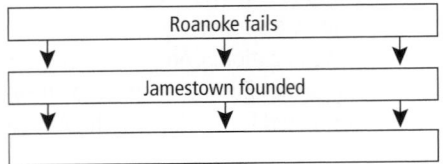

Why It Matters Neglected by the Spanish and French, the Atlantic coast remained open to English colonization during the 1580s. England's first attempts to establish a colony in North America failed, but in 1607 they succeeded in founding Jamestown, which became part of the colony of Virginia. By 1732, four more Southern Colonies had been established: Maryland, North Carolina, South Carolina, and Georgia. **Section Focus Question: What were the characteristics of the government and the economy in the Southern Colonies?**

England's First American Colonies

The first promoters of English colonies were wealthy gentlemen from southwestern England. They included Sir Walter Raleigh, a special favorite of Queen Elizabeth I. English patriots and devout Protestants, these men wanted to advance their fortunes and increase the power of England.

They promised that an American colony would solve England's problems: a growing population and increased poverty due to a stagnant economy. The promoters proposed shipping poor people across the Atlantic to work in a new colony. By mining for gold and silver and by raising plantation crops, these workers would generate new wealth for England.

Roanoke Colony Fails After obtaining a **charter,** or certificate of permission, from the king, the group formed a **joint-stock company.** This was a business venture founded and run by a group of investors who were to share in the company's profits and losses. During the 1580s, Raleigh twice tried to colonize Roanoke, a small island on the North Carolina coast (then considered part of Virginia). But English ships struggled to land supplies, and the sandy, infertile soil produced scanty crops. Raleigh's first colonists returned home in despair. The second set mysteriously vanished.

The Virginia Company Sends More Colonists The English tried again under the new leadership of the Virginia Company, a corporation of great merchants based in London. In 1607, the colonists proceeded to Chesapeake Bay, a superior location north of Roanoke. The Chesapeake offered many good harbors and navigable rivers—as well as more fertile land. But the colonists also had to deal with especially powerful Indians.

Although divided into 30 tribes, the region's 24,000 Indians shared an Algonquian language. They were also united by the rule of an unusually powerful chief named **Powhatan.** In his sixties, Powhatan impressed the English colonists with his dignity, keen mind, and powerful build.

Rather than confront the colonists at the risk of heavy casualties, Powhatan hoped to contain them and to use them against his own enemies, the Indians of the interior. He especially wanted to trade with the colonists for their metal weapons.

Chief Powhatan ▼

The colonists, however, wanted Indian lands. They refused to recognize that the Indians occupied, used, and had ancestral ties to these lands. Despite the many native villages and their large fields of maize, Captain **John Smith,** a colonist who emerged as a strong leader, described Virginia as "overgrowne with trees and weedes, being a plaine wilderness as God first made it." The English insisted on improving that "wilderness" into profitable farmland.

✓ **Checkpoint** How did Powhatan deal with the English colonists?

Jamestown Overcomes Hardships

The colonists founded a new settlement and named it Jamestown to honor King James I. The surrounding swamps defended the town from attack, but those swamps also bred mosquitoes that carried deadly diseases, especially malaria. The colonists also suffered from hunger, for they were often too weakened by disease to tend their crops. Between 1607 and 1622, the Virginia Company would transport some 10,000 people to the colony, but only 20 percent of them would still be alive in 1622.

Conflict With Native Americans In 1609, war broke out between the Indians and the starving colonists. In 1613, the English captured Powhatan's favorite daughter, Pocahontas. As an English captive, Pocahontas converted to Christianity and married a colonist named John Rolfe. Weary with war, Powhatan reluctantly made peace. When Powhatan died in 1618, power passed to his brother Opechancanough (oh PEHCH uhn kah noh), who hated the invaders from England.

The Tobacco Crop Saves the Colony By 1616, the Virginia Company had spent more than 50,000 English pounds—an immense sum for that time. Yet all it had to show for it was an unprofitable settlement of 350 diseased, hungry, and unhappy colonists. The company saved the colony by allowing the colonists to own and work land as their private property. As farmer-owners, rather than company employees, the colonists worked harder to grow the corn, squash, and beans that ensured their survival. But to make a profit, they still needed a commercial crop to market in England.

JAMESTOWN
A COLONY SURVIVES

The first group of English settlers arrived in Jamestown on May 13, 1607. They established what would become the first permanent English settlement in America. But settling the region proved troublesome, as the settlers searched in vain for gold and refused to farm. Indians attacked the settlers for attempting to take Indian lands and food. Suffering from disease, malnutrition, and Indian attacks, two thirds of the Jamestown settlers died within the first seven months. The future looked bleak for the surviving settlers.

Fort James ▲
Colonists built the fort soon after they arrived.

◄ **Trade** Jamestown colonists grew tobacco for export to England. They traded beads and other manufactured goods with Indians for food.

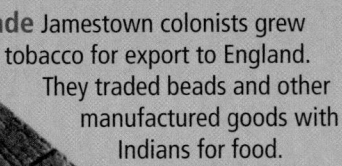

Starving Time During the ►
winter of 1609–1610, only 60 of about 200 settlers survived. In June, as the remaining colonists prepared to leave Virginia, a supply ship arrived.

Led by John Rolfe, the colonists learned how to cultivate tobacco in 1616. West Indian tobacco had become extraordinarily popular for smoking in Europe. King James fought a losing battle when he denounced smoking as "a custom loathsome to the eye, hateful to the nose, harmful to the brain, [and] dangerous to the lungs." Eventually, though, he learned to love the revenue that the Crown reaped by taxing tobacco imports.

Because tobacco plants need a long, hot, and humid growing season, the crop thrived in Virginia but not in England. That difference gave the colonial farmers an advantage. Their tobacco production surged from 200,000 pounds in 1624 to more than 1.5 million pounds in 1640. The Chesapeake region became the principal supplier of tobacco to Europe. The profits attracted more immigrants to Virginia.

Free Land Attracts Colonists to Virginia Beginning in 1619, the Virginia Company offered free land. Under the headright system, anyone who paid for passage to Virginia or who paid for another person's passage received 50 acres of land. This enabled the wealthiest colonists to acquire large plantations. To work those plantations, landowners imported workers from England. The population of Virginia began to grow.

The House of Burgesses The Virginia Company also granted political reforms. In 1619, it allowed the planters to create the **House of Burgesses,** the first representative body in colonial America. Male landowners over 17 years of age voted for two Burgesses to represent their settlement. The House of Burgesses had the power to make laws and raise taxes. It began a strong tradition of representative government in the English colonies.

Success By 1615, Jamestown was growing due to the leadership of John Smith and John Rolfe. Smith forced colonists to work hard. He also established trade with the Indians. Rolfe established tobacco as a crop in Jamestown, saving the colony from financial ruin.

▲ Captain John Smith

Thinking Critically
1. **Draw Inferences** Do you think Jamestown would have survived without John Smith's leadership? Why or why not?
2. **Draw Conclusions** What evidence is there that the Jamestown colonists were prepared to trade with the Indians?

History *Interactive* ★
For: More about Jamestown
Web Code: ncp-0205

In 1624, the Crown took over Virginia, making it the first royal colony in the English empire. During the seventeenth century, the English developed two types of colonial governments: royal and proprietary. The **royal colonies** belonged to the Crown, while the **proprietary colonies** belonged to powerful individuals or companies.

 Checkpoint What challenges did the Jamestown settlers overcome to survive?

The Effects of Expansion in Virginia

As the colonists expanded their tobacco plantations, they took more land from the Indians, who became enraged. In 1622, Opechancanough led a surprise attack that burned plantations and killed nearly a third of the colonists.

Wars With Algonquin Indians But counterattacks by the colonial survivors destroyed the Indian villages and their crops, reducing the natives to starvation. Defeated, Opechancanough made peace in 1632. The victors took more land and spread their settlements northward to the Potomac River.

With English settlements expanding, yet another war broke out between the colonists and Indians. In 1644, <u>intense</u> fighting killed hundreds of colonists and thousands of Indians, including Opechancanough. Disease and war reduced the Virginia Algonquins from 24,000 in 1607 to only 2,000 by 1670. The survivors became confined to small areas surrounded by colonial settlements. The number of settlers continued to surge, reaching 41,000 in 1670. The English had come to stay, to the alarm of Indians in the interior.

Vocabulary Builder
<u>intense</u>—(ihn TEHNS) *adj.* great, strong, or extreme in a way that can be felt

Bacon's Rebellion As the population of Virginia increased, settlers moved onto less fertile lands in the interior, where it cost more to transport their crops to market. They also faced greater danger from Indians angered by their intrusion.

The royal governor of Virginia, William Berkeley, worsened the growing crisis. Berkeley levied heavy taxes on the planters and used the proceeds to reward a few favorites from the wealthiest class, which dominated the House of Burgesses. He also expressed contempt for a free press and public education for common people. In 1671, he declared:

> **Primary Source** "I thank God, there are no free schools nor printing [in Virginia], and I hope we shall not have these [for a] hundred years; for learning has brought disobedience and heresy . . . into the world, and printing has divulged [spread] them, and libels [untruths] against the best government. God keep us from both!"
> —William Berkeley, 1671

In 1675, war erupted between the Indians and the settlers in the Potomac Valley. The settlers wanted to exterminate all of the colony's Indians. When Berkeley balked, the settlers rebelled under the leadership of the ambitious and reckless Nathaniel Bacon.

To popular acclaim, Bacon's men slaughtered Indians, peaceful as well as hostile. When Berkeley protested, Bacon marched his armed followers to Jamestown in a revolt called **Bacon's Rebellion.** In September 1676, they drove out the governor and burned the town. A month later, however, Bacon died suddenly of disease, and his rebellion collapsed. Berkeley regained power, but the rebellion had undermined his credibility. In 1677, the king appointed a new governor, and Berkeley returned to England.

Bacon's Rebellion showed that poorer farmers would not tolerate a government that catered only to the wealthiest colonists. The colony's leaders reduced the taxes paid by the farmers and improved their access to frontier land. But that frontier policy provoked further wars with the Indians of the interior.

✓ **Checkpoint** What were the causes of Bacon's Rebellion?

Other Southern Colonies

Virginia was the first of the Southern Colonies to be settled. During the seventeenth and eighteenth centuries, England established the Southern Colonies of Maryland, North Carolina, South Carolina, and Georgia.

Maryland In 1632, at the northern head of Chesapeake Bay, the English king established a second Southern Colony, named Maryland. The name honored Mary, the queen of the new monarch, Charles I (son of James). Charles gave Maryland to a favorite aristocrat, **Lord Baltimore,** who owned and governed it as a proprietary colony. Lord Baltimore founded Maryland as a colonial refuge for his fellow Catholics, who were discriminated against in England by the Protestant majority. Contrary to Lord Baltimore's hopes, however, more Protestants than Catholics immigrated to Maryland. Relations between the two groups deteriorated into armed conflict later in the century.

A Busy Port
Charles Town, South Carolina, was a center of trade and commerce by 1739. *How did Charles Town's location make it susceptible to attack?*

The Carolinas In 1670, the English established a new colony on the coast, north of Florida but south of Virginia. Called Carolina to honor King Charles II, the new colony included present-day North Carolina and South Carolina. The first settlement and capital was Charles Town, also named to honor the king. Carolina officially belonged to a group of English aristocrats—the Lords Proprietor—who remained in England, entrusting the colony's leadership to ambitious men from the West Indies. In 1691, the Lords Proprietor set aside the northern half of their territory as the distinct colony of North Carolina. In 1729, the North and South Carolinians rejected the control by the Lords Proprietor. The Carolinians demanded and received a Crown takeover. Thereafter, the king appointed their governors, who had to cooperate with elected assemblies in each colony.

Georgia In 1732, Georgia began as a proprietary colony intended to protect South Carolina against Spanish Florida. Led by **James Oglethorpe,** the Georgia trustees designed their colony as a haven for English debtors, who had been jailed because they could not pay their debts. Yet, most of Georgia's first colonists were poor English traders and artisans, or religious refugees from Switzerland and Germany.

Oglethorpe set strict rules for colonists. They could not drink alcohol and could not own slaves. Georgia's colonists had to work their own land and could therefore not own large plantations. These restrictions angered the colonists, who protested until the trustees surrendered to the Crown. Georgia became a royal colony in 1752.

✓ **Checkpoint** Why did Lord Baltimore establish Maryland?

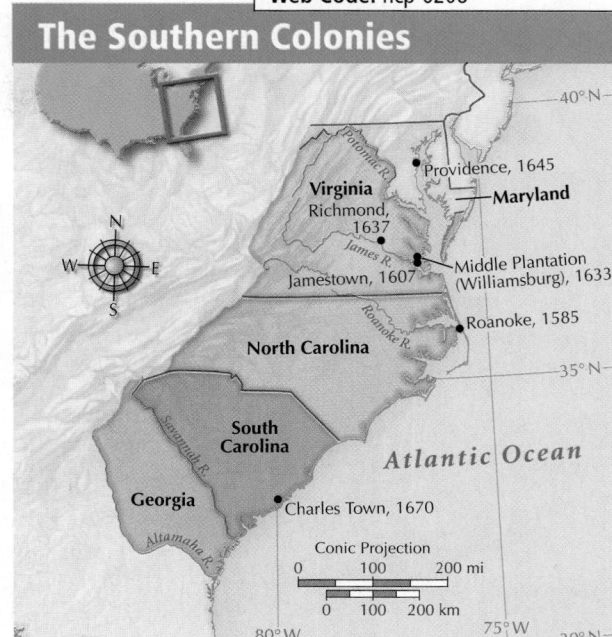

Geography *Interactive*
For: Interactive map
Web Code: ncp-0206

The Southern Colonies

Map Skills By 1732, there were five Southern Colonies.

1. **Locate:** (a) Jamestown, (b) Charles Town, (c) Altamaha River

2. **Place** Which rivers formed Georgia's borders?

3. **Draw Conclusions** Why do you think early settlements in the Americas were founded on or near bodies of water?

SECTION

3 Assessment

Progress Monitoring *Online*
For: Self-test with vocabulary practice
Web Code: nca-0207

Comprehension

1. **Terms and People** What do the terms and people below have in common? Explain.
   - charter
   - joint-stock company
   - Powhatan
   - John Smith
   - House of Burgesses
   - royal colony
   - proprietary colony
   - Bacon's Rebellion
   - Lord Baltimore
   - James Oglethorpe

2. **NoteTaking Reading Skill: Sequence** Use your flowchart to answer the Section Focus Question: What were the characteristics of the government and the economy in the Southern Colonies?

Writing About History

3. **Quick Write: Create a Flowchart** As you prepare to write a cause-and-effect essay, you need to decide how to organize it. To do this, create a flowchart that shows the causes and effects of Bacon's Rebellion. Decide whether you want to write about the events in chronological order or in order of importance.

Critical Thinking

4. **Draw Conclusions** What combination of geographic and economic circumstances allowed Jamestown to survive?

5. **Identify Central Issues** How did the House of Burgesses distinguish the English colony of Virginia from Spanish and French colonies in the Americas?

6. **Recognize Bias** How did colonists' attitudes toward Native Americans lead to Bacon's Rebellion?

▲ Settlers land at Plymouth Rock

WITNESS HISTORY 🔊 AUDIO

The Pilgrims Leave for America

John Robinson, a Puritan pastor, addressed the Puritans who were about to sail to America on the *Mayflower*. Robinson spoke to them about how they should choose those who would govern them. He told the Puritans:

“. . . whereas you are become a body politic, using amongst yourselves civil government, and are not furnished with any persons of special emiency above the rest, to be chosen by you into office of government; let your wisdom and godliness appear, not only in choosing such persons as do entirely love and will promote the common good, but also in yielding unto them all due honor and obedience in their lawful administrations. . . .”

—John Robinson, August 5, 1620

The New England Colonies

 Core Curriculum Objectives

- **2.I.A.2a** Relations between colonists and Native American Indians
- **2.I.A.2c** The peoples of the American colonies: Varieties of immigrant motivation, ethnicities, and experiences
- **2.I.A.3a** Colonial charters and self-government: Mayflower Compact

Terms and People

Puritan
Separatist
Pilgrim
Mayflower Compact
John Winthrop

Roger Williams
Anne Hutchinson
Pequot War
King Philip's War
Metacom

NoteTaking

Reading Skill: Recognize Multiple Causes
Create a chart to identify the reasons the Pilgrims left Europe.

Causes for Puritans' Emigration From England		
• Disagreements with Anglican Church	•	•

Why It Matters Far to the north of the Southern Colonies, the English founded another set of colonies during the 1600s. New England was a land of dense forests, rolling hills, and a short growing season. New England demanded hard labor to farm and offered little prospect of getting rich. Before long, however, trade and commerce would bring prosperity to New England. **Section Focus Question: What were the goals of the Plymouth and Massachusetts Bay colonies?**

Puritans and the Church of England

Most of the New England colonists were religious dissidents who disagreed with the established church. Known as **Puritans,** they wanted to purify the Church of England, or Anglican Church, the only official and legal church in that kingdom. The Puritans believed that the Anglican Church, although Protestant, retained too many ceremonies from the Catholic Church. And a Catholic-style hierarchy of bishops controlled the local congregations. While some Puritans sought to reform the Anglican Church, others known as **Separatists** began their own churches.

Puritan Beliefs and Values The Puritans followed the teachings of the theologian John Calvin. They believed that they could prepare for God's saving grace by leading moral lives, praying devoutly, reading the Bible, and heeding their ministers' sermons. But not even the most devout could claim salvation as a right and a certainty, for they believed God alone determined who was saved. Salvation depended on the will of God rather than good behavior or adherence to church rules.

Puritans came from all ranks of English society, including aristocrats. Most belonged to "the middling sort"—a term used to describe small-property holders, farmers, shopkeepers, and skilled artisans. Their modest properties put them economically ahead of much of the English population.

Puritanism reinforced the values of thrift, diligence, and morality. Puritans insisted that men honored God by working hard in their occupations. One Puritan explained, "God sent you unto this world as unto a Workhouse, not a Playhouse."

Puritans Challenge the Anglican Church
By challenging England's official church, the Puritans troubled the English monarchs, who led the Anglican Church. During the 1620s, King Charles I began to persecute the Puritans. His bishops dismissed Puritan ministers from their parishes and censored or destroyed Puritan books. Some Puritans sought a colonial refuge in North America, where they could escape the supervision of Anglican bishops. In their own colony, the Puritans could worship in their own churches and make their own laws, which they derived from the Bible. By living morally and prospering economically, they hoped to inspire their countrymen in England to adopt Puritan reforms.

✔ **Checkpoint** Why did Puritans challenge the Anglican Church?

Puritans Arrive in Massachusetts

In 1620, the first Puritan emigrants, who were later called **Pilgrims,** crossed the Atlantic in the ship the *Mayflower* to found the Plymouth Colony on the south shore of Massachusetts Bay. Before they disembarked, the group of about 100 made an agreement called the **Mayflower Compact.** The settlers agreed to form a government and obey its laws. This idea of self-government would later become one of the founding principles of the United States.

Massachusetts Bay Colony
In 1630, **John Winthrop** led a much larger group of Puritans to America. Winthrop exhorted his fellow Puritans to make their new colony "A City upon a Hill," an inspirational example for the people of England. Winthrop explained:

Primary Source "For we must consider that we shall be as a City upon a hill. The eyes of all people are upon us. [So] that if we shall deal falsely with our God in this work we have undertaken, and so cause him to withdraw his present help from us, we shall be made a story and a byword throughout the world."
—John Winthrop, 1630

Beginning with the town of Boston, these Puritans established the Massachusetts Bay Colony on the north shore of that broad bay. In Massachusetts, settlers established a republic, where the Puritan men elected their governor, deputy governor, and assembly. This was the most radical government in the colonies because it was the only one that elected its governor.

From the towns of Plymouth and Boston, colonists spread rapidly along the coast and into the interior. To the northeast, New

Plymouth Colony
Puritans established Plymouth Colony in 1620. They built English-style houses and survived due to help from Native Americans. *Why did the colonists build a stockade around their settlement?*

Hampshire and Maine emerged, where Puritans settled uneasily with fishing folk who were Anglicans. To the southeast, Rhode Island became a haven for especially radical Puritans. More conservative Puritans founded Connecticut along the Connecticut River and New Haven beside Long Island Sound. By the end of the seventeenth century, Massachusetts Bay Colony included Maine and Plymouth, while Connecticut absorbed New Haven.

Vocabulary Builder

toleration–(tahl uhr AY shuhn) *n.* government acceptance of religious beliefs and ideas that are different from established ones

Religious Dissenters Form New Colonies Most of the Puritans immigrated to New England to realize their own ideal society—and certainly not to champion religious toleration. A leading New Englander denounced "the lawlessnesse of liberty of conscience" as an invitation to heresy and anarchy. No Catholics, Baptists, or Quakers need come to New England—except to Rhode Island. Dissenters were given, in the words of one Puritan, "free Liberty to keep away from us." To make that point, the Massachusetts government executed four Quakers and burned their books. The Puritans feared that God would punish any people who tolerated individual choice in religion.

The Puritans also purged their own people for expressing radical religious opinions. During the 1630s, **Roger Williams** and **Anne Hutchinson** angered the authorities by arguing that Massachusetts had not done enough to break with Anglican ways. Williams argued that settlers had no right to take land from the Indians. He said they needed to purchase the land from the Indians.

As a woman, Hutchinson seemed doubly dangerous to Puritan leaders who insisted that only men should exercise public influence. Though she ably defended herself in a trial, John Winthrop banished Hutchinson from Massachusetts.

Prosecuted by the authorities, Williams fled to Rhode Island, where he founded Providence in 1636. Rhode Island was a rare haven for religious toleration in the colonial world. Hutchinson and her family moved to the colony after she was exiled from Massachusetts. Rhode Island attracted Baptists, Quakers, and Jews. Lacking a majority for any one faith, the Rhode Islanders agreed to separate church and state. They believed that mingling church and state corrupted religion.

Salem Witch Trials In addition to punishing religious dissenters, the New England Colonies prosecuted suspected witches. Whenever cattle and children sickened and died, the New Englanders suspected evil magic. For the safety of the community, witches had to be identified, prosecuted, and neutralized. The supposed victims of magic blamed neighbors who seemed to bear them ill will.

The most spectacular accusations occurred in and around Salem, Massachusetts, in 1692. The authorities there tried, convicted, and executed 19 suspected witches. But when the accusations reached members of prominent families, including the governor's wife, the judges dropped

HISTORY MAKERS

Roger Williams
(1603–1683)
Roger Williams, a Puritan minister, came to Massachusetts in 1631. He held that the king had no right to give to English colonists land that belonged to Native Americans. After a Massachusetts court banished him and his followers, Williams founded Providence, Rhode Island—on land purchased from Native Americans. He established religious freedom and separation of church and state. Williams also allowed all males who headed families the right to vote. In Massachusetts, only church members could vote.

Anne Hutchinson
(1591–1643)
Hutchinson arrived in Massachusetts in 1634, where she held meetings in her home to boldly promote her idea that God's grace alone was the key to salvation. But the colony's leaders opposed preaching by a woman. In 1637, they declared her ideas heresy and banished her. She moved first to Rhode Island and later to New Netherland, where she was killed in a Native American attack.

any further trials. Reassessed as a fiasco, the Salem mania ended the prosecution of witches in New England.

✓ **Checkpoint** Why did Rhode Island become a haven for people of various religious faiths?

Conflict With the Native Americans

The Puritans saw the Indians as lazy savages who accepted life in the wild, instead of laboring to conquer nature. The colonists remade the land to resemble England by clearing and fencing fields for cultivation in the English fashion. They built English-style houses, barns, mills, and churches. They introduced domesticated cattle, sheep, horses, and pigs. Colonists also killed wild animals that preyed on livestock.

The Pequot War By the 1630s, the Puritans of New England were engaged in a brisk fur trade with the Pequots and several other Indian nations. However, it was an uneasy relationship. Rivalry over control of the trade, coupled with Indian opposition to English territorial expansion, led to the outbreak of the **Pequot War.**

In 1636, Puritans accused the Pequots of murdering an English trader. But the Pequots denied the accusation. Allied with Narragansett and Mohegan Indians—enemies of the Pequots—the Puritans attacked several Pequot villages. In turn, the Pequots raided a Puritan village. Outraged, the Puritans burned a Pequot village filled with mostly women and children and killed most of its 600 to 700 inhabitants. The carnage was so complete that even the Puritans' Indian allies were shocked by the "manner of the Englishmen's fight . . . because it is too furious, and slays too many men." In 1638, by the Treaty of Hartford, the victorious English, Narragansetts, and Mohegans virtually eliminated the Pequot nation. The Pequots lost all their lands and surviving Pequots went to live among other Indian peoples.

Praying Towns After the Pequot War, the Puritans worked to convert and transform the Indians into replicas of English Christians. They pressured the Indians to move into special "praying towns," where they could be closely supervised by missionaries. By 1674, Massachusetts had 14 praying towns with 1,600 Indian inhabitants. After restricting the Indians to a few special towns, the Puritans claimed most of their lands for colonial settlement. The missionaries forced the praying-town Indians to abandon their traditional ways and to don English clothing. The missionaries insisted upon the English division of <u>gender</u> roles. They urged the Indian men to forsake hunting and fishing in favor of farming. The Indian women were supposed to withdraw from the cornfields to tend the home and to spin and weave cloth—just as English women did.

However, only a minority agreed to enter the praying towns. As the colonists continued to expand their settlements at the Indians' expense, most Native Americans despaired of keeping their lands without a war.

The Pequot War
In 1637, Puritans led an assault against the Pequot, destroying their villages. This woodcut shows Puritans and their Indian allies attacking a Pequot fort.

Vocabulary Builder
gender–(JEHN duhr) *n.* condition of being male or female, especially regarding how the condition affects social status

The New England Colonies

Geography *Interactive*
For: Interactive map
Web Code: ncp-0208

Area claimed by New York and New Hampshire

Maine (part of Mass.)

N.H.

Portland, 1633

Portsmouth, 1623

Salem, 1626

Massachusetts • Boston, 1630

Plymouth, 1620

Hartford, 1635 • Providence, 1636

Connecticut

New Haven, 1638

Newport, 1639

Rhode Island

Atlantic Ocean

Conic Projection

0   50   100 mi

0   50   100 km

70° W

Map Skills The New England colonists found a cool climate and a rocky terrain.

1. **Place** Which settlement was established three years after Plymouth?

2. **Draw Conclusions** How did New England's geography affect its economy?

King Philip's War In 1675, a massive Indian rebellion erupted. The colonists called it **King Philip's War,** after a chief named **Metacom** who was known to the colonists as "King Philip." They imagined that he plotted and led the rebellion. In fact, every Indian village fought under its own leader. Far from any masterful plot by Metacom, the uprising consisted of many angry groups of Indians acting separately but similarly.

With guns acquired from traders, the Indians at first devastated the New England settlements, destroying 12 towns. But the tide of war turned in 1676, when the rebels began to starve because their crops were destroyed by colonial counterattacks. The Indians also ran out of ammunition after losing their access to colonial traders. In August, Metacom died in battle, shot down by a praying-town Indian who served with the colonists. The war killed at least 1,000 English colonists and about 3,000 Indians.

The defeated Indians lost most of their remaining lands in southern New England. They survived only as a small minority on limited lands within a region dominated by the newcomers. In 1700, the 92,000 colonists outnumbered New England's 9,000 Indians.

Some of the defeated Indians fled northward to the French colony of Canada, where they found refuge. Whenever the French waged war on the English, the refugee Indians sought revenge by raiding the New England frontier. Those wars became frequent and bloody after 1689, as the English and the French escalated their struggle to dominate North America.

✓ **Checkpoint** How did Puritan praying towns compare with Spanish missions?

SECTION 4 Assessment

Progress Monitoring *Online*
For: Self-test with vocabulary practice
Web Code: nca-0209

Comprehension

1. **Terms and People** Write a sentence for each item below that explains how it is related to the founding of the New England Colonies.
   - Puritan
   - Separatist
   - Pilgrim
   - Mayflower Compact
   - John Winthrop
   - Roger Williams
   - Anne Hutchinson
   - Pequot War
   - King Philip's War
   - Metacom

2. **NoteTaking Reading Skill: Recognizing Multiple Causes** Use your chart to answer the Section Focus Question: What were the goals of the Plymouth and Massachusetts Bay colonies?

Writing About History

3. **Quick Write: List Effects** List the effects of one of the following events: the Mayflower Compact, the founding of Rhode Island, or the Salem witch trials. Then, rank the effects in order of importance.

Critical Thinking

4. **Identify Point of View** Read the following quotation and explain how it reflects Puritan values: "God sent you unto this world as unto a Workhouse, not a Playhouse."

5. **Make Comparisons** Compare the governments of the Virginia and Massachusetts colonies. How were the governments similar? How were they different?

6. **Recognize Bias** Consider the relationship between Indians and the following groups: Puritans, Virginians, Spanish colonists, and French colonists. How did each group's relationship with Native Americans reflect that group's bias toward Indians?

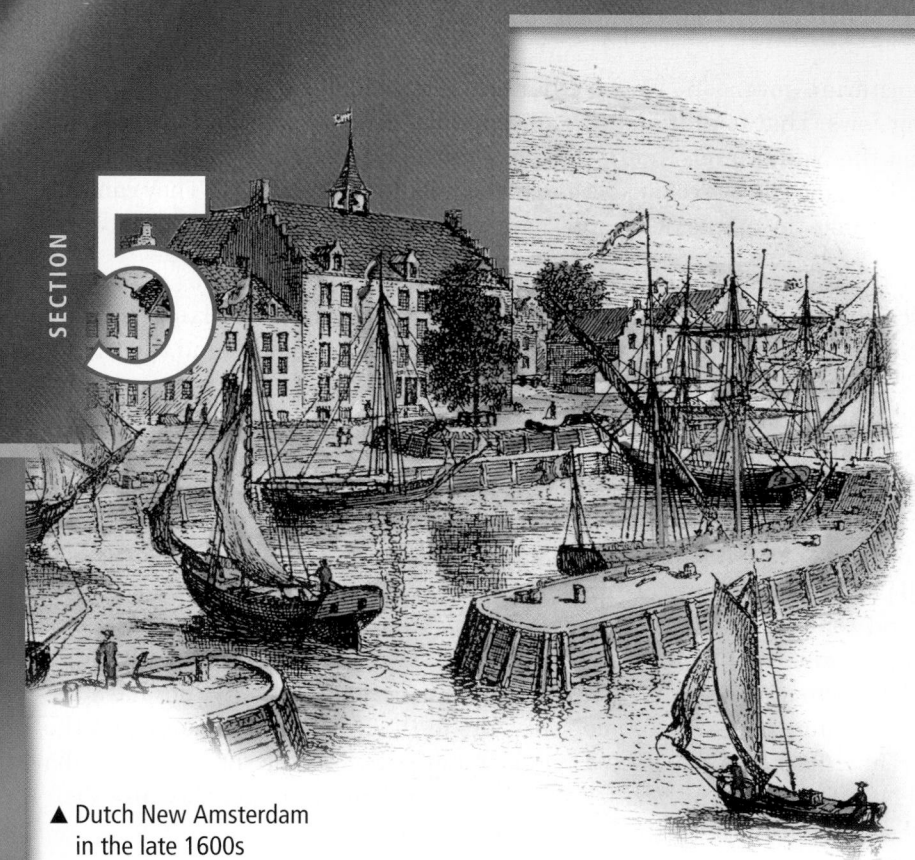

▲ Dutch New Amsterdam in the late 1600s

SECTION 5

WITNESS HISTORY AUDIO

The Dutch in New Amsterdam

At about the same time English colonists were establishing the Jamestown and Plymouth colonies, the Dutch founded New Netherland. New Amsterdam, the site of present-day Manhattan, was the Dutch capital. In the letter below, Peter Schaghen, an official of the Dutch West India Company, tells the directors of the purchase of Manhattan:

❝High and Mighty Lords,
Yesterday the ship the *Arms of Amsterdam* arrived here. It sailed from New Netherland . . . on the 23d of September. They report that our people are in good spirit and live in peace. The women also have borne some children there. They have purchased the Island Manhattes [Manhattan] from the Indians for the value of 60 guilders.❞

—Peter Schaghen, 1626

The Middle Colonies

 Core Curriculum Objectives

- **1.I.D.1d** Demographics: Religion
- **2.I.A.2** The peoples of the American colonies
- **2.I.A.3** Colonial experience: political rights and mercantile relationships

Key Terms and People

push factor   William Penn
pull factor   Quaker

NoteTaking

Reading Skill: Identifying Main Ideas and Details As you read this section, prepare an outline like the one below.

> I. The Dutch Establish New Netherland
>   A. Government in New Netherland
>   1. No elected assembly
>   2. Religious tolerance
>   3.
>   B. Push–Pull Factors

Why It Matters During the early seventeenth century, the English developed two distinct clusters of settlements along the Atlantic coast: the Chesapeake to the south and New England to the north. Along the mid-Atlantic coast, the Dutch and Swedes established their own small colonies. Growing English power threatened the Dutch and the Swedes. Soon, England would control most of the Atlantic seaboard. **Section Focus Question: What were the characteristics of the Middle Colonies?**

The Dutch Establish New Netherland

Beginning in 1609, Dutch merchants sent ships across the Atlantic and up the Hudson River to trade for furs with the Indians. In 1614, they founded a permanent settlement at Fort Nassau (later called Fort Orange) on the upper river. To guard the mouth of the river, the Dutch built New Amsterdam at the tip of Manhattan Island in 1625. With the finest harbor on the Atlantic coast, New Amsterdam served as the colony's largest town, major seaport, and government headquarters. Coming to trade or to farm, the Dutch—in contrast to the French, Spanish, and Puritan English—made virtually no missionary effort to convert the Indians.

Government in New Netherland The Dutch West India Company appointed the governor and an advisory council of leading colonists, but they did not permit an elected assembly. Although run by authoritarian governors, New Netherland tolerated various religious groups, including Jews. That toleration drew an especially diverse group of colonists, not only from the Netherlands, but also from France, Germany, and Norway. As in New England, most of the colonists were of the middle class and poor. They came as families—unlike the unmarried, young men who prevailed in the early Chesapeake.

Push-and-Pull Factors Despite an appealing location and religious toleration, the Dutch colony attracted few immigrants. In 1660, New Netherland had only 5,000 colonists—better than the 3,000 in New France, but far behind the 25,000 in the Chesapeake and the 33,000 in New England. Why did the colonization of New Netherland falter?

In mobilizing migration to the colonies, push factors were stronger than pull factors. **Push factors** motivate people to leave their home countries. For example, religious persecution pushed the Puritans out of England. **Pull factors** attract people to a new location. For example, the promise of a better life and fertile soil may pull people to a new land. During the seventeenth century, push was stronger in England than in the Netherlands. With the Netherlands' booming economy and a high standard of living, the Dutch had less cause to leave home than did the English, who suffered from a stagnant economy. The Dutch did not have the masses of roaming poor who became servants in the Southern Colonies. And the tolerant Dutch lacked a disaffected religious minority, such as the Puritans who founded New England. The English succeeded as colonizers largely because their troubled society failed to satisfy their people at home.

 Checkpoint Why did New Netherland have a diverse population?

New Sweden Is Founded

In 1638, traders founded New Sweden on the lower Delaware River, within the present state of Delaware. Settlers built Fort Christina at the site of present-day Wilmington. Like the Dutch colony, New Sweden had a dual economy: the fur trade with Indians and grain farming by colonists. Some of the colonists were Swedes, but most came from Finland, then under Swedish rule. Skilled at pioneer farming in heavily forested Scandinavia, these colonists adapted quickly to America. They introduced many frontier techniques that eventually became adopted in America, including the construction of log cabins.

Eventually, New Sweden extended to both sides of the Delaware River, into present-day New Jersey, Pennsylvania, and Maryland. Although highly skilled, the approximately 500 New Sweden colonists were too few to hold the land after a violent confrontation with their Dutch neighbors. In September 1655, the Dutch governor, Peter Stuyvesant, appeared with seven warships, compelling the Swedish commander to surrender.

 Checkpoint How did the Dutch take over New Sweden?

The English Conquest

Thinly populated, New Netherland suffered when the Dutch and English empires came to blows. The Dutch and English became violent rivals in global commerce during the 1650s and 1660s. The English leaders resented that the more efficient Dutch shippers captured most of the trade exporting Chesapeake tobacco and West Indian sugar.

New York Becomes an English Colony In 1664, an English expedition forced Governor Stuyvesant to surrender his colony. The English renamed it New

York, after the Duke of York, who received it as a proprietary colony. New Amsterdam became the city of New York, while Fort Orange became known as Albany. Victory secured the mid-Atlantic coast for the English, closing the gap between the Chesapeake Colonies to the south and the New England Colonies to the north. Under English rule, the conquered region became known as the Middle Colonies.

New Jersey Is Established In 1664, the Duke of York granted the lands between the Hudson and the Delaware rivers as a distinct new colony called New Jersey. Puritans and Scots settled the eastern half, while the western half attracted English Quakers. Relatively small and poor, New Jersey was dominated by its larger and wealthier neighbors: New York to the north and Pennsylvania to the west.

The Dutch Surrender New Amsterdam
As English warships approach, Peter Stuyvesant (center) readies for surrender.

✓ **Checkpoint** What colonies were established after the English took lands from the Dutch?

William Penn Founds Pennsylvania

Pennsylvania began as a debt paid to **William Penn** by King Charles II of England. Although the son of an admiral, Penn had embraced the Quaker faith, a <u>radical</u> form of Protestantism. As a wealthy gentleman, Penn was an unusual Quaker. Most Quakers were tradespeople, shopkeepers, and small farmers who distrusted rich and powerful men. In turn, the gentry of England generally despised the Quakers.

Quaker Beliefs In contrast to the Puritan emphasis on sacred scripture and sermons by ministers, the **Quakers** sought an "Inner Light" to understand the Bible. The Quakers did not have clergy, and considering women spiritually equal to men, Quakers established both men's and women's leadership for their meetings. Pacifists, the Quakers refused to bear arms. They also tolerated other faiths. Unlike Puritan Massachusetts, Pennsylvania would have no privileged church with tax support.

Pennsylvania Prospers In 1680, the king granted to Penn the land west of the Delaware River as the colony of Pennsylvania, which means "Penn's Woods." In 1682, Penn arrived with 23 ships bearing 2,000 colonists. For his capital, Penn established a city named Philadelphia, which means "City of Brotherly Love."

Thanks to a temperate climate, fertile soil, and a navigable river, the colonists prospered and multiplied, reaching 18,000 inhabitants by 1700. As with the New England Puritans—but unlike the Chesapeake colonists—most early Pennsylvanians came in freedom as families of middle-class means. Most were Quakers, but the colony also attracted Anglicans as well as German Baptists and Lutherans.

Cultivating peace with the local Indians, the Pennsylvanians avoided the sort of native rebellions that devastated Virginia, New England, and New Mexico. Called Delawares by the English, the local Indians were Algonquian speakers.

Vocabulary Builder
<u>radical</u>–(RAD ih kuhl) *adj.* favoring or making extreme changes in political, social, religious, or economic thought or practice

WILLIAM PENN'S
Holy Experiment

William Penn, a member of the aristocracy, became a Quaker as a young man. Persecuted in England for their religious beliefs, many Quakers were jailed—including Penn. In 1681, Penn founded Pennsylvania as a safe haven for Quakers. He called Pennsylvania a "holy experiment" because it was a place that guaranteed religious and political freedom for its inhabitants. This policy of toleration attracted Europeans with a variety of religious beliefs to immigrate to Pennsylvania, including Jews, Mennonites, Huguenots, and Lutherans.

Penn wrote a constitution for Pennsylvania that was unlike any other at the time. It guaranteed many fundamental liberties, limited the power of government, and contained provisions for amending the constitution. Many years later, these same ideas would appear in the U.S. Constitution.

A Planned Community ▲
Penn planned Philadelphia to include wide streets, parks, and hospitals.

Rights for Women ▶
Quakers encouraged women to speak during religious services and supported education for women.

▼ **Dealing Fairly With the Indians** Although Penn had been granted the land by the king of England, he purchased Pennsylvania from the Indians in the region and maintained good relations with them.

▲ **A New Kind of Colony** When he received the charter for Pennsylvania from King Charles, Penn envisioned his colony as one that would offer religious freedom. Penn also guaranteed many other freedoms.

Thinking Critically
1. **Analyze Information** Why did King Charles II give William Penn land in North America?

2. **Draw Conclusions** Why was Penn considered an unusual Quaker?

Unlike most other colonial leaders, Penn treated Native Americans with respect and paid fair prices for their land.

☑ **Checkpoint** How did William Penn's treatment of the Native Americans differ from the Puritans' treatment?

Diversity in the Middle Colonies

The Middle Colonies developed an ethnic and religious diversity greater than either the Chesapeake area or New England, where almost all of the white colonists came from England. The Middle Colonies included Dutch, Swedes, Finns, French Protestants, Germans, Norwegians, and Scots—as well as English. By faith, they were Quakers, Baptists, Anglicans, Presbyterians, Lutherans, Dutch Reformed, German Reformed, and Jews. No single ethnic group or specific religious denomination possessed a majority in any Middle Colony. In 1644, a Jesuit priest described New Amsterdam:

> **Primary Source** "No religion is publicly exercised but the Calvinist, and orders are to admit none but Calvinists, but this is not observed, for there are, besides Calvinists, in the Colony Catholics, English Puritans, Lutherans, Anabaptists, [etc.]"
> —Reverend Isaac Jogues, 1644

The diversity of the Middle Colonies violated the traditional belief that political order depended on ethnic and religious uniformity. Thrown together in unexpected combinations, the various colonists had to learn how to tolerate their differences. In their ethnic and religious pluralism, the Middle Colonies anticipated the American future.

☑ **Checkpoint** Why were the Middle Colonies more diverse than either the Southern or New England colonies?

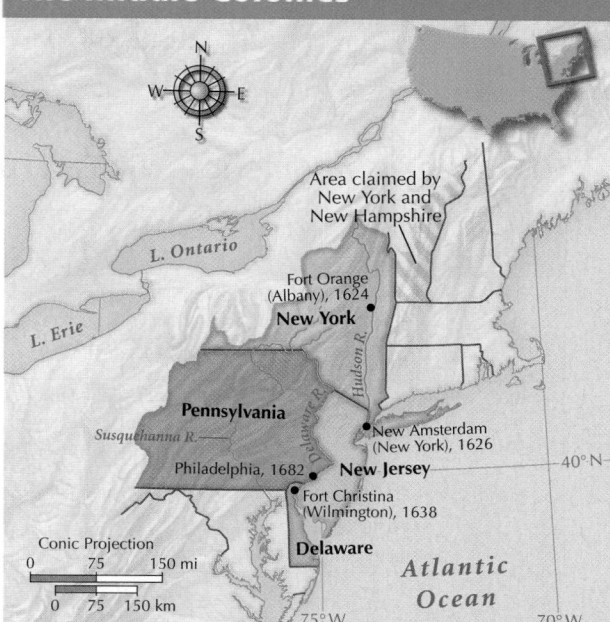

The Middle Colonies

Map Skills The Middle Colonies offered settlers fertile lands and a mild climate.
1. **Locate:** (a) Fort Orange, (b) New Amsterdam, (c) Philadelphia
2. **Interaction** Which rivers were important to settlers in the Middle Colonies? Explain.
3. **Compare and Contrast** How were the Middle Colonies similar to and different from the New England and Southern colonies?

SECTION 5 Assessment

Comprehension

1. **Terms and People** Write a sentence for each person or term below that tells how it contributed to the growth of the Middle Colonies.
   - push factor
   - pull factor
   - William Penn
   - Quaker

2. **NoteTaking Reading Skill: Identifying Main Ideas and Supporting Details** Use your completed outline to answer the Section Focus Question: What are the characteristics of the Middle Colonies?

Writing About History

3. **Quick Write: Provide Elaboration** Add interest to your cause-and-effect essay by finding supporting details, facts, and examples. Choose one of the events below and list as many specific details as possible. Then, write a paragraph using the details you listed to explain what caused the event.
   - The English defeat the Dutch and take over New Amsterdam.
   - William Penn gains a charter for Pennsylvania from King Charles II.

Critical Thinking

4. **Analyze Information** Why did fewer Dutch than English immigrate to the American colonies? Describe both the push factors and the pull factors that contributed to the difference.

5. **Draw Conclusions** How did geography help the colonies of New York and Pennsylvania prosper?

6. **Make Comparisons** How did religious toleration in the Middle Colonies differ from that in the New England Colonies?

Quick Study Guide

1.I.B.2,
1.I.D

Progress Monitoring *Online*
For: Self-test with vocabulary practice
Web Code: nca-0212

■ Europeans in America, 1600s–1700s

European Nation	Major Economic Activities	Government
Spain	• gold and silver mining • trading • farming	• Crown-appointed viceroys or governors • no elected officials
France	• fur trading • some farming	• Crown-appointed governors • no elected officials
England	• farming • fishing • trading	• Crown-appointed governors • elected assemblies

■ North America, 1753

Claimed by Britain
Claimed by France
Claimed by Spain

NEW FRANCE
Quebec
Montreal
Plymouth colony
13 COLONIES
Jamestown
Atlantic Ocean
NEW SPAIN
FLORIDA
St. Augustine
Mexico City
Pacific Ocean
Caribbean Sea

■ The 13 British Colonies

Colony	European Settlement
Southern Colonies	
Virginia	1607
Maryland	1632
Carolina	
North Carolina	1655
South Carolina*	1670
Georgia	1732
New England Colonies	
Massachusetts	1620
New Hampshire	1623
Connecticut	1634
Rhode Island	1636
Middle Colonies	
New York	1624
New Jersey	1630
Delaware	1638
Pennsylvania	1644

*North and South Carolina formed a single colony, Carolina, until they were separated in 1712.

☑ Quick Study Timeline

In America

1607	1608	1619	1620
English found Jamestown	**French found Quebec**	**House of Burgesses established**	**Pilgrims found Plymouth Colony**

Around the World

1500   **1600**   **1620**

1517
The Protestant Reformation begins

1519–1522
Magellan circumnavigates the world

1630s
Japan bars western merchants

American Issues
●–●–● **Connector**

By connecting prior knowledge with what you have learned in this chapter, you can gradually build your understanding of enduring questions that still affect America today. Answer the questions below. Then, use your American Issues Connector study guide (or go online: www.PHSchool.com **Web Code:** nch-6202).

Issues You Learned About

● **Global Interdependence** Events, ideas, and items that come from one region often reach and influence people in other regions.

1. Explain how religious conflicts that took place in Germany in the early 1500s impacted people throughout Europe.

2. Describe the economic relationship between French settlers and the Native Americans who lived around the St. Lawrence River.

3. How did global commerce affect events in New Netherland?

● **Church and State** In colonial days, religious beliefs had a strong influence on the development of society.

4. Why did the Puritans first come to North America? What religious groups were not welcome in Massachusetts?

5. Why did leaders of Massachusetts banish Roger Williams and Anne Hutchinson?

6. What vision did Lord Baltimore have for his Maryland colony? Did he achieve this vision?

7. How did the beliefs of the Quakers lead to separation between church and state in Pennsylvania?

● **American Indian Policy** From the moment that Europeans began settling in North America, they developed policies for dealing with the Native Americans who already lived on the land.

8. How did Spanish policy toward the Pueblos change after the Pueblo revolt?

9. What benefits did the Puritans gain from pressuring Indians to move into special "praying towns"?

10. Think about the different groups of European settlers who came to North America. Which group do you think changed the lives of American Indians the least? Explain your answer.

Connect to Your World	**New York**

Interaction with the Environment When the first Europeans arrived in the region that later became New York's capital, it was home to Mohican Indians who used the Hudson River as a major travel route. Because of its location on the west bank of the Hudson River near the Mohawk River, the area drew Dutch merchants who wanted a central location for their growing fur trade industry. They named the settlement Fort Orange. In 1664, the British took over the fort and renamed it Albany. Research the Port of Albany's activities today and create a chart detailing the exports and imports of the area.

History _Interactive_
For: Interactive timeline
Web Code: ncp-0213

| | 1664 New York and New Jersey become English colonies | 1671 Bacon's Rebellion | 1680 Pueblo Revolt | 1752 Georgia becomes a royal colony |

| **1640** | **1660** | **1680** | **1750** |

| 1642 English Civil War begins | 1652 Dutch build Cape Town in South Africa | 1682 Peter the Great becomes czar of Russia | |

Chapter Assessment

Terms and People

1. Define **viceroy**. Where did the viceroys have power?

2. Who was **Samuel de Champlain**? What relationship did he have with the Native Americans?

3. How did **royal colonies** differ from **proprietary colonies**? Give an example of each type.

4. What was the **Mayflower Compact**? What was its most important principle?

5. Who were the **Quakers**? What ideas did Quakers support?

Focus Questions

The focus question for this chapter is **How and why did European nations establish colonies in the Americas?** Build an answer to this big question by answering the focus questions for Sections 1 through 5 and the Critical Thinking questions that follow.

Section 1
6. How did Spain strengthen its colonies in the Americas?

Section 2
7. How did France's American colonies differ from Spain's American colonies?

Section 3
8. What were the characteristics of the government and the economy in the Southern Colonies?

Section 4
9. What were the goals of the Plymouth and Massachusetts Bay colonies?

Section 5
10. What were the characteristics of the Middle Colonies?

Critical Thinking

11. **Make Generalizations** What was life like for Native Americans who lived on or near Spanish missions?

12. **Categorize** How did colonists in Spanish America categorize members of society? Explain your answer.

13. **Explain Effects** What effect did the fur trade with Europe have on relations between Native American groups?

14. **Analyze Information** Why did the Spanish colonists begin importing enslaved Africans?

15. **Explain Causes and Effects** What were the causes and effects of Samuel Champlain's battle with the Iroquois in 1609?

16. **Identify Assumptions** What ideas did the English in Virginia and Massachusetts hold about the way that the Native Americans interacted with the land of North America? How does their treatment of Indians reflect their attitude?

17. **Draw Inferences** How did James Oglethorpe make Georgia different from other Southern Colonies?

18. **Recognize Cause and Effect** What led to the outbreak of King Philip's War? What results did it have?

19. **Make Comparisons** Was Rhode Island more similar to other colonies in New England or to those in the Middle Colonies? Give several reasons to support your answer.

20. **Compare and Contrast** How did colonial governments in New Spain, New France, and in the 13 British colonies differ? What similarities were there?

Writing About History

Expository Essay: Cause and Effect Choose one colony in North America and write an essay that explains the causes and effects of its founding.

Prewriting
- Consider what you know about the founding of each colony, and choose one that you think best shows cause and effect.
- Take time to research facts, descriptions, and examples to clearly illustrate the causes and effects in your essay.

Drafting
- Choose one of the following to organize the causes and effects in your essay: Show the chronological order of events, or order the events from the least important to the most important.
- As you draft your essay, illustrate each cause and effect with supporting facts and details.

Revising
- Review your entire draft to ensure that you show a clear relationship between the causes and effects.
- Analyze each paragraph to check that you have provided a thorough set of facts and details.
- Use the guidelines on page SH11 of the Writing Handbook to revise your report.

Regents DBQ Practice

European Motivations for Colonization

Why did European countries want colonies in North America? What motivated people to leave their homes to live on the edge of a distant continent they knew little about? Use your knowledge of colonial America and Documents A, B, and C to answer questions 1 through 4.

Document 1

"It will be a service to the Church of great consequence to carry the Gospel into those parts of the world. . . . The whole earth is the Lord's garden. . . . Why . . . suffer a whole continent as fruitful and convenient for the use of man to lie waste without any improvement? . . . What can be a better work, and more honorable and worthy of a Christian than to help rise and support a particular church while it is in its infancy, and to join his forces with such a company of faithful people, as by a timely assistance may grow strong and prosper. . . ."

—*John Winthrop,* Reasons for the Plantation in New England, *c. 1628*

Document 2

"Whereas . . . several lands, Islands, Places, Colonies, and Plantations have been obtained and settled in that Part of the Continent of America called New England, and thereby the Trade and Commerce there, hath been of late Years much increased: And whereas We have been informed by the hirable Petition of our Trusty and Well beloved John Winthrop [and others], being Persons principally interested in Our Colony or Plantation of Connecticut, in New England, that the same Colony . . . was Purchased and obtained for great and valuable Considerations, and some other Part thereof gained by Conquest . . . and at the only Endeavors . . . of theirs and their Associates . . . Subdued, and Improved, and thereby become a considerable Enlargement and Addition of Our Dominions and

Interest there. Now Know YE, That in consideration thereof . . . We have ordained . . . the said John Winthrop [and others] . . . One Body Corporate and politique, in Fact and Name, by the Name of, Governor and Company of the English colony of Connecticut in New-England, in America. . . ."

—*from the* Charter of Connecticut, *1662*

Document 3

"Carolina is a fair and spacious Province on the Continent of America. . . . This Province lying so neer Virginia, and yet more Southward, enjoys the fertility and advantages thereof; and yet is so far distant, as to be freed from the inconstancy of the Weather, which is a great cause of the unhealthfulness thereof. . . .

The Land is of divers sorts as in all Countryes of the world, that which lyes neer the Sea, is sandy and barren, but beareth many tall Trees, which make good timber for several uses; . . . up the River about 20 or 30 mile, where they have made a Town, called Charles-Town, there is plenty of as rich ground as any in the world. . . . The Woods are stored with Deer and Wild Turkeys, of a great magnitude, weighing many times above 50lbs a piece, and of a more pleasant tast than in England; . . . other sorts of Beasts in the Woods that are good for food; and also Fowls. . . . Here are as brave Rivers as any in the World, stored with great abundance of Sturgeon, Salmon, Bass, Plaice, Trout, and Spanish Mackrill, with many other most pleasant sorts of Fish, both flat and round, for which the English Tongue hath no name. . . . Last of all, the Air comes to be considered . . . and this is it which makes this Place so desireable, being seated in the most temperate Clime, where the neighbour-hood of the glorious Light of Heaven brings many advantages. . . . The Summer is not too hot, and the Winter is very short and moderate, best agreeing with English Constitutions. . . ."

—*Robert Horne,* A Brief Description of the Province of Carolina, *1666*

---

1. Document 3 suggests that England valued its New England Colonies for
   (1) commercial reasons.
   (2) religious reasons.
   (3) strategic reasons.
   (4) political reasons.

2. Which documents are most likely advertisements?
   (1) Document 1 only
   (2) Document 2 only
   (3) Document 3 only
   (4) Documents 1 and 2

3. Which documents suggest a religious motive for establishing colonies?
   (1) Document 1 only
   (2) Documents 2 and 3
   (3) Documents 1 and 3
   (4) Documents 1 and 2

4. **Writing Task** What role do you think economics played in the establishment of European colonies in North America? Use your knowledge of the colonial period and evidence from the sources above to explain your answer.

WITNESS HISTORY AUDIO

The Colonies Prosper

As the American colonies grew and prospered, England encouraged colonists to import English goods. Colonists eagerly purchased imported cloth, tea, furniture, books, and other items. And as manufacturing grew in England, colonists could buy a greater variety of goods at lower prices than ever before. One visitor to America noted:

“ . . . [colonists] import from London stuffs and every other article of English growth or manufacture, together with all sorts of foreign goods. England, and especially London, profits immensely by its trade with the American colonies; for not only New York but likewise all the other English towns on the continent, import so many articles from England that all their [currency] must go to Old England. . . . ”

—Peter Kalm, *Travels into North America*, 1748

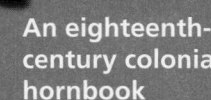

An eighteenth-century colonial hornbook

◀ Colonial artist Charles Willson Peale painted an image of his family that shows that they valued art and culture.

Colonists treasured pottery from England.

NY Core Curriculum Preview

Chapter Focus Question: What factors shaped life in colonial America in the seventeenth and eighteenth centuries?

Section 1
Immigration and Slavery 1.I.D.2, 2.I.A.2, 2.I.A.2b, 2.I.A.2c

Section 2
The American Colonies and England 1.I.B.3, 1.I.D.1d, 2.I.A.1, 2.I.A.1b

Section 3
Comparing Regional Cultures 1.I.A.2c, 2.I.A.3, 2.II.B.1a

Section 4
Wars of Empire 1.I.B.3, 1.I.B.4, 2.I.A.2a

JOIN, or DIE.

A political cartoon urges the 13 colonies to work together.

Use the ☑ **Quick Study Timeline** at the end of this chapter to preview chapter events.

Note Taking Study Guide Online
For: Note Taking and American Issues Connector
Web Code: nce-6301

65

WITNESS HISTORY AUDIO

New Arrivals

In the 1700s, thousands of European immigrants crossed the Atlantic Ocean, hoping to acquire land, earn a good living, and enjoy the freedoms that existed in colonial America. In 1739, a German immigrant noted that "Liberty of conscience [thought]" was the "chief virtue of this land. . . . But for this freedom, I think this country would not improve so rapidly."

Yet, there were others who crossed the Atlantic under drastically different circumstances. These were Africans, who were forced from their homeland and crammed onto slave ships. Thrust into a hostile world, they were expected to work from sunup to sundown under terrible conditions. Their experiences in North America were different in every way from that of European immigrants.

▲ James Oglethorpe, founder of Georgia, greets Scottish immigrants.

Immigration and Slavery

Core Curriculum Objectives

- **1.I.D.2** Immigration
- **2.I.A.2** The peoples of the American colonies
- **2.I.A.2b** Slave trade
- **2.I.A.2c** Varieties of immigrant motivation, ethnicities, and experiences

Terms and People

indentured servant
triangular trade

Middle Passage
Phyllis Wheatley

NoteTaking

Reading Skill: Identify Main Ideas As you read the section, use a concept web to list main ideas about population in the colonies.

Why It Matters As the colonies developed, Europeans began to arrive in greater numbers. At first, most immigrants were English, but during the 1700s larger numbers of Germans and Scotch-Irish arrived. Enslaved Africans were taken unwillingly from their home-lands and forced to work in a distant land. These newcomers would reshape American colonial society. **Section Focus Question: Which major groups of immigrants came to Britain's American colonies in the 1700s?**

Europeans Migrate to the Colonies

After a difficult start, England's American colonies grew steadily. By 1700, approximately 250,000 people of European background lived in the colonies. That number would rise tenfold during the next 75 years. Much of this growth came as a result of emigration from Europe.

Migration From England During the 1600s, about 90 percent of the migrants to the English colonies came from England. About half of these immigrants were **indentured servants**—poor immigrants who paid for passage to the colonies by agreeing to work for four to seven years. Instead of receiving a wage, indentured servants received basic food, clothing, and shelter—generally just enough to keep them alive. At the end of their term, they were supposed to receive clothes, tools, food, and sometimes land.

Developments in England caused the percentage of immigrants to drop dramatically. Prior to 1660, many English left their homeland because of religious and political turmoil. High unemployment and low wages in England added to the troubles. After 1660, however, the English economy improved and political and religious conflicts diminished. Increasingly, English people chose to stay in England.

The Scots and Scotch-Irish While English emigration shrank, Scottish emigration soared. Generally poorer than the English, the Scots had more reasons to seek their fortunes elsewhere. They also gained easier legal access to the colonies after 1707. In that year, Great Britain was formed by the union of England, Wales, and Scotland.

After the formation of Great Britain, many Scots became colonial officials. Some became royal governors. Scottish merchants also captured a growing share of the colonial commerce, especially the tobacco trade from the Chesapeake Bay.

The Scots immigrated to the 13 colonies in three streams. The first stream came from the Scottish lowlands. The second came from the Scottish highlands, and the third came from the province of Ulster in Northern Ireland. In the colonies, the Ulster Scots became known as the Scotch-Irish.

Nearly 250,000 Scotch-Irish people came to the colonies in the 1700s. They were descendants of Protestant Scots who had settled in Northern Ireland. The Scotch-Irish arrived in the American colonies in search of land. Many moved west to the mountainous "back country" that stretched from Pennsylvania to the Carolinas. There, they built farms on the frontier lands recently taken from the Indians.

The Germans Germans were second only to the Scotch-Irish as eighteenth-century emigrants from Europe to British America. Most of the 100,000 who immigrated to the colonies were Protestant. Almost all came from the Rhine Valley in southwestern Germany and northern Switzerland.

What factors explain the flood of German immigrants? They felt pushed by war, taxes, and religious persecution. During the 1700s, Germany was divided into many small principalities, frequently involved in wars. To build palaces and to wage war, German princes heavily taxed their people and forced young men to join the army. Most princes also demanded religious conformity. Germany also lacked enough farmland for its growing population.

In 1682, William Penn recruited a few Germans to settle in Pennsylvania, where they prospered. In letters to relatives and friends, immigrants reported that wages were high while land and food were cheap. In Pennsylvania, an immigrant could obtain a farm six times larger than a typical peasant holding in Germany. Pennsylvania demanded almost no taxes and did not force its young men to become soldiers.

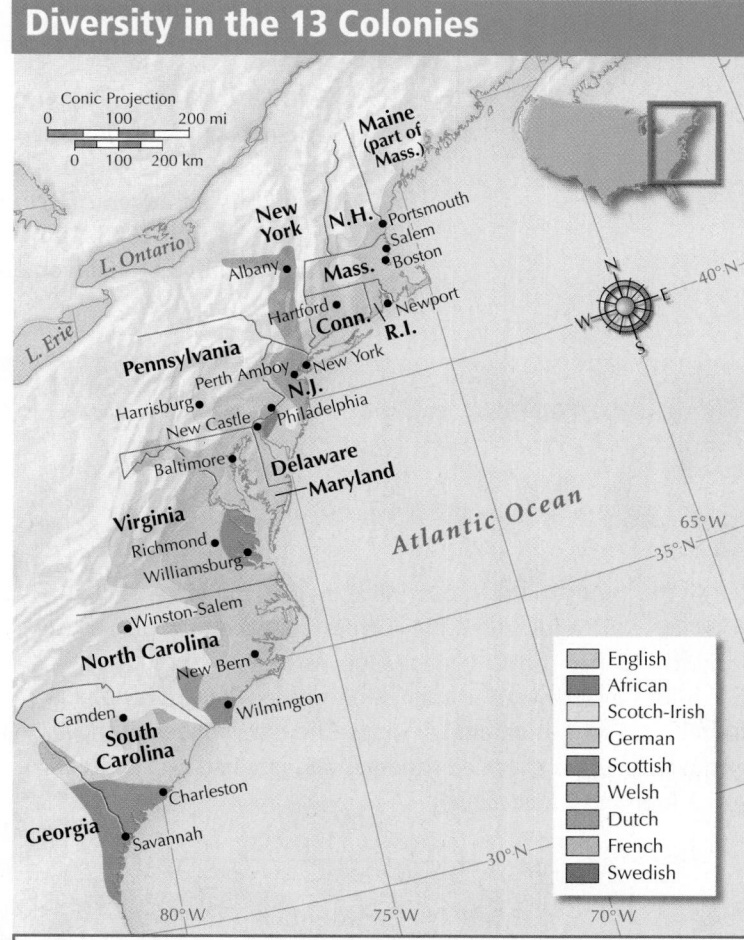

Geography *Interactive*
For: Interactive map
Web Code: ncp-0302

Diversity in the 13 Colonies

Map Skills Seeking land and liberty, Europeans from a number of nations immigrated to the 13 colonies during the 1700s. Hundreds of thousands of Africans were forced to migrate to the colonies.

1. **Locate:** (a) Pennsylvania, (b) Massachusetts, (c) South Carolina

2. **Region** Which colonies have the largest concentrations of people of African descent?

3. **Compare and Contrast** How does the diversity of the populations of New England and the Middle Colonies compare?

Immigration Brings Diversity Immigration brought changes to the colonies. In Pennsylvania, for instance, new waves of Scottish and German immigrants made the Quakers a minority in that colony. Although the different groups often distrusted one another at first, no group was large enough to impose its beliefs or to drive the others out of the colony. Instead, they all gradually accepted that a diverse society was an economic boon and the best guarantee for their own faith.

✔ **Checkpoint** Why did Scots and Germans emigrate from their homelands?

WITNESS HISTORY DVD

Watch *The Atlantic Slave Trade* on the **United States Witness History DVD** to explore the transatlantic slave trade.

Africans Are Transported to America

During the 1600s, landowning colonists in the Chesapeake region needed workers to raise crops. Indentured servants filled this need, and most early indentured servants were English. Yet, as English immigration began to decline in the late 1600s, the demand for labor in the colonies grew. As a result, many colonists began to turn to another source of labor: enslaved Africans.

Slavery in the Colonies Begins Early in the 1600s, colonists often treated African workers just as they treated indentured servants, giving them their freedom after several years of service. Freed blacks could own land, vote, and even buy enslaved Africans of their own.

By the mid-1600s, however, most colonies began to pass laws that supported the permanent enslavement of Africans. In 1705, Virginia's General Assembly

INFOGRAPHIC 🔊 AUDIO

The Middle Passage

From the 1400s to the 1800s, more than 10 million enslaved Africans made a forced journey across the Atlantic Ocean to the Americas. Called the Middle Passage, Africans endured horrific conditions as they were crammed onto ships "like herring in a barrel" and sent to unfamiliar lands. The drawing below shows enslaved Africans shackled together and jammed into spaces just 3 feet and 3 inches high.

Destinations of Enslaved Africans, 1500–1870

- 2.5% Non-Spanish Caribbean islands
- 41% Portuguese Brazil
- 37% Spanish America
- 15% British America
- 4.5% Europe and Asia

SOURCE: *World Civilizations*, Albert M. Craig

▲ The pie graph shows where slave traders sent captured Africans.

3 feet 3 in. high

declared that "All servants imported . . . who were not Christians in their native Country. . . shall be accounted and be slaves." Other laws stated that the children of enslaved African Americans were also enslaved. This change in legal <u>status</u> promoted the racist idea that people of African origin were inferior to whites.

Vocabulary Builder

<u>status</u>–(STAT uhs) *n.* legal position or condition of a person, group, country, etc.

The Transatlantic Slave Trade Once established, slavery expanded rapidly. During the 1700s, the British colonies imported approximately 1,500,000 enslaved Africans. The great majority went to the West Indies, but at least 250,000 came to the 13 colonies to labor on plantations and in homes.

Traders purchased slaves from African merchants and chiefs in the coastal kingdoms of West Africa. Most of those enslaved were kidnapped by armed men or taken in wars between kingdoms. Although they did not directly seize slaves, Europeans promoted the trade by offering high prices for captives.

Enslaved Africans came to the Americas as part of a three-part voyage called the **triangular trade.** Slave traders sailed from Europe to Africa, where they traded manufactured goods for enslaved Africans. Then, in the **Middle Passage,** shippers carried the enslaved Africans across the Atlantic to the American colonies. After selling the slaves for colonial produce, the traders returned to the mother country.

The brutality of the Middle Passage was extreme. On a voyage that lasted two months or more, enslaved Africans suffered the psychological trauma of separation from their families and villages—as they sailed toward a strange land and an unknown future. Slave traders branded their cargo with hot irons, placed them in shackles, and jammed them into dark holds so crowded that the slaves

▼ **Crossing the Atlantic** The voyage from West Africa to the Americas could take from three weeks to three months depending on the winds and the weather. The map shows where the enslaved came from and where they were going.

North America

13 Colonies 4.5%

Spanish America 15%

Atlantic Ocean

Europe 2.5%

Caribbean Sea

Non-Spanish Caribbean 41%

Africa

Guinea

Bight of Benin

Gulf of Guinea

Congo

South America

Brazil 37%

Angola

Miller Projection
0   1,000 miles
0   1,000 kilometers

▨ Area of origin of enslaved Africans
▬ Area of settlement of enslaved Africans
➤ Route of enslaved Africans

▼ Chains

▲ Shackles

A Forced Migration

Born in West Africa, Olaudah Equiano (1745–1797) was captured when he was 11 years old. In his memoir, he vividly described the ship that would take him across the Atlantic.

"I was soon put down under the decks, and there I received such a salutation in my nostrils as I had never experienced in my life: so that, with the loathsomeness of the stench, and crying together, I became so sick and low that I was not able to eat, nor had I the least desire to taste anything. I now wished for the last friend, death, to relieve me . . ."

—*The Interesting Narrative of the Life of Olaudah Equiano,* by Olaudah Equiano

Thinking Critically

1. **Compare Points of View** How might Equiano's memoir compare with the journal of the captain of a slave ship?

2. **Synthesize Information** Based on the map and the pie graph, from what region of Africa did most enslaved Africans come? To what region did most go?

could hardly move. The foul air promoted disease, and the ill might be thrown overboard to prevent the spread of disease. Some Africans, hoping for death, refused to eat. One ship's surgeon witnessed the following shocking scene:

Primary Source "Upon the Negroes refusing to take sustenance [food], I have seen coals of fire, glowing hot, put on a shovel and placed so near their lips as to scorch and burn them. And this has been accompanied with threats of forcing them to swallow the coals if they any longer persisted in refusing to eat."
—Alexander Falconbridge, 1788

Slave traders had an interest in delivering a large and healthy cargo. However, due to the conditions, at least 10 percent of those making the Middle Passage in the 1700s did not survive.

✓ **Checkpoint** How did the laws concerning enslaved Africans sent to the 13 colonies change in the 1700s?

Africans in the Americas

Following the ordeal of the Middle Passage, enslaved Africans faced a bleak future in America. At slave auctions, colonial buyers often broke up families to make it more difficult to plot escape or rebellion. The newly enslaved were ordered about in an unfamiliar language and put to work beside strangers who shared only their skin color. Arriving with distinct languages and identities as Ashantis, Fulanis, Ibos, and many others, the enslaved forged a new culture as African Americans.

Slavery in the North and the South Slavery varied considerably by region. In 1750, enslaved African Americans were small minorities in New England and the Middle Colonies. In those two regions, most enslaved African Americans labored as farmhands, dockworkers, sailors, and house servants.

Many more enslaved African Americans lived in the Southern Colonies, where they raised labor-intensive crops of tobacco, rice, indigo, or sugar. In the Chesapeake, they comprised 40 percent of the population. In coastal South Carolina, enslaved African Americans outnumbered the white population. To maximize their profits, masters demanded as much work as possible while minimizing the cost of feeding, clothing, and housing slaves. Most of the enslaved lived in crude huts with dirt floors, no windows, and few furnishings. Their work was long and hard: at least 12 hours a day, 6 days a week under the close supervision of a white overseer, who whipped those who resisted.

Developing a New Culture In the colonies, African Americans developed a rich culture based on African traditions and their circumstances in America. These traditions represented a blend of African cultures, as plantations, farms, and cities contained Africans from many different ethnic groups. Most African Americans adopted the Christianity of their masters, blending it with some African religious traditions. They modified African instruments, crafting banjos, rattles, and drums to create a music that emphasized rhythm and percussion.

This watercolor, painted on a South Carolina plantation in the late 1700s, shows a dance form and musical instruments that have their roots in Africa.

Rebels and Runaways Slaveholders could never break enslaved African Americans' longing to be free. In the South and especially in the West Indies, some enslaved African Americans rebelled. On the mainland, the largest uprising erupted in 1739 at Stono in South Carolina, where about 100 slaves killed 20 whites before suffering defeat and execution.

Running away was more common. In the West Indies and the Carolinas, enslaved African Americans became *maroons*, a name for those who hid in forests or swamps. Other runaways fled to remote Native American villages or to Florida, where the Spanish welcomed them with food, land, and freedom. The Spanish sought to weaken the British colonies and to strengthen their own frontier militia with freed African Americans. In the Chesapeake and northern colonies, runaways tried to fit into the small free black communities.

Many more of the enslaved, however, opted for a more subtle form of rebellion. They stayed on the plantations, but they resisted by working slowly, feigning illness, pretending ignorance, or breaking tools.

Free African Americans Although most African Americans remained slaves for life, a few did obtain their freedom. For example, an enslaved African American might manage to earn money and purchase his or her freedom or might be set free by a slave owner.

Free African Americans tended to live in cities, where they faced discrimination. A rare few managed to overcome enormous obstacles to distinguish themselves. One example was **Phillis Wheatley** of Boston (see the History Maker on this page).

✓ **Checkpoint** How did slavery differ in the North and the South?

HISTORY MAKERS

Phillis Wheatley
(1753?–1784)

Phillis Wheatley was the first African American to publish a book of poems. Captured at about age seven in West Africa, she was sold to John Wheatley, a Boston tailor. The Wheatleys allowed Phillis to learn to read, write, and study. She had her first poem published in 1767 in a Rhode Island newspaper. She won praise in the colonies and in Britain for her 1770 poem about the preacher George Whitefield. However, colonial publishers refused to publish a book of her poetry. Phillis and the Wheatleys found a London publisher to print her volume of poetry, *Poems on Various Subjects, Religious and Moral,* in 1773. That year the Wheatleys granted Phillis her freedom. She married in 1778 but lived in poverty until her death.

SECTION 1 Assessment

Progress Monitoring *Online*
For: Self-test with vocabulary practice
Web Code: nca-0303

Comprehension

1. Terms and People What is the relationship between each of the following terms and people and the population of the 13 colonies?
- indentured servant
- triangular trade
- Middle Passage
- Phillis Wheatley

2. NoteTaking Reading Skill: Main Ideas Use your concept web to answer the Section Focus Question: Which major groups of immigrants came to Britain's American colonies in the 1700s?

Writing About History

3. Quick Write: Define a Problem Choose one topic from this section that you could use to write a problem-and-solution essay. For example, you could write about the experiences of European immigrants, indentured servants, or enslaved Africans. Make a list of details, facts, and examples that define the problems one of these groups faced.

Critical Thinking

4. Understand Cause and Effect Based on the description of European immigration to the American colonies, what were the main causes of immigration to the Americas?

5. Analyze Why did slavery become a permanent condition in the colonies?

6. Draw Conclusions Why do you think enslaved African Americans living in the South were able to preserve parts of African culture as well as build a new African American culture?

American colonists imported English pottery. ▶

▲ At busy colonial ports, merchants shipped raw materials to England and received manufactured goods from England.

WITNESS HISTORY 🔊 AUDIO

An Illegal Trade

According to English law, the colonies could import manufactured goods only through English ports, where an additional tax was collected. Yet, the letter below holds that colonial importers evaded the law.

❝ . . . There has lately been carried on here a large illicit [illegal] trade. . . .

A considerable number of ships have . . . lately come into this country directly from Holland, laden . . . with reels of yarn or spun hemp, paper, gunpowder, iron, and goods of various sorts used for men and women's clothing. **❞**

—William Bollan, advocate general of Massachusetts, 1743

The American Colonies and England

Core Curriculum Objectives

- **1.I.B.3** Territorial expansion
- **1.I.D.1d** Religion
- **2.I.A.1** 17th- and 18th-century Enlightenment thought
- **2.I.A.1b** Key events (Magna Carta, habeas corpus, English Bill of Rights, Glorious Revolution)

Terms and People

Magna Carta	Navigation Acts
Parliament	mercantilism
English Bill of Rights	Enlightenment
habeas corpus	Benjamin Franklin
salutary neglect	Great Awakening

NoteTaking

Reading Skill: Identify Supporting Details Use the format below to outline the section's main ideas and supporting details.

```
I. Government in the Colonies
   A. Traditions of English government
      1. Magna Carta
      2.
   B.
   C.
II.
```

Why It Matters During the eighteenth century, the colonists looked to England as their model for literature, government, and their economy. Important English documents, such as the Magna Carta and the English Bill of Rights, were the basis of colonial government and law. In addition, the colonial economy was dependent on trade with England. Although the relationship between England and the 13 colonies was a close one, during the 1700s, the distant American colonies began to form their own ideas about government and the economy. **Section Focus Question: How did English ideas about government and the economy influence life in the 13 colonies?**

Government in the Colonies

England developed an empire of many disunited colonies during the 1600s. Lacking money, the English Crown granted charters to private companies or lords proprietors, individuals who supported the monarchy. Compared to the Spanish or French, the English monarch exercised little direct control over the colonists.

Traditions of English Government Also unlike the kings of France and Spain, the English monarchs were bound to uphold the provisions of the **Magna Carta,** a document English nobles forced King John to accept in 1215. The Magna Carta protected English nobles by limiting the king's ability to tax them and by guaranteeing due process, or the right to a trial. Before levying a tax, the king needed the consent of the nobles.

After the Magna Carta, a council of nobles continued to advise English monarchs. The nobles also maintained the right to approve taxes—one of their most important powers. During the 1300s, the council of nobles gained more power and evolved into the lawmaking body known as Parliament. The English **Parliament** became a bicameral, or two-house, legislature. Members of the House of Lords were nobles, who inherited their positions, and church leaders. Commoners elected members of the House of Commons. However, only men with property could vote. Although this limited the number of eligible voters, England allowed more people to vote than any other European nation at the time.

A Measure of Self-Rule in America Although they were thousands of miles away from their homeland, most settlers in the North American English colonies <u>asserted</u> that they were entitled to the same rights as any other English subject. Nevertheless, the type of government in the American colonies varied from region to region.

Vocabulary Builder
<u>assert</u>–(uh SURT) *v.* to state positively; declare

In New England, the Puritans established republics with elected governors. Elsewhere, the distant Crown or lords proprietors appointed the governor of a colony. But that governor had to share power with the propertied colonists. Those colonists refused to pay taxes unless authorized by their own elected representatives in a colonial assembly. Colonists also claimed they were protected by English common law, which emphasized individual liberties.

King James II Asserts Royal Power In 1685, James II became king of England and tried to rule without Parliament. An open Catholic, he alarmed the Protestant majority of England. The new king also tightened control over the New England Colonies by revoking their government charters. Then, he combined them with New York and New Jersey into a larger colony known as the Dominion of New England. The Dominion replaced the colonies' elected assemblies with a Crown-appointed governor-general and council. The Dominion angered the colonists, who insisted upon their right to refuse to pay taxes unless approved by their own elected representatives.

The Glorious Revolution Results in a Bill of Rights In 1689, the colonists learned that James II had been overthrown in England in a coup called the Glorious Revolution. The plotters replaced him with two Protestant monarchs, King William and Queen Mary. The new monarchs promised to cooperate with Parliament and to support the Anglican church. William and Mary also agreed to sign an **English Bill of Rights,** a document guaranteeing a number of freedoms and restating many of the rights granted in the Magna Carta. These rights included **habeas corpus,** the idea that no one could be held in prison without being charged with a specific crime. The English Bill of Rights also stated that a monarch could not keep a standing army in times of peace without Parliament's approval. (See the primary source at right.)

The English Bill of Rights
The Glorious Revolution ousted James II. King William and Queen Mary took the throne and signed the English Bill of Rights. A few of the provisions of the Bill of Rights appear below.

Primary Source ❝That levying money for or to the use of the Crown by pretence of prerogative, without grant of Parliament . . . is illegal;
That the raising or keeping a standing army within the kingdom in time of peace, unless it be with consent of Parliament, is against law;
That excessive bail ought not to be required, nor excessive fines imposed, nor cruel and unusual punishments inflicted;❞

—English Bill of Rights, 1689

ROOTS of DEMOCRACY

Although the United States is more than 200 years old, the ideas of democracy and representative government are far older. The roots of democracy reach back to civilizations in southwest Asia and Europe.

THE ENLIGHTENMENT ▲

Two Enlightenment philosophers who influenced American ideas about government were John Locke and Baron de Montesquieu. Locke stated that all people have natural rights and that if a monarch violates those rights, then the people have the right to overthrow the monarch. Montesquieu declared that the powers of government should be clearly defined and limited.

JUDEO~CHRISTIAN ROOTS ▲

The values found in the Bible, including the Ten Commandments and the teachings of Jesus, inspired American ideas about government and morality.

ENGLISH PARLIAMENTARY TRADITIONS ▼

Two key English documents inspired Americans. The Magna Carta (1215) and the English Bill of Rights (1689) guaranteed certain rights to citizens, including the right to trial by jury. The ideas of a two-house lawmaking body and voting rights also influenced Americans.

GRECO~ROMAN ROOTS ▶

Ancient Greek democracy and Roman republicanism have influenced American government.

Thinking Critically

1. **Draw Conclusions** How did the Magna Carta and the English Bill of Rights limit English monarchs?

2. **Make Inferences** What Enlightenment values appear in the Declaration of Independence?

History *Interactive* ✱
For: More about the roots of democracy
Web Code: nep-0114

News of the English upheaval inspired rebellions among colonists in Massachusetts, New York, and Maryland. In Boston, colonial militia arrested the king's appointed governor-general, the hated Sir Edmond Andros.

All the rebels claimed loyalty to the new monarchs. And Protestant rebels in Maryland were delighted when William and Mary converted their colony into a royal colony. The new monarchs merged the Massachusetts and Plymouth colonies into a single royal colony, called Massachusetts. The new charter provided a royal governor assisted by an appointed council and an elected assembly. The assembly was permitted to choose council members, subject to the governor's approval. The king let Rhode Island and Connecticut keep their old charters, which allowed them to elect their governors as well as their assemblies.

Compromise was harder in New York. There, the leader of the rebellion, Jacob Liesler, had seized the position of governor. Liesler, however, made many political enemies. When England appointed a new governor, Liesler was made to surrender. He was quickly tried, convicted, and executed in 1691. That hasty trial and execution left a bitter legacy. For the next generation, Liesler's supporters and enemies feuded, souring politics in New York.

The Glorious Revolution encouraged England to adopt a colonial policy that historians would later call **salutary neglect.** England allowed its colonies local self-rule. In return, the Crown expected colonial cooperation with its economic policies and assistance in the empire's wars against France and Spain.

Freedom of the Press About 50 years after the Glorious Revolution, conflict broke out between the English-appointed governor and colonists in New York City. In 1734, articles criticizing the governor appeared in the *New York Weekly Journal,* a newspaper printed by John Peter Zenger. Although Zenger did not write the articles, the governor had Zenger imprisoned for libel—printing falsehoods that are intended to damage a person's reputation. He sat in jail for eight long months awaiting trial. When Zenger came to trial, his lawyer argued that the articles were not libelous but truthful. The jury agreed and found Zenger not guilty. Today, Zenger's case is considered an early victory for freedom of the press.

✔ **Checkpoint** How did the Glorious Revolution affect the 13 colonies?

England's Economic Relationship With the Colonies

England's colonization of the Americas was driven in large part by financial concerns. The purpose of the English colonies was to increase the wealth and power of England—the mother country. The economic policy of mercantilism supported those ideas.

Mercantilism Drives the British Economy The policy of **mercantilism** holds that a nation or an empire could build wealth and power by developing its industries and exporting manufactured goods in exchange for gold and silver. This policy encouraged monarchs to minimize imports from rival empires and to drive those rivals out of colonial markets. By selling more than it purchased, the empire could build wealth in the form of gold or silver.

In general, the colonies fit nicely into the mercantile system because they offered different economic strengths to the empire. In England, land was scarce whereas people

Chart Skills The Navigation Acts were a series of laws that regulated trade between Britain and the colonies. *What benefits did the act passed in 1663 provide to Britain? How did it affect the colonies?*

Dried tobacco leaves

The Navigation Acts	
1651	Goods imported to England from Asia, Africa, and the Americas could be transported only in English ships.
1660	The American colonies could export sugar, tobacco, cotton, and indigo only to England.
1663	All foreign goods shipped to the colonies had to pass through English ports where a duty was collected.
1733	Duties were increased on sugar traded between the French Indies and the American colonies.

Brown rice

Sugar

were numerous, which meant that labor was cheap. Money for investment was abundant. This combination favored the development of industry. In the colonies, however, there was more land but fewer people and less money for investment. That combination favored agriculture. As a result, more than 90 percent of the colonists lived and worked on farms or plantations. They exported their produce in ships to buy tropical goods from Africa or the Caribbean or manufactured goods from England.

The Navigation Acts Regulate Trade The English regarded colonial commerce as the key to imperial power. By controlling colonial trade, they could collect more customs duties—taxes on imported goods. They used this money to build a stronger navy, which enabled them to defeat the Dutch and later the French. To obtain more sailors, ships, and trade, Parliament in the mid-1600s enacted a series of trade laws called the **Navigation Acts.**

The Navigation Acts stated that only English ships with English sailors could trade with English colonies. The acts also specified that especially valuable colonial goods, including tobacco and sugar, be shipped only to the mother country. Colonial ships were free to take their other products elsewhere. For example, New Englanders could export fish to Portugal and Spain.

Finally, the colonies had to import all their European goods via an English port, where they paid customs duties. For example, if a Virginian wanted a bottle of French wine, the wine had to come to America by way of an English port, rather than directly from France. Violators risked the confiscation of their ships and cargoes.

The Navigation Acts promoted the dramatic growth of English colonial commerce and the nation's prosperity. During the 1600s, English merchant shipping doubled. The value of imports and exports increased at least sixfold. In 1600, England had been a relatively poor nation, trading primarily with nearby northern Europe. By 1700, England's commerce was global, and London had become Europe's leading seaport.

At first, the Navigation Acts hurt the colonists economically because they had depended upon Dutch ships and Dutch manufactured goods. That changed by 1700. Protected by the Navigation Acts, British manufacturing and shipping improved in quality and quantity, outstripping the Dutch. The colonists could obtain better goods from British suppliers at lower costs. Thereafter, colonists often protested some particular feature of the Navigation Acts, but not the whole system.

The Consumer Revolution Most colonists lived on farms or plantations. There, they produced most of their own food, fuel, and homespun cloth. But no farm or plantation could produce everything that a family needed. The colonists wanted to purchase expensive imported goods, such as sugar from the West Indies, tea from India, and manufactured goods from Britain. To obtain those goods, every colonial farm and plantation needed to produce a surplus of produce that they could export.

The expanding transatlantic commerce produced a "consumer revolution" that brought more and cheaper goods to the colonies. Between 1720 and 1770, colonial imports per person increased by 50 percent. An immigrant from Germany marveled that "it is really possible to obtain all the things one can get in Europe in Pennsylvania, since so many merchant ships arrive there every year."

British manufacturers increasingly needed the growing American market. In 1700, the American colonies consumed about 10 percent of British exports. The rate of consumption rose to 37 percent by 1772.

Global Trade

This young colonial girl enjoys tea from India, sugar from the West Indies, and wears a dress of cloth made in England. *What products do people in the United States import in the twenty-first century?*

A sugar bowl

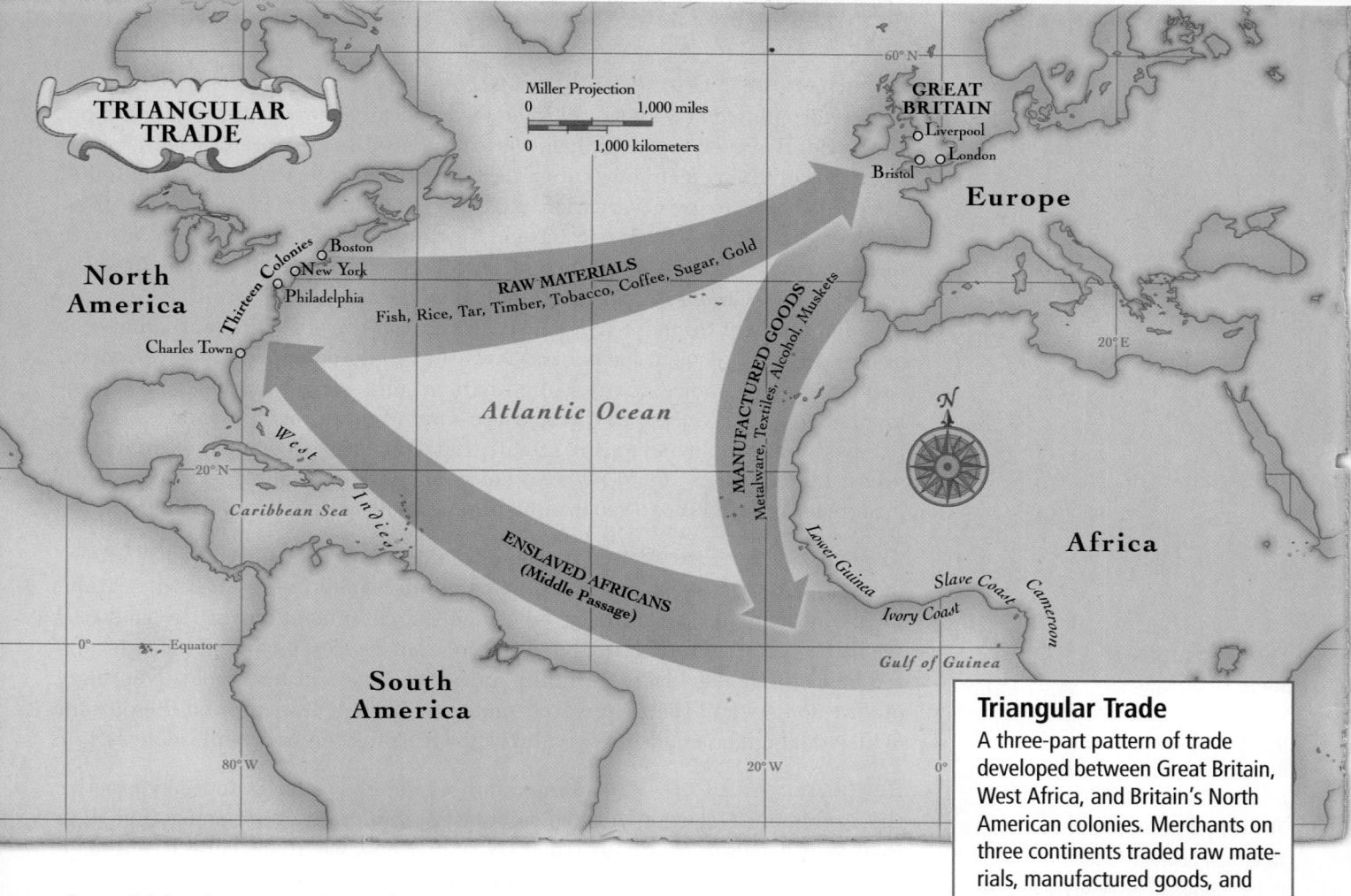

TRIANGULAR TRADE

Miller Projection

North America

Boston
New York
Philadelphia
Thirteen Colonies
Charles Town

RAW MATERIALS
Fish, Rice, Tar, Timber, Tobacco, Coffee, Sugar, Gold

Atlantic Ocean

West Indies

Caribbean Sea

South America

Equator

MANUFACTURED GOODS
Metalware, Textiles, Alcohol, Muskets

ENSLAVED AFRICANS
(Middle Passage)

GREAT BRITAIN
Liverpool
London
Bristol

Europe

Africa

Lower Guinea
Ivory Coast
Slave Coast
Cameroon
Gulf of Guinea

Triangular Trade
A three-part pattern of trade developed between Great Britain, West Africa, and Britain's North American colonies. Merchants on three continents traded raw materials, manufactured goods, and enslaved Africans. *What goods did England provide to West Africa? What did the colonies send to England?*

Grateful for the prosperity and consumer goods, the British as well as the colonists felt greater pride in their shared empire.

Both the middle class and the poorer class, however, bought more than they could afford. Americans suffered from a chronic trade imbalance, as they imported more than they exported. Most colonists bore mounting debts. The shortage of cash and the increasing debts fed a nagging unease at odds with the overall prosperity and general contentment with the empire.

Triangular Trade Route During the 1700s, a pattern of trade emerged that connected England, its colonies, and West Africa. Trade among the three continents had three main parts and formed a triangular shape (see the map on this page). On the first leg of the journey, British ships loaded with manufactured goods sailed to Africa's west coast. There, they swapped British manufactures—such as guns and cloth—for enslaved Africans. On the second, or middle, leg, the traders then carried the enslaved Africans to the American colonies. After selling the slaves for colonial raw material—such as sugar, timber, and tobacco—the traders returned to Europe.

✓ **Checkpoint** What was the purpose of the Navigation Acts?

New Ideas Affect the American Colonies

During the 1600s and 1700s, Europe experienced an intellectual movement known as the **Enlightenment**—a movement headed by thinkers who believed that all problems could be solved using human reason. The Enlightenment challenged old ways of thinking about science, religion, and government in Europe. Enlightenment thinkers changed the way many American colonists viewed the world as well.

Enlightenment Thinkers Offer New Worldviews Enlightenment philosophers formulated new ideas and suggested radically new ways of thinking about the world. However, these thinkers were influenced by the work of scientists who were part of a movement now called the Scientific Revolution. During the 1500s, scientists began to use observation and experimentation to learn about the physical world. Scientists, such as Sir Isaac Newton, used reason and observation to formulate new ideas about mathematics and physics. Those ideas challenged the traditional power of religious leaders to explain the physical world.

Enlightenment thinkers, like Rousseau and Voltaire of France and John Locke of Great Britain, looked for natural laws that could be applied to government, society, and economics. Many Enlightenment philosophers focused on government. Some, like Locke, challenged the unlimited power of monarchs. Locke believed that people had natural rights that came from God, and not from monarchs. Locke's ideas would have an enormous influence on American political leaders in the late 1700s. (See the infographic Roots of Democracy in this section.)

Impact on the Colonies A number of colonists were inspired by Enlightenment ideas. One such person was **Benjamin Franklin.** A successful printer, Franklin's hunger for knowledge embodied Enlightenment ideals. He conducted scientific experiments and invented a number of devices, including the lightning rod and bifocal eyeglasses. Franklin authored almanacs and books. Not many other colonists had the financial means to build their lives around the pursuit of knowledge. The majority knew little about Enlightenment philosophers.

Religion in the Colonies Many colonists came to America to freely practice their religions. However, most colonists were intolerant of religions other than their own. This was especially true in New England, where the church establishment was strongest. Because of its ethnic and religious diversity, many different churches were tolerated in the Middle Colonies.

Churches filled a key role in social life, especially in rural areas. Families who lived on widespread farms and plantations looked to the church as a place to gather with members of their community. Churches also served as a public space for reading government proclamations, for posting new laws, and for holding elections.

The Great Awakening During the mid-eighteenth century, a religious movement swept through the colonies. Known as the **Great Awakening,** it was a time when powerful evangelical preachers traveled from town to town giving emotion-packed sermons that deeply touched listeners. Hundreds, sometimes thousands, of people would come from miles around to be inspired by a preacher's words.

Preachers stressed that personal religious experience was important in seeking God's salvation. They rejected the Enlightenment view that everything in the world could be explained by natural law and logic. Jonathan Edwards of Massachusetts was a leading preacher during the period of the Great Awakening. Edwards used the vivid images of an angry God dangling unbelievers like a spider over a roaring fire to inspire listeners to repent of their sins. In his well-known sermon "Sinners in the Hands of an Angry God," Edwards urged people to ask forgiveness for their sins:

A Fiery Preacher
Jonathan Edwards's sermon "Sinners in the Hands of an Angry God" was reprinted many times. It warned readers to ask God's forgiveness.

Primary Source ❝O sinner! Consider the fearful danger you are in: it is a great furnace of wrath, a wide and bottomless pit, full of the fire of wrath, that you are held over in the hands that God, whose wrath is provoked and incensed as much against you, as against many of the damned in hell. You hang by a slender thread.❞
—Jonathan Edwards, 1741

In 1739, George Whitefield, England's most celebrated preacher, came to tour the colonies. For two years, he attracted large and enthusiastic crowds. Like Edwards, he promoted an emotional style of worship. Indeed, Whitefield urged common people to forsake ministers who favored a more subdued and rational style. Many other preachers copied Whitefield to spread the revivals. Indeed, the Great Awakening did much to inspire the American people with a sense of their own power as individuals.

Effects of the Great Awakening The Great Awakening had a profound impact on the colonies. Preaching that individuals could find their own salvation, the movement led to the formation of new churches in the colonies. Many Presbyterian, Dutch Reformed, and Congregationalist congregations were split between those who followed the preachers of the Great Awakening and those who did not. Eventually, the acceptance of the new churches contributed to an increase in tolerance. The movement also led to a rise in democratic belief in the colonies. Many preachers stressed that formal church rites were not as important as feeling God's spirit. Many colonists began to believe that if they could choose their method of worship, they could decide on their form of government.

HISTORY MAKERS

George Whitefield (1714–1770)
A celebrated preacher, George Whitefield moved audiences with his message—and his powerful voice—in both Great Britain and the American colonies. In school, Whitefield developed skill at speaking and a passion for the Bible. In college at Oxford, he met John and Charles Wesley, who founded the Methodist Church. Whitefield had a powerful conversion experience and devoted the rest of his life to preaching. He gave more than 18,000 sermons, sometimes speaking to crowds so large that the meetings had to be held outside. Along with travels across Britain, he journeyed to the colonies to preach, where the emotional power of his words and the message of salvation help launch the Great Awakening.

✔ **Checkpoint** What was the significance of the Great Awakening on the colonies?

Progress Monitoring Online
For: Self-test with vocabulary practice
Web Code: nce-0304

SECTION 2 Assessment

Comprehension

1. **Terms and People** For each term or name below, write a sentence explaining its impact on the political or economic life of the English colonies in North America.
   - Magna Carta
   - Parliament
   - English Bill of Rights
   - habeas corpus
   - salutary neglect
   - mercantilism
   - Navigation Acts
   - Enlightenment
   - Benjamin Franklin
   - Great Awakening

2. **NoteTaking Reading Skill: Identify Supporting Details** Use your completed outline to answer the Focus Question: How did English ideas about government and the economy influence life in the 13 colonies?

Writing About History

3. **Quick Write: Brainstorm for Possible Solutions** Choose one topic from this section, such as the Glorious Revolution, about which you could write a problem-solution essay. Use the text and your own knowledge to create a list of possible solutions to the problem that you have chosen to write about. Next, organize your list to rank the solutions from most effective to least effective.

Critical Thinking

4. **Make Inferences** How do you think England's policy of salutary neglect toward the 13 colonies would affect the colonies' future political and economic development?

5. **Summarize** How did England's economic policies serve the interests of the British as well as the American colonists?

6. **Recognize Cause and Effect** How did the ideas of the Enlightenment lead to the Great Awakening? How did the Great Awakening lead to the growth of democratic ideas in the 13 colonies?

Silver mug ▶

WITNESS HISTORY 🔊 AUDIO

Paul Revere: A Silversmith

Paul Revere is best remembered as a Patriot during the American Revolution. But even before the Revolution, Revere made outstanding contributions to the growing colonial economy. Like most boys, Revere learned a trade. His father taught him to be a silversmith, and when Revere achieved master craftsman status, he produced fine works of silver. Silver working was just one of his talents. Revere also learned to engrave copper plates for printing, make surgical instruments, clean teeth and replace missing teeth, and make and sell eyeglasses. After the American Revolution, Revere opened a hardware store, foundry, and a copper-rolling mill.

Clever and ambitious business owners like Revere contributed to a growing colonial economy. His contributions were acknowledged in his obituary, which read in part, "seldom has the tomb closed upon a life so honorable and useful."

▲ In a portrait by John Singleton Copley, Paul Revere holds a silver teapot.

Comparing Regional Cultures

NY Core Curriculum Objectives

- **1.I.A.2c** Agricultural areas
- **2.I.A.3** Colonial experience: political rights and mercantile relationships
- **2.II.B.1a** The growth of urban and industrial patterns of life in the North

Terms and People

staple crop   dame school
cash crop

NoteTaking

Reading Skill: Compare and Contrast

Complete a chart like this one comparing the three regions of the 13 colonies.

	New England	Middle Colonies	Southern Colonies
Economy	• Fishing •	• •	• •
Society	• •	• Religious diversity •	• •

Why It Matters By the early 1700s, the economic and social foundations of Britain's 13 colonies were in place. As the colonies developed, three distinct regions emerged, each with its own economic and social structure: New England, the Middle Colonies, and the South. Despite their differences, the regions were part of Britain's North American empire. Later in the eighteenth century, events would cause the colonies to unite against a common cause: British rule. **Section Focus Question: How did life differ in each of the three main regions of the British colonies?**

Regional Economic Patterns

The vast majority of people in the 13 colonies made their living as farmers. Other than shipbuilding and some ironworks, the colonies lacked industries. The few small cities were all seaports that focused on trade with England.

In spite of these broad similarities, the colonies had by the mid-1700s developed important regional distinctions. Variations in geography and climate helped explain the differences between life in New England, the Middle Colonies, and the South.

New England New England is an area with cold winters, a short growing season, and a rugged landscape. For these reasons, New Englanders could not raise the crops most in demand by Europeans: tobacco, sugar, rice, and indigo. Instead, most New Englanders worked small farms where they raised livestock and grew wheat, rye, corn, and potatoes for their own use. None of these commodities could profitably be shipped to England, where a similar climate permitted production of the same crops.

Vocabulary Builder
commodity–(kuh MAHD uh tee) *n.* anything bought or sold; any item that is traded

New Englanders did ship some products from their shores. They exported lumber from their forests and fish—especially cod—from the sea. They salted and then shipped the fish to Europe or to the West Indies to feed enslaved Africans working on sugar plantations. New Englanders also used wood harvested from regional forests to build ships.

The principal seaport in the region was Boston, which had about 16,000 people in 1750. There, merchants did a lively business carrying out the busy trade between the colonies and Great Britain.

The Middle Colonies As in New England, family farms prevailed in the Middle Colonies. But those farms were more prosperous than those in New England. With a more temperate climate, farmers in the Middle Colonies were able to produce more and better wheat than did the New Englanders.

Thanks to a growing export trade in wheat, the Middle Colonies boomed during the eighteenth century—while New England's economy stagnated. Philadelphia and New York became the two great seaports of the prospering Middle Colonies. Still, neither of these cities was large by today's standards. In 1760, Philadelphia had a population of only 25,000.

The South Because of an even warmer climate and longer growing season, the Southern Colonies could raise the most valuable and profitable colonial crops. In the Chesapeake colonies of Virginia and Maryland, planters raised staple crops of tobacco, though some in the 1700s were switching to wheat. **Staple crops** are crops that are in steady demand. These crops were also **cash crops,** crops grown for sale. North Carolina produced cattle and lumber, while South Carolina and Georgia harvested rice and indigo. (Cotton would not become an important crop until the 1790s.) Charleston, South Carolina, was the region's largest port. Near the coast, most of the population consisted of enslaved Africans working on plantations. In the hillier areas inland from the coast, white settlers and family farms prevailed.

✔ **Checkpoint** In what ways did agriculture differ in the three colonial regions?

Regional Social Patterns

The three colonial regions also varied in the shape and form of the social life that developed there. Factors such as availability of education and patterns of settlement helped create distinct differences between the regions.

Differences in Population In New England and the Middle Colonies, there were relatively few African Americans. In parts of the South, they formed the majority of the population.

The three regions also attracted different types of free settlers. During the seventeenth century, most immigrants to the South were poor, young, single men. Seeking work for the short term and a farm for the long term, they worked as indentured servants. In contrast, most of the immigrants to seventeenth-century New England were of the middle class and could pay their own way. They immigrated to the colony

Philadelphia was a large city by colonial standards.

Focus On Geography

Geography and Regional Economies

The geography of a region determines what type of housing people build, what type of clothing they wear, and how they make a living. Each region of the 13 colonies developed an economy based on its geography.

New England's geography lent itself to fishing, lumber, and small-scale farming. Trade and commerce took hold in the New England city of Boston and in other towns along the coast. For their thriving wheat, rye, and barley crops, the Middle Colonies became known as the "breadbasket" of colonial America. Flour and other products were shipped to England and the West Indies from busy ports in New York and Philadelphia. Large plantations in the South grew tobacco, rice, indigo, and eventually cotton. Enslaved Africans tended these labor-intensive crops. Backcountry farmers in the Middle and Southern colonies scratched out a living on small farms.

▲ **New England Colonies**
Fishing for cod off the coast of New England

Middle Colonies ▲
Family harvesting
its crop

◄ A grain shovel

▼ **Southern Colonies**
Virginia planter watching
enslaved Africans pack
tobacco leaves for export

FRENCH
TERRITORY

FRENCH
TERRITORY

SPANISH TERRITORY

Gulf of Mexico

Great Lakes

Maine
(part of Mass.)

N.H.

New
York   Mass.

Conn.

R.I.

Pennsylvania

N.J.

Md.   Del.

Virginia

North
Carolina

South
Carolina

Georgia

Atlantic Ocean

Distance in miles
0   100   200

0   100   200
Distance in kilometers

New England Colonies
Middle Colonies
Southern Colonies
Claimed by New Hampshire
and New York

Geography and History
- How did geography affect the economy in each of the three regions?
- How do you think geography affects your town or city?

as families, which meant a better balance between males and females. For example, in 1650, New England had six males for every four females, compared with four men for every woman in the Chesapeake area.

European immigrants seemed to prefer the Middle Colonies most of all. These colonies became the most ethnically and culturally diverse region in the entire British Empire. In addition to religious tolerance, the Middle Colonies offered immigrants greater economic opportunities.

Though a less desirable destination for immigrants than the other regions, New England provided a healthier environment. A hilly land with fast-flowing rivers and streams, New England was free of the malaria and dysentery that killed so many colonists elsewhere. In New England, people who survived childhood could expect to live to about 70 years, compared to 45 years in the Chesapeake region.

With a healthier environment and better balance between men and women, New England enjoyed rapid population growth. During the seventeenth century, New England received only 21,000 immigrants—a fraction of the 120,000 transported to the Chesapeake area. Yet in 1700, New England had 91,000 colonists, more than any other region.

Women in the Colonies By law and custom, there were few opportunities for women outside the home. Most women were legal dependents of men, and men held all the power in colonial households. Married women could not own property, could not vote, could not hold political office, and could not serve on a jury. Although women who were widowed could inherit a portion of their husband's property, they did not have any political rights.

Both men and women depended on one another to run farms, businesses, and households. Men generally did the work of planting, raising, and harvesting crops. Women usually managed the household duties, such as cooking, gardening, sewing, and child care.

Graph Skills As the graph illustrates, population in the American colonies grew steadily from the mid-1600s to the mid-1700s. *What was the white population in 1720? What were some of the reasons for the increase in both the white and African American populations?*

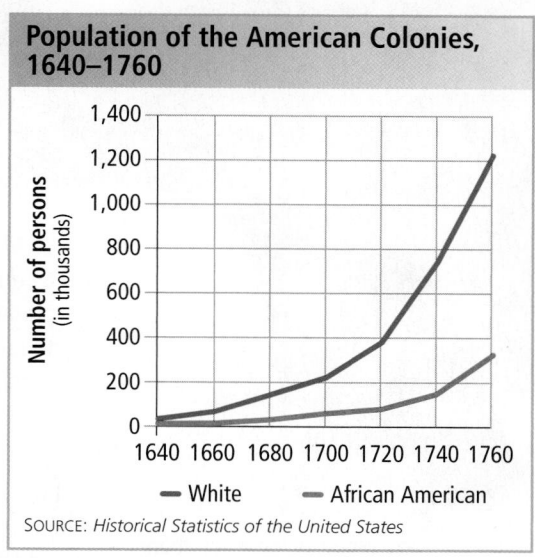

Population of the American Colonies, 1640–1760

SOURCE: *Historical Statistics of the United States*

Community Life The New England Colonies granted land to men who banded together to establish a town. New England leaders favored compact settlement in towns to support public schools and to sustain a local church. As a result, more adults were literate in New England than in the other colonial regions. In addition, while New England had fewer wealthy families than in the other regions, there was a greater degree of economic equality. Most men in New England owned their own farm, shop, or fishing boat.

In the Southern Colonies, the plantation economy based on slavery produced great profits. However, each large plantation was far from the next, and back-country farmers were excluded from plantation society. With a population that was spread far and wide, the southerners found it harder to sustain churches and schools. Illiteracy was more common in the South. Slavery also promoted greater economic inequality. A few white people became rich planters, but most remained common farmers.

Education As you have read, schooling was more available in New England than elsewhere in the colonies. By the mid-1600s, Massachusetts law required towns to provide schools where students could learn the basics of reading and writing. The goal was to enable students to read the Bible.

Larger New England towns offered a more advanced "grammar school" education—generally to boys only. Some girls did receive a grammar school education in **dame schools**—private schools operated out of a woman's home.

One-room schoolhouses were common in colonial New England. Hornbooks helped students learn to read.

Outside of New England, education was less widely available. Many colonists taught reading and mathematics to their own children. Wealthier families might hire a tutor to teach their children or send them to England to get an education.

Colleges were few, small, and very expensive. Most colonies had none, and only New Jersey had more than one—the College of New Jersey (Princeton) and Queens (Rutgers). Even the oldest and largest colleges—Harvard in Massachusetts, William and Mary in Virginia, and Yale in Connecticut—had fewer than 150 students. Only young men from prosperous families could attend. Most graduates became ministers.

During the colonial era, rules and regulations at colleges were quite strict. Students were expected to live moral and righteous lives, risking punishment or expulsion if they broke a rule. One rule stated:

Primary Source "If any scholar shall be guilty of profane swearing, cursing, vowing, any petty or implicit oath, profane . . . use of the [name of God], . . . fighting, striking, quarreling, challenging, turbulent words or behavior, . . . idleness, lying, defamation, talebearing, or any other suchlike immoralities, he shall be punished by fine, confession, . . . or expulsion, as the nature and circumstances of the case may require."
—Regulations at Yale College, 1745

The highly educated minority were expected to lead the common people. Although most colonists attended only grammar schools, most were better educated than their counterparts in Europe, many of whom were illiterate.

✔ **Checkpoint** How did education differ from one region to the other?

Progress Monitoring *Online*
For: Self-test with vocabulary practice
Web Code: nca-0306

Comprehension

1. **Terms and People** How does each term below relate to life in the colonies? Answer the question in one or two sentences that use each term.
   - staple crop
   - cash crop
   - dame school

2. **NoteTaking Reading Skill: Compare and Contrast** Use your completed chart to answer the Section Focus Question: How did life differ in each of the three main regions of the British colonies?

Writing About History

3. **Quick Write: Write a Thesis Statement** Immigrants to the colonies decided in which region they would live. Based on what you have read in this section, write a thesis statement for a problem-solution essay on deciding where to live from the point of view of a new immigrant.

Critical Thinking

4. **Compare and Contrast** In what ways were each of the major regions of the British colonies similar to one another, and in what ways were they different?

5. **Draw Conclusions** Why do you think more immigrants moved to the Middle Colonies and the Southern Colonies?

6. **Analyze** How do the goals and opportunities for education differ between colonial times and today?

▲ Rogers' Rangers

▲ Robert Rogers

Rogers' Rangers

The struggle for territory between England and France in North America broke into open conflict during the French and Indian War. From 1754 to 1763, the region between the Ohio Valley and Canada became a battlefield. To help win the war, England authorized units of Rangers—groups of colonial militiamen who served as scouts and soldiers—to aid English Crown soldiers. Rogers' Rangers, led by Robert Rogers of New Hampshire, became famous for including Indians and freed slaves in its ranks and for its unusual but highly effective tactics. As Rogers explained, his goals were:

❝ . . . from time to time, to use my best endeavours to distress the French and their allies, by sacking, burning, and destroying their houses, barns, barracks, canoes, . . . and by killing their cattle . . . and at all times to endeavor to way-lay, attack and destroy their convoys of provisions by land and water, in any part of the country where I could find them. ❞

—Robert Rogers, 1756

Wars of Empire

Core Curriculum Objectives

- **1.I.B.3** Territorial expansion
- **1.I.B.4** Impact during wartime
- **2.I.A.2a** Native American Indians (warfare)

Terms and People

George Washington
French and Indian War
Pontiac's Rebellion

Proclamation of 1763
Albany Plan of Union

NoteTaking

Reading Skill: Recognize Sequence As you read, keep track of the sequence of events that led to the French and Indian War.

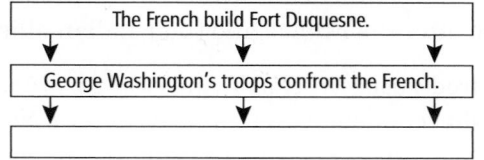

The French build Fort Duquesne.

↓

George Washington's troops confront the French.

↓

Why It Matters Conflict between the great European empires spread to the American colonies throughout the late seventeenth and early eighteenth centuries. The British and the colonists fought a series of wars against the French and their American Indian allies. In the process, however, the relationship between the British and their colonies became strained. **Section Focus Question: How did Great Britain's wars with France affect the American colonies?**

European Competition and the Colonies

By the mid-eighteenth century, England, France, Spain, and the Netherlands were locked in a worldwide struggle for empire. In North America, Britain's greatest rival was France. While Britain controlled the 13 colonies on the Atlantic seaboard, France controlled a vast territory that extended from the St. Lawrence River to the Gulf of Mexico.

Between 1689 and 1748, the British and the French fought a series of wars. Most of the fighting took place in Europe, but some spilled over into North America. Before long, British colonists were drawn into the war.

American Indians Affect the Balance of Power Each war between England and France was followed by a treaty that resolved nothing. Great Britain longed to drive the French from North America, and to accomplish this, the British needed to neutralize the great

French advantage: French support from most of the American Indians in the region. Native Americans dominated the forest passages between the frontiers of the rival empires.

The Indians benefited from their middle position between the competing empires. The British and French both gave generous gifts, especially of arms and ammunition, to woo the Indians. If one empire won a total victory, the Indians would lose their leverage and receive harsher treatment from the victors. They also were aware that the land they lived on was at stake. In the words of one Iroquois leader:

> **Primary Source** "We know our Lands are now become more valuable. The white People think we do not know their value; but we are sensible [aware] that the Land is everlasting, and the few Goods we receive for it are soon worn out that gone. . . . Besides, we are not well used [treated] with respect to the lands still unsold by us. Your people daily settle on these lands, and spoil our hunting. . . . Your horses and cows have eaten the grass our deer used to feed on."
>
> —Canasatego, Iroquois leader, July 7, 1742

Thus, the Indians recognized the importance of preserving the balance of power between the French and the British.

The Balance Shifts That balance began to tip as the British colonial population grew. In 1754, the 1,500,000 British colonists greatly outnumbered the 70,000 French. The increasingly powerful British often treated the Indians harshly and did little to stop settlers from taking Indian lands.

Compared to the British, the French were more <u>restrained</u>. Needing Indian allies, the French treated most Native Americans with respect and generosity. The outnumbered French worked with their Indian allies to resist British colonial expansion. The French built a string of small forts and trading posts along the Great Lakes and down the Ohio and Mississippi rivers. Lightly built and thinly manned, the posts depended upon the Indians for protection. Most Indians accepted these posts because, as one chief explained, "we can drive away the French when we please." That was not true of the British. Yet, while most Native Americans supported the French, some fought for the British.

✔ **Checkpoint** Why did the French and British fight frequently during the 1600s and 1700s?

The French and Indian War

One point of conflict between France and Great Britain was the fertile Ohio River valley, which was claimed by both countries but was largely unsettled. To discourage British colonists from moving into this area, the French built Fort Duquesne in what is now western Pennsylvania.

The new fort angered the British governor of Virginia, Robert Dinwiddie. In 1754, he sent colonial troops to evict the French. Dinwiddie entrusted the command to a young, ambitious Virginian named **George Washington.** His troops attacked and defeated a small French force. But Washington had to surrender when the French counterattacked. His defeat touched off a world war that eventually spread from America to Europe, Asia, Africa, and the West Indies. In Europe, the war was called the Seven Years' War. The British colonists called the conflict the **French and Indian War,** after the French and their Indian allies.

Early Battles At first, the British fared poorly in North America. In 1755, a combined British and colonial force did overwhelm two French forts near Nova Scotia. Those troops evicted the French settlers, known as Acadians, and gave

Vocabulary Builder
<u>restrain</u>–(rih STRAYN) *v.* to hold back from action

A young George Washington led British troops against the French in 1754.

their farms to New Englanders. But the British army suffered a disastrous defeat when General Edward Braddock marched into a French and Indian ambush near Fort Duquesne. Braddock died, but Washington led a skillful retreat that saved half of that army. Later, Washington recalled the battle in a letter to his mother:

Primary Source "... [We] were attacked by a body of French and Indians, whose number (I am certain) did not exceed 300 men. Ours consisted of about 1,300 well-armed troops, chiefly of the English soldiers, who were struck with such a panic that they behaved with more cowardice than it is possible to conceive. The officers behaved gallantly in order to encourage their men, for which they suffered greatly, there being near 60 killed and wounded—a large proportion out of the number we had!"

—George Washington, 1755

In 1756 and 1757, French General Louis-Joseph de Montcalm destroyed British forts on Lake Ontario and Lake George. Meanwhile, Indians raided British frontier settlements in Pennsylvania and Virginia.

The tide of war shifted in 1758 and 1759. The British managed to cut off French shipping to the Americas. As a result, many Indians deserted the French in favor of the better-supplied British. This allowed the British to capture Fort Duquesne. The British also seized the key French fortress of Louisbourg, which guarded the entrance to the St. Lawrence River. That victory cleared the way for General James Wolfe to attack the stronghold of Quebec in 1759. In a daring gamble, Wolfe's men used the cover of night to scale a cliff and occupy the Plains of Abraham, just outside the city walls. Marching out to attack, Montcalm suffered defeat and death.

In 1760, the British captured Montreal and forced the French governor general to surrender the rest of Canada, including the forts around the Great Lakes. The British had succeeded in their major North American goal.

British and French Wage War
The painting illustrates General Braddock's death after the battle at Fort Duquesne. The map shows the theater of war during the French and Indian War. *When did the British win Quebec and Montreal?*

North America, 1754–1763

Conic Projection
0   300   600 mi
0 300 600 km

1754

Hudson Bay

ROCKY MOUNTAINS

Missouri R.

Ohio R.

Mississippi R.

APPALACHIAN MTS.

St. Lawrence R.

Atlantic Ocean

Pacific Ocean

Gulf of Mexico

British claims
French claims
Spanish claims
Disputed territory

Conic Projection
0   300   600 mi
0 300 600 km

1763

Hudson Bay

Proclamation Line of 1763

ROCKY MOUNTAINS

Missouri R.

Ohio R.

Mississippi R.

APPALACHIAN MTS.

St. Lawrence R.

Atlantic Ocean

Pacific Ocean

Gulf of Mexico

Map Skills The French and Indian War changed the colonial boundaries of North America.

1. **Locate:** (a) Mississippi River, (b) Ohio River, (c) Appalachian Mountains

2. **Regions** How did British claims in North America change from 1754 to 1763?

3. **Analyze Information** Which nation was Britain's main rival in 1754? How might this have changed in 1763?

Treaty of Paris (1763) Fighting continued in other parts of the world. The British also won major victories in India, the Philippines, West Africa, and the West Indies. In 1763, the Treaty of Paris ended the war triumphantly for the British, who kept Canada, the Great Lakes country, the Ohio River valley, and Florida. They had driven the French from North America. Thereafter, the Mississippi River became the boundary between the British and the Spanish claims in North America.

✔ **Checkpoint** What was the outcome of the French and Indian War?

Pontiac's Rebellion

The conquest of Canada was dreadful news to Indians of the interior. No longer could they play the French and the British off against each other. Indeed, the British military commander Lord Jeffrey Amherst quickly cut off delivery of goods to Indians. British settlers flooded onto Indian lands in western Pennsylvania and Virginia.

The Indians affected included Mississauga, Ottawa, Potawatomi, Ojibwa, Wyandot, Miami, Kickapoo, Mascouten, Delaware, Shawnee, and Seneca. During the spring of 1763, members of these groups surprised and captured most of the British forts in the Ohio River valley and along the Great Lakes. Through the summer and fall, they also raided settlements of western Pennsylvania, Maryland, and Virginia. The British called this uprising **Pontiac's Rebellion,** after an Ottawa chief prominent in the attack on Detroit.

The Indians' goal was to weaken the British and lure the French back into North America. But they failed to capture the three largest and strongest British posts: Detroit, Niagara, and Fort Pitt (formerly Fort Duquesne).

During 1764, the Indian attackers ran short of gunpowder, shot, and guns. Without a European supplier, their rebellion fizzled. At the same time, the British government sought a quick end to the expensive war. The Crown blamed Amherst for the crisis, recalling him in disgrace. Thomas Gage, the new commander, recognized that respect for the Indians would cost less than military expeditions against them.

The various Indian nations made peace in return for British promises to restrain the settlers. The British rebuilt their forts, but they also tried to enforce the **Proclamation of 1763.** This document ordered colonial settlers to remain east of the Appalachian Mountains:

> **Primary Source** "And whereas it is just and reasonable, and essential to our Interest, and to the Security of our Colonies, . . . the several Nations or Tribes of Indians with whom We are connected, and who live under our Protection, should not be molested or disturbed in the Possession of such Parts of our Dominions and Territories as . . . are reserved to them, or any of them, as their Hunting Grounds."
> —Proclamation of 1763

The British troops, however, were too few to restrain the thousands of colonists who pushed westward. Troops burned a few log cabins, but the settlers simply rebuilt them. It was clear that the boundary set by the proclamation could not protect the Indians. At the same time, it irritated the colonists, who resented efforts to limit their expansion.

✓ **Checkpoint** What did the Indians involved with Pontiac's Rebellion hope to accomplish?

Aftermath of the War

The French and Indian War, as well as Pontiac's Rebellion, revealed the tensions between the British and their colonists. After investing so much blood and money to conquer North America, the British wanted greater control over their colonies. They also had a large war debt, plus the expensive job of guarding the vast territories taken from the French. The British thought that colonists should help pay these costs.

Bickering between the 13 colonies had also complicated the war effort and had angered the British. With British encouragement, colonial delegates had met in 1754 to review the **Albany Plan of Union.** Drafted by Benjamin Franklin, the plan called on the colonies to unite under British rule and to cooperate with one another in war. It created an American continental assembly that would include delegates from each colony. But, none of the colonies would accept the plan for fear of losing some of their own autonomy. The British also dropped the plan, fearing that 13 united colonies might be too difficult to manage.

During the 1760s, the British acted on their own to impose new taxes and new regulations on colonial trade. Those changes angered colonists who wanted to preserve the sort of loose empire that had, for so long, produced so many benefits at so little cost to them.

✓ **Checkpoint** What was the effect of the French and Indian War and Pontiac's Rebellion on the relationship between the colonies and Great Britain?

Benjamin Franklin supported the idea of colonial unity and created the "Join, or Die" political cartoon. *How is the idea of unity expressed in the political cartoon?*

Progress Monitoring *Online*
For: Self-test with vocabulary practice
Web Code: nee-0308

Comprehension

1. **Terms and People** How does each term below help explain how the relationship between Great Britain and its North American colonies began to change in the 1760s? For each term, write a sentence that explains your answer.
   • French and Indian War
   • Pontiac's Rebellion
   • Proclamation of 1763
   • Albany Plan of Union

2. **NoteTaking Reading Skill: Recognize Sequence** Use your completed flowchart to answer the Section Focus Question: How did Great Britain's wars with France affect the American colonies?

Writing About History

3. **Quick Write: Support a Solution** Based on what you have read, list supporting information for the following solution: What facts might Britain have used to support the decision to issue the Proclamation of 1763?

Critical Thinking

4. **Draw Conclusions** Why do you think French and British colonists in the Americas fought in the wars of their home countries?

5. **Compare and Contrast** How did the French and British differ in their efforts to gain control in North America?

6. **Make Inferences** What can you infer from the fact that the British were unable to enforce the Proclamation of 1763?

Quick Study Guide

2.I.A.2,
2.I.A.1

> **Progress Monitoring** *Online*
> **For:** Self-test with vocabulary practice
> **Web Code:** nca-0309

■ Diversity in the Colonies

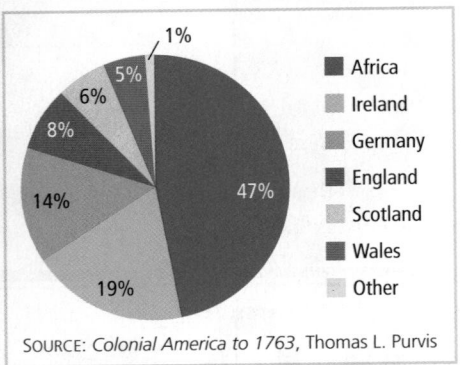

- Africa 47%
- Ireland
- Germany
- England
- Scotland
- Wales
- Other

1%, 5%, 6%, 8%, 14%, 19%

SOURCE: *Colonial America to 1763*, Thomas L. Purvis

■ English Ideas Influence the Colonies

English Ideas		
Magna Carta	**Parliament**	**English Bill of Rights**
• Limited monarch's right to tax • Guaranteed due process	• A bicameral legislature • An elected lower house • Power to tax	• Right to habeas corpus • Bars cruel or unusual punishment

■ The Three Regions of the 13 Colonies

Region	Climate	Economy	Population
New England Colonies	Cold winters; short growing season	Fishing; shipbuilding; trade; lumber; small subsistence farms	Few slaves or immigrants; more families; fast-growing population
Middle Colonies	Temperate; moderate growing season	Wheat, barley, and rye crops grown on moderate-sized farms; trade	Attractive to immigrants; tolerant of religious and ethnic differences
Southern Colonies	Warm climate; long growing season	Cash crops of tobacco, rice, and indigo grown on large plantations using slave labor	More men than women; indentured servants; enslaved African Americans a majority in some areas

■ The French and Indian War

Cause and Effect
Causes
• England and France vie for power in Europe • French and English make alliances with Indians • Conflict between French and English over territory in North America

↓

The French and Indian War

↓

Effects
• France loses colonies in North America • England gains Canada • Proclamation of 1763 limits colonial settlement

☑ Quick Study Timeline

In America

1705
Virginia introduces harsher slave codes

1735
John Paul Zenger's trial becomes foundation for freedom of the press

1700

1720

Around the World

1689
England's Glorious Revolution brings a bill of rights

1707
England, Scotland, and Wales join to form United Kingdom of Great Britain

1736
Qianlong becomes emperor of China

American Issues
●—●—●—● **Connector**

By connecting prior knowledge with what you have learned in this chapter, you can gradually build your understanding of enduring questions that still affect America today. Answer the questions below. Then, use your American Issues Connector study guide (or go online. www.PHSchool.com **Web Code:** nch-6302).

Issues You Learned About

● **America Goes to War** Since colonial days, people in North America have taken part in local as well as global skirmishes.

1. **The French and Indian War** Colonial troops participated in the French and Indian War, which was fought in North America in the mid-1700s. Write a summary of the war, including its key events, its outcome, and its aftermath. Consider:
   • the conflict over the Ohio River valley
   • the progress of the war
   • the Treaty of Paris
   • the settlement of the western lands
   • the reaction of American Indians
   • the Native American alliances and motives

● **Interaction With the Environment** The colonists relied on farming to provide for the needs of their families as well as to raise cash crops for export.

2. Farmers in the Middle Colonies and the South sold crops to England. Why were New Englanders unsuccessful in the export of farm products?

3. Why did the Middle Colonies economically boom during the eighteenth century?

4. Is the following statement true: All farmers grew crops only for subsistence. Explain your answer.

● **Church and State** Religion played a strong role in colonial government as well as in the daily lives of the colonists.

5. In which of the three colonial regions did organized religion and religious leaders have the most influence? Why?

6. Provide at least two examples of the ties between established churches in colonial America and the colonial governments.

7. How did Rhode Island and Pennsylvania differ from the other colonies in terms of religion?

Connect to Your World	**New York**

Migration and Urbanization When the Dutch settled New Netherland, many early settlers chose to use Africans as slaves to help develop the colony. Slaves were typically put to work clearing forests, building ports, clearing roads, and serving as household workers. Over time, some slaves eventually negotiated a type of "half-freedom" with the Dutch West India Company. "Half-free" slaves were left to work on their own farms in exchange for yearly tribute payments. The half-free slaves also agreed to provide labor to the Dutch West India Company when necessary. Find out more about the role African slaves played in New York's colonial history. Write a short report to summarize the results of your research.

1740 Great Awakening begins	1754 Benjamin Franklin draws up the Albany Plan of Union	1754–1763 French and Indian War	1763–1764 Pontiac's Rebellion

1740   **1760**

History Interactive
For: Interactive timeline
Web Code: ncp-0311

	1748 Montesquieu's *The Spirit of the Laws*	1760 George III becomes king of England	1763 Treaty of Paris ends war between French and British

Chapter Assessment

Terms and People

1. Define **indentured servant.** What future could an indentured servant expect?

2. What was the **Magna Carta**? What impact did it have on English political traditions?

3. What was the **Great Awakening**? What ideas did it stress?

4. What was the **French and Indian War**? How did it change North America?

5. What was **Pontiac's Rebellion**? How did this rebellion affect the colonies?

Focus Questions

The focus question for this chapter is **What factors shaped life in colonial America in the seventeenth and eighteenth centuries?** Build an answer to this big question by answering the focus questions for Sections 1 through 4 and the Critical Thinking questions that follow.

Section 1
6. Which major groups of immigrants came to Britain's American colonies in the 1700s?

Section 2
7. How did English ideas about government and the economy influence life in the 13 colonies?

Section 3
8. How did life differ in each of the three main regions of the British colonies?

Section 4
9. How did Great Britain's wars with France affect the American colonies?

Critical Thinking

10. **Draw Inferences** How did Britain's policy of mercantilism affect the colonies?

11. **Summarize** Identify the three cultural groups that dominated immigration to the colonies in the 1600s and 1700s, and briefly explain their reasons for coming to America.

12. **Evaluate Credibility of Sources** Do you think *The Interesting Narrative of Olaudah Equiano, or Gustavus Vassa the African* is a reliable source of information about the African American experience in colonial America? Why or why not?

13. **Categorize** Name the three colonial regions and their primary resources and economic activities.

14. **Make Comparisons** Compare and contrast the opportunities available to immigrants in the three colonial regions.

15. **Explain Causes** What caused the French and Indian War to erupt in 1754?

16. **Analyze Visuals** Study the political cartoon below, created by Benjamin Franklin, and then answer the questions.

What do the different parts of the snake represent? What does the cartoon's title mean? What do you think inspired Franklin to create this drawing?

17. **Synthesize Information** Do you think the Proclamation of 1763 ended the British policy of following salutary neglect when it came to governing the colonies? Explain your answer.

Writing About History

Writing a Problem-Solution Essay Immigrants in colonial America had to adapt to a diverse society, and they also had to deal with Native Americans who were defending their homelands.

Write a problem-solution essay about one of these topics, or choose your own topic relating to the content of this chapter.

Prewriting
- Choose the topic that interests you most. If you have a personal interest in a problem and its solution, your essay will be easier to develop.
- Narrow your topic.
- Make a list of details, facts, and examples that proves there is a problem. Then, identify the specific parts of your solution.

Drafting
- Develop a working thesis and choose information to support it.
- Organize the paragraphs in a logical order so that readers can understand the solution you propose.

Revising
- Use the guidelines on page SH11 of the Writing Handbook to revise your essay.

Regents DBQ Practice

Colonial Labor

The English colonists in North America faced many daunting tasks. They needed to fell timber, establish farms, and build settlements. The amount of work required was overwhelming. Who did that work? Use your knowledge of Colonial America and Documents 1, 2, and 3 to answer questions 1 through 4.

Document 1

"This Indenture, Made the Fourth Day of August in the Twenty-ninth Year of the Reign of our Sovereign Lord George the Second King of Great Britain, &, And in the Year of our Lord, One Thousand Seven Hundred and fifty five Between William Buckland of Baford Carpenter & Joiner of the one Part, and Thomson Mason of London, Esq. of the other Part,

Witnesseth, That the said William Buckland . . . shall and will, as a faithful Covenant Servant, well and truly serve the said Thomas Mason his Executors and assigns in the Plantation of Virginia beyond the Seas, for the Space of Four Years, next ensuing his Arrival in the said Plantation in the Employment of a Carpenter and Joiner. . . .

And the said Thomas Mason . . . shall and will at his . . . proper Costs and Charges, with what convenient Speed [he] may, carry and convey, or cause to be carried and conveyed over unto the said Plantation, the said Wm Buckland and from henceforth, and during the said Voyage, and also during the said Term, shall and will at the like Costs and Charges, provide for and allow the said Wm Buckland all necessary Meat, Drink, Washing, Lodging, fit and convenient for Wm as Covenant Servants in such Cases are usually provided for and allowed and pay and allow William Buckland Wages on Salary at the Rate of Twenty Pounds Sterling per Annum Payable Quarterly."

—*Indenture Contract of William Buckland, 1755*

Document 2

"Ran away from the Subscriber, living near James-Town, last Sunday was Fort-night, a Negroe Man, named Harry, who formerly belonged to Col. Grymes, of Richmond County: He is about 5 Feet 7 Inches high, thin visag'd, has small Eyes, and a very large Beard; is about 35 Years old; and plays upon the Fiddle. He had a dark-colour'd cloth Coat, double breasted, 2 cotton Jackets, dy'd of a dark Colour, a Pair of Buckskin Breeches, flourish'd at the Knees, and a blue Great Coat. It is suppos'd he is gone to Richmond County, where he has a Wife. Whoever apprehends him, so that he be brought to me near James-Town, shall have a Pistole [gold coin] Reward, besides what the Law allows. William Newgent. N.B. As he ran away without any Cause, I desire he may be punish'd by Whipping, as the Law directs."

—*advertisement in the* Virginia Gazette, *March 20 to March 27, 1746*

Document 3

"And as for the general sort that shall go to be planters, be they [very] poor, so they be honest, . . . the place will make them rich: all kinds of [workers] we must first employ, are carpenters, shipwrights, masons, sawyers, brick makers, bricklayers, plowmen, sowers, planters, fishermen, coopers, smiths, . . . tailors, turners, and such like, to make and fit all necessaries, for comfort and use of the Colony, and for such as are of no trades (if they be industrious) they shall have their employment enough, for there is a world of means to set many thousands to work, partly in such things as I mentioned before, and many other profitable works, for no man must lie idle there. . . ."

—*Virginia Company pamphlet recruiting Jamestown settlers, 1609*

---

1. Where was Document 1 probably written?
   (1) in England
   (2) aboard ship
   (3) in Virginia
   (4) in Jamestown

2. In Document 2, the advertiser states that Harry ran away "without any Cause." Yet the advertisement hints at a likely cause. What is it?
   (1) to escape whipping
   (2) to practice his trade
   (3) to enjoy stolen goods
   (4) to join his wife

3. What reasonable conclusion about Jamestown in 1611 might you draw from Document 3?
   (1) Jamestown needed new leadership.
   (2) Jamestown had no enslaved people.
   (3) Jamestown needed many types of workers.
   (4) Jamestown was moving from farming to industry.

4. **Writing Task** Based on Documents 1, 2, and 3, and on what you have learned in Chapter 3, write a letter from the point of view of an indentured servant in Jamestown. Use information from the documents and the chapter to give your family or friends an impression of what life as an indentured servant in Jamestown might have been like.

NY Connect to New York

George Clinton

Born: July 26, 1739, Little Britain, New York

In 1765, American colonists protested when Britain introduced new taxes. This anger swelled into a full-blown war—the American Revolution. By the war's end, America was established as a nation in its own right, independent of Britain. During these trying times, some of the country's most powerful minds went to work crafting a plan of government for their new country. One of these men was George Clinton, a New Yorker who played a significant role in the birth of the United States.

Clinton represented the state of New York at the Second Continental Congress, a meeting of the colonies' delegates in May 1775, just after the war started. Clinton and the other representatives debated how the country should be run, making important decisions on financial, diplomatic, and military issues.

In 1777, Clinton (often called "Father of New York State") was elected as the first governor of his home state of New York. Leaders of the new nation were struggling over an important question—how much power should the federal government have over each state? As a state politician and strong Antifederalist, George Clinton believed that the power of the national government should be limited. Clinton and another famous New Yorker, Alexander Hamilton, debated the issue of states' rights in a series of letters published in newspapers in the late 1780s.

> "The evils pointed out in the system are now within our power to remedy—but if we suffer ourselves to be influenced by specious [false] reasoning unsupported by example to an unconditional adoption of an imperfect government, the opportunity will be forever lost, for history does not furnish a single instance of a government once established, voluntarily yielding up its powers to secure the rights and liberties of the people."
>
> —George Clinton, 1788

Clinton served as New York's governor for more than two decades (from 1777 to 1795 and from 1801 to 1804). He also served as Vice President under Thomas Jefferson. Clinton's long political career, like that of many other statesmen, helped to shape the history of both his home state and the United States in their very first days.

CREATING THE AMERICAN REPUBLIC

CONTENTS

The Spirit of '76, by
Archibald M. Willard,
honors the heroes of the
American Revolution. ▶

A.M.Willard

4 The American Revolution
1765–1783

A Revolution of Ideas

Many years after the Revolutionary War ended, John Adams—a Patriot and the second President of the United States—reflected on the meaning of the Revolution. In his mind, the war itself was not the Revolution.

66What do we mean by the American Revolution? Do we mean the American war? The Revolution was effected before the war commenced. The Revolution was in the minds and hearts of the people. . . . This radical change in the principles, opinions, sentiments, and affections of the people was the real American Revolution.99

—John Adams, February 13, 1818

Listen to the Witness History *audio to hear more about the American Revolution.*

◄ In this nineteenth-century painting, General George Washington looks over his troops during the harsh winter at Valley Forge.

Teapot

Tricorn hat

Core Curriculum Preview

Chapter Focus Question: What aspects of the American Revolution were revolutionary?

Section 1
Causes of the Revolution 2.I.A.3a, 2.I.A.4a

Section 2
Declaring Independence 2.I.A.4, 2.I.A.4b, 2.I.A.4c

Section 3
Turning Points of the War 2.I.A.4, 2.I.A.4b, 2.I.A.4c

Section 4
War's End and Lasting Effects 2.I.A.4, 2.I.A.4b, 2.I.A.5d

Use the ☑ **Quick Study Timeline** at the end of this chapter to preview chapter events.

Snare drum

> **Note Taking Study Guide *Online***
> **For:** Note Taking and American Issues Connector
> **Web Code:** nce-6401

◄ George III, the king of England

A copy of
the Stamp
Act ►

WITNESS HISTORY 🔊 AUDIO

Rights of the Colonists

James Otis, a leading patriot, argued that British taxes threatened colonists' rights and would make them slaves to the king and Parliament.

❝I can see no reason to doubt but the imposition of taxes . . . in the colonies is absolutely irreconcilable with the rights of the colonists as British subjects and as men. . . .

We all think ourselves happy under Great Britain. We love, esteem, and reverence our mother country, and adore our King. And could the choice of independency be offered the colonies or subjection to Great Britain upon any terms above absolute slavery, I am convinced they would accept the latter.❞

—James Otis, from *The Rights of the British Colonies Asserted and Proved*, 1763

Causes of the Revolution

 Core Curriculum Objectives

- **2.I.A.3a** Colonial charters and self-government: Mayflower Compact, town meetings, House of Burgesses, local government, property rights, enforceable contracts, Albany Plan of Union
- **2.I.A.4a** Causes of the Revolution

Terms and People

Stamp Act	Boston Massacre
John Adams	committee of
Patrick Henry	correspondence
Sons of Liberty	Boston Tea Party
nonimportation	Intolerable Acts
agreement	First Continental
	Congress

<u>Note</u>Taking

Reading Skill: Recognize Sequence
Record the events that increased tension between Britain and its colonies.

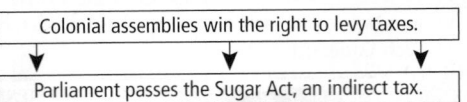

Why It Matters The American colonists enjoyed the protection of Britain during the Indian wars while paying very little of the cost. Meanwhile, they profited from trade within the British Empire. Most importantly, they cherished the political rights they enjoyed as British subjects. When Parliament began to tax the colonists to raise revenue, they protested. Eventually, the protests turned to rebellion and rebellion turned to war. **Section Focus Question: What caused the colonists to rebel against the British?**

The Colonists' Political Heritage

The colonists believed that Great Britain enjoyed the best government on Earth. British liberty included the due process of the common law, trial by jury, and freedom of the press from prior censorship. Above all, the colonists cherished the right to pay no tax unless it was levied by their representatives. Colonial governments followed the British model, but the colonists' protests of the 1760s revealed that there were some important differences.

British Government Is a Model The British government had three branches. Executive power belonged to the monarch. Legislative power was divided between two houses of Parliament: the House of Lords and the House of Commons. Aristocrats inherited seats in the House of Lords. Only the House of Commons depended on elections by a small percentage of the people.

Similarly, each colony except Pennsylvania had a two-house legislature: an elected assembly and a council of prominent colonists appointed to life terms by the governor. The governor was appointed by, represented, and served the king. Only Connecticut and Rhode Island elected their own governor, while Pennsylvania's entire assembly was elected. The colonists did not elect any members of British Parliament.

By modern standards, the British system was far from democratic. But democracy seemed foolish and dangerous in a society where people inherited wildly unequal property and status. In 1770, the British prime minister, Lord North, insisted, "I can never acquiesce in the absurd opinion that all men are equal." Most Britons and colonists agreed, and wealthy men controlled government in the colonies as in Great Britain.

Differences in Colonial Governments Despite the similarities, colonial politics differed from the British model in several ways. The British constitution was not a formal document but a collection of laws and traditions accumulated over centuries. In contrast, the colonists' rights had traditionally been spelled out in formal legal documents such as the royal charters of Maryland or South Carolina, as well as informal written agreements like the Mayflower Compact.

In addition, two thirds of free colonial men owned enough property to qualify to vote, compared to less than a fourth of British men. By 1760, political upheaval in Great Britain and European wars had allowed the elected colonial assemblies to increase their powers at the expense of the royal governors. Since the colonies lacked aristocrats with inherited titles, the leaders in both assembly and council were wealthy planters and merchants related by blood or marriage. The assemblies often withheld salaries from unpopular governors.

British officials hoped to change the situation by taxing the colonists to provide salaries to royal governors and judges. Crown salaries would make them less responsive to the assemblies and councils. But that prospect alarmed the colonists, who began to cherish their deviations from Britain as important advantages. Members of Parliament believed that they "virtually represented" every British subject, including the colonists. While Parliament expected the colonists to obey, the colonists saw themselves as equal members of the British political body. These differences quickly became a problem when Parliament tried to levy taxes on the colonies. The colonists believed that only their own elected officials had that right.

Vocabulary Builder
virtual—(VER choo uhl) *adv.* being such in practice or effect, though not in actual fact; implied

✔ **Checkpoint** How did colonial governments differ from the British government?

Comparing British and Colonial Governments	☑ Quick Study
Great Britain	**American Colonies**
King	**Governor**
• Inherited executive power	• Appointed by and served the king but paid by the colonial legislature
Parliament	**Colonial Legislatures**
House of Lords	**Upper House or Council**
• Aristocrats with inherited titles also inherited legislative power	• Appointed by governor • Prominent colonists but without inherited titles
House of Commons	**Lower House or Assembly**
• Elected by men who held significant amounts of property • Less than 1/4 of British men qualified to vote	• Elected by men who held property • About 2/3 of colonial men qualified to vote

New Taxes Upset Colonists

The Seven Years' War—called the French and Indian War in the colonies—nearly doubled Britain's national debt and greatly expanded its colonial territories. Parliament needed to raise money, both to pay the debt and to protect the colonies. People in Britain paid far more taxes than the colonists did. This imbalance seemed unfair, for the war had been fought largely to protect the colonists. Parliament decided that the colonists could and should pay more to help the Empire.

The Sugar, Quartering, and Stamp Acts Colonial merchants had grown rich from trade, often smuggling or bribing officials to avoid duties, or taxes, on imports. In 1764, the new prime minister, George Grenville, proposed raising money by collecting duties already in effect. The law, known as the Sugar Act when put into effect, actually lowered the duty on foreign molasses. However, it also assigned customs officers and created courts to collect the duties and prosecute smugglers. Grenville hoped that these measures would encourage colonists to pay the tax.

In early 1765, Parliament passed another unpopular law, the Quartering Act. This act required the colonies to provide housing and supplies for the British troops stationed there after the French and Indian War. Colonists complained but most went along with the changes because they accepted Parliament's right to regulate trade and provide for defense.

In March 1765, Parliament passed a bill intended to raise money from the colonies. The **Stamp Act** required colonists to pay a tax on almost all printed materials, including newspapers, books, court documents, contracts, and land deeds. This was the first time that Parliament had imposed a direct tax within the colonies.

Taxation Without Representation The colonists angrily protested the Stamp Act, which was to take effect in November. They claimed that it threatened their prosperity and liberty. Colonial leaders questioned Parliament's right to tax the colonies directly. They argued that the colonies had no representation in Parliament, so Parliament had no right to tax them. Some colonists believed that if they accepted this tax, Parliament would add ever more taxes, stripping away their property and political rights. Many colonists thought that the stamp tax revealed a conspiracy by British officials to destroy American liberties.

The colonists' arguments puzzled the members of Parliament. After all, most Britons paid taxes although they could not vote. Many large British cities did not elect representatives to Parliament, which claimed to represent everyone in the Empire. Parliament dismissed the colonial opposition as selfish and narrow-minded. The Empire needed money, and Parliament had the right to levy taxes anywhere in the Empire. Of course, Parliament's argument did not sway the colonists, who were appalled to discover that the British were denying their right to tax themselves.

✔ **Checkpoint** Why did the British impose new taxes on the colonies?

Colonial Protests Intensify

Tax resistance among the colonists took three forms: intellectual protest, economic boycotts, and violent intimidation. All three forms combined to force the British to back down. Colonial leaders wrote pamphlets, drafted resolutions, gave speeches, and delivered sermons to persuade colonists to defy the new taxes. The surge in political activity astonished **John Adams,** a prominent Massachusetts lawyer who observed "our presses have groaned, our pulpits have thundered, our legislatures have resolved, our towns have voted."

Symbols of New Taxes
Printed materials were supposed to be marked with stamps like these to show that the tax had been paid. *Why do you think there were stamps of different values?*

Enlightenment Ideas Colonial protests drew upon the liberalism of the Enlightenment. Europe's leading liberal writers included Baron de Montesquieu of France and John Locke of England. They argued that people had divinely granted natural rights, including life, liberty, and property. A good government protected these individual rights. Locke insisted that government existed for the good of the people. Therefore, people had the right to protest any government that violated this "social contract" by failing to protect their rights.

Patrick Henry, a young Virginia representative, used these ideas to draft a radical document known as the Virginia Resolves. He argued that only the colonial assemblies had the right to tax the colonists:

> **Primary Source** "Resolved therefore, That the General Assembly of this colony, together with his majesty or his substitutes have, in their representatives capacity the only exclusive right and power to lay taxes and imposts upon the inhabitants of this colony; and that every attempt to vest such power in any other person or persons whatever than the General Assembly aforesaid is illegal, unconstitutional, and unjust, and has a manifest tendency to destroy British as well as American liberty."
> —Patrick Henry, May 29, 1765

On May 30, 1765, the Virginia House of Burgesses accepted most of Henry's resolves, but rejected two—including the one above—because they were deemed too radical. Colonial newspapers, however, printed all six, believing that they had been accepted. Eight other colonies then adopted resolves similar to Henry's original proposal.

Patriot Leaders Emerge Colonists violently opposed the Stamp Act, which affected every colonist. In the months following the passage of the act, colonists began to work together to fight it, which created a new, but still fragile, sense of American unity. Those who opposed the British taxes called themselves "Patriots." In the seaport streets, people showed a powerful new interest in politics. To lead the popular protests, some men formed associations known as the **Sons of Liberty.** Their most famous leader was Boston's Samuel Adams, a cousin of John Adams.

As the protests continued, angry crowds assaulted colonists who supported or helped to collect the taxes. The crowds were especially violent in Boston. In August 1765, a mob led by the Sons of Liberty tore down the office and damaged the house of the stamp tax collector. The Massachusetts lieutenant governor, Thomas Hutchinson, denounced this riot. He insisted that the colonists had a legal duty to pay Parliament's taxes. Another mob destroyed Hutchinson's house. Thereafter, no one in Boston dared to voice support for the stamp tax. By the end of the year, every stamp collector in the colonies had resigned, leaving no one to collect the taxes.

Leaders Organize a Boycott Some colonial leaders opposed the tax but feared the violence of the crowds. To control and coordinate their protest activities, nine colonies sent delegates to a Stamp Act Congress held in New York City in October 1765. Members of this congress encouraged a consumer boycott of goods imported from Britain. Local committees enforced these **nonimportation agreements,** which threatened British merchants and manufacturers with economic ruin.

Tarring and Feathering
In this painting, Bostonians pour hot tea down the throat of a tax collector who has been tarred and feathered. *How do you think this type of artwork affected colonists still loyal to the British Crown?*

Women played an important economic role in the boycotts. When colonists stopped buying British goods, they needed "homespun" cloth to substitute for British-manufactured cloth. Gatherings of women to spin thread and weave cloth drew applause from spectators and from the Patriot newspapers. Women also gave up certain comforts when they pledged not to buy any manufactured British goods. Known as "Daughters of Liberty," these women won respect for their efforts in the political struggle.

The combination of tactics worked. Under pressure from British merchants and manufacturers, Parliament repealed the Stamp Act in 1766. But the struggle was not over, for Parliament also passed an act declaring its right to levy taxes on the colonists.

✔ **Checkpoint** What three tactics did colonists use to protest British taxes?

New Taxes Lead to New Protests

The Stamp Act crisis showed that the colonists would not accept a direct tax. But the British government still needed to raise money to pay its debt and support troops in the colonies. Charles Townshend, the Crown's chief financial officer, thought that colonists would accept indirect taxes on commerce. After all, they had long accepted customs duties in principle, though evading them in practice. In 1767, Parliament passed the Townshend Acts, which levied new import duties on everyday items such as glass, lead, paint, paper, and tea.

To Townshend's surprise, the colonists insisted that they would pay no new taxes of any sort to Parliament. They also resented Townshend's plans to use the money to pay the salaries of colonial governors and judges, making them more independent of the colonial assemblies. That prospect alarmed the colonists, who valued their financial control of the governors.

Violence Erupts in Boston In response to the Townshend Acts, the colonists revived their protests, boycotts, and street violence. Once again, the largest riots occurred in Boston, where many of the British customs officials abused their power. The Massachusetts legislature issued a circular letter denouncing the Townshend duties. Few other colonial legislatures paid attention to it until the governor dissolved the Massachusetts legislature in retaliation for their protest.

In an already tense situation, customs officers seized the merchant ship *Liberty* in June 1768 for smuggling. The ship belonged to John Hancock, a wealthy merchant and a prominent colonial politician. The seizure set off riots against the customs officers. To suppress the riots, the Crown sent 4,000 troops to occupy Boston, a city of only 16,000 people. For over a year, the presence of British troops inflamed popular anger, especially because the poorly paid soldiers competed with unskilled workers for jobs.

Analyzing Political Cartoons

Death of the Stamp Act This cartoon shows British government ministers mourning the end of the Stamp Act. George Grenville carries a coffin to a tomb containing the remains of other unpopular acts. In the background, warehouses are empty because the contents have quickly been shipped to America.
1. Why is Grenville portrayed as the father of a dead child?
2. What is the significance of the ships and warehouses?

One night in March 1770, a group of colonists hurled snowballs and rocks at British soldiers guarding the Customs House. The nervous soldiers fired into the crowd, killing five colonists. The dead included Crispus Attucks, a sailor who may have been an escaped slave of mixed Indian and African ancestry. Under the leadership of Samuel Adams, Patriots called the killings the **Boston Massacre.** Adams later organized a network of local **committees of correspondence** throughout Massachusetts. The committees provided leadership and promoted cooperation. By 1773, several other colonies had created committees, which helped build colonial unity.

Once again, Parliament backed down. The British withdrew troops from Boston and dropped most of the Townshend duties. But to preserve the principle of Parliamentary supremacy, Parliament kept the tax on tea. Therefore, colonists continued to boycott British tea and to drink smuggled Dutch tea.

The Boston Tea Party The tea boycott worsened financial problems for the already struggling British East India Company. To help the company and encourage the colonists to pay the tax, Parliament passed a law allowing the company to sell directly to the colonists. This made their tea cheaper than the smuggled tea, even with the tax.

Instead of buying the cheaper tea, the colonists protested that the British were trying to trick them into paying the tax. If the East India Company sold tea directly, it would also hurt the wealthy colonists who smuggled tea. On the night of December 16, 1773, Boston Patriots took matters into their own hands. Dressed as Indians, they boarded three British ships laden with tea and dumped the tea into the harbor. The event became known as the **Boston Tea Party.**

✓ **Checkpoint** How did tensions between the colonists and Britain escalate after 1767?

▼ A British soldier's cap badge

Colonists Unite Against Harsh Measures

The Bostonians' actions outraged Parliament and the Crown. To punish Boston, Parliament passed the Coercive Acts. They closed the port to trade until the inhabitants paid for the destroyed tea, including the tax. They also increased the power of the governor at the expense of the elected assembly and town meetings. To enforce these measures, the British sent warships and troops to Boston.

The Intolerable Acts The colonists were outraged. In addition to closing the port, the acts forced colonists to house British troops and allowed British officials to be tried in Britain for crimes committed in the colonies. In addition, the Quebec Act extended Canada's southern border, cutting off lands claimed by several colonies. The horrified colonists called the legislation the **Intolerable Acts.** They rejected the idea that the British could shut down trade and change colonial governments at will.

In rural Massachusetts, people reacted to the British actions with violence. Armed with clubs and guns, they forced the courts of law to shut down. They also assaulted anyone who accepted an office under the governor or spoke in favor of obeying Parliament. They coated some victims in hot tar and feathers—a punishment both humiliating and painful.

The Colonies Take Action Fortunately for Massachusetts, the other colonies also opposed the Coercive Acts and viewed them as a threat to their freedom.

In the fall of 1774, delegates from every colony except Georgia met in Philadelphia, Pennsylvania, for the **First Continental Congress.** Virginia's delegates included the fiery Patrick Henry, who became famous for declaring,

Soldiers Arrive in Boston

British troops row to shore from their ships in Boston Harbor (below). They were known as Redcoats because of their red jackets (above). *How does the artist use the size and placement of ships to convey the force used by the British in Boston?*

"Give me liberty, or give me death." He delighted the New England delegates by declaring, "The distinctions between Virginians, Pennsylvanians, New Yorkers, and New Englanders are no more. I am not a Virginian, but an American."

To pressure Parliament to withdraw the Coercive Acts, the delegates announced a boycott of all British imports. Throughout the colonies, the Patriots established local committees and provincial congresses to enforce the boycotts. In effect, the Patriots established new governments that bypassed Parliament and the Crown. By including common shopkeepers, artisans, and farmers, the committees expanded the ranks of the politically active. In the spring of 1775, a newly arrived immigrant marveled, "They are all liberty mad."

By 1774, Patriot John Adams had decided that he already lived in a new country named America. He also believed that Americans could unite to defeat the British. But Adams was ahead of most colonists, who still hoped to remain within the British Empire, provided that Parliament would revoke the Coercive Acts and stop trying to tax them. Far from blaming the king, most colonists still expected that he would side with them against Parliament. Within two years, however, events would prove Adams right.

▲ Patrick Henry, a radical Patriot, encouraged the Continental Congress to embrace independence as their goal.

✔ Checkpoint How did the Coercive Acts lead to colonial unity?

SECTION **1** Assessment

Progress Monitoring *Online*
For: Self-test with vocabulary practice
Web Code: nca-0402

Comprehension

1. **Terms and People** Explain how each term or person below increased tensions in the colonies or helped colonial leaders organize for action.
   - Stamp Act
   - John Adams
   - Patrick Henry
   - Sons of Liberty
   - nonimportation agreement
   - Boston Massacre
   - committee of correspondence
   - Boston Tea Party
   - Intolerable Acts
   - First Continental Congress

2. **NoteTaking Reading Skill: Recognize Sequence** Use your flowchart to answer the Section Focus Question: What caused the colonists to rebel against the British?

Writing About History

3. **Quick Write: Contrast** List each of the taxes levied by Parliament on the American colonists. Then, make a chart showing how the British justified the taxes and why the colonists protested it.

Critical Thinking

4. **Compare Points of View** Explain why Parliament did not understand the colonists' argument "no taxation without representation."

5. **Recognize Ideologies** Why did the colonists first accept and then later reject indirect taxes such as duties on trade?

6. **Determine Relevance** How did the Intolerable Acts aid Patriot leaders?

EXPERIENCE
THE ROAD TO REVOLUTION

WILLIAM JACKSON, an IMPORTER; at the BRAZEN HEAD, North Side of the TOWN-HOUSE, and Opposite the Town-Pump, in Corn-hill, BOSTON.

It is desired that the SONS and DAUGHTERS of LIBERTY, would not buy any one thing of him, for in so doing they will bring Disgrace upon themselves, and their Posterity, for ever and ever, AMEN.

Fighting between Patriots and the British did not begin until 10 years after the Stamp Act caused an uproar in the colonies. In 1765, not many colonists wanted independence from Britain. Over the next decade, a few organizers rallied colonists to join the Patriots. These printers, merchants, and lawyers used the language of the Enlightenment to attract converts to the cause of independence.

In response to British taxes, early Patriots began organizing the resistance. Samuel Adams created committees of correspondence in Massachusetts to inform the colony about events in Boston. Other colonies quickly followed. Later, Sons and Daughters of Liberty employed the masses of people in their anti-British actions.

BOSTON, September, 27, 1774.

GENTLEMEN,

THE committees of correspondence of this and several of the neighbouring towns, having taken into consideration the vast importance of withholding from the troops now here, labour, straw, timber, flitwork, boards, and in short every article excepting provisions necessary for their subsistance; and being under a necessity from their conduct of considering them as real enemies, we are fully satisfied that it is our bounden duty to withhold from them every thing but what meer humanity requires; and therefore we must beg your close and serious attention to the inclosed resolves which were passed unanimously; and as unanimity in all our measures in this day of severe trial, is of the utmost consequence, we do earnestly recommend your co-operation in this measure, as conducive to the good of the whole.

We are,

Your Friends and Fellow Countrymen,

Signed by Order of the joint Committee,

William Cooper Clerk.

Prominent Patriots joined ▶ the Sons and Daughters of Liberty and committees of correspondence.

On August 26, 1765, Boston colonists attacked the home of the Lieutenant Governor during riots opposing the Stamp Act. ▼

▲ James Otis was a leader of the Massachusetts committee of correspondence.

▲ Joseph Reed joined the Philadelphia committee of correspondence.

April 5, 1764

The Sugar Act lowers the tax on molasses, but increases penalties for smuggling, denying a jury trial to accused smugglers.

March 22, 1765

Passage of the Stamp Act results in riots and the formation of the Sons of Liberty.

June 29, 1767

Passage of the Townshend Acts leads to colonial nonimportation agreements.

▲ Printing presses were powerful tools for Patriots. The press for this paper had to be slipped out of Boston to prevent the British from destroying it.

▲ Pictures of these coffins, with the initials of colonists who died in the Boston Massacre, were printed in newspapers throughout the colonies.

▼ In response to the Tea Act, Boston Patriots dressed as Indians and dumped British tea into the harbor.

Thinking Critically
1. **Recognize Propaganda** How did newspapers win support for the Patriots?
2. **Identify Point of View** How would Parliament have interpreted the colonists' reactions?

Connect to Today Research a group that is working to gain support for a specific cause today. Write a report evaluating the tactics they use to spread their message.

History Interactive ✳

For: Experience the Road to Revolution activities
Web Code: ncp-0403

March 5, 1770
The Boston Massacre results in greater support for the Patriots, who use newspapers to advance their cause.

April 27, 1773
Parliament passes the Tea Act, leading to the Boston Tea Party in December.

April 1, 1774
Parliament closes the port of Boston; Virginia calls for every colony to create committees of correspondence.

The Spirit of Independence

In 1776, the Continental Congress decided to declare independence. But some colonists were hesitant.

❝Some people among us seem alarmed at the *name of Independence,* while they support . . . the *spirit* of it. Have we not made laws, . . . levied war, and regulated commerce, not only without his Majesty's intervention, but absolutely against his will? Are we not as criminal in the eyes of Britain for what we have done as for what we can yet do? If we institute any government at all, for heaven's sake let it be the best government we can. We shall be as certainly hanged for a bad as a good one. . . . If, therefore, we incur the danger, let us not decline the reward. . . .❞

—letter from a member of the Virginia Convention, February 10, 1776

◀ Signing the Declaration of Independence

Declaring Independence

Core Curriculum Objectives

- **2.I.A.4** The Revolutionary War and the Declaration of Independence
- **2.I.A.4b** Revolutionary ideology (republican principles, natural rights)
- **2.I.A.4c** Revolutionary leaders: Benjamin Franklin, George Washington, John Adams, Samuel Adams, Patrick Henry

Terms and People

militia
Loyalist
Second Continental
  Congress
Continental Army
George Washington

Thomas Paine
Declaration of
  Independence
Thomas Jefferson
natural rights

NoteTaking

Reading Skill: Recognize Sequence Use a timeline to keep track of events in this section.

April 18, 1775
Battles of Lexington
and Concord

July 4, 1776

Why It Matters In 1776, the colonists of British America made three important decisions. First, they declared independence from Britain. Second, they chose a republican model for their new government. Third, they confederated the 13 states as the United States of America. These decisions were unprecedented and risky. The colonists gambled their lives and property but found a strength that surprised and changed the world. **Section Focus Question: What events led the colonists to declare their independence from Britain?**

War Begins

In early 1775, the dispute between the British government and the colonists took a drastic turn. Following the passage of the Coercive Acts, in addition to being the military commander, General Thomas Gage had been named governor of Massachusetts. John Hancock, Samuel Adams, and other colonial leaders then convened a Provincial Congress to govern Massachusetts without Gage. They also began to stockpile arms and ammunition.

The Battles of Lexington and Concord On April 19, 1775, war erupted at Lexington and Concord, two country towns west of Boston. Gage provoked the battles by sending troops to arrest Hancock and Adams in Lexington and to seize Patriot weapons stockpiled in Concord. Tipped off by men, including Paul Revere, who had ridden into the countryside to warn of the approaching British troops, the local Patriots rallied to drive the troops back to Boston. The Patriot fighters were **militia,** full-time farmers and part-time soldiers.

By morning, about 70 Patriots had gathered on the Lexington Green. As the British soldiers, called Redcoats, marched into town at dawn, the British commander ordered the militia to disperse. As they did, someone fired a shot. When the shooting stopped, eight Patriots were dead. The Redcoats marched on to Concord. What happened next stunned the British. The British troops began their march back to Boston following a skirmish with Patriots in Concord. However, hundreds of minutemen, Patriot militia who earned their name by their ability to respond quickly to calls for soldiers, lined the roads, firing at the British from behind trees and stone walls. The Patriots killed or wounded more than 200 British soldiers.

Stunned and exhausted, the British reached the safety of Boston in the late afternoon. From throughout New England, thousands of Patriot militiamen rushed to confine the British troops in the city. Provincial assemblies of Patriots seized control of the New England colonies. **Loyalists,** or colonists who remained loyal to Britain, fled to take refuge in Boston. But would the rest of the colonies help New England fight the British?

The Second Continental Congress The answer came in May 1775 when delegates from all the colonies assembled in Philadelphia for the **Second Continental Congress.** To the relief of New Englanders, Congress assumed responsibility for the war. Armed volunteers from the Middle and Southern colonies marched north to join the Patriot siege of Boston. Congress gave the command of the new **Continental Army** to **George Washington.** Washington had served as a colonial officer in the French and Indian War and he came from Virginia, the largest and most powerful colony. New England needed Virginia's help to win the war.

Some radical members of the Continental Congress wanted to declare American independence from Britain, but they recognized that most of their constituents were not yet ready to do so. Most colonists still hoped to remain within the British Empire but without paying taxes to Parliament. In July 1775, after three months of bloodshed, Congress sent an "Olive Branch Petition" to King George III. The petition reaffirmed the colonists' allegiance to the king but not to Parliament. The king rejected the petition and sent more troops to Boston.

✓ **Checkpoint** What actions did the Second Continental Congress take in response to the outbreak of war with Britain?

The First Battle

The engraving below shows the battle on Lexington Green. Patriots hung the lantern below from the steeple in a Boston church to signal that British troops were on the move. *Based on this picture, does it seem likely that the Patriots would defeat the British?*

Patriots Abuse Loyalists

Loyalists were subjected to harsh treatment by their Patriot neighbors. In this picture, a Loyalist is paraded through town, followed by drummers. *Why did Patriots publicly humiliate Loyalists?*

Patriots and Loyalists Disagree

Most colonists supported the Continental Congress and the boycott of British imports, but a large minority preferred British rule. These colonists were later called Loyalists. Champions of law and order, many Loyalists dreaded the Patriot crowds and committees, viewing them as illegal and brutal. One Loyalist declared, "If I must be enslaved, let it be by a King at least, and not by a parcel of upstart, lawless committeemen. If I must be devoured, let me be devoured by the jaws of a lion, and not gnawed to death by rats and vermin."

Loyalists Fear Disorder Although many Loyalists opposed Britain's taxes, they felt that Parliament and the Crown must be obeyed as the legitimate government of the Empire. The Loyalists feared that the resistance would lead to a deadly and destructive war that Britain seemed certain to win. They doubted that the colonists could defeat an empire that had recently crushed the combined powers of France and Spain.

During the summer of 1774, two old friends and lawyers walked together to discuss the crisis: John Adams, a Patriot, and Jonathan Sewell, a Loyalist. During the conversation, Sewell warned Adams, "Great Britain is determined on her system. Her power is irresistible, and it will certainly be destructive to you, and all those who . . . persevere in opposition to her designs."

Adams boldly replied, "I know that Great Britain is determined in her system, and that . . . [has] determined me on mine. . . . Swim or sink, live or die, survive or perish with my country—that is my unalterable determination."

Loyalists Oppose the Patriots' Demands About a fifth of the colonists remained loyal, and many more wished to remain neutral. According to <u>stereotype</u>, Loyalists were wealthy elitists who sold out their fellow colonists to reap profitable offices in the British government. A few Loyalists did fit that description, but many more were ordinary farmers and artisans. Others belonged to cultural minorities who feared oppression by the Patriot majority.

Vocabulary Builder
<u>stereotype</u>–(STER ee uh tīp) *n.* an oversimplified image of a group of people

Loyalists disliked the taxes, oaths of allegiance, and militia drafts demanded by the new Patriot authorities to support the Patriots' war. They also resented the Patriots for shutting down Loyalist newspapers and for punishing people who criticized the Patriots' actions. Loyalists concluded that the Patriots demanded more in taxes and allowed less free speech than did the British.

Loyalism also appealed to Native Americans and to enslaved people. The Indians wanted British help to keep out the settlers pressing westward. Because slaveholders led the revolution in the Southern Colonies, their slaves saw the British as the true champions of liberty. Thousands of enslaved people sought their freedom by running away to join the British forces.

✔ **Checkpoint** Why did Loyalists oppose the Patriots' cause?

Opinion Swings Toward Independence

In January 1776, a short but powerful book swung popular opinion in the colonies in favor of independence. Entitled *Common Sense,* the book was by **Thomas Paine,** a recent immigrant from England who had been both an artisan and a tax collector. In *Common Sense*, many Americans read what they longed to believe but had not known how to express. Similar ideas would soon appear in a declaration of the colonists' independence.

Thomas Paine's Radical Proposal In simple but forceful and direct language, Paine proposed a radical course of action for the colonies: independence from Britain, republican state governments, and a union of the new states.

Paine denounced the king and aristocrats of Britain as frauds and parasites. He wanted the common people to elect all of their government, not just a third

WITNESS HISTORY DVD

Watch *The Enlightenment and the American Revolution* on the **United States Witness History DVD** to explore how European philosophers influenced the Patriots.

Thomas Paine's
Common Sense

The printing press was vital to Patriot success before and during the American Revolution. The book *Common Sense* (below right) was the first great American bestseller. At least 150,000 copies were produced, a stunning total for a population of only 2.5 million people.

Thomas Paine (right), the author of *Common Sense,* appealed to common people by writing more clearly and directly than any previous political writer had. John Adams later noted that no man had "more influence on [the world's] inhabitants or affairs for the last thirty years than Thomas Paine."

One of Jefferson's drafts of the
Declaration of Independence ▼

of it. Paine depicted the king, rather than Parliament, as the greatest enemy of American liberty. He hated the rigid class structure of Britain for smothering the hopes of common people without a noble title or money. A republic, he argued, would provide opportunities to reward merit rather than inherited privilege. Freed from the empire, Americans could trade with the entire world.

By uniting to create a republic, Americans could create a model that would inspire common people everywhere to reject kings and aristocrats. Paine concluded, "The cause of America is in a great measure the cause of all mankind." This view was new and powerful in 1776, when the revolution was a desperate gamble.

The Colonists Declare Independence By the spring of 1776, Paine's ideas had built momentum for American independence. Noting the shift in public opinion, Congress selected a committee to draft a document declaring American independence and explaining the reasons for it. On July 2, Congress voted that America was free. Two days later, they approved the **Declaration of Independence.**

Drafted by **Thomas Jefferson,** the Declaration drew upon Paine's ideas to denounce the king as a tyrant who made American independence necessary. Although primarily a long list of colonial grievances, the Declaration also advanced the bold idea that "all men are created equal." Congress embraced the Enlightenment ideas that all men are born with **natural rights** that cannot be taken away by a government. Jefferson called them "unalienable rights."

This sweeping statement was far ahead of the social and economic reality in the new United States. For example, many of the signers of the Declaration owned slaves. But the idea of equality would inspire future generations of Americans, including enslaved people, to make a better, more equal society.

Declaring independence on paper was one thing. Achieving it was another. The colonists faced many challenges before they could become an independent nation. No colony in the Americas had yet won independence from a European empire. Fighting the British for independence would pit the poorly organized colonists against the greatest military power on Earth.

✔ **Checkpoint** What ideas were expressed in the Declaration of Independence?

SECTION
2 **Assessment**

Progress Monitoring *Online*
For: Self-test with vocabulary practice
Web Code: nca-0404

Comprehension

1. **Terms and People** For each item below, write a sentence explaining its significance to the Revolutionary War.
   • militia
   • Loyalist
   • Second Continental Congress
   • Continental Army
   • George Washington
   • Thomas Paine
   • Declaration of Independence
   • Thomas Jefferson
   • natural rights

2. **NoteTaking Reading Skill: Recognize Sequence** Use your completed timeline to answer the Section Focus Question: What events led the colonists to declare their independence from Britain?

Writing About History

3. **Quick Write: Compare** Write a paragraph comparing the Patriot and Loyalist viewpoints. Explain their shared concerns and why they thought that the British or the Patriots were the best hope for America.

Critical Thinking

4. **Draw Inferences** Why did the Second Continental Congress send the Olive Branch Petition to the king?

5. **Recognize Ideologies** Why did Loyalists oppose independence from Britain?

6. **Recognize Bias** Why did Thomas Paine argue so forcefully for independence?

7. **Explain Effects** How did the Enlightenment affect the American Revolution?

In Congress, July 4, 1776

THE UNANIMOUS DECLARATION OF THE THIRTEEN UNITED STATES OF AMERICA,

When in the Course of human events, it becomes necessary for one people to dissolve the political bands which have connected them with another, and to assume among the powers of the earth, the separate and equal station to which the Laws of Nature and of Nature's God entitle them, a decent respect to the opinions of mankind requires that they should declare the causes which impel them to the separation.

We hold these truths to be self-evident, that all men are created equal, that they are endowed by their Creator with certain unalienable Rights, that among these are Life, Liberty and the pursuit of Happiness.—That to secure these rights, Governments are instituted among Men, deriving their just powers from the consent of the governed,—That whenever any Form of Government becomes destructive of these ends, it is the Right of the People to alter or to abolish it, and to institute new Government, laying its foundation on such principles and organizing its powers in such form, as to them shall seem most likely to effect their Safety and Happiness. Prudence, indeed, will dictate that Governments long established should not be changed for light and transient causes; and accordingly all experience hath shewn, that mankind are more disposed to suffer, while evils are sufferable, than to right themselves by abolishing the forms to which they are accustomed. But when a long train of abuses and usurpations, pursuing invariably the same Object evinces a design to reduce them under absolute Despotism, it is their right, it is their duty, to throw off such Government, and to provide new Guards for their future security.—Such has been the patient sufferance of these Colonies; and such is now the necessity which constrains them to alter their former Systems of Government. The history of the present King of Great Britain is a history of repeated injuries and usurpations, all having in direct object the establishment of an absolute Tyranny over these States. To prove this, let Facts be submitted to a candid world.

He has refused his Assent to Laws, the most wholesome and necessary for the public good.

He has forbidden his Governors to pass Laws of immediate and pressing importance, unless suspended in their operation till his Assent should be obtained; and when so suspended, he has utterly neglected to attend to them.

He has refused to pass other Laws for the accommodation of large districts of people, unless those people would relinquish the right of Representation in the Legislature, a right inestimable to them and formidable to tyrants only.

He has called together legislative bodies at places unusual, uncomfortable, and distant from the depository of their public Records, for the sole purpose of fatiguing them into compliance with his measures.

Commentary

◀ **Preamble**
The document first lists the reasons for writing the Declaration.

◀ **Protection of Natural Rights**
People set up governments to protect their basic rights. These rights are unalienable; they cannot be taken away. The purpose of government is to protect these natural rights. When a government does not protect the rights of the people, the people must change the government or create a new one. The colonists feel that the king's repeated usurpations, or unjust uses of power, are a form of despotism, or tyranny, that has denied them their basic rights.

◀ **Grievances Against the King**
The list of grievances details the colonists' complaints against the British government and King George III. The colonists have no say in determining the laws that govern them, and they feel King George's actions show little or no concern for the well-being of the people.

The colonists refuse to relinquish, or give up, the right to representation, which they feel is inestimable, or priceless.

Commentary

The king has refused to allow new legislators to be elected. As a result, the colonies have not been able to protect themselves against foreign enemies and convulsions, or riots, within the colonies.

The king has tried to stop foreigners from coming to the colonies by refusing to pass naturalization laws. Such laws set up the process for foreigners to become legal citizens.

The king alone has decided a judge's tenure, or term. This grievance later would result in Article 3, Section 1, of the Constitution, which states that federal judges hold office for life.

Forced by the king, the colonists have been quartering, or lodging, troops in their homes. This grievance found its way into the Constitution in the Third Amendment.

The king has taken away the rights of the people in a nearby province (Canada). The colonists feared he could do the same to the colonies if he so wished.

 Checkpoint

Why does the Declaration list the colonists' many grievances?

He has dissolved Representative Houses repeatedly, for opposing with manly firmness his invasions on the rights of the people.

He has refused for a long time, after such dissolutions, to cause others to be elected; whereby the Legislative powers, incapable of Annihilation, have returned to the People at large for their exercise; the State remaining in the mean time exposed to all the dangers of invasions from without, and convulsions within.

He has endeavored to prevent the population of these States; for that purpose obstructing the Laws for Naturalization of Foreigners; refusing to pass others to encourage their migration hither, and raising the conditions of new Appropriations of Lands.

He has obstructed the Administration of Justice, by refusing his Assent to Laws for establishing Judiciary powers.

He has made Judges dependent on his Will alone, for the tenure of their offices, and the amount and payment of their salaries.

He has erected a multitude of New Offices, and sent hither swarms of Officers to harass our people and eat out their substance.

He has kept among us in time of peace, Standing Armies, without the Consent of our legislatures.

He has affected to render the Military independent of and superior to the Civil power.

He has combined with others to subject us to a jurisdiction foreign to our constitutions, and unacknowledged by our laws; giving his Assent to their Acts of pretended Legislation:

For Quartering large bodies of armed troops among us:

For protecting them, by a mock Trial, from punishment for any Murders which they should commit on the Inhabitants of these States:

For cutting off our Trade with all parts of the world:

For imposing Taxes on us without our Consent:

For depriving us in many cases, of the benefits of Trial by Jury:

For transporting us beyond Seas to be tried for pretended offenses:

For abolishing the free System of English Laws in a neighbouring Province, establishing therein an Arbitrary government, and enlarging its Boundaries so as to render it at once an example and fit instrument for introducing the same absolute rule into these Colonies:

For taking away our Charters, abolishing our most valuable Laws, and altering fundamentally the Forms of our Governments:

For suspending our own Legislature, and declaring themselves invested with power to legislate for us in all cases whatsoever.

He has abdicated Government here, by declaring us out of his Protection, and waging War against us.

He has plundered our seas, ravaged our Coasts, burned our towns, and destroyed the lives of our people.

He is at this time transporting large Armies of foreign Mercenaries to compleat the works of death, desolation and tyranny, already begun with circumstances of Cruelty and perfidy scarcely paralleled in the most barbarous ages, and totally unworthy the Head of a civilized nation.

He has constrained our fellow Citizens taken Captive on the high Seas to bear Arms against their Country, to become the executioners of their friends and Brethren, or to fall themselves by their Hands.

He has excited domestic insurrections amongst us, and has endeavored to bring on the inhabitants of our frontiers the merciless Indian Savages, whose known rule of warfare, is an undistinguished destruction of all ages, sexes and conditions.

In every stage of these Oppressions We have Petitioned for Redress in the most humble terms: Our repeated Petitions have been answered only by repeated injury. A Prince, whose character is thus marked by every act which may define a Tyrant, is unfit to be the ruler of a free people.

Nor have We been wanting in attentions to our British brethren. We have warned them from time to time of attempts by their legislature to extend an unwarrantable jurisdiction over us. We have reminded them of the circumstances of our emigration and settlement here. We have appealed to their native justice and magnanimity, and we have conjured them by the ties of our common kindred to disavow these usurpations, which, would inevitably interrupt our connections and correspondence. They too have been deaf to the voice of justice and of consanguinity. We must, therefore, acquiesce in the necessity, which denounces our Separation, and hold them, as we hold the rest of mankind, Enemies in War, in Peace Friends.

We, therefore, the Representatives of the United States of America, in General Congress, Assembled, appealing to the Supreme Judge of the world for the rectitude of our intentions, do, in the Name, and by the Authority of the good People of these Colonies, solemnly publish and declare, That these United Colonies are, and of Right ought to be Free and Independent States; that they are Absolved from all Allegiance to the British Crown, and that all political connection between them and the State of Great Britain, is and ought to be totally dissolved; and that as Free and Independent States, they have full Power to levy War, conclude Peace, contract Alliances, establish Commerce, and to do all other Acts and Things which Independent States may of right do. And for the support of this Declaration, with a firm reliance on the protection of Divine Providence, we mutually pledge to each other our Lives, our Fortunes and our sacred Honor.

Commentary

The king has hired foreign mercenaries, or soldiers, to bring death and destruction to the colonists. The head of a civilized country should never act with the cruelty and perfidy, or dishonesty, that the king has.

The colonists have repeatedly asked the king to correct these wrongs. Each time, he has failed to do so. Because of the way he treats his subjects, the king is not fit to rule.

The colonists have appealed to the British people. They have asked their fellow British subjects to support them. However, like the king, the British people have ignored the colonists' requests.

◀ **Declaring Independence**
The resolution of independence boldly asserts that the colonies are now "free and independent states." The Declaration concludes by stating that these new states have the power to wage war, establish alliances, and trade with other countries.

✓ Checkpoint

What powers does the new nation have, now that it is independent?

Signatories of the Declaration of Independence

JOHN HANCOCK
PRESIDENT OF THE CONTINENTAL CONGRESS 1775–1777

NEW HAMPSHIRE
Josiah Bartlett
William Whipple
Matthew Thornton

MASSACHUSETTS BAY
Samuel Adams
John Adams
Robert Treat Paine
Elbridge Gerry

RHODE ISLAND
Stephen Hopkins
William Ellery

CONNECTICUT
Roger Sherman
Samuel Huntington
William Williams
Oliver Wolcott

NEW YORK
William Floyd
Philip Livingston
Francis Lewis
Lewis Morris

NEW JERSEY
Richard Stockton
John Witherspoon
Francis Hopkinson
John Hart
Abraham Clark

DELAWARE
Caesar Rodney
George Read
Thomas McKean

MARYLAND
Samuel Chase
William Paca
Thomas Stone
Charles Carroll
of Carrollton

VIRGINIA
George Wythe
Richard Henry Lee
Thomas Jefferson
Benjamin Harrison
Thomas Nelson, Jr.
Francis Lightfoot Lee
Carter Braxton

PENNSYLVANIA
Robert Morris
Benjamin Rush
Benjamin Franklin
John Morton
George Clymer
James Smith
George Taylor
James Wilson
George Ross

NORTH CAROLINA
William Hooper
Joseph Hewes
John Penn

SOUTH CAROLINA
Edward Rutledge
Thomas Heyward, Jr.
Thomas Lynch, Jr.
Arthur Middleton

GEORGIA
Button Gwinnett
Lyman Hall
George Walton

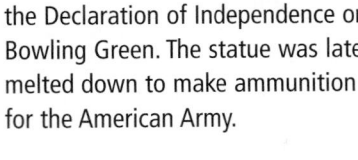

New Yorkers tear down a statue of King George III after a reading of the Declaration of Independence on Bowling Green. The statue was later melted down to make ammunition for the American Army.

Washington's canteen ▶

◀ Continental soldiers

SECTION 3

WITNESS HISTORY AUDIO

Could England Win the War?

During the war, Thomas Paine wrote several pamphlets supporting the Patriot cause. Paine directed this passage to Britain's commander, Lord Howe:

❝By what means, may I ask, do you expect to conquer America? If you could not effect it in the summer, when our army was less than yours, nor in the winter, when we had none, how are you to do it? . . . [Y]ou have been outwitted . . . your advantages turn out to your loss and show us that it is in our power to ruin you. . . . You cannot be so insensible as not to see that we have two to one the advantage of you, because we conquer by a drawn game, and you lose by it.❞

—Thomas Paine, *The American Crisis II*, 1777

Turning Points of the War

Core Curriculum Objectives

- **2.I.A.4** The Revolutionary War and the Declaration of Independence
- **2.I.A.4b** Revolutionary ideology (republican principles, natural rights)
- **2.I.A.4c** Revolutionary leaders: Benjamin Franklin, George Washington, John Adams, Samuel Adams, Patrick Henry

Terms and People

William Howe	Saratoga
mercenary	Marquis de Lafayette
Battle of Trenton	Benjamin Franklin
Charles Cornwallis	Valley Forge
Battle of Princeton	Monmouth

NoteTaking

Reading Skill: Summarize Record the British and Patriot strengths and weaknesses on a chart like the one below.

British	
Strengths	**Weaknesses**
•	•
•	•

Why It Matters To make their independence a reality, the Patriots had to win a hard and bloody war against the world's most powerful empire. Britain's population was nearly four times larger than the 2.5 million people in the colonies. And at least a fifth of the colonists were Loyalists. Another fifth were slaves, who were likely to join the British to escape enslavement. Many others remained neutral for as long as possible. **Section Focus Question: What factors helped the Patriots win the war?**

The Opposing Sides

At the beginning of the war, Britain seemed to have great advantages. A leader in manufacturing, Britain produced more ships and weapons than the colonists did. The British also had an established government, while the Americans were starting from scratch. Meanwhile, the Continental Congress struggled to pay for the war. Lacking the authority to collect taxes, Congress and the states printed paper money to pay their debts, producing inflation that damaged the economy. The Continental soldiers suffered from hunger and cold, while British troops were well trained and had plenty of supplies. The odds seemed slight that the Patriots could win.

The British Make Mistakes In 1775, the British did not take the Patriots seriously as an enemy. Two months after the defeat at Concord, they repeated their mistake at the Battle of Bunker Hill. By fortifying hills overlooking Boston, the Patriots hoped to drive the British from that seaport. To retake the hills, the new British commander, Lord **William Howe,** ordered a frontal assault by soldiers in the middle of the day. Carrying heavy packs and wearing red uniforms, his men marched uphill straight into a murderous fire from entrenched Patriots. Why did Howe put his soldiers in such a dangerous position?

Howe wanted to win the battle despite giving the Patriots every advantage. That would prove, in another general's words, "that trained troops are invincible against any numbers or any position of untrained rabble." Instead of proving Howe's point, the British suffered a bloodbath as two charges failed. A third charge captured the hills only because the Patriots ran out of ammunition. Technically, the British had won the battle, but they suffered more than twice the Patriot casualties. The Patriots had won a psychological victory.

In January 1776, six months after the Battle of Bunker Hill, Colonel Henry Knox arrived with cannons to reinforce the Patriots outside Boston. His men had hauled the cannons hundreds of miles from upstate New York, where Ethan Allen's men had captured them from Fort Ticonderoga. With Patriot cannons shelling both Boston and the British ships in the harbor, the British abandoned the city in March.

The British Misunderstand the Conflict Lord Howe continued to pursue a misguided strategy. The British thought that they were fighting a traditional European war. They believed that the Patriots would surrender if Howe could defeat the Continental Army and capture the major seaports, including Philadelphia, the Patriot capital. In fact, the British accomplished these goals but still lost the war.

The British never fully understood that they were fighting a different type of war, a revolutionary war. The Patriots understood that it was a struggle to win the hearts and minds of the civilian population. Instead of surrendering after setbacks, the Patriots kept on fighting. Thomas Paine wrote an inspiring series of essays, *The American Crisis,* which George Washington read to encourage his troops. Meanwhile, the British further angered colonists when they hired German **mercenaries,** or soldiers who fought for hire. These "Hessians," as they were called, had a particularly brutal reputation.

The Patriots' Strengths Patriot persistence owed much to Washington's leadership. He realized that to preserve his Continental Army from destruction, he could not risk all on a major battle under unfavorable conditions. Outnumbered and often outmaneuvered, Washington lost most of the battles, but his skillful retreats saved his army to fight another day. By preserving and inspiring his soldiers, Washington sustained them through incredible hardships. His small but committed army hung together despite the casualties and the soldiers' hunger and ragged clothing.

By preoccupying the British army, Washington's Continental Army freed the local militias to suppress the Loyalists in the countryside.

Colonists Endure Hard Times To succeed, the Continental Army needed aid and support from the civilian population. Throughout the war, women's work was crucial. Women freed their husbands and sons for military service by running farms and shops. They also made clothing, blankets, and shoes for the soldiers. Without these contributions, the Patriots could not have sustained their army.

On January 3, 1777, Washington attacked Cornwallis in Princeton, New Jersey. *How did the Patriots' tactics in this battle differ from the way they attacked the troops retreating from Concord in 1775?*

However, the British navy also blockaded the ports, making many items scarce and expensive. A few colonists took advantage of the shortages by profiteering, or selling rare items at a very high price. Furthermore, the Patriots caused inflation by issuing paper money, which means that the value of money decreased. If farmers sold their crops to the Patriots, they would be paid in "Continentals," paper money issued by the Continental Congress. It would be worth nothing if the Patriots lost. The British army, however, paid for their food in gold.

During the war, some women followed their husbands into the army. They received rations for maintaining the camps and washing clothing. A few women even helped fire cannons or served as soldiers by masquerading as men. For her service, Deborah Sampson later won a military pension from Congress. Another story says that Mary Hays became known as Molly Pitcher for delivering water to troops during the battle at Monmouth. Legend says that she stepped in and took her husband's place at the cannon.

✓ **Checkpoint** What were the Patriots' strengths?

The War Shifts to the Middle States

After the British left Boston in early 1776, they decided to attack New York City and cut off New England from the rest of the colonies. After winning a series of battles, Howe captured the city on September 15. About 30,000 British and German troops nearly crushed the poorly trained Continentals. Forced to retreat across New Jersey, Washington barely saved his little army and the Revolution by counterattacking on December 26. Crossing the Delaware River in the middle of Christmas night, he surprised a garrison of more than 1,000 German mercenaries at the **Battle of Trenton.** This modest victory raised the spirits of the troops and Patriot supporters at a critical moment.

Military Turning Points Washington began 1777 with another victory. Again moving his troops in the night, Washington inflicted heavy casualties on General **Charles Cornwallis**'s troops at the **Battle of Princeton.** During the remainder of 1777, however, Washington suffered more defeats. In the fall, he lost Philadelphia to Howe's army.

NoteTaking

Reading Skill: Recognize Sequence Use a timeline to record the sequence of important events and battles during the war.

September 15, 1776
British capture
New York City

Led by General John Burgoyne, another British army marched from Canada to invade New York's Hudson Valley. Falling into a Patriot trap at **Saratoga,** Burgoyne surrendered in October. The greatest Patriot victory yet, Saratoga suggested that the United States might just win the war.

European Allies Enter the War The victory at Saratoga took on greater importance because it encouraged France to recognize American independence and to enter the war. France welcomed the opportunity to weaken an old enemy, Britain. During the early years of the war, however, the French had doubted that the Patriots could win. Unwilling to risk an open alliance, they had limited their assistance to secret shipments of arms and ammunition. But that covert aid kept the Patriot army alive and fighting. Some French volunteers, including the aristocrat and Patriot general **Marquis de Lafayette,** also provided military expertise.

After Saratoga, the French risked an open alliance with the United States. Negotiated in February 1778, the alliance reflected the diplomatic genius of **Benjamin Franklin,** the leading American negotiator in Paris. A cunning gentleman, Franklin became popular in France by presenting himself in public as a simple American who loved the French. As the French army and navy began attacking the British, the war became more equal. Although the first joint operations failed miserably, the alliance would produce the biggest victory of the war in 1781.

The British suffered another blow in 1779 when Spain entered the war as a French <u>ally</u>. The Spanish also wanted to weaken the British, but they feared that American independence would inspire their own colonists to rebel against Spanish rule. Spain was not an official American ally, but the Spanish governor of Louisiana, Bernardo de Gálvez, provided money and supplies to the Patriots and prevented British ships from entering the Mississippi River at New Orleans.

Vocabulary Builder
<u>ally</u>– (AL ī) *n.* person, group, or country joined with another or with others to achieve a common purpose

The Continental Army Faces Challenges Back in Pennsylvania, Washington's army spent the harsh and hungry winter of 1777 to 1778 at **Valley Forge,** outside of Philadelphia. The soldiers suffered from a lack of supplies and food. Washington reported to Congress that nearly a third of his 10,000 soldiers had no coats or shoes.

Baron Von Steuben drills soldiers at Valley Forge.

Primary Source "Unless some great . . . change suddenly takes place . . . this Army must inevitably be reduced to one or other of these three things. Starve, dissolve, or disperse in order to obtain subsistence in the best manner they can."
—George Washington, Valley Forge, December 23, 1777

Despite their hardships, the soldiers improved from careful drilling supervised by a German volunteer, Baron Von Steuben, who had come to help the Patriots. In June 1778, the British evacuated Philadelphia, retreating across New Jersey to New York City. On the way, they fought off Washington's pursuit at **Monmouth,** New Jersey. The Continental soldiers demonstrated their improved discipline under fire.

Despite having won most of the battles, the British had little to show for it beyond their headquarters in New York City. Despairing of winning in the North, the British turned their attention to the South.

✓ **Checkpoint** Describe the course of the war in 1777 and 1778.

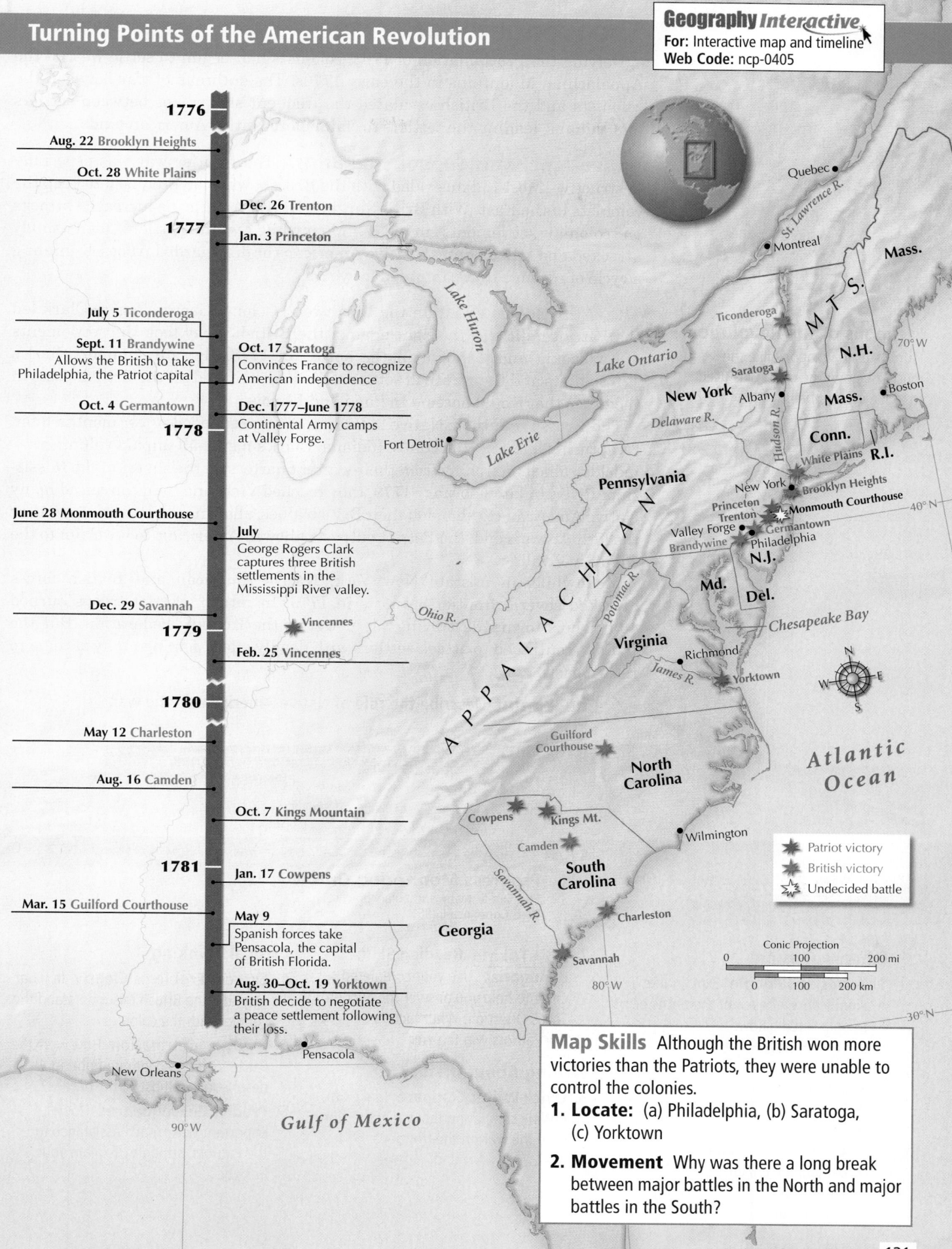

Turning Points of the American Revolution

Geography Interactive
For: Interactive map and timeline
Web Code: ncp-0405

1776

Aug. 22 Brooklyn Heights

Oct. 28 White Plains

Dec. 26 Trenton

1777

Jan. 3 Princeton

July 5 Ticonderoga

Sept. 11 Brandywine
Allows the British to take
Philadelphia, the Patriot capital

Oct. 17 Saratoga
Convinces France to recognize
American independence

Oct. 4 Germantown

Dec. 1777–June 1778
Continental Army camps
at Valley Forge.

1778

June 28 Monmouth Courthouse

July
George Rogers Clark
captures three British
settlements in the
Mississippi River valley.

Dec. 29 Savannah

1779

Feb. 25 Vincennes

1780

May 12 Charleston

Aug. 16 Camden

Oct. 7 Kings Mountain

1781

Jan. 17 Cowpens

Mar. 15 Guilford Courthouse

May 9
Spanish forces take
Pensacola, the capital
of British Florida.

Aug. 30–Oct. 19 Yorktown
British decide to negotiate
a peace settlement following
their loss.

Quebec
St. Lawrence R.
Montreal
Mass.
Lake Huron
Ticonderoga
N.H.
70° W
Lake Ontario
Saratoga
Boston
New York
Albany
Mass.
Delaware R.
Conn.
Hudson R.
Fort Detroit
Lake Erie
White Plains
R.I.
Pennsylvania
New York
Brooklyn Heights
Princeton
Monmouth Courthouse
40° N
Trenton
Valley Forge
Germantown
Brandywine
Philadelphia
N.J.
Md.
Del.
Chesapeake Bay
Ohio R.
Vincennes
Virginia
Richmond
Potomac R.
James R.
Yorktown
N
W   E
S
Guilford
Courthouse
North
Carolina
Atlantic
Ocean
Cowpens
Kings Mt.
Camden
Wilmington
Savannah R.
South
Carolina
Charleston
Georgia
Savannah
80° W

Patriot victory
British victory
Undecided battle

Conic Projection
0   100   200 mi
0   100   200 km

New Orleans
Pensacola
90° W
Gulf of Mexico
30° N

Map Skills Although the British won more
victories than the Patriots, they were unable to
control the colonies.
1. **Locate:** (a) Philadelphia, (b) Saratoga,
(c) Yorktown
2. **Movement** Why was there a long break
between major battles in the North and major
battles in the South?

121

The Frontier War

Defying the Proclamation of 1763, colonists had begun to settle west of the Appalachian Mountains in the early 1770s. The outbreak of war between the colonists and the British escalated the frequent skirmishes between settlers and Indians, leading the settlers to claim more Native American lands.

Native Americans Support the British The frontier war was especially destructive. Most Indians sided with the British, who had promised to keep the colonists in the East. With British urging, Native Americans increased attacks on colonial settlements in 1777. Meanwhile, white settlers increasingly attacked and killed neutral Native Americans or disregarded truces, beginning a cycle of revenge that continued for years.

The War Moves West In the Northwest, Colonel George Rogers Clark led the Patriot militia in the fight against the British. They took the settlements of Kaskaskia and Cahokia in the spring of 1778. By late summer, Clark's 175 soldiers and their French settler allies had captured all the British posts in the areas that would become Indiana and Illinois.

The British and their Native American allies responded a few months later, recapturing a fort at Vincennes, Indiana. Clark's men—all unpaid volunteers—quickly rallied, marching from their winter quarters on the shores of the Mississippi River. In late February 1779, they reached Vincennes and convinced many Native Americans to abandon their British allies, allowing the Patriots to recover the fort. At war's end, the Patriot outposts allowed Americans to lay claim to the Ohio River valley.

Meanwhile, in upstate New York, Native American and British forces attacked several frontier outposts in 1779. In return, Patriot troops burned 40 Iroquois towns, destroying the power of the Iroquois Federation. But the Indians continued to attack settlers with deadly effect, forcing many of them to return east.

✓ **Checkpoint** Describe the role of Native Americans in the war.

Weapons of the Revolution
Patriots used weapons like the musket below. The mold was used to make musket balls.

SECTION 3 Assessment

Progress Monitoring *Online*
For: Self-test with vocabulary practice
Web Code: nca-0406

Comprehension

1. **Terms and People** Explain the significance of each of the terms or people listed below.
   - William Howe
   - mercenary
   - Battle of Trenton
   - Battle of Princeton
   - Saratoga
   - Marquis de Lafayette
   - Benjamin Franklin
   - Valley Forge
   - Monmouth

2. **NoteTaking Reading Skill: Summarize** Use your completed chart to help you answer the Section Focus Question: What factors helped the Patriots win the war?

Writing About History

3. **Quick Write: Compare** Make an outline comparing the war in the North with the war on the frontier.

Critical Thinking

4. **Express Problems Clearly** In what ways did the British misunderstand the conflict with the colonies?

5. **Analyze Information** How were the Patriots able to continue fighting, despite losing most of the battles?

6. **Predict Consequences** How important was French assistance to the Patriots' struggle? Explain your answer.

Redcoats surrender at Yorktown ▶

Cornwallis Surrenders

More than 15 years after colonists began protesting new taxes, the Patriots defeated the British army.

❝I have the Honor to inform Congress, that a Reduction of the British Army under the Command of Lord Cornwallis, is most happily effected. The unremitting Ardor which actuated every Officer and Soldier in the combined Army on this Occasion, has principally led to this Important Event, at an earlier period than my most sanguine Hopes had induced me to expect.❞

—George Washington, October 19, 1781

War's End and Lasting Effects

 Core Curriculum Objectives

- **2.I.A.4** The Revolutionary War and the Declaration of Independence
- **2.I.A.4b** Revolutionary ideology (republican principles, natural rights)
- **2.I.A.5d** The abolition of slavery in the North

Terms and People

Kings Mountain
Yorktown

Treaty of Paris
manumission

NoteTaking

Reading Skill: Recognize Sequence Use a flowchart to record the events leading up to the Treaty of Paris.

Summer 1781: Washington marches south; requests French fleet

↓   ↓   ↓

Why It Matters By eighteenth-century standards, the American Revolution was very radical. For the first time, overseas colonies rejected their empire to create a republican union—something long dismissed as a dangerous fantasy. By defying the conventional wisdom of their time, the Patriots began an enormous experiment aimed at creating a more open and equal society. **Section Focus Question: What did the Revolution accomplish, and what ideas did it set in motion?**

The British Invade the South

As the war continued, the British expected Loyalist support in the South, especially among the farmers of North Carolina, South Carolina, and Georgia. But the British wasted this support by continuing their misguided strategy. Instead of supporting Loyalist militias, the British continued to wage a conventional war.

The British Win Early Victories In the South, as in the North, the British won most of the battles and captured the leading seaports. In late 1778, they seized Savannah, Georgia. During the spring of 1780, they captured Charleston, South Carolina—along with 5,000 Patriot soldiers. That summer, the British crushed another Patriot army at Camden, South Carolina.

Just as the British began their offensive in the South, Spanish forces under Bernardo de Gálvez made key attacks on British forts in the Gulf Coast region. In 1780, they captured the British fort at Mobile, Alabama. The next year, they took Pensacola, the capital of British

Benjamin Franklin (1709–1795)

A printer, author, scientist, and diplomat, Franklin was perhaps the best-known American of his time. He proposed the 1754 Albany Plan of Union and helped to draft the Declaration of Independence. He secured French assistance during the Revolutionary War and negotiated favorable terms for the United States upon war's end. In addition, he was instrumental in creating the new nation's Constitution.

As a scientist, Franklin is famous for his experiments with electricity. But he also invented bifocal glasses, a wood stove that was safer than an open fire, and other items still used today.

Vocabulary Builder
frustrated–(FRUHS trayt ehd)
adj. unable to achieve an objective

West Florida. These moves were intended to solidify Spanish power in North America, but they also diverted British troops from the offensive against the Patriots.

Patriots Drive the British Back Despite winning major battles, the British failed to control the southern countryside, where the Revolution became a brutal civil war between Patriot and Loyalist militias. Both sides plundered and killed civilians. A German officer in the British service observed, "This country is the scene of the most cruel events. Neighbors are on opposite sides, children are against their fathers."

In October 1780, at **Kings Mountain** in South Carolina, the Patriots crushed a Loyalist militia and executed many of the prisoners. As the Loyalists lost men and territory, neutral civilians swung over to the Patriot side. They increasingly blamed the British troops for bringing chaos into their lives. A disgusted Loyalist explained to a British officer, "The lower sort of People, who were . . . originally attached to the British Government, have suffered so severely, [and] been so frequently deceived, that Great Britain has now a hundred enemies, where it had one before." Instead of destroying the Patriots, the British army helped create more of them.

As the countryside became sympathetic to the Patriots, General Cornwallis became frustrated. The Continental Army in the South was small, but it was led by two superb new commanders, Nathanael Greene and Daniel Morgan. In early 1781, the Continental Army inflicted heavy losses on the British at the battles of Cowpens in South Carolina and Guilford Courthouse in North Carolina. Despairing of winning in the Carolinas, Cornwallis marched north into Virginia. But he was leading his troops directly into a trap.

✓ **Checkpoint** Describe the war in the South.

The War Ends

Although earlier it seemed unlikely, the Patriots won the war. Four main factors contributed to their success. First, the British made tactical mistakes because they initially underestimated the Patriots. Second, the British misunderstood the political nature of the conflict. Third, the Patriots were highly motivated and benefited from George Washington's shrewd leadership. Fourth, the Patriots received critical assistance from France.

Cornwallis Surrenders During the late summer of 1781, Washington boldly and rapidly marched most of his troops south. He planned to trap Cornwallis's army at **Yorktown,** Virginia. For the plan to work, however, Washington needed a French fleet to arrive at the right moment to prevent the British navy from evacuating their army by sea. Although Washington thought that a French fleet was on its way, he could not be certain when it would arrive.

The French fleet appeared at just the right moment to block the mouth of the Chesapeake Bay, trapping the British navy. Given the lack of efficient long-distance communication, this coordination was an incredible stroke of luck for the Patriots. Trapped by land and by sea, Cornwallis surrendered his army of 8,000 at Yorktown on October 19. The French had made the critical difference. At Yorktown, their soldiers and sailors outnumbered Washington's Americans.

The Treaty of Paris The loss of 8,000 soldiers was a crushing blow to the British war effort. After seven years of fighting, the British public was fed up with the casualties and with heavy taxes to pay for the war. In early 1782, a new administration came to power, determined to make peace. An American delegation, including Benjamin Franklin, negotiated a treaty with appealing terms. In 1783, the **Treaty of Paris** recognized American independence and granted generous boundaries to the United States. At the negotiating table, Franklin secured far more territory than the Patriots had won in the war. By making a

Events That Changed America

The Battle of Yorktown

The Battle of Yorktown was not a single battle, but a siege with many small confrontations. In July 1781, British troops under General Cornwallis marched to Yorktown, Virginia, expecting reinforcements from New York. French General Lafayette's smaller force trapped the British on the peninsula until the Continental Army and more French troops arrived in late August. Meanwhile, a French fleet prevented reinforcements from reaching Cornwallis by sea. The French and American forces forced Cornwallis to surrender his 8,000 troops on October 19. It was the last military confrontation of the war.

SIEGE OF YORKTOWN

American troops
American advance
French troops
French advance
British troops

A cannon from the battle ▶

Handbill announcing a celebration of the Patriot victory at Yorktown. ▼

Lord Cornwallis, the British commander at Yorktown ▶

The French fleet arrives at Yorktown. ▼

Illumination.

COLONEL TILGHMAN, Aid de Camp to his Excellency General WASHINGTON, having brought official acounts of the SURRENDER of Lord Cornwallis, and the Garrisons of York and Gloucester, those Citizens who chuse to ILLUMINATE on the GLORIOUS OCCASION, will do it this evening at Six, and extinguish their lights at Nine o'clock.

Decorum and harmony are earnestly recommended to every Citizen, and a general disf. countenance to the least appearance of riot.

October 24, 1781.

Thinking Critically
Explain how the Battle of Yorktown might be viewed either as a Patriot victory or as a British loss.

History Interactive ★
For: More about the Battle of Yorktown
Web Code: ncp-0407

NoteTaking

Reading Skill: Summarize Use a concept web to summarize how the Revolution affected different groups.

separate peace with the British, the Americans strained their alliance with the French, who had expected to control the negotiations.

✓ **Checkpoint** Explain how the Revolutionary War ended.

The Revolution Impacts Society

The Patriots promised liberty and opportunity, but some Americans won more than others. The greatest winners were Patriot men of at least modest prosperity. They secured political rights and the economic benefits of western expansion. The losers were Loyalists and Native Americans who had sided with the British.

The British Abandon Their Allies The British tried to protect their Loyalist allies by setting conditions in the treaty, but state laws and mob violence prevented most Loyalists from returning to their homes after the war. About 90,000—including 20,000 former slaves—became refugees. About half of them resettled in Britain's northern colonies. Many slaves were re-enslaved in the British West Indies. In effect, the American Revolution spawned two new nations: the American Republic and the future Dominion of Canada.

Native Americans were also stunned when the British abandoned them in 1783. The Treaty of Paris ignored the Indians, leaving them vulnerable to the American hunger for revenge and land. In treaties at Fort Stanwix in 1784 and Hopewell in 1785, the Patriots forced the Indians to give up massive tracts of land as the price of peace. Settlers surged westward. More than 100,000 Americans lived in Tennessee and Kentucky by 1790. The Revolution was a disaster for the Indians.

The Revolution Impacts Women Women gained few political or legal rights as a result of the war, but they won respect based on the new conception of women as "republican mothers." Abigail Adams and Judith Sargent Murray noted that the Republic needed virtuous citizens, who learned their virtue from their mothers. This invited women to speak out on issues that affected their ability to raise virtuous children.

The Revolution inspired some women to seek a larger voice in public affairs. In a famous letter of 1776, Abigail Adams asked her husband, John, to "remember the Ladies" in drafting the new nation's laws. In particular, she sought legal protection for wives beaten by their husbands. Although John Adams respected his wife, he dismissed her request.

The law reserved legal and political rights to husbands. Widows could vote in New Jersey but nowhere else. As was the norm in most of Europe at the time, wives could not own property or make contracts.

Changes for African Americans Slavery seemed inconsistent with the ideals of the Revolution, but in 1776, one of every five Americans was of African ancestry, and a majority of African Americans were enslaved. Most Americans—including some Patriot leaders—accepted slavery as natural. British and Loyalist critics mocked the Patriots as hypocrites who spoke of liberty while holding slaves. In 1778, the Patriot governor of New Jersey confessed that slavery was "utterly inconsistent with the principles of Christianity and humanity; and in Americans, who have idolized liberty, peculiarly odious and disgraceful."

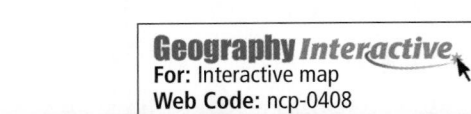

Geography *Interactive*
For: Interactive map
Web Code: ncp-0408

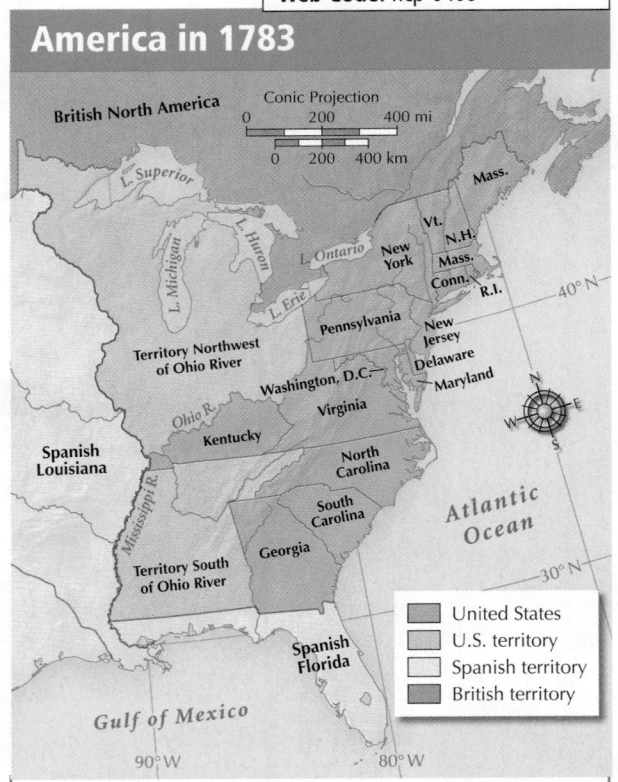

America in 1783

Map Skills This map shows the United States after the Treaty of Paris.
1. Why might the Spanish have been upset about the new borders?
2. What territory might the French have wanted?

The Revolution inspired many slaves to demand freedom. In the northern states, some slaves petitioned legislatures for emancipation and sued their owners in the courts. About 5,000 African Americans joined Patriot militias, the Continental Army, or the small Continental Navy in return for a promise of freedom. However, the southern states feared armed blacks as a threat to the slave system, so at least 50,000 southern slaves escaped to join the British.

The Revolution led to emancipation in the North, where slavery was not critical to the economy and slaves numbered only 5 percent of the population. Although laws eventually banned slavery in the northern states, many northern masters sold their slaves to the South before they could become free.

Emancipation failed in the South, where slaves amounted to about one third of the population and were essential to the plantation economy. In Maryland and Virginia, some planters voluntarily freed their slaves, a practice known as **manumission.** After 1800, however, southern states passed laws to discourage further manumissions. Southern whites feared that freed blacks would seek revenge for past treatment as slaves. However, by 1810, about 20,000 southern slaves had been freed, including 300 liberated by George Washington.

✓ **Checkpoint** How did the Revolutionary War affect Loyalists, Native Americans, women, and slaves?

This 1779 woodcut shows a female Continental soldier.

Revolutionary Ideas Spread

Perhaps the greatest effect of the Revolution was to spread the idea of liberty, both at home and abroad. The statement that "all men are created equal" was radical when Jefferson drafted the Declaration of Independence. Although Jefferson probably intended his statement to apply to white men, African Americans and women repeated those words to claim their rights.

Over the next three centuries, the Patriots' principles inspired revolutions around the world. Beginning with the French Revolution in 1789, European republicans cited the American precedent to overthrow kings and aristocrats. In the nineteenth century, independent republics emerged throughout Latin America. During the twentieth century, Africans and Asians began national liberation movements. As Thomas Paine had predicted, the American Revolution changed the world.

✓ **Checkpoint** How has the Revolution inspired other groups?

SECTION **4** Assessment

Progress Monitoring Online
For: Self-test with vocabulary practice
Web Code: nca-0409

Comprehension

1. **Terms and People** Explain the significance of each of the terms below.
   • Kings Mountain
   • Yorktown
   • Treaty of Paris
   • manumission

2. **NoteTaking Reading Skill: Summarize** Use your completed flowchart and concept web to answer the Section Focus Question: What did the Revolution accomplish, and what ideas did it set in motion?

Writing About History

3. **Quick Write: Compare and Contrast** Write a short essay comparing and contrasting the results of the Revolution for two of these groups: white Patriot men, women, African Americans, or Loyalists.

Critical Thinking

4. **Identify Central Issues** Why did the British lose the war?

5. **Summarize** Summarize the terms of the Treaty of Paris.

6. **Draw Inferences** Explain the effects of the Revolution on minority groups and women.

CHAPTER 4

Quick Study Guide

2.I.A.4,
2.I.A.3

Progress Monitoring *Online*
For: Self-test with vocabulary practice
Web Code: nca-0410

■ Key British Legislation, 1764–1774

Date	Act	Outcome
1764	Sugar Act	Although it reduced the tax on molasses, the Sugar Act was strictly enforced, so colonists ended up paying more taxes.
1765	Stamp Act	This tax on printed items was the first direct tax on the colonists. It added a fee to printed materials such as legal documents and newspapers.
1765	Quartering Act	Following the French and Indian War, Britain maintained a standing army in the colonies. This act required colonial assemblies to house and provision the soldiers.
1766	Declaratory Act	This act repealed the Stamp Act but asserted Parliament's right to rule the colonies as it saw fit.
1767	Townshend Acts	Import taxes on a variety of goods were collected to support royal officials in the colonies, removing the responsibility from the colonial assemblies. They were so unpopular that all the taxes were repealed, except the one on tea.
1773	Tea Act	This act was created to save the East India Tea Company. Although it lowered the price of tea, it gave the company a monopoly and threatened the business of colonial importers.
1774	Intolerable Acts	Officially called the Coercive Acts, these laws were meant to force Massachusetts to pay for the tea destroyed in the Boston Tea Party. The laws closed Boston Harbor and forced colonists to house British soldiers in their homes.

■ Major Events of the American Revolution

Date	Major Turning Point
1774	September 5, First Continental Congress meets
1775	April 19, Battles of Lexington and Concord May 10, Second Continental Congress meets June 17, Battle of Bunker Hill
1776	January 9, Paine publishes *Common Sense* July 4, Declaration of Independence
1777	October 17, Patriots win at Saratoga
Winter 1777–1778	Baron Von Steuben trains the Continental Army at Valley Forge, Pennsylvania
1778	February 6, France signs an alliance with the United States
1780	May, General Clinton captures 3,000 Patriot soldiers as he takes Charleston, South Carolina
1781	October 19, Cornwallis surrenders at Yorktown
1783	September 3, Treaty of Paris signed

☑ Quick Study Timeline

In America

1763
Proclamation of 1763 prohibits white settlement west of the Appalachian Mountains

1768
British troops land in Boston

1760

1765

Around the World

1763
Seven Years' War ends, giving Britain control of Canada

1768
War breaks out between Russia and the Ottomans

1769
James Watt patents a steam engine

American Issues
●—●—● Connector

By connecting prior knowledge with what you have learned in this chapter, you can gradually build your understanding of enduring questions that still affect America today. Answer the questions below. Then, use your American Issues Connector study guide (or go online: www.PHSchool.com **Web Code** nch-6402).

Issues You Learned About

● **America Goes to War** The American Revolution pitted the world's most powerful empire against a small group of dedicated colonists.

1. Write one or two paragraphs explaining how the Patriots were able to defeat Britain. Consider:
   - the Patriots' strengths
   - Britain's tactical strategy
   - Britain's understanding of the conflict
   - military turning points
   - the involvement of foreign nations

● **Women in American Society** The roles and responsibilities of women in America have changed over time.

2. Why was the support of women crucial to the effort of the Patriots, both before and during the war?

3. How did the idea of "republican motherhood" enhance women's status in society?

● **Global Interdependence** Foreign nations provided valuable assistance to the Patriots fighting the American Revolution.

4. Why did France enter the American Revolution on the side of the Patriots? What aid did France provide?

5. Although Spain entered the war as a French ally, the nation remained fearful of helping the Patriots. Why?

6. What events did the American Revolution inspire in other countries?

Connect to Your World	New York

America Goes to War Isaac Sears, a merchant sea captain, was an influential New York patriot during the Revolutionary War. He led the resistance against the Stamp Act in New York City as a member of the Sons of Liberty. When "King Sears," as he was called, was arrested in April 1775 for anti-British activities, his followers rescued him from the authorities. In November 1775, Sears led a raid on Loyalists' businesses and supplies in New York City. The raids made him popular among the New York citizenry even though various patriot organizations disapproved of his actions. After the war, he was elected to the New York state legislature in 1784 and 1786. Read more about Sears' fellow members of the Sons of Liberty. Write a short profile on one of them.

1770	1775	1776	1781
The Boston Massacre	George Washington becomes commander in chief of the Continental Army	Congress signs the Declaration of Independence	Cornwallis surrenders at Yorktown

1770	**1775**	**1780**

1770	1776	
Explorer James Cook claims Australia for Britain	Adam Smith publishes *The Wealth of Nations*	**History** *Interactive* **For:** Interactive timeline **Web Code:** ncp-0411

Chapter Assessment

Terms and People

1. What were the **Intolerable Acts**? How did colonists in Massachusetts and throughout the colonies respond to them?

2. What was the **Declaration of Independence**? What basic propositions did it make?

3. Define **natural rights.** How did Jefferson use this concept to justify the Declaration of Independence?

4. Who were **William Howe** and **Charles Cornwallis**? Who were their counterparts from the Continental Army?

5. What was the **Treaty of Paris**? What effect did it have on the territory of North America?

Focus Questions

The focus question for this chapter is **What aspects of the American Revolution were revolutionary?** Build an answer to this big question by answering the focus questions for Sections 1 through 4 and the Critical Thinking questions that follow.

Section 1
6. What caused the colonists to rebel against the British?

Section 2
7. What events led the colonists to declare their independence from Britain?

Section 3
8. What factors helped the Patriots win the war?

Section 4
9. What did the Revolution accomplish, and what ideas did it set in motion?

Critical Thinking

10. **Make Comparisons** In what ways were the colonial governments different from the British government?

11. **Recognize Propaganda** Study the illustration of the Boston Massacre earlier in the chapter. Then, answer the questions that follow: Why did Paul Revere create and circulate this engraving? Is it an accurate representation of what took place? Explain.

12. **Synthesize Information** How were the goals of the First and Second Continental Congresses related?

13. **Identify Central Issues** Briefly explain the proposals Thomas Paine put forth in *Common Sense.*

14. **Analyze Information** Why was the Battle of Bunker Hill a technical victory for the British but a real victory for the Patriots?

15. **Analyze Evidence** Think about the progress of the Revolutionary War in the South. How do the events that took place there support the idea held by many colonists that the 13 colonies would fail to unite into one republic?

16. **Determine Relevance** What was the significance of the Battle of Yorktown?

17. **Draw Conclusions** Think about the ideas expressed in the Declaration of Independence. Did the American Revolution succeed at living up to the ideals expressed in this document? Support your answer with information from the text.

Writing About History

Comparing and Contrasting The American Revolution was a complicated event having many players with differing viewpoints and desired outcomes. Native Americans also became involved in the conflict. Write an essay comparing and contrasting the viewpoints of pro-British Indians (such as the Shawnee, Mohawk, Seneca, Delaware, and Ottawa) and pro-Patriot Indians (such as the Oneida and Tuscarora).

Prewriting
• Write down some questions you have about the Indian involvement in the Revolutionary War.

• Use your questions to direct your research about several different Indian nations.

• Narrow your research by choosing two Indian nations on which to focus.

Drafting
• Make an outline that shows the specific points you are going to compare and contrast.

• Develop a working thesis based on the information in your outline.

• Write an introduction that explains what the actions of these Indian nations tell historians about the Revolutionary War. Then, write a body and conclusion.

Revising
• Use the guidelines on page SH22 of the Writing Handbook to revise your essay.

Regents DBQ Practice

Slavery and the American Revolution

The American Revolution was fought for the ideals of freedom and liberty. However, thousands of African Americans were enslaved. How did the colonists and enslaved people react to this incongruity, or inconsistency? Use your knowledge of the American Revolution and Documents 1, 2, 3, and 4 to answer questions 1 through 4.

Document 1

I wish most sincerely there was not a slave in the province—it allways appeard a most iniquitous [vicious] scheme to me. fight ourselfs for what we are daily . . . plundering from those who have as good a right freedom as we have—you know my mind upon this subject.

—*Abigail Adams, September 22, 1774*

Document 2

[I]n every human Breast, God has implanted a Principle, which we call Love of Freedom; it is impatient of Oppression. . . . I will assert, that the same Principle lives in us. God grant Deliverance [rescue] . . . and get him honour upon all those whose Avarice [greediness] impels them to countenance [allow] . . . Calamities [affliction] of their fellow Creatures. This I desire not for their Hurt, but to convince them of the strange Absurdity of their Conduct whose Words and Actions are so . . . opposite.

—*Phillis Wheatley, a black poet, March 11, 1774*

Document 3

[King George] has waged cruel war on human nature itself, violating its most sacred rights of life and liberty in the persons of a distant people who never offended him, captivating and carrying them into slavery in another hemisphere, or to incur miserable death in their transportation thither.

—*from a draft of the* Declaration of Independence

Document 4

The petition of A Great Number of Blackes detained in a State of slavery in the bowels of a free & Christian County Humbly sheweth that your Petitioners apprehend that they have in Common with all other men a Natural and Unalienable Right to . . . freedom . . . which they have Never forfeited by any Compact or agreement whatever. . . .

[T]hey therfor[e] humble Beseech your honours to . . . cause an act of the legislature to be pas[sed] Wherby they may be Restored to the Enjoyments of that which is the Natural right of all men—and their Children who wher Born in this Land of Liberty may not be held as Slaves after they arrive at the age of twenty one years so may the Inhabitance of this States No longer chargeable with the inconstancy of acting themselves that part which they condemn and oppose in others Be prospered in their present Glorious struggle for Liberty

—*letter to the Massachusetts House of Representatives, January 13, 1777*

---

1. Who is the writer of Document 4?
   (1) a group of white Patriot men
   (2) a group of black slaves
   (3) a group of British soldiers
   (4) a group of enslaved and free women

2. What assumption is included in Document 3?
   (1) Slavery is the colonists' fault.
   (2) Slavery is acceptable, but the slave trade is evil.
   (3) The slave trade is acceptable, but slavery is evil.
   (4) Slavery is fundamentally wrong.

3. The writer of Document 2 believes slavery is
   (1) natural.
   (2) ordained by God.
   (3) absurd.
   (4) honorable.

4. **Writing Task** In what ways do each of these writers agree? Which argument is most convincing? Consider the background of each writer and use your knowledge of the chapter content and specific evidence from the primary sources above to support your opinion.

Creating a Government for the New Nation

During the Revolutionary War, the Patriots knew they needed to create a national government to coordinate the colonies' actions. The challenge after the war was to establish what plan of government the new nation needed and how to go about creating it. After much debate, perseverance, and dedication, the United States Constitution became the blueprint for the government we know today. The following quote by statesman and constitutional lawyer Daniel Webster has been quoted by former President Reagan and other speakers at various celebrations of the Constitution.

66We may be tossed upon an ocean where we can see no land—nor, perhaps, the sun and stars. But there is a chart and a compass for us to study, to consult, and to obey. The chart is the Constitution.99
—Daniel Webster, American statesman

Listen to the Witness History *audio to hear more about the United States Constitution.*

◄ Delegates at the Constitutional Convention as visualized by artist J.H. Froelich, 1935

Ink and quill pen set used by the signers of the Constitution

Surveying compass

Benjamin Franklin ceramic figurine

 Core Curriculum Preview

Chapter Focus Question: What led to the creation of the United States Constitution, and what are its key principles?

Section 1
A Confederation of States   2.I.A.6, 2.I.A.7, 2.I.B.1, 2.I.B.2a, 2.I.E.1

Section 2
Drafting the Constitution   2.I.B.1a, 2.I.B.1b, 2.I.B.2

Section 3
Ratifying the Constitution   2.I.B.4, 2.I.B.4b, 2.I.E.1, 2.I.E.10

Use the ☑ **Quick Study Timeline** at the end of this chapter to preview chapter events.

Note Taking Study Guide *Online*
For: Note Taking and American Issues Connector
Web Code: nce-6501

▲ John Adams

WITNESS HISTORY ◀)) AUDIO

Creating a Republic

During the American Revolution, each state created its own constitution, or plan of government. But the states also needed some form of government to hold them together, however loosely. In 1777, John Adams wrote to Richard Henry Lee:

❝You and I, dear friend, have been sent into life at a time when the greatest lawgivers of antiquity would have wished to live. How few of the human race have ever enjoyed an opportunity of making election of government . . . for themselves or their children.❞

—John Adams

A Confederation of States

Core Curriculum Objectives

- **2.I.A.6** Articles of Confederation
- **2.I.A.7** Northwest Ordinance
- **2.I.B.1** Constitutional Convention: Representation and process
- **2.I.B.2a** Protecting liberty against abuses or power
- **2.I.E.1** Basic constitutional principles: National power—limits and potentials

Terms and People

republic
unicameral legislature
bicameral legislature
Articles of Confederation
John Dickinson
federal

Northwest Territory
Land Ordinance of
1785
Northwest Ordinance
of 1787
Shays' Rebellion

NoteTaking

Reading Skill: Identify Main Ideas Use a table to list characteristics of early state governments and characteristics of the national government under the Articles of Confederation.

Early State Governments	Early National Government
• All states established republics, in which voters chose representatives.	• Each state had one vote, regardless of size.
•	•

Why It Matters After the Revolutionary War, the Patriots feared creating another tyrannical or abusive parliament, so therefore they refused to entrust the new Union with much power. As a result, most authority remained with the states. Within a short time, the powerful states and weak national government faced severe problems. **Section Focus Question: What form of national government did the Patriots create initially, and what events revealed that a new government was necessary?**

Early State Governments

Upon declaring independence in 1776, the Congress invited each new state to create a constitution to establish a government. Although these documents varied, they all called for **republics,** or governments in which the people elect their representatives. But the Patriots disagreed over the proper design for those republics. Some Patriots, such as Thomas Paine, sought changes that would promote democracy by putting more power in the hands of the people. But more conservative Patriots distrusted the ability of the common people. They hoped instead to preserve many colonial institutions.

Some States Reject Executive Power The more democratic Patriots wanted to create state governments with strong legislatures and weak governors (or with no governor at all). Seeking greater rights for the people, these leaders preferred a **unicameral legislature,** or one with a single house, whose members were elected by the people. Pennsylvania and Georgia adopted these more democratic constitutions.

Most States Preserve Colonial Traditions Most states, however, including Massachusetts and New York, chose to create more conservative state constitutions. These state governments had a bicameral legislature and a strong governor. A **bicameral legislature** is a lawmaking body with two houses—a Senate and a House of Representatives. These constitutions counterbalanced the power of the common voters in the House with the power of wealthy, well-educated gentlemen in the Senate.

Democratic Gains Even the conservative constitutions, however, dramatically expanded the power of the common people. In contrast to the colonial era, voters chose the members of both houses of the new legislatures, rather than just the members of the lower house. Almost all of the states also enlarged their legislatures. Creating smaller districts and a greater number of representatives made representatives more accountable to their constituents, or voters. In almost all of the states, the voters also elected their governor—something only two colonies had previously done.

Still, democratic and conservative Patriots disagreed about who would vote. The democratic Patriots wanted equal political rights for almost all free men, even those who had little or no property. Pennsylvania's state constitution opened voting to all men over the age of 21 who paid any taxes.

In most of the states, however, the conservatives preserved the colonial property requirements to vote. Adams warned that allowing poor men to vote would "confound and destroy all distinctions, and prostrate all ranks to the common level." Valuing distinctions, he opposed political equality as foolish and unworkable. But even in the conservative states, most free men qualified to vote because owning farms was so widespread. Both theory and practice excluded slaves and women from voting.

Over time, in most states, the most democratic institution—the House of Representatives—gained power at the expense of the Senate and the governor. By the mid-1780s, this concentration of legislative power troubled conservative Patriots who feared the "tyranny of the majority."

Freedom of Religion Because the American Revolution promoted greater religious liberty, most states also guaranteed freedom of religion in their constitutions. Before this time, states collected taxes to support religious establishments. The freedom to choose among several faiths had been controversial. After the Revolution, however, religious liberty and pluralism became the norm. This came about with the passage of the Virginia Statute for Religious Freedom in 1786, drafted by Thomas

Election Day in Philadelphia, 1764

Pennsylvania was the first state to open voting to all men over the age of 21 who paid taxes, as seen in the engraving here where men in Philadelphia are voting. *Why did most states not want to grant poor men the right to vote?*

Religious Freedom
The Virginia Statute for Religious Freedom, still part of Virginia's constitution today, embraced the idea of religious liberty without state interference. Children often made needlework samplers (above) that included aspects of religion such as biblical stories or verses. *What was the significance of the Virginia Statute for Religious Freedom?*

Vocabulary Builder
implement–(IHM pluh mehnt)
v. to carry into effect

Jefferson. Massachusetts and Connecticut were exceptions. They kept their Congregational established churches, which continued to draw fire from Baptists and Methodists.

✔ **Checkpoint** Why did most states choose a bicameral legislature?

Congress Creates the Articles of Confederation

In 1777, the Continental Congress drafted the original constitution for the union of the states, known as the **Articles of Confederation.** A confederation is a league or alliance of states that agree to work together. Under the leadership of **John Dickinson** of Pennsylvania, the Congress designed a loose confederation of 13 states, rather than a strong and centralized nation. The Articles reflected the principles of the Declaration of Independence and rejected the centralized power of the British Empire as a threat to liberty. As Article II reads, "Each state retains its sovereignty, freedom, and independence, and every power, jurisdiction, and right, which is not by this Confederation expressly delegated to the United States, in Congress assembled."

The Structure of the New National Government The new **federal,** or national, government consisted of a congress of delegates, chosen by state legislatures rather than by voters. Although states could choose to send as many as seven delegates, each state—no matter how large or small—had a single vote. Enormous Virginia had no more power than tiny Rhode Island. The powers to make, <u>implement</u>, and enforce the laws were all placed with the Congress. The national government included no President or executive branch. Instead, executive power was spread among several committees of congressmen.

Powers of the National Congress The Articles granted certain limited powers to Congress. These powers were mostly external: to declare and conduct war and to negotiate peace, to regulate foreign affairs and to administer relations with Indian nations. The Congress had no power to raise money through taxes. Therefore, it relied on contributions from the states, which were unreliable.

On some minor issues, a majority of seven states could pass a law. But on the major issues, including declaring war and making treaties, two thirds of the states (nine) had to approve. Amending the Articles was almost impossible because all 13 states had to approve any change. In 1781, all states finally ratified the Articles.

✔ **Checkpoint** What was the structure of the new government under the Articles of Confederation?

Congress Creates a Plan for Western Lands

One of the most important accomplishments of the national Congress under the Articles of Confederation was the creation of plans for both settling and governing a vast territory that they had authority over. This territory, called the **Northwest Territory,** lay north of the Ohio River and west of Pennsylvania to the Mississippi River. By selling this land to speculators and farmers, the Congress hoped to raise revenue and extend America's republican society westward.

Distributing Western Lands Western settlement, however, threatened to escape the government's control. By 1784, hundreds of settlers had already crossed the Ohio River to make their own farms. This provoked war with the Native Americans, who defended their land. Already strapped for cash, the federal leaders could not afford to fight wars provoked by unregulated settlement. Congressmen also feared that the settlers would secede from the Union, form their own states, and turn to the British or the Spanish empire for protection. If deprived of the western lands, the federal government would be hard-pressed to pay its debts and would probably collapse. To save the Union, the federal leaders needed to regulate frontier settlement.

In ordinances, or laws, adopted in 1785 and 1787, the Congress defined a program for managing the Northwest Territory. In the **Land Ordinance of 1785,** the Congress designed a system for dispensing, or distributing, the public lands. By running a grid of lines north to south and east to west, federal surveyors divided the land into hundreds of townships, each six square miles. They then subdivided each township into 36 "sections" of one square mile (640 acres), to be sold for at least one dollar per acre.

Because ordinary farmers could not afford to pay $640, the price and size of the sections favored wealthy land speculators who had cash. To obtain land, ordinary settlers had to buy it from the speculators. The Congress sometimes broke its own rules to further benefit speculators. For example, in 1787, the Congress sold 1.5 million acres for a mere 10 cents per acre to the Ohio Company, a politically powerful group of land speculators and army officers from New England.

Governing Western Lands The **Northwest Ordinance of 1787** provided a government for the western territory based on Thomas Jefferson's ideas. At first, the Congress would appoint a territorial government led by a governor, secretary, and three judges. The citizens would enjoy freedom of religion, trial by jury, and the rights of common law, including habeas corpus. Once a territory had 5,000 men, they could establish an elected assembly—but the governor retained an absolute veto over its laws. When the population of a territory reached 60,000, the people could request admission to the Union as a state on equal terms with the original 13 states, provided the new state adopted a republican constitution. The Northwest Territory later formed the midwestern states of Ohio, Indiana, Illinois, Michigan, Wisconsin, and part of Minnesota.

The Northwest Ordinance of 1787 also barred slavery from this territory, which meant that the five new states would enter the Union as free states rather than slave states. This federal restriction set a precedent that would

Settling the Northwest Territory

This newspaper clipping spread the word to potential settlers with an early printed version of the Northwest Ordinance. Surveyors used instruments such as the compass shown here to divide land into areas of uniform size. *How do you think these ordinances in 1785 and 1787 affected the settlement and development of the territory?*

Settling the Northwest Territory

With the adoption of the Land Ordinance of 1785, Congress had an official plan for settling the Northwest Territory, a territory that belonged to the United States after the American Revolution. (Previously, individual states claimed the territory.) The plan under the ordinance was to divide public lands into uniform sizes that could be sold at standardized prices. The old system used natural features to mark off parcels of land in varying sizes and shapes.

Under the 1785 ordinance, surveyors first laid out a grid of lines spaced six miles apart, which resulted in a grid of squares. These squares represented individual townships. Then, each township was divided into 36 sections, and these 1-mile-square sections could be divided into smaller units for sale to farmers. The land and income from the sixteenth section of each township provided funding for public education.

▼ The rectangular grid established in 1785 remains visible in landscapes across the Midwest today.

CANADA

Lake Superior

Minnesota 1858

Wisconsin 1848

Lake Michigan

Lake Huron

Michigan 1837

Iowa

Lake Erie

NORTHWEST TERRITORY

Pennsylvania

Illinois 1818

Indiana 1816

Ohio 1803

Missouri

W. Va.

Virginia

Kentucky

CONIC PROJECTION
SCALE IN MILES
0   100   200
SCALE IN KILOMETERS
0   100   200

1803 Date of statehood
Present-day borders are shown.

Township and Range Lines

Ohio River

AREA OF
FIRST SURVEY

Township

6	5	4	3	2	1
7	8	9	10	11	12
18	17	16	15	14	13
19	20	21	22	23	24
30	29	28	27	26	25
31	32	33	34	35	36

6 miles

6 miles

Section

Half Section
320 Acres

Quarter Section
160 Acres

Half-Quarter Section
80 Acres

1 mile

1 mile

Quarter-Quarter Section
40 Acres

Geography and History How do the modern landscapes of states in the Midwest, such as Indiana and Ohio, reflect the system established by the Land Ordinance of 1785?

later alarm people in southern states who wanted to expand slavery throughout the territories.

By adopting the Northwest ordinances, the Congress discarded the British model of keeping colonies in permanent subordination. The Congress designed the territories to attract American settlers and to assure their acceptance of federal rule. In the wake of the Revolution, few Americans would settle where they could not enjoy basic freedoms, including the right to elect those who would set their taxes.

But freedom and opportunity for Americans came at the expense of the region's 100,000 Indians, who were expected to give up their lands and relocate elsewhere. During the mid-1780s, however, the Indians resisted, and the federal government lacked the means to defeat them. For want of money, the Confederation reduced its army to only 350 men who could barely defend themselves much less conquer the territory.

 Checkpoint What were the plans for settling and governing the Northwest Territory under the Articles of Confederation?

Conflicts With Spain and Britain

During the mid-1780s, the Spanish and British did not take the new United States seriously. To them, the republican Confederation seemed weak to the point of anarchy, or lawlessness.

The Spanish Forbid American Trade The Spanish had never liked American independence, and they distrusted American expansion westward because they feared it threatened their colonies of Louisiana and Mexico. To discourage settlements west of the Appalachian Mountains, the Spanish forbade American trade with New Orleans. American settlers expected to ship their produce down the Mississippi River to market in Spanish-held New Orleans. The Congress lost support from western settlers when it almost accepted the closure of New Orleans in return for commercial agreements to benefit northeastern merchants. George Washington observed, "The Western settlers . . . stand, as it were, upon a pivot; the touch of a feather would turn them any way."

Relations With Britain Deteriorate Relations with the British Empire were also strained. In the peace treaty that ended the American Revolution in 1783, the British had tried to cultivate American goodwill. A year later, the British abandoned that policy in favor of making the Americans pay for their independence. Rejecting the new doctrine of free trade championed by Adam Smith, the British renewed their traditional mercantilism as defined by the Navigation Acts.

This meant that Americans could only trade with the British Empire under rules that favored British interests. They could certainly import all the British manufactures that they wanted, but they could no longer freely send their ships to trade with the British West Indies—the most important market for American fish, lumber, and grains. During the 1780s, the British reserved this valuable trade for their ships to benefit their merchants. They alone could carry the American produce needed by West Indian consumers.

This restriction especially hurt Massachusetts, which had more ships than any other state and a greater need for the West Indian market for its fish and lumber. In retaliation, Massachusetts prohibited British ships from transporting its exports. But this retaliation did not work because the other states did not support Massachusetts. In addition, the Congress was too weak to coordinate a common front against

Tensions With Britain
The British retained their hold on forts such as Fort Michilimackinac (the sketch shown below) even after the forts rightfully belonged to the Americans. *What did this reveal about the organization of the United States government?*

Britain's mercantile policy. American merchants began to call for a stronger national government.

The British Empire also embarrassed the Confederation by keeping frontier forts on the American side of the boundary set by the peace treaty. To please the Indians, the British kept their forts at Niagara, Detroit, and Michilimackinac. For justification, the British cited American violations of the peace treaty. Contrary to the spirit of the treaty, some states had blocked attempts by British merchants to collect debts and attempts by Loyalists to reclaim their confiscated properties. The Congress could not make the states honor the treaty.

The British hold on the forts angered Americans, but they could do nothing because they could not afford an army. Like the merchants, many settlers wanted a national government strong enough to compel British respect on the frontier.

 Checkpoint What Spanish and British actions showed that they did not take the new American nation seriously?

Weaknesses of the Articles of Confederation

The fledgling government under the Articles of Confederation found itself facing a host of difficulties. It soon became clear to many that the Articles themselves were part of the problem.

Economic Weaknesses Under the Articles, the federal Congress could not establish a common currency, nor could it regulate interstate commerce or levy taxes. For financial support, the Congress relied solely on contributions from the states, which were unreliable. And the Congress could do nothing to compel states to pay their share. Without money, the federal government could not fund its immense war debts. Between 1781 and 1786, the Congress received only one sixth of what it requested from the states. By 1786, it needed $2.5 million to pay the interest on its debts but had only $400,000 on hand. The states had bankrupted the nation.

To survive, the Congress sought a constitutional amendment to permit a federal 5 percent duty on imported goods. Twice, that amendment failed when a single state balked: Rhode Island in 1782 and New York in 1786. If amending the Articles was so difficult, perhaps only a new constitution could save the Union.

Farmers Revolt in Massachusetts Meanwhile, a slowdown in the trading of goods increased unemployment in the seaports and reduced the prices paid to farmers for their produce. Without the West Indian market for their shipping, Americans could not pay for their imported manufactured goods. Their debts to British suppliers mounted. In 1785, those suppliers curtailed their credit and demanded payments from the American import merchants. These demands sent a shock wave through the weak American economy as the importers sought to collect from their own debtors in the countryside. Most Americans were farmers, and most farmers were in debt. They lacked the cash to pay their debts on short notice, especially when prices fell for their crops. Losing lawsuits for debt, they faced the loss of their crops, livestock, and even their farms to foreclosure.

In western Massachusetts in 1786, farmers took up arms to shut down the courts to block any foreclosure hearings. Farmers did not want to lose their property or go to prison, but they could not pay the higher taxes imposed by the Massachusetts government. One of their leaders was Daniel Shays, a veteran of the Revolutionary War. In 1787, he led about 1,000 farmers to seize

Weaknesses of the Articles of Confederation	☑ Quick Study

- Congress could not levy or collect taxes.
- Congress was powerless to regulate interstate commerce and foreign trade.
- Each state had only one vote in Congress, regardless of its size.
- A two-thirds majority (9 out of 13 states) was required to pass laws.
- Articles could only be amended with the consent of all states.
- No separate executive branch to enforce acts of Congress
- No system of federal courts

weapons from the Springfield Armory and again attempted to shut down the courts. But the elected leaders of Massachusetts insisted that the new Republic could not survive if people violently interfered with the courts. In eastern Massachusetts, the state raised an army, which marched west to suppress what became known as **Shays' Rebellion.**

Most other states avoided rebellion by satisfying their debtors with relief measures. Some states suspended lawsuits for debt until the depression lifted. More common were state laws to flood the money supply with paper money. Paper money made it easier for debtors to pay, while reducing the value that creditors could collect. Naturally, what relieved the debtors infuriated their creditors, who felt cheated.

Creditors blamed the relief measures on excessive democracy. They saw the state governments as too responsive to the opinion of the public, which had wanted debtor relief. James Madison agreed: "Liberty may be endangered by the abuses of liberty as well as [by] the abuses of power." Some thought of abandoning republicanism in favor of an American monarchy. But most hoped to save the Republic by establishing a stronger national government. This stronger government would therefore be capable of controlling the states whenever they threatened commercial property.

Shays' Rebellion

A woodcut made during Shays' march to Springfield, Massachusetts, depicts Shays and another leader of the rebellion, Job Shattuck. *What was the significance of Shays' Rebellion?*

✓ **Checkpoint** What events suggested that a stronger national government was necessary?

SECTION 1 Assessment

Progress Monitoring *Online*
For: Self-test with vocabulary practice
Web Code: nca-0502

Comprehension

1. **Terms and People** For each item listed below, write a sentence explaining its significance to the formation of a new national government.
   - John Dickinson
   - Northwest Territory
   - Land Ordinance of 1785
   - Northwest Ordinance of 1787
   - Shays' Rebellion

2. **NoteTaking Reading Skill: Identify Main Ideas** Use your completed table to answer the Section Focus Question: What form of national government did the Patriots create initially, and what events revealed that a new government was necessary?

Writing About History

3. **Quick Write: Combine Visuals to Synthesize** Based on the images in this section and the chart listing the weaknesses of the Articles, write a brief newspaper article summarizing the events that led many people to believe the nation needed a stronger national government.

Critical Thinking

4. **Make Comparisons** What were the similarities and differences among early state governments?

5. **Synthesize Information** In what ways was the early government under the Articles of Confederation tested?

6. **Identify Central Issues** What would you consider the greatest weakness of the Articles of Confederation? Explain.

◄ James Madison

▲ Inkstand and quill pen

WITNESS HISTORY 🔊 AUDIO

The Father of the Constitution

James Madison, often referred to as the Father of the Constitution, took detailed notes at the Constitutional Convention. After his death, his notes were published as *The Debates in the Federal Convention of 1787*. In the Preface, Madison describes the pressure on the delegates:

❝At the date of the Convention, the aspect & retrospect of the pol[itical] condition of the U.S. could not but fill the pub[lic] mind with a gloom which was relieved only by a hope that so select a Body would devise an adequate remedy for the existing and prospective evils so impressively demanding it.❞

—James Madison, Preface to *The Debates in the Federal Convention of 1787*

Drafting the Constitution

 Core Curriculum Objectives

- **2.I.B.1a** Framers of the Constitution (James Madison)
- **2.I.B.1b** Plans of government (Virginia Plan, New Jersey Plan, Connecticut Plan)
- **2.I.B.2** Conflict and compromise: seeking effective institutions

Terms and People

Alexander Hamilton
James Madison
Virginia Plan
New Jersey Plan

Great Compromise
federalism
Three-Fifths
   Compromise

NoteTaking

Reading Skill: Identify Supporting Details
In a concept web like the one below, write details about each plan or compromise that led to the creation of the United States Constitution.

Why It Matters After Shays' Rebellion, many Americans agreed that they needed a stronger federal government to preserve the Union. The Congress called for a convention to meet in Philadelphia in 1787 "for the sole and express purpose of revising the Articles of Confederation." Instead of revising the Articles of Confederation, however, the delegates created an entirely new constitution that replaced the confederation of the national Union. **Section Focus Question: What new system of national government did the delegates agree upon at the Constitutional Convention of 1787?**

The Constitutional Convention

By 1787, most Americans agreed that the Articles of Confederation were flawed and needed at least two major changes. First, almost everyone wanted Congress to have the power to regulate interstate and international commerce. Second, most Americans also supported granting Congress the power to tax the people. To draft proposed amendments to the Articles, 12 of the 13 states sent delegates to a special convention in Philadelphia in May 1787. (Rhode Island declined to participate.) Once done, the delegates were supposed to submit the proposed amendments to ratification by the 13 state legislatures.

The convention, then known as the Federal Convention, was slated to begin on May 14. However, only the delegates from Pennsylvania and Virginia made it there on time. More than a week would pass before there were enough delegates to begin the convention.

The Convention Begins The Federal Convention opened in the Pennsylvania State House, now known as Independence Hall, on May 25, when 29 delegates had finally arrived. Other delegates continued to arrive during the <u>subsequent</u> weeks and months. The proceedings of the convention were shrouded in secrecy so the delegates could speak freely. Because of this, the windows of the hall were often closed for privacy. It was an especially hot summer in 1787 so the delegates were frequently uncomfortable in their closed-off space.

Although Thomas Jefferson and John Adams were away in Europe serving as diplomats, the convention included most of the other leading statesmen of the day. Several leaders emerged, including Alexander Hamilton of New York and James Madison of Virginia. The eldest delegate was Benjamin Franklin of Pennsylvania, who added great prestige to the proceedings. Other leaders in attendance were Roger Sherman, Gouverneur Morris, James Wilson, Elbridge Gerry, William Paterson, John Dickinson, Charles Pinckney, Edmund Randolph, and George Mason. These delegates were not typical Americans. They were all white males, many were wealthy, and more than half of them were lawyers. Many of the delegates had helped to write their state constitutions, and seven had been state governors. Twenty-one had fought in the American Revolution, and eight had signed the Declaration of Independence. After reading the names of those in attendance, Jefferson remarked that it was "an assembly of demi-gods." The delegates unanimously elected George Washington as the president of the convention.

Hamilton and Madison The convention's leading thinkers were Alexander Hamilton and James Madison. Bold in action, **Alexander Hamilton** was very conservative in principles. Disliking democracy, he praised the British constitution, including its king and House of Lords, as "the best model the world has ever produced." He insisted that a balanced government should have elements of aristocracy and monarchy as well as of republicanism. Hamilton believed that such a government would have real power to command its citizens and impress foreign empires. Gouverneur Morris of Pennsylvania also advocated a strong central government at the Convention. Morris thought the President should hold office for life.

James Madison showed his eagerness to participate in the convention by arriving in Philadelphia 11 days early. He had also sent a letter to George Washington in April outlining his thoughts about what should be debated at the convention. Madison had concluded that only a strong nation could rescue the states from their own democratic excesses. Although a critic of democracy, Madison favored republicanism rather than a constitution modeled after the British system. His challenge was to design a government that was both strong and republican. Rejecting the old notion that a republic needed to be small and homogeneous, he insisted that a large republic with diverse interests would best preserve the common good. He reasoned that the numerous

Vocabulary Builder
subsequent–(SUHB sih kwehnt)
adj. following; coming after

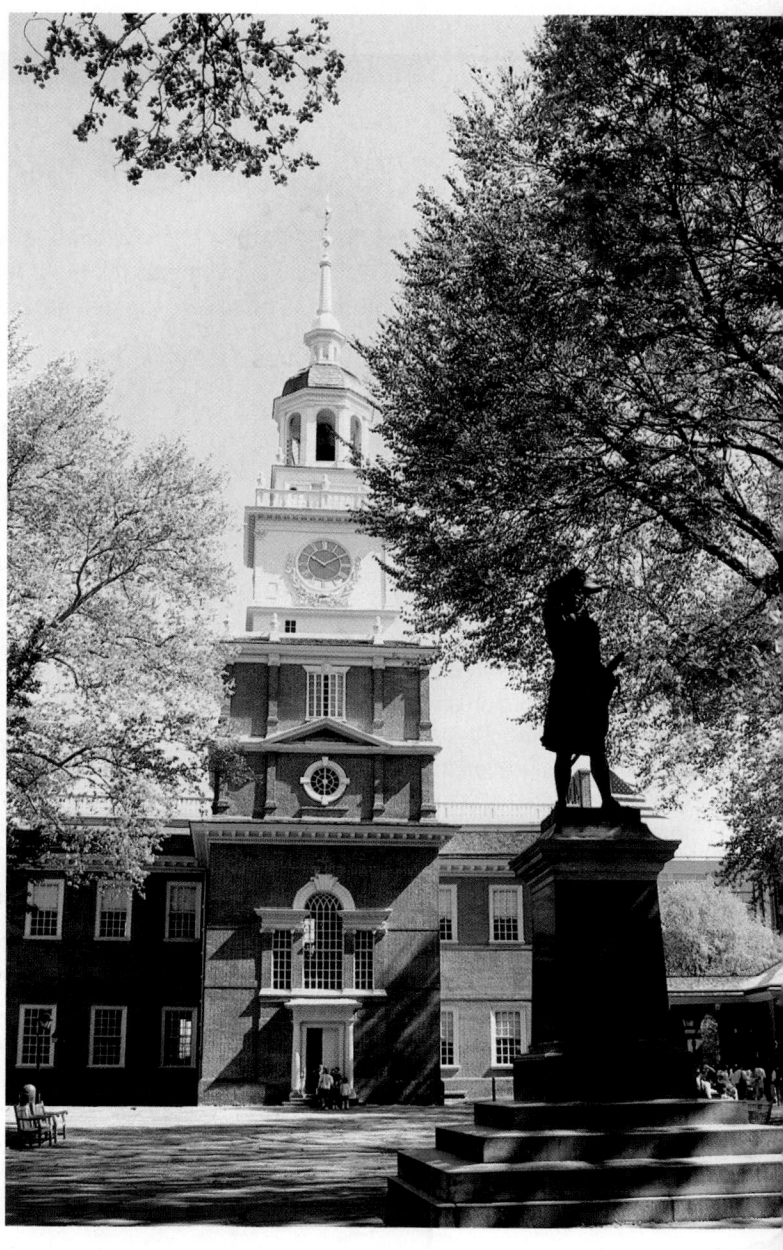

The Pennsylvania State House
Today, visitors can tour Independence Hall in Philadelphia, where the delegates met in 1787.

interests would "check" one another. Madison hoped that the nation's most learned men, rather than the many local political leaders he saw in the state legislatures, would govern the new national Republic. In addition to providing the basic blueprint for the Constitution, Madison kept the notes that are the best record of the convention.

✔ **Checkpoint** What were some of the characteristics of the delegates to the Constitutional Convention?

Rival Plans of Government

Before a constitution could be written and approved, the delegates needed to come to an agreement about what it should contain. To achieve this goal, they advanced and debated a number of proposals for several months.

The Virginia Plan Most of the delegates preferred an ambitious scheme proposed by Madison called the **Virginia Plan.** In addition to securing the power to

Meet the Framers

Who were the men who attended the Constitutional Convention during the steaming summer of 1787? They were some of the most famous and important men in America. According to one historian, the delegates were the "well-bred, well-fed, well-wed, and well-read."
In all, there were 55 who attended these secret proceedings, though they were never there all at once. The four illustrated here were among the most influential.

Alexander Hamilton
Hamilton was born on an island in the British West Indies. His thirst for education brought him to New York for schooling three years before the American Revolution. Not long after arriving in the United States, he picked up the Patriots' cause and served as a colonel during the Revolution on George Washington's staff. He and Washington developed a lifelong alliance. Hamilton was confident and was considered more ambitious than all the other delegates at the convention. He argued strongly for a powerful central government.

Benjamin Franklin
There was not much that Franklin had not crossed off his list by the time he arrived at the convention. He had started a newspaper, published a colonial bestseller, started a volunteer fire department, and was also a philosopher, scientist, inventor, and diplomat. Eighty-one years old at the time of the convention, Franklin was in poor health but nonetheless contributed his prestige, common sense, and wit to the proceedings. When the convention ended after four months of secrecy, a woman asked him what the delegates had produced. His reply? "A republic, if you can keep it."

tax and to regulate commerce, Madison proposed creating a government that divided power among three branches—the legislative, executive, and judicial branches. The plan proposed a bicameral legislature with a House of Representatives and a Senate. In both houses, the states with larger populations would have more members. Madison's plan also included a daring feature—the national Congress would have the power to veto any state law, just as Parliament had done with colonial laws.

The Virginia Plan also called for a strong President. The President would enjoy a relatively long term in office of seven years but could not be elected a second time. The President would command the armed forces and manage foreign relations. He would appoint all executive and judicial officers, subject only to approval by the Senate. A critic of the plan, Patrick Henry, worried that such a powerful President could "easily become a king."

The New Jersey Plan Some delegates advocated only modest changes to the Articles of Confederation. Favored by the small states, their proposal, introduced by William Paterson of New Jersey, became known as the **New Jersey Plan.** This

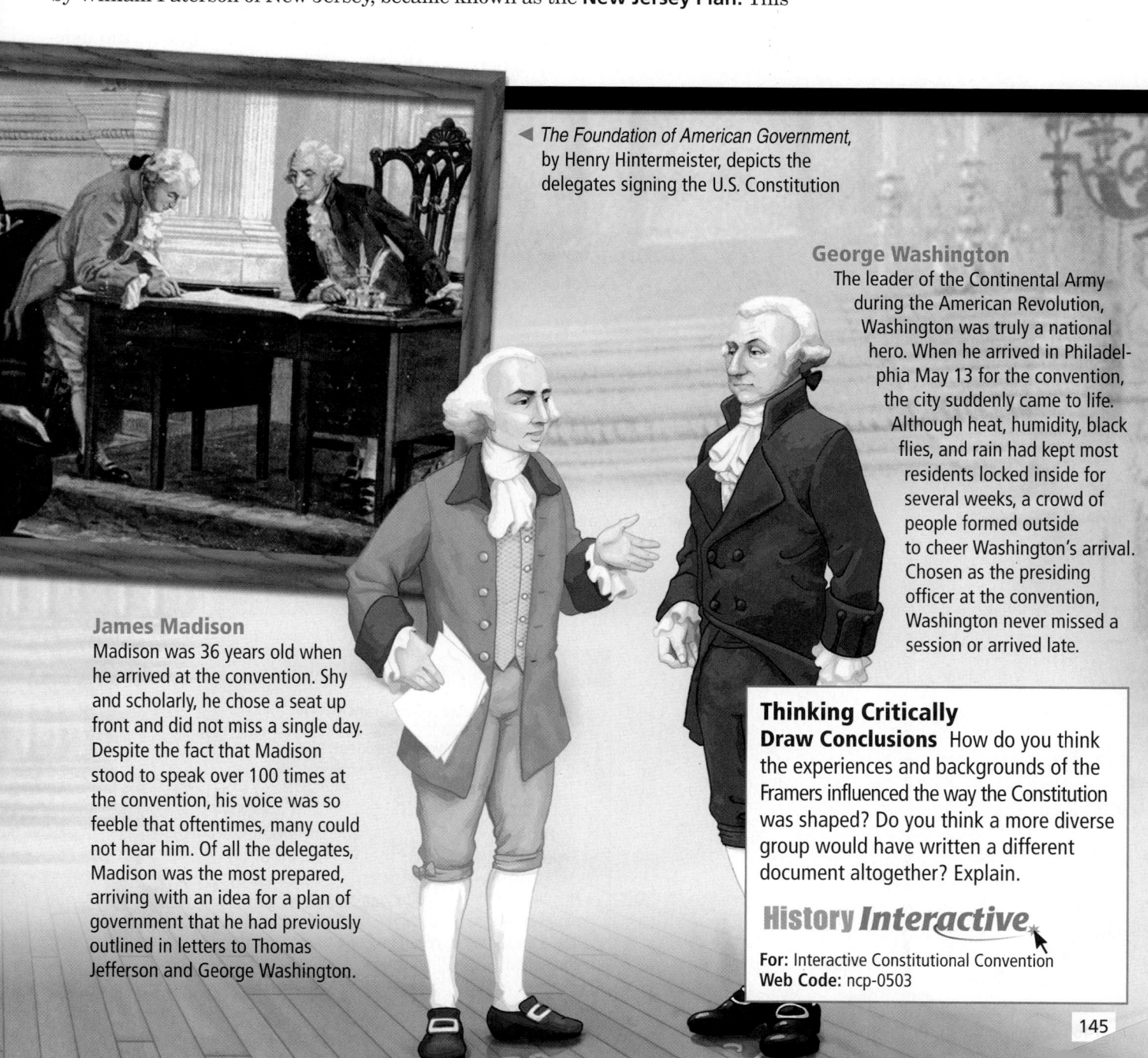

◀ *The Foundation of American Government,* by Henry Hintermeister, depicts the delegates signing the U.S. Constitution

George Washington
The leader of the Continental Army during the American Revolution, Washington was truly a national hero. When he arrived in Philadelphia May 13 for the convention, the city suddenly came to life. Although heat, humidity, black flies, and rain had kept most residents locked inside for several weeks, a crowd of people formed outside to cheer Washington's arrival. Chosen as the presiding officer at the convention, Washington never missed a session or arrived late.

James Madison
Madison was 36 years old when he arrived at the convention. Shy and scholarly, he chose a seat up front and did not miss a single day. Despite the fact that Madison stood to speak over 100 times at the convention, his voice was so feeble that oftentimes, many could not hear him. Of all the delegates, Madison was the most prepared, arriving with an idea for a plan of government that he had previously outlined in letters to Thomas Jefferson and George Washington.

Thinking Critically
Draw Conclusions How do you think the experiences and backgrounds of the Framers influenced the way the Constitution was shaped? Do you think a more diverse group would have written a different document altogether? Explain.

History *Interactive*

For: Interactive Constitutional Convention
Web Code: ncp-0503

plan gave Congress the powers to regulate commerce and to tax, but it kept the three chief principles of the Articles of Confederation. First, it retained a unicameral legislature representing the states as equals, no matter how large or small. Second, it preserved an executive committee rather than adopting a singular President. Third, the states remained sovereign except for those few powers specifically granted to the national government. Under the New Jersey Plan, the United States would remain a loose confederation.

✓ **Checkpoint** What were the differences between the Virginia and New Jersey plans?

Settling Differences Through Compromise

Something had to be done in order to prevent the convention from ending in a stalemate. The delegates were far from a unanimous decision concerning the structure of the new government, and without the compromises laid out below, they may never have reached an agreement.

The Great Compromise Led by Roger Sherman of Connecticut, the delegates reached a compromise between the Virginia and the New Jersey plans, known as the Connecticut Compromise, or the **Great Compromise.** John Dickinson

Diagram Skill The Great Compromise, calling for representation based on a state's population in the House and equal representation in the Senate, was critical to resolving the debate between the small states and the large states. As the diagram shows, the Constitution reflects characteristics of each plan because of the Great Compromise. *What was the main concern of the small states before a compromise was reached?*

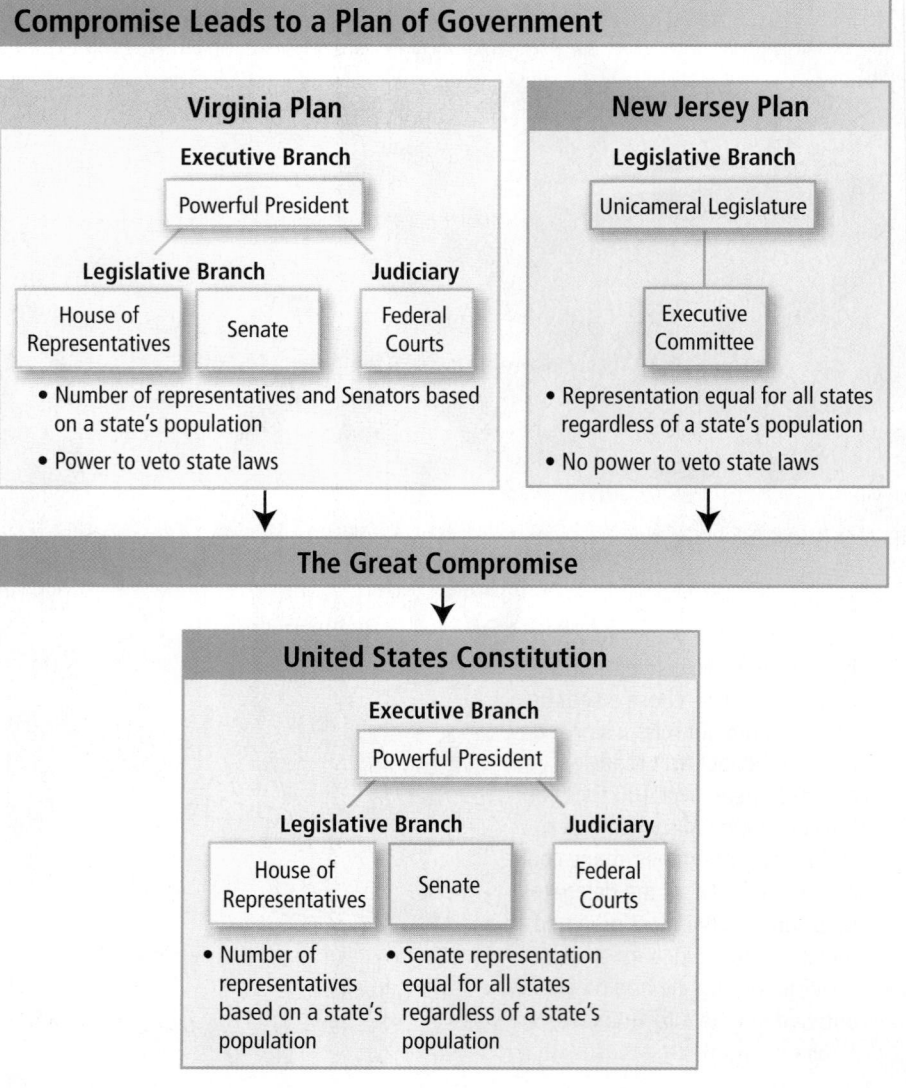

Compromise Leads to a Plan of Government

Virginia Plan

Executive Branch

Powerful President

Legislative Branch   Judiciary

House of Representatives   Senate   Federal Courts

• Number of representatives and Senators based on a state's population
• Power to veto state laws

New Jersey Plan

Legislative Branch

Unicameral Legislature

Executive Committee

• Representation equal for all states regardless of a state's population
• No power to veto state laws

The Great Compromise

United States Constitution

Executive Branch

Powerful President

Legislative Branch   Judiciary

House of Representatives   Senate   Federal Courts

• Number of representatives based on a state's population
• Senate representation equal for all states regardless of a state's population

of Delaware played a key role in creating this compromise, which made a concession to the small states: The Senate would equally represent every state, regardless of size, by allowing two senators per state. In keeping with the Virginia Plan, the House of Representatives would represent population, granting more power to the larger states.

Federal Power and States' Rights In another concession, Madison abandoned his cherished national veto over state laws. Instead, the compromise simply forbade the states from enacting the sorts of laws that offended many during the 1780s. For instance, the states could no longer issue their own money or provide debtor relief at creditors' expense. By compromising between Madison's plan and the New Jersey Plan, the delegates supported a system known as **federalism** that divided government power between the federal government and state governments.

Slavery and the Three-Fifths Compromise During the debates over the Constitution, the delegates discovered that their greatest division pitted the southern against the northern delegates. The southerners feared future domination by the northern states, which had more free people. They worried that northern domination would threaten the slave system, which they viewed as essential to the southern economy and society. The delegates from South Carolina and Georgia threatened to walk out unless provided constitutional protection for slavery.

The subject tore at Madison. On the one hand, he wanted a powerful nation, and he despised slavery as "the most oppressive dominion ever exercised by man over man." On the other hand, he owned slaves, and he knew that southern

Decision ● Point

Should Delegates to the Constitutional Convention Ratify the Constitution?

Delegates at the Constitutional Convention in 1787 debated the pros and cons of the new Constitution. In the end, at least 9 of the 13 states had to ratify the document. Read the options below. Then, you decide.

Patrick Henry Opposes Ratifying the Constitution

Primary Source

"I review . . . the subject . . . and . . . the dangers . . . in this new plan of government, and compare . . . my poor abilities to secure our rights, it will take much more time to traverse the objectionable parts of it. . . . [T]he change is dangerous . . . and the experiment ought not be made. . . ."

—Patrick Henry, June 9, 1788

Alexander Hamilton Favors Ratifying the Constitution

Primary Source

"The establishment of a Constitution, by the voluntary consent of a whole people, is a prodigy, to the completion of which I look forward. . . . I dread . . . the consequences of new attempts, because I know that powerful individuals, in this and other states, are enemies to a general national government in every possible shape."

—Alexander Hamilton, *The Federalist Papers*

You Decide
1. Why did Henry oppose ratifying the Constitution?
2. Why did Hamilton favor ratifying the Constitution?
3. What decision would you have made? Why?

voters would reject a constitution that threatened slavery. So he assured his constituents in Virginia that the Constitution offered slavery "better security than any that now exists."

That security took three forms. First, the Constitution forbade Congress from blocking the importation of slaves for twenty years. Georgia and South Carolina would import another 100,000 slaves by 1808. Second, a compromise known as the **Three-Fifths Compromise** counted each slave as three fifths of a person to be added to a state's free population in allocating representatives to the House of Representatives and electoral college votes. The three-fifths clause gave the southern states more seats in Congress and more power in presidential elections than they would have enjoyed had only free people been counted—as the northern delegates preferred. Third, the Constitution committed all states to return fugitive slaves to their owners. In other words, running away to a free state did not free a slave. Northerners were required to help enforce the slave system as the price of union.

Most state constitutions had adopted bills of rights to protect civil liberties from the power of government. But the federal delegates declined to include a bill of rights in their constitution. A South Carolina delegate, Charles C. Pinckney, explained, "such bills generally begin with declaring that all men are by nature born free." Such a declaration would come "with a very bad grace when a large part of our property consists in men who are actually born slaves." Unlike the Declaration of Independence, the Constitution did not proclaim that all men were born free and equal in their rights.

On September 17, the Constitutional Convention concluded with 42 delegates still present. Many, including Madison, disliked the compromises, but Franklin appealed to all to unite in support of the "federal experiment." Hamilton reluctantly accepted the Constitution as the only alternative to "anarchy and Convulsion." In the end, 39 delegates signed the document, while three refused to sign out of protest. George Mason and Edmund Randolph of Virginia and Elbridge Gerry of Massachusetts considered the document to be flawed. Next came the greater challenge of winning approval from the states.

✓ **Checkpoint** What was the significance of the Three-Fifths Compromise?

SECTION **2** Assessment

Progress Monitoring *Online*
For: Self-test with vocabulary practice
Web Code: nca-0504

Comprehension

1. **Terms and People** For each item listed below, write a sentence explaining its significance to the new Constitution.
   - Alexander Hamilton
   - James Madison
   - Virginia Plan
   - New Jersey Plan
   - Great Compromise
   - Three-Fifths Compromise

2. **NoteTaking Reading Skill: Identify Supporting Details** Use your completed concept web to answer the Section Focus Question: What new system of national government did the delegates agree upon at the Constitutional Convention of 1787?

Writing About History

3. **Quick Write: Combine Quotes and Visuals** Based on the quote by Madison and the images of the delegates in this section, what can you conclude about the characters of the delegates? Write one or two paragraphs with your conclusion.

Critical Thinking

4. **Determine Relevance** Why did leaders call for the Constitutional Convention?

5. **Identify Alternatives** In addition to the two proposed frameworks for a new constitution, what other plan might the delegates have considered?

6. **Compare Points of View** How did the Great Compromise satisfy both the small and the large states?

2.I.E(6)

John Locke:
Two Treatises of Government

The Framers of the Constitution relied upon the writings of Enlightenment philosophers Baron de Montesquieu, Jean Jacques Rousseau, and John Locke. English philosopher John Locke (1632–1704) published *Two Treatises of Government* in 1690. Locke believed that all people had the same natural rights of life, liberty, and property. In this essay, he states that the primary purpose of government is to protect these natural rights. He also states that governments hold their power only with the consent of the people.

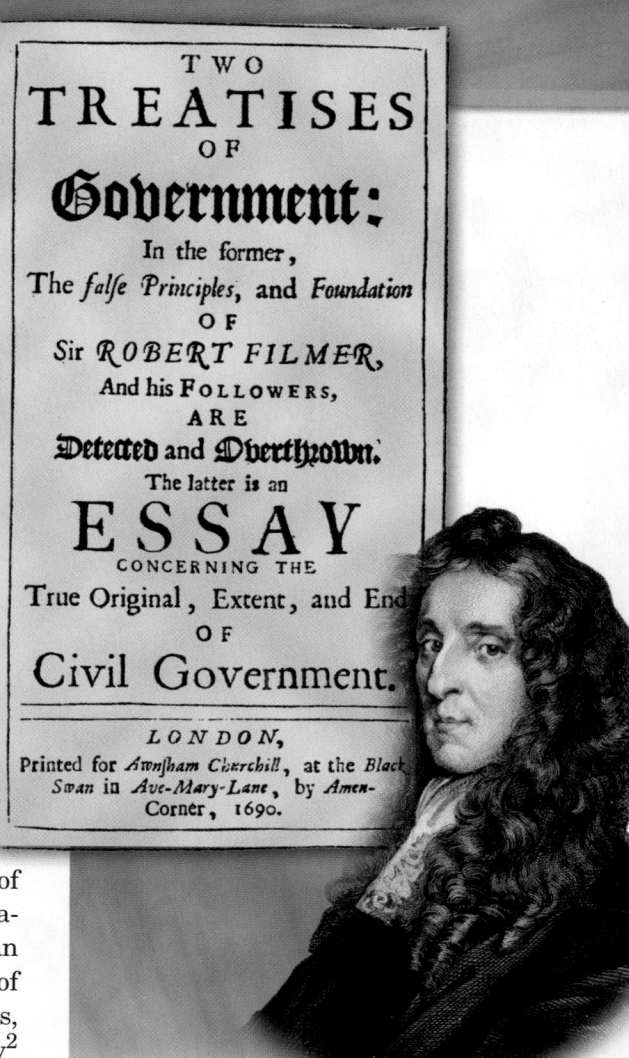

▲ John Locke and the title page of *Two Treatises of Government*

But though men, when they enter into society, give up the equality, liberty, and executive power they had in the state of nature, into the hands of society . . . the power of the society, or legislative constituted by them, can never be supposed to extend farther than the common good. . . . Whoever has the legislative or supreme power of any commonwealth, is bound to govern by established standing laws, promulgated[1] and known to the people, and not by extemporary[2] decrees, by indifferent and upright judges, who are to decide controversies by those laws; and to employ the force of the community at home only in the execution of such laws, or abroad to prevent or redress foreign injuries, and secure the community from inroads[3] and invasion. And all this to be directed to no other end but the peace, safety, and public good of the people. . . .

The reason why men enter into society, is the preservation of their property; and the end while they chuse [choose] and authorize a legislative, is, that there may be laws made, and rules set, as guards and fences to the properties of all the members of the society. . . .

Whensoever therefore the legislative [power] shall transgress[4] this fundamental rule of society; and either by ambition, fear, folly or corruption, endeavour to grasp themselves, or put into the hands of any other, an absolute power over the lives, liberties, and estates of the people; by this breach of trust they forfeit the power the people had put into their hands for quite contrary ends, and it devolves[5] to the people; who have a right to resume their original liberty, and, by the establishment of a new legislative, (such as they shall think fit) provide for their own safety and security. . . .

1. **promulgated** (PRAHM uhl gayt ihd) *v.* published or made known.
2. **extemporary** (ehk STEHM puh rer ee) *adj.* without any preparation.
3. **inroads** (IHN rohdz) *n.* advances at the expense of someone.
4. **transgress** (trans GREHS) *v.* to go beyond; break.
5. **devolves** (dih VAHLVZ) *v.* passes.

Thinking Critically
1. **Draw Inferences** According to Locke, how should a society be governed? Why do you think he felt this way?

2. **Identify Central Issues** What does Locke say can happen if a government fails to protect the rights of its people?

SECTION 3

WITNESS HISTORY AUDIO

A Hopeful Future

After the hard work was completed at the Constitutional Convention, the delegates set out to win approval of the document they had created from the states. With amendments, that document—the United States Constitution—has now endured for more than 200 years. At the time, however, the system of government established by the document was in no way secure. Benjamin Franklin wryly observed:

❝Our Constitution is in actual operation; everything appears to promise that it will last; but in this world nothing is certain but death and taxes.❞

—Benjamin Franklin, 1789

Ratifying the Constitution

Core Curriculum Objectives

- **2.I.B.4** Ratification of the Constitution
- **2.I.B.4b** Ratification: Federalist and Antifederalist arguments
- **2.I.E.1** National power—limits and potentials
- **2.I.E.10** Separation of powers

Terms and People

ratification	popular sovereignty
Federalist	limited government
Antifederalist	separation of powers
The Federalist	checks and balances
John Jay	electoral college
Bill of Rights	

NoteTaking

Reading Skill: Identify Main Ideas Use a table to record the arguments for and against ratification of the Constitution.

Ratification of the Constitution	
Arguments For	**Arguments Against**
• A strong central government would be able to handle the problems that faced the nation.	• A strong central government would undermine basic liberties.
•	•
•	•

Why It Matters The delegates to the Constitutional Convention had designed a strong federal government. As you learned, all but three delegates endorsed the new Constitution, despite the fact that many felt it was imperfect. After most of the delegates signed it, the proposed Constitution was printed, circulated, and hotly debated. The question remained whether the states would accept the proposed plan. If they did not, what would become of the new nation? **Section Focus Question: How did Americans ratify the Constitution, and what are its basic principles?**

The Struggle Over Ratification

By drafting a new Constitution, the delegates had exceeded their mandate. They were only supposed to propose amendments to the Articles of Confederation. Official approval, or **ratification,** of an entirely new constitution was doomed if all 13 states had to approve it as the Articles required. To improve the odds of ratification, the delegates arbitrarily decided to change the rules. They determined that approval by nine states would suffice. They also took the ratification decision away from the state legislatures, for they would most certainly oppose a new constitution that would deprive them of some power. Instead, the delegates ruled that specially elected conventions would determine a state's choice for or against the Constitution. Two groups soon emerged in the debate: the Federalists, who favored ratification, and the Antifederalists, who opposed it.

Federalists Favor Strong Government Those who favored ratification of the Constitution were known as **Federalists.** The group included George Washington, James Madison, and Alexander Hamilton. The Federalists stressed the weaknesses of the Articles. They argued that only a new government based on the proposed Constitution could overcome the difficulties facing the new nation.

Antifederalists Fear a Strong Government Critics of the Constitution, known as **Antifederalists,** denounced it as a retreat from the liberty won by the Revolution. The Antifederalists especially disliked the lack of a bill of rights that would provide basic liberties, protecting the people from the powers of the government. They noted that the Constitution greatly increased the powers of the central government and provided a more elitist government by concentrating power in relatively few hands at a great distance from most voters. The Antifederalists believed that liberty could not survive unless the federal government remained weak, which meant that most power would belong to the democratic state governments. One Antifederalist asked:

> **Primary Source** "What have you been contending for these ten years past? Liberty! What is Liberty? The power of governing yourselves. If you adopt this Constitution, have you this power? No: you give it into the hands of a set of men who live one thousand miles distant from you."
> —James Lincoln, South Carolina delegate

The Antifederalists included such leading Patriots as Samuel Adams and John Hancock of Massachusetts, George Clinton of New York, and Richard Henry Lee and Patrick Henry of Virginia. Successful state politicians, they distrusted the Federalist effort to subordinate the states to a stronger national Union.

The Federalists Gain Support Most farmers recognized that the Constitution threatened the state debtor-relief laws that had rescued their farms from foreclosure. Common farmers also distrusted the lawyers, merchants, and other wealthy men who promoted the Constitution, viewing them as aristocrats hostile to the Republic. In South Carolina, farmers protested by staging a mock funeral around a coffin with the word *Liberty* painted on the side. Because most citizens were farmers, the proposed Constitution lacked majority support in 1787.

However, the Constitution had the support of two of the most popular and trusted men in America—George Washington and Benjamin Franklin. Their support allayed the fears of many rural Americans. Some frontier farmers also endorsed the Constitution because they hoped that a stronger nation would defeat the Native Americans and take control of the British forts along the Great Lakes.

The Federalists also enjoyed popular support in key places—the seaports—which hosted most of the ratifying conventions. Unlike the common farmers, most urban artisans supported the Constitution. Hurt by the depression of the 1780s, the artisans hoped that a strong national government could expand American commerce. The seaports also had most of the nation's newspapers, the printers of which strongly endorsed the Constitution.

The Federalists were also better organized than the Antifederalists. Acting quickly after the Constitutional Convention, the Federalists built a nationwide network of support. Their national experience and connections gave them a great advantage in coordinating the first national political campaign. By contrast, the Antifederalists were state politicians who struggled to build alliances across state lines.

The Federalist Papers Outline Key Ideas The Federalists' case for ratification of the Constitution appeared in *The Federalist,* a series of 85 essays that came to be called the Federalist Papers. Three leading Federalists—Madison, Hamilton, and **John Jay**—wrote the essays, which were published in New York newspapers in 1787 and 1788, a time of heated debate in New York's ratifying convention. The essays argued that the separation of powers in three branches of government would prevent the concentration of power dreaded by the Antifederalists.

The authors were also eager for the United States to have a strong central government, as supported by Madison in *The Federalist,* No. 10. Federalist leaders feared that the United States would dissolve without a strong government. (See Primary Source at the end of the section.) They argued in *The Federalist,* No. 51, that the checks and balances in the Constitution prevented any of the three branches from gaining too much power. The authors insisted that the real threat to liberty came from the state legislatures, which lacked sufficient checks and balances. Hamilton wrote of the importance of a judicial branch in *The Federalist,* No. 78. Today, these essays help scholars, judges, and lawyers understand the meaning of the Constitution.

 Checkpoint Why did the Federalists have more support than the Antifederalists?

Ratifying Conventions

Exploiting their advantages, the Federalists pushed for quick ratifying conventions in five states. By mid-January 1788, the Federalists had won ratification in Delaware, Pennsylvania, New Jersey, Georgia, and Connecticut. These early victories created momentum. To complete ratification, the Federalists needed only four of the remaining eight states. But the Antifederalists mounted a stronger fight in those states.

The Federalists Triumph In Massachusetts, the Federalists faced defeat until they made two key concessions to sway the moderate Antifederalists, led

---

HISTORY MAKERS

James Madison (1751–1836)
Madison wrote 29 of the Federalist Papers, including three he wrote with Hamilton. He wrote the essays while he was living in New York and serving as a member of the Confederation Congress. After he returned home to Virginia in the spring of 1788, he was elected to the Virginia convention to ratify the Constitution that he played a large role in creating. Madison also helped frame the Bill of Rights.

Alexander Hamilton (1755–1804)
It was Hamilton's idea to write the essays that became known as the Federalist Papers. He came up with the idea in order to help win the ratification vote in New York. Hamilton wrote 51 of the 85 essays. In Federalist Paper No. 1, Hamilton laid out the plan for all the essays. In later essays, he tackled such topics as the office of the President and the authority of the Supreme Court to rule on the constitutionality of a law.

John Jay (1745–1829)
A successful New York attorney, John Jay wrote four of the first five Federalist Papers—Nos. 2, 3, 4, and 5. In them, he argued for a strong federal government to protect the Union from foreign force and influence. His contributions to the essays were cut short when he fell ill, though he wrote No. 64 when he recovered.

by Governor John Hancock. First, the Federalists appealed to Hancock's vanity. They hinted that he could become the nation's first Vice President by switching sides. Second, to make that switch easier, they promised to support key amendments to the Constitution. They would add a bill of rights but only after ratification—not as a condition for it. In early February, following Hancock's lead, the Massachusetts convention ratified the Constitution.

The promise of a bill of rights helped the Federalists win most of the remaining states. Maryland ratified in April; South Carolina, in May; and New Hampshire, in early June. They provided the winning nine, but the new nation would not last without the support of Virginia and New York. In late June, Virginia narrowly ratified, despite the forceful opposition of Patrick Henry, the greatest political orator of his generation. In July, New York also narrowly approved after Hamilton threatened New York City's secession from the state to join the Union if the state rejected the Constitution.

With the ratification of 11 states, the Congress of the Confederation made plans for the establishment of the new government and chose New York City as the temporary capital. The new Congress <u>convened</u> there on March 4, 1789, in Federal Hall. Plans for electing the nation's first President and Vice President were made. Within a short time, Rhode Island and North Carolina, which had previously rejected the Constitution, reconsidered and joined the Union.

Adding the Bill of Rights If the Federalists deserve credit for the Constitution, the Antifederalists deserve credit for the federal **Bill of Rights,** the first ten amendments to the Constitution. Only the forceful resistance of the Antifederalists obliged the Federalists to add a bill of rights.

In the newly elected Congress, Madison drafted the Bill of Rights. Many of these amendments relied on an earlier Virginia bill of rights. Madison limited the amendments to guarantees of individual rights, leaving the federal framework the same. He also avoided any sweeping preamble that declared all men equal in their creation and rights. That omission enabled slave owners to persist in denying rights to their slaves. The protected rights included freedom of religion, speech, press, assembly, and petition; protection from unreasonable searches and seizures; and the right to a speedy and public trial.

Madison feared that any finite list of rights would later be abused to deny any left unmentioned. So the Ninth Amendment provided: "The enumeration in the Constitution, of certain rights, shall not be construed to deny or disparage others retained by the people." That left open the subsequent development of additional rights. Congress passed the Bill of Rights in 1789.

✔ **Checkpoint** What was the importance of the inclusion of a bill of rights in the Constitution?

A Celebration
This engraving shows the celebration of New York's ratification of the Constitution. *Who is identified with the success of ratification here?*

Vocabulary Builder
<u>convene</u>–(kuhn VEEN) *v.* to meet or assemble

Principles of the New Constitution

The Republic established by the Constitution of the United States became a symbol of freedom not only to Americans but to countries in Europe and republics in Latin America as well. The authors of the Constitution established a representative government based on these basic principles: popular sovereignty,

Expanding and Protecting Civil Rights

 2.I.A.6

TRACK THE ISSUE

What should the federal government do to expand and protect civil rights?

The U.S. Constitution guarantees equal rights for all Americans. In 1789, though, African Americans, women, and Native Americans did not have the same rights given white males. Over the years, however, rights have been extended to these groups. A major question remains, though: How far should the government go to expand rights? Use the timeline below to explore this enduring issue.

1791 Bill of Rights
The first 10 amendments to the U.S. Constitution guarantee certain basic rights and freedoms.

1868 Fourteenth Amendment
Guarantees citizenship to everyone born or naturalized in the United States.

1920 Nineteenth Amendment
Women gain the right to vote.

1964 Civil Rights Act
Bans race or gender discrimination in public accommodations and jobs.

1990 Americans With Disabilities Act
Bans discrimination against people with disabilities.

The Bill of Rights

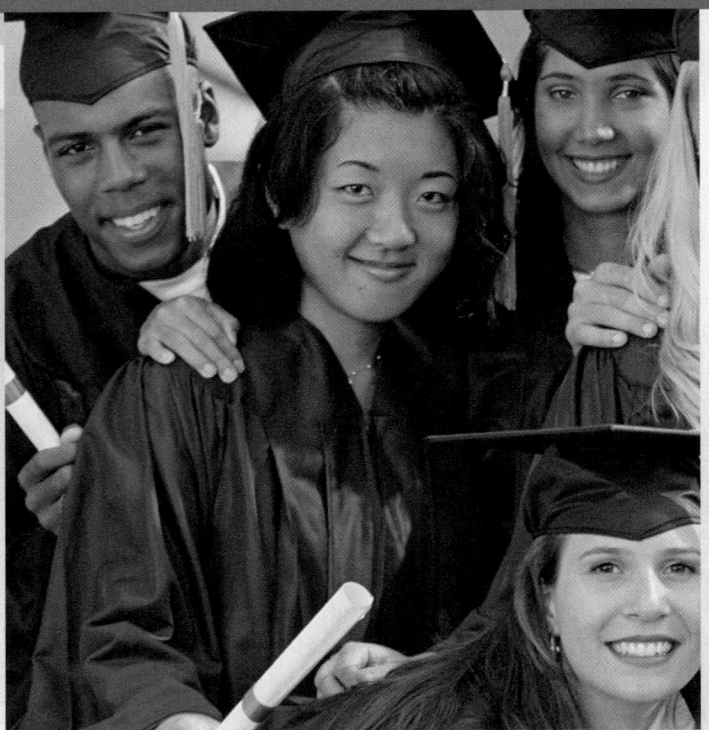

College graduates celebrate their achievements.

DEBATE THE ISSUE

Affirmative Action Some urge companies, colleges, and the government to use affirmative action programs to expand opportunities for women and minorities. Others argue that such steps are unfair.

"You do not take a man who for years has been hobbled by chains, liberate him, bring him to the starting line of a race, saying 'you are free to compete with all the others,' and still justly believe you have been completely fair. . . . We seek not just freedom but opportunity . . . not just equality as a right and a theory, but equality as a fact and as a result."

—President Lyndon Johnson, speech, June 4, 1965

"The civil rights laws themselves forbade employers to discriminate on the basis of race, sex, national origin, color, or religion. They didn't say anything about guaranteeing a certain number of slots to minorities or women. . . . The supporters of affirmative action everywhere seemed to believe that the only way to eliminate racial discrimination against blacks, Latinos, and women was to discriminate against white men."

—Linda Chavez, essay, October 2002

? TRANSFER Activities

1. **Compare** Choose a statement about affirmative action you disagree with. Explain why you disagree.

2. **Analyze** Do you think either Johnson or Chavez believed that affirmative action is a basic right? Why or why not?

3. **Transfer** Use the following Web site to see a video, try a WebQuest, and write in your journal. **Web Code:** neh-6502

limited government, separation of powers, federalism, checks and balances, and representative government.

Popular Sovereignty The Constitution abides by the principle of **popular sovereignty,** in which all government power comes from the people. In other words, the government derives its political authority from the people.

Limited Government Popular sovereignty ensures that a government's power is restricted, or limited. In a **limited government,** the Constitution specifically states what powers the government has. The principle of limited government also refers to the rule of law. Government leaders are not supposed to be above the law.

Separation of Powers The Constitution mandated the **separation of powers** within the federal government. The Constitution, therefore, defined distinct legislative, executive, and judicial branches with different responsibilities to prevent misuse of power by any of the three branches.

The Constitution assigns certain specific powers to each of the three branches of the federal government. The legislative branch, or Congress, enacts laws. The executive branch, headed by the President, carries out the laws, negotiates treaties, and commands the armed forces. The judicial branch interprets the Constitution and enforces the law. The Constitution established a Supreme Court and authorized Congress to establish other courts as needed.

Federalism Just as the Constitution divides power among the three branches of the federal government, it also divides power between the states and the nation, a division known as federalism. At the time, this meant that the states could no longer issue their own paper money or provide debtor relief at creditors' expense. These delegated powers belonged exclusively to the federal government. Federalism also reserves some powers to the state governments. For example, states regulate all elections. The federal and state governments also hold some overlapping concurrent powers, among them parallel court systems.

Principles of the Constitution	☑ Quick Study
Popular sovereignty	The people are the only source of the government's power.
Limited government	The government has only the powers that the Constitution gives it.
Separation of powers	The government's power is divided among three branches: the legislative, the executive, and the judicial branches.
Federalism	The federal government and the state governments share power.
Checks and balances	Each branch of government has the power to limit the actions of the other two.
Representative government	Citizens elect representatives to government to make laws.

Checks and Balances The Constitution also limits the power of government by creating a system of **checks and balances** designed to prevent the emergence of a single domineering center of power. For example, while only Congress has the power to enact laws, the President may veto them. However, a two-thirds majority in both houses of Congress can override the President's veto. The President nominates judges, but the Senate must approve them.

Representative Government The writers of the new Constitution had misgivings about the democratic rule of the majority. Many saw democracy as something that would lead to mob rule. Instead of creating a direct democracy in which all citizens vote on every matter, the writers created an indirect democracy in which voters elect representatives to govern.

For example, the Constitution stipulated that the citizens would directly elect only the representatives to the House of Representatives. The state legislatures, rather than the voters, would choose the members of the Senate (who would serve for six years, rather than the two years representatives served). Similarly, an **electoral college,** or group of persons chosen from each state, would indirectly elect the President. Each state legislature would determine whether to choose those electors or let the citizens elect them.

In addition, the indirectly elected President and senators would choose the least democratic branch of all: the judiciary. By giving the federal judges (including the Supreme Court Justices) life terms, the delegates meant to insulate them from democratic politics.

 Checkpoint What are the major principles of the Constitution?

The Constitution Endures

The Constitution became the supreme law of the land in 1789, and with amendments, it has endured for more than 200 years. At about 7,000 words, the Constitution is relatively brief and often ambiguous. Therefore, it invites debate. Some politicians, including Thomas Jefferson, argued that the Constitution should be interpreted narrowly and literally to restrict federal power. But most Federalists, including George Washington, insisted that the Constitution be read broadly to allow for the expansion of federal power when necessary.

How is it that a Constitution written when the nation was little more than a small colonial outpost continues to guide the actions of the government today? The Framers knew they could not anticipate future social, economic, or political events. They, therefore, worded parts of the Constitution to permit flexibility. The Constitution has survived and thrived in part because it provides a process for its own amendment, that is, for changes in its content. The Constitution makes amendment possible but difficult. Two thirds of both houses of Congress must approve an amendment, which becomes law only when ratified by three fourths of the states. Since the Bill of Rights, only 17 amendments have been added to the Constitution.

Checkpoint What has enabled the Constitution to endure for more than 200 years?

Progress Monitoring *Online*
For: Self-test with vocabulary practice
Web Code: nca-0505

Comprehension

1. **Terms and People** For each term listed below, write a sentence explaining why it is an important principle in the Constitution.
   - popular sovereignty
   - limited government
   - separation of powers
   - checks and balances

2. **NoteTaking Reading Skill: Identify Main Ideas** Use your completed table to answer the Section Focus Question: How did Americans ratify the Constitution, and what are its basic principles?

Writing About History

3. **Quick Write: Compare Evidence** Describe the relationship between the plans of government that were proposed at the Constitutional Convention and the plan that was chosen. Look at the diagram in the previous section on the plans of government as well as the chart of the principles of the Constitution in this section. Write your description in one or two paragraphs.

Critical Thinking

4. **Compare Points of View** What was the main argument of the Antifederalists?

5. **Summarize** Why did Madison feel it was necessary to add the Ninth Amendment?

6. **Draw Conclusions** Why do you think the delegates made amending the Constitution difficult?

2.I.B.4a

James Madison:
The Federalist, No. 10

One of the most notable essays in the Federalist Papers is *The Federalist,* No. 10. In it, Madison argues that a national government on a continental scale would strengthen rather than weaken liberty. He believed that in a large and diverse republic, no single faction, or interest group, could control the government because the numerous factions would check one another.

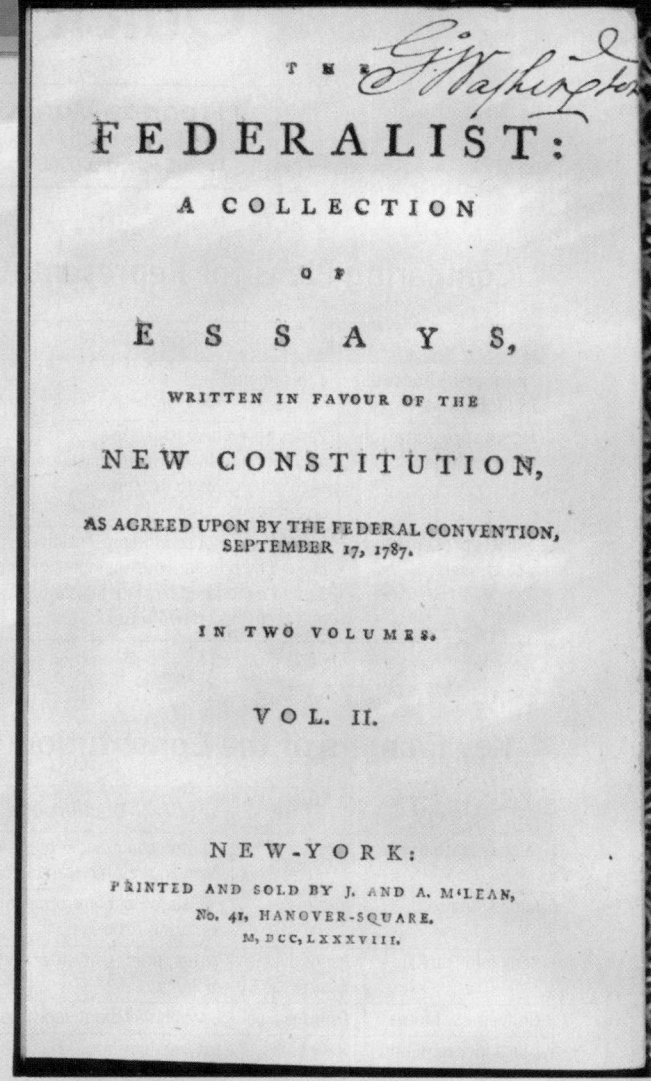

▲ Title page from *The Federalist* signed by George Washington

The latent causes of faction are thus sown in the nature of man; and we see them everywhere brought into different degrees of activity. . . . A zeal for different opinions concerning religion, concerning government, and many other points, . . . have, in turn, divided mankind into parties, inflamed them with mutual animosity, and rendered them much more disposed to vex and oppress each other than to cooperate for their common good. . . .

From this . . . it may be concluded that a pure democracy, by which I mean a society consisting of a small number of citizens, who assemble and administer the government in person, can admit of no cure for the mischiefs of faction. . . . Hence it is that such democracies have ever been spectacles of turbulence and contention; have ever been found incompatible with personal security or the rights of property; and have in general been as short in their lives as they have been violent in their deaths. . . .

A republic, by which I mean a government in which the scheme of representation takes place, opens a different prospect, and promises the cure for which we are seeking. Let us examine the points in which it varies from pure democracy, and we shall comprehend both the nature of the cure and the efficacy which it must derive from the Union. . . .

The two great points of difference between a democracy and a republic are: first, the delegation of the government, in the latter, to a small number of citizens elected by the rest; secondly, the greater number of citizens, and greater sphere of country, over which the latter may be extended. . . .

The influence of factious leaders may kindle a flame within their particular States, but will be unable to spread a general conflagration through the other States. A religious sect may degenerate into a political faction in a part of the Confederacy; but the variety of sects dispersed over the entire face of it must secure the national councils against any danger from that source. A rage for paper money, for an abolition of debts, for an equal division of property, or for any other improper or wicked project, will be less apt to pervade the whole body of the Union than a particular member of it; in the same proportion as such a malady is more likely to taint a particular county or district, than an entire State. . . .

Thinking Critically

1. According to Madison, what are the differences between a democracy and a republic? Which does he support and why?

2. Does Madison consider factions to be good or bad for the nation? Explain.

Quick Study Guide

Progress Monitoring *Online*
For: Self-test with vocabulary practice
Web Code: nca-0506

■ Comparing Plans for Representation in the New Federal Government

	Virginia Plan	New Jersey Plan	U.S. Constitution Provisions
Number of houses in legislature	2 (Bicameral)	1 (Unicameral)	2 (Bicameral)
How representation is determined	Varies based on each state's population or by the financial support each state gives to the central government	Equal representation for each state	Equal representation for each state in the Senate; representation in the House of Representatives varies based on each state's population
How representatives are chosen	Members of House of Representatives elected by popular vote; members of Senate nominated by state legislatures and then chosen by House	Elected by state legislatures	Members of House of Representatives elected by popular vote in each state; members of Senate chosen by state legislatures*

*Seventeenth Amendment later provided for popular election of senators

■ Key Framers of the Constitution

Name	State	Background
George Washington	Virginia	Planter; commander of the Continental Army in the American Revolution
James Madison	Virginia	Legislator; major proponent of replacing Articles
Benjamin Franklin	Pennsylvania	Writer; printer; inventor; legislator; diplomat
Gouverneur Morris	Pennsylvania	Lawyer; merchant; legislator
Alexander Hamilton	New York	Lawyer; legislator; champion of strong central government
Roger Sherman	Connecticut	Merchant; mayor of New Haven; legislator; judge
John Dickinson	Delaware	Lawyer; historian; major advocate of independence

■ The Bill of Rights

1st:	Guarantees freedom of religion, speech, press, assembly, and petition
2nd:	Guarantees right to bear arms
3rd:	Prohibits quartering of troops in private homes
4th:	Protects people from unreasonable searches and seizures
5th:	Guarantees due process for accused persons
6th:	Guarantees the right to a speedy and public trial in the state where the offense was committed
7th:	Guarantees the right to jury trial for civil cases tried in federal courts
8th:	Prohibits excessive bail and cruel and unusual punishments
9th:	Provides that people have rights beyond those stated in the Constitution
10th:	Provides that powers not granted to the national government belong to the states and to the people

☑ Quick Study Timeline

In America

1777
Continental Congress adopts the Articles of Confederation, which established a limited national government in 1781

1786
Shays' Rebellion breaks out

Presidential Terms

1775   **1780**   **1785**

Around the World

1782
James Watt builds first rotary steam engine

1784
Pitt's India Act establishes dual control of India

American Issues
•—•—• Connector

By connecting prior knowledge with what you have learned in this chapter, you can gradually build your understanding of enduring questions that still affect America today. Answer the questions below. Then, use your American Issues Connector study guide (or go online: www.PHSchool.com **Web Code:** nch-6503).

Issues You Learned About

● **Expanding and Protecting Civil Rights** Most democracies include safeguards to protect the individual rights and freedoms of their citizens.

1. How did the Federalists' promise to support a bill of rights influence the ratification battle?

2. What are some of the rights guaranteed to American citizens by the Bill of Rights?

3. What is the significance of the Ninth Amendment?

● **Checks and Balances** The federal Constitution provided a system of checks and balances to prevent any of the three branches from dominating the others.

4. Support or disprove this statement: The Articles of Confederation provided a strong system of checks and balances for the federal government.

5. What are the three branches of the federal government and their powers? Give an example of how one branch might check the power of another branch.

6. What prior experiences may have led the delegates at the Constitutional Convention to create a national government with a separation of powers and a system of checks and balances?

● **Federal Power and States' Rights** Questions about the power of the federal government versus the power of state governments date to the earliest days of the nation.

7. Under the Articles of Confederation, did the state governments or the federal government have more power? Explain.

8. Explain whether James Madison supported federal power or state power. Use evidence from the text to support your answer.

9. Why did the Antifederalists support a weak national government?

Connect to Your World — New York

Federal Power and States' Rights The New York State Constitution, drafted by the Federalist John Jay, was adopted in 1777. Like the United States Constitution, it created three branches of government: a bicameral legislature, a judiciary, and an executive branch. Other similarities included voting rights only for male land-owners, and legalized slavery. These aspects of the state's constitution were gradually removed through constitutional amendments. Find copies of New York State's first and latest constitutions. List three similarities and three differences between the documents.

1787
Constitutional Convention drafts a new plan of government; Northwest Ordinance passed

1791
Bill of Rights added to the Constitution

1792
George Washington unanimously wins reelection

History _Interactive_
For: Interactive timeline
Web Code: ncp-0508

George Washington 1789–1797

1790   **1795**   **1800**

1789
Parisians storm the Bastille, starting the French Revolution

1793
France declares war on Britain and Spain

1795
Russia, Prussia, and Austria divide Poland

1799
Napoleon seizes control of France

Chapter Assessment

Terms and People

1. Define **unicameral legislature** and **bicameral legislature.** Which type of legislature did most states have?

2. What was the **Land Ordinance of 1785**? What groups of Americans benefited from this land ordinance, and why?

3. What was the **Great Compromise**? What were its specific details?

4. Define **federalism.** How did the introduction of federalism affect the rights of the state governments?

5. What is the **Bill of Rights**? Who insisted on the creation of the Bill of Rights?

Focus Questions

The focus question for this chapter is **What led to the creation of the United States Constitution, and what are its key principles?** Build an answer to this big question by answering the focus questions for Sections 1 through 3 and the Critical Thinking questions that follow.

Section 1

6. What form of national government did the Patriots create initially, and what events revealed that a new government was necessary?

Section 2

7. What new system of national government did the delegates agree upon at the Constitutional Convention of 1787?

Section 3

8. How did Americans ratify the Constitution, and what are its basic principles?

Critical Thinking

9. **Compare Points of View** How did the views of democratic Patriots and conservative Patriots diverge regarding Americans and voting rights? How were they similar?

10. **Express Problems Clearly** Think about the challenges the United States faced with Britain in its early years of nationhood. Then, identify one challenge and explain why Congress failed to solve it.

11. **Recognize Causes** Why did the national government under the Articles of Confederation face bankruptcy?

12. **Draw Conclusions** Did the Virginia Plan or the New Jersey Plan represent a more radical departure from the Articles of Confederation? Explain.

13. **Identify Central Issues** How did the northern delegates at the Constitutional Convention convince the southern delegates to support the new Constitution?

14. **Analyze Political Cartoons** Study the political cartoon below, which shows the gradual ratification of the Constitution by the states. Then, answer the questions that follow.

To what does the cartoonist compare the ratification of the Constitution? What opinion do you think the artist had about the new Constitution?

15. **Categorize** Identify which branch of the federal government each official belongs to: the President, a senator, a Supreme Court Justice, and a member of the House of Representatives.

16. **Make Comparisons** How did the national government under the Constitution differ from the government under the Articles of Confederation?

Writing About History

Synthesis Writing Coming up with a plan for a new national government was a daunting task for the delegates at the Constitutional Convention. Consider the characters and events of the convention, and then write an essay that answers the following question: How did the Constitution reach its final form?

Prewriting

- Refresh your memory by flipping through the chapter or find other sources relating to the essay question. Compare visuals, quotes, and features.

- Using what you learn from the various sources, compile a list of significant people and events that shaped the plan that came to be the Constitution.

- Record similarities or differences among the various sources to help identify the main idea you will develop.

Drafting

- Develop a thesis statement that identifies the focus of your essay.

- Make an outline for your essay with facts and examples.

- Begin each paragraph with a clear sentence about the topic of the paragraph.

- Organize your essay so that your reader sees where information from sources overlap.

Revising

- Use the guidelines on page SH11 of the Writing Handbook to revise your essay.

Regents DBQ Practice

Religious Freedom in Early America

America was settled by colonists who had been subjected to religious discrimination in their native countries. How did the religious diversity of the nation influence the formation of state and federal governments? Use your knowledge of colonial society and Documents 1, 2, and 3 to answer questions 1 through 4.

Document 1

"Whereas Almighty God has created the mind free; that all attempts to influence it by temporal punishments . . . are a departure from the plan of the Holy author of our religion, . . . that to compel a man to furnish contributions of money for the propagation of opinions which he disbelieves, is sinful and tyrannical; . . . that our civil rights have no dependence on our religious opinions, any more than our opinions in physics or geometry. . . .

Be it enacted by the General Assembly, That no man shall be compelled to frequent or support any religious worship, place, or ministry whatsoever, nor shall be enforced, restrained, molested, or burthened in his body or goods, nor shall otherwise suffer on account of his religious opinions or belief; but that all men shall be free to profess, and by argument to maintain, their opinion in matters of religion, and that the same shall in no wise diminish, enlarge, or affect their civil capacities. . . . [Y]et we are free to declare, and do declare, that the rights hereby asserted are the natural rights of mankind, and that if any act shall hereafter be passed to repeal the present, or to narrow its operation, such act will be an infringement of natural right."

—*Thomas Jefferson*, Virginia Statute for Religious Freedom, *1786*

Document 2

"Congress shall make no law respecting an establishment of religion, or prohibiting the free exercise thereof; or abridging the freedom of speech, or of the press; or the right of the people peacefully to assemble, and to petition the government for a redress of grievances."

—*First Amendment to the United States Constitution, 1791*

Document 3

Religion in the Colonies, 1776

Denomination	Number of Congregations
Congregational	668
Presbyterian	588
Baptist	497
Episcopal	495
Quaker	310
German Reformed	159
Lutheran	120
Methodist	65
Catholic	56
Moravian	31
Separatist and Independent	27
Dunker	24
Mennonite	16
Huguenot	7
Sandemanian	6
Jewish	5
Total	**3,074**

SOURCE: *The Churching of America, 1776–2005,* Roger Finke and Rodney Stark

---

1. What civil right does Document 1 protect?
   (1) freedom of speech
   (2) freedom of the press
   (3) freedom of education
   (4) freedom of religion

2. What can you conclude about the growth of religion in the colonies based on Document 3?
   (1) By 1776, there were fewer than 2,000 congregations in America.
   (2) There were a variety of religious denominations in colonial America.
   (3) Most colonists did not practice their religion on a regular basis.
   (4) Most colonists belonged to two establishment churches.

3. How are Documents 1 and 2 related?
   (1) Both established the right of assembly.
   (2) Both prohibited the government from imposing religious taxes.
   (3) Both guaranteed the separation of church and state.
   (4) Both guaranteed freedom of the press.

4. **Writing Task** What effect did religious liberty have on the development of the new nation? Use your knowledge of the new government and specific evidence from the primary and secondary sources above to support your answer.

THE SIX BASIC PRINCIPLES

**The classic textbook *Magruder's American Government*
outlines the six basic principles of the Constitution.
Below is a description of these principles:**

1 Popular Sovereignty

The Preamble to the Constitution begins
with the bold phrase, "We the people . . ."
These words announce that in the United
States, the people are sovereign. The government receives its power from the people
and can govern only with their consent.

2 Limited Government

Because the people are the ultimate source
of all government power, the government
has only as much authority as the people
give it. Government's power is thus limited.
Much of the Constitution, in fact, consists
of specific limitations on government power.

3 Separation of Powers

Government power is not only limited, but
also divided. The Constitution assigns certain powers to each of the three branches:
the legislative (Congress), executive
(President), and judicial (federal courts).
This separation of government's powers
was intended to prevent the misuse of
power.

4 Checks and Balances

The system of checks and balances gives
each of the three branches of government
the ability to restrain the other two. Such a
system makes government less efficient but
also less likely to trample on the rights of
citizens.

5 Judicial Review

Who decides whether an act of government
violates the Constitution? Federal courts
have the power to review acts of the federal
government and to cancel any acts that are
unconstitutional, or violate a provision in
the Constitution.

6 Federalism

A federal system of government is one in
which power is divided between a central
government and smaller governments. This
sharing of powers is intended to ensure
that the central government is powerful
enough to be effective, yet not so powerful
as to threaten states or individuals.

PARTS OF THE CONSTITUTION

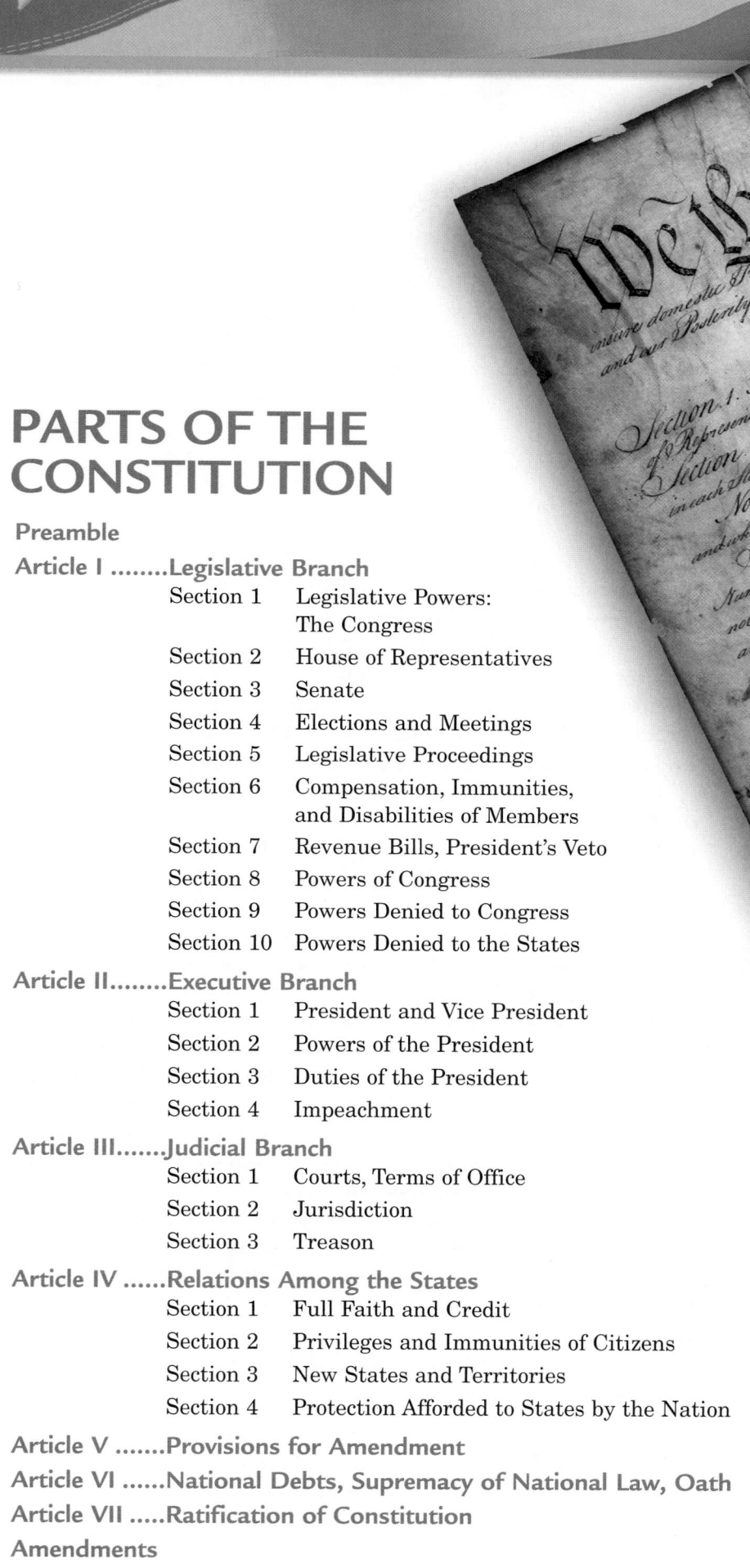

A Note on the Text of the Constitution

The complete text of the Constitution, including amendments, appears on the pages that follow. Portions of the Constitution altered by later amendments or that no longer apply have been crossed out. Commentary appears in the outside column of each page.

Commentary

The Preamble ▶

The Preamble describes the purpose of the government as set up by the Constitution. Americans expect their government to defend justice and liberty and provide peace and safety from foreign enemies.

Clause 4 ▶

Executive authority means the governor of a state. If a member of the House leaves office before his or her term ends, the governor must call a special election to fill the seat.

Preamble

We the People of the United States, in Order to form a more perfect Union, establish Justice, insure domestic Tranquility, provide for the common defence, promote the general Welfare, and secure the Blessings of Liberty to ourselves and our Posterity, do ordain and establish this Constitution for the United States of America.

Article I. Legislative Branch

Section 1. Legislative Powers; The Congress

All legislative Powers herein granted shall be vested in a Congress of the United States, which shall consist of a Senate and House of Representatives.

Section 2. House of Representatives

1. The House of Representatives shall be composed of Members chosen every second Year by the People of the several States, and the Electors in each State shall have the Qualifications requisite for Electors of the most numerous Branch of the State Legislature.

2. No Person shall be a Representative who shall not have attained to the Age of twenty-five Years, and been seven Years a Citizen of the United States, and who shall not, when elected, be an Inhabitant of that State in which he shall be chosen.

3. Representatives ~~and direct Taxes~~* shall be apportioned among the several States which may be included within this Union, according to their respective Numbers, ~~which shall be determined by adding to the whole Number of free Persons, including those bound to Service for a Term of Years and excluding Indians not taxed, three fifths of all other Persons.~~ The actual Enumeration shall be made within three Years after the first Meeting of the Congress of the United States, and within every subsequent Term of ten Years, in such Manner as they shall by Law direct. The Number of Representatives shall not exceed one for every thirty Thousand, but each State shall have at Least one Representative; ~~and, until such enumeration shall be made, the State of New Hampshire shall be entitled to choose three, Massachusetts eight, Rhode Island and Providence Plantations one, Connecticut five, New York six, New Jersey four, Pennsylvania eight, Delaware one, Maryland six, Virginia ten, North Carolina five, South Carolina five, and Georgia three.~~

4. When vacancies happen in the Representation from any State, the Executive Authority thereof shall issue Writs of Election to fill such Vacancies.

*Portions of the Constitution altered by later amendments or that no longer apply are crossed out.

5. The House of Representatives shall choose their Speaker and other Officers; and shall have the sole Power of Impeachment.

Section 3. Senate

1. The Senate of the United States shall be composed of two Senators from each State ~~chosen by the Legislature thereof~~ for six Years; and each Senator shall have one Vote.

2. Immediately after they shall be assembled in Consequences of the first Election, they shall be divided, as equally as may be, into three Classes. The Seats of the Senators of the first Class shall be vacated at the Expiration of the second Year; of the second Class, at the Expiration of the fourth Year; and of the third Class, at the Expiration of the sixth Year; so that one-third may be chosen every second Year; ~~and if Vacancies happen by Resignation, or otherwise, during the Recess of the Legislature of any State, the Executive thereof may make temporary Appointments until the next Meeting of the Legislature, which shall then fill such Vacancies.~~

3. No Person shall be a Senator who shall not have attained to the Age of thirty Years, and been nine Years a Citizen of the United States, and who shall not, when elected, be an Inhabitant of that State for which he shall be chosen.

Commentary

◄ **Clause 5** The House elects a Speaker. Also, only the House has the power to <u>impeach</u>, or accuse a federal official of wrongdoing.

◄ **Clause 1** Each State has two senators.

◄ **Clause 2** Every two years, one third of the senators run for reelection. The Seventeenth Amendment changed the way of filling <u>vacancies</u>, or empty seats. Today, the governor of a state must choose a senator to fill a vacancy that occurs between elections.

> ✔ **Checkpoint**
> **What is the main job of Congress?**

Separation of Powers

Legislative Branch (Congress)
Passes laws

- Can override presidential veto
- Approves treaties
- Can impeach and remove President and other high officials from office
- Prints and coins money

- Raises and supports armed forces
- Can declare war
- Regulates foreign and interstate trade

Executive Branch (President)
Carries out laws

- Proposes laws
- Can veto legislation
- Serves as commander in chief of armed forces

- Negotiates foreign treaties
- Appoints federal judges, ambassadors, and other high officials
- Can grant pardons to federal offenders

Judicial Branch
(Supreme Court and Other Lower Federal Courts)
Interprets Laws
- Can declare laws unconstitutional
- Can declare executive actions unconstitutional

Commentary

Clause 5 ►
The House elects a Speaker. Also, only the House has the power to impeach, or accuse a federal official of wrongdoing.

Clause 6 ►
The Senate acts as a jury if the House impeaches a federal official. The Chief Justice of the Supreme Court presides if the President is on trial. Two thirds of all senators present must vote for conviction, or finding the accused guilty. No President has ever been convicted.

 Checkpoint

Which branches are involved in presidential impeachment?

Clause 1 ►
Each state legislature can decide when and how congressional elections take place, but Congress can overrule these decisions. In 1842, Congress required each state to set up congressional districts with one representative elected from each district. In 1872, Congress decided that congressional elections must be held in every state on the same date in even-numbered years.

4. The Vice President of the United States shall be President of the Senate but shall have no Vote, unless they be equally divided.

5. The Senate shall choose their other Officers, and also a President pro tempore, in the Absence of the Vice President, or when he shall exercise the Office of President of the United States.

6. The Senate shall have the sole Power to try all Impeachments. When sitting for that Purpose, they shall be on Oath or Affirmation. When the President of the United States is tried, the Chief Justice shall preside: And no Person shall be convicted without the Concurrence of two thirds of the Members present.

7. Judgment in Cases of Impeachment shall not extend further than to removal from Office, and disqualification to hold and enjoy any Office of honor, Trust, or Profit under the United States: but the Party convicted shall nevertheless be liable and subject to Indictment, Trial, Judgment and Punishment, according to Law.

Section 4. Elections and Meetings

1. The Times, Places and Manner of holding Elections for Senators and Representatives, shall be prescribed in each State by the Legislature thereof; but the Congress may at any time by law make or alter such Regulations, except as to the Places of choosing Senators.

2. The Congress shall assemble at least once in every Year, ~~and such Meeting shall be on the first Monday in December, unless they shall by Law appoint a different Day.~~

Section 5. Legislative Proceedings

1. Each House shall be the Judge of the Elections, Returns and Qualifications of its own Members, and a Majority of each shall constitute a Quorum to do Business; but a smaller Number may adjourn from day to day, and may be authorized to compel the Attendance of absent Members, in such Manner, and under such Penalties, as each House may provide.

2. Each House may determine the Rules of its Proceedings, punish its Members for disorderly Behavior, and, with the Concurrence of two thirds, expel a Member.

3. Each House shall keep a Journal of its Proceedings, and from time to time publish the same, excepting such Parts as may in their Judgment require Secrecy; and the Yeas and Nays of the Members of either House on any question shall, at the Desire of one fifth of those Present, be entered on the Journal.

4. Neither House, during the Session of Congress, shall, without the Consent of the other, adjourn for more than three days, nor to any other Place than that in which the two Houses shall be sitting.

Section 6. Compensation, Immunities, and Disabilities of Members

1. The Senators and Representatives shall receive a Compensation for their Services, to be ascertained by Law, and paid out of the Treasury of the United States. They shall in all Cases, except Treason, Felony, and Breach of the Peace, be privileged from Arrest during their Attendance at the Session of their respective Houses, and in going to and returning from the same; and for any Speech or Debate in either House, they shall not be questioned in any other Place.

2. No Senator or Representative shall, during the Time for which he was elected, be appointed to any civil Office under the Authority of the United States, which shall have been created, or the Emoluments whereof shall have been increased during such time; and no Person holding any Office under the United States, shall be a Member of either House during his Continuance in Office.

Section 7. Revenue Bills, President's Veto

1. All Bills for raising Revenue shall originate in the House of Representatives; but the Senate may propose or concur with amendments as on other Bills.

2. Every Bill which shall have passed the House of Representatives and the Senate, shall, before it become a Law, be presented to the President of the United States: If he approve he shall sign it, but if not he shall return it, with his Objections to that House in which it shall have originated, who shall enter the Objections at large on their Journal, and proceed to reconsider it. If after such Reconsideration two thirds of the House shall agree to pass the Bill, it shall be sent, together with the Objections, to the other House, by which it shall likewise be reconsidered, and if approved by two thirds of that House, it shall become a Law. But in all such Cases the Votes of both Houses shall be determined by Yeas and Nays, and the Names of the Persons voting for and against the Bill shall be entered on the Journal of each House respectively. If any Bill shall not be returned by the President within ten Days

Commentary

◀ **Clause 4** Neither house can <u>adjourn</u>, or stop meeting, for more than three days unless the other house approves. Both houses must meet in the same city.

◀ **Clause 1** Tax bills must be introduced in the House, but the Senate can make changes in those bills.

◀ **Clause 2** A <u>bill</u>, or proposed law, that is passed by a majority of the House and Senate is sent to the President. If the President signs the bill, it becomes law. The President can <u>veto</u>, or reject, a bill by sending it back to the house where it was introduced. Congress can override the President's veto if each house of Congress passes the bill again by a two-thirds vote.

Commentary

✔ **Checkpoint**

What is the role of Congress and the President in making laws?

(Sunday excepted) after it shall have been presented to him, the Same shall be a law, in like Manner as if he had signed it, unless the Congress by their Adjournment, prevent its Return, in which Case it shall not be a Law.

3. Every Order, Resolution, or Vote to which the Concurrence of the Senate and House of Representatives may be necessary (except on a question of adjournment) shall be presented to the President of the United States; and before the Same shall take Effect, shall be approved by him, or, being disapproved by him, shall be repassed by two thirds of the Senate and House of Representatives, according to the Rules and Limitations prescribed in the Case of a Bill.

How a Bill Becomes a Law

Start: Senate

 Introduction
Bill introduced in Senate.

 Committee Action
Bill referred to standing committee. Moves to subcommittee for study, hearings, revisions, approval. Moves back to full committee for more hearings and revisions.

 Floor Action
Bill is debated, then passed or defeated. If passed, the bill goes to the House of Representatives. If the bill has already passed in House, the bill goes to Conference Committee.

 Conference Committee
Conference Committee resolves differences between House and Senate versions of the bill.

Congressional Approval
House and Senate vote on final passage. Approved bill is sent to the President.

 Presidential Action
President signs, vetoes, or allows the bill to become a law without signing. Vetoed bill returns to Congress. Veto may be overridden by two-thirds majority vote of each house.

 Floor Action
Bill is debated, then passed or defeated. If passed, the bill goes to Senate. If the bill has already passed through Senate, the bill goes to Conference Committee.

 Committee Action
Bill referred to standing committee. Moves to subcommittee for study, hearings, revisions, approval. Moves back to full committee for more hearings and revisions. Moves to Rules Committee to set conditions for debate and amendments.

 Introduction
Bill introduced in House

Start: House

Section 8. Powers of Congress
The Congress shall have Power

1. To lay and collect Taxes, Duties, Imposts and Excises to pay the Debts and provide for the common Defence and general Welfare of the United States; but all Duties, Imposts and Excises, shall be uniform throughout the United States;

2. To borrow Money on the credit of the United States;

3. To regulate Commerce with foreign Nations, and among the several States, and with the Indian Tribes;

4. To establish an uniform Rule of Naturalization, and uniform Laws on the subject of Bankruptcies throughout the United States;

5. To coin Money, regulate the Value thereof, and of foreign Coin, and fix the Standard of Weights and Measures;

6. To provide for the Punishment of counterfeiting the Securities and current Coin of the United States;

7. To establish Post Offices and post Roads;

8. To promote the Progress of Science and useful Arts, by securing for limited Times to Authors and Inventors the exclusive Right to their respective Writings and Discoveries;

9. To constitute Tribunals inferior to the supreme Court;

10. To define and punish Piracies and Felonies committed on the high Seas, and Offences against the Law of Nations;

Commentary

◀ **Section 8** The Constitution is our social contract in which the people consent to the form and powers of government. An important part of the contract is the enumeration of legislative powers which sets the scope and limits of government authority over the people. Article I, Section 8, lists most of the expressed powers of Congress. Numbered from 1 to 18, these powers are also known as enumerated powers.

◀ **Clause 1** <u>Duties</u> are tariffs, or taxes on imports. Imposts are taxes in general. <u>Excises</u> are taxes on the production or sale of certain goods.

◀ **Clause 4** <u>Naturalization</u> is the process whereby a foreigner becomes a citizen. <u>Bankruptcy</u> is the condition in which a person or business cannot pay its debts. Congress has the power to pass laws on these two issues.

◀ **Clause 6** <u>Counterfeiting</u> is the making of imitation money. <u>Securities</u> are bonds. Congress can make laws to punish counterfeiters.

Commentary

Clause 11 ▶

Only Congress can declare war. Declarations of war are granted at the request of the President. <u>Letters of marque and reprisal</u> were documents issued by a government allowing merchant ships to arm themselves and attack ships of an enemy nation. They are no longer issued.

 Checkpoint

Which powers of Congress relate to taking in and spending money?

Clause 18 ▶

Congress has the power to make laws as needed to carry out the previous 17 clauses. It is sometimes known as the "Necessary and Proper Clause."

Clause 1 ▶

<u>Such persons</u> means slaves. In 1808, as soon as Congress was permitted to abolish the slave trade, it did so.

Clause 2 ▶

A <u>writ of habeas corpus</u> is a court order requiring government officials to bring a prisoner to court and explain why he or she is being held. A writ of habeas corpus protects people from unlawful imprisonment. The government cannot suspend this right except in times of rebellion or invasion.

11. To declare War, grant Letters of Marque and Reprisal, and make Rules concerning Captures on Land and Water;

12. To raise and support Armies, but no Appropriation of Money to that Use shall be for a longer Term than two Years;

13. To provide and maintain a Navy;

14. To make Rules for the Government and Regulation of the land and naval Forces;

15. To provide for calling forth the Militia to execute the Laws of the Union, suppress Insurrections and repel Invasions;

16. To provide for organizing, arming, and disciplining the Militia, and for governing such Part of them as may be employed in the Service of the United States, reserving to the States respectively, the Appointment of the Officers, and the Authority of training the Militia according to the discipline prescribed by Congress;

17. To exercise exclusive Legislation in all Cases whatsoever, over such District (not exceeding ten Miles square) as may, by Cession of Particular States, and the Acceptance of Congress, become the Seat of the Government of the United States, and to exercise like Authority over all Places purchased by the Consent of the Legislature of the State in which the Same shall be, for the Erection of Forts, Magazines, Arsenals, Dockyards and other needful Buildings;—And

18. To make all Laws which shall be necessary and proper for carrying into Execution the foregoing Powers and all other Powers vested by this Constitution in the Government of the United States, or in any Department or Officer thereof.

Section 9. Powers Denied to Congress

1. ~~The Migration or Importation of such Persons as any of the States now existing shall think proper to admit, shall not be prohibited by the Congress prior to the Year one thousand eight hundred and eight, but a Tax or duty may be imposed on such Importation, not exceeding ten dollars for each Person.~~

2. The Privilege of the Writ of Habeas Corpus shall not be suspended, unless when in Cases of Rebellion or Invasion the public Safety may require it.

3. No Bill of Attainder or ex post facto Law shall be passed.

4. No Capitation, ~~or other direct, Tax~~ shall be laid, unless in Proportion to the Census of Enumeration hereinbefore directed to be taken.

5. No Tax or Duty shall be laid on Articles exported from any State.

6. No Preference shall be given by any Regulation of Commerce or Revenue to the Ports of one State over those of another: nor shall Vessels bound to, or from, one State, be obliged to enter, clear or pay Duties in another.

7. No Money shall be drawn from the Treasury, but in Consequence of Appropriations made by Law; and a regular Statement and Account of the Receipts and Expenditures of all public Money shall be published from time to time.

8. No Title of Nobility shall be granted by the United States: And no Person holding any Office of Profit or Trust under them, shall, without the Consent of the Congress, accept of any present, Emolument, Office, or Title, of any kind whatever, from any King, Prince, or foreign State.

Section 10. Powers Denied to the States

1. No State shall enter into any Treaty, Alliance, or Confederation; grant Letters of Marque and Reprisal; coin Money; emit Bills of Credit; make any Thing but gold and silver Coin a Tender in Payment of Debts; pass any Bill of Attainder, ex post facto Law, or Law impairing the Obligation of Contracts, or grant any Title of Nobility.

Commentary

◄ **Clause 3** A <u>bill of attainder</u> is a law declaring that a person is guilty of a particular crime without a trial. An <u>ex post facto</u> law punishes an act which was not illegal when it was committed.

◄ **Clause 1** The writers of the Constitution did not want the states to act like separate nations, so they prohibited states from making treaties or coining money. Some powers denied to the federal government are also denied to the states.

The Federal System

Powers of the National Government
• Regulate interstate and foreign trade
• Declare war
• Create and maintain armed forces
• Establish foreign policy
• Create federal courts
• Make copyright and patent laws
• Establish postal offices
• Coin money
• Set standard weights and measures
• Admit new states

Concurrent Powers
• Provide for public welfare
• Administer criminal justice
• Charter banks and borrow money
• Levy and collect taxes
• Borrow money

Powers Reserved to the States
• Regulate trade within state
• Maintain schools
• Establish local governments
• Make laws about marriage and divorce
• Conduct elections
• Provide for public safety
• Create corporation law

Commentary

Clauses 2, 3 ▶
Powers listed here are forbidden to the states, but Congress can pass laws that give these powers to the states. Clause 2 forbids states from taxing imports and exports without the consent of Congress.

Clause 3 ▶
This clause forbids states from keeping an army or navy without the consent of Congress. States cannot make treaties or declare war unless an enemy invades or is about to invade.

Clauses 2, 3 ▶
Some writers of the Constitution were afraid to allow the people to elect the President directly. Therefore, the Constitutional Convention set up the electoral college. Clause 2 directs each state to choose <u>electors</u>, or delegates to the electoral college, to vote for President. A state's electoral vote is equal to the combined number of senators and representatives. Each state may decide how to choose its electors. Members of Congress and federal officeholders may not serve as electors. This part of the original electoral college system is still in effect.

Clause 3 ▶
This clause called upon each elector to vote for two candidates. The candidate who received a majority of the electoral votes would become President. The runner-up would become Vice President. If no candidate won a majority, the House

2. No State shall, without the Consent of the Congress, lay any Imposts or Duties on Imports or Exports, except what may be absolutely necessary for executing its inspection Laws; and the net Produce of all Duties and Imposts, laid by any State on Imports or Exports, shall be for the Use of the Treasury of the United States; and all such Laws shall be subject to the Revision and Control of the Congress.

3. No State shall, without the Consent of Congress, lay any Duty of Tonnage, keep Troops, or Ships of War in time of Peace, enter into any Agreement or Compact with another State, or with a foreign Power, or engage in War, unless actually invaded, or in such imminent Danger as will not admit of delay.

Article II Executive Branch

Section 1. President and Vice President

1. The executive Power shall be vested in a President of the United States of America. He shall hold his Office during the Term of four Years, and, together with the Vice President, chosen for the same Term, be elected as follows:

2. Each State shall appoint, in such Manner as the Legislature thereof may direct, a Number of Electors, equal to the whole Number of Senators and Representatives to which the State may be entitled in the Congress: but no Senator or Representative, or Person holding an Office of Trust or Profit, under the United States, shall be appointed an Elector.

3. ~~The Electors shall meet in their respective States, and vote by Ballot for two Persons, of whom one at least shall not be an Inhabitant of the same State with themselves. And they shall make a List of all the Persons voted for, and of the Number of Votes for each; which List they shall sign and certify, and transmit sealed to the Seat of the Government of the United States, directed to the President of the Senate. The President of the Senate shall, in the Presence of the Senate and House of Representatives, open all the Certificates, and the Votes shall then be counted. The Person having the greatest Number of Votes shall be the President, if such Number be a majority of the whole Number of Electors appointed; and if there be more than one who have such Majority, and have an equal Number of Votes, then, the House of Representatives shall immediately choose by Ballot one of them for President; and if no Person have a Majority, then from the five highest on the List the said House shall in like Manner choose the President. But in choosing the President, the Votes shall be taken by States, the Representatives from each State having one Vote; a quorum for this Purpose shall consist of a Member or Members from two thirds of the States, and a Majority of~~

~~all the States shall be necessary to a Choice. In every Case, after the~~
~~Choice of the President, the Person having the greatest Number of~~
~~Votes of the Electors shall be the Vice President. But if there should~~
~~remain two or more who have equal Votes, the Senate shall choose~~
~~from them by Ballot the Vice President.~~

4. The Congress may determine the Time of choosing the Electors, and the Day on which they shall give their Votes; which Day shall be the same throughout the United States.

5. No Person except a natural born Citizen, or a Citizen of the United States, at the time of the Adoption of this Constitution, shall be eligible to the Office of President; neither shall any person be eligible to that Office who shall not have attained to the Age of thirty-five Years, and been fourteen Years a Resident within the United States.

6. ~~In Case of the Removal of the President from Office, or of his Death, Resignation, or Inability to discharge the Powers and Duties of the said Office, the Same shall devolve on the Vice President,~~ and the Congress may by Law provide for the Case of Removal, Death, Resignation or Inability, both of the President and Vice President, declaring what Officer shall then act as President, and such Officer shall act accordingly, until the Disability be removed, or a President shall be elected.

7. The President shall, at stated Times, receive for his Services, a Compensation, which shall neither be increased nor diminished during the Period for which he shall have been elected, and he shall not receive within that Period any other Emolument from the United States, or any of them.

8. Before he enter on the Execution of his Office, he shall take the following Oath or Affirmation:

"I do solemnly swear (or affirm) that I will faithfully execute the Office of President of the United States, and will to the best of my Ability, preserve, protect and defend the Constitution of the United States."

Section 2. Powers of the President

1. The President shall be Commander in Chief of the Army and Navy of the United States, and of the Militia of the several States, when called into the actual Service of the United States; he may require the Opinion, in writing, of the principal Officer in each of the executive Departments, upon any Subject relating to the Duties of their respective Offices, and he shall have Power to Grant Reprieves and Pardons for Offences against the United States, except in Cases of Impeachment.

Commentary

would choose the President. The Senate would choose the Vice President. The election of 1800, however, ended in a tie in the electoral college between Thomas Jefferson and Aaron Burr. The Twelfth Amendment changed the electoral college system so that this could not happen again.

 Checkpoint

Who may become President?

◀ **Clause 6** The powers of the President pass to the Vice President if the President leaves office or cannot discharge his or her duties. The Twenty-fifth Amendment clarifies this clause.

◀ **Clause 7** The President is paid a salary. It cannot be raised or lowered during his or her term in office. The President is not allowed to hold any other state or federal position while in office.

◀ **Clause 1** The President is the head of the armed forces and the state militias when they are called into national service. The military is under <u>civilian</u>, or nonmilitary, control. The President has the power to grant a <u>reprieve</u>, or pardon. A reprieve suspends punishment. A <u>pardon</u> prevents prosecution for a crime or overrides the judgment of a court.

Commentary

Clause 2 ▶
The President has the power to make treaties with other nations. Under the system of checks and balances, all treaties must be approved by two thirds of the Senate. The President has the power to appoint ambassadors to foreign countries and to appoint other high officials. The Senate must confirm, or approve, these appointments.

Section 4 ▶
Civil officers include federal judges and members of the Cabinet. High crimes are major crimes. Misdemeanors are lesser crimes. The President, Vice President, and others can be forced out of office if impeached and found guilty of certain crimes.

2. He shall have Power, by and with the Advice and Consent of the Senate, to make Treaties, provided two thirds of the Senators present concur; and he shall nominate, and by and with the Advice and Consent of the Senate, shall appoint Ambassadors, other public Ministers and Consuls, Judges of the supreme Court, and all other Officers of the United States, whose Appointments are not herein otherwise provided for, and which shall be established by Law: but the Congress may by Law vest the Appointment of such inferior Officers, as they think proper, in the President alone, in the Courts of Law, or in the Heads of Departments.

3. The President shall have Power to fill up all Vacancies that may happen during the Recess of the Senate, by granting Commissions which shall expire at the End of their next Session.

Section 3. Duties of the President

He shall from time to time give to the Congress Information of the State of the Union, and recommend to their Consideration such Measures as he shall judge necessary and expedient; he may, on extraordinary Occasions, convene both Houses, or either of them, and in Case of Disagreement between them, with Respect to the Time of Adjournment, he may adjourn them to such Time as he shall think proper; he shall receive Ambassadors and other public Ministers; he shall take Care that the Laws be faithfully executed, and shall Commission all the Officers of the United States.

Section 4. Impeachment

The President, Vice President and all Civil Officers of the United States, shall be removed from Office on Impeachment for and Conviction of, Treason, Bribery, or other high Crimes and Misdemeanors.

Article III Judicial Branch

Section 1. Courts, Terms of Office

The judicial Power of the United States, shall be vested in one supreme Court, and in such inferior Courts as the Congress may from time to time ordain and establish. The Judges, both of the supreme and inferior Courts, shall hold their Offices during good Behavior, and shall, at stated Times, receive for their Services, a Compensation, which shall not be diminished during their Continuance in Office.

Section 2. Jurisdiction

1. The judicial Power shall extend to all Cases, in Law and Equity, arising under this Constitution, the Laws of the United States, and Treaties made, or which shall be made, under their Authority;— to all Cases affecting Ambassadors, other public Ministers, and Consuls;— to all Cases of Admiralty and maritime Jurisdiction;— to Controversies to which the United States shall be a Party;— to Controversies between two or more States;— ~~between a State and Citizens of another State~~;— between Citizens of different States;— between Citizens of the same State claiming Lands under Grants of different States, and between a State, or the Citizens thereof, and foreign States, Citizens, or Subjects.

2. In all Cases affecting Ambassadors, other public Ministers and Consuls, and those in which a State shall be a Party, the supreme Court shall have original Jurisdiction. In all the other Cases before mentioned, the supreme Court shall have appellate Jurisdiction, both as to Law and Fact, with such Exceptions, and under such Regulations as the Congress shall make.

3. The trial of all Crimes, except in Cases of Impeachment, shall be by Jury; and such Trial shall be held in the State where the said Crimes shall have been committed; but when not committed within any State, the Trial shall be at such Place or Places as the Congress may by Law have directed.

Commentary

◀ **Clause 1** <u>Jurisdiction</u> refers to the right of a court to hear a case. Federal courts have jurisdiction over cases that involve the Constitution, federal laws, treaties, foreign ambassadors and diplomats, naval and maritime laws, disagreements between states or between citizens from different states, and disputes between a state or citizen and a foreign state or citizen.

◀ **Clause 2** <u>Original jurisdiction</u> means the power of a court to hear a case when it first arises. The Supreme Court has original jurisdiction over only a few cases, such as those involving foreign diplomats. More often, the Supreme Court acts as an <u>appellate court</u>. An appellate court considers whether the trial judge made errors during the trial or incorrectly interpreted or applied the law in reaching a decision.

Checks and Balances

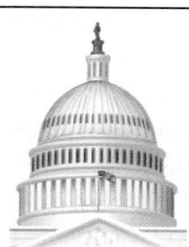

Courts may declare acts of Congress to be unconstitutional.

Congress creates lower courts and may remove judges through impeachment; Senate approves or rejects appointment of judges.

Judicial Branch
Interprets the law

Judges are appointed for life, free from executive control; courts may declare executive actions to be unconstitutional.

President appoints Supreme Court justices and other federal judges.

President may veto legislation, call special sessions, recommend legislation and appeal to the people.

Legislative Branch
Makes the law

Congress makes laws, creates agencies and programs, and appropriates funds to carry out laws and programs; it may override veto with two-thirds vote and may remove President through impeachment; Senate approves treaties and presidential appointments.

Executive Branch
Carries out the law

Commentary

 Checkpoint

How does the Constitution define treason?

Clause 2 ▶

The act of returning a suspected criminal or escaped prisoner to a state where he or she is wanted is called extradition. State governors must return a suspect to another state. However, the Supreme Court has ruled that a governor cannot be forced to do so if he or she feels that justice will not be done.

Clause 3 ▶

Persons held to service or labor refers to slaves or indentured servants. The Thirteenth Amendment replaces this clause.

Clause 1 ▶

Congress has the power to admit new states to the Union. Existing states cannot be split up or joined together to form new states unless both Congress and the state legislatures approve. New states are equal to all other states.

Section 3. Treason

1. Treason against the United States shall consist only in levying War against them, or in adhering to their Enemies, giving them Aid and Comfort. No Person shall be convicted of Treason unless on the Testimony of two Witnesses to the same overt Act, or on Confession in open Court.

2. The Congress shall have Power to declare the Punishment of Treason, but no Attainder of Treason shall work Corruption of Blood, or Forfeiture except during the Life of the Person attainted.

Article IV Relations Among the States

Section 1. Full Faith and Credit

Full Faith and Credit shall be given in each State to the public Acts, Records, and judicial Proceedings of every other State. And the Congress may by general Laws prescribe the Manner in which such Acts, Records and Proceedings shall be proved, and the Effect thereof.

Section 2. Privileges and Immunities of Citizens

1. The Citizens of each State shall be entitled to all Privileges and Immunities of Citizens in the several States.

2. A Person charged in any State with Treason, Felony, or other Crime, who shall flee from justice, and be found in another State, shall on Demand of the executive Authority of the State from which he fled, be delivered up, to be removed to the State having Jurisdiction of the Crime.

3. ~~No Person held to Service or Labor in one State, under the Laws thereof, escaping into another, shall, in Consequence of any Law or Regulation therein, be discharged from Service or Labor, but shall be delivered up on Claim of the Party to whom such Service or Labor may be due.~~

Section 3. New States and Territories

1. New States may be admitted by the Congress into this Union; but no new State shall be formed or erected within the Jurisdiction of any other State; nor any State be formed by the Junction of two or more States, or Parts of States, without the Consent of the Legislatures of the States concerned as well as of the Congress.

2. The Congress shall have Power to dispose of and make all needful Rules and Regulations respecting the Territory or other Property belonging to the United States; and nothing in this Constitution shall be so construed as to Prejudice any Claims of the United States, or of any particular State.

Section 4. Protection Afforded to the States by the Nation

The United States shall guarantee to every State in this Union a Republican Form of Government, and shall protect each of them against Invasion; and on Application of the Legislature, or of the Executive (when the Legislature cannot be convened) against domestic Violence.

Article V Provision for Amendments

The Congress, whenever two thirds of both Houses shall deem it necessary, shall propose Amendments to this Constitution, or, on the Application of the Legislatures of two thirds of the several States, shall call a Convention for proposing Amendments, which, in either Case, shall be valid to all Intents and Purposes, as Part of this Constitution, when ratified by the Legislatures of three fourths of the several States, or by Conventions in three fourths thereof, as the one or the other Mode of Ratification may be proposed by the Congress; Provided that no Amendment which may be made prior to the Year One thousand eight hundred and eight shall in any Manner affect the first and fourth Clauses in the Ninth section of the first Article; and that no State, without its Consent, shall be deprived of its equal Suffrage in the Senate.

Article VI National Debts, Supremacy of National Law, Oath

Section 1.

All Debts contracted and Engagements entered into, before the Adoption of this Constitution, shall be as valid against the United States under this Constitution, as under the Confederation.

Section 2.

This Constitution, and the Laws of the United States which shall be made in Pursuance thereof; and all Treaties made, or which shall be made, under the Authority of the United States, shall be the supreme Law of the Land; and the Judges in every State shall be bound thereby, anything in the constitution or Laws of any State to the Contrary notwithstanding.

Commentary

◀ **Article V** The Constitution can be amended, or changed, if necessary. An amendment can be proposed by (1) a two-thirds vote of both houses of Congress or (2) a national convention called by Congress at the request of two thirds of the state legislatures. (This second method has never been used.) An amendment must be ratified, or approved, by (1) three fourths of the state legislatures or (2) special conventions in three fourths of the states. Congress decides which method will be used.

◀ **Section 2** The "supremacy clause" in this section establishes the Constitution, federal laws, and treaties that the Senate has ratified as the supreme, or highest, law of the land. Thus, they outweigh state laws. A state judge must overturn a state law that conflicts with the Constitution or with a federal law.

Article VII ▶

During 1787 and 1788, states held special conventions. By October 1788, the required nine states had ratified the United States Constitution.

 Checkpoint

What had to happen before the Constitution would go into effect?

Section 3.

The Senators and Representatives before mentioned, and the Members of the several State legislatures, and all executive and judicial Officers, both of the United States and of the several States, shall be bound by Oath or Affirmation, to support this Constitution; but no religious Test shall ever be required as a Qualification to any Office or public Trust under the the United States.

Article VII Ratification of Constitution

The ratification of the Conventions of nine States, shall be sufficient for the Establishment of this Constitution between the States so ratifying the same.

Done in Convention by the Unanimous Consent of the States present the Seventeenth Day of September in the Year of our Lord one thousand seven hundred and Eighty seven and of the Independence of the United States of America the twelfth. In witness whereof We have hereunto subscribed our Names.

Attest: William Jackson, SECRETARY
George Washington, PRESIDENT and deputy from Virginia

New Hampshire
John Langdon
Nicholas Gilman

Massachusetts
Nathaniel Gorham
Rufus King

Connecticut
William Samuel Johnson
Roger Sherman

New York
Alexander Hamilton

New Jersey
William Livingston
David Brearley
William Paterson
Jonathan Dayton

Pennsylvania
Benjamin Franklin
Thomas Mifflin
Robert Morris
George Clymer
Thomas Fitzsimons
Jared Ingersoll
James Wilson
Gouverneur Morris

Delaware
George Read
Gunning Bedford, Jr.
John Dickinson
Richard Bassett
Jacob Broom

Maryland
James McHenry
Dan of St. Thomas Jenifer
Daniel Carroll

Virginia
John Blair
James Madison, Jr.

North Carolina
William Blount
Richard Dobbs Spaight
Hugh Williamson

South Carolina
John Rutledge
Charles Cotesworth Pinckney
Charles Pinckney
Pierce Butler

Georgia
William Few
Abraham Baldwin

AMENDMENTS

First Amendment Freedom of Religion, Speech, Press, Assembly, and Petition

Congress shall make no law respecting an establishment of religion, or prohibiting the free exercise thereof, or abridging the freedom of speech, or of the press; or the right of the people peaceably to assemble, and to petition the Government for a redress of grievances.

Second Amendment Bearing Arms

A well-regulated Militia being necessary to the security of a free State, the right of the people to keep and bear Arms, shall not be infringed.

Third Amendment Quartering of Troops

No Soldier shall, in time of peace be quartered in any house, without the consent of the Owner, nor, in time of war, but in a manner to be prescribed by law.

Commentary

The Amendments The Amendments are changes made to the Constitution, which has been amended 27 times since it was originally ratified in 1788. The first 10 amendments are referred to as the Bill of Rights.

◀ **First Amendment** The First Amendment protects five basic rights: freedom of religion, speech, the press, assembly, and petition. Congress cannot set up an established, or official, church or religion for the nation, nor can it forbid the practice of religion.

Congress may not <u>abridge</u>, or limit, the freedom to speak or write freely. The government may not censor, or review, books and newspapers before they are printed. This amendment also protects the right to assemble, or hold public meetings. <u>Petition</u> means ask. <u>Redress</u> means to correct. <u>Grievances</u> are wrongs. The people have the right to ask the government for wrongs to be corrected.

◀ **Second Amendment** The Supreme Court decision in the case of *District of Columbia* v. *Heller* in 2008 ruled that a ban on handguns in the District of Columbia violated the Second Amendment. This is the first case since *U.S.* v. *Miller* in which the Court moved to interpret the Second Amendment.

◀ **Third Amendment** In colonial times, the British could quarter, or house, soldiers in private homes without permission of the owners. The Third Amendment prevents such abuses.

Commentary

Fourth Amendment ▶

This amendment protects Americans from unreasonable searches and seizures. Search and seizure are permitted only if a judge issues a <u>warrant</u>, or written court order. A warrant is issued only if there is probable cause. This means an officer must show that it is probable, or likely, that the search will produce evidence of a crime.

Fifth Amendment ▶

This amendment protects the rights of the accused. <u>Capital crimes</u> are those that can be punished with death. <u>Infamous crimes</u> are those that can be punished with prison or loss of rights. The federal government must obtain an <u>indictment</u>, or formal accusation, from a <u>grand jury</u> to prosecute anyone for such crimes. A grand jury is a panel of between 12 and 23 citizens who decide if the government has enough evidence to justify a trial.

    <u>Double jeopardy</u> is forbidden by this amendment. This means that a person cannot be tried twice for the same crime. However, if a court sets aside a conviction because of a legal error, the accused can be tried again. A person on trial cannot be forced to <u>testify</u>, or give evidence, against himself or herself. A person accused of a crime is entitled to <u>due process of law</u>, or a fair hearing or trial.

    The government cannot seize private property for public use without paying the owner a fair price for it.

Fourth Amendment Searches and Seizures

The right of the people to be secure in their persons, houses, papers, and effects, against unreasonable searches and seizures, shall not be violated, and no Warrants shall issue, but upon probable cause, supported by Oath or affirmation, and particularly describing the place to be searched, and the persons or things to be seized.

Fifth Amendment Criminal Proceedings; Due Process; Eminent Domain

No person shall be held to answer for a capital, or otherwise infamous crime, unless on a presentment or indictment of a Grand Jury, except in cases arising in the land or naval forces, or in the Militia, when in actual service in time of War or public danger; nor shall any person be subject for the same offence to be twice put in jeopardy of life or limb; nor shall be compelled in any criminal case to be a witness against himself, nor be deprived of life, liberty, or property, without due process of law; nor shall private property be taken for public use, without just compensation.

Sixth Amendment Criminal Proceedings

In all criminal prosecutions, the accused shall enjoy the right to a speedy and public trial, by an impartial jury of the State and district wherein the crime shall have been committed, which district shall have been previously ascertained by law, and to be informed of the nature and cause of the accusation; to be confronted with the witnesses against him; to have compulsory process for obtaining witnesses in his favor, and to have the Assistance of Counsel for his defence.

Seventh Amendment Civil Trials

In Suits at common law, where the value in controversy shall exceed twenty dollars, the right of trial by jury shall be preserved, and no fact tried by a jury, shall be otherwise re-examined in any Court of the United States, than according to the rules of the common law.

Eighth Amendment Punishment for Crimes

Excessive bail shall not be required, nor excessive fines imposed, nor cruel and unusual punishment inflicted.

Ninth Amendment Unenumerated Rights

The enumeration in the Constitution, of certain rights, shall not be construed to deny or disparage others retained by the people.

Tenth Amendment Powers Reserved to the States

The powers not delegated to the United States by the Constitution, nor prohibited by it to the States, are reserved to the States respectively, or to the people.

Commentary

◀ **Sixth Amendment** In criminal cases, the jury must be impartial, or not favor either side. The accused is guaranteed the right to a trial by jury. The trial must be speedy. The accused must be told the charges and be allowed to question all witnesses. The accused must be allowed a lawyer.

◀ **Seventh Amendment** Common law refers to rules of law established by judges in past cases. An appeals court can set aside a verdict only if legal errors make the trial unfair.

◀ **Eighth Amendment** <u>Bail</u> is money that the accused leaves with the court as a pledge to appear for trial. If the accused does not appear, the court keeps the money. This amendment prevents the court from imposing bail or fines that are <u>excessive</u>, or too high. The amendment also forbids cruel and unusual punishments, such as physical torture.

◀ **Ninth Amendment** The rights of the people are not limited to those listed in the Bill of Rights. In the Ninth Amendment, the government is prevented from claiming these are the only rights people have.

◀ **Tenth Amendment** Powers not given to the federal government belong to the states. Powers reserved to the states are not listed in the Constitution.

Commentary

Eleventh Amendment ▶
A private citizen from one state cannot sue the government of another state in federal court. However, a citizen can sue a state government in a state court.

Twelfth Amendment ▶
This amendment changed the way the electoral college voted as outlined in Article II, Section 1, Clause 3. This amendment provides that each elector choose one candidate for President and one candidate for Vice President. If no candidate for President receives a majority of electoral votes, the House of Representatives chooses the President. If no candidate for Vice President receives a majority, the Senate elects the Vice President. The Vice President must be a person who is eligible to be President.

It is possible for a candidate to win the popular vote and lose the electoral college. This happened in 1888 and 2000.

Eleventh Amendment Suits Against States

The Judicial power of the United States shall not be construed to extend to any suit in law or equity, commenced or prosecuted against one of the United States by Citizens of another State, or by Citizens or Subjects of any Foreign State.

Twelfth Amendment Election of President and Vice President

The Electors shall meet in their respective States and vote by ballot for President and Vice President, one of whom, at least, shall not be an inhabitant of the same State with themselves; they shall name in their ballots the person voted for as President, and in distinct ballots the person voted for as Vice President, and they shall make distinct lists of all persons voted for as President, and of all persons voted for as Vice President, and of the number of votes for each, which lists they shall sign and certify, and transmit sealed to the seat of the government of the United States, directed to the President of the Senate;— The President of the Senate shall, in the presence of the Senate and the House of Representatives, open all the certificates and the votes shall then be counted;— the person having the greatest Number of votes for President shall be the President, if such number be a majority of the whole number of Electors appointed; and if no person have such a majority, then, from the persons having the highest numbers not exceeding three on the list of those voted for as President, the House of Representatives shall choose immediately, by ballot, the President. But in choosing the President, the votes shall be taken by States, the representation from each State having one vote; a quorum for this purpose shall consist of a member or members from two thirds of the States, and a majority of the States shall be necessary to a choice. ~~And if the House of Representatives shall not choose a President whenever the right of choice shall devolve upon them, before the fourth day of March next following, then the Vice President shall act as President, as in case of death or other constitutional disability of the President.~~ The person having the greatest number of votes as Vice President, shall be the Vice President, if such number be a majority of the whole number of Electors appointed, and if no person have a majority, then from the two highest numbers on the list, the Senate shall choose the Vice President; a quorum for the purpose shall consist of two thirds of the whole number of Senators, a majority of the whole number shall be necessary to a choice. But no person constitutionally ineligible to the office of President shall be eligible to that of Vice President of the United States.

Thirteenth Amendment Slavery and Involuntary Servitude

Section 1. Neither slavery nor involuntary servitude, except as a punishment for crime whereof the party shall have been duly convicted, shall exist within the United States, or any place subject to their jurisdiction.

Section 2. Congress shall have power to enforce this article by appropriate legislation.

Fourteenth Amendment Rights of Citizens

Section 1. All persons born or naturalized in the United States and subject to the jurisdiction thereof, are citizens of the United States and of the State wherein they reside. No State shall make or enforce any law which shall abridge the privileges or immunities of citizens of the United States; nor shall any State deprive any person of life, liberty, or property, without due process of law; nor deny to any person within its jurisdiction the equal protection of the laws.

Section 2. Representatives shall be apportioned among the several States according to their respective numbers, counting the whole number of persons in each State, excluding Indians not taxed. But when the right to vote at any election for the choice of electors for President and Vice President of the United States, Representatives in Congress, the Executive and Judicial officers of a State, or the members of the Legislature thereof, is denied to any of the male inhabitants of such State, being twenty-one years of age, and citizens of the United States, or in any way abridged, except for participation in rebellion, or other crime, the basis of representation therein shall be reduced in the proportion which the number of such male citizens shall bear to the whole number of male citizens twenty-one years of age in such State.

Section 3. No person shall be a Senator or Representative in Congress, or elector of President and Vice President, or hold any office, civil or military, under the United States, or under any State, who, having previously taken an oath, as a member of Congress, or as an officer of the United States, or as a member of any State legislature, or as an executive or judicial officer of any State, to support the Constitution of the United States, shall have engaged in insurrection or rebellion against the same, or given aid or comfort to the enemies thereof. But Congress may, by a vote of two thirds of each House, remove such disability.

Commentary

◄ **Thirteenth Amendment**
The Emancipation Proclamation (1863) freed slaves only in areas controlled by the Confederacy. This amendment freed all slaves. It also forbids involuntary servitude, or labor done against one's will. However, it does not prevent prison wardens from making prisoners work. Congress can pass laws to carry out this amendment.

◄ **Fourteenth Amendment, Section 1** This amendment defines citizenship for the first time in the Constitution. It was intended to protect the rights of the freed slaves by guaranteeing all citizens "equal protection under the law."

◄ **Fourteenth Amendment, Section 2** This section replaced the three-fifths clause. It provides that representation in the House of Representatives is decided on the basis of the number of people in the states. It also provides that states that deny the vote to male citizens aged 21 or over will be punished by losing part of their representation. This provision has never been enforced.

✓ **Checkpoint**

What is one key provision of the Fourteenth Amendment?

Commentary

Fifteenth Amendment, ▶
Section 1 This amendment gave African Americans the right to vote. In the late 1800s, however, southern states used grandfather clauses, literacy tests, and poll taxes to keep African Americans from voting.

Fifteenth Amendment, ▶
Section 2 Congress can pass laws to carry out this amendment. The Twenty-fourth Amendment barred the use of poll taxes in national elections. The Voting Rights Act of 1965 gave federal officials the power to register voters where there was voting discrimination.

Sixteenth Amendment ▶
Congress has the power to collect taxes on people's income. An income tax can be collected without regard to a state's population. This amendment changed Article I, Section 9, Clause 4.

Section 4. The validity of the public debt of the United States, authorized by law, including debts incurred for payment of pensions and bounties for services in suppressing insurrection or rebellion, shall not be questioned. But neither the United States nor any State shall assume or pay any debt or obligation incurred in aid of insurrection or rebellion against the United States, or any claim for the loss or emancipation of any slave; but all such debts, obligations and claims shall be held illegal and void.

Section 5. The Congress shall have power to enforce, by appropriate legislation, the provisions of this article.

Fifteenth Amendment Right to Vote—Race, Color, Servitude

Section 1. The right of citizens of the United States to vote shall not be denied or abridged by the United States or by any State on account of race, color, or previous condition of servitude.

Section 2. The Congress shall have power to enforce this article by appropriate legislation.

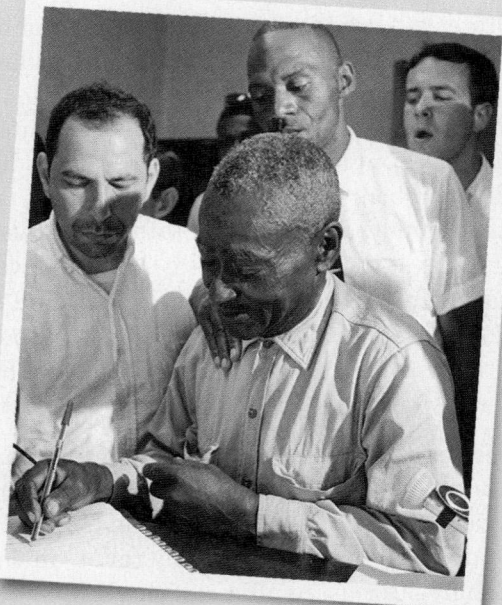

Sixteenth Amendment Income Tax

The Congress shall have power to lay and collect taxes on incomes, from whatever source derived, without apportionment among the several States, and without regard to any census or enumeration.

Seventeenth Amendment Popular Election of Senators

Section 1. The Senate of the United States shall be composed of two Senators from each State, elected by the people thereof, for six years; and each Senator shall have one vote. The electors in each State shall have the qualifications requisite for electors of the most numerous branch of the State legislatures.

Section 2. When vacancies happen in the representation of any State in the Senate, the executive authority of such State shall issue writs of election to fill such vacancies: *Provided,* That the legislature of any State may empower the executive thereof to make temporary appointments until the people fill the vacancies by election as the legislature may direct.

Section 3. ~~This amendment shall not be so construed as to affect the election or term of any Senator chosen before it becomes valid as part of the Constitution.~~

Eighteenth Amendment Prohibition of Alcoholic Beverages

Section 1. ~~After one year from the ratification of this article the manufacture, sale, or transportation of intoxicating liquors within, the importation thereof into, or the exportation thereof from the United States and all territory subject to the jurisdiction thereof for beverage purposes is hereby prohibited.~~

Section 2. ~~The Congress and the several States shall have concurrent power to enforce this article by appropriate legislation.~~

Section 3. ~~This article shall be inoperative unless it shall have been ratified as an amendment to the Constitution by the legislatures of the several States, as provided in the Constitution, within seven years of the date of the submission hereof to the States by Congress.~~

Nineteenth Amendment Women's Suffrage

Section 1. The right of citizens of the United States to vote shall not be denied or abridged by the United States or by any State on account of sex.

Section 2. Congress shall have power to enforce this article by appropriate legislation.

Commentary

◄ **Seventeenth Amendment**
This amendment replaced Article I, Section 3, Clause 2. Before it was adopted, state legislatures chose senators. This amendment provides that senators are elected directly by the people of each state.

◄ **Eighteenth Amendment**
This amendment, known as Prohibition, banned the making, selling, or transporting of alcoholic beverages in the United States. Later, the Twenty-first Amendment repealed, or canceled, this amendment.

◄ **Nineteenth Amendment**
Neither the federal government nor state governments can deny the right to vote on account of sex.

Twentieth Amendment, ▶
Section 1 The date for the inauguration of the President was changed to January 20, and the date for Congress to begin its term changed to January 3. Prior to this amendment, the beginning-of-term date was set in March. The outgoing officials with little or no influence on matters were not effective in office. Being so inactive, they were called "lame ducks."

Twentieth Amendment, ▶
Section 3 If the President-elect dies before taking office, the Vice President-elect becomes President. If no President has been chosen by January 20 or if the elected candidate fails to qualify for office, the Vice President-elect acts as President, but only until a qualified President is chosen. Finally, Congress has the power to choose a person to act as President if neither the President-elect nor the Vice President-elect is qualified to take office.

Twenty-first Amendment, ▶
Section 1 The Eighteenth Amendment is repealed, making it legal to make and sell alcoholic beverages. Prohibition ended on December 5, 1933.

Twentieth Amendment Presidential Terms; Sessions of Congress

Section 1. The terms of the President and Vice President shall end at noon on the 20th day of January, and the terms of Senators and Representatives at noon on the 3d day of January, of the years in which such terms would have ended if this article had not been ratified; and the terms of their successors shall then begin.

Section 2. The Congress shall assemble at least once in every year, and such meeting shall begin at noon on the 3d day of January, unless they shall by law appoint a different day.

Section 3. If, at the time fixed for the beginning of the term of the President, the President elect shall have died, the Vice President elect shall become President. If a President shall not have been chosen before the time fixed for the beginning of his term, or if the President elect shall have failed to qualify, then the Vice President elect shall act as President until a President shall have qualified; and the Congress may by law provide for the case wherein neither a President elect nor a Vice President elect shall have qualified, declaring who shall then act as President, or the manner in which one who is to act shall be selected, and such person shall act accordingly until a President or Vice President shall have qualified.

Section 4. The Congress may by law provide for the case of the death of any of the persons from whom the House of Representatives may choose a President whenever the right of choice shall have devolved upon them, and for the case of the death of any of the persons from whom the Senate may choose a Vice President whenever the right of choice shall have devolved upon them.

Section 5. ~~Sections 1 and 2 shall take effect on the 15th day of October following the ratification of this article.~~

Section 6. This article shall be inoperative unless it shall have been ratified as an amendment to the Constitution by the legislatures of three fourths of the several States within seven years from the date of its submission.

Twenty-first Amendment Repeal of Prohibition

Section 1. The eighteenth article of amendment to the Constitution of the United States is hereby repealed.

Section 2. The transportation or importation into any State, Territory, or possession of the United States for delivery or use therein of intoxicating liquors, in violation of the laws thereof, is hereby prohibited.

Section 3. ~~This article shall be inoperative unless it shall have been ratified as an amendment to the Constitution by conventions in the several States, as provided in the Constitution, within seven years from the date of the submission hereof to the States by the Congress.~~

Twenty-second Amendment Presidential Tenure

Section 1. No person shall be elected to the office of the President more than twice, and no person who has held the office of President, or acted as President, for more than two years of a term to which some other person was elected President shall be elected to the office of the President more than once. ~~But this Article shall not apply to any person holding the office of President, when this Article was proposed by the Congress, and shall not prevent any person who may be holding the office of President, or acting as President, during the term within which this Article becomes operative from holding the office of President or acting as President during the remainder of such term.~~

Section 2. ~~This article shall be inoperative unless it shall have been ratified as an amendment to the Constitution by the legislatures of three-fourths of the several states within seven years from the date of its submission to the States by the Congress.~~

Twenty-third Amendment Presidential Electors for The District of Columbia

Section 1. The District constituting the seat of Government of the United States shall appoint in such manner as the Congress may direct:

A number of electors of President and Vice President equal to the whole number of Senators and Representatives in Congress to which the District would be entitled if it were a State, but in no event more than the least populous State; they shall be in addition to those appointed by the States, they shall be considered, for the purposes of the election of President and Vice President, to be electors appointed by a State; and they shall meet in the District and perform such duties as provided by the twelfth article of amendment.

Section 2. The Congress shall have power to enforce this article by appropriate legislation.

Commentary

◀ **Twenty-second Amendment, Section 1** This amendment provides that no President may serve more than two terms. A President who has already served more than half of someone else's term can serve only one more full term. Before Franklin Roosevelt became President, no President served more than two terms in office. Roosevelt broke with this custom and was elected to four terms.

◀ **Twenty-third Amendment, Section 1** This amendment gives the residents of Washington, D.C., the right to vote in presidential elections. Until this amendment was adopted, people living in Washington, D.C., could not vote for President because the Constitution had made no provision for choosing electors from the nation's capital. Washington, D.C., has three electoral votes.

Commentary

Twenty-fourth Amendment, ▶
Section 1 A poll tax is a tax on voters. This amendment bans poll taxes in national elections. Some states used poll taxes to keep African Americans from voting. In 1966, the Supreme Court struck down poll taxes in state elections, also.

Twenty-fifth Amendment, ▶
Section 1 If the President dies or resigns, the Vice President becomes President. This section clarifies Article II, Section 1, Clause 6.

Twenty-fifth Amendment, ▶
Section 3 If the President declares in writing that he or she is unable to perform the duties of office, the Vice President serves as acting President until the President recovers.

Twenty-fifth Amendment, ▶
Section 4 Two Presidents, Woodrow Wilson and Dwight Eisenhower, fell gravely ill while in office. The Constitution contained no provision for this kind of emergency.

Twenty-fourth Amendment Right to Vote in Federal Elections

Section 1. The right of citizens of the United States to vote in any primary or other election for President or Vice President, for electors for President or Vice President, or for Senator or Representative in Congress, shall not be denied or abridged by the United States or any State by reason of failure to pay any poll tax or other tax.

Section 2. The Congress shall have power to enforce this article by appropriate legislation.

Twenty-fifth Amendment Presidential Succession; Vice Presidential Vacancy; Presidential Inability

Section 1. In case of the removal of the President from office or of his death or resignation, the Vice President shall become President.

Section 2. Whenever there is a vacancy in the office of the Vice President, the President shall nominate a Vice President who shall take office upon confirmation by a majority vote of both Houses of Congress.

Section 3. Whenever the President transmits to the President pro tempore of the Senate and the Speaker of the House of Representatives his written declaration that he is unable to discharge the powers and duties of his office, and until he transmits to them a written declaration to the contrary, such powers and duties shall be discharged by the Vice President as Acting President.

Section 4. Whenever the Vice President and a majority of either the principal officers of the executive departments or of such other body as Congress may by law provide, transmit to the President pro tempore of the Senate and the Speaker of the House of Representatives their written declaration that the President is unable to discharge the powers and duties of his office, the Vice President shall immediately assume the powers and duties of the office as Acting President.

Thereafter, when the President transmits to the President pro tempore of the Senate and the Speaker of the House of Representatives his written declaration that no inability exists, he shall resume the powers and duties of his office unless the Vice President and a majority of either the principal officers of the executive department or of such other body as Congress may by law provide, transmit within four days to the President pro tempore of the Senate and the Speaker of the House of Representatives their written declaration that the President is unable to discharge the powers and duties of his office. Thereupon Congress shall decide the issue, assembling within forty-eight hours for that purpose if not in session. If the Congress, within twenty-one days after receipt of the latter written declaration, or, if Congress is not in session, within twenty-one days after Congress is required to assemble, determines by two-thirds vote of both Houses that the President is unable to discharge the powers and duties of his office, the Vice President shall continue to discharge the same as Acting President; otherwise, the President shall resume the powers and duties of his office.

Twenty-sixth Amendment Right to Vote—Age
Section 1. The right of citizens of the United States, who are eighteen years of age or older, to vote shall not be denied or abridged by the United States or by any State on account of age.

Section 2. The Congress shall have the power to enforce this article by appropriate legislation.

Twenty-seventh Amendment Congressional Pay
No law varying the compensation for the services of the Senators and Representatives, shall take effect, until an election of Representatives shall have intervened.

Commentary

✔ Checkpoint
Why is the Twenty-fifth Amendment important?

◀ **Twenty-sixth Amendment, Section 1** In 1970, Congress passed a law allowing 18-year-olds to vote. However, the Supreme Court decided that Congress could not set a minimum age for state elections.

◀ **Twenty-seventh Amendment** If members of Congress vote themselves a pay increase, it cannot go into effect until after the next congressional election. This amendment was proposed in 1789. In 1992, Michigan became the thirty-eighth state to ratify it.

The First American President

On April 14, 1789, a horse and rider arrived at George Washington's home in Virginia, bearing a letter telling Washington that he had been unanimously elected President of the new United States. Washington spent eight days traveling to the capital at New York. So many people crowded the roads to see and applaud him that he said he could barely see through the dust they kicked up. Abigail Adams—the wife of John Adams, who would become Vice President—spoke for the nation when she described Washington as "polite with dignity . . . modest, wise, and good."

1789 button from Washington's inauguration

◄ Washington had to leave his comfortable estate at Mount Vernon, Virginia, and move to New York to assume the presidency of the United States.

 Core Curriculum Preview

Chapter Focus Question: How did the United States build a government, expand its territory, and conduct foreign policy in its early years?

Section 1
Government and Party Politics   2.I.F.1, 2.I.F.3b

Section 2
The Struggle Over Foreign Policy   2.I.A.2a, 2.I.F.3b

Section 3
The Age of Jefferson   2.I.F.4b, 2.I.F.4c, 2.II.A.3, 2.II.C.1

Section 4
The War of 1812   2.I.F.4c, 2.I.F.4d

The 1795 Treaty of Greenville signed between Native Americans and the United States

Thomas Jefferson's writing desk

Use the ☑ **Quick Study Timeline** at the end of this chapter to preview chapter events.

Note Taking Study Guide *Online*
For: Note Taking and American Issues Connector
Web Code: nce-6601

A button from Washington's inauguration ▶

▲ Women pay respect to the new President.

WITNESS HISTORY 🔊 AUDIO

The First Inaugural

When George Washington gave his Inaugural Address in 1789, he was well aware of the extraordinary responsibility of leading "the experiment entrusted to the hands of the American people." An official at the inauguration described the ceremony in a letter to his wife:

“It was with difficulty a passage could be made by the troops through the pressing crowds, who seemed to be incapable of being satisfied by gazing at this man of the people. . . . The streets were lined with the inhabitants as thick as the people could stand. . . . The houses were filled with gentlemen and ladies, the whole distance being half a mile, and the windows to the highest stories were illuminated by the sparkling eyes of innumerable companies of ladies, who seemed to vie with each other to show their joy on this great occasion.”

—Elias Boudinot, April 30, 1789

Government and Party Politics

Core Curriculum Objectives

- **2.I.F.1** Implementing the new constitutional principles: Creating domestic stability through sound financial policies: Hamilton's financial plans
- **2.I.F.3b** Suppressing dissent (the Whiskey Rebellion)

Terms and People

administration
precedent
Cabinet
tariff
loose construction

strict construction
Whiskey Rebellion
political party
Democratic Republican

NoteTaking

Reading Skill: Summarize Summarize information about the early American government in an outline like the one below.

> I. Building the Federal Government
>   A. Electing Washington as President
>   B. Forming the Cabinet
>   C. Setting up the Judiciary
> II.

Why It Matters In 1789, the leaders of the new federal government of the United States gathered in New York City. Besides ideals, they had very little to guide them. The newly ratified Constitution was clear on some points but vague on others. It was also entirely untested. Those who had written the Constitution, along with the new President, George Washington, knew full well that a good start would secure the daring experiment in republican union. But early mistakes could doom it. **Section Focus Question: How did debate over the role of government lead to the formation of political parties?**

Building the Federal Government

The new government started out with huge problems. It had inherited a national debt of $52 million from the Confederation—a huge burden for a nation with a farm economy and only about 3 million people. With no navy and an army of only around 400 men, the United States was not respected by other countries. At New Orleans, the Spanish closed the Mississippi River to American trade. Along the Great Lakes, the British kept forts within American territory.

Electing a President Fortunately, the new government enjoyed extraordinary leaders. In 1789, the new electoral college unanimously elected George Washington as President of the United States. As a revolutionary leader, Washington enjoyed widespread respect and popularity. Yet he took the difficult job reluctantly.

"About ten o'clock I bade farewell to Mount Vernon, to private life, and to domestic felicity, and with a mind oppressed with more anxious and painful sensations than I have words to express, set out for New York."

—George Washington, April 16, 1789

Massachusetts patriot John Adams was elected Vice President. Washington's **administration,** or the officials in the executive branch of government, began with just himself, Adams, and about a dozen clerks. Besides the newly elected Congress, there were few other federal officers. There were also few set rules to guide the administration. Quickly after taking office, Washington began setting important **precedents,** or acts or statements that become traditions to be followed.

Setting Up the Judiciary The Constitution called for one Supreme Court and several smaller ones, but intentionally left to Congress the details of organizing a federal court system. Madison, who had been elected to the House of Representatives in the first Congress, helped to pass the Judiciary Act of 1789. This act established a judiciary, or a system of courts. The U.S. judiciary was made up of thirteen federal district courts, one for each state. Three circuit courts would hear appeals from the state courts and a six-member Supreme Court would decide contested cases. The Supreme Court also served as a trial court in certain cases involving states or foreign affairs. The act also established the office of Attorney General to prosecute and defend cases on behalf of the federal government. Washington appointed John Jay as the first Chief Justice of the Supreme Court.

Setting Up the Cabinet One of Washington's most important precedents was the formation of a **Cabinet,** or the group of federal leaders who headed the major departments of the executive branch and advised the President. The first four executive departments were the departments of State, Treasury, and War, and the Attorney General. The State Department, led by Thomas Jefferson, conducted foreign policy. The War Department supervised national defense. The Secretary of the Treasury, Alexander Hamilton, managed the nation's finances. Nominated by the President, the Cabinet members were approved by the Senate. In 1907, the Cabinet was officially recognized by law.

✔ **Checkpoint** Why was setting up the Cabinet an important precedent?

Hamilton's Plans Stir Debate

Hamilton was tasked with paying off the young nation's immense debts and setting it on a course of economic security. An ardent Federalist, he believed that a strong, centralized government was necessary to preserve the Union. As he developed his plans, Hamilton faced fierce and vocal opposition from Antifederalists, who feared that a strong national government would threaten states' rights and people's freedoms. Their struggles and debates made clear that two very different views of government were solidifying in the new nation.

The First Cabinet

An engraving from the 1800s shows the first Cabinet. Henry Knox was the Secretary of War, and Edmund Randolph was the Attorney General.

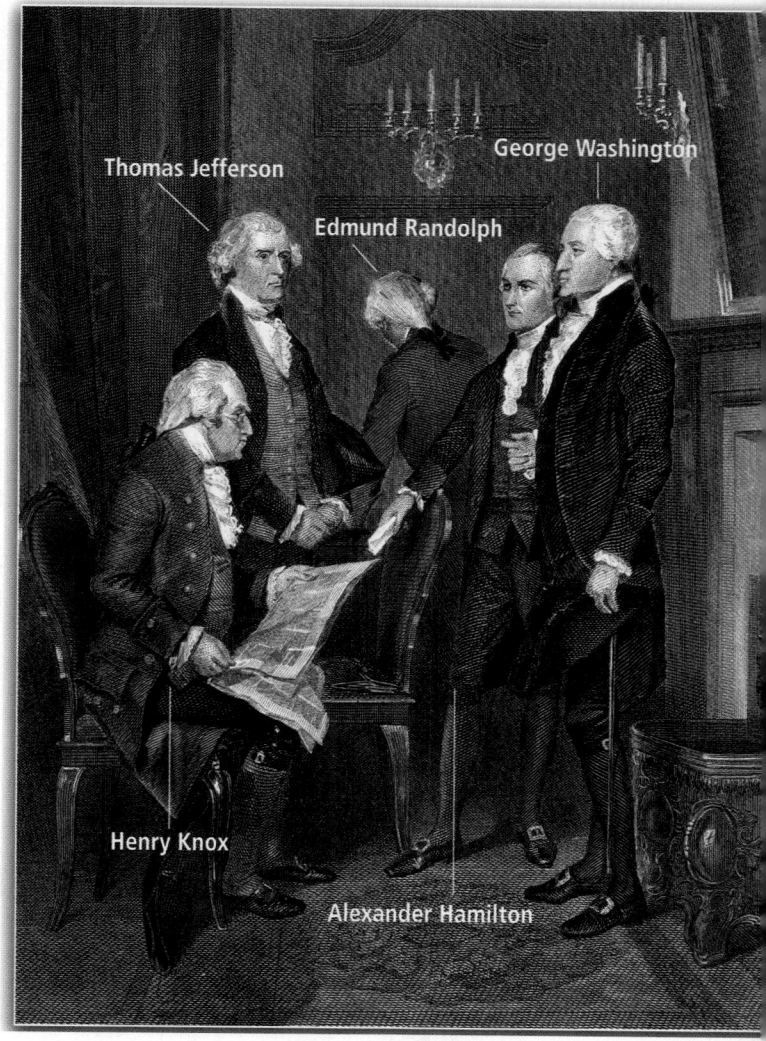

Thomas Jefferson

George Washington

Edmund Randolph

Henry Knox

Alexander Hamilton

Hamilton's Plan for Restructuring Debt

Action	Result	Lasting Legacy
Pay foreign debt and interest in full	Restore national credit	Established United States as trustworthy
Federal government assumes state debts	Bring stability to country; stimulate economy	Unified country
Impose excise taxes and tariffs	Pay debts and increase manufacturing	Established precedent of nation paying its debts
Create national bank and national currency	Help government regulate economy and commerce; generate income through loans	Created model on which today's Federal Reserve System is based

Stabilizing the Economy

Though Jefferson and Madison fiercely opposed Hamilton's plans, Congress eventually adopted them. The first bank of the United States, founded in 1791, stands in Philadelphia. The check above was drawn from the bank in 1794. *What did Hamilton plan to do about states' debts?*

Handling the National Debt Hamilton despised the nation's agricultural economy as backward. He wanted to quickly develop a commercial and industrial economy that could support a large federal government along with a strong army and navy. He saw the national debt of $52 million and the additional $25 million in debts owed by the individual states as assets. Rather than pay down those debts using cash reserves, he meant to fund them by selling government bonds, which would pay annual interest to the holders. Such bonds delighted investors, who welcomed an opportunity to reap annual profits.

To pay the annual interest on the bonds, Hamilton proposed new excise taxes and high **tariffs,** or taxes on imported goods, to raise <u>revenue</u> for the federal government and protect struggling American manufacturers from foreign competition. He also asked Congress to charter a Bank of the United States that could regulate state banks, strengthen the national government, and ensure that business interests were closely aligned with those of the government.

Hamilton's Strategy Hamilton saw three great benefits from his system. First, it would establish the nation's financial credibility, making it easier to borrow money in the future. Second, it would buy political support from the wealthiest Americans, which Hamilton believed was essential for the government's stability. Third, it would enrich investors, who could then build new ships, wharves, storehouses, and factories. In other words, his plan would promote the accumulation of capital needed for commercial and industrial growth.

Hamilton's program was intended to redistribute wealth in two ways: from farmers to merchants and from the South to the North. About eighty percent of the nation's debt was owed to merchants in the seaport cities of the Northeast. During the 1780s, they had bought up notes issued by the Congress or by the states. Those notes had lost most of their value but the merchants had bought them anyway as an investment. Because they paid only a fraction of the original value of the notes, and because Hamilton proposed paying them at full value, the merchants would profit under Hamilton's plan. But to pay those debts, the federal government would tax the American people, who were mainly farmers.

✔ **Checkpoint** Why did Hamilton want to add to the national debt?

Opposing Hamilton

The southern states, which were overwhelmingly agricultural, had done a better job of paying their own debts. Why, southerners wondered, should they pay federal taxes to bail out the northern states? And why should their tax dollars flow into the pockets of creditors in the Northeast? Opposition to Hamilton's plans grew steadily in the South.

Interpreting the Constitution To justify his ambitious program, Hamilton interpreted the Constitution broadly, relying on its "implied powers" and its clause empowering Congress to enact laws for the "general welfare." His broad interpretation, or **loose construction,** appalled his critics, including Jefferson and Madison. They favored a **strict construction,** or limiting the federal government to powers explicitly granted by the Constitution. They opposed Hamilton's plans for assuming state debts. Fearing that a national bank would benefit the North at the expense of the South, they also argued that the Constitution did not authorize Congress to charter one.

Compromise Over a National Capital As Americans aligned themselves either with Hamilton or with Madison and Jefferson, debate heated up. Jefferson declared that Hamilton's system "flowed from principles adverse to liberty and . . . calculated to undermine and demolish the republic." Jefferson and Madison insisted that Hamilton was betraying the American Revolution to establish a "kingly government." They pointed to Great Britain, where factories made owners wealthy but kept most of the workers in poverty. Fearing that industrial development led to greater inequality, they concluded that America needed to keep a farm economy in order to sustain the Republic.

In 1791, by a narrow vote, Congress approved full funding of the federal debt, the implementation of new excise taxes, and the creation of a national bank. But in order to get southerners to agree to the assumption of state debts, Hamilton promised that in ten years the national capital would move southward to the banks of the Potomac River, between Maryland and Virginia. To honor the first President, who was reelected in 1792, the new capital became known as Washington, District of Columbia.

The Whiskey Rebellion In western Pennsylvania, mountains made it difficult to transport bulky bushels of grain to eastern markets. So people distilled their grain into whiskey, which was more compact and of higher value. Rural farmers hated the excise tax on whiskey, which reminded them of the British taxes that had led to the Revolution. In 1794, farmers resisted the tax by intimidating and attacking tax collectors.

Hamilton welcomed the opportunity to demonstrate the new power of the nation by suppressing the **Whiskey Rebellion.** Washington agreed, observing, "We had given no testimony to the world of being able or willing to support our government and laws." Under Hamilton's command, 12,000 militiamen marched west into the troubled region. The rebellion quickly dissolved. Rather than resist such overwhelming force, most rebels stayed home or ran away. Hamilton arrested twenty suspects, but only two were convicted. Jefferson mocked that "an insurrection was announced and proclaimed and armed against, but could never be found."

Analyzing Political Cartoons

The Whiskey Rebellion A cartoon published in 1794 added to the intense debate over the Whiskey Rebellion.
1. Which figures in the cartoon are rebels? Which represent the government?
2. Does the cartoonist side with the government or the rebels? How can you tell?

✓ **Checkpoint** On what grounds did some people oppose Hamilton's plans?

A Two-Party System Emerges

The Whiskey Rebellion highlighted the growing division in American politics. The federal government, headed by Washington and Hamilton, sought to secure its power and authority. Meanwhile the opposition, led by Madison and Jefferson, grew stronger.

Debating the Whiskey Rebellion The Whiskey Rebellion, and its outcome, fueled disagreement. The Federalists blamed the rebellion in part on a set of political clubs known as the Democratic Societies. The clubs had formed to oppose the Federalists. Although these clubs were small and scattered, Washington

◀ An early political cartoon honors Washington and demonizes Jefferson.

▲ A farmer plows a North Carolina field in 1787.

▼ Wealthy merchants stroll along the harbor in New York City.

Political Parties Grow

With the ink barely dry on the Constitution, distinct political parties were already forming in the United States. The intense debate over ideas that had surrounded the writing of the Constitution shaped the rise of the Federalist and Democratic Republican parties in the new nation.

Federalists
- Led by Alexander Hamilton
- Favored a strong centralized government
- Wanted to base economy on industry and trade
- Were pro-British
- Supported a loose construction of the Constitution

Democratic Republicans
- Led by Thomas Jefferson
- Thought states should have more power
- Wanted to base economy on farming
- Were pro-French
- Supported a strict construction of the Constitution

Thinking Critically
1. **Contrast** What were the major differences between the Federalists and the Democratic Republicans?
2. **Draw Inferences** Though George Washington supported most Federalist beliefs, he refused to declare himself a Federalist. Why do you think this was so?

denounced them as "the most diabolical attempt to destroy the best fabric of human government and happiness." Jefferson and Madison defended the societies, fearing that aristocracy would triumph if leaders were immune from constant public scrutiny and criticism. They were alarmed that the Federalists had sent so many troops to <u>suppress</u> popular dissent in western Pennsylvania. As debate over the rebellion continued, the two sides gradually emerged as distinct political groups.

Political Parties Compete for Power The authors of the Constitution wanted to avoid organized **political parties,** or groups of people who seek to win elections and hold public office in order to shape government policy. They deemed these groups to be "factions" that threatened the unity of a republic. Despite these intentions, politicians decided to form two parties: the Federalists, led by Hamilton and John Adams, and the **Democratic Republicans,** led by Jefferson and Madison.

Northerners, especially merchants, tended to favor the Federalists. In contrast, southerners, especially farmers, voted mainly for the Democratic Republicans. Still, Federalists and Democratic Republicans could be found in every social class, in every type of community, in every region, and in every state. Political elections were closely contested most of the time.

The first two Presidents and most of the governors, state legislators, and congressmen were Federalists. Their electoral success indicates that many common voters shared Federalist values. Voters credited the Federalists with the new Constitution and with the nation's increased prosperity and stability during the 1790s.

But many common people continued to support the Democratic Republicans. They worried that the Federalists would concentrate wealth and power in the hands of the elite. Many voters also believed that the Democratic Republican Party offered more social mobility.

✔ **Checkpoint** Who were the leaders of the two emerging political parties?

Vocabulary Builder

<u>suppress</u>–(suh PREHS) *v.* to put an end to with force

SECTION **1** Assessment

Progress Monitoring *Online*
For: Self-test with vocabulary practice
Web Code: nca-0611

Comprehension

1. Terms and People For each term below, explain its impact on early American government.
- administration
- precedent
- Cabinet
- tariff
- loose construction
- strict construction
- Whiskey Rebellion
- political party
- Democratic Republican

2. NoteTaking Reading Skill: Summarize Use your completed outline to answer the Section Focus Question: How did debate over the role of government lead to the formation of political parties?

Writing About History

3. Quick Write: Frame Research Questions Choose an event from this section. Write two or three questions to generate ideas for a research paper. For example, if you choose the Whiskey Rebellion, you could ask, "Why was it in some people's interest to call this event a rebellion?"

Critical Thinking

4. Predict Consequences Would the federal government have survived if the first President had not had widespread respect? Explain.

5. Analyze Information Why did Hamilton believe that wealthy Americans were necessary to secure the nation's economic future?

6. Recognize Ideologies How did Americans structure their debates about the economy in terms of interpreting the Constitution?

7. Draw Conclusions Is it possible to govern a democracy without political parties? Explain.

WITNESS HISTORY ◀)) AUDIO

A Great Orator Speaks

In 1792, government officials met with Native Americans in Philadelphia to discuss treaty issues and continuing skirmishes between settlers and Indians in the Northwest. In response to a plea from President Washington for peace, a famous Seneca orator replied,

❝When you Americans and the king made peace [in 1783], he did not mention us, and showed us no compassion, notwithstanding all he said to us, and all we had suffered . . . he never asked us for a delegation to attend our interests. Had he done this, a settlement of peace among all the western nations might have been effected. . . .❞

—Red Jacket, 1792

▲ Washington presents Red Jacket with a peace medal (above right) at the 1792 meeting.

The Struggle Over Foreign Policy

Core Curriculum Objectives

- **2.I.A.2a** Native American Indians (relations between colonists and Native American Indians, trade, alliances, forced labor, warfare)
- **2.I.F.3b** Suppressing dissent (the Alien and Sedition Acts)

Terms and People

Little Turtle
Battle of Fallen Timbers
French Revolution
John Jay
XYZ Affair

Alien and Sedition Acts
Virginia and Kentucky resolutions
Aaron Burr

NoteTaking

Reading Skill: Identify Supporting Details Record details about early U.S. foreign policies in a chart like this one.

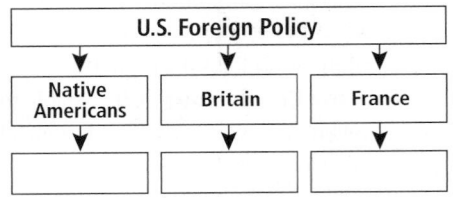

Why It Matters In addition to building a government, making peace with Native Americans, and maintaining control over expanded borders, the young United States had to establish itself in the international community during a volatile time. By 1793, Britain and France had resumed war, and both threatened efforts by the United States to stay neutral. Debate over America's response to a war and to a revolution in France affected the nation's foreign policy as well as its domestic structure. **Section Focus Question: How did foreign policy challenges affect political debate and shape American government?**

Conflict in the Ohio Valley

Although the United States had gained a vast new territory west of the Appalachians from the Treaty of Paris, the British kept their forts on the American side of the Great Lakes. Hoping to limit American settlement in the Northwest Territory, the British provided arms and ammunition to the Miami Indians and their allies, who were actively resisting American expansion into their lands. In 1790, Native Americans led by the war chief **Little Turtle** defeated a small force sent by President Washington to stop attacks against settlers. In 1791 in the Ohio Valley, British guns helped a confederacy of many Indian nations, again led by Little Turtle, to crush a larger American force commanded by General Arthur St. Clair.

But the tide turned in August 1794 when federal troops led by General Anthony Wayne defeated the Native American confederacy at the **Battle of Fallen Timbers,** named for the fallen trees that covered the battle site. Wayne's decisive victory forced the Native Americans to accept his peace terms. In the Treaty of Greenville, Native American leaders ceded most of the present state of Ohio to the U.S. government. This also opened the Northwest Territory to settlement.

 Checkpoint Why was the Battle of Fallen Timbers significant?

American Relations With Europe

While the British were helping Native Americans take a stand against the United States, the young nation struggled to chart a sure course in the area of foreign policy.

Responding to the French Revolution In 1789, Americans welcomed news of the **French Revolution,** a republican uprising in France. Grateful for French help during the American Revolution, Americans now saw the French as fellow republicans in a hostile world of aristocrats and kings. In 1793, however, leaders of the French Revolution began executing thousands of opponents, including the French king and his family. They also declared war on the monarchies of Europe, including Great Britain.

In response, Americans divided along party lines. The Democratic Republicans regretted the executions but still preferred the French Republic to its monarchical foes. Jefferson regarded the French Revolution as "the most sacred cause that ever man was engaged in." But the Federalists decided that the French revolutionaries were bloody anarchists out to destroy religion and social order. They suspected that the Democratic Republicans meant to do the same.

Proclaiming Neutrality By 1793, Britain and France were at war. Both American political parties agreed that the United States was too weak to get tangled in the war and too dependent on trade with Britain, which provided nearly 90 percent of American imports. That trade generated most of the federal revenue, which came primarily from tariffs and only secondarily from excise taxes.

Battle of Fallen Timbers
An engraving from the mid-1800s shows the 1794 battle that weakened Native American resistance. General Anthony Wayne, commander in chief of the United States Army, is shown below and on horse.

If the United States entered the conflict, it could bankrupt the federal government. In 1793, President Washington, therefore, issued a proclamation of American neutrality, which became a foundation of American policy toward Europe until the twentieth century. The powerful British navy tested that neutrality by seizing American ships trading with the French colonies in the West Indies. Those seizures added to American outrage at the British policy along the new nation's western frontier.

Signing Treaties With Britain and Spain To avoid war with Britain, Washington sent Chief Justice **John Jay** to London to negotiate a compromise with the British. In the Jay Treaty of 1794, the British gave up their forts on American soil, but they kept most of their restrictions on American ships. The treaty also required Americans to repay prewar debts to the British. Washington and the Federalists favored this compromise, but the Democratic Republicans denounced the Jay Treaty as a sellout. After a heated debate, the Senate narrowly ratified the treaty, keeping the peace.

In 1795, the United States also signed a treaty with Spain. American settlers needed to move their goods down the Mississippi River to New Orleans, where they could be shipped to markets in the East. But, Spain controlled the Mississippi River and New Orleans. To ensure a free flow of trade, an American diplomat, Thomas Pinckney, negotiated a favorable treaty with the Spanish, who feared that an Anglo-American alliance might threaten their American possessions. Pinckney's Treaty guaranteed Americans free shipping rights on

INFOGRAPHIC ◀)) AUDIO

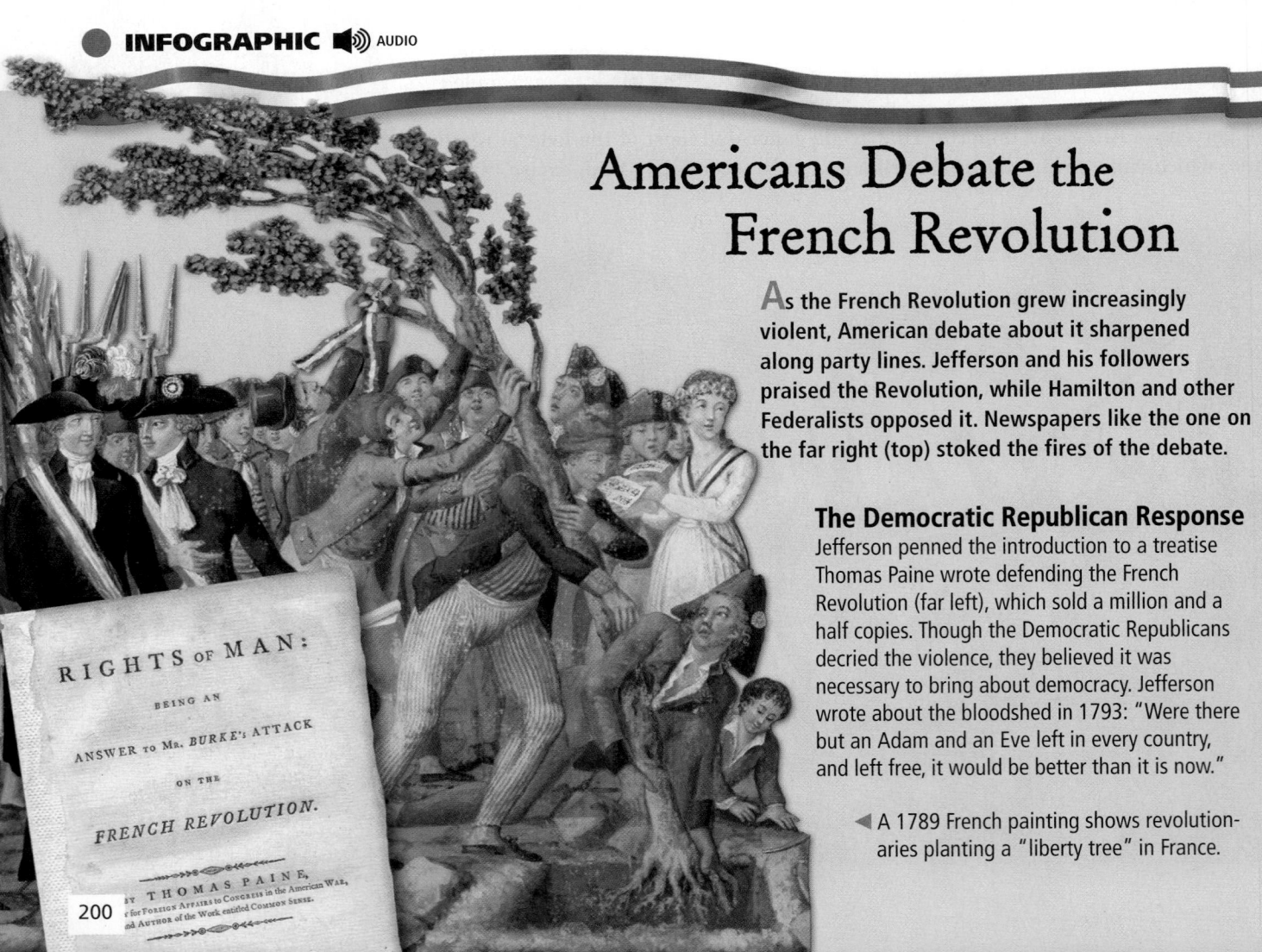

Americans Debate the French Revolution

As the French Revolution grew increasingly violent, American debate about it sharpened along party lines. Jefferson and his followers praised the Revolution, while Hamilton and other Federalists opposed it. Newspapers like the one on the far right (top) stoked the fires of the debate.

The Democratic Republican Response
Jefferson penned the introduction to a treatise Thomas Paine wrote defending the French Revolution (far left), which sold a million and a half copies. Though the Democratic Republicans decried the violence, they believed it was necessary to bring about democracy. Jefferson wrote about the bloodshed in 1793: "Were there but an Adam and an Eve left in every country, and left free, it would be better than it is now."

◀ A 1789 French painting shows revolutionaries planting a "liberty tree" in France.

RIGHTS OF MAN:

BEING AN

ANSWER TO MR. BURKE'S ATTACK

ON THE

FRENCH REVOLUTION.

BY THOMAS PAINE,
for Foreign Affairs to Congress in the American War,
and Author of the Work entitled Common Sense.

200

the Mississippi River and access to New Orleans. The treaty also established the northern boundary of Spanish Florida.

The removal of British forts, victories over Native Americans, and secure access to New Orleans encouraged thousands of Americans to move westward. By 1800, nearly 400,000 Americans lived beyond the Appalachian Mountains. By selling land to these settlers, the federal government gained revenue that helped to pay off the national debt.

Washington's Farewell In 1792, Washington had won reelection without opposition, but he declined to run again in 1796. In ailing health, he longed to escape the political turmoil by returning to his beloved plantation, Mount Vernon. He also recognized that the young nation needed him to set an example by walking away from power, proving that he was no king. His voluntary retirement after two terms set a precedent honored by all Presidents until the 1940s.

Washington retired with a record of astounding achievements. On the frontier, the Indians had been defeated, the western lands opened to settlement, and the Whiskey rebels suppressed. He had kept the nation out of the war in Europe. A booming foreign trade boosted tariffs, which funded the government and the national debt. Many historians have concluded that without Washington's skillful leadership, the nation may not have survived the harsh tests of the early 1790s. In a farewell address, Washington offered sound political advice for his successors, calling on them to temper their political strife in favor of national unity and to avoid "entangling alliances" that might lead to overseas wars.

✓ **Checkpoint** What treaties were signed during Washington's presidency?

THE PROVIDENTIAL DETECTION

The Federalist Response

While the Federalists sympathized with the French drive for democracy, they distrusted the common people who were bringing it about. Adams wrote that public affairs should be left to "the rich, the well-born and the able." In cartoons like the one above on the right, Federalists attacked Jefferson for worshiping the French and destroying the American Constitution.

Thinking Critically

1. **Identify Point of View** What do each of the paintings suggest about their authors' viewpoints toward the French Revolution?

2. **Recognize Ideologies** What did the parties' response to the Revolution reveal about their basic ideas regarding political power and government?

The Parties Debate Foreign Policy

The Federalist candidate, John Adams, narrowly defeated Thomas Jefferson in the 1796 presidential election. The nation voted along regional lines, with Jefferson winning most of the southern electoral votes and Adams carrying almost all of the northern states. Due to an awkward feature of the Constitution, Jefferson, as the second place finisher, became Adams's Vice President.

Adams Confronts Crisis With France Although honest and dedicated, Adams could also be stubborn and pompous. Lacking tact, he made few friends and many enemies. Those foes included Hamilton, who had retired from public office but who tried to control the Federalist Party and the national government from behind the scenes. His meddling weakened the Adams administration.

Vocabulary Builder
unify–(YOO nuh fī) *v.* to bring together; to make into one unit

A French crisis briefly <u>unified</u> the nation. The Jay Treaty of 1794 had offended the French as a betrayal of their 1778 treaty of alliance with the United States. To show their irritation, in 1796 the French began seizing American merchant ships. Adams sent envoys to Paris to negotiate peace. But three French officials—known in code as X, Y, and Z—demanded humiliating terms, including $250,000 in bribes. Adams broke off negotiations. Called the **XYZ Affair,** the insult roused public sentiment against France. In 1798, the Federalist majority in Congress expanded the army and authorized a small navy, which won some surprising victories over French warships. To pay for the expanded military, Congress imposed unpopular taxes on stamps and land.

The Alien and Sedition Acts The Federalists exploited the war fever by passing the controversial **Alien and Sedition Acts** in 1798. The Alien Act authorized the President to arrest and deport immigrants who criticized the federal government. Because most immigrants supported the Democratic Republicans, the Federalists made it difficult for them to become citizens. The Sedition Act made it a crime for citizens to publicly discredit the federal government. Arguing that criticism undermined trust in the government, the Federalists used this act to silence Democratic Republican opposition.

The Sedition Act did allow juries to acquit defendants who could prove the literal truth of their statements. But that still put the burden of proof on the defendants, reversing the tradition of presuming someone innocent until proven guilty. In the end, the federal government convicted ten men of sedition, including those in Massachusetts who erected a liberty pole comparing the Federalists to the Loyalists who had supported the British king.

Analyzing Political Cartoons

Fighting Over the Sedition Act A 1798 cartoon shows a fight that broke out in Congress between Federalist Roger Griswold (with cane) and Democratic Republican Matthew Lyon (with tongs). Lyon, the first person tried and jailed under the Sedition Act, was considered a Democratic Republican hero and won reelection while in his jail cell. *What is the cartoonist's view of Congress during the Adams administration? How can you tell?*

The Virginia and Kentucky Resolutions

In two Democratic Republican states, the state legislatures passed controversial resolves in response to the acts. Written by Jefferson and Madison in 1798 and 1799, the **Virginia and Kentucky resolutions** declared the Sedition Act unconstitutional. The resolves even hinted that states had the power to nullify federal laws that were unconstitutional. Though this doctrine of nullification threatened to dissolve the union, no other state legislatures adopted it. Instead, the presidential election of 1800 would decide the balance of federal power and states' rights.

 Checkpoint What was the XYZ Affair?

The Election of 1800

By 1800, the Sedition Act and the new federal taxes had become very unpopular. Sensing that trend, in 1799 Adams had suspended expansion of the army and sent new diplomats to France to seek peace. Those moves angered many Federalists, including Hamilton, who worked to undermine Adams's reelection. Adams lost the heated election to Jefferson.

Jefferson and his running mate, **Aaron Burr,** tied. The voters had meant for Jefferson to become President and Burr to become Vice President. But because the Constitution did not then allow a distinction between electoral votes, the House of Representatives had to decide between the two. Hamilton preferred Jefferson, so in early 1801 the Federalist congressmen allowed Jefferson to become President. This peaceful transfer of power from one party to another set a valuable precedent. To avoid another electoral crisis, in 1804 the Constitution was amended to require electors to vote separately for President and Vice President. Offended by Hamilton's criticism, Burr killed him in a duel in 1804.

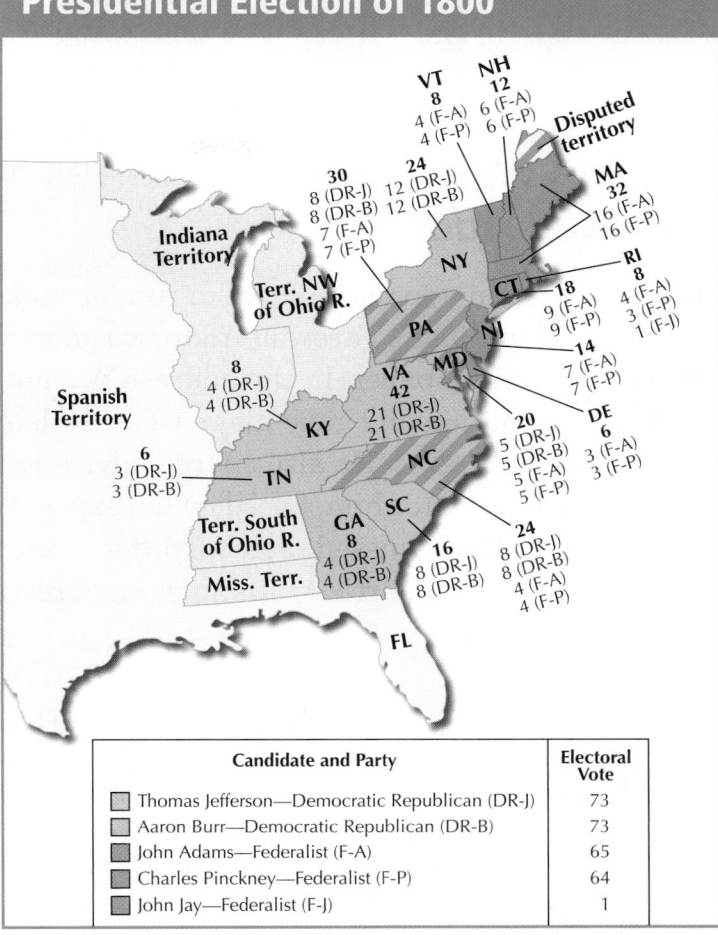

Presidential Election of 1800

Candidate and Party	Electoral Vote
Thomas Jefferson—Democratic Republican (DR-J)	73
Aaron Burr—Democratic Republican (DR-B)	73
John Adams—Federalist (F-A)	65
Charles Pinckney—Federalist (F-P)	64
John Jay—Federalist (F-J)	1

 Checkpoint Compare the election of 1796 to the election of 1800.

SECTION **2** **Assessment**

Progress Monitoring Online
For: Self-test with vocabulary practice
Web Code: nca-1621

Comprehension

1. Terms and People What is the relationship between each of the following terms or people and American foreign policy during the 1790s?
- Little Turtle
- Battle of Fallen Timbers
- French Revolution
- John Jay
- XYZ Affair
- Alien and Sedition Acts

2. NoteTaking Reading Skill: Identify Supporting Details Use your completed chart to answer the Section Focus Question: How did foreign policy challenges affect political debate and shape American government?

Writing About History

3. Quick Write: Narrow Your Topic Choose a topic from this section to research. Then, narrow it down by creating a concept web. Choose one of the outer circles as a manageable topic for a research paper.

Critical Thinking

4. Identify Central Issues Why did the British support Native American resistance to westward expansion in the United States?

5. Recognize Ideologies How did American debates about foreign policy in the 1790s reflect the beliefs of the political parties?

6. Draw Inferences Does having a President and Vice President from different parties help or hinder government? Explain.

NY 2.I.A.F.4

Washington asked Hamilton to revise his farewell address; Hamilton's version appears to the right. ▶

George Washington:
Farewell Address

In 1796, Washington decided not to run for reelection. On September 19, his Farewell Address ran in a Philadelphia newspaper. In the address Washington thanked the nation and gave his reasons for leaving office after two terms. He also offered advice to those who would come after him, based on his experience and observations. He discussed regional differences, foreign policy, and political parties with amazing foresight.

L et me now take a more comprehensive view, and warn you in the most solemn manner against the baneful[1] effects of the spirit of party generally.

This spirit, unfortunately, is inseparable from our nature, having its root in the strongest passions of the human mind. It exists under different shapes in all governments, more or less stifled, controlled, or repressed; but, in those of the popular form, it is seen in its greatest rankness,[2] and is truly their worst enemy. . . .

It agitates the community with ill-founded jealousies and false alarms, kindles the animosity of one part against another, foments[3] occasionally riot and insurrection. It opens the door to foreign influence and corruption, which finds a facilitated access to the government itself through the channels of party passions. Thus the policy and the will of one country are subjected to the policy and will of another. . . .

So likewise, a passionate attachment of one nation for another produces a variety of evils. Sympathy for the favorite nation, facilitating the illusion of an imaginary common interest in cases where no real common interest exists, and infusing into one the enmities of the other, betrays the former into a participation in the quarrels and wars of the latter without adequate inducement or justification. It leads also to concessions to the favorite nation of privileges denied to others which is apt doubly to injure the nation making the concessions. . . .

The jealousy of a free people ought to be constantly awake, since history and experience prove that foreign influence is one of the most baneful foes of republican government. But that jealousy to be useful must be impartial.[4] . . .

▲ George Washington, as painted by Gilbert Stuart in 1796

1. **baneful** (BAYN fuhl) *adj.* harmful; destructive.
2. **rankness** (RANGK nehs) *n.* state of being excessive and unpleasant.
3. **foments** (foh MEHNTS) *v.* stirs up.
4. **impartial** (ihm PAHR shuhl) *adj.* fair; not favoring one side.

Thinking Critically

1. **Synthesize Information** What does Washington say are the many "baneful effects" of political parties?

2. **Draw Inferences** What event was Washington thinking of when he warned about "foreign influence"?

◀ President Thomas Jefferson, with a banner
(right) from his 1800 presidential campaign

Jefferson Calls for Free Speech

In 1801, Thomas Jefferson became the nation's third
President. He emphasized that the federal government
should respect public opinion and should allow public
criticism—implying that the previous Federalist administration had fallen short on those scores. In an eloquent
Inaugural Address, Jefferson insisted that the Republic
needed free speech and constant debate.

❝If there be any among us who wish to dissolve the union,
or to change its republican form, let them stand undisturbed
as monuments of the safety with which error of opinion may
be tolerated where reason is left free to combat it.❞
—Thomas Jefferson, Inaugural Address, 1801

The Age of Jefferson

 Core Curriculum Objectives

- **2.I.F.4b** A new nation in a world at war
- **2.I.F.4c** Economic pressures as a tool of
  diplomacy
- **2.II.A.3** The Marshall Court
- **2.II.C.1** The Louisiana Purchase

Terms and People

bureaucracy	Lewis and Clark
John Marshall	Expedition
judicial review	Barbary War
Marbury v. *Madison*	impressment
Louisiana Purchase	embargo

NoteTaking

Reading Skill: Identify Main Ideas Record
main ideas about Jefferson's presidency in a
concept web like the one below.

Why It Matters In addition to capturing the presidency in 1800,
the Democratic Republicans won control of Congress and most of
the state governments. The Federalists would never reclaim
national power. Besides taking government in a new direction, the
Jefferson administration left a profound legacy with its acquisition
of new territory. **Section Focus Question: What were the successes and
failures of the Jefferson administrations?**

Pursuing Republican Principles

When the Democratic Republicans took power, they spoke of the
election as a "revolution." Jefferson insisted that "the Revolution of
1800 was as real a Revolution in the principles of our government as
that of 1776 was in its form." In that view, those in the Jefferson
administration set out to do things quite differently from their predecessors, who had copied the style of the British monarchy.

New Government Policies Jefferson encouraged Congress to
abandon the Alien and Sedition Acts, as well as the hated taxes on
stamps, land, and alcoholic spirits. Unlike Hamilton, Jefferson
wanted to retire the national debt by paying it down. Despite reducing taxes, he cut the national debt from $80 million when he took
office to $57 million in 1809. To do this he made major cuts to the
army and navy and streamlined the government's **bureaucracy,** or
the departments and workers that make up the government. He
also benefited when customs revenue from imports increased with
a dramatic growth in foreign trade. In addition, the westward movement of American farm families increased the sale of federal lands.
These two revenues drove down the federal debt.

A Change in Style The Federalists believed that expensive displays taught the public to respect their leaders. Without that respect, they did not think that the government could survive. But, the Democratic Republicans hated the Federalist displays of wealth as an aristocratic threat to the republic. Although Jefferson was a very wealthy, refined, and educated gentleman, he recognized the popularity of a common style. A friend described Jefferson in this way:

> **Primary Source** "If his dress was plain, unstudied, and sometimes old-fashioned in its form, it was always of the finest materials . . . and if in his manners he was simple, affable, and unceremonious, it was not because he was ignorant of but because he despised the conventional and artificial usages of courts and fashionable life."
> —Mrs. Samuel Harrison Smith, c. 1801

✓ **Checkpoint** Why was Jefferson's election considered a "republican revolution"?

John Marshall's Supreme Court

When Thomas Jefferson became President in 1801, **John Marshall** became Chief Justice of the Supreme Court. Although the two men were cousins, they were political enemies. Marshall was a Federalist, a last-minute appointee by the outgoing President, John Adams. Marshall's appointment had a major impact on the Supreme Court and on its relationship with the rest of the federal government. Over 35 years, he participated in more than 1,000 court decisions, writing over half of them—more than any other Supreme Court Justice in U.S. history.

Marshall's Four-Part Legacy Marshall applied four of Hamilton's principles to interpret the Constitution. First, his Supreme Court claimed the power to review the acts of Congress and of the President to determine if they were constitutional. This power is known as **judicial review.** Second, he insisted that federal laws were superior to state laws. Third, like Hamilton, Marshall broadly interpreted the Constitution to find implied powers for the national government. Fourth, he insisted upon the "sanctity of contracts." This limited the power of state governments to interfere with business.

Marbury* v. *Madison In 1803, Marshall first asserted the power of judicial review in the case of ***Marbury* v. *Madison.*** In early 1801, outgoing President John Adams had appointed William Marbury, a Federalist, a justice for the District of Columbia. The incoming Secretary of State, James Madison, refused to deliver the official papers of appointment. When Marbury complained to the Supreme Court, Marshall ruled in favor of Madison by declaring unconstitutional part of the Judiciary Act of 1789.

This ruling was a stroke of genius. Marshall gave the Democratic Republicans what they wanted by denying Marbury his appointment. But in doing so, Marshall claimed a sweeping power for the Supreme Court that the Democratic Republicans did not want that Court to have. After all, the Constitution was silent on what institution should judge the constitutionality of congressional actions. In the Kentucky and Virginia resolutions of 1798, Jefferson and Madison had claimed that power for the state legislatures. Because of Marshall, today we accept that the Supreme Court will review the constitutionality of federal laws.

Establishing Important Precedents After establishing the precedent of judicial review, Marshall never again ruled a federal law unconstitutional. Instead, most of his decisions overruled state laws, usually to defend businesses and interstate commerce from state interference, or strengthened judicial review.

NoteTaking

Reading Skill: Recognize Sequence As you read, trace events that led to the recognition that the Supreme Court would have the power to review federal laws.

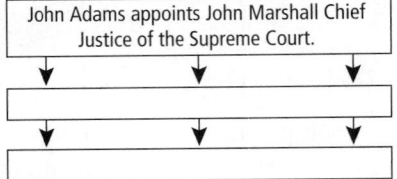

| John Adams appoints John Marshall Chief Justice of the Supreme Court. |

How Can the Supreme Court Declare Laws to Be Unconstitutional?

 2.II.A.3

The Constitution grants each branch of government certain powers. To prevent any one branch from becoming too powerful, a system of checks and balances is part of this framework. While the Constitution specifies balancing powers for the executive and legislative branches, it says little about the judicial branch. One challenge facing the young government was to decide how the judiciary could balance the powers of the President and the legislature.

▼ Chief Justice John Marshall, painted in 1840

Marbury v. *Madison* (1803)

The Facts	The Issue	The Decision
William Marbury asked the Supreme Court to grant him a job as a federal judge, which had been promised to him by the Adams administration but denied by the incoming Jefferson administration. He also sued Secretary of State James Madison.	Marbury argued that the Judiciary Act of 1789, gave the Supreme Court the power to make a government official perform a certain duty.	The Court ruled that in passing the 1789 law, Congress had exceeded the powers granted by the Constitution. Since the law was unconstitutional, the Supreme Court could not order Madison to grant Marbury his commission.

Why It Matters

Marbury v. *Madison* established the power of judicial review, ensuring that the Supreme Court had the final authority to interpret the meaning of the Constitution. In his majority opinion, Marshall wrote:
"It is emphatically the province and duty of the judicial department to say what the law is. Those who apply the rule to particular cases, must of necessity expound and interpret that rule. If two laws conflict with each other, the courts must decide on the operation of each."

Marbury v. *Madison* established the judiciary branch as an equal partner in government. Since 1803, the Supreme Court and other courts have used judicial review in thousands of cases.

Connect to Your World

Supreme Court Justices serve lifetime terms and are responsible for interpreting the Constitution. When one of the nine seats of the Supreme Court must be filled, the President nominates a replacement. Then, the Senate must approve the President's nomination with a vote. In this way, both the executive and legislative branches can check and balance the power of the judiciary.

Who are the judges that can declare laws to be unconstitutional in today's Supreme Court? Research the Court's current makeup. Create a Supreme Court profile, indicating which Justices were appointed by Democratic Presidents, which by Republican Presidents, and whether they can be described as strict or loose constructionists.

For: Supreme Court cases
Web Code: nce-0631

◀ Current Chief Justice John Roberts

These decisions set precedents critical to the development of the new nation's legal and economic systems. Like Hamilton, Marshall interpreted the Constitution broadly to find the implied powers needed for a strong national government.

✓ **Checkpoint** Why was *Marbury* v. *Madison* so important?

WITNESS HISTORY DVD

Watch *The Lewis and Clark Expedition* on the **United States Witness History DVD** to explore how this historic trip affected Jefferson and the country.

The Nation Expands

Jefferson insisted that farm ownership—which freed citizens from dependence on a landlord or on an employer—was essential to the freedom of white Americans. Yet without expansion there would not be enough farms for the rapidly growing population. With the population doubling every 25 years, the nation needed twice as much land every generation to maintain farm ownership.

Eyeing the Louisiana Territory To get more land, Jefferson wanted the United States to expand to the Pacific—despite the fact that much of the continent was already inhabited by Native Americans and European colonists. At first, Jefferson believed that Spain's vast Louisiana Territory west of the Mississippi River would be easy to conquer. He noted that the Spanish colonists were few, their empire was weak, and they were distracted by the war in Europe. Jefferson's plans went awry, however, when the United States got a new and far

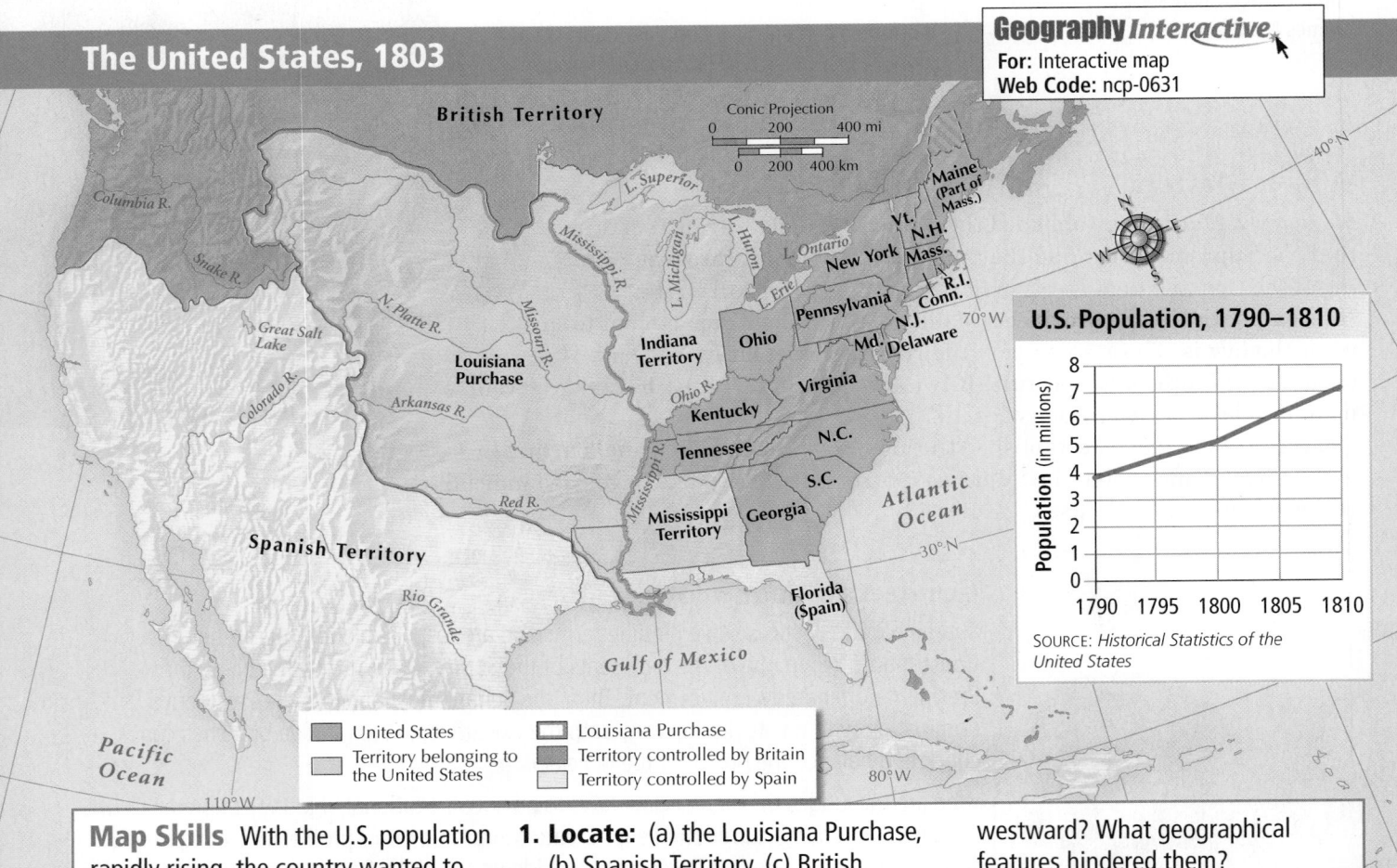

The United States, 1803

Geography *Interactive*
For: Interactive map
Web Code: ncp-0631

U.S. Population, 1790–1810

SOURCE: *Historical Statistics of the United States*

United States
Territory belonging to the United States
Louisiana Purchase
Territory controlled by Britain
Territory controlled by Spain

Map Skills With the U.S. population rapidly rising, the country wanted to expand its borders. In turn, the expansion of land brought about by the Louisiana Purchase encouraged population growth.

1. **Locate:** (a) the Louisiana Purchase, (b) Spanish Territory, (c) British Territory

2. **Movement** What geographical features helped settlers move westward? What geographical features hindered them?

3. **Predict** Describe the population growth in the years 1790–1810. How would this growth affect U.S. foreign relations?

more dangerous neighbor to the west. In 1801, France's military dictator, Napoleon Bonaparte, had forced Spain to give him the Louisiana Territory, including the strategic city of New Orleans. The French threatened to block American access to the market in New Orleans. An alarmed Jefferson considered joining the British in an alliance to fight France.

The Louisiana Purchase Jefferson reasoned that he could avoid war by offering to buy New Orleans from the French. When James Monroe and Robert Livingston, the American minister in France, approached Napoleon, they found him surprisingly receptive. Napoleon's imperial plans had been foiled by slave rebels in the Caribbean colony of Saint Domingue, which is now Haiti. Led by Toussaint L'Ouverture, the rebels defeated a French army sent to suppress them. Without that army to occupy Louisiana, and needing money to fight the British, Napoleon decided to sell all of the Louisiana Territory.

In the **Louisiana Purchase** of 1803, Jefferson obtained a vast territory extending from the Mississippi River to the Rocky Mountains. At about 828,000 square miles, the Louisiana Territory nearly doubled the size of the United States. For all of this, the United States paid only $15 million. Although a great bargain, the Louisiana Purchase was also something of an embarrassment, as it contradicted Jefferson's constitutional principles. He had long argued for a minimal federal government, and the Constitution did not authorize the federal government to buy territory from a foreign country. Jefferson confessed that he had "done an act beyond the Constitution."

In 1804, Jefferson sent Meriwether Lewis and William Clark to explore the new territory, in what became known as the **Lewis and Clark Expedition** (see American Experience feature in this chapter). The men were guided much of the way by a Shoshone woman, named Sacajawea, and her husband.

✓ **Checkpoint** How did the United States gain the Louisiana Territory?

Jefferson's Foreign Troubles

While Jefferson succeeded in his plans to expand to the west, he faced a number of significant challenges to solidifying the stability and economy of the United States.

Fighting the Barbary War The Barbary States of North Africa—Morocco, Algiers, Tunis, and Tripoli—were profiting by seizing American ships and sailors in the Mediterranean Sea. To buy immunity from that piracy, the Washington and Adams administrations had paid protection money to the Barbary States. Jefferson was willing to do the same until the ruler of Tripoli increased his price. In 1801, Jefferson sent the small American navy to blockade the port of Tripoli, winning a favorable peace in 1805, concluding the **Barbary War.**

Entering the Reexport Trade As the population grew and spread westward, the United States needed to expand overseas markets for the <u>surplus</u>

Thomas Jefferson
(1743–1826)
Along with being a statesman, Thomas Jefferson was an amateur scientist. His deep interest in plants and animals contributed to the Lewis and Clark Expedition. His plantation, Monticello, served as a laboratory for experimenting with plants. Jefferson grew hundreds of varieties of fruits and vegetables, recording their growth in detailed journals. He imported many plants from around the world, including Italian broccoli and Mexican peppers. Some plant samples Lewis and Clark brought back from the West ended up in his garden, where they still thrive today. Jefferson was an enthusiastic experimenter, trying new varieties of those plants that did not flourish. "The greatest service which can be rendered any country," he said, "is to add an useful plant to its culture."

▲ Portable writing desk designed by Jefferson

Vocabulary Builder
<u>surplus</u>–(SUHR pluhs) *adj.* more than is needed

produce raised on its new farms. From 1793 to 1807, war in Europe aided this goal. The dominant British navy quickly captured most of France's merchant ships. To supply food to the French colonies in the West Indies, and to export their sugar, the French turned to American ships. Because the British had banned direct American voyages between the French West Indies and France, American merchants picked up cargoes in the French colonies and took them to ports in the United States, where they unloaded them. Then the merchants reshipped the cargoes to France as if they were American products.

The value of this "reexport" trade soared from about $300,000 in 1790 to nearly $59 million in 1807, creating a boom for the American economy. To meet the new demand, American shipyards produced hundreds of new ships, tripling the size of the nation's merchant marine by 1807. Prosperous American merchants built new wharves, warehouses, and mansions, boosting the construction trades in seaport cities. Farmers also benefited by selling their produce to feed French soldiers in Europe and enslaved Africans and plantation owners in the West Indies.

The British hated the reexport trade for two reasons. First, it helped the French economy, which sustained Napoleon's army. Second, the new trade helped the United States become Britain's greatest commercial competitor. In 1805, as British merchants lost markets and profits to American shippers, British warships began to stop and confiscate growing numbers of American merchant ships for trading with the French.

Facing British Impressment The British navy also angered the United States by relying on **impressment,** or taking American sailors from their ships and forcing them to serve in the British navy. Engaged in a tough war, the British desperately needed sailors for their huge fleet. Britain insisted that anyone born within its empire was a British subject for life. Yet British naval officers also took American-born sailors. By 1812, about 6,000 American citizens had been impressed for the harsh duty of serving on a British warship.

At first, Federalist merchants were willing to regard the British abuses as unfortunate costs of doing business on the high seas. They

The Reexport Trade in Action

American ports like Philadelphia, shown here, thrived during the reexport trade. *Why couldn't American ships carry French goods directly to France?*

70° W   60° W

UNITED STATES

❺ Another U.S. ship is loaded with the same goods, now identified as American

❻ The ship is then allowed to pass through the blockade on its way to France

To France

30° N

Atlantic Ocean

❸ Ships redirected to the United States

To United States

❹ French goods are unloaded in America

West

❷ Ships blocked from crossing Atlantic by British warships

❶ American ships are loaded with French goods

To France

Indies

Caribbean Sea

Miller Projection
0   20   400 mi
0   20   400 km

British blockade

French goods (coffee, sugar, cotton, wine, spirits, tea, spices)

pointed out that the old trade with Great Britain remained even more valuable than the new reexport trade with France. But Democratic Republicans insisted that the British actions insulted the United States and threatened the country's economic growth. In 1807, when the British attacked an American warship, the *Chesapeake,* in order to take some of its sailors, many Americans—including many Federalists—were outraged.

Jefferson Asks for an Embargo The United States lacked a navy large enough to challenge the British fleet. Jefferson balked at the high cost of building a bigger navy, which would undermine his policies of reducing the national debt and keeping taxes low. He also worried that a large military would become a threat to the Republic.

As an alternative to war, in 1807 Jefferson persuaded Congress to declare an **embargo,** suspending trade by ordering American ships to stay in port. He expected the embargo to starve the British and close their factories, creating riots in the streets. Instead, the British found other markets in South America. Meanwhile, the embargo bankrupted American merchants, threw American sailors out of work, and hurt farmers, who could no longer export their crops. Exploiting voter anger, the Federalists gained support in the northern states, especially in New England.

Even Jefferson had to admit failure, lifting the embargo just before he retired from the presidency in 1809. Despite having been easily reelected in 1804, the embargo had caused his popularity to lag. Still, he was succeeded by his friend James Madison, who defeated a Federalist rival in the election of 1808.

✔ **Checkpoint** Why did Jefferson call for an embargo?

Attacking the *Chesapeake*
This engraving from 1816 shows British sailors taking over the *Chesapeake* and impressing the American sailors on board.

SECTION 3 Assessment

Progress Monitoring *Online*
For: Self-test with vocabulary practice
Web Code: nca-0631

Comprehension

1. **Terms and People** Explain the impact of the following people or terms on the development of the United States in the early 1800s.
   - bureaucracy
   - John Marshall
   - judicial review
   - *Marbury* v. *Madison*
   - Louisiana Purchase
   - Lewis and Clark Expedition
   - Barbary War
   - impressment
   - embargo

2. **NoteTaking Reading Skill: Identify Main Details** Use your completed chart to answer the Section Focus Question: What were the successes and failures of the Jefferson administrations?

Writing About History

3. **Quick Write: Develop a Thesis Statement** Introduce your topic by summarizing it in a single, clear statement. For example, if your topic for this section is John Marshall's Supreme Court, your thesis statement might be "John Marshall had a profound and lasting impact on the Supreme Court and its role in the federal government."

Critical Thinking

4. **Apply Information** How did Jefferson view the Supreme Court precedent of judicial review?

5. **Identify Central Issues** What was Jefferson's main reason for purchasing the Louisiana Territory from France?

6. **Recognize Cause and Effect** What was the impact of the embargo on the American economy?

EXPERIENCE LEWIS AND CLARK

Lewis and Clark discovered ▶ many species new to science, including 15 mammals, 16 birds, 7 fish, 7 reptiles, and dozens of plants.

In 1800, the lands west of the Appalachians were as foreign to Americans as the moon is to many people today. Therefore, when Thomas Jefferson sent Meriwether Lewis and William Clark on their expedition, he handed them a set of remarkable instructions. The President had spent years crafting them, and they reflected his own impressive range of scientific knowledge. Jefferson called for specific data such as local temperatures, when native plants flowered, and what Native Americans wore and ate. Jefferson named the group the "Corps of Discovery," and meant it literally. He saw the expedition as an unprecedented chance to combine scientific discovery with commercial knowledge that would stimulate the nation's growth. Jefferson spent two years as Lewis's mentor, hiring experts to train the expedition leader in botany, taxidermy, paleontology, and other related fields.

1 Meriwether Lewis   **2** William Clark   **3** The compass Clark carried on the expedition.   **4** A woodpecker species preserved by Lewis and named for him. **5** Clark's detailed diary of the expedition, including hundreds of sketches. **6** A sketch of a trout from Clark's diary.   **7** A drawing of a prairie bird.   **8** Black Moccasin, a Minitari chief who met Lewis and Clark and was painted by George Catlin three decades later.   **9** A peace medal that the expedition gave to Native American chiefs; Jefferson's likeness appears on the other side.

The Journeys of
Lewis & Clark
1803 to 1806

—— Westward routes (1803–1804)
- - - - Eastward routes (1806)
- - - - Lewis's return-route variation
- - - - Clark's return-route variation
—— Louisiana Purchase

BRITISH TERRITORY

Fort Clatsop

Columbia R.

Great Falls
Missouri R.
Yellowstone R.

Mandan/Minitari villages

OREGON COUNTRY

Lewiston

Snake R.

Great Salt Lake

N. Platte R.

LOUISIANA TERRITORY

Colorado R.

Rio Grande

Continental Divide

SPANISH TERRITORY

ROCKY MOUNTAINS

Cascade Range

Pacific Ocean

Distance in miles
0   100   200   300   400

0   100 200 500 400
Distance in kilometers

Great Lakes

Michigan Territory

Indiana Territory

St. Louis
Ohio R.
Louisville

Missouri R.

Mississippi R.

Mississippi Territory

Orleans Territory

Spanish Florida

Gulf of Mexico

UNITED STATES

Washington, D.C.

Atlantic Ocean

Thinking Critically

1. Analyze Visuals Analyze the map and the images. How do they reflect Jefferson's belief that the expedition was a "Corps of Discovery"?

2. Synthesize Information How did the expedition's charge to learn from Native Americans conflict with U.S. policy toward Native Americans in general?

Connect to Today Do research into modern explorations to little-known places. Does the government have a role in these explorations? How are they similar to and different from the Lewis and Clark Expedition?

History *Interactive* ★

For: To discover more about the Lewis and Clark Expedition
Web Code: ncp-0632

Burning the Capitol

In 1814, the British entered Washington, D.C., during the War of 1812. They drove President Madison and his Cabinet into the woods before burning the city. Madison's wife, Dolley, heroically saved a painting of George Washington before joining the others. Years later, a British officer described the scene:

"Of the Senate house, the President's palace, the barracks, the dockyard, etc., nothing could be seen except heaps of smoking ruins, and even the bridge, a noble structure upwards of a mile in length, was almost wholly demolished."

—George Robert Gleig, 1826

▲ A modern-day artist re-creates the burning of the White House by the British.

The War of 1812

 Core Curriculum Objectives

- **2.I.F.4c** Economic pressures as a tool of diplomacy
- **2.I.F.4d** The failure of Republican diplomacy: War of 1812

Terms and People

Tecumseh
Battle of Tippecanoe
War Hawks
War of 1812
Andrew Jackson
Francis Scott Key

"The Star-Spangled Banner"
Battle of New Orleans
Treaty of Ghent
Hartford Convention

NoteTaking

Reading Skill: Recognize Sequence Record the causes of the War of 1812 in a chart like this one.

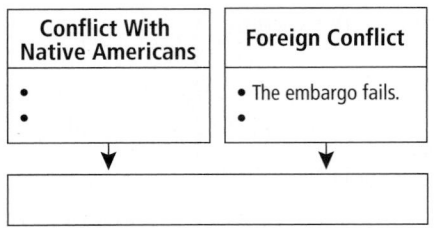

Conflict With Native Americans	Foreign Conflict
• •	• The embargo fails. •

Why It Matters Just a few decades after its founding, the United States found itself involved in a major war. The war tested not only the young nation's resources and strength but the solidarity of its people as well. Despite their political divisions, Americans managed both to fight a war and to get the country back on track in the war's aftermath. **Section Focus Question: Why did the United States go to war with Britain, and what was the outcome of that war?**

Gearing Up for War

Democratic Republicans felt humiliated by the failure of the 1807 embargo against Britain. With persistent British abuses on the oceans, and Native American resistance in the West, Americans increasingly blamed the British.

Replacing the Embargo In 1809, Congress replaced the embargo with the Nonintercourse Act. Aimed at Britain and France, the act stated that the United States would resume trade with whichever of those countries lifted their restrictions on American shipping. The following year, Congress passed legislation that went a step further. Macon's Bill No. 2 restored trade with both Britain and France but also promised that if either country actively recognized American neutrality, then the United States would resume trading sanctions against the other country. When France agreed to withdraw decrees against American shipping, President Madison ordered sanctions against the British. In the meantime, however, France continued to seize American ships.

Battling Native Americans On the western frontier, two Shawnee Indian brothers, the prophet Tenskwatawa and the warrior **Tecumseh,** wanted to preserve Native American culture and unite the Indian nations in armed resistance against American expansion. They were angered by the government's repeated use of dishonest treaties to take their lands. In late 1811, while Tecumseh was seeking allies in the South, Governor William Henry Harrison of the Indiana Territory led troops into the brothers' village of Prophetstown, along the Tippecanoe River. After the **Battle of Tippecanoe,** the Americans burned Prophetstown. The Native American movement lost some momentum, though most Native Americans escaped to fight again.

Vocabulary Builder
momentum–(moh MEHN tuhm)
n. force or speed of motion

The War Hawks Demand War In 1811 some aggressive young politicians, known as the **War Hawks,** took the lead in Congress. Representing farmers and settlers from the southern and western states, the War Hawks included John C. Calhoun of South Carolina and Henry Clay of Kentucky. Strongly nationalist, they denounced the impressments of American sailors and British support for Native Americans. The War Hawks pushed for a war against Britain to restore national honor. They insisted that invading British-held Canada would deprive the Indians of their main source of arms and drive the British out of North America. The War Hawks also believed that the British would make maritime concessions to get Canada back from the Americans. They underestimated the value that the British put on their domination of world trade.

✓ **Checkpoint** Why did many Americans blame Britain for their problems?

Decision ○ Point

Should the United States Declare War on Britain?

No American disputed the fact that Britain was interfering with American shipping. Yet while the War Hawks called for war, some people questioned their motives. Read the opinions below, and then decide whether war against Britain was justified.

Grundy Urges War

Primary Source

"What, Mr. Speaker, are we now called on to decide? It is, whether we will resist by force the attempt, made by [Britain], to subject our maritime rights to the arbitrary and capricious rule of her will. . . . Sir, I prefer war to submission. [This] unjust and lawless invasion of personal liberty, calls loudly for the interposition of this Government. . . ."

—Senator Felix Grundy (KY)
December 9, 1811

Randolph Opposes War

Primary Source

"Sir, if you go to war it will not be for the protection of, or defense of your maritime rights. Gentlemen from the North have been taken up to some high mountain and shown all the kingdoms of the earth; and Canada seems tempting to their sight. . . . Agrarian [greed], not maritime right, urges the war. [We hear] but one word— Canada! Canada! Canada!"

—Senator John Randolph (VA)
December 16, 1811

You Decide
1. What is Grundy's reason for war?
2. Does Randolph believe Grundy? Explain.
3. What decision would you have made? Why?

Tecumseh (1768–1813)

Tecumseh, a Shawnee warrior from the Ohio Valley, spearheaded a spiritual and military resistance movement among Native Americans. He called for them to return to traditional values as a way of preserving their culture. At the same time, he actively resisted the United States, fighting in battles, rejecting treaties, and traveling widely to convince Indian groups that they were all one people and that no one group had the right to make a treaty. He also mocked the very idea of owning land. Meeting with William Henry Harrison in 1810, he scoffed, "Sell a country! Why not sell the air, the clouds and the great sea, as well as the earth?"

War Breaks Out

Humiliated by British interference with American trade, impressments, and support for Indian attacks on settlers, President Madison urged Congress to declare war on Britain in June of 1812. Although the **War of 1812** deeply divided the nation, Madison narrowly won reelection later that year. Disunited, unprepared, and with only a small army and navy, the United States went to war once again with the world's greatest power.

The Invasion of Canada Fails Thomas Jefferson acted as adviser to Madison. He argued that with a population of 8 million, the United States could easily conquer Canada, which had only 250,000 people. Indeed, the prospects for a victory looked favorable. An overland invasion would save the cost of building a bigger navy to fight the British. In addition, Jefferson argued that the United States did not even need a professional army. The citizen militia of the states could do the job quickly and with little expense. He called the conquest of Canada "a mere matter of marching."

Jefferson's assumptions proved to be wrong. In fact, the small British and Indian forces in Canada repeatedly defeated the American invasion attempts in 1812 and 1813. Reliance on the state militias proved a disaster. Having had no professional training, many militiamen broke rank and ran when attacked. The American regular army performed almost as poorly. One blundering general, William Hull, surrendered Detroit to a much smaller British force commanded by Isaac Brock and assisted by Indians led by Tecumseh. Instead of bolstering American pride, the attempted invasion of Canada only further embarrassed the nation.

Defeating the Native Americans To the surprise of many Americans—and to the shock of the British—the little American navy performed well, capturing four British ships during 1812. On Lake Erie, American ships led by Oliver Hazard Perry defeated a British flotilla in 1813, enabling an American army, commanded by Harrison, to retake Detroit.

The Americans made little progress in conquering Canada, but they did defeat Britain's Indian allies within the United States. In October 1813, Harrison's army killed Tecumseh and scattered his supporters. In 1814, **Andrew Jackson** of Tennessee crushed the Creek Indians of Alabama, who had allied with the British. To make peace, the survivors surrendered most of their lands. Jackson then invaded the Spanish colony of Florida, defeating the Seminole Indians and seizing the Spanish fort at Pensacola.

The British Invade During 1812 and 1813, most of the British forces were in Europe fighting Napoleon. In early 1814, however, the French dictator's defeat freed thousands of British troops to fight in North America. During the summer and fall, the British took the offensive. While the British navy blockaded the coast, British forces invaded the United States. One army occupied eastern Maine, easily brushing aside the weak defense by local militia. From Montreal, a second army invaded northern New York, while a third British force landed in Maryland and marched on Washington, D.C. In late 1814, a British fleet carried a fourth army into the Gulf of Mexico to attack New Orleans.

On the defensive, the Americans fought better than they had when invading Canada. Except for the occupation of Maine, the British attacks ended in defeat. The British did capture the national capital, easily accessible by ship via the Chesapeake Bay, and burned the White House and Capitol in revenge for some American arson in Canada. But the British suffered defeat when they moved on to attack Baltimore. Lawyer **Francis Scott Key,** who observed the British attack on Fort McHenry, celebrated the American victory by writing a poem that later became the national anthem known as **"The Star-Spangled Banner."**

Primary Source

" O say, can you see, by the dawn's early light,
What so proudly we hail'd at the twilight's last gleaming,
Whose broad stripes and bright stars, thro' the perilous fight,
O'er the ramparts we watch'd, were so gallantly streaming? "
—Francis Scott Key, 1814

Meanwhile, on Lake Champlain near Plattsburgh, New York, American ships defeated a British fleet, forcing British troops to retreat to Canada.

✓ **Checkpoint** What were some American successes and failures during the war?

Geography Interactive
For: Interactive map
Web Code: ncp-0641

Major Battles of the War of 1812

Map Skills Though Americans claimed victory, neither side actually gained or lost any territory during the War of 1812.

1. **Locate:** (a) Fort McHenry, (b) New Orleans, (c) Lake Champlain

2. **Place** In what kinds of places were most of the major battles fought?

3. **Determine Relevance** How did the British naval blockade affect the outcome of the war?

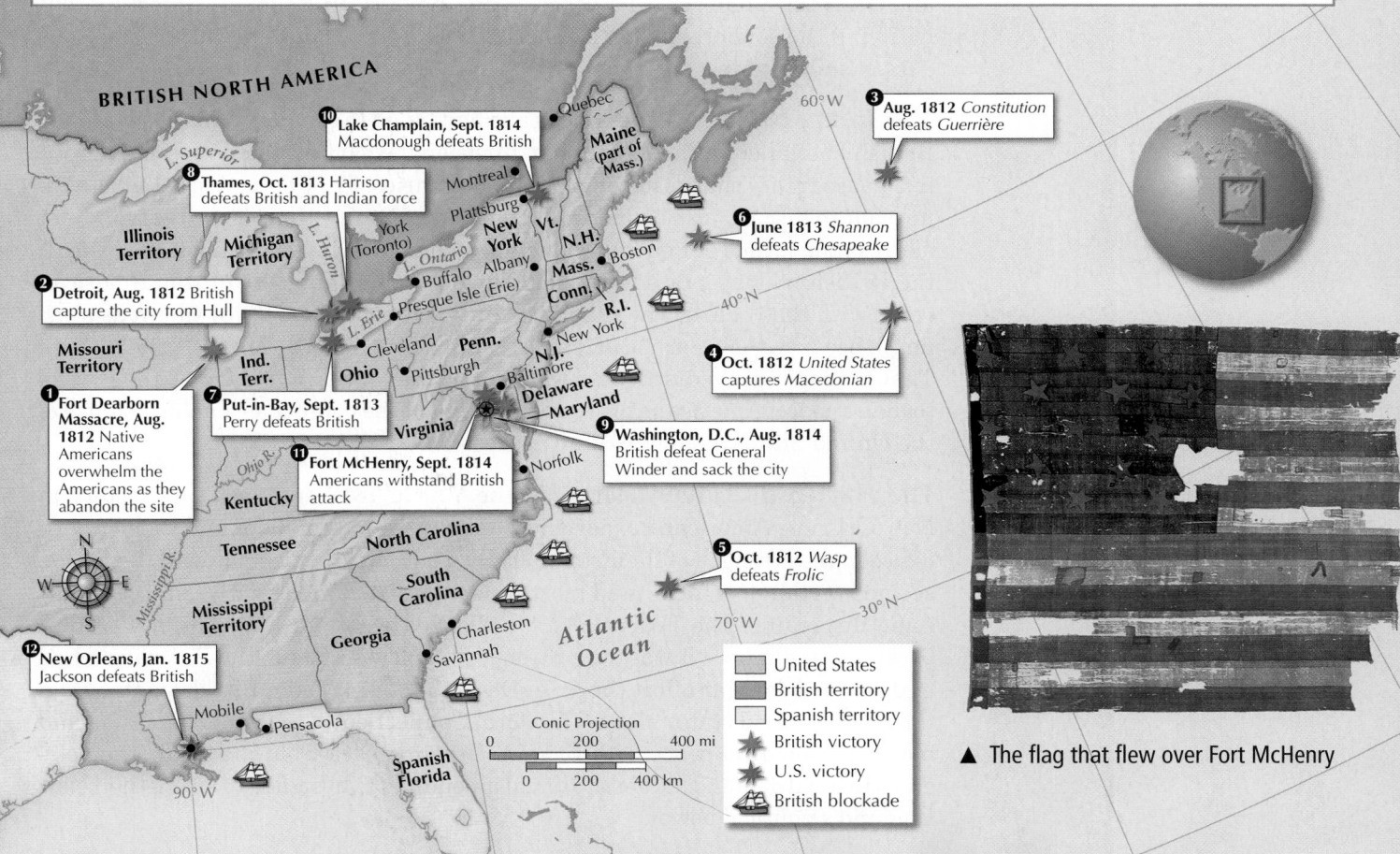

The flag that flew over Fort McHenry

Battle of New Orleans

This engraving from the 1800s depicts Andrew Jackson inspiring his soldiers to fight the British. *How does the engraving show that the United States lacked a regular standing army?*

War's Aftermath and Effects

The Americans won their greatest victory at the **Battle of New Orleans** in January 1815. From a strong and entrenched position, General Andrew Jackson routed the British attack. In this lopsided battle, the Americans suffered only 71 casualties, compared to 2,036 British casualties. The bloodshed at New Orleans was especially tragic because it came two weeks after the Americans and the British had signed a peace treaty at Ghent in Belgium. Unfortunately, notifying the soldiers in North America took over a month because of the slow pace of sailing ships.

The Treaty of Ghent The Americans had failed to conquer Canada, while the British had failed in their American invasions. Weary of war, both sides agreed to a peace treaty that restored prewar boundaries. They agreed to set up a commission to discuss any boundary disputes at a future time. The treaty did not address the issues of neutrality or impressments. But after Napoleon's defeat, the British no longer needed to impress American sailors or to stop American trade with the French. The Americans interpreted the **Treaty of Ghent** as a triumph because they learned of it shortly after hearing of Jackson's great victory. That sequence of events created the illusion that Jackson had forced the British to make peace. Americans preferred to think of the conflict as a noble defense of the United States against British aggression.

The Hartford Convention After the War of 1812 and Jackson's victory in New Orleans, Americans experienced a surge of nationalism and a new confidence in the strength of their republic. By weathering a difficult war, the nation seemed certain to endure, and most Americans were giddy with relief. The outcome discredited the Federalists, who looked weak for opposing a war that became popular once it was over. Strongest in New England, the Federalists had undermined the war effort there. In December 1814, Federalist delegates from the New England states met at Hartford, Connecticut, to consider secession and making a separate peace with Britain. Drawing back from the brink, the delegates instead demanded constitutional amendments designed to strengthen New England's political power.

Unfortunately for the delegates of the **Hartford Convention,** their demands reached Washington, D.C., at the same time as news of the peace treaty and Jackson's victory. That combination embarrassed the Federalists, who were mocked as defeatists and traitors. Madison ignored their demands, and the voters punished the Federalists in the elections that followed. By 1820 the Federalist Party was dead—a sad fate for the party that had created the federal government only to lose faith in it during the War of 1812.

The Nation Continues to Grow Events during the War of 1812 ended most Indian resistance east of the Mississippi River for the time being. As a result of various defeats of Native Americans in the South, millions of acres of southern land also opened up for settlement. Settlement in the South and West led to the establishment of the new states of Indiana (1816), Mississippi (1817), Illinois (1818), and Alabama (1819). The union became bigger and stronger.

Meanwhile, American settlers had been pouring into Spanish Florida, resulting in cross-border conflict among the region's Seminole Indians, Americans, and the Spanish. Fugitive slaves from the United States, seeking sanctuary in Florida, added to the tensions. Over the next decade, the conflict would contribute to Spain's decision to cede Florida to the United States. In return the United States renounced its claims to Texas, as part of the Adams-Onís Treaty signed in 1819.

✓ **Checkpoint** What was the Hartford Convention?

Cause and Effect

Causes
- British interfere with American shipping
- British interfere with American expansion into the western frontier
- Southerners want Florida, which is owned by Britain's ally Spain
- War Hawks want to expel Britain completely from North America

The War of 1812

Effects
- Revealed need for a strong standing army
- Encouraged American nationalism
- Brought end to the Federalist Party
- Shattered the strength of Native American resistance
- Paved the way for American acquisition of Florida

Analyze Cause and Effect Despite ending in stalemate, the War of 1812 had a major impact on the United States. *How did it affect American settlers?*

SECTION

4 Assessment

Progress Monitoring *Online*
For: Self-test with vocabulary practice
Web Code: nca-0641

Comprehension

1. **Terms and People** Write a sentence for each item below, explaining its relation to the War of 1812.
   - Tecumseh
   - Battle of Tippecanoe
   - War Hawks
   - Andrew Jackson
   - Francis Scott Key
   - "The Star-Spangled Banner"
   - Battle of New Orleans
   - Treaty of Ghent

2. **NoteTaking Reading Skill: Recognize Sequence** Use your completed chart to answer the Section Focus Question: Why did the United States go to war with Britain, and what was the outcome of that war?

Writing About History

3. **Quick Write: Give Details** Choose a topic for a research paper. Then, note the kinds of details that you should include to support a thesis. For example, if your thesis is that the American military was weaker than the British military during the War of 1812, you could include facts, statistics, quotations, and paraphrased information.

Critical Thinking

4. **Synthesize Information** Why were farmers and settlers especially likely to support the War of 1812?

5. **Make Comparisons** Compare American military strengths and weaknesses during the War of 1812 to those during the Revolutionary War.

6. **Identify Alternatives** What alternatives did Native Americans have during the war? Would the outcome have been different for them if they had chosen a different course of action?

Quick Study Guide

2.I.F.2,
2.I.F.4b

Progress Monitoring _Online_
For: Self-test with vocabulary practice
Web Code: nca-1651

■ Establishing Important Precedents

Date	Precedent
1789	**Cabinet** Washington sets up the group of federal leaders who head major departments and advise the President.
1789	**Judiciary** Judiciary Act establishes a Supreme Court, the federal court system, and the office of Attorney General.
Around 1792	**Political parties** A two-party system, made up of Federalists and Democratic Republicans, emerges.
1797	**Two terms for Presidents** Washington retires after two terms in office.
1801	**Peaceful transfer of power** With Jefferson's election, power transfers peacefully from one party to the other.
1803	**Judicial review** The Supreme Court case _Marbury_ v. _Madison_ establishes judicial review.

■ Major U.S. Conflicts, 1794–1812

Date	Event	Cause/Significance
1794	Whiskey Rebellion	People on frontier protest whiskey taxes; First challenge facing the new government
1794	Battle of Fallen Timbers	Native Americans resist American expansion, aided by the British; American victory opened Northwest Territory
1801	Barbary War	Barbary States seize American ships and sailors; First American victory overseas
1811	Battle of Tippecanoe	Native Americans led by Tecumseh resist American expansion; American victory weakens Native American movement
1812	War of 1812	Americans blame Britain for various problems; War strengthens national unity; defeat of Native Americans opens up vast lands for settlement

■ U.S. Territorial Expansion

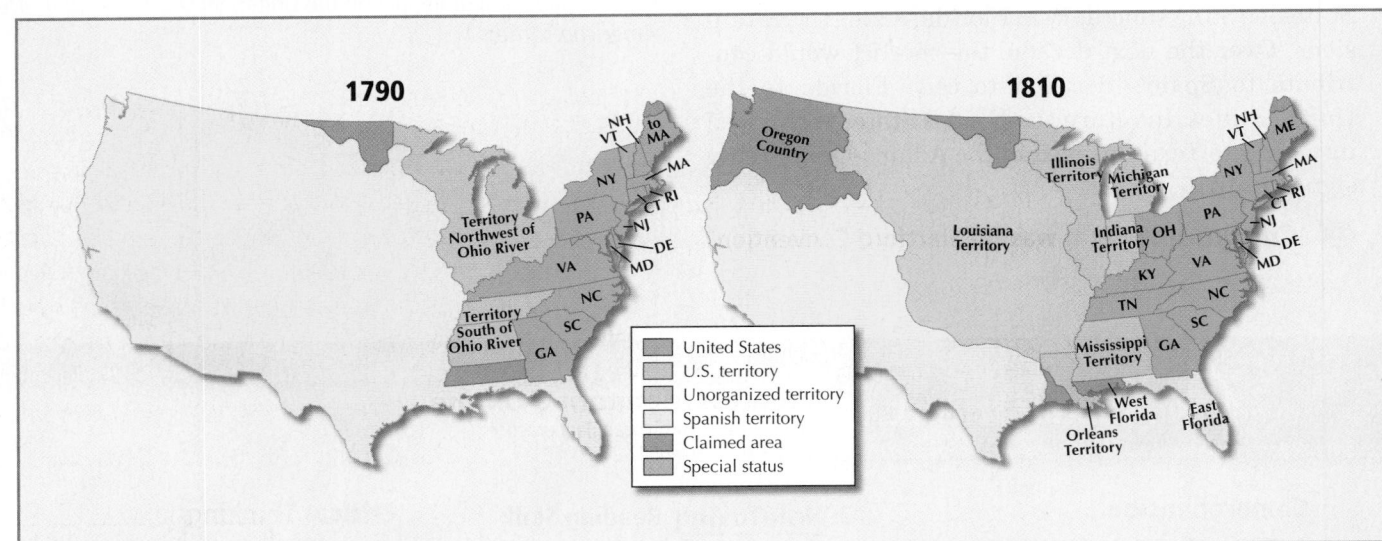

✔ Quick Study Timeline

In America

1789
Washington elected President

1795
Treaty of Greenville signed

Presidential Terms   George Washington 1789–1797   John Adams 1797–1801

| **1790** | **1795** | **1800** |

Around the World

1789
Revolution breaks out in France

1793
China rejects British diplomatic mission

1801
United Kingdom of Great Britain and Ireland established

American Issues
●—●—● Connector

 2.II.B.1b

By connecting prior knowledge with what you have learned in this chapter, you can gradually build your understanding of enduring questions that still affect America today. Answer the questions below. Then, use your American Issues Connector study guide (or go online: www.PHSchool.com **Web Code:** nch-6602).

Issues You Learned About

● **U.S. Foreign Policy** As a new nation, the United States had to establish a foreign policy. Deciding on foreign policies that are in the best interest of the nation has been an enduring issue.

1. In his Farewell Address, George Washington stated, "The great rule of conduct for us, in regard to foreign nations, is in extending our commercial relations to have with them as little political connection as possible." Write an evaluation of whether or not future Presidents followed Washington's advice and kept out of foreign alliances. Consider the following:
   - the funding of the military
   - laws and actions regarding trade with foreign nations
   - wars the United States has become involved in
   - international organizations the United States has become part of

● **Federal Power and States' Rights** The struggle for power between state governments and the federal government was sparked in the early years of the Republic.

2. According to Jefferson and Madison, what institution had the power to judge whether or not a federal law was constitutional?

3. Did Chief Justice John Marshall believe that federal laws were superior or inferior to state laws? Explain.

4. Would a strict constructionist be more likely to support a strong federal government or a weak federal government? Explain your answer.

● **Territorial Expansion of the United States** From its original 13 states along the eastern seaboard, the United States has expanded across the continent.

5. What were the results of the Treaty of Greenville?

6. What was the importance of the Louisiana Purchase?

7. How did the United States gain new land for settlement in Florida?

Connect to Your World	New York

Education in American Society In addition to shaping the United States government in its early years, New Yorker Alexander Hamilton helped found one of New York's oldest colleges, Hamilton College. Hamilton was a trustee when the institution was founded in 1793 under the name The Hamilton-Oneida Academy as a school for both Native American and settler children. In 1812, it became the third college to be established in the state, and is still thriving today. Find the ten oldest colleges or universities in the state, and write a brief history of one of them.

History *Interactive*
For: Interactive timeline
Web Code: ncp-0651

1803
Jefferson makes Louisiana Purchase

1807
Embargo Act passed

1814
Treaty of Ghent ends the War of 1812

Thomas Jefferson 1801–1809

James Madison 1809–1817

1805

1810

1815

1804
Haiti declares independence from France

1810
Colombia gains independence from Spain

1815
French leader Napoleon is defeated at Waterloo

Chapter Assessment

Terms and People

1. Define **tariff.** Why did Hamilton favor tariffs?

2. What do **loose construction** and **strict construction** mean? Explain which view Thomas Jefferson held, and why.

3. What was the **Battle of Fallen Timbers**? What was the result of this battle?

4. Define **judicial review.** Explain how the power of judicial review developed.

5. What was the **War of 1812**? Explain its major causes.

Focus Questions

The focus question for this chapter is **How did the United States build a government, expand its territory, and conduct foreign policy in its early years?** Build an answer to this big question by answering the focus questions for Sections 1 through 4 and the Critical Thinking questions that follow.

Section 1

6. How did debate over the role of government lead to the formation of political parties?

Section 2

7. How did foreign policy challenges affect political debate and shape American government?

Section 3

8. What were the successes and failures of the Jefferson administrations?

Section 4

9. Why did the United States go to war with Britain, and what was the outcome of that war?

Critical Thinking

10. **Decision Making** What was one of Washington's most important decisions in setting up the new federal government? Explain.

11. **Draw Conclusions** Would an American who supported a strong national government be more likely to vote for a Federalist or a Democratic Republican? Who would this American have likely voted for in the presidential election of 1800? Explain your answer.

12. **Draw Inferences** Why do you think Tecumseh had difficulty uniting Native Americans to resist the expansion of American settlers onto their lands?

13. **Make Inferences** Why did the Virginia and Kentucky resolutions threaten national unity?

14. **Analyze Information** How did John Marshall help establish the authority of the Supreme Court?

15. **Analyze Graphs** Describe the graph below. What event explains the data on the graph? What would cause exports to rise again in 1809?

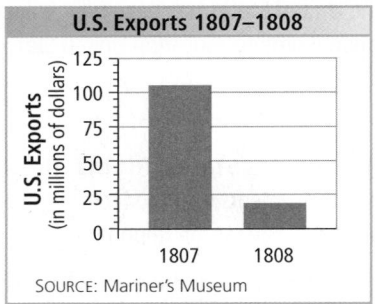

U.S. Exports 1807–1808

U.S. Exports (in millions of dollars)

125 — 100 — 75 — 50 — 25 — 0

1807   1808

SOURCE: Mariner's Museum

16. **Explain Effects** What effect did the War of 1812 have on political parties in the United States?

Writing About History

Writing a Research Paper The first few years of the United States were influential ones in the nation's history. Write a research paper that describes the importance of a person or an event in shaping the new republic. Choose your own topic or one of the following: George Washington, Thomas Jefferson, the Louisiana Purchase, the War of 1812.

Prewriting

• Choose the topic that most interests you, and create a set of questions about it.

• Narrow your topic to make it more manageable.

• Gather details and make a research plan.

Drafting

• Develop a thesis statement.

• Create an outline or graphic organizer to organize your information.

• Provide appropriate details from various sources.

Revising

• Use the guidelines on page SH14 of the Writing Handbook to revise your report.

Regents DBQ Practice

Settling the Northwest Territory

From 1787 on, huge numbers of American settlers poured into the Northwest Territory, frequently coming into conflict with the people who already lived there. How did the newcomers and the Native Americans interact? Use your knowledge of American western expansion and Documents 1, 2, 3, and 4 to answer questions 1 through 4.

Document 1

"The utmost good faith shall always be observed towards the Indians; their lands and property shall never be taken from them without their consent; and, in their property, rights, and liberty, they shall never be invaded or disturbed, unless in just and lawful wars authorized by Congress; but laws founded in justice and humanity, shall from time to time be made for preventing wrongs being done to them, and for preserving peace and friendship with them."

—*Northwest Ordinance of 1787, Section 14, Article 3*

Document 2

"At present, we do not think of ourselves perfectly secure from [the Indians] on account of a few lawless bandits made up of Mingos, Shawnees, and Cherokees, who reside at present on the waters of the Scioto [River]. These are a set of thievish, murdering rascals. . . . [L]et the treaty end how it may. . . . [The] little skulking parties of Indians, if they are never won over to be our friends, can never do us any considerable injury. On the other hand, should there be a general Indian war, this will be a place of general rendezvous for an army. So that, in all human probability, the settlement can never fail of the protection of government."

—*Rufus Putnam, Superintendent, Ohio Land Company, 1788*

Document 3

"A white man gathers from a field, a few times bigger than his room, bread enough for a whole year. If he adds to this a small field of grass, he maintains beasts . . . while we must have a great deal of ground to live upon. A deer will serve us a couple of days, and a single deer must have a great deal of ground to put him in good condition. If we kill two or three hundred a year, 'tis the same as to eat all the wood and grass of the land they live on and that is a great deal. No wonder the whites drive us every year further before them from the sea to the Mississippi. They spread like oil on a blanket; we melt like snow before the sun."

—*Little Turtle, Miami Chief, 1792*

Document 4

Movement into the Northwest Territory

1. Document 1 could best be described as a
   (1) treaty.
   (2) charter.
   (3) constitution.
   (4) law.

2. What can you conclude from Document 2?
   (1) Native Americans had varied reactions to settlers.
   (2) Rufus Putnam advocated "a general Indian war."
   (3) Soldiers were marching to Ohio.
   (4) Settlers lived along the Scioto River.

3. According to Document 3, Little Turtle thought American expansion
   (1) was due to missionary activity.
   (2) was fueled by racism.
   (3) could likely be halted.
   (4) was inevitable because of differences in land use.

4. **Writing Task** Did Americans in the Northwest Territory adhere to the provisions of the Northwest Ordinance of 1787 regarding native peoples? Use your knowledge of American history and evidence from the sources above to explain your answer.

NY Connect to New York

Susan B. Anthony

The first half of the 1800s was an era in which reformers tried to resolve the inequities they observed in American society.

> "Wherever, on the face of the globe or on the page of history, you show me a disfranchised class, I will show you a degraded class of labor. Disfranchisement means inability to make, shape or control one's own circumstances. The disfranchised must always do the work, accept the wages, occupy the position the enfranchised assign to them."
>
> —From a speech given by Susan B. Anthony

A notable New Yorker, Susan B. Anthony, an abolitionist and temperance movement worker turned women's rights advocate, put her mark on the cause of women's suffrage. You will read more about abolitionists (who worked to end slavery) and temperance workers (who wanted to moderate or end alcohol consumption) in the coming chapters.

Anthony, who was raised in the Quaker religion, grew up in Battenville, New York. As an adult she worked as a teacher in a Quaker boarding school in New Rochelle, New York. From 1846 to 1849, Anthony served as the head-mistress of Canajoharie Academy's female department in Rochester, New York.

In 1851, Anthony was attending a temperance convention in Seneca Falls, New York (the location of the famous women's rights convention three years earlier) when she met Amelia Bloomer, editor of the temperance newspaper *The Lily*, and Elizabeth Cady Stanton, a women's suffragist. Stanton and Anthony developed a lifelong friendship, and Anthony turned her attention toward the women's rights movement. In 1852, Anthony was told that women were not welcome to speak at a Sons of Temperance meeting in Albany. This slight led Anthony to form the Women's New York State Temperance Society.

Canvassing for women's rights was a difficult and often alienating job for Anthony. In 1872, to emphasize her position that women are guaranteed the right to vote in the Bill of Rights, she cast a vote in Rochester for the presidential election and was arrested. Though she did not see suffrage in her lifetime, she was honored for her efforts in 1979 when she was the first woman to be represented on U.S. currency.

EXPANSION AND REFORM

CONTENTS

A pioneer family builds a cabin in the early 1800s. ▶

Nationalism Revived

After the War of 1812, the United States experienced a period of growth and renewed nationalism. Expanding markets, along with thriving industries and businesses, transformed American life. The new nationalism was reflected not only in this industrial growth, but in Supreme Court rulings and domestic and foreign policies.

“The war [of 1812] has renewed and reinstated the national feelings and character which the Revolution had given, and which were daily lessened.”
—Albert Gallatin, 1816

Listen to the Witness History *audio to hear more about the nationalism characteristic of this time period.*

◀ New York Harbor, 1849

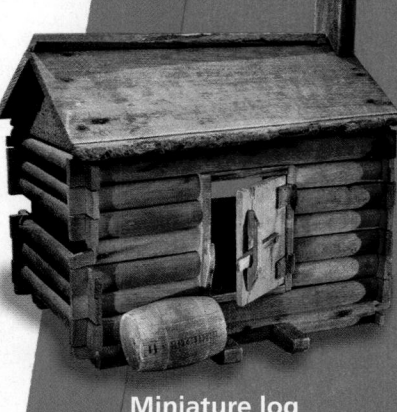

Miniature log cabin from the Election of 1840

Work schedule at the Holyoke Mills, 1853

 Core Curriculum Preview

Chapter Focus Question: How did nationalism and sectionalism affect the United States from the early 1800s to the mid-1800s?

Section 1
Industry and Transportation   3.II.B.1, 3.II.B.4, 3.III.D.2

Section 2
Sectional Differences   2.I.A.2c, 2.II.B.1a, 2.II.B.1d, 3.III.A.2c

Section 3
An Era of Nationalism   1.I.D.1e, 2.I.F.4e, 2.II.A.2, 2.II.A.3

Section 4
Democracy and the Age of Jackson   2.I.F.3, 2.II.B.2b, 3.III.D.3

Section 5
Constitutional Disputes and Crises   2.II.A.1, 2.II.B

Use the ☑ **Quick Study Timeline** at the end of this chapter to preview chapter events.

Cotton gin

Note Taking Study Guide *Online*
For: Note Taking and American Issues Connector
Web Code: nce-6701

Lowell girl lunch pail ▶

▲ Lowell girl weaving in textile mill

WITNESS HISTORY 🔊 AUDIO

Dawn of the Industrial Age

The United States experienced a revolution in the early 1800s—a revolution in the way many people lived and worked. This revolution introduced factory methods of production from Great Britain. Here, a Lowell mill girl writes to her father about her work schedule at the textile mill:

❝Dear Father, I am well which is one comfort. . . . At half past six [the bell] rings for the girls to get up and at seven they are called into the mill. At half past 12 we have dinner and are called back again at one and stay till half past seven. I get along very well with my work.❞
—Mary Paul, December 21, 1845

Industry and Transportation

Core Curriculum Objectives

- **3.II.B.1** Transportation: railroads and automobiles; urban transportation
- **3.II.B.4** Communications: telegraph, telephone
- **3.III.D.2** The impact of industrialization

Terms and People

turnpike
National Road
Erie Canal
Industrial Revolution
Samuel Slater

Francis Cabot Lowell
Lowell girl
interchangeable parts
Eli Whitney
Samuel F.B. Morse

NoteTaking

Reading Skill: Identify Causes and Effects
Fill in a table with the causes and effects of the transportation revolution and industrialization.

Transportation and Industry	
Causes	**Effects**
• Invention of commercial steamboat	• Drastically increased speed of traveling upstream
•	•
•	•

Why It Matters Developments in technology began to transform life in the United States in the early 1800s. New methods of transporting and manufacturing goods changed the way people lived and worked. The United States was set on a course of industrialization that would shape life in the nation for decades. **Section Focus Question: How did transportation developments and industrialization affect the nation's economy?**

The Transportation Revolution

The original 13 states hugged the Atlantic Coast, and all major settlements in the United States sprang up near a harbor or river because water provided the most efficient way to move people and goods. At the start of the nineteenth century, overland transportation consisted of carts, wagons, sleighs, and stagecoaches pulled by horses or oxen over dirt roads. Moving goods just a few dozen miles by road could cost as much as shipping the same cargo across the ocean.

Improving the Roads In an effort to improve overland transportation, some states chartered companies to operate **turnpikes**—roads for which users had to pay a toll. The term came from the turnpikes, or gates, that guarded entrances to the roads. Turnpike operators were supposed to use toll income to improve the roads and ease travel. But only a few turnpikes made a profit, and most failed to lower transportation costs or increase the speed of travel. The country's lone decent route, which was made of crushed rock, was the **National Road.** Funded by the federal government, this roadway extended west from Maryland to the Ohio River (in present-day West Virginia) in 1818.

The Steamboat Goes Commercial The first major advance in transportation was the development of the steamboat. By burning wood or coal, the engine boiled the water to create steam. The force of the steam turned a large, rotating paddle, which pushed the boat through the water. American Robert Fulton designed the first commercially successful steamboat—the *Clermont*.

The steamboat made it much easier to travel upstream against the current. For example, before the steamboat, it took about four months to travel the 1,440 miles from New Orleans to Louisville, Kentucky, along the Mississippi and Ohio rivers. In 1820, a steamboat made the same journey in just 20 days. By 1838, it took a steamboat only six days. Steamboats unlocked the great potential of the Mississippi River Basin for moving people and goods. The number of steamboats plying the rivers of that system grew from 230 in 1834 to nearly 700 in 1843.

Steam-powered ships also revolutionized transatlantic travel. By 1850, a steamship could cross the Atlantic in 10 to 14 days, compared to the 25 to 50 days for a sailing ship.

HISTORY MAKERS

Robert Fulton (1765–1815)

Although Fulton was born and raised in Pennsylvania, he spent much of his life in England and France. There, he worked first as a painter and then as an inventor and engineer, where he constructed canals and experimented with torpedoes and submarines. When he returned to the United States after 19 years, President Jefferson asked him to help build canals in the new Louisiana territory. Fulton declined, however, choosing to focus instead on the development of the steamboat. In 1807, Fulton's steamboat, the *Clermont*, successfully made its journey from New York to Albany, demonstrating to the world the possibilities of steam navigation. This success led Fulton and his business partner, Robert Livingston, to start the first commercial steamboat service.

Canals Boom A second transportation advance of the early 1800s was the construction of canals. The nation's canal network grew from 100 miles in 1816 to 3,300 miles in 1840. Mostly built in the Northeast, canals provided efficient water transportation that linked farms to the expanding cities.

The best-known canal of the era was the **Erie Canal.** Completed in 1825, it ran 363 miles across New York State from Lake Erie to the Hudson River. Before this canal went into service, it could cost $100 or more to ship a ton of freight overland from the city of Buffalo on the shores of Lake Erie to New York City. The canal lowered that cost to just $4.

By funneling western produce to the Hudson River, the Erie Canal helped make New York City the nation's greatest commercial center. As a result, the city grew quickly. From a population of 124,000 in 1820, its population surged to 800,000 in 1860. The canal also enhanced the value of farmland in the Great Lakes region, because farmers there now had easier access to eastern markets for their goods.

> **Primary Source** "The increase of commerce, and the growth of the country, have been very accurately measured by the growth of the business of the Canal. It has been one great bond of strength, infusing life and vigor into the whole. Commercially and politically, it has secured and maintained to the United States the characteristics of a homogeneous [sharing common features] people."
> —Report by the Secretary of the Treasury, 1853

Railroads Further Ease Transport The most dramatic advance in transportation in the 1800s was the arrival of a new mode of transportation—railroads. This technology, largely developed in Great Britain, began to appear in the United States in the 1820s. Horses pulled the first American trains. But clever inventors soon developed steam-powered engines, which could pull heavier loads of freight or passengers at higher speeds than horses could manage.

Geography *Interactive*
For: Interactive map
Web Code: ncp-0702

A Revolution in Transportation In the early 1800s, businesses were expanding and Americans needed more efficient and reliable transportation. Roads and canals provided a good start, but they soon proved too slow and limited for a nation on the move. Beginning in the late 1820s, iron rails were laid on long tracks to connect locations such as New York City and New Haven, Connecticut. Goods could be shipped faster and more easily on trains, and cities located along railroads prospered. Via the rails, vast regions gained access to expanding markets.

▼ Early American express train

Major Canals, Roads, and Railroads, 1840–1850

Geography and History
• What did the transportation developments that occurred during this time period have in common?
• In what part of the country were most of the railroads located in the mid-1800s? Why do you think this was the case?

Compared to canals, railroads cost less to build and could more easily scale hills. Trains moved faster than ships and carried more weight. Their introduction put a quick end to the brief boom in canal building. Meanwhile, the American rail network expanded from 13 miles of track in 1830 to 31,000 miles by 1860. In 1800, a journey from New York City to Detroit, Michigan, took 28 days by boat. In 1857, the same trip took only two days by train.

✓ **Checkpoint** What were the major developments in transportation between 1800 and 1860?

Technology Sparks Industrial Growth

Developments in technology also transformed manufacturing. This transformation became known as the **Industrial Revolution,** which changed not only the nation's economy but also its culture, social life, and politics.

The Industrial Revolution began in Great Britain during the 1700s, with the development of machines, powered by steam or flowing rivers, to perform work that had once been done by hand. The first machines spun thread and wove cloth more quickly and cheaply.

Slater Opens First Textile Mill To protect its industrial advantage, the British banned the export of machinery, as well as the emigration of workers with knowledge of the technology. However, a skilled worker named **Samuel Slater** defied that law and moved to the United States. Slater used his detailed knowledge of the textile machinery to build the nation's first water-powered textile mill in 1793 at Pawtucket, Rhode Island. The mill used the flowing Blackstone River to power its machinery, which produced one part of the textile: cotton thread. Slater and his business partners later built more factories along New England rivers. These factories used the so-called family system, in which entire families, including parents and children, were employed in the mills. Those families settled in villages owned by factory owners and located around the mills.

Lowell Builds Fully Operational Mill Boston merchant **Francis Cabot Lowell** developed another industrial system in Massachusetts. In 1811, he toured England's factory towns to gather secret information. Returning home, Lowell organized a company called the Boston Associates. In 1813, the associates built their first mill at Waltham, Massachusetts, in which all operations in the manufacture of cloth occurred—instead of just the production of thread. During the 1820s, they built more factories on the Merrimac River and established a new town called Lowell. Their system employed young, single women recruited from area farms. The company enforced strict rules of behavior and housed the **"Lowell girls"** in closely supervised boardinghouses. After a few years of work, most of the young women married and left the factories.

Factory Work Changes Lives The growth of factories changed more than the speed and volume of production. It changed the working lives of thousands of people. Machines increased the pace of work and divided labor into many small tasks done by separate workers. This process reduced the amount of skill and training required for individual jobs. Factory owners benefited because untrained workers were more numerous and less costly to employ. In some trades, owners achieved those benefits without adopting new machines. The manufacture of clothing and shoes are two examples.

As you have read, America's first factories produced thread or cloth rather than finished clothing. During the 1820s, a garment trade developed primarily in New York City. Contractors provided cloth to poor women who made the clothes in their homes without the help of machines. They earned about $1 per week.

Shoemaking followed a similar model. Lynn, Massachusetts, led the nation in this industry. A few men performed the skilled and better-paying tasks of cutting and shaping leather for the tops of the shoes. For less pay (about 50 cents a week), women sewed the shoes together.

✔ **Checkpoint** What changes occurred in the United States with the rise of industry in the early 1800s?

Inventions Transform Industry and Agriculture

A number of key innovations paralleled the revolutions in transportation and industry in the early 1800s. These also dramatically affected the American economy and society.

New Methods of Production To improve efficiency in factories, manufacturers designed products with **interchangeable parts,** identical

▼ Samuel Slater's textile mill, Pawtucket, Rhode Island

Vocabulary Builder
component–(kuhm POH nuhnt) *n.*
part; one of the parts of a whole

components that could be used in place of one another. Inventor **Eli Whitney** introduced this idea to the United States. Traditionally, items such as clocks and muskets were built one at a time by skilled artisans who made each part and assembled the device from start to finish by hand. As a result, a part that would work in one gun or clock might not work in any other. Whitney proposed making muskets in a new way—by manufacturing each part separately and precisely. Under Whitney's system, a part that would work in one musket would work in another musket. In other words, the parts would be interchangeable.

It took some years for American manufacturers to make interchangeable parts reliably. Yet the idea of interchangeable parts eventually made possible the much more efficient production of a wide range of manufactured goods. One of the products manufactured with interchangeable parts was the sewing machine. Invented by Elias Howe and improved by Isaac Singer, the sewing machine lowered the cost and increased the speed of making cloth into clothing.

Innovation Quickens Communication In 1837, American **Samuel F.B. Morse** invented the electric telegraph, which allowed electrical pulses to travel long distances along metal wires as coded signals. The code of dots and dashes is called Morse code after its inventor. Before the telegraph, a message could pass only as fast as a horse or a ship could carry a letter. By using Morse's invention, a message could be delivered almost instantly. By 1860, the nation had 50,000 miles of telegraph lines.

Agriculture Remains Strong Despite the growing size and power of the nation's factories, agriculture remained the largest industry in the United States. But change affected farming as well. American farms became more productive, raising larger crops for the market. In 1815, American farmers sold only about a third of their harvests. By 1860, that share had doubled. The gains came partly from the greater fertility of new farms in the Midwest. Farmers also adopted better methods for planting, tending, and harvesting crops and for raising livestock. After 1840, large farms also employed the steel plow invented by John Deere and the mechanical reaper developed by Cyrus McCormick.

▲ Samuel Morse's telegraph

✔ **Checkpoint** What were the key inventions between 1820 and 1860?

Progress Monitoring *Online*
For: Self-test with vocabulary practice
Web Code: nca-0703

Comprehension

1. Terms and People For each person below, write a sentence explaining the impact of his new invention or innovation on the economy of the United States.
- Samuel Slater
- Francis Cabot Lowell
- Eli Whitney
- Samuel F.B. Morse

2. NoteTaking Reading Skill: Identify Causes and Effects Use your completed table to answer the Section Focus Question: How did transportation developments and industrialization affect the nation's economy?

Writing About History

3. Quick Write: Choose a Topic Review your notes from this section to see what topics you would like to research further. Then, write a list of questions that you will research to find the answers.

Critical Thinking

4. Predict Consequences How might the United States have been different if transportation had not advanced during the 1800s?

5. Summarize How did textile mills develop in the United States?

6. Make Generalizations How was the development of interchangeable parts an example of the move to make work "less skilled" in the early 1800s?

◀ Northern factory

A Nation of Farming and Industry

Thomas Jefferson and the Democratic Republicans had once championed the idea of a nation of farmers. But Jefferson's own embargo of 1807 and the War of 1812 severely limited American access to British manufactured goods. Suddenly, Americans needed to develop factories.

❝We must now place the manufacturer by the side of the agriculturalist. . . . [S]hall we manufacture our own comforts or go without them at the will of a foreign nation? He, therefore, who is now against domestic manufactures must be for reducing us . . . to dependence on that nation. . . .❞

—Thomas Jefferson, in a letter to Benjamin Austin, 1816

▲ Southern cotton field

Sectional Differences

 Core Curriculum Objectives

- **2.I.A.2c** Varieties of immigrant motivation, ethnicities, and experiences
- **2.II.B.1a** The growth of urban and industrial patterns of life in the North
- **2.II.B.1d** Patterns of Southern development
- **3.III.A.2c** Working conditions: "wage slavery"

Terms and People

Tariff of 1816   nativist
capital   cotton gin
labor union

NoteTaking

Reading Skill: Compare and Contrast Use a Venn diagram like the one below to compare and contrast the North and the South.

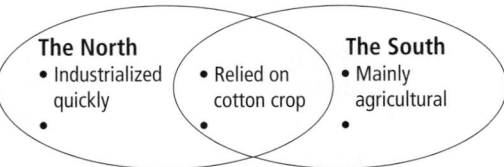

The North
- Industrialized quickly
-

• Relied on cotton crop
•

The South
- Mainly agricultural
-

Why It Matters Industrialization occurred mainly in the Northeast, where it changed the very structure of society. In the South, a boom in cotton production helped deepen the region's commitment to slavery. The two parts of the country developed in different ways—a fact that increasingly complicated politics in the United States. **Section Focus Question: How did the North and South differ during the first half of the 1800s?**

The North Embraces Industry

Thomas Jefferson had hoped to preserve the United States as a nation of farmers. Instead, between 1815 and 1860, the United States developed an industrial sector, or a distinct part of the economy or society dedicated to industry. Without intending to do so, Democratic Republican policies contributed to that industrial development.

Why Industrialization Spread The embargo of 1807 and the War of 1812 cut off access to British manufactured goods. Eager for substitutes, Americans built their own factories in the Northeast. After the war, however, British goods once again flowed into the United States, threatening to overwhelm fledgling American manufacturers. Congress could have let those industries wither from the competition. Instead, Congress imposed the **Tariff of 1816,** a tariff on imports designed to protect American industry. This tariff increased the price of imported manufactured goods by an average of 20 to 25 percent. The inflated price for imports encouraged Americans to buy products made in the United States. The tariff helped industry, but it hurt farmers, who had to pay higher prices for consumer goods.

Why the Northeast? Most of the new factories emerged in the Northeast. There were several reasons for this. One reason was greater <u>access</u> to **capital,** or the money needed to build factories or other productive assets. In the South, the land and the climate favored agriculture. Thus, people there invested capital in land and slave labor. The Northeast had more cheap labor to work in the factories. In addition, the Northeast had many swiftly flowing rivers to provide water power for the new factories.

 Checkpoint What factors contributed to industrialization in the early 1800s?

Social Change in the North

The arrival of industry changed the way many Americans worked by reducing the skill required for many jobs. This trend hurt highly skilled artisans, such as blacksmiths, shoemakers, and tailors, who could not compete with manufacturers working with many low-cost laborers. Most artisans suffered declining wages.

Workers Organize Troubled workers responded by seeking political change. During the 1820s, some artisans organized the Workingmen's Party to compete in local and state elections. They sought free public education and laws to limit the working day to ten hours versus the standard twelve.

The party also supported the right of workers to organize **labor unions**— groups of workers who unite to seek better pay and conditions. Most early labor unions focused on helping skilled tradesmen, such as carpenters or printers. Unions went on strike to force employers to pay higher wages, reduce hours, or improve conditions. In 1834 and 1836, for example, the Lowell mill girls held strikes when employers cut their wages and increased their charges for boarding. Singing "Oh! I cannot be a slave!" they left their jobs and temporarily shut down the factory. The Lowell strikes failed to achieve their goals, however. The women eventually returned to work and accepted the reduced pay.

Factory owners sometimes turned to the courts for protection. In 1835, a New York City court convicted 20 tailors of conspiracy for forming a union. Such convictions angered workers. But, neither the union movement nor the Workingmen's Party prospered in the early 1800s.

A Middle Class Emerges While hurting some working Americans, industrialization helped others. A middle class emerged, in which men helped manage businesses as bankers, lawyers, accountants, clerks, auctioneers, brokers, and retailers. The middle class stood above the working class of common laborers but below the upper class of wealthy business owners.

Most middle-class men worked in offices outside of their homes. They also began to move their homes away from the crowds, noise, and smells of the workshops and factories. Factory workers, however, could not afford that move. Neighborhoods, therefore, became segregated by class as well as by race. This contrasted with colonial cities and towns, where people of all social classes had to live close to one another.

For the middle class, work became separated from family life. These families expected wives and mothers to stay at home, tending those spaces as havens from the bustle of the working world, while the men went off to work and returned with the money to support the household. Working-class and farm families could not

▲ Glass cutters' trade union ribbon

afford such an arrangement. In those families, women and children also had to work.

Emigration From Ireland and Germany In the 1840s, the new middle class and most of the nation's farmers had been born in the United States. Increasingly, however, the working class was comprised of immigrants. Prior to 1840, immigration consisted mainly of Protestants from England or Scotland. During the 1830s, about 600,000 immigrants arrived. That number more than doubled to 1,500,000 during the 1840s and nearly doubled again to 2,800,000 in the 1850s.

This surge primarily came from Ireland and Germany, regions suffering from political upheavals, economic depressions, and rural famines. In Ireland, mass starvation occurred in the 1840s as a result of a fungus that destroyed the potato crop. The potato had been the primary food source for the Irish poor. A few historians suggest that the famine was an act of genocide. As hundreds of thousands of Irish were starving to death, huge amounts of livestock, corn, and other foods were being exported from Ireland to England. However, most historians dismiss this idea because there was no deliberate British policy to exterminate the Irish. In fact, the British government provided some relief with soup kitchens for the starving and work projects for the jobless. Even so, it is estimated that more than a million Irish people died of starvation or famine-related diseases. Another million or more left Ireland, immigrating to Australia or North America. Those who came to America joined many other Irish and German immigrants. Germans had fled their homeland during the same period when their political revolution failed.

Unlike most of their predecessors, the new immigrants tended to be Catholic or Jewish. In search of work, they arrived in the seaports of the Northeast. A small minority, mostly German, could afford to set up shops or move to the West to buy farmland. But most immigrants had to find work on the docks, in factories, at construction sites, or in middle-class homes as domestic servants.

Immigration boosted the Northeast's share of the nation's population. It also promoted urban growth. In 1860, immigrants comprised more than 40 percent of the population of New York City. Some working-class immigrants moved on to new cities in the Midwest, including Cincinnati, Chicago, Cleveland, and Detroit. Very few went to the South, which lacked factory jobs for wage workers.

The rapid influx of so many newcomers produced social and political strains. Poverty forced many immigrants to cluster in shabby neighborhoods. The newcomers competed for jobs and housing with free African Americans. Rioters attacked African Americans, killing some and burning others' homes.

Catholic immigrants also suffered contempt from the American-born Protestant majority. Protestants distrusted the Catholic Church, thinking it to be hostile to republican government. Protestant workers also resented the competition from newcomers who depressed wages offered by employers. Riots between Protestants and Catholics occurred in Philadelphia in 1844 and in Baltimore in 1854.

Some politicians, particularly in the Whig Party, exploited ethnic tensions. Called **nativists,** they campaigned for laws to discourage immigration or to deny political rights to newcomers. To defend their interests, many immigrants became active in the Democratic Party.

✓ **Checkpoint** How did industrialization change the experience of working people?

Irish Famine
Many Irish immigrants came to the United States in the 1840s to escape the famine. Today, there are several memorials in the United States commemorating those who suffered in Ireland. Pictured here (top) is the Irish Memorial located in Philadelphia. The etching (inset) shows a family that is homeless and starving as a result of the famine. *What drew Irish and German immigrants to the United States?*

Southern Agricultural Economy and Society

During the 1780s, Thomas Jefferson, James Madison, and George Washington hoped that slavery would gradually fade away. They thought that a shift from tobacco to wheat cultivation would slowly undermine the slave system, making it less profitable. Indeed, they saw some evidence of such a trend in Virginia and Maryland, where many slaves were freed during the 1780s.

That trend, however, did not affect the Deep South—the region to the south and southwest of Virginia. In fact, the trend did not last even in Virginia. Slavery became more profitable as cotton became the South's leading crop.

Cotton Production Surges In the Deep South, three developments worked together to boost cotton production: the cotton gin, western expansion, and industrialization.

In 1793, Eli Whitney invented the **cotton gin** while working in Georgia. This machine reduced the amount of time and the cost of separating the cotton seeds from the valuable white fiber. The cotton gin made cotton cultivation much more profitable. Previously a minor crop, cotton became the South's leading product. From 5 million pounds in 1793, cotton production surged to 170 million pounds in 1820.

In part, that surge came as planters in older states—Georgia, South Carolina, and North Carolina—switched to growing cotton. But mostly it came as planters moved west or south to make new plantations in Florida, Tennessee, Alabama, Mississippi, Arkansas, Louisiana, and east Texas. These areas offered fertile soil and a warm climate well suited for growing cotton.

The increase in the cotton supply filled a growing demand from textile factories in the Northeast and in Europe. By 1840, southern plantations produced 60 percent of the cotton used by American and European factories. Cotton and cotton textiles accounted for over half the value of all American exports. With good reason, Americans spoke of "King Cotton" as the ruler of their economy.

Cotton Boom Spreads Slavery Growing cotton required workers as well as land. Southern planters met this need with enslaved African Americans. After federal law abolished the overseas slave trade in 1808, illegal trade and interstate trade filled the gap. Many slaves came from the fading tobacco plantations of Virginia and Maryland, where planters who once grew crops now acquired their income from trading slaves.

Because cotton was so profitable, the demand for slaves soared. Slaves became more valuable to their owners. In 1802, a slave could sell for $600. By 1860, that price had tripled to $1,800. The total number of slaves increased from 1.5 million in 1820 to 4 million in 1860. Far from withering, slavery flourished and became more deeply entrenched in the southern economy.

Economic Consequences Although many plantation owners became rich, cotton production limited regional development. Most of the South became too dependent on one crop. That dependence paid off in most years, when cotton prices were high. But prices sometimes plummeted, forcing many planters into bankruptcy.

Another problem was that plantations dispersed the population. The South lost out on the urban growth needed for an industrial economy. Only one southern city, New Orleans, ranked among America's top fifteen cities in 1860. The South also lacked the commercial towns so common in the Northeast and Midwest. In 1860, a traveler in Alabama noted, "In fact the more fertile the land, the more destitute is the country of villages and towns."

The stunted commercial development in the South did not attract the immigrants who needed wage work. Consequently, the northern population grew much faster than the southern population. In 1850, the North had twice as many free people as did the South. That trend increased the political power of the North, especially in the House of Representatives. And that political trend alarmed southern whites who did not trust northerners to protect slavery.

The South also paid an economic price for keeping two fifths of its people in slavery. For lack of wages, most slaves were desperately poor and consumed very little. The South's limited consumer demand discouraged southern entrepreneurs from building factories. It was more profitable to buy a plantation.

Cultural Consequences A dispersed population and the burden of slavery affected the culture of the South. Planters opposed education for slaves and cared little about providing it to poor whites. The rate of southern white illiteracy was 15 percent—three times higher than what it was in the North and West.

Cotton Production and Slavery, 1800–1860

Slaves and bales of cotton (in millions)

— Cotton Production
— Number of Slaves

SOURCE: *Historical Statistics of the United States*

▲ With the invention of the cotton gin, a surge in cotton production brought about a corresponding growth in the use of slave labor.

THE COTTON GIN EXPANDS SLAVERY

Eli Whitney made cotton-growing big business with his invention of the cotton gin in 1793. Using a cotton gin, one person could clean about 50 times the amount of cotton in a day as someone working by hand. As a result, vast new areas in the South were planted with cotton, making the South the world's largest cotton supplier. But while the cotton gin decreased the amount of labor needed to remove seeds, the overall need for labor increased as cotton production went up.

◄ This ad for cotton thread illustrates the effects cotton production had on slavery and plantations in the South, as well as manufacturing towns in the North.

BLACK & COLORS—FOR HAND AND MACHINE.

J & P. COATS.

The cotton gin had spiked-teeth mounted ► on an enclosed revolving cylinder. Raw cotton was fed into the machine, and as the cylinder was turned, the seeds that were embedded in the plant were separated from the cotton fibers. Before the cotton gin, enslaved people performed this tedious task by hand.

Why It Matters
Enslaved people provided cheap labor, which led to a revitalization of slavery at a time when it was on the decline. Over time, this expansion of slavery increased tensions between the North and the South, eventually resulting in the Civil War.

Thinking Critically
1. **Identify Central Issues** Why did the invention of the cotton gin eventually cause further tensions between the North and the South?

2. **Predict Consequences** What might have happened to cotton as a commodity if the cotton gin had never been invented?

Although slavery was central to life in the South, slaveholders were a minority. No more than one fourth of white men had slaves in 1860. Three fourths of these held fewer than 10 slaves, and only about 3,000 white men owned 100 or more slaves. The typical slaveholder lived in a farmhouse and owned only four or five slaves.

Why, then, did southern whites so vigorously defend the slave system? Part of the answer lies in the aspirations of common farmers. They hoped some day to acquire their own slaves and plantations. Common whites also dreaded freeing the slaves for fear they would seek bloody revenge.

All classes of whites also believed that they shared a racial bond. Even the poorest whites felt a sense of racial superiority. They also reasoned that southern whites enjoyed an equality of rights impossible in the North, where poor men depended on wage labor from rich mill owners. Southern farmers took pride in their independence. They credited that independence to a social structure that kept slaves at the bottom.

By the 1850s, proslavery forces rejected the criticism of slavery once expressed by Jefferson, Madison, and Washington. They no longer defended slavery as a necessary evil but touted the institution as a positive good. They also insisted that slavery was kinder to African Americans than industrial life was to white workers:

> **Primary Source** "The negro slaves of the South are the happiest, and, in some sense, the freest people in the world. . . . The free laborer must work or starve. He is more of a slave than the negro, because he works longer and harder for less allowance than the slave."
>
> —George Fitzhugh, *Cannibals All! or, Slaves Without Masters,* 1857

Despite these claims, no northern workers fled to the South to become slaves, while hundreds of slaves ran away to seek wage work in the North.

✓ **Checkpoint** Why did slavery spread in the South, rather than fade away?

SECTION 2 Assessment

Progress Monitoring *Online*
For: Self-test with vocabulary practice
Web Code: nca-0704

Comprehension

1. **Terms and People** What is the relationship between each of the following terms and the impact of industrialization in the northeastern United States?
   - Tariff of 1816
   - capital
   - labor union

2. **NoteTaking Reading Skill: Compare and Contrast** Use your completed Venn diagram to answer the Section Focus Question: How did the North and South differ during the first half of the 1800s?

Writing About History

3. **Quick Write: Gather Details** When writing a research report, you should include facts, examples, descriptions, and other information to help explain your findings. Make a list of details about the sectional differences between the North and the South that you read about in this section.

Critical Thinking

4. **Recognize Cause and Effect** How did the physical geography of the Northeast help influence the spread of industry there?

5. **Draw Conclusions** What can you conclude about factory workers based on the fact that there was little public support for labor unions or the policies of the Workingmen's Party in the early 1800s?

6. **Express Problems Clearly** What was the relationship between the cotton gin and the growth of slavery in the South?

Sectionalism and National Politics

TRACK THE ISSUE

How do regional differences affect national politics?

Throughout U.S. history, people in different parts of the country have had different views on important national issues. These differences have sometimes divided American politics along regional lines. Use the timeline below to explore this enduring issue.

1787 Three-fifths Compromise
North and South disagree over how to count enslaved people for congressional representation.

1812 War of 1812
Western and southern farmers favor war.

1816–1832 Tariffs
North wants protective tariffs.

1861 Civil War
Disagreements between the North and the South lead to the Civil War.

1948 Dixiecrats
Southern Democrats split from their party over civil rights.

2004 Presidential Election
Election confirms division between Democratic and Republican states.

Henry Clay, a senator from the western state of Kentucky, supported the War of 1812.

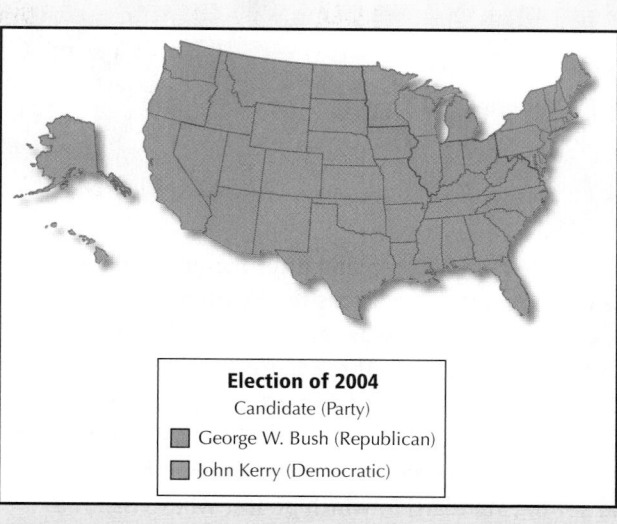

Election of 2004
Candidate (Party)
■ George W. Bush (Republican)
■ John Kerry (Democratic)

The presidential election of 2004

DEBATE THE ISSUE

Red and Blue States Recent presidential elections have revealed an alleged political divide between the states. "Red" states in the South, West, and Midwest have generally voted Republican. "Blue" states in the Northeast and Pacific West have generally voted Democratic. Are regional or sectional differences affecting voting patterns?

❝Democrats and Republicans once came from the same kinds of communities. Now they don't. . . . The nation has gone through a big . . . sifting of people and politics into what is becoming two Americas. One is urban and Democratic, the other Republican, suburban and rural.❞

—Bill Bishop, *Austin American-Statesman*

❝Very little in politics, very little in life is black and white, or in this case, red and blue. There's an awful lot of gray. . . . Truth be told, if we ask about core American values and core beliefs, about opportunity, equity and how we should go about living our lives, we see very little [if] any difference.❞

—Samuel Abrams, Harvard University researcher

 TRANSFER Activities

1. **Compare** In what way does Bishop believe the United States is split? How does Abrams see the red-blue divide?

2. **Analyze** How do you think each of the writers quoted above would respond to the regional differences of opinion regarding the War of 1812?

3. **Transfer** Use the following Web site to see a video, try a WebQuest, and write in your journal. **Web Code:** neh-6702

EXPERIENCE PLANTATION LIFE

During the decades before the Civil War, and after the invention of the cotton gin, large plantations sprang up across the South as far west as Texas and Arkansas. Contrary to popular belief, very few white southerners led lives of genteel ease on plantations. Three fourths of southern whites owned no slaves at all, and of those who did, most owned fewer than 10 slaves and lived on small farms rather than plantations. Despite being few in number, white plantation owners dominated the South's economic and political life and set the standard to which poorer whites aspired.

Of the 2.5 million enslaved Africans in the United States, 1.8 million of them lived and worked on cotton plantations. Treatment of slaves was often extremely harsh and included beatings, confinement, whippings, and humiliation. The use and threat of punishment was a constant part of life as a slave. Even in cases where an owner was less harsh, slaves did not have control of their lives—they could be sold at any time and taken away from their families.

▲ Some slaves worked in a specific trade on a plantation. For example, a slave who worked as a blacksmith made these garden tools—a pair of hedge clippers (above left) and a combination hoe/pitchfork (above right).

▼ There were many other jobs for slaves on a plantation. Some worked in the main house cooking and cleaning, and others worked as carpenters, coopers (those who make barrels), or meat curers. The vast majority of slaves, however, worked in the fields for 16 or more hours a day—planting, hoeing, weeding, and harvesting crops under backbreaking conditions. An overseer, who worked for the plantation owner, supervised them and was often demanding and brutal. Although at great human cost, plantation labor produced enormous staple crops such as cotton, sugar, and rice, which provided the backbone for the southern economy.

insisted that the tariff and "internal improvements" would work together to tie the different regions into a harmonious and prosperous whole.

Clay also favored reestablishment of a national bank. The charter for the first Bank of the United States, created during Washington's administration, expired in 1811. That freed private and state banks to print their own money, which caused widespread uncertainty about the value of money. A national bank, Clay argued, would provide federal control over the nation's money supply and banking practices. In 1816, Congress established the second Bank of the United States. But most congressmen opposed using federal funds for internal improvements.

Vocabulary Builder
advocate–(AD vuh kiht) *n.* a person who supports or urges something

Marshall and the Supreme Court Boost Federal Power Under John Marshall, who served as Chief Justice from 1801 to 1835, the Supreme Court favored a strong federal government and a national economy. Marshall applied several Federalist principles to interpret the Constitution. For example, the Marshall Court claimed the power to review the acts of Congress and of the President for their constitutionality. This was established in the landmark decision *Marbury* v. *Madison* (1803). Marshall also insisted upon the "sanctity of contracts." In *Dartmouth College* v. *Woodward* (1819) and *Fletcher* v. *Peck* (1810), the Marshall Court limited a state government's power to interfere in business contracts.

Further, the Marshall Court insisted that federal law was superior to state law. This point was famously established in *McCulloch* v. *Maryland* (1819). The case involved the renewed Bank of the United States. When it was reestablished in 1816, branches were placed in states across the country. In effect, the bank competed with and threatened many state and local banks. In Maryland, state officials tried to defend their banks by levying a tax on the operations of the Bank of the United States.

The Marshall Court struck down this Maryland law. Embracing a broad interpretation of the Constitution, Marshall insisted that Congress had the power to charter a national bank. Further, no state could destroy such a bank with taxes.

Finally, Marshall broadly interpreted the Constitution to give greater power to the national government. In the 1824 case *Gibbons* v. *Ogden*, Marshall rejected a steamboat monopoly granted by the state of New York. The monopoly threatened the business of a steamboat operator who had run a service between New Jersey and New York. Marshall ruled that steamboat traffic was "commerce" and that the power to regulate commerce involving more than one state—interstate commerce—belonged to the federal government. As in *McCulloch* v. *Maryland*, the ruling extended federal power by creating a broad definition of commerce and by asserting the supremacy of federal over state law.

In general, Marshall's Court encouraged the development of large, far-flung business corporations by freeing them from meddling by the states. (Think, for example, how difficult it might have been to build a railroad company that covered several states if each state had the power to establish its own monopolies within its borders.) Corporations took the place of the older, smaller, and simpler forms of business—single proprietorships and limited partnerships whose reach was confined to a small area. Due in part to the Marshall Court, the United States increasingly became one large integrated market.

Economy Experiences Panics As the national market emerged and more enterprises became interconnected over greater distances, the economy became subject to periodic shocks, or panics. These panics were the result of "busts" in a "boom-and-bust" cycle that is common in capitalism. In capitalism, individuals own most productive property—factories

Primary Source "The question is, in truth, a question of supremacy. And if the right of the states to tax the means employed by the general government be conceded [accepted], the declaration that the Constitution, and the laws made in pursuance thereof, shall be the supreme law of the land, is empty and unmeaning. . . ."

—John Marshall, *McCulloch v. Maryland*, 1819

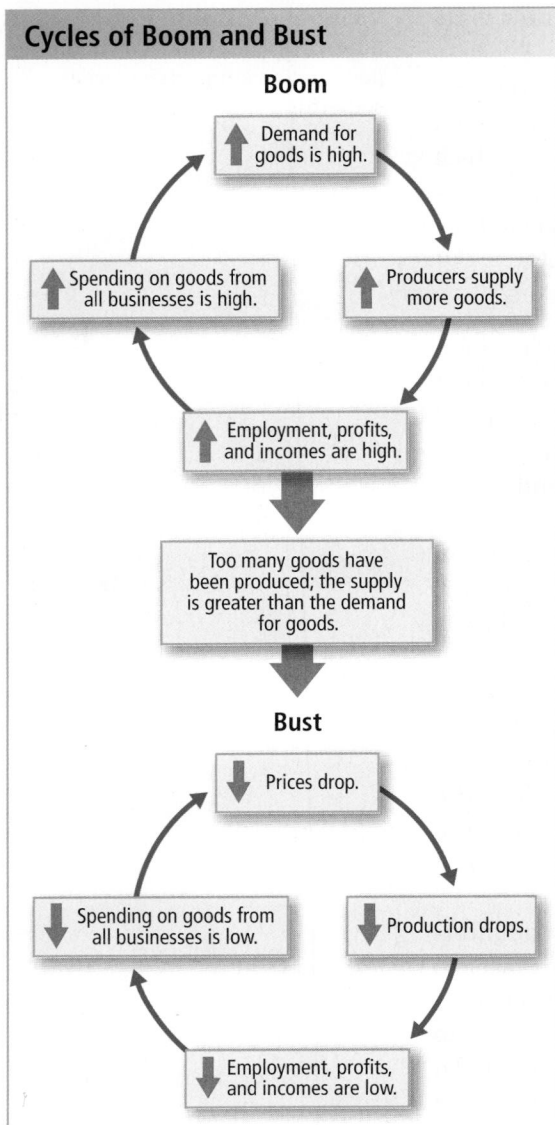

Cycles of Boom and Bust

Boom

Demand for goods is high.

Spending on goods from all businesses is high.

Producers supply more goods.

Employment, profits, and incomes are high.

Too many goods have been produced; the supply is greater than the demand for goods.

Bust

Prices drop.

Spending on goods from all businesses is low.

Production drops.

Employment, profits, and incomes are low.

Diagram Skill Market economies experience cycles of good times, called booms, and cycles of bad times, called busts. Typically, a sharp rise or drop in an economic variable will set off a series of events that brings about the next phase of the cycle. These variables include the amount of money businesses are willing to invest, interest rates, and economic shocks, such as wars, discovery of a new oil field, or a crop failure. *What happens when producers create more goods than buyers demand?*

Vocabulary Builder

episode—(EHP uh sohd) *n.* an event or incident

and farms—and markets set prices. During the "boom" phase, high consumer demand encourages owners to expand production. But once the expanded supply of goods exceeds demand, a "bust" follows. Prices fall and producers cut back on production, closing factories and firing workers. Those jobless workers then have less to spend, hurting other businesses.

Between 1815 and 1860, there were three great panics that occurred: 1819, 1837, and 1857. Thousands of factory workers lost their jobs. The panics also hurt farmers and planters as demand declined for their grain or cotton. When farm prices fell, many farmers and planters could not pay their debts. They, therefore, lost their properties to lawsuits and foreclosures.

Panics led many workers and farmers to doubt capitalism—or at least to blame the banks, especially the Bank of the United States. The panics lifted after a year or two, however, and "boom" times returned. These economic revivals quieted the doubts.

American Art and Literature Flourish Nationalism also influenced art and literature. Artists celebrated America's beautiful landscape, while novelists expressed pride in the nation's immense potential. A period known as the American Renaissance ensued, in which literature reflected the nationalistic spirit. James Fenimore Cooper of New York became the first American to make a career as a novelist. His most celebrated novels, a series known as *The Leatherstocking Tales,* created the genre of frontier adventure tales that persists to this day. There were also several regional voices in literature. For instance, Cooper influenced William Gilmore Simms, a southern writer who gave frontier stories a more southern voice.

✔ **Checkpoint** How did nationalism affect the economy starting in 1816?

Nationalism Influences Foreign Affairs

Nationalism also influenced the nation's foreign policy. A key figure in this development was **John Quincy Adams,** James Monroe's Secretary of State and the son of former President John Adams. Monroe and Adams hoped to reduce the nation's great regional tensions by promoting national expansion.

Expanding the United States In 1819, American pressure and Adams's diplomacy persuaded Spain to sell Florida to the United States. Spain had felt pressured to give up their claims by the First Seminole War that occurred in 1818. The Seminoles were an American Indian group from southern Georgia and northern Florida, an area that was then part of Spain. Seminoles clashed often with white settlers, who were upset with the Seminoles for providing safe havens for runaway slaves. American General Andrew Jackson led a force into Florida to fight the Seminoles and seized Spanish forts. Though Jackson had not been told to act against the Spanish, the episode made it clear that Spanish control of Florida was very weak. Ratified in 1821, the **Adams-Onís Treaty** also ended Spanish claims to the vast Pacific Coast territory of Oregon. The British also claimed Oregon, but in 1818, the United States and Great Britain agreed to share the contested territory. Following the Adams-Onís Treaty, Americans began to settle in Florida and pursue the fur trade in Oregon.

The Hudson River School

American art also reflected the spirit of nationalism. The majestic scenery of the landscape inspired a group of landscape painters known as the Hudson River School. These painters used realistic detail to reflect an enormous reverence toward nature. Their dramatic depictions of towering mountains, rushing waterfalls, and plummeting gorges presented a world in which tiny, humbled humans existed in harmony with nature.

▲ **Asher B. Durand,** *Kindred Spirits* (1849) **Natural Beauty** This tribute to Thomas Cole, one of the leaders of the Hudson River School, shows Cole sharing an awe-inspiring view with his friend, poet William Cullen Bryant.

◄ **Martin Johnson Heade,** *Haystacks on the Newburyport Marshes* (1862) **Light and Dark** Later members of the Hudson River School were known as Luminists because of their fascination with the effects of light. Here, Martin Johnson Heade captures the glow of a late afternoon sky as the sun sets.

▲ **Jasper Cropsey,** *Autumn—on the Hudson River* (1859)
New Colors The invention of chemical pigments gave artists an exciting new palette of intense, pure colors, which were used to maximum effect by Jasper Cropsey, who became known as "the painter of autumn." His brilliant foliage created a sensation.

Thinking Critically
1. **Analyze Art** Cole and Durand often included a broken stump in their paintings. What do you think it symbolizes?
2. **Make Inferences** How might Hudson River School paintings have helped lead to the creation of national and city parks?

The Monroe Doctrine Adams also formulated the famous foreign policy doctrine named for President Monroe—the **Monroe Doctrine.** This policy responded to threats by European powers, including France, to help Spain recover Latin American colonies that had declared their independence. Monroe and Adams were eager to protect those new republics. The British shared that goal and proposed uniting with the United States to warn the other European powers to stay out of Latin America. Adams and Monroe, however, preferred to act without a British partner. In 1823, Monroe issued a written doctrine declaring that European monarchies had no business meddling with American republics. In return, the United States promised to stay out of European affairs.

> **Primary Source** "... [T]he occasion has been judged proper for asserting, as a principle in which the rights and interests of the United States are involved, that the American continents, by the free and independent condition which they have assumed and maintain, are henceforth not to be considered as subjects for future colonization by any European powers. . . ."
> —James Monroe, address to Congress, December 2, 1823

The Monroe Doctrine meant little in 1823 when the Americans lacked the army and navy to enforce it. The Latin American republics kept their independence with British, rather than American, help. The doctrine did, however, reflect the nation's growing desire for power. The doctrine became much more significant in the 1890s and in the twentieth century, when the United States increasingly sent armed forces into Latin American countries.

✓ **Checkpoint** What foreign policy actions did John Quincy Adams take that reflected nationalism?

The Nation Compromises Over Slavery

The spirit of nationalism failed to suppress regional differences in the United States. Such differences made the nation more difficult to govern. In 1819, this difficulty became evident in a crisis over Missouri's admission to the Union as a new state. At that point, the Union had an equal number of slave and free states—which meant equal regional power in the United States Senate. If Missouri entered the Union as a slave state, it would tip the balance in favor of the South. This prospect alarmed northern congressmen. A New York congressman proposed banning slavery in Missouri as a price for joining the Union. The proposed ban outraged southern leaders, who claimed a right to expand slavery westward.

In 1820, after a long and bitter debate, Henry Clay crafted the **Missouri Compromise.** The northern district of Massachusetts would enter the Union as the free state of Maine to balance admission of Missouri as a slave state. To discourage future disputes over state admissions, the compromise also drew a line across the continent from the southwestern corner of Missouri to the nation's western boundary. Territories south of that line would enter as slave states. Those north of the line would become free states.

The compromise solved the short-term crisis. But that crisis had exposed the growing division between the North and the South over the expansion of slavery. Jefferson worried, "This momentous question, like a fire-bell in the night, awakened and filled me with terror. I considered it at once the [death] knell of the Union."

Southern whites felt insulted by the northern attacks on their region's reliance on slavery. They also felt threatened. In 1822, they blamed the Missouri

The Missouri Compromise

Geography *Interactive*
For: Interactive map
Web Code: ncp-0706

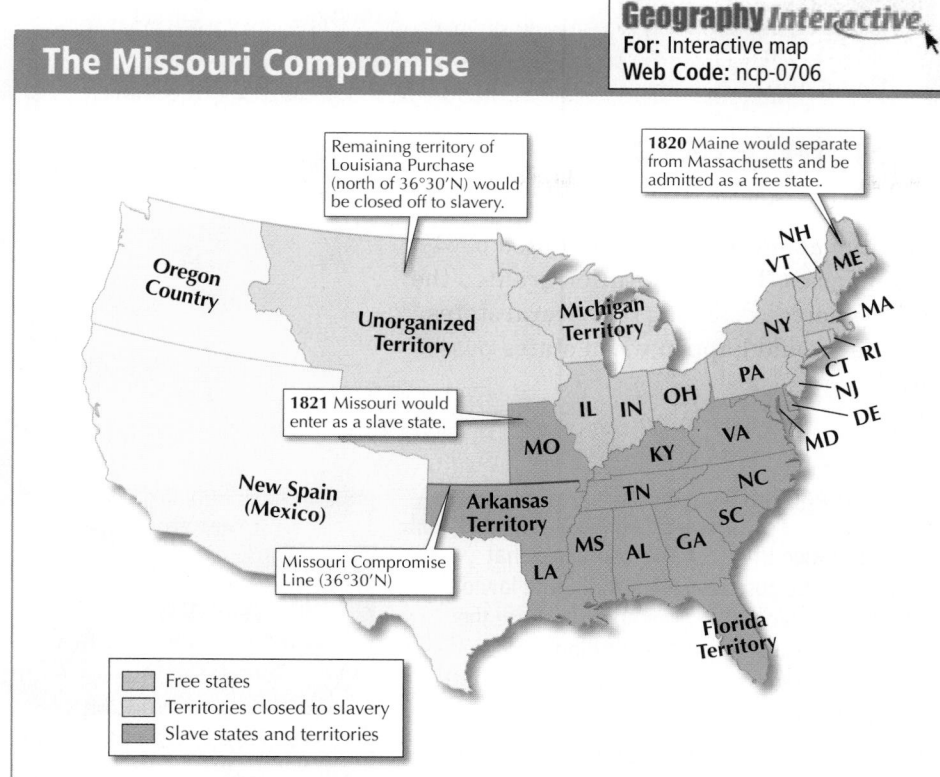

Remaining territory of Louisiana Purchase (north of 36°30′N) would be closed off to slavery.

1820 Maine would separate from Massachusetts and be admitted as a free state.

Oregon Country

Unorganized Territory

Michigan Territory

1821 Missouri would enter as a slave state.

New Spain (Mexico)

Arkansas Territory

Missouri Compromise Line (36°30′N)

Florida Territory

Free states
Territories closed to slavery
Slave states and territories

Map Skills The Missouri Compromise admitted Maine as a free state, Missouri as a slave state, and prohibited slavery north of 36°30′N latitude.

1. **Region** Which would cover more land under the compromise—new free states or new slave states?

2. **Draw Conclusions** What did the compromise reveal about the state of the Union?

debates for inspiring Denmark Vesey to plan a slave revolt. Vesey, a black freedman, prepared slaves to seize control of Charleston, South Carolina. The revolt, however, never took place because Charleston officials learned of the plot. These officials arrested, tried, convicted, and hanged Vesey and 34 others. Anxious over their close call, southern politicians insisted that their safety required northern silence on slavery.

✔ **Checkpoint** How did sectionalism threaten the expansion of the Union?

SECTION

3 Assessment

Progress Monitoring *Online*
For: Self-test with vocabulary practice
Web Code: nca-0707

Comprehension

1. **Terms and People** How does each term below demonstrate the increasing nationalism in the years following the War of 1812? Answer the question in a paragraph that uses each term.
   • American System
   • Adams-Onís Treaty
   • Monroe Doctrine

2. **NoteTaking Reading Skill: Understand Effects** Use your completed concept web to answer the Section Focus Question: How did domestic and foreign policies reflect the nationalism of the times?

Writing About History

3. **Quick Write: Write a Thesis** As in other types of essays and reports, the backbone for a research report is the thesis, or main idea. Reread the text in this section on Henry Clay's American System. Then, write a thesis statement for a research report on this topic.

Critical Thinking

4. **Recognize Sufficient Evidence** How did the fact that James Monroe won reelection in 1820 nearly unanimously reflect the nationalism of the era?

5. **Draw Conclusions** How did the spirit of nationalism contribute to the Monroe Doctrine?

6. **Analyze Information** What did the Missouri Compromise suggest about the limits of nationalism in the United States in the 1820s?

Who Has Power Over Interstate Commerce?

 2.II.A.3

Under the Articles of Confederation, the national government had limited power. States controlled business within their boundaries. The Constitution granted the national Congress the power to "regulate commerce . . . among the several states." But what exactly did that power mean? What would happen when states passed laws that affected business between states?

Gibbons v. *Ogden* (1824)

The Facts	The Issue	The Decision
• Aaron Ogden had a license from the state of New York to run steamboats between New York and New Jersey. • Thomas Gibbons had a license from the federal government to run steamboats in the same area. • A New York court ruled that Gibbons had to stop running his boats but Ogden could continue to operate his. • Gibbons appealed to the Supreme Court.	Gibbons argued that the commerce clause of the Constitution gave Congress the exclusive right to regulate business between states.	• The Court said that New York State law did not apply because the Constitution was the supreme law of the land. • The Court also ruled that interstate commerce includes any business that crosses state boundaries.

New-York and Brooklyn Ferry.

SUCH persons as are inclined to compound, agreeable to law, in the Steam Ferry-Boat, Barges, or common Horse Boats, will be pleased to apply to the subscribers, who are authorized to settle the same.

GEORGE HICKS, Brooklyn,
JOHN PINTARD, 52 Wall-st.

Commutation for a single person not
transferable, for 12 months, $10 00
Do. do. 8 months, 6 67
May 3, 1814 6m.

▲ Brooklyn steam ferry ad, 1814

Why It Matters

Gibbons v. *Ogden* clearly set forth the power of the national government to control commerce between states. It also did something much more far-reaching. Ogden had argued that Congress's power did not apply to the facts in this case because navigating boats on a river was not commerce. Only the buying and selling of goods, he said, should be affected by this power of Congress. John Marshall, writing the Court's decision, rejected that idea. Commerce, he said, was any kind of business interaction. It included the movement of people or goods by boat.

This decision opened broad areas of activity for the federal government. Congress has used this power to pass laws such as granting workers the right to form unions, setting limits on child labor, requiring companies to pay a minimum wage, and banning racial discrimination. Congress has also passed laws regulating radio and television, requiring that food and medicines are safe, and many others.

Connect to Your World

In recent years, the Court has moved to limit the power of Congress to use the commerce clause to pass certain laws. Research to find a case from the last 10 years involving the commerce clause. Read about the law under question and the Court's decision. Explain in one or two paragraphs whether you agree or disagree with the way the Court viewed the commerce clause.

For: Supreme Court cases
Web Code: nce-0708

◄ Today, the FCC (Federal Communications Commission) has regulations on cellphone usage.

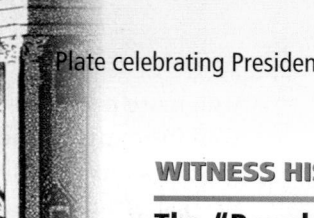

SECTION 4

WITNESS HISTORY ◀》 AUDIO

The "People's President"

After a disappointing loss in the election of 1824, Andrew Jackson rode a wave of popular support to the presidency in 1828. At his inauguration, many of those same voters caused a wild scene at the White House when they arrived in large numbers to celebrate the historic event.

❝Ladies fainted, men were seen with bloody noses and such a scene of confusion took place as is impossible to describe. . . . But it was the People's day, and the People's President, and the People would rule.❞

—Margaret Bayard Smith in a letter to Mrs. Kirkpatrick, March 11, 1829

▲ A crowd gathers for Jackson's inauguration

Democracy and the Age of Jackson

Core Curriculum Objectives

- **2.I.F.3** Establishing a stable political system
- **2.II.B.2b** The rise of mass politics (John Quincy Adams, Andrew Jackson, the spoils system, the bank war, Martin Van Buren)
- **3.III.D.3** Native American Indians

Terms and People

caucus
Andrew Jackson
Martin Van Buren
Jacksonian Democracy

spoils system
Indian Removal Act
Trail of Tears

NoteTaking

Reading Skill: Understand Effects Use a flowchart like the one below to record the effects of Jackson's presidency.

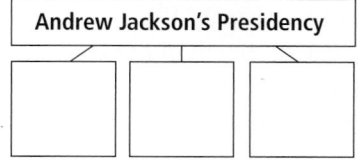

Andrew Jackson's Presidency

Why It Matters The election of 1824 signaled a shift in American political and social life. As a new political party emerged, the nation expanded its concept of democracy in some ways and narrowed it in others. The era became known for one of American history's towering and controversial figures—Andrew Jackson. **Section Focus Question: What changes did Andrew Jackson represent in American political life?**

The Election of 1824

As the presidential election of 1824 approached, two-term President James Monroe announced that he would not seek a third term. As you have read, his presidency was marked by what appeared to be general political harmony. There was only one major political party, and the nation seemed to be united in its purpose and direction. Beneath this surface, however, there were differences. These would become obvious in the election of 1824.

A Four-Way Race Four leading Democratic Republicans hoped to replace Monroe in the White House. John Quincy Adams, Monroe's Secretary of State, offered great skill and experience. A caucus of Democratic Republicans in Congress preferred William Crawford of Georgia. A **caucus** is a closed meeting of party members for the purpose of choosing a candidate. War hero **Andrew Jackson** of Tennessee and Henry Clay of Kentucky provided greater competition for Adams.

A Troubled Outcome The crowded race produced no clear winner. Jackson won more popular votes than did Adams, his next nearest competitor. Jackson did well in many southern states and in the western part of the country. Adams ran strongest in the Northeast. But neither won a majority of the electoral votes needed for election. As a result, for the second time in the nation's history (the first was in 1800), the House of Representatives had to determine the outcome of a presidential election. There, Clay threw his support to Adams, who became President. When Adams appointed Clay as Secretary of State, Jackson accused them of a "corrupt bargain," in which he thought Clay supported Adams in exchange for an appointment as Secretary of State.

Jackson's opposition weakened Adams's presidency. Taking a broad, nationalist view of the Constitution, Adams pushed for an aggressive program of federal spending for internal improvements and scientific exploration. Jackson and other critics denounced this program as "aristocratic" for allegedly favoring the wealthy over the common people. This would become a growing theme in national politics.

Jackson Begins His Next Campaign Much of the criticism of Adams's presidency came from Andrew Jackson. Indeed, Jackson and his supporters spent much of Adams's term preparing for the next election. Jackson especially relied upon New York's **Martin Van Buren,** who worked behind the scenes to build support for Jackson. Meanwhile, Jackson traveled the country drumming up support among the voters—a new practice.

Jackson hoped to exploit the increasingly democratic character of national politics. In the 1824 presidential election, a growing number of states had chosen their presidential electors based on popular vote. This was a shift from the method used in the first presidential elections, in which state legislatures chose electors. By 1836, every state but South Carolina was choosing electors based on the popular vote. Voters also had an increased role in choosing other state and local officials across the country. For example, the use of caucuses was replaced in many cases by more public conventions in which voters had a greater say in who became a candidate for office.

During the 1810s and 1820s, many states rewrote their constitutions. Those documents had originally restricted the right to vote and hold office to men who owned property. In 1776, about three fourths of all free men could meet the property-ownership requirement because they owned a farm or a shop. But that qualified proportion slipped as more men worked for wages in the expanding industries. Without their own farm or shop, they could not vote. The economic losses caused by the Panic of 1819 had also removed many voters from the rolls.

The new state constitutions expanded the electorate by abolishing the property requirement. In most states, any white man who paid a tax could vote and hold office. These changes increased participation in elections. Male voter turnout that had been less than 30 percent in the elections of the early 1800s reached almost 80 percent in 1840.

Unfortunately, the expansion of democracy did not benefit all Americans. Most of the new constitutions also took the vote away from free blacks—even those

Vocabulary Builder
exploit–(ehk SPLOYT) v. to take advantage of; utilize

HISTORY MAKERS

Andrew Jackson (1767–1845)
As a major general in the War of 1812, Andrew Jackson became a national hero when he defeated the British at New Orleans. Bitter over his defeat in the presidential election of 1824, Jackson came back four years later and won decisively, despite a campaign that was rife with personal attacks on his character and that of his wife. Elected by the "common man," Jackson was the first President who was not an aristocrat from Massachusetts or Virginia, but rather from the Tennessee frontier. His presidential victory was marred, however, when his wife Rachel died before he moved to Washington to assume office. Jackson believed in a strong presidency and used his power to veto 12 congressional acts—more than all the previous six Presidents combined.

with property. Nor did the new constitutions allow women to vote. (With the exception of New Jersey, in which a loophole in the state constitution allowed property-owning women to vote until 1807, no state had ever allowed women to cast a ballot.) In addition, American Indians, who were not citizens of the United States, were denied the vote. Democracy was limited to white men.

✓ **Checkpoint** How did Jackson respond to his defeat in the 1824 presidential election?

The Growing Electorate, 1824–1840	
Presidential Election	Total Popular Vote
1824	350,671
1828	1,155,350
1832	1,318,406
1836	1,500,802
1840	2,404,118

SOURCE: Encyclopædia Britannica

The Growing Electorate

Before 1824, presidential election results did not include a popular vote count. By 1840, the number of voters had skyrocketed. The painting, entitled *The County Election* by George Caleb Bingham, reflects this trend. *Which Americans were not represented on the table above?*

Jackson Emerges

During the mid-1820s, Andrew Jackson became the symbol of American democracy. Historians refer to the movement as **Jacksonian Democracy.** In his speeches and writings, Jackson celebrated majority rule and the dignity of the common people. He projected himself as a down-to-earth common man with humble roots, which contrasted with the image of the aristocratic leaders of the past.

Jackson's life reflected the nation's own story of expanding opportunity. He was born in a log cabin, orphaned as a boy, and wounded during the American Revolution. Moving west to the then-frontier, he had become a wealthy lawyer and planter in Tennessee. (In fact, Jackson was wealthier than Adams.) Jackson won military fame in the War of 1812 and in the wars against the Creeks and Seminoles.

The Election of 1828 By the election of 1828, Jackson's supporters called themselves Democrats, not Democratic Republicans. Jacksonian Democracy triumphed in the presidential election of 1828. With 56 percent of the popular vote and two thirds of the electoral votes, Jackson defeated Adams. A rowdy crowd attended Jackson's inauguration in Washington, D.C. Their raucous conduct symbolized the triumph of the democratic style over the alleged aristocracy represented by John Quincy Adams.

Jackson owed his victory to his campaign manager Martin Van Buren, who revived the Jeffersonian partnership of southern planters and northern common people. The party promised a return to Jeffersonian principles: strong states and a weak federal government that would not interfere in slavery. Only those principles, Van Buren argued, could keep sectional tensions from destroying the Union.

A New Party Structure While returning to old principles, the Democrats innovated in party structure. They developed a disciplined system of local and state committees and conventions. The party cast out anyone who broke with party discipline. While becoming more democratic in style, with carefully planned appeals to voters and great public rallies, elections also became the business of professional politicians and managers.

The new party rewarded the faithful with government jobs. Where Adams had displaced only a dozen government officials when he became President, Jackson replaced hundreds. He used the government jobs to reward Democratic activists. Van Buren's "reward" was appointment as Secretary of State, the coveted steppingstone to the presidency. The Democrats defended the use of jobs as rewards for political loyalty. Here, Senator William Learned Marcy of New York defended the Jacksonians:

> **Primary Source** "They boldly preach what they practice. When they are contending for victory, they avow [state] the intention of enjoying the fruits of it. If they are defeated, they expect to retire from office. If they are successful, they claim, as a matter of right, the advantages of success. They see nothing wrong in the rule, that to the victor belongs the spoils [loot] of the enemy."
> —Senator William Learned Marcy, speech before Congress, January 1832

Critics, however, denounced the use of political jobs as a reward for party loyalty, a practice they called the **spoils system**.

✓ **Checkpoint** How did Jackson's life mirror his political beliefs?

Native American Removal

Jackson's political base lay in the South, where he captured 80 percent of the vote. Those voters expected Jackson to help them remove the 60,000 American Indians living in the region. These Indians belonged to five nations: the Cherokee, Chickasaw, Creek, Choctaw, and Seminole.

Southern voters had good reason to expect Jackson's help with Indian removal. Jackson's victory in the Creek War of 1814 had led to the acquisition of millions of

● INFOGRAPHIC 🔊 AUDIO

THE TRAIL OF TEARS

In 1829, white settlers discovered gold on Cherokee lands in northwestern Georgia. It was only a matter of time before the government decided to relocate the Cherokees and other Native Americans living in the Southeast to other lands. In May 1838, soldiers forced more than 15,000 Cherokees into military stockades at bayonet point. Wahnenauhi, a Cherokee woman, wrote of the removal: "[P]erish or remove! It might be,—remove and perish! [A] long journey through the Wilderness,—could the little ones endure? [A]nd how about the sick? [T]he old people and infirm, could they possibl[y] endure the long tedious journey; Should they leave?"

But the Cherokees were not given a choice. The first leg of their journey began in October 1838. Their final destination lay 1,000 miles west in Indian Territory. The name of the route they followed is known as the "Trail of Tears," which comes from the Cherokee nunna-da-ul-tsun-yi, for the "trail where they cried."

◄ Cherokee bag, early nineteenth century

Creek acres in Georgia and Alabama. His war with the Seminoles in 1818 paved the way for the Adams-Onís Treaty and American control of Florida.

Still, many Native Americans had remained in the South. In many cases, they had even adopted white American culture. For example, many practiced Christianity, established schools, owned private property, and formed constitutional, republican governments. A Cherokee named Sequoyah invented a writing system for the Cherokee language so they could print their own newspaper and books. These Native Americans in the five southeastern tribes became known as the "five civilized tribes."

Many southern whites, however, denounced the Indian civilizations as a sham. Indians could never be civilized, southerners insisted. President Jackson agreed that the Indians should make way for white people. "What good man would prefer a country covered with forests and ranged by a few thousand savages to our extensive Republic?" he asked. Indeed, southern whites wanted the valuable lands held by the Indians. Between 1827 and 1830, the states of Georgia, Mississippi, and Alabama dissolved the Indian governments and seized these lands. In 1832, after the Indians appealed their case to the federal courts, John Marshall's Supreme Court tried to help the Indians. In *Worcester* v. *Georgia*, the Court ruled that Georgia's land seizure was unconstitutional. The federal government had treaty obligations to protect the Indians, the Court held, and federal law was superior to state law. President Jackson, however, ignored the Court's decision. "John Marshall has made his decision, now let him enforce it," Jackson boldly declared. Although often a nationalist, Jackson favored states' rights in this case.

▼ **Native American Removal, 1830–1840** The map below shows the relocation routes of Native Americans, including the Trail of Tears (in red).

▼ The journey west was a time of sadness and hardship. More than 4,000 Cherokees died of disease, cold, and starvation.

Thinking Critically

1. **Draw Inferences** Why do you think Americans were willing to give up new lands to the Indians?

2. **Identify Alternatives** Why did Jackson forcibly relocate Native Americans? What other action might he have taken to handle the conflict between the southern states and Native Americans?

Even before this ruling, Jackson had urged Congress to pass the **Indian Removal Act** of 1830. This act sought to peacefully negotiate the exchange of American Indian lands in the South for new lands in the Indian Territory (modern-day Oklahoma).

> **Primary Source** "Rightly considered, the policy of the General Government toward the red man is not only liberal, but generous. He is unwilling to submit to the laws of the States and mingle with their population. To save him from this alternative, or perhaps utter annihilation, the General Government kindly offers him a new home. . . ."
> —President Andrew Jackson, message to Congress, December 8, 1830

The Choctaws and Chickasaws reluctantly agreed to leave their southeastern homelands for new lands in the West. A few stayed behind, but they suffered violent mistreatment by whites.

The Jackson administration continued pressuring remaining Indian groups to sell their lands and move west. In 1835, a small group of Cherokees who did not represent their nation made an agreement with the government under which all Cherokees would leave the South for Oklahoma. Though the rest of the Cherokees protested, the federal government sought to enforce the treaty. In 1838, U.S. soldiers forced 16,000 Cherokees to walk from their lands in the Southeast to Oklahoma along what came to be called the **Trail of Tears.** At least 4,000 Cherokees died of disease, exposure, and hunger on their long, hard journey.

Some Indians in the South resisted removal. In 1836, after a number of violent conflicts with white settlers, troops forcibly removed the Creeks from their southern lands. In Florida, the Seminoles fought the Second Seminole War between 1835 and 1842. In the end, American troops forced most Seminoles to leave Florida.

Removal also affected Native Americans in the Midwest. In Illinois, a chief named Black Hawk led the resistance by the Sauk and Fox nations. In what became known as Black Hawk's War, they fought federal troops and local militia until crushed in 1832.

✓ **Checkpoint** Why did many white people want Native Americans removed from the southeastern United States?

SECTION **4** Assessment

Progress Monitoring Online
For: Self-test with vocabulary practice
Web Code: nca-0709

Comprehension

1. **Terms and People** How does each term or person below help reflect the role of Andrew Jackson in American political life in the 1820s and 1830s? For each name or term, write a sentence that explains your answer.
   - Martin Van Buren
   - Jacksonian Democracy
   - spoils system
   - Indian Removal Act

2. **NoteTaking Reading Skill: Understand Effects** Use your completed flowchart to answer the Section Focus Question: What changes did Andrew Jackson represent in American political life?

Writing About History

3. **Quick Write: Make an Outline** Create an outline for this section on the Age of Jackson. Identify each topic and subtopic in a single phrase. When you are ready to write your research report, you can then use the outline as a guide.

Critical Thinking

4. **Analyze Information** Why do you think the election of 1824 helped lead to change in national politics?

5. **Draw Conclusions** Why do you think Jackson favored and benefited from the democratic expansion that took place in the 1820s and 1830s?

6. **Summarize** What was the basic view of Jackson toward the Native Americans living in the southeastern United States in the early 1800s?

◄ John C. Calhoun

Debate Over States' Rights

In 1828, John C. Calhoun wrote an anonymous document in response to the high tariff Congress adopted that year. The tariff, known as the Tariff of Abominations to people in the South who adamantly opposed it, meant high prices for goods that southern planters needed.

❝So partial are the effects of the [Tariff] system that its burdens are exclusively on one side and its benefits on the other. It imposes on the agricultural interest of the South. . . . That the manufacturing States . . . bear no share of the burden of the Tariff . . .❞

—John C. Calhoun, *South Carolina Exposition and Protest*, 1828

Constitutional Disputes and Crises

 Core Curriculum Objectives

- **2.II.A.1** The first and second two-party systems
- **2.II.B** Constitutional stress and crisis

Terms and People

Tariff of Abominations   nullification
John C. Calhoun   Whig

NoteTaking

Reading Skill: Compare Fill in a table like the one below to compare the viewpoints of Jackson and Calhoun on the issue of nullification.

Nullification	
Andrew Jackson	**John C. Calhoun**
•	•
•	•
•	•

Why It Matters Jackson's presidency featured a number of conflicts and crises, and it helped bring about the formation of a rival political party. In spite of this, Jackson was able to secure the election of a handpicked successor. That administration was unable to survive its own crises and gave way to a Whig presidency. **Section Focus Question: What major political issues emerged during the 1830s?**

The Nullification Crisis

The protective tariffs had long been a topic of debate and discord in the United States. In general, the industrial North favored them, but the agricultural South disliked them.

In 1828, Congress adopted an especially high tariff. Southerners called it the **Tariff of Abominations.** This tariff had been designed by members of Congress not only to promote American industry but to embarrass President Adams and ensure a Jackson victory in that year's presidential election. In fact, Adams did sign the tariff, though reluctantly, and it did help bring about his defeat in 1828.

Calhoun Champions Nullification Jackson's Vice President, **John C. Calhoun** of South Carolina, violently opposed the tariff. During the War of 1812, he had been a strong nationalist. But his opinions changed after the the Missouri controversy of 1819 and 1820. This episode convinced him that the future of slavery, which he

The Nullification Crisis of 1833

1828 and 1832: Congress passes tariffs on imported goods, which benefit northern manufacturers but hurt southern planters.

↓ ↓ ↓

South Carolina votes to nullify, or void, both the 1828 and 1832 tariffs within the state's borders and threatens to secede from the Union if force is used against the state.

↓ ↓ ↓

Force Bill gives Jackson authority to use troops to enforce federal law in South Carolina.

↓ ↓ ↓

Congress reduces the tariffs on imports.

↓ ↓ ↓

South Carolina suspends its nullification of the tariffs but nullifies the Force Bill.

Diagram Skill The Nullification Crisis of 1833 was part of a power struggle between the states and the national government that had been present since the earliest days of the new nation. At issue was a state's power to challenge the authority of the federal government. Although the crisis was avoided, questions of nullification and secession remained. *How was the Nullification Crisis avoided?*

Vocabulary Builder
perpetual–(per PECH oo ehl) *adj.* ongoing; continuous

supported, required a stronger defense of states' rights. Toward that end, he began to champion the concept of **nullification,** which meant that states could nullify, or void, any federal law deemed unconstitutional.

Calhoun and his supporters expected Jackson to reject a protective tariff. After all, Jackson was not a supporter of the tariff, and they hoped he might take action against it on his own. He did modify the tariff rates, but not enough to satisfy Calhoun.

The Crisis Deepens In 1832, the South Carolina legislature nullified the protective tariff and prohibited the collection of federal tariff duties in South Carolina after February 1, 1833. Further, the state threatened to secede from the Union if the federal government employed force against South Carolina. Calhoun resigned the vice presidency and instead became a senator.

Jackson generally supported states' rights, and he wanted a lower tariff. He drew the line at nullification and secession, however. "Disunion by armed force is treason," Jackson thundered. He felt the Union must be <u>perpetual</u> and states must honor federal law.

> **Primary Source** "I can have within the limits of South Carolina fifty thousand men, and in forty days more another fifty thousand. . . . The Union will be preserved. The safety of the republic, the supreme law, which will be promptly obeyed by me."
>
> —President Andrew Jackson, December 9, 1832

Other state legislatures around the country supported him by passing resolutions rejecting nullification.

Webster Defends the Union In Congress, Daniel Webster of Massachusetts became the great champion of nationalism. In an 1830 debate over nullification, he had blasted the notion in a fiery speech. "Liberty *and* Union, now and forever, one and inseparable," he declared. Webster defined the Union as the creation of the American people rather than of the states. In 1833, Webster led the way in pushing for passage of a Force Bill, giving Jackson authority to use troops to enforce federal law in South Carolina.

The Crisis Avoided At the same time, with Jackson's support, Congress also reduced the tariff. This reduced South Carolina's militancy. In March, a special convention suspended that state's ordinance of nullification. Still, the convention made a political statement by nullifying the now-unnecessary Force Bill. The crisis passed. Jackson and Webster could declare victory. The difficult questions of nullification and secession, however, had been postponed rather than resolved.

✔ **Checkpoint** How did President Jackson view nullification?

The Bank War

Notwithstanding his fight over nullification, Jackson was a supporter of the agricultural South. Indeed, he longed to revive Jefferson's ideal of an agrarian republic, in which almost all white men owned farms and enjoyed a rough equality. But industrialization worked against that vision. Increasing numbers of Americans worked in cities for wages instead of on their own farms. In the cities, a gap widened between rich owners and poor workers. Wealth became more abstract and fluid since it was measured in bank stock versus land. The changes troubled many Americans.

Jackson Opposes the Bank Jacksonian Democrats suspected that the new economy encouraged corruption and greed. They howled when industry sought special advantages, such as protective tariffs or federal subsidies for roads and canals. Industry claimed these advantages promoted economic growth. To Jackson and his followers, they seemed mainly to enrich wealthy people at the expense of everyone else. Jacksonian Democrats promised to rescue the Republic from a new form of aristocracy they called the "Money Power."

Jacksonian Democrats especially disliked the second Bank of the United States, which had been chartered by Congress in 1816. They saw it as a dangerous, and perhaps even corrupt, special interest that favored rich investors. Many business leaders, on the other hand, valued the Bank. They believed it promoted economic growth by providing a stable currency—paper money—in which people could have confidence. They argued that a lack of confidence in the money supply could cause serious harm to the economy.

The Bank had many supporters in Congress. In 1832, they voted to renew the Bank's charter. Jackson, however, vetoed the renewal. He denounced the Bank as "unauthorized by the Constitution, subversive of the rights of the states, and dangerous to the liberties of the people." He opposed government action that led to "the advancement of the few at the expense of the many." He regretted "that the rich and powerful too often bend the acts of government to their selfish purposes." Jackson posed as the defender of "the humble members of society—the farmers, mechanics, and laborers."

The Whig Party Forms The Bank's supporters denounced Jackson as a power-hungry tyrant trampling on the rights of Congress. The veto shocked them because previous Presidents had so rarely used that power—only nine times in forty-two years.

Led by Henry Clay and Daniel Webster, in 1832 the Bank's friends formed a new political party known as the **Whigs.** (The name came from a British political party.) The Whigs were nationalists who wanted a strong federal government to manage the economy. Relying on a broad interpretation of the Constitution, they favored the American System of protective tariffs, internal improvements, and a national bank. Whigs also appealed to northern Protestants who wanted the government to promote moral reform.

The emergence of the Whigs renewed two-party politics in the United States. For the next twenty years, Whigs challenged Jackson's Democrats in local, state, and national elections. These close contests drew growing numbers of voters to the polls.

In the presidential election of 1832, the Whigs nominated Henry Clay. Voters, however, reelected the popular Jackson in a landslide. Longtime Jackson supporter Martin Van Buren became the new Vice President. Emboldened by the

Analyzing Political Cartoons

"King Andrew" Jackson exercised firm authority as President. He wielded such power that his critics sometimes referred to him as "King Andrew."
1. What details does the cartoonist use here to portray Jackson's use of power?
2. What does his trampling of the Constitution suggest?

Henry Clay (1777–1852)

Henry Clay was born in Virginia but made his home in Kentucky—and also in the U.S. Congress. In 1811, Clay was elected to the U.S. House of Representatives and, though only 34 years old, was named Speaker of the House. Clay served most of the next 40 years in the House or the Senate. Devoted to the Union, he crafted three major compromises to settle political crises that threatened to divide the nation: the Missouri Compromise, the compromise tariff in 1833, and the Compromise of 1850. In honor of these achievements, he was called "The Great Pacificator." Clay never achieved his dearest ambition, though—he wanted to be President of the United States.

Daniel Webster (1782–1852)

Daniel Webster gained fame for his skill as an orator and lawyer when he argued and won several cases before the Supreme Court. Like Clay, Webster spent most of the four decades from 1811 to 1850 in the U.S. House and Senate representing first New Hampshire and then Massachusetts. There, he spoke forcefully in favor of preserving the Union and backed Clay's compromise to end the nullification crisis in 1833 and the Compromise of 1850. He supported the 1850 plan saying that he spoke "not as a Massachusetts man, nor as a Northern man, but as an American." Like Clay, Webster was always frustrated by his inability to win the presidency.

public support, Jackson completed his attack on the second Bank of the United States by withdrawing federal funds and placing them in state banks. Though its charter still had several years to run, Jackson's action weakened it severely. As Secretary of the Treasury, Roger B. Taney managed Jackson's plan to undermine the Bank of the United States. When John Marshall died in 1835, Jackson rewarded Taney by appointing him Chief Justice of the United States.

 Checkpoint What did Jackson think of the second Bank of the United States?

Politics After Jackson

Jackson reveled in his victory, but the Bank's destruction weakened the economy. Relieved from federal regulation, state banks expanded, inflating prices with a flood of paper bank notes. The face value of bank notes exploded from $10 million in 1833 to $149 million in 1837. The inflation hurt the common people that Jackson had professed to help.

Van Buren's Presidency and the Panic of 1837 Economic trouble was still in the future when Jackson retired from politics in 1836. In that year's election, voters chose Martin Van Buren, Jackson's favorite, to become President.

Soon after Van Buren took office in 1837, the economy suffered a severe panic. A key trigger was Jackson's decision, taken months earlier, to stop accepting paper money for the purchase of federal land. The effect was a sharp drop in land values and sales. As a result, hundreds of banks and businesses that had invested in land went bankrupt. Thousands of planters and farmers lost their land. One out of three urban workers lost his or her job. Those who kept their jobs saw their wages drop by 30 percent. The Panic of 1837 was the worst depression suffered by Americans to that date.

The Whigs Taste Brief Victory in the Election of 1840 The depression in 1837 revived the Whigs. In 1840, they ran William Henry Harrison for President and John Tyler for Vice President. Harrison was known as "Old Tip" for his successes at the Battle of Tippecanoe against the Indians in 1811. The Whigs ran a campaign that was light on ideas but heavy on the sort of theatrics that would become common in American politics. For example, the Whigs organized big parades and coined a catchy slogan—"Tippecanoe and Tyler too"—to garner voters' attention. With more creativity than honesty, Whig campaign managers portrayed Harrison as a simple farmer who lived in a log cabin and drank hard cider instead of the expensive champagne favored by Van Buren. Turning the political tables, the Whigs persuaded voters that Van Buren was ineffective, corrupt, and an aristocrat who threatened the Republic. This helped Harrison win the presidency, and meant that the Whigs had succeeded in capturing Congress.

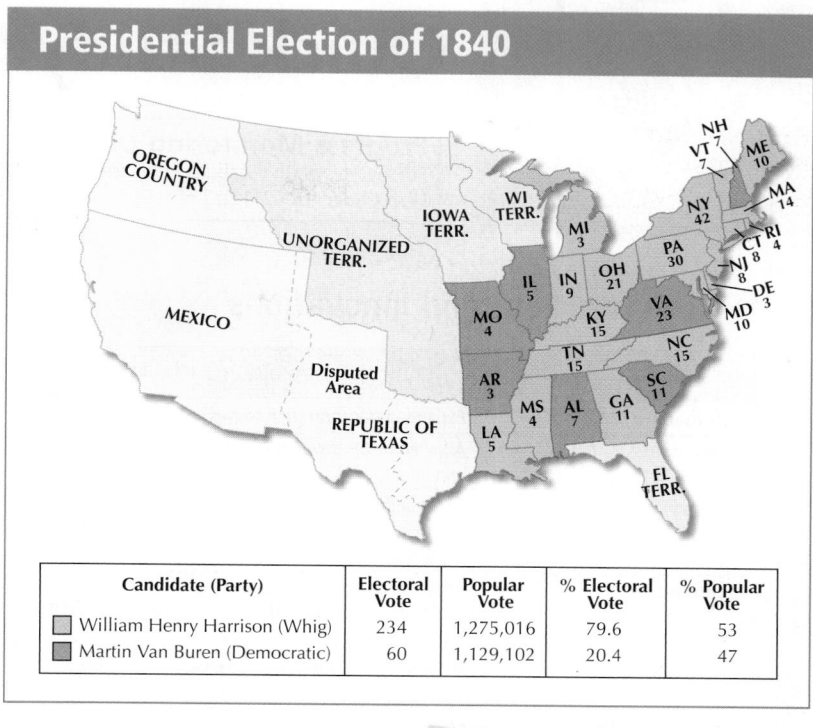

Presidential Election of 1840

Candidate (Party)	Electoral Vote	Popular Vote	% Electoral Vote	% Popular Vote
William Henry Harrison (Whig)	234	1,275,016	79.6	53
Martin Van Buren (Democratic)	60	1,129,102	20.4	47

The Whig victory proved brief, however. A month after assuming office, Harrison died of pneumonia. Vice President John Tyler of Virginia became the President. He surprised and horrified the Whigs by rejecting their policies. He vetoed Congress's legislation to restore the Bank of the United States and to enact Clay's American System. The Whigs would have to wait for a future election to exercise full control of the government.

✓ **Checkpoint** Who succeeded Jackson in the White House, and what happened to him?

Presidential Election of 1840
Whig Party flag picturing William Henry Harrison's log cabin

SECTION

5 Assessment

Progress Monitoring *Online*
For: Self-test with vocabulary practice
Web Code: nca-0710

Comprehension

1. **Terms and People** For each term or person below, write a sentence explaining the significance to national politics between 1828 and 1840.
   • Tariff of Abominations
   • John C. Calhoun
   • nullification
   • Whig

2. **NoteTaking Reading Skill: Compare and Contrast** Use your completed table to answer the Section Focus Question: What major political issues emerged during the 1830s?

Writing About History

3. **Quick Write: Write an Introduction** Research more about the nullification crisis that you learned about in this section. Then, write an introductory paragraph on the topic. This paragraph should introduce the topic and map out what you will discuss within the research report.

Critical Thinking

4. **Compare Points of View** Compare the viewpoints of President Jackson and John C. Calhoun on the Tariff of Abominations.

5. **Synthesize Information** How did the attack on the second Bank of the United States lead to the formation of the Whig Party?

6. **Recognize Cause and Effect** How did Jackson's economic policies affect Van Buren?

Quick Study Guide

2.II.B.1,
2.II.A

Progress Monitoring *Online*
For: Self-test with vocabulary practice
Web Code: nca-0711

■ Key Inventions and Innovations

Invention or Innovation	Political, Economic, or Social Effect(s)
Toll roads	Expanded transportation routes
Steamboats	Allowed faster travel, shipping, and upstream movement
Canals	Expanded transportation routes; improved commerce by linking farms to cities; opened new regions to settlement
Railroads	Cost less to build than canals and could move farther and faster, and carry more weight; connected East and West
Textile mills	Provided jobs; increased the speed of producing textiles
Interchangeable parts	Made possible the efficient production of a wide range of manufactured goods

■ Causes and Effects of the Cotton Boom

Cause and Effect
Causes
• Invention of the cotton gin • Available slave labor

↓

The Cotton Boom

↓

Effects
• Creation of the Cotton Belt in the South • Huge rise in cotton production • Creation of state economies based on cotton production • Westward spread of farming in the South • Expansion of slavery system • Slower urban growth in the South than in the North

■ Key Nationalist Supreme Court Cases

Case	Issues	Outcome of Decision
McCulloch v. *Maryland* (1819)	• Does the government have the power to create a national bank? • Do states have the right to tax institutions created by the federal government?	• Reinforced the principle of the power of the national government over state governments; states could not interfere with an agency of the national government and, therefore, could not tax the national bank
Gibbons v. *Ogden* (1824)	• Who has the power to regulate commerce: the states, the federal government, or both? • What if states passed laws that affected business between states?	• Established the federal government's right to regulate all aspects of interstate commerce

☑ Quick Study Timeline

In America

1814 Francis Cabot Lowell builds first centralized textile mill	1819 Florida ceded to United States	1820 Missouri Compromise passed	1823 President Monroe issues Monroe Doctrine

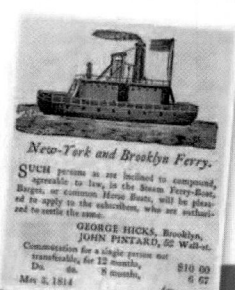

Presidential Terms James Madison 1809–1817   James Monroe 1817–1825   John Quincy Adams 1825–1829

1810   **1820**

Around the World

1811 Wars of independence begin in South America	1815 Napoleon defeated at Waterloo	1822 Brazil gains independence from Portugal

American Issues
●—●—● Connector

 2.II.B.1a

By connecting prior knowledge with what you have learned in this chapter, you can gradually build your understanding of enduring questions that still affect America today. Answer the questions below. Then, use your American Issues Connector study guide (or go online: www.PHSchool.com **Web Code:** nch-6703).

Issues You Learned About

● **Sectionalism and National Politics** Because the regions of the country had different economies and cultures they developed political differences.

1. How did sectionalism affect the nation's first political parties?

2. How did the Missouri Compromise reflect the sectionalism that divided the nation in the early 1800s?

3. Why did many political leaders in the North support the so-called Tariff of Abominations while nearly all of South Carolina's leaders opposed it?

● **American Indian Policy** The U.S. government generally denied American Indians the right to hold on to their homelands.

4. How did the U.S. government acquire American Indian lands?

5. Why did many American Indians in the Southeast adopt elements of white American culture?

6. How did the Supreme Court rule in *Worcester* v. *Georgia*? What effect did this ruling have on the American Indian nations that lived in the Southeast?

● **Technology and Society** Beginning in the early 1800s, new ways of transporting and manufacturing goods transformed the United States.

7. Summarize the advances in transportation that took place in the early 1800s.

8. What invention led to the development of "King Cotton" in the South? Why?

9. How did the Industrial Revolution change the way people lived and worked in the United States?

Connect to Your World	New York

Government's Role in the Economy The revolution in New York transportation in the 1800s was partly spurred by government funding. For example, the proposal for the Erie Canal was initiated by New York governor DeWitt Clinton. In 1817, the New York legislature agreed to provide $7 million to build the canal. Soon after its completion in 1825, New York City began a period of explosive economic growth as the port of New York transformed itself into a major center for trade and manufacturing. Research to find other government-funded transportation projects in New York (railroads, bridges, highways). Then write a short essay in which you discuss the advantages and disadvantages of government funding for transportation.

1830
Indian Removal Act passed

1838
Cherokees forcibly relocated westward on the Trail of Tears

1850
U.S. slave population exceeds 3 million; cotton crop tops one billion pounds

Andrew Jackson 1829–1837 | Martin Van Buren 1837–1841 | William Henry Harrison 1841 John Tyler 1841–1845 | James K. Polk 1845–1849

1830 | **1840** | **1850**

1833
Slavery abolished in the British Empire

1839
Opium Wars between Britain and China begin

1845
Irish potato famine begins

History Interactive
For: Interactive timeline
Web Code: ncp-0713

Chapter Assessment

Terms and People

1. Who was **Eli Whitney**? What were his main contributions to American society?

2. What was the **Tariff of 1816**? Why did Congress pass the tariff?

3. What was the **Monroe Doctrine**? How effective was this doctrine initially?

4. Define **caucus**. How did the use of caucuses change with the expansion of democracy?

5. Who were the **Whigs**? What policies did they support?

Focus Questions

The focus question for this chapter is **How did nationalism and sectionalism affect the United States from the early 1800s to the mid-1800s?** Build an answer to this big question by answering the focus questions for Sections 1 through 4 and the Critical Thinking questions that follow.

Section 1
6. How did transportation developments and industrialization affect the nation's economy?

Section 2
7. How did the North and South differ during the first half of the 1800s?

Section 3
8. How did domestic and foreign policies reflect the nationalism of the times?

Section 4
9. What changes did Andrew Jackson represent in American political life?

Section 5
10. What major political issues emerged during the 1830s?

Critical Thinking

11. **Explain Causes** What led to the rise of nativism in the United States in the early to mid-1800s?

12. **Categorize** Categorize and explain the factors that led to less industrial growth in the South than in the North.

13. **Make Generalizations** What domestic policies did the Marshall Court favor?

14. **Synthesize Information** How did nationalism influence domestic and foreign affairs?

15. **Draw Conclusions** Many called Andrew Jackson the "People's President." How accurate was this nickname? Explain your answer.

16. **Analyze Information** Was Jackson's refusal to uphold the Supreme Court's decision in the debate over the Cherokees a legitimate use of the system of checks and balances? Explain.

17. **Make Inferences** The Whigs supported a strong federal government to manage the economy. Could the same statement be said about the Jacksonian Democrats?

Writing About History

Writing a Research Report In this chapter, you learned about the sectionalism and nationalism that shaped the United States in the time period after the War of 1812 to the mid-1800s. Choose one of the following specific topics related to the chapter: steamboats on the Mississippi River; the Erie Canal; the Lowell mills; Irish immigration; James Fenimore Cooper; the First Seminole War; the Choctaw, Chickasaw, or Cherokee Indians. Do research at the library and online to gather additional information about the topic. Write a research report based on your findings.

Prewriting
- Review your notes and the chapter to identify links between your research topic and the contents of the chapter.
- Make a list of key ideas you want to address in your report.
- Research additional sources to gather facts. Organize your ideas and sources on note cards by topic and subtopic.

Drafting
- Write a thesis statement that reflects the main idea of your research report.
- Make an outline that breaks down the topics and subtopics.
- Write an introduction, at least three paragraphs, and a conclusion. Be sure to address all parts of your outline.

Revising
- Use the guidelines on page SH14 of the Writing Handbook to revise your report.

Regents DBQ Practice

The Monroe Doctrine

The Monroe Doctrine guided American foreign policy, to greater and lesser extents, throughout the nineteenth and into the twentieth centuries. Use your knowledge of the Monroe Doctrine and Documents 1, 2, 3, and 4 to answer questions 1 through 4.

Document 1

In the wars of the European powers in matters relating to themselves we have never taken any part, nor does it comport with our policy so to do. . . . With the movements in this hemisphere we are of necessity more immediately connected. . . . We owe it, therefore, to candor and to the amicable relations existing between the United States and those powers to declare that we should consider any attempt on their part to extend their system to any portion of this hemisphere as dangerous to our peace and safety.

—*James Monroe, address to Congress, December 2, 1823*

Document 2

The question presented by the letters you have sent me, is the most momentous which has ever been offered to my contemplation since that of Independence. . . . Our first and fundamental maxim should be, never to entangle ourselves in the broils of Europe. Our second, never to suffer Europe to intermeddle with [this side of the] Atlantic affairs. America, North and South, has a set of interests distinct from those of Europe, and peculiarly her own. She should therefore have a system of her own, separate and apart from that of Europe.

—*Thomas Jefferson, letter to James Monroe, October 24, 1823*

Document 3

AND IT LOOKED EASY, TOO.

—*Political cartoon, 1850s*

Document 4

Monroe essentially declared that the United States would not tolerate intervention in the Americas by European nations. Monroe also promised that the United States wouldn't interfere with already established colonies or with governments in Europe. In one sense, this declaration was an act of isolationism, with America withdrawing from the political tempests of Europe. . . . On the positive side, the Doctrine marked what might be called the last step in America's march to independence, which had begun in the Revolution and moved through post-independence foreign treaties, the Louisiana Purchase, the War of 1812, and the postwar agreements.

—*Kenneth Davis, historian*

---

1. How many principles of American foreign policy are expressed in Document 1?
   (1) one
   (2) two
   (3) three
   (4) four

2. Which of the following statements most accurately summarizes Thomas Jefferson's ideas as expressed in Document 2?
   (1) He supported the principles of the Monroe Doctrine.
   (2) He supported just one of the principles of the Monroe Doctrine.
   (3) He quietly opposed the principles of the Monroe Doctrine.
   (4) He vigorously opposed the principles of the Monroe Doctrine.

3. Which documents assert that the Monroe Doctrine had become a success?
   (1) Documents 1 and 2
   (2) Documents 2 and 3
   (3) Documents 3 and 4
   (4) Documents 4 and 1

4. **Writing Task** Did the Monroe Doctrine express a policy of isolationism? Use your knowledge of American history and specific evidence from the primary sources above to explain your answer.

Another Great Awakening

In the early 1800s, a wave of religious intensity once again swept the United States. Religious leaders organized meetings where people would camp out for days at a time to sing hymns and listen to ministers preaching:

❝There, on the edge of a prairie in Logan County, Kentucky, the multitudes came together and continued a number of days and nights encamped on the ground. . . . Many, very many, fell down as men slain in battle. . . . After lying there for hours, they obtained deliverance. The gloomy cloud that had covered their faces seemed gradually and visibly to disappear, and hope, in smiles, brightened into joy. They would rise, shouting deliverance . . .❞
—Reverend Barton W. Stone

Listen to the Witness History *audio to hear more about the Second Great Awakening.*

◀ A lively camp meeting spreads the religious revival of the early 1800s

 Core Curriculum Preview

Chapter Focus Question: How did the Second Great Awakening lead to several reform efforts, and what effect did those reform efforts have on American society?

Section 1
A Religious Awakening   1.I.D.1d, 2.I.A.5c

Section 2
A Reforming Society   2.II.B.2d

Section 3
The Antislavery Movement   2.II.B.2

Section 4
The Women's Movement   3.III.A.3, 4.I.B.2b, 4.I.C.4e

Use the ☑ **Quick Study Timeline** at the end of this chapter to preview chapter events.

1846 textbook

Statue honoring women's rights leaders

Shaker box

Note Taking Study Guide *Online*
For: Note Taking and American Issues Connector
Web Code: nce-6801

◀ Charles Grandison Finney

WITNESS HISTORY 🔊 AUDIO

Religious Revival

In the early 1800s, America experienced a second wave of religious enthusiasm. The famous preacher Charles Grandison Finney described the benefits of a religious revival:

❝Christians will have their faith renewed. While they are in their backslidden state they are blind to the state of sinners. . . . But when they enter into a revival, . . . they see things in that strong light which will renew the love of God in their hearts. This will lead them to labor zealously to bring others to him.❞

—Charles Grandison Finney,
Lectures on Revivals of Religion, 1835

A Religious Awakening

🅝🅨 Core Curriculum Objectives

- **1.I.D.1d** Religion
- **2.I.A.5c** Guaranteeing religious liberty (disestablishment of churches, the growth of religious pluralism)

Terms and People

Second Great
  Awakening
revivalist
Charles Grandison
  Finney
evangelical
Joseph Smith

Mormon
Unitarian
utopian community
Transcendentalist
Ralph Waldo Emerson
Henry David Thoreau

NoteTaking

Reading Skill: Identify Main Ideas Note the main ideas under each blue heading in a chart.

Religion in the Early 1800s		
Second Great Awakening	**Discrimination**	**Other Religious Movements**
• Camp meetings	•	•

Why It Matters By the early 1800s, the United States was well established as an independent, growing country. How their young country would develop was of keen interest to Americans. Many decided that the best future for the United States was one in which its citizens embraced religion. **Section Focus Question: How did the Second Great Awakening affect life in the United States?**

The Second Great Awakening Changes America

In the early 1700s, Americans had experienced a burst of religious energy known as the Great Awakening. Another revival of religious feeling called the **Second Great Awakening** swept the country beginning in the early 1800s and lasting for nearly half the century. Protestant preachers who believed that Americans had become immoral and that reviving religious participation was crucial to the country's future started and led the Second Great Awakening. These preachers were known as **revivalists,** because they wanted to revive, or reenergize, the role of religion in America.

The Second Great Awakening profoundly influenced American life. Church membership skyrocketed. Moreover, reawakened religious feeling moved Americans to work for a wide variety of social reforms.

Evangelical Revivals Fan Religious Fervor The Second Great Awakening began on the frontier in Kentucky and then spread north and south, reaching the cities of the Northeast in the 1820s.

Its religious inspiration was spread through outdoor services known as "revivals" or "camp" meetings that lasted for as long as a week. Plentiful food and lively religious music added to the appeal of the gatherings, which were often held in isolated rural areas.

One of the most influential revivalists was former attorney **Charles Grandison Finney.** In passionate sermons, Finney dramatically proclaimed his own faith and urged his listeners to do the same. This **evangelical** style of worship, designed to elicit strong emotions and attract converts, proved highly successful: At Finney's revivals, hundreds of people at a time declared their faith.

Another leading voice was Lyman Beecher, a Yale-educated minister. Like Finney, Beecher became known for his fiery sermons. Beecher also traveled widely, urging people to read the Bible, join a church, and embrace religion. In 1832, Beecher became president of the new Lane Theological Seminary in Cincinnati, Ohio, which trained more evangelical preachers to join the revival.

Many revivalists' sermons featured the idea that the United States was leading the world into the millennium, or the thousand years of glory following the Second Coming of Jesus. Called millennialism, the belief that the millennium was at hand inspired some reformers to try to ready their society by perfecting it through reform.

Tension Between Church and State During the Second Great Awakening, some Americans wanted the government to encourage public morality by supporting religion. Others disagreed with this aim, holding that the government should protect public life from religious control. An example of the tension between the two groups is the defeat of the Sabbatarian reform movement. The Sabbatarians wanted the federal government to uphold the Christian Sabbath (a special day of each week reserved for worship) as a day of rest by not allowing any business transactions or mail delivery on that day. Congress insisted it had no authority to interfere with trade and refused to ban commerce on the Sabbath. The debate over church and state continues to this day.

African Americans Embrace the Spirit Many preachers of the Second Great Awakening welcomed African Americans at their revivals. However, some African Americans established their own, separate churches. Led by a former slave named Richard Allen, a group of Philadelphians formed their own church in 1787. African Americans in several other cities did the same. In 1816, these churches united to become the African Methodist Episcopal (AME) Church. By 1826, the AME Church had nearly 8,000 members.

For enslaved African Americans, religion had a special significance. It offered the promise of eternal freedom after a lifetime of oppression. Religious folk songs, called spirituals, gave them strength to deal with the difficulties of their lives. For some, the contradiction between religious ideals and their cruel captivity inspired them to revolt against their oppressors. Indeed, many men who led slave revolts said they were called by God to lead enslaved people out of bondage.

New Religious Groups Form Heightened religious awareness also led to the formation of two new religious groups. In New York State,

A Religious Leader

The painted serving tray below commemorates the Congregationalist minister Lemuel Haynes. In 1785, he was perhaps the first African American to be ordained by a mainstream Protestant church.

Church and State

Students pray around a flagpole outside their school.

TRACK THE ISSUE

What is the proper relationship between government and religion?

The First Amendment says that government may not establish religion or interfere with the free exercise of religion. This is often referred to as "separation of church and state." But Americans differ over how these clauses interact to prevent government from establishing religion while protecting the religious liberties of individuals. Use the timeline below to explore this enduring issue.

1791 Bill of Rights
First Amendment bars government involvement in religion.

1840s Sabbatarian Controversy
Congress debates whether to ban commerce and mail delivery on Sundays.

1947 *Everson* v. *Board of Education*
Supreme Court affirms separation of government and religion.

1984 Federal Equal Access Act
Law allows students to form religious clubs at public high schools.

2000 *Mitchell* v. *Helms*
Ruling allows private schools to receive federal funds for educational materials.

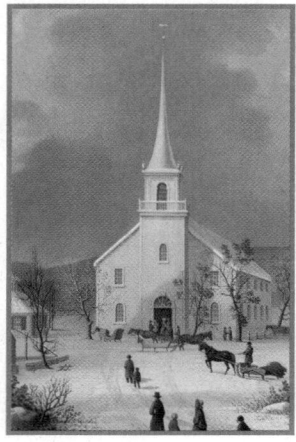

A church of the early 1800s

DEBATE THE ISSUE

Should prayer be allowed in public schools? One controversial topic in the church-state debate is the issue of prayer in public schools. Current law prohibits public school-sponsored prayers. Some Christians believe this ban violates their right to practice their beliefs.

"We're deeply religious. . . . And we believe that prayer in school is a necessity because, although yes, my children say blessings at home and pray at home and they learn to do that at church, most of their waking hours are spent in school. So why shouldn't they be able to pray, on the intercom, anywhere."

—Pat Mounce, high school parent, Pontotoc, Mississippi

"I'm a Catholic and I hope a devout one, but I think that the public school classroom is no place for me to try and impose my world formula for prayer on children who don't share it, and for that very reason, I don't want my children in a public school classroom to be exposed to someone else's religion or formula."

—Senator Phillip A. Hart, Michigan

TRANSFER Activities

1. **Compare** What views do Mounce and Hart share? On what point do they differ?

2. **Analyze** How do you think each of these two speakers would have reacted to the issue of outlawing commerce on Sunday?

3. **Transfer** Use the following Web site to see a video, try a WebQuest, and write in your journal. **Web Code:** neh-6802

Joseph Smith spoke and wrote of visions he said directed him to found a new religious group. In 1830, Smith and a few followers organized the Church of Jesus Christ of Latter-day Saints, whose members are commonly called the **Mormons.** The church grew rapidly, attracting more than 1,000 members in just a few months. It would grow to become one of the most influential religious groups in the country.

In New England, members of several Puritan or Congregational churches began to argue that, instead of seeing God as a "Trinity," people should see God as a single divine being—a unity. They organized themselves into a separate religious group called the **Unitarians,** after their belief. The Unitarians' views diverged from established religious creeds and a literal interpretation of the Bible. They reflected a growing Christian liberalism, which influenced many other religious groups in the nineteenth century.

✓ **Checkpoint** What was the Second Great Awakening?

Non-Protestants Suffer Discrimination

The preachers of the Second Great Awakening were Protestant. By the mid-1800s, well over half of all Americans were also Protestant. Non-Protestants were in the distinct minority and faced discrimination.

Mormons Are Persecuted Many Americans were wary of the new Mormon Church. Mormons isolated themselves in their own communities where they followed practices that were frowned upon by their neighbors, such as allowing men to have more than one wife. Further, the Mormons became economically powerful because they held land as a group rather than as individuals. They also voted as a group, which gave them political power.

The Mormons' power angered their neighbors. As a result, wherever they set up communities, their neighbors tried to chase them away, sometimes using violence. Mormons were chased out of Ohio, and then Missouri. They sought refuge in Illinois, founding the town of Nauvoo, which grew rapidly. In 1844, Joseph Smith declared his intention to run for President. Many non-Mormons were outraged. In the ensuing violent conflict, Smith was murdered.

The Mormons Leave Nauvoo
The Mormons were chased out of several states before finding a home in Utah. Below is a dramatic image of the Mormons being forced to leave Nauvoo, Illinois. *Looking at the map, why do you think the Mormons chose Salt Lake City as a site for resettlement?*

Mormon Migrations, 1830–1848

INFOGRAPHIC

Brook Farm

LIVING THE UTOPIAN DREAM

Brook Farm was founded in 1841 by a group of Transcendentalist thinkers led by George Ripley (left). At Brook Farm, Ripley hoped to "combine the thinker and the worker, as far as possible, in the same individual." He believed that physical labor, education, and a life lived close to nature would lead to well-rounded, healthy individuals, and through them, to a more perfect society. Although considered by many to have succeeded in some of these goals, Brook Farm was troubled by financial problems from the start, causing it to fail after just six years.

George Ripley hoped that Brook Farm would "impart a greater freedom, simplicity, truthfulness, refinement and moral dignity to our mode of life."

Vocabulary Builder
discrimination–(dih skrihm ih NAY shuhn) *n.* unfair bias in the treatment of a particular group

Smith's successor, Brigham Young, led the Mormons far west, to the Great Salt Lake valley in present-day Utah, then a part of Mexico. Here, Mormon communities thrived. They recruited new members from Europe and developed irrigation systems so they could farm the dry desert land.

Catholics and Jewish People Face Discrimination Members of the Roman Catholic Church faced particularly harsh discrimination in the early 1800s. Many Protestants viewed Catholicism as incompatible with American ideals of democracy. They believed that Catholics would choose loyalty to the Pope, the leader of the Roman Catholic Church, over loyalty to the United States. "Down with Popery" yelled Protestants in Philadelphia as they rioted against Catholic worshippers, echoing the sentiments of many Americans across the country.

Moreover, most Catholics of the time faced discrimination for another reason: their poverty. Many were poor immigrants from Ireland. Because they had little money, they would work for extremely low wages, which threatened other workers. Because Irish immigrants arrived in increasingly large numbers, many feared they were growing too powerful.

Jewish people also faced discrimination. Until late in the nineteenth century, state constitutions, from New England to the South, required public officials to be Christians, sometimes specifically Protestant. Jews were then barred from holding office. In the early 1800s, there were only about 2,000 Jewish people in America, mostly clustered in Rhode Island, New York, and Pennsylvania. In the 1840s, when Jewish people came to America in greater numbers to escape political unrest in Europe, Americans often ostracized them.

✔ **Checkpoint** Why did many Americans discriminate against Mormons, Catholics, and Jewish people?

Communal Societies Before 1860

◀ In the mid-1800s, some Americans tried to improve or perfect society by forming small, isolated societies based on experimental ideas.

- ● Utopian community
- ■ Shaker community

Map shows 1860 borders

Conic projection

Thinking Critically

1. **Recognize Ideologies** What were the goals of the Brook Farm utopia?

2. **Recognize Effects** Why did Brook Farm fail?

Several literary figures, including Nathaniel Hawthorne (right), called Brook Farm home for some length of time. Ralph Waldo Emerson, Horace Greeley, and Margaret Fuller visited the communal society.

Utopias and Transcendentalism

In the early 1800s, many Americans turned to Protestant churches, while some formed new religious groups. Still others sought different routes to try to fashion a more perfect society.

Utopian Communities Seek a Better Life During the early 1800s, dozens of groups of Americans sought to improve their lives in a unique way. They chose to distance themselves from society by setting up communities based on unusual ways of sharing property, labor, and family life. These settlements came to be called **utopian communities,** or utopias, because they aspired to be perfect communities. Organizers of utopias hoped their settlements would both engender virtue in their members and inspire those outside their communities.

Two well-known utopian communities were New Harmony, in Indiana, and Brook Farm, near Boston. In 1825, Robert Owen, a British social reformer, sought to have people from different backgrounds work together in a cooperative society at New Harmony. The society attracted some 1,000 people whom Owen described as "the industrious and well-disposed of all nations." At Brook Farm in 1841, George Ripley and 80 others sought to combine physical and intellectual labor. Brook Farm failed after only six years, while New Harmony lasted just two years. Most of the 50 or so other utopian communities were similarly short-lived.

The Shakers Succeed Another group that set up a chain of separate communal living societies was the United Society of Believers in Christ's Second Appearing, more commonly known as the Shakers. The Shakers had organized during the middle 1700s but reached their peak during the 1840s. Shakers set up independent villages in New Hampshire, New York, Ohio, and

HISTORY MAKERS

Henry David Thoreau
(1817–1862)
Henry David Thoreau is counted among the great American writers for his classic work, *Walden*. In *Walden*, he shares his experiences of subsisting alone in the woods for two years near Walden Pond in Massachusetts, living out the Transcendentalist theories of finding religious inspiration through nature and inside oneself.

Illinois. Men and women lived in separate housing and did not marry or have children. The communities grew only when adults joined, or when the group took in orphans. The economy flourished because of the Shaker's careful attention to high-quality crafts and farm produce. Remnants of their settlements still exist today.

Transcendentalists Advance New Ideas In New England, a group known as the **Transcendentalists** developed a new way to look at humanity, nature, and God, and the relationship among them. They were called the Transcendentalists because they believed that people could *transcend*, or go beyond, their senses to learn about the world. They believed that individuals should listen to nature and to their own consciences—instead of religious doctrines—to learn the truth about the universe.

Ralph Waldo Emerson, a former Unitarian minister, was the leading Transcendentalist. He celebrated the interplay between the individual and the universe in sermons, essays, and poems. "Within man," Emerson wrote, "is the soul of the whole; the wise silence; the universal beauty." Emerson gathered a group of men and women who met regularly in his Concord, Massachusetts, home to read and talk about ways to develop a rich spiritual life for individuals and for society. They published their ideas in their magazine, *The Dial*, which was edited by Margaret Fuller.

One of Emerson's most important followers was **Henry David Thoreau.** In 1846, Thoreau was jailed after refusing to pay taxes to support the Mexican-American War, which he viewed as immoral. Thoreau explained his thinking in a landmark essay, "Civil Disobedience," in which he argues that a person must be true to his or her own conscience, even if it means breaking the law. "Civil Disobedience" provided inspiration to later leaders who fought for civil rights around the world and is still widely read and admired.

 Checkpoint What did the Transcendentalists believe?

SECTION **1** Assessment

Progress Monitoring *Online*
For: Self-test with vocabulary practice
Web Code: nca-0802

Comprehension

1. Terms and People What role did each term or person below play in the Second Great Awakening? Write your answers in complete sentences.
- revivalist
- Charles Grandison Finney
- evangelical
- Mormon
- Unitarian

2. NoteTaking Reading Skill: Identify Main Ideas Use your chart to answer the Section Focus Question: How did the Second Great Awakening affect life in the United States?

Writing About History

3. Quick Write: Identify a Viewpoint Write a paragraph describing religion from the point of view of an evangelical preacher in the early 1800s. Include how religion would fit in with participation in the process of government.

Critical Thinking

4. Draw Inferences Why do you think the religious messages of the Second Great Awakening affected so many Americans?

5. Determine Relevance What factors led to discrimination against Irish immigrants in the early and middle 1800s?

6. Make Comparisons How did the methods of people who created utopian societies differ from those of other reformers?

Nature by Ralph Waldo Emerson

Ralph Waldo Emerson is considered the founder of Transcendentalism. His essay *Nature* (1836) was a statement of the movement's beliefs. Emerson came from a long line of ministers and became a Unitarian minister himself in 1829. However, he came to believe that people could get closer to God by transcending the material world and appreciating the beauties of nature rather than through following organized religion. In the excerpt below, Emerson expresses these Transcendentalist ideas.

▲ Ralph Waldo Emerson

The Notch of the White Mountains, Thomas Cole, 1839 ▼

In the woods, we return to reason and faith. There I feel that nothing can befall me in life—no disgrace, no calamity[1] (leaving me my eyes), which nature cannot repair. Standing on the bare ground—my head bathed by the blithe[2] air and uplifted into infinite space—all mean egotism[3] vanishes. I become a transparent eyeball; I am nothing; I see all; the currents of the Universal Being circulate through me; I am part or parcel of God. . . . I am the lover of uncontained and immortal beauty. In the wilderness, I find something more dear and connate[4] than in the streets or villages. In the tranquil landscape, and especially in the distant line of the horizon, man beholds somewhat as beautiful as his own nature. . . .

The waving of the boughs in the storm is new to me and old. It takes me by surprise, and yet is not unknown. Its effect is like that of a higher thought or a better emotion coming over me, when I deemed I was thinking justly or doing right.

Yet it is certain that the power to produce this delight does not reside in nature, but in man, or in a harmony of both.

1. **calamity** (kuh LAM uh tee) *n.* disaster
2. **blithe** (blīth) *adj.* carefree
3. **egotism** (EE goh tihz uhm) *n.* selfishness
4. **connate** (kuh NAYT) *adj.* existing naturally

Thinking Critically
1. **Draw Conclusions** What does Emerson mean by the phrase "I become a transparent eyeball"?

2. **Analyze Literature** What is the main point of this excerpt?

▲ A print promoting the temperance cause, 1855

WITNESS HISTORY 🔊 AUDIO

Improving Society

In the early and middle 1800s, Americans became involved in a wide variety of reform movements, ranging from helping society's disadvantaged to trying to control alcohol abuse. Ralph Waldo Emerson eloquently expressed the feelings of many:

❝[T]he idea which now begins to agitate society has a wider scope than our daily employments, our households, and the institutions of property. We are [going] to revise the whole of our social structure, the state, the school, religion, marriage, trade, science, and explore the foundations in our own nature. . . . What is a man born for but to be a Reformer, a Remaker . . .?❞

—Ralph Waldo Emerson,
"Man the Reformer," 1841

A Reforming Society

 Core Curriculum Objectives

- **2.II.B.2d** The birth of the American reform tradition (religious and secular roots; public schools; care for the physically disabled and the mentally ill; the problems of poverty and crime; antislavery; women's rights movement)

Terms and People

public school movement
Horace Mann
Dorothea Dix

penitentiary movement
temperance movement
Neal Dow

NoteTaking

Reading Skill: Understand Effects As you read, note the different problems facing society in the early 1800s, what reformers did to address each problem, and the effects of their efforts.

Causes	Efforts to Reform	Results
Educating all Americans		

Why It Matters Many Americans embraced religion during the Second Great Awakening. Soon, many of these people began to put their religious ideals into practice by working to reshape, or reform, parts of American life. Their efforts would impact several groups of the most disadvantaged Americans. **Section Focus Question: What were the main features of the public school, penitentiary, and temperance reform movements?**

Reforming Education

The leaders of the Second Great Awakening preached that their followers had a sacred responsibility to improve life on Earth through reform, especially for the disadvantaged. Not all reformers were motivated by religion. Many were simply moved by the suffering they saw. One of most popular reform movements was in the field of education.

Reformers Value Education Since colonial times, most American children had been taught at home by their parents. Some communities established schools. *The American Spelling Book,* created by Noah Webster in the 1780s, remained the most popular schoolbook. Webster developed special spelling forms that he felt were representative of America's honesty and directness, emphasizing America's differences from England.

Still, reformers saw education in America as woefully inadequate. Because there were no public schools that children were required by law to attend, most children did not go to school. Reformers who led the **public school movement,** also called the common school movement, sought to establish such a system of tax-supported public schools. They argued that expanding education would give Americans the knowledge and <u>intellectual</u> tools they needed to make decisions as citizens of a democracy. Education would promote economic growth by supplying knowledgeable workers and help keep wealthy, educated people from oppressing the uneducated poor.

Horace Mann Leads the Public School Reform Movement One of the greatest school reformers was **Horace Mann.** Mann grew up poor and had firsthand experience with inadequate schooling. He never forgot his humble beginnings. They inspired him to work to provide all children with a better education than he had received.

As a leader in the Massachusetts Senate, Mann championed the creation of a state board of education. He resigned from the Senate in 1837 to chair the first board. In this capacity, Mann advanced the idea of free public schools that all children were required by law to attend. He argued for state oversight of local schools, standardized school calendars, and adequate school funding. Mann also led the fight to abolish corporal, or physical, punishment. Further, he worked to establish training to create a body of well-educated, professional teachers.

Mann's influence was felt nationwide. Because of his work and the work of other school reformers, state legislatures across the country set aside funds to support free public schools. The reformers faced resistance from reluctant taxpayers and those who believed that education should include specific religious teaching. Despite opposition, within the next few decades, government-supported public schools became the norm across the nation. The percentage of American children attending school doubled.

Many women played key roles in the school reform movement. They petitioned their local legislatures to support public education and became teachers in the new schools. Catharine Beecher, a daughter of Lyman Beecher, and

A Place of Learning
During this period, more and more women moved into the classroom, both as students and as teachers. Students of both sexes learned from popular textbooks like the one above, which uses everyday items to illustrate the alphabet. *How does the classroom shown below differ from modern classrooms?*

Emma Willard established schools for women in Connecticut, Ohio, and New York. Elizabeth Blackwell and Ann Preston helped to establish medical training for women by the 1850s.

✓ **Checkpoint** What did the public school movement accomplish?

Helping the Ill and Imprisoned

Americans who had little or no voice in how they were treated were of special concern to many reformers. That was one reason why many reformers worked tirelessly to help Americans who were imprisoned or mentally ill.

Dorothea Dix Campaigns for Change One reformer who turned her religious ideals into action was **Dorothea Dix.** In 1841, she began teaching Sunday school in a Massachusetts prison. When she discovered that people suffering from mental illnesses were housed along with hardened criminals, she decided to act to change things.

Dix spent two years visiting every prison, almshouse (place for housing the poor), and hospital in Massachusetts. Then she wrote to the state legislature, vividly describing the horrors she had seen and demanding action:

> **Primary Source** ❝I tell what I have seen—painful and shocking as the details often are—that from them you may feel more deeply the imperative obligation which lies upon you to prevent the possibility of a repetition or continuance of such outrages upon humanity. . . . I come as the advocate of [the] helpless, forgotten, [and] insane. . . . Men of Massachusetts . . . raise up the fallen, succor the desolate, restore the outcast, defend the helpless.❞
> —Dorothea Dix, petition to the Massachusetts Legislature, 1843

Dix went on to campaign across the nation, encouraging other communities to build humane hospitals for people with mental illnesses. Her campaign was remarkably successful, leading directly to the creation of the first modern mental hospitals.

Reformers Target the Prison System Dix and others also worked to reform American prisons. Until that time, most people viewed prisons as a place to punish criminals. Prison reformers, however, thought that prisons should make criminals feel penitence, or sorrow for their crimes. The prison reform movement is thus sometimes called the **penitentiary movement.**

Two types of penitentiaries were proposed by reformers. The Pennsylvania System, advocated by the Philadelphia Society for Alleviating the Miseries of Public Prisons, was embodied in the Eastern State Penitentiary. In Eastern State, prisoners were urged to repent while they lived in complete solitary confinement, working alone in their cells and exercising in individual yards. The Pennsylvania System was expensive to run, and its complete isolation of prisoners came to be viewed as cruel. The second type of penitentiary was based on a system used in Auburn Prison, in Central New York, in the 1820s. In Auburn, prisoners worked with one another during the day in strict silence but slept in individual cells at night. Many American prisons followed the Auburn model.

✓ **Checkpoint** What motivated Dorothea Dix to campaign for reform?

HISTORY MAKERS

Dorothea Dix (1802–1887)
Dorothea Dix was an ordinary American who took extraordinary action to help other people. Despite persistent health problems, she campaigned for 40 years to win better, more humane treatment for people with mental illness—and met with amazing success. She helped to establish state mental hospitals in 15 states and Canada, and even spread her ideas in Europe. She also worked to improve prisons, favoring the Pennsylvania System of penitentiaries.

The Temperance Movement

When reformers surveyed American society, they saw a country in desperate need of reform. Ongoing industrialization caused rapid and unsettling changes. Crime, sickness, poverty, and neglected families and children seemed rampant. Many reformers attributed these problems to the widespread use of alcohol.

In response, reformers launched the **temperance movement,** an effort to end alcohol abuse and the problems created by it. Temperance means drinking alcoholic beverages in moderation. Some reformers believed in prohibition, or a complete ban, on alcohol consumption. Temperance reformers published pamphlets and posters warning that wasting money on liquor prevented people from buying food for their families. They argued that drinking alcohol led to violence and crime. The American Temperance Society, which had thousands of members in several states, held meetings where people were urged to pledge to refrain from drinking alcohol. The Washington Temperance Society sought to help drinkers through dramatic public confessions, discussion, and counseling.

However, the temperance movement had real success only when the reformers won changes in the law. **Neal Dow,** who earned a worldwide reputation for his lectures on alcohol abuse, became mayor of Portland, Maine, in 1851. He succeeded in securing the passage of the so-called "Maine Law," which restricted the sale of alcohol. Within a few years, a dozen states had passed similar temperance laws. Temperance would remain an enduring issue for the next hundred years.

✔ **Checkpoint** How successful was the temperance movement?

Analyzing Political Cartoons

The Root of All Evil? In the illustration above, alcohol is blamed for a number of problems, including epilepsy and cholera, two medical problems unrelated to alcohol usage.

1. By what reasoning is violence related to alcohol consumption?
2. What position on the temperance debate do you think the cartoonist holds?

SECTION 2 Assessment

Progress Monitoring *Online*
For: Self-test with vocabulary practice
Web Code: nca-0803

Comprehension

1. **Terms and People** Identify a leader and explain the goals of each of the following reform movements.
   • public school movement
   • penitentiary movement
   • temperance movement

2. **NoteTaking Reading Skill: Understand Effects** Use your table to answer the Section Focus Question: What were the main features of the public school, penitentiary, and temperance reform movements?

Writing About History

3. **Quick Write: State a Point of View** Write a paragraph defining the viewpoint of a mid-1800s reformer on the following issue: Should states pass laws to outlaw alcohol consumption? Give one argument someone might use to support that viewpoint.

Critical Thinking

4. **Recognize Cause and Effect** How did the Second Great Awakening lead to the launch of many reform movements?

5. **Draw Inferences** According to reformers, how would the public school movement help America's government and economy?

6. **Demonstrate Reasoned Judgment** How effective do you think the penitentiary movement was? Explain.

7. **Analyze Information** How did leaders of the temperance movement try to solve the problems of crime and poverty?

WITNESS HISTORY 🔊 AUDIO

The Evils of Slavery

In 1845, Frederick Douglass, an escaped slave, described his childhood in his autobiography. His powerful words gave many Americans their first understanding of—and compassion for—the lives of enslaved people in the South:

"I never saw my mother . . . more than four or five times in my life; and each of these times was very short in duration, and at night. She [worked] about twelve miles from my home. She made her journeys to see me in the night, traveling the whole distance on foot, after the performance of her day's work. She was a field hand, and a whipping is the penalty of not being in the field at sunrise, unless a slave has special permission from his or her master to the contrary—a permission which they seldom get. . . . I do not recollect of ever seeing my mother by the light of day. . . . She died when I was about seven years old. . . . I was not allowed to be present during her illness, at her death, or burial."

—Frederick Douglass, *Narrative of the Life of Frederick Douglass*

▲ Slaves toil at backbreaking labor in this illustration from an 1836 geography textbook.

The Antislavery Movement

Core Curriculum Objectives

• **2.II.B.2** Equal rights and justice: expansion of franchise; search for minority rights; expansion of slavery; abolitionist movement; the Underground Railroad; denial of Native American Indian rights and land ownership

Terms and People

freedman
Nat Turner
abolition movement

William Lloyd Garrison
Frederick Douglass
Gag Rule

NoteTaking

Reading Skill: Summarize Summarize what life was like for African Americans in the 1800s in a chart.

Lives of African Americans		
Daily Life	Ways of Surviving	Lives of Free Blacks
•	•	•

Why It Matters During the period of reform that swept the United States in the early and middle 1800s, reformers tried to improve life through campaigns to help children, families, and disadvantaged adults. Soon, reformers also set out to help another group of exploited people: enslaved African Americans in the South. **Section Focus Question: How did reformers try to help enslaved people?**

Life Under Slavery

Slavery, an American institution since colonial times, expanded across the South in the early 1800s with the growth of cotton farming. By 1830, from Maryland to Texas, some 2 million Africans and African Americans were held as slaves in the United States. About one third of these people were children under ten years of age. All of them struggled in their lives of captivity, knowing that they were at the mercy of slaveholders.

Suffering Cruel Treatment Most of these unfortunate men, women, and children labored from dawn to dusk at backbreaking tasks—cultivating fields of cotton, loading freight onto ships, or preparing meals in scorching hot kitchens. Their "overseers" maintained brutal work routines by punishing people physically with beatings, whipping, and maimings, and mentally, through humiliation and the threat of being separated from family members. The basics of life—food, clothing, and shelter—were barely adequate for most enslaved people.

The conditions under which enslaved people lived can be difficult to imagine. One glimpse of the heartbreak that tormented so many is provided by a letter from an enslaved woman, apparently pregnant, to her mother, who had been sold. She wrote to say that now her husband had also been sold:

> **Primary Source**   "A cloud has settled upon me and produced a change in my prospect, too great for words to express. My husband is torn from me, and carried away by his master. . . . I went to see him—tried to prevail on him not to carry my husband away . . . but mother—all my entreaties and tears did not soften his hard heart. . . . A time is fast approaching when I shalt want my husband and my mother, and both are gone!"
>
> —Emily, an enslaved African American, 1836

Such anguish was commonplace. This woman was relatively lucky—she could read and write, and managed to get a letter to a distant family member. More often, enslaved people were not allowed to learn to read, and family members who were separated never heard from each other again.

Surviving Through Spirit and Strength The miserable conditions forced on enslaved people took their inevitable toll. Some, losing all hope, took their own lives. Others simply toiled through a lifetime of pain and sadness.

But, in a remarkable triumph of spirit over hardship, most enslaved people maintained their hope and their dignity. They developed many ways of coping with their inhumane conditions. They worked to maintain networks of family and friends. Parents kept family traditions alive by naming children for beloved aunts, uncles, or grandparents, and by passing on family stories that their children could cherish wherever they might find themselves. Enslaved people took comfort in their religion, a unique mix of traditional African and Christian beliefs, which shone the light of hope in the midst of their difficult lives.

Resisting Slavery Many enslaved people did whatever they could to fight back against their oppressors. Resistance took many forms including sabotage, such as breaking tools or outwitting overseers, and the more direct method of escape. Tens of thousands of enslaved people fled to the North or to Mexico, where slavery was prohibited. A loose network of ever-changing escape routes called the Underground Railroad helped many reach freedom.

Some enslaved people decided not to run but to fight. Indeed, historians estimate that nearly 200 significant slave revolts took place in the first half of the 1800s. In 1822, Denmark Vesey planned what would have been the greatest slave revolt in American history in Charleston, South Carolina. Vesey was a **freedman,** or former slave. Traveling to Haiti as a ship's carpenter, he was inspired by the successful slave rebellion that had taken place there in the 1790s. Vesey nurtured

Families Separated
This engraving shows the anguish of a mother and daughter on the auction block, while an indifferent slave-owner looks on.

his dream of a revolt after becoming frustrated with his status as a second-class citizen in Charleston. When authorities shut down Vesey's church, he was prompted into action. Vesey gathered some five-dozen conspirators and plotted a slave uprising that would involve hundreds or even thousands of people. The plan called for slaves in the city and on surrounding plantations to seize weapons from guardhouses and arsenals and use them to destroy Charleston and free all of the slaves living nearby. His plan was thwarted, however, when news of it leaked. In the end, Vesey and dozens of his accomplices were hanged.

In 1831, a slave named **Nat Turner** was more successful in carrying out his plans for revolt. Turner had taught himself to read the Bible and believed that he had received a sign from God instructing him to lead his people to freedom. In August of 1831, he led followers through the countryside near Richmond, Virginia, intending to capture a nearby armory and gain more weapons. On their journey, Turner's group killed nearly 60 people before the local militia stopped their march. In the process of the manhunt that followed, the local militia killed dozens of African Americans. Turner was captured after six weeks. He and his associates were executed.

Terrified by the idea of a successful slave revolt, southerners reacted by passing much more stringent laws and controls regarding slavery. In some places, it became illegal to teach enslaved people to read. Often, they were forbidden to gather in groups unless an overseer was present. Yet, these restrictions did nothing to dampen the spirit of the enslaved people who were determined to resist their captivity—and they inspired free people in the North to work against slavery.

 Checkpoint How did enslaved people resist their captivity?

Nat Turner's Revolt

In this dramatic image, a slave hunter apprehends Nat Turner after his failed revolt in 1831. Turner is still a controversial historical figure. Depicted in several books and films, he is sometimes shown as a visionary resisting oppression against overwhelming odds; other times he is portrayed as a delusional murderer. *How would you describe this artist's depiction of Nat Turner?*

The Lives of Free African Americans

Not all people of African descent in the United States were held as slaves. Beginning with Massachusetts and Pennsylvania in the 1780s, northern states had gradually outlawed slavery by the 1840s. In Maryland and Virginia, many slaveholders were slowly manumitting, or officially freeing, their slaves. The net result was a large and growing population of free blacks. Despite their freedom, however, they suffered from persistent racial discrimination.

Moreover, the very existence of free African Americans concerned many white Americans, especially slaveholders. They felt that the large population of free African Americans made those still in bondage long all the more for freedom. In 1816, some of the South's most prominent slaveholders established the American Colonization Society (ACS). The goal of the ACS was to encourage the migration of free blacks to Africa. The ACS established Liberia, a colony on the west coast of Africa, and by 1830 some 1,100 people from the United States had been relocated there.

Most free African Americans were wary of the motives of the ACS. Most had been born in America, and they considered the United States their home. Moreover, they feared that colonization was just a plan to strengthen slavery by exiling the most able black leaders. Although several thousand free African Americans did eventually migrate to Liberia, most chose to stay in the country of their birth.

An illustration of ▶
an African American
man playing the
banjo from 1859

African American Spirituals Give Hope

Enslaved African Americans drew strength to endure their difficult lives from community, tradition, religion, and music. Combining all of these was the African American spiritual. In these religious songs, enslaved African Americans merged African musical traditions with biblical stories and Protestant hymns to create a unique form of music. Spirituals were rarely sung the same way twice, and their original versions were never recorded. Still, many of the songs survive in some form.

Go Down, Moses

Go down, Moses,
'Way down in Egypt land,
Tell ol' Pharaoh,
Let my people go!

One of the biblical stories that slaves most identified with was the story of Moses leading the Israelites out of slavery in Egypt. Egypt stood for the American South, the Israelites for enslaved African Americans, and the Pharaoh for a particular white master or white society in general.

When Israel was in Egypt's land,
Let my people go.
Oppressed so hard they could not stand,
Let my people go.

O let us all from bondage flee,
Let my people go.
And let us all in Christ be free,
Let my people go.

In the verses, the repetition of the phrase "Let my people go!" might have been sung in the traditional African call-and-response style. In this style, a soloist or small group would have improvised while singing the first and third lines, while a larger group responded with the repeating phrase.

A painting, circa 1860, showing an African American funeral gathering ▼

Thinking Critically

1. **Draw Inferences** In what way did African American spirituals combine African and European influences to create something new?

2. **Recognize Causes** Why do you think few African American spirituals survive in their original forms?

281

Garrison Founds *The Liberator*

In 1831, Boston printer William Lloyd Garrison founded *The Liberator,* a newspaper devoted to abolishing slavery. He proclaimed his mission to speak out against slavery on the front page of the paper's first issue:

Primary Source "On this subject, I do not wish to think, or to speak, or write, with moderation. No! no! . . . I am in earnest—I will not equivocate—I will not excuse—I will not retreat a single inch—AND I WILL BE HEARD."

—*William Lloyd Garrison,* The Liberator

Considered a dangerous radical, Garrison was dragged through the streets of Boston by a mob in 1835. However, he did not let such attacks stop him from fighting against the evils of slavery. **Why do you think Garrison refused to speak or write with moderation on the subject of slavery?**

Many free African Americans worked together to establish churches and schools. Some acted to try to change and improve the lives of enslaved African Americans. In Boston, a free African American named David Walker published a pamphlet that used religion as the base for a blistering attack on slavery:

Primary Source "You may do your best to keep us in wretchedness and misery, to enrich you and your children, but God will deliver us from under you. . . . Treat us then like men, and we will be your friends. And there is no doubt in my mind, but that the whole of the past will be sunk into oblivion, and we yet, under God, will become a united and happy people. The whites may say it is impossible, but remember that nothing is impossible with God."

—David Walker, *Appeal to the Colored Citizens of the World,* 1829

Walker's pamphlet was outlawed in the slaveholding South. Still, it reached a wide audience in the North, where more people were beginning to view slavery as fundamentally incompatible with the religious views they embraced during the Second Great Awakening.

✔ **Checkpoint** How did free blacks cope with discrimination in the mid-1800s?

The Fight Against Slavery

Misgivings about slavery had been spreading across the nation since Revolutionary times. Many northerners objected to it on moral grounds. By 1804, all states north of Maryland had passed legislation to end slavery. In 1807, bringing new slaves to any part of the United States from Africa was banned. Still, slavery was an established institution in the South, where slaves played an important role in the economy.

NoteTaking

Reading Skill: Contrast Use a chart like the one below to contrast the opinions held by those who supported slavery and abolitionists.

Debate Over Slavery	
Against	**For**
• Abolitionists believed that slavery was immoral.	• Slaveholders argued that slavery was justified because it formed the basis of the South's economy.
•	•

By the early 1800s, a growing number of Americans opposed to slavery began to speak out. Because they wanted slavery abolished, or ended, they became known as abolitionists. The great reform movement they led was the **abolition movement.**

Garrison Demands Emancipation A printer named **William Lloyd Garrison,** who lived in Boston, Massachusetts, became one of the leading abolitionists. Garrison began his antislavery career by working for Benjamin Lundy, a Baltimore Quaker who published America's first antislavery newspaper. In 1831, Garrison began publishing his own antislavery newspaper, *The Liberator.* Garrison used dramatic language to attract readers and convince them that slavery was morally wrong. This technique of trying to effect change by persuading people through moral arguments is called moral suasion. It was a favorite technique of leaders of many reform movements.

Garrison was in favor of emancipation, or the freeing of enslaved people. At first he thought, like most abolitionists, that this should be accomplished gradually over time to minimize economic and social disruption. But Garrison soon took the radical step of advocating immediate emancipation and the extension of full political and social rights to African Americans.

In cities across the Northeast and the Midwest, abolitionist societies, made up of people who shared Garrison's views, sprang up. Founded by Garrison in 1833, the American Anti-Slavery Society had over 150,000 members nationally by 1840. This group implemented moral suasion by printing antislavery pamphlets and distributing them to churches and other community organizations. The American Anti-Slavery Society and similar groups also supported a team of hundreds of lecturers who spoke against slavery at camp meetings and other public gatherings. They insisted that holding slaves was counter to most Americans' religious ideals.

Many Abolitionists Spread the Word Theodore Weld, a student at the Lane Theological Seminary in Ohio, became another leading abolitionist. Weld shared Garrison's belief in the power of moral suasion. However, whereas Garrison resorted to public confrontation, Weld chose to work through the churches. Weld married Angelina Grimké, the daughter of a southern slaveholder, who was so moved by the abolition movement that she went north to join it. She and her sister Sarah Grimké spoke and wrote against slavery. Another well-known abolitionist, and arguably the most eloquent, was **Frederick Douglass,** a former slave whose booming voice filled lecture halls with touching stories about the difficulty of his life as a slave.

 Checkpoint How did abolitionists attempt to bring about the end of slavery in the United States?

Working Against Abolition

Despite the growing call of abolitionists, most Americans continued to support slavery. The voices against abolition came from both the slave states of the South and the free states of the North.

HISTORY MAKERS

Frederick Douglass (1818?–1895)
Frederick Douglass was born a slave in Maryland and escaped to the North in 1838. In 1841, he spontaneously shared his experiences as a slave at an antislavery convention. His remarks so stirred his audience that he soon became a valued speaker for the abolitionist cause. His autobiography, *Narrative of the Life of Frederick Douglass,* first published in 1845, reached still more people. During the Civil War, Douglass, as an adviser to President Lincoln, convinced the President to allow freedmen to fight for the North. Douglass also lent strong support to the women's movement.

Should Slavery Be Abolished?

Although the answer to the question above is obvious now, debate raged on the issue in the mid-1800s. Advocates on both sides felt passionately that they were right.

ANGELINA GRIMKÉ

Southern-born Angelina Grimké, with her sister Sarah, was a dedicated abolitionist who worked to arouse moral outrage against slavery.

Primary Source

"Let every slaveholder apply these queries to his own heart: Am *I* willing to be a slave . . . Am *I* willing to see my mother a slave, or my father, my *white* sister, or my *white* brother? If *not,* then in holding others as slaves, I am doing what I would *not* wish to be done to me . . . and thus have broken this golden rule . . . "

—Appeal to Christian Women of the South, 1836

JOHN C. CALHOUN

One of the South's most distinguished statesman, Calhoun believed that slavery was vital to America's way of life.

Primary Source

"I hold that in the present state of civilization, where two races of different origin, and distinguished by color, and other physical differences, as well as intellectual, are brought together, the relation now existing in the slaveholding States between the two, is, instead of an evil, a good—a positive good. . . . [T]here never has yet existed a wealthy and civilized society in which one portion of the community did not . . . live on the labor of another."

—Speech to the Senate, February 6, 1837

Compare

1. What argument does Calhoun use to defend slavery?

2. Which quotation do you think is more effective? Why?

Southerners Cling to Slavery As abolitionists were developing their arguments against slavery, southern slaveholders intensified their arguments in support of it. They publicized their conviction that slavery was necessary because it formed the foundation of the South's agricultural economy. Moreover, they argued, slavery benefited the North, since the North's textile and shipping industries depended upon southern cotton.

They further maintained that a slave labor force was superior to the wage labor force of the North. They argued that northern employers and laborers would be inevitably at odds, since employers wanted workers to work more for less money while workers wanted to work less for more money. In contrast, such conflict was avoided in the South, where the well-being of slaves depended on their slaveholders' fortunes and slaveholders' fortunes depended on the well-being of their slaves.

But some southerners went even further, claiming that Christianity supported slavery, that enslaved people could not survive without slaveholders, and that the enslavement of Africans was historically inevitable. Such assertions were clearly racist, but many people of the time believed them.

Vocabulary Builder
inevitable–(ihn EHV ih tuh buhl) *adj.* impossible to prevent; unavoidable

As abolitionist rhetoric grew more strident, southern support for gradual manumission, or freeing, of slaves decreased. Southern spokespeople stepped up their arguments about the value of slavery, and southern slaveholders tried to prevent southerners from reading abolitionist publications. Post offices refused to deliver abolitionist newspapers. Southerners—even many of those who did not own slaves—embraced slavery as their preferred way of life, to be defended at all costs.

Northerners Resist Abolition Southerners were not alone in their resistance to abolition. Most northerners agreed with them. In Boston in 1835, Garrison was chased through the streets by an angry mob as a result of his antislavery views. In Philadelphia in 1838, the Grimké-Weld wedding, attended by both white and black guests, so infuriated local residents that they burned down the antislavery meeting hall. In Alton, Illinois, irate crowds destroyed abolitionist newspaper editor Elijah Lovejoy's printing press several times, killing Lovejoy himself in November 1837.

In city after city, white workers, fearing black competitors would take their jobs, launched stiff resistance to abolition. Wealthy industrialists resented the presence of black entrepreneurs in their midst. They also worried that the end of slavery would cut off the supply of southern cotton for northern textile mills.

Most white northerners disliked southerners, but they did not want to wrestle with the problems of African Americans either. They wanted to stay out of the controversy about slavery. When southern politicians pushed a **Gag Rule,** a law which prohibited debate and discussion in Congress on the subject of slavery, some northerners supported them. First passed in 1836, the Gag Rule was renewed annually for eight years.

Slavery Divides the Nation Although the abolition movement remained small and mostly confined to the North, it was vocal—and persistent. The debate over slavery divided Americans like no other issue. It widened regional cultural differences between the largely urban and industrialized North and the largely rural and agricultural South. Indeed, the divisive issue of slavery would soon prove to be a major factor in the division of the country itself.

✓ **Checkpoint** Why did many Americans oppose abolishing slavery?

SECTION

3 Assessment

Progress Monitoring *Online*
For: Self-test with vocabulary practice
Web Code: nca-0804

Comprehension

1. **Terms and People** Explain the role each of the following terms or people played in the debate over slavery.
   - freedman
   - Nat Turner
   - abolition movement
   - William Lloyd Garrison
   - Frederick Douglass
   - Gag Rule

2. **NoteTaking Reading Skill: Summarize** Use your charts to answer the Section Focus Question: How did reformers try to help enslaved people?

Writing About History

3. **Quick Write: Prioritize Arguments** List three arguments in favor of total emancipation for enslaved African Americans in 1845. Then, order the three arguments from most important to least important.

Critical Thinking

4. **Summarize** In what ways did enslaved people cope with their captivity?

5. **Identify Point of View** Why did most free African Americans not support the ACS?

6. **Draw Inferences** What role did religion play in the abolition movement?

7. **Recognize Cause and Effect** What led to the decline of manumission in the South?

▲ Woman who worked in the temperance reform movement, 1851

WITNESS HISTORY AUDIO

Equality for Women

The sisters Sarah Grimké and Angelina Grimké Weld were ardent abolitionists. Through their work on the behalf of slaves, they became interested in fighting for the rights of another oppressed group: women.

❝I am persuaded that the rights of woman, like the rights of slaves, need only be examined to be understood and asserted, even by some of those, who are now endeavouring to smother the irrepressible desire for mental and spiritual freedom which glows in the breast of many. . . .

Men and women were CREATED EQUAL; they are both moral and accountable beings, and whatever is *right* for man to do is *right* for woman.❞

—Sarah Grimké, *Letters on the Equality of the Sexes and the Condition of Women*, 1838

The Women's Movement

 ### Core Curriculum Objectives

- **3.III.A.3** Women, families, and work
- **4.I.B.2b** Women's rights and efforts for peace
- **4.I.C.4e** Women's suffrage amendment

Terms and People

matrilineal
Sojourner Truth
women's movement
Lucretia Mott
Elizabeth Cady Stanton

Seneca Falls Convention
Amelia Bloomer
suffrage
Married Women's
   Property Act

NoteTaking

Reading Skill: Identify Causes and Effects

Use a chart to record the causes and effects of the women's rights movement in the 1800s.

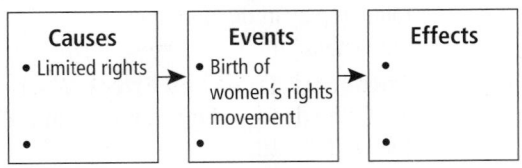

Causes	Events	Effects
• Limited rights	• Birth of women's rights movement	•
•	•	•

Why It Matters A spirit of reform permeated American life in the early and middle 1800s. Women took active roles in the abolition movement and other reform movements. Soon, some of these reformers began to work to gain equality for women as well. Their efforts would lay the groundwork for women's struggle for equal rights over the next hundred years. **Section Focus Question: What steps did American women take to advance their rights in the mid-1800s?**

Women Work for Change

In the 1800s, American women's freedoms and rights were sharply limited. Instead of taking a powerful role in public life, women were expected to make a difference privately, by influencing their husbands and raising their children to be good Americans. But this idealized influence was too limiting for women. Largely as a result of the Second Great Awakening, women of the early 1800s began to take on more active roles in public life.

Women Face Limits In the early 1800s, American women lacked many basic legal and economic rights. Under the British legal traditions that dominated the United States, women usually could not hold property or hold office or vote, and they usually were forbidden even to speak in public. Formal educational opportunities were virtually unheard of. In the rare instances of divorce, husbands generally gained custody of children.

Some of the groups living in America—certain Native Americans, African Americans, and Mexican Americans—had a tradition of affording women a significant amount of power. In these cultures, women controlled or influenced work patterns and family structures. Some cultures were **matrilineal,** that is, the inheritance of family names and property followed the female line in the family. Still, the legal and economic rights of the majority of American women lagged far, far behind those of American men.

Women Lead Reform Efforts The drive to reform American society created by the Second Great Awakening provided new opportunities for women. Many joined reform groups sponsored by their churches. Women played leading roles in all of the great reform movements of the day. Catharine Beecher, Emma Willard, Elizabeth Blackwell, and Ann Preston advanced education during the public school movement. Dorothea Dix almost single-handedly launched reforms in the way the country treated prisoners and people who suffered from mental illness. Most community leaders of the temperance movement were women; after all, they and their children were the primary victims of husbands' and fathers' abuse of alcohol.

The abolition movement attracted some of the most thoughtful women of the day, including Angelina and Sarah Grimké. Many abolitionist groups, like the Philadelphia Female Anti-Slavery Society, were made up entirely of women. One of the most effective abolitionist lecturers was **Sojourner Truth,** a former slave from New York who held audiences spellbound with her powerful speech and arguments.

Women Enter the Workplace In the 1820s and 1830s, the Northeast was rapidly industrializing. This provided the first real economic opportunity in the nation's history for women outside the home. Thousands of young women, who previously would have stayed in the family home, went to work in the new mills and factories. This gave many women a small degree of economic independence (although their wages were typically sent to their husbands or fathers) and a larger degree of social independence as they developed networks of friendships with other factory workers. By 1830, a few women's labor unions had formed, and women went on strike for better wages and working conditions.

✔ **Checkpoint** What led to women becoming leaders of various reform movements?

Chart Skills In the early 1800s, American women lacked many basic rights that are now taken for granted. Even the heavy and restrictive clothing women wore (below) limited what they could do. *How did the status of women in the 1800s go against the modern interpretation of the Constitution?*

Political and Economic Status of Women in the Early 1800s
Women could not vote.
Women could not hold public office.
Women could not serve on juries.
Few women received any level of higher education.
Women could not work in most trades or professions.
When they did work, women were paid less than men doing the same jobs, and their fathers or husbands often took what money they did earn.
Married women lost legal control of any money or property they owned before marriage to their husbands. Married women could not testify against their husbands in court, sue for divorce, or gain custody of their children.

Women Begin the Fight for Rights

Vocabulary Builder

virtually—(VUHR choo uh lee)
adv. not completely, but for all
practical purposes

Although many women became leading reformers, and many others entered the workforce, there had still been <u>virtually</u> no progress in women's rights. Real progress began only when two historical trends coincided in the 1830s. First, many urban middle-class northern women began to hire poor women to do their housework. This allowed the middle-class women more time to think about the society in which they wanted to raise their children. Second, women began to see their own social restrictions as being comparable to slavery.

The Origins of the Women's Rights Movement The parallels between the lack of power held by slaves and the lack of power held by women were hard to ignore. In fact, many women argued that their lack of rights made them almost the same as slaves. These women, along with a handful of men in the abolition movement, began to work for women's rights. They began the **women's movement,** a movement working for greater rights and opportunities for women, of the early and middle 1800s. This stage of the women's movement was active throughout the 1800s and into the early 1900s.

Women's rights reformers began to publish their ideas in pamphlets and books. One of these was the Transcendentalist Margaret Fuller, who believed that what women needed was not personal power but "as a nature to grow, as an intellect to discern, as a soul to live freely and unimpeded, to unfold such powers as were given her...". The Grimké sisters also published their ideas on women's rights. In *Letters on the Equality of the Sexes and the Condition of Women,* Sarah Grimké argued that God made men and women equal and that therefore men and women should be treated equally. Building on her sister's

● INFOGRAPHIC

History-Makers of the Early Women's Movement

Many women from different backgrounds and with different goals fought for women's rights in the mid-to late-1800s. Below are three early leaders.

◀ **Margaret Fuller** (1810–1850) took a key role in developing Transcendentalist thought. As an accomplished writer and thinker, she believed that women's powers of intellect were equal to those of men and that women should be able to pursue any career they chose. Her book *Woman in the Nineteenth Century* provided an intellectual basis for the budding women's rights movement.

"We would have every path open to woman as freely as to man."

Margaret Fuller

ideas, Angelina Grimké Weld defended the rights of both slaves and women on moral grounds:

Primary Source   "The investigation of the rights of the slave has led me to a better understanding of my own. . . . Human beings have *rights*, because they are *moral* beings. . . [I]f rights are founded on the nature of our moral being, then the *mere circumstance of sex* does not give to man higher rights and responsibilities, than to woman."

—Angelina Grimké, *Letters to Catherine E. Beecher*, 1838

Dozens of other women began to call for greater rights.

Women Disagree on Aims   The women who spoke up for full equality were a small minority, however. Even among abolitionists there was disagreement about how much public leadership women should take. When an international abolitionist convention met in London in 1840, the group fractured over whether women should be allowed to join in the men's business meetings. Some abolitionists thought that they should not. Two who thought they should were **Lucretia Mott** and **Elizabeth Cady Stanton.**

Both Mott and Stanton were active reformers, supporting particularly the temperance and abolitionist causes. Mott had helped found the American Anti-Slavery Society and the Philadelphia Female Anti-Slavery Society. Stanton was married to a leading abolitionist, Henry Stanton. (Both Elizabeth and Henry were already keenly interested in women's rights.) These two women, outraged that women were refused full participation at a meeting to discuss the promotion of human decency and equality, were inspired to take a dramatic step to advance women's rights.

✔ **Checkpoint**   What conditions led women to start to work to gain rights?

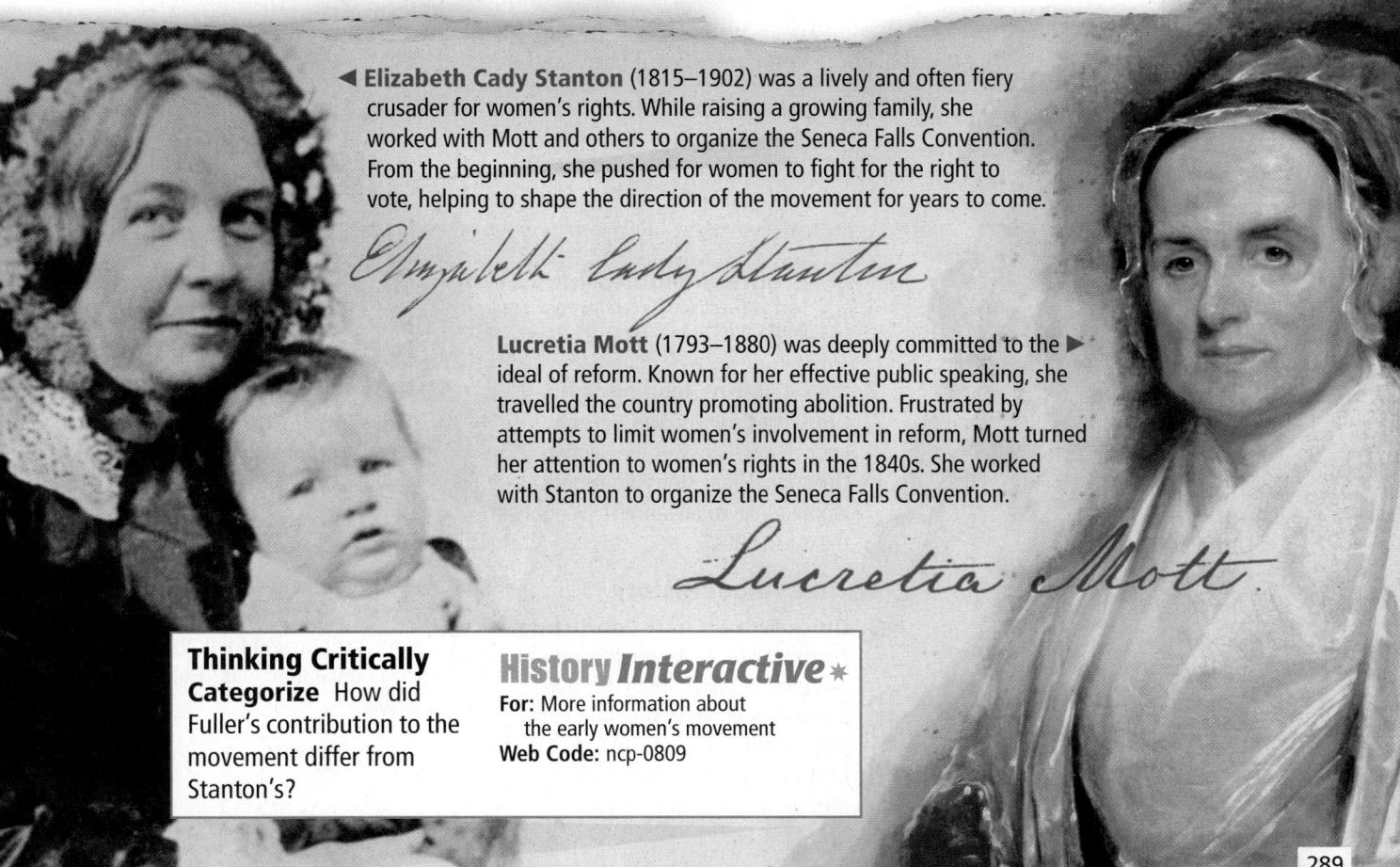

◄ **Elizabeth Cady Stanton** (1815–1902) was a lively and often fiery crusader for women's rights. While raising a growing family, she worked with Mott and others to organize the Seneca Falls Convention. From the beginning, she pushed for women to fight for the right to vote, helping to shape the direction of the movement for years to come.

Elizabeth Cady Stanton

Lucretia Mott (1793–1880) was deeply committed to the ► ideal of reform. Known for her effective public speaking, she travelled the country promoting abolition. Frustrated by attempts to limit women's involvement in reform, Mott turned her attention to women's rights in the 1840s. She worked with Stanton to organize the Seneca Falls Convention.

Lucretia Mott

Thinking Critically
Categorize How did Fuller's contribution to the movement differ from Stanton's?

History *Interactive* ★
For: More information about the early women's movement
Web Code: ncp-0809

Women Convene in Seneca Falls

In 1848, Mott and Stanton helped organize the nation's first Women's Rights Convention in Seneca Falls, New York. Often called the **Seneca Falls Convention,** the meeting attracted hundreds of men and women. One of the most illustrious attendees was Frederick Douglass. The delegates to the convention adopted a "Declaration of Sentiments," modeled after the language of the Declaration of Independence. The Declaration of Sentiments was ridiculed, and the convention resulted in few concrete improvements in women's rights. It did, however, mark the beginning of the women's movement in the United States.

The Seneca Falls Convention Inspires Women The Seneca Falls Convention inspired generations of young women. One of these was **Amelia Bloomer,** who actually attended the convention. While she remained relatively quiet there, she would soon become a leading voice for women's rights. In the following years, Bloomer published a newspaper, *The Lily,* in which she advocated equality of women in all things—including the right to wear pants instead of dresses.

Another woman who drew inspiration from the convention was Susan B. Anthony, whose involvement in the temperance and abolition movements led her to work for greater rights for women as well. Anthony would help lead the charge to win a single, critical right for women: the right to vote. This quest for **suffrage** would prove to be a long, hard fight.

Women Make Some Gains In 1848, the same year as the Seneca Falls Convention, the state of New York passed a law, the **Married Women's Property Act,** guaranteeing many property rights for women. Elizabeth Cady Stanton had worked hard for its passage. Twelve years later, the law was amended to make it more comprehensive. New York's efforts to advance property rights for women would become a model for similar laws in other states in the years to come.

By the middle 1800s, American women had laid the foundation for a future in which equality seemed a real possibility. They had become wage earners. They had become reformers. And they had started to voice their call for justice.

✓ **Checkpoint** What role did Lucretia Mott and Elizabeth Cady Stanton play in the women's rights movement?

A Radical Suggestion

In the mid-1800s, a number of women worked to reform the way women dressed. One of their innovations was the idea of wearing full-cut trousers under a short skirt rather than the long, heavy skirts of the day. Although she did not invent them, Amelia Bloomer wore the trousers publicly, and they were dubbed "bloomers" after her.

Progress Monitoring *Online*
For: Self-test with vocabulary practice
Web Code: nca-0805

Comprehension

1. **Terms and People** Explain the role each term or person listed below played in the early women's rights movement.
   - Lucretia Mott
   - Elizabeth Cady Stanton
   - Seneca Falls Convention
   - Amelia Bloomer
   - Married Women's Property Act

2. **NoteTaking** **Reading Skill: Identify Causes and Effects** Use your chart to answer the Section Focus Question: What steps did American women take to advance their rights in the mid-1800s?

Writing About History

3. **Quick Write: Chart Conflicting Arguments** Make a table with two columns. In one column, list two arguments in favor of fighting for female suffrage in the mid-1800s. In the other column, list two arguments against female suffrage.

Critical Thinking

4. **Draw Inferences** Why do you think women's rights were so limited in the early years of the country?

5. **Synthesize Information** Why did some abolitionists become outspoken advocates for women's rights?

6. **Determine Relevance** How significant do you think the Seneca Falls Convention was? Explain your answer.

NY 4.I.C.4e

The Declaration of Sentiments (1848)

Elizabeth Cady Stanton, along with four other women, created the Declaration of Sentiments to outline the aims of the Seneca Falls Convention. They purposely modeled the language of the Declaration of Sentiments on the Declaration of Independence as a potent reminder of the principles of equality upon which the United States was founded.

Notes taken at the Seneca Falls Convention (top), a statue honoring Elizabeth Cady Stanton and Lucretia Mott, as well as Susan B. Anthony

We hold these truths to be self-evident: that all men and women are created equal; that they are endowed by their Creator with certain inalienable rights; that among these are life, liberty, and the pursuit of happiness. . . .

The history of mankind is a history of repeated injuries and usurpations[1] on the part of man toward woman, having in direct object the establishment of an absolute tyranny over her. To prove this, let facts be submitted to a candid[2] world.

He has never permitted her to exercise her inalienable right to the elective franchise.

He has compelled her to submit to law in the formation of which she had no voice. . . .

He has made her, if married, in the eye of the law, civilly dead. He has taken from her all right in property, even to the wages she earns. . . .

He has denied her the facilities for obtaining a thorough education, all colleges being closed against her. . . .

He has endeavored, in every way that he could, to destroy her confidence in her own powers, to lessen her self-respect, and to make her willing to lead a dependent and abject[3] life.

Now, in view of this entire disfranchisement of one-half the people of this country, their social and religious degradation, in view of the unjust laws above mentioned, and because women do feel themselves aggrieved, oppressed, and fraudulently deprived of their most sacred rights, we insist that they have immediate admission to all the rights and privileges which belong to them as citizens of the United States.

1. **usurpations** (yoo suhr PAY shuhns) *n.* seizures
2. **candid** (KAN dihd) *adj.* fair
3. **abject** (AB jehkt) *adj.* miserable

Thinking Critically

1. **Synthesize Information** Based on the facts listed, what rights and privileges do the authors believe that women are being denied?

2. **Recognize Causes** Why do you think this declaration was modeled on the Declaration of Independence?

Quick Study Guide

2.II.B.2,
3.III.A.3

■ Effects of the Second Great Awakening

■ Major Reform Movements and Their Notable Leaders

Movement	Leader
School reform	Horace Mann
Prison reform	Dorothea Dix
Temperance	Neal Dow
Abolitionist	William Lloyd Garrison, Theodore Weld, Frederick Douglass, Angelina and Sarah Grimké
Women's rights	Sojourner Truth, Angelina Grimké, Margaret Fuller, Elizabeth Cady Stanton, Lucretia Mott, Susan B. Anthony

■ The Beginning of the Women's Rights Movement

Women lack basic civil rights and are excluded from public life.

↓ ↓ ↓

Religious inspiration and sympathy with human suffering cause women to become involved in reform movements.

↓ ↓ ↓

Women take active roles in various reform movements, particularly the temperance and abolitionist movements.

↓ ↓ ↓

Women use their experience fighting for other types of reform to begin the fight for their own rights.

☑ Quick Study Timeline

In America

1830
Charles Grandison Finney begins revivals in Rochester, New York

1838
Frederick Douglass escapes from slavery in Maryland

Presidential Terms   Andrew Jackson 1829–1837   Martin Van Buren 1837–1841

1830   **1835**

Around the World

1833
Slavery abolished in British West Indies

1837
Victoria becomes queen in Great Britain

American Issues
●━━●━━● **Connector**

 2.II.C.2

By connecting prior knowledge with what you have learned in this chapter, you can gradually build your understanding of enduring questions that still affect America today. Answer the questions below. Then, use your American Issues Connector study guide (or go online: www.PHSchool.com **Web Code:** nch-6803).

Issues You Learned About

● **Church and State** The United States follows a policy of keeping religion separate from matters of government.

1. What guarantees the American people the right to freedom of religion?

2. As you have read, many states had laws that barred Jewish people from holding public office. Evaluate these laws with regard to the Constitution's policy on religious freedom and the prohibition of religious practices in government.

3. Some communities and states have passed "blue laws" banning the sale of certain goods on Sundays. Do you think such laws violate the separation of church and state?

● **Social Problems and Reforms** The early 1800s initiated a period of tremendous efforts to improve different aspects of American society.

4. How is the work of Dorothea Dix still felt today?

5. What methods did abolitionists use to further their cause?

6. Identify two female reformers and explain what they did.

● **Education and American Society** The United States supports a public school system that has the goal of providing a quality education for all the country's children.

7. What would be the benefit of creating tax-supported public schools?

8. Why did reformers assert that a system of public education would be an important tool of democracy?

Connect to Your World	New York

Church and State Joseph Smith founded the Mormon church in 1830 in Fayette, New York. Soon afterwards, Smith and his followers moved west to Ohio, and the Mormon faith drew more followers as communities were founded within several Midwestern states. Upon Smith's death, the new Mormon leader, Brigham Young, led his followers to Salt Lake City, Utah, which today remains the center of the Mormon faith. Mormons continue to reside in western New York, and Mormon visitors from around the world come to visit Smith's boyhood home in Palmyra, New York. Each summer Palmyra's Hill Cumorah Pageant celebrates Mormonism at the place where Smith said an angel revealed to him the faith's essential texts. Conduct research to create a fact sheet about religious denominations in New York.

1843
Dorothea Dix seeks better treatment of people with mental illness

1848
Women's rights convention held in Seneca Falls, New York

William H. Harrison 1841 John Tyler 1841–1845	James K. Polk 1845–1849	Zachary Taylor 1849–1850 Millard Fillmore 1850–1853
1840	**1845**	**1850**

1839
Opium War between Great Britain and China begins

1845
Irish potato famine begins

History Interactive
For: Interactive Timeline
Web Code: ncp-0808

Chapter Assessment

Terms and People

1. Who were **Joseph Smith** and the **Mormons**? Why did many Americans distrust them?

2. What was the **temperance movement**? What measures brought the most success to the temperance movement?

3. Who were **William Lloyd Garrison** and **Frederick Douglass**? How did they help the abolitionist cause?

4. Define **matrilineal.** Was the United States mainly a matrilineal society in the early 1800s? Explain.

5. What is **suffrage**? Why did some women consider winning suffrage a critical step?

Focus Questions

The focus question for this chapter is **How did the Second Great Awakening lead to several reform efforts, and what effect did those reform efforts have on American society?** Build an answer to this big question by answering the focus questions for Sections 1 through 4 and the Critical Thinking questions that follow.

Section 1

6. How did the Second Great Awakening affect life in the United States?

Section 2

7. What were the main features of the public school, penitentiary, and temperance reform movements?

Section 3

8. How did reformers try to help enslaved people?

Section 4

9. What steps did American women take to advance their rights in the mid-1800s?

Critical Thinking

10. **Recognize Cause and Effect** Why did the Second Great Awakening begin? What were some of the ways that it changed American society?

11. **Analyze Information** What did the Transcendentalists and people who founded utopias have in common?

12. **Draw Conclusions** How might Horace Mann's experiences as a senator have made him an ideal leader for the school reform movement?

13. **Analyze Graphs** According to the graph below, how did the amount of alcohol consumed by Americans change from 1820 to 1860?

Annual Consumption of Alcohol per Person: 1820–1860

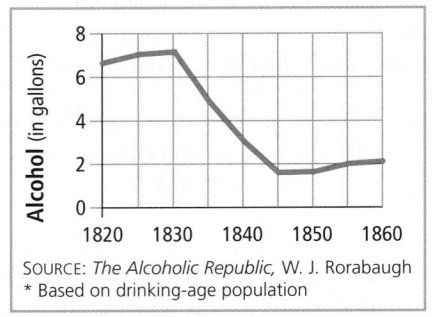

SOURCE: *The Alcoholic Republic,* W. J. Rorabaugh
* Based on drinking-age population

14. **Make Generalizations** What groups of people did reformers work hardest to help? Why?

15. **Problem Solving** How successful were slave revolts in helping enslaved African Americans resist slavery?

16. **Compare Points of View** What similar ideas did abolitionists and women's rights reformers hold?

Writing About History

Writing a Persuasive Essay In a persuasive essay, the writer identifies an issue and presents arguments that will persuade readers to support a particular viewpoint. Choose one of the reform movements described in this chapter. Write a three-paragraph essay in which you define the issue and give reasons in support of your viewpoint.

Prewriting

- Read the text in this chapter relating to the topic you have chosen.

- Use Internet or library sources to find additional descriptions and primary sources relating to your topic.

- Decide what viewpoint you wish to support.

- Make a list of arguments that might be used to support that viewpoint. Identify the two strongest arguments.

Drafting

- Make an outline identifying what aspects of your topic you want to describe.

- Write an opening paragraph in which you describe the issue and explain why it is important.

- Write two persuasive paragraphs. In each paragraph, use reasoned but forceful language that explains one of the arguments you have identified in your pre-writing. If possible, anticipate and counter possible objections to your arguments.

Revising

- Use the guidelines on page SH16 of the Writing Handbook to revise your writing.

Regents DBQ Practice

Nat Turner's Revolt Shakes the South

In August 1831, Nat Turner led one of the most deadly slave revolts in American history. He and about 50 followers killed nearly 60 white people in Southampton County, Virginia, in a bloody three-day rampage. Although Turner and many of his followers were quickly caught, tried, and executed, his revolt had far-reaching repercussions. Use your knowledge of this time period and Documents 1, 2, 3, and 4 to answer questions 1–4.

Document 1

"A fanatic preacher by the name of Nat Turner (Gen. Nat Turner) who had been taught to read and write, and permitted to go about preaching in the country, was at the bottom of this infernal brigandage. . . . We cannot say how long they were organizing themselves—but they turned out on last Monday early (the 22d) upon their nefarious expedition. . . . They were mounted to the number of 40 or 50; and with knives and axes— knocking on the head, or cutting the throats of their victims."

—*An account of the revolt from the newspaper* The Richmond Enquirer, *August 30, 1831*

Document 2

"I have received this day another number of *The Liberator,* a newspaper printed in Boston, with the express intention of inciting the slaves and free negroes in this and the other States to rebellion and to murder the men, women, and children of those states. Yet we are gravely told that there is no law to punish such an offence. . . . If this is not checked it must lead to a separation of these states."

—*Diary entry of Virginia Governor John Floyd, September 27, 1831*

Document 3

"Not far from this time Nat Turner's insurrection broke out; and the news threw our town [in North Carolina] into great commotion. . . . Those who never witnessed such scenes can hardly believe what I know was inflicted at this time on innocent men, women, and children, against whom there was not the slightest ground for suspicion. Colored people and slaves who lived in remote parts of the town suffered in an especial manner. . . . Every where men, women, and children were whipped till the blood stood in puddles at their feet. Some received five hundred lashes. . . . The dwellings of the colored people, unless they happened to be protected by some influential white person, who was nigh at hand, were robbed of clothing and every thing else the marauders thought worth carrying away."

—*Harriet Jacobs, from her slave narrative* Incidents in the Life of a Slave Girl, Written by Herself

Document 4

Some Measures Passed in Reaction to Nat Turner's Revolt	
States	**Measures**
Virginia	• Passed twenty new statutes regulating the lives of free and enslaved African Americans
Alabama, Maryland, Tennessee	• Forbade free blacks from moving to the state and settling there • Further restricted the ways African Americans could meet
Mississippi	• Required all free blacks to leave the state within ninety days
Alabama, South Carolina	• Punished anyone who attempted to teach enslaved African Americans to read or write
Georgia	• Offered a reward for the arrest of the publisher or anyone caught circulating *The Liberator* or other "seditious" written material

---

1. How might Nat Turner's role as a preacher have been to his advantage in planning the revolt?
   (1) It allowed him to meet with other slaves to plan the revolt.
   (2) It allowed him travel about the countryside freely.
   (3) It may have given him more influence over other slaves.
   (4) All of the above

2. What attitude towards William Lloyd Garrison's abolitionist newspaper *The Liberator* do both Documents 2 and 4 show?
   (1) It is a harmless scandal sheet.
   (2) It gives a good proslavery defense.
   (3) It contains dangerous, seditious propaganda.
   (4) It was of no consequence in the South.

3. How did Nat Turner's revolt affect Harriet Jacobs' town in North Carolina, according to Document 3?
   (1) Laws were passed restricting the movement of African Americans.
   (2) Whites beat and stole from African Americans, regardless of their guilt or innocence.
   (3) The commotion allowed Jacobs and other slaves to escape.
   (4) It had no effect.

4. **Writing Task** How did Nat Turner's revolt affect the lives of slaves and the ongoing debate about slavery in the United States? Summarize the effects of the revolt. Use your knowledge of the time period and the documents above to support your main points.

Westward Ho!

"Westward the course of empire takes its way," an Irish bishop wrote of North America in 1726. Little more than a century later, American empire builders fulfilled his prophecy. Thousands of pioneers moved westward along such routes as the Oregon Trail. This song of the 1850s captures their spirit:

❝The western fields give thousands wealth,
    Ho! Westward Ho!
And yield to all a glowing health,
    Ho! Westward Ho!
For all inclined to honest toil,
    Ho! Westward Ho!
Secure their fortunes from the soil,
    Ho! Westward Ho!❞
            —Ossian E. Dodge, "Ho! Westward Ho!"

Listen to the Witness History *audio to hear more about American pioneers in the West.*

◄ After traveling along the Oregon Trail in 1866, William Henry Jackson painted this view of wagon trains approaching Chimney Rock in Nebraska.

Flag of the Republic of Texas

 Core Curriculum Preview

Chapter Focus Question: What were the causes and effects of westward expansion in the early 1800s?

Section 1
Migrating to the West   2.II.C.2, 2.II.C.3

Section 2
Texas and the Mexican-American War
2.II.C.4, 2.II.C.5, 2.II.C.6

Section 3
Effects of Territorial Expansion   2.II.C.5, 2.II.C.6, 2.II.D.1

Use the ☑ **Quick Study Timeline** at the end of this chapter to preview chapter events.

U.S. Army hat from Mexican-American War

Equipment of California gold prospector

┌───┐
│ **Note Taking Study Guide** *Online*   │
│ **For:** Note Taking and American Issues Connector │
│ **Web Code:** nce-6901   │
└───┘

◀ Wagon train to the West

 WITNESS HISTORY 🔊 AUDIO

A Pioneer Woman Heads West

On April 9, 1853, Amelia Stewart Knight left Iowa with her family to join a wagon train headed for Oregon. Her diary describes many of the hazards of the five-month trek, from extreme heat or cold to poisonous water. It also reports encounters—some cordial and some tense—with Native Americans. In one entry, Knight wrote:

❝After looking in vain for water, we were about to give up as it was near night, when husband came across a company of friendly Cayuse Indians about to camp, who showed him where to find water, half mile down a steep mountain, and we have all camped together, with plenty of pine timber all around us. . . . We bought a few potatoes from an Indian, which will be a treat for our supper.❞
—Diary of Mrs. Amelia Stewart Knight, 1853

Migrating to the West

 Core Curriculum Objectives

- **2.II.C.2** Exploring and settling the West (explorers, naturalists, trappers and traders, trailblazers, missionaries, pioneers, the Mormon Church)
- **2.II.C.3** The Spanish, Mexican, and Native American West

Terms and People

Junípero Serra	Mountain Men
expansionist	Oregon Trail
Manifest Destiny	Brigham Young
Santa Fe Trail	Treaty of Fort Laramie

NoteTaking

Reading Skill: Identify Main Ideas Outline the main ideas relating to westward migration.

> I. Settling the Spanish Borderlands
>   A. Spain Settles New Mexico
>   1. Colony is sparsely populated
>   2.
>   B.
> II.

Why It Matters Since colonial times, Americans seeking economic opportunity had looked westward. By the 1840s, migrants were crossing the Rocky Mountains to Oregon and California. In time, these and other western lands would become part of the United States, helping the nation grow in both wealth and power. **Section Focus Question: What were the causes of westward migration?**

Settling the Spanish Borderlands

In 1830, what is now the U.S. Southwest was the Mexican North. Like the former British colonies in the East, this region had a long colonial history, one that dated back to the Spanish conquest of the Americas.

Spain Settles New Mexico Founded in 1598, New Mexico was the oldest colony along New Spain's northwestern frontier. Yet, by 1765, only about 9,600 Hispanics lived in New Mexico, half of them in the two major towns of El Paso and Santa Fe. The rest lived on farms and ranches scattered through the long Rio Grande valley. One factor discouraging further settlement was the threat of war with nomadic Native Americans in surrounding areas. Colonists depended for protection on an alliance with local Pueblo Indians. But disease steadily reduced the Pueblo population, from about 14,000 in 1700 to about 10,000 in 1765.

At the same time, the nomads of the Great Plains, known to the Spanish as Apaches, were becoming more powerful. The Apaches lived by hunting vast herds of buffalo. These hunts became easier after 1680 when the Apaches acquired horses from the Spanish. On horseback, men could see farther, travel faster, and kill their prey more quickly and in greater safety. At the same time, the nomads began to acquire firearms from French traders. The Indians continued to hunt with bows and arrows, but they used guns to wage war.

Warfare Threatens the Colony In 1800, a trader on the Great Plains remarked, "This is a delightful country and, were it not for perpetual wars, the natives might be the happiest people on earth." The conflict stemmed largely from competition for the buffalo herds. Well-armed groups, such as the Comanches of the Rocky Mountains and the Lakotas of the Mississippi Valley, spread at the expense of Apaches and other long-time residents of the Great Plains.

The defeated Apaches fled west into New Mexico, where they raided Pueblo and Spanish settlements, taking horses, sheep, cattle, and captives. Some Apaches found a haven in the canyons of northwest New Mexico, where they became known as Navajos. The Pueblos taught their Navajo neighbors how to weave, make pottery, grow corn, and herd sheep. But most Apaches remained nomadic hunters.

Raids on Spanish settlements became more frequent and destructive, for the Apaches were now armed, mounted, and desperate. The Comanches began to attack New Mexico as well. In 1777, a governor sadly reported that Indian raids had reduced his colony "to the most deplorable state and greatest poverty."

Spanish officials rescued New Mexico by building stronger frontier defenses and using more flexible diplomacy with the nomads. By providing gifts and weapons, the new officials found it cheaper to form bonds with some nomads than to fight them all. In general, Spain paid Comanche and Navajo allies to attack the Apaches. For the most part, the strategy worked.

Although most Apache groups remained defiant, some accepted peace on Spain's terms. And the alliance program did reduce raids on New Mexico. As the colony became safer, its population grew and its economy developed. By 1821, the Hispanic population had grown to about 40,000.

Texas Attracts Few Settlers New Mexico's growth and improved security did not extend to Texas, its sister colony to the east along the Gulf of Mexico. In Texas, the nomads were more formidable and the colony remained weaker.

The Spanish had founded Texas as a buffer zone to protect the valuable towns and mines of Mexico to the south. Like New Mexico, Texas was a mixture of ranches, missions, and military *presidios*. But Texas stagnated because few settlers felt attracted to such a distant and poor region subject to nomadic raiders. In 1760, only about 1,200 colonists lived in Texas, primarily in and around San Antonio. Ranchers drove longhorn cattle southward for sale in Mexico.

Missions Thrive in California In the 1760s, the Spanish extended their northern buffer zone to the west by colonizing the California coast. They were

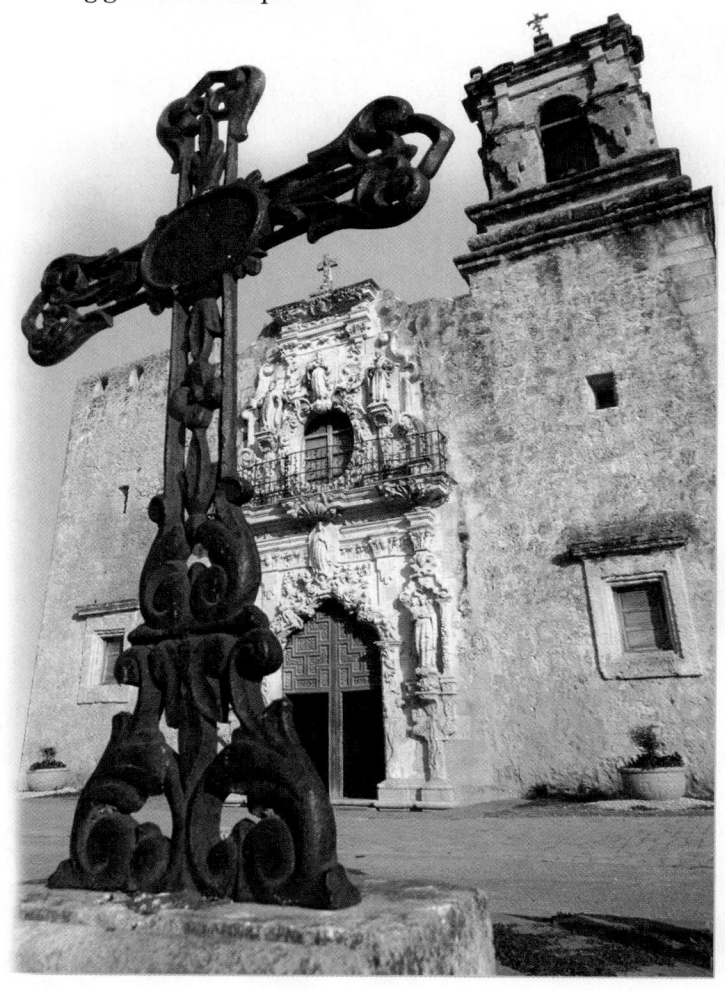

A Spanish Colonial Mission
Many of the oldest buildings in the Southwest are Spanish missions, like this one in Texas. Native Americans were forced to live and work on the mission grounds, where Spanish priests taught them about Christianity.

North America in 1820

British North America (Canada)

Oregon Country
(Occupied jointly by U.S. and Great Britain)

Unorganized Territory

Great Salt Lake

Michigan Territory

San Francisco
San Jose
Monterey
San Antonio de Padua
San Luis Obispo
Santa Barbara
San Gabriel
Los Angeles
San Juan Capistrano
San Diego

Taos
Santa Fe
Albuquerque

Spanish Territory

Tucson
Tubac
Janos
Carrizal
El Paso

Nacogdoches

Arkansas Territory

San Antonio

Laredo

Pacific Ocean

30°N

120°W

Gulf of Mexico

NY
PA
IL IN OH
VA
KY
TN
NC
SC
MS AL GA
LA
FL
ME

Conic Projection

0   200   400 mi

0   200   400 km

	United States
†	Mission
□	Presidio
●	Town
⛪	Mission and presidio
⊡	Presidio and town

Geography *Interactive*
For: Interactive map
Web Code: ncp-0902

Map Skills In 1820, most of the land that is now the American Southwest belonged to Spain. Mexico won independence the following year.

1. **Locate:** (a) Santa Fe, (b) San Antonio, (c) San Francisco, (d) Oregon

2. **Movement** What geographic and political obstacles did Americans moving westward face in the 1820s?

3. **Identify Alternatives** What methods might the United States have used to gain greater access to the Pacific coast?

This 1832 painting depicts a Native American buffalo hunt on the Great Plains. Nomadic hunters depended for survival on free movement across northern Mexico and the western U.S. territories.

afraid of losing the region to Russian traders probing south from Alaska. As in Texas, Spain had trouble attracting settlers to California. Potential settlers were daunted by California's isolation from Mexico. The distance to market discouraged the export of California's livestock and grains. The limited economy depended on royal money sent to supply and pay the soldiers.

Lacking colonists, the Spanish leaders sought to convert Indians to Christianity. Led by Father **Junípero Serra,** Franciscan priests set up a string of missions. The missions were more successful in California than in Texas or New Mexico. Because the local Indians lacked guns and horses, California missions suffered few raids. By the time of Father Serra's death in 1784, California had two agricultural towns (San Jose and Los Angeles), four *presidios,* and nine missions. In 1821, when Spanish rule ended, the system had grown to 20 missions housing more than 18,000 Native American converts. The Native Americans constructed buildings, dug irrigation ditches, erected fences, herded cattle, and cultivated grain. But large numbers died of diseases, and the Spanish had to round up more Indians to replace them.

✓ **Checkpoint** How did conflict develop between Spanish settlers and Native Americans in the Southwest?

Americans Look Westward

In 1821, a revolution toppled Spanish rule and established Mexico as an independent republic. The U.S. government officially recognized its fellow republic to the south. But American **expansionists,** people who favored territorial growth, soon began to covet New Mexico, Texas, and California. Thinly settled but rich in resources, the three provinces seemed ripe for American plucking.

Expansionists Seek Manifest Destiny
Expansionists justified their views by pointing to the weakness of the Mexican government and economy. They argued that the Mexicans, whom many Americans regarded as inferior, did not deserve to keep lands so badly needed for American settlement.

In 1845, journalist John L. O'Sullivan wrote an influential editorial in favor of expansion. He wrote:

> **Primary Source** "The American claim is by the right of our manifest destiny to overspread and possess the whole of the continent which Providence has given us for the development of the great experiment of liberty and . . . self-government entrusted to us."
>
> —John L. O'Sullivan, *New York Morning News,* December 27, 1845

Vocabulary Builder
manifest–(MAN uh fehst) *adj.* obvious; clear; plain

Expansionists were soon using the term **Manifest Destiny** to refer to the belief that God wanted the United States to own all of North America. But O'Sullivan envisioned liberty primarily for white men. Expansion would come at the expense of Indians and Mexicans. And southern expansionists hoped to add more slave states to strengthen their political position in Congress.

Americans Trade With Mexico
Mexican independence spurred American trade with northern Mexico. The Spanish had discouraged such contacts, but Mexican officials welcomed them. Indeed, trade and migration promoted economic growth in the border provinces. Still, as the Spanish had feared, American traders and settlers would come to threaten the security of Mexico's border.

Merchants from Missouri saw Mexican independence as an opportunity to open trade across the Great Plains with Santa Fe, the capital of New Mexico. Welcomed by the Mexican officials, the traders launched a growing commerce along what became known as the **Santa Fe Trail.** In exchange for American manufactured goods, the New Mexicans offered horses, mules, furs, and silver.

In the 1820s, mariners from the Northeast launched a more ambitious route. Sailing around South America to the California coast, they traded manufactured goods for tallow and hides from California ranches. Like New Mexico, California became economically dependent on commerce with the Americans.

Mountain Men Cross the Rockies
Other traders ventured up the Missouri River and into the Rockies, seeking valuable furs from the abundant beaver of the mountain streams. The daring young American trappers who hunted for beaver pelts in the Rockies were called **Mountain Men.** Most worked for two large fur companies, which provided their supplies.

Restless in pursuit of furs, the Mountain Men thoroughly probed the Rockies, making important discoveries. They blazed the best route through the mountains, via South Pass in what is now Wyoming. Some Mountain Men then pressed westward to the Great Salt Lake in the arid Great Basin of Utah. In 1826, Jedediah Smith crossed the Great Basin and the Sierra Nevada to reach California. In addition to trapping, he traded with the Mexican residents. Smith's trade and migration route became the California Trail, linking the United States with the Pacific coast.

Mountain Men
As this painting shows, Mountain Men lived a solitary, rugged existence as they hunted beaver in the Rocky Mountains. In time, they undermined their own way of life, killing beaver faster than the beaver could reproduce. *What dangers would Mountain Men face? Why do you think they were willing to face them?*

Trails to the West

During the 1840s alone, nearly 20,000 Americans migrated to California, Oregon, and Utah along the major overland trails. The trails also became trade routes, carrying merchants and goods in both directions.

◀ **Oregon Trail** Most emigrants on the Oregon Trail were farmers, and their final destination was the fertile land of the Willamette Valley. They packed their family and everything they could carry—from cast-iron stoves to the family Bible—onto covered wagons.

Missionaries Reach Oregon A variant of this trail turned northwest at South Pass to reach Oregon Country. In 1836, Marcus and Narcissa Whitman followed this route, which became known as the **Oregon Trail,** to found an Indian mission at Walla Walla.

The Whitman compound served as a magnet and way station for farm families bound farther west to the fertile Willamette Valley. In 1847, the Whitmans were killed by Native Americans who blamed them for a deadly measles epidemic. But by then, the tide of migration to Oregon was unstoppable.

✓ **Checkpoint** What role did the Mountain Men play in westward expansion?

The Journey Westward

In 1842, an official government expedition led by John C. Frémont set off across the western country, following trails blazed by the Mountain Men and the Whitmans. Although Frémont found little that was new, his vivid and romantic reports gave wider publicity to the fertility of the Far West. In the years that followed, the overland trails drew thousands of settlers west to California and Oregon.

◄ **Mormon Trail** The final destination for Mormon emigrants was the Great Salt Lake in present-day Utah. Through extensive irrigation and farming, Mormon settlers permanently altered their desert environment.

Westward Migration, 1840s

Western Trail	Number of Settlers	Where To	When
California Trail	2,700	California	1842–1848
Mormon Trail	4,600	Utah	1847–1848
Oregon Trail	11,500	Oregon	1842–1848

SOURCE: CIA World Factbook Online

Supplies for Travelers Forts along the overland trails provided more than protection. They were also homes to trading posts, where wagon trains could replenish their supplies. ▼

◄ **Donner Pass** For emigrants, mountain passes could be a gateway to their final destination—or a snowy tomb. The Donner Pass was named for a party who got trapped in the Sierra Nevadas in the winter of 1846–1847. Nearly half died of starvation, and the survivors resorted to eating their dead.

Geography and History
- How did the goals of travelers on the Oregon and Mormon trails differ? How were they similar?
- Do deserts and mountain passes still present a hazard to travelers today? Why or why not?

Wagon Trains Journey West <u>Commencing</u> in springtime at the western edge of Missouri, the demanding journey covered nearly 2,000 miles and took about five months to complete. Oxen pulled the emigrants' wooden wagons covered with canvas. For security and mutual help, most emigrants traveled in trains of from 10 to 100 wagons and from 50 to 1,000 people. Eager to get to the fertile and humid Pacific, the emigrants bypassed the Great Plains, which they considered little better than a desert, and the Great Basin, which truly was a desert. They were also in a hurry to get across two cold and lofty mountain chains, the Rockies and the Sierra Nevada.

Most of the emigrants were farm people from the Midwest. Men relished the journey as an adventure, while many women more keenly felt the hardships and anxieties. "What had possessed my husband, anyway, that he should have thought of bringing us away out through this God-forsaken country?" wrote one woman in her diary.

Indeed, the journey was a gamble that cost many their property and some their lives. Emigrants faced hunger, exposure, disease, poisoned streams—or worse. In 1846, the Donner Party got lost on the way to California. Trapped by snow in the Sierra Nevada, the starving survivors resorted to cannibalism.

Vocabulary Builder
<u>commence</u>–(kuh MEHNS) v. to begin a project or an enterprise

Brigham Young 1801–1877

"This is the place!" Brigham Young declared when he first spied the Great Salt Lake in July 1847. It was the end of a long journey that had begun 17 months earlier, when he led a Mormon party out of Illinois in the middle of a snowy, bitterly cold winter. During his next 30 years as president of the Mormon Church, Young provided the colony with tough, inspiring leadership. He also served eight years as the first governor of the Utah Territory.

Despite the dangers, the rewards of the journey could be great. Most of those who persevered gained bigger and better farms in Oregon or California than they had owned in the East or Midwest. Between 1840 and 1860, about 260,000 Americans crossed the continent to settle on the west coast.

Mormons Seek a Refuge One group of people preferred to settle along the way. These were the Mormons. As you read in the last chapter, Mormon founder Joseph Smith was killed in 1844 by a mob in Illinois.

Leadership passed to **Brigham Young,** a brilliant organizer with a powerful will. Convinced that the Mormons could not survive among hostile neighbors, Young organized an exodus. In 1847, he led Mormons across the Great Plains and the Rockies to establish the colony of New Zion on the eastern shore of the Great Salt Lake. Through hard work and cooperation, the Mormons made the arid land bloom by diverting water from mountain streams. By 1860, some 40,000 Mormons lived in the West.

Despite their achievements and their isolation, other Americans continued to distrust the Mormons. During the 1850s, after the territory had passed from Mexico to the United States, the government forced the Mormons to accept federal authority. New Zion became the federal territory of Utah.

Indians Face Restrictions So long as wagons kept moving west, Native Americans usually left them alone. Still, the federal government sought to protect migrants by restricting the Plains Indians. The 1851 **Treaty of Fort Laramie** bound the Indians to territories away from the major trails. But the Indians clung to their mobile way of life, pursuing buffalo across all artificial boundaries. As migration continued, the stage was set for future conflict.

✓ **Checkpoint** What difficulties and opportunities awaited migrants to the West?

SECTION **1** Assessment

Progress Monitoring *Online*
For: Self-test with vocabulary practice
Web Code: nca-0903

Comprehension

1. Terms and People Write a sentence explaining how each of the following was connected with westward migration.
- Manifest Destiny
- Santa Fe Trail
- Mountain Men
- Oregon Trail
- Brigham Young
- Treaty of Fort Laramie

2. NoteTaking Reading Skill: Identify Main Idea Use your outline to answer the Section Focus Question: What were the causes of westward migration?

Writing About History

3. Quick Write: Identify an Issue In the news media, an editorial is a statement supporting one view of a current issue. Choose a topic from this section as the subject for an editorial. Write a sentence explaining why people of the time might have held differing views on that issue.

Critical Thinking

4. Recognize Effects What long-term effects did the introduction of horses and firearms have on Native Americans in the West?

5. Recognize Viewpoints Who might have agreed with the idea of Manifest Destiny? Who might have disagreed?

6. Make Decisions If you were a poor farmer in 1850, would you have chosen to join a wagon train to the West? Why or why not?

SECTION **2**

▲ Texans defend the Alamo

WITNESS HISTORY 🔊 AUDIO

A Child at the Alamo

In March 1836, Mexican troops attacked the Alamo in San Antonio, Texas. Among those inside the old mission was eight-year-old Enrique Esparza. His father, Gregorio, was one of a group of Texans engaged in a struggle to win independence from Mexico. Some 70 years later, Esparza recalled hearing sounds of shooting at two in the morning:

❝I heard my mother say: 'Gregorio, the soldiers have jumped the wall. The fight's begun.' He got up and picked up his arms and went into the fight. I never saw him again. . . . It was so dark that we couldn't see anything, and the families that were in the quarters just huddled up in the corners. My mother's children were near her. Finally they began shooting through the dark into the room where we were. A boy who was wrapped in a blanket in one corner was hit and killed.❞
—Enrique Esparza, *San Antonio Express,* 1907

Texas and the Mexican-American War

🔵 **Core Curriculum Objectives**

- **2.II.C.4** Motives for and implications of expansion and western settlement
- **2.II.C.5** Politics of western expansion (Manifest Destiny, the Texas and Oregon questions, the Mexican War)
- **2.II.C.6** Impact of western expansion upon Mexicans and Native Americans

Terms and People

Stephen F. Austin	Alamo
Antonio López de Santa Anna	Sam Houston
	James K. Polk
autonomy	Zachary Taylor
Lone Star Republic	Winfield Scott

NoteTaking

Reading Skill: Recognize Sequence Look for the steps that led to war with Mexico.

Mexico encourages Americans to settle in Texas.
▼   ▼   ▼

Why It Matters With American expansionists seeking new territory and Mexico in control of most of the land to the south and west, conflict between the two nations seemed almost inevitable. The flashpoint for conflict became Texas. In time, that conflict would lead to a war that would vastly increase the size of the United States. **Section Focus Question: How did the revolution in Texas lead to war with Mexico?**

Texas Wins Independence

Of all the Mexican provinces, Texas was most vulnerable to U.S. expansion. Offering abundant, fertile land, Texas lay closest to the United States. And it had only a small Hispanic population, known as *Tejanos* (teh HAH nohs), to defend the province. In 1821, only about 4,000 Tejanos lived in Texas.

Americans Migrate to Texas To develop and defend the province, Mexico adopted a risky strategy: It agreed to allow Americans to settle in Texas. In return for cheap land grants, Americans had to agree to become Mexican citizens, to worship as Roman Catholics, and to accept the Mexican constitution, which banned slavery. Mexico hoped this strategy would convert American settlers from a potential threat to an economic asset.

WITNESS HISTORY DVD

Watch *The Alamo* on the **United States Witness History DVD** to explore one of the key battles of the Texas war for independence.

Led by **Stephen F. Austin,** American emigrants began to settle east of San Antonio, founding the town of Austin. Like settlers on other frontiers, these newcomers sought the economic opportunity of good farmland in large portions. Mostly coming from the southern United States, they raised corn, pigs, cattle, and cotton. By 1835, Texas was home to about 30,000 American settlers, known as Anglo-Texans. They outnumbered Tejanos by about six to one.

Tensions Build Relations between Anglo-Texans and the Mexican government soured by 1830. Despite their oaths of allegiance and their land grants, the settlers had not honored their part of the bargain. They remained Protestants and ignored Mexico's slavery ban by smuggling in enslaved African Americans to work their farms and plantations. In turn, the Anglo-Texans felt dismayed by the unstable Mexican government, which suffered from military coups.

In 1834, the charismatic but ruthless general **Antonio López de Santa Anna** seized power in Mexico City. Santa Anna favored a centralized, authoritarian government dominated by the military. His coup troubled those liberal Mexicans who preferred a decentralized federal system like that of the United States. Santa Anna's rule especially angered the people of Texas, both Anglo-Texans and Tejanos, who wanted greater **autonomy,** or independent control over their own affairs. One Anglo-Texan protested that Santa Anna would "give liberty to our slaves and make slaves of ourselves."

Texans Revolt In 1835, the Texans rebelled against Mexican rule. They seized the Mexican garrisons at Goliad and San Antonio. A year later, the Texans declared their independence and adopted a republican constitution. Their new nation became known as the **Lone Star Republic** because of the single star on its flag.

To crush the rebellion, Santa Anna led his army north into Texas. In March 1836, his forces attacked the small Texan garrison at the **Alamo,** a fortified former mission in San Antonio. After 12 days of cannon fire, Mexican troops overran the walls of the Alamo. Refusing to keep prisoners, Santa Anna ordered the defenders slaughtered. The victims included Anglo-Texans Jim Bowie and Davy Crockett, as well as a dozen Tejanos. A few weeks later, Santa Anna ordered a similar mass execution of Texan prisoners who had surrendered at Goliad.

Santa Anna expected the slaughter to frighten other Texans into surrendering. Instead, the fallen defenders of the Alamo became martyrs to the cause of Texan independence. The slogan "Remember the Alamo" rallied the Texans and attracted volunteers to their cause from the southern United States.

Led by **Sam Houston,** the Texans drew Santa Anna eastward into a trap. In April, they surprised and crushed the Mexican army at the Battle of San Jacinto. Houston's men killed 630 and captured 730 Mexicans, including Santa Anna himself, while suffering only 32 casualties.

Fearing execution, Santa Anna signed a treaty recognizing Texan independence. He conceded generous boundaries that stretched the new republic south and west to the Rio Grande. On paper, Texas even got half of New Mexico, including its capital of Santa Fe.

Of course, the government in Mexico City refused to honor a treaty forced on a captured and disgraced

HISTORY MAKERS

Sam Houston (1793–1863)

Sam Houston was the only American to serve as governor of two different states—first Tennessee, then Texas. In between, he was commander of the Texan army, president of the Republic of Texas, and U.S. senator from Texas.

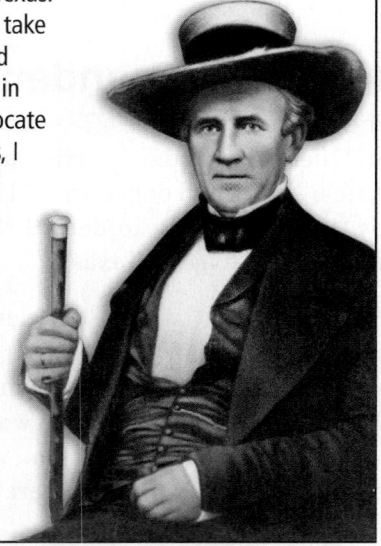

Houston was not afraid to take unpopular stands. An adopted Cherokee, he once said that "in presenting myself as the advocate of the Indians and their rights, I shall stand very much alone." In addition, though himself a slaveholder, he angered proslavery forces by opposing the spread of slavery into the West. Finally, in 1861, when Houston spoke out against Texas seceding from the Union, he was removed from the governorship of the state he had helped create.

Should the United States Annex Texas?

From the time it achieved independence, Texas sought U.S. statehood. America's leaders had to decide whether to annex Texas. The 1844 presidential rivals James Polk and Henry Clay disagreed on the issue. Read their views below. Then, you make the call.

Polk Favors Annexation

Primary Source

"None can fail to see the danger to our safety and future peace if Texas remains an independent state or becomes an ally or dependency of some foreign nation more powerful than herself. Is there one among our citizens who would not prefer perpetual peace with Texas to occasional wars, which so often occur between bordering independent nations?"

—James K. Polk, inaugural address, 1845

Clay Opposes Annexation

Primary Source

"Annexation and war with Mexico are identical. Now, for one, I certainly am not willing to involve this country in a foreign war for the object of acquiring Texas. . . . I regard all wars as great calamities, to be avoided, if possible, and honorable peace as the wisest and truest policy of this country."

—Henry Clay, "Raleigh Letter," 1844

You Decide

1. Why did Polk think annexation would promote peace?
2. Why did Clay think annexation would lead to war?
3. What decision would you have made? Why?

dictator. The Mexicans only would accept an independent Texas that remained within its traditional boundaries, which extended no farther south than the Nueces River. For the next decade, a border war persisted between Texas and Mexico.

 Checkpoint What issues led Anglo-Texans and Tejanos to seek independence from Mexico?

Americans Debate Expansion

Texans elected Sam Houston as their first president. He quickly asked the United States to annex Texas. President Jackson privately favored the request, but he could not overcome opposition in Congress. Northern representatives balked at adding another slave state, especially one so big and potentially powerful. For nearly a decade, Texas continued to apply in vain for annexation. Houston tried to pressure Congress by pretending to consider joining the British Empire. At the time, Britain and the United States jointly occupied the Oregon Territory in the Pacific Northwest. The prospect alarmed expansionists.

An Expansionist Becomes President The annexation of Texas became a key issue in the 1844 presidential election. Southern expansionists supported **James K. Polk** of Tennessee. A Jacksonian Democrat and a slaveholder, Polk devoutly believed in Manifest Destiny. Whig candidate Henry Clay opposed annexation.

Polk reasoned that northerners would accept the annexation of Texas if they got their own prize. He promised them the Oregon Territory. Polk threatened to fight Britain if it did not concede all of Oregon. Polk's vow to obtain both Texas and Oregon helped him win a decisive electoral victory.

Vocabulary Builder
reluctant–(rih LUHK tuhnt) *adj.*
unwilling; marked by mental
hesitation or reservations

Polk Compromises on Oregon However, northern Democrats soon felt betrayed by the new President. They had reluctantly supported annexing Texas because Polk had also vowed to grab all of Oregon. Instead, in June 1846 Polk compromised with the British, agreeing to split the Oregon Territory at the 49th parallel of latitude. The United States got the future states of Washington, Oregon, and Idaho. The British kept what became the Canadian province of British Columbia. An Ohio Democrat sputtered, "Our rights to Oregon have been shamefully compromised. The administration is Southern, Southern, Southern!"

Polk compromised because the nation could not afford two wars. He wanted to fight weak Mexico rather than powerful Britain. Indeed, by the time the Oregon compromise was completed, war with Mexico had already begun.

✓ **Checkpoint** What compromise did the United States and Britain reach regarding the Oregon Territory?

The Mexican-American War

A month before Polk took office, Congress narrowly voted to annex Texas, which entered the Union as a slave state in December 1845. Annexation inflamed the long-standing border dispute between Texas and Mexico. Polk endorsed the Texan claim to the land south and west of the Nueces River as far as the Rio Grande. This claim tripled the traditional size of Texas. Outraged, the Mexicans refused to recognize the annexation.

Congress Declares War Polk sent American troops led by General **Zachary Taylor** to occupy the contested borderland between the two rivers. While waiting for the inevitable conflict, Polk drafted a declaration of war. He did not have to wait long. In May 1846, a Mexican patrol clashed with American soldiers, killing eleven. Polk rushed his war message to Congress:

> **Primary Source** "We have tried every effort at reconciliation. . . . But now, after reiterated menaces, Mexico has passed the boundary of the United States, has invaded our territory and shed American blood upon the American soil."
> —James K. Polk, war message to Congress, May 11, 1846

Of course, the Mexicans saw the clash differently: To them it was an American invasion that shed Mexican blood on Mexican soil.

Democrats, especially those from the South, were enthusiastically in favor of war with Mexico. Most Whigs, especially those from the North, opposed war. They believed that Polk had deliberately provoked the war by sending troops to Texas. Whigs also feared that Polk would not settle for even the biggest version of Texas but planned to annex the adjacent northern Mexican provinces, including New Mexico and California. The conquered territories might then become slave states, increasing southern power in Congress.

Despite their suspicions, most Whigs did not dare block the declaration of war. They knew that the war had wide popular support—and they remembered the demise of the Federalist Party after it had opposed the War of 1812. On May 13, Congress voted overwhelmingly to declare war on Mexico.

U.S. Forces Sweep to Victory In the war, the United States had great advantages. It was much larger, wealthier, and more populous than Mexico. The Mexicans lacked the industries that so quickly and abundantly supplied the Americans with arms and ammunition. The Americans also had a larger and better navy and more advanced artillery. Above all, the United States enjoyed superb officers, well trained at the military academy at West Point. Generals Zachary Taylor and

The Mexican-American War

Geography *Interactive*
For: Interactive map
Web Code: ncp-0904

Oregon Country

40°N

Bear Flag Revolt
(June 14, 1846)
Sonoma
San Francisco

Unorganized Territory

Iowa

Fort Leavenworth

Missouri

Bent's
Old Fort

UNITED STATES

San Gabriel
(Jan. 8, 1847)
Los Angeles
San Pasqual (Dec. 6, 1846)
San Diego

Santa Fe

Colorado R.

*Pacific
Ocean*

Arkansas

El Brazito
(Dec. 25, 1846)
El Paso

30°N

MEXICO

Texas

Louisiana

Mississippi R.

Houston
San Antonio

New Orleans

Sacramento
(Feb. 28, 1847)

Rio Grande

Nueces R.

Corpus Christi
Palo Alto
(May 8, 1846)

Gulf of California

Matamoros (May 17–18, 1846)

Mazatlán

Buena Vista
(Feb. 22–23, 1847)

Monterrey
(Sept. 19–25,
1846)

Gulf of Mexico

120°W

110°W

Tampico

Cerro Gordo
(April 18, 1847)

Mexico City
(Sept. 14, 1847)

Chapultepec
(Sept. 13, 1847)

Veracruz (March 27, 1847)

Legend:
- Disputed territory
- American victory
- Mexican victory
- American forces
- Mexican forces
- Fort
- Blockade

Conic Projection
0   200   400 mi
0   200   400 km

Timeline:

1846

May Taylor crosses Nueces River

June Bear Flag revolt in California

August United States troops occupy Santa Fe

1847

February Battle of Buena Vista

March Scott captures Veracruz

September Battle of Chapultepec

September United States Army enters Mexico City

1848

Map Skills The Mexican-American War of 1846–1847 began in Texas. During the war, the United States won every major battle.

1. **Locate:** (a) Nueces River, (b) Rio Grande, (c) California, (d) Monterrey, (e) Veracruz, (f) Mexico City

2. **Region** What region on the map was the subject of the land dispute that sparked the war?

3. **Synthesize Information** Use the map and chart to describe U.S. troop movements in the final month of the war.

Battle of Monterrey
In September 1846, U.S. troops under General Zachary Taylor attacked Monterrey, Mexico. The plumed hat (above left) was part of the U.S. military uniform of the time.

Winfield Scott received exceptional support from their junior officers, including Robert E. Lee, Ulysses S. Grant, and William T. Sherman. (All these men would later play key roles in the U.S. Civil War.) Meanwhile, Mexicans were bitterly divided because Santa Anna had resumed his dictatorship.

In this one-sided war, the United States won every major battle. During the summer of 1846, General Stephen W. Kearny quickly conquered New Mexico. Meanwhile, the U.S. Navy helped American settlers, led by explorer John C. Frémont, to seize control of California. Until they could legally join the United States, these rebels organized the short-lived Bear Flag Republic. Frémont joined forces with Kearny to bring all of California under American control.

Taylor led another army deeper into northern Mexico, seizing the city of Monterrey in September. In February 1847, Santa Anna tried to retake the city. But Taylor's small army defeated the more numerous Mexicans at the bloody Battle of Buena Vista.

By early 1847, American forces had achieved all of Polk's war goals—but he wanted more. A New England critic of the war complained that with every victory, "Our Manifest Destiny higher and higher kept mounting." In March, the navy carried another American army, commanded by Winfield Scott, to the Mexican port city of Veracruz. After seizing the port, Scott boldly marched his men through 200 miles of rugged terrain to Mexico City.

Scott faced bitter resistance at Chapultepec (chah POOL tuh pehk), a fortress above Mexico City. The defenders included six young Mexican cadets—ranging in age from 13 to 19—who fought to the death. Today, Mexico honors the cadets who fell at Chapultepec as *Los Niños Héroes,* or the Child Heroes.

In September 1847, Scott captured Mexico City. After little more than a year and a half of fighting, the Mexican-American War had ended in a thorough American victory.

 Checkpoint What advantages did the United States have in the Mexican-American War?

SECTION **2 Assessment**

Progress Monitoring _Online_
For: Self-test with vocabulary practice
Web Code: nca-0905

Comprehension

1. **Terms and People** Write a sentence explaining how each of the following was connected with the conflict between the United States and Mexico.
   - Antonio López de Santa Anna
   - autonomy
   - Lone Star Republic
   - Alamo
   - Sam Houston
   - James K. Polk
   - Zachary Taylor

2. **NoteTaking Reading Skill: Recognize Sequence** Use your chart to answer the Section Focus Question: How did the revolution in Texas lead to war with Mexico?

Writing About History

3. **Quick Write: Express an Editorial Position** Imagine that you are the editor of either a southern Democrat or a northern Whig newspaper in 1844. Write a topic sentence for an editorial supporting either Polk or Clay for the presidency. Make sure your sentence clearly identifies your position.

Critical Thinking

4. **Recognize Causes** In what way was the fighting in Texas the responsibility of both the Anglo-Texans and the Mexican government?

5. **Make Decisions** Do you think Polk was right to compromise with Britain over Oregon? Explain.

6. **Draw Conclusions** Do you think the U.S. declaration of war against Mexico was justified? Why or why not?

▲ Chinese miners in California

Gold-mining tools ▶

Seeking a Mountain of Gold

By 1849, poor farmers in China had received word of a "mountain of gold" across the Pacific Ocean. Soon, thousands of Chinese men joined fortune seekers from all over the world in a rush to the gold fields of California. However, the Chinese newcomers often faced a hostile reception. In a letter home to his parents, one young American miner described the unfair treatment of Chinese miners:

❝They are coming by thousands all the time The miners in a great many plases will not let them work The miners hear drove off about 200 Chinamen about two weeks ago but they have com back about as thick as ever (I would not help drive them off as I thought they had no rite to drive them).❞

—Robert W. Pitkin, 1852

Effects of Territorial Expansion

🗽 Core Curriculum Objectives

- **2.II.C.5** Politics of western expansion (Manifest Destiny, the Texas and Oregon questions, the Mexican War)
- **2.II.C.6** Impact of western expansion upon Mexicans and Native Americans
- **2.II.D.1** United States society divided

Terms and People

Treaty of Guadalupe Hidalgo
Gadsden Purchase
Wilmot Proviso

California Gold Rush
forty-niners
placer mining
hydraulic mining

NoteTaking

Reading Skill: Understand Effects Trace the effects of the Mexican-American War.

Event		Effect
Mexican-American War	→	• Treaty of Guadalupe Hidalgo; United States gains territory • •

Why It Matters As a result of its quick victory in the Mexican-American War, the United States would finally achieve the expansionists' goal of Manifest Destiny. Yet, the long-term effects of the war served to highlight growing differences between North and South and set the stage for future conflict. **Section Focus Question: What were the effects of the Mexican-American War and the California Gold Rush?**

America Achieves Manifest Destiny

In February 1848, the defeated Mexicans made peace with the Americans. The **Treaty of Guadalupe Hidalgo** (gwah duh LOO pay ee THAHL goh) forced Mexico to give up the northern third of their country and added 1.2 million square miles of territory to the United States.

The United States Gains Territory In return for leaving Mexico City and paying $15 million, the victors kept New Mexico and California. They also secured the Rio Grande as the southern boundary of Texas.

The treaty disgusted and humiliated Mexicans, who continued for decades to feel bitterness toward the United States. The treaty also dismayed Polk, but for a different reason. After Scott captured Mexico City, the President decided that he wanted to keep more of Mexico. He blamed his negotiator, Nicholas Trist, for settling for too little. But Polk had no choice but to submit the treaty to Congress because northern public opinion would not support a longer war.

Geography Interactive
For: Interactive map
Web Code: ncp-0906

Conic Projection
0   200   400 mi
0   200   400 km

BRITISH TERRITORY

Ceded by Britain,
(Convention of 1818)

Disputed with Great
Britain until 1842

L. Superior

OREGON COUNTRY
(Agreement with
Britain, 1846)

Lake Ontario

L. Michigan

L. Huron

L. Erie

LOUISIANA PURCHASE
(Purchased from France, 1803)

THE UNITED STATES
(1783)

ORIGINAL 13 STATES

MEXICAN CESSION
(Treaty of Guadalupe
Hidalgo, 1848)

GADSDEN PURCHASE
(Purchased from
Mexico, 1853)

120° W

TEXAS ANNEXATION
(Annexed by Congress, 1845)

Atlantic
Ocean

30° N

Pacific
Ocean

(Annexed, 1812)

(Annexed, 1810)

FLORIDA
(Ceded by Spain, 1819)

MEXICO

Gulf of Mexico

80° W

—— Present-day state boundaries

110° W

90° W

Map Skills By 1853, the United States had achieved Manifest Destiny and stretched from the Atlantic to the Pacific.

1. **Locate:** (a) Oregon, (b) Texas, (c) Mexican Cession, (d) Gadsden Purchase

2. **Regions** What territory did the United States acquire as the result of war?

3. **Connect Past and Present** Is your own state on this map? If so, how and when was it acquired by the United States?

Vocabulary Builder
comprise–(kuhm PRīZ) v. to include; to make up

In the **Gadsden Purchase** of 1853, the United States obtained from Mexico another 29,640 square miles in southern Arizona and New Mexico. The Americans bought this strip to facilitate a railroad across the continent. Along with the annexation of Texas, the Treaty of Guadalupe Hidalgo and the Gadsden Purchase increased the area of the United States by about one third. Only the Louisiana Purchase had added more territory. The new lands <u>comprised</u> present-day New Mexico, California, Nevada, Utah, Arizona, and half of Colorado.

The Wilmot Proviso Divides Americans Even before the war ended, the prospect of gaining land from Mexico stirred fierce debate in the United States. In 1846, Whig congressman David Wilmot of Pennsylvania had proposed a law, known as the **Wilmot Proviso,** that would ban slavery in any lands won from Mexico. The proposal broke party unity and instead divided Congress largely along sectional lines. Most northern Democrats joined all northern Whigs to support the Wilmot Proviso. Southern Democrats joined southern Whigs in opposition. The Proviso passed in the House of Representatives, but it failed narrowly in the Senate.

The Wilmot Proviso would reappear in every session of Congress for the next 15 years. Repeatedly, it passed in the House only to fail in the Senate. The Proviso brought the slavery issue to the forefront and weakened the two major parties, which had long tried to avoid discussing the issue in Congress. Thus, the lands won from Mexico increased tensions between North and South.

✓ **Checkpoint** How did the Mexican-American War serve to heighten tensions over slavery?

The California Gold Rush

To most Americans, the new lands in the West seemed too distant for rapid settlement. But in early 1848, workers at John Sutter's sawmill found flecks of gold in the American River east of Sacramento, California.

Forty-Niners Flock to California By summer, news of the gold strike caused a sensation in the eastern United States. In a mass migration known as the **California Gold Rush,** some 80,000 fortune seekers headed for California in search of easy riches. About half of these **forty-niners** traveled by land trails. Another half went by ship around South America or via a short land passage at the Isthmus of Panama. The ships landed their human cargo in San Francisco.

The golden news also attracted miners from around the Pacific Rim. Many fortune seekers came from South America, especially Peru and Chile. Another 25,000 laborers migrated from China to California during the 1850s. From a mere 14,000 in 1847, California's population of outside settlers surged to 225,000 in just five years.

Miners Lead a Rough Life Forty-niners flocked to the gold fields with high hopes. One young man described the excitement of departing for California from Indiana:

> **Primary Source** "The diggings had been discovered but a twelve-month before, and the glowing tales of their marvelous richness were on every tongue. Our enthusiasm was wrought up to the highest pitch, while the hardships and perils . . . were scarcely given a passing thought."
> —David Rohrer Leeper, "The Argonauts of '49"

At first, the miners used cheap metal pans, picks, and shovels to harvest gold flecks from the sand along the banks and bottoms of rivers and streams. This process was known as **placer mining.** A few miners got rich, but most worked hard for little gain. Because food and clothing were so expensive, shrewd traders made more money selling goods to the miners than the miners made by panning for gold.

Conditions were hard in the crowded mining camps. Poor sanitation promoted diseases, especially cholera and dysentery, killing hundreds. In addition, life was cheap and law was scarce in the camps. Almost all of the inhabitants were men, who felt frustrated by their failure to find much gold and by their lack of family life. Competition and fights became common. One forty-niner noted, "It is surprising how indifferent people become to the sight of violence and bloodshed in this country."

In search of order, the miners carried out their own rough justice. Without official legal authority, they acted as judges, juries, and executioners.

Methods of Mining Change Placer mining soon gave way to more efficient methods that required more money and equipment. One method was to dam and divert rivers to expose their beds. Another method, **hydraulic mining,** employed jets of water to erode gravel hills into long lines of sluices to catch the gold. Hydraulic mining damaged the environment by leveling hills and clogging rivers with sediment.

The Lure of California Gold
The California gold fields attracted thousands of men and a smaller number of women (bottom). The poster (below, left) advertises ship passage to California. *What does the guidebook (below, right) suggest about the appeal of the California Gold Rush?*

Those with the most money turned to "hard rock mining," searching in the mountains for veins of quartz that contained gold. Miners extracted gold by digging deep tunnels and shafts braced with posts and beams and drained by pumps. One California newspaper complained that the new type of large-scale mining operation "<u>degrades</u> the sturdy miner into a drudge . . . while [mine owners] reap the great profit of his endeavor." The democratic age of placer mining was over. With few exceptions, wealthy investors rather than common miners owned the mines and enjoyed the profits.

Vocabulary Builder
<u>degrade</u>—(dee GRAYD) *v.* to reduce in status or rank

✓ **Checkpoint** What problems did forty-niners face in the California gold fields?

INFOGRAPHIC

San Francisco:
GROWTH OF A CITY

For those traveling by ship, San Francisco was the gateway to the California gold fields. It was also a place where miners could come to buy supplies, exchange gold for cash, or relax. Through migration and trade, San Francisco quickly became *the* major American city on the Pacific coast in the 1800s.

Before and After What happened to San Francisco between 1848 (above) and 1850 (below)? One word explains the rapid building boom: GOLD!

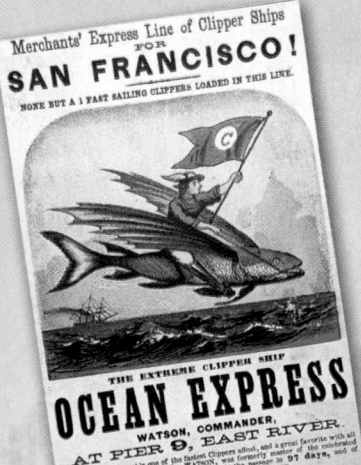

◀ **A Fast Trip West**
This 1851 advertisement promises a superfast trip from New York around the southern tip of South America to San Francisco—in as little as 97 days!

▼ **Street Scene**
This painting shows a busy street market in 1850 San Francisco.

Thinking Critically
1. **Draw Inferences** What kind of businesses do you think sprang up in San Francisco as a result of the Gold Rush?

2. **Draw Conclusions** What other circumstances might cause rapid changes in a city's population?

History *Interactive* ★

For: To discover more about the growth of San Francisco
Web Code: ncp-0910

Growth of San Francisco	
Year	Population
1848	800
1849	25,000
1852	36,000
1860	57,000

SOURCE: CIA World Factbook Online

Effects of the Gold Rush

Newcomers from the eastern United States quickly asserted their dominance over California. To discourage the Chinese, they levied a heavy tax on foreign miners.

Indians and Mexicans Face Discrimination

White miners also terrorized and killed Native Americans by the thousands. Losing their land, many surviving Indians became workers on farms and ranches.

Mob violence drove most Mexican Americans away from the gold fields. Those who stayed had to pay the foreign miners' tax, though Mexicans had been in California long before the new American majority. *Californios*, or Mexican Californians, also lost most of their land. Contrary to the Treaty of Guadalupe Hidalgo, the courts ignored land titles created under Mexican law.

California Seeks Statehood
The new Californians wanted quickly to organize a state and enter the union. In October 1849, their leaders held a convention and drew up a state constitution. The new constitution excluded African Americans, both slave and free. Most of the new Californians were northerners who did not want to compete with southern slaveholders who could use slave labor to seek gold. Nor did the miners want any free blacks to live in California.

California's application for statehood stirred discord between North and South. At the time, the Union was comprised of 15 free states and 15 slave states. Admission of a new free state would thus tip the delicate regional balance in the Senate. Over the next decade, debate over the spread of slavery into the lands won from Mexico would grow increasingly bitter. Thus, westward expansion became a major source of the division that ultimately led to the tragic Civil War.

✓ **Checkpoint** What impact did the settlement of California have on Mexicans already living there?

HISTORY MAKERS

Mariano Vallejo
(1808–1890)
Mariano Vallejo lived under Spanish, Mexican, and U.S. rule. The son of wealthy landowners, he became a general in the Mexican army. Critical of the Mexican government, Vallejo welcomed the arrival of U.S. settlers. Though he was briefly imprisoned during the Bear Flag revolt, he continued to support the American cause, serving as a delegate to the California constitutional convention and as a state legislator. But like many Californios, he lost most of his land to white settlers when the courts refused to recognize his family land grants. Vallejo lived his final years on a small fragment of his once large ranch.

SECTION **3** Assessment

Progress Monitoring *Online*
For: Self-test with vocabulary practice
Web Code: nca-0907

Comprehension

1. **Terms and People** Write a sentence explaining how each of the following was connected with westward expansion.
   - Treaty of Guadalupe Hidalgo
   - Gadsden Purchase
   - Wilmot Proviso
   - California Gold Rush
   - forty-niners
   - placer mining
   - hydraulic mining

2. **NoteTaking Reading Skill: Recognize Effects** Use your chart to answer the Section Focus Question: What were the effects of the Mexican-American War and the California Gold Rush?

Writing About History

3. **Quick Write: Write an Editorial** Write an editorial on the Wilmot Proviso that might have appeared in an 1846 newspaper. Define the issue and give reasons to support one position.

Critical Thinking

4. **Apply Information** How did the Treaty of Guadalupe Hidalgo settle the chief issues that led to the Mexican-American War?

5. **Draw Conclusions** Who benefited most from the California Gold Rush? Who benefited least?

6. **Evaluate Information** What do you think was the most important long-term result of the Mexican-American War? Explain.

Quick Study Guide

 2.II.C.5, 2.II.C.6

Progress Monitoring Online
For: Self-test with vocabulary practice
Web Code: nca-0908

■ Spain Settles the Southwest

The Spanish Borderlands		
New Mexico	**Texas**	**California**
• Oldest Spanish colony in borderlands • Warfare with Apache nomads discourages settlement • Spain builds defenses; some Apaches accept life on reservations • Hispanic population grows	• Settled by Spanish as buffer zone to protect Mexico • Warfare with Native Americans discourages settlement • Cattle ranching is central to economy	• Colonized to prevent Russian settlement • Distance from Mexico discourages settlement • Strong mission system; Native Americans forced to live and work on missions

■ Westward Migration

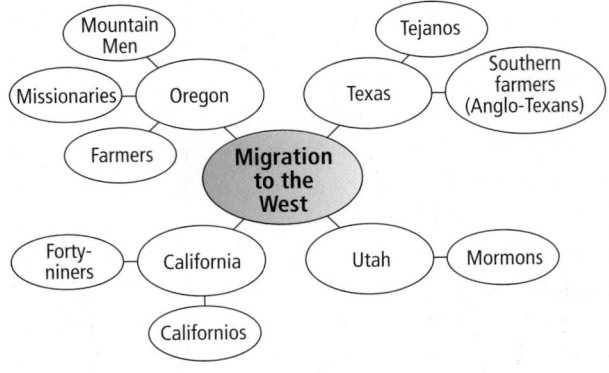

Mountain Men — Missionaries — Oregon — Farmers

Tejanos — Texas — Southern farmers (Anglo-Texans)

Migration to the West

Forty-niners — California — Californios

Utah — Mormons

■ The Mexican-American War

Cause and Effect
Causes
• Expansionists pursue Manifest Destiny. • Texas wins independence from Mexico. • Boundary dispute arises between Mexico and Texas. • United States annexes Texas. • President Polk sends U.S. troops into disputed area of Texas. • Mexican and U.S. troops clash in Texas.

Mexican-American War

Effects
• United States wins quick victory. • Treaty of Guadalupe Hidalgo cedes Southwest to United States. • Wilmot Proviso is proposed, then defeated in Congress. • Issue of slavery in West divides nation. • Mexican Americans in West lose many rights. • Americans migrate to California during Gold Rush.

☑ Quick Study Timeline

1826
Jedediah Smith blazes California Trail

1836
Texas declares independence

In America

Presidential Terms	James Monroe 1817–1825	John Quincy Adams 1825–1829	Andrew Jackson 1829–1837	Martin Van Buren 1837–1841

1820 **1830**

Around the World

1821
Mexico wins independence

1834
Santa Anna becomes dictator of Mexico

American Issues 2.II.C.5
●─●─● Connector

By connecting prior knowledge with what you have learned in this chapter, you can gradually build your understanding of enduring questions that still affect America today. Answer the questions below. Then, use your American Issues Connector study guide (or go online: www.PHSchool.com **Web Code:** nch-6902).

Issues You Learned About

● **America Goes to War** Events in Texas led the United States to go to war with Mexico, its neighbor to the south.

1. Prior to the Mexican-American War, what conflicts had the United States fought?

2. What justification did the United States make for declaring war on Mexico? What do you think Mexico thought about this reasoning?

3. What advantages did the United States have over Mexico in the Mexican-American War?

● **Territorial Expansion of the United States** The United States has gradually added territory through purchase and treaties and as a result of wars.

4. What was the importance of the Louisiana Purchase?

5. Would the Mexican-American War have occurred if expansionists had not hoped to gain control of Mexico's northern territories? Explain.

6. How did the settlement of California by gold seekers impact the lives of the people already settled there?

● **Sectionalism and Nationalism** People may hold political opinions that are based on the particular needs of the region in which they live.

7. What challenge caused the greatest debate between northerners and southerners during the early to mid-1800s? Give specific examples of issues that were part of this debate.

8. Was the balance of power in the Senate tipped by the admission of California into the Union? Explain.

Connect to Your World	New York

Territorial Expansion of the United States New York had its share of people who ventured west in search of land and fortune. Some of these settlers found their way to Texas, where conflict between Mexico and the United States led to the battle of the Alamo in 1836. Eleven New Yorkers fought to defend the Alamo, and all lost their lives. These New Yorkers are remembered in a room at the present-day site of the shrine at the Alamo. The room contains a semi-circle of state flags. Each flag honors the home state of the soldiers who died at the Alamo. Conduct research about migration into and out of New York. Choose one time period and write a brief essay describing the reasons that migrants decided to move to or leave the state.

History *Interactive*
For: Interactive timeline
Web Code: ncp-0909

	1846 Mexican-American War begins	1848 Gold is discovered in California	1851 Treaty of Fort Laramie	1853 Gadsden Purchase	1861 Civil War begins

William H. Harrison 1841 John Tyler 1841–1845	James K. Polk 1845–1849	Zachary Taylor 1849–1850 Millard Fillmore 1850–1853	Franklin Pierce 1853–1857	James Buchanan 1857–1861
1840		**1850**		**1860**

1846 Britain compromises with United States on Oregon	1849 Chinese immigration to America begins

Chapter Assessment

Terms and People

1. What was the chief goal of American **expansionists**?

2. What was the **Oregon Trail**? Which settlers traveled along this trail, and why?

3. What was the goal of the **Treaty of Fort Laramie**? How did it affect Native Americans?

4. Who were **Antonio López de Santa Anna** and **Sam Houston**? How were the two men linked?

5. How did **James K. Polk** encourage territorial expansion?

6. What was the **Gadsden Purchase**? Why did the United States seek this purchase?

7. What was the **Wilmot Proviso**? Did it unite or divide Congress? Explain.

8. What was the goal of the **forty-niners**?

Focus Questions

The focus question for this chapter is **What were the causes and effects of westward expansion in the early 1800s?** Build your answer to this big question by answering the focus questions for Sections 1 through 3 and the Critical Thinking questions that follow.

Section 1

9. What were the causes of westward migration?

Section 2

10. How did the revolution in Texas lead to war with Mexico?

Section 3

11. What were the effects of the Mexican-American War and the California Gold Rush?

Critical Thinking

12. **Identify Central Issues** Why was settlement so limited in Spain's northern territories? How successful was Spain's effort to encourage settlement?

13. **Identify Point of View** Did people who believed in Manifest Destiny support the acquisition of New Mexico, Texas, and California? Explain.

14. **Predict** Why might the role of the Mormon Church in the government of the Utah Territory become a source of future conflict with the federal government?

15. **Summarize** Present a brief history of Texas that spans the period from the 1700s through the mid-1800s. What do you think were the two most important turning points in Texas history?

16. **Compare Points of View** Why did most northerners tend to oppose the Mexican-American War while most southerners tended to support it?

17. **Explain Effects** How did the Oregon settlement and the Treaty of Guadalupe Hidalgo change the map of North America?

18. **Draw Conclusions** Why do you think so few women or families made their way west to live and work in the California mining camps?

19. **Explain Effects** Identify three effects of the California Gold Rush. Which effect do you think was most important in the long term? Explain.

20. **Categorize** Throughout the 1800s, farmers traveled west in search of land. What other specific groups of Americans made their way west in the 1800s, and why?

Writing About History

Writing an Editorial The purpose of an editorial, whether in a newspaper or in the broadcast media, is to influence public opinion on a current issue. Imagine that you are a newspaper editor in the mid-1800s. Write an editorial on one of the following topics: the idea of Manifest Destiny; the Texas war for independence; the Treaty of Guadalupe Hidalgo; California's application for statehood.

Prewriting

- Identify a specific issue connected with your topic. The issue should be one on which there might have been at least two possible opposing viewpoints.

- Choose a context for your editorial. For example, are you writing for a northern or southern newspaper? An Anglo-Texan or Mexican newspaper?

- Identify your editorial viewpoint on the topic. List reasons in favor of that viewpoint.

Drafting

- Write an opening statement in which you briefly but clearly define the issue.

- State your editorial opinion.

- Clearly state the reasons why you think your readers should support your position.

Revising

- Use the guidelines for revising your writing on page SH16 of the Writing Handbook.

Regents DBQ Practice

2.II.C.6,
2.II.C.5

New Settlement in the Mexican Cession

After the Mexican-American War, Mexico lost about one third of its territory to the United States. This land, called the Mexican Cession, attracted American settlers. What happened to the Mexicans who now found themselves living in a different country? Use your knowledge of American history and Documents 1, 2, 3, 4, and 5 to answer questions 1 through 4.

Document 1
The Mexican Cession

Entire State	Part of State
• Texas (Texas Annexation)	• Oklahoma (Texas Annexation)
• California (Mexican Cession)	• Kansas (Texas Annexation)
• Nevada (Mexican Cession)	• Colorado (Texas Annexation, Mexican Cession)
• Utah (Mexican Cession)	• Wyoming (Texas Annexation, Mexican Cession)
• Arizona (Mexican Cession, Gadsden Purchase)	
• New Mexico (Mexican Cession, Gadsden Purchase, Texas Annexation)	

Document 2

"Mexicans now established in territories previously belonging to Mexico . . . shall be free to continue where they now reside. . . . In the said territories, property of every kind, now belonging to Mexicans not established there, shall be inviolably respected. . . . The Mexicans who, in the territories aforesaid, shall not preserve the character of citizens of the Mexican Republic . . . shall be incorporated into the Union of the United States and be admitted at the proper time . . . to the enjoyment of all the rights of citizens of the United States, according to the principles of the Constitution; and in the mean time, shall be maintained and protected in the free enjoyment of their liberty and property, and secured in the free exercise of their religion without restriction."

— *Treaty of Guadalupe Hidalgo, 1848*

Document 3

"That ultimately the whole of Mexico will be embraced in our Union, there is very little room to doubt. That dislike to Americans of the North, which was a characteristic of the Mexicans, founded on prejudice, has to a very remarkable extent given way to admiration, and a desire for closer intimacy. . . ."

— *"Mexico and the Mexicans,"* The United States Democratic Review, *June 1850*

Document 4

"What a difference between the present time and those that preceded the Americans. If the Californios could all gather together to breathe a lament, it would reach heaven as a moving sigh which would cause fear and consternation in the Universe. What misery!"

— *Mariano Vallejo, late 1800s*

Document 5

"Unlike earlier [American] colonists, these new settlers came as conquerors. In most areas they were vastly outnumbered by Mexicans who had recently been given citizenship and, supposedly, equal rights. The Anglo settlers most likely felt insecure as a minority and so they, the conquerors, set out to subdue the conquered. Mexican Americans soon found that they were discriminated against and treated like aliens in lands they felt rightfully belonged to them. Their land was taken from them; their political power, or the potential for it, usurped, and their social position threatened."

— *A History of the Mexican-American People, Julian Samora, 1977*

---

1. According to Document 1, which of the following states was not affected by the Treaty of Guadalupe Hidalgo?
   (1) Oklahoma
   (2) Nevada
   (3) New Mexico
   (4) Wyoming

2. According to Document 2, Mexican residents in the Mexican Cession
   (1) were required to surrender to American forces.
   (2) were forced to sell their lands.
   (3) would enjoy equal rights.
   (4) would have to move to Mexico.

3. Which of the following pairs of documents express similar main ideas?
   (1) 2 and 4
   (2) 3 and 5
   (3) 3 and 4
   (4) 4 and 5

4. **Writing Task** What were the most important long-term consequences of the Mexican Cession? Use your knowledge of American history and evidence from the sources above to explain your answer.

NY Connect to New York

New York City and the Civil War

In the first half of the 1800s, disagreement between the Northern states and the Southern states over issues such as slavery, trade and tariffs, and states' rights was growing. By the 1850s, many in the North demanded an end to slavery, and some Southern states threatened to secede, or break away, from the rest of the country. Tensions reached their peak when Abraham Lincoln, who was against slavery, was elected president in late 1860. The South seceded and renamed itself the Confederate States of America. In 1861, fighting broke out between the Northern states, or the Union, and the Confederacy. The Civil War had begun.

In the years leading up to and including the Civil War, a group of northerners called "peace Democrats," or "Copperheads," argued that the North should try to settle its differences with the South without war. One leading Copperhead politician, Fernando Wood, served as Mayor of New York City. In 1861 he argued that New York should become a "free city" and refuse to fight the South.

> "If the Confederacy is broken up the Government is dissolved, and it behooves [is appropriate for] every distinct community, as well as every individual, to take care of themselves. When Disunion has become a fixed and certain fact, why may not New York disrupt the bands which bind her to a venal [dishonest] and corrupt master—to a people and a party that have plundered [stolen] her revenues, attempted to ruin her commerce, taken away the power of self-government, and destroyed the Confederacy of which she was the proud Empire City? Amid the gloom which the present and prospective condition of things must cast over the country, New York, as a *Free City*, may shed the only light and hope of a future reconstruction of our once blessed Confederacy."

Much of New York City's Irish population supported Wood because they feared that the abolition of slavery would lead to former slaves competing for their jobs. However, despite these fears, New York City did not follow through on Wood's idea, and more New Yorkers fought for the Union than residents of any other Northern city.

CIVIL WAR AND RECONSTRUCTION

CONTENTS

An African American regiment during the Civil War ▶

10

The Union in Crisis
1846–1861

Can Slavery Be Regulated in the Territories?

The slavery debate dominated American politics in the 1850s. Abraham Lincoln, the Republican candidate for the Illinois Senate seat, worried that federal legislation favored slavery by allowing slavery to exist until a territory became a state. Lincoln's opponent, Senator Stephen Douglas, explained how he thought that the people of a territory could close their region to slavery:

66[P]olice regulations can only be established by the local legislature, and if the people are opposed to slavery they will elect representatives to that body who will by unfriendly legislation effactually prevent the introduction of it into their midst. If, on the contrary, they are for it, their legislation will favor its extension. . . .99

—Stephen Douglas, August 27, 1858, Freeport, Illinois

Listen to the Witness History *audio to hear more from the Lincoln-Douglas debates.*

◀ Abraham Lincoln (standing) and Stephen Douglas (left) debated seven times while campaigning in 1858.

 Core Curriculum Preview

Chapter Focus Question: How did the nation's expansion lead to the Civil War?

Section 1
Slavery, States' Rights, and Western Expansion
2.I.A.5d, 2.II.B.3, 2.II.C.4

Section 2
A Rising Tide of Protest and Violence   2.II.B.2, 2.II.B.3, 2.II.D.1a

Section 3
Political Realignment Deepens the Crisis
2.II.D.1, 2.II.D.1b

Section 4
Lincoln, Secession, and War   2.II.D.1b, 2.II.D.2

Use the ☑ **Quick Study Timeline** at the end of this chapter to preview chapter events.

slave tags

John Calhoun

Lincoln 1860 campaign flag

FOR PRESIDENT,
ABRAHAM LINCOLN
VICE PRESIDENT,
HANNIBAL HAMLIN

┌─────────────────────────────────────┐
│ **Note Taking Study Guide** *Online* │
│ **For:** Note Taking and American Issues Connector │
│ **Web Code:** nce-7001 │
└─────────────────────────────────────┘

◄ Jefferson Davis

Why Limit Slavery Only in the Territories?

The Free-Soil Party argued that slavery should not expand into the territories. Senator Jefferson Davis questioned the new party's motives. Why would they only try to limit slavery in the territories but not in the states? Rather than true concern for the slaves, Davis believed they had another purpose.

❝It is not humanity that influences you. . . . It is that you may have an opportunity of cheating [the South] that you want to limit slave territory. . . . It is that you may have a majority in the Congress of the United States and convert the Government into an engine of northern aggrandizement. It is that your section may grow in power and prosperity upon treasures unjustly taken from the South. . . . [Y]ou want . . . to promote the industry of the New England states, at the expense of the people of the South and their industry.❞

—Senator Jefferson Davis of Mississippi

Slavery, States' Rights, and Western Expansion

Core Curriculum Objectives

- **2.I.A.5d** The abolition of slavery in the North
- **2.II.B.3** The great constitutional debates: states' rights versus federal supremacy
- **2.II.C.4** Motives for and implications of expansion and western settlement

Terms and People

Wilmot Proviso
Free-Soil Party
popular sovereignty

secede
Compromise of 1850
Fugitive Slave Act

NoteTaking

Reading Skill: Categorize Organize people, groups, and ideas by their position on slavery.

Position on Slavery		
For	Against	Compromise
•	• Wilmot Proviso	•
•	•	•

Why It Matters From the nation's earliest days, the issue of slavery divided Americans. As the nation expanded, the problem became more pressing. Should slavery be allowed in the new western territories? Southerners said yes; many northerners said no. **Section Focus Question: How did Congress try to resolve the dispute between North and South over slavery?**

Slavery Divides the Nation

After the American Revolution, the North and the South developed distinctly different ways of life. The North developed busy cities, embraced technology and industry, and built factories staffed by paid workers. As immigrants arrived in northern ports, the North became an increasingly diverse society.

The South, on the other hand, remained an agrarian, or agricultural, society. The southern economy and way of life was based largely on a single crop: cotton. To grow cotton, southern planters depended on the labor of enslaved African Americans.

By the mid-nineteenth century, cotton cultivation and slavery had spread across the Deep South—that is, through Florida and Alabama into Louisiana, Mississippi, and Texas. As the country continued to expand, Americans faced a crucial question: Should slavery be allowed to spread to new American territories west of the Mississippi River?

Wilmot Proviso Seeks to Limit Slavery Americans had long avoided the troubling issue of the expansion of slavery. But when the United States gained new territories as a result of the Mexican War in the late 1840s, the nation had to decide whether to admit these lands as slave territories or free territories. The delicate balance of power between North and South—free and slave—depended on this decision.

During the early days of the Mexican War, Pennsylvania congressman David Wilmot had predicted the dilemma. He proposed a law stating, "neither slavery nor involuntary servitude shall ever exist in any" lands won from Mexico. Southerners angrily denounced the **Wilmot Proviso.** The northern-dominated House of Representatives approved the law, but the Senate voted it down.

Northern Views of Slavery Slavery ended early in the North, but slowly. By 1800, there were about 50,000 enslaved people in the North, compared to nearly one million in the South. In 1860, there were still 18 slaves in New Jersey, but none in the other northern states. Most white northerners at the time viewed blacks as inferior. Laws in the northern states severely limited the rights of free African Americans and discouraged or prevented the migration of more. As a result, many white northerners had little personal experience with African Americans, slave or free, and only a few held strong opinions about slavery.

A vocal minority of northerners were abolitionists, or people who wanted to end slavery. They believed that slavery was morally wrong. Some abolitionists favored a gradual end, while others demanded that all slavery be outlawed at once.

Not all northerners wanted to end slavery. Some white northern bankers, mill owners, and merchants earned a lot of money on southern cotton and tobacco or by trading or transporting enslaved people. They were sympathetic to Southern plantation owners and did not want to abolish slavery. Some northern workers—especially those in unskilled, low-paying jobs—also opposed abolition, fearing that freed slaves might come north and compete with them for work.

Southern Views of Slavery Slavery was an integral part of southern life. Many southerners believed that God intended that black people should provide the labor for white "civilized" society. In a speech before Congress in 1837, planter John Calhoun of South Carolina firmly defended and even praised the virtues of slavery. "I hold it [slavery] to be a good . . . ," he said, " . . . and [it] will continue to prove so if not disturbed by the . . . spirit of abolition." Calhoun's words expressed the feelings of many white southerners.

By the 1850s, many southern politicians, journalists, and economists had begun to argue that the northern free labor system harmed society more than slavery did. Southerners claimed that enslaved people were healthier and happier than northern wage workers.

✓ **Checkpoint** How did northerners and southerners view slavery?

The Election of 1848

The Wilmot Proviso had given the nation's political parties a new focus. In the 1848 presidential campaign, both Democrats and Whigs split over the question of whether to limit the expansion of slavery. New political factions emerged, with slavery at the center of debate.

A Slave Auction
An 1861 English engraving depicts a slave auction. The horrors of slavery led to the growth of the antislavery movement.

Free-Soil Party Vows to Keep Territories Free Several factions united in support of the Wilmot Proviso to form the new **Free-Soil Party.** Pledged to a "national platform of freedom" that would "resist the aggressions of the slave power," they nominated New Yorker Martin Van Buren as their candidate for President. The Free-Soil Party promised "free soil, free speech, free labor, and free men." Their main goal was to keep slavery out of the western territories.

Whigs and Democrats Dodge the Slavery Issue For decades, the major parties—the Whigs and Democrats—had avoided the slavery issue, thus managing to win support in both the North and the South. In 1848, they hoped once again to attract voters from all sides of the slavery debate. But with the Free-Soilers calling for limits to slavery in the territories, the major parties were forced to take a stand.

Both Democrats and Whigs addressed the problem by embracing the idea of **popular sovereignty,** a policy stating that voters in a territory—not Congress—should decide whether or not to allow slavery there. This idea had wide appeal, since it seemed in keeping with the traditions of American democracy. Furthermore, it allowed Whigs and Democrats once again to focus on the personal exploits and triumphs of their candidates rather than on the issues.

Van Buren Runs as a Free-Soil Candidate

Former President Martin van Buren was the Free-Soil candidate for the presidency in 1848. *What do the pictures on this poster tell you about the party?*

The Whigs nominated Zachary Taylor, a general and a hero of the Mexican War. The Democrats put forward Governor Lewis Cass of Michigan. Cass opposed the Wilmot Proviso and supported popular sovereignty. Taylor, who was primarily a military man, revealed little of his political opinions. But Taylor was a slaveholding Louisiana planter, so many southern voters automatically assumed that he supported slavery.

When the votes were counted, Taylor won the election, with slim majorities in both northern and southern states. Van Buren did not carry any states, but he did draw sufficient votes to cause Cass to lose. The Free-Soil Party, which had won 10 percent of the vote with its antislavery platform, had clearly captured Americans' attention.

✔ **Checkpoint** What role did the Free-Soil Party play in the election of 1848?

A Compromise Avoids a Crisis

To expand slavery or restrict it—this dilemma came to haunt the rapidly growing nation. In 1848, gold was discovered in California, and soon thousands of adventurers were headed west to seek their fortune. Before long, the burgeoning western territories would petition for entry into the Union. Should these new states allow slavery? Who would decide?

California Statehood Threatens the Balance of Power "Gold fever," as it came to be known, drew people from all over the world. They literally dug into the western foothills of California's Sierra Nevada, setting up towns with names that reflected their hopes and their origins: Gold Run, Eldorado (Spanish for "gilded one"), Dutch Flats, Chinese Camp, French Corral, Negro Bar, Iowa Hill.

Within a year, more than 80,000 people had journeyed to California. As the influx continued without a letup, California became a wild and lawless place.

Californians recognized that they needed a government to bring order to the chaos. In 1849, they drafted a constitution and asked to be admitted to the Union as a free—nonslave—state.

California's request created an uproar in the nation. For years, the North and the South had accused each other of being "aggressors" on the issue of slavery. And for years, the two sides had maintained a delicate balance of slave and free states in Congress. Now, inflamed southerners angrily noted that admission of California would tip the balance in favor of the free states.

Other concerns simmered around the edges of the slavery issue, threatening to come to an explosive boil. Texas, a slave state, and the federal government were locked in a dispute over Texas's northwestern border. New Mexico and Utah were organizing to become territories but seemed likely to someday join the Union as free states. In the North, abolitionists seemed to be gaining ground in their bid to ban slavery in Washington, D.C.

In the meantime, southerners demanded that the federal government enforce the weak and often-neglected Fugitive Slave Law of 1793. The law stated that runaway slaves must be returned to their masters, but it provided no government aid to do so. The South felt that its property and its honor were at stake. Many northerners insisted that the federal government should not help to enforce slavery.

Clay Offers a Compromise

Since the War of 1812, the Senate had benefited from the leadership of three extraordinary statesmen: Daniel Webster from the North, John Calhoun from the South, and Henry Clay from the West. Clay's ability to work out compromises to the thorniest problems had earned him the title the "Great Pacificator." In the crisis now brewing, Clay, although in his seventies and ailing, once again came forward.

Clay urged the North and South to reach an agreement. He advanced a series of compromise resolutions, offering concessions to both the South and the North (see chart). The most significant proposed that Congress admit California as a free state but also enact a stricter fugitive slave law. Popular sovereignty would decide the slavery issue in the Utah and New Mexico territories. Clay's attempt at sectional justice garnered wide support.

Calhoun and Webster Speak

The Senate's other two giants—Calhoun and Webster—prepared long and deeply passionate responses to Clay's proposal. Calhoun was too sick and weak to deliver his own speech, but he watched defiantly from his seat as a younger colleague read it for him.

Calhoun's speech expressed his fear "that the agitation on the subject of slavery would, if not prevented by some timely and effective measure, end in disunion." But Calhoun did not believe that Clay's proposal gave the South enough protection. If the North would not submit to the South's demands, "let the states agree to separate and part in peace. If you are unwilling that we should part in peace, tell us so, and we shall know what to do." In other words, if the North did not agree, the South would **secede,** or break away, from the Union.

Daniel Webster, also ill and nearing the end of his life, tried to rally both northerners and southerners to the cause of unity. In an emotional speech, Webster urged senators to accept Clay's compromise. He suggested that the cotton and tobacco crops that flourished under slavery would not grow in California. Thus, he argued, popular sovereignty would allow the South to feel a measure of comfort but would not result in the spread of slavery to the West. (In fact, California eventually became a cotton-producing state—although a free one.)

Clay's Compromise of 1850
1. Congress would admit California as a free state.
2. The people of the territories of New Mexico and Utah would decide the slavery question by popular sovereignty.
3. The slave trade—but not slavery—would be ended in Washington, D.C.
4. Congress would pass a strict new fugitive slave law.
5. Texas would give up its claims to New Mexico in return for $10 million.

Clay Proposes a Compromise
Henry Clay urged the Senate to adopt a compromise on the slavery issue. It was one of his last major actions in the Senate.

Should the Union be saved?

The settling of the West made it impossible to maintain equal numbers of free and slave states. Western territories wanted to become free states. The argument over California statehood showed how the North and South were moving toward a civil war.

JOHN CALHOUN

Calhoun, from South Carolina, was a passionate supporter of slavery. As a senator, he argued that any state had the right to secede, or leave the Union, if it disagreed with national laws.

Primary Source

"[T]here is not a single Territory in progress in the Southern section, and no certainty that any additional State will be added to it. . . . [This destruction of the equilibrium] was caused by the legislation of this government, which was appointed as the common agent of all. . . .

If you admit [California] under all the difficulties that oppose her admission, you compel us to infer that you intend to exclude [the South] from the whole of the acquired Territories, with the intention of destroying . . . the equilibrium between the two sections."

—Senator John Calhoun,
March 4, 1850

DANIEL WEBSTER

Webster [shown here], from Massachusetts, was a strong nationalist. As a senator, he supported sectional compromise as a way to preserve the Union.

Primary Source

"I wish to speak to-day, not as a Massachusetts man, nor as a Northern man, but as an American, and a member of the Senate of the United States. . . . I speak to-day for the preservation of the Union. "Hear me for my cause." I speak to-day, out of a solicitous and anxious heart, for the restoration to the country of that quiet and that harmony which make the blessings of this Union so rich, and so dear to us all.

[T]he strength of America will be in the Valley of the Mississippi. [What can we] say about the possibility of cutting that river in two? I would rather hear of war, pestilence, and famine, than to hear talk of secession. . . . [T]o dismember this glorious country! . . . No, Sir!"

—Senator Daniel Webster,
March 7, 1850

Compare

1. What does Webster mean when he says "the strength of America will be in the Valley of the Mississippi"? What would cut the Mississippi River in two?

2. What does Calhoun accuse the U.S. government of doing?

Though some abolitionists felt betrayed by Webster's conciliatory three-hour speech, it persuaded many northerners to support the compromise.

 Checkpoint How did California statehood spark a new crisis over slavery?

Senate Adopts the Compromise of 1850

Over the years, Congress had adopted a variety of measures in order to preserve the Union. The Northwest Ordinance of 1787 had limited slavery. The Missouri Compromise of 1820 had maintained the balance between slave and free states. Now, in yet another effort to ward off division, the Senate adopted legislation based on Clay's proposals. It became known as the **Compromise of 1850.**

The debate over ratification of the compromise raged for months. Young northern radicals, like New York's William Seward, argued that the morality of God's "higher law" against slavery was more important than popular sovereignty or national unity. Equally radical southerners organized boycotts against northern goods, and a few even promoted separation from the Union.

The proceedings erupted into violence in the Senate when Senator Thomas Hart Benton of Missouri, who supported California's admission as a free state, denounced Mississippi senator Henry Foote, who opposed it. Furious, Foote rose from his seat and aimed a loaded revolver at Benton. The alarmed senators tried to restore order. But Benton was defiant, shouting "I am not armed! I have no pistols! I disdain to carry arms! Stand out of the way, and let the assassin fire!" At last, a senator from New York seized the revolver and locked it in a desk. Order was restored.

Still, debate dragged on. With dozens of speeches—one lasting two days—an exhausted Clay struggled to gain supporters for the compromise. But in the end, the young senator Stephen A. Douglas of Illinois took charge. Working tirelessly, Douglas steered each <u>component</u> of Clay's plan through the Congress, persuading the Senate to adopt each measure separately.

By September 1850, the obstacles to agreement had melted away: Both Calhoun and the slaveholding President Taylor were dead. Unlike Taylor, the new President, Millard Fillmore, supported the compromise. At last, the Senate passed the Compromise of 1850. California was admitted as a free state, and the policy of popular sovereignty was applied to the territory acquired from Mexico. Texas relinquished its claims on New Mexico in return for $10 million from the federal government with which to settle its debts.

One by one, the other provisions passed. Slavery would remain undisturbed in Washington, D.C., but the slave trade was prohibited. And a new **Fugitive Slave Act** added stringent amendments to the earlier law, including the requirement that private citizens assist with apprehending runaway slaves. Citizens who assisted a fugitive slave could be fined or imprisoned.

Most Americans, in both the North and South, breathed a sigh of relief that the crisis had been laid to rest. Though the Compromise of 1850 restored calm for the moment, it carried the seeds of new crises to come.

Vocabulary Builder
<u>component</u>–(kuhm POH nuhnt) *n.* piece or element

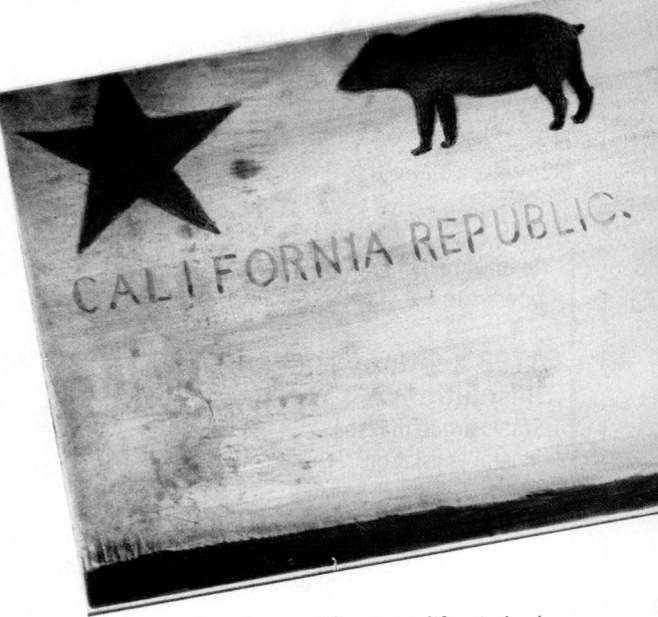

American settlers in California had declared independence from Mexico in 1846. Their symbol, the bear, later became the symbol on California's state flag.

✓ **Checkpoint** What were the provisions of the Compromise of 1850?

SECTION 1 Assessment

Progress Monitoring *Online*
For: Self-test with vocabulary practice
Web Code: nca-1002

Comprehension

1. Terms and People For each item below, write a sentence explaining its significance.
- Wilmot Proviso
- Free-Soil Party
- popular sovereignty
- secede
- Compromise of 1850
- Fugitive Slave Act

2. NoteTaking Reading Skill: Categorize Use your chart to answer the Section Focus Question: How did Congress try to resolve the dispute between North and South over slavery?

Writing About History

3. Quick Write: Gather Evidence Make a chart outlining arguments for and against adopting the Compromise of 1850. Your outline may include moral, economic, and political issues.

Critical Thinking

4. Compare Points of View How did the northern and southern views of slavery differ?

5. Make Generalizations What role did the issue of slavery play in the election of 1848?

6. Identify Central Issues Why did California's application for statehood cause a crisis?

7. Draw Conclusions How did the Compromise of 1850 appease both North and South?

Federal Power and States' Rights

NY 2.II.B.3

TRACK THE ISSUE

THE ESSENTIAL ?

How much power should the federal government have?

Under the Constitution, all powers not granted to the federal government belong to the states. Over time, however, the federal government has expanded its scope, especially in the area of social programs. Use the timeline below to explore this enduring issue.

1791 Bill of Rights
Tenth Amendment reserves most powers to the states.

1798 Kentucky and Virginia Resolutions
States argue that they can void federal legislation.

1831 Nullification Crisis
John C. Calhoun declares that states may overturn federal laws.

1857 *Dred Scott* v. *Sandford*
Supreme Court rules that federal government does not have power to outlaw slavery within territories.

1930s New Deal
Government expands power over economy and social services.

1965 Voting Rights Act
Law allows federal officers to register voters.

Dred Scott

Exhaust and waste gases from cars are just one of the many issues in the center of the continuing national debate about the environment.

DEBATE THE ISSUE

The Environment and States' Rights Since 1967, the Environmental Protection Agency (EPA) allowed California to make its own emissions rules. California is exempt from the Clean Air Acts as long as its rules are stricter than those of the Federal Government and it obtains a waiver from the federal government. In November 2007, Governor Arnold Schwarzenegger sued the Federal Government because the EPA denied California a waiver.

"The authority of the States to address greenhouse gas emissions from motor vehicles has been supported—by the Supreme Court [and] by a federal court here in California. On this issue, the . . . EPA . . . has failed to follow the States' lead . . . we are prepared to force it out of the way . . . to protect the environment."
—Governor Arnold Schwarzenegger, April 2, 2008

"I believe that Congress by passing a . . . federal standard of 35 mpg (miles per gallon) delivers significant reductions that are more effective than a state-by-state approach. This applies to all 50 states. . . . and that's great for the economy, for national security, and for the environment."
—Stephen L. Johnson, EPA Administrator

TRANSFER Activities
1. **Compare** Why does Governor Schwarzenegger feel California should oppose the federal government? Why does Stephen Johnson disagree?
2. **Analyze** Should a state have the right to determine its own environmental standards?
3. **Transfer** Use the following Web site to see a video, try a WebQuest, and write in your journal. **Web Code:** neh-7002

This image first appeared around 1835 and became an abolitionist symbol.

Tags used to identify slaves ▶

WITNESS HISTORY 🔊 AUDIO

Slavery and Union

By the time Congress debated the Compromise of 1850, white Boston abolitionist William Lloyd Garrison had been protesting against slavery for more than two decades and a growing number of Americans were joining his cause. He stated his resistance to compromise clearly:

❝I am for union! . . . [but] I am not for SLAVERY and UNION. . . . [T]his is the issue we make before the country and the world.❞

—William Lloyd Garrison, 1850

A Rising Tide of Protest and Violence

NY **Core Curriculum Objectives**

- **2.II.B.2** Equal rights and justice: expansion of franchise; search for minority rights; expansion of slavery; abolitionist movement
- **2.II.B.3** The great constitutional debates: efforts to address slavery issue
- **2.II.D.1a** The American Civil War: U.S. society divided: Kansas-Nebraska Act, John Brown's raid

Terms and People

personal liberty laws   Kansas-Nebraska Act
Underground Railroad   John Brown
Harriet Tubman   "Bleeding Kansas"
Harriet Beecher Stowe

NoteTaking

Reading Skill: Understand Effects Use a concept web to record the effects of the Fugitive Slave Act on different groups of people.

Why It Matters Americans had greeted the Compromise of 1850 with relief. But the ink on the document had barely dried before the issue of slavery resurfaced, this time with violent results. **Section Focus Question: How did the Fugitive Slave Act and the Kansas-Nebraska Act increase tensions between the North and the South?**

Resistance Against the Fugitive Slave Act

The Compromise of 1850 was meant to calm the fears of Americans. But one provision, the new Fugitive Slave Act, had the opposite effect. The law, which required citizens to catch and return runaway slaves, enraged many northerners. The anger was not restricted to abolitionists; it extended to other northerners who felt forced to support the slave system.

Northerners also resented what they saw as increasing federal intervention in the affairs of the independent states. A few northern states struck back, passing **personal liberty laws.** These statutes nullified the Fugitive Slave Act and allowed the state to arrest slave catchers for kidnapping. Many northerners agreed with abolitionist William Lloyd Garrison when he demanded "nothing less than . . . a Revolution in the Government of the country."

NORTH STAR.

ROCHESTER NEW YORK, THURSDAY, JULY 18, 1850

THE FUGITIVE SLAVE ACT

Before 1850, many white northerners assumed that slavery was not their problem. When a new Fugitive Slave Act forced them to participate in the slave system, they resisted. In several northern cities, crowds tried to rescue fugitive slaves from their captors.

The free black community also took action. The law meant that no African American could feel safe. Through urban networks known as "Vigilance Committees," and through antislavery newspapers, African Americans remained in constant communication. The committees looked out for slave hunters and helped fugitives avoid capture.

300 DOLLARS REWARD!

RUNAWAY from John S. Doak on the 21st inst., two NEGRO MEN; LOGAN 45 years of age, bald-headed, one or more crooked fingers; DAN 21 years old, six feet high. Both black.

Fugitive slaves were often aided by an informal network of abolitionists, known as the Underground Railroad. If fugitives were caught and returned to slavery, they could be forced to wear devices meant to prevent another escape, such as a collar with bells on it (above right).

Underground ▶ Railroad conductor Harriet Tubman

▲ The map above shows approximate routes of the Underground Railroad.

A MAN KIDNAPPED!

A PUBLIC MEETING AT

FANEUIL HALL!

WILL BE HELD

THIS FRIDAY EVEN'G,

May 26th, at 7 o'clock,

To secure Justice for A MAN CLAIMED AS A SLAVE by a

VIRGINIA KIDNAPPER!

Soldiers sometimes escorted ▶ slave hunters and their captives because crowds sometimes tried to free the captured men and women.

Thinking Critically

1. **Infer** Why might the Underground Railroad have been more active in free states than in slave states?

2. **Draw Conclusions** In what ways did the Fugitive Slave Act affect free African Americans?

Black Americans, of course, despised the law. Some of the captured "fugitive slaves" were really free people who had been kidnapped and sold into slavery. Although the imprisoned African Americans could appeal to a judge for their release, the law awarded $10 to judges who ruled in favor of slave owners but only $5 to those who ruled that the captive should be set free. Slaves, fugitives, and free black people plotted and carried out resistance. Through the succeeding decade, tempers flared and violence erupted as far north as Canada, as far west as Kansas, and as far south as Virginia.

Northern Blacks Mobilize In 1851, a small group of free African Americans gathered in a farmhouse in Christiana, Pennsylvania. Heavily armed, they had come to protect several fugitives from their Maryland master, who had brought a federal official to reclaim them. In the scuffle that followed, the slave owner was killed. White bystanders refused to <u>intervene</u> to help the slave-hunting party. Although more than 30 people were tried for conspiracy, none was found guilty. No one was tried for the murder of the slave owner.

The "Christiana Riot" was a dramatic enactment of a scene that was played out in many northern communities. In Vermont and New Hampshire, in New York City, in Oberlin, Ohio, and in Baltimore, Maryland, African Americans and white bystanders defied officials who tried to reclaim fugitives to slavery.

Underground Railroad to Freedom Northern abolitionists and free black people risked their lives and safety to help enslaved people escape to freedom through a loosely organized network known as the **Underground Railroad.** Although it was not underground and had no tracks or cars, this escape system used railroad terminology to describe its actions. A secret network of "conductors" hid runaway slaves in farm wagons and on riverboats and then moved them to destinations in the North or in Canada—sometimes even as far as England. Using complex signals and hiding places, the Underground Railroad carried its passengers over hundreds of miles of dangerous terrain.

Underground Railroad conductors had to be resourceful and daring. One of the most courageous was **Harriet Tubman,** a Maryland-born fugitive slave. She was known as "Black Moses" because, like Moses in the Bible, she led her people out of bondage. After her own escape in 1849, Tubman made almost two dozen trips into the South, guiding hundreds of slaves, including her own parents, to safety. Southern planters placed a large reward on her head, but she was never captured.

Several fugitive slaves published dramatic escape stories that inspired black Americans and struck fear in the hearts of white southerners. In one account, six-foot-tall Henry "Box" Brown described how he had himself packed into a small crate and shipped from Richmond, Virginia, to the Underground Railroad agents in Philadelphia. Light-skinned Ellen Craft and her husband, William, made their escape by posing as an invalid gentleman and his loyal servant.

Stowe and Delany Condemn Slavery In 1852, **Harriet Beecher Stowe** published *Uncle Tom's Cabin,* a powerful condemnation of slavery. Stowe's sympathetic main character, Uncle Tom, gave slavery a face for those who had never witnessed it firsthand. Set in the slave-owning South, Stowe's story features the gentle and patient Uncle Tom, a frightened slave mother, and both kind and cruel slave owners. Selling 300,000 copies in its first year, the novel spread compassion for enslaved people in the North, but it infuriated people in the South.

Black abolitionist Martin Delany also wrote an antislavery novel, called *Blake.* It is the story of an African American who chooses to rebel violently, rather than to submit like Uncle Tom. The protagonist, Blake, murders a white

Vocabulary Builder
intervene–(ihn tuhr VEEN) *v.* to get involved in a situation in order to prevent a certain outcome

slave owner in order to make his escape, a scenario that terrified slave owners. In the following excerpt, Blake stands up to his master's threat to whip him:

> **Primary Source**   "I won't be treated like a dog. You sold my wife away from me, after always promising that she should be free. . . . And now you talk about whipping me. Shoot me, sell me, or do anything else you please, but don't lay your hands on me, as I will not suffer you to whip me!"
>
> —Martin R. Delany, *Blake*

White southerners responded by writing their own versions of southern life. In these accounts, slaves were happy and carefree, gently cared for and taught Christianity by kind masters. They claimed that only mentally ill slaves ran away. A southern doctor even reported his discovery of a disease he called Drapetomania, which supposedly caused slaves to flee. "With the advantages of proper medical advice," he claimed "this troublesome practice" could be eliminated.

✓ **Checkpoint** How did northerners respond to the Fugitive Slave Act?

The Kansas-Nebraska Act Undoes the Missouri Compromise

Although Congress meant well, its repeated attempts to resolve the question of slavery resulted in a jumble of contradictory, and often unenforceable, policies. The Missouri Compromise, the Wilmot Proviso, the Compromise of 1850: Each seemed to offer the solution. But, in reality, the issue lay beyond the ability of patchwork legislation to resolve.

Douglas Presses for Popular Sovereignty It was Senator Douglas who forced the issue of slavery to the surface once again. In 1854, Douglas introduced a bill to set up a government in the Nebraska Territory. The area would be organized, Douglas proposed, according to the principle of popular sovereignty. That is, the people of the territory themselves would decide whether to allow slavery or outlaw it when they applied for statehood. On the surface, Douglas's plan made sense. In fact, it seemed to be a democratic solution. But would it work in practice?

Congress Debates the Kansas-Nebraska Act Once again, Congress was gripped in bitter debate. After pressure from the South, which feared Nebraska might decide to enter as a free state, Douglas amended the bill to divide the region into two distinct territories, Kansas and Nebraska. The idea was that Kansas would become a slave state and Nebraska would organize as a free state, but those assumptions were not written into the bill. In the spring of 1854, Congress accepted this proposal and passed the **Kansas-Nebraska Act.** Some northerners pointed out that, in effect, the Kansas-Nebraska Act nullified the Missouri Compromise by allowing slavery to spread to areas that had been free for more than 30 years.

✓ **Checkpoint** How did the Kansas-Nebraska Act revive the issue of slavery?

A Battle Rages in "Bleeding Kansas"

Most of the people who came to the newly opened territory of Kansas were farmers looking for land. But Kansas also attracted settlers—northern and southern—with political motives. Each group wanted to outnumber the other, so that when it came time to vote, they could control the government. Their competition to settle the territory would have deadly consequences.

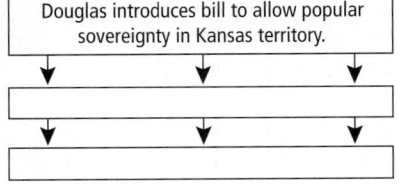

Territories Open to Slavery

Geography *Interactive*
For: Interactive map skills
Web Code: ncp-1003

Missouri Compromise, 1820

- Slavery prohibited in the Louisiana Territory north of 36°30′, except in Missouri
- Maine entered as a free state
- Missouri entered as a slave state

Significance: Sponsored by Henry Clay, the compromise preserved the balance of free and slave states in the Senate. However, it marked the beginning of the sectional conflict that would lead to civil war.

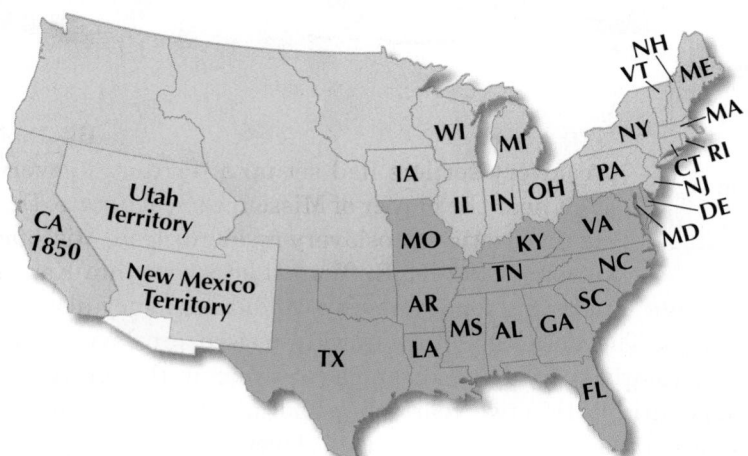

Compromise of 1850

- California entered as a free state
- Slavery issue to be decided by popular sovereignty in Utah and New Mexico territories
- New, stricter Fugitive Slave Act
- Slave trade but not slavery is ended in Washington, D.C.

Significance: Stephen Douglas steered each of the provisions though Congress as a separate bill. It showed that compromise was not a good solution to the sectional conflict, as it pushed many moderates toward more radical positions.

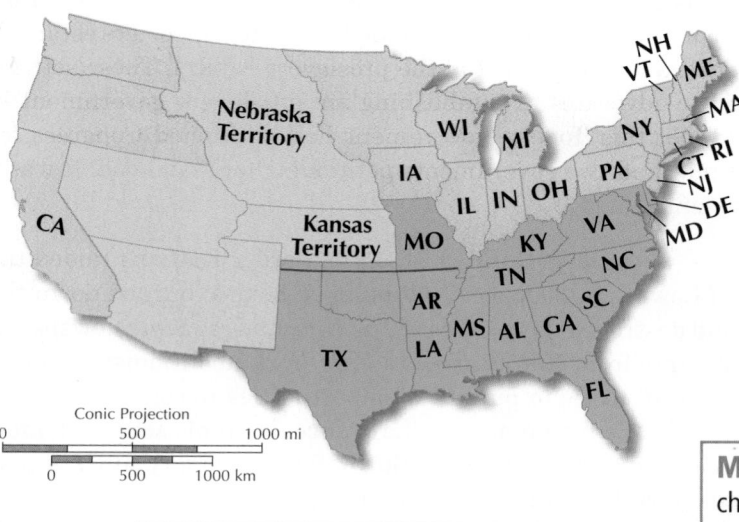

Kansas-Nebraska Act, 1854

- Created potential for slavery in Kansas and Nebraska territories by allowing for popular sovereignty

Significance: Sponsored by Stephen Douglas, this bill overturned the Missouri Compromise. Although it was meant to unite the nation, it caused further division and led to the creation of the Republican Party.

Conic Projection

0   500   1000 mi

0   500   1000 km

■ Slave states
□ Territories open to slavery by popular sovereignty
□ States and territories closed to slavery
— Missouri Compromise line (36°30′N)

Map Skills Between 1820 and 1854, three compromises changed the territories that were opened to slavery.

1. **Identify** Which territories were open to slavery after (a) the Missouri Compromise, (b) the Compromise of 1850, and (c) the Kansas-Nebraska Act?

2. **Analyze** Why were so many people upset by the Kansas-Nebraska Act?

Confrontation in Kansas

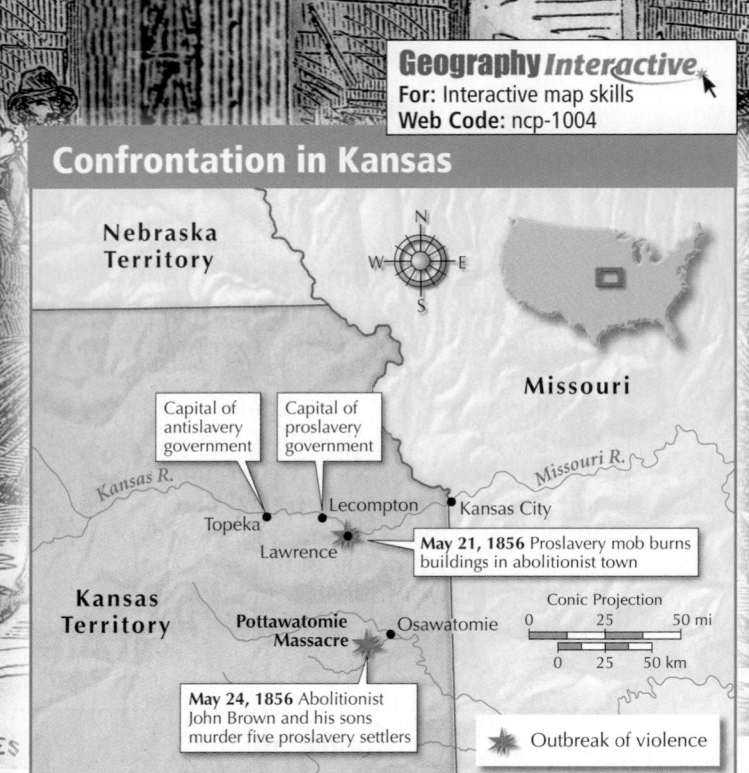

Nebraska Territory

Missouri

Capital of antislavery government

Capital of proslavery government

Kansas R.

Topeka

Lecompton

Kansas City

Lawrence

Missouri R.

May 21, 1856 Proslavery mob burns buildings in abolitionist town

Kansas Territory

Pottawatomie Massacre

Osawatomie

Conic Projection

0   25   50 mi

0   25   50 km

May 24, 1856 Abolitionist John Brown and his sons murder five proslavery settlers

⭐ Outbreak of violence

Map Skills Kansas became a battleground over slavery.

1. Locate: (a) Lawrence, (b) Missouri, (c) Topeka

2. Draw Conclusions What problems could result from having two governments in Kansas?

The Sack of Lawrence

On May 21, 1856, proslavery men attacked the Free-Soil town of Lawrence, Kansas. They burned the hotel and destroyed the newspaper. *Why did proslavery forces attack Lawrence?*

Two Governments Are Established By 1855, proslavery settlers had set up a territorial government near the border of Missouri, a slave state. During the election, proslavery residents from Missouri, known as Border Ruffians, had swept into Kansas and coerced local voters into voting for proslavery candidates. They also cast their own illegal votes. The new legislature quickly passed proslavery laws, including penalties for antislavery agitation and a requirement that officeholders take a proslavery oath. Within two years, they had called a convention and developed a constitution that would have legalized slavery and punished those who spoke or wrote against it.

Northern abolitionists also rushed into Kansas. The New England Emigrant Aid Society raised money to help several thousand free-state supporters establish the town of Lawrence, a few miles east of the proslavery capital. These settlers joined other free-state advocates in establishing an antislavery government in Topeka. By early 1856, this Topeka government had petitioned Congress for statehood. Kansas now had two governments petitioning for statehood. It was a sure setup for disaster.

Violence Grips the Territory On May 21, 1856, Border Ruffians raided the antislavery town of Lawrence, Kansas. They pillaged homes, burned down the Free State Hotel, and destroyed the presses of *The Kansas Free State* newspaper.

Swift retaliation came from **John Brown,** a New York abolitionist who had moved his family several times in pursuit of opportunities to confront slavery head-on and who now made his home near Lawrence. With his sons and a few friends, Brown carried out a midnight execution of five proslavery settlers near Pottawatomie Creek, about 20 miles south of Lawrence.

When stories of the incident reached the East, abolitionists were stunned. While they were outraged at the events that triggered it, they condemned Brown's massacre. In Kansas, both sides armed for battle. Throughout the fall of 1856, violent outbreaks occurred in various locales around Lawrence. Reporters characterized the territory as **"Bleeding Kansas."** By now, it was clear that popular sovereignty was not a solution to the slavery issue.

Over the next several years, the question of how to admit Kansas to the Union baffled local residents, political parties, the U.S. Congress, and the Supreme Court. Although the Border Ruffians had determined the outcome of the election, President Franklin Pierce urged Congress to admit Kansas as a slave state in 1858. However, Congress refused and Kansas submitted four constitutions before it finally entered as a free state in 1861, after the Civil War had already begun.

Violence Spreads to the Senate The violent battles over slavery were not limited to Kansas. Tempers ran high in Congress, and some members went to work armed not only with words but with pistols and canes. In May 1856, just as fighting broke out in Kansas, Massachusetts senator Charles Sumner delivered a blistering speech on the Senate floor, which came to be known as "The Crime Against Kansas." He blasted southerners for their bullying and fraud in the Kansas elections, and he referred to the Border Ruffians from Missouri as "hirelings, picked from the drunken spew and vomit of an uneasy civilization—in the form of men."

Then, Sumner invited trouble. He insulted South Carolina senator Andrew Butler, who was absent. But a few days later, Butler's nephew, South Carolina representative Preston Brooks, attacked Sumner in the Senate, beating him unconscious with a cane.

What happened next illustrates the division of the two sides. Congress tried to punish Brooks by removing him from office. His constituency simply reelected him and sent him back. Sumner was so badly injured that he could not return to the Senate for three years. The Massachusetts voters reelected him anyway, using his empty seat as a public reminder of southern treachery. The divide between North and South grew ever wider and deeper.

✔ **Checkpoint** Why did violence break out in Kansas?

SOUTHERN CHIVALRY — ARGUMENT versus CLUB'S.

Violence in the Senate
Representative Brooks beat Senator Sumner with a cane meant to train dogs. *What does this depiction tell you about the event?*

SECTION **2** Assessment

Progress Monitoring *Online*
For: Self-test with vocabulary practice
Web Code: nca-1005

Comprehension

1. **Terms and People** Place each of the items below into one of these two categories: advancing slavery or working against slavery
   - personal liberty laws
   - Underground Railroad
   - Harriet Tubman
   - Harriet Beecher Stowe
   - Kansas-Nebraska Act
   - John Brown
   - "Bleeding Kansas"

2. **NoteTaking Reading Skill: Understand Effects** Use your concept web to answer the Section Focus Question: How did the Fugitive Slave Act and the Kansas-Nebraska Act increase tensions between the North and the South?

Writing About History

3. **Quick Write: Outline an Argument** List points supporting or opposing the Kansas-Nebraska Act, and then rank them in order of importance.

Critical Thinking

4. **Recognize Effects** What were the consequences of the Fugitive Slave Act for slaveholders, white northerners, free African Americans, and fugitive slaves?

5. **Summarize** How did the Kansas-Nebraska Act undo the Missouri Compromise?

6. **Synthesize** How did "Bleeding Kansas" embody the slavery controversy?

2.I.A.4d

Uncle Tom's Cabin by Harriet Beecher Stowe

An early edition of
Uncle Tom's Cabin ▶

UNCLE TOM'S CABIN;

OR,

LIFE AMONG THE LOWLY.

BY

HARRIET BEECHER STOWE.

VOL. I.

...EDTH THOUSAND.

...TON:

...T & COMPANY

...D, OHIO:

...& WORTHINGTON.

...2.

In Harriet Beecher Stowe's controversial story, a kind Kentucky slave owner is forced by financial necessity to sell his slave, Tom. Tom remains kind and gentle, despite losing his family and ending up in the possession of a cruel man named Simon Legree. The story led many early readers to think of slaves as people, rather than as possessions, for the first time. In this excerpt, Tom is sold to Legree at an auction.

Various spectators, intending to purchase, or not intending, as the case might be, gathered around the group, handling, examining, and commenting on their various points and faces with the same freedom that a set of jockeys discuss the merits of a horse. . . .

Tom had been standing wistfully examining the multitude of faces thronging around him, for one whom he would wish to call master. And if you should ever be under the necessity, sir, of selecting, out of two hundred men, one who was to become your absolute owner and disposer, you would, perhaps, realize, just as Tom did, how few there were that you would feel at all comfortable in being made over to. . . .

A little before the sale commenced, a short, broad, muscular man . . . elbowed his way through the crowd, like one who is going actively into business; and, coming up to the group, began to examine them systematically. From the moment that Tom saw him approaching, he felt an immediate and revolting horror at him, that increased as he came near. He was evidently, though short, of gigantic strength. His round, bullet head . . . and stiff, wiry, sunburned hair, were rather unprepossessing items. . . . This man proceeded to a very free personal examination of the lot. He seized Tom by the jaw, and pulled open his mouth to inspect his teeth; made him strip up his sleeve, to show his muscle; turned him round, made him jump and spring to show his paces. . . .

Tom stepped upon the block, gave a few anxious looks round; all seemed mingled in a common, indistinct noise,—the clatter of the salesman crying off his qualifications in French and English, the quick fire of French and English bids; and almost in a moment came the final thump of the hammer, and the clear ring of the last syllable of the word *"dollars,"* as the auctioneer announced his price, and Tom was made over.—He had a master!

He was pushed from the block;—the short, bullet-headed man seizing him roughly by the shoulder, pushed him to one side, saying in a harsh voice, "Stand there, *you!*"

▲ Harriet Beecher Stowe

Thinking Critically

1. **Identify Point of View** Whose point of view is reflected in this selection?

2. **Demonstrate Reasoned Judgment** How accurately could a white northern woman portray the feelings of an enslaved person being auctioned? What parts of her story might have been written differently by someone who had been enslaved?

SECTION 3

"A ~~~~ ~~~~ ~~~~. I believe ~~~~ ~~~~ endure permanently half s~~~ ~~~ half free. I do not expect the Union to be dissolved—I do not expect the house to fall—but I do expect it will cease to be divided. It will become all one thing, or all the other."

—Abraham Lincoln, June 16, 1858

◄ Douglas and Lincoln debate

Political Realignment Deepens the Crisis

 Core Curriculum Objectives

- **2.II.D.1** United States society divided
- **2.II.D.1b** Abraham Lincoln, the secession crisis, and efforts at compromise (Lincoln-Douglas debates)

Terms and People

Know-Nothings
Republican Party
Dred Scott
Roger B. Taney

Abraham Lincoln
Stephen Douglas
Harpers Ferry

NoteTaking

Reading Skill: Sequence Use a timeline to record significant political events.

Early 1850s—Whig
Party disintegrates

1850	1852	1854	1856	1858

Why It Matters Americans had always lived with sectional differences, but they temporarily resolved those differences through negotiation and compromise. By the mid-1850s, however, the battle over slavery threatened to tear the nation apart. **Section Focus Question: What developments deepened the divisions between North and South?**

The Shifting Political Scene

Traditionally, American political parties extended across sectional lines. Democrats and Whigs came from the North, South, and West. Presidents, too, had come from all areas of the country. But in the 1840s, American politics increasingly reflected regional tensions, especially over the issue of slavery.

The Whig Party Disintegrates The Compromise of 1850, as well as the policies that grew out of it, caused political upheaval. Millard Fillmore—the last Whig President—angered the South with his support for California's entry as a free state. Northerners inflamed by his support of the Fugitive Slave Act and popular sovereignty left the party in large numbers.

For the 1852 presidential election, Whigs searched unsuccessfully for a candidate and a platform to unite their members. But with their two visionary leaders—Henry Clay and Daniel Webster—dead, the party fell back on Winfield Scott, a military hero. Deeply divided over the issues, the Whigs lost to the Democrats, who solidly endorsed the 1850 Compromise that they hoped and believed would preserve the Union. The Whigs would never again achieve enough harmony to mount a presidential campaign.

Know-Nothings Attract Support By the mid-1800s, a growing immigrant population was changing the country. For example, up to that time, Protestantism—which includes Baptists, Methodists, Presbyterians, and many other groups—had been the dominant American religion. By 1850, however, Americans of Irish and German descent and Spanish-speaking natives of lands ceded by Mexico had made Catholicism the nation's largest religious group. Many native-born white Protestants were alarmed by the change. These "nativists" raised questions that reflected their prejudices. Would Catholics bring ideas that would undermine America's religious freedom? Would the newcomers take jobs away from workers who were already here? Or, alternatively, would they be lazy, not work, and become paupers, weighing down society?

These concerns fueled the growth of an anti-immigrant movement. Dubbed **"Know-Nothings"** because members responded "I know nothing" when questioned about their nativist organization, the group quickly gathered momentum. By 1855, the Know-Nothings had abandoned secrecy to form the American Party. Like the Whigs, however, the American Party soon divided over the issue of slavery in the western territories.

The Republican Party Is Born As the old parties broke up, antislavery zeal gave rise to the new **Republican Party** in 1854. Opposition to slavery was the center of the Republican philosophy. Attracting antislavery Democrats, Whigs, Free-Soilers, and Know-Nothings, the Republican Party grew rapidly in the North. It included a coalition of businessmen who believed that slavery stifled industry, as well as moral leaders who feared that slavery encouraged vice. By 1856, it was ready to challenge the older, established parties.

 Checkpoint How did the rise and fall of political parties reflect divisions in the United States?

American Political Parties During the 1850s	
Democratic Party (1800–present)	• Opposed strong central government • Divided over slavery issue in the 1850s
Whig Party (1834–1852)	• Favored national economic development • Opposed Andrew Jackson • Antislavery members left in the 1850s
Know-Nothings or The American Party (1843–1856)	• Opposed to immigration • Joined by antislavery Whigs • Took a proslavery platform in 1856
Free-Soil Party (1847–1854)	• Worked to prevent slavery in the western territories • Formed by antislavery Democrats and Whigs • Absorbed into the new Republican Party
Republican Party (1854–present)	• Opposed to slavery • Opposed to Kansas-Nebraska Act

Sectional Divisions Intensify

For many years, the North and South tried to ignore or patch over their differences. But by the mid-1850s, the dispute over slavery caused sectional differences to intensify.

The Election of 1856 Causes Alarm Republicans, at their first national convention, nominated for President the abolitionist John C. Frémont, a colorful Mexican War hero who had helped win California's independence. The Democrats nominated James Buchanan of Pennsylvania, while the Know-Nothings put up former President Millard Fillmore.

"Free Soil, Free Labor, Free Men, Frémont!" Under this slogan, the Republican Party tried to

THE GREAT PRESIDENTIAL SWEEPSTAKES OF 1856.

Analyzing Political Cartoons

A Race for the Presidency In this cartoon, the Know-Nothing candidate Fillmore leads the race in the "American Express" carriage, which represents his anti-immigrant platform. The outgoing Democratic president, Franklin Pierce, carries Buchanan. The Republican Frémont is last, urged on by the abolitionist Horace Greeley (wearing a top hat).

1. Explain the cartoonist's stance on abolition.
2. Did the cartoonist correctly predict the election results?

rally Americans to reject popular sovereignty and to insist that slavery be excluded from the western territories. They also campaigned to admit Kansas as a free state.

But Buchanan, who promised that as President he would stop "the agitation of the slavery issue," won the election, supported by the large majority of southerners. His running mate from the South, John C. Breckinridge, further bolstered his campaign. Still, the Republican Frémont, with his solid abolitionist platform, made a strong showing, winning one third of the popular vote and 11 northern states.

The *Dred Scott* Decision Triggers Outrage While passions still ran high from the 1856 election, another event fueled the flames of division. In 1857, the U.S. Supreme Court ruled in the case of Missouri slave **Dred Scott,** who had sued for his freedom. Scott based his case on the fact that his master had taken him to the free state of Illinois and Wisconsin Territory, where slavery was outlawed by the Missouri Compromise. In other words, between 1834 and 1838, Scott had lived mostly on free soil while remaining enslaved.

With the help of abolitionists, Scott's case reached the Supreme Court under Chief Justice **Roger B. Taney.** In its decision handed down in March 1857, the Court ruled against Scott. In a controversial decision, the Court decided that slaves and their descendants were property, not citizens, and therefore were not entitled to sue in the courts. It also said that the Missouri Compromise was unconstitutional because it was illegal for Congress to deprive an owner of property—in this case, a slave—without due process of law.

Southerners celebrated the decision, but the North viewed it with alarm. Abolitionists labeled the ruling a southern conspiracy. Some suggested that the North should secede from the Union. Others insisted that the members of the Supreme Court should be impeached. Leading black abolitionist Frederick Douglass predicted that the decision would actually hasten the end of slavery:

Does Congress Have the Power to Limit Slavery?

 2.II.D.1a

One of the most divisive issues facing the country in the 1850s was the question of slavery in the territories. The Missouri Compromise had banned slavery from some areas and allowed it in others. The Kansas-Nebraska Act left the question up to those people living in a territory. But if the Constitution allowed slavery to exist, did Congress have the power to take these actions?

Dred Scott v. *Sandford* (1857)

The Facts	The Issue	The Decision
• Dred Scott, an African American slave, was taken north of the Missouri Compromise line, where slavery was banned.	Scott argued that since he had lived several years in a free state and several years in a free territory, he should be free.	• The Court stated that temporary residence in a free territory did not make Scott free. • It said that Scott was property, not a citizen, and therefore had no right to sue. • It further reasoned that no African American could be a citizen. • It stated that Congress could not ban slavery from any territory because doing so would take away slave owners' property without due process of law.

Chief Justice Roger B. Taney

Why It Matters

The *Dred Scott* decision deeply split an already divided country. Southerners applauded the Court for defending their rights to hold slaves. A South Carolina newspaper victoriously declared that the decision proves that "slavery is guaranteed by the constitutional compact." Many in the North viewed the decision with dismay, however. Republicans wanted to block the spread of slavery, and the Court's decision dashed their hopes. Abraham Lincoln expressed the fears of many that the Court would act even more boldly in the future. In an 1858 speech, he warned that the Court would next force slavery onto northern soil:

> "We shall lie down pleasantly dreaming that the people of Missouri are on the verge of making their state free and we shall awake to the reality instead, that the Supreme Court has made Illinois a slave state."

By further inflaming both North and South, the *Dred Scott* decision took the nation one step closer to a civil war.

Connect to Your World

The Court has made other controversial decisions over the years. Examples are *Engel* v. *Vitale* (1962), *Miranda* v. *Arizona* (1966), *Roe* v. *Wade* (1973), *Texas* v. *Johnson* (1989), and *Kelo* v. *New London* (2005). Read about the Court's decision in a controversial case and its aftermath. Analyze how people with different points of view have responded to the decision.

For: Supreme Court cases
Web Code: nce-1006

— Frederick Douglass, 1857

✓ **Checkpoint** What were the reactions to the *Dred Scott* decision?

The Lincoln-Douglas Debates

Throughout the 1850s, American attention was riveted on westward expansion. But no discussion of expansion, or any aspect of the nation's future, could get beyond the issue of slavery. In 1858, Stephen Douglas and Abraham Lincoln held a series of seven debates while competing for a seat in the U.S. Senate. Thousands of Americans attended the Lincoln-Douglas debates and listened raptly as the two candidates presented opposing views of slavery and its role in America.

Stephen A. Douglas, the "Little Giant" stood just over 5 feet tall. His opponent, Abraham Lincoln, was about 6 feet, 4 inches tall.

"Honest Abe" vs. "The Little Giant" Raised in rural poverty and largely self-taught, **Abraham Lincoln** began his political career at age 25, when he was elected to the Illinois state legislature as a Whig. By 1836, he had been admitted to the Illinois bar and was practicing law in Springfield. He soon gained a reputation for integrity and directness that earned him the title "Honest Abe." Lincoln seemed to be staunchly opposed to slavery, but his political life was marked by a desire to steer a middle course.

In the 1840s, Lincoln had served a short stint in the U.S. House of Representatives, supporting Zachary Taylor and his policy of admitting California as a free state. But Lincoln's real political career began with his opposition to the Kansas-Nebraska Act and its <u>implicit</u> support for the expansion of slavery promoted by rival Illinois politician **Stephen A. Douglas.**

Douglas was, in many ways, the opposite of Lincoln. Lincoln was tall, lanky, and slow of speech. Douglas was short, round, and filled with energy and a commanding voice. These qualities earned him the nickname the "Little Giant." His critics, however, questioned his motives and his sincerity. Unlike Lincoln, Douglas supported the annexation of Texas, and he promoted popular sovereignty as the solution to regional tensions. But many wondered if he promoted these policies because he believed in them or because he had a financial stake in the railroads that would profit from them.

Vocabulary Builder
<u>implicit</u>–(ihm PLIHS iht) *adj.* unspoken but understood

Douglas Backs Popular Sovereignty Douglas had supporters in both the North and the South. Though he was not a slaveholder, his wife had inherited slaves, and he was somewhat sympathetic to slavery. Popular sovereignty, he insisted, was the implied intent of the Constitution. He expressed this sentiment strongly in the seventh and last debate:

Primary Source "This Union was established on the right of each State to do as it pleased on the question of slavery, and every other question."
— Stephen A. Douglas, 1858

Douglas was seeking the support of both southern and northern Democrats. But while some southerners supported him, many northern Democrats distrusted what they believed were his self-serving motives.

Lincoln Wins a Reputation When Lincoln stood before these same audiences, he spoke of the "eternal struggle between right and wrong." He repeatedly

The Raid at Harpers Ferry

Marines led by Colonel Robert E. Lee smashed the armory door at Harpers Ferry and succeeded in capturing John Brown (pictured above) and his followers inside. No slaves joined Brown's rebellion. *Did John Brown's raid have a chance to succeed?*

referred to the *Dred Scott* decision as wrong. He attacked popular sovereignty as wrong. And he condemned slavery as a system whereby one person does the "work and toil to earn bread" and someone else does the eating. While Lincoln, like most white people of his day, ridiculed the idea of social and political equality with African Americans, he strongly affirmed the idea of their natural rights:

> **Primary Source** ❝There is no reason in the world why the negro is not entitled to all the natural rights enumerated in the Declaration of Independence—the right of life, liberty, and the pursuit of happiness. I hold that he is as much entitled to these as the white man. . . . In the right to eat the bread, without the leave of anybody else, which his own hand earns, he is my equal and the equal of Judge Douglas, and the equal of every living man.❞
>
> —Abraham Lincoln, 1858

The debates lasted for weeks. When they were over, Douglas won the election by a slim margin. But Lincoln had not really lost. As a result of the debates, Lincoln won a large following that would serve him well the next time he ran for national office.

✔ **Checkpoint** How did Lincoln and Douglas differ on the issue of slavery?

John Brown's Raid

Both Lincoln and Douglas believed the slavery crisis had to be resolved within the framework of the nation's laws. Abolitionist John Brown felt no such constraints. Brown viewed himself as an angel of God, avenging the evil of slavery. Even before one of his sons was killed in Bleeding Kansas, he had concluded that violence was the best way to reach his goal. By late 1857, Brown had begun planning his attack. For many months, he crisscrossed New England, the Midwest, and Canada, soliciting recruits and funds to mount an armed assault on slavery.

Brown Seizes the Arsenal at Harpers Ferry By the fall of 1859, Brown was ready. "Men, get your arms," he cried, "we will proceed to the ferry." Gathering his following of 21 men—including 5 free African Americans—Brown set out to seize the federal arsenal in **Harpers Ferry,** Virginia (now in West Virginia). He hoped to inspire local slaves to join a revolution that would destroy slavery in the South.

Brown had chosen Harpers Ferry because it was a hub of trains and canals, which would offer efficient escape routes. This locale was also near the borders of Pennsylvania, a free state, and Maryland, where there were many free African Americans. It seemed the ideal launching point.

But the effort failed. Few Americans—black or white—were prepared to join a rebellion organized by this intense, fanatical white man. Frederick Douglass, a close friend, refused to join, warning Brown that his mission "would array the whole country against us." A few black and white abolitionists sent money for guns, but in the end Brown's revolution came to naught. Local residents surrounded Brown's men in the arsenal, and federal troops soon arrived to arrest them. Two more of Brown's sons were killed in the fray, but a few of the rebels escaped to Canada. Brown and several others, however, went to the gallows.

Brown's Execution Deepens the Growing Divide Brown's attack increased the heat in already-boiling tempers. Similar to the *Dred Scott* decision, suspicion and rumors were widespread. Stephen Douglas accused the Republicans of instigating Brown's attack, and southern congressmen demanded an investigation. But when Abraham Lincoln and other Republicans condemned Brown, the rumors subsided. Yet, many congressmen still came armed to the Capitol. The uncertainty caused a steep drop in cotton prices, and many southerners prepared for war.

Many northerners thought abolitionist activism had gone too far. But others now saw Brown as a courageous martyr. They were moved to tears when he proclaimed his willingness to "mingle my blood . . . with the blood of my children and with the blood of millions in this slave country whose rights are disregarded by wicked, cruel, and unjust enactments."

Some admirers suggested that Brown should be buried at Boston's Bunker Hill, next to the heroes of the American Revolution. A popular song later immortalized him, celebrating the fact that "his soul goes marching on." On the morning of his execution, Brown made the prophetic prediction that "the crimes [of slavery] of this guilty land will never be purged away, . . . without very much bloodshed." Many Americans agreed with him.

✔ **Checkpoint** How did Americans respond to John Brown's raid and his execution?

SECTION

3 Assessment

Progress Monitoring *Online*
For: Self-test with vocabulary practice
Web Code: nca-1007

Comprehension

1. Terms and People For each item below, write a sentence that explains its significance.
- Know-Nothings
- Republican Party
- Dred Scott
- Roger B. Taney
- Abraham Lincoln
- Stephen A. Douglas
- Harpers Ferry

2. NoteTaking Reading Skill: Sequence Use your timeline to answer the Section Focus Question: What developments deepened the divisions between North and South?

Writing About History

3. Quick Write: Organize Your Ideas Write a short argument supporting a presidential candidate from the election of 1856. Explain why this candidate was the best person to lead the politically unstable nation.

Critical Thinking

4. Recognize Ideologies Why did the Republican Party form?

5. Recognize Effects How did the *Dred Scott* decision increase tensions between North and South?

6. Determine Relevance How successful was John Brown's raid on Harpers Ferry?

◀ President Buchanan

WITNESS HISTORY AUDIO

The President Falters

Outgoing President James Buchanan condemned South Carolina's secession from the Union but was unwilling to use force to stop it. Many northerners criticized his weak response to the crisis. In an address to Congress, he seemed almost baffled that the situation had deteriorated so far:

❝How easy it would be for the American people to settle the slavery question forever and to restore peace and harmony to this distracted country! . . . All that is necessary to accomplish the object, and all for which the slave States have ever contended, is to be let alone and permitted to manage their domestic institutions in their own way. As sovereign States, they, and they alone, are responsible before God and the world for the slavery existing among them.❞

—President Buchanan, December 3, 1860

Lincoln, Secession, and War

NY Core Curriculum Objectives

- **2.II.D.1b** Abraham Lincoln, the secession crisis, and efforts at compromise (election of 1860, secession, Fort Sumter)
- **2.II.D.2** The American Civil War: Wartime actions

Terms and People

Jefferson Davis
John C. Breckinridge
Confederate States of America

Crittenden Compromise
Fort Sumter

NoteTaking

Reading Skill: Identify Causes and Effects
Use a cause-and-effect chart to show the events that led to secession.

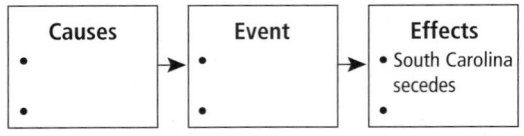

Causes	Event	Effects
•	•	• South Carolina secedes
•	•	•

Why It Matters Despite repeated attempts at compromise, disagreement between the North and the South over the issue of slavery continued to deepen. With the election of Republican President Abraham Lincoln in 1860, the crisis came to a head. The Union of states that had been formed less than a hundred years before was about to dissolve. **Section Focus Question: How did the Union finally collapse into a civil war?**

The Election of 1860

John Brown's raid and execution were still fresh in the minds of Americans as the 1860 presidential election approached. Uncertainty about Kansas—would it be a slave state or a free state?—added to the anxiety. In the North, loss of confidence in the Supreme Court resulting from the *Dred Scott* decision and rage about the Fugitive Slave Act's intrusion into the states' independence further aggravated the situation.

The issue of states' rights was on southern minds as well. Would northern radicals conspire to eliminate slavery not only in the territories but also in the original southern states? In the spring of 1860, Mississippi senator **Jefferson Davis** convinced Congress to adopt resolutions restricting federal control over slavery in the territories. The resolutions also asserted that the Constitution prohibited Congress or any state from interfering with slavery in the states where it already existed. Even southerners who did not own slaves felt that their way of life and their honor were under attack.

With ill will running so deep, the upcoming elections posed a serious dilemma. It was hard to imagine that either northerners or southerners would accept a President from the other region. Could the Union survive?

Democrats Split Their Support The Democrats held their nominating convention in Charleston, North Carolina. For ten days, they argued about the issue that had plagued the nation for decades: slavery. The southern Democrats called for a platform supporting federal protection of slavery in the territories. The northern Democrats, who backed Stephen Douglas, supported the doctrine of popular sovereignty. When the Douglas forces prevailed, the delegates from eight southern states walked out and formed a separate convention.

The Democrats were now split into two parties. The northern Democrats nominated Stephen A. Douglas. The southern Democrats nominated the Vice President, **John C. Breckinridge** of Kentucky. Breckinridge was committed to expanding slavery into the territories.

Whigs Make a Last Effort In the meantime, the few remaining Whigs teamed up with the Know-Nothings to create the Constitutional Union Party. They hoped to heal the split between North and South. Their candidate was John Bell, a little-known moderate from Tennessee. Their platform condemned sectional parties and promised to uphold "the Constitution of the country, the Union of the States and the enforcement of the laws."

Republicans Nominate Lincoln The Republicans, who had gained great strength since their formation, held their nominating convention in Chicago. After several ballots, they nominated Abraham Lincoln as their candidate. When the party convened, seasoned politician William H. Seward of New York had been the favorite to win the nomination. But when many delegates began to worry that Seward's antislavery views were too radical, the convention went with the more moderate Lincoln.

The Candidates for President

Abraham Lincoln
- Republican
- Illinois
- Platform:

Slavery must not be allowed in the territories.

Stephen Douglas
- Northern Democrat
- Illinois
- Platform:

Popular sovereignty should decide the issue of slavery in the territories when they become states.

John Bell
- Constitutional Unionist
- Tennessee
- Platform:

The federal government should support slavery and also defend the Union.

John Breckinridge
- Southern Democrat
- Kentucky
- Platform:

The federal government must protect slavery.

The Republican platform called for the end of slavery in the territories. At the same time, the Republicans defended the right of each state to control its own institutions and stipulated that there should be no interference with slavery in the states where it already existed. Abraham Lincoln—with his great debating skills, his moderate views, and his reputation for integrity—was seen as the ideal candidate to carry the Republican platform to victory.

Vocabulary Builder
stipulate–(STIHP yuh layt) *v.* to specify or indicate

Lincoln Wins the Election Benefiting from the fracturing among the other political parties, Lincoln won the election handily, with 40 percent of the popular vote and almost 60 percent of the electoral vote. Still, he did not receive a single southern electoral vote. In fact, he was not even on the ballot in most southern states.

Breckinridge was the clear favorite among southern voters, carrying every cotton state, along with North Carolina, Delaware, and Maryland. The border

Events That Changed America

THE ELECTION OF 1860

FOR PRESIDENT,
ABRAHAM LINCOLN
VICE PRESIDENT,
HANNIBAL HAMLIN

Ah! ha! Gentlemen! you need'nt think to catch me napping; for I am a regular Wide awake.

▲ Election propaganda for Lincoln and Douglas

The Election of 1860 The election of 1860 was a turning point for the United States. Looking at an election map shows clearly how the country was divided.

Look at the cartoon to the right to see one viewpoint of the campaign for the presidency. Try to figure out what the cartoonist thinks of each of these candidates. Lincoln is on the left, dressed as a member of a Republican support group called the "Wide Awakes." As he approaches the White House, the other candidates try to sneak in.

John Bell tells Stephen Douglas to hurry up. Douglas, meanwhile, tries to unlock the door with different keys, but none of them works. In the far right, the current President, Buchanan, tries to pull John Breckinridge in through the window.

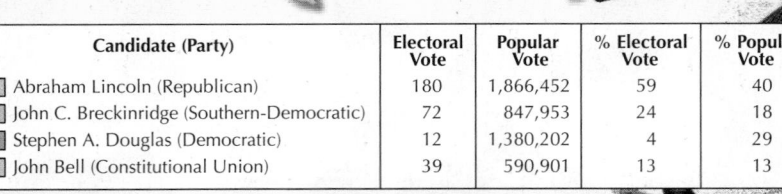

Candidate (Party)	Electoral Vote	Popular Vote	% Electoral Vote	% Popular Vote
Abraham Lincoln (Republican)	180	1,866,452	59	40
John C. Breckinridge (Southern-Democratic)	72	847,953	24	18
Stephen A. Douglas (Democratic)	12	1,380,202	4	29
John Bell (Constitutional Union)	39	590,901	13	13

Entered according to act of Congre

states of Virginia, Kentucky, and Tennessee—whose economic interests were not as closely tied to slavery as the cotton states were—gave their votes to Bell. Stephen A. Douglas, although running second to Lincoln in the popular vote, won only in Missouri and New Jersey.

The election of 1860 demonstrated that Americans' worst fears had come to pass. There were no longer any national political parties. Bell and Breckinridge competed for southern votes, while Douglas and Lincoln competed in the North and West. The North and South were now effectively two political <u>entities</u>, and there seemed no way to bridge the gap.

Vocabulary Builder
entity—(EHN tuh tee) *n.* something that exists as a single and complete unit

✔ **Checkpoint** How did Lincoln's election reflect the break between the North and the South?

▲ Election propaganda for Bell and Breckinridge

Why It Matters

The election of 1860 was the first national contest for the Republican Party, which became one of the two major political parties. More importantly, the election was the immediate cause for the secession of the southern states.

Thinking Critically

1. **Analyze** What is the meaning of the keys with which Douglas is trying to open the door?

2. **Make Comparisons** How is Lincoln portrayed in a different manner from the other candidates?

History *Interactive* ✶

For: More about the election of 1860
Web Code: ncp-1008

Long-term Causes of the Civil War

- Sectional economic and cultural differences
- Debate over expansion of slavery into the territories
- Political compromises failed to ease sectional differences and resolve question of expanding slavery
  —Missouri Compromise (1820)
  —Compromise of 1850
  —Kansas-Nebraska Act (1854)
- Laws and court decisions increased sectional tension
  —Fugitive Slave Act (1850)
  —Dred Scott decision
  —Tariff policy
- Growth of the antislavery movement
- *Uncle Tom's Cabin*

Short-term Causes of the Civil War

Kansas-Nebraska Act splits political parties

↓

Breakdown of the party system

↓

Lincoln elected President

↓

South Carolina secedes from the Union

The Union Collapses

Southerners were outraged that a President could be elected without a single southern vote. In the southerners' perception, the South no longer had a voice in the national government. They decided to act.

Southern States Leave the Union As soon as Lincoln's election was confirmed, the South Carolina legislature summoned a state convention. Meeting in Charleston on December 20, 1860, and without a dissenting vote, the convention declared that "the union now subsisting between South Carolina and the other States, under the name of the 'United States of America,' is hereby dissolved." They cited as their reason for seceding the election of a President "whose opinions and purposes are hostile to slavery." They further declared:

> **Primary Source** "On the 4th of March next, [a new administration] will take possession of the Government. It has announced . . . that a war must be waged against slavery until it shall cease throughout the United States. . . .
> The Guarantees of the Constitution will then no longer exist; the equal rights of the States will be lost. The slaveholding States will no longer have the power of self-government, or self-protection, and the Federal Government will have become their enemy."
> —Declaration of the Immediate Causes Which Induce and Justify the Secession of South Carolina From the Federal Union, December 20, 1860

In the next few weeks, six other states of the Deep South seceded from the Union. Sentiments favoring secession were not always unanimous, with the gravest doubts surfacing in Georgia. State senator Alexander H. Stephens, though alarmed by Lincoln's election, was devoted to the Union of states under the Constitution: "This government of our fathers, with all its defects, comes nearer the objects of all good government than any other on the face of the Earth," he said. But Georgia voted to secede anyway. Like delegates in the other slave-dependent, cotton-growing states, they believed they had to take this step to protect their property and way of life.

The Confederacy Is Formed In February 1861, the seven seceding states established the **Confederate States of America.** They then proceeded to frame a constitution for the new government. The Confederate constitution closely resembled the U.S. Constitution. However, it stressed the independence of each state and implied that states had the right to secede. It also guaranteed the protection of slavery. To win the support of Britain and France, which adamantly opposed the slave trade, it prohibited importing new slaves from other countries.

Not all southerners backed the Confederacy. Some large planters with economic ties to the North still hoped for a compromise. So, too, did many small farmers with no vested interest in slavery. To gain the loyalty of such citizens, the Confederacy chose former Mississippi senator Jefferson Davis as their president. Davis had supported the Compromise of 1850, but he had also insisted that the South should be left alone to manage its own culture and institutions—including slavery.

A Final Compromise Fails Some politicians sought a final compromise. Kentucky senator John Crittenden proposed a constitutional amendment allowing slavery in western territories south of the Missouri Compromise line. He also called for federal funds to reimburse slaveholders for unreturned fugitives.

Focus On Geography

Slavery and Secession

Cotton cultivation increased substantially in the nineteenth century. Harvesting cotton (right) was a time-consuming and difficult task that required a large labor force. This led planters to buy more enslaved people. In 1861, more than 50 percent of the population was enslaved in some areas of the Deep South. Tension built over extending slavery into the territories. The states with the largest slave populations seceded. Border states, which had fewer enslaved people, stayed in the Union.

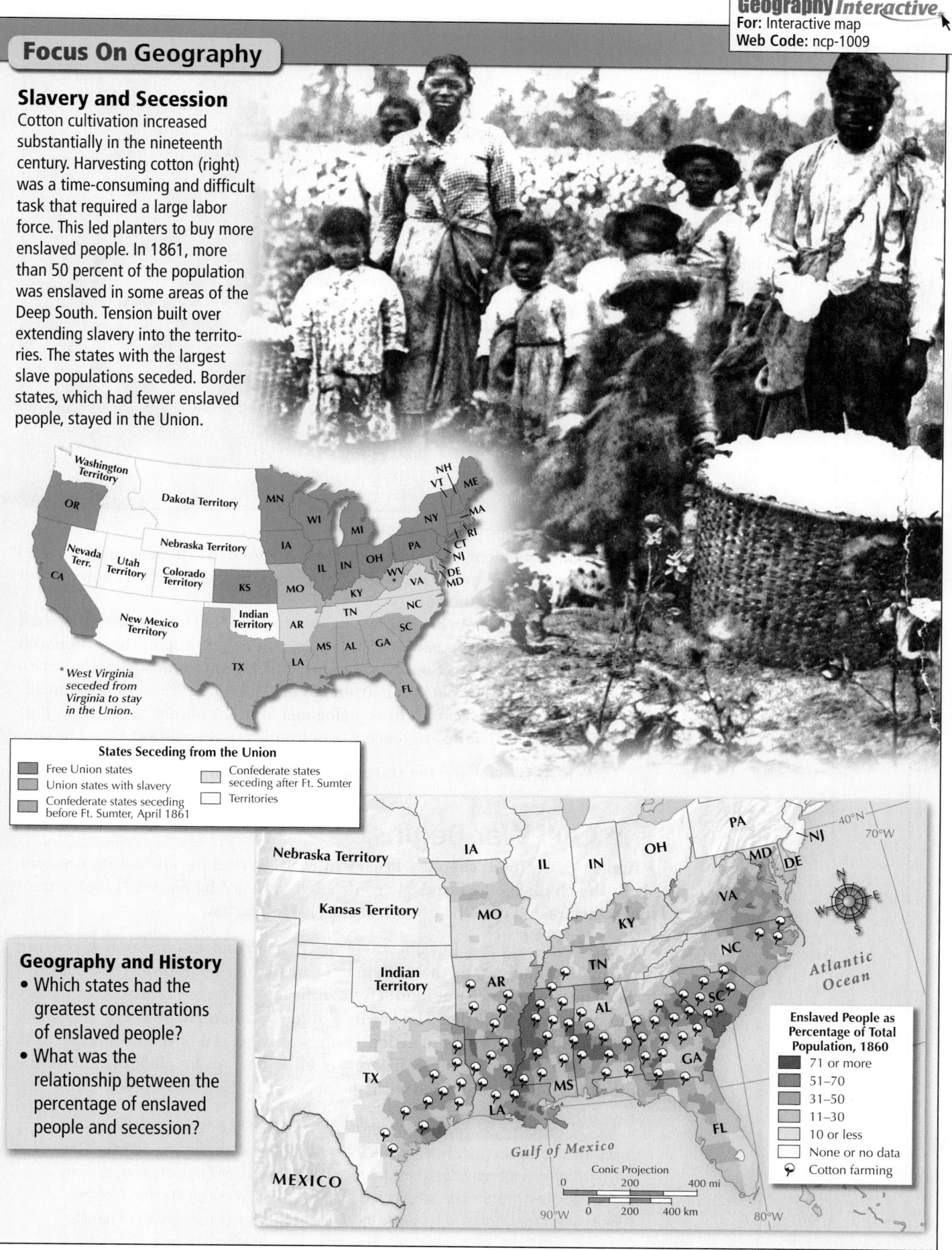

*West Virginia seceded from Virginia to stay in the Union.

States Seceding from the Union

- Free Union states
- Union states with slavery
- Confederate states seceding before Ft. Sumter, April 1861
- Confederate states seceding after Ft. Sumter
- Territories

Geography and History

- Which states had the greatest concentrations of enslaved people?
- What was the relationship between the percentage of enslaved people and secession?

Enslaved People as Percentage of Total Population, 1860

- 71 or more
- 51–70
- 31–50
- 11–30
- 10 or less
- None or no data
- Cotton farming

Conic Projection

0   200   400 mi

0   200   400 km

Abraham Lincoln (1809–1865)

Lincoln grew up on the Kentucky frontier and moved to Illinois as a young man. Although he had little formal education, he enjoyed reading and disliked farming. In 1836, he began practicing law in Illinois.

Lincoln began his political career as a Whig in the Illinois state legislature, later serving in the U.S. Congress. Although not an abolitionist, he opposed slavery. When the Whigs fell apart, he joined the new Republican Party.

Upon assuming the presidency, Lincoln faced tough challenges. Seven states had already left the Union. Lincoln won reelection as he steered the country through the Civil War. He is best remembered for ending slavery in the United States.

Jefferson Davis (1808–1889)

Davis is best known for his role as president of the Confederate States of America. Before the Civil War, he served in the U.S. House of Representatives in 1845 but left to join the army during the war with Mexico in 1846.

Returning home to Mississippi as a hero, Davis became a U.S. Senator and, later, the Secretary of War. He opposed South Carolina's secession, still hoping for a compromise. Even when his own Mississippi seceded a few weeks later, he left the Senate by appealing for peace.

Two weeks later, he became president of the Confederate States of America. Despite his strong leadership, the Confederacy lacked the manpower and manufacturing capability to defeat the Union. He was imprisoned for treason after the war but was never tried.

Lincoln, now President-elect, warned that Crittenden's plan would "lose us everything we gained by the election." A narrow margin of senators voted down this **Crittenden Compromise.**

President Buchanan, in his last few weeks in office, told Congress that he had no authority to prevent secession. He lamented the breakup of the Union and he sympathized with the South's concerns, but he made no serious effort to resolve the crisis. Other pacifying attempts also failed. A secret peace convention held in Washington, which drew delegates from the border states as well as the North and South, failed to reach a compromise that could save the Union.

 Checkpoint Why did the states of the Deep South leave the Union?

The Civil War Begins

Amid this turmoil, the new President took office. Lincoln had no illusions about the challenge he faced. He confronted "a task," he feared, "greater than that which rested upon [President George] Washington."

Lincoln Takes Office Lincoln was sworn in as President on March 4, 1861. In his inaugural address, he took a firm but conciliatory tone toward the South. "I have no purpose, directly or indirectly, to interfere with the institution of slavery in the states where it exists," he began. But he *did* intend to preserve the Union. "No state, upon its own mere action, can lawfully get out of the Union," he said. Still, he would avoid violence. There would be no war, he pledged, unless the South started it. He concluded with an appeal to the South to live in peace:

> **Primary Source** "We are not enemies, but friends. We must not be enemies. Though passion may have strained, it must not break our bonds of affection. The mystic chords of memory, stretching from every battle-field, and patriot grave, to every living heart and hearthstone, all over this broad land, will yet swell the chorus of the Union, when again touched, as surely they will be, by the better angels of our nature."
>
> —Abraham Lincoln, March 4, 1861

Lincoln Decides to Act When the southern states seceded, they seized the federal forts and arsenals within their borders. Only four forts remained in Union hands. The most important of these was **Fort Sumter,** which guarded the harbor at Charleston, South Carolina. In January 1861, President Buchanan tried to send troops and supplies to the fort, but the unarmed supply ship sailed away when Confederate guns fired on it. Upon taking office, Lincoln had to decide whether to take the risk required to hold on to these forts or yield to Confederate demands that they be surrendered.

By April, the troops at the fort desperately needed food and supplies. Lincoln, who still hoped to bring back the South without bloodshed, faced a dilemma. Should he try to resupply the fort? Or should he let the Confederates take it? Lincoln struggled to make a decision. During his inaugural address, he had promised southerners that "the government will not assail you." But as President, he was sworn to defend the property of the United States. A wrong move could touch off a war. At last, trying to steer a middle course, Lincoln notified South Carolina that he was sending supplies—food only, no arms—to the fort.

Fort Sumter Falls South Carolinians were suspicious of Lincoln's motives and ordered the Fort Sumter garrison to surrender to the Confederacy. When the Union troops refused, the Confederates fired on the fort. The Union troops eventually ran out of ammunition, forcing the commander to surrender.

Northerners responded to the attack on Fort Sumter with shock and anger. A few days later, on April 15, President Lincoln declared that "insurrection" existed and called for 75,000 volunteers to fight against the Confederacy.

The South responded just as strongly. At the outbreak of hostilities, the states of Virginia, Arkansas, Tennessee, and North Carolina joined the Confederacy. As in the North, the South raised troops quickly and struggled to equip and train them before sending them into battle.

Both sides predicted a short skirmish, with victory only a few days or months away. These predictions were unfounded. Americans faced years of terrible suffering before the fighting that had begun at Fort Sumter finally ended.

✔ **Checkpoint** What event led to the outbreak of war?

The flag above flew over Fort Sumter as Confederate troops attacked (pictured above).

SECTION **4** **Assessment**

Progress Monitoring *Online*
For: Self-test with vocabulary practice
Web Code: nca-1010

Comprehension

1. **Terms and People** For each item below, write a sentence explaining its significance.
   • Jefferson Davis
   • John C. Breckinridge
   • Confederate States of America
   • Crittenden Compromise
   • Fort Sumter

2. **NoteTaking Reading Skill:** Use your cause-and-effect chart to answer the Section Focus Question: How did the Union finally collapse into a civil war?

Writing About History

3. **Quick Write: Outline an Argument** Outline an answer to this question: Was secession the only option for the South?

Critical Thinking

4. **Recognize Effects** How did the election of 1860 increase sectional tensions?

5. **Recognize Causes** Why did the southern states secede?

6. **Demonstrate Reasoned Judgment** How could Buchanan have prevented war?

Quick Study Guide

2.II.D.1a,
2.II.D.2b

Progress Monitoring *Online*
For: Self-test with vocabulary practice
Web Code: nca-1011

■ Key Legislation Affecting Slavery

Legislation	Effect on Slavery
Missouri Compromise	Prohibited slavery in all federal territories north of 36° 30', except in Missouri
Compromise of 1850	Opened New Mexico and Utah territories to slavery by applying popular sovereignty, or letting the residents decide when they applied for statehood; ended the slave trade in Washington, D.C.
Fugitive Slave Act	Part of the Compromise of 1850, this law forced all Americans to return fugitive slaves to their masters or face arrest
Personal liberty laws	State laws passed in several northern states that allowed slave catchers to be arrested for kidnapping
Kansas-Nebraska Act	Opened Kansas and Nebraska territories to slavery by applying popular sovereignty

■ Proslavery and Antislavery Arguments

Proslavery Arguments
• Banning slavery would deprive slave owners of their property (their slaves)
• African Americans were better off enslaved than free because slave owners cared for them
• Free African Americans would compete with white laborers for jobs

Antislavery Arguments
• Slavery was morally wrong
• Slavery harmed society

■ Key People

Person	Significance
John Brown	Abolitionist who killed proslavery settlers in Kansas and tried to start a slave revolt in Virginia
James Buchanan	President from 1857–1861 who did not act to stop South Carolina's secession
Henry Clay	Kentucky senator who proposed the Compromise of 1850
John Calhoun	South Carolina senator who supported slavery and warned that the South would secede if slavery were threatened
Jefferson Davis	Mississippi senator who became president of the Confederacy
Stephen Douglas	Illinois Democrat who believed in popular sovereignty and steered the Compromise of 1850 through the Senate; he defeated Lincoln in the 1858 Senate race but lost to him in the 1860 presidential election
Frederick Douglass	Former slave and abolitionist who became the face of abolitionism
William Lloyd Garrison	White abolitionist and publisher of *The Liberator* who helped organize the American Anti-Slavery Society
Abraham Lincoln	Republican President whose election in 1860 caused South Carolina to secede
Dred Scott	The slave who sued for freedom after living in free states and a free territory; his loss in the Supreme Court outraged many northerners and pushed the nation toward war
Daniel Webster	Massachusetts senator and nationalist who supported the Compromise of 1850 to save the Union

✔ Quick Study Timeline

In America

1848
The Mexican War ends and northern Mexico is annexed to the United States

1850
Congress agrees to the Compromise of 1850

CALIFORNIA REPUBLIC

Presidential Terms   James K. Polk 1845–1849

Zachary Taylor 1849–1850
Millard Fillmore 1850–1853

1846　　　　　　　　　　**1849**　　　　　　　　　　**1852**

Around the World

1848
Revolutions take place through-out Europe

1850
Taiping Rebellion begins in China

American Issues

•—•—• Connector

By connecting prior knowledge with what you have learned in this chapter, you can gradually build your understanding of enduring questions that still affect America today. Answer the questions below. Then, use your American Issues Connector study guide (or go online: www.PHSchool.com **Web Code:** nch-7003).

Issues You Learned About

● **Federal Power and States' Rights** State governments and the federal government may disagree over legislation.

1. How did the system of popular sovereignty favor state power over federal power?

2. Why and how did some northern state legislatures reject the federal government's passage of the Fugitive Slave Act?

3. How did the constitution created by the Confederacy support states' rights over federal power?

● **Sectionalism and National Politics** During the mid-1800s, the South and North were split over the issue of slavery.

4. What incidents among members of Congress emphasized the emotional nature of the debate over slavery between North and South?

5. Which groups backed each of the four candidates for the presidency in 1860, and what positions did each hold?

6. Why was the result of the presidential election of 1860 unacceptable to the South?

● **America at War** By the mid-1800s, the United States had been involved in several wars, but never one that pitted citizens against each other.

7. How did Lincoln attempt to breach the divide between North and South in his inaugural address?

8. What caused Lincoln to call for troops to fight against the Confederacy?

Connect to Your World | New York

Sectionalism and National Politics As you have read, sectional differences between the North and the South led to the creation of the Republican Party. The name Republican was derived from, and paid tribute to, the ideals of founding father Thomas Jefferson's Democratic Republican party. Horace Greeley—founder, publisher, and editor of the influential newspaper the *New York Tribune*—popularized the term "Republican" in an 1854 editorial. The term, he wrote in the editorial, would "fitly designate those who had united to restore the Union to its true mission of champion and promulgator of Liberty rather than propagandist of slavery." Conduct research on Greeley's life. Write a brief essay discussing the influence that Greeley had on politics, both through his work as a newspaper editor and his career as a politician representing New York.

History Interactive
For: Interactive timeline
Web Code: ncp-1013

| 1854 Congress passes the Kansas-Nebraska Act | 1857 The Supreme Court rules against Dred Scott | 1860 Lincoln wins the presidential election, leading South Carolina to secede | 1861 The Civil War begins at Fort Sumter, South Carolina |

| Franklin Pierce 1853–1857 | James Buchanan 1857–1861 | Abraham Lincoln 1861–1865 |

| **1855** | **1858** | **1861** |

| 1854 Britain and France join the Crimean War against Russia | 1857 Hindu and Muslim soldiers in India rebel against British rule | 1861 Czar Alexander II emancipates Russian serfs |

Chapter Assessment

Terms and People

1. What was the **Fugitive Slave Act**? Under the Fugitive Slave Act, what would happen to people who assisted a fugitive slave?

2. What was the **Underground Railroad**? How did the Underground Railroad work?

3. Why was the territory called **"Bleeding Kansas"**? Why did Kansas become a battleground for proslavery and antislavery forces?

4. What was the strategic significance of **Harpers Ferry**? Why did abolitionists launch an attack there?

5. Who was **Jefferson Davis**? What point of view did he support on the slavery issue?

Focus Questions

The focus question for this chapter is **How did the nation's expansion lead to the Civil War?** Build an answer to this big question by answering the focus questions for Sections 1 through 4 and the Critical Thinking questions that follow.

Section 1

6. How did Congress try to resolve the dispute between North and South over slavery?

Section 2

7. How did the Fugitive Slave Act and the Kansas-Nebraska Act increase tensions between the North and South?

Section 3

8. What developments deepened the divisions between North and South?

Section 4

9. How did the Union finally collapse into a civil war?

Critical Thinking

10. **Explain Causes** Up until the 1840s, the Whigs and the Democrats had failed to declare an opinion on the slavery issue. What caused them to change this policy?

11. **Compare Points of View** How did Calhoun and Webster respond to Clay's proposed compromise? With which side did the majority of congressmen agree?

12. **Recognize Bias** What attitudes did abolitionist writers and proslavery writers portray in their novels?

13. **Analyze Information** In what ways did the Kansas-Nebraska Act support the expansion of slavery?

14. **Draw Conclusions** How did the Republican Party grow so rapidly that within two years its candidates were challenging the established parties?

15. **Predict Consequences** What did Frederick Douglass predict might happen as a result of the *Dred Scott* decision?

16. **Analyze Charts** Study the chart below. Then, answer the question that follows. Which candidate received the fewest electoral votes in comparison with his percentage of the popular vote? Explain.

Candidate	Percentage of Popular Vote	Number of Electoral Votes
Abraham Lincoln	39.9%	180
Stephen A. Douglas	29.4%	12
John C. Breckinridge	18.1%	72
John Bell	12.6%	39

17. **Identify Point of View** Why was the Crittenden Compromise unacceptable to Lincoln?

Writing About History

Debate a Topic The decades before the Civil War were filled with political compromises, new political parties, and feuding between different sections of the country. Prepare an argument that you would use to debate the question: Was the Civil War inevitable?

Prewriting

- Make a list of the arguments for each side of the debate.
- Rank each point from most to least important.
- Decide which side you are going to argue.

Drafting

- Develop a working thesis, and choose supporting information to support the thesis.
- Make an outline organizing your argument and addressing the points that the opposition might make.
- Write an introduction that explains your argument, provide a body of evidence, and end with a convincing conclusion.

Revising

- Using the guidelines on page SH16 of the Writing Handbook to revise your report. Review your argument and add information where it is not strong.

Regents DBQ Practice

John Brown's Raid

Abolitionist John Brown dedicated his life to ending slavery in the United States. He was a deeply religious man, but he did not hesitate to use violence to achieve his goals. To what extent was John Brown's raid at Harpers Ferry successful? Use your knowledge of the raid and its consequences along with Documents 1, 2, 3, and 4 to answer questions 1 through 4.

Document 1

"I John Brown am now quite certain that the crimes of this guilty land: will never be purged away; but with Blood. I had as I now think: vainly flattered myself that without very much bloodshed; it might be done."

—*John Brown, December 2, 1859*

Document 2

"Though it convert the whole Northern people, without an exception, into furious, armed abolition invaders, yet old Brown will be hung! That is the stern and irreversible decree, not only of the authorities of Virginia, but of the PEOPLE of Virginia, without a dissenting voice. And, therefore, Virginia, and the people of Virginia, will treat with the contempt they deserve, all the craven appeals of Northern men in behalf of old Brown's pardon. The miserable old traitor and murderer belongs to the gallows, and the gallows will have its own."

—*Richmond "Whig" newspaper editorial quoted in the* Liberator, *November 18, 1859*

Document 3

"But the question is, Did John Brown fail? . . . And to this I answer ten thousand times, No! . . . When John Brown stretched forth his arm the sky was cleared. The time for compromises was gone—the harmed hosts of freedom stood face to face over the chasm of a broken Union—and the clash of arms was at hand. The South staked all upon getting possession of the Federal Government, and failing to do that, drew the sword of rebellion and thus made her own, and not Brown's, the lost cause of the century."

—*Frederick Douglass, May 30, 1881*

Document 4

---

1. How do documents 1, 3, and 4 portray John Brown?
   (1) As a criminal who committed treason
   (2) As a martyr who died for a just cause
   (3) As an abolitionist who went too far
   (4) As the cause of the Civil War

2. What does Document 2 predict about Brown's execution?
   (1) It will turn southerners into abolitionists.
   (2) The people of Virginia will not support it.
   (3) People will quickly forget about Brown.
   (4) It will turn northerners into abolitionists.

3. According to Frederick Douglass, what did John Brown's raid achieve?
   (1) It pushed the nation toward the Civil War.
   (2) It made abolitionism a lost cause.
   (3) It helped the North to gain control of the government.
   (4) It achieved nothing of importance.

4. **Writing Task** To what extent was John Brown's raid on Harpers Ferry a success or failure? Consider different points of view when constructing your answer. Use your knowledge of the time period and specific evidence from the primary sources above to support your answer.

11 The Civil War
1861–1865

War Between the States

During the Civil War, soldiers sang marching songs to stir their spirits for battle. Union troops proclaimed:

❝The Union forever,
   Hurrah! boys, hurrah!
   Down with the traitors,
   Up with the stars!❞
                    — "The Battle Cry of Freedom"

But Confederates countered with their own battle cry:

❝But now, when Northern treachery
   Attempts our rights to mar,
   We hoist on high the Bonnie Blue Flag
   That bears a single star.❞
                    — "The Bonnie Blue Flag"

Listen to the Witness History *audio to hear more about the Civil War.*

◄ This painting by Don Troiani depicts the Battle of Gettysburg.

A tattered diary of a Civil War soldier

Cannonball from a battle between Union and Confederate ironclads

NY Core Curriculum Preview

Chapter Focus Question: What were the causes, key events, and effects of the Civil War?

Section 1
Resources, Strategies, and Early Battles
2.II.D.2a, 2.II.D.2c

Section 2
African Americans and the War   2.II.D.2d, 3.I.A.1

Section 3
Life During the War   3.I.B.1, 2.II.D.2b, 2.II.D.2c

Section 4
Turning Points of the War   3.I.B.1, 3.I.C.5, 3.I.E.4

Section 5
The War's End and Impact   3.I.E.1, 3.I.E.2, 3.I.E.3, 3.I.E.4, 3.I.E.5

Union drummer boy

Use the ☑ **Quick Study Timeline** at the end of this chapter to preview chapter events.

> **Note Taking Study Guide *Online***
> **For:** Note Taking and American Issues Connector
> **Web Code:** nce-7101

▲ An illustration shows Union volunteers, each dressed up like Uncle Sam, marching in a parade.

SECTION 1

Marching Off to War

When the war began, families on both sides watched as husbands and sons rushed to join the Union and Confederate armies. Often there were celebratory parades to cheer the soldiers on. As the men marched off, family members felt both sadness and pride. One Richmond resident noted these mixed emotions in her diary:

❝An old lady, the mother of several dearly loved sons, but echoed the almost universal sentiment when she said . . . 'War, I know is very dreadful, but if, by the raising of my finger, I could prevent my sons from doing their duty to their country now, though I love them as my life, I could not do it. I am no coward, nor have I brought up my boys to be cowards. They must go if their country needs them.'❞

—Sallie Brock Putnam, *Richmond During the War*

Resources, Strategies, and Early Battles

 Core Curriculum Objectives

- **2.II.D.2a** Wartime actions: Military strategy, major battles, and human toll
- **2.II.D.2c** Wartime actions: Government policy during the war

Terms and People

blockade	Stonewall Jackson
Robert E. Lee	George B. McClellan
Anaconda Plan	Ulysses S. Grant
border state	Shiloh

NoteTaking

Reading Skill: Categorize As you read, use a table to note the advantages of the North and the South at the beginning of the war.

Wartime Advantages	
Union	**Confederacy**
• Population	• Strong military tradition
•	•
•	•

Why It Matters In 1861, the long, bitter dispute over slavery and states' rights erupted into war. The first shots at Fort Sumter set the stage for a long, costly struggle. At stake was the survival of the United States. **Section Focus Question: How did each side's resources and strategies affect the early battles of the war?**

Union and Confederate Resources

As the Civil War began, each side possessed significant strengths and notable weaknesses. At first glance, most advantages appeared to add up in favor of the Union.

Advantages of the Union The North enjoyed a tremendous advantage in population. Some 22 million people lived in the states that stayed in the Union. By contrast, the Confederacy had a population of only 9 million, of whom 3.5 million were enslaved African Americans.

The industrialized North was far better prepared to wage war than the agrarian South. Most of the nation's coal and iron came from Union mines, and the vast West was a source of gold, silver, and other resources. The densely populated urban areas of the Northeast supported a wide variety of manufacturing. With mechanized factories and a steady flow of European immigrants seeking work, the Union could produce more ammunition, arms, uniforms, medical supplies, and railroad cars than the Confederacy could. In addition, the Union had a larger railroad network for moving troops and material.

The Union had a small but well-organized navy. By late 1861, the Union had launched more than 250 warships, with dozens more under construction. The South had no navy at all, leaving it vulnerable to a naval **blockade** in which Union ships prevented merchant vessels from entering or leaving the South's few good ports, <u>thereby</u> crippling southern trade.

Finally, while the Confederate government was new and inexperienced, the North had an established government and an outstanding leader in Abraham Lincoln. Not everyone recognized this fact at the outset of the war, but Lincoln's leadership would prove invaluable to the Union cause.

Advantages of the Confederacy Still, the North did have some distinct weaknesses compared to the South. One of the Confederacy's advantages was psychological. Many northerners were willing to let the slaveholding South go. To them, preserving the Union was not worth killing and dying for. But the Confederacy was fighting for survival. Although there were pockets of pro-Union feeling in places such as western Virginia, most southern whites believed passionately in the Confederate cause. Even those who were not slaveholders resented what they saw as northern efforts to dominate them.

When the war began, Union forces consisted of only 16,000 men. New recruits signed on for three months of service, hardly long enough to form an efficient fighting team. The South faced similar challenges in assembling its armies, but it had a strong military tradition and fine leaders like Virginia's **Robert E. Lee.** Lee, who had an outstanding record in the United States Army, actually opposed secession and slavery. Yet he turned down an offer to command Union forces. He wrote:

> **Primary Source** "With all my devotion to the Union, and the feeling of loyalty and duty of an American citizen, I have not been able to make up my mind to raise my hand against my relatives, my children, my home. I have therefore resigned my commission in the army, and save in defense of my native state . . . I hope I may never be called upon to draw my sword."
>
> —Robert E. Lee, letter to his sister, April 20, 1861

In fact, Lee did accept command of the Confederate army and provided the South with inspiring military leadership throughout the war. The North struggled to find a commander of such caliber.

Vocabulary Builder
<u>thereby</u>—(ther BĪ) *adv.* by or through that

Resources Compared
As fresh-faced soldiers marched off to war, each side's resources gave it advantages over the other. For example, in terms of population, the Union outnumbered the Confederacy by a ratio of 2.5 to 1. *Pick two pie graphs and explain what advantage those resources gave to the North or South.*

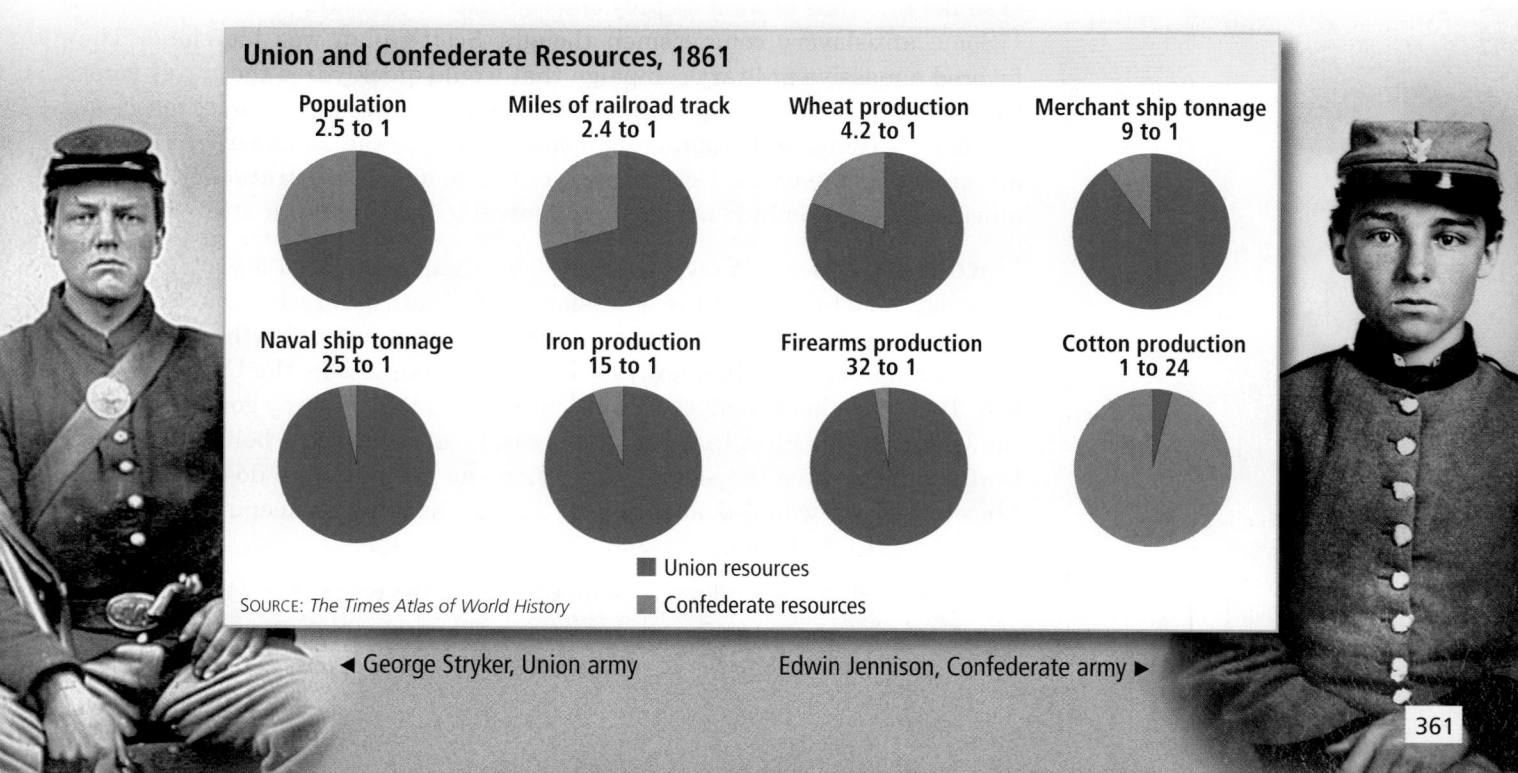

Union and Confederate Resources, 1861

Population 2.5 to 1	Miles of railroad track 2.4 to 1	Wheat production 4.2 to 1	Merchant ship tonnage 9 to 1

Naval ship tonnage 25 to 1	Iron production 15 to 1	Firearms production 32 to 1	Cotton production 1 to 24

■ Union resources
■ Confederate resources

SOURCE: *The Times Atlas of World History*

◄ George Stryker, Union army   Edwin Jennison, Confederate army ►

Finally, the Confederacy had a number of strategic advantages. It did not need to conquer the North; it simply had to avoid defeat, expecting that in time the North would give up the effort. By and large, southern forces would be fighting a defensive war on familiar, friendly ground while northern forces had to fight an offensive war in enemy territory. Union troops and supplies had to travel farther to reach the field of battle. The North also had to devote precious military resources to defending Washington, D.C. Only the Potomac River separated the Union capital from Confederate Virginia.

 Checkpoint What were some of the strengths and weaknesses of the Union and the Confederacy?

Confederate and Union Strategies

As the two sides prepared for war, Union and Confederate leaders contemplated their goals and how they might go about meeting them. While northerners hoped for a quick victory, southern strategists planned for a prolonged war.

The Confederacy Seeks Foreign Support The strategy of the Confederacy had two main thrusts. Militarily, the South hoped to preserve its small armies while doing enough damage to <u>erode</u> the Union's will to fight. Politically, it hoped to win formal recognition from Britain and France. Trade with these nations was crucial to the South, since the supply of manufactured goods from the North was now cut off. By the same token, the European textile industry was dependent on southern cotton. Confederate leaders reasoned that if the war dragged on, French and British mills would run out of raw cotton. Therefore, these countries might be willing to provide military aid to the South.

The Union Devises the Anaconda Plan The initial Union strategy was a two-part plan devised by General Winfield Scott, a Virginia-born hero of the Mexican-American War and the commander of all U.S. forces in 1861. First, the Union would blockade southern ports, starving the South of income and supplies. Then, Union forces would drive southward along the Mississippi River. Union control of the Mississippi would split the Confederacy in two, fatally weakening it. Scott's plan came to be known as the **Anaconda Plan,** after a type of snake that coils around its prey and squeezes it to death.

Some antislavery congressmen thought Scott's plan was too timid. They favored a massive military campaign that would quickly free the slaves across the South. Lincoln also hoped that a decisive victory over rebel forces massed in northern Virginia and around Richmond might lead the Confederacy to negotiate an end to the crisis. Despite such criticism and concentration on winning quickly, the Anaconda Plan remained central to the Union war strategy.

Lincoln Avoids the Slavery Issue The Union also faced a tricky political question: how to prevent the secession of Missouri, Kentucky, Delaware, and Maryland. Although these **border states** allowed slavery, they had not joined the Confederacy. Lincoln knew that if they chose to secede, the Union could be lost. To reduce this threat, the President insisted that his only goal was to save the Union. In his First Inaugural Address, he announced, "I believe I have no lawful right to [free the slaves], and I have no inclination to do so." Although Lincoln's stand troubled abolitionists, he did succeed in keeping the border states loyal to the Union.

 Checkpoint How did the Union strategy in the war differ from the Confederate strategy?

Vocabulary Builder
<u>erode</u>—(ee ROHD) *v.* to eat into; wear away

New Technology Changes Warfare

The Civil War revolutionized warfare. On water, new warships steamed into battle encased in thick armor plating. On land, the minié ball and the repeating rifle greatly improved soldiers' accuracy and firepower in battle. These changes resulted in staggering numbers of casualties on both sides. As the conflict dragged on, military commanders were forced to change their strategies to account for the deadly impact of new technology.

▲ Wooden ships were no match for ironclads like the Confederate *Virginia* and the Union *Monitor*.

▼ Cone-shaped minié balls were accurate at much greater ranges than round bullets.

This Henry repeating rifle could be fired 16 times before reloading.

▼ Most Civil War troops were arranged into tightly-packed formations prior to marching against an enemy position. New firearms and ammunition exacted a gruesome toll on the massed attackers.

▲ As casualties mounted, soldiers adapted their tactics and dug trenches for cover from enemy fire.

Thinking Critically

1. **Compare and Contrast** How did Civil War technology differ from earlier military technology?

2. **Draw Conclusions** How might future military tactics change because of lessons learned during the Civil War?

NoteTaking

Reading Skill: Recognize Sequence Use a timeline to note how the fighting developed during the early years of the Civil War.

July
Bull Run/Manassas

1861   1862   1863

Early Battles of the Civil War

The Civil War started slowly. The first large battle did not take place until three months after the firing on Fort Sumter. Ultimately, the conflict would span nearly four years and stretch across much of the continent.

Bull Run Shakes Union Confidence In July 1861, General Scott sent General Irvin McDowell and more than 30,000 Union troops to do battle with Confederate forces waiting outside Washington. The two armies met at Bull Run, a creek near Manassas, Virginia. In the battle's first hours, Union troops gained the upper hand. But a determined stand led by Confederate General Thomas J. Jackson sent them scrambling back to Washington. Confederates nicknamed their hero **Stonewall Jackson** in honor of his refusal to yield to the Union armies.

The battle, known as the Battle of Bull Run in the North and the Battle of Manassas in the South, proved a shock to those who had hoped the war would end quickly—and who were unprepared for the carnage modern warfare could produce. Lincoln responded by calling for additional troops and by replacing McDowell with General **George B. McClellan.**

Grant Fights in Tennessee While McClellan began to organize his Army of the Potomac, General **Ulysses S. Grant** pursued the Mississippi Valley wing of the Anaconda Plan. In February 1862, he directed the attack and capture of two Confederate strongholds—Fort Henry on the Tennessee River and Fort Donelson on the Cumberland River. His bold action drove Confederate forces from western Kentucky and much of Tennessee, and boosted northern morale. However, in April, Grant's troops fought a terrible battle in southwest Tennessee. In just two days of fighting, nearly 25,000 Union and Confederate soldiers were killed or wounded. The Battle of **Shiloh** horrified both the North and South and damaged Grant's rising reputation.

Union Forces Capture New Orleans While Shiloh shocked the public, it did not slow the course of the war. Just days later, Union ships under the command of David Farragut sailed through the Gulf of Mexico and seized the vital southern port of New Orleans at the mouth of the Mississippi. Emboldened by his success, Farragut continued to sail north, hoping to capture the Confederate stronghold of Vicksburg, Mississippi. The Confederates, however, stopped Farragut's fleet more than 50 miles from his goal. Meanwhile, pushing southward from Tennessee, Grant's land forces were also checked in their advance on Vicksburg. Complete Union control of the Mississippi would have to wait.

Fighting Spreads to the Southwest The American Southwest held strategic value to both sides in the Civil War. The region held rich gold mines and offered access to California and the Pacific Ocean. Despite its importance, neither side stationed many troops in the region.

Fighting did take place as far west as Arizona. But the most significant action occurred in New Mexico in early 1862, when a Confederate force marched up the Rio Grande from Texas. The goal was to

A Fierce Fight at Shiloh
Union troops fight off a Confederate charge into the "Hornet's Nest." This sunken road saw some of the heaviest casualties at Shiloh. *Why do you think soldiers called this position the "Hornet's Nest"?*

The Civil War, 1861–1862

Legend:
- Union state
- Confederate state
- Union forces
- Confederate forces
- Union victory
- Confederate victory
- Undecided battle
- Union blockade

drive Union troops from the Southwest and capture it for the Confederacy. The rebel troops were defeated in late March at Glorieta Pass, thanks in part to the destruction of their supply train by a Union force under Major John Chivington and Lt. Col. Manuel Chavez. The Confederates eventually retreated back into Texas, never to mount another threat to Union control of the Southwest.

The Union and Confederacy also vied for the loyalty of the Southwest's residents—many of whom in the past had been treated as outcasts. The Union got help from Mexican American militia in Texas, which worked to disrupt Confederate supply lines. Both sides also courted Native American groups throughout the entire West. The Cheyennes were able to bargain with the Union government for land in return for their aid. The Confederates persuaded the Creeks and Choctaws to support their cause. They also sought support from the Cherokee nation. The Cherokees, however, split over the question of which side to support. Such conflict within Native American groups was not uncommon as loyalties shifted during the course of the war.

The *Monitor* Battles the *Virginia* Few of the major battles of the Civil War took place at sea. However, one notable exception occurred in 1862 when the Union ship *Monitor* clashed with its Confederate opponent *Virginia* off the Virginia coast. The Union had hired a European engineer to design the *Monitor* as a model for a fleet of ships plated with iron armor. The Confederacy, meanwhile, had built the ironclad *Virginia* by refitting a Union ship previously known as the *Merrimack*. On March 9, the two ironclads met in battle. Though neither ship emerged the victor, the contest signaled the beginning of the end of wooden warships.

✔ **Checkpoint** What was the outcome and impact of the first major battle of the Civil War?

Map Skills In the early years of the war, most fighting took place in two distinct theaters of operation: one in Virginia and the other in the Mississippi River valley.

1. **Locate:** (a) Bull Run, (b) Richmond, (c) New Orleans, (d) Glorieta Pass

2. **Movement** What was McClellan's strategy for victory?

3. **Draw Inferences** How did the Union blockade affect the Confederate economy?

Geography *Interactive*
For: Interactive map
Web Code: ncp-1102

Stalemate Develops in the East

While Union and Confederate forces squared off in the Mississippi Valley and farther west, major fighting in the East focused on the state of Virginia. As elsewhere, the outcomes did not prove decisive for either side.

Lincoln Urges McClellan to Attack Since taking command of Union forces after Bull Run, General McClellan had been planning what he hoped would be a decisive drive on the Confederate capital at Richmond, Virginia. A skilled leader beloved by his troops, McClellan was also very cautious. He did not want to execute his plan until he felt his troops were ready.

McClellan's caution created friction with Lincoln, who was anxious for military victories. Yet, even as he pushed McClellan to act, the President was unwilling to give the general all the forces he asked for. Lincoln insisted on holding a large force near the capital to protect it from a Confederate attack. Stonewall Jackson's brilliant campaign in the spring of 1862 in the nearby Shenandoah Valley of Virginia increased Lincoln's concerns.

By midsummer, Lincoln insisted that McClellan take action. Reluctantly, McClellan sailed his army southward across Chesapeake Bay. The force landed on a peninsula southeast of Richmond and then began its march toward the capital. Thus, the action was called the Peninsular Campaign.

McClellan Fails to Take Richmond McClellan's army was actually larger than the force defending Richmond. But Confederate General Robert E. Lee led his troops skillfully. In a series of battles known as the Seven Days (June 26–July 2), Lee took advantage of McClellan's cautious style. The Union advance stalled and McClellan retreated to Washington.

After the retreat, Lincoln replaced McClellan. The move proved to be a mistake. At the Second Battle of Bull Run in late August, Lee's Confederates handed the Union a crushing defeat. Stonewall Jackson was instrumental in outmanuevering a larger Union force and nearly destroying it before the Federals could retreat. The victory, known in the South as the Second Battle of Manassas, energized Lee and led Lincoln to return McClellan to command. Lee and McClellan would soon face off in the single bloodiest day of the Civil War.

✔ **Checkpoint** Why did Lincoln and McClellan clash in early 1862?

This cannonball was fired from the *Monitor* during its contest against the *Virginia*. What does the photo suggest about the battle?

SECTION 1 **Assessment**

Progress Monitoring *Online*
For: Self-test with vocabulary practice
Web Code: nca-1103

Comprehension

1. **Terms and People** For each of the following items, write a sentence explaining its significance.
   - blockade
   - Robert E. Lee
   - Anaconda Plan
   - border state
   - Stonewall Jackson
   - George B. McClellan
   - Ulysses S. Grant
   - Shiloh

2. **NoteTaking Reading Skill: Categorize** Use your table to answer the Section Focus Question: How did each side's resources and strategies affect the early battles of the war?

Writing About History

3. **Quick Write: Plan a News Article** Review the information about the battle between the *Monitor* and the *Virginia*. Plan a news article you might write about the encounter by answering the questions required of every news article: *Who? What? When? Where? Why?*

Critical Thinking

4. **Predict Consequences** Which side do you think had the best long-term chances for victory at the start of the Civil War? Why?

5. **Identify Effects** Choose two battles discussed in this section and describe one effect of each.

6. **Contrast** Based on what you have read, how did Grant and McClellan differ as military leaders?

A Memorable Day

Frederick Douglass, the foremost African American abolitionist, journalist, and orator of his time, traveled the United States and spoke out against slavery. In his autobiography, he described his reaction to the Emancipation Proclamation:

❝The first of January, 1863, was a memorable day in the progress of American liberty and civilization. It was the turning-point in the conflict between freedom and slavery. A death blow was then given to the slave-holding rebellion. Until then the federal arm had been more than tolerant to that relic of barbarism. . . . We fought the rebellion, but not its cause. And now, on this day . . . the formal and solemn announcement was made that thereafter the government would be found on the side of emancipation. This proclamation changed everything.❞

—Frederick Douglass, *Life and Times of Frederick Douglass*

▲ Like the African Americans gathered in this postcard, Frederick Douglass celebrated the long-awaited Emancipation Proclamation

African Americans and the War

NY Core Curriculum Objectives

- **2.II.D.2d** Lincoln and Emancipation (the Emancipation Proclamation, the Gettysburg Address, African American participation in the war, the 13th Amendment)
- **3.I.A.1** Lincoln's plan for Reconstruction

Terms and People

contraband
Antietam
Emancipation
  Proclamation

Militia Act
54th Massachusetts
  Regiment

NoteTaking

Reading Skill: Identify Supporting Details As you read, use an outline to record details about African Americans during the war.

I. The Push Toward Emancipation
  A. Enslaved African Americans Seek Refuge
    1. Enslaved people come under Union control
    2.
  B.
II. Emancipation at Last

Why It Matters Despite Lincoln's efforts to downplay the slavery issue, abolitionists kept up the pressure to end slavery. Soon, Lincoln himself recognized the need to include freedom for enslaved Americans among the goals of the war. His actions helped bring about the beginning of the end of slavery in the United States. At the same time, African American soldiers joined the fight for freedom. **Section Focus Question: How did the Emancipation Proclamation and the efforts of African American soldiers affect the course of the war?**

The Push Toward Emancipation

Pressures at home and abroad urged Lincoln to address the issue of slavery. Abolitionists such as Frederick Douglass and William Lloyd Garrison, as well as the thousands who supported them, were impatient with Lincoln's policies. Another reason for Lincoln to act was that slavery was unpopular in Europe. Antislavery sentiment was one of the main reasons why Great Britain was reluctant to aid the Confederacy.

Enslaved African Americans Seek Refuge On the battlefield, Union officers faced a dilemma: what to do with enslaved African Americans who came under their control. It was absurd, argued these officers, to return slaves to their owners. Early on, Union General Benjamin Butler had gathered hundreds of black refugees into his camps and set them to manual labor. He declared the fugitives under his protection to be **contraband,** or captured war supplies. General John Frémont went a step further, declaring that enslaved people who came under his command in Missouri were free. Fearing retaliation from the border states, Lincoln reversed Frémont's order.

Lincoln's Plan Needs a Victory Lincoln realized he could not avoid the slavery issue for long. He secretly began working on a plan for the emancipation of enslaved African Americans living in Confederate states. In the summer of 1862, he shared his ideas with a surprised Cabinet. The members generally supported Lincoln's plan but agreed that its announcement should wait. After the Union failure at the Second Battle of Bull Run, such a proclamation might look like an act of desperation. What was needed was a major Union victory. Several weeks later, Lincoln got his opportunity.

Victory Comes at Antietam After his army's recent victories, General Lee was brimming with confidence. In early September 1862, he led his troops into Maryland, the border state where many favored the South. Lee hoped to inspire a pro-Confederate uprising. A victory on Union soil might also spur European recognition of the Confederacy. Lee also hoped to acquire an abundance of food supplies for his hungry army in an area unmolested by war.

Vocabulary Builder
ally–(uh LĪ) *v.* to unite or associate for a specific purpose

Lee's invasion did not go according to plan. On September 8, the general issued a "Proclamation to the People of Maryland" that invited them to <u>ally</u> themselves with the South. But Marylanders responded to the invitation with far less enthusiasm than Lee had anticipated. A few days later, Union soldiers found a copy of Lee's battle plan wrapped around some cigars at an abandoned rebel campsite. As a result, Lee lost the crucial element of surprise. When McClellan reviewed the orders, he exclaimed, "Here is a paper with which if I cannot whip Bobbie Lee, I will be willing to go home."

The two armies converged at Sharpsburg, Maryland, and McClellan's troops fanned out near Antietam Creek. On September 17, Union troops attacked Lee's army in three phases, moving from one side of the Confederate line to the other. By the end of the day, more than 23,000 soldiers lay dead or wounded. The Battle of **Antietam** marked the bloodiest single day of the Civil War. With his army exhausted and Maryland still in the Union, Lee retreated to Virginia. Though Union losses exceeded Confederate losses, Lincoln had the victory he needed to move forward with emancipation.

✔ **Checkpoint** Why did Lincoln decide to change his official stand on slavery?

Emancipation at Last

On September 22, 1862, Lincoln formally announced the **Emancipation Proclamation.** Issued as a military decree, it freed all enslaved people in states still in rebellion after January 1, 1863. It did not, however, apply to loyal border states or to places that were already under Union military control. Lincoln hoped the proclamation might convince some southern states to surrender before the January 1 deadline.

Many northerners responded to the Emancipation Proclamation with great excitement. "We shout for joy that we live to record this righteous decree," rejoiced Frederick Douglass. Some who had once criticized Lincoln for inaction now praised his name and held rallies in honor of the proclamation. An African American minister in Philadelphia said:

"The morning dawns! The long night of sorrow and gloom is past. . . . The Proclamation has gone forth, and God is saying . . . to this nation Man must be free. . . . Your destiny as white men and ours as black men are one and the same."

—Jonathan C. Gibbs, January 1, 1863

Others were less enthusiastic. William Lloyd Garrison grumbled that "what is still needed is a proclamation distinctly announcing the total abolition of slavery." British abolitionists applauded the President's move—but also wondered about Lincoln's conviction, since he attacked slavery only in areas over which he had no control. Lincoln also received criticism in Congress. Many Republicans felt the proclamation had not gone far enough, while many Democrats felt it was too drastic a step. The Proclamation may have been one factor leading to Democratic gains in the fall congressional elections.

Although the Emancipation Proclamation did not actually free a single slave, it was an important turning point in the war. For northerners, it redefined the war as being "about slavery." For white southerners, the call to free the slaves ended any desire for a negotiated end to the war. Confederate leaders now felt they must fight to the end.

For African Americans in the North, the proclamation made them eager to join the Union army and fight against slavery. Even before Lincoln's decree, growing demands by African Americans—and a growing need for soldiers on

Antietam: The Bloodiest Day of the War

The gruesome clash at Antietam claimed thousands of lives. Below, Confederate dead lie near the Dunker Church. Though the Union lost more men during the battle, Confederate losses amounted to a higher percentage of troop strength. *Why was Lincoln eager to claim victory in spite of Union losses?*

Casualties at Antietam				
	Union		Confederate	
Phase of the Battle	Troops Involved	Casualties*	Troops Involved	Casualties*
Morning	22,400	6,550	20,800	6,050
Midday	9,700	2,900	6,500	2,600
Afternoon	13,820	2,350	6,000	1,120

*Casualties include troops injured, captured, missing, or killed
SOURCE: National Park Service

BATTLE OF ANTIETAM

Union forces
Confederate forces

Potomac River
North Woods
East Woods
West Woods
Dunker Church
McClellan's Headquarters
Bloody Lane
Scale in Miles
0   ¼   ½
Lee's Headquarters
Antietam Creek
SHARPSBURG
Burnside's Bridge

This drummer had been enslaved prior to his service in the 79th U.S. Colored Infantry. ▼

COME AND JOIN US BROTHERS.

▲ Poster used to recruit African American regiments

The 54th Massachusetts Regiment storms Fort Wagner.

African Americans Display Courage in War

The photos and illustrations above testify to the dedication and bravery of African American soldiers during the war. The attack of the 54th Massachusetts on Fort Wagner was memorialized in both a monument and an award-winning film. *Why do you think these soldiers were so honored by succeeding generations of Americans?*

the frontlines—had led the Union to reconsider its ban on African American soldiers. Just two months before the proclamation, Congress had passed the **Militia Act,** mandating that black soldiers be accepted into the military.

✓ **Checkpoint** What were the effects of the Emancipation Proclamation?

African Americans Join the Fight

With the Emancipation Proclamation, the Union moved from allowing black troops to actively recruiting them. African American leaders were asked to seek volunteers. The abolitionist governor of Massachusetts enthusiastically supported the formation of the all-black **54th Massachusetts Regiment.** By war's end, more than 180,000 African American volunteers had served in the Union military. The Confederacy considered drafting slaves and free blacks in 1863 and 1864, but most southerners opposed the enlistment of African Americans.

African American Soldiers Fight Bravely Racist attitudes left many whites with low expectations for black troops. But performance in battle proved these expectations to be false. In June 1863, accounts appeared of a battle in Port Hudson, Mississippi—the first major test for African American soldiers. A Union officer declared that "my prejudices with regard to negro troops have been dispelled by the battle. . . . The brigade of negroes behaved magnificently."

A few weeks later, the 54th Massachusetts followed Robert Gould Shaw, their respected white officer, into battle at Fort Wagner in Charleston harbor. During the unsuccessful assault, Shaw and many of his men were killed. Nevertheless, the 54th had earned respect for its discipline and courage. One soldier received the Congressional Medal of Honor—the first of almost two dozen African American soldiers to be decorated for bravery.

Still, African American troops faced prejudice. They were usually assigned menial tasks, such as cooking, cleaning, or digging latrines. They often served the longest guard duty and were placed in exposed battle positions. It took a three-year effort to win equal pay. Black soldiers also knew that if captured, they would be killed. In one bloody incident, Confederates massacred more than 100 African American soldiers who were trying to surrender at Fort Pillow, Tennessee. Nevertheless, African Americans supported the Union in hundreds of battles, and some 70,000 lost their lives.

▲ Monument to the 54th Massachusetts Regiment in Boston

▲ Actor Denzel Washington in the 1989 movie *Glory*

Enslaved People Help the Union Cause Enslaved African Americans in the South also played an important role in the war, finding a variety of ways to passively or actively help the Union forces. White owners often abandoned plantations for the safety of southern cities, leaving trusted slaves to manage the farm. Advancing Union forces often enlisted these African Americans to produce food for the northern troops. Other African Americans used their familiarity with the terrain to serve as spies or scouts for Union armies. Sometimes, emancipated slaves organized their own military units. Regiments of former slaves appeared in such places as South Carolina, Kansas, and Missouri. Across the South, ambitious slaves seized the opportunity to begin to shape their own civilian lives. Some demanded, and got, wages for their work. Others simply abandoned their masters, fleeing to Union camps or to the North or West. They turned Lincoln's promise of freedom into a reality.

✔ **Checkpoint** How did African Americans respond to Union recruitment efforts after the Emancipation Proclamation?

---

2 Assessment

Progress Monitoring *Online*
For: Self-test with vocabulary practice
Web Code: nca-1104

Comprehension

1. Terms and People For each of the following terms, write a sentence explaining its significance.
- Antietam
- Emancipation Proclamation
- 54th Massachusetts Regiment

2. NoteTaking Reading Skill: Identify Supporting Details Use your outline to answer the Section Focus Question: How did the Emancipation Proclamation and the efforts of African American soldiers affect the course of the war?

Writing About History

3. Quick Write: Write Headlines Choose three events described in this section. Imagine you are writing a news article about each one. Write a headline for each article that will capture its main idea and attract the attention of readers.

Critical Thinking

4. Make Decisions Do you think Lincoln was right to wait so long before declaring emancipation? Why or why not?

5. Identify Effects What do you think was the most important effect of the Emancipation Proclamation?

6. Draw Inferences A corporal in the 54th Massachusetts wrote to President Lincoln: "Your Excellency, we have done a Soldier's Duty. Why can't we have a Soldier's pay?" What does this letter suggest about conditions for black soldiers in the Civil War?

Chapter 11 Section 2 371

2.II.D.2d

Abraham Lincoln:
The Emancipation Proclamation

Five days after the Union victory at Antietam, Abraham Lincoln issued the Emancipation Proclamation. The presidential decree freed all enslaved persons in states under Confederate control as of January 1, 1863. One of the most important documents in American history, the proclamation changed the nature of the Union cause and paved the way for the eventual abolition of slavery by the Thirteenth Amendment in 1865.

Whereas, on the twenty-second day of September, in the year of our Lord one thousand eight hundred and sixty-two, a proclamation was issued by the President of the United States, containing, among other things, the following, to wit:

That on the first day of January, in the year of our Lord one thousand eight hundred and sixty-three, all persons held as slaves within any State or designated part of a State, the people whereof shall then be in rebellion against the United States, shall be then, thenceforward,[1] and forever free; and the Executive Government of the United States, including the military and naval authority thereof, will recognize and maintain the freedom of such persons, and will do no act or acts to repress such persons, or any of them, in any efforts they may make for their actual freedom. . . .

And by virtue of the power, and for the purpose aforesaid, I do order and declare that all persons held as slaves within said designated States, and parts of States, are, and henceforward shall be free; and that the Executive government of the United States, including the military and naval authorities thereof, will recognize and maintain the freedom of said persons.

And I hereby enjoin upon the people so declared to be free to abstain from all violence, unless in necessary self-defence; and I recommend to them that, in all cases when allowed, they labor faithfully for reasonable wages.

And I further declare and make known, that such persons of suitable condition, will be received into the armed services of the United States to garrison[2] forts, positions, stations, and other places, and to man vessels of all sorts in said service.

And upon this act, sincerely believed to be an act of justice, warranted by the Constitution, upon military necessity, I invoke the considerate judgment of mankind, and the gracious favor of Almighty God. . . .

President Lincoln and the first page of his final draft of the proclamation ▶

1. **thenceforward** (thehns FOR werd) *adv.* from that time onward.

2. **garrison** (GAR uh suhn) *v.* to occupy and control by sending troops into.

Thinking Critically

1 **Draw Conclusions** How did the emotional effects of the proclamation differ from its actual effects?

2. **Explain Effects** How did the Emancipation Proclamation benefit the Union war effort?

SECTION 3

▲ Painting of a Confederate hospital scene

The Hardships of War

Mrs. Judith Brockenbrough McGuire, the wife of a high school principal from Alexandria, Virginia, kept a diary that describes daily life in the South throughout the Civil War. Her record of a people under siege highlights the hardships endured by her friends and neighbors as Union soldiers confiscated the supplies they so desperately needed:

❝February 11, 1863. For ten days past I have been at the bedside of my patient in Richmond. The physicians for the third time despaired of his life; by the goodness of God he is again [recovering his health]. Our wounded are suffering excessively for tonics, and I believe that many valuable lives are lost for the want of a few bottles of [medicine]. . . . Oh, how cruel it is that the Northern Government should have made medicines and the necessaries of life to the sick and wounded, contraband articles!❞

—Judith Brockenbrough McGuire, Civil War diary

Life During the War

NY Core Curriculum Objectives

- **3.I.B.1** Economic and technological impacts of the Civil War
- **2.II.D.2b** Impact of war on home front
- **2.II.D.2c** Government policy during the war

Terms and People

income tax
bond
Homestead Act
conscription

Copperhead
habeas corpus
inflation
Clara Barton

NoteTaking

Reading Skill: Compare and Contrast
Note the similarities and differences between the northern and southern home fronts during the war.

North
• Income tax to pay for the war
•

• Conscription to provide soldiers
•

South
• "Blockade runners" to deliver supplies
•

Why It Matters As African Americans rushed to join the Union ranks, the war dragged on. The fighting brought hard times to the home fronts of both North and South and helped transform many aspects of American life. Between 1861 and 1865, the economy and society of both regions underwent deep and lasting changes. These changes would help launch the North into the modern world, while the South suffered physical and social damage that persisted for decades. **Section Focus Question: How did the Civil War bring temporary and lasting changes to American society?**

The Home Front in the North

The war had a huge impact on northern industry. For example, the drop in southern cotton production severely damaged the large cotton textiles industry. At the same time, other industries boomed as demand for clothing, arms, and other supplies spiked. To meet the demand, industry became more mechanized.

War Transforms the Northern Economy Paying to supply the military was a major economic challenge. To help meet the cost, the Union government introduced a tax based on an individual's earnings. At first, the **income tax** was 3 percent on all income over $800 a year. As the war continued, the tax was increased. The Union also raised tariffs, which brought in revenue and helped northern industry by raising the cost of imported goods.

The biggest source of wartime funds came from the sale of government **bonds.** In return for the purchase price, the buyer received a certificate promising to pay the holder a larger amount of money at a future date. The Union sold billions of dollars worth of bonds to banks and individuals. Citizens were encouraged to buy bonds as an act of patriotism.

To increase the amount of cash in circulation and to help people buy war bonds, Congress passed the Legal Tender Act in 1862. This law allowed the Treasury to issue paper money, called "greenbacks" because of the color of the paper used. For the first time, the United States had a single, common currency that its citizens could use to purchase goods.

The Civil War also helped bring about far-reaching changes in the use of public land in the West. For years, the question of how to use this land had been dominated by the slavery issue. In addition, northern and southern companies squabbled over the route for a proposed rail line linking California to the East. With secession, however, these issues disappeared. In 1862, Congress passed the **Homestead Act,** making western land available at very low cost to those who would farm it. The war also resolved the argument over the route of the intercontinental railroad. The Pacific Railroad Act granted land to companies to build rail lines through Union territory.

The Draft Triggers Rioting In 1863, the Union instituted **conscription,** also called the draft, to meet the unending demand for fresh troops. Under this system, any white man between the ages of 20 and 45 might be called for required military service. However, a man could pay $300 to hire a replacement. Thus, at a time when laborers earned less than $2 per day, the burden of conscription fell mostly on recent immigrants and others who held low-paying jobs.

▼ Both the Union and the Confederacy initiated drafts to replenish the ranks of their depleted armies.

● INFOGRAPHIC

Troubles on the Home Fronts

▼ Northern anger over conscription led to violence. The worst incident was the New York Draft Riot of 1863, shown below.

The Civil War introduced civilians on both sides to the hardships of life during wartime. The effects were economic, political, and social. Across the divided nation, economic troubles, political turmoil, draft riots, and attacks on civil liberties disrupted life on the home fronts.

Some northern Democrats called for an immediate end to the fighting. Likening these politicians to poisonous snakes, their enemies called them "Copperheads." This cartoon shows Copperheads threatening the Union. ▼

Many working men resented the fact that the rich could pay to avoid the draft. They also worried about losing their jobs to African Americans, who were not subject to conscription. Anger over the draft led to violence. In the New York Draft Riot of July 1863, a mob of poor white working men went on a four-day rampage, damaging factories that made war supplies and attacking African Americans. Blacks were also targeted in similar race riots in other northern cities.

War Threatens Civil Liberties Draft rioters were not the only northerners angered by the war effort. A <u>faction</u> calling themselves "Peace Democrats" opposed Lincoln's conduct of the war and demanded an end to the fighting. Their opponents dubbed them **Copperheads,** after a type of poisonous snake found in the South. While some Copperheads promoted violence against the Union, most remained loyal to it and wanted only to end the war.

The President, however, viewed any effort to undermine the war effort as a grave threat to the nation. To deal with this crisis, he suspended the constitutional right of **habeas corpus,** which protects a person from being held in jail without being charged with a specific crime. Lincoln empowered the military to arrest people suspected of disloyalty to the Union, including some who had criticized the President and others who had participated in draft riots.

Vocabulary Builder
<u>faction</u>–(FAK shuhn) *n.* a group of people inside a political party or government, working in a common cause against other such groups or against the main body

✔ **Checkpoint** What was the response in the North to conscription?

The Home Front in the South

The Civil War made great economic demands on the South as well. But, unlike the North, the Confederacy lacked the resources to meet these demands. As the war dragged on, the South seemed in danger of collapse.

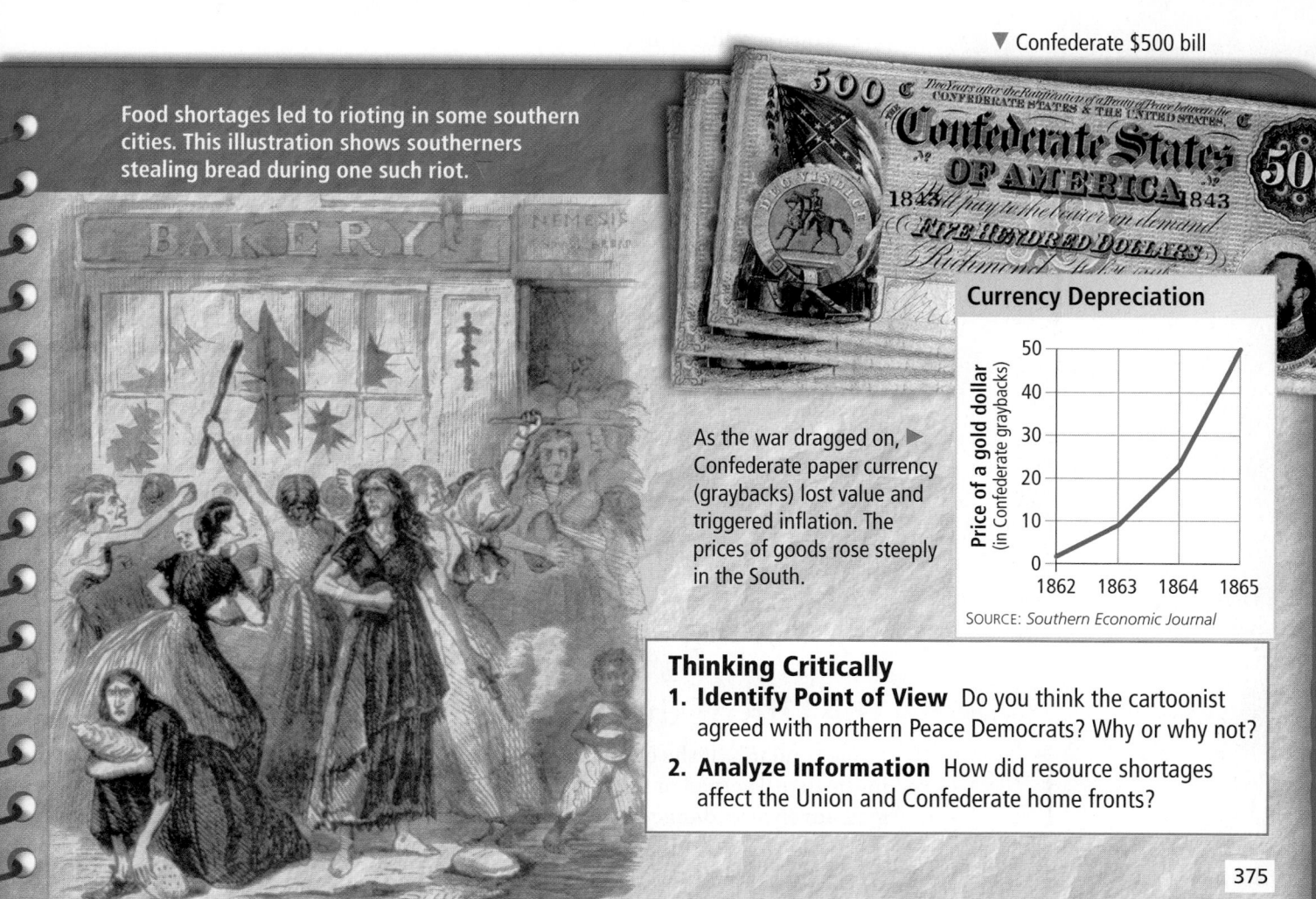

▼ Confederate $500 bill

Food shortages led to rioting in some southern cities. This illustration shows southerners stealing bread during one such riot.

As the war dragged on, ▶ Confederate paper currency (graybacks) lost value and triggered inflation. The prices of goods rose steeply in the South.

Currency Depreciation

Price of a gold dollar (in Confederate graybacks)

SOURCE: *Southern Economic Journal*

Thinking Critically
1. **Identify Point of View** Do you think the cartoonist agreed with northern Peace Democrats? Why or why not?

2. **Analyze Information** How did resource shortages affect the Union and Confederate home fronts?

375

Blockade Brings Hardships The most pressing threat was the Union blockade of southern ports. Small, swift ships known as "blockade runners" were initially effective at avoiding capture and delivering needed supplies to the South. However, by 1863, the Union blockade was about 80 percent effective. As a result, southerners were forced to depend almost entirely on their own farms and factories. This production was often complicated by nearby military operations. Even when farmers were able to harvest crops, they had difficulty getting the food to market or to the troops because rivers and rail lines were often blocked by Union forces.

Davis Struggles to Pay for War Much of the South's wealth was invested in land and in more than 3 million slaves. Most of that slave labor was devoted to producing market crops, such as cotton, tobacco, and sugar. The war drastically reduced the value of these assets, leaving President Jefferson Davis with few sources of money with which to finance the Confederate military effort.

The South used every opportunity to ease its economic squeeze. When possible, Confederate soldiers seized Union weapons, food, and supplies—often from bodies on the battlefields. Union shoes and boots were especially prized. Although Britain remained officially neutral, British shipyards helped the Confederacy build blockade runners. Entrepreneurs built ironworks in several southern cities. Still, the costs of the war quickly outran the South's resources. Duties on the South's few imports were hard to collect, and many southerners resisted the 10 percent tax on farm produce.

Like the Union, the Confederacy issued paper money, backed only by the government's promise to pay. Many doubted the value of Confederate money. Prices soared as those with items to sell demanded more and more Confederate cash. This **inflation,** combined with the shortage of food, led to riots in some parts of the South. In a note to North Carolina Governor Zebulon Vance, one woman reported on the dire conditions in that state:

> **Primary Source** "I have threatened for some time to write you a letter—a crowd of we poor women went to Greensborough yesterday for something to eat as we had not a mouthful [of] meat nor bread—what did they do but put us in jail—we women will write for our husbands to come home and help us."
> —Nancy Mangum, 1863

Southern Leaders Argue Hardships quickly began to weaken southern unity. As early as August 1861, Mary Boykin Chesnut of South Carolina wrote in her diary of "the rapid growth of the party forming against Mr. Davis." Indeed, Jefferson Davis found that his attempts to build unity were often hampered by his stubborn personality and by the fierce spirit of independence that had led to secession in the first place. Some states resisted sending troops outside their own borders or having their militia serve under commanders from other states.

As in the North, the Confederate government enacted conscription laws, seized private property in support of the war effort, and suspended habeas corpus. In response, some southerners called for Davis's impeachment. In Georgia, there was even talk of seceding from the Confederacy!

✔ **Checkpoint** Why did the Confederacy face severe economic problems during the Civil War?

The Life of the Soldier

Just under half the eligible men in the Union and four out of five eligible men in the South served in the military during the Civil War. Their experiences mingled adventure, danger, comradeship, pride, and terrible hardship.

The South in Distress
Although he criticized Lincoln for suspending habeas corpus in the North, President Jefferson Davis eventually did the same to keep order in the Confederacy.

Camp Life Offers New Experiences The Civil War gave many young men their first taste of travel. A typical regiment was comprised of recruits from the same town who had all joined up together. Still, soldiers were often homesick and bored. When not preparing for battle, they passed the time writing letters home, playing games, or attending religious revivals. One Confederate chaplain noted that many southern men "have come out of this war Christian soldiers."

In the border states especially, many families suffered divided loyalties, with brothers or sons fighting on different sides. Soldiers might find themselves far from home but camped across the battlefield from family. It was not uncommon for soldiers to exchange greetings with the "enemy" between engagements.

Soldiers Face Death in Many Forms As you have read, new technology used in the Civil War resulted in killing on a scale never before seen in America. Tens of thousands of soldiers died on the battlefields and many more were injured. Powerful new weapons caused gaping wounds, and the most frequent treatment was the amputation of limbs—sometimes without anesthesia. Doctors lacked modern knowledge about infection, so even minor wounds could prove deadly.

For those who survived the fighting, life in camp had its own dangers. Poor drinking water and lack of sanitation led to a rapid spread of illness in the ranks. For every soldier killed in battle, two died of disease.

Worse yet were the prison camps. On both sides, prisoners of war faced overcrowding and filth while in captivity. African American prisoners in Confederate camps were usually killed outright. The most notorious camp was the open-pen prison at Andersonville, Georgia. By the summer of 1864, some 33,000 Union prisoners had been crowded into its confines. With their own troops starving, Confederates had little incentive to find food for Union prisoners. During the 15 months that Andersonville remained in operation, more than 12,000 union prisoners died of disease and malnutrition.

✓ **Checkpoint** What were the greatest dangers faced by wounded and captured soldiers during the Civil War?

WITNESS HISTORY DVD

Watch **The Civil War** on the **United States Witness History DVD** to learn more about the lives of Civil War soldiers.

A soldier's tin cup

Camp Life During the Civil War

Union troops share a meal in 1863.

For most soldiers, army life was months of tedious marching and drilling punctuated by brief periods of fierce and deadly combat. To fight boredom in camp, troops engaged in many activities to entertain themselves and one another. One Confederate marveled at a "fellow by the name of Vaughn… [who] could sing funny Songs, dance clog, make funny speeches, play tricks, turn somersaults, and [do] other things [too] numerous to mention." *What does the quotation suggest about the soldiers' mood in camp?*

A bullet ripped through this war diary. ▶

◀ A Union surgeon's deck of cards

377

Clara Barton (1821–1912)

Alarmed by the casualties at the First Battle of Bull Run in July 1861, Clara Barton—then a clerk at the U.S. Patent Office in Washington, D.C.—quickly began collecting medical supplies. She carried them to the battlefield and began nursing the wounded soldiers. Barton continued this work for the rest of the war. In 1870, while in Europe on vacation, Barton nursed soldiers wounded in a war between France and Germany. She went on to found the American branch of the International Red Cross and served as its president for more than 20 years. During this time, Barton added disaster relief to the agency's mission.

Women and the War

Many women had long sought an active role in public life. The Civil War offered them new opportunities. Even women who did not choose new roles often were forced to assume unfamiliar responsibilities.

Women Do New Work The vast majority of women did not get close to military action, but many took over family businesses, farms, or plantations. With so many men away at the front, women made inroads into professions that had previously been dominated by men. By war's end, for example, most teaching jobs had been taken over by women.

A few white women from the North and the South masqueraded as men and marched into battle. More commonly, wives joined husbands in camps, cooking and doing laundry. Like their husbands and brothers, some African American women in the South served as spies and guides.

Nurses Care for the Sick and Wounded In both the North and South, the most notable military role for women was nursing. The development of nursing as a profession began slowly, as small groups of women formed organizations to assist returning soldiers and their families. Beginning in 1861, **Clara Barton** took the effort one step further. After collecting medical supplies in her Massachusetts community, she secured permission to travel with Union army ambulances and assist in "distributing comforts for the sick and wounded of both sides."

President Lincoln approved the formation of the United States Sanitary Commission, which authorized women to oversee hospitals and sanitation in military installations. This systematic program of federal responsibility for public health would be yet another lasting effect of the Civil War.

 Checkpoint How did women contribute to the war effort?

SECTION 3 Assessment

Progress Monitoring *Online*
For: Self-test with vocabulary practice
Web Code: nca-1105

Comprehension

1. **Terms and People** For each of the following items, write a sentence explaining its significance.
   - income tax
   - Homestead Act
   - conscription
   - Copperhead
   - habeas corpus
   - Clara Barton

2. **NoteTaking Reading Skill: Compare and Contrast** Use your Venn diagram to answer the Section Focus Question: How did the Civil War bring temporary and lasting changes to American society?

Writing About History

3. **Quick Write: Gather Information for a News Article** Gather information for a news article about the daily life of soldiers during the Civil War. List the relevant information, using phrases and sentences.

Critical Thinking

4. **Identify Central Issues** How did wartime needs lead to limitations on individual freedom in the North? Do you think such actions were justified?

5. **Compare and Contrast** How were the wartime economic problems of the North and South similar? How were they different?

6. **Analyze Information** Why do you think nursing came to be a profession dominated by women? Is this still true today?

NY 2.II.D

Julia Ward Howe ▶

Songs of the Civil War 🔊 AUDIO

Soldiers on both sides loved music during the war, from the rousing marching tunes they sang to summon courage in battle to the sentimental campfire songs that longed for the day "When This Cruel War Is Over." However, North and South each embraced its own anthem that lifted the spirits of soldiers fighting in the field.

The Battle Hymn of the Republic When abolitionist and poet Julia Ward Howe visited Washington, D.C., in 1861, she heard Union troops sing a marching song called "John Brown's Body." Later that night, the stirring tune still ringing in her ears, Howe composed lyrics she believed were better suited to the noble cause of ending slavery. The first time Abraham Lincoln heard "The Battle Hymn of the Republic," he stood up, tears running down his face, and called out over the cheering crowd: "Sing it again! Sing it again!"

Dixie The song that came to represent the South was actually written by a northern musician named Daniel Decatur Emmett in 1859. The origin of the song's title is uncertain—possibly it came from the Mason-Dixon line that separated North and South—but homesick Confederate soldiers took the tune as their own. When the war ended in 1865, Lincoln ended a celebratory address to a crowd outside the White House by asking a nearby band to play "Dixie."

◀ Civil War era homemade banjo

▼ A Union regimental band poses for a photograph in 1863.

Mine eyes have seen the glory of the coming of the Lord;

He is trampling out the vintage where the grapes of wrath are stored;

He hath loosed the fateful lightning of His terrible swift sword;

His truth is marching on.

Glory, glory, hallelujah!

Glory, glory, hallelujah!

Glory, glory, hallelujah!

His truth is marching on.

Oh, I wish I was in the land of cotton,
Cinnamon seed and sandy bottom,
Look away, look away, look away Dixie Land.
In Dixie Land, where I was born in,
Early on one frosty mornin',
Look away, look away, look away Dixie Land.
I wish I was in Dixie, Hooray! Hooray!
In Dixie Land I'll take my stand
To live and die in Dixie.
Away, away, away down south in Dixie.
Away, away, away down south in Dixie.

Thinking Critically
1. **Analyze Lyrics** Why do you think Union soldiers found "The Battle Hymn of the Republic" so inspiring?
2. **Draw Inferences** Why might Lincoln have asked for "Dixie" to be played when the war ended?

▲ Dead soldiers at Little Round Top

Drum from a Union regiment
that fought at Gettysburg ▶

WITNESS HISTORY 🔊 AUDIO

Gettysburg: A Soldier's Story

In early July 1863, North and South clashed near
Gettysburg, Pennsylvania. A young Union officer described
the fighting on a hill called Little Round Top:

❝As we reached the crest a never to be forgotten scene burst
upon us. A great basin lay before us full of smoke and fire, and
literally swarming with riderless horses and fighting, fleeing
and pursuing men. The air was saturated with the sulphurous
fumes of battle and was ringing with the shouts and groans of
the combatants. The wild cries of charging lines, the rattle of
musketry, the booming of artillery and the shrieks of the
wounded were the orchestral accompaniments of a scene like
very hell itself. . . .❞
—Lt. Porter Farley, 140th New York Infantry Regiment

Turning Points of the War

 Core Curriculum Objectives

- **3.I.B.1** Economic and technological impacts of the Civil War
- **3.I.C.5** The emerging debate over "proper" role of African Americans
- **3.I.E.4** War's impact on the development of the North as an industrial power

Terms and People

siege
Vicksburg
Gettysburg
George Pickett

Gettysburg Address
total war
William Tecumseh
  Sherman

NoteTaking

Reading Skill: Summarize As you read, use a
timeline to trace how the tide of the war turned
toward Union victory.

Summer
Gettysburg; Vicksburg

1863	1864	1865	1866

Why It Matters In the early stages of the war, the North had only
limited success in achieving its military goals. But after months of difficult fighting and military setbacks, the Union enjoyed some stunning military successes in 1863. Though there was much bloodshed to
come, that year marked the beginning of the end for the Confederacy.
**Section Focus Question: How did the Battles of Vicksburg and Gettysburg
change the course of the Civil War?**

Union Victory at Vicksburg

Although Union General U. S. Grant's troops battled the Confederates in Kentucky and central Tennessee in late 1862, the major focus
of the Union's western campaign remained the Mississippi River. The
Anaconda Plan depended on gaining control of the river and
cutting the South in half. Yet after two years of war, the Confederacy
still had strongholds at Port Hudson, Louisiana, and Vicksburg,
Mississippi. "Vicksburg is the key!" Lincoln proclaimed. "The war can
never be brought to a close until that key is in our pocket."

Grant Faces a Formidable Challenge Grant made several
attempts to fulfill Lincoln's goal, but it was a daunting task. The
mighty Vicksburg fortress towered high above the waters of the
Mississippi. Along the city's western edge, Confederate gunners
could rain deadly fire on any gunboats that might approach. In May
1862, they thwarted one such assault under Union Admiral David

Farragut. Grant even tried digging a canal so that Union ships could bypass the stretch of the river dominated by the Vicksburg batteries, but the attempt failed. Vicksburg's location also protected it from attack by land. A Union assault in late 1862 stalled out in the labyrinth of swamps, creeks, and woods guarding the northern approaches to the city.

Grant Initiates a Brilliant Plan In the spring of 1863, Grant devised a new plan to take the Confederate stronghold. First, he marched his troops southward through Louisiana to a point south of Vicksburg. At the same time, he ordered a cavalry attack on rail lines in central Mississippi to draw Confederate attention away from the city. On April 30, some 20,000 of Grant's men crossed the river and headed northeast to capture the Mississippi state capital at Jackson. After sacking that city, the Federals turned west toward Vicksburg, gaining control of the main rail line leading into the city and fortress. Vicksburg was completely cut off.

Grant launched two frontal assaults against the Confederates but failed to break their defenses. So, on May 22, he placed Vicksburg under **siege.** A siege is a military tactic in which an army surrounds, bombards, and cuts off all supplies to an enemy position in order to force its surrender. For over a month, Union guns kept up a steady fire from land and river. One astonished resident noted "ladies walk[ing] quietly along the streets while the shells burst above them, their heads meanwhile protected by parasol." The constant fire and lack of supplies gradually weakened Vicksburg's defenders. (See the American Experience feature at the end of this section.) Finally, on July 4, 1863, the Confederate commander concluded that his position was hopeless and ordered his forces to surrender. The siege of **Vicksburg** was over. Days later, after it learned of the Vicksburg surrender, the Confederate garrison at Port Hudson, Louisiana, also surrendered to the Union. With its last strongholds on the Mississippi in Union hands, the Confederacy was split in two.

✔ **Checkpoint** What was the outcome of the siege of Vicksburg?

Campaign for Vicksburg, March–July 1863

March 29 Grant moves main body of army south of Vicksburg

May 18–July 4 Siege of Vicksburg

May 19 and 22 Unsuccessful attacks on Vicksburg

May 15 Grant turns west to isolate and attack Vicksburg

April 16 Union navy passes Vicksburg

Champion Hill (May 16)

Jackson (May 14)

Raymond (May 12)

Bruinsburg

Port Gibson (May 1)

April 30 Union navy ferries army across the Mississippi

SOUTHERN R.R. OF MISSISSIPPI

Conic Projection
0   5   10 mi
0   5   10 km

Union advances
Union forces
Union gunboats
Confederate defenses
Union victory

Map Skills General Grant's plan to encircle and capture Vicksburg required rapid maneuvering and close coordination of Union forces.

1. **Locate:** (a) Vicksburg, (b) Bruinsburg, (c) Champion Hill

2. **Movement** How long did it take Grant's forces to reach Vicksburg once they crossed the Mississippi?

3. **Draw Inferences** Why did Grant take such an indirect route to Vicksburg when he had been so close in March?

Geography *Interactive.*
For: Interactive map
Web Code: ncp-1106

A Turning Point in the East

While Union troops advanced in the West, the situation was different in the East. Despite claiming victory at Antietam, Lincoln soon replaced General McClellan for failing to pursue the retreating Confederates. McClellan's <u>successor</u>, General Ambrose Burnside, headed south, hoping to win a decisive victory.

Lee Wins Two Victories and Pushes North The Army of the Potomac met General Lee's Army of Northern Virginia at Fredericksburg, Virginia, in December 1862. Burnside had 120,000 troops, while Lee had fewer than 80,000. But Lee, aided by generals Stonewall Jackson and James Longstreet, soundly defeated the new Union commander. Union casualties were more than double those of the Confederacy.

Lincoln replaced Burnside with General Joseph Hooker, who launched his own offensive against Lee in the spring. The two armies clashed at Chancellorsville, just west of Fredericksburg. Once again, the Confederates overwhelmed the Federals. The loss at the Battle of Chancellorsville was devastating to the Union. Upon hearing the news, President Lincoln paced the room, muttering "What will the country say? What will the country say?" Nevertheless, Lee paid dearly for his

Vocabulary Builder
successor–(suhk SEHS uhr) *n.* person or thing that succeeds, or follows, another

Focus On Geography

Battle of Fredericksburg

On December 13, 1862, Union forces attempting to smash Lee's army at Fredericksburg had to cross a canal ditch and 400 yards of open ground. The Confederates commanded Marye's Heights, a low hill that gave a clear view of the attackers. The rebels were further aided by the excellent cover offered by a sunken road and stone wall. "A chicken could not live on that field when we open on it," noted one Confederate artilleryman. Almost 9,000 Union soldiers were cut down before the wall. Many of the wounded lay on the battlefield through a cold snowy night.

Waves of Federal troops march ▶ against Marye's Heights.

Geography and History
How did human-environment interaction lead to the high number of Union casualties at Fredericksburg?

victory, losing the incomparable Stonewall Jackson during the fighting. After being accidentally shot by his own men, Jackson died a few days after the battle.

Though he was upset by the loss of Jackson, Lee sensed an opportunity to win international support for the Confederacy, demoralize the Union, and perhaps even force an end to the war. Once again, he decided to invade the North. In June 1863, Lee's army set off through Virginia's Shenandoah Valley and crossed into Union territory, eventually reaching Pennsylvania.

Union Troops Engage Lee at Gettysburg Lee's invasion caused great concern throughout the Union. The Army of the Potomac, now under the leadership of General George Meade, set out to engage the Confederates. Meanwhile, a Confederate unit headed for the town of Gettysburg, hoping to seize footwear from the shoe factory there. On the morning of July 1, Lee's men ran into several brigades of Union cavalry commanded by General John Buford. Buford's men spread out northwest of town and called for reinforcements. This was the start of the decisive Battle of **Gettysburg,** which would last for the next three days. (See the Events That Changed America feature on the following page.)

Lee Loses His "Right Arm"

After Stonewall Jackson was mistakenly shot by his own troops at Chancellorsville (above), doctors had to amputate his arm. Upon hearing the news, Lee lamented, "He has lost his left arm, but I have lost my right arm." *What do you think Lee meant?*

As the main bodies of both armies converged on Gettysburg, the first day of the fighting went to the Confederates. They pushed the smaller Union force back through the town and onto higher ground to the south. But nightfall halted the Confederate advance. This allowed General Meade to bring up the rest of his army and strengthen the Union position. Union troops dug in along a two-and-a-half mile defense line stretching from Culp's Hill and Cemetery Hill southward along Cemetery Ridge. The Federal line ended at two more rocky hills, Little Round Top and Big Round Top. Troubled that the Union now held the high ground, Confederate General James Longstreet regretted, "It would have been better had we not fought at all than to have left undone what we did."

Lee Is Defeated and Forced to Retreat As July 2 dawned, Lee's men prepared to assault both ends of the Union line. Lee ordered one force to move against the northern part of Meade's defenses while General Longstreet attacked the southern end of Cemetery Ridge. Late in the afternoon, Longstreet's troops charged against a large body of Union soldiers that had mistakenly abandoned Little Round Top and moved westward off Cemetery Ridge. The two sides hammered at each other for several hours in some of the fiercest fighting of the war. The rebels, however, failed to breach the Union line.

Meanwhile, Union troops had noticed the undefended position on Little Round Top. They hurried forward just in time to meet the gray tide of Confederates rushing uphill. Anchoring the Union defense of the hilltop was a Maine unit under Colonel Joshua L. Chamberlain. Chamberlain's men stood firm against numerous Confederate attacks, but their numbers and ammunition eventually dwindled. Chamberlain responded by ordering a bayonet charge that shocked and scattered his exhausted enemy. Hundreds of Confederates surrendered and the fighting drew to a close. Night fell and the Union still held the high ground.

Lee was not discouraged. Despite opposition from Longstreet—and believing that victory was still within reach—the Confederate commander attacked one more time. The result was disastrous. In the early afternoon of July 3, Lee commenced an artillery barrage aimed at the center of the Union line. He had hoped his cannon would break up the Union defenses in advance of an infantry attack on Cemetery Ridge. When Lee's men, including a division under General **George Pickett,** marched toward the ridge, thousands of Confederates were mowed down by Union rifle and cannon fire. After the failure of Pickett's Charge, Lee ordered the general to reposition his division. "General Lee," replied Pickett, "I have no division now." The Battle of Gettysburg was over. On the battlefield lay over 50,000 dead and wounded. About half of these were Confederates—nearly a third of Lee's fighting force. Lee abandoned his invasion of the North and led his limping army back into Virginia. The South had suffered a crushing defeat. It would never again attempt to fight on Union soil.

Lincoln Honors the Dead In November 1863, Lincoln came to the Gettysburg battlefield to dedicate a cemetery for the fallen soldiers. There, he delivered his

Events That Changed America

BATTLE OF GETTYSBURG

As the bloodiest battle ever fought on American soil, the Battle of Gettysburg marked a turning point in the Civil War. To halt a second Confederate invasion of the North, more than 90,000 Union soldiers faced off against General Robert E. Lee and 77,500 soldiers of the Army of Northern Virginia in early July 1863.

On July 1, Confederate troops collided with Union cavalry just outside the small Pennsylvania crossroads of Gettysburg. By the end of the day, the Confederates had routed the gathering force of Union troops and forced them onto higher ground south of town. For the next two days, Lee's army hammered at the Union lines as each side struggled to win the battle. Despite Confederate General George Pickett's heroic charge against Union positions on July 3, Lee's battered men ultimately lost the battle. They avoided destruction at the hands of the victorious Union army by retreating back to Virginia.

July 1 Late on the first day, ▶ Lee ordered General Richard Ewell to push onto Cemetery Hill "if practicable." Ewell famously decided not to press his attack, leaving the Union defenders to dig in.

The battle had begun when the Confederates attempted to raid a shoe factory in Gettysburg. ▼

July 1

GENERAL LEE

GENERAL MEADE

GETTYSBURG

Seminary Ridge

Cemetery Hill

Culp's Hill

Scale in Miles

0 ½ 1

N

Cemetery Ridge

Little Round Top

Big Round Top

Union positions
Union retreat
Confederate positions
Confederate advance
Road

July 2

GENERAL LEE

GETTYSBURG

Seminary Ridge

Cemetery Hill

Culp's Hill

GENERAL MEADE

Wheat Field

Cemetery Ridge

Little Round Top

GENERAL LONGSTREET

Devil's Den

Big Round Top

July 2 Union Colonel Joshua L. Chamberlain (right) commanded his regiment's desperate, bloody defense of Little Round Top.

Gettysburg Address. He described the Civil War as a struggle to fulfill the Declaration of Independence and to preserve a nation "dedicated to the proposition that all men are created equal." Today, the speech is recognized as an enduring statement of American values and goals. (See the Documents of Our Nation section at the back of this textbook.) The President concluded his speech by urging:

Primary Source "[W]e here highly resolve that these dead shall not have died in vain—that this nation under God, shall have a new birth of freedom—and that government of the people, by the people, for the people, shall not perish from the earth."
—Abraham Lincoln, November 19, 1863

✔ **Checkpoint** What was the outcome of the Battle of Gettysburg?

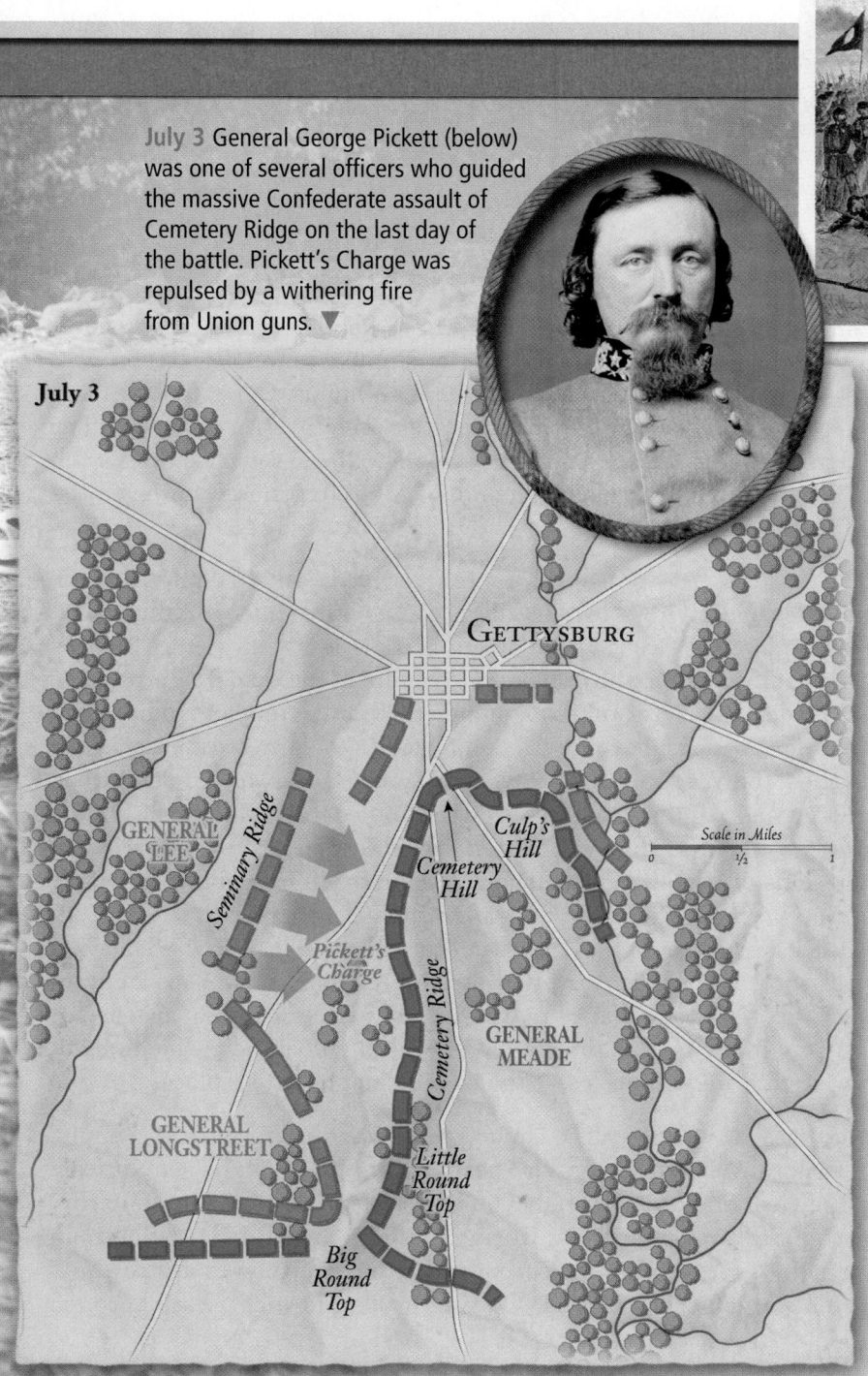

July 3 General George Pickett (below) was one of several officers who guided the massive Confederate assault of Cemetery Ridge on the last day of the battle. Pickett's Charge was repulsed by a withering fire from Union guns. ▼

▲ July 3 The peak moment of the Confederate charge came when General Lewis Armistead (above, with hat on sword) led his troops through a breach in the Union line. Armistead and many of his men were soon killed in the Union counterattack.

Why It Matters

Along with Vicksburg, Gettysburg turned the tide of the Civil War in favor of the Union. After its second invasion of the North was defeated, the Confederacy would fight the rest of the war on its own soil. Lincoln's immortal Gettysburg Address, delivered four months after the battle, motivated the Union to connect the massive human sacrifice to "a new birth of freedom" for the United States.

Thinking Critically

What might have happened if the South had won at Gettysburg? Describe a new course of events.

History Interactive ✷

For: To discover more about the Battle of Gettysburg
Web Code: ncp-1107

385

SHERMAN'S MARCH TO THE SEA

Atlanta, Sept. 2
GEORGIA R.R.
Eatonton
Milledgeville
Macon
Griswoldville, Nov. 22
Georgia
Statesboro
Waynesboro, Dec. 4
Millen
South Carolina
Charleston
Savannah, Dec. 21
Fort McAllister, Dec. 13
Atlantic Ocean

Union forces
Union victory
Fort
Railroad
Scale in Miles
0 25 50

Goals of Total War ☑ Quick Study

- Strike military <u>and</u> civilian targets.
- Destroy materials and crops that enemy forces might be able to use.
- Destroy railroads and factories to damage the local economy.
- Break the people's will to continue fighting.

Sherman Unleashes Total War

Soon after occupying Atlanta, William Tecumseh Sherman (see photo) abandoned his supply lines and set off to "make Georgia howl." Above, his troops ravage the Confederate countryside. *How do you think southerners felt about Sherman?*

The Union Presses the Advantage

Coming within a day of each other, the Union victories at Gettysburg and Vicksburg dealt a severe blow to the Confederacy. Lee's troops were in retreat and the Mississippi was in Union hands. Gone, too, was any hope for the Confederacy to win recognition from Britain or France. The war was not over—indeed, the Confederacy would still win some victories, such as that at Chickamauga, Georgia, in the fall of 1863. In general, however, the situation of the South was dire.

Grant Marches Toward Richmond Lincoln recalled General Grant from the Mississippi Valley in early 1864 to take charge of the entire Union military effort. The President knew that Grant would accept nothing less than victory. He was correct. Grant set his sites on the Confederate capital of Richmond. "I propose to fight it out," he declared, "if it takes all summer." Grant's campaign did last all summer and for months beyond. He engaged Lee's army in a series of ferocious battles: the Wilderness, Spotsylvania Court House, and Cold Harbor. Grant's strategy was to inflict more losses on the Confederates than their limited resources could withstand. The cost of Grant's relentless advance was horrifying. Tens of thousands of Union and Confederate soldiers fell on the battlefields of Virginia. In the North, public outrage began to grow.

Grant's attack did not target the South's military forces alone. He was following a strategy of **total war,** which involves striking civilian as well as military targets. The purpose of total war is to weaken not just an enemy's armies but also the economy that supports them and the overall will of the people to fight. The South was suffering serious losses that it could not hope to replace.

Sherman Drives to the Sea The Union's total-war strategy was also implemented by General **William Tecumseh Sherman.** In May 1864, he set out from the Tennessee-Georgia border with 60,000 troops on a 250-mile march to capture the port of Savannah, Georgia. During his "March to the Sea," Sherman ordered his men to get supplies by looting along the way, then to destroy anything of potential value left behind. Cutting a 60-mile-wide swath through

Georgia, Sherman's army tore up railroad tracks, destroyed buildings, and vandalized hundreds of private homes. With Union forces closing in on Atlanta, Confederate troops abandoned the city. Sherman's men occupied it on September 2 and forced the residents to leave. When the mayor asked Sherman to reconsider his order, the general responded:

Primary Source "You might as well appeal against the thunder-storm as against these terrible hardships of war. They are inevitable, and the only way the people of Atlanta can hope once more to live in peace and quiet at home is to stop the war. . . . We don't want your negroes or your horses or your houses or your lands . . . but we do want, and will have, a just obedience to the laws of the United States. That we will have, and if it involves the destruction of your improvements, we cannot help it."
—William T. Sherman, letter to James Calhoun, September 12, 1864

Once Atlanta was emptied, Union troops burned it to the ground. "Sherman the Brute," as southerners called him, continued eastward and captured Savannah in late December.

The Election of 1864 As 1864 drew to a close, Lincoln had much to celebrate. While his military commanders were winning victories on the battlefield, he had won reelection in November.

The campaign had been difficult. Lincoln had lost some support even in his own party. Some Republicans criticized the President for grasping too much authority; others charged that he was not fully committed to ending slavery. Democrats, fractured into several factions, finally nominated George McClellan, the popular former Union commander.

Lincoln's presidency had seemed in jeopardy. However, Union victories boosted his popularity. Many Union soldiers, loyal to Lincoln, were allowed to go home to vote. When the ballots were in, McClellan won 45 percent of the popular vote, but Lincoln received 212 of the 233 electoral votes. The reelection of Abraham Lincoln destroyed any last Confederate hopes that the North would cave in and negotiate a peace.

 Checkpoint What strategy did Grant follow as commander of Union forces?

SECTION 4 Assessment

Progress Monitoring Online
For: Self-test with vocabulary practice
Web Code: nca-1108

Comprehension

1. **Terms and People** For each of the following items, write a sentence explaining its significance.
   • siege
   • Vicksburg
   • Gettysburg
   • George Pickett
   • Gettysburg Address
   • total war
   • William Tecumseh Sherman

2. **NoteTaking Reading Skill: Summarize** Use your timeline to answer the Section Focus Question: How did the Battles of Vicksburg and Gettysburg change the course of the Civil War?

Writing About History

3. **Quick Write: Begin to Write a News Article** Choose a battle discussed in this section. Outline the article you would write about the battle, including how you would answer the five *W* questions. Write the headline for the article.

Critical Thinking

4. **Apply Information** Using examples from this section, write a general definition of the term *turning point*.

5. **Draw Inferences** In the Gettysburg Address, Lincoln stated that the purpose of the war was to ensure "that this nation . . . shall have a new birth of freedom—and that government of the people, by the people, for the people, shall not perish from the earth." What do you think he meant?

6. **Analyze Information** Why do you think General Sherman felt justified in destroying civilian property during his march through Georgia?

EXPERIENCE
THE SIEGE OF VICKSBURG

Not Safe at Home In her diary, Vicksburg resident Emma Balfour described a rain of death: "We have spent the last two nights in a cave, but tonight I think we will stay at home. It is not safe I know, for the shells are falling all around us. . . ." ▼

Shots rang out over the trenches. Artillery shells slammed into houses. Frightened civilians abandoned their homes. Burrowing into hillsides overlooking the Mississippi River, the citizens of Vicksburg built bomb shelters out of earth and wood. There, they waited as the Union encircled and bombarded one of the Confederacy's last remaining strong points in the West.

If the Union army could not capture this strategic outpost on the Mississippi, the Union would be hard-pressed to fulfill the Anaconda Plan and split the Confederacy in two. Facing many obstacles, General Ulysses S. Grant decided against a final frontal assault to take Vicksburg. Instead, beginning in May 1863, Grant surrounded the city hoping to bomb and starve it into submission. On July 4, after a six-week siege, Vicksburg surrendered. For Vicksburg's brave and battered citizens, their terrible ordeal was over. For the rest of the Confederacy, the fall of Vicksburg was a devastating loss.

A page from Emma Balfour's diary ▼

Life in a Bomb Shelter
Shell-shocked civilians tried to survive the bombardment by living in underground shelters like this one. ▼

Trophy of Victory
Union soldiers captured this Confederate flag at Vicksburg.

Smuggling in Supplies As supplies dwindled in Vicksburg, Lamar Fontaine (below) and other southerners smuggled food and ammunition into the city. ▼

Blasted to Freedom Escaping to freedom at Vicksburg, this enslaved man was blasted 300 yards across the lines when Union miners blew up a Confederate fortification. ▶

Thinking Critically
1. **Analyze Visuals** How did the civilians of Vicksburg respond to the Union attack on their city?

2. **Draw Conclusions** Do you think Grant's tactics at Vicksburg were warranted? Why or why not?

Connect to Today Do research to learn about recent natural disasters in the United States. How did those events impact Americans living in the areas where they occurred?

History *Interactive* ✳
For: To learn more about the siege of Vicksburg
Web Code: ncp-1109

Battle for the River
Confederate artillery in Vicksburg fire upon passing Union ships. The Confederates desperately hoped to maintain control of the Mississippi River. ▶

▲ Confederate soldiers roll up their flag after Lee's surrender

WITNESS HISTORY AUDIO

The South Surrenders

Confederate General John B. Gordon was with General Lee at Appomattox Court House when the Army of Northern Virginia surrendered to Union troops. Gordon later described the despair of his soldiers:

❝During these last scenes at Appomattox some of the Confederates were so depressed in spirit . . . that the future seemed to them shrouded in gloom. They knew that burnt homes and fenceless farms, poverty and ashes, would greet them on their return from the war. Even if the administration at Washington should be friendly, they did not believe that the Southern States could recover in half a century from the chaotic condition in which the war had left them.❞

—General John B. Gordon, *Reminiscences of the Civil War*

The War's End and Impact

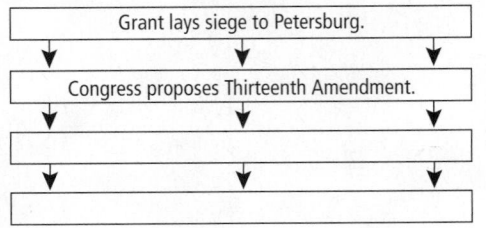 Core Curriculum Objectives

- **3.I.E.1** War's impact on political alignments
- **3.I.E.2** War's impact on citizenship
- **3.I.E.3** War's impact on federal-state relations
- **3.I.E.4** War's impact on the development of the North as an industrial power
- **3.I.E.5** War's impact on American society

Terms and People

Thirteenth Amendment   Mathew Brady
John Wilkes Booth   Land Grant College Act

NoteTaking

Reading Skill: Recognize Sequence As you read, use a flowchart to note what happened during the final days of the Civil War.

Grant lays siege to Petersburg.
↓   ↓   ↓
Congress proposes Thirteenth Amendment.
↓   ↓   ↓
↓   ↓   ↓

Why It Matters After four years of bitter struggle and sacrifice, the Confederacy stood on the brink of defeat. As Lee prepared to surrender to Grant, Lincoln began to plan for the future. The Civil War had lasting effects on both the North and the South. With the fighting over, Americans faced the difficult challenge of rebuilding their nation. **Section Focus Question: What was the final outcome and impact of the Civil War?**

The War's Final Days

In the summer of 1864, Grant continued his bloody drive toward Richmond. But at Petersburg, about 20 miles south of Richmond, the Confederates made a desperate stand. (See the map at the end of the section.) Petersburg was a vital railroad center. If Grant captured it, he could cut all supply lines to Richmond.

Grant Places Petersburg Under Siege As he had at Vicksburg, Grant turned to siege tactics. Throughout the summer and fall and into the winter, his forces tightened their grip around Petersburg. Both sides dug trenches and threw up fortifications to guard against attack. By March 1865, the two opposing lines of defense stretched for more than 30 miles around Petersburg.

Fighting was fierce. Union troops suffered more than 40,000 casualties. The Confederates lost 28,000 men. However, unlike Grant, Lee had no replacement troops in reserve. As the siege of Petersburg wore on, Union strength grew in comparison to the Confederate defenders.

Lincoln Looks to the Future With the Confederate position truly desperate, southerners began to talk of peace. In February 1865, a party led by Confederate Vice President Alexander Stephens met with Lincoln to discuss a <u>feasible</u> end to the war. However, these discussions produced no results. One reason for the failure was that the U.S. Congress, with Lincoln's support, had recently proposed the **Thirteenth Amendment** to the Constitution. If ratified, the amendment would outlaw slavery in the United States. The Confederate peace delegation was unwilling to accept a future without slavery. (The Thirteenth Amendment was ratified in December 1865.)

Despite the failure of the February meeting, Lincoln was confident of an eventual victory. He now began to turn his attention to the process of bringing the Confederate states back into the Union. This would be no easy task. Many northerners had a strong desire to punish the South harshly.

Lincoln had a different goal. While committed to the defeat of the Confederacy and an end to slavery, he believed that the Union should strike a more generous stance with the rebellious states. At the beginning of March, in his Second Inaugural Address, Lincoln declared his vision of a united and peaceful nation. "With malice toward none," Lincoln said, Americans should "do all which may achieve and cherish a just and lasting peace."

Lee Surrenders to Grant Several weeks later, the Confederates made a desperate attempt to break the siege of Petersburg. They failed. Recognizing that the situation was hopeless, Lee ordered a retreat from Petersburg on the night of April 2. Richmond, now defenseless, was evacuated and set aflame.

Lee's one hope was to join with Confederate forces in North Carolina. Setting out on the march, the men suffered from a lack of food and constant harassment by Union forces. Finally, Lee and his starving, exhausted soldiers were trapped at the town of Appomattox Court House, Virginia. On April 9, Lee formally surrendered to Grant. The Union general refused to allow his troops to gloat. "The war is over," he said, "the rebels are our countrymen again."

Lee's surrender did not officially end the war. The South still had some 170,000 soldiers under arms, and it took until June for other Confederate generals scattered around the South to complete similar surrenders. In Texas, African Americans celebrated June 19, 1865, as "Juneteenth," the day the news of surrender reached the Southwest.

Lincoln Is Assassinated On April 14, just days after Lee's surrender, Lincoln decided to relax by attending a new comedy, *Our American Cousin,* at nearby Ford's Theatre. During the performance, actor and Confederate supporter **John Wilkes Booth** approached the President's private box. Booth fired a single shot into the back of Lincoln's head. Leaping to the stage, he was heard to call out *"Sic semper tyrannis!"* ("Thus ever to tyrants," the motto of Virginia) and "the South is avenged." Mortally wounded, Lincoln died the next morning.

Booth became the target of a massive manhunt. After several days, he was shot and killed while hiding in a barn in Virginia. Soon, it was discovered that Booth had been part of a plot to kill not only Lincoln, but also the Vice President and the Secretary of State.

Vocabulary Builder
feasible–(FEE zuh buhl) *adj.*
possible; practical

▼ Lee surrenders to Grant at Appomattox Court House

HISTORY MAKERS

In May and June 1864, Robert E. Lee's Army of Northern Virginia beat back Ulysses S. Grant's Army of the Potomac in several fierce battles between Washington and Richmond. After each fight, Grant sidestepped Lee to march closer to the southern capital. However, as the Union army moved, Lee followed and set up strong defensive positions, which forced Grant to attack. Neither general could maneuver to win a decisive victory. In a month's time, the two armies suffered nearly 70,000 combined casualties. By late summer, the bloody contest had settled into a siege at Petersburg, south of Richmond. In early April 1865, Lee abandoned the city and eventually surrendered to Grant.

Ulysses S. Grant
(1822–1885)

Robert E. Lee
(1807–1870)

A "wanted" poster showing Booth at the top (center photo)

The assassin John Wilkes Booth levels a pistol at his unsuspecting victim.

The plotters hoped to cause chaos and panic in the North, thereby giving the South time to regroup and continue the war. Although Secretary of State William Seward was attacked and seriously injured by one of Booth's accomplices, Booth was the only man to carry out his part of the plot. Four of his accomplices were later hanged as coconspirators.

Lincoln's tragic death had a deep political impact. His murder united his northern supporters and critics, who now saw him as both a hero and a symbol of freedom. Gone was the strong, skilled leader who had guided the nation through its greatest crisis. As you will read in the next chapter, his presence would be greatly missed in the difficult days ahead.

The Death of a President

After Booth shot him, Lincoln was carried to a boardinghouse across the street from Ford's Theatre. There, doctors struggled to save his life but ultimately failed. When President Lincoln died, his Secretary of War, Edwin Stanton, plainly stated, "Now he belongs to the ages." *How do you think northerners reacted to Lincoln's assassination? How do you think southerners reacted?*

 Checkpoint What event marked the end of the Confederacy's hopes in the Civil War?

Why the North Won

With hindsight, it is tempting to claim that the Union victory had been certain from the outset, but that is not the case. When the war began, the South had confidence, outstanding military leadership, and a strong determination to defend its land. By contrast, many northerners were far less committed to the fight.

But as northerners warmed to the conflict, they were able to marshal their greater technological prowess, larger population, and more abundant resources. Moreover, the Union was able to develop new advantages, particularly brilliant and fearless military leaders, such as Grant and Sherman, who were willing to do everything it took to win the war. Meanwhile, the South used up its resources, unable to call upon fresh troops and supplies. According to historian Richard Current, the Confederacy's inability to gain a European ally and northern military superiority sealed the South's fate:

Primary Source

"[I]t seems to have become inevitable once two dangers for the Union had been passed. One of these was the threat of interference from abroad. The other was the possibility of military disaster resulting from the enemy's superior skill or luck on the battlefield. . . . Both dangers appear to have been over by midsummer, 1863. . . . Thereafter, month by month, the resources of the North began increasingly to tell, in what became more and more a war of attrition."

—Richard N. Current, in *Why the North Won the Civil War*

Lincoln's body was transported back to Springfield, Illinois, aboard a special funeral train. During the 12-day trip, thousands of Americans in cities and towns along the train route lined up to pay their respects to the fallen President.

The North also enjoyed the steady leadership of President Lincoln. At a time when opinion in the North was bitterly divided, he applied uncommon skill to the difficult task of keeping the nation together.

Finally, Lincoln's decision to proclaim emancipation was a fateful step that changed the nature of the war. Lincoln's determination—and the determination of thousands of African Americans in the North and South—sustained northern spirits, even as the war sapped southern resolve.

✔ **Checkpoint** **What were some of the reasons the North prevailed in the Civil War?**

Lincoln's funeral casket is displayed to mourners in Philadelphia, Pennsylvania.

The War's Lasting Impact

The United States had never experienced a war like the Civil War. Some individual battles produced casualties greater than the United States had previously sustained in entire wars. When the war was over, more than 600,000 Americans were dead. Hundreds of thousands more were maimed.

The Civil War ushered in the harsh reality of modern warfare. For the first time, ordinary citizens could see the carnage of the battlefield through the photographs of journalists such as **Mathew Brady.** His exhibition "The Dead at Antietam" provided graphic evidence of the terrible realities of war.

Effects on the Economy After the fighting ended, social and political disillusionment on both sides fed economic greed. The era following the war came to be labeled the Gilded Age—a term that suggested a superficial glitter and beauty covering up an underlying decay. Nevertheless, in the North, the industrial boom that was fueled by the war continued. In 1862, Congress passed both the **Land Grant College Act** and legislation authorizing a protective tariff. The Land Grant College Act gave money from the sale of public lands to states for the establishment of universities that taught "agriculture and mechanical arts." The tariff protected northern industry from foreign competition and raised much-needed revenue for the Union war effort. It also led to a surge in manufacturing that lasted far beyond the end of the war. After 1865, northern factories, banks, and cities underwent sweeping industrialization, helping the United States emerge as a global economic power.

In contrast, rebuilding the South was slow and tortured. Southern cities, such as Richmond and Atlanta, lay in ruins, as did many of the region's factories and railroads. The South struggled to regain its economic footing after the war, often

NoteTaking

Reading Skill: Understand Effects Use a concept web to identify the effects of the Civil War.

Effects of the War

Economic boom in the North

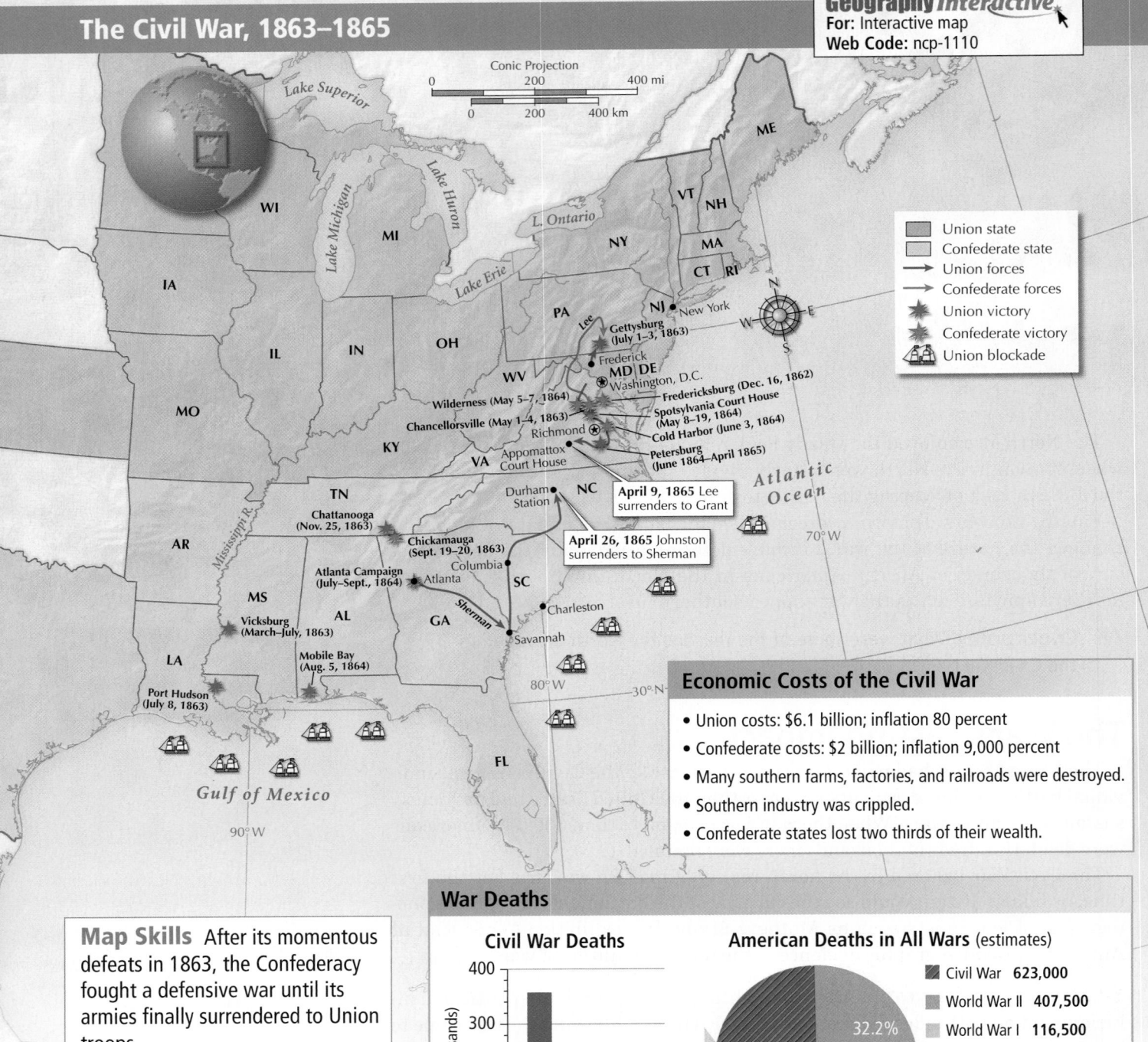

Geography *Interactive*
For: Interactive map
Web Code: ncp-1110

Legend:
- Union state
- Confederate state
- → Union forces
- → Confederate forces
- Union victory
- Confederate victory
- Union blockade

Map labels: Lake Superior, Lake Michigan, Lake Huron, L. Ontario, Lake Erie, WI, MI, ME, VT, NH, NY, MA, CT, RI, PA, NJ, New York, IA, IL, IN, OH, MO, KY, WV, MD, DE, Washington, D.C., Frederick, VA, Richmond, Appomattox Court House, TN, AR, MS, AL, GA, SC, NC, LA, FL, Atlantic Ocean, Gulf of Mexico, Mississippi R.

Gettysburg (July 1–3, 1863)
Fredericksburg (Dec. 16, 1862)
Wilderness (May 5–7, 1864)
Spotsylvania Court House (May 8–19, 1864)
Chancellorsville (May 1–4, 1863)
Cold Harbor (June 3, 1864)
Petersburg (June 1864–April 1865)
Chattanooga (Nov. 25, 1863)
Chickamauga (Sept. 19–20, 1863)
Atlanta Campaign (July–Sept., 1864)
Vicksburg (March–July, 1863)
Mobile Bay (Aug. 5, 1864)
Port Hudson (July 8, 1863)
Durham Station
Columbia
Charleston
Savannah
Atlanta
Sherman
Lee

April 9, 1865 Lee surrenders to Grant

April 26, 1865 Johnston surrenders to Sherman

Conic Projection
0 200 400 mi
0 200 400 km

90°W, 80°W, 70°W, 30°N

Economic Costs of the Civil War

- Union costs: $6.1 billion; inflation 80 percent
- Confederate costs: $2 billion; inflation 9,000 percent
- Many southern farms, factories, and railroads were destroyed.
- Southern industry was crippled.
- Confederate states lost two thirds of their wealth.

War Deaths

Civil War Deaths

Troops (in thousands)
0, 100, 200, 300, 400

Union | Confederacy

SOURCE: *Encyclopedia Britannica*

American Deaths in All Wars (estimates)

- Civil War **623,000** — 49.1%
- World War II **407,500** — 32.2%
- World War I **116,500** — 9.2%
- Vietnam War **58,000** — 4.6%
- Korean War **37,000** — 2.9%
- Mexican-American War **13,500** — 1.0%
- American Revolution **4,500** — 0.4%
- Other major wars **8,000** — 0.6%

0.6%

SOURCES: U.S. Military History Institute; Department of Defense

Map Skills

After its momentous defeats in 1863, the Confederacy fought a defensive war until its armies finally surrendered to Union troops.

1. **Locate:** (a) Gettysburg, (b) Petersburg, (c) Atlanta, (d) Appomattox Court House

2. **Regions** Where was most of the fighting concentrated after 1863? Why?

3. **Draw Conclusions** Which side do you think suffered the most as a result of the Civil War? Why?

▲ The Costs of War

The death toll from the Civil War was staggering. More than half a million soldiers died—nearly as many were killed as in all other American wars combined. Additionally, more than 500,000 soldiers were wounded in the fighting. The material devastation of the war would plague the South for decades after its defeat.

relying on northern investment and seeking ways to enter the modern cash economy. For many decades, agriculture would remain at the center of southern economy. Northerners, forgetting Sherman's destruction of southern assets, would often blame the slow recovery on southerners' own shortcomings.

Effects on Society As a result of the war, the southern landscape was in shambles. Many Confederate soldiers returned to find their homes and farms destroyed. Millions of dislocated white southerners drifted aimlessly about the South in late 1865. Defeat had shaken them to the very core of their beliefs. Some felt that they were suffering a divine punishment, with one southerner mourning, "Oh, our God! What sins we must have been guilty of that we should be so humiliated by Thee now!" Others, however, came to view the Civil War as a lost, but noble, cause. These white southerners kept the memory of the struggle alive and believed that, eventually, the South would be redeemed.

African Americans of the South were equally disoriented. But they also had a new sense of hope. Freedom promised them a new life with new opportunities, including a chance to own land and to control their own lives. Some headed west to take advantage of the Homestead Act. Black southerners eagerly joined the migration that would mark American society for many years. However, as Reconstruction began, most African Americans in the South found that freedom was a promise not fully delivered.

Effects on Government and Politics In many ways, the Civil War eased the history of disunity in American political life. While sectional differences remained strong, never again would such differences trigger threats of secession. Instead, over time, the economic, political, and social life of the nation's disparate regions would increasingly intertwine.

Debates over states' rights did not end with the Civil War. Still, the war helped cement federal authority. The government had fought a war to assert that individual states did not have the power to break the national bond forged by the Constitution. Increasingly, the federal government would come to play a larger role in Americans' lives. And more Americans would see themselves as citizens not just of a state but of a united nation.

Monument at Antietam National Battlefield

✔ **Checkpoint** What were some of the lasting effects of the Civil War?

SECTION **5** Assessment

Progress Monitoring *Online*
For: Self-test with vocabulary practice
Web Code: nca-1111

Comprehension

1. **Terms and People** For each of the following items, write a sentence explaining its significance.
   - Thirteenth Amendment
   - John Wilkes Booth
   - Mathew Brady
   - Land Grant College Act

2. **NoteTaking Reading Skill: Recognize Sequence** Use your flowchart to answer the Section Focus Question: What was the final outcome and impact of the Civil War?

Writing About History

3. **Quick Write: Draft a News Article** Outline the news article you would write about the surrender at Appomattox or the assassination of President Lincoln. Then, write the headline and the first two paragraphs.

Critical Thinking

4. **Identify Alternatives** What alternatives did the South face in February 1865? Do you think they made the right choice?

5. **Predict Consequences** What was Lincoln's attitude toward the defeated South? How do you think his death might have affected plans for reuniting the country?

6. **Draw Conclusions** Why do you think a larger percentage of American troops died in the Civil War than in any other American war?

Chapter 11 Section 5 **395**

Quick Study Guide

 2.II.D.2d, 2.II.D.2a

Progress Monitoring *Online*
For: Self-test with vocabulary practice
Web Code: nca-1112

■ Comparing North and South

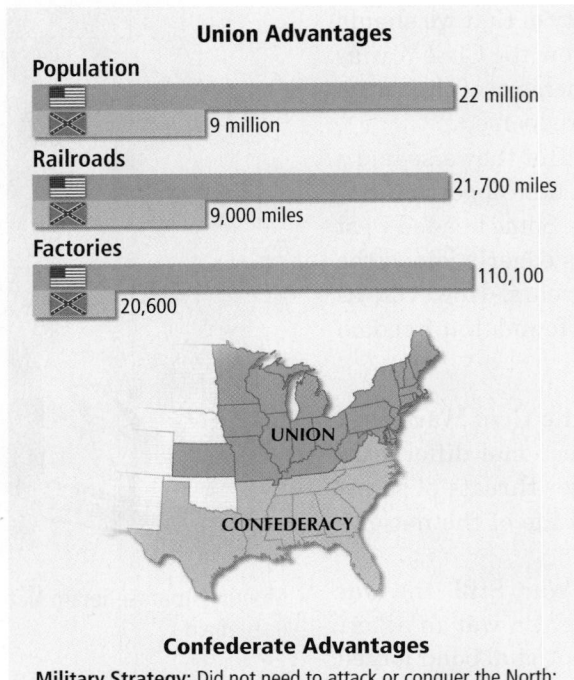

Union Advantages

Population
22 million
9 million

Railroads
21,700 miles
9,000 miles

Factories
110,100
20,600

UNION

CONFEDERACY

Confederate Advantages

Military Strategy: Did not need to attack or conquer the North; had only to avoid defeat in order to win the war

Leadership: Many United States Army officers sided with the South at the outbreak of the war (foremost among them was Robert E. Lee).

Morale: Most white southerners were willing to fight to protect their way of life.

■ Key Battles of the Civil War

Union Victories	Confederate Victories
• Glorieta Pass	• Fort Sumter
• Shiloh	• First Bull Run (First Manassas)
• New Orleans	• Seven Days
• Antietam	• Second Bull Run (Second Manassas)
• Perryville	• Sabine Pass
• Gettysburg	• Fredericksburg
• Vicksburg	• Chancellorsville
• Port Hudson	• Chickamauga
• Chattanooga	• Wilderness
• Atlanta	• Spotsylvania Court House
• Petersburg	• Cold Harbor

■ Extent of the Emancipation Proclamation, 1863

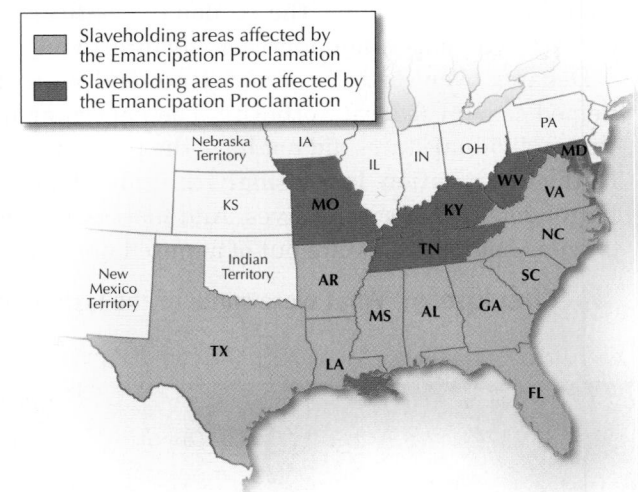

Slaveholding areas affected by the Emancipation Proclamation

Slaveholding areas not affected by the Emancipation Proclamation

☑ Quick Study Timeline

In America

1861
North and South clash at Bull Run

1862
Thousands die at Shiloh

January 1863
Emancipation Proclamation takes effect

Presidential Terms   Abraham Lincoln 1861–1865

1861   1862   18

Around the World

1861
Alexander II emancipates Russian serfs

1862
Victor Hugo publishes *Les Misérables*

1863
Ismail Pasha comes to power in Ottoman Egypt

American Issues
•—•—• Connector

2.II.D.2b

By connecting prior knowledge with what you have learned in this chapter, you can gradually build your understanding of enduring questions that still affect America today. Answer the questions below. Then, use your American Issues Connector study guide (or go online: www.PHSchool.com **Web Code:** nch-7102).

Issues You Learned About

● **Social Problems and Reforms** Initially, the North engaged in the Civil War to prevent the breakup of the United States. Over time, however, the nature of the northern war effort changed to focus more on abolishing slavery.

1. What was the practical effect of the Emancipation Proclamation? What was the emotional effect?

2. What new right was extended to African Americans in the North around the time of the Emancipation Proclamation?

3. Is it likely that the Thirteenth Amendment, ending slavery in the United States, would have passed in 1865 if the Civil War had not been taking place? Explain.

● **Women in American Society** As with previous conflicts and movements in American history, the Civil War encouraged women to assume new responsibilities.

4. What new roles did women take on during the American Revolution?

5. How did women contribute to the antislavery movement in the early nineteenth century?

6. How did the Civil War create new opportunities for women on both sides?

● **Government's Role in the Economy** The federal government may pass new laws in response to the economic impact of a war.

7. What measures did the federal government pass to increase war funds during the Civil War?

8. What was the Homestead Act? How did the Civil War contribute to its passage?

Connect to Your World | New York

Women in American Society Like Clara Barton and other nurses, New Yorker Mary Edwards Walker cared for sick and wounded soldiers during the Civil War. However, Walker was one of very few women to work as a doctor during that time. At the start of the war, she volunteered her services as an unpaid assistant surgeon, becoming the first female surgeon in the U.S. Army. In 1865, she became the first woman to receive the Congressional Medal of Honor for her work during the war. In addition to working as a doctor, Walker was a lifelong advocate of women's rights. Study enrollment patterns for women attending medical school in the 1800s and today; then write an essay comparing opportunities for women in medicine today compared to the 1800s.

July 1863
Union victories at Gettysburg and Vicksburg

1864
Sherman's March to the Sea; Lincoln reelected

1865
Lee surrenders to Grant; Lincoln assassinated

Andrew Johnson 1865–1869

1864   **1865**   **1866**

1864
Chinese government crushes Taiping Rebellion

1865
Joseph Lister founds modern antiseptic surgery

History *Interactive*
For: Interactive timeline
Web Code: ncp-1114

Chapter Assessment

Terms and People

1. Who was **Ulysses S. Grant**? Why was he important to the Union war effort?

2. What was the Battle of **Antietam**? What effect did it have on the North?

3. Define **conscription**. Which members of society did conscription fall most heavily on? Why?

4. Who were the **Copperheads**? Which people were most likely to be Copperheads, and why?

5. What were the siege of **Vicksburg** and the Battle of **Gettysburg**? What effects did they have on the progress of the war?

Focus Questions

The focus question for this chapter is **What were the causes, key events, and effects of the Civil War?** Build an answer to this big question by answering the focus questions for Sections 1 through 5 and the Critical Thinking questions that follow.

Section 1
6. How did each side's resources and strategies affect the early battles of the war?

Section 2
7. How did the Emancipation Proclamation and the efforts of African American soldiers affect the course of the war?

Section 3
8. How did the Civil War bring temporary and lasting changes to American society?

Section 4
9. How did the Battles of Vicksburg and Gettysburg change the course of the Civil War?

Section 5
10. What was the final outcome and impact of the Civil War?

Critical Thinking

11. **Analyze Evidence** Think about Robert E. Lee's reasons for turning down leadership of the Union forces and serving the South instead. What does this tell you about some of the difficulties the Civil War posed for all Americans?

12. **Analyze Information** How did African American soldiers surpass the initial expectations the Union had about them?

13. **Draw Conclusions** What is a possible explanation for Lincoln's refusal to obey the Supreme Court's ruling that only Congress had the right to suspend habeas corpus?

14. **Analyze Photographs** Study the image below of Richmond, Virginia, in 1865. What does the photograph suggest about the needs of the postwar period?

15. **Compare Points of View** How did Lincoln's ideas about the course the nation should take after the Civil War differ from those held by many northerners?

16. **Make Comparisons** Which side experienced more losses in the Civil War, the North or the South? Explain why this was the case.

Writing About History

Write a News Article People on both sides during the Civil War followed the war's events through news reports printed in local newspapers. Imagine that you are a reporter during the Civil War. Decide whether you are reporting from one of the national capitals or are traveling with one of the armies. Choose an event and write an article for your newspaper.

Prewriting
- Gather information about an event that interests you. Make sure you will be able to answer the five *W* questions: *Who? What? Where? When? Why?*
- Consider your audience and remember that a news article is an objective account of events.
- Gather additional information about the event from other sources.

Drafting
- Sort your information and write an outline of the article.
- Write the first paragraph, which should tell the most basic information about what happened.
- Write at least two more paragraphs, filling in further information. Newspaper articles include the least important information last.
- Write a headline that will help readers know what the article will be about.

Revising
- Use the guidelines on page SH11 of the Writing Handbook to revise your essay.

Regents DBQ Practice

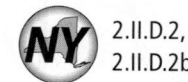
Total War

Union General William Tecumseh Sherman implemented a strategy of total war during his "march to the sea" in 1864. The concept of total war called for expanding military targets to include civilian economic resources. Use your knowledge of the Civil War and Documents 1, 2, 3, and 4 to answer questions 1 through 4.

Document 1

"Sherman's Atlanta campaign in May to September 1864 won the Confederate prize that ensured Lincoln's reelection that year. Sherman ordered a civilian evacuation of Atlanta, burned everything of any military value, and in November headed out of the city on his famous 'march to the sea.' More than any other Civil War commander, Sherman grasped the brutal logic of total war. In such a war, civilian morale and economic resources are as much military targets as the enemy's armies. For Sherman, war unleashed the fury of hell, and he refused to sentimentalize the killing and pillaging required for victory."

—*William L. Barney,* The Reader's Companion to American History

Document 2

CITIZENS OF ATLANTA LEAVING THE CITY IN COMPLIANCE WITH GENERAL SHERMAN'S ORDERS.

"Citizens of Atlanta leaving the City in Compliance With General Sherman's Orders."

Document 3

"Many people on both sides believed that the war would be short—one or two battles and the cowardly Yankees or slovenly rebels would give up. . . . Responsible leaders on both sides did not share the popular faith in a short war. Yet even they could not foresee the kind of conflict this war would become— a total war, requiring total mobilization of men and resources, destroying these men and resources on a massive scale, and ending only with unconditional surrender. In the spring of 1861 most northern leaders thought in terms of a limited war. Their purpose was not to conquer the South but to suppress insurrection and win back the latent loyalty of the southern people. The faith in southern unionism lingered long."

—*James M. McPherson,* Battle Cry of Freedom

Document 4

"William Tecumseh Sherman was considered one of the ablest generals in the Federal army, but he was a cruel one. . . . His celebrated march through Georgia put a stain upon his name that will cling to it as it is found upon the pages of history. . . . With his grand army of veterans, almost unopposed, he had overrun and desolated the fairest sections of the South, burning cities, towns, and country dwellings; had wantonly destroyed many millions of dollars worth of property, both public and private; had made thousands of women and children and aged men homeless and destitute by burning their homes and destroying their means of subsistence. And it was to glorify him for these deeds of barbarism that 'Marching through Georgia' was written, and it is for this that it is sung."

—*Milford Overley,* "What 'Marching Through Georgia' Means"

1. The authors of Documents 1 and 3 define total war as
   (1) total mobilization of men and resources against both military and civilian targets.
   (2) a diplomatic effort aimed at avoiding the outbreak of hostilities.
   (3) a military effort devoted almost entirely against civilian targets.
   (4) a policy for controlling the civilian populations of cities.

2. Which of the documents focuses on southerners reacting to total war?
   (1) Documents 1 and 2
   (2) Documents 2 and 3
   (3) Documents 2 and 4
   (4) Documents 1 and 4

3. According to Document 1, why might Sherman have refused to "sentimentalize" total war?
   (1) He wanted to protect Confederate government property.
   (2) He wanted captured Confederate soldiers to help rebuild war-torn areas.
   (3) He wanted more troops and supplies from Washington.
   (4) He wanted civilian suffering to speed the collapse of the Confederate war effort.

4. **Writing Task** What impact did the military strategy of total war have on the people of the South during the Civil War? Use your knowledge of the war and specific evidence from the primary sources above to support your opinion.

All Is Now Lost

At the end of the Civil War, much of the South was in ruins. As described below by a member of a southern plantation family, all southerners faced not only the reconstruction of their cities and homes, but the reconstruction of the South as a whole. *Listen to the* Witness History *audio to hear more about Reconstruction.*

❝Our losses have been frightful, and we have, now, scarcely a support. My Father had five plantations on the coast, and all the buildings were burnt, and the negroes . . . are roaming in a starving condition. Our farm near Charleston was abandoned. . . . All is now lost, and the negroes, left to themselves . . . seek a little food, about the city. Our Residence in the city, was sacked . . . and the house well riddled by shell & shot. Our handsome Residence in the country was burnt. The Enemy passed over all our property on the coast in their march from Savannah to Charleston, the whole country, down there, is now a howling wilderness. . . . [I]t will be many years, before this once productive country will be able to support itself.❞

—Edward Barnwell Heyward

◄ Young African Americans sitting amid the rubble and ruins of Charleston, South Carolina

Ticket to President Johnson's impeachment trial

A carpetbag suitcase

Lithograph with portraits of African American politicians

NY Core Curriculum Preview

Chapter Focus Question: What lasting consequences arose from the struggles over Reconstruction?

Section 1
Rival Plans for Reconstruction   3.I.A.1, 3.I.A.2, 3.I.C.3, 3.I.C.5

Section 2
Reconstruction in the South   3.I.C.1, 3.I.C.2a, 3.I.C.2b

Section 3
The End of Reconstruction   3.I.C.4, 3.I.D.1, 3.I.D.3

Use the ☑ **Quick Study Timeline** at the end of this chapter to preview chapter events.

Note Taking Study Guide *Online*
For: Note Taking and American Issues Connector
Web Code: nce-7201

Mary Chesnut and her husband, James ▶

WITNESS HISTORY AUDIO

Nothing Left But the Bare Land

Mary Chesnut was the wife of a wealthy and respected South Carolina planter and politician. During the Civil War, her husband resigned from the United States Senate to fight for the Confederacy. Now, at war's end, the family was penniless. The world they had known was gone. Mary Chesnut described the devastation.

66Mrs. Bartow drove me to our house at Mulberry. On one side of the house, every window was broken, every bell torn down, every piece of furniture destroyed, every door smashed in. . . . [The Yankee soldiers] carried off sacks of our books and our papers, our letters were strewed along the Charleston road. Potter's raid ruined us. He burned our mills and gins, and a hundred bales of cotton. Indeed nothing is left now but the bare land.99

—Mary Boykin Chesnut, May 1865

Rival Plans for Reconstruction

Core Curriculum Objectives

- **3.I.A.1** Lincoln's plan for Reconstruction
- **3.I.A.2** Congressional Reconstruction
- **3.I.C.3** Struggle for political control in the New South
- **3.I.C.5** The emerging debate over "proper" role of African Americans

Terms and People

Reconstruction	black code
Radical Republican	Civil Rights Act of 1866
Wade-Davis Bill	Fourteenth Amendment
Freedmen's Bureau	impeach
Andrew Johnson	Fifteenth Amendment

NoteTaking

Reading Skill: Identify Main Ideas Use a chart to record main ideas about Reconstruction.

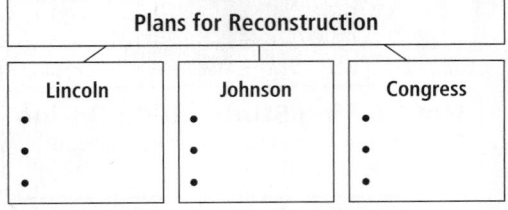

Why It Matters Even before the end of the Civil War, Congress and the President disagreed over how the seceded states would rejoin the Union. When the war ended, bitterness between the North and South was compounded by a power struggle between the executive and legislative branches of government. The issues that arose and how they were dealt with would have consequences for generations to come. **Section Focus Question: How did the Radical Republicans' plans for Reconstruction differ from Lincoln's and Johnson's?**

The Issues of Reconstruction

When the Civil War ended, parts of the South lay in ruins—homes burned, businesses closed, many properties abandoned. African Americans, though emancipated, lacked full citizenship and the means to make a living. During the era of **Reconstruction** (1865–1877), the federal government struggled with how to return the eleven southern states to the Union, rebuild the South's ruined economy, and promote the rights of former slaves.

How Will Southern States Rejoin the Union? To many Americans, the most important issue was deciding the political fate of Confederate states. Should Confederate leaders be tried for treason, or should they be pardoned so that national healing could proceed as quickly as possible? And what should be the process by which southern representatives could reclaim their seats in Congress?

The Constitution provided no guidance on secession or readmission of states. It was not clear whether Congress or the President should take the lead in forming Reconstruction policy. Some argued that states should be allowed to rejoin the Union quickly with few conditions. But many claimed that the defeated states should first satisfy certain <u>stipulations</u>, such as swearing loyalty to the federal government and adopting state constitutions that guaranteed freedmen's rights.

Vocabulary Builder

<u>stipulation</u>–(stihp yuh LAY shuhn) *n.* act of specifying a condition in an agreement

How Will the Southern Economy Be Rebuilt? The Civil War devastated the South's economy. Between 1860 and 1870, the South's share of the nation's total wealth declined from more than 30 percent to 12 percent. The Union army had destroyed factories, plantations, and railroads. Nearly half of the region's livestock and farm machinery were gone. About one fourth of southern white men between the ages of 20 and 40 had died in the war. In addition, more than 3 million newly freed African Americans were now without homes or jobs. After the war, the land was the South's most valuable asset, and arguments raged over who should control it.

During Reconstruction, some people proposed using the land to benefit former slaves. General William Tecumseh Sherman proposed that millions of acres abandoned by planters, or confiscated by the federal government, should be given to former slaves. "Forty acres and a mule," he suggested, would be sufficient to support a family. Many northerners thought this might also be a way to restore the South's productivity, reconstruct its economy, and provide employment as well as income for many African Americans.

Not everyone agreed. Southern landowners rejected the idea that the government could simply give away their land. Many white northerners worried that confiscating property violated the Constitution. Even some southern African Americans felt that the government should pay white southerners for farmland, and then sell it to former slaves on easy terms.

What Rights Will African Americans Have? The Thirteenth Amendment freed African Americans from slavery, but it did not grant them the privileges of full citizenship. The former slaves hoped that they would gain voting rights and access to education, benefits that most northern black people also did not have. Most leaders of the Republican Party, which at the time dominated the federal government, supported programs to extend full citizenship to African Americans. However, most white southerners opposed the idea. They feared it would undermine their own power and status in society.

✔ **Checkpoint** What were three major issues of Reconstruction?

Lincoln Sets a Moderate Course

Even while the war was in progress, Union politicians had debated programs for repairing the nation's political structure and economy. For President Lincoln, one of the first major goals was to reunify the nation.

Ten Percent Plan Offers Leniency Throughout the war, Lincoln had felt some sympathy for the South and hoped that southern states might easily rejoin the Union after the war. To this end, in 1863 he issued a Proclamation of Amnesty and Reconstruction, known as the "Ten Percent Plan." According to its terms, as soon as ten percent of a state's voters took a loyalty oath to the Union, the state could set up a new government. If the state's constitution abolished slavery and provided education for African Americans, the state would regain representation in Congress.

Destruction and Devastation
The destruction of the Richmond, Virginia, rail depot (below) and the many other stations and railroads during the Civil War contributed to the South's devastated economy during Reconstruction. *Why would destroying a region's rail system affect the local economy?*

Freedmen's Bureau

Freedmen's Bureau schools like this one brought new educational opportunities for African Americans. *How old do the students at this school appear to be?*

Vocabulary Builder

compensate–(KAHM puhn sayt) *v.* to make up for

Lincoln was generous in other ways to white southerners. He was willing to grant pardons to former Confederates, and he considered <u>compensating</u> them for lost property. In addition, Lincoln did not require a guarantee of social or political equality for African Americans. He recognized pro-Union governments in Arkansas, Louisiana, and Tennessee even though they denied African Americans the right to vote.

Lincoln took the position that the Union was unbreakable and therefore the southern states had never really left the Union. In his Second Inaugural Address, delivered a month before the war ended, Lincoln promised forgiveness:

> **Primary Source** "With malice toward none, and charity for all, with firmness in the right as God gives us to see the right, let us strive on to finish the work we are in, to bind up the nation's wounds . . . to do all which may achieve and cherish a just and a lasting peace among ourselves and with all nations."
>
> —Lincoln's Second Inaugural Address, March 1865

Radicals Oppose the Ten Percent Plan Members of Lincoln's own party opposed his plan. Led by Representative Thaddeus Stevens and Senator Charles Sumner, these "**Radical Republicans**" in Congress insisted that the Confederates had committed crimes—by enslaving African Americans and by entangling the nation in war.

The Radical Republicans advocated full citizenship, including the right to vote, for African Americans. They favored punishment and harsh terms for the South, and they supported Sherman's plan to confiscate Confederates' land and give farms to freedmen.

Rejecting Lincoln's Ten Percent Plan, Congress passed the **Wade-Davis Bill** in 1864. It required that a majority of a state's prewar voters swear loyalty to the Union before the process of restoration could begin. The bill also demanded guarantees of African American equality. President Lincoln killed this plan with a "pocket veto" by withholding his signature beyond the 10-day deadline at the end of the congressional session.

Government Aids Freedmen One Radical Republican plan did receive the President's support. This was the Bureau of Refugees, Freedmen, and Abandoned Lands, known as the **Freedmen's Bureau.** Created a few weeks before Lincoln's death, its goal was to provide food, clothing, healthcare, and education for both black and white refugees in the South.

The Freedmen's Bureau helped reunite families that had been separated by slavery and war. It negotiated fair labor contracts between former slaves and white landowners. By representing African Americans in the courts, the Bureau also established a precedent that black citizens had legal rights. The Freedmen's Bureau continued its efforts until 1872.

✔ **Checkpoint** How did Lincoln's goals differ from those of the Radical Republicans?

Johnson's Reconstruction Plan

Lincoln was assassinated in April 1865, just weeks after his second inaugural. Lincoln's death thrust his Vice President, **Andrew Johnson,** into the presidency.

Johnson Seeks to Restore the Union Like Lincoln, Johnson wanted to restore the political status of the southern states as quickly as possible. He offered pardons and the restoration of land to almost any Confederate who swore allegiance to the Union and the Constitution. His main requirement was that each state ratify the Thirteenth Amendment and draft a constitution that abolished slavery. However, Johnson resented wealthy planters and required that they and other Confederate leaders write to him personally to apply for a pardon.

Johnson's dislike of the planter class did not translate into a desire to elevate African Americans. Like many southerners, Johnson expected the United States to have a "government for white men." He did not want African Americans to have the vote. In fact, he had little sympathy for their plight. Johnson supported states' rights, which would allow the laws and customs of the state to outweigh federal regulations. States would, therefore, be able to limit the freedoms of former slaves.

By the time Congress reconvened in December 1865, most Confederate states had met Johnson's requirements for readmission. Radical and moderate Republicans were concerned about the lack of African American suffrage, but they remained hopeful that black political rights would soon follow.

Southerners Aim to Restore Old Ways That hope was soon dashed. Beginning with the state conventions required by Johnson, southern leaders proceeded to rebuild their prewar world. Many states specifically limited the vote to white men. Some states sent their Confederate officials to the United States Congress. All of the states instituted **black codes**—laws that sought to limit the rights of African Americans and keep them as landless workers.

The codes required African Americans to work in only a limited number of occupations, most often as servants or farm laborers. Some states prohibited African Americans from owning land, and all set up vagrancy laws. These laws stipulated that any black person who did not have a job could be arrested and sent to work as prison labor. Even though the South remained under Union military occupation, white southerners openly used violence and intimidation to enforce the black codes.

Congress Fights Back Both Radical and moderate Republicans were infuriated by the South's disregard of the spirit of Reconstruction. When the southern representatives arrived in Washington, D.C., Congress refused them their seats. Congress also created a committee to investigate the treatment of former slaves.

Through the spring of 1866, the political situation grew worse. While the Radicals claimed that federal intervention was needed to advance African American political and civil rights, President Johnson accused them of trying "to Africanize the southern half of our country." When Congress passed a bill to allow the Freedmen's Bureau to continue its work and provide it with authority to punish state officials who failed to extend civil rights to African Americans, Johnson vetoed it. Undaunted, Congress sought to overturn the black codes by passing the **Civil Rights Act of 1866.** This measure created federal guarantees of civil rights and superseded any state laws that limited them. But once again, Johnson used his veto power to block the law. Johnson was now openly defying Congress.

✓ **Checkpoint** How did the southern states try to reestablish conditions before the war?

Congressional Reconstruction

As violence against African Americans in the South increased, moderate and Radical Republicans blamed the rising tide of lawlessness on Johnson's lenient policies. Congress then did something unprecedented. With the required two-thirds majority, for the first time ever, it passed major legislation over a President's veto. The Civil Rights Act of 1866 became law.

Decision ● Point

Who Controls the Readmission of States?

Although their main purpose was to reunite the nation, Reconstruction policies actually created new divisions between the President and Congress. A critically divisive issue was how the southern states should be readmitted into the Union.

Johnson Opposes Tight Restrictions

Primary Source

"As eleven States are not at this time represented in either branch of Congress, it would seem to be [the President's] duty on all proper occasions to present their just claims to Congress. . . . [I]f they are all excluded from Congress, if in a permanent statute they are declared not to be in full constitutional relations to the country, they may think they have cause to become a unit in feeling and sentiment against the Government."

—President Andrew Johnson, 1866

Stevens Favors Tight Restrictions

Primary Source

"The late war between two acknowledged belligerents . . . broke all the ties that bound them together. The future condition of the conquered power depends on the will of the conqueror. . . . Hence a law of Congress must be passed before any new State can be admitted. . . . Until then no member can be lawfully admitted into either House. . . . Then each House must judge whether the members . . . possess the requisite qualifications."

—Thaddeus Stevens, 1865

You Decide
1. Why did Johnson favor immediate readmission?
2. Why did Stevens want tight restrictions?
3. What decision would you have made? Why?

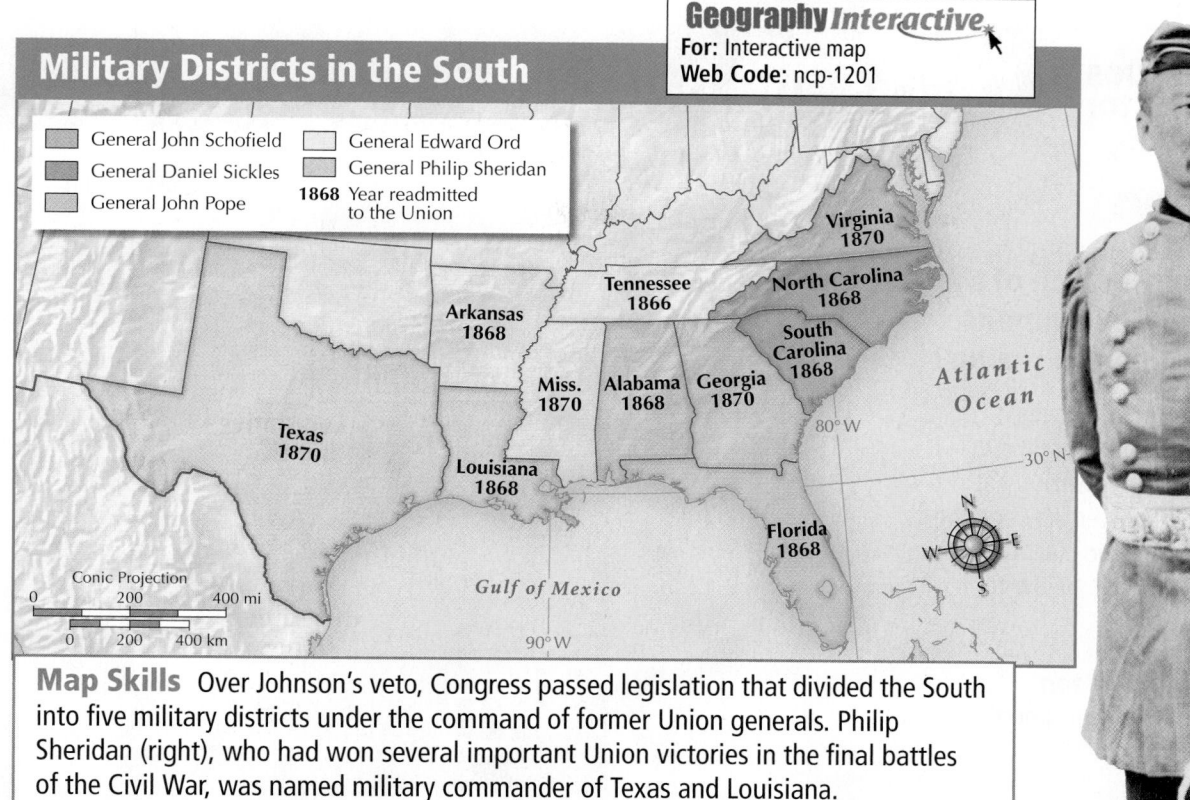

Military Districts in the South

Geography *Interactive*
For: Interactive map
Web Code: ncp-1201

General John Schofield
General Daniel Sickles
General John Pope
General Edward Ord
General Philip Sheridan
1868 Year readmitted to the Union

Virginia 1870
Tennessee 1866
North Carolina 1868
Arkansas 1868
South Carolina 1868
Miss. 1870
Alabama 1868
Georgia 1870
Texas 1870
Louisiana 1868
Florida 1868

Atlantic Ocean
80° W
30° N
Gulf of Mexico
90° W

Conic Projection
0   200   400 mi
0   200   400 km

Map Skills Over Johnson's veto, Congress passed legislation that divided the South into five military districts under the command of former Union generals. Philip Sheridan (right), who had won several important Union victories in the final battles of the Civil War, was named military commander of Texas and Louisiana.
Identify Points of View How do you think southerners felt about military rule by northern generals?

Radical Reconstruction Begins Feeling their strength in Congress, a coalition of Radical and moderate Republicans spent nearly a year designing a sweeping Reconstruction program. To protect freedmen's rights from presidential vetoes, southern state legislatures, and federal court decisions, Congress passed the **Fourteenth Amendment** to the Constitution. It guaranteed equality under the law for all citizens. Under the amendment, any state that refused to allow black people to vote would risk losing the number of seats in the House of Representatives that were represented by its black population. The measure also counteracted the President's pardons by barring leading Confederate officials from holding federal or state offices.

Congress again passed legislation over Johnson's veto with the ratification of the Military Reconstruction Act of 1867. The act divided the 10 southern states that had yet to be readmitted into the Union into five military districts governed by former Union generals (see map above). The act also delineated how each state could create their new state government and receive congressional recognition. In each state, voters were to elect delegates to write a new constitution that guaranteed suffrage for African American men. Then, once the state ratified the Fourteenth Amendment, it could reenter the Union.

Congress Impeaches the President The power struggle between Congress and the President reached a crisis in 1867. To limit the President's power, Congress passed the Tenure of Office Act. Under its terms, the President needed Senate approval to remove certain officials from office. When Johnson tried to fire Secretary of War Edwin Stanton, the last Radical Republican in his Cabinet, Stanton barricaded himself in his office for about two months.

Angrily, the House of Representatives voted to **impeach** Johnson, that is, to charge him with wrongdoing in office, for trying to fire Stanton. The trial in the

American Issues Connector

Checks and Balances

NY 2.I.D

TRACK THE ISSUE

? Does any branch of the federal government have too much power?

Our system of checks and balances is meant to prevent any branch of government from becoming too powerful. Yet at times the balance of power between the executive, legislative, and judicial branches has shifted. Use the timeline below to explore this enduring issue.

1803 *Marbury* v. *Madison*
John Marshall affirms Supreme Court's right of judicial review.

1830s Jackson Presidency
Andrew Jackson increases executive power.

1868 Johnson Impeachment
Congress tries to remove President Andrew Johnson from office.

1930s New Deal
Franklin D. Roosevelt boosts presidential power to fight the depression.

1960s Warren Court
Supreme Court under Earl Warren becomes a force for social reform.

1973 War Powers Act
Congress limits the President's power to wage war.

2000s War on Terrorism
Congress increases executive branch powers to combat terrorism.

Ticket to Andrew Johnson's trial

◄ **Judicial Branch**

▲ **Legislative Branch**

◄ **Executive Branch**

DEBATE THE ISSUE

Imbalance of Power? During the administration of President George W. Bush, much debate focused on the relative powers of the President and Congress.

"I do have the view that over the years there had been an erosion of presidential power. . . . I served in the Congress for 10 years. I've got enormous regard for the other body . . . but . . . the President of the United States needs to have his constitutional powers unimpaired, if you will, in terms of the conduct of national security policy."
—Vice President Richard Cheney, December 20, 2005

"During the early years of the post–World War II era, power was relatively well-balanced . . . but major shifts . . . have made Congress much weaker and the President dangerously stronger. . . . The Bush presidency has attained a level of power over Congress that undermines sound democratic governance."
—Walter Williams, *Seattle Times*, May 2004

? TRANSFER Activities

1. **Compare** When does Vice President Cheney feel the President should have more power? Why would Walter Williams disagree?

2. **Analyze** How did the administration of President Andrew Johnson reflect a similar power struggle?

3. **Transfer** Use the following Web site to see a video, try a WebQuest, and write in your journal. **Web Code:** neh-7202

Senate lasted through the spring of 1868. In the end, the Radicals failed—by only one vote—to win the two-thirds majority necessary in the Senate to remove Johnson from office. Several moderate Republicans backed away from conviction. They felt that using impeachment to get rid of a President who disagreed with Congress would upset the balance of power in the government. During his impeachment trial, Johnson had promised to enforce the Reconstruction Acts. In his remaining time in office, he kept that promise.

The Fifteenth Amendment Extends Suffrage In 1868, the Republican candidate, former Union general, Ulysses S. Grant was elected President. Although he won the electoral vote by a huge margin and had a significant lead in the popular vote, his opponent, Horatio Seymour, a Democrat from New York, received a majority of the white vote. Republican leaders now had another reason for securing a constitutional amendment that would guarantee black suffrage throughout the nation.

In 1869, Congress passed the **Fifteenth Amendment** forbidding any state from denying suffrage on the grounds of race, color, or previous condition of servitude. Unlike previous measures, this guarantee applied to northern states as well as southern states. Both the Fourteenth and Fifteenth amendments were ratified by 1870, but both contained loopholes that left room for evasion. States could still impose voting restrictions based on literacy or property qualifications, which in effect would exclude most African Americans. Soon the southern states would do just that.

Major Reconstruction Legislation, 1865–1870	☑ Quick Study

Legislation	Provisions
Freedmen's Bureau Acts (1865–1866)	Create a government agency to provide services to freed slaves and war victims
Civil Rights Act of 1866	Grants citizenship to African Americans and outlaws black codes
Reconstruction Act of 1867	Divides former Confederacy into military districts
Fourteenth Amendment (1868)	Guarantees citizenship to African Americans and prohibits states from passing laws to take away a citizen's rights
Fifteenth Amendment (1870)	States that no citizen can be denied the right to vote because of "race, color, or previous condition of servitude"
Enforcement Act of 1870	Protects voting rights by making intimidation of voters a federal crime

✔️ **Checkpoint** How did the Fourteenth and Fifteenth amendments extend the rights of African Americans?

Progress Monitoring *Online*
For: Self-test with vocabulary practice
Web Code: nca-1201

Comprehension

1. **Terms and People** For each item below, write a sentence explaining its significance:
   - Reconstruction
   - Radical Republican
   - Wade-Davis Bill
   - Freedmen's Bureau
   - Andrew Johnson
   - black code
   - Civil Rights Act of 1866
   - Fourteenth Amendment
   - impeach
   - Fifteenth Amendment

2. **NoteTaking Reading Skill: Identify Main Ideas** Use your chart to answer the Section Focus Question: How did the Radical Republicans' plans for Reconstruction differ from Lincoln's and Johnson's?

Writing About History

3. **Quick Write: Identify Audience and Purpose** Write a letter to your constituents about the passage of the Civil Rights Acts as if you were Thaddeus Stevens. Before you begin, consider your audience and the purpose of your letter—information, persuasion, or explanation.

Critical Thinking

4. **Predict Consequences** Why was Reconstruction of the South likely to be a difficult process?

5. **Draw Conclusions** Why do you think President Lincoln proposed generous terms for Reconstruction in 1863?

6. **Analyze Information** How did the Radical Republicans try to protect the rights of African Americans?

▲ Freedmen line up to vote.
◄ Portrait of Senator Hiram Revels

WITNESS HISTORY 🔊 AUDIO

An African American in the Senate

In 1861, Jefferson Davis left his seat in the U.S. Senate and became President of the Confederacy. In 1870, his unfinished term was resumed by Hiram Revels—an African American. A few months later, Senator Revels stood up to make his first speech. He answered those who charged that African Americans in the South were using their new political power to seek revenge on white southerners:

❝As the recognized representative of my downtrodden people, I deny the charge. . . . They bear toward their former masters no revengeful thoughts, no hatreds, no animosities. They aim not to elevate themselves by sacrificing one single interest of their white fellow-citizens. They ask but the rights which are theirs by God's universal law. . . . [to] enjoy the liberties of citizenship on the same footing with their white neighbors and friends.❞

—Hiram Revels, speech in the U.S. Senate, March 16, 1870

Reconstruction in the South

 Core Curriculum Objectives

- **3.I.C.1** Agriculture: land and labor (sharecropping and tenant farming)
- **3.I.C.2a** Status of freedmen: Economic, political, social, and educational experiences
- **3.I.C.2b** Status of freedmen: From exclusion to segregation

Terms and People

scalawag
carpetbagger
segregation
integration
sharecropping

share-tenancy
tenant farming
Ku Klux Klan
Enforcement Acts

NoteTaking

Reading Skill: Identify Main Ideas Use a chart like the one below to record details about changes in the South during Reconstruction.

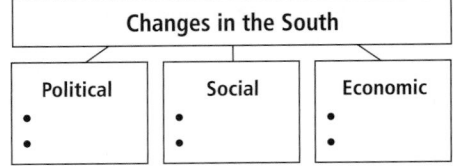

Changes in the South		
Political	**Social**	**Economic**
•	•	•
•	•	•

Why It Matters Before the Civil War, a limited number of powerful men had controlled the South. In the wake of the war, a very basic question needed to be resolved. Who would gain power and how would they use it? How this question was answered at the time would have both immediate and lasting consequences. **Section Focus Question: What were the immediate effects of Reconstruction?**

Republican Governments Bring Change

By 1870, all of the former Confederate states had met the requirements under Radical Reconstruction and rejoined the Union. Republicans dominated their newly established state governments.

African Americans Use Political Power Almost 1,500 black men—some born free, some recently released from slavery—helped usher the Republican Party into the South. These new black citizens served the South as school superintendents, sheriffs, mayors, coroners, police chiefs, and representatives in state legislatures. Six served as lieutenant governors. Two state legislatures—in Mississippi and South Carolina—had black Speakers of the House. Between 1870 and 1877, two African American senators and fourteen African American congressmen served in the United States Congress.

Most importantly, millions of southern African American men were now voters. Since the Radical Republicans required a loyalty oath, many white southerners were not eligible to vote, or chose to stay away from the constitutional conventions and from the elections that followed. Black men, however, quickly signed up to use their new right of suffrage. Thus, by 1868, many southern states had both African American elected officials and a strong Republican Party. Ironically, South Carolina—the state that had ignited the Civil War—became the one state where a black majority ruled the legislature, although only for a short time.

Scalawags and Carpetbaggers Take Part in Southern Politics

The Republican Party attracted not only black southerners but also others who sought change and challenge. **Scalawags,** as southern white critics called them, were white men who had been locked out of pre–Civil War politics by their wealthier neighbors. The new Republican Party invited them in.

Scalawags found allies in northern white or black men who relocated to the South. These northerners came seeking to improve their economic or political situations, or to help make a better life for freedmen. Many southern white people resented what they felt was the invasion of opportunists, come to make their fortunes from the South's misfortune. Southerners labeled the newcomers **"carpetbaggers,"** after the inexpensive carpet-cloth suitcases often carried by northerners.

For carpetbaggers, the opportunities in the new South were as abundant as those in the western frontier: new land to be bought, new careers to be shaped. The progress of Blanche K. Bruce presents an example. Born a slave in Virginia, Bruce learned to read from his owner's son. When the war began, Bruce left the plantation and moved to Missouri, where he ran a school for black children for a short time before moving on to Oberlin College in Ohio. In 1866, Bruce—now 25 years old—went south to Mississippi, where he became a prosperous landowner and was elected to several local political positions. In 1874, in his mid-thirties, Bruce was elected to the United States Senate.

Bruce's story highlights several characteristics of the carpetbaggers. First, they were often young. Second, since only the wealthy minority of white southerners were literate, a northerner with even a basic education had a real advantage. Finally, for African Americans, the South was the only place to pursue a political career. Even though the Fifteenth Amendment established suffrage nationally, no black congressman was elected from the North until the twentieth century.

Successes and Failures Result

On the other hand, the Republican Party did not support women's suffrage, arguing that they could not rally national support behind the essential goal of black suffrage if they tried to include women too. Even so, the Reconstruction South offered northern women—white and black—opportunities that they could not pursue at home. In medical facilities, orphanages, and other relief agencies, single women carved out new roles and envisioned new horizons. They also participated in

Analyzing Political Cartoons

The Burden of Reconstruction This cartoon appeared in a northern newspaper in the 1870s.

A President Grant

B Union soldiers

C the South

1. What do the weapons and soldiers in the cartoon represent?
2. What is the woman doing? Is her task easy or difficult?
3. What is this cartoonist's view of Reconstruction?

what was the most enduring development of the new South—the shaping of a public school system.

Mandated by Reconstruction state constitutions, public schools grew slowly, drawing in only about half of southern children by the end of the 1870s. Establishing a new school system was expensive. This was especially so since southerners opted for **segregation,** or separation of the races. Operating two school systems—one white, one black—severely strained the southern economy. A few of the most radical white Republicans suggested **integration**—combining the schools—but the idea was unpopular with most Republicans. <u>Nevertheless</u>, the beginning of a tax-supported public school system was a major Reconstruction success.

Despite these successes, the South still faced many challenges. Many southerners remained illiterate. The quality of medical care, housing, and economic production lagged far behind the North and, in some cases, behind the newly settled West. Legal protection for African Americans was limited, and racial violence remained a problem until well into the twentieth century.

A new reality was sweeping the country. Political offices, which were once an honor bestowed upon a community's successful business people, were becoming a route to wealth and power rather than a result of these attributes. However, conditions in the South were not unlike the rest of the country in that respect. Ambitious people everywhere were willing to bribe politicians in order to gain access to attractive loans or contracts.

Some of the most attractive arenas for corruption involved the developing railroads. Republicans were the party of African American freedom, but they were also the party of aggressive economic development. Building railroads had two big advantages. First, the construction of tracks and rail cars created jobs. Second, the rail lines would provide the means to carry produce and industrial goods to expanded markets. Hence, in many states across the nation, legislatures gave public land or lent taxpayers' money to railroad speculators.

In some cases, the speculators delivered on their promises and repaid the loans. But southern leaders, who had fewer resources and less financial expertise than their northern peers, found that a good number of their loans were stolen or mismanaged. Though northern white speculators defaulted, too, many Americans used these examples to argue that southern black politicians were dishonest or incompetent.

Vocabulary Builder
<u>nevertheless</u>–(nehv uhr thuh LEHS) *adv.* in spite of

Rebuilding the South

After the Civil War, the South faced the challenge of rebuilding. Some of its most important cities lay in ruins. *What evidence of rebuilding can you see in this photograph?*

✔ **Checkpoint** What new groups were active in politics under Republican governments?

Freed People Build New Communities

For newly freed African Americans, the importance of such issues as public corruption was matched by the importance of trying to work out new social institutions and economic relationships. Some freedmen deliberately moved away from the plantation, even if the owner had been a generous person. As one minister put it, "As long as the shadow of the great house falls across you, you ain't going to feel like no free man and no free woman."

Work and Family For the first time, many African American men and women could legalize and celebrate their marriages, create homes for their families, and make choices about where they would reside (though these choices were restricted by black codes limiting what work they might do). Life presented new problems and opportunities.

> **Primary Source** "I stayed on [the plantation] 'cause I didn't have no place to go. . . . Den I starts to feeling like I ain't treated right. So one night I just put that new dress in a bundle and set foot right down the big road, a-walking west!"
> —Mary Lindsey, age 19

Many African Americans headed for southern cities, where they could develop churches, schools, and other social institutions. They also hoped to find work. Skilled men might find work as carpenters, blacksmiths, cooks, or house servants; women took in laundry, or did child care or domestic work. However, most often, black workers had to settle for what they had had under slavery: substandard housing and poor food, in return for hard labor.

African American Farmers
Although some African Americans moved to southern cities after the Civil War, many remained in rural areas. *How do you think the lives of these freed African Americans compared to their lives during slavery?*

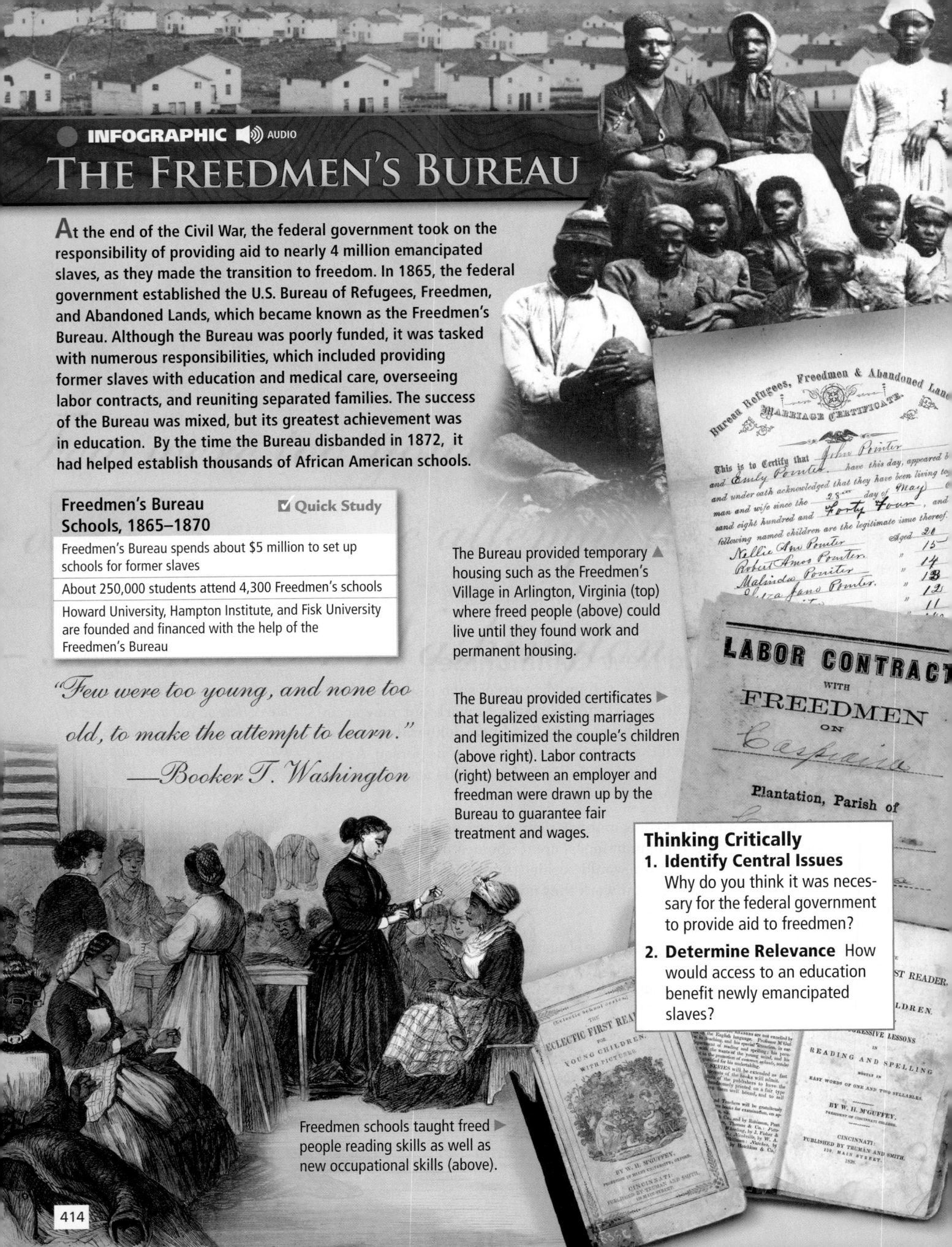

THE FREEDMEN'S BUREAU

At the end of the Civil War, the federal government took on the responsibility of providing aid to nearly 4 million emancipated slaves, as they made the transition to freedom. In 1865, the federal government established the U.S. Bureau of Refugees, Freedmen, and Abandoned Lands, which became known as the Freedmen's Bureau. Although the Bureau was poorly funded, it was tasked with numerous responsibilities, which included providing former slaves with education and medical care, overseeing labor contracts, and reuniting separated families. The success of the Bureau was mixed, but its greatest achievement was in education. By the time the Bureau disbanded in 1872, it had helped establish thousands of African American schools.

Freedmen's Bureau Schools, 1865–1870   ☑ Quick Study

Freedmen's Bureau spends about $5 million to set up schools for former slaves

About 250,000 students attend 4,300 Freedmen's schools

Howard University, Hampton Institute, and Fisk University are founded and financed with the help of the Freedmen's Bureau

"Few were too young, and none too old, to make the attempt to learn."
—*Booker T. Washington*

The Bureau provided temporary ▲ housing such as the Freedmen's Village in Arlington, Virginia (top) where freed people (above) could live until they found work and permanent housing.

The Bureau provided certificates ▶ that legalized existing marriages and legitimized the couple's children (above right). Labor contracts (right) between an employer and freedman were drawn up by the Bureau to guarantee fair treatment and wages.

Thinking Critically

1. **Identify Central Issues** Why do you think it was necessary for the federal government to provide aid to freedmen?

2. **Determine Relevance** How would access to an education benefit newly emancipated slaves?

Freedmen schools taught freed ▶ people reading skills as well as new occupational skills (above).

The majority of African American families remained in rural areas. There, they labored in such occupations as lumbering, railroad building, or farming land for landowners—white or black—who themselves were often poor.

Schools and Churches Freed people immediately realized the intrinsic value of learning to read and perform basic arithmetic. Only in this way could they vote wisely and protect themselves from being cheated. So the Freedmen's Bureau schools filled quickly. By 1866, there were as many as 150,000 African American students—adults and children—acquiring basic literacy. Three years later, that number had doubled. Tuition amounted to 10 percent of a laborer's wage, but attendance at Freedmen's schools represented a firm commitment to education.

Vocabulary Builder
intrinsic–(ihn TRIHN sihk) *adj.*
basic; essential

In addition to establishing its own schools, the Freedmen's Bureau aided black colleges. It also encouraged the many northern churches and charitable organizations that sent teachers, books, and supplies to support independent schools. Mostly these schools taught the basics of reading, writing, and math, but they also taught life skills such as health and nutrition, or how to look for a job.

The black church was an important component of Reconstruction education. Under slavery, slave owners sometimes allowed their slaves to hold their own religious services. Now, with freedom, black churches were established throughout the South and often served as school sites, community centers, employment agencies, and political rallying points. By providing an arena for organizing, public speaking, and group planning, churches helped develop African American leaders. A considerable number of African American politicians began their careers as ministers.

✔ **Checkpoint** Why were schools and churches important to freed people?

Remaking the Southern Economy

Many of the South's problems resulted from the uneven distribution of land. As an agricultural region, the South's wealth was defined by landownership. Yet, in 1860, the wealthiest 5 percent of white southerners owned almost half the region's land. Relatively few people held the rest of the land. In fact, more than 90 percent of southern land was owned by only 50 percent of the people. This meant that even before the war, the South had a large number of white citizens with little or no land. After the war, the millions of landless southern white people were competing with millions of landless black people for work as farm laborers on the land of others.

The plan developed by General Sherman and the Radical Republicans to give or sell land to freed people did not provide a solution. Congress had no interest in Thaddeus Stevens's radical suggestion that large plantations be confiscated from once-wealthy planters and redistributed to freedmen. A few African American men, however, were able to gather together the means to buy land. By 1880, about 7 percent of the South's land was owned by African Americans.

Systems For Sharing the Land Even large land owners had no money to purchase supplies or pay workers. As a result, many southerners adopted one of three arrangements: sharecropping, share-tenancy, or tenant-farming.

The first two of these systems could be carried out without cash. Under the **sharecropping** system, which embraced most of the South's black and white poor, a landowner dictated the crop and provided the sharecropper with a place to live, as well as seeds and tools, in return for a "share" of the harvested crop. The landowner often bought these supplies on credit, at very high interest, from a supplier. The landlord passed on these costs to the sharecropper. Hence, sharecroppers were perpetually in debt to the landowner, and the landowner was always in debt to the supplier.

One problem with this system was that most landlords, remembering the huge profits from prewar cotton, chose to invest in this crop again. Dishonest landowners could lie about the cost of supplies devaluing the sharecropper's harvest that now amounted to less than the season's expenses. Thus the sharecropper could never move, because he always owed the owner the labor for next year's crop.

Share-tenancy was much like sharecropping, except that the farmworker chose what crop he would plant and bought his own supplies. Then, he gave a share of the crop to the landowner. In this system, the farmworker had a bit more control over the cost of supplies. Therefore, he might be able to grow a variety of crops or use some of the land to grow food for his family. With these choices, it became more possible to save money.

Tenant Farmers The most independent arrangement for both farmer and landowner was a system known as **tenant farming.** In this case, the tenant paid cash rent to a landowner and then was free to choose and manage his own crop—and free to choose where he would live. This system was only viable for a farmer who had good money-management skills—and some good luck.

✓ **Checkpoint** What arrangements allowed landless people to farm?

Violence Undermines Reform Efforts

The struggle to make a living in a region devastated by war led to fierce economic competition. Economic uncertainty in turn fueled the fire of white southerners' outrage. Already resentful of the Republican takeover of local politics and of occupation by federal troops, white southerners from all economic classes were united in their insistence that African Americans not have full citizenship.

The Sharecropping System

In theory, sharecropping provided an opportunity for poor, landless freedmen and white southerners to save money to purchase their own land. However, as the chart at right illustrates, sharecropping proved to be an endless cycle of debt and poverty that southern farmers could rarely escape. As agriculture was key to the southern economy, the sharecropping system remained a major source of labor until the 1940s when mechanized farming reduced the need for human laborers.

Why was the sharecropping system considered an endless cycle for southern farmers?

◀ Cotton was the primary crop of sharecroppers.

Sharecropping Cycle of Poverty

1 Landowner provides land, seed, and tools to sharecropper in exchange for a large share of the harvested crop.

2 Sharecropper purchases supplies from landowner's store on credit, often at high interest rates.

3 Sharecropper plants and harvests the crop.

4 Landowner sells the crop and takes the predetermined share. The sharecropper's portion of the crop is worth less than the amount owed to the landowner.

5 Sharecropper must promise the landowner a larger share of the next year's crop and becomes trapped in a cycle of debt.

The Ku Klux Klan Strikes Back The more progress African Americans made, the more hostile white southerners became as they tried to keep freedmen in a subservient role. During Reconstruction, dozens of loosely organized groups of white southerners emerged to terrorize African Americans. The best known of these was the **Ku Klux Klan,** formed in Tennessee in 1866. Klan members roamed the countryside, especially at night, burning homes, schools, and churches, and beating, maiming, or killing African Americans and their white allies. Dressed in white robes and hoods, mounted on horses with hooves thundering through the woods, these gangs aimed to scare freed people away from voting.

The Klan took special aim at the symbols of black freedom: African American teachers and schools, churches and ministers, politicians, and anyone—white or black—who encouraged black people to vote. Unfortunately, often their tactics succeeded. In many rural counties, African American voters were too intimidated to go out to the polls.

The Federal Government Responds Racial violence grew even more widespread, in the North as well as in the South, after the Fifteenth Amendment guaranteed all American men the right to vote. In Arkansas, Republican legislators were murdered. In New Orleans, riots broke out. One freed woman from South Carolina reported that the Klan killed her husband, a sharecropper on the land of one Mr. Jones. The widow explained that Klan members were incensed because Mr. Jones had had "poor white folks on the land, and he [evicted them], and put all these blacks on the premises."

The United States Congress took action, passing **Enforcement Acts** (also known as Ku Klux Klan Acts) in 1870 and 1871. The acts made it a federal offense to interfere with a citizen's right to vote. Congress also held hearings inviting black politicians and other observers to describe the situation in the South. George Ruby of Texas told how he had been dragged into the woods and beaten

NoteTaking

Reading Skill: Identify Cause and Effect Use a chart like the one below to summarize the causes and effects of the Enforcement Acts.

Cause	Event	Effect
•	• Congress passes Enforcement Acts	•

To ensure a large harvest, sharecroppers ▶ used every inch of land to farm.

Percentage of sharecropped farms (by county)
- 0%–20%
- 21%–34%
- 35%–80%

Conic Projection
0   100   200 mi
0   100 200 km

VIRGINIA

TENNESSEE

NORTH CAROLINA

ARKANSAS

SOUTH CAROLINA

MISS.

ALABAMA

GEORGIA

TEXAS

LOUISIANA

Atlantic Ocean

FLORIDA

Gulf of Mexico

95° W   85° W

because he had opened a school in Louisiana. Emanuel Fortune, one of Florida's political organizers, reported that his "life was in danger at all times" because he was "a leading man in politics."

Racial violence at the polls was not limited to the South. In the 1870 election in Philadelphia, a company of marines was sent in to protect African American voters. When no such protection was supplied for the 1871 elections, an African American teacher, Octavius Catto, was killed in antiblack political riots. At a protest meeting that followed, one African American Philadelphian spoke out:

Primary Source ❝The Ku Klux of the South are not by any means the lower classes of society. The same may be said of the Ku Klux of the North. . . . Let no man think that we ask for people's pity or commiseration. What we do ask is fairness and equal opportunities in the battle of life.❞

—Isaiah Wears, 1871

Klan Spreads Terror
Ku Klux Klan members dressed in costumes to hide their identities. They used terror tactics to intimidate African Americans and their supporters, such as leaving miniature coffins as warnings.

Congress used the Ku Klux Klan Acts to indict hundreds of Klansmen throughout the South. After 1872, on account of the federal government's readiness to use legal action, there was a decline in violence against Republicans and African Americans. The hatred may have been contained, but it was far from extinguished. Smoldering beneath the surface, it would flare up in the coming decades.

✔ **Checkpoint** How did the federal government react to racial violence?

SECTION **2 Assessment**

Progress Monitoring *Online*
For: Self-test with vocabulary practice
Web Code: nca-1202

Comprehension

1. **Terms and People** For each of the following terms, write a sentence explaining its significance.
   - scalawag
   - carpetbagger
   - segregation
   - integration
   - sharecropping
   - share-tenancy
   - tenant farming
   - Ku Klux Klan
   - Enforcement Acts

2. **NoteTaking Reading Skill: Identify Main Ideas** Use your chart to answer the Section Focus Question: What were the immediate effects of Reconstruction?

Writing About History

3. **Quick Write: Write a Complaint Letter** Write to your supplier after a poor harvest as if you were a southern landowner during Reconstruction. Explain why you will have a problem paying for the supplies you bought at the beginning of the season.

Critical Thinking

4. **Analyze Information** How did Republican governments provide new opportunities in the South?

5. **Make Generalizations** How did social and economic life change for freed people?

6. **Summarize** Why did racial violence increase after 1870? How did the federal government respond?

▲ Wade Hampton

WITNESS HISTORY AUDIO

A Stormy Election

Wade Hampton was an old southern aristocrat from a long line of cotton planters and had been a Confederate general during the Civil War. In short, he was exactly the sort of man that Radical Republicans did not want to see in power.

In 1876, Hampton ran for governor of South Carolina. Across the state, huge crowds cheered his fiery speeches denouncing the carpetbaggers and scalawags who controlled the state government. Hampton won the election by a wide margin. But Radical Republicans charged fraud and refused to leave office. For four months, while federal troops barred Hampton from the statehouse, South Carolina had two separate governments. Not until the troops were withdrawn did Hampton take full possession of his office. The stormy election proved to be one of the last stands for Radical Republicans in the South.

The End of Reconstruction

NY **Core Curriculum Objectives**

- **3.I.C.4** Supreme Court interpretations of the 13th and 14th amendments
- **3.I.D.1** End of Reconstruction: Disputed election of 1876
- **3.I.D.3** Abridgment of rights of freed African Americans

Terms and People
Redeemer
Rutherford B. Hayes
Compromise of 1877

NoteTaking

Reading Skill: Identify Main Ideas Use a chart like the one below to record main ideas about the factors that led to the end of Reconstruction.

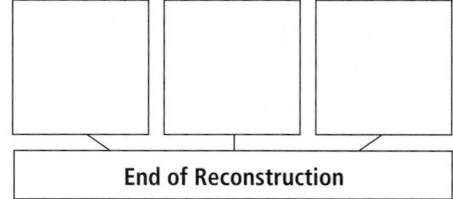

End of Reconstruction

Why It Matters In the end, most northerners came to realize what southerners already knew. The rebuilding of the politics, economy, and society of the South would not be easy, nor would it happen quickly. As reformers lost their resolve, old prejudices took new shapes. It would take generations of striving before some issues were resolved. **Section Focus Question: How and why did Reconstruction end?**

The Nation Considers Other Matters

By 1872, the nation had been focusing its energies on regional strife for almost two decades. Meanwhile, other social, political, and economic issues cried out for attention. European immigration had swelled the population in the North and West. Corruption and intrigue had become part of city politics. As new technologies spurred the growth of industry and provided new opportunities for huge profits, they also provided opportunities for major corruption.

Corruption Plagues Grant's Administration Ulysses S. Grant was a popular war hero but a disappointing President. Allied with the Radical Republicans, he promised to take a strong stand against southern resistance to Reconstruction. But Grant's ability to lead was marred by scandal. He gave high-level advisory posts to untrustworthy friends and acquaintances who used their positions

INFOGRAPHIC The Power of the Political Cartoon

Thomas Nast (1840–1902) (right) is considered by some to be the father of the American political cartoon. Through his drawings he attacked the major political and social issues of the post-Civil War period, including corruption, economic crisis, and inequality. Initially, political cartoons were drawn using the likeness of the subjects. However, Nast built on his skills of caricature and used this art form to clearly illustrate the intent of his imagery. In addition to his style, Nast's influence is still reflected in the political cartoons of today, as he is credited with popularizing such national symbols as the Democratic donkey, the Republican elephant, and Uncle Sam.

◄ "The Brains" 1871
Corruption in local and national government was a major problem during the 1870s. This drawing of New York City's Boss Tweed clearly communicates the issue. Tweed feared the power of Nast's drawings and attempted to bribe him to stop. In the end, Nast's cartoons were credited with Tweed's downfall.

Reconstruction Falters
- Economic problems divert attention.
- Corruption weakens federal and state government.
- Supreme Court decisions undermine African American freedoms.
- Democrats regain control of southern states.

to line their own pockets. His own Vice President, Schuyler Colfax, was investigated and implicated in a scheme to steal profits from the Union Pacific Railroad. A plan by railroad developer and financier Jay Gould to corner the gold market actually included President Grant's brother-in-law.

When Grant ran for reelection in 1872, some reform-minded Republicans withdrew their support and teamed up with some Democrats to create the Liberal Republican Party. The Liberal Republicans advocated civil service reform, removal of the army from the South, and an end to corruption in southern and national governments. Grant easily defeated their presidential candidate, the *New York Tribune* editor, Horace Greeley.

Not long after the election, however, Americans sensed the aura of greed surrounding American politics. When scandal swirled around the members of his administration including his private secretary, the Secretary of War, and members of Congress, Grant seemed to look the other way. Even though he had stated, "Let no guilty man escape," he seemed to lack the will to root out this corruption. Confidence in public officials plummeted.

Across the nation, local scandals came to light. Many city officials sold lucrative public construction contracts to their friends or diverted money from city accounts. The most notorious of these scandals involved a band of New York City Democratic politicians led by state senator William "Boss" Tweed. The "Tweed Ring," as it came to be known, plundered millions of dollars from the city's treasury. By 1873, when Tweed was convicted and sentenced to prison, the public's confidence in its leaders was at a low ebb.

"Worse Than Slavery" 1874 ▶
Nast was an advocate of black civil rights and drew many cartoons addressing the issue. Here he attacks the intolerable treatment of African Americans by Southern white supremacist groups.

◀ **"Out of the Ruins" 1873**
At the end of Reconstruction, the nation's economy was very unstable. Eventually, the many financial and industrial bankruptcies led to the Panic of 1873. In this cartoon, Nast illustrates the nation's financial crisis while alluding to a hopeful future.

Thinking Critically
1. **Draw Conclusions** Why do you think a cartoon such as "The Brains" would inspire fear in a political figure?
2. **Make Comparisons** How are the Nast cartoons similar to the political cartoons of today? How are they different?

History Interactive
For: To learn more about political cartoons
Web Code: ncp-1204

Economic Panic Leads to Depression The public's discontent was worsened by economic turmoil and uncertainty. In the fall of 1873, one of the nation's most influential banks failed, apparently as a result of overextended loans to the expanding railroad industry. Suddenly, the southern economy was not the only one in trouble.

Across the nation, bank failures, job losses, and the uncertain economy added to the array of concerns that preoccupied northerners. The stamina necessary to keep pressure on the South waned.

✓ **Checkpoint** Why did the public lose confidence in government?

Why Did Reconstruction End?

The end of Reconstruction did not come suddenly. However, ever since the Radical Republicans failed to convict President Johnson, their power and crusading zeal had faded.

Northern Support Evaporates As the 1860s ended, voters and politicians outside the South increasingly turned their attention to other pressing issues—reforming politics and the economy, among other things. Also, the continued cost of military operations in the South worried many. Gradually and quietly, beginning in 1871, troops were withdrawn from the South. In 1872, the Freedmen's Bureau was dissolved.

Vocabulary Builder
transition–(tran ZIHSH uhn) *n.*
process of moving from one stage
to another

The death of Radical Republican leader Charles Sumner in 1874 also symbolized an important <u>transition</u>. A generation of white reformers, forged by abolitionist fervor and anxious to carry that passion into the national politics of Reconstruction, had passed away. Without such leaders to temper it, northern racial prejudice reemerged.

Supreme Court Decisions Impede Equality

Vocabulary Builder
scope–(skohp) *n.* range covered by
a subject

The Thirteenth, Fourteenth, and Fifteenth amendments guaranteed African Americans' rights. Yet it was left to the courts to interpret how these new amendments would be applied.

In a series of landmark cases, the Supreme Court chipped away at African American freedoms in the 1870s. In what became known as the *Slaughterhouse Cases* (1873), the Court restricted the <u>scope</u> of the Fourteenth Amendment. It concluded that though a citizen had certain national rights, the federal government would have no control over how a state chose to define rights for the citizens who resided there. Three years later, the Supreme Court heard the case of *United States* v. *Cruikshank*. This case involved a white mob in Louisiana who had killed a large group of African Americans at a political rally. The Court ruled that the due process and equal protection clauses of the Fourteenth Amendment protected citizens only from the action of the state and not from the action of other citizens.

African Americans in Congress

The montage below shows the Mississippi delegates to the 44th U.S. Congress. Blanche K. Bruce (second row, right) was the first African American to serve a full term as a U.S. senator. After Bruce, no African American was elected to the U.S. Senate until the 90th Congress almost 100 years later.

Southern Whites Gain Power

While the Klan intimidated with violence and the courts with legal interpretation, some southern Democrats devised a more subtle strategy for suppressing black rights. They put together a coalition to return the South to the rule of white men. To appeal to small farmers, they emphasized how Republican programs like schools and road-building resulted in higher taxes. They compromised with local Republicans by agreeing to African American suffrage. In return, southern Republicans joined their Democratic neighbors in ostracizing white southerners who supported the Radical Republicans. Playing on the national sensitivity to corruption, the new coalition seized every opportunity to discredit black politicians as being both self-serving and incompetent. These Democrats and Republicans agreed that racial segregation should be the rule of the new South.

The main focus of their strategy was compromise: finding common issues that would unite white southerners around the goal of regaining power in Congress. These compromisers have become known as **Redeemers,** politicians who aimed to repair or "redeem" the South in the eyes of Congress. Sometimes their strategy is described as being designed to "redeem" or reclaim the South from northern domination. In either case, their plan brought some success. By 1870, Virginia, North Carolina, and Tennessee had reinstated wealthy white southern men as governors, and had sent Confederate leaders back to the United States Congress. Other Confederate states soon followed their lead. In the congressional elections of 1874, the Republicans lost their control over the House of Representatives.

Can the Federal Government Enforce Protection of Rights?

 3.I.C.4

After the Civil War, the Fourteenth Amendment declared that African Americans were citizens of the United States. Both the Fourteenth and Fifteenth amendments protected them from discrimination. But how were those rights to be enforced? Did they apply only to the federal government or also to the states?

United States v. *Cruikshank* (1875)

The Facts	The Issue	The Decision
• William J. Cruikshank belonged to a group that wanted to reestablish white government in Louisiana. • In Colfax, Louisiana, a clash between this group and some African Americans resulted in the deaths of 100 blacks. • Cruikshank was convicted of trying to take away the civil rights of African Americans.	Cruikshank claimed that his conviction was unconstitutional because his actions did not come under the authority of federal law.	The Court overturned Cruikshank's conviction saying that the Fourteenth Amendment did not apply to individuals but only to the actions of states, and that the charges did not specify that he intended to deprive African Americans of their rights.

Why It Matters

Cruikshank, along with several other Supreme Court rulings in the 1870s, severely limited the impact of the Fourteenth and Fifteenth amendments. Although Congress passed several civil rights laws giving the federal government the power to enforce the protections of these amendments, the Court stripped away the authority of those laws.

Not long after *Cruikshank,* army troops were withdrawn from the South, and the federal government abandoned its efforts to protect African Americans. In the aftermath, white southerners used unfair laws and violence to limit African Americans' right to vote and to take away other rights as well. Not until the middle of the twentieth century did federal courts begin to strike down these laws as unconstitutional.

▼ Gathering the wounded following the Colfax massacre.

Connect to Your World

Later Court decisions upheld the federal government's authority on the civil rights protections provided by the Fourteenth and Fifteenth amendments. For that reason, employers cannot turn down jobseekers, schools cannot deny admissions, and restaurants cannot refuse to serve people because of their race or religion. Write an essay explaining how significant the Fourteenth Amendment is to American society today.

For: Supreme Court cases
Web Code: nce-1202

◀ **Protection of Rights**
Today, through the Fourteenth Amendment, the federal government ensures equal protection of all citizens, which includes equal access to education.

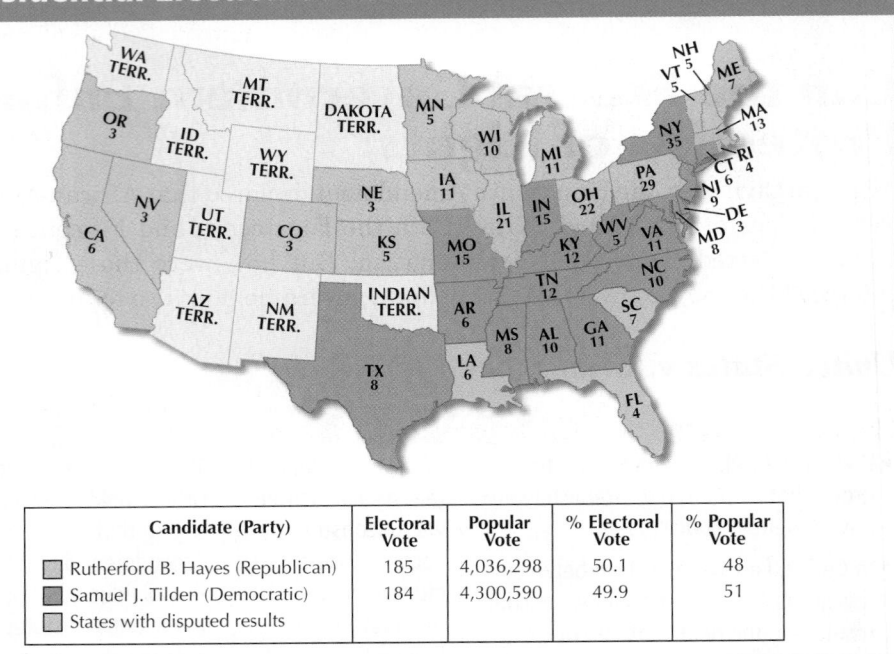

Presidential Election of 1876

Candidate (Party)	Electoral Vote	Popular Vote	% Electoral Vote	% Popular Vote
Rutherford B. Hayes (Republican)	185	4,036,298	50.1	48
Samuel J. Tilden (Democratic)	184	4,300,590	49.9	51
States with disputed results				

Map Skills Samuel Tilden won the popular vote in the 1876 election, but there were disputes about the electoral votes.

1. **Location:** In which southern states were election results disputed?

2. **Draw Inferences** Based on the map, do you think the Civil War brought an end to sectionalism?

Geography *Interactive*
For: Interactive map
Web Code: ncp-1202

Reconstruction Officially Ends With the Radical Republicans' loss of power, the stage was set to end northern domination of the South. The 1876 election pitted Ohio Republican **Rutherford B. Hayes** against New York Democrat Samuel Tilden. Hayes, a respected Union general, had served in the House of Representatives in 1866. He had resigned to become governor of Ohio, where he developed a reputation for honesty and reform-mindedness. Tilden had been active in fighting corruption in New York City. Both candidates, then, held appeal for voters who were tired of corrupt leadership.

Tilden received 51 percent of the popular vote and carried all of the southern states. However, Republicans claimed that the votes had been miscounted in three southern states, which happened to be states where Republicans controlled the reporting of ballots. Not surprisingly, in the recount, the Republicans found enough mistakes to swing the election to Hayes by one electoral vote.

When southern Democrats protested the results of this vote, Congress was charged with mediating the crisis. It created a commission of five senators (chosen by the Republican-dominated Senate), five representatives (chosen by the Democratic House of Representatives), and five Supreme Court Justices.

In what became known as the **Compromise of 1877,** Hayes was elected President. In return, the remaining federal troops were withdrawn from the South, a southerner was appointed to a powerful cabinet position, and southern states were guaranteed federal subsidies to build railroads and improve their ports.

Federal Reconstruction was over. The South and the millions of recently freed African Americans were left to negotiate their own fate.

✔ **Checkpoint** How did southern Redeemers gain power?

Evaluating Reconstruction's Effects

Was Reconstruction a "success" or a "failure"? There have been many different answers from southerners and northerners, black and white, then and now. All agree, however, that some things were forever changed when the victorious North tried to remake the vanquished South.

NoteTaking

Reading Skill: Identify Main Ideas Create a chart with information about the effects of Reconstruction.

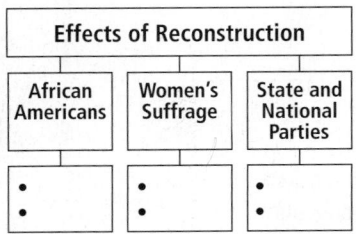

Effects of Reconstruction		
African Americans	Women's Suffrage	State and National Parties
• •	• •	• •

Among the enduring changes to the South were the introduction of a tax-supported school system and an infusion of federal money to modernize railroads and ports. In addition, the economy expanded from one crop—cotton—to a range of agricultural and industrial products. There was a gradual transition to a wage economy from a barter-and-credit system. But some historians say that these changes might have happened anyway, since southern planters were concerned about their debt-ridden society even before the war.

Reconstruction failed to heal the bitterness between North and South or to provide lasting protection for freed people. However, it did raise African Americans' expectations of their right to citizenship, and it placed before Americans the meaning and value of the right to vote.

Effects on African Americans Before the Civil War, no African American in the South, and only a small number in the North, had the right to vote. Few black southerners owned land. Most worked others' land, without pay, and without hope of improving their lot.

Reconstruction changed these things. By 1877, a few southern black Americans owned their own farms. That number would grow slowly through the next decades. Before the Civil War, most southern African Americans worked—involuntarily—in agriculture. Reconstruction began to give them choices. Perhaps most importantly, the Freedmen's Bureau helped reunite freed slaves with their families and promoted literacy within African American communities.

Though it fell short of its ambitious goals, Reconstruction opened new vistas for black Americans, North and South. The Thirteenth, Fourteenth, and Fifteenth amendments provided hope for full inclusion in American society, though it would take later generations to use them to gain racial equality.

Effects on Women's Suffrage Movement One of the ironies of Reconstruction is that it gave the vote to black American men, while fragmenting the women's movement that had often been supportive of black freedom. In the debate over the Fifteenth Amendment, there was disagreement about whether it should also include a clause giving women the right to vote. Some felt the Fifteenth Amendment could not get ratified if it included women's suffrage. Those who agreed with this position formed the American Woman Suffrage Association (AWSA) in 1869.

HISTORY MAKERS

Robert Smalls (1839–1915)

Born into slavery, Robert Smalls lived in Charleston, South Carolina, before the Civil War. During the war, he stole a Confederate boat full of military supplies and steamed it to a Union ship anchored in the harbor. The navy hired him as a pilot. After distinguished service in a battle, he became the first African American to command a navy ship. After the war, Smalls entered South Carolina's new state government and then was elected five times to the U.S. House of Representatives, a major post-Reconstruction achievement (see graph below). In the 1890s, he fought, unsuccessfully, against the movement in South Carolina to take away African Americans' civil rights.

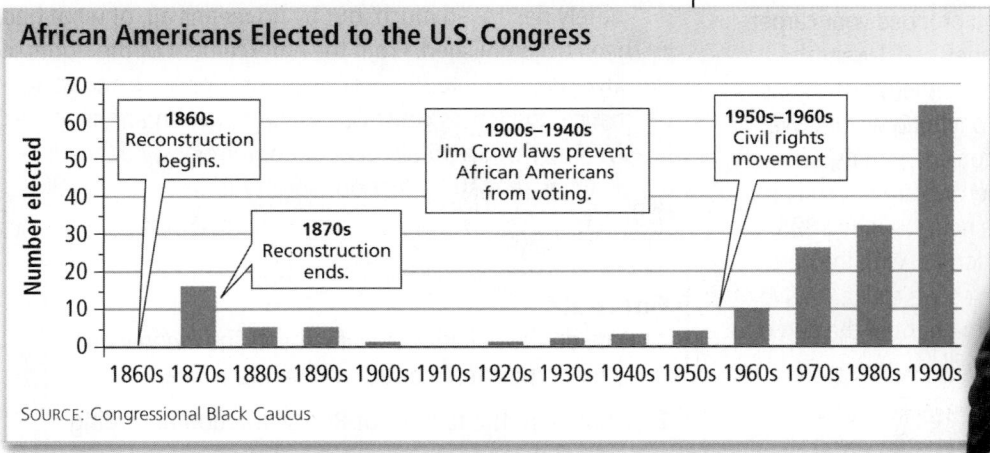

African Americans Elected to the U.S. Congress

1860s Reconstruction begins.

1870s Reconstruction ends.

1900s–1940s Jim Crow laws prevent African Americans from voting.

1950s–1960s Civil rights movement

SOURCE: Congressional Black Caucus

Was Reconstruction "Radical"?

After the Civil War, Congress passed a series of increasingly radical measures designed to rebuild the South. The effectiveness of these measures was hotly debated at the time, and the debate has continued into the present day. How radical was Reconstruction?

NORTHERN NEWSPAPER, 1865

Radical Republicans advocated harsh treatment for the South.

Primary Source

"There is one, and only one, sure and safe policy for the immediate future: namely: the North must remain the absolute Dictator of the Republic until the spirit of the North shall become the spirit of the whole country. . . . The South is still unpurged of her treason. Prostrate in the dust she is no less a traitor at this hour than when her head was erect. . . . They cannot be trusted with authority over their former slaves. . . . The only hope for the South is to give the ballot to the Negro and in denying it to the rebels."

—*The Independent*, May 5, 1865

THE "WEAK" GOVERNMENT 1877–1881.

HISTORIAN FRANCIS SIMKINS

Reconstruction neglected the economic needs of the former slaves.

Secondary Source

"A truly radical program would have called for the confiscation of land for the freedmen. Land was the principal form of Southern wealth, the only effective weapon with which the ex-slaves could have battled for economic competence and social equality. . . . The dominant Radicalism of the day naively assumed that a people's salvation could be obtained through the ballot and the spelling book. . . ."

—Francis Simkins, 1939

HISTORIAN ERIC FONER

Reconstruction set into motion the ongoing effort to address inequality.

Secondary Source

"Over a century ago . . . Americans made their first attempt to live up to the noble professions of their political creed. . . . The effort produced a sweeping redefinition of the nation's public life and a violent reaction that ultimately destroyed much, but by no means all, of what had been accomplished. From the enforcement of the rights of citizens to the stubborn problem of economic and racial justice, the issues central to Reconstruction are as old as the American republic, and as contemporary as the inequalities that still afflict our society today."

—Eric Foner, 2002

SOUTH CAROLINA SENATOR BENJAMIN TILLMAN

White southerners opposed northern domination and their ideas of equality.

Primary Source

"You had set us an impossible task. You had handcuffed us and thrown away the key, and you propped your carpetbag negro government with bayonets. . . . I want the country to get the full view of the Southern side of this question and the justification for anything we did. We were sorry we had the necessity forced upon us, but we could not help it, and as white men we are not sorry for it. . . . We did not disfranchise the negroes until 1895. . . . [W]e had a constitutional convention . . . with the purpose of disfranchising as many of them as we could. . . . We of the South have never recognized the right of the negro to govern white men, and we never will."

—Senator Benjamin Tillman, 1900

Compare

1. How do the opinions of Tillman and *The Independent* differ on northern control of the South?

2. What were the failures of Reconstruction according to Simkins and Foner?

Others, like Elizabeth Cady Stanton, believed that women and African Americans should get the vote immediately. They formed the National Woman Suffrage Association (NWSA). This group scored its first victory in 1869, when the Wyoming Territory became the first political unit to extend the vote to women. Both the NWSA and the AWSA included some black women. However, a further division occurred when a group of black women split off to form the Colored Women's Progressive Franchise association in 1880.

The Effects on State and National Politics American politics were irrevocably shaped by the Civil War and Reconstruction. The Republican Party, born out of the controversy over slavery, continued to be seen by many as "the party of Lincoln, that freed the slaves." White southerners therefore shunned it, while African Americans—in both the North and South—embraced it. Consequently, the Democratic Party came to dominate the white South.

Following Reconstruction, the national Republicans became the party of big business—a reputation that continues to the present. The national Democratic Party, which identified with industrial laborers, differed from the southern Democrats and had to maintain a delicate balance with the southern faction on this issue as well as on the question of race.

The Effects on State and Federal Power What political unit has more power—the federal government or the individual states? In cases of disputes of public policy, which branch of the federal government has the last word? These questions have perplexed American lawmakers since the Constitution's creation. During Reconstruction, they acquired deeper meaning as the federal government asserted its authority not only over southern states but over state laws in other regions as well.

In the end, American voters and their representatives in government opted for a balance of power, at the expense of protecting freed people in the South. With the demise of the Radical Republicans, most congressmen concluded that it was better to let the South attend to its own affairs than to leave a whole region under the control of federal military power and federal political control. That choice would have far-reaching social, political, and economic implications.

✔ **Checkpoint** What were the positive effects of Reconstruction?

Effects of Reconstruction	☑ Quick Study

- Union is restored.
- African Americans gain citizenship and voting rights.
- South's economy and infrastructure are improved.
- Southern states establish public school system.
- Ku Klux Klan and other groups terrorize African Americans.
- Sharecropping system takes hold in the South.

SECTION

3 Assessment

Progress Monitoring *Online*
For: Self-test with vocabulary practice
Web Code: nca-1203

Comprehension

1. **Terms and People** For each item below, write a sentence explaining its role in bringing Reconstruction to an end.
   - Redeemer
   - Rutherford B. Hayes
   - Compromise of 1877

2. **NoteTaking Reading Skill: Identify Main Ideas** Use your chart to answer the Section Focus Question: How and why did Reconstruction end?

Writing About History

3. **Quick Write: Write an E-mail** Historians who specialize in Reconstruction disagree about the main reason that Reconstruction ended. Write an email as if you were a historian expressing your point of view to a colleague. Identify the subject line you would use, and summarize the main point you would make. Use complete sentences and remember to follow proper e-mail etiquette.

Critical Thinking

4. **Identify Central Issues** What factors contributed to the refocusing of the nation away from the problems of the South?

5. **Recognize Cause and Effect** Why did the goals of the Republican Party change during the 1870s?

6. **Identify Point of View** From the perspective of an African American in the South, how was Reconstruction a success and how was it a failure?

Quick Study Guide

 3.I.A.2, 3.I.C.3

Progress Monitoring *Online*
For: Self-test with vocabulary practice
Web Code: nca-1204

■ Congressional Reconstruction

Cause and Effect

Causes

- Southern governments pass black codes.
- Violence against African Americans in the South increases.
- Southerners disregard spirit of Reconstruction.
- Johnson defies Congress and vetoes key bills.

↓

Congressional Reconstruction

↓

Effects

- Congress overrides president's veto.
- South put under military rule.
- Congress passes 15th Amendment.
- House impeaches Johnson.
- Republicans control southern state governments.

■ Democrats Regain Control

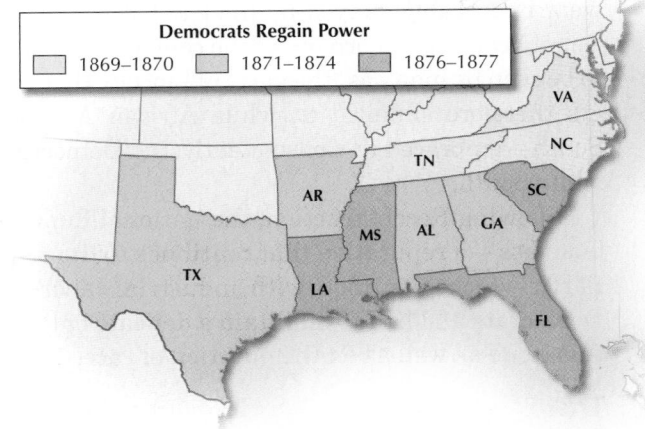

Democrats Regain Power

| | 1869–1870 | | 1871–1874 | | 1876–1877 |

■ Successes and Failures of Reconstruction

Successes	Failures
• The Union is restored. • Southern economic rebuilding begins. • African Americans are granted citizenship and voting rights. • Freedmen's Bureau helps African Americans get education, housing, and jobs. • Public school system develops in the South.	• Distribution of wealth and power in the South remains unchanged. • Many southerners are caught in a cycle of poverty. • Southern governments limit African American voting. • Racism continues in the North and South. • Many southerners remain bitter toward the federal government and Republican Party.

☑ Quick Study Timeline

In America	**1863** Lincoln issues Proclamation of Amnesty and Reconstruction	**1865** Freedmen's Bureau created	**1866** Ku Klux Klan forms in Tennessee	**1867** South placed under military rule

Presidential Terms Abraham Lincoln 1861–1865   Andrew Johnson 1865–1869

1862   **1865**   **1868**

Around the World	**1864** Taiping Rebellion ends	**1867** Russia sells Alaska to the United States	**1868** Japan's Meiji Restoration

American Issues
●—●—●—● Connector

By connecting prior knowledge with what you have learned in this chapter, you can gradually build your understanding of enduring questions that still affect America today. Answer the questions below. Then, use your American Issues Connector study guide (or go online: www.PHSchool.com **Web Code:** nch-7203).

Issues You Learned About

● **Checks and Balances** The Constitution gives each of the three branches of government the ability to check the powers of the other branches.

1. Think about the political clashes and events that surrounded Congressional Reconstruction. Then, write a paragraph that describes how the system of checks and balances worked to shape the Reconstruction era. Consider:
   • the Fourteenth Amendment
   • presidential vetoes
   • the Tenure of Office Act
   • President Johnson's impeachment trial

● **Expanding and Protecting Civil Rights** During Reconstruction, new legislation guaranteed African American civil rights.

2. Prior to the Civil War, how were the rights of free African Americans in the South restricted?

3. After the Thirteenth Amendment abolished slavery, southern states responded by passing "black codes." How did these codes affect African Americans' experience of freedom?

4. Why did Republicans in Congress believe that the Civil Rights Act of 1866 was an insufficient response to the "black codes" and work for passage of the Fourteenth Amendment?

● **Federal Power and States' Rights** In some cases, the federal government passes laws that are contrary to the laws a state would make.

5. What is the meaning of the term *states' rights*? Why was this an important issue prior to the Civil War? How was this an important issue during Reconstruction?

6. In the 1870s, the Supreme Court issued several rulings that allowed states the opportunity to undermine federal laws. What were these cases, and how did they limit federal power?

Connect to Your World | New York

Sectionalism and National Politics Just as it was nationally, the Reconstruction era in New York was a time of sectional division, often coinciding with conflict between the two main political parties. Just after the war, Republicans in control of the state government tried to gain more power over Democrat-controlled New York City. In 1865, the legislature passed a law that reformed New York City's fire department, placing it under state, not local, control. In 1866, another law created a state-controlled Metropolitan Board of Health. Eventually, the balance of power swung back to the Democrats, who gave control of both new bodies to the city. Research the relationship between the parties on the national and state level and write an essay summarizing the conflicts.

History *Interactive*
For: Interactive timeline
Web Code: ncp-1203

1870 Fifteenth Amendment gives African Americans the right to vote	**1876** Supreme Court rules in *Cruikshank* case	**1877** Reconstruction ends

Ulysses S. Grant 1869–1877

Rutherford B. Hayes 1877–1881

1871 — **1874** — **1877**

1869 Suez Canal opens

1871 Germany is unified

1873 Slave markets abolished in Zanzibar

1876 Diaz gains power in Mexico

Chapter Assessment

Terms and People

1. Who were the **Radical Republicans**? Identify two specific policies that they supported.

2. What was the **Wade-Davis Bill**? How did it differ from Lincoln's plan for Reconstruction?

3. Define **scalawag**. Which groups of people in the South welcomed scalawags, and which groups disliked them?

4. Define **segregation** and **integration**. Which policy was generally supported in the post–Civil War South?

5. Who were the **Redeemers**? What strategy did they follow, and how successful were they?

Focus Questions

The focus question for this chapter is **What lasting consequences arose from the struggles over Reconstruction?** Build an answer to this big question by answering the focus questions for Sections 1 through 3 and the Critical Thinking questions that follow.

Section 1
6. How did the Radical Republicans' plans for Reconstruction differ from Lincoln's and Johnson's?

Section 2
7. What were the immediate effects of Reconstruction?

Section 3
8. How and why did Reconstruction end?

Critical Thinking

9. **Recognize Bias** Think about the different policies that Johnson supported for Reconstruction. Which of his policies represent the beliefs of a typical white southerner? How did these beliefs shape his policies?

10. **Draw Conclusions** Why did most African American voters support the Republican Party? What is a likely explanation for the fact that southern African Americans were elected to Congress during Reconstruction but no northern African Americans were elected to Congress until 1928?

11. **Distinguish False From Accurate Images** Study the drawing of a carpetbagger at right. Does this drawing present a faithful representation? Which elements seem accurate and which seem biased?

12. **Determine Relevance** Analyze the role that the Freedmen's Bureau played in the lives of newly freed African Americans.

13. **Make Comparisons** Explain the differences between the three farming arrangements in the South after the Civil War. Which system was best for the farmer?

14. **Make Generalizations** How did many white southerners react to the new status of African Americans in society?

15. **Predict Consequences** How do you think passage of the Fifteenth Amendment would affect the future women's suffrage movement?

16. **Analyze Information** Historians disagree about whether Reconstruction was a success or a failure. Explain what you think were Reconstruction's greatest success and greatest failure using examples and details from the text.

Writing About History

Writing a Letter Reconstruction was a period of enormous change in the South. It was an era of physical rebuilding, of great economic changes, and of adjusting social relationships. Choose one aspect of Reconstruction in the South, and, as if you have been commissioned by Congress to visit the region and investigate, write a letter reporting your observations.

Prewriting
• Choose an aspect of Reconstruction that interests you, and gather information from the text and other sources about it.
• Consider your audience and what they will be interested in reading.
• Gather additional information that you might have observed had you actually traveled to the South during Reconstruction.

Drafting
• Members of Congress are very busy, so plan to include a summary of your observations in the first paragraph or two of your letter.
• Make an outline to organize your ideas.
• Write the introductory summary and then write the rest of the letter including more details.
• Use the structure of a formal letter.

Revising
• Use the guidelines on page SH11 of the Writing Handbook to revise your letter.

Regents DBQ Practice

The Freedmen's Bureau

Congress created the Freedmen's Bureau to help freed slaves in the South. What impact did the Bureau have on education? How did white southerners react to the work of the Freedmen's Bureau? Use your knowledge of the Freedmen's Bureau and Documents 1, 2, 3, and 4 to answer questions 1 through 4.

Document 1

"I am just returned from a tour through my district, and in reply to your note . . . have to say that at this place there are 366 colored children under 14 of which perhaps 200 might be gathered into a school. . . . The colored people here are anxious that a school may be established, and I heartily second their desire. Winchester also presents a favorable field for efforts in their behalf. There are 372 under 14, and a colored church that will accommodate about half of the pupils. . . . At Harpers Ferry I found a school of 40 pupils established by Miss Mann . . . and taught by her for four months under every discouragement illustrating heroic charity. She is about to accept a situation elsewhere, and was exceedingly anxious that the school should be continued. . . . I promised that the school should continue."
— *W. Storer How, August 31, 1865*

Document 2

Freedmen's Bureau school of Edisto Island, South Carolina

Document 3

Cartoon depicting President Johnson's veto of the Freedmen's Bureau bill.

Document 4

"We have pronounced ourselves distinctly in favor of the education of the Freedmen. . . . It is the interest of the whites and blacks alike that education should be generally diffused, and it will prepare both classes for the better performance of their duties. Therefore, let the people of the South, even the true, and, in fact, we think, only real friends of the negro move in the matter wisely and upon system. If the negro is to possess civil rights, and those are already accorded him, a certain amount of education will be indispensable. . . . The following . . . remarks show very clearly what difficulties are in the way of the system which has been established by those who are ignorant of the nature and character of the blacks. The Southern people must take the matter in their own hands."
— *J.D.B. DeBrow, Debow's Review, July 1866*

---

1. Which documents present a constructive view of the Freedmen's Bureau's efforts?
   (1) Documents 2 and 3
   (2) Documents 1 and 4
   (3) Documents 1 and 2
   (4) Documents 3 and 4

2. In Document 4, what is the author's view of educating freed slaves?
   (1) The job should be given to the Freedmen's Bureau.
   (2) Northern teachers should be trained for the job.
   (3) The job should be given to educated blacks.
   (4) Southerners who understand freed slaves should educate them.

3. Which document presents the conflict between President Johnson and Congress over the Freedmen's Bureau?
   (1) Document 1
   (2) Document 2
   (3) Document 3
   (4) Document 4

4. **Writing Task** How did the Freedmen's Bureau provide education for African Americans after the Civil War? Did everyone support its efforts to help freed slaves? Use your knowledge of the chapter content and specific evidence from the primary sources above to support your opinion.

NY Connect to New York

Cornelius Vanderbilt

Born: May 27, 1794, Staten Island, New York

In the second half of the 1800s and the beginning of the 1900s, the United States experienced a period of unprecedented industrial growth fueled by new technologies, an influx of immigrant workers, and an entrepreneurial spirit. New Yorker Cornelius Vanderbilt contributed to the country's industrial growth in the late 1800s and early 1900s through his involvement in the transportation industry.

Born to a poor family in Staten Island, New York, Cornelius Vanderbilt quit school at age 11 to begin working. At 16, he purchased a boat with borrowed money and started a business ferrying people between Staten Island and New York City. Over the next two decades, Vanderbilt gained control over virtually all boat traffic on the Hudson River, making him a millionaire. He expanded his business beyond the New York area, offering transportation from New York to Providence and Boston, and later from New York City to San Francisco.

In the 1850s, he began to expand his business to railroads. By 1867 he gained control of the New York Central Railroad. He consolidated it with other railroads he owned in the Midwest to offer the first rail service from New York City to Chicago in 1873.

"The largest employer of labor in the United States, he despised all routine office work, kept his figures in a vest-pocket book, ate sparingly, never speculated in stocks, never refused to see a caller, rose early, read Pilgrim's Progress every year, and, for diversion, played whist [a card game] and drove his trotters [type of horse] whenever he could."

—Description of Vanderbilt from Vanderbilt Mansion Web site

One of Vanderbilt's finest achievements was the construction of Grand Central Depot in New York City. The train station, today known as Grand Central Terminal, is a transportation hub for trains and subway cars and is one of New York City's most famous landmarks. The terminal features a hall named after Vanderbilt.

Along with J.P Morgan, Andrew Carnegie, John D. Rockefeller, and others, Cornelius Vanderbilt helped changed the face of the nation in the new industrial age.

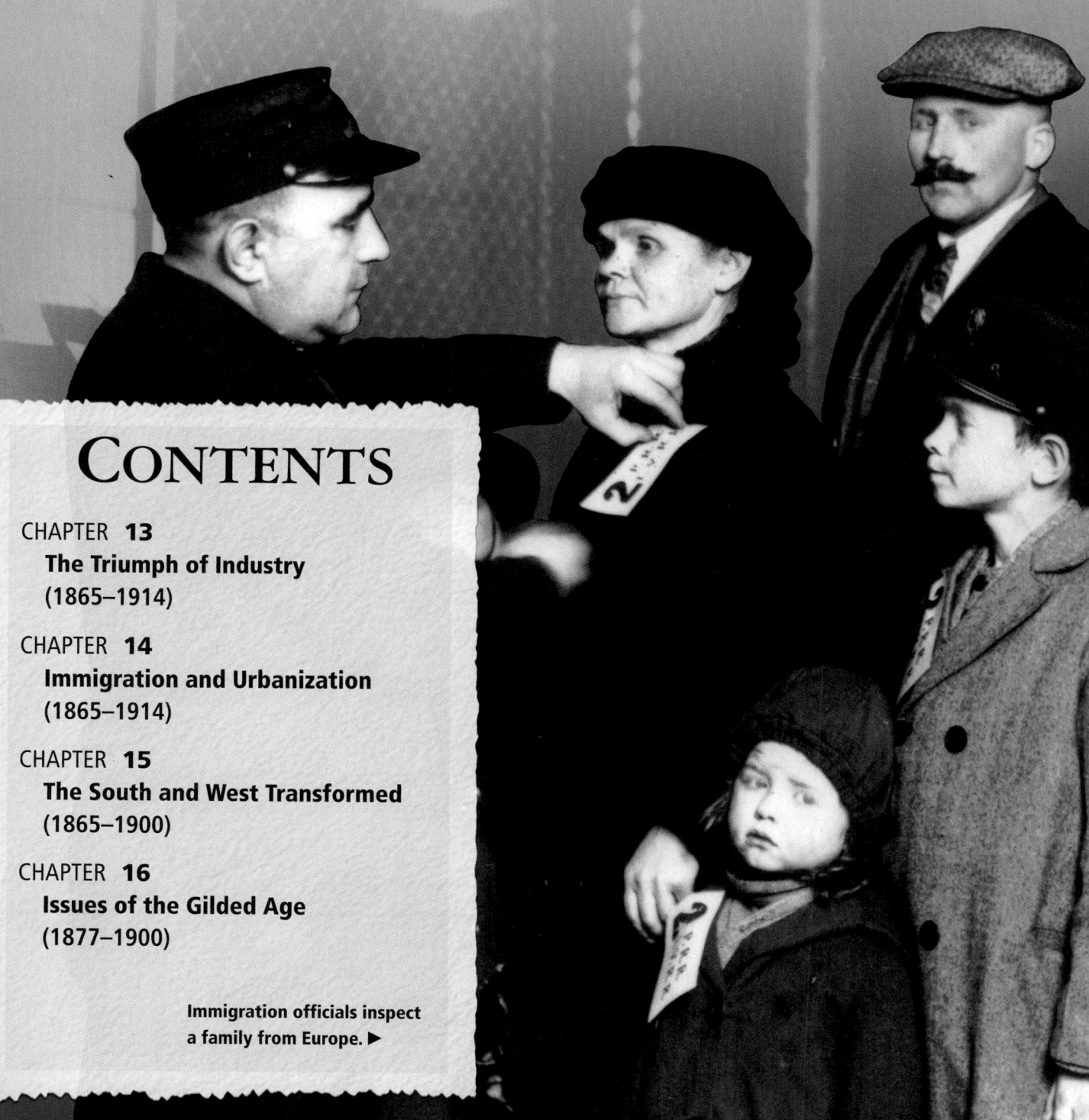

INDUSTRIALIZATION OF THE UNITED STATES

CONTENTS

**Immigration officials inspect
a family from Europe.** ▶

13 The Triumph of Industry

1865–1914

The March of American Progress

On May 24, 1883, the front page of the *Brooklyn Eagle* heralded the opening of the Brooklyn Bridge:

> "Proudly uprearing its mighty towers, secure in the integrity of its massive cables, spanning the graceful arch of its splendid superstructure the perilous rush of the swiftly flowing river, the great bridge . . . stands today a completed monument to human ingenuity, mechanical genius and engineering skill. . . . With its completing are realized the hopes of millions of people, the fruition of fourteen years of faithful and persistent toil. . . . Its opening to public use marks an enormous stride in the march of American progress . . ."

Listen to the Witness History *audio to hear more about the Brooklyn Bridge.*

◄ People take a tour on a high catwalk while work on the Brooklyn Bridge is in progress.

Early labor-union ribbon

Thomas Edison's light bulb

NY Core Curriculum Preview

Chapter Focus Question: How did the industrial growth of the late 1800s shape American society and the economy?

Section 1
Technology and Industrial Growth   3.III.A, 3.II.B, 3.II.C

Section 2
The Rise of Big Business   3.II.C.1, 3.II.C.3, 3.II.D.3

Section 3
The Organized Labor Movement   3.I.B.3, 3.II.E.1, 3.II.E.1d

Fireworks over the new Brooklyn Bridge

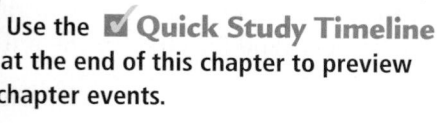

Use the ☑ **Quick Study Timeline** at the end of this chapter to preview chapter events.

Note Taking Study Guide *Online*
For: Note Taking and American Issues Connector
Web Code: nee-7301

435

Alexander Graham Bell's telephone ▶

WITNESS HISTORY 🔊 AUDIO

Celebrating the Nation's Centennial

On May 10, 1876, the United States celebrated its 100th anniversary by opening the Centennial Exhibition in Philadelphia. At a time when the total population of the country was only 46 million people, the exhibition drew nearly 9 million visitors. The event stunned Americans and foreign visitors alike with its demonstration of new technology, including an icemaker and a telephone. It also introduced the United States to the world as a new industrial and innovative powerhouse.

◀ President Grant and foreign visitors look in amazement at the Corliss steam engine, shown for the first time at the Centennial.

Technology and Industrial Growth

Core Curriculum Objectives

- **3.III.A** Impact of industrialization
- **3.II.B** Major areas of growth in business and industry
- **3.II.C** Representative entrepreneurs

Terms and People

entrepreneur
protective tariff
laissez faire
patent
Thomas Edison

Bessemer process
suspension bridge
time zone
mass production

NoteTaking

Reading Skill: Identify Causes and Effects
As you read, record the causes and effects of industrialization in a chart like the one below.

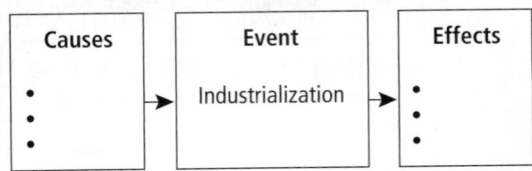

Why It Matters The end of the Civil War marked the beginning of a major transformation in American society. Americans enthusiastically embraced innovation and technology with the goals of expanding business and improving people's daily lives. American industrialization grew out of the English Industrial Revolution, but it had a distinctly American character. Backed by business leaders and shaped by a huge number of creative inventors and scientists, this "second industrial revolution" turned the United States into an industrial powerhouse. **Section Focus Question: How did industrialization and new technology affect the economy and society?**

Encouraging Industrial Growth

The Civil War challenged industries to make products more quickly and efficiently than they had been made before. Factories stepped up production, employing new tools and methods to produce guns, ammunition, medical supplies, and uniforms in large numbers. The food industry transformed itself, developing ways to process foods so they could be shipped long distances. Railroads expanded, and more efficient methods of creating power were developed. Meanwhile, the government encouraged immigration to meet the increasing demand for labor in the nation's factories.

Natural Resources Fuel Growth The country's growth was fueled, in part, by its vast supply of natural resources. Numerous coal mines along the eastern seaboard provided fuel to power steam locomotives and factories. Thick forests across the country were cut into lumber for construction. The nation's many navigable riverways transported these and other resources to cities and factories. Then, in 1859, Edwin Drake drilled what became the world's first oil well in Titusville, Pennsylvania. Before Drake's invention, oil, which was used for light and fuel, was mainly obtained from boiling down whale blubber. But whale hunting was time-consuming, and whales were becoming scarce. Drilled oil was relatively cheap to produce and easy to transport. The oil industry grew quickly after 1859 and encouraged the growth of related industries such as kerosene and gasoline.

The Workforce Grows After the Civil War, large numbers of Europeans, and some Asians, immigrated to the United States. They were pushed from their homelands by factors such as political upheaval, religious discrimination, and crop failures. In 1881 alone, nearly three quarters of a million immigrants arrived in America. That number climbed steadily, reaching almost one million per year by 1905. Immigrants were willing to work for low wages because competition for jobs was fierce. And they were prepared to move frequently in pursuit of economic opportunity. All of these factors meant that industries had a huge, and willing, workforce to fuel growth. The potential workforce grew even larger in the 1890s, when droughts and competition from foreign farmers drove American farmers in large numbers to seek jobs in the cities.

Capitalism Encourages Entrepreneurs In 1868, Horatio Alger published his first novel, *Ragged Dick, or Street Life in New York*. This wildly successful novel told the story of a poor boy who rose to wealth and fame by working hard. Alger's novels stressed the possibility that anyone could vault from poverty and obscurity to wealth and fame. In this excerpt, he describes how Ragged Dick starts his climb to success.

Doing Business
Store owners in 1896 seek to expand their business by advertising and offering delivery.

Primary Source

"Ten dollars a week was to him a fortune. . . . Indeed, he would have been glad, only the day before, to get a place at three dollars a week. . . . Then he was to be advanced if he deserved it. It was indeed a bright prospect for a boy who, only a year before, could neither read nor write. . . . Dick's great ambition to "grow up 'spectable" seemed likely to be accomplished after all."
—Horatio Alger, 1868

The "rags to riches" idea depended on the system of capitalism, or free enterprise, in which individuals own most businesses. The heroes of this system were **entrepreneurs,** or people who invest money in a product or enterprise in order to make a profit. Entrepreneurs fueled industrialization. The factories, railroads, and mines they established created jobs and also attracted foreign investment.

Government Policies Encourage Free Enterprise Government policies encouraged the success of businesses in the late 1800s. For example, the government gave railroad builders millions of acres of land in return for their promise to quickly link the East and West coasts. To encourage the buying of American goods, Congress enacted **protective tariffs,** or taxes that would make imported goods cost more than those made locally. The government also encouraged **laissez-faire** policies, which allowed businesses to operate under minimal government regulation. Such policies, along with a strong legal system that enforced private property rights, provided the predictability and security that businesses and industries needed to encourage investment and growth.

✓ **Checkpoint** What factors spurred industrial growth in the late 1800s?

Innovation Drives the Nation

By the late 1800s, the drive for innovation and efficiency seemed to touch every sphere of life in the United States. The number of patents increased rapidly during this time. A **patent** is a grant by the federal government giving an inventor the exclusive right to develop, use, and sell an invention for a set period of time. Businessmen invested heavily in these new innovations, hoping to create new industries and expand old ones.

Electricity Transforms Life In 1876, inventor **Thomas Edison,** supported by wealthy industrialists like J. P. Morgan, established a research laboratory at Menlo Park, New Jersey. Edison, a creative genius who had had only a few months of formal education, would receive more than 1,000 patents for new inventions. In 1880, for example, with the goal of developing affordable lighting for homes, Edison and his team invented the light bulb. Within a few years, they had also developed plans for central power plants to light entire sections of cities. Other inventors later improved upon Edison's work. George Westinghouse, for example, developed

Major Inventions of the 1800s

▲ **Telegraph** Samuel Morse's telegraph sends the first message from Washington, D.C., to Baltimore, Maryland, on May 24, 1844. Before the telegraph, messages were sent by horse and rider. In the early 1860s, the telegraph replaced the Pony Express—the long distance mail service in the West.

▼ **Sewing Machine** Elias Howe's sewing machine revolutionizes the way clothes are made in homes and factories. In his original design, a hand-turned wheel moved the needle up and down.

technology to send electricity over long distances. Electricity lit city streets and powered homes and factories, extending the number of hours in the day when Americans could work and play.

Revolutionizing Communications In 1844, inventor Samuel Morse perfected telegraph technology, or the process of sending messages over wire. In 1876, Alexander Graham Bell patented the telephone. Within a few years, 148 telephone companies had strung more than 34,000 miles of wire, and long-distance lines linked several cities in the Northeast and Midwest. By 1900, there were more than one million telephones in the United States, and more than 100,000 miles of telegraph wire linked users across the land. In 1896, Guglielmo Marconi invented the wireless telegraph. Future inventors would build on this innovation in developing the radio.

Steel: A Practical Wonder In the 1850s in England, a man named Henry Bessemer developed a process for purifying iron, resulting in strong, but lightweight, steel. American industries quickly adopted the **Bessemer process,** and by 1890 the United States was outproducing British steel manufacturers. Strong steel made possible a host of innovations, including skyscrapers and the elevators to service them. However, one of its most dramatic uses was in the construction of **suspension bridges,** bridges in which the roadway is suspended by steel cables. The first suspension bridge was the Brooklyn Bridge, spanning the East River in New York City. Completed in 1883, it was at the time of its construction the longest bridge in the world.

HISTORY MAKERS

Thomas Edison (1847–1931)
One of history's most prolific inventors, Thomas Edison lost much of his hearing as a child, which led to poor performance in school. He began working at an early age and by 16 was a telegraph operator. His hearing problems—and an interest in machines—led him to try to invent new equipment that relied on sight rather than sound. Edison produced his first major invention, a machine to report stock prices, at the age of 22. He used the money earned from selling this and other machines to build the Menlo Park complex, where he and his team of workers developed hundreds of new devices or improved old ones.

Safety Elevator Elisha Otis develops a safety mechanism to prevent elevator cars from suddenly falling. He demonstrates his invention at an exposition in New York.

Light Bulb Thomas Edison patents the electric light bulb. Within two years, he installs a street-lighting system in New York City.

Steam Boiler Furnace African American inventor Granville Woods invents an improved steam-powered furnace for running trains.

Establishing Time Zones
A map shows an early railroad route covering three time zones. *Why would making railroad schedules be difficult without time zones?*

Vocabulary Builder
stimulate—(STIHM yoo layt) *v.* to excite to action

Technology and Transportation As railroads expanded, they made use of new technologies and also encouraged innovation. George Westinghouse patented air brakes for trains in 1869, while Granville Woods patented a telegraph system for trains in 1887. Meatpacker Gustavus Swift developed refrigerated cars for transporting food. By 1883, there were three transcontinental railroad lines in the United States. The expanding transportation network caused some problems. Throughout most of the 1800s, most towns set their clocks independently. When trains started regular passenger service between towns, time differences made it hard to set schedules. In 1884, delegates from 27 countries divided the globe into 24 **time zones,** one for each hour of the day. The railroads adopted this system, which is still used today.

Technology affected how Americans traveled and where they lived. Electric streetcars, commuter trains, and subways appeared in major cities. As a result, Americans living in neighborhoods outside the city could commute to work. Factory production of automobiles with gas-powered engines began in 1902. The first successful airplane flight in 1903 by brothers Orville and Wilbur Wright, two bicycle manufacturers, marked the birth of a new industry.

A Spiral of Growth Railroads played a key role in transforming American industries and businesses. They could transport large amounts of goods quickly, cheaply, and efficiently. Because they linked the nation, they allowed businesses to obtain raw materials easily and to sell finished goods to larger numbers of people. They encouraged new methods for management and administration, which were soon adopted by the business community. In addition, the expanding railroad network <u>stimulated</u> innovation in many other industries.

An abundance of natural resources and an efficient transportation system to carry raw materials and finished goods set up a spiral of related growth. For example, factories turned out plate glass for windows of passenger rail cars. The factories needed freight cars to carry the windows to their destinations. Those freight cars were created in factories that used railroads to transport fuel to supply the furnaces that turned out more railroad cars. In this way, factory production generated more factory production. To meet the growing demand, factory owners developed systems for turning out large numbers of products quickly and inexpensively. Known as **mass production,** these systems depended upon machinery to carry out tasks that were once done with hand tools.

✓ **Checkpoint** How did new technologies shape industrialization?

The Impact of Industrialization

Industrialization touched every aspect of American life, from the way businesses and farms operated to the kinds of products Americans used. It also affected the country's relationship with the world and with its own environment.

Linking World Markets By the 1880s, American exports of grain, steel, and textiles dominated international markets. With almost as many miles of railroad track as the rest of the world combined, the United States could easily

Focus On Geography

The Railroads: Shaping American Cities More than any other factor, the growth of the United States in the mid-to late-1800s can be linked directly to the railroads. As the railroads expanded, they created some cities or greatly influenced the physical and economic growth of others.

Chicago, Illinois Within twenty years after the arrival of the railroads, Chicago had become the nation's main railroad hub. Livestock and grain came to Chicago from the West, while manufactured goods came from the East. Industries such as meatpacking flourished, in turn influencing the railroads. The need to keep meat fresh, for example, resulted in the development of the refrigerated train car. ▶

Pittsburgh, Pennsylvania ▶ With its extensive natural resources, Pittsburgh grew into an industrial powerhouse in the 1800s. Railroads shipped steel and other products to the rest of the country and brought immigrants into the city to begin new lives. With its strong steel-based economy, Pittsburgh became known as "The Steel City."

Geography and History
- Why is it accurate to refer to Chicago as a railroad "hub"?
- How did the railroads contribute to the growth of American cities?

Las Vegas, Nevada Once an army fort, new railroad track laid in the late 1800s turned Las Vegas into a bustling railroad town. The city's water resources allowed trains to refuel and served as a rest stop for passengers. In 1905, Las Vegas became a city. ▼

◀ **Atlanta, Georgia** Atlanta literally got its name from the railroads. It was founded in 1837 as a transportation hub where the Georgia and Atlantic rail lines began. Burned by Union forces during the Civil War, within thirty years Atlanta was once again the proud "railroad center of the southeast."

A Pleasant Scene

An attractive 1879 print of a Massachusetts factory gives no hint of the pollution the factory regularly produced.

transport goods from where they were made or grown to ports where they could be shipped around the world. Exports of food and goods greatly expanded the American economy. As the United States grew as a world economic power, it often clashed with the economic views and political policies of other countries.

Changing American Society Massive changes in industry altered how Americans lived and worked. Even farms became mechanized, meaning that fewer farm laborers were needed to feed the nation. Out-of-work farmers and their families moved to urban areas to find work, especially in the increasingly industrial North. Many moved to manufacturing centers that had sprung up around growing factories or industries. The mass production of goods meant that these new urban dwellers had easy access to clothing and supplies that they would have had to make by hand in the past. Yet they faced higher costs of living, were dependent upon cash wages to buy food, and performed repetitive work in factories.

Thinking About the Environment In the early 1800s, few worried about how industry might affect the environment. However, by the late 1800s, industrial waste had risen dramatically and mining had begun to destroy the land. In the Midwest, increasing agricultural production had led to soil erosion and dust storms. People began to raise concerns about protecting natural resources. Congress responded by setting aside protected lands that would eventually become part of the National Park Service. Its creation of Yellowstone Park in 1872 was one of the first federal responses to concerns about the environment.

✔ **Checkpoint** What impact did industrialization have on Americans?

Progress Monitoring Online
For: Self-test with vocabulary practice
Web Code: nca-1311

Comprehension

1. **Terms and People** For each item below, write a sentence explaining how it relates to industrialization.
   • entrepreneur
   • protective tariff
   • laissez faire
   • patent
   • Thomas Edison
   • Bessemer process
   • suspension bridge
   • time zone
   • mass production

2. **NoteTaking Reading Skill: Identify Causes and Effects** Use your completed chart to answer the Section Focus Question: How did industrialization and new technology affect the economy and society?

Writing About History

3. **Quick Write: Define Your Audience** Suppose that you are Thomas Edison writing a memo to J. P. Morgan requesting more financial support for work being done in your lab. Think about how much information Morgan needs to know, and summarize it in bullets.

Critical Thinking

4. **Recognize Ideologies** Would you characterize all of the government's policies in the late 1800s toward business as laissez faire? Explain your answer.

5. **Determine Relevance** How did the system of patents encourage innovation and investment?

6. **Distinguish Fact From Opinion** Explain why you agree or disagree with this statement: "The late 1800s was a time of great progress for all Americans."

WITNESS HISTORY 🔊 AUDIO

From Rags to Riches

In 1848, 12-year-old Andrew Carnegie and his poverty-stricken family immigrated to the United States. He immediately began work in a Pennsylvania textile factory. Two years later, he got a job in a railroad office. By the time he was 40, he was a wealthy investor and the nation's most successful steelmaker, famous for his commitment to innovation. Carnegie's "rags to riches" story did not end with wealth. Believing that "the man who dies rich thus dies disgraced," he established a number of charitable organizations in the United States and around the world.

◀ Young Andrew Carnegie (far left) worked as a "bobbin boy," winding cotton thread onto a bobbin like the one at left.

The Rise of Big Business

 Core Curriculum Objectives

- **3.II.C.1** Entrepreneurs: John D. Rockefeller: oil; Andrew Carnegie: steel; Ford: auto
- **3.II.C.3** Entrepreneurs: Conflict between public good and private gain
- **3.II.D.3** Competition and absorption; mergers and trusts; Sherman Antitrust Act, 1890 (*United States* v. *E.C. Knight,* 1895)

Terms and People

corporation	Andrew Carnegie
monopoly	vertical integration
cartel	Social Darwinism
John D. Rockefeller	ICC
horizontal integration	Sherman Antitrust Act
trust	

NoteTaking

Reading Skill: Identify Supporting Details Record supporting details about the rise of American big business in a chart like this one.

```
        Rise of Big Business

  Corporations          Debates

  [        ]          [        ]
```

Why It Matters The rapid industrial growth that occurred after the Civil War transformed American business and society. Yet it was only the beginning. The rise of big business, characterized by the investment of huge amounts of resources, turned the United States into one of the most economically powerful countries in the modern world. **Section Focus Question: How did big business shape the American economy in the late 1800s and early 1900s?**

Fighting for Profits

Until the mid-nineteenth century, most businesses were run by one person or family. This meant that no business could grow bigger than one family's ability to invest in it or run it. Businesses were also local, buying and selling to customers who lived nearby. Industrialization changed all this. Railroads provided businesses with access to raw materials and customers from farther and farther away. Business leaders, lured by the profits offered by these larger markets, responded by combining funds and resources.

The Corporation Develops To take advantage of expanding markets, investors developed a form of group ownership known as a **corporation.** In a corporation, a number of people share the ownership of a business. If a corporation experiences economic problems, the investors lose no more than they had originally invested in the business. The corporation was the perfect solution to the challenge of expanding business, especially for risky industries such as railroads

Structure of a Corporation

Public Shareholders
Give money to a company in exchange for share ownership

Board of Directors
Elected by shareholders to set business direction and to protect company

Managers
Hired by the board of directors. Run the company and hire workers

Employees
Carry out the company's jobs

Running a Corporation

Companies issue shares like those above to their investors. In every corporation, shareholders have the final say on how their money should be invested. *How does the role of director differ from that of manager?*

or mining. A corporation had the same rights as an individual: it could buy and sell property, and it could sue in the courts. If one person chose to leave the group, the others could buy out his interests.

Corporations were perfectly suited to expanding markets. They had access to huge amounts of capital, or invested money, allowing them to fund new technology, enter new industries, or run large plants across the country. Aided by railroads and the telegraph, corporations had the ability to operate in several different regions. After 1870, the number of corporations in America increased dramatically. They were an important part of industrial capitalism, or the economic free-market system centered around industries.

Gaining a Competitive Edge Corporations worked to maximize profits in several ways. They decreased the cost of producing goods or services by paying workers the lowest possible wages or paying as little as they could for raw materials. They tried to increase profits by advertising their products widely, thus increasing their potential customer base. Like J. P. Morgan, the heads of some corporations supported research laboratories where inventors could experiment with products and methods that might bring the corporations future profits. Others thought up new ways to make money. Cornelius Vanderbilt, a self-made businessman in the railroad industry, got his start in the steamboat business. He cleverly succeeded in getting his competitors to pay him to relocate because his low fares were driving them out of business.

Some corporations tried to gain a **monopoly,** or complete control of a product or service. To do this, a corporation either bought out its competitors or drove them out of business. Once consumers had no other choices for a given product or service, the sole remaining company was free to set its own prices. Other corporations worked to eliminate competition with other businesses by forming a **cartel.** In this arrangement, businesses making the same product agree to limit their production and thus keep prices high. Still other corporations came up with new methods. **John D. Rockefeller,** an oil tycoon, made deals with railroads to increase his profits:

Primary Source "[Rockefeller's company] killed its rivals, in brief, by getting the great trunk lines to refuse to give them transportation. Vanderbilt is reported to have said that there was but one man—Rockefeller—who could dictate to him."

—H. D. Lloyd, *The Atlantic,* 1881

Horizontal and Vertical Integration Businessmen continued to develop ever more effective ways to increase profits and decrease costs. One way was to create a giant company with lower production costs. This system of consolidating many firms in the same business is called **horizontal integration.** Rockefeller was one of the first businessmen to use this method. However, Ohio state law prevented one company from owning the stock of another, meaning that Rockefeller could not buy out his competitors. His lawyer had an idea to get around this law, called a **trust.** In a trust, companies assign their stock to a board of trustees, who combine them into a new organization. The trustees run the organization, paying themselves dividends on profits.

Rockefeller, steel tycoon **Andrew Carnegie,** and other businessmen also increased their power by gaining control of the many different businesses that make up all phases of a product's development. This process, called **vertical integration,** allowed companies to reduce costs and charge higher prices to competitors.

 Checkpoint What strategies did corporations use to decrease costs and increase profits?

Debating the Role of Big Business

Throughout the 1880s, business mergers created powerful empires for those who invested in steel, railroads, meat, farm equipment, sugar, lumber, and a number of other enterprises. However, while business leaders grew wealthy, many smaller companies and consumers began to question their goals and tactics.

Comparing Viewpoints

What is the Legacy of the Business Tycoons?

Business tycoons like Carnegie, Rockefeller, and Vanderbilt had a huge role in spurring America's industrial growth. Yet even today, historians debate the real legacy of those men.

MATTHEW JOSEPHSON

Josephson (1899–1978) was the political and economic historian who coined the phrase "robber barons."

Primary Source

"To organize and exploit the resources of a nation upon a gigantic scale . . . and to do this only in the name of an uncontrolled appetite for private profit—here surely is the great inherent contradiction whence so much disaster, outrage and misery has flowed."

BURTON W. FOLSOM, JR.

Folsom (born 1948) is a historian who has described the great businessmen of the time as entrepreneurs.

Primary Source

"In 1870, when Rockefeller founded Standard Oil, kerosene was 30 cents a gallon. Twenty years later, Rockefeller had almost a 90 percent market share and kerosene was only eight cents a gallon. Customers were the real winners here, because Rockefeller's size allowed him to cut costs. . . ."

Compare
1. What is the basic difference between Folsom's and Josephson's views of these businessmen?
2. What is Folsom's main defense of Rockefeller's tactics?

"Robber Barons" or "Captains of Industry"? Gradually, consumers, workers, and the federal government came to feel that systems like trusts, cartels, and monopolies gave powerful businessmen an unfair advantage. Most small businesses were bought up or squeezed out of competition. Small businesses that joined trusts found that they received few profits. Consumers were harmed by the unfairly high prices that monopolies and cartels set on their products. Because of their capacity to swindle the poor, shrewd capitalists became known as "robber barons."

At the same time, many people believed that business leaders served the nation positively, thus earning the nickname "captains of industry." Factories, steel mills, and railroads provided jobs for an ever-growing labor force. The development of efficient business practices and industrialists' support for developing technology benefited the nation's economy, stimulating innovation and shaping

Events That Changed America

NEW WAYS OF DOING BUSINESS

The rise of the Standard Oil Company marked the beginning of a brand new way of building and conducting business in America. Many, though not all, of John D. Rockefeller's business practices at Standard Oil are part of mainstream corporate culture in the U.S. today. In 1904, journalist Ida Tarbell wrote, "It was the first in the field, and it has furnished the methods, the charter, and the traditions of its followers." Believing that a mix of small and large companies produced chaos and instability in prices and supplies, Rockefeller pioneered new techniques for organizing the oil industry to create a more stable and seamless business environment.

Through creativity and hard work, Rockefeller rose from a ▶ modest background to become the world's first billionaire. From his first paycheck he gave 10 percent of his earnings to his church. By the time he died, he had given away hundreds of millions of dollars.

▲ Standard Oil became a dominant symbol of the bustling American economy. At its height, the company controlled 90 percent of the nation's oil industry.

HORIZONTAL INTEGRATION

Rockefeller bought up rival businesses in Ohio, Pennsylvania, and New York to gain more control of the oil-refining industry. One of Rockefeller's harshest critics led protests against the growing power of Standard Oil—only to take a job there years later.

Clark, Payne & Company, OH

Hanna, Baslington & Company, OH

Atlantic Refining Company, OH

Charles Pratt & Company, NY

Imperial Refining Company, PA

Chess, Carley & Company, KY

Purchased by Rockefeller

Standard Oil Company

the United States into a strong international leader. Furthermore, many business leaders, like Carnegie, Rockefeller, and Vanderbilt, were important philanthropists. They established universities, museums, and libraries, believing that such institutions made it possible for the disadvantaged to rise to wealth.

Social Darwinism Catches On In 1859, biologist Charles Darwin published *On the Origin of Species,* arguing that animals evolved by a process of "natural selection" and that only the fittest survived to reproduce. Yale professor William Graham Sumner soon applied this theory to the rough-and-tumble world of American capitalism, calling it **Social Darwinism.** He declared that wealth was a measure of one's inherent value and those who had it were the most "fit."

People used Social Darwinism to justify all sorts of beliefs and conditions. Supporters of the laissez-faire economic system argued that the government

VERTICAL INTEGRATION

Rockefeller next sought to turn Standard Oil into a kind of empire. He invested in industries related to oil production, including pipelines, tank cars, oil barrels, railroads, and marketing companies. By taking control of the entire supply chain, Rockefeller was able to exert almost complete control over competitors.

Oil wells/ Pipelines

Tank Cars/ Railroads

Retail outlets

Purchased by Rockefeller

Standard Oil Company

Why It Matters

Rockefeller's methods—from advertising (below) to buying out competitors—changed the American business climate. In turn, big business transformed American society itself in the twentieth century, becoming the accepted means for the nation to conduct its business and produce and sell its goods. It also ushered in the globalization that would become the striking characteristic of twenty-first century life.

Following in Rockefeller's ▶ footsteps, Microsoft's Bill Gates carried the torch of modern business leadership. While praised for his philanthropy, he has also been criticized for monopolistic techniques— just as Rockefeller was.

Thinking Critically

In the late 1800s, people debated the impact of corporations, calling their leaders either "robber barons" or "captains of industry." Are such debates still relevant today?

History *Interactive* ✶
For: More about big business
Web Code: ncp-1320

should stay out of private business, because interference would disrupt natural selection. Many Social Darwinists believed that the nation would grow strong by allowing its most vigorous members to rise to the top. Therefore, they felt that it was wrong to use public funds to assist the poor. Social Darwinism was often used to fuel discrimination. Social Darwinists pointed to the poverty-stricken condition of many minorities as evidence of their unfitness.

 Checkpoint What arguments did people use to support or oppose big business?

The Government Imposes Regulations

The great industrialists' methods and their stranglehold on the nation's economy worried some Americans. The railroad industry was renowned for unjust business practices, including random and unfair rates and the process of pooling rates and traffic.

Finally, in 1887, the United States Senate created the **Interstate Commerce Commission (ICC)** to oversee railroad operations. This was the first federal body ever set up to monitor American business operations. The ICC could only monitor railroads that crossed state lines, and it could not make laws or control the railroads' transactions. Still, the ICC could require the railroads to send their records to Congress, so that Congress could initiate investigations of unfairness. Over the next several decades, the government would set up many other federal bodies to regulate American businesses.

Similarly, the federal government slowly became involved in regulating trusts. In 1890, the Senate passed the **Sherman Antitrust Act,** which outlawed any trust that operated "in restraint of trade or commerce among the several states." For more than a decade, the provision was seldom enforced. In fact, the law was often used in the corporations' favor, as they argued that labor unions restrained trade. However, the ICC and the Sherman Antitrust Act began a trend toward federal limitations on corporations' power.

 Checkpoint How did the federal government regulate business?

NoteTaking

Reading Skill: Recognize Sequence As you read, record details about how the government gradually became involved in regulating industry.

Vocabulary Builder
restraint–(rih STRAYNT) *n.* holding back or checking of action

---

SECTION 2 Assessment

Progress Monitoring *Online*
For: Self-test with vocabulary practice
Web Code: nca-1321

Comprehension

1. Terms and People For each item below, write a sentence explaining how it relates to the rise of big business in the late 1800s.
- corporation
- monopoly
- cartel
- John D. Rockefeller
- horizontal integration
- trust
- Andrew Carnegie
- vertical integration
- Social Darwinism
- ICC
- Sherman Antitrust Act

2. NoteTaking Reading Skill: Identify Supporting Details Use your completed charts to answer the Section Focus Question: How did big business shape the American economy in the late 1800s and early 1900s?

Writing About History

3. Quick Write: Narrow Down the Topic You are the head of a corporation and need to write a memo to your shareholders about the company's financial situation. You want to make a positive impression. What kind of information should you include? What should be the subject line of the memo?

Critical Thinking

4. Identify Central Issues Why did business leaders create new forms of ownership like monopolies, cartels, and trusts?

5. Determine Relevance How accurate is it to describe business leaders like Rockefeller and Carnegie as both "robber barons" and "captains of industry"?

6. Draw Inferences What does the fact that government regulation of business was not very successful at first tell you about the relationship between government and big business?

3.II.C.1

Andrew Carnegie: *Wealth* (1889)

One of America's wealthiest tycoons, Andrew Carnegie was also a dedicated philanthropist. By the time he died, he had given away more than 80 percent—over $350 million—of his own fortune. Carnegie wrote frequently about the role of wealthy businessmen in the American economy. In *Wealth,* he wrote that people had the right to accumulate as much wealth as they could, but they also had the responsibility to give it away. His ideas became popularly known as the "gospel of wealth."

Carnegie (above) built more than 2,000 public libraries around the country. A letter he wrote to the director of the New York Public Library expresses his enthusiasm for the project.

It is well, nay, essential for the progress of the race, that the houses of some should be homes for all that is highest and best in literature and the arts, and the refinements of civilization, rather than none should be so. Much better this great irregularity than universal squalor. . . .[1]

The price which society pays for the law of competition, like the price it pays for cheap comforts and luxuries, is also great; but the advantages of this law are also greater still, for it is to this law that we owe our wonderful material development, which brings improved conditions in its train. But, whether the law be benign[2] or not, we must say of it, as we say of the change in the conditions of men to which we have referred: It is here; we cannot evade[3] it; no substitutes for it have been found; and while the law may be sometimes hard for the individual, it is best for the race, because it insures the survival of the fittest in every department. . . .

What is the proper mode of administering wealth after the laws upon which civilization is founded have thrown it into the hands of the few? . . .

Individualism[4] will continue, but the millionaire will be but a trustee for the poor; intrusted for a season with a great part of the increased wealth of the community, but administering it for the community far better than it could or would have done for itself. . . . The man who dies leaving behind him millions of available wealth, which was his to administer during life, will pass away "unwept, unhonored, an unsung," no matter to what uses he leaves the dross[5] which he cannot take with him. Of such as these the public verdict will then be: The man who dies rich thus dies disgraced.

1. **squalor** (SKWAHL uhr) *n.* state of filth or of being miserable
2. **benign** (bih NĪN) *adj.* favorable; doing no harm
3. **evade** (ee VAYD) *v.* to escape or avoid
4. **individualism** (ihn duh VIHJ oo uhl ihz uhm) *n.* self-interest
5. **dross** (drahs) *n.* waste or useless substances

Thinking Critically

1 **Analyze Information** Does Carnegie believe that there is anything wrong with amassing wealth? Why or why not?

2 **Synthesize Information** How does Carnegie use the doctrine of Social Darwinism to support his argument?

The Right to Strike

In 1890, labor leader Samuel Gompers testified before a government labor commission. Describing the condition of workers, he argued that unions and strikes were the only way workers' rights could be expanded.

❝We recognize that peaceful industry is necessary to successful civilized life, but the right to strike and the preparation to strike is the greatest preventive to strikes. If the workmen were to make up their minds to-morrow that they would under no circumstances strike, the employers would do all the striking for them in the way of lesser wages and longer hours of labor.❞
—Report on the (U.S.) Industrial Commission on Capital and Labor, 1890

◀ Immigrants paint machinery in a Cleveland, Ohio, factory.

The Organized Labor Movement

 Core Curriculum Objectives

- **3.I.B.3** Developing labor needs
- **3.II.E.1** Efforts at national labor unions: Knights of Labor (1869); AF of L (1881–1886); ILGWU (1900)
- **3.II.E.1d** Union leadership (Gompers, Debs)

Terms and People

sweatshop	Samuel Gompers
company town	AFL
collective bargaining	Haymarket Riot
socialism	Homestead Strike
Knights of Labor	Eugene V. Debs
Terence V. Powderly	Pullman Strike

NoteTaking

Reading Skill: Identify Main Ideas Record the main ideas about the rise of organized labor.

Why It Matters As industrialization intensified, the booming American economy relied heavily on workers to fuel its success. But struggles between business owners and workers also intensified, as workers rebelled against low pay and unsafe working conditions. To keep the economy thriving, Americans had to find ways to ease the tensions between business owners and workers. **Section Focus Question: How did the rise of labor unions shape relations among workers, big business, and government?**

Workers Endure Hardships

The industrial expansion in the United States made the American economy grow by leaps and bounds. Industrial growth produced great wealth for the owners of factories, mines, railroads, and large farms. It also brought general improvements to American society in the form of higher standards of living, wider availability of cheap goods, and access to public institutions like museums and schools. However, the people who actually performed the work in factories and industries struggled to survive. In addition, workers—especially immigrants, women, and minorities—often faced ridicule and discrimination.

Factory Work In the 1880s and 1890s, factory owners, seeking to maximize profits, employed people who would work for low wages. Immigrants made up a large percentage of the workforce. Far from home, lacking good English-speaking skills, and often very poor, immigrants would generally take almost any job. Factory workers toiled long hours—12 hours a day, 6 days a week—in small, hot, dark, and dirty workhouses known as **sweatshops.** These sweatshops employed thousands of people, mainly women, who worked for long hours on machines making mass-produced items. Owners ensured productivity by strictly regulating workers' days. Owners clocked work and break hours, and they fined workers for breaking rules or working slowly.

Factory work was often dangerous. Workspaces were poorly lit, often overheated, and badly ventilated. Some workers lost their hearing from the noisy machines. Accidents were common, both from faulty equipment and lack of proper training. Despite the harsh conditions, employers suffered no shortage of labor. There were always more people than jobs.

Families in the Workforce As industrialization advanced, more jobs opened up for women. They worked as laundresses, telegraph operators, and typists. But most women—and their families—worked in the factories. Since low wages meant that both parents needed jobs, bringing children to work kept them off the streets and close to their parents. It also meant that the children could earn a wage, which helped the family to survive. By the end of the 1800s, nearly one in five children between the ages of 10 and 16 worked rather than attending school. Conditions were especially harsh for these children. Many suffered stunted physical and mental growth. By the 1890s, social workers began to lobby to get children out of factories and into child care or schools. Eventually, their efforts prompted states to pass legislation to stop child labor.

Living in Company Towns Many laborers, especially those who worked in mines, were forced to live in isolated communities near their workplaces. The housing in these communities, known as **company towns,** was owned by the business and rented out to employees. The employer also controlled the "company store," where workers were forced to buy goods. The company store sold goods on credit but charged high interest. As a result, by the time the worker received wages, most of the income was owed back to the employer. Since workers could be arrested if they left their jobs before they repaid these loans, employers could hold workers to their jobs through a system that workers' advocates called "wage slavery." Through its management of the company town, employers could also reinforce ethnic competition and distrust. For example, Mexican, African American, or Chinese workers could be segregated in separate towns.

✔️ **Checkpoint** How did working conditions affect families?

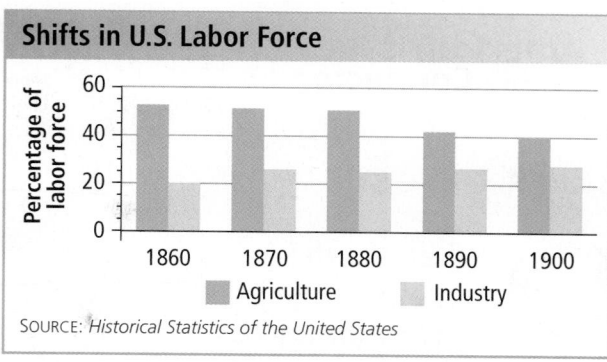

Shifts in U.S. Labor Force

SOURCE: *Historical Statistics of the United States*

A Changing Workforce

In the late 1800s, the number of Americans working in agriculture steadily declined. *Describe the growth in the industrial workforce between 1860 and 1900.*

Child Laborers

Adults supervise child workers in a textile factory circa 1890. A Pennsylvania job advertisement from the late 1800s called for workers "with large families."

Technology and Society

 1.I.C

TRACK THE ISSUE

What are the benefits and costs of technology?

Technology has had a great impact on American life. It has brought economic and social benefits for the nation, yet it has also had some negative effects. What are the benefits and costs of technological change? Use the timeline below to explore this enduring issue.

Late 1700s Factory System
Water-powered mills boost production but worsen conditions for workers.

1859 Oil Refining
Oil fuels industrial growth and raises standard of living but encourages American dependence on a single resource and worsens pollution.

1930s Polymers
Manufactured materials like plastics have many uses but also increase pollution.

1940s Nuclear Reactor
Nuclear energy holds promise but carries the threat of radioactive meltdown and nuclear waste.

2000s Genetic Engineering
Biotechnology offers benefits but may also have harmful effects.

Factory workers circa 1900

Nuclear power plant, Illinois

DEBATE THE ISSUE

Nuclear Energy Building more nuclear plants would help meet our energy needs and limit fossil-fuel emissions that contribute to global warming. But the radioactive material they produce may pose grave risks to human health and safety.

❝Nuclear energy supplies clean, reliable, affordable and safe electricity and is the only emission-free source that can be readily expanded to meet our nation's growing energy needs. . . . Nuclear power plants produce electricity that otherwise would be supplied by oil-, gas-, or coal-fired generating capacity, and thus *prevent* the emissions associated with that fossil-fueled capacity.❞

—John E. Kane, Senior Vice President, Nuclear Energy Institute

❝There is strong skepticism . . . [about] the promises of the nuclear industry. . . . This is an industry that on a daily basis, as a direct result of its work, generates the most toxic and long-lived substances known to humans. It is an industry that poses a grievous threat to the health of humans and to the wider biosphere.❞

—Dave Sweeney, nuclear campaigner, Australian Conservation Foundation

 TRANSFER Activities

1. **Compare** Why does Mr. Kane support nuclear energy? Why does Mr. Sweeney oppose it?

2. **Analyze** Which of the authors cited here would be more likely to question the factory system's impact on workers?

3. **Transfer** Use the following Web site to see a video, try a WebQuest, and write in your journal. **Web Code:** neh-7302

Labor Unions Form

Industrialization lowered the prices of consumer goods, but in the late 1800s most factory workers still did not earn enough to buy them. Increasingly, working men and women took their complaints directly and forcefully to their employers. Employers usually opposed the growing labor movement, which they saw as a threat to their businesses and profits.

Early Labor Protests As early as the 1820s, factory workers tried to gain more power against employers by using the technique of **collective bargaining,** or negotiating as a group for higher wages or better working conditions. One form of collective bargaining was the strike, in which workers agreed to cease work until certain demands were met. Some strikes were local, but often they involved workers in a whole industry across a state, a region, or the country.

The first national labor union was founded in 1834 as the National Trades Union, open to workers from all trades. It lasted only a few years, and no new unions formed in the wake of the depressions of the late 1830s. However, local strikes succeeded in reducing the factory workday in some regions. The 10-hour workday became the standard in most New England factories. Gradually, national unions began to reappear.

Socialism Spreads In the 1830s, a movement called **socialism** spread throughout Europe. Socialism is an economic and political philosophy that favors public, instead of private, control of property and income. Socialists believe that society at large, not just private individuals, should take charge of a nation's wealth. That wealth, they argue, should be distributed equally to everyone.

In 1848, the German philosophers Karl Marx and Friedrich Engels expanded on the ideas of socialism in a treatise titled *Communist Manifesto*. This pamphlet denounced capitalism and predicted that workers would overturn it. Most Americans rejected these ideas, believing that they threatened the American ideals of free enterprise, private property, and individual liberty. The wealthy in particular opposed socialism because it threatened their fortunes. But many labor activists borrowed ideas from socialism to support their goals for social reform.

Founding the Knights of Labor In 1869, Uriah Smith Stephens founded a labor union called the **Knights of Labor.** Stephens, a tailor who had lived and worked around the country, included all workers of any trade, skilled or unskilled, in his union. The Knights also actively recruited African Americans. Under Stephens, the union functioned largely as a secret society, devoted to broad social reform such as replacing capitalism with workers' cooperatives. The Preamble to the Knights' Constitution, written in 1878, read:

> **Primary Source** "The recent alarming development and aggression of aggregated wealth, which, unless checked, will inevitably lead to the pauperization and hopeless degradation of the toiling masses, render it imperative, if we desire to enjoy the blessings of life, that a check should be placed upon its power . . . and a system adopted which will secure to the laborer the fruits of his toil. . . ."

In 1881, **Terence V. Powderly** took on the leadership of the Knights. The son of Irish immigrants, Powderly had worked in a menial job on the railroad before rising to become mayor of Scranton, Pennsylvania, in the 1870s. He continued to pursue ideological reforms meant to lead workers out of the bondage of wage labor. He encouraged boycotts and negotiation with employers, but he abandoned the secretive nature of the union. By 1885, the Knights had grown to include some 700,000 men and women nationwide, of every race and ethnicity. By the 1890s, however, after a series of failed strikes, the Knights had largely disappeared.

Showing Loyalty

Early unions promoted loyalty—and spread recognition—by printing their names and locations on ribbons, buttons, and posters. *Do you think employers allowed workers to display such items at work? Explain.*

Forming the AFL In 1886, **Samuel Gompers** formed the **American Federation of Labor (AFL).** Gompers was a poor English immigrant who had worked his way up to head the local cigarmakers' union in New York. While the Knights of Labor were made up of all workers, the AFL was a craft union, a loose organization of skilled workers from some 100 local unions devoted to specific crafts or trades. These local unions retained their individuality but gained strength in bargaining through their affiliation with the AFL.

Gompers set high dues for membership in the AFL, pooling the money to create a strike and pension fund to assist workers in need. Unlike the Knights of Labor, the AFL did not aim for larger social gains for workers. Instead, it focused on very specific workers' issues such as wages, working hours, and working conditions. The AFL also pressed for workplaces in which only union members could be hired. Because of its narrow focus on workers' issues, the AFL was often called a "bread and butter" union.

The AFL was not as successful as the Knights in gaining membership, partly because of its own policies. It opposed women members, because Gompers believed their presence in the workplace would drive wages down. While it was theoretically open to African Americans, local branches usually found ways to exclude them.

 Checkpoint How did various labor unions differ in their goals?

Strikes Rock the Nation

As membership in labor unions rose and labor activists became more skilled in organizing large-scale protests, a wave of bitter confrontations between labor and management hit the nation. The first major strike occurred in the railroad industry in 1877. Striking workers, responding to wage cuts, caused massive property destruction in several cities. State militias were called in to protect strikebreakers, or temporary workers hired to perform the jobs of striking workers. Finally, the federal government sent in troops to restore order. In the decades to follow, similar labor disputes would affect businesses, the government, and the organization of labor unions themselves.

Violence Erupts in Haymarket Square On May 1, 1886, thousands of workers mounted a national demonstration for an eight-hour workday. Strikes erupted in several cities, and fights broke out between strikers and strikebreakers. Conflict then escalated between strikers and police who were brought in to halt the violence. On May 4, protesters gathered at Haymarket Square in Chicago. The diverse crowd included anarchists, or radicals opposed to all government. A frenzy broke out when a protester threw a bomb, killing a policemen. Dozens of people, both protesters and policemen, were killed. Eight anarchists were tried

Major Strikes of the Late 1800s		☑ Quick Study
Strike	**Cause**	**Effect**
Railroad strikes, 1877	Response to cuts in workers' wages	Set the scene for violent strikes to come
Haymarket Square, 1886	Part of a campaign to achieve an eight-hour workday	Americans became wary of labor unions; the Knights of Labor were blamed for the riot and membership declined.
Homestead Strike, 1892	Economic depression led to cuts in steelworkers' wages	After losing the standoff, steelworker unions lost power throughout the country.
Pullman Strike, 1893	Wages cut without a decrease in the cost of living in the company town	Employers used the courts to limit the influence of unions.

KNIGHTS OF THE NINETEENTH CENTURY.

for murder, and four were executed. The governor of Illinois, deciding that evidence for the convictions had been scanty, pardoned three of the others. The fourth had already committed suicide in jail.

The **Haymarket Riot** left an unfortunate legacy. The Knights of Labor fizzled out as people shied away from radicalism. Employers became even more suspicious of union activities, associating them with violence. In general, much of the American public at that time came to share that view.

Steelworkers Strike at Homestead

In the summer of 1892, a Carnegie Steel plant in Homestead, Pennsylvania, cut workers' wages. The union immediately called a strike. Andrew Carnegie's partner, Henry Frick, responded by bringing in the Pinkertons, a private police force known for their ability to break up strikes. The Pinkertons killed several strikers and wounded many others in a standoff that lasted some two weeks. Then, on July 23, an anarchist who had joined the protesters tried to assassinate Frick. The union had not backed his plan, but the public associated the two. Recognizing that public opinion was turning against unions, the union called off the strike in November. The **Homestead Strike** was part of an epidemic of steelworkers' and miners' strikes that took place as economic depression spread across America. In each case, troops and local militia were called in to suppress the unrest.

Workers Strike Against Pullman

In 1893, the Pullman Palace Car Company, which produced luxury railroad cars, laid off workers and reduced wages by 25 percent. Inventor George Pullman, who owned the company, required workers to live in the company town near Chicago and controlled their rents and the prices of goods. In May of 1894, workers sent a delegation to negotiate with Pullman. He responded by firing three workers and shutting down the plant.

Desperate, the workers turned to the American Railway Union (A.R.U.), led by **Eugene V. Debs.** Debs had begun work in a low-level railroad job while still a teenager, working his way up. He had condemned the railroad strike of 1877, which he said was a result of disorganization and corruption within the unions.

● INFOGRAPHIC

Pullman Workers Strike!

On May 11, 1894, workers of the Pullman Palace Car Company in Chicago went on strike, protesting wage cuts and worker layoffs. When the workers allied with the American Railway Union, the strike quickly spread. Railroad workers refused to service trains with Pullman cars, disrupting rail and mail service in several states. The strike grew increasingly violent, with workers destroying railroad equipment. When 12,000 federal troops were called in to end the strike, clashes between workers and troops broke out and led to riots, looting, and the deaths of over 30 people. The strike finally ended on August 3, with the arrest of Eugene Debs.

The Company Town

Pullman intended his clean, neat company town to protect workers from immoral influences—and to make a favorable impression on visitors. Life inside the town presented a different picture. Pullman owned the housing, stores, and churches, and charged steep rents for them all. Despite cutting wages several times, he never reduced rents or prices of goods. As a result, Pullman workers went further and further into debt.

After a deduction for rent, a worker's paycheck in the late 1800s totaled two cents (about forty cents in today's dollars). After the strike a worker testified that "I have seen men with families of eight or nine children crying because they got only three or four cents after paying their rent."

The Main Players

◀ **George Pullman** amassed a fortune in the railroad car business. A government investigation of the strike blamed Pullman and ruined his reputation.

Experienced labor leader and ARU head
◀ **Eugene Debs** spent six months in jail, where he read about European labor unions and became a Socialist.

Thinking Critically

1. **Distinguishing Fact From Opinion** A Pullman worker described life in the company town as "slavery worse than that of Negroes of the South." Is this factually accurate?

2. **Predict Consequences** How might the Pullman Strike have been avoided?

Debs organized the A.R.U. as an industrial union, grouping all railroad workers together rather than separating them by the job they held. He believed that industrial unions allowed groups to exert united pressure on employers.

The A.R.U. called for a nationwide strike. By June of 1894, nearly 300,000 railworkers had walked off their jobs. The **Pullman Strike** escalated, halting both railroad traffic and mail delivery. Railroad owners cited the Sherman Antitrust Act in its argument that the union was illegally disrupting free trade. On July 4, President Grover Cleveland sent in federal troops, ending the strike. When he refused the government's order to end the strike, Debs was imprisoned for conspiring against interstate commerce. Though Debs appealed the conviction, claiming that the government had no authority to halt the strike, the Supreme Court upheld it in the case *In re Debs* in 1895.

Effects on the Labor Movement The outcome of the Pullman Strike set an important <u>trend</u>. Employers appealed frequently for court orders against unions, citing legislation like the Sherman Antitrust Act. The federal government regularly approved these appeals, denying unions recognition as legally protected organizations and limiting union gains for more than 30 years. As the twentieth century opened, industrialists, workers, and government agencies lashed out at one another over numerous labor issues. Contract negotiations, strikes, and legislation would become the way of life for American industry.

In the decades after Pullman, the labor movement split into different factions, some increasingly influenced by socialism. By the end of the 1800s, Debs had become a Socialist. He helped organize the American Socialist Party in 1897, running for President in 1900. In 1905, he helped found the Industrial Workers of the World (IWW), or Wobblies. The IWW was a radical union of unskilled workers with many Socialists among its leaders. In the first few decades of the 1900s, the IWW led a number of strikes, many of them violent.

✔ **Checkpoint** Why did workers increasingly turn to the strike as a tactic to win labor gains?

Vocabulary Builder

<u>trend</u>–(trehnd) *n.* general course of events

SECTION

3 Assessment

Progress Monitoring *Online*
For: Self-test with vocabulary practice
Web Code: nca-1331

Comprehension

1. **Terms and People** For each item below, write a sentence explaining how it relates to the growing labor movement in the late 1800s.
   - sweatshop
   - company town
   - collective bargaining
   - socialism
   - Knights of Labor
   - Terence V. Powderly
   - Samuel Gompers
   - AFL
   - Haymarket Riot
   - Homestead Strike
   - Eugene V. Debs
   - Pullman Strike

2. **NoteTaking Reading Skill: Identify Main Ideas** Use your completed concept web to answer the Section Focus Question: How did the rise of labor unions shape relations among workers, big business, and government?

Writing About History

3. **Quick Write: Organize Information** Suppose you are a labor organizer writing a memo to union members proposing a strike. Decide on the kind of information you want to present in the main body of your memo. List the information you will cover and note what format it will be in, for example, bulleted lists, charts, and so on.

Critical Thinking

4. **Recognize Ideologies** What does the prevalence of child labor in the 1800s tell you about how society viewed children at the time?

5. **Identify Central Issues** Why were employers generally opposed to labor unions?

6. **Recognize Cause and Effect** Why did the major strikes of the late 1800s lead to a backlash against labor unions?

CHAPTER 13

Quick Study Guide

 3.II.E.1, 3.III.A

Progress Monitoring Online
For: Self-test with vocabulary practice
Web Code: nca-1341

■ Causes of Industrialization

Civil War	Natural Resources	Growing Workforce	Technology/Innovation	Government Policies
The war encouraged production, innovation, and expansion of railroads.	Ample natural resources, including oil, fueled growth.	Immigrants willing to work for low wages flowed into the country.	New technology and innovative business practices spurred growth.	Government policies encouraged investment in businesses and new technology.

↓ ↓ ↓ ↓ ↓

Industrialization

■ Influential Labor Unions

Name	Date Founded	Significance
National Trades Union	1834	First national union; open to workers from all trades
Knights of Labor	1869	Sought general ideological reform; open to workers from all trades
American Federation of Labor	1886	Focused on specific workers' issues; organization of skilled workers from local craft unions
American Railway Union	1893	First industrial union; open to all railway workers

■ Important People of the Late 1800s

Thomas Edison	Invented new technology, such as electric lighting, that stimulated business
Henry Bessemer	Developed process for creating strong, lightweight steel for use in construction and railroads
Andrew Carnegie	Use of vertical consolidation influenced the rise of big business; urged businessmen to also be philanthropists
John D. Rockefeller	Use of new business strategies, such as horizontal consolidation, influenced the rise of big business
Samuel Gompers	Formed the AFL, influencing the rise of labor unions
Eugene V. Debs	Challenged big business by orchestrating the Pullman Strike and helping to found the IWW

■ Important Government Policies of the Late 1800s

- **Protective tariffs** Congress enacted tariffs on imported goods to make them cost more than locally produced goods.
- **Laissez-faire policies** The government allowed businesses to operate under minimal government regulation.
- **Subsidizing railroads** The government gave railroad builders millions of acres of land.
- **Strike breaking** Government troops routinely helped break up strikes.
- **Antiunion actions** Courts used legislation like the Sherman Antitrust Act to order unions to stop disrupting free trade.

☑ Quick Study Timeline

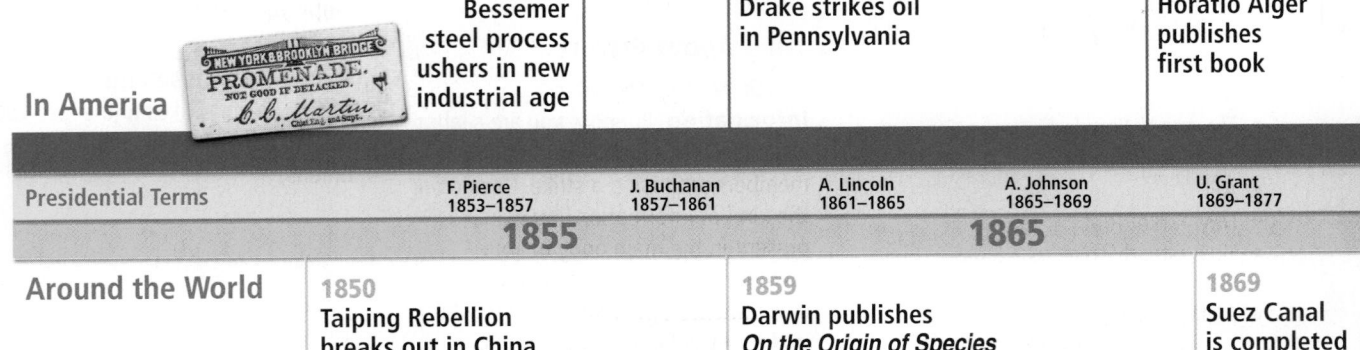

In America

| 1856 Bessemer steel process ushers in new industrial age | 1859 Drake strikes oil in Pennsylvania | 1868 Horatio Alger publishes first book |

Presidential Terms

| F. Pierce 1853–1857 | J. Buchanan 1857–1861 | A. Lincoln 1861–1865 | A. Johnson 1865–1869 | U. Grant 1869–1877 |

1855   1865

Around the World

| 1850 Taiping Rebellion breaks out in China | 1859 Darwin publishes *On the Origin of Species* | 1869 Suez Canal is completed |

American Issues
•—•—• Connector

By connecting prior knowledge with what you have learned in this chapter, you can gradually build your understanding of enduring questions that still affect America today. Answer the questions below. Then, use your American Issues Connector study guide (or go online: www.PHSchool.com **Web Code:** neh-7303).

Issues You Learned About

● **Technology and Society** New technology brings both positive and negative changes to a society.

1. The industrialization of the United States changed the way Americans worked and lived. Write a paragraph or two evaluating the benefits and drawbacks of technology on American society. Consider the following:
   - new inventions and innovations
   - the growth of railroads
   - the loss of traditional jobs and the development of new ones
   - the environment
   - the rise of big business and business tycoons

● **Government's Role in the Economy** The government may pass new laws regulating business in response to changes in the economy.

2. Identify and describe one way that the federal government contributed to the success of businesses in the late 1800s.

3. What problems caused the government to create the Interstate Commerce Commission and the Sherman Antitrust Act? What were the long-term effects of these laws?

4. How did corporations and businesses transform the Sherman Antitrust Act into a tool for their own benefit?

● **Social Problems and Reform** Labor unions first formed in the early 1800s to protect workers' rights, and by the late 1800s, several national organizations had developed.

5. According to Uriah Smith Stephens, what was the best solution for leading workers out of the bondage of labor?

6. What working conditions did labor unions seek to improve? What methods did they use to achieve their aims?

7. Overall, did the efforts of the labor unions have a positive impact on workers' lives and jobs? Explain.

Connect to Your World | New York

Technology in Society George Westinghouse was born in Central Bridge, New York in 1846. An inventor and businessman, Westinghouse received over 100 patents and started many companies. He worked with other inventors to develop a system for transmitting alternating current (AC) electricity, which we still use today. In 1893, Westinghouse's company, working with inventor Nikola Tesla, began to build generators to harness the energy of Niagara Falls and transmit it to distant destinations, using the AC system. The project was a great success, carrying electricity first to Buffalo, 20 miles away, and later all the way to New York City. Research the impact of Westinghouse's work in alternating currents, and write a paragraph explaining its significance.

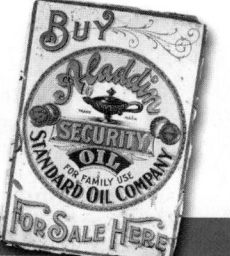

| 1877 Great Railroad Strike | 1882 Standard Oil Trust is formed | 1890 Congress passes Sherman Antitrust Act | 1894 Pullman Strike | **History Interactive** For: Interactive timeline Web Code: ncp-1341 |

| R. Hayes 1877–1881 | J. Garfield 1881 C. Arthur 1881–1885 | G. Cleveland 1885–1889 | B. Harrison 1889–1893 | G. Cleveland 1893–1897 | W. McKinley 1897–1901 |

1875   **1885**   **1895**

1876 Korea becomes an independent nation

1885 Congress Party is established in India

1899 Boer War breaks out in southern Africa

Chapter Assessment

Terms and People

1. What was the **Bessemer process**? What effect did it have on American industry?

2. Define **corporation**. List two methods that corporations used to maximize their profits.

3. Define **horizontal integration** and **vertical integration**. Identify a company or an entrepreneur that practiced each.

4. What was the **Haymarket Riot**? What impact did it have on the labor movement?

5. Who was **Eugene V. Debs**? How did the government respond to his actions in the Pullman Strike?

Focus Questions

The focus question for this chapter is **How did the industrial growth of the late 1800s shape American society and the economy?** Build an answer to this big question by answering the focus questions for Sections 1 through 3 and the Critical Thinking questions that follow.

Section 1

6. How did industrialization and new technology affect the economy and society?

Section 2

7. How did big business shape the American economy in the late 1800s and early 1900s?

Section 3

8. How did the rise of labor unions shape relations among workers, big business, and government?

Critical Thinking

9. **Analyze Causes and Effects** Was the idea of "rags to riches" a cause or a result of industrialization? Explain.

10. **Draw Inferences** Why did industrialists like J. P. Morgan support the work of inventors?

11. **Explain Effects** How did the growth of railroad technology change American society? How did it change businesses?

12. **Recognize Bias** What does the theory of Social Darwinism demonstrate about the way some Americans felt about wealth and poverty?

13. **Predict Consequences** What would a modern-day entrepreneur who believed in Carnegie's "gospel of wealth" do with his or her fortune?

14. **Analyze Information** Describe the system that critics of mining towns referred to as "wage slavery." Why did critics adopt this name?

15. **Recognize Ideologies** Would Marx and Engels have become entrepreneurs if they had lived in the United States? Explain.

16. **Analyze Charts** Mary Harris Jones played a prominent role in one of the labor unions below, traveling around the country and demanding rights for coal miners and other workers. Which union was it? Explain your answer using details from the chart.

Knights of Labor	American Federation of Labor
• Founded in 1869 by Uriah Smith Stephens	• Founded in 1886 by Samuel Gompers
• Included skilled and unskilled workers	• Included skilled workers who practiced specific crafts and trades
• Included women and members of all races and ethnicities	• Excluded women and African Americans as members
• Originally operated as a secret society	• Set high dues for membership
• Focused on achieving social reform	• Focused on addressing specific workers' issues

---

Writing About History

Writing a Memo In the age of industrialization and big business, long before there were cellphones and e-mail, people conveyed their ideas to one another by writing. Memos were one way to briefly convey information, such as company policy, legal matters, financial matters, and so on. Write a memo that one of the following people may have written in the late 1800s: John D. Rockefeller, Thomas Edison, Andrew Carnegie, Eugene V. Debs, Samuel Gompers, George Pullman.

Prewriting

• Use library or online resources to read about each of the people listed above.

• Choose the person who most interests you and note the kinds of information he or she would have wanted to convey.

• Choose a title line for your memo. If your topic cannot fit onto one line, it may be too broad for the purposes of a memo.

Drafting

• Present your main point as clearly and concisely as possible.

• Decide whether any of your information can be better conveyed as a chart, bulleted list, or other graphic organizer.

Revising

• Use the guidelines on page SH16 of the Writing Handbook to revise your memo.

Regents DBQ Practice

Attitudes Toward Organized Labor

Were labor unions successful in working out their disputes with big-business owners? Or did the federal government and the courts need to play a role in settling these disputes? Use your knowledge of the organized labor movement and Documents 1, 2, 3, and 4 to answer questions 1 through 4.

Document 1

"The workers at the blast furnaces in our steel-rail works once sent in a 'round-robin' stating that unless the firm gave them an advance of wages by Monday afternoon at four o'clock they would leave the furnaces. . . . Gentlemen of the Blast Furnace Committee, you have threatened our firm that you will break your agreement and that you will leave these blast furnaces . . . unless you get a favorable answer to your threat by four o'clock today. It is not three but your answer is ready. You may leave the blast furnaces. . . . The worst day that labor has ever seen in this world is that day in which it dishonors itself by breaking its agreement. You have your answer."

— The Autobiography of Andrew Carnegie,
August 1920

Document 2

"In the winter of 1893–1894 the employees of the Pullman Palace Car Company . . . joined the new American Railway Union . . . attempting to organize all workers connected with the railways. . . . The [Pullman] company refused to consider arbitration and the boycott went into effect. . . . Indictments charging Debs [president of the American Railway Union] and others of violations of the Sherman Act were secured. . . . As a result of the various injunctions, indictments, and the activities of federal troops which reached Chicago, following directions from President Cleveland, the strike and the consequent violence were practically at an end by the middle of July."

— Labor and the Sherman Act
by Edward Berman, 1930

Document 3

"There was a time when workmen were denied the right of leaving their employers, when they were part of the soil, owned by their employers. . . . Not many years ago, when workmen counseled with each other for the purpose of resisting a reduction in their wages or making an effort to secure an increase, it was held to be a conspiracy punishable by imprisonment. Through the effort of organized labor, an enlightened public sentiment changed all this until to-day the right to unite for material, moral, and social improvement on the part of workers is accepted by all."

— *Samuel Gompers to Editor,* Washington Evening Star,
May 15, 1900

Document 4

THE CHIVALRY OF MODERN KNIGHTS.
© 2001 HARPWEEK®

---

1. In Document 1, what view does Andrew Carnegie take toward organized labor?
   (1) Businesses should bargain with employees.
   (2) Workers should be paid fair wages.
   (3) Employees should honor their original work agreement.
   (4) Business owners should take workers' threats seriously.

2. Which document is a secondary source that describes how the Sherman Act was used as a legal tool to end a strike?
   (1) Document 4
   (2) Document 1
   (3) Document 2
   (4) Document 3

3. Who does the cartoonist ridicule in Document 4?
   (1) The government
   (2) The Knights of Labor
   (3) The Sherman Antitrust Act
   (4) George Pullman

4. **Writing Task** Who do you think was correct about the way to settle disputes between organized labor and big business: business owners, organized labor, or the government? Use your knowledge of the chapter content and specific evidence from the primary and secondary sources above to support your opinion.

14 Immigration and Urbanization

1865–1914

WITNESS HISTORY 🔊 AUDIO

The New American City

Midwestern clergyman Josiah Strong was both fascinated and distressed by rapid urban growth. Americans bought more than 130,000 copies of his 1885 book *Our Country: Its Possible Future and Its Present Crisis*. In it, Strong explains:

> ❝The city is the nerve center of our civilization. It is also the storm center. . . . During the half century preceding 1880, population in the city increased more than four times as rapidly as that of the village and country. In 1800 there were only six cities . . . which had a population of 8,000 or more. In 1880 there were 286. . . . The city has become a serious menace to our civilization, because . . . it has a peculiar attraction for the immigrant. . . . Our ten larger cities contain only nine per cent of the entire population, but 23 per cent of the foreign. . . . The rich are richer, and the poor are poorer, in the city than elsewhere; and, as a rule, the greater the city, the greater are the riches of the rich and the poverty of the poor.❞
> —Josiah Strong, *Our Country: Its Possible Future and Its Present Crisis*, 1885

Listen to the Witness History *audio to hear more about cities of the late eighteenth century.*

◀ This colorized photograph shows Mulberry Street in New York City's "Little Italy" around 1900.

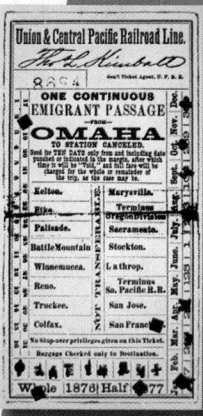

Immigrant train ticket to San Francisco

Early skyscraper

Ⓝⓨ Core Curriculum Preview

Chapter Focus Question: How did American urban life change between 1875 and 1914?

Section 1
The New Immigrants 1.I.D.2, 3.III.B.1, 3.III.C.1, 3.III.C.2

Section 2
Cities Expand and Change 3.III.A.1, 3.III.B.4

Section 3
Social and Cultural Trends 3.III.A.3, 3.III.A.4, 3.III.A.5

Use the ☑ **Quick Study Timeline** at the end of this chapter to preview chapter events.

Early bicycle

Note Taking Study Guide block

Note Taking Study Guide *Online*
For: Note Taking and American Issues Connector
Web Code: nee-7401

SECTION

1

WITNESS HISTORY 🔊 AUDIO

Looking Forward and Back

Life was difficult for many immigrants in the United States during the late 1800s, but it also offered freedoms they had never known in their homelands.

❝Not the looking forward made me go, but the looking backward made me search a new life and struggle a hard battle. . . . [I]t is hard still now to bear the homesickness, loneliness, among strange people not knowing the language doing hard [work] without a minute of joy. But when I look back into my childhood . . . , always under a terrible fear . . . I think that there is not anything harder. . . . America means for an Immigrant a fairy promised land that came out true, a land that gives all they need for their work, a land which gives them human rights, a land that gives morality through her churches and education through her free schools and libraries.❞

—young Russian Jewish woman

The New Immigrants

Core Curriculum Objectives

- **1.I.D.2** Immigration
- **3.III.B.1** Immigration, 1850–1924: New sources: eastern/southern Europe
- **3.III.C.1** Reactions to the "new" immigration: Cultural pluralism: assimilation
- **3.III.C.2** Reactions to the "new" immigration: Nativists' stereotyping and prejudice

Terms and People

"new" immigrant   Americanization
steerage   "melting pot"
Ellis Island   nativism
Angel Island   Chinese Exclusion Act

NoteTaking

Reading Skill: Identify Main Ideas Record the main ideas of each section in an outline.

| I. New Immigrants Come to America |
| A. |
| B. |
| II. Immigrants Decide to Leave Home |

Why It Matters Immigration has been a central theme in American history. However, when the foreign-born population of the United States nearly doubled between 1870 and 1900, some Americans feared that the newcomers would destroy American culture. Instead, Americans adopted parts of immigrant cultures, while immigrants adopted parts of American culture. **Section Focus Question: Why did immigrants come to the United States, and what impact did they have upon society?**

New Immigrants Come to America

Immigrants had always come to America for economic opportunity and religious freedom. Until the 1870s, the majority had been Protestants from northern and western Europe. They came as families to settle in the United States, often on farms with family or friends who had come before. Many had saved some money for the journey, had a skill or trade, or were educated.

Many German and Irish Catholics had immigrated in the 1840s and 1850s, and more arrived after the Civil War. Some Americans had prejudices against Catholics, but the Irish spoke English and the German Catholics benefited from the good reputation of their Protestant countrymen. Although they lacked skills and money, the children of these immigrants were often able to blend into American society. Beginning in the 1870s, Irish and Germans were joined by **"new" immigrants** from southern and eastern Europe. They arrived in increasing numbers until the outbreak of World War I.

In contrast to "old" immigrants who had come before the Irish and Germans, "new" immigrants were often unskilled, poor, Catholic or Jewish, and likely to settle in cities rather than on farms. Many came alone, planning to save some money in the United States and return home to live. They came from Italy, Greece, Poland, Hungary, and Russia. After 1900, immigrants from Southern and Eastern Europe made up more than 70 percent of all immigrants, up from about 1 percent at midcentury. Many native-born Americans felt threatened by these newcomers with different cultures and languages.

✓ **Checkpoint** Describe the "new" immigrants.

Immigrants Decide to Leave Home

Two types of factors lead to immigration. Push factors are those that compel people to leave their homes, such as famine, war, or persecution. Pull factors are those that draw people *to* a new place, such as economic opportunity or religious freedom. Many immigrants in the late nineteenth century had both push and pull factors that helped them decide to leave the familiar for the unknown.

Push Factors In the 1880s, farmers had a difficult time. In Mexico, Poland, and China, land reform and low prices forced many farmers off their land. Some chose to come to America to get a new start. Beginning in the 1840s, China and eastern Europe experienced repeated wars and political revolutions. These events disrupted economies and left political refugees. One of the largest groups to settle in America were Russian and eastern European Jews. Beginning in the 1880s, they fled religious persecution and came to the United States to achieve a better life.

Pull Factors In addition to a vague hope for opportunity, the United States offered special attractions, including plentiful land and employment. The 1862 Homestead Act and aid from railroad companies made western farmland inexpensive. The railroads even offered reduced fares to get there because they needed customers in the west for their own business to succeed. Until 1885, immigrants were recruited from their homelands to build railroads, dig in mines, work in oil fields, harvest produce, or toil in factories. Others hoped to strike it rich by finding gold.

Many others were "chain immigrants," joining family or friends who had already settled in America. The earlier arriving immigrants promised to help the newcomers find work and housing, and sometimes they even sent them tickets for the journey. Immigrants may have lured their families and friends with the promise of religious and political freedom. In America, one could worship and vote as one chose without fear of persecution by the government.

✓ **Checkpoint** List the push and pull factors for immigrants.

Reminders of Home
Immigrants often brought items of special significance, such as this Jewish prayer shawl from Russia. ▼

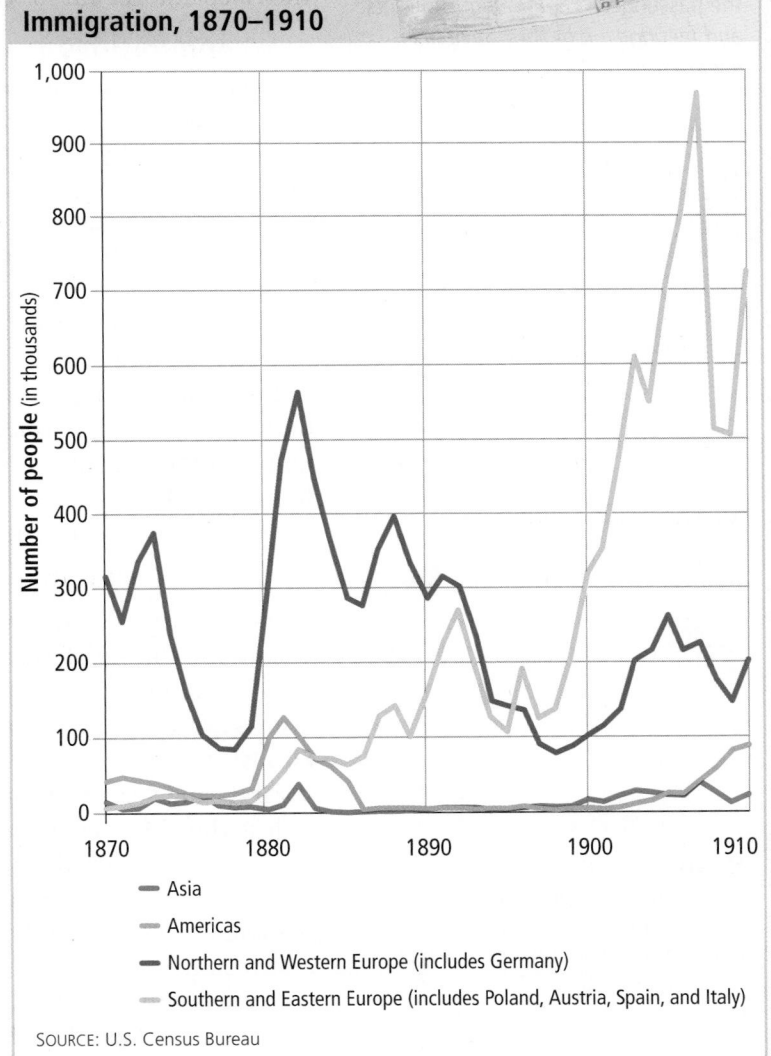

Immigration, 1870–1910

Number of people (in thousands)

- Asia
- Americas
- Northern and Western Europe (includes Germany)
- Southern and Eastern Europe (includes Poland, Austria, Spain, and Italy)

SOURCE: U.S. Census Bureau

Union & Central Pacific Railroad Line.

ONE CONTINUOUS
EMIGRANT PASSAGE
—FROM—
OMAHA
TO STATION CANCELED.

Arriving in America
Immigrants wait on the deck of the S.S. *Prince Frederick Wilhelm.* Look at the passengers' faces. *What thoughts and feelings might they have been experiencing? Why?*

The Immigrant Experience

Immigrant experiences varied greatly. However, there were common themes: a tough decision to leave home and family, a hard and costly journey with an uncertain end, and the difficulties of learning a new language and adjusting to a foreign culture. Millions of people decided that the possibilities outweighed the risks and set out for the United States.

The Long Journey Coming to America was a big task. Travelers needed money for passage and to make a new start, although some had only enough for a ticket. The immigrants' first task was to pack the items that would help them start a new life. Usually, they brought only what they could carry: clothes, maybe a photograph of loved ones, a cherished musical instrument, or the tools of their trade. Next, they made their way to a port of departure, hoping that a ship would be leaving soon. In war-torn areas, just getting to the ship could be dangerous.

By the 1870s, steamships made the trip across the Atlantic safer and faster than ever before. However, it could be an awful voyage. Most immigrants traveled in **steerage,** the worst accommodations on the ship. Located on the lower decks with no private cabins, steerage was crowded and dirty. Illness spread quickly, while rough weather could force seasick passengers to stay in cramped quarters for days at a time. Under these conditions, even healthy immigrants fell ill, while frail passengers sometimes died. Passengers on other voyages were fortunate to have beautiful weather and no illness onboard.

Immigrants Arrive at American Ports The first stop for ships at American ports was a processing station where immigration officials decided who could stay in the United States. To enter, immigrants had to be healthy and show that they had money, a skill, or a sponsor to provide for them. Most European immigrants arrived in New York Harbor. Beginning in 1892, they were processed at **Ellis Island.**

First- and second-class passengers were inspected on the ship and released, unless they had obvious medical problems. All third-class, or steerage, passengers were sent to Ellis Island. There, immigration officers conducted legal and medical inspections. Since the shipowners did a <u>preliminary</u> screening before passengers boarded, only about 2 percent of immigrants were denied entry; the rest took a ferry to New York City. In 1907, 10-year-old Edward Corsi arrived with his family from Italy. Years later, when he had become an immigration official, he remembered his first impressions:

—Edward Corsi, *In the Shadow of Liberty,* 1935

Chinese and other Asian immigrants crossed the Pacific Ocean, arriving in San Francisco Bay. They were processed at **Angel Island,** which opened in 1910. If Ellis Island was welcoming to some, Angel Island was always formidable and seemingly designed to filter out Chinese immigrants. After 1882, Chinese travelers were turned away unless they could prove that they were American citizens or had relatives living in America. Officials often assumed that Chinese newcomers would misrepresent themselves in order to gain entry. While most immigrants left Ellis Island within hours, Chinese immigrants at Angel Island were often held for weeks or even months in poor conditions.

✔ **Checkpoint** Describe what happened to immigrants when they arrived.

Opportunities and Challenges in America

Passing immigration inspections was just the first step. Once in America, immigrants immediately faced tough decisions such as where to settle and how to find work. On top of that, most had to learn a new language and new customs. Sometimes, immigrants worked with an agent who spoke their language for help finding work and housing, but many agents took advantage of the newcomers to make money. Lucky immigrants had contacts through family and friends who could help them navigate a new and strange world.

Immigrants Assimilate Into Society Most new immigrants stayed in cities, close to industrial jobs in factories. There, they often lived in ethnic neighborhoods, called ghettoes, with people who shared their native language, religion, and culture. Neighbors might have come from the same country, region, or even village.

Angel Island Poetry

Detained Chinese immigrants might have spent weeks or months waiting to find out if they would be allowed to stay in the United States. To pass the time and express their frustrations, many carved poems into the walls at Angel Island. What does the poem below tell you about the author?

Primary Source

66Lin, upon arriving in America,
Was arrested, put in a wooden building,
And made a prisoner.
I was here for one autumn.
The Americans did not allow me to land.
I was ordered to be deported.99

—*Taoist From the Town of Iron* AUDIO

By 1890, many cities had huge immigrant populations. In San Francisco and Chicago, they made up more than 40 percent of the population. Four out of five inhabitants of New York City were foreign born or had foreign-born parents. While exclusionist policies forced some people to live in ghettoes, these neighborhoods also provided familiarity. Specialty shops, grocers, and clothing stores provided a taste of the food and culture that immigrants had left behind.

In many cities, volunteer institutions known as settlement houses ran **Americanization** programs, helping newcomers learn English and adopt American dress and diet. At the same time, immigrants helped one another through fraternal associations, such as the Polish National Alliance and the Ancient Order of Hibernians. These organizations, based on ethnic or religious identity, provided social services and financial assistance. Settlement workers and immigrants alike believed that American society was a **"melting pot"** in which white people of all different nationalities blended to create a single culture. The term came from the name of a play that opened in 1908. This model excluded Asian immigrants, who became targets of social and legal discrimination.

Despite the hopes of settlement workers, immigrants often held on to their traditions. Their children, however, became more Americanized, without memories of homes and families left behind. Some adults dreamed of returning to their homelands, but few did. Instead, they established fraternal lodges and religious institutions that made them feel more comfortable in their new surroundings. Catholics, in particular, established churches and parochial schools. In many cities, Irish Catholic churches stood side by side with Italian Catholic churches—each built to serve the needs of its own community. The immigrants' churches, schools, and institutions reminded native-born Americans that new cultures were changing American society.

New Immigrants Face Hostility Accepting immigrants into American society was not always easy. Newcomers often faced **nativism,** which was a belief that native-born white Americans were superior to newcomers. During the economic recessions of the late nineteenth century, competition for jobs and housing fueled resentment, while religious and cultural differences sparked suspicion between native-born workers and immigrants, as well as between ethnic groups. Many workers worried that immigrants would work for lower pay.

Religion was also a big problem. Protestants were suspicious of Catholicism, the religion of many Irish, German, Italian, and Polish people. Some native-born white Protestants would not hire, vote for, or work with Catholics or Jews. Some Americans even signed restrictive contracts agreeing not to rent or sell property to Catholics, Jews, African Americans, or other groups they considered "non-native."

Nativist intellectuals backed up their prejudices with dubious scientific rhetoric that linked immigrants' physical characteristics to criminal tendencies or lower intellectual abilities. Extreme hostility toward Chinese laborers led Congress to pass the **Chinese Exclusion Act** in 1882. The act prohibited immigration by Chinese laborers, limited the civil rights of Chinese immigrants already in the United States, and forbade the naturalization of Chinese residents. Many Chinese dared not visit their families in China, fearing they would not be permitted to return. In 1898, a court case established that Chinese people born in America were United States citizens and could, therefore, come and go freely. However, many immigration officials ignored this ruling.

In the same year, Congress passed another act that prohibited the entry of anyone who was a criminal, immoral, a pauper, or likely to need public assistance. In practice, the law was used to bar many poor or handicapped immigrants. These acts marked the beginning of immigration restriction into the United States. Until then, everyone had been welcomed. Immigration became a constant topic of conversation throughout America.

✔ **Checkpoint** Why did some Americans want to restrict immigration?

Immigrants Change America

Despite opposition, immigrants transformed American society. They fueled industrial growth, acquired citizenship, elected politicians, and made their traditions part of American culture. Mexican Americans in the Southwest developed effective ranching techniques, while Chinese, Irish, and Mexican laborers built the railroads. Equally as important, immigrants labored in coal mines, steel mills, textile mills, and factories. Immigrant women worked in factories, as seamstresses, as laundresses, and doing piecework. Others became domestic servants. Though the conditions were harsh and they received few benefits, immigrants' labor helped the United States become a world power.

Increasingly, immigrants demanded a voice, becoming active in labor unions and politics. They lobbied for policies to protect the poor and powerless and used their votes to elect favorable governments. The political leaders they supported became powerful. Union leaders demanded reforms that helped immigrants as well as all laborers. Immigrants expanded the definition of *American*.

✔ **Checkpoint** How did immigrants assimilate to and change American culture?

Immigrant Contributions
Immigrants made many contributions to American culture. Composer Irving Berlin immigrated in 1893 and later wrote "God Bless America" and many other well-known songs. *Can you name any other famous immigrants?*

SECTION **1** Assessment

Progress Monitoring _Online_
For: Self-test with vocabulary practice
Web Code: nca-1402

Comprehension

1. **Terms and People** What do the terms below have in common?
   - "new" immigrant
   - steerage
   - Ellis Island
   - Angel Island
   - Americanization
   - "melting pot"
   - nativism
   - Chinese Exclusion Act

2. **NoteTaking Reading Skill: Main Ideas** Use your outline to answer the Section Focus Question: Why did immigrants come to the United States, and what impact did they have upon society?

Writing About History

3. **Quick Write: Outline a Proposal** Outline a plan for helping immigrants adjust to life in America. Consider cultural and language differences.

Critical Thinking

4. **Make Comparisons** How did new immigrants differ from old immigrants?

5. **Express Problems Clearly** What problems did immigrants face in coming to America?

6. **Draw Conclusions** In what ways did immigrants affect the American economy and culture?

IMMIGRANTS 1905

EXPERIENCE ELLIS ISLAND

▲ Ellis Island in 1926

▼ Immigrants arrive at Ellis Island carrying their belongings and a paper with their entry number.

By 1900, thousands of immigrants steamed past the Statue of Liberty and landed at Ellis Island each day. After checking their baggage, immigrants walked up a staircase toward the Great Hall on the second floor. Doctors watched closely, looking for signs of illness. At the top of the stairs, about one tenth of the immigrants were marked with chalk and sent for a closer examination. Some were quarantined on the island until they recovered their health. Others were sent home, their dreams crushed.

At the Great Hall, immigrants waited for an interview with a customs officer who checked paperwork and determined if immigrants would be able to support themselves. If they passed inspection, they could buy a train ticket before boarding a ferry for the mainland. Those with no money might stay in the dormitories until a sponsor arrived to vouch for them. Single women were detained until a relative collected them, or they could marry on the island. By 1954, more than 12 million immigrants had passed through Ellis Island on their way to a new life.

Causes of Immigration

Push Factors	Pull Factors
• Persecution	• Religious and political freedom
• Economic hardship	• Cheap land
• Lack of jobs	• Factory jobs
• War	• Family in the United States

GREAT HALL

MEDICAL EXAM

THE DINING ROOM

The passenger list (below right) included each passenger's name, gender, previous address, who paid for the tickets, and other information. Immigrants often brought keepsakes like this locket and sent postcards to announce their safe arrival.

Thinking Critically

1. **Analyze Visuals** Look at the photos on this page. In what ways might Ellis Island have been an intimidating place?

2. **Make Inferences** Why were single women not allowed to leave Ellis Island on their own?

Connect to Today Do research to learn about how immigrants legally enter the United States today. How are the experiences of today's immigrants similar to and different from those of the immigrants who arrived at Ellis Island?

History *Interactive* ★

For: Experience Ellis Island video, audio, and analysis
Web Code: ncp-1403

A Fiery Tide

As cities expanded, city services, such as fire departments, became more common. But that was not enough to save Chicago from a fire that left hundreds of thousands homeless.

❝The firemen were working with extraordinary perseverance. When it seemed impossible for a man to stand without suffocation they carried their hose, sprinkling the houses opposite and endeavoring to stop its spread in a westerly direction. But it was evident by midnight that human ingenuity could not stem that fiery tide.❞

—*Chicago Tribune*, October 11, 1869

▲ Firetruck around 1900

Cities Expand and Change

 Core Curriculum Objectives

- **3.III.A.1** Impact of industrialization: Urban growth
- **3.III.B.4** Immigration, 1850–1924: Urbanization: ghettos

Terms and People

urbanization
rural-to-urban migrant
skyscraper
Elisha Otis

mass transit
suburb
Frederick Law Olmsted
tenement

NoteTaking

Reading Skill: Identify Main Ideas Record the main ideas of this section in a flowchart.

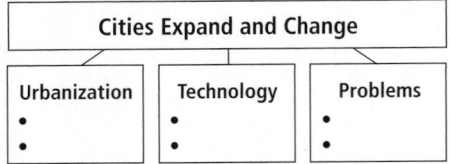

Why It Matters As one historian has noted, America was born on the farm and moved to the city. In 1860, most Americans lived in rural areas, with only 16 percent living in towns or cities with a population of 8,000 or more. By 1900, that percentage had doubled, and nearly 15 million Americans lived in cities with populations of more than 50,000. This period was the beginning of an upsurge in urbanization that both reflected and fueled massive changes in the way Americans lived. **Section Focus Question: What challenges did city dwellers face, and how did they meet them?**

America Becomes a Nation of Cities

In the late nineteenth century, America experienced a period of **urbanization** in which the number of cities and people living in them increased dramatically. Still, numbers and statistics do not tell the whole story of how Americans became city folk. Urban people lived differently from rural people. They worked on schedules, rode trolley cars, paid rents to live in apartment buildings, and interacted with many strangers. Over time, their urban values became part of American culture.

Cities Offer Advantages America's major cities were manufacturing and transportation centers clustered in the Northeast, on the Pacific Coast, and along the waterways of the Midwest. Connected

Growth of Cities, 1870–1900

Geography *Interactive*
For: Interactive map skills
Web Code: ncp-1404

Population in 1900 — Population in 1870

3,400,000 people —
250,000 people — 1,000,000 people
— 38,000 people

SOURCE: U.S. Census Bureau

Map Skills In 1900, more than six times as many people lived in cities of 25,000 or more than in 1870.

1. **Locate:** (a) New York, (b) Chicago, (c) San Francisco, (d) Minneapolis

2. **Describe** Which areas of the country were the most urbanized?

3. **Draw Conclusions** Who settled in cities?

by the new railroad lines, cities became magnets for immigrants and rural Americans. They were attracted by jobs in factories or the service industries. Those with a little money opened shops. The educated increasingly joined the new middle-class professions, working in downtown offices.

Women's opportunities, in particular, were dramatically expanded in urban areas. In addition to factory work, they could take in boarders, do piecework, or become domestic servants. Educated women found work as teachers or in offices as secretaries and typists.

While many city jobs offered only hard work for little reward, they were an improvement over the alternatives for many. Cities offered variety, promise, and even a bit of glamour. By saving part of their wages, city workers might attain some comforts or perhaps even move into the growing middle class. At the least, they could increase their children's opportunities by sending them to school. While some laborers were trapped in an endless cycle of poverty, only the very poorest were unable to enjoy a higher standard of living in the late nineteenth century.

Life was hard in the city, but most preferred it to the country. Horace Greeley, a politician and New York City newspaper editor, wrote in the 1860s, "We cannot all live in cities, yet nearly all seem determined to do so." City churches, theaters, social clubs, and museums offered companionship and entertainment. Transportation out of the city and to other cities was easily accessible. In this period of growth and expansion, some migrants moved from city to city, trying to improve their fortunes.

Immigrants Move In to Seize Opportunities By 1900, some urban areas had a population that was more than 40 percent foreign born. Some immigrants found their way to a city through happenstance, while others joined family

Trolleys brought commuters to the suburbs.

▲ Electric lights glowed in Times Square in New York City by 1910.

▲ Beginning in 1903, women in New York City could ride in female-only subway cars like this one.

members or were recruited by companies needing labor. In this way, neighborhoods, cities, regions, and industries often acquired a majority of workers from a particular locale. For example, employees at the steel mills of western Pennsylvania were predominantly Polish, while the textile factories of New York became a center for eastern European Jewish people. Domestic servants in the Northeast were primarily Irish women, while Scandinavians worked in the fish-packing industry of the Pacific Northwest.

Farmers Migrate From Country to City Many **rural-to-urban migrants** moved to cities in the 1890s. The move from farm to factory was wrenching. Former agricultural workers often found themselves working in dim light and narrow confines. The pace of work was controlled by rigid schedules, with no slow seasons. However, factory work paid wages in cash, which was sometimes scarce on family farms. The increasing difficulty of making a living on a farm, combined with the excitement and variety of city life, sparked a vigorous rural-to-urban migration.

Midwestern cities such as Minneapolis–St. Paul and Chicago exploded in the decade between 1880 and 1890. Many of the newcomers were immigrants or migrants from the rural West. They were attracted by land but also by economic opportunities. African Americans moving out of the South were also part of the migration, although on a smaller scale. The majority of these African Americans stayed in southern cities, but migrants to northern and western cities paved the way for a much larger migration after World War I.

✓ **Checkpoint** What were the advantages of city life?

Technology Improves City Life

As cities swelled in size, politicians and workers struggled to keep up with the demands of growth to provide water, sewers, schools, and safety. American innovators stepped up to the task by developing new technologies to improve living conditions. The middle and upper classes benefited most from the innovations, but every city dweller was affected. Electric trolleys and subways, building codes, and other innovations kept crowded cities from slipping into pollution and chaos.

Vocabulary Builder
innovation–(ihn uh VAY shuhn) *n.* new invention or way of doing things

▲ Trolley cars, trucks, and wagons pulled by horses create a traffic jam in Chicago in 1905.

Engineers Build Skyward The cities of the late nineteenth century began to take their modern form. For the first time, skylines became recognizable by their **skyscrapers.** These ten-story and taller buildings had steel frames and used artistic designs to magnify their imposing height. Inside, they provided office space in cities that had no room left on the ground. But tall buildings were only realistic because of other new technology. In the 1850s, **Elisha Otis** developed a safety elevator that would not fall if the lifting rope broke. Central heating systems were also improved in the 1870s.

In these years, architecture emerged as a specialized career. The American Institute of Architecture was established in 1857 to professionalize the practice. Its members encouraged specific education and official licensing in order to become an architect. These professionals designed the buildings that were quickly becoming hallmarks of urban life: public schools, libraries, train stations, financial institutions, office buildings, and residences.

Electricity Powers Urban Transit In 1888, Richmond, Virginia, introduced a revolutionary invention: streetcars powered by overhead electric cables. Within a decade, every major city followed. It was the beginning of a transportation revolution. **Mass transit**—public systems that could carry large numbers of people fairly inexpensively—reshaped the nation's cities. Commuter rail lines had carried people to areas in and around cities since the 1870s. However, they were powered by coal-driven steam engines, making them slow, unreliable, and dirty. Some cities used trolleys pulled by horses, which were slower and left horse waste all over the streets. Electricity, on the other hand, was quiet, clean, and efficient. Electric cars also ran on a reliable schedule and could carry many more people than horse-drawn carts.

Electric cable cars were not practical in every city, however. Cables strung in narrow streets could block fire trucks, and traffic congestion often prevented streetcars from running on schedule. In 1897, Boston solved this problem by running the cars underground in the nation's first subway system. New York City followed in 1904.

Technology Advances
1868 New York City installs elevated transit with steam-driven engines
1873 San Francisco installs steam-driven cable cars
1880 First practical lightbulb
1882 New York City installs first permanent commercial central power system
1888 Richmond, Virginia, introduces streetcars powered by overhead electric cables
1897 Boston opens public underground subway

WITNESS HISTORY DVD

Watch *The New American City* on the **United States Witness History DVD** to explore cities of the nineteenth century.

TENEMENT BUILDING

Dumbbell Tenement

Many urban workers, especially immigrants, lived in tenements with a design like the one above. The air shafts between buildings were too narrow to let in air or light. Several families often shared the same apartment, while the whole floor shared toilets located in dark, airless hallways. *What problems might tenement living cause?*

Middle and upper class people who could afford transit fares moved away from the noise and dirt of the industrial city. They built housing in the cleaner, quieter perimeter, known as streetcar **suburbs.** From there, they rode mass transit into the center of the city to work, shop, or be entertained, returning to their homes in the evening. Poorer people remained in city centers so that they could walk to work.

City Planners Control Growth As cities grew larger and more complex, architectural firms expanded to offer city-planning services designed to make cities more functional and beautiful, even as their populations skyrocketed. Architect Daniel Burnham designed his version of the ideal city for Chicago's 1893 World's Columbian Exhibition, a fair held to commemorate Columbus's arrival in the Americas. Called the White City, the integrated design included boulevards, parks, buildings, and even electric streetlights.

Mass transit allowed city planners to segregate parts of the city by zoning, or designating certain areas for particular functions. Through the 1890s, cities embraced designs that had separate zones for heavy industry, financial institutions, and residences. They also built public spaces, such as public libraries, government buildings, and universities.

Parks and recreational spaces were one of the most important aspects of city planning. Since the 1850s, cities had built parks as a solution to some of the problems of urban growth. Philadelphia purchased areas along the Schuylkill River to protect the city's water supply from industrial pollution. They hired landscape engineer **Frederick Law Olmsted** to design Fairmount Park. Olmsted had also designed New York City's Central Park and similar parks in Detroit, Michigan; Washington, D.C.; and Palo Alto, California.

✔ **Checkpoint** How did public transportation change urban areas?

Urban Living Creates Problems

Growing cities faced many problems caused by overcrowding and poverty. In 1890, New York's Lower East Side had a population of more than 700 people per acre. As immigrants and rural migrants arrived, they crowded into neighborhoods that already seemed to be overflowing.

Housing Conditions Deteriorate As newcomers moved into urban areas, those who could not afford to ride mass transit had to live within walking distance of the industrial plants and factories where they worked. Housing in densely populated neighborhoods was often aging and usually overcrowded. Most urban workers lived in **tenements:** low-cost multifamily housing designed to squeeze in as many families as possible. Sometimes, several families lived in one apartment or even one room. They used the space for sewing clothes or doing other piecework to earn money.

Tenement owners usually lived in the suburbs or in fashionable downtown areas, away from the industrial grime. However, they built apartments for desperate people who had little choice about where they lived. With few windows and little sanitation, tenements were unhealthy and dangerous. In 1890, journalist Jacob Riis drew attention to the plight of New York tenement dwellers:

Primary Source "Go into any of the 'respectable' tenement neighborhoods . . . you shall come away agreeing [that] . . . life there does not seem worth living. . . . [T]he airshaft. . . . seems always so busy letting out foul stenches . . . that it has no time to earn its name by bringing down fresh air. . . ."

—Jacob Riis, *How the Other Half Lives*

TRACK THE ISSUE

NY 3.III.B.4

How does migration affect patterns of settlement in America?

Several migration trends have shaped settlement patterns in the United States. One is the movement of people to the West and to the southern "Sunbelt." Another is the movement from rural to urban areas, which then developed suburbs. These migrations have had a great influence on American life. Use the timeline below to explore this enduring issue.

1862 Homestead Act
Offer of free land brings settlers to the Great Plains.

1880–1920 Urban Migration
Millions of Americans leave farms for the city. By 1920, urban population exceeds rural population.

1910–1930 Great Migration
Southern blacks move north, giving rise to African American neighborhoods.

1950s Suburban Flight
Mass movement from central cities to suburbs begins.

1970s–Present Sunbelt Growth
Sunbelt states grow rapidly as Americans move to the warmer, southern half of the country.

A modern suburb of Las Vegas, Nevada

A poster advertising a "streetcar suburb" of the late nineteenth century

DEBATE THE ISSUE

Expanding Suburbs American suburbs began in the 1800s but mushroomed after World War II. By 1990, nearly half of all Americans lived in suburbs. These communities offered many benefits. But critics say they have contributed to urban sprawl, traffic congestion, and other problems.

"Suburbanization represents a significant improvement in the quality of life for people who settle there. Most people who move out of their older homes do so because their needs have changed. Suburban and rural areas often meet these new needs better than older, more densely populated central cities."

—Samuel Staley, Reason Public Policy Institute

"Sprawling patterns of growth are an inefficient use of land that scatters jobs, houses, schools and shopping across the landscape. . . . It leaves people little choice but to use their auto for any trip. . . . It fragments the ecosystems that protect our drinking water and wildlife habitat and that provide recreational opportunities that we all enjoy."

—Robert J. Pirani, Regional Plan Association, New York

TRANSFER Activities

1. **Compare** How do the two quotations differ in their perspective on suburbs?

2. **Analyze** How did the growth of the suburbs affect urban life and growth?

3. **Transfer** Use the following Web site to see a video, try a WebQuest, and write in your journal. **Web Code:** neh-7402

City Workers
The street cleaner and police officer above worked for New York City around 1900. *Why were these city workers needed?*

Water and Sanitation Pose Risks Late nineteenth-century cities were filthy. Unpaved streets were snarled with ruts and littered with trash and even dead horses that were left to rot. Alleys between tenements were clogged with food waste and trash. Only the newest urban dwellings had indoor toilets, and the shared toilets in tenements often overflowed. These conditions were perfect for breeding epidemics, posing danger to everyone. Governments and city planners began to take steps to improve living conditions.

During the 1880s, planners attempted to regulate housing, sanitation, sewers, and public health. They began to take water from reservoirs that were separate from the polluted rivers and lakes. In the next decade, a new filtration system improved water quality even more. Private companies competed for lucrative contracts to manage water distribution. Especially in the Southwest, where water was in short supply, questions of who should profit from water delivery sent city planners into a frenzy.

Fire, Crime, and Conflict Even one careless act could have devastating consequences in crowded housing. Open fireplaces and gas lighting started fires that quickly swept through a city. A fire destroyed Chicago in 1871, killing between 200 to 300 people. It also left more than 100,000 people homeless. As the nineteenth century drew to a close, many cities developed professional firefighting teams.

At night, the streets were dangerous, yet many factory workers had to travel to and from work in the dark. In response to this challenge, professional, uniformed city police forces replaced the lone constable and the decentralized neighborhood watch. The new officers were civil servants who took exams and regularly patrolled city neighborhoods. They were aided in their task of ensuring safety by new electric streetlights.

However, the police were unable to overcome the challenge of tension between urban groups. In every big city, communities clashed along ethnic and racial fault lines. Police allowed immigrants to sleep in the station houses to avoid the violence in the streets. Even very young boys joined neighborhood gangs for safety. Race, class, and neighborhood loyalties and conflicts continued to define neighborhood life for many generations.

✔ **Checkpoint** Describe the problems created by urban living.

SECTION **2** **Assessment**

Progress Monitoring *Online*
For: Self-test with vocabulary practice
Web Code: nca-1406

Comprehension

1. **Terms and People** For each item below, write a sentence explaining its significance.
   - urbanization
   - rural-to-urban migrant
   - skyscraper
   - Elisha Otis
   - mass transit
   - suburb
   - Frederick Law Olmsted
   - tenement

2. **NoteTaking Reading Skill: Identify Main Ideas** Use your flowchart to answer the Section Focus Question: What challenges did city dwellers face, and how did they meet them?

Writing About History

3. **Quick Write: Write a Proposal** Write a proposal explaining how you would fix one urban problem of the late 1800s.

Critical Thinking

4. **Draw Inferences** Why did immigrants and rural migrants move to cities?

5. **Summarize** How did city planners try to improve city life?

6. **Analyze** Why did the cities of the late nineteenth century have many problems?

Skyscrapers

3.III.A.1c

By the 1870s and 1880s, cities had begun to expand upward. Architects experimented with designs for taller, stronger buildings. Finally, in 1885, William LeBaron Jenney designed the Home Insurance Company building in Chicago (right). It was the first building in which a steel frame supported the outside walls, allowing more space and windows on lower floors.

▲ The Home Insurance Building in Chicago

Other projects quickly followed as engineers perfected strong but lightweight Bessemer steel supports. Louis Sullivan, Jenney's student, designed and built St. Louis's Wainwright Building in 1890. Leading architects, including Sullivan, believed that buildings must be functional first, but also artistic. This group, known as the Chicago School, designed many of the nation's early skyscrapers.

Over time the look of skyscrapers changed as architects began to experiment with materials other than stone for outer walls. Some people thought that skyscrapers were ugly and would change cities for the worse. Some cities passed laws that limited the height of buildings, allowing light to reach the streets.

▲ Cartoon showing Manhattan sinking under the weight of its skyscrapers

▶ Construction workers high above New York City

Thinking Critically

1. **Analyze Visuals** How did tall buildings change the physical landscape of urban areas?

2. **Infer** What does the cartoon tell you about the perception of skyscrapers?

◀ An 1896 advertisement

▲ A family on a bicycle outing

America Takes to Wheels

In the 1880s, the "safety bicycle" gained popularity in the United States. Cheaper than a horse, it offered an easy mode of transportation in the period before automobiles and mass transit became widespread.

❝By 1893 a million bicycles were in use. It seemed as though all America had taken to wheels. . . . By physicians the therapeutic benefits were declared to be beyond compare, while dress reformers welcomed cycling as an aid to more rational fashions. . . . 'It is safe to say,' declared an expert of the census bureau in 1900, 'that few articles ever used by man have created so great a revolution in social conditions as the bicycle.'❞

—Arthur M. Schlesinger, Sr.,
The Rise of the City, 1878–1898

Social and Cultural Trends

Core Curriculum Objectives

- **3.III.A.3** Women, families, and work
- **3.III.A.4** The growing middle class (consumerism)
- **3.III.A.5** Art and literature

Terms and People

Mark Twain	Joseph Pulitzer
Gilded Age	William Randolph Hearst
conspicuous consumerism	Horatio Alger
mass culture	vaudeville

NoteTaking

Identify Main Ideas Record the main ideas of this section in a table.

Consumerism	Mass Culture	Entertainment
•	•	•
•	•	•

Why It Matters Novelist **Mark Twain** satirized American life in his 1873 novel, *The Gilded Age*. He depicted American society as gilded, or having a rotten core covered with gold paint. Most Americans were not as cynical. The dizzying array of things to do and buy convinced the growing middle class that modern America was in a true golden age. Still, Twain's label stuck, and historians refer to the last decades of the nineteenth century as "the **Gilded Age.**" The new lifestyle that middle-class Americans adopted during this period—shopping, sports, and reading popular magazines and newspapers—contributed to the development of a more commonly shared American culture that would persist for the next century. **Section Focus Question: What luxuries did cities offer to the middle class?**

Americans Become Consumers

Industrialization and urbanization changed the lives of American workers. More people began to work for wages rather than for themselves on farms. Some people worked in offices, drove trolleys, or became factory foremen. Even farmers made more cash as machinery improved and they sold more crops. At the same time, more products were available than ever before and at lower prices. This led to a culture of **conspicuous consumerism,** in which people wanted and bought the many new products on the market. All but the very poorest working-class laborers were able to do and buy more than they would have in the past.

Advertising Attracts Customers Rowland H. Macy opened what he called a department store in New York in 1858. It became the largest single store in America. Its sales methods—widespread advertising, a variety of goods organized into "departments," and high-quality items at fair prices—became the standard in large urban stores. By the 1870s, many big cities had department stores: Jordan Marsh in Boston, Marshall Field in Chicago, and Wanamaker's in Philadelphia.

John Wanamaker developed innovative ways to keep customers satisfied. He was the first to offer a money back guarantee. In addition, he placed large newspaper advertisements to attract customers. Later, Wanamaker became Postmaster General. In that position, he lowered the bulk shipping rates and began free delivery to rural areas, which led to a boom in the mail-order catalog business.

While department stores pioneered new marketing and sales techniques, companies began to create trademarks with distinctive logos that consumers would recognize. For the first time, consumers began to notice and buy brand-name goods. Long-distance shipping allowed consumers in Atlanta, Cincinnati, and San Francisco to purchase the same products.

Some Achieve Higher Standards of Living After the Civil War, Americans began to measure success by what they could buy. Equating purchasing power with a higher standard of living, middle-class and some working-class consumers rushed to modernize their homes and clothing styles. In this period, the cost of living decreased because manufactured products and new technology cost less. Better sanitation and medical care contributed to better health, causing life expectancy to climb. That was good news for most people.

The end of the nineteenth century is sometimes called the Victorian Era, after the queen of England. The rich were richer than ever before, and the middle class tried to imitate their lifestyle. Factory-produced clothing and prepackaged food gave homemakers a break from some activities, but rising expectations of cleanliness and more complicated meals meant that they spent more time on those tasks. Other luxuries, like indoor plumbing, also became common. On the other hand, many women had to work outside their homes to achieve a middle-class lifestyle.

Life changed for men, as well. Public transportation allowed families to live at a distance from the dirt, noise, and bustle of industry. However, it often meant that men became commuters, leaving home early in the morning and returning late in the evening. Still, their culture taught them that hard work would pay off.

✓ **Checkpoint** How did consumption patterns change in the late nineteenth century?

Mass Culture

One of the effects of the spread of transportation, communication, and advertising was that Americans all across the country became more and more alike in their consumption patterns. Rich and poor could wear the same clothing styles, although the quality of that

Changing Roles for Women
Women in the late 1800s were primarily responsible for housekeeping, though a growing number worked outside the home. *How might new appliances like these have changed women's work and expectations?*

NEW WAYS OF SHOPPING

Department stores made shopping into a form of entertainment for middle-class women. Enormous display windows gave shoppers a glimpse of what was inside—clothing, furnishings, toys, and other items—all under one roof. Well-groomed young women sold the merchandise, which the shopper could touch before buying. Different brands and styles were available for comparison. Stores aimed their advertising at women, realizing that they made the purchasing decisions.

Catalogs sold ▶ everything from houses to hats. This toothpaste advertisement is aimed at women.

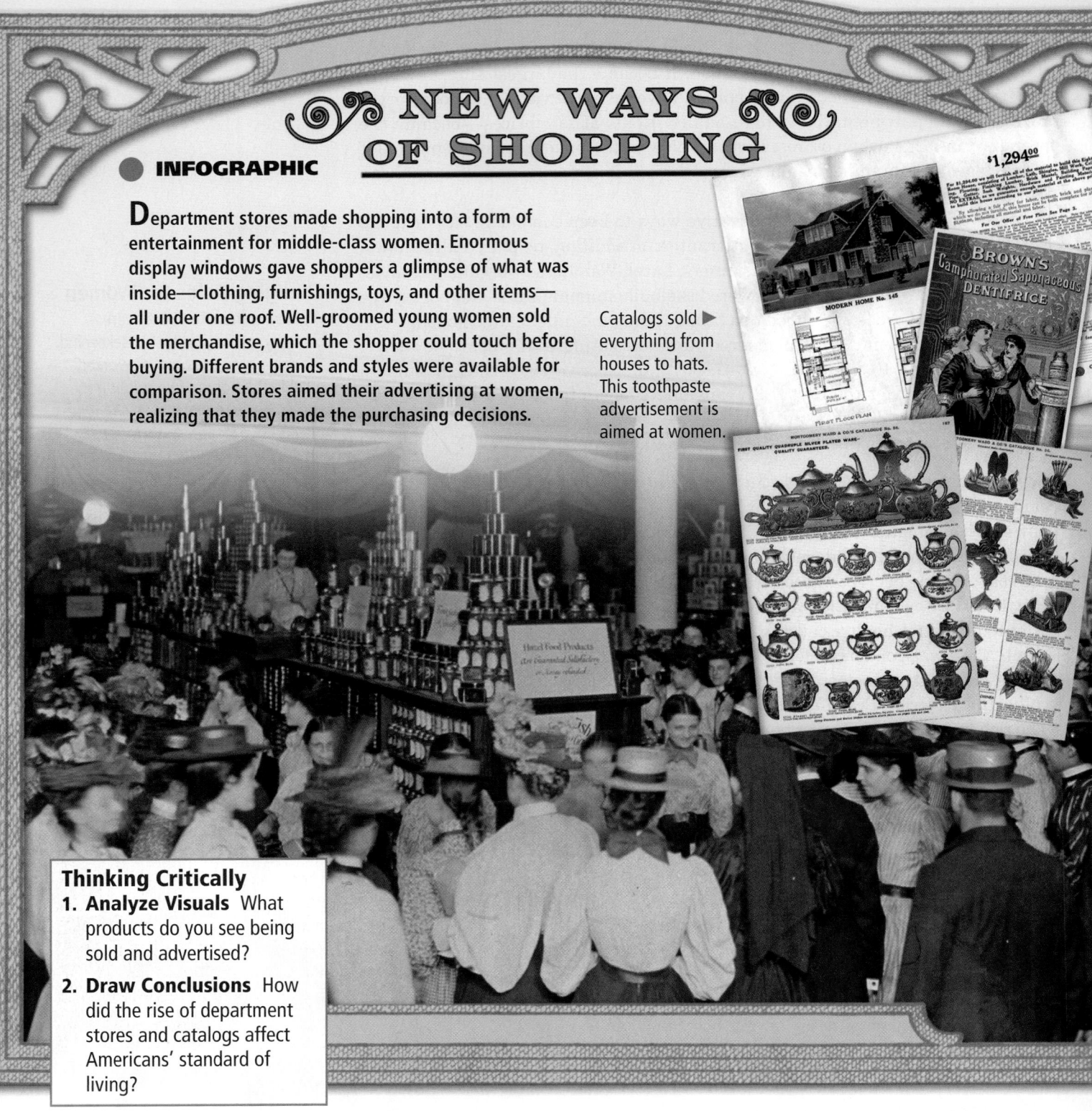

Thinking Critically

1. **Analyze Visuals** What products do you see being sold and advertised?

2. **Draw Conclusions** How did the rise of department stores and catalogs affect Americans' standard of living?

clothing varied. Household gadgets, toys, and food preferences were often the same from house to house. This phenomenon is known as **mass culture.**

Newspapers Circulate Far and Wide The newspapers of the Gilded Age both reflected and helped create mass culture. Between 1870 and 1900, the number of newspapers increased from about 600 to more than 1,600. No one knew more about newspapers than **Joseph Pulitzer,** a Hungarian immigrant who had fought in the Civil War. Active in Missouri politics in the 1870s, Pulitzer moved to New York in the 1880s, where he started a morning paper, the *World*. It was so successful that Pulitzer soon started publishing the *Evening*

World. The papers were inexpensive because they were supported in part by businesses that placed advertisements in their pages.

The job of a newspaper, Pulitzer believed, was to inform people and to stir up controversy. His newspapers were sensationalistic, filled with exposés of political corruption, comics, sports, and illustrations. They were designed to get the widest possible readership, rather than simply to report the news. Pulitzer soon found a competitor in **William Randolph Hearst,** whose *Morning Journal* employed the same tactics. Their sensational styles sold many papers.

At the same time, ethnic and special-interest publishers <u>catered</u> to the array of urban dwellers, especially immigrants. The Philadelphia *Tribune,* begun in the 1880s, targeted the African American market. In New York, there were six Italian-language papers by 1910. Each sold more than 10,000 copies daily.

Literature and the Arts Flourish Mark Twain was not the only author to take a critical look at society during the Gilded Age. Novels that explored harsh realities were popular. Stephen Crane exposed the slums of New York in his *Maggie: A Girl of the Streets* (1893). He later wrote *The Red Badge of Courage,* which explored the psychological aspects of war. Other novelists focused on moral issues. **Horatio Alger** wrote about characters who succeeded by hard work, while Henry James and Edith Wharton questioned a society based upon rigid rules of conduct. Playwrights such as John Augustin Daly mirrored Twain's disapproval of the Gilded Age.

The vitality of city life also inspired graphic artists. Philadelphia's Thomas Eakins painted a larger-than-life illustration of a medical operation, complete with exposed flesh. Painter Robert Henri and his associates developed a style of painting known as the Ashcan School which dramatized the starkness and squalor of New York City slums and street life.

Education Newspapers and literature flourished, in part, because more Americans could read. Public education expanded rapidly. Slowly in the South and rapidly in the North, grade-school education became compulsory. Many locales provided public high schools, although only a small percentage of young people attended. In 1870, the nation had only a few hundred high schools; in 1910, there were more than 5,000. Kindergartens also appeared as a way to help working-class mothers. As a result, the literacy rate climbed to nearly 90 percent by 1900.

Schools taught courses in science, woodworking, and drafting, providing skills that workers needed in budding industries. The curriculum also included civics and business training. Urban leaders counted on schools to help Americanize immigrants, teaching them English and shaping them into good citizens. Teacher-training schools responded to the call. Not only did they grow in number, but they also developed more sophisticated ideas about teaching and learning. Reformer John Dewey sought to enhance student learning by introducing new teaching methods.

Institutions of higher education also began to provide specialized training for urban careers. Today's liberal arts curriculum was largely designed during this era. A few of

Vocabulary Builder

cater–(KAYT uhr) *v.* to supply something that is wanted or needed by a particular group

HISTORY MAKERS

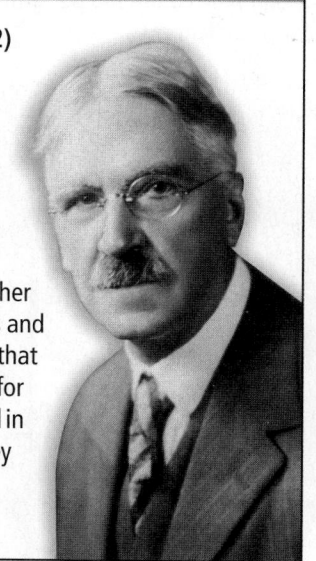

John Dewey (1859–1952)
Dewey was an influential philosopher, reformer, and professor. His child-centered philosophy shaped progressive education reform. He argued that students learn by doing activities that teach them to answer their own questions, rather than by memorizing from books and lectures. His opponents argued that orderly classrooms were better for learning. Dewey's ideas declined in popularity by the 1950s, but they remain influential today.

U.S. Literacy Rates, 1870–1920

Percentage of population that is literate

1870	1880	1890	1900	1910	1920
80.0%	83.0%	86.7%	89.3%	92.3%	94.0%

SOURCE: *Historical Statistics of the United States*

the new careers—teaching, social work, and nursing—were open to middle-class women. This led to an upsurge in women's colleges, since women were barred from many men's colleges. However, many state universities began to accept women into their classes.

Limited access to white institutions led to a growth in schools and colleges for African Americans. Across the South, the number of normal schools, agricultural colleges, and industrial-training schools mushroomed as the children of newly freed slaves set out to prepare to compete as free people.

✓ **Checkpoint** What factors contributed to mass culture?

New Forms of Popular Entertainment

Urban areas with thousands of people became centers for new types of entertainment in the Gilded Age. Clubs, music halls, and sports venues attracted large crowds with time and money to spend. The middle class began to take vacations at this time, while the working classes looked for opportunities to escape from the busy city, even if just for a day.

City Dwellers Escape to Amusement Parks In 1884, Lamarcus Thompson opened the world's first roller coaster. At ten cents a ride, Thompson averaged more than $600 per day in income. The roller coaster was the first ride to open at Coney Island—the nation's best-known amusement park—at the edge of the Atlantic Ocean in New York City. Soon, Coney Island added a hotel and a horse-racing track. Similar amusement parks, located within easy reach of a city, were built around the country.

Going to the Circus

Circuses such as the Ringling Brothers and the Barnum & Bailey began in the late nineteenth century, traveling around the country to perform before large audiences.

While earlier generations had enjoyed a picnic in the park, the new urbanite—even those with limited means—willingly paid the entry fees for these new, more thrilling, entertainments. Urban residents of all ethnicities and races could be found at these amusement spots, though each group was usually relegated to a particular area of the parks. The parks represented a day-long vacation for city laborers who could not afford to take the long seaside vacations enjoyed by the wealthy.

Outdoor Events Draw Audiences In 1883, "Buffalo Bill" Cody threw a Fourth of July celebration near his ranch in Nebraska. He offered prizes for competitions in riding, roping, and shooting. So many people attended that Cody took his show on the road, booking performances at points along railroad lines. Buffalo Bill's Wild West Show toured America and Europe, shaping the world's romantic notion of the American West. The show included markswoman Annie Oakley and the Sioux leader Sitting Bull, as well as displays of riding, roping, and horse-and-rider stunts.

Religious-inspired entertainment also grew in popularity. The Chautauqua Circuit, a kind of summer camp that opened in 1874, sponsored lectures and entertainment along New York's Chautauqua Lake. It began as a summer school for Methodist Sunday school teachers. Soon, Chautauqua leaders were transporting their tents to small towns all across America to deliver comic storytelling, bands and singers, and lectures on politics or morals. A family might stay at a camp for as long as two weeks. Many people saw their first "moving pictures," or movies, in a Chautauqua tent. Theodore Roosevelt called Chautauqua "the most American thing in America."

New Entertainment in the Cities Cities, with their dense populations, offered many glitzy shows and various types of entertainment. At first, **vaudeville** shows were a medley of musical drama, songs, and off-color comedy. In 1881, an entrepreneur named Tony Pastor opened a theater in New York, aiming to provide families with a "straight, clean variety show." By 1900, a few companies owned chains of vaudeville theaters, stretching all across the country.

Performance theater was not the only option. Movie theaters, called nickelodeons, soon introduced motion pictures, charging a nickel for admission. Films such as *The Great Train Robbery* became wildly popular. In music halls, ragtime bands created a style of music that would later evolve into jazz.

Some cities—including Philadelphia, Chicago, Atlanta, Buffalo, and Omaha—hosted exhibitions of new technology and entertainment. These extravaganzas stretched Americans' imaginations to see a future filled with machines and gadgets. Millions of visitors saw everything from steam engines to typewriters and telephones. In many ways, the new amusements mirrored urban life, filled with variety, drama, bright colors, and a very fast pace.

Spectator Sports Attract Fans Baseball—America's national sport—had been around for a number of years before the National League organized it into a business in 1876. Baseball soon became a public show. Major cities built stadiums that seated thousands, like Boston's Fenway Park. Billboards advertised everything from other sports to toothpaste and patent medicines. There were even baseball songs. The most famous—"Take Me Out to the Ball Game"—was written in 1908. Until 1887, teams sometimes included African American players. After the Chicago White Stockings refused to play against a team that had a black player, separate African American teams emerged by 1900.

Like baseball, horse racing, bicycle racing, boxing, and football became popular spectator sports. University football clubs formed on campuses around the country, but they faced a public outcry at the violence of the game. Rule changes made it into the sport we know today. Meanwhile, James Naismith invented basketball at the Springfield, Massachusetts, YMCA in 1891. Heroes emerged in major sports, particularly in boxing, as immigrants and ethnic Americans rooted for the boxers who shared their background.

✔️ **Checkpoint** What new forms of entertainment began in the late nineteenth century?

A Special Honor
This 1911 baseball card shows the pitcher Cy Young. He had the most wins of any pitcher in Major League history.

SECTION 3 Assessment

Progress Monitoring *Online*
For: Self-test with vocabulary practice
Web Code: nca-1407

Comprehension

1. **Terms and People** What do the following terms and people have in common?
   - Mark Twain
   - Gilded Age
   - conspicuous consumerism
   - mass culture
   - Joseph Pulitzer
   - William Randolph Hearst
   - Horatio Alger
   - vaudeville

2. **NoteTaking Reading Skill: Identify Main Ideas** Use your completed table to answer the Section Focus Question: What luxuries did cities offer to the middle class?

Writing About History

3. **Quick Write: Make a Plan** Write an itinerary for a weekend trip to a city in 1900. Consider what kinds of activities a first-time visitor from the country might like to experience.

Critical Thinking

4. **Analyze** What factors contributed to consumerism?

5. **Summarize** Describe middle-class entertainment.

6. **Make Comparisons** How did middle-class urban life differ from life for the urban poor?

Quick Study Guide

 3.III.B.1,
3.III.A.1

Progress Monitoring *Online*
For: Self-test with vocabulary practice
Web Code: nca-1408

■ Foreign-Born Population

City	1870	1890	1910
New York, NY	44.5%	42.2%	40.8%
Chicago, IL	48.4%	41.0%	35.9%
San Francisco, CA	49.3%	42.4%	34.1%
Boston, MA	35.1%	35.3%	36.3%
Cleveland, OH	41.8%	37.2%	35.0%
Philadelphia, PA	27.2%	25.7%	24.8%
St. Louis, MO	36.1%	25.4%	18.4%
Detroit, MI	44.5%	39.7%	33.8%
Milwaukee, WI	47.3%	38.9%	29.8%
Scranton, PA	45.3%	34.0%	27.0%

SOURCE: U.S. Census Bureau

■ Rural and Urban Population

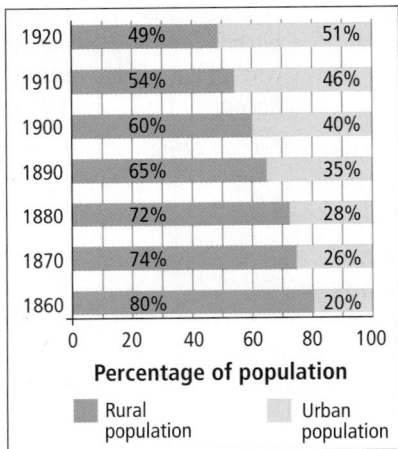

Year	Rural	Urban
1920	49%	51%
1910	54%	46%
1900	60%	40%
1890	65%	35%
1880	72%	28%
1870	74%	26%
1860	80%	20%

Percentage of population

■ Rural population ■ Urban population

SOURCE: U.S. Census Bureau

■ Urban Problems

Problem	→	Solution
Crowding	→	Skyscrapers, city planning, parks
Poor housing	→	Building codes
Danger	→	Streetlights and police forces
Potential for fire	→	Electric lights and fire departments
Poor sanitation	→	Public-health departments

■ Aspects of Mass Culture

Mass Culture
• Advertising
• Department stores and mail-order catalogs
• Factory-produced clothing
• Prepackaged food
• Newspapers
• Public education
• Entertainment

Entertainment
• Amusement parks
• Outdoor shows
• The Chautauqua Circuit
• Vaudeville shows
• Movie theaters
• Exhibitions and fairs
• Spectator sports

☑ Quick Study Timeline

In America

1871
Fire devastates Chicago

1882
Chinese Exclusion Act closes the door to new immigration from China

1892
A processing center for immigrants opens at Ellis Island

Presidential Terms U. S. Grant 1869–1877   R. Hayes 1877–1881   J. Garfield 1881   C. Arthur 1881–1885   G. Cleveland 1885–1889   B. Harrison 1889–1893

1870 **1880** **1890**

Around the World

1871
Britain legalizes labor unions

1881
The czar persecutes Jews in Russia

1894
Russia's last czar, Nicholas II, begins his reign

American Issues
•—•—•—• Connector

By connecting prior knowledge with what you have learned in this chapter, you can gradually build your understanding of enduring questions that still affect America today. Answer the questions below. Then, use your American Issues Connector study guide (or go online: www.PHSchool.com **Web Code:** neh-7403).

Issues You Learned About

● **Migration and Urbanization** Immigrants have overcome many obstacles in their quest to make better lives for themselves in the United States.

1. Millions of immigrants moved to American cities in the late 1800s and early 1900s. Write a short narrative describing the life of one of these immigrants. Consider the following:
- reasons for immigration
- the journey to America
- arrival at processing stations
- life in the United States
- the process of adopting American culture

● **Technology and Society** New technology that developed in the 1880s changed the landscape of cities.

2. How did skyscrapers reflect technology merged with art?

3. Explain the inventions that made skyscrapers a more practical form of construction.

4. Why were commuter rail lines that were powered by electricity an improvement over earlier forms of commuter rail lines?

● **Education and American Society** During the Gilded Age, education became available to more Americans.

5. What is a likely reason that the government decided to use tax dollars to support schools for all American children?

6. How might John Dewey have recommended that students at teacher-training schools study for their future careers?

7. Why was there a growth in women's colleges and African American colleges during this period?

Connect to Your World   New York

Migration and Urbanization As you have read, Jacob Riis exposed the difficult lives of New York City tenement dwellers to the world in 1890, but a decade later conditions had not improved significantly. The New York legislature then passed the Tenement House Act of 1901, requiring new and existing tenement houses to have proper ventilation, better lighting in apartments and hallways, more fire precautions, and indoor toilets. Some landlords and real estate companies criticized the law, fearing it would reduce the value of their property, but reluctantly complied. Many cities modeled their own housing laws after New York's 1901 Act. Research housing laws in other major cities during this time period, and make a chart that compares that city's standards with New York's.

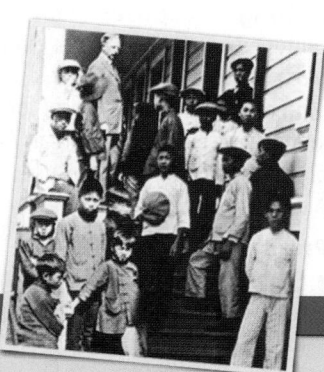

1897
Boston opens America's first subway system

1907
Immigration to the United States reaches an all-time high

1910
A processing center for immigrants opens at Angel Island in San Francisco Bay

G. Cleveland 1893–1897
W. McKinley 1897–1901
T. Roosevelt 1901–1909
W. Taft 1909–1913
W. Wilson 1913–1921

1900   **1910**   **1920**

1901
The first "foolproof" vacuum cleaner is invented in England

1910
The Mexican Revolution begins

1914
World War I begins in Europe

History Interactive
For: Interactive timeline
Web Code: ncp-1410

Chapter Assessment

Terms and People

1. Who were the **"new" immigrants**? What characteristics did they share?

2. What were **Ellis Island** and **Angel Island**? What happened at these locations?

3. Define **mass transit.** How did mass transit impact urban populations?

4. What was the **Gilded Age**? What ideas about American society did it express?

5. Who were **Joseph Pulitzer** and **William Randolph Hearst**? How did people respond to their work?

Focus Questions

The focus question for this chapter is **How did American urban life change between 1875 and 1914?** Build an answer to this big question by answering the focus questions for Sections 1 through 3 and the Critical Thinking questions that follow.

Section 1

6. Why did immigrants come to the United States, and what impact did they have upon society?

Section 2

7. What challenges did city dwellers face, and how did they meet them?

Section 3

8. What luxuries did cities offer to the middle class?

Critical Thinking

9. **Analyze Visuals** Study the photograph at right. Then, answer the question that follows: How do the activities of these immigrant children support the argument that newcomers were taught to feel patriotism toward their adopted country?

10. **Draw Conclusions** Do you think that immigrants who lived in urban ghettoes had a harder or an easier time adapting to American culture than immigrants in other locations?

11. **Compare Points of View** How did the views of settlement house workers differ from nativists over immigration?

12. **Explain Causes** What led many rural Americans to migrate to the cities in the 1890s?

13. **Problem Solving** What do you think was the most important step taken by city planners and government officials to improve city life? Explain your answer.

14. **Analyze Information** Could the United States between 1870 and 1914 be considered a "land of opportunity"? Explain your answer.

15. **Make Generalizations** What types of subjects did public high schools in the 1900s emphasize and why?

16. **Synthesize Information** Explain the relationship between the growth of the middle class, changes in the economy, and new forms of mass entertainment.

Writing About History

Writing a Proposal In the late nineteenth and early twentieth centuries, more immigrants than ever before arrived in America. Most of them settled in cities, although they usually came from rural areas. Write a proposal for a program that would help immigrants adjust to life in an American city in 1900. Focus on the most challenging aspect of an immigrant's life in an American city.

Prewriting

- Decide what type of organization will run your program. Will it be a local government, state government, federal government, or another organization?

- Decide what challenge(s) your program would address and which immigrants it would serve.

- Take notes about these topics.

- Gather additional resources.

Drafting

- Make an outline that includes the steps in your plan and explains why each step is necessary.

- Write an introduction that explains why the proposal is important, and then write a body and a conclusion.

Revising

- Use the guidelines on page SH16 of the Writing Handbook to revise your draft.

Regents DBQ Practice

The Impact of Immigration, 1870 to 1910

From 1870 to 1910, more than 20 million immigrants entered the United States from Europe. How did immigrants change American society? What impact did immigrants have on the United States economy? Use your knowledge of immigration and Documents 1, 2, 3, and 4 to answer questions 1 through 4.

Document 1
Occupations of Immigrants, 1901

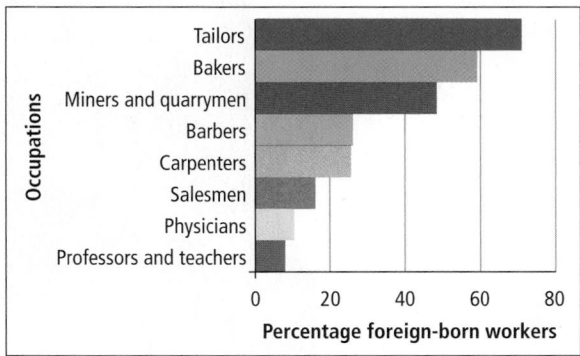

SOURCE: *Reports of the Industrial Commission on Immigration, 1901*

Document 2
Uncle Sam is a man of strong features.

Document 3

"At night we got homesick for our fine green mountains. We read all the news about home in our Lithuanian Chicago newspaper, *The Katalikas.* It is a good paper and gives all the news. . . . I joined the Cattle Butcher's Union. This union is honest and has done me a great deal of good. It has raised my wages. I am getting $11 [a week]. . . . It has given me more time to read and speak and enjoy life like an American. . . . With more time and more money I live much better and I am very happy. So is Alexandria. She came a year ago and has learned to speak English already. . . . [W]e belong to a Lithuanian society that gives two picnics in summer and two balls in winter. . . . I go one night a week to the Lithuanian Concertina Club. . . . The union is doing another good thing. . . . I help the movement by being an interpreter for the other Lithuanians who come in. . . ."

— *Antanas Kaztauskis, "From Lithuania to the Chicago Stockyards,"* Independent, *Aug. 4, 1904*

Document 4

"Upon taking control of the Commonwealth of Massachusetts, the American Party proposed and passed legislation aimed at restricting the strength of the growing Irish community in Boston. The most drastic measure proposed was a constitutional amendment requiring that immigrants wait 21 years after naturalization before they could become voting citizens of the Commonwealth. . . . The Know-Nothing General Court also proposed a legislative redistricting that would reduce the number of seats in predominantly immigrant Boston. This benefited the rural areas, which were predominantly populated by 'Yankee' descendents of English settlers."

— *Steven Taylor, "Progressive Nativism: The Know-Nothing Party in Massachusetts,"* Historical Journal of Massachusetts, *2000*

1. According to Document 1, which occupation employed the highest percentage of immigrants?
   (1) Teaching
   (2) Retail
   (3) Mining
   (4) Medicine

2. The caption for the cartoon in Document 2 reads "Uncle Sam is a man of strong features." What does that mean?
   (1) Only native-born white Protestants are really American.
   (2) People of many nationalities make America strong.
   (3) The government should restrict immigration.
   (4) Immigrants should try to blend in.

3. What can you conclude about the goal of the American Party in Massachusetts?
   (1) It passed laws to encourage Irish immigration.
   (2) It wanted immigrants to move from rural areas into cities.
   (3) It attempted to limit the political participation of Irish immigrants.
   (4) It proposed legislation to increase the number of legislative seats in Boston.

4. **Writing Task** How did immigrants change American society? What impact did immigrants have on the United States economy? Use your knowledge of the chapter content and specific evidence from the primary sources above to support your opinion.

15

The South and West Transformed

1865–1900

Businesses Running Full Blast

The lure of gold and silver in the American West attracted prospectors from all over the country and the world. As mining camps developed, the need for merchants, innkeepers, lawyers, and others arose. Tradesmen came to alleviate this need and to enjoy the benefits of the new frontier. The western boom was so great that towns grew up in the blink of an eye, as discovered by this late 1800s miner.

❝I know you won't believe it but it is true. I went out of town for five days and where the timber stood thick as I went out, when I came back it was all built up solid. On both sides of a street . . . there were stores selling goods, restaurants, boarding house, offices and all kinds of businesses running full blast, and not in tents, but in houses.❞

Listen to the Witness History *audio to hear more about the transformation of the West.*

◀ Main Street of Lower Creed, Colorado, *c.* 1880s

A buffalo hunt on an elk robe

Horse saddle, *c.* 1850s

 Core Curriculum Preview

Chapter Focus Question: How did the economy, society, and culture of the South and West change after the Civil War?

Section 1
The New South   3.I.C.1, 3.I.C.2a, 3.I.C.3, 3.I.D.3

Section 2
Westward Expansion and the American Indians
3.III.C.1, 3.III.C.2, 3.III.D.3

Section 3
Transforming the West   2.II.C.6, 3.III.D.1a, 3.III.D.1c

Poster advertising the Grand Opening of the Union Pacific Railroad

Use the ☑ **Quick Study Timeline** at the end of this chapter to preview chapter events.

Note Taking Study Guide *Online*
For: Note Taking and American Issues Connector
Web Code: nee-7501

▲ Workers in a Mississippi textile mill

WITNESS HISTORY AUDIO

Creating a "New South"

After the Civil War, forward-looking southern businessmen sought ways to diversify the southern economy and develop more industry. Henry Grady, editor of an Atlanta newspaper, described his vision of a "New South":

❝There was a South of slavery and secession—that South is dead. There is a South of union and freedom—that South, thank God, is living, breathing, growing every hour. . . . The old South rested everything on slavery and agriculture, unconscious that these could neither give nor maintain healthy growth. The new South presents a perfect democracy, . . . a social system compact and closely knitted, less splendid on the surface, but stronger at the core . . . and a diversified industry that meets the complex needs of this complex age.❞

—Henry Grady, 1886

The New South

NY Core Curriculum Objectives

- **3.I.C.1** The New South: Agriculture: land and labor (sharecropping and tenant farming)
- **3.I.C.2a** The New South: Status of freedmen
- **3.I.C.3** The New South: Struggle for political control
- **3.I.D.3** Restoration of white control and abridgment of freed African Americans' rights

Terms and People

cash crop
Farmers' Alliance

Civil Rights Act of 1875

NoteTaking

Reading Skill: Identify Supporting Details As you read, fill in a concept web like the one below with details about how the South changed after the Civil War. Add additional circles as needed.

Why It Matters After Reconstruction ended, the South struggled to develop its industry. Although there were pockets of success, the South was not able to overcome its economic and social obstacles to industrial development overall. As a result, the South remained largely agricultural and poor. **Section Focus Question: How did the southern economy and society change after the Civil War?**

Industries and Cities Grow

During the Gilded Age, many southern white leaders envisioned a modernized economy that included not only agriculture but also mills and factories. Henry Grady was among those who called for a "New South" that would use its resources to develop industry.

New Industries Spread Through the South Before the Civil War, the South had shipped its raw materials—including cotton, wood, and iron ore—abroad or to the North for processing into finished goods. In the 1880s, northern money backed textile factories in western North Carolina, South Carolina, and Georgia, as well as cigar and lumber production, especially in North Carolina and Virginia. Investment in coal-, iron-, and steel-processing created urban centers in Nashville, Tennessee, and Birmingham, Alabama.

During this time, farming also became somewhat more diversified, with an increase in grain, tobacco, and fruit crops. Even the landscape of farming changed as smaller farms replaced large plantations.

Railroads Link Cities and Towns A key <u>component</u> of industrialization is transportation. To meet this need, southern rail lines expanded, joining rural areas with urban hubs such as Mobile and Montgomery in Alabama and the bustling ports of New Orleans, Louisiana, and Charleston, South Carolina. Yet, by the 1880s, only two rail lines—from Texas to Chicago and from Tennessee to Washington, D.C.—linked southern freight to northern markets.

To combat economic isolation, southerners lobbied the federal government for economic help and used prison labor to keep railroad construction costs down. Gradually, rail connections supported the expansion of small hubs such as Meridian, Mississippi, and Americus, Georgia. The new cities of Atlanta, Dallas, and Nashville developed and began rivaling the old.

Southern Economic Recovery Is Limited Despite these changes, the southern economy continued to lag behind the rest of the country. While the North was able to build on its strong industrial base, the South first had to repair the damages of war. Moreover, industry rests on a three-legged stool: natural resources, labor, and capital investment. The South had plenty of the first but not enough of the second and third.

Sustained economic development requires workers who are well trained and productive as well as consumers who can spend. Public education in the South was limited. In fact, the South spent less than any other part of the country on education, and it lacked the technical and engineering schools that could have trained the people needed by industry. At the same time, low wages discouraged skilled workers from coming to the South, and the lure of higher wages or better conditions elsewhere siphoned off southern workers.

Additionally, very few southern banks had survived the war, and those that were functioning had fewer assets than their northern competitors. Most of the South's wealth was concentrated in the hands of a few people. Poor tenant farmers and low-paid factory workers did not have cash to deposit. With few strong banks, southern financiers were often dependent on northern banks to start or expand businesses or farms. The southern economy suffered from this lack of labor and capital.

✓ **Checkpoint** What factors limited southern economic recovery?

Vocabulary Builder

<u>component</u>—(kuhm POH nuhnt)
n. any of the main parts of a whole

**Industry Develops
in the South**

With large deposits of iron ore and coal, Alabama became a center of the steel industry in the late 1800s. This photograph shows workers outside the ironworks at Ensley, Alabama. *What evidence of a "New South" can you see in this photograph?*

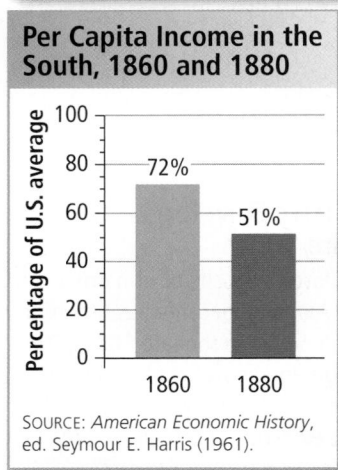

Wholesale Price of Cotton, 1865–1890

Cents per pound

SOURCE: *Historical Statistics of the United States*

Per Capita Income in the South, 1860 and 1880

Percentage of U.S. average

72%   51%

1860   1880

SOURCE: *American Economic History,* ed. Seymour E. Harris (1961).

Farming in the New South

After the Civil War, farmers in the South continued to rely heavily on cotton. This made them particularly vulnerable when pests such as the boll weevil threatened their crops. *What do the graphs indicate about the economic situation in the South after the Civil War?*

Southern Farmers Face Hard Times

Before the Civil War, most southern planters had concentrated on such crops as cotton and tobacco, which were grown not for their own use but to be sold for cash. The lure of the **cash crop** continued after the war, despite efforts to diversify. One farm magazine recommended that "instead of cotton fields, and patches of grain, let us have fields of grain, and patches of cotton."

Cotton Dominates Agriculture Cotton remained the centerpiece of the southern agricultural economy. Although at the end of the Civil War cotton production had dropped to about one third of its prewar levels, by the late 1880s, it had rebounded. However, during the war, many European textile factories had found suppliers outside the South, and the price of cotton had fallen. Now, the South's abundance of cotton simply depressed the price further.

Dependence on one major crop was extremely risky. In the case of southern cotton, it was the boll weevil that heralded disaster. The boll weevil, a beetle which could destroy an entire crop of cotton, appeared in Texas in the early 1890s. Over the next decade, the yield from cotton cultivation in some states dropped by more than 50 percent. By 1900, cotton's appeal and its problems dominated the southern economy, much as they had before the Civil War.

Farmers Band Together Faced with serious difficulties, Texas farmers in the 1870s began to organize and to negotiate as a group for lower prices for supplies. The idea spread. Local organizations linked together in what became known as the **Farmers' Alliance.** These organizations soon connected farmers not only in the South but also in the West. Farmers' Alliance members tried to convince the government to force railroads to lower freight prices so members could get their crops to markets outside the South at reduced rates. Because of regularly rising rates, the Alliances also wanted the government to regulate the interest that banks could charge for loans.

 Checkpoint Why did southern farmers face hard times?

Black Southerners Gain and Lose

The Thirteenth, Fourteenth, and Fifteenth amendments had changed African Americans' legal status. Over time, however, these legal gains were pushed back by a series of Supreme Court decisions.

Political and Economic Gains Citizenship afforded black southerners the right to vote in local and federal elections, and for a few black people it provided the means to serve their country in government or in the military. Some African Americans opened urban businesses or bought farmland. In developing the Farmers' Alliances, white leaders in some places invited black farmers to join, reasoning that the alliance would be stronger if all farmers took part. In this way, the Farmers' Alliances offered a glimpse of the political possibilities of interracial cooperation.

Perhaps the most important gain for southern African Americans, however, was access to education. Hundreds of basic-literacy schools and dozens of teachers' colleges, supported by the federal government or by northern philanthropists, enabled African Americans to learn to read and write.

White Backlash Begins Many realities of southern black lives did not change much, however. Some white southerners focused their own frustrations on trying to reverse the gains African Americans had achieved during Reconstruction.

Groups such as the Ku Klux Klan used terror and violence to intimidate African Americans. Meanwhile, many African American freedoms were whittled away. Churches that were once integrated became segregated. New laws supported the elimination of black government officials.

With Congress's enactment of the **Civil Rights Act of 1875,** they guaranteed black patrons the right to ride trains and use public facilities such as hotels. However, in a series of civil rights' cases decided in 1883, the Supreme Court ruled that decisions about who could use public accommodations was a local issue, to be governed by state or local laws. Southern municipalities took advantage of this ruling to further limit the rights of African Americans.

✔ **Checkpoint** How did southern blacks lose their rights?

Going to School
After the Civil War, African Americans for the first time had an opportunity to get an education, although usually in segregated classrooms like this one.

SECTION 1 Assessment

Progress Monitoring *Online*
For: Self-test with vocabulary practice
Web Code: nca-1501

Comprehension

1. **Terms and People** For each term below, write a sentence explaining its role in southern life.
   - cash crop
   - Farmers' Alliance
   - Civil Rights Act of 1875

2. **NoteTaking Reading Skill: Identify Supporting Details** Use your concept web to answer the Section Focus Question: How did the southern economy and society change after the Civil War?

Writing About History

3. **Quick Write: Define a Topic for an Oral Presentation** Begin planning an oral presentation on the economic recovery of the South after the Civil War. First, make a list of what you already know about that topic. Then, narrow down the list to focus on a specific topic. Describe this topic in one sentence.

Critical Thinking

4. **Categorize** What positive steps did the South take to industrialize after the Civil War?

5. **Recognize Cause and Effect** How did southern agriculture suffer from the domination of cotton?

6. **Make Comparisons** How did southern African Americans both gain and lose civil rights after the Civil War?

Painted buffalo hide ▶

WITNESS HISTORY AUDIO

My Heart Feels Like Bursting

Conflict between Native Americans and white settlers began almost from the moment the first Europeans arrived. The clash came to a head with the Indian Wars in the late 1800s. Satanta, a Kiowa chief, clearly expressed the Indian sentiment:

❝I don't want to settle. I love to roam over the prairies. There I feel free and happy, but when we settle down we grow pale and die. . . . A long time ago this land belonged to our fathers; but when I go up to the river I see camps of soldiers on its banks. These soldiers cut down my timber; they kill my buffalo; and when I see that my heart feels like bursting. . . . This is our country. . . . We have to protect ourselves. We have to save our country. We have to fight for what is ours.❞

—Chief Satanta, 1867

◀ A Native American warrior astride his war horse.

Westward Expansion and the American Indians

 Core Curriculum Objectives

- **3.III.C.1** Cultural pluralism: assimilation (Americanization)
- **3.III.C.2** Nativist reactions: stereotyping and prejudice
- **3.III.D.3** Native American Indians

Terms and People

reservation
Sand Creek Massacre
Sitting Bull
Battle of Little Big Horn
Chief Joseph

Wounded Knee
assimilate
Dawes General
  Allotment Act

NoteTaking

Reading Skill: Identify Supporting Details
As you read, fill in a concept web with details about Native Americans west of the Mississippi.

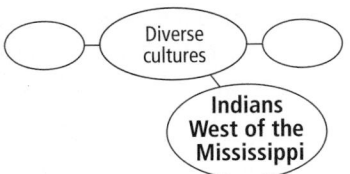

Why It Matters In 1787, the Constitution granted sole power for regulating trade with the Native Americans to the federal government. This is just one of many decrees that would establish the long, strained relationship between the federal government and Native Americans. During the 1830s, the federal government forced Native Americans from the East to resettle west of the Mississippi River and promised them the land there forever. In the 1840s through the 1860s, pressure from white settlers weakened this promise. In the ensuing contest, Native American cultures were irrevocably changed. **Section Focus Question: How did the pressures of westward expansion impact Native Americans?**

Cultures Under Pressure

By the end of the Civil War, about 250,000 Indians lived in the region west of the Mississippi River referred to as "The Great American Desert." While lumped together in the minds of most Americans as "Indians," Native Americans embraced many different belief systems, languages, and ways of life.

Diverse Cultures Geography influenced the cultural diversity of Native Americans. In the Pacific Northwest, the Klamaths, Chinooks, and Shastas benefited from abundant supplies of fish and forest animals. Farther south, smaller bands of hunter-gatherers struggled to exist on diets of small game, insects, berries, acorns, and roots. In the arid lands of New Mexico and Arizona, the Pueblos irrigated the land to grow corn, beans, and squash. They built adobe homes high in the cliffs to protect themselves from aggressive neighbors. The more mobile Navajos lived in homes made of mud or in hogans that could be moved easily. The most numerous and nomadic Native Americans were the Plains Indians, including the Sioux, Blackfeet, Crows, Cheyenne, and Comanches. The Plains Indians were expert horsemen and hunters. The millions of buffalo that roamed the Plains provided a rich source for lodging, clothing, food, and tools.

Indian cultures, however, shared a common thread—they saw themselves as part of nature and viewed nature as sacred. By contrast, many white people viewed the land as a resource to produce wealth. These differing views sowed the seeds of conflict.

Threatened by Advancing Settlers In the early 1800s, the government carried out a policy of moving Native Americans out of the way of white settlers. President Jackson moved the Cherokees off their land in Georgia and onto the Great Plains. To white settlers, Native Americans were welcome to this "Great American Desert," so called as it was thought to be uninhabitable. To limit conflict, an 1834 law regulated trade relations with Indians and strictly limited the access of white people to this Indian Territory. White settlement generally paused at the eastern rim of the territory and resumed in the Far West.

By the 1850s, however, federal policy toward Native Americans was again challenged: Gold and silver had been discovered in Indian Territory as well as settled regions further west. Americans wanted a railroad that crossed the continent. In 1851, therefore, the federal government began to restrict Indians to smaller areas. By the late 1860s, Indians were forced onto separate **reservations,** specific areas set aside by the government for the Indians' use. No longer free to roam the Plains, Indians faced suppression and poverty.

A Meeting of Cultures
Treaty signings such as this one between the Peace Commission and the Cheyenne and Arapaho Indians were a common occurrence during the late 1800s. *How does this photograph illustrate the cultural differences among the groups?*

Two more staggering blows threatened Native American civilizations: White settlers introduced diseases to which Indians had no immunity, and the vitally important buffalo herds were destroyed. In the 1870s, hunters slaughtered hundreds of buffaloes in a single day. They skinned the animals for their hides and left the meat to rot. Trainloads of tourists came to kill buffaloes purely for sport, leaving behind both the valuable meat and hides.

✓ **Checkpoint** What three circumstances hurt Native Americans?

New Settlers and Native Americans Clash

The rapid industrial development and expansion following the Civil War set Native Americans and white settlers on a collision course. Advances in communication and transportation that supported industrial growth also reinforced faith in manifest destiny. Horace Greeley, editor of the *New York Tribune*, encouraged the poor to move West:

> **Primary Source** "If you strike off into the broad, free West, and make yourself a farm from Uncle Sam's generous domain, you will crowd nobody, starve nobody, and neither you nor your children need evermore beg. . . ."
> —*New York Tribune*, February 5, 1867

Generally ignored was the fact that Native Americans inhabited half of the area of the United States. Indians fought to retain or regain whatever they could.

Rebellion and Tragedy on the Plains In 1862, while the Civil War raged in the East, a group of Sioux Indians had resisted threats to their land rights by attacking settlements in eastern Minnesota. In response, the government waged a full-scale war against the Sioux, who then were pushed west into the Dakotas.

The Sioux rebellion sparked a series of attacks on settlements and stagecoach lines as other Plains Indians also saw their way of life slipping away. Each battle took its toll, raising the level of distrust on all sides. In the fall of 1864, a band of Colorado militia came upon an unarmed camp of Cheyenne and Arapaho Indians, who were under U.S. Army protection, gathered at Sand Creek. The troops opened fire, killing many men, women, and children despite the Indians' efforts to signal their friendship by raising the American flag.

Praise turned to scorn for the commanding officer, John Chivington, when the facts of the encounter became known. The **Sand Creek Massacre** spawned another round of warfare as Plains Indians joined forces to repel white settlement.

Once the Civil War ended, regiments of Union troops—both white and African American—were sent to the West to subdue the Indians. Recruitment posters for volunteer cavalry promised that soldiers could claim any "horses or other plunder" taken from the Indians. The federal government defended its decision to send troops as necessary to maintain order.

Peace Plans Fail As the Plains Indians renewed their efforts to hold onto what they had, the federal government announced plans to build a road through Sioux hunting grounds to connect gold-mining towns in Montana. Hostilities intensified. In 1866, the legendary warrior Red Cloud and his followers lured Captain William Fetterman and his troops into an ambush, killing them all.

The human costs of the struggle drew a public outcry and called the government's Indian policy into question. As reformers and humanitarians promoted education for Indians, westerners sought strict controls over them. The government-appointed United States Indian Peace Commission concluded that lasting peace would come only if Native Americans settled on farms and adapted to the civilization of the whites.

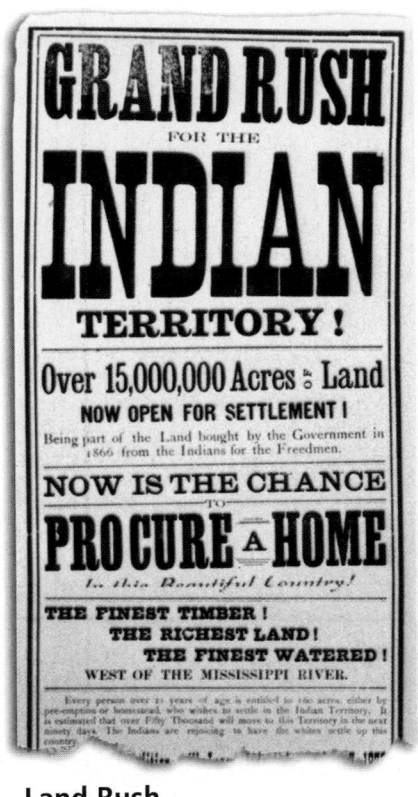

Land Rush
Posters like the one above advertised land to white settlers in areas previously promised to Native Americans.

NoteTaking

Reading Skill: Recognize Sequence Copy the timeline below, and use it to record important dates and events in the Indian Wars.

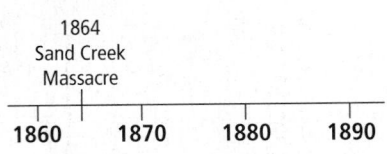

1864
Sand Creek
Massacre

1860   1870   1880   1890

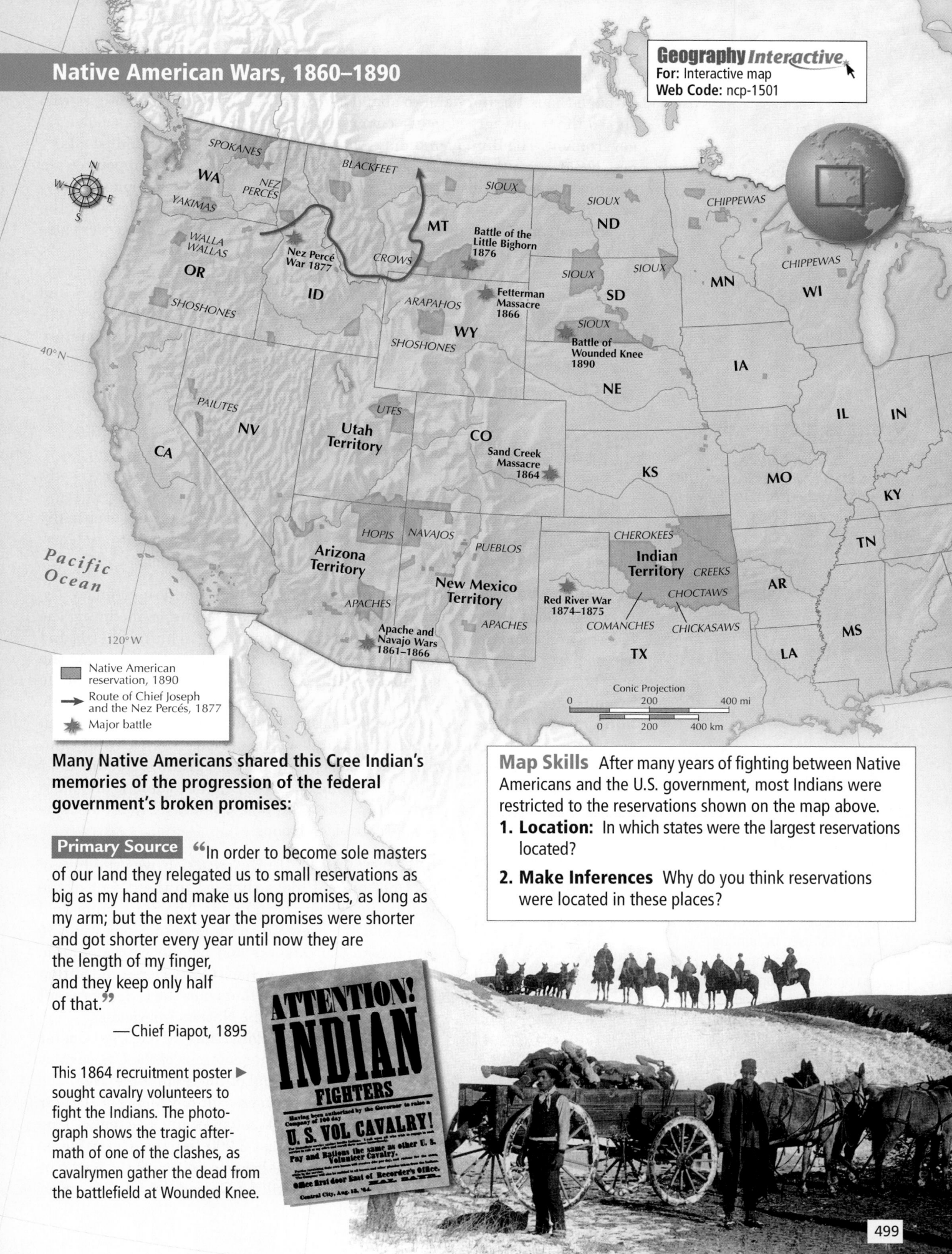

Geography *Interactive*
For: Interactive map
Web Code: ncp-1501

SPOKANES
WA
NEZ PERCÉS
YAKIMAS
WALLA WALLAS
OR
SHOSHONES
Nez Percé War 1877
ID
BLACKFEET
MT
CROWS
Battle of the Little Bighorn 1876
SIOUX
ND
SIOUX
CHIPPEWAS
ARAPAHOS
Fetterman Massacre 1866
SIOUX
SIOUX
SD
SIOUX
Battle of Wounded Knee 1890
MN
CHIPPEWAS
WI
WY
SHOSHONES
NE
IA
PAIUTES
UTES
Utah Territory
NV
CA
CO
KS
MO
IL
IN
KY
Sand Creek Massacre 1864
HOPIS
NAVAJOS
PUEBLOS
CHEROKEES
Arizona Territory
New Mexico Territory
APACHES
APACHES
Red River War 1874–1875
Indian Territory
CREEKS
CHOCTAWS
COMANCHES
CHICKASAWS
AR
TN
MS
Apache and Navajo Wars 1861–1866
TX
LA

Pacific Ocean

120°W
40°N

Legend:
- Native American reservation, 1890
- Route of Chief Joseph and the Nez Percés, 1877
- Major battle

Conic Projection
0   200   400 mi
0   200   400 km

Many Native Americans shared this Cree Indian's memories of the progression of the federal government's broken promises:

Primary Source "In order to become sole masters of our land they relegated us to small reservations as big as my hand and make us long promises, as long as my arm; but the next year the promises were shorter and got shorter every year until now they are the length of my finger, and they keep only half of that."

—Chief Piapot, 1895

This 1864 recruitment poster ▶ sought cavalry volunteers to fight the Indians. The photograph shows the tragic aftermath of one of the clashes, as cavalrymen gather the dead from the battlefield at Wounded Knee.

ATTENTION! INDIAN FIGHTERS
Having been authorized by the Governor to raise a Company of 100 day
U.S. VOL CAVALRY!
Pay and Rations the same as other U.S. Volunteer Cavalry.

Office first door East of Recorder's office.
Central City, Aug. 13, '64.

Map Skills After many years of fighting between Native Americans and the U.S. government, most Indians were restricted to the reservations shown on the map above.

1. Location: In which states were the largest reservations located?

2. Make Inferences Why do you think reservations were located in these places?

Vocabulary Builder
adequate–(AD ih kwuht) *adj.*
enough to meet a need

In an effort to pacify the Sioux and to gain more land, the government signed the Fort Laramie Treaty of 1868. The government agreed not to build the road through Sioux territory and to abandon three forts. The Sioux and others who signed the treaty agreed to live on a reservation with support from the federal government. The Bureau of Indian Affairs, established in 1824, handled affairs between Native Americans and the government. The agency appointed an agent who was responsible for distributing land and <u>adequate</u> supplies to anyone willing to farm as well as for maintaining peaceful relations between the reservation and its neighbors. A school and other communal buildings were also promised by the treaty.

As often happened, some Indians could not live within the imposed restrictions. Unfortunately, many Indian agents were unscrupulous and stole funds and resources that were supposed to be distributed to the Indians. Even the most well-meaning agents often lacked support from the federal government or the military to enforce the terms of the treaties that were beneficial to Native Americans.

✓ **Checkpoint** Why did tensions exist between settlers and Indians?

WITNESS HISTORY DVD

Watch **A Clash of Cultures** on the **United States Witness History DVD** to learn more about conflicts between white settlers and Native Americans in the West.

The End of the Indian Wars

The conditions facing Native Americans had all the ingredients for tragedy. Indians were confined to isolated and impoverished areas, which were regularly ravaged by poverty and disease. Promises made to them were eventually broken. Frustration, particularly among young warriors, turned to violence. Guns replaced treaties as the government crushed open rebellions.

Red River War The Red River War, a series of major and minor incidents, led to the final defeat of the powerful southern Plains Indians, including the Kiowas and Comanches. It marked the end of the southern buffalo herds and the opening of the western panhandle of Texas to white settlement. At the heart of the matter was the failure of the United States government to abide by and enforce the terms of the 1867 Treaty of Medicine Lodge. White buffalo hunters were not kept off Indian hunting grounds, food and supplies from the government were not delivered, and white lawlessness was not punished. Hostilities began with an attack by Indians on a group of Texans near the Red River in June 1874. They came to an end in June 1875 after the last Comanche holdouts surrendered to U.S. troops.

Battle of the Little Big Horn It was the lure of gold not animal hides that led to the defeat of the Indians on the northern Plains. The Black Hills Gold Rush of 1875 drew prospectors onto Sioux hunting grounds in the Dakotas and neighboring Montana. When the Sioux, led by chiefs Crazy Horse and **Sitting Bull,** assembled to drive them out, the U.S. Army sent its own troops against the Native Americans.

In June 1876, a colonel named George Custer rushed ahead of the other columns of the U.S. cavalry and arrived a day ahead of the main force. Near the Little Bighorn River, in present-day Montana, Custer and his force of about 250 men unexpectedly came upon a group of at least 2,000 Indians. Crazy Horse led the charge at what became known as the **Battle of the Little Big Horn,** killing Custer and all of his men.

HISTORY MAKERS

Sitting Bull (1831?–1890)
Sitting Bull belonged to the Hunkpapa band, one of seven Lakota Sioux groups that lived by hunting buffalo. A famed fighter, he was named Hunkpapa war chief in his late twenties. Trained as a holy man, he also became a spiritual leader. By the late 1860s, his reputation was so great that the Lakota chose him as the first-ever chief of all seven bands.

TRACK THE ISSUE

How should the federal government deal with Indian nations?

From its earliest days, the federal government has grappled with the issue of relations with Native Americans. Since Indians in the West were forced to move onto reservations, government policy has shifted several times. Use the timeline below to explore this enduring issue.

1787 U.S. Constitution
Federal government given power to regulate trade with Native Americans.

1824 Bureau of Indian Affairs
Agency created to handle relations with Native Americans.

1887 Dawes Act
Government divides reservations into individual land holdings.

1934 Indian Reorganization Act
Tribal governments gain more control over own affairs.

1975 Indian Self-Determination and Educational Assistance Act
Indians win control over schools and other government services.

Comanche girls, 1892

 7.III.B.6

Native Americans in traditional garb press for Indian rights in Washington, D.C.

DEBATE THE ISSUE

Native American Land Claims Today, several Native American nations have made claims to their original lands, arguing that old treaties were illegal. Opponents say that to recognize these claims after so many years would lead to injustice to the people now living on those lands.

❝For over 200 years, we have endured hardship and indignities from the unjust taking of our ancestral land. We have been confined to a small reservation. We have suffered the painful loss of our traditional way of life. . . . There will be no actions to evict our neighbors from their homes as we know all too well the pain and suffering displacement causes.❞

—Tadodaho (Sidney Hill) of the Onondaga Nation, March 10, 2005

❝Employing a unique body of laws, today's courts have decided to hear cases based on alleged violations of federal law that occurred over 200 years ago. Even more incredible than the ability and willingness of our judicial system to resurrect these ancient claims, is its [tendency] to apply modern legal interpretations to ancient events and blatantly disregard the historical record.❞

—Scott Peterman, May 25, 2002

 TRANSFER Activities

1. **Compare** How do Tadodaho and Peterman differ on the subject of land claims?

2. **Analyze** How do you think Tadodaho would view the Dawes Act?

3. **Transfer** Use the following Web site to see a video, try a WebQuest, and write in your journal. **Web Code:** neh-7502

Cries for revenge motivated army forces to track down the Indians. Sitting Bull and a small group of followers escaped to Canada. Crazy Horse and his followers surrendered, beaten by weather and starvation. By then, the will and the means to wage major resistance had been crushed.

Chief Joseph and the Nez Percés

Farther west, in Idaho, another powerful drama played out. In 1877, the federal government decided to move the Nez Percés to a smaller reservation to make room for white settlers. Many of the Nez Percés were Christians and had settled down and become successful horse and cattle breeders. They had pride in themselves and a great deal to lose.

Trying to evade U.S. troops who had come to enforce their relocation, the Nez Percés's leader **Chief Joseph** led a group of refugees on a trek of more than 1,300 miles to Canada. Stopped just short of the border, Chief Joseph surrendered with deeply felt words: "I will fight no more forever." Banished with his group to a barren reservation in Oklahoma, he traveled twice to Washington, D.C., to lobby for mercy for his people.

Wounded Knee

With the loss of many leaders and the destruction of their economy, Native Americans' ability to resist diminished. In response, many Indians welcomed a religious revival based on the Ghost Dance. Practitioners preached that the ritual would banish white settlers and restore the buffalo to the Plains. As the popularity of the movement spread, government officials became concerned about where it might lead.

In 1890, in an effort to curtail these activities, the government ordered the arrest of Sitting Bull. In the confrontation, he and several others were killed.

Vocabulary Builder
confrontation–(kahn fruhn TAY shuhn) *n.* hostile encounter

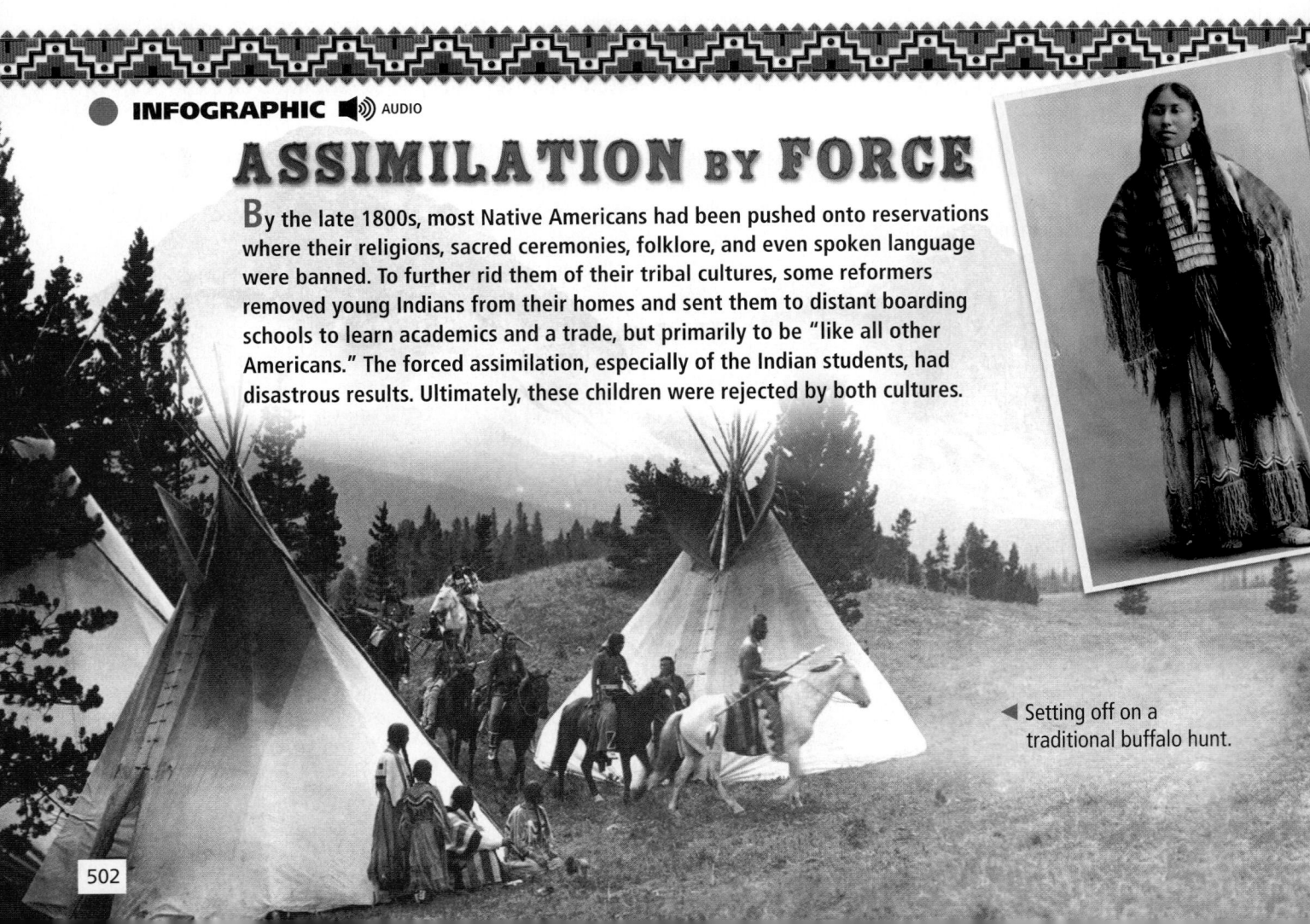

INFOGRAPHIC 🔊 AUDIO

ASSIMILATION BY FORCE

By the late 1800s, most Native Americans had been pushed onto reservations where their religions, sacred ceremonies, folklore, and even spoken language were banned. To further rid them of their tribal cultures, some reformers removed young Indians from their homes and sent them to distant boarding schools to learn academics and a trade, but primarily to be "like all other Americans." The forced assimilation, especially of the Indian students, had disastrous results. Ultimately, these children were rejected by both cultures.

◀ Setting off on a traditional buffalo hunt.

Troops then set out after the group of Indians as they fled. Hostilities broke out at Wounded Knee, South Dakota, when the well-armed cavalry met and outgunned the Indians. The ground was stained with the blood of more than 100 men, women, and children. The tragic end of the Ghost Dance War at **Wounded Knee** sealed the Indians' demise.

✔ **Checkpoint** What rebellions ended major Indian resistance?

The Government Promotes Assimilation

The reservation policy was a failure. Making Indians live in confined areas as wards of the government was costly in human and economic terms. Policy makers hoped that as the buffalo became extinct, Indians would become farmers and be **assimilated** into national life by adopting the culture and civilization of whites.

Reformers Criticize Government Policy A few outspoken critics defended the Indians' way of life. In *A Century of Dishonor*, Helen Hunt Jackson decried the government's treatment of Native Americans:

Primary Source "There is not among these three hundred bands of Indians one which has not suffered cruelly at the hands either of the Government or of white settlers. The poorer, the more insignificant, the more helpless the band, the more certain the cruelty and outrage to which they have been subjected. . . . It makes little difference where one opens the record of the history of the Indians; every page and every year has its dark stain. . . ."

—Helen Hunt Jackson, 1881

▼ Carlisle Indian Industrial School book cover

◄ A Native American bride in her tribe's traditional bridal dress (far left) and the same bride with her groom in "American" wedding attire (right).

Established in 1879, the Carlisle Indian Industrial School in Pennsylvania was one of the first boarding schools for Native Americans. Students there were required to change their traditional hairstyles, dress, and language to that of the white American culture

Thinking Critically
1. **Draw Conclusions** Why do you think it was difficult for assimilated Native Americans to be accepted by their own cultures?

2. **Synthesize Information** Why is forced assimilation destined to fail?

Helen Hunt Jackson
(1830–1885)
Helen Hunt Jackson grew up in Massachusetts. In the late 1870s, she heard some Native Americans speak about their peoples' plight. Deeply moved, she was determined to publicize their cause. In *A Century of Dishonor*, she sharply criticized the U.S. government's history of shattered treaties. She elaborated on the situation in a report on Indian policy written for the government and in the highly popular novel *Ramona*. Jackson's work helped build sympathy for the plight of Native Americans.

Susette La Flesche, the granddaughter of a French trader and an Omaha Indian woman, also used her writing and lecturing talents to fight for recognition of the Indians and Indian rights in the courts. Born on the Omaha reservation in Nebraska, she studied in the East and returned to the reservation to teach.

Congress Passes the Dawes Act In 1871, Congress had passed a law stating that "no Indian nation or tribe within the United States would be recognized as an independent nation, tribe or power with whom the United States may contract by treaty." Indians were now to be treated as individuals.

Partly in response to reformers like La Flesche and Jackson and partly to accelerate the process of assimilation, Congress passed the **Dawes General Allotment Act** (sometimes known as the Dawes Severalty Act) in 1887. The Dawes Act replaced the reservation system with an allotment system. Each Indian family was granted a 160-acre farmstead. The size of the farm was based on the eastern experience of how much land was needed to support a family. In the arid West, however, the allotment was not big enough.

To protect the new Indian owners from unscrupulous speculators, the Dawes Act specified that the land could not be sold or transferred from its original family for 25 years. Congress hoped that by the end of that time, younger Indians would embrace farming and individual landownership. To further speed assimilation, missionaries and other reformers established boarding schools, to which Indian parents were encouraged to send their children. Indian children were to learn to live by the rules and culture of white America. The struggle to retain their homeland, freedom, and culture proved tragic. Although Native Americans faced their enemy with courage and determination, tens of thousands died in battle or on squalid reservations. Only a small number were left to carry on their legacy.

✔ **Checkpoint** How did the Dawes Act change the way Indians were treated?

SECTION 2 Assessment

Progress Monitoring *Online*
For: Self-test with vocabulary practice
Web Code: nca-1502

Comprehension

1. Terms and People For each item below, write a sentence explaining its significance to the fate of Native Americans.
- reservation
- Sand Creek Massacre
- Sitting Bull
- Battle of the Little Big Horn
- Chief Joseph
- Wounded Knee
- assimilate
- Dawes General Allotment Act

2. NoteTaking **Reading Skill: Identify Supporting Details** Use your concept web and timeline to answer the Section Focus Question: How did the pressures of westward expansion impact Native Americans?

Writing About History

3. Quick Write: Research an Oral Presentation Use library or Internet resources to gather information on one of the battles in the Indian Wars. Afterward, list at least two written sources and two images that you might use in an oral presentation.

Critical Thinking

4. Recognize Cause and Effect Why did Native Americans and white settlers clash?

5. Analyze Information How did Native Americans try but fail to keep their land?

6. Identify Central Issues What steps were taken to foster assimilation of Native Americans?

Locusts were one of the challenges to farming on the Plains. ▶

A Test of Courage

Pioneer life in the West in the late 1800s was significantly different from daily life in the East. The challenges were great and survival often difficult. However, according to Lulu Fuhr, a Kansas pioneer, the pioneering spirit met these challenges head-on:

❝There were many tearful occasions for the tearful type. There were days and months without human fellowship, there were frightful blizzards, [drought] destroying seasons . . . and many pitiful depriva-tions, but there were also compensations for the brave, joyous, determined pioneer.❞

—Lulu Fuhr

◀ Pioneer woman gathers buffalo chips to use as fuel.

Transforming the West

Core Curriculum Objectives

- **2.II.C.6** Impact of western expansion upon Mexicans and Native Americans
- **3.III.D.1a** Land west of the Mississippi: Rolling plains and the Great American Desert
- **3.III.D.1c** The Homestead Act, 1862, and the settlement of the West

Terms and People

vigilante
transcontinental
  railroad
land grant

open range
Homestead Act
Exodusters

NoteTaking

Reading Skill: Identify Main Ideas Use a chart to record details about changes in the West.

Western Settlement			
Miners	Railroads	Ranchers	Farmers

Why It Matters The West was swept by enormous change after the Civil War. As railroads increased access, settlers, ranchers, and miners permanently transformed millions of acres of western land. **Section Focus Question: What economic and social factors changed the West after the Civil War?**

Miners Hope to Strike It Rich

Mining was the first great boom in the West. Gold and silver were the magnets that attracted a vast number of people. Prospectors from the East were just a part of a flood that included people from all around the world.

Mining Towns Spring Up From the Sierra Nevada to the Black Hills, there was a similar pattern and tempo to the development of mining regions. First came the discovery of gold or silver. Then, as word spread, people began to pour into an area that was ill prepared for their arrival. The discovery of gold at Pikes Peak in Colorado and the Carson River valley in Nevada are classic examples. Mining camps sprang up quickly to house the thousands of people who flooded the region. They were followed by more substantial communities. Miners dreamed of finding riches quickly and easily. Others saw an opportu-nity to make their fortune by supplying the needs of miners for food, clothing, and supplies.

A mechanized steam shovel for stripping copper

Mining
WEALTH

Most mining towns developed in regions with easily accessible mineral ores. Yet, some towns became cities due to the abundance of deep veins of less accessible precious metals. The desire to access these mother lodes led to new innovations in mining. And, as in most nineteenth-century industries, mechanized equipment was developed to speed up the process. Mines became caverns that ran for miles deep underground with railed trams hauling ore to the surface. Investments and investors were required to support this vast infrastructure, and mining moved out of the hands of the lone prospector and into the account books of big businesses.

Patent notice for a piece of mechanized mining equipment ▼

MINING MACHINERY DENVER COLO. U.S.A. No Leyner MAKERS
THE J. GEO. LEYNER ENGINEERING WORKS

▼ Mining during the late 1800s (far left) gave rise to the modern-day capital city of Helena, Montana (below).

Thinking Critically
1. **Draw Conclusions** Why do you think towns developed in mining regions?
2. **Recognize Cause and Effect** How did the discovery of natural resources contribute to the settlement of the West?

History *Interactive* ⋆
For: To learn more about industry in the West
Web Code: ncp-1504

The rough-and-tumble environment of these communities called out for order. To limit violence and <u>administer</u> justice in areas without judges or jails, miners set up rules of conduct and procedures for settling disputes. In extreme situations, self-appointed law enforcers known as **vigilantes** punished law-breakers. As towns developed, they hired marshals and sheriffs, like Wyatt Earp and Bat Masterson, to keep the peace. Churches set up committees to address social problems.

Some mining towns—like Leadville, Colorado, and Nevada City, Montana—were "boomtowns." They thrived only as long as the gold and silver held out. Even if a town had developed churches and schools, it might become a ghost town, abandoned when the precious metal disappeared. In contrast, Denver, Colorado; Boise, Idaho; and Helena, Montana, were among the cities that diversified and grew.

Vocabulary Builder
<u>administer</u>–(ad MIHN ihs tuhr) *v.* to manage or direct

Large Companies Make Mining Big Business The first western mining was done by individuals, who extracted the minerals from the surface soil or a streambed. By the 1870s, the remaining mineral wealth was located deep underground. Big companies with the capital to buy mining equipment took over the industry. Machines drilled deep mine shafts. Tracks lined miles of underground tunnels. Crews—often recruited from Mexico and China—worked in dangerous conditions underground.

The arrival of the big mining companies highlighted an issue that would relentlessly plague the West: water and its uses. Large-scale mining required lots of water pumped under high pressure to help separate the precious metals from silt. As the silt washed down the mountains, it fouled water being used by farmers and their livestock. Despite these concerns, the federal government continued to support large mining companies by providing inexpensive land and approving patents for new inventions. Mining wealth helped fuel the nation's industrial development.

Prosperity in the West
Transportation by railroad allowed industries and settlements to prosper throughout the West. *How does this image illustrate the growth of Jimtown, Colorado?*

✔ **Checkpoint** What were the two major phases of mining?

Railroaders Open the West

As industry in the West grew, the need for a railroad to transport goods increased as well. The idea of a **transcontinental railroad,** a rail link between the East and the West, was not new. Arguments over the route it should take, however, had delayed implementation. While the Civil War kept the South out of the running, Congress finally took action.

Building the Transcontinental Railroad Unlike Europe, where railroads were built and owned by governments, the United States expected its railroads to be built by private enterprise. Congress supported construction of the transcontinental railroad in two ways: It provided money in the form of loans and made **land grants,** giving builders wide stretches of land, alternating on each side of the track route.

Simultaneously in 1863, the Central Pacific started laying track eastward from Sacramento, California, while the Union Pacific headed westward from Omaha, Nebraska. Construction proved to be both difficult and expensive.

The Final Spike

In 1869, the Union Pacific and Central Pacific railroads came together at Promontory, Utah. A symbolic golden spike (above) was the final one driven in to mark the completion of the transcontinental railroad. *How does the photograph above illustrate the mood of this event?*

The human cost of building the railroad was also high. Starved for labor, the Central Pacific Company brought recruits from China and set them to work under harsh contracts and with little regard for their safety. Inch by inch, they chipped and blasted their way through the granite-hard Sierra Nevada and Rockies. Meanwhile, working for the Union Pacific, crews of Irish immigrants crossed the level plains from the East. The two tracks eventually met at Promontory, Utah, in 1869, the same year that the Suez Canal was completed in Egypt. The continent and the world were shrinking in size.

Railroads Intensify Settlement The effects of the railroads were far reaching. They tied the nation together, moved products and people, and spurred industrial development.

The railroads also stimulated the growth of towns and cities. Speculators vied for land in places where a new railroad might be built, and towns already in existence petitioned to become a stop on the western rail route. Railroads intensified the demand for Indians' land and brought white settlers who overwhelmed Mexican American communities in the Southwest. There was no turning back the tide as waves of pioneers moved west.

The addition of states to the Union exemplifies the West's growth. Requirements for statehood included a population of at least 60,000 inhabitants. Between 1864 and 1896, ten territories met those requirements and became states.

✓ **Checkpoint** How did the government encourage the development of a transcontinental railroad?

Ranchers Build the Cattle Kingdom

Cattle ranching fueled another western boom. This was sparked by the vast acres of grass suitable for feeding herds of cattle. Once the railroad provided the means to move meat to eastern markets, the race was on for land and water.

Vaqueros and Texas Longhorns Long before the arrival of eastern settlers in the West, Mexicans in Texas had developed an efficient system for raising livestock. The Texas longhorn, which originated in Mexico, roamed freely and foraged for its own feed. Each owner marked—or "branded"—the cattle so they could be identified. Under this **open-range system,** property was not fenced in. Though ranchers claimed ownership and knew the boundaries of their property, cattle from any ranch grazed freely across those boundaries. When spring came, the ranchers would hire cowboys to comb thousands of acres of open range, "rounding up" cattle that had roamed all winter. The culture of the cowboy owed its very existence to the Mexican *vaqueros* who had learned to train horses to work with cattle and had developed the roping skills, saddle, lariat, and chaps needed to do the job.

Cowboys and Cattle Drives Once cows were rounded up, cowboys began the long cattle drive to take the animals to a railroad that would transport them to eastern markets. The trek from Texas, Colorado, or Montana to the nearest junction on the transcontinental railroad could take weeks or even months.

Economic Development of the West

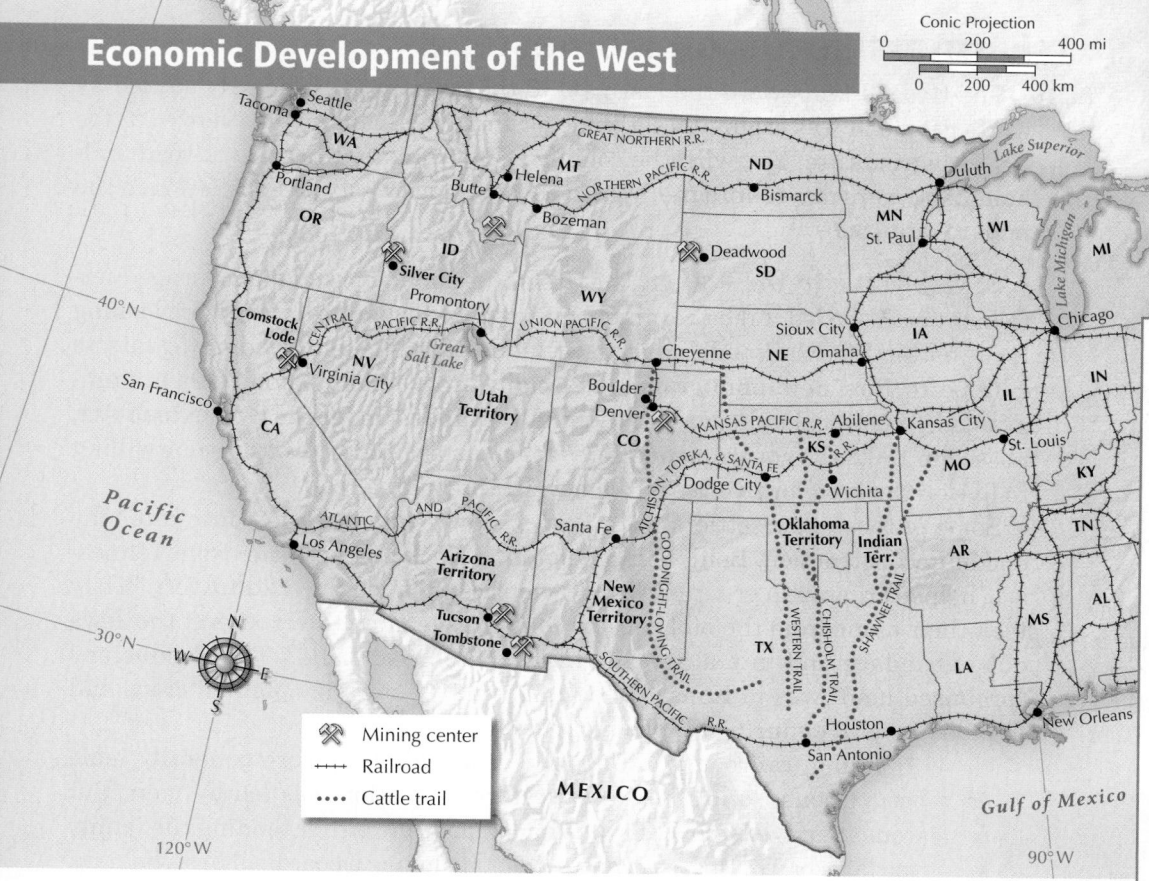

Conic Projection
0   200   400 mi
0   200   400 km

Map Skills Miners, ranchers, and railroads all played a role in the development of the West in the late 1800s.

1. **Locate:** (a) Promontory, (b) Helena, Montana, (c) Chisholm Trail

2. **Location:** Explain how the location of these cities enabled them to become centers of economic activity: Denver, Virginia City, Abilene, Omaha.

3. **Draw Conclusions** How did the railroads contribute to the growth and prosperity of the West?

Geography *Interactive*
For: Interactive map
Web Code: ncp-1502

The cowboys' work was hard, dangerous, low-paying, and lonely—often involving months of chasing cattle over the countryside. A band of cowboys often included a mix of white, Mexican, and African American men.

The Cow Towns Cattle drives concluded in such railroad towns as Dodge City, Kansas, where the cattle were sold and the cowboys were paid. These cow towns gave rise to stories about colorful characters such as Wild Bill Hickok, Doc Holliday, Wyatt Earp, and Jesse James. They were also the site of rodeos, competitions based on the cowboys' skills of riding, roping, and wrestling cattle. Bill Pickett, an African American cowboy, is credited with inventing bulldogging, in which a cowboy leaps from his horse onto a steer's horns and wrestles the steer to the ground.

The End of Open-Range Ranching Open-range ranching flourished for more than a decade after the Civil War. During that time, several million cattle were driven from Texas north to the railroad stops in Wyoming, Nebraska, and Kansas. But by the mid-1880s, however, the heyday of open-ranching came to an end.

Several factors contributed to the demise of the open range. The invention of barbed wire made it possible to fence in huge tracts of land on the treeless plains. The supply of beef exceeded demand, and the price of beef dropped sharply. Added to these factors was a period of extreme weather in the 1880s—brutally freezing winters followed by summer droughts. As springs dried up, herds of cattle starved. The nature of cattle ranching changed as ranchers began to raise hay to feed their stock, and farmers and sheepherders settled on what had been open range.

▲ Cattle branding irons

✔ **Checkpoint** How did the railroad affect the cattle industry?

Farmers Settle on Homesteads

The Great Plains were the last part of the country to be heavily settled by white people. It was originally set aside for Indians because it was viewed as too dry for agriculture. Yet, with the coming of the transcontinental railroad, millions of farmers moved into the West in the last huge westward migration in the mid- to late 1800s.

Farmers Move to the Plains The push-and-pull factors that encouraged settlement were varied. Like the miners and cattle ranchers, farmers were looking for a better life. Railroads advertised land for sale, even sending agents to Europe to lure new immigrants, especially from Scandinavia. Other immigrants fled political upheavals in their native lands. Under the **Homestead Act,** passed in 1862, the government offered farm plots of 160 acres to anyone willing to live on the land for five years, dig a well, and build a road.

Some of these new settlers were former slaves who fled the South after the end of Reconstruction. Benjamin Singleton, a black businessman from Tennessee, helped organize a group of African Americans called the "**Exodusters.**" They took their name from the biblical story of Moses leading the exodus of the Jews out of bondage and into a new life in the "Promised Land." The Exodusters' "promised land" was in Kansas and Oklahoma, where they planted crops and founded several enduring all-black towns.

Mining, railroad building, and cattle herding were generally male occupations, so much of the western migration was led by men. But women arrived, too. Everyone had a job to do, either tending the family and farm or working as an entrepreneur running a boardinghouse, laundry, or bakery.

Challenges Demand Solutions The life of homesteaders was hard. Windstorms, blizzards, droughts, plagues of locusts, and heart-rending

Farming the Plains

A family (bottom) poses with their prized possessions in front of their sod house. Some homeowners covered the inside walls with muslin (top) to help keep out the dirt and to prevent bugs, mice, or snakes from crawling in. *How did settlers adapt to the challenges of living on the Plains?*

loneliness tested their endurance. On the treeless plains, few new arrivals could afford to buy lumber to build a home. Instead, they cut 3-foot sections of sod and stacked them like bricks, leaving space for a door and one window. The resulting home was dark, dirty, and dingy.

Necessity is the mother of invention, and farmers on the Plains had many needs beyond housing. The development of barbed wire, a length of wire with twisted barbs, enabled a farmer to fence land cheaply to keep out wandering livestock. The development of a plow that could tackle the sod-covered land, the grain drill that opened furrows and planted seed, the windmill that tapped underground water, and dry-farming techniques were some of the innovations that enabled farmers to succeed. To spur development of better ways to farm, Congress passed the Morrill Act in 1862, which granted land to states for the purpose of establishing agricultural colleges.

Nothing, however, prepared farmers for a series of blizzards and droughts in the 1880s and 1890s that killed animals and ruined harvests. Some of the discouraged and ill-prepared settlers headed back east. The farmers who remained became more commercial and depended more on scientific farming methods.

✓ **Checkpoint** Why did farmers move to the Plains?

Competition, Conflict, and Change

There is a sharp contrast between the picture of the West depicted in novels and movies and the reality of life on the Plains. The West was a place of rugged beauty, but it was also a place of diversity and conflict.

Economic Rivalries The various ways that settlers sought to use western land were sometimes at odds with one another. Conflicts between miners, ranchers, sheepherders, and farmers led to violence and acts of sabotage. And no matter who won, Native Americans lost. Grazing cattle ruined farmers' crops, and sheep gnawed grass so close to the ground that cattle could not graze the same land. Although miners did not compete for vast stretches of grassland, runoff from large-scale mining polluted water that ran onto the Plains—and everyone needed water.

Early on, geologist John Wesley Powell recognized water as an important but limited resource. He promoted community control and distribution of water for the common good. Despite his efforts, water <u>usage</u> remained largely unregulated to the benefit of some but not all.

Vocabulary Builder
<u>usage</u>—(YOO sihj) *n.* the act or way something is used

Prejudices and Discrimination From the 1850s onward, the West had the widest diversity of people in the nation. With fewer than 20 percent of the nation's total population, it was home to more than 80 percent of the nation's Asian, Mexican and Mexican American, and Native American residents. Chinese immigrants alone accounted for 100,000 immigrants, almost all of them in the West.

Ethnic tensions often lurked beneath the surface. Many foreign-born white people sought their fortunes on the American frontier, especially in the years following the mid-century revolutions in Europe. Their multiple languages joined the mix of several dozen Native American language groups. Differences in food, religion, and cultural practices reinforced each group's fear and distrust of the others. But mostly it was in the larger cities or towns that discrimination was openly displayed. Chinese immigrants, Mexicans, and Mexican Americans were most often its targets.

Conflict came in many guises. For example, ranchers often belittled homesteaders, labeling them "sodbusters" to mock their work in the soil and their modest houses. Conflict also arose because the view of the ownership of natural

A Diverse Population
Economic opportunities attracted diverse groups to the West. Chinese workers were among the many immigrant groups hired to help build the transcontinental railroad.

resources varied. For many generations, Mexicans had mined salt from the salt beds of the El Paso valley. Mexicans viewed these areas as public property, open to all. However, when Americans arrived in the 1870s, they laid claim to the salt beds and aimed to sell the salt for profit. In 1877, in what became known as the El Paso Salt War, Americans and Mexicans clashed over access to this crucial commodity. When the battles ended, the salt beds were no longer communal property. Now, users would have to buy this natural product.

Closing of the Frontier The last major land rush took place in 1889 when the federal government opened the Oklahoma Territory to homesteaders. On April 22, thousands of "boomers" gathered along the border. When the signal was given, they charged in to stake their claims. However, they found that much of the best land had already been taken by "sooners," who had sneaked into the territory and staked their claims before the official opening.

The following year, the 1890 national census concluded that there was no longer a square mile of the United States that did not have at least a few white residents. The country, the report said, no longer had a "frontier," which at the time was considered an uninhabited wilderness where no white person lived. The era of free western land had come to an end.

However, the challenges and tensions were far from over. Controversies over Indians' land rights were still to come. So, too, were more battles over water and over the mistreatment of minority citizens—especially the Chinese and the Mexican Americans. One historian has described Mexican Americans as "foreigners in their own land." And as the number of African Americans increased in the West, they, too, would battle discrimination.

✓ **Checkpoint** What were some of the causes of prejudice and discrimination in the West?

SECTION **3** Assessment

Progress Monitoring Online
For: Self-test with vocabulary practice
Web Code: nca-1503

Comprehension

1. **Terms and People** For each of the following terms, write two or three sentences explaining its significance.
   - vigilante
   - transcontinental railroad
   - land grant
   - open-range system
   - Homestead Act
   - Exoduster

2. **NoteTaking Reading Skill: Identify Main Ideas** Use your chart to answer the Section Focus Question: What economic and social factors changed the West after the Civil War?

Writing About History

3. **Quick Write: Outline an Oral Presentation** Make an outline for an oral presentation on the challenges of farming on the Great Plains. Write your main ideas and supporting details on separate note cards. Determine the order in which you will likely deliver your speech, and number each card accordingly. Include any facts and quotations on the cards as well.

Critical Thinking

4. **Make Comparisons** How did mining in the West change over time?

5. **Recognize Cause and Effect** How did railroads contribute to the settlement and growth of the West?

6. **Express Problems Clearly** How did economic and cultural diversity cause conflicts in the West?

3.III.A.5

Picturing the West

Frederic Remington and Charles Russell were late-nineteenth-century artists who depicted life on the western frontier. Both went west as young men. Remington spent only a few months on a Kansas sheep farm, while Russell worked for nearly a decade as a cowhand. Their experiences on the frontier greatly influenced their art. Remington's and Russell's paintings and sculptures fascinated people on the East Coast and greatly influenced the public's image of the West. However, by the time Remington and Russell were painting, the life they were depicting was either already gone or disappearing swiftly.

▲ Russell, *Smoking Up*

◀ Remington, *The Outlier* (far left)

◀ Remington, *Vaquero* (left)

▼ Remington, *Dash for the Timber*

Thinking Critically
1. **Make Inferences** How do you think this artwork influenced the way people perceived Native Americans and the West?

2. **Connect to Today** How do photographs or paintings of different parts of the world today influence the way we conceive of a place or a culture?

513

Quick Study Guide

2.II.C.4,
3.III.D

Progress Monitoring *Online*
For: Self-test with vocabulary practice
Web Code: nca-1504

■ The New South

Economic Growth	Limits to Growth
• Development of new industries such as textiles, lumber, iron, steel • Expansion of rail lines • Some agricultural diversification to reduce dependence on cotton	• Shortage of skilled workers • Wealth concentrated in hands of a few • Few banks to finance business expansion

■ Transforming the West

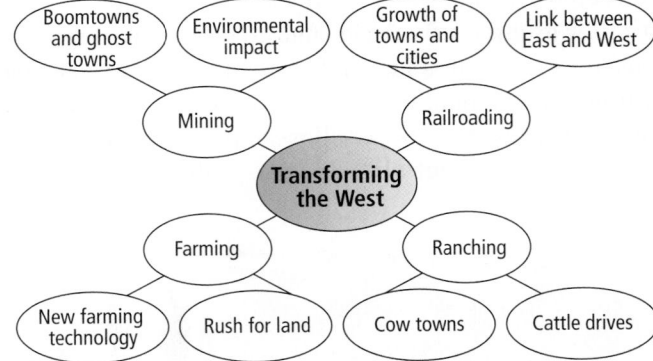

■ Key Events in the Indian Wars

Event	Description
Sand Creek Massacre, 1864	U.S. troops kill unarmed Cheyenne and Arapaho men, women, and children.
Fetterman Massacre, 1866	Sioux lure Captain William Fetterman and his troops into an ambush.
Red River War, 1874–1875	Series of conflicts ends with defeat of southern Plains Indians. Texas panhandle opened to white settlement.
Battle of the Little Bighorn, 1876	Colonel George Custer meets a huge Sioux force. Custer and all 250 of his men perish.
Nez Percé War, 1877	Rather than relocate to a reservation, Nez Percés flee more than 1,000 miles but are forced to surrender just short of the Canadian border.
Battle of Wounded Knee, 1890	Ghost Dance raises fears of Sioux uprising. More than 100 Sioux are killed at Wounded Knee.

☑ Quick Study Timeline

In America

1869 Transcontinental railroad connects East and West

1875 Black Hills gold rush

1876 Sioux defeat U.S. troops in Battle of the Little Bighorn

Presidential Terms	Andrew Johnson 1865–1869	Ulysses S. Grant 1869–1877	Rutherford B. Hayes 1877–1881

1865 **1870** **1875**

Around the World

1868 Meiji Restoration begins in Japan

1870 Franco-Prussian War begins

1871 Germany is unified

1876 Diaz gains power in Mexico

American Issues
●—●—●—● Connector

1.I.A.2d

By connecting prior knowledge with what you have learned in this chapter, you can gradually build your understanding of enduring questions that still affect America today. Answer the questions below. Then, use your American Issues Connector study guide (or go online: www.PHSchool.com **Web code:** neh-7503).

Issues You Learned About

● **American Indian Policy** As white settlers pushed west, the federal government backed policies to provide them with more land—the land upon which many Native American groups already lived.

1. Write an evaluation of how the U.S. government treated Native Americans in the mid- to late 1800s. Consider:
   - the creation of the reservation system
   - treaties between Native American groups and the federal government
   - clashes between U.S. soldiers and Native Americans
   - the Dawes Act

● **Expanding and Protecting Civil Rights** The struggle of a group of people to gain full civil rights may take decades to achieve.

2. What constitutional amendments improved the status of African Americans in the United States? What changes did these amendments bring?

3. How did white southerners in the late 1800s undermine the civil rights that African Americans had gained during Reconstruction?

● **Interaction With the Environment** The American West was a vast land filled with natural resources.

4. What natural resources drew pioneers to the West?

5. How did Native Americans and white settlers differ in their views of the natural environment?

6. What impact did white people have on the buffalo herds of the West?

Connect to Your World — New York

Interaction with the Environment In the late 1800s, mining companies, rather than individual miners, used their resources to pursue the dream of striking it rich in the West. New Yorkers who were shareholders in the New York Mining Company paid for expeditions to western mines, profiting if the expeditions found gold. Some shareholders even went to California themselves. Today, mining within New York itself is an important industry. Most of New York's mining is for sand, gravel, and limestone. New York also produces emery, wollastonite, garnet, zinc, and salt. Find out where in New York three different resources are mined. Create a symbol for each of these resources and use the symbols to illustrate the locations of mines on a New York state map.

History *Interactive*
For: Interactive timeline
Web Code: ncp-1503

| 1879 Exodusters from the South settle in Kansas and Oklahoma | 1883 Supreme Court overturns Civil Rights Act of 1875 | 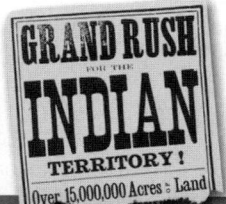 | 1887 Dawes Act breaks up Indian reservations | 1889 Oklahoma is opened to white settlement | 1890 Ghost Dance War marks end of Indian resistance |

James A. Garfield 1881   Chester A. Arthur 1881–1885   Grover Cleveland 1885–1889   Benjamin Harrison 1889–1893

1880   **1885**   **1890**

1884 **European nations divide Africa at Berlin Conference**

1889 **Brazil becomes a republic**

Chapter Assessment

Terms

1. Define **cash crop**. How did the South's emphasis on cash crops affect its agricultural development?

2. What was the **Sand Creek Massacre**? What effect did it have on the American West?

3. What occurred at **Wounded Knee**? Where and when did it take place, and how was this event significant in the lives of Native Americans?

4. What was the **transcontinental railroad**? What was its purpose, and how did it affect the settlement of the West?

5. What was the **Homestead Act**? What did a family have to do to qualify for the Homestead Act?

Focus Questions

The focus question for this chapter is **How did the economy, society, and culture of the South and West change after the Civil War?** Build an answer to this big question by answering the focus questions for Sections 1 through 3 and the Critical Thinking questions that follow.

Section 1

6. How did the southern economy and society change after the Civil War?

Section 2

7. How did the pressures of westward expansion impact Native Americans?

Section 3

8. What economic and social factors changed the West after the Civil War?

Critical Thinking

9. **Analyze Information** According to Henry Grady, what would characterize the "New South"? In the post–Civil War years, was Grady's vision realized?

10. **Analyze Information** How did Supreme Court rulings in the civil rights cases in 1883 affect the situation of African Americans in the post-Reconstruction South?

11. **Draw Inferences** Why did the federal government encourage Native Americans to assimilate?

12. **Summarize** Summarize the causes and effects of the Indian Wars.

13. **Recognize Cause and Effect** Why did the federal government encourage the construction of the transcontinental railroad? What effect did the new railroad have on the people and the land?

14. **Distinguish False From Accurate Images** The painting below was created in 1914. What emotions do you think the artist is attempting to evoke? Explain your reasoning.

Writing About History

Preparing for an Oral Presentation The post–Civil War years were a complex time in the South and the West, involving a variety of economic, social, and cultural changes. Choose a topic for an oral presentation on some aspect of these changes, and prepare an oral presentation that you might give to classmates to expand on the discussion in your textbook.

Prewriting

- Make a list of possible topics relating to the transformation of the South and the West. Narrow down your list and define a specific topic for your presentation.

- Use library and Internet resources to gather information on your topic. Include both written sources and images.

- Write main ideas and supporting details on note cards.

Drafting

- Develop a working thesis in which you clearly state the purpose of your presentation.

- Write an introduction that clearly defines your topic and what you hope to show.

- Use your note cards to make an outline for your presentation. Clearly indicate the images you would use and when.

- Write a concluding statement that sums up the main point of your presentation.

Revising

- Use the guidelines on page SH31 of the Writing Handbook to revise your presentation.

Regents DBQ Practice

U.S. Indian Policy

During the 1800s, most Native Americans were forced to move onto reservations. It was one of the greatest population displacements in modern history. What was the rationale behind this policy? What effects did it have? Use your knowledge of American history and Documents 1, 2, 3, and 4 to answer questions 1 through 4.

Document 1

". . . [I]t would be [foolish] to expect that the wild Indians will become industrious and frugal except through a severe course of industrial instruction and exercise, under restraint. The reservation system affords the place for thus dealing with tribes and bands. . . . [I]t is essential that the right of the Government to keep Indians upon the reservations assigned to them, and to arrest and return them whenever they wander away, should be placed beyond dispute. Without this, whenever these people become restive under compulsion to labor, they will break away in their old roving spirit, and stray off in small bands to neighboring communities, upon which they will prey in a petty fashion, by begging and stealing. . . ."

—*Annual Report of the Commissioner of Indian Affairs*, 1872

Document 2

Land Holdings in the U.S., 1871

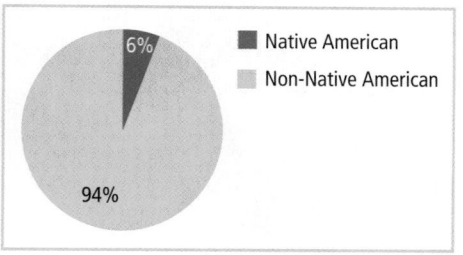

6%
94%
■ Native American
■ Non-Native American

Document 3

Navajo student of the Carlisle Indian Industrial School, 1882

Before

After

Document 4

"All men were made by the same Great Spirit Chief. They are all brothers. The earth is the mother of all people, and all people should have equal rights upon it. You might as well expect all rivers to run backward as that any man who was born a free man should be contented penned up and denied liberty to go where he pleases. If you tie a horse to a stake, do you expect he will grow fat? If you pen an Indian up on a small spot of earth and compel him to stay there, he will not be contented nor will he grow and prosper. I have asked some of the Great White Chiefs where they get their authority to say to the Indian that he shall stay in one place, while he sees white men going where they please. They cannot tell me."

—*Chief Joseph, Nez Percé*

---

1. Document 2 reflects data from the year 1871. How would it be different if it reflected data from a century earlier?
   (1) The percentage of non–Native American lands would be slightly higher.
   (2) The percentage of Native American lands would be slightly lower.
   (3) The percentage of non–Native American lands would be significantly lower.
   (4) The percentages of Native American and non–Native American lands would be approximately the same.

2. In Document 4, Chief Joseph likens a reservation to a
   (1) mother.
   (2) stake.
   (3) horse.
   (4) river.

3. Which term would a historian most likely use in reference to Document 3?
   (1) assimilation
   (2) coexistence
   (3) displacement
   (4) repatriation

4. **Writing Task** In Document 1, the Commissioner of Indian Affairs advocates "a severe course of industrial instruction and exercise." To what was he referring? Use your knowledge of American history and the sources above to develop your answer.

16

Issues of the Gilded Age

1877–1900

Paupers and Millionaires

In 1873, Mark Twain and Charles Dudley Warner published *The Gilded Age*. Disillusioned with the corruption, poverty, and dishonesty around them, Twain and Warner used the novel to express their views. Eventually, the term *Gilded Age* came to define an era in which excessive extravagance and wealth concealed mounting social problems, government corruption, and poverty.

Among the problems were those faced by farmers. In desperation, dissatisfied farmers joined the Populist Party. Ignatius Donnelly, a Populist delegate, addressed his party:

“We meet in the midst of a nation brought to the verge of moral, political, and material ruin. Corruption dominates the ballot box, the legislatures, the Congress. . . . The people are demoralized. . . . The fruits of the toil of millions are boldly stolen to build up the colossal fortunes. . . . We breed two great classes—paupers and millionaires.”

—Ignatius Donnelly, Preamble to the Omaha Platform, 1892

Listen to the Witness History *audio to hear more about the Issues of the Gilded Age.*

THE GILDED AGE
A Tale of Today

MARK TWAIN
& CHARLES DUDLEY WARNER

The Gilded Age

Button from 1896 presidential campaign

◀ Wealthy people had the pleasure of enjoying leisure time. This group takes a rest from an afternoon of golf.

(NY) Core Curriculum Preview

Chapter Focus Question: What political, social, and economic issues did the nation face during the late 1800s?

Section 1
Segregation and Social Tensions
3.I.C.2b, 3.II.E.1c, 4.I.B.2c

Section 2
Political and Economic Challenges
3.II.E.2d, 3.III.A.2b

Section 3
Farmers and Populism 3.II.F.1a, 3.II.F.1b, 3.II.F.1c

Use the ☑ **Quick Study Timeline** at the end of this chapter to preview chapter events.

Protesting for women's rights

Note Taking Study Guide *Online*
For: Note Taking and American Issues Connector
Web Code: nee-7601

▲ Frederick Douglass

WITNESS HISTORY AUDIO

Frederick Douglass Laments the Color Line

In 1883, Frederick Douglass, the famous black leader and former runaway slave, addressed a gathering of African Americans in Louisville, Kentucky. Twenty years had passed since Lincoln had issued the Emancipation Proclamation, yet, as Douglass observed, African Americans had not realized their hopes for equality.

❝Though we have had war, reconstruction and abolition as a nation, we still linger in the shadow and blight of an extinct institution. Though the colored man is no longer subject to be bought and sold, he is still surrounded by an adverse sentiment, which fetters all his movements. In his downward course he meets with no resistance, but his course upward is resented and resisted at every step of his progress. . . .❞

—Frederick Douglass, address in Louisville, Kentucky, 1883

Segregation and Social Tensions

Core Curriculum Objectives

- **3.I.C.2b** From exclusion to segregation
- **3.II.E.1c** Attitudes toward immigrants, African Americans, women
- **4.I.B.2c** The black movement and reform (Booker T. Washington and W.E.B. Du Bois)

Terms and People

Jim Crow laws
poll tax
literacy test
grandfather clause

Ida B. Wells
Booker T. Washington
W.E.B. Du Bois
Las Gorras Blancas

NoteTaking

Reading Skill: Summarize Record the ways in which different groups challenged Reconstruction.

Why It Matters During Reconstruction, the federal government sought to secure equal rights for African Americans. By the time of the Gilded Age (1877–1900), however, African Americans and other minorities experienced a narrowing of their rights. This turn away from equality for all had a lasting impact on society in the United States. **Section Focus Question: How were the civil and political rights of certain groups in America undermined during the years after Reconstruction?**

African Americans Lose Freedoms

Following the disputed presidential election of 1876, President Hayes removed federal troops from the South. This action allowed southern states to reassert their control over African Americans without concern about federal intervention. Southern governments enacted various measures aimed at disenfranchising, or taking away the voting rights of, African Americans and enacted **Jim Crow laws** that kept blacks and whites segregated, or apart.

States' Governments Limit Voting Rights The Fifteenth Amendment, which became part of the United States Constitution in 1870, prohibited state governments from denying someone the right to vote because of "race, color, or previous condition of servitude." After Reconstruction, southern states got around this amendment by passing a number of other restrictive measures. They enacted a **poll tax,** which required voters to pay a tax to vote. The tax, which began in Georgia, cost voters $1 or $2 to vote. Poor African Americans could scarcely afford such a fee. The states also required voters to pass **literacy tests** and "understanding" tests. Because African Americans had been <u>exploited</u> economically and denied an education, these restrictions disqualified many of them as voters.

Southern states also enacted **grandfather clauses,** which allowed a person to vote as long as his ancestors had voted prior to 1866. Of course, the ancestors of the black freedmen did not vote prior to 1866, but the ancestors of many whites did. In other words, grandfather clauses allowed poor and illiterate whites but not blacks to vote. Some southern states also established all-white primaries, meaning only whites had a voice in selecting who got to run in general elections.

In addition, whites resorted to violence to keep African Americans from participating in the political process. As South Carolina senator Ben Tillman put it: "We have done our level best. We have scratched our heads to find out how we could eliminate the last one of them [black voters]. We stuffed ballot boxes. We shot them."

As a result of these actions, throughout the Deep South, black participation in politics fell dramatically. In Louisiana, for example, the number of blacks registered to vote plummeted from 130,000 in 1894 to just over 1,300 in 1904. On the eve of World War II, in 1940, only 3 percent of all African Americans in the South could vote.

New Laws Force Segregation As the nineteenth century drew to a close, Jim Crow became a way of life in the South. Initially, some white southerners opposed Jim Crow laws on the grounds that if some aspects of life were segregated, in time all aspects of life would become segregated and this would impose an undue burden on society. "If there must be Jim Crow cars [railroad], there should be Jim Crow waiting saloons. And if there were Jim Crow saloons," stated a prominent Charleston newspaper writer, "then there would have to be Jim Crow jury boxes and a Jim Crow Bible for colored witnesses." The whole idea, he concluded, was "absurd."

Nevertheless, widespread segregation became a reality. In addition to Jim Crow railroad cars and waiting stations, southern states established Jim Crow jury boxes and Bibles, as well as cemeteries, restaurants, parks, beaches, and hospitals. Similarly, in northern states, including those that had civil rights laws that outlawed legal segregation, black migrants found many examples of de facto segregation—actual segregation, such as restrictions on where they were allowed to live and work.

During the 1870s, the Supreme Court ruled in cases that undermined the civil rights of African Americans. In *Plessy* v. *Ferguson* (1896), the Supreme Court upheld the constitutionality of Jim Crow laws. (See the feature page at the end of this section.) It did so by arguing that as long as states maintained "separate but equal" facilities, they did not violate the Fourteenth Amendment. Yet, in reality, separate

Vocabulary Builder

exploit–(ehk SPLOYT) *v.* to treat someone unfairly in order to earn money or gain an advantage

Rights Denied

As Jim Crow laws spread through the South, African Americans, as shown in the cartoon below, lost freedoms gained during Reconstruction. The change in African American voting patterns evident in South Carolina after 1876 was repeated in other southern states. The graph shows the effects of Jim Crow which kept African Americans from voting.

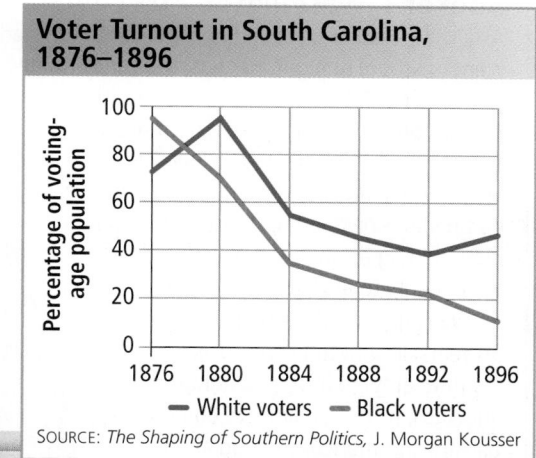

Voter Turnout in South Carolina, 1876–1896

SOURCE: *The Shaping of Southern Politics,* J. Morgan Kousser

THE POLITICAL PINKERTONS.

facilities were rarely equal. For instance, in 1915, South Carolina spent nearly 14 dollars for every white student but less than 3 dollars for every black student.

✓ **Checkpoint** In what ways were the rights of African Americans restricted?

African Americans Oppose Injustices

Even during the darkest days of Jim Crow, African Americans refused to accept their status as second-class citizens. They established black newspapers, women's clubs, fraternal organizations, schools and colleges, and political associations with the goal of securing their freedom. They did not always agree on the best strategies for achieving their goal. However, they were united in their determination to "never turn back" until they had equality.

Booker T. Washington Urges Economic Advancement The most famous black leader during the late nineteenth century was **Booker T. Washington.** Born a slave in 1856, Washington argued that African Americans needed to accommodate themselves to segregation, meaning they should *not* focus their energies on seeking to overturn Jim Crow. Instead, he called for blacks to "pull themselves up from their own bootstraps" by building up their economic resources and establishing their reputations as hardworking and honest citizens.

HISTORY MAKERS

Booker T. Washington (1856–1915)

As a child, Booker T. Washington worked by day and went to school at night. He was eventually trained as a teacher. After several years of teaching, he was chosen in 1881 to head a normal school, where teachers are trained, in Tuskegee, Alabama. When he arrived, the newly formed school had no buildings or students. Washington went to work finding a space—and persuading 40 students to attend.

Washington led the school for more than 30 years. In that time, the Tuskegee Institute grew to include a hundred buildings, a staff of almost 200 people— all African Americans—and about 1,500 students. It became a model for many similar schools established throughout the country. In the process, Washington became one of the leading figures in the African American community.

Primary Source "The wisest among my race understand that the agitation of questions of social equality is the extremest folly, and that progress in the enjoyment of all the privileges that will come to us must be the result of severe and constant struggle rather than artificial forcing. . . . It is important and right that all privileges of the law be ours, but it is vastly more important that we be prepared for the exercises of these privileges."
—Booker T. Washington, Atlanta Exposition address, 1895

In addition to speaking and writing, Washington poured his energies into the Tuskegee Institute, a school in Macon County, Alabama. Under Washington, Tuskegee became known for providing "industrial education," sometimes referred to as vocational education. Such an education, as Washington had suggested in his Atlanta Exposition address, would prepare African Americans to exercise the privileges of citizenship.

W.E.B. Du Bois Attacks Washington's Ideas A native of Great Barrington, Massachusetts, **W.E.B. Du Bois,** who earned his Ph.D. from Harvard University in 1896, criticized Washington's willingness to accommodate southern whites. Echoing the spirit of the abolitionists, he argued that blacks should demand full and immediate equality and not limit themselves to vocational education. Du Bois did not feel that the right to vote was a privilege that blacks needed to earn. He also argued that Washington wrongly shifted the burden of achieving equality from the nation to "Negro's shoulders" alone. You will learn more about the conflict between Washington and Du Bois in the next chapter.

Ida Wells Crusades Against Lynching One African American woman who fought for justice was **Ida B. Wells.** Born into slavery in 1862, Wells grew up in Holly Springs, Mississippi. Her father, James Wells, became a prominent local businessman and raised her to fight for the rights of African Americans. As a young adult, Wells moved to Memphis, Tennessee, where she worked as a schoolteacher and became active in the African Methodist Episcopal Church. Wells bought a local newspaper, renamed it *Free Speech*, and wrote numerous articles that condemned the mistreatment of blacks.

In 1892, after a mob attack on close friends in Memphis, she wrote an editorial attacking the practice of lynching in the South. "Eight Negroes lynched since last issue of the 'Free Speech,'" Wells declared. "If Southern white men are not careful, they will over-reach themselves and public sentiment will have a reaction."

Local whites responded to Wells's editorial by running her out of town. In exile, Wells embarked on a lifelong crusade against lynching. She wrote three pamphlets aimed at awakening the nation to what she described as the "southern horrors" of legalized murder. She also toured Europe and helped organize women's clubs to fight for African American rights.

✓ **Checkpoint** How did Wells, Washington, and Du Bois protest the mistreatment of African Americans?

Chinese Immigrants Face Discrimination

During the same time that Jim Crow arose in the South, Chinese immigrants faced racial prejudice on the West Coast. In 1879, California barred cities from employing people of Chinese ancestry. Several years later, San Francisco established a segregated "Oriental" school. Elsewhere, mobs of whites attacked Chinese workers, saying they had taken "white" jobs. Congress responded to these attacks by passing the Chinese Exclusion Act, which prohibited Chinese laborers from entering the country.

Like African Americans, brave Chinese immigrants challenged discrimination. Saum Song Bo questioned why he should support a fund-raising drive to build the Statue of Liberty. "That statue represents Liberty holding a torch which lights the passage of those of all nations who come into this country," Bo wrote in a letter published in *American Missionary* in 1898. "But are the Chinese allowed to come? As for the Chinese who are here, are they allowed to enjoy liberty as men of all other nationalities enjoy it?"

Chinese immigrants also turned to the federal courts to protect their rights but with mixed results. In 1886, in the case of *Yick Wo* v. *Hopkins,* the U.S.

Forging a New Life
Frequently faced with job discrimination, some Chinese immigrants, such as the ones shown here, managed to start their own businesses. These immigrants pose proudly in front of their own grocery store.

Supreme Court sided with a Chinese immigrant who challenged a California law that banned him and other Chinese from operating a laundry. In 1898, the Court ruled that individuals of Chinese descent, born in the United States, could not be stripped of their citizenship. Yet the Court upheld the Chinese Exclusion Act and several other discriminatory measures.

✓ **Checkpoint** How did Chinese immigrants use the court system to protest discrimination?

Mexican Americans Struggle in the West

Like African Americans and Asian Americans, Mexican Americans struggled against discrimination in the latter decades of the nineteenth century. At the center of their struggle stood land. The Treaty of Guadalupe Hidalgo, signed at the end of the Mexican-American War, guaranteed the property rights of Mexicans who lived in the Southwest prior to the war. Still, four out of five Mexican Americans who lived in New Mexico lost their land, as did Mexican Americans in other southwestern states.

Abuses and Discrimination Undermine Rights Many factors caused the Mexican Americans to lose most of their land. When Anglo Americans and Mexican Americans laid claim to the same land, U.S. courts put the burden of proof on Mexican Americans to show that they really owned the land. Differences in legal customs, and the fact that much of the land was held communally, not individually, made it difficult for many of them to do so.

In addition, Anglo Americans used political connections to take land away from Mexican Americans. The "Sante Fe Ring," an association of prominent

● **INFOGRAPHIC**

Discrimination in the West

America's move toward integration was neither smooth nor steady. African Americans were not the only group to suffer discrimination. Mexicans and Chinese immigrants also faced harsh and constant discrimination.

After the Treaty of Guadalupe Hidalgo, Mexicans were "thrown among those who were strangers to their language, customs, laws and habits." Although guaranteed the rights of U.S. citizens, Mexicans were subjected to laws limiting their rights as citizens and landowners.

The Burlingame Treaty signed in 1868 guaranteed government protection for Chinese immigrants. Yet, this was hardly the reality. Chinese immigrants were often victims of discrimination and random violence.

Both Mexicans and Chinese immigrants responded to the prejudice with group resistance, lawsuits, and labor strikes.

Surviving harsh conditions, these ▶
Mexican women in San Antonio, Texas,
prepare a meal outside their shack.

whites, got the federal government to grant the group control of millions of acres of land in New Mexico. Thousands of Mexican Americans had lived on and farmed this land for many years. Since New Mexico was a territory, not a state, however, Mexican Americans, who comprised the majority of the population, had no representatives in Washington, D.C., to challenge this deal.

Mexican Americans Fight Back Throughout the Southwest—in Texas, New Mexico, Arizona, and California—Mexican Americans fought to maintain their rights. Many Mexicans especially resented the loss of their land. One group, **Las Gorras Blancas,** targeted the property of large ranch owners by cutting holes in barbed-wire fences and burning houses. The group declared: "Our purpose is to protect the rights and interests of the people in general; especially those of the helpless classes." Supported by a national labor organization, the Knights of Labor, the group also had a newspaper to voice their grievances.

As anti-Mexican feelings increased, a group of Hispanic citizens in Tucson, Arizona, formed the Alianza Hispano-Americana in 1894 to protect the culture, interests, and legal rights of Mexican Americans. Within two years, new branches of the organization opened in other cities.

✔ **Checkpoint** Why did Mexican Americans lose rights to their land?

Women Make Gains and Suffer Setbacks

Before the Civil War, women played a prominent role in many reform movements, including the drive to abolish slavery. They even began to fight for their own right to vote, to own property, and to receive an education. In the decades that followed the Civil War, women continued to fight for these rights. In some cases, they were successful; in others, they were not.

▼ Violence against Chinese immigrants increased in the West throughout the 1870s and 1880s. In railroad towns and mining camps, angry whites looted and burned Chinese communities.

◀ Chinese immigration papers

Chinese laborers took on the most ▲ dangerous jobs while working on the transcontinental railroad.

Thinking Critically

1. **Analyze Information** Why did anti-Chinese feelings increase during the depression years of the 1870s?

2. **Draw Conclusions** Were Mexican protest groups such as Las Gorras Blancas effective? Explain.

History *Interactive* ✶

For: More about discrimination in the West
Web Code: ncp-1607

525

Women in American Society

 3.III.A.3

TRACK THE ISSUE

Why do Americans disagree over women's rights?

In early America, women had few legal rights. They could not vote, hold office, or work at most jobs. Married women could not own property and were under the legal authority of their husbands. The women's movement helped change all this. Nevertheless, Americans still remain divided over women's rights. Use the timeline below to explore this enduring issue.

1848 Seneca Falls Convention
Women meet in upstate New York to declare support for women's rights

1869 The National Woman Suffrage Association
Anthony and Stanton form organization to fight for women's suffrage

1920 Nineteeth Amendment
Women gain right to vote

1964 Title VII of the Civil Rights Act
Law protects women against job discrimination

1972 Title IX of the Education Codes
Law bans sex discrimination in schools

Supporters of women's suffrage gather in protest.

While many women today have successful careers, some still feel limited in their efforts to land higher positions in their chosen fields.

DEBATE THE ISSUE

Women in the Workplace On average, women earn less than men in the workplace. This wage gap has led to charges of sex discrimination. Feminists also argue that a "glass ceiling" keeps many women from rising to the top of their profession. But other factors may be involved, too.

❝The wage gap is the result of a number of factors in addition to discrimination, such as the differences in women's education, their shorter time in the workforce, and their concentration in a narrow range of jobs that are underpaid because women are in them. Nonetheless, a significant portion is attributable to discrimination.❞

—Sonia Pressman Fuentes, founding member, National Organization for Women

❝[Feminists] often portray working women as victims of rampant discrimination [which] [they say] . . . renders women powerless in the face of an impenetrable glass ceiling. While discrimination does exist in the workplace, levels of education . . . and time spent in the workforce play a far greater role in determining women's pay and promotion.❞

—Naomi Lopez, Director, Center for Enterprise and Opportunity

❓ *TRANSFER* Activities

1. **Compare** How do the two writers agree? How do they disagree?

2. **Analyze** Affirmative action makes it possible for women and minorities to compete in the workplace. Which of the two women quoted above might support it?

3. **Transfer** Use the following Web site to see a video, try a WebQuest, and write in your journal. **Web Code:** neh-7602

Fighting for a Constitutional Amendment

Expanding the rights of African Americans left some women's rights activists, such as Susan B. Anthony, angry. Anthony favored abolishing slavery. Yet she felt betrayed when Radical Republicans did not include women in the Fourteenth and Fifteenth amendments.

In 1869, Anthony and Elizabeth Cady Stanton formed the National Woman Suffrage Association to fight for a constitutional amendment that would grant women the right to vote. In 1872, Anthony voted in an election in Rochester, New York, an illegal act for which she was tried and ultimately convicted in federal court. While awaiting trial, Anthony toured the nation, delivering a speech titled "Is It a Crime for a Citizen of the United States to Vote?" Anthony declared, "Our . . . government is based on . . . the natural right of every individual member . . . to a voice and a vote in making and executing the laws." Anthony's address failed to convince the nation to enact a women's suffrage amendment. By the time of Anthony's death in 1906, only four western states—Wyoming, Utah, Colorado, and Idaho—had granted women the right to vote.

Breaking Down Other Barriers Women's rights activists, however, did achieve some of their other goals. The number of women attending college jumped. By 1900, one third of all college students, nationwide, were women.

Women also played an increasingly important role in a number of reform movements. Frances Willard led the Women's Christian Temperance Union (WCTU). While temperance, or the ban of the sale of liquor, remained Willard's primary goal, she also supported women's suffrage. She argued that women needed the vote to prohibit the sale of alcohol. Like many of WCTU's members, Willard also promoted other social causes, such as public health and welfare reform.

✓ **Checkpoint** What successes did women achieve in the years after Reconstruction?

HISTORY MAKERS

Susan B. Anthony (1820–1906)
Originally involved in the temperance movement, reformer Susan B. Anthony joined the fight for women's right to vote in the 1850s. Working closely with her friend Elizabeth Cady Stanton, Anthony spent five decades tirelessly pushing the cause by traveling, writing, speaking, and organizing. To challenge laws that barred women from voting, she cast a ballot in the presidential election of 1872 and then refused to pay the fine when found guilty. Shortly before her death, Anthony urged women to continue the struggle for voting rights with the words "Failure is impossible."

SECTION **1** Assessment

Progress Monitoring Online
For: Self-test with vocabulary practice
Web Code: nca-1602

Comprehension

1. **Terms and People** Explain how each person or group challenged discrimination.
   - Booker T. Washington
   - W.E.B. Du Bois
   - Ida B. Wells
   - Las Gorras Blancas

2. **NoteTaking Reading Skill: Summarize** Use your concept web to answer the Section Focus Question: How were the civil and political rights of certain groups in America undermined during the years after Reconstruction?

Writing About History

3. **Quick Write: Prepare an Outline** Write down notes to answer the following prompt: Explain how issues such as social reform, civil rights, and the economy dominated local politics in the late 1890s. Then, use your notes to prepare an outline to answer the prompt.

Critical Thinking

4. **Draw Conclusions** How did the *Plessy* v. *Ferguson* decision support the existence of Jim Crow laws?

5. **Recognize Cause and Effect** How did the Treaty of Guadalupe Hidalgo affect relations between Mexican Americans and white Americans in the Southwest?

6. **Analyze Information** Do you think women activists during the late 1800s had any effect on the political or social life of the country? Explain.

Can Separate Treatment Be Equal Treatment?

 3.I.D.4

The Fourteenth Amendment, passed during Reconstruction in 1866, guaranteed equal rights to all citizens. By 1890, civil rights and racial equality were not significant issues for whites in the North and South. Already, the Supreme Court was handing down decisions that overturned Reconstruction legislation and encouraged racial discrimination.

Plessy v. *Ferguson* (1896)

The Facts	The Issue	The Decision
• In 1890, Louisiana passed a law allowing railroads to provide "separate but equal" facilities. • Homer Plessy, an African American, sat in the car reserved for whites. • He was arrested when he refused to move to the "colored" car.	In his appeal to the Supreme Court, Plessy argued that the *Separate Car Act* violated the Fourteenth Amendment.	A 7 to 1 majority declared that state laws requiring separate but equal accommodations for whites and blacks did not violate the Fourteenth Amendment.

Why It Matters

The majority of the Supreme Court reasoned that the Constitution was not intended to protect social equality of race. This interpretation allowed southern states to make laws requiring separate but equal facilities. These racial discrimination laws, known as Jim Crow laws, lasted nearly 60 years before the Court reversed its decision in *Brown* v. *Board of Education* (1954). In this case, the Court ruled that separate but equal facilities violated the Fourteenth Amendment.

JIM CROW LAW.

UPHELD BY THE UNITED STATES SUPREME COURT.

Statute Within the Competency of the Louisiana Legislature and Railroads—Must Furnish Separate Cars for Whites and Blacks.

Washington, May 18.—The Supreme Court today in an opinion read by Justice Brown, sustained the constitutionality of the law in Louisiana requiring the railroads of that State to provide separate cars for white and colored passengers. There was no interstate commerce feature in the case for the railroad upon which the incident occurred giving rise to case—Plessey vs. Ferguson—East Louisiana railroad. was and is operated wholly within the State, to the laws of Congress of many of the States. The opinion states that by the analogy of the laws of Congress, and of many of states requiring establishment of separate schools for children of two races another similar laws—the

▲ An article from an 1896 newspaper reporting the *Plessy* v. *Ferguson* verdict

---

Connect to Your World

What does it mean to be treated equally? Are there instances where separate treatment is equal treatment? Consider the following situations. Decide what is equal treatment for the individuals in each case. Discuss your conclusions with the rest of the class.

• Two students enter their high school. One of them is confined to a wheelchair.

• Twelfth graders are required to pass algebra in order to graduate. One student has a documented learning disability in math; the other does not.

For: Supreme Court cases
Web Code: nee-1603

A young man in a wheelchair faces the difficulty of entering a building. ▶

◀ Mark Twain

The Gilded Age

The spoils system, or the practice of giving government positions to political supporters, was the accepted way of staffing federal offices. However, there were demands for reform. Mark Twain and Charles Dudley Warner give their view of the situation in *The Gilded Age*.

"Unless you can get the ear of a Senator . . . and persuade him to use his 'influence' in your behalf, you cannot get an employment of the most trivial nature in Washington. Mere merit, fitness and capability, are useless baggage to you without 'influence.' . . . It would be an odd circumstance to see a girl get employment . . . merely because she was worthy and a competent, and a good citizen of a free country that 'treats all persons alike.'**"**

—from *The Gilded Age* by Mark Twain and Charles Dudley Warner

THE GILDED AGE
A Tale of Today

MARK TWAIN
& CHARLES DUDLEY WARNER

Political and Economic Challenges

Core Curriculum Objectives

- **3.II.E.2d** Attitude and role of government
- **3.III.A.2b** Geographic, economic, social, and political considerations

Terms and People

spoils system   Pendleton Civil Service Act
civil service   gold standard

NoteTaking

Reading Skill: Identify Main Ideas As you read, describe the issues that dominated national politics in the 1870s and 1880s.

> I. Politics and Economics
>   A. Political Stalemate
>   B. Corruption in Politics
>   1.
>   2.

Why It Matters While Congress enacted many major reforms during Reconstruction, it passed very few measures between 1877 and 1900. Instead, inaction and political corruption characterized the political scene during the Gilded Age. This raised questions whether or not democracy could succeed in a time dominated by large and powerful industrial corporations and men of great wealth. **Section Focus Question: Why did the political structure change during the Gilded Age?**

Balance of Power Creates Stalemate

Party loyalties were so evenly divided that no faction or group gained control for any period of time. Only twice between 1877 and 1897 did either the Republicans or Democrats gain control of the White House and both houses of Congress at the same time. Furthermore, neither held control for more than two years in a row. This made it very difficult to pass new laws. Most of the elections were very close as well, allowing those who lost to block new legislation until they got back in power.

In comparison to Lincoln, the Presidents of the Gilded Age appeared particularly weak. They won by slim margins and seemed to lack integrity. Rutherford B. Hayes owed his election in 1876 to a secret deal. Benjamin Harrison became only the second President in history to lose the popular vote but win the electoral college vote.

Chester Arthur, who took the helm following James Garfield's assassination, upset so many of his fellow Republicans that he failed to win his own party's presidential nomination in 1884.

The most noteworthy President of the era was Grover Cleveland. In an era known for its corruption, Cleveland maintained a reputation for integrity. He once observed, "A Democratic thief is as bad as a Republican thief." Cleveland enjoyed an extremely rapid rise to political prominence. In 1881, running as a reformer, he won the race for mayor in Buffalo, New York. A year later, he became the governor of New York, and in 1884, he became the first Democrat to win the White House in 24 years. In 1888, even though he won the popular vote, Cleveland lost to Benjamin Harrison. But Cleveland came back to rewin the presidency in 1892.

✔ **Checkpoint** Why did the federal government fail to make significant political gains between 1877 and 1897?

Corruption Plagues National Politics

Grover Cleveland's reputation for honesty was the exception. Many government officials routinely accepted bribes. As Henry Adams, the great-grandson of John Adams, observed, "one might search the whole list of Congress, Judiciary, and Executive . . . [from] 1870 to 1895, and find little but damaged reputation."

Political Cartoonists Raise the Alarm Besides such writers as Mark Twain, political cartoonists expressed their concern about the damaging effects of corruption and big money.

"The Bosses of the Senate," one of the most famous political cartoons of the time, drawn by Joseph Keppler, showed a cluster of businessmen representing various trusts, glaring down on the chambers of the Senate.

Thomas Nast did a series of cartoons which exposed the illegal activities of William Marcy "Boss" Tweed, a powerful New York City politician. Eventually, Tweed was arrested. However, he escaped and fled to Spain. While there, Tweed was identified through one of Nast's cartoons.

Analyzing Political Cartoons

The Bosses of the Senate In this political cartoon, Joseph Keppler shows how corporate interests have taken over the business of the Senate.
1. Why do you think the businessmen are drawn so large?
2. How do you think most Americans responded to the political influence of corporations?

THE BOSSES OF THE SENATE.

The Spoils System Dominates the Government Political parties and the spoils system were central components of politics during the Gilded Age. Under the **spoils system,** which was first used by President Andrew Jackson, politicians awarded government jobs to loyal party workers, with little regard for their qualifications. Parties held elaborate rallies and parades to get out the vote. However, candidates for the presidency did not take part in the campaign. They felt it lowered the reputation of the presidency. Political parties developed sophisticated organizations that reached virtually into every ward, in every precinct, in every city in the nation.

The spoils system served as the glue that helped make the parties so powerful. The Postmaster General, who headed the U.S. Postal Service, for example, could reward thousands of supporters with jobs. Likewise, other officials could and did use federal contracts to convince people to vote for their candidates. Ironically, political participation probably got a boost from the spoils system and the fierce partisanship of the era. About 75 to 80 percent of all those who could vote did vote in presidential elections during the Gilded Age.

President Garfield Is Shot
Charles J. Guiteau, unsuccessful at getting a government position, shot President Garfield in a Washington, D.C., train station. *How did Garfield's assassination lead to a change in the civil service system?*

Civil Service Reform Promotes Honest Government The feeling that the spoils system corrupted government, or at least made it terribly inefficient, prompted a number of prominent figures to promote civil service reform. The **civil service** is a system that includes federal jobs in the executive branch. In a reformed system, most government workers would get their jobs due to their expertise and maintain them regardless of which political party won the election. Reforming the spoils system did cause controversy. Without the spoils system, politicians felt they would not attract the people needed to run their parties. Independent attempts by politicians to change the system failed. When Rutherford B. Hayes took office in 1877, he worked for civil service reform. He even placed well-known reformers in high offices. However, the Republican Party did not support his reform efforts. It took the assassination of President James Garfield by Charles J. Guiteau to make civil service reform a reality. Guiteau shot Garfield because he believed that the Republican Party had not fulfilled its promise to give him a government job.

Chester A. Arthur became President after the assassination of Garfield. While Arthur defended the spoils system, he supported the movement for civil service reform, which had been strengthened because of public indignation over Garfield's assassination. Arthur signed the **Pendleton Civil Service Act** in 1883. This act established a Civil Service Commission, which wrote a civil service exam. Individuals who wanted to work for the government had to take the exam, and getting a job depended on doing well on the exam, not on <u>manipulating</u> one's political connections. Initially, the act covered only a small percentage of federal employees, but its reach grew over time, reducing the power of the spoils system.

Vocabulary Builder
<u>manipulate</u>–(muh NIHP yoo layt) *v.* to exert influence or practice deception to obtain some advantage

✓ **Checkpoint** How did the spoils system lead to government corruption and, eventually, government reform?

Economic Issues Challenge the Nation

The tariff and monetary policy were critical economic issues during the Gilded Age. The tariff issue sharply divided the Democrats and Republicans. Monetary policy gave rise to independent political parties or movements that disagreed with the major parties' commitment to the **gold standard.** Using the gold standard meant that the government would use gold as the basis of the nation's currency.

Americans Debate the Tariff Question The debate over the tariff had deep roots in American history. The tax on imports of manufactured goods and some agricultural products was created to protect newly developed industries. Since then, the debate to lower or increase tariffs continued. Differences over the tariff had divided the Federalists and Jeffersonians and the Democrats and Whigs. During the Gilded Age, it divided the Republicans and Democrats. The tariff question became a major issue during the presidential election of 1888. The Republicans favored a high tariff, arguing that it would allow American industries to grow and promote jobs in manufacturing. Democrats countered that high tariffs increased the costs of goods to consumers and made it harder for American farmers to sell their goods abroad.

Conflicts Develop Over Monetary Policy Two related factors turned monetary policy into a bitter issue during the Gilded Age. During the Civil War, the federal government issued paper money, known as greenbacks. After the war, because they had contributed to wartime inflation (a rise in prices), the government retired, or got rid of, the greenbacks.

Around the same time, Congress passed the Coinage Act of 1873. This law reversed the government policy of making both gold and silver coins. Those who favored the minting of silver—in other words, considering silver as money—protested against what they termed the "Crime of 1873" and prompted Congress to mint silver dollars. Nonetheless, the debate over whether to consider both gold and silver as money or only gold as money continued.

Bankers and others involved in international trade feared that considering silver as money would undermine the economy. In contrast, most farmers favored coining silver to create inflation. They hoped the rise in prices would increase their income. You will read more about this dispute in the next section.

✔ **Checkpoint** Why did the Republicans and Democrats differ in their view of the tariff issue?

Silver and Gold
By the 1870s, the debate between supporters of the gold or the silver standard began to dominate national politics. At one time, however, the government used both metals to back national currency. Silver and gold certificates, as shown here, were widely circulated.

SECTION 2 Assessment

Progress Monitoring *Online*
For: Self-test with vocabulary practice
Web Code: nca-1604

Comprehension
1. **Terms and People** Explain how each of the following terms describes a political issue during the 1870s and 1880s.
   - spoils system
   - civil service
   - Pendleton Civil Service Act
   - gold standard

2. **NoteTaking Reading Skill: Identify Main Ideas** Use your outline to answer the Section Focus Question: Why did the political structure change during the Gilded Age?

Writing About History
3. **Quick Write: Examine the Question** Look for the key word that will tell you how to focus and organize your response: Summarize the importance of the tariff as a national issue. Write a brief paragraph.

Critical Thinking
4. **Draw Inferences** Why do you think Congress became the strongest branch of the government in the 1880s?

5. **Analyze Information** What were the positive and negative effects of the Pendleton Civil Service Act?

6. **Identify Point of View** President Cleveland called the high tariff "unjust taxation." Why do you think President Cleveland made this statement? Explain his point of view.

Black and White Together

In the late 1800s, a social and political movement made up largely of farmers arose in the South and West. Known as Populists, the biggest obstacle this group faced, especially in the South, was antagonism between blacks and whites. Populist leader Tom Watson tried to persuade the groups to work together.

❝The white tenant lives adjoining the colored tenant. . . . They are equally burdened with heavy taxes. They pay the same high rent. . . . They pay the same enormous prices for farm supplies. . . . Now the People's Party says to these two men, 'You are kept apart that you may be separately fleeced of your earnings. . . . You are deceived and blinded that you may not see how this race antagonism perpetuates a monetary system which beggars both.❞

—Thomas Watson, "The Negro Question in the South," 1892

▲ Farmers gather at a Populist rally. The inset photo shows the cover of a Farmers' Alliance songbook.

Farmers and Populism

NY Core Curriculum Objectives

- **3.II.Fa** Agrarian response to economic change: The Grange movement
- **3.II.Fb** Agrarian response to economic change: Populism, William Jennings Bryan
- **3.II.Fc** Agrarian response to economic change: National government response: Interstate Commerce Act

Terms and People

Oliver H. Kelley   William Jennings Bryan
Grange   William McKinley
Populist Party

NoteTaking

Reading Skill: Identify Causes and Effects
As you read, list the reasons that farmers in the South and West felt the need to organize and the effects of their effort.

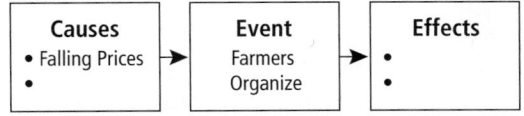

Causes	Event	Effects
• Falling Prices	Farmers Organize	•
•		•

Why It Matters Following the Civil War, millions of men and women migrated west in search of the American dream. However, in the late 1880s and early 1890s, their dream began to turn into a nightmare, which, in turn, sparked a social and political revolt known as populism. This movement displayed the dissatisfaction of millions of ordinary Americans—poor farmers, small landholders, and urban workers—and produced one of the largest third-party movements in American history. **Section Focus Question: What led to the rise of the Populist movement, and what effect did it have?**

Farmers Face Many Problems

The farmers of the West and the South were willing to accept the difficulties of farm life. Yet, farmers discovered that other enormous obstacles stood in the way of realizing their dreams. They received low prices for their crops, yet they had to pay high costs for transportation. Debts mounted while their influence on the political system declined.

Falling Prices and Rising Debt Between 1870 and 1895, farm prices plummeted. Cotton, which sold for about 15 cents a pound in the early 1870s, sold for only about 6 cents a pound in the mid-1890s. Corn and wheat prices declined nearly as rapidly. One study estimated

◀ A farmer plows through hard soil.

Plight of the Farmer

Banks considered mortgage loans a good investment. However, between 1889 and 1893, thousands of farms failed and banks foreclosed on mortgages. ▼

In the 1890s, farmers faced drought, poor harvests, debt, and a drop in the price of wheat, barley, and other crops. Oliver H. Kelley, who would eventually found the Grange organization, hoped to encourage farmers to feel their labor was "honorable" and "farming [was] the highest calling on earth." It was an ambitious goal, since farmers were a discontented group during the late 1800s. Furthermore, as the cartoon at the right shows, the government support that farmers sought was slow in coming. Farm reform was not a primary concern for most lawmakers.

Planting crops on tough prairie soil was hard work for this couple on their farm in Nebraska. ▼

Critical Thinking

1. **Synthesize Information** Why might farmers have readily joined forces with urban workers?

2. **Identify Point of View** Do you think most farmers felt that their work was "the highest calling on earth"? Explain.

that by the early 1890s, it was costing farmers more to produce corn than they could get by selling it, so they burned it and used it as fuel. Planting more crops did not help. On the contrary, the more crops farmers produced, the more prices declined.

During the same time period, the cost of doing business rose. To pay for new machinery, seed, livestock, and other needs, farmers went into debt. An increasing number of farmers mortgaged their farms to raise funds to survive and became tenant farmers—meaning they no longer owned the farm where they worked.

Big Business Practices Also Hurt Farmers blamed big business, especially the railroads and the banks, for their difficulties. They protested that railroads, as monopolies, charged whatever rates they wanted. Likewise, they complained that banks set interest rates at ridiculously high levels. Southern farmers, especially black sharecroppers, faced the added problem of having to deal with dishonest merchants and landlords who paid less for crops and charged more for supplies than promised.

In addition, farmers grew angry because they felt the nation had turned its back on them. The United States had a long tradition of electing leaders from farm states with agricultural backgrounds, like Thomas Jefferson. Yet, it now appeared that most of the nation's leaders came from urban industrial states. Moreover, farmers felt that they performed honest labor and produced necessary goods, while bankers and businessmen were the ones who got rich. One editor for a farmers' newspaper explained:

> **Primary Source** "There are three great crops raised in Nebraska. One is the crop of corn, one a crop of freight rates, and one a crop of interest. One is produced by farmers who sweat and toil to farm the land. The other two are produced by men who sit in their offices and behind their bank counters and farm the farmers."
> —*Farmers' Alliance,* 1890

Farmers, however, refused to accept these circumstances. They took action.

 Checkpoint What were the farmers' major grievances, or complaints?

Farmers Organize and Seek Change

Farmers created a <u>network</u> of organizations, first in the Midwest and then in the South and West, to address their problems. The Granger movement, also known as the "Patrons of Husbandry," was the first.

The Grange Tries Several Strategies Organized in 1867 by **Oliver H. Kelley**—a Minnesota farmer, businessman, journalist, and government clerk—the organization popularly known as the **Grange** attracted about a million members. The goals of the Grange included providing education on new farming techniques and calling for the regulation of railroad and grain elevator rates.

In the mid-1870s, the states of Illinois, Wisconsin, and Minnesota enacted laws that set maximum rates for shipping freight and for grain storage. The railroad companies challenged these "Grange Laws" in the courts, but the Supreme Court, in general, upheld them. The Grangers also prompted the federal government to establish the Interstate Commerce Commission (ICC) to oversee interstate transportation.

Farmers' Alliances Lead the Protest Although the Grange declined in the late 1870s, farm protest remained strong. Farmers' Alliances, such as the Southern Farmers' Alliance, became important reform organizations. These alliances formed cooperatives to collectively sell their crops, and they called on the federal

Vocabulary Builder
<u>network</u>–(NEHT werk) *n.* group of people, organizations, etc., that work together

government to establish "sub-treasuries," or postal banks, to provide farmers with low-interest loans. They hoped the cooperatives would push the costs of doing business down and the prices for crops up. Some of the cooperative efforts succeeded. The Georgia Alliance led a boycott against manufacturers who raised the price of the special cord that farmers used to wrap bundles of cotton.

The Southern Farmers' Alliance organized white farmers. However, there was an Alliance network for African American farmers. R. M. Humphrey, a white Baptist minister, headed the Colored Farmers' Alliance, which had been organized by African American and white farmers. Nearly one million African American farmers joined the group by 1891. The Colored Farmers' Alliance recognized that both white and African American farmers shared the same difficulties, but racial tensions prevented any effective cooperation between the groups.

✓ **Checkpoint** What reforms did the farmers' organizations introduce?

The Populist Party Demands Reforms

The spread of the Farmers' Alliances culminated with the formation of the **Populist Party,** or People's Party, in 1892. These Populists sought to build a new political party from the grass roots up. They ran entire slates of candidates for local, state, and national positions. Like a prairie fire, the Populist Party spread rapidly, putting pressure on the two major political parties to consider their demands.

Populists State Their Goals The Populist Party spelled out their views in their platform, which they adopted in Omaha, Nebraska, in July 1892. The platform warned about the dangers of political corruption, an inadequate monetary supply, and an unresponsive government. The Populist Party proposed specific remedies to these problems. To fight low prices, they called for the coinage of silver, or "free silver." To combat high costs, they demanded government ownership of the railroads. Mary Elizabeth Lease, a fiery Populist Party spokesperson, also advanced the cause of women's suffrage.

The Populist Party nominated James B. Weaver of Iowa as their presidential candidate and James Field of Virginia as his running mate. Both had risen to the rank of general in the United States and Confederate armies, respectively, and their nominations represented the party's attempt to overcome the regional divisions that had kept farmers apart since the end of the Civil War. (Southern whites had supported the Democrats; northerners, the Republicans.) The Populist Party also sought to reach out to urban workers, to convince them that they faced the same enemy: the industrial elite.

Populists Achieve Some Successes For a new political party, the Populists did quite well in 1892. Weaver won more than one million votes for the presidency, and the Populists elected three governors, five senators, and ten congressmen. In 1894, the Populist Party continued to expand its base, gaining seats in the state legislatures and prompting the major political parties to consider endorsing its ideas.

In the South, the Populist Party had to unite blacks and whites if it hoped to succeed politically. As noted above, Tom Watson, Georgia's most famous Populist Party leader, made a strong case for casting aside racial prejudice in favor of a political alliance between the races. However, the Democratic Party successfully used racist tactics, such as warning that a Populist victory would lead to "Negro supremacy," to diminish the appeal of the Populist Party.

✓ **Checkpoint** What were the goals of the Populist Party?

The Populist Party, 1890–1900

Geography *Interactive*
For: Interactive map skills
Web Code: ncp-1605

130° W

WA
MT
ND
MN
OR
ID
WY
SD
MI
WI
NY
ME
VT
NH
MA
CT
RI
NE
IA
PA
NJ
40° N
NV
Utah
Territory
CO
KS
IL
IN
OH
WV
VA
DE
MD
CA
MO
KY
NC
Pacific
Ocean
Arizona
Territory
New Mexico
Territory
Oklahoma
Territory
Indian
Terr.
AR
TN
SC
Atlantic
Ocean
30° N
MS
AL
GA
TX
LA
FL
120° W
Gulf of Mexico
90° W
80° W

Legend:
- Populist representatives in the U.S. Congress
- Populist governor and Congress representatives
- All or some electoral vote(s) to Populist presidential candidate

Conic Projection
0 200 400 mi
0 200 400 km

The Omaha Platform

Distressed farmers did not feel that either the Republican or Democratic parties addressed their problems. As a result, in 1892, farmers attended a convention in Omaha, Nebraska, to set forth their own party platform. Their demands, detailed in The Omaha Platform, are listed below.

- Unlimited coinage of silver
- Graduated income tax
- Government ownership of railroad and telegraph companies
- Bank regulations

Map Skills By the election of 1892, the Populist Party began to draw national attention.

1. **Region** Why did Populists fail to win support in northeastern states?

2. **Draw Conclusions** Based on the map, why might the Democratic and Republican parties have been concerned about the Populist Party in the elections after 1892?

Populist Party supporters wore silver badges to show their stand on free silver.

537

Economic Crisis and Populism's Decline

In 1893, a four-year-long depression began that not only worsened conditions for already-suffering farmers but for other Americans as well. Labor unrest and violence engulfed the nation. The major parties failed to satisfactorily respond to the nation's distress.

In the midst of national discontent, the Populist Party's dream of forging a broad coalition with urban workers grew. The Populists' relative success at the polls in 1892 and 1894 raised their hopes further. The decision of the Democratic Party to nominate **William Jennings Bryan** as their presidential candidate put the election for the Populists on an entirely different plane, leading some to believe they could win the White House that year.

Bryan and the Election of 1896 Born in Salem, Illinois, William Jennings Bryan moved to Lincoln, Nebraska, where he set up a law practice in 1887. He earned the nickname the "boy orator," in part by displaying his strong debating skills during his successful run for the United States Congress in 1890. In 1896, Bryan addressed the national Democratic convention on the subject of the gold standard, attacking Grover Cleveland and others in the party who opposed coining silver. The audience listened and cheered as Bryan spoke for "the plain people of this country," for "our farms" and declared "we beg no longer." The speech became known as the "Cross of Gold" speech because it ended with the following line: "You shall not press down upon the brow of labor this crown of thorns, you shall not crucify mankind upon a cross of gold."

The speech so moved the Democratic delegates that they nominated Bryan as their party's presidential candidate. He was just 36 years old and had not been a contender for the nomination until then. Bryan's advocacy of "free silver," or the coinage of silver as well as gold, and his support of a number of other Populist Party proposals, placed the Populists in a difficult situation. Holding their convention after the Democrats, the Populists had to decide whether to nominate their own presidential candidate and continue to focus on building a broad-based movement from the bottom up or to endorse Bryan with the hope that they could capture the White House in 1896. They chose the latter course.

Bryan's campaign was like none other before. For the first time, a presidential candidate toured the nation, speaking directly to the people. In contrast, **William McKinley,** the Republican candidate, accumulated approximately $15 million, 30 times the amount Bryan had, and allowed party regulars to do the campaigning for him. Marcus Hanna, the political powerhouse who orchestrated McKinley's run, cast Bryan and his Populist Party supporters as a potential dictator and a threat to the Republic. For instance, one cartoon published in the

Geography *Interactive.*
For: Interactive map skills
Web Code: ncp-1606

The Presidential Election of 1896

Candidate (Party)	Electoral Vote	Popular Vote	% Electoral Vote	% Popular Vote
William McKinley (Republican)	271	7,104,779	60.6	51.0
William Jennings Bryan (Democratic)	176	6,502,925	39.4	46.7
Other	—	314,226	—	2.3

Map Skills The election of 1896 changed the shape of national politics.

1. **Location** Which two states were split between Bryan and McKinley?

2. **Synthesize Information** Why could the election results be considered a victory of industry over agriculture?

pro-Republican *Los Angeles Times* depicted the Democratic-Populist coalition as a collection of evil witches, who fed the fires of sectionalism, discontent, and prejudice in order to win the election.

✓ **Checkpoint** How did the nomination of William Jennings Bryan affect the Populist Party?

Populism's Legacy

McKinley won the election of 1896 and went on to win reelection, again over Bryan, in 1900. Bryan's emphasis on monetary reform, especially free silver, did not appeal to urban workers, and the Populist Party failed to win a state outside of the South and West. Moreover, the decision to endorse Bryan weakened the Populists at the local and state levels, and the party never recovered from its defeat in 1896. The Populist Party lingered for nearly a decade. By the early 1900s, it had disappeared as a feasible alternative to the two major political parties. Most of the voters who supported the Populist Party returned to the Democratic Party in 1896.

Even though the Populist Party fell apart, many of the specific reforms that it advocated became a reality in the early decades of the twentieth century. As we shall see, the Progressives supported a graduated income tax, regulation of the railroads, and a more flexible monetary system. Moreover, populism had a lasting effect on the style of politics in the United States. For a brief time, there was even a coalition of whites and blacks in Texas. They were able to find a common political ground. Increasingly, candidates campaigned directly to the people, and, like Bryan, they emphasized their association with ordinary Americans.

✓ **Checkpoint** What happened to the Populist Party?

HISTORY MAKERS

William Jennings Bryan (1860–1925)

William Jennings Bryan practiced law before entering politics. Soon after moving to Nebraska, he was elected to the House of Representatives, where he served two terms. A gifted speaker, Bryan was called "the Great Commoner" because he favored the poor farmers over large corporations. Bryan also backed many Progressive causes, such as the direct election of senators, the adoption of an income tax, Prohibition, and women's suffrage. In 1913, President Woodrow Wilson named him Secretary of State. Committed to keeping peace, Bryan persuaded 31 countries to accept his idea of arbitrating international disputes instead of resorting to war. His hopes for peace were dashed, however, when World War I broke out.

SECTION 3 Assessment

Progress Monitoring *Online*
For: Self-test with vocabulary practice
Web Code: nea-1607

Comprehension

1. **Terms and People** Explain the significance of these terms and people in establishing support for farmers.
   - Oliver H. Kelley
   - Grange
   - Populist Party
   - William Jennings Bryan

2. **NoteTaking Reading Skill: Identify Causes and Effects** Use your cause-and-effect chart to answer the Section Focus Question: What led to the rise of the Populist movement, and what effect did it have?

Writing About History

3. **Quick Write: Support Your Ideas** Write a paragraph in response to the following: Explain how the election of 1896 ended the political stalemate that began in 1877. Keep in mind that each sentence should support your main idea.

Critical Thinking

4. **Determine Relevance** How did the deflation, or decrease, in the money supply in the late 1800s affect farmers?

5. **Synthesize Information** How did the Farmers' Alliances begin a crusade against big business?

6. **Make Comparisons** In what ways did McKinley represent the old way of politics? In what ways did Bryan represent the new way?

Quick Study Guide

 3.I.C.2b,
3.II.F

Progress Monitoring *Online*
For: Self-test with vocabulary practice
Web Code: nca-1608

■ Segregation and Discrimination

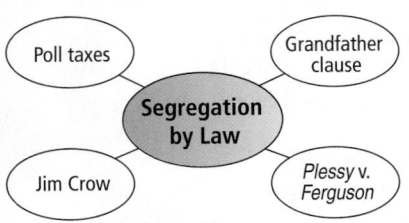

Poll taxes

Grandfather clause

Segregation by Law

Jim Crow

Plessy v. Ferguson

■ Gold or Silver?

Gold Bugs	Silverites
• Gold standard	• Bimetallism
• Supported by bankers and factory owners	• Supported by farmers and workers
• Effects	• Effects
–Prices fall	–Prices rise
–Less money in circulation	–More money in circulation

■ Wheat Prices, 1866–1896

SOURCE: *Historical Statistics of the United States*

■ Populist Party Platform

- Increase in money supply
- Graduated income tax
- Federal loan program for farmers
- Election of U.S. senators by popular vote
- Eight-hour workday
- Restriction on immigration
- Government ownership of railroads

☑ Quick Study Timeline

In America

1877
First Farmers' Alliance is established

1882
Congress passes Chinese Exclusion Act

Presidential Terms   Ulysses S. Grant 1869–1877

Rutherford B. Hayes 1877–1881

James A. Garfield 1881
Chester A. Arthur 1881–1885

1870   **1875**   **1880**

Around the World

1871
Labor unions legalized in Great Britain

1873
Slave markets abolished in Zanzibar

American Issues
•—•—• Connector

 3.II.Fa

By connecting prior knowledge with what you have learned in this chapter, you can gradually build your understanding of enduring questions that still affect America today. Answer the questions below. Then, use your American Issues Connector study guide (or go online: www.PHSchool.com **Web Code:** neh-7603).

Issues You Learned About

● **Women in American Society** Throughout our country's history, women have worked to bring positive change to society.

1. Describe the role that women played in the abolition movement. Why were some women reformers disappointed with the post-Civil War reforms?

2. On the eve of the Declaration of Independence, Abigail Adams wrote to her husband, John Adams: ". . . in the new code of laws . . . , I desire you would remember the ladies and be more generous and favorable to them. . . . Do not put such unlimited power into the hands of the husbands. . . . If . . . attention is not paid to the ladies, we are determined to foment [start] a rebellion, and will not hold ourselves bound by any laws in which we have no voice. . . ." Would Susan B. Anthony and Elizabeth Cady Stanton have agreed with Adams's views? Explain.

● **Expanding and Protecting Civil Rights** Minority groups have worked hard to gain their full civil rights.

3. What was the significance of the Thirteenth, Fourteenth, and Fifteenth amendments?

4. In what ways were African Americans' civil rights violated in the post-Civil War years?

5. How did Chinese immigrants use the legal system to challenge discrimination? How successful were these efforts?

● **Sectionalism and National Politics** Different regions of the country often have varying economic and political needs.

6. By the late 1800s, farmers in the South and Midwest had lost a great deal of their political power. How did this happen?

7. Why and how did the Populist Party seek to expand its message to urban voters?

8. Why was the Populist Party short-lived?

Connect to Your World	New York

Government's Role in the Economy Although the Grange movement was strongest in the Midwest, South, and West, it had a strong presence in New York as well. The New York State Grange, established in 1873, had 17,000 members by 1876. The organization worked to encourage state regulation of railroads and supported alcohol prohibition and women's suffrage. The group also organized cooperatives, which tried to help New York farmers save money on supplies and insurance. Today, the Grange is still active in New York, with over 9,000 members. Research the New York State Grange today. What recent economic legislation has the Grange supported? Write a brief mission statement that summarizes the organization's current goals.

1883
Civil Service Act establishes a merit system for government jobs

1888
Booker T. Washington opens Tuskegee Institute

1896
In *Plessy* v. *Ferguson*, Supreme Court rules separate but equal facilities legal

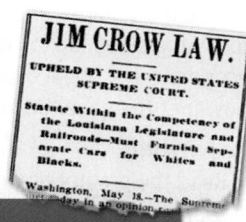

Grover Cleveland 1885–1889   Benjamin Harrison 1889–1893   Grover Cleveland 1893–1897

1885   **1890**   **1895**

1885
First Canadian transcontinental railroad completed

1893
Women gain right to vote in New Zealand

History *Interactive*
For: Interactive timeline
Web Code: ncp-1608

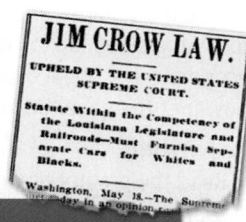

Chapter Assessment

Terms and People

1. Define **poll tax**. Why did poll taxes have a particularly negative effect on African Americans?

2. What was **Las Gorras Blancas**? What was its goal?

3. What was the **Pendleton Civil Service Act**? What led to its passage?

4. What was the **gold standard**? Which groups of Americans supported it, and which groups opposed it?

5. Who was **William Jennings Bryan**? Why did the Populist Party support him?

Focus Questions

The focus question for this chapter is **What political, social, and economic issues did the nation face during the late 1800s?** Build an answer to this big question by answering the focus questions for Section 1 through 3 and the Critical Thinking questions that follow.

Section 1

6. How were the civil and political rights of certain groups in America undermined during the years after Reconstruction?

Section 2

7. Why did the political structure change during the Gilded Age?

Section 3

8. What led to the rise of the Populist movement, and what effect did it have?

Critical Thinking

9. **Make Comparisons** How were the views of Booker T. Washington and W.E.B. Du Bois similar? How were they different?

10. **Analyze Information** Were the goals of Las Gorras Blancas and the Farmers' Alliance the same? Explain.

11. **Make Generalizations** How would you characterize the American political landscape during the Gilded Age?

12. **Evaluate Credibility of Sources** The *Farmers' Alliance* wrote in 1890 that there were three main ways that people earned money in Nebraska: by raising corn crops, by charging freight rates, and by charging interest on bank loans. Do you think this statement should be taken at face value? Explain.

13. **Analyze Maps** Answer the questions based on the map as well as your reading of this chapter. In the 1896 election, William J. Bryan won the most states but lost the election.
    (a) In which regions did McKinley win?
    (b) Why did the Populist Party fail to win the election?

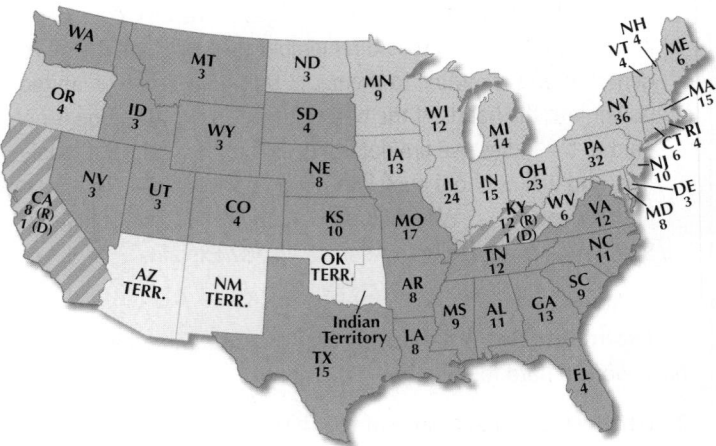

Candidate (Party)	Electoral Vote	Popular Vote	% Electoral Vote	% Popular Vote
McKinley (Republican)	271	7,104,779	60.6	51.0
Bryan (Democratic)	176	6,502,925	39.4	46.7

Writing About History

Writing for Assessment The depression of 1893 had lasting effects on the nation. However, the seeds for these effects began before the collapse of the economy. Write an answer to the following essay topic: Analyze how a demand for a better share of economic and social benefits led Americans to challenge the power of the government and big business before and after 1893.

Prewriting

- Read the prompt and determine what you know about the topic.
- Look for key words, such as "explain," that will tell you what kind of answer to provide.

Drafting

- Focus your time by allowing 10 minutes for prewriting, 20 minutes for drafting, and 10 minutes for revising your response.

- Develop a thesis for your essay, and make sure each piece of information supports it.

Revising

- Use the guidelines on page W22 of the Writing Handbook to revise your essay.

Regents DBQ Practice

Populism

What the Populist movement lacked in longevity—it lasted barely a decade—it made up for in passion. Populist fervor swept the country in the 1890s, and People's Party candidates won millions of votes. What made Populist ideas so attractive to so many Americans? Did this short-lived but spirited movement have a lasting effect on the American landscape?

Document 1

"The man who is employed for wages is as much a business man as his employer; . . . the merchant at the crossroads store is as much a business man as the merchant of New York; the farmer who goes forth in the morning and toils all day, . . . is as much a business man as the man who goes upon the Board of Trade and bets upon the price of grain; the miners who go down a thousand feet into the earth, or climb two thousand feet upon the cliffs, and bring forth from their hiding places the precious metals . . . are as much business men as the few financial magnates who, in a back room, corner the money of the world. We come to speak of this broader class of business men."

—William Jennings Bryan, Democratic National Convention, 1896

Document 2

"We realize that, while we [Americans] have political independence, our financial and industrial independence is yet to be attained by restoring to our country the Constitutional control and exercise of the functions necessary to a people's government, which functions have been basely surrendered by our public servants to corporate monopolies. . . ."

—Preamble from the People's Party platform, 1896

Document 3

A Box of Problems
—Los Angeles Times, September 14, 1896

Document 4

"As the People's party died, many of the disillusioned dropped out of politics. This is part of the reason the percent of eligible voters to cast ballots in presidential races dropped thirty percent between 1896 and 1924. Others continued the egalitarian struggle by joining Eugene V. Debs in the Socialist party. Many, however, returned to the reform wings of their old parties. Several farmer demands [later] became law, . . . namely monopoly regulation, banking/currency reform, and the graduated income tax. Populists had also advocated direct democracy with reforms such as the initiative and referendum. . . . America, however, adopted Populist reforms selectively and piecemeal. The result was hardly the egalitarian vision of Populism in its heyday."

—Worth Robert Miller, The Gilded Age: Essays on the Origin of Modern America

---

Reading, Analysis, and Writing Skills

Use your knowledge of Populism and Documents 1, 2, 3, and 4 to answer questions 1 through 4.

1. Which of the documents is a primary source that suggests that Populist ideas would unleash dangerous consequences for the United States?
   (1) Document 1
   (2) Document 2
   (3) Document 3
   (4) Document 4

2. Which primary source documents describe Populist ideas?
   (1) Documents 1 and 2
   (2) Documents 2 and 3
   (3) Documents 3 and 4
   (4) Documents 4 and 1

3. According to Document 4, what became of Populist supporters after the People's Party ceased to exist?
   (1) They formed a new Populist Party.
   (2) They re-created the People's Party with new leaders.
   (3) They joined different political parties.
   (4) They became farm reformers.

4. **Writing Task** How much did populism impact life in the United States? Use your knowledge of American history and evidence from the sources above to support your position.

NY Connect to New York

Theodore Roosevelt

Born: October 27, 1858, New York, New York

As America neared the end of the 1800s and looked ahead to the new century, a progressive spirit began to grow throughout the country, inspiring people to tackle social problems such as poverty, poor working conditions, and women's lack of rights. A major figure of the Progressive Era was Theodore Roosevelt, a politician from New York who would become one of the most influential Presidents in history.

Roosevelt's New York roots went back to the seventeenth century. His father, Theodore Roosevelt, Sr., "was one of the wealthy old Knickerbocker class, whose Dutch ancestors had been living on Manhattan Island since the 1640s." He was a successful glassware merchant.

Along with his reform-minded nature, Roosevelt is remembered for being a lifelong naturalist. He believed that New York's forests and other natural resources should be protected and conserved for future generations.

Roosevelt memorably said, "[T]he time has come to inquire seriously what will happen when our forests are gone; when the coal, the iron, and the oil and the gas are exhausted; when the soils shall have been still further impoverished and washed into streams."

Theodore Roosevelt first entered politics at the age of 23, serving on the New York State Assembly. In 1886, he unsuccessfully ran for mayor of New York City as the Republican candidate against Abram S. Hewitt and Henry George.

From 1889 to 1895 he served as president of the New York City Board of Police Commissioners. He was elected the state's 33rd governor in 1898. In this position he enacted many reforms, such as removing corrupt officials and enacting legislation to regulate corporations.

After two years of serving as governor, Roosevelt was elected Vice President on a ticket led by President William McKinley. Once he became president in 1901 upon McKinley's death, Roosevelt did not forget New York. His summer home, Sagamore Hill (now a National Historic Site), was located on Cove Neck, Oyster Bay, New York.

EMERGENCE OF THE MODERN UNITED STATES

CONTENTS

In France, a Red Cross nurse
tends American soldiers
wounded in World War I. ▶

Slum Sisters

In 1865, Methodist minister William Booth opened a street-corner mission in the slums of London. This was the beginning of the Salvation Army. By 1889, the Salvation Army had taken root in New York City. The Army sent pairs of women, known as 'slum sisters,' to visit tenement dwellers. Carrying mops and buckets along with religious pamphlets, these volunteers scrubbed floors, cooked meals, and cared for the sick. As cities grew and industry boomed, the slum sisters of the Salvation Army were just a few of the reformers who dedicated themselves to the needs of the poorest of the poor. *Listen to the* Witness History *audio to hear more about efforts to help the poor.*

◀ The Salvation Army delivers baskets of food to the poor in New York City on Christmas day.

The Jungle exposed the abuses of the meatpacking industry

NY Core Curriculum Preview

Chapter Focus Question: What were the causes and effects of the Progressive Movement?

Section 1
The Drive for Reform   4.I.A.1, 4.I.B.1a, 4.I.B.1b, 4.I.B.2a

Section 2
Women Make Progress   4.I.A.1, 4.I.B.2b

Section 3
The Struggle Against Discrimination   4.I.A.4, 4.I.B.2c, 4.I.B.2e

Section 4
Roosevelt's Square Deal   4.I.C.1, 4.I.C.2, 4.I.C.3a, 4.I.C.3c

Section 5
Wilson's New Freedom   4.I.C.4a, 4.I.C.4c, 4.I.C.4d

Use the ☑ **Quick Study Timeline** at the end of this chapter to preview chapter events.

1912 Progressive Party presidential campaign button

Women's suffrage statuette

Note Taking Study Guide *Online*
For: Note Taking and American Issues Connector
Web Code: nee-7701

▲ These boys toiled in a West Virginia coal mine.

WITNESS HISTORY AUDIO

Children in the Coal Mines

Progressive reformers were appalled by the child labor that was common in coal mines, textile mills, and other industries. John Spargo, a union organizer and socialist, sadly described the terrible conditions endured by boys working in the coal mines.

❝The coal is hard, and accidents to the hands, such as cut, broken, or crushed fingers, are common among the boys. Sometimes there is a worse accident: a terrified shriek is heard, and a boy is mangled and torn in the machinery, or disappears in the chute to be picked out later smothered and dead. Clouds of dust fill the breakers and are inhaled by the boys, laying the foundations for asthma and miners' consumption.❞

—John Spargo, *The Bitter Cry of the Children*, 1906

The Drive for Reform

 Core Curriculum Objectives

- **4.I.A.1** Progressives supported the use of government power for different reform purposes
- **4.I.B.1a** The "Muckrakers" and reform: Magazine writers
- **4.I.B.1b** The "Muckrakers" and reform: Novelists
- **4.I.B.2a** Social settlement movement and the problems of poverty (Jacob Riis, Jane Addams)

Terms and People

Progressivism	Jane Addams
muckraker	direct primary
Lincoln Steffens	initiative
Jacob Riis	referendum
Social Gospel	recall
settlement house	

NoteTaking

Reading Skill: Identify Details Fill in a chart like this one with details about Progressivism.

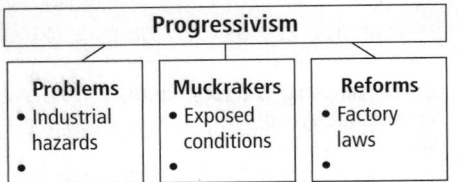

Why It Matters Industrialization, urbanization, and immigration brought many benefits to America, but they also produced challenging social problems. In response, a movement called **Progressivism** emerged in the 1890s. Progressives believed that new ideas and honest, efficient government could bring about social justice. Progressive ideas brought lasting reforms that still affect society today. **Section Focus Question: What areas did Progressives think were in need of the greatest reform?**

Origins of Progressivism

The people who made up the Progressive Movement came from many walks of life. They came from all political parties, social classes, ethnic groups, and religions. Many Progressive leaders emerged from the growing middle class, whose power and influence was rapidly spreading. Dissatisfied industrial workers also joined the Progressive Movement. So did a few wealthy Americans driven by a desire to act for the good of society.

Progressives Share Common Beliefs What the Progressives shared in common was a belief that industrialization and urbanization had created troubling social and political problems. Progressives wanted to bring about reforms that would correct these problems and injustices. They encouraged their state legislatures and the federal government to enact laws to address the issues faced by the poor. Progressives wanted to use logic and reason to make society work in a more efficient and orderly way. Many, motivated by religious faith, sought social justice.

Progressivism was similar to the Populist Movement of the late 1800s. Both were reform movements that wanted to get rid of corrupt government officials and make government more responsive to people's needs. Both sought to eliminate the abuses of big business. Still, the two movements differed. At the forefront of Progressivism were middle-class people. They believed that highly educated leaders should use modern ideas and scientific techniques to improve society. Leaders of the Populist Movement, on the other hand, consisted mostly of farmers and workers.

Progressives Target a Variety of Problems Some Progressives thought that political reform was the most urgent need. For many women, the number one goal was winning the right to vote. Other Progressives considered honest government to be the most important goal. Reformers targeted city officials who built corrupt organizations, called political machines. The bosses of these political machines used bribery and violence to influence voters and win elections. They counted on the loyalty of city workers who looked the other way when they took public money for themselves. Bosses also helped people solve personal problems, which often kept voters loyal.

Corrupt and ineffective government combined with the booming growth of cities produced other problems. The people living in America's crowded cities needed paved streets, safe drinking water, decent housing, and adequate municipal services. The lack of adequate services led to wretched living conditions for the urban poor. Too often, dishonest business owners and politicians controlled municipal services. Bribes and shady deals made them rich while conditions for urban residents remained unsafe and little changed.

While some Progressives focused on government, others were worried about big business. As you have learned, wealthy industrialists took over businesses and built huge trusts that limited competition and raised prices. Middle-class Progressives wanted the government to "bust the trusts" and so create more economic opportunities for smaller businesses. Progressives complained that the Sherman Antitrust Act of 1890 was inadequate and ineffective in limiting the abuses of big business.

Other Progressive reformers, often motivated by their religious faith, sought to reduce the growing gap between the wealthy and the poor. Progressives attacked the harsh conditions endured by miners, factory workers, and other laborers. They wanted better conditions for poor people living in city slums. They wanted social welfare laws to help children, as well as government regulations to aid workers and consumers.

✔ **Checkpoint** What problems did Progressive reformers hope to solve?

THE SHARP METHOD.—IT WORKS WITH ANY BOARD OF ALDERMEN.

Analyzing Political Cartoons

Business and Government Corruption In the 1880s, Jacob Sharp expanded his streetcar business by bribing New York City aldermen and other government officials.

1. What symbols represent the corruption of city government?
2. According to the cartoonist, what is the effect of the street railroad monopoly on the taxpayer?

Muckrakers Reveal the Need for Reform

Socially conscious journalists and other writers dramatized the need for reform. Their sensational investigative reports uncovered a wide range of ills afflicting America in the early 1900s. Even though Theodore Roosevelt agreed with much of what they said, he called these writers **muckrakers** because he thought them too fascinated with the ugliest side of things. (A muckrake is a tool used to clean manure and hay out of animals' stables.) The writers were angry at first but in time took up Roosevelt's taunting name as a badge of honor. The muckrakers' articles appeared in magazines and newspapers that entered millions of American homes. People across the nation were horrified by the conditions that were revealed to them.

Journalists Uncover Injustices One leading muckraker was **Lincoln Steffens,** managing editor at *McClure's,* a magazine known for uncovering social problems. In 1903, Steffens published *The Shame of the Cities,* a collection of articles on political corruption. His reports exposed how the government of Philadelphia let utility companies charge their customers excessively high fees. He showed how corrupt politicians won elections by bribing and threatening voters, and revealed how political corruption affected all aspects of life in a city.

Primary Source "The visitor [to St. Louis] is told of the wealth of the residents, of the financial strength of the banks, and of the growing importance of the industries; yet he sees poorly paved, refuse-burdened streets, and dusty or mud-covered alleys; he passes a ramshackle firetrap crowded with the sick and learns that it is the City Hospital. . . . Finally, he turns a tap in the hotel to see liquid mud flow into [the] wash basin or bathtub."

—Lincoln Steffens and Claude Wetmore, "Corruption and Reform in St. Louis," *McClure's Magazine,* October 1902

Jacob Riis ▼

● **INFOGRAPHIC**

EXPOSING HOW THE OTHER HALF LIVES

"Long ago it was said that 'one half of the world does not know how the other half lives.' . . . It did not know because it did not care." Jacob Riis, believing that the "poor were the victims rather than the makers of their fate," used images and words to make the public confront the conditions of New York City's tenement slums.

Riis's 1890 book ▼

▲ A horse lies dead in a New York City street as children play nearby. A lack of city services forced slum-dwellers to live in unsanitary conditions.

HOW THE OTHER HALF LIVES STVDIES AMONG THE TENEMENTS OF NEW YORK

Another influential muckraker was **Jacob Riis,** a photographer for the *New York Evening Sun*. Riis turned his camera on the crowded, unsafe, rat-infested tenement buildings where the urban poor lived. Between 1890 and 1903, he published several works, including *How the Other Half Lives* (see Infographic below), that shocked the nation's conscience and led to reforms.

Other outraged writers joined Riis and Steffens. In *The History of Standard Oil,* Ida Tarbell reported that John D. Rockefeller used ruthless methods to ruin his competitors, charge higher prices, and thereby reap huge profits. Others proclaimed the need to improve schools or warned of the breakdown of family life because mothers had to work long hours in factories. John Spargo focused attention on the dangerous and difficult lives of child workers. (See the Witness History at the beginning of this section.)

Novelists Defend the Downtrodden Fiction writers put a human face on social problems. They developed a new genre—the naturalist novel—that honestly portrayed human misery and the struggles of common people. Theodore Dreiser, a midwesterner raised in poverty, published *Sister Carrie* in 1900. His provocative novel traces the fate of a small-town girl drawn into the brutal urban worlds of Chicago and New York.

Naturalist novels became very popular. Frank Norris's *The Octopus* fascinated readers by dramatizing the Southern Pacific Railroad's stranglehold on struggling California farmers. In *The Jungle*, Upton Sinclair related the despair of immigrants working in Chicago's stockyards and revealed the unsanitary conditions in the industry. (See an excerpt from the novel at the end of this section.) African American author Frances Ellen Watkins portrayed some of the struggles of black Americans in her 1892 novel *Iola Leroy*.

✓ **Checkpoint** What role did journalists and other writers play in the Progressive Movement?

WITNESS HISTORY DVD

Watch *The Jungle: A View of Industrial America* on the **United States Witness History DVD** to learn more about city life in the industrial age.

▼ Adults and children sew knee-pants in a New York tenement, many of which served as both homes and workshops. "[F]rom earliest dawn until mind and muscle give out together," people toiled unprotected by the laws governing factory work.

▲ A New York City cobbler prepares for the Jewish Sabbath Eve dinner in a Ludlow Street coal cellar.

Thinking Critically
Analyze Visuals What do Riis's images reveal about the conditions of city slums?

History *Interactive* ✶
For: A look at tenement life
Web Code: nep-0403

Progressives Reform Society

The work of the muckrakers increased popular support for Progressivism. Progressive activists promoted laws to improve living conditions, public health, and schools. They urged government to regulate businesses. They believed that careful social planning would make American life better.

The Social Gospel Guides Reform Efforts Many reformers, like Walter Rauschenbusch, thought that Christianity should be the basis of social reform. A child of German immigrants, Rauschenbusch had become a Baptist minister. He blended ideas from German socialism and American Progressivism into a plan for building a better society. His book *Christianity and the Social Crisis* outlined what he called the **Social Gospel.** By following the Bible's teachings about charity and justice, he explained, people could make society "the kingdom of God."

Many Protestant leaders followed Rauschenbusch's program. They began to urge the end of child labor and a shorter workweek. They also pushed for the federal government to limit the power of corporations and trusts.

Settlement House Workers Aid the Urban Poor An important goal of many Progressives was to improve the lives of poor people in the cities. One approach was the **settlement house,** a community center that provided social services to the urban poor. Before settlement houses, there were private charities that helped poor people. Settlement house workers gave mothers classes in child care and taught English to immigrants. They ran nursery schools and kindergartens. They also provided theater, art, and dance programs for adults.

A young woman named **Jane Addams** became a leading figure in the settlement house movement. After graduating from college, she pursued several different careers. On a trip to Europe in 1888, however, she was inspired by the work at Toynbee Hall, a "settlement house" in London. In 1889, Addams opened Hull House, a settlement house in Chicago. Over the years, Hull House grew to include 13 buildings. Its success inspired other college-educated, middle-class women to become social workers. By 1911, the country had more than four hundred settlement houses.

The 1911 Triangle Shirtwaist Factory Fire

Victims of the Triangle Shirtwaist Factory fire lie at the feet of a police officer as he looks up at the deadly blaze. *How did the fire help or hurt Progressives' efforts to reform workplace conditions?*

Protecting Children and Improving Education Progressives also tried to help children. Leading the effort was a lawyer named Florence Kelley. Kelley helped convince the state of Illinois to ban child labor, and other states soon passed similar laws. In 1902, Kelley helped form the National Child Labor Committee, which successfully lobbied the federal government to create the U.S. Children's Bureau in 1912. This new agency examined any issue that affected the health and welfare of children. The agency still works to protect children today.

But progress in children's rights had a long way to go. In 1916, Congress passed the Keating-Owens Act, which banned child labor. However, two years later, the Supreme Court ruled the law unconstitutional. It was not until 1938 that Congress would end child labor for good.

Progressives also tried to better children's lives by improving education. A number of states passed laws that required children to attend school until a certain age. However, there were heated debates about what children should learn and how they should learn. Some argued that they should be taught only work skills. Others said they should learn to appreciate literature and music. Most educators agreed that girls should learn different things from boys.

Educator John Dewey criticized American schools for teaching children to memorize facts but not to think creatively. Dewey wanted schools to teach new subjects such as history and geography, as well as practical skills like cooking and carpentry. His ideas were not adopted at once, but in later years, many states put them into effect.

Progressives Help Industrial Workers In the early 1900s, the United States had the highest rate of industrial accidents in the world. Long hours, poor ventilation, hazardous fumes, and unsafe machinery threatened not only workers' health but also their lives. Each year some thirty thousand workers died on the job, while another half a million were injured.

In March 1911, a fire at the Triangle Shirtwaist Factory in New York City shocked Americans and focused attention on the need to protect workers. Workers in the factory had little chance to escape the raging fire because managers had locked most of the exits. The fire killed 146 workers, most of them young Jewish women. Many jumped from the windows in desperation. Inside the smoldering ruins, firefighters found many more victims, "skeletons bending over sewing machines."

After the blaze, outraged Progressives intensified their calls for reform. New York passed laws to make workplaces safer, and other cities and states followed suit. Many states also adopted workers' compensation laws, which set up funds to pay workers who were hurt on the job.

Progressives also persuaded some states to pass laws limiting the workday to 10 hours. However, their efforts suffered a blow in 1905 when the Supreme Court ruled in *Lochner* v. *New York* that such laws were unconstitutional.

✔ **Checkpoint** How did Progressives work to help the urban poor?

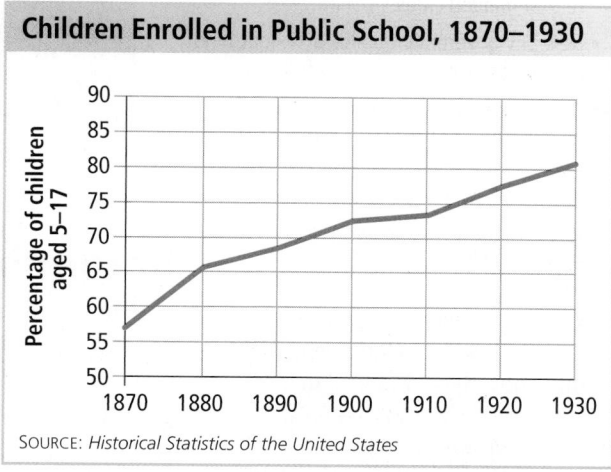

Children Enrolled in Public School, 1870–1930

SOURCE: *Historical Statistics of the United States*

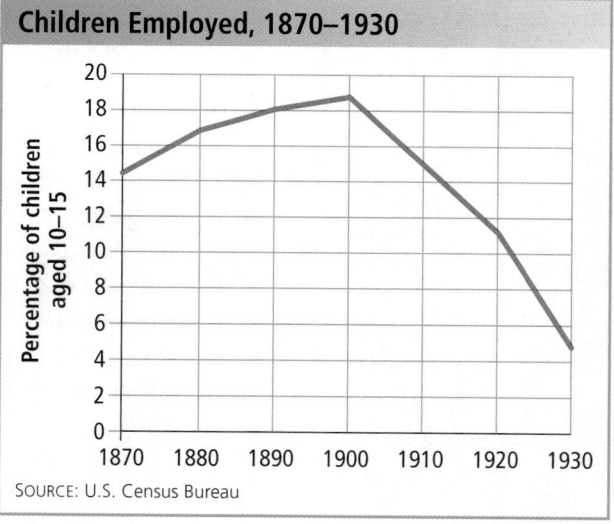

Children Employed, 1870–1930

SOURCE: U.S. Census Bureau

Graph Skills During the Progressive Era, child labor declined sharply while school enrollment increased. *According to the graphs, how did the percentage of children employed change from 1890 to 1920? How did school enrollment change during the same period?*

Post-Hurricane Reforms in Galveston

- Galveston adopts a new commission form of government that spreads to other reform-minded cities.
- New city government builds a 17-foot-high seawall as protection against future storms.
- City government uses landfill to raise low-lying neighborhoods above sea level.

Devastated Galveston

After the coastal city of Galveston, Texas, was hit by a powerful hurricane, it adopted the commission form of government to lead the rebuilding effort. *What features would a city government need to handle a reconstruction job of the scale seen here?*

Reforming Government

Progressive reformers realized that they needed to reform the political process in order to reform society. They would have to free government from the control of political bosses and powerful business interests. They wanted to give people more control over their government and make government more effective and efficient in serving the public.

Reformers Improve City Government Just as the Triangle Shirtwaist Factory fire spurred reformers to action, so did another disaster. In 1900, a massive hurricane left the city of Galveston, Texas, in ruins. The greatest national calamity in American history, the hurricane killed more than 8,000 people. As an emergency measure, Galveston replaced its mayor and board of aldermen with a five-person commission. The commission form of government proved very efficient as the city carried out a tremendous rebuilding effort. The following year, Galveston decided to permanently adopt the commission form of government.

Known as the Galveston plan, many other cities decided to take up the commission form of government. By 1918, nearly 500 cities had adopted some form of the Galveston plan. Dayton, Ohio, and other cities modified the plan by adding a city manager to head the commission. The new city governments curbed the power of bosses and their political machines. The reform governments purchased public utilities so that electric, gas, and water companies could not charge city residents unfairly high rates.

Progressives Reform Election Rules Progressives also pushed for election reforms, taking up some Populist ideas. Traditionally, it was the party leaders who picked candidates for state and local offices. But in Wisconsin, reform governor Robert M. La Follette established a **direct primary,** an election in which citizens themselves vote to select nominees for upcoming elections. By 1916, all but four states had direct primaries.

Progressives also wanted to make sure that elected officials would follow citizens' wishes. To achieve this goal, they worked for three other political reforms: the initiative, the referendum, and the recall. The **initiative** gave people the power to put a proposed new law directly on the ballot in the next election by collecting citizens' signatures on a petition. This meant that voters themselves could pass laws instead of waiting for elected officials to act. The **referendum** allowed citizens to approve or reject laws passed by a legislature. The **recall** gave voters the power to remove public servants from office before their terms ended.

Progressives won yet another political reform: They adopted the Populist call for the direct election of senators by voters, not state legislators. That reform became law in 1913 when the Seventeenth Amendment to the Constitution was approved.

Progressive Governors Take Charge <u>Dynamic</u> Progressives became the leaders of several states, and chief among them was Robert La Follette of Wisconsin. Elected governor in 1900, "Fighting Bob" won the passage of many reform laws. Under his leadership, the Wisconsin state government forced railroads to charge lower fees and pay higher taxes. La Follette helped his state to improve education, make factories safer, and adopt the direct primary. Progressives called Wisconsin the "laboratory of democracy."

Hiram Johnson, governor of California, shattered the Southern Pacific Railroad's stranglehold on state government. He put in place the direct primary, initiative, referendum, and recall. He also pushed for another goal of some Progressives—planning for the careful use of natural resources such as water, forests, and wildlife.

Other Progressive governors included Theodore Roosevelt of New York and Woodrow Wilson of New Jersey. Roosevelt worked to develop a fair system for hiring state workers and made some corporations pay taxes. Wilson reduced the railroads' power and pushed for a direct primary law. Both Roosevelt and Wilson later became President and brought reforms to the White House.

✓ **Checkpoint** How did Progressive reformers change local and state governments?

Vocabulary Builder
<u>dynamic</u>–(dī NAM ihk) *adj.*
energetic; relating to change or productive activity

SECTION

1 Assessment

Progress Monitoring *Online*
For: Self-test with vocabulary practice
Web Code: nea-0402

Comprehension

1. **Terms** Explain how each of the following terms is an example of a social or political reform.
   - settlement house
   - direct primary
   - initiative
   - referendum
   - recall

2. **NoteTaking Reading Skill: Identify Details** Use your flowchart to answer the Section Focus Question: What areas did Progressives think were in need of the greatest reform?

Writing About History

3. **Quick Write: Compare and Contrast Points of View** In a narrative essay, you may compare and contrast points of view on an issue through the opinions of various individuals. Compare and contrast Social Darwinism with Social Gospel through the personalities of William Graham Sumner, Billy Sunday, and Dwight L. Moody. Use library or Internet resources to complete this assignment.

Critical Thinking

4. **Recognize Cause and Effect** What problems did muckrakers expose and what effects did their work have on Progressive reform?

5. **Summarize** Describe Walter Rauschenbusch's ideas about Social Gospel and the Progressive Movement.

6. **Identify Points of View** Which groups in American society might have opposed Progressive reform? Explain.

The Jungle by Upton Sinclair

When Upton Sinclair published *The Jungle* in 1906, he meant to open America's eyes to the plight of workers in the filthy, dangerous Chicago stockyards. Instead, popular outrage focused on the wider-reaching threat of spoiled meat. Congress quickly passed the nation's first legislation regulating the meat, food, and drug industries. Sinclair, disappointed by his failure to provoke more sympathy for the overworked, underpaid workers, noted "I aimed at the public's heart, and by accident I hit it in the stomach."

There was never the least attention paid to what was cut up for sausage. . . . There would be meat that had tumbled out on the floor, in the dirt and sawdust, where the workers had tramped and spit uncounted billions of consumption [tuberculosis] germs. There would be meat stored in great piles in rooms; and the water from leaky roofs would drip over it, and thousands of rats would race about on it. It was too dark in these storage places to see well, but a man could run his hand over these piles of meat and sweep off handfuls of the dried dung of rats. These rats were nuisances, and the packers would put poisoned bread out for them; they would die, and then rats, bread, and meat would go into the hoppers together. This is no fairy story and no joke; the meat would be shoveled into carts, and the man who did the shoveling would not trouble to lift out a rat even when he saw one—there were things that went into the sausage in comparison with which a poisoned rat was a tidbit. There was no place for the men to wash their hands before they ate their dinner, and so they made a practice of washing them in the water that was to be ladled into the sausage. There were the butt-ends of smoked meat, and the scraps of corned beef, and all the odds and ends of the waste of the plants, that would be dumped into old barrels in the cellar and left there. Under the system of rigid economy which the packers enforced, there were some jobs that it only paid to do once in a long time, and among these was the cleaning out of the waste barrels. Every spring they did it; and in the barrels would be dirt and rust and old nails and stale water—and cartload after cartload of it would be taken up and dumped into the hoppers with fresh meat, and sent out to the public's breakfast.

Thinking Critically

1. **Analyze Literature** Describe the author's style in this excerpt.

2. **Evaluate Literature** How does Sinclair's way of writing boost his credibility?

◀ A woman working at a Pittsburgh cigar factory in 1909

Women at Work

As the Progressive Movement wore on, many reformers took up causes that affected women. Although women spearheaded a number of Progressive reforms, they did not have the right to vote in national elections. In workplaces like the Triangle Shirtwaist Factory, women endured the awful conditions described by one worker:

❝It was a world of greed; the human being didn't mean anything. The hours were from 7:30 in the morning to 6:30 at night when it wasn't busy. When the season was on we worked until 9:00. No overtime pay, not even supper money. . . . When you were told Saturday afternoon, through a sign on the elevator, 'If you don't come in on Sunday, you needn't come in on Monday,' what choice did you have? You had no choice.❞

—Pauline Newman, organizer of the International Ladies Garment Workers Union

▲ A week's wages—only $1.50!

Women Make Progress

Core Curriculum Objectives

- **4.I.A.1** Progressives supported the use of government power for different reform purposes
- **4.I.B.2b** Women's rights and efforts for peace

Terms and People

Florence Kelley	suffrage
NCL	Carrie Chapman Catt
temperance movement	NAWSA
Margaret Sanger	Alice Paul
Ida B. Wells	Nineteenth Amendment

NoteTaking

Reading Skill: Identify Main Ideas As you read this section, complete an outline like the one below to capture the main ideas.

> I. Women Expand Reforms
> A. Hardships for women
>   1.
>   2.
> B.

Why It Matters In the early 1900s, a growing number of women were no longer content to have a limited role in society. Women activists helped bring about Progressive reforms and won the right to vote. In the years ahead, women would continue the struggle to expand their roles and rights. **Section Focus Question: How did women of the Progressive Era make progress and win the right to vote?**

Progressive Women Expand Reforms

In the early 1900s, a growing number of women wanted to do more than fulfill their roles as wives and mothers. They were ready to move beyond raising children, cooking meals, keeping the home tidy, and caring for family members. They wanted to expand their role in the community.

Education helped women achieve their goals. By the 1890s, a growing number of women's colleges prepared them for careers as teachers or nurses. Some, such as Bryn Mawr College in Pennsylvania and the School of Social Work in New York, trained them to lead the new organizations working for social reform. Armed with education and modern ideas, many middle-class white women began to tackle problems they saw in society.

Working Women Face Hardships For most women, however, working outside the home meant difficult jobs, with long hours and dangerous conditions. And these women were usually expected to hand over their wages to their husbands, fathers, or brothers. Many women labored in factories that made cigars or clothing. Others toiled as laundresses or servants. Immigrants, African Americans, and women from rural areas filled these jobs, and most of them had little or no education. As a result, they could easily be cheated or bullied by their employers. Without being able to vote, women had little influence on the politicians who could expand their rights and look after their interests.

Reformers Champion Working Women's Rights A key goal of women reformers was to limit the number of work hours. They succeeded in several states. For example, a 1903 Oregon law capped women's workdays at ten hours. Five years later, in *Muller* v. *Oregon*, the Supreme Court reviewed that law. Lawyer Louis D. Brandeis argued that long working hours harmed working women and their families.

The Supreme Court agreed with Brandeis. Based on their role as mothers, it said, women could be "properly placed in a class" by themselves. As a result, laws could limit their work hours, even if similar laws would not be allowed for men. At the time, Progressives viewed this decision as a victory for women workers. In later years, however, this ruling was used to justify paying women less than men for the same job.

Florence Kelley believed that women were hurt by the unfair prices of goods they had to buy to run their homes. In 1899, she helped found the **National Consumers League (NCL),** which is still active today. The NCL gave special labels to "goods produced under fair, safe, and healthy working conditions" and urged women to buy them and avoid products that did not have these labels. The NCL pushed for other reforms as well. It backed laws calling for the government to inspect meatpacking plants, to make workplaces safer, and to make payments to the unemployed.

Florence Kelley also helped form the Women's Trade Union League (WTUL), another group that tried to improve conditions for female factory workers. It was one of the few groups in which upper-class and working-class women served together as leaders. The WTUL pushed for federal laws that set a minimum wage and an eight-hour workday. It also created the first workers' strike fund, which could be used to help support families who refused to work in unsafe or unfair conditions.

Women Work for Changes in Family Life A main goal of Progressive women was to improve family life. They pushed for laws that could help mothers keep families healthy and safe. One focus of this effort was the **temperance movement** led by the Women's Christian Temperance Union (WCTU). This group promoted temperance, the practice of never drinking alcohol. Members felt that alcohol often led men to spend their earnings on liquor, neglect their families, and abuse their wives. Formed in the 1870s, the WCTU gained strength during the Progressive Era. Their work led to the passage of the Eighteenth Amendment, which outlawed the production and sale of alcohol.

Nurse **Margaret Sanger** thought that family life and women's health would improve if mothers had fewer children. In 1916, Sanger, herself one of 11 children, opened the country's first birth-control clinic. Sanger was jailed several times as a "public nuisance." But federal courts eventually said doctors could give out information about family planning. In 1921, Sanger founded the American Birth Control League to make this information available to more women.

Women Campaign for Temperance

Minnesota women march to ban alcohol. The temperance movement gained a victory when Congress passed the 18th Amendment in 1917.

African American women also worked for social change. In 1896, **Ida B. Wells,** a black teacher, helped form the National Association of Colored Women (NACW). The group aimed to help families strive for success and to assist those who were less fortunate. With money raised from educated black women, the NACW set up day-care centers to protect and educate black children while their parents went to work.

✔ **Checkpoint** What steps did women take to win workers' rights?

Women Fight for the Right to Vote

One of the boldest goals of Progressive women was **suffrage**—the right to vote. They argued that this was the only way to make sure that the government would protect children, foster education, and support family life. As Jane Addams explained, women needed the vote because political issues reached inside people's homes.

> **Primary Source** ❝If the street is not cleaned by the city authorities no amount of private sweeping will keep the tenement free from grime; if the garbage is not properly collected and destroyed a tenement-house mother may see her children sicken and die of diseases from which she alone is powerless to shield them, although her tenderness and devotion are unbounded. She cannot even secure untainted meat for her household, . . . unless the meat has been inspected by city officials.❞
>
> —Jane Addams, *Ladies Home Journal,* 1910

Since the 1860s, reformers such as Susan B. Anthony and Elizabeth Cady Stanton had tirelessly struggled for the right for women to have a voice in political issues. They failed at the federal level, but by the end of the 1890s women in western states, such as Wyoming and Colorado, had won the right to vote.

Catt Takes Charge of the Movement In the 1890s, the national suffrage effort was reenergized by **Carrie Chapman Catt.** Catt had studied law and worked as one of the country's first female school superintendents. A captivating speaker, Catt traveled around the country urging women to join the **National American Woman Suffrage Association (NAWSA).** In 1900, she became the president of the NAWSA. Catt promoted what became known as her "winning plan," which called for action on two fronts. Some teams of women lobbied Congress to pass a constitutional amendment giving women the right to vote. Meanwhile, other teams used the new referendum process to try to pass state suffrage laws. By 1918, this <u>strategy</u> had helped women win the right to vote in New York, Michigan, and Oklahoma.

Catt introduced a "society plan" to recruit wealthy, well-educated women. She and her army of workers signed on women from all levels of society, including African Americans, Mexican Americans, and Jewish immigrants. All these women, called "suffragettes," helped promote suffrage in their own areas.

While the suffrage movement gained ground, some women worked against it. The National Association Opposed to Woman Suffrage (NAOWS) believed that the effort to win the vote would take women's attention away from family and volunteer work that benefited society in many ways. But as the pressure for women's suffrage grew stronger, the NAOWS faded away.

HISTORY MAKERS

Ida B. Wells (1862–1931)
Wells had gained fame for her campaign against the lynching of African Americans. But she was also a tireless worker for women's suffrage and joined in the famous 1913 march for universal suffrage that took place in Washington, D.C. Not able to tolerate injustice of any kind, Ida B. Wells, along with Jane Addams, successfully blocked the establishment of segregated schools in Chicago. In 1930, she ran for the Illinois State legislature, which made her one of the first black women to run for public office in the United States.

Vocabulary Builder
<u>strategy</u>—(STRAT uh jee) *n.* plan or an action based on a plan

Activists Carry on the Struggle Some women, known as social activists, grew more daring in their strategies to win the vote. **Alice Paul,** their best-known leader, was raised in a Quaker home where she was encouraged to be independent. Paul attended a Quaker college and the New York School of Social Work before earning a Ph.D. from the University of Pennsylvania in 1912. She believed that drastic steps were needed to win the vote. By 1913, she was organizing women to recruit others across the nation. They drew in women of many backgrounds, from Maud Younger, known as the "millionaire waitress" because she organized California's first waitresses' union, to Nina Otero-Warren, a Hispanic who headed New Mexico's State Board of Health.

By 1917, Paul formed the National Woman's Party (NWP), which used public protest marches. The NWP became the first group to march with picket signs

SUFFRAGISTS WIN THE VOTE

The National Woman's Party began picketing the White House, urging President Wilson to back the woman's suffrage amendment. Susan B. Anthony had introduced the amendment nearly 40 years earlier, but the Senate had rejected it twice. So when America entered World War I, and Wilson proclaimed, "The world must be made safe for democracy," the weary suffragists were astounded. They wondered how could America be a democracy if women could not vote?

Then, when envoys from Russia visited Wilson in June, Alice Paul and her activists saw a golden opportunity. The Russians had just overthrown the czar, established a republic, and granted women the right to vote. As the envoys neared the White House, the suffragists stunned and embarrassed Wilson by unveiling a new banner that claimed America was not a democracy. The women set in motion a series of events that would change America.

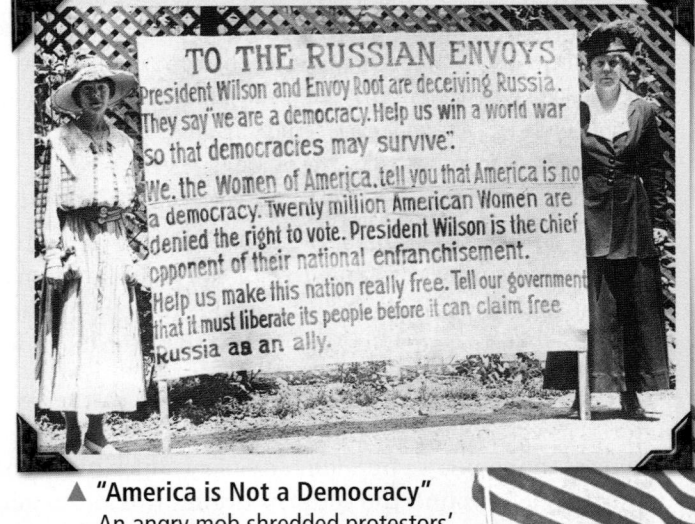

▲ **"America is Not a Democracy"** An angry mob shredded protestors' banners. The police warned the women not to return.

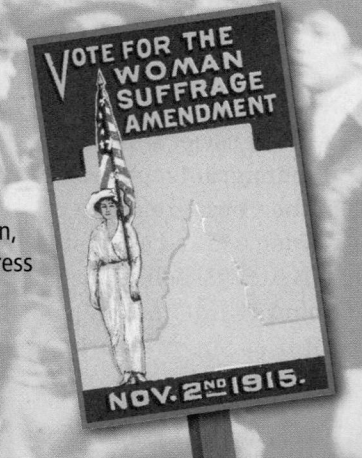

Suffrage Poster ▶ In marches on Washington, D.C., women urged Congress to vote for suffrage.

outside the White House. Hundreds of women were arrested in these protests. Some went on hunger strikes, refusing to eat until they could vote. The NWP methods angered many people, including women in other suffrage groups. Nevertheless, they did help win women the right to vote, because the NWP's actions made less-radical groups like the NAWSA look tame by comparison.

The Nineteenth Amendment Becomes Law When the United States entered World War I in 1917, Carrie Catt and Florence Kelley led the NAWSA to support the war effort. Their actions and those of the NWP convinced a growing number of legislators to support a women's suffrage amendment. In June 1919, Congress approved the **Nineteenth Amendment,** which stated that the right to vote "shall not be denied or abridged on account of sex." On August 18, 1920, the

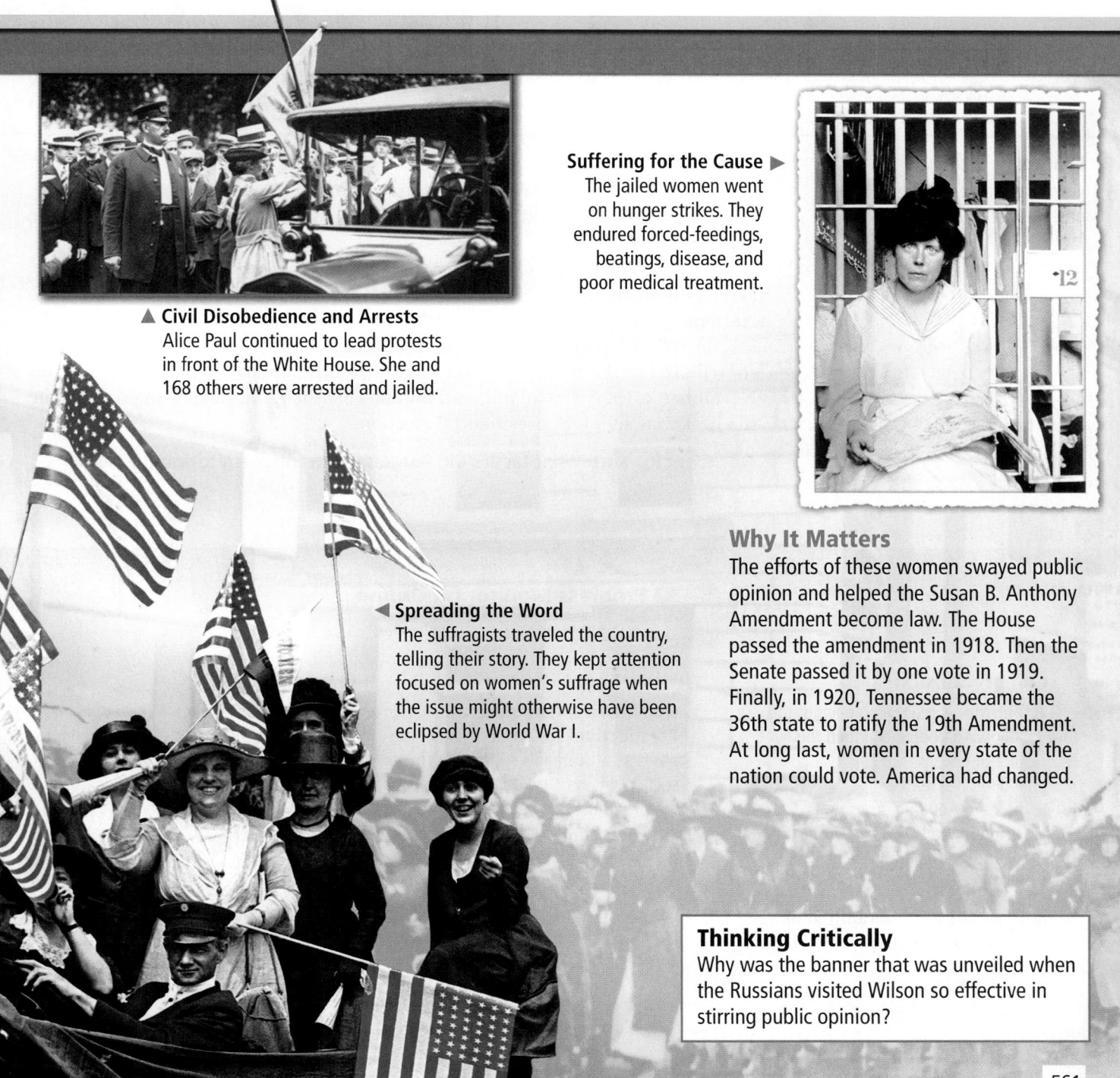

Suffering for the Cause ▶
The jailed women went on hunger strikes. They endured forced-feedings, beatings, disease, and poor medical treatment.

▲ Civil Disobedience and Arrests
Alice Paul continued to lead protests in front of the White House. She and 168 others were arrested and jailed.

◀ Spreading the Word
The suffragists traveled the country, telling their story. They kept attention focused on women's suffrage when the issue might otherwise have been eclipsed by World War I.

Why It Matters
The efforts of these women swayed public opinion and helped the Susan B. Anthony Amendment become law. The House passed the amendment in 1918. Then the Senate passed it by one vote in 1919. Finally, in 1920, Tennessee became the 36th state to ratify the 19th Amendment. At long last, women in every state of the nation could vote. America had changed.

Thinking Critically
Why was the banner that was unveiled when the Russians visited Wilson so effective in stirring public opinion?

561

Passage of Women's Suffrage

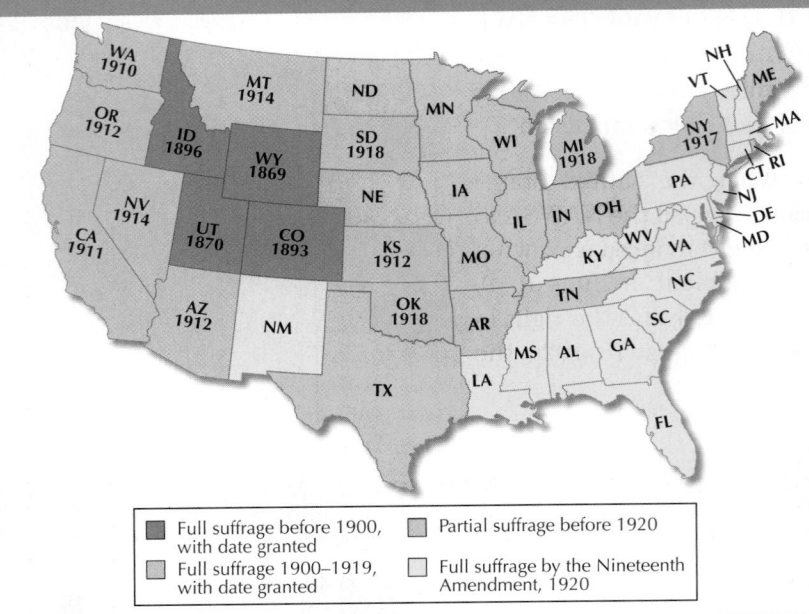

Full suffrage before 1900, with date granted
Full suffrage 1900–1919, with date granted
Partial suffrage before 1920
Full suffrage by the Nineteenth Amendment, 1920

Women's Suffrage

What pattern do you see in the passage of suffrage at the state level?

Tennessee State House of Representatives passed the amendment by one vote. With Tennessee's ratification, enough states had passed the amendment that it became official.

Alice Paul and Carrie Catt both claimed responsibility for the victory. In fact, according to historian Nancy Cott, "neither the shocking militancy of the National Women's Party nor the ladylike moderation of NAWSA was so solely responsible for victory as each group publicly claimed." The rival groups both contributed to the triumph of the women's suffrage movement. As a result, on November 2, 1920, Catt, Paul, and millions of other American women voted for the first time in a U.S. presidential election.

✓ **Checkpoint** What tactics did Progressive women use to win the right to vote?

SECTION

2 **Assessment**

Progress Monitoring *Online*
For: Self-test with vocabulary practice
Web Code: nea-0404

Comprehension

1. **People** Explain how each of the following people changed the lives of women.
   • Florence Kelley
   • Margaret Sanger
   • Ida B. Wells
   • Carrie Chapman Catt
   • Alice Paul

2. **NoteTaking Reading Skill: Identify Main Idea** Use your outline to answer the Section Focus Question: How did women of the Progressive Era make progress and win the right to vote?

Writing About History

3. **Quick Write: Communicate Perspective** Look at the map on the passage of women's suffrage in this section. In one paragraph, describe the map from the perspective of a supporter of suffrage for women. In a second paragraph, describe the map as viewed by a suffrage opponent.

Critical Thinking

4. **Draw Conclusions** Why would education have led middle-class women to address societal problems?

5. **Solve Problems** Choose one specific social problem and explain how Progressive women reformers proposed to solve that problem.

6. **Analyze Effects** How did suffragists' efforts at the state level affect their effort to win the right to vote at the national level?

TRACK THE ISSUE

What are the most pressing problems, and how can we solve them?

There have been many movements for social reform in the United States. But Americans do not always agree on the need for reform or on the best way to achieve it. In fact, some reform ideas face strong opposition. Why do some reform movements win support, while others do not? Use the timeline below to explore this enduring issue.

1790s–1820s
Second Great Awakening
Revival of Christian faith sparks moral and spiritual reform.

1830s–1850s Abolitionism
Antislavery forces demand an end to the slave system.

1890–1920 Progressivism
Reformers urge a broad range of social and political changes.

1950s–1960s Civil Rights
African Americans lead movement for racial equality.

1990s–2000s
Healthcare Reform
Reformers combat the spiraling costs of healthcare and insurance.

Young children line up to receive vaccinations in a school clinic.

NY 4.I.B.2

Healthcare costs are a major issue.

DEBATE THE ISSUE

Health Insurance Medical costs are soaring. Many Americans lack health insurance and cannot pay their bills. Some reformers want the government to provide universal health insurance, also known as a single-payer system. Others say this approach will cause more harm than good.

"... Everybody has ... to be covered. There's only three ways of doing it. You can have a single-payer system, you can require employers, or you can have individual responsibility. My plan combines employers and individual responsibility, while maintaining Medicare and Medicaid. The whole idea of universal health care is ... a core Democratic principle ..."

—Senator Hillary Clinton, 2008

"A single-payer system promotes higher taxes, limits technology, produces waiting lists, rations care, and prolongs suffering. ... A universal healthcare system run by government will reduce the quality and access to health care for all Americans. It's a prescription for disaster."

—Sally Pipes, President, Pacific Research Institute

 TRANSFER Activities

1. **Compare** Why does Hillary Clinton support universal health care? Why does Sally Pipes oppose it?

2. **Analyze** Do you think Sally Pipes would support the efforts of some Progressive Era city governments to purchase public utilities? Explain.

3. **Transfer** Use the following Web site to see a video, try a WebQuest, and write in your journal. **Web Code:** neh-7702

▲ Cuero family, Warner Springs, California, 1904

WITNESS HISTORY AUDIO

Voices of Protest

The sympathy that reformers felt for the plight of the poor did not often extend to minorities. In 1912, Progressive journalist Samuel Bryan wrote an investigative article about Mexican immigrants. Displaying a common bias, Bryan concluded that the immigrants did not work hard enough. Yet, he was forced to admit that Mexican Americans faced discrimination. He wrote:

❝[Mexican Americans] are now employed to a considerable extent in the coal mines of Colorado and New Mexico, in the ore mines of Colorado and Arizona, in the smelters of Arizona, in the cement factories of Colorado and California, . . . and in fruit growing and canning in California. . . . Where they are employed in other industries, the same wage discrimination against them as was noted in the case of railroad employees is generally apparent.❞

—Samuel Bryan, *The Survey,* September 1912

The Struggle Against Discrimination

 Core Curriculum Objectives

- **4.I.A.4** Increasing inequities between wealth and poverty
- **4.I.B.2c** The black movement and reform (Booker T. Washington, W.E.B. Du Bois, and the NAACP)
- **4.I.B.2e** Formation of Anti-Defamation League

Terms and People

Americanization
Booker T. Washington
W.E.B. Du Bois
Niagara Movement

NAACP
Urban League
Anti-Defamation League
mutualistas

NoteTaking

Reading Skill: Main Idea and Details
Outline the section's main ideas and details.

> I. The Struggle Against Discrimination
> A.

Why It Matters Prejudice and discrimination against minorities continued even as the Progressive Movement got underway. But in the spirit of Progressivism, African Americans, Latinos, Catholics, Jews, and new immigrant groups worked to help themselves. Their efforts paved the way for the era of civil rights that would follow decades later. **Section Focus Question: What steps did minorities take to combat social problems and discrimination?**

Progressivism Presents Contradictions

The Progressive Era was not so progressive for nonwhite and immigrant Americans. Most Progressives were white Anglo-Saxon Protestant reformers who were indifferent or actively hostile to minorities. They tried to make the United States a model society by encouraging everyone to follow white, middle-class ways of life.

Social Reform or Social Control? Settlement houses and other civic groups played a prominent role in the **Americanization** efforts of many Progressives. While they taught immigrants English, their programs also tried to change how immigrants lived. They advised immigrants how to dress like white middle-class Americans and pushed them to replace the foods and customs of their homelands with

Protestant practices and values. These reformers believed that assimilating immigrants into American society would make them more loyal and moral citizens.

Many Progressives found the immigrants' use of alcohol especially alarming. In many European countries, it was customary for families to serve wine or beer with meals. Many reformers, however, believed that these practices showed moral faults. As a result, prejudice against immigrants was one of the forces behind the temperance movement.

Racism Limits the Goals of Progressivism Many Progressives shared the same prejudice against nonwhites held by other white Americans of the time. They believed that some people were more fit than others to play a leading role in society. They agreed with <u>so-called</u> scientific theories that said that dark-skinned peoples had less intelligence than whites. In the late 1800s, southern Progressives used these misguided theories to justify the passage of laws that kept African Americans from voting. Some southern Progressives urged an end to the violence and terrorism waged against African Americans. Edgar Gardner Murphy, an Episcopal minister and a leading Alabama Progressive, advised that African Americans "will accept in the white man's country the place assigned him by the white man, . . . not by stress of rivalry, but by genial cooperation with the white man's interests."

After the Supreme Court issued its *Plessy* v. *Ferguson* decision, states across the North and the South had passed segregation laws. By 1910, segregation was the norm across the nation. After 1914, even the offices of the federal

Vocabulary Builder
so-called–(SOH kawld) *adj.* commonly named; falsely or improperly named

---

Comparing Viewpoints

How should we respond to discrimination?

African Americans were freed from slavery, but discriminatory laws and racist attitudes kept them oppressed and threatened. African Americans debated how they should respond to this discrimination.

BOOKER T. WASHINGTON

Washington (1856–1915) believed that African Americans had to achieve economic independence before civil rights. Black people must tolerate discrimination while they proved themselves equal to white people. Slowly, civil rights would come.

Primary Source

"[The Negro must] live peaceably with his white neighbors . . . the Negro [must] deport himself modestly . . . depending upon the slow but sure influences that proceed from the possessions of property, intelligence, and high character for the full recognition of his political rights."

W.E.B. DU BOIS

Du Bois (1868–1963) believed that black Americans had to demand their social and civil rights or else become permanent victims of racism. African Americans must fight every day for the rights given to them in the Constitution.

Primary Source

"We claim for ourselves every single right that belongs to a freeborn American . . . and until we get these rights we will never cease to protest. . . . How shall we get them? By voting where we may vote, by persistent, unceasing agitation, by hammering at the truth, by sacrifice and work."

Compare
1. How did the views of Washington and Du Bois about the nature of civil rights differ?
2. How do these leaders' opinions reflect the era in which they lived? Would leaders today make similar arguments? Explain.

government in Washington, D.C., were segregated as a result of policies approved by President Woodrow Wilson, a Progressive.

✓ **Checkpoint** What attitudes did most Progressives hold about minorities and immigrant groups?

African Americans Demand Reform

In the face of these injustices, the nation's most visible African American leader urged patience. **Booker T. Washington** told blacks to move slowly toward racial progress. By working hard and waiting patiently, he believed, African Americans would gradually win white Americans' respect and eventually would be able to exercise their full voting and citizenship rights.

Other African Americans rejected this view. The most outspoken among them were **W.E.B. Du Bois** and William Monroe Trotter. Both men had been raised in New England and educated at Harvard University. Both urged African Americans to demand immediately all the rights guaranteed by the Constitution.

African Americans Form the Niagara Movement Du Bois and Trotter were especially concerned that all across the South, black men were being denied the right to vote. In the summer of 1905, they and other leading African American thinkers met at Niagara Falls. They had to meet in Canada because no hotel on the New York side of the border would give them rooms.

The **Niagara Movement,** as the group called itself, denounced the idea of gradual progress. Washington, they said, was too willing to compromise African Americans' basic rights. They also condemned his notion of teaching only trade skills. This kind of education, Du Bois said, "can create workers, but it cannot make *men*." Talented blacks should be taught history, literature, and philosophy, so they could think for themselves.

Despite its bold ideas, the Niagara Movement never grew to more than a few hundred strong. To make a difference, African Americans needed a more powerful voice.

Riots Lead to Formation of NAACP In the summer of 1908, a white mob in Springfield, Illinois, attempted to lynch two African American prisoners in the city jail. Upon learning that the prisoners had been removed to safety, the rioters turned their anger against the city's black residents, killing two people and burning 40 homes. The Niagara Movement members were outraged that such an attack could happen in Abraham Lincoln's hometown.

Niagara Movement

The original leaders of the Niagara Movement met in response to W.E.B. Du Bois's call to "organize thoroughly the intelligent honest Negroes throughout the United States."

This lynching occurred during the 1908 Springfield, Illinois, riot.

The Springfield riot also got the attention of a number of white reformers. They now <u>acknowledged</u> the need to help African Americans protect their lives, win the right to vote, and secure their civil rights. In 1909, they joined with leaders of the Niagara Movement to form the **National Association for the Advancement of Colored People (NAACP).** The NAACP aimed to help African Americans be "physically free from peonage [forced, low-paid labor], mentally free from ignorance, politically free from disfranchisement, and socially free from insult."

NAACP leaders included white and black Progressives who had worked in other areas of social reform. Among them were Jane Addams, Ray Stannard Baker, and Florence Kelley. Ida B. Wells, owner of a Tennessee newspaper, used her publication to make clear the horror of lynching. She and the others planned the group's strategy—to use the courts to challenge unfair laws. In the early 1900s, the NAACP focused on the battle for equal access to decent housing and professional careers like teaching.

African Americans Form the Urban League Across the country, African Americans were migrating from rural to urban areas during this period. Local black clubs and churches set up employment agencies and relief efforts to help African Americans get settled and find work. In 1911, more than 100 of these groups in many cities joined into a network called the **Urban League.** While the NAACP helped middle-class blacks struggle for political and social justice, the Urban League focused on poorer workers. It helped families buy clothes and books and send children to school. It helped factory workers and maids find jobs. Both the NAACP and the Urban League still aid African Americans today.

✓ **Checkpoint** Why did African Americans and others decide it was time to organize against discrimination?

Reducing Prejudice and Protecting Rights

African Americans were not alone in seeking their rights. Individuals and organizations of diverse ethnic groups spoke out against unfair treatment and took action by creating self-help agencies. For example, in northern cities, Catholic parishes offered a variety of social services to immigrants. In Chicago, a network of Polish Catholic groups grew so strong that it earned the nickname American Warsaw.

The Anti-Defamation League Aids Jews Jews in New York had formed the B'nai B'rith in 1843 to provide religious education and to help Jewish families. In response to growing anti-Semitism, the group founded the **Anti-Defamation League** in 1913. Its goal was—and still is—to defend Jews and others against physical and verbal attacks, false statements, and "to secure justice and fair treatment to all citizens alike. . . ."

Mexican Americans Organize Mexican Americans also organized to help themselves. Those living in Arizona formed the Partido Liberal Mexicano (PLM), which offered Mexican Americans many of the same services that the Urban League gave to African Americans. In several states, Mexican Americans formed **mutualistas,** groups that made loans and provided legal assistance. The mutualistas also had insurance programs to help members if they were too sick to work.

Vocabulary Builder
acknowledge—(ak NAHL ihj) *v.* to admit to be true

HISTORY MAKERS

Octaviano Larrazolo (1859–1930)
Larrazolo was a Progressive governor in New Mexico who worked for many reforms. He helped make sure that New Mexico's first state constitution protected Latinos from discrimination. Elected governor in 1918, he pushed for laws aimed at helping children and improving public health. He also favored bilingual education and voting rights for women. That last stand cost him the support of his Republican Party, and he served only one term as governor.

Japanese Field Workers

Japanese immigrants, like those above, often found work tending the fruit orchards of California. Through hard work, many were later able to buy land and orchards of their own.

Many Mexican Americans were forced to sign unfair labor contracts that kept them in debt to people whose land they worked. In 1911, the Supreme Court struck down a law that enforced that system.

Native Americans Take Action Progressives did little to help Native Americans. The Dawes Act, passed in 1887, had divided reservations into plots for individuals to farm. But the law also said that lands not given to individual Indians could be sold to the general public. By 1932, nearly two thirds of the lands held by tribes in 1887 were in the hands of whites.

Carlos Montezuma, a Native American from Arizona, helped establish the Society of American Indians in 1911, the first organization for Indian rights to protest federal Indian policy. A doctor, Montezuma treated Native Americans living on reservations. He urged Native Americans to preserve their cultures and avoid being dependent on the government.

Asian Americans Fight Unfair Laws Asian Americans also had to protect themselves. A 1913 California law said that only American citizens could own land. Because Japanese immigrants could not become citizens, the law forced them to sell their land. Japanese Americans found a way around this, however, by putting the land in their children's names. Because their children had been born in the United States, they were American citizens.

Takao Ozawa fought the law in court that blocked Asian Americans from becoming citizens. In 1922, however, the Supreme Court ruled against him. A newspaper read by Japanese Americans commented, "The slim hope that we had entertained . . . has been shattered completely."

 Checkpoint What strategies did other minority groups use to defend their rights?

SECTION 3 Assessment

Progress Monitoring *Online*
For: Self-test with vocabulary practice
Web Code: nea-0406

Comprehension

1. **Terms and People** For each item below, write a sentence explaining its significance.
   - Booker T. Washington
   - W.E.B. Du Bois
   - Niagara Movement
   - NAACP
   - Urban League
   - Anti-Defamation League
   - mutualistas

2. **NoteTaking Reading Skill: Main Ideas and Details** Use your outline to answer the Section Focus Question: What steps did minorities take to combat social problems and discrimination?

Writing About History

3. **Quick Write: Gather Details** Suppose you want to write a narrative about the effect of the Urban League's work in the Progressive Era. Conduct research to find descriptions and images of African American life before and during this period.

Critical Thinking

4. **Analyze Information** How did Progressives' views about race and values foster prejudice?

5. **Draw Inferences** What do the differing approaches of Booker T. Washington and W.E.B. Du Bois suggest about their views of American society?

6. **Compare** Were the goals and actions of the mutualistas more similar to those of the Urban League or to those of the Anti-Defamation League? Explain.

▲ Theodore Roosevelt speaking in New York City

"Teddy" bear ▶

WITNESS HISTORY 🔊 AUDIO

A Bold Leader Takes Control

When Theodore Roosevelt entered the White House, never before had the country had so young a leader. He brought to the presidency tremendous energy, vision, and a willingness to expand presidential power in order to improve American lives. In a rousing speech, he urged some young supporters:

❝The principles for which we stand are the principles of fair play and a square deal for every man and every woman in the United States. . . . I wish to see you boys join the Progressive Party, and act in that part and as good citizens in the same way I'd expect any one of you to act in a football game. In other words, don't flinch, don't fold, and hit the line hard.❞

—Theodore Roosevelt, Address to Boy's Progressive League, 1913

Roosevelt's Square Deal

 Core Curriculum Objectives

- **4.I.C.1** Emerging Progressive movement: political reform
- **4.I.C.2** Theodore Roosevelt's Square Deal
- **4.I.C.3a** Theodore Roosevelt's concern for nature, land, and resources
- **4.I.C.3c** Roles of Gifford Pinchot and John Muir

Terms and People

Theodore Roosevelt
Square Deal
Hepburn Act
Meat Inspection Act
Pure Food and Drug Act
John Muir

Gifford Pinchot
National Reclamation
    Act
New Nationalism
Progressive Party

NoteTaking

Reading Skill: Identify Main Ideas As you read this section, use a concept web like the one below to record the main ideas.

Why It Matters In the late 1800s, the United States had several weak and ineffective Presidents. The arrival of Theodore Roosevelt, a charismatic figure who embraced Progressive ideals, ushered in a new era. Roosevelt passed Progressive reforms and expanded the powers of the presidency. He changed the way Americans viewed the roles of the President and the government. **Section Focus Question: What did Roosevelt think government should do for citizens?**

Roosevelt Shapes the Modern Presidency

In 1901, when **Theodore Roosevelt** became President of the United States, he was only 43 years old. However, Roosevelt had packed quite a lot into those years, gaining a reputation for being smart, energetic, and opinionated. The sickly child of wealthy parents, he had used his family's resources to develop both his strength and his mind. Observers said he generated so much energy that if you met him, you left the event with bits of his personality "stuck to your clothes."

Roosevelt Rises to the Presidency Roosevelt had graduated with honors from Harvard University in 1880. He spent only a few months studying law at Columbia University before being elected to the New York State Assembly. After three years' service there, and after the deaths of both his mother and his wife, Alice, Roosevelt retired to a ranch in the West. There he developed a love of the wilderness.

INFOGRAPHIC

A Rough Rider in the White House

Theodore Roosevelt's energetic leadership style enabled him to redefine the presidency. He took on industry and tackled tough issues. Roosevelt used his presidential power to bust illegal monopolies, reduce abusive business practices, and make a symbolic statement against segregation.

This 1909 cartoon shows ▶ Roosevelt's differing approaches to "good" and "bad" trusts.

Roosevelt could not remain long out of the spotlight, however. By 1889, he had returned to politics. As president of New York City's Board of Police Commissioners, he gained fame by fighting corruption. President William McKinley noticed him and named him Assistant Secretary of the Navy. When the Spanish-American War broke out in 1898, Roosevelt resigned the post to form the Rough Riders, a volunteer cavalry unit that became famous during the war.

After the end of the conflict, the young war hero was elected governor of New York, where he pushed for Progressive reforms. His reform efforts annoyed Republican leaders in the state, though. They convinced McKinley to choose Roosevelt as his running mate so Roosevelt would leave New York—and them—alone. McKinley was reelected President in 1900, but within a few months he was assassinated, and Roosevelt became President. Roosevelt soon <u>dominated</u> public attention. Journalists vied for interviews with him and children begged their parents for a teddy bear, the new stuffed animal named for him.

Roosevelt greatly expanded the power of the President. He used his office and its powers to convince Americans of the need for change and to push through his reform proposals. He called his program the **Square Deal,** and its goals were to keep the wealthy and powerful from taking advantage of small business owners and the poor. His idea of fair government did not mean that everyone would get rich or that the government should take care of the lazy. He compared his Square Deal to a hand of cards.

Vocabulary Builder
<u>dominate</u> – (DAHM ih nayt) *v.* to have a commanding place or position in

Primary Source ❝When I say I believe in a square deal, I do not mean to give every man the best hand. If good cards do not come to any man, or if they do come, and he has not got the power to play them, that is his affair. All I mean is that there shall be no crookedness in the dealing.❞

—Theodore Roosevelt, 1905

✓ **Checkpoint** What did Roosevelt want his Square Deal program to achieve?

The illustration shows that ▶ in 1901, Booker T. Washington accepted Roosevelt's invitation to dinner. Roosevelt's actions angered those who favored segregation.

◀ "Patent medications" sometimes made fraudulent claims or contained harmful chemicals. Roosevelt helped restore consumer confidence by supporting laws that regulated the food and drug industries.

Thinking Critically
1. **Analyze Visuals** Look at the image of Roosevelt's dinner with Washington. Why would the artist have placed a painting of Abraham Lincoln in the background?
2. **Make Generalizations** Using the information in these visuals, make one generalization about Theodore Roosevelt as President.

Trustbusting and Regulating Industry

Roosevelt often stepped in with the authority and power of the federal government. One example was in 1902, when Pennsylvania coal miners went on strike. The miners wanted a pay raise and a shorter workday. Roosevelt sympathized with the overworked miners, but he knew that a steady supply of coal was needed to keep factories running and homes warm. He wanted the strike ended quickly.

First, Roosevelt tried to get mine owners to listen to workers' concerns. When this failed, he threatened to send federal troops to take control of the mines and to run them with federal employees. His threat forced the mine owners to give the miners a small pay raise and a nine-hour workday. For the first time, the federal government had stepped in to help workers in a labor dispute.

The coal strike was one of many steps Roosevelt took to control the power of corporations. Within a year, Roosevelt convinced Congress to establish the Department of Commerce and Labor to monitor businesses engaged in interstate commerce and to keep capitalists from abusing their power.

Roosevelt Takes on the Railroads The cost of shipping freight on railroads had been an issue since the 1870s. Railroad companies could charge whatever they wanted. The railroads' power was especially troublesome for western farmers. They had no other way to move their products to eastern markets.

In 1887, Congress had created the Interstate Commerce Commission (ICC) to oversee rail charges for shipments that passed through more than one state. The ICC was supposed to make sure that all shippers were charged the same amounts. By 1900, though, the Supreme Court had stripped away most of the ICC's power. So Roosevelt pushed Congress to pass the Elkins Act in 1903, which imposed fines on railroads that gave special rates to favored shippers. In 1906, he got Congress to pass the **Hepburn Act,** which gave the ICC strong enforcement powers. This law gave the government the authority to set and limit shipping costs. The act also set maximum prices for ferries, bridge tolls, and oil pipelines.

Roosevelt Enforces the Sherman Antitrust Act It did not take long for the President and his administration to earn a reputation as "trustbusters." In response to an antitrust suit filed by Roosevelt's attorney general, the Supreme Court ruled in 1904 that the Northern Securities Company—a big railroad company—was an illegal trust. The decision forced the company to split into smaller companies. The next year, the Court found that a beef trust and several powerful agricultural companies broke antitrust laws.

Roosevelt was not interested in bringing down all large companies. He saw a difference between "good trusts" and "bad trusts." Big businesses could often be more efficient than small ones, he believed. Big business was bad, he said, only if it bullied smaller outfits or cheated consumers. So he supported powerful corporations as long as they did business fairly. His supporters called him a "trust-tamer," but some wealthy Progressives criticized his trustbusting.

Regulating Food and Drug Industries In 1906, Upton Sinclair published his novel *The Jungle*. His descriptions of the filthy, unhealthy conditions in meatpacking plants revolted the public and infuriated the President. Roosevelt urged Congress to pass the **Meat Inspection Act** that same year. It provided federal agents to inspect any meat sold across state lines and required federal inspection of meat-processing plants. Today, when we eat lunchmeat or grilled chicken, we trust that federal inspectors have monitored the plant where it is produced. If there is a serious problem, the government can force the meat-packer to pull the product off the shelves before many people become sick. This regulation is one lasting result of Progressives' insistence that the government take responsibility for food safety.

The **Pure Food and Drug Act** placed the same controls on other foods and on medicines. It also banned the interstate shipment of impure food and the mislabeling of food and drugs. Today, the Food and Drug Administration (FDA) still enforces this law and others. The FDA monitors companies to make sure people are not hurt by dangerous substances or dishonest labels. For example, before a drug can be sold, it must be tested and approved by the FDA.

 Checkpoint What impact did Roosevelt's actions have on the government's role in the economy?

The Government Manages the Environment

Roosevelt's deep reverence for nature also shaped his policies. The books he published on hunting and the rugged West reflected his fascination with the competition between humans and the wilderness. He was pleased that the federal government had established Yellowstone National Park in 1872 to protect wildlife, and he admired California naturalist **John Muir,** whose efforts had led Congress to create Yosemite National Park in 1890.

Should National Forests Be Conserved or Preserved? In 1891, Congress had given the President the power to protect timberlands by setting aside land as federal forests. Following Muir's advice, Roosevelt closed off more than 100 million acres of forestland. However, the President did not agree with Muir that all wild areas should be preserved, or left untouched. Some wild lands held valuable resources, and Roosevelt thought those resources were meant to be used. This view became clear in his forest policy. In typical Progressive style, he called on experts to draw up plans for both conserving and using the forests.

Roosevelt drew on the "rational use" ideas of **Gifford Pinchot,** who led the Division of Forestry in the U.S. Department of Agriculture. Pinchot recommended a different approach—that forests be preserved for public use. By this, he meant

Vocabulary Builder
rational – (RASH uhn uhl) *adj.* relating to or based on reason; reasonable

National Land Conservation

Geography *Interactive*
For: Interactive map
Web Code: nep-0407

Conic Projection

0   200   400 mi

0   200   400 km

CANADA

National Parks and Forests

Established before Roosevelt's presidency

Established during Roosevelt's presidency

Established after Roosevelt's presidency

WA — Mount Ranier

OR

ID

MT — Yellowstone

Grand Teton

WY

ND

SD

MN

WI

MI

NY

VT

NH

ME — Acadia

MA

CT

RI

40°N

NV

UT

CO — Rocky Mountain

NE

IA

IL

IN

OH

PA — Allegheny

NJ

MD — DE

70°W

CA — Yosemite, Sequoia

Grand Canyon

AZ

NM

KS

MO — Mark Twain

KY

WV

VA — Shenandoah

NC

Pacific Ocean

OK

AR

TN — Great Smoky Mountains

SC

Atlantic Ocean

MEXICO

Big Bend

TX

MS — Kisatchie

AL

GA

30°N

LA

FL

Gulf of Mexico

PR   VI — 18°N

66°W

RUSSIA   70°N

60°N

AK — Denali

CANADA

22°N

20°N

HI

Glacier Bay

50°N   170°W 160°W 150°W 140°W

Haleakala

80°W

90°W

In 1892, John Muir helped found the Sierra Club to help people enjoy California's wild places and to lobby for protection of natural resources.

Primary Source ❝Climb the mountains and get their good tidings, Nature's peace will flow into you as sunshine flows into trees. The winds will blow their own freshness into you and the storms their energy, while cares will drop off like autumn leaves. As age comes on, one source of enjoyment after another is closed, but nature's sources never fail.❞

—John Muir, *Our National Parks*, 1901

Map Skills The land conservation movement of the Progressive Era led to the conservation of millions of acres of United States land.

1. Human-Environment Interaction How does preserving land for national parks and forests benefit people?

2. Regions What region of the country has the greatest area of conservation lands? Why do you think this is so?

President Theodore Roosevelt and conservationist John Muir at California's Yosemite National Park in 1903

Los Angeles Aqueduct

Massive water projects carry water from reservoirs and lakes to distant cities and farmland. *Why would some people oppose redirecting water in such ways?*

that forests should be protected so that trees would have time to mature into good lumber. Then, the protected areas should be logged for wood to build houses and new areas placed under protection. "The object of our forest policy," explained Pinchot, "is not to preserve the forests because they are refuges for the wild creatures of the wilderness, but rather they are the making of prosperous homes." Pinchot's views came to dominate American policies toward natural resources.

Roosevelt Changes Water Policy A highly controversial natural resource issue was water. Over centuries, Native Americans had used various irrigation methods to bring water to the arid Southwest. The situation changed in the late 1800s, when prospectors began mining and farming in Utah, New Mexico, Colorado, Nevada, and California. Mining machinery required a great deal of water, and systems of sharing water used by Mexican Americans were fought by people and businesses moving into these states. Private irrigation companies came to the area, staked claims to sections of riverbeds and redirected the water so farmers could revive—or "reclaim"— dried-up fields. Bitter fights developed over who should own water rights and how the water should be shared.

Roosevelt sprang into action on this issue. He listened to Nevada representative Francis Newlands, who wanted the federal government to help western states build huge reservoirs to hold and to conserve water. Roosevelt pushed Congress for a law that would allow it.

In 1902, Congress passed the **National Reclamation Act,** which gave the federal government the power to decide where and how water would be distributed. The government would build and manage dams that would create reservoirs, generate power, and direct water flow. This would make water from one state's rivers and streams available to farmers in other states. The full effect of the Reclamation Act was felt over the next few decades, as water management projects created huge reservoirs and lakes where there had been dry canyons. Examples include the Salt Valley Project in Arizona and the Roosevelt Dam and Hoover Dam on the Colorado River.

✔ **Checkpoint** How did Roosevelt's policies affect the environment?

NoteTaking

Reading Skill: Compare and Contrast As you read, fill in the Venn diagram with similarities and differences between Roosevelt and Taft.

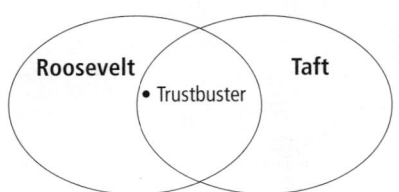

Roosevelt   Taft
• Trustbuster

Roosevelt and Taft Differ

Roosevelt left the presidency after two terms in office, saying he wished to enjoy private life. He was still a powerful force in the Republican Party, however, and he used that power to help Secretary of War William Howard Taft win the presidency in 1908. Roosevelt expected Taft to continue his programs of managing business and natural resources. Political cartoonists made caricatures of Roosevelt handing over what he called "my policies" to Taft, who seemed to have no ideas of his own.

Taft Takes His Own Course But Taft soon set his own agenda. He approved the Payne-Aldrich Act (1909), which did not lower tariffs as much as Roosevelt had wanted. He also pushed Congress to pass the Mann-Elkins Act (1910), which gave the government control over telephone and telegraph rates. He encouraged Congress to propose an income tax. Perhaps, most importantly, he dropped Roosevelt's distinction between good trusts and bad trusts.

Taft's Justice Department brought lawsuits against twice as many corporations as Roosevelt's had done. As a result, in 1911, the Supreme Court "busted" the trust built by the Standard Oil Company. But Taft also supported what the Court called its "rule of reason," which relaxed the hard line set by the Sherman Antitrust Act. The rule of reason allowed big monopolies so long as they did not "unreasonably" squeeze out smaller companies. Roosevelt publicly criticized these decisions. Then, Taft's attorney general sued to force U.S. Steel to sell a coal company it had bought. Roosevelt, who had approved the purchase of the company, fumed.

Taft further infuriated Roosevelt and other Progressives in the Republican Party when he fired Gifford Pinchot for publicly criticizing Secretary of the Interior Richard Ballinger. Pinchot charged that Ballinger, who opposed Roosevelt's conservation policies, had worked with business interests to sell federal land rich in coal deposits in Alaska.

Analyzing Political Cartoons

Taft in the White House Theodore Roosevelt looks on as President Taft is entangled in troubles.
1. What details illustrate Taft's troubles?
2. What does the cartoon suggest about Roosevelt's reaction to Taft's situation?

Roosevelt Strikes Back Roosevelt began traveling the country speaking about what he called the **New Nationalism**—a program to restore the government's trustbusting power. (See an excerpt from Roosevelt's New Nationalism speech at the end of this book.) Declaring himself as "strong as a bull moose," Roosevelt vowed to tackle the trusts in a third presidential term. The Taft-Roosevelt battle split the Republican Party as an election neared. Progressives bolted from the Republican party and set up the **Progressive Party.** Reformer Jane Addams nominated Roosevelt as the Progressive Party's candidate for the 1912 presidential election. The Republicans nominated Taft. A bitter election loomed.

✓ **Checkpoint** How did William Howard Taft's policies compare with Theodore Roosevelt's?

SECTION **4 Assessment**

Progress Monitoring Online
For: Self-test with vocabulary practice
Web Code: nea-0408

Comprehension

1. **Terms** Explain how each of the following acts and policies reflects Progressivism's influence.
   - Square Deal
   - Hepburn Act
   - Meat Inspection Act
   - Pure Food and Drug Act
   - National Reclamation Act
   - New Nationalism

2. **NoteTaking Reading Skill: Identify Main Ideas** Use your concept web to answer the Section Focus Question: What did Roosevelt think government should do for citizens?

Writing About History

3. **Quick Write: Present a Point of View** Choose one of the industries that President Roosevelt regulated. Imagine that you are a worker or business owner in the industry. In one or two paragraphs, describe your reaction to the President's actions. Use details to relate the effect of the government's actions on your work.

Critical Thinking

4. **Recognize Causes** Why might Theodore Roosevelt's push for reforms have angered some political leaders?

5. **Apply Information** How did Roosevelt's use of presidential and federal power differ from that of earlier Presidents? Give two examples.

6. **Analyze** How did Theodore Roosevelt's national forest policy reflect his ideas about conservation and preservation?

7. **Draw Conclusions** Do you think Roosevelt's public criticisms of Taft were justified? Why or why not?

WITNESS HISTORY 🔊 AUDIO

A History of Reform

Before becoming President of the United States, Woodrow Wilson was president of Princeton University in New Jersey. At the time, most Princeton students were sons of wealthy families. These students joined "eating clubs" that excluded poor students and other outsiders.

Wilson objected. The eating clubs, he said, made social life more important than learning. Furthermore, he said, the clubs were unfair and damaging to those students who were excluded. Wilson lost his fight to do away with the eating clubs. But he won a reputation as a high-minded reformer who would speak out against social injustice. Wilson's reform efforts would continue in his role as President of the United States.

▲ Wilson campaign button

Wilson's New Freedom

Core Curriculum Objectives

- **4.I.C.4a** Progressivism at its zenith; the 1912 election
- **4.I.C.4c** Clayton Antitrust Act and the Federal Trade Commission
- **4.I.C.4d** The Federal Reserve System (monetary controls)

Terms and People

Woodrow Wilson
New Freedom
Sixteenth Amendment
Federal Reserve Act

Federal Trade Commission
Clayton Antitrust Act

NoteTaking

Reading Skill: Identify Details As you read this section, fill in a concept web like the one below to record details from the section.

- Lowered tariffs
- Regulated banks
- **Wilson's New Freedom**

Why It Matters Republicans Theodore Roosevelt and William Howard Taft introduced the country to forceful Progressive Presidents. Democrat Woodrow Wilson used the expanded power of the presidency to promote a far-reaching reform agenda. Some of Wilson's economic and antitrust measures are still important in American life today. **Section Focus Question: What steps did Wilson take to increase the government's role in the economy?**

Wilson and the Democrats Prevail

In 1912, the Republican Party split over the issue of reform. Those who wanted a more active government formed the Progressive Party and chose Theodore Roosevelt as their candidate for President. Loyal Republicans gave the nod to President William Howard Taft.

The split created an opportunity for the Democrats and their candidate, **Woodrow Wilson,** to win the White House. Wilson's ideas had caught the attention of William Jennings Bryan, who helped Wilson win the Democratic nomination. As a student and later as a professor, Wilson had thought a great deal about good government. His doctoral thesis, *Congressional Government,* had launched him on a career teaching in college before he became the reforming governor of New Jersey.

Wilson shaped his ideas into a program he called the **New Freedom.** His plan looked much like Roosevelt's New Nationalism. It, too, would place strict government controls on corporations.

In a speech on the New Freedom, Wilson outlined his aim to provide more opportunities—more freedom—for small businesses.

Primary Source "The man with only a little capital is finding it harder and harder to get into the field, more and more impossible to compete with the big fellow. Why? Because the laws of this country do not prevent the strong from crushing the weak."

—Woodrow Wilson, "The New Freedom," 1913

Though he did not win the majority of the popular vote, Wilson received more than four times the number of Electoral College votes that went to Roosevelt or to Taft. The pious and <u>intellectual</u> son of a Virginia minister, Wilson was the first man born in the South to win the presidency in almost 60 years.

✔ **Checkpoint** How did Republican divisions help Wilson win the presidency?

Vocabulary Builder
intellectual–(ihn tuh LEHK choo uhl) *adj.* guided by thought; possessing great power of thought and reason

Wilson Regulates the Economy

President Wilson attacked what he called the "triple wall of privilege"—the tariffs, the banks, and the trusts—that blocked businesses from being free. Early in his first term, he pushed for new laws that would bring down those three walls and give the government more control over the economy.

Congress Lowers Tariffs and Raises Taxes First, Wilson aimed to prevent big manufacturers from unfairly charging high prices to their customers. One way to do this was to lower the tariffs on goods imported from foreign countries so, if American companies' prices were too high, consumers could buy foreign goods. Wilson called a special session of Congress and convinced its members to pass the Underwood Tariff Bill, which cut tariffs.

The Underwood Tariff Act of 1913 included a provision to create a graduated income tax, which the recently passed **Sixteenth Amendment** gave Congress the power to do. A graduated income tax means that wealthy people pay a higher percentage of their income than do poor people. The revenue from the income tax more than made up for the money the government lost by lowering tariffs on imports.

Federal Reserve Act Next, Wilson tried to reform the banking system. At the time, the country had no central authority to supervise banks. As a result, interest rates for loans could fluctuate wildly, and a few wealthy bankers had a great deal of control over the national, state, and local banks' reserve funds. This meant that a bank might not have full access to its reserves when customers needed to withdraw or borrow money.

Wilson pushed Congress to pass the **Federal Reserve Act** (1913). This law placed national banks under the control of a Federal Reserve Board, which set up regional banks to hold the reserve funds from commercial banks. This system, still in place today, helps protect the American economy from having too much

Progressive Party button

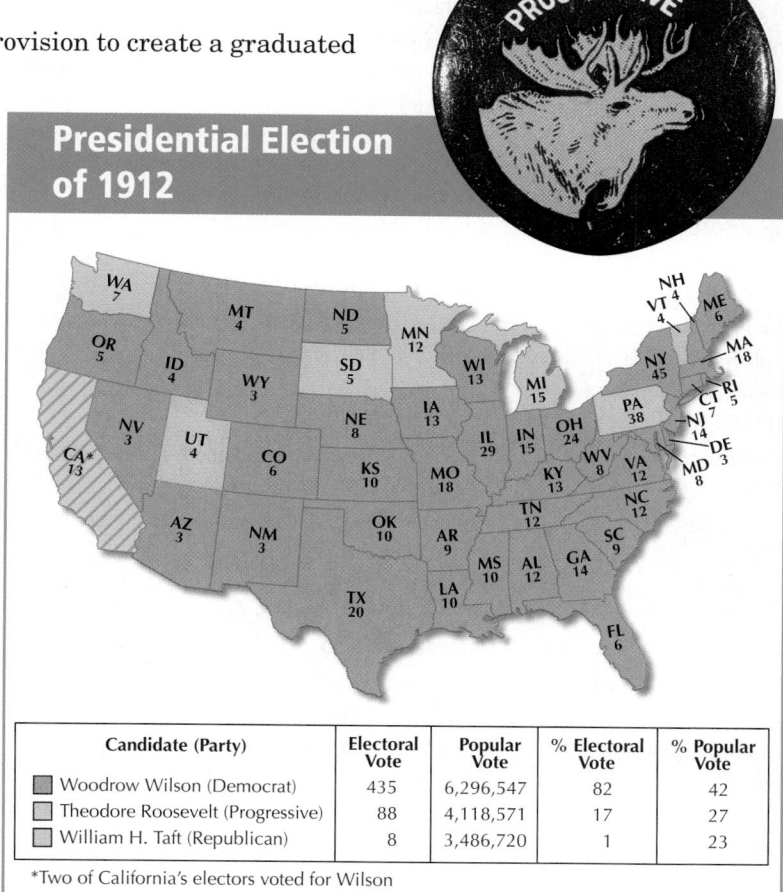

Presidential Election of 1912

Candidate (Party)	Electoral Vote	Popular Vote	% Electoral Vote	% Popular Vote
Woodrow Wilson (Democrat)	435	6,296,547	82	42
Theodore Roosevelt (Progressive)	88	4,118,571	17	27
William H. Taft (Republican)	8	3,486,720	1	23

*Two of California's electors voted for Wilson

money end up in the hands of one person, bank, or region. The Federal Reserve Board also sets the interest rate that banks pay to borrow money from other banks, and it supervises banks to make sure they are well run. Historians have called the Federal Reserve Act the most important piece of economic legislation before the 1930s.

Wilson Strengthens Antitrust Regulation Like Presidents before him, Wilson focused on trusts. Wilson agreed with Roosevelt that trusts were not dangerous as long as they did not engage in unfair practices. In 1914, he persuaded Congress to create the **Federal Trade Commission (FTC)**. Members of this group were named by the President to monitor business practices that might lead to monopoly. The FTC was also charged with watching out for false advertising or dishonest labeling. Congress also passed the **Clayton Antitrust Act** (1914), which strengthened earlier antitrust laws by spelling out those activities in which businesses could not engage.

These laws are still in effect today, protecting both businesses and consumers from abusive business activities. In recent years, the FTC has prosecuted companies that traded stocks dishonestly and fined companies that published false ads. The FTC also regulates buying on the Internet.

Progressive Era Legislation and Constitutional Amendments

Legislation/Amendment	Effect
Sherman Antitrust Act (1890)	Outlawed monopolies and practices that restrained trade, such as price fixing
National Reclamation Act (1902)	Provided for federal irrigation projects by using money from the sale of public lands
Elkins Act (1903)	Imposed fines on railroads that gave special rates to favored shippers
Hepburn Act (1906)	Authorized the federal government to regulate railroad rates and set maximum prices for ferries, bridge tolls, and oil pipelines
Meat Inspection Act (1906)	Allowed the federal government to inspect meat sold across state lines and required inspection of meat-processing plants
Pure Food and Drug Act (1906)	Allowed federal inspection of food and medicine and banned the shipment and sale of impure food and the mislabeling of food and medicine
Sixteenth Amendment (1913)	Gave Congress the power to collect taxes on people's income
Seventeenth Amendment (1913)	Instituted the direct election of senators by the people of each state
Underwood Tariff Act (1913)	Lowered tariffs on imported goods and established a graduated income tax
Federal Reserve Act (1913)	Created the Federal Reserve Board to oversee banks and manage reserve funds
Federal Trade Commission Act (1914)	Established the Federal Trade Commission to monitor business practices, false advertising, and dishonest labeling
Clayton Antitrust Act (1914)	Strengthened the Sherman Antitrust Act by spelling out specific activities businesses could not do
Eighteenth Amendment (1919)	Banned the making, selling, and transporting of alcoholic beverages in the United States
Nineteenth Amendment (1920)	Gave women the right to vote in all elections

Workers' Rights Protected The Clayton Antitrust Act also ushered in a new era for workers by protecting labor unions from being attacked as trusts. Now, workers could organize more freely. Samuel Gompers of the American Federation of Labor (AFL) praised the new law as the "Magna Carta" of labor.

On the heels of these protections came the Workingman's Compensation Act (1916), which gave wages to temporarily disabled civil service employees. That same year, Wilson pushed for the Adamson Act to prevent a nationwide railroad strike, which would have stopped the movement of coal and food, leaving millions of Americans cold and hungry. Railroad union leaders insisted on the eight-hour day, but railroad managers would not accept it. Wilson called many company leaders to the White House, pleading with them to change their minds and avert a strike. When those efforts failed, he worked with Congress to pass the Adamson Act, which limited railroad employees' workdays to eight hours.

However, Wilson did not always support organized labor, as a tragic incident known as the Ludlow Massacre showed. In the fall of 1913, coal miners in Ludlow, Colorado, demanded safer conditions, higher pay, and the right to form a union. When the coal company refused, they walked off the job. Evicted from company housing, the miners and their families set up in a tent city near the mines. The strike continued through the winter. Then, on April 20, 1914, the Colorado National Guard opened fire on the tent city and set fire to the tents, killing some 26 men, women, and children. In the end, Wilson sent federal troops to restore order and break up the strike. The miners' attempt to form a union had failed.

✓ **Checkpoint** What policies did Wilson pursue in support of his New Freedom program?

Progressivism Leaves a Lasting Legacy

The political reforms of the Progressives had a lasting effect on the American political system. The initiative, referendum, and recall and the Nineteenth Amendment expanded voters' influence. Progressive reforms also paved the way for future trends. Starting in this period, the federal government grew to offer more protection to Americans' private lives while at the same time, gaining more control over peoples' lives.

The American economy today showcases the strength of the Progressives' legacy. Antitrust laws, the Federal Reserve Board, and the other federal agencies watch closely over the economy. The controls that Roosevelt and Wilson put in place continue to provide consumer protections. In later years, the government built on those actions to extend regulation over other aspects of business.

The Progressive years also greatly expanded the government's role in managing natural resources. Especially in the West, federal action on dams, national parks, and resource use remain major areas of debate. Those debates and decisions affect people in other regions as well. For example, while farmers in California, Arizona, or New Mexico worry about getting enough water to grow crops, the rest of the nation awaits the delivery of the food they grow.

It is true that many of the problems identified by the Progressives still plague us today. There are still dishonest sellers, unfair employment practices, and problems in schools, cities, the environment, and public health. However, the Progressive reformers passed on the idea that government can take action to help people fix those problems.

✓ **Checkpoint** What was the long-term impact of the Progressive Era on American life?

SECTION **5** Assessment

Progress Monitoring _Online_
For: Self-test with vocabulary practice
Web Code: nea-0409

Comprehension

1. **Terms and People** For each item below, write a sentence explaining its significance.
   - Woodrow Wilson
   - New Freedom
   - Sixteenth Amendment
   - Federal Reserve Act
   - Clayton Antitrust Act

2. **NoteTaking Reading Skill: Identify Details** Use your flowchart to answer the Section Focus Question: What steps did Wilson take to increase the government's role in the economy?

Writing About History

3. **Quick Write: Use Vivid Language** Choose an event discussed in this section. In one or two paragraphs, retell a portion of the event. Be sure to use vivid language and include details. Do additional research if needed.

Critical Thinking

4. **Compare and Contrast** How were the goals and actions of Wilson's New Freedom similar to Roosevelt's New Nationalism? How were they different?

5. **Draw Conclusions** Describe how each of the following met Progressive goals: the Sixteenth Amendment; the Clayton Antitrust Act; the FTC.

6. **Demonstrate Reasoned Judgment** In which area do you think government reforms had the greatest impact? Why?

Quick Study Guide

NY 3.III.A.2,
3.III.A.2d

Progress Monitoring *Online*
For: Self-test with vocabulary practice
Web Code: nea-0410

■ Effects of Social Progressivism

Living Conditions	• Immigrants gain access to child care and English classes.
	• Municipal governments are pressured to improve sanitation and tenement safety.
	• Minority groups organize, create self-help agencies, and fight discrimination.
	• Immigrants are encouraged to become "Americanized."
	• Laws regulate safety of foods and medicine.
Working Conditions	• City and state laws improve workplace safety.
	• Workers' compensation laws provide for payments to injured workers.
	• Laws limit workday hours; Supreme Court upholds limits for women but not for men.
	• State and federal governments were urged to adopt minimum wage and make other reforms.
	• Strike fund aids workers who reject unsafe working conditions.
	• Minority job seekers gain access to more jobs.
Children	• State and federal laws ban child labor; Supreme Court overturns federal ban.
	• Compulsory-education laws require children to attend school.
	• Poor children gain access to nursery schools and kindergartens.

■ Progressive Organizations That Worked for Rights

NAACP — National Consumers League — Partido Liberal Mexicano — **Worked to Protect or Expand Rights** — National American Woman Suffrage Association — Anti-Defamation League — Urban League

■ Municipal Reforms

Government Reforms	Election Reforms
• Commission form of government	• Direct primary
• City managers	• Initiative
• Trained administrators	• Referendum
• City-owned public utilities	• Recall

☑ Quick Study Timeline

In America

1892	1899	1900	1902
John Muir helps found Sierra Club	Florence Kelley helps found National Consumers League	Hurricane devastates Galveston, Texas	President Roosevelt signs the National Reclamation Act

Presidential Terms   Grover Cleveland 1893–1897   William McKinley 1897–1901   Theodore Roosevelt 1901–1909

1895   **1900**

Around the World

1893	1900	1901
New Zealand becomes first nation to grant women the right to vote	Boxer Rebellion erupts in China	Britain outlaws employing children under the age of 12 in factories or workshops

American Issues
●—●—●—● Connector

By connecting prior knowledge with what you have learned in this chapter, you can gradually build your understanding of enduring questions that still affect America today. Answer the questions below. Then, use your American Issues Connector study guide (or go online: www.PHSchool.com **Web Code:** neh-7703).

Issues You Learned About

● **Social Problems and Reforms** Again and again, Americans have worked to reform problems that afflict society.

1. Think about the social problems that you have read about in this chapter. Identify the five problems that you think posed the biggest threat to society or to groups of Americans. Create a chart showing the following:
   - social problems
   - reform efforts
   - reformers involved
   - results of reform efforts

● **Voting Rights** Over the years, Americans have gradually expanded the democratic right to vote.

2. Who were some of the nineteenth-century leaders of the women's suffrage movement?

3. What methods did Carrie Chapman Catt use to help women win voting rights?

4. How did Alice Paul's methods differ from Catt's?

● **Government's Role in the Economy** Americans often debate the proper balance between free enterprise and government regulation of the economy.

5. What is a trust?

6. How did Roosevelt's and Taft's attitudes toward trusts differ?

7. What effect did Wilson have on trusts?

Connect to Your World	New York

Women in American Society Seneca Falls, New York, the site of the first Women's Rights Convention, is today home to the National Women's Hall of Fame. Many of the women you read about in this chapter have been inducted, including Jane Addams, Ida B. Wells, Alice Paul, and New Yorkers Margaret Sanger and Susan B. Anthony. Other New Yorkers in the Hall of Fame include Shirley Chisholm, the first African American woman elected to the United States Congress, and Hilary Rodham Clinton, the first female senator from New York. Research notable New York women who have not yet been inducted into the Hall of Fame, and nominate one you believe deserves the honor.

1906 Congress passes the Meat Inspection and Pure Food and Drug acts	1909 NAACP is formed	1913 Congress passes the Federal Reserve Act	1920 Nineteenth Amendment is ratified

William H. Taft 1909–1913   Woodrow Wilson 1913–1921

1905	1910	1915	1920

1910 Mexican Revolution begins

1914 World War I begins in Europe

History Interactive
For: Interactive timeline
Web Code: nep-0412

Chapter Assessment

Terms and People

1. Who were the **muckrakers**? Explain the effect the muckrakers had on American life.

2. Define **suffrage.** Why did Progressive women demand suffrage?

3. Who were **Booker T. Washington** and **W.E.B. Du Bois**? What different ideas did they hold?

4. What was the **Pure Food and Drug Act?** Which government agency enforces this act, and how does it do so?

5. Define the **Sixteenth Amendment.** How did it help the government?

Focus Questions

The focus question for this chapter is **What were the causes and effects of the Progressive Movement?** Build an answer to this big question by answering the focus questions for Sections 1 through 5 and the Critical Thinking questions that follow.

Section 1
6. What areas did Progressives think were in need of the greatest reform?

Section 2
7. How did women of the Progressive Era make progress and win the right to vote?

Section 3
8. What steps did minorities take to combat social problems and discrimination?

Section 4
9. What did Roosevelt think government should do for citizens?

Section 5
10. What steps did Wilson take to increase the government's role in the economy?

Critical Thinking

11. **Analyze Visuals** Study the photograph of the child coal miners on the opening page of Section 1. What does this image tell you about the life of young laborers?

12. **Identify Point of View** Explain the different points of view Progressives held on the education of children. What point of view did John Dewey hold?

13. **Draw Inferences** In what way did the Court ruling in *Muller* v. *Oregon* contradict the ideas behind the women's rights movement?

14. **Draw Inferences** What factors may have pushed African Americans to migrate from rural areas to urban areas?

15. **Make Generalizations** How did nonwhites and minority groups seek to better themselves during the Progressive Era?

16. **Determine Relevance** How important was Upton Sinclair's *The Jungle* to passage of the Meat Inspection Act? Explain.

17. **Explain Effects** How did the Progressive Party affect the presidential election of 1912?

18. **Analyze Information** Why do historians believe that the Federal Reserve Act was the most important piece of economic legislation before the 1930s?

19. **Analyze Ideas and Effects** Compare the Social Gospel Movement and its results with Social Darwinism, which you read about earlier.

20. **Predict Consequences** Do you think that either the NAWSA or the NWP could have succeeded in gaining suffrage for women on its own? Explain.

Writing About History

Writing a Narrative Essay Write a narrative essay that tells a story about one of the reform efforts of the Progressive Era in the United States. Tell the story from the point of view of a historical individual or a fictional character of the period.

Prewriting
- Choose a reform effort that interests you most. Take notes about the people and locations involved.
- Choose a purpose for your essay. For example, you may want to highlight a certain event or result that you think deserves attention.
- Gather the facts and details you will need to tell your story, including any historic background.

Drafting
- Identify the climax, or most important part, of your story. Then, decide what will happen in the beginning, middle, and end of the essay.

- Write an opening for the essay that will grab a reader's interest and make sure to include sensory details.
- Use many details to make the story vivid. Include dialogue when possible to convey the thoughts of your character.
- Write a conclusion that summarizes the significance of the experience to the character.

Revising
- Use the guidelines on page SH11 of the Writing Handbook to revise your narrative essay.

Regents DBQ Practice

Regulation of the Economy

During the Progressive Era, Presidents such as Theodore Roosevelt and Woodrow Wilson called for the federal government to take on a greater role in regulating the economy. But not all Americans approved of the expansion of federal power. Use your knowledge of the Progressive Era and Documents 1, 2, 3, and 4 to answer questions 1 through 4.

Document 1

"This country belongs to the people who inhabit it. Its resources, its businesses, its institutions, and its laws should be utilized, maintained, or altered in whatever manner will best promote the general interest. It is time to set the public welfare in the first place. . . .

We demand . . . that those who profit by control of business affairs shall justify that profit and that control by sharing with the public the fruits thereof. We therefore demand a strong national regulation of interstate corporations. . . .

We pledge our party to establish a Department of Labor, with a seat in the Cabinet, and with wide jurisdiction over matters affecting the conditions of labor and living."
— *Progressive "Bull Moose" Party Platform, 1912*

Document 2

Federal Reserve System

Board of Governors	• Appointed by the President; confirmed by the Senate • Sets cash-reserve requirements for member banks • Reviews the short-term rates set by reserve banks
12 Federal Reserve Banks	• Each serves one of 12 regional districts • Set short-term interest rates for member banks
All nationally chartered banks required to be members	

Document 3

"What effect is what you may do here going to have upon the future welfare, productiveness, and value of the greatest single industrial interest of the country?. . . . Gentlemen, you may pass an act that will so compromise the value of the property and the prosperity of the communities of this country that it will bring widespread disaster. . . .

What I say, gentlemen, is that [it] is a very, very serious moment when an Anglo-Saxon government undertakes the charge of the people's money and says how much they shall earn by the exercise of their constitutional rights of liberty and property. And it should be recognized that possibly we are at the parting of the ways, and that if this be done it will go on until those constitutional guarantees have but little value, and the only profession worth exercising in the country will be that of holding office in some administrative board."
— *David Wilcox, President of Delaware and Hudson Railroad, testimony to Congress, 1905*

Document 4

"We have studied, as perhaps no other nation has, the most effective means of production, but we have not studied cost or economy as we should either as organizers of industry, as statesmen, or as individuals. Nor have we studied and perfected the means by which government may be put to the service of humanity, in safeguarding the health of the nation, the health of its men and its women and its children, as well as their rights in the struggle for existence. . . .

The first duty of law is to keep sound the society it serves. Sanitary laws, pure-food laws, and laws determining conditions of labor, which individuals are powerless to determine for themselves, are intimate parts of the very business of justice and legal efficiency."
— *Woodrow Wilson, First Inaugural Address, 1913*

---

1. Which of the documents above most closely reflects a belief in laissez-faire economics?
   (1) Document 1
   (2) Document 2
   (3) Document 3
   (4) Document 4

2. Why does the Progressive Party platform favor the creation of a federal Department of Labor?
   (1) It would increase the profits of corporations.
   (2) It would promote the good of the people.
   (3) It would lead to the regulation of interstate commerce.
   (4) It would limit the growing power of the federal government.

3. Based on Document 2, how did the Federal Reserve Act increase the role of the federal government?
   (1) It gave a federal board greater power to regulate interest rates.
   (2) It increased the number of commercial banks.
   (3) It made the Board of Governors independent of the President and Senate.
   (4) It gave the people the right to elect the Board of Governors of the Federal Reserve.

4. **Writing Task** Should the federal government have broad power over the economy and people's lives? Use your knowledge of the Progressive Era and specific evidence from the primary sources above to support your opinion.

Americans Charge to Victory

When Theodore Roosevelt assumed command of the First U.S. Regiment of Volunteer Cavalry, the press nicknamed his new unit "Roosevelt's Rough Riders." On July 1, 1898, the Rough Riders, together with other units—including African American troops from the U.S. Ninth and Tenth Cavalries—stormed into battle outside Santiago, Cuba. A junior officer who would later become a decorated general remembered the unity of his fellow soldiers as the Americans charged up Spanish-held San Juan Hill:

❝White regiments, black regiments, regulars and Rough Riders, representing the young manhood of the North and South, fought shoulder to shoulder, unmindful of race or color . . . mindful only of their common duty as Americans.❞
—Lieutenant John J. Pershing

Listen to the Witness History *audio to hear more about America's rise to global power.*

◀ Future President Theodore Roosevelt poses with his victorious Rough Riders atop San Juan Hill.

Carving of Commodore Matthew Perry on an animal tusk

NY Core Curriculum Preview

Chapter Focus Question: How did the United States become a global power?

Section 1
The Roots of Imperialism 4.II.A.1a, 4.II.A.1b, 4.II.A.2c, 4.II.A.3

Section 2
The Spanish-American War 4.II.A.1, 4.II.A.3a, 4.II.A.3b

Section 3
The United States and East Asia 1.I.A.4, 4.II.A.1, 4.II.A.2a, 4.II.A.2b

Section 4
The United States and Latin America 4.II.A.4b, 4.II.A.4c

Use the ☑ **Quick Study Timeline** at the end of this chapter to preview chapter events.

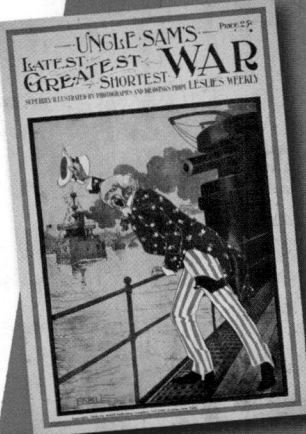

Poster from the Spanish-American War

Medal won by African American soldier in Spanish-American War

> **Note Taking Study Guide *Online***
> **For:** Note Taking and American Issues Connector
> **Web Code:** nee-7801

◀ John Stevens

WITNESS HISTORY 🔊 AUDIO

America Eyes Hawaii

"The Hawaiian pear is now fully ripe and this is the golden hour for the United States to pluck it." John Stevens, U.S. minister to Hawaii, was not talking about fruit when he sent this note to the Secretary of State in 1893. He was talking about the United States taking over the Hawaiian Islands—along with their rich fields of sugar cane and pineapples. And Stevens did more than just talk. He ordered the United States Marines to aid in a revolt against the queen of Hawaii.

Five years later, the Senate finally agreed to annex Hawaii. The "Hawaiian pear" became part of the United States.

◀ A Hawaiian plantation worker harvests pineapples.

The Roots of Imperialism

 Core Curriculum Objectives

- **4.II.A.1a** From old diplomacy to new: Role of increased American power
- **4.II.A.1b** Perry and the "opening" of Japan
- **4.II.A.2c** Other Pacific overtures: Acquisition of Hawaii
- **4.II.A.3** Imperialism: the Spanish-American War

Terms and People

imperialism
extractive economy
Alfred T. Mahan
Social Darwinism

Frederick J. Turner
Matthew Perry
Queen Liliuokalani

NoteTaking

Reading Skill: Identify Main Ideas As you read, fill in a concept web like the one below with the key events that marked America's first steps toward world power.

Why It Matters For most of its early history, America played a small role in world affairs. But in the late 1800s, this began to change. With leading spokesmen calling for the United States to join the ranks of the world's major powers, the United States began to acquire influence and territories outside its continental borders. The United States was abandoning isolationism and emerging as a new power on the global stage. **Section Focus Question: How and why did the United States take a more active role in world affairs?**

The Causes of Imperialism

During the Age of Imperialism, from the mid-1800s through the early 1900s, powerful nations engaged in a mad dash to extend their influence across much of the world. European nations added to colonies they had established during the Age of Exploration by acquiring new colonies in Africa and Asia. Following European success, Japan and the United States also began to consider the benefits of **imperialism,** the policy by which strong nations extend their political, military, and economic control over weaker territories.

Imperialists Seek Economic Benefits One reason for the rush to grab colonies was the desire for raw materials and natural resources. This was especially true for European nations and Japan. They sought colonies to provide tea, rubber, iron, petroleum, and other materials for their industries at home. These colonial economies were examples of **extractive economies.** The imperial country extracted, or removed, raw materials from the colony and shipped them to the home country. Possession of colonies gave nations an edge in the competition for global resources. In contrast to other world powers, the resource-rich United States had fewer concerns about shortages of raw materials in the nineteenth century.

For Americans, the problem was not a shortage of materials, but a surplus of goods. The booming U.S. economy of the late 1800s was producing more goods than Americans could consume. Farmers complained that excess production resulted in declining crop prices and profits. Industrialists urged expanding trade into new overseas markets where American <u>commodities</u> could be sold. Otherwise, they warned, American factories would close and unemployment would rise. Senator Albert J. Beveridge, a Progressive and friend of Theodore Roosevelt, explained why the United States needed to become a world power:

Vocabulary Builder
<u>commodity</u>—(kuh MAHD uh tee) *n.* anything bought or sold; any article of commerce

> **Primary Source** "Today we are raising more [crops] than we can consume. Today we are making more than we can use. . . . Therefore we must find new markets for our produce, new occupation for our capital, new work for our labor."
> —Senator Albert J. Beveridge, "The March of the Flag," 1898

Imperialists Stress Military Strength To expand and protect their interests around the world, imperialist nations built up their military strength. **Alfred T. Mahan,** a military historian and an officer in the United States Navy, played a key role in transforming America into a naval power. In *The Influence of Sea Power Upon History*, Mahan asserted that since ancient times, many great nations had owed their greatness to powerful navies. He called upon America to build a modern fleet. Mahan also argued that the United States would need to acquire foreign bases where American ships could refuel and gather fresh supplies. Influenced by the ideas of Mahan and others, the United States expanded and modernized its navy by building new steel-plated, steam-powered battleships such as the USS *Maine*. By 1900, the United States had the third largest navy in the world.

A Strong Navy
Prominent imperialists like Alfred T. Mahan called for a strong American navy to protect U.S. interests overseas. *How could a strong navy benefit American exporters?*

HISTORY MAKERS

Alfred T. Mahan (1840–1914)
Mahan, a naval officer and historian, urged American leaders to build a stronger navy and to obtain naval bases in Cuba, Hawaii, and the Philippines. He also argued that the United States should build a canal across Central America so its ships could move quickly between the Atlantic and Pacific oceans. American leaders eventually adopted all of Mahan's ideas to bolster the power of the United States Navy.

Imperialists Believe in National Superiority Imperialists around the world used ideas of racial, national, and cultural superiority to justify imperialism. One of these ideas was **Social Darwinism,** the belief that life consists of competitive struggles in which only the fittest survive. Social Darwinists felt that certain nations and races were superior to others and therefore were destined to rule over inferior peoples and cultures. Prominent Americans worried that if the United States remained isolated while European nations gobbled up the rest of the world, America would not survive.

One reason that these Americans embraced Social Darwinism was that they had long believed that God had granted them the right and responsibility to settle the frontier. They spoke of America's "Manifest Destiny" to expand all the way to the Pacific Ocean. In a best-selling work titled *Our Country,* Josiah Strong picked up on this theme. A religious missionary, Strong argued that Americans had a responsibility to spread their Western values. "God is training the Anglo-Saxon race," he asserted, "for its mission [to civilize] weaker races." American missionaries who shared Strong's belief journeyed to foreign lands to gain converts to Christianity.

In *The Significance of the Frontier in American History,* historian **Frederick Jackson Turner** noted that the frontier had been closed by gradual settlement in the nineteenth century. Throughout American history, he continued, the frontier had traditionally supplied an arena where ambitious Americans could pursue their fortunes and secure a fresh start. It had thus served as a "safety valve," siphoning off potential discontent. Now that America had spanned the continent, advocates of Turner's thesis urged overseas expansion as a way to keep the "safety valve" open and avoid internal conflict.

✓ **Checkpoint** What factors influenced Americans to play a more active role in the world?

America's First Steps Toward World Power

Beginning in the mid-1800s, with little fanfare, America focused more and more on expanding its trade and acquiring new territories. One of America's first moves toward world power came before the Civil War.

U.S. Power Grows in the Pacific In 1853, Commodore **Matthew Perry** sailed a fleet of American warships into present-day Tokyo Bay, Japan. Prior to Perry's arrival, Japan had denied the rest of the world access to its ports. In fact, because most Japanese people had never seen steamships before, they thought the ships in Perry's fleet were "giant dragons puffing smoke." Perry cleverly won the Japanese emperor's favor by showering him with lavish gifts. Japanese leaders also realized that by closing off their nation to the outside world, they had fallen behind in military technology. Within a year, Perry negotiated a treaty that opened Japan to trade with America.

Perry's journey set a precedent for further expansion across the Pacific Ocean. In 1867, the United States took possession of the Midway Islands. Treaties in 1875 and 1887 increased trade with the Hawaiian Islands and gave the United States the right to build a naval base at Pearl Harbor.

Seward Purchases Alaska In 1867, Secretary of State William Seward bought Alaska from Russia for $7.2 million. Journalists scoffed at the purchase and referred to Alaska as "Seward's Folly" and "Seward's Icebox." They wondered why the United States would want a vast tundra of snow and ice 1,000 miles north

Nationalism Fuels Pursuit of Empire

In the late nineteenth century, patriotic songs by composers such as John Philip Sousa reinforced Americans' widespread belief in the national superiority of the United States. *How did nationalism contribute to the rise of American imperialism?*

Causes of Imperialism	☑ Quick Study
Economic gain	• Industrialists want raw materials for industries in their home countries. • Entrepreneurs want to sell their goods and invest in new overseas markets.
Militarism	Colonial powers seek bases for naval forces that protect their global trade networks.
Nationalism and Social Darwinism	Imperialists feel a moral duty to spread their culture to peoples they consider inferior.

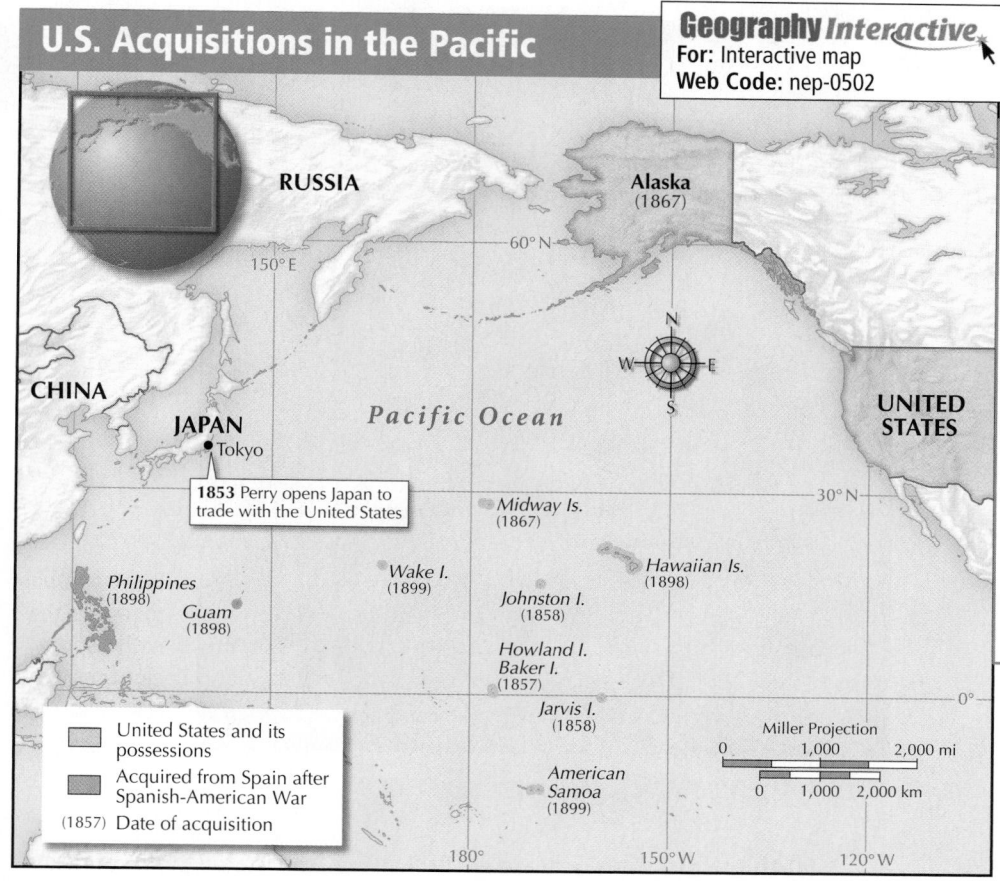

U.S. Acquisitions in the Pacific

Geography *Interactive*
For: Interactive map
Web Code: nep-0502

RUSSIA

Alaska
(1867)

60° N

150° E

CHINA

JAPAN
• Tokyo

Pacific Ocean

1853 Perry opens Japan to
trade with the United States

Midway Is.
(1867)

30° N

UNITED
STATES

Philippines
(1898)
Guam
(1898)

Wake I.
(1899)

Hawaiian Is.
(1898)

Johnston I.
(1858)

Howland I.
Baker I.
(1857)

Jarvis I.
(1858)

Miller Projection

0   1,000   2,000 mi

0   1,000   2,000 km

American
Samoa
(1899)

☐ United States and its
possessions
☐ Acquired from Spain after
Spanish-American War
(1857) Date of acquisition

180°   150° W   120° W

Map Skills Between 1853
and 1898, the United States
opened Japan to American trade
and gained valuable possessions
across the Pacific Ocean.

1. Locate: (a) Japan, (b) Alaska,
(c) Hawaiian Islands

2. Place Which islands lie about
halfway between the United
States and Japan?

3. Analyze Why were the
Hawaiian Islands important to
U.S. naval and merchant
ships?

of its border. But Seward's purchase almost doubled the country's size, and the "ice-box" turned out to be rich in timber, oil, and other natural resources. Alaska also greatly expanded America's reach across the Pacific. Scholars today see Seward's purchase as a key milestone on America's road to power.

Engraving of Matthew Perry on an
animal tusk

U.S. Influence in Latin America Grows U.S. businessmen saw Latin America as a natural place to expand their trade and investments. Secretary of State James Blaine helped them by sponsoring the First International Pan-American Conference in 1889. Blaine preached the benefits of economic cooperation to delegates of 17 Latin American countries. The conference also paved the way for the construction of the Pan-American Highway system, which linked the United States to Central and South America.

In 1895, tensions rose between America and Great Britain because of a border dispute between British Guiana and Venezuela. Claiming that Britain was violating the Monroe Doctrine, President Cleveland threatened U.S. intervention. After some international saber-rattling, the British accepted a growing U.S. sphere of influence in Latin America. Relations between Britain and the United States soon improved.

✔ **Checkpoint** Why did journalists criticize Seward for his purchase of Alaska?

The United States Acquires Hawaii

The Hawaiian Islands had been economically linked to the United States for almost a century. Since the 1790s, American merchant ships had stopped at Hawaii on their way to East Asia. Missionaries had established Christian churches and schools on the islands. Americans had also established sugar cane

Territorial Expansion of the United States

TRACK THE ISSUE

Should the United States expand its territory?

The United States has expanded its territory many times. It has done so through various means, including negotiation, treaty, annexation, and war. But territorial expansion has often aroused strong debate among Americans. Use the timeline below to explore this enduring issue.

1803 Louisiana Purchase
Jefferson buys Louisiana Territory despite doubts about constitutionality.

1845 Texas Annexation
Texas joins the Union despite opposition from Mexico and nonslave states.

1848 Mexican Cession
United States gains vast lands in the Southwest as a result of war with Mexico.

1867 Alaska Purchase
Critics say Alaska is an icebox and call the deal "Seward's Folly."

1893 Hawaiian Revolt
American planters overthrow Queen Liliuokalani and pave way to annexation in 1898.

1898 Spanish-American War
Victory over Spain puts Cuba, Puerto Rico, the Philippines, and Guam under U.S. control.

Queen Liliuokalani

Protesters want to restore the native sovereignty of the Hawaiian Islands.

DEBATE THE ISSUE

Native Hawaiian Sovereignty In 1898, the United States annexed Hawaii without the consent of native Hawaiians. In recent years, some Hawaiians have called for the return of native sovereignty. One possible solution is the establishment of some form of self-rule for natives, much like the "nation within a nation" status of Native Americans.

"For the overwhelming majority of Hawaiians, justice means political status and federal recognition, the restoration of our inherent sovereignty and redress from the United States for the illegal overthrow of the Kingdom of Hawaii. . . . Although there are more Hawaiians than . . . any other native peoples in the United States, Hawaiians have remained without recognition of our right to self-govern."

—Clayton Hee, Office of Hawaiian Affairs

"Would the citizens of [a] Native Hawaiian government—like reservation Indians—be immune from state laws, regulations and taxes? . . . If Congress were to create a separate tribal government for Native Hawaiians, it would be imposing just such a system on the people of Hawaii. Persons of different races, who live together in the same society, would be subject to different legal codes. This . . . is a recipe for permanent racial conflict."

—John Kyl, senator from Arizona

? TRANSFER Activities

1. **Compare** How do the two speakers differ on the issue of self-rule for Hawaiians?

2. **Analyze** If Native Hawaiians gain sovereignty, how would their lives change?

3. **Transfer** Use the following Web site to see a video, try a WebQuest, and write in your journal. **Web Code:** neh-7802

plantations there. In 1887, American planters convinced King Kalakaua (kah LAH kah oo ah) to amend Hawaii's constitution so that voting rights were limited to only wealthy landowners, who were, of course, the white planters.

American Planters Increase Their Power In the early 1890s, American planters in Hawaii faced two crises. First, a new U.S. tariff law imposed duties on previously duty-free Hawaiian sugar. This made Hawaiian sugar more expensive than sugar produced in the United States. The sugar-growers in Hawaii therefore feared that they would suffer decreasing sales and profits.

The other problem was that in 1891, Kalakaua died and his sister Liliuokalani (lih lee oo oh kah LAH nee) was his <u>successor</u>. A determined Hawaiian nationalist, **Queen Liliuokalani** resented the increasing power of the white planters, who owned much of the Hawaiian land. She abolished the constitution that had given political power to the white minority.

With the backing of U.S. officials, the American planters responded quickly and forcefully. In 1893, they overthrew the queen. John Stevens, U.S. minister to Hawaii, ordered United States Marines to help the rebels seize power. The new government, led by wealthy planter Sanford B. Dole, asked President Benjamin Harrison to annex Hawaii into the United States.

The United States Annexes Hawaii President Harrison signed the treaty of annexation but could not get the required Senate approval before Grover Cleveland became President. Cleveland ordered a full investigation, which revealed that the majority of the Hawaiian people did not approve of the treaty. Cleveland refused to sign the agreement and apologized for the "flagrant wrong" done by the "reprehensible conduct of the American minister."

However, American sentiment for annexation remained strong, especially on the West Coast, where California business interests had close ties with the planters in Hawaii. In 1897, a new President entered the White House. William McKinley's administration favored annexation, and in 1898, after the outbreak of the Spanish-American War, Congress proclaimed Hawaii an official U.S. territory.

Vocabulary Builder

<u>successor</u>–(suhk SEHS uhr) *n.* person or thing that succeeds, or follows, another

✔ **Checkpoint** How did American planters react to Queen Liliuokalani's actions when she gained power?

SECTION **1** Assessment

Progress Monitoring *Online*
For: Self-test with vocabulary practice
Web Code: nea-0504

Comprehension

1. **Terms and People** For each person listed below, write a sentence explaining his or her significance to American imperialism.
   - Alfred T. Mahan
   - Frederick J. Turner
   - Matthew Perry
   - Queen Liliuokalani

2. **NoteTaking Reading Skill: Identify Main Ideas** Use your concept web to answer the Section Focus Question: How and why did the United States take a more active role in world affairs?

Writing About History

3. **Quick Write: Choose a Topic** To write a narrative essay, start by choosing a topic. Suppose that you want to write a narrative from the perspective of the American imperialist Alfred T. Mahan. Make a list of topics that interest you, such as the construction of new battleships for the United States Navy or an account of a U.S. exploration for unclaimed territory in the Pacific Ocean. You may want to do research in books and on the Internet before you decide on a topic.

Critical Thinking

4. **Evaluate Information** Which of the motives for American imperialism do you think was the most important? Why?

5. **Compare Points of View** How did public opinion about the purchase of Alaska in 1867 differ from the view of historians today?

6. **Make Decisions** If you had been President in 1894, would you have supported or opposed the annexation of Hawaii? Give reasons for your answer.

1898 recruiting poster ▶

YOUR COUNTRY CALLS YOU

R·M·WRIGHT '98.

▲ Nameplate from the *Maine's* wreckage

WITNESS HISTORY AUDIO

Remember the *Maine*!

On February 15, 1898, an explosion ripped through the hull of the USS *Maine* in Havana harbor, in the Spanish colony of Cuba. More than 250 American sailors died. The incident ignited a furor as Americans clamored for war with Spain. In newspapers, speeches, and songs, patriots implored their fellow citizens to remember the *Maine:*

❝And shall our country let it pass, this deed of foul intent? And shall our country dare believe it was an accident? . . . Come arm, we all, and let us teach a lesson to bold Spain. We will avenge, by more than speech the destruction of the *Maine*!❞

—H. W. Petrie, lyrics from "The Wreck of the *Maine*," 1898

The Spanish-American War

NY **Core Curriculum Objectives**

- **4.II.A.1** From old diplomacy to new, 1865–1900
- **4.II.A.3a** Imperialism: Causes for the Spanish-American War
- **4.II.A.3b** Imperialism: United States empire—Cuba

Terms and People

José Martí
William Randolph Hearst
Yellow Press
jingoism

George Dewey
Emilio Aguinaldo
Rough Riders
Treaty of Paris

NoteTaking

Reading Skill: Identify Causes and Effects Note the causes, key events, and effects of the Spanish-American War.

Cause	Spanish-American War	Effect
• •	• Dewey destroys Spanish fleet	• U.S. acquires Philippines •

Why It Matters American power and economic interests around the world were growing. Still, the United States remained reluctant to risk war with other powers to acquire colonies. That changed, however, in 1898, when America went to war against Spain. The United States acquired colonies and became a world power. **Section Focus Question: What were the causes and effects of the Spanish-American War?**

Causes of the War

At the end of the nineteenth century, Spain was an imperial nation in decline. Its formerly vast empire had dwindled to a small number of possessions, including the Philippine Islands in the Pacific and the Caribbean islands of Puerto Rico and Cuba.

Cubans Rebel Against Spanish Rule By 1897, American entrepreneurs had invested $50 million in sugar cane plantations and other ventures in Cuba, which lay just 90 miles off the Florida coast. These businessmen saw Cuba as a growing market for American products. However, the island was very unstable. Yearning for freedom, the Cubans repeatedly rebelled against Spanish rule.

In 1895, Cuban patriot **José Martí** launched a war for independence from Spain. With cries of *"Cuba Libre!"* ("Free Cuba!"), rebel fighters used guerrilla tactics of hit-and-run raids against Spanish forces. In response, Spanish General Valeriano Weyler devised a

Rebellion in Cuba

Spain sent 150,000 troops and one of its best generals, Valeriano Weyler, to smash the uprising. Here, rebel cavalry forces charge into battle. *What attitude do you think the artist had toward the rebels? How can you tell?*

plan to deprive the rebels of food and recruits. He herded the rural population into reconcentration camps, where tens of thousands died from disease and starvation. Meanwhile, the Cubans and Spanish destroyed American property.

Many Americans favored the Cubans, whose struggle for freedom and democracy reminded Americans of their own revolutionary heritage. The brutality of Spanish tactics intensified American affection and sympathy for the rebels. But other Americans, especially business people, were worried about U.S. economic interests in Cuba and hoped that Spain would quickly put down the rebellion.

The Yellow Press Inflames Opinion Rival newspaper publishers Joseph Pulitzer and **William Randolph Hearst** heightened the public's dislike of the Spanish government. Their publications were called the **Yellow Press** because they featured a popular comic-strip character called The Yellow Kid. To boost readership, Pulitzer's *New York World,* Hearst's *New York Journal,* and similar newspapers pasted sensational headlines and pictures on their front pages. Their stories exaggerated Spanish atrocities and compared Cuban rebels to the patriots of the American Revolution.

President William McKinley warned the Spanish to quickly establish peace, or the United States would take whatever steps it "should deem necessary to procure this result." Spain recalled General Weyler and offered the Cuban rebels some reforms. But the rebels insisted on independence, which Spain refused to grant. McKinley ordered the battleship *Maine* to Havana harbor to protect American citizens in Cuba.

Then, in February 1898, the *Journal* published a private letter written by Enrique Dupuy de Lôme, Spain's ambassador to Washington, D.C. The letter, stolen by Cuban rebels and leaked to Hearst, called McKinley a weak and stupid politician. Hearst published the letter under the sensational headline, "Worst Insult to the United States in Its History." The letter fueled American **jingoism,** or aggressive nationalism, and inflamed relations with Spain.

The *Maine* Blows Up Soon after the *Journal* published de Lôme's letter, the *Maine* exploded in Havana harbor. Of the 350 officers and crew on board at the time, 266 died. The Yellow Press promptly accused Spain of blowing up the battleship. One *Journal* headline even declared: "War? Sure!"

But President McKinley did not ask Congress to declare war just yet. Instead, he ordered a special naval board of inquiry to investigate the cause of the explosion. On March 28, 1898, the board concluded that a mine had destroyed the battleship. Years later, follow-up investigations raised doubts about the naval board's findings, but, at the time, most people blamed Spain.

The Nation Goes to War War fever gripped the nation. In newspapers, speeches, and songs, patriotic Americans implored their fellow citizens to "Remember the *Maine*!" In response to American demands, Spain agreed to abolish the reconcentration camps and make other concessions, but it was too little too late. On April 11, 1898, McKinley asked Congress for the authority to use force against Spain to end the fighting in Cuba "in the name of humanity, in the name of civilization, in behalf of endangered American interests."

Eight days later, Congress enacted four resolutions that amounted to a declaration of war on Spain. The fourth resolution—the Teller Amendment—stipulated that the United States had no intention of annexing Cuba. The navy quickly blockaded Cuban ports, and McKinley called for more than 100,000 volunteers to join the army. In response, Spain declared war on the United States.

✔ **Checkpoint** Why did Americans object to Spanish actions in Cuba?

Vocabulary Builder
stipulate – (STIHP yuh layt) *v.* to include specifically in the terms of an agreement

Spanish misrule of Cuba and the sinking of the USS *Maine* moved the nation toward war with Spain. ▼

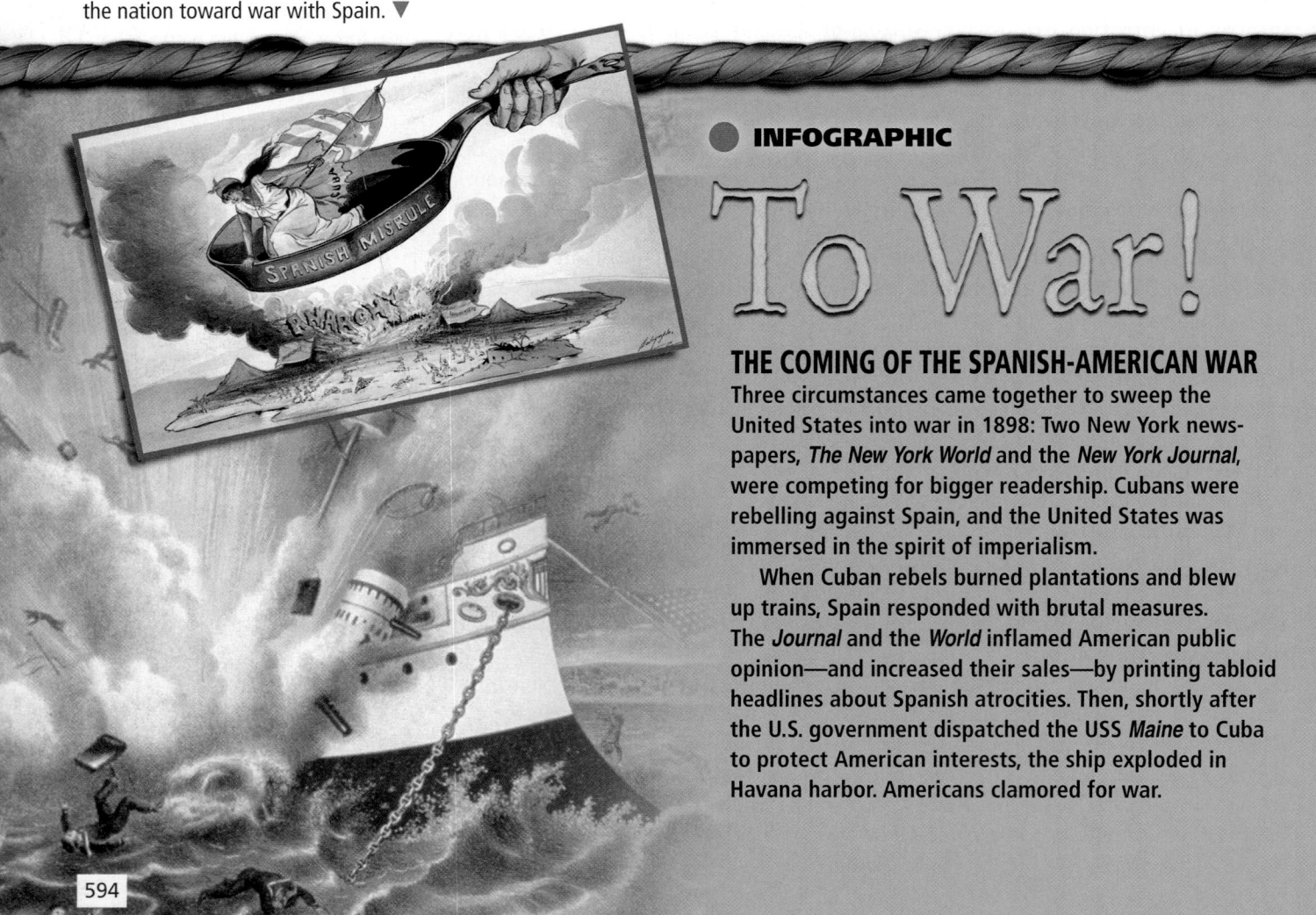

● **INFOGRAPHIC**

To War!

THE COMING OF THE SPANISH-AMERICAN WAR
Three circumstances came together to sweep the United States into war in 1898: Two New York newspapers, *The New York World* and the *New York Journal*, were competing for bigger readership. Cubans were rebelling against Spain, and the United States was immersed in the spirit of imperialism.

When Cuban rebels burned plantations and blew up trains, Spain responded with brutal measures. The *Journal* and the *World* inflamed American public opinion—and increased their sales—by printing tabloid headlines about Spanish atrocities. Then, shortly after the U.S. government dispatched the USS *Maine* to Cuba to protect American interests, the ship exploded in Havana harbor. Americans clamored for war.

American Troops Battle the Spanish

Americans responded enthusiastically to the war. About 200,000 men enlisted in the army, up from the 25,000 that enlisted at the beginning of 1898. In early May, as the United States Army prepared to attack, Americans heard news of a great naval victory over Spain. But, surprisingly, the victory was not in Cuba. Rather, it was in the Pacific Ocean, on the opposite side of the world.

Dewey Takes the Philippines On May 1, 1898, Commodore **George Dewey** steamed his squadron of vessels into Manila Bay, in the Spanish-held Philippines. The Americans completely surprised the Spanish fleet that was stationed in the bay. Upon issuing the order to "fire when ready," Dewey watched his ships quickly destroy the Spanish force. While no American died during the naval battle, nearly 400 Spanish sailors lost their lives. Americans gleefully received news of the victory and proclaimed Dewey a hero.

While Dewey was winning an astounding victory over the Spanish navy, Filipino nationalists led by **Emilio Aguinaldo** (ahg ee NAHL doh) were defeating the Spanish army. Like the Cubans, the Filipinos were fighting for freedom from Spain. In August, after some 15,000 U.S. soldiers had landed on the islands, Spanish troops surrendered to the United States.

U.S. Forces Win in Cuba Meanwhile, American troops landed in Cuba in June 1898. U.S. Marines captured Guantánamo Bay, and a force of 17,000 soldiers under U.S. Army General William Shafter stormed ashore east of Santiago.

In spite of their excitement for the war, the troops faced deplorable conditions. They were poorly trained and supplied. As they assembled for duty around

With each new headline, the Yellow Press sold more papers to Americans angry with Spain. ▼

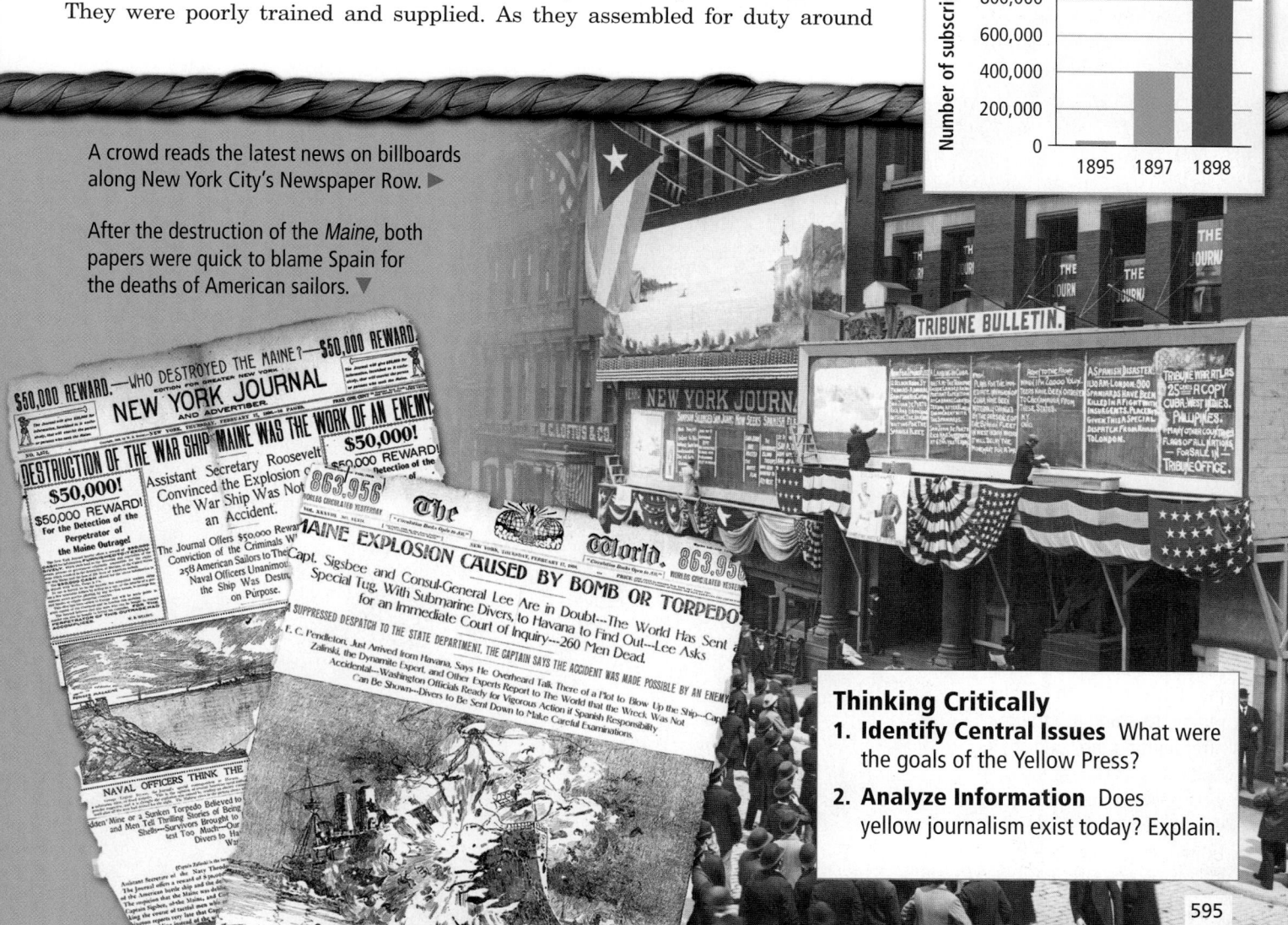

New York Journal Sales

A crowd reads the latest news on billboards along New York City's Newspaper Row. ▶

After the destruction of the *Maine*, both papers were quick to blame Spain for the deaths of American sailors. ▼

Thinking Critically
1. **Identify Central Issues** What were the goals of the Yellow Press?
2. **Analyze Information** Does yellow journalism exist today? Explain.

Tampa, Florida, the soldiers were issued <u>obsolete</u> weapons and heavy wool uniforms that were unsuitable for Cuba's tropical climate. Corrupt and inefficient officials provided the men with rotting and contaminated food.

General Shafter's army consisted of state National Guard units and regular army units, including the African American Ninth and Tenth Cavalry regiments from the western frontier. Another cavalry unit was organized and commanded by the future President Theodore Roosevelt. His **Rough Riders** consisted of rugged westerners and upper-class easterners who relished what Roosevelt called the "strenuous life."

The Rough Riders and Roosevelt gained fame for the role they played in the battles for Kettle and San Juan hills outside Santiago, Cuba. Joined by African American soldiers from the Ninth and Tenth Cavalries, the Riders stormed up those hills to secure high ground surrounding Santiago. One war correspondent described a charge of the African American soldiers:

> **Primary Source** "[T]hey followed their leader up the terrible hill from whose crest the desperate Spaniards poured down a deadly fire of shell and musketry. They never faltered. . . . [T]heir aim was splendid, their coolness was superb. . . . The war had not shown greater heroism."
>
> —War correspondent, 1898

Two days after the battle of San Juan Hill, the Spanish navy made a desperate attempt to escape from Santiago's harbor. U.S. forces, which had blockaded the harbor, destroyed the Spanish fleet as it tried to break out. Surrounded, outnumbered, and dispirited, Spanish forces in Santiago surrendered. Although a few battles followed when U.S. forces occupied the island of Puerto Rico, another Spanish

▼ Regimental flag carried by African American soldiers

African Americans Serve Their Country

African American soldiers of the Ninth and Tenth Cavalry regiments stand at attention after fighting the Spanish in Cuba. The medals above were won by Augustus L. Reed, an African American officer in the United States Navy.

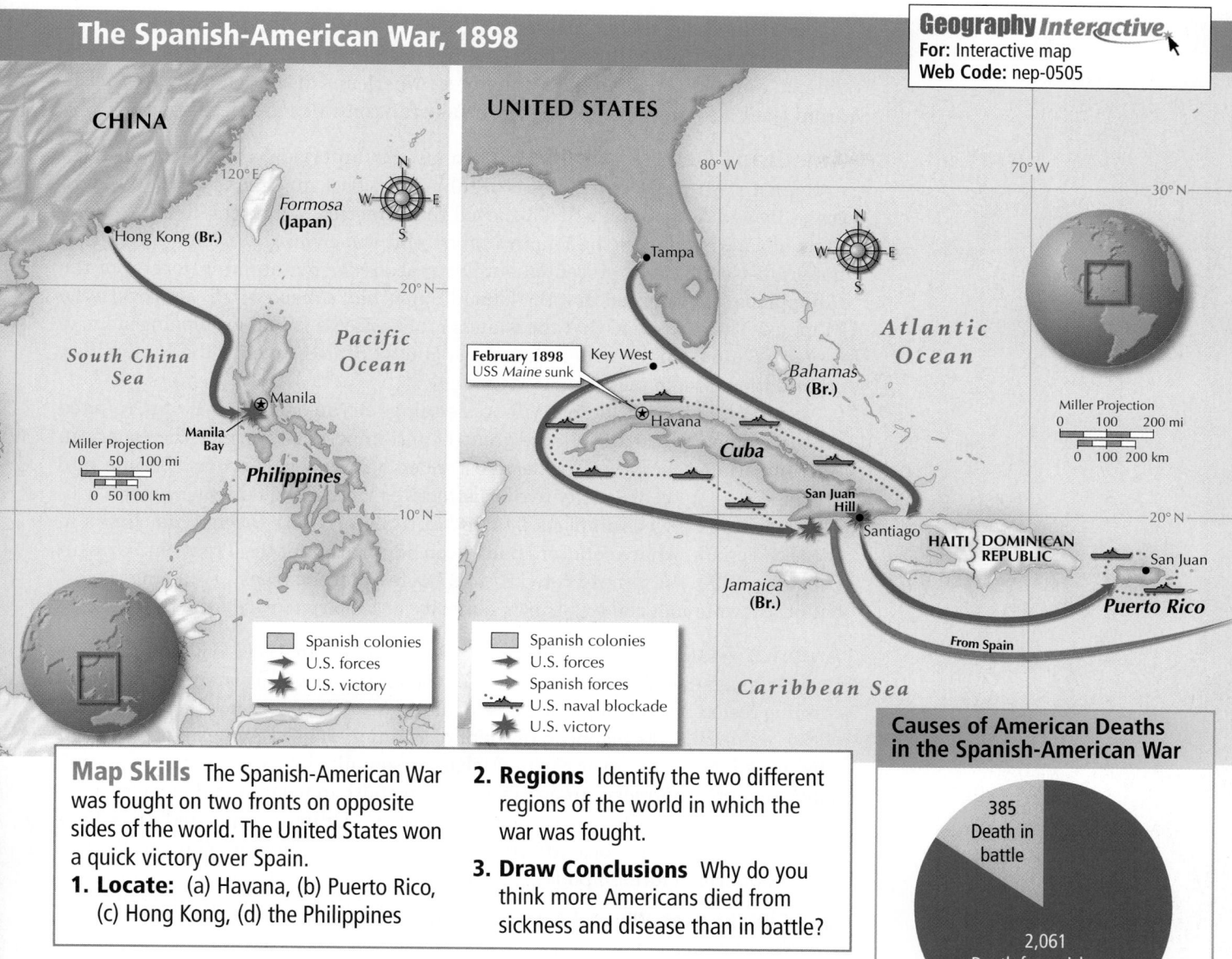

The Spanish-American War, 1898

Geography *Interactive*
For: Interactive map
Web Code: nep-0505

CHINA

Hong Kong (Br.)

Formosa
(Japan)

South China
Sea

Pacific
Ocean

Manila

Manila
Bay

Philippines

Miller Projection
0   50   100 mi

0 50 100 km

Spanish colonies
U.S. forces
U.S. victory

UNITED STATES

80° W   70° W

30° N

Tampa

February 1898
USS *Maine* sunk   Key West

Bahamas
(Br.)

Havana

Atlantic
Ocean

Cuba

20° N

10° N

San Juan
Hill

Santiago

HAITI DOMINICAN
REPUBLIC

San Juan

Jamaica
(Br.)

Puerto Rico

From Spain

Caribbean Sea

Miller Projection
0   100   200 mi

0 100 200 km

20° N

Spanish colonies
U.S. forces
Spanish forces
U.S. naval blockade
U.S. victory

Map Skills The Spanish-American War was fought on two fronts on opposite sides of the world. The United States won a quick victory over Spain.
1. Locate: (a) Havana, (b) Puerto Rico, (c) Hong Kong, (d) the Philippines

2. Regions Identify the two different regions of the world in which the war was fought.

3. Draw Conclusions Why do you think more Americans died from sickness and disease than in battle?

Causes of American Deaths in the Spanish-American War

385
Death in battle

2,061
Death from sickness and disease

SOURCE: *Historical Statistics of the United States*

possession, the fighting had come to an end. Although almost 3,000 Americans died during the war, only around 380 died in combat. Disease, especially malaria and yellow fever, caused most of the deaths.

✔ **Checkpoint** How did the Rough Riders and African American cavalry units contribute to the war effort?

Effects of the War

Secretary of State John Hay referred to the conflict with Spain as a "splendid little war" because of the ease and thoroughness of America's victory. Although the war may have been "splendid," it created a new dilemma for Americans: What should the United States do with Spain's former possessions?

The Treaty of Paris Signed by Spain and the United States in December 1898, the **Treaty of Paris** officially ended the war. Spain gave up control of Cuba, Puerto Rico, and the Pacific island of Guam. It also sold the Philippines to the United States for $20 million.

The Teller Amendment, passed by Congress when it declared war on Spain, prevented the United States from taking possession of Cuba. The amendment did not, however, apply to the Philippines. Americans disagreed over whether to grant the Philippines independence or take full control of the Pacific nation.

Americans Debate Imperialism In an 1899 interview, President McKinley explained, "We could not give [the Philippines] back to Spain—that would be cowardly and dishonorable." He believed that America had no choice but to "take them all, and to educate the Filipinos, and uplift and civilize . . . them." McKinley's imperialist supporters presented similar reasons for maintaining control of the Philippines. They argued that the United States had a responsibility to govern the Filipinos. They reasoned that the islands represented a valuable stepping stone to trade in China. They warned that if the United States gave up the Philippines, other nations would take control of them.

Anti-imperialists, including William Jennings Bryan and Mark Twain, rejected these arguments. In 1899, a large group of anti-imperialists formed the American Anti-Imperialist League. The league condemned imperialism as a crime and attacked it as "open disloyalty to the distinctive principles of our government."

The debate between imperialists and anti-imperialists reached its climax in the U.S. Senate, where senators had to consider ratifying the Treaty of Paris. In February 1899, the Senate voted 57 to 27 in favor of the treaty. By a single "yes" ballot, the vote met the two-thirds majority necessary to ratify the treaty.

America Assumes a New Role in the World In 1900, William Jennings Bryan ran against William McKinley for the presidency. To bolster his chances of winning reelection, the Republican McKinley named Theodore Roosevelt, the "hero of San Juan Hill," as his vice-presidential running mate. Emphasizing the overwhelming U.S. victory over Spain, McKinley soundly defeated Bryan. The President's reelection signaled America's continuing faith in his imperialist policies.

As a result of the Spanish-American War, the United States had an empire and a new stature in world affairs. The war marked a turning point in the history of American foreign policy.

✓ **Checkpoint** Why did American leaders think it was important to keep the Philippines?

SECTION **2 Assessment**

Progress Monitoring *Online*
For: Self-test with vocabulary practice
Web Code: nea-0506

Comprehension

1. **Terms and People** What do the following terms and people have in common?
   - José Martí
   - William Randolph Hearst
   - Yellow Press
   - jingoism

2. **NoteTaking Reading Skill: Identify Causes and Effects** Use your cause-and-effect chart to answer the Section Focus Question: What were the causes and effects of the Spanish-American War?

Writing About History

3. **Quick Write: Gather Details** When you write a narrative essay, you often need to gather details about your topic. Suppose that you want to write a narrative diary entry as a witness to the destruction of the USS *Maine*. Conduct research to find descriptions of the explosion and illustrations of the event from newspapers of the time. You may want to research particular newspapers such as the *New York World* and the *New York Journal*.

Critical Thinking

4. **Draw Conclusions** Do you think the United States would have gone to war with Spain without the explosion of the *Maine*? Why or why not?

5. **Identify Points of View** Who might agree with John Hay's opinion that the Spanish-American War was a "splendid little war"? Who might disagree? Why?

6. **Summarize** What were the principal issues dividing imperialists and anti-imperialists?

A Plea for Peace

Sixto Lopez, a leading Filipino spokesman, wrote to President McKinley to express his disapproval of America's decision to keep control of the Philippines. When he wrote the letter, many Filipinos had already taken up arms against the U.S. military.

❝I only know that the Filipino people are asking for [what] the American people have enjoyed for more than a hundred years. . . . At this season of peace I plead for peace. I plead on behalf of the wife and mother whose cheeks are coursing the silent tears . . . on behalf of the sad little faces, too young to realize what has happened. . . .**❞**

—Sixto Lopez, 1900

▲ An American soldier and two Filipino women

SECTION 3

The United States and East Asia

NY **Core Curriculum Objectives**

- **1.I.A.4** Barriers to expansion/development
- **4.II.A.1** From old diplomacy to new, 1865–1900
- **4.II.A.2a** Other Pacific overtures: United States and China; Boxer Rebellion
- **4.II.A.2b** Other Pacific overtures: The Open-Door policy

Terms and People

insurrection	Open Door Policy
guerrilla warfare	Russo-Japanese War
William Howard Taft	"Gentlemen's
sphere of influence	Agreement"
John Hay	Great White Fleet
Boxer Rebellion	

NoteTaking

Reading Skill: Recognize Sequence As you read, use a timeline to trace events and developments in East Asia that tested America's new global power.

Filipino insurrection begins

1898   1901   1904   1907

Why It Matters America's decision to keep the Philippines reflected a desire to expand its influence, compete with European colonial powers, and gain new trade in Asia. American leaders devised policies to open China and other Asian markets to U.S. producers. They also wanted to extend the benefits of American culture to the people of the region. Imperialism in East Asia brought greater power and wealth to Americans, but it also increased international tensions in Asia. **Section Focus Question: How did the United States extend its influence in Asia?**

Filipinos Rebel Against U.S. Rule

The Filipino nationalist leader Emilio Aguinaldo had thought that the United States was an ally in the Filipino struggle for independence. His forces had fought side by side with the Americans against the Spanish. However, after the United States decided to maintain possession of the Philippines, Aguinaldo grew disillusioned with America. He helped organize an **insurrection,** or rebellion, against U.S. rule. The rebels believed they were fighting for the same principle of self-rule that had inspired America's colonial patriots during the American Revolution.

Guerrilla War Erupts in the Philippines Outgunned by American troops, Filipino insurgents relied on **guerrilla warfare,** a form of non-traditional warfare generally involving small bands of fighters

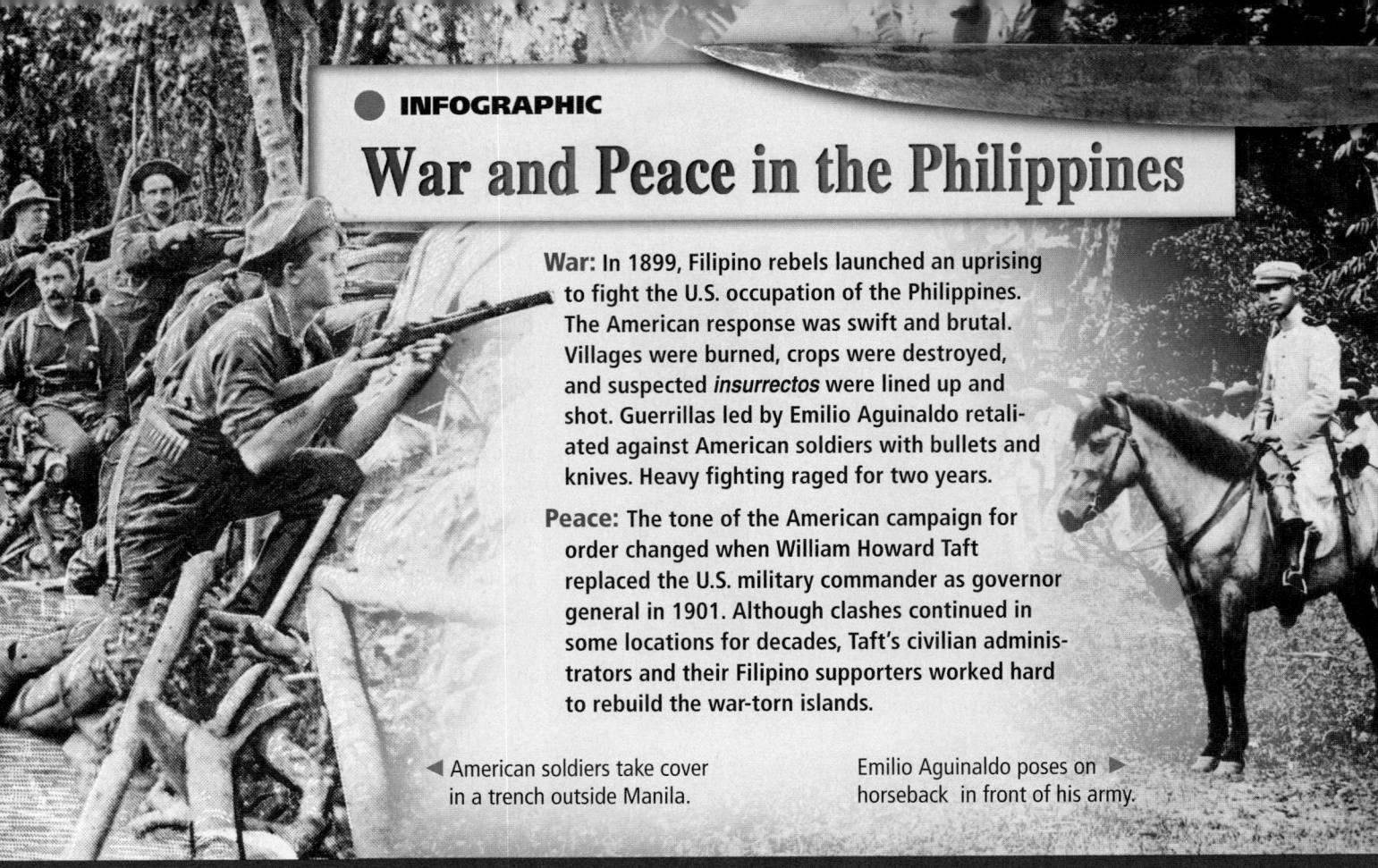

INFOGRAPHIC

War and Peace in the Philippines

War: In 1899, Filipino rebels launched an uprising to fight the U.S. occupation of the Philippines. The American response was swift and brutal. Villages were burned, crops were destroyed, and suspected *insurrectos* were lined up and shot. Guerrillas led by Emilio Aguinaldo retaliated against American soldiers with bullets and knives. Heavy fighting raged for two years.

Peace: The tone of the American campaign for order changed when William Howard Taft replaced the U.S. military commander as governor general in 1901. Although clashes continued in some locations for decades, Taft's civilian administrators and their Filipino supporters worked hard to rebuild the war-torn islands.

◄ American soldiers take cover in a trench outside Manila.

Emilio Aguinaldo poses on ► horseback in front of his army.

to attack behind American lines. In turn, the American military used extraordinary measures to crush the rebellion. Like the Spanish in Cuba, U.S. soldiers gathered civilians into overcrowded concentration camps. General Jacob Smith ordered his soldiers not to take prisoners. "I wish you to kill and burn, the more you kill and burn the better you will please me," he commented. A California newspaper defended such actions:

> **Primary Source** "Let us all be frank. WE DO NOT WANT THE FILIPINOS. WE DO WANT THE PHILIPPINES. All of our troubles in this annexation matter have been caused by the presence in the Philippine Islands of the Filipinos. . . . The more of them killed the better. It seems harsh. But they must yield before the superior race."
> —San Francisco *Argonaut,* 1902

In the spring of 1901, the Americans captured Aguinaldo. Although the fighting did not end immediately, his capture marked the beginning of the end of the insurrection. The war in the Philippines took more lives than the Spanish-American War. Nearly 5,000 Americans and 200,000 Filipinos died in the fighting. The U.S. government sent more than 100,000 troops to fight in the war and spent upwards of $400 million to defeat the insurgency. The conflict highlighted the <u>rigors</u> of fighting against guerrilla insurgents.

Reforms Lead to Promise of Self-Rule In 1901, **William Howard Taft**—a future President of the United States—became governor of the Philippines. Taft had large ambitions for helping the islands recover from the rebellion. He censored the press and placed dissidents in jail to maintain order and to win the support of the Filipino people. At the same time, he extended limited self-rule and ordered the construction of schools, roads, and bridges.

Vocabulary Builder
<u>rigor</u> – (RIHG uhr) *n.* extreme hardship or difficulty

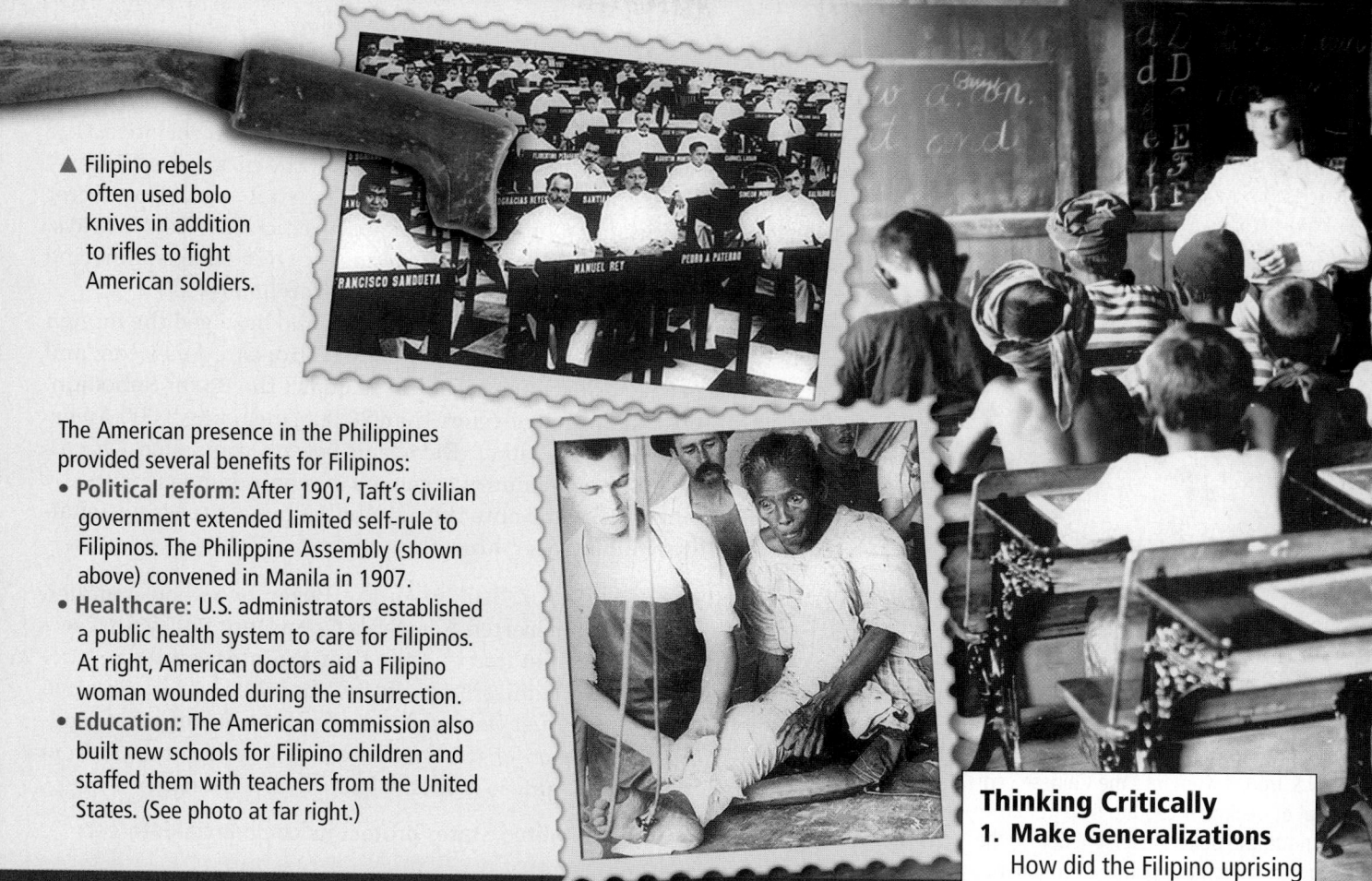

▲ Filipino rebels often used bolo knives in addition to rifles to fight American soldiers.

The American presence in the Philippines provided several benefits for Filipinos:

- **Political reform:** After 1901, Taft's civilian government extended limited self-rule to Filipinos. The Philippine Assembly (shown above) convened in Manila in 1907.
- **Healthcare:** U.S. administrators established a public health system to care for Filipinos. At right, American doctors aid a Filipino woman wounded during the insurrection.
- **Education:** The American commission also built new schools for Filipino children and staffed them with teachers from the United States. (See photo at far right.)

In 1916, Congress passed the Jones Act, which pledged that the Philippines would ultimately gain their independence. Thirty years later, after U.S. forces liberated the islands from Japanese occupation at the end of World War II, the Philippines finally became an independent nation.

✔ **Checkpoint** Why did hostilities erupt in the Philippines after the Spanish-American War?

The United States Pursues Interests in China

By 1899, once-mighty China had fallen into political, economic, and military disarray. Its huge population, however, was a tempting target for other nations' imported goods. Rather than compete for Chinese trade, Britain, France, Germany, and Russia carved China into distinct **spheres of influence.** Within its zone, each power had privileged access to Chinese ports and markets. Japan also expanded its regional influence, grabbing territory in China and Korea. Since the United States did not have a zone, this system of "special privileges" threatened to limit American trade in China.

America Declares Equal Trade in China In order to overcome these barriers, U.S. Secretary of State **John Hay** issued the first of a series of notes to foreign diplomats in 1899. He notified the leaders of imperialist nations that the United States expected "perfect equality of treatment for commerce" in China. Hay's note had little immediate impact on the actions of European nations or Japan. However, it served as a guiding principle of American foreign policy in Asia for years to come.

Thinking Critically
1. **Make Generalizations** How did the Filipino uprising present a new challenge to American soldiers?

2. **Explain Effects** What two things happened in 1901 that signaled a shift in the rebellion?

History *Interactive*
For: To discover more about the Filipino insurrection
Web Code: nep-0509

The U.S. Intervenes in the Boxer Rebellion In response to the growing influence of outsiders in their country, some Chinese joined secret societies. One such society, the Righteous and Harmonious Fists, won the nickname "Boxers" from Europeans because its members trained in martial arts. The secret societies celebrated traditional Chinese customs and criticized Western ways. They also condemned Chinese converts to Christianity. Over time, simmering anger exploded into an outright rebellion against the "foreign devils."

In May 1900, the Boxers killed foreign missionaries and besieged the foreign diplomats' district in Beijing. A multinational force of European, American, and Japanese troops was sent to the Chinese capital to quash the **Boxer Rebellion.** An initial force of 2,100 soldiers grew to more than 20,000, including 2,000 Americans. After putting down the rebellion, European powers compelled China's imperial government to pay an indemnity, or money to repair damage caused by the rebellion. This poured more fuel onto the nationalist fire. Chinese nationalists would eventually revolt and overthrow the emperor in 1911.

Hay Reaffirms the Open Door Policy As the Boxer Rebellion engulfed China, Secretary of State Hay reasserted America's **Open Door Policy.** In a second note to European powers, Hay stated that the United States wanted to "preserve Chinese territorial and administrative entity." In other words, America did not want colonies in China; it just wanted free trade there. As an act of goodwill, the United States used some of the indemnity money it received from China to fund scholarships for Chinese students to study in America.

✔ **Checkpoint** How did the United States protect its commercial interests in China?

Tensions Rise Between America and Japan

Like the United States, Japan wanted to expand its influence in China. Japan also disapproved of the European "carve-up" of the region. Furthermore, the Japanese took offense to the presence of Russian troops in Manchuria, a region of China that bordered Russia. In February 1904, without a declaration of war, Japan attacked and bottled up Russia's Pacific fleet stationed at Port Arthur, China. The Japanese followed up on this victory with a series of major land engagements in Manchuria that caused more than 100,000 Russian casualties. However, Japan also suffered heavy losses in the fighting.

American Soldiers Rescue Diplomats in China
U.S. troops went into the Chinese capital of Beijing in 1900 to help put an end to the Boxer Rebellion. Below, the troops march through the Forbidden City in close ranks.

Roosevelt Settles the Russo-Japanese War In 1905, representatives from Russia and Japan met in Portsmouth, New Hampshire, to negotiate an end to the **Russo-Japanese War.** When the talks stalled, President Theodore Roosevelt intervened and convinced the two sides to sign a peace treaty. (Roosevelt had become President when McKinley was assassinated in 1901.) For his efforts, Roosevelt won the Nobel Peace Prize. The President's intervention—and his receipt of the famous award—prominently displayed America's growing role in world affairs.

Anti-Asian Prejudice Troubles Relations Despite Roosevelt's achievement, America entered troubled waters in its relations with Japan. A root cause of this trouble was anti-Asian sentiment on the West Coast of the United States. In the fall of 1906, the San Francisco School Board banned Japanese, Chinese, and Korean children from attending public schools with white children. The incident drew Japan's immediate wrath. One Tokyo journal demanded that Japan retaliate. "Stand up Japanese nation! Our countrymen have been HUMILIATED on the other side of the Pacific," the newspaper cried out.

Roosevelt disapproved of the decision to segregate Asian children in the San Francisco schools. He understood Japan's anger with America. To calm tensions, he negotiated a **"Gentlemen's Agreement"** with Japan. According to the pact, the school board pledged to end its segregation policy. In return, Japan agreed to limit the emigration of its citizens to the United States.

The Great White Fleet Sets Sail While Roosevelt used diplomacy to ease tensions with Japan, he also promoted military preparedness to protect U.S. interests in Asia. Expressing rising concerns about Japan's territorial expansion at the expense of China, Korea, and Russia—the President won congressional support for a new force of navy ships, known as the **Great White Fleet.** In 1907, Roosevelt sent this armada of 16 white battleships on a "good will cruise" around the world. The voyage of the Great White Fleet demonstrated America's increased military power to the world.

A Mighty American Fleet
After stopping at several Latin American ports, the Great White Fleet moved on to Asia and made a friendly visit to the Japanese port city of Yokohama. *How do you think the Japanese felt about the U.S. warships' visit?*

✔ **Checkpoint** What were some of the difficulties America faced in maintaining good relations with Japan?

SECTION
3 Assessment

Progress Monitoring *Online*
For: Self-test with vocabulary practice
Web Code: nea-0507

Comprehension

1. **Terms and People** For each item below, write a sentence explaining its significance.
   - insurrection
   - guerrilla warfare
   - William Howard Taft
   - Boxer Rebellion
   - Open Door Policy

2. **NoteTaking Reading Skill: Recognize Sequence** Use your timeline to answer the Section Focus Question: How did the United States extend its influence in Asia?

Writing About History

3. **Quick Write: Write an Introduction** A narrative essay needs an introduction that "hooks" a reader and draws him or her into your story. Suppose that you want to write a narrative from the perspective of an American sailor aboard a battleship in the Great White Fleet. Draft an introduction that captures the excitement and purpose of the fleet's departure from America.

Critical Thinking

4. **Recognize Bias** Based on what you have read, what role do you think racial attitudes played in U.S. policy in the Philippines?

5. **Analyze Information** Identify two threats to U.S. interests in China, and describe how the U.S. government responded to those threats.

6. **Apply Information** How do President Roosevelt's actions toward Japan illustrate the use of diplomacy and compromise?

TAFT BIDS NATION BE WORLD POWER

DOLLARS VERSUS BULLETS

American Capital Must Be Employed if We Are to Get Our Share of Markets.

...CY ABOVE PARTIES

...Efficient Representatives and of Broad Policies ...place Expediency.

..., Dec. 3.—Declaring that ... on the threshold ... having ... the ...

◀ Newspaper announcing Taft's goal

▲ William Howard Taft

WITNESS HISTORY ◀)) AUDIO

Dollars for Bullets

Like President Roosevelt, President William Howard Taft stressed the need to assert American power around the world. Taft's "dollar diplomacy" aimed to expand American investments abroad:

❝The diplomacy of the present administration . . . has been characterized as substituting dollars for bullets. . . . It is [a policy] frankly directed to the increase of American trade upon the axiomatic principle that the government of the United States shall extend all proper support to every legitimate and beneficial American enterprise abroad.**❞**
—President William Howard Taft, 1912

The United States and Latin America

NY Core Curriculum Objectives

- **4.II.A.4b** Latin American affairs: West Indies protectorates ("the big stick")
- **4.II.A.4c** Latin American affairs: Panama Canal: acquisition and construction; Canal retrocession treaty

Terms and People

Foraker Act
Platt Amendment
"big stick" diplomacy
Panama Canal

Roosevelt Corollary
"dollar diplomacy"
"moral diplomacy"
Francisco "Pancho" Villa

NoteTaking

Reading Skill: Identify Supporting Details Complete a table like the one below to note how the U.S. dealt with Puerto Rico and Cuba.

American Policy After Spanish-American War	
Puerto Rico	**Cuba**
• Foraker Act establishes civil government in 1900	•
•	•

Why It Matters As the United States tentatively asserted its interests in East Asia, Americans called for a more aggressive role in Latin America. American entrepreneurs and government leaders viewed the region as the nation's backyard and as a sphere of influence from which other great powers should be excluded. American influence in Latin America brought obvious benefits to the United States, but it also contributed to anti-American hostility and instability in the region. **Section Focus Question: What actions did the United States take to achieve its goals in Latin America?**

U.S. Policy in Puerto Rico and Cuba

America's victory over Spain liberated the Puerto Rican and Cuban people from Spanish rule. But victory left the fates of these islands unresolved. Would Puerto Rico and Cuba become independent nations? Or would they become colonies of the United States? As questions lingered in the aftermath of war, the United States assumed control in Puerto Rico and Cuba.

Civil Government in Puerto Rico As the smoke from the Spanish-American War cleared, Puerto Rico remained under direct U.S. military rule. In 1900, Congress passed the **Foraker Act,** which established a civil government in Puerto Rico. The act authorized the President of the United States to appoint a governor and part of the Puerto Rican legislature. Puerto Ricans could fill the rest of the legislature in a general election.

Whether Puerto Ricans could enjoy citizenship rights in the United States, however, remained unclear. This unusual situation led to a series of court cases, known as Insular Cases, in which the Supreme Court determined the rights of Puerto Ricans. One case examined whether the U.S. government could <u>assess</u> taxes on Puerto Rican goods sold in the United States. The Supreme Court ruled the taxes legal and determined that Puerto Ricans did not enjoy the same rights as U.S. citizens.

In 1917, President Woodrow Wilson signed the Jones-Shafroth Act. It granted Puerto Ricans more citizenship rights and gave the islanders greater control over their own legislature. Still, many Puerto Ricans expressed their discontent because they did not enjoy all of the same rights as Americans.

Vocabulary Builder

<u>assess</u>—(uh SEHS) *v.* to impose a fine, tax, or special payment on a person or property

United States Establishes Cuban Protectorate

Although the Treaty of Paris granted Cuban independence, the United States Army did not withdraw from the island until 1902. But before the U.S. military left, Congress obliged Cuba to add to its constitution the **Platt Amendment.** The amendment restricted the rights of newly independent Cubans and effectively brought the island within the U.S. sphere. It prevented Cuba from signing a treaty with another nation without American approval. It also required Cuba to lease naval stations to the United States. Additionally, the Platt Amendment granted the United States the "right to intervene" to preserve order in Cuba.

Many Cubans strongly disliked the Platt Amendment but soon realized that America would not otherwise end its military government of the island. The United States, for its part, was unwilling to risk Cuba's becoming a base for a potentially hostile great power. Cuba thus added the Platt Amendment to its constitution as part of a treaty with the United States. The treaty made Cuba a protectorate of the United States and governed their relationship for decades.

✔ **Checkpoint** Why did Cubans dislike the Platt Amendment?

Roosevelt Pursues "Big Stick" Diplomacy

Upon assuming the presidency after McKinley's assassination, Theodore Roosevelt promoted a new kind of diplomacy based on America's success in the Spanish-American War. Beyond determining what would happen to Puerto Rico and Cuba, Roosevelt developed a broader policy for U.S. action in Latin America. Historians have called this Roosevelt's **"big stick" diplomacy** since it depended on a strong military to achieve America's goals. "Big stick" stemmed from the President's admiration for an old African saying, "Speak softly and carry a big stick; you will go far."

Roosevelt's view that America needed to carry a big stick during the Age of Imperialism flowed from his adherence to balance-of-power principles and from his view of the United States as a special nation with a moral responsibility to "civilize," or uplift, weaker nations. In this sense, the new President held beliefs similar to those of other imperial powers in Europe and Asia. Roosevelt also felt that America's elite—its statesmen and captains of industry—had to accept the challenge of international leadership.

HISTORY MAKERS

Theodore Roosevelt (1858–1919)

As a boy, Theodore Roosevelt suffered from asthma and poor eyesight. Determined not to be held back by physical limitations, he took on an active program of exercise that included boxing and horseback riding.

In 1898, when Roosevelt was Assistant Secretary of the Navy, he again showcased his determination. Two months before the United States declared war on Spain, he secretly ordered Commodore George Dewey to sail for Hong Kong, within striking distance of the Philippines. Thus, when the war began, U.S. ships were instantly ready to attack the Spanish fleet in Manila Bay. Soon after Dewey's victory, Roosevelt resigned from his post and organized the Rough Riders.

The Panama Canal

The construction of the Panama Canal was a monumental engineering feat. It fulfilled a vision of shortening the travel distance between the Atlantic and Pacific oceans that traced back to when the Spanish first began shipping gold and silver from the Americas in the 1500s. To complete the canal, workers built a series of locks to raise ships to the level of Gatún Lake, 85 feet above sea level, to cross the isthmus. (See the diagram below.) From 1904 to 1913, tens of thousands of laborers worked on the canal. In the end, the challenge of the landscape was overshadowed by the threat of the deadly mosquito, which spread yellow fever and malaria. "If we do not control malaria, our mortality is going to be heavy," warned Dr. William Gorgas, a United States Army surgeon. He convinced the chief engineer that fighting the mosquito was vital to keeping American steam shovels in action.

▲ In 1898, the U.S. battleship *Oregon* raced around South America to fight the Spanish in Cuba. Without a Central American canal to shorten its voyage to Florida, the *Oregon* spent more than two months at sea.

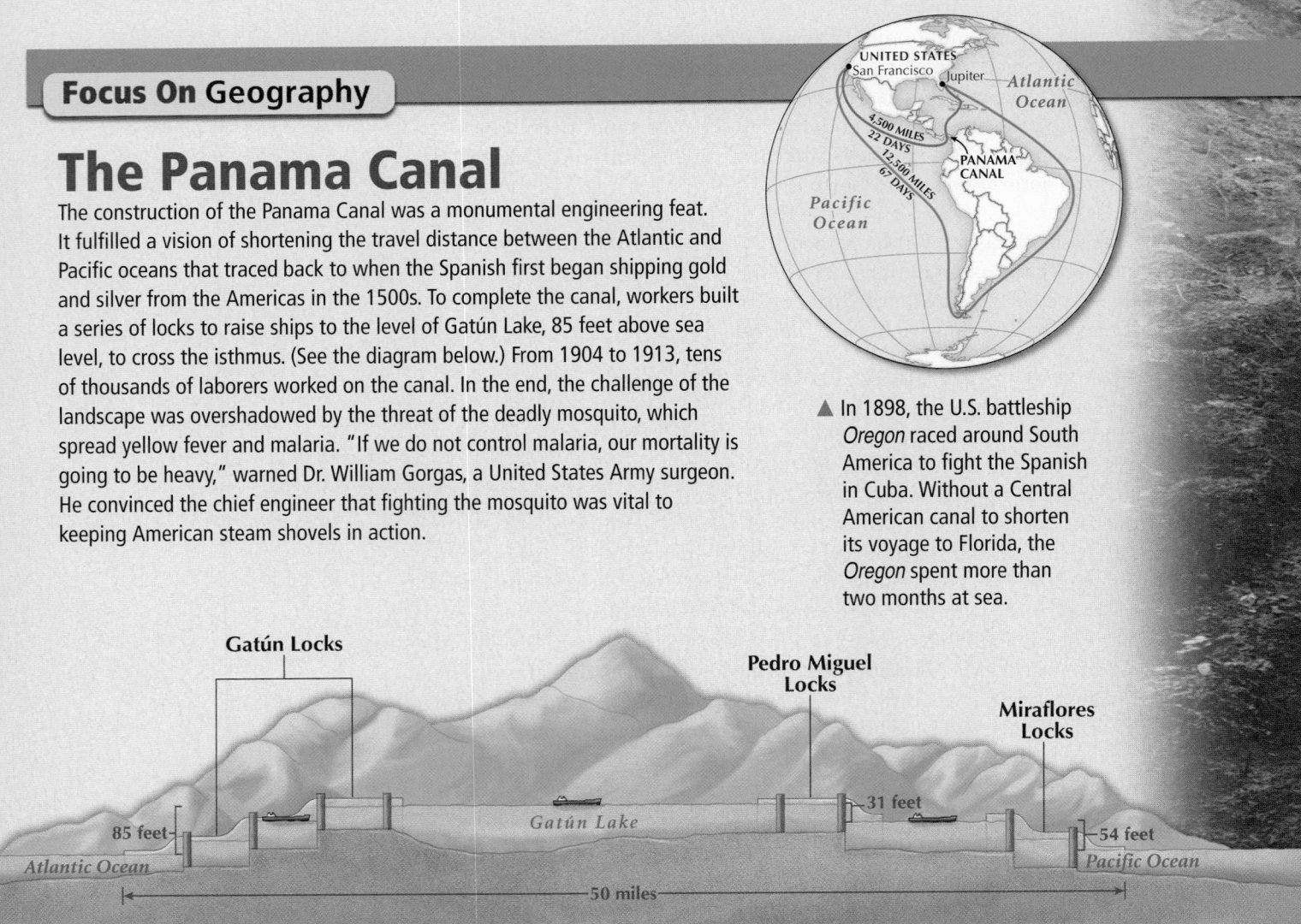

Gatún Locks

Pedro Miguel Locks

Miraflores Locks

Gatún Lake

85 feet

31 feet

54 feet

Atlantic Ocean

Pacific Ocean

50 miles

Vocabulary Builder

nevertheless–(nehv er thuh LEHS) *adv.* in spite of that; however

America Builds the Panama Canal Although the plan to dig a canal across Central America did not originate with Roosevelt, he <u>nevertheless</u> played a crucial role in its history. In the late 1800s, a French company had tried to link the Atlantic to the Pacific across the Isthmus of Panama but failed. Afterward, some suggested building a canal through Nicaragua. However, those plans came to nothing. Eventually, an agent from the French company that had abandoned its canal attempt convinced the United States to buy the company's claim. In 1903, the U.S. government bought the Panama route for $40 million.

Before it could build a canal through Panama, however, the United States needed the consent of the Colombian government. At that time, Panama was part of independent Colombia. American efforts to negotiate a purchase of land across the isthmus stalled when Colombia demanded more than the United States was willing to provide.

So Roosevelt stepped in. The President dispatched U.S. warships to the waters off Panama to support a Panamanian rebellion against Colombia. The appearance of the United States Navy convinced the Colombians not to suppress the uprising. Panama soon declared its independence from Colombia. The new nation immediately granted America control over the "Canal Zone." To secure this land for its vital trade link, America agreed to pay Panama $10 million and an annual rent of $250,000.

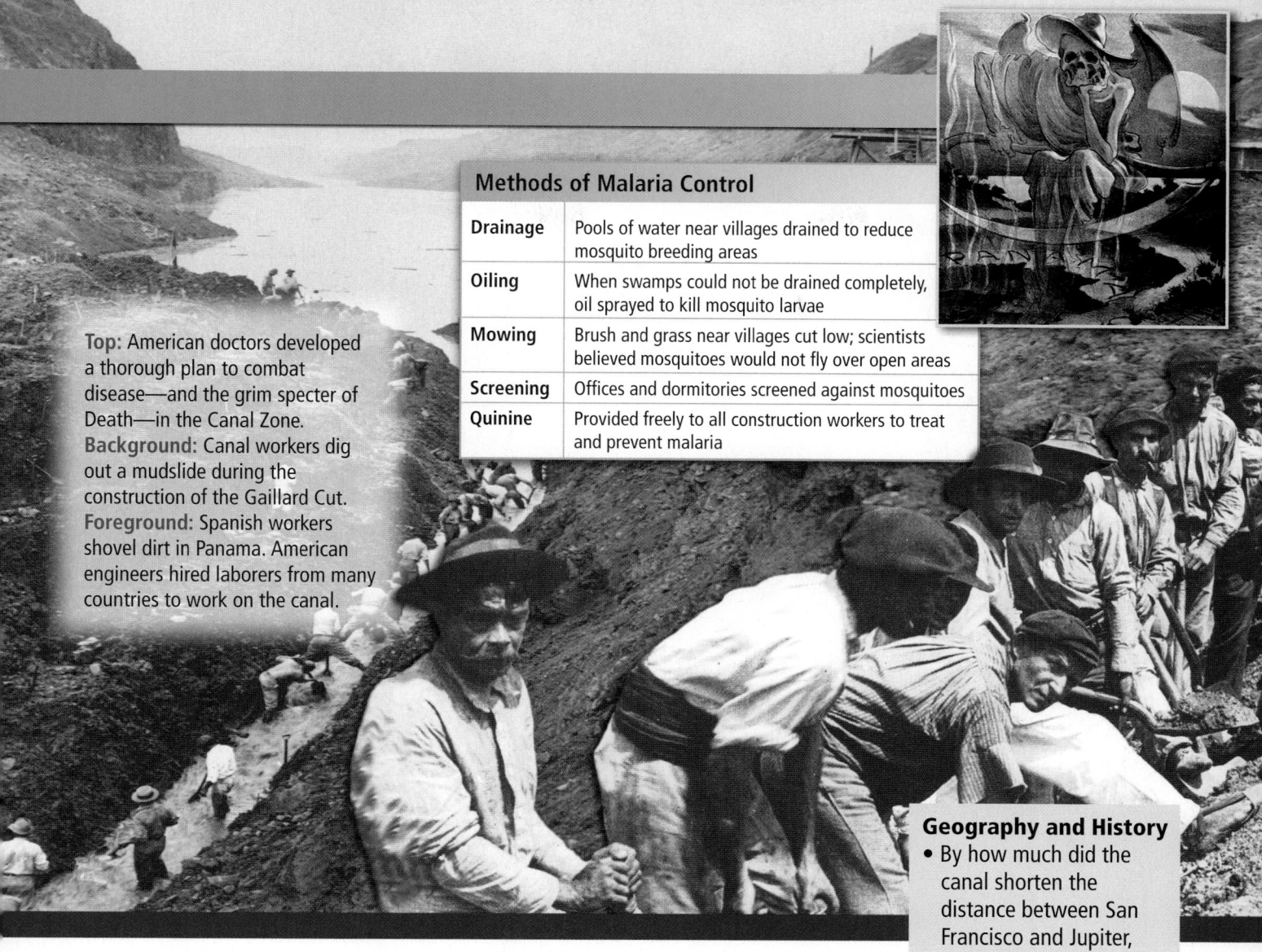

Methods of Malaria Control	
Drainage	Pools of water near villages drained to reduce mosquito breeding areas
Oiling	When swamps could not be drained completely, oil sprayed to kill mosquito larvae
Mowing	Brush and grass near villages cut low; scientists believed mosquitoes would not fly over open areas
Screening	Offices and dormitories screened against mosquitoes
Quinine	Provided freely to all construction workers to treat and prevent malaria

Top: American doctors developed a thorough plan to combat disease—and the grim specter of Death—in the Canal Zone.
Background: Canal workers dig out a mudslide during the construction of the Gaillard Cut.
Foreground: Spanish workers shovel dirt in Panama. American engineers hired laborers from many countries to work on the canal.

Geography and History
- By how much did the canal shorten the distance between San Francisco and Jupiter, Florida?
- Which methods of malaria control involved direct changes to the physical environment of the Canal Zone?

More than 35,000 workers helped dig the **Panama Canal,** often in very difficult conditions. Completion of the canal depended on scientific breakthroughs by doctors as they learned how to combat tropical diseases. Still, more than 5,000 canal workers died from disease or accidents while building the canal. When the finished waterway opened in 1914, it cut some 8,000 nautical miles off the trip from the west coast to the east coast of the United States.

Roosevelt Updates the Monroe Doctrine In the early 1900s, the inability of Latin American nations to pay their debts to foreign investors raised the possibility of European intervention. In 1903, for example, Germany and Britain blockaded Venezuelan ports to ensure that debts to European bankers were repaid. Roosevelt concluded: "If we intend to say hands off to the powers of Europe, then sooner or later we must keep order ourselves." So in a 1904 message to Congress, he announced a new Latin American policy.

The President's **Roosevelt Corollary** updated the Monroe Doctrine for an age of economic imperialism. In the case of "chronic wrongdoing" by a Latin American nation—the kind that Europeans might use to justify military intervention—the United States would assume the role of police power, restoring order and depriving other creditors of the excuse to intervene. This change, Roosevelt argued, merely reasserted America's long-standing policy of keeping the Western Hemisphere free from European intervention.

U.S. Interventions in Latin America

Geography Interactive
For: Interactive map
Web Code: nep-0508

UNITED STATES

U.S. expeditionary force 1916–1917

MEXICO

U.S. expeditionary force 1914

Mexico City

Veracruz

Gulf of Mexico

U.S. troops 1898–1902, 1906–1909, 1912, 1917–1922

Havana

CUBA

Guantanamo

Bahamas (Br.)

U.S. troops 1915–1934

U.S. troops 1916–1924

HAITI

DOMINICAN REPUBLIC

Atlantic Ocean

Purchased from Denmark 1917

Puerto Rico

Antigua (Br.)

Virgin Is.

Jamaica (Br.)

U.S. leased naval base 1903

Acquired from Spain 1898

Guadeloupe (Fr.)
Dominica (Br.)
Martinique (Fr.)
St. Lucia (Br.)
Grenada (Br.)
Barbados (Br.)

British Honduras (Br.)

GUATEMALA

HONDURAS

EL SALVADOR

NICARAGUA

U.S. troops 1909–1910, 1912–1925, 1926–1933

Caribbean Sea

Pacific Ocean

U.S. troops 1924–1925

COSTA RICA

PANAMA

Trinidad (Br.)

VENEZUELA

Miller Projection
0   200   400 mi
0   200   400 km

U.S. acquired Canal Zone 1904; Canal completed 1914

COLOMBIA

30° N

20° N

10° N

100° W   90° W   80° W   70° W

Map Skills The United States repeatedly intervened in the affairs of its Latin American neighbors from the time of the Spanish-American War through the early 1900s.

1. Locate: (a) Cuba, (b) Mexico, (c) Veracruz, (d) Nicaragua, (e) Panama Canal Zone

2. Place Why was Panama an ideal place for the construction of a canal?

3. Analyze Why was Cuba vital to U.S. operations in Central America and the Caribbean?

THE BIG STICK

PANAMA

◄ **Wielding the Big Stick**

With his update to the Monroe Doctrine, Roosevelt wanted only "to see neighboring countries stable, orderly, and prosperous." But if those governments were to collapse, the United States stood ready to restore order and prevent European intervention.

Latin Americans React to the Roosevelt Corollary Many Latin Americans resented America's role as the hemisphere's police force. They disagreed with Roosevelt's belief that Latin Americans could not police themselves. Francisco García Calderón, a Peruvian diplomat, contended that the Monroe Doctrine had taken on an "aggressive form with Mr. Roosevelt." Like Calderón, Nicaraguan spokesman Augusto Sandino felt that the United States threatened the "sovereignty and liberty" of his people. Sandino eventually led an army of guerrillas against U.S. Marines in Nicaragua in the 1920s.

Taft Switches to Dollar Diplomacy Roosevelt handpicked William Howard Taft to succeed him as the Republican candidate for President in 1908. Taft shared Roosevelt's basic foreign policy objectives. After defeating William Jennings Bryan in the general election, Taft wanted to maintain the Open Door Policy in Asia and ensure ongoing stability in Latin America. The new President pursued both goals with the aim of expanding American trade.

Taft hoped to achieve these ends by relying less on the "big stick" and more on **"dollar diplomacy."** As Taft commented in 1912, he looked to substitute "dollars for bullets." The policy aimed to increase American investments in businesses and banks throughout Central America and the Caribbean. Americans busily invested in plantations, mines, oil wells, railways, and other ventures in those regions. Of course, "dollar diplomacy" sometimes required a return to the "big stick" and military intervention. Such was the case when President Taft dispatched troops to Nicaragua in 1909—and again in 1912—to protect the formation of a pro-American government there.

✔ **Checkpoint** What were Roosevelt's most important foreign-policy initiatives in Latin America?

Wilson Pursues Moral Diplomacy

During the 1912 presidential election campaign, Democratic candidate Woodrow Wilson criticized the foreign policies of his Republican predecessors Theodore Roosevelt and William Howard Taft. After his election victory, Wilson appointed the anti-imperialist William Jennings Bryan as Secretary of State, which sent a strong message to the American people.

The U.S. Supports Honest Government in Latin America The new President intended to take U.S. foreign policy in a different direction. He promised that the United States would "never again seek one additional foot of territory by conquest" but would instead work to promote "human rights, national integrity, and opportunity." Wilson spelled out his new **"moral diplomacy"** in a message to the American people:

> **Primary Source** "We must prove ourselves [Latin America's] friends and champions upon terms of equality and honor. . . . We must show ourselves friends by comprehending their interest, whether it squares with our own interest or not. . . . Comprehension must be the soil in which shall grow all the fruits of friendship. . . . I mean the development of constitutional liberty in the world."
> —Woodrow Wilson, October 27, 1913

In spite of his stated preference for "moral diplomacy" over "big stick" or "dollar diplomacy," Wilson used the military on a number of occasions to guide Latin Americans in the directions that he thought proper. In 1915, Wilson sent marines to Haiti to protect American investments and to guard against the potential of German or French aggression in the nation. Wilson prodded the government of Haiti to sign an agreement that essentially gave the United

NoteTaking

Reading Skill: Compare As you read, compare Wilson's moral diplomacy with the foreign policies of Roosevelt and Taft by completing a flowchart like the one below.

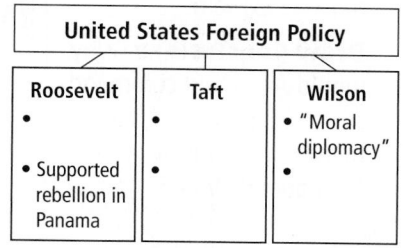

United States Foreign Policy		
Roosevelt	**Taft**	**Wilson**
•	•	• "Moral diplomacy"
• Supported rebellion in Panama	•	•

INTERVENTION IN MEXICO:
THE HUNT FOR PANCHO VILLA

On March 9, 1916, the Mexican rebel Francisco "Pancho" Villa and his gang of outlaws attacked Columbus, New Mexico, killing 18 Americans. An enraged President Wilson dispatched General John J. Pershing to hunt Villa down. Equipped for the first time with airplanes such as the Curtiss JN-3 to support its movements in the field, the U.S. Army pushed 400 miles into Mexico. The Americans chased Villa for 11 months in spite of protests from the Mexican government and occasional clashes with the Mexican army. Preoccupied more by the ongoing war in Europe than by the apprehension of Villa, Wilson ultimately withdrew Pershing's army in early 1917.

▲ Painting of a Curtiss JN-3

New Mexico

Columbus

① Villa raids Columbus and kills 18 Americans

Ascension

② Pershing gives chase as Villa flees south

Dublan

Carrizal

⑤ U.S. troops fight Mexican government soldiers

MEXICO

Río Grande

N W E S

▲ General Pershing leads American cavalry in Mexico in 1916.

UNITED STATES
Map area
MEXICO

Guerrero   Agua Caliente

Temochic

Ojos Azules

④ U.S. troops kill most of Villa's men but Villa escapes

Valle de Zaragoza

◄ Pancho Villa was eventually killed by unknown assassins in 1923.

Parral

③ U.S. troops repel attack by Mexican government forces

→ Villa's route
→ Pershing's route
✹ Villa's raid
⚔ Skirmish

0 ————— 50 miles
0 ————— 50 kilometers

Thinking Critically

1. **Analyze Information** Do you think Pershing's expedition violated the ideals of "moral diplomacy"? Explain.

2. **Draw Conclusions** Why would American commanders be eager to test new military technology in the field against Villa?

States the right to control its financial and foreign affairs. The marines did not leave until 1934. Under Wilson, U.S. soldiers and sailors also intervened in the Dominican Republic and in Mexico.

Revolution Grips Mexico For decades, Mexican dictator Porfirio Díaz had benefited his country's small upper class of wealthy landowners, clerics, and military men. With Díaz's encouragement, foreign investments in Mexico grew. As a result, American business people owned large portions of Mexico's industries. While foreign investors and Mexico's aristocracy grew rich, Mexico's large population of farmers struggled in poverty.

In 1911, Francisco Madero led the Mexican Revolution that toppled Díaz. Madero was committed to reforms but was a weak administrator. In 1913, General Victoriano Huerta seized power and executed Madero. Under "dollar diplomacy," Taft probably would have recognized Huerta as the leader of Mexico because Huerta pledged to protect American investments. But under "moral diplomacy," Wilson refused to do so, declaring that he would not accept a "government of butchers." Instead, Wilson favored Venustiano Carranza, another reformer, who had organized anti-Huerta forces.

Wilson Sends U.S. Troops Into Mexico In 1914, the President used the Mexican arrest of American sailors as an opportunity to help Carranza attain power. Wilson sent marines to occupy the Mexican port of Veracruz. The action caused Huerta's government to collapse, and Carranza assumed the presidency.

Huerta's fall from power cheered many Mexicans and appeared to validate Wilson's "moral diplomacy." However, Wilson soon discovered that he faced more trouble in Mexico. The new Carranza government was slow in bringing about reforms, and rebels again rose up, this time under the leadership of **Francisco "Pancho" Villa.** For a while, Wilson courted Villa. After American support disappeared in 1916, Villa's forces crossed into New Mexico and raided the town of Columbus, leaving 18 Americans dead. President Wilson responded by sending General John J. Pershing and more than 10,000 troops on a "punitive expedition" to Mexico.

Pershing's forces chased Villa for several months but failed to capture the rebel leader. Wilson eventually withdrew American troops from Mexico in 1917, mostly because of his concerns about World War I raging in Europe. Not long afterward, the United States declared war on Germany. Free from hunting Villa, Pershing took command of the American Expeditionary Force in France.

A generation earlier, few would have believed it possible that more than one million American troops would engage in a large-scale war in Europe. But the triumph over Spain and U.S. actions in Asia and Latin America demonstrated that America had emerged as a world power. Now, World War I would test that new global strength.

✔ **Checkpoint** What was "moral diplomacy"?

Progress Monitoring Online
For: Self-test with vocabulary practice
Web Code: nea-0510

Comprehension

1. **Terms and People** Define each term below. How are they similar? How are they different?
   - "big stick" diplomacy
   - "dollar diplomacy"
   - "moral diplomacy"

2. **NoteTaking Reading Skill: Identify Supporting Details** Use your table to answer the Section Focus Question: What actions did the United States take to achieve its goals in Latin America?

Writing About History

3. **Quick Write: Write a Conclusion** A narrative essay should include a conclusion that wraps up the events described in your story. Suppose that you want to write a narrative from the perspective of United States Army General John J. Pershing as he pursued "Pancho" Villa through northern Mexico. Write a conclusion to the story Pershing would tell of the pursuit.

Critical Thinking

4. **Analyze Geography** What impact did the building of the Panama Canal have on American trade?

5. **Identify Assumptions** How do the Platt Amendment and the Roosevelt Corollary reflect similar assumptions about the governments of Latin American nations?

6. **Draw Conclusions** Do you think Woodrow Wilson succeeded in carrying out the principle of "moral diplomacy" in Latin America? Explain.

CHAPTER

18

Quick Study Guide

 4.II.A.3,
4.II.A.4c

Progress Monitoring *Online*
For: Self-test with vocabulary practice
Web Code: nea-0511

■ Cause and Effect: American Imperialism

Causes

- Industrialized nations compete for raw materials and markets.
- Nations seek overseas bases to support naval and commercial interests.
- Imperialists believe in a superior American culture.

American Imperialism

Effects

- The United States purchases Alaska from Russia in 1867.
- American planters, supported by U.S. Marines, overthrow Hawaii's Queen Liliuokalani in 1893; the United States annexes Hawaii in 1898.
- The United States wins the Spanish-American War and acquires colonies in the Caribbean Sea and in the Pacific.
- In 1899, U.S. Secretary of State John Hay establishes the Open Door Policy to protect American trading rights in China.
- Panama rebels against Colombian rule; President Roosevelt acquires land for the construction of the Panama Canal.
- President Wilson sends U.S. troops on a "punitive expedition" into Mexico to hunt and capture the rebel Pancho Villa.

■ The Panama Canal

■ U.S. Interventions in Latin America

Country	Type of Intervention	Year
Cuba	Occupation	1898–1902, 1906–1909, 1912, 1917–1922
Dominican Republic	Military intervention Occupation	1905–1907 1916–1924
Haiti	Occupation	1915–1934
Mexico	Military intervention	1914, 1916–1917
Nicaragua	Occupation	1912–1925, 1927–1933
Panama	Acquisition of Canal Zone	1904
Puerto Rico	Military invasion and territorial acquisition	1898

☑ Quick Study Timeline

In America

1890
Mahan publishes
The Influence of Sea Power Upon History

1898
United States annexes Hawaii; Spanish-American War

Presidential Terms	Benjamin Harrison 1889–1893	Grover Cleveland 1893–1897	William McKinley 1897–1901

1890   **1895**   **1900**

Around the World

1893
Americans overthrow Queen Liliuokalani in Hawaii

1899
Filipino insurrection

1900
Boxer Rebellion

American Issues
●━━●━━● Connector

4.II.A.1a

By connecting prior knowledge with what you have learned in this chapter, you can gradually build your understanding of enduring questions that still affect America today. Answer the questions below. Then, use your American Issues Connector study guide (or go online: www.PHSchool.com **Web Code:** neh-7803).

Issues You Learned About

● **Territorial Expansion of the United States** The United States has acquired land inside and outside of the continental United States.

1. Think about the events that led to the annexation of Hawaii. Write a paragraph explaining whether you think the United States had the right to take control of Hawaii. Consider the following:
   • the initial status of the Hawaiian Islands
   • changes made to the Hawaiian constitution by the monarchy
   • the role of American planters in Hawaii's government and society
   • the reasons that some Americans sought annexation
   • the Senate's initial response to the treaty of annexation

● **America and the World** At times, the United States chooses to get involved in the affairs of other countries.

2. Who proclaimed the Monroe Doctrine, and why?

3. How did the Roosevelt Corollary demonstrate Roosevelt's belief in "big stick" diplomacy?

4. What policies did Taft and Wilson develop for their involvement in Latin American affairs?

● **America Goes to War** The United States sometimes becomes involved in regional conflicts in other parts of the world.

5. Why did many Americans favor the Cuban revolutionaries in their struggle for freedom from Spain?

6. What event caused President McKinley and Congress to prepare for war with Spain?

Connect to Your World   New York

America Goes to War When Alfred T. Mahan called for a stronger navy in the late 1800s, New York was already prepared. The federal government founded the New York Naval Shipyard, popularly known as the Brooklyn Navy Yard, in 1801. Located in Brooklyn on Wallabout Bay, a semicircular section of the East River, it was once known as the country's best shipbuilding facility. Many historic vessels were launched there, including the USS *Maine*, the destruction of which served as a catalyst for the Spanish-American War. In 1966 the Navy sold the shipyard to the city of New York, and today it is a private industrial park with over 4,500 workers. Learn more about the United States Navy in New York today, and create a graphic organizer to display your findings.

| 1907 Great White Fleet | 1908 President Taft embraces "dollar diplomacy" | | 1916 Pershing hunts Pancho Villa in Mexico |

Theodore Roosevelt 1901–1909   William H. Taft 1909–1913   Woodrow Wilson 1913–1921

1905   **1910**   **1915**   **1920**

1904 U.S. gains control of Canal Zone in Panama

1910 Mexican Revolution begins

1914 World War I breaks out in Europe

History Interactive
For: Interactive timeline
Web Code: nep-0513

Chapter Assessment

Terms and People

1. Define **Social Darwinism.** How did some imperialists make use of this concept?

2. Who was **Queen Liliuokalani**? What changes did she bring to her country?

3. What was the **Treaty of Paris**? What were its terms?

4. Define **guerrilla warfare.** Who relied on guerrilla warfare?

5. Define the **Foraker Act** and **Platt Amendment.** Did they settle the debate over U.S. policy in Puerto Rico and Cuba?

Focus Questions

The focus question for this chapter is **How did the United States become a global power?** Build an answer to this big question by answering the focus questions for Sections 1 through 4 and the Critical Thinking questions that follow.

Section 1
6. How and why did the United States take a more active role in world affairs?

Section 2
7. What were the causes and effects of the Spanish-American War?

Section 3
8. How did the United States extend its influence in Asia?

Section 4
9. What actions did the United States take to achieve its goals in Latin America?

Critical Thinking

10. **Recognize Ideologies** How did U.S. expansion in the late nineteenth century extend and change the principle of Manifest Destiny?

11. **Make Comparisons** Choose two of the following: Commodore Perry's mission to Japan; the revolt in Hawaii; the Open Door Policy; the building of the Panama Canal. Explain how the two were similar yet different in terms of U.S. goals and actions.

12. **Recognize Propaganda** How did the Yellow Press contribute to U.S. actions against Spain?

13. **Compare Points of View** Explain the different opinions held by imperialists and anti-imperialists in the debate over the Philippines.

14. **Analyze Line Graphs** How were growing tensions with Japan linked to the trend shown on the graph below?

U.S. Navy Yearly Federal Budget, 1898–1908

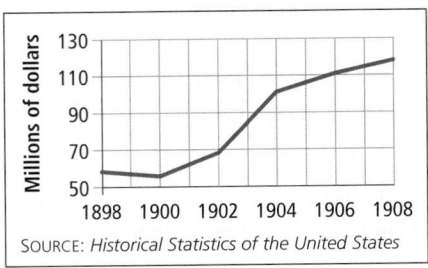

SOURCE: *Historical Statistics of the United States*

15. **Draw Conclusions** What was the goal of U.S. policy toward China? Why do you think Hay did not favor establishing colonies in China?

16. **Predict Consequences** If Wilson had been President when the United States was seeking to build the Panama Canal, do you think he would have supported Panama's rebellion against Colombia? Justify your answer.

Writing About History

Write a Narrative Essay Write a narrative essay telling a story about America's emergence as a global power in the late 1800s and early 1900s. Write your essay from the point of view of an imperialist or an anti-imperialist. Consult page SH11 of the Writing Handbook for additional help.

Prewriting
• Choose a chapter event that interests you most to write about.

• Choose a purpose for your essay. You might highlight a certain aspect of the event that you think deserves attention.

• Gather details related to your essay topic.

Drafting
• Identify the climax, or the most important part, of your story. Then, decide what will happen in the beginning, middle, and end of the essay.

• Write an introduction for the essay that will grab a reader's interest.

• Use many details to make the story vivid. When possible, include dialogue to convey the thoughts of the character.

• Write a conclusion that summarizes the significance of the experience to the character.

Revising
• Use the guidelines on page SH11 of the Writing Handbook to revise your essay.

YOUR COUNTRY CALLS YOU

Regents DBQ Practice

American Imperialism

Should the United States annex territories in order to establish a global empire? Or should it honor American roots by granting self-rule to the native peoples of those lands? Use your knowledge of the debate over American imperialism and the following documents to answer questions 1 through 4.

Document 1

Uncle Sam Wrestles With Filipino Insurgency

Document 2

The taking of the Philippines does not violate the principles of the Declaration of Independence, but will spread them among a people who have never known liberty and who in a few years will be unwilling to leave the shelter of the American flag. . . . The form of government natural to the Asiatic has always been despotism. . . . [T]o abandon those islands is to leave them to anarchy, [and] to short-lived military dictatorships. . . .

Senator Henry Cabot Lodge, March 1900

Document 3

I wanted the American eagle to go screaming into the Pacific. It seemed tiresome and tame for it to content itself with the Rockies. Why not spread its wings over the Philippines, I asked myself? And I thought it would be a real good thing to do. . . . But I have thought some more, since then, and I have read carefully the treaty of Paris, and I have seen that we do not intend to free, but to subjugate the people of the Philippines. We have gone there to conquer, not to redeem. . . . And so I am an anti-imperialist. I am opposed to having the eagle put its talons on any other land.

Mark Twain, October 1900

Document 4

WELL, I HARDLY KNOW WHICH TO TAKE FIRST!

---

1. Which of the documents is a primary source that supports the maintenance of American control over the Philippines to ensure a stable government there?
   (1) Document 1
   (2) Document 2
   (3) Document 3
   (4) Document 4

2. According to Document 1, how did the cartoonist choose to portray the Filipino population?
   (1) Filipinos are resisting the American presence in the Philippines.
   (2) Filipinos are cooperating with American officials to maintain U.S. control.
   (3) Filipinos are fleeing their homes in fear of American soldiers.
   (4) Filipinos are celebrating their independence from Spain.

3. Mark Twain most closely agrees with which of the other documents?
   (1) Documents 1 and 4
   (2) Documents 1 and 2
   (3) Document 2
   (4) Document 4

4. **Writing Task** How did the principles of the American Revolution influence the debate over American imperialism in the Philippines? Use your knowledge of the aftermath of the Spanish-American War and specific evidence from the primary sources above to support your opinion.

American Soldiers Arrive "Over There"

During World War I, nearly 4 million American soldiers went "over there"—to France—to help the Allies win the war. A British volunteer nurse working near the front in France described the arrival of the new American troops:

American soldier's helmet

66I pressed forward with the others to watch the United States physically entering the War, so god-like, so magnificent, so splendidly unimpaired in comparison with the tired, nerve-racked men of the British Army. So these were our deliverers at last, marching up the road to Camiers in the spring sunshine!99
—Vera Brittain, *Testament of Youth*

Listen to the Witness History *audio to learn more about America in World War I.*

◄ A French couple greets American soldiers in France in 1918.

 Core Curriculum Preview

Chapter Focus Question: What caused the United States to become involved in World War I, and how did the United States change as a result of its involvement?

Section 1
From Neutrality to War   4.II.A.1a, 4.II.B.1a, 4.II.B.1b, 4.II.B.1c

Section 2
The Home Front   4.I.C.5, 4.II.B.1c, 4.II.C.1, 4.II.C.2

Section 3
Wilson, War, and Peace   4.II.D.1, 4.II.D.2, 4.II.D.3, 4.II.D.4

Section 4
Effects of the War   4.II.C.4, 5.I.A.1, 5.I.A.3, 5.I.B.4

Use the ☑ **Quick Study Timeline** at the end of this chapter to preview chapter events.

American recruitment poster

World War I–era airplane

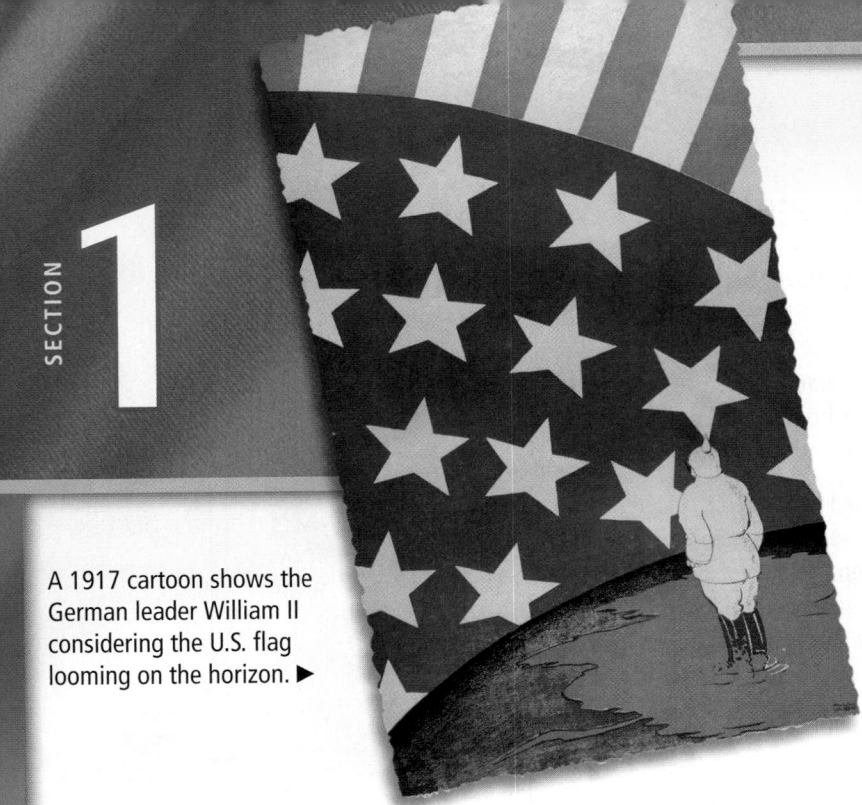

A 1917 cartoon shows the German leader William II considering the U.S. flag looming on the horizon. ▶

WITNESS HISTORY 🔊 AUDIO

To Fight or Not to Fight?

When war broke out in Europe in 1914, the United States decided to stay neutral. However, incidents like the senseless destruction of Louvain, a medieval university town in Belgium, by German troops turned American opinion against Germany.

❝For two hours on Thursday night I was in what for six hundred years had been the city of Louvain. The Germans were burning it . . . the story . . . was told to us by German soldiers incoherent with excesses; and we could read it in the faces of the women and children being led to concentration camps and of the citizens on their way to be shot.❞

—American journalist Richard Harding Davis, August 1914

From Neutrality to War

 Core Curriculum Objectives

- **4.II.A.1a** An emerging global involvement: Role of increased American power
- **4.II.B.1a** Restraint and involvement: United States' efforts at neutrality
- **4.II.B.1b** Restraint and involvement: Causes of United States' entry into World War I
- **4.II.B.1c** Restraint and involvement: United States' role in the war

Terms and People

Alsace-Lorraine	casualty
militarism	contraband
Francis Ferdinand	U-boat
William II	*Lusitania*
Western Front	Zimmermann note

NoteTaking

Reading Skill: Identify Causes As you read, identify the causes of World War I, the conditions facing soldiers, and the reasons for U.S. involvement.

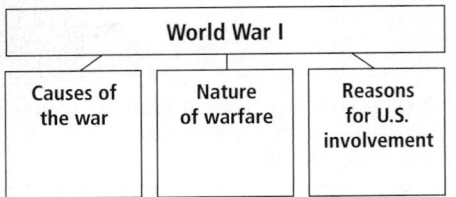

Why It Matters In 1914, nationalism, militarism, imperialism, and entangling alliances combined with other factors to lead the nations of Europe into a brutal war. The war quickly stretched around the globe. The United States remained neutral at first but ended up abandoning its long tradition of staying out of European conflicts. **Section Focus Question: What caused World War I, and why did the United States enter the war?**

What Caused World War I?

Until 1914, there had not been a large-scale European conflict for nearly one hundred years. However, bitter, deep-rooted problems simmered beneath the surface of polite diplomacy. Europe was sitting on a powder keg of nationalism, regional tensions, economic rivalries, imperial ambitions, and militarism.

Nationalism and Competition Heighten Tension Nationalism, or devotion to one's nation, kick-started international and domestic tension. In the late 1800s, many Europeans began to reject the earlier idea of a nation as a collection of different ethnic groups. Instead, they believed that a nation should express the nationalism of a single ethnic group. This belief evolved into an intense form of nationalism that heightened international rivalries. For example, France longed to avenge its humiliating defeat by a collection of German states in 1871 and regain **Alsace-Lorraine,** the territory it lost during that conflict. Nationalism also threatened minority groups within nation-states. If a country existed as the expression of "its people," the majority ethnic group, where did ethnic minorities fit in?

The spread of the theory of Social Darwinism did not help soothe the competitive instinct. Social Darwinism applied biologist Charles Darwin's ideas of natural selection and "survival of the fittest" to human society. Social Darwinists believed that the best nation would come out ahead in the constant competition among countries.

Nationalism also destabilized old multinational empires such as Austria-Hungary and the Ottoman Empire. This was particularly true in the Balkan region of southeastern Europe. For example, when Serbia emerged as an independent nation in 1878, it challenged the nearby empire of Austria-Hungary in two ways: by trying to gain territory controlled by the empire, where Serbs lived, and by the example it offered to Austria-Hungary's diverse peoples.

The nationalist sentiments of the period sometimes spilled over into the economic goals of each nation. Industrial output, trade, and the possession of an overseas empire were the yardsticks of wealth and greatness. The leading industrial nations competed for lands rich in raw materials as well as for places to build military bases to protect their empires. Britain already had a large empire, and France commanded a smaller one. But Germany, Italy, Belgium, Japan, and the United States also rushed to join the imperial race. Together, industrialized nations jostled among themselves as they carved colonies out of Africa, claimed islands in the Pacific, and began to nibble away at China.

Militarism Produces an Arms Race For some European leaders, the question was not so much *if* a great war would start but *when*. To prepare, leaders increased the size of their armies and stockpiles of weapons. No nation readied its war machinery more than Germany. By 1914, it had a huge standing army and the largest, deadliest collection of guns in the world. It also built up its navy enough to rival Britain's, the world's strongest at that time. To keep up, Britain, too, increased the size of its navy. A spirit of **militarism,** or glorification of the military, grew in the competing countries and fueled this arms race even more.

The contest between Germany and Britain at sea and between Germany, France, and Russia on land guaranteed one important thing: The next major war would involve more troops and more technologically advanced weapons than ever before. Machine guns, mobile artillery, tanks, submarines, and airplanes would change the nature of warfare.

Building the War Machine
In the early 1900s, European countries raced to keep up with one another's military might. Below, workers build artillery in Essen, a German city, in 1904. *According to the chart, which country had the largest army in 1914? Which had the largest navy?*

Military Strength, 1914

Germany	
Austria-Hungary	
Russia	
France	
Britain	
United States	

🚶 200,000 troops   🚢 2 large warships

SOURCE: *Encyclopædia Britannica Online*, 2005; *The Pity of War*, Niall Ferguson

World War I, 1914–1917

Geography *Interactive*
For: Interactive map
Web Code: nep-0602

Allies, 1917
Central Powers, 1917
Neutral countries, 1917
Front line, 1914
Front line, 1915–1916
Front line, 1917
Russian offensive, June–September 1916
Battle site

Occupied by Central Powers at end of 1915

Conic Projection

Map Skills The war on most fronts was a stalemate by 1916.

1. **Locate:** (a) Belgium, (b) Western Front, (c) Battle of Verdun

2. **Location** What challenge did Germany's location present to its pursuit of victory in the war?

3. **Synthesize Information** Describe the movement of the opposing lines of the Western Front between 1914 and 1917.

Vocabulary Builder

ally–(AL ī) *n.* person, nation, or group joined with another for a common purpose

Alliances Make Nations Overconfident and Reckless European leaders also prepared for war by forming alliances. Before 1914, two major ones emerged. Germany, Austria-Hungary, and Italy joined together in the Triple Alliance (although Italy never fought with it). Opposed to the Triple Alliance was the Triple Entente, made up of France, Russia, and Great Britain. Alliances emboldened leaders to act recklessly. They knew that if they did declare war, powerful <u>allies</u> were obligated to fight along with them. No country wanted to be seen as an unreliable partner. As years passed, European leaders thought less of the advantages of peace and more of the possible benefits of war. Some also hoped that a foreign war would help to smooth over domestic problems.

Assassination Hurtles Europe Toward World War On June 28, 1914, Archduke **Francis Ferdinand,** heir to the throne of Austria-Hungary, and his wife Sophie left for what they thought would be a routine visit to Sarajevo (sar uh YAY voh), the capital city of the Austro-Hungarian province of Bosnia. But a handful of young Bosnians had other plans for the archduke and his wife. These men were ethnic Serbs who believed that Bosnia rightfully belonged to Serbia, and they saw Francis Ferdinand as a tyrant. After the archduke's driver made a wrong turn, Gavrilo Princip, one of the conspirators, noticed the couple in the car, pulled a pistol from his pocket, and fired it twice. First Sophie and then Francis Ferdinand died. People around the world were shocked by the senseless murders. But no one expected that they would lead to a great world war.

✓ **Checkpoint** How did nationalism and militarism both work to push Europe toward war?

The Fighting Begins

Everything was in place for a great conflict—nationalist ambitions, large armies, stockpiles of weapons, alliances, and military plans. The nations of Europe were hurtling like giant trains toward a great collision. Archduke Francis Ferdinand's assassination was the incident that triggered this conflict.

Alliances Cause a Chain Reaction Soon after the assassination, Kaiser **William II,** the German emperor, assured Austria-Hungary that Germany would stand by its ally if war came. Confident in Germany's support, Austria-Hungary then sent a harsh ultimatum to Serbia demanding Serbia's total cooperation in an investigation into the assassination. When Serbia did not agree to all of the demands, Austria-Hungary declared war on July 28, 1914.

Because of the alliance system, what otherwise might have been a localized quarrel quickly spread. In early August, Russia mobilized for war to help its ally Serbia against Austria. This caused Germany to declare war against Russia. France, Russia's ally, promptly declared war against Germany. The very next day, Germany declared war against neutral Belgium, so that it could launch an invasion of France through that small country. Great Britain, which had treaties with France and Belgium, immediately declared war against Germany. In less than one week, the Central Powers of Germany and Austria-Hungary were at war against the Allied Powers of Britain, France, Russia, and Serbia. The Ottoman Empire later joined the Central Powers.

German soldiers fought through Belgium and moved southwest into France, toward Paris. Then in September, with the German advance only 30 miles from Paris, the French and the British counterattacked and stopped the German forces near the Marne River.

Deadly Technology Leads to Stalemate After the Battle of the Marne, the Germans settled onto high ground, dug trenches, and fortified their position. When the French and British attacked, the German troops used machine guns and artillery to kill thousands of them. The French and British then dug their own trenches and used the same weapons to kill thousands of counterattacking Germans. Soon, 450 miles of trenches stretched like a huge scar from the coast of Belgium to the border of Switzerland. Although fighting went on in Eastern Europe, the Middle East, and in other parts of the world, this **Western Front** in France became the critical battle front. The side that won there would win the war.

The war dragged on for years, and it was hideously deadly—much more so than anyone had expected. The primary reason for the length of the war and its deadly nature was the simple fact that the defensive weapons of the time were better and more devastating than the offensive ones. Generals on each side threw their soldiers into assaults against the enemy without fully considering the new technology. Charging toward trenches that were defended by artillery, machine guns, and rifles was futile. In virtually every battle on the Western Front, the attacking force suffered terribly. Even the use of poison gas did nothing to benefit the offense, despite its horrifying effects. Ineffective offensives and effective defensives produced only a deadly stalemate.

War in the Trenches

German soldiers hunker down in a shallow trench that stretches into the distance to protect themselves from enemy fire. *How did new technology make defenses such as trenches necessary?*

WITNESS HISTORY DVD

Watch *World War I: A New Kind of War* on the **United States Witness History DVD** to learn more about the nature of warfare during World War I.

Horror of Modern Warfare

Although gas masks were soon developed to counter poison gas, gas attacks were still particularly horrifying to soldiers. *According to the chart, which type of weapon caused the most casualties?*

The Reality of Trench Warfare The stalemate led to gruesome conditions for the men in the trenches of the Western Front. The soldiers battled the harsh conditions of life often as fiercely as they attacked the enemy. They developed "trench foot" from standing for hours in wet, muddy trenches. They contracted lice from the millions of rats that infested the trenches. Dug into the ground, the soldiers lived in constant fear, afraid to pop their heads out of their holes and always aware that the next offensive might be their last.

Even on a quiet day, soldiers could be killed by snipers or a surprise gas attack, like the one described by French officer Paul Truffaut at Verdun:

> **Primary Source** "The special shells the men call "shells on wheels" [shells filled with poison gas] are whizzing by continuously. They explode silently and have no smell but can be deadly. They killed several men yesterday. One of my men refused to put his mask on because he couldn't smell anything. All of a sudden, he was dizzy, foaming at the mouth and his skin went black, then he went rigid and died."
> —Paul Truffaut, March 5, 1917

In between enemy lines was an area known as "no man's land." Artillery barrages had blasted no man's land until any fields, trees, or homes, that had once existed there, were charred beyond recognition. Soldiers went "over the top" of their trenches into this muddy, nearly impassable wasteland when they attempted to attack the entrenched enemy.

Casualties—or soldiers killed, wounded, and missing—mounted first in thousands, then hundreds of thousands, and finally in millions. Almost one million French soldiers were killed or wounded in just the first three months of the war. The Germans lost only slightly fewer. In two battles in 1916—Verdun (ver DUHN) and the Somme (suhm)—the British, French, and Germans sustained more than 2 million casualties. The British suffered 60,000 casualties on the first day alone at the Somme and achieved virtually nothing. And still the stalemate dragged on.

✓ **Checkpoint** Why did both sides embrace trench warfare as a strategy to win the war?

Deadly Technology of World War I	✓ Quick Study
Machine guns	Improved machine guns could fire 600 bullets per minute.
Artillery field guns	These long-range cannons caused more casualties than any other type of weapon.
Poison gas	Gases such as chlorine, phosgene, and mustard gas could kill, blind, or burn their victims.
Submarines	German U-boats, or submarines, used torpedoes as well as on-deck guns to sink ships.
Tanks and armored cars	Both sides tried to develop vehicles that could go over the rough ground and barbed-wire barricades of no man's land, with limited success.
Airplanes	Planes were used for reconnaissance, bombing, and fighting but did not prove decisive.

Wilson Urges Neutrality

As the war spread in Europe, President Woodrow Wilson called for Americans to be "impartial in thought as well as action." In a "melting pot" nation that tried to make Americans of peoples from diverse origins, Wilson did not want to see the war set Americans against one another. At first, most Americans viewed the conflict as a distant European quarrel for land and influence. Unless the nation's interests were directly threatened, Americans wanted no part of it. They preferred to maintain what they viewed as traditional American isolation from European disputes. Still, many Americans felt the war's effects and few were truly impartial in thought. Most held a preference for one or another combatant, and many businesses benefited from the increased demand by warring nations for American goods.

Americans Have Divided Loyalties In 1914, one third of Americans were foreign-born. Many still thought of themselves in terms of their former homelands—as German Americans, Irish Americans, Polish Americans, and so on. With relatives in Europe, many people supported the nation in which they were born.

Some German Americans in the Midwest and some Irish Americans along the East Coast felt strongly that the Central Powers were justified in their actions. Many Americans had emigrated from Germany or Austria-Hungary. Millions of Irish Americans harbored intense grudges over the centuries of Great Britain's domination of their homeland. They hoped that Ireland would gain its independence as Britain became entangled in the war. Many Jewish Americans who had fled Russia to escape the Czarist regimes' murderous pogroms against Jews hoped for Russia's defeat.

Most Americans, however, sided with Britain and France, both of which had strong historic ties with the United States. America's national language was English, its cultural heritage was largely British, and its leading trading partner was Britain. France had aided the American cause during the Revolutionary War.

Stop!

American Opinion Crystallizes No event at the beginning of the war swayed American opinion more than the vicious German invasion of neutral Belgium. German soldiers marching through Belgium committed numerous atrocities, killing unarmed civilians and destroying entire towns. British journalists and propagandists stressed, and sometimes exaggerated, the brutality of the Germans' actions. Americans might have only dimly understood the causes of the war, but they clearly perceived the human cost of the war for Belgium.

Eventually, three distinct positions on the war crystallized among Americans. One group, the isolationists, believed that the war was none of America's business and that the nation should isolate itself from the hostilities. A second group, the interventionists, felt that the war did affect American interests and that the United States should intervene in the conflict on the side of the Allies. A third group, the internationalists, occupied the middle ground. Internationalists believed that the United States should play an active role in world affairs and work toward achieving a just peace but not enter the war.

✓ **Checkpoint** Why did President Wilson fear that the war would set Americans against one another?

Neutrality Gives Way to War

An internationalist, President Wilson sincerely desired peace in his country and around the world. Between the start of the war in 1914 and America's entry into it in 1917, Wilson attempted to use his influence to end the conflict among the warring countries. He failed in this great effort. Ultimately, he also failed to keep the United States out of the war.

Britain Blockades Germany Early in the war, British leaders decided to use their navy to blockade Germany to keep essential goods from reaching the other country. International law generally allowed **contraband** goods, usually defined as weapons and other articles used to fight a war, to be confiscated legally by any belligerent nation. Noncontraband goods, such as food, medical supplies, and other nonmilitary items, could not be confiscated. Britain, however, contested the definition of noncontraband articles. As the war continued, Britain expanded its definition of contraband until it encompassed virtually every product, including gasoline, cotton, and even food—in spite of international law.

German Submarines Violate Neutral Rights Germany responded by attempting to blockade Britain—even though it lacked the conventional naval forces to do so. Instead, in February 1915, Germany began sinking Allied ships using its **U-boats,** or submarines. The reality of the German blockade struck America on May 7, 1915, when a German U-boat sank the British passenger liner *Lusitania* off the coast of Ireland. German officials correctly claimed that

INFOGRAPHIC 🔊 AUDIO

Ships Sunk by U-boats, May 1917–Jan. 1918

- Ship sunk

Conic Projection
0   50   100 mi
0 50 100 km

North Sea

Edinburgh

Belfast

Dublin

UNITED KINGDOM

Queenstown

London

Portsmouth   Dover

Falmouth

Atlantic Ocean

Le Havre
Cherbourg

Brest

FRANCE

During World War I, German U-boats, like the *U-166* shown below, destroyed more than 11 million tons of Allied shipping and killed nearly 14,000 people.

U-Boats
Sink American Neutrality

On May 7, 1915, the British passenger ship *Lusitania* cruised off the coast of Ireland. The German submarine *U-20*, lurking underwater, sighted the ship and fired a torpedo into its starboard side. It sank within 20 minutes, killing nearly 1,200 passengers. Among the dead were 128 Americans.

The sinking of the *Lusitania* was part of Germany's submarine blockade of Britain. The sinking of passenger ships carrying American neutrals angered the United States when it occurred in 1915 and again in 1916. Nonetheless, in early 1917, desperate German leaders declared unrestricted submarine warfare—causing the United States to enter the war.

the ship was carrying ammunition and other contraband. Americans protested that an unarmed and unresisting ship should not be sunk without first being warned and provided with safety for its passengers. President Wilson was stunned but still wanted peace. "There is such a thing as a man being too proud to fight," he told his fellow citizens. "There is such a thing as a nation being so right that it does not need to convince others by force that it is right."

Germany helped to keep the United States out of the war by eventually promising not to sink any more passenger ships. But in 1916, Germany violated that promise by sinking the unarmed French passenger ship *Sussex*. Another storm of protest erupted in America. Again, Germany pledged not to sink unarmed ships. This promise, called the Sussex Pledge, would not last long.

Wilson Prepares for War President Wilson wanted to remain at peace, but even he must have realized the futility of that hope. At the end of 1915, Wilson began to prepare the nation for war. Many believed that "preparedness" was a dangerous course that could actually provoke war. Even so, Congress passed two pieces of legislation in 1916 to prepare for the possibility of U.S. involvement. The National Defense Act expanded the size of the army, and the Naval Construction Act ordered the building of more warships.

Still, Wilson hoped to avoid the conflict. In 1916, he ran for reelection with the slogan, "He kept us out of war." It was a close election, but Wilson won a narrow victory over Republican Charles Evans Hughes.

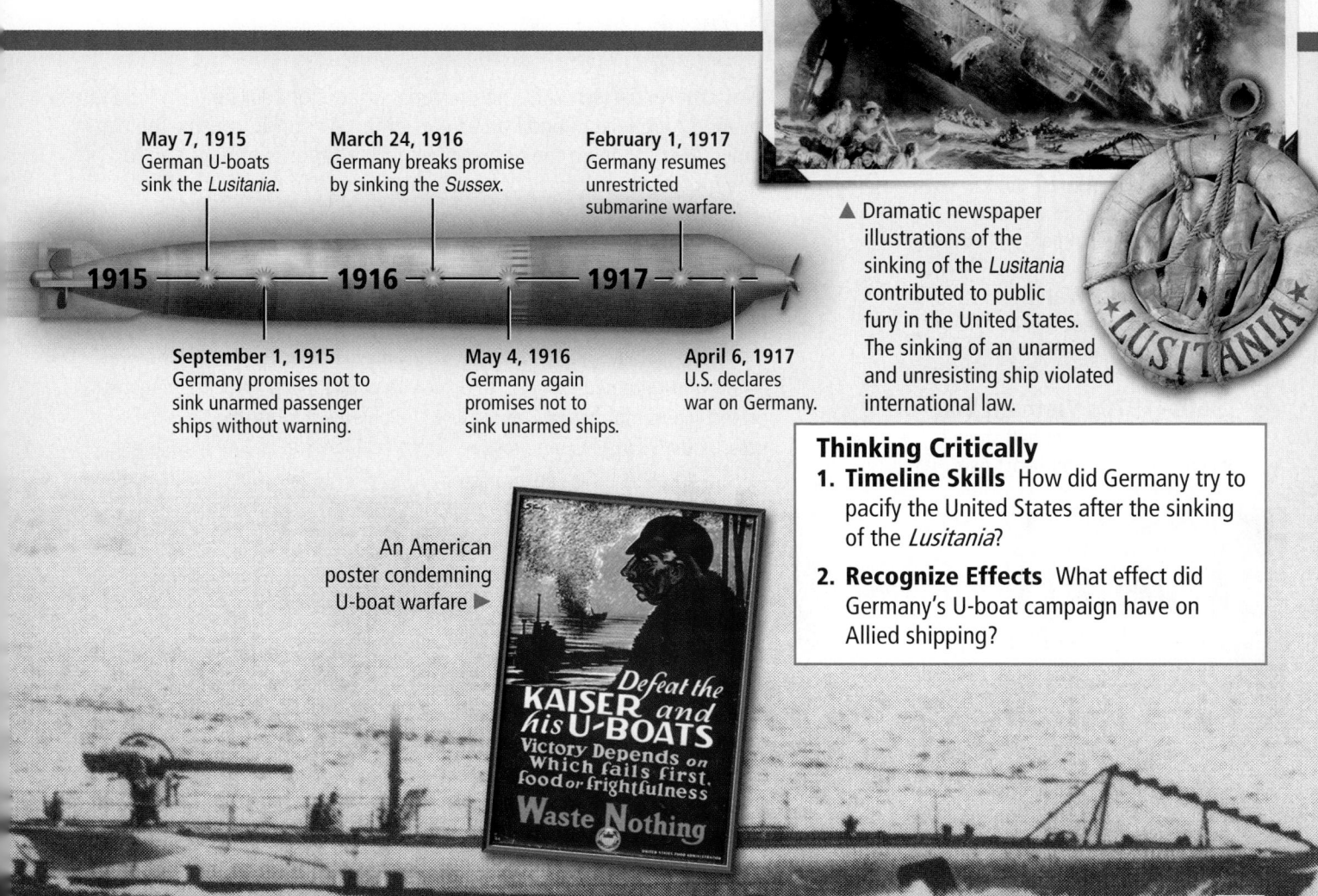

May 7, 1915
German U-boats sink the *Lusitania*.

March 24, 1916
Germany breaks promise by sinking the *Sussex*.

February 1, 1917
Germany resumes unrestricted submarine warfare.

1915 — **1916** — **1917**

September 1, 1915
Germany promises not to sink unarmed passenger ships without warning.

May 4, 1916
Germany again promises not to sink unarmed ships.

April 6, 1917
U.S. declares war on Germany.

▲ Dramatic newspaper illustrations of the sinking of the *Lusitania* contributed to public fury in the United States. The sinking of an unarmed and unresisting ship violated international law.

An American poster condemning U-boat warfare ▶

Defeat the **KAISER** *and his* **U-BOATS**
Victory Depends on Which fails first. food or frightfulness
Waste Nothing

Thinking Critically

1. **Timeline Skills** How did Germany try to pacify the United States after the sinking of the *Lusitania*?

2. **Recognize Effects** What effect did Germany's U-boat campaign have on Allied shipping?

America Goes to War

 4.II.B.1

TRACK THE ISSUE

When should America go to war?

Over the years, the United States has had many motives for going to war. The nation has gone to war to protect itself, gain economic benefits, aid its allies, expand its borders, or increase its power and influence. Under what circumstances is war justified? Americans debate this issue each time the country fights. Use the timeline below to explore this enduring issue.

1812 War of 1812
Americans fight to stop Britain from seizing American ships and sailors.

1860s Civil War
North and South fight over slavery, states' rights, and preservation of the Union.

1917–1918 World War I
United States goes to war after Germany violates American neutrality.

1940s World War II
The Japanese attack on Pearl Harbor draws America into the conflict.

1960s–1970s Vietnam War
United States fights to halt spread of communism in Southeast Asia.

U.S. soldiers patrol the streets in Baghdad, Iraq.

DEBATE THE ISSUE

War on Terrorism After the terrorist attacks of 2001, the United States invaded Afghanistan and Iraq as part of the War on Terrorism. The war aimed to track down the perpetrators of the terrorist attacks and to prevent future attacks by promoting democracy in the Middle East.

"The use of military force against terrorist networks and regimes abetting their crimes is certainly justifiable. . . . Our leaders are, in my judgment, morally obligated to use as much force as necessary . . . to protect innocent Americans and other potential victims of terrorism."
—Robert P. George, professor, Princeton University

"When you make the argument that there is a 'just war,' what you are saying is that there is an aggression, a major offense is being committed and you do not have any other way to protect people from that aggression except to use force."
—Reverend J. Brian Hehir, Catholic theologian

A newspaper announces America's entry into World War I on April 6, 1917.

 TRANSFER Activities

1. **Compare** Why does Professor George support the War on Terrorism? Why does Reverend Hehir oppose it?

2. **Analyze** Do you think Hehir would have supported the decision to enter World War I? Explain.

3. **Transfer** Use the following Web site to see a video, try a WebQuest, and write in your journal. **Web Code:** neh-7902

America Enters the War Wilson did not have much time to enjoy his victory. In early 1917, two events occurred that helped to push the United States into the war. American trade with the Allies had sustained Britain and France in the war, while the British blockade of Germany had stopped the flow of American goods to the Central Powers. As far as Germany was concerned, desperate times demanded desperate measures.

In January 1917, suffering severe supply shortages due to the blockade, Germany took action. First, German Foreign Minister Arthur Zimmermann sent a telegram to Mexico. The **Zimmermann note** proposed an alliance with Mexico, stating that if the United States declared war on Germany, Mexico should declare war on the United States. In return, after a German victory, Mexico would get back the states of Texas, New Mexico, and Arizona, which it had lost in 1848 after its defeat in the Mexican-American War. The telegram was intercepted by the British, who gave it to American authorities. Next, Germany once again announced unrestricted submarine warfare against Britain.

Although most leaders knew Mexico had no intention of attacking the United States, Americans were shocked by the publication of the Zimmermann note. Even Wilson no longer called for peace. On April 2, 1917, he asked Congress for a declaration of war against Germany:

> **Primary Source** ❝The world must be made safe for democracy. Its peace must be planted upon the tested foundations of political liberty. . . . We are but one of the champions of the rights of mankind. We shall be satisfied when those rights have been made as secure as the faith and the freedom of nations can make them.❞
> —Woodrow Wilson, April 2, 1917

Congress responded on April 6, 1917, with a declaration of war. Wilson's long struggle to keep America at peace was over.

✔ **Checkpoint** What German actions led the United States to enter World War I?

HISTORY MAKERS

Jeannette Rankin (1880–1973)
In 1916, Jeannette Rankin became the first woman elected to Congress. Committed to women's rights, she was also a dedicated pacifist. She and 49 other members of Congress voted against declaring war on Germany in 1917. Twenty-four years later, in 1941, she was the only member of Congress to vote against the declaration of war against Japan. "As a woman," Rankin said, "I can't go to war, and I refuse to send anyone else." She lost her bid for reelection in the election years that followed both votes.

SECTION 1 Assessment

Progress Monitoring Online
For: Self-test with vocabulary practice
Web Code: nea-0603

Comprehension

1. **Terms and People** For each item below, write a sentence explaining its significance to the outbreak and course of World War I.
   - militarism
   - Francis Ferdinand
   - William II
   - casualty
   - U-boat
   - *Lusitania*

2. **NoteTaking Reading Skill: Identify Causes** Use your chart to answer the Section Focus Question: What caused World War I, and why did the United States enter the war?

Writing About History

3. **Quick Write: Identify Causes** List each cause of U.S. entry into World War I, and then organize them in order of importance. Finally, turn your list into a paragraph describing the causes of U.S. involvement in the war.

Critical Thinking

4. **Draw Conclusions** Why did a stalemate develop on the Western Front?

5. **Compare Points of View** Compare the three positions Americans took on the issue of whether or not the United States should enter the war.

6. **Synthesize Information** Why did the United States decide to enter the war and fight on the side of the Allies?

Supporting the War

While soldiers trained to fight in the war, Americans on the home front supported the war by working in war industries, lending money to the government, and conserving food to feed the troops abroad.

Little AMERICANS *Do your bit*

Eat Oatmeal-Corn meal mush- Hominy - other corn cereals- and Rice with milk. *Save the wheat for our soldiers.* Leave nothing on your plate

UNITED STATES FOOD ADMINISTRATION

"Perhaps it will not be long before we will read each day long lists of American boys killed or wounded in the trenches of France. There will be boys in those lists that you know, boys that I know. And as our eyes film over with tears it will be at least some comfort to us to be able to say, 'I am helping too. I am saving food for the boys who are fighting.'"

—Committee on Public Information bulletin, July 1917

▲ Girl Scouts collect peach pits to be used in gas-mask filters.

The Home Front

Core Curriculum Objectives

- **4.I.C.5** World War I: effect on domestic reform
- **4.II.B.1c** United States role in the war
- **4.II.C.1** War opposition and patriotism: the draft issue
- **4.II.C.2** Espionage and Sedition acts

Terms and People

Selective Service Act	conscientious objector
Bernard Baruch	Espionage Act
CPI	Great Migration
George Creel	

NoteTaking

Reading Skill: Summarize As you read, summarize the key points made in the section in a chart like the one below.

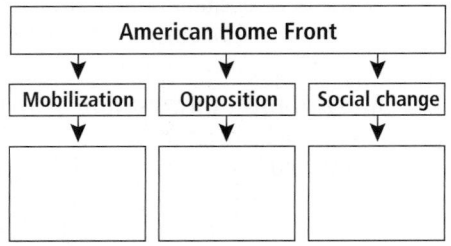

American Home Front
→ Mobilization → Opposition → Social change

Why It Matters Before the war, the federal government played a minor role in the daily lives of most Americans. But during World War I, the government assumed new powers. It regulated industrial and agricultural production, worked to shape public opinion, and established a new military draft. While war required sacrifice, it also brought new economic opportunities and many Americans migrated to other parts of the country in search of these opportunities. The war permanently changed Americans' relationship with their government. **Section Focus Question: How did the war affect Americans at home?**

America Mobilizes for War

War affects many things, but its greatest impact is on the lives of ordinary people. People fight, sacrifice, and sometimes die in war. People work to produce the food that soldiers eat and the guns that soldiers fire. People shape the information that others receive about the war. War may be the result of conflicts between nations, but it touches the lives of millions of individuals.

Building an Army When the United States entered World War I, the United States Army was only a fraction of the size of European armies. To build the army, President Wilson encouraged Americans to volunteer for service and pushed Congress to pass the **Selective Service Act.** The act, which Congress passed in May 1917, authorized a draft of young men for military service in Europe. On the first day of its enactment, June 5, 1917, more than 9.6 million Americans registered for the draft and were assigned a number. The government held a "great national lottery" in July to decide the order in which the first draftees would be called into service. Blindfolded, Secretary of War Newton D. Baker pulled number 258 out of a jar. The group of men assigned that number became the very first draftees.

Over the course of the war, more than 24 million Americans registered for the draft. Of these, about 2.8 million were actually drafted into the armed forces. Including volunteers, the total number of American men in uniform during World War I reached nearly 4.8 million. More than 4 million of these were sent to help the Allies in France.

Constructing a War Economy While the Selective Service Commission raised an army, President Wilson worked to shift the national economy from peacetime to wartime production. This process proved slow and frustrating. First, the Council of National Defense, which was formed in August 1916, created an array of new federal administrative agencies to oversee different phases of the war effort. Individual agencies regulated food production, coal and petroleum distribution, and railway use. In practical terms, this meant that the government determined what crops farmers grew, what products industries produced, and how supplies moved around on the nation's trains.

Problems and administrative overlap soon led to the creation of the War Industries Board (WIB). The WIB eventually became independent of the Council of National Defense. Headed by **Bernard Baruch** (buh ROOK), an influential Wall Street investment broker who reported directly to the President, the WIB regulated all industries engaged in the war effort. Baruch's agency determined what products industries would make, where those products went, and how much they would cost. The system of free enterprise was curtailed to fulfill the nation's acute need for war materials. Americans realized that they had to cooperate rather than compete in order to defeat the Central Powers.

What Baruch did for industry, future U.S. President Herbert Hoover achieved for agriculture. As head of the Food Administration, he set prices high for wheat and other foodstuffs to encourage farmers to increase production. He also asked

Wartime Production

These women worked during the war inspecting bullets for rifles. *According to the graph, by what percentage did manufacturing increase between 1915 and 1918?*

Rising U.S. Production, 1915–1918

Percentage of increase over 1914 production levels

Textiles · Manufacturing · Agriculture

* In 1916, agricultural output did not increase above the 1914 levels.
SOURCE: *The American Home Front*, James L. Abrahamson

Americans to <u>conserve</u> food as a patriotic gesture. If the American people ate less, then more food could be shipped to American and other Allied soldiers fighting the war overseas. To this end, Hoover instituted wheatless Mondays and Wednesdays, meatless Tuesdays, and porkless Thursdays and Saturdays.

Shaping Public Opinion Hoover's efforts would have been fruitless if the American people did not believe in supporting the war. Most Americans did not understand the reasons for the war in 1914, and many questioned why the United States became involved in 1917. It was the job of the **Committee on Public Information (CPI)** to educate the public about the causes and nature of the war. The CPI had to convince Americans that the war effort was a just cause.

Wilson appointed **George Creel** as the director of the CPI. A former journalist and a passionate admirer of American institutions, Creel combined education and a widespread advertising campaign to "sell America." The CPI distributed 75 million pamphlets and 6,000 press releases, and it assembled an army of 75,000 speakers who gave lectures and brief speeches on America's war aims and the nature of the enemy. In addition, the CPI designed, printed, and distributed millions of posters that dramatized the needs of America and its allies. The CPI also stressed the cruelty and wickedness of the enemy, particularly Germany, which in some cases aggravated resentment toward German Americans. Still, using these methods, Creel and the CPI earned widespread support for the American war effort.

✔ **Checkpoint** How did the United States ready its military, economy, and people for war?

Opposition and Its Consequences

The CPI's work was important because Americans did not always peacefully agree with one another about the war. Members of two large ethnic groups, German Americans and Irish Americans, tended to oppose the Allies for different reasons. Swept up in patriotic fervor, some people treated German Americans with prejudice, or intolerance. Other Americans were pacifists who opposed war for any reason. To quiet dissent, or differing opinions, the government acted in ways that sometimes trespassed on individual liberties.

Noble Goals
Postcards like this one emphasized Wilson's goal of making the world "safe for democracy."

Resistance to the Draft Without a doubt, the draft created controversy. Some Americans believed it was an illegal intrusion of the federal government into their private lives. Some men refused to cooperate with the Selective Service process. They were often court-martialed and imprisoned. Others simply tried to avoid the draft. Perhaps as many as 12 percent of men who received draft notices never responded to them.

Another group resisted the draft by becoming **conscientious objectors,** people whose moral or religious beliefs forbid them to fight in wars. In theory, the Selective Service Act exempted from combat service members of "any well recognized religious sect or organization . . . whose existing creed or principles forbid its members to participate in war." In practice, this policy was widely ignored. Some conscientious objectors were treated badly by their local draft boards, and others were humiliated in training camps. As America's participation in the war increased, however, the government improved its treatment of conscientious objectors.

"To make the World Safe for Democracy"

● **INFOGRAPHIC**

HE'S IN THE ARMY NOW!

While the presence of millions of American soldiers in France helped the Allies, their absence at home had dramatic consequences. Families lived in constant fear for their fathers, husbands, brothers, or sons overseas, some of whom would never return. Many people had to take on the jobs of the absent soldiers. Meanwhile, the government encouraged Americans to go to work in war industries, conserve food and other goods, and buy Liberty bonds to support the war effort.

Effects of the War on the Workforce

Workers Lost	Workers Gained
In addition to the millions of workers who went into the military, immigrants from Europe, who had swelled the workforce in the early 1900s, dropped from one million in 1914 to only 31,000 in 1918.	Nearly 500,000 women joined the workforce for the first time, 400,000 African Americans left the rural South for industrial jobs in the North, and nearly 240,000 Mexicans immigrated to the United States, filling mainly agricultural jobs in the Southwest.

Result: Despite gains, the United States still faced a shortage of workers when it joined the war in 1917.

SOURCE: *The American Home Front*, James L. Abrahamson

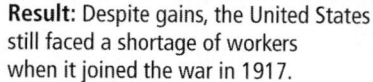

Private T. P. Loughlin says goodbye to his family (above right). A poster with a stirring message urges Americans to buy Liberty bonds (far right). Two women deliver ice, a job formerly done by men (left).

OVER THE TOP
FOR YOU

Buy U.S. Gov't Bonds
THIRD LIBERTY LOAN

Women Work for Peace Some American women also opposed the war. Before the war, a number of leading American feminists, including reformer Jane Addams, formed the Women's Peace Party and, with pacifist women from other countries, the Women's International League for Peace and Freedom. Jeannette Rankin, the first woman to serve in the U.S. House of Representatives, voted against the declaration of war. After America joined the Allies, some women continued to oppose the war, but most supported American war efforts. For example, the influential National American Woman Suffrage Association (NAWSA) dropped its initial peace initiatives and supported America's war <u>objectives</u>. After adopting this new policy, NAWSA doubled in size.

Thinking Critically
1. **Draw Conclusions** How did conserving food on the home front help the war effort?

2. **Predict Consequences** What do you think will happen to the women and African Americans who took new jobs during the war when the war ends?

Vocabulary Builder
objective–(uhb JEHK tihv) *n.* something worked toward; goal

The Government Cracks Down on Dissent The work of the CPI created a mood in America that did not welcome open debate. Some felt the CPI stifled the free expression of controversial opinions and worried about the impact of a rigorous military campaign on democracy. They did not want the freedoms that Americans held most dear to become victims of the conflict. As in previous and future wars, the government navigated a difficult path between respecting and restricting individual rights. Authorities tended to treat harshly individuals who worked against the goal of winning the war.

In June 1917, Congress passed the **Espionage Act,** allowing postal authorities to ban treasonable or seditious newspapers, magazines, or printed materials from the mail. It also enacted severe penalties for anyone engaged in disloyal or treasonable activities. Anyone found obstructing army recruiters, aiding the enemy, or generally interfering with the war effort could be punished with up to a $10,000 fine and 20 years of imprisonment.

In 1918, Congress limited freedom of speech even further with the passage of the Sedition Act. The act made it unlawful to use "disloyal, profane, scurrilous, or abusive language" about the American form of government, the Constitution, or the military forces. The government employed the Sedition Act to prosecute socialists, political radicals, and pacifists. Eugene V. Debs, the leader of the Socialist Party in America, was imprisoned under the act. For his crime—giving a mildly antiwar speech to a convention of socialists in Canton, Ohio—he was sentenced to a 10-year term in a federal prison.

The Supreme Court upheld the constitutionality of the Sedition Act in the case of *Schenck* v. *United States* (1919). The Court ruled that there are times when the need for public order is so pressing that First Amendment protections of speech do not apply. The Debs case and others like it show that the war did lead to some suppression of personal freedoms and individual rights.

Prejudice Against German Americans Sometimes, the war enthusiasm created by the CPI and other groups took an ugly turn. Some German Americans were treated harshly during the war. Americans regarded Germany—with its arrogant kaiser, ruthless generals, and spike-helmeted soldiers—as the primary foe among the Central Powers. Popular movies, such as *The Kaiser, the Beast of Berlin*, as well as some CPI posters and speeches intensified this feeling by portraying Germany as a cruel enemy. Some Americans wrongly generalized that if Germany was cruel, then all German people were cruel.

As a result, Americans stopped teaching German in public schools and discontinued playing the music of Beethoven and Brahms. They renamed German measles "liberty measles," cooked "liberty steaks" instead of hamburgers, and walked their "liberty pups" instead of dachshunds. German Americans were pressured to prove their loyalty to America by condemning the German government, giving up speaking German and reading German-language newspapers, and participating enthusiastically in any patriotic drive. Occasionally, hatred of the German enemy boiled over into violence against German Americans. Some German Americans were harassed, others were beaten, and a few were killed for no other reason than they were born in Germany or spoke with a German accent.

✓ **Checkpoint** Compare and contrast the reasons some Americans did not support the war.

Eugene V. Debs Protests

In June 1918, Socialist leader Eugene V. Debs was arrested for making an antiwar speech in Canton, Ohio (below). While in prison, Debs accepted the Socialist Party's nomination for President and won more than 900,000 votes in the 1920 election.

The War Changes American Society

The war not only changed the economic and political lives of Americans, but it also brought substantial social changes. New opportunities opened up for women, African Americans, and Mexican Americans. Some left their homes to seek new ones where they could take advantage of these opportunities.

Women Embrace New Opportunities Before the war, some American women campaigned for women's suffrage. They won the vote in several western states and still hoped to gain the franchise nationally. Many feared that the war would draw attention away from their efforts. In fact, the war gave women new chances and won them the right to vote.

As men entered the armed forces, many women moved into the workforce for the first time. Women filled jobs that were vacated by men who had gone to fight. They worked in munitions factories, on the railroads, as telegraph operators and trolley conductors, and in other jobs that were previously open only to men. Others labored on farms. Some joined the Red Cross or the American Women's Hospital Service and went overseas. They worked as doctors, nurses, ambulance drivers, and clerks. Thousands enlisted when the Army Corps of Nurses was created in 1918. Women proved that they could succeed in any type of job, regardless of difficulty or risk.

By their efforts and sacrifices during the war, women convinced President Wilson to support their suffrage demands. He contended that granting the vote to women was "vital to winning the war." If women could do the work of men, they certainly deserved the same voting privileges as men. Finally, in 1919, Congress passed the Nineteenth Amendment giving the vote to women. The required two thirds of states ratified the amendment in the summer of 1920, a victory more than 70 years in the making.

Nursing the Wounded

Red Cross workers were a symbol of caring in the midst of fear during World War I. About 18,000 American Red Cross nurses cared for wounded soldiers and civilians during the war. Their job was difficult and often dangerous—nearly 300 nurses lost their lives.

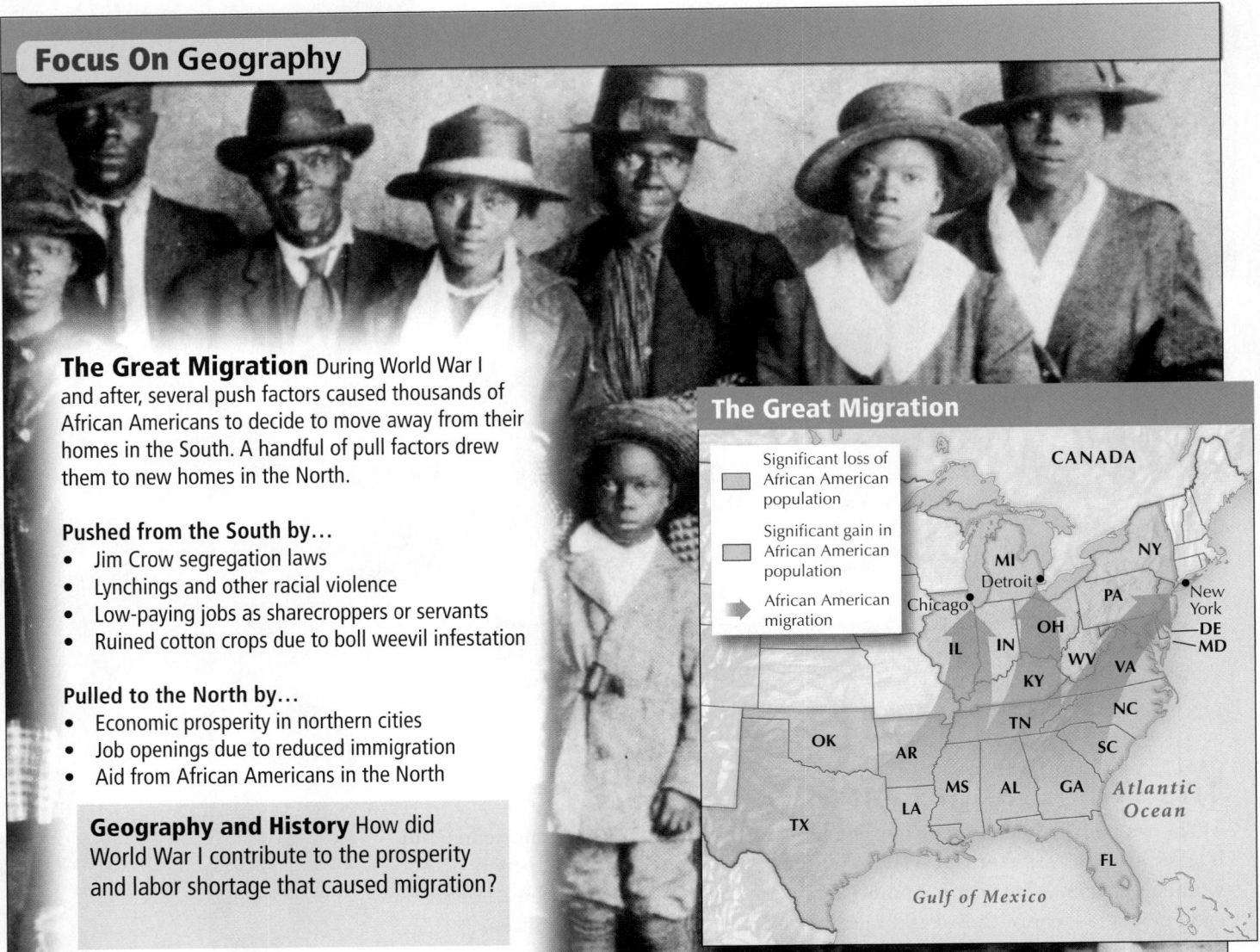

The Great Migration During World War I and after, several push factors caused thousands of African Americans to decide to move away from their homes in the South. A handful of pull factors drew them to new homes in the North.

Pushed from the South by...
- Jim Crow segregation laws
- Lynchings and other racial violence
- Low-paying jobs as sharecroppers or servants
- Ruined cotton crops due to boll weevil infestation

Pulled to the North by...
- Economic prosperity in northern cities
- Job openings due to reduced immigration
- Aid from African Americans in the North

Geography and History How did World War I contribute to the prosperity and labor shortage that caused migration?

The Great Migration

- Significant loss of African American population
- Significant gain in African American population
- → African American migration

CANADA · Detroit · Chicago · MI · NY · PA · New York · OH · DE · MD · IL · IN · WV · VA · KY · NC · TN · SC · OK · AR · MS · AL · GA · Atlantic Ocean · LA · TX · FL · Gulf of Mexico

African Americans Follow Opportunity North The war similarly presented new opportunities to African Americans. From the outset, most African American leaders supported the war. "If this is our country, then this is our war," wrote African American leader W.E.B. Du Bois. He viewed the struggle as an excellent opportunity to show all Americans the loyalty and patriotism of African Americans. Thousands of them enlisted or were drafted into the army and sailed for the battlefields of France. On the battlefield, they fought in segregated units under the command of white officers. Altogether, 367,000 African Americans served in the military. Hundreds died for their country.

Meanwhile, a great movement of African Americans from the rural South to the industrial North was taking place. This movement to the "Land of Hope," as many African Americans referred to the North at that time, is called the **Great Migration.** African Americans left their homes in the South for many reasons. Some hoped to escape the violent racism of the South. Others desired better jobs and a chance for economic advancement, which wartime industry in the North offered. Still others dreamed of a better future for their children. Between 1910 and 1920, more than 1.2 million African Americans moved to the North.

Some whites in the South tried to get blacks to stay in the region of their birth, using methods that ranged from persuasion to violence. Meanwhile, African

Americans who already lived in the North encouraged migration. Newspapers in the North, such as the Chicago *Defender,* an African American newspaper that was widely read in the South, pushed home this point:

Primary Source   "I beg you, my brother, to leave the benighted land. . . . Get out of the South. . . . Come north then, all you folks, both good and bad. . . . The *Defender* says come."

—*Chicago Defender*

African Americans moved to Chicago, as the *Defender* encouraged, where they found work in meatpacking plants. They migrated to Detroit, where they obtained jobs in auto factories. They traveled to smaller industrial towns in the Midwest and to the giant cities of the Northeast. Millions eventually made the exodus, and although they did not entirely escape discrimination, many did forge better futures. The Great Migration was one of the most important episodes in African American history.

Mexican Americans Move North Some of the same reasons that led African Americans to move north caused Mexicans to cross the border into the United States. Many Mexicans also faced violence and desperate poverty, and they also wanted better lives for themselves and their children. Most immigrated to the American West, where they sought work on large ranches and farms in Texas and along the Pacific Coast. Increased demands for food and a decrease in American farmworkers created jobs that Mexican migrants filled.

Some of the Mexican migration was seasonal. Many workers crossed the border to harvest fruits or grains or to pick cotton while each crop was in season, then crossed back into Mexico. But others stayed and made the United States their home. Some Mexican workers migrated first to the Southwest and then to the northern states in search of factory jobs, but a large population stayed in California. They formed *barrios* (BAHR ee ohz), or Hispanic neighborhoods, in Los Angeles and in smaller cities in California's Imperial Valley. California had always had a rich Hispanic heritage, but these new immigrants added an important economic dimension to that heritage.

✓ **Checkpoint** How did the war provide new opportunities for women, African Americans, and Mexican Americans?

SECTION

2 Assessment

Progress Monitoring *Online*
For: Self-test with vocabulary practice
Web Code: nea-0604

Comprehension

1. Terms and People For each item below, write a sentence explaining how it affected the American home front during World War I.
- Selective Service Act
- Bernard Baruch
- CPI
- George Creel
- conscientious objector
- Espionage Act
- Great Migration

2. NoteTaking **Reading Skill Summarize** Use your chart to answer the Section Focus Question: How did the war affect Americans at home?

Writing About History

3. Quick Write: Identify Multiple Effects Write a paragraph describing three effects that World War I had on the American home front. Think about economic and social changes caused by the war. Be sure to include at least one example of each effect to support your statements.

Critical Thinking

4. Categorize In what ways did Americans support the war effort?

5. Identify Point of View How did the Supreme Court justify the restrictions of the Sedition Act?

6. Predict Consequences How do you think returning soldiers reacted to changes at home when the war ended?

What Are the Limits of Free Speech?

 4.II.C.3

The First Amendment guarantees that each person has the right to free speech, both spoken and written. It protects the right of people to have their say and to hear what others have to say. But can the government limit freedom of speech in order to protect the rights or safety of individuals and the nation?

Schenck v. *United States* (1919)

The Facts	The Issue	The Decision
• During World War I, Charles Schenck was convicted of violating the Espionage Act of 1917, which made it a crime to cause refusal of duty in the military. • Schenck had distributed pamphlets urging men to resist the military draft.	Schenck's appeal to the Supreme Court argued that his actions were protected by the First Amendment.	The Court unanimously upheld Schenck's conviction and said that in times of war the government may place reasonable limitations on freedom of speech.

Why It Matters

The Supreme Court reasoned that there are limits to freedom of speech. Justice Oliver Wendell Holmes pointed out that one does not have the right to falsely shout "Fire!" in a crowded theater and cause a panic. He then set his famous "clear and present danger" test for determining the limits of the First Amendment protection of speech.

▲ A World War I–era poster

> "The question in every case is whether the words used are used in such circumstances and are of such a nature as to create a clear and present danger that they will bring about the substantive evils that Congress has a right to prevent."

Over the years, the Supreme Court has protected the individual's right to express unpopular ideas. But the Court has also said that free speech is limited. Restricted speech includes obscenities, libel, slander, words that incite violence, and words that pose an immediate threat to the rights of individuals or national security.

Connect to Your World

What are the limits of free speech in schools? Select one of the cases below. Research and summarize the facts of the case, the Court's decision, and the reasoning behind the decision. Explain why you agree or disagree with the decision.

- *Tinker* v. *Des Moines School District* (1969)
- *Hazelwood School District* v. *Kuhlmeier* (1988)

For: Supreme Court cases
Web Code: nee-0613

◄ **Free Speech in School**
In 1969, Mary Beth Tinker went to the Supreme Court to test her right to protest the Vietnam War in school.

WITNESS HISTORY 🔊 AUDIO

War Enthusiasm

Although the first American troops arrived in France in 1917, American soldiers did not reach France in great numbers until 1918. George M. Cohan's song "Over There" was used effectively to recruit troops and raise morale.

❝Over there, over there.
Send the word, send the word over there,
That the Yanks are coming,
The Yanks are coming . . .
So prepare, say a pray'r,
Send the word, send the word to beware.
We'll be over, we're coming over,
and we won't come back till it's over
Over there.❞

—From the song "Over There," written by George M. Cohan in 1917

▲ "Over There" sheet music

▲ American troops disembark in France.

Wilson, War, and Peace

NY Core Curriculum Objectives

- **4.II.D.1** The peace movement: Women's International League for Peace and Freedom
- **4.II.D.2** War aims: The Fourteen Points
- **4.II.D.3** Treaty of Versailles: Wilson's role
- **4.II.D.4** League of Nations: Henry Cabot Lodge and the United States Senate rejection

Terms and People

convoy
Vladimir Lenin
John J. Pershing
Fourteen Points
self-determination
League of Nations
Henry Cabot Lodge
reparations
"irreconcilables"
"reservationists"

NoteTaking

Reading Skill: Sequence As you read, sequence the events leading to the end of World War I in a timeline.

U-boat war intensifies.   Armistice ends war.

```
    March                          Nov.
    1917                           1918
```

Why It Matters When the United States entered World War I in the spring of 1917, the conflict had become a deadly, bloody stalemate. The war would be won or lost on the Western Front in France. Since 1914, both sides had tried desperately to break the stalemate there—and failed. The American entry into the war would play a key role in the Allied victory. **Section Focus Question: How did Americans affect the end of World War I and its peace settlements?**

America Gives the Allies the Edge

To European leaders, the United States was a great unknown. Ethnic divisions in America raised questions about how committed American troops would be in combat. Some doubted that the United States could raise, train, equip, and transport an army fast enough to influence the outcome of the war. Desperate German military leaders renewed unrestricted submarine warfare, hoping to end the conflict before the Americans could make a difference.

Allied Convoys Protect Shipping The Allies immediately felt the impact of the renewed unrestricted submarine warfare. German U-boats sank merchant ships in alarming numbers, faster than replacements could be built. As one merchant ship after another sank to the bottom of the sea, the Allies lost crucial supplies.

Together, the Allies addressed the problem of submarine warfare by adopting an old naval tactic: convoying. In a **convoy,** groups of

Vocabulary Builder
mutual–(MYOO choo uhl) *adj.*
shared

merchant ships sailed together, protected by warships. The arrangement was designed to provide <u>mutual</u> safety at sea. Convoys made up of British and American ships proved to be an instant success. Shipping losses from U-boat attacks fell as sharply as they had risen. Germany's gamble had failed.

The Allies Struggle Meanwhile, the situation on land began to swing in favor of the Central Powers. The Allies were exhausted by years of combat. Russia was torn by revolutions. In March 1917, a moderate, democratic revolution overthrew Czar Nicholas II but kept Russia in the war. In November 1917, radical communists led by **Vladimir Lenin** (LEHN ihn) staged a revolution and gained control of Russia. Russia stopped fighting in mid-December, and on March 3, 1918, the Treaty of Brest-Litovsk ended the war between Russia (soon to become the Soviet Union) and Germany. The end of the war on the Eastern Front allowed Germany to send more soldiers to the Western Front.

In the spring of 1918, Germany launched an all-out offensive on the Western Front. The fierce attacks threatened to break through Allied defenses and open a path to Paris. The hard-pressed Allies organized a joint command under French General Ferdinand Foch (fawsh).

American Troops Join the Fight General **John J. Pershing,** the commander of American forces in Europe, arrived in France in June 1917, with a small American force. However, it was not until early 1918 that American troops began arriving in larger numbers. At about the same time, the German offensive began to stall. By the end of March 1918, Allied counterattacks and German exhaustion ended the great German offensive.

More fighting followed, and with each passing week, American troops assumed more of the burden on the battlefield. Germany launched several more offensives. Allied defenses buckled and stretched but did not break. Each failed offensive weakened Germany a bit more and raised Allied hopes.

American Troops Distinguish Themselves American troops called "doughboys," saw significant action in the late spring and summer of 1918. Americans fought on the defensive along with the French at the Second Battle of the Marne and on the offensive at the Battle of Cantigny (kahn tee NYEE), where they dislodged a large German force from fortified positions. They battled valiantly at Château-Thierry (sha TOH tir EE) and Belleau (beh LOH) Wood, Meuse-Argonne (myooz ahr GAHN) and Saint-Mihiel (mee YEHL). Although it took some time, American troops learned quickly and fought bravely.

One of America's greatest war heroes was Alvin York of Tennessee. On October 8, 1918, York was one of thousands of Americans fighting in the Meuse-Argonne region of northeastern France. Trapped behind enemy lines, York and 16 other Americans took cover from blistering machine-gun fire. As half of the American force fell to German bullets, York took aim with his rifle and silenced a nearby German machine-gun nest. He then dodged a flurry of bullets to attack several other machine gunners and even charged one German position with only a pistol! When the firefight died down, York and the surviving Americans had taken the German position against amazing odds. York's battlefield heroics earned him a Congressional Medal of Honor.

HISTORY MAKERS

John J. Pershing (1860–1948)
John J. Pershing was an experienced soldier and leader who had fought in several wars before the beginning of American involvement in World War I. After the U.S. declaration of war, Pershing guided the creation of the American Expeditionary Force. He faced the difficult task of turning millions of untrained men into an effective fighting force. He then led this force in France. His skill in doing so helped the Allies win the war.

American Involvement in World War I, 1918

Geography *Interactive*
For: Interactive map
Web Code: nep-0605

Allies, 1918
Central Powers, 1918
Neutral countries, 1918
Allied front line, July 1918
Armistice line, November 1918
American offensives
British offensives
French offensives
Battle, 1918

North Sea

NETHERLANDS

52°N

UNITED KINGDOM

London

GERMANY

English Channel

Brussels

BELGIUM

Meuse River

Rhine River

0°

50°N

1 **Late May–July 1918**
Americans help stop the German advance at Cantigny, Château-Thierry, Belleau Wood, and the Second Battle of the Marne.

Amiens

Cantigny

LUX.

Moselle River

4 **Late September–November 11, 1918**
Americans attack through the Argonne Forest, reaching the Germans' vital railway line as the armistice brings the war to an end.

Aisne River

Oise R.

Seine River

Belleau Wood

Marne

Argonne

Paris

Château-Thierry

Saint-Mihiel

Marne River

2 **Late July–Early September 1918**
American forces help the Allies launch counteroffensives at the Marne and Amiens.

3 **Mid-September 1918**
American forces and French forces attack the Germans at Saint-Mihiel.

Miller Projection
0   50   100 mi
0   50   100 km

FRANCE

SWITZERLAND

When the American General Pershing reached France, he is said to have remarked "Lafayette, we are here!" He was referring to the French General Marquis de Lafayette, who aided the American cause during the Revolutionary War. Now was the time for America to repay that debt.

Map Skills American troops helped their allies stop the German offensive and launch successful counteroffensives.

1. **Locate:** (a) Allied front line, (b) Second Battle of the Marne, (c) armistice line

2. **Region** In what region of France did American troops have their greatest impact?

3. **Summarize** Describe the American contribution to the Allied victory on the Western Front.

The Convoy System in World War I

A cruiser directed the convoy.

Destroyers, or fast, armed ships, protected the merchant ships.

Armed trawlers and torpedo boats provided close protection and detected torpedoes.

Merchant ships, sometimes camouflaged, carried vital war supplies.

Alvin York was only one of thousands of heroes, many of whom died and most of whom were never recognized for their deeds. They followed orders, fought bravely, and made great sacrifices. Although African American soldiers often faced discrimination in the United States Army, they demonstrated their patriotism in dozens of engagements. For example, an entire African American unit, the 369th Infantry Regiment, received the *Croix de Guerre*, a French award for bravery, for its members' actions in the Meuse-Argonne campaign. By the end of the war, 1.3 million American soldiers had served on the front, more than 50,000 had lost their lives, and about 230,000 had been wounded.

The War Ends The American troops, added to those of France, Britain, and Italy, gave the Allies a military advantage. By the fall of 1918, the German front was collapsing. Both the German and Austro-Hungarian armies had had enough. Some men deserted, others mutinied, and many refused to fight. Their leaders faced little choice but to surrender. On November 11, 1918, Germany surrendered to the Allies in a railway car in Compiegne (kohn PYEHN), France.

The war was over. Of the millions of soldiers who mobilized to fight, almost 5 million Allied and 8 million Central Power troops were dead. Nearly 6.5 million civilians were also dead, victims of the terrible conflict. It was left to the peacemakers to determine whether the results would justify the costs.

✓ **Checkpoint** How did American involvement help the Allies win World War I?

● **INFOGRAPHIC**

American Voices From the Western Front

▲ American doughboy helmet, worn by a member of the first U.S. division in France

In 1918, Americans fought alongside other Allied troops in several key battles on the Western Front, including Belleau Wood, Château-Thierry, the Second Battle of the Marne, Saint-Mihiel, and Argonne Forest. Although all of these battles were Allied victories, they were nonetheless deadly. Machine-gun barrages and exploding artillery shells filled with shrapnel or deadly gas killed or wounded thousands of American troops. One soldier wrote home to his mother: "Don't worry. I am alright and it is worthwhile…we are blocking the road to Paris. So we don't die in vain."

"Our division, which went into action yesterday morning at practically full strength, has lost half its men. …I am just beginning to realize what war really is."

—John Clark, fighting in the Second Battle of the Marne, July 19, 1918

American machine-gunners at Belleau Wood

Wilson Promotes Peace Without Victory

Vladimir Lenin, leader of the communist revolution in Russia, maintained that the entire war was nothing more than an imperialistic land-grab. Once in power, he exposed secret treaties that Russia had made with the other Allies in which they agreed to divide among themselves the empires of their enemies. These revelations undercut the morality of the Allied cause in the war.

For President Woodrow Wilson, however, the war was not about acquisitions and imperialism—it was about peace and freedom. In January 1917, Wilson had introduced the idea of a "peace without victory" in an address to Congress:

Primary Source "Only a tranquil Europe can be a stable Europe. . . . [There] must be a peace without victory. . . . Victory would mean peace forced upon the loser, a victor's terms imposed upon the vanquished. It would be accepted in humiliation . . . and would leave a sting, a resentment, a bitter memory upon which terms of peace would rest, not permanently, but only as upon quicksand."
—Woodrow Wilson, "Peace Without Victory" speech, January 22, 1917

In another address to Congress in January 1918, Wilson answered Lenin's charges about the nature of the conflict by outlining America's war aims in what became known as the **Fourteen Points.** At the heart of the Fourteen Points was his idea of "peace without victory." Wilson proposed a peace inspired by noble ideals, not greed and vengeance.

Military Casualties of World War I

Troops (in millions)

Russia, British Empire, France, Italy, United States, Germany, Austria-Hungary

Allies — Central Powers

☐ Troops mobilized
▨ Troops killed, wounded, or missing

SOURCE: *Encyclopædia Britannica Online*

"Sept 29 at 5.50 A.M. Several men were gassed before we went over. Advanced to top of ridge. Capt. Smith killed. 1st Lt. McKory and 2nd Lt. Kerr killed later. No officers left. Piece of shrapnel hit helmet and went through canister of my gas mask."

—Corporal Wilfred H. Allen, fighting in late September 1918

Private Martin P. Coogan
75th Field Artillery

Gas mask ▶

American soldiers bandaged after a gas attack ▼

Devastated battlefield near Ypres

Thinking Critically
Why do you think American casualties were relatively few compared with the casualties of the other combatants?

History *Interactive* ✦
For: Interactive content
Web Code: nep-0611

NoteTaking

Reading Skill: Summarize As you read, summarize Wilson's goals for peace and whether or not each goal was fulfilled.

Wilson's Ideas for Peace	Decision Made at Paris Peace Conference
Peace without victory	Great Britain and France make Germany pay reparations.
Open diplomacy	
Freedom of seas and free trade	
Move toward ending colonialism	
Self-determination	
League of Nations	

The Fourteen Points sought to fundamentally change the world by promoting openness, encouraging independence, and supporting freedom. Critical of all secret treaties, Wilson called for open diplomacy. He insisted on freedom of the seas, free trade, a move toward ending colonialism, and a general reduction of armaments. He also championed national **self-determination,** or the right of people to choose their own form of government. This would lead to the creation of several new, independent states, but also raised many questions of which populations would achieve statehood and under what circumstances. Finally, he asked for a **League of Nations** to secure "mutual guarantees of political independence and territorial integrity to great and small states alike."

In early 1919, the victorious Allies held a peace conference in Versailles (ver SĪ), a suburb of Paris, in the former palace of Louis XIV. President Wilson believed that the peace conference was too important to be left to career diplomats and lesser politicians, so he crossed the Atlantic Ocean himself to represent the United States at the conference, something no President had ever done.

Wilson did not invite any leading Republicans to join him in his peace delegation. Senator **Henry Cabot Lodge,** a Republican foreign policy expert, was left behind because Wilson disliked him intensely. Wilson's decision angered Republicans, who had won control of Congress in the 1918 elections. However, when the American President arrived in France, adoring crowds greeted him. "Never has a king, never has an emperor received such a welcome," wrote one journalist.

 Checkpoint Why did Wilson believe that a "peace without victory" would help avoid future wars?

Wilson at the Paris Peace Conference

Wilson's idealism did not inspire the other Allied leaders at the peace conference. They blamed Germany for starting the war, reminded Wilson that they had suffered more in the war than the United States, and insisted that Germany make **reparations,** or payment for war damages. They wanted to weaken Germany so that it would never threaten Europe again.

Allied Leaders Reject Wilson's Ideas British prime minister David Lloyd-George and French premier Georges Clemenceau (klay mahn SOH) knew that the citizens of their countries expected both peace and victory. Lloyd-George insisted on protecting the existing colonial status quo and punishing Germany. Clemenceau wanted to make Germany pay dearly for what it had done to France. In addition to reparations, he demanded the return of Alsace-Lorraine and several key German colonies. Besides Britain and France, other Allies also had goals of their own and were skeptical of Wilson's grand vision.

Allies Create a League of Nations Once the Versailles conference began, Clemenceau, Lloyd-George, Italian Premier Vittorio Orlando, and other Allied leaders started to chip away at Wilson's Fourteen Points. Onto the scrap heap of failed proposals they piled freedom of the seas, free trade, the liberation of colonial empires, a general disarmament, and several other ideas.

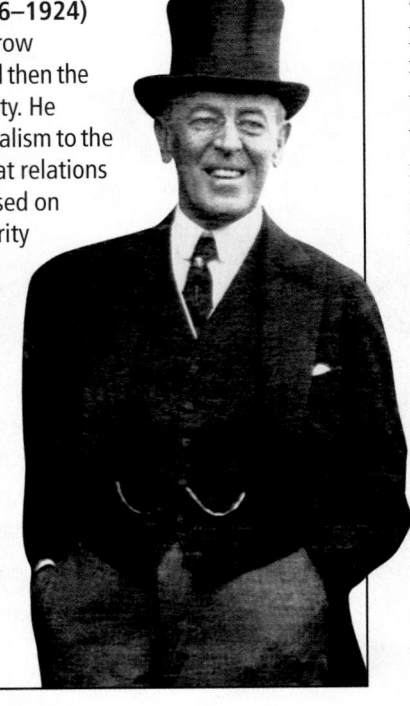

HISTORY MAKERS

Woodrow Wilson (1856–1924)
Before entering politics, Woodrow Wilson was first a professor and then the president of Princeton University. He brought his intellect and his idealism to the presidency. Wilson believed that relations between nations should be based on the principles of collective security and the common good. During the Paris Peace Conference, he urged other nations to form an international organization that could be used to promote peace. Although the League of Nations was ultimately unable to ensure peace in Europe, it laid the groundwork for the United Nations, which the United States took an active role in creating after World War II.

Territorial Changes After World War I

Geography *Interactive*
For: Interactive map
Web Code: nep-0606

Legend:
- New states
- British mandate
- French mandate
- Austro-Hungarian Empire, 1914
- German Empire, 1914
- Ottoman Empire, 1914
- Russian Empire, 1914

Map Skills Several of Wilson's Fourteen Points were violated when the map of Europe was redrawn after the war.

1. **Locate:** (a) Alsace-Lorraine, (b) Austro-Hungarian Empire, (c) Yugoslavia, (d) Iraq

2. **Region** Which of the four former empires lost the most territory as a result of the war?

3. **Identify Central Issues** How did the establishment of mandates violate the principle of self-determination?

Wilson lost a number of battles but kept fighting to salvage a League of Nations, a world organization where countries could gather and peacefully resolve their quarrels. On this point, Wilson refused to compromise. The other delegates finally voted to make the League of Nations part of the treaty.

Problems With the Peace In the end, the various peace treaties created almost as many problems as they solved. In the new map that emerged from the conference, national self-determination was violated almost as often as it was confirmed. In Europe, several populations of Germans found themselves attached to non-German nations. The same was true of several Austrian populations.

Furthermore, in the Middle East, the breakup of the Ottoman Empire led to new states in which ethnic groups were clustered together randomly. To form Iraq, for example, the Versailles peacemakers threw together three provinces of the defeated Ottoman Empire—Basra, Baghdad, and Mosul. But Basra had natural links to the Persian Gulf and India, Baghdad to Persia, and Mosul to Turkey and Syria. The various regions had no sense of Iraqi nationalism. In addition, Iraq, like other holdings in the Middle East, Asia, and Africa, was not allowed to practice self-determination. It was attached to Britain as a mandate, or territory overseen by another nation.

✓ **Checkpoint** How did the decisions at the Paris Peace Conference violate the Fourteen Points?

Should the United States Join the League of Nations?

After the Paris Peace Conference, the United States had to decide whether to join the League of Nations. The League's purpose was to help maintain peace in the world. In the political cartoon below, Wilson overloads a dove, a symbol of peace, with a large, heavy branch representing the League of Nations. Read the options below. Then you make the call.

President Wilson Favors Joining

Primary Source

❝A general association of nations must be formed . . . for the purpose of affording mutual guarantees of political indepen-dence and territorial integrity to great and small states alike. . . . It is the principle of justice to all peoples . . . and their right to live on equal terms . . . with one another, whether they be strong or weak.❞

—President Woodrow Wilson,
January 8, 1918

Senator Borah Opposes Joining

Primary Source

❝Mr. President, there is another reason . . . why I shall record my vote against this treaty. It imperils what I conceive to be the underlying, the very first principles of this Republic. It is in conflict with the right of our people to govern themselves free from all restraint, legal or moral, of foreign powers. It challenges every tenet of my political faith.❞

—Senator William Borah,
November 19, 1919

You Decide
1. Why did Wilson favor joining the League of Nations?
2. Why did Borah oppose joining?
3. What decision would you have made? Why?

America Rejects the Treaty

When Wilson left Versailles to return to the United States, he knew the treaty was not perfect. But he believed that over time the League could correct its prob-lems. He still thought that a lasting peace could emerge.

Wilson Faces Troubles at Home Wilson did not leave his problems in France when he boarded a ship bound for the United States. German Americans thought the treaty was too harsh toward Germany, especially the "war guilt clause" that suggested that Germany had caused the war. Irish Americans crit-icized the failure to create an independent Ireland. Most importantly, however, the treaty would need to be submitted to the Republican-controlled Senate For-eign Relations Committee and then ratified, or approved, by the Republican-controlled Senate. In both bodies, as well as in his own Democratic Party, Wilson faced stiff opposition.

A handful of senators believed that the United States should not get entangled in world politics or involved in world organizations. Known as **"irreconcilables,"** these isolationist senators opposed any treaty that had a League of Nations folded into it. They particularly disliked Article 10 of the League covenant. Article 10 called for mutual defense by the signers of the treaty, a pledge that each nation would "respect and preserve . . . the territorial integrity and existing polit-ical inde-pendence of all the Members of the League."

A larger group of senators, led by Henry Cabot Lodge and known as **"reservationists,"** were opposed to the treaty as it was written. Some wanted only small changes, while others demanded larger ones. For example, many felt

Article 10 could lead the United States into a war without the consent of Congress, which was unconstitutional. Reservationists believed that the language of the article was too vague and demanded that it not <u>contradict</u> the power of Congress to declare war. But with some changes, the reservationists were prepared to vote for the Treaty of Versailles. They knew that polls indicated that the American people favored the League of Nations.

Wilson had compromised in Versailles, but he was not ready to compromise in Washington, D.C. When the Senate delayed its ratification vote, Wilson took his case directly to the people. The League of Nations had become his personal crusade. Even though he was ill and weak, he set himself the grueling task of crossing the country and giving 32 addresses in 33 days. But his health failed on September 25, 1919, in Pueblo, Colorado. He was rushed back to Washington, D.C., but suffered a debilitating stroke a few days later. As the Senate prepared to vote on the treaty, Wilson lay close to death, barely able to speak.

The Senate Rejects the Versailles Treaty In November 1919, one year after the war ended, a treaty revised to eliminate the complaints of the reservationists reached the Senate for a vote. Wilson would not compromise and told his Democratic supporters to vote with the irreconcilables against it. They did, and it was defeated. Next, the Senate voted on the treaty without any changes. The Democrats voted for it, but the combined strength of the irreconcilables and reservationists defeated it. Once more it was voted on, this time with only modest changes. Again, Wilson told his followers to vote against it. Although some Democrats voted for it, the combination of Wilson Democrats and irreconcilables defeated the treaty.

The problem was not that most of the Senate was isolationist. Except for the irreconcilables, most senators wanted the United States to participate in world affairs. They differed slightly on what form that participation would take. However, at a moment that demanded compromise, Wilson and his opponents refused to put aside personal and political differences for the good of the country. The tragedy of the failed votes was that without full American support, the League of Nations proved unable to maintain peace among nations.

✓ **Checkpoint** What reservations did Henry Cabot Lodge and his followers have about the peace treaty?

Vocabulary Builder
<u>contradict</u>–(kahn truh DIHKT) v. to go against

SECTION

3 Assessment

Progress Monitoring *Online*
For: Self-test with vocabulary practice
Web Code: nea-0607

Comprehension

1. **Terms and People** For each item below, write a sentence explaining why it is significant to the end of World War I.
   - convoy
   - Fourteen Points
   - self-determination
   - League of Nations
   - Henry Cabot Lodge
   - reparations
   - "irreconcilables"
   - "reservationists"

2. **NoteTaking Reading Skill: Sequence** Use your timeline and chart to answer the Section Focus Question: How did Americans affect the end of World War I and its peace settlements?

Writing About History

3. **Quick Write: Create an Effects Diagram** Predict at least three problems that could stem from the Treaty of Versailles. Create a diagram showing these effects.

Critical Thinking

4. **Summarize** Describe America's contributions to the Allied war effort.

5. **Express Problems Clearly** What problems did the peace treaties solve? What problems did they create?

6. **Draw Conclusions** Why did the United States Senate ultimately reject the peace treaty and the League of Nations?

4.II.D.2

Woodrow Wilson:
The Fourteen Points

In a speech to Congress on January 8, 1918, President Wilson laid out America's war aims and his vision for peace after the war. His speech included fourteen key points upon which he believed that the peace following the war must be based. However, not all of Wilson's ideas were adopted at the Paris Peace Conference.

What we demand in this war, therefore, is nothing peculiar to ourselves. It is that the world be made fit and safe to live in; and particularly that it be made safe for every peace-loving nation which, like our own, wishes to live its own life, [and] determine its own institutions. . . . The program of the world's peace, therefore, is our only program; and that program, the only possible program as we see it, is this:

1. Open covenants[1] of peace, openly arrived at, after which there shall be no private international understandings of any kind but diplomacy shall proceed always frankly and in the public view.

2. Absolute freedom of navigation upon the seas, outside territorial waters, alike in peace and in war, except as the seas may be closed in whole or in part by international action for the enforcement of international covenants.

3. The removal, so far as possible, of all economic barriers and the establishment of an equality of trade conditions among all the nations consenting to the peace and associating themselves for its maintenance.

4. Adequate guarantees given and taken that national armaments will be reduced to the lowest point consistent with domestic safety.

5. A free, open-minded, and absolutely impartial adjustment of all colonial claims, based upon a strict observance of the principle that in determining all such questions of sovereignty the interests of the populations concerned must have equal weight with the equitable claims of the government whose title is to be determined. . . .

14. A general association of nations must be formed under specific covenants for the purpose of affording mutual guarantees of political independence and territorial integrity to great and small states alike.

Summary of the Fourteen Points

1.	Make no secret diplomatic agreements.
2.	Allow freedom of the seas in peace and war.
3.	Remove as many economic trade barriers as possible between countries.
4.	Reduce stockpiles of military armaments to lowest point needed for domestic safety.
5.	Adjust colonial claims, giving more weight to the views of the colonized peoples.
6.	Evacuate and restore Russian territories seized during the war.
7.	Restore and protect Belgium's sovereignty.
8.	Restore French territory and settle the debate over Alsace-Lorraine.
9.	Adjust Italy's boundaries according to the nationalities of populations living there.
10.	Allow the peoples of the former Austro-Hungarian Empire to choose their own governments.
11.	Redraw boundaries of Balkan states based on nationalities and historical allegiances.
12.	Separate the Ottoman Empire into independent countries according to nationality; guarantee all nations access to the Dardanelles.
13.	Restore and protect Poland as a sovereign state with access to the sea.
14.	Establish an association of nations to provide collective security and to ensure peace.

▼ President Wilson giving a speech in 1916

Thinking Critically

1. **Make Inferences** Why does President Wilson think that the Fourteen Points are "the only possible program" for the world's peace?

2. **Synthesize Information** Which of the Fourteen Points introduced the idea of the League of Nations?

1. **covenant** (KUHV uh nuhnt) *n.* formal agreement.

SECTION

4

WELCOME HOME

▲ Members of the famous 369th Infantry Regiment are welcomed home in New York City, 1919.

A Difficult Transition

The service of African Americans during the war renewed hopes for equal rights for African Americans. However, the reality changed little.

❝It is necessary now as never before that the black man press his claims as an American citizen. . . . The Government laid claim to him, both body and soul, and used him as freely as if he were the equal of any other man behind the guns. . . . The path he had to walk was just as rough, the load he had to carry was just as heavy, and the life he gave just as sweet, as that of any other man who laid his all upon the altar. He should contend, therefore, for every privilege, every comfort, every right which other men enjoy.❞

—Dr. A. A. Graham, African American leader

Effects of the War

 Core Curriculum Objectives

- **4.II.C.4** Red Scare, 1918–1919
- **5.I.A.1** War's effects on gender roles, on African Americans, and other minority groups
- **5.I.A.3** Return to "normalcy"
- **5.I.B.4** Problems on the farm

Terms and People

influenza	Nicola Sacco
inflation	Bartolomeo Vanzetti
Red Scare	Warren G. Harding
Palmer Raids	creditor nation

NoteTaking

Reading Skill: Identify Main Ideas As you read, identify and record the main ideas of this section in a concept web like the one below.

Why It Matters The end of World War I produced an unstable international order. The loss of territory and the harsh reparations imposed by the Allies encouraged a strong desire for revenge in Germany. Meanwhile, Lenin's Soviet Russia threatened revolution throughout the industrial world. In the United States, the horrors of the war along with widespread fear of communists and radicals led Americans to question their political, if not their economic, role in the world. **Section Focus Question: What political, economic, and social effects did World War I have on the United States?**

America Adjusts to Peace

World War I produced significant economic, social, political, and cultural changes in America and throughout the world. This led to important, occasionally painful, adjustments.

Flu Epidemic Grips the Nation The movement from war to peace would have been difficult even in the best of times. But the end of 1918 and 1919 were not the best of times. In September 1918, an unusually deadly form of the **influenza,** or flu, virus appeared. Research in recent years shows that the 1918 influenza virus was originally a bird flu that mutated to spread to humans. Many historians now believe that the virus originated in the United States, then traveled around the world. Once the virus began, it spread like a wildfire and killed millions worldwide like a predator feasting on its prey. The great influenza pandemic, coming on the heels of the Great War, gave a sense of doom and dread to people around the globe.

The Influenza Pandemic Hits the United States

The influenza attack of 1918 was a pandemic, an epidemic that affects many people all over the world. Oddly, the virus hit men and women in their twenties and thirties the hardest, rather than children and the elderly. The flu pandemic killed 550,000 Americans, including 50,000 soldiers. Worldwide, it probably claimed between 50 and 100 million lives. **Describe how the influenza virus spread in the United States.**

People who contracted the influenza virus (above) often complained of "body aches so intense they felt like bones breaking." Many people avoided public places, and others, like these ballplayers (right), wore masks when they went outside.

The Spread of Influenza in the United States

■	Before September 14
▨	September 14–September 21
□	After September 21

Most of the virus' victims in the United States died between mid-September and early December 1918.

Women and African Americans Confront New Realities Women and African Americans made significant advances during the war. However, the end of the war also spelled the end of wartime economic opportunities for both groups. A postwar recession, or economic slowdown, created a competitive job market. By 1920, there were fewer women in the workforce than there had been in 1910.

In northern industrial cities, African American workers vied with returning soldiers for jobs and housing. During the hot summer of 1919, race riots erupted in cities throughout the country. The worst, in Chicago, was triggered by the drowning of a young black man by whites, and went on for 13 days. In 1921, violence erupted in Tulsa, Oklahoma, when armed African American men—many of them returning veterans—tried to protect a young black man from lynching. By the time the Tulsa race riots were over, at least 10 whites and 26 African Americans were dead. In one African American neighborhood, white rioters burned 35 city blocks to the ground.

Inflation Leads to Labor Unrest During the war, **inflation,** or rising prices, had been held in check. After the conflict, Americans rushed to buy consumer goods rather than war bonds. The scarcity of these goods, coupled with widespread demand, caused inflation. During the war, the price of corn, wheat, cotton, cattle, and other agricultural goods had risen, encouraged by Hoover's policies. After the war, prices fell sharply, making it difficult for farmers to pay their mortgages or buy what they needed for the next growing season. This began a long period of tough times for farmers.

Industrial workers also felt the pain of inflation when their wages did not buy as much as they had during the war. In 1919, more than 4 million workers, or 20 percent of the workforce, went on strike at one time or another. Demanding rewards for their wartime patriotism, workers struck for higher wages and shorter workdays. In Boston, even the police force struck. The workers won some of the strikes, but they lost far more. When some strikes turned violent, the pro-management press blamed the presence of radicals among the strike leaders.

✔ **Checkpoint** How did the economic situation after the war lead to labor unrest?

The Red Scare

The reaction against labor was partly spurred by a wave of fear of radicals and communists. The <u>emergence</u> of the Soviet Union as a communist nation, which began in 1917, fed these fears. Communist ideology called for an international workers' revolution as a prelude to the death of capitalism. To this end, Soviet leader Vladimir Lenin encouraged and supported revolutions outside of his country. In Central and Eastern Europe, a series of communist revolts did break out, making it seem like the worldwide revolution was starting.

Fear of Communism Starts the Red Scare This revolutionary activity abroad, coupled with strikes across the United States, prompted the first American **Red Scare,** a wave of widespread fear of suspected communists and radicals thought to be plotting revolution within the United States. Real revolutionary activity inside America gave substance to the scare. Authorities discovered bombs mailed to important industrialists and government officials, including Attorney General A. Mitchell Palmer. Suspected anarchists, members of a radical political movement, exploded bombs in cities across America.

As the leading law-enforcement official, Palmer mounted a broad offensive against radicals in the United States in 1919 and 1920. In a series of raids in early 1920, known as the **Palmer Raids,** police arrested thousands of people, some who were radicals and some who were simply immigrants from southern or Eastern Europe. Most were never charged or tried for a crime. The government then deported hundreds of radicals.

To many, these actions seemed to attack the liberties that Americans held most dear. A group of people in New York City formed the American Civil Liberties Union (ACLU) in 1920 to protect these liberties. The ACLU tried to do this by becoming involved in important court cases. To this end, the ACLU became involved in one of America's most controversial court cases: the trial of Nicola Sacco and Bartolomeo Vanzetti.

Sacco and Vanzetti Are Executed **Nicola Sacco** (SAH koh) and **Bartolomeo Vanzetti** (van ZEHT ee) were Italian immigrants and known anarchists. They were charged with shooting and killing two men during a holdup at a shoe factory in a town

Vocabulary Builder
<u>emergence</u>–(ee MER juhns) *n.* rise or development

Guilty or Innocent?
Rosina Sacco visits her husband, Nicola Sacco, and Bartolomeo Vanzetti as the two men wait in the prisoners' dock during their famous trial. Debate whether both were truly guilty still continues.

The Wall Street Bombing

On September 16, 1920, just days after Sacco and Vanzetti's murder indictment, a horsecart filled with dynamite exploded in the financial heart of New York City. The explosion and flying debris killed about 40 people and caused the New York Stock Exchange to close early that day. Investigators suspected that anarchists had staged the bombing, but the culprits were never found.

near Boston. Eyewitnesses of the event said the robbers "looked Italian." Sacco and Vanzetti were arrested and charged with the crime. Even though the ACLU provided defense counsel, the two men were found guilty in a swift and decisive trial, despite the fact that there was little hard evidence against them. Some prominent legal scholars, intellectuals, and liberal politicians charged that the convictions were based more on Sacco and Vanzetti's ethnicity and political beliefs than on the facts of the crime. Nevertheless, on August 23, 1927, the two men were put to death in the electric chair.

At its worst, hysteria accompanied by violence characterized the Red Scare. Mobs attacked suspected radicals, abused immigrants, and committed crimes in the name of justice. But eventually, the great fear ended. Americans saw that democracy and capitalism were more powerful in the United States than Lenin's call for worldwide revolution. By the summer of 1920, the Red Scare hysteria, like the great influenza, had run its course.

 Checkpoint How did the rise of communism in the Soviet Union contribute to the Red Scare?

Americans Embrace Normalcy

Woodrow Wilson hoped that the presidential election of 1920 would prove that Americans supported both the League of Nations and his vision of the role the United States should play in the world. He suggested that electing Democratic presidential candidate James M. Cox of Ohio would show support for the League. The election of Republican candidate **Warren G. Harding** of Ohio would serve as a final rejection of the League.

Harding had a different view of the presidential race. He knew that national elections seldom turned on a single issue. Harding campaigned for a rejection of Wilsonian idealism. He was tired of progressive reforms and foreign crusades. Harding called for a return to "normalcy," by which he meant the "normality" of what he believed had been a simpler time before Wilson took office in 1913. Harding won in a landslide, and Republicans won control of Congress, as well. Americans had decisively rejected Wilson's ideas.

A Quiet American Giant Despite Harding's election and all it implied, the United States did not plan to totally withdraw from world affairs. By 1920, the United States was an economic giant. It was the richest, most industrialized country in the world. Even before the war, America led all other nations in industrial output. Now, British and French demands for American goods created an immense trade imbalance. Europeans had to borrow money from American bankers and obtain lines of credit with American business firms to pay for the goods.

This situation fundamentally changed America's economic standing in the world. The United States was now the largest **creditor nation** in the world, meaning that other countries owed the United States more money than the United States owed them. World War I shifted the economic center of the world from London to New York City. The United States embraced its new role as a quiet giant. A world without America playing a major economic role had become simply impossible to conceive.

The World Adjusts to a New Order World War I had caused sweeping changes around the globe. German and Russian monarchies toppled, and new forms of government were created. The Austro-Hungarian and Ottoman empires ceased to exist. Britain and France emerged from the war victorious but economically and politically weakened. In contrast, the victorious United States came out of the war strong, confident, and prosperous.

An old order five hundred years in the making had collapsed in just a few years. It was as if the world's compass was out of whack and no one knew where to turn for directions. The United States was unsure of the requirements of its new status. Could America retreat into isolationism in political but not economic affairs? After rejecting the League of Nations, how could it exert its moral authority in the world? Americans would wrestle with these questions—and many others—in the decades ahead.

✔ **Checkpoint** Why did the United States become the leading economic power after World War I?

A Return to "Normalcy"
The election of 1920 was the first presidential election in which women were allowed to vote under the Nineteenth Amendment. American voters overwhelmingly elected Warren G. Harding, who promised a return to simpler days.

Progress Monitoring *Online*
For: Self-test with vocabulary practice
Web Code: nea-0608

Comprehension

1. **Terms and People** For each item below, write a sentence explaining its significance to events in the United States after World War I.
   - influenza
   - inflation
   - Red Scare
   - Palmer Raids
   - Nicola Sacco
   - Bartolomeo Vanzetti
   - Warren G. Harding

2. **NoteTaking Reading Skill: Summarize** Use your concept web to answer the Section Focus Question: What political, economic, and social effects did World War I have on the United States?

Writing About History

3. **Quick Write: Write a Thesis Statement** Write a thesis statement for a cause-and-effect essay on the effects of World War I on the United States. Your thesis statement should state a point you will argue.

Critical Thinking

4. **Analyze Information** How did the influenza pandemic make the transition from war to peace more difficult?

5. **Determine Relevance** How does the Sacco and Vanzetti case demonstrate the mindset of the Red Scare?

6. **Draw Inferences** How did Americans both reject and embrace the new global influence of the United States?

Quick Study Guide

Progress Monitoring *Online*
For: Self-test with vocabulary practice
Web Code: nea-0609

■ Causes and Effects of America's Entry into World War I

Causes
- Many Americans have cultural ties with Britain and France.
- Reports of German atrocities in Belgium outrage Americans.
- Germany continues its policy of unrestricted submarine warfare, despite promises to stop.
- In the Zimmermann note, Germany offers Mexico the chance to regain lost U.S. territory.

America's Entry Into World War I

Effects
- The Allies defeat the Central Powers.
- The Government's role in daily life increases.
- African Americans and Mexican Americans migrate north.
- More women enter the workforce.
- The United States refuses to join the League of Nations.
- The United States becomes a leading economic power.

■ Views on America's Decision to Fight or Not to Fight

Isolationists	Believed the United States should isolate itself from all foreign conflicts
Internationalists	Believed the United States should actively work for peace but not enter the war
Interventionists	Believed the United States should intervene in the war on the side of the Allies, protect U.S. interests, and fulfill U.S. obligations

■ Key Military Engagements Involving American Troops

- Cantigny
- Château-Thierry
- Belleau Wood
- Second Battle of the Marne
- Amiens
- Saint-Mihiel
- Meuse-Argonne Offensive

☑ Quick Study Timeline

In America

1914
President Wilson announces American neutrality in World War I

1915
Sinking of the *Lusitania* angers Americans

Presidential Terms   **Woodrow Wilson 1913–1921**

Around the World

1914
Assassination of Austrian archduke triggers World War I

1915
Poison gas first used on Western Front

1916
More than 2 million casualties suffered in battle of Verdun and battle of the Somme on Western Front

American Issues
⬤–⬤–⬤ Connector

By connecting prior knowledge with what you have learned in this chapter, you can gradually build your understanding of enduring questions that still affect America today. Answer the questions below. Then, use your American Issues Connector study guide (or go online: www.PHSchool.com **Web Code:** neh-7903).

Issues You Learned About

⬤ **America Goes to War** The United States has been involved in two global conflicts.

1. How has the United States made the decision to declare war in past conflicts?

2. In 1916, Wilson won reelection using the campaign slogan "He kept us out of war," but less than a year later, the United States joined World War I. What happened to change Wilson's mind?

3. Why did some Americans oppose American involvement in World War I?

⬤ **Civil Liberties and National Security** At times, Americans' civil liberties are curtailed, resulting in major debates over constitutional rights and powers.

4. How does the Constitution guarantee that accused criminals will receive fair trials?

5. Why did some people protest the execution of Sacco and Vanzetti?

6. Describe another event during the Red Scare that seemed to curtail civil liberties.

⬤ **Checks and Balances** Responsibilities are shared among the three branches of the federal government.

7. Which branch of the government has the power to make treaties?

8. How did the battle over the Treaty of Versailles demonstrate the ways in which the different branches of the federal government may void one another's decisions?

Connect to Your World   New York

New York Goes to War New York played an important role in World War I, both as an industrial center and by sending soldiers overseas. New York City has numerous World War I memorials. One memorial located in Brooklyn's Prospect Park is a sculpture of an angel supporting a weary soldier and features the names of people from Brooklyn who were killed in the war. In Manhattan, a large plaque and bust in Central Park are dedicated to John Purroy Mitchel, a former New York City mayor who died while serving in the Army Air Corps. Research war memorials in your area of New York, and write a description of one you find. Then write a proposal for a new one, including a design, possible location, and text.

1917
United States declares war on Germany

1919
United States Senate rejects membership in League of Nations

History *Interactive*
For: Interactive timeline
Web Code: nep-0610

| 1917 | 1918 | 1919 | 1920 |

1918
Armistice with Germany ends war

1918–1919
Deadly influenza pandemic sweeps across the world

Chapter Assessment

Terms and People

1. Define **Western Front.** What characterized this region during World War I?

2. Who was **George Creel**? What methods did he introduce to "sell America"?

3. What was the **League of Nations**? How successful was the League of Nations?

4. Define **reparations.** What stance did Britain and France take on reparations?

5. Define **influenza.** What effect did it have on the world's population immediately after World War I?

Focus Questions

The focus question for this chapter is **What caused the United States to become involved in World War I, and how did the United States change as a result of its involvement?** Build an answer to this big question by answering the focus questions for Sections 1 through 4 and the Critical Thinking questions that follow.

Section 1
6. What caused World War I, and why did the United States enter the war?

Section 2
7. How did the war affect Americans at home?

Section 3
8. How did Americans affect the end of World War I and its peace settlements?

Section 4
9. What political, economic, and social effects did World War I have on the United States?

Critical Thinking

10. **Recognize Causes** Identify and explain the causes of World War I.

11. **Analyze Credibility** How do you know the Zimmermann note was a reliable source? Explain.

12. **Distinguish False From Accurate Images** Is the image to the right an accurate or inaccurate image of Germans during World War I? Why do you think the artist chose this representation?

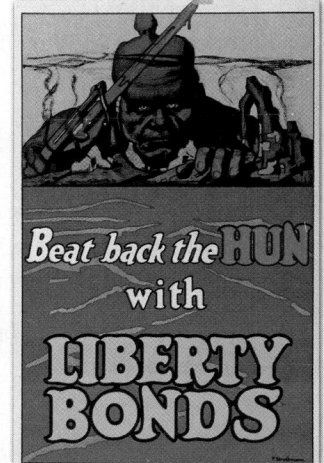

13. **Draw Conclusions** How did Wilson arrive at the decision that women deserved the right to vote?

14. **Summarize** What was the main goal that Wilson wanted to accomplish with the Fourteen Points?

15. **Categorize** Who were the main groups of senators opposed to the Versailles Treaty, and what positions did they hold? Who supported the treaty?

16. **Express Problems Clearly** What problems led to a weak postwar economy?

17. **Determine Relevance** How did the presidential election of 1920 show Americans' rejection of Wilson's ideas?

Writing About History

Write a Cause-and-Effect Essay World War I both caused and affected many different events around the world. Write an essay in which you explain how several different causes led to an event or trend that occurred during World War I. Consider one of the following topics: the stalemate on the Western Front, the increased role of women in the war effort, or the defeat of the Treaty of Versailles in the United States.

Prewriting
• Choose the topic above that interests you the most. Consider what caused the event in question.

• List the multiple causes. Conduct research if necessary to gather more information.

Drafting
• Develop a thesis that clearly states the causal relationship between your event and its main causes.

• Choose an organizational structure for your essay.

• Write an introduction, several body paragraphs, and a conclusion.

Revising
• Use the guidelines on page SH11 of the Writing Handbook to revise your essay.

Regents DBQ Practice

Americans for and Against the War

Both before and after the U.S. entry into World War I, Americans differed in their opinions about the war. While most Americans demonstrated their patriotism with enthusiasm by buying war bonds, conserving food, and enlisting in the army, others, including Quakers and pacifists, continued to oppose the war. Use your knowledge of Americans' opinions on World War I and the following documents to answer questions 1 through 4.

Document 1

"I find myself a soldier among millions of others in the great Allied Armies, fighting for all I believe to be right and civilized and humane against a power which is evil and which threatens the existence of all the rights we prize and the freedom we enjoy, although some of you in California as yet fail to realize it. It may seem to you that for me this is all quite uncalled for, that it can only mean the supreme sacrifice for nothing or some of the best years of my life wasted, but I tell you that not only am I willing to give my life to this enterprise . . . but that I firmly believe if I live through it to spend a useful lifetime with you, that never will I have an opportunity to gain so much honorable advancement for my own soul, or to do so much for the cause of the world's progress. . . ."

—*Harry Butters, an American volunteering with the Allies in 1915*

Document 2

"I could not look at those long lines of fine looking men, marching so gaily along, and with so little realization of what it all means, without a fresh outburst of tears. How little they realized that they were endorsing a system which means that great armies of splendid manhood shall go forth and slay other great armies. And why? Because stupid diplomats were too avaricious [greedy], too selfish, too ambitious to sanely handle the affairs entrusted to their care. . . . And yet we, blind and stupid as we are, are rushing into the same horrible cataclysm [disaster]."

—*Lella Secor*

Document 3

"It was quite black out there on the Atlantic and in the blackness the [*Lusitania*'s] life-boats alternately rose on the crests of the waves and sank into the black valley between. The boats carried women and children whose hair hung in icicles over their shoulders. . . . Now and then a half-dead passenger uttered a shriek of pain or of anguish as she realized that a friend or relative had died in her arms. . . . Meanwhile, in the dark hull of the German submarine, the captain watching through the periscope finally turned his head away. Even this man, agent of Prussian cruelty, had witnessed a scene upon which he did not care to gaze."

—*Wesley Frost, giving a speech sponsored by the Committee on Public Information*

Document 4

MAY THE SPARKS NEVER REACH IT!

1. Which of the documents above reflects the views of a pacifist opposed to the war?
   (1) Document 1
   (2) Document 2
   (3) Document 3
   (4) Document 4

2. The speech in Document 3 is designed to promote
   (1) sympathy for the sailors on the German U-boats.
   (2) sympathy for the innocent victims of a U-boat attack.
   (3) support for pacifists.
   (4) support for the British.

3. What point of view does Document 4 express?
   (1) Interventionist
   (2) Internationalist
   (3) Isolationist
   (4) Pacifist

4. **Writing Task** Why did some Americans support the war effort while others opposed it? Use your knowledge of World War I and specific evidence from the documents to support your answer.

NY Connect to New York

Francis Perkins

Born: April 10, 1882, in Boston, Massachusetts

In the 1920s, Americans were prosperous and optimistic. Then the 1930s brought the Great Depression, a period of nationwide economic struggle. Frances Perkins, a politician who made a name for herself in New York, assisted President Franklin D. Roosevelt with his response to the economic crises of the 1930s.

Perkins began her political career in New York, serving on state committees from 1910 to 1919. Deeply affected by witnessing the tragic Triangle Shirtwaist Fire in New York City in 1911, in which over 100 young seamstresses died, she worked to improve safety in factories.

She was appointed by Governor Alfred E. Smith to the New York State Industrial Commission in 1919, and went on to chair the State Industrial Board in 1926. The next governor of New York, future president Franklin D. Roosevelt, appointed Perkins as state industrial commissioner in 1929. In all these positions, Perkins worked to secure unemployment insurance and develop the government's role in fiscal policies.

When President Roosevelt appointed Perkins Secretary of Labor in 1933, she became the first woman to serve in a Cabinet position. She served in the position for 12 years.

About her first Cabinet meeting, she said:

> "I was apprehensive and on guard at the first official Cabinet meeting. As the only woman member, I did not want my colleagues to get the impression that I was too talkative. I resolved not to speak unless asked to do so . . . My colleagues looked at me with tense curiosity. I think some weren't sure I could speak."
>
> —from Perkins's book *The Roosevelt I Knew*

As she had in New York, Perkins worked in the Cabinet to alleviate the hardships of working people, pushing for fair and safe labor practices, such as a minimum wage, a standardized workweek, and laws barring the hiring of children. She was involved in many aspects of Roosevelt's New Deal, such as the establishment of Social Security and the Civilian Conservation Corps.

After serving as Secretary of Labor, Perkins worked on the U.S. Civil Service Commission under President Truman. She retired from government service in 1952, lecturing and teaching until her death in 1964.

PROSPERITY AND DEPRESSION

CONTENTS

Construction of the Dam,
by William Gropper,
celebrates American
workers who struggled
through hard times. ▶

Kings of Jazz

When he was 14 years old, Louis Armstrong began to haunt the jazz clubs of New Orleans, Louisiana. King Oliver, an experienced musician, took the boy under his wing and bought him his first cornet. Before long, young Armstrong—nicknamed Satchmo—was making a name for himself playing in clubs and on riverboats.

Then, he got a telegram from King Oliver asking him to come to Chicago to join his Creole Jazz Band. Armstrong was scared, but he made the move north. Satchmo would become America's ambassador of jazz, and jazz would become the music that made the "Roaring Twenties" roar. *Listen to the* Witness History *audio to hear more about jazz.*

 King Oliver's Creole Jazz Band, left, helped create the jazz sound.

Dancing the Charleston

 Core Curriculum Preview

Chapter Focus Question: How did the United States experience both economic growth and social change in the decade after World War I?

Section 1
A Booming Economy   5.I.B.5, 5.I.C.1a, 5.I.C.1b

Section 2
The Business of Government   4.II.D.6, 5.I.A.3, 5.I.B.2, 5.I.B.3

Section 3
Social and Cultural Tensions   5.I.C.2a, 5.I.C.2b, 5.I.C.2c

Section 4
A New Mass Culture   5.I.C.1d, 5.I.C.3b, 5.II.B.7c

Section 5
The Harlem Renaissance   5.I.C.3c(2), 5.II.B.7b

Use the ☑ **Quick Study Timeline** at the end of this chapter to preview chapter events.

Campaign button for Warren G. Harding

Ford Model T

Note Taking Study Guide *Online*
For: Note Taking and American Issues Connector
Web Code: nee-8001

659

The gift that simplifies housekeeping
... and safeguards health

GENERAL ELECTRIC
Refrigerator

"Makes it Safe to be Hungry"

GENERAL ELECTRIC COMPANY · HANNA BUILDING · CLEVELAND, OHIO

▲ Will Rogers

◄ 1920s magazine ad

WITNESS HISTORY 🔊 AUDIO

Paying for It?

Folksy comedian Will Rogers was one of the most beloved entertainers of his day. Whether standing onstage twirling a rope or chatting on the radio, he could always be counted on to deliver good-natured, amusing comments on the American scene. In the 1920s—with the nation in the midst of a giant economic boom—Rogers turned his keen eye on Americans' passion for buying things:

❝No nation in the history of the world was ever sitting as pretty. If we want anything, all we have to do is go and buy it on credit. So that leaves us without any economic problems whatsoever, except perhaps some day having to pay for them. But we are certainly not thinking of that this early.❞
—Will Rogers, radio commentary, 1928

A Booming Economy

Core Curriculum Objectives

- **5.I.B.5** 1920s Economy: Speculative boom: the "big bull market"
- **5.I.C.1a** Mass consumption: The automobile: new industries, products, and services
- **5.I.C.1b** Mass consumption: Installment buying

Terms and People

Henry Ford	consumer revolution
mass production	installment buying
Model T	bull market
scientific management	buying on margin
assembly line	

NoteTaking

Reading Skill: Identify Supporting Details
Note specific economic changes of the 1920s.

Why It Matters In the decade after World War I, the American economy experienced tremendous growth. Using revolutionary mass-production techniques, American workers produced more goods in less time than ever before. The boom fundamentally changed the lives of millions of people and helped create the modern consumer economy. **Section Focus Question: How did the booming economy of the 1920s lead to changes in American life?**

The Automobile Drives Prosperity

Rarely, if ever, has the nation enjoyed such an economic boom as it did in the 1920s. The recession that had followed World War I quickly ended. All signs pointed to economic growth. Stock prices rose rapidly. Factories produced more and more goods and, with wages on the rise, more and more people could afford to buy them.

Much of this explosive growth was sparked by a single business: the automobile industry. Carmaker **Henry Ford** introduced a series of methods and ideas that revolutionized production, wages, working conditions, and daily life.

Ford Pioneers Mass Production Ford did not originate the idea of **mass production,** the rapid manufacture of large numbers of identical products. It had been used, for example, to make sewing machines and typewriters. But such products involved only hundreds of parts—not the thousands that go into the production of cars. Ford brought mass production to new heights.

Early in the century, only wealthy city dwellers could afford cars. The automobile was often seen as a symbol of the class divisions in the country. City drivers who ventured out onto country roads frightened horses and cows, coated crops with dust, and rutted dirt roads. "To the countryman," said Woodrow Wilson in 1906, cars "are a picture of the arrogance of wealth."

Ransom Olds had introduced a less expensive car, the Oldsmobile in 1901. But it was Henry Ford who truly brought the automobile to the people. In 1908, he introduced the **Model T,** a reliable car the average American could afford. The first Model T sold for $850. Soon after, Ford opened a new plant on the Detroit River. The Detroit location gave Ford easy access to steel, glass, oil, and rubber manufactured in Pennsylvania, Ohio, Indiana, and Illinois.

Ford hired **scientific management** experts to improve his mass-production techniques. Scientific management was a relatively new method of improving efficiency, in which experts looked at every step of a manufacturing process to find ways to reduce time, effort, and expense. Ford also studied the techniques of Chicago meatpacking houses, where beef carcasses were moved on chains past a series of meat cutters, each of whom cut off a specific part of the carcass. Ford reversed the process. He put his cars on moving **assembly lines.** At each step, a worker added something to construct the automobile. In two years, assembly line techniques reduced the time it took to manufacture a Model T— from more than 12 hours to just 90 minutes.

The assembly line allowed Ford to keep dropping the sale price. The cost of a Model T fell to $350 by 1916 and to $290 by 1927. It was slow, dull, and available only in black. But the Model T was the first car that ordinary people could afford. In 1919, only 10 percent of American families owned an automobile. By 1927, 56 percent did.

Graph Skills The economic boom of the 1920s was reflected in many aspects of the economy, from wages to industrial production to stock prices. *By how much did wages increase between 1910 and 1925? During what years did stock prices soar the most?*

Average Price of Selected Stocks, 1921–1929

SOURCE: *Standard and Poor's*

Earnings of Nonagricultural Employees, 1910–1930

SOURCE: *Historical Statistics of the United States*

Gross Domestic Product

Year	Value of goods produced (in millions of dollars)
1921	68,355
1923	82,994
1925	87,359
1927	94,161
1929	101,444

SOURCE: *National Bureau of Economic Research*

◀ The automobile gave Americans new freedom to enjoy picnics, camping, and Sunday drives.

Impact of the *Automobile*

YELLOWSTONE PARK

Henry Ford made the automobile affordable for the average American. By the 1920s, the growing "car culture" was changing the nation in deeper ways than even Ford might have imagined.

The Gas Station ▶
Automobiles encouraged the growth of related industries—especially the oil industry. The gas station—and gas fumes—became a permanent feature of the U.S. landscape.

STANDARD

US 66

U.S. HIGHWAY SYSTEM
1926

Pacific Ocean

Atlantic Ocean

— Major U.S. highway

◀ The Highway System
By 1925, states had built hundreds of highways, and the federal government organized them into a numbered system. One of the first federal highways was Route 66, which ran from Illinois to California.

Advertising ▶
Ads stressed what cars gave their owners—speed, status, and a new sense of freedom.

CADILLAC
A NOTABLE PRODUCT OF GENERAL MOTORS

◀ Vacation Industry
Americans used their new cars and expanded leisure time to travel. Motels and motor camps sprung up all over the nation.

Enjoy our Southern Hospitality
HARBIN'S TOURIST COURT
MEMPHIS, TENN.
U.S. HIGHWAY 51 SOUTH.
4 MILES SOUTH OF CITY LIMITS

Connect to Your World
Which of the features of "car culture" shown here are still part of American life today?

History *Interactive* ✶
For: More on the automobile
Web Code: nep-0712

When it came to managing the men who worked along his assembly lines, Ford also proved that he was not afraid of <u>innovation</u>. In 1914, he more than doubled the wages of a large number of his workers, from $2.35 to $5 a day. He also reduced their workday from 9 hours to 8 hours. In 1926, he became the first major industrialist to give his workers Saturday and Sunday off. Before Ford, the idea of a "weekend" hardly existed. Ford shrewdly realized that if workers made more money and had more leisure time, they would become potential customers for his automobiles. The combination of the Model T and the "five-dollar day, forty-hour week" made Ford not only a very rich man but also one of the shapers of the modern world.

The Automobile Changes America The boom in the automotive industry <u>stimulated</u> growth in other industries related to car manufacture or use. The steel, glass, rubber, asphalt, wood, gasoline, insurance, and road-construction industries all benefited. For example, one seventh of all steel output was used to make automobiles. The need for gasoline prompted a nationwide search for oil deposits. Oil discoveries in California, Texas, New Mexico, and Oklahoma brought workers and money to the Southwest.

Road construction boomed, especially when the federal government introduced the system of numbered highways in 1926. The millions of cars on American roads led to the rapid appearance of thousands of service stations, diners, and motor hotels (a term later shortened to *motels*). The growth in all these industries created new and often better-paying jobs, spurring national prosperity.

The automobile caused additional economic effects. Other forms of ground transportation, such as railroads and trolleys, suffered a decline in use. With cars, people could go where they wanted, when they wanted. They did not have to travel along set tracks on set schedules.

The automobile prompted a new sense of freedom and prosperity. Never had Americans been so mobile. Entire families crowded into their cars for cross-country vacations or Sunday drives to the country. Ownership of an automobile came to symbolize participation in the American dream of success.

Finally, automobiles altered residential patterns. The ability to drive to work permitted people to live farther from their places of employment. This led to the development of suburban communities linked to cities by arteries of highways and roads. Los Angeles, one of the first cities whose growth was influenced by the automobile, developed in a sprawling, haphazard fashion. It became, according to one observer, "a series of suburbs in search of a city."

✔ **Checkpoint** How did Henry Ford increase the production and sale of automobiles?

A Bustling Economy

The 1920s saw what has been called a **consumer revolution,** in which a flood of new, affordable goods became available to the public. The widespread availability of electrical power supported the consumer revolution. Electric washing machines, vacuum cleaners, and irons made housekeeping easier and less time-consuming. Accessible electricity also contributed to radio and refrigerator sales.

Advertising and Credit Build a Consumer Culture The growing advertising industry also played its part. Using new "scientific" techniques and psychological research, advertisers were able to sell more products to more Americans than ever before. Magazine and newspaper ads often focused on the desires and fears of Americans more than on what people really needed.

Vocabulary Builder
<u>innovation</u>–(ihn uh VAY shuhn) *n.* change in the way of doing something; act of introducing such a change

Vocabulary Builder
<u>stimulate</u>–(STIHM yuh layt) *v.* to excite to action; to cause to grow or act

Advertisers celebrated consumption as an end in itself, convincing people that they could be the person they wanted to be just by buying the right products. From Kleenex to Listerine, Americans bought products that years earlier they could never have imagined they needed.

Finally, new ways of buying fueled the consumer revolution. People who did not have enough ready cash could buy what they wanted on credit. **Installment buying,** in which a consumer would make a small down payment and then pay off the rest of the debt in regular monthly payments, allowed Americans to own products they might otherwise have had to save up for years in order to buy.

The Big Bull Market Makes Fortunes Consumers were not the only Americans buying and selling in a big way. During the 1920s, the stock market enjoyed a dizzying **bull market,** a period of rising stock prices. More and more Americans put their money into stocks in an effort to get rich quick. By 1929, around 4 million Americans owned stocks.

The pounding desire to strike it rich often led investors to ignore financial risks. As the market soared, people began **buying on margin**—another form of buying on credit. By purchasing stock on margin, a buyer paid as little as 10 percent of the stock price upfront to a broker. The buyer then paid the broker for the rest of the stock over a period of months. The stock served as collateral, or security, for the broker's loan. As long as the price of the stock rose, the buyer had no trouble paying off the loan and making a profit. But if the price fell, the buyer still had to pay off the loan. Buyers gambled that they would be able to sell the stock at a profit long before the loan came due.

In truth, the big bull market stood on very shaky ground. But most people ignored the dangers. By the middle of 1929, economic authorities proclaimed that America and the stock market had entered a "new era." Stock prices would continue their march upward, they said, while boom-and-bust economics would become a thing of the past.

✔ **Checkpoint** How did buying on margin allow more people to invest in the stock market?

Cities, Suburbs, and Country

The economic boom did not affect all parts of the nation equally. While urban and suburban areas prospered, rural Americans faced hardships.

People Flock to Cities In the 1920s, the movement of people was toward cities. Immigrants settled in cities. Farmers left their fields for cities. The direction of the African American Great Migration was toward northern cities. Mexican Americans crossing the border relocated to southwestern cities.

As in the late nineteenth century, cities grew and changed shape. In addition, the adoption of skyscraper technology caused cities to stretch skyward. Steel-framed skyscrapers with light coverings of masonry and glass began to dominate the skylines of the nation's cities. New York's Empire State Building, finished in 1931, symbolized the power and majesty of the United States.

The Suburbs Grow Improved mass transportation and the widespread use of automobiles caused cities to expand outward. More urban workers moved to the suburbs. Western and southern cities, developed after the automobile revolution, encompassed suburban areas as well as inner cities. Suburbs mushroomed, growing much faster than inner cities.

Urban Growth
Built by automaker Walter P. Chrysler in 1928, New York's Chrysler Building (below) was the world's tallest skyscraper—but only for a short time. *Look at the table below. Why do you think Detroit grew so fast after 1910?*

Population of Selected U.S. Cities, 1910–1930			
City	1910	1920	1930
New York	4,766,883	5,620,048	6,930,446
Chicago	2,185,283	2,701,705	3,376,478
St. Louis	687,029	772,897	821,960
Los Angeles	319,198	576,673	1,238,048
Detroit	465,766	993,078	1,568,662

SOURCE: U.S. Census Bureau

Slowly at first, but more rapidly as the century progressed, suburbs drained people and resources from the cities. Catering to middle- and upper-class residents, suburbs tended to be more conservative and Republican. Meanwhile, the inner cities at the heart of older urban areas began a slow but steady decline.

Many Americans Face Hardship In the cities and suburbs, Americans enjoyed prosperity and the fruits of growth. They participated in the consumer economy and in the joys of automobile ownership. The wealthiest urban residents—owners and managers of businesses—reaped fabulous rewards, which they often pumped back into the bull market. But there were problems looming ahead. America's wealth was poorly distributed. Industrial wages rose at a much slower rate than corporate salaries.

Worst yet, farm incomes declined during the decade. Many people living in the country did not participate in the consumer benefits and economic gains of the decade. They formed part of another America—poorer and outside the economic boom. In particular, farmers suffered from growing debt and falling farm prices. A protest song of 1928 expressed their frustration:

Earnings of Agricultural Employees, 1918–1928

SOURCE: *Historical Statistics of the United States*

Rural Struggles
American farmers did not share in the prosperity of the 1920s. *Compare this graph to the economic graphs at the beginning of this section and make a generalization about farm wages versus nonfarm wages in the 1920s.*

Primary Source

❝'Leven-cent cotton, forty-cent meat,
How in the world can a poor man eat?
Mule's in the barn, no crop's laid by,
Corncrib empty and the cow's gone dry.❞
—Bob Miller and Emma Dermer,
"Eleven Cent Cotton"

If the wealthy believed that the country had entered an age of permanent prosperity, the "other Americans" saw things differently.

✔ **Checkpoint** What impact did the development of suburbs have on American society?

Assessment

Progress Monitoring *Online*
For: Self-test with vocabulary practice
Web Code: nea-0702

Comprehension

1. **Terms and People** For each of the following, write a sentence explaining how that person or item was connected with the changing economy of the 1920s.
   • Henry Ford
   • mass production
   • assembly line
   • consumer revolution
   • installment buying
   • bull market
   • buying on margin

2. **NoteTaking Reading Skill: Identify Supporting Details** Use your concept web to answer the Section Focus Question: How did the booming economy of the 1920s lead to changes in American life?

Writing About History

3. **Summarize a Historical Interpretation** Using information from the text, write a paragraph summarizing the reasons for the historical viewpoint that Henry Ford was one of the chief makers of the modern world.

Critical Thinking

4. **Analyze Effects** How is the rise of the automobile an example of technology affecting attitudes or values?

5. **Draw Conclusions** Why do you think many advertisers began to focus on the benefits of their products rather than on the products themselves?

6. **Predict Consequences** Identify two potential signs of weakness in the economy of the 1920s, and predict what might happen if those problems are not solved.

Harding campaign button ▶

▲ President Harding joins a parade.

A Fun-Loving President

In 1920, voters turned from the intellectualism and rigid idealism of Woodrow Wilson to someone who presented himself as an average American, Warren G. Harding. "I am a man of limited talents from a small town," Harding admitted. "I don't seem to grasp that I am President." The genial politician from Marion, Ohio, got more pleasure from golf, poker, and music. He once claimed that he could play every band instrument "but the slide trombone and the e-flat cornet." But what Harding loved most was shaking hands with tourists who visited the White House:

❝I love to meet people. It is the most pleasant thing I do; it is really the only fun I have. It does not tax me, and it seems to be a very great pleasure to them.❞

—Warren G. Harding, U.S. President

The Business of Government

 Core Curriculum Objectives

- **4.II.D.6** Reparations and war debts (United States as a world banker)
- **5.I.A.3** Return to "normalcy": 1918–1921
- **5.I.B.2** Avarice and scandal: Teapot Dome
- **5.I.B.3** Coolidge prosperity; not for everyone

Terms and People

Andrew Mellon	Washington Naval
Herbert Hoover	Disarmament
Teapot Dome scandal	Conference
Calvin Coolidge	Kellogg-Briand Pact
	Dawes Plan

NoteTaking

Reading Skill: Compare and Contrast
Note similarities and differences between Presidents Harding and Coolidge.

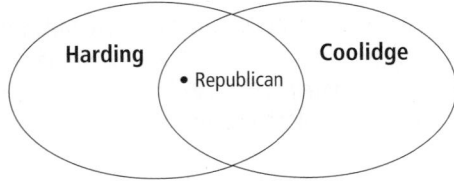

Why It Matters In 1920, Warren G. Harding was elected President on a pledge of a "return to normalcy." Rather than pursue reform, as the Progressives had done, Harding and his successor, Calvin Coolidge, favored more conservative policies that aided the growth of business. This pattern—a period of activism followed by a more laissez-faire approach—would repeat itself in the 1950s and 1980s. **Section Focus Question: How did domestic and foreign policy change direction under Harding and Coolidge?**

The Harding Administration

What exactly did a "return to normalcy" mean? Different voters saw different things in the vague phrase. Some saw it as a retreat from involvement in world affairs, others as a rejection of Progressive reform efforts or a swing back to laissez-faire economics. Once in office, however, Harding had to give substance to his promise.

New Policies Favor Big Business Harding signaled the economic direction of his administration by naming wealthy banker **Andrew Mellon** Secretary of the Treasury. Mellon's idea of prudent economic policy was to support legislation that advanced business interests. He disliked the relatively new income tax, favoring instead low taxes on individuals and corporations. Mellon also cut the fat from the budget. By 1925, Congress had reduced spending from a wartime high of $18 billion to $3 billion. Instead of sinking deeper into debt, the Treasury actually showed a surplus.

Harding signed a bill raising protective tariff rates by about 25 percent. The tax on imports made it easier for American producers to sell goods at home. However, in retaliation, European nations also hiked tariffs, making American goods harder to sell overseas. This tariff war weakened the world economy.

Under the Progressive leadership of Roosevelt and Wilson, the federal government had passed laws to break up monopolies, protect workers, and restrict the absolute freedom of business leaders. By contrast, Harding favored a return to a more traditional laissez-faire approach. He and Mellon worked to reduce government regulation of business.

Still, the Harding administration did not abandon social goals. Harding's thoughtful and energetic Secretary of Commerce, **Herbert Hoover,** worked with business and labor leaders to achieve voluntary advancements. What the Progressives hoped to achieve through legislation, Hoover attempted to attain with the cooperation of interest groups. He enjoyed great successes at getting people to work together instead of battling one another.

The Ohio Gang Cashes In Harding was a kind, likable man, but he was not especially intelligent. Perhaps no President was friendlier, and few had less sense of what was expected of a President. Faced with a tax issue, Harding lamented, "I listen to one side and they seem right . . . I talk to the other side, and they seem just as right, and here I am where I started. . . . What a job!"

Rather than struggle to master the complexities of the job, Harding trusted others to make decisions. Many were his close friends, men he enjoyed relaxing and gambling with at late-night poker games. Known as the Ohio Gang, they were not honest public servants like Mellon and Hoover. They were mostly greedy, small-minded men who saw government service as a chance to get rich at the expense of the very citizens they were supposed to serve.

Charles Forbes, head of the Veterans' Bureau, practiced graft on an immense scale and wasted hundreds of millions of taxpayers' dollars. For example, his department bought $70,000 worth of floor cleaner—enough to last 100 years—at more than 24 times the fair price. Another Harding pal, Attorney General Harry Daugherty, used his position to accept money from criminals.

The Teapot Dome Scandal Explodes The worst scandal involved Secretary of the Interior Albert Fall. In 1921, Fall arranged to transfer oil reserves in Elk Hills, California, and Teapot Dome, Wyoming, from the Navy Department to the Interior Department. The oil reserves were intended for the navy's use in time of emergency. Harding signed the transfer.

Once Fall had control of the oil, he forgot about the needs of the navy. He leased the properties to private oilmen in return for "loans"—which were actually bribes. Rumors of the deal led to a Senate investigation, and, by 1924, the entire

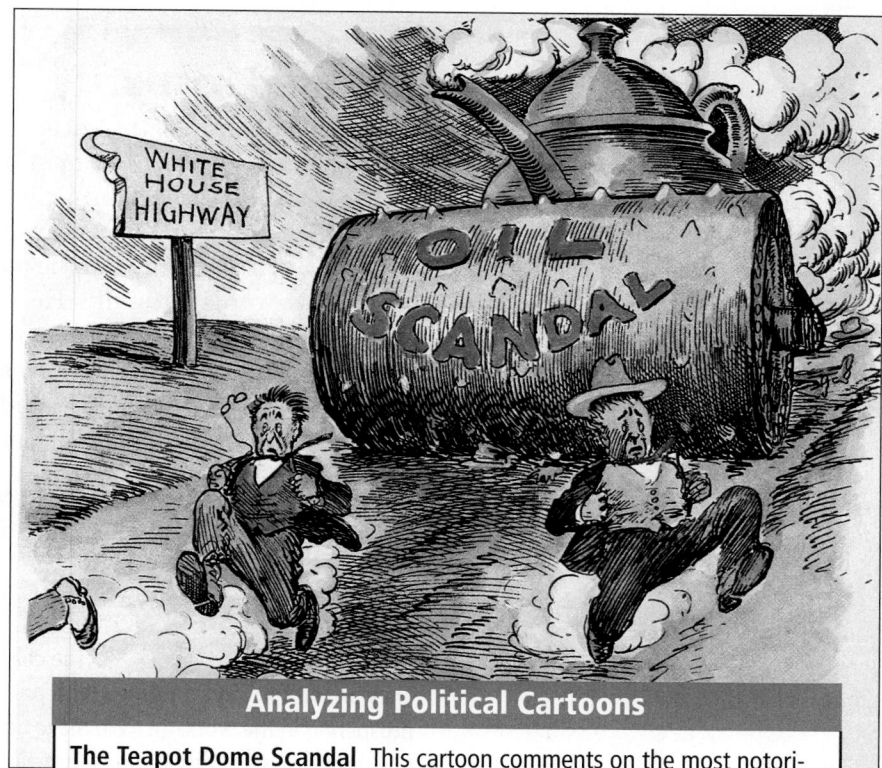

Analyzing Political Cartoons

The Teapot Dome Scandal This cartoon comments on the most notorious scandal of the Harding administration.
1. What object is used to represent the scandal? Why?
2. According to the cartoon, what is the impact of the scandal?

Silent Cal

In the picture (above right), President Coolidge reenacts the scene when his father swore him in as President. At above left, Coolidge wears a proper business suit to go fishing.

sordid affair was revealed to the public. Later, the oil reserves were returned to the government. Fall was sentenced to a year in prison.

Harding himself never saw the full extent of the **Teapot Dome scandal.** In fact, he only had a growing suspicion that his friends were up to no good. But that was enough, as he said, to keep him "walking the floor nights." In July 1923, he visited Alaska during a speaking tour. On his return voyage, he suffered a heart attack and died on August 2. Americans mourned Harding as they had mourned no other President since Lincoln. When the full extent of the scandals emerged, however, the public formed a different opinion of him.

✓ **Checkpoint** What were the causes and effects of the Teapot Dome scandal?

Coolidge Prosperity

News of Harding's death reached Vice President **Calvin Coolidge** during a visit to his father's Vermont farm. Almost immediately, the elder Coolidge, a justice of the peace, used the family Bible to swear in his son as President.

In personality, Coolidge was far different from the outgoing, back-slapping Harding. Known as Silent Cal, he was quiet, honest, and frugal—a man who measured his words carefully. He placed his trust in business, and put his administration in the hands of men who held to the simple virtues of an older America. Political sharpies out to make a quick buck had no place in the Coolidge administration. Neither did Progressives who believed in an activist government bent on sweeping reforms.

Silent Cal Supports Big Business Coolidge admired productive business leaders. "The man who builds a factory," Coolidge once said, "builds a temple." He believed that the creation of wealth benefited the nation as a whole. In 1925, he expressed this view in his best-known speech:

> **Primary Source** "The chief business of the American people is business. They are profoundly concerned with producing, buying, selling, investing, and prospering in the world. . . . We make no concealment of the fact that we want wealth, but there are many other things that we want very much more. We want peace and honor, and that charity which is so strong an element of all civilization. The chief ideal of the American people is idealism."
> —Calvin Coolidge, speech to the American Society of Newspaper Editors

Coolidge's statement of values and principles has often been oversimplified as "the business of America is business."

In his approach to the economy, Coolidge continued to follow the goals of Secretary of the Treasury Mellon by reducing the national debt, trimming the federal budget, and lowering taxes to give <u>incentives</u> for businesses. Coolidge thus oversaw a spectacular boom in the national economy. For almost six years, the economy soared, generating industrial profits, spectacular growth in the stock market, and general prosperity, especially for urban Americans.

Troubles Brew Beneath the Surface Yet, there were grave problems breeding in the nation. Farmers struggled to keep their land as the prices of their goods fell. Labor unions demanded higher wages and better working conditions. African Americans faced severe discrimination, especially in the South, where Jim Crow laws made enforced segregation a way of life. African American leaders urged Congress to pass an antilynching law. In the Southwest, Mexican Americans confronted shamefully low wages and efforts to force them to return to Mexico.

To all of these concerns, Silent Cal remained silent. Like Harding, he mistrusted the use of legislation to achieve social change. Unlike Progressive Presidents, he believed that it was not the business of the federal government to help create an ideal nation.

✔ **Checkpoint** What policies did Calvin Coolidge favor to support economic growth?

Vocabulary Builder
<u>incentive</u>–(ihn SEHNT ihv) *n.* something intended to encourage someone to take action or work harder

America's Role in the World

Under both Harding and Coolidge, America continued to play an increasingly important role in world business and trade. Beyond that, U.S. foreign policy was largely shaped by reaction to World War I. No previous war had been as deadly. Citizens of all nations agreed: It must never happen again. But how could this goal be achieved?

Seeking an End to War One solution was to avoid another arms race, such as the naval rivalry between Germany and Britain that had contributed to the outbreak of the war. In 1921 and 1922, diplomats gathered in Washington, D.C., to halt another naval arms race before it got out of control. World leaders agreed to limit construction of large warships and hammered out a settlement on several problems between Japan and the West. This **Washington Naval Disarmament Conference** did not end the world's naval problems, but it raised hopes that nations could solve disagreements without resorting to war.

A later attempt to prevent war was the **Kellogg-Briand Pact** of 1928. Secretary of State Frank B. Kellogg and French Foreign Minister Aristide Briand

The United States in International Affairs, 1920–1929		✔ **Quick Study**
	Goal	**U.S. Action**
League of Nations	To prevent war and settle disputes between nations	U.S. membership favored by Wilson; rejected by Senate
World Court	To make judgments in international disputes voluntarily submitted by nations	U.S. participation favored by Harding; rejected by Senate
Washington Naval Conference	To reduce arms race and size of navies of major powers	U.S. agreed with leading naval powers to limit construction of warships.
Kellogg-Briand Pact	To "outlaw war … as an instrument of national policy"	U.S. agreed with many other nations to renounce war as a means of settling international disputes.

(bree AHN) drew up a treaty to "outlaw" war "as an instrument of national policy." Eventually, 62 nations ratified the pact. But, in reality, the pact was unenforceable. Kellogg knew it, Briand knew it, and so did the rest of the diplomats. No sooner was the ink dry than everyone involved forgot about it.

Although Congress applauded the useless Kellogg-Briand Pact, it refused to join the World Court, an international body which at least promised to help <u>mediate</u> international disputes. As much as possible, most American leaders in the 1920s hoped to avoid another war by keeping the rest of the world at arm's length.

Collecting War Debts

Money issues were another matter. The United States insisted that Britain and France repay their huge war debts to the United States. For this to happen, though, Germany had to make the reparation payments to Britain and France imposed by the Treaty of Versailles. The complex financial issue threatened to undermine the international economy. Some statesmen suggested reducing or even canceling both war debts and reparations. But the frugal Coolidge insisted that a debt was a debt and had to be paid.

In 1924, an agreement known as the **Dawes Plan** arranged U.S. loans to Germany. By enabling Germany to make reparation payments to Britain and France, the Dawes Plan helped Britain and France to repay their debts to the United States. Of course, the entire scheme was financed by U.S. money. After the stock market crash of 1929, however, the well of U.S. money went dry. Germany stopped reparation payments, and Britain and France ended war-debt payments to the United States.

In the end, the war-debt situation damaged America's reputation in the eyes of the world. People from England and France thought that it was heartless for American bankers and politicians to insist on repayment of debts and not to take into account the human costs of the war. In the next war, the United States would take a more flexible approach to war loans.

 Checkpoint How did the United States support world peace efforts during the 1920s?

Vocabulary Builder

<u>mediate</u>–(MEE dee ayt) *v.* to bring about the settlement of a dispute between two parties

---

SECTION **2** Assessment

Progress Monitoring *Online*
For: Self-test with vocabulary practice
Web Code: nea-0703

Comprehension

1. **Terms and People** For each of the following, write a sentence explaining its importance to national politics of the 1920s.
   - Teapot Dome scandal
   - Washington Naval Disarmament Conference
   - Kellogg-Briand Pact
   - Dawes Plan

2. <u>Note</u>Taking **Reading Skill: Compare and Contrast** Use your Venn diagram to answer the Section Focus Question: How did domestic and foreign policy change direction under Harding and Coolidge?

Writing About History

3. **Comparing Historical Interpretations** Some people view Coolidge as a moral, idealistic President who restored integrity to government and promoted prosperity. Others see him as a stiff, unimaginative President who retreated from the idealism of the Progressive Era and cared only for the interests of business. Make a Venn diagram comparing these differing historical interpretations.

Critical Thinking

4. **Make Comparisons** How did the approach to government of Harding and Coolidge differ from that of the Progressives?

5. **Draw Conclusions** Do you think that Harding should be held responsible for the scandals in his administration? Why or why not?

6. **Evaluate Information** Many Americans in the 1920s seemed to support both isolationism and an active role in international affairs. Do you agree?

◄ Billy Sunday

▲ Crowd at a Billy Sunday revival meeting

WITNESS HISTORY 🔊 AUDIO

Kicking, Fighting, Butting, and Biting

In a time of rapid social change, with a deadly war behind them, many Americans sought a return to more traditional values. They found comfort and strength in the words of preachers such as Billy Sunday. A former pro baseball player, Sunday never lost the dynamic energy of an athlete. Arms flailing, fists punching the air, he railed against the evils of greed, card playing, dancing, and, especially, drinking. He liked to tell audiences:

❝I'm against sin. I'll kick it as long as I've got a foot, and I'll fight it as long as I've got a fist. I'll butt it as long as I've got a head. I'll bite it as long as I've got a tooth. And when I'm old and fistless and footless and toothless, I'll gum it 'till I go home to Glory.❞

—Billy Sunday, sermon

Social and Cultural Tensions

 Core Curriculum Objectives

- **5.I.C.2a** Threats to civil liberties: Red Scare, Ku Klux Klan, and Sacco and Vanzetti
- **5.I.C.2b** Prohibition
- **5.I.C.2c** Science, religion, and education: the Scopes trial

Terms and People

modernism	Ku Klux Klan
fundamentalism	Prohibition
Scopes Trial	Eighteenth Amendment
Clarence Darrow	Volstead Act
quota system	bootlegger

NoteTaking

Reading Skill: Contrast As you read, look for issues that divided Americans in the 1920s.

Differing Viewpoints	
Education	• Viewpoint 1 • Viewpoint 2
Evolution	

Why It Matters In the 1920s, while many city dwellers enjoyed a rising standard of living, most farmers suffered through hard times. Conflicting visions of what the nation should be heightened the urban-rural division. Some of these issues, such as immigration policy and teaching the theory of evolution, still divide Americans today. **Section Focus Question: How did Americans differ on major social and cultural issues?**

Traditionalism and Modernism Clash

The 1920 census reported that, for the first time in American history, more people lived in urban areas than in rural regions. This simple fact had profound consequences. The nation had been divided before, but usually along north-south or east-west lines. In the 1920s, however, the split was between urban America and rural America. On virtually every important social and cultural issue, the two groups were divided.

Urban Americans enjoyed new consumer products and a wide array of leisure activities. They generally showed an openness toward social change and the new discoveries of science. The growing trend to emphasize science and secular values over traditional ideas about religion became known as **modernism.**

By contrast, rural Americans did not participate fully in the consumer bonanzas, and they missed out on many of the new forms of leisure. People in the country generally embraced a more traditional view of religion, science, and culture.

High School Education, 1900–1930	
Year	High School Graduates (percentage of 17-year-olds)
1900	6.3
1910	8.6
1920	16.3
1930	28.8

SOURCE: U.S. Census Bureau

Americans Go to School

Although school attendance grew steadily, fewer than half of American children graduated from high school by 1930. *How much did the high school graduation rate increase during the 1920s?*

Education Becomes More Important Rural and urban Americans differed in their attitudes toward formal education. In rural America, prolonged formal education had not seemed vital. Farmers expected their children to master the "Three R's"—reading, writing, and arithmetic. But beyond that, education collided with the many farm tasks that needed to be done. Muscle, endurance, and knowledge of crops and animals seemed more important to farmers than "book learning."

Formal education took on more importance in urban America. Mental ability, not muscular fitness, was seen as the essential ingredient for success. Mastery of mathematics and language could spell the difference between a low-paying, unskilled job and a higher-paying position as an office worker. By 1930, more American teens were graduating from high school, and more Americans than ever before went to college.

Religious Fundamentalism Grows In the 1920s, many devout Americans believed that Christianity was under siege throughout the world. They pointed to Soviet communist attacks on the Orthodox Church in Russia and to the Mexican revolutionary assaults on the Roman Catholic Church in Mexico.

At home, a growing number of Christians were upset by what they saw as secular trends in religion and culture. They reaffirmed their belief in the fundamental, or basic, truths of their religion. This approach, often called **fundamentalism,** emphasized Protestant teachings and the belief that every word in the Bible was literal truth. Fundamentalists believed that the answer to every important moral and scientific question was in their holy book. Their ideas took root all over the country but were especially strong in rural America.

Americans Clash Over Evolution Fundamentalism and modernism clashed head-on in the **Scopes Trial** of 1925. At issue was the theory of evolution, developed by English scientist Charles Darwin. Darwin believed that complex forms of life, such as human beings, had developed gradually from simpler forms of life. This theory clashed with the description of creation in the Bible.

In 1925, Tennessee passed a law making it illegal to teach Darwin's theory in the state's public schools. The American Civil Liberties Union convinced John Scopes, a high school biology teacher in Dayton, Tennessee, to challenge the law. When Scopes taught evolution in his classroom, he was promptly arrested.

The Scopes Trial drew nationwide attention. Journalists flocked to Dayton to cover the emotionally charged event, which many dubbed the "Monkey Trial" because of the mistaken belief that Darwin claimed that human beings descended from monkeys. **Clarence Darrow,** the most celebrated defense attorney in America, traveled from his home in Chicago to defend Scopes. Three-time presidential candidate William Jennings Bryan, a long-time defender of rural values, served as an expert for the prosecution.

The highlight of the trial came when Darrow called Bryan to the stand as an expert on the Bible. Bryan affirmed that the Bible stated the literal truth. He testified that he believed that God created Adam and Eve and that Joshua made the sun stand still. Darrow tried to use science to cast doubt on such beliefs, but Bryan firmly stated, "I accept the Bible absolutely."

Scopes was found guilty of breaking the law—a fact that was never in question—and fined $100. While the Scopes Trial showcased a major cultural and religious division, it did not heal the conflict or answer its central questions. When the trial was over, each side still believed in the truth of its position. The conflict over evolution continues today.

 Checkpoint How did the Scopes Trial illustrate the urban-rural split in the 1920s?

Restricting Immigration

Another cultural clash involved the ongoing boom in immigration. As in the past, Americans known as nativists argued that the new arrivals took jobs away from native-born workers and threatened American religious, political, and cultural traditions.

Nativists Oppose Immigration Although nativist politicians had been able to restrict immigration from China in 1882, they had failed to push through laws to restrict immigration from southern and eastern Europe. On the eve of World War I, however, Congress did pass a law requiring immigrants to take a literacy test. Immigrants who could not read or write their own language were prohibited from entering the United States. President Wilson vetoed the law, but Congress overrode Wilson's veto.

During the postwar Red Scare, fear that communists and socialists from eastern Europe were traveling to the United States with their revolutionary doctrines added an emotional edge to the debate. The problem that confronted nativists was traditional immigration policy. All Americans who could trace their ancestry back far enough discovered foreign origins. Many viewed the immigration experience as part of what made an American an American.

Quota Laws Limit Newcomers World War I, the Russian Revolution, and the Red Scare strengthened the nativist position. Two important laws—the Emergency Quota Act of 1921 and the National Origins Act of 1924—established a **quota system** to govern immigration from specific countries.

Comparing Viewpoints

Should a State Ban Teaching of Darwin's Theory of Evolution?

The Scopes Trial of 1925 revolved around a Tennessee law that banned the teaching of Darwin's theory of evolution. The deeper issue involved a clash between traditional religious beliefs and modern science.

THE PROSECUTION

William Jennings Bryan believed that Tennessee had a right to protect its children from ideas that violated biblical teachings.

Primary Source

"Science is a magnificent force, but it is not a teacher of morals. . . . In war, science has proven itself an evil genius; it has made war more terrible than it ever was before."

"It is for the jury to determine whether this attack upon the Christian religion shall be permitted in the public schools of Tennessee by teachers employed by the state."

"When Shall We Three Meet Again?"

THE DEFENSE

Dudley Field Malone, who joined Clarence Darrow in the defense of Scopes, argued against a state determining what should be taught.

Primary Source

"We feel we stand with progress. We feel we stand with science. We feel we stand with intelligence. We feel we stand with fundamental freedom in America."

"Let the children have their minds kept open. Close no doors to their knowledge. Shut no door from them. Make the distinction between theology and science. Let them have both. Let them be taught both. Let them both live."

Compare
1. How does Bryan's view of science differ from that of Malone?
2. What does each man feel should happen when science clashes with religion?

U.S. Immigration Policy

TRACK THE ISSUE

How should government regulate immigration?

The first major effort to limit immigration to the United States came in the late 1800s. By then, immigrants were streaming into the country. Many Americans worried about losing their jobs or their sense of national identity. Since then, immigration and immigration policy have remained controversial issues. Use the timeline below to explore this enduring issue.

1882 Chinese Exclusion Act
Federal government makes first law to exclude a specific national group.

1924 National Origins Act
Law sets quotas on numbers of immigrants from each country.

1952 McCarran-Walter Act
Law establishes political beliefs as criteria for exclusion.

1965 Immigration Act Amended
Congress abolishes national quotas but sets ceiling for each hemisphere.

1986 Immigration Reform and Control Act
Law offers amnesty to some illegal aliens.

2004 Guest Worker Program
President Bush proposes law allowing temporary foreign workers.

Immigrants enter New York's Ellis Island in the 1920s.

Immigrants and foreign visitors go through a careful check before they are allowed to enter the country.

DEBATE THE ISSUE

Amnesty for Illegal Immigrants In recent years, Americans have hotly debated the question of amnesty for illegal immigrants. Some Americans favor laws providing a legal route to citizenship. Critics say that laws curbing further illegal immigration would be more effective.

"Amnesty combined with serious penalties for employers that hire undocumented workers . . . is the only real way out of [this] situation. . . . It . . . is . . . the option most likely to secure the border and end the system of undocumented worker exploitation—which is precisely why our well-funded leaders in Washington have no intention of pursuing it."

—Tom Head, author

"Amnesty for illegal aliens is simply a reward for law-breaking. No system depending on a strict regard for the rule of law can treat law-breaking so casually. Amnesty will be a magnet for further illegal immigrants, who hope to be future recipients of the nation's compassion."

—Edward J. Erler, Senior Fellow, Claremont Institute

TRANSFER Activities

1. **Compare** Why does Tom Head support amnesty? Why does Erler oppose it?

2. **Analyze** How does the issue debated today differ from the issues that led to the passage of the National Origins Act?

3. **Transfer** Use the following Web site to see a video, try a WebQuest, and write in your journal. **Web Code:** neh-8002

The National Origins Act set up a simple formula: The number of immigrants of a given nationality each year could not exceed 2 percent of the number of people of that nationality living in the United States in 1890. The year 1890 was chosen because it came before the great wave of immigration from southern and eastern Europe. For example, the act permitted about 65,721 immigrants from England and Northern Ireland to come to America every year, but it allowed only about 5,802 immigrants from Italy. The act also continued to exclude most Asian immigrants. America had closed its "golden door" to many of the people trying to enter.

More Mexicans Come North The quota system did not apply to Mexico, which was still reeling from the chaos of the 1910 revolution. Mexicans settled in sparsely populated regions of the Southwest and made major contributions to the local economies. Most Mexican newcomers found work harvesting crops in Texas and California. A smaller number sought jobs in the factories and farms of the North or Midwest.

Many Mexican immigrants faced discrimination and hostility in their new homes. They often competed with native-born Americans for jobs and were frequently subjected to brutality and violence.

 Checkpoint How did new laws change U.S. immigration policy in the 1920s?

The New Ku Klux Klan

Immigration restriction was an attempt to turn back the clock to what many saw as a simpler, better time—a time before the nation became ethnically diverse. As rural Americans saw the country become increasingly urban and their own position in the nation slip in relative importance, many lashed out against symbols of change. Some even turned to organizations that supported doctrines of hate and employed violence and terror to achieve their ends.

The Klan Rises Again In 1915, on Stone Mountain in Georgia, a group of angry men revived the **Ku Klux Klan.** The original Klan had been formed in the South during Reconstruction largely to terrorize African Americans who sought to vote. Although the revived Klan continued to promote hatred of African Americans, it was also aimed at the new America taking shape in the cities. It targeted Jews, Catholics, and immigrants. The Klan also claimed to stand against lawbreaking and immorality. One of their leaders claimed that "every criminal, every gambler . . . every crooked politician . . . is fighting the Klan."

At its height, the Klan's "Invisible Empire" had perhaps 4 to 5 million members. Most were in the South, but there were also branches in the Midwest, Northeast, and West—in both rural areas and in small industrial cities. One center of Klan strength was Indiana, where Klan leader David Stephenson ruled with an iron fist and controlled numerous politicians. They burned crosses, boycotted businesses owned by anyone who was Jewish, Catholic, or African American, and terrorized citizens in the darkness of night. Klansmen

The New Ku Klux Klan
In 1925, thousands of Klansmen (below) staged a huge march in Washington, D.C.

usually wore masks to conceal their identities, met to wave flags and preach hate, and followed leaders with such titles as Grand Dragon and Imperial Wizard. But behind the Klan's confident facade were Americans fearful of change.

Americans Oppose the Klan Individuals, as well as organizations such as the NAACP and the Jewish Anti-Defamation League, battled against the Klan and its values. They embraced the idea of racial, ethnic, religious, and cultural diversity. For them, the notion of the "melting pot" was as old as America itself, and they drew strength from American traditions and saw hope in the American future. Journalist William Allen White noted:

> **Primary Source** "To make a case against a birthplace, a religion, or a race is wickedly un-American and cowardly. The whole trouble with the Ku Klux Klan is that it is based upon such deep foolishness that it is bound to be a menace to good government in any community."
> —William Allen White, letter to the editor of the *New York World,* 1921

The Klan itself became thoroughly corrupt. Its leaders bribed politicians, stole from its members' dues, and lied to its members. Stephenson ended up going to prison for assault and second-degree murder. By the late 1920s, the Klan stood exposed. Although it never disappeared, it withered in importance.

✔ **Checkpoint** How did the goals of the new Ku Klux Klan differ from those of the old Klan?

● **INFOGRAPHIC**

PROHIBITION AND CRIME

Supporters of Prohibition rightly pointed out that alcohol was at the root of many social ills, from child abuse to lost productivity on the job. Sadly, the attempt to ban alcohol opened the door to a new set of social problems.

During Prohibition, many ordinary Americans—rich and poor—became lawbreakers. Ignoring the Volstead Act, they found creative ways to hide alcohol. This woman has a flask hidden in her boot. ▼

Federal agents destroy a still used to manufacture illegal alcohol. Although these "feds" worked tirelessly, there were not enough of them to enforce Prohibition effectively. ▼

Prohibition and Crime

Another divisive issue was **Prohibition,** the banning of alcohol use. Since the early 1800s, temperance reformers had crusaded against alcohol. By 1917, some 75 percent of Americans lived in "dry" counties that had banned liquor. World War I increased support for temperance. It seemed unpatriotic to use corn, wheat, and barley to make alcohol when soldiers overseas needed bread.

Government Bans Alcoholic Beverages In 1919, the states ratified the **Eighteenth Amendment** to the Constitution. It forbade the manufacture, distribution, and sale of alcohol anywhere in the United States. The amendment had been passed largely on the strength of rural votes. Congress then passed the **Volstead Act,** a law that officially enforced the amendment.

Advocates of Prohibition, known as "drys," called it a "noble experiment." They argued that Prohibition improved individuals, strengthened families, and created better societies. In fact, drinking—as well as alcoholism and liver disease caused by drinking—did decline during Prohibition.

Opponents of Prohibition, dubbed "wets," countered that the ban on alcohol did not stop people from drinking. Instead, they argued, Prohibition helped create an atmosphere of hypocrisy and increased organized crime.

Americans Break the Law As the wets noted, the Volstead Act did not stop Americans from drinking, but it did prevent them from purchasing drinks

Vocabulary Builder

advocate–(AD vuh kiht) *n.* supporter; one who argues in favor of something

Critics of Prohibition ▶ argued that it encouraged political corruption. In this cartoon, a row of officials from federal agents to judges hold their hands out for bribe money.

◀ Prohibition encouraged a new breed of organized crime. Racketeers like Al Capone (left) and his rival, Bugs Moran, thumbed their nose at the law and ruthlessly murdered their competitors (below).

7 CHICAGO GANGSTERS SLAIN BY FIRING SQUAD OF RIVALS SOME IN POLICE UNIFORM

cial to The New York Times.
CAGO, Feb. 14.—Chicago gang-
aders observed Valentine's
th machine guns and a stream
result seven mem—

VICTIMS LINED UP IN

Hands Up Faces to Wall

Thinking Critically
1. **Summarize** What three types of lawbreaking are illustrated here?
2. **Analyze** How were these three types of lawbreaking related to one another?

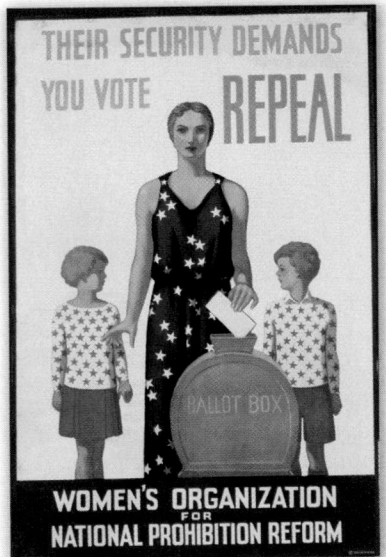

Wets Seek Repeal
Supporters of the Eighteenth Amendment had often used images of mothers and children to press for a ban on alcohol. This propaganda poster uses similar images to press for the repeal.

legally. The gap between the law and individual desires was filled by a large illegal network. People made alcohol in homemade stills or smuggled it in from other countries. **Bootleggers** sold illegal alcohol to consumers. In cities, secret drinking establishments, known as speakeasies, attracted eager customers.

Government agents worked tirelessly to stop the flow of illegal liquor. However, they were short-handed, and the demand for alcohol was too great. There were millions of dollars to be made by both organized and unorganized criminals. Particularly in cities, policemen and politicians tended to look the other way when liquor was concerned. They rationalized their actions by saying that if people wanted to drink they would drink.

Al Capone, a Chicago gang leader, was the most famous criminal of the Prohibition era. He defended his illegal actions:

> **Primary Source** "I make my money from supplying a public demand. If I break the law, my customers, who number hundreds of the best people in Chicago, are as guilty as I am. The only difference between us is that I sell and they buy. Everybody calls me a racketeer. I call myself a businessman."
> —Al Capone, quoted in *Era of Excess* (Sinclair)

The problem was that under the guise of providing a glass of beer or scotch, organized crime spread into other areas of society. Capone's other "businesses" included prostitution, drugs, robbery, and murder. Thus, Prohibition contributed to the growth of organized crime in America.

Prohibition Divides the Nation By the mid-1920s, most city politicians clamored for the repeal of the Eighteenth Amendment. But to many rural Americans, liquor and crime were tied to other divisive cultural issues of the day. Thus, like immigration and evolution, the debate over Prohibition became part of a battle over the future of America.

In the culturally divided 1920s, Americans could not reach a satisfactory settlement on the issue. Not until 1933 did the Twenty-first Amendment finally repeal Prohibition.

✓ **Checkpoint** What were the effects of the Eighteenth Amendment and the Volstead Act?

SECTION 3 Assessment

Progress Monitoring *Online*
For: Self-test with vocabulary practice
Web Code: nea-0705

Comprehension

1. **Terms and People** For each of the following, write a sentence explaining its importance to the social and cultural clashes of the 1920s.
   • modernism
   • fundamentalism
   • Scopes Trial
   • quota system
   • Ku Klux Klan
   • Prohibition
   • Eighteenth Amendment
   • Volstead Act
   • bootlegger

2. **NoteTaking Reading Skill: Contrast** Use your table to answer the Section Focus Question: How did Americans differ on major social and cultural issues?

Writing About History

3. **Compare and Contrast** Write the opening paragraph for an essay comparing supporters and opponents of Prohibition. Use the information in this section as well as your own thoughts. Consider the goals and values that wets and drys might have had in common as well as the ways in which they differed.

Critical Thinking

4. **Recognize Ideologies** How did the two sides in the Scopes Trial represent conflicting value systems? What did each side value most?

5. **Identify Points of View** Why did both supporters and opponents of immigration quotas believe they were defending American traditions and values?

6. **Draw Conclusions** Why do you think the revived Ku Klux Klan was able to spread beyond the South and even into some urban areas?

◀ Couple dancing to phonograph music

Couple dancing to phonograph music

SECTION 4

WITNESS HISTORY AUDIO

"Ain't We Got Fun?"

The phonograph had come a long way from that day in 1877 when inventor Thomas Edison had recorded himself reciting "Mary Had a Little Lamb." By the 1920s, Americans were buying thousands of phonographs and millions of shiny phonograph records. In the comfort of their living rooms, they listened and danced to popular songs that reflected the carefree spirit of the age. One hit tune of 1921 told of a young couple who were determined to enjoy themselves even though they didn't have much money:

❝Night or daytime, it's all playtime,
Ain't we got fun?
Hot or cold days, any old days,
Ain't we got fun?
If wifie wishes to go to a play,
Don't wash the dishes, just throw them away!❞

—Gus Kahn and Raymond B. Egan,
"Ain't We Got Fun?"

A New Mass Culture

 Core Curriculum Objectives

- **5.I.C.1d** Entertainment: radio; motion pictures; advertising and cultural homogenization
- **5.I.C.3b** Women's changing roles
- **5.II.B.7c** Art: WPA, fine arts, Hollywood, comic books

Terms and People

Charlie Chaplin
The Jazz Singer
Babe Ruth
Charles Lindbergh
flapper

Sigmund Freud
"Lost Generation"
F. Scott Fitzgerald
Ernest Hemingway

NoteTaking

Reading Skill: Summarize Look for ways in which culture changed during the 1920s.

Why It Matters The automobile reshaped American culture, creating new forms of recreation and making it easier for people to travel. Other factors also contributed to changing ways of daily life. Americans listened to the radio, went to the movies, and followed the exploits of sports heroes. In the process, a new mass culture emerged—one whose shape and character closely resemble our own. **Section Focus Question: How did the new mass culture reflect technological and social changes?**

New Trends in Popular Culture

The 1920s was in many respects the first decade of our modern era. Even as cultural issues divided Americans from different regions or economic levels, technology was beginning to break down other barriers. Nowhere is this more evident than in the leisure interests of the American people.

Americans Enjoy More Leisure Time The growth of cities changed leisure patterns. On farms, people worked from dawn to dusk, with little time to spare. In the evenings, a farm family might play games, read, or sing together around the piano. Occasionally, they joined other farm families and townsfolk for picnics or a game of baseball. They did not have the time or the money for more extensive leisure pursuits.

City life was different. The average workweek in all industries fell from 70 hours in 1850 to 55 in 1910 to 45 by 1930. The workweek itself also changed from seven days a week to six and at last to five. At the same time, salaries and wages were on the rise.

▼ **Charlie Chaplin,** the comic "common man"

▲ **Douglas Fairbanks,** athletic star of adventure movies

► **Lon Chaney,** star of horror films like *The Phantom of the Opera*

▲ **Mary Pickford,** known as America's Sweetheart

Silent Movie Stars

Each silent movie star had his or her own special appeal. The four shown above were among the most popular not only in the United States but around the world.

Americans Flock to the Movies With more free time and disposable income, urban and suburban Americans looked to new sources of entertainment. Motion pictures helped supply that demand.

The technology to make motion pictures had been around for a generation, but the movie industry rose to new heights in the 1920s. A handful of huge studios in Hollywood, California, established monopolies that controlled the production, distribution, and exhibition of movies. During the 1920s, from 60 to 100 million Americans went to the movies each week. Ornate movie palaces or small local theaters became America's cultural classrooms.

For most of the decade, the studios made silent pictures. They were an ideal entertainment at a time when millions of immigrants spoke little English. Motion pictures transcended languages and even literacy, treating universal themes in familiar ways that allowed any viewer to follow the stories. Motion pictures became America's democratic art. Unlike theatrical productions or classical concerts, movies were available to anyone with a few cents to spare. In addition, the fact that movies were silent made it easier for them to cut across geographic boundaries. Hollywood's biggest movies and stars became nearly as popular in far corners of the world as they were at home.

Many stars of the silent era portrayed ordinary folks. Comedian **Charlie Chaplin,** the most popular silent film star, played the Little Tramp. The character was equal parts hobo, dreamer, and poet but an eternal optimist in his ability to charm his audience and continually reinvent himself. Other stars played more romantic types. Handsome Rudolph Valentino was the sheik, as exotic to ordinary Americans as the deserts of Arabia. William S. Hart was a steely-eyed cowboy who came into town to restore law and order.

In 1927, film history changed, suddenly and forever, with the release of ***The Jazz Singer,*** the first movie with sound synchronized to the action. Audiences were amazed when Al Jolson said—not pantomimed—"You ain't heard nothin' yet" and then launched into a song. Silent pictures quickly faded out, replaced by "talkies." But whether silent or sound, movies spoke directly to the desires, needs, fears, and fantasies of millions of people in the United States and around the world.

The Radio and Phonograph Break Barriers Like the movies, the phonograph and the radio also became powerful instruments of mass popular culture. Each was the result of both technological advances and business enterprise. Millions of radios and phonographs (as well as phonograph records) were marketed in the 1920s. On a deeper level, the phonograph and radio helped produce a standardized culture. Americans in the East and West and North and South listened to the same songs, learned the same dances, and shared the same popular culture as they never had before.

The radio, or wireless, had been developed in the 1890s by Italian inventor Guglielmo Marconi. Before the 1920s, the radio had been an innovation for a small group of military technicians, telephone operators, and amateur "wireless" operators. Then, in 1920, an executive of the Westinghouse company started radio station KDKA in Pittsburgh, Pennsylvania. It was an immediate success. Within three years, there were almost 600 licensed stations broadcasting to more than 600,000 radio sets. Americans listened to music, educational lectures and religious sermons, and news and weather reports. They also heard commercials for a wide variety of consumer products.

Radios brought distant events into millions of homes in a way unmatched by newspapers or magazines. In 1927, much of America listened to a championship boxing match between Gene Tunney and Jack Dempsey. That night, theaters and movie houses played to empty seats as Americans huddled next to their sets. Even the men on death row at Sing Sing prison listened to the broadcast. Before the 1920s, such coverage of an event had been impossible.

The phonograph allowed people to listen to the same music they heard on the radio, but whenever they wanted. Early phonographs employed difficult-to-use wax cylinders and suffered from poor sound quality. In the 1920s, grooved disc recordings and superior sound reproduction improved the sound of the earlier machines. Recordings helped spread country and western music from the South and West to the North and East, while pop tunes from New York City's Tin Pan Alley traveled in the other direction. As they listened to the same songs, Americans also learned the same fashionable dances, from the fox trot to the Charleston.

✔ **Checkpoint** How did movies and the radio cut across geographic barriers?

An Age of Heroes

Hollywood's chief rivals for the creation of heroes were the nation's baseball parks, football fields, and boxing rings. Before the 1920s, there were relatively few nationally famous athletes, such as boxer John L. Sullivan and all-around athlete Jim Thorpe. Most sports stars were local heroes. This changed by the 1920s, often called the Golden Age of Sports.

Sports Heroes Win Fans Thanks to increased newspaper readership and the rise of radio coverage, every major sport boasted nationally famous performers. Perhaps the leading sports hero was baseball home-run king **Babe Ruth**. Others included Red Grange in football, Jack Dempsey in boxing, Bobby Jones in golf, and Bill Tilden in tennis. Women athletes, too, gained fame, from tennis player Helen Wills to Gertrude Ederle, the first woman to swim the English Channel.

HISTORY MAKERS

Babe Ruth (1895–1948)
Babe Ruth—also known as the Bambino and the Sultan of Swat—towered over major league baseball, not only while he was playing but for decades after. Originally a standout pitcher for the Boston Red Sox, Ruth gained fame as a slugging outfielder for the New York Yankees. In 1920, baseball was suffering from a gambling scandal. Ruth's amazing home runs and great appeal helped the sport win back fans. His record for most home runs in a season stood for more than 30 years, and his record for most home runs in a career lasted even longer.

Why did athletes reach such heights of popularity? Part of the answer is that the Golden Age of Sports was also the Golden Age of the Sportswriter. Such journalists as Damon Runyon and Grantland Rice captured the excitement of sports events in their colorful prose. Turning the finest athletes into seemingly immortal gods, the sportswriters nicknamed Babe Ruth the Sultan of Swat and dubbed Notre Dame's football backfield the Four Horsemen.

The other part of the answer is that the decade needed heroes. World War I had shattered many Americans' faith in progress, making the world seem cheap and flawed. Athletic heroes reassured Americans that people were capable of great feats and lofty dreams. If in our heroes we see our idealized selves, the sports heroes of the 1920s gave Americans a sense of hope.

Lucky Lindy Crosses the Atlantic Even the biggest sports stars could not match the adoration given aviator **Charles Lindbergh.** In the 1920s, the airline industry was in its infancy. Flying aces had played a role in World War I, and a few small domestic airlines carried mail and passengers. But airplanes were still a novel sight to most Americans. The pilot became a new breed of hero, a romantic daredevil who risked death with every flight.

Lindbergh outdid them all. In May 1927, he took off from Long Island, New York, in his tiny single-engine plane, the *Spirit of St. Louis*, and headed east— to Paris, France. Other pilots had flown across the Atlantic Ocean before, but Lindbergh was the first to do it solo and non-stop. The flight took more than 33 hours, and the lone pilot had to stay awake the entire time. He also recalled, "In the daytime I knew where I was going, but in the evening and at night it was largely a matter of guesswork."

When Lindbergh landed in Paris, he became an instant media celebrity, dubbed Lucky Lindy and the Lone Eagle. The radio reported on his landing, and movie newsreels showed his triumphant return home. The modest young man from the Midwest became the greatest hero of his time.

Lucky Lindy Crosses the Atlantic

"Well, I made it," Charles Lindbergh said simply as he landed his airplane, the *Spirit of St. Louis,* in Paris. Moments later, soldiers had to rescue him from the thousands of well-wishers who crowded the airfield.

 Checkpoint How did the new mass media contribute to the popularity of heroes?

NoteTaking

Reading Skill: Summarize As you read, classify the various types of changes that took place in women's lives in the 1920s.

Women in the 1920s		
Social Changes	Political Changes	Economic Changes

Women Assume New Roles

In a 1931 book, *Only Yesterday*, journalist Frederick Lewis Allen attempted to make sense of the fads, heroes, and problems of the 1920s. Featured prominently was the New Woman. During the decade, many women challenged political, economic, social, and educational boundaries, to prove that their role was as vital outside the home as inside it.

Flappers Challenge Older Limits During the Victorian Age of the late 1800s and early 1900s, women had been expected to center their lives on the home and family. The New Woman of the 1920s, noted Allen, was more liberated. She wore dresses with shorter hemlines, put on more makeup, danced to the latest crazes, and generally assumed that she had the same political and social rights as any man.

THE NEW Woman?

What was new about the "New Woman" of the 1920s? The flapper—exciting to some and shocking to others—became the most familiar symbol of women's new freedom. But for most women, change came more slowly and subtly.

◀ **New Products for the Housewife**
Even for the majority of women who stayed at home to care for the house and children, life changed. New consumer products such as dishwashers and vacuum cleaners made housework easier.

The Flapper ▲
"Flappers are we/ Flappers wild and free," crowed a song of the 1920s. "Never too slow/ All on the go." But although flappers influenced styles and attitudes, relatively few women were full-fledged flappers.

"Firsts" for American Women, 1920s

Florence Allen	First woman state judge (1920)
Marie Luhring	First woman automotive engineer (1920)
Rebecca Felton	First woman in U.S. Senate (1922)
Nellie Tayloe Ross	First woman governor (1924)
Gertrude Ederle	First woman to swim English Channel (1926)
Dorothy Arzner	First woman to direct a talking movie (1927)
Phoebe Omlie	First woman to earn a federal pilot's license (1927)

◀ **Women Pioneers**
In the 1920s, individual women seized opportunities to blaze new trails in fields from politics to auto mechanics.

Office Workers The trend toward more women entering the workforce continued throughout the decade. Some white-collar jobs, such as stenographers and telephone
◀ operators, became predominantly female.

Thinking Critically

1. **Evaluate Information** Why were the "Firsts" shown on the table at left important?

2. **Draw Conclusions** Why do you think the flapper became a major symbol even though relatively few women were flappers?

Vocabulary Builder

sociological–(soh see uh LAH jih kuhl) *adj.* having to do with the study of human society and social relations

Popular magazines, <u>sociological</u> studies, novels, and movies all echoed Allen's observations. The rejection of Victorian morality seemed so total and the New Woman so novel that the change amounted to a "revolution in manners and morals." The symbol of all these changes was the **flapper,** a young woman with short skirts and rouged cheeks who had her hair cropped close in a style known as a bob.

There was only a germ of truth in the various observations. The Victorian code of separate spheres for men and women was disappearing but not as rapidly or as completely as Allen indicated. The flapper was undoubtedly more publicized than imitated. Still, the image of the flapper underscores an important aspect of the decade. Not all women aspired to be flappers, but many wanted more control over their lives—and got it.

Women Make Strides The great fight for suffrage had been won with the passage of the Nineteenth Amendment. What was the next step? Some groups, such as the National American Woman Suffrage Association, called on women to work in reform movements, run for office, or fight for laws to protect women and children in the workplace. Some women had success in public life. In 1925, Nellie Tayloe Ross of Wyoming and Miriam Ferguson of Texas became the first women elected as their state's governor.

The National Women's Party took a more militant position, demanding complete economic, social, and political equality with men. Their primary goal was the passage of an Equal Rights Amendment. Most women, though, believed that a new constitutional amendment was premature. They set more achievable goals and made significant strides in employment. Although most working women continued to toil in domestic service and manufacturing, others moved into clerical, sales, and management positions. Women also won jobs in journalism, aviation, banking, and the legal and medical professions.

Family Life Changes Perhaps the most widespread revolution taking place in women's lives was a quiet one. During the decade, women tended to live longer, marry later, and have fewer children, freeing their time to pursue other interests. Some entered the workforce, others devoted more time to charitable work, and still others joined clubs that discussed books and ideas. All these pursuits enlarged the intellectual world of women.

The consumer economy of the 1920s benefited women. Electric vacuum cleaners and irons took some of the labor and drudgery out of household chores. Of course, not all women shared in the blessings of technology. Many homes in rural America had no access to electricity. For women in these regions, household labor continued to involve intense, even painful, work. They drew and carried water from wells, heated irons on stoves, and washed clothes by hand. Here again, the split between urban and rural Americans was distinct.

 Checkpoint What political gains did American women make during the 1920s?

Modernism in Art and Literature

No area of American life, however, reflected the impact of World War I more than literature and the arts. The war altered the way writers and artists viewed the world, changed the way they approached their craft, and inspired them to experiment with new forms and fresh ideas.

The Arts Reflect a Mood of Uncertainty During the Victorian era, most poets and novelists had expressed a belief in progress, placing boundless faith in human potential. But World War I called the notion of progress into question.

How could a society ruled by the idea of progress embark on a war that killed millions of people, destroyed monuments of civilization, and left survivors hungry, homeless, and hopeless? This was not an action of a rational people, a new generation of writers argued, but the irrational exploits of civilization without a sense of direction. This pessimistic, skeptical worldview sparked an artistic movement known as modernism.

The theories of Austrian <u>psychologist</u> **Sigmund Freud** (SIHG muhnd froid) also contributed to literary and artistic modernism. Freud argued that much of human behavior is driven not by rational thought but by unconscious desires. To live in society, people learn to suppress these desires. But the tension between outward behavior and the subconscious, said Freud, could lead to mental and even physical illness. Freud's theories led writers and artists to explore the subconscious mind.

Modern Painting Challenges Tradition Modernism clashed head-on with traditionalism most dramatically in the field of modern art. Since the late 1800s, European painters had led the way in seeking a fresh visual idiom, or language. They moved away from representational paintings that simply reproduced real life and experimented with more abstract styles.

Modern Art

By the 1920s, many artists had broken away from purely representational styles. The two American artists shown here used vastly different methods in their work. *How do these paintings reflect the changing world of the 1920s? How do they express differing moods?*

Edward Hopper: *Automat*
Basically realistic, Edward Hopper's works often reflect the loneliness and anonymity of urban life. In this 1927 painting, a woman dressed in flapper style eats in a restaurant where even the food is dispensed by machine.

Joseph Stella: *Brooklyn Bridge*
Joseph Stella was one of the few American painters to follow a European style called futurism, which celebrated change and technology. This 1920 painting is more abstract than Hopper's, but the subject matter is still recognizable.

685

▼ Willa Cather

American Postwar Novelists

Novelist	Major Themes	Representative Work
Willa Cather (1873–1947)	Frontier life on the Great Plains	*My Ántonia* (1918) depicts the passing of the American frontier through the life of an immigrant girl in Nebraska.
William Faulkner (1897–1962)	Life in the South; inner workings of mind	*The Sound and the Fury* (1929) uses different narrators to tell the story of the complex inner workings of a Southern family.
F. Scott Fitzgerald (1896–1940)	The Jazz Age	*The Great Gatsby* (1925) shows the emptiness of the Jazz-Age world of flappers and bootleggers.
Ernest Hemingway (1899–1961)	Disillusionment of postwar generation	*A Farewell to Arms* (1929) tells the story of doomed love between a cynical American ambulance driver and a nurse during World War I.
Sinclair Lewis (1885–1951)	Small-town life in the Midwest	*Main Street* (1920) paints a satirical portrait of small-minded people in an American town.
Edith Wharton (1862–1937)	Life among the rich in New York	*The Age of Innocence* (1920) depicts a wealthy young man prevented by social conventions from marrying the woman he loves.

▲ Original cover of *Main Street*

Most Americans got their first real glimpse of the new European approach at a major art show at New York's 69th Infantry Regimental Armory in 1913. Traditionalists were outraged by the Armory Show, and Theodore Roosevelt said that most of it represented the "lunatic fringe" of the art world. But many American painters were inspired by the bold new styles. They began their own search for artistic honesty in abstract patterns. In the 1920s, paintings by Edward Hopper, Man Ray, Joseph Stella, and Georgia O'Keeffe demonstrated the richness and varied styles of American artists. At the same time, the works of artists such as Archibald Motley and William H. Johnson portrayed African American perspectives on modern life.

Postwar American Literature Flowers American writers of the 1920s are often referred to as the **"Lost Generation"** because they no longer had faith in the cultural guideposts of the Victorian era. But many were inspired by their "lost" condition to search for new truths and fresh ways of expressing those truths. Never in American history had one decade seen the emergence of so many great literary talents. A list of writers who rose to distinction in the 1920s includes F. Scott Fitzgerald, Ernest Hemingway, Edith Wharton, Sinclair Lewis, William Faulkner, Gertrude Stein, Eugene O'Neill, and T. S. Eliot. Each of these writers remains today on any list of distinguished American authors.

Novelist **F. Scott Fitzgerald** explored the reality of the American dream of wealth, success, and emotional fulfillment. In *This Side of Paradise*, he wrote that his generation had "grown up to find all Gods dead, all wars fought, and all faiths in man shaken." In *The Great Gatsby* (1925), his most accomplished work, Fitzgerald showed the American dream ending in nightmare. In the novel, through hard work and careful planning, James Gatz re-creates himself as Jay Gatsby, a successful tycoon. Gatsby fills his home with wild parties, dancing, bootleg liquor, and endless activity:

> **Primary Source** "In the main hall a bar with a real brass rail was set up, and stocked with gins and liquors and with cordials so long forgotten that most of his female guests were too young to know one from another. By seven o'clock the orchestra had arrived, no thin five-piece affair, but a whole pitful of oboes and trombones and saxophones. . . . People were not invited—they went there. They got into automobiles which bore them out to Long Island, and somehow they ended up at Gatsby's door."
> —F. Scott Fitzgerald, *The Great Gatsby*

But in the end, Gatsby is destroyed by the very things he hoped to achieve. His lofty dreams end in a violent, meaningless death.

Fitzgerald's fellow novelist and good friend **Ernest Hemingway** explored similar themes but in a new idiom. Hemingway felt betrayed, not only by the American dream, but also by literary language itself. In *A Farewell to Arms*, his 1929 novel about World War I, Hemingway's narrator says:

> **Primary Source** "I was always embarrassed by the words sacred, glorious, and sacrifice. . . . I had seen nothing sacred, and the things that were glorious had no glory and the sacrifices were like the stockyards at Chicago if nothing was done with the meat except to bury it. . . . Abstract words such as glory, honor, courage, or hallow were obscene beside the concrete names of villages, the numbers of roads, the names of rivers, the numbers of regiments and the dates."
> —Ernest Hemingway, *A Farewell to Arms*

HISTORY MAKERS

Gertrude Stein (1874–1946)
Gertrude Stein lived for a while in Europe as a child and returned there after college. A poet and writer, her poetry was highly experimental and often difficult to understand. But her Paris home became a gathering place for writers and artists. She supported new styles and encouraged several American writers, including Ernest Hemingway and F. Scott Fitzgerald. It was Stein who called this group the "Lost Generation."

In his short stories and novels, Hemingway worked to develop a writing style that reflected his insights. He wrote in unadorned sentences, stripped of vague adjectives and adverbs. He created a style that was as concrete and as powerful as a rifle shot.

Influenced by Freud, other writers explored the subconscious mind. Playwright Eugene O'Neill experimented with techniques that put the subconscious right on stage. In *The Emperor Jones*, the title character gets lost in a jungle and is attacked by imaginary beings called Little Formless Fears. In *Strange Interlude*, characters turn away from their conversations with other people on stage and speak their thoughts directly to the audience.

Certainly, many poets and novelists of the decade were disillusioned. Like Hemingway and Fitzgerald, they wrestled with the meaning of the war and life itself. But in the end, their efforts resulted in the creation of literary masterpieces, not worthless products of aimless despair.

✓ **Checkpoint** What impact did World War I have on postwar American literature?

SECTION 4 Assessment

Progress Monitoring *Online*
For: Self-test with vocabulary practice
Web Code: nea-0706

Comprehension

1. **Terms and People** For each of the following, write a sentence explaining the importance of that person or item to American culture of the 1920s.
   - Charlie Chaplin
   - *The Jazz Singer*
   - flapper
   - Sigmund Freud
   - "Lost Generation"
   - F. Scott Fitzgerald
   - Ernest Hemingway

2. **NoteTaking Reading Skill: Summarize** Use your concept web to answer the Section Focus Question: How did the new mass culture reflect technological and social changes?

Writing About History

3. **Compare** Write a paragraph comparing the mass culture of today with the mass culture of the 1920s. Consider: What technologies form part of the mass culture? What role do they play in our lives?

Critical Thinking

4. **Analyze Information** How did the increased popularity of sports heroes and the disillusionment of the "Lost Generation" writers represent different responses to the same events?

5. **Identify Main Ideas** How did the political role of American women change in the years after World War I?

6. **Analyze Literature** Reread the selection from *The Great Gatsby*, on the previous page. How does it reflect other information you have learned about the society of the 1920s?

EXPERIENCE THE ROARING TWENTIES

Turn on the radio! Let's go to the movies! In the 1920s, Americans were having fun in ways that hadn't even been invented half a century earlier. And, with new forms of mass communication, fads and entertainment were spreading faster and wider than ever before. For a few pennies, a farmer in Indiana could go to the movies and enjoy the same laughs and thrills as a factory worker in New York or a businessman in San Francisco. Practically every American knew ballplayer Ty Cobb, actress Mary Pickford, and singer Rudy Vallee.

Today, the technology and the fads have changed. But the age of mass culture has never left us. ◀)) AUDIO

◀ **The Charleston**
No fad symbolizes the Roaring Twenties more than the Charleston. Here, two young people demonstrate the wild, loose-limbed dance that swept the nation.

Saturday Night at the Movies ▼
By the 1920s, Americans were going to the movies so often that attendance at other forms of public entertainment, such as theater, suffered. Decades later, the rise of television would have the same effect on movie attendance.

Average Weekly Movie Attendance, 1922–1930

People per week (in millions)

100
75
50
25
0

1922 1924 1926 1928 1930

SOURCE: *Historical Statistics of the United States*

Households With Radios, 1922–1930

SOURCE: *Historical Statistics of the United States*

▲ **Radio Days**
As more radios were sold, the radio became the centerpiece of millions of American living rooms. At first, headsets were required to listen to broadcasts.

▲ **Casual Reading**
Mass-market magazines with eye-catching covers were more popular than ever. This *Life* magazine cover (left) highlights the growing popularity of golf among both men and women. *Amazing Stories* (right) was the first "pulp" magazine devoted exclusively to science fiction.

The Great American Pastime
Baseball remained America's favorite sport, but mass media brought it to an entirely new audience. Here, veteran superstar Ty Cobb (below) of the Detroit Tigers greets some young fans. ▼

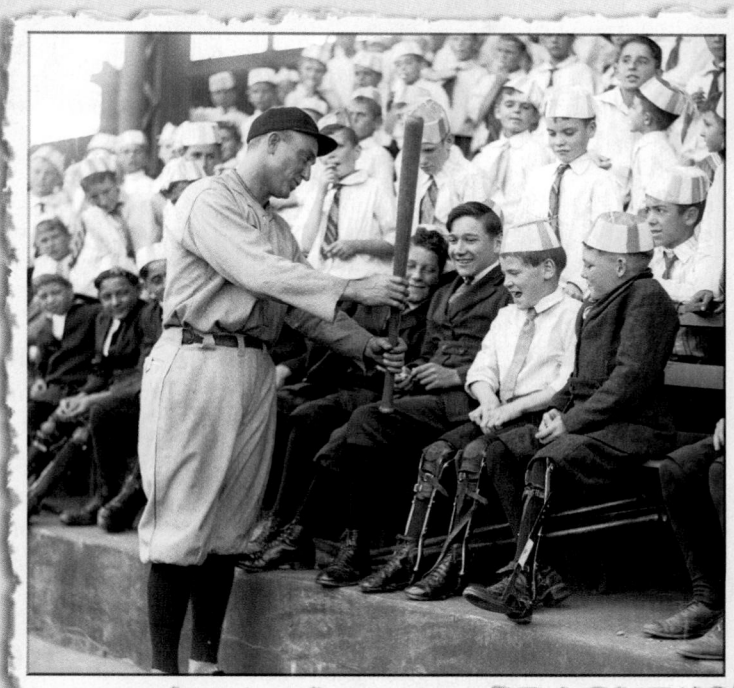

Thinking Critically
1. **Analyze Visuals** Identify two ways that technology affected leisure activities.

2. **Draw Conclusions** Do you think mass entertainment, such as movies and radio, would promote greater understanding and unity among Americans? Explain.

Connect to Today Many people worry that some of today's leisure activities, such as video games and the Internet, have a negative impact on family togetherness. Do you agree or disagree? Give reasons for your answer.

History *Interactive* ✳

For: Experience the Mass Culture of the 20s video, audio, and analysis
Web Code: nep-0707

OPPORTUNITY
A JOURNAL OF NEGRO LIFE

JUNE 1926

◀ Magazines like this one focused on African American culture and history.

WITNESS HISTORY AUDIO

The Excitement of Harlem

In the early 1920s, the New York City neighborhood known as Harlem was the most vibrant African American community in the nation. Teeming with people and teeming with activity, it was also, as one observer noted, "a great magnet for the Negro intellectual." Among those who were drawn to Harlem was a young Missouri-born poet named Langston Hughes. He later recalled what he felt like as he stepped off the subway:

❝I can never put on paper the thrill of the underground ride to Harlem. I went up the steps and out into the bright September sunlight. Harlem! I stood there, dropped my bags, took a deep breath and felt happy again.❞

—Langston Hughes, *The Big Sea*

The Harlem Renaissance

Core Curriculum Objectives

- **5.I.C.3c(2)** Shifting cultural values: The literary scene: The Harlem Renaissance
- **5.II.B.7b** Culture of the Depression: Music: jazz, swing

Terms and People

Marcus Garvey
jazz
Louis Armstrong
Bessie Smith

Harlem Renaissance
Claude McKay
Langston Hughes
Zora Neale Hurston

NoteTaking

Reading Skill: Identify Main Ideas As you read, identify the main ideas.

> I. New "Black Consciousness"
>   A. New Chances, New Challenges
>   1. Migration to North continues
>   2.
>   B.
> II.

Why It Matters As a result of World War I and the Great Migration, millions of African Americans relocated from the rural South to the urban North. This mass migration continued through the 1920s and contributed to a flowering of music and literature. Jazz and the Harlem Renaissance made a lasting impact, not only on African Americans but on the culture all Americans share. **Section Focus Question: How did African Americans express a new sense of hope and pride?**

A New "Black Consciousness"

Like the immigrants who traveled from Europe and Asia, African Americans who left the South dreamed of a better future. They had heard stories of economic opportunity, social advancement, and greater political rights. The South, they reasoned, was a dead end. Locked into low-paying rural jobs, barred from decent schools, faced with the reality of Jim Crow oppression and the threat of lynching, they pointed their compasses north.

Migrants Face Chances and Challenges Most African American migrants to the north probably found a better life. Wages in a Detroit auto plant or a Pittsburgh steel mill were far better than what a sharecropper earned in the South. In such cities as New York, Chicago, Pittsburgh, and Cleveland, African Americans had a growing political voice. In those towns, there also existed black middle and upper classes. African American ministers, physicians, lawyers, teachers, and journalists practiced their professions and served as role models to the younger generation.

But in coming North, African Americans had certainly not escaped racism and oppression. On average, they were forced to live in the worst housing and labor in the lowest paying jobs. In addition, as the race riots of the summer of 1919 demonstrated, violence was a threat to African Americans north as well as south of the Mason-Dixon line. After World War I, African Americans increased their demand for a real solution to the country's racial problems.

New York City's Harlem became the focal point for the aspirations of hundreds of thousands of African Americans. Some 200,000 blacks settled in Harlem. Migrants from the South mixed with recently arrived immigrants from Caribbean islands, such as Jamaica. This dynamic blend of different cultures and traditions bred new ideas.

Garvey Calls for Racial Pride The most prominent new African American leader to emerge in the 1920s was **Marcus Garvey.** Born in Jamaica, Garvey traveled widely before immigrating to Harlem in 1916. From his travels, Garvey drew one important conclusion: Everywhere blacks were exploited. To combat the problem, he promoted the idea of universal black nationalism and organized a "Back to Africa" movement. Unlike Booker T. Washington or W.E.B. Du Bois, Garvey did not call for blacks and whites to work together to improve America. Instead, Garvey advocated the separation of the races.

Garvey's message found willing converts in American cities. By the mid-1920s, his Universal Negro Improvement Association boasted almost 2.5 million members and sympathizers. His advocacy of black pride and black support of black-run businesses won considerable support.

Garvey's movement fell apart in the second half of the decade. The federal government sent him to prison for mail fraud and then deported him to Jamaica. Without his powerful leadership, the Universal Negro Improvement Association lost its focus and appeal.

Although Garvey's movement died, his ideas did not fade. The nationalist and separatist aspects of the Nation of Islam and the Black Power movement in the 1960s owed much to Garvey. So, too, did later appeals to black pride, self-reliance, and cultural ties to Africa. Harlem's major newspaper, the *Amsterdam News*, later wrote, "In a world where black is despised, he taught [African Americans] to admire and praise black things and black people."

 Checkpoint How did Marcus Garvey encourage African American pride?

Marcus Garvey
Dressed in a ceremonial uniform, Marcus Garvey rides in a New York City parade on the opening day of a 1922 convention of a group called Negro Peoples of the World.

The Jazz Age

It was F. Scott Fitzgerald who called the 1920s the "Jazz Age." However, it was African Americans who gave the age its jazz. A truly <u>indigenous</u> American musical form, **jazz** is a musical form based on improvisation. Jazz musicians creatively recombine different forms of music, including African American blues and ragtime, and European-based popular music.

A Unique American Music Emerges Jazz emerged in the South and Midwest, particularly New Orleans, where different cultures and traditions came together and influenced each other. Early jazz artists won fame playing in

Vocabulary Builder
<u>indigenous</u>—(ihn DIHJ uh nuhs) *adj.* native to; growing out of a particular region or country

Storyville, a section of New Orleans known for its night life. From the South, it spread north with the Great Migration of African Americans.

Trumpet player **Louis Armstrong** became the unofficial ambassador of jazz. After playing with King Oliver's band in New Orleans and Chicago and with Fletcher Henderson's orchestra in New York, Armstrong began to organize his own groups. His ability to play the trumpet and his subtle sense of improvisation made him a legend and influenced the development of jazz. After Armstrong, all jazz bands featured soloists. Many also began to feature vocal soloists, such as **Bessie Smith,** the "Empress of the Blues."

Jazz Wins Worldwide Popularity Jazz was more than a musical style. It was also a symbol of the Roaring Twenties. It was part of the Prohibition era, played in speakeasies and nightspots in New York, Chicago, St. Louis, and Los Angeles. It was the sound of the Cotton Club, one of Harlem's most famous attractions, where African Americans played African American music to all-white audiences. Phonograph records and radio spread the influence of jazz across the country and beyond. By the end of the decade, the popularity of jazz had spread to Europe as well.

But jazz was still more. It was a demonstration of the depth and richness of African American culture. Gerald Early, a modern scholar of English and African American studies, predicted that, in the future, America will be best remembered for three great contributions—the Constitution, baseball, and jazz. All three enriched lives, opened windows to new possibilities, and lifted the human spirit. Jazz announced that the United States was a land of shared cultures and traditions, a place where people came together and created something greater than their parts.

Jazz quickly bridged the races. Trumpeter Bix Beiderbecke (BĪ der behk) became the first white musician to contribute to the styles and popularity of jazz. Jazz sounds influenced such white songwriters and composers as Cole

Stars of the Jazz Age 🔊)) AUDIO

Not only was Louis Armstrong (below left) an influential trumpeter, he also pioneered "scat," a style in which the singer improvises meaningless syllables that mimic the sounds of musical instruments. The recordings and concerts of blues singer Bessie Smith (below right) made her the highest-paid African American entertainer of the 1920s.

Porter, Irving Berlin, and George Gershwin, whose jazz-inspired orchestral work *Rhapsody in Blue* premiered in 1924. The title of a song by African American band leader Duke Ellington best captures how jazz changed popular music: "It Don't Mean a Thing If It Ain't Got That Swing."

✓ **Checkpoint** How did jazz spread from its roots in the South to the North in the 1920s?

The Harlem Renaissance

Jazz and blues were expressions of the African American experience. The pain of the African American experience can be heard in the blues, and the joy of that experience in the soaring notes of jazz. The range of such African American musicians as Duke Ellington and Cab Calloway speaks to the varieties of African American life. But in the 1920s, there were other expressions of African American culture. Novelists, poets, and artists celebrated their culture and explored questions of race in America. This flowering of African American culture became known as the **Harlem Renaissance.** The Harlem Renaissance helped give a new vocabulary and dynamic to race relations in the United States.

African American Literature Flowers In the 1920s, the term the "New Negro" entered the American vocabulary. It suggested a radical break with the past. No longer would African Americans silently endure the old ways of exploitation and discrimination. The new mood was most vividly expressed in Harlem, which attracted African American novelists, essayists, poets, and journalists from all over the country and beyond. In their work, these writers explored the pains and joys of being black in America, leaving a literary legacy that spoke to all Americans of all times.

Jean Toomer's *Cane* (1923) set the tone for the Harlem Renaissance. A collection of short stories, poems, and sketches, *Cane* presented African American life and folk culture in all its richness. It was not a blueprint for where African Americans needed to move politically in the future, but a plea to remember and preserve the past.

Soon, other African American writers joined Toomer at the forefront of the Harlem Renaissance. Jamaican immigrant **Claude McKay** was the most militant of these writers. In his novels and poems, McKay showed ordinary African Americans struggling for dignity and advancement in the face of discrimination and economic hardships. A poem that McKay wrote after Chicago was stricken by violent race riots captured his sense of anger and militancy:

HISTORY MAKERS

Duke Ellington (1899–1974)
Duke Ellington became one of the most important early figures in jazz and probably its greatest composer. He gained fame in the 1920s, when his band played in Harlem nightclubs. Hiring many skilled musicians, he arranged his music to showcase their talents. Ellington wrote or arranged about two thousand pieces of music that range from popular songs to ballets and movie music. Before his death, he had been awarded the highest honors from the governments of both the United States and France.

Primary Source

"If we must die—let it not be like hogs,
Hunted and penned in an inglorious spot.
While round us bark the mad and hungry dogs,
Marking their mark at our accursed lot. . . .
What though before us lies the open grave?
Like men we will face the murderous, cowardly pack,
Pressed to the wall, dying but fighting back!"
—Claude McKay, "If We Must Die"

McKay represented the political and ideological left wing of the Harlem Renaissance. More in the center was **Langston Hughes,** probably the most powerful African American literary voice of his time. For Hughes, the force of the movement was not politics but a celebration of African American culture and life. (See the American Literature feature on the next page.) In more than 50 works of fiction, poetry, journalism, and criticism, he captured the remarkable diversity of everyday African American life. In the last line of his autobiography *The Big Sea*, Hughes wrote, "Literature is a big sea full of many fish. I let down my nets and pulled. I'm still pulling."

Another powerful voice was **Zora Neale Hurston.** Hurston traveled the rural back roads of her native Florida, collecting folk tales in books such as *Mules and Men*. But Hurston also looked to the future. Her 1937 novel *Their Eyes Were Watching God* expressed the new longing for independence felt by many women, black and white.

The Harlem Renaissance Has Lasting Impact The Harlem Renaissance gave a voice to African American culture, just as jazz and blues gave it a tune. It altered the way many white Americans viewed African American culture, and even the way African Americans viewed themselves. James Weldon Johnson, poet and secretary of the NAACP, noted:

> **Primary Source** "A great deal has been accomplished in this decade of 'renaissance.' . . . Today, one may see undesirable stories, but one may also read stories about Negro singers, Negro actors, Negro authors, Negro poets. The connotations of the very word *Negro* have changed. A generation ago many Negroes were half or wholly ashamed of the term. Today, they have every reason to be proud of it."
> —James Weldon Johnson, article in *Harper's* magazine, 1928

The Harlem Renaissance ended with the national financial collapse that also ended the nation's decade of prosperity. But the sense of group identity and African American solidarity that it created would become part of the bedrock on which the later civil rights movement would be constructed.

✓ **Checkpoint** What themes did Langston Hughes and Zora Neale Hurston explore?

▲ Zora Neale Hurston

SECTION **5** Assessment

Progress Monitoring *Online*
For: Self-test with vocabulary practice
Web Code: nea-0708

Comprehension

1. **Terms and People** For each of the following, write a sentence explaining the importance of that person or item to the development of African American culture.
   - Marcus Garvey
   - jazz
   - Louis Armstrong
   - Bessie Smith
   - Harlem Renaissance
   - Claude McKay
   - Langston Hughes
   - Zora Neale Hurston

2. **NoteTaking Identify Main Ideas** Use your section outline to answer the Section Focus Question: How did African Americans express a new sense of hope and pride?

Writing About History

3. **Compare and Contrast** Write a thesis statement and introductory paragraph for an essay in which you compare the influence of jazz to the influence of the Harlem Renaissance. Consider both the similarities and differences in the two cultural developments.

Critical Thinking

4. **Identify Points of View** Why do you think Marcus Garvey rejected the goals of earlier African American leaders such as Washington and Du Bois?

5. **Analyze Information** How did jazz blend cultural influences and cross-cultural divides?

6. **Identify Main Ideas** Restate the main idea of Claude McKay's poem "If We Must Die" in your own words.

NY 5.I.C.3c(2)

Two Poems by Langston Hughes

Langston Hughes wrote about how it felt to be African American, from the pain of racial prejudice to his deep pride in his culture and heritage. The two poems below are among his most famous.

▲ Langston Hughes

The Negro Speaks of Rivers

I've known rivers:
I've known rivers ancient as the world and older than the flow of human
    blood in human veins.

My soul has grown deep like the rivers.

I bathed in the Euphrates when dawns were young.[1]
I built my hut near the Congo and it lulled me to sleep.
I looked upon the Nile and raised the pyramids above it.
I heard the singing of the Mississippi when Abe Lincoln went down to
    New Orleans, and I've seen its muddy bosom turn all golden in the
    sunset.

I've known rivers:
Ancient, dusky rivers.

My soul has grown deep like the rivers.

My People

The night is beautiful,
So the faces of my people.

The stars are beautiful,
So the eyes of my people.

Beautiful, also, is the sun.
Beautiful, also, are the souls of my people.

Harlem street scene,
1920s ▶

Thinking Critically

1. **Analyze Literature** In "The Negro Speaks of Rivers," what point do you think Hughes is making when he names four rivers at four different periods of history?

2. **Make Inferences** How would you describe the speaker's attitude toward being African American in these poems?

---

1. The Euphrates is a river in the Middle East. The Nile and the Congo are rivers in Africa.

Quick Study Guide

5.I.C.1,
5.I.C.3

Progress Monitoring Online
For: Self-test with vocabulary practice
Web Code: nea-0709

■ Rise of the Automobile

- Decline of railroads, trolleys
- Mass production; lower prices
- Higher wages for auto workers
- **Rise of the Automobile**
- Growth of suburbs
- Greater freedom
- Highway system
- Growth in related industries

■ Urban and Rural Population, 1900–1930

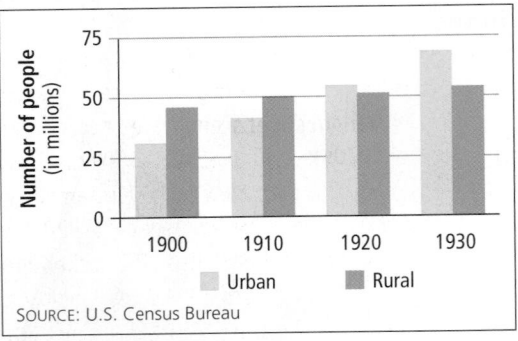

Number of people (in millions)

SOURCE: U.S. Census Bureau

■ Urban ■ Rural

■ Economic Policies of Harding and Coolidge

Goal: Support Economic Growth		
Policy: Raise Tariffs	**Policy: Cut Government Spending**	**Policy: Support Business**
• Increased sales of domestic goods • Led to tariff war with foreign nations	• Cut national debt • Created federal budget surplus	• Encouraged business growth through tax incentives and reduced regulations • Caused organized labor to lose ground

■ New Cultural Trends

Mass culture	Radio and movies unite people of different regions.
Prohibition	Crime rises as people find ways to avoid the ban on alcohol.
Fundamentalism	Many Christians promote a literal interpretation of the Bible and return to traditional values.
Modernism	Literature and art depict postwar disillusionment and the influence of the subconscious on human behavior.
Jazz	Musical style blends elements of African American and European forms.
Harlem Renaissance	Literature and art express pride and aspirations of African Americans.

✓ Quick Study Timeline

In America

1919
Eighteenth Amendment is ratified

1920
Warren Harding elected President

1922
Investigations into Teapot Dome scandal begin

Presidential Terms	Woodrow Wilson 1913–1921	Warren Harding 1921–1923	
	1919	**1921**	**1923**

Around the World

1919
Paris peace conference meets

1921
World Court is founded in the Netherlands

1923
Reparations contribute to inflation in Germany

American Issues
•—•—• Connector

 5.I.C.1c

By connecting prior knowledge with what you have learned in this chapter, you can gradually build your understanding of enduring questions that still affect America today. Answer the questions below. Then, use your American Issues Connector study guide (or go online: www.PHSchool.com **Web Code:** neh-8003).

Issues You Learned About

● **U.S. Immigration Policy** The U.S. government makes decisions about how many immigrants to allow into the country.

1. In the mid-1800s, the United States experienced a wave of immigration. From which countries did the majority of these immigrants come?

2. What measures had been taken to restrict immigration before the 1920s?

3. Was the National Origins Act biased? Explain.

● **Women in American Society** Women's roles in society continue to change and evolve, allowing women greater opportunities.

4. What amendment gave women the right to vote, and when was it ratified?

5. What immediate changes were the result of women's winning the right to vote?

6. How did the role of women in society change in the 1920s?

● **Technology and Society** New technological developments continually change the way Americans work and play.

7. Prior to the automobile, what inventions in transportation transformed the way people and goods traveled in the United States?

8. What social changes did the automobile bring to America?

9. What other technological changes affected American culture in the 1920s?

Connect to Your World | New York

Technology and Society By the early 1920s, increasing numbers of Americans were using cars to get around. To ease travel between New Jersey and New York, the two states worked together to build the Holland Tunnel, which connected New York City and Jersey City. Clifford Holland, for whom the tunnel is named, engineered and directed the project, which began in 1920 and was completed in 1927. Running under the Hudson River, the tunnel is more than a mile and a half long. Nearly 52,000 vehicles passed through it the day it opened in November 1927. Research other ways New York changed in the 1920s because of increased automobile use. Use your findings to create a presentation on the effect of cars on New York.

History *Interactive*
For: Interactive timeline
Web Code: nep-0711

1924
National Origins Act sets up quota system for immigration

1925
Scopes trial begins in Tennessee

1927
***The Jazz Singer,* first talking movie, opens**

1929
Stock market crash marks end of 1920s prosperity

Calvin Coolidge 1923–1929

Herbert Hoover 1929–1933

1925

1927

1929

1924
Stalin comes to power in the Soviet Union

1927
Civil war begins in China

1928
Major nations sign Kellogg-Briand Pact to ban war

Chapter Assessment

Terms and People

1. Define **bull market**. How did it affect the investment activities of Americans?

2. Who was **Andrew Mellon**? What economic goals did he achieve?

3. What was the **Eighteenth Amendment**? Which lawmakers supported it?

4. Define **modernism**. Explain how modernist ideas could be viewed in literature.

5. What was the **Harlem Renaissance**? Name and describe the accomplishments of two people who took part in it.

Focus Questions

The focus question for this chapter is **How did the United States experience both economic growth and social change in the decade after World War I?** Build an answer to this big question by answering the focus questions for Sections 1 through 5 and the Critical Thinking questions that follow.

Section 1
6. How did the booming economy of the 1920s lead to changes in American life?

Section 2
7. How did domestic and foreign policy change direction under Harding and Coolidge?

Section 3
8. How did Americans differ on major social and cultural issues?

Section 4
9. How did the new mass culture reflect technological and social changes?

Section 5
10. How did African Americans express a new sense of hope and pride?

Critical Thinking

11. **Analyze Evidence** What evidence supports the conclusion that Henry Ford cared about the quality of life of his workers?

12. **Predict Consequences** What likely happened in the 1930s to people who, in the 1920s, bought goods they could not afford on the installment plan?

13. **Analyze Information** Did Harding show good leadership of the country? Explain.

14. **Draw Inferences** Why did Congress support the Kellogg-Briand Pact even when lawmakers knew that its provision could not be enforced?

15. **Summarize** How could you describe the cultural differences between rural and urban Americans in the 1920s? What issues led to cultural clashes between the two groups?

16. **Analyze Information** What did athletes represent for Americans in the 1920s?

17. **Evaluate Information** List four changes that affected women in the 1920s. Which of these do you think had the most immediate effect? Which do you think was most important in the long term?

18. **Identify Central Issues** What did southern African Americans hope to find by moving north? Did they achieve their goals?

Writing About History

Writing a Comparison-and-Contrast Essay Evaluations and interpretations of historical eras often change over time or differ from historian to historian. Write the introductory paragraph and outline for an essay comparing two historical views on one of the following topics: the prosperity of the 1920s; the presidency of Calvin Coolidge; the role of the United States in world affairs after World War I; the "New Woman."

Prewriting
- Use Internet or library sources to find two different interpretations or descriptions of one of the topics above. You may use this textbook as one of your sources.
- Make a Venn diagram to identify similarities and differences in the two articles.

Drafting
- Develop a working thesis in which you define the differences between the two historical interpretations.
- Write an opening paragraph in which you introduce the topic and summarize the major differences between your two sources.
- Make an outline organizing your supporting details.

Revising
- Use the guidelines on page SH11 of the Writing Handbook to revise your writing.

Regents DBQ Practice

Scientific Management and Mass Production

The legacy of Henry Ford included not only the popularly priced automobile but techniques of mass production. What were his goals in introducing these techniques, and what impact did they have? Use your knowledge of the chapter material and Documents 1, 2, 3, and 4 to answer questions 1 through 4.

Document 1

"If you and your workman have become so skillful that you and he together are making two pairs of shoes in a day, while your competitor and his workman are making only one pair, it is clear that after selling your two pairs of shoes you can pay your workman much higher wages than your competitor who produces only one pair of shoes is able to pay his man, and that there will still be enough money left over for you to have a larger profit than your competitor. . . . The greatest permanent prosperity for the workman, coupled with the greatest prosperity for the employer, can be brought about only when the work of the establishment is done with the smallest combined expenditure of human effort, plus nature's resources, plus the cost for the use of capital in the shape of machines, buildings."

—*Frederick Taylor*, Principles of Scientific Management, *1911*

Document 2

"[In 1914], Ford announced that he would nearly double the minimum salary paid to his 13,600 workers to $5 a day, and reduce the workday from nine hours to eight. In a stroke, he transformed the people who manufacture automobiles into the people who buy them. . . . The reaction from business thinkers was generally negative. 'He's crazy, isn't he?' asked Adolph Ochs, publisher of the *New York Times*. . . . The *Wall Street Journal* went even further, accusing Ford of having 'committed economic blunders, if not crimes' and applying 'spiritual' principles where they don't belong.'"

—*Kevin Baker*, "Ford's Paradox," *2000*

Document 3

Assembly line at Ford auto plant, 1928

Document 4

"We have decided upon and at once put into effect through all the branches of our industries the five day week. Hereafter there will be no more work with us on Saturdays and Sundays. These will be free days, but the men, according to merit, will receive the same pay equivalent as for a full six day week. . . . It does not pay to put men at work, excepting in continuous operations, from midnight until morning. As a part of low cost production—and only low cost production can pay high wages—one must have a big investment in machinery and power plants. Expensive tools cannot remain idle. They ought to work twenty-four hours a day, but here the human element comes in, for although many men like to work all night and have part of their day free, they do not work so well and hence it is not economical, or at least that is our experience, to go through the full twenty-four hours."

—*Henry Ford*, "Why I Favor Five Days' Work With Six Days' Pay," *1926*

---

1. Documents 3 and 4 provide evidence that Henry Ford
   (1) applied the principles described in Document 1.
   (2) disagreed with the principles described in Document 1.
   (3) had influenced the writer of Document 1.
   (4) had listened to the criticisms of the business leaders quoted in Document 2.

2. According to Document 2, why did many business leaders disapprove of Ford's wage plan?
   (1) It did not take the well-being of his workers into account.
   (2) It was not based on accepted business principles.
   (3) It violated antitrust laws.
   (4) It would give Ford an unfair advantage over his competitors.

3. According to Document 4, why did Ford institute the five-day workweek?
   (1) If his machinery was not used over the weekend, it would last longer.
   (2) His company would save money if he could pay his workers for only five days' work instead of six.
   (3) He was giving in to the demands of labor unions for a shorter workweek.
   (4) The five-day workweek would allow maximum productivity and efficiency.

4. **Writing Task** Who was right: Henry Ford or his critics? Use your knowledge of the chapter content and specific evidence from the primary sources above to support your opinion.

The Depression Descends on America

No one who lived through the Great Depression ever forgot it. Panicked investors watched their fortunes dwindle to nothing overnight. Jobless men trudged anywhere and everywhere looking for work. The hungry lined up for handouts from churches and charitable organizations. Misery stalked Americans at virtually every turn. One survivor of the Depression remembered:

“There were many beggars, who would come to your back door, and they would say they were hungry. I wouldn't give them money because I didn't have it. But I did take them in and put them in my kitchen and give them something to eat.”
—Kitty McCulloch

Listen to the Witness History *audio to hear more about the Great Depression.*

◄ A poor family from rural Maryland poses for a photograph.

Stock ticker machine

Magazine cover from the early 1930s

NY Core Curriculum Preview

Chapter Focus Question: How did the Great Depression happen and how did Americans respond to it?

Section 1
Causes of the Depression 5.II.A.1a, 5.II.A.1b, 5.II.A.2

Section 2
Americans Face Hard Times 5.II.A.4

Section 3
Hoover's Response Fails 5.II.A.3a, 5.II.A.3b, 5.II.A.4

Use the ☑ **Quick Study Timeline** at the end of this chapter to preview chapter events.

World War I victory medal worn by Bonus Army veteran

Note Taking Study Guide *Online*
For: Note Taking and American Issues Connector
Web Code: nee-8101

An affluent middle-class family, 1925

▲ Stock ticker tape

WITNESS HISTORY ◀)) AUDIO

Stock Market Prosperity

As the 1920s roared along, millions of Americans poured their savings into the soaring "bull" market. Excited investors bought and sold stocks based on "tips" from friends or brokers. Many investors amassed huge fortunes on the strength of rising stock prices. Families who had to scrimp and save at the beginning of the decade found themselves fabulously wealthy by its end. In 1929, a prominent magazine printed a poem that captured the essence of America's market fever:

❝Oh, hush thee, my babe, granny's bought some more shares,
Daddy's gone out to play with the bulls and the bears,
Mother's buying on tips and she simply can't lose,
And baby shall have some expensive new shoes!❞
—*The Saturday Evening Post*, 1929

Causes of the Depression

 Core Curriculum Objectives

- **5.II.A.1a** Weakness in the economy: Overproduction/underconsumption
- **5.II.A.1b** Weakness in the economy: Overexpansion of credit
- **5.II.A.2** The stock market crash

Terms and People

Herbert Hoover	business cycle
speculation	Great Depression
Black Tuesday	Hawley-Smoot Tariff

NoteTaking

Reading Skill: Recognize Multiple Causes
Identify the causes of the Great Depression.

Uneven distribution of wealth

Depression Causes

Why It Matters During the Roaring Twenties, many Americans enjoyed what seemed like an endless era of prosperity. Then, in October 1929, the mighty bull market crashed. As production fell and unemployment rose, the U.S. economy lurched into a period of dramatic decline. Years after the Great Depression began, many Americans came to see this contraction as a regular feature of the nation's business cycle. **Section Focus Question: How did the prosperity of the 1920s give way to the Great Depression?**

Prosperity Hides Troubles

In 1928, Republican leaders exuded confidence about both their party and their country. The Roaring Twenties had been a Republican decade. In 1920, Americans sent Warren G. Harding to the White House, and four years after that they sent Calvin Coolidge. Neither election had been close.

Once in office, both Presidents watched the country grow increasingly prosperous. As the decade passed, consumption went up, the gross national product went up, and the stock market went up. No matter what index an economist chose to consult, the conclusion was always the same: Times were good in America—and they were getting better. Republicans took credit for the bullish economy, and Americans heartily agreed.

Optimism Sweeps Hoover to Victory When the Republicans met at their 1928 nominating convention, they chose **Herbert Hoover**—an accomplished public servant—to run for the White House. Born in Iowa, Hoover was orphaned as a child. But he overcame this personal tragedy and eventually graduated from Stanford University with a degree in geology. He became a mining engineer and worked all over the world. By 1914, after amassing a vast fortune, he retired from engineering and devoted himself to public service.

Herbert Hoover came to the attention of Americans during World War I, first as the brilliant coordinator of the Belgium relief program and then as head of the Food Administration. During the Harding and Coolidge administrations, Hoover served as Secretary of Commerce. His philosophy was simple but effective. He stressed the importance of competition, but he also believed in voluntary cooperation between labor and management. American greatness showed itself, Hoover maintained, when owners, workers, and government officials <u>converged</u> on common goals.

With a solid record of accomplishments behind him and seemingly endless prosperity in front of him, Hoover was a formidable presidential candidate in 1928. While his campaign ads noted how Republicans had "put the proverbial 'chicken in every pot,'" Hoover spoke glowingly of ending poverty in America:

> **Primary Source** "By adherence to the principles of decentralized self-government, ordered liberty, equal opportunity, and freedom to the individual, our American experiment in human welfare has yielded a degree of well-being unparalleled in all the world. It has come nearer to the abolition of poverty, to the abolition of fear of want, than humanity has ever reached before."
>
> —Herbert Hoover, campaign speech, 1928

Hoover's contest with Democratic nominee Alfred E. Smith of New York was, in the end, no contest at all. Americans voted overwhelmingly for Hoover, prosperity, and the continuation of Republican government. When the new President took office in March 1929, America was awash in a sea of confidence. Few imagined that an economic disaster lay just seven months in the future.

But even as Hoover delivered his victory speeches, economic troubles were beginning to worry some Americans. The prosperity of the 1920s was not as deep or as sturdy as Hoover claimed. Throughout the U.S. economy, there were troubling signs.

Problems Plague the Agricultural Sector American farmers faced difficult times during the 1920s. Farmers made up one fourth of the American workforce during the decade. To meet the unprecedented crop demands created by World War I, they had increased harvest yields and bought more land to put under the plow. They also bought costly tractors and other mechanized farm equipment. Farmers contracted huge debts doing this, and the additional mortgage payments followed them into the 1920s.

After the war, the demand for American crops fell sharply. Despite this drop, postwar production remained high because of increasingly mechanized farm equipment and more intensive farming methods. Farms were getting bigger and yielding bumper crops at harvest. However, farmers were failing to sell off their huge crop surpluses and to pay the debts they owed banks and other institutions.

The result was a rural depression that affected millions of Americans. Hard-pressed to pay their debts, forced to sell in a glutted and competitive world market, and confronted by several natural disasters, farmers did not share in the boom times of the 1920s. They did not have the cash to buy the new consumer goods produced by

Vocabulary Builder
converge—(kuhn VERJ) *v.* to move or be directed toward the same purpose or result

Farmers Struggle to Get By
Farmers who could not meet their debts faced bank foreclosures on their land, equipment, and livestock. Here, a horse is paraded in front of prospective buyers at a Missouri farm sale.

Causes of the Great Depression

Lured by luxury and easy credit, many Americans bought expensive new cars during the 1920s. ▼

History remembers the 1920s as a decade of bull markets and new fortunes. However, by 1929, the surging American economy was on the brink of financial collapse. Soaring stock prices made rich people richer and concentrated more wealth into fewer hands. Excited by a stream of new products and buyer-friendly payment plans, consumers piled up huge debts as they purchased goods on credit. Everywhere, the economy expanded, soaring toward its peak in the summer of 1929 and then pausing on the verge of contraction—and economic chaos. (See the diagram below.)

The Business Cycle

Peak — Expansion — Contraction — Peak — Expansion — Contraction — Expansion

Declining production, employment, and income — Trough

Rising production, employment, and income — Trough

Consumer Debt, 1921–1929

Dollars (in billions)

8
6
4
2
0

1921   1923   1925   1927   1929

SOURCE: *Historical Statistics of the United States*

▲ American consumers racked up more than $6 billion of debt by 1929—more than double what they owed at the beginning of the decade.

American industries. They lived largely on credit from month to month, often teetering on the brink of financial ruin. Any downward slide in the economy was likely to hit America's struggling farmers first and hardest.

Wealth Is Distributed Unevenly Unlike farmers, industrial workers participated in the great national success story. During the 1920s, their wages rose steadily, as did their disposable income. Many purchased Model T Fords along with a variety of other consumer products. Though they were certainly not wealthy, industrial laborers were in a better financial position than their fathers had been a generation before.

But the problem was that while wages rose gradually, worker productivity increased astronomically. Between 1923 and 1929, output per person-hour jumped 32 percent, but workers' wages inched up only 8 percent. During that same period, corporate profits from worker output skyrocketed 65 percent. All these figures pointed to the fact that during the 1920s, the rich became much, much richer, while industrial workers simply became less poor. In few periods of the country's history have so small a number of rich Americans dominated such a large percentage of the country's total wealth. In 1929, for example, the wealthiest 1 percent of the population earned about the same amount of money as the bottom 42 percent.

This uneven distribution of the nation's wealth created economic problems. More than 60 percent of all American families had yearly incomes of less than $2,000 per year. Twenty-four thousand of the country's wealthiest families enjoyed annual incomes of more than $100,000, which was 50 times more than what most families were earning. But these wealthy families did not eat 50 times more food than lower-income families. The wealthiest households did not

As the pie chart below shows, income was distributed unevenly among Americans in the 1920s. The wealthiest 1 percent of the population, like the women at right, could afford luxurious homes and expensive clothing. But most Americans earned considerably less. The poorest segment of the population was sometimes reduced to begging for money, like the man below.

Income Distribution, 1929

1%
5%
29%
65%

■ $1,999 and under   ■ $5,000–$9,999
■ $2,000–$4,999   ■ $10,000 and over

SOURCE: *Historical Statistics of the United States*

Stock Prices, 1923–1929

Standard and Poor's index of common stocks

26.25
22.50
18.75
15.00
11.25
7.50
3.75
0

1923 1925 1927 1929

SOURCE: *Historical Statistics of the United States*

Easy credit and a steep rise in stock prices encouraged investors to borrow money to buy stock on margin.

---

purchase 50 times more automobiles or radios or ovens. The rich undoubtedly spent a lot on consumer products. The problem was that the wealthiest few did not buy enough to keep the economy booming.

A healthy economy needs more people to buy more products, which in turn creates even more wealth. In this way, a healthy economy avoids underconsumption that can limit economic growth. The uneven distribution of wealth in the 1920s pointed to an uncertain future for the American economy.

From the overproduction of the struggling farmer to the underconsumption of the lower-income industrial worker, deep-seated problems created economic instability. Too many Americans did not have enough money to buy what they needed or wanted.

Easy Credit Hides Problems For a time, the expansion of credit partially hid this problem. Americans bought automobiles, appliances, radios, and other goods on credit. Using the installment plan, they paid a small percentage down and the rest over a period of months or years. By the end of the decade, 80 percent of radios and 60 percent of cars were purchased on installment credit. Americans even bought stock on credit, making such stock purchases on margin. Every year, Americans accumulated more debt. In the past, they had feared debt and put off buying goods until they had the cash to pay for those items. However, easy credit changed this behavior during the 1920s. The growing credit burden could mask the problem of Americans living beyond their means for only so long before the economy imploded.

✔ **Checkpoint** What economic problems lurked beneath the general prosperity of the 1920s?

Thinking Critically

1. **Make Generalizations** Is it fair to suggest that the American economy stood "on thin ice" in 1929? Why or why not?

2. **Analyze Costs and Benefits** How did easy credit and buying stock on margin provide both costs and benefits to the U.S. economy?

The Stock Market Crashes

By 1929, some economists observed that soaring stock prices were based on little more than confidence. Prices had no basis in reality. Although other experts disagreed, it became clear that too much money was being poured into stock **speculation.** Investors were gambling, often with money they did not even have, on stock increases to turn quick profits. If the market's upward climb suddenly reversed course, many investors would face economic devastation.

On September 3, 1929, the stock market began to sputter and fall. Prices peaked and then slid downward in an uneven way. At the end of October, however, the slide gave way to a free fall. After the Dow Jones average dropped 21 points in one hour on October 23, many investors concluded that the boom was over. They had lost confidence—the very thing that had kept the market up for so long.

The next day, October 24, came to be known as Black Thursday. With confidence in the stock market failing, nervous investors started to sell. Stock in General Electric that once sold at $400 a share plunged to $283. Across the United States, investors raced to pull their money out of the stock market. On October 29, **Black Tuesday,** the bottom fell out. More than 16 million shares were sold as the stock market collapsed in the Great Crash. Billions of dollars were lost. Whole fortunes were wiped out in hours. Many speculators who had bought stock on margin lost everything they had. President Hoover tried to soothe Americans by insisting that the "business of the country is on a sound and prosperous basis." But by November 13, the Dow Jones average had dropped like a brick from its September high of 381 to 198.7. The Great Crash represented another hallmark of the nation's **business cycle,** which explained the periodic growth and contraction of the economy.

✔ **Checkpoint** **What happened on October 29, 1929?**

The Panic Spreads

The sudden collapse of stock prices sent brokers and investors into a panic throughout New York's financial district and across the country. A cartoonist for the *New York World* captured the feelings of many Americans in the aftermath of the Great Crash.

The Great Depression Begins

The stock market crash marked the beginning of the **Great Depression,** a period lasting from 1929 to 1941 in which the economy faltered and unemployment soared. Though it did not start the depression by itself, the crash sparked a chain of events that quickened the collapse of the U.S. economy.

The Banks Collapse One of the first institutions to feel the effects of the stock market crash was the country's banking system. The crisis in confidence continued as frightened depositors feared for their money and tried to withdraw it from their banks. Few banks could survive a sustained "run" of requests by depositors for their money. In 1929, 641 commercial banks failed. A year later, 1,350 failed. And a year after that, 1,700 went under. By 1932, many Americans believed that no banks would be left standing.

Another cause of many bank failures was misguided monetary policy. During the 1920s, the Federal Reserve, which regulates the amount of money in circulation, cut interest rates to stimulate economic growth. But in 1929, worried about investor overspeculation, the "Fed" limited the money supply to discourage lending. As a result, there was too little money in circulation to help the economy after the stock market crash. When plummeting stock prices sent investors to the banks to secure whatever hard money they had left, the banks were cleaned out of currency and forced to close.

Businesses Close and Unemployment Rises

Banks were not the only institutions to face the harsh financial realities of the depression. The collapse of stock prices, combined with reduced consumer spending, spelled trouble for American businesses. Business leaders believed that the survival of their companies depended on production cutbacks, to maintain price levels, and layoffs, to reduce payroll. While their stocks were still falling, companies began closing plants and forcing workers onto the growing lists of the unemployed. In August 1931, Henry Ford closed several of his Detroit automobile factories, putting nearly 75,000 people out of work.

Like a snowball rolling down a hill, the problem of production cuts kept getting bigger and bigger. As businesses closed plants and fired workers to save money, more Americans lost their jobs. As unemployment grew and incomes shrank, consumers spent less money. So businesses cut production even more, closing more plants and firing more workers. By 1933, nearly 25 percent of all American workers had lost their jobs.

Tariffs Add to the Woes

Hoping to reverse the downward slide, the government moved to protect American products from foreign competition. In June 1930, Congress passed the **Hawley-Smoot Tariff,** which raised prices on foreign imports to such a level that they could not compete in the American market. The tariff inspired European countries to retaliate and enact protective tariffs of their own.

Far from solving the problems of the depression, the Hawley-Smoot Tariff added to them. At a time when American manufacturers and farms had a glut of unsold products, the international move toward high protective tariffs closed markets. This closure was not just harmful to American producers. It was equally disastrous to the global economy. The ripple effect caused by the Hawley-Smoot Tariff helped to destroy international trade.

The Depression Goes Global

The Hawley-Smoot Tariff was only one of the causes of a depression spreading across the globe. As we saw earlier, the European problems of reparation payments, war debt payments, and international imbalance of trade had already created a shaky economic structure. In the early 1930s, the structure collapsed. Germany ceased their reparation payments, and the United States agreed to suspend France and Britain's war debt payments. The international economy had largely been funded by American loans to Europe, but the crisis in the United States drastically curtailed those loans. As a result, European nations

NoteTaking

Reading Skill: Recognize Sequence Use a flowchart to note what happened in the wake of the stock market crash.

| Stock market crashes |
| Commercial banks fail |
| |
| |

Banks Fail

In 1931, more than 1,500 banks ran out of money and closed their doors. Depositors lost untold savings. Here, a crowd gathers outside the closed doors of a bank in New York City. *How might Americans react today if hundreds of banks failed?*

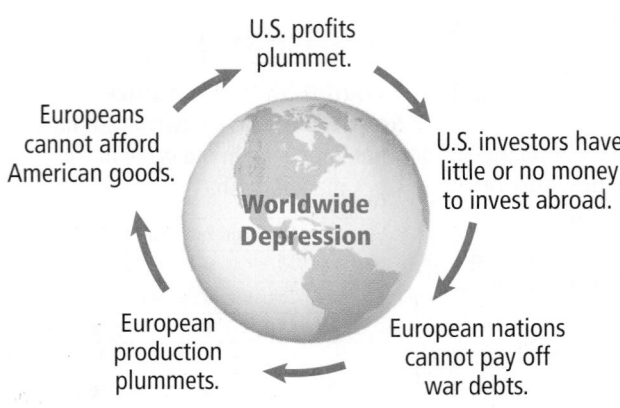

U.S. profits plummet.

Europeans cannot afford American goods.

Worldwide Depression

U.S. investors have little or no money to invest abroad.

European production plummets.

European nations cannot pay off war debts.

Diagram Skills The diagram above shows how the stock market collapse contributed to a global economic crisis. *How did European war debts affect the U.S. economy?*

experienced the same cycle of business failures, bank collapses, and high unemployment as the United States. The depression had become a global nightmare.

 Checkpoint How did the stock market crash contribute to the onset of the depression?

What Caused the Great Depression?

Historians and economists disagree on the exact causes of the Great Depression. Some have stressed a single root cause in their explanations of the financial crisis. Milton Friedman, one economist, believed that the depression resulted from a contraction in the money supply. The twin events of the stock market crash in 1929 and the run of bank failures in 1930 left too little money in circulation for the nation's economic needs.

John Maynard Keynes was one of the most influential economists of the depression. He argued that the lack of government interference in the economy led to the depression. Critical problems in money supply, distribution of wealth, stock speculation, consumer spending, productivity, and employment could have been controlled, he said, by proactive government policies. Keynes's work points to a fundamental difference between many economists regarding the depression. While Keynes recommended that governments spend more money to keep people employed when the economy slows, other noted economists like Ludwig von Mises and Friedrich von Hayek criticized centralized economic planning and management.

There will never be a fully accepted answer to the question of what caused the Great Depression. But clearly, problems in consumption contributed heavily to it. Economic hardships before 1929 in Europe and rural America, coupled with an uneven distribution of wealth and overspeculation in the stock market, created dangerous economic conditions. When this was combined with poor or misinformed economic decisions by Congress and President Hoover, the Great Depression resulted.

 Checkpoint What were the primary causes of the Great Depression?

Progress Monitoring *Online*
For: Self-test with vocabulary practice
Web Code: nea-0802

Comprehension

1. **Terms** For each term below, write a sentence explaining its significance.
   - speculation
   - business cycle
   - Great Depression
   - Hawley-Smoot Tariff

2. **NoteTaking Reading Skill: Recognize Causes** Use your concept web to answer the Section Focus Question: How did the prosperity of the 1920s give way to the Great Depression?

Writing About History

3. **Quick Write: Define a Problem** Choose one topic from this section that you could use to write a problem-solution essay. For example, you could write about the weaknesses in the agricultural sector of the economy. Make a list of details, facts, and examples that define the problems that this weakness poses to a stable economy.

Critical Thinking

4. **Explain Causes** How did the uneven distribution of the nation's wealth weaken the American economy?

5. **Analyze Information** Why was recovery so difficult after the stock market crash?

6. **Draw Conclusions** Do you think the nation would have experienced an economic depression even if the stock market had not crashed? Why or why not?

◀ Hobos walk along a railroad line.

WITNESS HISTORY AUDIO

Riding the Rails

As the country plunged deeper into the Great Depression, many young people left home, either out of necessity or to follow their dreams of a better life. Nearly a quarter million teenagers hit the road during the early 1930s, jumping freight trains to ride from town to town. Some looked for work, others thirsted for adventure, but all faced the dangers of the hobo life. Charley Bull, who left his California home at 18, recalled:

❝You could ride on top of a freight car and then you just had to be careful. If a train is going sixty or seventy miles an hour and hits a curve and you're walking and your back's to the turn and you don't see it coming—a little tiny turn can throw you right off the train. A lot of people have been killed like that.❞

—Charley Bull, from a PBS presentation "The American Experience—Riding the Rails"

Americans Face Hard Times

 Core Curriculum Objectives

• **5.II.A.4** The Great Depression: Unemployment

Terms and People

bread line
Hooverville
tenant farmer

Dust Bowl
Okies
repatriation

NoteTaking

Reading Skill: Categorize As you read, use a Venn diagram to note how the Great Depression affected both urban and rural America.

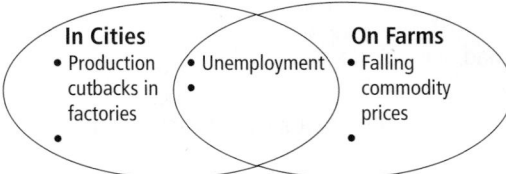

In Cities	Unemployment	On Farms
• Production cutbacks in factories •	•	• Falling commodity prices •

Why It Matters The stock market crash signaled the end of boom times and the beginning of hard times. As investors mourned their losses, Americans watched the economy stagger into the Great Depression. In the cities and on the farms, desperate poverty gripped the nation. Even after prosperity returned, those who lived through the crisis would remember the pain and worries of the depression. Tested by extreme hardship, this generation of Americans forged a character and will strong enough to overcome economic ruin and restore prosperity. **Section Focus Question: How did the Great Depression affect the lives of urban and rural Americans?**

Misery and Despair Grip America's Cities

The Great Depression had a deep and lasting impact on the lives of the people who lived through it. Few Americans grasped the underlying problems of the 1920s economy or the subtle reasons for the stock market crash. Fewer still comprehended how the crash led to the Great Depression. But they did understand the *impact* of the economic crisis. Workers understood having a job one day and being unemployed the next. Whole families knew the shame and fear of losing their homes.

The Great Depression touched every American because every American either experienced or knew someone who experienced the hardships and loss caused by the economic catastrophe. For many, their lives were never the same again.

Bank Failures

Business Failures

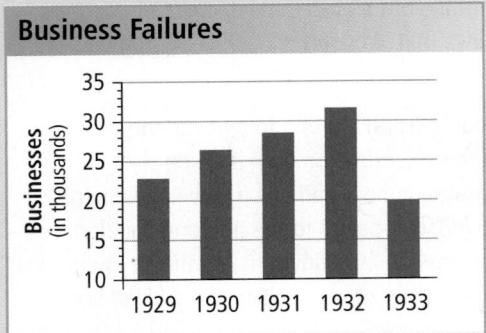

Per Capita Income and Spending

SOURCE: *Historical Statistics of the United States*

Graph Skills The year 1929 marked the start of a pronounced downturn in the American economy. *In what year did the largest number of banks fail? By roughly how much did Americans' average yearly income decrease between 1929 and 1933?*

Searching for a Job and a Meal The threat of unemployment and destitution haunted workers in cities and towns across the United States. Between 1921 and 1929, annual average unemployment rates had never risen above 3.7 percent. But then, the depression hit, and the rate shot up. By 1933, it had climbed to a shocking 24.9 percent.

Despite this high rate, millions of workers were able to keep their jobs. However, most had their wages or hours cut. Many workers brought home paychecks that were 10, 20, sometimes 30 percent less than their pre-depression checks.

Yet statistics tell only part of the story. The human drama of unemployment unfolded over and over again, in city after city across the nation. For a man employed as a factory worker, the 1920s had promised a chance at upward economic mobility. He had been able to provide for his family, enjoy a decent standard of living, and save something for retirement. Then, the depression hit. The man saw his hours cut and his workweek shortened. Eventually, he was laid off. Looking for another job, he trudged from one factory to the next. "No help wanted here" or "We don't need nobody" greeted him at every turn. The man's clothes began to look worn. His collars and cuffs became frayed, and his pants became shiny at the knees. He said less, stared more, moved slower.

Maybe his wife was able to find work washing and ironing clothes or laboring as a maid. But those jobs were hard to find, too. At home, children ate smaller meals. Water replaced milk. Meat disappeared from the table. Hunger lurked about the home like an unwanted guest. Sometimes, the parents and children received free meals in public soup kitchens. Often, the only place for the family to get a free scrap of food was in a **bread line,** where people lined up for handouts from charities or public agencies.

Descending Into Poverty Men like the factory worker just described moved from unemployed to unemployable. Whole families descended into hunger and homelessness. Their dreams of success and prosperity turned into nightmares of failure and poverty.

This feeling of loss—this sense of the "American Dream" betrayed—wove through the cultural fabric of the Great Depression. The widespread despair found expression in an early-1930s song by E. Y. Harburg. It tells the story of an American "Everyman," a worker who labored to build the country and a citizen soldier who fought to defend it. However, the depression has left him out of work, out of money, and out of dreams:

Primary Source

"They used to tell me I was building a dream
And so I followed the mob.
When there was earth to plow or guns to bear,
I was always there, right on the job.
They used to tell me I was building a dream
With peace and glory ahead—
Why should I be standing in line,
Just waiting for bread?
Once I built a railroad, I made it run,
Made it run against time.
Once I built a railroad, now it's done—
Brother can you spare a dime?"

—song lyrics, "Brother Can You Spare a Dime?"

Effects of the Great Depression

After the stock market crash, the American economy slowed to a crawl in the face of a devastating global Depression. Bank failures more than quadrupled from 1929 to 1933. Companies fired thousands of workers to keep from going out of business. As a result, unemployment soared, condemning a quarter of the American workforce to poverty. (See the line graph below.) Jobless people crowded outside employment offices, clamoring for work to put food on their tables. Life became a daily struggle for many Americans during these lean times.

Unemployed men wait for a chance to register for municipal jobs in New York City in 1933. ▼

Top: Women and children wait in a bread line set up by a religious mission.
Center: This 1932 cartoon summarized the feelings of many depositors when their banks failed.
Bottom right: Unable to support their families, some men gave in to despair.

Unemployment, 1928–1933

People (in millions)

3% of workforce

25% of workforce

1928 1929 1930 1931 1932 1933

SOURCE: *Historical Statistics of the United States*

Thinking Critically

1. **Analyze Information** How did the shrinking economy lead to increased layoffs of workers?

2. **Draw Conclusions** What effect might a high unemployment rate have on the wages of Americans who still had jobs?

Harburg said the song asked a simple question about the nature of the depression. "This is a man who says: I built the railroads. . . . I fought your wars. . . . [Why] should I be standing in line now? What happened to all this wealth I created?"

Looking for a Place to Live As Americans lost their jobs and ran through their savings, they had to scrounge wherever they could to keep from going hungry. They sold furniture, pawned jewelry, and moved to cheaper lodgings—anything to keep their pantries stocked and rents paid. In many cities, they ran out of money, were evicted from their homes, and ended up on the streets.

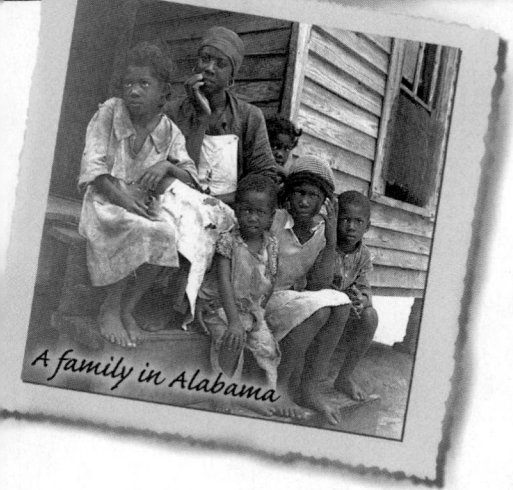

A field-worker's home in California

A family in Alabama

Americans Face Hard Times

Photographs of the 1930s conveyed the gritty realism of daily life under the boot heels of hunger, homelessness, and destitution. Cartoonists of the time criticized political leaders, President Hoover foremost among them, for the parts they played in bringing about, or failing to prevent, the depression. *Judging from these images, what would it have been like to live in a Hooverville?*

Homeless people slept on park benches, in empty railway cars, or in cardboard boxes. Many grouped together in **Hoovervilles,** makeshift shantytowns of tents and shacks built on public land or vacant lots. Homeless people, some of whom had worked as skilled carpenters before the crisis, cobbled houses together out of lumber scraps, tar paper, tin, and glass. One of the largest Hoovervilles in the country sprang up in the middle of Central Park in New York City. There, the homeless covered themselves with newspapers, called Hoover blankets, to stay warm at night. They walked around looking for jobs with their empty pants pockets turned inside out, a sign of poverty known as Hoover flags.

Despite the difficulties of life during the depression, many Americans did what they could to boost morale and help their neighbors. During a New York City newspaper strike, Mayor Fiorello LaGuardia read comic strips to children over the radio. In Reading, Pennsylvania, members of the Taxpayers Protection League staged nonviolent protests to thwart evictions. Nevertheless, thousands of other Americans found no such escapes from their misery.

✓ **Checkpoint** How did the Great Depression affect American cities in the early 1930s?

Poverty Devastates Rural America

In cities and towns across the nation, Americans faced a terrible plight. The numbers of the unemployed, homeless, and hopeless increased like a casualty list in some great war. In rural America, people fared no better. In fact, sometimes their condition was even worse. Farmers had been suffering even before the Great Depression. Falling commodity prices and accumulating debt had made it a struggle for farmers to keep their heads above water. Many failed to stay afloat and sank so deep that they lost their farms.

Commodity Prices Plunge But then the bottom fell out of the economy and the depression added more woes. Crop prices fell even further, and new debts were added to old debts. To make matters even worse, the Great Plains was suffering through a choking drought, an ecological disaster that lasted for years. As a result, many more farmers lost their farms and moved. They traveled about the country, looking for work and fighting for survival.

A sprawling Hooverville in Seattle, Washington

▲ A 1935 political cartoon criticizing Hoover

The basic reality of farm life was the low prices paid to farmers for crops they grew for market. In 1919, a bushel of wheat sold for $2.16; in 1932, it sold for 38 cents. A pound of cotton fetched 35.34 cents in 1919; the same pound fetched 6.52 cents in 1932. The sharp fall in prices was evident with other farm products—corn and beans, cattle and hogs. The income farmers generated was not enough to allow them to continue farming. They could not pay their debts, purchase more seed, repair equipment, and buy what their families needed to survive. Overburdened by the diminishing returns for their labor, some farmers buckled under the stress.

In Sioux City, Iowa, in 1932, the Sioux City Milk Producers Association threatened to strike if its members did not see higher profits for their milk. When the association's threats were ignored by local storeowners, farmers dumped 1,000 gallons of milk on a road outside the city. Despite such a drastic—and for many Americans unthinkable—action like this, farmers everywhere feared losing everything.

Farmers Lose Their Farms Between 1930 and 1934, nearly one million farmers failed to pay their mortgages and lost their farms. Banks foreclosed on their lands and houses and repossessed their farming equipment. The bankers sold what they could at public auctions. Some farmers remained on the land as **tenant farmers,** working for bigger landowners rather than for themselves. Others drifted away from their communities, looking for some other kind of work.

Cesar Chavez, who later became a well-known labor organizer, recalled the troubles his proud father had during the depression. A California bank repossessed his father's small ranch, and the family was evicted from their house. Chavez remembered how it felt to lose his home:

> **Primary Source** "We had been poor, but we knew every night there was a bed *there*, and *this* was our room. . . . But that all of a sudden changed. When you're small, you can't figure these things out. You know something's not right and you don't like it, but you don't . . . let that get you down. You sort of just continue to move."
> —Cesar Chavez

Like the Chavez family, other farmers moved on after their losses. But for those who remained, Mother Nature dealt a cruel blow to already cruel times.

History Interactive
For: To learn more about the Dust Bowl
Web Code: nep-0809

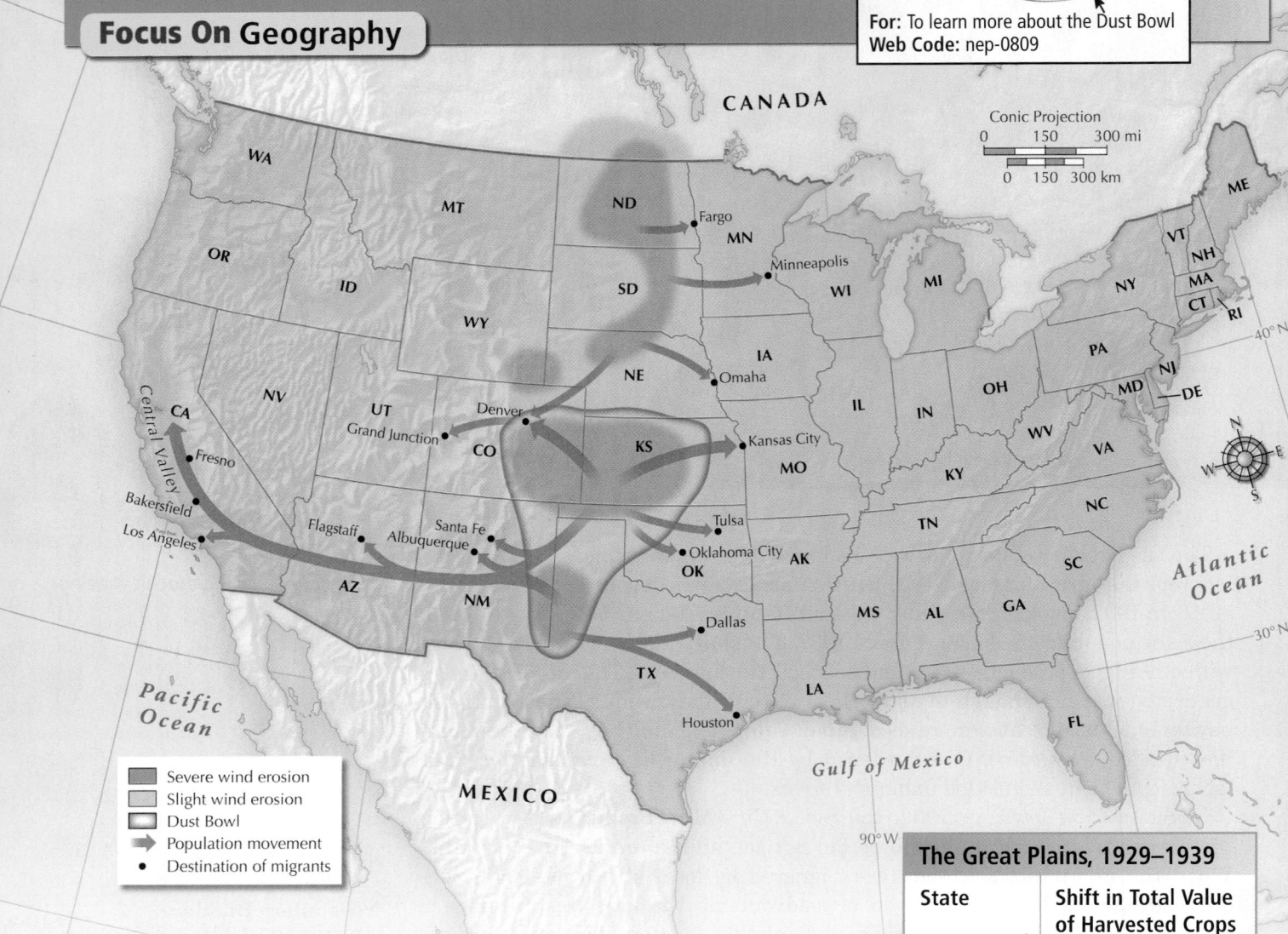

Map Legend:
- Severe wind erosion
- Slight wind erosion
- Dust Bowl
- Population movement
- Destination of migrants

The Great Plains, 1929–1939	
State	**Shift in Total Value of Harvested Crops**
Colorado	−51%
Kansas	−53%
Nebraska	−61%
New Mexico	−32%
North Dakota	−47%
Oklahoma	−49%
South Dakota	−57%
Texas	−45%
Wyoming	−40%

The Dust Bowl

By the middle of the 1930s, drought and wind had cut a huge swath of destruction down the middle of the continental United States. The "black blizzards" of the Dust Bowl soared to heights of 8,000 feet and swept like waves across towns and farms. Outside, rabbits, birds, and field mice suffocated and died in the swirling dust. Inside, dirt seeped through every crack and covered everything and everyone in layers of grit. "We live with the dust, eat it, sleep with it," observed one witness. A single storm could carry more than 300 million tons of dust, and constant storms in the "dirty thirties" destroyed as many as 5 million acres of wheat. Much of the Great Plains "breadbasket" simply blew away.

Whole harvests could be destroyed wherever dust storms struck. Many farmers went out of business as a result of their crop failures. ▶

A massive dust storm threatens the town of Stratford, Texas, in this photograph from 1935. ▼

Geography and History
How did environmental change affect farmers living on the Great Plains during the 1930s?

The Great Plains Becomes a Dust Bowl Farmers who survived the tumble in prices were still not safe. Through the mid-1930s, a drought in the Great Plains added to their problems. Water was a constant problem in the region. Normal rainfall seldom exceeded the 20 inches a year that traditional American agricultural practices demanded. As a result, droughts on the Great Plains were often more devastating than those in the East and Midwest. In the years before America's western rivers were dammed and irrigation practices became widespread, there were few answers to the drought threat.

New farming methods made drought conditions worse. Intensive farming came to prominence throughout the region in the late nineteenth and early twentieth centuries. Farmers then had moved onto the plains and plowed under much of the natural grasses in order to plant oceans of winter wheat. The landscape shift tipped the ecological balance of the region. In the past, plains grasses prevented the topsoil from blowing away during periods of drought. By the early 1930s, that dwindling grassy safety net could no longer do the job.

By 1932, the combination of drought, loose topsoil, and high winds resulted in disaster on the Great Plains. The winds kicked up towering dust storms that began to blow east. These gigantic clouds of dust and dirt could rise from ground level to a height of 8,000 feet. The dust storms moved as fast as 100 miles per hour and blotted out the sun, plunging daylight into darkness.

Most of the dust storms started in the southern Great Plains, especially the high plains regions of Texas, Oklahoma, Kansas, New Mexico, and Colorado. This swath of parched earth became known as the **Dust Bowl.** For people living in these hardest hit regions, depression and dust storms defined the misery of the "dirty thirties."

Those unfortunate enough to be caught in a dust storm were temporarily choked and blinded by the swirling dirt. The storms killed cattle and birds, blanketed rivers, and suffocated fish. Dirt seeped into houses, covering everything with a thick coat of grime. Some dust clouds blew east as far as the Atlantic coast, dumping acres of dirt on Boston, New York, and Washington. Altogether, dust storms displaced twice as much dirt as Americans had scooped out to build the Panama Canal.

Desperation Causes Migration Many farm families trapped in the Dust Bowl had no choice but to migrate out of the region. They had lost their farms to the banks. Dust storms had destroyed most remaining opportunities. They were low on everything except despair. Although only some came from Oklahoma, Dust Bowl refugees were generally referred to as **Okies,** regardless of their states of origin.

Okie families packed onto rickety trucks and headed toward California or Oregon or Washington, any place where a job might be found. Before the pace slowed, 800,000 people migrated out of Missouri, Arkansas, Oklahoma, and Texas alone.

Agricultural collapse and the Great Plains Dust Bowl forced millions of Americans to leave the midwestern and southern regions where they had been born. Many moved to California, lured by the promise of jobs, but were crushed when that promise too often proved empty. Others headed to the cities of the Northeast and Midwest, again looking for jobs, shelter, and relief. As a result of the migration, rural states lost population while states with large cities gained population.

WITNESS HISTORY DVD

Watch **The Dust Bowl** on the **United States Witness History DVD** to learn more about the causes and effects of the Dust Bowl.

Okies Flee the Dust Bowl
The Okie exodus from the Great Plains carried thousands of Americans west to the rich farmlands of California. Okies also packed up and headed east to great industrial centers like Chicago, Pittsburgh, and New York. Here, a migrant family arrives in California.

There were other effects of the Dust Bowl. The farmers best able to survive the Great Depression were the ones with the biggest operations. They often bought repossessed land at rock-bottom prices and expanded their holdings into large commercial farms. The Dust Bowl also motivated the government to help Great Plains farmers. After the initial crisis, immense federal projects dammed western rivers. Dams eventually provided irrigation that made farm profits possible on the Great Plains.

✓ **Checkpoint** How did the Dust Bowl make life even more difficult for farmers on the Great Plains?

Fierce Job Competition in California

As Okies flowed into California, Mexican and Mexican American migrants already there faced stiff new competition for scarce jobs. Here, a family of migrant farmworkers gathers outside their home in California's Imperial Valley. *What does the photograph suggest about the economic status of migrant workers in California?*

Few Americans Escape Hard Times

One of the ironies of the depression was the word itself. In the nineteenth and early twentieth centuries, an economic slump was called a "panic" or a "crisis." President Hoover used the word *depression* to describe the state of affairs because he thought it sounded less severe than the other terms. But before long, Hoover's "depression" gave way to the "Depression" and then the "Great Depression." The term described not only a state of mind, but also an economic reality. It showed a despondent America, filled with people overwhelmed by seemingly inescapable poverty. Not only did the depression make victims of the men and women who lost jobs, it also was an economic and emotional crisis that profoundly affected Americans in all walks of life.

The Depression Attacks Family Life For millions of Americans, the depression was an intensely personal affair. Men who lost their jobs and could not find other work often felt that they had betrayed their families. They had been the "breadwinners," the providers, the ones whose paychecks fed and clothed the family and kept a roof over everyone's head. The loss of a job meant a reduction in status. Different men reacted differently to unemployment. Many labored tirelessly to find a new job, while others sank into shame and despair. Some even deserted their families.

The unemployed were not the only ones who suffered. Men lucky enough to have jobs lived in constant fear that the next paycheck would be their last. They often felt guilty for being employed while so many of their relatives and friends were suffering. Few Americans were spared from the crisis.

Wives and children experienced the pain of their husbands and fathers. Birthrates plummeted to the lowest marks in American history—a sure sign of family distress. Mothers worked constantly to stretch meager family incomes. They sewed clothes, searched for odd jobs, and valiantly tried to meet their families' needs. With both parents preoccupied with making something out of nothing, family discipline often declined. Some children quit school. Others ran away from home. Families coped with the depression as best they could. Some huddled together, working to survive the hard times. Others broke apart, making those times even harder and lonelier.

Minorities Suffer Hardships The depression affected everyone, but it did not affect them equally. Americans on the bottom rung of the economic ladder—the poorest of the poor, often minorities with no financial resources—felt the sting of the depression the keenest. A Howard University sociologist noted early in the crisis that African Americans were "the last to be hired and the first to be fired." In the South, landowners threw African American sharecroppers off the plots they had been farming. Many of these workers migrated to northern cities, but there were no jobs waiting there. Only more poverty greeted them. In 1932, unemployment among African Americans hovered around 50 percent, nearly double the national rate.

However, African Americans had long stood firm against the challenges of poverty. They relied on the emotional resources of family and religion to cope with grim times. During his interview with a depression historian, an African American man explained what the depression meant to African Americans:

> **Primary Source** "The Negro was born in depression. It didn't mean too much to him, The Great American Depression, as you call it. There was no such thing. The best he could be was a janitor or a porter or shoeshine boy. It only became official when it hit the white man."
>
> —Clifford Burke, quoted in *Hard Times*, 1970

Hard times came upon Mexican Americans as well. As more Okies headed west out of the Dust Bowl, the competition for jobs between those migrants and Mexican American farmworkers in states like California heated up. A flood tide of workers struggled to find and keep farm jobs. Often, Mexican Americans faced the additional burden of discrimination when competing with white farmhands for those jobs. In the Southwest, many white Americans clamored for Mexican American **repatriation.** Repatriation involved efforts by local, state, and federal governments to encourage or coerce Mexican immigrants and their naturalized children to return to Mexico. Hundreds of thousands of people of Mexican ancestry—many of them U.S. citizens—were pushed out of the United States. Even so, many more remained. By the end of the 1930s, Mexican Americans were working in most industries of the Southwest, including farming, ranching, and industry.

✓ **Checkpoint** How did the depression take a toll on women, children, and minorities in America?

Poverty in the South
African Americans who had long faced discrimination and segregation were especially hard-hit by the depression. Many moved from the South to seek jobs in the North. Here, a man sits forlornly outside his home in Atlanta, Georgia.

SECTION 2 Assessment

Progress Monitoring *Online*
For: Self-test with vocabulary practice
Web Code: nea-0803

Comprehension

1. **Terms and People** What do each of the following terms have in common? Explain.
   - bread line
   - Hooverville
   - tenant farmer
   - Okies

2. **NoteTaking Reading Skill: Categorize** Use your Venn diagram to answer the Section Focus Question: How did the Great Depression affect the lives of urban and rural Americans?

Writing About History

3. **Quick Write: Brainstorm for Possible Solutions** Choose one topic from this section, such as skyrocketing unemployment in American cities, about which you could write a problem-solution essay. Use the text and your own knowledge to list possible solutions to the problem. Next, organize your list by ranking the solutions from most effective to least effective.

Critical Thinking

4. **Compare and Contrast** How were the experiences of the urban unemployed and the rural poor similar? How were they different?

5. **Recognize Effects** How do you think the arrival of so many Okies affected native Californians?

6. **Draw Inferences** Where might Americans have laid the blame for their difficulties during the early 1930s?

EXPERIENCE THE GREAT DEPRESSION

Moviegoers cheered as Shirley Temple sang "Prosperity Is Just Around the Corner." Salvation Army volunteers handed out clothing and food to the needy. While some of the unemployed sold apples on sidewalks, others rioted in the streets.

There were many reactions to the Great Depression, some hopeful and some desperate, but everywhere Americans struggled to ease the daily burden of their poverty. The mayor of Youngstown, Ohio, captured the universality of the Depression when he described its victims laid low in his city: "These were old men gnarled by heavy labor, young mechanics tasting the first bitterness of defeat, clerks and white-collar workers learning the equality of misery, derelicts who fared no worse in bad times than in good, Negroes who only a short time before had come from Southern cotton fields, immigrants who had been lured to [the] 'land of youth and freedom'—each one a personal tragedy, and all together an overwhelming catastrophe for the nation. . . ."

As unemployment soared, the jobless often demonstrated against their former employers. A protest at a Ford Motor Company plant in March 1931 erupted in violence that left four workers dead. Here, a man is carried off during a demonstration in New York City. ▼

DEMOCRACY

Fred Bell, like his cartoon counterpart above, lost millions of dollars in the stock market crash and then sold apples on the street.

Despite their own hardships, ▶ many Americans volunteered in soup kitchens and at bread lines. Here, relief-agency workers help hand out potatoes to the hungry.

SHIRLEY TEMPLE
IN
"Bright Eyes"
with JAMES DUNN
FOX

During the Depression, trips to the movies helped people forget their troubles. Shirley Temple cheered crowds, as did the Marx Brothers and the Three Stooges. ▶

▲ As the Depression worsened, many sharecroppers like the Arkansas family shown here were evicted by landowners across the South.

Thinking Critically

1. **Analyze Visuals** What were some of the positive ways in which people responded to the Depression? What were some of the negative responses?

2. **Draw Conclusions** How did apple selling and riding the rails help men cope with losing their jobs?

Connect to Today Do research to learn about the nation's business cycle. How are the peaks and valleys of the modern American economy different from those of the late 1920s and early 1930s?

History *Interactive* ∗
For: To discover more about the Great Depression
Web Code: nep-0804

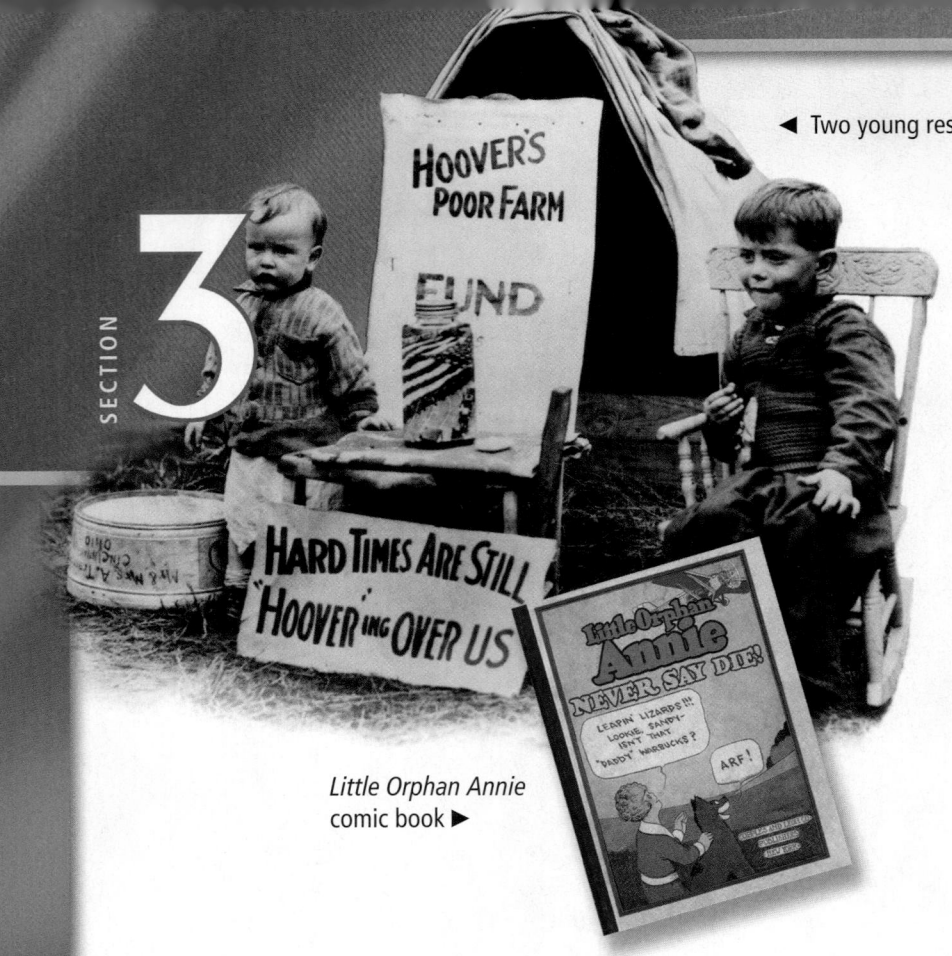

◀ Two young residents of a Hooverville, 1932

Little Orphan Annie comic book ▶

WITNESS HISTORY 🔊 AUDIO

Rugged Individualism

Despite their suffering during the 1930s, children remained important symbols of hope and resilience. Harold Gray's *Little Orphan Annie,* one of the most popular comic strips of the time, entertained millions of children with stories of a strong-willed orphan and her sidekick dog Sandy. Gray depicted Annie's many adventures and described her determination in the face of various challenges.

Although much of his young audience did not realize it, the conservative Gray was preaching a philosophy of "rugged individualism" through *Little Orphan Annie.* He summed up his heroine's message of self-reliance when he noted that "Annie is [tough], with a heart of gold and a fast left, [and] can take care of herself because she has to."

Hoover's Response Fails

 Core Curriculum Objectives

- **5.II.A.3a** President Hoover's response: Rugged individualism; "trickle-down" economics
- **5.II.A.3b** President Hoover's response: Reconstruction Finance Corporation
- **5.II.A.4** Unemployment, the Bonus Army, Hoovervilles

Terms and People

localism	Hoover Dam
Reconstruction Finance	Bonus Army
Corporation	Douglas MacArthur
trickle-down economics	

NoteTaking

Reading Skill: Identify Supporting Details
As you read, fill in the outline with details about President Hoover's response to the depression.

> I. Cautious Response to Depression Fails
> A. Hoover Turns to Volunteerism
>   1. Calls on business leaders to maintain employment, wages, prices
>   2.
> B. Volunteerism Fails to Bring Relief
>   1.
> II. Hoover Adopts More Activist Policies

Why It Matters From big cities to small towns, the Great Depression spread misery far and wide across America. The unemployed and the homeless crowded into shantytowns. Giant dust storms swallowed the Great Plains. Yet as the crisis deepened, Herbert Hoover struggled to respond to the nation's problems. As a result of Hoover's failed response, in 1932 Americans would turn to a new leader and increased government intervention to stop the depression. **Section Focus Question: Why did Herbert Hoover's policies fail to solve the country's economic crisis?**

Cautious Response to Depression Fails

Herbert Hoover did not cause the Great Depression. But Americans looked to him as their President to solve the crisis. He tried. Hoover was an intelligent man, familiar with business methods and economic theory. He labored long hours, consulted a wide range of experts, and tried to marshal the resources of the country to solve the problems of the depression. As the economic situation worsened, he tried several different approaches. In the end, he failed to discover the right formula, but it was not because of a lack of effort.

Hoover Turns to Volunteerism At the start of the economic downturn, Hoover followed a hands-off policy. Like most economists of the day, Hoover viewed the upswings and downswings of business cycles as natural occurrences. He felt that government should not interfere with such events. Periodic depressions were like storms. They could not be avoided, but strong businesses could weather them without the support of the government.

A policy of doing nothing, however, was no policy at all. Hoover soon recognized this fact and turned to a policy he had used in the past. As Secretary of Commerce during the 1920s, Hoover had motivated businessmen and laborers to voluntarily work toward common goals. To address the current crisis, he asked business and industrial leaders to keep employment, wages, and prices at current levels. He <u>simultaneously</u> called for the government to reduce taxes, lower interest rates, and create public-works programs. The plan was to put more money into the hands of businesses and individuals to encourage more production and consumption. This, Hoover said, would reverse the cycle that led to the depression.

Vocabulary Builder
<u>simultaneously</u>—(sī muhl TAY nee uhs lee) *adv.* done at the same time

Lastly, Hoover requested that wealthier individuals give more money to charity. Millions of Americans gave money, clothing, and food to private and religious charities, which in turn distributed the goods to those in need. The idea was for all Americans to voluntarily join forces to combat the depression.

Volunteerism Fails to Bring Relief Although the ideas behind the plan were sound, Hoover's program relied too much on voluntary cooperation. The President believed he could persuade Americans to act not in their own best interests but in those of the country as a whole. He was cautious to encourage, not legislate, America's recovery. But volunteerism did not work. Businesses cut wages and laid off workers because it was in their own best interests. Farmers boosted production because it was in the best interests of their families. Most Americans followed individual, not cooperative, courses.

Hoover had also asked state and local governments to provide more jobs and relief measures. He had faith in **localism,** the policy whereby problems could best be solved at local and state levels. However, towns and states simply did not have the financial or human resources to successfully combat the crisis. Making matters worse, the President strongly resisted using federal resources to provide direct relief to individuals. Believing it to be unconstitutional, Hoover opposed public assistance and instead favored "rugged individualism" so that people could better themselves through their own efforts. Yet as the months wore on, unemployment increased, charities ran low on money, and local and state governments could no longer plug the leaks in the economy. The crisis demanded decisive federal action.

✓ **Checkpoint** Why was Hoover reluctant to have the federal government interfere with the economy?

Hoover Adopts More Activist Policies

With Hoovervilles and homelessness on the rise, the President's failed policies were laid bare. Poor Americans called trucks pulled by horse or mule "Hoover wagons," campfires "Hoover heaters," and cardboard boxes "Hoover houses." The association of the President's name with suffering and want indicated Americans' negative feelings about their leader.

HISTORY MAKERS

Herbert Hoover (1874–1964)
After the depression hit, President Hoover eventually embraced an active economic plan. He urged Congress to fund construction projects that would provide jobs and pushed for legislation that would loan money to businesses to kick-start the economy. Yet at the same time, Hoover insisted that local governments and charities should provide direct aid to people out of work. "Economic depression cannot be cured by legislative action or executive pronouncement," he said. As a result, many Americans blamed him for their troubles.

Hoover Dam Energy Use

Arizona 19%

Nevada 24%

California 57%

SOURCE: U.S. Bureau of Reclamation

Hoover Dam Powers the West

Hoover Dam contains 325 million cubic yards of concrete—enough to pave a highway 16 feet wide from New York City to San Francisco—and provides power to more than a million people each year. It also irrigates millions of acres of farmland in western states.

Hoover decided to reverse course and use federal resources to battle the depression. Believing the economy suffered from a lack of credit, Hoover urged Congress to create the **Reconstruction Finance Corporation (RFC).** Passed in 1932, the RFC gave more than a billion dollars of government loans to railroads and large businesses. The act also lent money to banks so that they could extend more loans to struggling businesses. Hoover believed that if the government lent money to bankers, they would lend it in turn to businessmen. Businessmen would then hire workers, production and consumption would increase, and the depression would end. This theory, known as **trickle-down economics,** held that money poured into the top of the economic pyramid will trickle down to the base.

Although the RFC put the federal government at the center of economic life, it did not work well under Hoover's guidance. The RFC lent out billions, but all too often bankers did not increase their loans to businesses. Additionally, businesses often did not use the loans they received to hire more workers. In the end, the money did not trickle down to the people who needed it the most.

Despite the failings of the RFC, Hoover succeeded with one project that made a difference. During the 1920s, Secretary of Commerce Hoover had called for the construction of a dam on the Colorado River. By the time Hoover became President in 1929, Congress had approved the project as part of a massive public-works program. Workers broke ground on Boulder Dam (later renamed **Hoover Dam**) in 1930. Construction brought much-needed employment to the Southwest during the early 1930s.

 Checkpoint What actions did Herbert Hoover take to fight the effects of the depression?

Americans Protest Hoover's Failures

From the Oval Office, Hoover worked hard to end the depression. But to many out-of-work Americans, the President became a symbol of failure. Some people blamed capitalism, while others questioned the responsiveness of democracy. Many believed the American system was due for an overhaul.

Some Urge Radical Change Some Americans thought the answer to the country's problems was the rejection of capitalism and the acceptance of socialism or communism. They argued that capitalism created great inequities of wealth and an unhealthy atmosphere of competition in society. In fact, they saw the depression as a sign that capitalism was about to collapse. Looking at the Soviet Union, they maintained that a state-run economy was the only avenue out of the depression. Even during the worst of the crisis, though, communist calls for revolution proved no match for American dreams of progress, opportunity, and individual freedom.

Fascist appeals from the political right also failed to hold any attraction. Economic troubles in Europe contributed to the rise to power of fascist leaders like Benito Mussolini in Italy and Adolf Hitler in Germany. Despite this political shift abroad, no fascist gained power in the United States. Although some questioned the ability of America's capitalistic and democratic institutions to overcome the crisis, most Americans never lost faith in their country.

The Bonus Army Marches on Washington Most Americans did not want a revolution, but many did desire substantial changes. In 1932, one such group arrived in Washington, D.C., demanding a solution to their particular problem. From across the country came World War I veterans seeking the bonus Congress had promised them. They became known as the **Bonus Army.** In 1924, Congress had passed the Adjusted Compensation Act, which provided for a lump-sum payment to the veterans in 1945. But in 1931, many veteran groups began to call for an early payment of the bonus, arguing that out-of-work vets needed the money to support themselves. Congress agreed and passed a bill to provide for early payment of the bonuses. However, President Hoover vetoed the bill, saying that many of the vets did not need the early payment.

▼ The Bonus Army gathers on Capitol Hill.

● **INFOGRAPHIC** 🔊 AUDIO

THE BONUS ARMY

During the economic boom of the 1920s, Congress promised a bonus to World War I veterans to be paid out in 1945. In the summer of 1932, as the nation struggled in the grasp of the Depression, the "Bonus Expeditionary Force" of veterans converged on Washington, D.C., seeking immediate payment. When the Senate rejected their demands, President Hoover called upon the army to keep order. General Douglas MacArthur brought in troops to drive the protesters out of the city. Evalyn McLean, a Washington, D.C., resident, remembered the federal action: "I saw in a news reel the tanks, the cavalry, and the gas-bomb throwers running those wretched Americans out of our capital. I was so raging mad . . . ." Memories of the event influenced the next presidential election.

Honorary medal given to veterans of World War I ▼

◀ U.S. troops set fire to the Bonus Army camps after driving out the protesters.

General MacArthur (left) and his aide, ▶ Colonel Dwight Eisenhower (right), supervise the removal of the Bonus Army.

Thinking Critically
1. **Identify Points of View** How might the veterans and regular soldiers have felt about one another during the standoff?

2. **Make Generalizations** Was the Bonus Army justified in its protest? Why or why not?

723

In protest, veteran groups marched on Washington. In the summer of 1932, almost twenty thousand veterans arrived in the capital, setting up camps and occupying empty government buildings. A riot broke out in July when police tried to evict the marchers from their makeshift settlements.

Hoover Orders the Bonus Army Out Although President Hoover sympathized with the marchers, he called for General **Douglas MacArthur** and federal troops to "[s]urround the affected area and clear it without delay." MacArthur exceeded his order, deciding to move the marchers out of the city altogether. He ordered his troops to ready tear gas and fix bayonets.

The Army force that pushed the marchers out included not only MacArthur but also the future World War II generals Dwight Eisenhower and George Patton. While Eisenhower regretted the use of the Army to solve a political problem, Patton ordered his troops to brandish their sabers in a show of force. Force, perhaps excessive, was exactly what MacArthur used. More than one thousand marchers were tear-gassed, and many were injured, some very badly.

After the removal, MacArthur said that the marchers were a gang of revolutionaries bent on taking over the government:

> **Primary Source** "They had come to the conclusion, beyond a shadow of a doubt, that they were about to take over . . . direct control of the government. . . . It is my opinion that had the president let it go on another week the institutions of our government would have been very severely threatened."
> —Douglas MacArthur, 1932

The Aftermath Dooms Hoover Hoover had not ordered the use of such force against the veterans. Nevertheless, photographs of American troops marching with fixed bayonets against ragged veterans shocked the nation. Any chance that Hoover had for winning reelection in November ended after the summer of 1932. With unemployment nearing 25 percent, stomachs grumbling from hunger, and the number of homeless people increasing every day, Hoover's policies had failed completely. Americans were ready for a change.

 Checkpoint Why did Hoover order the removal of the Bonus Army from its camps?

SECTION 3

Assessment

Progress Monitoring Online
For: Self-test with vocabulary practice
Web Code: nea-0805

Comprehension

1. **Terms and People** For each of the following terms, write a sentence explaining its significance.
   - localism
   - RFC
   - Hoover Dam
   - Bonus Army

2. **NoteTaking Reading Skill: Identify Supporting Details** Use your outline to answer the Section Focus Question: Why did Herbert Hoover's policies fail to solve the country's economic crisis?

Writing About History

3. **Quick Write: Analyze Solutions** Based on what you have read, list supporting information—such as details, data, and facts—for the following thesis statement of a problem-solution essay: Although President Hoover responded to the developing economic crisis, he ultimately failed to stop it.

Critical Thinking

4. **Recognize Ideologies** How did Hoover's views on government influence his response to the depression? Give two examples.

5. **Analyze Evidence** What facts show that Hoover's policies to reverse the depression failed?

6. **Recognize Effects** How did MacArthur's tactics in removing the Bonus Army affect Hoover's political future?

5.II.B.7a

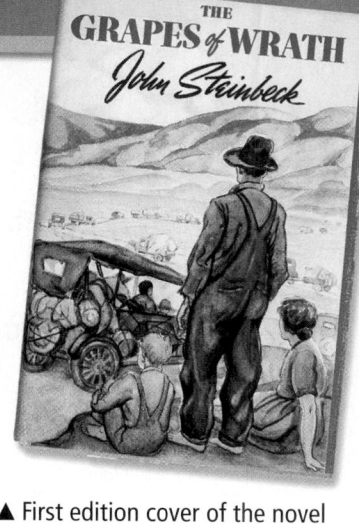

The Grapes of Wrath by John Steinbeck

Published during the depths of the depression, *The Grapes of Wrath* won its author the Pulitzer Prize in 1940. Steinbeck's sympathetic portrayal of dispossessed Okies, along with his searing criticism of the rich and powerful who profited from their plight, caused an immediate sensation. The novel tells the story of the Joad family, hardy Dust Bowl farmers who are forced off their land by the bank. The Joads join the mass migration west, to the "promised land" of California. There, instead of opportunity, they find low wages, harsh conditions, discrimination—and finally, after years of drought, the cruel irony of a killing flood.

▲ First edition cover of the novel

In the barns, the people sat huddled together; and the terror came over them, and their faces were gray with terror. The children cried with hunger, and there was no food.

Then the sickness came, pneumonia, and measles that went to the eyes and to the mastoids.[1]

And the rain fell steadily, and the water flowed over the highways, for the culverts[2] could not carry the water.

Then from the tents, from the crowded barns, groups of sodden men went out, their clothes slopping rags, their shoes muddy pulp. They splashed out through the water, to the towns, to the country stores, to the relief offices, to beg for food, to cringe and beg for food, to beg for relief, to try to steal, to lie. And under the begging, and under the cringing, a hopeless anger began to smolder. And in the little towns pity for the sodden men changed to anger, and anger at the hungry people changed to fear of them. Then sheriffs swore in deputies in droves, and orders were rushed for rifles, for tear gas, for ammunition. Then the hungry men crowded the alleys behind the stores to beg for bread, to beg for rotting vegetables, to steal when they could.

Frantic men pounded on the doors of the doctors; and the doctors were busy. And sad men left word at country stores for the coroner to send a car. The coroners were not too busy. The coroners' wagons backed up through the mud and took out the dead.

And the rain pattered relentlessly down, and the streams broke their banks and spread out over the country.

▲ The Joads, from the 1940 film *The Grapes of Wrath*, starring Henry Fonda

Thinking Critically

1. **Draw Inferences** Why did the townspeople's pity for the hungry migrant workers change to anger and then to fear?

2. **Analyze Literature** Notice the words Steinbeck uses to describe the rain and flooding. What might the flood symbolize in the story?

---

1. **mastoids** (MAS toidz) *n.* infection-prone areas of the skull behind the ears.
2. **culverts** (KUHL vertz) *n.* drainage ditches crossing under roads.

Quick Study Guide

 5.II.A.1,
5.II.A.4

Progress Monitoring *Online*
For: Self-test with vocabulary practice
Web Code: nea-0806

■ The Cycle of Production Cutbacks

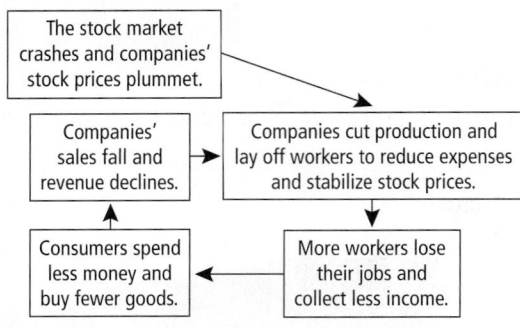

- The stock market crashes and companies' stock prices plummet.
- Companies cut production and lay off workers to reduce expenses and stabilize stock prices.
- Companies' sales fall and revenue declines.
- More workers lose their jobs and collect less income.
- Consumers spend less money and buy fewer goods.

■ Cause and Effect: The Great Depression

Causes
- Overproduction and underconsumption of agricultural crops
- Uneven distribution of income
- Gradual accumulation of consumer debt
- Widespread stock market speculation

The Great Depression

Effects
- Banks and businesses fail.
- Unemployment soars.
- Personal incomes shrink.
- Countries enact high tariffs to protect their products from foreign competition; world trade declines.
- American loans to Europe dry up.

■ Causes of the Dust Bowl

Severe drought scorches the land.

Farmers plow deep-rooted grasses to plant crops.

Livestock overgraze the land.

Windstorms blow topsoil away.

☑ Quick Study Timeline

In America

1928
Hoover elected President

October 1929
Stock market crashes

June 1930
Hawley-Smoot Tariff

Presidential Terms	Calvin Coolidge 1923–1929	Herbert Hoover 1929–1933	
	1928	**1929**	**1930**

Around the World

1928
Stalin launches first Five-Year Plan in the Soviet Union

1930
Haile Selassie becomes emperor of Ethiopia

American Issues
●—●—● Connector

By connecting prior knowledge with what you have learned in this chapter, you can gradually build your understanding of enduring questions that still affect America today. Answer the questions below. Then, use your American Issues Connector study guide (or go online: www.PHSchool.com **Web Code:** neh-8102).

Issues You Learned About

● **Government's Role in the Economy** Like other Presidents, Hoover sought the right balance between free enterprise and government intervention in the economy.

1. Think about the problems that emerged in society during the Great Depression and Hoover's response to them. Write a paragraph suggesting what Hoover might have done to improve the nation's economic situation and morale. Consider the following:
   - the depression's impact on families, businesses, industries, agriculture, and the banking system
   - the rising unemployment rate
   - the falling prices for farm products
   - Hoover's belief in volunteerism
   - responses to Hoover's policies

● **Migration and Urbanization** Economic changes often lead to migration around the country.

2. Why did thousands of people who lived in the Great Plains leave the region in the 1930s?

3. How did the drought on the Great Plains change population distribution in the country?

4. What other migrations took place as a result of the Great Depression?

● **Global Interdependence** The economies of nations around the world are impacted by distant events.

5. What economic practice of the 1920s contributed to the weakening of European economies?

6. What happened to European economies as a result of the Great Depression in the United States?

Connect to Your World | New York

Poverty and Prosperity The stock market crash of 1929 created a frantic atmosphere in New York City's financial district. Crowds gathered on the street outside the New York Stock Exchange, and extra policemen were ordered to the neighborhood to keep order. Buses gave sightseeing tours of the area to tourists interested in seeing, as one tour bus conductor put it, "where all that money was lost last week." Restaurants stayed open well past their usual hours to feed the brokers and clerks who worked late into the night to deal with the repercussions of the crash. Find out more about the mood in New York City after the stock market crash, and write a first-person account as though you witnessed these events.

1931
Bank failures cause panic

January 1932
Congress sets up the RFC

July 1932
Bonus Army driven from Washington, D.C.

History *Interactive*
For: Interactive timeline
Web Code: nep-0808

Franklin D. Roosevelt 1933–1945

1931

1932

1933

1931
Japanese troops occupy Manchuria

1932
Britain and France agree to suspend German reparations

1933
Hitler becomes chancellor of Germany

Chapter Assessment

Terms and People

1. Who was **Herbert Hoover**? What did he represent to the American people in 1928?

2. What is the **business cycle**? If you were to chart the business cycle of 1929, how would you represent the period from mid-October through mid-November?

3. Define **bread line.** Who ran bread lines during the depression?

4. What was Mexican American **repatriation**? How did Mexican Americans respond to this effort?

5. Define **trickle-down economics.** Explain how the depression proved whether or not this theory worked.

Focus Questions

The focus question for this chapter is **How did the Great Depression happen, and how did Americans respond to it?** Build an answer to this big question by answering the focus questions for Sections 1 through 3 and the Critical Thinking questions that follow.

Section 1
6. How did the prosperity of the 1920s give way to the Great Depression?

Section 2
7. How did the Great Depression affect the lives of urban and rural Americans?

Section 3
8. Why did Herbert Hoover's policies fail to solve the country's economic crisis?

Critical Thinking

9. **Identify Central Issues** What weaknesses existed in the U.S. economy before the stock market crash?

10. **Recognize Causes** How did the Dust Bowl cause Okies to prefer life in California over life on the Great Plains?

11. **Analyze Line Graphs** Based on the graph below, between which two years did unemployment rise the most? Based on your reading, explain why the increase was especially great during this period.

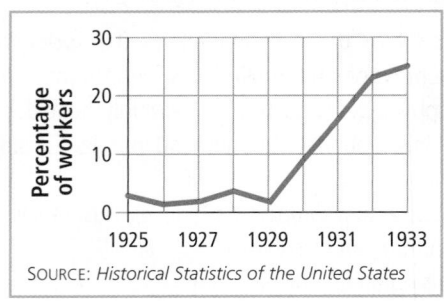

U.S. Unemployment Rate, 1925–1933

SOURCE: *Historical Statistics of the United States*

12. **Synthesize Information** Why did some men find their role in the family diminished during the depression? What were some of the different ways these men reacted?

13. **Identify Central Issues** Do you think the depression changed people's goals and expectations? Why or why not?

14. **Draw Conclusions** Why did Hoover turn from volunteerism and localism to more activist policies to fight the depression?

15. **Identify Fact Versus Opinion** What demands did the Bonus Army make? What did General MacArthur think about the Bonus Army?

Writing About History

Writing a Problem-Solution Essay Throughout its history, the United States has experienced periods of economic decline. However, not all these downturns ended in a general depression. In 1929, underlying problems surfaced to sink the American economy in the wake of the stock market crash. Write a problem-solution essay about one of these causes of the depression or choose your own topic relating to the content in this chapter.

Prewriting
• Choose the topic that interests you the most. If you have a personal interest in a problem and its solution, your essay will be easier to develop.

• Narrow your topic.

• Make a list of details, facts, and examples that prove there is a problem. Then, identify the specific parts of your solution.

Drafting
• Develop a working thesis and choose information to support it.

• Organize the paragraphs in a logical order so that readers can understand the solution you propose.

Revising
• Use the guidelines on page SH16 of the Writing Handbook to revise your essay.

Regents DBQ Practice

Worldwide Depression

In 1929, the stock market crash echoed across the Atlantic Ocean to a European continent still suffering the aftereffects of war. Use your knowledge of the Great Depression and the following documents to answer questions 1 through 4.

Document 1

"Values decreased, prices fell, production lessened. The American faith began its decline as extremely as had its illusions been created. Simultaneously, with the misfortunes of business in America came the catastrophes of Europe. . . . The [American] government made unheard-of efforts in the last three years to contain the avalanche. . . . But they made the big mistake of believing they could save the nation in isolation."

—El Sol, *Madrid newspaper, March 7, 1933*

Document 2

Nations indebted to the United States, 1914–1925
Loans given by the United States, 1914–1918
Loans given by the United States for reconstruction, 1919–1925
$160 Total debt (in millions of dollars)
*Debt repudiated in 1918

Document 3

"The Hawley-Smoot Tariff went into effect in June 1930, in the full blast of the depression. Under the circumstances there was great indignation and resentment on the part of the majority of the countries of the world, but that of the debtor countries of Europe was extreme. This intense indignation, coupled with the absolute necessity of securing a favorable trade balance, could result in but one course of action: retaliatory tariff increases against the United States."

—Joseph M. Jones, Jr., Tariff Retaliation: Repercussions of the Hawley-Smoot Bill

Document 4

PASSING THE BUCK.

---

1. Which of the documents is a primary source that explains how the stock market crash snowballed into an international economic crisis?
   (1) Document 1
   (2) Document 2
   (3) Document 3
   (4) Document 4

2. In Document 4, how did the cartoonist choose to portray the problem of reparations after World War I?
   (1) The United States does not need its loans repaid.
   (2) Germany has plenty of money available to repay Britain and France.
   (3) Britain and France cannot repay U.S. loans because Germany is bankrupt.
   (4) The United States is loaning more money to Germany.

3. According to Joseph Jones, which of the following statements is an accurate assessment of the Hawley-Smoot Tariff?
   (1) It caused European countries to pass their own protective tariffs.
   (2) It opened international markets and stimulated world trade.
   (3) It put limits on Allied war debts.
   (4) It established the funds for the Reconstruction Finance Corporation.

4. **Writing Task** How did the structure of loans to rebuild Europe after World War I collapse under the weight of economic depression? Use your knowledge of the war, the Great Depression, and specific evidence from the primary sources above to support your opinion.

A New Beginning

Still suffering through the worst economic crisis in the nation's history, depression-weary Americans anxiously awaited Franklin D. Roosevelt's Inaugural Address.

"Saturday, March 4, 1933.

Turn on the radio. It's time for the inauguration.

There is a tension in the air today—a sense of momentousness and of expectation. When you went downtown this morning you found the banks shut. . . . But what next? . . . The one thing you want to hear, that everybody wants to hear, is the Inaugural Address. All over the country people are huddled round their radios, wondering what Roosevelt's answer to disaster will be.**"**

—Frederick Lewis Allen, *Since Yesterday: The 1930s In America*

Listen to the Witness History *audio to learn more about FDR's inauguration.*

◀ On the campaign trail in West Virginia, Governor Roosevelt greets a coal miner.

Movie poster for *King Kong*

1932 presidential campaign button

 Core Curriculum Preview

Chapter Focus Question: How did the New Deal respond to the ravages of the Depression and change the role of the federal government?

Section 1
FDR Offers Relief and Recovery 5.II.B.1a, 5.II.B.1b, 5.II.B.1c

Section 2
The Second New Deal 5.II.B.1c, 5.II.B.3c, 5.II.B.3d, 5.II.B.4, 5.II.B.5a

Section 3
Effects of the New Deal 5.II.B.6b, 5.II.B.6d, 5.II.B.6e, 5.II.B.6f

Section 4
Culture of the 1930s 5.II.B.7a, 5.II.B.7b, 5.II.B.7c

Use the ☑ **Quick Study Timeline** at the end of this chapter to preview chapter events.

The CCC provided government jobs for unemployed young men.

Note Taking Study Guide *Online*
For: Note Taking and American Issues Connector
Web Code: nee-8201

▼ Franklin Delano Roosevelt

▼ Roosevelt campaign banner

VELT FOR PRESIDENT

WITNESS HISTORY 🔊 AUDIO

Overcoming Fear

Franklin D. Roosevelt's March 1933 inauguration came at a somber moment in American history. The U.S. economy had hit rock bottom. Many Americans wondered if they would ever find work again. With the first words of his Inaugural Address, FDR reassured the American people:

❝This is preeminently the time to speak the truth, the whole truth, frankly and boldly. Nor need we shrink from honestly facing conditions in our country today. This great Nation will endure as it has endured, will revive and will prosper. So, first of all, let me assert my firm belief that the only thing we have to fear is fear itself—nameless, unreasoning, unjustified terror which paralyzes needed efforts to convert retreat into advance.❞

—*Franklin D. Roosevelt, First Inaugural Address, March 4, 1933*

FDR Offers Relief and Recovery

 Core Curriculum Objectives

- **5.II.B.1a** New Deal relief of suffering: Bank "holiday"; Emergency Banking Act
- **5.II.B.1b** New Deal relief of suffering: Federal Emergency Relief Act
- **5.II.B.1c** New Deal relief of suffering: Unemployment

Terms and People

Franklin D. Roosevelt	CCC
Eleanor Roosevelt	NRA
New Deal	PWA
fireside chat	Charles Coughlin
FDIC	Huey Long
TVA	

NoteTaking

Reading Skill: Connect Ideas Fill in a chart like the one below with the problems that FDR faced and the steps he took to overcome them.

FDR Tackles Tough Problems	
Problem	**FDR's Policy**
Failing banks	

Why It Matters The Great Depression challenged the faith of Americans that democracy could handle the crisis. Faced with similar circumstances, people in Germany, Italy, and Japan had turned to dictators to deliver them from despair. The New Deal had great significance because America's response to the Great Depression proved that a democratic society could overcome the challenges presented by the severe economic crisis. **Section Focus Question: How did the New Deal attempt to address the problems of the depression?**

Roosevelt Takes Charge

In 1928, Herbert Hoover had almost no chance of losing his bid for the presidency. In 1932 however, Hoover had almost no chance of winning reelection. The depression had taken its toll. About 25 percent of the population was unemployed. Bank failures had wiped out peoples' savings. The hungry waited on long lines at soup kitchens.

Americans were ready for a change. In July of 1932, the relatively unknown governor of New York, **Franklin D. Roosevelt,** accepted the Democratic Party's nomination for President.

Roosevelt Overcame Obstacles Strangely enough, Americans had chosen a presidential candidate who had never known economic hardship. As a child, Franklin Delano Roosevelt had enjoyed all the privileges of an upper-class upbringing, including education at elite schools and colleges. From his parents and teachers, FDR gained a great deal of self-confidence and a belief that public service was a noble calling.

In 1905, Franklin married his distant cousin **Eleanor Roosevelt.** President Theodore Roosevelt, Eleanor's uncle and Franklin's fifth cousin gave the bride away. In time, Eleanor would become deeply involved in public affairs.

Like Teddy Roosevelt, Franklin rose quickly through the political ranks. After election to the New York State Senate, he served as Woodrow Wilson's Assistant Secretary of the Navy. In 1920, Roosevelt was the Democratic Party's vice presidential nominee. Although the Democrats lost the election, many considered him the rising star of the party.

Then, in the summer of 1921, tragedy struck. While vacationing, FDR slipped off his boat into the chilly waters of the North Atlantic. That evening, he awoke with a high fever and severe pains in his back and legs. Two weeks later, Roosevelt was diagnosed with polio, a dreaded disease that at the time had no treatment. He never fully recovered the use of his legs.

FDR did not allow his physical disability to break his spirit. With Eleanor's encouragement, Roosevelt made a political comeback. In 1928, he was elected governor of New York and earned a reputation as a reformer. In 1932, he became the Democrat's presidential candidate, pledging "a new deal for the American people."

Voters Elect a New President When FDR pledged a **"New Deal,"** he had only a vague idea of how he intended to combat the depression. Convinced that the federal government needed to play an active role in promoting recovery and providing relief to Americans, he experimented with different approaches to see which one worked best.

> **Primary Source** "The country needs and, unless I mistake its temper, the country demands bold, persistent experimentation. It is common sense to take a method and to try it. If it fails, admit it frankly and try another. But above all, try something!"
> —Franklin D. Roosevelt, speech at Oglethorpe University, May 22, 1932

The 1932 election campaign pitted Roosevelt against President Herbert Hoover. The two men advocated very different approaches to the problems of the Great Depression. Hoover believed that depression relief should come from state and local governments and private agencies. Roosevelt believed that the depression required strong action and leadership by the federal government. As Hoover noted, "This campaign is more than a contest between two men. . . . It is a contest between two philosophies of government."

Hoover's popularity declined as the Great Depression worsened. Even longtime Republicans deserted him. FDR—with the support of those who embraced his ideas as well as those who opposed Hoover's approach—won a landslide presidential victory, defeating Hoover by more than 7 million votes.

Americans had to wait four long months between Roosevelt's election, in November 1932, and his inauguration, in March 1933. Meanwhile, they watched helplessly as thousands of banks collapsed and unemployment soared. What would Roosevelt do to combat the depression? Even the experts did not know what to expect.

Putting Together a Winning Team To help him plan the New Deal, FDR sought the advice of a diverse group of men and women. Among the most influential was a group of professionals and academics whom the press nicknamed the

FDR Not Slowed by Polio

Despite the debilitating effects of polio, FDR continued to serve in public office. *How do you think FDR's earlier jobs and experiences prepared him to serve as President?*

- **1903** Earned BA in history from Harvard University
- **1910** Elected to the New York State Senate
- **1913** Appointed Assistant Secretary of the Navy
- **1920** Campaigned as Democratic nominee for Vice President
- **1921** Contracted polio, which paralyzed his legs
- **1928** Elected governor of New York State
- **1933** Inaugurated as President of the United States

"Brain Trust." Roosevelt, a Democrat, displayed his openness by nominating two Republicans, Henry Wallace and Harold Ickes (IHK uhs), to serve as his Secretary of Agriculture and Secretary of Interior. Roosevelt also nominated Frances Perkins, a social worker, to serve as his Secretary of Labor. She became the first woman Cabinet member in U.S. history.

Throughout his presidency, FDR depended heavily on his wife, Eleanor. She traveled widely, interacting with the American people and serving as FDR's "eyes and ears." For example, in 1933, the Bonus Army, which had marched on Washington, D.C., in 1932, returned to the capital, seeking an early payment of its bonus for World War I service. Like Hoover, FDR informed the marchers that the government could not afford to pay them their bonus. But unlike Hoover, who had sent the army to evict the Bonus Army, FDR sent Eleanor. She sang songs with the veterans and made them feel that the government cared.

✓ **Checkpoint** How did FDR's background and actions help build confidence among the American people?

The First Hundred Days Provide Instant Action

During his first hundred days in office, Roosevelt proposed and Congress passed 15 bills. These measures, known as the First New Deal, had three goals: relief, recovery, and reform. Roosevelt wanted to provide relief from the immediate hardships of the depression and achieve a long-term economic recovery. He also instituted reforms to prevent future depressions.

FDR Swiftly Restores the Nation's Confidence Roosevelt wasted no time dealing with the nation's number one crisis. Late in 1932, banks had begun to

---

RELIEF, RECOVERY, AND REFORM
THE FIRST 100 DAYS

Working together, President Roosevelt and Congress quickly passed many new laws to provide job relief, speed economic recovery, and reform business practices. These New Deal programs marked the beginning of the federal government's increasingly active role in shaping the economy and society.

▲ FDR used his first "fireside chat" to explain reform measures taken to end bank runs.

▼ Low-interest HOLC loans helped people meet mortgage payments, stimulating the housing industry.

Achievements of the First Hundred Days
Federal Deposit Insurance Corporation (FDIC)
National Recovery Administration (NRA)
Civilian Conservation Corps (CCC)
Public Works Administration (PWA)
Agricultural Adjustment Act (AAA)
Tennessee Valley Authority (TVA)
Home Owners' Loan Corporation (HOLC)

fail in great numbers. A banking panic gripped the nation as frightened depositors lined up outside banks, trying to withdraw their savings.

The day after his inauguration, Roosevelt called Congress into a special session and convinced them to pass laws to shore up the nation's banking system. The Emergency Banking Bill gave the President broad powers—including the power to declare a four-day bank "holiday." Banks all over the country were ordered to close. The closings gave banks time to get their accounts in order before they reopened for business.

Eight days after becoming President, Roosevelt delivered an informal radio speech to the American people. This was the first of many presidential **fireside chats.** They became an important way for Roosevelt to communicate with the American people. In the first fireside chat, FDR explained the measures he had taken to stem the run on banks. His calming words reassured the American people. When the bank holiday ended, Americans did not rush to their banks to withdraw their funds. Roosevelt had convinced them that the banks were a safe place to keep their money.

Reforming the Financial System A number of Roosevelt's proposals sought to reform the nation's financial institutions. One act created the **Federal Deposit Insurance Corporation (FDIC),** which insured bank deposits up to $5,000. In the following year, Congress established the Securities and Exchange Commission (SEC) to regulate the stock market and make it a safer place for investments.

These financial reforms helped restore confidence in the economy. Runs on banks ended, largely because Americans now had confidence that they would not lose their lifetime savings if a bank failed. The stock markets also stabilized as regulated trading practices reassured investors.

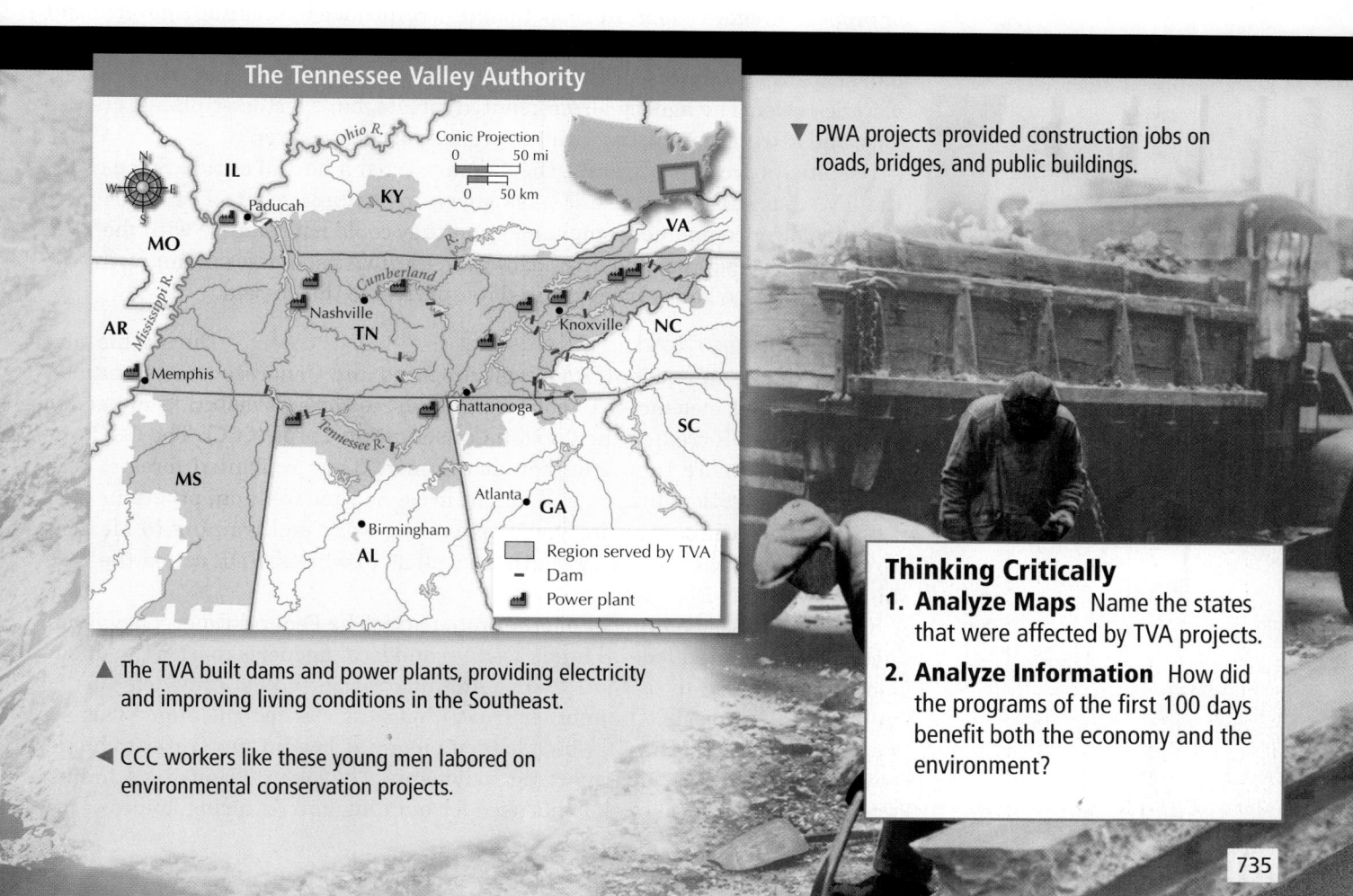

The Tennessee Valley Authority

▼ PWA projects provided construction jobs on roads, bridges, and public buildings.

▲ The TVA built dams and power plants, providing electricity and improving living conditions in the Southeast.

◄ CCC workers like these young men labored on environmental conservation projects.

Thinking Critically
1. **Analyze Maps** Name the states that were affected by TVA projects.
2. **Analyze Information** How did the programs of the first 100 days benefit both the economy and the environment?

Government Puts People to Work

The Works Progress Administration poster (above) promoted the benefits of putting people to work. These TVA workers (right) assembled generators at the Cherokee Dam in Tennessee. *If you had been out of work during the depression, what effect might these images have had on you? Why?*

Helping Farmers A number of New Deal programs aimed at easing the desperate plight of American farmers. For years, the supply of crops grown by American farmers had far exceeded demand. Prices dropped to the point where it was no longer profitable to grow some crops. To counter this, Congress passed the Agricultural Adjustment Act (AAA), which sought to end overproduction and raise crop prices. To accomplish these goals, the AAA provided financial aid, paying farmers subsidies not to plant part of their land and to kill off excess livestock. Many Americans believed it was immoral to kill livestock or destroy crops while people went hungry. However, by 1934, farm prices began to rise.

The TVA Aids Rural Southerners Americans living in the Tennessee River valley were among the poorest in the nation. Few had electricity, running water, or proper sewage systems. In 1933, Congress responded by creating a government agency called the **Tennessee Valley Authority (TVA).** The TVA built a series of dams in the Tennessee River valley to control floods and to generate electric power. The agency also replanted forests, built fertilizer plants, created jobs, and attracted industry with the promise of cheap power.

Despite its accomplishments, the TVA attracted a host of critics. Some called the TVA "socialist," because it gave government direct control of a business. Private power companies complained that they could not compete with the TVA, because the agency paid no taxes. However, the TVA's successes in improving life in the Tennessee Valley have ensured its survival to the present.

Providing Relief and Promoting Industrial Recovery During his first hundred days as President, Roosevelt proposed and Congress enacted numerous other relief measures. To counter the depression's devastating impact on young men, FDR created the **Civilian Conservation Corps (CCC).** The CCC provided jobs for more than 2 million young men. They replanted forests, built trails, dug irrigation ditches, and fought fires. As time went on, programs such as the CCC became more inclusive, extending work and training to Mexican American and other minority youth, as well as to whites. FDR called the CCC his favorite New Deal program.

Congress passed a number of other relief acts. The Federal Emergency Relief Act (FERA) granted federal funds to state and local agencies to help the unemployed. The short-lived Civil Works Administration (CWA) provided jobs on public-works projects. On another front, Congress created the Home Owners Loan Corporation (HOLC), which loaned money at low interest rates to homeowners who could not meet mortgage payments. The Federal Housing Administration (FHA) insured bank loans used for building and repairing homes.

These New Deal measures marked a clear break from the policies of the Hoover administration, which had disapproved of direct relief to individuals. The $500 million appropriated for FERA represented the largest peacetime expenditure by the federal government to that time.

The centerpiece of the early New Deal's recovery program was the National Industrial Recovery Act, which established the **National Recovery Administration (NRA).** Roosevelt called the NIRA "the most important and far-reaching legislation ever enacted by the American Congress." Working with business and labor leaders, the NRA developed codes of fair competition to govern whole industries. These codes established minimum wages for workers and minimum prices for the goods that businesses sold. The idea behind these codes was to increase the wages of workers so they could buy more goods and raise prices so companies could make a profit.

Another New Deal legislative achievement was the **Public Works Administration (PWA),** which built bridges, dams, power plants, and government buildings. The PWA was responsible for building many important projects still in use today, such as New York City's Triborough Bridge, the Overseas Highway linking Miami and Key West, and the Bonneville Dam on the Columbia River in the Pacific Northwest. These public-works projects improved the nation's infrastructure and created millions of new jobs for workers.

 Checkpoint **What actions did Roosevelt take during his first hundred days in office?**

Opposition to the New Deal Emerges

While Roosevelt had little difficulty gaining support from Congress for his proposals, a minority of Americans expressed their opposition to the New Deal. Some thought the changes it brought were too radical. Others thought that the New Deal was not radical enough. Several of FDR's critics attracted mass followings and made plans to challenge him for the presidency in 1936.

The Right Says "Too Much" The chief complaint against the New Deal was that it made the government too powerful. Critics contended that the government was telling business how to operate, spending large sums of money, and piling up a huge national debt.

To many conservatives, the New Deal was destroying free enterprise and undermining individualism. In a 1934 book entitled *The Challenge to Liberty*, former President Herbert Hoover described the New Deal as "the most stupendous invasion of the whole spirit of liberty" in the nation's history. Robert Taft, the son of former President William Howard Taft and a leading Republican in Congress, claimed Roosevelt's programs threatened individual freedom.

In 1934, these critics formed the American Liberty League. Supporters included prominent business leaders, such as Alfred Sloan and William Knudsen of General Motors. Leading Democrats, such as John W. Davis, the Democrat's presidential nominee in 1924, and Al Smith, the nominee in 1928, joined the Liberty League because they felt Roosevelt had deserted the Democratic Party's principles of a limited federal government.

Analyzing Political Cartoons

The Galloping Snail This cartoon represents the relationship between President Roosevelt and Congress during FDR's first hundred days in office.

 President Roosevelt

 Congress

C Roosevelt's New Deal agenda

1. Why did the cartoonist use a snail to represent Congress?
2. What is the cartoonist saying about the relationship between the President and Congress?

The New Deal: Too Much—or Not Enough?

Franklin Roosevelt's New Deal raised the issue of how involved the government should be in the economy and in the lives of its citizens. This question divided many Americans.

ALFRED E. SMITH

Smith (1873–1944) served as governor of New York and ran for President in 1928. He believed the New Deal made the government too powerful and described it as a "trend toward Fascist control" and "the end of democracy."

Primary Source

"... Something has taken place in this country—there is a certain kind of foreign 'ism' crawling over [it]. ... There can be only one Capitol, Washington or Moscow! There can be only one atmosphere of government, [the] clear, pure, fresh air of free America, or the foul breath of Communistic Russia."

FRANCIS TOWNSEND

Townsend (1867–1960) was a medical doctor who felt the New Deal did not do enough to help older Americans devastated by the depression. He proposed a pension plan funded by a national sales tax.

Primary Source

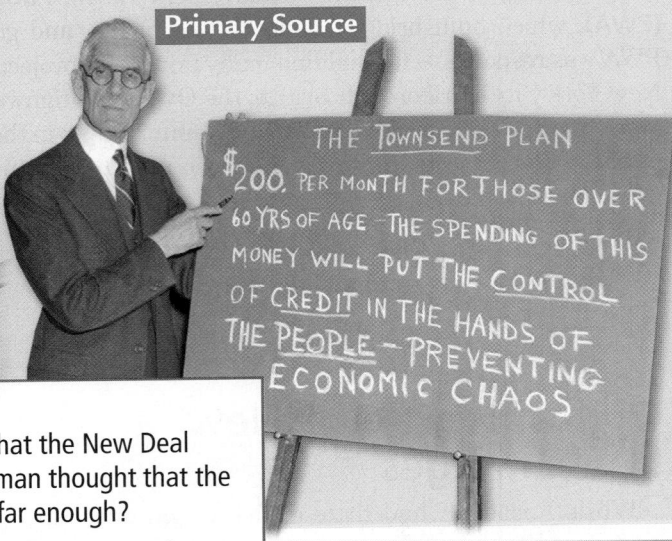

THE TOWNSEND PLAN
$200, PER MONTH FOR THOSE OVER 60 YRS OF AGE – THE SPENDING OF THIS MONEY WILL PUT THE CONTROL OF CREDIT IN THE HANDS OF THE PEOPLE – PREVENTING ECONOMIC CHAOS

Compare
1. Which man thought that the New Deal went too far? Which man thought that the New Deal did not go far enough?
2. Why does each oppose the New Deal?

Vocabulary Builder

ensure–(ehn SHUR) *v.* to make safe; guarantee

The Left Says "Not Enough" While conservatives accused FDR of supporting socialism, some leading socialists charged that the New Deal did not do enough to end the depression. Norman Thomas, the Socialist Party's presidential candidate, claimed that FDR's only concern was saving the banking system and ensuring profits for big business. The American Communist Party described the New Deal as a "capitalist ruse."

Populist Critics Challenge FDR The most significant criticism of FDR came from a cluster of figures whose roots were in the Populist movement. They saw themselves as spokesmen for poor Americans, challenging the power of the elite. Roosevelt's strongest critics were Francis Townsend, Father Charles Coughlin, and Huey Long.

Townsend, a doctor from California, had a simple program. It called for the federal government to provide $200 a month to all citizens over the age of 60. These funds, he argued, would filter out to the rest of society and produce an economic recovery. To promote this plan, he established "Townsend Clubs" and held meetings that resembled old-time church revivals.

Father **Charles Coughlin** presented an even bigger challenge to FDR. Coughlin, a Roman Catholic priest, had attracted millions of listeners to his weekly radio show. At first, Coughlin supported the New Deal, but in time he broke with FDR, accusing him of not doing enough to fight the depression. Coughlin said that Roosevelt had "out-Hoovered Hoover" and called the New Deal "the raw deal."

Coughlin mixed calls for the nationalization of industry with anti-Semitic remarks and attacks on "communists" who, he charged, were running the country. By the early 1940s, Coughlin's views became so extreme that Roman Catholic officials forced him to end his broadcasts.

Canadian by birth, Coughlin could not run against FDR in the 1936 election. However, he threatened to throw his support behind an even more popular New Deal critic, Senator **Huey Long** of Louisiana. Long was an expert performer whose folksy speeches delighted audiences. Long's solution to the depression was his "Share Our Wealth" program that proposed high taxes on the wealthy and large corporations, and the redistribution of their income to poor Americans.

> **Primary Source** "God invited us all to come and eat and drink all we wanted. He smiled on our land and we grew crops of plenty to eat and wear. . . . [But then] Rockefeller, Morgan, and their crowd stepped up and took enough for 120,000,000 people and left only enough for 5,000,000 for all the other 125,000,000 to eat. And so the millions must go hungry and without those good things God gave us unless we call on them to put some of it back."
>
> —Huey Long radio broadcast, 1934

Roosevelt viewed Long as a serious political threat. But unlike Roosevelt, Long did not have a deep faith in democracy. Ruling Louisiana as if he owned the state, he made many enemies. In 1935, a political enemy assassinated Long, ending the most serious threat to Roosevelt's presidency.

✔ **Checkpoint** What were the two major criticisms of FDR's New Deal economic policies?

Huey Long Challenges the Roosevelt Administration
Huey Long used his Share Our Wealth Society to promote the redistribution of wealth in the country. *How might Long's efforts have influenced FDR's policies?*

SECTION **1** Assessment

Progress Monitoring *Online*
For: Self-test with vocabulary practice
Web Code: nea-0902

Comprehension

1. **Terms and People** For each item below, write a sentence explaining how it affected the lives of people during the New Deal.
   - Eleanor Roosevelt
   - fireside chat
   - TVA
   - PWA
   - Charles Coughlin
   - Huey Long

2. **NoteTaking Reading Skill: Connect Ideas** Use your problem-solution table to answer the Section Focus Question: How did the New Deal attempt to address the problems of the depression?

Writing About History

3. **Quick Write: Identify Main Ideas** Before you can synthesize, you must understand the main idea, or thesis, of each source. Study the political cartoon in this section and write a sentence summarizing its main idea about FDR. Then, review the Alfred E. Smith primary source quote. Write a sentence summarizing Smith's view of FDR.

Critical Thinking

4. **Draw Inferences** Why did President Roosevelt need his wife, Eleanor, to serve as his "eyes and ears"?

5. **Make Comparisons** How did FDR's economic policies differ from those of Herbert Hoover?

6. **Identify Central Issues** Why do you think the depression led to the development of some extreme proposals?

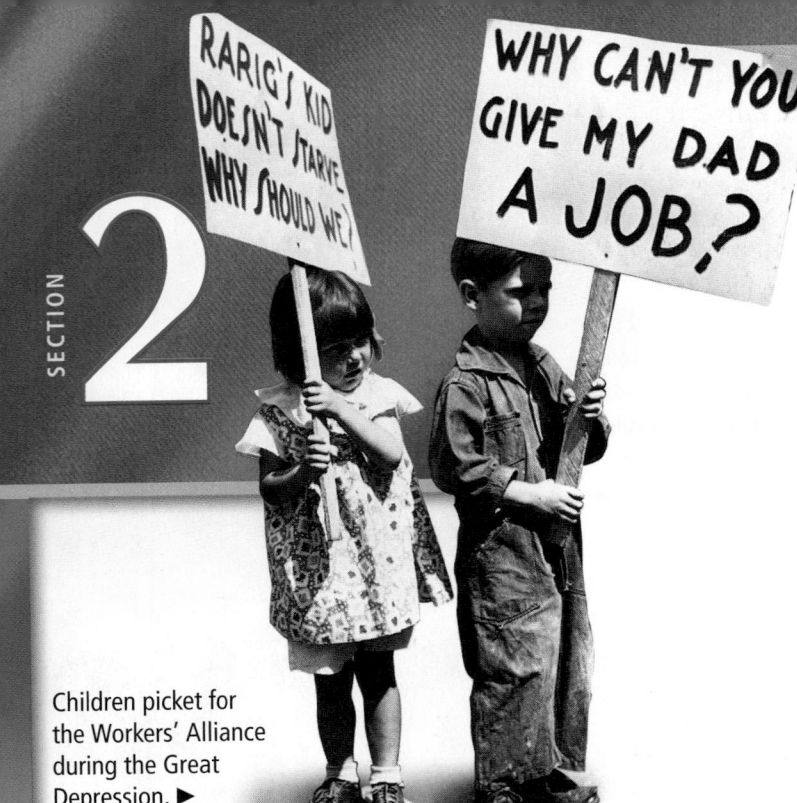

Children picket for the Workers' Alliance during the Great Depression. ▶

WITNESS HISTORY 🔊 AUDIO

Trying to Survive

During the Great Depression, people found themselves desperate for work. Daily visits to the unemployment office and workplaces often turned up nothing. Some of the jobless lost their homes. Others could not feed their children. One 12-year-old boy wrote to President Roosevelt to ask for help for his family.

❝My father hasn't worked for 5 months. . . . Please you do something. . . . We haven't paid the gas bill, and the electric bill, haven't paid grocery bill. . . . I have a sister she's twenty years, she can't find work. My father he staying home. All the time he's crying because he can't find work.❞

—Anonymous 12-year-old boy, Chicago, 1936

The Second New Deal

NY Core Curriculum Objectives

- **5.II.B.1c** New Deal relief of suffering: Unemployment
- **5.II.B.3c** Social Security Act
- **5.II.B.3d** Labor reform
- **5.II.B.4** Labor's response: Formation of CIO
- **5.II.B.5a** New Deal controversy: Constitutional issues

Terms and People

Second New Deal
WPA
John Maynard Keynes
pump priming
Social Security Act
Wagner Act

collective bargaining
Fair Labor Standards Act
CIO
sit-down strikes
court packing

NoteTaking

Reading Skill: Connect Ideas Complete a table like the one below to record problems and the second New Deal's solutions.

The Second New Deal	
Problem	**Solution**
Unemployment	

Why It Matters FDR's goals for the first New Deal were relief, recovery, and reform. Progress had been made, but there was still much work that needed to be done. Beginning in early 1935, Roosevelt launched an aggressive campaign to find solutions to the ongoing problems caused by the Great Depression. This campaign, known as the Second New Deal, created Social Security and other programs that continue to have a profound impact on the everyday lives of Americans. **Section Focus Question: What major issues did the Second New Deal address?**

Extending Social and Economic Reform

In his fireside chats, press conferences, and major addresses, Roosevelt explained the challenges facing the nation. He said that the complexities of the modern world compelled the federal government to "promote the general welfare" and to intervene to protect citizens' rights. Roosevelt used legislation passed during the **Second New Deal** to accomplish these goals. The Second New Deal addressed the problems of the elderly, the poor, and the unemployed; created new public-works projects; helped farmers; and enacted measures to protect workers' rights. It was during this period that the first serious challenges to the New Deal emerged.

New Programs Provide Jobs In the spring of 1935, Congress appropriated $5 billion for new jobs and created the **Works Progress Administration (WPA)** to administer the program. Roosevelt placed his longtime associate Harry Hopkins in charge. The WPA built or improved a good part of the nation's highways, dredged rivers and harbors, and promoted soil and water conservation. The WPA even provided programs in the arts for displaced artists. As Hopkins explained, artists "have to eat just like other people."

By 1943, the WPA had employed more than 8 million people and spent about $11 billion. Its workers built more than 650,000 miles of highways and 125,000 public buildings. Among the most famous projects funded by the WPA were the San Antonio River Walk and parts of the Appalachian Trail.

All of these programs were expensive, and the government paid for them by spending money it did not have. The federal deficit—$461 million in 1932—grew to $4.4 billion in 1936. The enormous expenditures and growing debt led many to criticize the government's public-works projects as wasteful. Some economists disagreed. British economist **John Maynard Keynes** argued that deficit spending was needed to end the depression. According to Keynes, putting people to work on public projects put money into the hands of consumers who would buy more goods, stimulating the economy. Keynes called this theory **pump priming.**

Social Security Eases the Burden on Older Americans The United States was one of the few industrialized nations in the world that did not have some form of pension system for the elderly. During the depression, many elderly people had lost their homes and their life savings and were living in poverty. On January 17, 1935, President Roosevelt unveiled his plans for Social Security.

In addition to creating a pension system for retirees, the **Social Security Act** that Congress enacted established unemployment insurance for workers who lost their jobs. The law also created insurance for victims of work-related accidents and provided aid for poverty-stricken mothers and children, the blind, and the disabled.

The Social Security Act had many flaws. At first, it did not apply to domestics or farmworkers. Since African Americans were disproportionately employed in these fields, they were not eligible for many of the benefits of Social Security. Widows received smaller benefits than widowers, because people presumed that elderly women could manage on less money than elderly men. Despite these shortcomings, Social Security proved the most popular and significant of the New Deal programs.

More Aid Goes to Farmers The Second New Deal included further help for farmers. When the depression began, only 10 percent of all farms had electricity, largely because utility companies did not find it profitable to run electric lines to communities with small populations. To bring farmers into the light, Congress established the Rural Electrification Administration (REA). The REA loaned money to electric utilities to build power lines, bringing electricity to isolated rural areas. The program was so successful that by 1950, more than 80 percent of American farms had electricity.

New Deal programs changed the relationship of the federal government to the American farmer. The government was now committed to providing price supports, or subsidies, for agriculture. Critics attacked price supports for undermining the free market. Others observed that large

Electricity Comes to Rural Farms

The success of the REA allowed farm families to light their homes, pump water, and run radios, refrigerators, and washing machines.

Farms With Electricity, 1930–1950

Percentage of farms

SOURCE: *Statistical Abstract of the United States*

farms, not small farmers, benefited most from federal farm programs. Even during the 1930s, many noticed that tenant farmers and sharecroppers, often African Americans, did not fully share in the federal programs. Yet farm prices stabilized, and agriculture remained a productive sector of the economy.

Water Projects Change the Face of the West Many of the New Deal public-works water projects had an enormous impact on the development of the American West. The government funded the complex Central Valley irrigation system in California. The massive Bonneville Dam in the Pacific Northwest controlled flooding and provided electricity to a vast number of citizens. In 1941, the Department of the Interior's Bonneville Power Administration (BPA) hired folk singer Woody Guthrie for one month to write songs for a movie they had made

Milestones in SOCIAL SECURITY

During the Great Depression, many elderly Americans had lost their life savings and were struggling to survive. The 1935 Social Security Act created a pension system as well as unemployment insurance for workers who had lost their jobs. Financed through a payroll tax on employers and workers, Social Security is one of the country's most important legislative achievements.

1935–1950 The Social Security program was expanded in 1939 to pay benefits to the widows and young children of deceased workers. In 1950, amendments to the Social Security Act increased benefit payments and extended coverage to more workers. As a result, almost all working Americans now contribute to Social Security and are eligible for benefits.

◄ Since 1940, senior citizens have depended on their monthly Social Security retirement checks.

Social Security benefits ► helped widows feed their children.

promoting the benefits of electricity. Guthrie's song, "Roll on, Columbia," pays tribute to the projects that harnessed the power of the Columbia River.

Primary Source

"Your power is turning our darkness to dawn,
And on up the river is the Grand Coulee Dam,
The Mightiest thing ever built by a man,
To run the great factories and water the land."
—Woody Guthrie, "Roll On, Columbia," 1941

✓ **Checkpoint** Why did the onset of the depression make it essential to have some form of Social Security?

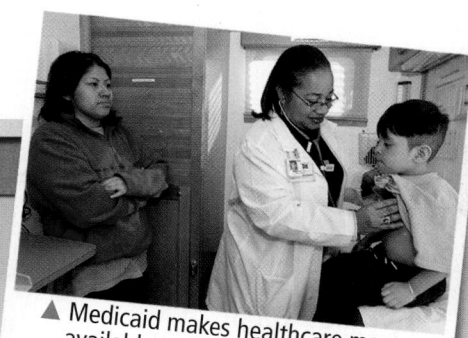
▲ Medicaid makes healthcare more available to low-income families.

1950–1970 During the 1950s and 1960s, Social Security expanded to provide benefits to people with disabilities. In 1965, two new Social Security programs, Medicare and Medicaid, were introduced. Medicare is a health-insurance program for Americans age 65 and older, and Medicaid provides health insurance to needy persons of any age.

1970–Today The Supplemental Social Security Income (SSI) program, begun in 1974, provides monthly payments to the needy elderly and to people who are blind or who have a disability. The Medicare Prescription Drug program, passed in 2003, provides Medicare recipients with voluntary prescription-drug coverage and discounts. President George W. Bush's proposal to allow younger workers to invest Social Security tax money in personal retirement accounts was rejected by the public in 2005.

The Elderly and Poverty, 1940–2000

Percentage living in poverty (y-axis: 0 to 100)
Years (x-axis): 1940, 1960, 1980, 2000

SOURCE: U.S. Census Bureau

▼ Supplemental Security Income benefits help people who are blind.

The Medicare Prescription ▶ Drug program helps seniors manage rising drug costs.

Why It Matters

For more than 70 years, Social Security has provided basic economic security to millions of Americans. Social Security programs act as a safety net for senior citizens, the poor, and others in financial need. Popular support for Social Security continues, although concern mounts over the program's long-term funding.

Thinking Critically

Describe four different kinds of benefits that the Social Security system provides today.

History *Interactive*

For: More about Social Security
Web Code: nep-0903

Labor Unions Find a New Energy

Vocabulary Builder

upsurge–(UHP serj) *n.* a sudden, rapid increase

Even before the Great Depression, most industrial workers labored long hours for little pay. Few belonged to labor unions. However, during the Great Depression, there was an upsurge in union activity. New unions enlisted millions of workers from the mining and automobile industries.

Granting New Rights to Workers Roosevelt believed that the success of the New Deal depended on raising the standard of living for American industrial workers. This, he believed, would improve the entire economy. The National Labor Relations Act was the most important piece of New Deal labor legislation. Called the **Wagner Act,** it recognized the right of employees to join labor unions and gave workers the right to **collective bargaining.** Collective bargaining meant that employers had to negotiate with unions about hours, wages, and other working conditions. The law created the National Labor Relations Board (NLRB) to look into workers' complaints.

The **Fair Labor Standards Act** of 1938 provided workers with additional rights. It established a minimum wage, initially at 25 cents per hour, and a maximum workweek of 44 hours. It also outlawed child labor. The minimum wage remains one of the New Deal's most controversial legacies. In the years ahead, the minimum wage would be gradually raised. Today, whenever a raise in the minimum wage is proposed, economists and political leaders debate the wisdom of such an increase.

Workers Use Their Newfound Rights The upsurge in union activity came at the same time as a bitter feud within the major labor federation, the American Federation of Labor (AFL). The AFL represented skilled workers—such as plumbers, carpenters, and electricians—who joined trade or craft unions. Few workers in the major industries belonged to the AFL, and the union made little effort to organize them.

Fed up with the AFL's reluctance to organize, John L. Lewis, the president of the United Mine Workers, and a number of other labor leaders, established the **Congress of Industrial Organizations (CIO).** The workers targeted by the CIO-organizing campaigns tended to be lower paid and ethnically more diverse than those workers represented by the AFL.

Sit-Down Strikes Lead to Union Gains

The success of the UAW's sit-down strike against General Motors led the U.S. Steel Company to recognize the steelworkers' union. *How do you think strikes affected union membership?*

Labor Union Membership, 1920–1960

20				
15				
10				
5				
0				
1920	1930	1940	1950	1960

Union members (in millions)

SOURCE: *Historical Statistics of the United States*

The Second New Deal

Program	Year	Effects
Social Security Act (SSA)	1935	Established a pension system and unemployment insurance; provided payments to workers injured on the job, the poor, and people with disabilities
Works Progress Administration (WPA)	1935	Employed millions of people on government projects ranging from highway construction to arts programs
Rural Electrification Administration (REA)	1935	Provided loans to electric companies to build power lines, bringing electricity to isolated rural areas
National Labor Relations Act (Wagner Act)	1935	Outlawed unfair labor practices; granted workers the right to organize unions and to bargain collectively; created the National Labor Relations Board
National Youth Administration (NYA)	1935	Trained and provided jobs and counseling for unemployed youth between the ages of 16 and 25
Banking Act of 1935	1935	Finalized the creation of the FDIC and made insurance for bank deposits permanent; created a board to regulate the nation's money supply and interest rates on loans
United States Housing Authority (USHA)	1937	Subsidized construction of low-cost public housing by providing federal loans
Fair Labor Standards Act	1938	Banned child labor, established a minimum hourly wage, and set the workweek at 44 hours
Food, Drug, and Cosmetic Act	1938	Prohibited the mislabeling of food, drugs, and cosmetics, and ensured the safety and purity of these products

This commemorative postage stamp honors the many programs of FDR's New Deal. Critics mocked the abbreviated titles, or acronyms, of the New Deal programs as "alphabet soup." *Use the chart to identify five programs from the second New Deal that helped workers.*

In December 1936, members of the CIO's newly formed United Automobile Workers Union (UAW) staged a **sit-down strike,** occupying one of General Motors' most important plants in Flint, Michigan. In a sit-down strike, workers refuse to leave the workplace until a settlement is reached. When the police and state militia threatened to remove them by force, the workers informed Michigan governor Frank Murphy that they would not leave.

> **Primary Source** "We fully expect that if a violent effort is made to oust us many of us will be killed and we take this means of making it known to our wives, to our children, to the people of the State of Michigan and the country, that if this result follows from the attempt to eject us, you are the one who must be held responsible for our deaths!"
>
> —Auto workers sit-down committee, Flint, Michigan, January 1936

The strike lasted for 44 days until General Motors, then the largest company in the world, agreed to recognize the UAW. This union success led to others. By 1940, 9 million workers belonged to unions, twice the number of members in 1930. Just as important, union members gained better wages and working conditions.

✓ **Checkpoint** How did the New Deal affect trade unions?

Challenges to the New Deal

Franklin Roosevelt won an overwhelming victory in the presidential election of 1936. He received 61 percent of the vote, compared to just 37 percent for his Republican challenger, Alfred M. Landon. Roosevelt carried every state but Maine and Vermont. FDR entered his second term determined to challenge the group that he considered the main enemy of the New Deal—a Supreme Court that had struck down many of his programs.

The Supreme Court Opposes the New Deal A year before the 1936 election, the Supreme Court had overturned one of the key laws of Roosevelt's first hundred days. In the case of *Schechter Poultry* v. *United States,* the Supreme Court unanimously ruled that since the President has no power to regulate interstate commerce, the National Industrial Recovery Act was unconstitutional. One pro–New Deal newspaper captured the mood of many Democrats: "AMERICA STUNNED; ROOSEVELT'S TWO YEARS' WORK KILLED IN TWENTY MINUTES."

Not long afterward, the Court ruled a key part of the Agricultural Adjustment Act unconstitutional. Roosevelt charged that the Court had taken the nation back to "horse-and-buggy" days. He expected the Court to strike down other New Deal measures, limiting his ability to enact new reforms.

FDR Proposes "Packing" the Court So on February 5, 1937, in a special address to Congress, FDR unveiled a plan that would dilute the power of the sitting Justices of the Supreme Court. He called for adding up to six new Justices to the nine-member Court. He justified his proposal by noting that the Constitution did not specify the number of judges on the Court. He added that many of the Justices were elderly and overworked. Critics, recognizing that Roosevelt's new appointees would most likely be New Deal supporters, called his plan **court packing.** They accused him of trying to increase presidential power and upsetting the delicate balance between the three branches of the federal government. Some critics urged Americans to speak out.

> **Primary Source** "If the American people accept this last audacity of the President without letting out a yell to high heaven, they have ceased to be jealous of their liberties and are ripe for ruin."
>
> —Dorothy Thompson, newspaper columnist, 1937

Given Roosevelt's enormous popularity, he might have convinced Congress to enact his plan but he did not have to because the Court began to turn his way. On March 29, 1937, the Court ruled 5 to 4 in favor of a minimum wage law. Two weeks later, again by a vote of 5 to 4, the Supreme Court upheld the constitutionality of the Wagner Act. In both cases, Justice Owen J. Roberts provided the deciding vote. Pundits called it the "switch in time to save nine," because Roberts had previously voted against several New Deal programs. Roberts's two votes in support of the New Deal removed FDR's main reason for packing the Court.

Shortly after this switch, Judge Willis Van Devanter, who had helped strike down several New Deal programs, resigned from the Court. This enabled FDR to nominate a Justice friendlier to the New Deal. With more retirements, Roosevelt nominated a number of other new Justices, including Felix Frankfurter, one of his top advisers.

Indeed, 1937 marked a turning point in the history of the Court. For years to come, the Court more willingly accepted a larger role for the federal government. Yet the court-packing incident weakened FDR politically. Before the court-packing plan, FDR's popularity prevented critics from challenging him. Now that Roosevelt had lost momentum, critics felt free to take him on. And even though the Court did not strike down any more laws, after 1937 Roosevelt found the public much less willing to support further New Deal legislation.

THE INGENIOUS QUARTERBACK!

Analyzing Political Cartoons

The Ingenious Quarterback! This 1937 cartoon makes fun of FDR's court-packing plan.
1. Why did the cartoonist make FDR the quarterback and Congress the referee?
2. What is the cartoonist's message?

A New Downturn Spurs Conservative Gains The turmoil over the Supreme Court had barely faded when the Roosevelt administration faced another crisis. During 1935 and 1936, economic conditions had begun to improve. Unemployment had fallen 10 percent in four years. With the economy doing better, FDR cut back on federal spending in order to reduce the rising deficit. But he miscalculated.

While Roosevelt reduced federal spending, the Federal Reserve Board raised interest rates, making it more difficult for businesses to expand and for consumers to borrow to buy new goods. Suddenly, the economy was in another tailspin. Unemployment soared to more than 20 percent. Nearly all of the gains in employment and production were wiped out.

Largely because of the downturn, the Democrats suffered a setback in the 1938 congressional elections. Republicans picked up 7 Senate and 75 House seats. Although Democrats still maintained a majority in both houses of Congress, Roosevelt's power base was shaken because many southern Democrats were lukewarm supporters of the New Deal. Needing their support for his foreign policies, FDR chose not to try to force more reforms through Congress.

✓ **Checkpoint** What setbacks did Roosevelt face during his second term as President?

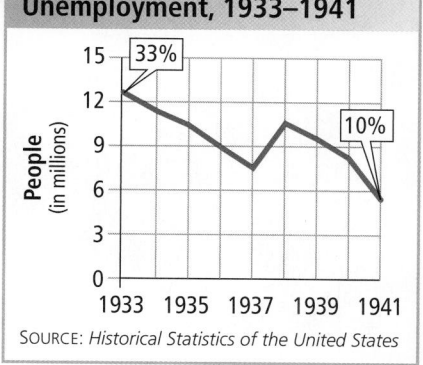

Unemployment, 1933–1941

SOURCE: *Historical Statistics of the United States*

Millions Look for Jobs
While New Deal programs employed many Americans, millions of others continued to search for work. *What happened to the unemployment rate in 1937?*

---

2 Assessment

Progress Monitoring *Online*
For: Self-test with vocabulary practice
Web Code: nea-0904

Comprehension

1. **Terms** For each act or New Deal agency below, explain how it eased conditions during the depression.
   - WPA
   - Social Security Act
   - Wagner Act
   - Fair Labor Standards Act

2. **NoteTaking Reading Skill: Connect Ideas** Use your table to answer the Section Focus Question: What major issues did the second New Deal address?

Writing About History

3. **Quick Write: Compare and Contrast** In order to synthesize, you need to compare and contrast different sources. List some emotions expressed by the photos on the first and last pages of this section. Do these images convey the same idea as the graph above? Explain in one or two sentences.

Critical Thinking

4. **Identify Central Issues** What were the most important reforms of the Second New Deal?

5. **Make Comparisons** Why did American labor make greater progress during the 1930s than during the prosperous 1920s?

6. **Demonstrate Reasoned Judgment** Do you think that FDR's court-packing plan was justified? Explain your answer.

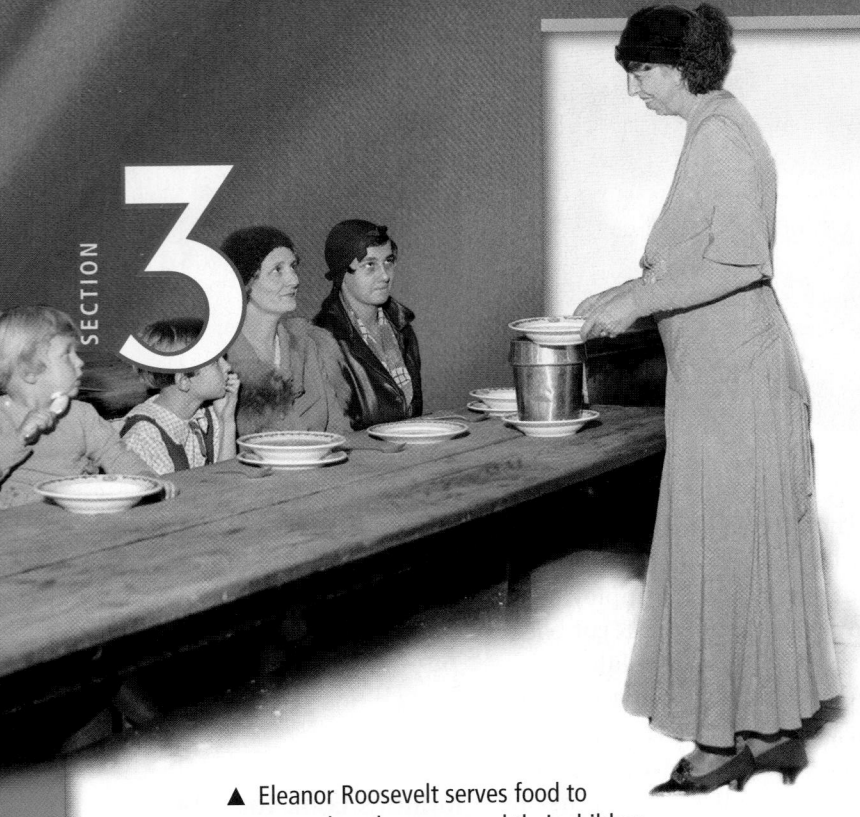

▲ Eleanor Roosevelt serves food to unemployed women and their children.

WITNESS HISTORY AUDIO

The Caring First Lady

Eleanor Roosevelt played a crucial role in the New Deal. She traveled to places FDR could not, advised her husband, and served as an inspiration to millions of Americans. Mrs. Roosevelt also corresponded with thousands of citizens. The following letter reflects the affection that many citizens felt for the first lady.

❝Ridley Park, Pennsylvania
 Dear Mrs. Roosevelt:
. . . Just to look at your picture and that of our President seems to me like looking at the picture of a saint. So when you answered my letter and promised to have some one help me it only proved that you are our own Mrs. Roosevelt. I have told everyone what you have done for me. I want them to know you are not too busy to answer our letters and give us what help and advice you can. You hold the highest place any woman can hold still you are not to[o] proud to befriend the poor. . . . Thank you and God bless you both.❞
—Letter to Eleanor Roosevelt, September 1, 1935

Effects of the New Deal

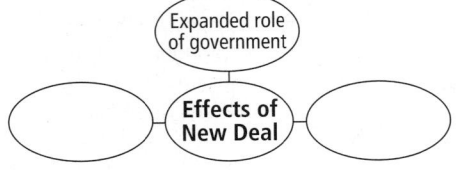

Core Curriculum Objectives

- **5.II.B.6b** Eleanor Roosevelt as the President's eyes and ears
- **5.II.B.6d** The New Deal and women
- **5.II.B.6e** The New Deal and minorities
- **5.II.B.6f** Indian Reorganization Act

Terms and People

Black Cabinet
Mary McLeod Bethune
Indian New Deal

New Deal coalition
welfare state

NoteTaking

Reading Skill: Identify Main Ideas As you read, identify the lasting effects of the New Deal upon American society.

```
        ┌──────────────┐
        │ Expanded role │
        │ of government │
        └──────────────┘
   ┌────────┐  │  ┌────────┐
   │        │──┤  │        │
   └────────┘ Effects of └────────┘
            New Deal
```

Why It Matters The New Deal provided desperately needed relief from the depression and enacted reforms that guarded against economic catastrophe. It did not end the depression. World War II, with its massive military spending, would do that. Yet, the New Deal mattered enormously because it brought fundamental changes to the nation. It changed the role of the federal government in the economy, the power of the presidency, and the relationship of the American people to their government. **Section Focus Question: How did the New Deal change the social, economic, and political landscape of the United States for future generations?**

Women Help Lead the New Deal

The New Deal provided some women with the opportunity to increase their political influence and to promote women's rights. Foremost among them was Eleanor Roosevelt, who transformed the office of First Lady from a largely ceremonial role to a position of action and deep involvement in the political process. Representing the President, she toured the nation. She visited farms and Indian reservations and traveled deep into a coal mine. She helped FDR on his campaigns and offered advice on policy issues. In her newspaper column, "My Day," she called on Americans to live up to the goal of equal justice for all.

"Eleanor Roosevelt is the First Lady of Main Street," explained magazine writer Margaret Marshall. "She occupies the highest social position in the land. Yet she makes friends on a plane or a train even as you and I." Mrs. Roosevelt's causes included advancing public health and education, promoting the arts in rural areas, and even addressing flood control. She exhibited boundless energy, traveling more than 60,000 miles in two years.

Molly Dewson, head of the Women's Division of the Democratic Party, observed that Eleanor Roosevelt provided women with an unprecedented access to the President. "When I wanted help on some definite point, Mrs. Roosevelt gave [me] the opportunity to sit by the President at dinner and the matter was settled before we finished our soup."

The Roosevelt Administration included the first female Cabinet member, Secretary of Labor Frances Perkins. She played a leading role in establishing Social Security. Perkins also helped win approval of the Fair Labor Standards Act, which ended child labor and established a minimum wage.

However, the New Deal did not fight to end gender discrimination in the workplace. Indeed, some historians have argued that a number of New Deal programs reinforced traditional <u>gender</u> differences. The WPA and other relief programs employed women but made a much greater effort to provide work to men first. For example, women were not eligible to work for the CCC. However, the increased homeownership and insured savings accounts brought by the New Deal were of special benefit to the widows of men who were covered.

Vocabulary Builder
<u>gender</u>–(JEHN der) *n.* a person's sex

✔ **Checkpoint** What impact did the New Deal have on women?

African Americans Make Advances and Face Challenges

When the depression hit, African American workers were often the first to lose their jobs. By 1934, the unemployment rate for African Americans was almost 50 percent, more than twice the national average. Eleanor Roosevelt and others urged the President to improve the situation of African Americans.

As the New Deal progressed, Eleanor Roosevelt increasingly used her position to protest against racial discrimination. At a meeting held by the Southern Conference on Human Welfare, a biracial group that sought to promote racial reforms, the first lady sat with the black delegates—a daring move in segregated Birmingham, Alabama. When a white police officer told her that she was violating local segregation laws, Mrs. Roosevelt moved her chair to the space between the black and white sides. She then delivered a rousing and provocative keynote address in favor of racial reform.

Primary Source ❝We are the leading democracy of the world and as such must prove to the world that democracy is possible and capable of living up to the principles upon which it was founded. The eyes of the world are upon us, and often we find they are not too friendly eyes.❞
—Eleanor Roosevelt, November 22, 1938

HISTORY MAKERS

Frances Perkins (1882–1965)
After graduating from college, Frances Perkins earned her master's degree in economics. From 1912, until being named Secretary of Labor, she held various jobs in New York State government. She was a strong voice for consumers and workers, especially working women and children.

Mary McLeod Bethune (1875–1955)
Mary McLeod Bethune was a teacher who worked to improve educational opportunities for African Americans. Bethune served as FDR's special adviser on minority affairs. As the director of Negro Affairs of the National Youth Administration, Bethune was the first black woman to head a federal agency.

The President invited many African American leaders to advise him. These unofficial advisers became known as the **Black Cabinet.** They included Robert Weaver and William Hastie, Harvard University graduates who rose to high positions within the Department of the Interior. Hastie later became a federal judge, and Weaver was the first African American Cabinet member.

Mary McLeod Bethune was another member of the Black Cabinet. The founder of what came to be known as Bethune Cookman College, she was a powerful champion of racial equality. In her view, the New Deal had created a "new day" for African Americans. She noted that African Americans gained unprecedented access to the White House and positions within the government during Roosevelt's presidency.

Nevertheless, Roosevelt did not always follow the advice of his Black Cabinet. Racial discrimination and injustice continued to plague African Americans. When the NAACP launched an energetic campaign in favor of a federal antilynching law, the President refused to support it. FDR told black leaders that he could not support an antilynching law, because if he did, southern Democrats "would block every bill I ask Congress to pass." Hence, no civil rights reforms became law during the 1930s.

Several New Deal measures also unintentionally hurt African Americans. Federal payments to farmers to produce fewer crops led white landowners to evict unneeded black sharecroppers from their farms. Even though they benefited from the WPA and other relief measures, African Americans often did not receive equal wages. Social Security and the Fair Labor Standards Act exempted domestic workers and farm laborers, two occupations in which African Americans were employed in great numbers.

 Checkpoint How did the New Deal affect African Americans?

Native Americans Benefit From Building Projects

Navajo medicine men attend the opening of a new hospital in Fort Defiance, Arizona, in 1938. *How was this project part of the Indian New Deal?*

The New Deal Affects Native Americans

Attempting to improve the lives of Native Americans, the Roosevelt administration made major changes in long-standing policies. The 1887 Dawes Act had divided tribal lands into smaller plots. By the early 1930s, it was clear that the act had worsened the condition of the people it was designed to help. Of the original 138 million acres American Indians had owned in 1887, only 48 million remained in American Indian hands, and much of it was too arid to farm. John Collier, the New Deal's Commissioner of Indian Affairs, warned that the Dawes Act was resulting in "total landlessness for the Indians."

To prevent further loss of land and improve living conditions for Native Americans, Collier developed the **Indian New Deal,** a program that gave Indians economic assistance and greater control over their own affairs. Collier got funding from New Deal agencies for the construction of new schools and hospitals and to create an Indian Civilian Conservation Corps. In addition, the Bureau of Indian Affairs, in a reversal of previous policies, encouraged the practice of Indian religions, native languages, and traditional customs. Collier also convinced Congress to pass the Indian Reorganization Act of 1934, considered the centerpiece of the Indian New Deal. This law restored tribal control over Native American land.

Although it did not immediately improve their standard of living, the Indian Reorganization Act gave Native Americans greater control over their destiny. But some New Deal measures actually hurt Native Americans. For example, federal authorities determined that large herds of sheep tended by the Navajos were causing soil erosion on the Colorado Plateau. As a result, the federal government enacted a Navajo Livestock Reduction program, which mandated that the Navajo sell or kill thousands of sheep. The Navajo deeply resented this act. They did not believe that their sheep threatened the soil and they did not trust the motives of government agents.

✔ **Checkpoint** In what ways did the New Deal alter the U.S. policies toward Native Americans?

The New Deal Creates a New Political Coalition

By the time he died in 1945, Roosevelt had been elected to four terms as President. His legendary political skills had united an unlikely group of Americans into a strong political force called the **New Deal coalition.** This coalition brought together southern whites, northern blue-collar workers—especially those with immigrant roots—poor midwestern farmers, and African Americans.

African American voting patterns show the importance of the New Deal coalition. Before the New Deal, most African Americans voted Republican, the party of Abraham Lincoln. Responding to the efforts of Franklin and Eleanor Roosevelt, African Americans began to vote Democratic during the 1930s. This trend was strongest in the West and the North. For example, in 1934, Arthur W. Mitchell, an African American Democrat, defeated Oscar De Priest, an African American Republican, to represent the largely black south side of Chicago. Mitchell became the first African American Democrat elected to Congress.

The New Deal coalition gave the Democratic Party a sizable majority in both houses of Congress. Before FDR's election, the Democrats had been the minority party in the House of Representatives for all but eight years since 1895. But from 1932 to 1995, the Democrats controlled the majority of seats in the House of Representatives for all but four years. The coalition that elected Roosevelt in 1932 went on to secure the White House for the Democrats in six of the next eight presidential elections.

African Americans Join New Deal Coalition

In Atlanta, African Americans register to vote in a Democratic primary election. *What percentage of African American voters voted Democratic in 1932? What was the percentage in 2004?*

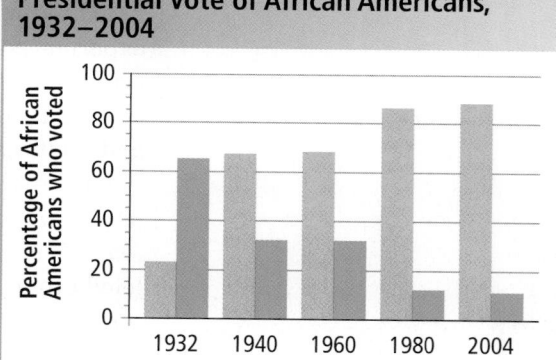

Presidential Vote of African Americans, 1932–2004

Percentage of African Americans who voted

100, 80, 60, 40, 20, 0

1932   1940   1960   1980   2004

■ Democrat   ■ Republican

SOURCES: Joint Center for Political and Economic Studies; Donald L. Grant, *The Way It Was in the South: The Black Experience in Georgia*; Sean J. Savage, *Roosevelt: The Party Leader, 1932–1945*; CNN.com

Besides forging a powerful political coalition, Roosevelt and the New Deal helped to unify the nation. Social and <u>ethnic</u> divisions, so much a part of the 1920s, diminished significantly during the 1930s. Immigrant communities, in particular, gained a greater sense of belonging to the mainstream. Programs such as the CCC and WPA allowed individuals of varied backgrounds to get to know one another, breaking down regional and ethnic prejudices. As one CCC worker observed:

Primary Source "The Civilian Conservation Corps is a smaller melting pot within the big one. We are thrown together in such a way that we have to get acquainted whether or not we want to. . . . Different races and nationalities look each other in the face, work and eat together for the first time. And it is a safe bet, we think, that this process many times results in the elimination of traditional prejudices based on ignorance and misinformation."

—C. W. Kirkpatrick, CCC worker

✓ **Checkpoint** How did New Deal policies affect ethnic and social divisions?

The Role of Government Expands

New Deal programs greatly increased the size and scope of the federal government. "For the first time for many Americans," writes historian William Leuchtenburg, "the federal government became an institution that was directly experienced. More than the state and local governments, it came to be *the* government." Moreover, the government began to do things it had never done before, from withdrawing taxes directly from workers' paychecks to distributing benefits to the elderly.

Though the New Deal did not end the depression, it did help restore the American economy. It created the foundation for sustained and stable growth. According to Pulitzer Prize–winning historian David Kennedy, "the unparalleled economic vitality of the post-1940 decades was attributable to many factors. But the [economic expansion] . . . owed much to the New Deal."

Playing a Larger Role in the Economy With the New Deal, the federal government broke from the tradition of laissez faire, or leaving the economy alone, which had characterized most of American history. Now the federal government accepted responsibility for spurring economic growth, or pump priming. For the first time, the government had acted as an employer of the unemployed and a sponsor of work projects. FDR accepted the idea that the federal government had to do something to get the economy going again, and Democrats and many Republicans agreed.

FDR's rejection of laissez-faire policies led a number of New Deal critics to accuse him of promoting socialism. However, many New Deal measures actually strengthened capitalism and helped make possible the economic boom of the post–World War II era. The FDIC and SEC restored Americans' trust in banks and the stock market. The Federal Housing Authority (FHA) provided low-interest loans, increasing homeownership.

The New Deal affected millions of workers and their families. The Wagner Act boosted union membership, which continued to grow after World War II. Minimum wage increases improved the purchasing power of minorities and those at the bottom rung of the economic ladder. New Deal legislation created child labor laws, workers' compensation laws, and unemployment insurance, programs that had important and enduring impacts on the U.S. economy.

TRACK THE ISSUE

THE ESSENTIAL?

What is the proper balance between free enterprise and government regulation of the economy?

In theory, a free-enterprise system should function with little government interference. In practice, though, our government often plays a strong economic role. How much government regulation of the economy is appropriate? Use the timeline below to explore this enduring issue.

1890 Sherman Antitrust Act
Congress tries to curb the power of monopolies.

1906 Pure Food and Drug Act
Progressive law regulates the safety of food and medicine.

1913 Federal Reserve Act
Federal Reserve system is established to control the money supply.

1933 Agricultural Adjustment Act
New Deal law pays farmers to reduce production, causing higher crop prices and farm profits.

2001 Tax Cuts
Government lowers taxes in an effort to promote economic growth.

Federal Social Welfare Spending

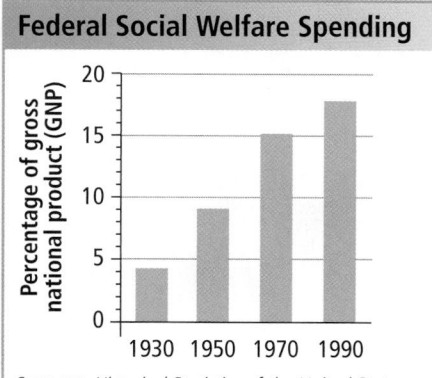

SOURCES: *Historical Statistics of the United States*; *Social Security Bulletin*; *Statistical Abstract of the United States*

 5.II.B.5

Activists protest plans to privatize Social Security.

DEBATE THE ISSUE

Social Security's Effectiveness The government manages retirement accounts for millions of Americans through the Social Security system. But with the coming retirement of millions of baby boomers, some people believe that Social Security can no longer achieve its original goals.

"Well, the system is facing serious financial problems, but more than that it has become an increasingly bad deal for today's workers. Workers are paying 12 1/2 percent of their income into a system that is providing a poorer and poorer return. It's a system in which workers don't own their assets, have no legal rights to their benefits, don't control their money, and a system that penalizes groups like African Americans and working women."

—Michael Tanner, Cato Institute

"Social Security is one of the most successful government programs. It has consistently provided a safety net for seniors so that retirees are able to support themselves through their retirement and pay for food, housing, and medical costs. By helping to support the elderly and vulnerable among us, Social Security provides Americans with the guarantee of security for life."

—Center for American Progress

 TRANSFER Activities

1. **Compare** Do you think that today's Center for American Progress would support or oppose New Deal laws like the AAA?

2. **Analyze Costs and Benefits** Compare the data on this page to the data in the Section 2 Social Security feature. Do you think that the costs of Social Security outweigh the benefits?

3. **Transfer** Use the following Web site to see a video, try a WebQuest, and write in your journal. **Web Code:** neh-8202

The New Deal had a great impact on rural Americans. Regional public-works projects, such as the TVA and Bonneville Dam, reduced flooding and provided water for irrigation. Along with the Rural Electrification Administration, these dams brought electricity to farmers in the Southeast and the Northwest. Rose Dudley Scearce of Shelby, Kentucky, recalled what the REA meant to her farm family:

Primary Source 66The first benefit we received from the REA was light, and aren't lights grand? My little boy expressed my sentiments when he said, 'Mother, I didn't realize how dark our house was until we got electric lights.' . . . Like the rest of the people, we changed our storage-battery radio into an electric radio. . . . Next we bought an electric refrigerator. . . . The next benefit we received from the current was our electric stove. . . . Now with a vacuum cleaner, I can even dust the furniture before I clean the carpet, the carpet gets clean, and I stay in good humor.99
—Rose Dudley Scearce, "What the REA Service Means to Our Farm House"

● **INFOGRAPHIC**

P·W·A and W·P·A PROJECTS

The Public Works Administration (PWA) and the Works Progress Administration (WPA) were New Deal government agencies that provided work relief for people who had lost their jobs during the depression.

Both agencies focused on large public-works projects that benefited local communities across the nation. Their combined efforts produced thousands of schools, hospitals, parks, bridges, dams, housing developments, libraries, and other public buildings. They also built or improved thousands of miles of roads and highways, installed sewer systems, and conducted environmental-conservation projects.

Thinking Critically
Analyze Besides giving jobs to the unemployed, describe other ways that PWA and WPA projects might have helped local economies.

Montana School for the Deaf and Blind

WA

Bonneville Dam

ID

Great Falls

MT

ND

Grand Coulee Dam

OR

Reforestation (Yellowstone National Park)

Denver Water Tunnel

WY

Pacific Ocean

Water Supply System (Eureka)

Golden Gate Bridge (San Francisco)

State Supreme Court (Carson City)

NV

Utah Highway Tunnel

CO

CA

UT

Central Valley Irrigation Project

Hoover Dam

Window Rock

Santa Fe Courthouse

AZ

Navajo Capital/ Indian Council

NM

Los Angeles Aqueduct

TX

San Antonio River Walk

Distance in miles
0   100   200   300   400

Creating a Welfare State "We are going to make a country in which no one is left out," Franklin Roosevelt once told Frances Perkins. The many programs he enacted to realize this goal led to the rise of a **welfare state** in the United States, a government that assumes responsibility for providing for the welfare of children and the poor, elderly, sick, disabled, and unemployed.

The creation of the American welfare state was a major change in government policy. With the exception of military veterans, most Americans had never received any direct benefits from the federal government. State and local governments, private charities, and families had long served as the safety net for needy Americans. True, the New Deal did not achieve FDR's goal of "a country in which no one is left out," because it exempted many Americans from Social Security and other programs. Still, the New Deal established the principle that the federal government was responsible for the welfare of all Americans. In the latter half of the twentieth century, the reach of government programs would grow greatly.

Cause and Effect

Causes

- Stock market crash
- Failure of farms and businesses
- Sharp decline in prices and production
- Failure of banks
- Massive unemployment and low wages
- Homelessness and Hoovervilles
- Drought, crop failures, and Dust Bowl

The New Deal

Effects

- Millions employed in new government programs
- Banking system is stabilized
- Regulated stock market restores confidence
- Social-insurance programs aid elderly and poor
- Agricultural subsidies help farmers
- Government takes more active role in economy

Connections to Today

- Social Security and other New Deal programs still exist
- Size and role of federal government still debated
- Costs and benefits of social welfare programs still debated

Analyze Cause and Effect The New Deal brought dramatic changes to the United States. *Identify one economic and one political effect of the New Deal.*

New Deal reforms provided the framework for the debate over the proper role of the federal government in the private lives of Americans. It energized liberals who would push for an even greater role for the federal government in future years. But it troubled conservatives who would argue that the expansion of the federal government limited American rights. Indeed, this very debate divides liberals and conservatives to this day.

Restoring the Environment Reared in New York State's beautiful Hudson River valley, Franklin Roosevelt had a great love of nature. As a child, FDR also loved outdoor sports and became an expert swimmer and sailor. A number of his New Deal programs, such as the CCC, aimed at restoring forests and preserving the environment. Other federal agencies started soil conservation efforts. Perhaps most visibly, New Dealers worked hard to end the Dust Bowl, a symbol of the degraded state of the land at the beginning of the depression.

Franklin Roosevelt also continued the conservation work of his cousin, President Theodore Roosevelt. Although funds were short, the government set aside about 12 million acres of land for new national parks, including Shenandoah National Park in Virginia, Kings Canyon National Park in California, and Olympic National Park in Washington State.

However, not all New Deal programs helped the environment. Several of the large public-works projects, such as the TVA and the string of dams along the Columbia River, had a mixed impact. The dams controlled floods, generated electric power, and provided irrigation, but they also upset the natural habitats of some aquatic life. Massive reservoirs created by these projects also displaced some people and destroyed some traditional Native American burial, hunting, and fishing grounds.

Changing the Nature of the Presidency In no area did FDR have a greater impact than on the office of the President itself. The expanding role of the government, including the creation of many new federal agencies, gave the executive branch much more power. New Deal administrators, such as Harry Hopkins, head of the WPA, commanded large bureaucracies with massive budgets and little supervision by Congress. Their authority increased Roosevelt's influence. Indeed, some commentators even began to speak of the rise of an imperial presidency, an unflattering comparison to the power exercised in the past by rulers of great empires.

FDR also affected the style of the presidency. His mastery of the radio captivated Americans. His close relations with the press assured a generally popular response to his projects from the major media. Because he served for such a long time and was such an outstanding communicator, FDR set a standard that future Presidents had a hard time fulfilling.

Later, during World War II, FDR's presidential power grew even greater. As commander in chief of the nation's armed forces, he exercised enormous authority over many aspects of life. Most Americans accepted the President's increased

FDR's Effect on the Presidency ☑ Quick Study

- Increased power of the President and the executive branch
- Made mass media, such as radio, an essential tool in advertising and promoting policies
- Expanded role of the President in managing the economy
- Expanded role of the President in developing social policy
- Won third and fourth terms, leading to passage of Twenty-second Amendment, which limited Presidents to two consecutive terms

authority as a necessary condition of wartime. But after the war, they sought to protect the delicate balance between the different branches of government and between the federal and state governments.

One way that Americans sought to guard against the growing power of the President was by amending the Constitution. When Roosevelt ran for an unprecedented third term in 1940, he knew that he had broken an unwritten rule, established by George Washington, that Presidents should serve only two terms. He won that election and then ran and won again in 1944. But after Roosevelt's death in 1945, there was a growing call for limiting a President's term in office. In 1951, the Twenty-second Amendment was ratified, limiting the President to two consecutive terms.

The Presidency After Roosevelt

Franklin Roosevelt had a dramatic impact on the role of the presidency. *Was FDR's impact positive or negative?*

✓ **Checkpoint** In what ways did the role of the federal government grow during Franklin Roosevelt's presidency?

SECTION 3 Assessment

Progress Monitoring *Online*
For: Self-test with vocabulary practice
Web Code: nea-0906

Comprehension

1. **Terms and People** What is the relationship between each of the following terms or people and the enduring significance of the New Deal?
   - Black Cabinet
   - Mary McLeod Bethune
   - Indian New Deal
   - New Deal coalition
   - welfare state

2. **NoteTaking Reading Skill: Identify Main Ideas** Use your concept web to answer the Section Focus Question: How did the New Deal change the social, economic, and political landscape of the United States for future generations?

Writing About History

3. **Quick Write: Draw Conclusions** After comparing information from different sources, the next step in synthesizing is to draw conclusions. Compare the photograph of Eleanor Roosevelt with the primary source on the section's opening page. Write a paragraph that describes Mrs. Roosevelt's personality.

Critical Thinking

4. **Recognize Cause and Effect** Why do you think African Americans suffered more extensive discrimination during the depression than during more prosperous times?

5. **Determine Relevance** Has the New Deal coalition affected politics in your community today? Explain your answer.

6. **Synthesize Information** Did the growth in the powers of the federal government during the New Deal benefit the nation? Explain your answer.

▲ The Wizard of Oz's
Dorothy, Tin Man,
and Scarecrow

SECTION

4

WITNESS HISTORY 🔊 AUDIO

"Somewhere Over the Rainbow"

Americans eager to escape the gloom of the depression regularly sought refuge in the fantasy world presented by the movies. One of their favorites was *The Wizard of Oz,* which opened in 1939. In an early scene, the farm girl Dorothy sings of better times:

❝Somewhere over the rainbow
Way up high,
There's a land that I've heard of
Once in a lullaby.

Somewhere over the rainbow
Skies are blue,
And the dreams that you dare to dream
Really do come true.

Some day I'll wish upon a star
And wake up where the clouds are far behind me.
Where troubles melt like lemon drops
Away above the chimney tops
That's where you'll find me.❞
— "Over the Rainbow," E. Y. Harburg, 1939

Culture of the 1930s

Core Curriculum Objectives

- **5.II.B.7a** Culture of the Depression: Literature
- **5.II.B.7b** Culture of the Depression: Music
- **5.II.B.7c** Culture of the Depression: Art

Terms and People

Frank Capra
Federal Art Project
mural

Dorothea Lange
John Steinbeck
Lillian Hellman

NoteTaking

Reading Skill: Identify Main Ideas and Details Complete a table like the one below to record examples of cultural or popular media.

Cultural or Popular Media	Example
Movies	

Why It Matters Mass entertainment, such as *The Wizard of Oz,* flourished during the New Deal years as Americans sought escape from the worries of the depression. And, for the first time, the government played an active role in the arts, creating programs that put artists to work. It was a golden age for entertainment, and the movies, music, and works of literature produced during this era hold a unique place in American culture. **Section Focus Question: How did the men and women of the depression find relief from their hardships in the popular culture?**

Movies and Radio Captivate Americans

Entertainment became big business during the 1930s. Large radio networks, such as NBC and CBS, were broadcasting giants while a cluster of film companies—including MGM, Warner Brothers, Twentieth Century Fox, and Paramount—dominated the silver screen. By 1935, two in three homes owned a radio; by the end of the decade, about nine in ten did. In 1939, nearly two thirds of all Americans attended at least one movie a week. Stars in both industries made fortunes and attracted loyal followings. Glossy fan magazines tracked the stars' personal and professional lives.

Enjoying Escapism Above all, when Americans went to the movies during the Great Depression, they did so as a means of escapism. They sought relief from their concerns through a good laugh, a good cry, a lyrical song, or by seeing good triumph over evil. *The Wizrd of Oz,* one of the most memorable depression-era films, delivered all four. It promised weary audiences that their dreams really would come true.

The big movie studios churned out musicals, romantic comedies, and gangster films. Children marveled at the colorful animation of Walt Disney's *Snow White and the Seven Dwarfs.* For a good scare, teens and young adults flocked to *Frankenstein.* Adults watched dancers Fred Astaire and Ginger Rogers glide effortlessly across the ballroom floor in *Top Hat.* And millions wept as they watched the stormy love affair between Clark Gable and Vivien Leigh in the Civil War epic *Gone With the Wind.*

Providing Social Commentary In the early 1930s, many films reflected the public's distrust of big business and government. Gangster movies, such as *Public Enemy* starring James Cagney, were very popular. These films showed a declining faith in government and law enforcement, with characters turning to crime to survive the depression. But as the New Deal restored confidence, the government regained its glow, and movies began portraying government officials as heroes. In 1935, Cagney portrayed an FBI agent who captured the bad guys in *G-Men.*

Other films focused on the strength of average Americans. Director **Frank Capra** was a leader of this genre. The characters in his films were everyday people struggling with the hardships of the time. In Capra's *Mr. Smith Goes to Washington,* actor James Stewart plays a junior senator who fights against the greed and corruption he finds in the nation's capital. Depression-era audiences cheered Capra's films, which celebrate American idealism and the triumph of the common man over the forces of adversity.

Radio's Golden Age The success of the movie industry was matched by that of radio. The national radio networks broadcast popular shows starring comedians such as Bob Hope and Jack Benny. Americans avidly followed soap operas,

Radio Captures the Nation
Americans united in their love for the radio and its stars, including mainstays George Burns and Gracie Allen (below).

variety shows, and humorists, such as Will Rogers. Dramatic shows were also popular. *The Lone Ranger* started its run in 1933 and ran for more than 20 years. The detective serial *The Shadow* began each thrilling episode with the haunting line, "Who knows what evil lurks in the hearts of men?"

In addition to providing entertainment, the family radio provided information. FDR used his fireside chats to explain and promote his New Deal programs. Newscasters delivered the daily news and political commentary.

On at least one occasion, radio listeners had a hard time recognizing the difference between news and entertainment. It happened on the night of October 30, 1938, when millions of Americans tuned in to a drama called *War of the World,* directed by Orson Welles. The Mercury Theatre broadcast was so realistic that many people believed that Martians were actually invading. Panic gripped areas of the country until announcers insisted that it was all make-believe.

Swinging to the Sounds of the Era Like films and radio shows, music provided a diversion from hard times. Whether listening to the radio at home or dancing in nightclubs, Americans enjoyed the popular music of the day. "Swing" music played by "big bands" topped the charts. Duke Ellington, Benny Goodman, Artie Shaw, Glenn Miller, and Jimmy and Tommy Dorsey were some of the top swing musicians, a term probably derived from Ellington's tune "It Don't Mean a Thing If It Ain't Got That Swing." *Your Hit Parade* and *Make Believe Ballroom*—the program that introduced disc jockeys—were just two of the radio shows that brought the latest tunes to listeners. The most popular vocalist of the era was Bing Crosby.

Latin music was very popular. The rhythms of the rumba and the samba had a special appeal for dancers, and Latin bands were prominently featured in films and on the radio. Folk and ethnic music also gained a following during the 1930s. Black singers focused on the harsh conditions faced by African Americans. Huddie Ledbetter, a folk singer known as Leadbelly, described experiences of African Americans with the songs "Cotton Fields" and "The Midnight Special." Woody Guthrie wrote ballads about the Okies, farmers who fled Dust Bowl states and headed to California. Guthrie's song "Dust Bowl Refugee" helped listeners understand the Okies' plight.

✓ **Checkpoint** **What were some of the most important popular cultural trends of the 1930s?**

Funding the Arts

The Federal Art Project poster (below) promotes an exhibition of works by WPA artists. William Gropper's mural, *Construction of a Dam,* was a tribute to the strength and dignity of labor inspired by the construction of two western dams.

The New Deal and the Arts

During the New Deal, the federal government provided funding for the arts for the first time in American history. Recognizing that many artists and writers faced dire circumstances, WPA administrator Harry Hopkins established a special branch of the WPA to provide artists with work. Programs such as the **Federal Art Project,** the Federal Writers' Project, and the Federal Theater Project offered a variety of job opportunities to artists.

In federally funded theaters, musicians and actors staged performances that were often free to the public. In a series of new state guidebooks, WPA writers recorded the history and folklore of the nation. Artists painted huge, dramatic **murals** on public buildings across the nation. These paintings celebrated the accomplishments of the workers who helped build the nation. Many of the murals can still be seen in public buildings today.

Photographers also benefited from federal arts programs. The Resettlement and Farm Security Administration (FSA) sought to document the plight of America's farmers. Roosevelt's top aide, Rexford Tugwell, told the head of the FSA, "Show the city people what it's like to live on the farm." Walker Evans and **Dorothea Lange** were among the FSA photographers who created powerful images of impoverished farmers and migrant workers, including Lange's famous photo "Migrant Mother."

Primary Source ❝When Dorothea took that picture that was the ultimate. She never surpassed it. . . . She has all the suffering of mankind in her but all the perseverance too. A restraint and a strange courage.❞
—Roy Stryker, FSA, on Dorothea Lange's "Migrant Mother"

Some members of Congress attacked the Federal Art programs for promoting radical values. Congressman J. Parnell Thomas described the Federal Writers' and Theater projects as "a hotbed for Communists." Eleanor Roosevelt and others defended the Federal Art programs on the grounds that they did not "believe in censoring anything." Nonetheless, congressional support for the programs declined. Although the Federal Art programs ceased to exist in the early 1940s, they set a precedent for further federal funding of the arts and humanities in the 1960s.

✓ **Checkpoint** In what ways did the New Deal support American arts?

California

One of several WPA murals in San Francisco's Coit Tower, *California* was painted by Maxine Albro, an artist who painted many scenes of Mexican life after studying with noted Mexican muralist Diego Rivera.

The Literature of the Depression

The literature of the 1920s, from authors such as F. Scott Fitzgerald and Ernest Hemingway, sometimes overshadowed the literature of the 1930s. Still, the depression era produced some memorable works.

During the depression, many writers drifted to the left and crafted novels featuring working-class heroes. They believed that the American economic system no longer worked and they blamed this failure on political and business leaders. Many artists of the 1930s saw "ordinary Americans" as the best hope for a better day.

The most famous novel of the 1930s was **John Steinbeck**'s *The Grapes of Wrath*. Steinbeck follows the fictional Joad family from their home in Oklahoma, which has been ravaged by Dust Bowl conditions, to California, where they hope to build a better life. But instead of the Promised Land, the Joads encounter exploitation, disease, hunger, and political corruption.

African American writers captured the special plight of blacks, facing both the depression and continuing prejudice. Richard Wright's *Native Son* explored racial prejudice in a northern urban setting. Wright was an outspoken critic of racial discrimination.

In New York, some important playwrights had their first successes during the New Deal period. **Lillian Hellman,** a New Orleans native, wrote several plays featuring strong roles for women. Hellman's plays *The Children's Hour, The Little Foxes,* and *Watch on the Rhine* are also notable for their socially conscious subject matter. Clifford Odets was another dramatist who achieved prominence in the 1930s. His plays *Waiting for Lefty* and *Awake and Sing!* chronicle the struggles of the working class during the Great Depression.

On a lighter note, many Americans devoured comic strips and comic books during the 1930s. Among the most popular comic strips were *Flash Gordon,* a science-fiction saga; *Dick Tracy,* a detective story; and *Superman,* the first great "superhero" comic. The success of *Superman,* which began in 1938, quickly led to a radio show and later to a popular television series and several feature films. *Superman* reassured Americans that ordinary citizens, like mild-mannered Clark Kent, could overcome evil.

 Checkpoint Describe the most notable works of literature of the 1930s.

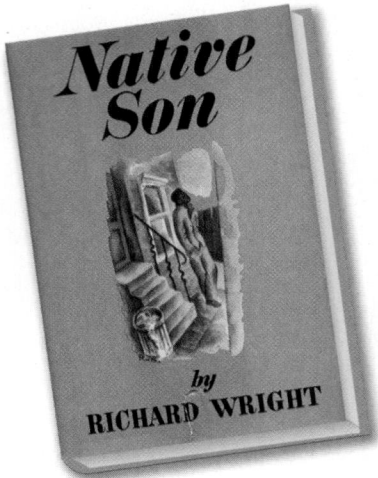

Native Son
Richard Wright's novel about the psychological pressures that lead a young black man to commit murder sold more than 200,000 copies in one month. During the 1930s, the author worked as a writer and editor for the Federal Writers' Project in Chicago.

SECTION 4 Assessment

Progress Monitoring *Online*
For: Self-test with vocabulary practice
Web Code: nea-0907

Comprehension

1. **Terms and People** For each item below, write a sentence explaining how it affected the people of the era.
   - *The Wizard of Oz*
   - Frank Capra
   - *War of the Worlds*
   - Federal Art Project

2. **NoteTaking Reading Skill: Identify Main Ideas and Details** Use your table to answer the Section Focus Question: How did the men and women of the depression find relief from their hardships in the popular culture?

Writing About History

3. **Quick Write: Make Generalizations** Compare *The Wizard of Oz* and *War of the Worlds.* Write a few sentences describing how both were escapist fare that helped people forget their troubles.

Critical Thinking

4. **Make Generalizations** What values did the movies and other popular entertainment of the depression reinforce for Americans?

5. **Identify Effects** How did federal support of the arts benefit both artists and the public?

6. **Identify Point of View** How did the work of New Deal era artists and writers contribute to our appreciation today of the New Deal?

5.II.B.7c

The Golden Age of Hollywood

The 1930s were a Golden Age for Hollywood—and for moviegoers. Depression-era audiences watched the latest Hollywood spectacles in beautiful theaters that were a far cry from today's multiplexes. Advancements in color and sound added even more realism to movies that depicted lives of glamour and adventure unknown to most Americans. But it was the outstanding quality of the movies that made the 1930s Hollywood's Golden Age.

▲ *King Kong* (1933)
King Kong was the thrilling adventure tale of a giant ape and the woman he loved. The film's innovative special effects helped make it a huge box-office hit.

◄ *Gone With the Wind* (1939)
Clark Gable was Rhett Butler, and Vivien Leigh was Scarlett O'Hara in the Civil War saga adapted from Margaret Mitchell's Pulitzer Prize–winning novel.

▲ *Swing Time* (1936)
Fred Astaire and Ginger Rogers became one of the silver screen's legendary teams as they danced their way through a series of popular musicals.

▼ *Dead End* (1937)
A gritty social drama about life in a Manhattan slum, *Dead End* starred Humphrey Bogart and introduced the Dead End Kids.

Thinking Critically

1. **Make Inferences** Why would people who were struggling just to get by enjoy films portraying extravagant upper-class lifestyles?

2. **Connect to Today** Do you think Hollywood movies give an accurate picture of contemporary American life? Explain.

Quick Study Guide

Progress Monitoring *Online*
For: Self-test with vocabulary practice
Web Code: nea-0908

■ New Deal Legislation

New Deal Program	Effects
Federal Deposit Insurance Corporation (FDIC), 1933	Guaranteed bank deposits up to $5,000 to ease banking crisis
National Recovery Administration (NRA), 1933	Established codes to regulate wages and prices, stimulate consumer activity, and promote fair competition
Securities and Exchange Commission (SEC), 1934	Regulated the stock market and restored investor confidence
Civilian Conservation Corps (CCC), 1933	Provided jobs for millions of young, single men on conservation projects
Public Works Administration (PWA), 1933	Sponsored large-scale government construction projects to create new jobs and improve the nation's infrastructure
Agricultural Adjustment Act (AAA), 1933	Paid subsidies to lower production on farms and raise crop prices
Tennessee Valley Authority (TVA), 1933	Built dams and hydroelectric plants in the Tennessee River valley to control flooding, generate power, and attract industry to the South
Home Owners' Loan Corporation (HOLC), 1933	Provided low-interest loans to homeowners who were unable to make mortgage payments

■ Effects of the New Deal

Immediate Effects
• Banking system is stabilized.
• Federal payments help farmers.
• Work-relief programs provide jobs.
• Social Security provides safety net.
• New Deal helps to unify the nation.

Long-term Effects
• Power of the presidency increases.
• Government takes active role in economy.
• New Deal coalition is powerful political force.
• Wagner Act protects workers and raises standard of living.
• Minorities and women gain positions in government.

■ Opposition to the New Deal

On the Left	On the Right
• New Deal does not do enough to end the depression.	• New Deal makes government too powerful.
• FDR's only concern is saving banks and big business.	• Increased government role in economy equals socialism.
• New Deal does not address redistribution of wealth.	• New Deal destroys free enterprise and individual freedom.
• New Deal does not help the elderly.	• New Deal creates huge national debt.

☑ Quick Study Timeline

	1932 More than 5,000 banks close	1933 FDR begins New Deal	1934 Dust Bowl worsens	1935 Social Security Act passed
In America				

Presidential Terms Herbert Hoover 1929–1933   Franklin D. Roosevelt 1933–1945

1932   **1935**

Around the World	1932 Aldous Huxley's *Brave New World* is published	1933 Nazis begin burning of books	1935 Italy invades Ethiopia

American Issues
•—•—• Connector

By connecting prior knowledge with what you have learned in this chapter, you can gradually build your understanding of enduring questions that still affect America today. Answer the questions below. Then, use your American Issues Connector study guide (or go online: www.PHSchool.com **Web Code:** neh-8203).

Issues You Learned About

● **Government's Role in the Economy** Political leaders disagree on how much control the government should have over the national economy.

1. Do you agree with the statement that many Americans probably thought that Herbert Hoover should have let his administration take a greater role in the economy? Explain.

2. Following the tradition of laissez faire, how did the federal government respond to the downturn of the economy under Hoover? How did it respond under Roosevelt?

● **American Indian Policy** The U.S. government has followed different policies toward Native Americans.

3. What did the Indian Removal Act demand? What action did some Indian tribes, that did not want to follow the Indian Removal Act, take?

4. What was the Dawes Act? Did it achieve its goals?

5. How did John Collier bring changes to American Indian life and culture?

● **Federal Power and States' Rights** At times, the national government may seem to go beyond its constitutional rights.

6. According to the Constitution, what powers does the national government have over trade? What powers does each state government have?

7. In response to the Supreme Court ruling in *Schechter Poultry* v. *United States,* one newspaper proclaimed this headline: "ROOSEVELT'S TWO YEARS' WORK KILLED IN TWENTY MINUTES." What did the headline mean?

Connect to Your World | New York

Government's Role in the Economy The Civilian Conservation Corps (CCC) worked on approximately 200 projects in New York in the 1930s. One of these was Gilbert Lake State Park, north of Oneonta, New York. When the camp opened in 1933, the area around Gilbert Lake was almost entirely wilderness. About 200 men worked to build walkways, roads and trails, cabins with stone fireplaces, picnic grounds, and dams to create lakes. The CCC workers lived in drafty tents and wooden barracks, receiving $30 a month, $25 of which was sent home to their families. Visitors to Gilbert Lake today can still enjoy the projects they completed. Research another site in New York that the CCC worked on, and create a brochure of its history.

1936
UAW stages sit-down strike

1939
Gone With the Wind breaks box-office records

1940
FDR reelected to third term

History *Interactive*
For: Interactive timeline
Web Code: nep-0910

1938

1941

1936	**1937**	**1939**	**1941**
Spanish Civil War begins	Pablo Picasso paints *Guernica*	Radio broadcasts WWII events	Japanese attack Pearl Harbor

Chapter Assessment

Terms and People

1. What was the **CCC**? How did it help individual Americans as well as the country?

2. Define **pump priming**. Give an example of pump priming in the second New Deal.

3. Define **collective bargaining** and **sit-down strikes**. How effective did workers find these methods?

4. Who was **Mary McLeod Bethune**? How did she feel about the New Deal?

5. What were the Federal Theater Project, the Federal Writers' Project, and the **Federal Art Project**? When and why did they come to an end?

Focus Questions

The focus question for this chapter is **How did the New Deal respond to the ravages of the depression and change the role of the federal government?** Build an answer to this big question by answering the focus questions for Sections 1 through 4 and the Critical Thinking questions that follow.

Section 1
6. How did the New Deal attempt to address the problems of the depression?

Section 2
7. What major issues did the second New Deal address?

Section 3
8. How did the New Deal change the social, economic, and political landscape of the United States for future generations?

Section 4
9. How did the men and women of the depression find relief from their hardships in the popular culture?

Critical Thinking

10. **Analyze Information** The first New Deal had three goals: relief, recovery, and reform. Choose one of the laws or programs created by the first New Deal and explain how the program met one, two, or all of these goals.

11. **Compare Points of View** Why did both the right and the left protest the New Deal?

12. **Summarize** What impact did New Deal programs and legislation have on the lives of industrial workers?

13. **Analyze Graphs** Study the graph below.

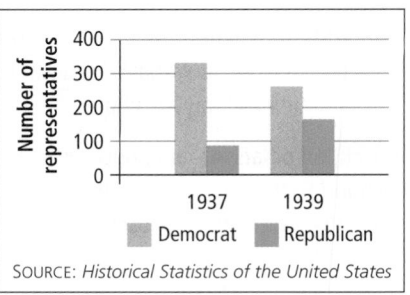

SOURCE: *Historical Statistics of the United States*

What political shift does this graph show? What caused this change?

14. **Draw Inferences** Why did New Deal work programs place a greater emphasis on employing men than women?

15. **Determine Relevance** What does the creation of a welfare state say about the changing priorities of the United States? Does this principle still hold today? Give examples to support your answer.

16. **Identify Point of View** Why might filmmakers have chosen to produce movies that drew on America's historical past?

17. **Evaluate Credibility of Sources** Do you think the work of depression-era writers can be read for historical value? Explain.

Writing About History

Synthesize Information In this chapter there are different images of President Roosevelt. One photograph might present FDR as weak, while another shows him as strong and confident. A cartoon might praise or criticize him. Write a few paragraphs in which you compare several different viewpoints on FDR, and then draw your own conclusion about him.

Prewriting
- Find four different images of Roosevelt that you will compare and contrast.
- Identify the main idea or viewpoint that is conveyed by each photograph or cartoon.

Drafting
- For each image, write a brief paragraph describing the main idea of the image.

- Then, write a paragraph in which you point out how the portrayals of FDR are similar and different.

- Finally, write a concluding paragraph in which you draw your own conclusions and make some generalizations about the nature of FDR.

Revising
- Use the guidelines on page SH11 of the Writing Handbook to revise your essay.

Regents DBQ Practice

The Tennessee Valley Authority

Was the Tennessee Valley Authority (TVA) a federal program that would bring jobs and electricity to rural towns in the region? Or was it an expensive, poorly planned federal program that taxpayers would have to shoulder and that would also cause many environmental problems? Use your knowledge of the TVA and Documents 1, 2, 3, and 4 to answer questions 1 through 4.

Document 1

". . . The continued idleness of a great national investment in the Tennessee Valley leads me to ask Congress for legislation necessary to enlist this project in the service of the people. It is clear that the Muscle Shoals development is but a small part of the potential public usefulness of the entire Tennessee River. Such use, if envisioned in its entirety, transcends mere power development; it enters the wide fields of flood control, soil erosion, afforestation, elimination from agricultural use of marginal lands, and distribution and diversification of industry."

—President Franklin D. Roosevelt, April 10, 1933

Document 2

Document 3

". . . The TVA has therefore appeared to be on the side of the angels in the controversy between it and the utilities. But the conservation program of the TVA is only a masquerade. It has no functional connection with the power program of the Authority, and the amount spent on it is only an insignificant portion of the Authority's total expenditures. Other departments of government, both state and national, are charged with the duty of caring for soil erosion and are doing such work effectively without the building of dams and power facilities. . . . The American people are paying more than half a billion dollars for eleven dams, chiefly designed to supply power to one area. But this power is to be supplied to this area at less than cost. . . . [The] TVA will operate annually at a deficit, and these deficits must . . . be paid for out of the pockets of the taxpayers."

—From "Political Power" by Wendell L. Willkie from *Atlantic Monthly* 160 (August 1937) pp. 211–214

Document 4

"One of TVA's original missions was to manage the region's natural resources, but the agency has long invoked the ire of environmentalists. TVA . . . was the leading promoter of destructive coal strip-mining. . . . TVA still remains the nation's worst violator of the Clean Air Act. The agency, in fact, is the largest emitter among eastern utilities of nitrogen oxide (NOx), which causes smog. It is the third largest emitter of sulfur dioxide (SO_2) and carbon dioxide (CO_2), which has been identified as the leading cause of global warming. TVA's nuclear program has been so plagued with safety and economic problems that consumer activist Ralph Nader in 1998 declared: 'The TVA . . . has the most expensive set of nuclear reactors, has a debt of $29 billion, has the poorest safety record with TVA reactors spending more time on the Nuclear Regulatory Commission's watch list than any other utility.'"

— "Restructure TVA: Why the Tennessee Valley Authority Must Be Reformed" by Richard Munson (September 17, 2001)

---

1. Which document is a secondary source that criticizes the environmental impact of the Tennessee Valley Authority?
(1) Document 1
(2) Document 2
(3) Document 3
(4) Document 4

2. According to Documents 2 and 3, why were taxpayers concerned about the Tennessee Valley Authority?
(1) It provided cheap electricity only to people in Tennessee.
(2) Taxpayers demanded an investigation because it operated at a deficit.
(3) Taxpayers in Tennessee wanted the government to promise better flood control.
(4) It did not build enough dams to provide adequate electricity.

3. In Document 1, what message is President Roosevelt trying to convey to Congress?
(1) He wanted Congress to view the TVA as a way to control the region's environmental problems.
(2) He wanted Congress to build the TVA only to provide electricity.
(3) He wanted Congress to provide money to the region's farmers.
(4) He wanted Congress to plan many additional watershed projects throughout the country.

4. Writing Task Who was right about the impact of the Tennessee Valley Authority: President Roosevelt or his critics? Use your knowledge of the chapter and evidence from the primary sources above to support your opinion.

NY Connect to New York

The United States Military Academy at West Point

In 1802, President Thomas Jefferson signed an act of Congress establishing the United States Military Academy along the Hudson River in West Point, New York. Originally founded as a school for military engineers, the West Point Academy has developed into one of the most famous military schools in the world. Some of West Point's most noted alumni played key roles in World War II.

George S. Patton, a 1909 graduate, was one of the first members of the United States Tank Corps in World War I. He enthusiastically supported the use of the new tank technology in warfare. Particularly famous are the victories of the Third Army armored units under Patton's leadership, which achieved many high-profile victories against the Germans. The Third Army liberated 81,522 square miles of territory in Europe over the course of the war.

Dwight D. Eisenhower, who graduated in 1915, directed the Allied Forces landing in North Africa in November 1942. In this unit, you will learn about Eisenhower's command of the Allied landing in France on D-Day, one of the turning points of the war. He went on to become the thirty-fourth president of the United States, leading the nation from 1953 to 1961.

Early in his military career, Eisenhower had served under yet another important World War II figure who attended West Point—Douglas MacArthur, a 1903 graduate. MacArthur served in World War I, and then returned to West Point as superintendent, where he worked to improve the school's curriculum, teaching methods, and standards. During World War II, he led America and its allies in the Pacific to victory over Japan.

These men came from different backgrounds, but they all trained for their pivotal roles in American history at the prestigious West Point Academy in New York, overlooking the scenic Hudson River. West Point celebrated its bicentennial in 2002, and continues to train future military leaders.

The leaders mentioned above are just a few of the Americans you will learn about who used their skills and strength to confront the challenge of fighting the most deadly conflict the world has seen—World War II. The United States would step onto the center stage of world events in fighting this war and forging a future in its aftermath.

WORLD WAR II AND POSTWAR AMERICA

CONTENTS

This famous photo, taken in New York City's Times Square, captured the nation's joy at the end of World War II. ▶

A Rendezvous With Destiny

In the 1930s, Adolf Hitler, a ruthless dictator, rose to power in Germany. Early in 1939, American President Franklin Roosevelt contrasted American life with life under a dictatorship like Hitler's:

"Dictatorship, however, involves costs which the American people will never pay: The cost of our spiritual values. . . . The cost of having our children brought up, not as free and dignified human beings, but as pawns molded and enslaved by a machine. . . . Once I prophesied that this generation of Americans had a rendezvous with destiny. That prophecy comes true. To us much is given; more is expected."

—Franklin Roosevelt, State of the Union Address, January 4, 1939

Listen to the Witness History *audio to hear more about World War II.*

◀ German dictator Adolf Hitler at a Nazi Party rally in the 1930s

Button for the America First Committee, an isolationist group

Japanese "Zero" plane

Core Curriculum Preview

Chapter Focus Question: What events caused World War II, and how did the United States become involved?

Section 1

Dictators and War 4.II.D, 5.I.B.1, 6.I.A.3, 6.I.B.1, 6.I.B.2

Section 2

From Isolation to Involvement 6.I.A.1, 6.I.A.4, 6.I.B.3, 6.I.B.4

Section 3

America Enters the War 6.I.C.1, 6.I.C.2a, 6.I.C.2b, 6.I.C.2c, 6.I.C.2f

Use the ☑ **Quick Study Timeline** at the end of this chapter to preview chapter events.

Board game that spread Nazi ideals to German children

Note Taking Study Guide *Online*
For: Note Taking and American Issues Connector
Web Code: nee-8301

▲ Hitler's manifesto, *Mein Kampf*

WITNESS HISTORY AUDIO

Hitler's Brutal Determination

For the German dictator Adolf Hitler, war was an ennobling experience. War united a nation, demanded righteous sacrifices, and culminated in territorial acquisitions. Hitler believed that there was no morality in war, just victory and defeat. He instructed his generals:

❝The victor will not be asked afterwards whether he told the truth or not. When starting and waging a war it is not right that matters, but victory. Close your hearts to pity. Act brutally. Eighty million people [Germans] must obtain what is their right. Their existence must be made secure. The stronger man is right.❞
—Adolf Hitler, August 1939

◄ Hitler speaks to the German people.

Dictators and War

 Core Curriculum Objectives

- **4.II.D** The search for peace and arms control: 1914–1930
- **5.I.B.1** Post-World War I recession
- **6.I.A.3** Spanish Civil War: war technology
- **6.I.B.1** Aggressions of Japan, Germany, Italy: 1932–1940
- **6.I.B.2** Appeasement: The Munich Conference (1938)

Terms and People

totalitarianism
Joseph Stalin
Benito Mussolini
Adolf Hitler
antisemitic

Spanish Civil War
appeasement
Anschluss
Munich Pact

NoteTaking

Reading Skill: Summarize As you read, summarize the actions in the 1930s of each of the countries listed in the table below.

Soviet Union	Italy	Germany	Japan

Why It Matters The effects of World War I and the Great Depression touched almost every corner of the world. In some countries, these upheavals led to the rise of a new kind of brutal dictatorship—the totalitarian state. Led by aggressive dictators, these states would destroy the peace established after World War I and spark a new, even deadlier, global conflict. **Section Focus Question: Why did totalitarian states rise after World War I, and what did they do?**

A Bitter Peace Unravels

In November 1918, World War I ended when Germany surrendered to the Allies. In 1919, delegates from 27 nations met in Versailles to hammer out a peace agreement, but only Britain, France, and the United States had a real say in most of the important decisions. Germany and Russia were not even present. From the first, many Germans resented the resulting Treaty of Versailles. Other nations also grumbled over the peace settlements. Italy and Japan, both Allies, had expected far more land for their sacrifices. The war that American President Woodrow Wilson had called "a war to end all wars" had left behind a mountain of bitterness, anger, frustration, and despair, often capped by a burning desire for revenge.

During the 1920s many nations, new and old, moved steadily toward democracy and freedom. Others, however, took the opposite direction, embracing repressive dictatorships and **totalitarianism,** a theory of government in which a single party or leader controls the economic, social, and cultural lives of its people. Throughout history ideologies, but his sharpest assaults were against communists and Jews. Hitler was violently **anti-Semitic,** or prejudiced against Jewish people. Anti-Semitism had troubled Europe for centuries, mainly motivated by religious intolerance and economic resentment. In the late nineteenth century, new pseudo-scientific theories about Jews as a race, along with the rise of nationalism, caused Jews to be marginalized as ethnic outsiders. Hitler believed and spread this type of thinking. He preached that the greatest threat confronting Germany was the Jewish people who lived there. In *Mein Kampf,* which quickly became a national bestseller, Hitler presented a blueprint of his hatreds and plans for world domination.

Hitler Seizes Power The shattered German economy—the widespread unemployment, homelessness, and hunger—played into the Nazis' hands. Recognizing the power of Hitler's party, in January 1933, the president of the Weimar Republic appointed Hitler chancellor of Germany. Over the next two years, Hitler became president as well as chancellor, consolidated his power, and ruled unchecked by the Reichstag (RĪKS tahg), or the German parliament. By 1935, the democratic institutions of the Weimar Republic were silenced, and Hitler spoke alone as the voice of Germany.

Like Stalin and Mussolini, Hitler was the symbol of his totalitarian regime. Aided by a secret police that crushed all opposition, a state-controlled press that praised his accomplishments, and a state-controlled educational system that

Vocabulary Builder

ideology—(ī dee AHL uh jee) *n.* a system of ideas that guides an individual, movement, or political program

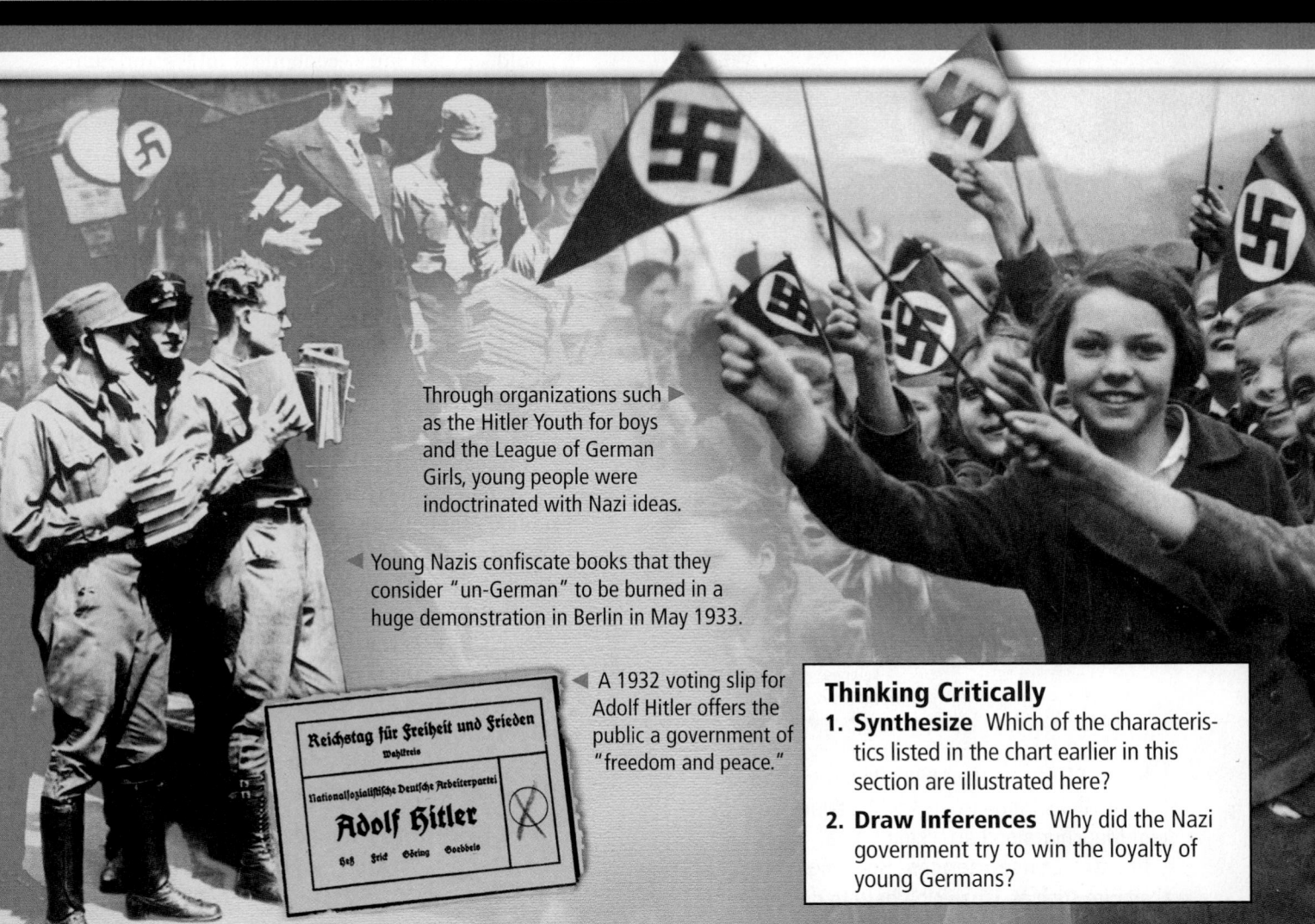

Through organizations such as the Hitler Youth for boys and the League of German Girls, young people were indoctrinated with Nazi ideas.

Young Nazis confiscate books that they consider "un-German" to be burned in a huge demonstration in Berlin in May 1933.

A 1932 voting slip for Adolf Hitler offers the public a government of "freedom and peace."

Reichstag für Freiheit und Frieden
Wahlkreis

Nationalsozialistische Deutsche Arbeiterpartei

Adolf Hitler ☒

Heß   Frick   Göring   Goebbels

Thinking Critically
1. **Synthesize** Which of the characteristics listed in the chart earlier in this section are illustrated here?

2. **Draw Inferences** Why did the Nazi government try to win the loyalty of young Germans?

indoctrinated the young, Hitler assumed a godlike aura. One German described the emotions of seeing Hitler address a crowd:

Primary Source "There stood Hitler in a simple black coat and looked over the crowd. . . . How many look up to him with a touching faith! As their helper, their savior, their deliverer from unbearable distress—to him who rescues . . . the scholar, the clergyman, the farmer, the worker, the unemployed, who leads them from the [jumbled political] parties back into the nation."
—Louise Solmitz, a schoolteacher who observed an early Nazi rally

By the late 1930s, Hitler's economic policies, including rearmament and massive public-works projects, had ended the depression in Germany. Many Germans followed his lead and cheered for him at Nazi rallies. Meanwhile, his political initiatives restricted freedom. He openly attacked Jewish people, communists, and socialists.

Militarists Gain Power in Japan In Japan, as in Germany, the 1920s was a period of increased democracy and peaceful change. The Japanese government reduced the power of the military, passed laws to give all men the right to vote, legalized trade unions, and allowed several diverse political parties to be established. This period ended when the Great Depression discredited Japan's civilian leaders in the 1930s.

Reasserting their traditional powers, military leaders argued that expansion throughout Asia would solve Japan's economic troubles and guarantee future security. Throughout the 1930s, the military played a significant role in shaping Japanese civilian and military policy.

Japan, however, did not become a totalitarian dictatorship. No charismatic leader like Stalin or Hitler emerged. Instead, Japan continued as a constitutional monarchy headed by a mainly aloof emperor.

The Japanese Expand Their Empire As the power shifted toward military control, Japan started on a course of aggressive military expansion. In 1931, Japan attacked Manchuria (man CHUR ee uh), a region in northeastern China, and established a puppet state. The new nation was named Manchukuo (man choo kwoh). Japan controlled its domestic and foreign policies, as well as its abundant natural resources. In 1937, Japan moved against China, gaining control over major Chinese railroad links and coastal areas. In the then-capital city of Nanjing, Japanese soldiers acted with such brutality—murdering more than 200,000 residents and burning a large section of the city—that the incident became known as the "Rape of Nanjing."

✔ **Checkpoint** How did the Great Depression affect political life in Germany and Japan?

Geography *Interactive*
For: Interactive map
Web Code: nep-1002

Japanese Expansion, 1931–1939

SOVIET UNION

Miller Projection
0   200   400 mi
0   200 400 km

MONGOLIA

Manchuria
(Manchukuo)

Beijing

Korea   Sea of Japan   JAPAN

Huang River

Yellow Sea

Tokyo

Osaka

CHINA   Nanjing

Chang River   Shanghai

Pacific Ocean

Taiwan

Hong Kong
(Britain)

South China Sea

	Japanese Empire, 1930
	Japanese sphere of influence, 1930
	Japanese conquests, 1931–1933
	Japanese conquests, 1937–1939

Map Skills In the 1930s, Japan tried to increase its influence in Asia by taking control of Manchuria and attacking China.
Predict Consequences How might an empire such as Japan's be hard to defend?

Dictators Turn to Aggression

In the 1930s, Italy and Germany resorted to acts of aggression similar to those of Japan in Asia. Throughout the decade, neither the League of Nations nor democratic nations succeeded in stopping the aggression. It was a time that recalled a line from Irish poet William Butler Yeats: "The best lack all conviction and the worst are full of passionate intensity."

Weakness of the League of Nations In many ways, the League of Nations never recovered from America's refusal to join it. The League was also handicapped by its own charter. It had no standing army and no real power to enforce its decrees. It was only as strong as its members' resolve, and during the worldwide depression of the 1930s, those members lacked resolve. When aggressive nations began to test the League, they discovered that the organization was long on words and short on action.

Hitler and Mussolini Threaten the Peace From the first, Hitler focused on restoring Germany's strength and nullifying the provisions of the Treaty of Versailles. From 1933 to 1936, he rebuilt the German economy and dramatically enlarged the army, navy, and air force in direct defiance of the Treaty of Versailles. In the mid-1930s, Hitler began to move toward his goal of reunifying all Germanic people into one Reich, or state. He spoke often of the need for Germany to expand to gain *Lebensraum* (LAY buhns rowm), or living space, for its people. In 1935, he reclaimed the Saar (sahr) region from French control. In 1936, in a direct challenge to the League, he sent German troops into the Rhineland. The League failed to respond.

Meanwhile, Mussolini commenced his own imperial plans. In 1935, Italy invaded Ethiopia, an independent country in east Africa. Its emperor, Haile Selassie (HĪ luh suh lah SEE), appealed to the League of Nations for support. The organization did almost nothing, and Ethiopia fell.

Fighting Breaks Out in Spain Fascists were also victorious in the **Spanish Civil War,** a bloody conflict that raged from 1936 until 1939. The Nationalists, who had fascist tendencies, rebelled against Spain's democratic Republican government. Both Hitler and Mussolini sent military and economic aid to the Nationalist leader, General Francisco Franco, using the conflict to test some of their new military technology. Though the Soviet Union provided some support for the Republican side, France, Britain, and the United States remained largely on the sidelines, deploring the bloodshed but refusing to provide weapons to the Republican forces.

> ✓ **Checkpoint** Why did the League of Nations fail to halt German and Italian aggression?

Aggression Goes Unchecked

The policy that France and Britain pursued against aggressive nations during the 1930s is known as **appeasement.** It is a policy of granting concessions to a potential enemy in the hope that it will maintain peace. Unfortunately,

---

HISTORY MAKERS

Benito Mussolini (1883–1945)
Adolf Hitler (1889–1945)
Benito Mussolini's involvement in radical politics began when he was a young man. In 1919, he formed the Fascist Party and quickly gained followers with his powerful speaking style and by terrorizing opponents. Other world leaders criticized him when he sent Italian armies to invade Ethiopia in 1935. Only Germany's Adolf Hitler supported the move, and the two leaders became allies.

Before World War I, Adolf Hitler lived in Vienna and tried to make his living as an artist. During the war, he fought for Germany and was wounded several times. In 1933, Hitler became head of the German government. He quickly took absolute power using propaganda and violence. Though never close, he and Benito Mussolini supported each other in their efforts to control Europe.

NoteTaking

Reading Skill: Identify Main Ideas Use a concept web like the one below to record the main ideas about the policies of Great Britain, France, and the United States toward aggressive nations.

Appeasement at Munich

British prime minister Neville Chamberlain greets Hitler at the Munich Conference in 1938. Historians still debate why Britain and France pursued the policy of appeasement leading up to World War II.

appeasement only spurred the fascist leaders to become more bold, adventurous, and aggressive.

Why did France and Britain appease the fascist powers? There were a number of reasons. World War I was so horrible that some leaders vowed never to allow another such war to break out. Other leaders believed that the Soviet Union posed a greater threat than Nazi Germany. They maintained that a strong Germany would provide a buffer against the Soviet menace. Still other leaders questioned the resolve of their own people and their allies—particularly the United States.

The United States played an important role in this appeasement policy. Although, in the 1930s, President Franklin Roosevelt pursued a Good Neighbor policy with Latin America and improved relations with the Soviet Union, he did not take a forceful line against German aggression. Instead, the country concerned itself with its own economic troubles and embraced a policy of isolationism.

Hitler took advantage of the lack of commitment and unity among France, Britain, and the United States. In the spring of 1938, he brought Austria into his Reich. Austria was given little choice but to accept this union, called the **Anschluss** (AHN shloos). In the fall, Hitler turned toward the Sudetenland, a portion of western Czechoslovakia that was largely populated by ethnic Germans.

Many people expected the conflict over the Sudetenland to lead to a general war. But once again, Britain and France appeased Germany. At the Munich Conference with Hitler, British prime minister Neville Chamberlain and French premier Edouard Daladier sacrificed the Sudetenland to preserve the peace. On his return to London, Chamberlain told a cheering crowd that the **Munich** (MYOO nihk) **Pact,** the agreement reached at the conference, had preserved "peace for our time." He was wrong. It merely postponed the war for 11 months.

 Checkpoint Why did Britain, France, and the United States not stop fascist aggression in the 1930s?

SECTION 1 Assessment

Progress Monitoring *Online*
For: Self-test with vocabulary practice
Web Code: nea-1003

Comprehension

1. **Terms and People** Write several sentences describing what the items listed below have in common.
   - totalitarianism
   - Joseph Stalin
   - Benito Mussolini
   - Adolf Hitler
   - anti-Semitic
   - Anschluss

2. **NoteTaking Reading Skill: Summarize** Use your table and concept web to answer the Section Focus Question: Why did totalitarian states rise after World War I, and what did they do?

Writing About History

3. **Quick Write: Analyze Primary Sources** Reread the Primary Source in this section describing the crowd at one of Hitler's speeches. Write one paragraph analyzing the source. Consider the following questions: What key words are used to describe Hitler? What do these words suggest about how the crowd viewed Hitler?

Critical Thinking

4. **Recognize Effects** How did World War I contribute to the rise of dictators in Europe?

5. **Make Comparisons** How were Germany and Japan similar in the 1930s? How were they different?

6. **Express Problems Clearly** How did the policy of appeasement encourage aggression?

▲ Women protesting the Lend-Lease Act

WITNESS HISTORY 🔊 AUDIO

An Isolationist Voice

As war erupted in Europe, Americans debated what stance the United States should take on the global conflict. Charles A. Lindbergh, the popular aviation hero, felt strongly that it would be a mistake for the United States to enter the new war in Europe:

❝We must band together to prevent the loss of more American lives in these internal struggles of Europe. . . . Modern war with all its consequences is too tragic and too devastating to be approached from anything but a purely American standpoint. We should never enter a war unless it is absolutely essential to the future welfare of our nation. . . . Our safety does not lie in fighting European wars. It lies in our own internal strength, in the character of the American people and of American institutions.❞

—Charles Lindbergh, radio address,
September 15, 1939

From Isolation to Involvement

 Core Curriculum Objectives

- **6.I.A.1** Isolation: causes of disillusion and pacifism
- **6.I.A.4** FDR's quarantine speech
- **6.I.B.3** German attack on Poland; start of World War II in Europe
- **6.I.B.4** Gradual United States involvement

Terms and People

blitzkrieg	Neutrality Act of 1939
Axis Powers	Tripartite Pact
Allies	Lend-Lease Act
Winston Churchill	Atlantic Charter

NoteTaking

Reading Skill: Sequence Sequence the major events described in the section in a timeline.

Germany invades Poland.   Atlantic Charter issued.

Sept. 1939   Aug. 1941

Why It Matters While Britain and France appeased the dictator in Germany at Munich, American President Franklin Roosevelt condemned aggression in Asia but did little to stop it. As war exploded in Europe, it became increasingly difficult for the United States to maintain its neutrality. Once again, Americans would have to decide what role they were willing to play in shaping world events. **Section Focus Question: How did Americans react to events in Europe and Asia in the early years of World War II?**

Roosevelt Opposes Aggression

The unrestrained violence of the 1937 Japanese attack on China shocked Americans, even before the notorious Rape of Nanjing in December 1937. Japan attacked without a declaration of war. Its planes rained terror on Chinese cities, especially Shanghai and Nanjing. The Japanese had even killed three American sailors when Japanese warplanes sank the United States gunboat *Panay* on the Chang River.

In the midst of these bloody events, President Franklin Roosevelt criticized Japan's aggression in a speech in Chicago on October 5, 1937. He lamented the "reign of terror and international lawlessness," the bombing of civilian populations, and the horrible acts of cruelty. Speaking in a city where American isolationist sentiments were strong, Roosevelt suggested that no part of the world was truly isolated from the rest of the world. He warned:

> **Primary Source**   **"**When an epidemic of physical disease starts to spread, the community approves and joins in a quarantine of the patients in order to protect the health of the community against the spread of the disease. . . . War is a contagion, whether it be declared or undeclared. It can engulf states and peoples remote from the original scene of hostilities. We are determined to keep out of war, yet we cannot insure ourselves against the disastrous effects of war and the dangers of involvement.**"**
> —President Franklin Roosevelt, Quarantine speech, October 5, 1937

Roosevelt's solution for stopping aggression involved an informal alliance of the peace-loving nations, but he did not suggest what steps the peaceful nations should take in quarantining the aggressive ones. Roosevelt's speech was widely criticized, and for a time, the President backed away from his more interventionist stance. The speech did, however, alert some Americans to the threat Japan posed to the United States.

✔ **Checkpoint** How did President Roosevelt react to Japan's aggression in China in the late 1930s?

War Erupts in Europe

Roosevelt's words failed to prevent Japan from extending its control over much of China. Similarly, France and Britain's efforts to appease Hitler in Europe failed to limit the dictator's expansionist plans. By the end of 1938, even the leaders of France and Britain realized that Hitler's armed aggression could only be halted by a firm, armed defense. The urgency of the situation grew in the spring of 1939 when Hitler violated the Munich Pact by absorbing the remainder of Czechoslovakia into his German Reich.

Hitler Launches a Blitzkrieg Against Poland Finally, British and French leaders saw the need to take action. They vowed not to let Hitler take over another country without consequences. Realizing that Hitler's next move would be against Poland, Britain and France signed an alliance with Poland, guaranteeing aid if Hitler attacked. Hitler, however, was more concerned about war with the Soviet Union than with Britain and France. Not wanting to fight a war on two fronts, Germany signed the Nazi-Soviet Nonaggression Pact with the Soviets on August 23, 1939. The two former rivals publicly promised not to

The German Juggernaut Rolls Through Europe

As the map on the next page shows, the Nazi war machine rampaged through Europe from 1939 through 1941. Below, victorious German troops parade through the Arc de Triomphe in Paris, France (left), after Nazi tanks had rolled through Belgium (right).

attack one another. Secretly, they agreed to invade and divide Poland and recognize each other's territorial ambitions. The public agreement alone shocked the West and guaranteed a German offensive against Poland.

War came to Europe in the early hours of September 1, 1939, when a massive German **blitzkrieg** (BLIHTS kreeg), or sudden attack, hit Poland from three directions. *Blitzkrieg* means "lightning war." It was a relatively new style of warfare that emphasized the use of speed and firepower to penetrate deep into the enemy's territory. The newest military technologies made it devastatingly effective. Using a coordinated assault by tanks and planes, followed by motorized vehicles and infantry, Germany broke through Poland's defenses and destroyed its air force. The situation became even more hopeless on September 17 when the Soviet Union invaded Poland from the east. Although France and Britain declared war against Germany, they did nothing to help save Poland. By the end of the month, a devastated Poland fell in defeat.

France Falls to the Axis Powers Europe was at war, just as it had been 21 years earlier. The **Axis Powers** eventually included Germany, Italy, Japan, and several other nations. The **Allies** included Britain, France, and eventually many other nations, including the Soviet Union, the United States, and China. But after the Polish campaign, the war entered an eight-month period of relative quiet, known in Britain as the "phony war." Things would not remain quiet for long, however.

The next storm erupted with raging fury in the spring of 1940. Germany's nonaggression pact with the Soviet Union freed Hitler to send his army west. On April 9, 1940, Germany attacked Denmark and Norway. The two countries fell almost immediately. On May 10, he sent his blitzkrieg forces into the

A woman weeps as she salutes her new rulers.

German Aggression, 1936–1941

Geography *Interactive*
For: Interactive map
Web Code: nep-1004

Legend:
- Axis Powers
- Areas taken over by Germany, 1936–1939
- Areas under Axis control, 1941
- Areas under Allied control, 1941
- Neutral nations
- Axis troop movements
- Maginot Line
- Major site of German bombing during the Battle of Britain
- 1937 borders

Conic Projection
0   200   400 mi
0   200   400 km

Map Skills In 1939, Hitler used force, rather than diplomatic gymnastics to add territory to the German Reich.

1. **Locate:** (a) Sudetenland, (b) Poland, (c) Vichy France

2. **Location** What made Poland a difficult ally for France and Britain to protect?

3. **Synthesize Information** How does this map illustrate the dire situation of the Allies in 1941?

Netherlands, Belgium, and Luxembourg. The small nations fell like tumbling dominoes. Hitler seemed invincible; his army unstoppable.

Hitler next set his sights on France. France had prepared for Germany's invasion by constructing an interconnected series of fortresses known as the Maginot Line along its border with Germany. Additionally, France had stationed its finest armies along its border with Belgium—the route that Germany had used to attack France in 1914. In between the Maginot Line and Belgium lay the Ardennes, a hilly, forested area that military experts considered invasion proof.

But once again the military experts were wrong. In early May 1940, German tanks rolled through the Ardennes, ripped a hole in the thin French line there, and raced north toward the English Channel. The German plan involved attacking the French and British forces from the front and the rear and trapping them against the channel. It almost worked. Only a few tactical German mistakes gave Britain enough time to evacuate its forces from the French port of Dunkirk. Some 338,000 British and French troops escaped, to Britain. Had they not escaped, it is doubtful if Britain could have remained in the war.

The Miracle of Dunkirk was a proud moment for Britain, but as the new prime minister **Winston Churchill** cautioned Parliament, "wars are not won by evacuations." Although the British army escaped, the Germans took Paris and forced the French to surrender in the same railway car that the French had used for the German surrender in 1918. France was then divided into two sections: a larger northern section controlled by the Germans and known as Occupied France, and a smaller southern section administered by the French and known as Unoccupied France, or Vichy France, after its capital city. Although Vichy France was officially neutral, it collaborated with the Nazis.

The Battle of Britain Is Fought in the Air France had fallen to Hitler in just 35 days. Hitler next turned his fury on Britain. After the evacuation at Dunkirk, Churchill made it clear that he had no intention of continuing the policy of appeasement. He told his nation:

> **Primary Source** "We shall go on to the end. We shall fight in France, we shall fight on the seas and oceans, we shall fight with growing confidence and growing strength in the air, we shall defend our island, whatever the cost may be, we shall fight on the beaches, we shall fight on the landing grounds, we shall fight in the fields and in the streets, we shall fight in the hills; we shall never surrender."
>
> —Winston Churchill, June 4, 1940

Churchill's words stirred his nation as the British readied themselves for battle. Hitler's plan to invade Britain, codenamed Operation Sea Lion, depended upon Germany's Luftwaffe, or air force, destroying the British Royal Air Force and gaining control over the skies above the English Channel. The Battle of Britain, then, was an air battle, fought over the English Channel and Great Britain. It began in July 1940. The British lost nearly 1,000 planes, the Germans more than 1,700. Germany bombed civilian as well as military targets, destroying houses, factories, and churches and conducted a months-long bombing campaign against London itself, known as "the blitz." But the British held on and, sensing failure, Hitler made a tactical decision to postpone the invasion of Britain indefinitely.

✓ **Checkpoint** Which side seemed to be winning the war at the end of 1940?

The Miracle of Dunkirk

Almost cut off from escape by the German army, British and French troops evacuated from Dunkirk using almost any sailing vessel available, including private yachts and fishing boats as small as 14 feet long! Some of the small boats were used to get close to shore to pick up men and then ferry them to larger naval vessels waiting in deeper waters. *Why do you think the evacuation from Dunkirk raised morale in Britain?*

Edward R. Murrow Reports on the Blitz

American news correspondent Edward R. Murrow (above) broadcast live from London as the Luftwaffe bombed the city. He described the purpose of his reports: "I have an old-fashioned belief that Americans like to make up their own minds on the basis of all available information." ◀◉ AUDIO
How do you think Murrow's reports influenced Americans?

A milkman (above) delivers milk as usual in October 1940 amid the devastation of an air raid. Londoners (left) take refuge in an underground train station converted into an air-raid shelter.

Americans Debate Involvement

Winston Churchill referred to the United States in many of his speeches during the crisis in France and the Battle of Britain. The fight against Hitler, Churchill implied, was more than simply a European struggle. Nazi aggression threatened the freedoms and rights cherished by democratic nations everywhere. The contest was between ideologies as well as nations.

America Favors Isolation President Roosevelt shared Churchill's concerns, but at the beginning of the war in Europe he understood that the majority of Americans opposed U.S. intervention. The severe economic crisis of the Great Depression had served to pin the nation's attention firmly on domestic affairs throughout the 1930s. In addition, many believed that U.S. involvement in World War I had been a deadly, expensive mistake. The rise of fascism in Europe made the sacrifices of World War I seem even more pointless.

In the 1930s, numerous books and articles presented a new theory about why the United States had become involved in World War I that disturbed many Americans. The theory held that big business had conspired to enter the war in order to make huge fortunes selling weapons. In 1934, a senate committee chaired by Gerald Nye of South Dakota looked into the question. Although the Nye Committee discovered little hard evidence, its findings suggested that "merchants of death"—American bankers and arms manufacturers—had indeed pulled the United States into World War I. The committee's findings further reinforced isolationist sentiments.

In order to avoid making the "mistakes" that had led to U.S. involvement in World War I, Congress passed the Neutrality Acts of 1935, 1936, and 1937.

The acts imposed certain restrictions on Americans during times of war. For example, Americans were prohibited from sailing on ships owned by belligerents or nations at war. The acts also prevented Americans from making loans to belligerents or selling them arms and munitions. The acts did not distinguish between aggressors like Germany and Italy and victims like Poland, or their allies, France and Britain.

Interventionists Urge Support for the Allies Once war began in Europe, Roosevelt felt confined by the limitations of the Neutrality Acts. Though he issued a proclamation of American neutrality, he was firmly anti-Nazi and wanted to aid the democracies of Europe. In the end, Congress agreed and passed the **Neutrality Act of 1939,** which included a cash-and-carry provision. This provision allowed belligerent nations to buy goods and arms in the United States if they paid cash and carried the merchandise on their own ships. Since the British navy controlled the seas, cash-and-carry in effect aided the Allies.

Many Americans disagreed with Roosevelt's openly pro-Allies position. They argued that FDR's policies violated American neutrality and threatened to push the United States into the war. Between early 1940 and late 1941, a great debate raged in America between isolationists and interventionists. The debate became particularly heated after the fall of France left Britain standing by itself in Europe against Germany. Interventionist organizations such as the Committee to Defend America by Aiding the Allies claimed that Britain was fighting for free countries everywhere. Sending aid to Britain was a way for America to stay out of the conflict.

Isolationists Argue for Neutrality Isolationists countered by claiming that giving aid to the Allies was automatically harming the Axis and would culminate with the United States entering the conflict. They argued that the only way to keep America safe was to follow a policy of complete neutrality. The America First Committee, an isolationist group, held rallies and sponsored speeches that criticized Roosevelt's openly pro-British policies. Charles Lindbergh became the leading isolationist voice. Lindbergh believed that the real threats to America were the Soviet Union and Japan, and he did not want to see his country weaken itself fighting in Western Europe to save Britain. Lindbergh's addresses were measured and clear. He appealed to Americans' minds but not their hearts.

Roosevelt Inches Toward Involvement Events in Europe shocked Americans out of strict neutrality. Reports by Edward R. Murrow, a CBS reporter stationed in London, during the blitz brought the war into American living rooms. His frequent live radio reports, which began with the words "This is London," emphasized that the Germans were bombing not armies or military sites but civilians—grandparents, parents, and children.

These reports and the turn of events in Europe against the Allies convinced many Americans that the United States needed to at least prepare to defend itself. Shortly after the fall of France in September 1940, Germany, Italy, and Japan signed the **Tripartite Pact** and became

The Only Way We Can Save Her

"STAY OUT! STAY OUT FOR MY SAKE, AS WELL AS YOUR OWN!"

WAR MAD EUROPE

DEMOCRACY

AMERICA, THE LAST REFUGE OF DEMOCRACY

Analyzing Political Cartoons

The Only Way to Save Democracy? In this cartoon, a figure symbolizing democracy begs Uncle Sam to stay out of the war in Europe.
1. What does this cartoonist think has happened to democracy in Europe?
2. According to this cartoonist's vision, how will the United States be able to save democracy?

Isolationist Viewpoint	Interventionist Viewpoint
• The United States should avoid alliances with other nations.	• The United States should work with other nations to promote collective security.
• Americans should focus on issues at home, such as the depression.	• Axis aggressions were wrong and threatened American interests.
• Complete neutrality was the way to keep the United States safe.	• The United States should aid the Allies, who were fighting for democracy and freedom.
• Intervention in a foreign war would be a mistake, just as World War I was.	• The United States should put pressure on the Axis Powers and prepare for war.

allies. In that same month, after a heated debate between isolationists and interventionists, Congress passed a Selective Service Act—a peacetime draft—providing for the military training of 1.2 million troops and 800,000 reserve troops each year.

At the same time, President Roosevelt took an additional step to strengthen Britain. He gave Britain 50 World War I–era battleships in exchange for eight British defense bases. Britain needed the destroyers to convoy goods across the Atlantic. Believing the act to be an emergency measure, Roosevelt made the transfer without the consent of Congress.

The American people <u>evaluated</u> FDR's leadership the next month in the presidential election. Roosevelt ran for an unprecedented third term against Republican nominee Wendell L. Willkie of Indiana. Willkie was critical of FDR's handling of both the economy and foreign affairs but not of the President's basic positions on either. Given such little differences between candidates, Americans voted overwhelmingly not to change leaders in the middle of a crisis.

✔ **Checkpoint** According to interventionists, how would aiding the Allies actually keep the United States out of the war?

America Takes Steps Toward War

Once safely reelected, President Roosevelt increased his support of Britain. When Britain began to run short on funds to purchase cash-and-carry goods in the United States, FDR took the opportunity to address Congress. On January 6, 1941, he spoke about "four freedoms"—freedom of speech, freedom of worship, freedom from want, and freedom from fear—that were threatened by Nazi and Japanese militarism. Roosevelt believed that the best way to stay out of the conflict with Germany was to aid Britain.

Lend-Lease Gives Aid to the Allies Roosevelt compared America's situation to the scenario of a fire in a neighbor's home. If a neighbor asked to borrow your fire hose to put out the fire, you would not debate the issue or try to sell the hose. Extending help was both being a good neighbor and acting to keep the fire from spreading to your own home.

Britain, Roosevelt said, needed American aid, and it had run out of money to pay for it. The President called for America to become "the great arsenal for democracy." Once again, America answered Britain's plea for help. In March 1941, Congress approved the **Lend-Lease Act,** symbolically numbered 1776, after another heated debate between isolationists and interventionists. The act authorized Roosevelt to

Aid to Britain
The president of Bundles for Britain (above) collects money for her organization, which sent food and clothing to help British people suffering from the effects of the war. *Is Bundles for Britain an example of the interventionist or isolationist viewpoint?*

Vocabulary Builder
<u>evaluate</u>—(ee VAL yoo ayt) *v.* to judge or find the value of

Roosevelt and Churchill
President Roosevelt (left) met with British prime minister Winston Churchill (right) in August 1941. Although the United States was still not at war with Germany, the two leaders set out some common goals in the Atlantic Charter. *How did President Roosevelt's actions reveal his interventionist stance?*

"sell, transfer title to, exchange, lease, lend, or otherwise dispose of, to any such government any defense article" whenever he thought it was "necessary in the interests of the defense of the United States." By 1945, the United States had sent more than $40 billion of Lend-Lease aid to the Allies, including the Soviet Union. The Lend-Lease Act was nothing less than an economic declaration of war against Germany and the Axis Powers.

The Atlantic Charter Reinforces America's Support of Britain In August 1941, President Roosevelt and prime minister Churchill met secretly on a warship off the misty coast of Newfoundland. They talked not only about Britain's problems in the war but also about their hopes for the world after Hitler's defeat. On board the ship they signed the **Atlantic Charter,** a document that endorsed national self-determination and an international system of "general security." The signing of the Atlantic Charter signaled the deepening alliance between the two nations.

U.S. Navy Battles German U-Boats Hitler was not blind to America's actions in support of the Allies. Nor did he fail to notice the fact that the United States had begun to escort arms shipments to Iceland, where the British picked them up and transported them to England.

In the fall of 1941, he ordered his German U-boats, or submarines, to attack American ships. The U-boats shot at the USS *Greer,* hit the USS *Kearny,* and sunk the USS *Reuben James,* killing more than a hundred sailors. The attacks shocked and angered Americans, moving them closer to declaring war on Germany. Though the United States was still officially a neutral nation, Roosevelt gave orders to the navy to attack German U-boats on sight. In June 1941, Germany had gone to war against the Soviet Union, and by November, war against the United States seemed inevitable.

 Checkpoint How did the United States support the Allies after Roosevelt's reelection?

Progress Monitoring *Online*
For: Self-test with vocabulary practice
Web Code: nea-1005

Comprehension

1. **Terms and People** For each item below, write a sentence explaining its significance.
   - blitzkrieg
   - Axis Powers
   - Allies
   - Winston Churchill
   - Neutrality Act of 1939
   - Tripartite Pact
   - Lend-Lease Act
   - Atlantic Charter

2. **NoteTaking Reading Skill: Sequence** Use your timeline to answer the Section Focus Question: How did Americans react to events in Europe and Asia in the early years of World War II?

Writing About History

3. **Quick Write: Compare Points of View** Compare the image of the women protesting the Lend-Lease Act to the excerpt from Roosevelt's Quarantine speech in this section. Write a paragraph summarizing the two different points of view presented by these two documents.

Critical Thinking

4. **Summarize** Describe the course of World War II in Europe until the end of 1940.

5. **Identify Point of View** Why did members of the America First Committee believe that the United States should avoid war with Germany?

6. **Recognize Causes** Why did the United States give more and more help to the Allies?

6.I.B.4

Franklin Delano Roosevelt: The "Four Freedoms" Speech

In his State of the Union address to Congress on January 6, 1941, President Roosevelt stressed the danger that aggressive fascist powers presented to the United States. He urged the American people to support those "who are resisting aggression and are thereby keeping war away from our Hemisphere"—namely the Allies. Congress passed the Lend-Lease Act three months later to do just that. Finally, Roosevelt set out the ideals that he believed Americans should fight for: the Four Freedoms.

I address you, the Members of the Seventy-Seventh Congress, at a moment unprecedented[1] in the history of the Union. I use the word "unprecedented" because at no previous time has American security been as seriously threatened from without as it is today. . . .

In the future days, which we seek to make secure, we look forward to a world founded upon four essential human freedoms.

The first is freedom of speech and expression—everywhere in the world.

The second is freedom of every person to worship God in his own way—everywhere in the world.

The third is freedom from want—which, translated into world terms, means economic understandings which will secure to every nation a healthy peace time life for its inhabitants—everywhere in the world.

The fourth is freedom from fear—which, translated into world terms, means a worldwide reduction of armaments to such a point and in such a thorough fashion that no nation will be in a position to commit an act of physical aggression against any neighbor—anywhere in the world.

That is no vision of a distant millennium. It is a definite basis for a kind of world attainable in our own time and generation. That kind of world is the very antithesis[2] of the so-called new order of tyranny which the dictators seek to create with the crash of a bomb. . . . The world order which we seek is the cooperation of free countries, working together in a friendly, civilized society.

This nation has placed its destiny in the hands and heads and hearts of its millions of free men and women; and its faith in freedom under the guidance of God. Freedom means the supremacy of human rights everywhere. Our support goes to those who struggle to gain those rights and keep them. Our strength is our unity of purpose.

To that high concept there can be no end save victory.

1. **unprecedented** (uhn PREHS uh dehn tihd) *adj.* new, having no previous example.
2. **antithesis** (an TIHTH uh sihs) *n.* exact opposite.

SAVE FREEDOM OF SPEECH

BUY WAR BONDS

Inspired by Roosevelt's speech, the illustrator Norman Rockwell created four paintings, each illustrating one of the Four Freedoms. In *Freedom of Speech,* Rockwell shows a man speaking at his town meeting.

Thinking Critically

1. **Summarize** What are the Four Freedoms?

2. **Predict Consequences** How do you think an isolationist would respond to Roosevelt's speech?

A Date Which Will Live in Infamy

In December 1941, the Japanese mounted a surprise attack on the U.S. naval base at Pearl Harbor, Hawaii. The next day Franklin Delano Roosevelt spoke to the shocked American public:

❝Yesterday, December 7, 1941—a date which will live in infamy—the United States of America was suddenly and deliberately attacked by naval and air forces of the Empire of Japan. . . . The facts of yesterday speak for themselves. The people of the United States have already formed their opinions and well understand the implications to the very life and safety of our nation. . . . No matter how long it may take us to overcome this premeditated invasion, the American people in their righteous might will win through to absolute victory.❞
—Franklin Roosevelt, Message Asking for War Against Japan, December 8, 1941

▲ President Roosevelt addresses Americans after the attack on Pearl Harbor

America Enters the War

 Core Curriculum Objectives

- **6.I.C.1** Pearl Harbor
- **6.I.C.2a** The "arsenal of democracy"
- **6.I.C.2b** Role of women: WACs; Rosie the Riveter; return of the retired
- **6.I.C.2c** Mobilizing for war: minority issues
- **6.I.C.2f** Experiences of men and women in the military

Terms and People

Hideki Tojo	Douglas MacArthur
Pearl Harbor	Bataan Death March
WAC	Battle of Coral Sea

NoteTaking

Reading Skill: Identify Causes and Effects
As you read, record the causes and effects of the attack on Pearl Harbor, as well as details about the attack itself, in a chart like the one below.

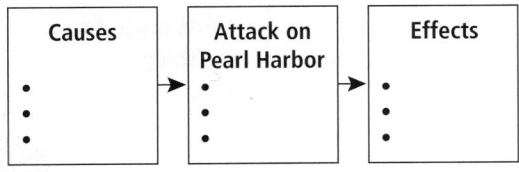

Why It Matters In the beginning of December 1941, the United States had engaged in warlike activity but had yet to commit itself. A surprise attack on Pearl Harbor, an American naval base in Hawaii, ended all debate and brought the United States into the war. The participation of the United States in this war, as in World War I, would decide the struggle's conclusion. **Section Focus Question: How did the United States react to the Japanese attack on Pearl Harbor?**

Japan Attacks the United States

Although Japan and the United States had been allies in World War I, conflict over power in Asia and the Pacific had been brewing between the two nations for decades prior to 1941. Japan, as the area's industrial and economic leader, resented any threats to its authority in the region. America's presence in Guam and the Philippines and its support of China posed such a threat. Yet Japan relied on trade with the United States to supply much-needed natural resources.

Trouble in the Pacific As war broke out in Europe, the Japanese Empire continued to grow in China and began to move into Indochina. President Roosevelt tried to stop this expansion, in July of 1940, by placing an embargo on important naval and aviation supplies to Japan, such as oil, iron ore, fuel, steel, and rubber. After Japan signed the Tripartite Pact in 1940 with Germany and Italy, FDR instituted a more extensive embargo. The embargo slowed, but did not stop, Japanese expansion as the Japanese were able to secure the resources they needed within their new possessions.

In 1941, General **Hideki Tojo** (hī DEHK ee TOH joh) became the Japanese prime minister. Known as "the Razor" for his sharp mind, he focused intently on military expansion but sought to keep the United States neutral. Throughout the summer of 1941, Japan and the United States attempted to negotiate an end to their disagreement, but with little success. Japan was bent on further expansion, and the United States was firmly against it. Finally, in late November 1941, Cordell Hull, the U.S. Secretary of State, rejected Japan's latest demands. Formal diplomatic relations continued for the next week, but Tojo had given up on peace. By the beginning of December he had made the decision to deliver a decisive first blow against the United States.

The Japanese Attack Pearl Harbor As Japanese diplomats wrangled in the U.S. capital, Japan's navy sailed for **Pearl Harbor,** Hawaii, the site of the United States Navy's main Pacific base. The forces that Tojo sent from Japan under the command of Vice Admiral Chuichi Nagumo (joo EE chee nah GOO moh) included 6 aircraft carriers, 360 airplanes, an assortment of battleships and cruisers, and a number of submarines. Their mission was to eradicate the American naval and air presence in the Pacific with a surprise attack. Such a blow would prevent Americans from mounting a strong resistance to Japanese expansion.

The attackers struck with devastating power, taking the American forces completely by surprise. A sailor aboard the hospital ship USS *Solace* recalled the destruction of the USS *Arizona:*

> **Primary Source** "I saw more planes coming in, passing over Battleship Row dropping bombs. I remember very clearly what looked like a dive-bomber coming in over the *Arizona* and dropping a bomb. I saw that bomb go down through what looked like a stack, and almost instantly it cracked the bottom of the *Arizona*, blowing the whole bow loose. It rose out of the water and settled. I could see flames, fire, and smoke coming out of that ship, and I saw two men fling through the air and the fire, screaming as they went."
> —Corpsman James F. Anderson, aboard the USS *Solace* in Pearl Harbor

Results of the Attack The Americans suffered heavy losses: nearly 2,500 people killed, 8 battleships severely damaged, 3 destroyers left unusable, 3 light cruisers damaged, and 160 aircraft destroyed and 128 more damaged. The U.S. battlefleet was knocked out of commission for nearly six months, allowing the Japanese to freely access the needed raw materials of their newly conquered territories, just as they had planned.

Despite these losses, the situation was not as bad as it could have been. The most important ships—aircraft carriers—were out at sea at the time of the attack and survived untouched. In addition, seven heavy cruisers were out at sea and also avoided detection by the Japanese. Of the battleships in Pearl Harbor, only three—the USS *Arizona,* the USS *Oklahoma,* and the USS *Utah*—suffered irreparable damage. American submarine bases also survived the morning, as did important fuel supplies and maintenance facilities. In the final analysis, Nagumo proved too conservative. He canceled a third wave of bombers, refused to seek out the aircraft carriers, and turned back toward home because he feared an American counterstrike. The American Pacific Fleet survived.

America Declares War As the news about Pearl Harbor spread across the nation and FDR prepared to address Congress, Americans rallied together. Many did not know what to expect, but they anticipated monumental changes. Journalist Marquis Child recalled thinking, "Nothing will ever be the same," and added, "it never was the same."

Japanese Ambitions

In late 1941, General Hideki Tojo (below) decided to stage a surprise attack on American forces. Items like this matchbook (below left) glorified Japan's military might. On the matchbook, planes emerge from a Japanese flag and fly in the direction of the flags of Britain and the United States.

The attack on Pearl Harbor left little doubt about declaring war on Japan. The Soviet Union's conversion to the Allied side, following Germany's invasion in June 1941, made some Americans doubt the wisdom of supporting the Allies. The attack on Pearl Harbor changed that. It made the necessity of declaring war on Japan clear and ended any continuing political divisions between isolationists and interventionists. After President Roosevelt's speech, the House voted 388 to 1 to declare war, and the Senate joined them unanimously. True to their military commitments with Japan, Germany and Italy declared war on America. Both Democrats and Republicans put aside their political differences to unify the nation in facing the task of winning a global war.

✓ **Checkpoint** What did the Japanese military leaders hope to achieve by attacking Pearl Harbor? Were they successful in this goal?

Events That Changed America

SURPRISE ATTACK! PEARL HARBOR

December 7, 1941, dawned an overcast day in Pearl Harbor, Hawaii. The members of the U.S. military stationed there went about their usual Sunday activities. About half of the United States Navy's Pacific Fleet, including eight huge battleships, sat clustered in the harbor. At nearby Hickam Field and other airfields, American planes sat quietly wing-to-wing in perfect rows.

Then, at just after 6 A.M., hundreds of Japanese planes poured through a break in the clouds and into the central valley of Oahu. Over the next several hours, Japanese bombers torpedoed the moored ships, while fighters and dive-bombers machine-gunned and bombed ship decks and airfields. American military forces, caught completely by surprise, attempted to ward off the attackers with little effect. The scene was one of utter destruction.

◀ The USS *Arizona* sank during the attack. Nearly 1,200 sailors and marines died on this ship alone.

Sailors at Ford Island Naval Air Station are stunned by the wreckage around them. ▼

Mobilizing for War

Following the Japanese attack, a spirit of patriotism and service swept across the country. Americans looked for ways to contribute to the war effort. They joined the military, volunteered with the Red Cross and other organizations, and moved into new jobs to help.

Responding to the Call During the course of the war, more than 16 million Americans served in the military. From 1941 to 1942 alone, the army grew from about 1.4 million to more than 3 million, the navy increased from under 300,000 to more than 600,000, and the marines expanded from only about 54,000 to almost 150,000. Americans from all ethnic and racial backgrounds joined the fight. Approximately 300,000 Mexican Americans and 25,000 Native Americans

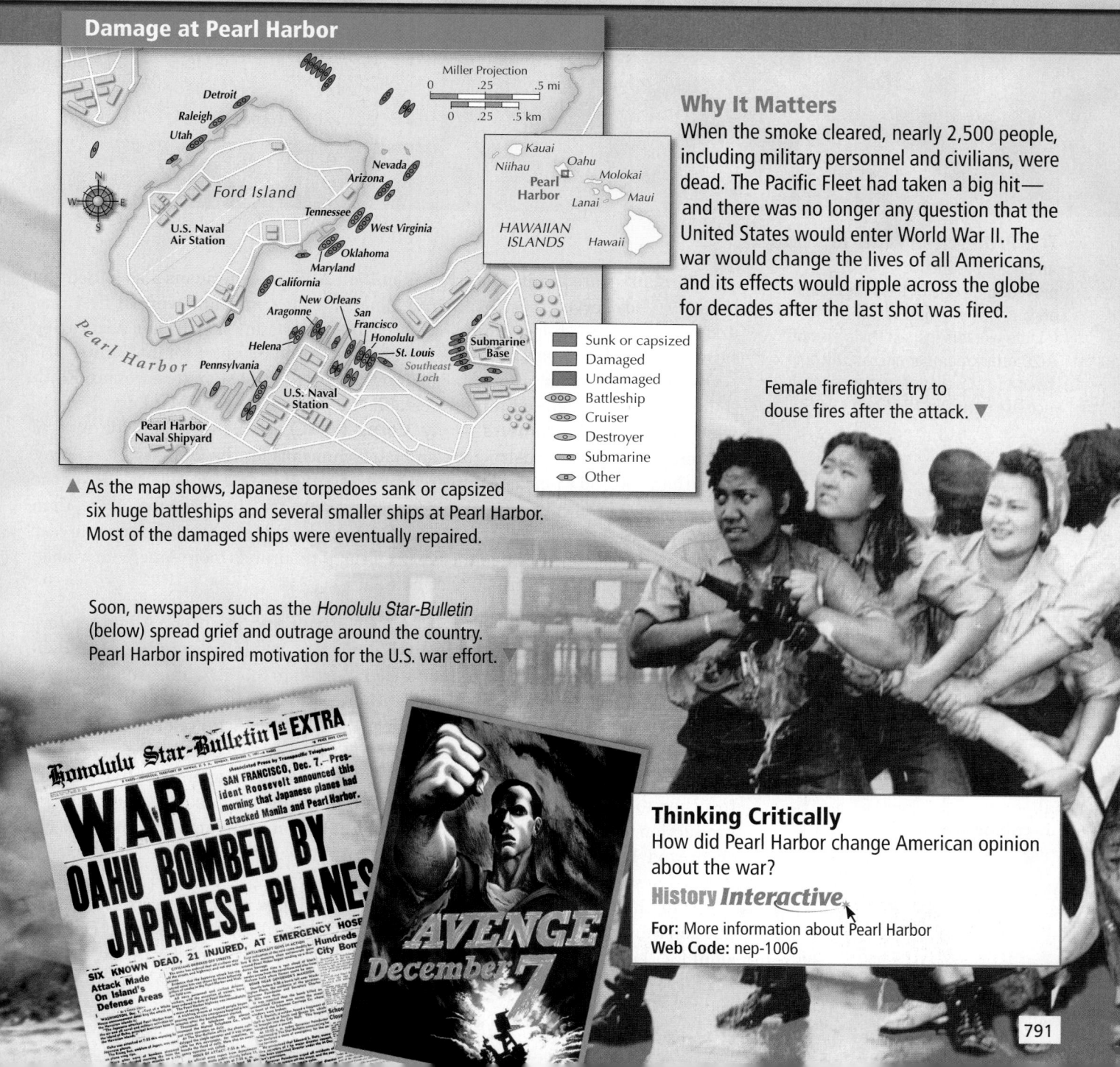

Damage at Pearl Harbor

▲ As the map shows, Japanese torpedoes sank or capsized six huge battleships and several smaller ships at Pearl Harbor. Most of the damaged ships were eventually repaired.

Soon, newspapers such as the *Honolulu Star-Bulletin* (below) spread grief and outrage around the country. Pearl Harbor inspired motivation for the U.S. war effort.

Why It Matters

When the smoke cleared, nearly 2,500 people, including military personnel and civilians, were dead. The Pacific Fleet had taken a big hit— and there was no longer any question that the United States would enter World War II. The war would change the lives of all Americans, and its effects would ripple across the globe for decades after the last shot was fired.

Female firefighters try to douse fires after the attack. ▼

Thinking Critically
How did Pearl Harbor change American opinion about the war?

History *Interactive*

For: More information about Pearl Harbor
Web Code: nep-1006

World War II Aircraft Production

SOURCE: U.S. Department of Defense

Legend: United States, Germany, Great Britain, Japan, Soviet Union

The Production Miracle

America's productive capability proved to be one of the Allies' main advantages in World War II. Above, female workers inspect the noses of A-20 attack bomber aircraft. *By how much did U.S. aircraft production increase between 1941 and 1944?*

Vocabulary Builder

allocate—(AL oh kayt) *v.* to distribute according to a plan

served in integrated units. Nearly one million African Americans also joined the military. They served mostly in segregated units, however, and were at first limited to supporting roles. However, as casualties mounted, African Americans saw more active combat, and some eventually served in white combat units.

Over 350,000 women also responded to the call. In 1941, Congresswoman Edith Nourse Rogers introduced a bill to establish a Women's Army Auxiliary Corps— which became the **Women's Army Corps (WAC)** in 1943—to provide clerical workers, truck drivers, instructors, and lab technicians for the United States Army. More than 150,000 women volunteered for the service; 15,000 served abroad over the course of the war and over 600 received medals for their service. More than 57,000 nurses served in the Army Nurse Corps, putting themselves in danger to care for the wounded in Europe and the Pacific. Tens of thousands more American women joined similar navy and Coast Guard auxiliaries.

Mobilizing Industry From the start, Roosevelt and the other Allied leaders knew that American production would play a key role in helping the Allies win the war. Although America's industry had started to mobilize in response to the Lend-Lease Act, American production still needed to increase the rate at which it churned out war materials. In January 1942, the government set up the War Production Board (WPB) to oversee the conversion of peacetime industry to war industry. Later, the government created a host of other agencies that worked together to <u>allocate</u> scarce materials into the proper industries, regulate the production of civilian goods, establish production contracts, negotiate with organized labor, and control inflation, with the Office of War Mobilization (OWM) to supervise all of these efforts.

Under the direction of the government, Americans worked to create a "production miracle." The massive defense spending finally ended the Great Depression; for the first time in more than a decade there was a job for every worker. Each year of the war, the United States raised its production goals for military materials, and each year it met these goals. The Ford Motor Company poured all of its resources into war production, building over 8,000 B-24 Liberator bombers. Henry J. Kaiser's shipyards produced large merchant "Liberty Ships" in as little as four and a half days. In 1944, American production levels were double those of all the Axis nations put together, giving the Allies a crucial advantage. In a toast at a wartime conference, even Joseph Stalin, an Allied leader, praised American production: "To American production, without which the war would have been lost."

✔ **Checkpoint** What were the first actions taken by the United States once war was declared?

Fierce Fighting in the Pacific

With Pearl Harbor smoldering, the Japanese knew they had to move fast to gain important footholds in Asia and the Pacific. Although Japan's population was smaller than America's, the Japanese did have military advantages, including technologically advanced weapons and a well-trained and highly motivated military. At the start of the Pacific war the outlook was grim for America.

Japanese Forces Take the Philippines In December 1941, General **Douglas MacArthur,** commander of United States Army forces in Asia, struggled to hold the U.S. positions in the Philippines with little support. This task grew even more daunting when the Japanese destroyed half of the army's fighter planes in the region and rapidly took Guam (gwahm), Wake Island, and Hong Kong. The main land attack came on December 22. MacArthur positioned his forces to repel the Japanese invasion, but he badly miscalculated the strength of the enemy and was forced to retreat. U.S. forces fell back from Manila to the Bataan (buh TAN) Peninsula and a fortification on Corregidor (kuh REHG uh dor) Island, where they dug in for a long siege. Trapped in Corregidor, Americans suffered, lacking necessary military and medical supplies and living on half and quarter rations.

Although MacArthur was ordered to evacuate to Australia, the other Americans remained behind. They held out until early May 1942, when 75,000 Allied soldiers surrendered. Japanese troops forced the sick and malnourished prisoners of war, or POWs, to march 55 miles up the Bataan Peninsula to reach a railway that took them inland where they were forced to march 8 more miles. More than 7,000 American and Filipino troops died during the grueling journey, which is known as the **Bataan Death March.**

Japanese Forces Advance Throughout the Pacific, Japanese forces attacked and conquered. These advances secured important oil and rubber supplies for Japan, and brought Southeast Asia and the western Pacific securely under Japanese control. By the summer of 1942, Japan appeared ready to dominate the Indian Ocean, Australia, New Zealand, and the central Pacific. If the Allies did not regroup quickly, they would have little hope of victory in the Pacific.

NoteTaking

Reading Skill: Sequence
Sequence the fighting that followed Pearl Harbor in a table like the one below.

Early War in the Pacific	
May 1942	The Philippines fall to the Japanese.

America Mobilizes
These young men train to fight abroad. Training went on for months before soldiers were considered ready for combat.

Japanese Aggression, December 1941–June 1942

Geography *Interactive*
For: Interactive map
Web Code: nep-1007

SOVIET UNION

MONGOLIA

Manchuria (Manchukuo)

Vladivostok

Beijing

CHINA

Korea

Sea of Japan

JAPAN

Yellow Sea

Tokyo

Shanghai

Doolittle Raid Successful American raid on Tokyo shocks the Japanese in April 1942.

Burma (U.K.)

French Indochina

Hong Kong (U.K.)

South China Sea

Manila Japanese forces land near Manila in late December 1941. American forces hold out in the Bataan Peninsula until April 9 and on Corregidor Island until May 5.

Bangkok

THAILAND

Manila

Philippines (U.S.)

Mariana Islands

Saipan

Guam (U.S.)

Caroline Islands

Midway Island (U.S.)

Wake Island (U.S.)

Hawaiian Islands (U.S.)

30° N

Pearl Harbor Japan attacks Pearl Harbor in Hawaii, Wake Island, Midway Island, Guam, the Philippines, and Hong Kong on December 7 and 8, 1941.

Marshall Islands

Pacific Ocean

Malaya (U.K.)

Singapore

Borneo

Celebes

Dutch East Indies

Java Sea

Batavia Java

Sumatra

Gilbert Islands (U.K.)

New Guinea Rabaul

Solomon Islands (U.K. & Aust.)

Battle of Coral Sea Outcome of battle between Allied aircraft carriers and Japanese aircraft carriers is inconclusive, but Japan calls off attack on New Guinea in 1942.

0°

Indian Ocean

Darwin

Coral Sea Coral Sea

180°

Miller Projection

0   500   1,000 mi

0   500   1,000 km

120° E

Aleutian Islands (U.S.)

Kuril Islands

AUSTRALIA

Extent of Japanese control, December 1941
Extent of Japanese control, June 1942
Areas under Japanese control, 1942
Japanese advance, December 1941
Japanese advance, January–May 1942
Major battle
Route of Doolittle Raid

Map Skills By mid-1942, the Japanese controlled much of Southeast Asia and the Pacific region.

1. **Locate: (a)** Philippines, **(b)** New Guinea, **(c)** Wake Island, **(d)** Pearl Harbor

2. **Movement** What targets other than Pearl Harbor did the Japanese attack in December 1941?

3. **Recognize Cause and Effect** Why did the Doolittle Raid shock the citizens of Tokyo?

Prisoners of War on the Bataan Peninsula American and Filipino troops surrender to the Japanese after holding out for months with little food. They did not yet know that this would be only the beginning of their ordeal.

America Strikes Back With the Doolittle Raid After Pearl Harbor, FDR wanted America to retaliate against Japan. American military leaders devised a plan for a nighttime bombing raid from the deck of the aircraft carrier USS *Hornet,* led by Colonel James Doolittle. While still 800 miles away from mainland Japan, the *Hornet* was detected, so rather than wait for night, Doolittle led a force of 16 B-25 bombers against Tokyo. They delivered their payload on the Japanese capital just after noon.

The raid killed 50 Japanese people and damaged 100 buildings. The pilots then flew to China, where they crash-landed. Doolittle's Raid proved a <u>minimal</u> military gain, but it bolstered American morale for the long fight ahead.

Vocabulary Builder
minimal–(MIHN uh muhl) *adj.* smallest or least amount possible

The Battle of Coral Sea Gives Hope A second event, the **Battle of Coral Sea,** also helped to kindle hope for the American military in the Pacific. In early May 1942, the Japanese moved to take Port Moresby in New Guinea. From that position they could threaten Australia and protect their important military bases at Rabaul (also in New Guinea). To counter Japan's move, the United States sent two aircraft carriers, the USS *Lexington* and USS *Yorktown*, along with support vessels.

On May 7 and 8, in the middle of a Pacific storm, Japanese and U.S. aircraft carriers engaged in battle. It was the first sea fight in which enemy warships never sighted one another. Instead, U.S. airplanes attacked Japanese ships and vice versa. Although technically the Battle of Coral Sea proved a draw, strategically it was a victory for the United States because it forced the Japanese to call off their attack on New Guinea. It marked a shift in momentum toward the Americans. From that day on, the Pacific theater of battle would be won or lost on the strength of aircraft carriers and planes—and here, America's productive capacity gave Americans a marked advantage over their adversaries.

The Battle of Coral Sea and the Doolittle Raid gave the United States a renewed sense of confidence. The war would last three more years, but the dark days of early 1942 were over.

 Checkpoint What military advantages did the United States have over Japan?

Progress Monitoring *Online*
For: Self-test with vocabulary practice
Web Code: nea-1008

Comprehension

1. **Terms and People** For each item below, write a sentence explaining how it related to the entry of the United States into World War II.
   • Hideki Tojo
   • Pearl Harbor
   • WAC
   • Douglas MacArthur
   • Bataan Death March
   • Battle of Coral Sea

2. <u>NoteTaking</u> **Reading Skill: Identify Causes and Effects** Use your chart and table to answer the Section Focus Question: How did the United States react to the Japanese attack on Pearl Harbor?

Writing About History

3. **Quick Write: Compare Primary Sources** Compare the primary source describing the attack on Pearl Harbor to the images of the attack in this section. Write one paragraph describing what information both sources convey about the event.

Critical Thinking

4. **Identify Points of View** Was the Japanese attack on Pearl Harbor a success or failure from the Japanese point of view? Explain.

5. **Predict Consequences** What role do you think the productive capacity of the United States played in World War II?

6. **Draw Conclusions** Why was the Battle of Coral Sea a turning point for the Allies?

23

Quick Study Guide

NY 6.I.B, 6.I.C

Progress Monitoring *Online*
For: Self-test with vocabulary practice
Web Code: nea-1009

■ Key Causes of World War II

Destruction caused by World War I	Failure of World War I peace settlements	Global economic Depression

↓ ↓ ↓

Causes of World War II

↑ ↑ ↑ ↑

Weakness of the League of Nations	Militaristic, nationalist leaders in Germany, Italy, and Japan	Acts of aggression by Axis Powers	British and French appeasement

■ Key Allied Powers and Axis Powers and Their Leaders

Allies	Leaders
Great Britain	Winston Churchill, prime minister
France	Charles de Gaulle, leader of French not under German control
Soviet Union	Joseph Stalin, communist dictator
United States	Franklin D. Roosevelt, President

Axis Powers	Leaders
Germany	Adolf Hitler, Nazi dictator
Italy	Benito Mussolini, fascist dictator
Japan	Hideki Tojo, army general and prime minister; Hirohito, emperor

■ Steps Toward American Entry Into World War II

1935–1937	Congress passes Neutrality Acts to help prevent the United States from being drawn into any foreign wars.
1939	The Neutrality Act of 1939 allows belligerent nations to buy supplies from the United States on a cash-and-carry basis; The act favors the Allies.
September 1940	Roosevelt tightens trade embargo against Japan; Congress passes Selective Service Act, instituting a peacetime draft.
March 1941	Congress passes the Lend-Lease Act, allowing the United States to give aid to the Allies.
August 1941	Roosevelt and Churchill issue the Atlantic Charter.
Summer 1941	Japanese and American diplomats try to resolve differences.
October–November 1941	German U-boats sink United States Navy ships; U.S. merchant ships are armed and given permission to sink U-boats.
December 1941	Japan attacks Pearl Harbor; the United States declares war on Japan and later on Germany and Italy.

☑ Quick Study Timeline

In America

1933 Nearly one in four American workers is unemployed	1934–1936 Nye Committee scrutinizes reasons for U.S. involvement in World War I	1935 Congress bans the sale of arms to countries at war

Presidential Terms — Franklin D. Roosevelt 1933–1945

1931   **1933**   **1935**

Around the World

1931 Japanese army overruns Manchuria	1933 Hitler becomes chancellor of Germany	1935 Italy invades Ethiopia

American Issues
●─■─■─● **Connector**

By connecting prior knowledge with what you have learned in this chapter, you can gradually build your understanding of enduring questions that still affect America today. Answer the questions below. Then, use your American Issues Connector study guide (or go online: www.PHSchool.com **Web Code:** neh-8302).

Issues You Learned About

● **America and the World** Americans debated involvement in World War II.

1. What viewpoint on the war did isolationists hold? What viewpoint did interventionists hold?

2. Write a speech as if you were a Congress member who is either an isolationist or an interventionist. In your speech, you should express your view and attempt to persuade others to believe as you do. Consider the following:
- the spread of fascist governments
- the aggression of Japan, Italy, and Germany
- the lessons of World War I
- the Neutrality Acts
- the Tripartite Pact

● **Global Interdependence** Countries develop specific policies about ways to deal with other countries' aggressive acts.

3. What was decided at the Munich Conference?

4. What happened after Hitler absorbed Czechoslovakia into the German Reich in the spring of 1939?

5. Did the appeasement policies of Britain and France prove to be effective? Explain.

● **America Goes to War** The United States became involved in World War II after an attack on its own soil.

6. What earlier global conflict had the United States been involved in? Why did the country get involved in that conflict?

7. How did the attack on Pearl Harbor draw the United States into war with Germany and Italy?

Connect to Your World	New York

New York Goes to War While many soldiers from New York fought overseas in World War II, other New Yorkers contributed to the war effort at home. Nearly 30 factories in Rochester each contributed parts toward the B-29 Superfortress, a powerful plane used by the United States Army, among others. Rochester's factories also produced innovative optical equipment, such as spy cameras and aiming devices for guns. In Bethpage on Long Island, the Grumman Aircraft Engineering Corporation was famous for its high quality navy planes. Research other New York companies or factories that helped to make America's "production miracle" a reality during World War II. Choose one key product, and write a paragraph explaining how it was used during the war.

1937
Roosevelt condemns aggression in Quarantine speech

1940
Roosevelt wins third term

1941
Pearl Harbor is attacked

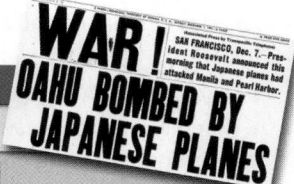

1937

1939

1941

1938
Germany annexes Austria

1939
Germany invades Poland, beginning World War II

1941
Germany invades the Soviet Union

History *Interactive*
For: Interactive timeline
Web Code: nep-1010

Chapter Assessment

Terms and People

1. Who was **Adolf Hitler**? How did he rise to power?
2. What was the **Spanish Civil War**? Describe other European countries' involvement in that war.
3. What was the **Lend-Lease Act**? How did it involve the United States in World War II?
4. What happened as a result of Japan's attack on **Pearl Harbor**?
5. Who was General **Douglas MacArthur**? What happened to him and his soldiers in the Philippines?

Focus Questions

The focus question for this chapter is **What events caused World War II, and how did the United States become involved?** Build an answer to this big question by answering the focus questions for Sections 1 through 3 and the Critical Thinking questions that follow.

Section 1
6. Why did totalitarian states rise after World War I, and what did they do?

Section 2
7. How did Americans react to events in Europe and Asia in the early years of World War II?

Section 3
8. How did the United States react to the Japanese attack on Pearl Harbor?

Critical Thinking

9. **Make Comparisons** What did the governments in Italy and Germany in the 1930s have in common?
10. **Draw Conclusions** Do you think the League of Nations followed a policy of appeasement toward aggressors? Explain.
11. **Recognize Causes** Why do you think Germany wanted to sign a nonaggression pact with the Soviet Union?
12. **Draw Inferences** Why did Hitler decide to call off Operation Sea Lion?
13. **Determine Relevance** When did the United States declare war on Japan? How much Lend-Lease aid had the United States provided to Allies by this time?

Lend-Lease Aid Given by the United States

Year	To British Empire	To Soviet Union
1941 (March–December)	$1.1 billion	$20.0 million
1942	$4.8 billion	$1.4 billion
1943	$9.0 billion	$2.4 billion
1944	$10.8 billion	$4.1 billion
1945 (January–August)	$4.4 billion	$2.8 billion
Total	**$30.1 billion**	**$10.7 billion**

SOURCE: *British War Economy*, W. K. Hancock and M. M. Gowing

14. **Predict Consequences** Do you think the United States would have eventually joined World War II if the Japanese had not attacked Pearl Harbor?
15. **Identify Central Issues** What was Japan's primary goal in taking part in World War II?
16. **Summarize** Describe the war in the Pacific from December 1941 through May 1942.

Writing About History

Analyzing Point of View Between early 1940 and late 1941, a great debate raged in America between isolationists and interventionists. Go online to **www.PHSchool.com** and enter **Web Code: nep-1012** to read a series of primary sources on the Lend-Lease Act, each reflecting a different point of view. Then, write an essay comparing and contrasting the different viewpoints on the act.

Prewriting
- On note cards, summarize each of the primary sources in your own words focusing on the writer's particular argument(s) in support of or opposed to the Lend-Lease Act.
- Organize your summaries into two piles: those supporting and those opposing the Lend-Lease Act.

Drafting
- Develop a working thesis and choose information to support the thesis.
- Make an outline organizing your essay.
- Write an introduction in which you point out what you think were the strongest arguments of both sides of the debate.
- Write a body and a conclusion. Be sure to include and cite quotes from the primary sources to support your main points.

Revising
- Use the guidelines on page SH11 of the Writing Handbook to revise your essay.

Regents DBQ Practice

American Contributions to the War Effort

Both prior to and during World War II, Americans mobilized to produce the material needed to win the war. Factories quickly converted from producing consumer goods to military goods, and each year the country increased and met its production goals. The following documents illustrate the role of American industrial output during the war. Use your knowledge of American production during World War II and Documents 1, 2, 3, and 4 to answer questions 1 through 4.

Document 1

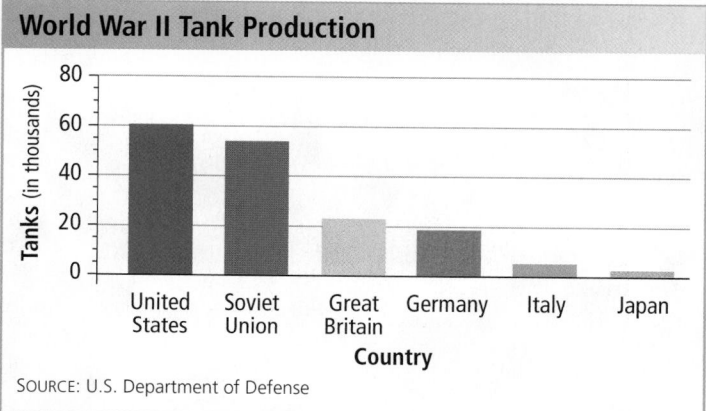

World War II Tank Production

SOURCE: U.S. Department of Defense

Document 2

"The superiority of the United Nations [Allies] in munitions and ships must be overwhelming—so overwhelming that the Axis nations can never hope to catch up with it. In order to attain this overwhelming superiority the United Nations must build planes and tanks and guns and ships to the utmost limit of our national capacity. . . . This production of ours in the United States must be raised far above its present levels. . . . Let no man say it cannot be done. It must be done—and we have undertaken to do it."

President Franklin D. Roosevelt, Annual Message to Congress, January 6, 1942

Document 3

The Liberty Ship Robert E. Peary *was built in a matter of days.*

Document 4

"The reliance on American aid indicates just how much the Allied war effort owed to the exceptional material and logistical strength of the United States.

The ability of the world's largest industrial economy to convert to the mass production of weapons and war equipment is usually taken for granted. Yet the transition from peace to war was so rapid and effective that the USA was able to make up for the lag in building up effectively trained armed forces by exerting a massive material superiority.

This success owed . . . a great deal to the character of American industrial capitalism, with its 'can-do' ethos, high levels of engineering skill and tough-minded entrepreneurs. After a decade of recession the manufacturing community had a good deal of spare, unemployed capacity to absorb. . . ."

From World War Two: How the Allies Won, *Professor Richard Overy*

---

1. According to Document 1, which of the following countries produced the most tanks during World War II?
   (1) Germany and Italy
   (2) Italy and Japan
   (3) the United States and the Soviet Union
   (4) the Soviet Union and the United Kingdom

2. In Document 2, President Roosevelt is calling for
   (1) the immediate recruitment of troops.
   (2) a dramatic increase in the production of armaments.
   (3) a dramatic increase in the workforce.
   (4) production levels to match those of the Axis Powers.

3. According to the author of Document 4,
   (1) the Allied victory is often taken for granted.
   (2) America's transition to war production was slow but effective.
   (3) Allied success was partly a result of American know-how and effort.
   (4) the training of American troops was superior to that of the enemies' troops.

4. **Writing Task** Do you agree that America's role in the war was crucial to the Allies eventual success? Why? Use your knowledge from the chapter and specific evidence from the documents to support your view.

The Slow March to Victory

In June 1944, Allied troops landed in German-held France and began their push toward the defeat of Hitler. An American soldier later described his memories:

❝Trying to stay clean, trying to rest when possible, eating when possible. . . . Feeling very thankful that one of the guys just looking upwards into a tree observed a German and without hesitation fired his rifle from the hip—Hollywood fashion—killing the German, who no doubt was waiting for the last GI in the platoon to pass by and would then open fire from the rear. . . . On the move constantly, pushing inland, small villages with buildings burning.❞
—Dick Biehl, quoted in *June 6, 1944: The Voices of D-Day*

Listen to the Witness History *audio to hear more about American soldiers in France.*

◀ Near a French village, an American soldier fires a cannon at retreating German soldiers in 1944.

Navajos in the United States Marines sent coded messages in their native language.

NY Core Curriculum Preview

Chapter Focus Question: What impact did World War II have on America and the world?

Section 1
The Allies Turn the Tide 6.I.C.2a, 6.I.C.3b, 6.I.C.3c

Section 2
The Home Front 6.I.C.2b, 6.I.C.2d, 6.I.C.2e, 6.I.C.5a

Section 3
Victory in Europe and the Pacific 6.I.C.3c, 6.I.C.4a, 6.I.C.4b

Section 4
The Holocaust 6.I.C.5c

Section 5
Effects of the War 6.I.C.4d, 6.I.C.5d, 6.II.A.1, 6.II.A.2a, 6.II.B.1

Use the ☑ **Quick Study Timeline** at the end of this chapter to preview chapter events.

Patch commemorating the Battle of Guadalcanal

American tank

Note Taking Study Guide *Online*
For: Note Taking and American Issues Connector
Web Code: nee-8401

▲ American marines on Guadalcanal

Guadalcanal patch ▶

WITNESS HISTORY 🔊)) AUDIO

Spiders as Big as Your Fist

World War II placed U.S. soldiers in a dazzling variety of settings, from mountains to deserts to forests to tropical isles. One marine described the ordeal of fighting on a Pacific island:

❝It was beautiful, but beneath the loveliness . . . Guadalcanal was a mass of slops and stinks and pestilence; of scum-crusted lagoons and vile swamps inhabited by giant crocodiles; a place of spiders as big as your fist and wasps as long as your finger . . . of ants that bite like fire, of tree leeches that fall, fasten and suck; of scorpions, of centipedes whose foul scurrying across human skin leaves a track of inflamed flesh, of snakes and land crabs, rats and bats and carrion birds and of a myriad of stinging insects.❞
—Robert Leckie, *Delivered From Evil: The Saga of World War II*

The Allies Turn the Tide

NY **Core Curriculum Objectives**

- **6.I.C.2a** The "arsenal of democracy"
- **6.I.C.3b** Allied strategy and leadership: Europe first
- **6.I.C.3c** Allied strategy and leadership: A two-front war

Terms and People

Dwight Eisenhower	strategic bombing
George S. Patton, Jr.	Tuskegee Airmen
unconditional surrender	Chester Nimitz
saturation bombing	Battle of Midway

NoteTaking

Reading Skill: Summarize List the ways in which the Allies turned back the Axis advance.

Turning Back the Axis	
In Europe	**In the Pacific**
• Battle against U-boats in Atlantic	•
•	•

Why It Matters The attack on Pearl Harbor brought America into World War II on the Allied side. In 1942, the Allies began to stop the seemingly unstoppable Axis onslaught. Though years of fighting lay ahead, the most aggressive threat to world peace and democracy in modern times had been halted. **Section Focus Question: How did the Allies turn the tide against the Axis?**

Axis and Allies Plan Strategy

By June 1942, the Allies were battered but still fighting. As you have read, British pilots had fought off a Nazi invasion of their island, while at the Battle of Coral Sea, the U.S. Navy had frustrated Japanese plans to extend their domination in the Pacific. Although the war was not close to being over, the Allies spied signs of hope.

The Axis Powers never had a coordinated strategy to defeat the Allies. Germany, Italy, and Japan shared common enemies but nurtured individual dreams. Hitler wanted to dominate Europe and eliminate "inferior" peoples. Mussolini harbored dreams of an Italian empire stretching from the eastern Adriatic to East Africa. Tojo sought Japanese control of the Western Pacific and Asia.

The Allies shared more unified goals. Roosevelt, Churchill, and Stalin considered Germany the most dangerous enemy. None felt Japan or Italy posed a serious long-term threat. Only Germany had the resources to bomb Britain, fight U.S. and British navies on the

Atlantic, and invade the Soviet Union across a 1,200-mile front. Thus, although their <u>ultimate</u> goal was to fight and win a two-front war, the Allies agreed to pursue a "Europe First" strategy. Until Hitler was defeated, the Pacific would be a secondary theater of war.

 Checkpoint Why did the Allies decide to concentrate first on the war in Europe?

Vocabulary Builder
<u>ultimate</u>–(UHL tuh miht) *adj.*
final; most advanced

Turning the Tide in Europe

The first blow America struck against the Axis was by fulfilling FDR's promise to be the "arsenal of democracy." American industries turned out millions of tons of guns, tanks, and other supplies—enough to keep the Soviets and British battling Germany for years. The problem was delivering the supplies.

Allies Battle U-Boats in the Atlantic Hitler was determined to cut the sea lines between the United States and Europe before American aid could make a difference. "Wolf packs" of German U-boats patrolled the Atlantic and Caribbean, sinking more than 3,500 merchant ships and killing tens of thousands of Allied seamen. "The only thing that ever really frightened me during the war was the U-boat peril," Churchill later wrote.

Finally, in mid-1943, the Allies began to win the war in the North Atlantic. As in World War I, convoys of escort carriers protected Allied shipping. A new invention, radar, helped Allied vessels locate U-boats on the surface at night. Long-range aerial bombers and underwater depth charges allowed Allied forces to sink U-boats faster than Germany could manufacture them.

Soviets Turn Back Nazis at Stalingrad Germany had attacked Russia in June 1941, sending one army north toward Leningrad, a second east toward Moscow, and a third south toward Stalingrad. Although Hitler's forces penetrated deep into Soviet territory, killing or capturing millions of soldiers and civilians, they did not achieve their main objective of conquering the Soviet Union. Soviet resistance and a brutal Russia winter stopped the German advance.

In 1942, Hitler narrowed his sights and concentrated his armies in southern Russia. His goal this time was to control the rich Caucasus oil fields. To achieve this objective, he would have to capture the city of Stalingrad.

The struggle for Stalingrad was especially ferocious. German troops advanced slowly, fighting bitter block-by-block, house-by-house battles in the bombed-out buildings and rubble. Soviet troops then counterattacked, trapping the German forces. Yet Hitler refused to allow his army to retreat. Starving, sick, and suffering from frostbite, the surviving German troops finally surrendered on January 31, 1943.

The battle of Stalingrad was the true turning point of the war in Europe. It ended any realistic plans Hitler had of dominating Europe. Nazi armies were forced to retreat westward back toward Germany. Instead, it was the Soviet Union that now went on the offensive.

Surrender at Stalingrad
The long Battle of Stalingrad ended in January 1943 with the surrender of German troops like these. Of the 91,000 prisoners taken by the Soviets, only about 5,000 eventually survived and returned to Germany.

Desert Warfare American soldiers had to fight in many unfamiliar types of terrain. But the Sahara of North Africa—the world's largest desert—presented special challenges:

- In hot, dry weather, sandstorms choked and blinded troops.
- In wet weather, mud halted machinery.
- The high visibility of the desert terrain made it difficult for troops to move without being seen.
- Poisonous reptiles, ants, and scorpions added to the problems.

Brilliant tank strategists like Patton and Rommel were able to overcome such challenges. But the tanks themselves caused other problems, such as kicking up enormous dust clouds that could be seen miles away.

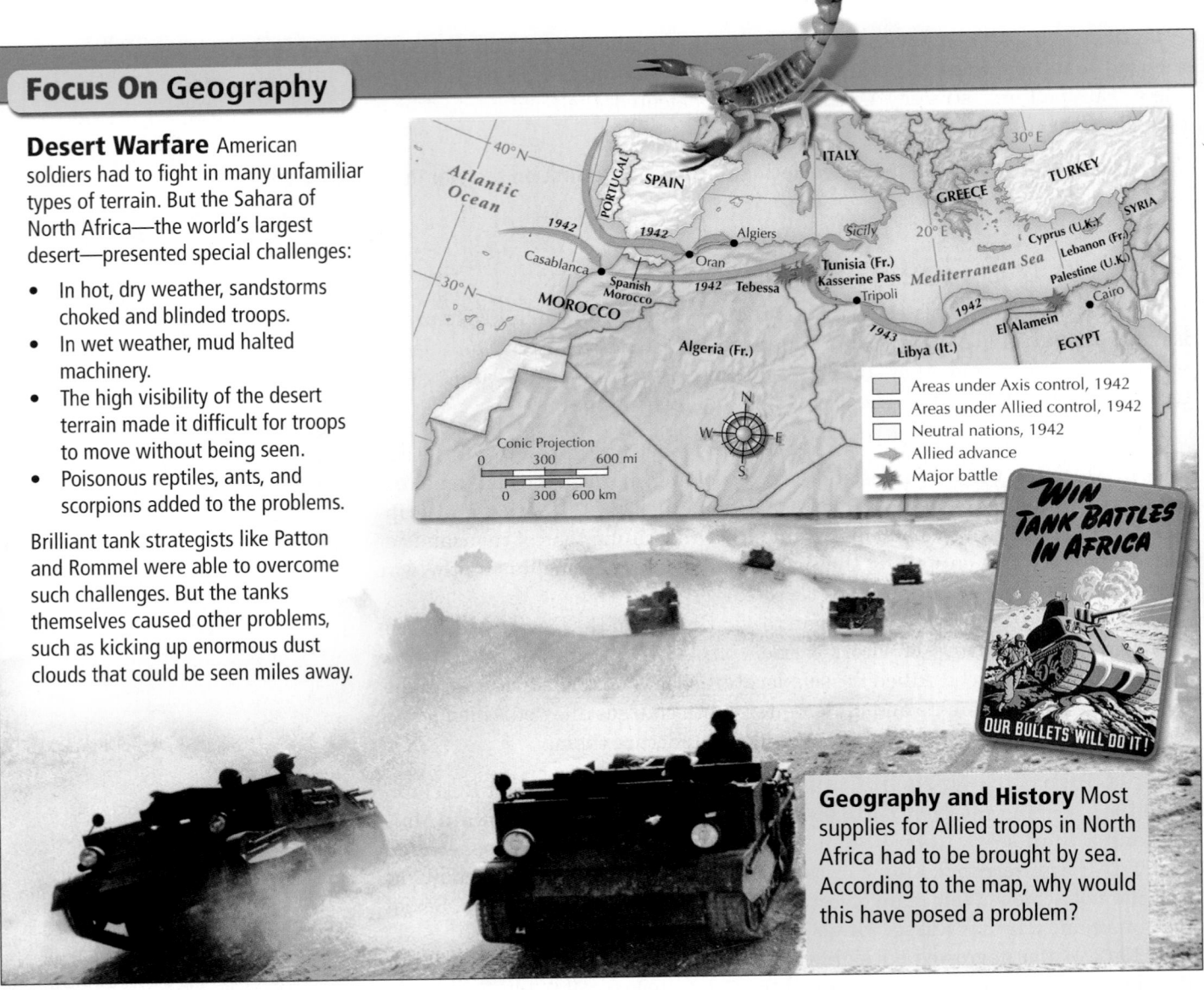

Geography and History Most supplies for Allied troops in North Africa had to be brought by sea. According to the map, why would this have posed a problem?

Allies Drive Germans Out of North Africa Meanwhile, another important campaign was taking place in the deserts and mountains of North Africa, where the British had been fighting the Germans and Italians since 1940. Several goals motivated the Allied campaign in North Africa. Stalin had wanted America and Britain to relieve the Soviet Union by establishing a second front in France. However, FDR and Churchill felt they needed more time to prepare for an invasion across the English Channel. An invasion of North Africa, however, required less planning and fewer supplies. In addition, forcing Germany out of North Africa would pave the way for an invasion of Italy.

In October 1942, the British won a major victory at El Alamein (ehl al uh MAYN) in Egypt and began to push westward. The next month, Allied troops landed in Morocco and Algeria and began to move east toward key German positions. An energetic American officer, General **Dwight Eisenhower**—known as Ike—commanded the Allied invasion of North Africa.

In February 1943, German general Erwin Rommel (known as the Desert Fox) led his Afrika Korps against the Americans at the Kasserine Pass in Tunisia. Rommel broke through the American lines in an attempt to reach the Allied supply base at Tebessa in Algeria. Finally, American soldiers stopped the assault. Lack of supplies then forced Rommel to retreat.

The fighting at the Kasserine Pass taught American leaders valuable lessons. They needed aggressive officers and troops better trained for desert fighting. To that end, Eisenhower put American forces in North Africa under the command of **George S. Patton, Jr.,** an innovative tank commander. A single-minded general known as Blood and Guts, Patton told his junior officers:

> **Primary Source** ❝You usually will know where the front is by the sound of gunfire, and that's the direction you should proceed. Now, suppose you lose a hand or an ear is shot off, or perhaps a piece of your nose, and you think you should walk back to get first aid. If I see you, it will be the last . . . walk you'll ever take.❞
> —George S. Patton, Jr., 1943

Patton's forces advanced east with heightened confidence. Simultaneously, the British pressed westward from Egypt, trapping Axis forces in a continually shrinking pocket in Tunisia. Rommel escaped, but his army did not. In May 1943, German and Italian forces—some 240,000 troops—surrendered.

✓ **Checkpoint** Why was the Battle of Stalingrad a turning point in World War II?

Increasing the Pressure on Germany

Germany was now on the defensive, and the Allies planned to keep it that way. In January 1943, Roosevelt and Churchill met in Casablanca, Morocco, to plan their next move. The conference resulted in two important decisions. First, the Allies decided to increase bombing of Germany and invade Italy. Second, FDR announced that the Allies would accept only **unconditional surrender,** or giving up completely without any concessions. Hitler, Mussolini, and Tojo could not hope to stay in power through a negotiated peace.

Allies Invade Italy The Allies next eyed Italy. Situated across the Mediterranean from Tunisia and 2 miles from the Italian mainland, Sicily was the obvious target for an invasion. The Allies could invade Sicily without great risk from U-boats and under the protection of air superiority. In July 1943, British and American armies made separate landings in Sicily and began to advance across the island before joining forces in the north. Once again, Eisenhower commanded the joint American-British forces.

Ike hoped to trap Axis forces on Sicily, but they escaped to the Italian mainland. Still, the 38-day campaign achieved important results: It gave the Allies complete control of the western Mediterranean, paved the way for an invasion of Italy, and ended the rule of Benito Mussolini. On September 3, 1943, Italy surrendered to the Allies and five weeks later declared war on Germany.

But Hitler was not through with Italy. After a small German airborne force rescued Mussolini from a mountaintop fortress, Hitler installed him as head of a puppet state in northern Italy. In the south, German military forces continued the fight against the Allies.

On the Beach at Sicily
Using only a small foldable shovel, an American soldier digs himself a foxhole on the beach at Sicily.

The invasion of Italy was a slow, grinding slog. Italy was crisscrossed with mountains and rivers. Heavy rains and mountain snows made combat difficult and painful. Men fought in ankle-deep mud. In the mountains, where tanks and heavy artillery were useless, Allied forces depended on mules to haul supplies up slippery and steep roads. To make matters worse, the Germans occupied the best defensive positions. Fighting continued into 1945. The Allies won battles, but none were important enough to alter the basic German defensive policy.

Bombers Batter Germany Stalin continued his demand that Roosevelt and Churchill open a second front in France. While the Allies did not launch a massive invasion of France until 1944, they did open a second front of another kind in early 1942. From bases in England, Allied bombers launched nonstop attacks against Germany. Flying by night in order to avoid being shot down in large numbers, British planes dropped massive amounts of bombs on German cities. The goal of this **saturation bombing** was to inflict maximum damage.

By day, American bombers targeted Germany's key political and industrial centers. The goal of this campaign of **strategic bombing** was to destroy Germany's capacity to make war. A Nazi official later commented that "the fleets of bombers might appear at any time over any large German city or important factory."

An African American fighter squadron known as the **Tuskegee Airmen** played a key role in the campaign, escorting bombers and protecting them from enemy fighter pilots. In more than 1,500 missions over enemy territory in Europe, the Tuskegee Airmen did not lose a single bomber.

Overall, though, the bombing missions cost the Allies dearly. Bomber crews suffered an incredibly high 20 percent casualty rate. But they successfully

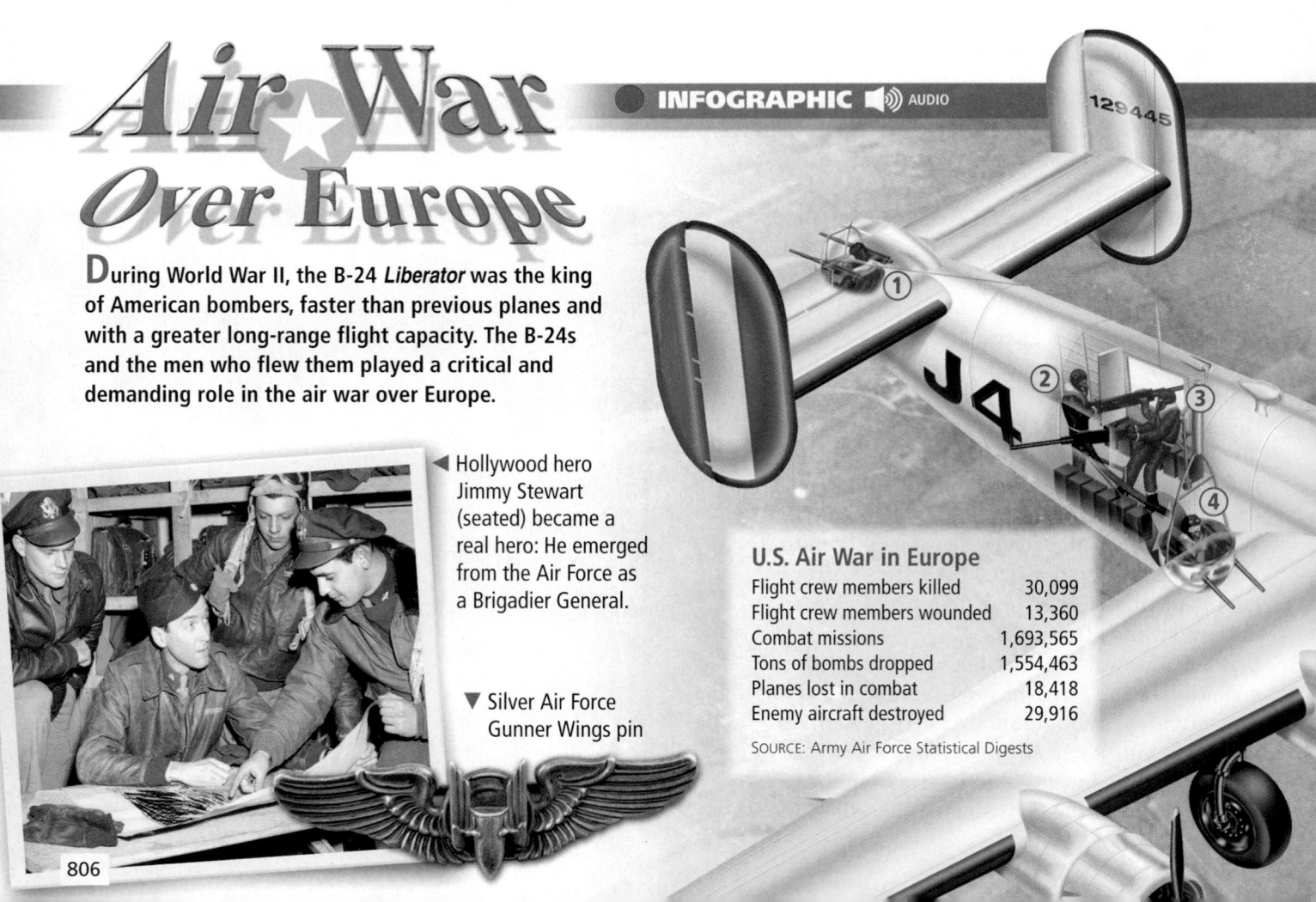

Air ★ War Over Europe

INFOGRAPHIC 🔊 AUDIO

During World War II, the B-24 *Liberator* was the king of American bombers, faster than previous planes and with a greater long-range flight capacity. The B-24s and the men who flew them played a critical and demanding role in the air war over Europe.

◀ Hollywood hero Jimmy Stewart (seated) became a real hero: He emerged from the Air Force as a Brigadier General.

▼ Silver Air Force Gunner Wings pin

U.S. Air War in Europe

Flight crew members killed	30,099
Flight crew members wounded	13,360
Combat missions	1,693,565
Tons of bombs dropped	1,554,463
Planes lost in combat	18,418
Enemy aircraft destroyed	29,916

SOURCE: Army Air Force Statistical Digests

carried the war into Germany, day after day and night after night. This second front in the sky did indeed relieve some of the pressure on the Soviet armies on the Eastern Front and helped pave the way for an all-out Allied offensive.

✔ **Checkpoint** What were the goals of British and American bombing runs over Germany?

Turning the Tide in the Pacific

While the Allies pursued their "Europe First" strategy, they did not ignore the Pacific. Through May 1942, Japanese forces continued to advance with seemingly unstoppable <u>momentum</u>. They had attacked American, British, and Dutch colonies, winning control of the Philippines, Malaya, Dutch East Indies, Hong Kong, Wake Island, Guam, and Burma. Then, the United States struck back. As you have read in the last chapter, the Battle of Coral Sea served as a warning that America might be down in the Pacific, but it was not out.

Vocabulary Builder
<u>momentum</u>–(moh MEHN tuhm) *n.* forward motion; push

Turning Point: Americans Triumph at Midway Admiral Yamamoto, commander of Japanese forces in the Pacific, knew that the United States Navy was still a powerful threat. Before the Americans could retaliate for Pearl Harbor, Yamamoto sought to destroy American aircraft carriers in the Pacific. He turned his attention to Midway, an American naval base in the Central Pacific that was vital to the defense of Hawaii. Losing Midway would force American defenses back to the California coast. Yamamoto's ambitious plan entailed taking Midway and establishing a military presence in the Aleutians, a string of islands off the coast of Alaska.

The B-24 took more crew members to operate than any flying machine ever built. Each member of the 10-man crew had a vital job. (1, 2, 3, 4, 5, 10) **Gunners:** defend the B-24 from attacking enemy planes coming from any direction (5) **Flight Engineer:** handles any mechanical problems; doubles as gunner (6) **Radio Operator:** communicates with ground, other planes (7) **Pilot:** responsible for entire mission (8) **Co-pilot:** assists pilot in flying plane (9) **Navigator:** plots course of plane; also doubles as Bombardier in charge of aiming and dropping bomb

Tuskegee Airmen Rather than carrying bombs, some planes escorted and protected the planes that did. The most celebrated of these escort crews were the Tuskegee Airmen, a special unit of African American pilots. In more than 1,500 missions over Europe, the Tuskegee Airmen did not lose a single bomber.

Thinking Critically
1. **Draw Inferences** Which members of the flight crew carried out the main objective of the mission? What was the chief job of the other members?
2. **Synthesize Information** How did the Tuskegee Airmen affect the casualty figures listed in the chart at left?

What Yamamoto did not realize was that Admiral **Chester Nimitz,** commander of the United States Navy in the Pacific, knew the Japanese plans. Navy code breakers had intercepted Japanese messages. To meet the expected assault, Nimitz sent his only available aircraft carriers to Midway. The Japanese navy was stretched out across more than a thousand miles, from the Aleutians to well west of Midway. American forces were all concentrated near Midway.

The Japanese commenced their attack on June 4, 1942. In the most important naval battle of World War II, the United States dealt Japan a decisive defeat. Torpedo planes and dive bombers sank 4 Japanese aircraft carriers, along with all 250 aircraft on board and many of Japan's most experienced pilots. America lost only one aircraft carrier.

The **Battle of Midway** was the turning point of the war in the Pacific, ending the seemingly unstoppable Japanese advance. Japan still had a powerful navy, committed troops, and fortified positions. But it would never again threaten Hawaii or Pacific domination. Japan was now on the defensive end of the war.

Americans Take the Offensive The first American offensive in the Pacific took place in August 1942, with an assault on Guadalcanal in the Solomon Islands. (See the Witness History at the beginning of this section.) After three months of intense fighting, the United States Marines drove the Japanese off the island.

Guadalcanal was the first leg in a strategy to approach Japan from both the southwest Pacific and the central Pacific, using combined U.S. Marine, Navy, and Army forces. The logic behind the dual offensives was to force Japan to fight a two-front war and to capture bases from which to bomb the Japanese home islands. In jungles and coral reefs, under torrential monsoons and the blistering sun, fighting for every new piece of territory, American servicemen began their slow, painful trek toward Japan.

The Battle of Midway

Midway was a new kind of naval battle. Instead of armed ships facing each other directly, the fighting was carried on by swift airplanes that took off from the decks of aircraft carriers to bomb vessels many miles away.

 Checkpoint What impact did the Battle of Midway have on Japanese expansion in the Pacific?

SECTION **1** Assessment

Progress Monitoring _Online_
For: Self-test with vocabulary practice
Web Code: nea-1102

Comprehension

1. **Terms and People** Write a sentence explaining how each of the following was connected with the Allied effort to turn back the Axis offensive.
   - Dwight Eisenhower
   - George S. Patton, Jr.
   - unconditional surrender
   - saturation bombing
   - strategic bombing
   - Tuskegee Airmen
   - Chester Nimitz
   - Battle of Midway

2. **NoteTaking Reading Skill: Summarize** Use your table to answer the Section Focus Question: How did the Allies turn the tide against the Axis?

Writing About History

3. **Quick Write: Describe a Photograph** Look at the photograph from Stalingrad in this section. Write a two-sentence factual description of what is happening in the picture. Use at least one descriptive adjective and one action verb.

Critical Thinking

4. **Analyze Causes** Why did Roosevelt support a "Europe First" strategy even though it was Japan that had first attacked the United States?

5. **Evaluate Information** Was the Allied invasion of Italy a success? Give reasons for your answer.

6. **Apply Information** How does the Battle of Midway illustrate the importance of intelligence gathering and espionage in modern warfare?

◀ Workers in an aircraft plant

WITNESS HISTORY AUDIO

Rosie the Riveter

Who was Rosie the Riveter? The image of a muscular, determined worker, hair tucked under a kerchief, graced countless magazines and posters. And several real-life Rosies won nationwide publicity, including Rose Hicker, a worker in a Tarrytown, New York, aircraft plant, who set a record for driving rivets into the wing of a bomber. But, in fact, Rosie was not based on one woman. The name was first used in a 1942 song:

❝All the day long, whether rain or shine,
She's a part of the assembly line.
She's making history,
Working for victory,
Rosie the Riveter.❞

—Redd Evans and John Jacob Loeb,
"Rosie the Riveter"

◀ "Rosie the Riveter" poster

The Home Front

Core Curriculum Objectives

- **6.I.C.2b** Role of women in the war
- **6.I.C.2d** Financing the war: War bonds; Hollywood goes to war
- **6.I.C.2e** Rationing
- **6.I.C.5a** War's impact on minorities: Incarceration of Japanese-Americans

Terms and People

A. Philip Randolph
Executive Order 8802
bracero program
internment

442nd Regimental
  Combat Team
rationing
OWI

NoteTaking

Reading Skill: Identify Main Ideas As you read, identify the major effects of World War II on the home front.

The Home Front, World War II		
Economy	**Effects on Women**	**Effects on Minorities**
• War bonds • Wage controls	• •	• •

Why It Matters World War II engaged the peoples and resources of the countries involved. The war effort stirred patriotism and promoted economic recovery. And, while wartime fears and tensions tested civil liberties, new opportunities for women and minorities would spur stronger efforts to ensure equal rights after the war was over. **Section Focus Question: How did the war change America at home?**

New Economic Opportunities

American industry quickly converted to war production to meet the nation's military needs. Once industry exhausted the available men, women found more jobs for the taking. Government and industry launched an all-out publicity campaign urging women to do their part to meet wartime production quotas. In time, women made up one third of the wartime workforce.

Women Work for Victory A woman working outside the home was nothing new, but wartime pressures created two sharp breaks from the past. Many women found jobs, especially in heavy industry, that fell outside the traditional realm of women's work. The need for labor also weakened the common practice that a woman quit her job once she married. Three fourths of women working in war industries were married, and 60 percent were older than 35 years.

The image of Rosie the Riveter's rolled up sleeves, red kerchief, and rivet gun gave Americans an enduring image of women in wartime production. Still, women labored in both blue-collar and white-collar jobs. Most factory owners expected women to step aside

WITNESS HISTORY DVD

Watch *Women in World War II* on the **United States Witness History DVD** to explore the varied contributions of American women to the Allied victory in World War II.

once men returned home at war's end. In white-collar settings, however, the war accelerated long-term trends toward increased employment. During the 1940s, the number of women employed in secretarial and clerical work increased five-fold.

The benefits that women gained from wartime work cannot be underestimated. They earned paychecks, formed new and different relationships, and gained organizational experience. "I decided that if I could learn to weld like a man," noted one laborer, "I could do anything it took to make a living." The confidence and knowledge women developed enriched their postwar experiences and helped create opportunities for their daughters in the years ahead.

With fathers in the military and mothers in the workplace, children's lives began to change. The federal government spent $50 million building day-care centers for children of working mothers. Still, only about 130,000 kids ended up in day-care centers. Many women preferred to leave their children in the care of neighbors or relatives.

African Americans Demand Fair Employment Many African American leaders hoped the war might provide jobs and alleviate their dismal economic situations. However, few found meaningful employment with national defense employers. Out of 100,000 Americans working in the aircraft industry in 1940, for example, only 240 were African Americans. Even jobs provided by the government and military remained segregated.

African American leaders stressed the need for a "Double V" campaign—victory against fascism abroad and victory against discrimination at home. The charismatic and savvy labor leader **A. Philip Randolph** asserted that African Americans would no longer accept second-class citizenship. "We loyal Negro American citizens demand the right to work and fight for our country," he proclaimed. Randolph presented President Roosevelt a list of demands, including the end of discriminatory practices in government-funded training, employment, and the armed services. He also took steps to organize a massive protest march on Washington, D.C.

FDR had hoped to put civil rights reform on the back burner while fighting the Axis Powers. But Randolph persisted in his plans. Roosevelt feared that the sight of a huge protest march on the nation's capital would undermine wartime unity and provide ammunition for enemy propaganda. So, under pressure, he issued **Executive Order 8802.** This measure assured fair hiring practices in any job funded with government money and established the Fair Employment Practices Committee to enforce these requirements.

Such victories encouraged African Americans to join organizations dedicated to promoting equal rights. The NAACP grew to 500,000 members. In 1942, civil rights leaders founded the Congress of Racial Equality (CORE), an organization that sought to apply non-violent protest as a means of fighting segregation. Although segregation still prevailed in the military, the South, and other parts of the nation, wartime developments helped set the agenda for the civil rights struggles of the coming decades.

Checkpoint How did the war create new opportunities for African Americans?

HISTORY MAKERS

A. Philip Randolph (1889–1979)

In 1925, A. Philip Randolph became head of the Brotherhood of Sleeping Car Porters. At the time, virtually all the nation's porters were African American. The Pullman Corporation, which employed them, refused to deal with labor unions. In fact, the Brotherhood had to be organized in secret. For 12 years, the company fired or threatened union members and attacked Randolph as a dangerous radical. But Randolph refused to give up. Finally, in 1937, the Pullman company gave in and signed the first contract in history between a major company and an African American labor union.

Workers on the Move

Wartime needs encouraged migration as people moved in search of work. California alone gained 2 million new residents seeking work in the state's many shipyards and other wartime industries. Although the South lost residents in its rural areas, it grew by a million new people as a whole. Older industrial cities in the North, such as Detroit, Gary, Chicago, and Cleveland, also boomed.

The Population Starts to Shift
The ebb and flow of people fostered long-term changes. After receiving billions of dollars to fund industry, the South and Southwest became a growing cultural, social, economic, and political force. This trend continues to this day.

To alleviate the rural population drain, especially in the West, the United States partnered with Mexico to operate the **bracero program,** bringing laborers from Mexico to work on American farms. During the war years, several hundred thousand braceros migrated to the United States. Although they often faced discrimination, they contributed greatly to the war effort. In the long term, the bracero program <u>initiated</u> decades of migratory labor in the West.

Migration Triggers Conflict
In the summer of 1943, wartime migration led to racial violence in a number of cities. The worst occurred in Detroit, Michigan, where conflict erupted over the construction of housing for black workers drawn north to defense plants. Finally, some 100,000 whites and blacks broke into scattered fights at a city park. By the next morning, full-scale riots erupted in which 34 people were killed. Federal troops ended the violence, but nobody found a real resolution to the city's problems.

Mexican Americans had long dealt with similar tensions. Few had mastered the English language, and many languished in slums while struggling to find work. A violent incident highlighted the problems. In the Los Angeles area, many Mexican and Mexican American youths dressed in stylish "zoot suits" with baggy pants and long jackets. In June 1943, mobs of off-duty sailors roamed through the Mexican sections of Los Angeles, attacking "zooters." Once the fighting ended, police arrested the zoot-suited victims, not their attackers.

Vocabulary Builder
initiate–(ih NIHSH ee ayt) *v.* to begin or originate

After the Zoot Suit Riots
Los Angeles police arrest a group of young Mexican Americans after a spate of violence in June 1943. Some, like the second prisoner from the right, wear the flashy, baggy zoot suits that gave the incident its name.

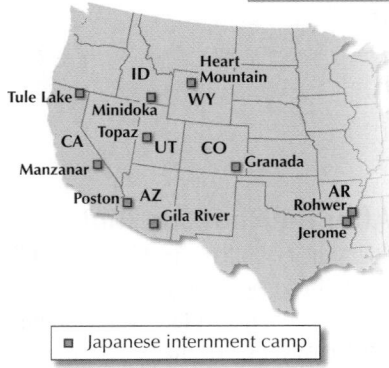

Japanese internment camp

Manzanar Internment Camp

At the Manzanar internment camp in California's Owens Valley (above, right), Japanese Americans lived in bleak barracks, subject to heat and dust storms. Above, a mother and her children await relocation. *Which western states housed internment camps?*

After the riots, an indignant Governor Earl Warren formed a committee to investigate the causes of the outbreak and demanded that the guilty parties be punished. Although the committee blamed the lack of sufficient recreation for the violence, long-brewing racial tensions acted as the true spark.

✓ **Checkpoint** How did the war affect the location of industries and workers in the United States?

A Challenge to Civil Liberties

The attack on Pearl Harbor spread fear across America. The federal government began drafting policies toward immigrants and aliens from the Axis nations. All resident "enemy aliens" were required to register with the government, submit to fingerprinting, and list their organizational affiliations.

Aliens Face Restrictions Originally, laws made no distinction among nationalities. German, Italian, and Japanese aliens were subject to arrest or deportation if deemed dangerous to national security. Some 11,000 German immigrants and hundreds of Italian immigrants were held in camps; others faced curfews or travel restrictions. Federal orders also forced all three groups to vacate the West Coast temporarily in the winter of 1942. Once public fears subsided, FDR removed Germans and Italians from the enemy aliens list.

Japanese aliens and Japanese American citizens received no such respite. Believing Japanese Americans to be inherently disloyal, West Coast leaders pressed FDR to address the "threat." In February 1942, the President issued Executive Order 9066, designating certain areas as war zones from which anyone might be removed for any reason. By September, the government evacuated more than 100,000 Japanese Americans on the West Coast. Evacuees—including both Issei, Japanese immigrants, and Nisei, native-born American citizens of Japanese descent—were forced to sell their property at a loss and allowed to take only necessary items.

Why did Japanese Americans generally face harsher treatment than Italian or German Americans? Several factors help explain the difference: racism, the smaller numbers of Japanese Americans, their lack of political clout, and their relative isolation from other Americans. In Hawaii, where Japanese Americans comprised one third of a multiracial society, they escaped a similar fate.

Vocabulary Builder
comprise–(kuhm PRĪZ) *v.* to include; to make up

Japanese Americans Are Interned The first orders stipulated only that Japanese Americans must leave designated military zones, but leaders in interior states objected. The governor of Arizona insisted his state did not want to become a "dumping ground for enemy aliens." The War Department then initiated a policy of **internment,** or temporary imprisonment of members of a specific group. Japanese American men, women, and children were transported to camps in isolated locations such as Poston, Arizona, and the Gila River Indian Reservation. With few exceptions, Nisei and Issei remained in the camps for the duration of the war.

Families huddled into stark one-room shacks, while single people were herded into drafty bunkhouses. Camp schools were hopelessly underfunded. Internees often suffered from food shortages and substandard medical care. The psychological effects could be just as severe. One internee reported:

> **Primary Source** ❝The resettlement center is actually a jail—armed guards in towers with spotlights and deadly tommy guns, fifteen feet of barbed-wire fences, everyone confined to quarters at nine. . . . What really hurts [is being called] 'Japs.' 'Japs' are the guys we are fighting.❞
> —Ted Nakashima, *The New Republic,* June 5, 1942

Some Japanese Americans went to court to seek their rights. In the 1944 case of Korematsu v. United States, the Supreme Court upheld the government's wartime internment policy. (See Landmark Decisions of the Supreme Court at the end of this section.) Not until 1988 did the government offer an apology and $20,000 payments to surviving internees.

Japanese Americans also faced another form of discrimination. At first, they were not accepted into the armed forces. But after the government lifted the ban in early 1943, many eagerly enlisted. The all-Nisei **442nd Regimental Combat Team** fought in the Italian campaign and became the most decorated military unit in American history. The 442nd helped counter the notion that Japanese Americans were not loyal citizens.

✔ **Checkpoint** Why were Japanese Americans interned during World War II?

Supporting the War Effort

The war eventually cost Americans $330 billion, which was double the total amount of federal expenditures since the founding of the nation. In six years, the national debt skyrocketed from $42 billion to $269 billion. To help raise funds, Congress levied a 5 percent tax on all working Americans. In addition, millions of Americans bought war bonds to save income and invest in the war effort. The government reminded Americans that every dollar spent on war bonds meant another bullet or bomb and another step closer to victory. (See the American Experience feature at the end of this section.)

The Government Manages the Economy Increased production of war goods created a scarcity of consumer products. As shortages led to price increases, many feared that inflation

The Cost of Waging War

The cost of building arms and paying and equipping military personnel caused the federal budget to skyrocket. *Based on the combined information on the two graphs, approximately how much was spent on national defense in 1945?*

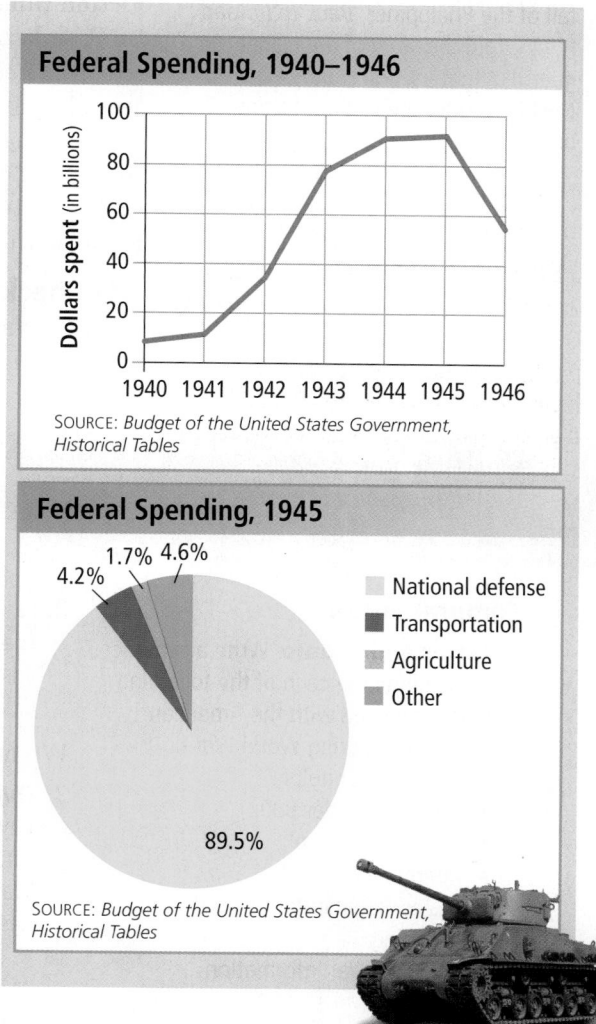

Federal Spending, 1940–1946

Dollars spent (in billions)

1940 1941 1942 1943 1944 1945 1946

SOURCE: *Budget of the United States Government, Historical Tables*

Federal Spending, 1945

- 4.2%
- 1.7%
- 4.6%
- 89.5%

- National defense
- Transportation
- Agriculture
- Other

SOURCE: *Budget of the United States Government, Historical Tables*

Sherman tank ▶

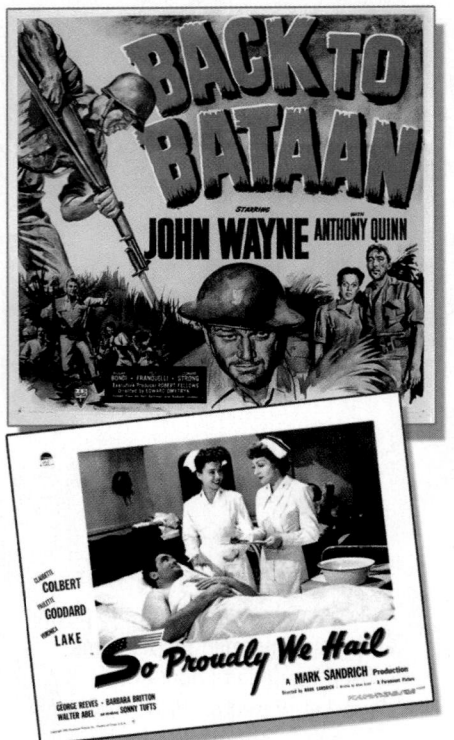

Hollywood Goes to War
The two films above dealt with the fall of the Philippines. *Back to Bataan* (1945) told the story of anti-Japanese guerrilla fighters. *So Proudly We Hail* (1943) paid tribute to the courage of army nurses.

would run wild. To manage this problem, FDR created the Office of Price Administration, which had the authority to control wages and set maximum prices. Another form of economic control was **rationing.** Americans were issued coupon books that limited the amount of certain goods, such as butter and tires, that they could buy. Rationing ensured that raw materials such as rubber and oil found their way into war production.

Although most Americans accepted the need for wartime controls, others resented the restrictions. Unscrupulous profiteers manipulated the ration coupon system to create a "black market," an illegal underground network for the sale of restricted goods. Because the government restricted job mobility to ensure constant production and because wages lagged behind rising prices and profits, some workers accused their employers of unfair practices. Still, Americans created a powerful industrial network that contributed to victory and carried long-term consequences.

Media Boosts Morale Sacrifices on the home front took a toll on morale. The federal **Office of War Information (OWI)** worked closely with the media to encourage support of the war effort. The OWI tried to spotlight common needs, minimize racial and economic divisions, and downplay problems of poverty and crime. The radio, print, and film industries reminded Americans that they were in a struggle between dictatorship and democracy.

Hollywood proved a capable and willing ally in this cause. Documentaries like Frank Capra's *Why We Fight* series highlighted the need to defeat fascism. Fiction films showed patriotic Americans pitching in overseas or on the home front and stirred hatred of the enemy with stereotypical portrayals of treacherous Japanese and brutal Germans. Movie stars and popular singers volunteered their time to sell war bonds and entertain the troops.

Encouraged by government and media, Americans voluntarily contributed to the war effort in dozens of large and small ways. They planted victory gardens and collected paper, scrap metal, and fat. Instead of buying new, many people followed the motto "Use it up, wear it out, make it do, and do without."

☑ **Checkpoint** How did the federal government control resources needed for the war effort?

SECTION 2 Assessment

Progress Monitoring *Online*
For: Self-test with vocabulary practice
Web Code: nea-1103

Comprehension
1. **Terms and People** Write a sentence explaining how each of the following was connected with the American home front during World War II.
   • A. Philip Randolph
   • Executive Order 8802
   • bracero program
   • internment
   • 442nd Regimental Combat Team
   • rationing
   • Office of War Information

2. **NoteTaking** Reading Skill: **Identify Main Ideas** Use your table to answer the Section Focus Question: How did the war change America at home?

Writing About History
3. **Quick Write: Describe a Scene** Review the text relating to Japanese American internment during World War II. Write a two-sentence factual description of what you might witness as a family is being sent to a camp. Use at least one descriptive adjective and one action verb.

Critical Thinking
4. **Predict Consequences** Predict two possible consequences for wartime women factory workers when men began to return from overseas after the war.

5. **Compare** How were the causes of the Detroit race riots and the Los Angeles Zoot Suit Riots similar?

6. **Draw Conclusions** Do you think the federal government was justified in limiting individual freedom by imposing wage and price controls and by rationing during wartime? Why or why not?

Can government limit a group's liberties during wartime?

NY 6.I.C.5a

Because some leaders feared that some Japanese Americans might be disloyal, the government took action against the whole group. How should national security be balanced against civil rights?

Korematsu v. United States (1944)

The Facts	The Issue	The Decision
• In 1942, President Roosevelt ordered that select people could be banned from war zones. • The army relocated Japanese Americans on the West Coast to internment camps. • Fred Korematsu was arrested for resisting the army's order.	Korematsu argued that he was denied equal protection under the law simply because he was a Japanese American.	The Court held that the military order was justified for security reasons. Three judges dissented. Justice Frank Murphy wrote that internment "falls into the ugly abyss of racism."

Why It Matters

Most experts today agree with Murphy that the *Korematsu* case was a triumph of prejudice over justice. In recent years, the war on terrorism has revived talk of *Korematsu* in discussions of "racial profiling." Racial profiling is a law enforcement technique in which police or federal investigators single out members of a particular racial or ethnic group for questioning. Defenders of profiling argue that, because several deadly terrorist attacks were carried out by radical Muslims, it is only logical for law enforcement officials to pay special attention to Muslims. Critics insist that racial profiling is a form of prejudice that violates the civil rights of individuals.

▲ A Japanese American is arrested in 1943.

Connect to Your World

Discussing racial profiling in 2004, Fred Korematsu warned, "No one should ever be locked away simply because they share the same race, ethnicity, or religion as a spy or terrorist. If that principle was not learned from the internment of Japanese Americans, then these are very dangerous times for our democracy." Write an editorial agreeing or disagreeing with Fred Korematsu's position.
For: Supreme Court cases
Web Code: neh-1115

◄ Americans today protest against racial profiling by law enforcement officials.

EXPERIENCE THE WORLD WAR II HOME FRONT

While fathers, sons, husbands, and brothers were serving overseas, their families served on the home front. Every American was expected to help boost morale and make sacrifices to shoulder the cost of the war.

Since World War II, the United States has not experienced a war that required so much of Americans on the home front. However, soldiers today continue to face combat, homesickness, and occasional boredom. That is why the USO and ordinary citizens still work to provide support for America's troops. ◀))) AUDIO

▲ **Collecting Scrap**
Here, children collect junk metal that might be turned into bullets or old clothes that could be recycled into blankets and uniforms.

▼ **Victory Gardens**
With so much farm produce going to feed the troops, people planted "victory gardens" in vacant lots (below) or in their backyards.

▲ **Rationing**
Households were issued ration books and stamps, which told them how much of certain items, such as sugar or butter, they were allowed to buy. The above poster explains how the rationing system worked.

▼ USO
Through the United Service Organizations (USO), volunteers boosted the morale of those who were fighting the war. At the USO's Hollywood Canteen in Los Angeles, a soldier could get a hot meal served by a celebrity or dance with their favorite movie star. Here, servicemen pose with glamorous actress Hedy Lamarr.

War Bonds Poster ▶

They're fighting harder than ever

are you buying MORE WAR BONDS THAN EVER?

Thinking Critically
1. **Analyze Visuals** Choose one of the posters shown on this spread and describe what message it gave to people.
2. **Draw Conclusions** Do you think the effort on the home front helped to win the war? Explain.

Connect to Today How do Americans today give support and encouragement to people serving in the military?

History Interactive ✴
For: More about the home front in World War II.
Web Code: nep-1115

Lieutenant
Audie
Murphy ▶

WITNESS HISTORY 🔊 AUDIO

Audie Murphy, American Hero

Audie Murphy received more medals than any other American in World War II. In January 1945, his squad was set upon by German troops near Holtzwihr, France. Ordering his men to withdraw, Murphy climbed atop a burning tank that was in danger of exploding. For an hour, the young lieutenant used the tank's machine gun to hold off the enemy on three sides:

❝Germans reached as close as 10 yards, only to be mowed down by his fire. He received a leg wound, but ignored it and continued the single-handed fight until his ammunition was exhausted. He then made his way to his company, refused medical attention, and organized the company in a counterattack.❞

—Medal of Honor Citation for Audie Murphy

Victory in Europe and the Pacific

 Core Curriculum Objectives

- **6.I.C.3c** Allied strategy and leadership: A two-front war
- **6.I.C.4a** Atomic bomb: The Manhattan project
- **6.I.C.4b** Truman's decision to use the atomic bomb against Japan: Hiroshima and Nagasaki

Terms and People

D-Day	kamikaze
Battle of the Bulge	Albert Einstein
Harry S. Truman	Manhattan Project
island hopping	J. Robert Oppenheimer

NoteTaking

Reading Skill: Recognize Sequence
Identify the steps that led to the Allied victory.

Europe	The Pacific
• Allies land at Normandy on D-Day	•
•	•

Allies Win World War II

Why It Matters In 1942 and 1943, the Allies turned back the Axis advances. In the last two years of the war, 1944 and 1945, they delivered the final, crushing blow. They attacked Germany from the west and east, and the United States advanced across the Pacific to the doorstep of Japan. In the process, Americans created a new form of weapon that would change both warfare and global politics. **Section Focus Question: How did the Allies defeat the Axis Powers?**

Planning Germany's Defeat

Throughout 1943, Roosevelt, Churchill, and Stalin squabbled over when they would start a second front in France. Up to that point, Soviet troops had done most of the fighting in Europe. Stalin insisted that Britain and the United States carry more of the military burden by attacking Germany in the west, thereby forcing Germany to divide its troops.

Roosevelt sympathized with Stalin's position, but Churchill hesitated and delayed. Recalling the slaughter of British troops on the Western Front in World War I, he was not anxious to see history repeat itself. He argued that the German U-boat presence was too great in the English Channel and that the Allies needed more landing craft, more equipment, and better-trained soldiers.

In November 1943, Roosevelt and Churchill traveled to Teheran, Iran, for their first face-to-face meeting with Stalin. Churchill continued to voice reservations about a cross-channel invasion, but

FDR sided with Stalin. Reluctantly, Churchill agreed. After years of war, British and American soldiers would invade France and begin their march toward Germany. At the end of the Teheran Conference, the Big Three issued a joint statement that gave no hint of their earlier disagreements:

Primary Source "We have reached complete agreement as to the scope and timing of the operations to be undertaken from the east, west and south. The common understanding which we have here reached guarantees that victory will be ours. . . . No power on earth can prevent our destroying the German armies by land, their U Boats by sea, and their war planes from the air."
—Declaration of the Three Powers, December 1, 1943

Six months after the Teheran Conference, the plan to open a second front in France became reality. The massive Allied invasion of France was given the code name Operation Overlord.

✓ **Checkpoint** On what issues did Stalin, Roosevelt, and Churchill disagree?

D-Day Invasion of Normandy

Overlord involved the most experienced Allied officers in Europe. American General Dwight D. Eisenhower again served as Supreme Commander. British General Bernard Montgomery served as commander of the ground forces, while General Omar Bradley led the United States First Army.

Eisenhower Plans the Invasion Overlord involved landing 21 American divisions and 26 British, Canadian, and Polish divisions on a 50-mile stretch of beaches in Normandy. The fleet was the largest ever assembled, comprising more than 4,400 ships and landing crafts.

The plan dictated striking five beaches in Normandy (code-named Utah, Omaha, Gold, Juno, and Sword), but it also involved an elaborate deception. The Allies created a fictional army under General Patton. Although the army existed only on paper, the Allies set up fake headquarters in southeast England across the English Channel from Calais, equipped with wood and cardboard tanks, useless ships, and detectable radio traffic. The Allies hoped to convince the Germans that the Allied attack would come at Calais, not farther west in Normandy. In the end, the deception worked. Hitler ordered his top tank division to Calais.

Heroes Storm the Beaches On June 6, 1944—known as **D-Day**—the Allies hit Germany in force. More than 11,000 planes prepared the way, attempting to destroy German communication and transportation networks and soften Nazi beach defenses. At 6:30 A.M., after a rough crossing of the English Channel, the first troops landed.

On four of the beaches, the landings were only lightly opposed and casualties relatively low. But at Omaha, one of the two beaches assigned to American forces, the Germans offered stiff opposition. On the cliffs overlooking the beach, the Germans had dug trenches and built small concrete pillbox structures from which heavy artillery could be fired. They had the beach covered with

HISTORY MAKERS

Dwight D. Eisenhower (1890–1969)
As a young man, Dwight Eisenhower had not been considered a brilliant student at the U.S. Military Academy at West Point. During the 1930s, though, his career rose due to his organizational skill and ability to work with others. In 1942, Ike was given command of all American forces in Europe—even though more than 350 other generals had more seniority. After strong performances in North Africa and Italy, he was made Supreme Commander of Allied Forces. His skillful handling of the D-Day invasion and the drive to Germany won wide respect. Eisenhower went on to serve two terms as President before retiring.

a wide variety of deadly guns. They had also heavily mined the beaches. When the first American soldiers landed, they stepped out of their landing crafts into a rainstorm of bullets, shells, and death. Some crafts dumped their occupants too far from the beach; soldiers, weighted down by heavy packs, drowned.

One writer called D-Day "the longest day." For many Americans, it was a very short day—and their last on Earth. Some fought bravely and died. Others fought bravely and survived. By the end of the day, the Allies had gained a toehold in France. Within a month, more than one million Allied troops had landed at Normandy. Berlin, the capital of Germany, was still a long road ahead, but the Allies had taken the first, and most important, step on that road.

✓ **Checkpoint** What was the primary objective of the D-Day invasion at Normandy?

THE ALLIES LAND ON D-DAY

"You are about to embark upon the Great Crusade, toward which we have striven these many months." General Eisenhower gave this message to Allied troops on the morning of June 6, 1944. "You will bring about the destruction of the German war machine, the elimination of Nazi tyranny over oppressed peoples of Europe, and security for ourselves in a free world." That day, Allied troops stormed the beaches of Normandy, paving the way for the liberation of France and the final defeat of the Nazis. But victory came at a tremendous cost. Wave after wave of soldiers were mowed down by German fire. One American later recalled, "As our boat touched sand and the ramp went down, I became a visitor to hell."

"The carnage on the beach was indescribable.... Although many wounded men were crying for help, aid-men were scarce and others could not help because they had an assigned task to accomplish."
—**Thomas E. Herring, C Company**

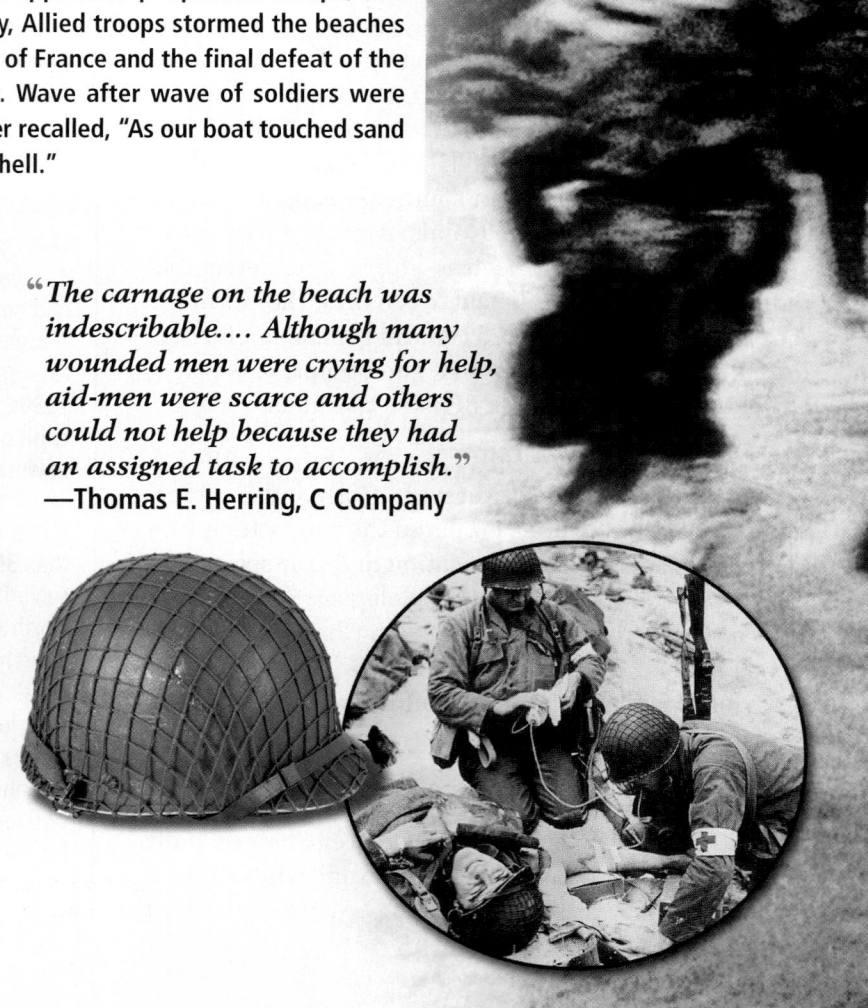

▲ The invasion of Normandy was truly a massive international effort. U.S., Canadian, and British forces were assigned to different beaches. Members of the French Underground were waiting to offer aid and support.

Liberation of Europe

After D-Day, Germany faced a hopeless two-front war. Soviet soldiers were advancing steadily from the east, forcing German armies out of Latvia, Romania, Slovakia, and Hungary. Mile by mile, Germany lost the lands it had once dominated and the natural resources it had once plundered.

Allies Advance Allied armies were also on the move in the west. In August 1944, the Allies liberated Paris. Hitler had ordered his generals to destroy the French capital, but they disobeyed him, leaving the "City of Lights" as beautiful as ever. As Parisians celebrated, Allied troops kept advancing.

As a mood of hopelessness fell over Germany, Rommel and other leading generals plotted to overthrow Hitler. On July 20, 1944, an officer planted a bomb at Hitler's headquarters. The explosion killed or wounded 20 people, but Hitler

"I remember the bullets flying over our craft and seeing the ricochets of the bullets hitting the water. The landing craft's door fell open and we ran into the surf. We were in very deep water and I thought I was either going to drown or be shot before getting to land. By the grace of God, I made it ashore and started running through the deep water toward the seawall."
—Jack Fox, combat medic

▲ Sixty years after D-Day, an American veteran revisits the cemetery in Normandy where so many of his comrades are buried.

Why It Matters

Six decades later, Americans still take pride in the young heroes who secured Omaha Beach. Whether they died on the blood-soaked sands or survived against impossible odds, the D-Day invaders helped create an enduring standard of courage, sacrifice, and patriotism. Books like Tom Brokaw's *The Greatest Generation* and movies like Steven Spielberg's *Saving Private Ryan* honor their memory.

Thinking Critically

Why do you think a veteran of D-Day would choose to return to a place where so many people died?

History *Interactive* ✶

For: Eyewitness accounts of D-Day
Web Code: nep-1105

World War II in Europe, 1942–1945

Geography *Interactive*
For: Interactive map
Web Code: nep-1106

Legend:
- Axis Powers, 1942
- Greatest extent of Axis control, 1942
- Allied territory, 1942
- Neutral nations, 1942
- Allied advance
- Major battle

Map labels: FINLAND, Leningrad, NORWAY, SWEDEN, Moscow, North Sea, DENMARK, Baltic Sea, SOVIET UNION, Stalingrad, 1943, Kursk, 1943, 1944, Warsaw, 1945, Berlin, 1945, 1945, GERMANY, 1944, IRELAND, UNITED KINGDOM, NETH., London, BELG., 1944, D-Day, NORMANDY, Paris, FRANCE, 1944, SWITZ., 1944, SLOVAKIA, 1945, HUNGARY, 1944, ROMANIA, Yalta, Black Sea, Atlantic Ocean, Vichy, Vichy France, ITALY, 1944, CROATIA, SERBIA, MONT., BULGARIA, ALB., GREECE, TURKEY, SYRIA, PORTUGAL, SPAIN, Rome, Anzio, 1944, 1943, Salerno, Palermo, Sicily, Mediterranean Sea, Tunis, 1943, Lebanon (Fr.), Battle of the Bulge (see below)

Scale: Conic Projection, 0 200 400 mi, 0 200 400 km

Winston Churchill gave U.S. forces full credit for the Allied victory at the Battle of the Bulge:

Primary Source "The United States troops have done almost all the fighting and have suffered almost all the losses. They have suffered losses almost equal to those of both sides at the Battle of Gettysburg. . . . [The Battle of the Bulge] will, I believe, be regarded as an ever-famous American victory."

—Winston Churchill, Address to the House of Commons, January 18, 1945

Map Skills In the final phases of the war in Europe, the Allies hemmed in Germany from the east, west, and south.
1. **Locate:** (a) Stalingrad, (b) Sicily, (c) Normandy, (d) Berlin
2. **Movement** Describe American and German troop movements at the Battle of the Bulge.
3. **Draw Conclusions** Why do you think there was no Allied attempt to approach Germany from the north?

Battle of the Bulge

Map labels: Meuse R., BELGIUM, St. Vith, Prüm, Ciergnon, La Roche, Rochefort, Ourthe R., Houffalize, Our R., GERMANY, Clervaux, St. Hubert, Bastogne, Wiltz, Vianden, Libramont, Neufchâteau, Echternach, LUXEMBOURG, Trier, Luxembourg, Moselle R., FRANCE

Scale: Conic Projection, 0 10 20 mi, 0 10 20 km

Legend:
- Axis control, Dec. 15, 1944
- Allied control, Dec. 15, 1944
- German offensive
- Allied counterattack
- Front line, Dec. 16, 1944
- Front line, Dec. 25, 1944
- Front line, Jan. 16, 1945

Battle of the Bulge ▲
The Battle of the Bulge was the last Nazi offensive of the war. After its failure, the German armies were in constant retreat.

survived. Rommel took poison to escape being put on trial. Claiming that fate was on his side, Hitler refused to surrender to the advancing troops.

Germany Counterattacks In December 1944, Hitler ordered a counterattack. With Allied troops strung out between the English Channel and the Alps, German forces massed near the Ardennes. Hitler's <u>scenario</u> called for English-speaking German soldiers in U.S. uniforms to cut telephone lines, change road signs, and spread confusion. German tanks would then secure communication and transportation hubs.

The counterattack, known as the **Battle of the Bulge,** almost succeeded. The Germans caught the Allies by surprise, created a bulge in the American line, and captured several key towns. Snowy, cloudy skies prevented the Allies from exploiting their air superiority. But at the Belgian town of Bastogne (bas TOHN), American forces held despite frostbite and brutal German assaults. Then, on December 23, the skies cleared and Allied bombers attacked German positions. After reinforcements arrived, the Allies went back on the offensive, steadily pushing the Germans out of France.

The Battle of the Bulge was a desperate attempt to drive a wedge between American and British forces. Instead, it crippled Germany by using its reserves and demoralizing its troops. Ultimately, it shortened the time Hitler had left.

Allies Push to Victory By January, the Soviet Army had reached the Oder River outside Berlin. The Allies also advanced northward in Italy. In April 1945, Mussolini tried to flee to Switzerland but was captured and executed. By this time, American and British troops had crossed the Rhine River into Germany. In April, a U.S. army reached the Elbe River, 50 miles west of Berlin. Allied forces were now in position for an all-out assault against Hitler's capital.

Hitler was by now a physical wreck: shaken by tremors, paranoid from drugs, and kept alive by mad dreams of a final victory. He gave orders that no one followed and planned campaigns that no one would ever fight. Finally, on April 30, he and a few of his closest associates committed suicide. His "Thousand Year Reich" had lasted only a dozen years.

On May 7, in a little French schoolhouse that had served as Eisenhower's headquarters, Germany surrendered. Americans celebrated V-E (Victory in Europe) Day. Sadly, FDR did not see the momentous day. He had died a few weeks earlier. It would be up to the new President, **Harry S. Truman,** to see the nation through to final victory.

✔ **Checkpoint** What were the results of the Battle of the Bulge?

Advancing in the Pacific

While war still raged in Europe, American forces in the Pacific had been advancing in giant leaps. They followed an **island-hopping** strategy, capturing some Japanese-held islands and ignoring others in a steady path toward Japan. From Tarawa and Makin in the Gilbert Islands, American forces jumped ahead to Eniwetok and Kwajalein in the Marshall Islands. Then, they took another leap to Saipan, Tinian, and Guam in the Mariana Islands.

Japanese Troops Fight to the Death American forces took each island only after a nearly unbelievable life-and-death struggle. Time and again, Japanese defenders fought

Vocabulary Builder
scenario–(suh NAIR ee oh) *n.* outline for a proposed series of events; script

Navajo Code Talkers
Navajo troops played a vital role in the Pacific island-hopping campaign. Using a code based on their own language—which was a mystery to the Japanese—Navajo radio operators sent critical messages from island to island. *What other special ethnic units played a role in the American war effort?*

World War II in the Pacific, 1942–1945

Areas under Japanese control, 1942
Extent of Japanese control, June 1942
Extent of Japanese control, June 1944
Allied advance
Atomic bomb target
Major battle

SOVIET UNION

MONGOLIA

Manchuria (Manchukuo)

Vladivostok

Beijing

Korea

CHINA

Yellow Sea

Shanghai

Hiroshima (Aug. 1945)

Tokyo

JAPAN

Sea of Japan (East Sea)

Kuril Islands

Aleutian Islands (U.S.)

Pacific Ocean

Nagasaki (Aug. 1945)

East China Sea

Okinawa (April–June 1945)

Iwo Jima (Feb.–March 1945)

Midway (June 1942)

Hawaiian Islands (U.S.)

INDIA

Burma (U.K.)

French Indochina

Hong Kong (U.K.)

South China Sea

Bangkok

Philippine Sea (June 1944)

Mariana Islands

Manila

Philippines (U.S.)

Wake Island (U.S.)

Saipan (June–July 1944)

Guam (July–Aug. 1944)

Marshall Islands (U.S.)

THAILAND

Leyte Gulf (Oct. 1944)

Caroline Islands

Malaya (U.K.)
Singapore

Sumatra

Borneo

Celebes

Tarawa (Nov. 1943)

Gilbert Islands (U.K.)

Batavia
Java

Dutch East Indies

New Guinea

Rabaul

New Britain (Dec. 1944)

Solomon Islands (U.K./Aust.)

Guadalcanal (Aug. 1942–Feb. 1943)

Eastern Solomons (Aug. 1942)

Santa Cruz (Oct. 1942)

Coral Sea

Darwin

Coral Sea (May 1942)

Indian Ocean

AUSTRALIA

Miller Projection
0   500   1,000 mi
0   500   1,000 km

Map Skills The island-hopping strategy brought U.S. forces closer and closer to the Japanese home islands, but it took even more drastic measures to bring the war in the Pacific to an end.

1. Locate: (a) Guadalcanal, (b) Okinawa, (c) Iwo Jima, (d) Hiroshima, (e) Nagasaki

2. Movement Describe the two separate island-hopping paths that brought American marines to Okinawa.

3. Predict Consequences What might have happened in the Pacific if Japan had been able to take Midway and Hawaii early in the war?

virtually to the last man. Rather than surrender, many Japanese troops readily killed themselves. At the same time, Japanese **kamikaze** (kah muh KAH zee) pilots deliberately crashed their planes into American ships. By the end of the war, more than 3,000 Japanese pilots had died in kamikaze missions. Their deaths, however, did not prevent General Douglas MacArthur from retaking the Philippines or the United States Navy from sinking Japanese ships.

American Forces Near Japan One of the fiercest battles in the island-hopping campaign took place in February and March 1945. On Iwo Jima (EE woh JEE muh), a 5-mile-long island 650 miles southeast of Tokyo, United States Marines faced a dug-in, determined enemy. In 36 days of fighting, more than 23,000 marines became casualties. But they took the island. The famous photograph of six marines (including Native American Ira Hayes) planting the American flag on Iwo Jima symbolized the heroic sacrifice of American soldiers.

The fight for Okinawa (oh kuh NAH wuh) in April 1945 was even deadlier. Only 340 miles from Japan, Okinawa contained a vital air base, necessary for the planned invasion of Japan. Taking Okinawa was the most complex and costly operation in the Pacific campaign, involving half a million troops and 1,213 warships. U.S. forces finally took Okinawa but at a cost of roughly 50,000 casualties.

From Okinawa and other Pacific bases, American pilots could bomb the Japanese home islands. Short on pilots and aircraft, low on fuel and ammunition, Japan was virtually defenseless. American bombers hit factories, military bases, and cities. In a single night in March 1945, B-29 bombers destroyed 16 square miles of Tokyo. The raid killed over 83,000 Japanese—more than either of the later atomic bombs—and injured 100,000 more.

✔ **Checkpoint** Why was the island-hopping campaign in the Pacific so deadly to both sides?

The Atomic Bomb Ends the War

Advances in technology, as well as the troops, helped determine the outcome of World War II. (See the Quick Study chart.) Allied and Axis scientists labored to make planes faster, bombs deadlier, and weapons more accurate. The most crucial scientific development of all was the atomic bomb.

▼ A soldier reading a radar screen

The Manhattan Project Develops the A-Bomb The atomic bomb began with an idea. In the early 1930s, scientists learned how to split the nuclei of certain elements. They also discovered that this process of nuclear fission released tremendous energy. Over the next decade, they learned more about the nature of the atom, the effect of a chain reaction, and the military uses of uranium.

Science and Technology of World War II		☑ Quick Study
Advance	**Military Use in WWII**	**Civilian Applications**
Radar	Detected objects such as bombs, incoming gunfire, or enemy ships	Used to track weather systems and monitor automobile speed
Calculating machines	Allowed cryptographers to break enemy codes by detecting letter patterns and frequencies	Developed into small personal computers
Jet engines	Enabled planes to fly much faster than non-jet-powered planes	Used in commercial airplanes
Penicillin	Cured soldiers' infected wounds, saving many lives	Used to treat bacterial infections

Vocabulary Builder

priority—(prī AHR uh tee) *n.*
degree of importance or urgency

Early in the war, **Albert Einstein,** the world's most famous scientist, signed a letter that alerted President Roosevelt about the need to proceed with atomic development. In 1942, FDR gave the highest national priority to the development of an atomic bomb. The program, code-named the **Manhattan Project,** cost several billion dollars and employed tens of thousands of people.

The two primary leaders of the project were General Leslie Groves and physicist **J. Robert Oppenheimer.** Groves was responsible for building facilities, acquiring the necessary materials, recruiting scientists, and providing security. Oppenheimer ran the scientific aspect of the project from the construction site in Los Alamos, New Mexico. Scientists working on the project included many refugees from Europe, including Enrico Fermi, developer of the first atomic reactor. Security on the Manhattan Project was tight. People worked on small parts of the puzzle, little realizing the whole picture.

On the morning of July 16, 1945, in a barren area outside of Alamogordo, New Mexico, the first atomic bomb was tested. The flash of light was clearly visible 180 miles away, and the sound was heard at a distance of 100 miles. Watching the blast, Oppenheimer recalled the following line from a Hindu poem: "Now I am become Death, the destroyer of Worlds."

The general's thoughts were less poetic. Turning to an aide, Groves said, "The war's over. One or two of those things and Japan will be finished."

Truman Makes His Decision The decision to use the bomb fell directly on the narrow shoulders of Harry Truman. The new President fully understood the ethical issues presented by using the bomb, especially against civilians. At the same time, he also knew that the Axis Powers had nuclear scientists, and there was no way to tell how close they were to developing their own bomb. Ultimately, Truman's chief priority was to save American lives. His military advisers predicted that, in light of the ferocious defense waged by Japanese soldiers during

Decision ⬤ Point

Should the United States Drop the Atomic Bomb?

President Truman had to decide whether to drop the bomb on Japan. Read the options below. Then, you decide.

Truman Favors Using the Bomb

Primary Source

"I asked Gen. Marshall what it would cost in lives to land . . . in Japan. It was his opinion that 1/4 million casualties would be the minimum cost. . . . I asked Sec. Stimson which cities in Japan were devoted exclusively to war production. He . . . named Hiroshima and Nagasaki. We sent an ultimatum to Japan. It was ignored. I ordered atomic bombs dropped on the two cities. . . . Dropping the bombs ended the war, saved lives and gave the free nations a chance to face the facts."

—President Harry S. Truman

Scientists Advise Caution

Primary Source

"We the undersigned scientists . . . believe that the United States ought not resort to the use of atomic bombs in the present phase of the war, at least not unless . . . Japan is given an opportunity to surrender. . . . A nation which sets the precedent of using these newly liberated forces of nature for purposes of destruction may have to bear the responsibility of opening the door to an era of devastation on an unimaginable scale."

—Scientist Leo Szilard

You Decide
1. Why did Truman decide to drop the bomb?
2. What course of action did Szilard favor?
3. What decision would you have made? Why?

the island-hopping campaign, an invasion of Japan might cost as many as 1,000,000 American casualties.

In truth, Truman did not agonize over the decision to use the atomic bomb against Japan. For the President, abstract ethical issues did not outweigh very real American lives and an opportunity to end the war. Later, some critics would condemn Truman's decision. But in the late summer of 1945, no one close to him did so.

Hiroshima and Nagasaki Are Destroyed On August 6, 1945, U.S. pilots dropped an atomic bomb on Hiroshima. It exploded at 9:14 A.M. One survivor of the blast later recalled the first moments:

Primary Source ❝After I noticed the flash, white clouds spread over the blue sky. It was amazing. It was as if blue morning-glories had suddenly bloomed up in the sky. . . . Then came the heat wave. It was very, very hot. Even though there was a window glass in front of me, I felt really hot. It was as if I was looking directly into a kitchen oven.❞

—Isao Kita, *Hiroshima Witness*

Within two minutes, more than 60,000 of Hiroshima's 344,000 residents were dead or missing.

Over the next three days, Japanese leaders debated whether to surrender or continue to fight. Then, on August 9, two events rocked Japan. First, the Soviet Union declared war against Japan and invaded Manchuria. Next, the United States dropped a second atomic bomb on Nagasaki, killing 35,000 residents.

Debate continued at the highest levels of Japanese government. Finally, Emperor Hirohito made the decision to surrender. On August 15, the Allies celebrated V-J (Victory in Japan) Day. Japan officially surrendered on September 2 aboard the USS *Missouri*. The most costly war in history was over. As many as 60,000,000 people, mostly civilians, had died in the conflict.

✔ **Checkpoint** What were the consequences of the decision to bomb Hiroshima and Nagasaki?

Hiroshima
This 1945 photograph shows the effects of just one atomic bomb on the city of Hiroshima. The heat was so intense that it melted this bottle (right).

SECTION 3 Assessment

Progress Monitoring *Online*
For: Self-test with vocabulary practice
Web Code: nea-1108

Comprehension

1. **Terms and People** Write a sentence explaining how each of the following was connected with the Allies' final push toward victory in World War II.
   - D-Day
   - Battle of the Bulge
   - Harry S. Truman
   - island hopping
   - kamikaze
   - Manhattan Project
   - J. Robert Oppenheimer

2. **NoteTaking Reading Skill: Recognize Sequence** Use your table to answer the Section Focus Question: How did the Allies defeat the Axis Powers?

Writing About History

3. **Quick Write: Identify Impressions** Review the text description of the D-Day landings, including the Events That Changed America feature. Then, make a list of sights, sounds, and smells associated with the event.

Critical Thinking

4. **Summarize** Summarize the arguments for and against an Allied invasion of France before 1944.

5. **Compare and Contrast** How were the final phases of the war in Europe similar to the final phases of the war in the Pacific? How were they different?

6. **Predict Consequences** What effect do you think possession of the atomic bomb will have on the role of the United States in the postwar world?

SECTION 4

▲ These starving prisoners at the Ebensee death camp in Austria were liberated by American soldiers.

"I Have No Words"

On April 15, 1945, American radio listeners sat stunned as newsman Edward R. Murrow told of a horror beyond belief. Murrow was reporting about his visit to the Nazi concentration camp at Buchenwald. He described the emaciated, hollow-eyed prisoners, the stink which was "beyond all description," the children with identification numbers tattooed on their arms, and the hundreds of "bodies stacked up like cordwood." Toward the end of his report, Murrow said:

❝I pray you to believe what I have said about Buchenwald. I have reported what I saw and heard, but only part of it. For most of it I have no words. Dead men are plentiful in war, but the living dead, more than twenty thousand of them in one camp. . . . If I've offended you by this rather mild account of Buchenwald, I'm not in the least sorry.❞
—Edward R. Murrow, CBS Radio Broadcast, April 15, 1945

The Holocaust

 Core Curriculum Objectives

- **6.I.C.5c** The Nazi Holocaust: United States and world reactions

Terms and People

Holocaust	genocide
anti-Semitism	concentration camp
Nuremberg Laws	death camp
Kristallnacht	War Refugee Board

NoteTaking

Reading Skill: Recognize Sequence As you read, identify the steps that led to Hitler's attempt to exterminate European Jews.

> 1933: Hitler becomes dictator of Germany; begins persecution of Jews

Why It Matters From the time he came to power, Adolf Hitler had targeted Jews for persecution. By the end of the war, the Nazis had murdered 6 million Jews and 5 million other people they considered inferior. Today, we continue to remember this tragedy and seek ways to prevent anything like it from ever happening again. **Section Focus Question: How did the Holocaust develop and what were its results?**

Roots of the Holocaust

What Edward R. Murrow saw at Buchenwald was just a fragment of the most horrific chapter of the Nazi era. In 1945, there was no word for it. Today, it is called the **Holocaust,** the Nazi attempt to kill all Jews under their control. The mass murders of Jews, as well as other "undesirables," were a direct result of a racist Nazi ideology that considered Aryans (white gentiles, especially those of Germanic, Nordic, and Anglo-Saxon blood) superior to other people.

Hitler Preaches Hate From the start, the Nazi movement trafficked in hatred and **anti-Semitism.** Hitler blamed Jews for all the ills of Germany, from communism to inflation to abstract painting—and, especially, for the defeat of Germany in World War I.

Other extremists influenced Hitler's ideas and shared his prejudices. In the 1920s, his was just another angry voice in the Weimar Republic, advancing simplistic answers for the nation's grave economic, political, and social troubles. In 1933, however, Hitler became chancellor of Germany.

Nazis Begin the Persecution
Hitler's persecution of the Jews began as soon as he came to power. At first, his focus was economic. He urged Germans to boycott Jewish-owned businesses, and he barred Jews from jobs in civil service, banking, the stock exchange, law, journalism, and medicine. In 1935, Hitler moved to a broader legal persecution. The **Nuremberg Laws,** named for the city that served as the spiritual center of Nazism, denied German citizenship to Jews, banned marriage between Jews and non-Jews, and segregated Jews at every level of society. Yet even these measures were not enough for Hitler. He hinted that, in the future, there might be what he called the "Final Solution to the Jewish question."

Hitler employed the full power of the state in his anti-Semitic campaigns. Newspapers printed scandalous attacks against Jews. Children in schools and the Hitler Youth movement were taught that Jews were "polluting" German society and culture. Comic books contained vile caricatures of Jews.

Violence Erupts on Kristallnacht
Acts of violence against Jews were common. The most serious attack occurred on November 9, 1938, and is known as **Kristallnacht** (KRIHS tahl nahkt), or the "Night of the Broken Glass." After a Jewish refugee killed a German diplomat in Paris, Nazi officials ordered attacks on Jews in Germany, Austria and the Sudetenland. Secret police and military units destroyed more than 1,500 synagogues and 7,500 Jewish-owned businesses, killed more than 200 Jews, and injured more than 600 others. The Nazis arrested thousands of Jews.

Jewish Refugees Face Obstacles
Between 1933 and 1937, about 129,000 Jews fled Germany and Nazi-controlled Austria. They included some of the most notable figures in the scientific and artistic world, including physicist Albert Einstein.

More Jews would have left, but they were not generally welcomed into other countries. During the Great Depression, with jobs scarce, the United States and other countries barred their doors to many Jews. In 1939, the ocean liner *St. Louis* departed Germany for Cuba with more than 900 Jewish refugees on board. Only 22 of the passengers received permission to stay in Cuba. U.S. officials refused to accept any of the refugees. The ship returned to Germany. Almost 600 of the Jews aboard the *St. Louis* later died in Nazi concentration camps.

✓ **Checkpoint** How did Hitler enforce anti-Semitism as chancellor of Germany?

German Jews Face Persecution
In Nazi Germany, Jews were forced to wear yellow stars (below right) with the word *Jude* ("Jew"). By the time of Kristallnacht (below left), Hitler's policy of anti-Semitism had progressed from discrimination to organized violence—but there was even worse to come.

● **INFOGRAPHIC**

CONCENTRATION CAMP

Auschwitz . . . Buchenwald . . . Dachau . . . The names of these and other concentration camps are a roll call of horror. Above, the motto over the gate at Auschwitz reads "Work makes you free." It gave no hint of what prisoners faced inside. Whether they died of disease or starvation, survived, or were murdered, all were dehumanized by a regime that treated them as less than human.

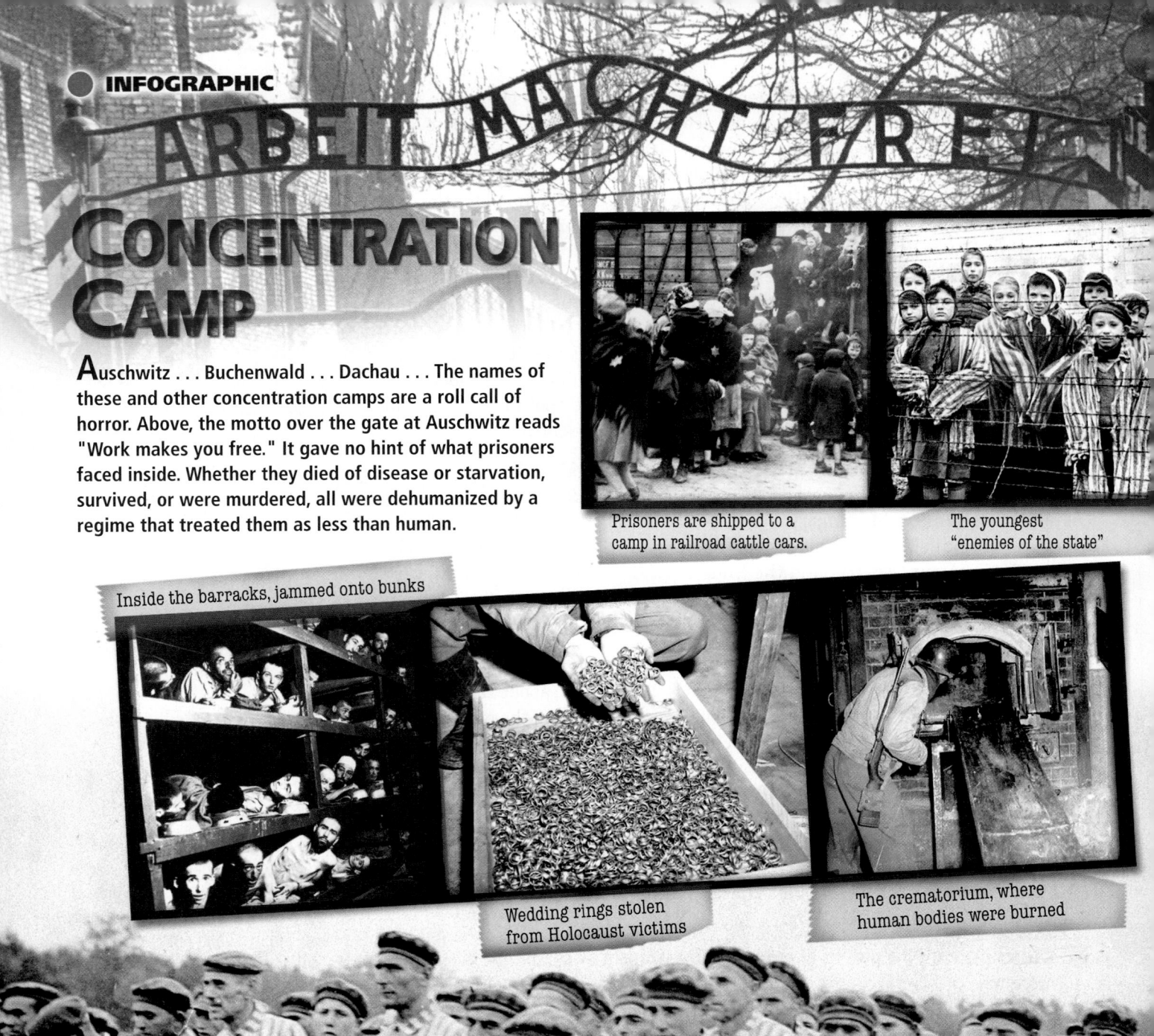

Prisoners are shipped to a camp in railroad cattle cars.

The youngest "enemies of the state"

Inside the barracks, jammed onto bunks

Wedding rings stolen from Holocaust victims

The crematorium, where human bodies were burned

Prisoners wore triangular, color-coded patches like these (left) from Dachau.
Yellow: Jew
Purple: Jehovah's Witness
Pink: homosexual
Red: political prisoner
Blue: immigrant
Green: criminal
Black: "antisocial"

Thinking Critically
1. **Identify Central Issues**
   How did Nazi Germany use concentration camps to carry out genocide?

2. **Predict Consequences**
   After the war, what do you think will happen to the Nazi officials who ran the camps?

Nazis Adopt the "Final Solution"

Since 1933, the Nazis had denied Jews the rights of citizenship and committed acts of brutality against them. These acts of persecution were steps toward Hitler's "Final Solution to the Jewish question": nothing short of the systematic extermination of all Jews living in the regions controlled by the Third Reich. Today, we call such willful annihilation of a racial, political, or cultural group **genocide.**

Nazis Build Concentration Camps In 1933, the year he became chancellor, Hitler opened the first Nazi **concentration camps,** where members of specially designated groups were confined. The earliest camps included Dachau, Sachsenhausen, and Buchenwald. Later, Ravensbruck, not far from Berlin, was opened for female prisoners.

In theory, the camps were designed not to kill prisoners, but to turn them into "useful members" of the Third Reich. The Nazis imprisoned political opponents such as labor leaders, socialists, and communists, as well as anyone— journalists or novelists, ministers or priests—who spoke out against Hitler. Many Jews as well as Aryans who had intimate relations with Jews were sent to camps. Other groups targeted as "undesirable" included Gypsies, Jehovah's Witnesses, homosexuals, beggars, drunkards, conscientious objectors, the physically disabled, and people with mental illness.

Camp administrators tattooed numbers on the arms of prisoners and dressed them in vertically striped uniforms with triangular insignias. For example, political prisoners wore red insignias, homosexuals pink, Jews yellow, and Jehovah's Witnesses purple. Inside the walls of the concentration camps, there were no real <u>restraints</u> on sadistic guards. They tortured and even killed prisoners with no fear of reprisals from their superiors.

Death by starvation and disease was an everyday occurrence. In addition, doctors at camps such as Dachau conducted horrible medical experiments that either killed inmates or left them deformed. Prisoners were made subjects of bogus experiments on oxygen deprivation, hypothermia, and the effects of altitude. Bodies were mutilated without anesthesia. Thousands of prisoners died in agonizing pain, including some 5,0[...] disabled children.

Nazi Concentration Camps

The Nazi system of concentration and slave labor camps extended over several countries. The six death camps in Poland were designed specifically for the extermination of Jewish prisoners.

Concentration Camps in Europe

Death camp

Major concentration or forced-labor camp

Vocabulary Builder
<u>restraint</u>–(rih STRAYNT) *n.*
control; something that holds someone back from action

Mili[...]
ar[...]

prisoners into death chambers and pumped in carbon monoxide or crammed the prisoners into showerlike facilities and released the insecticide Zyklon B.

Some concentration camps that the Nazis converted into death camps did not have gassing equipment. In these camps, Nazi guards shot hundreds of thousands of prisoners. Nazi "Action Groups" that followed the army into Eastern Europe also shot several million Jews and buried them in ditches.

In fully functioning death camps, the bodies of murdered prisoners were further desecrated. Human fat was turned into soap; human hair was woven into wigs, slippers, and mattresses; cash, gold fillings, wedding rings, and other valuables were stripped off the victims. After the Nazis had taken what they wanted, they burned the bodies in crematoriums.

By 1945, about 6 million European Jews had been murdered. But Jews were not the only victims. As many as 5 million others lay dead, including nearly 2 million non-Jewish Poles. While many survivors lived with constant nightmares of the experience, or with the sorrow and guilt of being the last members of their families, many others determined to rebuild their lives and families in the United States, Israel, or elsewhere and continue to be productive citizens.

 Checkpoint What actions did the Nazis take to carry out Hitler's "Final Solution"?

The Allies and the Holocaust

The inevitable question about the Holocaust is: Could it have been prevented? Could the nations in the democratic West—especially Britain, France, and the United States—have intervened at some point and stopped the slaughter of millions of innocent people? There are no simple answers to these questions. However, many people today believe that the West could have done more than it did.

Early Response Was Weak Before the war, the United States (as well as other countries) could have done more if it had relaxed its immigration policy. It could have accepted more Jewish refugees and saved the lives of many German and Austrian Jews. However, the State Department at first made a conscious effort to block Jewish immigration. Later commentators have blamed this failure to help European Jews on a variety of factors: anti-Semitism, apathy, preoccupation with the problems of the Great Depression, and a tendency to underestimate Hitler's genocidal plans.

NoteTaking

Reading Skill: Summarize As you read, identify different ways in which the United States and other nations responded to the treatment of Jews in Nazi Germany before, during, and after the war.

Response to the Holocaust

United States recognizes

...ed news of the
...d a
...ed

some 6,000 mentally or physically...

Millions Are Murdered in Death Camps

When Germany invaded Poland and the Soviet Union, the Nazis gained control of large territories that were home to millions of Jews. Under Nazi rule, Jews in Warsaw, Lodz, and other Polish cities were forced to live in crowded, walled ghettos. Nazis also constructed additional concentration camps in Poland and Eastern Europe.

At first, the murder of Jews and other prisoners tended to be more <u>arbitrary</u> than systematic. But at the Wannsee Conference in January 1942, Nazi leaders made the decision to move toward Hitler's "Final Solution." Reinhard Heydrich, an SS leader known as "the man with an iron heart," outlined a plan to exterminate about 11,000,000 Jews. Although the minutes of the meeting do not use the word "kill," everyone there understood that killing was their goal.

Many concentration camps, especially in Poland, were designated as **death camps,** where prisoners were systematically exterminated. The largest death camp was Auschwitz in southern Poland. Others included Treblinka, Maidenek, Sobibor, Belsec, and Chelmno. Prisoners from various parts of the Reich were transported by trains to the death camps and murdered. Nazis forced

Vocabulary Builder
<u>arbitrary</u>–(AR buh trer ee) *adj.*
not following any fixed rule or plan; random

American Government Takes Action Once the war started, news of mass killings had filtered to the West. By the end of 1942, the allies issued a statement acknowledging that Jews were being taken to Poland and killed there. In April 1943, British and American officials hosted the Bermuda Conference to discuss the possibility of rescuing the surviving Jewish refugees from Europe. However, no concrete action was taken.

By early 1944, however, FDR began to respond to the reports. He established the **War Refugee Board,** which worked with the Red Cross to save thousands of Eastern European Jews, especially in Romania and Hungary.

Tragically, too few were saved. Of the Allies, the Soviet Union was closest to the death camps, but Stalin showed no concern. Britain and the United States expressed sympathy, but their resources and strategy were focused on defeating Hitler not on stopping his genocidal campaign. They might have bombed railway lines to the death camps, but the camps were not military targets. A War Department official told the Refugee Board that bombing the railway lines "could be executed only by the diversion of considerable air support essential to the success of our forces now engaged in decisive operations elsewhere." The Allies also refused to pressure countries within the Nazi sphere of influence to stop the transportation of Jews to Germany.

Allied Soldiers Liberate the Camps For most Americans, the enormity of the Nazi crime became real only when soldiers began to liberate the concentration camps that dotted the map of Germany. When they saw it all—the piles of dead bodies, the warehouses full of human hair and jewelry, the ashes in crematoriums, the half-dead emaciated survivors—they realized as never before that evil was more than an abstraction.

Hardened by war, accustomed to the sight and smell of death, the soldiers who liberated the camps were nevertheless unprepared for what they saw. Major Richard Winters—who had parachuted behind enemy lines on D-Day, defended Bastogne at the Battle of the Bulge, and risked his life in a number of other engagements—was stunned almost beyond belief:

> **Primary Source** "The memory of starved, dazed men, who dropped their eyes and heads when we looked at them through the chain-link fence, in the same manner that a beaten, mistreated dog would cringe, leaves feelings that cannot be described and will never be forgotten. The impact of seeing those people behind that fence left me saying, only to myself, 'Now I know why I'm here.'"
> —Richard Winters, quoted in *Band of Brothers* (Ambrose)

The liberation of the camps led to an outpouring of American sympathy and sincere longing to aid the victims. Many survivors found temporary or permanent homes in the United States.

The revelation of the Holocaust also increased demand and support for an independent Jewish homeland. In 1948, when the Jewish community in Palestine proclaimed the State of Israel, President Truman immediately recognized the new nation. The United States became perhaps the staunchest ally of the new Jewish State.

✔ **Checkpoint** How did the U.S. government respond to the German campaign against European Jews?

A Survivor Bears Witness
This 90-year-old Holocaust survivor continues to speak to young Germans about his time in the Auschwitz death camp. He still bears a physical reminder of his suffering: the identification number tattooed on his arm.

SECTION 5

▲ Defendant Hermann Goring (right) at the Nuremberg Trials

WITNESS HISTORY 🔊 AUDIO

Nazism on Trial

In October 1945, a historic trial unlike any other began. The 21 defendants were the cream of the Third Reich, leaders of Hitler's war machine and architects of the Holocaust. Robert Jackson, the American prosecutor, scoffed as men like Hermann Goring, Hitler's handpicked successor, claimed to be tools of Hitler, unaware of his true plans. In his closing speech, Jackson turned the spotlight not on the defendants alone, but on the future of humanity:

❝No half-century ever witnessed slaughter on such a scale, such cruelties and inhumanities. . . . If we cannot eliminate the causes and prevent the repetition of these barbaric events, it is not an irresponsible prophecy to say that this twentieth century may yet succeed in bringing the doom of civilization.❞

—Robert Jackson, closing speech, Nuremberg War Crimes Trials, 1946

Effects of the War

 Core Curriculum Objectives

- **6.I.C.4d** Japanese war crime trials
- **6.I.C.5d** Nuremberg war crimes trials
- **6.II.A.1** Formation of the United Nations
- **6.II.A.2a** Universal Declaration of Human Rights: Eleanor Roosevelt's role
- **6.II.B.1** Summitry: Yalta and Potsdam

Terms and People

Yalta Conference
s___ower

Universal Declaration of Human Rights

Why It Matters World War II changed the nation in profound ways. Many Americans came home determined to extend the ideals of democracy and freedom at home as well as abroad. In addition, the United States emerged from the war prepared to take on the complex and vital role in world affairs that it still holds today. **Section Focus Question: What were the major immediate and long-term effects of World War II?**

Allies Set Postwar Goals

World War II differed from World War I in several ways. One major ... 19, the Kaiser

Roosevelt and Churchill were not in a good position to press Stalin too hard. The Red Army already occupied much of Eastern Europe, and Roosevelt wanted Soviet help in the war against Japan. Vague promises were about as much as Stalin would give.

Truman Faces Stalin at Potsdam A dramatically altered Big Three met in July 1945 in the Berlin suburb of Potsdam. Although Stalin remained in power in the Soviet Union, Harry S. Truman had become U.S. President upon the death of FDR. After the start of the conference, Clement Atlee replaced Churchill as prime minister of Britain.

While in Potsdam, Truman learned of the successful test of the atomic bomb. But he was more focused on Europe and the Soviet Union than on Asia. At the meeting, the Big Three formalized the decision to divide Germany into four zones of occupation: Soviet, American, British, and French. They agreed to new borders and free elections for Poland, and they recognized the Soviets' right to claim reparations for war damages from the German sector they controlled. Stalin also reaffirmed his Yalta pledge to enter the war against Japan.

✓ **Checkpoint** What goals did the Allies set for Eastern Europe at the Yalta Conference?

A New World Takes Shape

After the war ended in August 1945, plans for the postwar world had to be turned into realities. However, the changes that took place were not often what the Allies had envisioned at Yalta and Potsdam.

The World Map Changes World War II altered the political realities of the world. The borders of Poland, for example, shifted slightly to the west. In time, as you will read in the next chapter, differences between the Soviet Union and its former Allies led to the division of Germany into two countries: communist East Germany and noncommunist West Germany. Nearly all the nations of Eastern Europe became communist states under Soviet control.

Other countries experienced profound political changes. Communist and non-communist interests clashed in Eastern Europe. In China, a long-standing civil war between Nationalists and communists resumed.

In Japan, General Douglas MacArthur headed an American military occupation and supervised the writing of a new constitution. It abolished the armed forces except for purposes of defense, gave women the right to vote, enacted democratic reforms, and established the groundwork for full economic recovery.

Imperialism Goes Into Decline The war also marked the end of Western European domination of the world.

The Big Three at Yalta

This famous photo shows (left to right) Churchill, Roosevelt, and Stalin at the Yalta Conference. Their glum looks seem to say: Here are not victors, but potential enemies. In addition, FDR looks ill and tired—he died only months after this picture was taken.

The Decline of Imperialism, 1945–1989

Geography *Interactive*
For: Interactive map
Web Code: nep-1110

Legend:
- Gained independence, 1945–1949
- Gained independence, 1950–1959
- Gained independence, 1960–1969
- Gained independence, 1970–1989

Robinson Projection
0   2,000 mi
0   2,000 km

Map Skills In the decades following World War II, the Age of Imperialism ended as colony after colony won independence.

1. Locate: (a) Europe, (b) Africa, (c) Asia, (d) the Soviet Union

2. Regions On what continent did the largest number of nations win independence?

3. Predict Consequences How might the appearance of so many new nations affect the balance of power in the postwar world?

Vocabulary Builder
predominant–(pree DAHM uh nuhnt) *adj.* having the greatest amount of authority or dominance

Since the 1500s, nations such as Britain, France, and Spain had exerted paramount influence on global developments. They colonized much of Africa, the Middle East, Asia, and the Americas. They had controlled world trade and finance, led the industrial revolution, and stood at the forefront of world military power.

The aggressive acquisition of territories by Japan and Germany underscored the abuses of imperialism. After World War II, colonial peoples renewed their drive for independence from European powers. Freed from Japanese domination, the East Indies had no interest in returning to Dutch colonial status. Nor did Indochina want to see the return of French rule. India, Burma, colonies in the Middle East and Africa—all had their sights set on independence.

By the end of the war, it was clear that the Age of Imperialism was in the twilight of its existence. The British Empire, the <u>predominant</u> power of the nineteenth century, came out of the war suffering severe economic shortages and, within decades, would see the loss of most of its colonies.

The Balance of Power Shifts
Into the power vacuum stepped the United States and the Soviet Union. They had played the most decisive roles in defeating the Axis Powers, and they emerged from the war confident and strong. Indeed, they so dominated the postwar world that they became known as **superpowers.**

Of the two superpowers, the United States was clearly the stronger. Except for the attack on Pearl Harbor, no major battle had been fought on U.S. soil. In addition, American industry had boomed during the war. By 1945, America was wealthy, militarily powerful, and confident. By contrast, much of the war had been fought on Soviet soil. Its industries, cities, and peoples had suffered terribly. Still, the Red Army controlled most of Eastern Europe and threatened to move farther west. Militarily, although the Americans had the atomic bomb, the Soviets had the Red Army, the world's largest military force.

✔ **Checkpoint** What impact did World War II have on the relative roles of the United States and Britain in the world?

International Cooperation

Americans were quick to recognize that their nation had taken on a new position in the world. After World War I, the Senate had rejected the Treaty of Versailles and refused to join the League of Nations. Many Americans now viewed these decisions as mistakes that contributed to the rise of fascism and the outbreak of another war. As World War II drew to a close, Americans were ready to embrace the idea of world organizations.

A New World Economy Takes Shape The United States took on major responsibilities in shaping the postwar world economy. After meeting in 1944 with the Allies in Bretton Woods, New Hampshire, the U.S. government pushed for establishment of the International Monetary Fund and the World Bank. The United States provided most of the working capital for these new organizations, which worked to foster global economic and financial stability. The United States also signed the **General Agreement on Tariffs and Trade (GATT),** a 1948 treaty designed to expand world trade by reducing tariffs.

The United Nations Is Formed Even more importantly, the United States led the charge for the establishment of the **United Nations (UN),** an organization that, many hoped, would succeed where the League of Nations had failed. In April 1945, delegates from 50 nations met in San Francisco to write the charter for the UN. The Senate overwhelmingly ratified the charter, and the UN later set up its permanent home in New York City.

The United Nations was organized on the basis of cooperation between the Great Powers, not on the absolute equality of all nations. All member nations sat on the General Assembly. However, the five major World War II Allies—the United States, the Soviet Union, Britain, France, and China—were assigned permanent seats on the most powerful arm of the UN, the Security Council.

Over the next decades, the UN aided the move away from colonialism, helped to create the Jewish state of Israel, mediated regional conflicts, and provided food and other aid to much of the world. The UN also issued the **Universal Declaration of Human Rights** in 1948. This idealistic document states:

Primary Source "Recognition of the inherent dignity and of the equal and inalienable rights of all members of the human family is the foundation of freedom, justice and peace in the world. . . . All human beings are born free and equal in dignity and rights. They are endowed with reason and conscience and should act toward one another in a spirit of brotherhood."
—Universal Declaration of Human Rights

HISTORY MAKERS

Eleanor Roosevelt (1884–1962)
As First Lady, Eleanor Roosevelt had been a valuable, if unofficial, part of her husband's presidential administration. After FDR's death, President Truman named her to represent the United States at the United Nations. As elected chair of the Commission on Human Rights, she guided the drafting of the Universal Declaration of Human Rights, which she hoped would "become the international Magna Carta for all men everywhere." Her work on behalf of human rights won Roosevelt the nickname First Lady of the World. Shortly before her death, President John F. Kennedy named Roosevelt to head his Commission on the Status of Women.

Causes

- Europe suffers massive destruction in World War I
- Germans and Italians resent Versailles Treaty
- Great Depression leads to rise of fascist dictators
- European appeasement fails to end Axis aggression
- Japanese attack on Pearl Harbor

World War II

Effects

- Europe and Japan lay in ruins
- European colonies gradually gain independence
- Soviets dominate Eastern Europe
- Cold War between United States and Soviet Union begins
- America becomes a world power
- African Americans gain momentum to pursue civil rights

Connections to Today

- United States remains a global superpower
- U.S. government plays a large role in guiding the nation's economy

Analyze Cause and Effect In its overall impact, World War II is often considered the single most important event of the twentieth century. *How did World War II contribute to the two effects listed above under Connections to Today?*

The Declaration condemns slavery and torture, upholds freedom of speech and religion, and affirms that "everyone has the right to a standard of living adequate for the health and well-being of himself and his family." Though the document sets lofty goals it has proved difficult to enforce.

War Criminals Go on Trial In the effort to create a better world, the Allies did not forget to punish the people who had caused so much destruction and death. During the war, the Axis Powers had repeatedly violated the **Geneva Convention,** an international agreement governing the humane treatment of wounded soldiers and prisoners of war.

The Allies tried more than a thousand Japanese citizens for committing atrocities in China, Korea, and Southeast Asia and brutally mistreating prisoners of war. Hundreds were condemned to death, including Prime Minister Hideki Tojo and the general responsible for the Bataan Death March.

Americans more closely followed the **Nuremberg Trials,** in which the Allies prosecuted Nazis for war crimes. The trials turned a glaring spotlight on the evils of the Third Reich. The first of the Nuremberg Trials involved key leaders of Nazi Germany, such as Hermann Goring. Day by day, prosecutors described their crimes, detailing especially the horrors of the Holocaust. Most of the defendants pleaded that they were just following orders, that Hitler was the source of all the crimes. The judges at Nuremberg did not accept their excuses. Some of the Nazis were hanged; others received long prison terms.

In the following decades, Allied or Israeli authorities captured and tried such other Nazis as Adolf Eichmann, a leading architect of the "Final Solution." The periodic trials kept alive the memory of the Nazi crimes against humanity.

 Checkpoint What steps did the United States take to increase its role in the postwar world?

A New American Identity

A new American identity rose from the ashes of World War II, one formed as the antithesis of the Nazi ideal. Americans regarded the Nazis as totalitarian, racist, and warlike. They defined themselves as democratic, tolerant, and peaceful. During the war, U.S. leaders and American popular culture had emphasized these positive themes, repeating constantly that the Allies were fighting a "people's war" for tolerance, freedom, democracy, and peace. Although many Americans felt that their country had not always lived up to that ideal, they hoped that the postwar period would usher in significant changes.

The United States Assumes Global Leadership Millions of Americans had spent several years closely following the war. They had attached world maps to their walls and traced the paths of U.S. troops in the deserts of North Africa, the forests of Europe, and the coral islands of the Pacific. For this generation of Americans, the world had somehow become a smaller, more interconnected place. They had learned to think in global terms.

Few Americans called for a return to a policy of isolationism or retreat from their global responsibilities. They recognized that what happened in the far reaches of the globe affected them, that the economic and political health of

America was tied to world peace and economic development. They knew that America's national security involved world security.

Commitment to Civil Rights Grows African American soldiers in World War II had clearly believed they were fighting two foes: dictatorship overseas and racism in the United States. As the great African American poet Langston Hughes put it:

Primary Source

"You tell me that Hitler
Is a mighty bad man.
I guess he took lessons
From the Ku Klux Klan."
—Langston Hughes, quoted in *The Fight of the Century* (Hietala)

World War II gave renewed vigor to the fight for civil rights. In this battle, African Americans were not alone. A growing number of white Americans also called for the nation to fully live up to its promise as a beacon of freedom, democracy, and justice.

The Nation Prospers World War II ended the Great Depression and ushered in decades of economic growth. It also redistributed wealth across the country. Defense industries and military bases in the South and West spurred people to move to these regions, which in turn created more wealth and encouraged further migration.

The driving force for all the jobs and prosperity was the federal government. Like other wars, World War II led to a greater governmental influence in economic affairs. From the collection of raw materials to attempts to control inflation, the government had made the important decisions to guide the economy. In the process, it established the expanded economic role that government would play in postwar America.

✔ **Checkpoint** How did World War II foster support for civil rights?

A Hero Comes Home
For millions of Americans, World War II was not truly over until their loved ones came home from overseas. Here, a wounded G.I. embraces his parents.

SECTION 5 Assessment

Progress Monitoring *Online*
For: Self-test with vocabulary practice
Web Code: nea-1111

Comprehension

1. Terms and People For each term below, write a sentence explaining how it was connected with the building of the postwar world.
- Yalta Conference
- superpower
- GATT
- United Nations
- Universal Declaration of Human Rights
- Geneva Convention
- Nuremberg Trials

2. NoteTaking Reading Skill: Understand Effects Use your concept web to answer the Section Focus Question: What were the major immediate and long-term effects of World War II?

Writing About History

3. Quick Write: Write a Descriptive Paragraph Write a paragraph describing the look and feel of the Nuremberg Trials. Describe both what you might see and the emotional mood in the room.

Critical Thinking

4. Predict Consequences Identify one possible postwar consequence of the Allied disagreements at Yalta and Potsdam.

5. Recognize Causes and Effects Why do you think Americans supported participation in the UN after World War II when they had opposed participation in the League of Nations after World War I?

6. Compare In what way were both the Universal Declaration of Human Rights and the postwar push for civil rights reactions to the war?

Quick Study Guide

 6.I.C.3, 6.I.C.5

Progress Monitoring Online
For: Self-test with vocabulary practice
Web Code: nea-1112

■ Allied Leaders, World War II

World Political	U.S. Military
• Winston Churchill, Britain • Joseph Stalin, Soviet Union • Franklin D. Roosevelt, United States • Harry S. Truman, United States	**In Europe** • Dwight Eisenhower • George S. Patton • Omar Bradley **In the Pacific** • Douglas MacArthur • Chester Nimitz

■ World War II Home Front

More women work in industry and offices.

Many Japanese Americans are interned.

Government works to boost morale, control war economy.

World War II Home Front

German and Italian Americans register as enemy aliens.

Mexican workers move north.

African Americans seek fairer employment.

■ Five Turning Points of World War II

1942	**Battle of Midway** halts Japanese expansion in Pacific.
1942–1943	**Battle of Stalingrad** ends Nazi advances in Europe.
1942	**Battle of El Alamein** begins Allied offensive against Axis Powers in North Africa.
1944	**D-Day** invasion opens second front in Europe, paving way for final defeat of Germany.
1945	**Manhattan Project** develops atomic bomb, used to end war in Pacific.

■ World War II Deaths, Selected Nations

Country	Military Deaths	Civilian Deaths
Axis		
Germany	3,500,000	780,000
Italy	242,000	153,000
Japan	1,300,000	672,000
Allies		
France	213,000	350,000
Britain	264,000	93,000
China	1,310,000	1,000,000
Soviet Union	7,500,000	15,000,000
United States	292,000	6,000

SOURCES: Henri Michel, *Encyclopaedia Britannica; Harper Encyclopedia of Military History*
All figures are estimates.

✓ Quick Study Timeline

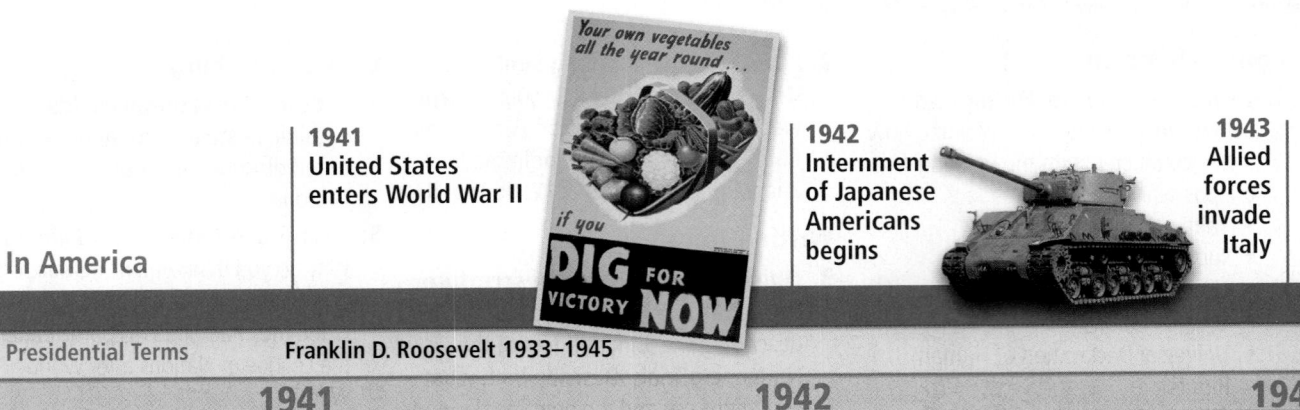

In America

1941
United States enters World War II

1942
Internment of Japanese Americans begins

1943
Allied forces invade Italy

Your own vegetables all the year round ...
if you
DIG FOR NOW
VICTORY

Presidential Terms   Franklin D. Roosevelt 1933–1945

1941	1942	1943

Around the World

1941
Germany invades Soviet Union

1942
Battle of Midway

1943
Germans surrender at Stalingrad

American Issues
●—●—●—● Connector

 6.II.A.1

By connecting prior knowledge with what you have learned in this chapter, you can gradually build your understanding of enduring questions that still affect America today. Answer the questions below. Then, use your American Issues Connector study guide (or go online: www.PHSchool.com **Web Code:** neh-8402).

Issues You Learned About

● **Protecting and Expanding Civil Rights** Americans may organize to demand fair treatment and civil rights.

1. Why did Roosevelt decide to issue an executive order assuring fair hiring practices in any job funded by the government?

2. What was the NAACP, when was it founded, and why did its membership grow during the war years?

3. How did World War II motivate African Americans' fight for civil rights? What do you think African Americans did after the war ended to win more civil rights?

● **Civil Liberties and National Security** During wartime, the government has often taken steps to suspend civil liberties.

4. During World War I, which groups of people suffered from persecution? Did the U.S. government violate these groups' civil liberties? Explain.

5. How did the United States defend its internment of Japanese Americans? How did some Japanese Americans respond?

6. Was there any evidence that Japanese Americans threatened national security? Present evidence that supports or weakens this claim.

● **Technology and Society** New technological developments can hurt society as well as help it.

7. What new technology contributed to the high casualties of World War I?

8. What was the atomic bomb? How powerful was the first one that was tested?

9. What effect did the dropping of atomic bombs on Hiroshima and Nagasaki have on the progress of World War II?

Connect to Your World — New York

America and the World At one of its early meetings, the United Nations General Assembly decided to locate its headquarters in New York City. The UN headquarters was built on 18 acres of land on the east side of Manhattan, and the complex includes the General Assembly building, the 39-floor Secretariat skyscraper, a conference building, and the Dag Hammarskjold Library. The site is an international territory—it is neither a part of the United States nor the state of New York. The flags of all member nations fly outside, and guided tours are offered to the public in over 20 languages. Conduct research on an international issue and then discuss as a class how the UN could play a role in solving this issue.

1944
D-Day landing in France

1945
World War II ends

Harry S. Truman 1945–1953

1944   **1945**   **1946**

1945
Nazi death camps liberated

1946
Nuremberg war crimes trials

History *Interactive*
For: Interactive timeline
Web Code: nep-1114

Chapter Assessment

Terms and People

1. Who were **Dwight D. Eisenhower** and **George S. Patton, Jr.**? How were the two men linked?
2. What Americans were sent to **internment camps**? What were conditions like in these camps?
3. Define **D-Day**. What was the result of this strategy?
4. What was the goal of the **Manhattan Project**?
5. Define **genocide**. How did Hitler attempt to accomplish genocide?
6. What was the purpose of the **Nuremberg Trials**?

Focus Questions

The focus question for this chapter is **What impact did World War II have on America and the world?** Build an answer to this big question by answering the focus questions for Sections 1 through 5 and the Critical Thinking questions that follow.

Section 1
7. How did the Allies turn the tide against the Axis?

Section 2
8. How did the war change America at home?

Section 3
9. How did the Allies defeat the Axis Powers?

Section 4
10. How did the Holocaust develop and what were its results?

Section 5
11. What were the major immediate and long-term effects of World War II?

Critical Thinking

12. **Recognize Effects** Explain the significance of Allied victories at Stalingrad and in North Africa.
13. **Evaluate Information** The Americans who fought in World War II have been called the "Greatest Generation." What do you think this means? What evidence supports this claim?
14. **Summarize** Summarize the contributions of two of these groups to the war effort: women, Mexican Americans, African Americans, Navajos.
15. **Interpreting a Political Cartoon** What is the main point of the cartoon below? How do you think American soldiers reacted to this cartoon?

"America is a myth, the superiority of her war potential is a legend, and the arsenal of democracy is a bogey for scared Europeans."
DR. OTTO DIETRICH, OCT. 29, 1942

16. **Make Decisions** Do you think Truman's decision to drop the atomic bomb was justified at the time? Was it justified in light of future events?
17. **Recognize Propaganda** How did Hitler use propaganda in his campaign against German Jews?
18. **Synthesize Information** **(a)** How do the meetings at Yalta and Potsdam reflect a new balance of global power? **(b)** What type of relationship do you think the United States and the Soviet Union will have in the post–World War II years?

Writing About History

Writing a Descriptive Essay In a descriptive essay, you try to convey in words the look, sound, and mood of an event. Write a three-paragraph descriptive essay on one of the following topics: an American flight crew making a bombing run over Germany; women going to work in defense industries during World War II; soldiers walking on Omaha Beach after D-Day; American soldiers liberating a concentration camp.

Prewriting
- Look at the pictures and read the text in this chapter relating to the topic you have chosen.
- Use Internet or library sources to find additional pictures and descriptions relating to your topic.
- Make a list of sights, sounds, impressions, and connections to your topic.

Drafting
- Make an outline identifying what aspects of your topic you want to describe.
- Write an opening paragraph in which you introduce the topic and identify the setting.
- Write descriptions using precise adjectives and specific action verbs. Avoid generalizations that are too broad or too vague.

Revising
- Use the guidelines on page SH8 of the Writing Handbook to revise your writing.

Regents DBQ Practice

The Battle of Midway

The Battle of Midway is considered a major turning point of World War II. But why was it so important? How was it viewed by the participants? Use your knowledge of the chapter material and Documents 1, 2, 3, and 4 to answer questions 1 through 4.

Document 1

War in Asia and the Pacific, December 1941–August 1942	
December 7, 1941	Japan bombs Pearl Harbor.
December 23, 1941	Japan captures Wake Island.
December 25, 1941	Japan captures Hong Kong.
February 15, 1942	Japan captures Singapore.
April 8, 1942	Japan captures Bataan, Philippines.
May 4, 1942	Japanese offensive stalls at Battle of the Coral Sea.
May 20, 1942	Japan drives British out of Burma.
June 4–7, 1942	United States Navy wins Battle of Midway.
August 7, 1942	Americans begin assault on Guadalcanal.

Document 2

"In numerous and widespread engagements lasting from the 3rd to 6th of June, with carrier based planes as the spearhead of the attack, combined forces of the Navy, Marine Corps and Army in the Hawaiian Area defeated a large part of the Japanese fleet and frustrated the enemy's powerful move against Midway that was undoubtedly the keystone of larger plans. All participating personnel, without exception, displayed unhesitating devotion to duty, loyalty and courage. This superb spirit in all three services made possible the application of the destructive power that routed the enemy. . . . These results were achieved at the cost of the *Yorktown* and *Hamman* sunk and about 150 planes lost in action or damaged beyond repair. Our total personnel losses were about ninety-two (92) officers and two hundred and fifteen (215) men."

—*Admiral Chester A. Nimitz, official report of the Battle of Midway, filed June 28, 1942*

Document 3

"Had Yamamoto fulfilled his projects of taking Midway and destroying Nimitz's carriers, the next program on his agenda was to turn to the Australian campaign. And with the aerial striking power of the U.S. Pacific Fleet out of the running, there would have been precious little to stop him. . . . And in the meantime, possession of Midway would have given Japan the means to harass at least the Hawaiian Islands and even the West Coast. . . . At Midway, the United States laid aside the shield and picked up the sword, and through all the engagements to follow, never again yielded the strategic offensive."

—*Gordon W. Prange,* Miracle at Midway, *1982*

Document 4

"It was Japan that had attacked the United States, and it was Japan on which the anger of the American people had focused. . . . Had it not been for Midway, Roosevelt could not have persevered with a Europe-first policy. Public opinion would not have allowed it. . . . Through an extraordinary combination of the skill and courage of our pilots, splendid intelligence, prudent risk-taking by our commanders that paid off, and sheer good luck, the apparently inferior American forces were victorious. This victory occurred despite the inferiority of our aircraft, the ineffectiveness of our torpedoes, the substantial absence of backup surface ships, and our overall numerical inferiority. You know the rest! Four Japanese carriers had been sunk. . . . The Japanese offensive had now been blunted. The Japanese fleet turned back toward the Home Islands and the opportunity for victory had been lost forever. . . . After Midway, the United States could, to the chagrin of Douglas MacArthur, turn its primary attention back to the European theatre."

—*Former Secretary of Defense James R. Schlesinger, June 5, 2003*

---

1. Which conclusion is best supported by Document 1?
   - **(1)** Japan lost the war as a direct result of the Battle of Midway.
   - **(2)** Before the Battle of Midway, Japan had been on the offensive.
   - **(3)** The Japanese invasion of Burma led to the Battle of Bataan.
   - **(4)** The Battle of Midway was the last Japanese victory in the Pacific.

2. On what point do Document 2 and Document 3 agree?
   - **(1)** The Battle of Midway was a setback for Japan.
   - **(2)** The Battle of Midway was a setback for the United States.
   - **(3)** The Battle of Midway was equally damaging to both sides.
   - **(4)** U.S. forces were undamaged at the Battle of Midway.

3. According to Document 4, how did the Battle of Midway make it easier for Roosevelt to pursue a "Europe First" strategy?
   - **(1)** It convinced Americans that Japan was no longer a threat.
   - **(2)** It roused public anger against Germany.
   - **(3)** It satisfied immediate public demand for action against Japan.
   - **(4)** It showed that the United States could not win in the Pacific unless it conquered Germany first.

4. **Writing Task** What might have happened if Japanese forces had won the Battle of Midway? Use your knowledge of the chapter content and specific evidence from the primary sources above to support your opinion.

25

The Cold War
1945–1960

Preparing for Attack

June 15, 1955—Wailing sirens announce that Soviet nuclear weapons are on the way. Their targets are New York, Los Angeles, and dozens of other U.S. cities. Schoolchildren duck for cover under their desks. People flee their homes and offices and rush to underground shelters. President Eisenhower is whisked away to a secret mountain location. Millions of casualties are expected. . . .

But this was only a drill. Called Operation Alert, it was one of numerous drills that took place during the Cold War, when the United States was locked in a desperate worldwide struggle against communism and the Soviet Union. *Listen to the* Witness History *audio to hear more about Operation Alert.*

◄ Schoolchildren try to stay calm during a "duck and cover" nuclear air-raid drill.

Korean War medal

Sign marking a nuclear bomb fallout shelter

Core Curriculum Preview

Chapter Focus Question: What were the causes, main events, and effects of the early Cold War?

Section 1
The Cold War Begins 6.II.B.1, 6.II.B.3a, 6.II.B.3b, 6.II.B.3d, 6.II.D.4

Section 2
The Korean War 6.II.C.2, 6.II.C.4a, 6.II.C.4b, 6.II.C.4c, 7.II.B.5

Section 3
The Cold War Expands 6.II.C.3, 7.II.B.2, 7.II.B.6, 7.II.B.7, 7.II.B.8

Section 4
The Cold War at Home 3.III.C.6, 6.II.D.1, 6.II.D.2, 6.II.D.3

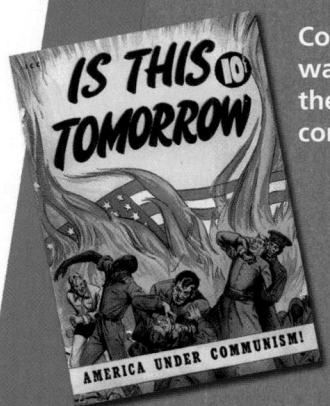

Comic book warning about the threat of communism

Use the ☑ **Quick Study Timeline** at the end of this chapter to preview chapter events.

Note Taking Study Guide *Online*
For: Note Taking and American Issues Connector
Web Code: nee-8501

◀ General George Patton

▲ U.S. and Soviet soldiers celebrate the Allied victory.

WITNESS HISTORY 🔊 AUDIO

A New Enemy

After World War II, U.S. General George Patton administered western Germany, while Soviet officials governed eastern Germany. Patton looked to the east and proclaimed:

❝Russia knows what she wants. World domination! . . . Let's keep our boots polished, bayonets sharpened, and present a picture of force and strength to the Russians. This is the only language that they understand and respect. If we fail to do this, then I would like to say that we have had a victory over the Germans and have disarmed them, but we have lost the war.❞
—General George S. Patton, October 1945

The Cold War Begins

 Core Curriculum Objectives

- **6.II.B.1** Summitry: Potsdam
- **6.II.B.3a** The Truman Doctrine: Greece and Turkey
- **6.II.B.3b** The Marshall Plan
- **6.II.B.3d** Formation of NATO alliance
- **6.II.D.4** Politics of the Cold War

Terms and People

satellite state	containment
Cold War	Marshall Plan
iron curtain	Berlin airlift
Truman Doctrine	NATO
George F. Kennan	Warsaw Pact

NoteTaking

Reading Skill: Contrast As you read, contrast the conflicting goals of the United States and the Soviet Union.

American Goals	Soviet Goals

Why It Matters In the 1930s, the policies of isolationism and appeasement had contributed to the rise of dictatorships and the outbreak of global war. After World War II, U.S. leaders viewed these past policies as mistakes. They sought new ways to keep the United States safe and to protect its interests around the world. **Section Focus Question: How did U.S. leaders respond to the threat of Soviet expansion in Europe?**

Roots of the Cold War

When Franklin Roosevelt died in April 1945, the nation was at a critical point. The United States was still at war. In addition, relations with the Soviet Union—one of the most important wartime allies—were beginning to break down.

American and Soviet Systems Differ The United States and the Soviet Union had been united only in their opposition to Nazi Germany. Beyond that, they had little in common. The United States was a capitalist democracy. Its citizens believed in free elections, economic and religious freedom, private property, and respect for individual differences. The Soviet Union was a dictatorship. Under Joseph Stalin, the Communist Party made all key economic, political, and military decisions. The Soviet people could not worship as they pleased, own private property, or express their views freely. Those who opposed or questioned Stalin risked imprisonment and death.

Allies Disagree on Future of Eastern Europe By the time Roosevelt, Stalin, and Churchill met at Yalta in February 1945, it was clear that the Allies would defeat Germany. But it was unclear how Germany and the nations of Eastern Europe would be governed after the war. Soviet troops already occupied much of Eastern Europe and some of Germany.

Stalin wanted to keep Germany weak and divided. He also wanted Eastern Europe to remain under the control of the Soviet Union. The United States and Great Britain sought a stronger, united Germany and independent nations in Eastern Europe. At the conference, Stalin agreed to establish "broadly representative" governments and free elections in Eastern Europe and to divide Germany only temporarily into zones of occupation.

Despite Stalin's promises, nearly all of the lands occupied by the Soviet Red Army in the spring of 1945 remained under Soviet control after the war. The Eastern European countries of Poland, Czechoslovakia, Hungary, Romania, and Bulgaria, as well as the eastern portion of Germany, became **satellite states** controlled by the Soviet Union.

Truman and Stalin Clash at Potsdam By the time Soviet, British, and U.S. leaders met at Potsdam in the summer of 1945, Harry Truman had succeeded Roosevelt as President. Truman and Clement Attlee, the new British prime minister, hoped that Stalin would confirm the decisions made at Yalta. However, Stalin refused to make a commitment to allow free elections in Eastern Europe.

Comparing Viewpoints

What Will Happen to Postwar Europe?

The Soviet Union and United States disagreed on what should happen to Europe after World War II. The disagreement had much to do with the conflicting values of the two countries and their leaders.

JOSEPH STALIN

Stalin was a dictator who ruled the Soviet Union from the 1920s to the 1950s. His policy of collectivizing land led to famine and to the death of millions. He also ordered the execution of thousands of communist officials.

Primary Source

"To choose one's victims, to prepare one's plan minutely, to slake an implacable vengeance, and then to go to bed . . . there is nothing sweeter in the world."

"This war is different from all earlier ones; the conqueror of a region imposes his own social system on it."

HARRY S. TRUMAN

As President from 1945 until 1953, Truman tried to stop the spread of communism. He promoted a "Fair Deal" program that included more social security benefits, public health insurance, and an end to racial discrimination.

Primary Source

"I would rather have peace in the world than be President."

"The American people desire, and are determined to work for, a world in which all nations and all peoples are free to govern themselves as they see fit, and to achieve a decent and satisfying life."

Compare
1. How did Truman's views on power differ from those of Stalin?
2. How did the two leaders disagree on the issue of self-government in Eastern Europe?

Truman left Potsdam believing that the Soviet Union was "planning world conquest" and that the alliance with the Soviet Union was falling apart. With the Soviet Red Army at his command, Stalin seemed to present a real threat. Thus, the stage was set for a worldwide rivalry between the United States and the Soviet Union. The 46-year struggle became known as the **Cold War** because the two superpowers never faced each other directly in a "hot" military conflict.

✔ **Checkpoint** How did the goals of U.S. and Soviet foreign policy differ after World War II?

Meeting the Soviet Challenge

President Truman was not the only world leader who believed that Stalin had <u>aspirations</u> toward world domination. Winston Churchill also spoke out forcefully against the Soviet Union. On March 5, 1946, he gave an important speech at Fulton College in Missouri, Truman's home state. Referring to a map of Europe, Churchill noted that "an **iron curtain** has descended across the Continent." (See the Primary Source on the opposite page.) East of that iron curtain, the Soviet Union was gaining more control by installing communist governments and police states and by crushing political and religious dissent. In addition, Churchill feared, the Soviets were attempting to spread communism to Western Europe and East Asia. The only solution, Churchill said, was for the United States and other democratic countries to stand firm.

Truman Faces a Crisis Truman shared Churchill's beliefs. Born in a small town in Missouri, Truman had been too poor to attend college. He was the only president in the twentieth century with no college education. Instead, he worked the family farm, fought in France during World War I, and eventually began a political career. His life was a testament to honesty, integrity, hard work, and a willingness to make difficult decisions. "The buck stops here," was his motto as President. It meant that the person sitting in the Oval Office had the obligation to face problems head-on and make hard decisions.

In 1947, no issue was more weighty than the growing crisis between the United States and the Soviet Union. After the war, a number of European and Asian countries were struggling against communist movements supported by the Soviets. In particular, the governments of Greece and Turkey were battling communist forces seeking to gain control. Greece and Turkey needed aid, and in 1947 the United States was the only country with the resources to help them.

The Truman Doctrine Opposes Communist Expansion On March 12, 1947, President Truman addressed both houses of Congress. With emotion in his voice, Truman described the plight of the Greek and Turkish people. The fight they were waging, he said, was the fight that all free people had to confront. Truman requested money from Congress "to support free peoples who are resisting attempted subjugation [conquest] by armed minorities or by outside pressures." If the United States retreated into isolationism, he warned, the peace of the world and the welfare of the nation would be in danger.

Congress responded by voting to give $400 million in aid for Greece and Turkey. President Truman's promise to aid nations struggling against communist movements became known as the **Truman Doctrine,** and it set a new course for American foreign policy.

✔ **Checkpoint** What events caused President Truman to propose what became known as the Truman Doctrine?

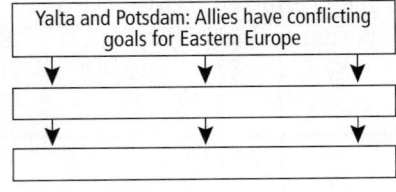

Cold War Europe, 1949

Geography *Interactive*
For: Interactive map
Web Code: nep-1202

Map Legend
- Communist nations
- Annexed by Soviet Union, 1939–1945
- Noncommunist nations
- —— Iron curtain

Conic projection

0   200   400 mi
0   200   400 km

[Map of Europe showing labels: NORWAY, FINLAND, SWEDEN, ESTONIA, LATVIA, LITHUANIA, IRELAND, UNITED KINGDOM, NETH., DENMARK, Baltic Sea, North Sea, London, BELGIUM, EAST GER., POLAND, SOVIET UNION, Moscow, LUX., WEST GERMANY, CZECHOSLOVAKIA, Paris, FRANCE, SWITZ., AUST., HUNG., ROMANIA, Atlantic Ocean, PORTUGAL, SPAIN, ITALY, YUGOSLAVIA, BULGARIA, Black Sea, Rome, ALB., GREECE, TURKEY, Mediterranean Sea]

In his speech at Fulton, Missouri, Winston Churchill described the extent of the Soviet "iron curtain," shown on the map above.

Primary Source "From Stettin in the Baltic to Trieste in the Adriatic, an iron curtain has descended across the Continent. Behind that line lie all the capitals of . . . Central and Eastern Europe. . . . The Communist parties, which were very small in all these Eastern States of Europe, have been raised to pre-eminence and power far beyond their numbers and are seeking everywhere to obtain totalitarian control."

— "Iron Curtain" speech, Winston Churchill, March 5, 1946

Map Skills Europe became a divided continent as the Cold War developed after World War II.

1. **Region** Why did the Soviet Union support the creation of communist states in Eastern Europe?

2. **Draw Conclusions** Based on the map, in what ways might the Soviet Union have benefited from gaining control of Greece and Turkey?

Churchill and the Iron Curtain

The day after Churchill gave his "Iron Curtain" speech, this cartoon appeared in a British newspaper. It shows Churchill peeping under the barrier built by "Joe" Stalin.

Containing Soviet Expansion

In the July 1947 issue of the magazine *Foreign Affairs*, a writer who called himself "X" published an article titled "The Sources of Soviet Conduct." The author was really **George F. Kennan,** an American diplomat and a leading authority on the Soviet Union. His article presented a blueprint for the American policy that became known as **containment** because its goal was to keep communism contained within its existing borders.

Kennan Argues for Containment Kennan contended that while Stalin was determined to expand the Soviet empire, he would not risk the security of the Soviet Union for expansion. In Kennan's view, the Soviet Union would only expand when it could do so without serious risks. Stalin would certainly not chance war with the United States—a war that might destroy his power in the Soviet Union—just to spread communism.

Kennan cautioned his readers that there would be no quick, easy solution to the Soviet threat. Containment would require a full commitment of American economic, political, and military power:

> **Primary Source** "We are going to continue for a long time to find the Russians difficult to deal with. It does not mean that they should be considered as embarked upon a do-or-die program to overthrow our society by a given date. . . . In these circumstances, it is clear that the main element of any United States policy toward the Soviet Union must be that of long-term, patient but firm and vigilant containment of Russian expansive tendencies."
> —George Kennan, "The Sources of Soviet Conduct"

The Marshall Plan Aids Europe's Economies The containment policy's first great success was in Western Europe. After World War II, people there confronted severe shortages of food, fuel, and medical supplies, as well as brutally cold winters. In this environment of desperate need, Secretary of State George C. Marshall unveiled a recovery plan for Europe. In a speech at Harvard University, he warned that without economic health, "there can be no political stability and no assured peace."

In early 1948, Congress approved the **Marshall Plan.** Over the next four years, the United States gave about $13 billion in grants and loans to nations in Western Europe. The program provided food to reduce famine, fuel to heat houses and factories, and money to jump-start economic growth. Aid was also offered to the Soviet satellite states in Eastern Europe, but Stalin refused to let them accept it.

The Marshall Plan provided a vivid example of how U.S. aid could serve the ends of both economic and foreign policy. The aid helped countries that desperately needed assistance. The prosperity it stimulated then helped the American economy by increasing trade. Finally, the good relationships that the aid created worked against the expansion of communism.

✓ **Checkpoint** Why did George Kennan think that containment would work against Soviet expansion?

The Cold War Heats Up

The front lines of the Cold War were located in Germany. The zones that were controlled by France, Britain, and the United States were combined to form West Germany. West Germany was bordered on the east by the Soviet-controlled East Germany. The Allies also controlled the western part of Berlin, a city tucked deep inside communist East Germany. (See the map on the opposite page.)

Marshall Plan Aids European Recovery

These Greek children benefited from U.S. aid designed to promote stable democracies in Europe. *According to the pie chart, what portion of U.S. aid was devoted to reducing famine?*

Shipments Financed by the Marshall Plan, 1948–1951

- Other 1%
- Machines and Vehicles 14%
- Raw Materials 38%
- Fuel 16%
- Food and Other Produce 32%

Berlin Airlift Saves West Berlin West Berlin was, as one Soviet leader later described it, "a bone in the throat" of the Soviet Union. Its relative prosperity and freedom stood in contrast to the bleak life of East Berliners. Stalin was determined to capture West Berlin or win other concessions from the Western allies. In June 1948, he stopped all highway, railway, and waterway traffic from western Germany into West Berlin. Without any means of receiving aid, West Berlin would fall to the communists.

Stalin was able to close roads, stop barges, and block railways, but he could not blockade the sky. For almost a year, the United States and Britain supplied West Berlin through a massive airlift. Food, fuel, medical supplies, clothing, toys—everything the residents of West Berlin needed was flown into the city.

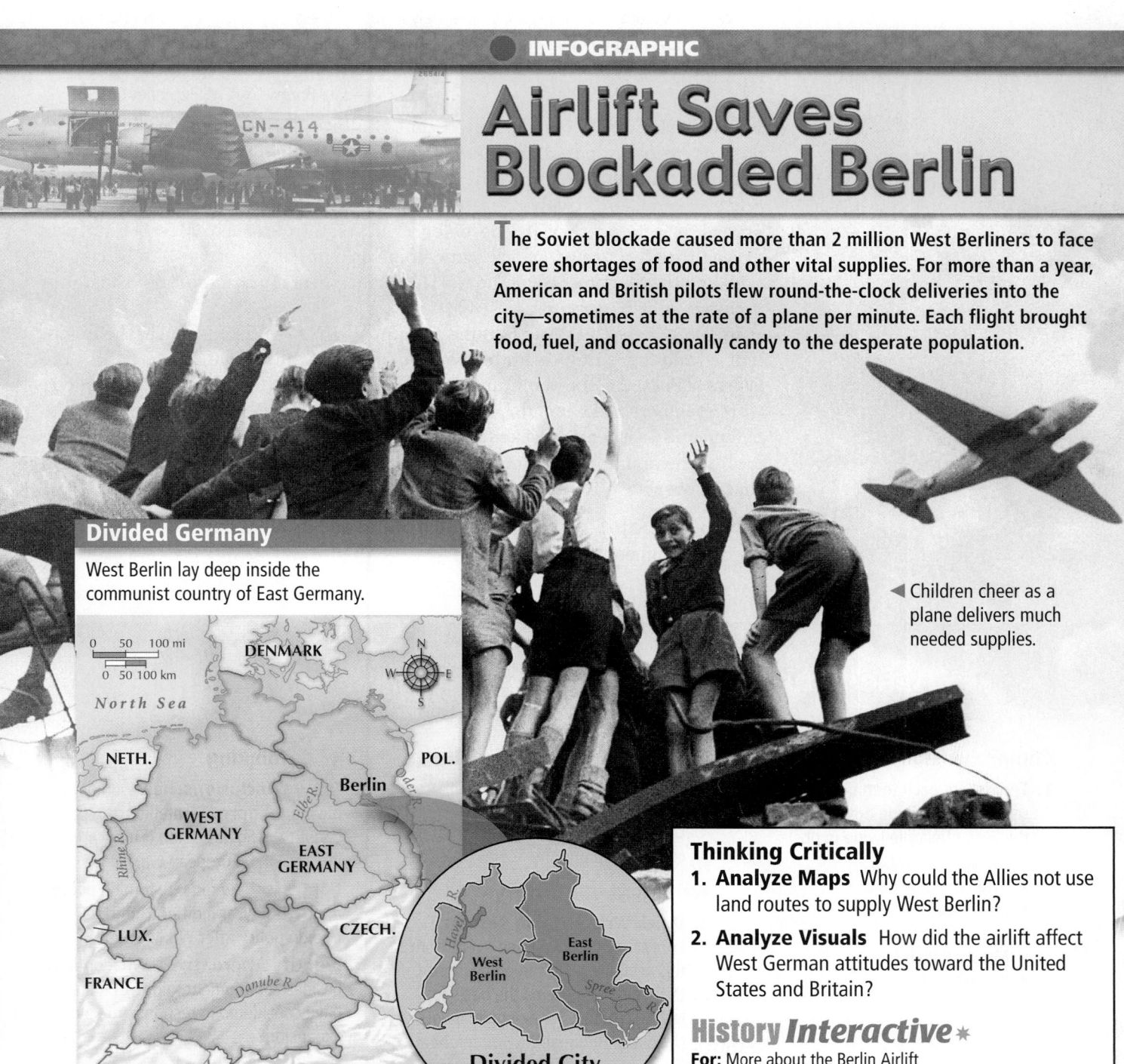

● INFOGRAPHIC

Airlift Saves Blockaded Berlin

The Soviet blockade caused more than 2 million West Berliners to face severe shortages of food and other vital supplies. For more than a year, American and British pilots flew round-the-clock deliveries into the city—sometimes at the rate of a plane per minute. Each flight brought food, fuel, and occasionally candy to the desperate population.

◄ Children cheer as a plane delivers much needed supplies.

Divided Germany

West Berlin lay deep inside the communist country of East Germany.

0 50 100 mi
0 50 100 km

DENMARK
North Sea
NETH.
POL.
Berlin
WEST GERMANY
EAST GERMANY
LUX.
CZECH.
FRANCE
Danube R.
Elbe R.
Rhine R.
SWITZ.
AUSTRIA

Divided City of Berlin

Havel R.
West Berlin
East Berlin
Spree R.

Thinking Critically
1. **Analyze Maps** Why could the Allies not use land routes to supply West Berlin?
2. **Analyze Visuals** How did the airlift affect West German attitudes toward the United States and Britain?

History *Interactive* ★

For: More about the Berlin Airlift
Webcode: nep-1213

Even through rain and snow, goods arrived regularly. The **Berlin airlift** demonstrated to West Berlin, the Soviet Union, and the world how far the United States would go to protect noncommunist parts of Europe and contain communism.

Vocabulary Builder
acknowledge–(ak NAHL ihj) *v.* to admit or recognize

Cold War Rivals Form Alliances In May 1949, Stalin was forced to acknowledge that his attempt to blockade Berlin had failed. The Berlin airlift was a proud moment for Americans and Berliners and a major success for the policy of containment. One Berlin resident later recalled her feelings when the blockade was finally lifted:

> **Primary Source** "Sheer joy—nothing else. Nothing else. Joy, and [the feeling that], 'We have done it! And it works!' . . . That was so very important. The West has won! I say this quite deliberately in such a crass way because you wanted to know how I felt emotionally. The West—well, we have succeeded. And the West has won and the others have not!"
> —Ella Barowsky, CNN interview, 1996

The Berlin airlift demonstrated that Stalin could be contained if Western nations were prepared to take forceful action. The **North Atlantic Treaty Organization (NATO),** formed in 1949, provided the military alliance to counter Soviet expansion. Twelve Western European and North American nations agreed to act together in the defense of Western Europe. Member nations agreed that "an armed attack against one or more of them . . . shall be considered an attack against all of them." This principle of mutual military assistance is called collective security.

In 1955, West Germany became a member of NATO. In response, the Soviet Union and its satellite states formed a rival military alliance, called the **Warsaw Pact.** All the communist states of Eastern Europe except Yugoslavia were members. Like members of NATO, nations of the Warsaw Pact pledged to defend one another if attacked. Although members agreed on paper not to interfere in one another's internal affairs, the Soviet Union continued to exert firm control over its Warsaw Pact allies.

✔ **Checkpoint** How did the United States and its allies apply the containment policy in Europe?

SECTION **1** Assessment

Progress Monitoring *Online*
For: Self-test with vocabulary practice
Web Code: nea-1203

Comprehension

1. **Terms** For each term below, write a sentence explaining how it changed the lives of people living in post-World War II Europe.
   - satellite state
   - iron curtain
   - Truman Doctrine
   - Marshall Plan
   - Berlin airlift
   - NATO

2. **NoteTaking Reading Skill: Contrast** Use your chart to answer the Section Focus Question: How did U.S. leaders respond to the threat of communism and the Soviet Union?

Writing About History

3. **Quick Write: Frame Research Questions** Choose one event from this section. Write three questions that you could use as the basis for a research paper. For example, if you chose the Berlin airlift, you might ask, "How much food was flown into Berlin?"

Critical Thinking

4. **Draw Conclusions** How would having control over satellite states benefit the Soviet Union if it became involved in a European war?

5. **Contrast** How did U.S. foreign policy after World War II differ from U.S. foreign policy after World War I?

6. **Identify Alternatives** What options besides containment might Truman have considered in response to Soviet expansion?

6.II.B.3a

Harry S. Truman:
The Truman Doctrine

In this address to Congress, President Truman stressed the duty of the United States to combat totalitarian regimes worldwide. His March 12, 1947, speech called for $400 million in aid to Greece and Turkey, both of which he said were threatened by communism. Congress approved the financial aid as well as the commitment of U.S. troops to administer postwar reconstruction.

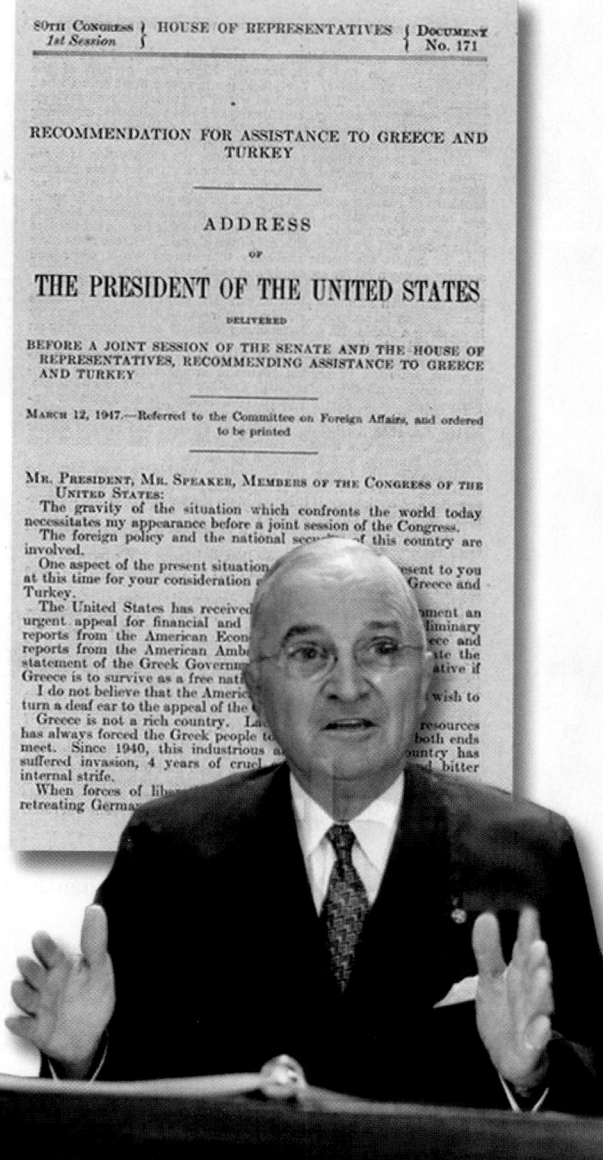

▲ President Truman delivering a speech

The peoples of a number of countries of the world have recently had totalitarian regimes forced upon them against their will. The government of the United States has made frequent protests against coercion[1] and intimidation, in violation of the Yalta agreement, in Poland, Romania, and Bulgaria. I must also state that in a number of other countries there have been similar developments.

At the present moment in world history nearly every nation must choose between alternative ways of life. The choice is too often not a free one. One way of life is based upon the will of the majority, and is distinguished by free institutions, representative government, free elections, guarantees of individual liberty, freedom of speech and religion, and freedom from political oppression. The second way of life is based upon the will of a minority forcibly imposed upon the majority. It relies upon terror and oppression, a controlled press and radio, fixed elections and the suppression of personal freedoms.

I believe that it must be the policy of the United States to support free peoples who are resisting attempted subjugation[2] by armed minorities or by outside pressures.

I believe that we must assist free peoples to work out their own destinies in their own way.

I believe that our help should be primarily through economic and financial aid which is essential to economic stability and orderly political processes. . . .

The seeds of totalitarian regimes are nurtured by misery and want. They spread and grow in the evil soil of poverty and strife. They reach their full growth when the hope of a people for a better life has died. We must keep that hope alive.

The free peoples of the world look to us for support in maintaining their freedoms. If we falter in our leadership, we may endanger the peace of the world—and we shall surely endanger the welfare of our own nation.

Thinking Critically
1. **Make Inferences** What is President Truman referring to when he mentions the two "alternative ways of life"?

2. **Recognize Causes and Effects** According to Truman, how would economic aid support freedom in Greece and Turkey?

1. **coercion** (koh ER zhuhn) *n.* government by force.
2. **subjugation** (suhb juh GAY shuhn) *n.* condition of being under the control of a conqueror.

Korean War Medal of Honor ▶

▲ American machine-gunners in Korea

WITNESS HISTORY 🔊 AUDIO

They Won't Escape This Time

General Lewis B. Puller was the only U.S. marine in history to win five Navy Crosses. Since the time he enlisted in 1918, Puller had fought in Haiti and Nicaragua, commanded marines in China, and waded ashore island after island in the Pacific during World War II. Pinned down by a surprise communist Chinese attack into North Korea, badly outnumbered, and cut off from reinforcement, Puller retained his courage and humor. He informed his regiment:

❝The enemy is in front of us, behind us, to the left of us, and to the right of us. They won't escape this time.❞

—Lewis "Chesty" Puller, November 1950

The Korean War

 Core Curriculum Objectives

- **6.II.C.2** The United States and China
- **6.II.C.4a** Korean War: China enters the war
- **6.II.C.4b** United Nations Efforts: MacArthur, Truman and limited war
- **6.II.C.4c** Korean War: stalemate and truce
- **7.II.B.5** Establishment of SEATO

Terms and People

Jiang Jieshi
Mao Zedong
38th parallel

Douglas MacArthur
limited war
SEATO

NoteTaking

Reading Skill: Categorize As you read, note problems and the steps that President Truman took to solve them. Use a problem-solution table like the one below.

Problem	Solution
Communists threaten takeover of China	

Why It Matters Europe had been the first focus of the Cold War. But in the early 1950s, U.S. involvement in the Korean War made East Asia the prime battleground in the long, hard Cold War struggle. The division between North and South Korea remains a source of international tension today. **Section Focus Question: How did President Truman use the power of the presidency to limit the spread of communism in East Asia?**

Communists Gain Control of China

Since the time of the Russian Revolution in 1917, the Soviets had hoped to spread communism to every corner of the world, training foreigners in Marxist theory and revolutionary strategy. The Soviets were confident that communism would reach worldwide influence. In 1949, events in China seemed to justify their confidence.

Civil War Divides China Before Japan invaded China in 1937, Nationalist leader **Jiang Jieshi** (zhee AHNG zhī SHEE), known in the United States as Chiang Kai-shek, had been fighting a civil war against communists led by **Mao Zedong** (mow zeh DUHNG). Although Jiang and Mao temporarily joined forces in an uneasy alliance to fight Japan, the civil war resumed with a new fury after the war ended.

The Soviet Union supported Mao, while the United States sent several billion dollars in aid to Jiang. American leaders feared that Jiang's defeat would create a communist superpower spanning most of Asia.

Jiang's regime proved unequal to the task. Nationalist generals were reluctant to fight. And, while masses of Chinese people faced starvation, corrupt officials diverted U.S. aid dollars into their own pockets. By promising to feed the people, Mao won increased support.

Communists Win in China In 1948, Mao's forces dominated the war. Jiang appealed for American military intervention. However, the U.S. government had no intention of sending American troops to support the corrupt Jiang. In 1949, Jiang fled the Chinese mainland, taking control of the large offshore island of Taiwan. Mao's communists then took control of the world's most populous country, renaming it the People's Republic of China.

Mao's victory was an immense shock to Americans. Not only was China under the control of sworn enemies of the United States, but communist regimes controlled about one fourth of the world's landmass and one third of its population. "Who lost China?" Americans asked. Many critics blamed the Truman administration, saying that the United States had failed to give enough support to Jiang. But Secretary of State Dean Acheson argued:

Communist Victory in China
Carrying hundreds of pictures of their leader, Mao Zedong, these Chinese communists celebrate the defeat of Jiang Jieshi in 1949.

Primary Source ❝The unfortunate but inescapable fact is that the ominous result of the civil war in China was beyond the control of the government of the United States. Nothing that this country did or could have done within the reasonable limits of its capabilities could have changed the result.❞
—Secretary of State Dean Acheson, "White Paper on China," August 1949

✔ **Checkpoint** Why were the communists able to win the Chinese Civil War?

Americans Fight in Korea

The focus of attention turned to the peninsula of Korea, separated from northeast China by the Yalu River. Once controlled by Japan, Korea had been divided into two independent countries by the United States and the Soviet Union after World War II. The dividing line was set at the **38th parallel** of latitude. In North Korea, the Soviets installed a communist government and equipped its armed forces. The United States provided smaller amounts of aid to noncommunist South Korea.

North Korea Invades South Korea American occupation troops remained in South Korea until June 1949. Their departure coincided with the communist victory in China. Soon after, North Korea began a major military buildup.

On June 25, 1950, North Korean forces attacked across the 38th parallel. The 90,000 North Korean troops were armed with powerful tanks and other Soviet weapons. Within days, the northerners overtook the South Korean capital city of Seoul and set out after the retreating South Korean army.

U.S. Forces Defend South Korea President Truman remembered how the policy of appeasement had failed to check the German aggression that sparked World War II. Determined that history would not repeat itself, he announced that the United States would aid South Korea.

Within days, the UN Security Council unanimously voted to follow Truman's lead, recommending that "the Members of the United Nations furnish such assistance to the Republic of Korea as may be necessary to repel the armed attack and to restore international peace and security in the area." Undoubtedly, the Soviet Union would have used its veto power to block the UN resolution if it had been present for the vote. However, it had been boycotting Security Council sessions because the UN had refused to seat Mao's People's Republic of China.

WITNESS HISTORY DVD

Watch *A Land Divided: The Korean War* on the **United States Witness History DVD** to explore how Cold War rivalries brought the United States into a deadly armed conflict.

Truman did not ask Congress for a formal declaration of war, as required by the Constitution. However, supported by the UN resolution, Truman ordered American troops who were stationed in Japan to move to South Korea. The soldiers were mainly occupation troops who had not been trained for forced marches in monsoon rains or heavy combat in rice paddies, nor did they have the military equipment needed to stop the invasion. Soon, they joined their South Korean allies in retreating to the southeast corner of the peninsula near the city of Pusan. There, the allies held fast. As fresh supplies and troops arrived from Japan, soldiers from other UN countries joined the American and South Korean forces.

MacArthur Drives Back the North Koreans By September 1950, the UN forces were ready to counterattack. General **Douglas MacArthur,** the World War II hero, had a bold plan to drive the invaders from South Korea. He suspected that the rapid advance of North Korean troops had left North Korea with limited supply lines. He decided to strike at this weakness by launching a surprise attack on the port city of Inchon, well behind enemy lines. Because Inchon was such a poor landing site, with swift currents and treacherous tides, MacArthur knew that the enemy would not expect an attack there.

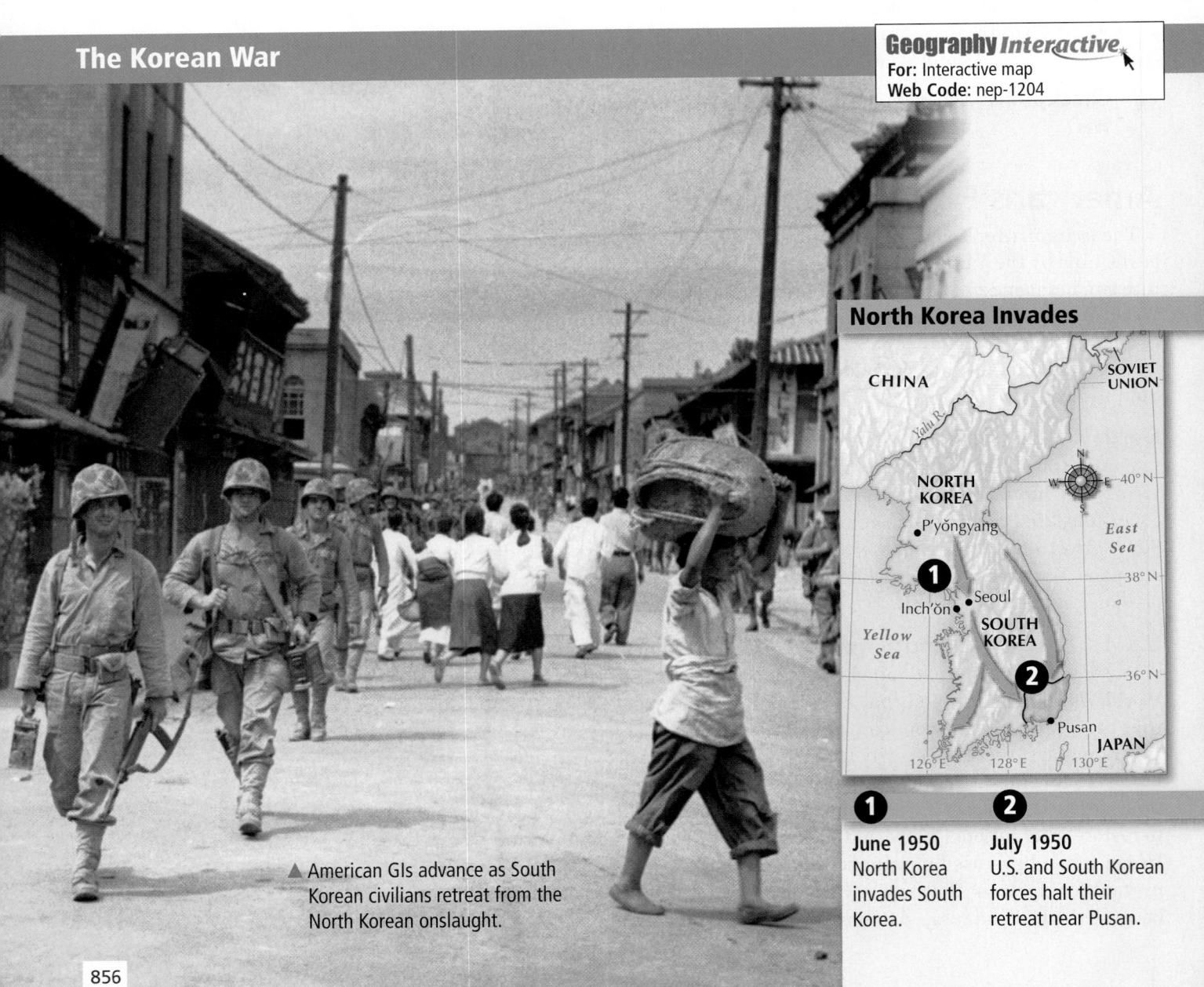

The Korean War

Geography *Interactive*
For: Interactive map
Web Code: nep-1204

North Korea Invades

CHINA

SOVIET UNION

Yalu R.

NORTH KOREA

• P'yŏngyang

East Sea

40° N

38° N

Inch'ŏn •

• Seoul

1

SOUTH KOREA

Yellow Sea

2

36° N

• Pusan

JAPAN

126° E   128° E   130° E

1
June 1950
North Korea invades South Korea.

2
July 1950
U.S. and South Korean forces halt their retreat near Pusan.

▲ American GIs advance as South Korean civilians retreat from the North Korean onslaught.

MacArthur's bold gamble paid off handsomely. On the morning of September 15, 1950, U.S. Marines landed at Inchon and launched an attack into the rear guard of the North Koreans. Communist forces began fleeing for the North Korean border. By October 1950, the North Koreans had been driven north of the 38th parallel.

With the retreat of North Korean forces, U.S. officials had to decide what to do next. Should they declare their UN mandate accomplished and end the war? Or should they send their forces north of the 38th parallel and punish the communists for the invasion? Truman was concerned about the action China would take if the United States carried the war into North Korea. Chinese leaders publicly warned the Americans not to advance near its borders. But MacArthur did not take this warning seriously. He assured Truman that China would not intervene in the war. Based on this advice, the United States pushed a resolution through the UN, calling for a "unified, independent, and democratic" Korea.

China Forces a Stalemate Highly confident, MacArthur attacked north of the 38th parallel. Despite mountainous terrain and freezing temperatures, by Thanksgiving the Allied advance had reached the Chinese border at the Yalu River. Then, on November 25, 1950, some 300,000 Chinese soldiers attacked

Vocabulary Builder
intervene–(ihn ter VEEN) v. to become involved in; to take action to settle a dispute or influence a course of action

---

Map Skills During the Korean War, UN troops supported South Korea, while China backed North Korea. Advantage seesawed between the two sides.

1. **Locate:** (a) 38th parallel, (b) Pusan, (c) Inchon, (d) Yalu River

2. **Movement** Describe the movement of communist troops after November 1950.

3. **Compare** How does the first map differ from the last one?

☐ North Korean control
↤ Communist attack
☐ South Korean control
➤ UN attack
— Line of control
Conic Projection
0   100 mi
0   100 km

UN Fights Back	**China Enters the War**	**Stalemate**

3
Sept. 15, 1950
UN forces land at Inchon and break out of Pusan.

4
Nov. 24, 1950
MacArthur starts offensive toward Yalu River.

5
Nov. 25, 1950
Chinese attack. UN and South Korean forces retreat.

6
Jan. 10, 1951
Communists push UN forces to 37th parallel.

7
Jan. 16, 1951
UN forces push communists back to 38th parallel.

8
June 27, 1951
Cease-fire is signed, with border at 38th parallel.

South Korean and U.S. positions. Badly outnumbered, the UN troops were forced back.

With China now in the war, the United States <u>confronted</u> a major land war in Asia. It was possible that this war could not be won without huge commitments of troops and even atomic weapons. Truman steadfastly ruled out both of these options. MacArthur, who favored an invasion of China, was enraged. He distrusted Truman's policy of a **limited war** fought to achieve only specific goals. As a soldier, MacArthur favored total victory.

Unable to sway Truman, the general sent a letter to the House Republican leader attacking the President's policies. After the letter became public, Truman fired MacArthur for insubordination. There was a huge outcry in the United States, and MacArthur returned home a national hero.

✓ **Checkpoint** How did President Truman react to the North Korean invasion of South Korea?

The Korean War Has Lasting Effects

By the spring of 1951, Allied forces had regrouped and stabilized their position near the 38th parallel. The stalemate lasted until 1953. During that time, the two sides fought small, bloody battles with limited results. At the same time, diplomats tried to devise an acceptable peace agreement.

The War Becomes a Political Issue The stalemate was a key issue in the presidential election of 1952. Republican candidate Dwight D. Eisenhower promised that if elected he would end the war. Upon his election, he visited Korea, spoke with the troops, and studied the enemy's fortifications.

Decision ● Point

Should the United States Invade China?

China's troops advanced, driving U.S. soldiers and marines back into South Korea.
General Douglas MacArthur favored a strong response that included an invasion of China.
President Truman disagreed. Read the options below. Then, you decide.

MacArthur Favors Invasion

Primary Source

❝I made it clear that if not permitted to destroy the enemy built-up bases north of the Yalu, if not permitted to utilize the friendly Chinese force of some 600,000 men on Formosa [Taiwan], if not permitted to blockade the China coast . . . the position of the command from the military standpoint forbade victory.❞

—General Douglas MacArthur, April 19, 1951

Truman Opposes Invasion

Primary Source

❝We do not want to see the conflict in Korea extended. We are trying to prevent a world war—not to start one. . . . Why can't we take other steps to punish the aggressor? Why don't we bomb Manchuria and China itself? Why don't we assist Chinese Nationalist troops to land on mainland China? If we were to do these things we would . . . become entangled in a vast conflict on the continent of Asia. . . .❞

—President Truman, April 11, 1951

You Decide
1. Why did MacArthur want to invade China?
2. Why did Truman oppose invasion?
3. What decision would you have made? Why?

Korean War's Impact on America		✔ Quick Study
Immediate Effects	**Long-Term Effects**	
• 37,000 Americans killed • 103,000 Americans wounded • Relations with China worsen • Armed forces racially integrated	• Military spending increases • Military commitments increase worldwide • Relations with Japan improve • Future presidents send military into combat without Congressional approval	

U.S. Troops Remain in Korea
American soldiers have stayed in Korea since the war. They patrol the border between the Koreas to prevent another North Korean invasion of South Korea.

Eisenhower became convinced that only strong action would break the stalemate. When peace talks threatened to fail, he hinted that he might introduce nuclear weapons into the conflict. That warning, along with the death of Joseph Stalin, convinced the communists to settle the conflict. On July 27, 1953, after slightly more than three years of fighting, the two sides signed a cease-fire. That cease-fire is still in effect today.

Examining the Lessons of the Korean War There was no victory in the Korean War. North Korea remained a communist country allied to China and the Soviet Union, and South Korea stayed a noncommunist country allied to the United States and the major democracies. The two Koreas remained divided at about the 38th parallel.

Yet, the war had an important long-term result. Truman had committed U.S. troops to battle without a congressional declaration of war. This set a precedent that future Presidents would follow. The Korean War also led to increased military spending. By 1960, military spending accounted for nearly half of the federal budget. More than a million U.S. soldiers were stationed around the world.

A new alliance underscored U.S. interest in Asia. Like NATO, the **Southeast Asia Treaty Organization (SEATO)** was a defensive alliance aimed at preventing the spread of communism. Its members included Pakistan, Thailand, the Philippines, Australia, New Zealand, France, Britain, and the United States.

✔ **Checkpoint** What were the most important results of U.S. participation in the Korean War?

SECTION

2 Assessment

Progress Monitoring *Online*
For: Self-test with vocabulary practice
Web Code: nea-1205

Comprehension

1. **Terms and People** What is the relationship between each of the following items and American policy in East Asia?
   • Jiang Jieshi
   • Mao Zedong
   • 38th parallel
   • limited war
   • SEATO

2. **NoteTaking Reading Skill: Categorize** Use your problem-solution table to answer the Section Focus Question: How did President Truman use the power of the presidency to limit the spread of communism in East Asia?

Writing About History

3. **Quick Write: Plan an Interview** Suppose that you were going to interview some American veterans of the Korean War. Write five questions that you might ask about their experiences and their views of the war.

Critical Thinking

4. **Identify Central Issues** Why did American aid to Jiang's Nationalists fail to prevent Mao's communists from taking control of China?

5. **Demonstrate Reasoned Judgment** How did General MacArthur's decision to advance toward the Yalu River change the course of the Korean War?

6. **Identify Central Issues** How did the way in which Truman handled the Korean crisis affect the powers of the presidency?

It can happen Here

JOIN

CIVIL DEFENSE

Civil defense poster ▶

Nuclear fallout shelter sign ▶

WITNESS HISTORY AUDIO

The Threat of War

After the Soviet Union tested an atomic bomb in 1949, President Truman reported to the nation that the nature of war had forever changed:

❝[W]ar has undergone a technological change which makes it a very different thing from what it used to be. War today between the Soviet empire and the free nations might dig the grave not only of our Stalinist opponents, but of our own society. . . . Such a war is not a possible policy for rational men.❞

—President Harry S. Truman

The Cold War Expands

Core Curriculum Objectives

- **6.II.C.3** USSR tests an A-bomb
- **7.II.B.2** John Foster Dulles, the domino theory and massive retaliation
- **7.II.B.6** Aswan Dam and Suez Canal
- **7.II.B.7** Polish and Hungarian uprisings
- **7.II.B.8** Eisenhower Doctrine: intervention in Lebanon

Terms and People

arms race
mutually assured
  destruction
John Foster Dulles
massive retaliation
brinkmanship

Nikita Khrushchev
nationalize
Suez crisis
Eisenhower Doctrine
CIA
NASA

NoteTaking

Reading Skill: Identify Main Ideas Identify the tactics used to wage the Cold War.

Why It Matters By 1950, the United States and the Soviet Union were the two most powerful nations in the world. The conflicting ideologies and goals of these rival nations led to a worldwide struggle for influence. The policies followed by the two superpowers helped shape the modern history of much of the world, from Latin America to the Middle East. **Section Focus Question: What methods did the United States use in its global struggle against the Soviet Union?**

The Arms Race Heightens Tensions

A change in the balance of world power is usually gradual, taking place over decades or even centuries. But sometimes, the shift happens in a blink of an eye. Such a major shift in the balance of power in the Cold War took place on September 2, 1949. Instruments in an American B-29 aircraft flying over Alaska detected unusual atmospheric radiation. The radiation cloud was drifting eastward from the direction of Siberia.

American nuclear scientists analyzed the data that the aircraft had gathered. They then reached an inescapable conclusion: The Soviet Union had set off an atomic bomb.

Communist Advances Shock the Nation The news shook U.S. leaders. They had believed that the Soviet Union was years away from developing an atomic bomb. Now, the Americans no longer had a monopoly on atomic weaponry.

The news that the Soviets had the bomb was followed the next month by news of the communist takeover of China. In a very short time, Americans sensed that the world was a much more dangerous and threatening place.

Nuclear Arsenals Expand Three months later, Truman ordered the Atomic Energy Commission to produce a hydrogen bomb. Developers predicted that the H-Bomb would be 1,000 times as powerful as an atomic bomb. They hoped it would restore the United States advantage over the Soviets.

Some scientists, such as J. Robert Oppenheimer and Albert Einstein, opposed developing the H-Bomb, claiming it would only lead to a <u>perpetual</u> **arms race.** Others argued that Stalin would continue to develop more powerful weapons no matter what the United States did.

In 1952, the United States tested the first hydrogen bomb. The next year, the Soviets tested one of their own. More bombs and tests followed. Most of these tests were conducted aboveground, spewing radioactive waste into the atmosphere. Atomic testing in the American west, at sites such as the Nevada desert, led to increased atmospheric radiation and long-range health problems for people living downwind of the test sites.

During the next four decades, the United States and the Soviet Union developed and stockpiled increasingly powerful nuclear weapons. They armed planes, submarines, and missiles with nuclear warheads powerful enough to destroy each other many times over. Both sides hoped that this program of **mutually assured destruction** would prevent either country from actually using a nuclear device against the other. Still, the threat of nuclear destruction seemed to hang over the world like a dark cloud.

✔ **Checkpoint** Why did the United States government decide to build a hydrogen bomb?

Vocabulary Builder
<u>perpetual</u>–(per PEHCH oo uhl) *adj.* constant; continuing without interruption

Eisenhower Introduces New Policies

President Dwight Eisenhower knew firsthand the horrors of war and the need to defend democracy. He had led the World War II Allied invasions of North Africa, Italy, and Normandy. Having worked with top military and political leaders during the war, he was capable of speaking the language of both.

Eisenhower accepted much of Truman's foreign policy. He believed strongly in a policy to actively contain communism. Eisenhower's secretary of state, **John Foster Dulles,** was an experienced diplomat who had helped organize the United Nations after World War II. Dulles endorsed the President's vision of the role the United States should play in the world.

In their approach toward foreign policy, Eisenhower and Dulles differed significantly from Truman and his Secretary of State, Dean Acheson. Both teams of men considered the spread of communism the greatest threat to the free world. But Eisenhower believed that Truman's approach to foreign policy had dragged the United States into an endless series of conflicts begun by the Soviet Union. These limited, regional conflicts threatened to drain the country's resources.

Eisenhower Favors Massive Retaliation Eisenhower opposed spending billions of dollars on conventional forces, such as troops, ships, tanks, and artillery. Instead, he focused on stockpiling nuclear weapons and building the planes, missiles, and submarines needed to deliver them. He assumed that if there were a major war, it would be nuclear.

Ike's new policy drew some criticism: Conservatives felt that downgrading conventional forces would weaken American defense, while liberals feared that preparing for nuclear

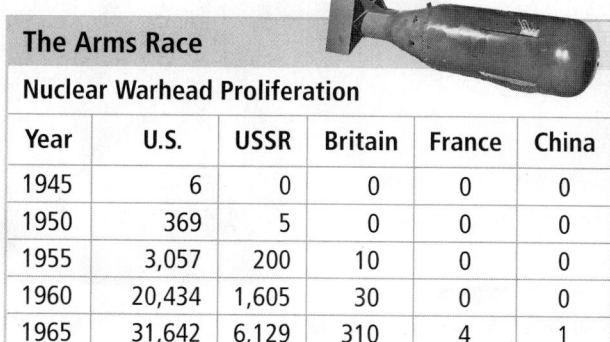

The Arms Race

Nuclear Warhead Proliferation

Year	U.S.	USSR	Britain	France	China
1945	6	0	0	0	0
1950	369	5	0	0	0
1955	3,057	200	10	0	0
1960	20,434	1,605	30	0	0
1965	31,642	6,129	310	4	1

Chart Skills The chart above shows effects of the arms race. *How did the Soviet Union's development of nuclear weapons affect U.S. defense spending? How did Eisenhower's policies affect defense spending? Explain.*

SOURCE: *Bulletin of the Atomic Scientists*

war made such a war more likely. Still, Eisenhower's approach did save money by providing a "bigger bang for the buck." In 1953, the defense budget was $50.5 billion; in 1955, it dropped down to $35.8 billion.

In 1954, Dulles announced the policy of **massive retaliation.** The United States would respond to communist threats to its allies by threatening to use crushing, overwhelming force, perhaps even nuclear weapons.

> **Primary Source** "A potential aggressor must know that he cannot always prescribe battle conditions to suit him. . . . The way to deter aggression is for the free community to be willing and able to respond vigorously at places and with means of his choosing."
>
> —John Foster Dulles, 1954

Dulles believed that only by going to the brink of war could the United States protect its allies, discourage communist aggression, and prevent war. "You have to take some chances for peace, just as you must take chances in war," he said in 1956. Dulles's approach became known as **brinkmanship.**

INFOGRAPHIC

Domestic Uses Of
COLD WAR Technology

To give their nations a military advantage, Cold War scientists rushed to invent advanced weaponry, transportation, and communication. Inventions whose origins go back to the Cold War include space travel, satellites, the Internet, and more.

▲ 5-FOOT-TALL MICROWAVE!
In 1946, a scientist working on radar-related military research noticed that the candy bar in his pocket had melted. Knowing a good thing when he saw it, he eventually invented the "Radarange." The early model above was about 5 feet tall.

▲ MONSTER COMPUTERS!
This 1946 computer calculated artillery trajectories and other military computations. Unlike today's laptop, it filled an entire room, required extensive wiring, and weighed about 30 tons.

Military Technology Led to These Inventions

1946	• Microwave oven
1946	• Computer
1948	• Hang glider
1958	• Nuclear energy plant
1960	• Communications satellite
1970s	• Smoke detector
1980s	• Global Positioning System

Connect to Your World
How did military technology indirectly affect the way of life in American homes?

Stalin's Death Eases Tensions On March 5, 1953, Joseph Stalin died, setting off a short power struggle. **Nikita Khrushchev** soon emerged as the new head of the Soviet Union. Although a communist and a determined opponent of the United States, Khrushchev was not as suspicious or as cruel as Stalin. He condemned the excesses of the Stalin regime and inched toward more peaceful relations with the democratic West.

In July 1955, Khrushchev met with Eisenhower at a conference in Geneva, Switzerland. Although the meeting yielded few significant results, it did seem to be a small move toward "peaceful co-existence" of the two powers.

✓ **Checkpoint** How was Eisenhower's approach to foreign affairs different from that of Truman?

The Cold War Goes Global

Peaceful co-existence was easier to imagine than it was to practice. The United States and the Soviet Union remained deeply divided. The Soviet Union would not allow free elections in the areas it controlled, and it continued to attempt to spread communism around the world. Dulles talked about "rolling back" communism and liberating the countries under Soviet rule.

Unrest Explodes Behind the Iron Curtain American talk of "rolling back" communist borders and Khrushchev's talk of "peaceful co-existence" were taken seriously by people in Soviet-dominated countries behind the iron curtain. People in Poland, Hungary, and Czechoslovakia resented the control exerted by the Soviet Union. Many hungered for more political and economic freedom.

In 1956, two uprisings shook Eastern Europe. First, workers in Poland rioted against Soviet rule and won greater control of their government. Since the Polish government did not attempt to leave the Warsaw Pact, Soviet leaders permitted the actions.

Then, encouraged by Khrushchev's words and Poland's example, Hungarian students and workers organized huge demonstrations. They demanded that pro-Soviet Hungarian officials be replaced, that Soviet troops be withdrawn, and that noncommunist political parties be organized. Khrushchev responded brutally, sending Soviet soldiers and tanks to crush the Hungarian revolution. The Soviets executed many of the revolution's leaders, killed hundreds of other Hungarians, and restored hard-line communists to power.

Americans could only watch these events in horror. Eisenhower's massive retaliation approach was powerless. The United States would not use nuclear weapons—or any other weapons—to guarantee Hungarian independence from the Soviet Union.

The Hungarian revolt added a new level of hostility to international relations. At the 1956 Olympic Games, held that November in Melbourne, Australia, the bitter feelings surfaced. A water-polo match between the Soviet Union and Hungary turned violent. Sportswriters called it the "blood in the water" match.

The U.S. Defuses the Suez Crisis The United States found itself involved in another world conflict, this time in the Middle East. As Cold War tensions increased, Egypt's president Gamal Abdel Nasser tried to use the U.S.–Soviet rivalry to his advantage.

Nasser wanted to construct a dam on the Nile River at Aswan. The United States and Britain initially offered to fund the project, but when Nasser recognized the People's Republic of China and

Revolt in Hungary
Americans admired the brave men and women who sacrificed their lives fighting against Soviet domination in Hungary. *Time* magazine even chose the Hungarian Freedom Fighter as its "Man of the Year" for 1956.

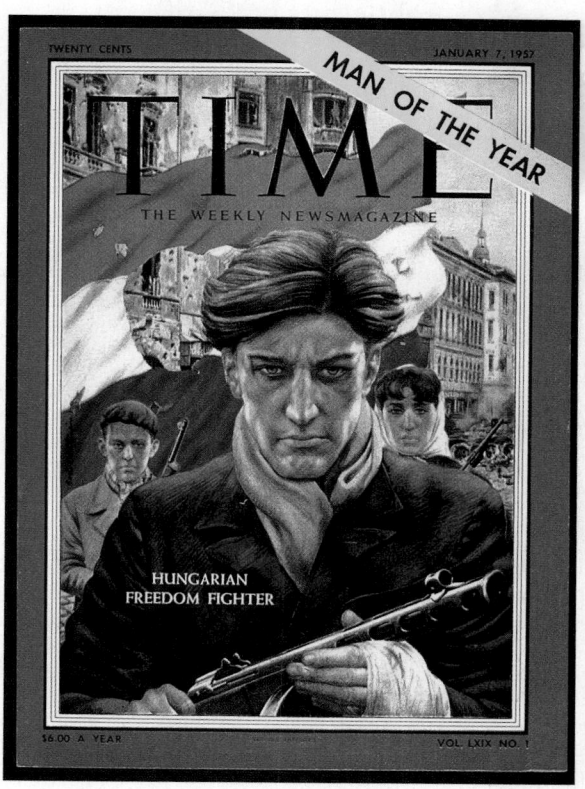

opened talks with the Soviet Union, the Eisenhower administration withdrew its offer. In response, Nasser **nationalized** the Suez Canal, placing it under government control. The canal, which connects the Mediterranean Sea with the Red Sea, had originally been managed by a British-French company and was protected by British armed forces.

Nasser's action threatened the flow of Middle Eastern oil to Europe. Without consulting with Eisenhower, Britain and France plotted to get the canal back into Western hands. They joined forces with Israel, a young nation that had long suffered from raids along its border with Egypt. Britain and France used the **Suez crisis** as an excuse to seize control of the Suez Canal.

President Eisenhower was outraged by these actions. Rather than support his Western allies, Ike criticized them and refused to supply them with U.S. oil. The three nations had counted on Eisenhower's support, and when it did not come, they were forced to withdraw their troops from Egypt.

Eisenhower Promises Strong Action In response to Soviet influence in the Middle East and elsewhere, the President made a statement in January 1957 that became known as the **Eisenhower Doctrine.** Eisenhower announced that the United States would use force to help any Middle Eastern nation threatened by communism. Eisenhower used his doctrine in 1958 to justify

Geography *Interactive*
For: Interactive map
Web Code: nep-1206

Global Cold War, 1946–1956

Map Skills The Cold War spread globally as the United States and the Soviet Union formed alliances and competed for power around the world. NATO and the Warsaw Pact were the two strongest alliances.

1. **Region** Identify a region where there were many Cold War hot spots. Why do you think there were so many conflicts in that region?

2. **Compare** How was Latin America important to the United States in the same way that Eastern Europe was important to the Soviet Union?

sending troops to Lebanon to put down a revolt against its pro-American government.

The Eisenhower administration also used the **Central Intelligence Agency (CIA)** in its struggle against communism. Congress had created the CIA in 1947 as an intelligence-gathering organization. Eisenhower gave it a new task. He approved covert, or secret, CIA operations to protect American interests. In 1953, the CIA aided a coup that installed a new government in Iran. In 1954, it accomplished a similar mission in Guatemala. While both operations helped to place anticommunist leaders in power, they also created long-term resentment against the United States.

Russians Succeed in Space
The dog Laika, aboard *Sputnik 2*, was the first living creature to orbit Earth. He was hailed as a Soviet hero.

The Cold War Blasts Off Into Space Although the United States successfully contained the spread of communism on the ground, it did suffer a setback in outer space. On October 4, 1957, the Soviet Union launched a 184-pound steel ball containing a small transmitter into an orbit of Earth. The Soviets named the tiny satellite *Sputnik 1*. The following month they launched a much larger satellite. It carried a dog, named Laika, to see how a living creature would react to life in outer space. Since there was no way to return the satellite to Earth, Laika died in orbit.

The launches shocked many Americans, who had long believed that superior technology would keep the United States ahead of the Soviet Union. Would Soviet space technology give them the rocket power to launch missiles onto American cities?

In a state of crisis, Congress quickly approved the National Defense Education Act, a $1 billion program intended to produce more scientists and teachers of science. The act authorized money for loans to enable high school and college graduates to continue their education in science. In addition, Congress created the **National Aeronautics and Space Administration (NASA)** to coordinate the space-related efforts of American scientists and the military.

✓ **Checkpoint** How did the Hungarian and Suez crises of 1956 raise Cold War tensions?

SECTION 3 Assessment

Progress Monitoring *Online*
For: Self-test with vocabulary practice
Web Code: nea-1207

Comprehension

1. **Terms** For each term below, write a sentence explaining its importance to the United States during the Cold War.
   • arms race
   • mutually assured destruction
   • massive retaliation
   • brinkmanship
   • Eisenhower Doctrine

2. **NoteTaking Reading Skill: Identify Main Ideas** Use your completed charts to answer the Section Focus Question: What methods did the United States use in its global struggle against the Soviet Union?

Writing About History

3. **Quick Write: Identify Sources** Identify two sources you might use to find answers to research questions about the arms race. One source should be a book from your school or public library. The other should be a reliable site on the Internet.

Critical Thinking

4. **Identify Point of View** Do you think that the massive retaliation policy favored by John Foster Dulles successfully deterred the Soviet Union? Explain your answer.

5. **Contrast** How were the covert operations of the CIA in Guatemala and Iran different from the military operations of the United States Army in Korea?

6. **Demonstrate Reasoned Judgment** Were Americans justified in being alarmed when the Soviets launched *Sputnik 1*? Explain.

EXPERIENCE THE COLD WAR

Fathers built bomb shelters in backyards, mothers stocked survival kits in basements, and children practiced ducking under their school desks. Across the nation, Americans prepared for the possibility that the Soviet Union might launch nuclear weapons against American cities. This was all part of the civil defense system of the early Cold War.

Throughout the 1950s and early 1960s, the civil defense system shaped American attitudes about their country and the Cold War. As the Cold War ended, civil defense became less important. But since 2001 and the rise of terrorism, it reemerged in a new form known as homeland security.

▼ Stay Tuned!
Emergency information would be broadcast on AM radio stations.

▶ Duck and Cover!
Schoolchildren were taught to "duck and cover" under their desks during nuclear air-raid drills.

▲ Evacuate!
In 1955, wailing sirens signaled a simulated nuclear attack and sent New Yorkers scurrying into underground fallout shelters. Similar drills took place across the nation.

ATTEND A HOME PREPAREDNESS WORKSHOP

Earn this award

this HOME is prepared

FOR SURVIVAL YOU WILL NEED

food and water ..enough for at least 14 days

first aid and home care of the sick ..when there is no trained medical help

sanitation ..safeguard your family's health

firefighting and rescue ..self-reliance for safety

Conelrad, utilities ..a guide to family action

receive this CITATION

by acquiring FAMILY FALLOUT SHELTER and completing the READINESS REQUIREMENTS

Kidde Kokoon

CANNED FOOD

CANNED WATER

DO YOU QUALIFY AS A RADEF VOLUNTEER?

IF YOU DO, YOU MAY BECOME A NUCLEAR AGE MINUTEMAN

▲ **Be Prepared!**
The Civil Defense Administration taught Americans how to survive a nuclear attack.

◄ **Take Shelter!**
Homeowners built backyard bomb shelters stocked with radiation suits and medical kits.

◄ **Volunteer!**
Citizens monitored the skies for enemy planes, stocked air-raid shelters, and maintained emergency equipment.

Thinking Critically

1. **Analyze Visuals** How did civil defense literature appeal to Americans' sense of duty and citizenship?

2. **Draw Conclusions** Do you think the civil defense program made Americans feel safer or more fearful? Explain.

Connect to Today Do research to learn about today's homeland security system. How are the methods and goals of this system similar to and different from the civil defense system of the 1950s?

History *Interactive* ✴

For: To discover more about the Cold War
Web Code: nep-1208

IS THIS TOMORROW

AMERICA UNDER COMMUNISM!

▲ Anticommunist comic

WITNESS HISTORY 🔊 AUDIO

Battling the Communist Menace

In the 1950s, Americans were alarmed by charges that communists had infiltrated their government and other institutions. Cold War themes made their way into movies, television shows, and novels. Even comic-book heroes like Superman battled the communist menace. In a 1952 comic book, a character states the concerns of many Americans:

❝Today's headlines shout of battles with Communist hordes in Korea—of Red riots in Rome and Paris and Berlin! But there's another secret battle taking place—right here, right now! A [secret] underground fight between Communism and democracy for the youth of America.❞

— "Backyard Battleground," in
Daring Confessions, 1953

The Cold War at Home

 Core Curriculum Objectives

- **3.III.C.6** The Red Scare
- **6.II.D.1** Truman and government loyalty checks
- **6.II.D.2** The case of Robert Oppenheimer
- **6.II.D.3** McCarthyism

Terms and People

Red Scare	Alger Hiss
Smith Act	Julius and Ethel
HUAC	Rosenberg
Hollywood Ten	Joseph R. McCarthy
blacklist	McCarthyism

NoteTaking

Reading Skill: Identify Causes and Effects
List efforts taken to protect Americans from communism and how these policies affected rights.

Anticommunist Policy	Effect on Rights

Why It Matters Americans have often faced the difficult task of balancing the need to provide national security with the need to protect people's rights and freedoms. In times of crisis, rights have sometimes been limited. Beginning in the late 1940s, the Cold War dominated American life. For some of those years, the nation was in the grip of a new Red Scare. The hunt for communists netted some spies, but it also disrupted the lives of thousands of innocent Americans. **Section Focus Question: How did fear of domestic communism affect American society during the Cold War?**

Worrying About Communists at Home

The Cold War influenced many aspects of American life. American soldiers fought and died in Korea. Industries hummed with activity, turning out weapons and supplies. Americans read newspaper articles about who "lost" China or who was winning the "space race." Popular culture reflected an us-versus-them attitude—democrats versus totalitarians, capitalists versus communists, the West versus the East. In the end, the Cold War was turning out to be every bit as global and as encompassing as World War II had been.

Truman Roots Out Communists The fear that communists both outside and inside America were working to destroy American life created a reaction known as a **Red Scare.** This fear was not unique to the late 1940s and 1950s. The 1917 Russian Revolution and the communists' call for worldwide revolution had led to a similar Red Scare in 1919 and 1920. However, the Red Scare that followed World War II went deeper and wider—and lasted far longer—than the earlier Red Scare. Truman's Attorney General, J. Howard McGrath, expressed the widespread fear of communist influence when he warned that communists "are everywhere—in factories, offices, butcher stores, on street corners, and private businesses. And each carries in himself the death of our society."

The spread of communism into Eastern Europe and Asia raised concerns that American communists, some in influential government positions, were working for the enemy. In truth, some American communists were agents of the Soviet Union, and a handful of them held high-ranking positions in government. However, overwhelmingly, government officials were loyal to the United States.

Recognizing public concern about domestic communism, President Truman created a Federal Employee Loyalty Program in March 1947. The order permitted the FBI and other government security agencies to screen federal employees for signs of political disloyalty. About 3,000 federal employees either were dismissed or resigned after the investigation. The order also empowered the Attorney General to compile a list of "totalitarian, fascist, or subversive organizations" in the United States. Americans who belonged to or supported organizations on the Attorney General's list were singled out for more intense scrutiny. Many were labeled "security risks" and dismissed from their jobs.

The Truman administration also used the 1940 **Smith Act** to cripple the Communist Party in the United States. This act made it unlawful to teach or advocate the violent overthrow of the U.S. government. In 1949, a New York jury found 11 communists guilty of violating the Smith Act and sent them to prison.

Congress Hunts Communists Congress joined in the search for communists. In 1938, the House of Representatives had created the **House Un-American Activities Committee (HUAC)** to investigate possible subversive activities by fascists, Nazis, or communists. After the war, the committee conducted several highly publicized hearings on communist activities in the United States. HUAC investigators probed the government, armed forces, unions, education, science, newspapers, and other aspects of American life.

The best-known HUAC hearings targeted the movie industry in 1947. The HUAC investigations uncovered people who were, or had been, communists during the 1930s and 1940s. A group of left-wing writers, directors, and producers known as the **Hollywood Ten** refused to answer questions, asserting their Fifth Amendment rights against self-incrimination. The hearings turned into a war of attacks and counterattacks as committee members and witnesses yelled at each other and pointed accusatory fingers.

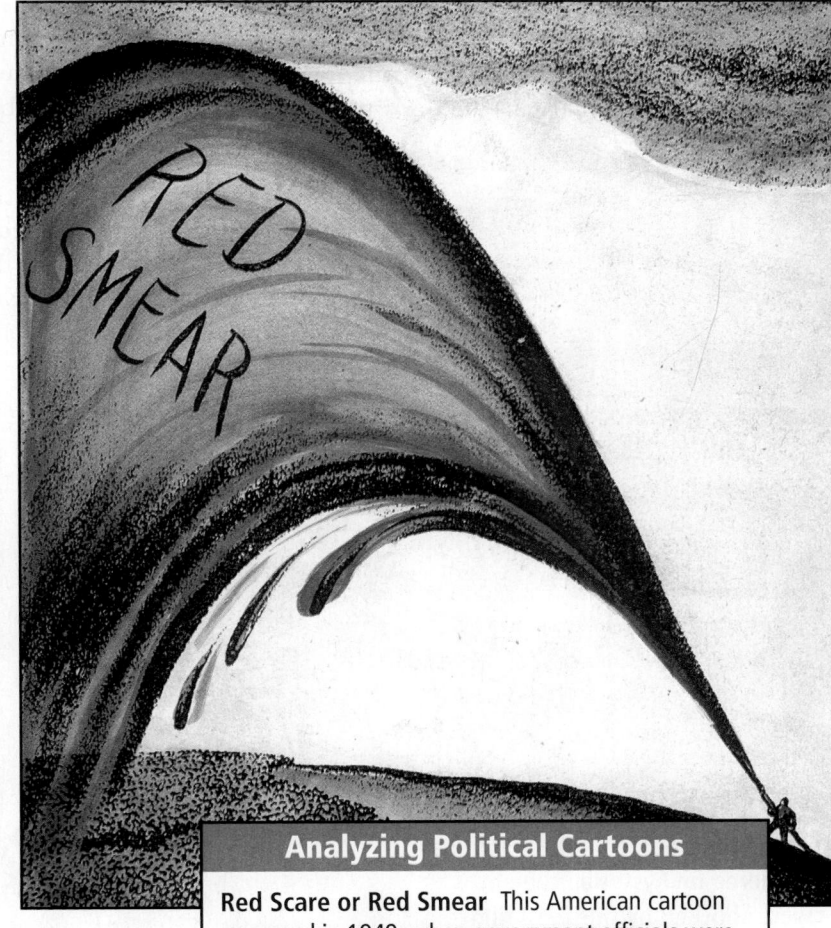

Analyzing Political Cartoons

Red Scare or Red Smear This American cartoon appeared in 1949, when government officials were prosecuting communists and others for subversive activities.

1. What is the cartoonist's attitude toward the attempt to uncover communists?
2. How do you think President Truman might have responded to this cartoon?

After the hearings, the Hollywood Ten were cited for contempt of Congress and were tried, convicted, and sent to prison. Movie executives circulated a **blacklist** of entertainment figures who should not be hired because of their suspected communist ties. The careers of those on the list were shattered. Not until the case of *Watkins* v. *United States* (1957) did the Supreme Court decide that witnesses before HUAC could not be forced to name radicals they knew.

The HUAC investigation had a powerful impact on filmmaking. In the past, Hollywood had been willing to make movies about controversial subjects such as racism and anti-Semitism. Now, most producers concentrated only on entertainment and avoided addressing sensitive social issues.

Freedom of Speech Takes a Hit The case of the Hollywood Ten demonstrated that in the mood of fear created by Soviet aggression, freedom of speech was not guaranteed. Americans lost their jobs because they had belonged to or contributed to an organization on the Attorney General's list. Others were fired for associating with people who were known communists or for making remarks that were considered disloyal. Teachers and librarians, mail carriers and longshoremen, electricians and construction workers—people from all walks of life—might be accused and dismissed from their jobs.

The effort to root out communist influence from American life cut across many levels of society. Communists were exposed and blacklisted in the country's <u>academic</u> institutions, labor unions, scientific laboratories, and city halls.

Government Investigates Oppenheimer The case of J. Robert Oppenheimer illustrates the difficulty of distinguishing loyalty from disloyalty. During World War II, Oppenheimer had led the Manhattan Project, which developed the atomic bomb. After the war, he became chairman of the General Advisory Committee of the U.S. Atomic Energy Commission (AEC). However, Oppenheimer

Vocabulary Builder
<u>academic</u>–(ak uh DEHM ihk) *adj.* related to education

INFOGRAPHIC 🔊 AUDIO

RED SCARE
CULTURE

Pop culture reflected the fears of the time. Some books and films bordered on hysteria. Audiences were shocked by the 1950 film *I Married a Communist,* but they cheered when John Wayne starred as Big Jim McClain, a two-fisted HUAC investigator chasing communists in Hawaii.

THEY PUSH A BUTTON AND VAST CITIES VANISH BEFORE YOUR VERY EYES!

CAPTAIN AMERICA...COMMIE SMASHER!
CAPTAIN AMERICA
"CAPTAIN AMERICA STRIKES!" "THE BETRAYERS!"

INVASION U.S.A.
GERALD MOHR • PEGGIE CASTLE • DAN O'HERLIHY
Screenplay by ROBERT SMITH • Produced by ALBERT ZUGSMITH and ROBERT SMITH • Directed by ALFR
COPYRIGHT 1952 MUTUAL PRODUCTIONS OF THE WEST   COUNTRY OF ORIGIN U.S.A.

▲ This comic book enlisted a popular hero in the fight against communism.

▲ Some novels and movies predicted a devastating atomic war between the United States and the Soviet Union.

had ties to people who belonged to the Communist Party, including his wife and brother.

In 1954, the AEC denied Oppenheimer access to classified information. Although the AEC had no evidence that Oppenheimer himself had ever been disloyal to the United States, it questioned whether his communist ties disqualified him from holding this position.

✔ **Checkpoint** What steps did Truman and Congress take to investigate communist influence in the United States?

Spy Cases Worry Americans

Two sensational spy trials drew the nation's attention to the threat posed by communist agents working to subvert the United States. The accused in the two cases could not have been more different. **Alger Hiss** had been educated at Johns Hopkins University and Harvard Law School. **Julius and Ethel Rosenberg** were from the poor, lower east side of Manhattan. Although Hiss and the Rosenbergs never met, their crimes and their trials have linked them in the public's imagination.

Whittaker Chambers Accuses Alger Hiss Until 1948, Alger Hiss's career seemed flawless. A seemingly dedicated government servant, Hiss had worked on several important New Deal agencies and helped to organize the United Nations. But a man named Whittaker Chambers disrupted Hiss's image.

As a young man, Chambers had become a communist espionage agent. But Chambers later turned against communism because of the brutality of Stalin's rule. Chambers began writing compellingly about the evils of communism. In 1948, he testified before HUAC about his

NoteTaking

Reading Skill: Compare and Contrast As you read, identify similarities and differences between the Hiss case and the Rosenberg case. Consider both the facts and the impact of the two spy cases.

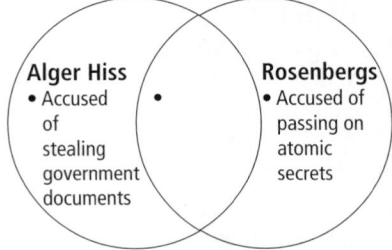

Alger Hiss
• Accused of stealing government documents

Rosenbergs
• Accused of passing on atomic secrets

◀ *I Was a Communist for the F.B.I.* thrilled movie-goers in 1951.

In this science-fiction classic, aliens invade Earth and take over people's minds. Many viewed this as a warning about communist influence. ▶

Thinking Critically

1. **Draw Conclusions** Do you think the investigations of the HUAC influenced the nature of pop culture? Explain.

2. **Recognize Cause and Effect** Do you think the culture of the 1950s made Americans feel safe? Explain.

871

NY 2.I.E.4

TRACK THE ISSUE

THE ESSENTIAL ?Q

What is the proper balance between national security and civil liberties?

The Constitution guarantees rights and freedoms to all American citizens. But during war and other crises, government leaders have limited such civil liberties in order to protect citizens' lives. Should they? Use the timeline below to explore this enduring issue.

1790s Undeclared War With France
Alien Act allows President to imprison or deport resident aliens. Sedition Act limits freedoms of speech and press.

1860s Civil War
Lincoln suspends the right of habeas corpus.

1940s World War II
Government sends more than 100,000 Japanese Americans into internment camps.

1950s Cold War
Anticommunist investigations violate some people's rights.

2001 War on Terrorism
Patriot Act helps catch terrorists but may reduce privacy rights.

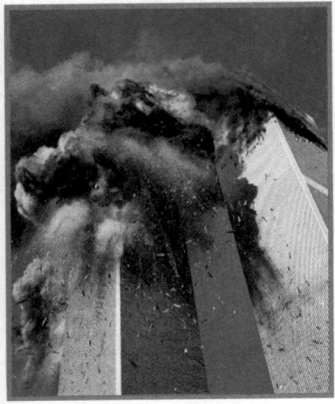

The World Trade Center towers in New York City burn after the September 11, 2001, terrorist attacks.

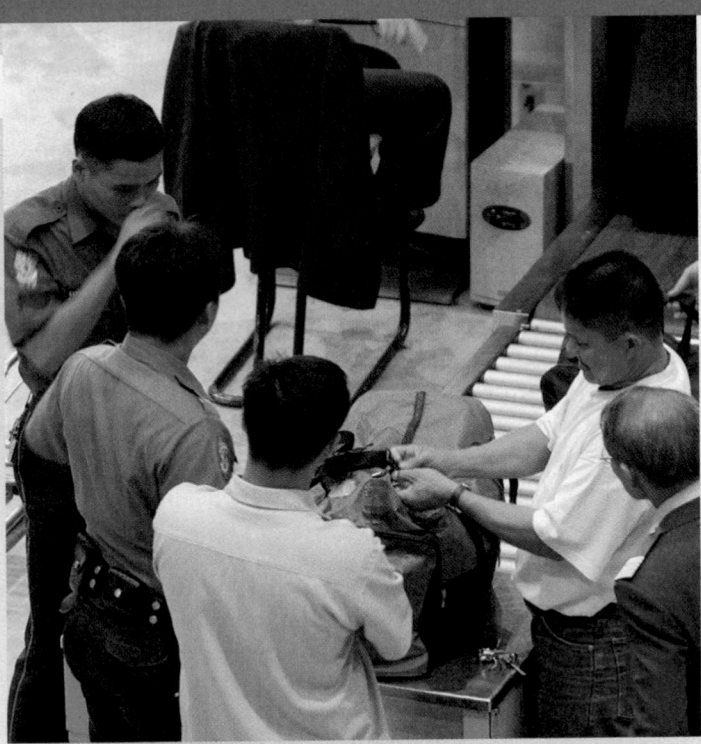

A traveler has his baggage searched at an airport security checkpoint.

DEBATE THE ISSUE

Terrorism and the Patriot Act After the devastating terrorist attacks of September 11, 2001, the United States declared a "War on Terrorism." Congress passed the Patriot Act to help law enforcement agencies prevent future terrorist attacks. The Act was to expire in 2005. In spite of controversy regarding it, Congress voted to extend the provisions of the Patriot Act to 2009.

❝I have a lot of problems with the Patriot Act. . . . It gives the government the ability to spy on its citizens and on foreign nationals without probable cause of a crime, to get wiretaps and warrants. It gives them the ability to get records from libraries and bookstores on people who are not targets of any criminal investigation.❞

—David Cole, professor, Center for Constitutional Rights

❝Right after 9-11, the President turned to the Attorney General and said very simply, "John, you make sure this does not happen again." Preventing another catastrophic attack on the American homeland would have been extremely difficult if not impossibly so without the tools that Congress provided in the USA Patriot Act.❞

—Viet Dinh, Assistant U.S. Attorney General

 TRANSFER Activities

1. **Compare** Why does Professor Cole oppose the Patriot Act? Why does the Assistant Attorney General support it?

2. **Analyze** Which of the two people above would have been more likely to oppose the work of HUAC during the Cold War? Why?

3. **Transfer** Use the following Web site to see a video, try a WebQuest, and write in your journal. **Web Code:** neh-8502

communist past and named Alger Hiss as one of his contacts in the federal government.

Hiss soon appeared before HUAC. He denied that he was a communist and an espionage agent, and he denied that he even knew Whittaker Chambers. But Richard Nixon, a young member of Congress from California, convinced the other committee members to press the case. Slowly, Hiss's story began to unravel. Chambers proved that he did know Hiss and that Hiss had given him confidential government documents. Chambers had even kept a microfilm copy of some of those documents, storing them in a hollowed-out pumpkin on his Maryland farm.

Hiss was tried for perjury. The first trial ended in a hung jury. At his second trial, he was found guilty and sentenced to five years in prison. Even after his conviction, many Americans continued to believe that Hiss was innocent. However, as years passed, the evidence grew overwhelmingly against him. The fact that someone as influential as Hiss was a communist agent raised serious concerns. The Hiss case had another unexpected effect. The congressional hearings thrust Richard Nixon into the national spotlight. In 1952, he was named Eisenhower's running mate and would later become President.

The Rosenbergs Are Executed Nothing created more concern about internal security than the charge that some Americans had helped the Soviets build an atomic bomb. The case began when a scientist named Klaus Fuchs was charged with sending atomic secrets to the Soviet Union. The investigation against Fuchs ultimately led to the arrest of Ethel and Julius Rosenberg in 1950. The Rosenbergs were charged with conspiring to pass secret information about nuclear science to Soviet agents.

The trial of the Rosenbergs generated intense controversy in America and around the world. The case against them was based largely on the word of one confessed spy. Pleading innocent, the Rosenbergs claimed that they were being persecuted for being Jewish and for holding unpopular beliefs. In the end, both were found guilty and sentenced to death. Many believed that the harsh sentence was intended as a lever to force them to identify other members of the alleged spy ring. But the Rosenbergs claimed they had no such information.

After 26 months on death row, the Rosenbergs were electrocuted in 1953. Years of debate followed the executions. Some believe that anti-Semitic sentiment did influence the outcome. In the 1990s, <u>tangible</u> evidence emerged indicating that Julius Rosenberg was guilty. Ethel Rosenberg appears to have played only a minor role in the espionage. Many people continue to believe that the death penalty was too severe for the little involvement she may have had.

✓ **Checkpoint** Why did the Rosenberg case attract nationwide attention and controversy?

0068310   ROSENBERG EXECUTION, 1953.
Credit: The Granger Collection, New York

Rosenbergs Executed
Julius and Ethel Rosenberg were executed after being found guilty of spying for the Soviet Union.

Vocabulary Builder
<u>tangible</u>—(TAN juh buhl) *adj.*
solid; definite; capable of being felt or understood

McCarthy Uses Ruthless Tactics

The early Cold War years saw one ominous event after another. The fall of China, Soviet nuclear bombs, and the exposure of Soviet agents in the United States all undermined American confidence. At that time, as Americans worried about the nation's security, a clever and unscrupulous man began to take advantage of this sense of fear and helplessness. He suggested that these set-backs were really caused by the work of traitors inside the United States.

McCarthy Makes Accusations In February 1950, a little-known senator from Wisconsin made a speech in Wheeling, West Virginia. The senator, **Joseph R. McCarthy,** charged that the State Department was infested with communist agents. He waved a piece of paper, which, he said, contained the names of State Department employees who were secretly communists.

> **Primary Source** "The reason why we find ourselves in a position of [weakness] is not because the enemy has sent men to invade our shores, but rather because of the traitorous actions of those who have had all the benefits that the wealthiest nation on earth has had to offer—the finest homes, the finest college educations, and the finest jobs in Government we can give. . . . I have here in my hand a list of 205 [individuals] that were known to the Secretary of State as being members of the Communist Party and who nevertheless are still working and shaping the policy of the State Department."
>
> —Joseph McCarthy, February 9, 1950

The charge provoked a furor. When challenged to give specific names, McCarthy said he had meant that there were "205 bad security risks" in the department. Then, he claimed that 57 employees were communists. Over the next months, the numbers on his list changed. McCarthy never did produce the list of communists. Still, with the outbreak of the Korean War in June 1950, McCarthy's accusations grabbed the attention of the American public.

At the time of the above speech, McCarthy was finishing his first term in the Senate. He had accomplished very little in that term and was looking for a popular issue on which to focus his 1952 reelection campaign. Anticommunism seemed to be just the issue. McCarthy was easily reelected to a second term.

McCarthy's Power Increases In the following four years, McCarthy put forward his own brand of anticommunism—so much so that the term **McCarthyism** became a catchword for extreme, reckless charges. By making irresponsible allegations, McCarthy did more to discredit legitimate concerns about domestic communism than any other single American.

Between 1950 and 1954, McCarthy was perhaps the most powerful politician in the United States. Piling baseless accusations on top of charges that could not be proved, McCarthy became chairman of an investigations subcommittee. Merely being accused by McCarthy caused people to lose their jobs and destroyed their reputations. He attacked ruthlessly. When caught in a lie, he told another. When one case faded, he introduced a new one.

Confident because of his increasing power, McCarthy took on larger targets. He attacked former Secretary of State George Marshall, a national hero and author of the Marshall Plan. Even other senators came to fear McCarthy. They worried that he would brand them as communist sympathizers.

McCarthy Falls From Power In 1954, McCarthy went after the United States Army, claiming that it, too, was full of communists. Army leaders responded that McCarthy's attacks were personally motivated.

HISTORY MAKERS

Margaret Chase Smith (1897–1995)

In 1950, Margaret Chase Smith of Maine was the only woman in the U.S. Senate. Like McCarthy, Smith was a Republican, but she strongly opposed her colleague's tactics. In June 1950, she spoke out, delivering what she called her "Declaration of Conscience" on the Senate floor. "Those of us who shout the loudest about Americanism in making character assassinations," she said, "are all too frequently those who . . . ignore some of the basic principles of Americanism: the right to criticize, the right to hold unpopular beliefs, the right to protest."

Her stand against McCarthyism won Smith nationwide attention. In 1964, she ran for president—the first woman nominated for that office at the convention of a major party. She finally retired in 1972 after 32 years in the Senate.

Finally, the Senate decided to hold televised hearings to sort out the allegations. For weeks, Americans were riveted to their television sets. Most were horrified by McCarthy's bullying tactics. For the first time, the public saw McCarthy badger witnesses, twist the truth, and snicker at the suffering of others. It was an upsetting sight for many Americans.

By the time the hearings ended in mid-June, the senator had lost many of his strongest supporters. The Senate formally censured, or condemned, him for his reckless accusations. Although McCarthy continued to serve in the Senate, he had lost virtually all of his power and influence.

The end of the Korean War in 1953 and McCarthy's downfall in 1954 signaled the decline of the Red Scare. The nation had been damaged by the suppression of free speech and by the lack of open, honest debate. However, Americans had come to realize how important their democratic institutions were and how critical it was to preserve them.

✓ **Checkpoint** What events led to Senator McCarthy being censured by the U.S. Senate?

Progress Monitoring *Online*
For: Self-test with vocabulary practice
Web Code: nea-1209

Comprehension

1. **Terms and People** For each of the following items, write a sentence explaining its significance.
   - HUAC
   - blacklist
   - Alger Hiss
   - Julius and Ethel Rosenberg
   - McCarthyism

2. **NoteTaking Reading Skill: Identify Causes and Effects** How did fear of domestic communism affect American society during the Cold War?

Writing About History

3. **Quick Write: Plan Research** Choose one specific topic from this section as the basis for a possible research paper. Write a paragraph describing how you would begin doing research on this topic. Identify one question you would like to answer. Then, describe how you would try to find the information. Be specific about the steps you would take in your research.

Critical Thinking

4. **Identify Central Issues** Were Americans correct in worrying that domestic communists endangered their security?

5. **Draw Conclusions** How effective was McCarthy's campaign against communists in government?

6. **Identify Points of View** How do movies reflect the values of a society?

Quick Study Guide

 6.II.D.4, 7.II.B

Progress Monitoring *Online*
For: Self-test with vocabulary practice
Web Code: nea-1210

■ Early Cold War Flashpoints

Flashpoint	Action and Reaction
Poland	• U.S. urges democratic elections. • USSR installs communist government.
Turkey	• USSR demands territory from Turkey and communist rebels threaten Greece. • U.S. approves Truman doctrine to aid Turkey, Greece, and other states resisting communism.
Berlin	• USSR blockades West Berlin. • U.S., Britain, and France airlift supplies to the city.
Korea	• North Korea invades South Korea. • U.S. and UN enter war on South Korean side. • China enters war on North Korean side.
Europe	• U.S. forms NATO for mutual defense. • USSR forms Warsaw Pact for mutual defense.

■ Cold War at Home

Loyalty Review Board — Smith Act — Hollywood blacklists — **Cold War at Home** — Oppenheimer case — Senator McCarthy — Spy cases

■ Divided Europe

Noncommunist
Communist

■ Cold War Alliances, 1955

NATO		Warsaw Pact
Belgium	Netherlands	Albania
Canada	Norway	Bulgaria
Denmark	Portugal	Czechoslovakia
France	Turkey	East Germany
Greece	United Kingdom	Hungary
Iceland	United States	Poland
Italy	West Germany	Romania
Luxembourg		Soviet Union

☑ Quick Study Timeline

In America

1947
Truman proposes the Truman Doctrine to fight communism

1948
Marshall Plan brings relief to Europe

1949
United States joins NATO

Presidential Terms   Harry S. Truman 1945–1953

1945   1947   1949

Around the World

1945
United Nations is established

1948
State of Israel is established

1949
China becomes a communist nation

Soviet Union tests an atomic bomb

American Issues
●─●─●─● **Connector**

6.II.D.3

By connecting prior knowledge with what you have learned in this chapter, you can gradually build your understanding of enduring questions that still affect America today. Answer the questions below. Then, use your American Issues Connector study guide (or go online: www.PHSchool.com **Web Code:** neh-8503).

Issues You Learned About

● **Civil Liberties and National Security** From the beginning of the American republic, Americans have debated to what extent individual freedom should be limited when the safety of the nation is at stake.

1. How does the Bill of Rights guarantee the rights of people accused of crimes?

2. During the Civil War, what action did President Lincoln take that limited these guaranteed rights? Why?

3. During the Cold War, what effect did the actions of HUAC and Senator McCarthy have on individual rights?

● **Balance of Power in Government** The balance of power in American government changes over time.

4. According to the Constitution, which branch of government has the power to declare war?

5. How did U.S. soldiers fight in Korea without a declaration of war?

6. How did Truman's actions affect the balance of power between the executive and legislative branches of the government?

● **America Goes to War** During times of conflict, Americans debate whether U.S. entry into war is justified.

7. What were arguments in favor of the United States going to war against North Korea?

8. What were arguments against U.S. entry into the Korean War?

Connect to Your World	**New York**

Civil Liberties and National Security Arthur Miller (1915–2005) is one of America's most famous playwrights. Born and raised in New York City, he began writing plays in college, and soon his work was featured on Broadway. One of his most famous plays, *The Crucible,* retells the story of the Salem Witch Trials. Miller felt the hysteria and false accusations of the Salem Witch Trials were similar to anti-communist persecution by Senator McCarthy. In 1956, Miller was called before the House Un-American Activities Committee. He was convicted of contempt because he refused to name people he had seen while attending an alleged communist meeting. Read more about the Salem Witch Trials, and then write an essay on whether you think Miller's comparison is valid.

1950
Senator McCarthy starts an anticommunist campaign

1954
Senate censures McCarthy

1957
Eisenhower Doctrine combats Soviet influence in the Middle East

Dwight D. Eisenhower 1953–1961

1951   **1953**   **1955**

1950
United States and China clash in Korea

1954
CIA helps over-throw Guatemala's government

1956
Soviets crush the Hungarian uprising

History *Interactive*
For: Interactive timeline
Web Code: nep-1212

Chapter Assessment

Terms and People

1. Define **satellite state.** Why did the Soviets want satellite states?

2. Define the **Truman Doctrine.** How was it implemented in Berlin?

3. Who were **Jiang** and **Mao**? What role did the United States play in their conflict?

4. Define **arms race.** How did the nuclear arms race promote the Red Scare in the United States?

5. What was the **HUAC**? How did its tactics help lead to McCarthyism?

Focus Questions

The focus question for this chapter is **What were the causes, main events, and effects of the early Cold War?** Build an answer to this big question by answering the focus questions for Sections 1 through 4 and the Critical Thinking questions that follow.

Section 1

6. How did U.S. leaders respond to the threat of Soviet expansion in Europe?

Section 2

7. How did President Truman use the power of the presidency to limit the spread of communism in East Asia?

Section 3

8. What methods did the United States use in its global struggle against the Soviet Union?

Section 4

9. How did fear of domestic communism affect American society during the Cold War?

Critical Thinking

10. **Explain Causes** What were the causes of the Cold War?

11. **Problem Solving** What problem did the Marshall Plan help solve?

12. **Compare and Contrast** How were Soviet activities in Berlin and Hungary similar? How were they different?

13. **Decision Making** Identify two key decisions made by President Truman regarding the Korean War. Explain the reasons that Truman had for his decisions. Explain the significant effects of each decision.

14. **Analyzing Tables** The table below shows Korean war casualties. Did communists or non-communists suffer more casualties? What are some possible reasons for the difference between communist and noncommunist losses?

Country or Organization	Total Killed and Wounded
China	900,000
South Korea	843,572
North Korea	520,000
United States	157,530
United Nations	15,465

SOURCE: U.S. Department of Defense

15. **Explain Effects** How did the arms race affect the United States economy?

16. **Compare** How was the Eisenhower Doctrine similar to the Truman Doctrine?

17. **Explain Effects** How did the Cold War affect freedom of speech and freedom of the press in the United States?

Writing About History

Writing a Research Report The early Cold War includes many stories of great courage and personal sacrifice. Write a research report that describes the actions of the person or group and explains why their actions were heroic. Write your report on one of the following topics: Pilots in the Berlin airlift, U.S. troops at Inchon, Senator Margaret Chase Smith opposing Senator McCarthy.

Prewriting

• Choose the topic that most interests you, and create a set of questions about the topic.

• Take notes about the people involved and the personal risks they took.

• Gather additional resources.

Drafting

• Develop a working thesis, and choose supporting information to support the thesis.

• Make an outline to organize the report.

• Write an introduction that explains why the topic is interesting, and then write a body and a conclusion.

Revising

• Use the guidelines on page SH14 of the Writing Handbook to revise your report.

Regents DBQ Practice

Analysis of Senator McCarthy

Was Senator McCarthy a power-hungry politician who deliberately misled and manipulated people? Or was he a product of the time, working like other officials to defend the American people against the threat of communism? Use your knowledge of the Cold War and Documents 1, 2, 3, and 4 to answer questions 1 through 4.

Document 1

In my opinion the State Department, which is one of the most important government departments, is thoroughly infested with communists. I have in my hand 57 cases of individuals who would appear to be either card-carrying members or certainly loyal to the Communist Party, but who nevertheless are still helping to shape our foreign policy.

Senator Joseph McCarthy, February 1950

Document 2

Document 3

[He] was in many ways the most gifted demagogue ever bred on these shores. No bolder seditionist ever moved among us—nor any politician with a surer, swifter access to the dark places of the American mind. The major phase of McCarthy's career was mercifully short. It began in 1950, three years after he had taken his seat in the Senate, where he had seemed a dim and inconsiderable figure. . . . If he was anything at all in the realm of ideas, principles, doctrines, he was a species of nihilist; he was an essentially destructive force, a revolutionist without any revolutionary vision, a rebel without a cause.

Richard H. Rovere, Senator Joe McCarthy

Document 4

Emotions ran very, very high about how to conduct the Cold War, about how to deal with the threat of Stalinism, both abroad but also at home. You had American soldiers dying in Korea. The Korean War formed the vivid backdrop for all of McCarthy's career. There was a bitter, bitter partisan battle in which people were prepared to say almost anything to blacken the reputations and to smear their political opponents. McCarthy did it, and his Republican allies did it. You also have to remember that the Democrats were quite prepared to do the same thing, and often did against McCarthy, calling him a Nazi sympathizer, talking about his investigations as posing a threat to American democracy and so on, charges which really don't, in the light of historical evidence and historical perspective, hold any kind of water.

Arthur Herman, The Rise and Fall of Joseph McCarthy

---

1. Which of the documents is a secondary source that claims that McCarthy was like other politicians of his time and not a significant threat to the American political system?
   (1) Document 1
   (2) Document 2
   (3) Document 3
   (4) Document 4

2. According to Richard Rovere, which of the following statements is the most accurate assessment of McCarthy?
   (1) He was a power-hungry politician who destroyed people without good reason.
   (2) He was a gifted politician who protected Americans from destructive forces.
   (3) He was a man with high ideals whose career in politics was too short.
   (4) He was evil, but he helped defeat communism.

3. The political cartoon most closely agrees with which of the other documents?
   (1) Documents 1 and 4
   (2) Documents 3 and 4
   (3) Document 3
   (4) Document 4

4. **Writing Task** With which of the historians quoted in the documents above do you most strongly agree? Use your knowledge of the Cold War, the Red Scare, and specific evidence from the primary sources above to support your opinion.

Postwar Prosperity

World War II was over, and Americans wanted nothing more than to put it and all its horrors behind them. Government spending helped new families make ends meet and helped change the economy from making bombs and warplanes to making cars and refrigerators. Americans were eager to buy these newly available items. They bought houses in the suburbs, cars, washing machines, automatic mixers, radios, and cameras. The future seemed rosy. *Listen to the* Witness History *audio to hear more about the prosperity and anxiety of the nation after World War II.*

◀ A favorite family pastime was taking a long afternoon drive in the family car.

1950s car ad

A cosmetic container served as an Eisenhower campaign item.

 Core Curriculum Preview

Chapter Focus Question: How did social and economic changes after World War II affect Americans?

Section 1
An Economic Boom   6.I.C.6a, 6.I.C.6b, 6.I.C.6c, 6.I.C.6f, 6.I.C.6g

Section 2
A Society on the Move   7.I.A.4, 7.I.A.5, 7.II.C.1b, 7.II.D.1b, 7.II.D.2

Section 3
Mass Culture and Family Life   7.II.D.1a, 7.II.D.1c, 7.II.D.2a

Section 4
Dissent and Discontent   6.I.C.6e, 7.II.D.1, 7.II.D.2b

Use the ☑ **Quick Study Timeline** at the end of this chapter to preview chapter events.

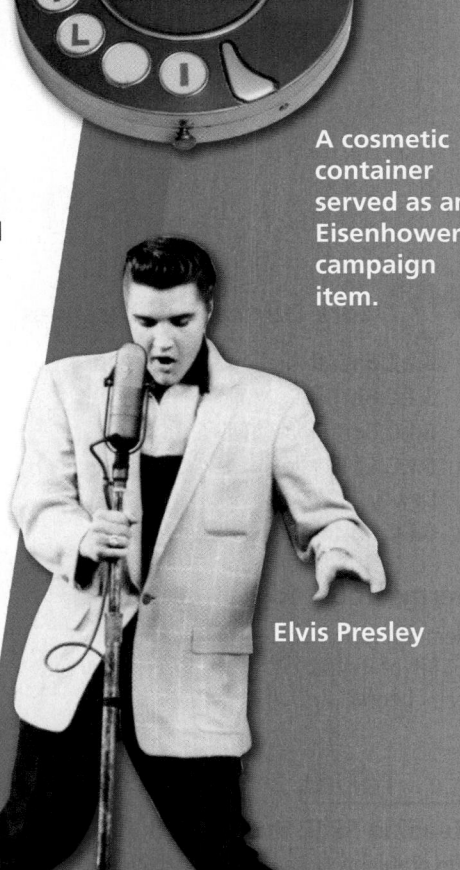

Elvis Presley

Note Taking Study Guide *Online*
For: Note Taking and American Issues Connector
Web Code: nee-8601

▼ Returning veterans, aided by the GI Bill of Rights, filled university classrooms.

WITNESS HISTORY AUDIO

The GI Bill of Rights

Passed in 1944, the Serviceman's Readjustment Act, known as the GI Bill of Rights, was intended to ease the soldier's transition from wartime to peacetime. One veteran remembers how the GI Bill affected his life:

❝You were able to go to any school that accepted you . . . So I . . . found the best school that I [could] go to, regardless of tuition, which was Columbia in New York, and they accepted me. I graduated [with] a Bachelor of Science in Business Administration and they accepted me into the Master's program in business at Columbia and I was amazed that [the government] paid the entire tuition. . . . [It] was a revolution that all these people, who never would go to college, went to college because of the GI Bill.❞

—Interview with Harvey S. Lowy, Rutgers Oral History Archives of World War II

An Economic Boom

 Core Curriculum Objectives

- **6.I.C.6a** Inflation and strikes
- **6.I.C.6b** The G.I. Bill
- **6.I.C.6c** Truman's Fair Deal
- **6.I.C.6f** Election of 1948: Truman versus Dewey
- **6.I.C.6g** Truman and civil rights

Terms and People

demobilization
GI Bill of Rights
baby boom
productivity
Taft-Hartley Act
Fair Deal

NoteTaking

Reading Skill: Understand Effects List the problems raised by the shift to a peacetime economy and the steps taken to solve them.

United States After WWII	
Problem	**Solution**
• Returning soldiers need jobs	• GI Bill

Why It Matters After World War II, many Americans worried that the war's end would bring renewed economic depression. Numerous economists shared this pessimistic view of the future, predicting that the American economy could not produce enough jobs to employ all those who were returning from the military. Yet, instead of a depression, Americans experienced the longest period of economic growth in American history, a boom that enabled millions of Americans to enter the middle class. This era of sustained growth fostered a widespread sense of optimism about the nation's future. **Section Focus Question: How did the nation experience recovery and economic prosperity after World War II?**

The Nation Recovers From War

At the end of the war in August 1945, more than 12 million Americans were in the military. Thousands of American factories were churning out ships, planes, tanks, and all the materials required to help fight the war in the Pacific. Virtually overnight, both the need for such a huge military machine and the focus on war production came to an end. Orders went out from Washington, D.C., canceling defense contracts, causing millions of defense workers to lose their jobs. Wartime industries had to be converted to meet peacetime needs.

As Americans set about enjoying the fruits of peace, President Harry Truman responded to calls to "bring the boys home for Christmas" by starting the **demobilization,** or sending home members, of the army. By July 1946, only 3 million remained in the military.

Americans were happy that the war was over, but they retained some sense of unease about the future. One poll taken in the fall of 1945 showed that 60 percent of Americans expected their earnings to fall with the return of a peacetime economy. "The American soldier is . . . worried sick about postwar joblessness," *Fortune* magazine observed.

The GI Bill Aids Returning Soldiers

To help deal with this anxiety, the federal government enacted a law popularly known as the **GI Bill of Rights.** It granted veterans a variety of benefits. It provided a year of unemployment payments to veterans who were unable to find work. Those who attended college after the war received financial aid. The act also entitled veterans to government loans for building homes and starting businesses.

The GI bill had an enormous impact on American society. Home loans to veterans fueled an <u>upsurge</u> in home construction, which led to explosive growth in suburban areas. Perhaps the greatest contribution of the GI bill came in education. The average soldier was inducted into the armed forces at the time when he or she would have been finishing high school. The bill encouraged veterans to enter or return to college. Each veteran was eligible to receive $500 a year for college tuition. The bill also provided $50 a month for living expenses and $75 a month for married veterans. Eight million veterans eventually took advantage of the education benefits.

A Baby Boom Fills Classrooms

Upon their return, soldiers quickly made up for lost time by marrying and having children. Americans had put off having children because of the depression and war. Now, confident that the bad times were behind them, many married couples started families. This led to what population experts termed a **baby boom.** In 1957, at the peak of the baby boom, one American baby was born every 7 seconds, a grand total of 4.3 million for the year. One newspaper columnist commented, "Just imagine how much these extra people . . . will absorb—in food, in clothing, in gadgets, in housing, in services. . . ." Between 1940 and 1955, the U.S. population experienced its greatest increase, growing 27 percent from about 130 to about 165 million.

Converting From a Wartime Economy

Fortunately, unemployment did not materialize, nor did a depression return. However, Americans experienced some serious economic problems. The most painful was skyrocketing prices. With war's end, the federal government ended rationing and price controls, both of which had helped keep inflation in check during the war. A postwar rush to buy goods created severe inflationary pressures. There was just too much money to spend on too few goods. Overall, prices rose about 18 percent in 1946. The price of some products, such as beef, nearly doubled within a year.

New Families

Marriage rates soared as soldiers returned home. Confident that the bad times were behind them, newly wed couples bought new homes and started families. The increase in the birthrate began in 1946 and slowed by 1964.

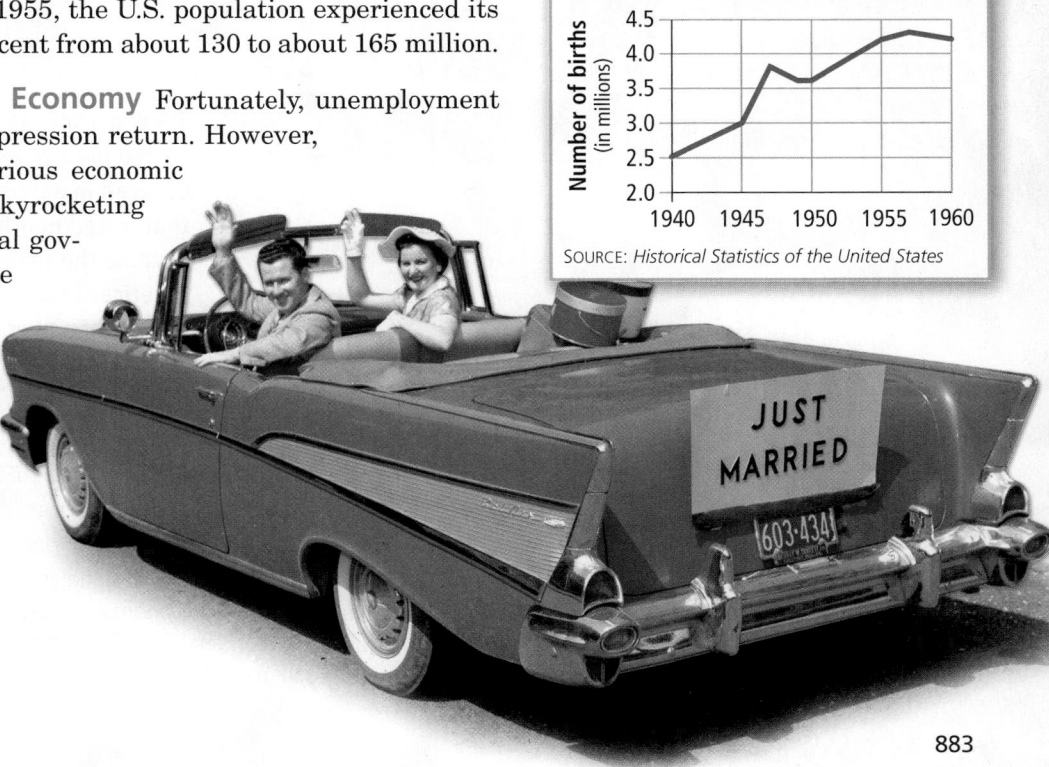

Birthrate, 1940–1960

SOURCE: *Historical Statistics of the United States*

The U.S. Dominates the World Economy During the depression, Americans could not buy the goods they desired. The economy improved during the war, but wartime restrictions kept spending down and limited economic growth. The end of wartime restrictions finally opened the floodgates to consumer purchases. As demand soared, businesses employed more people to produce goods. This created a cycle in which people bought new goods, leading businesses to hire more workers, who in turn bought more goods.

At the end of World War II, the United States was the only developed nation untouched by the devastation. Although it had only 6 percent of the world's population, the United States produced about 50 percent of the world's total output. This allowed Americans to enjoy a higher standard of living than any other nation in the world.

Technological Progress Boosts Productivity The American economy benefited from numerous technological advances during the postwar period. Some developments, such as the use of atomic energy, were the result of war research. The use of computers increased, and businesses gradually began to depend on them. Worker **productivity**—the rate at which goods are produced or services performed—continued to improve, largely because of new technology.

Government Spending Supports Growth Increased government spending boosted the economy, too. With the outbreak of the Korean War, the United States once again committed a significant part of its budget to defense spending. Military spending led to the development of new technologies and new materials, such as plastics and new light metal alloys, that found widespread use outside the military. Other large federal spending programs, such as the Marshall Plan, underlined foreign demand for goods made in the United States.

Vocabulary Builder
initiate–(ih NIHSH ee ayt) *v.* to arrange for something to start

✔ **Checkpoint** What did many Americans expect to happen to the American economy after World War II?

INFOGRAPHIC

AMERICA
Returns to
WORK

When World War II ended, nearly everyone feared hard times. However, the postwar years ushered in a period of domestic prosperity that lasted nearly 20 years. The United States became the richest country in the world. Many Americans found that they had greater buying power than ever before.

◀ By 1950, 3 out of 10 women were in the workforce.

The rise in the GNP signaled ▶ the nation's economic success. Between 1945 and 1960, the GNP more than doubled.

U.S. GNP, 1945–1960

Billions of dollars

600
400
200
0

1945   1950   1955   1960

SOURCE: USInfo.State.Gov

884

Truman Overcomes Huge Obstacles

On April 12, 1945, when Franklin Roosevelt died, Harry S. Truman had been Vice President for only 4 months. When Eleanor Roosevelt told him that her husband had died, Truman responded "Is there anything I can do for you?" She replied, "Is there anything we can do for you? For you are the one in trouble now."

Eleanor Roosevelt's remark captured Harry Truman's predicament. He had to preside over one of the more difficult times in American history. The postwar years saw the beginning of the Cold War and communist takeovers in Europe and Asia. At home, there was inflation and labor unrest. Communist advances and a troubled domestic economy created a sense of deep unrest in the American public during the Truman years.

Grappling With Congress and Labor From the first days of his presidency, Truman faced a double-barreled challenge: a restless labor movement and a combative Republican Party. Trade unionists demanded pay increases to keep up with inflation. When employers refused to meet labor's demands, millions of steel, coal, railroad, and automotive workers went on strike.

The wave of strikes was one of the largest in American history. It prompted Congress to enact the **Taft-Hartley Act,** a law that outlawed the closed shop—a workplace in which only union members can be hired. Taft-Hartley rolled back some of the rights that labor unions had gained during the New Deal. Although Truman vetoed the Taft-Hartley Act, Congress overrode his veto.

Angering Segregationists Unlike FDR, who feared challenging the power of white southern senators and representatives, Truman refused to remain passive. He established a special committee on civil rights to investigate race relations. The committee made several recommendations for civil rights reforms. However, Congress rejected the recommendations

American families wanted their own homes. Home construction contributed to the booming economy. ▼

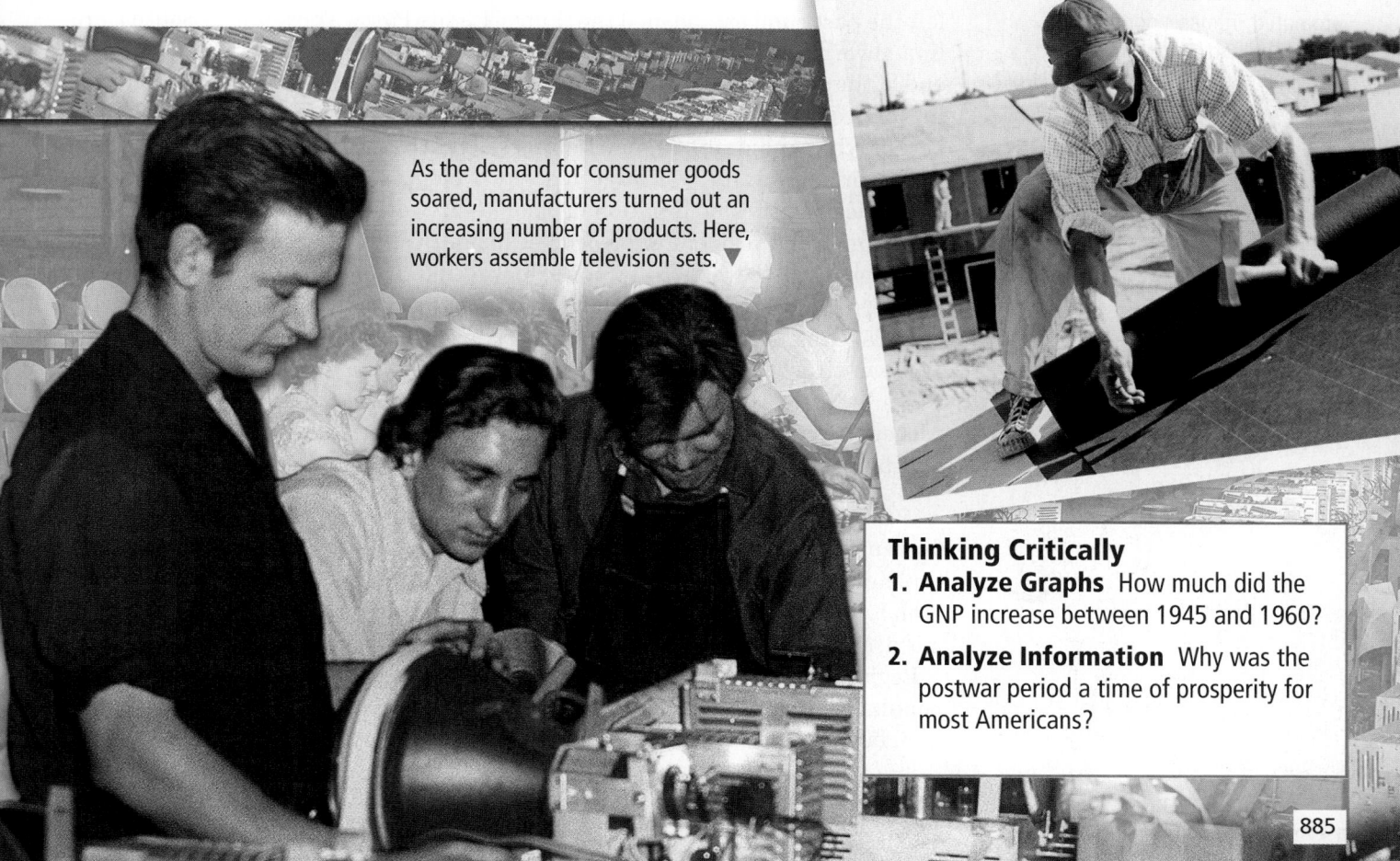

As the demand for consumer goods soared, manufacturers turned out an increasing number of products. Here, workers assemble television sets. ▼

Thinking Critically
1. **Analyze Graphs** How much did the GNP increase between 1945 and 1960?

2. **Analyze Information** Why was the postwar period a time of prosperity for most Americans?

Candidate (Party)	Electoral Vote	Popular Vote	% Electoral Vote	% Popular Vote
Truman (Democratic)	303	24,105,182	57	50
Dewey (Republican)	189	21,970,065	36	46
Thurmond (States' Rights)	39	1,169,063	7	2
Wallace (Progressive)	—	1,157,172	—	2

*One of Tennessee's electors voted for Thurmond

A Truman Victory

Despite the mistaken headline, Truman defeated Dewey in a close election. The Democrats won with a popular vote of 24 million to the Republicans' popular vote of nearly 22 million. The campaign button promoted Truman's opponents, Thurmond and Wright from the States' Rights Party. *What role should the media have in elections?*

and did not pass any meaningful civil rights reforms until the late 1950s. Truman also issued an executive order desegregating the military. This was more successful. By 1951, most units had been integrated.

Truman Upsets Dewey By the spring of 1948, Truman's standing had sunk so low that he faced challenges from both the right and the left in his own Democratic Party. Southern Democrats, angry at Truman's support for civil rights, left the party and established the States' Rights Party. They named South Carolina governor Strom Thurmond as their candidate for President. At the other end of the political spectrum, Henry Wallace, who had been Vice President during FDR's third term, broke with Truman over foreign policy issues. Wallace became the candidate of a new Progressive Party.

The breakaway of two large blocs of Democrats was accompanied by the Republican Party's nomination of Thomas Dewey, the well-known governor of New York, for President. Few people thought that Truman had any chance of winning the 1948 election. Truman, however, did not see it that way. He staged an energetic "whistle stop" train tour of the nation, delivering over 300 speeches and traveling 31,000 miles in a matter of weeks. At train stops in small towns, Truman attacked the current Congress as "do nothing" and the worst in history. "Give 'em hell, Harry!" some in the crowd would cry out during his speeches. Although every political poll predicted that Dewey would win easily, Truman won by a narrow victory. He had managed the political upset of the century.

Truman Proposes a Fair Deal Shortly after the election, Truman announced a far-ranging legislative program, which he called the **Fair Deal.** The Fair Deal, he explained, would strengthen existing New Deal reforms and establish new programs, such as national health insurance. But Congress was not in a reforming mood, and Truman failed to win approval for most of his Fair Deal proposals.

Legislative failure and a stalled war in Korea contributed to Truman's loss of popularity. He chose not to seek the 1952 Democratic nomination. His reputation, however, has improved through the years. Today, many historians applaud him for his common-sense approach, as the first President to challenge public discrimination and as a determined opponent of communist expansion.

 Checkpoint Why were workers dissatisfied during the postwar period?

Eisenhower Charts a Middle Path

The 1952 election was hardly a contest. The Republican candidate, Dwight Eisenhower, was so popular that both the Democratic and Republican parties had wanted him as their presidential candidate. Eisenhower, whose nickname was Ike, charmed the public with his friendly smile, reassuring personality, and record of service and honesty. The Democratic candidate, Adlai Stevenson, a senator from Illinois, failed to catch the popular imagination the way Eisenhower did.

Dwight Eisenhower had spent nearly his entire adult life in the military and had never held a political office before 1952. Thus, Americans could not know for certain which way he would guide the nation upon taking office. However, most Americans believed that Eisenhower's calm personality mirrored his political views and that he would keep to the "middle road," achieving a balance between liberal and conservative positions.

Eisenhower charted a middle course as President. While he shared the conservative view that the federal government had grown too strong, he did not repeal existing New Deal programs, such as Social Security and the minimum wage. Federal spending actually increased during his presidency. Eisenhower even introduced several large new programs. For example, he created an interstate highway system and began to spend federal dollars for education, specifically to train more scientists.

One reason for Eisenhower's popularity was the strength of the American economy during the 1950s. His presidency was one of the most prosperous, peaceful, and politically tranquil in the twentieth century.

Dwight Eisenhower

 Checkpoint Why did federal spending increase during Eisenhower's presidency?

SECTION **1** **Assessment**

Progress Monitoring *Online*
For: Self-test with vocabulary practice
Web Code: nea-1302

Comprehension

1. **Terms and People** Explain how each of the following changed the lives of Americans during the postwar years.
   - GI Bill of Rights
   - baby boom
   - productivity
   - Fair Deal

2. **NoteTaking Reading Skill: Understand Effects** Use your problem-and-solution chart to answer the Section Focus Question: How did the nation experience recovery and economic prosperity after World War II?

Writing About History

3. **Quick Write: Gather Information** Use the library and reliable Internet sources to find information about the Taft-Hartley Act. Use the words *Taft-Hartley Act* as key words to begin a search. Once you have found several sites, create note cards to gather the information you have found.

Critical Thinking

4. **Identify Assumptions** Why was the government willing to give billions of dollars in assistance to returning World War II veterans?

5. **Draw Conclusions** After the war, Truman faced challenges with labor unions. Would you consider Truman as working for or against organized labor? Explain.

6. **Synthesize Information** How did the baby boom impact the postwar economy?

WITNESS HISTORY 🔊 AUDIO

Homes for Veterans

In 1949, developer William Levitt purchased thousands of acres of farmland in Hempstead, on Long Island, New York. Drawing on modern production techniques, he constructed thousands of homes that he sold for just under $8,000 each. Advertisements for Levittown captured the mood of the country as it stood poised to begin an era of unprecedented prosperity.

❝This is Levittown! All yours for $58 [a month]. You're a lucky fellow, Mr. Veteran. Uncle Sam and the world's largest builder have made [it] possible for you to live in a charming house in a delightful community without having to pay for them with your eyeteeth.❞

—Advertisement for Levittown homes,
The New York Times, March 1949

▲ Moving vans line the street of a new suburban neighborhood.

A Society on the Move

 Core Curriculum Objectives

- **7.I.A.4** Corporate structures: multinational corporations
- **7.I.A.5** Employment: industry to service
- **7.II.C.1b** Interstate Highway Act
- **7.II.D.1b** New educational opportunities
- **7.II.D.2** Migration and immigration

Terms and People

Interstate Highway Act
Sunbelt
service sector
information industry
franchise business
multinational corporation
AFL-CIO
California Master Plan

NoteTaking

Reading Skill: Identify Main Ideas
Complete a chart like the one below to capture the main ideas.

```
              Postwar Changes
    ┌─────────────┬──────────────┬────────────┐
    │   Society   │   Economy    │ Education  │
    ├─────────────┼──────────────┼────────────┤
    │ • Growth of │ • Service    │ •          │
    │   suburbs   │   economy    │            │
    └─────────────┴──────────────┴────────────┘
```

Why It Matters Since the first colonists arrived in Jamestown, Virginia, Americans have been on the move. In the years following World War II, mobility became especially important. People moved to the suburbs and to the Sunbelt. They also moved into white-collar jobs. At the same time, the American economy was changing. The impact of these changes still affects us today. **Section Focus Question: What social and economic factors changed American life during the 1950s?**

Americans Move to the Suburbs

Between 1940 and 1960, more than 40 million Americans moved to the suburbs, one of the largest mass migrations in history. Rural regions suffered the most dramatic decline in population, but people also came by the thousands from older industrial cities, seeking, as one father put it, a place where "a kid could grow up with grass stains on his pants." During the same time period, many older industrial cities lost population.

Suburbs Attract Young Americans People flocked to the suburbs in part because the nation suffered from a severe shortage of urban housing. During the depression and World War II, new housing construction had come to a near standstill. At war's end, as Americans married and formed families, they went in search of a place they could call their own.

Fortunately, at this time of peak demand, developers figured out how to build affordable housing in a hurry. William Levitt became a leader in mass producing suburban homes. Entire rows of houses in Levittown were built using the same plan. This method enabled workers to build houses in weeks rather than in months. On the installment plan, buyers could pay $58 a month toward the cost of a home. Demand for the homes was so great that Levitt built two other Levittowns—one outside Philadelphia, Pennsylvania, and the other in New Jersey. These houses were ideal for young couples starting out because they were affordable and comfortable. Other developers adopted Levitt's techniques, and suburbs were soon springing up across the country.

Suburban development depended on help from the government. State and federal governments constructed thousands of miles of highways that linked the suburbs to cities. New home buyers benefited from the GI bill and the Federal Housing Administration (FHA), which provided low-interest loans. FHA-backed loans allowed home buyers to pay as little as 5 to 10 percent of the purchase price and to pay off their mortgages over 30 years.

Residents of new suburbs faced the challenge of establishing new towns with churches and schools and police and fire departments. Through these institutions, the suburbanites forged a sense of community. During the 1950s, the suburbs became increasingly self-contained. While suburban residents of earlier generations had depended on the city for entertainment and shopping, the postwar suburban dweller could find a vast array of goods and services in nearby shopping centers.

The "Car Culture" Takes Over During the 1920s, automobile ownership had soared in the United States. With the explosion of suburban growth in the 1950s, Americans grew even more dependent upon their cars. The number of registered automobiles jumped from 26 million in 1945 to 60 million in 1960.

The Car Culture
The automobile industry thrived and, as a result, led to new businesses. As shown here, Americans were happy to spend leisure time in their cars and watch a movie at the local drive-in theater. The number of families that owned cars increased drastically between 1950 and 1960. *Do you think increased car ownership may have had negative effects?*

Car Ownership, 1950–1965

SOURCE: *Historical Statistics of the United States*

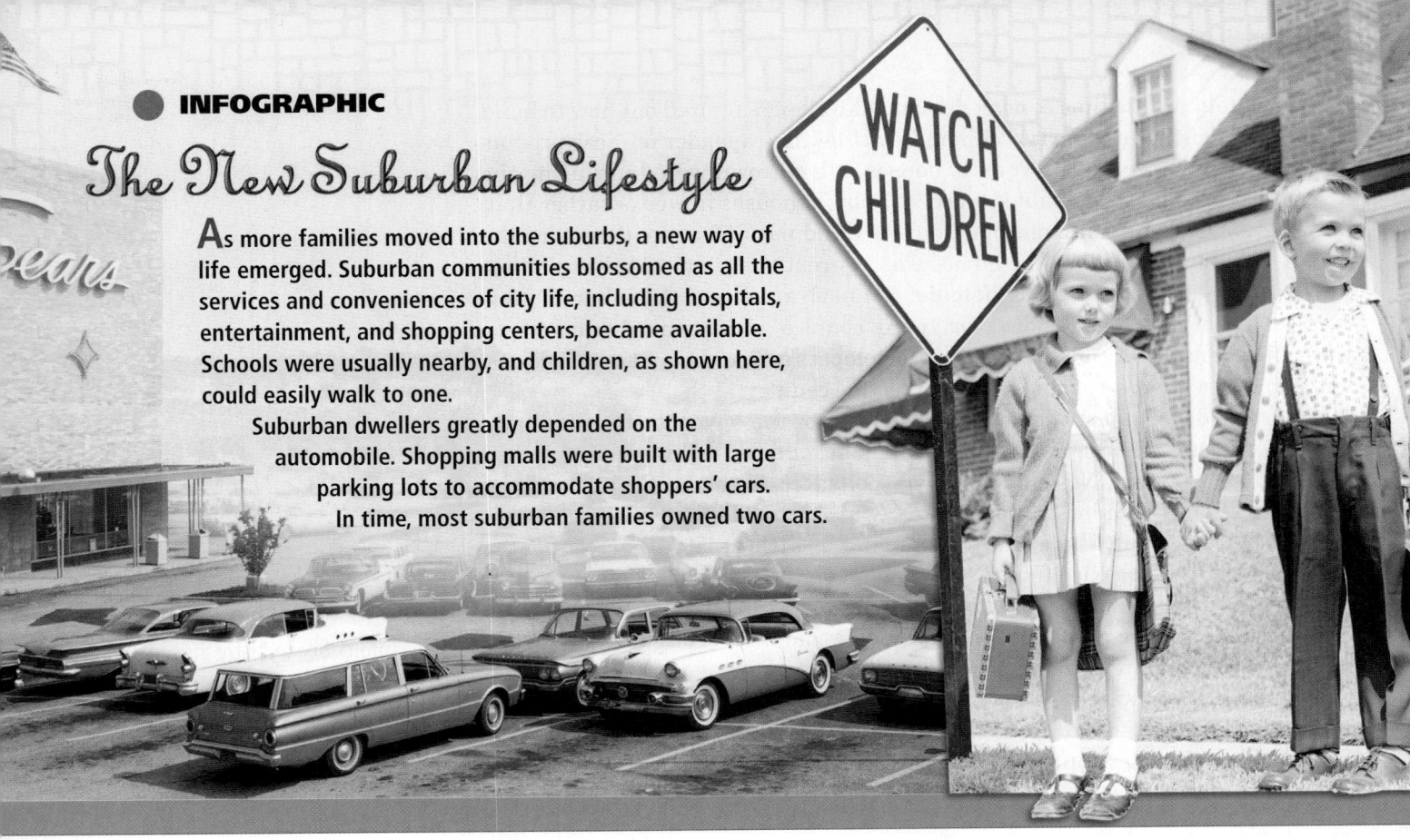

The New Suburban Lifestyle

As more families moved into the suburbs, a new way of life emerged. Suburban communities blossomed as all the services and conveniences of city life, including hospitals, entertainment, and shopping centers, became available. Schools were usually nearby, and children, as shown here, could easily walk to one.

Suburban dwellers greatly depended on the automobile. Shopping malls were built with large parking lots to accommodate shoppers' cars. In time, most suburban families owned two cars.

These new automobiles tended to have big engines and enormous horsepower. They came with the newest technology, such as power steering and brakes and automatic transmission. Harley Earl of the Ford Motor Company captured the mood of the 1950s by designing cars with lots of chrome that reminded people of jet planes.

While some suburbanites rode the train or other forms of mass transportation, Americans increasingly depended upon their cars to commute to work. Suburbanites also needed their cars to shop at suburban shopping malls. Entrepreneurs opened fast-food restaurants and drive-in movie theaters, both of which catered to the car culture. While these businesses flourished, many older businesses, often located in older city neighborhoods, struggled to survive.

✓ **Checkpoint** How did Americans living in the suburbs benefit from the "car culture"?

Eisenhower Interstate Highway System

The scale of suburban growth would not have been remotely possible without a massive federal program of highway building. Committed to the idea of easing automobile travel, President Eisenhower authorized the first funding of the interstate system in 1953. Further legislation passed by Congress in 1956 resulted in the **Interstate Highway Act,** which authorized funds to build 41,000 miles of highway consisting of multilane expressways that would connect the nation's major cities. This represented the biggest expenditure on public works in history, bigger by far than any project undertaken during the New Deal. In 1990, further recognition of President Eisenhower's role in establishing the massive highway system led to a renaming of the highways. It became the Dwight D. Eisenhower System of Interstate and Defense Highways.

Vocabulary Builder
undertake–(uhn der TAYK) v. to take upon oneself; agree to do

Suburban dwellers began to spend more time taking ▶
care of their lawns and gardens. As a result, lawn
mowers became increasingly popular. The young man
here is using his new lawn mower.

◀ Families tended to
spend more time
together. Backyard
cookouts were popular
pastimes. Usually,
hamburgers or frankfurt-
ers were prepared on
outdoor grills.

Thinking Critically
1. **Recognize Cause and Effect** How did the growth of the
   suburbs affect Americans?
2. **Draw Conclusions** One author described suburban living as
   "a life of dreariness." Do you agree? Explain.

History *Interactive* ✦
For: More about suburban life in the 1950s
Web Code: nep-1310

Besides easing commutes from suburbs to cities, the new highways boosted
the travel and vacation industries. Families traveled to national and state parks,
to the beach, and to new destinations, such as Las Vegas. With more money and
more children, American families avidly sought entertainment and leisure
activity. Walt Disney met this demand by building an extraordinary amusement park in Southern California. Disneyland exhibits excited the imagination
with spectacular visions of the future, including make-believe rides in space
and a special exhibit based on the movie *20,000 Leagues Under the Sea.*

✓ **Checkpoint** How did the Interstate Highway System spur the growth
of the suburbs?

Migrating to the Sunbelt

In 1958, the Brooklyn Dodgers and the New York Giants, two well-known
baseball teams, moved from New York City to Los Angeles and San Francisco,
respectively. Their move reflected another crucial trend of the postwar era, the
growth of the **Sunbelt,** the name given to the southern and western states. By
the mid-1960s, California passed New York as the state with the largest population. The migration to Sunbelt cities, such as Houston, Texas, and Los Angeles, California, continued for the rest of the twentieth century.

Seeking the Benefits of the Sunbelt Many factors played a role in attracting so many people to the Sunbelt. California, which added more than 5 million
new residents in the 1940s and 1950s, had both an appealing climate and a
large number of jobs in defense industries. The explosive growth of the aerospace and electronics industries also attracted newcomers to the Sunbelt. The
booming petrochemical industry boosted Houston's population. The development of air conditioning made it easier to live in hotter climates, too.

NoteTaking

**Reading Skill: Identify Causes
and Effects** As you read, identify
the effects of the population shift to
the Sunbelt.

Moving to the Sunbelt	
Causes	Effects
• Jobs	•
•	•

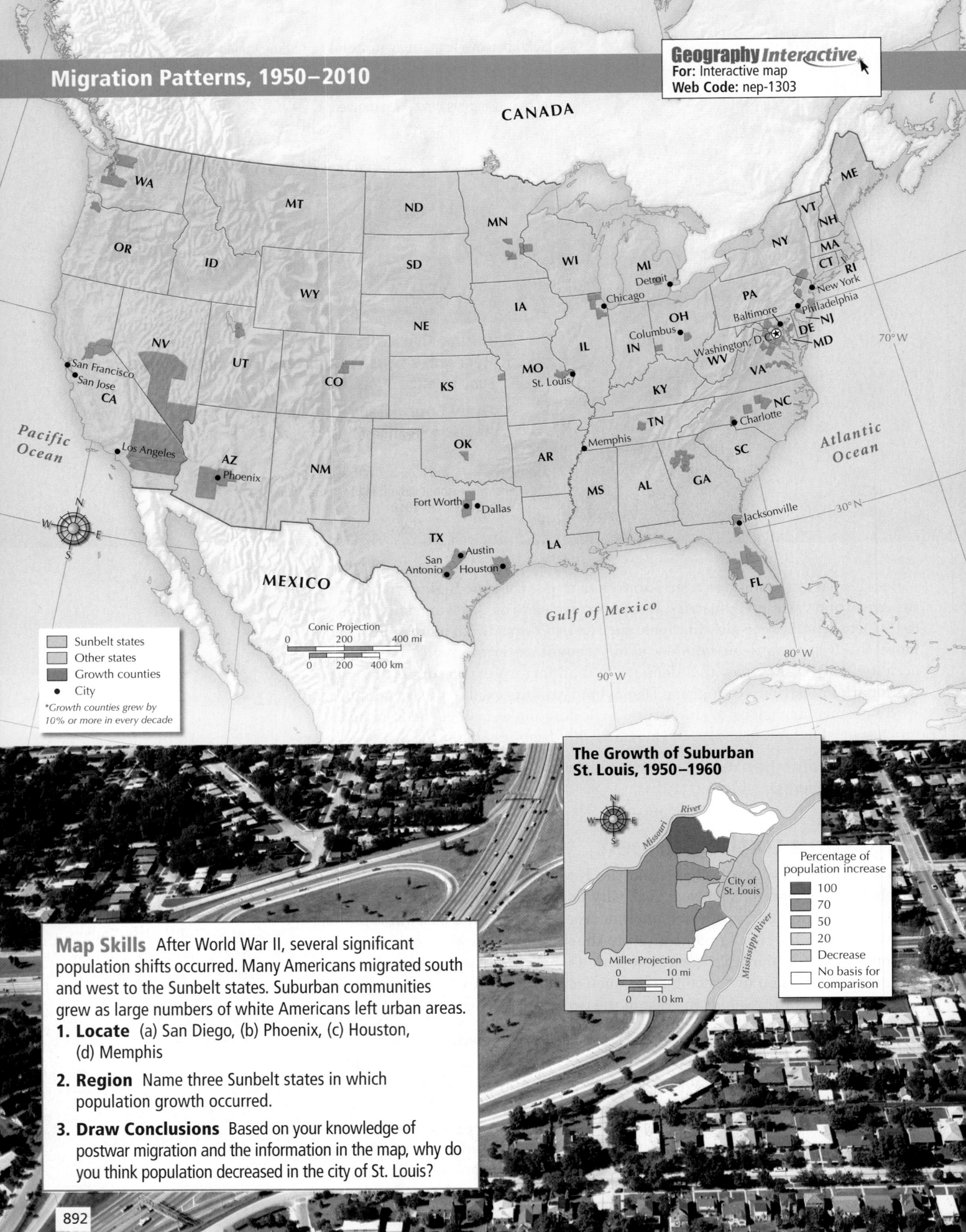

Migration Patterns, 1950–2010

CANADA

WA
MT
ND
MN
OR
ID
SD
WI
MI
  Detroit
NY
VT
NH
ME
MA
CT
RI
New York
WY
NE
IA
Chicago
OH
PA
Baltimore
Philadelphia
NJ
DE
MD
NV
UT
CO
IL
IN
Washington, D.C.
WV
VA
70° W
San Francisco
San Jose
CA
KS
MO
St. Louis
KY
NC
Charlotte
SC
Atlantic Ocean
Los Angeles
OK
AR
Memphis
TN
Pacific Ocean
AZ
Phoenix
NM
GA
MS
AL
Fort Worth
Dallas
TX
San Antonio
Austin
Houston
LA
Jacksonville
30° N
MEXICO
FL
Gulf of Mexico
80° W
90° W

Conic Projection
0   200   400 mi
0   200   400 km

Legend:
- Sunbelt states
- Other states
- Growth counties
- City

*Growth counties grew by 10% or more in every decade

The Growth of Suburban St. Louis, 1950–1960

Missouri River
City of St. Louis
Mississippi River

Miller Projection
0   10 mi
0   10 km

Percentage of population increase
- 100
- 70
- 50
- 20
- Decrease
- No basis for comparison

Map Skills After World War II, several significant population shifts occurred. Many Americans migrated south and west to the Sunbelt states. Suburban communities grew as large numbers of white Americans left urban areas.

1. **Locate** (a) San Diego, (b) Phoenix, (c) Houston, (d) Memphis

2. **Region** Name three Sunbelt states in which population growth occurred.

3. **Draw Conclusions** Based on your knowledge of postwar migration and the information in the map, why do you think population decreased in the city of St. Louis?

Latinos contributed to the growth of the Sunbelt. In the late 1950s and early 1960s, many Cubans, who were escaping the new regime of Fidel Castro, made Miami, Florida, their new home. Prior to World War II, most Mexican Americans lived in rural areas. However, by the 1960s, the majority of them migrated to urban areas, such as Los Angeles, El Paso, and Phoenix.

Impact of Migration The shift to the suburbs and the Sunbelt had a momentous impact on American society. As people moved, their political power went with them. Thus, suburbs and the Sunbelt gained representation. Urbanites in the Northeast and Midwest lost political power. California's representation in the House of Representatives, for example, more than doubled between 1948 and 1998.

Urban and suburban growth created environmental concerns, ranging from traffic jams and smog to water shortages. In the 1960s and 1970s, environmental groups would begin to grapple with some of the byproducts of this growth.

✔ **Checkpoint** What motivated so many Americans to migrate to the Sunbelt?

The American Economy Changes Focus

These important postwar population shifts were matched by equally groundbreaking structural changes in the American economy. For the first time in American history, more people found employment in the **service sector,** businesses that provide services, such as healthcare, law, retail, banking, or insurance, than in the manufacturing sector. These shifts led some to describe the United States as a postindustrial society.

The Service Sector Grows Between 1947 and 1957, the percentage of the American workforce employed in industrial or blue-collar jobs declined 4 percent. During the same time period, employment in the service sector, or white-collar jobs, rapidly grew. The new workforce included many who worked in **information industries,** including those who built or operated the first computers. These computers were enormous. One of the first, named ENIAC, short for Electronic Numerical Integrator and Computer, took up roughly 18,000 square feet, or the size of three basketball courts! Despite its size, it was less powerful than today's desktop computer.

Still, ENIAC was a remarkable advance. By the 1960s, the government and private industry had found many uses for the computer. Hotels used computers to help make reservations, and banks used them to keep track of accounts. Industries started using computers to automate work or perform jobs once done by people.

Meanwhile, the number of women in the labor force continued to grow, doubling between 1940 and 1960. Many of these women worked part time. Few pursued long-term careers and most remained underpaid. Yet, without their paychecks, their families would have found it difficult to remain in the middle class.

While the service sector grew rapidly, both the number and percentage of Americans who made a living by farming continued to decline. In 1935, one fourth of the nation's families lived on farms. By 1960, less than one in ten families did. At the same

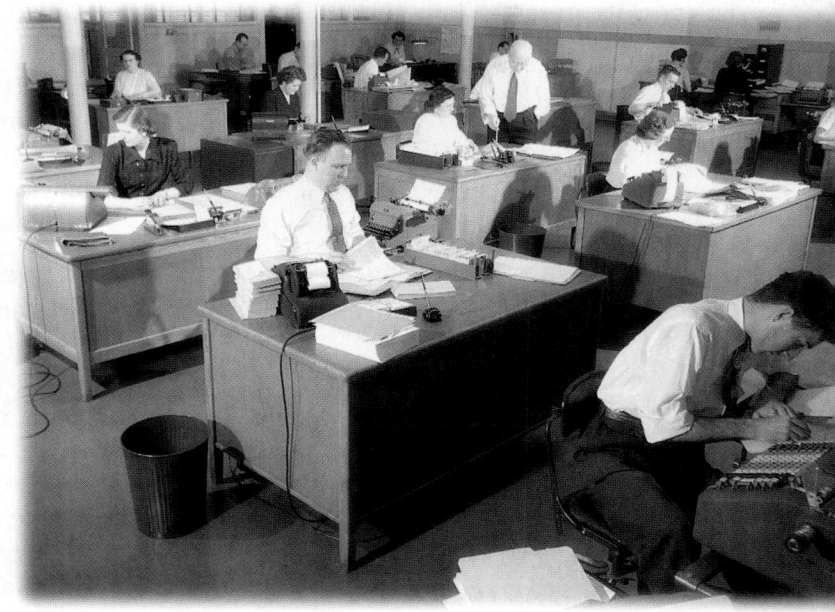

White-Collar Jobs
The number of white-collar workers, such as the office workers shown here, greatly increased in the 1950s.

time, improvements in technology, ranging from mechanical cotton pickers to chemical pesticides, made agriculture much more productive. This allowed fewer workers to grow even more food. New irrigation systems helped transform much of the land in the Southwest from arid to fertile fields.

Entrepreneurs Start Businesses At home, the postwar era saw the rise of **franchise businesses.** A franchise business allows a company to distribute its products or services through retail outlets owned by independent operators. Franchises were attractive to consumers because they stressed quality and sameness, no matter where one was in the United States. The Holiday Inn franchise came into existence following a trip that home builder Kemmons Wilson took to Washington, D.C., with his family of five children. Frustrated, Wilson found hotels difficult to locate, overpriced, and lacking adequate parking facilities. As he traveled, according to author David Halberstam, "Wilson became more irritated until he turned to his wife and announced that he was going into the hotel business. Everyone in this country, he thought, had a car and a family, and sooner or later everyone had to go somewhere." Today, there are tens of thousands of Holiday Inn hotels all over the world.

Many postwar critics lamented the growth of franchise businesses. For them, the franchises represented a growing lack of originality, evidence that the United States was becoming a "bland" nation in which people ate bland food, lived in bland look-a-like houses, and watched bland television shows that followed the same plot line.

American Corporations Go Multinational As the postwar economy expanded, so did **multinational corporations,** companies that produced and sold their goods and services all over the world and established branches abroad. General Motors, General Electric, and IBM, produced a larger and larger share of all of the goods sold. Many of these corporations earned large portions of their profits abroad. Coca Cola, for instance, sold its soft drinks all over the globe. Hollywood movies found eager audiences in Tokyo, Mexico City, and Germany.

Unions Consolidate Their Gains The prosperity of the 1950s was reflected in generally good times for the labor movement. In 1955, the AFL and the CIO, which had split in the mid-1930s, united to form the **AFL-CIO.** The new organization enjoyed a good deal of political clout, especially within the Democratic Party. Yet, trade unions also lost some momentum during the late 1940s and early 1950s. Most of the new white-collar workers did not join unions, and labor's image was tarnished by a corruption scandal involving the Teamsters Union. Government investigators accused the Teamsters, who represented truck drivers, of illegally using their members' funds.

✔ **Checkpoint** In what ways did American businesses change during the postwar period?

Vocabulary Builder
frustrate–(FRUHS trayt) *v.* to annoy; disappoint

Labor Leader
George Meany served as the first president of the AFL-CIO.

Educational Opportunities Expand

As the economy grew, so too did opportunities for Americans to attain higher education. A more educated workforce boosted economic productivity. In 1940, only about 15 percent of college-age Americans attended college. By the early 1960s, however, close to 40 percent did. The percentage of Americans who completed high school also rose sharply. "The astonishing growth of education in the late

1940s (and thereafter)," wrote historian James Patterson, "seemed yet another sign that the American Dream was well and alive."

Government Provides Funding for Education Large sums of money were needed to meet the education needs of the baby-boom generation. In the 1950s and early 1960s, California opened a new school about once a week. Most of the funding for education came from local and state governments, but after the Soviet Union launched *Sputnik 1* in 1957, many Americans called for more federal funds for education.

In a mood of crisis, Congress quickly approved the National Defense Education Act. Its $1 billion program was aimed at producing more scientists and science teachers. The act authorized money for loans to high school and college graduates to continue their scientific education.

Education Is "Democratized" The postwar era saw the stirrings of a movement to make education more accessible. Many states poured funds into their public universities, making it easier for ordinary Americans to attend college. California, for example, established a **California Master Plan,** which called for three tiers of higher education: research universities, state colleges, and community colleges. All of them were to be accessible to all of the state's citizens. Other states also built or expanded their college systems. On another front, in 1954, the Supreme Court ruled in *Brown* v. *Board of Education of Topeka* that segregated schools were unconstitutional. However, it would be years before many schools were actually integrated.

Growing Classrooms
Class sizes increased as baby-boom children reached school age. The number of high school and college graduates soared.

✔ **Checkpoint** How did American education change in the years following World War II?

Progress Monitoring *Online*
For: Self-test with vocabulary practice
Web Code: nea-1303

SECTION 2 Assessment

Comprehension

1. **Terms and People** What is the relationship between each of the following terms and the social and economic changes that took place in the postwar period?
   - Interstate Highway Act
   - Sunbelt
   - service sector
   - information industries
   - franchise business

2. **NoteTaking Reading Skill: Identify Main Ideas** Use your chart to answer the Section Focus Question: What social and economic factors changed American life during the 1950s?

Writing About History

3. **Quick Write: Evaluate Sources** Choose a topic from this section for further research. Use the Internet or the library to find one source that provides information about your selected topic. Determine the reliability of the source. Consider the following:
   - Is it a primary or secondary source?
   - Is the information supported by the evidence?
   - Is the information mostly facts or mostly opinions?
   - If you are using the Internet, is the information from a Web site that is known for being reliable?

Critical Thinking

4. **Draw Conclusions** What were the benefits of the Interstate Highway Act? What were the disadvantages?

5. **Demonstrate Reasoned Judgment** Do you think it was easy for people in declining manufacturing industries to switch into the service sector? Explain your answer.

6. **Synthesize Information** How did the Sunbelt states benefit from the growth of the automobile and air conditioning industries?

Baby-boomer fads were often based on popular television shows.

The Latest Fad

As baby boomers went to school, new fads came and went with amazing speed. One such fad revolved around a popular television show about the American folk hero Davy Crockett. Steven Spielberg, who later would become one of Hollywood's most successful movie directors, recalled the craze.

❝I was in third grade at the time. Suddenly, the next day, everybody in my class but me was Davy Crockett. And because I didn't have my coonskin cap and my powder horn, or Old Betsy, my rifle, and my chaps, I was deemed the Mexican leader, Santa Anna. And they chased me home from school until I got my parents to buy me a coonskin cap.❞

—Steven Spielberg, recalling the Davy Crockett craze of 1955

Mass Culture and Family Life

NY Core Curriculum Objectives

- **7.II.D.1a** Postwar consumption: homes, autos, and television
- **7.II.D.1c** The baby boom and its effects
- **7.II.D.2a** Suburbanization

Terms and People

consumerism   Benjamin Spock
median family income   rock-and-roll
nuclear family   Elvis Presley

•NoteTaking

Reading Skill: Identify Main Ideas Identify postwar changes in daily life and popular culture.

> I. The Culture of Consumerism
>   A. Americans spend more
>   1. Increased family income
>   2.

Why It Matters During the 1950s, the ideal family was one in which men worked and supported their families and women stayed home and reared their children. Television and other forms of mass culture suggested that this ideal was the norm. Whether most American families actually lived like the ones they saw on prime-time television, however, remains unclear. The family values of the 1950s still affect who we are and who we want to be. **Section Focus Question: How did popular culture and family life change during the 1950s?**

The Culture of Consumerism

For much of our history, Americans had been taught to save their money. "A penny saved is a penny earned," advised Benjamin Franklin. However, as the U.S. economy began to boom in the postwar era, Americans were caught up in a wave of **consumerism,** buying as much as they could, much of it on credit. What accounted for this spending spree?

Spending Is Easy One reason Americans spent more was that they had more money to spend. During the 1950s, **median family income,** or average family income, rose from $3,319 to $5,417. The average American family now had twice as much real income as the average family had during the prosperous years of the 1920s. Consumer-oriented companies found new and innovative ways to encourage buying on credit. For example, General Motors advertised its cars with the slogan "Buy Now, Pay Later." The Diner's Club introduced the first credit card.

Buying New Conveniences Home appliances topped the list of the goods that Americans bought. Families purchased electric washing machines and dryers, refrigerators and ranges. These labor-saving appliances helped transform housework, lessening the physical demands of everything from washing clothes to preserving foods.

With money to spend, easy credit, and new goods to buy, shopping became a new pastime for Americans. Supermarkets, where customers could buy everything from milk to mops, appeared. Shopping centers sprouted all over suburbia.

One product that Americans bought in record numbers was a television. In 1946, manufacturers produced fewer than 6,000 TV sets. Seven years later, Americans purchased 7 million sets and by the end of the decade, 90 percent of all households owned a television.

✔ **Checkpoint** What were some reasons why consumer spending skyrocketed in the postwar era?

Family Life in the Fifties

During World War II, many women—including married women with children—had gone off to work in factories. In 1943, women made up 25 percent of the workers in the wartime auto industry. With the war's end, however, most of the women who had entered the workforce returned to being homemakers. Now, a more traditional image of the family took hold, one in which women stayed home and men served as "breadwinners." Women who wanted a career outside the home faced social pressures to rethink their decisions.

Portraying the "Ideal" Family In the popular magazines of the postwar era, social scientists and other opinion makers described the **nuclear family,** or a household consisting of a mother and father and their children, as the backbone of American society. For the nuclear family to function smoothly, experts claimed, women had to accept their role as homemakers. Television shows and movies made similar assertions. For example, in the 1955 Hollywood movie *The Tender Trap,* actress Debbie Reynolds declared, "A woman isn't a woman unless she's been married and had children."

As the 1950s progressed, however, more women were willing to challenge the view that a woman could not have a career outside the home. By 1960, women held one third of the nation's jobs. Approximately half of these women workers were married.

Children Are the Focus More so than in the past, family life revolved around children. Not surprisingly, the best-selling book of the era was Dr. **Benjamin Spock**'s *Common Sense Book of Baby and Child Care.* Parents bought and read his book because they wanted expert advice on how to raise their children. Spock emphasized the importance of nurturing children, from their earliest days as infants through their teen years. Mothers, Spock suggested, should not

The Homemaker
The ideal housewife stayed at home and raised the children. She used the latest appliances, dressed well, and took advantage of faster ways to prepare meals. The ad is for a convenience food—rice that can be prepared in a few minutes.

Vocabulary Builder
nevertheless–(nehv er thuh LEHS)
adv. in spite of that; however

Vocabulary Builder
recur–(rih KUHR) *v.* to happen or
occur again, especially after some
lapse of time

worry about spoiling their children because children could not get too much comfort and love. Some criticized Spock for promoting what they called "a permissive culture." Nevertheless, Spock's book remained extremely popular for several decades.

Another sign of the degree to which family life revolved around children was the amount of money parents spent on their children. Some parents even defended their spending by arguing that such spending guaranteed against the recurrence of another depression.

As baby boomers became teens, their impact on the economy and American culture became even more noticeable. While as children they received toys, such as Davy Crockett caps and Barbie dolls, as teens they purchased very expensive items. As *LIFE* magazine observed:

Primary Source "The time is past when a boy's chief possession was his bike and a girl's party wardrobe consisted of a fancy dress worn with a string of dime-store pearls. . . . Today's teenagers surround themselves with a fantastic array of garish and often expensive baubles and amusements. They own 10 million phonographs, over a million TV sets, 13 million cameras."
—*LIFE*, August 31, 1959

Celebrating a Religious Revival The 1950s also witnessed a revival of religion in the United States. Organized religious groups became more powerful and more church buildings were built. Regular church attendance rose from about 50 million in 1940 to about 80 million in 1958. The increased number of churches in suburban communities across the country helped to strengthen community ties. The evangelist Billy Graham attracted millions to religious revivals that he held around the nation. Roman Catholic bishop Fulton Sheen effectively used television to reach audiences estimated at 10 million a week. During the 1950s, Congress added the words "In God We Trust" to the dollar bill and "under God," to the Pledge of Allegiance. These additions were aimed at making clear the contrast between the centrality of religion in American society and the atheist basis of communist societies.

Improved Healthcare Benefits Baby Boomers During the 1950s, American families benefited from numerous advances in medicine. In 1954, Dr. Jonas Salk developed a vaccine against polio, the disease that had struck down Franklin Roosevelt and that, in 1952 alone, had crippled tens of thousands and killed 1,400, mostly children. By 1960, the widespread distribution of Salk's new vaccine and an oral vaccine developed by Albert Sabin had nearly eliminated the disease.

At the same time, antibiotics, such as penicillin, came into widespread use. The antibiotics helped control numerous infectious diseases caused by bacteria, such as whooping cough and tuberculosis. As a result of these medical advances and a better understanding of the importance of diet, children born after 1946 had a longer life expectancy than those born before 1946.

✔ **Checkpoint** In what ways did family life revolve around children during the 1950s?

HISTORY MAKERS

Jonas Salk (1914–1995)
As a doctor, Salk showed early interest in developing vaccines. In the late 1940s, he turned his attention to polio, which was becoming an alarmingly serious problem. Some researchers thought a polio vaccine would have to use live virus cells, which carried risks. Salk believed dead cells could be used and succeeded in 1952 in developing such a vaccine. When tests proved it successful, the vaccine was ordered for all American children. Eventually, it was used around the world and contributed to eliminating polio.

Television Takes Center Stage

In 1938, when television was still just a curiosity, E. B. White, author of *Charlotte's Web,* wrote that it "is going to be the test of the modern world. . . . We shall stand or fall by the television." While White's view may have been exaggerated, clearly television has had an enormous impact on American society.

Between 1945 and 1960, Americans purchased television sets at a faster pace than they had bought either radios or cars during the 1920s. The popularity of this new technology threatened the movie industry because families stayed home to watch TV rather than go out to watch movies at the theater.

● **INFOGRAPHIC**

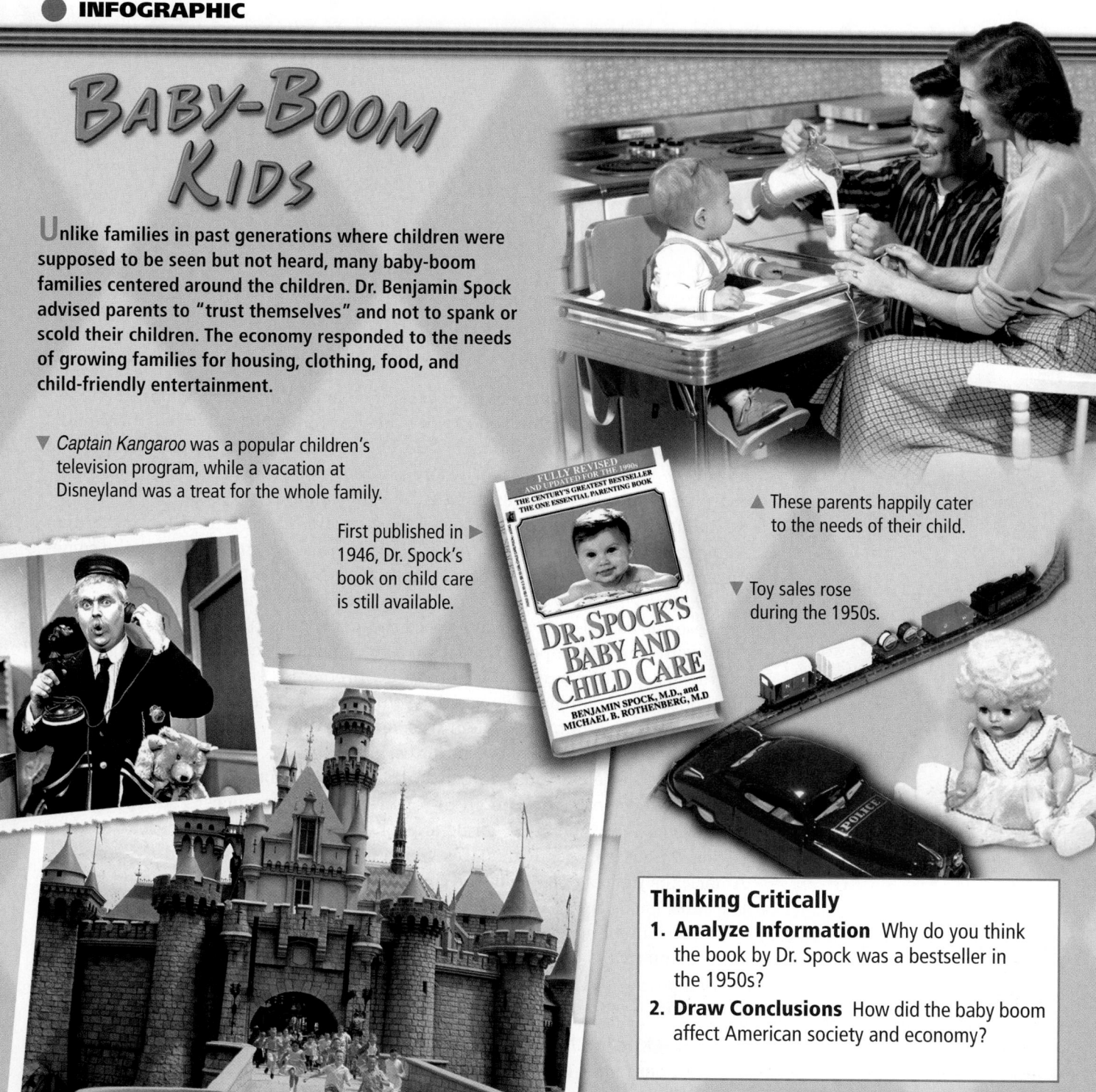

BABY-BOOM KIDS

Unlike families in past generations where children were supposed to be seen but not heard, many baby-boom families centered around the children. Dr. Benjamin Spock advised parents to "trust themselves" and not to spank or scold their children. The economy responded to the needs of growing families for housing, clothing, food, and child-friendly entertainment.

▼ *Captain Kangaroo* was a popular children's television program, while a vacation at Disneyland was a treat for the whole family.

First published in ▶ 1946, Dr. Spock's book on child care is still available.

FULLY REVISED AND UPDATED FOR THE 1990s
THE CENTURY'S GREATEST BESTSELLER
THE ONE ESSENTIAL PARENTING BOOK

DR. SPOCK'S BABY AND CHILD CARE

BENJAMIN SPOCK, M.D., and MICHAEL B. ROTHENBERG, M.D

▲ These parents happily cater to the needs of their child.

▼ Toy sales rose during the 1950s.

Thinking Critically

1. **Analyze Information** Why do you think the book by Dr. Spock was a bestseller in the 1950s?

2. **Draw Conclusions** How did the baby boom affect American society and economy?

A New Entertainment

Each week, families gathered to watch their favorite television shows. Viewers followed the adventures of a masked Lone Ranger and his Indian companion Tonto. The beloved sitcom "I Love Lucy," starring Lucille Ball, ran for nearly six years. "Beat the Clock," a popular game show, challenged participants to engage in unusual stunts. Ads such as the one below urged Americans to keep buying televisions.

◀ Lucille Ball

◀ The Lone Ranger and Tonto

▲ Beat The Clock

Give your family a new thrill this Christmas morning

Motorola TV

Although television attracted viewers of all ages, it had a special influence on children. Baby boom children rushed home from school to watch the *Howdy Doody Show* or the *Mickey Mouse Club*. Children also watched hours of cartoons and shows featuring their favorite superheroes, such as the Lone Ranger. Westerns were especially popular during the 1950s and early 1960s.

Among the most memorable shows were sitcoms about families. Fifty million Americans tuned in each week to watch the *I Love Lucy* show, starring the comedic actress Lucille Ball. Other popular family sitcoms included *Leave It to Beaver, The Adventures of Ozzie and Harriet,* and *Father Knows Best.*

These shows reflected and reinforced the ideal of the 1950s family. None of the family sitcoms had important African American characters. None of the major characters got divorced. Major real-life problems, such as mental illness, alcoholism, and personal depression, rarely, if ever, appeared. Writes David Halberstam, "No family problem was so great that it could not be cleared up within the allotted twenty-two minutes."

Even before television emerged in the 1950s, a mass national culture had begun to develop in the United States. Nationally broadcast radio programs, Hollywood films, and other forms of popular culture had helped erode distinct regional and ethnic cultures. Television sped up and reinforced this process. Americans in every region of the country watched the same shows and bought the same goods they saw advertised.

Television changed political campaigns. During the 1952 presidential campaign, Americans could see the candidates in action. Usually, candidates with more money could buy more advertising time. The impact of television on elections continues today.

✔ **Checkpoint** How did television reflect and reinforce the ideal of the nuclear family in the postwar period?

Rock-and-Roll Shakes the Nation

In the summer of 1951, a relatively unknown white disc jockey named Alan Freed began broadcasting what commonly had been called "race" music to listeners across the Midwest. Renaming the music **rock-and-roll,** Freed planted the seed for a cultural revolution that would blossom in the mid-1950s.

Drawing on African American Roots Rock music originated in the rhythm and blues traditions of African Americans. As African Americans began to move north, they brought their musical traditions with them. Independent recording companies began recording rhythm and blues (R&B) music. Rock-and-roll borrowed heavily from rhythm and blues. As Chuck Berry, known as the pioneer of rock-and-roll, put it, "It used to be called boogie-woogie, it used to be called blues, used to be called rhythm and blues. . . . It's called rock now."

Attracting a Wider Audience Live performances of rhythm and blues music was long kept separate from whites by Jim Crow laws in the South or by more subtle forms of segregation in the North. Through the radio, it began to attract a wider white audience in the postwar era. For example, a young **Elvis Presley** listened to a Memphis radio station that played African American gospel tunes. He began to integrate those tunes into the music he played. Meanwhile, in the early 1950s, Sam Phillips set up a recording studio in Memphis to record and play the music of some of Memphis's best African American blues performers, such as B. B. King. One day Phillips heard Presley and almost immediately recognized that he had found the person he had been looking for.

Presley's arrival set off the new rock craze. His first hit, "Heartbreak Hotel," sold in the millions and his success sparked popularity for rock music.

Yet, not everyone liked Elvis or the new rock craze. When Ed Sullivan, the host of a famous TV variety show, invited Elvis to sing on his show, he directed cameramen to show Elvis only from the waist up, because many parents objected to Elvis's gyrating hips and tight pants. Ministers complained about the passions that rock music seemed to unleash among so many youngsters. Congress held hearings on the subversive nature of rock music. Nonetheless, it became a symbol of the emerging youth culture and of the growing power of youth on mass culture.

 Checkpoint How did rock-and-roll gain popularity?

Popular Music
The record business boomed during the 1950s. Phonograph records, such as the one shown here, were made from vinyl, a plastic material. Listeners could enjoy nearly 30 minutes of music on each side.

SECTION **3** Assessment

Progress Monitoring Online
For: Self-test with vocabulary practice
Web Code: nea-1304

Comprehension

1. **Terms and People** For each item below, write two or three sentences explaining its significance.
   - consumerism
   - median family income
   - Benjamin Spock
   - Elvis Presley

2. **NoteTaking Reading Skill: Identify Main Ideas** Use your outline about changes in daily life and popular culture to answer the Section Focus Question: How did popular culture and family life change during the 1950s?

Writing About History

3. **Quick Write: Create an Annotated Bibliography** Choose one topic from this section, such as family life in the 1950s or the impact of suburban growth on the nation. Using the library or the Internet, find three or more sources on your chosen topic. Use these sources to prepare an annotated bibliography in which you record the information each source provides.

Critical Thinking

4. **Make Comparisons** In what ways was the mood of the 1950s different from the mood of the 1930s?

5. **Identify Point of View** Why do you think the nuclear family became more important during the 1950s?

6. **Identify Central Issues** Why was television a better medium than radio for consumerism?

History *Interactive* ◀))) AUDIO
For: To discover more about American music during the 1950s
Web Code: nep-1305

Rock-and-Roll

NY 7.I.A

Rock-and-roll music burst on the scene in the 1950s, thrilling teenagers and horrifying their parents. A faster version of the rhythm and blues played by B. B. King and other Memphis musicians, rock-and-roll made stars of singers such as Little Richard and Chuck Berry. The biggest rock-and-roll idol was Elvis Presley. Girls screamed and fainted at the sight of Elvis, and his concerts were mobbed. He sold 40 million records in two years. Critics said the new music was just a fad, but disc jockeys and TV hosts such as Dick Clark, whose *American Bandstand* got 45,000 fan letters a week, knew rock-and-roll was here to stay.

Elvis Presley and fans

On his hit television show, Dick Clark (above) played the records of Little Richard, Chuck Berry (top), and other rock-and-roll stars.

Thinking Critically

1. **Make Inferences** Why would Elvis Presley have achieved greater success than African American musicians in the 1950s?

2. **Connect to Today** How do reactions to current music resemble the early responses to rock-and-roll?

▼ Claude Brown, author of *Manchild in the Promised Land*

WITNESS HISTORY AUDIO

Troubles in the Promised Land

In the twentieth century, millions of African Americans left the rural South and migrated to cities in the North and West. Yet, many of these migrants were disappointed. Claude Brown, who grew up in Harlem, wrote about their disillusionment in his novel *Manchild in the Promised Land*.

❝The children of these disillusioned colored pioneers inherited the total lot of their parents— their disappointments, the anger. To add to their misery, they had little hope of deliverance. For where does one run to when he's already in the Promised Land?❞

—Claude Brown, *Manchild in the Promised Land*

Dissent and Discontent

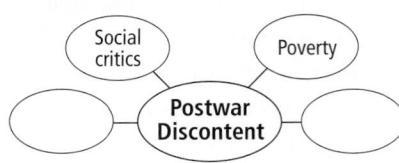

Core Curriculum Objectives

- **6.I.C.6e** Discrimination against minorities for housing, employment, education
- **7.II.D.1** Prosperity and conservatism
- **7.II.D.2b** Migration and Immigration: decline of cities

Terms and People

beatnik

urban renewal

inner city

termination policy

NoteTaking

Reading Skill: Identify Main Ideas Record the main ideas and supporting details.

Social critics

Poverty

Postwar Discontent

Why It Matters Despite the prosperity of the 1950s, not all people benefited. Some, such as Claude Brown, were left out and had little hope of deliverance. Others, who had benefited, wondered whether all of the material things they acquired had actually led to a better life. The discontents of the 1950s would manifest the first signs of the dissent that would dominate the 1960s. **Section Focus Question: Why were some groups of Americans dissatisfied with conditions in postwar America?**

Critics Reject the Fifties Culture

The failure of society to provide equal opportunities to minorities was one source of discontent during the postwar era. Another was the belief that while material conditions were better in the 1950s, the *quality* of life had not improved. Many intellectuals and artists did not consider homes in the suburbs, shopping centers, and an unending supply of new gadgets as representing a better life.

Objecting to Conformity Many social critics complained about an emphasis on conformity. In a book called *The Lonely Crowd*, sociologists David Riesman and Nathan Glazer lamented that Americans had sacrificed their individualism in order to fit into the larger community. They also criticized the power of advertising to mold public tastes. The theme of alienation, or the feeling of being cut off from mainstream society, dominated a number of the most popular novels of the era. The bestseller *The Man in the Gray Flannel Suit*, by Sloan

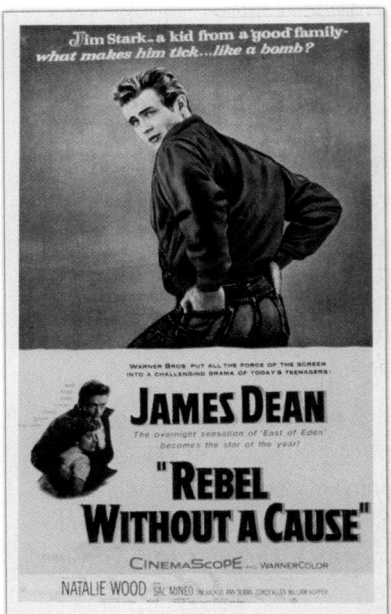

The Rebel
James Dean starred in the movie *Rebel Without a Cause*, which seemed to symbolize the way many young people felt at the time.

Vocabulary Builder
affluence–(AF loo uhns) *n.*
abundance or riches; wealth

Wilson, followed a World War II veteran who could not find real meaning in life after the war. Holden Caulfield, the main character in J. D. Salinger's *Catcher in the Rye*, a favorite among many teens, mocked what Salinger saw as the phoniness of adult society.

Although published in 1963, Betty Friedan's *The Feminine Mystique* would describe the plight of the suburban housewife during the 1950s. By the 1960s, Friedan would be at the forefront of a movement to change the social and political status of women in American society.

The Beats Reject Middle-Class Life An additional critique of American society came from a small group of writers and artists called **beatniks,** or the beats. The beats refused to conform to accepted ways of dressing, thinking, and acting. Conformity, they insisted, stifled individualism. They displayed their dislike of American society by careless dress and colorful jargon.

In their poems, such as Allen Ginsberg's "Howl," and novels, such as Jack Kerouac's *On the Road*, the beats lambasted what they saw as crass materialism and conformity of the American middle class. Many Americans, in turn, were outraged by their behavior.

✓ **Checkpoint** Why did many intellectuals and artists criticize American culture during the 1950s?

Rural and Urban Poverty

Hidden behind the new household appliances, the spreading suburbs, the burgeoning shopping malls, and the ribbons of highways was a very different United States. It was a nation of urban slums, desperate rural poverty, and discrimination. People who were poor and dispossessed were well hidden.

In an influential 1962 book entitled *The Other America*, Michael Harrington shocked many Americans by arguing that poverty was widespread in the United States. Harrington claimed that 50 million Americans, one fourth of the nation, lived in poverty. Despite American affluence, Harrington said, poverty plagued African Americans in the inner cities, rural whites in areas such as Appalachia, and Hispanics in migrant farm labor camps and urban barrios. Harrington argued that Americans could not afford to ignore the existence of the poor:

> **Primary Source** "The poor live in a culture of poverty. [They] get sick more than anyone else in the society. . . . Because they are sick more often and longer than anyone else, they lose wages and work and find it difficult to hold a steady job. And because of this, . . . their prospect is to move to an even lower level . . . toward even more suffering."
> —Michael Harrington, *The Other America*, 1962

Cities Suffer a Decline During the decades that followed World War II, African Americans and other nonwhite minorities moved in great numbers from rural areas to cities. Most migrated in search of better economic opportunities. In the same period, however, American cities were suffering a severe decline as middle-class white families moved to the suburbs.

The loss of the middle class hurt cities economically because the middle class paid a large share of the taxes. It hurt them politically, as well, because as the suburbs gained population, they also gained representation in state legislatures and the national government. This combination of declining economic and political power put a serious strain on cities, leading to a deterioration of services, such as garbage removal and street repair. In turn, as the conditions worsened and crime increased in what was now called the **inner city,** more of the middle class decided to move to the suburbs. Inner city refers to the older, central part of a city with crowded neighborhoods in which low-income, usually minority, groups live. Inner cities are often plagued with problems such as inadequate housing and schools, as well as crime.

Federal, state, and local governments tried to reverse the downward <u>trend</u> in American cities by developing **urban renewal** projects. With these projects, the government cleared large tracts of older housing and built freeways and developments which, it was hoped, would "revitalize" downtown areas. Unfortunately, the projects often backfired. Urban renewal drove people from their homes to make room for the new projects and highways. The poor were forced to seek housing in neighborhoods that were already overcrowded and overburdened. One resident of East Harlem, New York, who lost his home to an urban renewal project observed:

> **Primary Source** "Nobody cared what we wanted when they built this place. They threw our houses down and pushed us there and pushed our friends somewhere else. We don't have a place around here to get a cup of coffee or a newspaper even, or borrow fifty cents."
>
> —*America's History Since 1865*

The federal government tried to ease the shortage of affordable housing by constructing public housing. At the time, these housing projects seemed a godsend to those who lived there. Rent was cheap and the residents often enjoyed certain services, like hot running water, for the first time in their lives. Yet, since the public housing was often built in poor neighborhoods, the projects led to an even greater concentration of poverty. This, in turn led to other problems, such as crime.

The Rural Poor Also Suffer The plight of the rural poor was just as bad if not worse than that of the urban poor. Mississippi Delta sharecroppers, coal

Vocabulary Builder
<u>trend</u>–(trehnd) *n.* general or prevailing course, as of events, a discussion, etc.

The Faces of Poverty
As revealed in Michael Harrington's *The Other America,* poverty existed in urban and rural America. Crowded city tenements, such as the one shown at left below, were usually homes to large numbers of poor African Americans. In rural areas, poor whites and blacks endured lives of hardship. Below, a mother and her children stand in the doorway of a ragged shack.

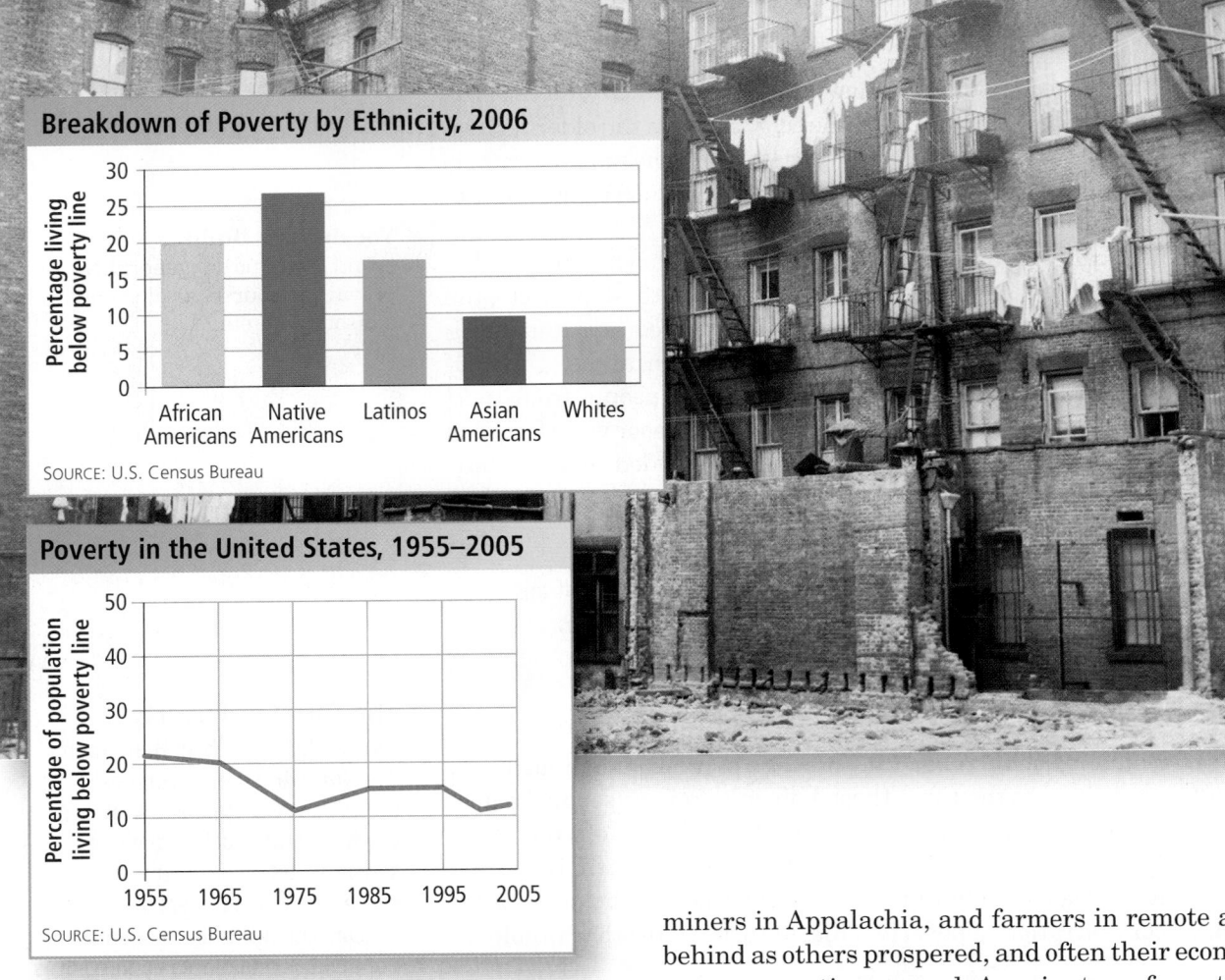

Breakdown of Poverty by Ethnicity, 2006

Percentage living below poverty line

SOURCE: U.S. Census Bureau

Poverty in the United States, 1955–2005

Percentage of population living below poverty line

SOURCE: U.S. Census Bureau

Graph Skills The number of people living below the poverty line decreased between 1955 and 2005. However, many Americans continue to struggle to find the steady jobs and decent housing that will help them break through the poverty cycle. *What percentage of Americans lived below the poverty line in 1965? Why do you think the poverty rate remains higher among minorities?*

miners in Appalachia, and farmers in remote areas were left behind as others prospered, and often their economic situation got worse as time passed. A major transformation in farming was taking place. Corporations and large-farm owners came to dominate farm production. Many independent small-farm owners found it difficult to compete with the large farms and slipped into poverty.

Many farmers responded by leaving their rural communities behind, joining the waves of the poor who relocated to the city. Others remained behind, wondering if they would ever get to enjoy the benefits of the new economy.

✔ **Checkpoint** How did the federal government respond to the decline of American cities?

"Other Americans" Face Injustice

During the postwar years, the battle for civil rights in the South began to gain headlines. Yet, in the same time period, African Americans and other minorities also fought for equality in the urban north and west. Central to their struggles were efforts to overcome housing and employment discrimination.

Puerto Ricans Latinos from Puerto Rico and Mexico and Native Americans faced many of the same problems that African Americans encountered in the years following World War II. Puerto Rican migrants to New York City, for example, often found themselves clustered together in many of the poorest inner city neighborhoods with employment opportunities limited by both formal and informal forms of discrimination. As newcomers whose native language was not English, they enjoyed little political power. Thus, they received little help from city governments in getting better services, education, or an end to discriminatory practices.

Mexicans Both Mexicans and Mexican Americans faced a similar situation in the United States. During World War II, the U.S. government had established the bracero program as a means to address the shortage of agricultural workers. *Braceros* was a term for Mexican migrant farmworkers in the United States. The program gave temporary visas to Mexican immigrants. By 1964, 3 million Mexicans had worked in the United States under the program, most of them as farm laborers. Many were exploited and cheated by their employers. Mexican workers followed crops from state to state. Often, children worked alongside their parents. The migrants had little power to oppose the exploitation, for if they complained about conditions, employers threatened to deport them back to Mexico. One U.S. Department of Labor official called the program "legalized slavery."

One champion of the rights of Mexican migrant workers, Ernesto Galarza, joined the effort to organize unions for Mexican farm laborers.

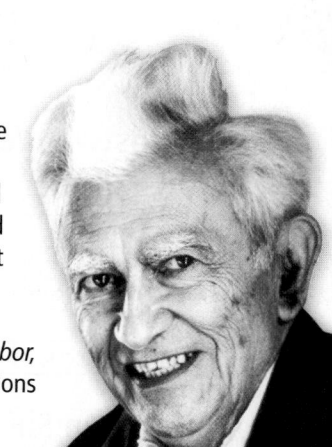

HISTORY MAKERS

Ernesto Galarza
(1905–1984)
Born in Mexico, Galarza came with his family to Sacramento, California, at age six. For a time, he worked as a farm laborer. More fortunate than most Mexican American children, he succeeded in school and eventually received a Ph.D. He began to help migrant farmworkers—many of them Mexican Americans—organize unions. His book, *Merchants of Labor*, exposed the poor working conditions of the braceros.

Native Americans In 1953, the federal government enacted the **termination policy,** a major change in the rules governing Native Americans. The law sought to end tribal government and to relocate Native Americans to the nation's cities. It also terminated federal responsibility for the health and welfare of Native Americans. Proponents of the policy argued that it would free American Indians to assimilate, or merge, into American society. While some Native Americans praised the intent of the program, most came to agree with Senator Mark Hatfield of Oregon who argued that it made things worse for them. "[T]he social and economic devastation which these policies have wrought upon many groups has been tremendous. . . . While these problems were already severe among Indian societies generally, they have become epidemic among terminated Indians."

✓ **Checkpoint** What were some of the problems that minorities had to overcome in the postwar era?

SECTION

4 Assessment

Progress Monitoring *Online*
For: Self-test with vocabulary practice
Web Code: nea-1306

Comprehension

1. Terms and People Explain how each term below relates to problems or issues in the 1950s.
- beatnik
- urban renewal
- termination policy

2. NoteTaking Reading Skill: Identify Main Ideas Use your concept web to answer the Section Focus Question: Why were some groups of Americans dissatisfied with conditions in postwar America?

Writing About History

3. Quick Write: Credit Sources When you use quotes or ideas from sources in your research paper, you must provide proper credit. One way to do this is to list the author and page number of the material you have used in parentheses following the statement. If you have used the Internet, list the Web site. Research a topic from this section and write a paragraph using two sources. Credit the sources where appropriate and list them at the end.

Critical Thinking

4. Summarize Summarize the arguments made by critics who rejected the culture of the fifties.

5. Synthesize Information During the 1950s, many middle-class Americans were unaware of poverty. Are poor people invisible today? Explain.

6. Draw Conclusions Why would the bracero program attract Mexican workers? What disadvantages did these workers face compared with other workers in the United States?

26 Quick Study Guide

6.I.C.6,
7.I.A

Progress Monitoring *Online*
For: Self-test with vocabulary practice
Web Code: nea-1307

■ The Postwar Years

Worker productivity improves.
Wages increase.
Consumerism rises.
Baby boom boosts population.
GI Bill helps veterans.
Government spending increases.

■ Population Shifts, 1950–1970

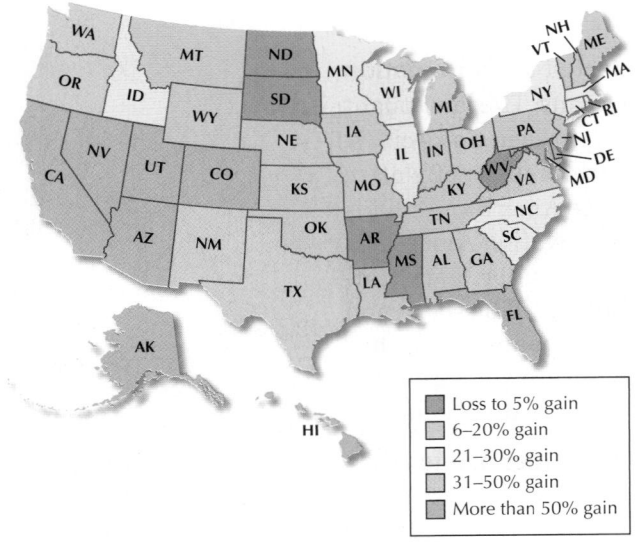

■ Loss to 5% gain
■ 6–20% gain
□ 21–30% gain
■ 31–50% gain
■ More than 50% gain

■ Life in America, 1950s

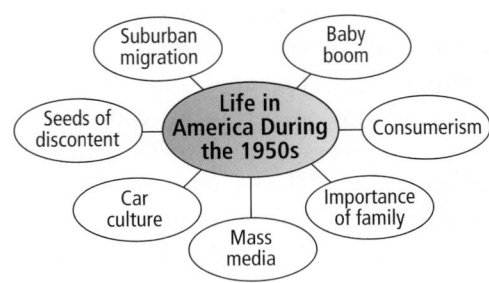

■ Causes of Discontent

Farmers suffer hardships and begin to migrate to cities.
Cities experience political and economic decline.
African Americans, Latinos, and Native Americans continue to suffer discrimination.
Poverty is widespread among Americans in urban and rural areas.
Writers and artists protest values of life in the 1950s.

✔ Quick Study Timeline

1944
GI Bill helps returning veterans

1947
Taft-Hartley Act limits power of unions

1951
Levittown, the first postwar suburb, is built on Long Island

In America

Presidential Terms   Harry S. Truman 1945–1953

1945   **1950**

Around the World

1945
World War II ends

1950
Korean War begins

American Issues
•—•—•—• Connector

By connecting prior knowledge with what you have learned in this chapter, you can gradually build your understanding of enduring questions that still affect America today. Answer the questions below. Then, use your American Issues Connector study guide (or go online: www.PHSchool.com **Web Code:** neh-8602).

Issues You Learned About

● **Poverty and Prosperity** Not all Americans have shared in the nation's more prosperous times.

1. In the postwar decades, some Americans enjoyed new prosperity while others sank deeper into poverty. Write a paragraph contrasting the haves and have nots in American postwar society.

● **Technology and Society** New technological advances impact American cultural life.

2. How did technology change American society in the 1950s? What were the effects of these inventions?

3. What view of American society did television programs of the 1950s present? How accurate was this view?

4. How did Elvis Presley's appearance on Ed Sullivan's TV variety show reflect the clash of values among Americans in the 1950s?

● **Migration and Urbanization** Americans are constantly moving, leading to the rise and fall of populations in cities, states, and regions.

5. In the 1950s and 1960s, more and more Americans moved to the Sunbelt. Describe another specific migration movement in the United States.

6. Why might the Brooklyn Dodgers have made the decision to relocate to Los Angeles in 1958?

Connect to Your World — New York

Migration and Urbanization Levitt & Sons, Inc. built the first Levittown in western Long Island, New York, 25 miles east of New York City, to take advantage of the demand for housing following World War II. The first Levittown had more than 17,000 affordable homes. Residents were guaranteed access to the development's schools, community halls, playgrounds, swimming pools, and shopping centers. Although William Levitt's communities were innovative, his developments excluded African Americans and were criticized as being soullessly uniform. Many of the New York Levittown homes were later remodeled or redesigned. Research new ideas about planning suburban development and draw a diagram that represents a different model of suburban development.

History *Interactive*
For: Interactive timeline
Web Code: nep-1309

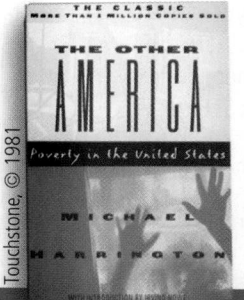
Touchstone, © 1981

1954
Salk develops polio vaccine

1956
Interstate Highway Act expands highway construction

1962
Michael Harrington's *The Other America* defines poverty in America

Dwight D. Eisenhower 1953–1961

John F. Kennedy 1961–1963

1955

1960

1965

1955
Soviet Union establishes Warsaw Pact

1959
Fidel Castro gains power in Cuba

1963
Military coup ends Diem government in South Vietnam

Chapter Assessment

Terms and People

1. Define **baby boom**. Explain the effect of the baby boom on American life.

2. What was the **Interstate Highway Act**? How did it help boost the postwar economy?

3. Who was **Benjamin Spock**? What different ideas did he have that changed people's views?

4. Define **beatnik**. Why was such a person dissatisfied?

Focus Questions

The focus question for this chapter is **How did social and economic changes after World War II affect Americans?** Build an answer to this big question by answering the focus questions for Sections 1 through 4 and the Critical Thinking questions that follow.

Section 1
5. How did the nation experience recovery and economic prosperity after World War II?

Section 2
6. What social and economic factors changed American life during the 1950s?

Section 3
7. How did popular culture and family life change during the 1950s?

Section 4
8. Why were some groups of Americans dissatisfied with conditions in postwar America?

Critical Thinking

9. **Analyze Information** How did the development of the interstate highway contribute to postwar prosperity?

10. **Synthesize Information** What measures did the government take to spark the economy after the war?

11. **Explain Effects** How did automobile production affect the economy?

12. **Draw Conclusions** How did technology both help and harm the farming industry?

13. **Analyzing Visuals** Study the visual below. In which election was this campaign button used? What voters would have supported these candidates and political party? Why?

14. **Identify Point of View** When describing company workers during the 1950s, one sociologist said, "When white-collar people get jobs, they sell not only their time and energy but their personalities as well." Why do you think some people agreed with this point of view?

15. **Analyze Information** Do you think life in the suburbs became the model for the American dream? Explain.

Writing About History

Writing a Research Report Musicians were not the only artists who responded to the changing culture of the postwar years. Painters experimented and began to record their vision of the postwar culture. Write a research report in which you choose two artists and explain the significance of their works. Here are some possible choices: Jackson Pollock, Romare Bearden, Willem de Kooning, Mark Rothko, Robert Rauschenberg, John T. Biggers.

Prewriting
- Do online research to read about the artists.
- Choose two artists. Gather information about the artists and their works.
- Create a set of questions about the artists you have chosen. Gather any additional information you need.

Drafting
- Develop a working thesis, and choose supporting information to support the thesis.
- Make an outline to organize the report.
- Write an introduction that explains why the topic is interesting, and then write a body and a conclusion.

Revising
- Use the guidelines on page SH14 of the Writing Handbook to revise your report.

Regents DBQ Practice

Impact of the Suburbs

During the postwar era, the population began to shift from the cities to the suburbs. What impact did this population shift have on American life? What impact did it have on the economy? Use your knowledge of the postwar era and Documents 1, 2, 3, and 4 to answer questions 1 through 4.

Document 1

Document 2

* The first year in which Hawaii and Alaska are included
SOURCE: *Historical Statistics of the United States*

Document 3

This is the way you live at LEVITTOWN

Document 4

"William Levitt . . . looked upon a green expanse of woods . . . in . . . Bucks County, Pa., and dreamed of instant suburbia. . . . When he marketed his mass-produced homes in beautiful color brochures, thousands of young families wanted to buy. . . . They came to escape crowded cities like Trenton . . . or Philadelphia. . . . They came to own their own home, cook with their own appliances, mow their own lawn. They had GI loans in hand, babies on the way, and a '50s brand of pioneering spirit. . . . 'We were young, all of us who moved to Levittown, and we thought Bill Levitt was the greatest man in the world. Imagine it—$10 deposit, $90 at settlement, and you had a house of your own!' . . . Levittown was a fresh marvel of modern planning to a Northeast corridor bursting at its seams in the early 1950s. . . . It took only $100 . . . to make a down payment on a Levittown home. Levitt, . . . said . . . 'that every family in the United States is entitled to decent shelter.'"

"1951: American dream houses, all in a row"
—by Jon Blackwell, *The Trentonian,* June 20, 1999

---

1. According to Document 4, what caused the shift of population from the cities to the suburbs?
   (1) The availability of affordable housing.
   (2) Fewer apartment buildings were built.
   (3) People saved more money to buy a home.
   (4) Cities provided good public transportation.

2. Which document most clearly explains the impact of housing on natural environment?
   (1) Document 4
   (2) Document 1
   (3) Document 3
   (4) Document 2

3. What can you conclude about life in the postwar era from Documents 1 and 3?
   (1) Most people wanted homes close to the city.
   (2) People looked at cheap houses as a way to escape crowded cities.
   (3) Most Americans could not afford new houses.
   (4) Cities were attractive and affordable places to live.

4. **Writing Task** What role did home ownership play in the population shift from cities to suburbs? What impact did it have on the economy? Use your knowledge of the chapter content and specific evidence from the primary sources above to support your opinion.

NY Connect to New York

The Hudson River

The Hudson River has been important to both the history of New York and the United States as a whole. Henry Hudson, an English explorer, discovered the river that bears his name, and his explorations led to the Dutch settling in New York. The Hudson River has remained important to the cultural and economic development of the state, and in the 1960s and 1970s, as many New Yorkers demanded social change and political reform, the river became a focal point for the development of the modern environmentalist movement.

In 1962, a company called Consolidated Edison wanted to build a pumped storage hydroelectric plant into the face of Storm King Mountain, along the west bank of the Hudson River near Cornwall, New York. Shortly after hearing of the company's proposal, a small group of local citizens formed the Scenic Hudson Preservation Conference. The group was concerned that building the storage project would threaten Cornwall's water supply and compromise the natural beauty of Storm King Mountain and the Hudson River.

Led by local New York residents, the Scenic Hudson Preservation Conference began to grow through letter-writing campaigns and fundraising drives. Eventually, the group mounted legal action to stop Consolidated Edison's plans. The legal struggle went on for 17 years and gained national prominence. Finally, in 1980, Consolidated Edison agreed to abandon their proposed plant and donated the land to be made into a public park.

The people who fought to save Storm King Mountain did more than preserve the environment in their area—they are credited with establishing the precedent for the National Environmental Policy Act (NEPA) of 1969, an important program that helps public officials make decisions that help to protect the environment.

Establishing new environmental policies was only one of many actions taken by the United States government to address important issues in the 1950s, 1960s, and 1970s. As you will read, reforms to achieve racial equality and further women's rights were also central to this era.

CHALLENGES AND CHANGE

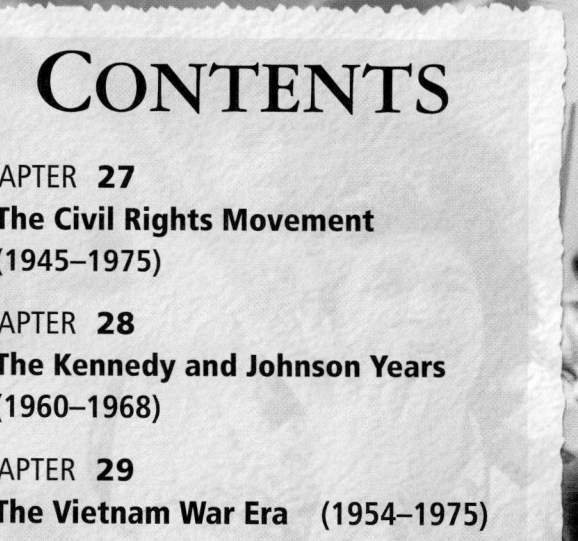

CONTENTS

Cesar Chavez leads a United Farm Workers rally in 1966. ▶

27

The Civil Rights Movement

1945–1975

Human Chain of Freedom

In the 1950s and 1960s, African Americans intensified their efforts to gain equal rights. During civil rights marches, peaceful protesters had to find the strength to face taunts and violence. Often, they found that strength in music. Hand in hand, they would face their opponents and sing. In the stirring civil rights anthem "Eyes on the Prize," they proclaimed:

❝Freedom's name is mighty sweet,
Soon one day we're gonna meet. . . .
The only thing we did wrong,
Stayed in the wilderness a day too long.
But the one thing we did right,
Was the day we started to fight.❞
—Alice Wine, "Eyes on the Prize"

Listen to the Witness History *audio to hear more about the civil rights movement.*

◄ Protesters hold hands and sing during a 1965 civil rights march in Selma, Alabama.

Sign protesting segregated restaurants

James Meredith, first black student at the University of Mississippi

Core Curriculum Preview

Chapter Focus Question: What were the causes, main events, and effects of the civil rights movement?

Section 1
Early Demands for Equality 7.II.C.2a, 7.II.C.2b, 7.II.C.2c

Section 2
The Movement Gains Ground 7.III.A.1a, 7.III.B.3a, 7.III.B.3b

Section 3
New Successes and Challenges 7.III.B.3a, 7.III.B.3b, 7.III.B.3c

Use the ☑ **Quick Study Timeline** at the end of this chapter to preview chapter events.

Button of a militant African American organization

Note Taking Study Guide *Online*
For: Note Taking and American Issues Connector
Web Code: nee-8701

◀ Medgar Evers

◀ Sign at a segregated bus station

WITNESS HISTORY 🔊 AUDIO

A Different Kind of Enemy

After serving in the army in Europe in World War II, Medgar Evers returned home to the South, where he faced a different kind of enemy: discrimination. When he and some other African American veterans tried to register to vote, a mob of armed whites blocked their way. "All we wanted to be was ordinary citizens," Evers later said, frustrated to find his life at risk in his own country. "We fought during the war for America, Mississippi included." Evers retreated that day, but he did not give up on his goal. He became an active member of the NAACP and a leader in the fight for civil rights.

Early Demands for Equality

NY **Core Curriculum Objectives**

- **7.II.C.2a** Jackie Robinson breaks the color barrier
- **7.II.C.2b** *Brown* v. *Board of Education of Topeka*
- **7.II.C.2c** Beginnings of modern civil rights movement: Montgomery bus boycott, Civil Rights Act, school desegregation

Terms and People

de jure segregation
de facto segregation
Thurgood Marshall
Earl Warren
Civil Rights Act of 1957
Rosa Parks
Montgomery bus boycott
Martin Luther King, Jr.

NoteTaking

Reading Skill: Summarize Copy the timeline below and fill it in with events of the early civil rights movement. When you finish, write two sentences that summarize the information in your timeline.

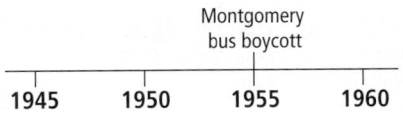

Montgomery
bus boycott

1945   1950   1955   1960

Why It Matters The postwar period brought prosperity to many, but most African Americans were still treated as second-class citizens. The civil rights movement, a broad and diverse effort to attain racial equality, compelled the nation to live up to its ideal that all are created equal. The movement also demonstrated that ordinary men and women could perform extraordinary acts of courage and sacrifice to achieve social justice, a lesson that continues to inspire people around the world today. **Section Focus Question: How did African Americans challenge segregation after World War II?**

Segregation Divides America

African Americans had a long history of fighting for their rights. After World War II, the struggle intensified, as African Americans grew increasingly dissatisfied with their second-class status.

Jim Crow Laws Limit African Americans In the South, Jim Crow laws enforced strict separation of the races. Segregation that is imposed by law is known as **de jure segregation.** In 1896, in *Plessy* v. *Ferguson,* the Supreme Court had ruled that such segregation was constitutional as long as the facilities for blacks and whites were "separate but equal." But this was seldom the case. The facilities for African Americans were rarely, if ever, equal.

In the South and elsewhere, segregation extended to most areas of public life. Officials enforced segregation of schools, hospitals, transportation, restaurants, cemeteries, and beaches. One city even forbade blacks and whites from playing checkers together.

Segregation Prevails Around the Nation In the North, too, African Americans faced segregation and discrimination. Even where there were no explicit laws, **de facto segregation,** or segregation by unwritten custom or tradition, was a fact of life. African Americans in the North were denied housing in many neighborhoods. They faced discrimination in employment and often could get only low-paying jobs.

Jim Crow laws and more subtle forms of discrimination had a widespread and severe impact on African Americans. Black Americans occupied the bottom rungs of the economic ladder. Compared to white Americans, they had significantly higher rates of poverty and illiteracy, as well as lower rates of homeownership and life expectancy. Although African Americans living in the North could vote, most who lived in the South could not. Very few African Americans held public office.

In the West and Southwest, Asian Americans and Mexican Americans, too, faced de facto segregation and, in some cases, legal restrictions. (Their struggle for equality will be discussed in a later chapter.)

The Civil Rights Movement Grows In many ways, World War II set the stage for the rise of the modern civil rights movement. President Roosevelt banned discrimination in defense industries in 1941. Gunnar Myrdal's publication in 1944 of *An American Dilemma* brought the issue of American prejudice to the forefront of public consciousness. Lastly, after risking their lives defending freedom abroad, African Americans were unwilling to accept discrimination at home.

In the 1940s, new efforts arose to try to bring an end to racial injustice. James Farmer and several others founded the Congress of Racial Equality (CORE). Its members were deeply influenced by Henry David Thoreau and Mohandas Gandhi. They became convinced that African Americans could apply direct non-violent methods to gain civil rights. CORE organized protests against segregation in Chicago, Detroit, Denver, and other northern cities.

Success was limited, but one highly visible break in the wall of segregation did take place in 1947. Jackie Robinson joined the Brooklyn Dodgers, becoming the first African American to play major league baseball. Robinson braved death threats and rough treatment, but throughout his career he won the hearts of millions and paved the way for integration of other sports.

Nevertheless, African Americans continued to face discrimination and felt that racial equality was long overdue.

African Americans Are Segregated

In some parts of the country, even drinking fountains were segregated (below, left). On public buses, African Americans had to sit in the back. *Were the separate facilities for African Americans shown here "equal"?*

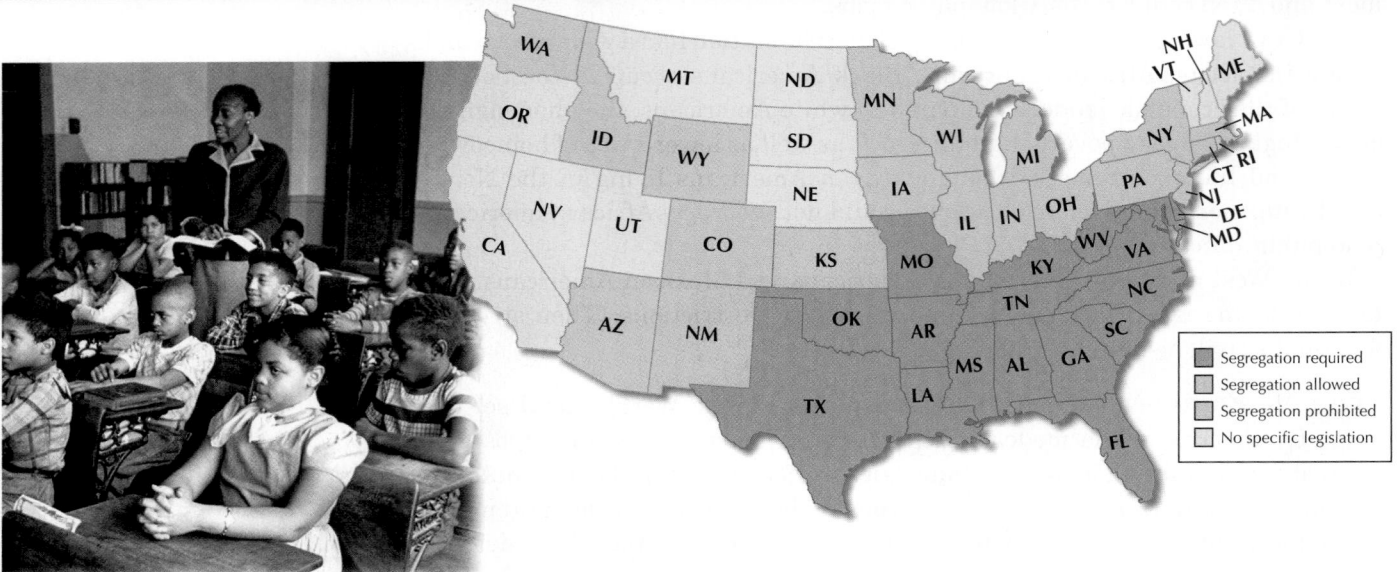

Geography Interactive
For: Interactive map
Web Code: nep-1402

Segregation required
Segregation allowed
Segregation prohibited
No specific legislation

Map Skills Before the *Brown* decision, many states had laws mandating segregation in public schools. Even in states that had no laws regarding segregation, there was de facto segregation in schools. The photograph shows Linda Brown, the student at the center of the *Brown* case, in her classroom in Topeka, Kansas.

1. Region Which states had laws requiring school segregation? What was the status of segregation in the state where Linda Brown lived?

2. Draw Conclusions Why did school segregation exist even where it was not mandated by law?

However, the vast majority of white Americans took the opposite view. Racial violence erupted in the South, sometimes against veterans who were just trying to register to vote.

In the wake of this violence, President Truman appointed a Committee on Civil Rights to investigate race relations. In its report, the committee recommended a number of measures to ensure equal opportunity for all Americans, including an antilynching law and federal protection of voting rights. Unfortunately, Truman was unable to win congressional support for these initiatives. However, in 1948, he did use his executive power to order the desegregation of the military. Over time, the U.S. armed forces would become one of the most integrated institutions in the United States.

 Checkpoint How did segregation affect the lives of African Americans?

Brown v. Board of Education

Although the civil rights movement had made some gains in the 1940s, it stalled in the early 1950s. Feeling that the executive and legislative branches of government were unwilling to promote additional reforms, the NAACP decided to turn to the federal courts to attain its goals.

The NAACP Challenges Segregation By the end of World War II, the NAACP had become the largest and most powerful civil rights organization in the nation. It attracted a wide array of individuals, both black and white, including a number of lawyers. In the 1940s, a team of NAACP attorneys pursued a strategy to challenge in the courts the legality of segregation. **Thurgood Marshall,** an African American lawyer from Baltimore, Maryland, headed the legal team that mounted this challenge.

In 1950, the NAACP won a number of key cases. In *Sweatt* v. *Painter*, the Supreme Court ruled that the state of Texas had violated the Fourteenth Amendment by establishing a separate, but unequal, all-black law school. Similarly, in the *McLaurin* v. *Oklahoma State Regents*, the Court ruled that the state of Oklahoma had violated George McLaurin's constitutional rights. Even though McLaurin had been admitted to the graduate school of the University of Oklahoma, he was denied equal access to the library, dining hall, and classrooms. According to the Supreme Court, a truly equal education involved more than simply admitting African Americans to previously all-white universities.

The Court Strikes Down Segregated Schools Not long after it won these cases, the NAACP mounted a much broader challenge to segregated public education at all grade levels. This challenge became known as *Brown* v. *Board of Education, Topeka, Kansas*. In the *Sweatt* and *McLaurin* cases, the NAACP had asserted that Texas and Oklahoma had failed to provide equal educational experiences. In the *Brown* case, however, the NAACP challenged the "separate but equal" principle itself, which had been established in the 1896 *Plessy* v. *Ferguson* case.

The Supreme Court agreed with the NAACP's argument that segregated public education violated the U.S. Constitution. All nine of the Court's Justices supported the *Brown* decision, which was written by newly appointed Chief Justice **Earl Warren.** "Does segregation of children in public schools solely on the basis of race . . . deprive the children of the minority group equal education opportunities?" Warren asked in his decision. "We believe that it does." The Chief Justice and the Court declared, "in the field of public education the doctrine of 'separate but equal' has no place."

In the same month as the *Brown* decision, the Supreme Court decided another civil rights case, this time involving Mexican Americans. In *Hernandez* v. *Texas*, the Court ended the exclusion of Mexican Americans from trial juries. The *Hernandez* decision was the first Supreme Court ruling against discrimination targeting a group other than African Americans.

Reaction to *Brown* The *Brown* decision was one of the most significant and controversial in American history. Because public education touched so many Americans, it had a much greater impact than cases involving only professional and graduate schools. Moreover, by overturning the principle of "separate but equal," the Court lent its support to the views of many civil rights advocates that all forms of segregation were wrong.

In a separate ruling, known as *Brown II,* the Court called for the implementation of its decision "with all deliberate speed" across the nation. However, most southerners had no intention of desegregating their schools without a fight. In 1956, about 100 southern members of Congress endorsed "The Southern Manifesto." They pledged to oppose the *Brown* ruling through all "lawful means," on the grounds that the Court had misinterpreted the Constitution.

More ominously, the Ku Klux Klan staged a revival. Many prominent white southerners and businessmen

HISTORY MAKERS

Thurgood Marshall (1908–1993)
An excellent student, Thurgood Marshall applied to the University of Maryland Law School but was turned down because he was an African American. He went to the law school at Howard University, an historically all-black school. The law school dean, Charles Hamilton Houston, trained the students to use the law to fight segregation, and in 1936, Marshall joined the NAACP legal team. *Brown* v. *Board of Education* was just one victory among many that he won. From 1965 until 1991, Marshall himself was a Justice on the Supreme Court.

organized "White Citizens Councils" that declared that the South would not be integrated. The Citizens Councils imposed economic and political pressure against those who favored compliance with the Supreme Court's decision.

✔ **Checkpoint** Why was the *Brown* v. *Board of Education* decision important?

Federal and State Governments Clash

Historically, education had been a state matter. States and local school boards ran the schools, and the federal government had little involvement. Local and state officials resisted the *Brown* decision's order to desegregate, and clashes with the federal government resulted. The most famous battle took place in 1957 in Little Rock, Arkansas.

A Conflict Erupts in Little Rock The Little Rock school board had established a plan to gradually desegregate its schools, beginning with Central High School. Nine young African American students volunteered to enroll. But Arkansas governor Orval Faubus announced his opposition to integration and called out the Arkansas state National Guard. When the nine students arrived at Central High, the soldiers blocked their way.

One of the nine, Elizabeth Eckford, has described the scene. An angry white mob began to approach her, with some screaming, "Lynch her! Lynch her!" Eckford sought out a friendly face, someone who might help. "I looked into the face of an old woman and it seemed a kind face," she recalled, "but when I looked at her again she spat on me." Fortunately, another white woman whisked Eckford away on a public bus before the mob could have its way. None of the nine African American students gained entrance to the school that day.

Up until the Little Rock crisis, President Eisenhower had provided little leadership on the civil rights front. Following the *Brown* decision, he did not urge the nation to rapidly desegregate its schools. Privately, he expressed his misgivings

Integrating Little Rock Schools

Angry white students surrounded Elizabeth Eckford (below, right) as she tried to enter Central High in Little Rock. *How is Eckford responding to the white students?*

about the ruling. But when Governor Faubus resisted the will of the federal courts, Eisenhower realized he had to act. He sent federal troops to Little Rock to protect the students and to enforce the Court's decision. Eisenhower explained this action in a nationally televised address:

Primary Source ❝It is important that the reasons for my action be understood by all our citizens. . . . A foundation of our American way of life is our national respect for law. . . . If resistance to the federal court orders ceases at once, the further presence of federal troops will be unnecessary and the City of Little Rock will return to its normal habits of peace and order and a blot upon the fair name and high honor of our nation in the world will be removed.❞

—President Dwight D. Eisenhower, "Address on Little Rock," 1957

For the entire school year, federal troops stayed in Little Rock, escorting the nine students to and from Central High and guarding them on the school-grounds. On the last day of class, Ernest Green, the one senior of the nine, became the first African American to graduate from Central High School. The showdown demonstrated that the President would not tolerate open defiance of the law. Still, most southern states found ways to resist full <u>compliance</u> with the Court's decision. Many years would pass before black and white children went to school together.

Vocabulary Builder
<u>compliance</u>–(kuhm PLĪ uhns) *n.* the act of obeying a rule or law

Congress Passes a Civil Rights Law Civil rights forces enjoyed a small victory when Congress passed the **Civil Rights Act of 1957** and President Eisenhower signed it into law. This law established the United States Civil Rights Commission, which had the power to investigate violations of civil rights. The law also gave the U.S. Attorney General greater power to protect the voting rights of African Americans. But overall, the law lacked teeth. Its main significance was that it was the first civil rights bill passed by Congress since Reconstruction.

 Checkpoint Why did President Eisenhower send federal troops to Little Rock?

The Montgomery Bus Boycott

In addition to legal efforts during this era, some civil rights activists took direct action to end segregation. On December 1, 1955, **Rosa Parks,** an African American seamstress, boarded a bus in Montgomery, Alabama, and sat down in an empty seat. Several stops later, the bus driver requested that she give up her seat to a white passenger. Montgomery law required African American passengers to give up their seats to whites. After Rosa Parks refused to obey the law, she was arrested. "The [policemen] asked if the driver had asked me to stand up, and I said yes, and they wanted to know why I didn't," Parks later recalled. "I told them I didn't think I should have to stand up. After I had paid my fare and occupied a seat, I didn't think I should have to give it up."

Rosa Parks Launches a Movement Parks's action set in motion a chain of events that transformed the civil rights movement. Over the next few days, a core of civil rights activists in Montgomery organized a one-day bus boycott. They called upon the black community

HISTORY MAKERS

Rosa Parks (1913–2005)
On December 1, 1955, in Montgomery, Alabama, Rosa Parks was arrested for refusing to give up her bus seat to a white passenger. African Americans responded with a boycott of city buses that lasted more than a year. Parks later moved to Detroit and worked for many years for Representative John Conyers, an African American member of Congress. She founded a nonprofit institute whose goal was to help young people improve their school, work, and inter-personal skills. When she died in 2005, her body was laid in honor at the Capitol in Washington, D.C., making her the first woman ever to be recognized in this way.

to refuse to ride the buses as a way to express their opposition to Parks's arrest, in particular, and segregation, in general. Meanwhile, during the **Montgomery bus boycott,** the NAACP began preparing a legal challenge.

For a long while, many people thought that Parks had refused to give up her seat simply because she was tired after a long day of work. But, in reality, Parks had a record of fighting for civil rights. She had been active in the Montgomery chapter of the NAACP for years. This does not mean that she set out to get arrested and spark a movement. But Parks and other activists welcomed the chance to use the incident to protest bus segregation.

● **INFOGRAPHIC**

King's Philosophy of
NONVIOLENT PROTEST

For Martin Luther King, Jr., the strategy of nonviolent protest had diverse roots. As the son and grandson of Baptist preachers, King absorbed the teachings of Jesus at an early age. Later, a deep interest in philosophy led him to explore the writings of the American author Henry David Thoreau, who advocated civil disobedience, or refusing to obey unjust government or laws. Mohandas Gandhi was another critical influence on King. During India's struggle for independence from British rule, Gandhi expanded on Thoreau's approach, preaching nonviolence as the only way to achieve victory against much stronger foes.

King was a Baptist preacher with a deep faith in God and in the teachings of Jesus. ▼

"In the midst of ... dangers I have felt an inner calm and known resources of strength that only God could give.... I have felt the power of God transforming the fatigue of despair into the buoyancy of hope."

King read Thoreau's *Essay on Civil Disobedience.* ▶

CIVIL DISOBEDIENCE
SOLITUDE AND LIFE WITHOUT PRINCIPLE

HENRY DAVID THOREAU

LITERARY CLASSICS

"Fascinated by the idea of refusing to cooperate with an evil system, I was so deeply moved that I reread the work several times. This was my first intellectual contact with the theory of nonviolent resistance."

Gandhi's tactics inspired King. ▶

"It was in this Gandhian emphasis on love and nonviolence that I discovered the method for social reform that I had been seeking."

Thinking Critically
1. **Apply Information** How did King put his belief in nonviolence into practice in the Montgomery bus boycott?
2. **Draw Conclusions** What are the advantages and disadvantages of nonviolent protest?

Martin Luther King Urges Nonviolence On the evening following the boycott, the Montgomery Improvement Association (MIA), the organization that sponsored the bus boycott, held a meeting. Dr. **Martin Luther King, Jr.,** a Baptist minister, addressed the group. Though he had had little time to prepare, King delivered an inspirational speech that brought the audience to its feet. Noting that African Americans were tired of segregation and oppression, King declared that there was no alternative but to protest. However, he called for the protest to be nonviolent. He urged them not to become resentful, which would lead to hatred toward whites, but rather to follow Christian doctrine and love them.

After King spoke, the MIA vowed to continue the boycott and chose King as its leader. For more than a year, African Americans in Montgomery maintained their boycott of the buses. They did so despite economic pressures from their employers and threats of violence by the Ku Klux Klan. King himself survived a bombing of his house. Fortunately, his wife and baby daughter were not home at the time. Finally, in 1956, the Supreme Court ruled that the Montgomery city law that segregated buses was unconstitutional. After more than a year, the MIA ended its boycott, and African Americans began to ride the buses again.

Ministers Form the SCLC The bus boycott represented a tremendous victory for African Americans in Montgomery and across the nation. The boycott revealed the power that African Americans could have if they joined together. The protest also elevated King and his philosophy of nonviolence into a prominent position within the civil rights movement.

After the boycott, King and another Montgomery minister, Ralph Abernathy, established the Southern Christian Leadership Conference (SCLC) to continue the struggle for civil rights. Made up largely of southern African American ministers, the SCLC advocated nonviolent resistance to fight injustice. The SCLC went on to organize a series of protests, including a Prayer Pilgrimage in Washington, D.C., in 1957, which helped convince Congress to pass civil rights legislation. Still, discrimination and segregation remained widespread.

✔ **Checkpoint** What role did Rosa Parks and Martin Luther King, Jr., play in the Montgomery bus boycott?

SECTION **1** Assessment

Progress Monitoring _Online_
For: Self-test with vocabulary practice
Web Code: nea-1403

Comprehension

1. **Terms and People** For each item below, write a sentence explaining its significance:
   - de jure segregation
   - de facto segregation
   - Thurgood Marshall
   - _Brown v. Board of Education_
   - Earl Warren
   - Civil Rights Act of 1957
   - Rosa Parks
   - Montgomery bus boycott
   - Martin Luther King, Jr.

2. **NoteTaking Reading Skill: Summarize** Use your timeline to answer the Section Focus Question: How did African Americans challenge segregation after World War II?

Writing About History

3. **Quick Write: Identify Questions** Historical research begins with identifying unanswered questions. Such questions often relate to the causes of an event or development. Reread this section and identify two events or developments that raise unanswered questions in your mind. Try to write questions that begin with _Why_ or _How_.

Critical Thinking

4. **Recognize Cause and Effect** Why did the struggle for equal rights intensify after World War II?

5. **Analyze Information** How did the _Brown_ decision lead to conflict between federal and state governments?

6. **Synthesize Information** Why is the Montgomery bus boycott considered a turning point in the civil rights movement?

How Does Segregation Affect Education?

Until the 1950s, public schools throughout the United States were segregated by race. This separation of students was legal because of the 1896 *Plessy* v. *Ferguson* decision, in which the Supreme Court ruled that "separate but equal" facilities did not violate the Constitution. However, many believed that segregated schools could never provide an equal education.

▼ Linda Brown

Brown v. *Board of Education* (1954)

The Facts	The Issue	The Decision
• Linda Brown was an African American student in the segregated school district of Topeka, Kansas. • Linda's parents tried to enroll her in an all-white school closer to home, but school officials denied the application on the basis of race. • The NAACP filed a lawsuit against the Board of Education on behalf of the Browns and several other black families.	The NAACP argued that segregated schools deprived African American students the equal protection of the law required by the Fourteenth Amendment.	The Supreme Court ruled unanimously that segregated schools were inherently unequal and violated the Fourteenth Amendment.

Why It Matters

Brown v. *Board of Education* was a major legal victory in the civil rights movement. This landmark decision brought America one step closer to securing equal rights for all. Chief Justice Earl Warren declared that segregation in education was unconstitutional because it prevented an equal education for all races:

"In these days, it is doubtful that any child may reasonably be expected to succeed in life if he is denied the opportunity of an education. Such an opportunity . . . is a right which must be made available to all on equal terms. . . . To separate them [children in grade and high schools] from others of similar age and qualifications solely because of their race generates a feeling of inferiority . . . that may affect their hearts and minds in a way unlikely to ever be undone. . . ."

▼ Students at a high school in Texas

Connect to Your World

Use the data in the table to create a graph, and describe the trend that you see. Then, research school segregation today. Have schools become more or less segregated since 2001? What might explain this change?

School Desegregation After *Brown*				
(Percentage of African American students in 90 percent minority schools)				
	1968	1988	1991	2001
South	78	24	26	31
Northeast	43	48	50	51
Midwest	58	42	40	47
West	51	29	27	30

SOURCE: *National Center for Education Statistics Common Core of Data*

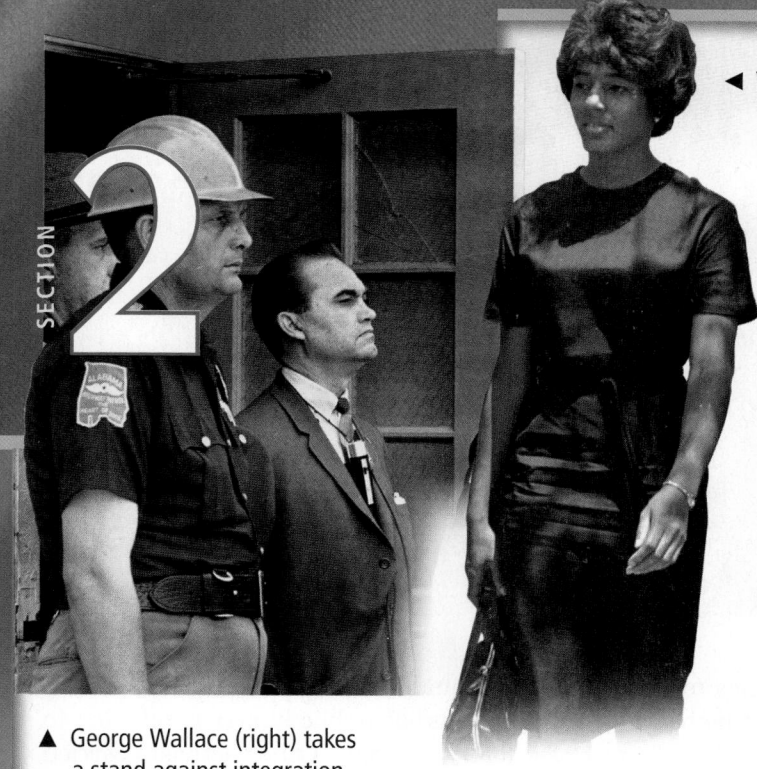

◀ Vivian Malone

▲ George Wallace (right) takes a stand against integration.

WITNESS HISTORY 🔊 AUDIO

Blocking the Schoolhouse Door

Alabama governor George Wallace made it clear where he stood on civil rights: "I say segregation now! Segregation tomorrow! Segregation forever!" Wallace vowed to stand "in the schoolhouse door" and personally block any attempt to integrate Alabama schools. On June 11, 1963, he got his chance. As federal marshals escorted two African American students to register at the University of Alabama, Wallace stood on the steps of the school. He proclaimed the right of states to regulate their own schools. One of the students later recalled:

❝I didn't feel I should sneak in. I didn't feel I should go around the back door. If [Wallace] were standing in the door, I had every right in the world to face him and to go to school.❞

—Vivian Malone Jones, 2003

The Movement Gains Ground

🟦NY Core Curriculum Objectives

- **7.III.A.1a** Civil rights actions: James Meredith at the University of Mississippi, Birmingham protest, March on Washington
- **7.III.B.3a** Black protest, pride, and power: NAACP
- **7.III.B.3b** Case studies of the civil rights movement: SNCC, SCLC, CORE

Terms and People

sit-in	Medgar Evers
SNCC	March on Washington
freedom ride	filibuster
James Meredith	Civil Rights Act of 1964

NoteTaking

Reading Skill: Summarize Use a concept web like the one below to record information about the civil rights protests of the 1960s.

Why It Matters Despite the *Brown* decision and other civil rights victories, little changed in the everyday lives of most African Americans. Nonetheless, activists continued to struggle for civil rights. In the early 1960s, the movement experienced a groundswell of support. This surge produced a dramatic shift in race relations, led to the passage of landmark civil rights legislation in 1964, and set the stage for future reforms. **Section Focus Question: How did the civil rights movement gain ground in the 1960s?**

Student Activists Make a Difference

After the *Brown* decision, many black youths expected that their schools would integrate quickly and that other racial reforms would follow. Change was not quick to come, however. Disappointed by the lack of progress, young African Americans began to challenge segregation with new vigor and determination.

Sit-ins Challenge Segregation On February 1, 1960, four African American college students ordered doughnuts and coffee at a Woolworth's lunch counter in Greensboro, North Carolina. As they expected, the white waitress refused to serve them. In the South, nearly all restaurants that served whites refused to serve blacks. To protest this discrimination, the four students sat down on the stools at the lunch counter, where they stayed until closing time.

Word of the Greensboro **sit-in** spread rapidly, sparking a wave of similar protests across the nation. In Nashville, Tennessee, for instance, students led by the Reverend James Lawson staged sit-ins

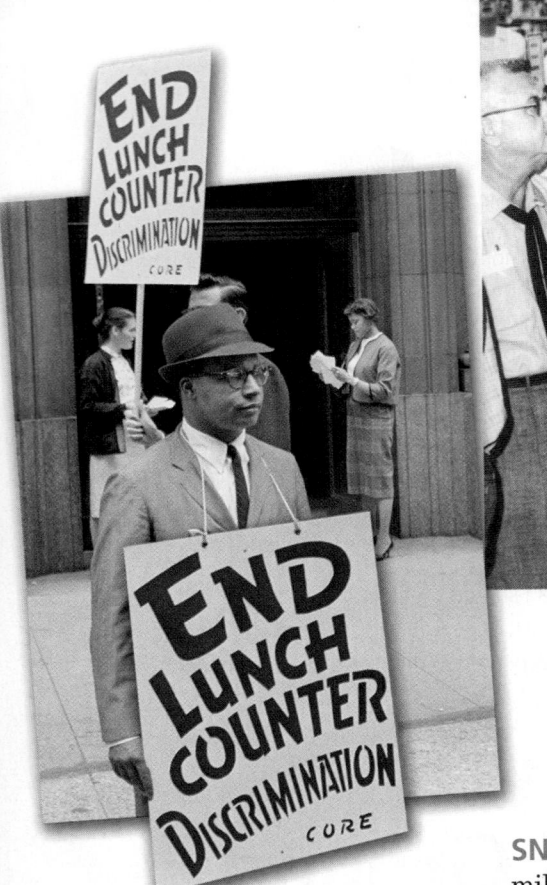

Protesting Segregation

Protesters challenged segregation at lunch counters by picketing (above, left). Later activists held sit-ins, like the one (above, right) in Jackson, Mississippi. Sit-in participants were trained not to react, even when hostile onlookers dumped food on them. *How would you describe the atmosphere at this lunch counter?*

and, later, marches to protest racial inequality. Elsewhere, protesters held "wade-ins" at public beaches and "read-ins" at public libraries, refusing to leave beaches or libraries reserved for whites only. Other activists carried picket signs in demonstrations and wrote letters to newspapers and government officials to express their support of the protests in the South.

SNCC Promotes Nonviolent Protest The sit-ins marked the birth of a new militancy, especially among young African Americans. To build on the momentum they had gained, about 175 students from 30 states met at Shaw University, in Raleigh, North Carolina. There, on Easter weekend in 1960, they listened to James Lawson deliver an inspiring address:

> **Primary Source** "We who are demonstrators are trying to raise what we call the 'moral issue.' That is, we are pointing to the viciousness of racial segregation and prejudice and calling it evil or sin. . . . [We are also] asserting, 'get moving.' The pace of change is too slow. At this rate it will be another generation before the major forms of segregation disappear. . . . Most of us will be grandparents before we can live normal human lives."
>
> —James Lawson, "From a Lunch Counter Stool," 1960

Ella Baker, a veteran of the struggle for civil rights, had organized the meeting. The granddaughter of enslaved African Americans, Baker had been active in the NAACP and SCLC. She helped the young activists to establish a new civil rights organization, the **Student Nonviolent Coordinating Committee**, or **SNCC**. Its goal was to create a grass-roots movement that involved all classes of African Americans in the struggle to defeat white racism and to obtain equality.

✔ **Checkpoint** How did young people energize the civil rights movement in the 1960s?

Riding for Freedom

The next battleground was interstate transportation. Activists targeted this industry because they knew that travel between states was subject to federal rather than state regulation. In fact, the Supreme Court had recently ruled in *Boynton* v. *Virginia* (1960) that segregation on interstate buses and in waiting rooms was illegal. Civil rights activists were now going to test the federal government's willingness to enforce the law.

Freedom Riders Face Angry Mobs In the spring of 1961, CORE staged a **"freedom ride"** through the Deep South. Riders set off in two separate buses from Washington, D.C., bound for New Orleans. En route, they defied segregationist codes. African Americans sat in the front of the bus and used "white" restrooms in bus stations.

In Alabama, the trip took a dangerous turn. After departing from Anniston, prosegregationists firebombed one of the buses. When the second bus arrived in Birmingham, a white mob attacked the riders.

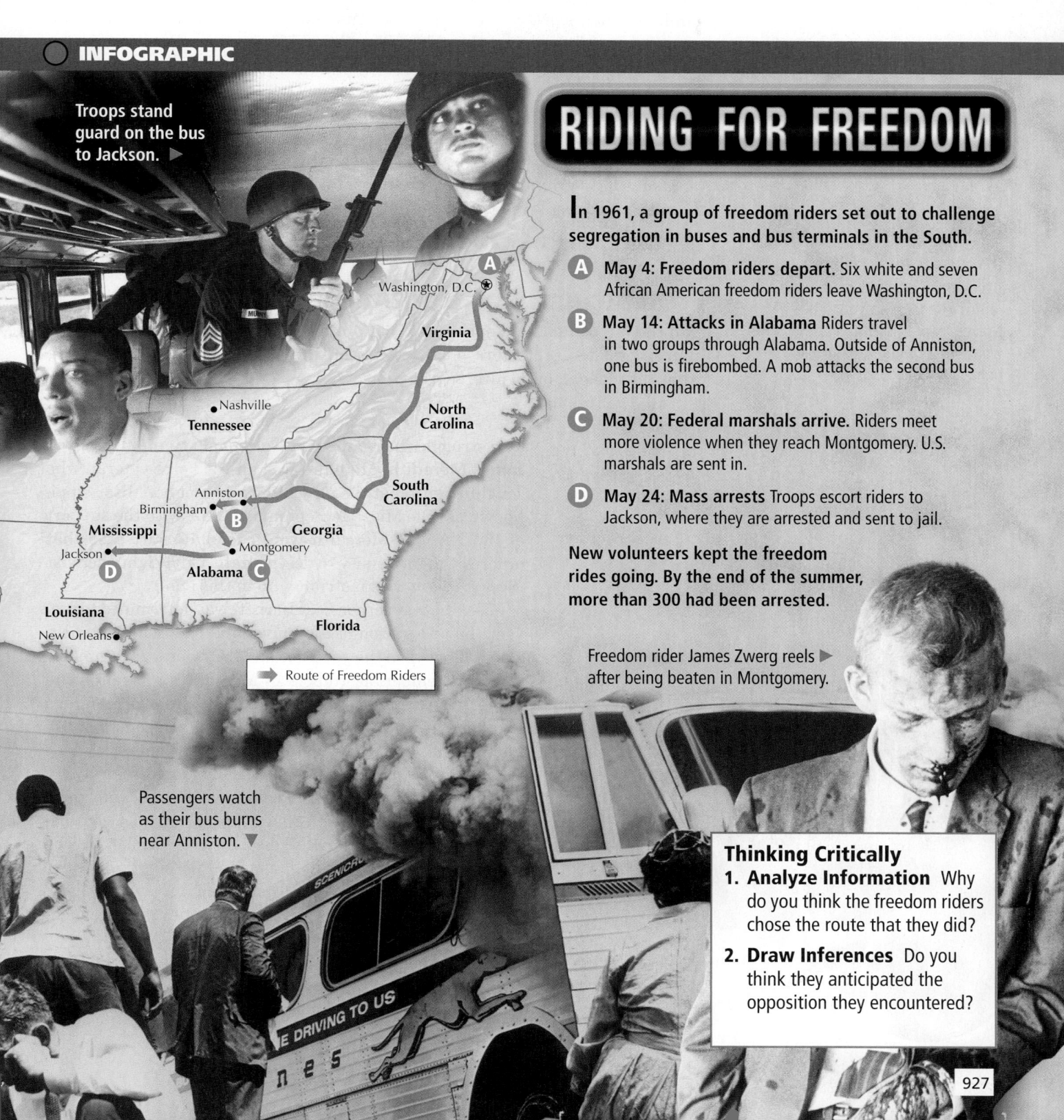

INFOGRAPHIC

Troops stand guard on the bus to Jackson. ▶

RIDING FOR FREEDOM

In 1961, a group of freedom riders set out to challenge segregation in buses and bus terminals in the South.

A **May 4: Freedom riders depart.** Six white and seven African American freedom riders leave Washington, D.C.

B **May 14: Attacks in Alabama** Riders travel in two groups through Alabama. Outside of Anniston, one bus is firebombed. A mob attacks the second bus in Birmingham.

C **May 20: Federal marshals arrive.** Riders meet more violence when they reach Montgomery. U.S. marshals are sent in.

D **May 24: Mass arrests** Troops escort riders to Jackson, where they are arrested and sent to jail.

New volunteers kept the freedom rides going. By the end of the summer, more than 300 had been arrested.

Washington, D.C.

Virginia

Nashville
Tennessee

North Carolina

South Carolina

Anniston
Birmingham
B

Mississippi

Georgia

Jackson
D

Montgomery

Alabama **C**

Louisiana

Florida

New Orleans

➡ Route of Freedom Riders

Freedom rider James Zwerg reels ▶ after being beaten in Montgomery.

Passengers watch as their bus burns near Anniston. ▼

SCENICR

E DRIVING TO US

Thinking Critically
1. **Analyze Information** Why do you think the freedom riders chose the route that they did?

2. **Draw Inferences** Do you think they anticipated the opposition they encountered?

President Kennedy Takes Action Photographs of the bombed-out bus and the injured riders appeared in newspapers and on television screens around the world, prodding President John F. Kennedy to intervene. Kennedy had intervened before. The previous year, when he was running for the presidency, Kennedy had helped to win Martin Luther King's release from a Georgia prison after state officials had sentenced King to 6 months in jail for a traffic violation. King was freed and Kennedy, with the help of African American voters, went on to win the presidential election of 1960.

Kennedy now took action to stem the violence against the freedom riders. His administration worked out a deal with Mississippi's leaders. Police and state troopers agreed to protect the riders. The Federal Transportation Commission also issued an order mandating the desegregation of interstate transportation. In exchange, the Kennedy administration agreed not to intervene when Mississippi authorities arrested the activists and sentenced them to jail for disturbing the peace.

The freedom riders achieved their immediate goal. They compelled a reluctant federal government to act. By refusing to allow violent mobs to deter them, the riders also displayed that intimidation would not defeat the movement.

✓ **Checkpoint** What did the freedom rides accomplish?

Protests and Confrontations Intensify

In the fall of 1962 and spring of 1963, protests against racial discrimination intensified. The protesters put pressure on the federal government to help break down legal, or de jure, segregation.

Integrating Ole Miss
Accompanied by federal marshals, James Meredith arrived at the University of Mississippi in 1962. He went on to graduate from the university in 1963.

Meredith Integrates the University of Mississippi One struggle that gained international attention involved **James Meredith.** Meredith was an Air Force veteran who sought to enroll at the all-white University of Mississippi, known as "Ole Miss." In September 1962, with the support of the NAACP, Meredith won a federal court case that ordered the university to desegregate. Civil rights activist **Medgar Evers** was instrumental in this effort.

Mississippi governor Ross Barnett was determined to prevent the integration of the university. The issue became a standoff between the governor and the federal government.

On September 30, rumors of Meredith's arrival on the university's campus began to spread. Federal marshals had been assigned to protect him. Over the course of the night, a full-scale riot erupted, with federal marshals battling white protestors intent on scaring Meredith away.

As the rioting took place, President Kennedy addressed the nation on television. "Americans are free . . . to disagree with the law but not to disobey it," he declared. "For any government of laws . . . , no man, however prominent and powerful . . . is entitled to defy a court of law." The rioting went on throughout the night. By the time it ended, 160 people had been injured and 2 men had been killed.

The following morning, Meredith registered as a student and took his first class. He graduated from Ole Miss in 1963 and went on to obtain his law degree from Columbia University in New York City. Tragically, Medgar Evers was assassinated, on his front doorstep, in June 1963. Three years later, Meredith himself was shot and nearly killed. Both shootings stand as historical reminders of the high costs of fighting racial discrimination.

King Campaigns in Birmingham In the spring of 1963, Martin Luther King, Jr., and the SCLC targeted Birmingham, Alabama, for a major civil rights campaign. They chose Birmingham because of its reputation as the most segregated city in the South.

The campaign began nonviolently at first with protest marches and sit-ins. City officials got a court order prohibiting the demonstrations. On Good Friday, April 12, 1963, King decided to violate the order and join the demonstration personally, even though he knew it would lead to his arrest. From his jail cell, King wrote a letter explaining why he and other civil rights activists were tired of waiting for reform: "For years now I have heard the word 'wait!' It rings in the ear of every Negro with piercing familiarity. This 'Wait!' has almost always meant 'Never.'"

One of the most poignant passages of the letter describes King's concern about the impact of discrimination on his children:

> **Primary Source** "Perhaps it is easy for those who have never felt the stinging darts of segregation to say, 'Wait.' But . . . when you suddenly find your tongue twisted and your speech stammering as you seek to explain to your six-year-old daughter why she can't go to the public amusement park that has just been advertised on television, and see tears welling up in her eyes when she is told that Funtown is closed to colored children. . . . Then you will understand why we find it difficult to wait."
> —Martin Luther King, Jr., "Letter From Birmingham Jail," 1963

After King was released from jail, the SCLC increased the frequency of the demonstrations. For the first time, schoolchildren joined the "freedom marches." Finally, Birmingham's Public Safety Commissioner, T. Eugene "Bull" Connor, would not <u>tolerate</u> the demonstrations any longer. He used police dogs and fire hoses on the protesters. Many Americans were shocked by photographs and news coverage of nonviolent protesters set upon by dogs and overwhelmed by the powerful jets of water from fire hoses. They sent telegrams and letters by the thousands to the White House, calling on the President to act.

Kennedy Backs Civil Rights In addition to the conflict in Birmingham, civil rights protests were taking place in cities from Jackson, Mississippi, to Cambridge, Maryland. President Kennedy became convinced that he had to take a more active role in promoting civil rights.

On June 11, 1963, Kennedy delivered a moving televised address. Calling civil rights a "moral issue," he declared that the nation had an obligation to "fulfill its promise" of giving all Americans "equal rights and equal opportunities." President Kennedy sent to Congress a proposal for sweeping civil rights legislation. His brother, Attorney General Robert F. Kennedy, led the charge for passage of the bill.

✓ **Checkpoint** How did James Meredith and Martin Luther King, Jr., prompt President Kennedy to promote civil rights?

Clash in Birmingham
Police in Birmingham, Alabama, used police dogs to break up civil rights marches in 1963. *How do you think Americans reacted when they saw images like these on television and in newspapers?*

Vocabulary Builder
tolerate–(TAHL er ayt) *v.* to allow or put up with

The Movement Marches on Washington

To put pressure on Congress to pass the new civil rights bill, supporters made plans for a massive demonstration in Washington, D.C. The event brought together the major civil rights groups—including the NAACP, SCLC, and SNCC—as well as labor unions and religious groups.

The **March on Washington** took place on August 28, 1963. Organizers had hoped for 100,000 demonstrators. More than double that number showed up, having made the journey to the capital from around the country. Before the march, there had been some concern about maintaining order at such a huge demonstration. Yet despite the massive numbers, the day was peaceful and even festive. Popular celebrities and entertainers were on hand to perform for the crowd.

The main rally took place in front of the Lincoln Memorial, where a distinguished roster of speakers addressed the crowd. The highlight of the day came

Events That Changed America

THE MARCH ON WASHINGTON

The March on Washington drew more than 200,000 people to Washington, D.C. The demonstrators were a diverse group from all parts of the country. They were young and old and came from various classes and religious backgrounds. More than a quarter of them were white.

The Washington Monument was the starting point for the day's events. Prominent singers performed songs, including the civil rights movement's unofficial anthem, "We Shall Overcome." Then, the throng marched to the Lincoln Memorial for the main rally. A. Philip Randolph, the elder statesman of the civil rights movement, gave the opening remarks, followed by representatives of various religious and labor groups. The final speaker was Martin Luther King, Jr., whose moving speech enthralled the crowd—and the millions more watching on television.

▼ King addresses the crowd around the reflecting pool between the Lincoln Memorial and Washington Monument.

when Martin Luther King, Jr., took the podium. King held the audience spellbound as he described his dream of a colorblind society "when all God's children" would be free and equal. Millions more watched King's address live on television. This powerful and eloquent speech has come to be known as the "I Have a Dream" speech. (You will read an excerpt from the "I Have a Dream" speech later in this chapter.)

Behind the scenes, there was some tension between the organizations that had planned the March. SNCC, in particular, had wanted to stage a more militant protest, to show its dissatisfaction with the pace of change. Yet for the public at large and for most who took part, the March on Washington represented a magical moment in American history.

✓ **Checkpoint** What is considered the highlight of the March on Washington?

▲ Button from the march urging interracial cooperation

Why It Matters
The March on Washington was one of the largest political demonstrations in U.S. history. Widely covered in the media, the march increased awareness of the movement and built momentum for the passage of civil rights legislation. Despite the huge numbers and the emotional intensity of the day, the march remained orderly and is considered a model for peaceful protest. The March on Washington has come to symbolize the civil rights movement itself.

▼ The crowd erupts in cheers after hearing King's speech.

Thinking Critically
Why was the March on Washington a symbolic and appropriate choice for a civil rights demonstration?

History Interactive

For: More on the March on Washington
Web Code: nep-1405

MARCH ON WASHINGTON FOR JOBS AND FREEDOM
AUGUST 28, 1963

LINCOLN MEMORIAL PROGRAM

1. The National Anthem — Led by Marian Anderson.
2. Invocation — The Very Rev. Patrick O'Boyle, Archbishop of Washington.
3. Opening Remarks — A. Philip Randolph, Director March on Washington for Jobs and Freedom.
4. Remarks — Dr. Eugene Carson Blake, Stated Clerk, United Presbyterian Church of the U.S.A.; Vice Chairman, Commission on Race Relations of the National Council of Churches of Christ in America.
5. Tribute to Negro Women Fighters for Freedom — Mrs. Medgar Evers
   Daisy Bates
   Diane Nash Bevel
   Mrs. Medgar Evers
   Mrs. Herbert Lee
   Rosa Parks
   Gloria Richardson
6. Remarks — John Lewis, National Chairman, Student Nonviolent Coordinating Committee.
   Walter Reuther, President, United Automobile, Aerospace and Agricultural Implement Workers of America, AFL-CIO; Chairman, Industrial Union Department, AFL-CIO.
7. Remarks — James Farmer, National Director, Congress of Racial

Congress Passes the Civil Rights Act of 1964

On September 15, 1963, less than three weeks after the march, a bomb exploded in the Sixteenth Street Baptist Church in Birmingham. The church had been the SCLC's headquarters earlier that spring. Four young African American girls, all dressed in their Sunday best, were killed in the bombing.

Two months later, on November 22, 1963, President John F. Kennedy was assassinated in Dallas, Texas. Vice President Lyndon B. Johnson assumed the presidency.

Johnson was a southerner with an undistinguished record on racial matters. However, he surprised many Americans by immediately throwing his support behind the cause of civil rights. "No eulogy could more eloquently honor President Kennedy's memory," Johnson told Congress and the nation, "[than the] earliest passage of the civil rights bill for which he fought so long."

The civil rights bill faced strong opposition in Congress, but Johnson put his considerable political skills to work for its passage. The bill passed in the House of Representatives, but it faced a more difficult fight in the Senate, where a group of southern senators attempted to block it by means of a **filibuster.** This is a tactic by which senators give long speeches to hold up legislative business. The filibuster went on for more than 80 days until supporters finally put together enough votes to overcome it. In the end, the measure passed in the Senate, and President Johnson signed the **Civil Rights Act of 1964** into law in July.

The act banned segregation in public accommodations and gave the federal government the ability to compel state and local school boards to desegregate their schools. The act also allowed the Justice Department to prosecute individuals who violated people's civil rights and outlawed discrimination in employment on account of race, color, sex, or national origin. It also established the Equal Employment Opportunity Commission (EEOC), which is responsible for enforcing these provisions and investigating charges of job discrimination.

 Checkpoint How did the Civil Rights Act of 1964 try to end discrimination?

SECTION

2 Assessment

Progress Monitoring Online
For: Self-test with vocabulary practice
Web Code: nea-1406

Comprehension

1. **Terms and People** For each item below, write a sentence explaining its significance:
   - sit-in
   - SNCC
   - freedom ride
   - James Meredith
   - Medgar Evers
   - March on Washington
   - filibuster
   - Civil Rights Act of 1964

2. **NoteTaking Reading Skill: Summarize** Use your concept web to answer the Section Focus Question: How did the civil rights movement gain ground in the 1960s?

Writing About History

3. **Quick Write: Construct a Hypothesis** After identifying an unanswered question, a historian might form a hypothesis, an unproven answer to that question. Write a one-sentence hypothesis to answer the following question: Why was Johnson more successful than Truman in getting civil rights legislation passed? Remem- ber, your statement is not a fact but a theory that might or might not be supported by further research. The sentence you write could later become the thesis statement for a research paper.

Critical Thinking

4. **Draw Conclusions** Why were sit-ins often a successful tactic?

5. **Analyze Information** Why did the freedom rides lead to violence?

6. **Recognize Cause and Effect** What events led to passage of the Civil Rights Act of 1964?

7.III.A.1a

Martin Luther King, Jr.:
I Have a Dream

Martin Luther King, Jr., delivered the closing address at the March on Washington. For approximately 20 minutes, he mesmerized the crowd with one of the most powerful speeches ever delivered. In this excerpt, King speaks of his dream for America:

I say to you today, my friends, that in spite of the difficulties and frustrations of the moment I still have a dream. It is a dream deeply rooted in the American dream.

I have a dream that one day this nation will rise up and live out the true meaning of its creed[1]: "We hold these truths to be self-evident; that all men are created equal."

I have a dream that one day on the red hills of Georgia the sons of former slaves and the sons of former slaveowners will be able to sit down together at the table of brotherhood.

I have a dream that one day even the state of Mississippi . . . will be transformed into an oasis of freedom and justice.

I have a dream that my four little children will one day live in a nation where they will not be judged by the color of their skin but by the content of their character.

I have a dream today.

I have a dream that one day the state of Alabama . . . will be transformed into a situation where little black boys and black girls will be able to join hands with little white boys and girls and walk together as sisters and brothers. . . .

This is our hope. This is the faith with which I return to the South. With this faith we will be able to hew[2] out of the mountain of despair a stone of hope. With this faith we will be able to transform the jangling discords of our nation into a beautiful symphony of brotherhood. . . .

This will be the day when all of God's children will be able to sing with new meaning, "My country 'tis of thee, sweet land of liberty, of thee I sing. Land where my father died, land of the Pilgrims' pride, from every mountainside, let freedom ring." . . .

When we let freedom ring, when we let it ring from every village and every hamlet, from every state and every city, we will be able to speed up that day when all of God's children, black men and white men, Jews and Gentiles[3], Protestants and Catholics, will be able to join hands and sing in the words of the old Negro spiritual, "Free at last! Free at last! Thank God Almighty, we are free at last!"

▲ Martin Luther King, Jr., at the March on Washington

---

1. **creed** (kreed) *n.* beliefs or principles
2. **hew** (hyoo) *v.* carve
3. **Gentiles** (JEHN tīlz) *n.* non-Jews

Thinking Critically
1. **Identify Central Issues** What is the "American dream" to which King refers?

2. **Draw Inferences** How well does King think the nation has lived up to its promises?

EXPERIENCE
NONVIOLENT PROTEST

College students held sit-ins at lunch counters. African Americans boycotted buses. Groups of demonstrators knelt in prayer. Protesters in the civil rights movement used many different nonviolent methods to make it clear that they would no longer tolerate segregation and voter discrimination. These protests eventually led to the passage of the Civil Rights Act and the Voting Rights Act.

Since the 1960s, America has made great strides in truly embodying the Declaration of Independence statement that "All men are created equal." However, certain groups still struggle to have their rights recognized. For example, individuals with disabilities worked to gain passage of the landmark Americans With Disabilities Act. This law requires that people with disabilities have equal access to public facilities and equal employment opportunities.

Pickets ▲
A woman carries a picket sign outside a segregated lunch counter. Picketers tried to discourage people from patronizing businesses that did not treat black and white customers equally.

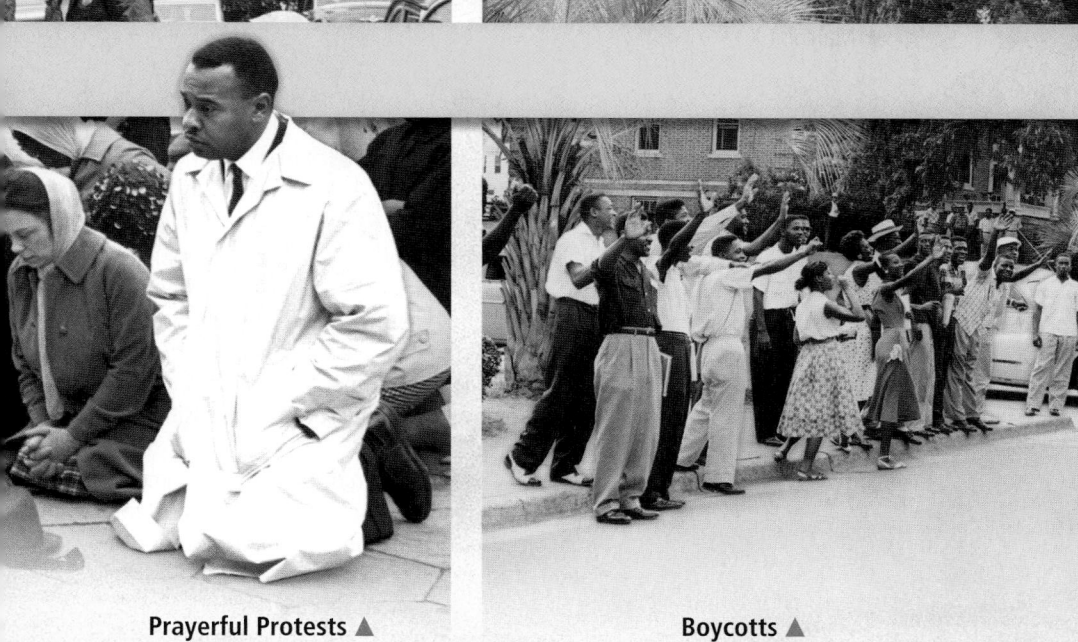

Prayerful Protests ▲
A group of demonstrators kneel in prayer during a hearing for arrested freedom riders in Albany, Georgia, in 1961. Nonviolent protests often took the form of prayer vigils like this.

Wade-ins ▼
Black protesters march onto a "whites only" public beach, ready to swim. Whites who did not want the beach desegregated face off against them as police stand guard.

Boycotts ▲
African American students at Florida A&M College jeer at a nearly empty city bus as it passes through the campus. Protesters in Tallahassee were boycotting the buses to protest segregation on the bus lines.

Thinking Critically

1. **Analyze Visuals** How did whites support or oppose black protesters?

2. **Draw Conclusions** Do you think the civil rights movement would have been as effective if protesters had not used peaceful protest methods?

Connect to Today Do research to learn about the passage of the Americans With Disabilities Act. How were the methods and goals of that movement similar to and different from the movement for racial equality in the 1960s? Did the bill succeed in gaining equal rights and opportunities for people with disabilities?

History *Interactive* *

For: Learn more about civil rights tactics
Web Code: nep-1407

◄ Malcolm X

▲ Button honoring Malcolm X

WITNESS HISTORY 🔊 AUDIO

Entering a New Era

Although the Civil Rights movement was making headway, many black activists were impatient with King's nonviolent methods and his emphasis on integration. Some believed that integration was not the solution. Others felt that more needed to be done to remove what they saw as oppression by white society.

Malcolm X (also known by his religious name, el-Hajj Malik el-Shabazz) became one of the most prominent voices for this faction. As a minister of the Nation of Islam, he preached a message of self-reliance and self-protection. He called for black pride and spread the idea of black nationalism, a belief in the separate identity and racial unity of the African American community. Malcolm was a "charismatic speaker who could play an audience as great musicians play instruments." His dynamic speeches won many adherents to his cause. The Civil Rights Movement had entered a new era.

New Successes and Challenges

NY Core Curriculum Objectives

- **7.III.B.3a** Black protest, pride, and power
- **7.III.B.3b** Case studies of the civil rights movement: Black Muslims, Malcolm X, civil unrest
- **7.III.B.3c** Legislative impact of the civil rights movement: Civil Rights Act, 24th Amendment, Voting Rights Act, Fair Housing Act

Terms and People

Freedom Summer
Fannie Lou Hamer
Voting Rights Act
Twenty-fourth
 Amendment

Kerner Commission
Malcolm X
Nation of Islam
black power
Black Panthers

NoteTaking

Reading Skill: Summarize Complete an outline to summarize the contents of this section.

> **I. Push for Voting Rights**
> **A. Freedom Summer**
> 1.
> 2.

Why It Matters During the 1950s and 1960s, the civil rights movement made great strides forward. Yet racial injustice was not fully eradicated. Frustration with this situation led some African Americans to turn to more radical and sometimes violent methods. African Americans achieved further successes, but for some the radicalism of the times left a bitter legacy. **Section Focus Question: What successes and challenges faced the civil rights movement after 1964?**

The Push for Voting Rights

None of the federal court decisions or civil rights measures passed through 1964 fundamentally affected the right to vote. The problem was a southern political system that used literacy tests, poll taxes, and intimidation to keep blacks from voting. In Mississippi, in 1964, for instance, not a single African American person was registered to vote in five counties that had African American majorities. All of the major civil rights organizations sought to overcome these political injustices.

SNCC Stages Freedom Summer SNCC had spent several years organizing voter education projects in Mississippi. It met with little success and a great deal of violent opposition. But in 1964, it called for a major campaign, known as **Freedom Summer.** About 1,000 volunteers, mostly black and white students, were to flood Mississippi. They would focus on registering African Americans to vote. They would also form the Mississippi Freedom Democratic Party (MFDP), an alternative to the state's all-white regular Democratic Party.

Even before most of the volunteers had arrived, three civil rights workers—Michael Schwerner, James Chaney, and Andrew Goodman—disappeared. SNCC claimed that they had been murdered; state authorities denied these charges. President Johnson ordered a massive search for the three, which ended when their bodies were found buried in an earthen dam. All had been shot at point-blank range. Yet, despite the obvious dangers, almost all of the other volunteers remained in the state.

After Freedom Summer ended in August 1964, an MFDP delegation traveled to the Democratic Convention in New Jersey, seeking to be recognized as Mississippi's only Democratic Party. At the convention, **Fannie Lou Hamer,** one of the MFDP's leaders, gave powerful testimony. She described how she and other activists had been beaten, fired from their jobs, and displaced from their homes all because, as she put it, they wanted "to register" and "live as decent human beings."

Despite Hamer's testimony, the Democrats refused to seat the MFDP. Instead, party officials offered a compromise: They would seat two MFDP members as "at-large delegates" and reform the nomination rules to guarantee greater minority representation in the future. The MFDP rejected this offer. Ironically, Mississippi's regular Democratic delegation left the convention in protest because the national party had made the offer to the MFDP.

Marching on Selma Early in 1965, Martin Luther King, Jr., and the SCLC organized a major campaign in Selma, Alabama, to pressure the federal government to enact voting rights legislation. The protests climaxed in a series of <u>confrontations</u> on the Edmund Pettus Bridge, on the main route from Selma to Montgomery. The first of these confrontations took place on March 7, 1965, a day that became known as "Bloody Sunday." Heavily armed state troopers and other authorities attacked the marchers as they tried to cross the bridge. Sheyann Webb, a six-year-old girl at the time, recalled the scene:

> **Primary Source** "I heard all of this screaming and . . . somebody yelled, 'Oh God, they're killing us!' . . . And I looked and I saw the troopers charging us . . . swinging their arms and throwing canisters of tear gas. . . . Some of them had clubs and others had ropes and whips. . . . It was like a nightmare. . . . I just knew then that I was going to die."
>
> —Sheyann Webb, *Selma, Lord, Selma*

Vocabulary Builder
<u>confrontation</u>–(kahn fruhn TAY shuhn) *n.* situation in which there is angry disagreement between opposing people or groups

Standoff in Selma
Police officers block the path of protesters attempting to march to Selma, Alabama.

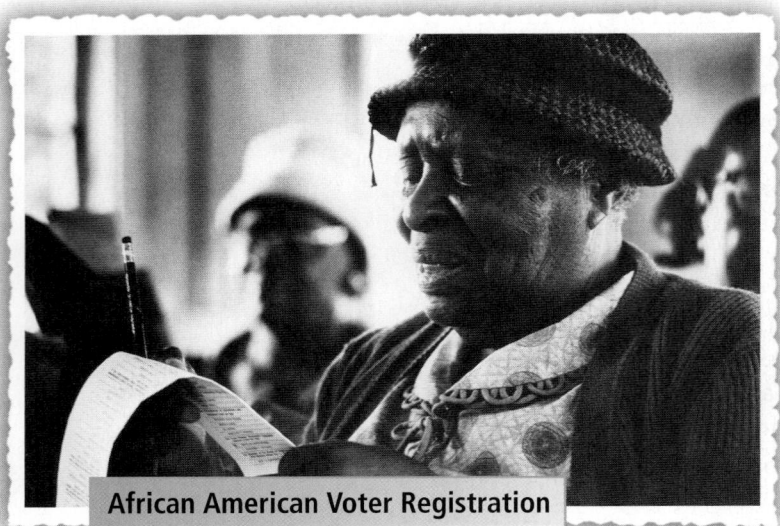

African American Voter Registration

(Percentage of voting-age African Americans)

State	1964	1968
Alabama	23.0	56.7
Louisiana	32.0	59.3
Mississippi	6.7	59.4
Texas	57.7	83.1
Virginia	45.7	58.4

SOURCE: Stanley, Harold W. *Voter Mobilization and the Politics of Race: The South and Universal Suffrage, 1952–1984*

Voting Rights Legislation Takes Effect

The table shows voter registration rates in some southern states before and after the Voting Rights Act of 1965. The women shown above are learning how to mark the ballot at a voter education class in Alabama in 1966. *Which state listed in the table had the greatest increase in voter registration between 1964 and 1968?*

Webb survived, but the rampage continued. Television coverage of the violence outraged the nation. On March 15, President Johnson went on national television and called for a strong federal voting rights law. Historically, regulation of voting rights had been left to the states, but Johnson argued that "it is wrong to deny any of your fellow citizens the right to vote." He added, "Their cause is our cause too, because it is not just Negroes, but really it is all of us, who must overcome the crippling legacy of bigotry and injustice. And, *we shall overcome.*"

New Legislation Guarantees Voting Rights Spurred by the actions of protesters and the words of the President, Congress passed the **Voting Rights Act** of 1965. The act banned literacy tests and empowered the federal government to oversee voting registration and elections in states that had discriminated against minorities. In 1975, Congress extended coverage to Hispanic voters in the Southwest.

Another legal landmark was the **Twenty-fourth Amendment** to the Constitution, ratified in 1964. It banned the poll tax, which had been used to keep poor African Americans from voting. In addition, the federal courts handed down several important decisions. *Baker* v. *Carr* and *Reynolds* v. *Simms* limited racial gerrymandering, the practice of drawing election districts in such a way as to dilute the African American vote, and established the legal principle of "one man, one vote."

These laws and decisions had a profound impact. Particularly in the Deep South, African American participation in politics skyrocketed. In Mississippi, the percentage of African Americans registered to vote jumped from just under 7 percent in 1964 to about 70 percent in 1986. Nationwide, the number of African American elected officials rose from fewer than 100 to more than 6,000 by the mid-1980s.

 Checkpoint What impact did the protests in Selma, Alabama, have on the nation?

Frustration Explodes Into Violence

Many celebrated the passage of the Voting Rights Act of 1965. Yet for some African Americans, things had not changed much. In many urban areas, there was anger and frustration over continuing discrimination and poverty. That anger exploded into violence in several cities.

Racial Violence Plagues Cities Less than a week after Johnson signed the Voting Rights Act, one of the worst race riots in American history erupted in the predominantly African American neighborhood of Watts in Los Angeles. Violence, looting, and arson spread for several days before National Guard troops restored order.

Watts was one of many race riots that erupted in the 1960s. The worst violence occurred in Newark, New Jersey, and Detroit, Michigan, in the summer of 1967. In Detroit, 43 people died, and property damage reached $50 million. The outbursts frightened many white Americans. In most previous race riots, whites had used violence to keep African Americans "in their place." But now, blacks were using violence against police and white business owners in black neighborhoods.

Voting Rights

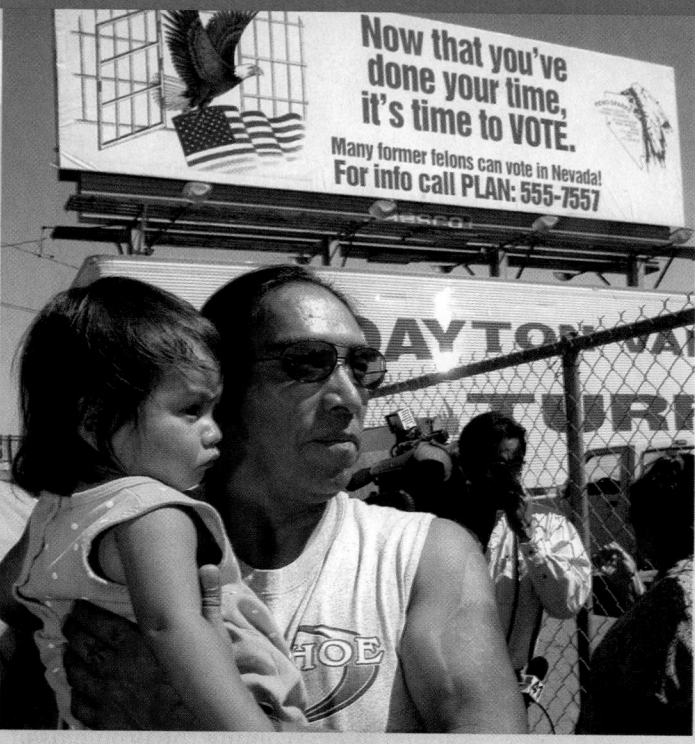

NY 2.I.E.4

TRACK THE ISSUE

What should the government do to promote voting rights?

Although the right to vote is a cornerstone of American democracy, many restrictions have been placed on voting rights over the years. As the history of the civil rights movement shows, gaining full electoral rights has been a struggle. How can the government ensure fair and free suffrage in America? Use the timeline below to explore this enduring question.

1820s–1830s Age of Jackson
States move toward universal white male suffrage.

1870 Fifteenth Amendment
Vote is extended to African American men, but this right is often violated.

1920 Nineteenth Amendment
Women's suffrage becomes law.

1965 Voting Rights Act
Law strengthens African American voting rights.

1971 Twenty-sixth Amendment
Voting age is lowered from 21 to 18.

2000 Presidential Election
Polling-place irregularities lead some states to reform voting process.

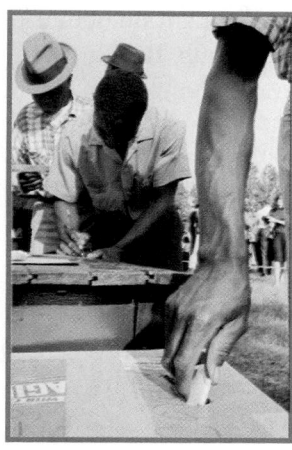

African Americans in Alabama voting for the first time after passage of the Voting Rights Act

A voter registration drive for ex-felons

DEBATE THE ISSUE

Voting Rights for Convicted Felons Most states do not allow felons to vote while they are in prison. In some states, this ban continues even after they are released. Should ex-convicts have their voting rights restored?

❝About 4.7 million Americans, more than 2 percent of the adult population, are barred from voting because of a felony conviction. Denying the vote to ex-offenders is antidemocratic and undermines the nation's commitment to rehabilitating people who have paid their debt to society.❞

—*The New York Times,* editorial

❝Individuals who have shown they are unwilling to follow the law cannot claim the right to make laws for the rest of us. We don't let everyone vote—not children, for instance, or noncitizens. . . . We have . . . standards of trustworthiness before we let people participate in the serious business of self-government, and people who commit serious crimes don't meet those standards.❞

—Roger Clegg, General Counsel, Center for Economic Opportunity

TRANSFER Activities

1. **Compare** How do these two views of felon voting rights differ?

2. **Contrast** How does the issue of voting rights for felons differ from the issue of voting rights in the 1960s?

3. **Transfer** Use the following Web site to see a video, try a WebQuest, and write in your journal. **Web Code:** neh-8702

Increasing Militancy
Black Panthers (above) demonstrated outside the courthouse where Huey Newton was on trial, charged with killing a police officer.

The Kerner Commission Seeks the Cause To determine the causes of the riots, President Johnson established the National Advisory Commission on Civil Disorders, known as the **Kerner Commission.** It concluded that long-term racial discrimination stood as the single most important cause of violence. The commission also recommended establishing and expanding federal programs aimed at overcoming the problems of America's urban ghettos.

> **Primary Source** ❝Our nation is moving toward two societies, one black, one white, separate and unequal. . . . Segregation and poverty have created the racial ghetto and a destructive environment totally unknown to most Americans.❞
> —National Advisory Commission on Civil Disorders, *Report,* 1967

The Kerner Commission's findings proved highly controversial. A number of conservative commentators argued against expanding federal spending. They said that this amounted to rewarding the rioters. Others noted that the black-white split that the report described ignored other minorities.

President Johnson did not follow up on the commission's recommendations, largely because the Vietnam War was consuming enormous sums of federal money. The riots also fueled a white backlash. Many whites opposed further reforms.

✔ **Checkpoint** Why was the Kerner Commission formed?

New Voices for African Americans

The racial rioting of the mid-1960s coincided with the radicalization of many African Americans, particularly young urban African Americans. Rather than advocating nonviolence and integration, they called for another approach.

Malcolm X Offers a Different Vision The most well-known African American radical was **Malcolm X,** who was born Malcolm Little in Omaha, Nebraska, in 1925. He adopted the *X* to represent his lost African name. Little, he argued, was his slave name. Malcolm had a difficult childhood. In his teens, Malcolm moved to Boston and then to New York City, where he became involved in drugs and crime and landed in prison on burglary charges at age 21.

While in prison, Malcolm became a convert to the **Nation of Islam,** a religious sect headed by Elijah Muhammad. The group prescribed strict rules of behavior, including no drugs or alcohol, and demanded a separation of the races.

After his release from prison, Malcolm became the Nation of Islam's most prominent minister. In 1964, however, he broke away from the Nation of Islam and formed his own organization. He then made a pilgrimage to Mecca, the holy city of Islam. Returning to the United States, he seemed willing to consider limited acceptance of whites. In February 1965, however, Malcolm X was shot and killed. Three members of the Nation of Islam were convicted of the murder.

Young Leaders Call for Black Power Many young African Americans saw themselves as heirs of the radical Malcolm X. They began to move away from the principle of nonviolence. They also began to question the goal of integration. As SNCC leader Stokely Carmichael put it:

> **Primary Source** "Integration . . . has been based on complete acceptance of the fact that in order to have a decent house or education, blacks must move into a white neighborhood or send their children to a white school. This reinforces the notion . . . that 'white' is automatically better and 'black' is by definition inferior."
> —"What We Want," 1966

Carmichael first used the term **"black power"** in 1966. In that year, James Meredith had set off on a "March Against Fear" across the state of Mississippi to encourage African Americans to register and vote. Meredith traveled only 20 miles before he was shot and left for dead by a white supremacist. SNCC, CORE, and SCLC members vowed to continue the march.

When they reached Greenwood, Mississippi, Carmichael and some other marchers were arrested. After his release, Carmichael told a crowd that African Americans needed "black power!" He later said that black power meant African Americans should collectively use their economic and political muscle to gain equality. Yet, many white Americans felt threatened. They believed that black power meant black violence.

Militants Form the Black Panthers Not long after Carmichael's "black power" speech, Huey Newton and Bobby Seale formed the Black Panther Party in Oakland, California. Almost overnight, the **Black Panthers** became the symbol of young militant African Americans. The Black Panthers organized armed patrols of urban neighborhoods to protect people from police abuse. They also created antipoverty programs, such as free breakfasts for poor African American children. The Black Panthers gained national attention when they entered the state

Olympic Protest
At the 1968 Summer Olympics, U.S. athletes Tommie Smith and John Carlos raised gloved fists in protest against discrimination.

Turbulent Times

The civil rights movement reached its peak in the 1960s but at a terrible cost. During the "long, hot summers" of 1965 to 1968, pent-up anger and frustration exploded into riots in African American communities across the nation. By the time the violence had subsided, hundreds of people had been killed, thousands were wounded, and neighborhoods lay in rubble. In addition to this heavy toll, assassins' bullets claimed the lives of key figures in the civil rights movement. Malcolm X was slain in 1965. Three years later, the assassination of Martin Luther King, Jr., shocked and grieved the nation.

King's funeral procession in Atlanta (above). A woman weeps as she pays her final respects. ▶

Long, Hot Summers	
Six days of arson, looting, and rioting rock the Watts section of Los Angeles.	**1965**
Riots break out in Chicago, San Fransisco, and other cities.	**1966**
Unrest continues. Riots occur in Detroit and Newark within a week of each other in July.	**1967**
King's assassination triggers riots in more than 100 cities, the worst in Washington, D.C.	**1968**

A pall of smoke ▲ envelops a city street during riots in Detroit in 1967.

Thinking Critically

1. **Recognize Cause and Effect** What factors contributed to the outbreak of riots in the 1960s?

2. **Predict Consequences** How do you think the events depicted here affected the civil rights movement?

capitol in Sacramento carrying shotguns and wearing black leather jackets and berets to protest attempts to restrict their right to bear arms.

The Panthers' style appealed to many young African Americans, who began to wear their hair in "Afros" and to refer to themselves as "black" rather than "Negro" or "colored." Some, following the lead of Malcolm X, changed their name and celebrated their African heritage. At the same time, the Panthers' militancy often led to violent confrontations with police. Each side accused the other of instigating the violence.

 Checkpoint What impact did Malcolm X have on the civil rights movement?

Martin Luther King's Final Days

Martin Luther King understood the anger and frustration of many urban African Americans whose lives had changed little despite the civil rights reforms of the 1960s. However, he disagreed with the call for "black power" and sought a nonviolent alternative to combat economic injustice. After spending about a year in Chicago's slums to protest conditions there, King made plans for a massive "Poor People's Campaign." The campaign's goal was to pressure the nation to do more to address the needs of the poor.

As part of this effort, King journeyed to Memphis, Tennessee, in early April 1968. There, he offered his assistance to sanitation workers who were striking for better wages and working conditions.

On April 3, King addressed his followers. He referred to threats that had been made against his life. "Like anybody, I would like to live a long life," King declared. "But I'm not concerned about that now. I just want to do God's will."

The following day, as King stood on the balcony outside his motel room, he was struck by a shot from a high-powered rifle. He died at a hospital shortly afterward, at the age of 39. James Earl Ray, a white ex-convict, was later charged with King's murder.

Robert F. Kennedy was campaigning for the presidency in Indianapolis when he heard of King's death. RFK stopped his campaign speech to give the audience the sad news. He reminded them that he had lost his own brother to an assassin's bullet. Kennedy asked those assembled to honor King's memory by replacing their anger and desire for revenge "with an effort to understand with compassion and love." Despite Kennedy's plea, riots broke out in hundreds of cities after King's assassination. Two months later, Robert Kennedy's life, too, was cut short by an assassin.

 Checkpoint Why did King go to Memphis in 1968?

WITNESS HISTORY DVD

Watch *Civil Rights Martyrs* on the **United States Witness History DVD** to learn more about some of those who lost their lives in the struggle for equal rights.

Significant Gains and Controversial Issues

King's assassination marked an important turning point. The protests for black freedom and racial equality that began in the mid-1950s crested in the late 1960s around the time of King's death. By then, the civil rights movement had made significant gains. Yet, white racism and the social and economic gap between many blacks and whites remained. New measures aimed at closing this gap tended to provoke more controversy than consensus in America.

Civil Rights Are Advanced The civil rights movement of the 1950s and 1960s succeeded in eliminating legal, or de jure, segregation and knocking down barriers to African American voting and political participation. During the same period, African American poverty rates fell and the median income of African American men and women rose rapidly, as did the number of African

Americans who graduated from high school. One symbol of the progress that had been made was the appointment of Thurgood Marshall as the first African American Supreme Court Justice in 1967. The following year, in the wake of King's murder, Congress passed one final civil rights measure, the Fair Housing Act, which banned discrimination in housing.

Controversial Issues Remain Attempts to increase the economic opportunities for African Americans and to integrate neighborhoods and schools encountered more difficulties. To achieve desegregated schools, the federal courts had ordered the use of forced busing. Richard Nixon, who succeeded Lyndon Johnson, criticized busing as a means of attaining racial balance.

At the same time, the Nixon administration formally established affirmative action as a means of closing the economic gap between blacks and whites. In a short period of time, colleges and universities, businesses, and local and state governments followed the federal government's lead and implemented their own affirmative action plans to increase African American representation in schools and the workforce.

Affirmative action proved controversial almost from the start. Some whites argued that it constituted reverse discrimination and violated the goal of creating a colorblind society. Justice Thurgood Marshall disagreed. "Three hundred and fifty years ago, the Negro was dragged to this country in chains to be sold into slavery," Marshall wrote. "The position of the Negro today in America is the tragic but inevitable consequence of centuries of unequal treatment."

Until the nation addressed the legacy of this unequal treatment, Marshall asserted, it would not fulfill its promise of providing equal rights and opportunities to all. This debate or controversy, as you will see in future chapters, remained unresolved.

✔ **Checkpoint** What gains did the civil rights movement make by the early 1970s?

SECTION 3 Assessment

Progress Monitoring _Online_
For: Self-test with vocabulary practice
Web Code: nea-1409

Comprehension

1. Terms and People For each of the items below, write a sentence explaining its significance:
- Freedom Summer
- Fannie Lou Hamer
- Voting Rights Act
- Twenty-fourth Amendment
- Kerner Commission
- Malcolm X
- Nation of Islam
- black power
- Black Panthers

2. NoteTaking Reading Skill: Summarize Use your outline to answer the Section Focus Question: What successes and challenges faced the civil rights movement after 1964?

Writing About History

3. Quick Write: Identify Sources After constructing a hypothesis, historians look for evidence that might either prove or disprove the hypothesis. List three sources of information that you might use to test the following hypothesis: The drive for voting rights in the South could have succeeded without the involvement of the federal government.

Critical Thinking

4. Recognize Cause and Effect How did the Selma march help lead to the passage of civil rights legislation?

5. Make Comparisons How did Malcolm X's views differ from Martin Luther King, Jr.'s views?

6. Identify Points of View Why did Justice Thurgood Marshall support affirmative action?

3.I.C.2b

A Raisin in the Sun
by Lorraine Hansberry

The 1940s and 1950s brought an explosion of literature that exposed the harsh discrimination African Americans faced. One of the most powerful writers of the period was the playwright Lorraine Hansberry. Her most famous work, *A Raisin in the Sun,* focuses on the struggles of a black family living in the South Side of Chicago.

In this excerpt, Lindner—a white man—tries to dissuade the family from moving into his neighborhood.

▲ Scene from a production of *A Raisin in the Sun*

LINDNER: I am sure you people must be aware of some of the incidents which have happened in various parts of the city when colored people have moved into certain areas—Well—because we have what I think is going to be a unique type of organization in American community life—not only do we deplore that kind of thing—but we are trying to do something about it. We feel—we feel that most of the trouble in this world, . . . exists because people just don't sit down and talk to each other.

RUTH: You can say that again, mister.

LINDNER: That we don't try hard enough in this world to understand the other fellow's problems. The other guy's point of view.

RUTH: Now that's right.

LINDNER: Yes—that's the way we feel out in Clybourne Park. And that's why I was elected to come here this afternoon and talk to you people. Friendly like, you know, the way people should talk to each other. . . . As I say, the whole business is a matter of *caring* about the other fellow. Anybody can see that you are a nice family of folks, hard working and honest I'm sure. Today everybody knows what it means to be on the outside of *something*. And of course, there is always somebody who is out to take the advantage of people who don't always understand."

WALTER: What do you mean?

LINDNER: Well—you see our community is made up of people who've worked hard as the dickens for years to build up that little community. They're not rich and fancy people; just hard-working, honest people who don't really have much but those little homes and a dream of the kind of community they want to raise their children in. Now I don't say we are perfect and there is a lot wrong in some of the things they want. But you've got to admit that a man, right or wrong, has the right to want to have the neighborhood he lives in a certain kind of way. And at the moment the overwhelming majority of our people out there feel that people get along better, take more of a common interest in the life of the community, when they share a common background. I want you to believe me when I tell you that race prejudice simply doesn't enter into it. It is a matter of the people of Clybourne Park believing, rightly or wrongly, as I say, that for the happiness of all concerned that our Negro families are happier when they live in their *own* communities.

BENETHEA: This, friends, is the Welcoming Committee!

Thinking Critically

1. **Synthesize Information** What reasons did Lindner give for not wanting the family to move into his neighborhood?

2. **Make Inferences** What obstacles did African Americans face in gaining social equality in the 1950s?

CHAPTER 27

Quick Study Guide

7.II.C.2,
7.III.A.1a

Progress Monitoring *Online*
For: Self-test with vocabulary practice
Web Code: nea-1410

■ Struggle for Equality

Little Rock Central High — Integration of public schools — Brown v. Board of Education

Struggle for Equality

Montgomery bus boycott

Voter registration drives — Voting rights — Equal access to public facilities — Sit-ins

Selma March

Freedom rides

■ Civil Rights Legislation

Civil Rights Act of 1964	• Banned segregation in public accommodations • Increased federal authority to enforce school desegregation • Outlawed discrimination in employment on basis of race, color, and sex
Twenty-fourth Amendment (1964)	• Eliminated poll tax as voting requirement
Voting Rights Act of 1965	• Banned literacy tests as voting requirement • Empowered the federal government to supervise voter registration and elections
Fair Housing Act of 1968	• Banned discrimination in housing

■ Civil Rights Organizations

Organization and Date Founded	Key People	Key Features
National Association for the Advancement of Colored People (NAACP) 1909	Thurgood Marshall	Focused on legal cases to end segregation and gain legal equality
Nation of Islam 1930	Elijah Muhammad; Malcolm X	Advocated separation of the races
Congress of Racial Equality (CORE) 1942	James Farmer	Organized peaceful protests to gain civil rights
Southern Christian Leadership Conference (SCLC) 1957	Martin Luther King, Jr.; Ralph Abernathy	Church-based group dedicated to nonviolent resistance; organized demonstrations and protest campaigns
Student Nonviolent Coordinating Committee (SNCC) 1960	James Lawson; Ella Baker; Stokely Carmichael	Grass-roots movement of young activists; organized voter education projects in the South
Black Panther Party 1966	Huey Newton; Bobby Seale	Militant group advocating armed confrontation; organized antipoverty programs

☑ Quick Study Timeline

1954
Supreme Court rules school segregation unconstitutional

1955
Bus boycott begins in Montgomery, Alabama

1957
Desegregation of Central High in Little Rock, Arkansas

In America

Presidential Terms Harry S. Truman 1945–1953   Dwight D. Eisenhower 1953–1961

1953   **1956**   **1959**

Around the World

1956
Crisis over Suez Canal

1959
Castro comes to power in Cuba

American Issues
●─●─● **Connector**

By connecting prior knowledge with what you have learned in this chapter, you can gradually build your understanding of enduring questions that still affect America today. Answer the questions below. Then, use your American Issues Connector study guide (or go online: www.PHSchool.com **Web Code:** neh-8703).

Issues You Learned About

● **Voting Rights** Minority groups in America sometimes have had to fight for their political rights.

1. Do you think the Voting Rights Act of 1965 did enough to ensure that African Americans would be allowed to exercise their voting rights? Consider the following:
   • the results of Freedom Summer
   • the number of African American elected officials before and after 1965
   • the percentage of southern African Americans registered to vote before and after 1965
   • the black power movement

● **Federal Power and States' Rights** The national government and the state governments sometimes disagree over the delegation of power.

2. *Brown* v. *Board of Education* sparked a clash between the federal government and several southern state governments. Describe an earlier incident in which the federal government and state government disagreed over the authority of the federal government.

3. How did Arkansas governor Orval Faubus attempt to assert his authority over that of the Supreme Court? How did President Eisenhower respond on behalf of the federal government?

● **Sectionalism and National Politics** Different regions of the country often respond to events in contradictory ways.

4. Why was the civil rights movement centered in the South?

5. How do you think the South and the North responded to the Voting Rights Act of 1965? Explain.

Connect to Your World	**New York**

Women in American Society At a time when African Americans across the nation were fighting for civil rights, New Yorker Shirley Chisholm made her voice heard. Born in Brooklyn in 1924 to immigrant parents, Chisholm worked as a teacher and education consultant and participated in community and political groups in her district. From 1964 to 1968, she represented Brooklyn in the New York state legislature. In 1968, she began her service in the U.S. House of Representatives, becoming the first African American woman to be elected to Congress. Research other twentieth-century women who have taken leadership roles in New York and create a profile of one woman whose actions you find inspiring.

History *Interactive*.
For: Interactive timeline
Web Code: nep-1412

1960
Greensboro sit-ins

1963
King speaks at March on Washington

1965
Riots break out in Watts section of Los Angeles

1968
Martin Luther King, Jr., is assassinated

John F. Kennedy 1961–1963

Lyndon B. Johnson 1963–1969

1962

1965

1968

1961
East Germany builds the Berlin Wall

1962
Mandela is jailed in South Africa

1966
Cultural Revolution in China

Chapter Assessment

Terms and People

1. Who was **Martin Luther King, Jr.**? What did he achieve in his lifetime?

2. Define **sit-ins.** What response did the first sit-in of the civil rights movement—at a Woolworth's lunch counter in 1960—provoke throughout the South?

3. What did the **Civil Rights Act of 1964** accomplish? Who worked to push this bill through Congress?

4. What did the **Twenty-fourth Amendment** do? How did it help African Americans?

5. What was the **Kerner Commission**? What recommendations did it make?

Focus Questions

The focus question for this chapter is **What were the causes, main events, and effects of the civil rights movement?** Build an answer to this big question by answering the focus questions for Sections 1 through 3 and the Critical Thinking questions that follow.

Section 1
6. How did African Americans challenge segregation after World War II?

Section 2
7. How did the civil rights movement gain ground in the 1960s?

Section 3
8. What successes and challenges faced the civil rights movement after 1964?

Critical Thinking

9. **Decision Making** What reasoning did the Supreme Court apply in the *Brown* v. *Board of Education* ruling?

10. **Analyze Maps** Study the map below. What civil rights campaign does this map show? Was this campaign successful?

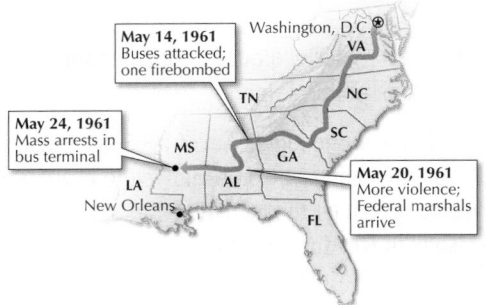

May 14, 1961 Buses attacked; one firebombed

Washington, D.C.

VA

TN

NC

May 24, 1961 Mass arrests in bus terminal

MS

SC

GA

LA

AL

May 20, 1961 More violence; Federal marshals arrive

New Orleans

FL

11. **Categorize** In what general areas did civil rights activists focus their efforts? List at least three general categories along with their key victories.

12. **Analyze Information** What role did television play in the civil rights movement of the 1950s and early 1960s? Do you think television contributed to the success of the movement? Explain.

13. **Comparing Points of View** How did Stokely Carmichael's and Martin Luther King, Jr.'s attitudes toward the civil rights movement differ?

14. **Express Problems Clearly** Why was affirmative action begun? Explain the controversy surrounding it.

Writing About History

Writing a Research Paper Write a hypothesis about one of the following aspects of the civil rights movement: the growth of de facto segregation in the North; the Montgomery bus boycott; the role of northern volunteers in the southern civil rights movement; the urban riots of the 1960s; the conflict between Malcolm X and Martin Luther King, Jr. Use your hypothesis as the basis of an essay that tests the hypothesis.

Prewriting
- Identify an unanswered question about the topic you have chosen.
- Write a one-sentence hypothesis that provides a possible answer to the question.
- Use the library or Internet to find three different sources of information that can be used to support or disprove your hypothesis.

Drafting
- Write an introductory paragraph in which you identify the question you are trying to answer and propose one hypothesis. Use your hypothesis as a thesis statement for the paragraph.
- In separate paragraphs, explain how each piece of evidence you have found either supports or disproves your hypothesis.
- Write a concluding paragraph in which you restate, modify, or reject your original hypothesis.

Revising
- Use the guidelines on page SH14 of the Writing Handbook to revise your writing.

Regents DBQ Practice

Civil Disobedience

During the 1960s, Martin Luther King, Jr., advocated the use of civil disobedience to end segregation in the South. What forms of civil disobedience were effective tools in ending segregation? Was nonviolence more effective than violence in achieving civil rights for African Americans? Use your knowledge of the civil rights movement and Documents 1, 2, 3, and 4 to answer questions 1 through 4.

Document 1

". . . Unjust laws exist; shall we be content to obey them, or shall we endeavor to amend them, and obey them until we have succeeded, or shall we transgress them at once? Men generally, under such a government as this, think that they ought to wait until they have persuaded the majority to alter them. They think that, if they should resist, the remedy would be worse than the evil. But it is the fault of the government itself that the remedy *is* worse than the evil. It makes it worse. Why is it not more apt to anticipate and provide for reform? Why does it not cherish its wise minority? Why does it cry and resist before it is hurt? Why does it not encourage its citizens to be on the alert to point out its faults, and do better than it would have them?"

—*Henry David Thoreau,* Civil Disobedience, *1849*

Document 2

"The only time I hear people talk about nonviolence is when black people move to defend themselves against white people. . . . White people beat up black people every day— Don't nobody talk about nonviolence. But as soon as black people start to move, the double standard comes into being. . . . We are on the move for our liberation. . . . We are concerned with getting the things we want, the things that we have to have to be able to function. . . . The question is, Will white people overcome their racism and allow for that to happen in this country? If that does not happen, brothers, and sisters, we have no choice but to say very clearly, 'Move over, or we're going to move on over you.'"

—*Stokely Carmichael speech, 1966*

Document 3

Birmingham, 1963

Document 4

"Oppressed people cannot remain oppressed forever. The yearning for freedom eventually manifests itself, and that is what has happened to the American Negro. . . . If one recognizes this vital urge that has engulfed the Negro community, one should readily understand why public demonstrations are taking place. The Negro has many pent-up resentments and latent frustrations, and he must release them. So let him march; let him make prayer pilgrimages to the city hall; let him go on freedom rides—and try to understand why he must do so. If his repressed emotions are not released in nonviolent ways, they will seek expression through violence; this is not a threat but a fact of history. So I have not said to my people: 'Get rid of your discontent.' Rather, I have tried to say that this normal and healthy discontent can be channeled into the creative outlet of nonviolent direct action."

—*Martin Luther King, Jr.,* "Letter From Birmingham Jail," *1963*

---

1. Which document advocates the use of violence if racism against African Americans is not ended?
   (1) Document 1
   (2) Document 2
   (3) Document 3
   (4) Document 4

2. According to Document 4, how does Martin Luther King, Jr., describe demonstrations such as freedom rides?
   (1) unjust laws
   (2) expression through violence
   (3) nonviolent direct action
   (4) discrimination

3. According to Document 1, what does Thoreau think about the role of government in addressing unjust laws?
   (1) The government should listen only to the majority viewpoint.
   (2) The government should listen to the minority viewpoint.
   (3) Violence should be used as an option to end oppression.
   (4) The public should be content with the laws.

4. **Writing Task** What do you think about the role of government depicted in Document 3? How does that image contrast with the ideas of King, Thoreau, and Carmichael? Use your knowledge of the chapter content and evidence from the primary sources above to support your opinion.

28 The Kennedy and Johnson Years

1960–1968

The Trumpet Summons Us

On January 20, 1961, John F. Kennedy was sworn in as President of the United States. His stirring Inaugural Address announced the dawn of a new era and rallied the nation to battle against the common enemies of man.

> "Now the trumpet summons us again—not as a call to bear arms, though arms we need—not as a call to battle, though embattled we are—but a call to bear the burden of a long twilight struggle, year in and year out, 'rejoicing in hope; patient in tribulation,' a struggle against the common enemies of man: tyranny, poverty, disease, and war itself. . . .
> And so, my fellow Americans, ask not what your country can do for you; ask what you can do for your country."
> —John F. Kennedy, Inaugural Address

The challenge of fulfilling these goals would inspire the agenda of President Kennedy and that of his successor, Lyndon B. Johnson. *Listen to the* Witness History *audio to learn more about the Kennedy and Johnson years.*

◄ Senator John F. Kennedy, the 1960 Democratic presidential candidate, is greeted by his supporters.

Kennedy campaign button

Peace Corps logo

 Core Curriculum Preview

Chapter Focus Question: How did the policies of Presidents Kennedy and Johnson affect the nation?

Section 1
Kennedy and the Cold War   6.II.D.4, 7.III.A.2, 7.III.A.2a, 7.III.A.2c, 7.III.A.2f

Section 2
Kennedy's New Frontier   7.III.A.1, 7.III.A.1a, 7.III.A.2g, 7.III.A.4

Section 3
Johnson's Great Society   7.II.C.1d, 7.III.B.1, 7.III.B.3c(1)

Use the ☑ **Quick Study Timeline** at the end of this chapter to preview chapter events.

The space rocket *Saturn V*

Note Taking Study Guide *Online*
For: Note Taking and American Issues Connector
Web Code: nee-8801

Kennedy campaign posters

The Democratic Candidate

During the election of 1960, John F. Kennedy's Catholicism became an important issue. Some Americans openly questioned whether a Catholic was independent enough from his church to serve as President. Kennedy dismissed such questions, insisting that a candidate's religion should not be a factor in running for office:

❝I am not the Catholic candidate for President. I am the Democratic Party's candidate for President, who happens also to be a Catholic.**❞**

—John F. Kennedy, address to Southern Baptist Leaders, 1960

Kennedy and the Cold War

Ⓝ Core Curriculum Objectives

- **6.II.D.4** Politics of the Cold War
- **7.III.A.2** Foreign policy and Cold War crises
- **7.III.A.2a** Bay of Pigs invasion
- **7.III.A.2c** Cuban missile crisis
- **7.III.A.2f** Peace Corps

Terms and People

John F. Kennedy	Bay of Pigs invasion
Richard M. Nixon	Nikita Khrushchev
Fidel Castro	Cuban missile crisis
flexible response	hot line
Peace Corps	Nuclear Test Ban Treaty
Alliance for Progress	Berlin Wall

NoteTaking

Reading Skill: Understand Effects As you read, list the Cold War crises Kennedy faced and the effects of each event.

Cold War Crisis	Result
Bay of Pigs Invasion	

Why It Matters As the Cold War continued into the 1960s, Kennedy took office facing the spread of communism abroad and the threat of nuclear war. Determined to succeed where he felt Eisenhower had failed, Kennedy's enthusiasm and commitment to change offered the hope that with hard work and persistence the United States could win the Cold War. **Section Focus Question: How did Kennedy respond to the continuing challenges of the Cold War?**

Kennedy Defeats Nixon in 1960

For eight years, President Dwight Eisenhower had presided over a nation that had generally enjoyed peace and prosperity. But even so, there were a number of issues that caused Americans grave concern. The launch of *Sputnik 1* showed that the rivalry between the United States and the Soviet Union was still intense. The U-2 spy plane incident demonstrated that the Cold War might heat up at a moment's notice. The Montgomery bus boycott provided clear evidence that the *Brown* decision had not ended racial discrimination in the land. Deep, unsettled problems remained—problems for a new decade and a new generation of political leadership.

The Candidates In the presidential election of 1960, Democrat **John F. Kennedy** and Republican **Richard M. Nixon** were quite similar in a variety of ways. For the first time in U.S. history, both candidates had been born in the twentieth century, Nixon in 1913 and Kennedy in 1917. Both had served in the navy during World War II.

Both had been elected to Congress in 1946 and to the Senate in the early 1950s. Both were passionate about foreign affairs and supported the Cold War fight against communism. Young and energetic, intelligent and hard-working, both wanted to be the first of their generation to lead the country.

Their differences, however, were as significant as their similarities. Kennedy was the son of a wealthy Boston businessman. His grandfather had been a state senator, and his father had served as the ambassador to Great Britain. Kennedy attended Harvard University. Although he was a Catholic and his religion was an issue in the election, he insisted that what church he attended should not be a factor.

Nixon, born in California, did not enjoy the advantages of a wealthy upbringing. His father struggled to make a living. As a young man, Nixon had to balance his time between his school studies and work to help support the family. Many voters, however, respected him for his experiences as Vice President under Eisenhower.

Televised Debates Make the Difference The 1960 election highlighted the growing power and influence of television. The candidates agreed to four televised debates. During the campaign, Nixon was hospitalized with a knee infection. After getting out of the hospital, he committed himself to a grueling schedule of public appearances. By the time of the first debate, held in late September in Chicago and watched by about 70 million people, Nixon looked pale and exhausted. Nixon arrived at the television studio an hour early, but he refused the offer to have makeup applied to hide his newly-growing beard. By contrast, Kennedy, tanned from open-air campaigning in California, looked healthy and confident. His relaxed manner, easy charm, and quick sense of humor added to his appeal.

In many ways, the debate boiled down to how the candidates looked and spoke, rather than what they said. Most Americans who listened to the debate on radio believed that Nixon had won. But the larger audience who watched the debate on television concluded that Kennedy was the clear victor. Although Nixon tried to change his image in the later debates, he was unable to significantly alter the country's initial impression of him. Kennedy's "victory" in the Chicago debate proved crucial in the election.

Kennedy Wins a Close Election Kennedy not only looked better on television, he also demonstrated an ability to react more quickly to unexpected events. For example, several weeks before the election, civil rights leader Martin Luther King, Jr., and a group of African American students were imprisoned during a protest in Atlanta, Georgia. Nixon said nothing publicly about the episode. Kennedy, however, telephoned King's wife, Coretta Scott King, to express his concern. He also worked behind the scenes to obtain King's release on bail. Kennedy's actions attracted the strong support of African Americans in the election.

The election of 1960 was the tightest presidential election since 1888.

Televised Debate
Richard Nixon (left) and John Kennedy (right) face each other in a televised debate. Kennedy won the election by a slim margin. *How did TV change political campaigns?*

The Presidential Election of 1960				
Candidate	Electoral Vote	Popular Vote	% Electoral Vote	% Popular Vote
John Kennedy (Democrat)	303	34,227,096	56.4	49.7
Richard Nixon (Republican)	219	34,107,646	40.8	49.6

In an election that witnessed the largest voter turnout in the country's history, Kennedy won by less than 120,000 of the 68 million popular votes cast. Had a few thousand people voted differently in Illinois and Texas, the election would have gone to Nixon. Kennedy's electoral victory was more convincing. He carried enough states to give him 303 electoral votes to Nixon's 219.

✓ **Checkpoint** How did the television debates affect the 1960 presidential election?

Kennedy Launches New Cold War Strategies

John Kennedy's 1960 campaign stressed the need for the United States to move forward with vigor and determination. Kennedy argued that during the Eisenhower years America had lost ground in the Cold War struggle against communism. He pointed to the new communist regime under **Fidel Castro** in Cuba and charged that there was now a "missile gap" that left the U.S. nuclear missile force inferior to that of the Soviet Union. The first goal of the Kennedy administration would be to build up the nation's armed forces.

Nowhere was the difference between Eisenhower and Kennedy more evident than in two important 1961 addresses. In his Farewell Address, Eisenhower counseled caution in foreign affairs. "The potential for the disastrous rise of misplaced power exists and will persist," he said.

Comparing Viewpoints

How Should the United States Fight the Cold War?

Both Presidents Eisenhower and Kennedy were strongly committed to containing communism. Their differences lay in their beliefs about the amount of military spending needed to carry out their goals.

DWIGHT D. EISENHOWER

In spite of numerous Cold War challenges, Eisenhower prided himself on having maintained peace. In his Farewell Address, he warned Americans about the effects of heavy defense spending.

Primary Source

"We annually spend on military security more than the net income of all United States corporations. . . . This . . . immense military establishment . . . is new in the American experience. We recognize the . . . need for this development. Yet we must not fail to comprehend its grave implications. Our toil, resources and livelihood are all involved."

JOHN F. KENNEDY

Determined to prepare the United States against nuclear attack, Kennedy supported programs that resulted in a $6 billion rise in defense spending. He defends his action in a State of the Union address:

Primary Source

"Our moral and physical strength begins at home. . . . But it includes our military strength as well. . . . [W]e must arm to deter others from aggression. We have increased the previous defense budget . . . not in the expectation of war but for the preservation of peace."

Compare
1. How does Eisenhower's plan for containing communism differ from Kennedy's?
2. Which plan may have prevented an attack on the United States? Explain.

As the first President born in this century, Kennedy proclaimed that a "new generation of Americans" was ready to meet any challenge. In his Inaugural Address, Kennedy warned his country's enemies:

Primary Source "Let every nation know, whether it wishes us well or ill, that we shall pay any price, bear any burden, meet any hardship, support any friend, oppose any foe to assure the survival and the success of liberty."
—John F. Kennedy, Inaugural Address, January 20, 1961

Kennedy issued a challenge to Americans: "Ask not what your country can do for you; ask what you can do for your country."

Building the Nation's Military Eisenhower's defense policy of "massive retaliation" had emphasized the construction of nuclear weapons. Although Kennedy did not ignore the possibility of a nuclear war, he wanted to make sure that the United States was prepared to fight both conventional wars and conflicts against guerrilla forces. Kennedy therefore gave increased funding to conventional United States Army and Navy forces as well as to Army Special Forces, such as the Green Berets. He wanted a **"flexible response"** defense policy, one that prepared the United States to fight any type of conflict.

Pursuing New Initiatives in the "Third World" The "Third World," as it was known at the time, was the developing nations in Africa, Asia, and Latin America that did not <u>align</u> with the United States or the Soviet Union. According to Soviet propaganda, Western capitalism created poverty and inequalities in the Third World, whereas communism promoted equality.

Like previous American leaders, Kennedy believed that democracy combined with prosperity would contain or limit the spread of communism. Therefore, he initiated programs to economically and politically strengthen the Third World. The **Peace Corps,** created in 1961, sent American volunteers around the world on "missions of freedom" to assist developing countries. They worked to provide technical, educational, and health services. Other programs stressed purely economic development. The **Alliance for Progress** promised to resurrect America's Good Neighbor policy toward Latin America. During the 1950s, many Latin Americans had grown increasingly resentful of the United States, claiming that it had too much influence in their region. Kennedy hoped to change that view with this program. It promoted economic assistance to Latin America. Unlike the Peace Corps, the Alliance for Progress was not successful.

✔ **Checkpoint** What strategies did Kennedy use to improve relations between the United States and developing countries?

Kennedy's Plan
Special fighting forces (left), such as the Green Berets, were ready at all times for any attack. But Kennedy's Cold War strategy also involved creating goodwill among nations. The establishment of the Peace Corps (right) fulfilled that goal. *How could the Peace Corps help America win the Cold War?*

Vocabulary Builder
<u>align</u>—(uh LiN) *v.* to decide to publicly support or not support a political group or country

Confronting Communism in Cuba

Vocabulary Builder

regime–(ruh ZHEEM) *n.*
particular administration or
government

In 1959, Cuban revolutionary Fidel Castro had succeeded in overthrowing the regime of Fulgencio Batista. Initially, the United States attempted to cultivate good relations with Castro. However, it soon became clear that the Cuban leader was determined to nationalize land held by private U.S. citizens, enforce radical reform measures, and accept Soviet economic and military aid. Thousands of wealthy and middle-class Cubans fled their country, many settling in Miami and southern Florida. Proud of their heritage and deeply anticommunist, they made new lives for themselves and their families in the United States.

Bay of Pigs Invasion After breaking diplomatic relations with Cuba in 1961, the Eisenhower administration authorized the Central Intelligence Agency (CIA) to plan an invasion of Cuba to overthrow Castro. The CIA recruited Cuban exiles and trained them in Guatemala. But when Eisenhower left office, the invasion plan was still that—an unexecuted, untried plan.

Pressured by members of the CIA and his own aides, Kennedy decided to implement the plan. On April 17, 1961, a CIA-led force of Cuban exiles attacked Cuba in the **Bay of Pigs invasion.** The invasion was badly mismanaged. The poorly equipped forces landed at the site with no protective cover. All but 300 of the 1,400 invaders were killed or captured. Not only did the Bay of Pigs invasion fail, it probably strengthened Castro's position in Cuba. It also turned many Cuban Americans against Kennedy.

Kennedy took personal responsibility for the failed invasion. However, he emphasized that the United States would continue to resist "communist penetration" in the Western Hemisphere.

Effects of the Cuban Missile Crisis ☑ Quick Study

- The Soviet Union removes missiles from Cuba.
- The United States removes missiles from Turkey.
- The United States and the Soviet Union avoid nuclear war.
- Kennedy and Khrushchev establish a "hot line" telephone system to keep communications open.
- In 1963, the United States, Great Britain, and the Soviet Union sign the Nuclear Test Ban Treaty.

WITNESS HISTORY DVD

Watch *Showdown: The Cuban Missile Crisis* on the **United States Witness History DVD** to explore the tense confrontation between the United States and the Soviet Union that nearly resulted in a nuclear war.

The Cuban Missile Crisis Kennedy's efforts to contain communism were severely threatened during the **Cuban missile crisis.** In August and September of 1962 U.S. intelligence discovered that the Soviets were building nuclear missile sites in Cuba, apparently to protect Castro from another American invasion. When the sites were completed, major East Coast cities and the Panama Canal would be in range of the missiles.

Kennedy demanded the removal of the missiles. In a dramatic television address on October 22, 1962, he blamed **Nikita Khrushchev,** the Soviet premier, for causing a "reckless and provocative threat to world peace." He also announced that he had approved a naval quarantine (blockade) of Cuba to prevent the Soviets from completing the bases. Behind the scenes, however, Kennedy worked toward a diplomatic settlement. He indicated that he would remove U.S. missiles in Turkey and Italy if the Soviets removed their missiles in Cuba.

After six tense days when nuclear war seemed a real possibility, Khrushchev agreed to honor the blockade and remove the missiles. As Secretary of State Dean Rusk later told a reporter, "Remember, when you report this, that, eyeball to eyeball, they blinked first."

The Results of the Crisis During the Cuban missile crisis, Kennedy and Khrushchev stood on the edge of a nuclear war and then slowly backed away. In the Soviet Union, Khrushchev lost prestige and more hard-line leaders chipped away at his power. In the United States, Kennedy emerged as a more mature and thoughtful leader, one who had faced a frightening test and had remained calm and resolute. The crisis prompted both leaders to move toward détente. They installed a **"hot line"** telephone system between Moscow and Washington, D.C.,

The Cuban Missile Crisis

Geography *Interactive*
For: Interactive map
Web Code: nep-1502

Gulf of Mexico

84°W   80°W   76°W

24°N

Havana

San Cristobal

Isle of Pines

Bay of Pigs site

Santa Clara

Trinidad

CUBA

Caribbean Sea

20°N

Guantanamo Bay

	Soviet missile base
	U.S. naval blockade
	U.S. naval base

Miller Projection

0   50   100 mi

0   50   100 km

Aerial photographs such as the one below, taken by an American U-2 spy plane, revealed the presence of Soviet missile bases in Cuba.

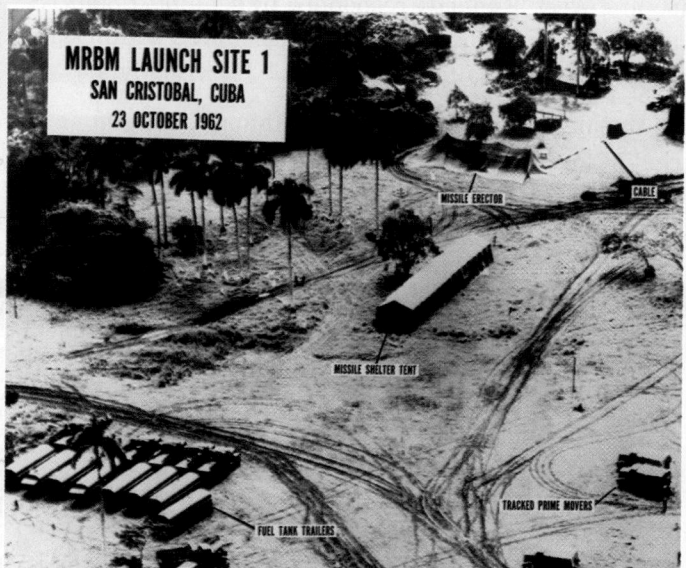

MRBM LAUNCH SITE 1
SAN CRISTOBAL, CUBA
23 OCTOBER 1962

MISSILE ERECTOR

CABLE

MISSILE SHELTER TENT

FUEL TANK TRAILERS

TRACKED PRIME MOVERS

Cuban Missile Bases

Conic Projection

0   250   500 mi

0   250 500 km

2,000 miles, 17 minutes

Chicago

New York

Washington, D.C.

UNITED STATES

Los Angeles

2,299 miles

1,500 miles, 15 minutes

1,000 miles, 12 minutes

Atlanta

761 miles

1,333 miles

1,139 miles

1,317 miles

CUBA

The location of missile bases in Cuba posed an immediate threat to several major American cities.

Map Skills Kennedy, aware of the Soviet arms buildup in Cuba, faced a difficult crisis.

1. **Place** Which U.S. city shown on the map was in the greatest danger from a nuclear attack? How long would it take a missile to reach that city?

2. **Draw Conclusions** How did the crisis affect U.S. relations with Cuba and the Soviet Union?

to improve communication. In 1963, the year after the crisis, the United States, Great Britain, and the Soviet Union signed the **Nuclear Test Ban Treaty,** the first nuclear-weapons agreement, which ended aboveground nuclear tests. Thirty-six other nations soon signed the agreement.

✔ **Checkpoint** Why was the United States concerned about the missile sites in Cuba?

The Berlin Crisis

Since 1958, Khrushchev wanted to sign a peace treaty that would put the western zones of Berlin under control of East Germany. His actions were motivated by the steady flow of skilled East German workers into West Berlin. Desiring to show his strength, Kennedy stood firm on America's commitment to defending the rights of West Berliners and West Germans. At a conference in Vienna in June 1961, Kennedy and Khrushchev focused on Berlin as the key issue. Khrushchev called the present situation "intolerable." He demanded that the United States recognize the formal division of Germany and end its military presence in West Berlin. Kennedy refused. He did not want to give up occupation rights he considered critical to defending Western Europe. In a tense atmosphere, Khrushchev said, "I want peace, but if you want war, that is your problem." Kennedy answered, "It is you, not I who wants to force a change." The meeting ended abruptly. The conference, meant to relax Cold War tensions, only increased them.

After returning home, both world leaders made moves that threatened the peace. Kennedy asked Congress to dramatically increase military spending. Khrushchev ordered the construction of a wall between East and West Berlin. The **Berlin Wall** became a visible symbol of the reality of the two Germanys and the gulf between the communist East and democratic West. Kennedy responded by sending 1,500 U.S. troops to West Berlin. For a time, Russian and American tanks moved within sight of each other. Yet, neither side could fully claim a victory.

✔ **Checkpoint** How did the meeting in Vienna affect relations between Kennedy and Khrushchev?

SECTION 1 Assessment

Progress Monitoring Online
For: Self-test with vocabulary practice
Web Code: nea-1503

Comprehension

1. **Terms and People** For each item below, explain its significance to the relations between the United States and the Soviet Union.
   - John F. Kennedy
   - Fidel Castro
   - Bay of Pigs invasion
   - Cuban missile crisis
   - Nikita Khrushchev
   - Berlin Wall

2. **Note****Taking Reading Skill: Understand Effects** Use your chart to answer the Section Focus Question: How did Kennedy respond to the continuing challenges of the Cold War?

Writing About History

3. **Quick Write: Support a Point of View** Identify one point of view regarding President Kennedy's actions in starting the Peace Corps. List three arguments in favor of this point of view. Then, prioritize them by identifying the most persuasive argument.

Critical Thinking

4. **Draw Conclusions** Television played an important role in the 1960 presidential election. How influential is television in presidential elections today? Explain.

5. **Synthesize Information** The flexible response policy increased the military budget. How do you think this affected the nuclear arms race?

6. **Identify Point of View** How did the Cuban missile crisis affect public opinion about President Kennedy?

SECTION 2

▲ President Kennedy with prominent civil rights and labor leaders in 1963. Dr. Martin Luther King, Jr., is at the far left.

WITNESS HISTORY   AUDIO

Civil Rights

Although Kennedy did not have a strong civil rights record while in the Senate, he did portray himself as a crusader for African American rights during his campaign. Toward the end of his presidency, he abandoned his cautious approach. In a special report to the American people on civil rights, he talked about the racial inequality that had long endured in the nation:

❝It ought to be possible for American students of any color to attend any public institution. . . . It ought to be possible for American consumers of any color to receive equal service in places of public accommodation . . . and it ought to be possible for American citizens of any color to register and to vote in a free election. . . . We preach freedom around the world, and we mean it, and we cherish it here at home, but are we to say to the world and, much more importantly, to each other that this is the land of the free except for the Negroes . . .?❞

—John F. Kennedy, June 11, 1963

Kennedy's New Frontier

NY **Core Curriculum Objectives**

- **7.III.A.1** The New Frontier: dreams and promises
- **7.III.A.1a** Civil rights actions
- **7.III.A.2g** Launching the race to the Moon
- **7.III.A.4** Assassination in Dallas

Terms and People

New Frontier
Equal Pay Act
deficit spending

space race
Warren Commission

NoteTaking

Reading Skill: Identify Main Ideas List the characteristics of John F. Kennedy's style that appealed to the American people.

The Kennedy Image
• Youthful
•
•

Why It Matters Kennedy's determination to change life at home resulted in his domestic agenda called the New Frontier. Faced with a conservative Congress, Kennedy met with opposition as he fought to turn his vision into a reality. Still, he had some success in making changes in Social Security benefits, dealing with poverty and racial discrimination, and spurring new interest and expectations for the space program. **Section Focus Question: What were the goals of Kennedy's New Frontier?**

The Kennedy Style

As John Kennedy showed in his 1960 campaign and in his Inaugural Address, he had a special quality—or charisma—that separated him from other politicians. With his exquisitely tailored clothes, quick smile, and sense of humor, he seemed closer to a movie star than to a run-of-the-mill politician. Although he suffered many health problems, he projected youthful health and energy.

He surrounded himself with other distinguished men. Reporters dubbed them "the best and the brightest." They came from some of the country's most prestigious businesses and universities. Robert McNamara, president of Ford Motor Company, agreed to serve as Secretary of Defense. Dean Rusk, president of the Rockefeller

The Kennedy Family
The new First Family charmed Americans with their youth and energy. Often, the President's children, Caroline and John, Jr., visited their father in the Oval Office.

Foundation, signed on as Secretary of State. Arthur Schlesinger, Jr., a Pulitzer Prize-winning historian, worked at the White House as a spokesperson for liberal causes and was a source of ideas for the President.

President Kennedy promised Americans that his administration would blaze a **"New Frontier."** The term described Kennedy's proposals to improve the economy, education, healthcare, and civil rights. He also hoped to jump-start the space program. In his presidential acceptance speech on July 15, 1960, in Los Angeles, California, Kennedy said,

> **Primary Source** "I stand tonight facing west on what was once the last frontier. . . . From the lands that stretch three thousand miles behind me, the pioneers of old gave up their safety, their comforts and sometimes their lives to build a new world here in the West. . . . But the problems are not all solved and the battles are not all won, and we stand today on the edge of a new frontier—the frontier of the 1960s—the frontier of unknown opportunities and perils—a frontier of unfulfilled hopes and threats."
>
> —John F. Kennedy, July 15, 1960

✓ **Checkpoint** Why did people feel that Kennedy was a different kind of politician?

Kennedy's Domestic Program

Early in his presidency, occupied by events in Cuba and Berlin, Kennedy devoted most of his attention to foreign affairs. But by 1963 he had become more concerned about pressing problems at home.

Kennedy—like millions of other Americans—was troubled by the high levels of poverty in the United States. *The Other America*, Michael Harrington's best-selling and influential 1962 exposé of poverty in America, shocked Kennedy and many other Americans.

While Kennedy failed to get Congress to accept his more ambitious social programs, he did push through an increase in the minimum wage, an extension in Social Security benefits, and improvements in the welfare system.

In addition, in 1962 Kennedy established the President's Commission on the Status of Women, a blue-ribbon panel that studied how poverty and

NoteTaking

Reading Skill: Identify Main Ideas As you read, identify details of Kennedy's domestic program.

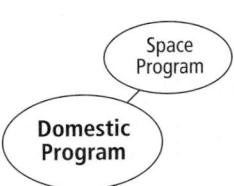

Space Program

Domestic Program

discrimination affected women. The differences in wages received by men and women for the same work was an especially glaring problem. The **Equal Pay Act** (1963) required equal wages for "equal work" in industries engaged in commerce or producing goods for commerce. Although it contained various loopholes, the law was a <u>crucial</u> step on the road to fair and equal employment practices. The next year Congress would prohibit discrimination by employers on the basis of race, color, religion, national origin, or sex.

Vocabulary Builder
<u>crucial</u>–(CROO shuhl) *adj.* of vital importance

Stimulating a Sluggish Economy Kennedy believed that increased prosperity would help to eliminate some of the nation's social problems. When he became President, the country was suffering from a high unemployment rate and a sluggish economy. To help the sagging economy, Kennedy proposed tax credits to encourage business investment in new factory equipment. At the same time, increased military spending created new jobs and boosted the economy. Finally, Kennedy accepted the "new economics" of theorist John Maynard Keynes that <u>advocated</u> **deficit spending** to stimulate the economy. Deficit spending is the government practice of borrowing money in order to spend more than is received from taxes. In 1963, Kennedy called for dramatic tax cuts for middle-class Americans as a way to put more money in the pockets of more people. At the same time, he increased the tax burden on wealthier citizens. Kennedy's economic initiatives jump-started the tremendous economic growth of the late 1960s.

Vocabulary Builder
<u>advocate</u>–(AD vuh kayt) *v.* to speak or write in support of; be in favor of

Moving Cautiously on Civil Rights Kennedy pursued a timid approach toward civil rights. He had narrowly won the 1960 election, and he had little real influence in Congress or even complete partisan support. He did not want to anger conservative, white southern members of Congress in his own party. They stood ready to block any civil rights legislation.

While Kennedy remained largely passive on civil rights issues, African Americans and their white allies challenged segregation in the South. In 1961, they took "freedom rides" to desegregate interstate bus travel. In 1963, Martin Luther King, Jr., took the civil rights struggle to Birmingham, Alabama. Such actions took courage and were met by angry, oftentimes violent, responses by white southerners.

In early 1963, Kennedy introduced a civil rights bill that demanded prosecution for voting-rights violations and federal money to aid school desegregation. Further violence in the South prompted Kennedy to introduce stronger civil rights legislation.

Racing Into Space The launching of the satellite *Sputnik 1* by the Soviet Union in 1957 called into question American technological superiority. Although Congress created the National Aeronautics and Space Administration (NASA) in 1958, the Soviets' space program remained several steps ahead of the American program. In April 1961, for example, the Soviet cosmonaut Yuri Gagarin became the first human to orbit Earth.

Kennedy recognized that the United States and the Soviet Union were locked in a **"space race."** *Space race* was the term used to describe the competition between the Soviet Union and the United States to develop technology to successfully land on the moon. In May 1961, NASA put astronaut Alan Shepard into a suborbital space flight aboard the Project Mercury space capsule *Freedom 7*. Encouraged by the success of Project Mercury, Kennedy committed the United States to landing a man on the moon by 1970.

---from <u>Straight Herblock</u>
(Simon & Schuster, 1964)

Analyzing Political Cartoons

Civil Rights This cartoon, titled "Eclipse," appeared in 1963, at a time when the civil rights struggle reached national prominence.
1. Define *eclipse*. Why do you think the cartoonist chose this title?
2. Do you think all Americans responded the same way to this cartoon? Explain.

SPACE EXPLORATION

After the successful space flight of Soviet cosmonaut Yuri Gagarin in April 1961, President Kennedy announced the goal of the United States to place a man on the moon before the end of the decade. In July 1969, the launching of the *Apollo 11* (shown left) was the first successful manned mission to land on the moon. Nearly forty years later, President Bush would announce his vision for the program—continued missions to the moon and further exploration of Mars.

Ed White ▶ floats outside *Gemini 4* during a mission in 1965.

▲ President Kennedy congratulates Alan Shepard.

▲ By 1995, Soviet and American crew members worked together on MIR, the Russian space station.

October 1958 NASA is created.

May 1961 Alan Shepard becomes the first American to make a space flight.

February 1962 John Glenn is the first American to orbit Earth.

January 1967 Fire kills *Apollo* astronauts Roger Chaffee, Virgil Grissom, and Edward White.

July 1969 *Apollo 11* astronauts successfully land on the moon.

June 1976 *Viking 1* transmits the first close-up images of Mars.

January 1986 Spacecraft *Challenger* explodes 73 seconds after takeoff. Seven astronauts are killed.

April 1990 Hubble Space Telescope is launched.

April 1997 *Pathfinder* lands on Mars.

November 1998 Construction of the International Space Station begins.

November 2000 The first crew takes residence in the International Space Station.

Edwin Aldrin stands ▶ on the surface of the moon next to the American flag in 1969.

Thinking Critically

1. **Identify Causes** How did international competition lead to space exploration?

2. **Identify Central Issues** How did the loss of *Challenger* lead Americans to reexamine the costs and benefits of the space program?

America's quest to reach the moon was punctuated by enormous successes and heartbreaking failures. Astronaut John Glenn became the first American to orbit Earth in February 1962. But astronauts Virgil Grissom, Edward White, and Roger Chaffee burned to death when their docked capsule exploded in fire during a routine test. Finally, in July of 1969, astronaut Neil Armstrong left his spacecraft *Columbia*'s landing vehicle and became the first man to step on the moon. The mission was a successful completion of Kennedy's bold dream.

✔ **Checkpoint** Why did Kennedy change the way in which he addressed civil rights issues?

The President Is Assassinated

During his first two and a half years in office, Kennedy made the transition from politician to national leader. In foreign affairs he confronted Soviet challenges, made hard decisions, and won the respect of Soviet leaders and American citizens. He also spoke eloquently about the need to move toward a peaceful future. In domestic affairs he finally came to the conclusion that the federal government had to lead the struggle for civil rights. Added to his new maturity was his ability to inspire Americans to dream noble dreams and work toward lofty ends.

In November 1963, Kennedy traveled to Dallas, Texas, to mend political fences for his 1964 reelection bid. He never lived to see 1964. While his motorcade moved through the city, assassin Lee Harvey Oswald, perched by a window on the sixth floor of the Texas School Book Depository, fired three shots at the President. The third shot hit Kennedy in the back of his head. A half hour later, doctors at Parkland Memorial Hospital pronounced him dead. Texan Lyndon B. Johnson, Kennedy's Vice President, was sworn in as the new President. Although many people would later question whether Oswald acted alone, the **Warren Commission,** which conducted the official investigation of the assassination, described Oswald as the "lone killer."

The senseless murder deeply saddened Americans across the nation. Millions of people watched Kennedy's funeral procession on television, and many reacted as if they had lost a family member. It seemed as if part of America's innocence had died with him.

✔ **Checkpoint** What was the purpose of the Warren Commission?

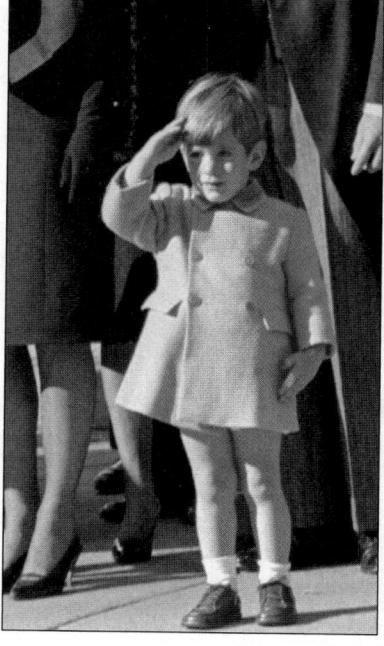

A Son's Farewell
John F. Kennedy, Jr., salutes his father's casket as it passes by in the funeral procession.

SECTION **2** **Assessment**

Progress Monitoring Online
For: Self-test with vocabulary practice
Web Code: nea-1504

Comprehension

1. **Terms and People** Discuss how each of the following terms met a goal of Kennedy's domestic program.
   • New Frontier
   • Equal Pay Act
   • deficit spending

2. **NoteTaking Reading Skill: Identify Main Ideas** Use your concept web to answer the Section Focus Question: What were the goals of Kennedy's domestic program?

Writing About History

3. **Quick Write: Identify Counterarguments** Identify one point of view regarding President Kennedy's decision to move cautiously on civil rights. Then, identify one argument that someone might use *against* this point of view. Remember, an effective counterargument does not simply state that the original argument was wrong but gives specific reasons for the opposing point of view.

Critical Thinking

4. **Analyze Information** Why did Kennedy consider foreign policy to be the most important issue of his administration?

5. **Draw Inferences** Why do you think Kennedy called his domestic program the New Frontier?

6. **Draw Conclusions** Was Kennedy's commitment to the space program an extension of the Cold War? Explain.

Can a Poor Person Get a Fair Trial?

7.III.B.7b

The Sixth Amendment gives a person accused of a crime the right to "the assistance of counsel." But what about poor defendants? They don't have the money to pay for a lawyer. If a poor person goes to trial without a lawyer and is convicted, was justice done?

Gideon v. *Wainwright* (1963)

The Facts	The Issue	The Decision
• Clarence Gideon was tried in a Florida court for breaking into a building. • Gideon said he was too poor to afford a lawyer and asked the court to appoint one. • After the judge refused, Gideon defended himself and was found guilty.	Gideon claimed he had been denied his rights to an attorney and to due process.	The Supreme Court ruled unanimously that Florida should have provided an attorney for Gideon.

Why It Matters

The Court's ruling in *Gideon* was forceful. All nine justices agreed that Florida should have given Gideon an attorney. They clearly stated why having an attorney is so important:

▲ Clarence Gideon

> "Any person hauled into court, who is too poor to hire a lawyer, cannot be assured a fair trial unless counsel is provided for him. This seems to us to be an obvious truth."

The decision had a tremendous impact on the country's legal system. Public defenders are state-paid officials who defend people who are too poor to hire their own lawyers.

But has the promise of *Gideon* been fulfilled? Critics say problems still remain. Many states do not fully fund the public defenders' offices that furnish lawyers for poor defendants. These defenders are overworked and underpaid, making it harder for them to do their job well. They lack the resources to hire experts to evaluate evidence. Many public defenders are not brought into a case as soon as a charge is made. This prevents them from properly advising their clients. Finally, public defenders do not have the time or resources to effectively carry out appeals to higher courts.

Connect to Your World

Research the use of public defenders in your state or community. Then, write an essay titled "*Gideon* Today," in which you explain whether you think the justice system is fair for poor people or not.

For: Supreme Court cases
Web Code: nee-1509

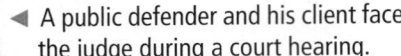

◀ A public defender and his client face the judge during a court hearing.

WITNESS HISTORY AUDIO

President Johnson's Hopes for America

In 1965, President Lyndon B. Johnson addressed a joint session of Congress. In the speech he talked about some of his hopes for America and how he wished to be remembered by history. He explained,

❝I do not want to be the President who built empires, or sought grandeur, or extended dominion. I want to be the President who educated young children . . . who helped to feed the hungry . . . who helped the poor to find their own way. . . .❞
—President Johnson, speech before Congress, March 15, 1965

◀ Lyndon Johnson is sworn in as President, in 1963, after Kennedy's assassination.

Johnson's Great Society

 Core Curriculum Objectives

- **7.II.C.1d** The Warren Court
- **7.III.B.1** Expanding on the Kennedy social programs: war on poverty, Medicare, education, environmental concerns
- **7.III.B.3c(1)** Legislative Impact: Civil Rights Act of 1964

Terms and People

Lyndon B. Johnson	Medicare
Civil Rights Act	Medicaid
War on Poverty	Immigration and
Economic Opportunity	Nationality Act of
Act	1965
Great Society	Warren Court

NoteTaking

Reading Skill: Identify Main Ideas Identify details about the Great Society programs.

The Great Society			
Education	Healthcare	Immigration	Poverty
•	• Medicare	•	•

Why It Matters **Lyndon B. Johnson,** who became President after Kennedy's assassination, shared the same goals as his predecessor. These goals shaped the purpose of Johnson's Great Society program. A seasoned politician, Johnson successfully pushed through significant domestic legislation that he hoped would become the first step to achieving the quality of life he thought all Americans should enjoy. **Section Focus Question: How did Johnson's Great Society programs change life for most Americans?**

Johnson's Rise to Leadership

Born in Stonewall, Texas, Lyndon B. Johnson was raised in the Hill Country town of Johnson City. He attended Southwest Texas State College and then taught for several years in Cotulla, Texas. There, at a tiny segregated school for Mexican Americans, he confronted firsthand the challenges faced by poverty-stricken minority students, and the lessons he learned remained with him for the rest of his life.

A Determined Texan After teaching for several years, Johnson entered politics—first as a Texas congressman's secretary and then as the head of the Texas National Youth Administration.

In 1937, Johnson was elected to Congress, and during the next several decades he became the most powerful person on Capitol Hill. Elected to the Senate in 1948, Johnson proved himself a master of party politics and rose to the position of Senate majority leader in 1955. In the Senate, he was adept at avoiding conflict, building political coalitions, and working out compromises. His skill was instrumental in pushing the 1957 Civil Rights Act through Congress.

In 1960, he hoped to be chosen by the Democratic Party to run for President, but when Kennedy got the nomination Johnson agreed to join him on the ticket as the vice presidential nominee. A New Englander and a Catholic, Kennedy needed Johnson to help carry the heavily Protestant South. Johnson was also popular both with Mexican American voters and in the Southwest. He was an important part of Kennedy's victory in 1960.

The Kennedy Legacy On becoming President after Kennedy's assassination, Johnson radiated reassurance and strength. His every action indicated that he was ready for the job and that the government was in good hands. Less than a week after the assassination, Johnson addressed a joint session of Congress.

> **Primary Source** "... [N]o memorial oration or eulogy could more eloquently honor President Kennedy's memory than the earliest possible passage of the Civil Rights Bill for which he fought so long."
> —President Johnson, speech before a Joint Session of Congress, 1963

With Johnson's ability to build consensus, or agreement on an issue by a group, the **Civil Rights Act** became law in the summer of 1964. It outlawed discrimination in voting, education, and public accommodations. The act demanded an end to discrimination in hospitals, restaurants, theaters, and other places open to the public. It also created the Equal Employment Opportunity Commission to fight discrimination in hiring. African Americans and Mexican Americans who faced almost daily discrimination benefited immeasurably from the legislation. Finally, Title VII of the 1964 Civil Rights Act prohibited discrimination on the basis of sex.

Johnson Declares a War on Poverty Johnson had made his intentions clear in his first State of the Union address when he said it was time to "declare an unconditional war on poverty." The new President planned to fuse his own dreams for America onto Kennedy's legislative agenda. Although Kennedy had failed to get Congress to approve his tax bill calling for dramatic tax cuts for middle-class Americans, Johnson was able to maneuver it through. In addition, he had added a billion-dollar **War on Poverty** to the bill.

Johnson's War on Poverty introduced measures to train the jobless, educate the uneducated, and provide healthcare for those in need. The 1964 **Economic Opportunity Act** created the Job Corps to train young men and women between the ages of 16 and 21 in the work skills they needed to acquire better jobs and move out of poverty. The act also established Volunteers in Service to America, or VISTA, patterned after Kennedy's Peace Corps, which sent American volunteers into poverty-stricken American communities in an effort to solve the country's pressing economic, educational, and medical problems. The volunteers served in inner-city schools and on Indian reservations. They worked in rural health clinics and urban hospitals.

Job Training
President Johnson visits a job training center in Texas. The success of Johnson's antipoverty programs is reflected in the declining numbers of Americans living below the poverty line.

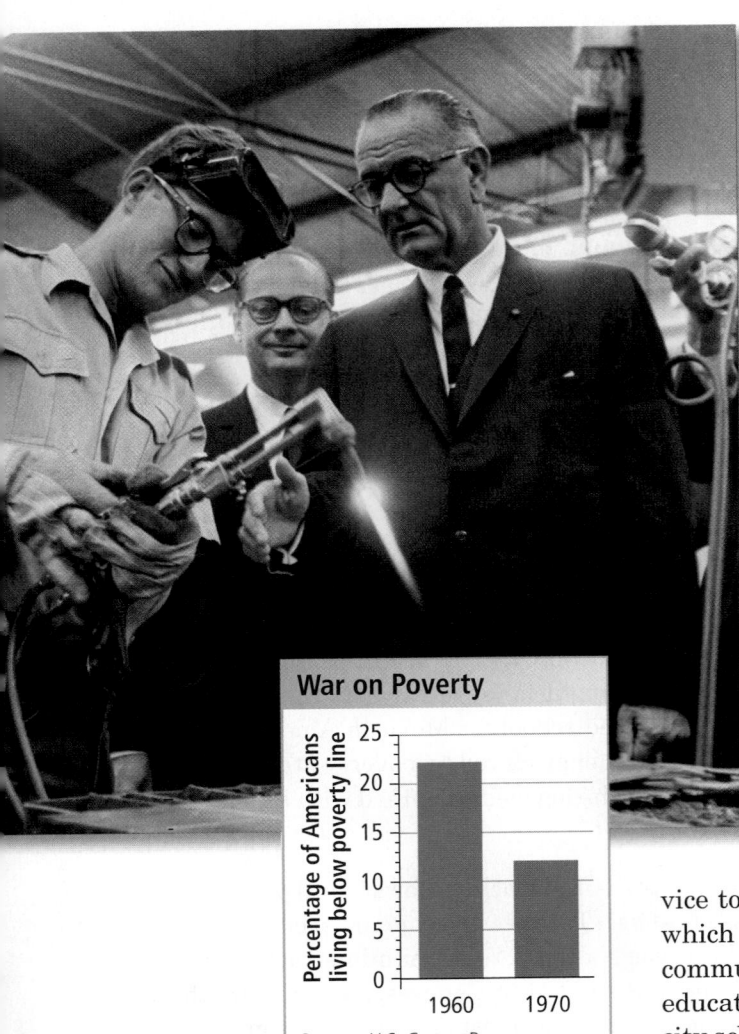

War on Poverty

Percentage of Americans living below poverty line

1960	1970
22	12

SOURCE: U.S. Census Bureau

Poverty and Prosperity

TRACK THE ISSUE

THE ESSENTIAL ?

How should Americans deal with the gap between rich and poor?

Over the years, Americans have tried to balance the extremes of wealth and poverty in society. Some have favored private charity to help the poor, while others have backed government policies to distribute wealth. Still, the gap remains. Use the timeline below to explore this enduring issue.

1800s Community Aid
Private charities provide aid for the poor.

1900 Poverty Level
An estimated 40 percent of Americans live in poverty.

1933 New Deal
Federal government provides aid for the poor.

1964 War on Poverty
President Johnson expands programs to reduce poverty.

1980s Reaganomics
President Reagan promotes business growth to reduce poverty.

1996 Welfare Reform
Government limits welfare programs.

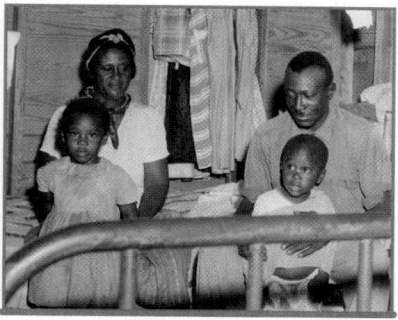

Migrant farm family in Virginia

Many workers, such as the grocery clerk shown here, hold minimum-wage jobs.

DEBATE THE ISSUE

The Minimum Wage The government has tried to reduce poverty for working people by setting a minimum wage. Supporters say this wage is too low to provide a decent living. Critics say an increase would hurt employers and make it harder for them to provide low-level jobs.

"We all lose when American workers are underpaid. It's a myth that small businesses can't pay a higher minimum wage. . . . When businesses don't pay a living wage, all society pays. We pay through poverty . . . [and] needless disease. . . . We pay as businesses and communities suffer economic decline."
—Margot Dorfman, CEO, U.S. Women's Chamber of Commerce

"Decades of economic research confirm that increasing the minimum wage destroys jobs for low-skilled workers while doing little to address poverty. When faced with higher labor costs, employers tend to hire fewer, more highly-skilled and experienced employees. That leaves unskilled or low-skilled workers . . . out in the cold."
—from The Economics Policy Institute

? TRANSFER Activities

1. **Compare** Why does Margot Dorfman support the minimum wage? Why does the Economic Policy Institute oppose it?

2. **Analyze** Would a minimum wage help reduce poverty? Explain.

3. **Transfer** Use the following Web site to see a video, try a WebQuest, and write in your journal. **Web Code:** neh-8802

Perhaps the most successful element of the Economic Opportunity Act was the Head Start program. Funds were provided for play groups, day care, and activities designed to help underprivileged children get ready for elementary school. Head Start enjoyed bipartisan support for decades.

Johnson Defeats Goldwater If Johnson was to continue his War on Poverty and other social goals, he needed to win the 1964 presidential election. In that year, the Republicans nominated Arizona senator Barry Goldwater, whose economic and social views were directly opposed to Johnson's. Whereas Johnson believed the federal government could best regulate the economy and promote social justice, Goldwater maintained that the federal government was the problem not the solution. According to Goldwater, social and economic issues, such as racism and poverty, should not be addressed by the federal government.

If elected, Goldwater would rein in the federal government by reducing its size and restricting its activities. He favored significant tax cuts and right-to-work laws, and he opposed social welfare legislation and government spending on educational, public housing, and urban renewal programs.

In 1964, most Americans were not ready either for Goldwater's belligerent tone or his conservative message. Johnson's campaign played up Goldwater's extremism, suggesting that his election would ensure the repeal of civil rights legislation and economic ruin.

Johnson had prosperity on his side, as well as his own impressive legislative record and the legacy of Kennedy. In the November election, he won a landslide

History *Interactive*

For: To discover more about the Great Society programs
Web Code: nep-1509

● **INFOGRAPHIC**

The Great Society
Arts and Education

At a 1965 news conference, President Johnson declared, "When I was young, poverty was so common that we didn't know it had a name. And education was something you had to fight for . . . ." Seemingly inspired by his own upbringing, Johnson set out to create the Great Society. The program included support for education and the arts.

▲ President Johnson signs the Higher Education Act on November 8, 1965, at the one-room schoolhouse near Stonewall, Texas, where his own education began.

▼ Project Head Start and the Elementary and Secondary Education Act committed the federal government to providing resources for individuals and schools. At left, a teacher works with students at a preschool program. Below, students work together in a school library.

victory, capturing more than 60 percent of the popular vote and carrying all but six states. Goldwater carried only Arizona and five southern states—Louisiana, Mississippi, Alabama, Georgia, and South Carolina. Furthermore, the <u>outcome</u> of the election was significant. The South was no longer solidly Democrat. Not only had Johnson won a ringing victory, but Democrats had captured both houses of Congress.

Vocabulary Builder
<u>outcome</u>–(OWT kuhm) *n.* final result of a meeting, process, or series of events

✓ **Checkpoint** How did Johnson continue Kennedy's plan to eliminate poverty in the United States?

The Great Society

In the spring of 1964, in a speech at the University of Michigan, Johnson outlined his vision for America, calling it the **Great Society.** He said that during the previous several centuries, Americans had spread across the continent, developed industrially, and created great wealth. But the work of America was not complete. He added,

> **Primary Source** "The challenge of the next half century is whether we have the wisdom to use that wealth to enrich and elevate our national life, and to advance the quality of our American civilization. . . . [W]e have the opportunity to move not only toward the rich society and the powerful society, but upward to the Great Society."
> —President Johnson, University of Michigan, May 22, 1964

For Johnson, the Great Society demanded "an end to poverty and racial injustice" and opportunity for every child.

◀ Public radio and television gained support through the sponsorship of the Corporation for Public Broadcasting. *Sesame Street*, featuring Big Bird and the Muppets, combines education and entertainment for children.

▲ The National Endowment for the Arts financially assists artists, arts education, and arts organizations. Wynton Marsalis (above) and Helen Frankenthaler (left) each won the National Medal of Honor.

Thinking Critically
1. **Draw Inferences** How might education programs be used to create a great society?
2. **Identify Point of View** Should the government provide funds to support the arts? Explain.

Healthier Citizens

President Johnson gave healthcare special attention. With Medicare and Medicaid, more Americans could receive basic healthcare.

Vocabulary Builder

overall–(OH ver awl) *adj.* including or considering everything

Healthcare Insurance In the first half of 1965, Congress passed parts of Johnson's Great Society legislation. Kennedy had supported similar legislation that failed to win congressional support. Johnson's agenda amended the Social Security Act by adding the Medical Care for the Aged Program, or **Medicare** as it was more popularly called. Medicare provided basic hospital insurance for Americans in the Social Security system who were age 65 and older. It also included a **Medicaid** feature that provided basic medical services to poor and disabled Americans who were not part of the Social Security system.

Johnson signed the bill into law in Independence, Missouri, home of former President Harry Truman, who had called for a national health insurance program almost 20 years earlier.

Education Along with health, education was one of the centerpieces of the Great Society program. Improved healthcare and education were necessary steps toward the goal of ending poverty. The 1965 Elementary and Secondary Education Act was designed to aid schools in poorer communities. It provided federal funds to improve school libraries, learning centers, language laboratories, and services in impoverished school districts. The act dramatically increased funding for Indian, inner city, and Mexican American schools.

Protecting the Environment and the Consumer The Great Society program extended to improving the overall quality of American life. In the early 1960s, several best-selling books raised Americans' awareness about environmental and consumer problems. Rachel Carson's *Silent Spring* (1962) detailed how chemical fertilizers and pesticides were damaging the fragile ecosystem. Ralph Nader's *Unsafe at Any Speed* (1965) attacked the automotive industry for its lack of concern for passenger safety.

Both these books helped to foster environmental and consumer activity and led to several important pieces of legislation. The Water Quality Act (1965) and the Clean Water Restoration Act (1966) aimed at improving water and air standards in the country. The National Traffic and Motor Vehicle Safety Act (1966) established safety standards for automotive vehicles.

New Immigration Policies Meanwhile, the civil rights movement was raising questions about America's long-standing immigration policy. The National Origins Acts of 1921 and 1924 had established a quota system that favored Western European immigrants and limited immigrants from other parts of the world. Such a discriminatory policy was clearly out of touch with the mood of the country in the early 1960s.

The **Immigration and Nationality Act of 1965** altered America's quota system. Nearly 170,000 immigrants from the Eastern Hemisphere were allowed into the country. Nearly 120,000 immigrants from the Western Hemisphere were welcomed. Immigrants from Latin America, Central America, the Caribbean, and Asia soon began to pour into the United States, providing the country with a pool of ideas, talent, and skills. During the 1960s and 1970s, millions of immigrants would arrive on American shores. Once again, the doors of America were open to immigrants from around the world. As in the late nineteenth and early twentieth centuries, New York and the urban East and West coasts attracted many of the country's newest immigrants.

The Legacy While the Great Society programs did not completely alter America, they did improve the lives of millions of individual Americans. Poverty and infant mortality rates declined. Medicare and Medicaid delivered needed healthcare to millions of elderly and poor Americans. Head Start and other anti-poverty programs provided the educational tools many underprivileged Americans needed to escape poverty. Furthermore, Congress also provided artists and scholars with assistance through the National Endowment for the Arts and Humanities, created in 1965. The Great Society victories may not have been as grandiose as Johnson predicted, but they were victories. The simple fact that 22.2 percent of all Americans lived below the poverty line in 1960 and 12.6 percent lived below the poverty line in 1970 says something about the triumphs of the Great Society.

✓ **Checkpoint** Which immigrant groups were affected by the Immigration and Nationality Act of 1965?

The Supreme Court and Reform

During the 1960s, the Supreme Court demonstrated a willingness to take the lead on controversial social, religious, and political issues. Led by Chief Justice Earl Warren, the Supreme Court at this time—often called the **Warren Court**—became the most liberal in American history. Its decisions supported civil rights, civil liberties, voting rights, and personal privacy.

Congressional Districts and Voters' Rights In several decisions the Supreme Court ruled in favor of the "one man, one vote" principle. The problem was one of apportionment of seats in state legislatures. During the twentieth century, large numbers of voters moved from rural to urban areas, but many state governments had not changed, or reapportioned, electoral districts to reflect the new conditions. This led to an electoral imbalance. In many states, rural areas had more power and urban areas had less power than their populations actually mandated.

In *Baker* v. *Carr* (1962), the Supreme Court ruled in favor of reapportionment on the basis of "one man, one vote." Electoral districts, it said, had to reflect the numbers of people in those districts. In *Reynolds* v. *Sims* (1964), the Court reaffirmed its decision, adding that any arrangement other than "one man, one vote" violated the equal protection clause of the Fourteenth Amendment.

HISTORY MAKERS

Earl Warren (1891–1974)
One of the country's most influential Chief Justices, Earl Warren was governor of California before being named to head the Supreme Court. As Chief Justice, he guided the Court to a unanimous ruling outlawing school segregation in *Brown* v. *Board of Education*. The Warren Court issued many landmark rulings in the areas of civil rights, criminal justice, First Amendment issues, and legislative districting. These decisions led many Americans to call for Warren's removal, though he remained on the Court until retiring in 1969.

Rights of the Accused The Warren Court also showed a heightened concern for the constitutional rights of accused lawbreakers. In four landmark cases, the Court broadened the individual rights of accused criminals and narrowed those of federal, state, and local government officials. In *Mapp* v. *Ohio* (1961), the Court ruled that evidence obtained illegally violated the Fourth Amendment and had to be excluded from federal and state trials. In *Gideon* v. *Wainwright* (1963), the Court decided that all accused criminals had the right to a lawyer whether or not they could pay for one. In *Escobedo* v. *Illinois* (1964), the Warren Court expanded on *Gideon* v. *Wainwright* by adding that every accused lawbreaker had to be offered access to a lawyer before questioning, and all evidence obtained from a suspect who had not been informed of his or her right to a lawyer could not be used in court. Finally, in *Miranda* v. *Arizona* (1966), the Court ruled that an accused criminal had to be informed of his or her Fifth and Sixth Amendment rights before being questioned.

Critics of these decisions argued that the Warren Court had tipped the balance of justice in favor of the rights of accused criminals. Today, many conservative justices still side with this opinion. The majority of the members of the Warren Court, however, have countered that the rights of individuals had to be protected, especially when freedom hung in the balance.

Separation of Church and State The Warren Court addressed the separation of church and state in the case of *Engel* v. *Vitale* (1962). The case involved whether or not a public school could require students to recite a state-sanctioned prayer. The Court ruled that school prayer was a violation of the First Amendment and an attempt by a governmental body to promote religion. The next year, the Court ruled in *Abington* v. *Schempp* that Bible reading in public schools also violated the First Amendment. The two decisions divided religious groups and the American people. Some welcomed the rulings, saying the government should have no say in personal religious matters. Others insisted the decisions were hostile to religion. The two decisions ignited, and continue to ignite, controversy. For more than 40 years, various religious groups have railed against these decisions.

 Checkpoint What major court ruling gave a person accused of a crime the right to have a lawyer?

Progress Monitoring *Online*
For: Self-test with vocabulary practice
Web Code: nea-1505

Comprehension

1. **Terms and People** Explain the relationship of the following terms to social reform.
   - War on Poverty
   - Great Society
   - Medicare
   - Medicaid

2. **NoteTaking Reading Skill: Identify Main Ideas** Use your chart to answer the Section Focus Question: How did Johnson's Great Society programs change life for most Americans?

Writing About History

3. **Quick Write: Chart Arguments and Counterarguments** Identify one point of view regarding the use of government funds to support massive social programs. Then, make a chart with two columns. In the first column, list two arguments in favor of that point of view. In the second column, list two arguments against that point of view.

Critical Thinking

4. **Make Comparisons** Were there differences in the goals of the New Frontier and the Great Society? Explain.

5. **Recognize Cause and Effect** How do you think the Immigration and Nationality Act of 1965 changed political activity in the nation?

6. **Identify Point of View** Why did some Americans feel that Supreme Court decisions during the 1960s considered only the rights of the poor?

What Rights Should an Accused Person Have?

Police officers try to obtain confessions from suspects. Yet, the Fifth Amendment protects people from self-incrimination—stating facts that will result in their being accused of a crime. The Sixth Amendment gives them the right to an attorney. How do those guaranteed rights come into play when a person is being questioned by police?

▲ A suspect is advised of his Miranda rights.

Miranda v. *Arizona* (1966)

The Facts	The Issue	The Decision
• Ernesto Miranda, under questioning by police, confessed that he had kidnapped and assaulted a woman. • Miranda was convicted in state court of the crimes in part because of the confession.	Miranda claimed the confession should not be used because police had not warned him of his right to avoid self-incrimination or to have a lawyer present.	A 5:4 majority ruled that the conviction should be thrown out because police had violated Miranda's rights when it obtained the confession.

Why It Matters

The majority based its reasoning on "the necessity for procedures which assure" the protection of Fifth Amendment rights. It spelled out those procedures:

“Prior to any questioning, the person must be warned that he has a right to remain silent, that any statement he does make may be used as evidence against him, and that he has a right to the presence of an attorney.”

That statement is familiar to many Americans from hearing it on television crime dramas. The majority also ruled that people who request a lawyer must be provided with one, even if they are too poor to pay for one themselves.

The decision has had a profound effect on the criminal justice system. Police officers must inform suspects of their rights. Only then can statements made by the suspect be used in a trial.

Connect to Your World

The Court addressed the issue of confessions by minors in *Yarborough* v. *Alvarado* (2004). Research the case. Write a summary that explains the facts, the Court's decision, Justice Sandra Day O'Connor's concerns about the rights of minors, and the views of the dissent.

For: Supreme Court Cases
Web Code: nee-1508

 7.III.B.7c

◀ A police officer holds the Miranda Warning card.

Quick Study Guide

7.II.C.1d,
7.III.A.1

Progress Monitoring *Online*
For: Self-test with vocabulary practice
Web Code: nea-1506

■ The New Frontier Paves the Way

New Frontier
• Anti-poverty legislation
• Peace Corps, Alliance for Progress
• Education legislation
• Healthcare legislation
• Civil rights goals

→

Great Society
• Economic Opportunity Act
• Volunteers in Service to America
• Head Start
• Medicare, Medicaid
• Civil Rights Act, 1964

■ NASA Spending 1950–1965

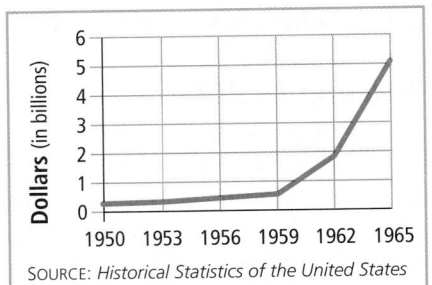

SOURCE: *Historical Statistics of the United States*

■ The Warren Court

Baker v. Carr

Mapp v. Ohio

Engel v. Vitale

Miranda v. Arizona

The Warren Court

Gideon v. Wainwright

Escobedo v. Illinois

Reynolds v. Sims

Abington v. Schempp

■ Cold War Challenges

Bay of Pigs	Berlin	Cuban Missile Crisis
• American CIA arms and trains anti-Castro forces.	• Kennedy meets with Khrushchev in Vienna.	• United States discovers Soviet missile sites in Cuba.
• Bay of Pigs invasion fails.	• East Germans and Soviets build Berlin Wall.	• Kennedy imposes blockade of Cuba.
• Soviets suspect weakness in Kennedy.	• In West Berlin, Kennedy delivers speech assuring West Germans of continued U.S. support.	• Khrushchev removes missiles from Cuba.

☑ Quick Study Timeline

In America

1961
Peace Corps established

1962
Cuban missile crisis

1963
President Kennedy assassinated

Presidential Terms   John F. Kennedy 1961–1963   Lyndon B. Johnson 1963–1969

1960   **1963**

Around the World

1961
Berlin Wall is built

1963
Civil War breaks out in Cyprus between Greeks and Turks

American Issues
•—•—•—• Connector

By connecting prior knowledge with what you have learned in this chapter, you can gradually build your understanding of enduring questions that still affect America today. Answer the questions below. Then, use your American Issues Connector study guide (or go online: www.PHSchool.com **Web Code:** neh-8803).

Issues You Learned About

● **Poverty and Prosperity** While some people find America to be a true "land of opportunity," others face a daily struggle to make ends meet.

1. What was revealed in Michael Harrington's book *The Other America*? How did Kennedy respond to this book?

2. Did Kennedy's new tax policies benefit upper-class Americans? Explain.

3. What did Johnson hope to accomplish with his War on Poverty? Describe one new program that was part of this effort.

● **America and the World** As part of the Cold War, the United States combated communism in Latin America.

4. What was the Cold War, and when and why did it begin?

5. Did the Peace Corps serve as a tool for promoting democracy or for helping developing nations? Explain.

6. Why do you think that the U.S. government was willing to invade communist Cuba in hopes of overthrowing its leader, but was not willing to invade other communist countries?

● **Social Problems and Reforms** In the 1960s, the government grew concerned with social problems and made efforts to fix them.

7. In 1963, Kennedy told the nation in a televised address that civil rights was a "moral issue . . . as clear as the American Constitution." Did Kennedy always hold this belief about civil rights? Explain.

8. List at least five different areas in which reform legislation was passed in the 1960s. Which was the most significant? Explain your choice.

Connect to Your World | New York

Poverty and Prosperity Daniel Patrick Moynihan (1927–2003), a scholar and politician from New York, experienced poverty firsthand as a child, working at the New York City piers while still in school. As part of the Department of Labor in the 1960s, he was a key player in the preparation of President Johnson's War on Poverty legislation. He caught the attention of the nation in 1965 when he co-wrote what later came to be known as the Moynihan Report—a study on the problems of poor African American families in the nation's cities that remains controversial today. From 1977 until 2001, he served in the U.S. Senate representing New York. Research the Moynihan report. Summarize Moynihan's position, and then offer your own opinion.

1965
Immigration and Nationality Act

1966
Miranda v. *Arizona* protects rights of the accused

History *Interactive*
For: Interactive timeline
Web Code: nep-1507

1966

1969

1965
India and Pakistan fight over control of Kashmir

1968
Fighting breaks out between Catholics and Protestants in Northern Ireland

Chapter Assessment

Terms and People

1. Define a "**flexible response**" defense policy. How did this defense policy differ from Eisenhower's defense policy?

2. What was the **Nuclear Test Ban Treaty**? Why was it so important?

3. What was the **Warren Commission**? What were its findings?

4. What was the purpose of **Medicare** and **Medicaid**? Who led the campaign for this legislation, and which legislation were they part of?

5. What was the **Immigration and Nationality Act of 1965**? Where did most of the new immigrants come from?

Focus Questions

The focus question for this chapter is **How did the policies of Presidents Kennedy and Johnson affect the nation?** Build an answer to this big question by answering the focus questions for Sections 1 through 3 and the Critical Thinking questions that follow.

Section 1
6. How did Kennedy respond to the continuing challenges of the Cold War?

Section 2
7. What were the goals of Kennedy's New Frontier?

Section 3
8. How did Johnson's Great Society programs change life for most Americans?

Critical Thinking

9. **Identify Central Issues** How did the education legislation passed during the Great Society build upon the War on Poverty's education program?

10. **Investigate Problems** How did the issues surrounding East and West Germany contribute to Cold War tensions between the United States and the Soviet Union?

11. **Analyze Information** The Equal Pay Act of 1963 required that women be paid the same wages as men for "equal work." Do you think this legislation had an effect on the passage of the Civil Rights Act of 1964? Explain.

12. **Analyze Charts** The chart below shows successful space launches. Use the chart, as well as your reading of the chapter, to describe the progress of the space race for the years shown. According to one source, the space program is a way to "unite" all nations. Do you agree or disagree? Explain.

Country	1957–1964	1965–1969	1970–1974
Soviet Union	82	302	405
United States	207	279	139
Japan			5
China			2
France			3
United Kingdom			1
Total	289	581	555

13. **Analyze Information** In what ways might Johnson's career as a teacher have made him aware that the nation faced serious social problems that needed to be addressed and reformed?

Writing About History

Writing a Persuasive Essay An effective persuasive essay does not simply argue its own point of view. It also anticipates and counters arguments that might be used by the other side. Write a three-paragraph persuasive essay on the subject of the Warren Court and its decisions regarding the rights of the accused.

Prewriting
- Identify the point of view that you will take in your essay.
- List any arguments you can think of in favor of your point of view. Prioritize them from the most persuasive to the least persuasive.
- Make a chart listing the two most persuasive arguments in one column and a possible counterargument to each argument in the other.

Drafting
- Write an introductory paragraph in which you define the issue and state your viewpoint.
- In the first paragraph, state your most persuasive argument.
- In the second paragraph, identify a counterargument to your argument. Give specific reasons why you disagree with the counterargument.
- Throughout your essay, use clear, direct language that makes your argument sound both reasonable and forceful. Remember, overly emotional language and name-calling can sometimes make your argument seem less persuasive not more persuasive.

Revising
- Use the guidelines on page SH22 of the Writing Handbook to revise your writing.

Regents DBQ Practice

The Effectiveness of President Johnson's Great Society Programs

In 1964, President Johnson proposed his vision for the United States called the Great Society. Johnson's goal was to end poverty and racial injustice and to give every child an opportunity to receive a good education. Would President Johnson's Great Society programs meet his goals or would they become a burden to taxpayers? Use your knowledge of Johnson's Great Society legislation and Documents 1, 2, and 3 to answer questions 1 through 4.

Document 1

"Project Head Start was created during the heady, idealistic days of the mid-1960s. President Lyndon Johnson believed that it was the nation's duty to provide not just legal equality but also equality of opportunity. In his 1965 commencement address at Howard University, he called for the 'next and the more profound stage' in the civil rights struggle. 'We seek not just freedom but opportunity.' . . . Johnson's War on Poverty would include a host of initiatives designed to bring blacks and other disadvantaged Americans to what he called 'the starting line' of American life with the skills and abilities necessary to compete on a level playing field. The War on Poverty focused on education as a tool for upward mobility, and Head Start was to become one of the cornerstones of the federal effort."

—"Competing Visions," Ron Haskins, 2004

Document 2

Head Start Budget, 1965–2005

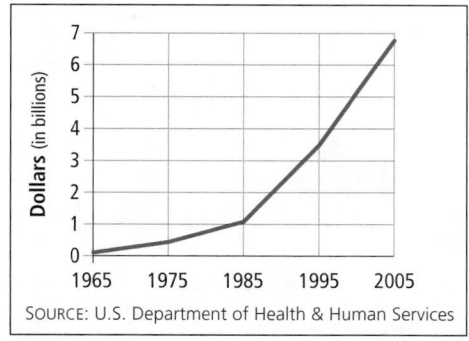

SOURCE: U.S. Department of Health & Human Services

Document 3

"On many domestic issues, [Senator] Dirksen continued the balancing act so central to his effectiveness, as he saw it: maintain a constructive relationship with the opposition and the loyalty of the Republican troops. He took issue with Medicare, for example: 'I would be eligible,' he said indignantly. 'Why should I be allowed to use dollars the government is taking from some young factory worker in Cleveland in the promise of providing for his old age?' The accumulation of Great Society spending programs appalled Dirksen. The taxpayers would have to come up with nearly $160 billion to fund them. Moreover, the programs brought with them an expanding federal bureaucracy and increasing centralization. To Dirksen, the Great Society was a misguided attempt at creating an immediate, utopian 'blueprint for paradise.'"

—*The Education of a Senator,* Frank H. Mackaman, 1998

---

1. According to Document 1, why did President Johnson use Head Start as part of his War on Poverty?
   (1) He wanted to use Head Start to provide legal equality for disadvantaged Americans.
   (2) He wanted to create Head Start for Americans with exceptional abilities.
   (3) He wanted to use Head Start as a tool to help people achieve upward mobility.
   (4) He wanted to use Head Start to maintain a constructive relationship with the Republicans.

2. Which documents imply that the Great Society had a positive effect on the lives of Americans?
   (1) Documents 1 and 3
   (2) Documents 2 and 3
   (3) Documents 1 and 2
   (4) Documents 1, 2, and 3

3. In Document 3, what viewpoint does Senator Dirksen take toward the Great Society programs?
   (1) He believed that Medicare would not help him.
   (2) He opposed the Republican view of the Great Society programs.
   (3) He proposed his own Great Society programs.
   (4) He believed that the Great Society programs would lead to an expanding federal government.

4. **Writing Task** Would President Johnson's Great Society programs meet his goals, or would they become a burden to taxpayers? Use your knowledge of the chapter content and specific evidence from the primary sources above to support your opinion.

29 The Vietnam War Era
1954–1975

War in Vietnam

During the Vietnam War, the United States Army used helicopters to transport troops. One helicopter pilot remembered a mission to evacuate injured soldiers:

❝We landed in front of the Jeep, or what was left of it. It was twisted like a child's discarded toy. . . . A sergeant ran up to my door. He told me through my extended microphone that two of the guys in the back were still alive. . . . They started loading up. The two wounded were unconscious, torn and bloody and gray.**❞**
—Captain Robert Mason, First Air Cavalry Division, 1965

Listen to the Witness History *audio to hear more about the Vietnam War Era.*

◀ U.S. troops evacuate a wounded American soldier from a firefight during the Vietnam War.

Ping-pong paddles commemorating Nixon's trip to China

Core Curriculum Preview

Chapter Focus Question: How did the United States confront communism in East Asia after the Korean War?

Antiwar poster

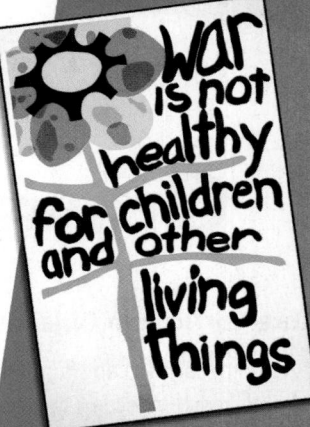

Land mine used against American soldiers

Use the ☑ **Quick Study Timeline** at the end of this chapter to preview chapter events.

Note Taking Study Guide *Online*
For: Note Taking and American Issues Connector
Web Code: nee-8901

▲ Ho Chi Minh depicted in a Vietnamese propaganda poster

WITNESS HISTORY ◀))) AUDIO

Hope for Independence

After World War II, a spirit of nationalism and revolution spread among European colonies around the world. As colonial peoples strived for independence, their struggles sometimes became mixed up with the Cold War conflict between communist states and western democracies. Such was the case in French Indochina, which consisted of the lands of Laos, Cambodia, and Vietnam. Unaware of the long and bloody war that lie ahead, a Vietnamese communist named Ho Chi Minh dreamed of a Vietnam free from French rule:

❝The oppressed the world over are wresting back their independence. We should not lag behind. . . . Under the Vietminh banner, let us valiantly march forward!❞

—Ho Chi Minh, 1945

Origins of the Vietnam War

 Core Curriculum Objectives

- **7.IV.A** Vietnam: sacrifice and turmoil
- **7.IV.A.1** The French-Indochinese War: early United States involvement; Truman, Eisenhower, and Kennedy policies
- **7.IV.A.2** United States and the spread of communism; domino theory; credibility of other United States commitments

Terms and People

Ho Chi Minh
domino theory
SEATO

Vietcong
Gulf of Tonkin Resolution

NoteTaking

Reading Skill: Summarize As you read, describe the Vietnam policies of Presidents Truman, Eisenhower, Kennedy, and Johnson.

U.S. Policy in Vietnam		
Truman/Eisenhower	**Kennedy**	**Johnson**
• •	• •	• • Gulf of Tonkin Resolution

Why It Matters Presidents Kennedy and Johnson shared a vision for a better America in the 1960s. They also shared a vision for a better world in which America would emerge victorious from its Cold War struggle against global communism. As part of this strategic and ideological battle, the United States established a new line of defense against communism in Vietnam. The conflict in Southeast Asia would grow to be one of the costliest wars in American history. **Section Focus Question: Why did the United States become involved in Vietnam?**

America and the War in Indochina

Situated far away in Southeast Asia, Vietnam did not attract significant American attention until the 1960s. Television news shows rarely mentioned it, and most Americans could not locate it on a map. But over a span of more than ten years, the United States sent several million soldiers to fight in Vietnam. America's involvement in Vietnam had roots in European colonialism, Cold War politics, and Vietnamese calls for national independence.

France Rules Indochina in Southeast Asia In the 1800s, French military forces established control over Indochina, a peninsula in Southeast Asia that includes the modern countries of Vietnam, Cambodia, and Laos. Slightly larger than the state of Texas, Indochina included almost 27 million people by the end of World War II. French colonial officials ruled Vietnam with an iron fist. They transplanted French laws into Vietnam and imposed high taxes. French business people acquired large rice and rubber

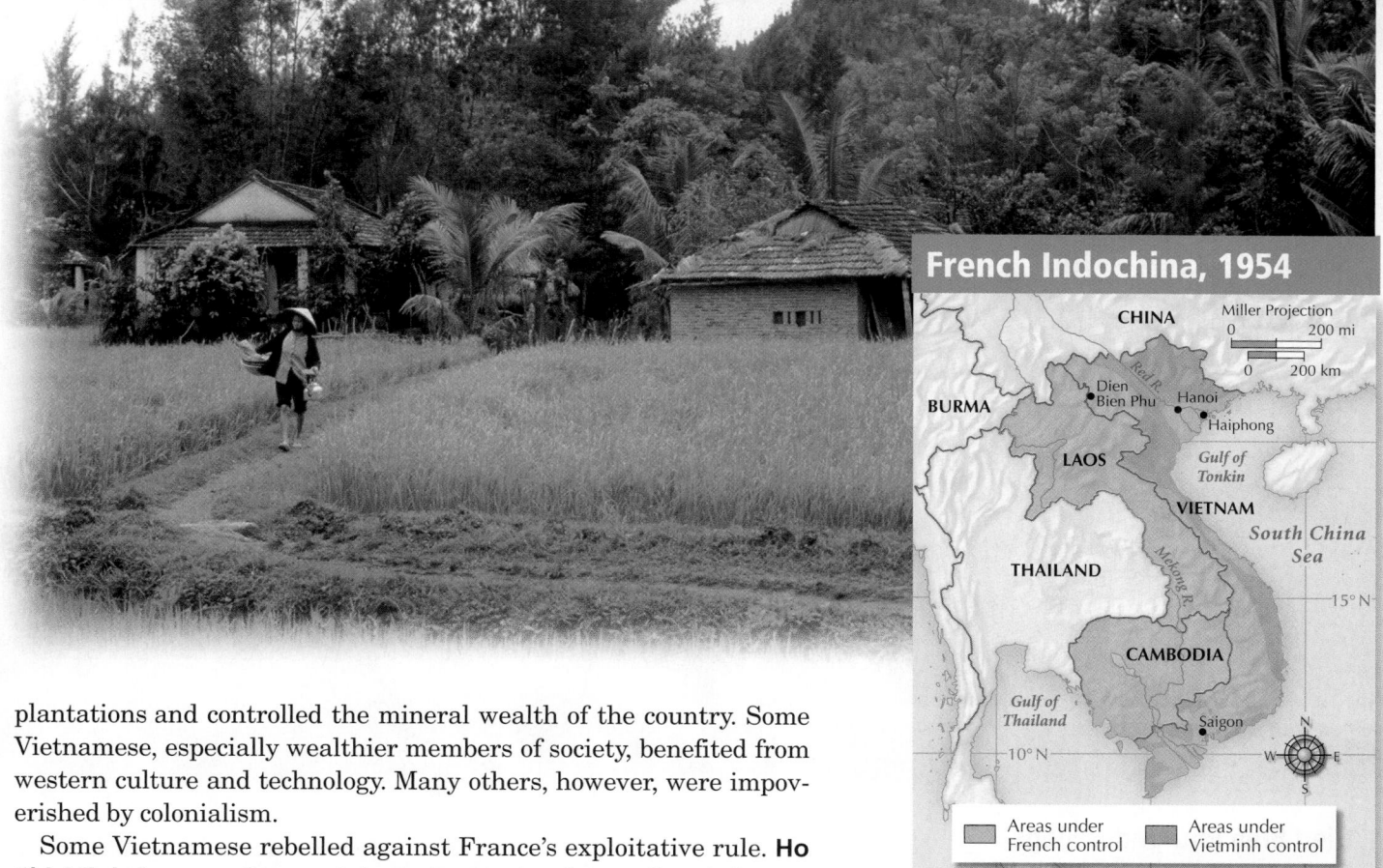

French Indochina, 1954

CHINA

Miller Projection
0   200 mi
0   200 km

BURMA

Dien Bien Phu • Hanoi
Haiphong

LAOS

Gulf of Tonkin

VIETNAM

South China Sea

THAILAND

Mekong R.

15° N

CAMBODIA

Gulf of Thailand

Saigon

10° N

Areas under French control   Areas under Vietminh control

105° E   110° E

plantations and controlled the mineral wealth of the country. Some Vietnamese, especially wealthier members of society, benefited from western culture and technology. Many others, however, were impoverished by colonialism.

Some Vietnamese rebelled against France's exploitative rule. **Ho Chi Minh** became the most important voice demanding independence for Vietnam. Born in 1890, Ho became involved in anti-French organizations as a young man and fled Vietnam in 1912. He traveled the world, visiting American ports and living periodically in London, Paris, and Moscow. During his 30-year absence, Ho constantly thought and wrote about Vietnam, and he searched for westerners who would support his plans for Vietnamese independence. Ho embraced communism, and eventually Soviet communists rallied to his cause.

The French Battle Nationalism and Communism During World War II, Japan had undermined French control over Vietnam. But when the conflict ended, France reasserted its colonial aims there. France's problem, however, was that colonialism was a dying institution. World War II had strengthened nationalist movements while weakening the economic and military positions of traditional European powers. In Vietnam, Ho Chi Minh clamored for independence as France struggled to maintain its dwindling global power.

Meanwhile, the United States faced a difficult decision. On the one hand, it supported decolonization. On the other hand, America wanted France as an ally in its Cold War effort to contain the Soviet Union. President Harry S. Truman believed that if he supported Vietnamese independence, he would weaken anticommunist forces in France. So, to ensure a strong, anticommunist Western Europe, Truman sacrificed his own anticolonial sentiments.

Vietnam thus became a pawn in Cold War politics. To <u>ensure</u> French support in the Cold War, Truman agreed to aid France's efforts to regain control over Vietnam. After communist forces won the civil war in China in 1949, America increased its aid to the French in Vietnam. Truman did not want to see another communist victory in Asia. Between 1950 and 1954, the United States contributed $2.6 billion to France's war efforts. Containing Ho Chi Minh's communist Vietminh—an abbreviation of the League for the Independence of Vietnam—became a national priority.

Vietnam Under French Rule

During the French colonial era, rural villagers failed to see the same profits as French plantation owners. Ho Chi Minh found many supporters for his anticolonial efforts in villages like the one above. *In 1954, what regions of Indochina were under communist control?*

Vocabulary Builder
ensure–(en SHOR) *v.* to guarantee; secure

Dien Bien Phu Under Siege

For almost two months, Vietminh soldiers hammered at French military positions around Dien Bien Phu. At left, Vietnamese communists take cover in a trench during the siege. At right, French troops guard Vietminh soldiers taken captive during the fighting.

The Domino Theory and Dien Bien Phu When President Dwight D. Eisenhower took office in early 1953, he continued Truman's policies toward Vietnam. He sent monetary aid to the French, arguing that by battling Ho Chi Minh, they were containing the spread of communism. Eisenhower told a journalist that the fight in Vietnam involved more than the future of just one country:

> **Primary Source** "You have a row of dominos set up, you knock over the first one, and what will happen to the last one is the certainty that it will go over very quickly. So you could have a beginning of a disintegration that would have the most profound influences."
>
> —Dwight D. Eisenhower, 1954

The **domino theory** was the idea that if Vietnam fell to communism, its closest neighbors would follow. This in turn would threaten Japan, the Philippines, and Australia. In short, stopping the communists in Vietnam was important to the protection of the entire region.

In 1954, however, the French lost their eight-year struggle to regain Vietnam. The Vietminh trapped a large French garrison at Dien Bien Phu, a military base in northwest Vietnam, and laid siege to it for 55 days. During the siege, which one Frenchman described as "hell in a very small place," Vietminh troops destroyed the French airstrip, cut French supply lines, and dug trenches to attack key French positions. Finally, on May 7, 1954, after suffering some 15,000 casualties, the French surrendered.

The very next day at an international peace conference in Geneva, Switzerland, France sued for peace. According to the Geneva Accords, France granted independence to Vietnam, Laos, and Cambodia. The accords also divided Vietnam at the seventeenth parallel into two countries, North Vietnam and South Vietnam. Ho Chi Minh's communist forces ruled in North Vietnam, and an anticommunist government, supported by the United States, assumed power in South Vietnam. The accords also called for free elections in 1956 to unify Vietnam.

✔ **Checkpoint** Why did Presidents Truman and Eisenhower support French efforts against Ho Chi Minh?

America Opposes Communism in Vietnam

During the Battle of Dien Bien Phu, France appealed to the United States for military support. President Eisenhower was willing to supply money but not soldiers. Ike would not commit American troops to defend colonialism in Asia. Nevertheless, the President firmly supported the new anticommunist government of South Vietnam.

The United States Aids South Vietnam America channeled aid to South Vietnam in different ways. In 1954, the United States and seven other countries formed the **Southeast Asia Treaty Organization (SEATO).** Similar to NATO, SEATO's goal was to contain the spread of communism in Southeast Asia.

The United States provided economic and military aid to the South Vietnamese government led by Ngo Dinh Diem. Diem was an ardent nationalist and anticommunist. Although he lacked popular appeal, his anticommunism guaranteed American support. When it came time for the 1956 unification elections, American intelligence analysts predicted that Diem would lose to the more popular Ho Chi Minh. Rather than risk losing, Diem refused to participate in the elections, a move made under the <u>auspices</u> of the United States government.

Communist Opposition Grows By 1957, a communist rebel group in the South, known as the National Liberation Front (NLF), had committed themselves to undermining the Diem government and uniting Vietnam under a communist flag. NLF guerrilla fighters, called **Vietcong,** launched an insurgency in which they assassinated government officials and destroyed roads and bridges. Supplied by communists in North Vietnam, the Vietcong employed surprise hit-and-run tactics to weaken Diem's hold on South Vietnam.

Diem's own policies also weakened his position in South Vietnam. A devout Roman Catholic in an overwhelmingly Buddhist nation, Diem did little to build a broad political base. Instead, he signed anti-Buddhist legislation and refused to enact significant land reforms. His lack of popular support hurt him in the civil war against North Vietnam. Only the support of the United States kept the unpopular leader in power.

Kennedy Sends U.S. Troops to Vietnam After his election in 1960, President John F. Kennedy took a more aggressive stand against the communists in Vietnam. Beginning in 1961, he sent Special Forces troops to South Vietnam to advise the Army of the Republic of Vietnam (ARVN) on more effective ways to fight the communist forces. By 1963, more than 15,000 American "advisers" were fighting in Vietnam.

Although U.S. advisers fought bravely and achieved some success, Diem continued to alienate South Vietnamese citizens. By late 1963, his regime was in shambles. Buddhists protested his restrictive policies, occasionally by setting themselves on fire. The Kennedy administration eventually concluded that South Vietnam needed new leadership. Working behind the scenes, Americans plotted with anti-Diem generals to overthrow Diem's government. On November 1, 1963, Diem was removed from power and later assassinated.

✔ **Checkpoint** How did the United States help the South Vietnamese government resist communism?

WITNESS HISTORY DVD

Watch *Causes of the Vietnam War* on the **United States Witness History DVD** to learn more about how the United States became involved in Vietnam.

Vocabulary Builder
auspices–(AWS puh sihz) *n.* approval and support

▼ A Buddhist monk sets himself on fire in Saigon to protest the Diem regime.

Analyzing Political Cartoons

The Opposing Forces Early in the war, this American cartoon focused on the technological differences between the two opposing forces.

1. Is the cartoon an accurate or exaggerated representation of the technological differences? Explain.

2. Who do you think the cartoonist expected to win the war? Why?

Johnson Leads the Nation Into War

Three weeks after Diem's fall, an assassin's bullet struck down President Kennedy. Vice President Lyndon B. Johnson was sworn in as the new President. Johnson was a Cold War traditionalist who held a monolithic view of communism. For this "Cold Warrior," communism in the Soviet Union, China, and Vietnam were all the same. He did not recognize subtle differences. He also knew that the American people expected victory in Vietnam.

North Vietnamese and U.S. Forces Clash In 1964, President Johnson faced his first crisis in Vietnam. On August 2, North Vietnamese torpedo boats fired on the American destroyer USS *Maddox* as it patrolled the Gulf of Tonkin off the coast of North Vietnam. The *Maddox* was not hit, and it returned fire on the North Vietnamese boat. Johnson promptly responded to the attack and to other North Vietnamese provocations. He announced that "aggression by terror against peaceful villages of South Vietnam has now been joined by open aggression on the high seas against the United States of America." Troubled by increasing strikes against an American ally, Johnson ordered an airstrike against North Vietnam.

Congress Gives Johnson Broad Military Powers The President next asked Congress to authorize the use of force to defend American troops. With little debate and only two senators voting against it, Congress agreed to Johnson's request and passed the **Gulf of Tonkin Resolution.** The resolution authorized the President "to take all necessary measures to repel any armed attack against the forces of the United States and to prevent further aggression." The resolution gave Johnson tremendous war powers. It allowed him to commit U.S. troops to South Vietnam and fight a war against North Vietnam without ever going back to Congress to ask for a declaration of war.

✓ **Checkpoint** What was the significance of the Gulf of Tonkin Resolution?

SECTION 1

Assessment

Progress Monitoring *Online*
For: Self-test with vocabulary practice
Web Code: nea-1602

Comprehension

1. **Terms and People** For each item below, write a sentence explaining its significance.
   • Ho Chi Minh
   • domino theory
   • Vietcong
   • Gulf of Tonkin Resolution

2. **NoteTaking** **Reading Skill: Summarize** Use your flowchart to answer the Section Focus Question: Why did the United States become involved in Vietnam?

Writing About History

3. **Quick Write: Generate an Argument** Choose a topic from this section that could be the subject of a persuasive essay. For example, you might choose the domino theory. Then, write a thesis statement arguing in favor of or against U.S. intervention in Southeast Asia. Make sure that the argument clearly explains your opinion on the topic.

Critical Thinking

4. **Identify Central Issues** Identify one argument for and one argument against Truman's decision to support the French rather than the Vietnamese nationalists.

5. **Make Decisions** What goals motivated President Kennedy's policy decisions regarding Vietnam?

6. **Recognize Cause and Effect** How did the *Maddox* incident contribute to the outbreak of war? How did it lead to a change in the balance of power in the American government?

◀ A young American soldier in Vietnam

WITNESS HISTORY 🔊 AUDIO

American Soldiers on Patrol

The war in Vietnam was different from previous wars. There were no front lines—the enemy was everywhere. The terrain was difficult and littered with mines and booby traps. Drenched in sweat, the men waded through flooded rice paddies and along tangled paths, stopping occasionally to pick leeches out of their boots. One soldier recalled the difficulties of maneuvering in the overgrown and disorienting jungle during the war:

❝You carried 50 to 70 pounds of equipment, and it was tough going, particularly in forested areas. Often you'd have to pull yourself along from one tree branch to the next, or we'd have to help each other by gripping hands. And you couldn't see anything, so you didn't know what was there around you.❞

—Sergeant William Ehrhart,
United States Marines

▲ Vietcong land mine used against American soldiers

U.S. Involvement Grows

NY **Core Curriculum Objectives**

- **7.IV.A.3** Civil war in South Vietnam; concept of guerilla warfare
- **7.IV.A.4** LBJ and the Americanization of the war

Terms and People

William Westmoreland   hawk
napalm   dove

NoteTaking

Reading Skill: Identify Supporting Details
As you read, fill in the outline with details about the escalation of the American war effort.

> I. "Americanizing" the War
>   A.
>   1.
>   2.

Why It Matters After the Gulf of Tonkin Resolution, President Johnson began to shift U.S. military efforts in Vietnam into high gear. But America's leaders and soldiers soon found themselves stuck in a deadly quagmire with no quick victory in sight. The war began to weaken the economy, divide the American people, and erode the nation's morale. **Section Focus Question: What were the causes and effects of America's growing involvement in the Vietnam War?**

"Americanizing" the War

In February 1965, President Johnson dramatically altered the U.S. role in the Vietnam War. In response to a Vietcong attack that killed American troops at Pleiku, Johnson ordered the start of Operation Rolling Thunder, the first sustained bombing campaign against North Vietnam. Johnson hoped that this new strategy of intensive bombing would convince North Vietnam to stop reinforcing the Vietcong in South Vietnam.

The bombs rained down destruction, but they failed to convince North Vietnam to make peace. As the communist forces continued to fight, the United States committed more troops to battle them on the ground. American soldiers moved beyond their adviser roles and assumed greater military responsibilities, while South Vietnamese troops accepted a secondary, more limited role in the war. U.S. military and civilian leaders hoped that American airstrikes, along with the troops on the ground, would eventually force the communists to the peace table.

American Assumptions and Strategies Johnson's change in strategy in 1965 stemmed primarily from the counsel of Secretary of Defense Robert McNamara and General **William Westmoreland,** the American commander in South Vietnam. These two advisers believed that the United States needed to increase its military presence in Vietnam and do more of the fighting in order to win the war. Operation Rolling Thunder and increased troop commitments fulfilled this need to "Americanize" the war effort.

Beginning in March 1965, U.S. airstrikes hammered North Vietnam and Vietcong strong points in South Vietnam. Between 1965 and 1973, American pilots dropped more than 6 million tons of bombs on enemy positions—almost three times the tonnage dropped by all the combatants during World War II. In addition to conventional bombs, American pilots dropped napalm and sprayed Agent Orange. **Napalm** is a jellied gasoline which was dropped in large canisters that exploded on impact, covering large areas in flames. It clung to anything it touched and was difficult to extinguish. Agent Orange is an herbicide meant to kill plant life. Almost half of South Vietnam's forested areas were sprayed at least once, and the ecological impact was devastating. U.S. forces used it to defoliate the countryside and disrupt the enemy's food supply. Many scientists believe that Agent Orange causes cancers and other physical problems.

As airstrikes intensified, American ground troops landed in South Vietnam. On March 8, 1965, U.S. Marines arrived to defend the airbase at Da Nang. They were soon followed by other troops. The soldiers accepted a wide range of missions. Some guarded bases. Others conducted search-and-destroy missions to kill as many Vietcong guerrillas as they could. Helicopters ferried commandos to and from remote locations for quick strikes against enemy positions.

An Elusive and Determined Enemy Large-scale battles against Vietcong or North Vietnamese Army units were not typical of America's strategy in Vietnam. American soldiers generally fought lightly armed Vietcong guerrillas in small engagements. Ho Chi Minh's military doctrine hinged on fighting only when victory was assured, which meant never fighting on his opponents' terms. He compared his troops to a tiger, while the Americans were like an elephant. If the tiger stands still, the elephant will crush it. But if the tiger keeps moving and occasionally jumps on the elephant to take a bite out of it, the elephant will slowly bleed to death.

During the war, the Vietcong behaved like Ho's tiger. They traveled light, often carrying just a rifle and a few handfuls of rice. They dug tunnels to hide in during the day and emerged at night to ambush American patrols. They infiltrated American bases and set off explosives. They set booby traps that maimed and crippled American troops. Their strategy was to wear the American elephant down. The leaders of North Vietnam and the Vietcong remained convinced that if they could avoid losing the war, the Americans would eventually leave.

A Costly and Frustrating War American strategy during this stage of the war yielded limited results. U.S. bombers did disrupt North Vietnamese industry and slow the movement of supplies to the Vietcong. But when the communists did not sue for peace, American troop commitments and battlefield deaths escalated rapidly. By the end of 1965, there were 184,300 U.S. troops in Vietnam and only 636 American soldiers had died in the war. Three years later, there were more than half a million U.S. troops in Vietnam and the number of American dead had risen to more than 30,000.

Vocabulary Builder
doctrine–(DAHK trihn) *n.* teachings

Vietnam War, 1963–1967

CHINA

BURMA

NORTH VIETNAM

Dien Bien Phu

Hanoi

Haiphong

Gulf of Tonkin

LAOS

Mekong R.

Vientiane

Red R.

Ho Chi Minh Trail

2. August 1964
Gulf of Tonkin incident escalates war

4. March 1965
Operation Rolling Thunder

South China Sea

3. February 1965
Vietcong attack at Pleiku

Hué

Da Nang

5. March 1965
First U.S. combat troops arrive

THAILAND

6. December 1967
More than 480,000 U.S. soldiers in South Vietnam

N
W E
S

15° N

CAMBODIA

SOUTH VIETNAM

Phnom Penh

Gulf of Thailand

1. November 1963
Diem government overthrown

Saigon

Mekong Delta

100° E   110° E   115° E   10° N

20° N

Miller Projection
0   100   200 mi
0   100   200 km

The Vietnam War Escalates

Year	Event
1961	President Kennedy sends military advisers to train South Vietnamese troops.
1963	More than 10,000 American military advisers train and fight in South Vietnam.
1964	Gulf of Tonkin Resolution passes; Number of U.S. troops doubles to more than 20,000.
1965	President Johnson authorizes bombing of North Vietnam; more than 180,000 U.S. troops are in South Vietnam.
1966–1967	Number of American soldiers in South Vietnam rises to nearly half a million.

Map Skills The Vietcong were resupplied with weapons, food, and fighters along the Ho Chi Minh Trail.

1. **Locate:** (a) Saigon, (b) Hanoi, (c) Ho Chi Minh Trail

2. **Movement** Through what countries did the Vietcong travel as they moved supplies from North Vietnam to South Vietnam?

3. **Draw Conclusions** Why might a U.S. attack against the Ho Chi Minh Trail cause an international backlash against the United States?

The Hardships of War in Vietnam

By 1968, the morale of American troops in Vietnam was on the wane. Units would fight to drive the Vietcong out of a village only to return weeks later to do the same job all over again. In a land where anyone could be the enemy, U.S. soldiers lived in a state of constant tension. Survival demanded remaining on the lookout for snipers, ambushes, and booby traps. The amount of rice cooking in a pot could be a clue to an impending attack. Was there just enough food for the people in view, or had others disappeared as the Americans approached? A moment of inattention could spell disaster.

Concealed entrance under cooking pot

Upper trench

Vent

Lower tunnel and hiding place

▲ Vietcong guerrillas relied on large tunnel networks to hide from—and launch surprise attacks against—American forces.

Each year, the war cost more American dollars and claimed more American lives. But at the end of each year, the United States seemed no closer to success. America's mission was to help South Vietnam build a stable noncommunist nation and thereby win the "hearts and minds" of its citizens. But corruption plagued the South Vietnamese administrative structure. Outside of the major cities, the government enjoyed little real support. Although American forces won most of the larger battles, they did not achieve a successful end to the war. By 1967, the war had devolved into a stalemate. Some U.S. critics of the war compared it to a quagmire—muddy terrain that sinks underfoot and is difficult to exit.

✔ **Checkpoint** What was the strategic aim of Operation Rolling Thunder?

Patriotism, Heroism, and Sinking Morale

For American soldiers in the field, the Vietnam War presented difficult challenges that demanded courage and patience. Unlike World War II, the Vietnam War did not emphasize territorial acquisition. The United States and its allies did not invade North Vietnam, march on Ho Chi Minh's capital of Hanoi, or attempt to destroy the communist regime. As in the Korean War, the United States was fearful of triggering both Chinese and Soviet entry into the conflict. Instead, American forces supported the survival and development of South Vietnam, which was besieged by the Vietcong and their North Vietnamese allies. In this fight, U.S. troops could never fully tell their friends from their enemies. Yet from the outset, they faced the dangers of Vietnam's battlefields with dedication and bravery.

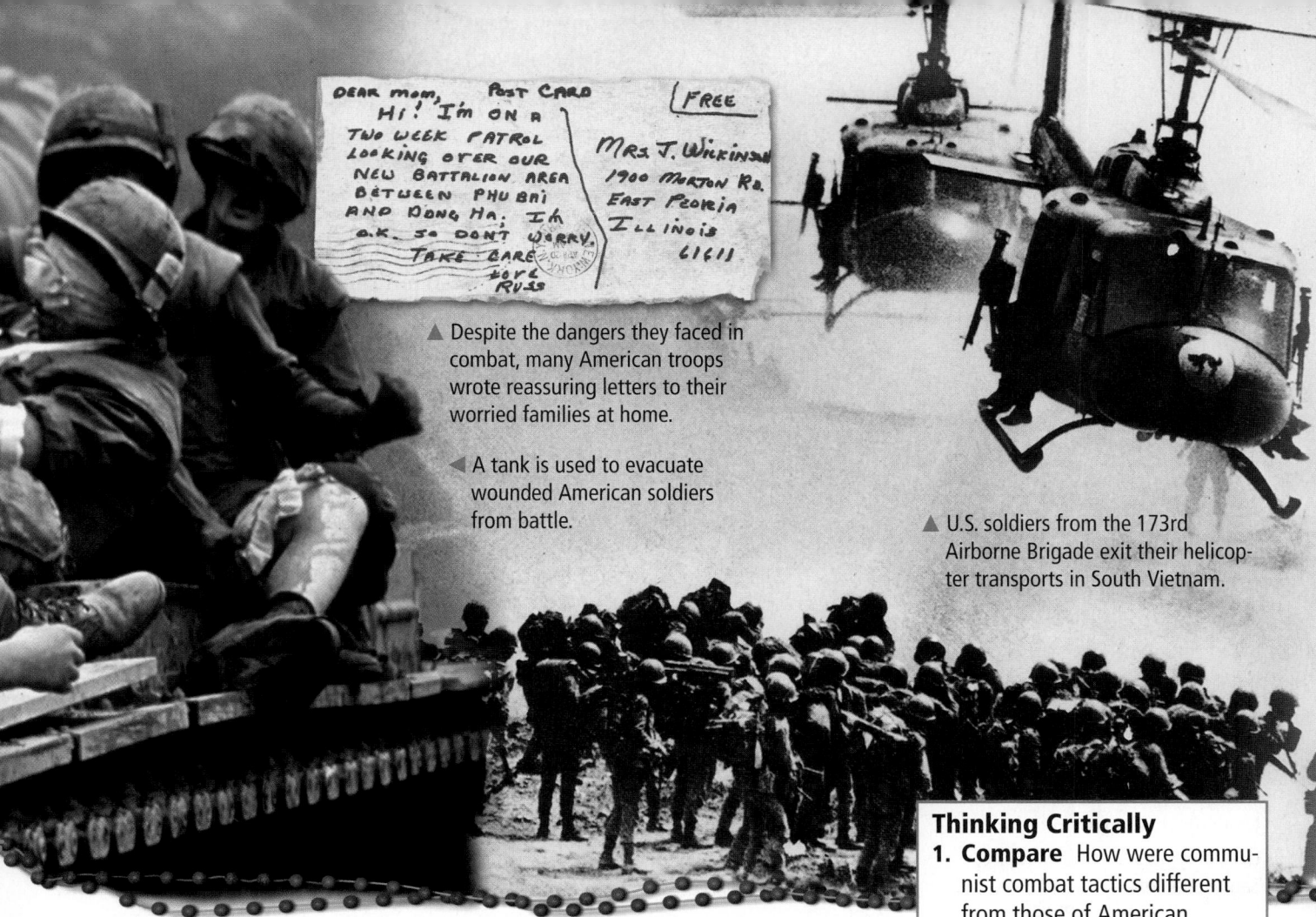

DEAR MOM, POST CARD
HI! I'm ON A
TWO WEEK PATROL
LOOKING OVER OUR
NEW BATTALION AREA
BETWEEN PHU BAI
AND DONG HA. I'M
O.K. SO DON'T WORRY.
TAKE CARE
LOVE
RUSS

FREE

MRS J. WILKINSON
1900 MORTON RD.
EAST PEORIA
ILLINOIS
61611

▲ Despite the dangers they faced in combat, many American troops wrote reassuring letters to their worried families at home.

◀ A tank is used to evacuate wounded American soldiers from battle.

▲ U.S. soldiers from the 173rd Airborne Brigade exit their helicopter transports in South Vietnam.

Thinking Critically

1. **Compare** How were communist combat tactics different from those of American troops?

2. **Draw Conclusions** How did images such as these, shown on television news shows, affect the home front?

History *Interactive* ★

For: To learn more about the hardships of the Vietnam War
Web Code: nep-1606

Danger on a New Battlefield Although American troops won numerous battles, they could not win the war outright. The problem was that the Vietcong and North Vietnamese avoided significant engagements. Rather than expose themselves to superior American firepower, the communists fought smaller skirmishes where their small-unit abilities and their knowledge of the landscape bettered their chances for victory.

U.S. forces often had no alternative but to fight indecisive battles in the jungles, rice paddies, and mountains of Vietnam. Most of these battlefields abounded with natural cover. Clad in black pajamas, Vietcong gunmen would spring out of the dense foliage, attack with automatic rifles and grenades, and disappear back into the landscape. Much of this fighting took place at night, which reduced the effectiveness of American planes, artillery, and troop tactics.

American Soldiers Fulfill Their Duty Despite the trials of war, American soldiers adapted to adverse conditions in Vietnam and fought with the same intensity that U.S. forces had shown in World Wars I and II. Many fought to prevent the spread of communism. Some fought to protect villagers in South Vietnam and win their trust and respect. Others fought because their country was at war and they felt it was their duty. A medic in the First Infantry Division explained his reason for going to Vietnam:

Primary Source ❝I volunteered. . . . Ever since the American Revolution my family had people in all the different wars, and that was always the thing—when your country needs you, you go. You don't ask a lot of questions. . . .❞
—David Ross, United States Army medic

Later, many did ask questions about America's involvement in the war, but overwhelmingly while they were in Vietnam, the soldiers met their duties with courage. More than 58,000 of them gave their lives for their country.

Women also displayed courage and valor. About 10,000 American military women served in Vietnam during the war. Most female military personnel were nurses. Not only did they face danger working close to the front, but they also had to cope with the emotional toll of constantly working with injured and dying soldiers and civilians.

Lynda Van Devanter volunteered to go to Vietnam and spent a year there as a nurse. Like other nurses, she confronted war and death on a daily basis. However, on one occasion she had to deliver a baby. She later recalled:

> **Primary Source** "It was creation of life in the midst of all that destruction. And creation of life restored your sanity. . . . Those were the things that kept you going. That there was life coming. There was still hope."
>
> —Lynda Van Devanter, United States Army nurse

Nurses in Vietnam

U.S. Army nurses Capt. Gladys E. Sepulveda, left, of Puerto Rico, and 2nd Lt. Lois Ferrari of Pittsburgh, rest on sandbags at Cam Ranh Bay in South Vietnam on July 14, 1965. They were awaiting transportation to Nha Trang where they were set to work in the 8th field hospital.

Morale Declines as War Wears On As the war lengthened, many Americans began to question U.S. involvement. The earliest soldiers in Vietnam had been volunteers, men committed to the fight against communism. But by the end of 1965, most American soldiers in Vietnam had been drafted into military service, and they were not as certain that preserving the government in South Vietnam was crucial to American interests. They sensed that many South Vietnamese people were indifferent—if not openly hostile—to their own nation. Increasingly, it seemed that Americans were dying to defend a nation whose people were unwilling to die to defend themselves.

✔ **Checkpoint** Why did the morale of American troops decline as the war continued?

Doubt Grows on the Home Front

The lack of progress toward victory in Vietnam also led to doubt in the United States. When President Johnson had begun to send troops to war, Americans had expected a relatively quick victory. After all, the United States was a militarily powerful, technologically advanced country, and North Vietnam was a poor country with comparatively little technology. Over the next few years, the Johnson administration kept <u>asserting</u> that an American victory was close at hand. But when that did not come, many began to question the President's foreign policy.

Vocabulary Builder
<u>assert</u>—(uh SERT) *v.* to state positively; declare

The War Weakens the Economy The war strained government finances. President Johnson's Great Society plan called for enormous domestic spending to eliminate poverty, improve education and medical care, and fight racial discrimination. The costs of fighting a war on the other side of the world were just as mammoth. Although massive government spending lowered the unemployment rate, it also led to rising prices and inflation. The combination of heavy government spending, rising prices, and inflation forced Johnson to raise taxes.

Ultimately, Johnson had to cut back on his Great Society reform initiatives to help pay for the war.

Antiwar Movement Begins to Emerge As long as America's involvement in Vietnam had been small and relatively inexpensive, few politicians voiced serious opposition. Despite its bipartisan support for the Vietnam policies of Johnson's predecessors, after the Gulf of Tonkin Resolution, Congress soon split over the President's escalation of the war.

Beginning in 1967, Congress—and eventually most of America—divided into two camps: hawks and doves. The mostly conservative **hawks** supported Johnson's war policy. Believing strongly in the containment of communism and the domino theory, they accepted rising troop levels, escalating costs, and increasing numbers of battlefield deaths. For the hawks, Vietnam was a crucial front in the Cold War. **Doves,** however, broke with Johnson's war policy. A diverse group of liberal politicians, pacifists, student radicals, and civil rights leaders, doves questioned the war on both moral and strategic grounds. For them, the conflict was a localized civil war, not a vital Cold War battleground.

Senator J. William Fulbright, chairman of the Senate Foreign Relations Committee, emerged as the early leader of the doves in Congress. A Democrat who had supported the Gulf of Tonkin Resolution, Fulbright soon came to believe that the war in Vietnam was a national civil war, not a Cold War conflict whose shots were called in Moscow or Beijing. In 1967 and 1968, Fulbright held public hearings on the war, providing a platform for critics of the conflict.

✓ **Checkpoint** What were the opposing viewpoints of hawks and doves?

Onward And Upward And Onward And—

Analyzing Political Cartoons

The Bombing Campaign U.S. officials promised that increased bombing would bring America closer to victory.
1. Does the emotion on the person's face suggest that the plan is working? Explain.
2. Do you think the cartoonist was a hawk or a dove? Explain.

Progress Monitoring *Online*
For: Self-test with vocabulary practice
Web Code: nea-1604

Comprehension
1. **Terms and People** For each item below, write a sentence explaining its significance.
   • William Westmoreland
   • napalm
   • dove

2. **NoteTaking Reading Skill: Identify Supporting Details** Use your outline to answer the Section Focus Question: What were the causes and effects of America's growing involvement in the Vietnam War?

Writing About History
3. **Quick Write: Support an Opinion With Evidence** Consider the following topic from the section: America's escalation of the war in Vietnam. Gather and present evidence from the text that supports the Americanization of the war effort.

Critical Thinking
4. **Evaluate Information** What military strategies did the United States employ in Vietnam? How successful were these strategies?

5. **Summarize** What difficulties did American soldiers face in Vietnam? What effect did these difficulties have?

6. **Contrast** How did the disagreements between hawks and doves reflect different views about war and world politics?

▲ Walter Cronkite

◀ A Vietnam veteran protests the war in 1970.

WITNESS HISTORY AUDIO

The "Living-Room War"

Walter Cronkite, the anchor of the CBS Evening News, was the most respected television journalist of the 1960s. His many reports on the Vietnam War were models of balanced journalism and inspired the confidence of viewers across the United States. But during the Tet Offensive, Cronkite was shocked by the disconnect between Johnson's optimistic statements and the gritty reality of the fighting. After visiting Vietnam in February of 1968, he told his viewers:

❝We have been too often disappointed by the optimism of the American leaders, both in Vietnam and Washington, to have faith any longer in the silver linings they find in the darkest clouds. . . . [I]t seems now more certain than ever that the bloody experience of Vietnam is to end in stalemate.❞

—Walter Cronkite, 1968

The War Divides America

Core Curriculum Objectives

- **7.IV.A.4b** Escalation of the war; Tet offensive
- **7.IV.A.5** Student protests at home: draft protests, Students for a Democratic Society
- **7.IV.A.6** 1968: A year of turmoil: President Johnson's decision not to seek reelection, assassinations of Dr. Martin Luther King, Jr. and Robert Kennedy, the Democratic Convention

Terms and People

draftee
SDS
"credibility gap"

Tet Offensive
Eugene McCarthy
Robert Kennedy

NoteTaking

Reading Skill: Recognize Sequence Note the events leading up to the 1968 election.

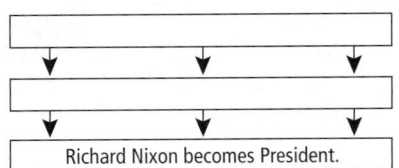

Richard Nixon becomes President.

Why It Matters President Johnson sent more American troops to Vietnam in order to win the war. But with each passing year, casualty lists got longer and victory seemed further away. As soldiers died abroad and hawks and doves argued at home, the Vietnam War opened up a deep emotional rift in American society. After the war ended, it would take years for the country to heal itself.

Section Focus Question: How did the American war effort in Vietnam lead to rising protests and social divisions back home?

Antiwar Protests Increase

The war in Vietnam divided Americans more deeply than any conflict since the Civil War. Although most Americans initially supported President Johnson's bombings and troop deployments, by 1966 critics began speaking out. Senator Fulbright's opposition to the war hurt Johnson in Congress, and the senator was soon joined by like-minded activists who believed that American soldiers were dying in a war that had little to do with American interests.

The Draft Becomes Increasingly Unpopular By 1965, most of the troops sent to Vietnam were no longer volunteers who had enlisted in the army. Instead, they were **draftees**—young men drafted into military service—who had been assigned a tour in Vietnam. In accordance with the Selective Service Act of 1948, the government drafted more than 1.5 million men into military service during the Vietnam War. All males had to register for the draft when they turned 18, and the Selective Service System called up draftees based on projected military needs.

Critics of the Selective Service System argued that the draft was not fair. The system gave local draft boards considerable influence in selecting men for service, and it also granted deferments to college students and men who worked in certain designated occupations. Most of the 2.5 million men who served in Vietnam came from working-class and poor backgrounds.

During the Johnson presidency, the number of African American troops fighting and dying in Vietnam was also disproportionately high. At the beginning of the war, African Americans suffered more than 20 percent of the total combat deaths, roughly twice their percentage of the U.S. population. Additionally, African American soldiers were more likely to serve in combat positions and less likely to become commissioned officers.

Civil rights leader Martin Luther King, Jr., spoke out against the added war burden shouldered by African American soldiers. Speaking at a New York church in 1967, King said that the war was hurting both poor blacks and whites. Vietnam was drawing human and economic resources away from America's other wars on poverty and discrimination. He added that it hindered poor Americans in other more direct ways:

Primary Source "It was sending their sons and their brothers and their husbands to fight and to die in extraordinary high proportions relative to the rest of the population. . . . [W]e have been repeatedly faced with the cruel irony of watching Negro and white boys on TV screens as they kill and die together for a nation that has been unable to seat them together in the same schools."

—Martin Luther King, Jr., 1967

Perceived inequities in the draft led to widespread resistance. Antiwar advocates sponsored a Stop-the-Draft week in October 1967, and some draft-eligible males burned their draft cards in protest. Finally, in 1969, the Selective Service System adopted a lottery that was designed to eliminate deferment abuses and create a more diverse army of draftees.

Vocabulary Builder
deferment–(dee FER muhnt) *n.*
postponement

African American Soldiers in Battle

The Vietnam War witnessed the highest proportion of African Americans ever to serve in an American war. Here, an African American Marine ducks behind a wall for cover while firing on an enemy position. *Based on the line graph, why might African American recruits be unhappy with the draft?*

African Americans and the Vietnam War

Percentage of African Americans

— African American combat deaths (U.S. Army)
— African Americans in U.S. population

SOURCES: Department of Defense; *Historical Statistics of the United States*

Activism Spreads on College Campuses Across America, college campuses became centers of antiwar sentiment. Professors and students criticized the war for a variety of reasons, ranging from pacifism and the war's effects on the economy to a personal desire to avoid military service. Antiwar activity on college campuses did not, however, reflect the attitudes of Americans as a whole. In fact, many professors remained vocal in their defense of the war effort during lectures and at protest rallies. For the most part, though, colleges and universities represented the extreme antiwar opinion.

Antiwar activities were part of more significant changes taking place on college campuses. Never before the 1960s had so many Americans entered colleges and universities. Between 1946 and 1970, the number of students enrolled in institutions of higher education increased from 2 million to 8 million. Many college students became a class unto themselves—segregated from the workforce, free from many adult responsibilities, and encouraged by their professors to think critically. Most of the students who embraced the antiwar cause came from upper-middle-class families. Students from working-class families were less likely to protest against the war.

The University of Michigan and the University of California at Berkeley became important hubs of the antiwar movement. The **Students for a Democratic Society (SDS)** was founded in 1960 at the University of Michigan. Originally formed to campaign against racism and poverty, the SDS soon began campaigning to end the war in Vietnam. By 1964, SDS had organized campus "teach-ins" and demonstrations against the war and encouraged draft-age males to sign "We Won't Go" petitions.

Students Clash With Authorities Student activism led to a clash with administrators and police in 1964. Students at the University of California at Berkeley protested against the school's decision not to allow them to use university grounds to organize off-campus political activities. The students formed the Free Speech Movement to contest the decision. When protesters occupied a university building, the police arrested them. In response, students cut classes to march in support of the FSM. University officials eventually relented and allowed students to engage in free speech activities on school grounds. The victory by students at Berkeley led to challenges at other colleges and universities.

More and More Americans Oppose the War Outside college campuses, other Americans soon enlisted in the antiwar cause. The war in Vietnam was the first "living-room war." Americans watched the progress—or lack of it—in their living rooms on nightly newscasts. The intimacy of television made news of the war unavoidable. But unlike World War II, there was no march to victory. Americans could not put maps of Vietnam on their walls and trace the routes the troops were taking to Hanoi.

Hawks and doves drifted farther apart. More groups organized against the war, their names corresponding with whom they represented—Vietnam Veterans Against the War, Catholic Peace Fellowship, Another Mother for Peace. Antiwar Americans—rich and poor, black and white—read reports from war correspondents who questioned U.S. progress in Vietnam. They watched government officials issue optimistic statement after optimistic statement. Soon, a *"credibility gap"* emerged between what the Johnson administration said and what many journalists reported. This gap referred to the American public's growing distrust of statements made by the government.

✔ **Checkpoint** Why did the antiwar movement grow across the nation?

Hawks Respond to Protests

Despite doves' vocal opposition to the war, hawks organized their own demonstrations to support U.S. policy in Vietnam. Below, New York City union members rally behind the American war effort in 1967.

Tet Offensive Is the Turning Point

In November 1967, President Johnson brought General Westmoreland home from Vietnam to address the nation's concerns about the war. Westmoreland said that the Vietcong were declining in strength and could no longer mount a major offensive. As Westmoreland made his claims, however, the North Vietnamese and Vietcong were planning just such an attack.

Communist Assault Shocks Americans

In early 1968, U.S. officials anticipated a communist offensive. As expected, on January 21, the North Vietnamese Army hit Khe Sanh in northwest South Vietnam. However, nine days later, the communists expanded their attack by hitting U.S. and ARVN positions throughout South Vietnam. The **Tet Offensive**—named after the Vietnamese lunar new year—was a coordinated assault on 36 provincial capitals and 5 major cities, as well as the U.S. embassy in Saigon.

The communists planned to take and hold the cities until the urban population took up arms in their support. They thought the Tet Offensive had a good chance of ending the war. The fighting was fierce, but in the end, American and South Vietnamese forces repelled the offensive and there was no popular uprising against the government of South Vietnam. Although U.S. forces won a tactical victory by preventing the Vietcong and North Vietnamese Army from achieving their primary objectives, the Tet Offensive was a strategic blow to the Americans. It demonstrated that the communists had not lost the will or the ability to fight on.

Tet Offensive, 1968

CHINA

NORTH VIETNAM

Hanoi

Gulf of Tonkin

LAOS

Mekong R.

South China Sea

THAILAND

—20° N

January–June 1968 Battle of Khe Sanh

—15° N

CAMBODIA

Gulf of Thailand

SOUTH VIETNAM

January 31, 1968 American embassy attacked

Saigon

Attack during Tet Offensive

Ho Chi Minh Trail

Miller Projection

0   100   200 mi

0   100   200 km

105° E   110° E

Map Skills In launching the Tet Offensive, the Vietcong and North Vietnamese Army wanted to demoralize South Vietnam and deal American forces a devastating blow.

1. **Regions** Identify two regions of South Vietnam that were hard-hit by the Tet Offensive.

2. **Draw Conclusions** How do you think the Tet Offensive affected the morale of North Vietnam? Explain.

War's End Is Nowhere in Sight

After the Tet Offensive, American military leaders seemed less confident of a quick end to the war. When Westmoreland requested more troops, President Johnson asked his new Secretary of Defense Clark Clifford to take an objective look at the military and political situation in Vietnam. The deeper Clifford delved into the matter, the more pessimistic he became. Sending more troops would <u>inevitably</u> require raising taxes, increasing draft rolls, and calling up reserves. It would lead to increased casualties in the field and dissent at home. And it still might not lead to victory. Clifford concluded that the President should radically shift U.S. policy from one that pursued victory to one that pursued a negotiated peace.

Johnson Steps Down

While Clifford deliberated, many Americans began to turn dramatically against the war. Some marched in protest and engaged in antiwar activities. Others registered their disapproval at the polls. In early

Vocabulary Builder
<u>inevitable</u>–(ihn EHV ih tuh buhl)
adj. certain to happen

Can the United States Win the War in Vietnam?

Despite the war's growing unpopularity, Johnson was reluctant to withdraw from Vietnam. Some urged him to get out of "Kennedy's war." His own Cabinet was divided on the issue.

DEAN RUSK

Citing Chamberlain and Hitler as an example, Secretary of State Rusk opposed appeasement. He supported increased bombing and troops to force North Vietnam to negotiate a peace.

Primary Source

"If . . . North Vietnam will stop [its] campaign to destroy the Republic of Vietnam, the measures we are taking to assist South Vietnam . . . will no longer be necessary. . . . We see no necessity for international negotiations. . . . [W]e cannot [think of] any points that would be negotiable."

—Dean Rusk, 1963

GEORGE BALL

Undersecretary of State Ball urged President Johnson in 1965 to stop sending U.S. soldiers to Vietnam.

Primary Source

"No one can assure you that we can beat the Viet Cong . . . no matter how many . . . troops we deploy. No [ground forces] of whatever size can win a guerrilla war—which is at the same time a civil war . . . in jungle terrain in the midst of a population that refuses cooperation. . . ."

—George Ball, 1965

Compare
1. According to Rusk, when should the United States end its participation in the war?
2. Why does Ball think that Rusk's strategy will not work?

1968, Minnesota senator **Eugene McCarthy,** the antiwar candidate for the Democratic Party nomination, made a surprisingly strong showing in the New Hampshire primary. Sensing that Johnson was in a politically weakened position, New York's Democratic senator **Robert Kennedy** announced his candidacy for the presidency. Both McCarthy and Kennedy believed that the war had divided America and drained resources away from the fights against poverty and discrimination. What Johnson feared most was happening: The war was undermining his presidency.

On March 31, 1968, two months after the Tet Offensive, the President addressed the nation on television. He announced that America would limit its bombing of North Vietnam and seek a negotiated settlement to the war. Johnson then shocked the nation by announcing that he would not run for another term as President. The speech marked another turning point in the war. The fight for victory was over. Peace was now the official government policy.

 Checkpoint How was the Tet Offensive both a victory and a defeat for the United States?

Violence Rocks 1968 Presidential Race

Johnson's decision not to seek reelection in 1968 threw the presidential race wide open. Many Americans believed it provided an opportunity to enact fundamental political and social changes. They argued that the future of the country was at stake. It was a time of new ideas and new plans. But the optimism and high hopes of the early campaign would soon die amidst political infighting, violence, and assassination.

Chicago 1968: Politics and Protest

As Democrats prepared to select a new presidential candidate at their convention in Chicago (see campaign artifacts at left), antiwar activists converged on the city in August 1968. Inside the main hall, dissension between hawks and doves in the party sparked angry outbursts. On the streets outside, violent clashes broke out between antiwar protesters and the Chicago police. The crowds chanted, "The whole world is watching! The whole world is watching!" And indeed it was. Television viewers saw a vivid display of the political strife and social unrest besieging America.

Opposition to the Vietnam War

In view of the developments since we entered the fighting in Vietnam, do you think the United States made a mistake sending troops to fight in Vietnam?

	March 1966	April 1967	April 1968
Yes	26%	37%	48%
No	59%	50%	40%
Don't Know	16%	13%	12%

SOURCE: American Institute of Public Opinion (Gallup Poll)

◄ As U.S. combat deaths in Vietnam increased from roughly 5,000 in 1966 to more than 14,000 in 1968, American public opinion turned against the war.

▲ Chicago mayor Richard J. Daley shouts insults at Senator Abraham Ribicoff during the senator's speech criticizing the tactics of the Chicago police.

Many protesters sought only to exercise their right to free speech. Others, eyeing the ever-present television cameras, sought—and succeeded in attracting—a police response. Here, a melee erupts outside a hotel where delegates are gathered. ▶

Thinking Critically

1. **Analyze Information** How did American casualties in Vietnam affect public opinion back home?

2. **Draw Conclusions** How do you think events in Chicago affected the U.S. soldiers in Vietnam?

Geography *Interactive*
For: Interactive map
Web Code: nep-1607

Candidate (Party)	Electoral Vote	Popular Vote	% Electoral Vote	% Popular Vote**
Richard M. Nixon (Republican)	301	31,710,470	56	43.6
Hubert H. Humphrey (Democratic)	191	30,898,055	36	42.5
George C. Wallace (American Independent)	46	9,906,473	8	13.6

*One Nixon elector voted outside the party's endorsement
**Minor parties received 0.3% of the popular vote

Map Skills In 1968, Richard Nixon defeated Vice President Hubert Humphrey and third-party candidate George Wallace, who had split from the Democratic Party.

1. **Regions** From where did Wallace draw most of his support?

2. **Draw Conclusions** What might have happened if Wallace had renounced his candidacy and rejoined the Democratic ranks?

Two Leaders Fall In the spring and summer of the campaign season, bullets struck down two Americans who spoke out eloquently for peace in Vietnam and peaceful change in American society. Martin Luther King, Jr., the most prominent leader of the civil rights movement, had publicly turned against the war in 1967. He contributed compelling social and moral reasons to the argument for peace. But his voice was tragically silenced on April 4, 1968, when a racist assassin shot and killed him in Memphis, Tennessee.

Robert Kennedy was the next leader to fall. He had based his campaign for the presidency on compassion and idealism, and millions of Americans rallied to his camp. On June 5, 1968, at a rally celebrating his victory in the California primary, Kennedy asserted that "we are a great country, an unselfish country, a compassionate country," and that he intended "to make that the basis of my running." Minutes later, a Palestinian immigrant named Sirhan Sirhan shot Kennedy in the head, killing him instantly. Sirhan may have wanted revenge for America's support for Israel in that country's war with Egypt the year before.

Protesters Disrupt Chicago Democratic Convention The murders of King and Kennedy cast a dark shadow over the election campaigns. In August 1968, the Democrats convened in Chicago to choose a presidential candidate to represent their party in the November election. As the delegates arrived, so too did antiwar protesters. Chicago's mayor deployed police and members of the National Guard to prevent any outbreaks of violence.

Inside the convention, the Democrats angrily debated placing an antiwar plank in the party platform. They chose Hubert Humphrey, Johnson's Vice President, over Eugene McCarthy, who had garnered support from many antiwar groups. As the delegates cast their votes, violence erupted outside the convention between police and protesters. After police beat activists with nightsticks, some protesters retaliated by throwing rocks and bottles at the onrushing tide of police.

The television coverage of the fierce fighting in the streets and bitter arguments on the convention floor shocked Americans. Chaos and civil disorder appeared to have replaced civil debate in the political arena. The divisions and violence in Chicago mirrored the deep divisions in American politics and the heartbreaking violence on the front lines in Vietnam.

Richard Nixon Wins the Presidency At a much more peaceful convention in Miami, Republicans nominated Richard M. Nixon, who promised if elected he would deliver "peace with honor." He wanted the United States out of Vietnam, but he also demanded honorable peace terms. He promised to listen to "the great, quiet forgotten majority—the nonshouters and the nondemonstrators." This large group of Americans, described by one commentator as "the young, the unblack, and the unpoor," was dubbed the "silent majority." Throughout his campaign, Nixon used a "southern strategy" of courting more conservative southern voters with appeals to law and order, striving to pull them away from their traditional support of the Democratic Party.

Alabama governor George Wallace also ran for the presidency on a third-party ticket. A lifelong Democrat prior to his entry into the race, Wallace said that neither of the traditional political parties represented southern voters who were unsettled by the cultural and social changes in the country. He had no sympathy for the demands of antiwar radicals, counterculture hippies, or African American militants. He represented the "white backlash" against the civil rights movement and the desire to press forward to victory in Vietnam.

The combination of Nixon's "southern strategy" and Wallace's third-party candidacy siphoned traditionally Democratic votes away from Humphrey. In a close election, Nixon captured victory by winning 43.6 percent of the popular vote and 301 electoral votes. Humphrey received 42.5 percent of the popular vote and Wallace 13.6 percent. The election marked the end of the Democratic "Solid South" and signaled significant changes in the nation's political landscape. Richard Nixon's ascendancy marked a new Republican domination of the American presidency.

✔ **Checkpoint** What happened at the 1968 Democratic Convention in Chicago?

"Silent" Supporters

In 1969, President Nixon called his supporters the "silent majority." Especially strong in the South and West, the silent majority consisted of patriotic veterans of World War II and the Korean War, middle class blue-collar workers, conservative young Americans, and many others.

SECTION 3 Assessment

Progress Monitoring *Online*
For: Self-test with vocabulary practice
Web Code: nea-1608

Comprehension

1. **Terms and People** For each item below, write a sentence explaining its significance.
   - draftee
   - "credibility gap"
   - Tet Offensive
   - Eugene McCarthy

2. **NoteTaking Reading Skill: Recognize Sequence** Use your flowchart to answer the Section Focus Question: How did the American war effort in Vietnam lead to rising protests and social divisions back home?

Writing About History

3. **Quick Write: Answer Opposing Arguments** To write a strong persuasive essay, you need to address arguments that could be raised to refute your own position. Choose a topic from this section, such as whether Johnson made the right decision by withdrawing from the 1968 presidential race. Then, create a chart listing arguments on both sides of the debate.

Critical Thinking

4. **Evaluate Information** Identify three factors that led to the growth of the antiwar movement. Which do you think was the most important?

5. **Identify Effects** How did the military outcome of the Tet Offensive differ from its impact on the American people?

6. **Draw Conclusions** What were the chief weaknesses of the Democrats in the 1968 election? How did these weaknesses aid the election of Richard Nixon?

▲ Antiwar demonstrators march in Washington, D.C.

WITNESS HISTORY 🔊 AUDIO

Antiwar Protests Spread

As Richard Nixon entered the White House in January 1969, students across the country continued to protest the war. And their words were starting to reach ordinary Americans, not just "long-haired radicals." In late 1969, antiwar protesters organized a series of peaceful demonstrations called "moratoriums." On October 15, the mayor of New York City addressed a crowd of these protesters:

❝We cannot [accept] the charge from Washington that this peaceful protest is unpatriotic. We heard that charge five years ago and three years ago. . . . The fact is that this dissent is the highest form of patriotism. It is the peaceful American way to turn the nation away from a self-defeating course.❞
—New York mayor John Lindsay, 1969

The War's End and Impact

Core Curriculum Objectives

- **7.IV.A.6d** Impact of the Vietnam War on society
- **7.V.A.2a(1)** Withdrawal from Vietnam and Cambodia; peace talks and signing of Paris Peace Accords (Pentagon papers, *New York Times* v. *United States*)

Terms and People

Vietnamization
My Lai
Pentagon Papers

Paris Peace Accords
War Powers Act

NoteTaking

Reading Skill: Compare and Contrast
Note the similarities and differences between Nixon's Vietnam policy and that of Lyndon Johnson.

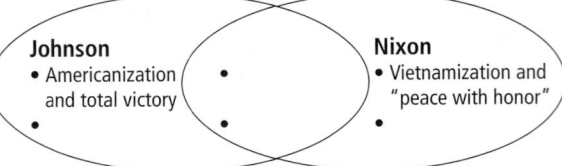

Why It Matters As a presidential candidate, Richard Nixon promised "peace with honor" and an end to a war that had fractured American society. Nixon did indeed withdraw American troops, and the Vietnam War finally ended. But the impact of the war endured. As the nation recovered from war, Americans reexamined the struggle against communism, the power of the presidency, and America's role in the world. **Section Focus Question: How did the Vietnam War end, and what were its lasting effects?**

Nixon Starts the Pullout

Nixon's defenders argued that he was a hard-working patriot with a new vision for America. His critics charged that he was a deceitful politician bent on acquiring power and punishing his enemies. There were elements of truth to both views. But defenders and critics alike agreed that Richard Nixon was a determined man with abundant political talent. From his first day in office, the new President realized that ending the Vietnam War was the key to everything else he hoped to achieve.

Peace Talks Stall Though formal peace talks between the warring parties had begun in May 1968, they were bogged down from the outset by disagreements and a lack of compromise. When Richard Nixon took office in January 1969, his peace delegation firmly believed they could break the impasse. The Americans and South Vietnamese wanted all communist troops out of South Vietnam.

They also wanted prisoners of war (POWs) returned. Meanwhile, the North Vietnamese demanded an immediate American withdrawal from Vietnam and the formation of a coalition government in South Vietnam that would include representatives from the Vietcong. Still hoping to win the war in the field, North Vietnam refused to budge from its initial position. And South Vietnam refused to sign any agreement that compromised its security.

Nixon's Plan: Vietnamization and Peace With Honor President Nixon refused to accept the North Vietnamese peace terms. He was committed to a policy of "peace with honor" and believed that there were still military options. He continued a gradual pullout of American troops, and expressed faith in the ability of the Army of the Republic of Vietnam to assume the burden of war. He called his approach **Vietnamization**—U.S. forces would withdraw as ARVN troops assumed more combat duties. The hope was that with continued American aid behind the front lines, the ARVN would fight its own battles to secure South Vietnam.

To reduce the flow of communist supplies to the Vietcong, Nixon ordered the secret bombing of the Ho Chi Minh Trail in Cambodia. This was a controversial move because it widened the scope of the war and helped to undermine the neutral government in Cambodia. In the end, neither Vietnamization nor secret bombings dramatically improved South Vietnam's chances of winning a war against the communists.

 Checkpoint How did Vietnamization differ from the war policies of Nixon's predecessors?

Troubles on the Home Front Intensify

Nixon inherited two things from Lyndon Johnson: an unpopular war and a vocal American opposition to it. The new President wanted "peace with honor," security for America's ally South Vietnam, and international respect for U.S. foreign policy. Antiwar activists wanted the war ended and American troops out of Vietnam—on any terms. Nixon found it increasingly difficult to achieve his goals and satisfy the snowballing antiwar movement.

American Troops in Cambodia More than a year into office, Nixon had grown impatient with the snail's pace of the peace negotiations. In 1970, he attempted to break the stalemate by ordering a ground attack on North Vietnamese Army and Vietcong bases in Cambodia. Nixon also hoped to aid the pro-American Cambodian government in its fight against the Khmer Rouge, a communist movement supported by North Vietnam.

On the evening of April 30, Nixon addressed the American people, informing them of his decision to carry the war into Cambodia. He stressed that the war had become a measure of how committed the United States was to preserving freedom around the world:

Primary Source "If, when the chips are down, the world's most powerful nation, the United States of America, acts like a pitiful, helpless giant, the forces of totalitarianism and anarchy will threaten free nations . . . throughout the world."
—President Richard Nixon, 1970

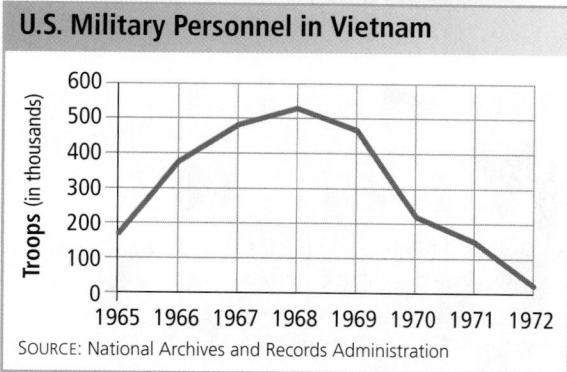

U.S. Military Personnel in Vietnam

SOURCE: National Archives and Records Administration

Vietnamizing the War
The United States scaled back its commitment of ground troops to Vietnam after 1968. However, while more American troops left for home, U.S. air forces dropped more bombs on communist targets in North Vietnam and along the Ho Chi Minh Trail. *How did the shift in American tactics ensure Nixon's "peace with honor"?*

The next morning, U.S. and ARVN forces crossed the border into Cambodia. These soldiers captured large stockpiles of weapons and supplies, but they did not break the stalemate. North Vietnam remained determined to have peace on its terms or no peace at all.

Violence Erupts at Kent State The Cambodian incursion had a profound impact on the peace movement at home. It stirred antiwar activists, who argued that Nixon had widened the war and made the world a more dangerous place. Throughout the country, college campuses erupted with protests. Several demonstrations prompted the police and National Guard to step in to preserve order.

On two campuses, confrontations between students and armed authorities led to deaths. Four days after Nixon's speech, demonstrators at Kent State University in Ohio threw rocks and bottles at members of the National Guard. When one guardsman thought he heard a sniper's shot, he fired his rifle. The shot prompted other National Guardsmen to discharge a volley of gunfire into a group of protesters, killing four youths. The Kent State killings led to demonstrations on other campuses. At Jackson State University, a traditionally African American college in Mississippi, a confrontation between students and police ended with two students dead.

College demonstrations against the war sometimes prompted counterprotests by Americans who supported the President. In response to a May 8, 1970, antiwar rally in downtown New York City, construction workers decided to demonstrate, carrying American flags and chanting "All the Way USA." Believing that some anti-

Protest and Death in Ohio
A student photographer at Kent State snapped this photograph moments after the Ohio National Guard opened fire on student protesters on May 4, 1970. *How do you think people reacted to seeing this photograph in the newspaper?*

war demonstrators had spit on the American flag, they pushed into the crowd and started hitting protesters. The clash drew national attention. Days later, thousands of construction workers, businessmen, secretaries, and housewives marched peacefully through Manhattan's streets in support of Nixon and the war effort. One man expressed his feelings about the march:

Primary Source   66I'm very proud to be an American, and I know my boy that was killed in Vietnam would be here today if he was alive, marching with us. . . . I know he died for the right cause, because in his letters he wrote to me he knew what he was fighting for: to keep America free. . . .99

—Robert Geary, May 20, 1970

As the fighting continued in Vietnam, the American home front became its own physical and emotional battlefield.

American Soldiers Kill Civilians at My Lai In 1971, two events increased the pressure on Nixon to pull U.S. troops out of Vietnam. The first event had roots in a U.S. action in South Vietnam three years earlier. On March 16, 1968, American forces searching for enemy troops in an area with a strong Vietcong presence came upon the village of **My Lai.** By this point in the war, many American troops had been injured and killed by Vietcong fighters posing as civilians. It was a recipe for disaster at My Lai, where Lieutenant William Calley's unit began shooting and killing unarmed civilians. During the assault, U.S. soldiers killed between four and five hundred Vietnamese.

Lt. Calley later maintained that he was following orders, but many of the soldiers present did not participate in the massacre. At least one risked his own life to stop it. The tragedy was made even worse by an inadequate military investigation of the incident. *Life* magazine eventually published photos taken during the event, and in March 1971, a military court convicted Lt. Calley of his participation in the attack. News of the My Lai massacre, the coverup, and Calley's trial shocked many Americans and added fuel to the burning antiwar fire.

Pentagon Papers Undermine Public Trust On the heels of My Lai came the 1971 publication of the **Pentagon Papers** in *The New York Times*. The term referred to a classified government history of America's involvement in Vietnam. The study was leaked to *The Times* by one of its coauthors, Daniel Ellsberg. Nixon tried to block the full publication, but in *New York Times* v. *United States*, the Supreme Court ruled against the administration. The study revealed that American leaders involved the U.S. in Vietnam without fully informing the American people and occasionally even lied to Congress.

✓ **Checkpoint** What happened at Kent State and Jackson State universities in 1970?

Slaughter and Coverup in South Vietnam

A photographer captured the terror in the village of My Lai as American troops were killing hundreds of civilians. The massacre was followed by a military investigation, but only Lt. William Calley was convicted. *Why were many Americans dissatisfied with the result of the military investigation?*

The War Finally Ends

The failings of Vietnamization and growing dissent at home forced President Nixon to search for some final way out of the conflict. A 1971 public-opinion poll revealed that two thirds of Americans favored withdrawing American troops, even if it meant a communist takeover of South Vietnam. Sensitive to the public mood, Congress pressed Nixon to bring the troops home. Many believed that to win reelection in 1972, he had to end the war.

American Troops Leave Vietnam In October 1972, the United States and North Vietnam came to terms on a peace settlement. One month later, with lasting peace almost at hand, Nixon easily defeated the antiwar Democrat George McGovern for reelection. But Nixon's triumph was short-lived. The Vietnamese peace fell apart when North Vietnam refused to sign the agreement. Talks broke off, but renewed American bombing in North Vietnam finally <u>induced</u> the North Vietnamese to resume negotiations.

At last, in January 1973, the United States, South Vietnam, North Vietnam, and the Vietcong signed the **Paris Peace Accords.** The parties agreed to a cease-fire and a U.S. troop withdrawal from South Vietnam. POWs would be exchanged, but North Vietnamese troops would remain in South Vietnam. The National Liberation Front would become a legitimate political party in South Vietnam, and South Vietnam's noncommunist government would remain in power pending a political settlement. With the war ended, the last American troops came home. Among the returning soldiers were more than 550 POWs, most of whom were pilots shot down during the war.

Saigon Falls For the United States, the war in Vietnam was over. For the Vietnamese, however, it continued. Neither North nor South Vietnam honored the cease-fire or worked toward a diplomatic settlement of their differences. In the spring of 1975, minor fighting escalated when North Vietnam launched an offensive against the South. Without American aid and ground support, the ARVN was no match for the Soviet-supplied North Vietnamese Army. By the end of April, the communists had taken Saigon. After decades of fighting and millions of deaths, Vietnam was unified under one flag.

✓ **Checkpoint** What did the signing parties agree to in the Paris Peace Accords?

Vocabulary Builder
<u>induce</u>–(ihn DOOS) *v.* to bring about; cause

◄ A Purple Heart is awarded to members of the U.S. armed forces who are wounded or killed by an enemy in combat.

⬤ **INFOGRAPHIC**

America's Veterans Return From Vietnam

In April 1973, a plane carrying the last American prisoners of war from Vietnam touched down in Hawaii. The flight marked the end of an era that had seen hundreds of thousands of American troops deployed to fight in the Vietnam War. The homecoming for many of these soldiers had been bittersweet. While some came home to exuberant family reunions and community parades, many Vietnam veterans received little or no public acknowledgment of their sacrifices. It was not until nearly a decade later that the nation dedicated the Vietnam Veterans Memorial (see photo at far right) to honor these brave Americans.

◄ A Vietnam veteran takes part in a 1973 parade in New York City to honor those who served in the war.

Some veterans, like this ► man in San Francisco in 1994, faced hard times after they reentered American society.

•HOMELESS
RESPECTFULLY· ASKING
"PLEASE HELP"
·DONATION · FOOD ·
THANK YOU
GOD BLESS
·VIETNAM ·VETERAN·
SEMPER FIDELIS
U.S.M.C.
BRAVO 19 ● 3RD. DIV.
CHULAI ·69· DANANG
- 0311-

The Vietnam War Has a Lasting Impact

More than 58,000 American soldiers gave their lives serving their country in Vietnam; another 300,000 were wounded. Although figures are not exact, the Vietnamese death toll most likely exceeded 2 million. Peace, however, did not mean the end of pain and hardship. The end of the war created other problems in Southeast Asia. The war also affected American attitudes toward world affairs.

Southeast Asia Suffers Further Turmoil Many foreign-policy experts in the United States had predicted that if North Vietnam won the Vietnamese civil war, communism would spread to other nations in Southeast Asia. In a limited sense, they were right. Communist regimes eventually came to power in both Laos and Cambodia. In Cambodia, the ruling Khmer Rouge unleashed a genocide on the populace, killing everyone who had ties to the West or previous Cambodian governments. Between 1975 and 1979, upwards of 2 million Cambodians were executed or died in labor camps.

In an expanded sense, however, many American foreign-policy strategists misjudged the spread of communism. They concluded it was a monolithic global movement controlled by Moscow and Beijing. However, as the war's aftermath would attest, communist movements in Southeast Asia were nationalistic and intolerant of outside influences. After the Vietnam War ended, Vietnamese communists went to war against the Khmer Rouge, who in turn received help from Chinese communists to battle the Vietnamese. In this conflict, the United States supported the Chinese.

Veterans Return Home to Mixed Reactions The war and the peace divided Americans. Some argued that the United States should never have entered the war and that their leaders had lied to them. Others countered that the war was part of an ongoing struggle against communism and that in the

The families of Americans still missing after the Vietnam War hope that those prisoners and missing will one day be returned to them. ▼

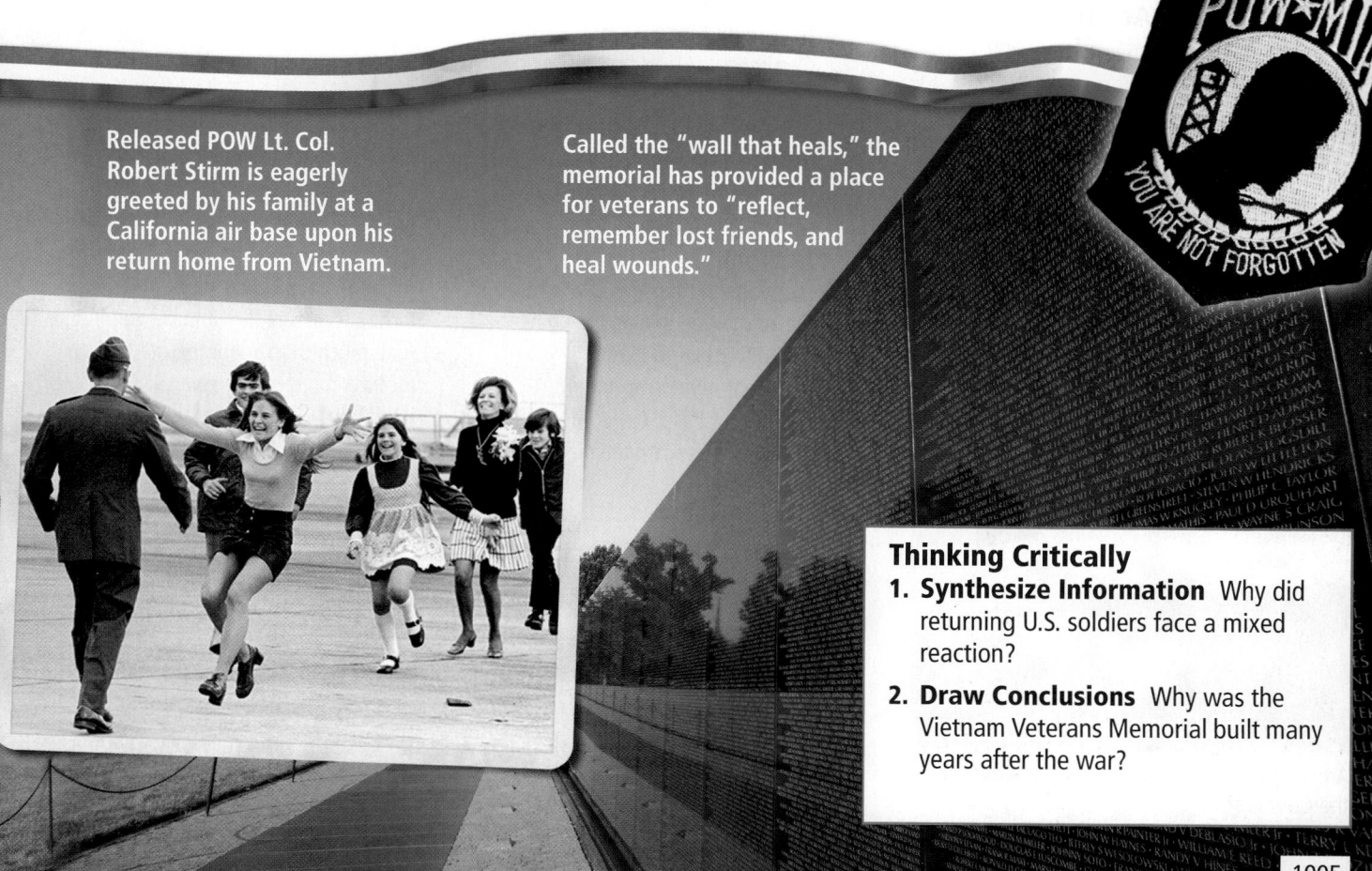

Released POW Lt. Col. Robert Stirm is eagerly greeted by his family at a California air base upon his return home from Vietnam.

Called the "wall that heals," the memorial has provided a place for veterans to "reflect, remember lost friends, and heal wounds."

Thinking Critically

1. **Synthesize Information** Why did returning U.S. soldiers face a mixed reaction?

2. **Draw Conclusions** Why was the Vietnam Veterans Memorial built many years after the war?

TRACK THE ISSUE

What is America's role in the world?

At times throughout its history, the United States has tried to avoid getting involved in other countries' affairs. At other times, it has played an active part in world affairs. Today, America is deeply involved around the world. But what should its role be? Use the timeline below to explore this enduring issue.

1796 Washington's Farewell Address
President Washington warns against foreign alliances.

1823 Monroe Doctrine
President Monroe tells Europe to stay out of the Americas.

1898 Spanish-American War
The United States defeats Spain and expands overseas.

1940s–1980s Cold War
The United States tries to stop the spread of communism around the world.

2000s War on Terrorism
The United States works with other countries to fight global terrorism.

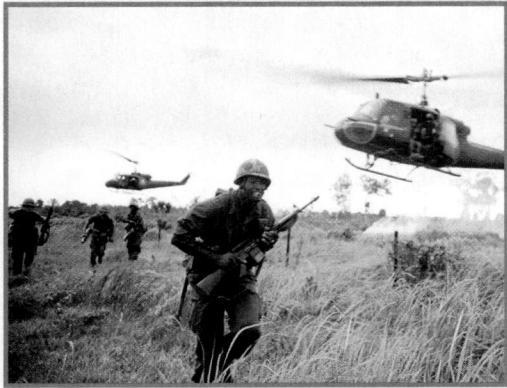

American soldiers fought in Vietnam during the Cold War.

NY 7.V.B.3

Since 2001, Afghanistan has labored to remake its government into a stable democracy.

DEBATE THE ISSUE

Intervention and Democracy In 2001, the United States invaded Afghanistan. It toppled the Taliban government and ended its support for terrorism. Since then, the United States has helped to rebuild Afghanistan. Can intervention bring progress to a country?

"The United States and Afghanistan have made great progress. . . . Together we have . . . worked to ensure that Afghanistan will never again be a safe haven for terrorists. The United States has supported the Afghan people as they have established a moderate, representative government."

—Joint Declaration of the United States-Afghanistan Strategic Partnership

"The [George W.] Bush administration has consistently labeled the invasion of [Afghanistan] a success. But reports from humanitarian organizations, United Nations officials and Afghanis themselves paint a very different picture—warlords dominate much of the country, the Taliban is still a force in many parts, and the illegal drug trade is flourishing."

—Seymour Hersh, journalist for *The New Yorker*

 TRANSFER Activities

1. **Compare** What does the first quotation say about the results of intervention? What does the second quotation say?

2. **Analyze** What kinds of challenges might leaders from both countries face as they work to create a functioning democratic government?

3. **Transfer** Use the following Web site to see a video, try a WebQuest, and write in your journal. **Web Code:** neh-8902

end, the United States betrayed South Vietnam. An unfortunate result of the controversy was that the nation never fully expressed its appreciation to the returning veterans.

Overwhelmingly, the 2.5 million enlisted men who served in Vietnam did so with honor and distinction. Yet, unlike the soldiers that returned to the United States after World Wars I and II—the famed Doughboys and G.I. Joes—few Vietnam vets enjoyed the warmth and adulation of victory parades. In addition to the indifference that some veterans encountered, some also suffered from physical and psychological ailments for years when they returned home.

Not until almost a decade after the end of the war did Americans begin to fully honor the courage and sacrifice of these veterans. The Vietnam Veterans Memorial, dedicated in Washington, D.C., in 1982, stands as an eloquent testament to the men and women who served and died in Vietnam.

Vietnam Changes American Policies The war was costly both monetarily and in the human toll of shattered lives. The war also altered American domestic and foreign policies. Lyndon Johnson's Great Society campaign against poverty and racism fell victim to the conflict. Increasingly, between 1964 and 1968, Johnson could not pay for both the Vietnam War and the Great Society. Paying for more guns left less money to pay for textbooks, school lunches, and prenatal care.

Additionally, the war undermined Americans' trust in their leaders and fragmented the Cold War consensus on foreign affairs. In 1973, Congress passed the **War Powers Act.** The act restricted the President's war-making powers by requiring him to consult with Congress within 48 hours of committing American forces to a foreign conflict. The act was a congressional attempt to check the unilateral formation of American foreign policy and stop the growth of the "imperial presidency."

Finally, the Vietnam War made Americans more suspicious of foreign commitments and less likely to intervene in the affairs of other countries. For the next 30 years, many Americans would view conflicts in Central America, Africa, the Balkans, and the Middle East through a lens tinted by the Vietnamese quagmire. The fear of "another Vietnam" had profound effects on American foreign policy in the postwar world.

✔ **Checkpoint** What did the War Powers Act do?

NoteTaking

Reading Skill: Recognize Effects As you read, use a concept web to identify the effects of the Vietnam War.

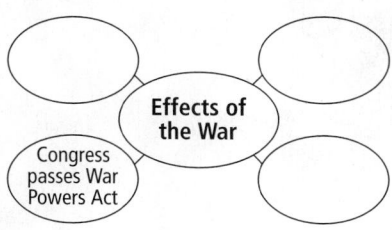

Effects of the War

Congress passes War Powers Act

SECTION 4 Assessment

Progress Monitoring *Online*
For: Self-test with vocabulary practice
Web Code: nea-1610

Comprehension

1. **Terms and People** For each term below, write a sentence explaining its significance.
   - Vietnamization
   - Paris Peace Accords
   - War Powers Act

2. **NoteTaking Reading Skill: Compare and Contrast** Use your Venn diagram to answer the Section Focus Question: How did the Vietnam War end, and what were its lasting effects?

Writing About History

3. **Quick Write: Choose Strongest Argument** Consider this thesis statement: Richard Nixon won the Vietnam War. List possible arguments for a persuasive essay that supports this thesis. Review each argument and choose the strongest one. Make sure that factual points from the text support your argument.

Critical Thinking

4. **Synthesize Information** How did Nixon redirect the peace process when he became President? Did his plan have the desired result?

5. **Explain Effects** What impact did the events of 1970 and 1971 have on Nixon's actions in Vietnam?

6. **Draw Conclusions** Which two effects of the Vietnam War do you think had the biggest long-term impact? Explain.

▲ Nixon and Zhou shake hands in China in 1972.

SECTION

5

WITNESS HISTORY 🔊 AUDIO

A New Era Begins

When Richard Nixon visited the People's Republic of China in February of 1972, Premier Zhou Enlai greeted the President as he landed in Beijing. Once on the wind-swept tarmac, Nixon walked toward his host with his arm outstretched. Recalling John Foster Dulles's refusal to shake Zhou's hand at the Geneva Conference in 1954, Nixon made certain not to repeat the insult to the Chinese leader. Nixon remembered the occasion in his memoir:

❝When I reached the bottom step, therefore, I made a point of extending my hand as I walked toward him. When our hands met, one era ended and another began.❞

—Richard Nixon

Nixon and the Cold War

 Core Curriculum Objectives

- **7.V.A** Nixon as President, 1969–1974
- **7.V.A.2a** Henry Kissinger and realpolitik: Opening to China and Detente: SALT

Terms and People

Henry Kissinger	Strategic Arms
realpolitik	Limitation Treaty
Zhou Enlai	détente

NoteTaking

Reading Skill: Categorize As you read, describe Nixon's Cold War foreign policies in dealing with China and the Soviet Union.

Nixon's Cold War Policies	
China	**Soviet Union**
• Normalization of relations will drive wedge between China and Soviet Union.	• Diplomacy with China will create Soviet fear of isolation.
•	•
•	•

Why It Matters As a presidential candidate, Richard Nixon had promised to end U.S. military involvement in the Vietnam War. Recognizing the potency of Soviet power and the increasing unwillingness of many Americans to pay the costs of containing communism everywhere, Nixon developed a new approach to the Cold War. His bold program redefined America's relations with the two titans of global communism, China and the Soviet Union. **Section Focus Question: How did Richard Nixon change Cold War diplomacy during his presidency?**

Nixon Redefines American Foreign Policy

During his years in office, Richard Nixon fundamentally reshaped the way the United States approached the world. Before Nixon took office, most American leaders shared a common Cold War ideology. They stressed that there existed a basic conflict between democratic, capitalist countries and totalitarian, communist ones. They divided the world into "us" and "them," and they established policies based on an assumption commonly held that "the enemy of my enemy is my friend." Therefore, a country opposed to communism was, by this definition, a friend of the United States. Nixon and **Henry Kissinger,** his leading adviser on national security and international affairs, altered this Cold War policy approach.

At first glance, Richard Nixon's partnership with Henry Kissinger seemed improbable. Nixon was a conservative California Republican, suspicious of the more liberal East Coast Republicans and exhausted with the political and strategic theories of Ivy League intellectuals. Kissinger was a Harvard-educated Jewish émigré from Germany and a prominent figure in East Coast intellectual circles. In several prior presidential campaigns, Kissinger had actually worked against Nixon. However, both men were outsiders, equipped with an outsider's readiness to question accepted orthodoxy.

In foreign affairs, Nixon and Kissinger embraced the idea of **realpolitik,** a German word meaning "real politics." According to realpolitik, political goals should be defined by concrete national interests instead of abstract ideologies. The two statesmen argued that if Americans would put aside their Cold War biases and look at the world with fresh eyes, U.S. global interests could be surveyed not in black and white but in shades of gray. For example, China and the Soviet Union—America's ideological enemies—could actually become excellent trading partners. At the same time, West Germany and Japan—America's ideological friends—were fast developing into economic rivals.

Nixon and Kissinger also questioned some lingering Cold War assumptions. For instance, they concluded that there was no united worldwide communist movement, as Lyndon Johnson and other Presidents had believed. There were important differences between the unique ideologies of the Soviet Union and China and other communist countries, such as Yugoslavia, North Korea, and North Vietnam, which often behaved quite independently. As President, Nixon insisted on a flexible, <u>pragmatic</u> foreign policy that avoided ideological absolutes.

 Checkpoint How did Nixon and Kissinger reshape America's approach to foreign affairs?

Vocabulary Builder
<u>pragmatic</u>–(prag MAT ihk) *adj.* practical; having to do with real actions and results rather than ideas and theories

Playing the China Card

From his first days in office, Nixon seemed determined to leave his mark on the nation's international affairs. Lyndon Johnson focused primarily on domestic affairs—the nuts and bolts of legislation and political deal-making. Nixon was more a man of the world, fascinated by global politics and shifting alliances. Johnson believed his Great Society would solidify his reputation as a great President. In stark contrast, Nixon thought his reorientation of American foreign policy would cement his legacy in the annals of United States history.

Reasons for Reaching Out to China "You're not going to believe this," a Nixon aide told a journalist in 1969, "but Nixon wants to recognize China." It was an odd, almost unbelievable, statement. At the time, the communist People's Republic of China was the most populous country in the world, but it was not officially recognized by the United States. Nor had it been admitted to the United Nations. The China that the United States recognized as the official representative body of the Chinese people was the Nationalist Chinese government exiled on the island of Taiwan. Nixon built his impressive career as a hard-line "Cold Warrior," a vigilant opponent of communism. He was the last politician Americans could imagine to extend the olive branch of recognition—and thus peace—to the communists.

Ever the political realist, Nixon knew that the People's Republic of China could not be ignored forever. He recognized that establishing diplomatic relations with the Chinese communists would benefit the United States. From an economic standpoint, improved relations would

HISTORY MAKERS

Henry Kissinger (b. 1923)
Born in Germany, Henry Kissinger came to the United States in 1938 when his family decided to flee the Nazis' growing persecution of Jews. After serving in the United States Army during World War II, he went to college. A brilliant student, Kissinger earned his bachelor's degree with highest honors and gained a Ph.D. at Harvard in just four years. Kissinger became a noted expert on national security and defense issues and soon impressed Richard Nixon with his foreign-policy analysis. When Nixon became President, he named Kissinger as his top national security adviser. The two worked closely together to end the Vietnam War, open relations with communist China, and shape the new diplomacy of détente with the Soviet Union. Nixon eventually named Kissinger his Secretary of State in 1973.

bring significant trade agreements, especially benefiting California and the Pacific Coast. Politically, U.S. normalization would drive a wedge between China and the Soviet Union, who had strayed from their traditional alliance and become rivals for territory and diplomatic influence. Finally, if the United States forged stronger relations with the Chinese, they might pressure North Vietnam to accept a negotiated peace to end the conflict still raging at the time.

Nixon Normalizes Relations With China With so much to gain and so little to lose, Nixon quietly pushed ahead with his plans. In public, the Chinese made symbolic overtures toward a meeting. In April 1971, China invited an American table-tennis team to play against its athletes. This small action demonstrated China's willingness to talk. Henry Kissinger worked behind the scenes, talking with Chinese leaders and ironing out sensitive issues with Premier **Zhou Enlai.** Then, in July 1971, Nixon announced that he would make an official state visit to China.

In February 1972, the President made the trip and toured the Great Wall, the Imperial Palace, and other historic sites. Nixon sat down for lengthy talks with Zhou Enlai and Communist Party Chairman Mao Zedong. He even learned enough Chinese to make a toast in the language of his host country. The visit was a great success and an important step toward normalizing diplomatic relations with China. The following year, American tourists started visiting and American companies set up a thriving trade with China. Nixon's China trip was the high point of his presidency. It bridged, as Zhou Enlai said, "the vastest ocean in the world, twenty-five years of no communication." In 1979, the United States and China established full diplomatic relations.

✓ **Checkpoint** Why did Nixon reach out to China?

Détente With the Soviet Union

Nixon's trip to the People's Republic of China prompted an immediate reaction from the Soviet Union, which had strained relations with both countries. Soviet leader Leonid Brezhnev feared that improved U.S.-Chinese relations would isolate Russia. Therefore, he invited Nixon to visit Moscow. Nixon made the trip in May 1972. Afterward, the President reported to Congress that he and Brezhnev had reached agreements in a wide variety of areas:

> **Primary Source** "Recognizing the responsibility of the advanced industrial nations to set an example in combating mankind's common enemies, the United States and the Soviet Union have agreed to cooperate in efforts to reduce pollution and enhance environmental quality. We have agreed to work together in the . . . conquest of cancer and heart disease."
>
> —Richard Nixon, speech to Congress, June 1, 1972

Nixon also announced plans to conduct a joint U.S.-Soviet space mission.

However, by far the high point of the summit was the signing of the first **Strategic Arms Limitation Treaty.** Otherwise known as SALT I, the treaty froze the deployment of intercontinental ballistic missiles (ICBMs) and placed limits on antiballistic missiles (ABMs), but it did not alter the stockpiling of the more dangerous multiple independent reentry vehicles (MIRVs). SALT I did not end the arms race between the United States and the Soviet Union. But it was a giant step toward that goal.

The importance of SALT I stemmed first and foremost from U.S. and Soviet efforts to reduce tensions between them. A policy aimed at easing Cold War tensions, **détente** had replaced previous diplomatic efforts based on suspicion and

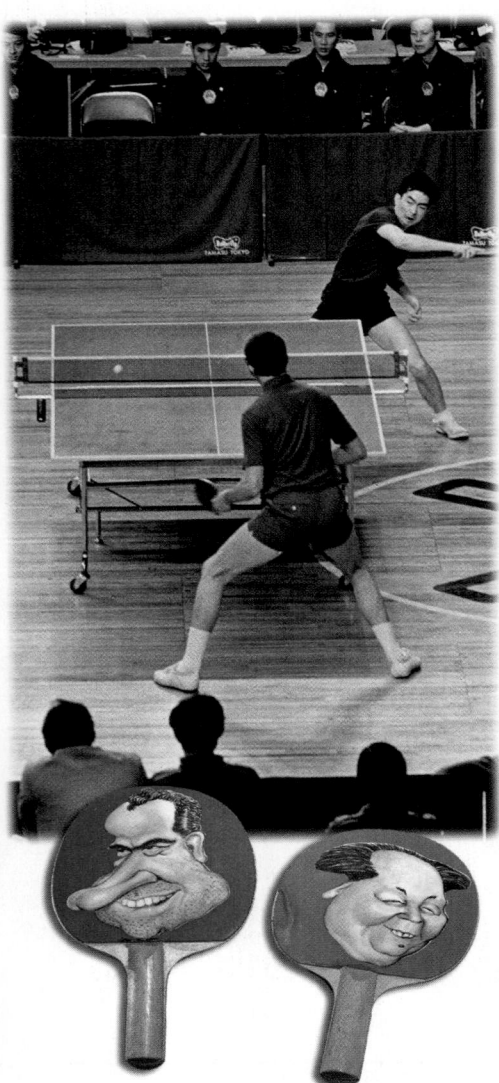

Ping-Pong Diplomacy
Nine American table-tennis players journeyed to China in 1971 to play matches against Chinese competitors. Americans commemorated the event with special ping-pong paddles fashioned after Nixon and Chinese leader Mao Zedong.

Nuclear Arms Treaty

As Leonid Brezhnev (seated, right) looks on, President Nixon signs the SALT I treaty during his historic visit to Moscow.

distrust. With his visits to China and the Soviet Union, coming within six months of each other, Richard Nixon dramatically altered America's global strategy. He relaxed the nation's inflexible stance toward communism and applied a more pragmatic approach to foreign policy. In the short term, the new relationships he forged helped the United States to end the Vietnam War. In the long term, Nixon's foreign-policy breakthroughs moved the world a step closer to the end of the Cold War.

✔ **Checkpoint** How did SALT I support Nixon's new policy for dealing with the Soviet Union?

Assessment

Progress Monitoring *Online*
For: Self-test with vocabulary practice
Web Code: nea-1611

Comprehension

1. **Terms and People** For each item below, write a sentence explaining its significance.
   - Henry Kissinger
   - realpolitik
   - Zhou Enlai
   - détente

2. **NoteTaking Reading Skill: Categorize** Use your table to answer the Section Focus Question: How did Richard Nixon change Cold War diplomacy during his presidency?

Writing About History

3. **Quick Write: Write the Essay Body** Choose a topic from the section on which you might write a persuasive essay. For example, you might discuss whether Nixon was a better Cold War President than his predecessors. Write the body of your essay, using a list of points you have made to guide you. Remember to open and close the body of the essay with strong arguments.

Critical Thinking

4. **Apply Information** How did Nixon's policy toward China reflect the philosophy of realpolitik?

5. **Draw Conclusions** Why did Nixon and Kissinger believe détente was a beneficial foreign policy?

6. **Predict Consequences** Did Richard Nixon position the United States to win the Cold War? Why or why not?

CHAPTER 29

Quick Study Guide

 NY 7.IV.A,
7.IV.A.1

Progress Monitoring *Online*
For: Self-test with vocabulary practice
Web Code: nea-1612

■ Roots of the U.S. Action in Vietnam

French Surrender at Dien Bien Phu	
Before	**After**
• **French-Indochinese War:** French forces battle Vietnamese communists under Ho Chi Minh.	• **Geneva Accords:** France grants independence to former colonies; Vietnam divided.
• **Cold War:** Truman helps France in order to maintain Cold War alliance against the Soviets.	• **SEATO:** U.S. assembles coalition to oppose spread of communism in Southeast Asia.
• **Domino Theory:** Eisenhower continues aid to French to prevent communist victory.	• **U.S. Intervention:** U.S. supports anticommunist Diem regime and sends troops to Vietnam.

■ Arms Control Agreements

Year	Agreement	Effect
1963	Nuclear Test Ban Treaty	Banned testing of nuclear weapons in the atmosphere
1972	SALT I Interim Agreement	Froze existing number of weapons held by each side
1972	SALT I Anti-Ballistic Missile Treaty	Set strict limits on missiles that could shoot down missiles from the other side
1979	SALT II Treaty	Set absolute limit on number of weapons each side could hold

■ The Vietnam War, 1969–1972

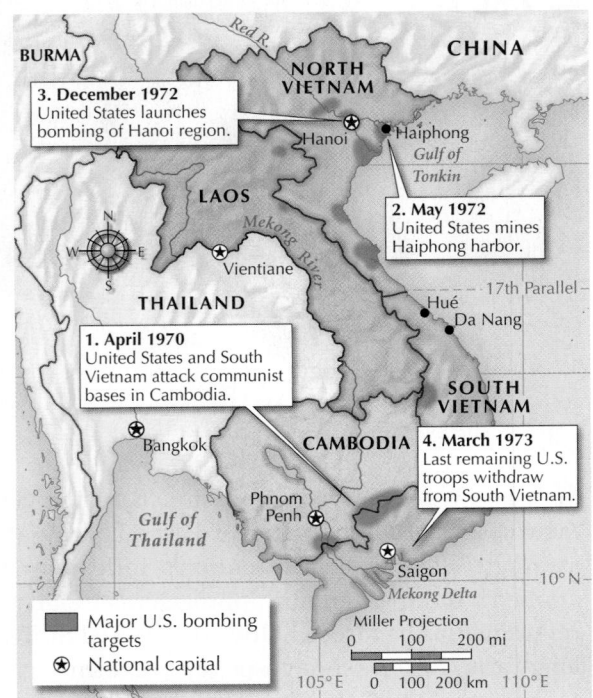

3. December 1972 United States launches bombing of Hanoi region.

2. May 1972 United States mines Haiphong harbor.

1. April 1970 United States and South Vietnam attack communist bases in Cambodia.

4. March 1973 Last remaining U.S. troops withdraw from South Vietnam.

■ Major U.S. bombing targets
⊛ National capital

Miller Projection

✔ Quick Study Timeline

In America			
	1950–1954 United States aids French war effort in Indochina	**1954** United States supports South Vietnam; SEATO forms	**1963** American involvement in South Vietnam increases; Kennedy assassinated

Presidential Terms	Harry S. Truman 1945–1953	Dwight D. Eisenhower 1953–1961	John F. Kennedy 1961–1963

1950   **1955**   **1960**

Around the World	**1950–1953** Korean War	**1954** Dien Bien Phu falls; Geneva Accords		**1963** South Vietnamese citizens protest Diem regime

American Issues
●—●—●—● **Connector**

By connecting prior knowledge with what you have learned in this chapter, you can gradually build your understanding of enduring questions that still affect America today. Answer the questions below. Then, use your American Issues Connector study guide (or go online: www.PHSchool.com **Web Code:** neh-8903).

Issues You Learned About

● **America and the World** During the Cold War, the United States tried to spread democracy, increase American power around the world, and limit the expansion of communism.

1. Think about the reasons for U.S. involvement in the Vietnam War and the reasons for opposition to America's role in the war. Then, write your own evaluation of whether the United States made the best decision in taking an active role in the Vietnam War. Consider the following:
   • domino theory and its validity
   • Gulf of Tonkin incident
   • implementation of the draft
   • conflict between hawks and doves
   • total of American casualties

● **America Goes to War** Again and again, Americans have faced the tough decision of whether or not to go to war.

2. What steps are usually followed before committing U.S. forces to war? Was this process followed in the Vietnam War? Explain.

3. Why did Johnson follow a policy of "Americanizing" the war effort? How did the war escalate under Johnson?

4. Why did President Nixon order bombing attacks on neighboring Cambodia? Why was this move controversial?

● **Global Interdependence** U.S. leaders often use diplomacy to improve relations with our friends and to reduce tensions with our rivals.

5. How did Nixon's China policy affect relations between the United States and the Soviet Union?

6. Explain the importance of SALT I.

Connect to Your World	**New York**

Education and American Society Although their demonstrations did not attract as much attention as those at Kent State, students in New York also protested U.S. foreign policy. In 1966, more than 100 New York University students walked out of the school's graduation ceremonies to protest the Vietnam War. At the State University of New York at Buffalo, students occupied one of the school's buildings in 1969 to protest the war. More protests at this university began a year later with an anti-war sit-in that led to nearly a month of unrest and protests, turning violent when protesters clashed with city police. Research student activism in New York during this time. Then write a newspaper article describing one particular protest or demonstration.

1964 Gulf of Tonkin Resolution	1968 Violence erupts at Democratic National Convention	1972 Nixon visits China

Lyndon B. Johnson 1963–1969   Richard M. Nixon 1969–1974

1965   **1970**   **1975**

1965 Operation Rolling Thunder	1968 Tet Offensive	1973 Paris Peace Accords

History *Interactive*
For: Interactive timeline
Web Code: nep-1614

Chapter Assessment

Terms and People

1. Who was **Ho Chi Minh**? What role did he play in Vietnam's history?
2. Define **hawks** and **doves**. What generalizations can you make about each group?
3. What was the **Tet Offensive**? Why was it a tactical victory for the Americans but a strategic victory for the communists?
4. Define the **Gulf of Tonkin Resolution** and the **War Powers Act**. What was the relationship between them?
5. Define **realpolitik**. Give an example of realpolitik in the 1970s.

Focus Questions

The focus question for this chapter is **How did the United States confront communism in East Asia after the Korean War?** Build an answer to this big question by answering the focus questions for Sections 1 through 5 and the Critical Thinking questions that follow.

Section 1
6. Why did the United States become involved in Vietnam?

Section 2
7. What were the causes and effects of America's growing involvement in the Vietnam War?

Section 3
8. How did the American war effort in Vietnam lead to rising protests and social divisions back home?

Section 4
9. How did the Vietnam War end and what were its lasting effects?

Section 5
10. How did Richard Nixon change Cold War diplomacy during his presidency?

Critical Thinking

11. **Compare** Compare the involvement of Presidents Truman, Eisenhower, Kennedy, Johnson, and Nixon in Vietnam.
12. **Explain Effects** What impact did the Vietnam War have on the United States domestic economy?
13. **Evaluate Credibility of Sources** In February 1968, a television journalist reported to his viewers that there was a "credibility gap" between Johnson's statements about the war and the reality of the fighting. Why did Americans come to doubt the word of their President?
14. **Analyze Charts** Study the chart below. Why were casualties the highest between 1967 and 1969? Why were casualties much lower in 1972?

American Casualties in Vietnam

Year	Killed in Action	Wounded in Action	Missing in Action
1961–1965	1,864	7,337	18
1966	5,008	29,992	61
1967	9,378	56,013	113
1968	14,594	87,388	176
1969	9,414	55,390	112
1970	4,221	24,835	101
1971	1,380	18,109	16
1972	300	3,936	11

SOURCE: National Archives and Records Administration

15. **Categorize** In his efforts to end the Vietnam War, Nixon followed some policies that seemed to lessen U.S. involvement and some that seemed to increase U.S. involvement. Give examples of each type of policy.
16. **Identify Assumptions** Before Nixon took office, what did Cold War foreign-policy strategists believe about the spread of communism? What assumptions did Nixon and Kissinger make when it came to foreign affairs?

Writing About History

Writing a Persuasive Essay From 1954 to 1975, the United States supported South Vietnam in an ultimately losing battle against communist forces from North Vietnam. Write a persuasive essay in which you argue for or against the following thesis: The Vietnam War could have been won by the United States and South Vietnam. Consult page SH16 of the Writing Handbook for additional help.

Prewriting
- Choose a side of the argument.
- Collect evidence, using a graphic organizer to list points on both sides of the issue.
- Research Internet or print sources to find materials that analyze your position from both sides. Take notes on relevant details, events, and people.

Drafting
- Clearly state the position that you will argue in a thesis statement. Use the rest of your introduction to provide necessary context about the issue.
- Make an outline to organize your argument and its supporting details. Then, choose information from your research that supports each part of your outline.

Revising
- Use the guidelines on page SH16 of the Writing Handbook to revise your essay.

Regents DBQ Practice

The 1968 Presidential Race

After the Tet Offensive showed the United States sinking deeper into a stalemate in Vietnam, the antiwar movement took center stage during the race for the White House. Use your knowledge of the election and the following documents to answer questions 1 through 4.

Document 1

"The feud that helped define the public lives of LBJ and RFK also helped shape the two greatest national undertakings of their times—the war on poverty and the war in Vietnam. Consumed by contempt for Kennedy, Johnson transformed a potential ally into an archenemy. . . . As Johnson and Kennedy became ever more bitter enemies, they divided constituencies they once shared, weakening their party by forcing its members to choose between them. They exposed and exacerbated the growing divide within the Democratic Party and American politics in general."

—*Jeff Shesol,* Mutual Contempt

Document 2

"[I]t is true that a house divided against itself by the spirit of faction, of party, of region, of religion, of race, is a house that cannot stand. There is division in the American house now. . . . I should not permit the Presidency to become involved in the partisan divisions that are developing in this political year. With America's sons in the fields far away, with America's future under challenge right here at home, with our hopes and the world's hopes for peace in the balance every day, I do not believe that I should devote an hour or a day of my time to any personal partisan causes or to any duties other than the awesome duties of this office—the Presidency of your country. Accordingly, I shall not seek, and I will not accept, the nomination of my party for another term as your President."

—*President Lyndon B. Johnson, March 31, 1968*

Document 3

Chicago police remove an antiwar protester from a demonstration during the 1968 Democratic National Convention.

Document 4

"For four years America's fighting men have set a record for courage and sacrifice unsurpassed in our history. . . . Never has so much military and economic and diplomatic power been used so ineffectively. . . . I say the time has come for the American people to turn to new leadership not tied to the mistakes and policies of the past. That is what we offer to America. And I pledge to you tonight that the first priority foreign policy objective of our next Administration will be to bring an honorable end to the war in Vietnam. We shall not stop there. We need a policy to prevent more Vietnams."

—*Republican Presidential Nominee Richard M. Nixon, August 8, 1968*

---

1. According to Document 2, Johnson has chosen not to run for reelection because he
   (1) does not believe he can win.
   (2) is tired of trying to lead a divided nation.
   (3) has more vital duties to perform.
   (4) thinks the nation needs new leadership.

2. Which of the documents focus primarily on the causes of divisions within the Democratic Party?
   (1) Documents 2 and 4
   (2) Documents 1 and 4
   (3) Documents 3 and 4
   (4) Documents 1 and 3

3. The speakers in Documents 2 and 4 would most likely agree that
   (1) ending the Vietnam War is a top priority for the President.
   (2) the Vietnam War has been badly managed.
   (3) the United States is on the verge of winning in Vietnam.
   (4) the United States should pull its troops out of Vietnam immediately.

4. **Writing Task** What were the most important factors that led to the defeat of the Democrats in 1968? Write a paragraph answering this question, using your knowledge of the chapter content and specific evidence from the primary sources above.

The Hippie Experience

Many young Americans in the 1960s identified with a cultural movement that rejected the social conventions of their parents' generation. Their long hair and flowing clothes set them apart from mainstream America. So did their name—hippies. One journalist and social commentator explains what it meant to be a hippie:

<blockquote>
❝The word 'hip' translates roughly as 'wise' or 'tuned-in.' A hippy is somebody who 'knows' what's really happening, and who adjusts or grooves with it. Hippies despise phoniness; they want to be open, honest, loving and free.❞

—Hunter S. Thompson, "The 'Hashbury' Is the Capital of the Hippies"
</blockquote>

Listen to the Witness History *audio to hear more about the hippie experience.*

◀ A hippie woman dances at the Woodstock music festival in New York, 1969.

Early logo of the National Organization for Women

A Beatles album released in 1969

Core Curriculum Preview

Chapter Focus Question: How did the counterculture and the expanding rights revolution of the 1960s and 1970s influence American society?

Section 1
The Counterculture 5.I.C.3, 7.II.D.1c, 7.IV.A.5c

Section 2
The Women's Rights Movement 3.III.A.3, 7.III.B.4, 7.III.B.4a, 7.III.B.4b

Section 3
The Rights Revolution Expands 7.III.A.3, 7.III.B.5, 7.III.B.6, 7.V.A.1d

Section 4
The Environmental Movement 7.V.A.1a, 7.V.A.1c, 7.V.B.2c(1)

Protesters holding up a peace sign

Use the ☑ **Quick Study Timeline** at the end of this chapter to preview chapter events.

> **Note Taking Study Guide *Online***
> **For:** Note Taking and American Issues Connector
> **Web Code:** nee-9001

◀ Some audience members make their own music.

SECTION 1

◀ A 1969 poster promises "3 days of peace & music" at the Woodstock concert.

WITNESS HISTORY AUDIO

Remembering Woodstock

In the summer of 1969, hundreds of thousands of people gathered for a rock concert in Bethel, New York. Most of the media criticized the three-day event because of the concertgoers' widespread use of drugs and open displays of "free love." The people who went to Woodstock felt differently. For them, Woodstock showed that close to half a million people could come together peacefully. Twenty-five years later, many who attended Woodstock still remember their experiences vividly.

❝Woodstock was a time of social changes in human freedom and expression. . . . We learned not to be ashamed of our bodies. . . . We spent time with our kids. . . . That festival set the standards for peace, music, people and expression and showed to the world that all was not just violence and hatred . . . it was LIFE!❞

—Juan C. Morales

The Counterculture

(NY) **Core Curriculum Objectives**

- **5.I.C.3** Shifting cultural values
- **7.II.D.1c** The baby boom and its effects
- **7.IV.A.5c** Cultural radicals: hippies and communalists

Terms and People

counterculture
generation gap
Beatles

commune
Timothy Leary

NoteTaking

Reading Skill: Identify Main Ideas As you read, use a concept web like the one below to record main ideas about the counterculture.

Youth generation

The Counterculture

Why It Matters Woodstock was a dynamic expression of a **counterculture** that arose in the 1960s. Members of the counterculture adopted values that ran counter to mainstream culture. They rebelled against long-standing customs in dress, music, and personal behavior. The counterculture both challenged the values of mainstream American society and unleashed a movement to reassert traditional values. **Section Focus Question: What was the counterculture, and what impact did it have on American society?**

The Counterculture Rises

The counterculture was rooted in the social and political events of the 1950s. The Beat movement had emphasized freedom from materialism and the importance of personal experience. The civil rights movement introduced the idea of social and political protest, which stimulated the Vietnam antiwar movement. Both movements prompted many people to question traditional boundaries, whether restrictions on rights or cultural norms in dress or hairstyles. It also heightened distrust of authority, leading some in the counterculture to declare, "Don't trust anyone over 30."

Members of the counterculture valued youth, spontaneity, and freedom of expression. Also called hippies, these young people promoted peace, love, and freedom. They experimented with new styles of dress and music, freer attitudes toward sexual relationships, and the recreational use of drugs. Their values were so different from traditional ones that many social analysts described the resulting situation as a **generation gap,** in which there was a lack of understanding and communication between the older and younger generations. Jerry Rubin, a political activist, described how long hair divided parents from their children:

Primary Source "Young kids identify short hair with authority, discipline. . . . Wherever we go, our hair tells people where we stand on Vietnam, Wallace, campus disruption, dope. . . . Yesterday I was walking down the street. A car passed by, parents in the front seat and a young kid, about eight, in the back seat. The kid flashed me the clenched fist sign. [Meaning: He identified with Rubin's long hair.]"
—Jerry Rubin, *America in the Sixties*

The baby boom that followed World War II resulted in a huge student population in the 1960s. By sheer numbers, the baby boomers became a force for social change. The music industry rushed to produce the music they liked; clothing designers copied the styles they introduced; universities were forced to change college courses and rules to accommodate them.

✔ **Checkpoint** What factors influenced the rise of the counterculture?

Defining the Counterculture

Many people have used the so-called trinity of the counterculture—sex, drugs, and rock-and-roll—to define the youth generation. But the counterculture was also marked by an interest in spirituality.

Music and Art Shape Youth Culture By the 1960s, rock-and-roll had become a defining characteristic of the baby-boom generation. When the **Beatles** made a triumphant visit to the United States in 1964, more than 70 million Americans watched the English rock band perform on Ed Sullivan's television show. The Beatles also had an impact on folk musicians like Bob Dylan, whose protest songs highlighted the civil rights and peace movements. As radical musician John Sinclair put it, rock became "a weapon of cultural revolution," urging listeners to reject conventions and, in many cases, the political policies of the government. Even after the counterculture had declined in significance, rock music remained popular among baby-boomers as well as their children.

The art and literature of the 1960s and 1970s also displayed a rebellious side. Andy Warhol's realistic paintings of common items of American culture, such as Campbell soup cans, questioned satirically what was "real." In literature, the novels of Tom Wolfe and Hunter S. Thompson blurred the lines between reporting and political activism.

The Sexual Revolution Members of the counterculture rejected many traditional restrictions on sexual behavior in what became known as the "sexual revolution." They called for the separation of sex from traditional family life and often advocated new living patterns. For example, many hippies lived together in **communes,** or small communities in which the people have common interests and share resources. The sexual revolution was one of the strongest indicators of the generation gap. One poll showed that nearly two thirds of all Americans over the age of 30 opposed premarital sex, whereas a majority of those under age 29 did not. Eventually, however, the sexual revolution led to a more open discussion of sex in the mainstream media.

Rock Art
The pop art that decorated concert posters, such as this one from the late 1960s, often challenged tradition.

The Generation Gap

In the 1960s and 1970s, many parents and their children had little in common apart from their genes. Parents of boomer children were heavily influenced by the two major events of their own childhoods, the depression and World War II. Part of what was called the "silent generation," they sought stability by conforming, and they started adulthood early, marrying young. In contrast, their baby-boomer children rejected tradition and authority in favor of individuality. Boomers did not want to fit in; they wanted to stand out.

THE BOOMER GENERATION

Teens during the 60s and 70s grew up in a time of prosperity. Many embraced activism and symbols of peace, such as flowers and pins. Rock-and-roll music shaped their worldviews and set them apart from their parents. The boomer generation also expressed a new distrust toward tradition and authority, reflected in popular magazines like *MAD*.

THE SILENT GENERATION

Parents of boomers grew up in a different world from their children. They had learned to live frugally through years of rationing during the depression and war. As teens, they had listened and danced to the big-band music that their parents had enjoyed. They valued loyalty, authority, and had respect for the military and veterans.

Age Breakdown, 1964

1964

Under age 17 36%

Over age 17 64%

SOURCE: Federal Interagency Forum on Child and Family Statistics

◄ The boomers' sheer numbers emphasized the growing generation gap. While today youths make up about a quarter of the population, in the mid-1960s they made up more than a third.

Thinking Critically

Draw Inferences Why do you think the generation of people born between 1925 and 1942 has been called the "silent generation"?

History *Interactive* ✶

For: More about the generation gap
Web Code: nep-1711

Life in Haight-Ashbury In 1967, as many as 2,000 people flocked to the Haight-Ashbury district of San Francisco, a center of the counterculture. Hippies there experimented with drugs, wore unconventional clothing, and listened to rock music and speeches by political radicals like Timothy Leary, a one-time Harvard researcher. He preached that drugs could free the mind, and he encouraged American youths to "tune in," "turn on" to drugs, and "drop out" of mainstream society. The hippies of San Francisco attracted a great deal of media attention, much of it critical of the lifestyles they advocated. Life in Haight-Ashbury did prove to have unwanted effects. As in other enclaves of hippie culture, it experienced high rates of drug abuse which led to increased crime.

Exploring Different Routes to Spirituality Some members of the counterculture sought spiritual enlightenment outside of the Judeo-Christian traditions in which they had been raised. Many explored Buddhism and other Eastern religions, while others sought spirituality by living in harmony with nature. Particularly in the late 1960s and early 1970s, some hippies established rural communes, seeking to live off the land as Native Americans had in the past. These beliefs had a lasting impact on the budding environmental movement.

 Checkpoint What characteristics define the counterculture?

The Counterculture Ends

By the end of the 1960s, many people, even those within the counterculture, had become disillusioned with some of its excesses. The utopian urge to discover a more authentic way of living had an unfortunate underside. Drug addictions and deaths from overdoses rose. A number of rock musicians, most famously Jimi Hendrix and Janis Joplin, died of drug overdoses while only in their twenties. The downward spiral continued in 1969 with a tragedy at a music festival sponsored in Altamont, California. While the Rolling Stones played, members of the Hells Angels, a motorcycle gang that had been hired to provide security, stabbed to death a black man who had approached the stage. The ugly violence <u>contradicted</u> the values of "peace and love" that many hippies embraced.

At the same time, the movement's values were becoming increasingly shallow and self-centered. When the counterculture fell apart, most hippies abandoned their social experiments and melted right back into the mainstream. Still, the seeds of protest they had sown would influence the growing "rights revolution."

Vocabulary Builder
contradict–(kahn truh DIHKT) v. to go against expressed views

 Checkpoint Why did the counterculture fall apart?

SECTION **1** **Assessment**

Progress Monitoring Online
For: Self-test with vocabulary practice
Web Code: nea-1711

Comprehension

1. Terms and People For each item below, write a sentence explaining how it influenced the counterculture.
- generation gap
- Beatles
- commune
- Timothy Leary

2. NoteTaking Reading Skill: Identify Main Ideas Use your concept web to answer the Section Focus Question: What was the counterculture, and what impact did it have on American society?

Writing About History

3. Quick Write: Identify Issues You are a teenager in the 1960s, and you've been invited to your father's club to give a speech about the values of the youth generation. Identify the issues that you will address, keeping your audience in mind.

Critical Thinking

4. Identify Assumptions What assumptions about mainstream culture were made by the counterculture?

5. Analyze Information Explain whether you agree with the following statement: "The counterculture was a form of protest."

6. Recognize Cause and Effect How did trends within the counterculture movement contribute to its downfall?

▲ National Organization for Women button

▲ Civil rights leader Coretta Scott King speaks to a group of feminists at a National Women's Conference.

WITNESS HISTORY 🔊 AUDIO

Challenging a Stereotype

❝The unspoken assumption is that women are different. They do not have executive ability, orderly minds, stability, leadership skills, and they are too emotional. It has been observed before, that society for a long time discriminated against another minority, the blacks, on the same basis—that they were different and inferior. The happy little homemaker and the contented "old darkey" on the plantation were both produced by prejudice. As a black person, I am no stranger to race prejudice. But the truth is that in the political world I have been far oftener discriminated against because I am a woman than because I am black.❞

—Shirley Chisholm, Address to the United States House of Representatives, May 21, 1969

The Women's Rights Movement

 Core Curriculum Objectives

- **3.III.A.3** Women, families, and work
- **7.III.B.4** Demands for equality: women
- **7.III.B.4a** The modern women's movement: Civil Rights Act, NOW
- **7.III.B.4b** Issues of the women's movement

Terms and People

feminism	ERA
Betty Friedan	Gloria Steinem
NOW	Phyllis Schlafly

NoteTaking

Reading Skill: Identify Causes and Effects
Record the causes, effects, and main figures of the women's movement in a chart like this one.

The Women's Movement		
Causes	Proponents/ Opponents	Effects
•	•	•
•	•	•

Why It Matters Following World War II, most women gave up their jobs to returning servicemen and went back to their homes to take care of their families. Social analysts and popular culture portrayed women, especially suburban housewives, as the personification of America's achievement of the good life. By the end of the 1960s, however, a broad-based movement to attain sexual equality had arisen. The women's movement fundamentally changed American life—from family and education to careers and political issues. **Section Focus Question: What led to the rise of the women's movement, and what impact did it have on American society?**

A Women's Movement Arises

Historians often refer to the women's movement of the 1960s and 1970s as the second wave of **feminism,** or the theory of political, social, and economic equality of men and women. They want to emphasize that the struggle for women's rights has had a long history, going back at least to the 1840s, when women drafted the Declaration of Sentiments at Seneca Falls, New York. The phrase *second wave of feminism* also reminds us that the first wave, which culminated with women's winning the right to vote in 1920, ended well before the nation addressed the call for full equality. In the decades that followed, women made little legal or social headway. Several factors influenced the rebirth of the women's movement in the 1960s and 1970s.

Seeking to Redefine Traditional Roles The civil rights struggle prompted women to look at the ways in which society judged and discriminated against them as a group. As Casey Hayden and Mary King, two veterans of that movement, put it: "Sex and caste. There seem to be many parallels that can be drawn between the treatment of Negroes and the treatment of women in society as a whole." The civil rights movement both inspired women to demand <u>gender</u> equality and taught them ways to get it. It also brought black and white women together, strengthening their shared cause.

Vocabulary Builder
<u>gender</u>—(JEHN der) *n.* a person's sex

Women also wanted to redefine how they were viewed. Many women objected to the inaccuracy of the housewife stereotype. Some needed to work to support themselves or their families. Others wanted more opportunities than their lives as housewives could offer. **Betty Friedan** powerfully articulated this message in her groundbreaking book *The Feminine Mystique.*

> **Primary Source**   "The problem lay buried, unspoken, for many years in the minds of American women. It was a strange stirring, a sense of dissatisfaction. . . . Each suburban wife struggled with it alone. As she made the beds, shopped for groceries, matched slipcover material, ate peanut butter sandwiches with her children, chauffeured Cub Scouts and Brownies, lay beside her husband at night—she was afraid to ask even of herself the silent question—'Is this all?'"
> —Betty Friedan, *The Feminine Mystique,* 1963

Looking for Better Work Despite the stereotypes, the number of women in the workforce grew throughout the 1950s and 1960s. Yet working women often found themselves in deadend jobs. Even those with training and education had their access to careers or advancement blocked, in many cases, by blatantly discriminatory employers. Sandra Day O'Connor, who ultimately became the first female Supreme Court Justice, graduated near the top of her class at Stanford Law School in the early 1950s. Yet while she found few employment opportunities upon graduation, her male counterparts won job offers at prestigious law firms. Facing such restrictions, women increasingly demanded equal treatment in the workplace.

✔ **Checkpoint** How did the women's movement of the 1960s begin?

Women Find Their Voices

Several years after she wrote *The Feminine Mystique,* Betty Friedan helped establish the **National Organization for Women (NOW).** The organization—which dedicated itself to winning "true equality for all women" and to attaining a "full and equal partnership of the sexes"—galvanized the women's movement.

NOW's Goals and Tactics NOW set out to break down barriers of discrimination in the workplace and in education. It attacked stereotypes of women in the media and called for more balance in roles in marriages. It had two major priorities. The first was to bring about passage of the **Equal Rights Amendment (ERA),** an amendment to the Constitution that would guarantee gender equality under the law. The ERA initially had been proposed in the early 1920s but had never passed. The second was to protect reproductive rights,

HISTORY MAKERS

Betty Friedan (1921–2006)
Educated at Smith College, where she edited the school newspaper, Betty Friedan did graduate work in psychology before becoming a journalist. She married in 1947 and was fired from her job when she became pregnant with her second child. Friedan raised three children and occasionally wrote articles for magazines. As she was working on one article, she realized that many educated women who had become housewives shared the uneasiness she felt about her life. This led her to write *The Feminine Mystique* in 1963, which helped launch the women's movement by inspiring women to join in the struggle for equal rights. In a later book, *The Second Stage* (1981), she criticized the direction of the women's movement, arguing that it had become too hostile to families.

A Diverse Movement

Women take part in a NOW rally in Washington, D.C., in 1970. A *Ms.* magazine cover from 1972 shows that women from all different backgrounds participated in the women's movement. *What women's issues might have been especially important to women in the military?*

especially the right to an abortion. NOW worked within the existing political system, lobbying for political reforms and readying court cases to compel the government to enforce existing legislation that banned discrimination. For some women, NOW seemed too extreme; for others, it was not extreme enough. Still, NOW served as a rallying point to promote equality for all women.

Raising Society's Awareness Finding NOW too tame, radical feminists sought a more fundamental restructuring of society. Rather than seeking legislative change, these protesters sought to show the way society trapped women into adopting restrictive roles. In addition to public protests of the Miss America Pageant, radical feminists engaged in small-scale consciousness-raising efforts. Other feminists sought to raise public awareness by making personal issues political. Charlotte Bunch, for example, wrote that "there is no private domain of a person's life that is not political and there is no political issue that is not ultimately personal."

Some feminists, like **Gloria Steinem,** tried to change awareness through the mass media. After graduating from college, Steinem worked as a freelance writer, including a stint of undercover work at a club run by *Playboy* magazine. While society tended to view Playboy bunnies in glamorous terms, Steinem revealed how much humiliation they had to endure to make a living. In 1972, she helped co-found *Ms.*, a feminist magazine. Its title meant to protest the social custom of identifying women by their marital status rather than as individuals.

Opposing the Women's Movement Some Americans—both men and women—openly challenged the women's movement. **Phyllis Schlafly,** for example, is a conservative political activist who denounced women's liberation as "a total assault on the family, on marriage, and on children." She worked hard to defeat the ERA, arguing that the act would compel women to fight in the military, end sex-segregated bathrooms, and hurt the family. Her argument resonated with many conservatives. With their support, the ERA fell three states short of becoming a constitutional amendment.

✔ **Checkpoint** What were the various goals of the women's movement?

Lasting Effects of the Women's Movement

The women's movement affected all aspects of American society. Women's roles and opportunities expanded. Women gained legal rights that had been denied them. And feminists sparked an important debate about equality that continues today. Yet the issues they raised continue to divide Americans. Some say that women haven't made enough gains. Others fear that the movement has actually harmed society.

Making Legal Headway Before the 1960s, there were no federal laws prohibiting gender discrimination. The Civil Rights Act of 1964, however, gave feminists a legal tool. It included a clause, called Title VII, that outlawed discrimination on the basis of sex. The clause was actually inserted by civil rights opponents, who thought it was so outlandish that it would make the entire bill look ridiculous. When the bill actually passed, however, women used Title VII to challenge discrimination. The bill also set up the Equal Employment Opportunity Commission (EEOC) to enforce the federal prohibition on job discrimination.

Enforcing Title VII, even with the EEOC, was often difficult. Still, NOW and other feminist organizations tirelessly filed suits against employers who refused to hire women or to pay them fairly, compelling the federal government to act. President Kennedy established the Commission on the Status of Women in 1961 to examine workplace discrimination. Title IX of the Higher Education Act of 1972 banned discrimination in education. The Equal Credit Opportunity Act, passed in 1974, made it illegal to deny credit to a woman just because of her gender.

Comparing Viewpoints

Do Women Need to Fight for Equal Rights?

Inspired by the successes of the civil rights movement, many American women in the late 1960s renewed their own demand for equal rights. Other women, however, argued that their demand was destructive.

PHYLLIS SCHLAFLY

Schlafly (born 1924) is a lawyer and political organizer who first became famous for her anticommunist views. She became an opponent of feminism.

Primary Source

"Feminism is doomed . . . because it [attempts] to repeal and restructure human nature."

"Women have babies and men provide support. If you don't like the way we're made you've got to take it up with God."

GLORIA STEINEM

Steinem (born 1934) is a journalist who founded political organizations to help women lobby for equal rights. She became the most famous feminist leader of the 1970s.

Primary Source

"Sex and race, because they are easily visible differences, have been the primary ways of organizing human beings into superior and inferior groups, and into the cheap labor on which this system still depends."

Compare

1. What do you think each woman would say about the role that biology plays in women's lives?

2. What is unusual about Schlafly's insistence that women should devote themselves to staying home and raising a family?

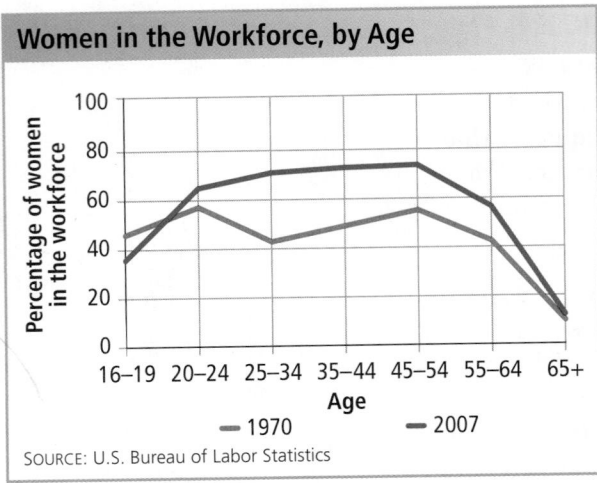

Women in the Workforce, by Age

SOURCE: U.S. Bureau of Labor Statistics

Graph Skills Compare the lines for 1970 and 2007 on the graph. Notice that the 1970 line makes the shape of a letter *m*. What factors explain this? Why is the 2007 line different?

Some feminists considered their most important legal victory to be the 1973 Supreme Court decision in *Roe* v. *Wade,* which assured women the right to legal abortions. Prior to *Roe,* most states outlawed or severely restricted abortion. Some women turned to illegal and often dangerous ways to end their pregnancies. The case and its decision was highly controversial at the time and still is today.

The Workplace Slowly Changes The women's movement fostered a shift in attitudes among both men and women, and the American workplace today reflects this change. The percentage of women in the workforce has grown, from about 30 percent in 1950 to more than 60 percent in 2000. So, too, has the number of married female workers. Fields long closed or severely limited to women—such as medicine, law, and accounting—have opened up as well. The general shift in attitudes symbolized by these changes has created a world of possibilities for many young women who never knew a time when women were not allowed to do these things.

Despite these gains, the average woman still earns less than the average man, partly because many women continue to work in fields that pay less. Some people have referred to this situation as a "pink collar ghetto." Whether this is because of discrimination, or because women who shoulder family responsibilities often have limited job choices, remains a matter of debate. Many studies suggest that a "glass ceiling" exists, limiting the advancement of even the most highly educated and skilled women workers.

Most troubling, the United States has witnessed a feminization of poverty over the past 30 years. This means that the majority of the nation's poor people are single women. These are the women in the lowest-paying jobs, with the fewest benefits. Many of these poor women are single mothers, who must bear the costs and responsibilities of raising children alone while also working.

 Checkpoint What legal and social gains has the women's movement made?

SECTION **2 Assessment**

Progress Monitoring Online
For: Self-test with vocabulary practice
Web Code: nea-1721

Comprehension

1. Terms and People What is the relationship between each of the following items and the women's movement?
- feminism
- Betty Friedan
- NOW
- ERA
- Gloria Steinem
- Phyllis Schlafly

2. NoteTaking Reading Skill: Identify Causes and Effects Use your cause-and-effect chart to answer the Section Focus Question: What led to the rise of the women's movement, and what impact did it have on American society?

Writing About History

3. Quick Write: Identify Arguments Suppose that you are either Betty Friedan or Phyllis Schlafly and you are giving a speech about women's roles in society. Identify and list the main arguments that would support your position.

Critical Thinking

4. Draw Inferences Why did so much time elapse between the first and second waves of feminism?

5. Identify Assumptions What beliefs led women to support the women's movement? What beliefs led women to oppose it?

6. Formulating Questions Make up two or three questions that will help you decide whether American women have made significant strides toward equality.

Esmeralda Santiago: *Almost a Woman*

As more Latinos arrived in America, their similar experiences as immigrants drew them together despite having come from many different countries. As Latinos, they faced common challenges: discrimination, lack of opportunity, and a mainstream society in which their differences were ignored and their voices often unheard. In this excerpt from her memoir *Almost a Woman,* Esmeralda Santiago tells what happened to her the first day after her family moved from Puerto Rico to New York.

Esmeralda Santiago

There was no horizon in Brooklyn. Everywhere I looked, my eyes met a vertical maze of gray and brown straight-edged buildings with sharp corners and deep shadows. Every few blocks there was a cement playground surrounded by [a] chain-link fence. And in between, weedy lots mounded with garbage and rusting cars.

A girl came out of the building next door, a jump rope in her hand. She appraised me shyly. I pretended to ignore her. She stepped on the rope, stretched the ends overhead as if to measure their length, and then began to skip, slowly, grunting each time she came down on the sidewalk. Swish splat grunt swish, she turned her back to me; swish splat grunt swish, she faced me again and smiled. I smiled back, and she hopped over.

"*¿Tú eres hispana?*" she asked, as she whirled the rope in lazy arcs.

"No, I'm Puerto Rican."

"Same thing. Puerto Rican, Hispanic. That's what we are here." She skipped a tight circle, stopped abruptly, and shoved the rope in my direction. "Want a turn?"

"Sure." I hopped on one leg, then the other. "So, if you're Puerto Rican, they call you Hispanic?"

"Yeah. Anybody who speaks Spanish."

I jumped a circle, as she had done, but faster. "You mean, if you speak Spanish, you're Hispanic?"

"Well, yeah. No . . . I mean your parents have to be Puerto Rican or Cuban or something."

I whirled the rope to the right, then the left, like a boxer. "Okay, your parents are Cuban, let's say, and you're born here, but you don't speak Spanish. Are you Hispanic?"

She bit her lower lip. "I guess so," she finally said. "It has to do with being from a Spanish country. I mean, you or your parents, like, even if you don't speak Spanish, you're Hispanic, you know?" She looked at me uncertainly. I nodded and returned her rope.

But I didn't know. I'd always been Puerto Rican, and it hadn't occurred to me that in Brooklyn I'd be someone else.

Girls skip rope in a city playground.

Thinking Critically
1. **Make Inferences** Reread the first paragraph. How does Esmeralda feel about her new surroundings?

2. **Interpret the Literature** What would it mean to come to a new country and be "someone else"?

WITNESS HISTORY 🔊 AUDIO

From Graffiti to Art

Judith Baca, the daughter of Mexican immigrants, taught art in public schools in a rough Los Angeles neighborhood in the early 1970s. Between her classes, she watched young Latinos hanging out in parks and writing graffiti on the walls. Intrigued by the kids' graffiti, she developed the idea of channeling their creative energy into painting murals. Her idea spread to other U.S. cities, where kids used murals to document and celebrate Latino culture and history. Their work was just one part of a growing movement that sought to educate, respect, and politically organize American Latinos.

◀ A mural from the Philadelphia Mural Arts Program, begun in 1984, honors the great Mexican muralist, Diego Rivera (seated at center).

The Rights Revolution Expands

 Core Curriculum Objectives

- **7.III.A.3** Movement for rights of disabled citizens
- **7.III.B.5** Rising consciousness of Hispanic-Americans
- **7.III.B.6** Demands for equality: American Indian Movement and other protests
- **7.V.A.1d** American Indian self-determination

Terms and People

Cesar Chavez	AIM
migrant farmworker	Japanese American
UFW	Citizens League
Chicano movement	Ralph Nader

NoteTaking

Reading Skill: Compare and Contrast
Create a Venn diagram to compare and contrast the Latino and Native American rights movements.

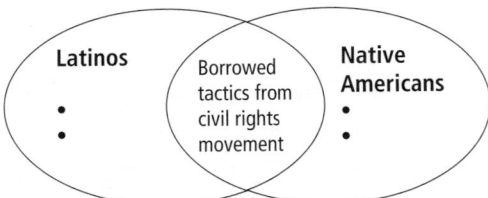

Why It Matters Successes in the civil rights and women's movements signaled a growing rights revolution in the United States. Latinos, Native Americans, and Asian Americans engaged in their own struggles for equality during the 1960s and 1970s, fighting to influence laws and government. Meanwhile, activists worked to expand rights for two broad groups: consumers and people with disabilities. **Section Focus Question: How did the rights movements of the 1960s and 1970s expand rights for diverse groups of Americans?**

The Latino Population Grows

After World War I, the United States passed legislation limiting European immigration. Yet during and after World War II, the country faced a growing demand for cheap labor. At the same time, the populations of Mexico and other Latin American nations grew steadily while job opportunities there declined. The combination of these factors created a steady stream of new immigrants to the United States.

A Spanish-Speaking Population People whose family origins are in Spanish-speaking Latin America are called Latinos or Hispanics. They come from many different places, but they share the same language and some elements of culture. Spanish-speaking people lived in many parts of the western United States before settlers from the United States arrived, and their numbers have grown steadily. Mexican Americans, known as Chicanos, have always made up the largest group of U.S. Latinos.

Mexican Americans Farm the Land Beginning in 1942, Mexican immigrants came to the United States under the *bracero*, or farmhand, program. This program granted Mexican migrants temporary guest worker status, and over a period of 25 years, more than 4 million of them entered the U.S. The *braceros* played a crucial role in sustaining American agriculture during and after World War II.

Along with Mexicans who had migrated to the U.S. illegally in search of work, *braceros* who had outstayed their permits were targeted for deportation in the 1950s. In 1965, however, the government passed the Immigration and Nationality Act Amendments, eliminating national-origin quotas for immigrants. In the decades that followed, the number of legal Mexican and Asian immigrants surged. More than 400,000 Mexicans arrived during the 1960s, another 630,000 in the 1970s, and more than 1.5 million in the 1980s.

Emerging Latino Communities on the East Coast After World War II, large numbers of Puerto Ricans, Dominicans, and Cubans migrated to the United States. As citizens of a United States territory, Puerto Ricans came legally, leaving their homeland in search of better-paying jobs. In contrast, most Cuban and Dominican immigrants came to America as political refugees, fleeing their countries to escape the harsh rule of dictators. Most Puerto Rican, Cuban, and Dominican immigrants settled in urban areas, especially in New York City and Miami, Florida.

✓ **Checkpoint** Why did Mexicans and immigrants from other Latin American countries migrate to the United States?

United States Latino Population

Latino population (in millions)

Year	Population	Percentage
1970	~9	4.5%
1980	~13	6.4%
1990	~20	8.8%
2000	~31	12.5%
2010*	~47	15.4%
2020*	~60	18.0%

* Projected growth
Percentages indicate proportion of total U.S. population that is Latino.
SOURCE: U.S. Census Bureau; Pew Hispanic Center

Graph Skills Describe the growth of the Latino population from 1970 to 2020.

Pressing for Equal Rights

Like other minorities, Latinos had long faced discrimination. After World War II, Latino veterans began agitating for equal treatment. Veteran Hector Garcia, for example, formed the American G.I. Forum to battle discrimination. In the 1960s and 1970s, influenced by the growing civil rights movement, Latinos increasingly fought for equal rights. They demanded better working conditions, salaries, and educational opportunities. Like African Americans, they sought federal protection of their right to vote and campaigned to elect politicians who represented their interests.

Cesar Chavez Organizes Farmworkers The most influential Latino activist was **Cesar Chavez.** Chavez fought for rights for farm laborers, who were among the most exploited workers in the nation. Because they migrated from farm to farm—and often from state to state—to pick fruits and vegetables, they were known as **migrant farmworkers.** They labored for long hours in deplorable conditions, with no benefits.

In 1962, Chavez organized a farmworkers' union in Delano, California. In the late 1960s, he merged his union with a separate union of Filipino farm laborers to form what became the **United Farm Workers (UFW).**

HISTORY MAKERS

Cesar Chavez (1927–1993)
Cesar Chavez spent his childhood and youth toiling, like his parents, as a migrant farmworker. In the 1950s, he trained to be a community organizer. His skills led him to be named chief of the group doing the training. In 1962, he formed the National Farm Workers Association. Migrant workers had tried to form unions before and failed; Chavez made the effort succeed. In an impassioned letter to the grape industry, he expressed the workers' suffering and determination. "We are men and women who have suffered and endured much," he wrote. "Generation after generation have sought to demoralize us, to break our human spirit. But God knows that we are not beasts of burden, agricultural implements or rented slaves; we are men."

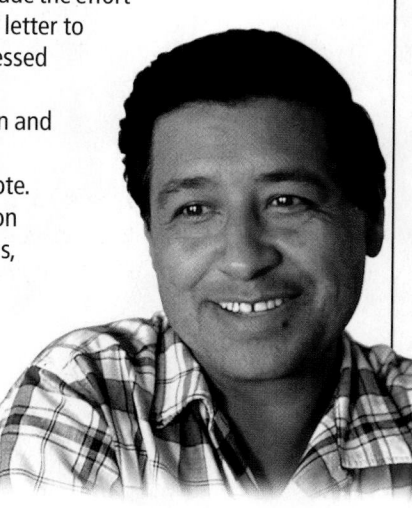

Vocabulary Builder
implement – (IHM pluh mehnt) *v.*
to bring about

Committed to nonviolent tactics, the UFW implemented a workers' strike and consumer boycott of table grapes. With the help of Dolores Huerta, Chavez's top aide, the UFW urged people across the nation to boycott California grapes in order to win recognition from the growers. In 1975, California passed a law requiring collective bargaining between growers and union representatives. Farmworkers finally had a legal basis to ask for better working conditions.

The Chicano Movement Grows While Chavez focused on farmworkers' rights, a broader Mexican American social and political effort grew, which came to be known as the **Chicano movement.** Part of it was dedicated to increasing Latinos' awareness of their history and culture. At California colleges and high schools, and in other states with a Mexican American population, Chicano students demanded that educators teach more about their heritage. Others in the movement focused on quality of life issues. For example, the National Council of La Raza was founded in 1968 with the goal of reducing poverty and discrimination and providing better opportunities for Latinos.

Much of the movement's energy was concentrated on attaining political strength for Latinos, or what some called "brown power." José Angel Gutiérrez organized the political party La Raza Unida in Texas. The party worked for better housing and jobs, and it successfully supported Latino political candidates. By 1980, six Hispanics sat in Congress, representing districts from New York to California. Moreover, Hispanics gained greater representation in state, county, and city governments.

✓ **Checkpoint** What were some of the demands of Latino groups in the 1960s and 1970s?

A worker picks strawberries at a California farm in 1963. ▼

INFOGRAPHIC 🔊 AUDIO

Migrant Workers
Seek A Living

In the 1960s, many Americans took for granted the availability of fresh fruits and vegetables in their supermarkets, even during the winter. This luxury was made possible by a group of hardworking and largely silent migrant farmworkers. Moving from farm to farm with the seasons, migrant farmworkers performed back-breaking labor for extremely low wages. They often worked in harsh conditions, without medical care, education for their children, or vacation. Even today, the majority of farmwork is done by migrant workers, often under similar conditions (see table above right).

Labels on produce crates showed stereotypical images of the Mexican farmworkers who harvested the crops. ▶

COMACHO

PACKED BY LLOYD H. DIEBERT MADERA, CA

Native Americans and Asian Americans Battle Discrimination

Native Americans had a long history of discrimination and suffered high rates of poverty, unemployment, and suicide. Inspired by the struggle for civil rights, they forged their own protest movements in the 1960s and 1970s. At the same time, Asian Americans fought long-standing discrimination.

Activist Groups Form As with the civil rights movement, the young took the lead in demanding change for American Indians. In 1961, the National Indian Youth Council (NIYC) formed, with the goal of preserving native fishing rights in the Northwest. Over time, the group expanded its aims to include broad civil rights for Native Americans. In 1968, the Chippewa activists Dennis Banks and George Mitchell founded the **American Indian Movement (AIM)**. At first, AIM focused on helping Indians living in urban ghettos. Before long, however, AIM was addressing all civil rights issues, particularly the securing of land, legal rights, and self-government for Native Americans.

Confronting the Government As Indians' dissatisfaction with the government grew, their activism became more militant. In late 1969, a group of American Indians occupied the island of Alcatraz, the site of a federal prison in San Francisco Bay that had closed in 1963. Members of the Sioux tribe asserted that the island belonged to them under a treaty provision granting them unused federal land. About 100 American Indians representing 50 tribes joined the occupation. In spite of efforts by the Coast Guard and other federal authorities to evict them, the Indians maintained control of the island until mid-1971.

The 1970s saw another series of confrontations. Led by Dennis Banks and Russell Means, AIM orchestrated a "long march" from San Francisco to Washington, D.C., in 1972. Upon arriving in the capital, they took control

Migrant Farmworkers Today

- 81 percent are foreign-born; of these, 77 percent are Mexican.
- 52 percent are illegal immigrants.
- The average migrant farmworker is a 31-year-old Spanish-speaking male.
- Half of all migrant farmworkers live far below the poverty level.
- The life expectancy for a migrant farmworker is 49 years.

SOURCE: U.S. Department of Labor; ERIC Digest

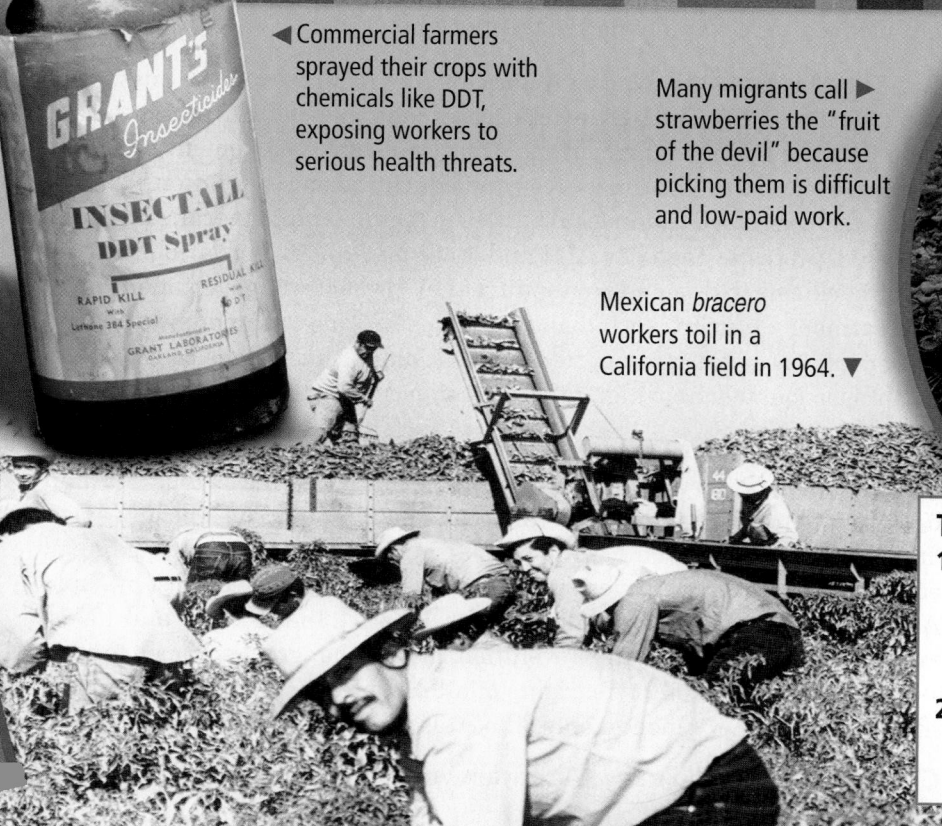

◄ Commercial farmers sprayed their crops with chemicals like DDT, exposing workers to serious health threats.

Many migrants call ► strawberries the "fruit of the devil" because picking them is difficult and low-paid work.

Mexican *bracero* workers toil in a California field in 1964. ▼

Thinking Critically

1. **Synthesize Information** Study the table and the images. Why might the average lifespan of migrant farmworkers be only 49 years today?

2. **Contrast** How does the produce crate label contrast with the actual conditions of migrant farmworkers?

1031

Daniel Inouye (born 1924)

When Hawaii became a state in 1959, Daniel Inouye was elected its first representative to Congress. Three years later, he became the Senate's first Asian American. The son of Japanese immigrants, Inouye entered the army after the bombing of Pearl Harbor. He lost an arm in combat and received the Medal of Honor. Inouye graduated from law school before entering public office. In more than forty years in the Senate, Inouye, a Democrat, has championed the interests of Hawaiians as well as healthcare and education for all children.

Ben Nighthorse Campbell (born 1933)

The son of a Portuguese immigrant mother and a Cheyenne Indian father, Ben Nighthorse Campbell joined the Air Force and served in the Korean War before entering college. In 1982, he was elected to the Colorado State Legislature. He went on to careers as a U.S. representative and then a senator. He did not run for reelection in 2005. Throughout his years in Congress, he worked for Native American rights and on policy relating to natural resources. Originally a Democrat, Campbell became a Republican in 1995.

of the Bureau of Indian Affairs building. They temporarily renamed it the Native American Embassy, suggesting Native Americans are treated as foreigners.

Siege at Wounded Knee In 1970, Dee Brown published *Bury My Heart at Wounded Knee,* about the 1890 massacre of Sioux at Wounded Knee, South Dakota. Brown noted that in all the history of the American West,

Primary Source ❝Only occasionally was the voice of an Indian heard, and then more often than not it was recorded by the pen of a white man. The Indian was the dark menace of the myths, and even if he had known how to write in English, where would he have found a printer or a publisher?❞

The best-selling book raised public consciousness about the historic mistreatment of Native Americans. Building on this momentum, AIM planned a dramatic confrontation at Wounded Knee. In late February of 1973, AIM took over the village and refused to leave until the government agreed to investigate the condition of reservation Indians. Federal authorities put Wounded Knee under siege, and two AIM members died in the resulting gunfire. The standoff ended in May when the government pledged to reexamine native treaty rights.

Making Legal Headway Native American activism spurred the passage of several laws in the 1970s. The Indian Self-Determination Act of 1975, for instance, fulfilled one of the main demands of the American Indian movement by granting tribes greater control over resources and education on reservations. Native Americans also continued to win legal battles to regain land, mineral, and water rights. Yet the protests staged by AIM and other militant groups also provoked a political backlash with some contending that the federal government gave special treatment to American Indians. While politicians debated how the government should treat Native Americans, the Indians themselves continued to suffer disproportionately from high rates of unemployment and other social ills.

Asian Americans Fight Discrimination Prejudice against people of Japanese and Chinese ancestry, who had come to the United States as laborers, had long been part of the American social and economic climate. The **Japanese American Citizens League,** founded in 1929 to protect Japanese Americans' civil rights, worked for decades to receive government compensation for property lost by Japanese Americans interned in camps during World War II. In the 1960s and 1970s, in the wake of the expanding rights revolution, many other groups formed to combat discrimination and protect the rights of all Asian Americans. The Immigration and Nationality Act Amendments (1965) also aided Asian immigrants.

NoteTaking

Reading Skill: Identify Causes
Identify causes of expanding rights for Asian Americans, consumers and those with disabilities.

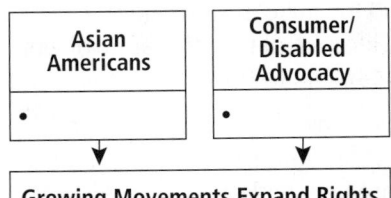

Asian Americans	Consumer/ Disabled Advocacy
•	•

Growing Movements Expand Rights

✔ **Checkpoint** Why did Native Americans work to expand their rights?

New Rights for Consumers and the Disabled

In the same way that many activists worked to extend rights to women and minorities and to protect the environment, others worked to protect the rights of consumers and Americans with disabilities.

During the Progressive Era, reformers had pushed for measures to protect consumers, ranging from the Pure Food and Drug Act to the Meat Inspection Act. The consumer rights movement reemerged during the 1960s and 1970s. It was led by **Ralph Nader,** a lawyer who began to investigate whether flawed car designs led to increased traffic accidents and deaths. His book, *Unsafe at Any Speed* (1965), attacked automakers whose thirst for profits produced unsafe vehicles that endangered the public. Nader's best-selling book stirred the nation and prompted Congress to pass the National Traffic and Motor Vehicle Safety Act in 1966. Among other things, the act made safety belts standard equipment in all cars. Nader went on to form several consumer advocacy groups. Under his influence, consumer advocacy adopted many of the practices that shape it today, including research and government lobbying. Advocacy for workers began to gain more prominence as well. The Nixon administration proposed the idea for the Occupational Safety and Health Administration (OSHA), which mandated workplace safety regulations.

Historically, the nation had treated people with disabilities as defective. FDR hid the fact that he could not walk because he did not want society to assume he was incapable of serving as President. Yet by the 1970s, Americans with disabilities were making great strides toward expanding their rights. Disabled veterans from the Korean and Vietnam wars took part in this activism. The Kennedy administration called for change by establishing the Panel on Mental Retardation in 1961 to explore ways for the government to help people with intellectual disabilities. The next year, Eunice Shriver, Kennedy's sister, began an athletic camp for young people with disabilities that eventually became the Special Olympics. Over the next few years, the government passed several laws guaranteeing equal access to education for people with disabilities.

A Winner
A girl shows her sister the gold medal she won at a 2003 Special Olympics event in South Carolina.

✔ **Checkpoint** How did rights for consumers and people with disabilities expand during the 1960s and 1970s?

SECTION 3 Assessment

Progress Monitoring *Online*
For: Self-test with vocabulary practice
Web Code: nea-1731

Comprehension

1. **Terms and People** What is the relationship of each of the items below to Latino, Native American and Asian American movements for equality?
   - Cesar Chavez
   - migrant farmworker
   - UFW
   - Chicano movement
   - AIM
   - Japanese American Citizens League

2. **NoteTaking Reading Skill: Compare and Contrast** Use your completed Venn diagram to answer the Section Focus Question: How did the rights movements of the 1960s and 1970s expand rights for diverse groups of Americans?

Writing About History

3. **Quick Write: Anticipate Opposing Arguments** Suppose that you are going to give a speech in support of making migrant farmworkers legal citizens with full benefits. Anticipate any opposing arguments, and note ways to address them in your speech.

Critical Thinking

4. **Draw Inferences** How did the government make immigration for Latinos and Asians easier in the 1960s?

5. **Identify Central Issues** Why was it particularly important to Latino activists to gain political rights?

6. **Draw Comparisons** How and why was the Native American struggle for equality different from that of Latinos?

7. **Predict Consequences** Do you think rights for people with disabilities would have been achieved earlier if FDR had openly shown his disability? Explain.

▲ Rachel Carson

A 1962 cartoon shows a man choking on fumes from a pesticide he uses to kill a fly. ▶

WITNESS HISTORY 🔊 AUDIO

An Environmental Wake-up Call

❝There once was a town in the heart of America where all life seemed to live in harmony with its surroundings. . . . Then a strange blight crept over the area and everything began to change. Mysterious maladies swept across the flocks of chickens; the cattle and sheep sickened and died. . . . There was a strange stillness. The birds, for example—where had they gone? . . . On the mornings that had once throbbed with the dawn chorus of robins, catbirds, doves, jays, wrens, and scores of other bird voices there was now no sound; only silence lay over the fields and woods and marsh. . . . No witchcraft, no enemy action had silenced the rebirth of new life in this stricken world. The people had done it to themselves. ❞
—Rachel Carson, *Silent Spring*, 1962

The Environmental Movement

NY **Core Curriculum Objectives**

- **7.V.A.1a** Modifications to Great Society programs (OSHA, Clean Air Act)
- **7.V.A.1c** Environmental Protection Agency (1970)
- **7.V.B.2c(1)** Environmental concerns: Three Mile Island

Terms and People

Rachel Carson
toxic waste
Earth Day
EPA

Clean Air Act
Clean Water Act
Endangered Species
 Act

NoteTaking

Reading Skill: Recognize Sequence As you read, record major events in the environmental movement in a flowchart like the one below.

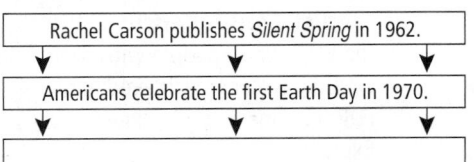

| Rachel Carson publishes *Silent Spring* in 1962. |
| Americans celebrate the first Earth Day in 1970. |

Why It Matters The "rights revolution" of the 1960s and 1970s eventually influenced all aspects of American life—including people's right to a clean and safe environment. The story told by **Rachel Carson** pointed out that human actions were harming not only the environment but people themselves. Public awareness of environmental issues prompted an important debate about the government's role in environmental regulations. **Section Focus Question: What forces gave rise to the environmental movement, and what impact did it have?**

Environmental Activists Speak Out

In the 1920s, Progressives had worked to conserve public lands and parks. But no one thought to worry much about the ill effects of industrialization. In 1952, however, a blanket of deadly smog, caused by coal fires, engulfed the city of London, killing some 12,000 people. Ten years after the London smog, a book sparked the modern environmental movement.

Silent Spring **Sparks a Movement** Coal smog is just one kind of **toxic waste,** or poisonous byproduct of human activity. Another is acid rain, or moisture in the air caused by the mixing of water with chemicals produced by the burning of fossil fuels. Toxic wastes are also produced when nuclear power is generated. Throughout the 1960s and 1970s, scientists learned more about toxic wastes and other environmental threats.

In 1962, biologist Rachel Carson's book *Silent Spring* described the deadly impact that pesticides were having on birds and other animals. Her book caused a sensation. Though the chemical industry fought back, the public was convinced by her argument. Carson did more than point to the dangers of chemicals and toxic waste. She also insisted that human activity drastically altered the environment and that humans had a responsibility to protect it. Her work eventually <u>compelled</u> Congress to restrict the use of the pesticide DDT. It also spurred widespread environmental activism among Americans.

When a fire erupted on the Cuyahoga River in Cleveland, Ohio, in 1969, activists instantly spoke out. The fire occurred when a spark ignited floating oil and debris—byproducts of industrialization—on the river's surface. *Time* magazine reported that the river "oozes, rather than flows." Even more luridly, the magazine remarked that in the Cuyahoga, a person "does not drown but decays."

Inaugurating Earth Day Events like the Cuyahoga fire seemed to confirm the dire predictions of *Silent Spring*. One response to growing environmental concerns was a nationwide protest called **Earth Day.** Wisconsin senator Gaylord Nelson, who played the leading role in organizing the protest, wanted "to shake up the political establishment and force this issue [environment] onto the national agenda." On April 22, 1970, close to 20 million Americans took part in Earth Day events across the nation. The yearly event attracted the support of many of the same people who had advocated civil and women's rights. It was also backed by a number of grassroots groups, including the Sierra Club, founded by John Muir in 1892, and the Wilderness Society, established in 1935. Historically, these groups had focused on conservation. With the rise of the environmental movement, however, they called for broader environmental protections.

Vocabulary Builder
<u>compel</u>–(kuhm PEHL) *v.* to force someone to do something

Earth Day, Then and Now
Students march through the streets of St. Louis on the first Earth Day to protest pollution caused by cars (left); students on Earth Day in 2005 rush to break a world record for the most trees planted in an hour.

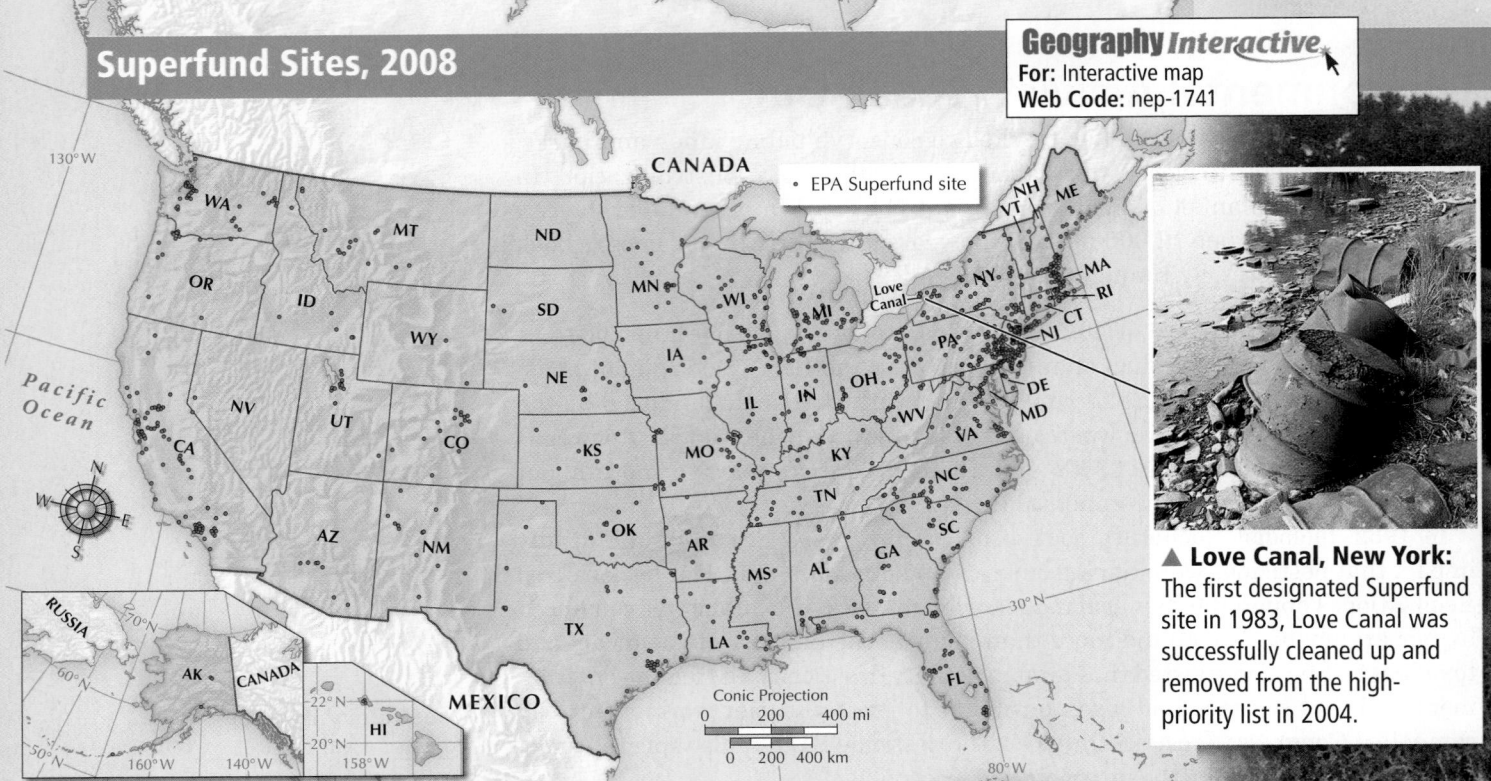

Superfund Sites, 2008

• EPA Superfund site

▲ **Love Canal, New York:** The first designated Superfund site in 1983, Love Canal was successfully cleaned up and removed from the high-priority list in 2004.

Conic Projection
0   200   400 mi
0   200   400 km

Map Skills In 1980, Congress established Superfund, a program financed by taxes on oil and certain chemicals, to clean up sites that had extreme environmental pollution. Today, more than 1,500 sites remain on the high-priority list.

1. **Identify** In general, where are most Superfund sites located? Why do you think this is so?

2. **Draw Inferences** Do sites in urban areas pose greater risks than sites in rural areas? Explain.

3. **Synthesize Information** Study the bar graph. What varied benefits does repurposing Superfund sites bring that would not be accomplished by just cleaning up the sites?

A President Turns Environmentalist In 1969, President Nixon declared that the 1970s "must be the years when America pays its debts to the past by reclaiming the purity of its air, its water and our living environment." Nixon had not come into office as an environmental activist. But the public's increasing concern with protecting the environment convinced him to support environmental reforms.

Under Nixon's leadership, Congress created the **Environmental Protection Agency (EPA)** in 1970. This federal agency's mission was to protect the "entire ecological chain." In addition to cleaning up and protecting the environment, the EPA sought to limit or to eliminate pollutants that posed a risk to the public's health, such as toxic substances that cause cancer. Nixon also signed a number of environmental laws. The **Clean Air Act** (1970) combated air pollution by, among other things, limiting the emissions from factories and automobiles. The **Clean Water Act** (1973) sought to limit the pollution of water by industry and agriculture. The **Endangered Species Act** (1973) promoted the protection of endangered plants and animals.

President Gerald Ford continued in Nixon's footsteps. In 1974, he created the Nuclear Regulatory Commission to make sure nuclear materials would be handled safely without harmful impacts on people or the environment.

✓ **Checkpoint** How did the modern environmental movement grow?

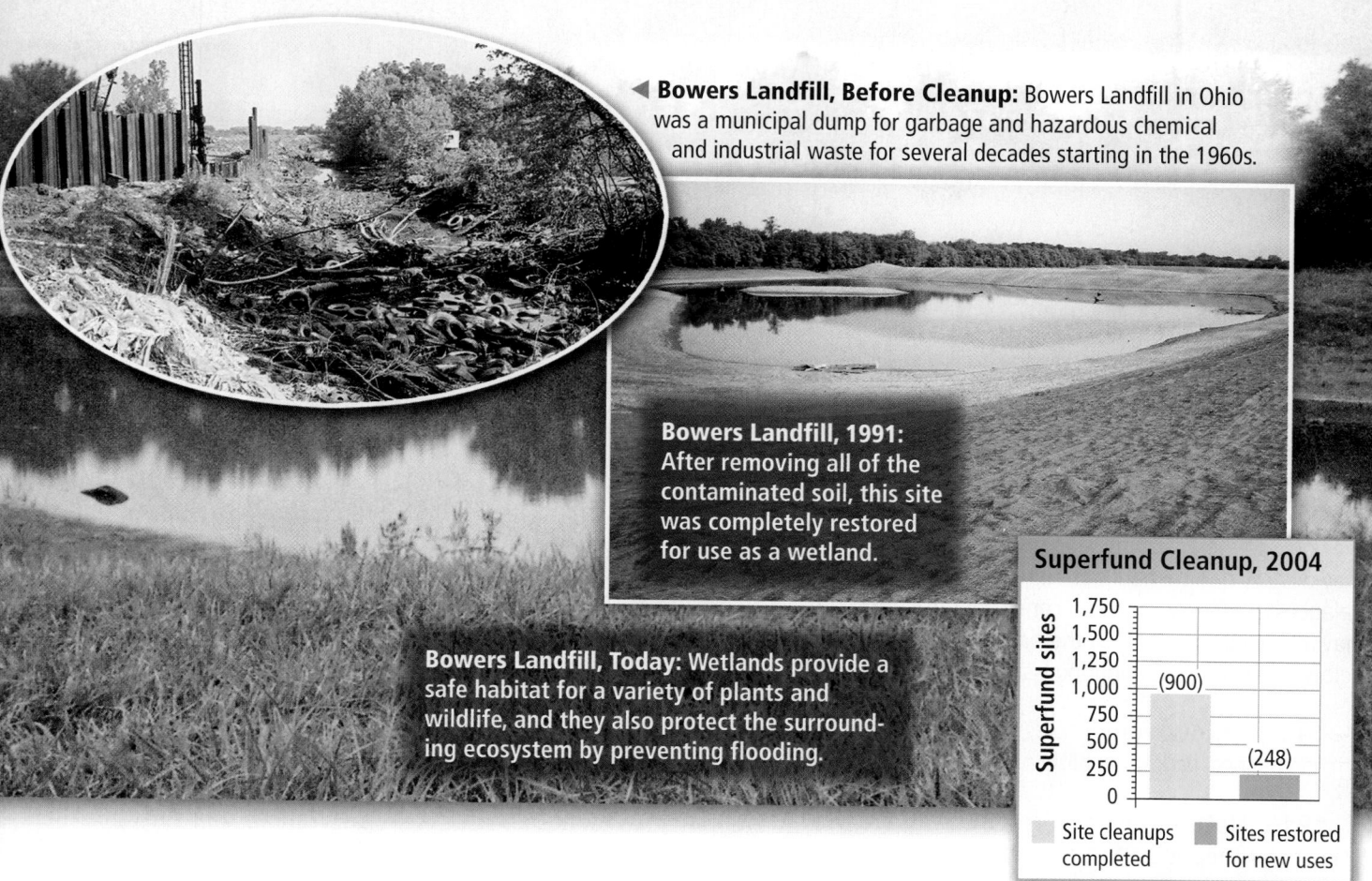

Bowers Landfill, Before Cleanup: Bowers Landfill in Ohio was a municipal dump for garbage and hazardous chemical and industrial waste for several decades starting in the 1960s.

Bowers Landfill, 1991: After removing all of the contaminated soil, this site was completely restored for use as a wetland.

Bowers Landfill, Today: Wetlands provide a safe habitat for a variety of plants and wildlife, and they also protect the surrounding ecosystem by preventing flooding.

Superfund Cleanup, 2004

Superfund sites

- (900) Site cleanups completed
- (248) Sites restored for new uses

One of Superfund's goals is to restore sites in ways that provide economic or environmental benefits to communities.

Environmental Setbacks

As the 1970s drew to a close, a series of environmental crises made the headlines. They reinforced the public's concern about the environment and produced calls for even more far-reaching actions. Yet, at the same time, a number of people began to wonder if the government had enacted too many regulations. Rather than calling for more federal action, they tried to limit the government's role in environmental protection.

The EPA Investigates Love Canal In 1978, a resident of Love Canal, a community near Niagara Falls in upstate New York, hung a sign from his home that read: "Give me Liberty. I've Already Got Death." This sign referred to the fact that residents of the community had exceptionally high rates of birth defects and cancer. Newspaper reporters and EPA investigators determined that these illnesses were caused by thousands of tons of toxic chemicals, which industries had been dumping in the ground for decades. One EPA administrator recalled the scene he witnessed following a heavy rain that sent toxic chemicals percolating up through the ground.

Primary Source "I visited the canal area at that time. Corroding waste-disposal drums could be seen breaking up through the grounds of backyards. Trees and gardens were turning black and dying. . . . Puddles of noxious substances were pointed out to me by the residents. Some of these puddles were in their yards, some were in their basements, others yet were on the school grounds. Everywhere the air had a faint, choking smell. Children returned from play with burns on their hands and faces."
—Eckhardt Beck, *EPA Journal*, 1979

The Love Canal contamination, along with other events involving hazardous waste, prompted Congress to establish Superfund (see feature at top) in 1980.

Interaction With the Environment

 7.III.B.1d

TRACK THE ISSUE

THE ESSENTIAL

How can we balance economic development and environmental protection?

The goals of economic growth and environmental protection are often in conflict. For example, power plants provide energy, but they pollute the air. Dams supply water, but they destroy natural habitats. Finding a balance between growth and conservation may involve trade-offs. Use the timeline below to explore this enduring issue.

1872 Yellowstone
First national park is established.

1916 National Park Service
Congress creates the National Park System.

1962 *Silent Spring*
Rachel Carson's book exposes dangers of pesticides.

1970 Clean Air Act
Congress establishes air quality standards.

1973 Endangered Species Act
Law offers protection for threatened species.

1997 Kyoto Protocol
United States signs international agreement on CO_2 emissions, but Congress fails to ratify it.

A view of Yellowstone's Grand Canyon painted in 1872

A herd of caribou grazes on a plain near an oil-drilling facility in Alaska.

DEBATE THE ISSUE

The Search for Oil Alaska's Arctic National Wildlife Refuge (ANWR) is a large nature preserve with an abundance of wildlife. It may also contain large deposits of crude oil. Some people want to drill for this oil, while others believe oil drilling would ruin the pristine wilderness.

" . . . There are good reasons . . . to permit ANWR drilling. . . . It could be done without wrecking the environment. . . . Only 2,000 acres of the 19 million-acre ANWR refuge would be subject to drilling. . . . Drilling could create 250,000 to 735,000 jobs nationwide. . . . [Drilling] in an environmentally sensitive fashion is important insurance against future energy shocks."

—Editorial, *USA Today*, 2005

"Drilling in the Arctic Refuge is not a path to energy independence or lower prices at the pump. The United States Geological Survey estimates that the Refuge has less than a single year's supply of oil that would not reach the market for at least 10 years. Meanwhile, the harm to wildlife and to our greatest wildlife refuge would be irreparable."

—Defenders of Wildlife

 TRANSFER Activities

1. **Compare** Why does the first source support drilling in the arctic refuge? Why does Defenders of Wildlife oppose it?

2. **Analyze** How might the first source have responded to the creation of the National Park Service in 1916? Explain.

3. **Transfer** Use the following Web site to see a video, try a WebQuest, and write in your journal. **Web Code:** neh-9002

Meltdown at Three Mile Island Shortly after the investigation at Love Canal, an accident occurred in the nuclear energy industry. On March 28, 1979, the core of the nuclear reactor at Three Mile Island outside Harrisburg, Pennsylvania, began to melt after the reactor malfunctioned. When the plant threatened to release radioactive gas, the governor declared a state of emergency and shut it down. To reassure the public that plant managers had contained the accident, President Jimmy Carter and his wife traveled to Three Mile Island and toured the reactor.

Even though the incident was contained and there proved to be no health risks, it had profound effects on America's energy policy. In the wake of the accident, Americans opposed nuclear energy, fearful of possible disasters. The government temporarily stopped building new nuclear power plants. Even though it later lifted the ban, no new American nuclear plants were ordered for more than a quarter of a century. In the 2000s, with energy shortages, many Americans began to call for building new nuclear plants.

Questioning Environmental Regulation As more environmental regulations were passed, opposition to them grew. Conservatives complained that they stripped individuals of their property rights by restricting what they could or could not do with their land. Some argued that private property owners would do a better job of protecting the environment than the government because the owners had an interest in preserving the profitability of their land. Many people—and especially industry leaders—also worried that too much environmental regulation would hamper business and jobs by diverting funds to cleaning up the air and water. Therefore, as the 1970s came to a close, Americans remained divided about what role the government should play in regulating industry and protecting the environment.

✓ **Checkpoint** Why did some people oppose the environmental movement?

Progress Monitoring *Online*
For: Self-test with vocabulary practice
Web Code: nea-1741

Comprehension

1. **Terms and People** For each item below, write a sentence explaining how it helped expand a right or provide a protection.
   - Rachel Carson
   - Earth Day
   - EPA
   - Clean Air Act
   - Clean Water Act
   - Endangered Species Act

2. **NoteTaking Reading Skill: Recognize Sequence** Use your completed flowchart to answer the Section Focus Question: What forces gave rise to the environmental movement, and what impact did it have?

Writing About History

3. **Quick Write: Organize the Material** You need to give a speech describing environmental problems in your region and how they could affect the local economy. Outline topics and arguments, remembering to begin with a strong argument or a personal story and to end with your most compelling argument.

Critical Thinking

4. **Recognize Cause and Effect** How did Rachel Carson's concern about DDT spark the environmental movement?

5. **Make Comparisons** How did the goals and tactics of the environmental movement compare with those of the women's movement?

6. **Identify Assumptions** What basic assumptions about the environment did opponents to environmental regulation have?

Progress Monitoring *Online*
For: Self-test with vocabulary practice
Web Code: nea-1751

■ Rights-Expanding Legislation

Equal Rights Amendment (ERA) (First proposed 1921; never passed)	Proposed constitutional amendment to guarantee gender equality
Panel on Mental Retardation (1961)	Explored ways the government could help people with disabilities
Title VII of the Civil Rights Act (1964)	Outlawed sex-based discrimination
Immigration and Nationality Act (1965)	Eased restrictions, making immigration easier for Latinos and Asians
National Traffic and Motor Vehicle Safety Act (1966)	Mandated safety equipment in cars
Environmental Protection Agency (1970)	Established to clean up degraded environments and to prevent further contamination
Clean Air Act (1970)	Limited emissions from factories and cars
Clean Water Act (1973)	Limited pollution of water by industry and agriculture
Endangered Species Act (1973)	Protected endangered plants and animals
Indian Self-Determination Act (1975)	Gave Native Americans control over resources on reservations

■ Major Activists and Groups

Activist/Group	Goal
Betty Friedan/National Organization of Women (NOW)	Win true equality for all women; pass ERA; make abortion legal
Phyllis Schlafly	Defeat the ERA
Cesar Chavez/United Farm Workers	Obtain better working conditions for migrant farmworkers
National Council of La Raza	Reduce Latino discrimination
La Raza Unida	Support Latino political candidates; obtain better jobs and housing for Latinos
Dennis Banks/American Indian Movement (AIM)	Secure legal rights and self-government for Native Americans
Rachel Carson	Publicize dangers of chemicals to environment
Ralph Nader	Enact legislation and regulations to protect consumers
Japanese American Citizens League	Secure civil rights for Japanese Americans

■ Influence of the Civil Rights Movement

The Civil Rights Movement

- African Americans push for legal and social equality.
- Groups use different tactics, including protesting, raising social consciousness, and working for political and legal change.
- Important legislation is passed, including the Civil Rights Act of 1964.

The Civil Rights Movement Influences Other Protest Movements

Goals
- Women, Latinos, Native Americans, Asian Americans, and people with disabilities push for legal and social equality.
- Environmental and consumer groups demand legal changes.

Tactics
- Women, Latinos, Native Americans, and environmentalists use civil rights protest tactics to support their own causes.

☑ Quick Study Timeline

In America

1962	1963	1966		1969
Rachel Carson's *Silent Spring* launches environmental movement	Betty Friedan publishes *The Feminine Mystique*	United Farm Workers union is formed		Woodstock festival celebrates the counter-culture

Presidential Terms John F. Kennedy 1961–1963   Lyndon B. Johnson 1963–1969

1960	**1964**	**1968**

Around the World

1960	1963	1966
Ceylon (now Sri Lanka) elects world's first female prime minister	**Soviet cosmonaut Valentina Tereshkova becomes first woman in space**	**Indira Gandhi becomes India's first female prime minister**

American Issues
●—●—●—● Connector

By connecting prior knowledge with what you have learned in this chapter, you can gradually build your understanding of enduring questions that still affect America today. Answer the questions below. Then, use your American Issues Connector study guide (or go online: www.PHSchool.com Web Code: neh-9003).

Issues You Learned About

● **Interaction With the Environment** The federal government seeks to balance environmental conservation with development.

1. How did John Muir and Theodore Roosevelt contribute to the early conservation movement in the United States?

2. Give three examples of human activities that have harmed the environment.

3. Give three examples of the way individuals or the government have tried to protect the environment.

● **Women in American Society** Women's movements have organized to demand greater equality in American society.

4. Describe the first wave of feminism, including its leaders and its goals.

5. Explain the goals of the second wave of feminism.

6. What are some reasons that the average woman continues to earn less than the average man?

● **U.S. Immigration Policy** The country's immigration laws change over time, often in response to outside influences.

7. In the past, Congress has passed laws preventing people from certain countries from immigrating to the United States. Identify one of these laws, its provisions, and the people against whom it was directed.

8. Why was the *bracero* program initiated in 1942?

9. What happened as a result of the Immigration and Nationality Acts Amendments?

Connect to Your World | New York

Interaction with the Environment The dumping of over 20,000 tons of toxic waste in the Love Canal neighborhood of Niagara Falls, New York is considered one of the worst environmental disasters in United States history. This disaster spurred the establishment of the federal Superfund program. Approximately 90 sites in New York are still on the Environmental Protection Agency's National Priorities List of Superfund sites. Locate the Superfund sites in your county. Choose one site and then put together a fact sheet about the site, including the source of the problem and what steps are being taken to address the environmental hazard.

1970
EPA is established

1973
Supreme Court legalizes abortion in *Roe* v. *Wade*; AIM confronts government at Wounded Knee

1979
Nuclear disaster occurs at Three Mile Island

Richard M. Nixon 1969–1974 | Gerald R. Ford 1974–1977 | Jimmy Carter 1977–1981

1972 | **1976** | **1980**

1971
Environmental group Greenpeace founded in Vancouver, Canada

1973
American involvement in Vietnam War ends

History *Interactive*
For: Interactive timeline
Web Code: nep-1751

Chapter Assessment

Terms and People

Match the following definitions with the items below.

counterculture   migrant farmworker
generation gap   Chicano movement
feminism   toxic waste

1. The _____ sought to raise cultural awareness among Latinos.

2. Members of the _____ promoted the sexual revolution.

3. Acid rain and the byproducts of nuclear power are examples of _____.

4. The baby boomers' rejection of traditional values set them apart from the older generation, creating a _____.

5. Phyllis Schlafly opposed _____ because she believed it hurt families.

6. Cesar Chavez led a movement to improve working conditions for the _____.

Focus Questions

The focus question for this chapter is **How did the counterculture and the expanding rights revolution of the 1960s and 1970s influence American society?** Build an answer to this big question by answering the focus questions for Sections 1 through 4 and the Critical Thinking questions that follow.

Section 1
7. What was the counterculture, and what impact did it have on American society?

Section 2
8. What led to the rise of the women's movement, and what impact did it have on American society?

Section 3
9. How did the rights movements of the 1960s and 1970s expand rights for diverse groups of Americans?

Section 4
10. What forces gave rise to the environmental movement, and what impact did it have?

Critical Thinking

11. **Recognize Ideologies** How did rock and folk music become, in the words of the musician John Sinclair, "a weapon of cultural revolution"?

12. **Synthesize Information** What underlying problem in American society did the rights movements of the 1960s and 1970s address?

13. **Make Comparisons** How were the lasting effects of the counterculture similar to and different from those of the other rights movements discussed in this chapter?

14. **Analyzing Visuals** Use information from the chapter to explain the data on the graph below.

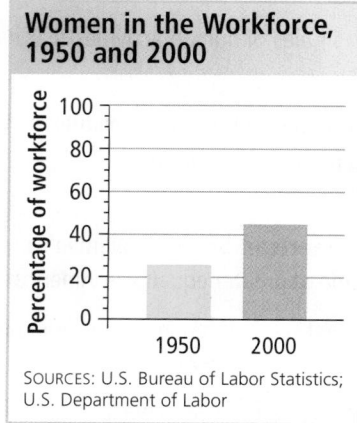

Women in the Workforce, 1950 and 2000

Percentage of workforce

SOURCES: U.S. Bureau of Labor Statistics; U.S. Department of Labor

15. **Predict Consequences** Would the rights movements of the 1960s and 1970s have been as successful without the examples of civil rights activists? Explain.

16. **Geography and History** Why was geography a central issue of the Native American movement but not of the other rights movements?

Writing About History

Writing a Persuasive Speech During the 1960s, many people used speeches to draw attention to their causes. Write a persuasive speech from the point of view of one of these people discussed in the chapter: Betty Friedan, Phyllis Schlafly, Cesar Chavez, Dennis Banks, Ralph Nader, or Rachel Carson. Deliver your completed speech to a classmate or to the entire class.

Prewriting
• Choose the person who most interests you. Take notes about the person's motivations and methods.

• Identify the venue where the speech will be delivered, as well as its audience.

Drafting
• Develop a thesis, and choose information to support it.

• List arguments that support your thesis, and answer opposing arguments.

• Write the speech, remembering to open with an attention-grabbing statement and to end with your strongest argument.

Revising
• Use the guidelines on page SH16 of the Writing Handbook to revise your speech.

Regents DBQ Practice

The Voting Rights Act

In 1965, Congress passed the Voting Rights Act, removing the barriers that had kept African Americans disenfranchised. In 1975, Congress amended the act to address voting barriers related to Latino and Native American voters. Section 203 of the law required that voting materials be published in languages other than English in certain areas. Section 5 required that certain counties with a history of discrimination pre-clear any voting changes with the U.S. Department of Justice. Use your knowledge of the civil rights movement and Documents 1, 2, 3, and 4 to answer questions 1 through 4.

Document 1

Citizens of language minorities have been effectively excluded from participation in the electoral process. Among other factors, the denial of the right to vote of such minority group citizens is ordinarily directly related to the unequal educational opportunities afforded them resulting in high illiteracy and low voting participation. . . . The requirements of the law are straightforward: all election information that is available in English must also be available in the minority language so that all citizens will have an effective opportunity to register, learn the details of the elections, and cast a free and effective ballot.

—From Section 203 of the Voting Rights Act, 1975

Document 2

I'm a naturalized citizen now, born in the Philippines and it just put a smile to my face as well as the rest of the people in our household when we get those ballots in Tagalog. We DON'T even have those in the country I came from so the more I appreciate all the efforts of you guys put into making sure every eligible citizen [is] able to understand and get informed with regards to all the candidates and all the measures by sending them tools in their native languages. America is truly the best country in the world to live in. . . . Proud to be a U.S. Citizen. . . . Thanks to all of you and keep up the good work.

—A voter from San Diego County, California

Document 3

This nation is still subject to the problem that Section 5 was developed to address. Even today, many jurisdictions still respond to growth in minority political power by restricting minority political opportunity. In Texas and Arizona, for example, the Justice Department continues to interpose a significant number of objections; the deterrent effect of Section 5 stops many discriminatory election changes before they are enacted by covered jurisdictions. Despite what you may hear from opponents of the Voting Rights Act, the emergency that led to the adoption of Section 5 has not passed. Latino voters have not yet closed the gap in voter registration and turnout in the Southwest. . . . I urge you today to reauthorize Section 5 with language clarifying congressional intent to prohibit intentional discrimination and to restore ability to elect. . . .

—Nina Perales, counsel to the Mexican American Legal Defense and Education Fund, 2005

Document 4

---

1. Document 2 supports the purpose and outcome of which other document?
   (1) Document 1
   (2) Document 3
   (3) Document 4
   (4) none of the documents

2. In Document 3, a lawyer testifies before Congress, urging it to
   (1) change key provisions of the Voting Rights Act.
   (2) disallow the Voting Rights Act.
   (3) reauthorize the Voting Rights Act.
   (4) amend the Voting Rights Act so that it applies only to Native Americans.

3. In Document 4, what is the cartoonist's opinion about American political parties and Latino voting rights?
   (1) The Democrats alone are concerned about Latino voting rights.
   (2) The Republicans alone are concerned about Latino voting rights.
   (3) Both parties are concerned about Latino voting rights.
   (4) Neither party is concerned about Latino voting rights.

4. **Writing Task** Explain why Latinos have focused on expanding voter participation, the obstacles they have faced, and the successes they have had. Use the documents on this page, along with material from the chapter, to support your assessment.

A Long National Nightmare

In the late summer of 1974, President Richard Nixon's resignation ended the drawn-out Watergate scandal. However, the nation still reeled from the shadow that Watergate had cast on its President. New President Gerald Ford attempted to set a new tone for the troubled nation:

❝My fellow Americans, our long national nightmare is over. Our Constitution works; our great Republic is a government of laws and not of men. . . . As we bind up the internal wounds of Watergate, more painful and more poisonous than those of foreign wars, let us restore the golden rule to our political process, and let brotherly love purge our hearts of suspicion and of hate.❞

—President Gerald Ford, August 9, 1974

Listen to the Witness History *audio to learn more about Nixon's resignation.*

◀ Two tourists in front of the White House read headlines announcing Nixon's intention to resign on August 8, 1974.

Yellow ribbon symbolizing the hope that hostages held in Iran would return home safely

Tape recorder used by President Nixon in the Oval Office

🅝🅨 Core Curriculum Objectives

Chapter Focus Question: What caused Americans to suffer a crisis of confidence during the 1970s?

Section 1
Nixon and the Watergate Scandal   7.V.A.1, 7.V.A.3b, 7.V.A.3c, 7.V.A.3d

Section 2
The Ford and Carter Years   7.V.B, 7.V.B.2a, 7.V.B.2b

Section 3
Foreign Policy Troubles   7.V.B.3, 7.V.B.3c, 7.V.B.3e

Sign on a Volkswagen Beetle announces a gas shortage

Use the ☑ **Quick Study Timeline** at the end of this chapter to preview chapter events.

Note Taking Study Guide *Online*
For: Note Taking and American Issues Connector
Web Code: nee-9101

▲ Nixon and aide H. R. Haldeman

The Watergate Tapes

Not long after President Nixon's 1972 reelection, the huge Watergate scandal began to unfold. The root of the scandal was a break-in at the Democratic Party's headquarters in Washington, D.C. Tapes of White House conversations later revealed that Richard Nixon and his top aides had tried to cover up the break-in:

❝H. R. Haldeman [assistant to the President]: Now, on the investigation, you know, the Democratic break-in thing, we're back to the—in the problem area because the FBI is not under control, because [FBI Director L. Patrick] Gray doesn't exactly know how to control them [his agents]. . . . [The] way to handle this now is for us to have [Deputy CIA Director] Walters call Pat Gray and just say, 'Stay . . . out of this.' . . . **President Nixon:** You call them in. . . . Play it tough. That's the way they play it and that's the way we are going to play it.❞

—Taped conversation, Oval Office, White House, June 23, 1972

Nixon and the Watergate Scandal

 Core Curriculum Preview

- **7.V.A.1** Nixon as President: domestic policies and events
- **7.V.A.3b** Watergate affair and its constitutional implications
- **7.V.A.3c** *United States* v. *Nixon*, 1974
- **7.V.A.3d** The impeachment process and resignation

Terms and People

silent majority	affirmative action
stagflation	Watergate
OPEC	Twenty-fifth Amendment
southern strategy	executive privilege

NoteTaking

Reading Skill: Identify Main Ideas Record Nixon's major domestic policies and goals in a chart like the one below.

Nixon's Domestic Policies and Strategies	
New Federalism	**Southern Strategy**

Why It Matters President Richard Nixon stood at the summit of his long government career when he was reelected President in a landslide in November 1972. Yet, less than two years later, Nixon left office in disgrace, the first time a President of the United States had resigned. The Watergate scandal gripped the nation and shaped the values and attitudes toward government that many Americans hold today. **Section Focus Question: What events led to Richard Nixon's resignation as President in 1974?**

Nixon's Policies Target Middle America

Richard Nixon's political career had more ups and downs than a roller coaster ride. Brought up in hard times, he worked his way through college and law school. After service in the navy during World War II, Nixon was elected to the House of Representatives in 1946 and then to the Senate in 1950. As Dwight Eisenhower's running mate in 1952, he became Vice President with Eisenhower's victory. Nixon was not yet 40 years old.

Then came the defeats. In 1960, Nixon narrowly lost to John F. Kennedy in the race for the White House. Two years later, Nixon's career hit bottom when he lost an election to become governor of California. In 1968, however, Nixon made a dramatic comeback, narrowly defeating Democrat Hubert Humphrey to win the presidency.

Nixon Calls for a "New Federalism" During the campaign for President, Nixon cast himself as the spokesperson for those he called Middle Americans, or the **silent majority.** As Nixon put it at the 1968 Republican convention, he sought to speak for the "non-shouters, the non-demonstrators," the men and women who "work in America's factories . . . run America's businesses . . . serve in the Government . . . provide most of the soldiers . . . [and] give life to the American dream."

Winning the support of Middle America proved a tricky task. Nixon believed that Americans had tired of the "big" government of Lyndon Johnson's Great Society. However, he also believed that the American people still wanted the government to address various social ills, ranging from crime to <u>pollution</u>.

Nixon's solution was to call for the establishment of a "new federalism." As he explained in his 1971 State of the Union address, the nation needed "to reverse the flow of power and resources from the States and communities to Washington and start power and resources flowing back from Washington to the States and communities." Nixon proposed revenue sharing with the states. Under revenue sharing, the federal government gave the states the money to fund social programs. The states then controlled the operations of these programs.

Nixon Expands the Government's Role However, while returning power and money to the states, Nixon also sponsored many programs that increased the size and role of the federal government. During his presidency, a number of powerful new federal agencies and laws came into existence. The Occupational Safety and Health Administration (OSHA) regulates workplaces to make them safer for workers. The DEA, or Drug Enforcement Administration, administers the federal war against illegal drugs. The Environmental Protection Agency (EPA) enforces federal environmental standards. The Clean Air Act, signed into law in 1970, gives the EPA the power to set air quality standards.

Nixon's welfare policies also reflected his complicated domestic strategy. To decrease the power of the federal government, Nixon began to dismantle the Office of Economic Opportunity, the cornerstone of Lyndon Johnson's "war on poverty." Yet, Nixon also proposed creating a Family Assistance Plan (FAP), which called for providing a guaranteed or minimum income to every American family. Although the FAP did not become law, federal spending on other social welfare programs, such as Medicare and public housing, grew steadily, especially during Nixon's early years.

The Economy Struggles As his presidency progressed, Nixon grappled with an increasingly troublesome economy. After decades of strong growth and low inflation, the U.S. economy experienced both recession and inflation at the same time. These symptoms began during the Johnson administration, but they grew stronger during the Nixon years. The combination of recession and inflation baffled economists and led them to coin a new term, **stagflation,** to describe the dual conditions of a stagnating economy and inflationary pressures.

Stagflation had several causes. Expanding federal budget deficits caused by the Vietnam War produced inflation. Another cause was rising foreign competition, which cost thousands of Americans their jobs. Heavy industries such as steel and auto production, which had enjoyed a dominant position since World War II, proved especially vulnerable to foreign competition. Yet

Vocabulary Builder
<u>pollution</u>–(puh LOO shuhn) *n.* environmental contamination

An Overwhelming Wave
While inflation drove prices up, most workers' wages stayed the same, causing the money they earned to buy fewer necessary goods. *How would high unemployment make the situation shown in the cartoon even worse?*

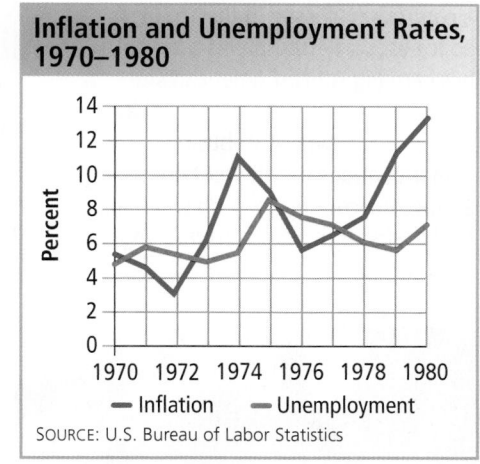

Inflation and Unemployment Rates, 1970–1980

SOURCE: U.S. Bureau of Labor Statistics

THE NIXON WAVE

the factor that caused most Americans pain was the rapid increase in the price of oil.

During the 1973 war between Israel and its Arab neighbors, the **Organization of Petroleum Exporting Countries (OPEC),** a group of mostly Arab countries that sells oil to other nations and cooperates to regulate the price and supply of oil, placed an embargo on Israel's allies, including the United States. Dependent on imports for nearly one-thirds of their energy, Americans soon felt the sting of this embargo as oil prices skyrocketed 400 percent in a single year. The embargo lasted until the spring of 1974 and resulted in gas lines at the pumps that stretched for blocks. With the end of the embargo, gas prices remained high.

Nixon fought stagflation in a variety of ways. Most dramatically, in August 1971, he placed a 90-day freeze on all wages and prices. The controls worked for a short time, causing a spurt of economic growth. However, price controls do not work well in a free economy, and the economy went into a tailspin in the mid-1970s.

 Checkpoint What was the goal of President Nixon's "new federalism"?

Nixon Follows a Southern Strategy

Having narrowly won the presidency in 1968, Richard Nixon set out to expand his base of support. He targeted blue-collar workers and southern whites, both of whom had traditionally voted for Democrats. By winning the support of southern whites, Nixon hoped to make the Republican Party a powerful force in the South. Commentators called this Nixon's **southern strategy.**

Controversy Rages Over Busing As part of his southern strategy, Nixon tried to place a number of conservative southerners as judges in federal courts. Most prominently, he nominated Clement Haynsworth and G. Harrold Carswell to serve on the U.S. Supreme Court. Both men failed to win Senate confirmation, in part because both had supported segregation in the past.

Criticizing court-ordered busing of children to schools outside their neighborhood was another way Nixon reached out to southern whites and urban blue-collar workers. For years, many school districts in both the South and the North had resisted desegregation. In 1971, federal courts ordered school districts to bus students to achieve greater racial balance. Recognizing the unpopularity of busing, Nixon made a nationally televised address in which he called for a moratorium, or freeze, on court-ordered busing. By speaking forcefully, Nixon won the support of many busing opponents.

Nixon Proposes New Civil Rights Initiatives Yet, as with much else that he did, Nixon's stance on civil rights was mixed. In 1969, the Nixon administration initiated the Philadelphia Plan, a program

Turmoil Over Busing

Court-ordered busing continued to be a controversial issue in the 1970s. A police escort (left) protects a school bus carrying African American students into a white neighborhood as part of the busing. Anti-busing demonstrations (right) went on around the country. *Why do you think that busing provoked such a strong reaction?*

that required labor unions and federal contractors to submit goals and timetables for the hiring of minorities. It was a type of **affirmative action,** a policy that gives special consideration to women and minorities in the fields of education and employment, in order to make up for past discrimination. Nixon's Assistant Secretary of Labor, Arthur Fletcher, who designed the Philadelphia Plan, argued:

> **Primary Source** "The Federal Government has an obligation to see that every citizen has an equal chance at the most basic freedom of all—the right to succeed. . . . Segregation didn't occur naturally—it was imposed. . . . The gap . . . between black and white . . . was growing wider and wider. . . . Visible, measurable goals to correct [these] imbalances are essential."
> —Arthur Fletcher, Assistant Secretary of Labor, speech on affirmative action, 1969

Nixon's Strategy Succeeds By the 1972 election, Nixon enjoyed high approval ratings. Some of this popularity was based on his trips to the Soviet Union and China. Some was based on his domestic policies.

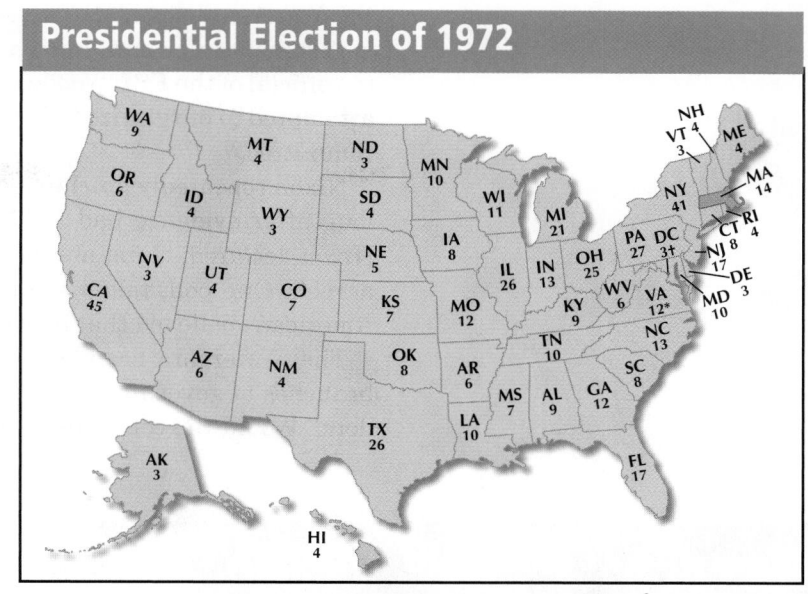

Presidential Election of 1972

Candidate (Party)	Electoral Vote	Popular Vote	% Electoral Vote	% Popular Vote
Richard M. Nixon (Republican)	520	46,740,323	96.7	60.7
George S. McGovern (Democratic)	17	28,901,598	3.1	37.5
Other	1	1,341,502	0.2	1.7

*One elector from Virginia voted for John Hospers (Libertarian)
†McGovern received 3 electoral votes from Washington, D.C.

Nixon ran a masterful political campaign in 1972, positioning himself as a moderate. He portrayed his opponents—George McGovern, an antiwar senator from South Dakota, and Alabama governor George Wallace—as extremists. (Wallace's campaign was cut short when he was shot and left paralyzed by a would-be assassin.) Nixon and his Vice President, Spiro Agnew, successfully cast themselves as spokespersons for the silent majority. On election day, Nixon won almost 61 percent of the popular vote and nearly all of the electoral votes. He became the first Republican presidential candidate to sweep the entire South.

✔ **Checkpoint** In what ways did Nixon appear to send mixed messages about civil rights?

The Watergate Scandal Brings Nixon Down

As a triumphant Richard Nixon stood before the cameras on election night 1972, he had no idea that the seeds of his downfall had already begun to sprout. The botched burglary of Democratic Party headquarters at the Watergate complex in June 1972 received little attention at first. But as investigators began to unravel the connections between the burglars and the White House, **Watergate,** as the scandal become known, came to dominate the national news.

The Watergate burglars were tried in 1973. After the trial, one of them, James McCord, charged that administration officials had been involved in the break-in. This led to a Senate investigation and to televised hearings, where numerous witnesses charged that the President and his top aides had taken part in a coverup. From the first news of the break-in, President Nixon denied any wrongdoing. Yet, as time went on, investigators discovered important links between the burglars and top Nixon administration officials.

Watergate Goes Public Two young *Washington Post* journalists, Bob Woodward and Carl Bernstein, played a <u>crucial</u> role in lifting the veil of secrecy from

NoteTaking

Reading Skill: Identify Causes and Effects Use a chart like the one below to record the causes and effects of the Watergate crisis.

Watergate Crisis	
Causes	**Effects**
• Break-in at Democratic Party headquarters	• Connections revealed between burglars and White House
•	•

Vocabulary Builder
<u>crucial</u>–(KROO shuhl) *adj.* of vital importance

the Watergate scandal. The two reporters followed tips provided by a secret government informant known as "Deep Throat," who was later revealed to be a top official of the FBI. Woodward and Bernstein reported that the men, who had attempted to burglarize the Watergate hotel, had close ties to Nixon's reelection committee.

Nixon repeatedly proclaimed his innocence. For example, in November 1973, long after evidence had implicated his top aides and forced them to resign, Nixon declared, "I am not a crook." Yet the polls indicated that the public disagreed. One poll, taken the next month, showed that fewer than one in five Americans believed that he was being honest about the Watergate affair.

The Watergate scandal created a historic showdown between the three branches of government. How far would Congress go to investigate the President? Would the courts demand that the President turn over information that

WATERGATE FORCES NIXON FROM OFFICE

One of the biggest political scandals in American history, Watergate has become synonymous with corruption and abuse of power. It began when President Nixon's reelection committee tried to record the conversations of political opponents, led to a string of coverups at the highest levels of the U.S. government, and ultimately forced Nixon from office. Nixon's role in the coverup shocked the nation.

The public might never have learned of the President's actions without the investigative reporting of journalists Bob Woodward and Carl Bernstein of the *Washington Post,* who broke the story in a series of articles. Their revelations, and those of other reporters, may have left the American people's faith in government shaken, but the aftermath reinforced the public's trust in the constitutional system.

June 1972
Five men linked to President Nixon's reelection campaign are arrested for trying to bug the offices of the Democratic National Committee in the Watergate complex (shown here) in Washington, D.C.

April 1973 Nixon denies knowledge of the Watergate break-in or any coverup.

May 1973 Archibald Cox is named as the Justice Department's special prosecutor for Watergate. The Senate Watergate Committee begins nationally televised hearings.

June 1973
Former White House counsel John Dean (right) tells investigators that Nixon authorized a coverup.

◀ Members of Congress hold a news conference about the scandal in May 1974.

might implicate him? And if the courts sided with Congress, would the President comply with its decisions?

Revealing the White House Tapes The Watergate scandal came to a climax with a dizzying array of developments. In the fall of 1973, Vice President Spiro Agnew resigned in the face of an unrelated corruption scandal. According to the procedures established by the **Twenty-fifth Amendment**, which deals with presidential succession, Nixon nominated Gerald Ford to become his new Vice President. Nixon's troubles multiplied when, in the summer of 1973, it was revealed that he had been secretly taping Oval Office conversations for many years. Many commentators speculated that these tapes would show that the President had played a leading role in trying to cover up the break-in.

▼ James McCord demonstrates a phone wiretap.

July 1973 Nixon, claiming executive privilege, refuses to release the tapes of secretly recorded Oval Office conversations.

October 1973 Nixon offers investigators summaries of tapes, which Special Prosecutor Cox refuses. Nixon fires Cox. This triggers other firings and resignations in what becomes known as the Saturday Night Massacre.

March 1974 Former Nixon administration officials are indicted on charges of conspiracy in the Watergate break-in. Richard Nixon is named as an "unindicted co-conspirator."

July 1974 The Supreme Court rules unanimously that Nixon must surrender all of the White House recordings requested by the new special prosecutor. The House Judiciary Committee recommends impeachment.

August 1974 Transcripts of tapes show that Nixon ordered a coverup of the Watergate break-in. On August 9, Nixon becomes first U.S. President to resign.

Why It Matters
While Watergate damaged the public's trust of government officials, the U.S. government's system of checks and balances withstood the crisis. Lawmakers passed laws to prevent similar abuses from happening. The role of the press in bringing the scandal to light reminded the public of the importance of a free press in a democratic society.

FROM THE WHITE HOUSE TO THE BIG HOUSE
IMPEACH NIXON NOW

Journalists Bernstein ▶ (left) and Woodward (right) with *Washington Post* publisher Katharine Graham

Thinking Critically
How did Congress and the Supreme Court balance the role of the executive branch during the Watergate crisis?

History *Interactive* ✶
For: More information about Watergate
Web Code: nep-1802

Public Trust in the Federal Government, 1964–1992

Percentage of Americans who trust the federal government*

80
60
40
20
0

1964 1968 1972 1976 1980 1984 1988 1992

SOURCE: The American National Election Studies
*Most of the time

Nixon refused to turn over these tapes to the special prosecutor investigating the scandal. The President justified withholding the tapes by claiming **executive privilege.** Executive privilege is the principle that the President has the right to keep certain information confidential. It took almost a year for the courts to sort out the matter. On July 24, 1974, in the case of *United States* v. *Nixon,* the Supreme Court disagreed that the tapes fell under the principle of executive privilege and ordered Nixon to turn them over. Chief Justice Warren Burger made it clear that the Court rejected Nixon's claim of executive privilege in this instance:

Primary Source "The expectation of a President to the confidentiality of his conversations and correspondence . . . has all the values to which we accord deference for the privacy of all citizens. . . . But this presumptive privilege must be considered in light of our historic commitment to the rule of law [the principle that all citizens are bound by the same laws]. . . . The very integrity of the judicial system and public confidence in the system depend on full disclosure of all the facts, within the framework of the rules of evidence."

—U.S. Supreme Court, *United States* v. *Nixon,* 1974

Nixon Resigns When investigators listened to the tapes, they found that crucial parts of the conversations were missing. Nixon claimed his secretary had mistakenly erased them. Still, the tapes provided enough evidence of Nixon's involvement in the coverup to lead the Judiciary Committee of the House of Representatives to vote to impeach the President. The committee charged Nixon with obstructing justice in the coverup of the Watergate break-in, misuse of power, and refusing to comply with House subpoenas. A number of Republican committee members joined the Democrats in voting for impeachment.

Recognizing that the full House of Representatives would vote in favor of impeachment and that many Republicans would vote to convict him in a trial in the Senate, Nixon decided to resign. In a speech to the American public on August 8, 1974, Nixon informed the nation that he would step down the following day in the hope that he "will have hastened the start of that process of healing which is so desperately needed in America." The long ordeal of Watergate had finally come to an end. With it, Nixon became the first and only President to resign the presidency.

Historians disagree about whether Nixon knew beforehand of the decision to burglarize Democratic Party headquarters. However, few doubt that he took part in the coverup. Testimony by his top aides, the Watergate tapes, and evidence gathered in the prosecution of the burglars all show that the President sought to quash the investigation.

Moreover, investigations revealed that Nixon had committed other abuses of presidential power. His reelection team had engaged in dirty tricks to secure his election. He had developed an "enemies list" and used federal agencies to go after his enemies. The President had ordered the FBI to place wiretaps on the telephones of those government employees and reporters he suspected of leaking information unfavorable to the administration.

Watergate Has a Lasting Impact In pursuit of personal power, Richard Nixon damaged the reputation of the

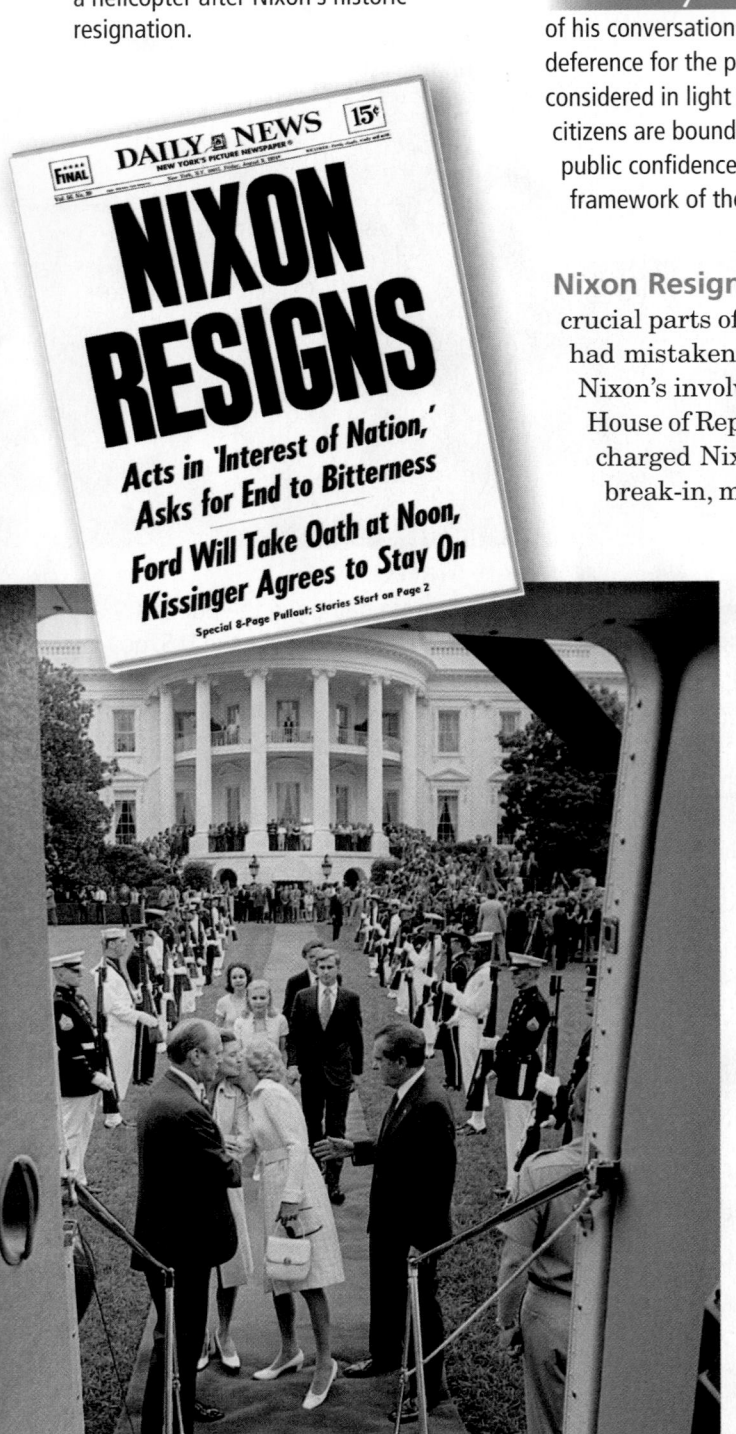

Nixon Quits
Nixon and his family bid goodbye to Gerald and Betty Ford as they board a helicopter after Nixon's historic resignation.

DAILY NEWS 15¢
FINAL
NIXON RESIGNS
Acts in 'Interest of Nation,'
Asks for End to Bitterness
Ford Will Take Oath at Noon,
Kissinger Agrees to Stay On
Special 8-Page Pullout; Stories Start on Page 2

presidency and shook the public's confidence in government. One conservative commentator, formerly a supporter of Nixon, echoed the disillusionment of many Americans:

Primary Source "The lies, the lies, the lies! . . . What a pity, what a pity! Here was a President who got us out of Vietnam, ended the draft . . . and by his bold overtures to Red China opened new avenues toward world peace. Now the good vanishes in the wreckage of the bad. The swearing-in of Gerald Ford cant come one hour too soon."
—James J. Kilpatrick, *National Review,* August 30, 1974

Polls revealed that from the late 1950s to the mid-1970s, the percentage of Americans who believed in the truth of government statements plummeted from 80 percent to 33 percent.

In the wake of Watergate, Congress enacted numerous reforms to try to restore the public's confidence in government and to prevent abuses of power in the future. It established a procedure for naming an independent counsel to investigate charges against the White House. The Federal Election Campaign Act of 1974 sought to limit the amount of money that individuals could give candidates, in order to prevent the corruption of the political process.

Yet, the Watergate affair also demonstrated that the nation could weather such a crisis. It showed the strength of the system of checks and balances. Both Congress and the Supreme Court had successfully checked the power of the President. According to *Time* magazine, Nixon's resignation represented an "extraordinary triumph of the American system." Watergate demonstrated that no person, not even a President, is above the law. As Gerald Ford said when he became President: "Our great republic is a government of laws and not of men."

✔ **Checkpoint** What role did Richard Nixon and his top aides play in the Watergate scandal?

Post-Watergate Government Reforms

Federal Election Campaign Act Amendments (1974)	Set limit on campaign contributions, provided partial federal funding for presidential campaigns, created the Federal Election Commission to enforce these laws
Freedom of Information Act Amendments (1974)	Penalized government officials who withheld documents illegally
Government in the Sunshine Act (1976)	Opened meetings of many government agencies to the public. By 1977, all states had passed sunshine laws.
Ethics in Government Act of 1978	Required financial disclosure forms from public officials, restricted government officials' ability to lobby, created the office of special prosecutor

A Breach of Faith
The laws and measures listed above were passed after Watergate to make government more transparent. *Do you think these laws helped to restore the public's faith in government? Explain.*

Assessment

Progress Monitoring *Online*
For: Self-test with vocabulary practice
Web Code: nea-1803

Comprehension

1. **Terms and People** For each term below, write a sentence explaining its relationship to the domestic policy record of the Nixon administration.
   • silent majority
   • stagflation
   • affirmative action
   • Watergate
   • executive privilege

2. **NoteTaking Reading Skill: Identify Main Ideas** Use your chart to answer the Section Focus Question: What events led to Richard Nixon's resignation as President in 1974?

Writing About History

3. **Quick Write: Write a Resumé** Conduct research on Richard Nixon's life and career, and then create a resumé for the former President that lists his educational background, work experience, and any awards he received.

Critical Thinking

4. **Summarize** How did Nixon respond to the economic problems he faced as President?

5. **Synthesize Information** In the long run, how successful was Richard Nixon's southern strategy?

6. **Draw Inferences** Opinion polls taken before and after Watergate showed a sharp drop in people's confidence in government. List two other results of the scandal.

What Are the Limits of Executive Privilege?

The President's power to keep certain communications with his advisers confidential is called executive privilege. This power is based on the idea that members of the executive branch should be able to advise the President without worrying that their opinions will be revealed to other branches of government or to the public.

United States v. Nixon (1974)

The Facts	The Issue	The Decision
• Congressional investigation revealed that President Richard Nixon and his aides may have committed illegal acts. • Taped Oval Office conversations between President Nixon and his aides were sought as evidence. • President Nixon refused to surrender the tapes to the Department of Justice.	President Nixon argued that executive privilege gave him the absolute right to withhold the tapes from the Department of Justice.	The Supreme Court ruled that executive privilege has limits. They said that executive privilege could not protect the President from the judicial process. Nixon must surrender the tapes to prosecutors.

Why It Matters

Although not specifically granted by the Constitution, Presidents have long assumed that executive privilege is implied by the constitutional separation of powers. *United States v. Nixon* was the test case that allowed the Supreme Court to define executive privilege and to set limits on its use.

In his written opinion, Chief Justice Burger recognized that there is a need for confidentiality in the executive branch, particularly when "military, diplomatic or sensitive national security secrets" must be protected. Under those conditions, the President has the absolute right to keep communications confidential. However, communications between the President and his advisers often concern policy that has nothing to do with national security. In those cases, Burger said, executive privilege is limited. A judge can decide that there is overwhelming government interest in obtaining the President's privileged communications. The due process of law in a criminal case is one example of overwhelming government interest.

A few days after the decision in *United States v. Nixon*, President Nixon resigned from office. The Court's ruling had proved that the President is not above the law.

▲ In this cartoon, the executive and legislative branches fight for power. In *United States v. Nixon,* the judicial branch backed the legislative branch.

Connect to Your World

Consider the limits of executive privilege outlined in *United States v. Nixon*. During their respective terms in office, recent Presidents Bill Clinton and George W. Bush have applied executive privilege in controversial situations. Research one example and then write a paragraph either defending or arguing against this use of executive privilege.

For: Supreme Court cases
Web Code: nee-1804

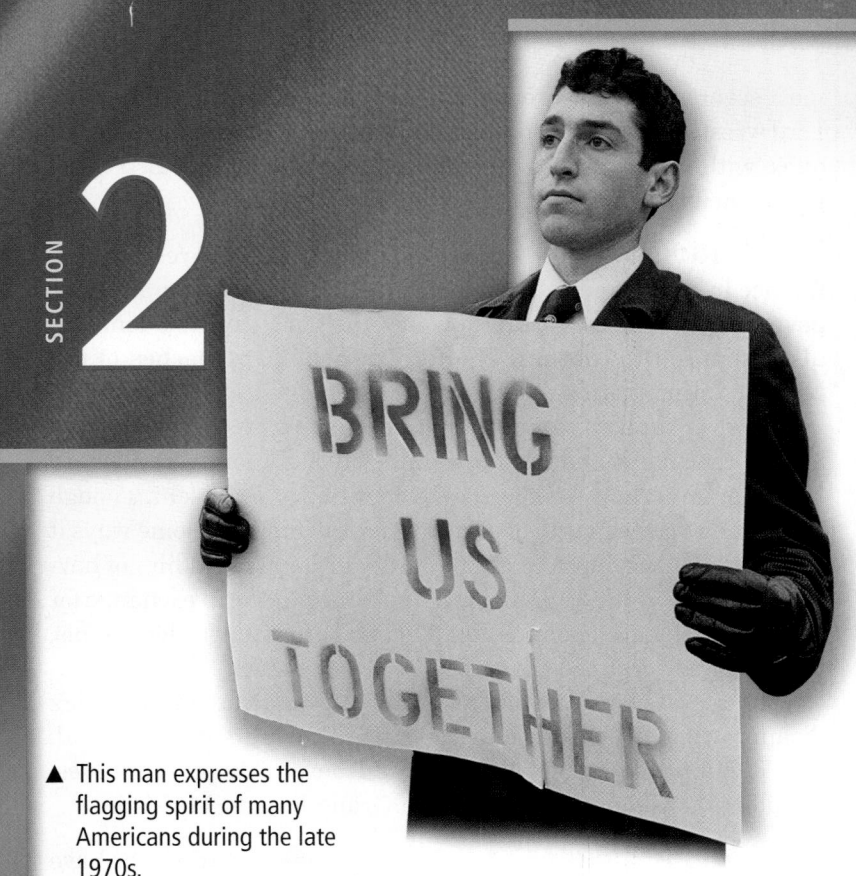

▲ This man expresses the flagging spirit of many Americans during the late 1970s.

WITNESS HISTORY AUDIO

A Crisis of Confidence

On July 4, 1976, the United States celebrated its bicentennial, or two hundredth anniversary. By the end of the decade, however, the celebratory mood had evaporated in the face of a series of crises that tested the nation's spirit. President Jimmy Carter took note of what he called the nation's crisis of confidence.

❝The symptoms of this crisis of the American spirit are all around us. For the first time in the history of our country a majority of our people believe that the next five years will be worse than the past five years. Two thirds of the people do not even vote. The productivity of workers is actually dropping. . . . There is a growing disrespect for government and for churches and for schools. . . . This is not a message of happiness or reassurance, but it is the truth and it is a warning.❞

—President Jimmy Carter, "Crisis of Confidence" speech, 1979

The Ford and Carter Years

 Core Curriculum Objectives

- **7.V.B** The Ford and Carter Presidencies
- **7.V.B.2a** Pardon for Nixon and amnesty for draft evaders
- **7.V.B.2b** Oil crisis: shifting energy priorities

Terms and People

Gerald Ford
pardon
Jimmy Carter

Christian fundamentalist
amnesty
televangelist

NoteTaking

Reading Skill: Identify Main Ideas Create an outline like the one below to record the political, economic, and social problems of the era and their impact on American society.

> I. Gerald Ford's Presidency
> A. Major Domestic Issues
> 1.
> 2.
> B.

Why It Matters In 1982, historian Peter Carroll published a history of the 1970s entitled *It Seemed Like Nothing Happened*. Compared to the turbulent 1960s, indeed, the 1970s appeared mostly uneventful. Yet, the decade witnessed significant social, economic, and cultural changes. These changes contributed to a growing sense among Americans that something had gone wrong, that the nation had gotten off the right track. This sense of disquiet is even now a part of the nation's political dialogue. **Section Focus Question: What accounted for the changes in American attitudes during the 1970s?**

Ford Faces Political and Economic Woes

Gerald Ford brought a long record of public service to the presidency. A star football player at the University of Michigan, Ford enlisted in the United States Navy and fought in World War II. Following the war, Ford successfully ran for a seat in the U.S. Congress, where he served for 25 years, rising to the position of House Minority Leader in 1965. Democrats as well as Republicans supported Ford's nomination for Vice President because he had a stellar reputation for hard work, integrity, and dependability.

Ford stepped into a delicate situation when he became President after Richard Nixon's resignation. Watergate had scarred the public's faith in government. Furthermore, the nation struggled with the

WIN Fails
Despite enthusiastic campaigning by Ford, his WIN plan failed to tame inflation.

most severe economic problems it had faced since the depression. Ford wrestled with these problems but not very successfully. He left office with the economy still suffering and the public's distrust of government still high.

Ford Pardons Nixon Ford moved quickly to try to restore confidence in government. He selected Nelson Rockefeller, a former governor of New York State, to serve as his Vice President. He also promised to continue the foreign policy approaches of the Nixon administration.

Whatever support he gained from these steps was lost when Ford announced that he had **pardoned,** or officially forgiven, Richard Nixon for any crimes he may have committed as President. Though the pardon was meant to heal the nation's wounds, in some ways it achieved just the opposite effect. Ford's critics accused him of having made a secret deal, promising Nixon the pardon in exchange for the vice presidential nomination. Though Ford strongly denied this, his popularity declined dramatically.

The congressional election results of 1974 indicated the public's disapproval of the pardon and the impact of Watergate in general. The Republicans lost 48 seats in the House of Representatives, including Ford's longtime district in Grand Rapids, Michigan.

Stagflation Plagues the Nation President Ford might have overcome this backlash if not for the troubled economy. Inflation hit double digits in 1974 and early 1975. To fight skyrocketing prices, Ford promoted a mostly voluntary plan known as WIN, or Whip Inflation Now. Unfortunately, WIN was a clear failure. Instead of improving, the economy took a turn for the worse. Factories closed down, consumer demand for goods dropped sharply, and the rate of unemployment rose steadily. Ford's popularity plummeted.

✓ **Checkpoint** How did President Ford's WIN program try to address inflation, and how successful was it?

WITNESS HISTORY DVD

Watch *The Presidency in Crisis* on the **United States Witness History DVD** to explore what some saw as a crisis in the presidency during the 1970s.

A Washington "Outsider" Becomes President

Prior to the mid-1970s, few Americans outside Georgia had ever heard of **Jimmy Carter,** a one-time governor of that state. But on election day 1976, Americans elected Carter President of the United States. He won a slim popular majority, receiving slightly more than 50 percent of the vote to Ford's 48 percent. In the electoral college, Carter won 297 votes compared to 240 for Ford.

Carter's rise was the result of several factors. Most important was the turmoil of the 1960s and Watergate, which created a backlash against professional politicians. Carter seized this opportunity by casting himself as a fresh face, with no ties to Washington, D.C. A born-again Christian who taught Sunday school, Carter won the support of many **Christian fundamentalists,** people who believe in a strict, literal interpretation of the Bible as the foundation of the Christian faith. This group became increasingly involved in politics in the 1970s.

Carter Pays a Price for Inexperience From the beginning of his presidency, Jimmy Carter sought to portray himself as a "citizens' President." He became the first President since William Henry Harrison to walk all the way from the Capitol to the White House during the inaugural parade. He held town meetings, wore casual clothes, and carried his own suitcase.

However, Carter's inexperience, which helped him get elected, hurt him during the early days of his presidency. As an outsider, he did not have close ties with the Democratic leadership in Congress. He submitted numerous bills to Congress, but few of them passed without major changes by his own party.

Just one day after his inauguration, Carter fulfilled one of his campaign pledges by granting **amnesty,** or political pardons, to Americans who had evaded the draft during the Vietnam War. Carter hoped this act would help the nation move beyond the divisions caused by that war. Yet the war remained an emotional issue, and many Americans criticized the President for forgiving those who had refused to fight. Republican senator Barry Goldwater called the amnesty "the most disgraceful thing that a President has ever done."

Problems Sap the Nation's Confidence Like Ford, Carter <u>contended</u> with the energy crisis and severe inflation. Inflation ate away at people's savings, raised the prices of necessities, and made American goods more costly abroad. The U.S. automobile industry, long a symbol of the nation's economic power, became a symbol of its ills. Japanese car companies vastly expanded their sales in the United States by selling better-built and more fuel-efficient cars at reasonable prices. The situation grew so bad that Chrysler, one of the three major American automobile companies, needed a federal loan to survive.

At the center of the nation's economic ills lay the ongoing energy crisis. In 1973, a gallon of gas cost about 40 cents. By the end of the decade, it cost close to $1.20. To make matters worse, the winter of 1976 to 1977 was an especially bitter one in parts of the United States, increasing the need for heating oil. Fuel shortages caused factory closings and business losses.

Vocabulary Builder
<u>contend</u>–(kuhn TEHND) *v.* to fight

In 1974, gas stations all over the country ran out of gas to sell motorists.

AM TO   PM
SORRY!
We're Dry!

RUNNING OUT OF GAS

The energy crisis of the 1970s rocked the American economy and stumped the best efforts of three Presidents to stop it. It made Americans feel powerless and angry, and added to the general crisis of confidence. **Why did the scarcity of oil in the 1970s have such a strong impact on the United States?**

WAIT HERE

ODD NUMBER LICENSE PLATE   10 GALS ONLY

HALF TANK OR LESS

Price of Imported Crude Oil, 1970–1980

Dollars per barrel (in 2005 constant dollars)

100
80
60
40
20
0

1970 1972 1974 1976 1978 1980

SOURCE: U.S. Energy Information Administration

The price of gas continued to increase in leaps and bounds throughout the 1970s.

At gas stations that had gas, people waited for hours in long lines that snaked for blocks.

Immigration to the United States, 1971–1980

Country of Origin	Number of Immigrants
Mexico	640,294
Philippines	354,987
Korea	267,638
Cuba	264,863
Vietnam	172,820
India	164,134
Dominican Republic	148,135
Jamaica	137,577
United Kingdom	137,374
Italy	129,368
China	124,326
Hong Kong	113,467

SOURCE: U.S. Office of Immigration Statistics

Immigration Changes America

In the 1970s, immigration continued from Southeast Asia and Latin America. Girls from families of Cuban refugees (above) attend a Catholic school in Miami, Florida. *From which region did more people emigrate in the 1970s—Southeast Asia or Latin America?*

Carter responded to the oil crisis by calling on Americans to conserve and by asking Congress to raise taxes on crude oil, which he hoped would encourage conservation. However, the bill that finally passed in the Senate had few of the President's ideas in it. Critics saw this as one more example of Carter's poor leadership skills.

Carter did implement several domestic policies that his successors would build on during the 1980s. To fight inflation, Carter nominated Paul Volcker to head the Federal Reserve Board. Under Volcker's lead, the Federal Reserve began raising interest rates. In the long term, this policy helped to bring an end to the inflation that had plagued the nation for so long.

✔ **Checkpoint** What challenges did President Carter face?

Changing Values Stir Unease

Social and cultural changes that had begun in the 1950s and 1960s continued unabated in the 1970s. As a result, by the end of the decade, the United States was a very different society from the one it had been a generation earlier. These differences gave rise to an ongoing debate about the nation's values.

Demography Affects Politics The migration of Americans to the Sunbelt and the continued growth of the suburbs, both of which had begun in the post–World War II years, continued during the 1970s. As northern industries suffered, many blue-collar workers and their families moved from the Rust Belt states of the Northeast and Midwest to the Sunbelt of the South and West. They sought work in the oil fields of Texas and Oklahoma and in the defense plants of southern California, the Southwest, and the Northwest. These trends changed the face of the United States.

The elections of Richard Nixon and Jimmy Carter demonstrated the growing political power of the Sunbelt. Earlier in the century, Presidents tended to come from the large northern industrial states, such as New York and Ohio. In the latter decades of the twentieth century, Presidents tended to come from the Sunbelt.

The influx of immigrants from Latin America and Asia represented a different kind of demographic change. Even before the 1970s, hundreds of thousands of Cubans, Puerto Ricans, and Mexicans had migrated to the United States. This migration, especially from Mexico and other Latin American countries, continued to be strong in the 1970s. The growing power of the Latino vote did not escape the notice of politicians. Richard Nixon was the first presidential candidate to seriously court the Spanish-speaking vote.

The "Me Generation" Comes of Age During the 1960s, radicals had challenged many of society's traditional values. They questioned restrictions on premarital sex and drug use. They sported casual clothing and long hairstyles that many of their parents' generation found improper. Yet the counterculture remained a relatively isolated phenomenon during the 1960s. By the end of the 1970s, in contrast, these behaviors had become more common. Nationwide, the

Focus On Geography

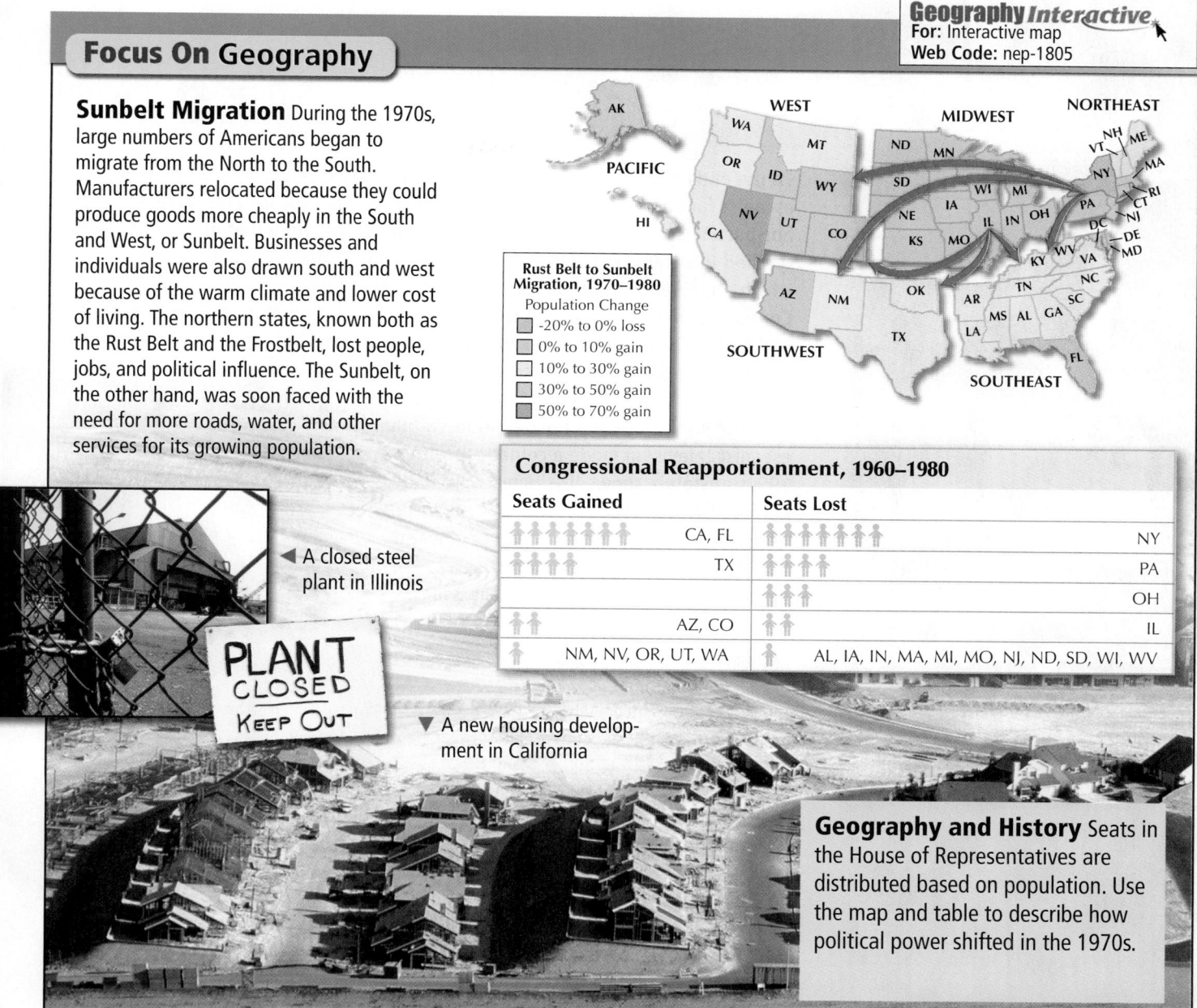

Sunbelt Migration During the 1970s, large numbers of Americans began to migrate from the North to the South. Manufacturers relocated because they could produce goods more cheaply in the South and West, or Sunbelt. Businesses and individuals were also drawn south and west because of the warm climate and lower cost of living. The northern states, known both as the Rust Belt and the Frostbelt, lost people, jobs, and political influence. The Sunbelt, on the other hand, was soon faced with the need for more roads, water, and other services for its growing population.

Rust Belt to Sunbelt Migration, 1970–1980
Population Change
- -20% to 0% loss
- 0% to 10% gain
- 10% to 30% gain
- 30% to 50% gain
- 50% to 70% gain

◀ A closed steel plant in Illinois

Congressional Reapportionment, 1960–1980

Seats Gained		Seats Lost	
𝕚𝕚𝕚𝕚𝕚𝕚𝕚𝕚	CA, FL	𝕚𝕚𝕚𝕚𝕚𝕚𝕚𝕚	NY
𝕚𝕚𝕚𝕚	TX	𝕚𝕚𝕚𝕚	PA
		𝕚𝕚𝕚	OH
𝕚𝕚	AZ, CO	𝕚𝕚	IL
𝕚	NM, NV, OR, UT, WA	𝕚	AL, IA, IN, MA, MI, MO, NJ, ND, SD, WI, WV

▼ A new housing development in California

Geography and History Seats in the House of Representatives are distributed based on population. Use the map and table to describe how political power shifted in the 1970s.

---

divorce rate had more than doubled between 1965 and 1979, and twice as many children were born out of wedlock. To some Americans, the new ways were a sign of troubled times.

Some critics called the 1970s the "me decade" because many Americans appeared to be absorbed with improving themselves. This trend was reflected in the rise of movements like Transcendental Meditation (TM), a practice based in Eastern religious ideas. Those who practiced TM sought to find inner relaxation and vitality by chanting their personal mantras for about half an hour twice a day.

The seventies also witnessed an increasing interest in personal fitness and health. Millions began to jog for exercise and to eat natural, or less processed, foods. In 1970, just over 100 men and women ran in the New York City Marathon. Ten years later, more than 14,000 ran in the race. Body building took off, too, largely due to the influence of Arnold Schwarzenegger. A charismatic personality, Schwarzenegger went on to become one of Hollywood's most popular actors and, later, governor of California.

TV Breaks New Ground

In the early 1970s, the face of television began to change. Shows based on escapist fantasy or nostalgia gave way to shows that focused on current, hot-button issues and featured more minorities. The show that most typified this trend was the situation comedy, or sitcom, *All in the Family*, which remained the number one television show from 1971 through 1976. Conflicts between the central character—blue-collar bigot Archie Bunker—and his liberal, hippie son-in-law Michael (below left) brought debates over national issues onto the TV screen.

Toward the end of the decade, perhaps as a result of Watergate and the defeat in Vietnam, escapist television made a comeback with 1950s nostalgia shows like *Happy Days* and *Laverne & Shirley*. The rising popularity of the newsmagazine *60 Minutes*, however, showed that Americans were still interested in tuning in to learn about relevant issues.

M*A*S*H* ❶, a comedy about a mobile hospital unit during the Korean War, resonated with viewers who were used to watching news reports on the Vietnam War. Shows like *Sanford and Son* ❷ and *Chico and the Man* ❸ proved that viewers would tune in to shows featuring minority characters. *60 Minutes* ❹ was the first television newsmagazine. *Roots* ❺, a graphic historical miniseries that followed the life of a slave and his descendants, fascinated more than 100 million viewers.

Happy Days (top) was about a teenager growing up in the 1950s, while its spin-off, *Laverne & Shirley* (bottom), followed two lifelong friends living and working together in Milwaukee.

Thinking Critically
1. **Identify Central Issues** How did television change in the 1970s?
2. **Determine Relevance** How did these changes reflect broader changes taking place in American culture?

Conservatives Reassert Traditional Values The 1970s witnessed a resurgence of fundamental Christianity, partly as a response to the shift in values. To some commentators, it seemed as if the nation was experiencing another Great Awakening, like the great religious movements of the eighteenth and nineteenth centuries. Although the total number of Americans who attended church on a regular basis did not change much, the number of men and women who belonged to evangelical churches rose rapidly. One in five Americans considered himself or herself a religious fundamentalist by 1980.

Evangelical ministers used the media to gain a broader audience. Those who preached on television—known as **televangelists**—such as Jerry Falwell, Oral Roberts, and Marion "Pat" Robertson, reached millions of viewers. Falwell's daily radio broadcasts were carried by 280 radio stations, and his weekly television show was broadcast to 1.5 million viewers.

Religious conservatives firmly opposed many of the social changes begun in the 1960s that had gone mainstream in the 1970s. They opposed the Supreme Court's rulings that legalized abortion and restricted prayer in school. Falwell formed a prominent Christian conservative organization known as the Moral Majority in 1979. He voiced the concerns of many fundamentalists:

> **Primary Source** "We must reverse the trend America finds herself in today. Young people . . . have been born and reared in a different world than Americans of past worlds. . . . They have learned to disrespect the family as God has established it. . . . They have been taught that the Bible is just another book of literature. . . . They have been introduced to the drug culture."
>
> —Reverend Jerry Falwell, *Listen America*, 1980

During the 1970s, religious conservatives began forming alliances with other conservatives. They worked with economic conservatives, who sought to cut taxes and government spending, as well as with supporters of a stronger foreign policy, who favored increasing defense spending. Together, they began forging a new political majority. By 1980, Ronald Reagan, another political outsider, would use this alliance to win election to the White House.

 Checkpoint In what ways did the United States change socially and culturally during the 1970s?

SECTION

2 Assessment

Progress Monitoring *Online*
For: Self-test with vocabulary practice
Web Code: nea-1806

Comprehension

1. Terms and People For each item below, write a sentence explaining its effect on social and economic conditions in the 1970s.
- Gerald Ford
- pardon
- Jimmy Carter
- Christian fundamentalist
- amnesty
- televangelist

2. NoteTaking Reading Skill: Identify Main Ideas Use your outline to answer the Section Focus Question: What accounted for the changes in American attitudes during the 1970s?

Writing About History

3. Quick Write: List Qualifications Suppose that you are Gerald Ford applying for the position of Vice President in the mid-1970s. Research Ford's background and skills. Then, list the qualifications that you would highlight to try to get the position.

Critical Thinking

4. Demonstrate Reasoned Judgment Should Gerald Ford have pardoned Richard Nixon?

5. Identify Point of View What arguments would you expect people to give for and against President Carter's decision to grant amnesty to Americans who had evaded the draft?

6. Draw Inferences How do you think Watergate affected social trends in the 1970s?

Are Affirmative Action Programs Fair?

NY 7.V.C.5

In the 1970s, the government urged employers and schools to adopt affirmative action programs. These programs aimed to increase the number of women and minority group members in college, postgraduate schools, and higher-paying jobs. The goal was to make up for past discrimination against these groups. Did those programs now discriminate against white males?

Regents of the University of California v. *Bakke* (1978)

The Facts	The Issue	The Decision
• Allan Bakke, a white man, was twice denied admission to a University of California medical school. • Bakke had a stronger academic record than 16 minority group applicants that the school had accepted under a special program.	Bakke claimed that his rights under the equal protection clause of the Fourteenth Amendment had been violated.	• Five Justices agreed that racial quotas violated Bakke's rights. • One of those Justices and four others agreed that race could be a factor in admissions decisions.

Why It Matters

Some people predicted that *Bakke* would end affirmative action. That did not happen, however. Justice Lewis Powell was the key figure in the Court's complex statements on the issue. He agreed with four Justices that quotas were not acceptable, but he also agreed with the other four that using race as a factor in admissions was acceptable. Powell favored using race as a "plus factor," just like artistic or musical ability, athletic talent, or other factors.

After the Court's decision, universities dropped quota systems. Many also followed Powell's opinion by setting up programs that consider a person's race as one factor among many.

▲ Protesters in Michigan support the University of California.

Connect to Your World

In 2003, the Court visited the issue again. In *Grutter* v. *Bollinger,* a 5-to-4 majority ruled that a law school's admissions policy met the standards of *Bakke* by using race as part of the process but not as a deciding factor. Read more about the case, then take the role of a newspaper editor and write an editorial agreeing or disagreeing with the Court's decision.

For: Supreme Court cases
Web Code: nee-1807

◄ Today's college classrooms reflect a greater gender and ethnic diversity in part because of affirmative action policies.

SECTION 3

▲ President Carter and Panama's leader General Omar Torrijos in 1978

Human Rights and American Foreign Policy

As President, Jimmy Carter sought to center America's foreign policy on human rights rather than on anticommunism. Carter outlined his views in 1977:

❝For too many years, we've been willing to adopt the flawed and erroneous principles and tactics of our adversaries, sometimes abandoning our own values for theirs. We've fought fire with fire, never thinking that fire is better quenched with water. . . . [I] believe that it is a mistake to undervalue the power of words and of the ideas that words embody.❞

—President Jimmy Carter, Commencement Address at Notre Dame University, 1977

Foreign Policy Troubles

 Core Curriculum Objectives

- **7.V.B.3** Foreign policy issues: the United States after Vietnam
- **7.V.B.3c** Middle East mediation: Camp David Accords
- **7.V.B.3e** Iranian hostage crisis: 1979–1981

Terms and People

Helsinki Accords	sanctions
human rights	developing world
SALT II	Camp David Accords
boat people	Ayatollah Khomeini

NoteTaking

Reading Skill: Identify Supporting Details Use a concept web like the one below to record the main ideas and details about the foreign policies of presidents Ford and Carter.

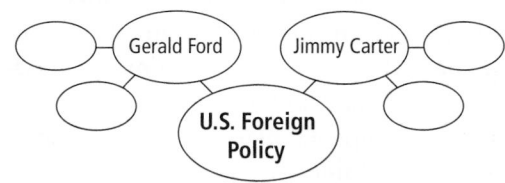

Why It Matters The ordeal of the Vietnam War led many to question the direction of American foreign policy. They asked: Why was the United States so concerned with fighting communism that it ended up supporting oppressive anticommunist governments? Should the United States continue to pursue détente with the Soviets? Or should it instead demand that the Soviet government grant its people more freedoms? The echoes of these debates continue to be heard today. **Section Focus Question: What were the goals of American foreign policy during the Ford and Carter years, and how successful were Ford's and Carter's policies?**

Ford Continues Nixon's Foreign Policies

Relations with the Soviet Union remained central to U.S. foreign policy during the Ford and Carter administrations. Upon assuming the presidency, Gerald Ford made clear that his foreign policy would differ little from that of Richard Nixon's. Ford retained Henry Kissinger as his Secretary of State and continued to pursue détente with the Soviet Union and China.

Pursuing Détente Ford and Soviet leader Leonid Brezhnev met in late 1974 and again the next year, when the two leaders endorsed the **Helsinki Accords.** This document put the nations of Europe on record in favor of **human rights,** or the basic rights that every human being is entitled to have. Some thought that President Ford

Vietnamese Boat People

These Vietnamese refugees wait in their rickety boat in Hong Kong's harbor in September 1979, having survived the voyage from Vietnam.

would try to compel the Soviet Union to allow more political freedoms, but Ford decided to put arms control ahead of human rights. At his direction, the United States continued disarmament talks with the Soviets. These talks led to an agreement known as **SALT II,** in which the two nations pledged to limit nuclear arms production.

Trouble in Southeast Asia Under Ford, the United States sought to put the turmoil of the Vietnam War behind it. When the communist Khmer Rouge government of Cambodia began a genocidal slaughter of civilians, killing about 1.5 million people between 1975 and 1979, the United States did not intervene. The main exception to this policy of noninvolvement came in May 1975, when the Khmer Rouge seized an American merchant ship, the *Mayaguez*, which had been steaming just outside Cambodian waters. Ford responded by sending in some United States Marines, who freed the ship.

During Ford's presidency, South Vietnam fell to North Vietnam. As the communists took over, hundreds of thousands of Vietnamese, many of whom had worked with the United States, tried to escape. Many refugees took to the seas in rickety, unseaworthy boats. These **boat people** represented the largest mass migration of humanity by sea in modern history. Over a 20-year period, more than one million men, women, and children braved storms, pirates, and starvation in search of refuge abroad. Their immediate destinations were in other nations of Southeast Asia, but many eventually found that refuge in the United States and Canada.

✔️ **Checkpoint** How did Ford approach foreign policy challenges during his presidency?

Carter Changes Course

Early in his presidency, Jimmy Carter proclaimed that as much as possible, American foreign policy would be guided by a concern for human rights. Carter hoped to make his foreign policy into a tool to end acts of political <u>repression</u> such as torture, murder, and imprisonment without trial. This policy direction helped reaffirm the position of the United States as a nation of freedom and justice. However, it undercut the goal of better relations with the Soviet Union.

Relations With the Soviet Union Cool At first, Carter continued Nixon's and Ford's policies toward the Soviet Union. He worked to achieve détente. He continued efforts at arms control, meeting with Leonid Brezhnev in June 1979 and signing the SALT II treaty.

However, relations between the two superpowers soon took a decidedly frosty turn. The SALT II treaty was bitterly debated in the United States Senate, where its opponents argued that it put the national security of the United States in jeopardy. Then, in December 1979, the Soviet Union invaded the neighboring country of Afghanistan to prop up a tottering communist government. Carter responded by withdrawing the SALT II treaty from Senate consideration and by imposing **sanctions,** or penalties, on the Soviets. The sanctions included a U.S. boycott of the 1980 Summer Olympic Games held in Moscow as well as a suspension of grain sales to the Soviet Union.

Vocabulary Builder
repression—(rih PREHSH uhn) *n.* the act of suppressing or keeping down

Carter Supports Human Rights in the Developing World Since the end of World War II, American Presidents had tended to see the **developing world**—the poor nations of Asia, Africa, and Latin America—as another stage for the Cold War. Carter broke with that approach and insisted that foreign policy toward the developing world should revolve around the expansion of human rights. Carter believed that U.S. relations with foreign countries should be determined by how a country treated its citizens.

Carter's <u>emphasis</u> on human rights led him to alter the U.S. relationship with a number of dictators. In Nicaragua, the Somoza family had ruled the country with an iron grip since the mid-1930s, most of the time with the support of the United States. In 1978, a leftist group known as the Sandinistas began a rebellion against the country's ruler, General Anastasio Somoza. His brutal response to the rebellion helped convince Carter to withdraw U.S. support. Without U.S. aid, General Somoza had to flee Nicaragua, and the Sandinistas came to power.

Carter's Policies Get Mixed Results in Latin America The Carter administration briefly sought to improve relations with Cuba, ruled by communist Fidel Castro since 1959. However, U.S.-Cuban relations soured in 1980 when Castro announced that any Cuban could leave the island from the port of Mariel for the United States. However, Castro insisted that any boats headed to the United States would also have to take criminals from the island's prisons. Because of this condition, the Mariel boatlift developed a bad reputation in the eyes of many Americans. Fewer than 20 percent of the people transported had spent time in prison, and many of those were political prisoners. Still, Americans were repelled by Castro's lack of concern for the welfare of the emigrants and by the idea that he would send criminals to the United States.

Carter's most controversial foreign policy move involved his decision to return the Panama Canal Zone to Panama. You will recall that Panama had given the United States control of a wide strip of land across the middle of the country in 1903 that later became the site of the Panama Canal. In 1977, Carter negotiated a set of treaties to return the Canal Zone to Panama by 1999. Many Americans worried that the loss of control over the canal would threaten American shipping and security. Nonetheless, the United States Senate narrowly ratified the treaties in 1978, and all control of the canal was ultimately turned over to Panama.

> ✔ **Checkpoint** In what ways did President Carter's policies differ from those of Ford?

Success and Setback in the Middle East

Carter's greatest achievement in foreign policy came in the region that also saw his greatest setback. He helped negotiate a historic peace agreement between Israel and Egypt, but he failed to win the release of Americans held hostage by Iranian radicals.

Israel and Egypt Agree to Peace Egypt had opposed Israel's existence since Israel's founding in 1948. As recently as 1973, the two nations had fought a bitter war. By 1977, eager to improve relations, Egyptian President Anwar el-Sadat and Israeli prime minister Menachem Begin met in Jerusalem to negotiate a peace agreement. To help continue the negotiations, Carter invited the two leaders to Camp David, the presidential retreat. For

Vocabulary Builder
<u>emphasis</u>–(EHM fuh sihs) *n.* special attention

HISTORY MAKERS

Jimmy Carter (born 1924)
A former navy officer and peanut farmer, Jimmy Carter's presidency began with high hopes and calls for a new emphasis on human rights. Carter lost his bid for reelection but continued to work to promote human rights and democracy around the world. He set up an organization called the Carter Center that promotes peace and human rights, and he has helped several countries' efforts to hold free and fair elections. He even joined Habitat for Humanity to help poor people build and afford new homes.

IRAN HOSTAGE CRISIS

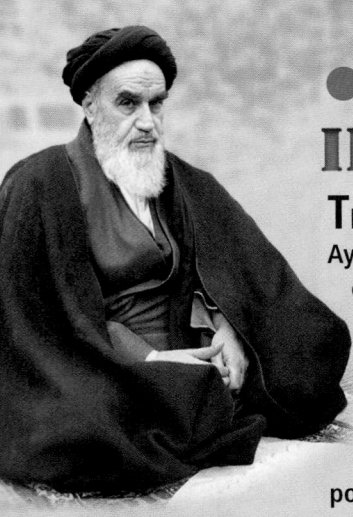

The Iranian Revolution, which toppled the Shah and brought the Ayatollah Khomeini to power in 1979, had a strong anti-American component. The United States had supported Mohammad Reza Shah Pahlavi, Iran's Shah, to secure a firm ally against communism in the region. However, the Shah's rule grew more oppressive after 1953, when the CIA had helped him control a challenge to his power. Resentment over political interference and foreign involvement in Iran's oil industry boiled over when the deposed Shah entered the United States for medical treatment. Outraged Iranians seized 66 American hostages and held 52 of them for 444 days.

▲ The Ayatollah Khomeini

A blindfolded American ▶ hostage is shown to the press.

The Crisis Unfolds

- **January 1979** The Iranian Revolution forces the Shah into exile.
- **February 1979** Ayatollah Khomeini returns to Iran after 15 years in exile.
- **April 1979** Khomeini takes power.
- **October 1979** The Shah enters the United States.
- **November 1979** Militant students take 66 Americans hostage. Carter halts oil imports and freezes Iranian assets in the United States.
- **April 1980** Carter severs diplomatic relations with Iran and imposes an economic embargo. A military mission to free the hostages ends in disaster.
- **January 1981** On the day of Reagan's inauguration, the hostages are released in exchange for $8 billion in frozen assets and a promise to lift trade sanctions against Iran.

nearly two weeks, the three leaders carried on the difficult negotiations that produced what is known as the **Camp David Accords.** These agreements provided the framework for a peace treaty in which Egypt formally recognized the nation of Israel, becoming the first Arab nation to do so. In return, Israel withdrew its troops from the Sinai Peninsula, which it had occupied since the 1967 war. The preamble to the Accords states:

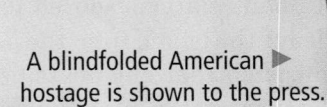

> **Primary Source** "After four wars during 30 years, despite intensive human efforts, the Middle East, which is the cradle of civilization and the birthplace of three great religions, does not enjoy the blessings of peace. . . . [Israel and Egypt] recognize that for peace to endure, it must involve all those who have been most deeply affected by the conflict. They therefore agree that this framework, as appropriate, is intended by them to constitute a basis for peace not only between Egypt and Israel, but also between Israel and each of its other neighbors. . . ."
>
> —Camp David Accords, September 19, 1978

Iran Seizes American Hostages Carter hoped that the Camp David Accords would usher in a new era of cooperation in the Middle East. Yet, events in Iran showed that troubles in the region were far from over. Since the 1950s, the United States had supported the rule of the Shah, or emperor, of Iran. In the 1970s, however, opposition to the Shah began to grow within Iran.

Dying of cancer, the Shah fled from Iran in January 1979. Fundamentalist Islamic clerics, led by the **Ayatollah Khomeini** (ī yuh TOH luh koh MAYN ee), took power. Carter allowed the Shah to enter the United States to seek medical treatment. Enraged Iranian radical students invaded the U.S. Embassy and took 66 Americans as hostages. The Khomeini government then took control of both the embassy and the hostages to defy the United States.

The hostage crisis consumed the attention of Carter during the last year of his presidency. To many Americans, Carter's failure to win all of the hostages' release was evidence of American weakness. As Peter Bourne put it in his biography of

Iranian students burn an American flag at the U.S. embassy in Tehran; protesters call for the CIA to stop interfering in Iran (right).

▲ The freed hostages arrive in the United States after their ordeal finally ends in January 1981.

Thinking Critically

1. **Recognize Causes** What event triggered the seizure of the American hostages in Iran?

2. **Synthesize Information** What actions did Carter take to try to get the hostages released?

Jimmy Carter, "Because people felt that Carter had not been tough enough in foreign policy . . . some bunch of students could seize American diplomatic officials and hold them prisoner and thumb their nose at the United States."

The hostage crisis began to change the way Americans viewed the world outside their borders. Nuclear war between the two superpowers was no longer the only threat to the United States. Although the Cold War still concerned Americans, the threats posed by conflicts in the Middle East threatened to become the greatest foreign policy challenge of the United States.

✔ **Checkpoint** How did the seizure of the U.S. Embassy by Iranian students affect Americans' view of the world?

SECTION **3** Assessment

Progress Monitoring *Online*
For: Self-test with vocabulary practice
Web Code: nea-1808

Comprehension

1. **Terms and People** For each item below, write a sentence explaining the way it affected U.S. foreign policy.
   - human rights
   - SALT II
   - boat people
   - sanctions
   - developing world
   - Camp David Accords
   - Ayatollah Khomeini

2. **NoteTaking Reading Skill: Identify Supporting Details** Use your concept web to answer the Section Focus Question: What were the goals of American foreign policy during the Ford and Carter years, and how successful were Ford's and Carter's policies?

Writing About History

3. **Quick Write: Present Skills** Put yourself in the place of someone applying to be the U.S. Ambassador to Panama in the mid-1970s. Write a paragraph describing the key qualities needed for the job.

Critical Thinking

4. **Draw Conclusions** What do you think were the most important foreign policy accomplishments of Gerald Ford and Jimmy Carter?

5. **Draw Inferences** What did Carter's inability to secure the release of the hostages in Iran symbolize to many Americans?

Chapter 31 Section 3 1067

31

Quick Study Guide

7.V.A.3c,
7.V.B.2

■ Watergate in Review

Issues	Consequences
• Presidential abuse of power (FBI wiretaps of "enemies") • Limits of executive privilege • Supreme Court's power to rule on presidential actions • Willingness of Congress to confront presidential power	• Shook public confidence in government • Damaged the reputation of the presidency • Confirmed the independent power of legislative and judicial branches • Demonstrated strength of checks and balances system • Prompted laws to govern independent counsel investigations and reform election finance practices

■ Economic Problems of the 1970s

Slow economic growth
Inflation
Energy crisis
Foreign competition

■ International Relations in the 1970s

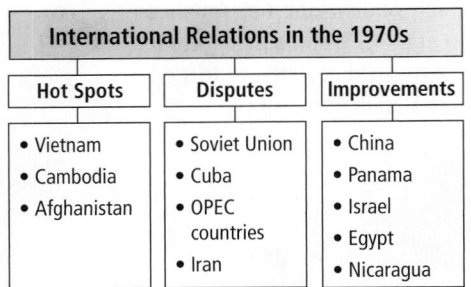

International Relations in the 1970s

Hot Spots	Disputes	Improvements
• Vietnam • Cambodia • Afghanistan	• Soviet Union • Cuba • OPEC countries • Iran	• China • Panama • Israel • Egypt • Nicaragua

■ Domestic Controversies in the 1970s

Court-ordered busing · Changing values · **Domestic Controversies of the 1970s** · Antiwar demonstrations · Affirmative action · Vietnam War · *Bakke* case · Nixon's Philadelphia Plan · Amnesty for draft resisters

☑ Quick Study Timeline

In America

1970
Clean Air Act becomes law

1973
OPEC oil embargo causes U.S. energy prices to soar

1974
Nixon resigns in wake of Watergate scandal; Ford becomes President

Presidential Terms Richard M. Nixon 1969–1974   Gerald R. Ford 1974–1977

1970   **1972**   **1974**

Around the World

1970	1971	1972	1975
United States invades Cambodia	**Idi Amin takes power in Uganda**	**Terrorists kill Israeli athletes at Munich Olympics**	**South Vietnam surrenders to North Vietnam**

American Issues
●━●━●━● Connector

1.I.B

By connecting prior knowledge with what you have learned in this chapter, you can gradually build your understanding of enduring questions that still affect America today. Answer the questions below. Then, use your American Issues Connector study guide (or go online: www.PHSchool.com **Web Code:** neh-9102).

Issues You Learned About

● **Checks and Balances** Political leaders disagree on how much authority each branch can exert over the others.

1. Why is the principle of checks and balances important to the U.S. government? Give an example of checks and balances at work.

2. Describe the role of the judicial branch and the legislative branch in the move to impeach President Nixon. What did *Time* magazine mean when it called Nixon's resignation an "extraordinary triumph of the American system"?

● **Church and State** The First Amendment of the United States Constitution, known as the Establishment Clause, calls for the separation of church and state.

3. Read the 1787 Virginia Statute for Religious Freedom, which appears in the documents section at the end of this book. What was the importance of this document?

4. Since the 1960s, the Supreme Court has made a number of rulings limiting prayers and religious readings in public schools. Why do you think that the Supreme Court banned prayer in public schools?

● **Sectionalism and National Politics** Different regions of the country often can be defined by their political beliefs.

5. Why did southern states traditionally vote for Democrats? What was remarkable about Nixon's presidential victory in 1972?

6. How did Nixon expand his base of support from the 1968 election? What was this strategy called?

7. Why did the Sunbelt gain political power in the 1970s?

Connect to Your World | New York

Migration and Urbanization As a part of the Rust Belt, the city of Buffalo, New York was strongly affected by migration to the Sunbelt in the 1970s. In the 1950s, the Buffalo area was a thriving manufacturing center, with major factories producing many products, including jet turbines, electronic equipment, iron, and steel. But over the next few decades, many of these factories were forced to close, and almost half of the population left the area. Since the 1970s, Buffalo has been trying to attract new businesses and residents by improving the downtown business district and focusing on new industrial fields, such as life science research. Research Buffalo today and create a brochure to attract new businesses to the city.

1976
America celebrates Bicentennial

1977
President Carter pardons Vietnam War draft evaders

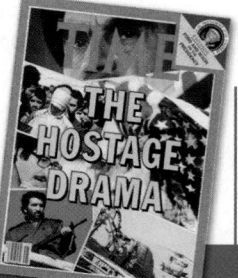

1979
Protesters seize U.S. embassy and hostages in Tehran

History *Interactive*
For: Interactive timeline
Web Code: nep-1811

Jimmy Carter 1977–1981

Ronald Reagan 1981–1989

1976   **1978**   **1980**

1978
Egypt and Israel sign Camp David Accords

1979
Soviet Union invades Afghanistan

1980
Iraq invades Iran

1981
Egyptian President Anwar Sadat is assassinated

Chapter Assessment

Terms and People

1. Define **stagflation.** What were the causes of stagflation in the early 1970s?
2. Define **executive privilege.** How did the Supreme Court rule on executive privilege in *United States* v. *Nixon*?
3. What is **amnesty**? Why did Carter's granting of amnesty to draft evaders anger some Americans?
4. What is the **developing world**? How did Carter change U.S. foreign policy toward the developing world?
5. Who was the **Ayatollah Khomeini**? How did his actions affect the Carter presidency?

Focus Questions

The focus question for this chapter is **What caused Americans to suffer a crisis of confidence during the 1970s?** Build an answer to this big question by answering the focus questions for Sections 1 through 3 and the Critical Thinking questions that follow.

Section 1
6. What events led to Richard Nixon's resignation as President in 1974?

Section 2
7. What accounted for the changes in American attitudes during the 1970s?

Section 3
8. What were the goals of American foreign policy during the Ford and Carter years, and how successful were Ford's and Carter's policies?

Critical Thinking

9. **Synthesize Information** Think about Nixon's approach to new programs and policies designed to ease racial inequality. Would you call him a supporter or an opponent of civil rights? Explain.
10. **Analyze Political Cartoons** Study the political cartoon in the Landmark Decisions of the Supreme Court feature about executive privilege that appears earlier in this chapter. Explain the political issue depicted in the cartoon and the cartoonist's view of it.
11. **Recognize Cause and Effect** Why did Ford pardon Nixon for any crimes he may have committed as President? What effect did this pardon have on American politics over the next few years?
12. **Analyze Information** How did Carter's role as a political outsider both help and hinder him in Washington, D.C.?
13. **Summarize** Summarize the responses of Nixon, Ford, and Carter to the downturn of the American economy, and explain what impact these measures had.
14. **Compare Points of View** Compare Ford's and Carter's foreign policy toward the Soviet Union.
15. **Identify Central Issues** Identify and describe two regions in the world in which Carter's policies had a major impact.

Writing About History

Applying for a Job Throughout American history, many talented individuals have worked in the federal government to try to address the energy and economic problems that have troubled the nation. Write an essay from the point of view of a college graduate in 1977 trying to get a job in the newly established Department of Energy. Explain what your qualifications are and how they are a good fit with the job's needs.

Prewriting
- Research the skills needed to fill a job in the Department of Energy in 1977.
- Develop the character of a 1977 college graduate based on those skills.

Drafting
- Write a thesis statement that expresses the key qualifications, skills, and qualities that you (as the college graduate) possess that suit the Department of Energy job.
- Expand upon these positive factors in the body of your essay.
- Close with an effective and well-worded conclusion.

Revising
- Use the guidelines on page SH16 of the Writing Handbook to revise your essay.

Regents DBQ Practice

Anatomy of a Scandal

President Richard Nixon's administration was marred by a political scandal, called Watergate, that led to his resignation. What were the roles of the Congress, the press, and the courts in investigating President Nixon's unchecked presidential power? Use your knowledge of the Watergate scandal and Documents 1, 2, and 3 to answer questions 1 through 4.

Document 1

Document 2

"If the president, for example, approves something because of the national security, or in this case because of a threat to internal peace and order of significant magnitude, then the president's decision in that instance is one that enables those who carry it out, to carry it out without violating a law. Otherwise they're in an impossible position. . . . [It] has been however argued that as far as a president is concerned, that in war time, a president does have certain extraordinary powers which would make acts that would otherwise be unlawful, lawful if undertaken for the purpose of preserving the nation and the Constitution, which is essential for the rights we're all talking about."

—*President Nixon, from an interview with British TV host, David Frost, May 19, 1977*

Document 3

"The Constitution charges the president with the task of taking care that the laws be faithfully executed, and yet the president has counseled his aides to commit perjury, willfully disregard the secrecy of grand jury proceedings, conceal surreptitious entry, attempt to compromise a federal judge, while publicly displaying his cooperation with the processes of criminal justice. . . . Has the president committed offenses, and planned, and directed, and acquiesced in a course of conduct which the Constitution will not tolerate? That's the question. It is reason, and not passion, which must guide our deliberations, guide our debate, and guide our decision."

—*Barbara Jordan, statement at the U.S. House Judiciary Committee Impeachment Hearings, Washington, D.C., July 25, 1974*

---

1. What point of view does Document 1 present?
   (1) The judicial viewpoint
   (2) The executive viewpoint
   (3) The viewpoint of Congress
   (4) The viewpoint of the press

2. Document 2 shows the role of the press in the Watergate scandal because it shows
   (1) that Nixon was accountable to the press.
   (2) how reporters began to investigate the story.
   (3) how Nixon was forced to confess his role in the scandal.
   (4) Nixon's willingness to accuse others of committing minor crimes.

3. In Document 3, what was the purpose of Barbara Jordan's statement?
   (1) It defended the actions of the President.
   (2) It tried to determine the grounds for impeachment.
   (3) It clarified Congress's role in the Watergate scandal.
   (4) It explained that the Constitution tolerated the President's conduct.

4. **Writing Task** Did Congress, the press, and the courts successfully do their jobs in investigating the Watergate scandal that led to President Richard Nixon's resignation? Use your knowledge of the chapter content and specific evidence from the primary sources above to support your opinion.

NY Connect to New York

Immigration to New York Today

When people talk about New York and immigration, you might think of Ellis Island, one of the main places where immigrants entered the United States in the late nineteenth and early twentieth centuries. However, today New York City is still a major entry point for immigrants, though most arrive by plane rather than by ocean liner or steamer.

Immigration has played a huge role in New York's history in the second half of the twentieth century. A large percentage of New York City residents have parents who are immigrants and an estimated 40 percent are themselves immigrants. Many are from Italy, parts of the former Soviet Union, Poland, Germany, Ireland, the United Kingdom, and Canada. There are also several hundred thousand Puerto Ricans living in the city, as well as many new residents from other parts of Latin America, India, China, and Korea. These immigrants, to New York and the rest of the country, have helped diversify our nation.

> "Our nation is the enduring dream of every immigrant who ever set foot on these shores, and the millions still struggling to be free. This nation, this idea called America, was and always will be a new world—our new world."
> —George H.W. Bush, State of the Union Address, January 31, 1990

The majority of immigrants to New York have followed the official immigration process to become citizens. However, an estimated 16 percent of immigrants have come to New York without following the proper procedures. Nationally, illegal immigration has become a controversial topic and an important issue for President George W. Bush.

On May 1, 2006, thousands of immigrants across the nation attended demonstrations to protest tighter restrictions on immigration that were proposed in Congress. Many did not go to work that day, in an effort to illustrate the importance of immigrants to the economy. In New York City, about 12,000 people joined hands to form eight human chains in four different neighborhoods, symbolizing their solidarity. The federal government continues to work to address this complicated and emotional issue.

Like immigration, many issues, including economic problems, cultural changes, and America's relationship with the rest of the world, continue to challenge the people of the United States. As you will read, Americans wrestled with these problems as the nation entered the twenty-first century.

CHANGING AND ENDURING ISSUES

CONTENTS

In classrooms across
the country, today's
students prepare to be
tomorrow's leaders. ▶

A New Agenda

Americans were tired of the prolonged economic and foreign policy problems of the 1970s. Many looked to Ronald Reagan, the Republican candidate for President in 1980:

66 I cannot and will not stand by and see this great country destroy itself. . . . I don't agree that our nation must resign itself to inevitable decline, yielding its proud position to other hands. . . . The crisis we face is not the result of any failure of the American spirit; it is the failure of our leaders to establish rational goals and give our people something to order their lives by. If I am elected, I shall regard my election as proof that the people of the United States have decided to set a new agenda. . . . 99

—Ronald Reagan, November 13, 1979

Listen to the Witness History *audio to learn more about Ronald Reagan.*

◀ Reagan on the campaign trail in 1980

1980 campaign pin

Piece of the Berlin Wall after its fall

NY Core Curriculum Preview

Chapter Focus Question: What was the conservative resurgence, and how did it affect the domestic and foreign policy of the United States?

Linda Evans and John Forsythe, stars of television's *Dynasty*

Use the ☑ **Quick Study Timeline** at the end of this chapter to preview chapter events.

> **Note Taking Study Guide *Online***
> **For:** Note Taking and American Issues Connector
> **Web Code:** nee-9201

Backlash Against Liberal Programs

By 1980, public discontent with liberal programs, from welfare to school busing, had grown considerably. Many middle- and working-class Americans, in particular, felt that the reforms enacted during the 1960s and carried out in the 1970s threatened the American dream.

❝If, during the 1960s and 1970s, there was an elite wisdom that shaped the directions of social policy, there was also a popular wisdom that explained why things were falling apart. . . . The popular wisdom is characterized by hostility toward welfare (it makes people lazy), toward lenient judges (they encourage crime), and toward socially conscious schools (too busy busing kids to teach them to read).**❞**

—Charles Murray, *Losing Ground,* 1984

Frustration over ▶ controversial issues in the 1970s, such as the busing battle featured on this cover of *Time* from 1975, lingered into the 1980s.

The Conservative Movement Grows

 Core Curriculum Objectives

- **2.I.E.1** Basic constitutional principles: limits and potentials of national power
- **7.V.B.3** Foreign policy issues: the United States after Vietnam
- **7.V.C** Reagan and Bush, the "new" federalism and growth of conservatism

Terms and People

liberal	unfunded mandate
conservative	Moral Majority
New Right	Ronald Reagan

NoteTaking

Reading Skill: Summarize As you read, summarize the rise of the conservative movement in an outline. Use the one below as a starting point.

> I. Two Views: Liberal and Conservative
>   A. Liberal ideas and goals
>   1.
>   2.

Why It Matters The 1964 election marked a low point for conservatives in the post–World War II era. Barry Goldwater, favorite of the conservative movement, lost the election in a landslide. Nonetheless, conservatives were not defeated by this loss at the polls. On the contrary, they set out to build an organization and to put forth a clear vision of their goals and values that would enable them to win in the future. By 1980, their plan had worked: Ronald Reagan, the new hero of the conservatives, was elected President. The modern conservative movement spearheaded by Ronald Reagan deeply affected the nation's policies for decades. **Section Focus Question: What spurred the rise of conservatism in the late 1970s and early 1980s?**

Two Views: Liberal and Conservative

The two major political parties in the United States in the late twentieth century were the Democrats, many of whom were "liberals," and the Republicans, who were often labeled "conservatives." **Liberals** generally favored government intervention to help the needy, whereas **conservatives** generally favored allowing the free market, private organizations, and individuals to do that. Although the two parties did agree on many basic issues, including core American values such as freedom and equality, they diverged on many others. In addition, individual members within both parties did not always conform to their party's majority.

The Ideas and Goals of Liberalism In the late 1970s, liberals tended to believe that the federal government should play a significant role in improving the lives of all Americans. They valued social programs that helped the poor, unemployed, elderly, and others. They also sponsored laws that protected the rights of minorities and women, especially in the post–World War II period. They supported greater government regulation of industry. In the foreign policy realm, liberals tended to favor cooperating with international organizations like the United Nations.

The Ideas and Goals of Conservatism In contrast, some conservatives felt that a large central government endangered economic growth and individual choice. They felt the liberal policies of the 1960s amd 1970s left a legacy of rising inflation and enormous waste. Futhermore, some conservatives criticized the liberal solution of "throwing money" at social problems. They sought to reduce taxes and limit government regulation of industry in order to promote economic growth. As conservative economist Milton Friedman and his wife Rose Friedman wrote in their book *Free to Choose*, "The story of the United States is the story of an economic miracle. . . . What produced this miracle? Clearly not central direction by government."

Other conservatives, neoconservatives or traditionalists, warned about the dangers posed to society by abandoning traditional values in favor of the new freedoms exemplified by the counterculture and advertised by the mass media. This concern with the perceived <u>degeneration</u> of modern youth dovetailed with many conservatives' religious beliefs.

Vocabulary Builder
<u>degeneration</u>–(dee jehn er AY shuhn) *n.* declining in quality

Anticommunism formed the third leg of modern conservatism. Most anticommunists focused on the dangers posed to the United States by the Soviet Union. They questioned the wisdom of the détente policy followed by Presidents Nixon, Ford, and Carter. They also fought against the SALT II treaty in the Senate.

✓ **Checkpoint** How was conservatism different from liberalism in the early 1980s?

The Conservative Movement Gains Strength

During the 1940s and 1950s, the lines separating Republicans and Democrats had blurred. The two parties had developed a bipartisan foreign policy aimed at containing communism. Both favored a relatively significant role for the government in domestic affairs. However, during the 1960s and 1970s, many Republicans became increasingly critical of the liberal policies of the Democrats. They advanced a new conservative agenda. The differences between the two major parties grew more pronounced. The **New Right,** as the resurgent conservative movement was called, grew rapidly and was a coalition of several different groups with varying ideas and goals.

Two Viewpoints: Liberal and Conservative		☑ Quick Study
Issue	**Liberal Viewpoint**	**Conservative Viewpoint**
Role of government in the economy	Favored more government involvement to lessen extreme economic inequalities through • social programs (often leading to higher taxes) • government regulation of industry	Favored limited government involvement in order to stimulate economic growth by • reducing taxes • decreasing regulation of industry
Foreign policy	Favored international diplomacy to combat communism in other countries	Favored relying on our own national defense and actively fighting against communism in other countries

Liberalism Loses Its Appeal

One reason for the revival of the Republican Party was the unraveling of the Democratic Party. The Vietnam War and urban riots of the 1960s divided the same people who had rallied around President Johnson's vision of the Great Society. The rise of the counterculture had alienated many midwestern Americans and white conservative Christians in the South. Watergate, the oil crises of the 1970s, and the Iran hostage crisis further weakened the public's faith in the federal government.

Just as importantly, the shifts in the economy of the 1970s, including the decline in northern industries, dampened America's optimism about the future. America had supported the Great Society, in part, because Johnson had suggested that the war on poverty and other new programs would not demand higher taxes. When the economy stagnated, liberal ideas lost their pull and conservative beliefs became more attractive.

The New Right Criticizes Liberal Programs

Many conservatives believed that liberal policies were responsible for stagflation and other economic problems of the late 1970s. They believed that the government taxed citizens and businesses too heavily and spent too much on the wrong programs. They complained about **unfunded mandates,** programs required but not paid for by the federal government.

Some conservatives also criticized federal welfare programs, arguing they rewarded lack of effort. Furthermore, they thought that the Great Society had made the problem of poverty worse not better. They believed that welfare contributed to the rise in the number of children born out of wedlock and therefore encouraged the decline of the traditional family, consisting of a married father and mother and their children. They also felt that affirmative action programs went too far and contributed to reverse discrimination.

Another group that supported the conservative platform was the "sagebrush rebels." Sagebrush rebels were activists who believed that the federal government controlled too much land in the western states. They thought the federal government should give control of this land to the states, to be used to their best economic advantage. Most environmentalists opposed the movement, not wanting to expose preserved lands to possible development.

Religious Participation Rises

At the same time, concern with cultural change caused more religious groups to become actively involved in politics. The **Moral Majority,** founded by Reverend Jerry Falwell in 1979, was a political organization working to fulfill religious goals. It also worried about the decline of the traditional family. The Moral Majority opposed the 1962 Supreme Court decision *Engel* v. *Vitale,* which forbade religious teaching in schools, as well as the historic 1973 *Roe* v. *Wade* decision, which legalized abortion. It condemned the Equal Rights Amendment and homosexuality.

The Moral Majority boosted the Republican Party's chances of winning the presidency by reaching out to Americans who had traditionally not participated in the political process. With other groups like it, the Moral Majority registered at least 2 million new voters before the 1980 presidential election. One of their tactics was to distribute Moral Majority "report cards" on candidates, which almost always favored Republicans.

Politics and Religion Meet
Reverend Jerry Falwell, founder of the Moral Majority, stands in front of his home church in Lynchburg, Virginia, in August 1980. A banner on top of the church's sign encourages members to register to vote. *How was the Moral Majority different from traditional religious groups?*

Population Trends Boost Conservatism Demographic, or population, trends also strengthened the conservative movement. Historically, northern cities stood as the stronghold of liberal Democrats. When an increasing number of Americans moved to the suburbs, their attachment to liberalism waned as they struggled financially during the tough economic days of the late 1970s. At the same time, Republicans emphasized issues that they believed would convince moderate liberals to switch their party allegiance. For instance, Republicans attacked school busing as a form of social engineering that threatened the long-cherished ideal of neighborhood schools.

Republicans also benefited from the migration from the Rust Belt to the Sunbelt, which took place in the 1970s, and a historical realignment of white voters in the Deep South. Since the Civil War, most white southerners had voted for the Democratic Party. Following the enactment of civil rights legislation in the mid-1960s, however, many white southerners began to shift their party allegiance. By the 1980s, the Republicans had become the dominant political party in the region.

✔ **Checkpoint** What were some of the forces that helped the Republican Party grow during the 1970s?

Reagan Wins the Presidency

The growing conservative movement swept the Republican presidential candidate, a man named **Ronald Reagan,** to victory in the 1980 election. Much more charismatic and polished than Goldwater, Reagan made clear his opposition to big government, his support for a strong military, and his faith in traditional values. Just as importantly, he radiated optimism, convincing Americans that he would usher in a new era of prosperity and patriotism.

Reagan's Path to the White House Born in Tampico, Illinois, in 1911, Reagan suffered the hardships of the Great Depression as a young adult before landing a job in Hollywood as a movie actor. Never a big star, Reagan appeared in many "B" or low-budget films. His most famous starring role was in *Knute Rockne,* a film based on the life of Notre Dame's legendary football coach.

When his acting career began to wane, Reagan became a spokesperson for General Electric and toured the nation giving speeches. Although once a staunch New Dealer, Reagan had become a Goldwater conservative. In these speeches he began to criticize big government and high taxes and warned of the dangers of communism. In 1964, near the end of Goldwater's presidential campaign, Reagan delivered a nationally televised address in which he spelled out these views:

> **Primary Source** "This is the issue of this election, whether we believe in our capacity for self-government or whether we abandon the American Revolution and confess that a little intellectual elite in a far-distant capital can plan our lives for us better than we can plan them ourselves."
> —Ronald Reagan, "A Time for Choosing," 1964

HISTORY MAKERS

Ronald Reagan (1911–2004)
Ronald Reagan's easy communication style, which appealed so much to his supporters, was rooted in his background as an entertainer. After graduating from college, he worked as a radio sports announcer until, in 1937, he signed a contract with a movie studio. In 1954, he began hosting a television show sponsored by General Electric. Soon, he was touring the country for the company, giving speeches that promoted traditional values and American business. As Reagan's views became more conservative, he switched from the Democratic to the Republican Party. He gained political fame in 1964 with a speech supporting conservative senator Barry Goldwater's run for the presidency.

While the speech failed to bolster Goldwater's campaign, it won the admiration of many conservatives. Two years later, Reagan won the governorship of California. He served for two terms as governor and nearly won the Republican presidential nomination in 1976. In 1980, he won the nomination by a landslide. His opponent was Jimmy Carter, the Democratic incumbent.

Reagan Wins a Close Election As the election approached, Carter looked like a lame duck. Persistent inflation, the Iran hostage crisis, and the Soviet invasion of Afghanistan made it easy for Reagan to cast the Carter presidency in a negative light. "Are you better off than you were four years ago?" Reagan asked audiences on the campaign trail, knowing that most Americans would say, "No."

The race remained relatively close until about one week before the election, when Reagan and Carter held their only presidential debate. In this debate, Reagan's gifts as a communicator shone. He appeared friendly and even-tempered and calmed fears that he did not have enough experience to serve as President. On Election Day, Reagan won 50.6 percent of the popular vote. Because most states award electoral votes on a "winner-takes-all" basis, Reagan won an overwhelming majority of electoral college votes despite the narrow margin by which he won the popular vote. Even though the Democrats maintained control of the House of Representatives, Republicans captured the U.S. Senate for the first time since 1955. The conservatives were back.

 Checkpoint What did Ronald Reagan promise to do if elected to the presidency?

The Presidential Election of 1980

Candidate (Party)	Electoral Vote	Popular Vote	% Electoral Vote	% Popular Vote
Ronald Reagan (Republican)	489	43,642,639	90.9	50.6
James Carter (Democratic)	49	35,480,948	9.1	41.2
John Anderson (Independent)	—	5,719,437	—	6.6

Comprehension

1. **Terms and People** For each item below, write a sentence explaining how it related to the rise of conservatism in the late 1970s.
   - liberal
   - conservative
   - New Right
   - unfunded mandate
   - Moral Majority
   - Ronald Reagan

2. **NoteTaking Reading Skill: Summarize** Use your outline to answer the Section Focus Question: What spurred the rise of conservatism in the late 1970s and early 1980s?

Writing About History

3. **Quick Write: Choose a Topic** Choose a topic from this section, such as Ronald Reagan's path to the White House, that would suit the creation of a multimedia presentation. Keep in mind that a multimedia presentation is an oral report that is enhanced with artwork, charts, music, videos, and so on.

Critical Thinking

4. **Compare Points of View** Describe one major difference between liberals and conservatives in the early 1980s.

5. **Identify Central Issues** What policies did members of the New Right criticize?

6. **Summarize** How did the Moral Majority help strengthen the Republican Party?

7. **Draw Conclusions** Why did Americans elect Ronald Reagan to the presidency in 1980?

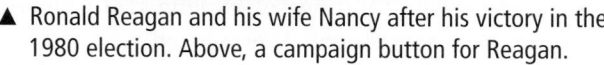

▲ Ronald Reagan and his wife Nancy after his victory in the 1980 election. Above, a campaign button for Reagan.

Reagan's Vision

During his eight years as President, Ronald Reagan earned a reputation as the "Great Communicator" because of his speaking abilities. In his farewell speech, he expressed his satisfaction with what he had accomplished:

❝After 200 years, two centuries, . . . [America is] still a beacon, still a magnet for all who must have freedom. . . . We've done our part. And as I walk off into the city streets, a final word to the men and women of the Reagan revolution, the men and women across America who for eight years did the work that brought America back. My friends: We did it.❞

—Ronald Reagan, Farewell Address, January 11, 1989

The Reagan Revolution

Core Curriculum Objectives

- **7.V.C.1** Supply-side economics
- **7.V.C.2** Tax policy and deficits
- **7.V.C.5** The Supreme Court and the schools
- **7.V.F.1** Trade imbalance with Japan

Terms and People

supply-side economics	Savings and Loan crisis
deregulation	voucher
budget deficit	AIDS
national debt	

NoteTaking

Reading Skill: Identify Main Ideas Identify the main ideas behind Reagan's policies.

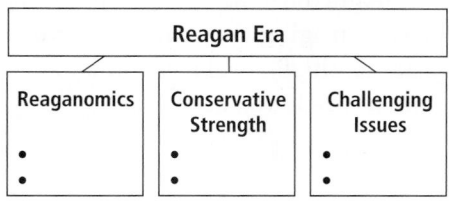

Why It Matters Conservatives celebrated Ronald Reagan's election as the fulfillment of their dreams. Some even referred to his coming to power as the "Reagan Revolution." The Reagan Revolution would bring a significant shift in the political direction of the nation. **Section Focus Question: What were the major characteristics of the conservative Reagan Revolution?**

Reaganomics Guides the Economy

Reagan and his advisers based their economic policies on the theory of "supply-side economics," sometimes called "Reaganomics." The theory of **supply-side economics** rests on the assumption that if taxes are reduced, people will work more and have more money to spend, causing the economy to grow. The government will then collect more in taxes. To cut taxes while still balancing the federal budget, however, Reagan also needed to reduce federal spending on programs favored by both Democrats and Republicans.

New Policies to Boost the Economy Congress approved most of Reagan's plan to institute supply-side economics by passing the Economic Recovery Act of 1981, which reduced taxes by 25 percent over three years. The richest Americans received the largest tax cuts. Reagan justified this move by saying that the wealthy would use the money they saved to invest in new businesses, which would

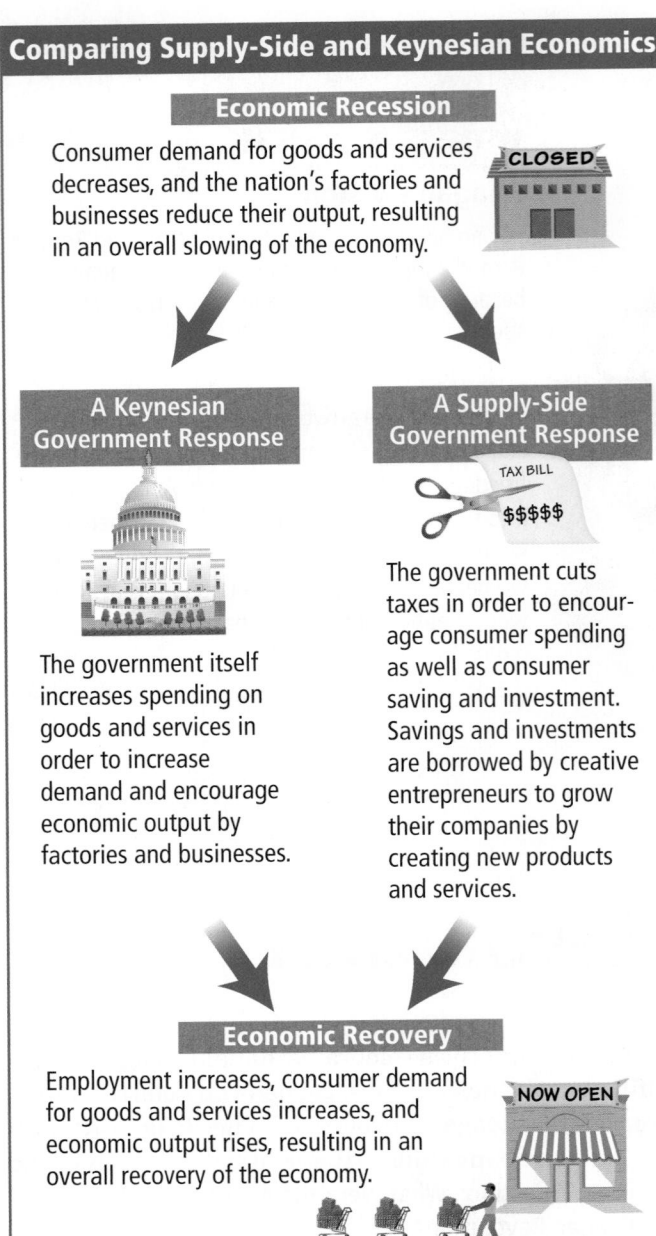

Comparing Supply-Side and Keynesian Economics

Economic Recession

Consumer demand for goods and services decreases, and the nation's factories and businesses reduce their output, resulting in an overall slowing of the economy.

CLOSED

A Keynesian Government Response

The government itself increases spending on goods and services in order to increase demand and encourage economic output by factories and businesses.

A Supply-Side Government Response

TAX BILL

$$$$$

The government cuts taxes in order to encourage consumer spending as well as consumer saving and investment. Savings and investments are borrowed by creative entrepreneurs to grow their companies by creating new products and services.

Economic Recovery

Employment increases, consumer demand for goods and services increases, and economic output rises, resulting in an overall recovery of the economy.

NOW OPEN

Diagram Skills Can you predict what might be the upsides and downsides of both of the responses shown above?

help everyone. Reagan also convinced Congress to cut about $40 billion from the federal budget, mostly by cutting spending for social programs.

In addition to cutting taxes, Reagan also reduced the government's role in the economy by calling for **deregulation,** or the removal of government control over industry. By the mid-1980s, Congress had deregulated the airline, telecommunications, and banking industries. The Reagan administration also cut funding for federal agencies that oversaw many other industries.

Recession and Recovery Despite Reagan's economic policies, the economy experienced a severe recession from 1980 to 1982. Unemployment rose to more than 10 percent in 1982. The recession hit blue-collar workers particularly hard. Many farmers, facing overseas competition, lost their farms. The policies that Paul Volcker, as head of the Federal Reserve Board, had introduced to tame the great inflation of the 1970s contributed to the recession in the early 1980s. Beginning in early 1983, however, the economy began to turn around. Inflation fell dramatically. The Gross National Product, or the annual income earned by Americans and American businesses, expanded at a healthy pace. America's economy seemed revitalized.

Despite this, the number of poor people, including the working poor, actually increased. In addition, immigrants from Latin America and Asia continued to pour into the United States. More than 7.3 million legal immigrants and hundreds of thousands of undocumented immigrants entered the country in the 1980s. Many of these newcomers worked in low-paying jobs and struggled to make ends meet. Meanwhile, the richest percentage of Americans grew richer.

Problems With Budget Deficits Reagan increased defense spending but failed to win huge cuts in government spending in other areas. This caused the federal **budget deficit,** or the shortfall between the amount of money spent and the amount taken in by the government, to skyrocket from about $79 billion in 1981 to more than $221 billion in 1986. The **national debt,** the amount of money the federal government owes to owners of government bonds, rose to $2.5 trillion.

In response to persistent budget deficits, Congress passed the Gramm-Rudman-Hollings Act in 1985. The act sought to balance the budget by 1990 by requiring automatic cuts in federal spending if the deficit exceeded a certain amount. However, the federal budget deficit set new records into the early 1990s.

The **Savings and Loan, or S&L, crisis** in 1989 exacerbated deficit problems. In the late 1980s, about 1,000 Savings and Loan banks failed, some because of fraudulent behavior and others because they made too many risky loans. Critics blamed Reagan's deregulation policies for encouraging the banks to invest in riskier propositions. To prevent a broader panic, the federal government spent upwards of $200 billion to bail out depositors at the failed banks.

✓ **Checkpoint** What was supply-side economics?

Conservative Strength Grows

Despite budget and debt problems, the economic recovery improved the national mood and helped Ronald Reagan's popularity. Reagan used his time in office to strengthen the conservative cause.

Reagan Wins Reelection in 1984 During the 1984 presidential campaign, Reagan used the phrase "It is morning in America" as a campaign slogan:

> **Primary Source** "It's morning again in America. In a town not too far from where you live, a young family has just moved into a new home. . . . Right down the street one of the neighbors has just bought himself a new car, with all the options. The factory down the river is working again. . . . Life is better, America is back. And people have a sense of pride they never felt they'd feel again."
> —Campaign commercial for the reelection of Ronald Reagan, 1984 ◀》 AUDIO

This theme dovetailed nicely with Reagan's upbeat spirit, which he displayed even in his darkest moments. For example, on March 30, 1981, a disturbed man named John Hinckley, Jr., tried to assassinate the President. One bullet from Hinckley's gun lodged in Reagan's chest. According to one account, Reagan joked to his doctors, "I hope you are all Republicans."

Americans voted overwhelmingly to reelect Reagan in 1984. He easily defeated Walter Mondale, the Democratic presidential nominee, and his running mate, Geraldine Ferraro, the first woman to be nominated for Vice President by a major political party. However, Reagan's <u>momentum</u> did not lead to a total triumph for conservatives, as Democrats retained control of the House of Representatives.

Vocabulary Builder
<u>momentum</u>–(moh MEHN tuhm)
n. forward motion; push

Conservative Supreme Court Justices and the Equal Access Act
During his two terms, Reagan appointed judges who he hoped would reverse the liberal drift of the federal courts. He appointed three new Justices—Sandra Day O'Connor, Antonin Scalia, and Anthony Kennedy—to the Supreme Court and elevated William Rehnquist, a well-known conservative, to the position of Chief Justice in 1986. Sandra Day O'Connor, nominated in 1981, was the first female Justice and a moderate conservative. Although she voted with other conservatives on many issues, she consistently voted to uphold *Roe* v. *Wade,* which Reagan opposed.

Near the end of Reagan's first term, Congress passed the Equal Access Act. This act required public secondary schools to allow any group equal access to school facilities. Conservative Christian groups supported the act's passage because many public schools did not allow religious groups to meet on school property. The Supreme Court confirmed the constitutionality of the Equal Access Act in 1990 in *Board of Education of Westside Community Schools* v. *Mergens.*

George H.W. Bush Becomes President Reagan used his personal popularity to promote George H.W. Bush, his Vice President for eight years, as Bush campaigned for the presidency against Massachusetts governor Michael Dukakis in 1988. Bush called for a "kinder, gentler nation," yet both candidates attacked the other using negative campaign ads. Bush cemented his support among conservatives by promising not to raise taxes and by casting himself as a defender of

HISTORY MAKERS

Sandra Day O'Connor (born 1930)

After getting her law degree in 1952, Sandra Day O'Connor served as a lawyer for many years before becoming involved in Arizona state politics in the late 1960s. She was serving as a judge on the Arizona Court of Appeals when she was nominated to the Supreme Court in 1981.

O'Connor sat on the Supreme Court for nearly 25 years. Her vote was the tiebreaker on several influential court cases, causing her to be called one of the most powerful women in the United States.

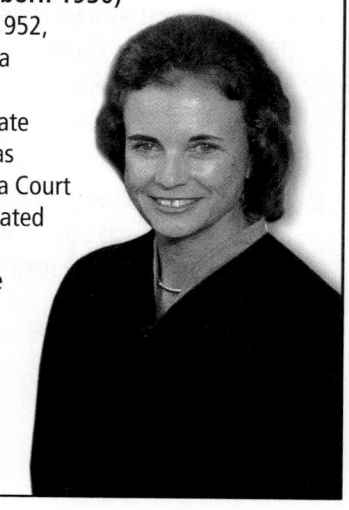

TIMES of the Eighties

A SNAPSHOT OF THE REAGAN YEARS

TV Review

Dynasty: Living large and behaving badly

Fans love the Wednesday night favorite, *Dynasty*, featuring Linda Evans as Krystle Carrington and John Forsythe as Blake Carrington. ■ See p. B6

Personal Computers: Hot item. ■ See p. A12

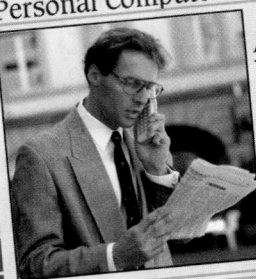

Are you a Yuppie?

If you're under 30, live in a city, and work in an office, then *yes*—you're a Young Urban Professional, or Yuppie.
■ See p. A7

In the Economy

Trade Imbalance With Japan Deepens

Japan's import restrictions are keeping American goods off of Japanese store shelves.

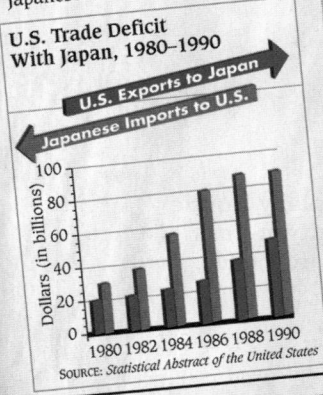

U.S. Trade Deficit With Japan, 1980–1990

U.S. Exports to Japan
Japanese Imports to U.S.

SOURCE: *Statistical Abstract of the United States*

ADA Passed!

■ The Americans With Disabilities Act (ADA) was passed by Congress and signed into law by President George H.W. Bush in July 1990.

■ The act will ensure that Americans with disabilities will receive the same opportunities in employment and access to public transportation and public places as other Americans.

■ The act benefits more than 43 million people and is another stride forward in the quest to protect the rights of all Americans.

Trend Spotting

VCRs Bring Fitness Craze Home

Videotapes of popular exercise programs, such as Judi Missett's Jazzercise fitness plan, are flying off the shelves.

Space Shuttle Challenger Explodes

Reagan Comforts the Nation

CAPE CANAVERAL, FLORIDA On January 28, 1986, the long-awaited launch of the space shuttle *Challenger* ended in tragedy when the shuttle exploded 73 seconds after take-off. The shuttle carried seven astronauts, including New Hampshire schoolteacher Christa McAuliffe. Her flight would have been the first time a private citizen entered space.

President Reagan spoke to the nation following the tragedy:

Primary Source "For the families of the seven [astronauts], we cannot bear, as you do, the full impact of this tragedy. But we feel the loss, and we're thinking about you so very much. Your loved ones were daring and brave, and they had that special grace, that special spirit that says, 'Give me a challenge and I'll meet it with joy.' They had a hunger to explore the universe and discover its truths. They wished to serve, and they did. They served all of us."

The space shuttle *Challenger* exploded shortly after lifting off from Kennedy Space Center. Inset: Schoolteacher Christa McAuliffe (far left) and six career astronauts died aboard the shuttle.

Thinking Critically

1. **Draw Conclusions** How do you think the trade imbalance with Japan affected the American economy?

2. **Summarize** How did new technologies help advance the personal fitness craze?

---

traditional values. However, Democrats won a majority of seats in both houses of Congress.

President Bush sought to control federal spending by encouraging Americans to volunteer. Government, he asserted, could take a smaller role in daily life if, "like a thousand points of light," community organizations and volunteers provided more help to the disabled, illiterate, and poor.

✔ **Checkpoint** How did Reagan try to build upon conservative gains during his presidency?

Confronting Challenging Issues

Despite Reagan and Bush's successes, the nation continued to face a number of pressing problems. In 1981 when thousands of air-traffic controllers went on strike, Reagan refused to negotiate with the Professional Air Traffic Controllers Organization (PATCO) and fired the striking workers because they were violating a law forbidding federal employees from striking. Many Americans admired Reagan's strong, decisive stance. Some union supporters, however, claimed that Reagan's action represented an assault on the labor movement.

In the 1980s, the rising cost of Social Security caused concern. As the number of elderly people in America grew, the Social Security system began to collect less money than it paid out. In 1983, Reagan signed the Social Security Reform Act, which raised the minimum retirement age and increased payroll taxes for Social Security. It provided a temporary fix but did not solve the long-term problems of the Social Security program.

Many Americans also worried about the state of America's public education system. In 1983, the Department of Education issued *A Nation at Risk*. This study showed that students were consistently scoring lower on standardized tests as time passed. The report argued that America's schools failed to prepare students adequately to compete with students around the globe.

Even before the report appeared, conservatives called for providing **vouchers,** or government checks, that could be used by parents to pay tuition at private schools. Conservatives argued that vouchers would force public schools to improve in order to attract and retain students. Liberals in Congress argued that vouchers would take much-needed money away from public schools.

In addition, the nation faced the threat of a new disease, **Acquired Immunodeficiency Syndrome (AIDS),** which first appeared in 1981. AIDS is the last stage of the Human Immunodeficiency Virus (HIV), which attacks the immune system of its victims. There is no known cure. At first, AIDS spread mainly among homosexual men and intravenous drug users. Later, the virus infected different groups of people. By 1994, AIDS had killed more than 250,000 Americans. President Reagan responded slowly to the AIDS epidemic. During George H.W. Bush's presidency, funding for research on the disease rose substantially.

✔ **Checkpoint** What were some of the challenges that the nation faced during the 1980s and early 1990s?

The AIDS Quilt
When the AIDS Quilt was displayed in Washington, D.C., in October 1988, it consisted of 8,288 panels, each created in the memory of a person who had died of AIDS. Today, the quilt has more than 44,000 memorial panels.

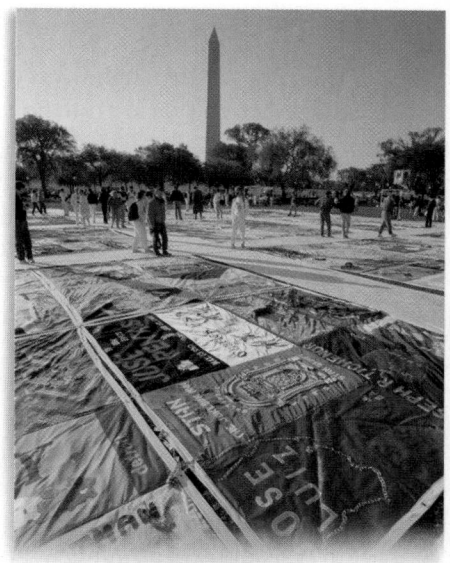

SECTION 2 Assessment

Progress Monitoring *Online*
For: Self-test with vocabulary practice
Web Code: nea-1903

Comprehension
1. **Terms and People** For each term below, write a sentence explaining its significance to the Reagan era.
   - supply-side economics
   - deregulation
   - budget deficit
   - national debt
   - Savings and Loan crisis
   - AIDS

2. **NoteTaking Reading Skill: Identify Main Ideas** Use your chart to answer the Section Focus Question: What were the major characteristics of the conservative Reagan Revolution?

Writing About History
3. **Quick Write: Create a Storyboard** Create a storyboard that illustrates one of the challenges facing Americans during this period. Use a combination of words and images to express your points.

Critical Thinking
4. **Summarize** In what ways did Reagan try to fulfill the goal of less government involvement in the economy?

5. **Draw Conclusions** How did Reagan strengthen the conservative cause?

6. **Identify Central Issues** How did Reagan address problems with Social Security?

Ronald Reagan: *Tear Down This Wall*

On June 12, 1987, President Reagan spoke at the Brandenburg Gate, near the Berlin Wall, in West Berlin, Germany. His speech acknowledged the new Soviet leader Mikhail Gorbachev's efforts at reform in the Soviet Union. However, Reagan was not satisfied with Gorbachev's limited measures. He challenged the Soviet leader to show a real commitment to reform by tearing down the Berlin Wall that had stood between East and West Berlin since 1961. This wall symbolized the division between communism and democracy.

In the 1950s, Khrushchev predicted: "We will bury you." But in the West today, we see a free world that has achieved a level of prosperity and well-being unprecedented in all human history. In the Communist world, we see failure, technological backwardness, declining standards of health, even want of the most basic kind—too little food. Even today, the Soviet Union still cannot feed itself. After these four decades, then, there stands before the entire world one great and inescapable conclusion: Freedom leads to prosperity. Freedom replaces the ancient hatreds among the nations with comity [courtesy] and peace. Freedom is the victor.

And now the Soviets themselves may, in a limited way, be coming to understand the importance of freedom. We hear much from Moscow about a new policy of reform and openness. Some political prisoners have been released. Certain foreign news broadcasts are no longer being jammed. Some economic enterprises have been permitted to operate with greater freedom from state control.

Are these the beginnings of profound changes in the Soviet state? Or are they token gestures, intended to raise false hopes in the West, or to strengthen the Soviet system without changing it? We welcome change and openness; for we believe that freedom and security go together, that the advance of human liberty can only strengthen the cause of world peace. There is one sign the Soviets can make that would be unmistakable, that would advance dramatically the cause of freedom and peace.

General Secretary Gorbachev, if you seek peace, if you seek prosperity for the Soviet Union and Eastern Europe, if you seek liberalization: Come here to this gate! Mr. Gorbachev, open this gate! Mr. Gorbachev, tear down this wall!

Reagan speaking at the Brandenburg Gate (above); the western side of the Berlin Wall before its fall (below)

Thinking Critically

1. **Demonstrate Reasoned Judgment** How does Reagan support his statement "Freedom is the victor"?

2. **Identify Central Issues** How does Reagan challenge Gorbachev to prove that his reforms are not "token gestures"?

WITNESS HISTORY ◀))) AUDIO

A Strong Approach to Communism

During the first term of his presidency, Ronald Reagan challenged the Soviet Union by building up America's military and casting the Cold War as a struggle between good and evil:

❝But if history teaches anything, it teaches that simpleminded appeasement or wishful thinking about our adversaries is folly. . . . I urge you to speak against those who would place the United States in a position of military and moral inferiority . . . beware the temptation . . . to ignore the facts of history and the aggressive impulses of an evil empire, to simply call the arms race a giant misunderstanding and thereby remove yourself from the struggle between right and wrong and good and evil.❞
—President Ronald Reagan, March 8, 1983

▲ A soldier trains at Fort Dix in New Jersey in the 1980s.

The End of the Cold War

Core Curriculum Objectives

- **7.V.E.1** Renewed United States power: Central America and the Caribbean
- **7.V.E.2** Middle East: war and hostages
- **7.V.G** United States–Soviet relations
- **7.VI.A.3a** Dissolution of the Soviet Union
- **7.VI.A.3b** Fall of the Berlin Wall and German reunification (1990)

Terms and People

Strategic Defense Initiative
Contras
Mikhail Gorbachev
glasnost
perestroika
Iran-Contra affair

NoteTaking

Reading Skill: Sequence As you read this section, use a flowchart like the one below to sequence major events related to the fall of communism in Europe and the Soviet Union.

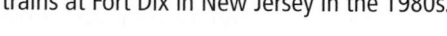

Why It Matters President Ronald Reagan believed that the United States had lost its way in the wake of the Vietnam War. Rather than détente, he felt the United States should seek to roll back Soviet rule in Eastern Europe and elsewhere. Reagan believed that peace would come through strength. Although they initially increased tensions between the two superpowers, Reagan's foreign policies contributed to the end of the Cold War. **Section Focus Question: What were Reagan's foreign policies, and how did they contribute to the fall of communism in Europe?**

Reagan Challenges Communism

President Reagan believed that the United States needed to weaken communism by challenging it as much as possible without provoking war. To this end, he devised policies aimed at toppling communist nations, ranging from building new nuclear missile systems to funding covert operations against Soviet troops and allies around the globe.

Reagan Builds Up the U.S. Military Under Reagan, the United States committed itself to the largest peacetime military buildup in its history. Reagan dedicated billions of dollars to the development and production of B-1 and B-2 bombers, MX missile systems, and other projects. In spite of massive protests by the nuclear freeze movement in the United States and abroad, the Reagan administration placed a new generation of nuclear missiles in Europe.

Reagan supported this massive military buildup, in part, because he did not believe that the Soviet Union could afford to spend as much on defense as the United States could. Reagan felt this

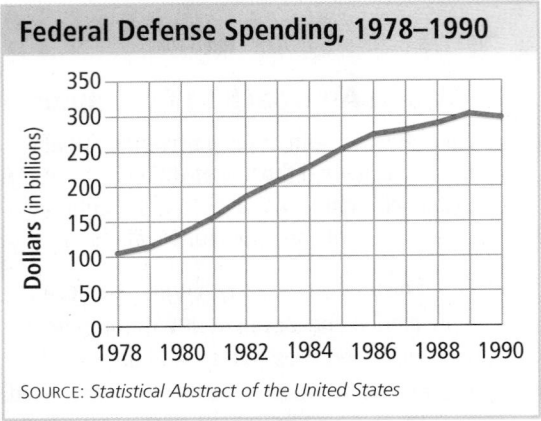

Federal Defense Spending, 1978–1990

SOURCE: *Statistical Abstract of the United States*

Graph Skills Reagan's foreign policy stance caused defense spending to increase dramatically. *How much did defense spending increase between 1978 and 1988?*

The Contras in Nicaragua

After coming to power in 1939, Nicaragua's socialist Sandinista government accepted aid from Cuba and the Soviet Union, alarming the United States. Below, a group of Contras review a map at a base camp along the San Juan River. Contras opposed the Sandinista government. *How did a socialist government in Nicaragua alarm foreign policy officials in the United States?*

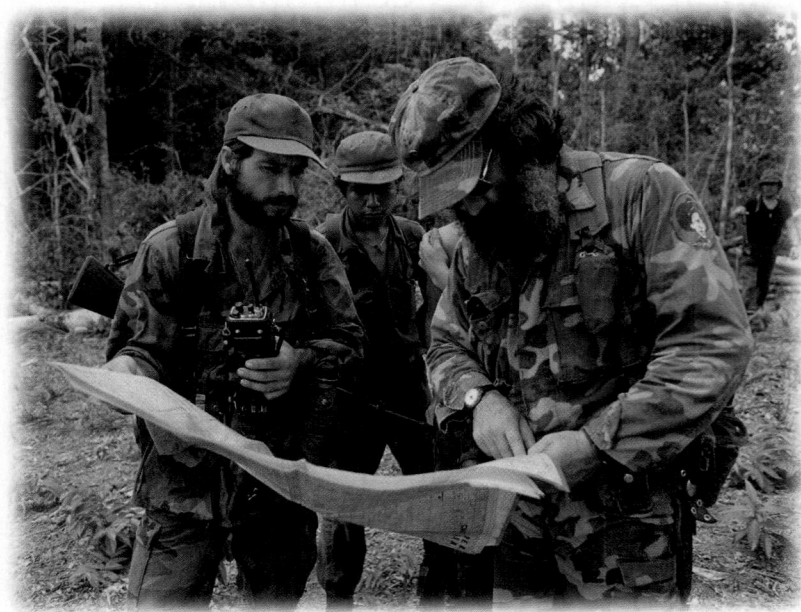

applied particularly to the **Strategic Defense Initiative (SDI),** a proposed program in which land- and space-based lasers would destroy any missiles aimed at the United States before they could reach their targets. Some dubbed the missile program "Star Wars," after the popular science-fiction movie trilogy, and claimed that it was unrealistic.

Reagan Aids Anticommunists Reagan also sought to weaken the Soviet Union by supporting anticommunist rebellions around the globe. To this end, the United States funded and trained the mujahadeen (moo jah huh DEEN), anti-Soviet rebels in Afghanistan. Reagan's advisers believed that with U.S. help, these guerrillas could drive the Soviets out of Afghanistan. In 1988, Soviet forces finally began to withdraw after years of fierce Afghan resistance.

Closer to home, Secretary of State Alexander Haig feared that the newly formed Sandinista government in Nicaragua provided the Soviets with a "safe house" in America's backyard. To counter this threat, the administration backed a group of anticommunist counterrevolutionaries, known as the **Contras.** At the same time, the United States supported a right-wing government in El Salvador as it battled leftist rebels. Many human rights activists strongly objected to this policy; even U.S. Ambassador Robert White described the legal system in El Salvador as "rotten" and called for the United States to suspend aid to the nation. Instead, Congress made funding for El Salvador's government dependent on the nation making progress on human rights.

In 1983, Reagan acted to counter another perceived threat in the Western Hemisphere. Members of a radical leftist movement, with some help from Cuba, had violently ousted the Grenadian prime minister. On October 25, 1983, U.S. troops invaded Grenada to prevent the island nation from becoming a communist outpost and to protect the lives of American medical students. Even though the legal grounds for this invasion proved questionable, most Americans approved of Reagan's decision.

Gorbachev Pursues Reform In 1985, **Mikhail Gorbachev** (mee kah EEL GOR buh chawf) became the President of the Soviet Union. Gorbachev ushered in a new Soviet era by pursuing the twin policies of *glasnost* and *perestroika*. **Glasnost** meant "a new openness," and **perestroika** stood for reforming the Soviet system—for instance, by moving away from a socialist or state-controlled economy. Gorbachev's reforms created an opening for a shift in relations between the two superpowers.

Gorbachev started these reforms mostly because the Soviet Union's economy lay in shambles. The nation faced regular shortages of food. Its factories and workers could not compete with their Western counterparts. A huge chunk of the Soviet economy's money went toward paying for the military. The war in Afghanistan had drained Soviet resources. Gorbachev realized that his nation could not match the military buildup initiated by the Reagan administration.

The Two Leaders Meet Gorbachev's policies and personality helped soften the Soviet Union's international image. Reagan responded to this change by moderating his own stance toward the Soviet Union. While the two nations had held no summits during Reagan's first four years in office, their leaders met four times between 1985 and 1989. During their final meeting in Moscow, Reagan and Gorbachev toasted each other at a state dinner, toured the sights like old friends, and held a joint press conference. At the press conference, a reporter asked Reagan about his description of the Soviet Union as an "evil empire." Reagan responded, "I was talking about another era." Then, Gorbachev allowed President Reagan to address students at Moscow State University on the benefits of the free-enterprise system and democracy:

Analyzing Political Cartoons

A Bumpy Ride? In this cartoon, the communist bloc, or the group of Soviet-dominated communist nations in Eastern Europe, is represented by a rickety car headed down the bumpy road of reform.

1. What does the cartoonist seem to think perestroika will do to the communist bloc?
2. Why might economic reforms like perestroika lead to bumpy, or troubled, times?

> **Primary Source** "Your generation is living in one of the most exciting times in Soviet history. It is a time when the first breath of freedom stirs the air and the heart beats to the accelerated rhythm of hope, when the accumulated spiritual energies of a long silence yearn to break free. . . . We do not know what the conclusion of this journey will be, but we're hopeful that the promise of reform will be fulfilled . . . leading to a new world of reconciliation, friendship, and peace."
> —Ronald Reagan, May 31, 1988

Even before this summit, the two nations had signed a historic nuclear arms pact and had begun negotiations on the START I Treaty, which would reduce the number of nuclear weapons in the world.

 Checkpoint What policies toward communism did President Reagan pursue?

The Cold War Ends

In a little over three years' time after Reagan's speech in Moscow, the Cold War had come to an end. The Berlin Wall came down; Poland, Czechoslovakia, and Hungary held democratic elections; and the Soviet Union disintegrated into numerous separate republics. *Time* magazine observed: "It was one of those rare times when the tectonic plates of history shift beneath men's feet, and nothing after is quite the same."

Communism Ends in Eastern Europe More so than any other event, the fall of the Berlin Wall symbolized the end of communism in Europe. For decades, the wall had blocked travel from communist East Berlin to democratic West Berlin. Guards shot those who attempted to escape over the wall to West Berlin. Then, in November 1989, following the fall of East Germany's communist government, East German authorities opened the wall's gates. Thousands climbed atop the wall; some even took sledgehammers and chipped away at the barricade. Within a year, East and West Germany would reunite as one single nation. Communists also lost power in Poland, Hungary, Czechoslovakia, Bulgaria, and Romania in 1989; in Albania in 1990; and in Yugoslavia in 1991.

WITNESS HISTORY DVD

Watch *Reagan and the End of the Cold War* on the **United States Witness History DVD** to explore Reagan's role in the end of the Cold War.

America's buildup of weapons, such as long-range nuclear missiles, threatens the Soviet Union.

The Soviet Union Breaks Apart In August 1991, hard-liners in the Soviet Union attempted to stage a coup in a last-gasp attempt to maintain communist rule. But when millions of Russians, led by Boris Yeltsin, rallied in the streets of Moscow in support of Gorbachev, the coup fell apart. Not long afterward, the Communist Party lost power, and the Soviet Union separated into 15 independent republics. Boris Yeltsin became the new leader of the largest new republic, the Russian Federation.

Historians do not totally agree on what caused the Soviet Union to collapse. Most acknowledge that Gorbachev's policy of *glasnost* opened the floodgates to rebellions against Soviet domination of Eastern Europe. Likewise, they note that his policy of *perestroika* fostered a challenge to communist rule within the Soviet Union. Yet, a number of scholars give Reagan credit for bringing an end

Events That Changed America

THE FALL OF COMMUNISM IN EUROPE

In the early 1980s, Ronald Reagan began to build up the American military. Knowing that the struggling Soviet economy could not match this buildup, Mikhail Gorbachev began reforms in the Soviet Union and sought a better relationship with the United States.

Then came 1989, the "year of the miracle." In that year, the nations of Eastern Europe experienced a series of bloodless revolutions. In June 1989, Solidarity, Poland's anticommunist reform party, swept into power. Its leader, Lech Walesa, was elected President in 1990. In November 1989, the Berlin Wall fell. People were allowed to travel freely from East to West Berlin for the first time in nearly 40 years. Next, massive demonstrations by university students in Czechoslovakia ended communist rule there. Finally, in August 1991, following a failed coup against Gorbachev, millions of Russians led by Boris Yeltsin protested against the central Soviet government, breaking its power. Not long afterward, the Soviet Union ceased to exist. President George H.W. Bush and Boris Yeltsin, the President of the new Russian Federation, established a friendly relationship between their nations.

▲ An American game about the Soviet policy of *glasnost*

▼ Reagan shares a friendly moment with Soviet leader Mikhail Gorbachev.

Lech Walesa, head of Poland's Solidarity movement, kisses the Polish flag as he takes his oath as President. ▼

to the Cold War. By dedicating America to a massive arms buildup, they argue, he hastened the collapse of the Soviet economy. In turn, this compelled Gorbachev to promote reform at home and relinquish control of Eastern Europe.

The key rival, competitor, and enemy of the United States for so many years had suddenly disappeared. President George H.W. Bush met and signed agreements with first Gorbachev and then Yeltsin to scale down and even eliminate certain types of nuclear weapons. Bush and Yeltsin issued a joint statement in 1992 pledging friendship and cooperation. The long Cold War, which had absorbed so much of the energy and resources of the Soviet Union and the United States since 1945, was finally over.

✔ **Checkpoint** What key actions and events brought about the end of the Cold War?

Why It Matters

Although communism survived in China, Cuba, and a few other nations, the fall of communism in Eastern Europe and the Soviet Union ended the Cold War. American leaders now faced new challenges and daunting questions: Should military spending be decreased? What new direction should American foreign policy take in the post–Cold War world?

◄ West Germans celebrate the fall of the Berlin Wall and the reunification of Berlin.

▲ Bush and Yeltsin meet at Camp David to discuss joint foreign-policy proposals.

◄ Thousands of Czechs hold peaceful protests and candlelight vigils to protest Czechoslovakia's communist regime.

A child plays on a statue of Stalin that has been knocked down in Gorky Park in Moscow. ▼

Thinking Critically
How did Reagan end up influencing Soviet policy in the mid-1980s?

History *Interactive*

For: More images from the fall of communism in Eastern Europe and the Soviet Union
Web Code: nep-1904

Trouble in the Middle East

Vocabulary Builder
contradict–(kahn truh DIHKT) *v.*
to go against

Trouble Persists in the Middle East

Even as the Soviet Union collapsed, the United States continued to confront problems in the Middle East. In 1982, Reagan sent a group of 800 United States Marines to Lebanon as part of an international force trying to bring peace to a nation torn by civil war. On October 23, 1983, a truck loaded with thousands of pounds of explosives smashed through barriers at the headquarters of the United States Marines in Beirut (bay ROOT), Lebanon's capital, and into a four-story building that housed hundreds of military personnel. The explosion killed 241 marines. Reagan withdrew the remaining marines in February 1984. The incident illustrated, once again, the complicated nature of Middle Eastern politics.

During the 1980s, the United States often clashed with Libya. Led by Muammar al-Qaddafi (MOO uh mahr al kuh DAH fee), whom Reagan described as "the mad dog of the Middle East," Libya supported terrorist groups. In 1986, following a terrorist attack on a Berlin nightclub, which Reagan blamed on Qaddafi, U.S. warplanes bombed Libya. The air raid killed one of Qaddafi's daughters. Even though Qaddafi was unharmed, his criticism of the United States dwindled.

Reagan's presidency had started with a breakthrough in the Middle East. Twenty minutes after he took the oath of office on January 20, 1981, Iran released all 52 Americans it had held hostage since 1979. But during his second term, the Iran-Contra affair badly tarnished Reagan's reputation.

The **Iran-Contra affair** began when the United States sold weapons to Iran in 1985 in exchange for Iran's promise to pressure terrorist groups in Lebanon to release some American hostages. The plan didn't work, and it <u>contradicted</u> the administration's policy of refusing to negotiate with terrorists. Then, the administration used the money from the sale to fund the Contras in Nicaragua, despite the fact that in 1983 Congress had banned sending funds to the Contras. News of these deals came out in 1986. Although President Reagan accepted responsibility for the actions of his administration, he never admitted to ordering his aides to support the Contras. Ultimately, several leading administration officials and a top aide, Oliver North, were convicted on charges stemming from the scandal, although many of the convictions were later overturned on technical grounds. In spite of this, Reagan left office with extremely high approval ratings.

 Checkpoint What was the Iran-Contra scandal?

SECTION **3 Assessment**

Progress Monitoring *Online*
For: Self-test with vocabulary practice
Web Code: nea-1905

Comprehension

1. **Terms and People** For each item below, write a sentence explaining how the term or person related to the fall of communism in Europe and the Soviet Union in the late 1980s and early 1990s.
   - Strategic Defense Initiative
   - Mikhail Gorbachev
   - *glasnost*
   - *perestroika*

2. **NoteTaking** **Reading Skill: Sequence** Use your flowchart to answer the Section Focus Question: What were Reagan's foreign policies, and how did they contribute to the fall of communism in Europe?

Writing About History

3. **Quick Write: Choose Images** Using library books or approved Internet sources, select images and write captions to create a multimedia presentation about the fall of the Berlin Wall.

Critical Thinking

4. **Draw Inferences** How did Reagan's foreign policy differ from that of Carter?

5. **Identify Point of View** During his first term, Reagan called the Soviet Union an "evil empire," but in his second term, he developed a working relationship with Gorbachev. What accounts for this change in strategy?

6. **Synthesize Information** Why did Reagan order an air raid on Libya?

WITNESS HISTORY 🔊 AUDIO

A New World Order

Less than two years after the Berlin Wall fell, the United States found itself involved in another war after Iraq invaded its neighbor Kuwait. President George H.W. Bush spoke about his vision for this war:

❝We stand today at a unique and extraordinary moment. The crisis in the Persian Gulf, as grave as it is, also offers a rare opportunity to move toward a historic period of cooperation. Out of these troubled times . . . a new world order can emerge; a new era—freer from the threat of terror, stronger in the pursuit of justice; and more secure in the quest of peace, an era in which the nations of the world, East and West, North and South, can prosper and live in harmony.❞

—George Herbert Walker Bush, Address to Congress, September 11, 1990

▲ President Bush and his wife, Barbara, visiting troops in Saudi Arabia during the Persian Gulf War

Foreign Policy After the Cold War

Core Curriculum Objectives

- **7.V.F.2** United States and South Africa
- **7.VI.A** The Bush Presidency
- **7.VI.A.3** Foreign policy issues
- **7.VI.A.3d** Persian Gulf crisis

Terms and People

Manuel Noriega	divest
Tiananmen Square	Saddam Hussein
apartheid	Operation Desert Storm
Nelson Mandela	

NoteTaking

Reading Skill: Summarize Use a chart like the one below to summarize Bush's major foreign-policy decisions.

Post-Cold War Foreign Policy	
America's new role in the world	Persian Gulf War
•	•
•	•

Why It Matters When the Cold War came to an end, many Americans hoped that a new era of peace would dawn. Yet, America's foreign policy during the Bush years demonstrated that the end of the Cold War would not lead to a new era of peace, but instead to a dangerous era of regional conflicts. **Section Focus Question: What actions did the United States take abroad during George H.W. Bush's presidency?**

A New Role in the World

When the Soviet Union collapsed, the United States became the only unopposed superpower poised to take a leading role in world affairs under the leadership of President George H.W. Bush. Few leaders entered the White House with as much foreign policy experience as Bush. A graduate of Yale and a veteran of World War II, Bush had served as the U.S. Ambassador to the United Nations, as director of the CIA, and as Ronald Reagan's Vice President. His experience would be put to the test as America faced a series of difficult international crises during the late 1980s and early 1990s.

Latin America and the War on Drugs In the late 1980s and early 1990s, Latin America experienced a wave of democracy. In Central America, a peace plan devised by Costa Rican leader Oscar Arias (AH ree uhs) brought free elections in Nicaragua and the end of a long civil war in El Salvador. In Chile, the notorious military dictator Augusto Pinochet (ah GOO stoh pee noh SHAY) gave up power.

Foreign Policy Under Bush

President Bush faced several foreign-policy challenges. He adjusted his policy depending on each situation. **How did Bush's approach in Somalia differ from his approach in Panama?**

▲ **Promoting Democracy in South Africa**
Bush greets South African leader Nelson Mandela soon after Mandela's release from prison in 1990.

Not all developments in Latin America, however, pleased the Bush administration. Since the Nixon administration, the government had been waging a "war on drugs," or an attempt to stop illegal drug use by going after both sellers and users. Groups of racketeers in Latin America supplied a significant amount of the illegal drugs in the United States. The Bush administration arrested and tried several international drug figures, including Eduardo Martinez Romero, the reputed financier of a Colombian drug cartel. Even more spectacularly, in December 1989, Bush sent more than 12,000 U.S. troops to invade Panama and arrest Panama's dictator **Manuel Noriega.** Brought to the United States for trial, Noriega was convicted of several charges of drug trafficking and sentenced to 40 years in prison.

China Cracks Down on Critics Meanwhile, in the spring of 1989, Chinese students captured the world's attention by staging prodemocracy protests in **Tiananmen Square** in the heart of Beijing. Many Americans hoped that these protests might result in the fall of communism in China. Instead, on June 4, Chinese tanks rolled into Beijing, killed hundreds of protesters, crushed the demonstrations, and imprisoned many prodemocracy activists.

The Bush administration condemned this action and suspended arms sales to China. However, Bush did not believe that stiffer penalties would influence Chinese leaders. He made the pragmatic choice to remain engaged with China economically and diplomatically, rather than cut off ties with the country.

Change Comes to South Africa While China resisted changes, long overdue ones were taking place in South Africa. For years, the South African government, controlled by whites, had maintained an oppressive system of rigid segregation known as **apartheid.** The leader of the antiapartheid movement, **Nelson Mandela** (man DEHL uh), had been imprisoned since 1962. In the late 1980s, protests against apartheid within South Africa and around the globe grew. In the United States, many private firms **divested,** or withdrew investments, from South Africa. Congress imposed economic sanctions instead of fully divesting, not wanting to destabilize the struggling nation. President Bush met with Mandela after his release from jail in 1990 and endorsed the drive to bring democracy to South Africa. Soon after, apartheid began to be dismantled, and South Africans elected Mandela as their leader in 1994 in their first free elections.

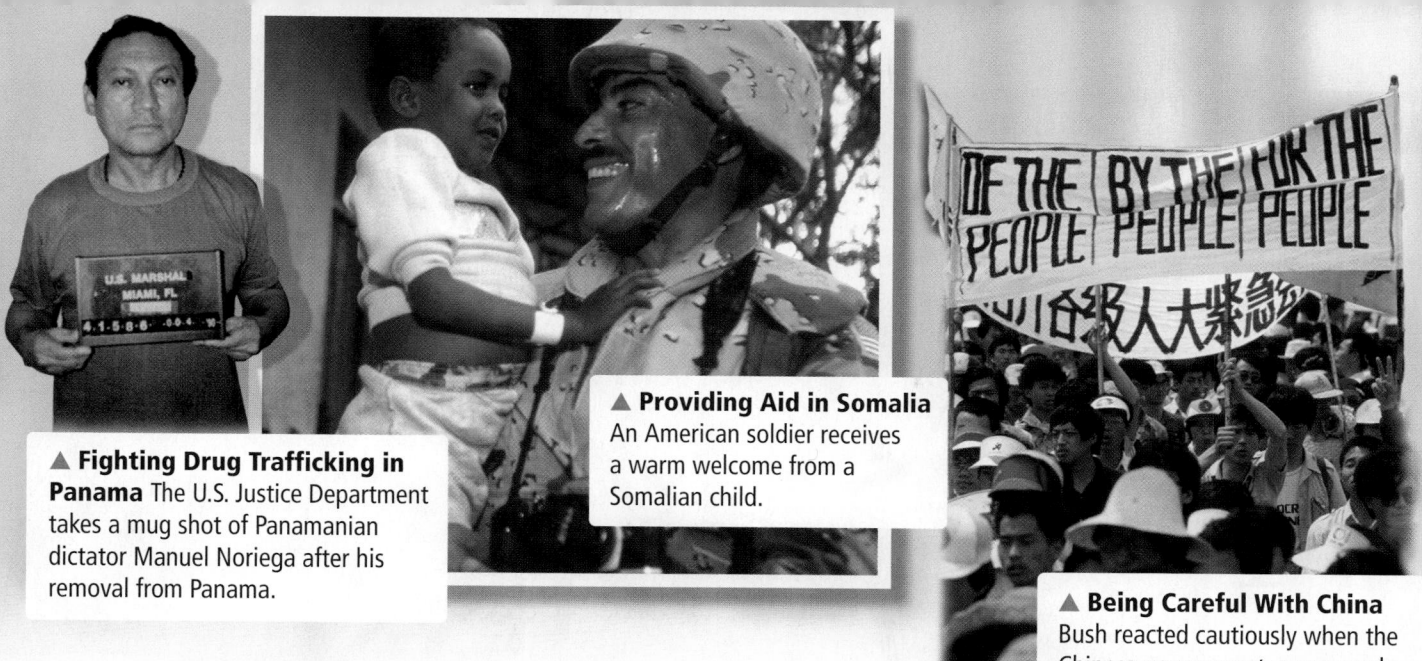

▲ **Fighting Drug Trafficking in Panama** The U.S. Justice Department takes a mug shot of Panamanian dictator Manuel Noriega after his removal from Panama.

▲ **Providing Aid in Somalia** An American soldier receives a warm welcome from a Somalian child.

▲ **Being Careful With China** Bush reacted cautiously when the Chinese government suppressed prodemocracy protests in Tiananmen Square.

Peacekeeping and Police Actions With the fall of communism in 1991, the nation of Yugoslavia disintegrated into a bloody civil war. Bush chose not to send troops because he feared that the tangled conflict could embroil the United States in another Vietnam. Not until 1992, however, did he back a modest UN plan to restore peace in Bosnia, one of the new republics carved out of Yugoslavia. By then, more than 150,000 civilians had died.

The Bush administration acted more swiftly to protect human rights in Somalia. As part of "Operation Restore Hope," United States Marines landed in this East African nation in December 1992 to help establish a cease-fire between rival warlords and to deliver food to hundreds of thousands of starving people. The American humanitarian mission reinforced UN efforts at peacekeeping and relief. Even some of Bush's most persistent critics applauded his decision to intervene in Somalia.

✔ **Checkpoint** What domestic problems caused President Bush to order the invasion of Panama?

The Persian Gulf War

The most important foreign-policy challenge faced by the Bush administration took place in the Persian Gulf. On August 2, 1990, Iraq invaded its tiny neighbor Kuwait. Nearly 150,000 Iraqi troops quickly overran Kuwaiti forces.

Causes of the War **Saddam Hussein,** Iraq's ruthless dictator, had run the Middle Eastern nation with an iron fist since 1979. By invading Kuwait, Hussein sought to take over Kuwait's rich oil deposits. With Kuwait in his power, Hussein would control nearly 20 percent of the oil produced around the world. The United States feared how Hussein would use the influence that controlling such a large amount of oil would give him. In addition, nearby Saudi Arabia possessed even more massive oil reserves. The United States did not want Hussein to seek to gain control of those reserves next. President Bush made it clear that he would not <u>tolerate</u> Iraq's aggression against its neighbor. He worked to build an international coalition and backed a UN resolution demanding that Iraqi troops withdraw.

Vocabulary Builder
<u>tolerate</u>–(TAHL er ayt) *v.* to put up with

The Persian Gulf War, 1991

Geography *Interactive*
For: Interactive map
Web Code: nep-1906

Legend:
- Allied air base
- Iraqi air base
- U.S. naval forces
- Allied air attacks
- Allied ground attacks
- Iraqi invasion of Kuwait
- Iraqi Scud attacks
- Iraqi retreat

Map labels: TURKEY, Incirlik, Mosul, SYRIA, CYPRUS, Mediterranean Sea, LEBANON, Beirut, Damascus, Euphrates River, Tigris River, IRAQ, Baghdad, IRAN, Haifa, ISRAEL, Tel Aviv, Amman, Jerusalem, JORDAN, Basra, Kuwait City, KUWAIT, SAUDI ARABIA, Hafar al Batin, Persian Gulf, EGYPT, Red Sea, Dhahran, Riyadh, 35° N, 35° E, 50° E, 25° N

Miller Projection
0   100   200 mi
0   100   200 km

Major Gulf War Coalition Members, 1991

Country*	Flag	Country*	Flag
Bahrain		Pakistan	
Canada		Qatar	
Egypt		Saudi Arabia	
France		Syria	
Germany		Turkey	
Japan		United Arab Emirates	
Kuwait		United Kingdom	
Netherlands		United States	
Oman			

*Other coalition members who made smaller contributions:
Argentina, Australia, Bangladesh, Belgium, Czechoslovakia, Denmark, Greece, Italy, Morocco, New Zealand, Niger, Norway, Poland, Portugal, Senegal, South Korea, Spain

Map Skills The Persian Gulf War consisted mainly of aerial bombardment, with only a brief ground war.
1. **Locate:** (a) Kuwait, (b) Saudi Arabia, (c) Baghdad
2. **Location** Why was Saudi Arabia a strategic ally?
3. **Synthesize Information** From what points did the Allied forces launch air attacks?

As they retreated, Iraqi troops set fire to Kuwait's oil wells, causing great environmental harm (below). General Norman Schwarzkopf, the commander of the coalition's forces in the Persian Gulf, consults with a soldier (right).

Operation Desert Storm By late fall, about 700,000 troops had assembled in Saudi Arabia, including nearly 500,000 American forces. Britain, France, Egypt, and Saudi Arabia, among others, also sent troops. Other nations, for example Japan, agreed to help pay for the costs of the operation. Initially, Bush hoped that the presence of these troops, along with the economic sanctions against Iraq, would convince Hussein to withdraw his soldiers. At the same time, the President asked for and received from Congress the authority to use force, if necessary, to back up the UN's resolution that Iraq leave Kuwait.

Operation Desert Storm, the name given to the American-led attack on Iraqi forces, began on January 16, 1991. General Colin Powell, the Chairman of the Joint Chiefs of Staff, and General Norman Schwarzkopf devised and executed a strategy that began with five weeks of devastating aerial bombardment on Iraqi forces. Iraq countered by launching Scud missiles on both coalition forces and Israel. Although, these missiles did little serious damage, they struck terror in the hearts of many who feared they were armed with chemical warheads.

On February 23, coalition troops stormed into Kuwait. Easily overmatched, Iraqi troops surrendered or fled, setting fire to Kuwaiti oil rigs along the way. Less than five days after the ground war began, Iraq agreed to a UN cease-fire. It had lost an estimated 25,000 soldiers. American deaths totaled 148. "We've kicked the Vietnam syndrome once and for all," proclaimed Bush. He then chose to limit American actions to enforcing the UN resolution. The coalition's forces would compel Iraq to leave Kuwait but would not continue on to Baghdad, Iraq's capital, to topple Saddam Hussein. As a result, Hussein and his regime survived the war. Bush's public approval rating skyrocketed.

HISTORY MAKERS

Colin Powell (born 1937)
The son of Jamaican immigrants, Colin Powell joined the army after college and served two tours of duty in Vietnam. He held several jobs in the army and in the government during the 1970s and 1980s. In 1989, President George H.W. Bush named General Powell Chairman of the Joint Chiefs of Staff. From that post, he guided the American victories in Panama and the Persian Gulf War. Powell later served as Secretary of State under President George W. Bush.

 Checkpoint What strategic political and economic interests caused the United States to become involved in the Persian Gulf War?

Progress Monitoring *Online*
For: Self-test with vocabulary practice
Web Code: nea-1907

Comprehension

1. **Terms and People** For each item below, write a sentence explaining how the term or person demonstrated the new role of the United States after the end of the Cold War.
   - Manuel Noriega
   - Tiananmen Square
   - apartheid
   - Nelson Mandela
   - divest
   - Saddam Hussein
   - Operation Desert Storm

2. **NoteTaking Reading Skill: Summarize** Use your chart to answer the Section Focus Question: What actions did the United States take abroad during George H.W. Bush's presidency?

Writing About History

3. **Quick Write: Create a Timeline** Plan, draft, and create a multimedia timeline featuring American foreign policy after the Cold War. Consider using a slideshow computer application to present your timeline.

Critical Thinking

4. **Draw Inferences** Why did President Bush respond differently to the crisis in Somalia than he did to the crisis in China?

5. **Compare** How was the Persian Gulf War fought differently from the Vietnam War?

6. **Draw Conclusions** Why did the U.S.-led coalition decide not to invade Baghdad or try to oust Hussein after driving Iraq out of Kuwait?

Quick Study Guide

7.V.C.1,
7.VI.A.3

Progress Monitoring *Online*
For: Self-test with vocabulary practice
Web Code: nea-1908

■ Key Policies and Actions of Ronald Reagan

Domestic
Supported tax cuts and deregulation to stimulate demand under the theory of supply-side economics
Took a strong stance on air-traffic controllers' strike
Appointed conservative Justices to the Supreme Court
Reformed Social Security
Increased defense spending

Foreign
Pressured the Soviet Union by building up the American military, including the Strategic Defense Initiative program
Aided anticommunist forces in several countries, including Afghanistan and Grenada
Signed arms control agreements with Soviet leader Mikhail Gorbachev
Sent peacekeeping force to Lebanon
Ordered an air raid on Libya because of Libyan leader Muammar al-Qaddafi's involvement in terrorist attacks

■ Key Events in George H.W. Bush's Presidency

- Signed Americans With Disabilities Act into law
- Forged friendly relationship between the United States and the new Russian Federation
- Continued the war on drugs by invading Panama and arresting Panamanian dictator Manuel Noriega on drug-trafficking charges
- Sent humanitarian mission to Somalia
- Headed an international coalition of forces in the Persian Gulf War

■ The Fall of Communism in Eastern Europe and the Soviet Union

☑ Quick Study Timeline

In America

1981
Hostages in Iran
released on first day
of Reagan's presidency

1983
Economy starts to
recover from recession

Presidential Terms	Ronald Reagan 1981–1989	
1980	**1982**	**1984**

Around the World

1982
Argentina and Great
Britain battle for control
of Falkland Islands

1984
Indira Gandhi,
prime minister of
India, is assassinated

American Issues
●—●—● Connector

By connecting prior knowledge with what you have learned in this chapter, you can gradually build your understanding of enduring questions that still affect America today. Answer the questions below. Then, use your American Issues Connector study guide (or go online: www.PHSchool.com **Web Code:** neh-9202).

Issues You Learned About

● **America and the World** The Cold War dominated American foreign policy for half a century, starting in the 1940s.

1. When and why was the Berlin Wall constructed? How did the United States respond at the time?

2. Why did Reagan's attitude toward Soviet leader Gorbachev change? What events and policies demonstrated this change?

3. What role do some historians believe the United States played in the fall of the Soviet Union?

● **Sectionalism and National Politics** Most politicians in the United States are members of a political party.

4. What were the first two major political parties in the United States, and what policies did they generally favor? In the late twentieth century, what were the country's two major political parties, and what policies did they generally favor?

5. What complaints did Republicans lodge against Democratic economic policies in the late 1970s?

6. Why had many white southerners changed their historical allegiance from the Democratic Party to the Republican Party by the 1980s?

● **Government's Role in the Economy** Different administrations back their own economic policies, such as raising or lowering taxes and increasing or decreasing funds for government programs.

7. What is supply-side economics? What changes did Reagan's application of supply-side economics bring to taxpayers?

8. What steps did Reagan take to lessen the federal government's role in the economy?

Connect to Your World	New York

New York Goes to War In 1991, hundreds of soldiers from New York's 42nd Infantry Division, a National Guard unit headquartered in Troy, volunteered to serve in the Persian Gulf War. Known as the "Rainbow Division," the 42nd Division had fought in Europe during both World Wars. The Rainbow soldiers had also helped solve problems at home — providing relief to New Yorkers after a major hurricane in 1972, and briefly taking over the state's prison system during a corrections officers' strike in 1979. In 2001, they responded quickly to the emergency created by the September 11 attacks on the World Trade Center in New York City. Research the 42nd Infantry Division and create a timeline of its major accomplishments.

1987
Reagan and Gorbachev sign treaty agreeing to eliminate some nuclear missiles

1991
United States leads coalition of forces in Persian Gulf War

George H. W. Bush 1989–1993

1986   **1988**   **1990**   **1992**

1988
Soviet forces begin to pull out of Afghanistan

1989
Berlin Wall falls

1991
Soviet Union breaks up; Cold War ends

History *Interactive*
For: Interactive timeline
Web Code: nep-1909

Chapter Assessment

Terms and People

1. What was the **New Right**? Give two reasons for the rise of the New Right.

2. What was the **Savings and Loan crisis**? How did the federal government respond to this crisis?

3. What is **AIDS**? How did Reagan and Bush react to the increase of AIDS in the United States?

4. What were *glasnost* and *perestroika*? What effect did they have on the Soviet Union?

5. Define **apartheid**. What actions did the United States take to end apartheid?

Focus Questions

The focus question for this chapter is **What was the conservative resurgence, and how did it affect the domestic and foreign policies of the United States?** Build an answer to this big question by answering the focus questions for Sections 1 through 4 and the Critical Thinking questions that follow.

Section 1

6. What spurred the rise of conservatism in the late 1970s and early 1980s?

Section 2

7. What were the major characteristics of the conservative Reagan Revolution?

Section 3

8. What were Reagan's foreign policies, and how did they contribute to the fall of communism in Europe?

Section 4

9. What actions did the United States take abroad during George H.W. Bush's presidency?

Critical Thinking

10. **Categorize** Identify the goals of the conservative movement in the early 1980s.

11. **Analyze Charts** Study the chart below. Use it, along with your reading of this chapter, to explain how the conservative movement affected Congress.

Composition of Congress, 1979–1983

Year	House of Representatives			Senate		
	Dem.	Rep.	Ind.	Dem.	Rep.	Ind.
1979	276	157	0	58	41	1
1981	243	192	0	46	53	1
1983	269	165	0	46	54	0

12. **Recognize Effects** Think about the economic policies that Reagan followed. Then, identify and describe one positive and one negative effect that his policies had on the economy.

13. **Identify Central Issues** In the Iran-Contra affair, what actions of several members of Reagan's administration went against the policies of the federal government?

14. **Make Generalizations** Describe the political policies that led to U.S. involvement in Afghanistan, Nicaragua, El Salvador, and Grenada.

15. **Synthesize Information** Reagan's foreign policy was directed at stopping communism. What was the basis of Bush's foreign policy? Give one specific example of this foreign policy.

16. **Draw Inferences** How did George H.W. Bush approach the war against Iraq in 1991?

Writing About History

Create a Multimedia Presentation In the late 1980s and early 1990s, sweeping changes happened in Europe and other places around the world. These changes affected the United States in subtler but still significant ways. Choose one of these changes, and create a multimedia presentation showing what happened and how it affected the United States.

Prewriting

- Go online to PHSchool.com and enter **Web Code: nep-1911** to review several presentations that use different types of media to make their points.

- Brainstorm topics and choose the one that you think lends itself best to a multimedia format.

- Outline the main points you would like to make and choose the type of media you will use to make each point.

Drafting

- Write a draft of your presentation.

- Search for or create images and artwork to enhance your presentation.

- Create storyboards showing how you will blend the text and images in your presentation.

- Consider using a computer application to put together the final presentation.

Revising

- Use the guidelines on page SH31 of the Writing Handbook to revise your work.

Regents DBQ Practice

Is the National Debt a Problem?

During the 1980s, the Reagan administration lowered tax rates, hoping to pull the economy out of a recession. At the same time, defense spending increased. These factors, in part, led to annual budget deficits that added substantially to the national debt. There remains substantial debate about the costs and benefits of national debt. Use your knowledge of Ronald Reagan's economic policies and Documents 1, 2, and 3 to answer questions 1 through 4.

Document 1
Budget Surpluses and Deficits, 1950–2006

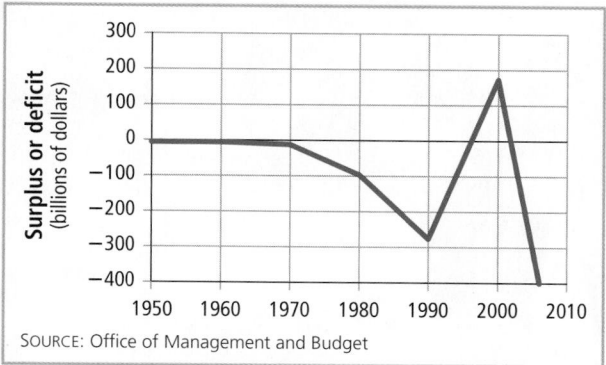

SOURCE: Office of Management and Budget

Document 2
National Debt as a Percentage of GDP, 1940–2010

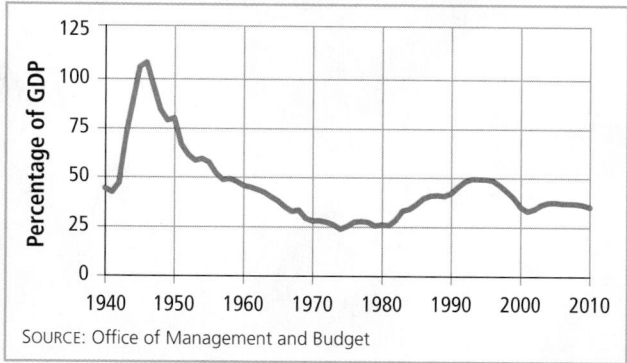

SOURCE: Office of Management and Budget

Document 3

"Large deficits and rising federal debt constrain future economic growth and living standards by reducing the amount of saving in the United States available for private investment. Federal borrowing to finance deficits may also put upward pressure on interest rates, which increases household borrowing costs for such things as homes, cars, and college loans.

In addition to these economic consequences, the budgetary effects of deficits and growing debt reduce the federal government's flexibility in funding various programs and activities. . . . In fiscal year 2003, net interest spending was the sixth largest item in the federal budget—about 7 percent of total federal spending was primarily used to pay interest on debt held by the public rather than to finance other public priorities. . . .

Federal borrowing has both advantages and disadvantages. . . . Borrowing, in lieu of higher taxes or lower government spending, may be viewed as appropriate during times of economic recession, war, and other temporary challenges. . . . Borrowing for such short-term circumstances can permit the government to hold tax rates relatively stable and avoid economic disruptions. Federal borrowing might also be viewed as appropriate for federal investment, such as building roads, training workers, and conducting scientific research, contributing to the nation's capital stock and productivity. . . . In concept, federal spending that is well chosen . . . could ultimately contribute to producing a larger economy from which to pay the interest and principal on the borrowed funds. However, in practice, [the Congressional Budget Office] concluded that many federal investments might not significantly increase economic growth because some are selected for political or other noneconomic reasons and others displace more productive investments by the private sector or state and local governments."

—*from* Federal Debt: Answers to Frequently Asked Questions, *U.S. Government Accountability Office, 2004*

---

1. According to Document 1, annual budget deficits
   (1) remained relatively low during the 1980s.
   (2) increased dramatically during the 1980s.
   (3) decreased dramatically during the 1980s.
   (4) disappeared during the 1980s.

2. According to Document 2, national debt
   (1) was at its lowest point ever during the 1980s.
   (2) was at its highest point ever during the 1980s.
   (3) increased during the 1980s.
   (4) decreased during the 1980s.

3. According to Document 3, federal debt
   (1) makes it easier for individual citizens and companies to borrow money.
   (2) makes it more difficult for the government to fund other public priorities.
   (3) is never desirable.
   (4) always increases economic growth.

4. **Writing Task** Do you think benefits of the increased national debt during the 1980s and 1990s outweighed the costs? Why or why not? Use evidence from the documents and the chapter to support your answer.

33

Into a New Century
1992–Today

Becoming American Citizens

Every year, hundreds of thousands of immigrants change their lives by taking part in naturalization ceremonies to become U.S. citizens. After declaring their commitment to this nation and renouncing allegiance to their home countries, they join other Americans in lending their talents, skills, and dreams to their new country. President George W. Bush has described citizenship in this way:

66America has never been united by blood or birth or soil, we are bound by ideals that move us beyond our backgrounds. . . . Every immigrant by embracing these ideals makes our country more, not less, American.99

Listen to the Witness History *audio to hear more about American citizenship.*

◀ Immigrants wait to be sworn in as U.S. citizens during a ceremony in Los Angeles, California, in February 2005.

Saddam Hussein's statue being toppled in Iraq

A simple "W '04" declares Bush's reelection campaign

NY Core Curriculum Preview

Chapter Focus Question: What political, social, technological, and economic trends have shaped American life since 1990?

Section 1
The Computer and Technology Revolutions 7.I.A, 7.I.A.3, 7.I.A.4, 7.I.A.5

Section 2
The Clinton Presidency 7.VI.B, 7.VI.B.1a, 7.VI.B.1c(2), 7.VI.B.1d

Section 3
Global Politics and Economics 7.VI.B.2, 7.VI.B.2a, 7.VI.B.2b, 7.VI.B.2c

Section 4
The George W. Bush Presidency 1.I.D.1, 2.I.E.4, 2.I.E.9, 7.V.C.2

Section 5
Americans Look to the Future 1.I.D.2, 2.I.E.6, 7.V.D.3, 7.V.D.4

Use the ✔ **Quick Study Timeline** at the end of this chapter to preview chapter events.

NASA rover exploring Mars

> **Note Taking Study Guide** *Online*
> **For:** Note Taking and American Issues Connector
> **Web Code:** nee-9301

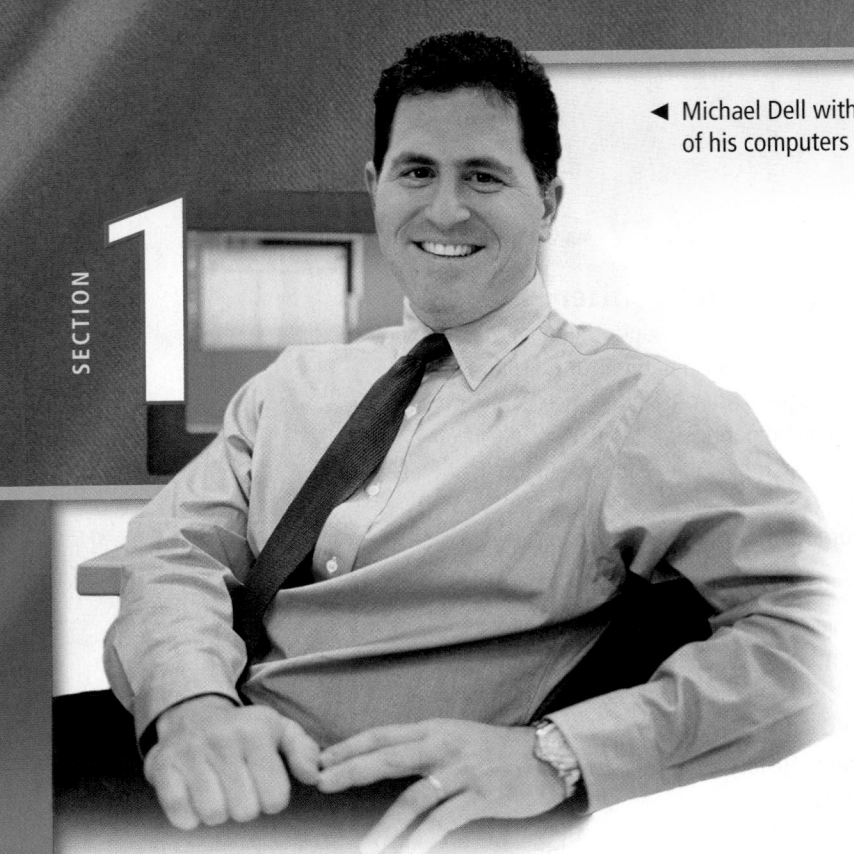

◀ Michael Dell with one of his computers

WITNESS HISTORY 🔊 AUDIO

A Young Entrepreneur

In 1980, a Texas teenager named Michael Dell bought his first computer. He immediately took the computer apart to see if he could rebuild it. Though Dell entered college intending to become a doctor, his real interest lay in the computer company he started from his college dorm room. By 2003, that small company had grown into a global corporation called Dell Inc.—the most profitable company in the computer industry.

❝There were obviously no classes on learning how to start and run a business in my high school, so I clearly had a lot to learn. And learn I did, mostly by experimenting and making a bunch of mistakes.❞

—Michael Dell, 1999

The Computer and Technology Revolutions

 Core Curriculum Objectives

- **7.I.A** Changes within the postindustrial United States
- **7.I.A.3** Technology (computers)
- **7.I.A.4** Corporate structures (multinational corporations)
- **7.I.A.5** Nature of employment

Terms and People

personal computer
biotechnology
satellite
Internet

globalization
multinational corporation
service economy

NoteTaking

Reading Skill: Categorize As you read, fill in a flowchart like this one to help you categorize technological changes and their impact.

Technology Revolution		
Computers	Communications	Globalization
• •	• •	• •

Why It Matters During the twentieth century, the rate of technological change sped up dramatically. New technology touched every aspect of life, including how Americans worked, played, and communicated. At the same time, globalization transformed the American economy, bringing both new challenges and new opportunities. **Section Focus Question: How have technological changes and globalization transformed the American economy?**

Technology Changes American Life

The 1900s was a century of unparalleled change. In 1903, Orville Wright flew the first airplane. Less than 70 years later, astronaut Neil Armstrong walked on the moon. During that same span of time, television went from a novelty at a World's Fair to a standard household possession, and sophisticated microscopes and telescopes unveiled previously hidden worlds. One of the most important innovations was the development of the computer.

Developing the Modern Computer Intense rivalry between enemies during World War II brought about a life-and-death race to develop new technologies, such as the computer. The U.S. government funded research that led to the creation of the first modern computer in 1946. This huge machine occupied the entire basement of the research lab. It calculated artillery ranges and performed computations for the atomic bomb.

Soon after World War II, universities and corporations joined government agencies to develop smaller, faster, more powerful computers that could perform a range of functions. The IBM company developed one of the first commercially successful computers in 1954. In the 1960s, a few companies located south of San Francisco, California, focused on developing improved technology for running the computer. Their efforts led to the microchip, a tiny fragment of silicon containing complex circuits, and the microprocessor, a silicon chip that held a central processing unit. These chips made possible the development of small computers, called **personal computers.**

Transforming Business and Industry At first, personal computers were a novelty item, used mainly by hobbyists. But by the 1980s, computers were transforming industries, research labs, and businesses. Personal computers could perform many different tasks but were small and simple enough for the average person to use. The technology that created them eventually spread to many other industries. Video games, cellular telephones, and other electronics all depended on microchips and microprocessors. Entrepreneurs played a large role in accelerating the use of personal computers. Steve Jobs's Apple Computers and Bill Gates's Microsoft made computers and software affordable for millions of Americans. Jeff Bezos's Amazon.com ushered in buying and selling products by computer. Like Andrew Carnegie and John D. Rockefeller a century before, these men amassed great fortunes by pioneering new technologies.

Revolutions in Science and Agriculture Medical science also moved ahead by gigantic leaps in the twentieth century, often aided by computer technology. Scientists developed drugs that extended patients' lives, reduced pain, and battled a huge number of diseases. They made artificial hearts and learned how to successfully transplant body organs. Such advancements, along with **biotechnology,** or the use of living organisms in the development of new products, have produced a level of healthcare unknown to any previous generation.

Advances in agricultural technology, including improved machinery, irrigation techniques, and growing methods, have brought profound changes to American society. While farms have grown larger and more productive, fewer people are needed to work them. In 1900, 50 percent of the labor force worked on farms. At the end of the century, only 2 percent did.

✔ **Checkpoint** What was the impact of the personal computer?

A Communications Revolution

Late in the twentieth century, commentators began to describe their times as the "information age." Access to information, they claimed, was access to power. Computers, cellphones, e-mails, and instant messaging became the tools of the information age. Entrepreneurs who could control these tools became wealthy—and powerful. For example, media executives who decide what gets on television can exert influence on political elections and controversial topics. But computer and communication technologies also have a democratic leveling effect. Anyone with access to a computer can acquire information that was once available only to a few, well-connected leaders.

A New Form of I.D.
A vet implants a tiny microchip (inset) into a puppy. If the dog is lost, a simple scan of the chip will reveal its name and its owner's address.

Satellite Technology Satellite technology increased the speed of global communications. **Satellites** are mechanical devices that orbit Earth in space, receiving and sending information-filled signals that are then relayed to televisions, telephones, and computers. Originally developed for military purposes during the Cold War, satellite technology was used in the 1970s by businessman Ted Turner to run the first "superstation," broadcasting into cable-equipped households across the country. In 1980, Turner began the 24-hour-per-day, all-news Cable News Network (CNN). Cellular telephones used similar satellite technology, allowing people to communicate away from their homes.

The Internet Is Born In the 1970s, various branches of the U.S. government along with groups in several American universities led efforts to link computer systems together via cables and satellites. By the 1980s, the **Internet,** or World Wide Web, had been born, reaching the general public in the 1990s. The Web made communication and access to information almost instantaneous. This breakthrough completely and profoundly transformed commerce, education, research, and entertainment. E-mail provided great advantages over the delays of postal mail and the expense of telephones. The impact has been especially great on people living in rural areas. The Internet's immense storage capacity also changed the world of research. In the 1980s, scientists and scholars primarily used the Internet to share information. By the early 1990s, they were using it as a research tool and an online database.

Households With Computers and Internet Access

Percentage of households

— Computer — Internet access

SOURCE: U.S. Census Bureau

Graph Skills The graph shows how Americans' access to computers and the Internet has changed over the past two decades. Describe the change. Note that the data for Internet access do not begin until 1997. Why might this be so?

✔ **Checkpoint** How did new technology revolutionize communications?

A Changing American Economy

All of these technological changes had a dramatic effect on the American economy. New technology influenced how and where people did their jobs. In this changing economy, one sector—the service industry—grew rapidly. A lower percentage of Americans than ever before worked on assembly lines or on farms. Instead, they provided services.

The Impact of Globalization New communications infrastructures—especially satellites and computers—have made it easier for companies to do global business. This has increased **globalization,** or the process by which national economies, politics, cultures, and societies become integrated with those of other nations around the world. **Multinational corporations** are one example. Such a corporation might have its financial headquarters in one country and manufacturing plants in several others, and may obtain its raw materials from many different places. The company then sells the products it makes to a worldwide market.

Globalization has made more products and services available to greater numbers of people, often at lower prices. It has hastened the development of some nations. But it has also had some drawbacks. Industrial nations have seen their manufacturing jobs flow out to less developed nations. Steel that was once manufactured in Pittsburgh, for example, might now be made in South Korea. In less developed nations, workers often do not enjoy the protections that workers have in industrial nations. Finally, the interconnection of world economies almost guarantees that economic problems in one region will be felt in others.

Computers Transform Workplaces Computer technology has also changed the nature of the American economy. Many workers have found that they need computer skills to get jobs. Banking, stockbroking, programming, and the many other occupations dependent on information and computers have added millions of jobs to the service economy. Many white-collar workers in the information economy have seen their jobs radically change. Professional workers are

INFOGRAPHIC

The Global Reach of E-commerce

Global communications, especially the Internet, have reshaped ways of doing business. Just 15 years ago, shoppers bought almost everything they needed at local stores, and most things they bought were made in the country where they lived. The Internet and e-commerce—electronic commerce, or business conducted over the Internet—have helped to change that. This illustration shows an example of e-commerce in progress.

1 A woman in Minneapolis, MN, shops for a pair of snowshoes online. She has questions about a model she likes and requests to speak with customer service on the Web site.

2 A customer-service representative in Bangalore, India, types answers to her questions in real-time.

3 The customer's order is received and processed by a computer at the sporting-goods company in Stockholm, Sweden. The computer sends messages to two locations.

4 A message to the Swedish company's U.S. warehouse in Los Angeles, CA, tells workers there to ship the shopper a pair of snowshoes.

5 Another message to a factory in Shanghai, China, tells workers there to produce more snowshoes and ship them to Los Angeles, CA.

Thinking Critically
Synthesize Information Use the illustration above to describe the impact of globalization.

History Interactive ✳
For: More about e-commerce
Web Code: nep-2011

Occupations Predicted to Grow the Fastest, 2004–2014

- Home health aides
- Network systems analysts
- Medical assistants
- Computer software engineers
- Physical therapist assistants
- Dental hygienists

SOURCE: U.S. Department of Labor

Chart Skills Americans' occupations in the next few years will be dramatically different from what they were 100 years ago. *Which two fields are projected to grow the fastest in the next few years?*

linked by a network of computers, fax machines, television screens, and cell phones. They often telecommunicate, holding meetings that involve participants sitting in offices around the world.

The Service Sector Expands With the production of services increasing faster than the production of goods, some economists say that America now has a **service economy.** Jobs in the service sector vary widely. Lawyers, teachers, doctors, research analysts, police officers, professional athletes, and movie stars are all service workers, as are salespeople and the people behind fast-food counters. Service workers are among the lowest paid and the highest paid people in the United States.

The transition from an industry-based economy to a service-based one has created opportunities for entrepreneurs. For example, Californians Richard and Maurice McDonald opened their new restaurant in 1948. The brothers emphasized efficiency, low prices, high volume, and quick service. They did away with anything that slowed down the process, including plates, glasses, dishwashing, and tipping. In 1955, Ray Kroc began to franchise the McDonald's system and name. By the end of the century, McDonald's had become the most successful food service organization in history, and the name McDonald's came to stand for low-priced, standardized-quality food.

Other entrepreneurs' names also came to symbolize their businesses. For example, Wal-Mart, a discount merchandising business founded by Sam Walton, became one of the most successful businesses in the late twentieth century.

Organized Labor Declines The rise of the service economy and the decline in American coal mining, steelmaking, and automobile manufacturing has had a strong impact on organized labor. At its peak in 1945, about 35 percent of all American workers belonged to unions. In 2000, less than 15 percent of workers did. Blue-collar jobs, once the mainstay of American labor, declined dramatically in the second half of the twentieth century. As a result, the political power of labor unions, as well as farm organizations, has fallen. At the same time, workers' average wages—especially those of nonprofessional workers—have fallen.

 Checkpoint How has globalization affected the American economy?

SECTION **1** Assessment

Progress Monitoring *Online*
For: Self-test with vocabulary practice
Web Code: nea-2011

Comprehension

1. **Terms and People** For each term below, write a sentence explaining its effect on American society or the economy.
   - personal computer
   - biotechnology
   - satellite
   - Internet
   - globalization
   - multinational corporation
   - service economy

2. **NoteTaking Reading Skill: Categorize** Use your flowchart to answer the Section Focus Question: How have technological changes and globalization transformed the American economy?

Writing About History

3. **Quick Write: Choose a Topic** Recall all the American issues you have studied in this course. Identify an issue that comes into play in this section, and explain how.

Critical Thinking

4. **Draw Inferences** Why are new technologies often developed as a result of waging war?

5. **Recognize Cause and Effect** How has the computer sped up the pace of globalization?

6. **Test Conclusions** Cite evidence to support or refute this statement: A service economy provides more opportunities to entrepreneurs than does an industrial economy.

▲ Sixteen-year-old Bill Clinton meets President Kennedy on July 26, 1963. A campaign button proclaims his own presidential bid nearly 30 years later.

Becoming President

In 1963, a high school student named Bill Clinton from Hope, Arkansas, went to the White House as part of a youth leadership conference. He was first in line to shake President Kennedy's hand. Thirty years later, Clinton was sworn in as President of the United States.

❝Thomas Jefferson believed that to preserve the very foundation of our nation, we would need dramatic change from time to time. Well, my fellow citizens, this is our time. . . . And so today, we pledge an end to the era of deadlock and drift—a new season of American renewal has begun.**❞**

—Bill Clinton, First Inaugural Address, 1993

The Clinton Presidency

Core Curriculum Objectives

- **7.VI.B** The Clinton Presidency
- **7.VI.B.1a** Clinton: Social concerns
- **7.VI.B.1c(2)** Clinton: Gun control
- **7.VI.B.1d** Clinton: Impeachment and acquittal

Terms and People

William Jefferson Clinton
H. Ross Perot
Family Medical Leave Act
Brady Bill
Newt Gingrich
Contract With America
Kenneth Starr
impeachment

NoteTaking

Reading Skill: Summarize Create an outline like the one below as you read to summarize information about the Clinton presidency.

> I. The 1992 Election
>   A. Bush's popularity plummets
>   B. Clinton runs as "New Democrat"
>   C. Clinton carries the election
> II. Clinton's Domestic Policies
>   A.

Why It Matters The conservative revolution of the 1980s had kept Republicans in the White House for 12 straight years and influenced every branch of government. The election of Bill Clinton to the presidency in 1992 signaled that Americans were ready for a change. Clinton's position as a moderate, practical Democrat had broad appeal for a wide range of voters. **Section Focus Question: What were the successes and failures of the Clinton presidency?**

The 1992 Election

After the 1991 Persian Gulf War ended, President George H.W. Bush's approval rating reached 91 percent. In less than one year, however, public opinion had changed. Saddam Hussein had stayed in power, continuing to threaten peace in the Middle East. The American economy had gone into recession and the federal deficit had risen. People were angered by Bush's betrayal of his 1988 campaign pledge not to raise taxes. Bush's sinking popularity opened up the way for the Democratic challenge.

Clinton Raises the Challenge The Democrats nominated **William Jefferson Clinton,** governor of Arkansas, as their presidential candidate. Clinton was born in 1946 into a humble home and had worked his way through college and law school before being elected governor of Arkansas in 1978. To widen his appeal and distance himself from traditional "tax and spend" liberals, Clinton promoted himself as a "New Democrat." New Democrats were centrists who sought to

Celebrating Victory
Newly elected President Bill Clinton, Vice President Al Gore, and their families greet supporters in Arkansas on November 3, 1992.

reconcile liberal and conservative ideals. They believed in strong national defense, tough stands on crime, free trade, welfare reform, and closer ties with corporations. They believed that government was necessary and important but that it had grown large and inefficient. Clinton's centrist position attracted conservative and liberal Democrats as well as moderate Republicans.

Winning the White House By 1992, Clinton was poised to capitalize on Bush's political problems. He entered the presidential race along with Texas billionaire **H. Ross Perot,** who led a self-funded independent party and promised to govern by sound business principles. Clinton's campaign focused on economic and social opportunity. Clinton charged that Bush's economic policies had made the rich richer. He also pointed out that, unlike Bush, he came from a family that had struggled through hard times and knew what it was like to worry about paying bills. Bush responded by attacking Clinton's character. Republicans accused the governor of draft-dodging, marital infidelity, and other moral laxities. Bush also suggested that Clinton and his vice presidential candidate Al Gore were too inexperienced to lead the nation.

In the end, Clinton's message carried the election. In the largest voter turnout since 1960, more than one hundred million Americans turned out at the polls. Clinton received 43 percent of the popular vote to Bush's 37 percent and Perot's 19 percent. Democrats also retained control of the House of Representatives and the Senate.

 Checkpoint How did Clinton use his stance as a moderate to attract voters?

Clinton's Domestic Policies

When Bill Clinton took the presidential oath of office on January 20, 1993, he faced a great challenge. Since 1968, Americans had chosen Republican Presidents in five out of six elections. The Republican argument that government was the problem, not the solution, resonated with many Americans. Clinton therefore needed to chart a middle course between the limited role for government advocated by Republicans and the traditional Democratic reliance on government programs to address social problems.

Signing New Laws Early in his presidency, Clinton signed the **Family Medical Leave Act,** which had been vetoed by President Bush despite having bipartisan support. The act guaranteed most full-time employees 12 workweeks of unpaid leave each year for the birth and care of a newborn child, to recover from a serious illness, or to care for an immediate family member with one. The Clinton administration also raised the minimum wage, increased access to college loans, and expanded tax credits for higher education.

Healthcare Reform Fails Healthcare reform headed Clinton's list of priorities. The United States was the only developed country without national healthcare. Though Clinton did not advocate socialized medicine, he wanted a program that would guarantee care for all Americans. His wife, Hillary Clinton, was appointed to head a healthcare task force to investigate the issue. The task force conducted highly publicized hearings and produced a long, detailed proposal that attracted immediate criticism from diverse interest groups. The bill never won congressional support and was <u>ultimately</u> dropped after about a year of debate.

Clinton had miscalculated Americans' faith in the federal government to solve the country's social problems. Millions of Americans simply did not feel that enlarging the federal bureaucracy and allowing the government to run healthcare was a good idea.

Dealing With Violence Clinton also tried to address the issue of violence in American society. In 1993, he signed the **Brady Bill,** a gun-control act named for presidential aide James Brady, who had been wounded in the 1981 assassination attempt on Ronald Reagan. Under Clinton, Congress also passed a $30 billion anticrime bill that increased funding for police and banned several kinds of assault weapons.

Still, violence continued to haunt the nation. In 1995, Americans were horrified by the bombing of a government building in Oklahoma City that killed 168 people and injured more than 800 others. The mass murder was committed, not by foreign terrorists, but by home-grown anti-government extremists. To deal with the threat of terrorism, federal buildings in major cities were surrounded with barriers to ward off similar attacks. New laws were passed to deter terrorism and impose stiffer penalties.

In 1999, yet another act of senseless violence stirred nationwide debate. At Colorado's Columbine High School, two heavily armed students killed 12 fellow students and a teacher, as well as wounding 24 others. In the aftermath of this tragedy, schools across the nation installed metal detectors and other security measures. Many schools instituted new anti-bully policies and "zero tolerance" approaches to school violence.

✓ **Checkpoint** What were Clinton's legislative successes and failures?

The Republicans Galvanize

After two years in office, Clinton had achieved a few lasting legislative victories. Yet the failure of his healthcare initiative signaled that his popularity, and his control of Congress, was waning. With the 1994 midterm elections approaching, congressional Republicans seized the opportunity to advance their own ideas.

Vocabulary Builder
ultimately – (UHL tuh miht lee) *adv.* in the end; finally

Oklahoma City Bombing
The Oklahoma City bombing of April 1995 was the worst act of domestic terrorism in American history. The victims included a number of children in a day care center.

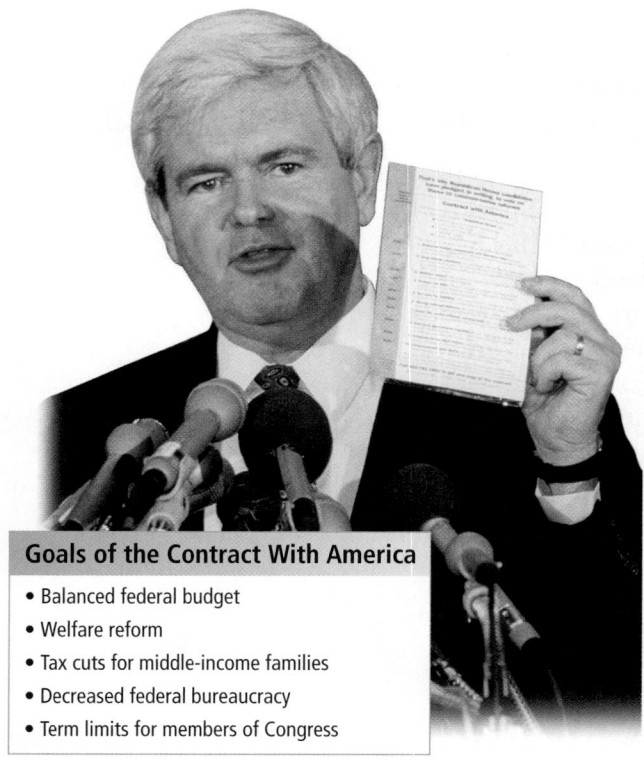

Goals of the Contract With America
• Balanced federal budget
• Welfare reform
• Tax cuts for middle-income families
• Decreased federal bureaucracy
• Term limits for members of Congress

The "Gingrich Revolution"
Gingrich explains his Contract with America at a press conference in January 1994. *How did his goals attract voters who were opposed to "big government"?*

Gingrich's Contract With America Georgia congressman **Newt Gingrich** led the opposition to Clinton. Gingrich was bold and aggressive and not interested in compromising with the Democrats: "We will cooperate, but we won't compromise." Many people thought that Gingrich's goal of the Republicans gaining control of the House of Representatives in 1994 was a nearly impossible task. After all, the Democrats had controlled the House for 58 of the previous 62 years.

Gingrich, however, galvanized Republicans around his **Contract With America,** a plan that attacked big government and emphasized patriotism and traditional values. The Contract With America called for congressional term limits, reduction of the federal bureaucracy, a balanced budget amendment to the Constitution, and large tax cuts, as well as increased defense spending, significant welfare reform, and tough anticrime legislation. The idea was to capture the votes of Americans who felt the federal government was too big, too wasteful, and too liberal.

Capturing the 1994 Elections Although most eligible voters did not vote in 1994, there was a strong turnout among Republicans. For the first time in 40 years, the Republicans won control of the House. They also captured the Senate and most of the governorships. *Newsweek* magazine observed:

> **Primary Source** "Last week in one of the most profound electoral routs in American history, Republicans won the right to occupy the Capitol and mount what their . . . commanders think of as a counter-revolution: a full-scale attack on the notion that a central government should play a central role in the life of the nation."

Once in office, Republicans passed most of Gingrich's program, but their attempts to slash Medicare and other government programs proved unpopular. Many Americans were also upset when the government shut down in 1995 because Congress would not pass Clinton's budget. Meanwhile, Clinton incorporated some of the conservative agenda into his own 1996 reelection bid. He signed a bill to reform welfare, passed legislation that appropriated more money for law enforcement, and called for stiffer sentencing for criminals. Finally, he made balancing the budget and reducing the federal deficit a priority.

Clinton Wins Reelection Beginning in the mid-1990s, the American economy broke out of recession and began to soar, starting the longest period of sustained growth in the country's history. Americans benefited from low unemployment, low inflation levels, and the government's efforts to balance the budget and reduce the deficit. In 1994, Clinton's disapproval rating had exceeded 60 percent, and few expected him to win a second term. As the 1996 election approached, however, the booming economy meant that few Americans had a compelling reason to change leadership.

The Republicans nominated Senate Majority Leader Robert Dole, a World War II hero and a moderate Republican. H. Ross Perot entered the race as the Reform Party candidate. Clinton skillfully captured the middle ground, labeling Dole as an out-of-touch conservative and Perot as a political quack. On election day, Americans chose Clinton by a wide margin. The House of Representatives and Senate, however, retained their Republican majorities.

✔ **Checkpoint** How did the Republicans take control of Congress?

Scandals, Impeachment, and Trial

President Clinton had dodged scandals from his first days in office. One, a sexual harassment suit, had stemmed from his years as governor of Arkansas. Another concerned investments that Bill and Hillary Clinton had made in the Whitewater Development Corporation, an Arkansas real estate company, in the 1970s and 1980s.

Prosecuting Clinton A special prosecutor appointed by Attorney General Janet Reno investigated the Whitewater investment case and recommended that no criminal charges be filed. However, in July Congress passed a new law requiring that special prosecutors be selected by a three-judge panel from the U.S. Court of Appeals. As a result, in August of 1994 special prosecutor **Kenneth Starr** was appointed to investigate the case again. In seven years of investigation Starr failed to uncover any conclusive evidence of the Clintons' guilt, though some of their associates were convicted.

In the process of prosecuting Whitewater, Starr began investigating Clinton's relationship with a White House intern. Clinton had denied under oath that the two had an affair. Eventually, Clinton admitted that he had lied. The Whitewater case was quickly overshadowed by the new scandal. In 1998, Starr recommended **impeachment** proceedings on a number of counts, all related to the intern scandal rather than to Whitewater.

Impeaching the President Most Americans condemned Clinton's actions but opposed impeachment. Congressional Democrats, similarly, did not believe his behavior met the standard of "Treason, Bribery, or other high Crimes and Misdemeanors" required by the Constitution for the impeachment and removal of a President. Nevertheless, the House of Representatives, led by the Republican majority, impeached Clinton on the charges of perjury and obstruction of justice.

In January 1999, the Senate tried the President. The removal of a President requires a two-thirds majority of senators, and from the beginning it was clear that Clinton's opposition did not have the necessary votes. After a short trial, the President was acquitted on both counts on February 12.

✔ **Checkpoint** What was the outcome of the Clinton impeachment?

SECTION 2 Assessment

Progress Monitoring Online
For: Self-test with vocabulary practice
Web Code: nea-2021

Comprehension

1. **Terms and People** For each item below, write a sentence explaining how it relates to Clinton's presidency.
   - H. Ross Perot
   - Family Medical Leave Act
   - Brady Bill
   - Newt Gingrich
   - Contract With America
   - Kenneth Starr
   - impeachment

2. **NoteTaking Reading Skill: Summarize** Use your completed outline to answer the Section Focus Question: What were the successes and failures of the Clinton presidency?

Writing About History

3. **Quick Write: Form a Main Idea** This section touches on the American issue of social problems and reforms. Compare the scandals surrounding Clinton to historical scandals you have read about. Write down a main idea that you will present in your response.

Critical Thinking

4. **Identify Central Issues** How did Clinton position himself ideologically in order to win over both Democrats and Republicans in the 1992 election?

5. **Recognize Ideologies** On what domestic issues did Democrats and Republicans differ during Clinton's presidency?

6. **Synthesize Information** Why did Clinton win reelection?

7. **Summarize** Summarize the events surrounding Clinton's impeachment.

WITNESS HISTORY 🔊 AUDIO

Calling for a "Shared Future"

In 2000, the United Nations launched the Millennium Summit. The three-day event, held in New York City, was the largest gathering of world leaders in history. In the Millennium Declaration, they stated:

❝We believe that the central challenge we face today is to ensure that globalization becomes a positive force for all the world's people. For while globalization offers great opportunities, at present its benefits are very unevenly shared, while its costs are unevenly distributed. . . . [O]nly through broad and sustained efforts to create a shared future, based upon our common humanity in all its diversity, can globalization be made fully inclusive and equitable.❞
—Millennium Declaration, September 8, 2000

▲ Former White House official John Sununu meets with Saudi Arabian government leaders at a dinner during the Millennium Summit in New York City in 2000.

Global Politics and Economics

 Core Curriculum Objectives

- **7.VI.B.2** Clinton: Foreign policy issues
- **7.VI.B.2a** United States–Middle East relations
- **7.VI.B.2b** United States in the global economy: NAFTA, GATT
- **7.VI.B.2c** Intervention in Somalia, Haiti, Bosnia, and Yugoslavia

Terms and People

EU	WTO
NAFTA	ethnic cleansing
GATT	al Qaeda

NoteTaking

Reading Skill: Identify Main Ideas
Complete a flowchart like this one to help you identify main ideas about global politics and economics.

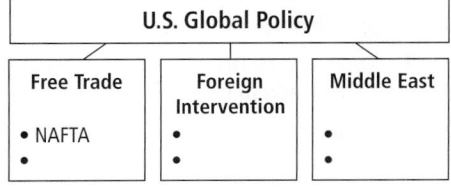

Why It Matters With the end of the Cold War, the United States was the sole superpower in a dramatically changing world. No longer defined by its opposition to communism, the United States had to carve out new roles for itself in a world of globalization and increasing regional conflict. President Clinton, the nation's first baby-boomer President, ushered in this new period of American soul-searching. **Section Focus Question: What role did the United States take on in global politics and economics following the Cold War?**

Competing in the Global Economy

In the 1990s, the United States was both an important promoter of global trade and an example for newly industrializing nations. As more nations participated in economic globalization, the United States tinkered with its own policies to ensure it remained an economic powerhouse.

The Role of Free Trade As an economic leader, America has had a major role in globalization. Free trade—the guiding principle of globalization—has been hotly debated in American politics. Americans want the lower costs that free trade creates but worry about the loss of American jobs to other countries. Generally, Republicans have supported the interests of big business and free trade agreements. Democrats have been more sympathetic to labor interests and have often opposed legislation that would cost American workers' jobs. Depending on which party has been in power, free trade has either been encouraged or hindered.

Bill Clinton challenged the traditional Democratic thinking by supporting free trade blocs, which in theory would increase the economic prosperity of particular regions. Europe was an example of such a bloc. In 1993, a number of European nations established the **European Union (EU)** to coordinate monetary and economic policies. By the end of the century, the EU had adopted a single currency, the euro, to promote economic efficiency. The EU's combined resources both encouraged trade among its members and challenged the economic leadership of the United States. North American free trade proponents believed a similar bloc would stimulate their own region.

America Joins NAFTA The **North American Free Trade Agreement (NAFTA),** a direct response to the EU was originally proposed during the Bush administration. President Bush and leaders of the other nations signed the agreement in 1992, but Congress blocked it. It called for a gradual removal of trade restrictions among the United States, Canada, and Mexico. NAFTA's supporters maintained that creating a free trade zone in North America would promote economic growth, reduce prices, increase exports, and encourage economic investment. Most labor leaders, environmentalists, and liberal Democrats argued that NAFTA would force American manufacturers to relocate to Mexico, where wages were lower and environmental controls were less rigid. They feared that hundreds of thousands of American jobs would be lost. President Clinton embraced NAFTA and pushed it through Congress. It went into effect in 1994, and since then the three countries have also signed agreements covering environmental protection, safety standards, and workers' rights.

Fourteen years later, with the removal of remaining trade restrictions between the United States and Mexico, the final provisions of NAFTA went into effect in January 2008.

Expanding Global Trade Clinton signed a total of 270 free trade agreements, including the revision of the **General Agreement on Tariffs and Trade (GATT)** in 1994 and the accords of the **World Trade Organization (WTO)** in 1995. GATT's goal was to reduce tariffs to promote free trade. The WTO replaced GATT, expanding the organization's authority to negotiate trade agreements, settle disputes, and enforce compliance with them. Clinton also continued the strong U.S. support of the World Bank.

Critics complain that the WTO and World Bank favor business interests over environmental concerns and workers' rights. At the 1999 WTO meeting in Seattle, protesters filled the streets, disrupting the proceedings. Yet most people agree that economic globalization has often had positive effects by exposing people to new ideas, technology, and communications. Nations involved in free trade have often become more democratic. Normalizing trade—engaging in free trade with countries rather than imposing sanctions based on disagreements—can strengthen economic ties. For example, normalizing trade with China has encouraged that country to adopt free market reforms.

Analyzing Political Cartoons

This political cartoon appeared as part of an intense national debate about the United States joining NAFTA.
1. What is the cartoonist's opinion about joining NAFTA?
2. Based on the cartoon, how would joining NAFTA affect the United States?

 Checkpoint Which trade blocs has the United States become involved with?

Americans on the Global Stage

When Bill Clinton became President, the more than 40-year-old American foreign policy of fighting communism had just ended. The United States needed to develop a role for itself in the post–Cold War world. Americans were willing to provide economic aid, as they did to nations of the former Soviet Union. But many of them questioned military <u>intervention</u> abroad, fearing a costly commitment like the Vietnam War. With violence surging in regional conflicts throughout the world, however, Clinton found it necessary to intervene. He did so with mixed success.

Vocabulary Builder
<u>intervention</u>–(ihn tuhr VEHN shuhn) *n.* becoming involved in the affairs of another nation, often by force

INFOGRAPHIC ◀))) AUDIO

The World Bank

The World Bank was founded in 1944 to help rebuild war-torn Europe. It still handles reconstruction efforts, as it did in India following a 2001 earthquake. ❶ Yet it has increasingly focused on issues facing developing countries, such as healthcare, human rights, debt relief, economic growth, and poverty. In Latin America, the Bank gives loans to people like this Peruvian man so they can own their own homes and businesses. ❷ Throughout the developing world, the Bank works to promote education for people like this Bulgarian girl. ❸

The U.S. has taken a primary role in the financing and management of the Bank. The Bank has its headquarters in Washington, D.C. As one of the Bank's most important partners, the U.S. has long seen the Bank and its work as integral to the American economy. Forty-five percent of U.S. exports go to developing countries in which the Bank is active, supporting American jobs. The U.S. also believes that strong and stable developing countries are vital to its own security.

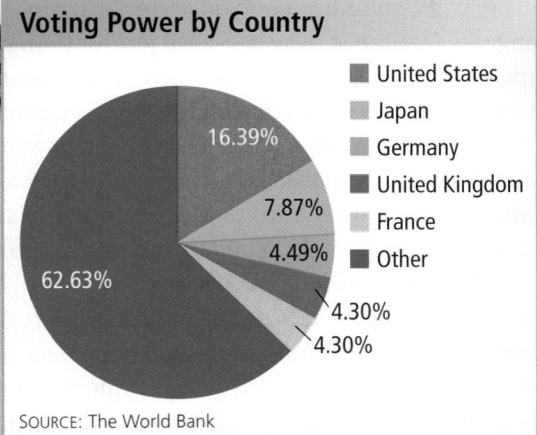

Voting Power by Country

- United States — 62.63%
- Japan — 16.39%
- Germany — 7.87%
- United Kingdom — 4.49%
- France — 4.30%
- Other — 4.30%

SOURCE: The World Bank

▲ Five of the Bank's 184 member countries take the lead in setting its direction. The chart shows the voting power for the Bank's Reconstruction and Development department. As with the World Bank's four other departments, the United States has the most voting power.

▼ A Senegalese family picks tomatoes on land that used to be plagued by drought. The Bank worked with governments and local communities to make the land usable and promote agriculture.

Thinking Critically

1. **Analyze Information** What kinds of work does the World Bank do?

2. **Draw Inferences** Why is it in America's interest to support the World Bank?

Intervening in Somalia and Haiti In the late 1980s, civil war broke out in Somalia. By 1991, the government had disintegrated and the fighting had caused widespread famine. In 1992, the United States led a multinational force, later joined by the UN, to bring about peace and distribute food. The coalition fell apart in 1994 when several countries, including the United States, suffered steep casualty rates and withdrew their troops. Eventually, the UN also withdrew, and civil war dragged on for several more years in the devastated country.

Meanwhile, conflict was simmering in Haiti. In 1990, Haitians brought Jean-Bertrand Aristide to the presidency, in the nation's first free elections. Less than a year later, a military coup overthrew Aristide, plunging the country into turmoil. Thousands of Haitians left the country by boat to immigrate to the United States as political refugees. Many were sent back by American immigration officials, causing a public outcry. In 1994, Clinton sent American troops to Haiti to restore Aristide to power. Although American action improved the situation, within a decade Haiti faced a sinking economy and rising rates of disease and crime.

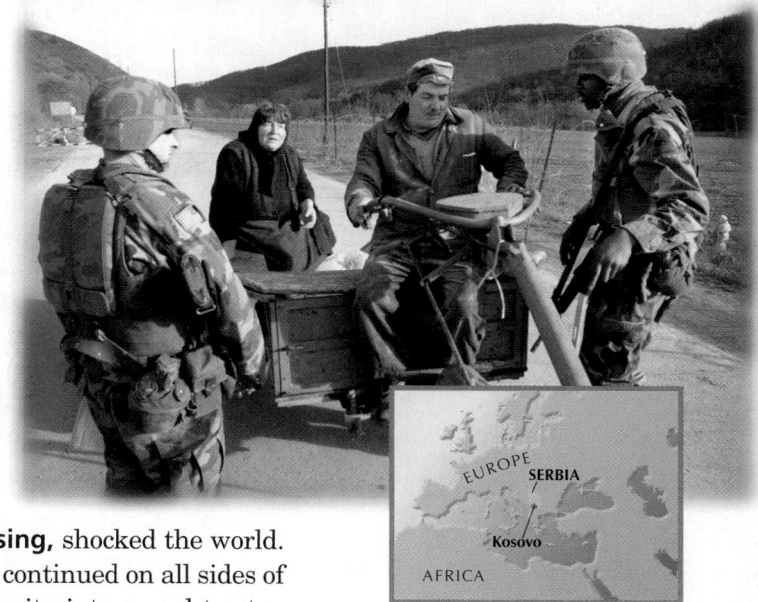

NATO in the Balkans
American soldiers monitor a border crossing between Serbia and Kosovo in 2001.

Fighting Ethnic Cleansing in Eastern Europe
In the Balkans, the collapse of communism broke up the country of Yugoslavia. For decades, the communist leader Tito had contained ethnic and religious strife. But his death in 1980, and the collapse of communism in 1989, left the country with no unifying forces. Soon, four of Yugoslavia's six major republics formed their own states, and long-suppressed ethnic and religious hostilities came boiling to the surface.

In newly independent Bosnia, ethnic and religious rivalries among Eastern Orthodox Serbs, Catholic Croats, and Bosnian Muslims eventually led to civil war. Serbs, with the help of Serbia-dominated Yugoslavia, attacked Bosnians and Croats. In many cases, they forcibly removed Bosnians and Croats from their homes and later murdered them. This state-sanctioned mass murder, violence, and rape, known as **ethnic cleansing,** shocked the world. The UN intervened with humanitarian aid. Yet atrocities continued on all sides of the struggle, and years went by before the world community intervened to stop the slaughter.

Galvanizing NATO Forces Finally, in the late summer of 1995, Clinton encouraged NATO to bomb Serbian strongholds. This was the first time the organization had gone into combat, and its use of force quickly brought about a cease-fire. In December 1995, the Dayton Accords established a federated, multinational Bosnia. Although the ethnic cleansing had ended, the enforced peace had not solved the problems of the region. In 1998, violence flared up anew— this time in Kosovo, a Serbian province on the Adriatic Sea. The fighting once again involved ethnic cleansing and also spread to the neighboring countries of Macedonia and Albania. NATO forced Serbs to withdraw from Kosovo.

✓ **Checkpoint** How did Clinton involve the United States in foreign conflicts?

America and the Middle East

In the 1990s, disputes and fighting between Israelis and Palestinians grew increasingly fierce. The conflict had increased instability in the region as a whole. As Clinton worked to address it, violence originating in the region spread outward, with the United States increasingly a target.

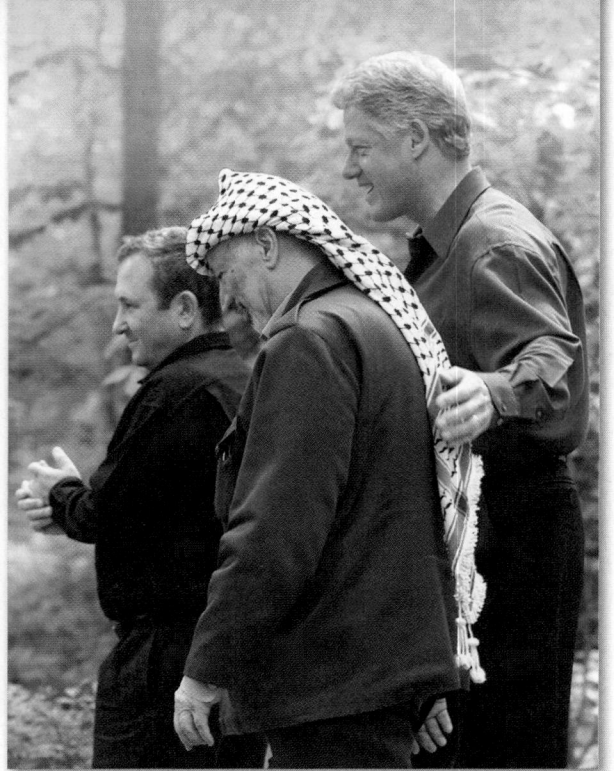

Camp David Talks
President Clinton walks with Ehud Barak and Yasir Arafat in the woods of Camp David in July 2000.

Trying for Peace in Israel In 1993, Palestinians and Israelis conducted secret negotiations in Oslo, Norway. The resulting Declaration of Principles promised Palestinian self-rule in Jericho and the Gaza Strip, as well as security for the Israelis. The declaration did not address Israeli settlement of the West Bank, a major issue that led to chronic violence, nor did it in any way placate extremists on both sides who had no interest in compromising. Israeli prime minister Yitzhak Rabin, who had signed the declaration, fell victim to the fury in 1995 when an Israeli religious fundamentalist assassinated him.

In 2000, Clinton invited Palestinian leader Yasir Arafat and Israeli prime minister Ehud Barak to Camp David to work on a peace agreement. They came close to signing one, but Arafat was not satisfied with any of the proposals. Back in Israel, Barak was ousted by Ariel Sharon, a "hawk" who opposed any concessions to the Palestinians. Palestinian suicide bombings increased, and with them so did crackdowns by the Israeli military.

Dealing With Terrorism In 1993, a terrorist group called **al Qaeda** exploded a bomb in the World Trade Center in New York City, killing six people and injuring more than one thousand others. Al Qaeda was led by a wealthy Saudi businessman named Osama bin Laden. Bin Laden had fought in Afghanistan in the 1980s on the side of Islamic fundamentalists who sought to expel the Soviet Union. By the late 1990s, he had formed al Qaeda with the purpose of ending American involvement in Muslim countries. Five years after the U.S. bombing, al Qaeda set off car bombs at American embassies in Nairobi, Kenya, and in Dar es Salaam, Tanzania. The blasts killed 225 people and injured more than 5,500 others. In 2000, al Qaeda bombed the USS *Cole,* an American warship anchored off the coast of Yemen, killing 17 American sailors. These attacks angered Americans and frustrated politicians, who were learning that fighting terrorism would be extremely difficult.

✔ **Checkpoint** What strategic, political, and economic interests did the United States have in the Middle East?

---

3 Assessment

Progress Monitoring *Online*
For: Self-test with vocabulary practice
Web Code: nea-2031

Comprehension

1. **Terms and People** For each term below, write a sentence describing what effect it has on the global economy or global society.
   - EU
   - NAFTA
   - GATT
   - WTO
   - ethnic cleansing
   - al Qaeda

2. **NoteTaking Reading Skill: Identify Main Ideas** Use your completed flowchart to answer the Section Focus Question: What role did the United States take on in global politics and economics following the Cold War?

Writing About History

3. **Quick Write: Plan a Structure** Compare the issue of America and the world in the context of this section with how it related to an earlier period in American history. Choose the best way to structure your comparison, such as point by point or topic by topic.

Critical Thinking

4. **Identify Central Issues** Why have efforts to reduce tariffs and trade barriers often been controversial in the United States?

5. **Identify Assumptions** What basic assumption about the U.S. role as sole superpower underlies American peacekeeping efforts of the 1990s?

6. **Analyze Information** For what various reasons has the United States become involved in Middle Eastern affairs?

1118   Into a New Century

WITNESS HISTORY 🔊 AUDIO

A Two-Term President

In 2005, George W. Bush was sworn in as President for a second term. In his inaugural address, he alluded to a remarkable shift in traditional American foreign policy, saying that the cause of advancing freedom and democracy abroad was sufficient reason for the United States to involve itself in conflict overseas.

❝All who live in tyranny and hopelessness can know: the United States will not ignore your oppression, or excuse your oppressors. When you stand for your liberty, we will stand with you.❞

—George W. Bush, Second Inaugural Address, 2005

▲ Bush's casual style attracted voters in both of his presidential races. By his reelection in 2004, he was often referred to simply as "W."

The George W. Bush Presidency

Core Curriculum Objectives

- **1.I.D.1** U.S. demographics: characteristics
- **2.I.E.4** Civil liberties—balance between government and the individual
- **2.I.E.9** Presidential power in wartime and in foreign affairs
- **7.V.C.2** The growth of conservatism: tax policy and deficits

Terms and People

George W. Bush
Bush v. *Gore*
No Child Left Behind Act
Afghanistan

Taliban
Patriot Act
Department of Homeland Security
WMD

NoteTaking

Reading Skill: Recognize Sequence Record the sequence of events in Bush's presidency in a flowchart like the one below.

> The 2000 election is disputed but leads to victory for George W. Bush.

> Bush launches an ambitious agenda including tax cuts and education legislation.

Why It Matters The election of **George W. Bush** to the presidency assured Republican domination of the White House and Congress. When the United States was attacked on September 11, 2001, Bush would use this unity—along with the support of a galvanized American public—to move the nation in a new direction. **Section Focus Question: What was the impact of Bush's domestic agenda and his response to the terrorist attack against the United States?**

An Election Controversy

The year 2000 brought an end to Clinton's two terms as President. Clinton's legacy of a strong economy coupled with personal scandal polarized voters. As candidates geared up for the 2000 presidential race, it promised to be a close election.

Three Candidates Run Clinton's Vice President, Al Gore, Jr., of Tennessee, ran for the Democrats. Gore selected Connecticut senator Joseph Lieberman as his Vice President, making Lieberman the first Jewish person to be on the ticket of a major party. Gore tried to associate himself with the economic record of the Clinton administration while distancing himself from Clinton's personal scandals.

The Republicans chose George W. Bush as their candidate. A son of George H.W. Bush and a former governor of Texas, Bush was popular with party leaders, conservatives, and Christian fundamentalists. As governor of Texas, he had been adept at working with Democrats as well as Republicans. Although he was not a gifted orator, he struck many Americans as down-to-earth and sincere.

Consumer advocate Ralph Nader ran for the Green Party. Saying that corporate interests controlled the two major parties, he claimed he alone represented all Americans.

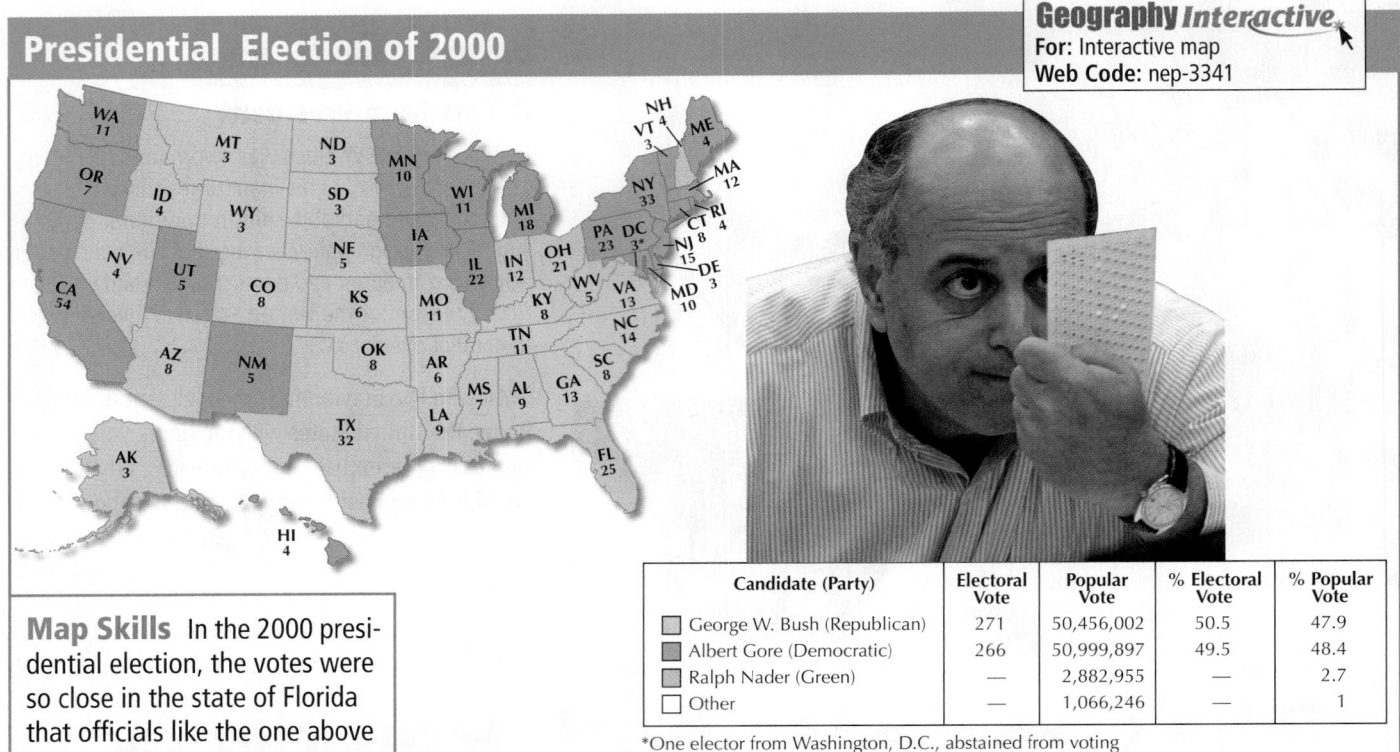

Presidential Election of 2000

Candidate (Party)	Electoral Vote	Popular Vote	% Electoral Vote	% Popular Vote
George W. Bush (Republican)	271	50,456,002	50.5	47.9
Albert Gore (Democratic)	266	50,999,897	49.5	48.4
Ralph Nader (Green)	—	2,882,955	—	2.7
Other	—	1,066,246	—	1

*One elector from Washington, D.C., abstained from voting

Map Skills In the 2000 presidential election, the votes were so close in the state of Florida that officials like the one above recounted ballots by hand. Although Al Gore wound up winning the popular vote, George Bush captured a greater number of electoral votes, winning him the presidency.

1. **Identify** In general, which regions voted for Bush? Which voted for Gore?

2. **Predict Consequences** How might the dispute over the 2000 election affect future elections?

A Tight Race The campaigns focused mainly on how to spend the federal budget surplus. Bush wanted to use it to institute widespread tax cuts, while Gore proposed strengthening Social Security and paying down the national debt. Bush also said that a Republican President would restore morality to the White House. None of the candidates had the appeal of former Presidents Reagan or Clinton. Bush tended to mispronounce words, and Gore appeared dull and cold. On election night, Americans voted mainly by party affiliation.

The vote margin in the Electoral College was razor thin. Although Gore received a half million more votes than Bush, he fell short of winning the 270 electoral votes needed to capture the presidency. So did Bush. The issue was Florida's 25 electoral votes. Gore ran strong in the cities and along the coast, but Bush won the suburbs and the center of the state. The popular vote in Florida was so close that a state law mandated an automatic statewide recount of votes. Bush led by a margin of 327 popular votes. He was awarded a total of 271 electoral votes, one more than was needed to win the election.

The Supreme Court Intervenes Given the extreme closeness of the votes, Democrats demanded a hand, rather than machine, recount in several Florida counties. Republicans countered by suing in a Miami district court to prevent the hand recount. For more than a month, confusion reigned as each charge prompted a countercharge. Finally, the Supreme Court ruled on the issue. In the case of Bush v. Gore, the court ended the re-recounting by a 5-to-4 decision. On December 12, 2000, Gore conceded defeat, and Bush delivered a conciliatory victory speech. The election showed an interesting geographical pattern. The Democrats captured votes in their traditional strongholds such as the two coasts and large cities. The Republicans had extended their influence, winning voters in a large bloc that included most of the Midwest and the South.

✔ **Checkpoint** Why did the Supreme Court decide the 2000 presidential election?

Bush Launches an Ambitious Agenda

Once in office, Bush turned to the domestic issues that most concerned him, including using Clinton's budget surplus to finance tax cuts. Like most Republicans, Bush believed that tax cuts would stimulate the economy. He felt they would provide Americans with more disposable income, leading to greater spending, heavier investment, and the creation of new jobs. In 2001, Bush successfully pushed a $1.3 trillion tax cut through Congress. The cut was highly controversial. It did put more money in the hands of consumers. Yet coming on the heels of a declining economy, it also increased federal budget deficits.

Bush's other domestic priority was education. He favored legislation that tied the federal funding of schools to demonstrable academic success. The 2002 **No Child Left Behind Act,** which attracted bipartisan support, held schools accountable by penalizing those that did not reach federal performance standards. It also called for improving teacher quality and for making information about schools more readily available to parents.

Bush also addressed the concern of older Americans who were caught between their relatively fixed incomes and the rising costs of prescription drugs. In 2003, Congress extended Medicare to cover prescription drugs for senior citizens. Like his tax cuts, the measure was controversial. It was expensive, creating further budget deficits, and many seniors found its provisions confusing and its coverage inadequate.

✓ **Checkpoint** What were Bush's domestic priorities?

Comparing Viewpoints

Should President Bush's Tax Cuts Be Passed?

President Bush's tax cuts sharply divided Americans into two camps—those who agreed with the cuts and those who opposed them.

Primary Source

Primary Source

Compare

1. In the cartoon on the left, the artist mocks Democrats for overreacting to the tax cuts. How does he do this?

2. Who does the artist of the cartoon on the right imply is the main beneficiary of Bush's tax cuts?

The United States Is Attacked

Bush had been in office less than a year when the United States was attacked by a foreign enemy for the first time since Pearl Harbor. Following the hijacking and crashing of four commercial airplanes on September 11, 2001, millions of Americans rushed to donate money, supplies, services, and their own blood. As it became clear that the crashes were part of an organized terrorist attack on the United States, Americans responded as they had after Pearl Harbor—as a unified, determined nation. The attack challenged the new President in unforeseen ways and led to a major shift in American foreign policy. On the day of the attacks, President Bush addressed the nation:

Events That Changed America

The Terrorist Attacks of 9/11

Shortly before 9 A.M. Eastern time on September 11, 2001, American Airline Flight 11 slammed into the north tower of the World Trade Center in New York City. The crash was the first of four airplane crashes in an orchestrated attack against the United States. Just over an hour after the first crash, the World Trade Center began to collapse, trapping the hundreds of firefighters and police who had gone into rescue people. Meanwhile, passengers on another hijacked plane, after learning of the crashes on their cell phones, bravely stormed the cockpit to prevent hijackers targeting another building.

This attack was the first on American soil since the Japanese bombed Pearl Harbor 50 years ago. More than 3,000 Americans died in the attacks. American's confidence in their nation's power and safety was deeply shaken.

◀ Terrified workers run away from the collapsing World Trade towers.

Thinking Critically
1. **Expressing Problems Clearly** Why was September 11, 2001, an "event that changed America"?
2. **Draw Inferences** After the attacks, a French newspaper declared "We are all Americans." What was meant by this statement?

"Today, our fellow citizens, our way of life, and our very freedom came under attack in a series of deliberate and deadly terrorist acts. . . . Thousands of lives were suddenly ended by evil, despicable acts of terror. . . . These acts of mass murder were intended to frighten our nation into chaos and retreat. But they have failed. . . . Terrorist attacks can shake the foundations of our biggest buildings, but they cannot touch the foundation of America. These acts shatter steel, but they cannot dent the steel of American resolve."

—President George W. Bush, September 11, 2001

✓ **Checkpoint** **What was the significance of September 11, 2001?**

America's War on Terrorism

In the wake of September 11, Bush and his advisers agreed that the most important priority should be finding and prosecuting the people behind 9/11. This would be just the first step in what Bush called the "war on terrorism."

Invading Afghanistan American government officials quickly determined that Osama bin Laden's al Qaeda network had been behind the September 11 attacks. Bin Laden opposed the presence of American troops in Saudi Arabia, the U.S. economic boycott against Iraq, and U.S. support for Israel. He also opposed any governments in the Middle East that he felt were pro-Western. Bin Laden and other al Qaeda leaders were believed to be hiding in Afghanistan, where the Islamic fundamentalist **Taliban** government allowed them to operate training camps for terrorists.

Bush believed that any government that sponsored terrorism, even if it did not itself commit terrorist acts, should be held accountable. He immediately demanded that the Taliban turn over bin Laden to U.S. custody. When the Taliban refused, he quickly sent American forces, joined by Great Britain and other allies, into Afghanistan. Joined by Afghan rebels, the allied forces overthrew the Taliban within three months. Although American troops captured several of al Qaeda's leaders, bin Laden himself escaped. While Afghanistan held its first free elections and wrote a new constitution, the United States still faced the threat of terrorism elsewhere.

Improving National Security Bush also moved quickly on the home front to prevent future terrorist attacks. Soon after September 11, Congress passed the **Patriot Act** to give law enforcement broader powers to monitor suspected terrorists. Congress also approved Bush's call for the creation of a new Cabinet-level **Department of Homeland Security** to coordinate domestic security matters among a number of federal, state, and local agencies. Some critics charged that the Patriot Act violated civil liberties, but most Americans were willing to give up some freedoms in return for improved protection against attack.

Launching Operation Iraqi Freedom Bush next turned his attention to Iraq. In the decade after the first Gulf War, Iraqi dictator Saddam Hussein had defied UN weapons inspectors. Many people both inside and outside of the Bush administration believed that Saddam was constructing and stockpiling nuclear, biological, and chemical **Weapons of Mass Destruction (WMD)**. Bush contemplated invading Iraq as part of his wider war on terrorism.

Despite many Americans' belief that UN weapons inspectors should be allowed to continue their search for WMD, in October of 2002 Congress authorized Bush to use American military forces against Iraq. On March 19, 2003, American and British military forces invaded Iraq in Operation Iraqi Freedom.

The United States and the Middle East

War in Iraq, 2003

April 14, 2003 Tikrit falls. Pentagon announces that major combat operations are over.

April 9, 2003 Fall of Baghdad

March 20, 2003 Explosions in Baghdad mark the beginning of U.S.-led operations.

March 23, 2003 First significant casualties during battle in An Nasiriyah.

Predominately Kurdish

Predominately Sunni Arab

Predominately Shia Arab

→ Advance by the U.S. and allies

✸ Major bombing target

Miller Projection
0   100   200 mi
0   100 200 km

War in Afghanistan, 2001–2002

November 9, 2001 Battle for Mazar-e Sharif.

December 7, 2001 Kandahar, the last Taliban controlled city, falls.

October 7, 2001 U.S. and British forces begin aerial bombing campaign of Taliban sites.

→ Advance by the U.S.

→ Advance by the Northern Alliance

✸ Major bombing target

Miller Projection
0   100   200 mi
0   100 200 km

U.S. ally

Unstable relations with United States

Miller Projection
0   250   500 mi
0   250 500 km

Map Skills

In the early 2000s, the United States waged two wars in the Middle East.

1. **Locate:** (a) Baghdad, (b) Kabul, (c) Pakistan, (d) Syria

2. **Location** Describe the location of Baghdad. What difficulty might a Baghdad-based government have keeping peace?

3. **Draw Inferences** Notice the location of Pakistan. Why is it important to the United States that Pakistan remain a reliable ally?

Geography *Interactive*

For: Interactive map
Web Code: nep-2043

Saddam's forces collapsed almost immediately. As the Iraqi capital of Baghdad fell, Saddam and the other Iraqi leaders went into hiding. Bush gave a victory speech on May 1, 2003, in front of a banner reading "mission accomplished." In the months that followed, Saddam and many of his supporters were captured.

✓ **Checkpoint** How did Bush combat terrorism?

Bush's Second Term

The Iraq war, terrorism, and the budget weighed heavily on Americans' minds as they cast their votes in the 2004 election.

Bush relied heavily on his image as a "war president," saying that the lack of an attack on American soil since 9/11 proved his competency as commander in chief. The Democratic candidate, Massachusetts senator John F. Kerry, was a decorated Vietnam veteran with many more years of political experience than Bush. His message never fully resonated with Americans, however, and Bush defeated Kerry by a comfortable margin. Once again, the U.S. electoral map indicated what many began to call a "red state, blue state" divide, with people along the coasts and in the big cities voting Democratic, and people in the South, Midwest, and rural areas voting Republican.

Iraq remained the major focus of Bush's second term. Saddam's brutal rule kept fighting among Iraq's three major groups: Sunnis, Shi'a, and Kurds in check. With Saddam's overthrow, these groups fought bitterly for power. By the end of 2005, Iraq had written a new constitution and established the beginnings of a democracy. But the chaos continued. Saddam went into hiding, but was soon captured. After a lengthy trial, Iraq's High Tribunal sentenced him to death for crimes against humanity. Saddam was executed in 2006.

By early 2004, the United Nations had determined that Saddam had never possessed nuclear weapons or the materials to make them. Critics of Bush charged that he had exaggerated evidence of WMD and misled Congress and the American people in his effort to win support for the war. Even those who agreed that the war was necessary worried that the United States had gotten itself into a quagmire.

Meanwhile, Bush faced serious domestic challenges. With so much money being spent on Iraq, the federal deficit grew larger. In August of 2005, Hurricane Katrina hit the Gulf Coast, destroying much of the city of New Orleans. The government response to Katrina, which largely affected poor people, was slow. National discontent was reflected in the 2006 Congressional elections in which Democrats, for the first time in 12 years, won control of both the House and the Senate.

During the final two years of his second term, Bush's approval ratings fell dramatically. By 2008 Americans faced serious problems. Wars in Afghanistan and Iraq, possible spread of nuclear weapons, and the continuing threat of terrorists stretched American resources. At home, healthcare concerns, the cost of oil, immigration problems, and the economy added to American worries.

✓ **Checkpoint** What challenges did Bush face in his second term?

The 2008 Election

The 2008 election broke new ground in America's political landscape. In the primary campaign, Senator Hillary Rodham Clinton became the first woman to win a major party's presidential primary. She came close to winning the Democratic nomination for president. Meanwhile, Democrat Barack Obama became the first African American to be nominated for president by a major party. Finally, Governor Sarah Palin of Alaska was the second woman, since Geraldine Ferraro in 1984 to be selected as a Vice Presidential running mate.

The Candidates In the 2008 presidential race, Republican John McCain and Democrat Barack Obama advanced different solutions to key issues such as the wars in Iraq and Afghanistan, the economy, healthcare, and energy policy. But they shared a firm belief in service to their country. McCain, the son and grandson of navy admirals, served as a pilot in the Vietnam War. He also endured six years as a prisoner of war in North Vietnam after his plane was shot down. After his release, he entered politics to continue to serve his country.

After graduating from Columbia University and Harvard Law School, Obama worked as a community organizer on the south side of Chicago. He set up programs to aid minorities and the poor. Like McCain,

HISTORY MAKERS

Condoleezza Rice (born 1954)
Condoleezza Rice grew up in segregated Birmingham, Alabama. At age 15, she entered college intending to become a concert pianist but graduated at age 19 with a degree in political science instead. By age 30, she had earned a Ph.D., served as an intern in the Carter administration, and held a professorship at Stanford University. In 2000, Rice was tapped by George W. Bush to become National Security Advisor. In 2004, she became the first African American woman to be named Secretary of State. Dr. Rice has taken an active role in the U.S. rebuilding of Iraq.

In a decisive victory, Barack Obama became the nation's first African American President.

he entered politics to fulfill a commitment to solving America's foreign and domestic problems.

An Historic Moment On January 20, 2009, Barack Obama became the 44th President and the first African American to hold the office. Speaking at a huge rally in Chicago after winning the race, his words defined the historic moment. "If there is anyone out there who still doubts that America is a place where all things are possible, who still wonders if the dream of our founders is alive in our time, who still questions the power of our democracy, tonight is your answer."

Obama's victory not only marked a shift in American politics but reflected the changed national mood. The election drew a huge voter turnout, with an unexpectedly large participation of young voters. Along with the economic crisis—nearly 62% of voters cited the economy as a major concern—and with the low approval ratings of President Bush, a Republican victory seemed almost impossible.

In Congress, the Democratic Party, which won a majority of seats in 2006, expanded its majority in the 2008 election.

Banking Crisis

During the last month of the 2008 campaign both candidates faced a disturbing, and potentially disastrous, economic crisis centered on Wall Street and in the banking industry. The causes of the crisis that flared up stemmed from a series of risky bank loans and a general decline in the value of many American homes. As a result, millions of Americans could not pay their home mortgages. Several important banking and investment firms who had engaged in the risky lending policies were either forced out of business or bought by other firms. Congress passed legislation that attempted to solve the problem but the crisis defied any quick-fix solutions. By the time of the election the crisis had spread around the world. The situation was so serious that many people considered it to be the worst economic crisis since the Great Depression.

 Checkpoint Why was the 2008 election significant?

SECTION 4 Assessment

Progress Monitoring *Online*
For: Self-test with vocabulary practice
Web Code: nea-2041

Comprehension

1. **Terms and People** Using complete sentences, relate each of the following items to the presidency of George W. Bush.
   - No Child Left Behind Act
   - Taliban
   - Patriot Act
   - Department of Homeland Security
   - WMD

2. **NoteTaking Reading Skill: Recognize Sequence** Use your completed flowchart to answer the Section Focus Question: What was the impact of Bush's domestic agenda and his response to the terrorist attack against the United States?

Writing About History

3. **Quick Write: Provide Details** Choose an American issue that has relevance both to the Bush presidency and to an earlier period of American history. Analyze the issue in both time periods, including details that define the issue and support your points.

Critical Thinking

4. **Compare Points of View** Compare how Democrats and Republicans viewed the initial results of the 2000 election.

5. **Analyzing Effects** Why do you think the economic crisis in the United States in 2008 had a global effect? Explain.

6. **Identify Assumptions** What assumptions about the United States were conveyed in Bush's speech to the nation on September 11?

7. **Recognize Cause and Effect** How did the September 11 attacks influence American policy in the Middle East?

WITNESS HISTORY 🔊 AUDIO

Finding the American Dream

In 1990, Eddie (Duc) and Linda (Lieu) Tran left Vietnam with their young son to start over in Columbus, Ohio. Sponsored by Linda's brother, who had fled Vietnam by boat during the fall of Saigon in 1975, the Trans were aware of the obstacles that faced them in their new country.

❝Learning the English language and finding jobs were our biggest challenges. We listened to the radio and tried to converse as much as possible with our co-workers to learn English. Everyone was helpful. And we were determined never to receive welfare. Linda got a job as a tailor ten days after we arrived. I owned a manufacturing business in Vietnam, but it took me six months to get employed here. Times were hard, and we still work 12-hour days in our restaurant now. But the best thing about this country is freedom. If you work hard, you can achieve the American dream.❞

—Eddie and Linda Tran, 2005

▲ The Trans today (above) with their sons and at their wedding in Vietnam (left).

Americans Look to the Future

 Core Curriculum Objectives

- **1.I.D.2** Immigration
- **2.I.E.6** Equality—its historic and present meaning as a constitutional value
- **7.V.D.3** The "new" immigrants (Immigration Reform and Control Act of 1986)
- **7.V.D.4** Changing demographic patterns (growing numbers of elderly)

Terms and People

Immigration Act of 1990
bilingual education
Immigration and Control Act of 1986

affirmative action
Violence Against Women Act
privatize

NoteTaking

Reading Skill: Identify Supporting Details
Record supporting details about the changing American society in a table like this one.

A Changing Society	
Immigration	**Demographics**
• Immigration policies relax	• Family structures change
•	•

Why It Matters As the twenty-first century dawned, American society looked very different from the way it had during the previous century. It also faced different challenges. As the nation entered the new millennium, it sought ways to preserve its heritage while at the same time adapting to rapid social, political, and technological change. **Section Focus Question: How was American society changing at the beginning of the twenty-first century?**

Immigrants Shape a Nation

For two centuries, American protection of religious and personal freedom, along with opportunities for social and economic mobility, has attracted huge numbers of immigrants. Over time, however, the nature of immigration has changed.

Immigration Policies Change For years, the government limited immigration to mainly northern and western Europeans. In the 1960s, however, laws began to relax immigration limitations. The **Immigration Act of 1990** increased quotas by 40 percent and eased most remaining restrictions. As a result, the period from the 1990s to the 2000s saw the largest numbers of immigrants in the country's history. During that time, almost one million immigrants arrived in America each year from all over the globe, representing a wide variety of cultures and religions. Today, immigrants account for more than 10 percent of the total American population.

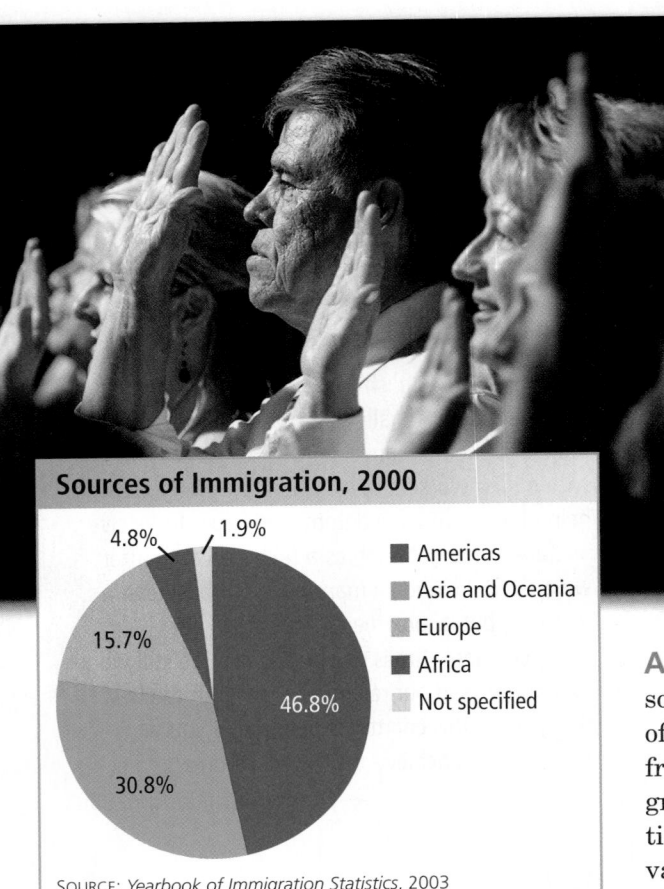

Sources of Immigration, 2000

- 4.8%
- 1.9%
- 15.7%
- 46.8%
- 30.8%

Legend:
- Americas
- Asia and Oceania
- Europe
- Africa
- Not specified

SOURCE: *Yearbook of Immigration Statistics*, 2003

U.S. Population by Race, 2000

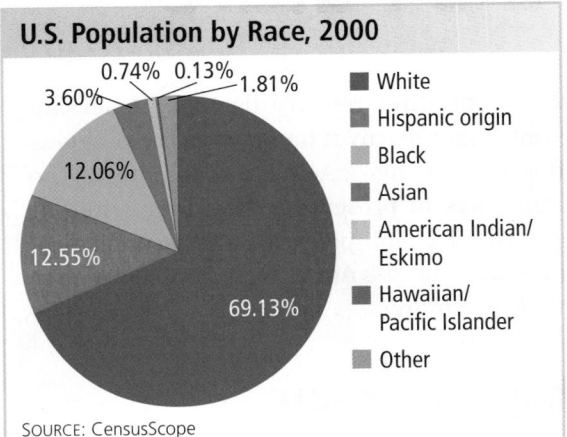

- 0.74%
- 0.13%
- 1.81%
- 3.60%
- 12.06%
- 12.55%
- 69.13%

Legend:
- White
- Hispanic origin
- Black
- Asian
- American Indian/ Eskimo
- Hawaiian/ Pacific Islander
- Other

SOURCE: CensusScope

Graph Skills Every year, people from all backgrounds are sworn in as U.S. citizens. Study the two pie charts. What was the largest minority group in 2000? How does the Sources of Immigration graph support the data in the U.S. Population by Race graph?

Latinos Exert Their Influence Most of the new immigrants were Latinos. In 2000, 27 percent of the total immigrant population were Mexicans, with people from the Caribbean and Central America making up almost 17 percent. Mexicans and Central Americans settled largely in the South and Southwest. Caribbean immigrants, many of them Cubans, settled in Florida. The census of 2000 showed that a third or more of the residents of Texas, New Mexico, Arizona, and California were Latinos.

Like all immigrants, Latinos have varying educational and employment backgrounds. Often they are forced to take lower-paying jobs with no healthcare benefits. However, Latino immigrants have had a profound social, cultural, and political impact. By 2001, Latinos held about 5,000 political offices and 4 percent of the seats in Congress, primarily as Democrats. Cuban Americans in Florida, generally Republican, have had an enormous influence on American political policy concerning Cuba.

A Surging Asian Population Asians make up the second-largest source of the new immigration. In 2000, they were nearly 23 percent of the total immigrant population, with the largest numbers coming from China, the Philippines, and India. The majority of Asian immigrants have settled in California, adding to the large Asian population in that state. As a group, Asian immigrants have had widely varying backgrounds, but overall they have the highest level of education. Some came to America with college degrees and marketable skills and found professional jobs. Others came from war-torn countries, with very little education.

Debating Immigration Immigration has long been debated in this country. People who would restrict it worry that immigrants take jobs and social services away from native-born Americans. They generally oppose **bilingual education,** in which students are taught in their native languages as well as in English, saying that immigrants must learn English in order to assimilate into American society. Proponents point out that immigrants contribute to the economy, often by taking jobs no one else wants. They also argue that with the U.S. birthrate falling immigrants help the country by maintaining its population.

Much of the debate concerns illegal immigrants. A large number of immigrants to the United States, especially Latinos, have come illegally. They labor in low-paying jobs, such as migrant farmwork, and receive no benefits. The **Immigration Reform and Control Act of 1986** hoped to stop the flow of illegal immigrants by penalizing employers who hired them and by granting resident status to those residing in the United States since 1982. But illegal immigrants still regularly cross U.S. borders. How to treat these illegal—but often necessary—workers is an ongoing debate. In 2008, the Bush administration proposed changes that would make it easier for farm employers to legally hire immigrant workers. He also proposed a process by which illegal immigrants could eventually gain citizenship.

✓ **Checkpoint** How has immigration to America changed over time?

Changing American Demographics

At the beginning of 2000, Americans were on the move more than ever. Coastal cities as well as the Sunbelt, or the region of warm southern and southwestern states, saw rapid population and economic growth as people left the cold Northeast and the Rust Belt. Meanwhile, the family itself was changing.

The Changing Family In 1960, more than 70 percent of American households were headed by a working father and a nonworking mother, neither of whom had ever been divorced. By 2000, fewer than 15 percent of households fit this model. In 2000, one out of every two marriages ended in divorce, and in a high percentage of households both parents worked outside the home. Single-parent households were far more common, with a quarter of all children growing up in a single-parent household. The number of children born to unmarried mothers also rose. In 1960, only 5 percent of children were born out of wedlock. In 2000, one out of every four white babies, one out of every three Latino babies, and two out of every three African American babies were born to unmarried mothers.

Debating Affirmative Action In the 1960s, President Johnson introduced the idea of **affirmative action,** or improving opportunities for women and minorities by giving preference to them in school admissions and job applications. Since that time, affirmative action has been hotly debated. Proponents argue that without such initiatives, minorities cannot overcome generations of <u>discrimination</u>. Opponents say that the policy is unfair and discriminates against nonminorities. In 1996, Californians voted to end affirmative action in state hiring and education. That same year, a federal court struck down an affirmative action admissions program at the University of Texas. In 2003, however, the Supreme Court decided in two cases involving the University of Michigan that while race could not be the deciding factor in admissions, it could be one of several factors.

Vocabulary Builder
discrimination–(dih skrihm ih NAY shuhn) *n.* unfair bias in the treatment of a particular group

Expanding Rights for All At the turn of the new century, African Americans and women continued to make social and political gains. By 2002, 33 percent of African American families enjoyed incomes of at least $50,000, placing them in the middle class. Also in 2002, 17 percent of African Americans over the age of 25 held bachelor's degrees. At the same time, legislation to enforce equal pay for equal work, address child care needs for working women, and end sexual harassment in the workplace has improved the lives of working women. Outside of the world of work, women have also achieved victories. Issues such as spouse abuse and date rape are now widely discussed. Incidents of violence against women are more often reported and more often punished than ever before.

Graph Skills While the income gap is slowly narrowing, wages among ethnic groups still vary widely. Study the graph. Which group enjoyed the highest income in the period shown? What might explain this?

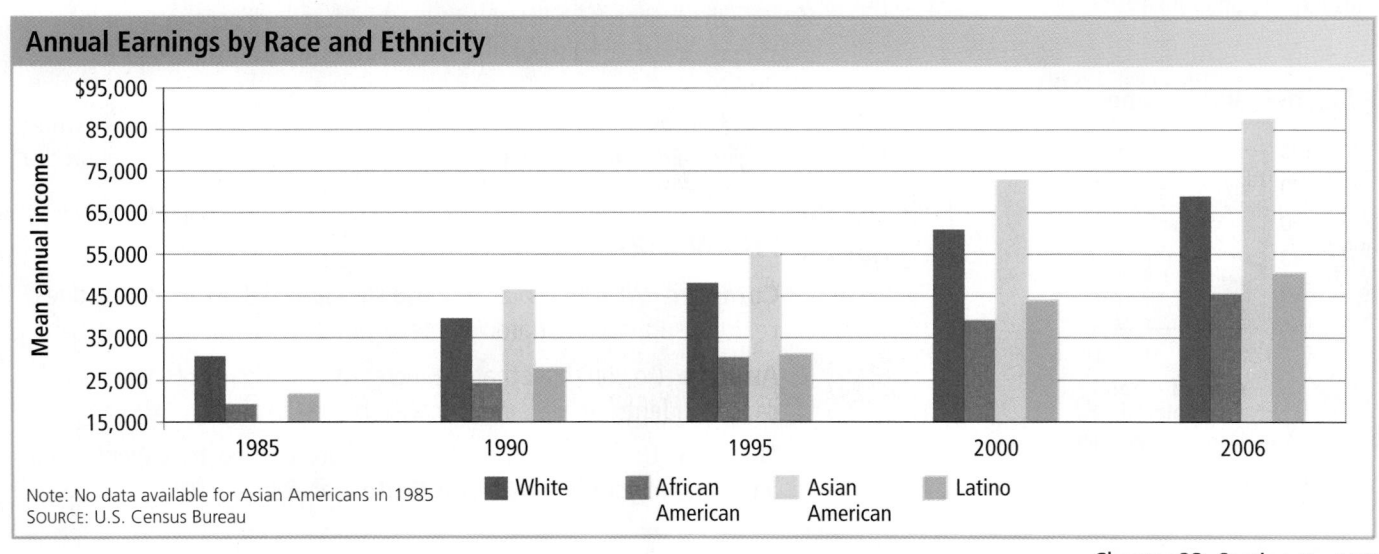

Annual Earnings by Race and Ethnicity

Mean annual income

Note: No data available for Asian Americans in 1985
SOURCE: U.S. Census Bureau

■ White　■ African American　■ Asian American　■ Latino

Education and American Society

TRACK THE ISSUE

THE ESSENTIAL ?

What should be the goals of American education?

Over time, the purpose of American education has changed. From an early focus on religion, schools turned to the promotion of democratic values. Today, they are placing a strong emphasis on performance standards. Use the timeline below to explore this enduring issue.

1600s–1700s Colonial Education
Schools emphasize religious study.

1852 Public Schools
Massachusetts passes first compulsory school attendance law in the United States.

1903 Du Bois-Washington Debate
Scholars debate the role of education in improving African Americans' lives.

1926 Scholastic Aptitude Test
The Scholastic Aptitude Test (SAT) is first administered.

2001 No Child Left Behind Act
Federal law tries to raise student performance through standardized testing and other measures.

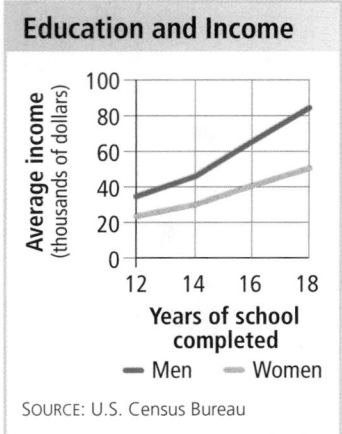

Education and Income

Average income (thousands of dollars) vs. Years of school completed

— Men — Women

SOURCE: U.S. Census Bureau

Students taking a standardized test

DEBATE THE ISSUE

Standardized Testing Standardized tests are used both to assess students and to hold teachers accountable for meeting standards. But critics argue that an emphasis on testing is hurting American schools.

❝We have learned a great deal about the nature of teaching and learning, and we know that students need to have opportunities to construct knowledge and connect that knowledge to what they already know. However, many . . . [standardized tests] still continue to focus on the memory of isolated facts which are destined to be forgotten.❞

—Marilyn Bizar, North Central Regional Educational Laboratory

❝You can't figure out whether schools are doing a good job unless you have some way of measuring how much their students are learning. . . . A guarantee by the national government of a decent education for every child is a noble cause, and so is the idea that all Americans will acquire a common body of skills and knowledge as they come of age.❞

—Nicholas Lemann, writer, *The New Yorker*

TRANSFER Activities

1. **Compare** Why does Bizar oppose standardized testing? Why does Lemann support standardized testing?

2. **Analyze** Do you think that the increase in standardized testing will cause students' achievement scores to rise? Explain.

3. **Transfer** Use the following Web site to see a video, try a WebQuest, and write in your journal. **Web Code:** neh-9302

The 1994 **Violence Against Women Act** increased federal resources to apprehend and prosecute men guilty of violent acts against women.

America Grows Older While the life expectancy of an American born in 1900 was less than 50 years, an American born in 2000 can expect to live to age 77. By 2000, older Americans tended to retire earlier, live longer, and exert more political influence. These factors have strained the country's social welfare system, especially Social Security and Medicare. In 1960, the federal government spent less than $100 billion on social welfare. By 2003, the amount had increased to $1.4 trillion.

With the large baby-boom generation reaching retirement age, the issue of elder care has become critical. Falling birthrates over the past two decades have meant that when the huge population of baby boomers retires, there will not be enough workers to cover their Social Security benefits. Politicians have been debating how to deal with this impending reality. In his second term, President Bush called for **privatizing** Social Security by allowing younger workers to invest some of their earnings in individual retirement accounts. Critics defeated the measure, saying that it would put younger workers at the mercy of fluctuating stock market returns without addressing the shortfall of funds. As Americans get older, the debate continues.

Facing the Future As the new millennium began, Americans looked back at a century of great change and technological progress. Looking forward, immense challenges remain. Americans still struggle with basic problems with which societies throughout history have struggled, as well as some new problems unique to the time. Yet with its greatest resource—the American people—the United States faces this new century with strength and optimism.

✔ **Checkpoint** What challenges have changing American demographics brought?

HISTORY MAKERS

George H. W. Bush (born 1924) and William Jefferson Clinton (born 1946)

Both presidents Bush and Clinton (below with the president of Indonesia) have spent much of their lives as public servants. Former political opponents, the two men formed an organization to bring relief to Southeastern Asians in the wake of the 2004 Asian tsunami. Touring the United States, the men raised millions of dollars by appealing to Americans to contribute to tsunami relief. A year later, Bush and Clinton went into action again in the wake of Hurricane Katrina. The former Presidents raised $100 million dollars and immediately set to work rebuilding and providing economic and educational opportunities to Americans devastated by the disaster. At the end of 2005, the former Presidents remarked that "the generosity of people never ceases to amaze us."

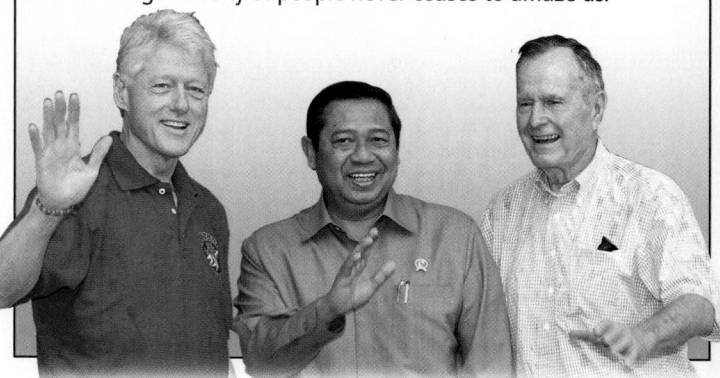

Progress Monitoring *Online*
For: Self-test with vocabulary practice
Web Code: nea-2051

Comprehension

1. **Terms and People** For each term below, write a sentence explaining its significance to American society in the twenty-first century.
   - Immigration Act of 1990
   - bilingual education
   - Immigration and Control Act of 1986
   - affirmative action
   - Violence Against Women Act
   - privatize

2. **NoteTaking Reading Skill: Identify Supporting Details** Use your completed table to answer the Section Focus Question: How was American society changing at the beginning of the twenty-first century?

Writing About History

3. **Quick Write: List Details** You are writing an essay that analyzes the American issue of education and American society. List details from this section that support your analysis.

Critical Thinking

4. **Draw Inferences** How can a nation's immigration policies affect its economy?

5. **Identify Central Issues** Why is an aging population a problem for a society?

Quick Study Guide

NY 7.VI.B.1, 7.VI.B.2

Progress Monitoring *Online*
For: Self-test with vocabulary practice
Web Code: nea-2061

■ World Trade Organization Members and Observers

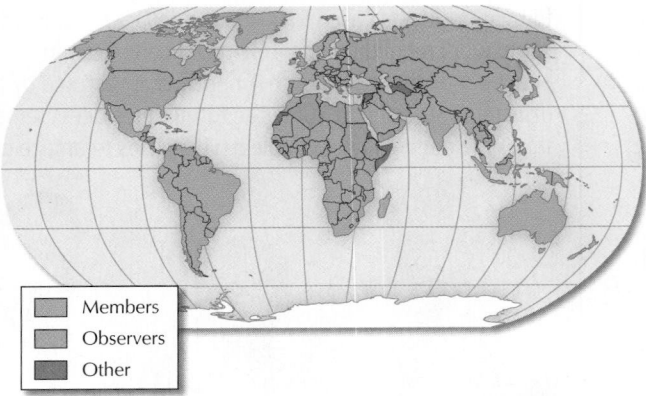

- Members
- Observers
- Other

■ Major Issues of American Society in the New Millennium

Technology—Computers, satellites, and advances in agriculture raise productivity and efficiency, but challenge many workers and industries.

Globalization—Globalization brings consumers more choices and opportunities, but can result in the loss of American jobs.

Terrorism—After September 11, government must work to make America more secure.

Immigration—Immigrants continue to enrich American society and fuel its economy, but their increasing numbers spark debate.

Demographics—Federal and local governments must find ways to support older Americans, Americans on the move, and nontraditional families.

■ Major Events in the Clinton and Bush Presidencies

President	Event
Clinton	**1992** Signed NAFTA; sent forces into Somalia
	1993 Signed Brady Bill; helped negotiate Declaration of Principles
	1994 Sent troops to Haiti
	1995 Sent forces into Bosnia as part of NATO
	1996 Signed bill to reform welfare
	1999 Impeached; cleared of charges
Bush	**2001** Pushed for major tax cuts; sent troops to war in Afghanistan; signed Patriot Act
	2002 Signed No Child Left Behind Act
	2003 Sent troops to war in Iraq
	2004 Bush reelected

✓ Quick Study Timeline

In America

1992 Bill Clinton is elected President	1994 Republicans win control of Congress	1996 Congress passes Welfare Reform Act	1998 President Clinton is impeached

Presidential Terms   George H. W. Bush 1989–1993   William J. Clinton 1993–2001

1992	1994	1996	1998

Around the World

1993 European Union forms	1994 Mandela is elected President of South Africa	1995 NATO forces restore order in Bosnia; WTO is established	1998 Indonesian dictator Suharto steps down

American Issues
●—●—●—● Connector

By connecting prior knowledge with what you have learned in this chapter, you can gradually build your understanding of enduring questions that still affect America today. Answer the questions below. Then, use your American Issues Connector study guide (or go online: www.PHSchool.com **Web Code:** neh-9303).

Issues You Learned About

● **Education and American Society** American leaders continually try to find new ways to improve the quality of the American education system.

1. Name and describe an educational reform in the United States that you have already learned about.

2. Why do you think the No Child Left Behind Act attracted the support of both Republicans and Democrats?

3. As part of the No Child Left Behind Act, schools must demonstrate success in order to receive federal funding. What are some ways that schools can demonstrate success?

● **Technology and Society** The development of the modern computer has changed the way people live, work, and play.

4. Prior to the computer, what do you think was the most important technological development, and why?

5. What spurred the development of the modern computer?

6. What are some ways that you use personal computers?

● **Global Interdependence** The United States economy depends on trade with countries around the world.

7. What are some of the issues that have caused a debate in the United States over free trade?

8. Why was Clinton's support of NAFTA controversial?

9. What are some of the benefits and drawbacks of globalization?

Connect to Your World   New York

Technology and Society The New York Stock Exchange (NYSE), founded in 1792, is the world's largest marketplace for stocks and bonds. Its headquarters are in the heart of New York City's Financial District. Though many other major stock exchanges operate electronically, most of the NYSE's business is still conducted face to face by people called floor traders. However, in 1999 investors began trading outside normal business hours by computer. Today, floor traders can receive information directly from investors through an electronic system called DOT (Designated Order Turnaround) rather than through a stockbroker hired by the investor. Research the NASDAQ, another famous stock market, and write a paragraph that compares and contrasts it with the NYSE.

2001
Terrorists attack United States. The United States invades Afghanistan

2003
War in Iraq begins

George W. Bush 2001–2009				Barack Obama 2009–
2000	**2002**	**2004**	**2006**	**2008**

2000
Putin is elected President of Russia

2002
Al Qaeda car bombs kill more than 200 people in Indonesia

History Interactive
For: Interactive timeline
Web Code: nep-2061

Chapter Assessment

Terms and People

1. Define **satellite.** What role does satellite technology play in everyday life?

2. Who is **Newt Gingrich**? What were some of his specific proposals during the Clinton presidency?

3. Define **ethnic cleansing.** Where was it used, and by whom?

4. What was the **Patriot Act**? What caused Congress to pass this legislation?

5. What is **bilingual education**? Why are some people opposed to it?

Focus Questions

The focus question for this chapter is **What political, social, technological, and economic trends have shaped American life since 1990?** Build an answer to this question by answering the focus questions for Sections 1 through 5 and the Critical Thinking questions that follow.

Section 1
6. How have technological changes and globalization transformed the American economy?

Section 2
7. What were the successes and failures of the Clinton presidency?

Section 3
8. What role did the United States take on in global politics and economics following the Cold War?

Section 4
9. What was the impact of Bush's domestic agenda and his response to the terrorist attack against the United States?

Section 5
10. How was American society changing at the beginning of the twenty-first century?

Critical Thinking

11. **Identify Central Issues** How did the rise of the service sector benefit some Americans and harm others?

12. **Draw Inferences** In the 1988 presidential election, 57.4 percent of Americans voted; in 1992, 61.3 percent voted, and in 1996, 54.2 percent voted. What may have contributed to the 1992 spike in voter participation?

13. **Analyze Evidence** In 1996, during his reelection campaign, Clinton announced, "The era of big government is over." Cite evidence supporting or refuting this statement.

14. **Synthesize Information** What foreign policy did the United States adopt in the post Cold War world?

15. **Determine Relevance** How helpful was the Declaration of Principles at resolving problems in the Middle East?

16. **Analyze Visuals** Study the visual below. What event are these newspaper headlines describing?

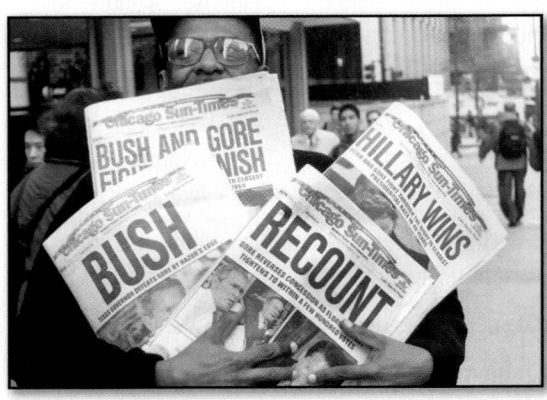

17. **Analyze Information** Did Operation Iraqi Freedom succeed at improving the lives of the Iraqi people?

18. **Explain Causes** Why was affirmative action first introduced in the United States?

Writing About History

Writing for Assessment As Americans head into the new millennium, many of the major issues that have been part of American history for over two centuries remain relevant. Write an essay that traces an important American issue over time. Explain why it became an American issue and how its relevance has changed or remained the same over time.

Prewriting
- Go online to www.PHSchool.com and enter **Web Code: neh-2061** to find a list of American issues.
- Eliminate issues about which you are unsure. Choose the one for which you have the most background information or ideas.
- Identify the focus of your essay by forming a main idea.

Drafting
- Sketch out an organizational plan for your essay. Consider using an outline or other graphic organizer to help you.
- Provide details that define, explain, support, or illustrate your points.
- Strengthen your introduction by including an interest-grabbing sentence.

Revising
- Use the guidelines on page SH11 of the Writing Handbook to revise your report.

Regents DBQ Practice

Media Influence on Political Issues

News coverage of the war in Iraq became news in itself. While editorial writers strongly supported or opposed American policy, other journalists questioned the way the war was being reported. Was the media too critical—or not critical enough? Use your knowledge of media coverage of the war in Iraq and Documents 1, 2, 3, and 4 to answer questions 1 through 4.

Document 1

"Mr. Bush's 'Plan for Victory' speech was, of course, the usual unadulterated nonsense. Its overarching theme—'We will never accept anything less than complete victory'—was being contradicted even as he spoke by rampant reports of Pentagon plans for stepped-up troop withdrawals between next week's Iraqi Elections and the more important (for endangered Republicans) American Election Day of 2006. The specifics were phony, too. Once again inflating the readiness of Iraqi troops, Mr. Bush claimed that the recent assault on Tal Afar 'was primarily led by Iraqi security forces'—a fairy tale immediately unmasked by Michael Ware, a Time reporter embedded in the battle's front lines, as 'completely wrong.'"

—*Frank Rich,* The New York Times, *December 11, 2005*

Document 2

Over the past few years, the Iraq war has morphed from a war of liberation against Saddam into a civil conflict between Sunnis and Shiites. . . . But the best news out of Iraq last week was that the Sunnis voted joyfully and in large numbers. In what they said and the way they acted, both the Sunnis and Shiites made it clear that while they are engaged in a fierce rivalry, they fervently believe in a democratic and unified Iraq. This is not yet a to-the-death struggle. . . . That's why it's necessary to have a third party—in Iraq, the United States—to cajole the two sides toward the settlement, to enforce the agreement afterward, to nurture a functioning social contract after that, and to prevent

hostile outside powers from spoiling the deal. That's why, again, it is essential that the U.S. remain in Iraq long enough to deescalate the conflict.

—*David Brooks,* The New York Times, *December 18, 2005*

Document 3

Document 4

Fairness and Accuracy in Reporting did a study. In the week leading up to General Colin Powell going to the Security Council to make his case for the invasions and the week afterwards—this was the period where more than half of the people in this country were opposed to an invasion—they did a study of CBS *Evening News,* NBC *Nightly News,* ABC *World News Tonight,* and the *NewsHour with Jim Lehrer* on PBS. The four major newscasts. Two weeks. Three hundred and ninety-three interviews on war. Three were anti-war voices. Three of almost four hundred, and that included PBS. . . . [T]hey have to provide the diversity of opinion that fully expresses the debate and the anguish and the discussions that are going on all over this country. That is media serving a democratic society.

—*Amy Goodman, "Independent Media in a Time of War," April 21, 2003*

---

1. Which of the documents is critical of the government's positive assessment of the war in Iraq?
   - **(1)** Document 1
   - **(2)** Document 2
   - **(3)** Document 3
   - **(4)** Document 4

2. According to Amy Goodman, which of the following statements is the most accurate assessment of media coverage of the invasion of Iraq?
   - **(1)** All the major newscasts tried to present both points of view about the invasion.
   - **(2)** The media coverage resulted in a national debate about the invasion.
   - **(3)** Media coverage favored opponents of the war.
   - **(4)** Media coverage did not reflect the diversity of opinion about the war.

3. What is the main point of the cartoon in Document 3?
   - **(1)** People generally do not trust the mainstream media.
   - **(2)** Although people claim to distrust the media, they still rely on it for information.
   - **(3)** The mainstream media is biased.
   - **(4)** The mainstream media is unbiased.

4. **Writing Task** Think about the political perspectives on the war in Iraq expressed in the media. Do you think the media has played an influential role in shaping American foreign policy in Iraq? Use your knowledge of media coverage of the war, key events in the war, and specific evidence from the primary sources above to support your opinion.

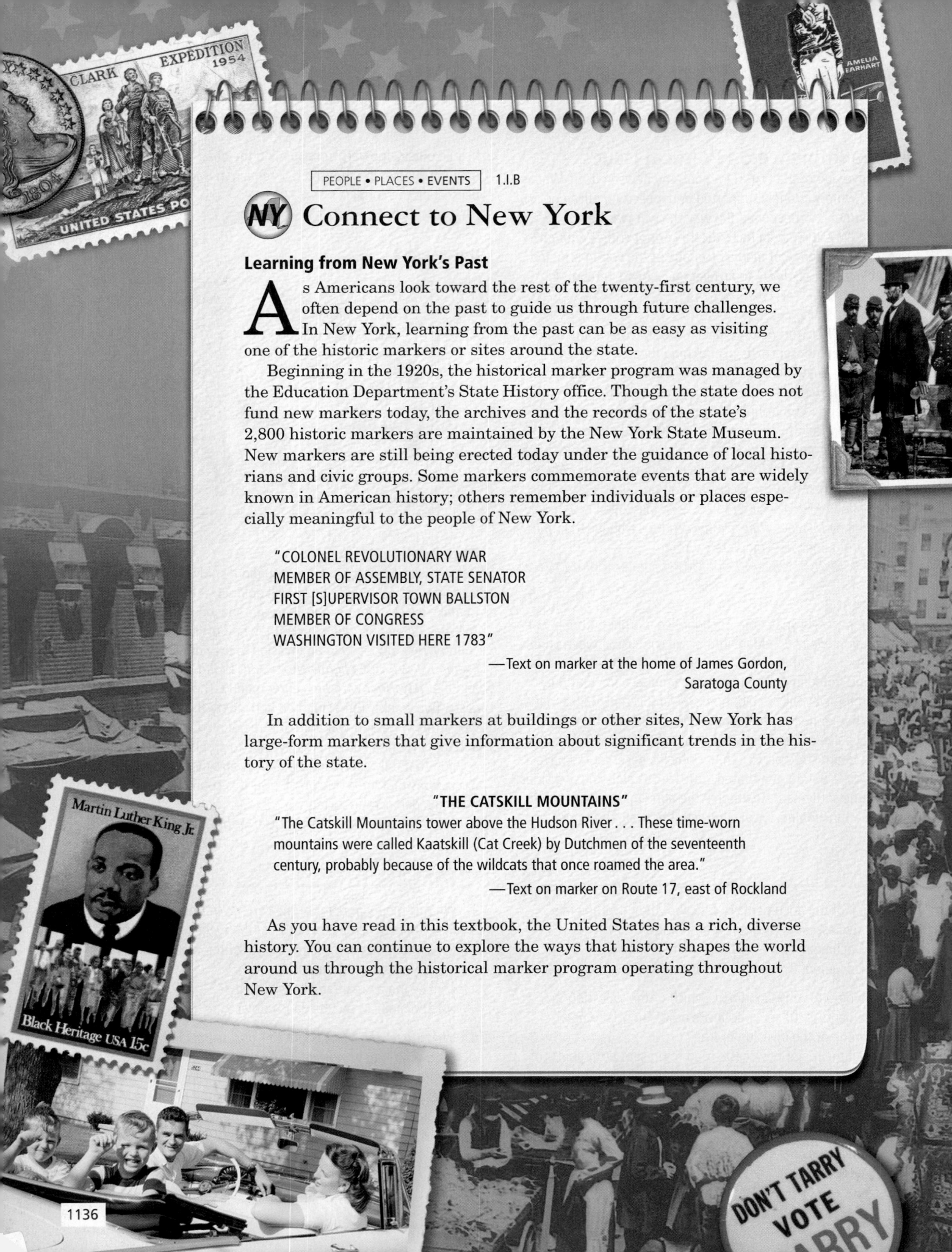

NY Connect to New York

Learning from New York's Past

As Americans look toward the rest of the twenty-first century, we often depend on the past to guide us through future challenges. In New York, learning from the past can be as easy as visiting one of the historic markers or sites around the state.

Beginning in the 1920s, the historical marker program was managed by the Education Department's State History office. Though the state does not fund new markers today, the archives and the records of the state's 2,800 historic markers are maintained by the New York State Museum. New markers are still being erected today under the guidance of local historians and civic groups. Some markers commemorate events that are widely known in American history; others remember individuals or places especially meaningful to the people of New York.

> "COLONEL REVOLUTIONARY WAR
> MEMBER OF ASSEMBLY, STATE SENATOR
> FIRST [S]UPERVISOR TOWN BALLSTON
> MEMBER OF CONGRESS
> WASHINGTON VISITED HERE 1783"
>
> —Text on marker at the home of James Gordon,
> Saratoga County

In addition to small markers at buildings or other sites, New York has large-form markers that give information about significant trends in the history of the state.

> **"THE CATSKILL MOUNTAINS"**
>
> "The Catskill Mountains tower above the Hudson River . . . These time-worn mountains were called Kaatskill (Cat Creek) by Dutchmen of the seventeenth century, probably because of the wildcats that once roamed the area."
>
> —Text on marker on Route 17, east of Rockland

As you have read in this textbook, the United States has a rich, diverse history. You can continue to explore the ways that history shapes the world around us through the historical marker program operating throughout New York.

Reference Section

Five Themes of Geography

The five themes of geography are tools you can use to analyze geographic information given in photographs, charts, maps, and text. Use these themes to determine the role of geography in U.S. history.

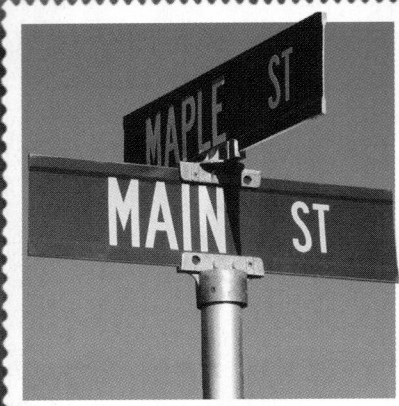

Location answers the question, Where is it? The answer might be an absolute location, such as 167 River Lane, or a relative location, such as six miles west of Mill City.

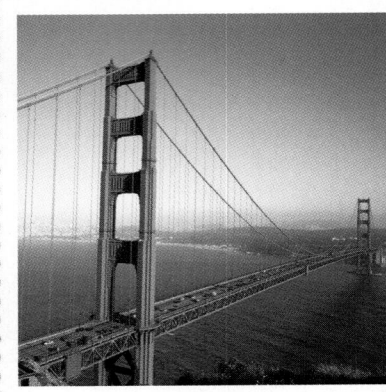

Place identifies natural and human features that make one place different from another. Landforms and buildings are features that can be used to identify a specific place.

Movement answers the question, How do people, goods, and ideas move from place to place?

Human-Environment Interaction explores the relationship between people and the natural world. Humans often modify their environment, and the environment affects how they live.

Regions are areas that share at least one common feature. Climate, culture, and government are features that can be used to define regions.

Profile of the Fifty States

State	Capital	Entered Union	Population (2005)	Population Rank	Land Area (Sq. Mi.)	Electoral Votes
Alabama	Montgomery	1819	4,557,808	23	50,744	9
Alaska	Juneau	1959	663,661	47	571,951	3
Arizona	Phoenix	1912	5,939,292	17	113,635	10
Arkansas	Little Rock	1836	2,779,154	32	52,068	6
California	Sacramento	1850	36,132,147	1	155,959	55
Colorado	Denver	1876	4,665,177	22	103,718	9
Connecticut	Hartford	1788	3,510,297	29	4,845	7
Delaware	Dover	1787	843,524	45	1,954	3
District of Columbia	——	——	550,521	——	——	3
Florida	Tallahassee	1845	17,789,864	4	53,927	27
Georgia	Atlanta	1788	9,072,576	9	57,906	15
Hawaii	Honolulu	1959	1,275,194	42	6,423	4
Idaho	Boise	1890	1,429,096	39	82,747	4
Illinois	Springfield	1818	12,763,371	5	55,584	21
Indiana	Indianapolis	1816	6,271,973	15	35,867	11
Iowa	Des Moines	1846	2,966,334	30	55,869	7
Kansas	Topeka	1861	2,744,687	33	81,815	6
Kentucky	Frankfort	1792	4,173,405	26	39,728	8
Louisiana	Baton Rouge	1812	4,523,628	24	43,562	9
Maine	Augusta	1820	1,321,505	40	30,862	4
Maryland	Annapolis	1788	5,600,388	19	9,774	10
Massachusetts	Boston	1788	6,398,743	13	7,840	12
Michigan	Lansing	1837	10,120,860	8	56,804	17
Minnesota	St. Paul	1858	5,132,799	21	79,610	10
Mississippi	Jackson	1817	2,921,088	31	46,907	6
Missouri	Jefferson City	1821	5,800,310	18	68,886	11
Montana	Helena	1889	935,670	44	145,552	3
Nebraska	Lincoln	1867	1,758,787	38	76,872	5
Nevada	Carson City	1864	2,414,807	35	109,826	5
New Hampshire	Concord	1788	1,309,940	41	8,968	4
New Jersey	Trenton	1787	8,717,925	10	7,417	15
New Mexico	Santa Fe	1912	1,928,384	36	121,356	5
New York	Albany	1788	19,254,630	3	47,214	31
North Carolina	Raleigh	1789	8,683,242	11	48,711	15
North Dakota	Bismarck	1889	636,677	48	68,976	3
Ohio	Columbus	1803	11,464,042	7	40,948	20
Oklahoma	Oklahoma City	1907	3,547,884	28	68,667	7
Oregon	Salem	1859	3,641,056	27	95,997	7
Pennsylvania	Harrisburg	1787	12,429,616	6	44,817	21
Rhode Island	Providence	1790	1,076,189	43	1,045	4
South Carolina	Columbia	1788	4,255,083	25	30,110	8
South Dakota	Pierre	1889	775,933	46	75,885	3
Tennessee	Nashville	1796	5,962,959	16	41,217	11
Texas	Austin	1845	22,859,968	2	261,797	34
Utah	Salt Lake City	1896	2,469,585	34	82,144	5
Vermont	Montpelier	1791	623,050	49	9,250	3
Virginia	Richmond	1788	7,567,465	12	39,594	13
Washington	Olympia	1889	6,287,759	14	66,544	11
West Virginia	Charleston	1863	1,816,856	37	24,078	5
Wisconsin	Madison	1848	5,536,201	20	54,310	10
Wyoming	Cheyenne	1890	509,294	50	97,100	3

SOURCES: U.S. Census Bureau, U.S. National Archives, *World Almanac*

The World: Political

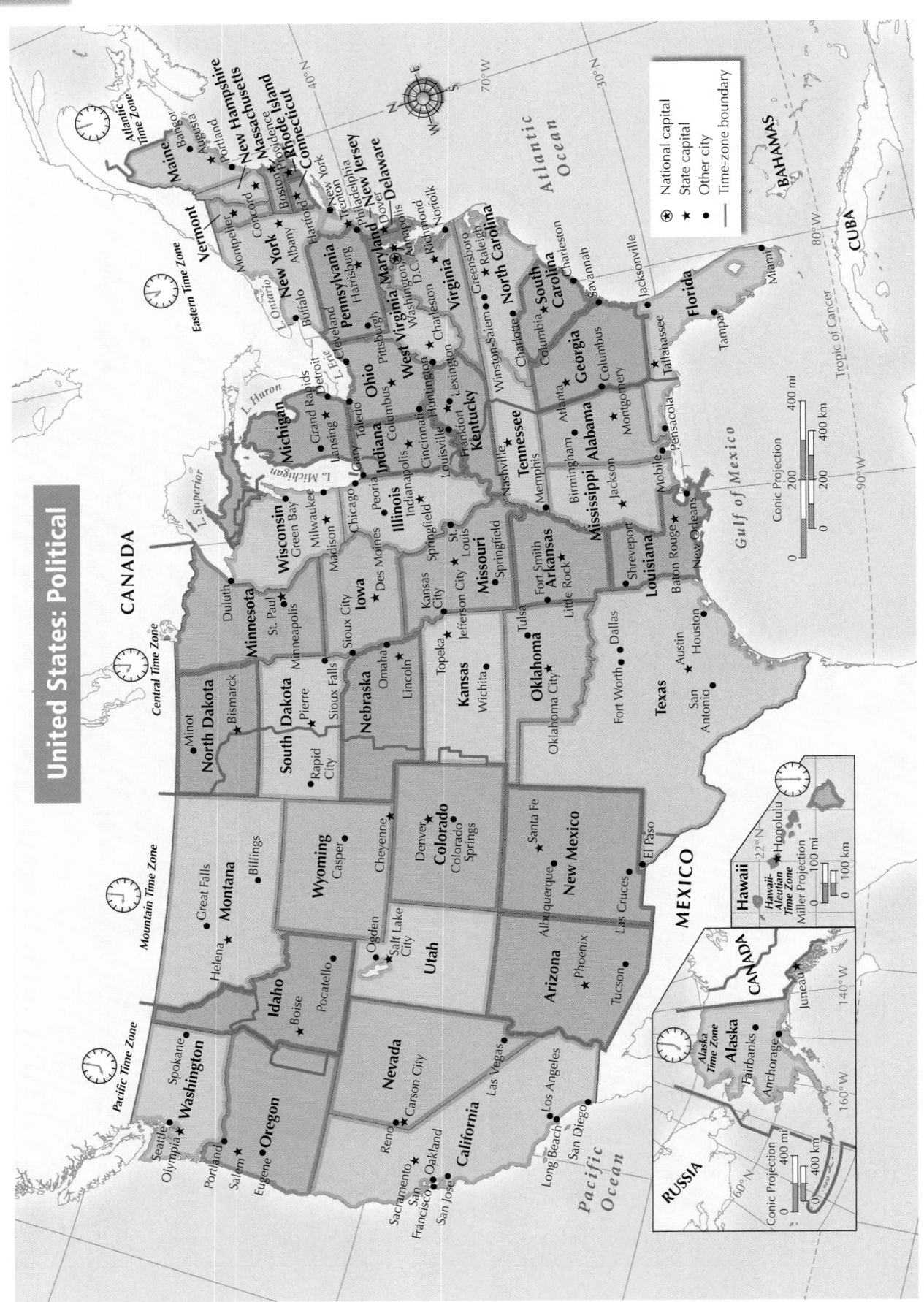

United States: Political

CANADA

Legend:
- ⊛ National capital
- ★ State capital
- • Other city
- — Time-zone boundary

Atlantic Time Zone

Eastern Time Zone

Central Time Zone

Mountain Time Zone

Pacific Time Zone

Maine — Bangor, Augusta, Portland
New Hampshire — Concord
Vermont — Montpelier
Massachusetts — Boston
Rhode Island — Providence
Connecticut — Hartford
New York — Albany, Buffalo, New York
New Jersey — Trenton
Pennsylvania — Harrisburg, Philadelphia, Pittsburgh
Delaware — Dover
Maryland — Annapolis
Washington, D.C.
West Virginia — Charleston, Huntington
Virginia — Richmond, Norfolk
North Carolina — Raleigh, Greensboro, Charlotte
South Carolina — Columbia, Charleston
Georgia — Atlanta, Columbus, Savannah
Florida — Tallahassee, Jacksonville, Tampa, Miami
Ohio — Columbus, Cleveland, Toledo, Cincinnati
Michigan — Lansing, Detroit, Grand Rapids
Indiana — Indianapolis, Gary
Kentucky — Frankfort, Louisville, Lexington
Tennessee — Nashville, Memphis
Alabama — Montgomery, Birmingham, Mobile
Mississippi — Jackson
Illinois — Springfield, Chicago, Peoria
Wisconsin — Madison, Milwaukee, Green Bay
Minnesota — St. Paul, Minneapolis, Duluth
Iowa — Des Moines, Sioux City
Missouri — Jefferson City, St. Louis, Springfield, Kansas City
Arkansas — Little Rock, Fort Smith
Louisiana — Baton Rouge, New Orleans, Shreveport
North Dakota — Bismarck, Minot
South Dakota — Pierre, Rapid City, Sioux Falls
Nebraska — Lincoln, Omaha
Kansas — Topeka, Wichita
Oklahoma — Oklahoma City, Tulsa
Texas — Austin, Dallas, Fort Worth, Houston, San Antonio, El Paso
Montana — Helena, Great Falls, Billings
Wyoming — Cheyenne, Casper
Colorado — Denver, Colorado Springs
New Mexico — Santa Fe, Albuquerque, Las Cruces
Idaho — Boise, Pocatello
Utah — Salt Lake City, Ogden
Arizona — Phoenix, Tucson
Washington — Olympia, Seattle, Spokane
Oregon — Salem, Portland, Eugene
Nevada — Carson City, Reno, Las Vegas
California — Sacramento, San Francisco, Oakland, San Jose, Los Angeles, Long Beach, San Diego

Gulf of Mexico — Pensacola

MEXICO

Atlantic Ocean
Pacific Ocean

BAHAMAS
CUBA

Tropic of Cancer

Conic Projection
0 200 400 mi
0 200 400 km

Hawaii — Honolulu
Hawaii–Aleutian Time Zone
Miller Projection
0 100 mi
0 100 km

Alaska — Juneau, Fairbanks, Anchorage
Alaska Time Zone
Conic Projection
0 400 mi
0 400 km

CANADA
RUSSIA

L. Superior, L. Huron, L. Michigan, L. Erie, L. Ontario

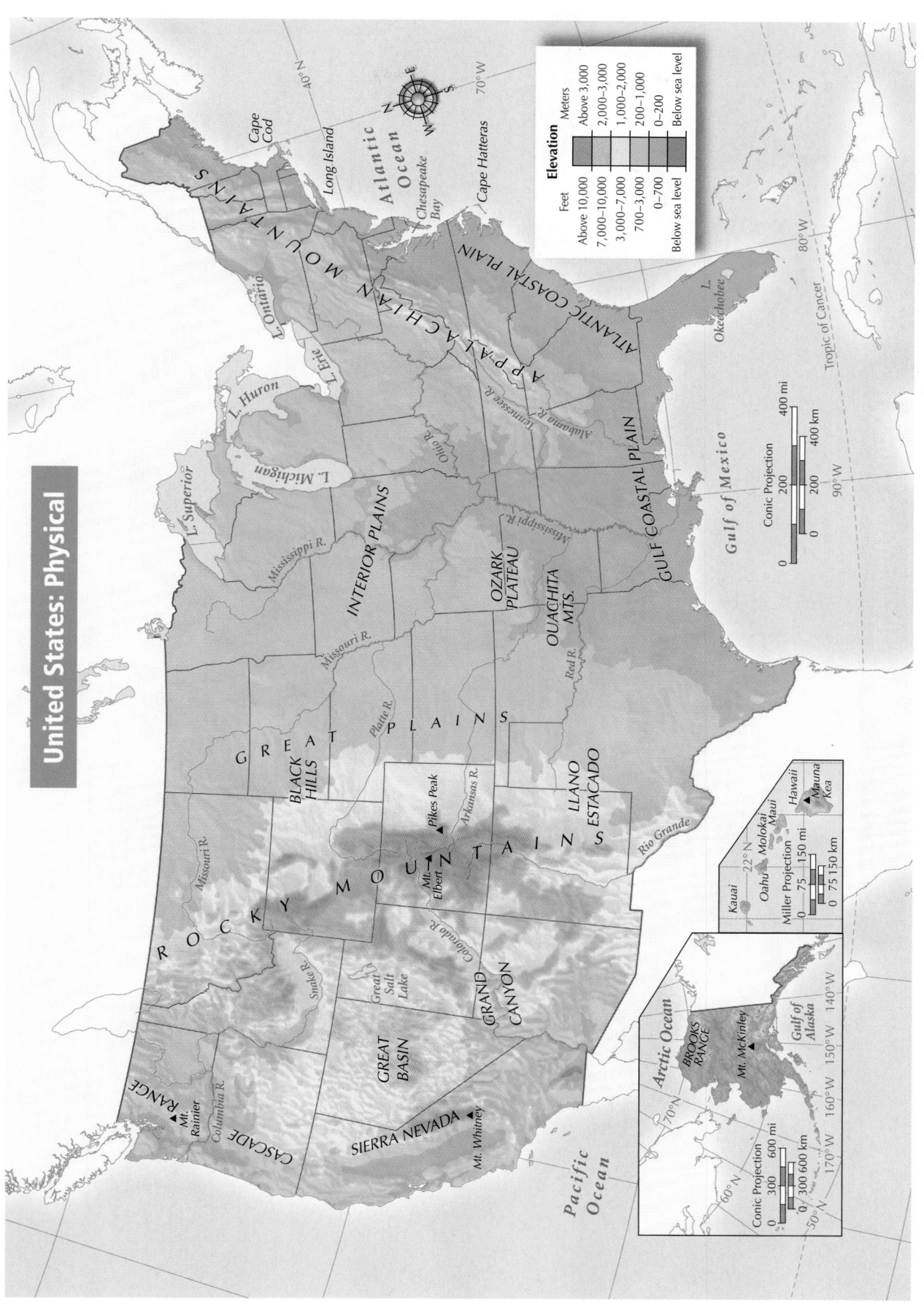

United States: Physical

Elevation

Feet	Meters
Above 10,000	Above 3,000
7,000–10,000	2,000–3,000
3,000–7,000	1,000–2,000
700–3,000	200–1,000
0–700	0–200
Below sea level	Below sea level

Cape Cod

Long Island

Atlantic Ocean

Cape Hatteras

Chesapeake Bay

APPALACHIAN MOUNTAINS

ATLANTIC COASTAL PLAIN

L. Ontario

L. Erie

L. Huron

L. Michigan

L. Superior

Tennessee R.

Alabama R.

Ohio R.

Mississippi R.

INTERIOR PLAINS

Missouri R.

OZARK PLATEAU

OUACHITA MTS.

Mississippi R.

Red R.

GULF COASTAL PLAIN

Gulf of Mexico

L. Okeechobee

Tropic of Cancer

GREAT PLAINS

BLACK HILLS

Platte R.

Pikes Peak

Arkansas R.

LLANO ESTACADO

Rio Grande

Missouri R.

Mt. Elbert

ROCKY MOUNTAINS

Colorado R.

Great Salt Lake

GRAND CANYON

Snake R.

GREAT BASIN

SIERRA NEVADA

Mt. Whitney

Columbia R.

CASCADE RANGE

Mt. Rainier

Pacific Ocean

Conic Projection
0   200   400 mi
0   200   400 km

Arctic Ocean

BROOKS RANGE

Mt. McKinley

Gulf of Alaska

70° N

60° N

50° N

170° W   160° W   150° W   140° W

Conic Projection
0   300   600 mi
0   300   600 km

Kauai

Oahu   Molokai   Maui

Hawaii

Mauna Kea

22° N

Miller Projection
0   75   150 mi
0   75   150 km

40° W

70° W

80° W

90° W

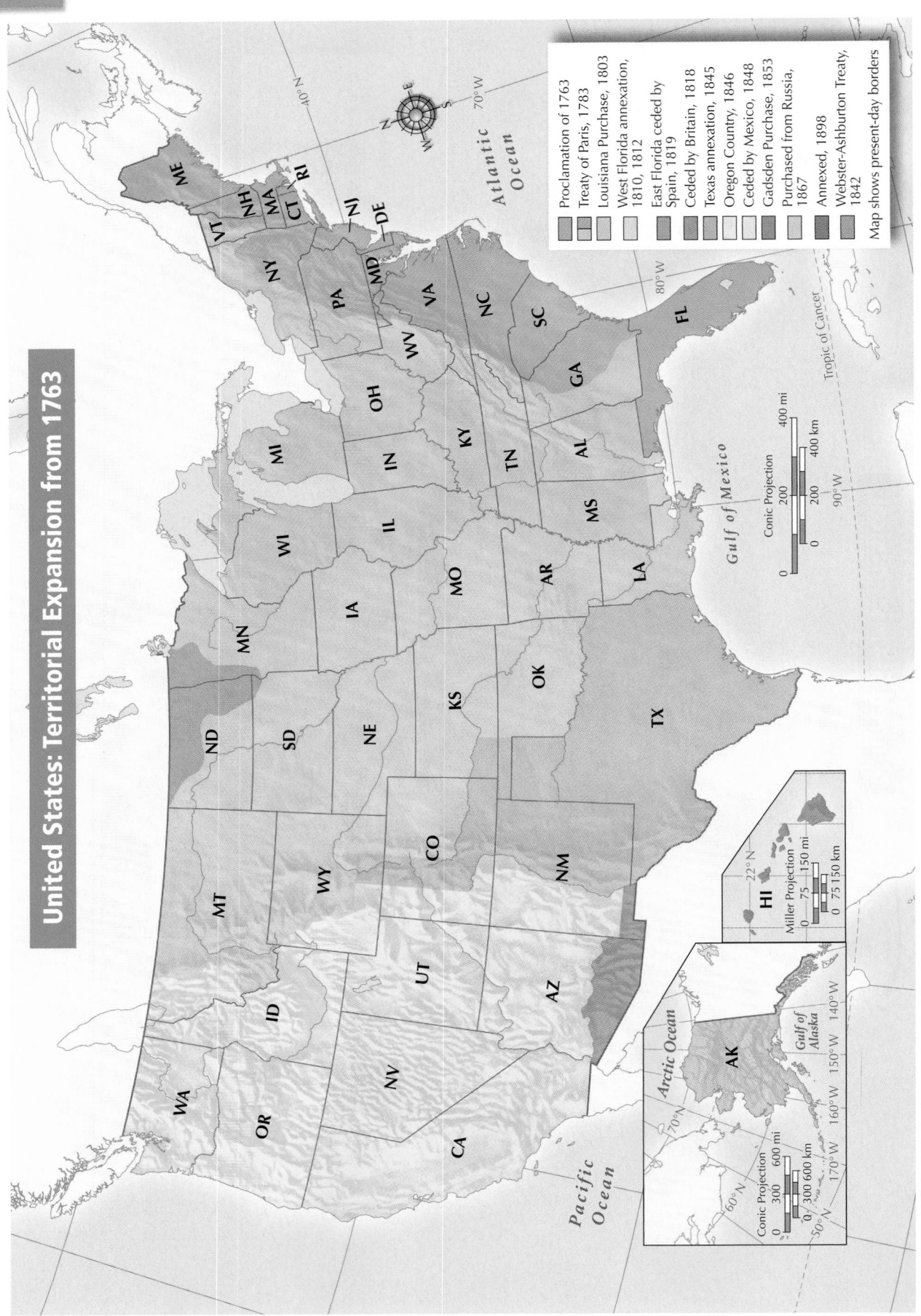

United States: Territorial Expansion from 1763

Legend:
- Proclamation of 1763
- Treaty of Paris, 1783
- Louisiana Purchase, 1803
- West Florida annexation, 1810, 1812
- East Florida ceded by Spain, 1819
- Ceded by Britain, 1818
- Texas annexation, 1845
- Oregon Country, 1846
- Ceded by Mexico, 1848
- Gadsden Purchase, 1853
- Purchased from Russia, 1867
- Annexed, 1898
- Webster-Ashburton Treaty, 1842
- Map shows present-day borders

Atlantic Ocean

Gulf of Mexico

Tropic of Cancer

Conic Projection
0   200   400 mi
0   200   400 km

Pacific Ocean

Arctic Ocean

Gulf of Alaska

AK

Conic Projection
0   300   600 mi
0   300   600 km

HI

Miller Projection
0   75   150 mi
0   75   150 km

United States: Climates

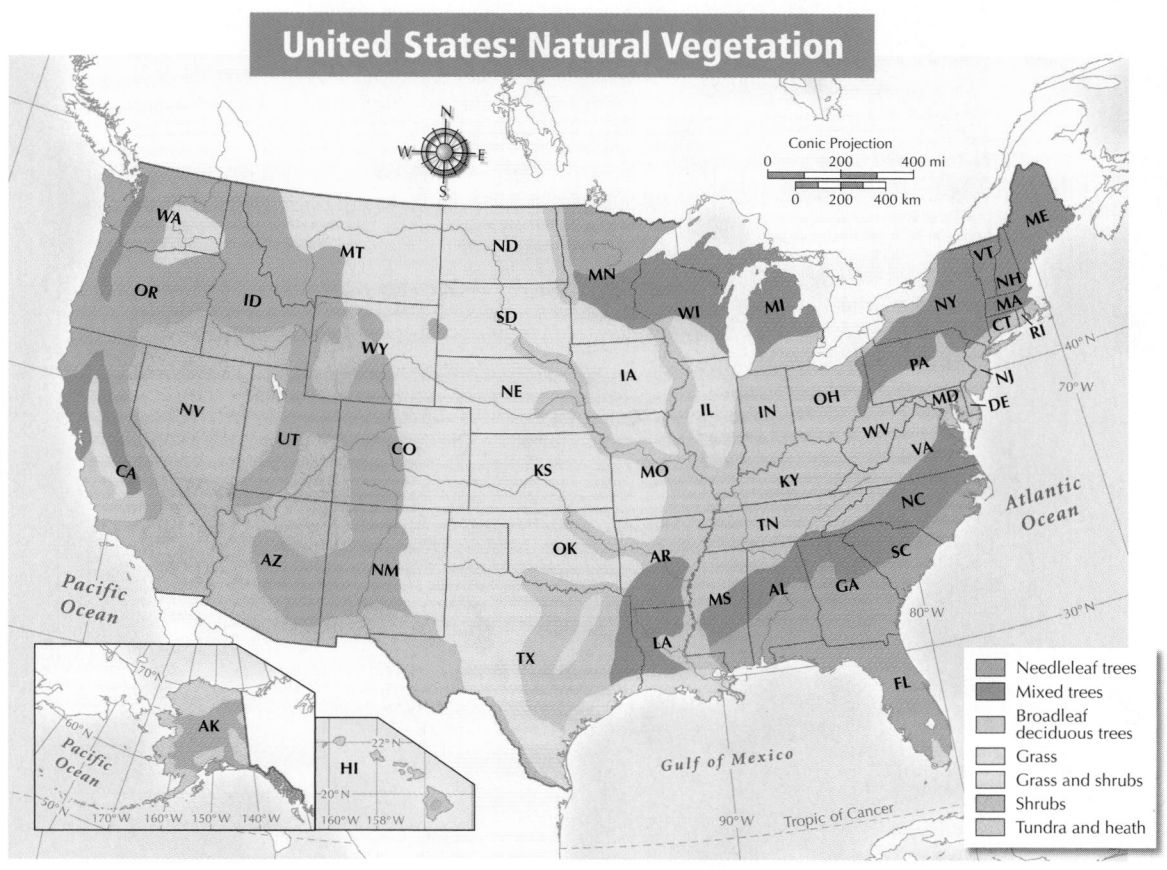

Tropical
- Tropical rain forest
- Savanna

Dry
- Semiarid
- Arid

Mild
- Mediterranean
- Humid subtropical
- Marine

Continental
- Warm summer
- Cool summer
- Subarctic

Polar
- Tundra

High Elevations
- Highland (varies with latitude and elevation)

Conic Projection
0   200   400 mi
0   200   400 km

WA, MT, ND, MN, WI, MI, ME, VT, NH, MA, CT, RI, NY, PA, NJ, DE, MD, OR, ID, WY, SD, IA, IL, IN, OH, WV, VA, NV, UT, CO, NE, KS, MO, KY, NC, CA, AZ, NM, OK, AR, TN, SC, MS, AL, GA, TX, LA, FL

Pacific Ocean

Atlantic Ocean

Gulf of Mexico

AK, HI

70°N, 60°N, 50°N, 22°N, 20°N, 170°W, 160°W, 150°W, 140°W, 158°W

40°N, 70°W, 80°W, 30°N, 90°W, Tropic of Cancer

United States: Natural Vegetation

Conic Projection
0   200   400 mi
0   200   400 km

- Needleleaf trees
- Mixed trees
- Broadleaf deciduous trees
- Grass
- Grass and shrubs
- Shrubs
- Tundra and heath

WA, MT, ND, MN, WI, MI, ME, VT, NH, MA, CT, RI, NY, PA, NJ, DE, MD, OR, ID, WY, SD, IA, IL, IN, OH, WV, VA, NV, UT, CO, NE, KS, MO, KY, NC, CA, AZ, NM, OK, AR, TN, SC, MS, AL, GA, TX, LA, FL

Pacific Ocean

Atlantic Ocean

Gulf of Mexico

AK, HI

70°N, 60°N, 50°N, 22°N, 20°N, 170°W, 160°W, 150°W, 140°W, 158°W

40°N, 70°W, 80°W, 30°N, 90°W, Tropic of Cancer

United States: Land Use and Land Cover

Farming
Grazing
Forestry
Park, military use
Urban
Desert
Wetland

Atlantic Ocean

Gulf of Mexico

Pacific Ocean

Tropic of Cancer

Conic Projection

400 mi
400 km
200
200
0
0

ME
NH
VT
NY
MA
CT
RI
New York
Philadelphia
NJ
DE
PA
Pittsburgh
MD
Washington, D.C.
WV
VA
NC
SC
GA
Atlanta
FL
Miami
OH
Cincinnati
KY
TN
AL
MS
New Orleans
IN
Detroit
MI
L. Michigan
L. Huron
L. Erie
L. Ontario
L. Superior
WI
Chicago
IL
MO
AR
LA
Houston
TX
Dallas
OK
KS
NE
IA
MN
Minneapolis
SD
ND
CO
Denver
WY
MT
UT
NM
AZ
Phoenix
NV
Los Angeles
CA
San Francisco
OR
WA
Seattle
Boston

Miller Projection
HI
75 150 mi
0 75 150 km
22° N

AK
Conic Projection
0   300 600 km
0   300   600 mi
70° N
60° N
50° N
170° W
160° W
150° W
140° W

40° N
30° N
70° W
80° W
90° W

United States: Natural Resources

Legend:
- Oil field
- Gas field
- Coal field
- Al Bauxite
- Co Cobalt
- Cu Copper
- Au Gold
- Fe Iron ore
- Pb Lead
- Mn Manganese
- Hg Mercury
- Mo Molybdenum
- Ag Silver
- S Sulfur
- U Uranium
- Zn Zinc

Atlantic Ocean

Gulf of Mexico

Pacific Ocean

Tropic of Cancer

Conic Projection
0 200 400 mi
0 200 400 km

HI
Miller Projection
0 75 150 mi
0 75 150 km

AK
Conic Projection
0 300 600 mi
0 300 600 km

United States: Population Density

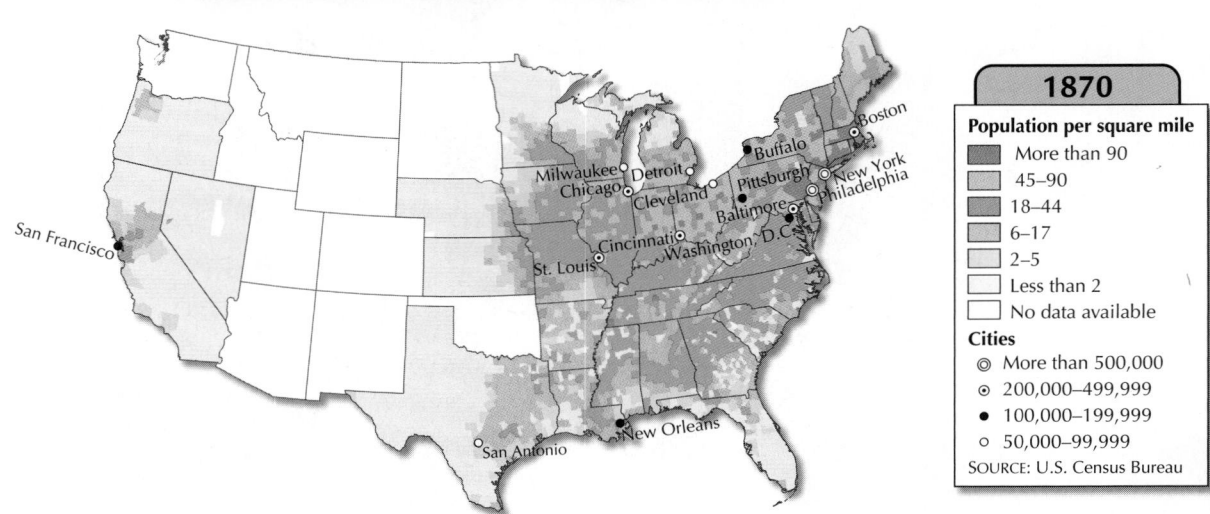

1870

Population per square mile

- More than 90
- 45–90
- 18–44
- 6–17
- 2–5
- Less than 2
- No data available

Cities

- ◎ More than 500,000
- ⊙ 200,000–499,999
- ● 100,000–199,999
- ○ 50,000–99,999

SOURCE: U.S. Census Bureau

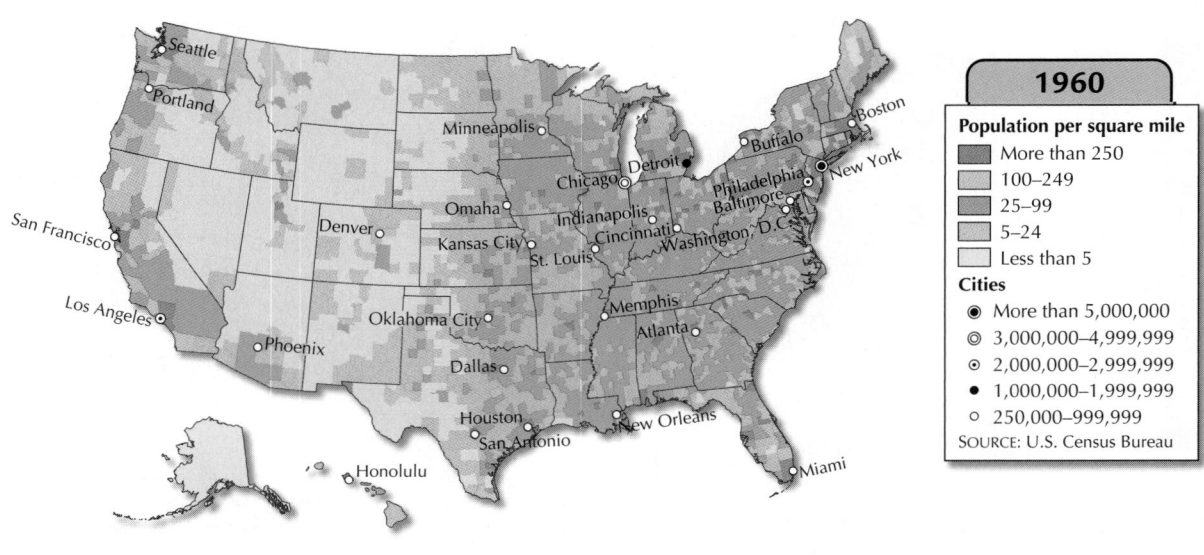

1960

Population per square mile

- More than 250
- 100–249
- 25–99
- 5–24
- Less than 5

Cities

- ◉ More than 5,000,000
- ◎ 3,000,000–4,999,999
- ⊙ 2,000,000–2,999,999
- ● 1,000,000–1,999,999
- ○ 250,000–999,999

SOURCE: U.S. Census Bureau

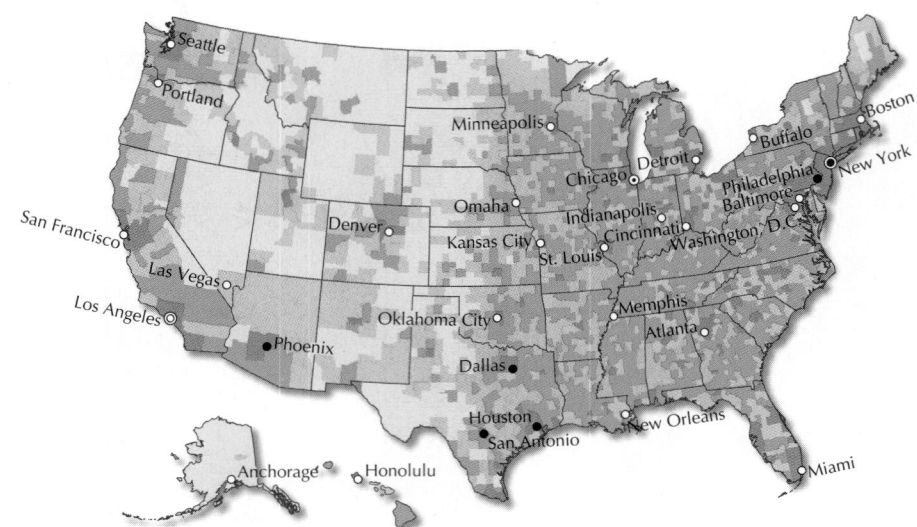

2000

Population per square mile

- More than 250
- 100–249
- 25–99
- 5–24
- Less than 5

Cities

- ◉ More than 5,000,000
- ◎ 3,000,000–4,999,999
- ⊙ 2,000,000–2,999,999
- ● 1,000,000–1,999,999
- ○ 250,000–999,999

SOURCE: U.S. Census Bureau

Presidents of the United States

1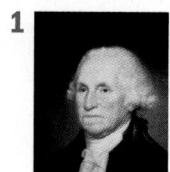
George Washington
(1732–1799)

Years in Office: 1789–1797
No political party

Elected from: Virginia
Vice President: John Adams

2
John Adams
(1735–1826)

Years in Office: 1797–1801
Federalist

Elected from: Massachusetts
Vice President: Thomas Jefferson

3
Thomas Jefferson
(1743–1826)

Years in Office: 1801–1809
Democratic Republican

Elected from: Virginia
Vice Presidents: Aaron Burr,
George Clinton

4
James Madison
(1751–1836)

Years in Office: 1809–1817
Democratic Republican

Elected from: Virginia
Vice Presidents: George
Clinton, Elbridge Gerry

5
James Monroe
(1758–1831)

Years in Office: 1817–1825
National Republican

Elected from: Virginia
Vice President: Daniel Tompkins

6
John Quincy Adams
(1767–1848)

Years in Office: 1825–1829
National Republican

Elected from: Massachusetts
Vice President: John Calhoun

7
Andrew Jackson
(1767–1845)

Years in Office: 1829–1837
Democrat

Elected from: Tennessee
Vice Presidents: John Calhoun,
Martin Van Buren

8
Martin Van Buren
(1782–1862)

Years in Office: 1837–1841
Democrat

Elected from: New York
Vice President: Richard Johnson

9
William Henry Harrison*
(1773–1841)

Year in Office: 1841
Whig

Elected from: Ohio
Vice President: John Tyler

10
John Tyler
(1790–1862)

Years in Office: 1841–1845
Whig

Elected from: Virginia
Vice President: none

11
James K. Polk
(1795–1849)

Years in Office: 1845–1849
Democrat

Elected from: Tennessee
Vice President: George Dallas

12
Zachary Taylor*
(1784–1850)

Years in Office: 1849–1850
Whig

Elected from: Louisiana
Vice President: Millard Fillmore

13
Millard Fillmore
(1800–1874)

Years in Office: 1850–1853
Whig

Elected from: New York
Vice President: none

14
Franklin Pierce
(1804–1869)

Years in Office: 1853–1857
Democrat

Elected from: New Hampshire
Vice President: William King

15
James Buchanan
(1791–1868)

Years in Office: 1857–1861
Democrat

Elected from: Pennsylvania
Vice President: John
Breckinridge

16
Abraham Lincoln**
(1809–1865)

Years in Office: 1861–1865
Republican

Elected from: Illinois
Vice Presidents: Hannibal
Hamlin, Andrew Johnson

17

Andrew Johnson
(1808–1875)

Years in Office: 1865–1869
Democrat†

Elected from: Tennessee
Vice President: none

18

Ulysses S. Grant
(1822–1885)

Years in Office: 1869–1877
Republican

Elected from: Illinois
Vice Presidents: Schuyler Colfax, Henry Wilson

19

Rutherford B. Hayes
(1822–1893)

Years in Office: 1877–1881
Republican

Elected from: Ohio
Vice President: William Wheeler

20

James A. Garfield**
(1831–1881)

Year in Office: 1881
Republican

Elected from: Ohio
Vice President: Chester A. Arthur

21

Chester A. Arthur
(1830–1886)

Years in Office: 1881–1885
Republican

Elected from: New York
Vice President: none

22

Grover Cleveland
(1837–1908)

Years in Office: 1885–1889
Democrat

Elected from: New York
Vice President: Thomas Hendricks

23

Benjamin Harrison
(1833–1901)

Years in Office: 1889–1893
Republican

Elected from: Indiana
Vice President: Levi Morton

24

Grover Cleveland
(1837–1908)

Years in Office: 1893–1897
Democrat

Elected from: New York
Vice President: Adlai Stevenson

25

William McKinley**
(1843–1901)

Years in Office: 1897–1901
Republican

Elected from: Ohio
Vice Presidents: Garret Hobart, Theodore Roosevelt

26

Theodore Roosevelt
(1858–1919)

Years in Office: 1901–1909
Republican

Elected from: New York
Vice President: Charles Fairbanks

27

William Howard Taft
(1857–1930)

Years in Office: 1909–1913
Republican

Elected from: Ohio
Vice President: James Sherman

28

Woodrow Wilson
(1856–1924)

Years in Office: 1913–1921
Democrat

Elected from: New Jersey
Vice President: Thomas Marshall

29

Warren G. Harding*
(1865–1923)

Years in Office: 1921–1923
Republican

Elected from: Ohio
Vice President: Calvin Coolidge

30

Calvin Coolidge
(1872–1933)

Years in Office: 1923–1929
Republican

Elected from: Massachusetts
Vice President: Charles Dawes

31

Herbert C. Hoover
(1874–1964)

Years in Office: 1929–1933
Republican

Elected from: New York
Vice President: Charles Curtis

32

Franklin D. Roosevelt*
(1882–1945)

Years in Office: 1933–1945
Democrat

Elected from: New York
Vice Presidents: John Garner, Henry Wallace, Harry S. Truman

33

Harry S. Truman
(1884–1972)

Years in Office: 1945–1953
Democrat

Elected from: Missouri
Vice President: Alben Barkley

34

Dwight D. Eisenhower
(1890–1969)

Years in Office: 1953–1961
Republican

Elected from: New York
Vice President: Richard M. Nixon

35

John F. Kennedy**
(1917–1963)

Years in Office: 1961–1963
Democrat

Elected from: Massachusetts
Vice President: Lyndon B. Johnson

36

Lyndon B. Johnson
(1908–1973)

Years in Office: 1963–1969
Democrat

Elected from: Texas
Vice President: Hubert Humphrey

37

Richard M. Nixon***
(1913–1994)

Years in Office: 1969–1974
Republican

Elected from: New York
Vice Presidents: Spiro Agnew, Gerald R. Ford

38

Gerald R. Ford
(1913–2006)

Years in Office: 1974–1977
Republican

Elected from: Michigan
Vice President: Nelson Rockefeller

39

James E. Carter
(1924–)

Years in Office: 1977–1981
Democrat

Elected from: Georgia
Vice President: Walter F. Mondale

40

Ronald W. Reagan
(1911–2004)

Years in Office: 1981–1989
Republican

Elected from: California
Vice President: George H. W. Bush

41

George H. W. Bush
(1924–)

Years in Office: 1989–1993
Republican

Elected from: Texas
Vice President: J. Danforth Quayle

42

William J. Clinton
(1946–)

Years in Office: 1993–2001
Democrat

Elected from: Arkansas
Vice President: Albert Gore, Jr.

43

George W. Bush
(1946–)

Years in Office: 2001–2009
Republican

Elected from: Texas
Vice President: Richard Cheney

44

Barack H. Obama
(1961–)

Years in Office: 2009–
Democrat

Elected from: Illinois
Vice President: Joseph R. Biden

Presidents

* Died in office
** Assassinated
*** Resigned
† Elected Vice President on the coalition Union Party ticket

Key Economic Questions

In every society, people have access to resources such as water, soil, and human labor. Yet all resources are limited. Economics is the study of how people choose to use their limited resources to meet their wants and needs. Every society must answer three basic economic questions. How a society answers these questions depends on how much it values different economic goals.

Economic Goals

Economic efficiency	Making the most of resources
Economic freedom	Freedom from government intervention in the production and distribution of goods and services
Economic security and predictability	Assurance that goods and services will be available, payments will be made on time, and a safety net will protect individuals in times of economic disaster
Economic equity	Fair distribution of wealth
Economic growth and innovation	Innovation leads to economic growth, and economic growth leads to a higher standard of living.
Other goals	Societies pursue additional goals, such as environmental protection.

Three Key Economic Questions

What goods and services should be produced?	How should goods and services be produced?	Who consumes the goods and services?
How much of our resources should we devote to national defense, education, public health, or consumer goods? Which consumer goods should we produce?	Should we produce food on large corporate farms or on small family farms? Should we produce electricity with oil, nuclear power, coal, or solar power?	How do goods and services get distributed? The question of who gets to consume which goods and services lies at the very heart of the differences between economic systems. Each society answers the question of distribution based on its combination of social values and goals.

Choices About How to Produce Goods
This wind farm illustrates a society's decision to produce electricity using the power of the wind. What do you think are the benefits and drawbacks of wind power?

Economic Systems

An economic system is the method used by a society to produce and distribute goods and services. A society's economic system reflects how that society answers the three key economic questions and what its economic goals are. Different systems produce different results in terms of productivity, the welfare of workers, and consumer choice.

Modern Economic Systems

	Description	Origin	Location Today
Market (Capitalist, Free-Enterprise)	Economic decisions are made in the marketplace through interactions between buyers and sellers according to the laws of supply and demand. Individual capitalists own the means of production. Government regulates some economic activities and provides such "public goods" as education.	Capitalism has existed since the earliest buying and selling of goods in a market. The market economic system developed in response to Adam Smith's ideas and the shift from agriculture to industry in the 1800s.	Canada, Germany, Japan, United States, and many other nations
Centrally Planned (Command, Socialist, Communist)	Central government planners make most economic decisions for the people. In theory, the workers own the means of production. In practice, the government does. Some private enterprise, but government dominates.	In the 1800s, criticism of capitalism by Karl Marx and others led to calls for distributing wealth according to need. After the 1917 Russian Revolution, the Soviet Union developed the first command economy.	Communist countries, including China, Cuba, and North Korea
Mixed (Social Democratic, Liberal Socialist)	A mix of socialism and free enterprise in which the government plays a significant role in making economic decisions.	The Great Depression of the 1930s ended laissez-faire capitalism in most countries. People insisted that government take a stronger role in fixing economic problems. The fall of communism in Eastern Europe in the 1990s ended central planning in most countries. People insisted on freer markets.	Most nations, including Brazil, France, India, Italy, Poland, Russia, Sweden, and the United Kingdom

Buyers and Sellers in a Free Market

In a market economy, buyers and sellers make decisions on the basis of their own self-interest. They may freely buy and sell goods. In a voluntary exchange, both parties expect to gain from the transaction.

The American Economy

For centuries, people have considered the United States to be a land of opportunity where anyone from any background could achieve success through hard work. Why has the United States been such an economic success? Certainly the open land, natural resources, and uninterrupted flow of immigrant labor have all contributed. But a key factor has also been the tradition of free enterprise—the social and political commitment to giving people the freedom to compete in the marketplace.

Constitutional Protections of Free Enterprise

Property Rights

Property rights are protected by the Fifth Amendment: "No person shall be deprived of life, liberty, or property, without due process; nor shall private property be taken for public use, without just compensation." The Fourteenth Amendment places the same limitation on state governments.

Taxation

Congress can only tax individuals and businesses in the ways the Constitution allows. Article 1 gives Congress the power to levy taxes, but Sections 2 and 9 require that direct taxes be apportioned according to population. The Sixteenth Amendment gave Congress the right to set taxes based on income.

Binding Contracts

Article 1, Section 10, guarantees people and businesses the right to make binding contracts.

▲ Free enterprise in the United States is founded on ideas so basic to our culture that we tend to take them for granted.

Flow of Goods, Services, and Money in a Market Economy

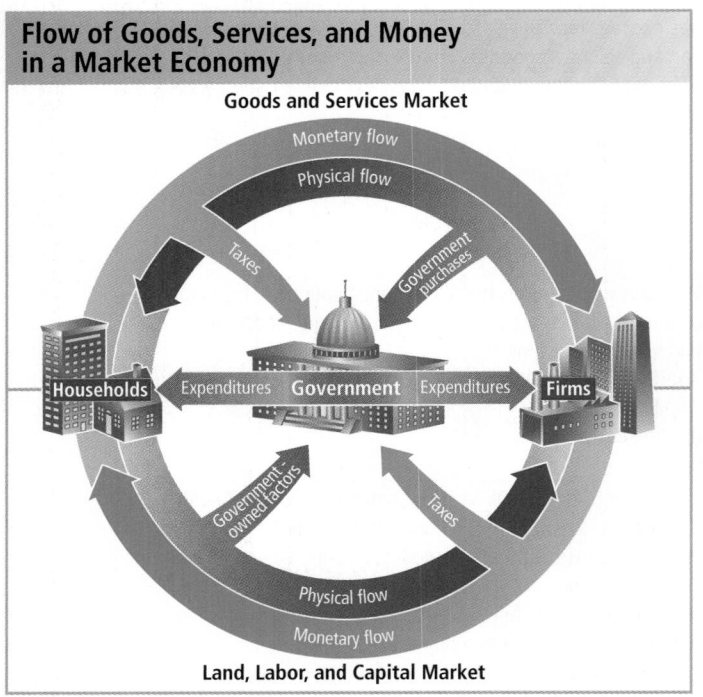

▲ This circular flow model shows how government typically interacts with households and businesses in the marketplace.

United States Workforce, by Occupation, 2005*

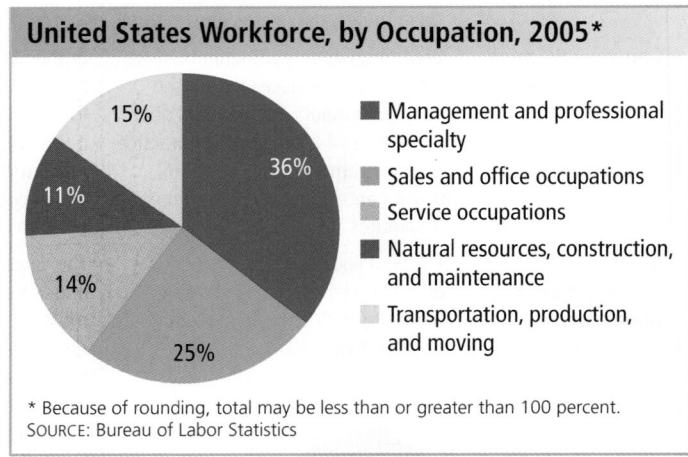

- Management and professional specialty
- Sales and office occupations
- Service occupations
- Natural resources, construction, and maintenance
- Transportation, production, and moving

* Because of rounding, total may be less than or greater than 100 percent.
SOURCE: Bureau of Labor Statistics

▲ How do you think this snapshot of the United States labor force would have looked in 1800? In 1900?

Key Events in American Economic History

1791
First Bank of the United States chartered

1834
Mill girls in Lowell, Massachusetts, protest wage cuts

1867
Knights of Labor formed

1886
American Federation of Labor formed

1780

1820

1860

1835
Strike for 10-hour workday in Philadelphia

1869
Financial panic sweeps nation

1892
Homestead Strike in Pennsylvania

Measuring the Economy's Performance

A modern industrial economy repeatedly experiences cycles of economic growth and decline. Business cycles are of major interest to macroeconomists, who study their causes and effects. Economists use many tools to predict changes in business cycles. The leading indicators are a set of key economic variables including stock prices, interest rates, and manufacturers' new orders for goods.

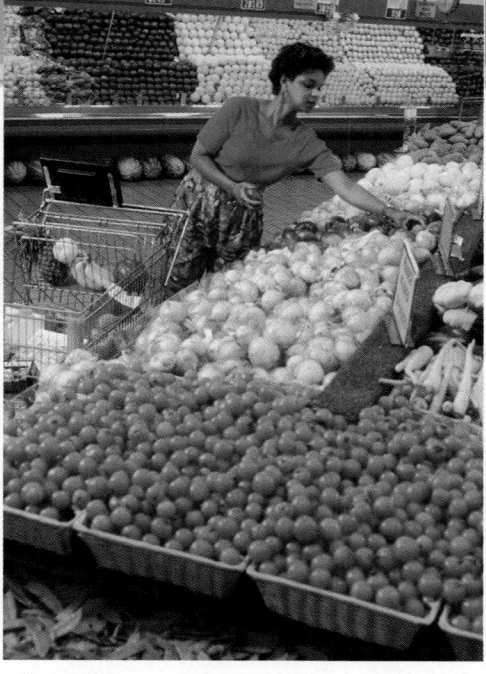

▲ **Food Prices** An increase in the price of food can signal inflation. What impact do rising food prices have on families?

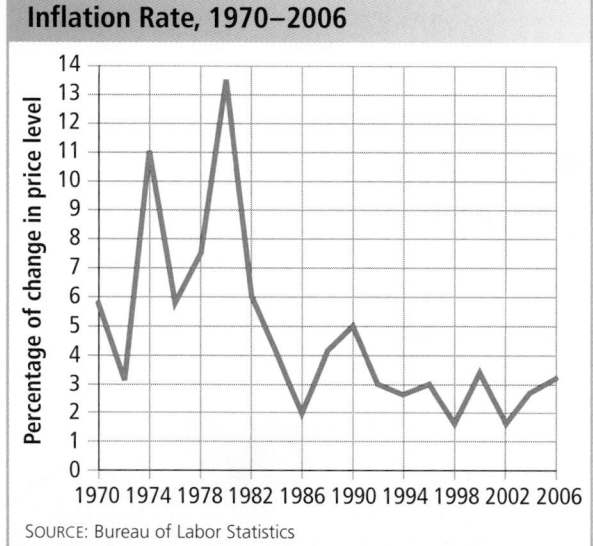

Inflation Rate, 1970–2006

SOURCE: Bureau of Labor Statistics

▲ One of the economic indicators economists look at is the economy's level of inflation. Inflation is a general increase in prices. As prices rise, the purchasing power of money declines.

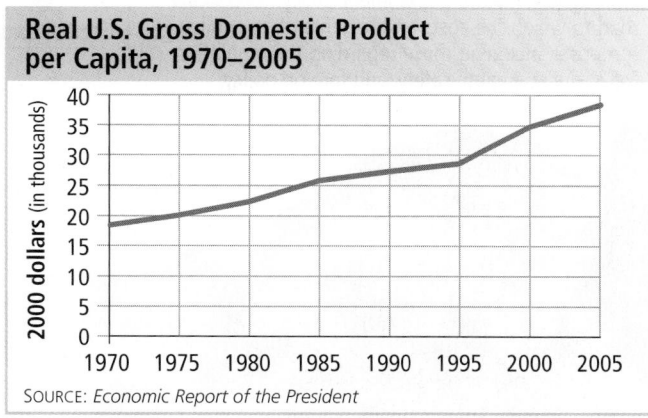

Real U.S. Gross Domestic Product per Capita, 1970–2005

SOURCE: *Economic Report of the President*

▲ Gross Domestic Product is the dollar value of all final goods and services produced within a country's borders in a given year. GDP per capita equals the GDP divided by the country's total population. Long-term increases in GDP allow an entire society to improve its standard of living.

Economics Handbook

1913	1929	1947	1955	1980	2008
Federal Reserve System created	Stock market crash	Taft-Hartley Act	AFL and CIO merge	Savings and Loan crisis begins	Mortgage crisis leads to increase in home foreclosures

1900	1940	1980	2020

1930	1933	1963	1997	2001
Great Depression begins	Federal Deposit Insurance Corporation (FDIC) created	Equal Pay Act	More than 160,000 ATMs operate in United States	Office of Faith-Based and Community Initiatives established

Analyzing Costs and Benefits

Economists point out that all individuals, businesses, and large groups of people make decisions that involve trade-offs. Trade-offs are all the alternatives that we give up whenever we choose one course of action over another. One alternative, though, is usually more desirable than all the others. The most desirable alternative given up as the result of a decision is called the opportunity cost. At times, a decision's opportunity cost may be unclear or complicated. Nonetheless, consumers, businesses, and governments must carefully consider trade-offs and opportunity costs before making a decision.

Safety Versus Cost and Convenience Tens of thousands of people are killed every year in auto accidents in the United States. Safety features like antilock brakes, air bags, and seatbelts may save lives, but they also make cars more expensive. Throughout history, government policymakers have had to weigh the costs and benefits of any policy proposal, including those regarding the regulation of business, health, safety, and foreign policy.

Costs of Auto Safety	
Saftey Feature	**Cost**
Antilock brakes	$600.00
Side-impact air bags	$350.00
Traction control	$1,200.00

The Federal Budget

The federal budget is a written document indicating the amount of money the government expects to receive during a certain year and authorizing the amount the government can spend that year. Government officials who take part in the budgeting process debate how much should be spent on specific programs such as defense, education, and scientific research.

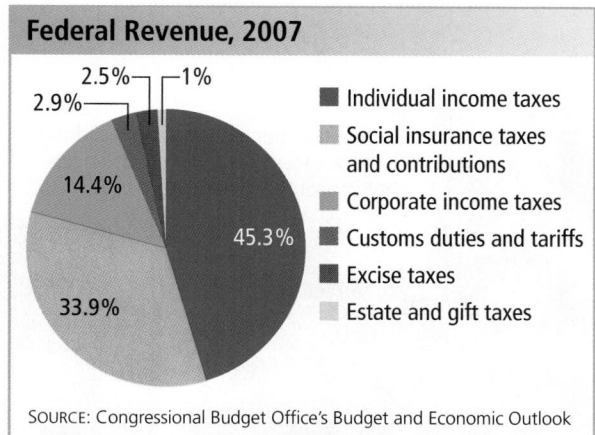

Federal Revenue, 2007

2.5% — 1%
2.9%
14.4%
45.3%
33.9%

- ■ Individual income taxes
- ■ Social insurance taxes and contributions
- ■ Corporate income taxes
- ■ Customs duties and tariffs
- ■ Excise taxes
- ■ Estate and gift taxes

SOURCE: Congressional Budget Office's Budget and Economic Outlook

▲ This graph shows the sources of government revenue. What are the largest sources of federal income?

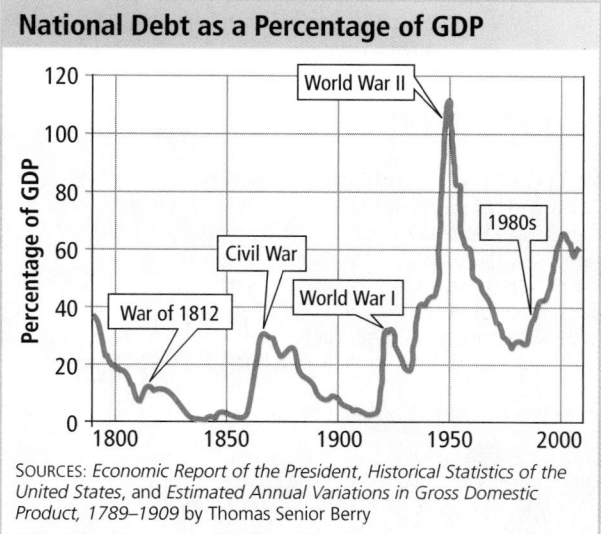

National Debt as a Percentage of GDP

World War II

Civil War

War of 1812

World War I

1980s

Percentage of GDP

1800   1850   1900   1950   2000

SOURCES: *Economic Report of the President, Historical Statistics of the United States,* and *Estimated Annual Variations in Gross Domestic Product, 1789–1909* by Thomas Senior Berry

▲ If the federal government's spending is greater than its income in any given year, then the budget is said to be in deficit. The government must then borrow money to pay the shortfall. The total of the government's borrowed money over time is added together to form the national debt.

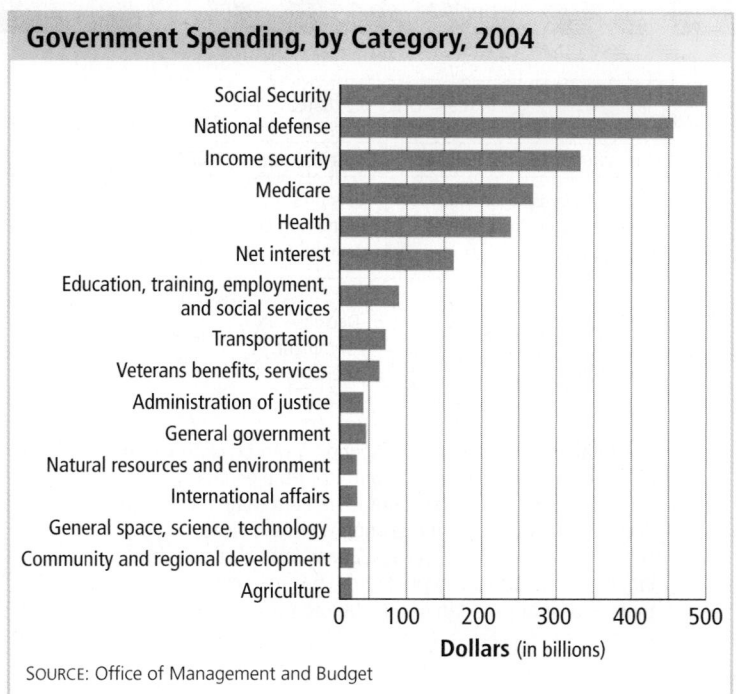

Government Spending, by Category, 2004

Social Security
National defense
Income security
Medicare
Health
Net interest
Education, training, employment, and social services
Transportation
Veterans benefits, services
Administration of justice
General government
Natural resources and environment
International affairs
General space, science, technology
Community and regional development
Agriculture

0   100   200   300   400   500
Dollars (in billions)

SOURCE: Office of Management and Budget

◀ This graph shows how the government spends its money. What are the largest areas of federal spending?

Tools for Moderating the Business Cycle: Fiscal Policy

The federal government takes in money to pay for its spending through taxation and borrowing. The decisions the government makes about taxing and spending can have a powerful impact on the overall economy. Fiscal policy is the use of government spending and revenue collection to influence the economy. Fiscal policies are used to achieve economic growth, full employment, and price stability.

▼ Cutting government spending is difficult because some voters will object to cuts that impact their interests.

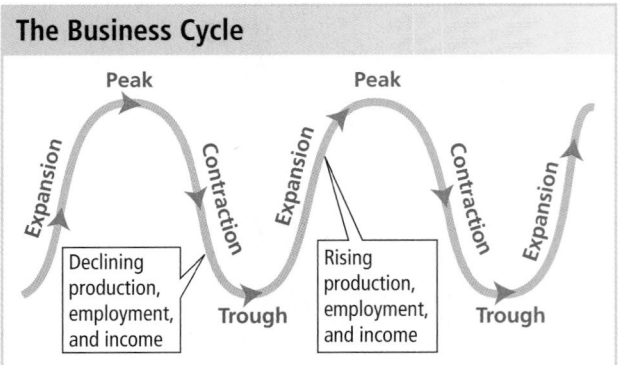

The Business Cycle

Peak — Peak

Expansion — Contraction — Expansion — Contraction — Expansion

Declining production, employment, and income — Trough

Rising production, employment, and income — Trough

▲ In a business cycle, a period of rising real GDP reaches a peak, then falls into a contraction. When the contraction reaches the low point, or trough, a new expansion begins. From 1854 to 1991, the United States experienced 31 business cycles. Excluding wartimes, the cycles averaged 48 months.

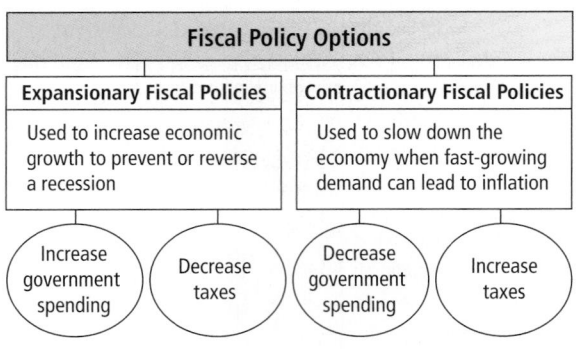

Fiscal Policy Options

Expansionary Fiscal Policies	Contractionary Fiscal Policies
Used to increase economic growth to prevent or reverse a recession	Used to slow down the economy when fast-growing demand can lead to inflation

Increase government spending — Decrease taxes — Decrease government spending — Increase taxes

▲ The total level of government spending can be changed to help increase or decrease the output of the economy. Similarly, taxes can be raised or lowered to help increase or decrease the output of the economy. Fiscal policies are difficult to put into practice because many laws dictate spending. Also, it is difficult to predict the business cycle, and there is a significant lag in time before policies take effect.

Tools for Moderating the Business Cycle: Monetary Policy

After the charter of the Second Bank of the United States expired, states chartered some banks while the federal government chartered others. Reserve requirements—the amount of money that banks are required to keep on hand—were difficult to enforce, and bank runs often led to panic. After the Panic of 1907, Congress responded with the Federal Reserve Act of 1913. This act created the Federal Reserve System—a group of twelve independent banks that could lend to other banks in times of need. Monetary policy refers to the actions the Federal Reserve Board takes to influence the level of real GDP and the rate of inflation in the economy.

Money Creation

$1,000 + $900 + $810 = $2,710

You deposit $1,000 into your checking account.

Your $1,000 deposit minus $100 in reserves is loaned to Elaine, who gives it to Joshua.

Joshua's $900 deposit minus $90 in reserves is loaned to another customer.

At this point, the money supply has increased by $2,710.

$100 held in reserve
$900 available for loans

$90 held in reserve
$810 available for loans

◄ The Federal Reserve is best known for its role in regulating the nation's money supply. Too much money in the economy leads to inflation. This diagram shows how money is created. By altering the amount of money banks are required to keep in reserve, the Fed can increase or shrink the money supply.

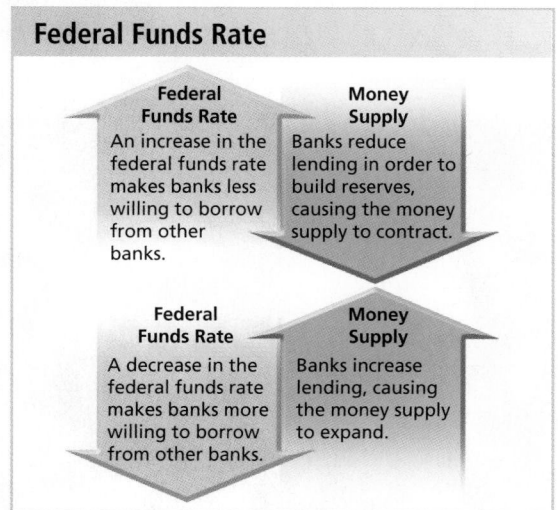

Federal Funds Rate

Federal Funds Rate
An increase in the federal funds rate makes banks less willing to borrow from other banks.

Money Supply
Banks reduce lending in order to build reserves, causing the money supply to contract.

Federal Funds Rate
A decrease in the federal funds rate makes banks more willing to borrow from other banks.

Money Supply
Banks increase lending, causing the money supply to expand.

▲ The federal funds rate is the interest rate that banks charge each other when they lend each other reserves. An increase in the federal funds rate makes borrowing more costly, and the monetary supply contracts. Banks are more willing to borrow and lend money when the federal funds rate is low.

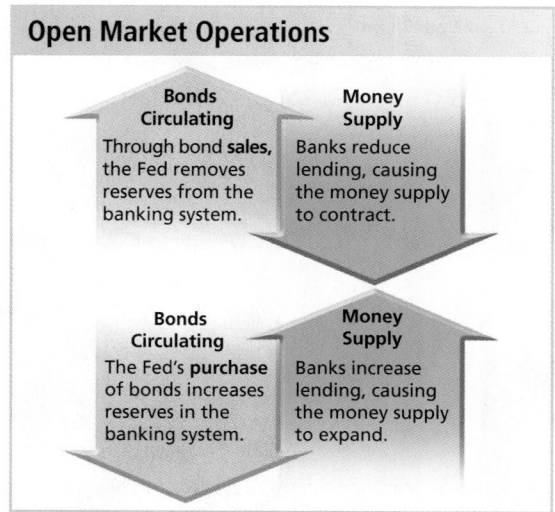

Open Market Operations

Bonds Circulating
Through bond **sales**, the Fed removes reserves from the banking system.

Money Supply
Banks reduce lending, causing the money supply to contract.

Bonds Circulating
The Fed's **purchase** of bonds increases reserves in the banking system.

Money Supply
Banks increase lending, causing the money supply to expand.

▲ When the Fed purchases government bonds on the open market, the bond seller deposits the money from the bond sale in the bank. In this way, funds enter the banking system, setting in motion money creation. When the Fed sells government bonds that it holds, bond buyers pay for the bonds using money from their bank accounts. When the Fed receives this money, it is taken out of circulation.

U.S. Foreign Trade

Foreign trade has played an important role in the U.S. economy. A free-trade zone is a region where a group of countries agrees to reduce or eliminate trade barriers, such as tariffs or taxes on imports. The North American Free Trade Agreement (NAFTA) set the goal of eliminating all tariffs and trade barriers between Canada, Mexico, and the United States by 2009. Supporters of NAFTA point to increased trade among the countries. About 100 regional trading organizations operate in the world today. Many goods are produced globally by multinational corporations, with parts produced in one country and assembled in another.

U.S. Exports and Imports, by Major Trading Partners, August 2006–August 2007

SOURCE: U.S. Census Bureau

Specialization and Trade International trade occurs when one country provides resources that another country needs. By specializing in the production of certain goods and services, nations can use their resources more efficiently. Do research at the library or online to learn more about absolute and comparative advantage to understand why specialization and trade can benefit all nations—even those with few resources.

Balance of Trade

The **balance of trade** is the relationship between a nation's imports and exports.

Historical Context: According to the theory of mercantilism, a nation could increase its wealth by protecting its own industries from foreign competition through tariffs, or taxes on imports, and by striving to export more than it imports. The American colonies provided a market for British-made goods. American colonists were not permitted to trade with countries other than Britain or to manufacture their own goods.

Today: In recent decades, the United States has had an unfavorable balance of trade. It has imported more than it has exported and experienced annual trade deficits. A trade imbalance can be corrected by limiting imports or increasing exports.

Major Exports and Imports, 2007

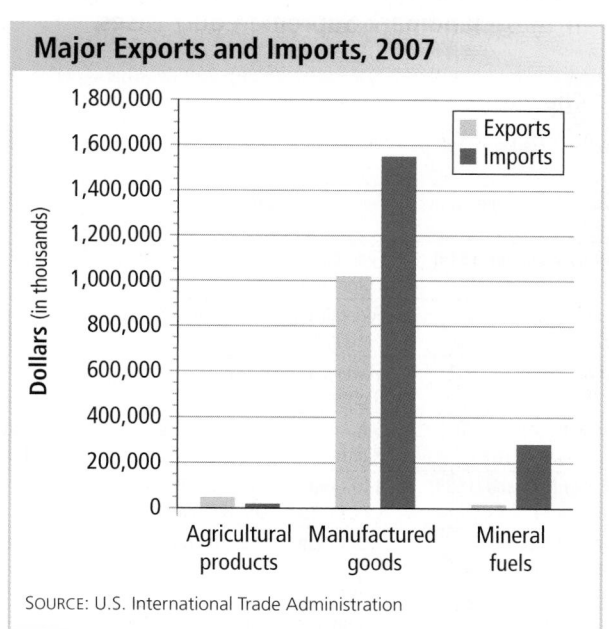

SOURCE: U.S. International Trade Administration

Major Trade Organization Members

Asia-Pacific Economic Cooperation (APEC)

Caribbean Community and Common Market (CARICOM)

European Union (EU)

North American Free Trade Agreement (NAFTA) and APEC

Southern Common Market (MERCOSUR)

Landmark Decisions of the Supreme Court

The table below lists key Supreme Court cases, issues, and decisions that have had a lasting impact on the course of the nation's history. Following the table, you will find a more detailed summary of each of these landmark Supreme Court cases.

The Case	The Issues	The Supreme Courts Decision
Marbury v. *Madison* (1803)	Judicial Review, Checks and Balances	First decision to assert judicial review: the power of the Court to interpret the constitutionality of a law
McCulloch v. *Maryland* (1819)	Federalism, States' Rights	Upheld the power of the national government and denied the right of a state to tax a federal agency.
Gibbons v. *Ogden* (1824)	Federalism, States' Rights, Interstate Commerce	Upheld broad congressional power to legislate and regulate commerce between states.
Worcester v. *Georgia* (1832)	Federalism, States' Rights; Native American Sovereignty	Ruled that Georgia had no power to pass laws affecting the Cherokees because federal jurisdiction over the Cherokees was exclusive.
Dred Scott v. *Sandford* (1857)	Slavery, 5th Amendment, Citizens' Rights	Ruled that slaves were property, not citizens and, therefore, Dred Scott was not entitled to use the courts.
Munn v. *Illinois* (1876)	5th Amendment, Public Interest; States' Rights	Upheld an Illinois law regulating railroad rates because the movement of grain was closely related to public interest.
Civil Rights Cases (1883)	14th Amendment Equal Protection Clause, Racial Discrimination	Stated that the 14th Amendment only applied to discriminatory action taken by states, not to discriminatory actions taken by individuals.
Wabash, St. Louis & Pacific R.R. v. *Illinois* (1886)	Federalism, Interstate Commerce	Struck down an Illinois law regulating interstate railroad rates, ruling that it infringed on the federal government's exclusive control over interstate commerce.
United States v. *E.C. Knight Co.* (1895)	Sherman Antitrust Act, Federalism, States' Rights	The Sherman Antitrust Act does not apply to manufacturers located within a single state, because under the 10th Amendment, states have the right to regulate "local activities."
In Re Debs (1895)	Labor Strikes, Interstate Commerce	Ruled that the federal government had the authority to halt a railroad strike because it interfered with interstate commerce and delivery of the mail.
Plessy v. *Ferguson* (1896)	Segregation, 14th Amendment Equal Protection Clause	Permitted segregated public facilities, arguing that separate but equal accommodations did not violate the equal protection clause of the 14th Amendment.
United States v. *Wong Kim Ark* (1898)	Immigration, citizenship,14th Amendment	Affirmed that under the 14th Amendment, all persons born in the United States are citizens of the United States.
Northern Securities Co. v. *United States* (1904)	Sherman Antitrust Act, Interstate Commerce	Sherman Antitrust Act could apply to any company that sought to eliminate competition in interstate commerce, including companies chartered within a single state.
Lochner v. New York (1905)	Labor conditions, property rights, 14th Amendment	Struck down a state law setting a 10-hour day for employees because the law interfered with an employee's right to contract with an employer and violated the protection of liberty guaranteed by the 14th Amendment.
Muller v. *Oregon* (1908)	Women's rights, Labor Conditions, 14th Amendment	In a departure from the *Lochner* case, the Court upheld a state law limiting women's work hours, viewing women as a special class needing special protections.
Standard Oil of New Jersey v. *United States* (1911)	Antitrust	Ruled that Standard Oil was an illegal monopoly and ordered that it be dissolved into smaller, competing companies.
American Tobacco v. *United States* (1911)	Antitrust	Ruled that American Tobacco was an illegal monopoly and ordered that it be dissolved into smaller, competing companies.
Schenck v. *United States* (1919)	1st Amendment freedom of speech, national security	The Court limited free speech in time of war, reasoning that freedom of speech can be limited if the words present a "clear and present danger" to the country.
Abrams v. *United States* (1919)	1st Amendment freedom of speech, national security	Upheld the convictions of persons who distributed antigovernment literature in violation of the Espionage Act. But Justices Holmes and Brandeis dissented, urging more stringent protection of the 1st Amendment.
Gitlow v. *New York* (1925)	1st Amendment freedoms of speech and press, 14th Amendment	Ruled that the freedoms of speech and press were "incorporated" and protected from impairment by the states by the due process clause of the 14th Amendment.
Stromberg v. *California* (1931)	1st Amendment freedom of speech, 14th Amendment	Overturned an anticommunist law that banned the public display of a red flag. This was the first time the Supreme Court struck down a state law under the 1st Amendment as applied to the states by the 14th Amendment.
Near v. *Minnesota* (1931)	1st Amendment freedom of speech, 14th Amendment	The Supreme Court struck down a Minnesota state law, ruling that it infringed upon freedom of the press, guaranteed by the due process clause of the 14th Amendment.

The Case	The Issues	The Supreme Court's Decision
Schechter Poultry Corporation v. United States (1935)	New Deal, separation of powers, interstate commerce	The Court held that Congress, not the President, has the power to regulate interstate commerce. The National Industrial Recovery Act was declared unconstitutional for exceeding the commerce power that the Constitution had given to Congress.
West Coast Hotel v. Parrish (1937)	Minimum wage laws, 5th Amendment	Ruled that the Constitution allowed the restriction of liberty of contract by state law where such restriction protected the community, health, safety, or vulnerable groups.
West Virginia State Board of Education v. Barnette (1943)	Pledge of Allegiance, 1st Amendment	The Court found that a state law requiring students to pledge allegiance to the flag violated freedom of speech and freedom of religion.
Hirabayashi v. United States (1943)	5th Amendment, civil liberties, national security	The Supreme Court upheld the legitimacy of travel restrictions imposed on Japanese Americans during World War II.
Korematsu v. United States (1944)	5th Amendment, civil liberties, national security	Ruled that the internment of Japanese Americans during World War II did not violate the Constitution.
Everson v. Board of Education (1947)	1st Amendment, establishment clause	The New Jersey law allowing reimbursement of money to parents whose children attended Catholic schools did not violate the 1st amendment. Some services "are separate from the religious function."
Dennis v. United States (1951)	1st Amendment, civil liberties, national security	The Court ruled that the Smith Act, which prohibited advocation of the overthrow of the U.S. government by force and violence, did not violate the 1st Amendment.
Brown v. Board of Education of Topeka (1954)	School segregation, 14th Amendment	The Court found that segregation itself was a violation of the Equal Protection Clause, commenting that "in the field of public education the doctrine of 'separate but equal' has no place."
Watkins v. United States (1957)	Rights of the accused, 5th Amendment	The Bill of Rights is applicable to congressional investigations, as it is to all forms of governmental action.
Yates v. United States (1957)	1st Amendment freedom of speech, national security	Ruled that the Smith Act did not forbid persons from advocating forcible overthrow of the government; it only forbade actions to achieve that goal.
Cooper v. Aaron (1958)	School segregation, 14th Amendment	The Court ruled unanimously against the Little Rock School Board's efforts to not comply with the Brown decision.
Mapp v. Ohio (1961)	Search and seizure 4th and 14th amendments	Ruled that evidence obtained by searches and seizures in violation of the Constitution is inadmissible.
Baker v. Carr (1962)	Legislative reapportionment, 14th Amendment	Ruled that federal Courts could direct that election-district boundaries be redrawn to ensure citizens' political rights.
Engel v. Vitale (1962)	1st Amendment, establishment clause	Ruled that the recitation of a prayer in a public classroom was a violation of the establishment clause of the 1st Amendment.
Gideon v. Wainwright (1963)	Rights of the accused, 6th and 14th amendments	The Court said that all states must provide an attorney in all felony and capital cases for people who cannot afford one themselves.
Reynolds v. Sims (1964)	Legislative reapportionment, 14th Amendment	Extended the one-person, one-vote principle of *Wesberry v. Sanders* (1964) to states, ruling that state legislative districts should be roughly equal in population so that every voter has an equally weighted vote.
Heart of Atlanta Motel v. United States (1964)	Racial segregation, interstate commerce	Racial segregation of private facilities engaged in interstate commerce was found unconstitutional.
Miranda v. Arizona (1966)	Rights of the accused, 5th, 6th, and 14th amendments	Before questioning suspects held in custody, police must inform suspects that they have the right to remain silent, that anything they say may be used against them, and that they have the right to counsel.
Swann v. Charlotte-Mecklenburg Board of Education (1971)	School desegregation, busing	Ruled that busing students to various schools is an acceptable way to integrate segregated school systems. The Court said school districts had broad powers to find solutions to the problem of segregation.
Tinker v. Des Moines (1969)	Students' rights, 1st Amendment freedom of speech	Students in school may exercise freedom of speech as long as they do not disrupt classwork, create substantial disorder, or interfere with the rights of others.
New York Times v. United States (1971)	1st Amendment freedom of the press	The Court limited censorship through "prior restraint" of the press, noting that it is the obligation of the government to prove that actual harm to the nation's security would be caused by the publication.
Roe v. Wade (1973)	Abortion, 9th Amendment, "right to privacy"	Decided that states could regulate abortions only in certain circumstances but otherwise a woman's right to an abortion was protected by her right to privacy.
United States v. Nixon (1974)	Executive privilege, separation of powers	Executive privilege was subordinate to "the fundamental demands of due process of law in the fair administration of criminal justice." President Nixon had to surrender audiotapes to a special prosecutor.
Regents of the University of CA v. Bakke (1978)	Affirmative action, 14th Amendment,	The Court held that a university could consider an applicant's race in making admissions decisions, but the use of strict racial quotas in affirmative action programs was not permissible.
New Jersey v. T.L.O. (1985)	Students' rights, 4th and 14th amendments	School officials, unlike the police, need only "reasonable suspicion" to search students when they believe illegal activity is occurring.
Texas v. Johnson (1989)	1st Amendment freedom of speech	Ruled that desecrating the flag as an act of protest is an act of expression protected by the 1st Amendment.
Cruzan v. Director, Missouri Department of Health (1990)	"Right to die," 9th Amendment, 14th Amendment	Individuals have the right to refuse medical treatment, but the State can preserve life unless there is "clear and convincing" evidence that the patient desires the withdrawal of medical treatment.

Supreme Court Cases

Supreme Court Cases

The Case	The Issues	The Supreme Court's Decision
Board of Education of Westside Community Schools v. Mergens (1990)	1st Amendment, Establishment Clause	Allowing students to meet in noncurricular clubs on campus and discuss religion is constitutional because it does not amount to state sponsorship of a religion.
Planned Parenthood of Southeastern Pennsylvania, et al. v. Casey (1992)	Abortion, 14th Amendment, "right to privacy"	The Court upheld a woman's "liberty" to have an abortion but also allowed for restrictive state regulations as long as they did not create an "undue burden" or "substantial obstacle" for a woman.
Vernonia School District v. Acton (1995)	Students' rights, 4th Amendment search and seizure	The Court decided that drug testing of student athletes was constitutional; students' rights can be lessened at school if it is necessary to maintain student safety.
Reno v. American Civil Liberties Union (1997)	Internet, 1st Amendment, freedom of Speech	Ruled that the 1996 Federal Communications Decency Act violated the 1st Amendment's right to freedom of speech by not clearly defining which Internet materials were "indecent."
Bush v. Gore (2000)	Election rules, 14th Amendment	Following the controversial 2000 presidential election, the Supreme Court held that the Florida Supreme Court's plan for recounting ballots was unconstitutional.
Mitchell v. Helms (2000)	1st Amendment, Establishment Clause	Ruled that a federal law providing funds for educational materials to public and private schools, including Catholic parochial schools, does not violate the 1st Amendment's Establishment Clause.
District of Columbia v. Heller (2008)	2nd Amendment	The Court rules that a ban on handguns in the District of Columbia violated the 2nd Amendment right to bear arms.

Abrams v. United States (1919)
(1st Amendment freedom of speech, national security) Jacob Abrams and others distributed leaflets attacking the U.S. decision to send troops to Russia, which was experiencing revolution and civil war. They were found guilty of violating the Espionage Act. The Supreme Court upheld the convictions citing Holmes's "clear and present danger" test. But Justices Holmes and Brandeis published a powerful dissenting opinion. Holmes argued that the "silly leaflet" of "poor and puny anonymities" posed no real danger to U.S. efforts, and thus failed to present a "clear and present danger." He urged his colleagues to enforce the 1st Amendment more stringently.

American Tobacco v. U.S. (1911)
(antitrust) Federal regulators filed an antitrust suit against American Tobacco, controlled by James Buchanan "Buck" Duke. The company controlled more than 90 percent of the world tobacco market. In 1911, the Supreme Court declared the company was a monopoly in violation of the Sherman Antitrust Act and ordered it to be split into five smaller competing companies.

Baker v. Carr (1962)
(legislative reapportionment, 14th Amendment) Rapid population growth had occurred in Tennessee's cities, but the rural-dominated Tennessee legislature did not redraw state legislature districts. Cities with larger populations were underrepresented, while rural communities with smaller populations held the majority of representation. Mayor Baker of Nashville asked for federal court help. The Supreme Court ruled that the apportionment of state legislative districts is within the jurisdiction of federal courts. The Court directed a trial to be held in a Tennessee federal court. The case led to the 1964 *Wesberry* decision, which affirmed voters' right to the equal protection guaranteed by the 14th Amendment and established the principle of "one man, one vote" for the apportionment of congressional districts.

Board of Education of Westside Community Schools v. Mergens (1990)
(1st Amendment, establishment clause) A request by Bridget Mergens to form a student Christian religious group at school was denied by an Omaha high school principal. Mergens took legal action, claiming that a 1984 federal law required "equal access" for student religious groups. The Court ordered the school to permit the club, stating that "a high school does not have to permit any extracurricular activities, but when it does, the school is bound by the . . . [Equal Access] Act of 1984. Allowing students to meet on campus and discuss religion is constitutional because it does not amount to 'State sponsorship of a religion.'"

Brown v. Board of Education of Topeka (1954)
(school segregation, 14th Amendment) Probably no twentieth-century Supreme Court decision so deeply stirred and changed life in the United States as *Brown*. An eight-year-old girl from Topeka, Kansas, was not permitted to attend her neighborhood school because she was an African American. The Court found that segregation was a violation of the Equal Protection Clause, commenting that "in the field of public education the doctrine of 'separate but equal' has no place. . . . Segregation is a denial of the equal protection of the laws." The decision overturned *Plessy*, 1896.

Bush v. Gore (2000)
(election rules, 14th Amendment) Following the controversial 2000 presidential election, the Florida Supreme Court ordered that every county in Florida had to manually recount some ballots. George Bush

filed a request for review in the U.S. Supreme Court. The Supreme Court held that the Florida court's plan for recounting ballots was unconstitutional, noting that the Equal Protection Clause guarantees individuals that their ballots cannot be devalued by "later arbitrary and disparate treatment." The Court reasoned that there were too many procedural differences among the various counties for a fair recount to be conducted by the deadline date set by law.

Civil Rights Cases (1883)

(14th Amendment Equal Protection Clause, racial discrimination) The Civil Rights Act of 1875 included punishments for businesses that practiced discrimination. The Court ruled on a number of cases involving the acts in 1883, finding that the Constitution, "while prohibiting discrimination by governments, made no provisions . . . for acts of racial discrimination by private individuals." The decision limited the impact of the Equal Protection Clause, giving tacit approval for segregation in the private sector.

Cooper v. Aaron (1958)

(school segregation, 14th Amendment) President Eisenhower sent troops to Little Rock, Arkansas, to protect black students and enforce court-ordered school integration. But the local school board and state government continued to use delaying tactics. Arkansas officials even claimed that a state governor had the same power as the Supreme Court to interpret the Constitution. African American students appealed to the Supreme Court. The Court reaffirmed the *Brown* ruling that segregation was unconstitutional and boldly affirmed the Supreme Court's authority as the ultimate interpreter of the Constitution.

Cruzan v. Director, Missouri Department of Health (1990)

("right to die," 9th Amendment, 14th Amendment) After Nancy Beth Cruzan was left in a "persistent vegetative state" by a car accident, Missouri officials refused to comply with her parents' request that the hospital terminate life-support. The Court upheld the State policy under which officials refused to withdraw treatment, rejecting the argument that the Due Process Clause of the 14th Amendment gave the parents the right to refuse treatment on their daughter's behalf. Although individuals have the right to refuse medical treatment, "incompetent" persons are not able to exercise this right; without "clear and convincing" evidence that Cruzan desired the withdrawal of treatment, the State could legally act to preserve her life.

Dennis v. United States (1951)

(1st Amendment, civil liberties, national security) Eugene Dennis, a leader of the Communist Party in the United States, was arrested for violation of the Smith Act, which prohibited advocacy of the overthrow of the U.S. government by force and violence. Dennis claimed that the law violated his 1st Amendment right to free speech. Reasoning that the Communist Party is a conspiratorial organization with "evil" intent, the Supreme Court upheld the Smith Act and Dennis's conviction. The Court ruled that free speech may be limited if it presents a clear and present danger to overthrow the government of the United States by force or violence.

District of Columbia v. Heller (2008)

(2nd Amendment, right to bear arms) The Supreme Court upheld a Court of Appeals decision overturning a District of Columbia law that made it illegal for private citizens to own handguns. The law also required that other firearms be kept either unassembled or with trigger locks in place, thus rendering them unusable. The Court ruled, 5–4, that this law violated a person's Second Amendment right to lawfully own a firearm. Justice Antonin Scalia stated in the Court's opinion "Few laws in the history of our Nation have come close to the severe restriction of the District's handgun ban. . . . Undoubtedly some think that the Second Amendment is outmoded in a society . . . where gun violence is a serious problem. That is perhaps debatable, but what is not debatable is that it is not the role of this Court to pronounce the Second Amendment extinct."

Dred Scott v. Sandford (1857)

(slavery, 5th Amendment, citizens' rights) This decision upheld property rights over human rights by saying that Dred Scott, a slave, could not become a free man just because he had traveled in "free soil" states with his master. A badly divided nation was further fragmented by the decision. "Free soil" federal laws and the Missouri Compromise line of 1820 were held unconstitutional because they deprived a slave owner of the right to his "property" without just compensation. This narrow reading of the Constitution, a landmark case of the Court, was most clearly stated by Chief Justice Roger B. Taney, a states' rights advocate.

Engel v. Vitale (1962)

(1st Amendment establishment clause) The State Board of Regents of New York required the recitation of a nonsectarian prayer at the beginning of each school day. A group of parents filed suit against the required prayer. The Supreme Court ruled that the recitation of a prayer in a public classroom was a violation of the establishment clause of the 1st Amendment. The Court ruled New York's action unconstitutional, observing, "There can be no doubt that . . . religious beliefs [are] embodied in the Regents' prayer."

Everson v. Board of Education (1947)

New Jersey allowed for the reimbursement of transportation costs to parents whose children attended private schools, including parochial Catholic schools. Arch Everson, a taxpaying resident of Ewing Township, sued the local school district, insisting that this reimbursement violated both the New Jersey State Constitution and the First Amendment. In a 5–4 ruling, the Supreme Court upheld the law, stating that the "First Amendment has erected a wall between church and state. . . . New Jersey has not breached it here."

Gibbons v. Ogden (1824)

(federalism, states' rights, interstate commerce) Aaron Ogden's exclusive New York ferry license gave him the right to operate steamboats to and from New York. Thomas Gibbons was operating steamboats between New York and New Jersey under a U.S. federal license. Ogden obtained an injunction from a New York court ordering Gibbons to stop operating his boats in New York waters. The Supreme Court invalidated the New York licensing regulations, holding that federal regulations should take precedence under the Constitution's Supremacy Clause (Article VI, Section 2). The decision strengthened the power of the United States to regulate interstate business. Federal regulation of the broadcasting industry, oil pipelines, and banking are all based on *Gibbons*.

Gideon v. Wainwright (1963)

(rights of the accused, 6th and 14th amendments) Gideon was charged with breaking into a poolroom. He could not afford a lawyer, and Florida refused to provide counsel for trials not involving the death penalty. Gideon defended himself poorly and was sentenced to five years in prison. The Court called for a new trial, arguing that the Due Process Clause of the 14th Amendment applied to the 6th Amendment's guarantee of counsel for all poor persons facing a felony charge. Gideon later was found not guilty with the help of a court-appointed attorney.

Gitlow v. New York (1925)

(1st Amendment freedoms of speech and press, 14th Amendment) Gitlow was convicted for distributing a manifesto that called for the establishment of socialism through strikes and other actions. The Supreme Court considered whether the 1st and 14th amendments had influence on state laws. According to what came to be known as the "incorporation" doctrine, the Court argued that the provisions of the 1st Amendment were "incorporated" by the 14th Amendment. The New York law was not overruled, but the decision clearly indicated that the Court could make such a ruling. Later cases extended the incorporation doctrine. Today, the Supreme Court holds that almost every provision of the Bill of Rights applies to both the federal government and the states.

Heart of Atlanta Motel v. United States (1964)

(racial segregation, interstate commerce) The Civil Rights Act of 1964 outlawed racial discrimination in "public accommodations," including motels that refused rooms to blacks. Although local desegregation appeared to fall outside federal authority, the government argued that it was regulating interstate commerce. The Court agreed, declaring, "The power of Congress to promote interstate commerce also includes the power to regulate the local incidents thereof, including local activities . . . which have a substantial and harmful effect upon that commerce." Racial segregation of private facilities engaged in interstate commerce was found unconstitutional.

Hirabayashi v. United States (1943)

(5th Amendment, civil liberties, national security) After the Japanese attack on Pearl Harbor, President Roosevelt issued executive orders to protect the West Coast from espionage and sabotage. As a result of these orders, curfews were established, and Japanese Americans were evacuated to relocation centers. Gordon Kiyoshi Hirabayashi, a student at the University of Washington, was convicted of violating a curfew and relocation order. Did the government policies violate the 5th Amendment rights of Americans of Japanese descent? The Supreme Court upheld the curfew, but evaded ruling on the relocation. The Court considered the vulnerability of military installations on the West Coast and the "solidarity" that persons of Japanese descent felt with their motherland, and reasoned that restrictions served an important national interest. Racial discrimination was justified since "in time of war residents having ethnic affiliations with an invading enemy may be a greater source of danger than those of a different ancestry."

In Re Debs (1895)

(labor strikes, interstate commerce) Eugene V. Debs, a leader of the 1894 Pullman Railroad Car workers' strike, refused to halt the strike as ordered by a federal court. Debs appealed his "contempt of court" conviction. Citing Article 1, Section 8 of the Constitution, the Supreme Court ruled that the government had a right to regulate interstate commerce and ensure the operations of the Postal Service. The federal court had a right to stop the strike because the strikers interfered with the railroad's ability to provide interstate commerce and deliver the mail, which benefited the needs and "general welfare" of all Americans.

Korematsu v. United States (1944)

(5th Amendment, civil liberties, national security) After the Japanese attack on Pearl Harbor, President Roosevelt issued executive orders to protect the West Coast from acts of espionage and sabotage. As a result of these orders, more than 110,000 Japanese Americans living on the West Coast were forced to abandon their property and live in primitive camps far from the coast. Korematsu refused to report to an assembly center and was arrested. The Court rejected his appeal, noting that "pressing public necessity [World War II] may sometimes justify restrictions which curtail the civil rights of a single racial group" but added that "racial antagonism" never can justify such restrictions. The *Korematsu* decision has been widely criticized, particularly since few Americans of German or Italian descent were interned. In 1988, the U.S. government officially apologized for the internment and paid reparations to survivors.

Lochner v. New York (1905)

(labor conditions, property rights, 14th Amendment) A New York law limited bakery employees' working hours to no more than 10 hours a day or 60 hours a week. Lochner claimed that the law infringed on his right to make employer/employee contracts and violated the Due Process Clause of the 14th Amendment. The Supreme Court struck down the New York law, arguing that states have the power to regulate health, safety, and public welfare, but that the New York law was not within the limits of these "police powers." The New York law interfered with citizens' property rights, guaranteed by the 14th Amendment.

Mapp v. Ohio (1961)

(search and seizure, 4th and 14th amendments) Admitting evidence gained by illegal searches was permitted by some states before *Mapp*. Cleveland police raided Dollree Mapp's home without a warrant and found obscene materials. She appealed her conviction, saying that the 4th and 14th amendments protected her against improper police behavior. The Court agreed, extending "exclusionary rule" protections to citizens in state courts, saying that the prohibition against unreasonable searches would be "meaningless" unless evidence gained in such searches was "excluded." *Mapp* developed the concept of "incorporation" begun in *Gitlow* v. *New York*, 1925.

Marbury v. Madison (1803)

(judicial review, checks and balances) After defeat in the 1800 election, President Adams appointed many Federalists to the federal courts, but James Madison, the new Secretary of State, refused to deliver the commissions. William Marbury, one of the appointees, asked the Supreme Court to enforce the delivery of his commission based on a provision of the Judiciary Act of 1789 that allowed the Court to hear such cases on original jurisdiction. The Court refused Marbury's request, finding that the relevant portion of the Judiciary Act was in conflict with the Constitution. This decision, written by Chief Justice Marshall,

established the evaluation of federal laws' constitutionality, or "judicial review," as a power of the Supreme Court.

McCulloch v. Maryland (1819)

(federalism, states' rights) Called the "Bank of the United States" case. A Maryland law required federally chartered banks to use only a special paper to print paper money, which amounted to a tax. James McCulloch, the cashier of the Baltimore branch of the bank, refused to use the paper, claiming that states could not tax the federal government. The Court declared the Maryland law unconstitutional, commenting ". . . the power to tax implies the power to destroy."

Miranda v. Arizona (1966)

(rights of the accused; 5th, 6th, and 14th amendments) Arrested for kidnapping and sexual assault, Ernesto Miranda signed a confession including a statement that he had "full knowledge of [his] legal rights. . . ." After conviction, he appealed, claiming that without counsel and without warnings, the confession was illegally gained. The Court agreed with Miranda that "he must be warned prior to any questioning that he has the right to remain silent, that anything he says can be used against him in a court of law, that he has the right to . . . an attorney and that if he cannot afford an attorney one will be appointed for him. . . ." Although later modified by *Nix* v. *Williams*, 1984, and other cases, *Miranda* firmly upheld citizen rights to fair trials in state courts.

Mitchell v. Helms (2000)

(1st Amendment Establishment Clause) Chapter 2 of the Education Consolidation and Improvement Act of 1981 provides for the allocation of funds for educational materials and equipment to public and private schools to implement "secular, neutral, and nonideological" programs. In Jefferson Parish, Louisiana, about 30 percent of Chapter 2 funds are allocated for private schools, most of which are Catholic. Mary Helms and other public school parents filed suit alleging that the policy violated the 1st Amendment's Establishment Clause. The Supreme Court disagreed, ruling that Chapter 2, as applied in Jefferson Parish, is not a law respecting an establishment of religion, noting that "the religious, irreligious, and areligious are all alike eligible for governmental aid."

Muller v. Oregon (1908)

(women's rights, labor conditions, 14th Amendment) In 1903, Oregon enacted a law prohibiting women from working in factories or laundries more than 10 hours in any day. After a conviction, Curt Muller claimed that the law violated his freedom of contract, protected by the 14th Amendment. The Court upheld the law, viewing women as a special class that needed special protections. The Court noted that "woman's physical structure and the functions she performs . . . justify special legislation restricting the conditions under which she should be permitted to toil."

Munn v. Illinois (1876)

(5th Amendment, public interest, states' rights) Responding to farmers' complaints about the exorbitant rates they were paying, Illinois passed laws that set maximum rates that railroads and grain storage companies could charge. Munn, a partner in a Chicago warehouse firm, appealed his conviction, contending that the Illinois regulation constituted a taking of property without due process of law. The Supreme Court upheld the Illinois laws, arguing that states may regulate the use of private property "when such regulation becomes necessary for the public good." The case established as constitutional the principle of public regulation of private businesses involved in serving the public interest.

Near v. Minnesota (1931)

(1st Amendment freedom of speech, 14th Amendment) Jay Near published a Minneapolis newspaper whose articles charged that local government and police officials were implicated with gangsters. A local official filed a complaint against Near under a Minnesota law that provided permanent injunctions against those who created a "public nuisance," by publishing, selling, or distributing a "malicious, scandalous and defamatory newspaper." The Supreme Court held that the Minnesota law was an infringement of freedom of the press guaranteed by the Due Process Clause of the 14th Amendment.

New Jersey v. T.L.O. (1985)

(students' rights, 4th and 14th amendments) After T.L.O., a New Jersey high school student, denied an accusation that she had been smoking in the school lavatory, a vice principal searched her purse and found cigarettes, marijuana, and evidence that T.L.O. had been involved in marijuana dealing at the school. T.L.O. was then sentenced to probation by a juvenile court but appealed on the grounds that the evidence against her had been obtained by an "unreasonable" search. The Court rejected T.L.O.'s arguments, stating that the school had a "legitimate need to maintain an environment in which learning can take place," and that to do this "requires some easing of the restrictions to which searches by public authorities are ordinarily subject." The Court thus created a "reasonable suspicion" rule for school searches, a change from the "probable cause" requirement in the wider society.

New York Times v. United States (1971)

(1st Amendment, freedom of the press) In 1971, *The New York Times* obtained copies of classified Defense Department documents, later known as the "Pentagon Papers," which revealed instances in which the Johnson administration had deceived Congress and the American people regarding U.S. policies during the Vietnam War. A U.S. district court issued an injunction against the publication of the documents, claiming that it might endanger national security. On appeal, the Supreme Court cited the 1st Amendment guarantee of a free press and refused to uphold the injunction against publication. The Court noted that it is the obligation of the government to prove that actual harm to the nation's security would be caused by the publication. The decision limited "prior restraint" of the press.

Northern Securities Co. v. United States (1904)

(Sherman Antitrust Act, interstate commerce) In 1901, financiers formed the Northern Securities Company as a holding company that controlled the stock of the Great Northern Railway, Northern Pacific Railway, the Chicago, Burlington & Quincy Railroad, and other railroads. Fearing a monopoly, President Theodore Roosevelt's trust-busting government applied the Sherman Antitrust Act. In response to the question of whether the Sherman Act applied to a company chartered by one of the states, the Supreme Court ruled "It cannot be said that any state may give a corporation, created under its laws, authority to restrain interstate or international commerce. . . . Every corporation created by a state is necessarily subject to the supreme law of the land."

Planned Parenthood of Southeastern Pennsylvania, et al. v. Casey (1992)

(abortion, 14th Amendment, "right to privacy") The Pennsylvania legislature enacted new regulations limiting abortion. Physicians had to provide patients with antiabortion information and wait at least 24 hours before performing an abortion. In most cases, minors needed the consent of a parent, and married women had to notify their husbands of their intention to abort the fetus. The Supreme Court reaffirmed a woman's "liberty" to have an abortion as it had in the *Roe* decision. However, it upheld most of Pennsylvania's provisions, reasoning that they did not create an "undue burden" or "substantial obstacle" for women seeking an abortion. Under this new "undue burden" test, the only provision to fail was the husband notification requirement.

Plessy v. Ferguson (1896)

(segregation, 14th Amendment equal protection) A Louisiana law required separate seating for white and African American citizens on public railroads, a form of segregation. Herman Plessy argued that his right to "equal protection of the laws" was violated. The Court held that segregation was permitted if facilities were equal. The Court interpreted the 14th Amendment as "not intended to give Negroes social equality but only political and civil equality. . . ." The Louisiana law was seen as a "reasonable exercise of (state) police power. . . ." Segregated public facilities were permitted until *Plessy* was overturned by the *Brown* v. *Board of Education* case of 1954.

Regents of the University of California v. Bakke (1978)

(affirmative action, 14th Amendment) Under an affirmative action program, the medical school of the University of California at Davis reserved 16 of 100 slots in each class for "disadvantaged citizens." When Bakke, a white applicant, was not accepted by the school, he claimed racial discrimination in violation of the 14th Amendment. The Court ruled narrowly, requiring Bakke's admission but not overturning affirmative action, preferring to review such questions on a case-by-case basis.

Reno v. American Civil Liberties Union (1997)

(Internet 1st Amendment, freedom of speech) Seeking to protect minors, the 1996 Federal Communications Decency Act made it a crime to transmit obscene or indecent messages over the Internet. The Supreme Court ruled that the "indecent transmission" provision and the "patently offensive display" provision of the Communications Decency Act violated the 1st Amendment's freedom of speech. The Court reasoned the act did not clearly define "indecent." The Internet does not have the special features (such as historical governmental oversight, limited frequencies, and "invasiveness") that have justified allowing greater regulation of content in radio and television.

Reynolds v. Sims (1964)

(legislative reapportionment, 14th Amendment) Voters of Jefferson County, Alabama, filed a suit challenging the apportionment of the Alabama legislature, which was still based on the 1900 federal census. The Supreme Court extended the "one person, one vote" principle that emerged from *Baker* v. *Carr* (1962) and *Wesberry* v. *Sanders* (1964) and applied it to this case, calling for reapportionment based on current census data. Applying the Equal Protection Clause of the 14th Amendment, the Court ruled that state legislative districts should be roughly equal in population so that every voter has an equally weighted vote.

Roe v. Wade (1973)

(abortion, 9th Amendment, "right to privacy") A Texas woman challenged a state law forbidding the artificial termination of a pregnancy, saying that she "had a fundamental right to privacy." The Court upheld a woman's right to choose in this case, noting that the state's "important and legitimate interest in protecting the potentiality of human life" became "compelling" at the end of the first trimester, and that before then,

". . . the attending physician, in consultation with his patient, is free to determine, without regulation by the state, that . . . the patient's pregnancy should be terminated." The decision struck down the state regulation of abortion in the first three months of pregnancy and was modified by *Planned Parenthood of Southeastern Pennsylvania* v. *Casey*, 1992.

Schechter Poultry Corporation v. United States (1935)

(New Deal, separation of powers, interstate commerce) As part of the New Deal, the National Industrial Recovery Act (NIRA) gave the President authority to regulate aspects of interstate commerce. The government convicted Schechter for not observing minimum wage and hour provisions, selling uninspected chickens, and other violations. The Supreme Court ruled that Congress, not the President, has the power to regulate interstate commerce, and that Congress cannot delegate that power to the President. The Court reversed the conviction of Schechter because his business, which operated almost exclusively in New York State, only indirectly affected interstate commerce. The Court also declared the NIRA to be unconstitutional because it exceeded the commerce power that the Constitution had given to Congress.

Schenck v. United States (1919)

(1st Amendment freedom of speech, national security) Schenck, a member of an antiwar group, urged men drafted into military service in World War I to resist and to avoid induction. He was charged with violating the Espionage Act of 1917, which outlawed active opposition to the war. The Court limited free speech in time of war, stating that Schenck's words presented a "clear and present danger. . . ." Although later decisions modified this one, the *Schenck* case created a precedent that 1st Amendment rights are not absolute.

Standard Oil of New Jersey v. United States (1911)

(antitrust) The Standard Oil Company of New Jersey, controlled by John D. Rockefeller, owned virtually all the oil-refining companies in the United States and was extending its stranglehold over oil exploration and retail distribution of refined products. The government therefore prosecuted Standard Oil under the Sherman Antitrust Act. The Supreme Court found Standard Oil to be an illegal monopoly that restrained free competition. It fined Rockefeller and others, and ordered that the company be dissolved into smaller, competing companies.

Stromberg v. California (1931)

(1st Amendment freedom of speech, 14th Amendment) A California state law, enacted in 1919, prohibited the public display of a red flag. Yetta Stromberg, a member of the Young Communist League and a counselor at a camp for working-class children, was arrested for violating the law. Stromberg had led the youth in raising and pledging allegiance to "the workers' red flag." The Court struck down the law, concluding that a law that permitted the punishment of peaceful opposition exercised in accordance with legal means and constitutional limitations was "repugnant to the guarantee of liberty contained in the 14th Amendment."

Swann v. Charlotte-Mecklenburg Board of Education (1971)

(school desegregation, busing) After the *Brown* decision, school desegregation advanced very slowly. The NAACP took the *Swann* case to the Supreme Court on behalf of six-year-old James Swann and other students in the Charlotte-Mecklenburg, North Carolina, school system where the vast majority of black students attended all-black schools. The Court held that all schools in a district need not reflect the district's racial composition, but that the existence of all-white or all-black schools must be shown not to result from segregation policies. It stated that busing students to various schools is an acceptable way to integrate segregated school systems. The Court said school districts had broad powers to find solutions to the problem of segregation.

Texas v. Johnson (1989)

(1st Amendment freedom of speech) To protest national policies, Johnson doused a U.S. flag with kerosene and burned it outside the 1984 Republican National Convention in Dallas. He was arrested and convicted under a Texas law prohibiting the desecration of the Texas and U.S. flags. The Court ruled that the Texas law placed an unconstitutional limit on "freedom of expression," noting that ". . . nothing in our precedents suggests that a state may foster its own view of the flag by prohibiting expressive conduct relating to it."

Tinker v. Des Moines (1969)

(students' rights, 1st Amendment freedom of speech) Marybeth and John Tinker violated a school rule and wore black armbands to school in protest against the Vietnam War. They were suspended. The Tinkers claimed that their freedom of speech had been violated. The Supreme Court agreed, saying that students do not "shed their constitutional rights to freedom of speech or expression at the schoolhouse gate." Students may express personal opinions as long as they do not disrupt classwork, create substantial disorder, or interfere with the rights of others. Since the wearing of black armbands was a "silent, passive expression of opinion" without these side effects, the Tinkers' action was protected by the 1st Amendment.

United States v. E. C. Knight Co. (1895)

(Sherman Antitrust Act, federalism, states' rights) After gaining control of the E. C. Knight Company, the American Sugar Refining Company controlled more than 90 percent of the American sugar-refining industry. The federal government sued the Knight Company under the provisions of the Sherman Antitrust Act. The Court ruled that the Sherman Antitrust Act does not apply to manufacturers located within a single state, because under the 10th Amendment, states have the right to regulate "local activities," such as manufacturing. In later cases, the Court modified its position and permitted Congress greater power to limit monopolies.

United States v. Nixon (1974)

(executive privilege, separation of powers) During the investigation of the Watergate scandal, journalists discovered that President Nixon had recorded all of his conversations in the White House, including some with administration officials accused of illegal activities. A special prosecutor subpoenaed the tapes. Nixon refused to release them, citing separation of powers, his need for confidentiality, and executive privilege to immunity from court demands for information. The Supreme Court rejected his arguments and ordered him to surrender the tapes. Executive privilege was subordinate to "the fundamental demands of due process of law in the fair administration of criminal justice."

United States v. Wong Kim Ark (1898)

(immigration, citizenship, 14th Amendment) The Chinese Exclusion Act of 1882 denied citizenship to Chinese immigrants. Wong Kim Ark was born in 1873 in California to Chinese parents who were resident aliens. In 1894, Ark visited China. When he returned to the United States, he was denied entrance on grounds that he was not a U.S. citizen. The Supreme Court ruled in favor of Ark. Under the 14th Amendment, all persons born in the United States are citizens of the United States. Since he was born in the United States, Ark was a citizen. The Chinese Exclusion Act could not apply to him because he was a citizen by birth.

Vernonia School District v. Acton (1995)

(students' rights, 4th Amendment, search and seizure) The Vernonia school district of Oregon established a student-athlete drug policy that authorized urinalysis drug testing of student athletes. James Acton refused the urinalysis test and was therefore not allowed to participate in the school's junior high football program. Did the school policy violate the 4th Amendment protection against unreasonable search and seizure? The Supreme Court ruled that the school policy was constitutional. The reasonableness of a search is judged by "balancing the intrusion on the individual's 4th Amendment interests against the promotion of legitimate governmental interests." The school's concern over the safety of students under their supervision overrides the minimal intrusion in student-athletes' privacy.

Wabash, St. Louis & Pacific R.R. v. Illinois (1886)

(federalism, interstate commerce) An Illinois law regulated railroad rates on the intrastate (within one state) portion of an interstate (two or more states) journey. The Supreme Court declared the state law to be invalid, ruling that continuous transportation across the country is essential and that states should not impose restraints on the freedom of commerce. The Court stated that the regulation of interstate railroad rates is a federal power and that states cannot enact statutes interfering or seriously affecting interstate commerce. Soon afterward, Congress created the Interstate Commerce Commission (ICC).

Watkins v. United States (1957)

(rights of the accused, 5th Amendment) In 1954, John Watkins testified in hearings conducted by the House Committee on Un-American Activities. Watkins answered questions about himself but refused to give information on individuals who had left the Communist Party, arguing that such questions were beyond the authority of the committee. After being convicted for refusing to answer the committee's questions, Watkins appealed, arguing that his conviction was a violation of the Due Process Clause of the 5th Amendment. The Supreme Court overturned Watkins's conviction. The Court said that congressional committees had to clearly define the specific purposes of their investigations. Congressional committees must abide by the Bill of Rights. No witness can be made to testify on matters outside the defined scope of a committee's investigation.

West Coast Hotel v. Parrish (1937)

(minimum wage laws, 5th Amendment) The case involved Elsie Parrish, an employee of the West Coast Hotel Company, who received wages below the minimum wage fixed by Washington State law. The issue was whether minimum wage laws violated the liberty of contract as construed under the 5th Amendment and applied by the 14th Amendment. The Supreme Court upheld the constitutionality of the minimum wage legislation, ruling that the Constitution allowed the restriction of liberty of contract by state law where such restriction protected the community, health, safety, or vulnerable groups, as in the case of *Muller* v. *Oregon*, 1908.

West Virginia State Board of Education v. Barnette (1943)

("Pledge of Allegiance," 1st Amendment) The West Virginia Board of Education required that all teachers and pupils salute the flag. Some children did not comply, saying the requirement went against their religious beliefs. The Court held that compelling public schoolchildren to salute the flag was unconstitutional. "Compulsory unification of opinion," the Court held, was antithetical to 1st Amendment values. The decision noted that Americans could not be forced to demonstrate their allegiance to "what shall be orthodox in politics, nationalism, religion, or other matters of opinion."

Worcester v. Georgia (1832)

(federalism, states' rights, Native American sovereignty) Two missionaries were convicted for violating a Georgia law requiring all whites living in Cherokee Indian Territory to obtain a state license. The Supreme Court overturned their convictions, ruling that the state had no power to pass laws affecting the Cherokees because federal jurisdiction over the Cherokees was exclusive. Chief Justice John Marshall argued, "The Cherokee nation, then, is a distinct community occupying its own territory in which the laws of Georgia can have no force. The whole intercourse between the United States and this nation, is, by our constitution and laws, vested in the government of the United States."

Yates v. United States (1957)

(1st Amendment, freedom of speech, national security) In 1951, fourteen members of the Communist Party in California were convicted of violating the Smith Act, which said it was illegal to advocate or organize the forceful overthrow or destruction of the U.S. government. Yates claimed that the law violated his 1st Amendment right to freedom of speech. The Supreme Court reversed the convictions, saying that to violate the Smith Act, a person must urge others to do something, not just believe in something. The Court distinguished between speech promoting an idea and speech advocating direct action.

Documents of Our Nation

The Mayflower Compact

▲ Signing of the Mayflower Compact

The Pilgrims arrived at Massachusetts in 1620. Before disembarking, they signed a covenant that established a basis for self-government derived from the consent of the governed. Forty-one men signed the compact, agreeing to abide by the laws of the government. Women, who did not enjoy equal rights, were not asked to sign.

In the name of God, Amen. We, whose names are underwritten, the loyal subjects of our dread Sovereign Lord King James, by the grace of God, of Great Britain, France and Ireland king, defender of the faith, etc. Having undertaken, for the glory of God, and advancement of the Christian faith, and honor of our king and country, a voyage to plant the first colony in the Northern parts of Virginia, do by these presents solemnly and mutually in the presence of God and one of another, covenant and combine ourselves together into a civil body politick, for our better ordering and preservation, and furtherance of the ends aforesaid; and by virtue hereof to enact, constitute, and frame such just and equal laws, ordinances, acts, constitutions and offices, from time to time, as shall be thought most meet and convenient for the general good of the Colony unto which we promise all due submission and obedience.

In witness whereof we have hereunder subscribed our names at Cape Cod the eleventh of November, in the year of the reign of our Sovereign Lord, King James, of England, France and Ireland, the eighteenth, and of Scotland the fifty-fourth. Anno Dom. 1620.

Patrick Henry
"Liberty or Death"

▲ Patrick Henry addresses fellow Virginians.

On March 23, 1775, Patrick Henry urged a Virginia convention to prepare for war against British forces. Decades later, from the recollections of men like Thomas Jefferson, William Wirt wrote a biography of Henry, including the speech below. Henry's passionate speech caused quite a stir, even if we cannot be certain of his exact words.

. . . It is now too late to retire from the contest. There is no retreat but in submission and slavery! Our chains are forged! Their clanking may be heard on the plains of Boston! The war is inevitable—and let it come! I repeat it, sir, let it come!

It is in vain, sir, to extenuate the matter. Gentlemen may cry, Peace, Peace—but there is no peace. The war is actually begun! The next gale that sweeps from the north will bring to our ears the clash of resounding arms! Our brethren are already in the field! Why stand we here idle? What is it that gentlemen wish? What would they have? Is life so dear, or peace so sweet, as to be purchased at the price of chains and slavery? Forbid it, Almighty God! I know not what course others may take; but as for me, give me liberty or give me death!

Thomas Paine
Common Sense

*I*n 1776, after the battles at Lexington and Concord, Thomas Paine published a fiery fifty-page pamphlet that challenged the authority of the British government and the royal monarchy. Paine appealed to the people of America to seek independence from Great Britain.

. . . As to government matters, it is not in the power of Britain to do this continent justice: The business of it will soon be too weighty, and intricate, to be managed with any tolerable degree of convenience, by a power, so distant from us, and so very ignorant of us. . . .

For as in absolute governments the King is law, so in free countries the law ought to be King; and there ought to be no other. But lest any ill use should afterwards arise, let the crown at the conclusion of the ceremony be demolished, and scattered among the people whose right it is.

A government of our own is our natural right: And when a man seriously reflects on the precariousness of human affairs, he will become convinced, that it is infinitely wiser and safer, to form a constitution of our own in a cool deliberate manner, while we have it in our power, than to trust such an interesting event to time and chance. . . .

▲ Abigail Adams

Abigail Adams
"Remember the Ladies"

*J*ohn and Abigail Adams spent long periods of time apart during the Revolution and the formation of the United States. During this time, they frequently wrote letters to each other, many discussing the politics of the day. In the following letter, written March 31, 1776, Abigail urges her husband to consider the role of women in the new nation.

. . . I long to hear that you have declared an independency—and by the way in the new Code of Laws which I suppose it will be necessary for you to make I desire you would Remember the Ladies, and be more generous and favorable to them than your ancestors. Do not put such unlimited power into the hands of the Husbands. Remember all Men would be tyrants if they could. If particular care and attention is not paid to the Ladies we are determined to foment a Rebellion, and will not hold ourselves bound by any Laws in which we have no voice, or Representation. . . .

John Adams
"Free and Independent States"

On July 2, 1776, the Second Continental Congress approved a resolution asserting the right of the colonies to be independent of Great Britain. Two days later, Congress would ratify the official Declaration of Independence. In between these two events, John Adams, a member of the Declaration of Independence draft committee, wrote to his wife expressing his excitement.

▲ John Adams

Yesterday the greatest question was decided, which ever was debated in America, and a greater, perhaps, never was or will be decided among men. A Resolution was passed without one dissenting Colony "that these United Colonies are, and of right ought to be, free and independent States, and as such they have, and of right ought to have, full power to make war, conclude peace, establish commerce, and to do all the other acts and things which other States may rightfully do." You will see, in a few days, a Declaration setting forth the causes which have impelled us to this mighty revolution, and the reasons which will justify it in the sight of God and man. A plan of confederation will be taken up in a few days.

Thomas Jefferson
Virginia Statute for Religious Freedom

Thomas Jefferson took great pride in drafting this law in 1777, but it was James Madison who skillfully secured its adoption by the Virginia legislature in 1786. The statute was the basis for the Religion Clauses in the Constitution's Bill of Rights.

. . . Be it enacted by the General Assembly, That no man shall be compelled to frequent or support any religious worship, place, or ministry whatsoever, nor shall be enforced, restrained, molested, or burthened in his body or goods, nor shall otherwise suffer on account of his religious opinions or belief; but that all men shall be free to profess, and by argument to maintain, their opinion in matters of religion, and that the same shall in no wise diminish, enlarge, or affect their civil capacities. . . .

◀ Bruton Parish Church in Virginia

The Northwest Ordinance

Adopted in 1787 by the Second Continental Congress, the Northwest Ordinance created a method for admitting new states to the Union. While the Articles of Confederation lacked a bill of rights, the Ordinance provided one that included many of the basic liberties that would later be included in the Constitution's Bill of Rights.

. . . **ART. 1.** No person, demeaning himself in a peaceable and orderly manner, shall ever be molested on account of his mode of worship or religious sentiments, in the said territory.

ART. 2. The inhabitants of the said territory shall always be entitled to the benefits of the writ of habeas corpus, and of the trial by jury. . . .

ART. 3. Religion, morality, and knowledge, being necessary to good government and the happiness of mankind, schools and the means of education shall forever be encouraged. . . .

ART. 6. There shall be neither slavery nor involuntary servitude in the said territory, otherwise than in the punishment of crimes whereof the party shall have been duly convicted: Provided, always, That any person escaping into the same, from whom labor or service is lawfully claimed in any one of the original States, such fugitive may be lawfully reclaimed and conveyed to the person claiming his or her labor or service as aforesaid.

▲ Settlers moving to the Ohio Territory

The Federalist, No. 51

This Federalist paper was probably written either by James Madison or Alexander Hamilton. It argues that the federal system and the separation of powers proposed in the Constitution provides a system of checks and balances that will protect the rights of the people.

. . . In order to lay a due foundation for that separate and distinct exercise of the different powers of government, which to a certain extent is admitted on all hands to be essential to the preservation of liberty, it is evident that each department should have a will of its own. . . .

But the great security against a gradual concentration of the several powers in the same department, consists in giving to those who administer each department the necessary constitutional means and personal motives to resist encroachments of the others. . . . Ambition must be made to counteract ambition. . . .

The constant aim is to divide and arrange the several offices in such a manner as that each may be a check on the other. . . .

In the compound republic of America, the power surrendered by the people is first divided between two distinct governments, and then the portion allotted to each subdivided among distinct and separate departments. Hence a double security arises to the rights of the people. . . .

Thomas Jefferson
First Inaugural Address

*A*fter the hotly contested presidential election of 1800, some expected that Jefferson's inaugural address would attack the defeated Federalists and their policies. Instead, he extended an olive branch of reconciliation. Jefferson praised a society in which people have full freedom to differ. He urged abidance with the will of the majority and respect for the rights of the minority.

Friends and Fellow Citizens:

. . . All . . . will bear in mind this sacred principle, that though the will of the majority is in all cases to prevail, that will, to be rightful, must be reasonable; that the minority possess their equal rights, which equal laws must protect, and to violate which would be oppression. Let us, then, fellow citizens, unite with one heart and one mind. . . . We have called by different names brethren of the same principle. We are all Republicans—we are all Federalists. If there be any among us who would wish to dissolve this Union or to change its republican form, let them stand undisturbed as monuments of the safety with which error of opinion may be tolerated where reason is left free to combat it. . . .

Still one thing more, fellow citizens—a wise and frugal government, which shall restrain men from injuring one another, which shall leave them otherwise free to regulate their own pursuits of industry and improvement, and shall not take from the mouth of labor the bread it has earned. This is the sum of good government. . . .

You should understand what I deem the essential principles of our government, and consequently those which ought to shape its administration. . . . Equal and exact justice to all men, of whatever state or persuasion, religious or political; peace, commerce, and honest friendship, with all nations— entangling alliances with none; the support of the state governments in all their rights . . . absolute acquiescence in the decisions of the majority. . . .

◀ Campaign banner promoting the election of Thomas Jefferson for President

Francis Scott Key
"The Star-Spangled Banner"

During the War of 1812, a Maryland attorney named Francis Scott Key witnessed the British attack on Fort McHenry, near Baltimore. In the morning, Key was so delighted to see the American flag still flying over the fort that he composed a poem to commemorate the event. Set to the music of a popular folk tune, "The Star-Spangled Banner" was officially made the national anthem by Congress in 1931.

▲ Flag that flew over Fort McHenry during the British attack

O say, can you see, by the dawn's early light,
What so proudly we hail'd at the twilight's last gleaming?
Whose broad stripes and bright stars, thro' the perilous fight,
O'er the ramparts we watch'd, were so gallantly streaming?
And the rockets' red glare, the bombs bursting in air,
Gave proof thro' the night that our flag was still there.
O say, does that star-spangled banner yet wave
O'er the land of the free and the home of the brave?

▲ Frederick Douglass

Frederick Douglass
Independence Day Speech

In 1852, Douglass accepted an invitation from the leading citizens of Rochester, New York, to speak at their Fourth of July celebration. Douglass delivered a scathing speech in which he attacked the hypocrisy of celebrating independence and freedom in a nation where millions of people were enslaved.

Fellow citizens, pardon me, allow me to ask, why am I called upon to speak here today? What have I, or those I represent, to do with your national independence? Are the great principles of political freedom and of natural justice, embodied in that Declaration of Independence, extended to us? . . .

What, to the American slave, is your Fourth of July? I answer: a day that reveals to him, more than all other days in the year, the gross injustice and cruelty to which he is the constant victim. To him, your celebration is a sham; your boasted liberty, an unholy license; your national greatness, swelling vanity; your sounds of rejoicing are empty and heartless; your denunciation of tyrants, brass-fronted impudence; your shouts of liberty and equality, hollow mockery; your prayers and hymns, your sermons and thanksgivings, with all your religious parade and solemnity, are, to Him, mere bombast, fraud, deception, impiety, and hypocrisy—a thin veil to cover up crimes which would disgrace a nation of savages. There is not a nation of savages. There is not a nation on the earth guilty of practices more shocking and bloody than are the people of the United States at this very hour. . . .

Sojourner Truth
"Ain't I a Woman?"

Sojourner Truth, an African American woman prominent in both the abolitionist and early feminist movements, delivered her famous speech at a women's rights convention in Akron, Ohio, in 1851. The version below was first published twelve years later in the Anti-Slavery Standard by Frances Gage, a celebrated antislavery fighter and president of the Convention. Although recent scholarship questions the exact wording of the speech, it made a great impact at the time and has endured as a classic statement of women's rights.

▲ Sojourner Truth

. . . I think that 'twixt the Negroes of the South and the women at the North, all talking about rights, the white men will be in a fix pretty soon. But what's all this here talking about?

That man over there says that women need to be helped into carriages, and lifted over ditches, and to have the best place everywhere. Nobody ever helps me into carriages, or over mud-puddles, or gives me any best place! And ain't I a woman? Look at me! Look at my arm! I have ploughed and planted, and gathered into barns, and no man could head me! And ain't I a woman? I could work as much and eat as much as a man—when I could get it—and bear the lash as well! And ain't I a woman? I have borne thirteen children, and seen most all sold off to slavery, and when I cried out with my mother's grief, none but Jesus heard me! And ain't I a woman? . . .

Elizabeth Cady Stanton
Address to the Legislature of New York

In 1854, Elizabeth Cady Stanton presented this speech to the New York State Legislature. She addressed the inequalities faced by all women under the state laws and discussed the specific challenges met by mothers, wives, and widows.

. . . Gentlemen, in republican America, in the nineteenth century, we, the daughters of the revolutionary heroes of '76, demand at your hands the redress of our grievances—a revision of your State Constitution—a new code of laws. Permit us then, as briefly as possible, to call your attention to the legal disabilities under which we labor.

1st. Look at the position of woman as woman. . . . We are persons; native, free-born citizens; property-holders, tax-payers; yet are we denied the exercise of our right to the elective franchise. We support ourselves, and, in part, your schools, colleges, churches, your poor-houses, jails, prisons, the army, the navy, the whole machinery of government, and yet we have no voice in your councils. We have every qualification required by the Constitution, necessary to the legal voter, but the one of sex. . . .

2nd. Look at the position of woman as wife. . . . The wife who inherits no property holds about the same legal position that does the slave on the Southern plantation. She can own nothing, sell nothing. She has no right even to the wages she earns; her person, her time, her services are the property of another. . . .

Abraham Lincoln
The Gettysburg Address

*A*t the Battle of Gettysburg, more than 51,000 Confederate and Union soldiers were listed as wounded, missing, or dead. President Lincoln gave this brief speech at the dedication of The Gettysburg National Cemetery on November 19, 1863. The five known manuscript copies of the speech differ slightly and historians debate which version Lincoln actually delivered. But the address is considered one of the most eloquent and moving speeches in American history. As Lincoln described the significance of the war, he invoked the Declaration of Independence and its principles of liberty and equality, and he spoke of "a new birth of freedom."

Four score and seven years ago our fathers brought forth on this continent, a new nation, conceived in Liberty, and dedicated to the proposition that all men are created equal.

Now we are engaged in a great civil war, testing whether that nation, or any nation so conceived and so dedicated, can long endure. We are met on a great battle-field of that war. We have come to dedicate a portion of that field, as a final resting place for those who here gave their lives that the nation might live. It is altogether fitting and proper that we should do this.

But, in a larger sense, we can not dedicate—we can not consecrate—we can not hallow—this ground. The brave men, living and dead, who struggled here, have consecrated it, far above our poor power to add or detract. The world will little note, nor long remember what we say here, but it can never forget what they did here. It is for us the living, rather, to be dedicated here to the unfinished work which they who fought here have thus far so nobly advanced. It is rather for us to be here dedicated to the great task remaining before us—that from these honored dead we take increased devotion to that cause for which they gave the last full measure of devotion—that we here highly resolve that these dead shall not have died in vain—that this nation, under God, shall have a new birth of freedom—and that government of the people, by the people, for the people, shall not perish from the earth.

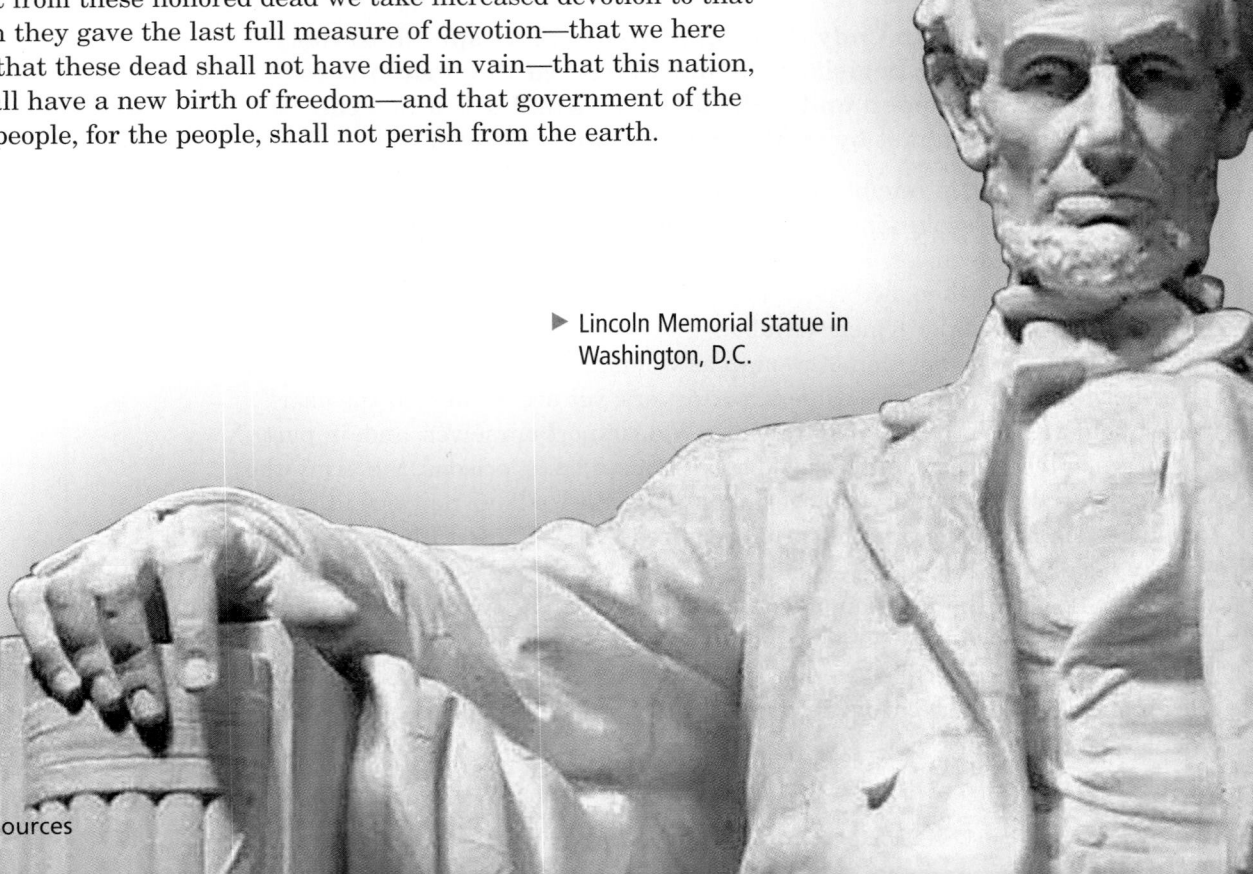

▶ Lincoln Memorial statue in Washington, D.C.

Abraham Lincoln
Second Inaugural Address

Lincoln delivered his second inaugural address just over a month before his death. He spoke about the war, slavery, and the need "to bind up the nation's wounds." The speech's closing words of reconciliation and healing are today carved in the walls of the Lincoln Memorial.

... On the occasion corresponding to this four years ago all thoughts were anxiously directed to an impending civil war. All dreaded it, all sought to avert it. While the inaugural address was being delivered from this place, devoted altogether to saving the Union without war, insurgent agents were in the city seeking to destroy it without war—seeking to dissolve the Union and divide effects by negotiation. Both parties deprecated war, but one of them would make war rather than let the nation survive, and the other would accept war rather than let it perish, and the war came.

One-eighth of the whole population were colored slaves, not distributed generally over the Union, but localized in the southern part of it. These slaves constituted a peculiar and powerful interest. All knew that this interest was somehow the cause of the war. To strengthen, perpetuate, and extend this interest was the object for which the insurgents would rend the Union even by war, while the Government claimed no right to do more than to restrict the territorial enlargement of it. Neither party expected for the war the magnitude or the duration which it has already attained. Neither anticipated that the cause of the conflict might cease with or even before the conflict itself should cease. Each looked for an easier triumph, and a result less fundamental and astounding. Both read the same Bible and pray to the same God, and each invokes His aid against the other.... Fondly do we hope, fervently do we pray, that this mighty scourge of war may speedily pass away. Yet, if God wills that it continue until all the wealth piled by the bondsman's two hundred and fifty years of unrequited toil shall be sunk, and until every drop of blood drawn with the lash shall be paid by another drawn with the sword, as was said three thousand years ago, so still it must be said "the judgments of the Lord are true and righteous altogether."

With malice toward none, with charity for all, with firmness in the right as God gives us to see the right, let us strive on to finish the work we are in, to bind up the nation's wounds, to care for him who shall have borne the battle and for his widow and his orphan, to do all which may achieve and cherish a just and lasting peace among ourselves and with all nations.

Chief Joseph
"I Will Fight No More Forever"

▲ Chief Joseph

In 1877, after being ordered to a reservation, Chief Joseph led some 800 of his Nez Percé people in an attempted escape to Canada. They fled more than 1,000 miles across Idaho and Montana, battling the U.S. Army all along the way. Finally, with fewer than 500 of his people remaining and only 40 miles from Canada, Chief Joseph surrendered. General O.O. Howard reported Chief Joseph's poignant words.

I am tired of fighting. Our chiefs are killed. . . . The old men are all dead. . . . It is cold and we have no blankets. The little children are freezing to death. My people, some of them, have run away to the hills, and have no blankets, no food; no one knows where they are—perhaps freezing to death. I want to have time to look for my children and see how many of them I can find. Maybe I shall find them among the dead. Hear me, my chiefs. I am tired; my heart is sick and sad. From where the sun now stands I will fight no more forever.

Preamble to the Constitution of the Knights of Labor

The Knights of Labor, which adopted its constitution in 1878, was a national labor union that sought the eight-hour day, abolition of child labor, and equal pay for equal work. The organization grew to more than 700,000 workers, but rapidly declined due to unsuccessful strikes and the formation of the American Federation of Labor in 1886.

The recent alarming development and aggression of aggregated wealth, which, unless checked, will inevitably lead to the pauperization and hopeless degradation of the toiling masses, renders it imperative, if we desire to enjoy the blessings of life, that a check should be placed upon its power and upon unjust accumulation, and a system adopted which will secure to the laborer the fruits of his toil; and as this much-desired object can only be accomplished by the thorough unification of labor, and the united efforts of those who obey the divine injunction that "In the sweat of thy brow shalt thou eat bread," we have formed the Noble Order of the Knights of Labor with a view of securing the organization and direction, by co-operative effort, of the power of the industrial classes; and we submit to the world the objects sought to be accomplished by our organization, calling upon all who believe in securing "the greatest good to the greatest number" to aid and assist us. . . .

Preamble to the Platform of the Populist Party

*T*he People's, or Populist, Party adopted its party platform in 1892 at its national convention in Omaha, Nebraska. The movement, which emerged from the Farmer's Alliance in the 1880s, sought political reforms and a redistribution of political and economic power.

The conditions which surround us best justify our co-operation; we meet in the midst of a nation brought to the verge of moral, political, and material ruin. Corruption dominates the ballot-box, the Legislatures, the Congress, and touches even the ermine of the bench. . . . The fruits of the toil of millions are boldly stolen to build up colossal fortunes for a few, unprecedented in the history of mankind; and the possessors of these, in turn, despise the Republic and endanger liberty. From the same prolific womb of governmental injustice we breed the two great classes—tramps and millionaires. . . .

We have witnessed for more than a quarter of a century the struggles of the two great political parties for power and plunder, while grievous wrongs have been inflicted upon the suffering people. We charge that the controlling influences dominating both these parties have permitted the existing dreadful conditions to develop without serious effort to prevent or restrain them. . . .

We believe that the power of government—in other words, of the people—should be expanded . . . to the end that oppression, injustice, and poverty shall eventually cease in the land. . . .

Emma Lazarus
"The New Colossus"

*A*t the dedication of the Statue of Liberty in 1886, President Grover Cleveland spoke of the Statue of Liberty as a symbol of Franco-American friendship and American ideals. But Jewish American poet Emma Lazarus saw the statue as a shining beacon to the millions who were migrating to the United States. The poem that she wrote to help raise money for the statue's pedestal is today carved on that pedestal for all to read.

Not like the brazen giant of Greek fame,
With conquering limbs astride from land to land;
Here at our sea-washed, sunset gates shall stand
A mighty woman with a torch, whose flame
Is the imprisoned lightning, and her name
Mother of Exiles. From her beacon-hand
Glows world-wide welcome; her mild eyes command
The air-bridged harbor that twin cities frame,
"Keep, ancient lands, your storied pomp!" cries she
With silent lips. "Give me your tired, your poor,
Your huddled masses yearning to breathe free,
The wretched refuse of your teeming shore,
Send these, the homeless, tempest-tossed to me,
I lift my lamp beside the golden door!"

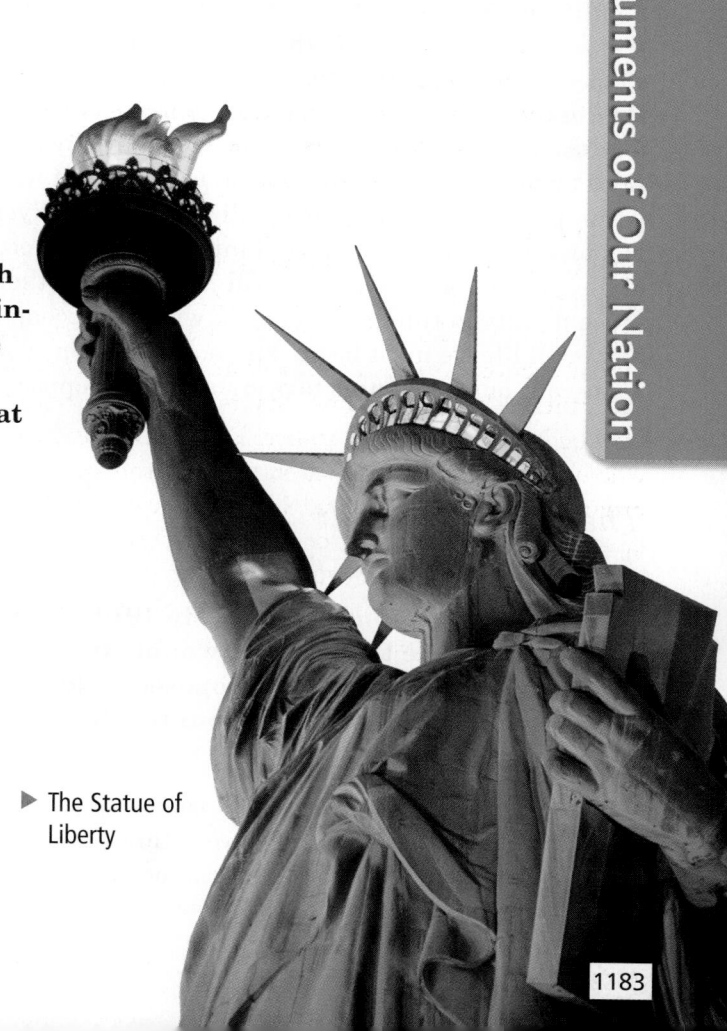

▶ The Statue of Liberty

Booker T. Washington
The Atlantic Exposition Address

*I*n 1895, African American leader Booker T. Washington addressed a predominantly white audience in Atlanta. He urged fellow blacks to build friendly relations with whites and to start "at the bottom" by working at "the common occupations of life." Other black leaders rejected Washington's plan and called it the "Atlanta Compromise."

. . . Ignorant and inexperienced, it is not strange that in the first years of our new life we began at the top instead of at the bottom; that a seat in Congress or the state legislature was more sought than real estate or industrial skill; that the political convention or stump speaking had more attractions than starting a dairy farm or truck garden. . . .

To those of my race who depend on bettering their condition in a foreign land or who underestimate the importance of cultivating friendly relations with the Southern white man, who is their next-door neighbor, I would say: "Cast down your bucket where you are"— cast it down in making friends in every manly way of the people of all races by whom we are surrounded.

Cast it down in agriculture, mechanics, in commerce, in domestic service, and in the professions. And in this connection it is well to bear in mind that whatever other sins the South may be called to bear, when it comes to business, pure and simple, it is in the South that the Negro is given a man's chance in the commercial world. . . . Our greatest danger is that in the great leap from slavery to freedom we may overlook the fact that the masses of us are to live by the productions of our hands, and fail to keep in mind that we shall prosper in proportion as we learn to dignify and glorify common labour, and put brains and skill into the common occupations of life. . . . No race can prosper till it learns that there is as much dignity in tilling a field as in writing a poem. It is at the bottom of life we must begin, and not at the top. Nor should we permit our grievances to overshadow our opportunities. . . .

▲ Booker T. Washington

Theodore Roosevelt
"The New Nationalism"

*A*t Ossowatomie, Kansas, in 1910, Theodore Roosevelt formulated the themes that would guide his 1912 campaign for the presidency. He proposed a New Nationalism that would promote human welfare and counter the power of big business.

. . . Now, this means that our government, National and State, must be freed from the sinister influence or control of special interests. Exactly as the special interests of cotton and slavery threatened our political integrity before the Civil War, so now the great special business interests too often control and corrupt the men and methods of government for their own profit. . . .

It has become entirely clear that we must have government supervision of the capitalization, not only of public-service corporations, including, particularly, railways, but of all corporations doing an interstate business. . . .

Combinations in industry are the result of an imperative economic law which cannot be repealed by political legislation. The effort at prohibiting all combination has substantially failed. The way out lies, not in attempting to prevent such combinations, but in completely controlling them in the interest of the public welfare. . . .

This New Nationalism regards the executive power as the steward of the public welfare. It demands of the judiciary that it shall be interested primarily in human welfare rather than in property, just as it demands that the representative body shall represent all the people rather than any one class or section of the people. . . .

Woodrow Wilson
"Peace Without Victory"

O**n January 22, 1917, before the United States entered World War I, President Wilson spoke to the U.S. Senate about his vision for the future. He called for a "peace without victory." His ideas would later influence international cooperation in the League of Nations.**

. . . It must be a peace without victory. . . . Victory would mean peace forced upon the loser, a victor's terms imposed upon the vanquished. It would be accepted in humiliation, under duress, at an intolerable sacrifice, and would leave a sting, a resentment, a bitter memory upon which terms of peace would rest, not permanently but only as upon quicksand. Only a peace between equals can last. . . .

No peace can last, or ought to last, which does not recognize and accept the principle that governments derive all their just powers from the consent of the governed, and that no right anywhere exists to hand peoples about from sovereignty to sovereignty as if they were property. . . .

There can be no sense of safety and equality among the nations if great preponderating armaments are henceforth to continue here and there to be built up and maintained. The statesmen of the world must plan for peace, and nations must adjust and accommodate their policy. . . .

I am proposing that all nations henceforth avoid entangling alliances which would draw them into competitions of power, catch them in a net of intrigue and selfish rivalry, and disturb their own. . . . There is no entangling alliance in a concert of power. When all unite to act in the same sense and with the same purpose, all act in the common interest and are free to live their own lives under a common protection. . . .

▲ Theodore Roosevelt delivering a campaign speech

Franklin D. Roosevelt
First Inaugural Address

*B*y 1933, the depression had reached its depth. Roosevelt's first inaugural address outlined in broad terms how he hoped to govern. He advised Americans "that the only thing we have to fear is fear itself." He reminded Americans that the nation's "common difficulties" concerned "only material things."

▲ Franklin D. Roosevelt greets supporters.

. . . This great Nation will endure as it has endured, will revive and will prosper. So, first of all, let me assert my firm belief that the only thing we have to fear is fear itself—nameless, unreasoning, unjustified terror which paralyzes needed efforts to convert retreat into advance. In every dark hour of our national life a leadership of frankness and vigor has met with that understanding and support of the people themselves which is essential to victory. I am convinced that you will again give that support to leadership in these critical days. . . .

I am prepared under my constitutional duty to recommend the measures that a stricken nation in the midst of a stricken world may require. These measures, or such other measures as the Congress may build out of its experience and wisdom, I shall seek, within my constitutional authority, to bring to speedy adoption.

But in the event that the Congress shall fail to take one of these two courses, and in the event that the national emergency is still critical, I shall not evade the clear course of duty that will then confront me. I shall ask the Congress for the one remaining instrument to meet the crisis—broad Executive power to wage a war against the emergency, as great as the power that would be given to me if we were in fact invaded by a foreign foe. . . .

George Kennan
"The Sources of Soviet Conduct"

*G*eorge Kennan published this article anonymously in the July 1947 issue of *Foreign Affairs*. He opposed appeasement and promoted firm opposition to the expansion of communism. His ideas on "containment" became the basis for U.S. policy toward the Soviet Union during the Cold War.

. . . In these circumstances it is clear that the main element of any United States policy toward the Soviet Union must be that of long-term, patient but firm and vigilant containment of Russian expansive tendencies. . . .

The Soviet pressure against the free institutions of the western world is something that can be contained by the adroit and vigilant application of counter-force at a series of constantly shifting geographical and political points, corresponding to the shifts and maneuvers of Soviet policy, but which cannot be charmed or talked out of existence. The Russians look forward to a duel of infinite duration, and they see that already they have scored great successes. . . .

The issue of Soviet-American relations is in essence a test of the overall worth of the United States as a nation among nations. To avoid destruction the United States need only measure up to its own best traditions and prove itself worthy of preservation as a great nation. . . .

The Pledge of Allegiance

*T*he Pledge of Allegiance was first written in 1892. It was revised twice before 1954, when the words "under God" were added, and it became the version that is still recited today.

I pledge allegiance to the Flag of the United States of America, and to the Republic for which it stands, one Nation under God, indivisible, with liberty and justice for all.

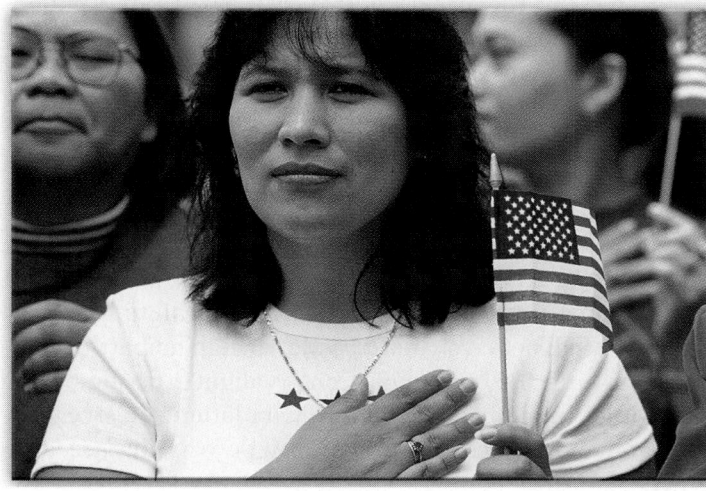

▲ A new citizen salutes the flag.

Dwight D. Eisenhower Farewell Address

*O*n January 17, 1961, President Eisenhower delivered his farewell to the American people on national television. To the surprise of the American people, the general who had led America to victory in World War II issued a strong warning about the dangers of the "military-industrial complex."

. . . Until the latest of our world conflicts, the United States had no armaments industry. American makers of plowshares could, with time and as required, make swords as well. But now we can no longer risk emergency improvisation of national defense; we have been compelled to create a permanent armaments industry of vast proportions. . . .

This conjunction of an immense military establishment and a large arms industry is new in the American experience. The total influence—economic, political, even spiritual—is felt in every city, every state house, every office of the Federal government. We recognize the imperative need for this development. Yet we must not fail to comprehend its grave implications. . . .

We must never let the weight of this combination endanger our liberties or democratic processes. We should take nothing for granted. Only an alert and knowledgeable citizenry can compel the proper meshing of huge industrial and military machinery of defense with our peaceful methods and goals, so that security and liberty may prosper together. . . .

John F. Kennedy
Inaugural Address

On January 20, 1961, President John F. Kennedy delivered his inaugural address in which he announced to the world that "we shall pay any price, bear any burden, meet any hardship, support any friend, oppose any foe, in order to assure the survival and success of liberty."

. . . Let the word go forth from this time and place, to friend and foe alike, that the torch has been passed to a new generation of Americans—born in this century, tempered by war, disciplined by a hard and bitter peace, proud of our ancient heritage—and unwilling to witness or permit the slow undoing of those human rights to which this Nation has always been committed, and to which we are committed today at home and around the world.

Let every nation know, whether it wishes us well or ill, that we shall pay any price, bear any burden, meet any hardship, support any friend, oppose any foe, in order to assure the survival and the success of liberty. . . .

Now the trumpet summons us again—not as a call to bear arms, though arms we need; not as a call to battle, though embattled we are—but a call to bear the burden of a long twilight struggle, year in and year out, "rejoicing in hope, patient in tribulation"—a struggle against the common enemies of man: tyranny, poverty, disease, and war itself. . . .

In the long history of the world, only a few generations have been granted the role of defending freedom in its hour of maximum danger. I do not shrink from this responsibility—I welcome it. . . .

And so, my fellow Americans: ask not what your country can do for you—ask what you can do for your country.

My fellow citizens of the world: ask not what America will do for you, but what together we can do for the freedom of man. . . .

▲ President Kennedy giving his Inaugural Address

Martin Luther King, Jr.
Letter from Birmingham Jail

In 1963, King led a campaign of nonviolent protest against segregation and discrimination in Birmingham, Alabama. Rather than obey a court order to desist, King went to jail. From there, he wrote a response to white Alabama clergymen who were urging King to be more moderate in his struggle. King responded that the wait for civil rights had been too long and that civil disobedience against unjust laws was needed to achieve social justice.

My Dear Fellow Clergymen,

While confined here in the Birmingham City Jail, I came across your recent statement calling our present activities "unwise and untimely." . . .

We have waited for more than 340 years for our constitutional and God-given rights. The nations of Asia and Africa are moving with jetlike speed toward the goal of political independence, and we still creep at horse and buggy pace toward the gaining of a cup of coffee at a lunch counter.

I guess it is easy for those who have never felt the stinging darts of segregation to say wait. But when you have seen vicious mobs lynch your mothers and fathers at will and drown your sisters and brothers at whim; when you have seen hate-filled policemen curse, kick, brutalize, and even kill your black brothers and sisters with impunity; when you see the vast majority of your 20 million Negro brothers smothering in an airtight cage of poverty in the midst of an affluent society; when you suddenly find your tongue twisted and your speech stammering as you seek to explain to your six-year-old daughter why she can't go to the public amusement park that has just been advertised on television, and see the tears welling up in her little eyes when she is told that Funtown is closed to colored children, . . . then you will understand why we find it difficult to wait. . . .

You express a great deal of anxiety over our willingness to break laws. . . . The answer is found in the fact that there are two types of laws: There are just and there are unjust laws. I would agree with Saint Augustine that "An unjust law is no law at all." . . .

All segregation statutes are unjust because segregation distorts the soul and damages the personality. It gives the segregator a false sense of superiority, and the segregated a false sense of inferiority. . . .

Let us all hope that the dark clouds of racial prejudice will soon pass away and the deep fog of misunderstanding will be lifted from our fear-drenched communities and in some not too distant tomorrow the radiant stars of love and brotherhood will shine over our great nation with all their scintillating beauty.

Yours for the cause of Peace and Brotherhood,
Martin Luther King, Jr.

▲ A reflective King in his Birmingham jail cell

Betty Friedan
The Feminine Mystique

*B*etty Friedan's book exploded onto the American scene in 1963. Her work sparked a national debate about women's roles and was a pivotal event in the modern women's movement.

. . . It . . . is time to stop giving lip service to the idea that there are no battles left to be fought for women in America, that women's rights have already been won. It is ridiculous to tell girls to keep quiet when they enter a new field, or an old one, so the men will not notice they are there. In almost every professional field, in business and in the arts and sciences, women are still treated as second-class citizens. . . . A girl should not expect special privileges because of her sex, but neither should she "adjust" to prejudice and discrimination.

She must learn to compete then, not as a woman, but as a human being. Not until a great many women move out of the fringes into the mainstream will society itself provide the arrangements for their new plan. . . .

◀ Betty Friedan

Lyndon Johnson
Voting Rights

President Johnson made this speech to Congress on March 15, 1965, a week after deadly racial violence erupted in Selma, Alabama. He used the phrase "we shall overcome," borrowed from African American leaders struggling for equal rights.

. . . There is no Negro problem. There is no Southern problem. There is no Northern problem. There is only an American problem. And we are met here tonight as Americans—not as Democrats or Republicans—we are met here as Americans to solve that problem. . . .

Many of the issues of civil rights are very complex and most difficult. But about this there can and should be no argument. Every American citizen must have an equal right to vote.

Yet the harsh fact is that in many places in this country men and women are kept from voting simply because they are Negroes. . . .

Wednesday I will send to Congress a law designed to eliminate illegal barriers to the right to vote. . . .

But even if we pass this bill, the battle will not be over. What happened in Selma is part of a far larger movement which reaches into every section and State of America. It is the effort of American Negroes to secure for themselves the full blessings of American life.

Their cause must be our cause too. Because it is not just Negroes, but really it is all of us, who must overcome the crippling legacy of bigotry and injustice.

And we shall overcome. . . .

Richard Nixon
Resignation Speech

In the shadow of the Watergate scandal, President Nixon delivered his resignation speech on August 8, 1974. The next morning, he signed the resignation documents, made a final speech to his staff, and stepped onto the Marine One helicopter for the last time, to begin a trip to California as an ex-President.

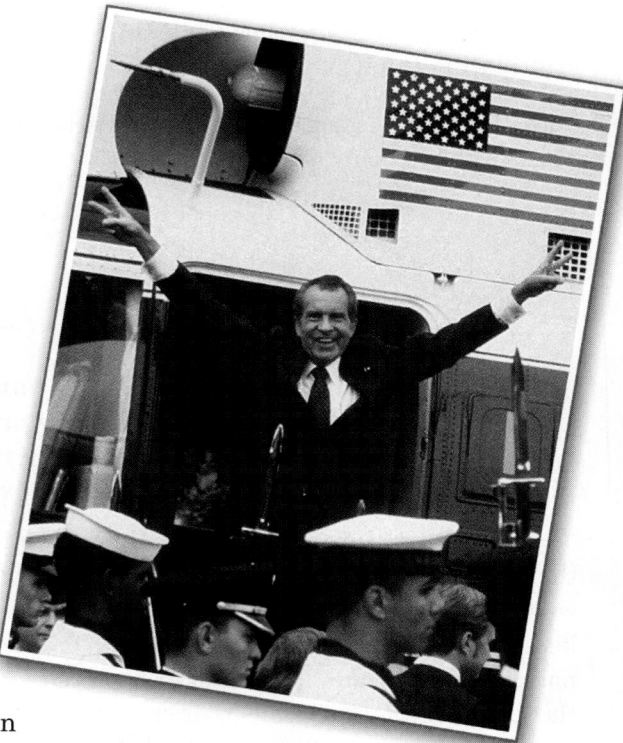

▲ Richard Nixon leaves the White House after resigning from the presidency.

. . . I have concluded that because of the Watergate matter I might not have the support of the Congress that I would consider necessary to back the very difficult decisions and carry out the duties of this office in the way the interests of the Nation would require. . . .

To continue to fight through the months ahead for my personal vindication would almost totally absorb the time and attention of both the President and the Congress in a period when our entire focus should be on the great issues of peace abroad and prosperity without inflation at home.

Therefore, I shall resign the Presidency effective at noon tomorrow. Vice President Ford will be sworn in as President at that hour in this office. . . .

Jimmy Carter
"Crisis of Confidence"

*I*n the 1970s, Americans struggled with the aftermath of the Vietnam War and the Watergate scandal. Economic problems and an energy crisis added to the malaise. On July 15, 1979, in a nationally televised address, President Carter identified what he believed to be a "crisis of confidence" among the American people.

. . . I want to talk to you right now about a fundamental threat to American democracy. . . . It is a crisis of confidence . . . that strikes at the very heart and soul and spirit of our national will. We can see this crisis in the growing doubt about the meaning of our own lives and in the loss of a unity of purpose for our nation. . . .

In a nation that was proud of hard work, strong families, close-knit communities, and our faith in God, too many of us now tend to worship self-indulgence and consumption. Human identity is no longer defined by what one does, but by what one owns. But we've discovered that owning things and consuming things does not satisfy our longing for meaning. . . .

As you know, there is a growing disrespect for government and for churches and for schools, the news media, and other institutions. This is not a message of happiness or reassurance, but it is the truth and it is a warning. . . .

Cesar Chavez
Commonwealth Club Address

*T*he Commonwealth Club of California, the nation's oldest public affairs forum, has hosted diverse speakers, including Theodore Roosevelt, Martin Luther King, Jr., Ronald Reagan, and Bill Gates. In 1984, Cesar Chavez spoke about the United Farm Workers and progress for Latinos.

▲ Cesar Chavez

. . . The United Farm Workers is first and foremost a union. . . . But the UFW has always been something more than a union. . . .

The UFW's survival . . . was not in doubt . . . after the union became visible, when Chicanos started entering college in greater numbers, when Hispanics began running for public office in greater numbers, when our people started asserting their rights on a broad range of issues and in many communities across this land. The union survival, its very existence, sent out a signal to all Hispanics that we were fighting for our dignity, that we were challenging and overcoming injustice, that we were empowering the least educated among us, the poorest among us.

The message was clear. If it could happen in the fields, it could happen anywhere: in the cities, in the courts, in the city councils, in the state legislatures. I didn't really appreciate it at the time, but the coming of our union signaled the start of great changes among Hispanics that are only now beginning to be seen. . . .

Like the other immigrant groups, the day will come when we win the economic and political rewards, which are in keeping with our numbers in society. . . .

William Clinton
Second Inaugural Address

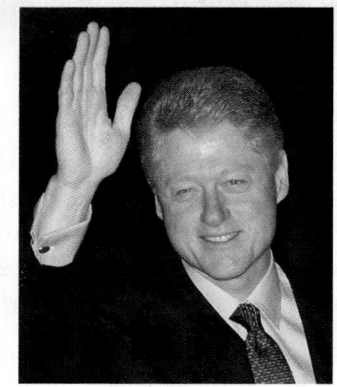

◀ President William Clinton

President Clinton took the oath of office for a second term on January 20, 1997. This was the last inaugural address of the twentieth century, and Clinton looked optimistically to the challenges that lay ahead in the next century.

. . . The world is no longer divided into two hostile camps. Instead, now we are building bonds with nations that once were our adversaries. Growing connections of commerce and culture give us a chance to lift the fortunes and spirits of people the world over. And for the very first time in all of history, more people on this planet live under democracy than dictatorship. . . .

Our land of new promise will be a nation that meets its obligations, a nation that balances its budget, but never loses the balance of its values. A nation where our grandparents have secure retirement and health care, and their grandchildren know we have made the reforms necessary to sustain those benefits for their time. A nation that fortifies the world's most productive economy even as it protects the great natural bounty of our water, air, and majestic land. . . .

George W. Bush
War on Terror Speech

▼ President Bush addresses rescue work at the World Trade Center site.

On September 11, 2001, terrorists hijacked and crashed passenger jets into the World Trade Center in New York City and the Pentagon Building in Washington, D.C. On September 20, President Bush addressed a joint session of Congress and announced to the nation a war on terrorism.

. . . Americans have known surprise attacks, but never before on thousands of civilians. All of this was brought upon us in a single day, and night fell on a different world, a world where freedom itself is under attack. . . .

The evidence we have gathered all points to a collection of loosely affiliated terrorist organizations known as al Qaeda.

The terrorists practice a fringe form of Islamic extremism that has been rejected by Muslim scholars and the vast majority of Muslim clerics; a fringe movement that perverts the peaceful teachings of Islam. . . .

Our war on terror begins with al Qaeda, but it does not end there. It will not end until every terrorist group of global reach has been found, stopped and defeated.

Americans are asking "Why do they hate us?" They hate what they see right here in this chamber: a democratically elected government. Their leaders are self-appointed. They hate our freedoms: our freedom of religion, our freedom of speech, our freedom to vote and assemble and disagree. . . .

Our response involves far more than instant retaliation and isolated strikes. Americans should not expect one battle, but a lengthy campaign unlike any other we have ever seen. . . .

We will rally the world to this cause by our efforts, by our courage. We will not tire, we will not falter and we will not fail. . . .

A

abolition movement nineteenth century movement that sought an end to slavery (p. 283)

movimiento de abolición movimiento del siglo XIX que buscaba suprimir la esclavitud

Acquired Immunodeficiency Syndrome (AIDS) a disease with no known cure that attacks the immune system. It began spreading in the early 1980s and remains a serious global health crisis today (p. 1085)

Síndrome de Inmunodeficiencia Adquirida (SIDA) una enfermedad para la que no se conoce cura que ataca el sistema inmunitario de sus víctimas; empezó a extenderse a principios de la década de 1980 y aún hoy sigue representando una seria crisis de salud mundial

Adams-Onís Treaty 1819 treaty in which Spain ceded Florida to the United States (p. 244)

Tratado Adams-Onís tratado de 1819 en el que España cedió Florida a Estados Unidos

administration staff of the executive branch (p. 193)

administración personal del poder ejecutivo

adobe sun-dried brick made from earth, water, and straw (p. 6)

adobe ladrillos hechos de tierra, agua y paja, secados al sol

affirmative action policy that gives special consideration to women and minorities to make up for past discrimination (pp. 1049, 1129)

acción afirmativa política que da trato especial a las mujeres y minorías para resarcirlas de la discriminación del pasado

AFL-CIO in 1955, the American Federation of Labor (AFL) and the Congress of Industrial Organization (CIO) labor unions united (p. 894)

AFL-CIO en 1955 los sindicatos de trabajadores, Federación Estadounidense del Trabajo (AFL) y el Congreso de Organización Industrial (CIO), se unieron

Alamo fortified former mission in San Antonio was the site of the 1836 defeat and slaughter of Texans by Mexican troops (p. 306)

El Álamo antigua misión fortificada en San Antonio, que fue el sitio de la derrota de 1836 y la matanza de tejanos a manos de tropas mexicanas

Albany Plan of Union Benjamin Franklin's 1754 proposal to create one government for the 13 colonies (p. 89)

Plan de la Unión de Albany propuesta de Benjamín Franklin de 1754 para crear un gobierno para las 13 colonias

Alien and Sedition Acts 1798 laws that allowed the government to imprison or deport aliens, and to prosecute its critics (p. 202)

Leyes de Extranjería y Sedición leyes de 1798 que permitieron que el gobierno arrestara o deportara a extranjeros y enjuiciara a sus críticos

Alliance for Progress President Kennedy's program which gave economic aid to Latin America (p. 955)

Alianza para el Progreso programa del presidente Kennedy que daba asistencia económica a América Latina

Allies group of countries led by Britain, France, the United States, and the Soviet Union that fought the Axis Powers in World War II (p. 781)

Aliados grupo de países encabezado por Gran Bretaña, Francia, Estados Unidos, y la Unión Soviética que peleó contra los Poderes del Eje en la Segunda Guerra Mundial

al Qaeda terrorist group established by Osama bin Laden to rid Muslim countries of Western influence (p. 1118)

al Qaida grupo terrorista establecido por Osama bin Laden para eliminar la influencia occidental en los países musulmanes

Alsace-Lorraine territory lost to Germany by France in 1871 (p. 618)

Alsacia y Lorena territorio que Francia perdió ante Alemania en 1871

American Federation of Labor (AFL) labor union that organized skilled workers in a specific trade and made specific demands rather than seeking broad changes (p. 454)

Federación Estadounidense del Trabajo sindicato de trabajadores que organizó a los trabajadores calificados en oficios específicos e hizo pequeñas demandas en lugar de buscar cambios amplios

American Indian Movement (AIM) group that focused on helping Indians, including the securing of legal rights, land, and self-government for Native Americans (p. 583)

Movimiento de Indígenas Estadounidenses grupo que se concentró en ayudar a los indígenas, incluyendo velar por sus derechos legales, tierra y de autodeterminación

American System Henry Clay's federal program designed to stimulate the economy with internal improvements and create a self-sufficient nation (p. 242)

Sistema Estadounidense programa federal de Henry Clay diseñado para estimular la economía con mejoras internas y crear una nación autosuficiente

Americanization belief that assimilating immigrants into American society would make them more loyal citizens (p. 468)

americanización creencia que sostenía que la asimilación de los inmigrantes por la sociedad estadounidense los haría ciudadanos más leales

amnesty general pardon for certain crimes (p. 1057)

amnistía perdón general de ciertos delitos

Anaconda Plan northern Civil War strategy to starve the South by blockading seaports and controlling the Mississippi River (p. 362)

Plan Anaconda estrategia del Norte en la Guerra Civil de llevar al Sur a la rendición por inanición al bloquear los puertos marinos y controlar el río Mississippi

Angel Island immigrant processing station that opened in San Francisco Bay in 1910 (p. 467)

Isla Ángel estación de procesamiento de inmigrantes que abrió sus puertas en la bahía de San Francisco en 1910

Anschluss union of Germany and Austria in 1933 (p. 778)

Anschluss unión de Alemania y Austria en 1933

Anti-Defamation League organization formed in 1913 to defend Jews against physical and verbal attacks and false statements (p. 119)

Liga Antidifamación organización formada en 1913 para defender a los judíos contra los ataques verbales y las falsas declaraciones

English/Spanish Glossary

Antietam 1862 Civil War battle in which 23,000 troops were killed or wounded in one day (p. 368)
   Antietam batalla de la Guerra Civil de 1862 en la que murieron o resultaron heridos 23,000 miembros de las tropas en un día de lucha

Antifederalist one who opposed ratification of the Constitution (p. 151)
   antifederalista quien se opuso a la ratificación de la Constitución

anti-Semitism prejudice and discrimination against Jewish people (pp. 775, 828)
   antisemítismo prejuicios contra las personas judías

apartheid political system of strict segregation by race in South Africa (p. 1094)
   apartheid sistema político de segregación intransigente basada en la raza, en Sudáfrica

appeasement policy of granting concessions in order to keep the peace (p. 777)
   apaciguamiento política de otorgar concesiones para que mantener la paz

arms race contest in which nations compete to build more powerful weapons (p. 861)
   carrera armamentista competencia en la que las naciones se enfrentan para construir armas más poderosas

Articles of Confederation original federal constitution drafted by the Continental Congress in 1777 (p. 136)
   Estatutos de la Confederación constitución federal original preparada por el Congreso Continental en 1777

assembly line arrangement of equipment and workers in which work passes from operation to operation in direct line until the product is assembled (p. 661)
   línea de ensamblaje organización de equipos y trabajadores en la que el trabajo pasa de una operación a otra en una línea directa hasta que el producto queda ensamblado

assimilate to be absorbed into the main culture of a society (p. 503)
   asimilarse ser absorbido por la cultura dominante de una sociedad

Atlantic Charter joint declaration made by Great Britain and the United States during World War II that endorsed national self-determination and an international system of general security (p. 786)
   Carta del Atlántico declaración conjunta entre Gran Bretaña y Estados Unidos durante la Segunda Guerra Mundial que aprobaba la autodeterminación nacional y un sistema internacional de seguridad general

autonomy independent control over one's own affairs (p. 306)
   autonomía control independiente sobre los asuntos propios

Axis Powers group of countries led by Germany, Italy, and Japan that fought the Allies in World War II (p. 781)
   Poderes del Eje grupo de países encabezado por Alemania, Italia y Japón que peleó contra los Aliados en la Segunda Guerra Mundial

B

baby boom increase in births between 1945 and 1964 (p. 435)
   baby boom aumento de nacimientos entre 1945 y 1964

Bacon's Rebellion Virginia farmers clashed with both Indians and the colonial government over frontier expansion in 1675 (p. 48)
   Rebelión de Bacon Conflicto entre los agricultores de Virginia, los indígenas y el gobierno colonial a causa de la expansión fronteriza en 1675

Barbary War war between the Barbary States and the United States (p. 209)
   Guerra Berberisca guerra entre los Estados de Berbería y Estados Unidos

Bataan Death March during World War II, the forced march of American and Filipino prisoners of war under brutal conditions by the Japanese military (p. 793)
   Marcha de la Muerte de Batán durante la Segunda Guerra Mundial, la marcha forzada de prisioneros de guerra estadounidenses y filipinos en condiciones brutales impuestas por los militares japoneses

Battle of the Bulge in December 1944, Hitler ordered a counterattack on Allied troops in Belgium, but it crippled Germany by using up reserves and demoralizing its troops (p. 375)
   Batalla de las Ardenas en diciembre de 1944, Hitler ordenó un contraataque contra las tropas aliadas en Bélgica, pero esto debilitó a Alemania al usar todas sus reservas y desmoralizar a sus tropas

Battle of Coral Sea World War II battle that took place between Japanese and American aircraft carriers (p. 795)
   batalla del Mar del Coral batalla entre aviones japoneses y estadounidenses, durante la Segunda Guerra Mundial, ocurrida en mayo de 1942 en el escenario del Pacífico

Battle of Fallen Timbers 1794 battle in which federal troops defeated the Miami Confederacy of Native Americans (p. 198)
   Batalla de Fallen Timbers batalla ocurrida en 1794 en que las tropas federales derrotaron a la Confederación Miami de Indígenas

Battle of Gettysburg battle in 1863 in which Confederate troops were prevented from invading the North and which resulted in more than 50,000 casualties (p. 383)
   Batalla de Gettysburg batalla durante 1863 en la que se evitó que las tropas Confederadas invadieran el Norte y que produjo más de 50,000 bajas

Battle of the Little Big Horn 1876 battle in which the Sioux defeated U.S. Army troops (p. 500)
   Batalla del Little Big Horn batalla de 1876 durante la cual los sioux derrotaron a las tropas del Ejército de Estados Unidos

Battle of Midway turning point of World War II in the Pacific, in which the Japanese advance was stopped (p. 808)
   Batalla de Midway momento decisivo de la Segunda Guerra Mundial en el Pacífico, en que se detuvo el avance de los japoneses

Battle of New Orleans War of 1812 battle when the United States defeated the British in January of 1815 (p. 218)
   Batalla de Nueva Orleáns batalla de la Guerra de 1812 en la que Estados Unidos derrotó a los británicos en enero de 1815

Battle of Princeton 1777 Revolutionary War battle in New Jersey, won by the Continental Army (p. 119)

Batalla de Princeton batalla de la Guerra de Independencia ocurrida en Nueva Jersey en 1777 que ganó el Ejército Continental

Battle of Tippecanoe 1811 battle in the Indiana Territory between Native Americans and United States troops in which the Native Americans were defeated (p. 215)

Batalla de Tippecanoe batalla de 1811 en el Territorio de Indiana entre los indígenas y las tropas de Estados Unidos en que los indígenas resultaron derrotados

Battle of Trenton 1776 Revolutionary War battle in New Jersey, won by the Continental Army (p. 119)

Batalla de Trenton batalla de la Guerra de Independencia ocurrida en Nueva Jersey en 1776 que ganó el Ejército Continental

Bay of Pigs invasion 1961 failed invasion of Cuba by a CIA-led force of Cuban exiles (p. 956)

invasión de Bahía de Cochinos invasión de 1961 por exilados cubanos encabezados por la CIA que fracasaron al tratar de invadir Cuba

beatniks small group of writers and artists, in the 1950s and early 1960s, who were critical of American society (p. 456)

beatniks pequeño grupo de escritores y artistas en la década de 1950 y principios de los 1960 que criticaban a la sociedad estadounidense

Berlin airlift program in which U.S. and British pilots flew supplies to West Berlin during a Soviet blockade (p. 852)

puente aéreo de Berlín programa en el que pilotos estadounidenses y británicos volaban llevando suministros a Berlín Occidental durante un bloqueo soviético

Berlin Wall dividing wall built by East Germany in 1961 to isolate West Berlin from Communist-controlled East Berlin (p. 958)

Muro de Berlín pared divisoria construida por Alemania Oriental en 1961 para aislar a Berlín Occidental del Berlín Oriental controlado por los comunistas

Bessemer process method developed in the mid-1800s for making steel more efficiently (p. 439)

proceso Bessemer método desarrollado a mediados del siglo XIX para fabricar más eficientemente el acero

bicameral legislature lawmaking body made up of two houses (p. 135)

legislatura bicameral cuerpo legislativo compuesto de dos cámaras

"big stick" diplomacy Theodore Roosevelt's policy of creating and using, when necessary, a strong military to achieve America's goals (p. 605)

diplomacia de "mano dura" política seguida por Teodoro Roosevelt según la cual se organizaría y usaría, cuando fuera necesario, una fuerza militar poderosa para lograr los objetivos de Estados Unidos

bilingual education system in which students are taught in their native languages as well as in English (p. 1128)

educación bilingüe sistema en el que se enseña a los estudiantes en su idioma nativo así como en inglés

Bill of Rights first ten amendments to the Constitution; written list of freedoms guaranteed to citizens by the government (p. 153)

Declaración de Derechos primeras diez enmiendas a la Constitución; listado escrito de las libertades que el gobierno garantiza a sus ciudadanos

biotechnology application of technology to solving problems affecting living organisms (p. 1105)

biotecnología aplicación de la tecnología para resolver problemas que afectan a los organismos vivos

Black Cabinet group of African American leaders who served as unofficial advisers to Franklin D. Roosevelt (p. 302)

Gabinete Negro grupo de líderes afroestadounidenses que fungieron como consejeros extraoficiales de Franklin D. Roosevelt

black code laws that restricted African Americans' rights and opportunities (p. 405)

códigos negros leyes que restringían los derechos y oportunidades de los afroestadounidenses

blacklist list of persons who were not hired because of suspected communist ties (p. 870)

lista negra lista de personas que no fueron contratadas por sospechas de vínculos comunistas

Black Panthers organization of militant African Americans founded in 1966 (p. 941)

Panteras Negras organización de militantes afroestadounidenses fundada en 1966

black power movement in the 1960s that urged African Americans to use their collective political and economic power to gain equality (p. 941)

poder negro movimiento de la década de 1960 que exhortó a los afroestadounidenses a usar su poder político y económico colectivo para lograr la igualdad

Black Tuesday October 29, 1929, when stock prices fell sharply in the Great Crash (p. 706)

Martes Negro 29 de octubre de 1929, el día en que los precios de las acciones cayeron precipitadamente en la Gran Caída de la Bolsa

"Bleeding Kansas" term used to describe the 1854–1856 violence between proslavery and antislavery supporters in Kansas (p. 336)

"Kansas Sangrante" término usado para describir la violencia de 1854 a 1856 entre los que apoyaban la esclavitud y los que estaban en contra de la esclavitud en Kansas

blitzkrieg "lightning war" that emphasized the use of speed and firepower to penetrate deep into the enemy's territory (p. 781)

blitzkrieg "guerra relámpago" que enfatiza el uso de velocidad y capacidad bélica para penetrar muy adentro en el territorio enemigo

blockade military tactic in which a navy prevents vessels from entering or leaving its enemy's ports (p. 361)

bloqueo táctica militar en la que una fuerza naval evita que los buques entren o salgan de los puertos enemigos

boat people refugees who leave their country by boat (p. 1064)

balseros refugiados que dejan su país en bote

bond certificate bought from the government that promises to pay the holder back the purchase amount plus interest at a future date (p. 374)

bono certificado comprado al gobierno que promete al titular pagar con intereses el monto de la compra en una fecha posterior

Bonus Army group of World War I veterans who marched on Washington, D.C., in 1932 to demand early payment of a bonus promised them by Congress (p. 723)

Ejército del Bono grupo de veteranos de la Primera Guerra Mundial que marcharon sobre Washington, D.C., en 1932, para exigir el pago anticipado de un bono que les prometiera el Congreso

bootlegger one who sells illegal alcohol (p. 678)

contrabandista quien vende alcohol ilegalmente

border state during the Civil War, the states that allowed slavery but remained in the Union: Delaware, Kentucky, Maryland, and Missouri (p. 362)

estados colindantes durante la Guerra Civil, estados donde se toleraba la esclavitud aunque quedaron parte de la Unión: Delaware, Kentucky, Maryland, y Missouri

Boston Massacre incident on March 5, 1770, in which British soldiers killed five colonists in Boston (p. 103)

Masacre de Boston incidente del 5 de marzo de 1770, durante el cual soldados británicos mataron a cinco colonos en Boston

Boston Tea Party December 16, 1773 protest against British taxes in which Bostonians disguised as Native Americans dumped tea into the harbor (p. 103)

Fiesta del Te de Boston protesta del 16 de diciembre de 1773 contra los impuestos británicos en la cual los ciudadanos de Boston disfrazados como nativos estadounidenses botaron te al mar en el puerto

Boxer Rebellion violence started by members of a secret society in China, which prompted the governments of Europe and America to send troops to squash the rebellion (p. 602)

Rebelión de los Bóxer actos de violencia iniciados por miembros de una sociedad secreta en China, que provocó los gobiernos de Europa y América enviaran tropas para sofocar la rebelión

bracero program plan that brought laborers from Mexico to work on American farms (p. 811)

programa de braceros plan que trajo trabajadores de México a trabajar en granjas estadounidenses

Brady Bill law passed in 1993 requiring a waiting period on sales of handguns, along with a criminal background check on the buyer (p. 1111)

Ley Brady ley aprobada en 1993 que exige un período de espera de cinco días para la venta de revólveres, junto con una verificación de los antecedentes delictivos del comprador

bread line line of people waiting for food handouts from charities or public agencies (p. 710)

cola de alimentación fila de personas que esperan alimentos gratuitos de obras caritativas o agencias públicas

brinkmanship belief that only by going to the brink of war could the United States protect itself against communist aggression (p. 862)

política arriesgado creencia según la que sólo estando al borde de la guerra Estados Unidos podía protegerse contra la agresión comunista

budget deficit shortfall between the amount of money spent and the amount taken in by the federal government (p. 1082)

déficit presupuestario faltante entre la cantidad de dinero gastado y la cantidad de dinero captado por el gobierno federal

bull market period of rising stock prices (p. 664)

mercado alcista perfodo durante el cual suben los precios de las acciones

bureaucracy group of departments and officials that make up an organization, such as a government (p. 205)

burocracia grupo de departamentos y personeros que componen una organización, tal como el gobierno

business cycle periodic growth and contraction of the economy (p. 706)

ciclo commercial crecimiento y contracción periódicos de la economía

buying on margin system of buying stocks in which a buyer pays a small percentage of the purchase price while the broker advances the rest (p. 664)

comprando por margen sistema de compra de acciones en el que el comprador paga un pequeño porcentaje del precio de compra mientras que el corredor anticipa el resto

C

Cabinet group of senior officials appointed by the President that heads the executive departments and advises the President (p. 193)

gabinete grupo de personeros de más alto rango nombrados por el presidente que encabezan los departamentos ejecutivos y aconsejan al presidente

California Gold Rush mass migration to California after the discovery of gold in 1848 (p. 313)

Fiebre del Oro de California migración masiva a California después que se descubriera oro en 1848

California Master Plan called for three tiers of higher education: research universities, state colleges, and community colleges, all of which were to be accessible to all of the state's citizens (p. 895)

Plan Maestro de California hizo un llamado para la creación de tres niveles de educación superior: universidades de investigación, universidades estatales, y centros educacionales comunitarios, los cuales deberían ser accesibles para todos los ciudadanos del estado

Camp David Accords 1978 agreement brokered by President Jimmy Carter between Egyptian and Israeli leaders that made a peace treaty between the two nations possible (p. 1066)

Acuerdos de Camp David acuerdo de 1978 agenciado por el presidente Jimmy Carter, entre los lideres de Egipto e Israel que hizo posible un tratado de paz entre ambas naciones

capital money or wealth used to invest in business or enterprise (p. 234)

capital dinero o bienes usados para invertir en un negocio o empresa

carpetbagger negative term for Northerners who moved to the South after the Civil War (p. 411)

carpetbagger término negativo para referirse a norteños que se trasladó al Sur después de la Guerra Civil

cartel association of producers of a good or service that prices and controls stocks in order to monopolize the market (p. 444)

cartel asociación de productores de un bien o servicio que coordina los precios y la producción

cash crop crop grown for sale (p. 494)

cultivo comercial cosecha cultivada para la venta

casualties soldiers killed, wounded, and missing (p. 622)

bajas soldados muertos, heridos y desaparecidos

caucus closed meeting of party members for the purpose of choosing a candidate (p. 249)

comité electoral reunión cerrada de miembros de un partido para efectos de elegir a un candidato

Central Intelligence Agency (CIA) U.S. intelligence-gathering organization (p. 865)

Agencia Central de Inteligencia organización estadounidense para la recolección de inteligencia

charter legal document giving certain rights to a person or company (p. 44)

carta constitucional documento legal que otorga derechos a una persona o compañía

checks and balances system in which each branch of the government has the power to monitor and limit the actions of the other two (p. 155)

controles y equilibrios sistema por el cual cada rama del gobierno tiene el poder de vigilar y limitar las acciones de las otras dos

Chicano movement movement that focused on raising Mexican American consciousness (p. 1030)

movimiento chicano movimiento enfocado en despertar la conciencia de los estadounidenses de origen mexicano

Chinese Exclusion Act 1882 law that prohibited the immigration of Chinese laborers (p. 468)

Ley de Exclusión de Chinos ley de 1882 que prohibía la inmigración de trabajadores chinos

Christian fundamentalist individual who believes in a strict, literal interpretation of the Bible as the foundation of the Christian faith (p. 1056)

fundamentalista cristiano persona que cree en la interpretación estricta y literal de la Biblia como el fundamento de la fe cristiana

Civilian Conservation Corps (CCC) New Deal program that provided young men with relief jobs on environmental conservation projects, including reforestation and flood control (p. 736)

Cuerpos de Conservación Civil programa del Nuevo Trato que proporcionaba ayuda a los jóvenes con trabajo en proyectos de conservación del medio ambiente, incluyendo reforestación y control de inundaciones

Civil Rights Act of 1866 law that established federal guarantees of civil rights for all citizens (p. 406)

Ley de Derechos Civiles de 1866 ley que estableció las garantías federales de los derechos civiles para todos ciudadanos

Civil Rights Act of 1875 law that banned discrimination in public facilities and transportation (p. 495)

Ley de Derechos Civiles de 1875 ley que prohibió la discriminación en instalaciones y transporte públicos

Civil Rights Act of 1957 law that established a federal Civil Rights Commission (p. 921)

Ley de Derechos Civiles de 1957 ley que estableció una Comisión Federal de Derechos Civiles

Civil Rights Act of 1964 outlawed discrimination in public places and employment based on race, religion, or national origin (pp. 932, 966)

Ley de Derechos Civiles de 1964 conjunto de leyes que prohibió la discriminación en lugares y empleos públicos con base en la raza, religión, o nacionalidad

civil service government departments and their nonelected employees (p. 531)

servicio civil departamentos gubernamentales y sus empleados que no son de elección popular

Clayton Antitrust Act 1914 law that strengthened the Sherman Antitrust Act (p. 130)

Ley Clayton Antimonopolio ley de 1914 que fortalecía la Ley Sherman Antimonopolio

Clean Air Act act passed in 1970 that lessened air pollution by limiting the emissions from factories and automobiles (p. 1036)

Ley para el Aire Puro ley aprobada en 1970 que buscaba disminuir la contaminación del aire al limitar las emisiones de fábricas y automóviles

Clean Water Act 1973 law that restricted the pollution of water by industry and agriculture (p. 1036)

Ley para el Agua Limpia ley aprobada en 1973 que buscaba restringir la contaminación industrial y agrícola del agua

Cold War worldwide rivalry between the United States and the Soviet Union (p. 848)

Guerra Fría rivalidad mundial entre Estados Unidos y la Unión Soviética

collective bargaining process in which employers negotiate with labor unions about hours, wages, and other working conditions (p. 453)

negociación colectiva proceso en el que los patronos negocian con los sindicatos sobre los horarios, salarios, y otras condiciones de trabajo

Columbian Exchange the global exchange of goods and ideas between Europe, Africa, and the Americas after Columbus made his first transatlantic voyage in 1492 (p. 25)

intercambio colombino intercambio global de bienes e ideas entre Europa, Africa y las Americas posterior al primer viaje transatlántico de Colón en 1492

Committee on Public Information (CPI) government agency created during World War I to encourage Americans to support the war (p. 630)

Comité de Información Pública organización creada por el gobierno durante la Primera Guerra Mundial para animar al público estadounidense a apoyar la guerra

committees of correspondence network of local groups that informed colonists of British measures and the opposition to them in the years before the Revolutionary War (p. 103)

comités de correspondencia red organizada de grupos locales que informaban a los colonos de las medidas británicas y la oposición a éstas antes de la Guerra Revolucionaria

commune small communities where people share resources (p. 1019)

comunas pequeñas comunidades en las que las personas comparten los recursos

company town community whose residents rely upon one company for jobs, housing, and shopping (p. 451)

pueblo de compañía comunidad cuyos residentes dependen de una compañía para obtener empleo, vivienda, y compras

Compromise of 1850 political agreement that allowed California to be admitted as a free state by allowing popular sovereignty in the territories and enacting a stricter fugitive slave law (p. 328)

English/Spanish Glossary

Acuerdo de 1850 acuerdo político que permitió la admisión de California como estado libre al permitir la soberanía popular en los territorios y aplicar una ley más estricta a los esclavos fugitivos

Compromise of 1877 agreement by which Rutherford B. Hayes won the 1876 presidential election and in exchange agreed to remove the remaining federal troops from the South (p. 424)

Acuerdo de 1877 acuerdo por el cual Rutheford B. Hayes ganó las elecciones presidenciales de 1876 y a cambio aceptó retirar las tropas federales que permanecían en el Sur

concentration camp camps used by the Nazis to imprison "undesirable" members of society (p. 831)

campo de concentración campos usados por los Nazis para encarcelar a miembros "indeseables" de la sociedad

Confederate States of America government of 11 southern states that seceded from the United States and fought against the Union in the Civil War (p. 350)

Estados Confederados de América gobierno de 11 estados sureños que se separó de Estados Unidos y peleó contra la Unión en la Guerra Civil

Congress of Industrial Organization (CIO) labor organization founded in the 1930s that represented industrial workers (p. 744)

Congreso de Organización Industrial organización de trabajadores fundada en la década de 1930 que representa a los trabajadores industriales

conquistador Spanish conqueror (p. 23)

conquistador conquistador español

conscientious objector person whose moral or religious beliefs forbid him or her to fight in wars (p. 630)

objetor de conciencia persona que rehúsa pelear en una guerra por convicciones morales o religiosas

conscription drafting of citizens into military service (p. 374)

conscripción reclutamiento de ciudadanos en el servicio militar

conservative person who tends to support limited government involvement in the economy, community help for the needy, and traditional values (p. 1076)

conservador persona que tiende a apoyar una participación gubernamental limitada en la economía, favorece la ayuda comunitaria para los necesitados, y mantiene los valores tradicionales

conspicuous consumerism purchasing of goods and services for the purpose of impressing others (p. 480)

consumismo llamativo compra de bienes y servicios para efectos de impresionar a los demás

consumerism large-scale buying, much of it on credit (p. 896)

consumismo compras a gran escala, la mayoría de éstas a crédito

consumer revolution flood of new, affordable goods in the decades after World War I (p. 663)

revolución de consumo flujo de bienes nuevos y asequibles durante las decadas posteriores a la Primera Guerra Mundial

containment policy of keeping communism contained within its existing borders (p. 850)

contención política de mantener el comunismo contenido dentro de sus fronteras existentes

Continental Army army that represented the colonies during the Revolutionary War (p. 109)

Ejército Continental ejército que representó a las colonias durante la Guerra de Independencia

Contract With America Republican plan headed by Newt Gingrich that focused on scaling back the government, balancing the budget, and cutting taxes (p. 1111)

Contrato con Estados Unidos plan republicano encabezado por Newt Gingrich enfocado en la reducción del gobierno, el equilibrio del presupuesto y la reducción de los impuestos

contraband supplies captured from an enemy during wartime (pp. 368, 624)

contrabando suministros confiscados al enemigo en tiempos de guerra

Contras anticommunist counterrevolutionaries who opposed the Sandinista government in Nicaragua in the 1980s (p. 1088)

Contras contrarrevolucionarios anticomunistas opuestos al gobierno Sandinista de Nicaragua en la década de 1980

convoy group of merchant ships sailing together, protected by warships (p. 637)

convoy grupo de buques mercantes que navegan juntos bajo la protección de buques de guerra

Copperhead negative term given to antiwar northern Democrats during the Civil War (p. 375)

Copperheads término peyorativo que se daba a los demócratas del Norte durante la Guerra Civil

corporation company recognized as a legal unit that has rights and liabilities separate from each of its members (p. 443)

corporación compañía reconocida como entidad legal con derechos y responsabilidades separados de los de cada uno de sus miembros

cotton gin machine invented in 1793 to separate the cotton fiber from its hard shell (p. 236)

desmotadora máquina inventada en 1793 para separar la fibra del algodón de la cáscara

counterculture movement that upheld values different from those of mainstream culture (p. 1018)

contracultura movimiento que mantuvo valores diferentes a los de la cultura tradicional

coureurs de bois from the French for "runner of the woods," French colonists who lived in the woods as fur traders (p. 42)

coureurs de bois expresión en francés que significa "corredor de los bosques," que designa a los colonos franceses habitantes de los bosques que comerciaban con pieles

court packing FDR plan to add up to six new justices to the nine-member Supreme Court after the Court had ruled that some New Deal legislation was unconstitutional (p. 746)

plan para llenar las cortes plan de FDR para agregar seis nuevos magistrados a los nueve miembros de la Corte Suprema luego de que la Corte dictaminó que algunas leyes del Nuevo Trato eran inconstitucionales

"credibility gap" American public's growing distrust of statements made by the government during the Vietnam War (p. 994)

"brecha de credibilidad" creciente desconfianza del público estadounidense ante declaraciones del gobierno durante la Guerra de Vietnam

creditor nation country which is owed more money by other countries than it owes other countries (p. 651)

nación acreedora país al que otros países le deben más dinero del que éste les debe

Crittenden Compromise 1861 proposed constitutional amendment that attempted to prevent secession of the southern states by allowing slavery in all territories south of the Missouri Compromise line (p. 352)

Acuerdo Crittenden enmienda constitucional propuesta en 1861 para intentar evitar la secesión de los estados del Sur al proponer que se permitiera la esclavitud en todos los territorios al sur de la línea del Acuerdo de Missouri

Cuban missile crisis 1962 conflict between the U.S. and the Soviet Union resulting from the Soviet installation of nuclear missiles in Cuba (p. 956)

crisis de los misiles de Cuba conflicto entre Estados Unidos y la Unión Soviética en 1962 como resultado de la instalación de misiles nucleares en Cuba por parte de los soviéticos

D

dame school elementary school during colonial times, often operated out of a woman's home (p. 83)

escuela de damas escuela primaria en la época colonial, a menudo con sede en la casa de una mujer

Dawes General Allotment Act 1887 law that divided reservation land into private family plots (p. 504)

Ley de Asignación General Dawes ley de 1887 que dividió las tierras de las reservaciones en parcelas familiares privadas

Dawes Plan agreement in which the United States loaned money to Germany, allowing Germany to make reparation payments to Britain and France (p. 670)

Plan Dawes acuerdo en el que Estados Unidos prestó dinero a Alemania, permitiéndole a ésta hacer pagos de reparación a Gran Bretaña y Francia

D-Day June 6, 1944, the day Allies landed on the beaches of Normandy, France (p. 819)

Día D 6 de junio de 1944, el día en que los Aliados desembarcaron en las playas de Normandía, Francia

death camp Nazi camp designed for the extermination of prisoners (p. 832)

campo de la muerte campo diseñados por los Nazis para el exterminio de prisioneros

Declaration of Independence document drawn up by the Second Continental Congress that announced American independence and the reasons for it (p. 112)

Declaración de Independencia documento redactado por el Segundo Congreso Continental que anunció la independencia de Estados Unidos y las razones para la misma

de facto segregation segregation by unwritten custom or tradition (p. 916)

segregación de facto segregación basada en la costumbre o la tradición no escrita

deficit spending practice of a nation paying out more money than it is receiving in revenues (p. 961)

déficit de gastos práctica de las naciones que gastan más de lo que reciben por ingresos

de jure segregation segregation imposed by law (p. 916)

segregación de iure segregación impuesta por ley

demobilization sending home members of the army (p. 883)

desmovilización enviar a los miembros del ejército de vuelta a casa

Democratic Republican led by Jefferson, one of the first political parties in the United States (p. 197)

Republicano Democrático encabezado por Jefferson, uno de los primeros partidos políticos en Estados Unidos

Department of Homeland Security department created by President Bush to coordinate domestic security efforts (p. 1125)

Departamento de Seguridad Nacional departamento creado por el presidente Bush para coordinar los esfuerzos de seguridad doméstica

deregulation reduction or removal of government controls over an industry (p. 1082)

desregulación reducción o eliminación de los controles gubernamentales en una industria

détente flexible diplomacy adopted by Richard Nixon to ease tensions between the United States, the Soviet Union, and the People's Republic of China (p. 1010)

distensión diplomacia flexible adoptada por Richard Nixon para aliviar las tensiones entre Estados Unidos, la Unión Soviética, y la República Popular China

developing world countries that are less economically advanced than developed countries such as the United States (p. 1065)

mundo en desarrollo países que son menos avanzados económica que los países desarrollados como Estados Unidos

direct primary election in which citizens themselves vote to select nominees for upcoming elections (p. 554)

primarias directas elecciones en las que los ciudadanos votan directamente para elegir los candidatos para las siguientes elecciones.

divest to take away or rid oneself of (p. 1094)

desposeer quitarse o librarse de algo

"dollar diplomacy" President Taft's policy of expanding American investments abroad (p. 609)

"diplomacia del dólar" política exterior del presidente Taft de expandir las inversiones estadounidenses en el exterior

domino theory idea that if a nation falls to communism, its closest neighbors will also fall under communist control (p. 982)

teoría dominó idea que estipulaba que si una nación cae ante el comunismo, sus vecinos más cercanos también caerán bajo el control comunista

dove person who opposed U.S. involvement in the Vietnam War (p. 991)

paloma persona opuesta a la participación estadounidense en la Guerra de Vietnam

draftee young American man drafted into military service (p. 992)

conscripto varón estadounidense joven reclutado para el servicio militar

Dust Bowl term used for the central and southern Great Plains during the 1930s when the region suffered from drought and dust storms (p. 715)

Cuenco de Polvo término usado para describir las Grandes Planicies, durante la década de 1930 cuando la región quedó desolada por la sequía y las tormentas de polvo

E

Earth Day annual event of environmental activism and protest, begun in 1970 (p. 1035)
Día de la Tierra evento anual de activismo y protesta ambiental, empezó en 1970

Economic Opportunity Act law passed in 1964 creating antipoverty programs (p. 966)
Ley de Igualdad de Oportunidades ley aprobada en 1964 que creo programas contra la pobreza

Eighteenth Amendment constitutional amendment banning the manufacture, distribution, and sale of alcohol in the United States (p. 677)
Decimoctava Enmienda enmienda constitucional que prohibió la fabricación, distribución y venta de alcohol en Estados Unidos

Eisenhower Doctrine policy of President Eisenhower that stated that the United States would use force to help any nation threatened by communism (p. 864)
doctrina Eisenhower política del presidente Eisenhower que indicaba que Estados Unidos usaría la fuerza para ayudar a cualquier nación amenazada por el comunismo

electoral college group of persons chosen from each state to indirectly elect the President and Vice President (p. 155)
colegio electoral grupo de personas escogidas de cada estado para elegir el presidente y vicepresidente indirectamente

Ellis Island island in New York Harbor that served as an immigration station for millions of immigrants arriving to the United States (p. 466)
Isla Ellis isla en el puerto de Nueva York que se usó como puesto de migración para millones de inmigrantes que llegaron a Estados Unidos

Emancipation Proclamation decree by President Lincoln that freed enslaved people living in Confederate states still in rebellion (p. 368)
Proclamación de Emancipación decreto del presidente Lincoln que liberó a los esclavos en los territorios confederados aún en rebelión

embargo official ban or restriction on trade (p. 211)
embargo prohibición o restricción oficial del comercio

Endangered Species Act law passed in 1973 to protect endangered plants and animals (p. 1036)
Ley de Especies en Peligro de Extinción ley aprobada en 1973 con el propósito de proteger las plantas y animales en peligro de extinción

Enforcement Acts 1870 and 1871 laws that made it a federal offense to interfere with a citizen's right to vote (p. 417)
Leyes de Aplicación leyes de 1870 y 1871 que hicieron una ofensa federal la interferencia con el derecho de un ciudadano de emitir el voto

English Bill of Rights document signed in 1689 that guaranteed the rights of English citizens (p. 73)
Declaración de Derechos Inglesa documento firmado en 1689 que garantizó los derechos de los ciudadanos ingleses

Enlightenment eighteenth-century movement during which European philosophers believed that society's problems could be solved by reason and science (p. 77)
Ilustración movimiento del siglo XVIII según el cual los filósofos europeos creían que los problemas de la sociedad se podían resolver mediante la razón y la ciencia

entrepreneur person who invests money in a product or business with the goal of making a profit (p. 437)
empresario persona que invierte dinero en un producto o empresa con el fin de obtener una ganancia

Environmental Protection Agency (EPA) government agency committed to cleaning up and protecting the environment (p. 1036)
Agencia de Protección Ambiental agencia gubernamental comprometida con la limpieza y protección del ambiente

Equal Pay Act 1963 law that required both men and women to receive equal pay for equal work (p. 961)
Ley de Pago Equitativo ley de 1963 que exigió que hombres y mujeres reciban la igual paga por un trabajo igual

Equal Rights Amendment (ERA) proposed amendment to the Constitution to guarantee gender equality (p. 1023)
Enmienda de Igualdad de Derechos enmienda propuesta a la Constitución garantizar la igualdad entre los sexos

Erie Canal canal completed in 1825 that connected Lake Erie to the Hudson River (p. 229)
Canal Erie canal terminado en 1825 que conecta el lago Erie con el río Hudson

Espionage Act act passed by Congress in 1917 enacting severe penalties for anyone engaged in disloyal or treasonable activities (p. 632)
Ley de Espionaje ley aprobada por el Congreso en 1917 que estableció penas severas para cualquiera que participara en actividades desleales o de traición

ethnic cleansing systematic effort to purge an area or society of an ethnic group through murder or deportation (p. 1117)
limpieza étnica esfuerzo sistemático para purgar una zona o sociedad de un grupo étnico mediante el asesinato o la deportación

European Union (EU) economic and political union of European nations established in 1993 (p. 1115)
Unión Europea unión económica y política de las naciones europeas establecida en 1993

evangelical style of worship meant to elicit powerful emotions to gain converts (p. 267)
evangélico estilo de culto cuyo fin es suscitar emociones fuertes para atraer conversos

Executive Order 8802 World War II measure that assured fair hiring practices in any job funded by the government (p. 810)
Orden Ejecutiva 8802 medida durante la Segunda Guerra Mundial que garantizaba prácticas justas de empleo en cualquier puesto financiado por el gobierno

executive privilege principle that the President has the right to keep certain communications between himself and other members of the executive branch private (p. 1052)
privilegio ejecutivo principio que indica que el presidente tiene derecho a mantener en privado ciertas comunicaciones con otros miembros del poder ejecutivo

Exodusters African Americans who migrated from the South to the West after the Civil War (p. 510)
Exodusters grupo de afroestadounidenses que emigraron al Oeste después de la Guerra Civil

expansionist person who favors expanding the territory or influence of a country (p. 300)
expansionista persona que favorece la expansión del territorio o influencia de un país

extractive economy economy in a colony where the colonizing country removed raw materials and shipped them back home to benefit its own economy (p. 586)
economía de extracción economía de una colonia donde el país colonizador extraía materias primas y las enviaba a la madre patria para beneficiar su propia economía

F

Fair Deal President Truman's program to expand New Deal reforms (p. 886)
Trato Justo programa del presidente Truman para expandir las reformas del Nuevo Trato

Fair Labor Standards Act 1938 law that set a minimum wage, a maximum workweek of 44 hours, and outlawed child labor (p. 744)
Ley de Normas Laborales Justas ley de 1938 que estableció el salario mínimo, una semana laboral de un máximo de 44 horas, y prohibió el trabajo infantil

Family Medical Leave Act law guaranteeing most full-time employees 12 workweeks of unpaid leave each year for personal or family health reasons (p. 1110)
Ley de Permiso Médico Familiar ley que garantiza a la mayoría de los empleados de tiempo completo 12 semanas laborales de permiso sin goce de sueldo cada año por razones personales o de salud familiar

Farmers' Alliance network of farmers' organizations that worked for political and economic reforms in the late 1800s (p. 494)
Alianza de Granjeros red de organizaciones agrícolas que lucho por alcanzar reformas políticas y económicas a finales del siglo XIX

federal national (p. 136)
federal nacional

Federal Art Project division of the Works Progress Administration that hired unemployed artists to create artworks for public buildings and sponsored art-education programs and exhibitions (p. 761)
Proyecto Federal de Arte división de la Administración de Progreso de Obras que contrató artistas desempleados para crear obras de arte en edificios públicos y patrocinó programas educativos y exhibiciones artísticos

Federal Deposit Insurance Corporation (FDIC) government agency that insures bank deposits, guaranteeing that depositors' money will be safe (p. 735)
Corporación Federal de Aseguramiento de Depósitos agencia gubernamental que asegura los depósitos bancarios, garantizando que el dinero de los depositantes estará seguro

federalism political system in which power is shared between the national government and state governments (p. 147)

federalismo sistema político en el cual el poder se comparte entre el gobierno nacional y los gobiernos estatales

Federalist one who favored ratification of the Constitution (p. 151)
federalista quien favoreció la ratificación de la Constitución

The Federalist series of 85 essays written by Madison, Hamilton, and Jay that explained and defended the Constitution (p. 151)
El Federalista conjunto de 85 ensayos escritos por Madison, Hamilton, y Jay que explicaba y defendía la Constitución

Federal Reserve Act 1913 law that placed national banks under the control of a Federal Reserve Board, which runs regional banks that hold the reserve funds from commercial banks, sets interest rates, and supervises commercial banks (p. 577)
Ley de Reserva Federal ley de 1913 que sometió a todos los bancos del país bajo el control de una Junta de Reserva Federal, que opera los bancos regionales que mantienen un fondo de reserva de los bancos comerciales, fija tasa de intereses, y supervisa a los bancos comerciales

Federal Trade Commission (FTC) government agency established in 1914 to identify monopolistic business practices, false advertising, and dishonest labeling (p. 578)
Comisión Federal de Comercio agencia gubernamental establecida en 1914 para identificar las prácticas comerciales monopolistas, falsa propaganda, y rótulos deshonestos

feminism theory that women and men should have political, social, and economic equality (p. 1022)
feminismo teoría que las mujeres y los hombres deben tener igualdad politíca, social, y económica

Fifteenth Amendment 1870 constitutional amendment that guaranteed voting rights regardless of race or previous condition of servitude (p. 409)
Decimoquinta Enmienda enmienda constitucional de 1870 que garantizó el derecho al sufragio independiente-mente de la raza o condición relacionada a la servitud

54th Massachusetts Regiment all-black unit led by Union Colonel Robert Gould Shaw during the Civil War (p. 370)
Regimiento 54o de Massachusetts escuadrón de la Unión dirigido por el coronel Robert Gould Shaw durante la Guerra Civil, compuesto totalmente de soldados negros

filibuster tactic by which senators give long speeches to hold up legislative business (p. 932)
obstruccionismo táctica empleada por los senadores que consistió en hacer prolongados discursos para detener los asuntos legislativos

fireside chat informal radio broadcast in which FDR explained issues and New Deal programs to average Americans (p. 735)
charla junto a la hoguera transmisión informal de radio en que FDR explicaba asuntos y programas del Nuevo Trato a los estadounidenses promedio

First Continental Congress group of delegates that met in 1774 and represented all the American colonies, except Georgia (p. 104)

Primer Congreso Continental grupo de delegados que se reunió en 1774 y representaba a todas las colonias estadounidenses, excepto Georgia

First Seminole War 1817–1818 war between U.S. soldiers and Seminole Indians in Florida (p. 244)

Primera Guerra Seminole guerra de 1817 a 1818 entre soldados estadounidenses e indígenas seminoles en Florida

flapper young woman from the 1920s who defied traditional rules of conduct and dress (p. 684)

chica flapper mujer joven de la década de 1920 que desafiaba las reglas tradicionales de conducta y atuendo

flexible response defense policy allowing for the appropriate action in any type of conflict (p. 955)

respuesta flexible política de defensa que permite acciones apropiadas en conflictos de cualquier tipo

Foraker Act law establishing a civil government in Puerto Rico (p. 604)

Ley Foraker ley que estableció un gobierno civil en Puerto Rico

Fort Sumter federal fort located in Charleston, South Carolina, where the first shots of the Civil War were fired (p. 353)

Fuerte Sumter fuerte federal ubicado en Charleston, Carolina del Sur, donde se dispararon las primeras balas de la Guerra Civil

forty-niners miners who went to California after the discovery of gold in 1848 (p. 313)

forty-niners mineros que se dirigieron a California después del descubrimiento de oro en 1848

442nd Regimental Combat Team World War II unit made up of Japanese American volunteers (p. 813)

Equipo de Combate del Regimiento 442 unidad de la Segunda Guerra Mundial compuesta por voluntarios estadounidenses de origen japonés

Fourteen Points list of terms for resolving World War I and future wars outlined by American President Woodrow Wilson (p. 641)

Catorce Puntos lista de condiciones planteada por el presidente estadounidense Woodrow Wilson para resolver la Primera Guerra Mundial y guerras futuras

Fourteenth Amendment 1868 constitutional amendment which defined citizenship and guaranteed citizens equal protection under the law (p. 407)

Decimocuarta Enmienda enmienda constitucional de 1868 que definió la ciudadanía y garantizó a los ciudadanos protección igual por la ley

franchise business to allow a company to distribute its products or services through retail outlets owned by independent operators (p. 894)

franquicias comerciales permitir que una compañía distribuya sus productos o servicios por medio de establecimientos minoristas y independientes

freedman person who has been freed from slavery (p. 279)

liberto esclavo que ha ganado la libertad

Freedmen's Bureau federal agency designed to aid freed slaves and poor white farmers in the South after the Civil War (p. 405)

Oficina de Hombres Libres agencia federal diseñada para ayudar a los esclavos liberados y los pobres granjeros blancos del Sur luego de la Guerra Civil

freedom ride 1961 protest by activists who rode buses through southern states to test their compliance with the ban on segregation on interstate buses (p. 927)

viaje por la libertad protesta de activistas que en 1961 viajaron en autobuses a través de los estados sureños para probar si acataban la prohibición contra la segregación en autobuses interestatales

Freedom Summer 1964 effort to register African American voters in Mississippi (p. 936)

Verano de Libertad esfuerzo de 1964 por empadronar a votantes afroestadounidenses en Mississippi

Free-Soil Party antislavery political party of the mid-1800s (p. 326)

Partido Tierra Libre partido político antiesclavista de mitad del siglo XIX

French and Indian War war fought from 1754 to 1763 in which Britain and its colonies defeated France and its Indian allies, gaining control of eastern North America (p. 86)

Guerra Franco-Indígena guerra peleada desde 1754 a 1763 en la que Gran Bretaña y sus colonias derrotaron a Francia y sus ailados indígenas, obteniendo el control de la región este de América del Norte

French Revolution republican uprising against the French monarchy that began in 1789 (p. 199)

Revolución Francesa levantamiento republicano contra la monarquía francesa que empezó en 1789

Fugitive Slave Act law that required all citizens to aid in apprehending runaway slaves (p. 329)

Ley de Esclavos Fugitivos ley que obligaba a todos los ciudadanos a aprehender a los esclavos escapados

fundamentalism movement or attitude stressing strict and literal adherence to a set of basic principles (p. 672)

fundamentalismo movimiento o actitud que enfatiza un cumplimiento estricto y literal a un conjunto de principios básicos

G

Gadsden Purchase 1853 purchase of land (present-day Arizona and New Mexico) from Mexico (p. 312)

Compra Gadsden compra que hizo Estados Unidos a México en 1853 de tierras que son actualmente Arizona y Nuevo México

Gag Rule rule lasting from 1836 to 1844 that banned debate about slavery in Congress (p. 285)

Ley de la Mordaza reglamento que prohibía debatir el tema de la esclavitud en el Congreso entre 1836 y 1844

General Agreement on Tariffs and Trade (GATT) international agreement first signed in 1947 aimed at lowering trade barriers (p. 1115)

Acuerdo General sobre Aranceles y Comercio tratado internacional firmado originalmente en 1947 diseñado para disminuir las barreras comerciales

generation gap lack of understanding and communication between older and younger members of society (p. 1019)

brecha generacional falta de entendimiento y comunicación entre los miembros más viejos y los más jóvenes de la sociedad

Geneva Convention international agreement governing the humane treatment of wounded soldiers and prisoners of war (p. 838)

Convención de Ginebra acuerdo internacional que regula el tratamiento humanitario de soldados heridos y prisioneros de guerra

genocide willful annihilation of a racial, political, or cultural group (p. 831)

genocidio aniquilación intencional de un grupo racial, político, o cultural

"Gentlemen's Agreement" pact between the United States and Japan to end segregation of Asian children in San Francisco public schools; in return, Japan agreed to limit the immigration of its citizens to the United States (p. 603)

"Pacto entre Caballeros" acuerdo entre Estados Unidos y Japón para terminar la segregación de niños asiáticos en las escuelas públicas de San Francisco; cambio, Japón aceptó limitar la migración de sus ciudadanos hacia Estados Unidos

Gettysburg Address speech by President Lincoln in which he dedicated a national cemetery at Gettysburg and reaffirmed the ideas for which the Union was fighting (p. 385)

Discurso de Gettysburg discurso del presidente Lincoln durante la inauguración del cementerio nacional en Gettysburg y que reafirmó las ideas por las que la Unión estaba en lucha

Ghana prominent kingdom in West Africa, known for its wealth and trade in gold, lasting from A.D. 800 to A.D. 1200 (p. 16)

Ghana importante reino en África Occidental, conocido por sus riquezas y comercio en oro, existente desde el siglo IX d. C. hasta el siglo XIII d. C

GI Bill of Rights eased the return of World War II veterans by providing education and employment aid (p. 883)

Declaración de Derechos de los Soldados ley que facilitó el retorno de los veteranos de la Segunda Guerra Mundial al brindarles educación y empleo

Gilded Age term coined by Mark Twain to describe the post-Reconstruction era which was characterized by a façade of prosperity (p. 480)

Edad Dorada término usado para describir la era después de la Reconstrucción que se caracterizó por una fachada de prosperidad para el país

glasnost Russian term for "new openness," a policy in the Soviet Union in the 1980s calling for open discussion of national problems (p. 640)

glasnost palabra rusa que significa "apertura", política de la Unión Soviética de finales de la década de 1980 con un llamado a la apertura y discusión de los problemas nacionales

globalization process by which national economies, politics, cultures, and societies mix with those of other nations around the world (p. 1106)

globalización proceso mediante el cual las economías, políticas, culturas, y sociedades de naciónes se mezclan con las de las otras naciones de todo el mundo

gold standard policy of designating monetary units in terms of their value in gold (p. 532)

estándar oro política de designar las unidades monetarias en términos de su valor en oro

grandfather clause law to disqualify African American voters by allowing the vote only to men whose fathers and grandfathers voted before 1867 (p. 521)

cláusula del abuelo ley para descalificar a los votantes afroestadounidenses que permitía votar sólo a los hombres cuyos padres y abuelos habían votado antes de 1867

Grange farmers' organization formed after the Civil War (p. 535)

Grange organización de granjeros formada después de la Guerra Civil

Great Awakening religious movement in the English colonies during the 1730s and 1740s, which was heavily inspired by evangelical preachers (p. 78)

Gran Despertar movimiento religioso en las colonias inglesas durante las décadas de 1730 y 1740, fuertemente inspirado por los predicadores evangélicos

Great Compromise compromise between the Virginia and New Jersey plans for a bicameral legislature; each state would have equal representation in the Senate and varied representation in the House of Representatives based on the state's population (p. 146)

Gran Acuerdo acuerdo mutuo entre los planes de Virginia y Nueva Jersey según el que cada estado tendría una representación equitativa en el Senado y una representación variada en la Casa de Representantes con base en la población del estado

Great Depression period lasting from 1929 to 1941 in which the U.S. economy faltered and unemployment soared (p. 706)

Gran Depresión período entre 1929 y 1941 durante el cual la economía de Estados Unidos falló y el desempleo creció

Great Migration movement of African Americans in the twentieth century from the rural South to the industrial North (p. 634)

Gran Migración desplazamiento de afroestadounidenses durante el siglo XX desde las zonas rurales del Sur hacia las zonas industrializadas del Norte

Great Society President Johnson's goals in the areas of health care, education, the environment, discrimination, and poverty (p. 969)

Gran Sociedad objetivos del presidente Johnson en las áreas de salud, educación, ambiente, discriminación, y pobreza

Great White Fleet battleships sent by Roosevelt in 1907 on a "good will cruise" around the world (p. 603)

Gran Flota Blanca barcos de guerra enviada por Roosevelt en 1907 en una "misión de buena voluntad" alrededor del mundo

guerrilla warfare nontraditional combat methods (p. 599)

guerra de guerrillas método de combate no tradicional constituido por ataques de retirada rápida realizados por grupos pequeños de guerreros

Gulf of Tonkin Resolution 1964 congressional resolution that authorized President Johnson to commit U.S. troops to South Vietnam and fight a war against North Vietnam (p. 984)

Resolución del Golfo de Tonkin resolución del Congreso de 1964 que autorizó al presidente Johnson a enviar tropas estadounidenses a Vietnam del Sur y entrar en guerra contra Vietnam del Norte

English/Spanish Glossary

habeas corpus constitutional guarantee that no one can be held in prison without charges being filed (pp. 73, 375)
hábeas corpus garantía constitucional para que nadie permanezca en prisión sin que hayan presentado cargos en su contra

Harlem Renaissance period during the 1920s in which African American novelists, poets, and artists celebrated their culture (p. 693)
Renacimiento de Harlem período durante la década de 1920 en el que los novelistas, poetas, y artistas afroestadounidenses celebraron su cultura

Harpers Ferry town in Virginia (now in West Virginia) where abolitionist John Brown raided a federal arsenal in 1859 (p. 344)
Harpers Ferry pueblo en Virginia (ahora en Virginia Occidental) donde el abolicionista John Brown asaltó un arsenal federal en 1859

Hartford Convention 1814 meeting of Federalists from New England who opposed the War of 1812 and demanded constitutional amendments to empower their region (p. 219)
Convención de Hartford reunión de 1814 de los federalistas de Nueva Inglaterra opuestos a la Guerra de 1812 y que exigió enmiendas constitucionales que daban poder a su región

hawk a person who supported U.S. involvement in the Vietnam War (p. 991)
halcón persona que apoyó la participación estadounidense en la Guerra de Vietnam

Hawley-Smoot Tariff protective import tax authorized by Congress in 1930 (p. 707)
Arancel Hawley-Smoot impuesto de importaciones protector aprobado por el Congreso en 1930

Haymarket Riot 1886 labor-related protest in Chicago which ended in deadly violence (p. 455)
revuelta de Haymarket protesta de 1886 de origen laboral ocurrida en Chicago que terminó con muertes violentas

Helsinki Accords agreement made in 1975 among the United States, Canada, and European nations, including the Soviet Union, in which all nations agreed to support human rights (p. 1063)
Acuerdos de Helsinki acuerdo realizado en 1975 entre Estados Unidos, Canadá, y las naciones de Europa, incluyendo la Unión Soviética, en que todos países acordaron apoyar los derechos humanos

Hepburn Act 1906 law that gave the government the authority to set railroad rates and maximum prices for ferries, bridge tolls, and oil pipelines (p. 571)
Ley Hepburn ley de 1906 que otorgó al gobierno la autoridad de fijar y limitar las tarifas ferroviarias y fijar los precios máximos para trasbordadores, peaje de puentes, y oleoductos

Hollywood Ten group of movie writers, directors, and producers who refused to answer HUAC questions about communist ties (p. 869)
diez de Hollywood grupo de guionistas, directores, y productores que se rehusaron a contestar preguntas del HUAC sobre vínculos comunistas

Holocaust name now used to describe the systematic murder by the Nazis of Jews and others (p. 828)
Holocausto nombre que se usa actualmente para describir el asesinato sistemático de judíos y otros por los Nazis

Homestead Act 1862 law that gave 160 acres of land to citizens willing to live on and cultivate it for five years (pp. 374, 510)
Ley de Repartición de Tierras ley de 1862 que otorgó 160 acres de terreno a los ciudadanos deseosos de habitarlo y cultivarlo por cinco años

Homestead Strike 1892 strike against Carnegie's steelworks in Homestead, Pennsylvania (p. 455)
huelga de Homestead huelga de 1892 contra la acería Carnegie en Homestead, Pennsylvania

Hoover Dam dam on the Colorado River that was built during the Great Depression (p. 722)
Represa Hoover represa en el río Colorado construida durante la Gran Depresión

Hooverville term used to describe makeshift shantytowns set up by homeless people during the Great Depression (p. 712)
Hooverville término usado para describir las barriadas de casuchas establecidas por los desposeídos durante la Gran Depresión

horizontal integration system of consolidating many firms in the same business (p. 445)
integración horizontal sistema de consolidación de muchas empresas en el mismo ramo de negocios

hot line direct telephone line between the White House and the Kremlin set up after the Cuban missile crisis (p. 956)
línea caliente línea de comunicación telefónica directa entre la Casa Blanca y el Kremlin establecida luego de la crisis de los misiles de Cuba

House of Burgesses representative assembly of colonial Virginia formed in 1619 (p. 46)
Cámara Baja de Virginia asamblea de representantes en la Virginia colonial formada en 1619

House Un-American Activities Committee (HUAC) congressional committee that investigated possible subversive activities within the United States (p. 869)
Comité de la Casa de Representantes de Actividades Anti-Estadounidenses comité del congreso que investigó posibles actividades subversivas dentro de Estados Unidos

human rights basic rights automatically held by every human being, including religious freedom, education, and equality (p. 1063)
derechos humanos derechos básicos que tiene todo ser humano automáticamente y que incluyen la libertad religiosa, la educación, y la igualdad

hydraulic mining use of water to erode gravel hills into long sluices to catch any gold (p. 313)
minería hidráulica uso de agua para erosionar la grava de las laderas y hacer que corra hacia largas esclusas para atrapar el oro

Ice Age period in Earth's history with low global temperatures and glaciers covering large areas (p. 4)
edad del hielo período en la historia de la Tierra caracterizado por bajas temperaturas globales y glaciares que cubrieron grandes áreas

Immigration Act of 1990 law that increased the number of immigrants allowed in the U.S. per year (p. 1127)

Ley de Migración de 1990 ley que aumenta el número de inmigrantes permitidos en Estados Unidos cada año

Immigration and Control Act of 1986 legislation that granted resident status to illegal immigrants residing in the United States since 1982 and penalized employers who hired illegal immigrants (p. 1128)

Ley de Migración y Control de 1986 legislación que otorgó la condición de residente a los inmigrantes ilegales que vivían en Estados Unidos desde 1982 y penaliza a los patronos que contratan inmigrantes ilegales

Immigration and Nationality Act of 1965 law that changed the national quota system to limits of 170,000 immigrants per year from the Eastern Hemisphere and 120,000 per year from the Western Hemisphere (p. 971)

Ley de Migración y Nacionalidad de 1965 ley que cambió el sistema de cuotas nacionales para limitar a 170,000 por año los inmigrantes del hemisferio oriental y 120,000 por año los del hemisferio occidental

impeachment accusation against a public official of wrongdoing in office (pp. 407, 1113)

impugnación acusación contra un empleado público de cometer delitos en la función pública

imperialism political, military, and economic domination of strong nations over weaker territories (p. 586)

imperialismo dominio político, militar y económico de naciones poderosas sobre territorios más débiles

impressment policy of seizing people or property for military or public service (p. 210)

requisa política de capturar personas o propiedades para el servicio militar o público

income tax tax that must be paid by individuals and corporations based on money earned (p. 373)

impuesto sobre la renta impuesto que deben pagar tanto individuos y corporaciones de acuerdo a los ingresos devengados

indentured servant individual who agreed to work without wages for a period of time in exchange for transportation to the colonies (p. 66)

sirviente obligado por contratado persona que aceptaba trabajar sin salario por un tiempo a cambio de transporte a las colonias

Indian New Deal 1930s legislation that gave Indians greater control over their affairs and provided funding for schools and hospitals (p. 751)

Nuevo Trato Indígena legislación de 1930 que otorgó mayor control a los indígenas estadounidenses sobre asuntos y financió escuelas y hospitales

Indian Removal Act act passed by Congress in 1830 that allowed the federal government to negotiate land trades with the Indians in the Southeast (p. 254)

Ley de Remoción de Indígenas ley aprobada por el Congreso en 1830 que permitió al gobierno negociar intercambios de tierras con los indígenas del Sudeste

Industrial Revolution shift from manual labor to mechanized work that began in Great Britain during the 1700s and spread to the United States around 1800 (p. 230)

Revolución Industrial cambio del trabajo manual al trabajo mecanizado que empezó en Gran Bretaña durante el siglo XVIII y llegó a Estados Unidos a principios del siglo XIX

inflation rising prices (pp. 376, 648)

inflación aumento de los precios

influenza flu virus (p. 647)

influenza virus de la gripe

information industry businesses that provide informational services (p. 893)

industrias de la información empresas que brindan servicios de información

initiative process in which citizens put a proposed new law directly on the ballot (p. 555)

iniciativa proceso en el que los ciudadanos proponen directamente una nueva ley en la papeleta de una elección

inner city the older, central part of a city with crowded neighborhoods in which low-income, usually minority groups, live (p. 905)

centro de la ciudad la parte más vieja y central de una ciudad con vecindarios muy poblados en los que viven grupos de bajos recursos, usualmente minorías

installment buying method of purchase in which buyer makes a small down payment and then pays off the rest of the debt in regular monthly payments (p. 664)

plan de pago a plazos método de compra mediante el cual el comprador paga un pequeño enganche y luego paga el resto de la deuda con abonos mensuales regulares

insurrection rebellion (p. 599)

insurrección rebelión

integration process of bringing people of different races, religions, and social classes together (p. 412)

integración proceso de acercar a personas de diferentes razas, religiones, y clases sociales

interchangeable parts identical components that can be used in place of one another (p. 232)

partes intercambiables componentes idénticos que se pueden sustituir unos a otros

Internet a computer network that links people around the world, also called World Wide Web (p. 1106)

Internet red de computadoras que enlaza a personas de todo el mundo, también llamada Red Mundial

internment temporary imprisonment of members of a specific group (p. 813)

reclusión encarcelamiento temporal para miembros de un grupo específico

Interstate Commerce Commission (ICC) first federal agency monitoring business operations, created in 1887 to oversee interstate railroad procedures (p. 448)

Comisión Interestatal de Comercio primera agencia federal en vigilar las operaciones comerciales, creada en 1887 para supervisar los procedimientos del ferrocarril interestatal

Interstate Highway Act 1956 law that authorized the spending of $32 billion to build 41,000 miles of highway (p. 890)

Ley de Carreteras Interestatales ley de 1956 que autorizó el gasto de $32 mil millones para construir 41,000 millas de carreteras

Intolerable Acts American name for the Coercive Acts, which Parliament passed in 1774 to control the colonies (p. 104)

Leyes Intolerables nombre estadounidense para las Leyes Coercitivas que aprobó el Parlamento en 1774 para controlar a las colonias

English/Spanish Glossary

Iran-Contra affair political scandal under President Reagan involving the use of money from secret arms sales to Iran to illegally support the Contras in Nicaragua (p. 1092)

incidente Irán-Contras escándalo político en la administración del presidente Reagan que involucró el uso de dinero procedente de la venta secreta de armas a Irán para apoyar ilegalmente a los Contras en Nicaragua

iron curtain term coined by Winston Churchill to describe the border between the Soviet satellite states and Western Europe (p. 848)

cortina de hierro término acuñado por Winston Churchill para describir la frontera entre los estados satélites soviéticos y Europa Occidental

Iroquois League confederation made up of five Iroquois peoples: the Mohawks, Oneidas, Onondagas, Cayugas, and Senecas (p. 9)

Liga Iroquesa confederación compuesta por los cinco pueblos iroquois: los mohawks, oneidas, onondagas, cayugas y sénecas

"irreconcilables" isolationist senators who opposed any treaty ending World War I that had a League of Nations folded into it (p. 644)

"irreconciliables" senadores aislacionistas opuestos a cualquier tratado para finalizar la Primera Guerra Mundial que involucrara una Sociedad de las Naciones

island hopping World War II strategy that involved seizing selected Japanese-held islands in the Pacific while bypassing others (p. 825)

salto de islas estrategia durante la Segunda Guerra Mundial que involucraba capturar islas selectas que mantenía Japón en el Pacífico a la vez que se evitaban otras

J

Jacksonian Democracy Andrew Jackson and his followers' political philosophy concerned with the interests of the common people and limiting the role of the federal government (p. 251)

Democracia de Jackson filosofía política de Andrew Jackson y sus seguidores que velaba por los intereses de la gente común y la limitación del papel del gobierno federal

jazz American musical form developed by African Americans, based on improvisation and blending blues, ragtime, and European-based popular music (p. 243)

jazz forma musical estadounidense creada por los afroestadounidenses y europeos, basada en la improvisación y la mezcla de el blues, ragtime y música popular de origen europeo

Jazz Singer, The the first movie with sound synchronized to the action (p. 232)

El Cantante de Jazz primera película con sonido y acción sincronizados

Jim Crow Laws segregation laws enacted in the South after Reconstruction (p. 520)

Leyes Jim Crow leyes segregacionistas implantabas en el Sur después de Reconstrucción

jingoism aggressive nationalism; support for warlike foreign policy (p. 145)

patrioterismo nacionalismo agresivo; apoyo a una política exterior belicosa

joint-stock company a company run by a group of investors who share the company's profits and losses (p. 44)

sociedad comanditaria por acciones compañía dirigida por un grupo de inversionistas que se reparten las ganancias y pérdidas de la empresa

judicial review power of the Supreme Court to decide whether the acts of a president or laws passed by Congress are constitutional (p. 206)

revisión judicial poder que le permite a la Corte Suprema decidir si los actos del presidente o las leyes aprobadas por el Congreso son constitucionales

K

kamikazes Japanese pilots who deliberately crashed planes into American ships during World War II (p. 825)

kamikazes pilotos japonéses que deliberadamente chocaban aviones contra buques estadounidenses durante la Segunda Guerra Mundial

Kansas-Nebraska Act 1854 law that divided the Nebraska Territory into Kansas and Nebraska giving each territory the right to decide whether or not to allow slavery (p. 334)

Ley Kansas-Nebraska ley de 1854 que dividió el territorio de Nebraska en Kansas y Nebraska, dándole a cada territorio el derecho de decidir si permitiría la esclavitud o no

Kellogg-Briand Pact 1928 agreement in which many nations agreed to outlaw war (p. 669)

Pacto Kellogg-Briand acuerdo de 1928 en el que los delegados de muchas naciones estuvieron anuentes a prohibir la guerra

Kerner Commission group set up to investigate the causes of race riots in American cities in the 1960s (p. 940)

Comisión Kerner grupo que se formó para investigar las causas de los disturbios raciales en las ciudades estadounidenses en la década de 1960

King Philip's War conflict between English colonists and Native Americans in New England (p. 53)

Guerra del Rey Felipe conflicto que surgió entre los colonos ingleses y los indígenas de Nueva Inglaterra

Kings Mountain a 1780 Revolutionary War battle in South Carolina in which Patriots defeated a Loyalist militia (p. 124)

Kings Mountain batalla de la Guerra de Independencia de 1780 en Carolina del Sur en la cual los patriotas derrotaron a una milicia leal a la corona

Knights of Labor labor union that sought to organize all workers and focused on broad social reforms (p. 453)

Caballeros del Trabajo sindicato de trabajadores que procuró organizar a todos los trabajadores y se enfocó en reformas sociales amplias

Know-Nothings political party of the mid-1800s, officially known as the American Party, that opposed immigration (p. 340)

Know-Nothings partido político efímero a mediados del siglo XIX, oficialmente conocido como el Partido Estadounidense, opuesto a la inmigración

Kristallnacht "Night of the Broken Glass," organized attacks on Jewish communities in Germany on November 9, 1938 (p. 829)

Kristallnacht "noche de los cristales rotos," ataques organizados contra comunidades judías en Alemania, el 9 de noviembre de 1938

L

Ku Klux Klan organization that promotes hatred and discrimination against specific ethnic and religious groups (pp. 417, 675)
Ku Klux Klan organización que promueve el odio y discriminación contra grupos étnicos y religiosos específicos

labor union organization of workers (p. 234)
sindicato de trabajadores organización de trabajadores

laissez-faire lenient, as in the absence of government control over private business (p. 438)
laissez-faire indulgente, por ejemplo, la ausencia de control gubernamental sobre las empresas privadas

land grant land designated by the federal government for building schools, roads, or railroads (p. 507)
tierras en concesión tierras designadas por el gobierno federal para la construcción de escuelas, carreteras, o ferrocarriles

Land Grant College Act 1862 law that made money available to states to establish universities that taught agriculture and mechanical engineering (p. 393)
Ley de Cesión de Terrenos para Universidades ley de 1862 que puso dinero a disposición de los estados para que establecieran universidades que enseñaran agricultura e ingeniería mecánica

Land Ordinance of 1785 law which designed a system for managing and settling lands in the Northwest Territory (p. 137)
Ordenanza de Tierras de 1785 ley mediante la cual designó un sistema para la administración y ocupación de tierras en el Territorio Noroeste

Las Gorras Blancas (the White Caps) group of Mexican Americans living in New Mexico who attempted to protect their land and way of life from encroachment by white landowners (p. 525)
Las Gorras Blancas grupo de estadounidenses de origen mexicano radicados en Nuevo México que intentaron proteger sus tierras y estilo de vida de la expansión de los terratenientes blancos

League of Nations world organization established after World War I to promote peaceful cooperation between countries (p. 642)
Sociedad de las Naciones organización mundial establecida después de a la Primera Guerra Mundial para promover la cooperación pacífica entre los países

Lend-Lease Act act passed in 1941 that allowed President Roosevelt to sell or lend war supplies to any country whose defense he considered vital to the safety of the United States (p. 785)
Ley de Préstamo-Arrendamiento ley aprobada por el Congreso en 1941 que permitió al presidente Franklin Roosevelt vender o prestar suministros bélicos a cualquier país cuya defensa se considerara vital para la seguridad de Estados Unidos

Lewis and Clark Expedition 1804 expedition sent by President Jefferson to explore the newly-acquired Louisiana Purchase (p. 209)
expedición de Lewis y Clark expedición de 1804 mandó por presidente Jefferson a explorar la recién adquirida Compra de Luisiana

liberal a person who tends to support government intervention to help the needy and favor laws protecting the rights of women and minorities (p. 1076)
liberal persona que tiende a apoyar la intervención gubernamental en la ayuda a los necesitados y favorece las leyes que protegen los derechos de las mujeres y las minorías

limited government principle stating that the government has only as much authority as the people give it and, therefore, its power is limited (p. 155)
gobierno limitado principio que declara que el gobierno sólo tiene tanta autoridad como la que le otorga el pueblo y por tanto su poder es limitado

limited war war fought to achieve only specific goals (p. 858)
guerra limitada guerra peleada para alcanzar objetivos específicos

literacy test reading and writing test formerly used in some southern states to prevent African Americans from voting (p. 521)
prueba de alfabetismo prueba de lectura antiguamente usada en algunos estados sureños para evitar que los afroestadounidenses votaran

localism policy relied on by President Hoover in the early years of the Great Depression whereby local and state governments act as primary agents of economic relief (p. 721)
localismo política de la que dependió el presidente Hoover a principios de la Gran Depresión para que los gobiernos locales y estatales actuaran como los principales agentes de asistencia económica

Lone Star Republic nation formed in 1835 by Texans who declared independence from Mexico (p. 306)
República de la Estrella Solitaria nación formada en 1835 por tejanos que le declararon la independencia a México

loose construction belief that the government has any power not forbidden by the Constitution (p. 195)
interpretación libre creencia en que el gobierno tiene cualquier poder que no le prohíba la Constitución

"Lost Generation" term for American writers of the 1920s marked by disillusion with World War I and a search for a new sense of meaning (p. 686)
"Generación Perdida" término usado para referirse a escritores estadounidenses de la década de 1920 marcados por su desilusión con la Primera Guerra Mundial y la búsqueda de un nuevo sentido de la vida

Louisiana Purchase 1803 purchase from France by the United States of the territory between the Mississippi River and the Rocky Mountains (p. 209)
Compra de Luisiana compra que hiciera Estados Unidos en 1803 del territorio entre el río Mississippi y las montañas Rocosas

Lowell girl young woman who worked in the textile mills in Lowell, Massachusetts, in the early 1800s (p. 231)
chica de Lowell mujer joven que trabajaba en las fábricas de textiles de Lowell, Massachusetts, a principios del siglo XIX

Loyalist colonist who remained loyal to Britain during the Revolution (p. 109)
leal a la corona colono que permaneció leal a Gran Bretaña durante la Guerra de Independencia

English/Spanish Glossary

Lusitania British passenger liner sunk by a German U-boat during World War I (p. 624)
Lusitania trasatlántico británico hundido por un submarino alemán durante la Primera Guerra Mundial.

M

Magna Carta English document from 1215 that limited the power of the king and provided basic rights for citizens (p. 72)
Carta Magna documento inglés de 1215 que limitó el poder del rey y dio derechos básicos a los ciudadanos

Mali West African empire lasting from A.D. 1200 to A.D. 1400 that prospered from the gold trade (p. 16)
Malí imperio del África Occidental existente desde el siglo XIII d. C. hasta el siglo XV que prosperó gracias al comercio del oro

Manhattan Project code name of the project that developed the atomic bomb (p. 826)
Proyecto Manhattan nombre en clave del proyecto que desarrolló la bomba atómica

Manifest Destiny 19th century doctrine that westward expansion of the United States was not only inevitable but a God-given right (p. 301)
Destino Manifiesto doctrina del siglo XIX que establecía que la expansión hacia el Oeste de Estados Unidos no sólo era inevitable sino un derecho Divino

manumission the act of freeing someone from slavery (p. 127)
manumisión acto de liberar a alguien de la esclavitud

Marbury v. Madison 1803 Supreme Court case that established the principle of judicial review (p. 206)
Marbury contra Madison caso presentado ante la Corte Suprema en 1803 que estableció el principio de revisión judicial

March on Washington 1963 demonstration in which more than 200,000 people rallied for economic equality and civil rights (p. 930)
Marcha en Washington manifestacíon en 1963 de más de 200,000 personas que marcharon a favor de la igualdad económica y los derechos civiles

Married Women's Property Act 1848 New York State law that guaranteed greater property rights for women; used as a model in other states (p. 290)
Ley del Patrimonio de las Casadas ley aprobada en 1848 en el estado de Nueva York que otorgaba mayores derechos sobre la propiedad a la mujer; sirvió de modelo en otros estados

Marshall Plan foreign policy that offered economic aid to Western European countries after World War II (p. 850)
Plan Marshall política económica y exterior que ofreció ayuda a los países de Europa Occidental después de la Segunda Guerra Mundial

mass culture similar cultural patterns in a society as a result of the spread of transportation, communication, and advertising (p. 482)
cultura de masas patrones similares de cultura en una sociedad como resultado de la propagación del transporte, comunicación, y publicidad

mass production production of goods in large numbers through the use of machinery and assembly lines (pp. 440, 660)
producción en masa producción de bienes en grandes cantidades mediante el uso de maquinaria y líneas de ensamblaje

massive retaliation policy of threatening to use massive force in response to aggression (p. 862)
represalia masiva política de amenazar con el uso de fuerza masiva en respuesta a una agresión

mass transit public transportation systems that carry large numbers of people (p. 475)
transporte de masas sistemas de transporte público que llevan a grandes cantidades de personas

matrilineal when inheritance is passed down through the female side of the family (p. 287)
matrilineal cuando los bienes se heredan por el lado materno de la familia

Mayflower Compact framework for self-government of the Plymouth Colony signed on the ship the *Mayflower* in 1620 (p. 51)
Pacto del Mayflower documento para establecer el sistema de autogobierno de la colonia de Plymouth firmado en el barco *Mayflower* en 1620

McCarthyism negative catchword for extreme, reckless charges of disloyalty (p. 874)
McCarthyismo lema negativo que expresa acusaciones extremas e irresponsables de deslealtad

Meat Inspection Act 1906 law that allowed the federal government to inspect meat sold across state lines and required federal inspection of meat processing plants (p. 572)
Ley de Inspección de Carnes ley de 1906 que permitió al gobierno federal inspeccionar la carne vendida entre los estados y que exigió la inspección federal de las plantas de procesamiento de carne

median family income measure of average family income (p. 896)
mediana del ingreso familiar medida del ingreso familiar promedio

Medicaid federal program created in 1965 to provide low-cost health insurance to poor Americans of any age (p. 970)
Medicaid programa federal creado en 1965 para brindar seguro de salud de bajo costo a los estadounidenses de escasos recursos de cualquier edad

Medicare federal program created in 1965 to provide basic hospital insurance to most Americans over the age of sixty-five (p. 970)
Medicare programa federal creado en 1965 para brindar seguro hospitalario básico a la mayoría de los estadounidenses mayores de sesenta y cinco de edad

melting pot society in which people of different nationalities assimilate to form one culture (p. 468)
crisol de razas una sociedad en la que las personas de diferentes nacionalidades se asimilan para formar una cultura

mercantilism economic policy under which a nation accumulates wealth by exporting more goods than it imports (p. 75)
mercantilismo filosofía económica que sostiene que una nación acumula riquezas al exportar más bienes de los que importa

mercenary professional soldier who is paid to fight in a foreign army (p. 118)
  mercenario soldado profesional a quien se le paga por pelear en un ejército extranjero

mestizo person in Spanish colonial America who was of European and Native American descent (p. 35)
  mestizo en la Hispanoamérica colonial, persona descendiente de europeo e indígena

metis person in French colonial America who was of French and Native American descent (p. 42)
  metis habitante de las colonias francesas en América descendiente de francés e indígena

Middle Ages period in European history from the 5th century through the 14th century (p. 11)
  Edad Media período en la historia de Europa que se inicia en el siglo V y termina en el siglo XIV

Middle Passage the forced transport of enslaved Africans from West Africa to the Americas (p. 69)
  Travesía Intermedia transporte forzado de esclavos desde África Occidental a las Américas

migrant farmworker person who travels from farm to farm to pick fruits and vegetables (p. 1029)
  trabajador agrícola migratorio persona que viaja de una granja a otra para la recolección de frutas y vegetales

militarism glorification of the military (p. 619)
  militarismo glorificación de lo militar

Militia Act 1862 law that allowed African American soldiers to serve in the Union military (p. 370)
  Ley de Alistamiento ley aprobada en 1862 que permitió a los soldados afroestadounidenses prestar servicio militar en los militares de la Unión

militia trained citizens who serve as soldiers during an emergency (p. 108)
  milicia ciudadanos entrenados que fungieron como soldados durante una emergencia

mission religious settlement usually run by Catholic priests and friars in colonial Spanish America (p. 37)
  misión asentamiento religioso generalmente manejado por sacerdotes y frailes católicos en la Hispanoamérica colonial

missionary person sent to a foreign country in order to convert others to their religion (p. 35)
  misionero persona enviada al país extranjero para convertir a otros a su credo

Missouri Compromise 1820 agreement calling for the admission of Missouri as a slave state and Maine as a free state, and banning slavery in the Louisiana Purchase territory north of the 36°30'N latitude (p. 246)
  Acuerdo de Missouri acuerdo de 1820 que hacía un llamado a la admisión de Missouri como estado esclavista y a Maine como estado libre, prohibiendo la esclavitud en el territorio de la Compra de Louisiana al norte de la latitud 36°30'

model T automobile manufactured by Henry Ford to be affordable on the mass market (p. 661)
  modelo T automóvil fabricado por Henry Ford para que fuera asequible en el mercado masivo

modernism artistic and literary movement sparked by a break with past conventions (p. 671)
  modernismo moda que daba énfasis a la ciencia y los valores seculares por sobre las ideas religiosas tradicionales

Monmouth 1778 Revolutionary War battle site in New Jersey where neither side won a clear victory (p. 120)
  Monmouth batalla de la Guerra de Independencia de 1778 en Nueva Jersey en la cual ninguno de los bandos obtuvo una victoria clara

monopoly exclusive control by one company over an entire industry (p. 444)
  monopolio control completo de una compañía de una industria

Monroe Doctrine foreign policy doctrine set forth by President Monroe in 1823 that discouraged European intervention in the Western Hemisphere (p. 246)
  Doctrina Monroe doctrina de política exterior establecida por el presidente Monroe en 1823 que desalentaba la intervención Europea en el hemisferio Occidental

Montgomery bus boycott 1955–1956 protest by African Americans in Montgomery, Alabama, against racial segregation in the bus system (p. 922)
  boicot de los autobuses de Montgomery protesta de 1955 a 1956 de los afroestadounidenses en Montgomery, Alabama, contra la segregación en el sistema de autobuses

"moral diplomacy" Woodrow Wilson's statement that the U.S. would not use force to assert influence in the world, but would instead work to promote human rights (p. 609)
  "diplomacia moral" aseveración de Woodrow Wilson en cuanto a que Estados Unidos no usaría la fuerza para ejercer su influencia en el mundo, sino que trabajaría en la promoción de los derechos humanos

Moral Majority political organization established by Reverend Jerry Falwell in 1979 to advance religious goals (p. 1078)
  Mayoría Moral organización política establecida por el reverendo Jerry Falwell en 1979 para promover objetivos religiosos

Mormon member of the Church of Jesus Christ of Latter-Day Saints, which was organized in 1830 by Joseph Smith (p. 269)
  mormón miembro de la Iglesia de Jesucristo de los Santos de los Últimos Días, fundada en 1830 por José Smith

Mountain Men American trappers who explored the Rocky Mountains area in the early 1800s (p. 301)
  montañeses tramperos estadounidenses que exploraron el área de las montañas Rocosas a principios del siglo XIX

muckraker writer who uncovers and exposes misconduct in politics or business (p. 550)
  muckraker escritores que descubren y exponen la mala conducta de políticos o empresas

multinational corporation companies that produce and sell their goods and services all over the world (pp. 894, 1106)
  corporaciones multinacionales compañías que producen y venden sus bienes y servicios alrededor del mundo

Munich Pact agreement made between Germany, Italy, Great Britain, and France in 1938 that sacrificed the Sudetenland to preserve peace (p. 778)
  Pacto de Munich acuerdo de 1938 entre Alemania, Italia, Gran Bretaña, y Francia que sacrificó los Sudetes para preservar la paz

mural a large picture painted directly on a wall or ceiling (p. 761)

English/Spanish Glossary

mural pintura de grandes dimensiones realizada directamente sobre una pared o cielo raso

mutualistas organized groups of Mexican Americans that make loans and provide legal assistance to other members of their community (p. 567)

mutualistas grupos organizados de estadounidenses de origen mexicano para ofrecer préstamos y asistencia legal a miembros de su comunidad

mutually assured destruction policy in which the United States and the Soviet Union hoped to deter nuclear war by building up enough weapons to destroy one another (p. 861)

destrucción mutua asegurada política con la que Estados Unidos y la Unión Soviética esperaban evitar la guerra nuclear al acumular suficientes armas para destruirse mutuamente

My Lai village in South Vietnam where in 1968 American forces opened fire on unarmed civilians; U.S. soldiers killed between 400 and 500 Vietnamese (p. 1003)

My Lai villa en Vietnam del Sur donde en 1968 fuerzas estadounidenses dispararon contra civiles desarmados; los soldados estadounidenses mataron entre 400 y 500 vietnamitas

N

napalm jellied gasoline dropped in canisters that explode on impact and cover large areas in flames; dropped by U.S. planes during the Vietnam War (p. 986)

napalm gasolina gelatinizada lanzada en latas que explotaban al impactar y dejaban en llamas grandes áreas; lanzadas por aviones estadounidenses durante la Guerra de Vietnam

national debt total amount of money that the federal government owes to the owners of government bonds (p. 1082)

deuda interna cantidad total de dinero que el gobierno federal debe a los dueños de bonos de gobierno

National Aeronautics and Space Administration (NASA) government agency that coordinates U.S. efforts in space (p. 865)

Administración Nacional de Aeronáutica y del Espacio agencia gubernamental formada para coordinar los esfuerzos estadounidenses en el espacio

National American Woman Suffrage Association (NWSA) group founded in 1890 that worked on both the state and national levels to earn women the right to vote (p. 559)

Asociación Nacional para el Sufragio de las Mujeres Estadounidenses grupo fundado en 1890 que funcionó a nivel tanto estatal como nacional para que se otorgara a las mujeres el derecho al voto

National Association for the Advancement of Colored People (NAACP) interracial organization founded in 1909 to abolish segregation and discrimination and to achieve political and civil rights for African Americans (p. 567)

Asociación Nacional para el Avance de los afroestadounidenses organización fundado en 1909 para suprimir la segregación y la discriminización y avanzar los derechos políticos y civiles de los afroestadounidenses

National Consumers League (NCL) group organized in 1899 to investigate the conditions under which goods

were made and sold and to promote safe working conditions and a minimum wage (p. 558)

Liga Nacional de Consumidores grupo organizado en 1899 para investigar las condiciones en que se fabricaban y vendían los bienes, así como promover condiciones seguras de trabajo y un salario mínimo

nationalism loyalty and devotion to one's nation (p. 242)

nacionalismo lealtad y devoción hacia la patria

nationalize to place a resource under government control (p. 864)

nacionalización poner un recurso bajo control gubernamental

National Organization for Women (NOW) organization established by Betty Friedan to combat discrimination against women (p. 1023)

Organización Nacional para Mujeres organización establecida por Betty Friedan para derribar las barreras de la discriminación contra mujeres

National Reclamation Act 1902 law that gave the federal government the power to decide where and how water would be distributed through the building and management of dams and irrigation projects (p. 574)

Ley Nacional de Reclamaciones ley de 1902 que otorgó al gobierno federal el poder para decidir adónde y cómo se distribuiría el agua, mediante la construcción y administración de represas y proyectos de irrigación

National Recovery Administration (NRA) New Deal agency that promoted economic recovery by regulating production, prices, and wages (p. 737)

Administración para la Recuperación Nacional agencia del Nuevo Trato que promovió la recuperación económica al instaurar nuevos códigos para controlar la producción, precios y salarios

National Road road built by the federal government in the early 1800s that extended from Maryland to Illinois (p. 228)

Carretera Nacional carretera construida por el gobierno a principios del siglo XIX que se extendía desde Maryland hasta Illinois

Nation of Islam African American religious organization founded in 1930 that advocated separation of the races (p. 940)

Nación Islámica organización afroestadounidense religiosa fundada en 1930 que abogó por la separación de las razas

nativism belief that native-born white Americans are superior to newcomers (p. 468)

nativismo creencia en que los blancos nacidos en Estados Unidos son superiores a los recién llegados

nativist person who favors native-born inhabitants over immigrants (p. 235)

nativista persona que favorece a los habitantes nativos sobre los inmigrantes

natural rights universal rights, such as life and liberty that, according to philosophers, derive from nature rather than a government (p. 112)

derechos naturales derechos universales, como la vida y la libertad, que según los filósofos, se derivan de la naturaleza y no de un gobierno

Navigation Acts British trade laws enacted by Parliament during the mid-1700s that regulated colonial commerce (p. 76)

Leyes de Navegación leyes comerciales británicas establecidas por el Parlamento a mediados del siglo XVIII que regulaban el comercio con las colonias

Neutrality Act of 1939 act that allowed nations at war to buy goods and arms in the United States if they paid cash and carried the merchandise on their own ships (p. 784)

Ley de Neutralidad de 1939 ley que permitió que las naciones en guerra compraran bienes y armas en Estados Unidos si pagaran en efectivo y transportaran la mercadería en sus propios barcos

New Deal programs and legislation enacted by Franklin D. Roosevelt during the Great Depression to promote economic recovery and social reform (p. 733)

Nuevo Trato programas y leyes establecidos por Franklin D. Roosevelt durante la Gran Depresión para promover la recuperación económica y reforma social

New Deal coalition political force formed by diverse groups who united to support Franklin D. Roosevelt and his New Deal (p. 751)

coalición del Nuevo Trato fuerza política formada por grupos diversos unidos para apoyar a Franklin D. Roosevelt y su Nuevo Trato

New Freedom Woodrow Wilson's program to place government controls on corporations in order to benefit small businesses (p. 576)

Nueva Libertad programa de Woodrow Wilson para establecer controles gubernamentales sobre las corporaciones a fin de brindar más oportunidades a las pequeñas empresas

New Frontier President Kennedy's plan aimed at improving the economy, fighting racial discrimination, and exploring space (p. 960)

Nueva Frontera plan del presidente Kennedy dirigido a mejorar la economía, al combatir discriminación racial, y avanzar el programa espacial

"new" immigrant Southern and Eastern European immigrant who arrived in the United States in a great wave between 1880 and 1920 (p. 464)

"nuevos" inmigrante inmigrante del Sur y Este de Europa que llegaró a Estados Unidos en una gran oleada entre 1880 y 1920

New Jersey Plan William Paterson's proposal for a unicameral legislature with each state having one vote (p. 145)

Plan de Nueva Jersey propuesta de William Paterson que requería una legislatura unicameral donde cada estado tendría un voto

New Nationalism President Theodore Roosevelt's plan to restore the government's trust-busting power (p. 575)

Nuevo Nacionalismo plan del presidente Teodoro Roosevelt para restaurar el poder del gobierno de disolver monopolios

New Right political movement supported by reinvigorated conservative groups in the latter half of the twentieth century (p. 1077)

Nueva Derecha movimiento político apoyado por grupos conservadores revigorizados durante la última mitad del siglo XX

Niagara Movement group of African American thinkers founded in 1905 that pushed for immediate racial reforms, particularly in education and voting practices (p. 566)

Movimiento Niágara grupo de pensadores afroestadounidenses fundado en 1905 que presionó para obtener reformas raciales inmediatas, particularmente en cuanto a la educación y el voto

Nineteenth Amendment constitutional amendment that gave women the right to vote (p. 561)

Décimonovena Enmienda enmienda constitucional que otorgó a las mujeres el derecho al voto

No Child Left Behind Act 2002 law aimed at improving the performance of primary and secondary schools particularly through mandated sanctions against schools not reaching federal performance standards (p. 1121)

Ley Que Ningún Niño Se Quede Atrás ley del año 2000 destinada a mejorar el desempeño de escuelas primarias y secundarias particularmente mediante sanciones por mandato contra las escuelas que no cumplan las normas federales de desempeño

nonimportation agreements colonial consumer boycotts of British exports as a response to taxes passed by Parliament (p. 101)

acuerdos de no importación boicots de los consumidores coloniales contra las exportaciones británicas como respuesta a los impuestos aprobados por el Parlamento

North American Free Trade Agreement (NAFTA) agreement signed in 1993 calling for the removal of trade restrictions among Canada, Mexico, and the United States (p. 1115)

Tratado de Libre Comercio de América del Norte (TLCAN) acuerdo firmado en 1993 para la remoción de las restricciones comerciales entre Canadá, México y Estados Unidos

North Atlantic Treaty Organization (NATO) military alliance formed to counter Soviet expansion (p. 852)

Organización del Tratado del Atlántico Norte (OTAN) alianza militar formada parar la expansión soviética

Northwest Ordinance of 1787 law which provided a basis for governing the Northwest Territory (p. 137)

Ordenanza del Noroeste de 1787 ley que estableció la base para el gobierno del Territorio del Noroeste

Northwest Territory vast territory north of the Ohio River and west of Pennsylvania as far as the Mississippi River (p. 136)

Territorio Noroeste vasto territorio al norte del río Ohio y al oeste de Pennsylvania hasta llegar al río Mississippi

nuclear family ideal or typical household with a father, mother, and children (p. 897)

núcleo familiar hogar ideal o típico con un padre, una madre, y niños

Nuclear Test Ban Treaty 1963 nuclear-weapons agreement, which banned aboveground nuclear tests (p. 958)

Tratado de Prohibición de Pruebas Nucleares acuerdo de 1963 sobre armas nucleares que prohibió las pruebas nucleares en la superficie de la Tierra

nullification concept in which states could nullify, or void, any federal law they deemed unconstitutional (p. 256)

anulación concepto por el que los estados podrían anular o vetar cualquier ley federal que consideraran inconstitucional

Nuremberg Laws laws enacted by Hitler that denied German citizenship to Jews (p. 829)

Leyes de Nuremberg leyes impuestas por Hitler que negaban la ciudadanía alemana a los judíos

Nuremberg Trials trials in which Nazi leaders were charged with war crimes (p. 838)

Juicios de Nuremberg juicios en los que se acusó a los líderes Nazis de crímenes de guerra

O

Office of War Information (OWI) government agency that encouraged support of the war effort during World War II (p. 814)

Oficina de Información de Guerra agencia gubernamental que animaba el apoyo al esfuerzo bélico durante la Segunda Guerra Mundial

Okies general term used to describe Dust Bowl refugees (p. 715)

Okies término general usado para describir a los refugiados del Cuenco de Polvo

Open Door Policy American statement that the government did not want colonies in China, but favored free trade there (p. 602)

política de puertas abiertas declaración estadounidense que proclamaba que el gobierno no deseaba colonias en China, pero favorecía el libre comercio ahí

open range vast area of grassland on which livestock roamed and grazed (p. 508)

praderas vastas áreas de pastizales en las que el ganado paseaba y pastaba

Operation Desert Storm 1991 American-led attack on Iraqi forces after Iraq refused to withdraw its troops from Kuwait (p. 1097)

Operación Tormenta del Desierto ataque que comandaron los estadounidenses en 1991 contra las fuerzas iraquíes luego que Irak rehusó a retirar sus tropas de Kuwait

Oregon Trail trail from Independence, Missouri, to Oregon that was used by pioneers in the mid-1800s (p. 302)

Sendero de Oregón ruta desde Independence, Missouri, hasta Oregón usada por los pioneros a mediados del siglo XIX

Organization of Petroleum Exporting Countries (OPEC) group of countries which sell oil to other nations and cooperate to regulate the price and supply of oil (p. 1048)

Organización de Países Exportadores de Petróleo grupo de países que venden petróleo a otras naciones y que coopera en la regulación del precio y suministro del crudo

P

Palmer Raids the series of raids in the early 1920s initiated by Attorney General A. Mitchell Palmer, against suspected radicals and communists (p. 201)

Redadas Palmer redadas de principios de la década de 1920 iniciadas por el fiscal general del estado A. Mitchell Palmer contra personas sospechosas de ser radicales o comunistas

Panama Canal human-made waterway linking the Atlantic to the Pacific across the Isthmus of Panama (p. 607)

Canal de Panamá vía acuática hecha por los humanos que une el Atlántico y el Pacífico a través del istmo de Panamá

pardon official forgiveness of a crime and its punishment (p. 1056)

indulto perdón oficial de un delito y su castigo

Paris Peace Accords 1973 peace agreement between the United States, South Vietnam, North Vietnam, and the Vietcong that effectively ended the Vietnam War (p. 1004)

Acuerdos de Paz de París acuerdo de paz de 1973 entre Estados Unidos, Vietnam del Sur, Vietnam del Norte, y el Vietcong que de hecho finalizó la Guerra de Vietnam

parliament legislative body of a country (p. 73)

parlamento entidad legislativa de un país

patent official rights given by the government to an inventor for the exclusive right to develop, use, and sell an invention for a set period of time (p. 438)

patente derechos oficiales otorgados por el gobierno a un inventor para que tenga los derechos exclusivos para desarrollar, usar, y vender un invento durante un plazo determinado

Patriot Act law passed following September 11, 2001, giving law enforcement broader powers in monitoring possible terrorist activities (p. 1125)

Ley Patriótica ley aprobada después del 11 de septiembre del 2001 que otorgó mayores poderes a los agentes de la ley para vigilar posibles actividades terroristas

Peace Corps American government organization that sends volunteers to provide technical, educational, and medical services in developing countries (p. 955)

Cuerpo de Paz organización del gobierno de Estados Unidos que envía voluntarios para que brinden servicios técnicos, educativos, y médicos en países en vías de desarrollo

Pearl Harbor American military base attacked by the Japanese on December 7, 1941 (p. 789)

Pearl Harbor base militar estadounidense atacada por los japoneses el 7 de diciembre de 1941

Pendleton Civil Service Act 1883 law that created a civil service system for the federal government in an attempt to hire employees on a merit system rather than on a spoils system (p. 531)

Ley Pendleton del Servicio Civil ley de 1883 que creó un sistema de servicio civil para el gobierno federal en un intento por contratar empleados con un sistema de méritos en lugar del clientelismo

penitentiary movement movement aimed at structuring prisons so that prisoners will feel penitent for their crimes (p. 276)

movimiento penitenciario movimiento encaminado a estructurar las prisiones de tal modo que los presos se sientan arrepentidos por los delitos cometidos

Pentagon Papers classified U.S. government study that revealed American leaders intentionally involved the United States in Vietnam without fully informing the American people; leaked to *The New York Times* in 1971 (p. 1003)

Documentos del Pentágono estudio clasificado del gobierno estadounidense que reveló que los líderes estadounidenses intencionalmente involucraron a Estados

Unidos en Vietnam sin haber informado completamente a la ciudadanía estadounidense; lo filtró al *The New York Times* en 1971

Pequot War war between Puritans and Pequot tribe in 1636 over trade rights and territorial expansion (p. 53)

Guerra de los Pequot guerra que ocurrió en 1636 entre los puritanos y la tribu Pequot, debido a los derechos comerciales y la expansión de territorio

perestroika a policy in the Soviet Union in the late 1980s calling for restructuring of the stagnant Soviet economy (p. 1088)

perestroika política de la Unión Soviética de finales de la década de 1980 que abogó por la reestructuración de la estancada economía soviética

personal computer small computer intended for individual use (p. 1105)

computadora personal computadora pequeña destinada al uso personal

personal liberty laws laws enacted by northern states to counteract the Fugitive Slave Act by granting rights to escaped slaves and free blacks (p. 331)

leyes de libertad individual leyes instauradas por los estados del Norte para contrarrestar la Ley de Esclavos Fugitivos, al otorgar derechos tanto a los esclavos escapados como a los negros libertos

Pilgrims English Puritans who sought religious freedom and founded Plymouth Colony in 1620 (p. 51)

peregrinos puritanos ingleses que buscaban la libertad de credo y que fundaron la colonia de Plymouth en 1620

placer mining use of metal pans, picks, and shovels to harvest gold from the banks and bottoms of rivers and streams (p. 313)

minería de placer uso de bandejas de metal, picos y palas para extraer el oro de las márgenes y fondos de ríos y arroyos

Platt Amendment set of conditions under which Cuba was granted independence in 1902, including restrictions on rights of Cubans and granting to the U.S. the "right to intervene" to preserve order in Cuba (p. 605)

Enmienda Platt grupo de condiciones con las que se le otorgó la independencia a Cuba en 1902, que incluían restricciones de los derechos de los cubanos y que otorgaban a EE.UU. el "derecho de intervenir" a fin de conservar el orden en Cuba

political party organization of people that seeks to win elections and hold public office in order to shape government policy (p. 197)

partido político organización de personas que busca ganar elecciones y ocupar puestos públicos a fin de dirigir las políticas gubernamentales

poll tax sum of money to be paid before a person could vote (p. 521)

impuesto electoral suma de dinero a pagar antes que una persona pudiera votar

Pontiac's Rebellion uprising in 1763 by Indians in the Great Lakes region (p. 88)

Rebelión de Pontiac levantamiento en 1763 de los indígenas en la región de los Grandes Lagos

popular sovereignty principle in which the people are the only source of government power (p. 155)

soberanía popular principio por el cual las personas son la única fuente de poder gubernamental

popular sovereignty political policy that permitted the residents of federal territories to decide on whether to enter the union as free or slave states (p. 326)

soberanía popular doctrina política que permitió a los residentes de los territorios federales decidir si ingresaban a la unión como estados libres o esclavistas

Populist Party People's Party; political party formed in 1891 to advocate a larger money supply and other economic reforms (p. 536)

Partido Populista Partido del Pueblo; partido político formado en 1891 para abogar por un mayor suministro de dinero y otras reformas económicas

precedent act or statement that becomes an example, rule, or tradition to be followed (p. 193)

precedente acción o declaración que se convierte en el ejemplo, regla o tradición a seguir

presidio fort built by the Spanish in colonial America, usually in what is today the U.S. Southwest and California (p. 35)

presidio fortín construido por los españoles en la América colonial, usualmente situado en lo que hoy día son el Sudoeste de Estados Unidos y California

privatize to transfer from governmental ownership or control to private interests (p. 1131)

privatizar transferir la propiedad o control gubernamental a intereses privados

Proclamation of 1763 declaration by the British king ordering all colonists to remain east of the Appalachian Mountains (p. 88)

Proclamación de 1763 declaración del rey de Gran Bretaña para que los colonos permanecieran al este de los montes Apalaches

productivity the rate at which goods are produced or services performed (p. 884)

productividad velocidad a la que se producen bienes o se brindan servicios

Progressive Party political party that emerged from the Taft-Roosevelt battle that split the Republican Party in 1912 (p. 575)

Partido Progresivo partido político surgido de la batalla entre Taft y Roosevelt que dividió al Partido Republicano en 1912

Progressivism movement that responded to the pressures of industrialization and urbanization by promoting reforms (p. 548)

Progresivismo movimiento surgido como respuesta a las presiones de la industrialización y urbanización, que promovía nuevas ideas y reformas políticas

Prohibition the forbidding by law of the manufacture, transport, and sale of alcohol (p. 677)

Prohibición ley para prohibir la fabricación, transporte, y venta de alcohol

proprietary colony English colony granted to an individual or group by the Crown (p. 47)

colonia concedida colonia inglesa cedida por la Corona a un individuo o grupo

protective tariff tax on imported goods making the price high enough to protect domestic goods from foreign competition (p. 438)

arancel proteccionista impuesto sobre bienes importados que sube lo suficiente su precio a fin de proteger a los bienes domésticos de la competencia extranjera

English/Spanish Glossary

public school movement movement aimed at providing greater educational opportunities through the establishment of tax-supported public schools (p. 275)

movimiento de educación pública movimiento orientado a ofrecer mayores oportunidades educativas mediante la fundación de escuelas públicas financiadas con los impuestos

Public Works Administration (PWA) New Deal agency that provided millions of jobs constructing public buildings (p. 737)

Administración de Obras Públicas agencia del Nuevo Trato que brindó millones de empleos en la construcción de obras públicas

pull factor factors that attract people to a new location (p. 56)

factor de atracción causa que atrae a la población hacia una nueva ubicación

Pullman Strike violent 1894 railway workers' strike which began outside of Chicago and spread nationwide (p. 457)

huelga de Pullman violenta huelga de los trabajadores ferrocarrileros de 1894 que empezó en las afueras de Chicago y se extendió por todo el país

pump priming economic theory that favored public works projects because they put money into the hands of consumers who would buy more goods, stimulating the economy (p. 741)

cebado de bomba teoría económica que favorece los proyectos de obras públicas porque ponen dinero en manos de los consumidores que comprarán más bienes, estimulando así la economía

Pure Food and Drug Act 1906 law that allowed federal inspection of food and medicine and banned the interstate shipment and sale of impure food and the mislabeling of food and drugs (p. 572)

Ley de Alimentos y Fármacos Puros Ley de 1906 que permitió la inspección federal de los alimentos y medicinas y prohibió el transporte y venta interestatal de alimentos impuros así como el rotulado erróneo de alimentos y fármacos

Puritans English Protestants who believed in strict religious discipline and the simplification of worship; settlers of the Massachusetts Bay Colony (p. 50)

puritanos protestantes ingleses que observaban una disciplina religiosa estricta y profesaban la simplificación del culto; pobladores de la Colonia de la Bahía de Massachusetts

push factor factors that motivate people to leave their home countries (p. 56)

factor de empuje causa que hace que la población deje su país de origen

Q

quota system arrangement that limited the number of immigrants who could enter the United States from specific countries (p. 673)

sistema de cuotas acuerdo que limitó el número de inmigrantes provenientes de países específicos que podían ingresar a Estados Unidos

R

Radical Republicans congressmen who advocated full citizenship rights for African Americans along with a harsh Reconstruction policy toward the South (p. 404)

Republicanos Radicales congresistas que abogaban por derechos ciudadanos íntegros para los afroestadounidenses junto con una política dura de Reconstrucción en el Sur

ratification official approval (p. 150)

ratificación aprobación oficial

rationing government-controlled limits on the amount of certain goods that civilians could buy during wartime (p. 814)

racionamiento límites controlados por el gobierno sobre la cantidad de ciertos bienes que podían comprar los civiles en tiempos de guerra

realpolitik a foreign policy promoted by Henry Kissinger during the Nixon administration based on concrete national interests instead of abstract ideologies (p. 1009)

realpolitik política exterior promovida por Henry Kissinger durante la administración Nixon con base en intereses nacionales concretos en lugar de ideologías abstractas

recall process by which voters can remove elected officials from office before their terms end (p. 555)

destitución proceso por el cual los electores pueden remover a funcionarios electos antes de terminar su período

Reconquista battle, ending in 1492, that reestablished Spanish Christian rule on the Iberian Peninsula after 700 years of Muslim dominance (p. 14)

la Reconquista batalla, finalizada en 1492, que volvió a establecer el poder cristiano español en la península Ibérica después de 700 años de dominio musulmán

Reconstruction program implemented by the federal government between 1865 and 1877 to repair damage to the South caused by the Civil War and restore the southern states to the Union (p. 402)

Reconstrucción programa implementado por el gobierno federal entre 1865 y 1877 para reparar los daños al Sur que causó la Guerra Civil y reincorporar los estados sureños a la Unión

Reconstruction Finance Corporation (RFC) federal agency set up by Congress in 1932 to provide emergency government credit to banks, railroads, and other large businesses (p. 722)

Corporación de Financiamiento para la Reconstrucción agencia federal establecida por el Congreso en 1932 para brindar créditos gubernamentales de emergencia a los bancos, ferrocarriles, y otras grandes empresas

Redeemer term for white southern Democrats who returned to power after 1870 (p. 422)

redentores término usado para los demócratas blancos sureños que regresaron al poder después de 1870

Red Scare fear that communists were working to destroy the American way of life (pp. 649, 868)

miedo rojo miedo a que los comunistas están empeñados en destruir la forma de vida estadounidense

referendum process that allows citizens to approve or reject a law passed by a legislature (p. 555)

referendo proceso que permite que los ciudadanos aprueben o rechacen una ley que ha aprobado por una legislatura

Renaissance period in European history lasting from the fourteenth to the sixteenth century, which ushered in a more secular age and encouraged freedom of thought, the importance of the individual, and renewed interest in classical learning (p. 13)

Renacimiento período en la historia de Europa que cubre desde el siglo XIV hasta el siglo XVI y que introdujo una edad más secular, alentó la libertad de pensamiento y la importancia del individuo, y renovó el interés en la educación clásica

reparations payment for war damages (p. 642)

reparaciones pago por los daños causados por la guerra

repatriation process by which Mexican Americans were encouraged, or forced, by local, state, and federal officials to return to Mexico during the 1930s (p. 717)

repatriación proceso por el cual los estadounidenses de origen mexicano fueron animados, o forzados, por los oficiales locales, estatales, y federales para que regresaran a México durante la década de 1930

republic form of government in which officials are elected by the people (p. 134)

república forma de gobierno en la que el pueblo elige a los funcionarios

Republican Party political party established around an antislavery platform in 1854 (p. 340)

Partido Republicano partido político establecido en 1854 en torno a una plataforma antiesclavista

reservationists a group of Senators, led by Henry Cabot Lodge, who opposed the Treaty of Versailles, to end World War I, unless specific changes were included (p. 196)

reservasionistas grupo de senadores encabezados por Henry Cabot que se oponía a terminar la Primera Guerra Mundial con el Tratado de Versalles a menos que éste inlcuyera ciertos cambios

reservation public lands where Native Americans were forced to live by the federal government (p. 497)

reservación tierras públicas donde el gobierno federal obligó a vivir a los indígenas

revivalist preacher who works to renew the importance of religion in American life (p. 266)

renovador de la fe predicador dedicado a renovar la importancia de la religión en el modo de vida estadounidense

rock-and-roll music originated in the gospel and blues traditions of African Americans (p. 901)

rock-and-roll música originada en las tradiciones del gospel y blues de los afroestadounidenses

Roosevelt Corollary President Theodore Roosevelt's reassertion of the Monroe Doctrine to keep the Western Hemisphere free from intervention by European powers (p. 607)

Corolario Roosevelt replanteamiento del presidente Teodoro Roosevelt de la Doctrina Monroe, según la cual la política de Estados Unidos era mantener al hemisferio occidental libre de la intervención de las potencias europeas

Rough Riders group of men, consisting of rugged westerners and upper-class easterners who fought during the Spanish-American War (p. 596)

jinetes rudos grupo de hombres fuertes provenientes del Oeste y de la clase alta del Este que pelearon durante la Guerra entre España y Estados Unidos

royal colony English colony that was under direct control of the Crown (p. 47)

colonia real colonia inglesa controlada directamente por la Corona

rural-to-urban migrant a person who moves from an agricultural area to a city (p. 474)

inmigrante del campo a la ciudad persona que se traslada de las áreas rurales a la ciudad

Russo-Japanese War a war between Japan and Russia in 1904 over the presence of Russian troops in Manchuria (p. 603)

Guerra Ruso-Japonesa guerra entre Japón y Rusia durante 1904 por la presencia de tropas Rusas en Manchuria

S

salutary neglect British policy in early 1700s which allowed the colonies virtual self-rule as long as Great Britain was gaining economically (p. 75)

negligencia benigna política británica de principios del siglo XVIII que permitió que las colonias virtualmente se autogobernaran en tanto que Gran Bretaña tuviera ganancias económicas

sanctions penalties (p. 1064)

sanciones castigos

Sand Creek Massacre 1864 incident in which Colorado militia killed a camp of Cheyenne and Arapaho Indians (p. 498)

Masacre de Sand Creek incidente de 1864 durante el cual una milicia de Colorado asesinó a un campamento de indígenas cheyene y arapaho

Santa Fe Trail trail developed by traders in the mid-1800s, connecting Independence, Missouri, to Santa Fe, New Mexico (p. 301)

Sendero de Santa Fe ruta creada por comerciantes a mediados del siglo XIX que unía a Independence, Missouri, con Santa Fe, Nuevo México

Saratoga 1777 Revolutionary War battle considered to be the turning point in the war because the Patriot win convinced the French to aid the United States (p. 120)

Saratoga una batalla en 1777 de la Guerra de Independencia considerada el punto crucial de la guerra porque el triunfo de los patriotas convenció a Francia de reconocer a Estados Unidos como nación

satellite a mechanical device that orbits Earth receiving and sending communication signals or transmitting scientific data (p. 1106)

satélite dispositivo mecánico que orbita la Tierra y que recibe y envía señales de comunicación o transmite datos científicos

satellite state independent nation under the control of a more powerful nation (p. 847)

estado satélite nación independiente bajo el control de una nación más poderosa

saturation bombing tactic of dropping massive amounts of bombs in order to inflict maximum damage (p. 807)

saturación de bombardeos táctica de dejar caer cantidades masivas de bombas a fin de infligir el máximo daño

English/Spanish Glossary

Savings and Loan crisis the failure of about 1,000 savings and loan banks as a result of risky business practices (p. 1082)

crisis financiera fracaso de cerca de 1,000 bancos de ahorro y préstamo como resultado de prácticas comerciales riesgosas

scalawag negative term for a southern white who supported the Republican Party after the Civil War (p. 411)

scalawag término negativo para referirse a un blanco sureño que apoyó al Partido Republicano después de la Guerra Civil

scientific management approach to improving efficiency, in which experts looked at every step of a manufacturing process, trying to find ways to reduce time, effort, and expense (p. 661)

administración científica enfoque para mejorar la eficiencia, en el que los expertos observaban cada paso de un proceso de manufactura y buscaban formas de reducir el tiempo, esfuerzo, y costo

Scopes Trial 1925 trial of a Tennessee schoolteacher for teaching Darwin's theory of evolution (p. 672)

Juicio Scopes juicio al que fue sometido, en 1925, un maestro de Tennessee por enseñar la teoría de Darwin sobre la evolución

secede to withdraw formally from a membership in a group or an organization (p. 327)

separarse retirir formalmente de la membresía en un grupo u organización

Second Continental Congress assembly of delegates representing every colony that met in 1775 in Philadelphia (p. 109)

Segundo Congreso Continental asamblea de delegados con representación de cada colonia que se reunió en 1775 en Filadelfia

Second Great Awakening religious revival movement in the first half of the 1800s (p. 266)

Segundo Gran Despertar movimiento de renovación religiosa que se dio en la primera mitad del siglo XIX

Second New Deal legislative activity begun by Franklin D. Roosevelt in 1935 to solve problems created by the Great Depression (p. 740)

Segundo Nuevo Trato actividad legislativa iniciada por Franklin D. Roosevelt en 1935 para lidiar con los problemas creados por la Gran Depresión

segregation forced separation, oftentimes by race (p. 412)

segregación separación forzada, a menudo con base en la raza

Selective Service Act act passed by Congress in 1917 authorizing a draft of men for military service (p. 628)

Ley de Servicio ley aprobada por el Congreso en 1917 que autorizó el reclutamiento de hombres para el servicio militar

self-determination the right of people to choose their own form of government (p. 642)

autodeterminación derecho de las personas de elegir su propia forma de gobierno

Seneca Falls Convention held in New York in 1848, the first women's rights convention in the United States (p. 290)

Convención de Seneca Falls la primera convención sobre los derechos de la mujer realizada en Estados Unidos, celebrada en Nueva York en 1848

separation of powers principle that divides power among the executive, legislative, and judicial branches of government (p. 155)

separación de poderes principio que divide el poder entre las ramas ejecutiva, legislativa, y judicial

Separatists groups who wished to separate from the Anglican Church to begin their own churches (p. 50)

separatistas grupos que querían separarse de la iglesia Anglicana para fundar sus propias iglesias

service economy an economic system focused on the buying and selling of services (p. 1108)

economía de servicio sistema económico enfocado en la compra y venta de servicios

service sector businesses that provide services rather than manufactured goods (p. 893)

sector de servicios empresas que brindan servicios en lugar de fabricar bienes

settlement house community center organized at the turn of the twentieth century to provide social services to the urban poor (p. 552)

casa de asentamiento centro comunal organizado a inicios del siglo XX para ofrecer servicios sociales a los pobres de la ciudad

sharecropping system in which a farmer tended a portion of a planter's land in return for a share of the crop (p. 415)

aparcería sistema en el cual un granjero atiende una porción de la tierra del propietario a cambio de una parte de la cosecha

share-tenancy much like sharecropping, except that the farmer chose what crop he would plant and bought his own supplies (p. 416)

arrendamiento por aparcería similar a la aparcería, excepto que el granjero elige qué cultivar y compra sus propios ínsumos

Shays' Rebellion farmers' rebellion led by Daniel Shays against higher taxes in Massachusetts (p. 141)

Rebelión de Shays rebelión de granjeros conducida por Daniel Shays en contra del aumento de impuestos en Massachusetts

Sherman Antitrust Act 1890 law banning any trust that restrained interstate trade or commerce (p. 448)

Ley Antimonopolios Sherman ley de 1890 que prohibió los consorcios que restringían el comercio o negocios interestatales

Shiloh 1862 Civil War battle where nearly 25,000 Union and Confederate troops were killed or wounded (p. 364)

Shiloh batalla de 1862 de la Guerra Civil en la que cerca de 25,000 miembros de las tropas de la Unión y la Confederación murieron o fueron heridos

siege military tactic in which an enemy is surrounded and all supplies are cut off in an attempt to force a surrender (p. 381)

sitio táctica militar según la cual se rodea al enemigo cerrando por completo el acceso de abastecimientos a fin de obligarlo a rendirse

silent majority phrase introduced by President Richard Nixon to refer to a significant number of Americans who supported his policies but chose not to express their views (p. 1047)

mayoría silenciosa frase introducida por el presidente Richard Nixon para referirse a un número significativo de estadounidenses que apoyaban sus políticas pero eligieron no expresar su opinión

sit-down strike labor protest in which workers stop working and occupy the workplace until their demands are met (p. 745)

   huelga de brazos caídos protesta laboral en que los trabajadores dejan de trabajar y ocupan el lugar de trabajo hasta que se satisfacen sus demandas

sit-in form of protest where participants sit and refuse to move (p. 925)

   sentada forma de protesta en que los participantes se sientan y rehúsan moverse

Sixteenth Amendment 1913 constitutional amendment that gave Congress the authority to levy an income tax (p. 577)

   Décimosexta Enmienda enmienda constitucional de 1913 que otorgó al Congreso la autoridad para establecer un impuesto a las rentas

skyscraper very tall building (p. 475)

   rascacielos edificio muy alto

Smith Act law that made it unlawful to teach or advocate the violent overthrow of the United States government (p. 869)

   Ley Smith ley que prohibió la enseñanza o defensa de un derrocamiento violento del gobierno estadounidense

Social Darwinism the belief held by some in the late nineteenth century that certain nations and races were superior to others and therefore destined to rule over them (p. 447)

   darwinismo social creencia de algunos a finales del siglo XIX según la que algunas naciones o razas eran superiores a otras y por lo tanto estaban destinadas a gobernar

Social Gospel reform movement that emerged in the late nineteenth century that sought to improve society by applying Christian principles (p. 552)

   Evangelio Social movimiento reformista surgido a finales del siglo XIX cuyo fin era mejorar la sociedad al aplicarse principios cristianos

socialism system or theory under which the means of production are publicly controlled and regulated rather than owned by individuals (p. 453)

   socialismo sistema o teoría según la cual los medios de producción son controlados y regulados públicamente en lugar de ser propiedad de individuos

Social Security Act 1935 law that set up a pension system for retirees, established unemployment insurance, and created insurance for victims of work-related accidents. It also provided aid for poverty-stricken mothers and children, the blind, and the disabled (p. 741)

   Ley del Seguro Social ley de 1935 que crea un sistema de pensión para jubilados, establece un seguro de desempleo y crea seguros para las víctimas de accidentes laborales. También suministra ayuda a las madres y niños pobres, ciegos, y discapacitados

Songhai large West African empire lasting from 1400 to 1600 (p. 16)

   Songhai gran imperio del África Occidental existente entre el siglo XV d. C. y el siglo XVII d. C.

Sons of Liberty organization of colonists formed in opposition to the Stamp Act and other British laws and taxes (p. 101)

   Hijos de la Libertad organización de colonos formada para oponerse a la Ley del Timbre y otras leyes e impuestos británicos

Southeast Asia Treaty Organization (SEATO) defensive alliance aimed at preventing communist aggression in Asia (pp. 859, 983)

   Organización del Tratado del Sudeste Asiático alianza defensiva orientada a prevenir la agresión comunista en Asia

southern strategy tactic of the Republican Party for winning presidential elections by securing the electoral votes of southern states (p. 1048)

   estrategia sureña táctica del Partido Republicano para ganar las elecciones presidenciales al asegurarse los votos electorales de los estados del Sur

"space race" the competition between the United States and the Soviet Union to develop the technology to successfully land on the moon (p. 961)

   "carrera espacial" competencia entre Estados Unidos y la Unión Soviética en el desarrollo de la tecnología para aterrizar exitosamente en la Luna

Spanish Civil War Nationalist forces led by General Francisco Franco rebelled against the democratic Republican government of Spain (p. 777)

   Guerra Civil Española conflicto en España, en el que las fuerzas Nacionalistas dirigidas por el General Francisco Franco se rebelaron contra el gobierno democrático Republicano

speculation practice of making high-risk investments in hopes of obtaining large profits (p. 706)

   especulación la práctica de hacer inversiones de alto riesgo con la esperanza de obtener grandes ganancias

sphere of influence a region dominated and controlled by an outside power (p. 601)

   esfera de influencia región dominada y controlada por un poder externo

spoils system practice of the political party in power giving jobs and appointments to its supporters, rather than to people based on their qualifications (pp. 252, 531)

   clientelismo práctica del partido político en el poder de asignar los puestos y nombramientos a sus seguidores en lugar de basarlos en las calificaciones

Square Deal President Theodore Roosevelt's program of reforms to keep the wealthy and powerful from taking advantage of small business owners and the poor (p. 570)

   Trato Justo programa de reformas del presidente Teodoro Roosevelt para evitar que los ricos y poderosos se aprovecharan de los propietarios de pequeñas empresas y de los pobres

stagflation term for the economic condition created in the late 1960s and 1970s by high inflation combined with stagnant economic growth and high unemployment (p. 1047)

   estanflación término para la condición económica creada a finales de las décadas de 1960 y 1970 por una alta inflación combinada con el estancamiento del crecimiento económico y el alto desempleo

Stamp Act 1765 law passed by Parliament that required colonists to pay taxes on printed materials (p. 100)

   Ley del Timbre ley de 1765 aprobada por el Parlamento para exigir a los colonos el pago de impuestos sobre los materiales impresos

"Star-Spangled Banner" poem written by Francis Scott Key in 1814 that became the national anthem in 1931 (p. 217)

"Bandera de Estrellas Centelleantes" poema escrito por Francis Scott Key en 1814 que se convirtió en el himno nacional en 1931

steerage third-class accommodations on a steamship, which were usually overcrowded and dirty (p. 466)

compartimento de tercera clase alojamiento de tercera clase en un buque de vapor que usualmente era hacinado y sucio

Strategic Arms Limitation Treaty (SALT I) 1972 treaty between the United States and the Soviet Union that froze the deployment of intercontinental ballistic missiles and placed limits on antiballistic missiles (p. 1010)

Tratado de Limitación de Armas Estratégicas tratado de 1972 entre Estados Unidos y la Unión Soviética que congeló el despliegue de misiles balísticos intercontinentales y puso límites a los misiles antibalísticos

Strategic Arms Limitation Treaty II (SALT II) proposed agreement between the United States and the Soviet Union to limit certain types of nuclear arms production; it was never ratified by the United States Senate (p. 1064)

Tratado de Limitación de Armas Estratégicas II acuerdo propuesto entre Estados Unidos y la Unión Soviética para limitar la producción de ciertos tipos de armas nucleares; no lo fué ratificado nunca por el Senado de Estados Unidos

strategic bombing tactic of dropping bombs on key political and industrial targets (p. 807)

bombardeo estratégico táctica de dejar caer bombas en blancos políticos e industriales clave

Strategic Defense Initiative (SDI) nicknamed "Star Wars," President Reagan's plan to develop innovative defenses to guard the United States against nuclear missile attacks (p. 1088)

Iniciativa de Defensa Estratégica apodada "Guerra de las Galaxias," plan de 1983 del presidente Reagan para financiar el desarrollo de defensas innovadoras para salvaguardar a Estados Unidos contra ataques con misiles nucleares

strict construction belief that the government is limited to powers clearly stated in the Constitution (p. 195)

interpretación estricta creencia en que el gobierno está limitado a los poderes claramente establecidos en la Constitución

Student Nonviolent Coordinating Committee (SNCC) grass-roots movement founded in 1960 by young civil rights activists (p. 926)

Comité Estudiantil Coordinador de la No Violencia movimiento de base compuesto fundado en 1960 por jóvenes activistas a favor de los derechos humanos

Students for a Democratic Society (SDS) organization founded in 1960 at the University of Michigan to fight racism and poverty (p. 994)

Estudiantes a Favor de una Sociedad Democrática organización fundada en 1960 en la Universidad de Michigan para combatir el racismo y la pobreza

suburb residential areas surrounding a city (p. 476)

suburbios áreas residenciales que rodean una ciudad

Suez crisis attempt by France and Great Britain to seize control of the Suez Canal in 1956 (p. 864)

crisis de Suez intento de Francia y Gran Bretaña por apoderarse del control del Canal de Suez en 1956

suffrage the right to vote (p. 290)

sufragio derecho al voto

Sunbelt name given to the region of states in the South and the Southwest (p. 891)

Cinturón del Sol nombre dado a la región de los estados del sur y suroeste

superpower powerful country that plays a dominant economic, political, and military role in the world (p. 836)

superpotencia país poderoso que juega un papel económico, político, y militar dominante en el mundo

supply-side economics economic theory that held that the government should increase the supply of labor and goods to achieve long-term growth, rather than increasing demand through government spending (p. 1081)

economía de la oferta teoría económica que mantiene que el gobierno debe aumentar la oferta de trabajo y bienes para alcanzar el crecimiento a largo plazo, en lugar de aumentar la demanda por medio del gasto gubernamental

suspension bridge bridge that has a roadway suspended by cables (p. 439)

puente colgante puente cuya carretera está suspendida por cables

sweatshop small factory where employees have to work long hours under poor conditions for little pay (p. 451)

taller del sudor fábrica pequeña donde los empleados deben trabajar muchas horas en condiciones deficientes a cambio de poca paga

T

Taft Hartley Act a law that restricted the power of labor unions (p. 885)

Ley Taft Hartley ley que restringió el poder de los sindicatos de trabajadores

Taliban Islamic fundamentalist faction that controlled most of Afghanistan from 1996–2001 (p. 1124)

Talibán fracción fundamentalista islámica que controló la mayor parte de Afganistán entre 1996 a 2001

tariff tax on imported goods (p. 194)

arancel impuesto sobre bienes importados

Tariff of Abominations 1828 protective tariff, so-named by its southern opponents (p. 255)

Arancel de Abominaciones arancel protector de 1828, llamado así por sus oponentes sureños

Tariff of 1816 protective tariff established by Congress to encourage Americans to buy goods made in the United States (p. 233)

Arancel de 1816 arancel protector establecido por el Congreso para estimular a los estadounidenses a comprar bienes hechos en Estados Unidos

Teapot Dome scandal scandal during the Harding administration in which the Secretary of the Interior leased government oil reserves to private oilmen in return for bribes (p. 668)

escándalo Teapot Dome escándalo durante la administración Harding en que el secretario del interior arrendó las reservas de petróleo del gobierno a petroleros privados a cambio de un soborno

televangelist minister who uses the television format to preach to millions of people (p. 1061)

teleevangelista pastor que usa el formato televisivo para predicar a millones de personas

temperance movement movement aimed at stopping alcohol abuse and the problems created by it (p. 277)

movimiento de temperancia movimiento encausado a eliminar el abuso del alcohol y los problemas que éste genera

tenant farming system in which a farmer paid rent to a landowner for the use of the land (p. 416)

agricultura de arrendamiento sistema en el que un agricultor paga un alquiler por el uso de la tierra a un propietario

tenement multistory building divided into apartments to house as many families as possible (p. 476)

vecindad edificio de varios pisos dividido en departamentos para albergar a varias familias

Tennessee Valley Authority (TVA) government agency that built dams in the Tennessee River valley to control flooding and generate electric power (p. 736)

Autoridad del Valle del Tennessee agencia gubernamental que construye represas en el valle del río Tennessee para controlar las inundaciones y generar energía eléctrica

termination policy ended all programs monitored by the Bureau of Indian Affairs. It also ended federal responsibility for the health and welfare of Native Americans (p. 907)

política de terminación política que cerró todos los programas a cargo de la Oficina de Asuntos Indígenas. También dio por terminada la responsabilidad federal en cuanto a la salud y bienestar de los indígenas estadounidenses

Tet Offensive communist assault on a large number of South Vietnamese cities in early 1968 (p. 995)

Ofensiva Tet asalto comunista contra un gran número de ciudades de Vietnam del Sur a principios de 1968

Thirteenth Amendment 1865 constitutional amendment that abolished slavery (p. 391)

Decimotercera Enmienda enmienda constitucional de 1865 que abolió la esclavitud

38th parallel dividing line between North and South Korea (p. 855)

paralelo 38 línea divisoria entre Corea del Norte y Corea del Sur

Three-Fifths Compromise compromise in which each enslaved person would be counted as three fifths of a person for the purposes of legislative representation (p. 148)

Acuerdo de Tres Quintos acuerdo según el que cada esclavo se contaría como tres quintos de una persona para efectos de la representación legislativa

Tiananmen Square site in Beijing where Chinese students' prodemocracy protests were put down by the Chinese government in 1989 (p. 1094)

Plaza Tiananmen lugar en Pekín donde las protestas de los estudiantes chinos a favor de la democracia fueron aplacadas por el gobierno chino en 1989

time zone any of the 24 longitudinal areas of the world within which the same time is used (p. 440)

huso horario cualquiera de las veinticuatro zonas del mundo en la que se usa la misma hora

totalitarianism a theory of government in which a single party or leader controls the economic, social, and cultural lives of its people (p. 772)

totalitarismo teoría de gobierno según la que un solo partido o líder controla la vida económica, social, y cultural de la población

total war military strategy in which an army attacks not only enemy troops but the economic and civilian resources that support them (p. 386)

guerra total estrategia militar en la cual, además de atacar a las tropas enemigas, un ejército arremete también contra los recursos económicos y civiles que las sostienen

toxic waste poisonous byproducts of human activity (p. 1035)

desechos tóxicos productos de desecho venenosos resultantes de la actividad humana

Trail of Tears forced march of the Cherokee Indians to move west of the Mississippi in the 1830s (p. 254)

Sendero del Llanto marcha forzada de los indígenas cherokee para mudarlos al oeste del Mississippi en la década de 1830

Transcendentalist person who follows the literary and philosophical movement based on finding spiritual reality through nature and consciousness of self (p. 272)

trascendentalista seguidor del movimiento literario y filosófico que buscaba hallar la realización espiritual a través de la naturaleza y la consciencia del propio ser

transcontinental railroad rail link between the eastern and the western United States (p. 507)

ferrocarril transcontinental enlace ferroviario entre el este y el oeste de los Estados Unidos

Treaty of Fort Laramie 1851 treaty that restricted Indians to specific areas away from the major trails (p. 304)

Tratado del Fuerte Laramie tratado de 1851 que restringía a los indígenas a áreas específicas alejadas de los senderos mayores

Treaty of Ghent 1814 agreement that ended the War of 1812 (p. 218)

Tratado de Gante acuerdo de 1814 que finalizó la Guerra de 1812

Treaty of Guadalupe-Hidalgo 1848 treaty ending the Mexican-American War (p. 311)

Tratado Guadalupe-Hidalgo tratado de 1848 que finalizó la Guerra México-Estadounidense

Treaty of Paris 1783 peace treaty that ended the Revolutionary War and affirmed American independence (p. 125)

Tratado de París tratado de paz de 1783 que dió por finalizada la Guerra de Independencia y estableció la independencia de Estados Unidos

Treaty of Paris an agreement signed by the United States and Spain in 1898, which officially ended the Spanish-American War (p. 597)

Tratado de París acuerdo firmado por Estados Unidos y España en 1898 que marcó el final oficial de la Guerra entre España y Estados Unidos

triangular trade three-way pattern of trade that involved England, English colonies in the Americas, and West Africa (p. 69)

comercio triangular patrón trilateral de comercio que involucró a Inglaterra, las colonias inglesas en las Américas, y África Occidental

English/Spanish Glossary

trickle-down economics economic theory that holds that money lent to banks and businesses will trickle down to consumers (p. 722)
economía por goteo teoría económica que mantiene que el dinero prestado a los bancos y empresas llegará a los consumidores

Tripartite Pact agreement that created an alliance between Germany, Italy, and Japan during World War II (p. 784)
Pacto Tripartito acuerdo que creó una alianza entre Alemania, Italia, y Japón durante la Segunda Guerra Mundial

Truman Doctrine President Truman's promise to help nations struggling against communist movements (p. 848)
doctrina Truman promesa del Presidente Truman de ayudar a las naciones en lucha contra los movimientos comunistas

trust group of separate companies that are placed under the control of a single managing board in order to form a monopoly (p. 445)
trust grupo de distintas compañías bajo el control de una sola junta administrativa

turnpike road that requires users to pay a toll (p. 228)
autopista de peaje carretera que exige el pago de una cuota a sus usuarios

Tuskegee Airmen African American squadron that escorted bombers in the air war over Europe during World War II (p. 807)
Aviadores de Tuskegee escuadrón de afroestadounidenses que escoltaba a los bombarderos en la guerra aérea en cielos de Europa durante la Segunda Guerra Mundial

Twenty-fifth Amendment constitutional amendment ratified in 1967 that deals with presidential succession, vice presidential vacancy, and presidential inability (p. 1051)
Vigésima Quinta Enmienda enmienda constitucional ratificada en 1967 que trata de la sucesión presidencial, vacantes de vicepresidentes, e incapacidad presidencial

Twenty-fourth Amendment constitutional amendment that banned the poll tax as a voting requirement (p. 938)
Vigésima Cuarta Enmienda enmienda constitucional que prohibió el impuesto electoral como requisito para votar

U

U-boat German submarine (p. 624)
buque submarino U submarino alemán

unconditional surrender giving up completely without any concessions (p. 805)
rendición incondicional darse por vencido completamente sin concesiones

Underground Railroad system that existed before the Civil War, in which black and white abolitionists helped escaped slaves travel to safe areas, especially Canada (p. 333)
Ferrocarril Subterráneo sistema que existió antes de la Guerra Civil en el que negros y blancos abolicionistas socorrían a los esclavos escapados a llegar a zonas seguras, especialmente Canadá

unfunded mandate program or action required but not paid for by the federal government (p. 1078)
mandatos sin fondos programas o acciones requeridos pero que no paga el gobierno federal

unicameral legislature lawmaking body made up of a single house (p. 134)
legislatura unicameral cuerpo legislativo compuesto de una sola cámara

Unitarian members of the Unitarian religion, which is based on the belief that God is a single divine being rather than a trinity (p. 269)
unitarios miembros del unitarismo, una religión basada en la creencia en que Dios es un ser único divino y no una trinidad

United Farm Workers (UFW) labor union of farm workers that used nonviolent tactics, including a workers' strike and a consumer boycott of table grapes (p. 1029)
Trabajadores Agrícolas Unidos sindicato de trabajadores agrícolas que usó tácticas pacíficas, incluyendo una huelga de trabajadores y un boicot por los consumidores de uvas

United Nations (UN) organization founded in 1945 to promote peace (p. 837)
Naciones Unidas (ONU) organización fundada en 1945 para promover la paz

Universal Declaration of Human Rights document issued by the UN to promote basic human rights and freedoms (p. 837)
Declaración Universal de los Derechos Humanos documento emitido por la ONU para promover los derechos y libertades humanos básicos

urbanization expansion of cities and/or an increase in the number of people living in them (p. 472)
urbanización expansión de ciudades y/o aumento del número de sus habitantes

Urban League network of churches and clubs that set up employment agencies and relief efforts to help African Americans get settled and find work in the cities (p. 567)
Liga Urbana red de iglesias y clubes que estableció agencias de empleo y esfuerzos de asistencia para ayudar a que los afroestadounidenses se asentaran y encontraran empleo en las ciudades

urban renewal government programs for redevelopment of urban areas (p. 905)
renovación urbana programas gubernamentales para el desarrollo de las áreas urbanas

utopian community separate settlement established with the goal of moral perfection (p. 271)
comunidad utópica asentamiento independiente fundado para alcanzar la perfección moral

V

Valley Forge location in Pennsylvania where Washington's army spent a difficult winter in 1777–1778 (p. 120)
Valle Forge lugar en Pennsylvania donde el ejército de Washington pasó un invierno difícil de 1777 a 1778

vaudeville type of show, including dancing, singing, and comedy sketches, that became popular in the late nineteenth century (p. 485)
vodevil tipo de espectáculo que incluye baile, canto, y comedia que se popularizó a finales del siglo XIX

vertical integration system of consolidating firms involved in all steps of a product's manufacture (p. 445)

integración vertical sistema de consolidación de empresas involucradas en todos los pasos de la manufactura de un producto

viceroy in colonial Spanish America, king-appointed official who governs a province, colony, or country (p. 35)

virrey en la Hispanoamérica colonial, funcionario nombrado por el rey para gobernar una provincia, colonia, o país

Vicksburg Confederate stronghold on the Mississippi River that surrendered to Union forces in 1863 after a siege (p. 381)

Vicksburg baluarte confederado en el río Mississippi que se rindió a las fuerzas de la Unión en 1863 luego de un sitio

Vietcong South Vietnamese communist rebels that waged a guerrilla war against the government of South Vietnam throughout the Vietnam War (p. 983)

Vietcong rebeldes comunistas sudvietnamitas que hicieron guerra de guerrillas contra el gobierno de Vietnam del Sur durante la Guerra de Vietnam

Vietnamization President Nixon's plan for gradual withdrawal of U.S. forces as South Vietnamese troops assumed more combat duties (p. 1001)

vietnamización plan del presidente Nixon para terminar gradualmente la participación estadounidense en Vietnam, a medida que las tropas sudvietnamitas asumían más deberes de combate

vigilante self-appointed law enforcer (p. 507)

vigilante persona autonombrada para hacer cumplir la ley

Violence Against Women Act law passed in 1994 that increased federal resources to apprehend and prosecute men guilty of violent acts against women (p. 1131)

Ley contra la Violencia hacia las Mujeres ley aprobada en 1994 que aumentó los recursos federales para arrestar y enjuiciar a los hombres culpables de actos violentos contra las mujeres

Virginia and Kentucky resolutions state resolutions passed in 1798 declaring the Alien and Sedition Acts unconstitutional (p. 202)

resoluciones de Virginia y Kentucky resoluciones estatales aprobadas en 1798 que declararon inconstitucionales las Leyes de Extranjería y Sedición

Virginia Plan James Madison's proposal for a bicameral legislature with representation based upon population (p. 144)

Plan de Virginia propuesta de James Madison para legislatura bicameral con representación basada en la cantidad de habitantes

Volstead Act law enacted by Congress to enforce the Eighteenth Amendment (p. 677)

Ley Volstead ley impuesta por el Congreso para hacer cumplir la Decimoctava Enmienda

Voting Rights Act law that banned literacy tests and empowered the federal government to oversee voter registration (p. 938)

Ley de Derechos Electorales ley que prohibió las pruebas de alfabetismo y dio poder al gobierno federal de vigilar el empadronamiento de los votantes

voucher certificates or other documents that can be used as money (p. 1085)

vales certificados u otros documentos que pueden ser usados como dinero

W

Wade-Davis Bill required that a majority of prewar voters in the Confederate states swear loyalty to the Union before restoration could begin (p. 404)

Proyecto de Ley Wade-Davis proyecto de ley que requería a los votantes de los estados Confederados de antes de la guerra jurar lealtad a la Unión para que comenzara la restauración

Wagner Act New Deal law that abolished unfair labor practices, recognized the right of employees to organize labor unions, and gave workers the right to collective bargaining (p. 744)

Ley Wagner ley que abolió las prácticas laborales injustas, reconoció el derecho de los trabajadores de organizar sindicatos, y dió a los trabajadores el derecho a las negociaciones colectivas

War Hawks members of Congress who pushed for war against Great Britain beginning in 1810 (p. 215)

halcones de guerra miembros del Congreso que presionaron por una guerra contra Gran Bretaña a partir de 1810

War of 1812 war between the United States and Great Britain (p. 216)

Guerra de 1812 guerra entre Estados Unidos y Gran Bretaña

War on Poverty President Johnson's programs aimed at aiding the country's poor through education, job training, proper health care, and nutrition (p. 966)

Guerra Contra la Pobreza programas del presidente Johnson enfocados en ayudar a los pobres de la nación mediante la educación, entrenamiento laboral, servicios de salud, y nutrición adecuados

War Powers Act 1973 law passed by Congress restricting the President's war-making powers; the law requires the President to consult with Congress before committing American forces to a foreign conflict (p. 1007)

Ley de Poderes Bélicos ley aprobada por el Congreso en 1973 que restringió los poderes bélicos del presidente; la ley exige que el presidente consulte con el Congreso dentro de un período de 48 horas antes de comprometer fuerzas estadounidenses en un conflicto extranjero

War Refugee Board U.S. government agency founded in 1944 to save Eastern European Jews (p. 833)

Junta de Refugiados de Guerra agencia del gobierno de Estados Unidos fundada en 1944 para salvar a los judíos de Europa Oriental

Warren Commission committee that investigated the assassination of President Kennedy (p. 963)

Comisión Warren comité que investigó el asesinato del presidente Kennedy

"Warren Court" Supreme Court of the 1960s under Chief Justice Earl Warren, whose decisions supported civil rights (p. 971)

"Corte Warren" Corte Suprema de la década de 1960 bajo el mandato del presidente de los magistrados Earl Warren, cuyas decisiones apoyaron los derechos civiles, libertades civiles, derecho al sufragio y privacidad personal

Warsaw Pact military alliance of the Soviet Union and its satellite states (p. 852)

Pacto de Varsovia alianza militar de la Unión Soviética y sus estados satélites

Washington Naval Disarmament Conference meeting held in 1921 and 1922 where world leaders agreed to limit construction of warships (p. 669)

Conferencia de Desarme Naval de Washington reunión realizada en 1921 y 1922 durante la cual los líderes mundiales acordaron limitar la construcción de buques de guerra

Watergate political scandal involving illegal activities that ultimately led to the resignation of President Nixon in 1974 (p. 1049)

Watergate escándalo político que involucró actividades ilegales que al final condujeron a la renuncia del presidente Nixon en 1974

Weapons of Mass Destruction (WMD) nuclear, biological, and chemical weapons intended to kill or harm on a large scale (p. 1125)

armas de destrucción masiva armas nucleares, biológicas, y químicas destinadas a matar o lesionar a gran escala

welfare state government that assumes responsibility for providing for the welfare of the poor, elderly, sick, and unemployed (p. 755)

estado de bienestar gobierno que asume la responsabilidad de velar por el bienestar de los pobres, ancianos, enfermos, y desempleados

Western Front battle front between the Allies and Central Powers in western Europe during World War I (p. 621)

Frente Occidental frente de batalla entre los Aliados y los Poderes Centrales en Europa occidental durante la Primera Guerra Mundial

Whig member of the nationalist political party formed in 1832 in opposition to the Democrats (p. 257)

Whig miembro del partido político nacionalista formado en 1832 en oposición a los demócratas

Whiskey Rebellion 1794 uprising in western Pennsylvania that opposed the federal excise tax on whiskey (p. 195)

Rebelión del Whiskey levantamiento de 1794 al oeste de Pennsylvania en oposición al impuesto federal indirecto sobre el whiskey

Wilmot Proviso proposed, but rejected, 1846 bill that would have banned slavery in the territory won from Mexico in the Mexican War (pp. 312, 325)

Condición Wilmot ley propuesta pero rechazada de 1846 que habría prohibido la esclavitud en los territorios ganados a México en la Guerra México-Estadounidense

Women's Army Corps (WAC) U.S. Army group established during World War II so that women could serve in noncombat roles (p. 792)

Cuerpo Femenino del Ejército grupo del Ejército de Estados Unidos establecido durante la Segunda Guerra Mundial para que las mujeres pudieran dar servicio en papeles no combativos

women's movement movement beginning in the mid-1800s in the United States that sought greater rights and opportunities for women (p. 288)

movimiento femenino movimiento iniciado a mediados del siglo XIX en Estados Unidos que buscaba conquistar mayores derechos y oportunidades para las mujeres

Works Progress Administration (WPA) key New Deal agency that provided work relief through various public-works projects (p. 292)

Administración del Progreso de Obras agencia clave del Nuevo Trato que brindó ayuda laboral a través de varios proyectos de obras públicas

World Trade Organization (WTO) international organization formed in 1995 to encourage the expansion of world trade (p. 667)

Organización Mundial del Comercio (OMC) organización internacional formada en 1995 para estimular la expansión del comercio mundial

Wounded Knee 1890 confrontation between U.S. cavalry and Sioux that marked the end of Indian resistance (p. 503)

Wounded Knee enfrentamiento de 1890 entre la caballería de Estados Unidos y los sioux que marcó el fin de la resistencia indígena

X

XYZ Affair diplomatic controversy in 1798 in which French officials demanded bribes of American negotiators (p. 202)

Asunto XYZ controversia diplomática en 1798 en la cual oficiales franceses exigieron sobornos de los negociadores estadounidenses

Y

Yalta Conference 1945 strategy meeting between Roosevelt, Churchill, and Stalin (p. 834)

Conferencia de Yalta reunión sobre estrategia realizada en 1945 entre Roosevelt, Churchill, y Stalin

Yellow Press newspapers that used sensational headlines and exaggerated stories in order to promote readership (p. 594)

prensa amarillista periódicos que utilizaban titulares sensacionales e historias exageradas para promover su circulación

Yorktown site in Virginia where Cornwallis's army surrendered to Washington (p. 124)

Yorktown lugar en Virginia donde el ejército de Cornwallis se rindió ante Washington

Z

Zimmermann note telegram written by German Foreign Minister Zimmermann proposing an alliance between Germany and Mexico against the United States during World War I (p. 627)

telegrama de Zimmermann telegrama escrito por el ministro del exterior alemán Zimmermann en el que proponía una alianza entre Alemania y México contra Estados Unidos en la Primera Guerra Mundial

Index

Index

Index

Index

Index

Index

Index

Index

Index

Index

Index

Acknowledgments

Staff Credits

The people who make up the **United States History** team—representing design services, editorial, editorial services, education technology, manufacturing and inventory planning, market research, marketing services, planning and budgeting, product planning, production services, project office, publishing processes, and rights and permissions—are listed below. Bold type denotes core team members.

Ernie Albanese, Mary Aldridge, Diane Alimena, Leann Davis Alspaugh, Michele Angelucci, Jasjit Arneja, **Margaret Antonini,** Rosalyn Arcilla, Alan Asarch, Helene Avraham, Penny Baker, Renée Beach, Peter Brooks, Lois Brown, Kerry Buckley, Pradeep Byram, Rui Camarinha, Lisa Carrillo, Sarah Carroll, Kerry Cashman, Justin Contursi, Jason Cuoco, Harold DelMonte, **James Doris,** Laura Edgerton-Riser, Leanne Esterly, Anne Falzone, Libby Forsyth, Phillip Gagler, Doreen Galbraith, Joe Galka, Kathy Gavilanes, Julie Gecha, Allen Gold, Holly Gordon, Mary Ann Gundersen, Mary Hanisco, Rick Hickox, Karen Holtzman, **Kristan Hoskins,** Beth Hyslip, Katharine Ingram, Linda Johnson, **John Kingston,** Stephanie Krol, Courtney Lane, Mary Sue Langan, Julian Libysen, **Salena LiBritz,** Marian Manners, Grace Massey, Patrick McCarthy, John McClure, Mike McLaughlin, Rich McMahon, Kathleen Mercandetti, Art Mkrtchyan, Karyl Murray, Ken Myett, Deborah Nicholls, Xavier W. Niz, Kim Ortell, Jennifer Paley, Ray Parenteau, **Judi Pinkham,** Linda Punskovsky, Matthew J. Raycroft, Maureen Raymond , **Ryan Richards,** Bruce Rolff, **Laura Ross,** Robyn Salbo, Donna Schindler, Gerry Schrenk, Mildred Schulte, **Melissa Shustyk,** Siri Schwartzman, Ann Shea, Robert Siek, **Laurel Smith,** Lisa Smith-Ruvalcaba, Kara Stokes, Frank Tangredi, Elizabeth Torjussen, Humberto Ugarte, Ellen Welch Granter, Rachel Winter

Additional Credits

Steve Apple, Karen Beck, Meg Ceccolini, Donna DiCuffa, Lynette Haggard, Stuart Kirschenbaum, Beth Kun, Carol Maglitta, Karen Mancinelli-Paige, Caroline McDonnell, Lesley Pierson, Rachel Ross, Ted Smykal, Alfred Voto, Marc Wezdecki

Art Credits

Kerry Cashman SH12, 7, 19, 26, 28–29, 37, 38, 44, 46, 51, 60–61, 68–69, 75, 83, 92–93, 102–103, 112–113, 115, 122–123, 132–133, 142, 146–147, 152–153, 158–159, 162, 164–165, 171, 176–177, 178, 183, 186, 192–193, 204–205, 214, 226, 228–229, 235, 240–241, 248–249, 256–257, 263, 266, 270–271, 275, 278–279, 285, 294–295, 305, 316–317, 326–327, 342–343, 348–349, 356, 358–359, 368–369, 372–373, 382, 392–393, 403, 414, 418–419, 422–423, 424, 428–429, 436–437, 442–443, 451, 460–461, 474, 479, 482–483, 486–487, 491, 494, 498–499, 514, 519, 520–521, 526–527, 540–541, 549, 556–557, 558, 564–565, 572, 582–583, 590, 592–593, 602–603, 612, 618–619, 620–621, 634, 636, 642–643, 650–651, 668, 674–675, 682, 684–685, 706–707; Ellen Welch Granter 398, 402, 406, 411, 412, 413, 420, 428, 430; Hefflin Agency/Ilene Winn-Lederer 10; Kevin Jones Associates 358–359; Steve McEntee 659; Rich McMahon C3, C6, C9, C12, C14, C17, 92, 443, 598, 601, 607, 615, 620, 640, 707, 708, 709, 710, 711, 712, 713; Jen Paley, SH11, SH12, SH13, SH14, SH15, SH16, SH17, SH18, SH19, SH20, SH21, SH26, SH27, SH28, SH31, 4, 9, 13, 15, 18, 20, 21, 28, 29, 31, 34, 35, 42, 48, 50, 54, 55, 59, 60, 62, 66, 73, 80, 87, 92, 100, 105, 106, 109, 116, 121, 126, 128, 130, 132, 135, 138, 140, 144, 147, 149, 151, 156, 159, 161, 164, 165, 166, 170, 174, 180, 181, 183, 189, 193, 194, 198, 199, 204, 212, 213, 216, 217, 218, 221, 223, 224, 231, 234, 235, 237, 238, 240, 241, 242, 248, 254, 256, 257, 259, 260, 261, 262, 263, 266, 272, 274, 278, 280, 284, 286, 292, 293, 295, 296, 297, 299, 300, 303, 305, 308, 309, 310, 316, 318, 324, 325, 329, 331, 337, 340, 344, 345, 348, 350, 351, 354, 358, 361, 365, 370, 377, 380, 384, 386, 390, 392, 395, 400, 423, 428, 434, 435, 437, 440, 441, 448, 455, 458, 460, 463, 468, 476, 477, 488, 490, 496, 498, 504, 505, 508, 511, 512, 517, 518, 526, 528, 529, 532, 537, 539, 544, 545, 549, 552, 553, 559, 560, 564, 566, 570, 572, 574, 578, 580, 581, 583, 584, 586, 589, 592, 594, 599, 603, 605, 609, 610, 611, 613, 628, 629, 633, 639, 644, 645, 648, 650, 652, 653, 656, 658, 660, 661, 663, 664, 666, 668, 671, 678, 679, 680, 681, 682, 684, 691, 704, 705, 706, 710, 714–715, 751, 906, 1026, 1101, 1129, 1154–1155, 1157, 1160, 1161; XNR Productions, Inc. SH22, 5, 11, 13, 24, 26, 28, 40, 46, 53, 85, 114, 125, 129, 141, 149, 158, 160, 162, 164, 172, 176, 186, 191, 195, 200, 214, 266, 281, 287, 306–307, 328, 333, 343, 346, 356, 364, 372, 374, 376, 383, 388, 401, 403, 408, 409, 416, 428, 438, 444, 460, 470, 479, 500, 509, 533, 539, 547, 550, 564, 565, 588, 601, 611, 632, 646, 648, 650, 669, 672, 676, 684, 692, 693, 694, 695, 696, 697, 698, 699, 700, 713, 892, 1036, 1132

Photo Credits

FrontEnd: L, Library of Congress; R, head, Stockdisc/Getty Images; Body Dirk Anschutz/Getty Images; **vi:** The Granger Collection, New York; **vii:** National Archives and Records Administration; **viii:** *Haystacks on the Newburyport Marshes, 1862* (oil on canvas) by Martin Johnson Heade (1819–1904) ©Walters Art Museum, Baltimore, USA/The Bridgeman Art Library; **ix:** Library of Congress; **x:** Frederic Remington, *A Dash for the Timber,* Oil on canvas, 1889. 1961. 381, Amon Carter Museum, Fort Worth, Texas; **xi:** Inset, Judith Miller/©Dorling Kindersley/Larry & Dianna Elman; T, ©Bettmann/CORBIS; **xii:** L, Getty Images; M, Getty Images; ML, Tim Ridley ©Dorling Kindersley/collection of the Louisiana State Museum, Gift of the New Orleans Jazz Club; R, © Bettmann/CORBIS; **xiii:** ©A724/GAMMA; **xiv:** L, ©Charles Gatewood/The Image Works; M, Prentice Hall; R, Time Life Pictures/Getty Images; **xv:** L, ©Peter Turnley/CORBIS; R, ©Reuters/CORBIS; **xvi:** John Dominis/Time Life Pictures/Getty Images; **xviii:** The New York Public Library/Art Resource, NY; **xix:** Photofest; **xxxii:** L, Library of Congress; R, head: Stockdisc/Getty Images; Body: Dirk Anschutz/Getty Images.

SH1: ©Darius Ramazani/zefa/CORBIS; **SH2:** Jose Luis Pelaez, Inc./CORBIS; **SH6:** Tom Stewart/CORBIS; **SH12:** Inset, Fox Photos/Getty Images; **SH19:** ©Charles Gupton/CORBIS; **SH23:** ©Bettmann/CORBIS; **SH24:** The Granger Collection/New York; **SH26** Library of Congress; **SH30:** ©Dynamic Graphics Group/IT Stock Free/ Alamy; **SH32:** Background, The Art Archive/National Archives Washington D.C.; BL, ©Bettmann/CORBIS; BR, ©Bettmann/CORBIS; ML, The Granger Collection, New York; MR, ©Bettmann/CORBIS; TL, ©Reuters/CORBIS; TM, The Granger Collection, New York; TR, The Granger Collection, New York; **01:** SuperStock, Inc.; **02–03:** The Granger Collection, New York; **03:** B, ©Richard A. Cooke/CORBIS; M, Peabody Essex Museum, Salem, Massachusetts, USA/The Bridgeman Art Library International; T, African, Nigeria, Edo peoples, court of Benin, Saltcellar: Portuguese Figure, 15th–16th century, Ivory, H. 7–1/8 in. (18.1 cm), The Metropolitan Museum of Art, Louis V., Bell and Rogers Funds, 1972. (1972.63ab) Photograph by Stan Reis. Photograph ©1984 The Metropolitan Museum of Art; **04:** Smithsonian American Art Museum, Washington, D.C./Art Resource, NY; **07:** BR, David Muench/CORBIS; L, George H.H. Huey/CORBIS; TR, Ira Block/National Geographic Image Collection; **09:** The Art Archive/British Museum/Eileen Tweedy; **11(2):** The Granger Collection, New York; **12:** akg-images; **14:** The Granger Collection, New York; **15:** HIP/Art Resource, NY; **17:** B, Nik Wheeler/CORBIS; Background, Getty Images; TL, photocuisine/CORBIS; TR, Getty Images; **19:** B, ©North Wind Picture Archives; T, Werner Forman/Art Resource, NY; **20:** ©Bettmann/CORBIS; **22:** The Granger Collection, New York; **23:** The Art Archive/Army Museum Madrid/Dagli Orti; **25:** BL, Courtesy of the Bancroft Library, University of California, Berkeley; BR, Chas Howson ©The British Museum/©Dorling Kindersley; MR, SSPL/The Image Works; TL, The Granger Collection, New York; TR, The Granger Collection, New York; **27:** B, The Granger Collection, New York; T, Sherwin Crasto/Reuters/CORBIS; **28:** L, David Muench/CORBIS; R, HIP/Art Resource, NY; **29:** L, ©Underwood & Underwood/CORBIS; R, The Granger Collection, New York; **30:** B, Chas Howson ©The British Museum/©Dorling Kindersley; T, Antiquarian Images; **32–33:** The Granger Collection, New York; **33:** T, ©Bettmann/CORBIS; B, Ashmolean Museum, University of Oxford; M, Courtesy of the Pilgrim Society, Plymouth, Massachusetts; **34:** Background, The Granger Collection, New York; Inset, ©Bettmann/CORBIS; **35:** MR, akg-images/Gilles Mermet; **37:** ©North Wind Picture Archives; **38:** Background, inset, & M, Mission San Luis, Florida Division of Historical Resources; TR, Courtesy of the Florida Museum of Natural History Historical Archaeology Collections; **39:** AP/Wide World Photos/Jeff Geissler; **40:** L, ©Bettmann/CORBIS; R, Tom McHugh/Photo Researchers, Inc.; **41:** Erich Lessing/Art Resource, NY; **42:** Wisconsin Historical Society #2784; **43:** Mary Evans Picture Library; **44:** ©Bettmann/CORBIS; **45:** ©Bettmann/CORBIS; **46:** BL, ©Jeremy Horner/CORBIS; Inset, BR, ©North Wind Picture Archives/Alamy; Inset, TR, ©MPI/Getty Images; ML, & TL, Courtesy of APVA Preservation Virginia; **47:** Background, ©MPI/Getty Images; R, *Captain John Smith, 1st Governor of Virginia, c.1616* (oil on canvas), English School, (17th century) Private Collection/The Bridgeman Art Library; **48:** The Granger Collection, New York; **50:** The Granger Collection, New York; **51:** ©Kevin Fleming/CORBIS; **52:** L, ©North Wind Picture Archives; R, ©North Wind Picture Archives; **53:** ©North Wind Picture Archives; **55:** The Granger Collection, New York; **57:** Library of Congress; **58:** B, Giraudon/Art Resource, NY; Inset, Collection of the New York Historical Society; MR, lower, ©Private Collection/©John Noott Galleries, Broadway, Worcestershire, UK/The Bridgeman Art Library; MR, upper Hulton Archive/Getty Images; TR, The New York Public Library/Art Resource, NY; **60:** *Captain John Smith, 1st Governor of Virginia, c.1616* (oil on canvas), English School, (17th century) Private Collection/The Bridgeman Art Library; **62:** L, ©North Wind Picture Archives; R, AP/Wide World Photos/Jeff Geissler; **63:** ©Bettmann/CORBIS; **64–65:** Collection of the New York Historical Society; **65:** B,M, & T, The Granger Collection, New York; **66:** The Granger Collection, New York; **68:** Louie Psihoyos/ CORBIS; **69:** B, Wilberforce House Museum, Hull City Council, UK/Dorling Kindersley; BL, Set of anklets, from West Africa (iron), African, (19th century), Private Collection, ©Michael Graham-Stewart/The Bridgeman Art Library; T, Royal Albert Memorial Museum, Exeter, Devon, UK/The Bridgeman Art Library; **70:** The Granger Collection, New York; **71:** B, The Granger Collection, New York; T, Title page and frontispiece to "Poems on Various Subjects, Religious and Moral" by Phillis Wheatley (1753–1784) published in London, 1773 (engraving), English School, (18th century) ©Massachusetts Historical Society, Boston, MA, USA, Bridgeman Art Library; **72:** L, Saint James United Methodist Church; R, The Granger Collection, New York; **73:** ©Michael Nicholson/CORBIS; **75:** BL, Martin Cameron ©Dorling Kindersley; BR, Philip Dowell ©Dorling Kindersley; M, Alex Wilson ©Dorling Kindersley, Courtesy of the Charlestown Shipwreck and Heritage Centre, Cornwall; **76:** T, Courtesy of S.J. Shrubsole, New York; B, The Granger Collection, New York; **78:** B, Rare Books Division, The New York Public Library, Astor, Lenox and Tilden Foundations; T, The Granger Collection, New York; **79:** The Granger Collection, New York; **80:** L, The Granger Collection, New York; R, Courtesy of S.J. Shrubsole, New York; **81:** The Granger Collection, New York; **82:** B, The Granger Collection, New York; M lower, From the Collections of The New Jersey Historical Society, Newark, New Jersey; M upper, The Granger Collection, New York; T, ©North Wind Picture Archives/North Wind Picture Archive; **84:** B, The Granger Collection, New York; T, The Granger Collection, New York; **85:** L, "Rogers Rangers Toward Ticonderoga" ©2006 John Buxton, licensed by The Greenwich Workshop, Inc.; R, ©CORBIS; **86:** The Granger Collection, New York; **87:** Paramount Press Inc. & Collection of the Westmorland Foundation, Gift of the Colonies Foundation; **89:** B, The Granger Collection, New York; T, The Philadelphia Museum of Art/Art Resource,NY; **90:** Louie Psihoyos/CORBIS; **91:** The Granger Collection, New York; **92:** B & T, The Granger Collection, New York; **95:** SuperStock, Inc; **96–97:** Courtesy of The American Revolution Center at Valley Forge; **97:** B, Guilford Courthouse National Military Park; M, Courtesy of the National Park Service, Museum Management Program and Morristown National Historical Park; T, Colonial Williamsburg Foundation; **98:** TL, Library of Congress; TR, Allan Ramsay (1713–1784),

Scottish, PG 216 *George III* (1738–1820), 18th century. Oil on canvas, 249.7 x 163 cm. Scottish National Portrait Gallery, Edinburgh, Scotland. The Bridgeman Art Library; **100:** ML & BL, ©Bettmann/ CORBIS; MR, ©North Wind Picture Archives; T, Library of Congress; TL & BR, ©North Wind Picture Archives; TR, Courtesy of The Bostonian Society Old State House; **101:** ©Christie's Images, Inc. 2004; **102:** The Granger Collection, New York; **103:** Collection of the New York Historical Society (#INV.6195.34); Library of Congress; **104:** B, ©Bettmann/CORBIS; T, Dumbarton House/The National Society of The Colonial Dames of America; **105:** The Granger Collection, New York; **106:** BL, The Granger Collection, New York; BR, Hulton Archive/Getty Images; MR lower, Hulton Archive/Getty Images; MR upper, ©North Wind Picture Archives/ North Wind Picture Archives; T, MPI/Getty Images; **107:** B, ©Bettmann/CORBIS; TL, Library of Congress; TR, ©North Wind Picture Archives/North Wind Picture Archives; **108:** ©Bettmann/ CORBIS; **109:** B, *The Battle of Lexington, April 19th 1775,* from Connecticut Historical Collections, by John Warner Barber, engraved by A. Doolittle, 1832 (engraving), American School, (19th century) Private Collection, Bridgeman Art Library; T, Photograph courtesy of the Concord Museum, Concord, MA and the archives of the Lexington Historical Society, Photo by Chip Fanelli; **110:** ©North Wind Picture Archives/North Wind Picture Archives; **111:** BR, Christie's Images; L, MPI/Getty Images; TR, The Granger Collection, New York; **112:** Library of Congress; **116:** The Art Archive; **117:** L, Courtesy of The Valley Forge Historical Society; R, Courtesy of the National Park Service, Museum Management Program and Morristown National Historical Park; Canteen, 18th Century carried by Isaac Whitehead during the Revolutionary War, MORR 2022; **118:** Getty Images, Inc., Hulton Archive Photos; **119:** *Battle of Princeton on 3rd January 1777* (oil on canvas) by William Mercer, (c.1773–c.1850) ©Atwater Kent Museum of Philadelphia/Courtesy of the Historical Society of Pennsylvania Collection/ Atwater Kent Museum of Philadelphia/The Bridgeman Art Library; **120:** The Granger Collection, New York; **122:** Courtesy National Park Service, Museum Management Program and The George C. Neumann Collection, Valley Forge National Historical Park. VAFO 1788; **123:** The Granger Collection, New York; **124:** Art Resource, N.Y.; **125:** Background, Bibliotheque Nationale, Paris, France/Lauros/Giraudon/The Bridgeman Art Library; TM, Christine Pemberton/ Omni-Photo Communications, Inc.; BR, MPI/Getty Images; BL, The Granger Collection, New York; **127:** The Granger Collection, New York; **128:** L, Allan Ramsay (1713–1784), Scottish, PG 216, *George III* (1738– 1820), 18th century. Oil on canvas, 249.7 x 163 cm. Scottish National Portrait Gallery, Edinburgh, Scotland, The Bridgeman Art Library; R, Dumbarton House/The National Society of The Colonial Dames of America; **130:** Courtesy of the National Park Service, Museum Management Program and The George C. Neumann Collection, Valley Forge National Historical Park; **132–133:** John H. Froelich, "The Adoption of the Constitution," The State Museum of Pennsylvania, Pennsylvania Historical and Museum Commission, (detail); **133:** Collection of The New York Historical Society; M, National Museum of American History, Smithsonian Institution; T, National Park Service; **134:** White House Collection, ©White House Historical Association; **135:** *Election Day in Philadelphia, 1764* (engraving), American School, (18th century) Private Collection, Peter Newark American Pictures/Bridgeman Art Library; **136:** Photo Courtesy of Stephen & Carol Huber, Old Saybrook, CT; **137:** BR, National Museum of American History, Smithsonian Institution; B, Ohio University Mahn Center for Archives and Special Collections; BL, Ohio University Mahn Center for Archives and Special Collections; **138:** Jim Wark/Airphoto; **139:** Clements Library, University of Michigan; **141:** Smithsonian Institution/Art Resource, NY; **142:** B, National Park Service; T, The Granger Collection, New York; **143:** Corel Professional Photos CD-ROM™; **144–145:** Library of Congress; **147:** R, ©Archivo Iconografico, S.A./CORBIS; L, ©Bettmann/CORBIS; **149:** B, The Granger Collection, New York; T, The Granger Collection, New York; **150:** L, ©Bettmann/ CORBIS; R, National Archives and Records Administration; **152:** L, The Art Archive/Chateau de Blerancourt/Dagli Orti; M, ©Bettmann/CORBIS; R, *John Jay* (1745–1829) *1786* (oil on canvas), Wright of Derby, Joseph (1734–1797) ©New York Historical Society, New York, USA/ Bridgeman Art Library; **153:** The Granger Collection, New York; **154:** B, Hulton Archive/Getty Images; T, Getty Images; **157:** The Pierpont Morgan Library/Art Resource, NY; **158:** Smithsonian Institution/Art Resource, NY; **159:** Brooklyn Museum of Art/CORBIS; **160:** T, ©Bettmann/CORBIS; B, John H. Froelich, "The Adoption of the Constitution," The State Museum of Pennsylvania, Pennsylvania Historical and Museum Commission, (detail); **162:** *The Signing of the Constitution of the United States in 1787,* 1940, Howard Chandler Christy (1873–1952) Hall of Representatives, Washington, D.C., USA/Bridgeman Art Library; **163:** The Art Archive/ National Archives Washington, D.C.; **164:** L, ©Swim Ink 2, LLC/CORBIS; R, ©Royalty-Free/ CORBIS; **166:** Courtesy New York State Historical Association; **169:** B, ©Bettmann/CORBIS; Inset, R, The Granger Collection, New York; T, The Granger Collection, New York; **180:** B, © Royalty-Free/CORBIS; T, ©Michael Kelley/Getty Images; **184:** ©Bettmann/CORBIS; **190–191:** National Gallery of Art, Washington. Gift of Edgar Williams & Bernice Chrysler Garbisch **191:** B, The Granger Collection, New York; M, The Granger Collection, New York; T, Courtesy of J. Harold CobbCollection; **192:** L, The Granger Collection, New York; R, Courtesy of J. Harold Cobb Collection; **193:** The Granger Collection, New York; **194:** B, Federal Reserve Bank of Richmond; T, Lee Snider/Photo Images/CORBIS; **195:** The Granger Collection, New York; **196** B, The Granger Collection, New York; T, Private Collection, Giraudon/The Bridgeman Art Library; **196:** TL, The Granger Collection, New York; **198:** L, ; R, Buffalo and Erie County Historical Society; **199:** B, The Granger Collection, New York; T, Kevin Fleming/CORBIS; **200:** Background, Giraudon/Art Resource, NY; Inset, Courtesy of Archiving Early America; **201:** B, *Taking of the Tuileries, Court of the Carrousel, 10th August 1792* (oil on canvas), Duplessi-Bertaux, Jean (1747–1819)/

Chateau de Versailles, France,/The Bridgeman Art Library; M, Library Company of Philadelphia; T, ©American Antiquarian Society; **202:** The Granger Collection, New York; **204:** B, Brooklyn Museum of Art/CORBIS; T, Library of Congress; **205:** L, The Granger Collection, New York; R, The Granger Collection, New York; **207:** B, Getty Images; T, Stapleton Collection/CORBIS; **209:** B, The Granger Collection, New York; T, Monticello/Thomas Jefferson Memorial Foundation, Inc.; **210:** The Granger Collection, New York; **211:** Leonard de Selva/CORBIS; **212:** #1, ©Royal Geographical Society, London, UK/The Bridgeman Art Library; #2, ©Royal Geographical Society, London, UK/The Bridgeman Art Library; #3, ©National Museum of American History, Smithsonian Institution; #4, From the Archives of the Ernst Mayr Library of the Museum of Comparative Zoology, Harvard University; #6, ©North Wind/North Wind Picture Archive; MR, Steve Hurst @ USDA-NRCS PLANTS Database; TR, ©Royalty-Free/CORBIS; **212–213:** #5, ©North Wind Picture Archives/ Alamy; **213:** #7, ©North Wind/North Wind Picture Archive; #8, Smithsonian American Art Museum, Washington, D.C./Art Resource, NY; #9, Photo by Siri Schwartzman, ©Prentice Hall; **214:** From the Collection of Mac G. and Janelle C. Morris; **215:** L, Stapleton Collection/CORBIS; R, ©CORBIS; **216:** The Granger Collection, New York; **217:** ©National Museum of American History, Smithsonian Institution, 2004; **218:** The Granger Collection, New York; **220:** L, Courtesy of the J. Harold Cobb Collection; R, The Granger Collection, New York; **221:** Composite photograph of the almost 200-year-old Star-Spangled Banner, the flag that inspired the national anthem. ©National Museum of American History, Smithsonian Institution, 2004; **222:** Brooklyn Museum of Art/CORBIS; **224:** Background, The Art Archive/National Archives Washington, D.C.; BL, ©Bettmann/CORBIS; BR, ©Bettmann/CORBIS; ML, The Granger Collection, New York; MR, ©Bettmann/CORBIS; TL, ©Reuters/CORBIS; TM, The Granger Collection, New York; TR, The Granger Collection, New York; **225:** The Granger Collection, New York; **226–227:** ©Bettmann/CORBIS; **227:** B, ©Bettmann/CORBIS; M, The Granger Collection, New York; T, ©National Museum of American History, Smithsonian Institution; **228:** TL, ©North Wind Picture Archives; TR, American Textile History Museum; **229:** B, ©Bettmann/CORBIS; T, ©SSPL/The Image Works; **230:** Robertstock; **231:** ©Bettmann/CORBIS; **232:** ©Bettmann/CORBIS; **233:** B, Hulton Archive/Getty Images, Inc.; Inset, Library of Congress; **234:** ©National Museum of American History, Smithsonian Institution; **235:** Inset, The Granger Collection, New York; T, Tzaud photo, photographersdirect.com; **237:** Background, ©Bettmann/ CORBIS; L, The Granger Collection, New York; R, ©Bettmann/CORBIS; **239:** The Granger Collection, New York; **240:** T, Old Slave Mart Museum; **240–241:** The Warner Collection of Gulf States Paper Corporation, Tuscaloosa, Alabama; **241:** MR, Richard Cummins/CORBIS; T, Owaki/Kulla/CORBIS; **242:** L, ©National Museum of American History, Smithsonian Institution; R, ©Bettmann/CORBIS; **245:** B, The Granger Collection, New York; M, *Haystacks on the Newburyport Marshes, 1862* (oil on canvas) by Martin Johnson Heade (1819–1904) © Walters Art Museum, Baltimore, USA/The Bridgeman Art Library; T, The Granger Collection, New York; **248:** B, ©Bob Daemmrich/The Image Works; MR, The Granger Collection, New York; **249:** Bridgeman Art Library/©New York Historical Society, New York, USA; L, Courtesy of the Library of Congress; TR, Bridgeman Art Library/©New York Historical Society, New York, USA; **250:** *Portrait of Andrew Jackson (1767–1845) 7th President of the United States, 1858* (oil on canvas), Sully, Thomas (1783–1872) Private Collection, ©Christie's Images/The Bridgeman Art Library; **251:** The Granger Collection, New York; **252:** L, Courtesy of the National Museum of the American Indian, Smithsonian Institution (17/9690), Photo by David Heald; **252–253:** The Granger Collection, New York; **255:** ©Photo by Seny Norasingh/Courtesy of Clemson University; **257:** The Granger Collection, New York; **258:** L, The Granger Collection, New York; R, The Granger Collection, New York; **259:** The Granger Collection, New York; **260:** The Granger Collection, New York; **261:** Bridgeman Art Library/©New York Historical Society, New York, USA; **262:** ©North Wind Picture Archives; **263:** Picture History; **264–265:** TR, The Granger Collection, New York; **265:** B, ©Judith Miller/Dorling Kindersley/Wallis and Wallis; M, Architect of the Capitol; T, Ames Historical Society; **266:** ©Bettmann/CORBIS; **267:** The Granger Collection, New York; T, Getty Images; **268:** B, The Granger Collection, New York; **269:** The Granger Collection, New York; **270:** Hulton Archive/Getty Images; **271:** Background, Courtesy of the Massachusetts Historical Society; Inset, Peabody Essex Museum, Salem, Massachusetts, USA/ Bridgeman Art Library; **272:** Getty Images; **273:** B, The Granger Collection, New York; T, Lebrecht Music & Arts Photo Library; **274:** Library of Congress; **275:** B, The Granger Collection, New York; T, Ames Historical Society; **276:** Library of Congress; **277:** ©Bettmann/CORBIS; **278:** The Granger Collection, New York; **279:** The Granger Collection, New York; **280:** ©CORBIS; **281:** B, The Historic New Orleans Collection, Museum/Research Center, Acc. No. 1960.46; T, Virginia Historical Society, Richmond, Virginia; **282:** L, Courtesy of the National Park Service, Museum Management Program and Frederick Douglass National Historic Site, FRDO 3124; *William Lloyd Garrison* (Black and white engraving by J. Sartain); R, ©Bettmann/CORBIS; **283:** The Granger Collection, New York; **284:** L, The Granger Collection, New York; R, ©Bettmann/CORBIS; **286:** Library of Congress; **287:** ©Bettmann/CORBIS; **288:** (2), The Granger Collection, New York; **289:** L, ©CORBIS; BM, Mary Evans Picture Library; R, National Portrait Gallery, Smithsonian Institution/Art Resource, New York; TM, Courtesy of the Elizabeth Cady Stanton Trust; **290:** Library of Congress; **291:** B, Architect of the Capitol; T, Dept. of Rare Books & Special Collections, Rush Rhees Library of the University of Rochester; **292:** The Granger Collection, New York; **293:** Library of Congress; **294:** The Granger Collection, New York; **296–297:** Scotts Bluff National Monument; **297:** B, Courtesy of The Oakland Museum of California; M, Chicago Historical Society; T, Courtesy of the Texas Memorial Museum; **298:** Hulton Archive/Getty Images, Inc.; **299:** Richard Cummins/CORBIS; **300:** The Granger Collection, New York; **301:** *Trapper Crossing the Mountains,* William T.

Acknowledgments

Ranney, The Anschutz Collection; **302:** Travelsite/Global/The Picture Desk; **303:** BL, ©North Wind Picture Archives/Nancy Carter/North Wind Picture Archives; BR, James L. Amos/National Geographic Society; T, Mary Evans Picture Library 2005; **304:** ©Bettmann/CORBIS; **305:** L, ©Bettmann/CORBIS; R, Courtesy of the Texas Memorial Museum; **306:** ©Bettmann/CORBIS; **307:** L, The Granger Collection, New York; R, ©Bettmann/CORBIS; **310:** B, Chicago Historical Society; T, Hulton Archive/Getty Images, Inc.; **311:** L, California State Library; R, Courtesy of The Oakland Museum of California; **313:** B, Seaver Center for Western History Research, Natural History Museum of Los Angeles County, Museum Collection Number 277; M, Courtesy of the California History Room, California State Library, Sacramento, California; T, ©Bettmann/CORBIS; **314:** BL, The Art Archive/E.B. Crocker Art Gallery Sacramento/Laurie Platt Winfrey; BR, SuperStock, Inc./SuperStock; ML, Private Collection/Peter Newark American Pictures/The Bridgeman Art Library; TL, Pascal Goetgheluck/Photo Researchers, Inc.; TR, Private Collection/Peter Newark Western Americana/The Bridgeman Art Library; **315:** Courtesy of the Vallejo Naval and Historical Museum; **316:** L, *Trapper Crossing the Mountains*, William T. Ranney, The Anschutz Collection; R, Courtesy of the Texas Memorial Museum; **317:** Hulton Archive/Getty Images, Inc.; **318:** ©Bettmann/CORBIS; **320:** Background, The Art Archive/ National Archives Washington, D.C.; BL, ©Bettmann/CORBIS; BR, ©Bettmann/CORBIS; ML, The Granger Collection, New York; MR, ©Bettmann/CORBIS; TL, ©Reuters/CORBIS; TM, The Granger Collection, New York; TR, The Granger Collection, New York; **321:** Library of Congress; **322–323:** Courtesy of the Abraham Lincoln Presidential Library and Museum; **323:** B, The Granger Collection, New York; M, The Granger Collection, New York; T, Courtesy of The Charleston Museum, Charleston, South Carolina; **324:** The Granger Collection, New York; **325:** B, Brown Brothers; T, The Granger Collection, New York; **326:** The Granger Collection, New York; **327:** The Granger Collection, New York; **328:** The Granger Collection, New York; **329:** Courtesy of the California History Room, California State Library, Sacramento, California; **330:** B, The Granger Collection, New York; T, Wrangler/Shutterstock, Inc.; **331:** L, The Granger Collection, New York; R, Courtesy of The Charleston Museum, Charleston, South Carolina; **332:** BL, The Granger Collection, New York; BR, ©North Wind Picture Archives; Lower M, The Art Archive/Culver Pictures; MR, The Granger Collection, New York; T, Library of Congress; TR, Collection of the Louisiana State Museum; Upper M, ©SuperStock, Inc./SuperStock; **336:** The Granger Collection, New York; **337:** The Granger Collection, New York; **338:** B, The Granger Collection, New York; T, The Granger Collection, New York; **339:** The Granger Collection, New York; **341:** The Granger Collection, New York; **342:** The Granger Collection, New York; **343:** L, The Granger Collection, New York; R, Library of Congress; **344:** (3), The Granger Collection, New York; **346:** The Granger Collection, New York; **347:** (4), The Granger Collection, New York; **348:** TL, The Granger Collection, New York; TR, Cornell University, Carl A. Kroch Library; **348–349:** Library of Congress; **349:** BR, Library of Congress; TR, Cornell University, Carl A. Kroch Library; **351:** Collection of The New York Historical Society; **352:** L, ©Bettmann/CORBIS; R, ©CORBIS; **353:** TL, United States Dept. of the Interior; TR, The Granger Collection, New York; **354:** Courtesy of the California History Room, California State Library, Sacramento, California; **355:** The Granger Collection, New York; **356:** The Granger Collection, New York; **357:** The Granger Collection, New York; **358–359:** Painting by Don Troiani, historicalartprints.com; **359:** B, ©CORBIS; M, Dave King/Dorling Kindersley, ©US Army Military History Institute; T, Courtesy of the National Park Service, Museum Management Program and Gettysburg National Military Park, Blood-stained diary of Alfred S. Rowe, Company C, 6th Maryland, GETT 7304; **360:** Library of Congress; **361:** L, Library of Congress; R: ©Bettmann/CORBIS; **363:** B, From the collection of the Behringer-Crawford Museum, Covington, KY; TM, Prentice Hall; BM, Military History/Smithsonian Institution; MR, Medford Historical Society Collection/ CORBIS; TL, Civil War Minie Ball Scottsville Museum; Scottsville, VA; TR, ARPL/HIP/The Image Works; **364:** Library of Congress; **366:** Dave King/Dorling Kindersley ©US Army Military History Institute; **367:** L, Library of Congress; R, ©Bettmann/CORBIS; **368–369:** ©Bettmann/CORBIS; **370:** Background, © CORBIS; L, ©CORBIS; R, Courtesy of the Chicago Historical Society; **371:** L, Library of Congress; M, Angus Oborn ©Rough Guides; R, ©Columbia TriStar/Photofest; **372:** B, Library of Congress; **373:** L, The Granger Collection, New York; R, National Museum of American History, Smithsonian Institution; **374:** BL, ©Bettmann/CORBIS; BR, The Granger Collection, New York; TL, Ohio Historical Society; **375:** BL, Library of Congress; TR, The British Museum/ Topham-HIP/The Image Works; **376:** Library of Congress; **377:** BL, Courtesy of the National Park Service, Museum Management Program and Gettysburg National Military Park, "Union Playing Cards" used by Assistant Surgeon Platte Brush, 104th Pennsylvania Volunteer Infantry, GETT 26941, http://www.cr.nps.gov/museum/exhibits/gettex/frame%20pages/frame.html; BR, Courtesy of the National Park Service, Museum Management Program and Gettysburg National Military Park, Blood-stained diary of Alfred S. Rowe, Company C, 6th Maryland, GETT 7304, http://www.cr.nps.gov/musum/exhibits/gettex/frame%20pages/frame.html; TL, Library of Congress; TR, Courtesy of the National Park Service, Museum Management Program and Gettysburg National Military Park, Tin Cup, GETT 3471,http://www.cr.nps.gov/museum/exhibits/gettex/frame%20pages/frame.html; **378:** Library of Congress; **379:** B, ©CORBIS; BR, Culver Pictures, Inc.; L, Gettysburg National Military Park; MR, Culver Pictures, Inc.; TR, ©Bettmann/CORBIS; **380:** L, B, Courtesy of the National Park Service, Museum Management Program and Gettysburg National Military Park, Drum carried by John Unger, Company B, 40th Regiment New York, Veteran Volunteer Infantry Mozart Regiment, December 20, 1863, GETT 32847 http://www.cr.nps.gov/museum/exhibits/gettex/frame%20pages/frame.html; **382:** MPI/Getty Images; **383:** The Granger Collection, New York; **384:** BL, Museum of the Confederacy; BR, ©CORBIS; T, www.sonofthesouth.net; **385:** L, Library of Congress; R, Getty Images ; **386:** Background, Culver Pictures, Inc.; Inset, ©CORBIS; **388:** BL, www.sonofthe-south.net; M, Collection of State Historical Museum/Mississippi Department of Archives and History; TR, Sharon Kay Humble; **388–389:** Getty Images; **389:** BR, Greenwich Workshop, Inc.;

M, The Museum of the Confederacy, Richmond, Virginia.; TL, Old Court House Museum, Vicksburg, MS; TR, L. M. Strayer Collection; **390:** Snark/Art Resource, NY; **391:** BR, ©CORBIS; BL, ©Hulton-Deutsch Collection/CORBIS; T, Smithsonian American Art Museum, Washington, D.C./Art Resource, NY; **392:** L, ©CORBIS; M, Library of Congress; **392–393:** M, ©CORBIS; **393:** R, ©Bettmann/CORBIS; **395:** ©Paul A. Souders/CORBIS; **396:** R, Library of Congress; **397:** L, ©CORBIS; R, Smithsonian American Art Museum, Washington, D.C./Art Resource, NY; **398:** B, ©CORBIS; T, Library of Congress; **399:** The New York Public Library/Art Resource, NY; **400–401:** ©Bettmann/CORBIS; **401:** B, Library of Congress; M, Antique Textile Resource; T, The Granger Collection, New York; **402:** The Granger Collection, New York; **403:** Library of Congress; **404:** Library of Congress; **405:** Getty Images; **406:** Library of Congress; **407:** ©CORBIS; **408:** B, The Granger Collection, New York; ML, istockphoto.com; MR, Corel Professional Photos CD-ROM™; T, Corel Professional Photos CD-ROM™; **410:** B, Library of Congress; T, The Granger Collection, New York; T, The Granger Collection, New York; **411:** B, The Granger Collection, New York; **412:** AP/Wide World Photos; **412–413:** Brown Brothers; **414:** BL, The Granger Collection, New York; BR, The McGuffy Museum; MR lower, LSU Shreveport Archives-Noel Memorial Library; MR upper, National Archives; T, Background, Hulton Archive/Getty Images; TR, Hulton Archive/Getty Images; **416:** Hargrett Rare Book and Manuscript Library/The University of Georgia Libraries; **417:** Brown Brothers; **418:** B, Collection of State Historical Museum/Mississippi Department of Archives and History; T, Picture History; **419:** Library of Congress; **420:** L, Library of Congress; R, National Archives; **420–421:** Library of Congress; **421:** R, The Granger Collection, New York; **422:** The Amistad Center for Art & Culture, Simpson Collection; **423:** B, David Pollack/CORBIS; T, ©CORBIS; **425:** Library of Congress; **426:** The Granger Collection, New York; **428:** ©CORBIS; **429:** The Granger Collection, New York; **430:** B, Library of Congress; T, ©Bettmann/CORBIS; **431:** B, ©CORBIS; T, Picture History; **432:** Background, The Art Archive/National Archives Washington, D.C.; BL, ©Bettmann/CORBIS; BR, ©Bettmann/CORBIS; ML, The Granger Collection, New York; MR, ©Bettmann/CORBIS; TL, ©Reuters/CORBIS; TM, The Granger Collection, New York; TR, The Granger Collection, New York; **433:** Getty Images; **434–435:** Museum of the City of New York/Getty Images; **435:** B, Museum of the City of New York; M, ©Bettmann/CORBIS; T, Collection of Ralph Brunke; **436:** L, The Granger Collection, New York; R, ©Bettmann/CORBIS; **437:** Brown Brothers; **438:** L, ©Bettmann/CORBIS; R, ©Bettmann/CORBIS; **439:** BL, ©Bettmann/CORBIS; BM, ©Bettmann/CORBIS; BR, no credit necessary; TR, Brown Brothers; **440:** Rand McNally and Company, "Burlington Route," 1892, Map Collections: 1544–1999, Library of Congress; **441:** BL, Library of Congress; BR, ©CORBIS; M, ©CORBIS; TR, Library of Congress; **442:** ©Bettmann/CORBIS; **443:** L, The Granger Collection, New York; R, American Textile History Museum, Lowell, Massachusetts; **444:** Background, ©Bettmann/CORBIS; L, ©Mary Evans Picture Library/The Image Works; R, ©Bettmann/CORBIS; **445:** ©Bettmann/CORBIS; **446:** ©CORBIS; TL, ASSOCIATED PRESS; TR, Underwood & Underwood/CORBIS; **447:** B, Getty Images; T, Getty Images; **449:** BL, ©Bettmann/CORBIS; BR, ©Bettmann/CORBIS; T, Carnegie Autograph Collection, Manuscripts and Archives Division, The New York Public Library, Astor, Lenox and Tilden Foundations; **450:** Brown Brothers; **451:** Hulton Archive/Getty Images; **452:** T, © Royalty-Free/Corbis; B, The Granger Collection, New York; **453:** ; **455:** Special Collections & Archives, Georgia State University Library; **456:** BL, Getty Images; BR, ©CORBIS; M, Library of Congress; T, Mary Evans Picture Library/The Image Works; **458:** Culver Pictures, Inc.; **459:** ©CORBIS; **460:** Brown Brothers; **461:** Provided courtesy HarpWeek, LLC; **462–463:** Library of Congress; **463:** B, ©CORBIS; M, ©Bettmann/CORBIS; T, Private Collection, Peter Newark American Pictures/Bridgeman Art Library; **464:** ©Bettmann/CORBIS; **465:** The Jewish Museum, NY/Art Resource, NY; **466:** Background, ©Bettmann/CORBIS; Inset, Private Collection, Peter Newark American Pictures/Bridgeman Art Library; **467:** The Granger Collection, New York; **468:** The New York Public Library/Art Resource, NY; **469:** B, The New York Public Library/Art Resource, NY; T, Brown Brothers; **470:** B, ©Topham/HIP/The Image Works; Inset, L, ©Topham/The Image Works; **470–471:** T, Photo by Lewis W. Hine/Museum of the City of New York/Getty Images; **471:** Background, B, ©Prentice Hall; Background, T, Courtesy of the National Park Service, Statue of Liberty National Monument; BR, ©Prentice Hall; BR (locket), Photo by Siri Schwartzman ©Prentice Hall; M, ©Prentice Hall; TL, ©Bettmann/CORBIS; TM, Photo by Siri Schwartzman ©Prentice Hall; TR, ©Bettmann/CORBIS; **472:** Brown Brothers; **474:** B, ©Bettmann/CORBIS; TL, Brown Brothers; **474–475:** TM, ©Bettmann/CORBIS; **475:** TR, © Bettmann/CORBIS; **477:** B, Library of Congress; T, ©Bettmann/CORBIS; **478:** ©Bettmann/ CORBIS; **479:** B, Brown Brothers; M, The Granger Collection, New York; T, ©Bettmann/CORBIS; **480:** B, ©Bettmann/CORBIS; T, ©CORBIS; **481:** B, ©Schenectady Museum Hall of Electrical History Foundation/CORBIS; T, Image courtesy of The Advertising Archives; **482:** Background, Museum of the City of New York/Byron Collection/Getty Images; Border, ©Cynthia Hart Designer/CORBIS; Inset, B, Prentice Hall; Inset, MR, ©Swim Ink 2, LLC/CORBIS; Inset, TR, Courtesy Sears Archives; **483:** ©CORBIS; **484:** B, Photo by Wallace G. Levison/Time Life Pictures/Getty Images; T, ©CORBIS; **485:** Library of Congress; **486:** Brown Brothers; **487:** The Granger Collection, New York; **488:** B, ©Bettmann/CORBIS; T, Getty Images; **489:** Chermayeff & Geismar; **490–491:** From the collections of Henry Ford Museum & Greenfield Village; **491:** B, Union Pacific Museum; M, Geoff Brightling/©Dorling Kindersley; T, Courtesy of The National Museum of the American Indian/Smithsonian Institution; **492:** University of South Alabama Archives; **493:** Getty Images, Inc.; **494:** ©CORBIS; **495:** The Granger Collection, New York; **496:** L, Brown Brothers; R, Courtesy of The National Museum of the American Indian/Smithsonian Institution, (099830.000), Photo by Carmelo Guadagno; **497:** Hulton Archive/ Getty Images, Inc.; **498:** Brown Brothers; **499:** L, Getty Images; R, Copyright ©1995–2005, Denver Public Library, Colorado Historical Society, and Denver Art Museum; **500:** B, The Granger Collection, New York; T, The Granger Collection, New York; **501:** B, The Granger Collection, New York; T, AP/Wide World Photos; **502:** B, ©Bettmann/CORBIS; **502–503:** Eastern Washington State Historical Society; **503:** B, The

Granger Collection, New York; T: Cumberland County Historical Society; **504:** Helen Hunt Jackson, CA. 1875. William S. Jackson Photograph Collection, pp 85–30s, Part 3, Folder 1, Photo 2, Photographed by Marshall, Boston Special Collections, Colorado College, Colorado Springs, Colorado **505:** L, U.S. Department of Agriculture; R, Frank Greenaway/©Dorling Kindersley; **506:** Background, ©Bettmann/CORBIS; BL, ©Bettmann/ CORBIS; BR, Courtesy of www. westernmininghistory.com; T, Dave Johnson; **507:** Copyright ©1995– 2005, Denver Public Library, Colorado Historical Society, and Denver Art Museum; **508:** B, The Granger Collection, New York; T, ©Bettmann/CORBIS; **509:** Geoff Brightling/ ©Dorling Kindersley; **510:** B, ©Bettmann/CORBIS; T, Philip Gould/CORBIS; **512:** SuperStock, Inc.; **513:** B, Frederic Remington, *A Dash for the Timber*, Oil on canvas, 1889. 1961. 381, Amon Carter Museum, Fort Worth, Texas; ML, Frederic Remington (American, 1861– 1909), *The Outlier, 1909*, Oil on Canvas, Brooklyn Museum of Art, New York, USA, Bequest of Miss Charlotte R. Stillman/Bridgeman Art Library; MR, Frederic Remington ©Christie's Images/CORBIS; T, Judith Miller/©Dorling Kindersley/The Coeur d'Alene Art; **514:** The Granger Collection, New York; **515:** L, Brown Brothers; R, Frank Greenaway/©Dorling Kindersley; **516:** B, U.S. Department of Agriculture; T, *The Navajo* (oil on canvas), Maynard Dixon (1875– 1946) Private Collection, ©Christie's Images/The Bridgeman Art Library; **517:** L, Cumberland County Historical Society; R, Cumberland County Historical Society; **518–519:** The Granger Collection, New York; **519:** B, ©Bettmann/CORBIS; M, ©David J. & Janice L. Frent Collection/ CORBIS; T, Meridian Book ©1994, Cover design by Robin Locke Monda; **520:** Border, J.R. Eyerman/Time Life Pictures/ Getty Images; Inset, The Granger Collection, New York; **521:** Museum of American Political Life, Photo by Steve Laschever; **522:** Brown Brothers; **523:** ©North Wind Picture Archives; **524:** Image by ©CORBIS; **524–525:** Border, The New York Public Library/Art Resource, NY; **525:** Background, California Historical Society, FN-21136; Inset, L, Courtesy of the Arizona Historical Society/Tucson AHS#B3102; Inset, R, ©North Wind Picture Archives; **526:** B, ©Bettmann/CORBIS; T, ©Royalty-Free/Corbis; **527:** The Granger Collection, New York; **528:** B, ©Royalty-Free/Superstock; TR, The Granger Collection, New York; **529:** L, The Image Works; R, Meridian Book ©1994, Cover design by Robin Locke Monda.; **530:** The Granger Collection, New York; **531:** The Granger Collection, New York; **532:** ©Federal Reserve Bank, USA; **533:** Background, Kansas State Historical Society; Inset, Cover illustration, Farmer's Alliance Songs, by E.O. Excell and Dr. Reid Parker, Chicago, IL: E.O. Excell, Publisher, ©1890, Elias Carr Papers (#160.29.c.); **534:** B, ©Bettmann/CORBIS; ML, Photo by Russ Lappa ©Prentice Hall; MR, lower, The Granger Collection, New York; MR, upper, ©Minnesota Historical Society/CORBIS; T, ©Alland/The Image Works; **537:** ©David J. & Janice L. Frent Collection/CORBIS; **539:** ©CORBIS; **540:** Cover illustration, Farmer's Alliance Songs, by E.O. Excell and Dr. Reid Parker, Chicago, IL: E.O. Excell, Publisher, ©1890, Elias Carr Papers (#160.29.c.); **541:** L, Brown Brothers; R, The Granger Collection, New York; **542:** Kansas State Historical Society; **543:** *Los Angeles Times;* **544:** Background, The Art Archive/National Archives Washington, D.C.; BL, ©Bettmann/CORBIS; BR, ©Bettmann/CORBIS; ML, The Granger Collection, New York; MR, ©Bettmann/CORBIS; TL, ©Reuters/CORBIS; TM, The Granger Collection, New York; TR, The Granger Collection, New York; **545:** ©CORBIS; **546–547:** Brown Brothers; **547:** B, The Granger Collection, New York; M, Getty Images; T, Dartmouth College Library; **548:** ©Bettmann/CORBIS; **549:** ©Bettmann/CORBIS; **550:** T, The Granger Collection, New York; B, The Granger Collection, New York; BR, The Granger Collection, New York; TL, Library of Congress; **551:** B, Hulton-Deutsch Collection/CORBIS; TR, The Granger Collection, New York; **552:** L, Underwood & Underwood/CORBIS; M, The Granger Collection, New York; R, Brown Brothers; **554:** Courtesy of The Rosenberg Library, Galveston, TX; **556:** B, Brown Brothers; TR, Dartmouth College Library; **557:** TL, Prentice Hall School Division; TR, Lewis W. Hine/George Eastman House/Getty Images, Inc.; **558:** Minnesota Historical Society/CORBIS; **559:** The Granger Collection, New York; **560:** BL, ©David J. & Janice L. Frent Collection/CORBIS; TR, Underwood & Underwood/CORBIS; **560–561:** Background, Library of Congress; Foreground, ©Bettmann/CORBIS; **561:** TL, Courtesy of the Historic National Woman's Party, Sewall-Belmont House and Museum, Washington, D.C.; TR, ©Bettmann/CORBIS; **562:** Brown Brothers; **563:** B, National Archives and Records Administration; T, Ariel Skelley/CORBIS; **564:** ©San Diego Historical Society, E.H. Davis Collection; **565:** L, ©Bettmann/CORBIS; R, Culver Pictures, Inc.; **566:** B, Courtesy of the Abraham Lincoln Presidential Library; T, The Granger Collection, New York; **567:** Library of Congress; **568:** Brown Brothers; **569:** L, Brown Brothers; R, Paul & Rosemary Volpp, ©Dorling Kindersley; **570:** T, ©Bettmann/CORBIS; TL, ©Bettmann/CORBIS; TR, The Granger Collection, New York; **571:** BR, Courtesy of the Kansas State Historical Society; BR, Science Museum/SSPL/The Image Works; L, The Granger Collection, New York; R, ©Bettmann/CORBIS; **573:** Library of Congress; **574:** Brown Brothers; **575:** The Granger Collection, New York; **576:** L, Judith Miller/©Dorling Kindersley/Larry & Dianna Elman; R, Brown Brothers; **577:** Getty Images; **578:** The Granger Collection, New York; **580:** Library of Congress; **581:** L, Culver Pictures, Inc.; R, The Granger Collection, New York; **582:** ©David J. & Janice L. Frent Collection/CORBIS; **584–585:** © Bettmann/CORBIS; **585:** B, Schomburg Center/Art Resource, NY; M, The Granger Collection/ New York; T, Getty Images; **586:** L, Brown Brothers; R, Brown Brothers; **587:** BR, ©CORBIS; LL, Brown Brothers; **588:** Library of Congress; **589:** Getty Images; **590:** B, ©CORBIS; T, Victor Jose Cobo/AP/Wide World Photos; **592:** L, ©Bettmann/CORBIS; R, Smithsonian Institution; **593:** Pearson Education/PH School; **594:** B, Chicago Historical Society; T, The Granger Collection, New York; **595:** BL, The New York Historical Society; BM, The New York Historical Society; BR, ©Bettmann/CORBIS; **596:** L, ©2002 The Museum of Fine Arts, Houston; M, Schomburg Center/Art Resource, NY; R, ©CORBIS; **599:** Library of Congress; **600:** L, Getty Images; R, ©Bettmann/CORBIS; **600–601:** TL, Prentice Hall; **601:** BM, U.S. Library of Congress; R, Duke University; TM, U.S. Library of Congress; **602:** ©Bettmann/CORBIS; **603:** The Granger Collection, New York;

604: L, ©Bettmann/CORBIS; **605:** ©Bettmann/CORBIS; **607:** BR, ©Bettmann/CORBIS; L, ©CORBIS; TR, The Granger Collection, New York; **608:** ©Bettmann/CORBIS; **610:** B, The Art Archive/Culver Pictures; M, Getty Images; T, Photograph by kind permission of Peter R. Westacott and The United States Air Force Art Program; **612:** L, ©CORBIS; R, ©Bettmann/ CORBIS; **613:** L, The Granger Collection, New York; R, Getty Images; **614:** ©Bettmann/ CORBIS; **615:** B, The Granger Collection/New York; T, The Granger Collection/New York; **616–617:** National Archives and Records Administration; **617:** B, Brown Brothers; M, Library of Congress; T, ©Prentice Hall; **618:** Mary Evans Picture Library; **619:** The Granger Collection, New York; **621:** ©Bettmann/CORBIS; **622:** Hulton-Deutsch Collection/CORBIS; **623:** The Granger Collection, New York; **624:** T, The Art Archive/Imperial War Museum/Eileen Tweedy; **624–625:** B, Courtesy of Motorbuch Verlag and Eberhard Moeller, Photo from *The Encyclopedia of U-Boats, From 1904 to the Present*; **625:** B, Library of Congress; M, Gary Ombler/Imperial War Museum ©Dorling Kindersley; TR, Three Lions/Getty Images; **626:** B, ©Bettmann/CORBIS; T, Ceerwan Aziz/Reuters/CORBIS; **627:** Hulton Archive/Getty Images, Inc.; **628:** L, Library of Congress; R, Stock Montage, Inc.; **629:** Brown Brothers; **630:** Rykoff Collection/CORBIS; **631:** BL, ©CORBIS; BR, The Granger Collection, New York; R, ©Bettmann/CORBIS; TL, Library of Congress; **632:** ©Bettmann/ CORBIS; **633:** B, Culver Pictures, Inc.; T, The Granger Collection, New York; **634:** Stock Montage, Inc./Historical Pictures Collection; **636:** B, ©Bettmann/CORBIS; T, Library of Congress; **637:** L, Library of Congress; R, The Granger Collection, New York; **638:** The Granger Collection, New York; **640:** B, ©Bettmann/CORBIS; T, Prentice Hall; **640–641:** BL, The Art Archive; **641:** BR, Ann Ronan Picture Library/HIP/The Image Works; M, The National World War I Museum, Kansas City, Missouri ; T, Prentice Hall; **642:** ©CORBIS; **644:** Library of Congress; **646:** Brown Brothers; **647:** L, Library of Congress; R, National Archives and Records Administration; **648:** L, Getty Images; R, Underwood & Underwood/CORBIS; **649:** ©Bettmann/CORBIS; **650:** Brown Brothers; **651:** B, ©Bettmann/CORBIS; T, ©Bettmann/CORBIS; **652:** The National World War I Museum, Kansas City, Missouri; **653:** L, ©Bettmann/CORBIS; R, Library of Congress; **654:** B, The Granger Collection, New York; T, Library of Congress; **655:** The Granger Collection, New York; **656:** Background, The Art Archive/National Archives, Washington D.C.; BL, ©Bettmann/CORBIS; BR, ©Bettmann/CORBIS; ML, The Granger Collection, New York; MR, ©Bettmann/CORBIS; TL, ©Reuters/CORBIS; TM, The Granger Collection, New York; TR, The Granger Collection, New York; **657:** The Art Archive/Laurie Platt Winfrey; **658–659:** Getty Images; **659:** B,The Granger Collection/New York; M, Getty Images; T, ©Bettmann/ CORBIS; **660:** L, Brown Brothers; R, Image courtesy of The Advertising Archives; **661:** ©Bettmann/ CORBIS; **662:** BL, Lake County Museum/CORBIS; BR, Image courtesy of The Advertising Archives; Inset, M, Visions of America, LLC/Alamy; Inset, TL, Blue Lantern Studio/CORBIS; M, ©Bettmann/CORBIS; T, ©CORBIS; **664:** Museum of the City of New York/CORBIS; **665:** USDA; **666:** L, ©Bettmann/CORBIS; R, Getty Images; **667:** The Granger Collection, New York; **668:** L, Brown Brothers; R, ©Bettmann/CORBIS; **671:** L, Library of Congress; R, Getty Images; **672:** Brown Brothers; **673:** The Granger Collection, New York; **674:** B, ©Bettmann/CORBIS; T, Ramin Talaie/CORBIS; **675:** Library of Congress; **676:** BL, ©Bettmann/CORBIS; BR, Library of Congress; T, Drug Enforcement Administration; **677:** BL, Dave King ©Dorling Kindersley, Courtesy of the New York City Police Museum; BM, from *The New York Times* 2/15 ©1929 All Rights Reserved; TL, The Art Archive/National Archives Washington, D.C.; TR, Library of Congress; **678:** K.J. Historical/CORBIS; **679:** L, Schenectady Museum, Hall of Electrical History Foundation/ CORBIS; R, The Granger Collection, New York; **680:** Louie Psihoyos/CORBIS; L, Image courtesy of The Advertising Archives; ML, Image courtesy of The Advertising Archives; MR, ©Bettmann/CORBIS; R, ©Bettmann/CORBIS; **681:** L, Smithsonian Institution Collections, National Museum of American History, Behring Center; R, Underwood & Underwood/CORBIS; **682:** B, ©Bettmann/CORBIS; T, The Art Archive/Culver Pictures; **683:** B, The Art Archive/Culver Pictures; M, The Granger Collection, NY; TL, ©Bettmann/CORBIS; TR, The Jewish Museum, NY/Art Resource, NY; **685:** L, ©Francis G. Mayer/CORBIS; R, The Newark Museum/Art Resource, NY; **686:** B, AP/Wide World Photos; T, Getty Images ; **687:** Getty Images ; **688:** B, John Springer Collection/CORBIS; M, ©Bettmann/CORBIS; **688–689:** T, ©Bettmann/CORBIS; **689:** BL, Sarah Fabian-Baddiel/HIP/The Image Works; BM, The Granger Collection, New York; MR, ©Bettmann/CORBIS; **690:** Schomburg Center, The New York Public Library/Art Resource, NY; **691:** ©Bettmann/CORBIS; **692:** L, Getty Images ; M, Tim Ridley ©Dorling Kindersley/ collection of the Louisiana State Museum, Gift of the New Orleans Jazz Club; R, Getty Images; **693:** Getty Images; **694:** The Granger Collection, New York; **695:** B, Brown Brothers; T, Winold Reiss, Portrait of Langston Hughes (1902–1967), ©1925, National Portrait Gallery, Washington, D.C., USA, Art Resource, NY; **696:** L, ©Bettmann/CORBIS; R: Getty Images; **697:** L, ©Bettmann/CORBIS; R, The Granger Collection, New York; **698:** The Jewish Museum, NY/ Art Resource, NY; **699:** Hulton Archive/Getty Images Inc.; **700–701:** ©CORBIS; **701:** B, © Prentice Hall; M, Conde Nast Publications, Inc.; T, Getty Images; **702:** L, Getty Images; R, Brown Brothers; **703:** The Granger Collection, New York; **704:** ©Bettmann/CORBIS; **705:** L, Minnesota Historical Society/CORBIS; R, Condé Nast Archive/CORBIS; **706:** B, The Granger Collection, New York; T, Getty Images; **707:** ©Bettmann/CORBIS; **709:** Brown Brothers; **711:** B, ©Bettmann/CORBIS; BR, Horace Bristol/CORBIS; M, The Granger Collection, New York.; T, ©Bettmann/CORBIS; **712:** B, ©CORBIS; TL, Library of Congress; **712– 713:** T, Museum of History and Industry/CORBIS; R, The Granger Collection; **714:** AP/Wide World Photos; **715:** The Granger Collection, New York; **716:** Copyright the Dorothea Lange Collection, Oakland Museum of California, City of Oakland, Gift of Paul S. Taylor; **717:** Library of Congress; **718:** B, ©Mary Evans Picture Library/The Image Works; **718–719:** AP/Wide World Photos; **719:** BL, ©CORBIS; BR, Prentice Hall; TL, The Granger Collection, New York; TR, AP/Wide World Photos; **720:** B, Prentice Hall; T, Hulton Archive/Getty Images, Inc.; **722:** ©CORBIS; **723:** B,

AP/Wide World Photos; BR, ©Bettmann/CORBIS; M, Prentice Hall; T, Hulton/Getty Images; **725:** B, Getty Images; T, Peter Anderson/©Dorling Kindersley; **726:** ©CORBIS; **727:** The Granger Collection, New York; **728:** Minnesota Historical Society/CORBIS; **730–731:** ©CORBIS; **731:** B, ©David J. & Janice L. Frent Collection/CORBIS; M, Blank Archives/Getty Images; T, The Granger Collection, New York; **732:** L, The Granger Collection, New York; R, Hulton Archive/Getty Images; **733:** *New York Daily News;* **734:** BL, ©CORBIS; M, The Granger Collection, New York; R,©CORBIS; TL, Topham/The Image Works; **735:** ©Bettmann/CORBIS; **736:** L, ©CORBIS; **737:** The Granger Collection, New York; **738:** L, ©Bettmann/CORBIS; R, ©Bettmann/CORBIS; **739:** T, AP/Wide World Photos; **740:** Minnesota Historical Society/CORBIS; **741:** ©CORBIS; **742:** BL, Associated Press, AP; BR, ©Bettmann/CORBIS; TL, © Bettmann/CORBIS; TR, Library of Congress; **743:** BR, Dennis MacDonald/PhotoEdit; L, Michael Newman/PhotoEdit; M, Mark Antman/The Image Works; TR, Monika Graff/The Image Works; **744:** B, ©Bettmann/CORBIS; Inset, ©CORBIS; **745:** *Celebrate the Century, 1930s, FDR's New Deal,* ©1998 Used with permission, All rights reserved. **746:** Library of Congress; **747:** AP/ Wide World Photos; **748:** ©Bettmann/CORBIS; **749:** L, ©CORBIS; R: Library of Congress; **750:** AP/Wide World Photos; **751:** AP/Wide World Photos; **753:** Tim Boyle/Getty Images; **757:** White House Photo Office; **758:** MGM/The Kobal Collection; **759:** BL, Getty Images; BR, ©Bettmann/CORBIS; M, The Advertising Archive; **760:** BL, ©CORBIS; **760–761:** B, Smithsonian American Art Museum, Washington, D.C./Art Resource, NY; **761:** BR, Kelly-Mooney Photography/CORBIS; ML, Selznick/MGM/The Kobal Collection; MR, Everett Collection; TR, The Granger Collection, New York; **762:** The Granger Collection, New York; **763:** BL, United Artists/Photofest; ML, Selznick/MGM/The Kobal Collection; MR, Everett Collection; TR, The Granger Collection, New York; **764:** L, Hulton Archive/Getty Images; R, ©Bettmann/CORBIS; **765:** L, ©CORBIS; R: Selznick/MGM/The Kobal Collection; **766:** ©CORBIS; **767:** *International Herald Tribune;* **768:** Background, The Art Archive/National Archives Washington, D.C.; BL, ©Bettmann/CORBIS; BR, ©Bettmann/CORBIS; ML, The Granger Collection, New York; MR, ©Bettmann/CORBIS; TL, © Reuters/CORBIS; TM, The Granger Collection, New York; TR, The Granger Collection, New York; **769:** Alfred Eisenstaedt/Pix Inc./Time Life Pictures/Getty Images; **770–771:** Hulton-Deutsch Collection; **771:** B, Deutsches Historisches Museum, Berlin; M, Philip Makanna/GHOSTS; T, The Art Archive/Imperial War Museum; **772:** L, The New York Public Library/Art Resource, NY; R, ©Bettmann/CORBIS; **773:** Getty Images; **774:** L, akg-images; M, ©Bettmann/CORBIS; R, akg-images; **775:** L, ©Bettmann/CORBIS; M, Mary Evans Picture Library 2005; R, ©Bettmann/CORBIS; **777:** ©Bettmann/CORBIS; **778:** ©CORBIS; **779:** ©Bettmann/CORBIS; **780:** L, ©Bettmann/CORBIS; R, ©Bettmann/CORBIS; **781:** ©Bettmann/CORBIS; **782:** © CORBIS; **783:** L, ©Bettmann/CORBIS; M, ©Bettmann/CORBIS; R, Hulton-Deutsch Collection/ CORBIS; **784:** The Granger Collection, New York; **785:** B, ©Bettmann/CORBIS; T, Time Life Pictures/Getty Images; **786:** AP/Wide World Photos; **787:** Printed by permission for the Norman Rockwell Family Agency Copyright ©1943, the Norman Rockwell Family Entities/ CORBIS; **788:** ©Bettmann/CORBIS; **789:** B, ©Bettmann/CORBIS; T, The Art Archive/Imperial War Museum; **790:** BL, AP/Wide World Photos; TL, Philip Makanna/GHOSTS; **790–791:** BR, Naval Historical Center # NH97379; **791:** L, Photo by Three Lions/Getty Images; M, SuperStock, Inc./ SuperStock; R, Photo by Three Lions/Getty Images; **792:** Courtesy of the National Archives and Records Administration, College Park, Maryland, photo no. (NWDNS-208-AA-352QQ (5); **793:** Brown Brothers; **794:** Getty Images; **796:** ©Bettmann/CORBIS; **797:** L, ©Bettmann/ CORBIS; R, Photo by Three Lions/Getty Images; **798:** ©Bettmann/CORBIS; **799:** ©CORBIS; **800–801:** ©CORBIS; **801:** B, Peter Wilson/©Dorling Kindersley, Courtesy of the Museum of the Regiments, Calgary; M, Getty Images; T, AP/Wide World Photos; **802:** L, Getty Images; R, Getty Images; **803:** ©CORBIS; **804:** Background, AP/Wide World Photos; R, National Archives; T, Dragesco-Joffe, Alain/Animals Animals, Earth Scenes; **805:** BR, ©Bettmann/CORBIS; **806:** L, AP/Wide World Photos; R, Prentice Hall; **806–807:** Background, National Archives and Records Administration; **807:** R, ©A724/GAMMA; **808:** Brown Brothers; **809:** B, Time Life Pictures/National Archives/Getty Images, Inc.; T, Library of Congress; **810:** Hulton Archive/Getty Images, Inc.; **811:** ©CORBIS; **812:** L, ©Bettmann/CORBIS; R, AP/Wide World Photos; **813:** Peter Wilson/©Dorling Kindersley, Courtesy of the Museum of the Regiments, Calgary; **814:** B, Everett Collection; T, Everett Collection; **815:** B, AP/Wide World Photos; T, Brown Brothers; **816:** Background, B, AP/Wide World Photos; BR, AP/Wide World Photos; Inset, BL, SuperStock, Inc.; MR, The Granger Collection, New York; TL, National Archives; TR, Library of Congress; **817:** Background, AP/Wide World Photos; R, SuperStock, Inc./SuperStock; **818:** L, Brown Brothers; R, Time Life Pictures/Getty Images; **819:** ©Bettmann/CORBIS; **820:** BL, Prentice Hall; BR, Keystone-France/ImageState; TL, Courtesy of Julie Fulmer, Prentice Hall.; **820–821:** Background, by Robert Capa ©2001 By Cornell Capa/Magnum Photos; **821:** T, Mychele Daniau/AFP/Getty Images; **823:** B, AP/Wide World Photos; T, ©Bettmann/ CORBIS; **825:** Brown Brothers; **826:** U.S. Air Force; **827:** B, Andy Crawford/Dorling Kindersley, copyright by kind permission of The Trustees of the Imperial War Museum, London; T, ©Bettmann/CORBIS; **828:** ©CORBIS; **829:** L, ©Bettmann/CORBIS; R, Andy Crawford/Dorling Kindersley, ©Imperial War Museum, London; **830:** B, USHMM, Courtesy of Robert A. Schmuhl; Background, T, Keystone/Getty Images; Inset, B, USHMM, Courtesy of KZ Gedenkstaette Dachau; M, U.S. Holocaust Memorial Museum. The views or opinions expressed in this book and the context in which the image is used, do not necessarily reflect the views or policy of, not imply approval or endorsement by, The United States Holocaust Memorial Museum.; M, U.S. National Archives/Roger-Viollet/The Image Works; ML, ©CORBIS; TL, akg-images; TR, Topham/The Image Works; **832:** Vincent Kessler/CORBIS; **834:** LEONE, ullstein bild/The Granger Collection, New York; **835:** ©Bettmann/CORBIS; **837:** ©Bettmann/ CORBIS; **839:** Brown Brothers; **840:** L, SuperStock, Inc.; R, Peter Wilson/©Dorling Kindersley, Courtesy of the Museum of the Regiments, Calgary; **841:** R, ©CORBIS; L, ©Bettmann/CORBIS; **842:** T, Used with permission from the *Stars and Stripes* a DoD publication, ©2005 *Stars and Stripes;* B: Keystone-France/ImageState; **844–845:** ©Bettmann/CORBIS

845: B, Conelrad Collection; M, Getty Images; T, William A. Bake/CORBIS; **846:** L, Getty Images; R, Getty Images; **847:** ©Bettmann/CORBIS; **849:** Solo Syndication/Associated Newspapers; **850:** ©Bettmann/CORBIS; **851:** B, ©Bettmann/CORBIS; T, Keystone/Getty Images; **853:** B, © Bettmann/CORBIS; T, www.ourdocuments.gov/NARA; **854:** L, ©CORBIS; R, William A. Bake/ CORBIS; **855:** AP/Wide World Photos; **856:** ©Bettmann/CORBIS; **858:** ©Bettmann/CORBIS; **859:** John Nordell/The Image Works; **860:** L, Conelrad Collection; R, Getty Images; **862:** BL, Jerry Cooke/CORBIS; MR, ©Bettmann/CORBIS; TL, ©Bettmann/CORBIS; TR, Jerry Cooke/CORBIS; **863:** Time Inc./Time Life Pictures/Getty Images; **865:** B, Getty Images; T, Sovfoto/Eastfoto; **866:** BL, ©Bettmann/CORBIS; BR: ©Bettmann/CORBIS; M: ©CORBIS; T: Conelrad Collection; **866–867:** AP/Wide World Photos; **867:** BL, Conelrad Collection; TR, Civil Defense Museum; **868:** Conelrad Collection; **869:** The Granger Collection, New York; **870:** Background, T, Conelrad Collection; Inset, Image courtesy The Advertising Archives/©2006 Marvel Characters, Inc. Used with permission; **870–871:** Conelrad Collection; B, Conelrad Collection; L, Courtesy of the Everett Collection/Everett Collection; R, Allied Artists/The Kobal Collection; **872:** B, Time Life Pictures/Getty Images; T, AFP/Getty Images; **873:** The Granger Collection, New York; **874:** Marvin Koner/CORBIS; **875:** Time Life Pictures/Getty Images; **876:** L, ©Bettmann/CORBIS; R, ©Bettmann/CORBIS; **877:** B, The Image Works; T, Time Life Pictures/Getty Images; **878:** ©CORBIS; **879:** The Granger Collection, New York; **880–881:** Getty Images; **881:** B, ©Bettmann/CORBIS; M, Dwight D. Eisenhower Library, Bob Paull, Staff Photographer; T, The Granger Collection, New York; **882:** Indiana U. Archives & Photographic Services (#47-1082); **883:** Hulton Archive/Getty Images, Inc.; **884:** Underwood & Underwood/CORBIS; **885:** L, Associated Press, AP; R, Ewing Galloway/Index Stock Imagery, Inc.; **886:** Inset, no credit; TL, W. Eugene Smith/Time Life Pictures/Getty Images; **887:** ©Bettmann/ CORBIS; **888:** Inset, Richard Wurts/National Building Museum; TL, Photo by J. R. Eyerman/ Time LifePictures/Getty Images; **889:** ©Bettmann/CORBIS; **890:** L, H. Armstrong Roberts/ Robertstock; R, H. Armstrong Roberts/Robertstock; **891:** L, H. Armstrong Roberts/Robertstock; R, Philip Gendreau/Corbis; **892:** R. KRUBNER/H. Armstrong Roberts; **893:** ©CORBIS; **894:** ©Bettmann/CORBIS; **895:** Brown Brothers; **896:** Inset, Smithsonian Institution Collections, National Museum of American History, Behring Center.; John Dominis/Time Life Pictures/Getty Images; **897:** BR, Tom Kelley/Hulton Archive/Getty Images; Inset, The Granger Collection, New York; **898:** ©Bettmann/CORBIS; **899:** BL, Time Life Pictures/Getty Images; BR, Getty Images; M, Penguin USA; TL, CBS Photo Archive/Getty Images; TR, H. Armstrong Roberts/Robertstock; **900:** M, Image courtesy of The Advertising Archives; TL, Wrather Corp/ Apex Film Corp/The Kobal Collection; TM, Getty Images; TR, CBS Photo Archive/Getty Images; **901:** Dunigan/H. Armstrong Roberts; **902:** B, Don Wright/Time Life Pictures/Getty Images; ML, The Everett Collection, Inc.; MR, Aardman Animations, Ltd.; T, Michael Ochs Archives.Com; **903:** Inset, Photo by Bob Adelman/Magnum Photos; ©Bettmann/CORBIS; **904:** Photofest; **905:** L, Bruce Davidson/ Magnum Photos; R, AP/Wide World Photos; **906:** ©Bettmann/CORBIS; **907:** Library of Congress; **908:** L, Library of Congress; R, Richard Wurts/National Building Museum; **909:** Photo by Eugene Richards/Magnum Photo, © 1981; **910:** B, Michael Ochs Archives.Com; **911:** L, AP/Wide World Photos; R, Collection of the State Museum of Pennsylvania; **912:** Background, The Art Archive/ National Archives Washington, D.C.; BL, ©Bettmann/CORBIS; BR, ©Bettmann/CORBIS; ML, The Granger Collection, New York; ML, The Granger Collection, New York; MR, ©Bettmann/CORBIS; TL, ©Reuters/CORBIS; TM, The Granger Collection, New York; TR, The Granger Collection, New York; **913:** ©1978/George Ballis/Take Stock; **914–915:** Photofest; **915:** T, ©Bettmann/CORBIS; M, ©Bettmann/CORBIS; B , ©David J. & Janice L. Frent Collections/CORBIS; **916:** B, ©CORBIS; T, AP/Wide World Photos; **917:** L, Magnum Photos; R, ©Bettmann/CORBIS; **918:** Time Life Pictures/Getty Images; **919:** Time Life Pictures/Getty Images; **920:** AP/ Wide World Photos; **921:** ©Bettmann/CORBIS; **922:** B, Time Life Pictures/Getty Images; M, The Granger Collection, New York; T, Prentice Hall; **924:** B, Bob Daemmrich/The Image Works; M, Time Life Pictures/Getty Images; T, ©CORBIS; **925:** L, AP/Wide World Photos; R, AP/Wide World Photos/Montgomery Advertiser; **926:** L, ©Bettmann/CORBIS; R, ©Bettmann/CORBIS; **927:** Background, ©Bettmann/CORBIS; BR, ©Bettmann/CORBIS; T, Bruce Davidson/ Magnum Photos; **928:** B, AP/Wide World Photos; T, AP/Wide World Photos; **929:** AP/Wide World Photos; **930:** Photo by Francis Miller/Time Life Pictures/Getty Images; **930–931:** Background, Flip Schulke/ Black Star; **931:** BL, John F. Kennedy Library, National Archives, document MS 2003-036; BR, Flip Schulke/CORBIS; TR, National Museum of American History, Smithsonian Institution; **933:** B, Time Life Pictures/Getty Images; T, Flip Schulke/CORBIS; **934:** L, AP/Wide World Photos; **934–935:** B, AP/Wide World Photos; T, ©Bettmann/CORBIS; **935:** TR, ©Bettmann/CORBIS; **936:** L, ©David J. & Janice L. Frent Collections/CORBIS; R, Time Life Pictures/Getty Images; **937:** AP/Wide World Photos; **938:** Flip Schulke/CORBIS; **939:** B, Flip Schulke/CORBIS; T, AP/ Wide World Photos; **940:** B, ©David J. & Janice L. Frent Collections/CORBIS; **940–941:** TL, ©Bettmann/CORBIS; **941:** TR, AP/Wide World Photos; **942:** B, POPPERFOTO/Alamy; Background, T, AP/Wide World Photos; TR, Bob Adelman/Magnum Photos; **945:** Photofest; **946:** L, Time Life Pictures/Getty Images; R, AP/Wide World Photos; **947:** L, ©Bettmann/CORBIS; R, Time Life Pictures/Getty Images; **948:** AP/Wide World Photos; **949:** AP Photo/Bill Hudson; **950–951:** ©Bettmann/Sygma/CORBIS; **951:** B, Time Life Pictures/Getty Images; M, The Peace Corps; T, ©David J. and Janice L. Frent Collection/CORBIS; **952:** ©David J. and Janice L. Frent Collection/CORBIS; **953:** Getty Images; Inset, ©Bettmann/CORBIS; **954:** ©CORBIS; **955:** L, JP Laffont/Sygma/CORBIS; R, Paul Conklin Photography/PhotoEdit; **957:** ©CORBIS; **959:** © Bettmann/CORBIS; **960:** B, ©CORBIS; T, ©Bettmann/CORBIS; **961:** "Eclipse," from *Straight Herblock* (Simon & Schuster, 1964); **962:** B, GRIN Great Images in NASA; ML, GRIN Great Images in NASA; MR, NASA; TL, NIX/NASA Image Exchange; TR, GRIN Great Images in NASA; **963:** ©Bettmann/CORBIS; **964:** B, Larry Kolvoord/The Image Works; T, stockphoto.com; **965:** ©Bettmann/CORBIS; **966:** ©Bettmann/CORBIS; **967:** B, ©Bettmann/CORBIS; T, James

Leynse/CORBIS; **968:** B, Banana Stock/AGE Fotostock; BL, Marty Heitner/The Image Works; T, AP/Wide World Photos; **969:** B, Hulton Archive/Getty Images; TL, Sesame Street and associated characters, trademarks, and design elements are owned and licensed by Sesame Workshop, ©2006 Sesame Workshop. All rights reserved.; TR, ArenaPal/Topham/The Image Works; **970:** L, Getty Images; R, Yoav Levy/Phototake; **971:** ©Bettmann/CORBIS; **973:** B, AP/Wide World Photos; T, Paul S. Conklin/PhotoEdit; **974:** L, The Peace Corps; R, National Portrait Gallery, Smithsonian Institution/Art Resource, NY; **975:** AP/Wide World Photos; **976:** © Bettmann/CORBIS; **978–979:** The Granger Collection, New York; **979:** B, West Point Museum Collection; M, Library of Congress; T, National Museum of American History, Smithsonian Institution; **980:** Topham/The Image Works; **981:** WolfgangKaehler/CORBIS; **982:** TL, AFP/AFP/Getty Images; TR, Topham/The Image Works; **983:** AP/Wide World Photos; **984:** Pierre-Aux wcoutes, Paris/Rothco Cartoons; **985:** TL, Photo by Chris Bain/West Point Museum Collection; TR, National Archives and Records Administration, Records of the U.S. Marine Corps; **987:** AP/Wide World Photos; **988:** BL, AP/Wide World Photos; R, Time Life Pictures/Getty Images; TL, National Archives; **989:** M, Associated Press, AP; R, Ullstein Bild/The Granger Collection, New York; **990:** Associated Press/Wide World Photos; **991:** T, "Onward And Upward And Onward And—," from *The Herblock Gallery* (Simon & Schuster, 1968); **992:** TV, Getty Images; L, CBS Photo Archive/ Getty Images; **992:** R, Leif Skoogfors/CORBIS; **993:** Topham/The Image Works; **994:** Bernard Gotfryd/Getty Images; **996:** Basset/National Archives and Records Administration; **997:** ML, Getty Images; B, ©Bettmann/CORBIS; MR, ©Bettmann/CORBIS; TL, Time Life Pictures/Getty Images; TR, Associated Press, AP; **998:** Photo by Bob Peterson/Time Life Pictures/Getty Images; **999:** ©David J. & Janice L. Frent Collections; **1000:** L, Leif Skoogfors/CORBIS; R, ©David J. & Janice L. Frent Collection/CORBIS; **1001:** AP/Wide World Photos/USAF; **1002:** Getty Images; **1003:** B, Time Inc./Time Life Pictures/Getty Images; T, Photo by Ronald S. Haeberle/Time Life Pictures/Getty Images; **1004:** BL, Getty Images; BR, Charles E. Pefley/Mira.com; TL, AbsoluteStockPhoto.com/Alamy; **1005:** BR, Brand X Pictures/Alamy; BL, Associated Press, AP; TR, Prentice Hall; **1006:** B, stockphoto.com; T, Ahmad Masood/Reuters/Corbis; **1008:** L, ©Bettmann/CORBIS; R, Corel Professional Photos CD-ROM™; **1009:** ©Bettmann/CORBIS; **1010:** B, National Museum of American History, Smithsonian Institution; T, AP/Wide World Photos; **1011:** Dirck Halstead/Liaison/Getty Images; **1012:** AP Photo/Malcolm Browne; **1013:** L, Photo by Terry Ashe/Time Life Pictures/Getty Images; R, Corel Professional Photos CD-ROM™; **1014:** stockphoto.com; **1015:** AP/Wide World Photos; **1016–1017:** Time Life Pictures/Getty Images; **1017:** B, Wally McNamee/CORBIS; M, Blank Archives/Getty Images; T, Charles Gatewood/The Image Works; **1018:** Background, Time Life Pictures/Getty Images; L, Getty Images; R, John Dominis/The Image Works; **1019:** B, ©Wes Wilson; **1020:** Background, & flowers, Prentice Hall; BL, Henry Diltz/CORBIS; BM, The Granger Collection, New York; BML, *Mad* cover #140, image courtesy of Doug Gilford's *Mad* Cover Site, collectmad.com/madcoversite; BR, Jason Reed/ Reuters/Corbis; TL, Prentice Hall; TML, Blank Archives/Getty Images; TMR, J.R. Eyerman/Getty Images, Inc./Time Life Pictures/; TR, H. Armstrong Roberts/Robertstock; **1022:** L, Charles Gatewood/The Image Works; R, ©Bettmann/CORBIS; **1023:** ©Bettmann/CORBIS; **1024:** L, ©*Ms. Magazine*; R, AP/Wide World Photos; **1025:** L, ©Bettmann/CORBIS; R, AP/Wide World Photos; **1027:** B, Mary Kate Denny/ PhotoEdit; T, ©Frank Cantor; **1028:** Tribute to Diego Rivera/©1998 & 2006 Philadelphia Mural Arts Program/Jane Golden/Delia King/Photo by Jack Ramsdale/Reprinted by permission; **1029:** B, Time Life Pictures/Getty Images; T, AP Photo/Barry Sweet; **1030:** L, AP Photo; R, Prentice Hall; **1031:** L, Galen Rowell/ CORBIS; R, Ed Kashi/CORBIS; **1032:** Rick Smolan/Against All Odds; **1033:** AP Photo/*The Post and Courier*, Mic Smith; **1034:** TL, Photofest; TR: Library of Congress; **1034–1035:** BL, ©Bettmann/CORBIS; **1035:** BR, AP Photo/Nature Consortium, Ron Wurzer; **1036:** Inset, ©CORBIS; **1036–1037:** Background, Ohio EPA; **1037:** Ohio EPA; **1038:** B, Thomas Moran, *The Grand Canyon of the Yellowstone, 1872*, The U.S. Department of the Interior Museum, Washington, D.C.; T, Copyright ©John Warden/Alaska Stock LLC; **1040:** Time Life Pictures/ Getty Images; **1041:** Henry Diltz/CORBIS; **1042:** Photofest; **1043:** ©1998 by Lalo Alcaraz, All Rights Reserved; **1044–1045:** ©Bettmann/CORBIS; **1045:** B, Dennis Brack/Black Star/ stockphoto.com; M, AP/Wide World Photos; T, Connie Ricca/CORBIS; **1046:** ©CORBIS; **1047:** Pelican Publications Company, Inc.; **1048:** L, ©Bettmann/CORBIS; R, ©Bettmann/ CORBIS; **1050:** BL, AP/Wide World Photos; BR, Mark Godfrey/The Image Works; MR, © Bettmann/CORBIS; T, Prentice Hall; **1051:** BL, Charles Gatewood/The Image Works; BR, Mark Godfrey/The Image Works; TL, AP Photo/National Archives; TR, ©Bettmann/CORBIS; **1052:** L, Nixon Presidential Materials Project, National Archives and Records Administration, Photo by Oliver F. Atkins; T, *New York Daily News*; **1054:** Courtesy of the *Worchester (Mass) Telegram*; **1055:** Mark Godfrey/The Image Works; **1056:** B, ©Bettmann/CORBIS; T, ©Bettmann/CORBIS; **1057:** B, Larry Lee Photography/CORBIS; TR, Black Star; **1058:** Nathan Benn/ CORBIS; **1059:** Background, Mark Richards/PhotoEdit; Inset, L, Jeffrey D. Smith/Woodfin Camp; Inset, R, Cleo Photography/PhotoEdit; **1060:** #1, CBS/Landov; #2, Courtesy of the Everett Collection/Everett Collection; #3, Courtesy of the Everett Collection/Everett Collection; #4, CBS/Landov; #5, ©ABC-TV/The Kobal Collection; B, ©Bettmann/CORBIS; BR, ©Paramount Television/The Kobal Collection; TR, Courtesy of the Everett Collection/Everett Collection; **1062:** B, Michael Pole/CORBIS; T, ©Bettmann/CORBIS; **1063:** AP/Wide World Photos; **1064:** ©Bettmann/CORBIS; **1065:** Mark Peterson/CORBIS; **1066:** L: Roger-Viollet/The Image Works; R, Kaveh Kazemi/CORBIS; **1066–1067:** ©Bettmann/CORBIS; **1067:** M, Wally McNamee/CORBIS; R, AP/Wide World Photos; **1068:** L, Black Star; R, Wally McNamee/CORBIS; **1069:** Time Life Pictures/Getty Images; **1070:** Dennis Brack/Black Star/stockphoto.com; **1071:** from *Herblock: A Cartoonist's Life* (Time Books, 1998); **1072:** Background, The Art Archive/National Archives Washington, D.C.; BL, ©Bettmann/CORBIS; BR, ©Bettmann/CORBIS; ML, The Granger

Collection, New York; ML, The Granger Collection, New York; MR, © Bettmann/CORBIS; TL, ©Reuters/CORBIS; TM, The Granger Collection, New York; TR, The Granger Collection, New York; **1073:** Jose L. Pelaez/CORBIS; **1074–1075:** ©CORBIS; **1075:** B, SPELLING/ABC/The Kobal Collection; M, ©Bettmann/Corbis; T, Pearson Education/Prentice Hall School; **1076:** Photo by Time Life Pictures/*Time Magazine*, Copyright Time Inc./Time Life Pictures/Getty Images; **1078:** Wally McNamee/CORBIS; **1079:** ©Bettmann/CORBIS; **1081:** L, Courtesy Ronald Reagan Library; R, Pearson Education/Prentice Hall School; **1083:** AP/ Wide World Photos/Ron Edmonds; **1084:** BL, Judi Sheppard Missett; BR, Photos12.com/Polaris; M, AP Photo/Barry Thumma; MR, AP Photo/Bruce Weaver; TL, SPELLING/ABC/The Kobal Collection; TR, STOCKFOLIO/Alamy; **1085:** AP/Wide World Photos/Charles Tasnadi; **1086:** B, Time Life Pictures/Getty Images; T, AP/Wide World Photos; **1087:** Leif Skoogfors/CORBIS; **1088:** Bill Gentile/CORBIS; **1089:** ©Wright, *Providence Journal Bulletin*; **1090:** BL, AFP/Getty Images; BR, UK-PRESS/GAMMA; M, Prentice Hall; T, ©CORBIS; **1091:** BL, Charles Steiner/The Image Works; BR, AP Photo/Lionel Cironneau; TL, Peter Turnley/CORBIS; TR, AP Photo/Doug Mills; **1093:** J. L. Atlan/Sygma/Corbis; **1094:** Time Life Pictures/Getty Images; **1095:** L, ©Bettmann/ Corbis; M, Betty Press/Woodfin Camp; R, Jacques Langevin/CORBIS SYGMA; **1096:** L, Ben Gibson-Katz/Woodfin Camp; R, ©David Turnley/CORBIS; **1097:** J.A. Giordano/CORBIS SABA; **1098:** Courtesy of the Ronald Reagan Library; **1099:** B, ©Bettmann/CORBIS; T, AFP/Getty Images; **1100:** AP Photo/Lionel Cironneau; **1102–1103:** AP/Wide World Photos/Ann Johansson; **1103:** B, NASA/Photo Researchers, Inc.; M, Mark Avery/Orange Country Register/CORBIS; T, Patrick Robert/CORBIS; **1104:** T, Courtesy of Dell, Inc.; **1105:** B, AP Photo/*The Fort Wayne Journal Gazette*, Samuel Hoffman; T, AP Photo/Steven Senne; **1109:** L, Arnie Sachs/CORBIS; R, Pearson Education/PH School Division; **1110:** AP/Wide World Photos/Susan Ragan; **1111:** ©Reuters/CORBIS; **1112:** B, Najlah Feanny/CORBIS; T, AP/Wide World Photos/ Joe Marquette; **1114:** AP/Wide World Photos/Robert Mecea; **1115:** Whittemore-Rothco Cartoons; **1116:** 1, ARKO DATTA/AFP/Getty Images; 2, ©Scott Wallace/World Bank; 3, ©Scott Wallace/World Bank; B, ©Scott Wallace/World Bank; T, Ariadne Van Zandbergen/Lonely Planet/Getty Images; **1117:** Tore Bergsaker/Sygma/CORBIS; **1118:** ©Reuters/CORBIS; **1119:** L, Kevin Lamarque/Reuters/CORBIS; R, Mark Avery/*Orange Country Register*/CORBIS; **1120:** Rhona Wise/AFP/Getty Images; **1121:** L, By Permission of Steve Kelley and Creators Syndicate, Inc.; R, ©2001. All rights reserved. Reprint permission provided by Mike Peters in conjunction with the Cartoonist Group; **1122:** Background, AP/Wide World Photos; Inset, Reuters/Sean Adair/Files SV; **1125:** Martin H. Simon/CORBIS; **1126:** Morry Gash/Associated Press; **1127:** L, Courtesy of Linda and Eddie Tran; R, Courtesy of Linda and Eddie Tran; **1128:** AP Photo/Matt York; **1130:** Bob Daemmrich/The Image Works; **1131:** SUPRI/Reuters/CORBIS; **1132:** AP/Wide World Photos/Susan Ragan; **1133:** L, Mario Tama/Getty Images; R, Christophe Calais/In Visu/CORBIS; **1134:** B, AP Photo/ Matt York; T, AP/Wide World Photos; **1135:** ©Dan Wasserman, 2005, Courtesy of Tribune Media Services; All rights reserved Reprinted with Permission; **1136:** Background, The Art Archive/National Archives Washington, D.C. ; BL, ©Bettmann/CORBIS; BR, ©Bettmann/COR-BIS; ML, The Granger Collection, New York; MR, ©Bettmann/CORBIS; TL, ©Reuters/CORBIS; TM, The Granger Collection, New York; TR, The Granger Collection, New York; **1137:** Richard Rowan/Photo Researchers, Inc.; **1138:** B, Jeff Greenberg/Omni-Photo Communications, Inc.; M, Copyright ©DEAN RIGGOTT/Grant Heilman Photography, All rights reserved; TL, Joseph Sohm, ChromoSohm Media Inc./Photo Researchers, Inc.; TM, ©Royalty-Free/CORBIS; TR, ©Jim Corwin/The Stock Connection; **1149:** #1, ©National Portrait Gallery, Smithsonian Institution/Art Resource, NY; #2, ©National Portrait Gallery, Smithsonian Institution/Art Resource, NY; #3, White House Collection, copyright White House Historical Association; #4, ©National Portrait Gallery, Smithsonian Institution/ Art Resource, NY; #5, ©National Portrait Gallery, Smithsonian Institution/Art Resource, NY; #6, ©National Portrait Gallery, Smithsonian Institution/Art Resource, NY; #7, White House Collection, copyright White House Historical Association; #8, White House Collection, copyright White House Historical Association; #9, ©National Portrait Gallery, Smithsonian Institution/Art Resource, NY; #10, ©National Portrait Gallery, Smithsonian Institution/Art Resource, NY; #11, White House Collection, copyright White House Historical Association; #12, ©National Portrait Gallery, Smithsonian Institution/Art Resource, NY; #13, White House Collection, copyright White House Historical Association; #14, ©National Portrait Gallery, Smithsonian Institution/Art Resource, NY; #15, ©National Portrait Gallery, Smithsonian Institution/Art Resource, NY; #16, National Portrait Gallery, Smithsonian Institution/Art Resource, NY; #17, White House Collection, copyright White House Historical Association; #18, ©National Portrait Gallery, Smithsonian Institution/Art Resource, NY; #19, White House Collection, copyright White House Historical Association; #20, ©National Portrait Gallery, Smithsonian Institution/Art Resource, NY; #21, © National Portrait Gallery, Smithsonian Institution/Art Resource, NY; #22, White House Collection, copyright White House Historical Association; #23, White House Collection, copyright White House Historical Association; #24, White House Collection, copyright White House Historical Association; #25, White House Collection, copyright White House Historical Association; #26, ©National Portrait Gallery, Smithsonian Institution/Art Resource, NY; 1150 #27 © National Portrait Gallery, Smithsonian Institution/Art Resource, NY; #28, White House Collection, copyright White House Historical Association; #29, White House Collection, copyright White House Historical Association; #30, White House Collection, copyright White House Historical Association; #31, White House Collection, copyright White House Historical Association; #32, White House Collection, copyright White House Historical Association; Background, Corel Professional Photos CD-ROM™; **1151:** #33, White House Collection, copyright White House Historical Association; #34, ©National Portrait Gallery, Smithsonian

United States History and Government

Unit One: Introduction

I. Geography

Content	Concepts/Themes	Connections

A. The physical/cultural setting in the Americas
  1. Size and location
  2. Major zones/areas
    a. Climate zones
    b. Vegetation zones
    c. Agricultural areas
    d. Natural resources
  3. Factors that shaped the identity of the United States
    a. Major mountain ranges
    b. Major river systems
    c. Great Plains
    d. Atlantic/Pacific oceans
    e. Coastlines
    f. Climate
    g. Abundance of natural resources
  4. Barriers to expansion/development
    a. Climate
    b. Mountain ranges
    c. Arid lands
    d. Great Plains
	Places and Regions
	
	Physical Systems
	
	Physical Systems
		Note:
		Sections A-1 to A-3 are suggested as a combination review and overview of United States geography that should introduce this course of study. Sections A-4 to D-5 are incorporated into the content outline of this core curriculum at the appropriate historical points. The Connections column suggests where these geographic concepts and themes can be integrated into the study of United States history and government. Use climate and physical feature maps to illustrate physical setting, regions, and features of different places in the United States.

B. Role/influence of geography on historical/cultural development
  1. Influences on early Native American Indians
  2. Influence on colonization patterns and colonial development
  3. Territorial expansion
  4. Impact during wartime
  5. Effect of location on United States foreign policy
	Environment
	Human Systems
		Use maps showing the stages of the expansion of the United States to demonstrate the importance of strategic location and to explain economic need to secure the port of New Orleans in the Louisiana Purchase (1803) or the need to obtain a natural boundary to the West such as the Mississippi River in the Treaty of Paris (1783). (Study in greater detail in UNIT TWO.)
		
		Discuss the influence of geography on settlement/demographic patterns in the United States, e.g.,
		  • the fact that the Great Plains area was settled in the period after the Civil War (UNIT THREE);
		  • lack of settlement in the arid lands of the Mexican Cession (UNIT TWO and UNIT THREE);
		  • influence of mountain ranges such as Appalachians and Rocky Mountains on westward travel and settlement (UNIT TWO and UNIT THREE);

Content	Concepts/ Themes	Connections
		• midwestern: effect of the Dust Bowl on agriculture (UNIT FIVE);
		• impact of the energy crisis of the 1970s on the development and demographic growth of the Southeast and Southwest (UNIT SEVEN).
		• lure of the so-called sun belt states for the increasing numbers of retired people (UNIT SEVEN)
		Illustrate the importance of strategic location in foreign policy discussions, e.g.,
		• interest in protecting the Western Hemisphere with Monroe Doctrine (UNIT TWO) and Roosevelt Corollary (UNIT FOUR);
		• interest in building the Panama Canal to link the Atlantic and Pacific trade (UNIT FOUR);
		• annexation of Hawaii as a potential naval base (UNIT FOUR);
		• acquisition of the Philippines in relation to China trade (UNIT FOUR);
		• Gulf War in terms of protecting oil resources of the Persian Gulf region (UNIT SEVEN).

C. Geographic issues today
  1. Waste disposal
  2. Water/air pollution
  3. Shifting populations
  4. Energy usage
  5. Urban problems/challenges
D. Demographics
  1. Characteristics
    a. Gender
    b. Age
    c. Ethnicity
    d. Religion
    e. Economic variables
    f. Nature of household
    g. Marital status
  2. Immigration
  3. Migration
  4. Population relationships/trends since 1865
    a. Population growth
    b. Distribution
    c. Density
  5. Current issues
    a. Graying of America
    b. Effects of the baby boom generation
    c. Changing composition of populations
	Science and Technology
	
	Human Systems Change
	
	Immigration and Migration
	
	Diversity
		Discuss these geographic issues as they relate to the United States' adjustment to industrial and demographic change (UNITS THREE – SEVEN). Consider demographic change in discussing stages of settlement and impacts of new waves of immigrants (UNITS THREE – SEVEN).
		
		Consider the impact of demographic change and political, economic, and social life, for example:
		• implications of baby boom generation at the early stages of their life cycle (increased demands for housing after WWII);
		• pressure on educational resources of the 1950s, 1960s, and 1970s;
		• graying of the population and its effects on Social Security and Medicare (UNIT SIX and UNIT SEVEN).

Unit Two: Constitutional Foundations for the United States Democratic Republic

I. The Constitution: The Foundation of American Society

Content	Concepts/ Themes	Connections
A. Historical foundations		
1. 17th- and 18th-century Enlightenment thought	Citizenship Civic Values	Students should understand that American political rights and institutions are derived from (1) British political traditions, (2) 18th-century Enlightenment thought, and (3) developments during the colonial period.
a. European intellectuals (Locke, Montesquieu, Voltaire, Rousseau)		
b. Key events (Magna Carta, habeas corpus, English Bill of Rights, Glorious Revolution)		
2. The peoples and peopling of the American colonies (voluntary and involuntary)		
a. Native American Indians (relations between colonists and Native American Indians, trade, alliances, forced labor, warfare)		
b. Slave trade	Civic Values	<u>Suggested Documents</u>: Mayflower Compact, Albany Plan of Union, Declaration of Independence, New York State Constitution
c. Varieties of immigrant motivation, ethnicities, and experiences		
3. Colonial experience: political rights and mercantile relationships	Government	
a. Colonial charters and self-government: Mayflower Compact, town meetings, House of Burgesses, local government, property rights, enforceable contracts, Albany Plan of Union		
b. Native American governmental systems		
c. Colonial slavery (evolution and variation of slavery in Chesapeake, South Carolina and Georgia, lower Mississippi Valley, middle colonies, and the North; slave resistance; influence of Africa and African-American culture upon colonial cultures; contradiction between slavery and emerging ideals of freedom and liberty)		
d. Freedom of the press: the Zenger case		
e. Salutary neglect, rights of English citizens in America		
4. The Revolutionary War and the Declaration of Independence	Civic Values Change	Students should understand the American Revolution as the result of colonial resistance to changes in British imperial policy after 1763. To what extent did the Declaration of Independence reflect Enlightenment thought and colonial experiences? <u>Suggested Document</u>: Thomas Paine, *Common Sense*
a. Causes of the Revolution		
b. Revolutionary ideology (republican principles, natural rights)		
c. Revolutionary leaders: Benjamin Franklin, George Washington, John Adams, Samuel Adams, Patrick Henry		
d. Slavery, African-Americans, and the outcome of the American Revolution (African-American role in the Revolution, growth of the "free black" population)		

New York Core Curriculum

Content	Concepts/ Themes	Connections
5. New York State Constitution based on republican principles 　**a.** New York State Constitution 　**b.** State constitutions (ratification by the people, unicameral versus bicameral legislatures, branches of government) 　**c.** Guaranteeing religious liberty (disestablishment of churches, the growth of religious pluralism) 　**d.** The abolition of slavery in the North	Civic Values	• What features from state constitutions, including New York's, were incorporated into the United States Constitution?
6. Articles of Confederation		• Why was this time called the "critical period"? • Why were the powers of the national government purposely limited? What were the major strengths and weaknesses of the government under the Articles? How did the authors of the Constitution remedy these weaknesses?
7. Northwest Ordinance **B.** Constitutional Convention 　**1.** Representation and process 　　**a.** Framers of the Constitution (James Madison) 　　**b.** Plans of government (Virginia plan, New Jersey plan, Connecticut plan)		Students should understand that the Philadelphia convention addressed weaknesses of the Articles while at the same time trying to avoid a tyrannical national government. • What kinds of men were delegates? Why?
2. Conflict and compromise: seeking effective institutions 　**a.** Protecting liberty against abuses or power 　**b.** Power separated and balanced 　**c.** The Constitution, slavery, and fear of tyrannical powers of government **3.** The document: structure of government	Government	• Why were no women or African-Americans included? How does this help to explain some of the resulting provisions? • Upon what principles of government did the authors agree? disagree? • What were the important compromises reached? • How did the compromises deal with slavery issues? • How was the national government under the Constitution different from that under the Articles?
4. Ratification 　**a.** The Federalist Papers—a New York activity with widespread influence 　**b.** The debate: Federalist and Anti-Federalist arguments	Civic Values	Students should understand the major arguments expressed in the Federalist Papers to gain support for the proposed Constitution. Students could examine Federalist Papers 51 and 78 and write a paper in support of ratification.
C. The Bill of Rights		Students should understand why the Bill of Rights was added to the Constitution, what the contents of the various amendments are, and how the Supreme Court has interpreted and applied the wording in specific cases. (Note: Teachers might consider discussing Bill of Rights cases listed later in the core curriculum while studying the Bill of Rights provisions.) • How did the Bill of Rights satisfy the Anti-Federalist argument? • What specific provisions have been interpreted by the Supreme Court?
D. Basic structure and function: three branches and their operation	Government	Students should understand the powers of the three branches of government as well as the system of checks and balances.

Content	Concepts/Themes	Connections

E. Basic constitutional principles
   1. national power—limits and potentials
   2. federalism—balance between nation and state
   3. the judiciary—interpreter of the Constitution or shaper of public policy
   4. civil liberties—protecting individual liberties from governmental abuses; the balance between government and the individual
   5. criminal procedures—the balance between the rights of the accused and protection of the community and victims
   6. equality—its historic and present meaning as a constitutional value
   7. the rights of women under the Constitution
   8. the rights of ethnic and racial groups under the Constitution
   9. Presidential power in wartime and in foreign affairs
  10. the separation of powers and the capacity to govern
  11. avenues of representation
  12. property rights and economic policy
  13. constitutional change and flexibility
	
	Diversity
		Students could list the powers of each branch and explain current examples of checks and balances.
		
		Students should understand basic constitutional principles and monitor their application throughout the course. After completing work on sections A-E, students could prepare a chart of several specific ideas expressed in the original Constitution and Bill of Rights. For each of these ideas, the students should (1) explain the meaning of the idea, (2) identify its historical origin(s), and (3) cite specifically where that idea is found in the Constitution and/or Bill of Rights.
		
		<u>Suggested Documents</u>: Federalist Papers, United States Constitution, Bill of Rights

F. Implementing the new constitutional principles
   1. Creating domestic stability through sound financial policies: Hamilton's financial plans
   2. Development of unwritten constitutional government under Washington, Adams, and Jefferson: cabinet, political parties, judicial review, executive and Congressional interpretation, lobbying; the Marshall Court (*Marbury* v. *Madison*, 1803, *McCulloch* v. *Maryland*, 1819, and *Gibbons* v. *Ogden*, 1824)
   3. Establishing a stable political system
     a. The Federalist and Republican parties (philosophies of Hamilton and Jefferson)
     b. Suppressing dissent (the Whiskey Rebellion, the Alien and Sedition Acts)
	Government	Students should understand that the Constitution provided only the basic framework for our government. In the early years under the Constitution, several important practical details of government were added.
		
		• How did Hamilton's financial plans contribute to economic growth?
		
		• How did Jefferson's and Madison's opposition to Hamilton's plans contribute to the rise of political parties?
		
		• How did the different geographic regions react to the economic debate?
		
		• How was the "necessary and proper" clause involved in the debate? How has this clause been used throughout our nation's history?

Content	Concepts/Themes	Connections
4. Neutrality and national security, Washington through Monroe: foreign affairs, establishing boundaries **a.** Neutrality: A key element of American foreign policy—influence of geography **b.** A new nation in a world at war **c.** Economic pressures as a tool of diplomacy **d.** The failure of Republican diplomacy: War of 1812 (significance of the War for Native American Indians, Spain, the growth of industry) **e.** Monroe Doctrine	Foreign Policy	• What roles did Washington, Adams, and Jefferson play in shaping the office of President which had been vaguely defined in the Constitution? • How did the rulings of the Marshall Court in *Marbury* v. *Madison, McCulloch* v. *Maryland,* and other cases strengthen the power of the Supreme Court compared to the other two branches? How did the Marshall Court influence the elements of federalism? • What motives influenced the conduct of United States foreign policy in the following periods? Federalist Era: 1789–1800; 1801–1812; Post War of 1812; Monroe Doctrine, Manifest Destiny • How did geography contribute to each of these foreign policy decisions? • How did the debate over foreign policy influence the development of political parties? • How did Jefferson, a strict constructionist and a devotee of limited government and frugality in terms of government spending, justify the purchase of Louisiana? • Was the War of 1812 a "second war for independence," a war of expansion, or a war for maritime rights? • To what extent did the Monroe Doctrine reflect isolationist/neutrality sentiment? United States national concerns? the concerns of the new Latin American republics? • To what extent was Manifest Destiny a philosophical justification for other, more complex social, political, and economic motives? • What regional tensions are evident in the debate over such issues as the Louisiana Purchase, Embargo Act of 1807, War of 1812, and Manifest Destiny? • In the attempt to obtain more secure national boundaries, what areas were acquired by war? by treaty and purchase? • What geographic factors were involved in acquisition and settlement of new territories?

II. The Constitution Tested: Nationalism and Sectionalism

Content	Concepts/ Themes	Connections

A. Factors unifying the United States, 1789–1861
  1. The first and second two-party systems
  2. The market economy and interstate commerce
  3. The Marshall Court
	Diversity	Students should understand that there were forces contributing to national unity as well as sectionalism.
		  ● What factors contributed to the growing economic interdependence of the United States at this time?
		  ● How did the further development of political parties reflect the growing economic and regional differences?
		  ● How did the rulings of the Marshall Court help to strengthen the national government and thereby help to unite the country?

B. Constitutional stress and crisis
  1. Developing sectional differences and philosophies of government
    a. The growth of urban and industrial patterns of life in the North
      1) the transportation revolution (Erie Canal, rise of the port of New York, New York City's rise as a trade and manufacturing center)
      2) the introduction of the factory system
      3) working conditions
      4) women and work
      5) urban problems
    b. Middle-class and working-class life in the pre–Civil War North (families, gender roles, schooling, childhood, living conditions, status of free blacks)
    c. Foreign immigration and nativist reactions (Jews; Irish mass starvation, 1845–1850; Germans; 1848 refugees; Know Nothings)
    d. Patterns of Southern development (growth of cotton cultivation, movement into the Old Southwest, women on plantations)
    e. Life under slavery (slave laws; material conditions of life; women and children; religious and cultural expression; resistance)
	Government
	
	Factors of Production
	
	Immigration and Migration
	Diversity
		● What geographic and economic factors contributed to sectional differences?
		● How did the question of the admission of new territories such as Missouri and later the Mexican Cession threaten national unity?
		● How was the character of America altered by conquest and annexation of the (1) Louisiana Purchase and (2) Mexican Cession?
		● What compromises were reached in 1820, 1833, and 1850 to resolve these sectional differences and avertconstitutional crisis?
		● What characterized the early immigrant experience?
		● What roles did these immigrant groups play in pre–Civil War American society—Irish, German, Scandinavian, and Chinese?
		● Where did these immigrant groups settle and why?
		● How did new arrivals change the composition of a region?

Content	Concepts/ Themes	Connections

2. Equal rights and justice: expansion of franchise; search for minority rights; expansion of slavery; abolitionist movement; the underground railroad; denial of Native American Indian rights and land ownership
  a. Political democratization: national political nominating convention, secret ballot
  b. The rise of mass politics (John Quincy Adams, Andrew Jackson, the spoils system, the bank war, Martin Van Buren)
  c. Native Americans
    1) History of Indian relations from 1607
    2) Native American cultural survival strategies (cultural adaptation, cultural revitalization movements, Pan-Indian movements, resistance)
    3) The removal policy: *Worcester* v. *Georgia*, 1832
  d. The birth of the American reform tradition (religious and secular roots; public schools; care for the physically disabled and the mentally ill; the problems of poverty and crime; antislavery; women's rights movement)
3. The great constitutional debates: states' rights versus federal supremacy (nullification); efforts to address slavery issue (Missouri Compromise, Compromise of 1850, fugitive slave law, *Dred Scott* v. *Sanford*, 1857); preservation of the Union
	Civic Values
	
	Reform Movement
		Students should understand the causes (push and pull factors) of Irish immigration to the United States during this period and the impacts of that migration on both Ireland and the United States.
		Students should understand that the Age of Jackson led to a series of democratic/humanitarian reform movements.
		• To what extent were reforms realized in the areas of voting rights, the abolition of slavery, women's rights, and property rights for Native American Indians?
		<u>Suggested Documents</u>: Seneca Falls Declaration and Resolutions on Woman's Rights, 1848
		
		• Did the Supreme Court ruling in *Dred Scott* v. *Sanford* make a civil war inevitable? Was "compromise" possible?
		• Why did Southerners see the election of Lincoln in 1860 as such a threat?
		• On what basis did Southerners justify their secession? How did this viewpoint compare with that of the Founding Fathers?
		• How did Lincoln and Buchanan differ regarding their constitutional powers as President?
		• In addition to slavery, what factors contributed to the Civil War?
		<u>Suggested Document</u>: *Dred Scott* v. *Sanford*, 1857

C. Territorial expansion through diplomacy, migration, annexation, and war; Manifest Destiny **1.** The Louisiana Purchase **2.** Exploring and settling the West (explorers, Lewis and Clark expedition, naturalists, trappers and traders, trailblazers, missionaries, pioneers, the Mormon Church **3.** The Spanish, Mexican, and Native American West **4.** Motives for and implications of expansion and western settlement **5.** Politics of western expansion (Manifest Destiny, the Texas and Oregon questions, the Mexican War) **6.** Impact of western expansion upon Mexicans and Native Americans	Immigration and Migration	

Content	Concepts/ Themes	Connections

D. The Constitution in jeopardy: The American Civil War
 	
1. United States society divided
 	
    a. Party disintegration and realignment and sectional polarization (Kansas-Nebraska Act, disintegration of the Whig Party and the rise of the Republican Party, *Dred Scott* decision, John Brown's raid)
 	
    b. Abraham Lincoln, the secession crisis, and efforts at compromise (Lincoln-Douglas debates, election of 1860, secession, compromise plans, Fort Sumter)
 	
2. Wartime actions
 	
    a. Military strategy, major battles (Antietam, Gettysburg), and human toll
 	
    b. Impact of war on home front (civil liberties during the Civil War, women's roles)
 	
    c. Government policy during the war (wartime finances, creating a national currency, transcontinental railroad, Homestead Act)
 	
    d. Lincoln and Emancipation (the Emancipation Proclamation, the Gettysburg Address, African-American participation in the Civil War, the 13th Amendment)
	Civic Values
	Constitutional Principles
	
	Change
		• Was the Civil War necessary to resolve the conflict over federalism?
		• To what extent were the powers of the President expanded as Lincoln attempted to deal with the crisis of civil war?
		
		<u>Suggested Documents</u>: The Emancipation Proclamation, the Gettysburg Address

New York Core Curriculum

Unit Three: Industrialization of the United States

I. The Reconstructed Nation

Content	Concepts/ Themes	Connections

A. Reconstruction plans
  1. Lincoln's plan
  2. Congressional Reconstruction
  3. Post-Civil War amendments (13th, 14th, and 15th)
  4. Impeachment of Andrew Johnson
  5. The reconstructed nation and shifting relationships between the federal government, state governments, and individual citizens
	Change
	Constitutional Principles
	Citizenship
		• In what ways were the Congressional Republican plans for Reconstruction more "radical" than those of Abraham Lincoln and Andrew Johnson? What were their views on secession, amnesty and pardon, and procedures for readmission of the Confederate states?
		• How might the debate over Reconstruction have been seen as an attempt to restore the balance of power between Congress and President that had been eroded by Lincoln's wartime measures?
		• Why did the Radical Republicans want to impeach Andrew Johnson? What are the constitutional grounds for impeachment? Had Johnson been removed from office through the impeachment process, how might our government system have changed?
		• What are the specific provisions of the 13th, 14th, and 15th amendments? In spite of the passage of these amendments, how did the Southern states deprive African-Americans of these rights for over 100 years?
		• What impact did the withdrawal of federal support for enforcement of these amendments have upon the status of freedmen?

B. The North
  1. Economic and technological impacts of the Civil War
  2. Expanding world markets
  3. Developing labor needs
	Factors of Production	• In what ways did the North benefit economically from the Civil War?

C. The New South
  1. Agriculture: land and labor (sharecropping and tenant farming)
  2. Status of freedmen
    a. The economic, political, social, and educational experiences of formerly enslaved African-Americans
    b. From exclusion to segregation
  3. Struggle for political control in the New South
  4. Supreme Court interpretations of the 13th and 14th amendments (*Civil Rights Cases*, 1883)
  5. The emerging debate over "proper" role of African-Americans
	Places and Regions
	
	Change
		Students should understand what economic changes were brought about in the South in the years after the Civil War.
		• What new forms of economic and political discrimination developed in the years following the Civil War?
		• In what ways did the Freedmen's Bureau benefit freed slaves?
		• What were the successes and failures of Reconstruction?
		• How did the Supreme Court rulings in the Civil Rights Cases narrow the meaning of the 14th Amendment?
		• Students might use excerpts from speeches and writings of Booker T. Washington and W. E. B. DuBois to compare and contrast the strategies of each to achieve equal rights. Ask students to evaluate the effectiveness of each strategy.

Content	Concepts/Themes	Connections

D. End of Reconstruction
  1. Disputed election of 1876
  2. End of military occupation
  3. Restoration of white control in the South (1870s and 1880s) and abridgment of rights of freed African-Americans
  4. *Plessy* v. *Ferguson*, 1896: "separate but equal"
E. The Impact of the Civil War and Reconstruction: Summary
  1. On political alignments
  2. On the nature of citizenship
  3. On federal-state relations
  4. On the development of the North as an industrial power
  5. On American society
	Citizenship
	
	Environment
		• How did the Compromise of 1877 contribute to segregation?
		• Why did the Northern Republicans and Congressional leaders abandon African-Americans in the 1870s?
		• Use excerpts from the Supreme Court's ruling in *Plessy* v. *Ferguson* to demonstrate that the Court's interpretation of the 14th Amendment established a legal basis for segregation.
		• How successful were the Radical Republicans in achieving their Reconstruction goals?
		• How and why did the "Solid South" emerge?
		• What issues became the primary concerns of the Republican Party after 1877?
		• What major civil rights issues remained unresolved?
		• How were economic development and expansion of the United States affected by the Civil War and Reconstruction?
		• Did the Compromise of 1877 make the end of the Civil War a "draw" rather than a "victory" for the North?

New York Core Curriculum

II. The Rise of American Business, Industry, and Labor, 1865–1920

Content	Concepts/Themes	Connections
A. Economic transformation and the "search for order"	Factors of Production	Students should understand the elements and implications of the expansion and consolidation of American business following the Civil War.
1. Business response to change: organize and rationalize	Factors of Production	• What are the advantages of corporations over proprietorships and partnerships?
2. Organizational responses	Human Systems	• What methods did business leaders use to maximize profits, reduce costs, and/or eliminate competition?
a. From proprietorships and partnerships to the rise of monopolies		
b. Incorporation		
c. Capital concentration; consolidation		
d. Expanding markets: national and international		
e. Merchandising changes, department stores, mail order catalogs		
B. Major areas of growth in business and industry	Science and Technology	Students should understand the geographic effects of the railroads on the United States.
1. Transportation: railroads and automobiles; urban transportation		
2. Building materials: steel		
3. Energy sources: coal, oil, electricity		
4. Communications: telegraph, telephone	Physical Systems	
C. Representative entrepreneurs: Case studies in concentrated wealth and effort (other personalities may be substituted; local examples of enterprise should also be used)		
1. John D. Rockefeller: oil; Andrew Carnegie: steel; Ford: auto		• For the various business leaders studied, what benefits did each individual's success bring to American society? How did these "captains of industry" build great fortunes? How did they use their wealth? What effects did the practices employed by these business leaders have upon competition? Were these business leaders "captains of industry" or "robber barons"?
2. Work ethic: Cotton Mather to Horatio Alger		• How do the prominent business leaders of the late-19th century compare with prominent contemporary business leaders?
3. Conflict between public good and private gain, e.g., use of resources		• What examples of philanthropic contributions exist in your community?
D. New business and government practices: Popular and government responses		Students should note that while the government basically pursued a policy of laissez-faire, there were many government policies that encouraged business development at this time.
1. Laissez-faire and government support; interpretation of 14th Amendment by Supreme Court		• What is meant by "laissez-faire"?
2. Railroad "pooling"; rate inequities (*Wabash, St. Louis, and Pacific Railway* v. *Illinois*, 1886); railroad regulation: state and national ICC.		• How did land grants, subsidies to railroads, tariff and monetary policies, military interventions to break strikes, injunctions, and immigration policies aid the development of business and industry?
3. Competition and absorption; mergers and trusts; Sherman Antitrust Act, 1890 (*United States* v. *E.C. Knight*, 1895)	Economic Systems	• How did Supreme Court rulings affect efforts to regulate business?
		• To what extent was the Sherman Antitrust Act effective in protecting competition?
		• How did groups such as farmers, consumers, workers, and company stockholders react to railroad practices during this time period?

Content	Concepts/ Themes	Connections

E. Labor's response to economic change: Organize
  1. Efforts at national labor unions: Knights of Labor (1869); AF of L (1881–1886); ILGWU (1900)
    a. "Bread and butter" objectives
    b. Unions and social issues (education)
    c. Attitudes toward immigrants, African-Americans, women
    d. Union leadership (Gompers, Debs)
  2. Struggle and conflict
    a. Major strikes: gains and losses—Homestead, Pullman (*In Re Debs,* 1895), Lawrence
    b. Management's position
    c. Weapons or tactics employed in disputes between labor and management
    d. Attitude and role of government
F. Agrarian response to economic change: Organize and protest
    a. The Grange movement as agrarian protest
    b. Populism: a political response—William Jennings Bryan and the election of 1896
      1) Case study: The Populists as a grassroots political party
    c. National government response: Interstate Commerce Act, 1887
	Factors of Production
	Human Systems
	
	Diversity
	
	Government
		• How effective was government regulation of railroads at the state level? national level?
		Students should understand that poor working conditions led to the formation of labor unions.
		• How did the AF of L and Knights of Labor differ in terms of types of workers organized; their views of immigrants, African-Americans, Chinese and women workers; union leadership; their positions on strikes and reform agendas?
		• How do the goals of labor unions in the late-19th century compare with goals today?
		• For the following three strikes, chart (a) conditions that led to the strike, (b) tactics used by both sides, (c) union leadership, (d) role of state or federal government, and (e) outcome of the strike:
		    (1) Homestead
		    (2) Pullman
		    (3) Lawrence
		
		Students should understand the problems faced by farmers in an expanding industrial economy and assess various efforts to resolve these problems.
		• What were the problems experienced by small farmers?
		• Compare the problems of farmers in the 1890s, 1920s, 1950s, 1980s.
		• What economic solutions were proposed by the Grangers?
		• To what extent was the Populist party successful in resolving the problems of farmers? What aspects of the Populist agenda were eventually legislated?
		• Was the Populist party a "typical" third party?

New York Core Curriculum

III. Adjusting Society to Industrialism: American People and Places

Content	Concepts/Themes	Connections

A. Impact of industrialization
  1. Urban growth
    a. Attractions: jobs, education, culture, public education system
    b. Problems (slums, increased crime, inadequate water and sanitation services)
    c. Skyscrapers and elevators; tenements and walk-ups
    d. Social Darwinism, increased class division, conspicuous consumption, social conscience, philanthropy
	Culture and Intellectual Life	Students should understand the economic, social, and political implications of rapid industrial growth and the shift from a rural to an urban way of life.
		  • What transformations did your own community undergo during this time period?

2. Work and workers
    a. Factories and people—immigrant patterns of settlement
    b. Geographic, economic, social, and political considerations
    c. Working conditions: "wage slavery"
    d. Living conditions: company towns and urban slums
    e. The Great Migration: The migration of African-Americans to the North
	Factors of Production
	
	Diversity
		Students should contrast the views of Social Darwinists like Carnegie, Russell Conwell, Vanderbilt, Rockefeller, and Morgan with the views of labor leaders, Populists, and Progressive reformers.
		  • Use political cartoons to illustrate the images of big business and the call for reforms.
		  • How were the lives of working-class women and children affected by industrialization? How did this reality compare with the Victorian view of traditional roles in society?
		  • What insights about the nature of child labor can be drawn from John Spargo's *The Bitter Cry of the Children*?

3. Women, families, and work
    a. Traditional roles—Victorian ideal and reality
    b. Outside and inside their homes: double drudgery
    c. Jobs for domestics, laundresses, and textile workers; technology brought jobs as telephone operators and typists
    d. Emerging family patterns: two wage earners, broken homes
    e. Problems of child labor, elderly, disabled, and African-American women
      1) Case study: child labor
    f. Role of religion in a pluralistic society
      1) Religious tolerance develops slowly
      2) Puritan beliefs and values influenced our historical development
      3) Religion and party politics to 1896
  4. The growing middle class (consumerism and its material benefits and effects)
  5. Art and literature (Mark Twain and penny dailies)
	Culture and Intellectual Life
	
	Diversity
		Describe the effects of internal migration on different regions of the United States.
		  • How was the class structure altered by industrialization?

B. Immigration, 1850–1924
  1. New sources: eastern/southern Europe; Asia—the "new ethnicity"
    a. Case studies: Italian immigration, Chinese immigration (1850–1924, West to East migration), Russian/Jewish immigration
  2. The impulses abroad
  3. The attractions here: labor shortages, liberty, and freedoms
	Change	Students should understand the characteristics that distinguished the new immigrants (1850–1924) from the earlier immigrant groups. What difficulties did they face? In what specific ways did they contribute to the shaping of American society?

Content	Concepts/ Themes	Connections

4. Urbanization: ghettos
5. "Americanization" process
6. Impacts on family, religion, education, and politics
7. Contributions to American society
  a. Diversity of the United States population
C. Reactions to the "new" immigration
  1. Cultural pluralism: assimilation (Americanization), acculturation ("melting pot" or cultural pluralism), or both
  2. Nativist reactions: stereotyping and prejudice
    1) Case study: Irish immigration
  3. Impact on African-Americans and other established minorities
  4. "Yellow Peril," West Coast restrictions
  5. Literacy testing, 1917
  6. The Red Scare
  7. Quota acts of 1921 and 1924
D. The frontier (1850–1890)
  1. Land west of the Mississippi
    a. Rolling plains and the Great American Desert
    b. Native American Indian nations; concept of oneness with the environment
    c. The Homestead Act, 1862, and the settlement of the West
  2. The impact of industrialization
    a. Improved transportation facilitated shipping of foodstuffs and migration of population
    b. Western migration of immigrants
    c. Potential for investment: development of key urban centers
  3. Native American Indians
    a. Pressures of advancing white settlement: differing views of land use and ownership
    b. Treaties and legal status
    c. The Indian wars: 1850–1900
    d. Legislating Indian life: reservations; Dawes Act (1887)
    e. Indian civil rights laws—legal status of Native American Indians, 1887–1970: citizenship, 1924; self-government, 1934; self-determination, 1970
	Culture and Intellectual Life
	
	Citizenship
	
	Environment
	
	Human Systems
	
	Science and Technology
	
	Diversity
	
	Human Systems
	Citizenship
		• Use cartoons from Thomas Nast to illustrate the negative reactions to these new immigrants.
		  - Compare and contrast the following:
		  - nativist movement of 1850s
		  - Ku Klux Klan of 1860s and 1870s
		  - Ku Klux Klan of 1920s
		• What conflicts between American ideals and reality are illustrated in a study of immigration laws such as (1) Chinese Exclusion Act, (2) Gentlemen's Agreement, (3) Literacy Test (1917), (4) Emergency Quota Act (1921), (5) Immigration Restriction Act (1924), (6) the McCarran-Walter Act (1952), and (7) immigration legislation of 1965, 1986, and the 1990s?
		• Locate the concentrations of different ethnic groups in the United States at the turn of the 20th century.
		
		• Use an excerpt from Frederick Jackson Turner's frontier thesis and an excerpt from one of his critics to illustrate conflicting views about the role of the frontier in the making of American democracy.
		• What are the geographic differences between the Great Plains, the Southwest, and the Rocky Mountains regions of the West?
		• What role did government policies play in the settling of the West?
		Have students consider the Homestead Act, land grants and subsidies to transcontinental railroads, and liberal immigration policy.
		• How did the Industrial Revolution contribute to the economic development of the Great Plains?
		
		Students should understand the clash that occurred between Native American Indians and advancing white settlers.
		• How did the Native American Indians' concepts of land ownership and respect for the natural environment compare with that of the white settlers?
		• Were the Indian wars a case study of genocide?
		• Evaluate the federal government's attempts to address Native American Indian rights from 1887 to the present.

Unit Four: The Progressive Movement: Responses to the Challenges Brought About by Industrialization and Urbanization

I. Reform in America

Content	Concepts/Themes	Connections
A. Pressures for reform 　**1.** Progressives supported the use of government power for different reform purposes 　**2.** Effects of developing technologies and their social, ethical, and moral impacts 　**3.** Struggle for fair standards of business operation and working conditions (*Lochner v. New York,* 1905; *Muller v. Oregon,* 1908) 　**4.** Increasing inequities between wealth and poverty 　**5.** Rising power and influence of the middle class	Science and Technology	• What specific political, economic, and social problems in late-19th-century America led to the call for reform?
B. Progress: Social and economic reform and consumer protection 　**1.** The "Muckrakers" and reform 　　**a.** Magazine writers (Steffens, Tarbell) 　　**b.** Novelists (Norris, Sinclair) 　　**c.** Legislation (Pure Food and Drug Act, 1906, Meat Inspection Act, 1906) 　**2.** Other areas of concern 　　**a.** Social settlement movement and the problems of poverty (Jacob Riis, Jane Addams) 　　**b.** Women's rights and efforts for peace 　　　**1)** The suffrage movement (Elizabeth Cady Stanton, Susan B. Anthony); Seneca Falls 　　　**2)** Beginnings of fight for birth control (Margaret Sanger) 　　　**3)** Peace movement 　　**c.** The black movement and reform (Booker T. Washington and W.E.B. DuBois) 　　　**1)** Formation of NAACP (1912) 　　　**2)** Ida Wells (anti-lynching) 　　　**3)** Marcus Garvey 　　**d.** Temperance/prohibition 　　**e.** Formation of Anti-Defamation League (1913)	Culture and Intellectual Life Diversity	• Have students define the concept of "muckraker" by compiling newspaper articles, editorials, and political cartoons in which the media is currently exposing some evil in business, government, or society. • Have students complete two charts illustrating specific examples of Progressive reforms. One chart should deal with the goals of Progressive reform; the other should deal with the means by which these Progressive reforms were achieved. Possible *means* might include (1) Presidential actions, (2) Congressional legislation, (3) Supreme Court rulings, (4) constitutional amendments, (5) state government actions, (6) local government actions, and (7) actions of individuals and groups outside the government. • Students could compare developments of the Progressive period with those of the New Deal and the Great Society. Topics could include goals, leadership, and the accomplishments of various groups. Groups could include farmers, women, labor, African-Americans, and Native American Indians.
C. Progressivism and government action 　**1.** Emerging Progressive movement: political reform 　　**1)** Influence of America's urban middle class 　　**a.** Municipal and state reform 　　　**1)** Municipal reform: response to urban problems 　　　**2)** Sudden growth and needed services 　　**b.** Progressive state reform: e.g., Wisconsin (Robert LaFollette); New York (Theodore Roosevelt); Massachusetts (initiative, referendum, recall); economic, social, environmental reforms	Government Civic Values	• How were the powers of the Presidency influenced by the reforming role played by Theodore Roosevelt and Woodrow Wilson? • How did the Supreme Court both aid and retard Progressive reform at this time?

I. Reform in America, continued

Content	Concepts/ Themes	Connections
2. Theodore Roosevelt and the Square Deal	Government	
a. The stewardship theory of the Presidency		
b. Legislation strengthening railroad regulation and consumer protection		
c. "Trust-busting" court cases (*Northern Securities Co.* v. *United States,* 1904); rule of reason: Standard Oil		
3. Conservation		
a. Theodore Roosevelt's concern for nature, land, and resources		
b. Federal legislation and projects: effects on states' limits		
c. Roles of Gifford Pinchot and John Muir		
4. Woodrow Wilson and the New Freedom		
a. Progressivism at its zenith; the 1912 election: Taft, Roosevelt, Wilson	Environment	
b. The Underwood Tariff and the graduated income tax		
c. Clayton Antitrust Act and the Federal Trade Commission		
d. The Federal Reserve System (monetary controls)	Civic Values	
e. Women's suffrage amendment		
5. World War I: effect on domestic reform		

II. The Rise of American Power

Content	Concepts/ Themes	Connections
A. An emerging global involvement	Places and Regions	Students should understand that United States imperialist designs in Asia and Latin America represent the second phase of Manifest Destiny.
1. From old diplomacy to new, 1865–1900		• Compare and contrast the motives and policies of the period 1890–1914 with those of the 1840s.
a. Role of increased American power		
1) Communications technology		• How was Social Darwinism reflected in United States foreign policy from 1890 to 1914?
2) American attitudes toward international role		
3) Growth of naval power		
b. Perry and the "opening" of Japan (1854)		
2. Other Pacific overtures		
a. United States and China; the Chinese perspective (Boxer Rebellion)		
b. The Open-Door policy		
c. Acquisition of Hawaii	Change	• Students should analyze headlines in Pulitzer and Hearst newspapers from 1897 to 1898 to illustrate Social Darwinism and the role of the press in shaping public opinion.
d. Naval bases: Samoa		
3. Imperialism: the Spanish-American War		
a. Causes for war		• To help students understand the opposing arguments of the imperialists and anti-imperialists regarding annexation of the Philippines, conduct a simulated Senate Foreign Relations Committee hearing on the proposed 1898 Treaty of Paris.
b. United States empire—Puerto Rico; Cuban protectorate (the Platt Amendment)		
1) Acquisition of the Philippines: "the great debate"		
2) Disposition of territories		
3) Constitutional issues		

Content	Concepts/ Themes	Connections

4. Latin American affairs
  a. Monroe Doctrine update (Roosevelt corollary): the view from Latin America
  b. West Indies protectorates ("the big stick")
  c. Panama Canal: acquisition and construction; Canal retrocession treaty
  d. Taft and dollar diplomacy
B. Restraint and involvement: 1914–1920
  1. United States involvement
    a. Efforts at neutrality and "preparedness"
    b. Causes of United States entry into World War I
    c. United States role in the war
    d. United States reaction to the Russian Revolution
C. Wartime constitutional issues
  1. War opposition and patriotism: the draft issue
  2. Espionage and Sedition acts
  3. *Schenck* v. *United States*, 1919; clear and present danger doctrine
  4. Red Scare, 1918–1919
D. The search for peace and arms control: 1914–1930
  1. The peace movement: Women's International League for Peace and Freedom
  2. War aims: The Fourteen Points
  3. Treaty of Versailles: Wilson's role
  4. League of Nations: Henry Cabot Lodge and the United States Senate rejection
  5. Washington Naval Disarmament Conference (1920s)
  6. Reparations and war debts (United States as a world banker)
  7. Kellogg-Briand Pact (1928)
  8. Establishment of the World Court
	
	Change
	
	Citizenship
	
	Government
	
	Human Rights
	Civic Values
		• Were United States actions in Latin America during this period a continuation of or a departure from previous American policy?
		• In what ways did United States policy from 1914 to 1917 violate Wilson's promise of neutrality in thought and actions? How did this action lead the United States into war?
		
		Students should understand how the rights of citizens are limited during wartime.
		• How did World War I restrictions on civil liberties compare with those imposed during the Civil War? World War II? (see *Schenck* v. *United States*, 1919 and *Debs* v. *United States*, 1919)
		• Why weren't the provisions of the Treaty of Versailles based more fully on Wilson's Fourteen Points?
		• What factors contributed to the Senate's failure to ratify the Treaty of Versailles?
		• To what extent did the Treaty of Versailles and subsequent diplomacy from 1920 to 1933 reflect Wilsonian principles?
		• Ask students to nominate individuals for the Nobel Peace Prize for actions taken during the period 1914–1930. More recently?

Unit Five: At Home and Abroad: Prosperity and Depression, 1917–1940

I. War and Prosperity: 1917–1929

Content	Concepts/ Themes	Connections
A. Impact of war	Diversity	• What important social changes took place both during and after World War I?
1. War's effects on gender roles, on African-Americans, and other minority groups		• What did the American public perceive "normalcy" to mean? (Apply the concept to both foreign and domestic affairs.)
2. Case study: Movement of African-Americans from the South to northern cities		• Investigate the causes and effects of the South-to-North migration during this time period.
3. Return to "normalcy": 1918–1921		• How did the economic policies of the 1920s contribute to the Great Depression?
B. The twenties: Business boom or false prosperity?		• What scandals arose during the Harding administration? What scandals have plagued subsequent administrations?
1. Post–World War I recession		
2. Avarice and scandal: Teapot Dome		
3. Coolidge prosperity; not for everyone	Factors of Production	
4. Problems on the farm		
a. Expansion, mortgages, and advancing technology		
b. Farmers and minorities fail to share in economic benefit		
5. Speculative boom: the "big bull market"		
C. Mass consumption and the clash of cultural values	Culture and Intellectual Life	• How did the growth of the automobile industry stimulate the growth of other industries? How did it influence United States politics and lifestyles?
1. Mass consumption		
a. The automobile: new industries, products, and services	Factors of Production	Have students compare the attitudes of the 1920s with those of the 1950s relative to: (1) restrictions on immigration, (2) anti-communist hysteria, (3) religion and morality, (4) role of women, (5) civil rights, (6) new forms of entertainment, (7) growth of suburbia, (8) transportation improvements, and (9) consumer attitudes.
b. Installment buying: consumer durable goods (appliances)		
c. Real estate boom and suburban development; its economic and geographic implications: decline of trolleys and trains, improvement of roads		
1) The emergence of new regional, political, and economic units	Science and Technology	
d. Entertainment: radio; motion pictures; advertising and cultural homogenization		

Content	Concepts/Themes	Connections
2. Constitutional and legal issues		
a. Threats to civil liberties: Red Scare, Ku Klux Klan, and Sacco and Vanzetti	Citizenship	
b. Prohibition (18th Amendment) and the Volstead Act: stimulus to crime, public attitudes, repeal (21st Amendment)		
c. Science, religion, and education: the Scopes trial (1925)		
d. Restrictions on immigration: closing the "golden door"		
3. Shifting cultural values		
a. Revolution in morals and manners: fads, flappers, and Freud	Culture and Intellectual Life	
b. Women's changing roles	Diversity	
1) Effect of World War I		
2) Involvement in the political process: the 19th Amendment		
3) Health and working conditions		
4) Women in the workforce		
5) Emerging role: emphasis on wife rather than mother		
c. The literary scene		
1) Sinclair Lewis, Ernest Hemingway, Edith Wharton, Willa Cather, and F. Scott Fitzgerald		
2) The Harlem Renaissance: Duke Ellington, Langston Hughes, Bessie Smith		

II. The Great Depression

Content	Concepts/ Themes	Connections
A. Onset of the Depression	Factors of Production	Students should understand that the basic weaknesses in the economy contributed to both the stock market crash and the general economic collapse that became known as the Great Depression.
1. Weakness in the economy		
a. Overproduction/underconsumption (maldistribution of wealth)		
b. Overexpansion of credit (e.g., buying stock on margin)		• Compare and contrast the responses of Presidents Herbert Hoover and Franklin Delano Roosevelt to the Depression.
2. The stock market crash	Economic Systems	
a. Worldwide nature—Growing financial interdependence		
b. Interdependent banking systems		
c. International trade		
d. Political repercussions		
3. The Hoover response	Diversity	
a. Rugged individualism; "trickle down" economics		
b. Reconstruction Finance Corporation		
4. Unemployment, the Bonus Army, Hoovervilles; impact on women and minorities		
B. Franklin D. Roosevelt and the New Deal: Relief, recovery, and reform programs	Government	Students should compare and contrast the New Deal with the Progressive and Great Society reform movements in terms of goals, leadership, and accomplishments.
1. Relief of human suffering		
a. Bank "holiday"; Emergency Banking Act		
b. Federal Emergency Relief Act		
c. Unemployment: WPA, PWA, CCC; troubling equity issues		
2. Recovery of the United States economy		
a. NRA: "codes of fair competition"		
b. Mortgage relief: HOLC, FHA		
c. First and second AAA, scarcity and parity		
3. Search for effective reform (program examples)		
a. Banking: Glass-Steagall Act (FDIC)	Economic Systems	
b. Stock market: SEC		
c. Social Security		
d. Labor		
1) Wagner Act (NLRB)		
2) Labor Standards Act		
4. Labor's response: Formation of CIO		
5. Controversial aspects of the New Deal		
a. Constitutional issues		
1) Supreme Court and the NRA (*Schechter Poultry Corp.* v. *United States,* 1935)		Students should understand that even though the New Deal did much to alleviate the effects of the Depression, the New Deal raised controversy. Some felt that it was leading to socialism, destroying checks and balances, and violating the two-term Presidential tradition. (see *United States* v. *Butler,* 1936)
2) Supreme Court and the AAA	Government	
3) TVA: model yardstick or creeping socialism		

Content	Concepts/Themes	Connections

b. 1936 election "mandate"
c. Roosevelt's "Court-packing" proposal: failure and success
d. 1940: third-term controversy (the unwritten constitution)
e. Passage of the 22nd Amendment (1951)
6. The human factor
  a. FDR as communicator and his efforts to restore public confidence; press conferences, "fireside chats," and effective use of the radio
  b. Eleanor Roosevelt as the President's eyes and ears
  c. The Dust Bowl and the Okies
  d. The New Deal and women (Frances Perkins)
  e. The New Deal and minorities (shift in African-American vote): discriminatory results
  f. Indian Reorganization Act (1934)
7. Culture of the Depression
  a. Literature: John Steinbeck and Langston Hughes
  b. Music: jazz, swing (big bands)
  c. Art: WPA, fine arts, Hollywood, comic books
8. Opposition to the New Deal: Al Smith, Norman Thomas, Huey Long, Father Coughlin, Dr. Townsend
	Culture and Intellectual Life
	
	Diversity
	
	Culture and Intellectual Life
		• Have students analyze the political impact of the "Court packing" proposal by comparing the anti-New Deal decision in *United States* v. *Butler,* 1936 with the pro–New Deal decision in *National Labor Relations Board* v. *Jones & Laughlin Steel Corp.,* 1937.
		• Why did Eleanor Roosevelt play such a substantive role as First Lady? How do her actions as First Lady compare with the actions of more recent First Ladies?
		• Why did African-American voters increasingly change political allegiance from the Republican Party to the Democratic Party after 1934?
		• How did the Depression and New Deal programs affect women and the nuclear family?
		• What geographic/environmental conditions contributed to the migration from the Dust Bowl to the West?
		• How do the problems of farmers in the 1920s and 1930s compare with those of the 1880s, 1950s, and 1980s?
		• How did the Indian Reorganization Act of 1934 compare with the Dawes Act of 1887 in terms of (1) goals and (2) Native American Indian reactions?
		• How did the New Deal support the fine arts?
		• Why did "escapist" movies become popular at this time?
		• What New Deal projects were completed in your own community?
		• What are the themes of the literature of John Steinbeck and the photographs of Margaret Bourke-White?

Unit Six: The United States in an Age of Global Crisis: Responsibility and Cooperation

I. Peace in Peril: 1933–1950

Content	Concepts/Themes	Connections
A. Isolation and neutrality	Interdependence	• To what extent did the isolationist policies of the 1930s reflect a desire to avoid a repeat of the conditions that drew us into World War I?
1. Causes of disillusion and pacifism		
2. Neutrality Acts of 1935–37		
3. Spanish Civil War: testing war technology and ideology		
4. FDR's "quarantine" speech (1937)		
B. Failure of peace; triumph of aggression		• In what sense was the United States "involved" in World War II before the Pearl Harbor attack and the Congressional declaration of war in December 1941?
1. Aggressions of Japan, Germany, Italy: 1932–1940		
2. Appeasement: The Munich Conference (1938)		
3. German attack on Poland; start of World War II in Europe	Places and Regions Interdependence	
4. Gradual United States involvement		
a. Neutrality Act of 1939 ("cash and carry")		
b. Lend-Lease Act and 50 overage destroyers deal		
c. The moral dimension: The Atlantic Charter (August 1941)		
C. The United States in World War II		
1. Pearl Harbor		
2. The human dimensions of the war	Culture and Intellectual Life	• How did the need to wage "total war" alter the nature of American society? • How did United States domestic policies during World War II compare with those of World War I?
a. The "arsenal of democracy" (feats of productivity)		
b. Role of women: WACs; Rosie the Riveter; return of the retired		
c. Mobilization: the draft; minority issues		
d. Financing the war: war bond drives; Hollywood goes to war		
e. Rationing		
f. Experiences of men and women in military service		
3. Allied strategy and leadership		Students should compare the role of the United States in World War I and World War II in terms of (1) the arsenal of democracy, (2) United States military leadership and strategy, and (3) role of the President in planning the peace.
a. Assistance to Soviet Union		
b. Europe first		
c. A two-front war		
4. The atomic bomb	Science and Technology	Students should understand that there were several moral issues that grew out of the war experience. These include (1) rights of Japanese-Americans, (2) integration of African-Americans, (3) United States reactions to the Nazi Holocaust, (4) morality of nuclear warfare, and (5) treatment of war criminals.
a. The Manhattan Project (role of refugees)		
b. Truman's decision to use the atomic bomb against Japan: Hiroshima and Nagasaki		
c. United States occupation of Japan; the "MacArthur constitution"		
d. Japanese war crime trials	Diversity	• Students should study the origins of these concerns and the ways in which they have been addressed in the postwar period.
5. The war's impact on minorities		• The Nuremberg trials established the concept of "crimes against humanity." What are some more current examples?
a. Incarceration of West Coast Japanese-Americans; Executive Order 9066; *Korematsu* v. *United States* (1944)		

I. Peace in Peril: 1933–1950, continued

Content	Concepts/ Themes	Connections
b. Extent of racially integrated units in the military	Civic Values Constitutional Principles	
c. The Nazi Holocaust: United States and world reactions		
d. The Nuremberg war crimes trials; later trials of other Nazi criminals, e.g., Eichmann, Barbie		
6. Demobilization	Change	• How did the economic, social, and political problems of adjusting to the end of World War II compare with those after World War I? Consider inflation, strikes, Presidential policies, political control of Congress, ways of dealing with communist threats, immigration policies, and opportunities for veterans.
a. Inflation and strikes		
b. The G.I. Bill; impact on education and housing		
c. Truman's Fair Deal		
d. Partisan problems with Congress		
e. Minorities continued to find it difficult to obtain fair practices in housing, employment, education	Diversity	• How did Truman enhance the civil rights of African-Americans? Why did he use executive power rather than Congressional legislation?
f. Upset election of 1948; Truman versus Dewey		
g. Truman and civil rights		

II. Peace with Problems: 1945–1960

Content	Concepts/ Themes	Connections
A. International peace efforts	Civic Values	Students should understand the role played by the United States in securing peace: (1) formation of the United Nations, (2) relief and refugee efforts, and (3) economic assistance to war-torn economies and societies.
1. Formation of the United Nations		
2. United Nations Universal Declaration of Human Rights		
a. Eleanor Roosevelt's role		
b. Senate response		
3. Displaced persons: refugee efforts		
B. Expansion and containment: Europe	Places and Regions	• How did the United States respond to the expansion of communism in Europe? in Asia?
1. Summitry: Yalta and Potsdam, establishing "spheres of influence"		• Compare and contrast the international role of the United States following World War II and World War I.
2. The Iron Curtain: Winston Churchill		
3. Postwar uses for United States power	Interdependence	• How might the situation in Europe be different today if the United States had not applied the Truman Doctrine? extended Marshall Plan aid? conducted the Berlin airlift? formed NATO?
a. The Truman Doctrine: Greece and Turkey		
b. The Marshall Plan		
1) Aid for Europe		
2) The Common Market		
3) European Parliament		
c. Berlin airlift		
d. Formation of NATO alliance		
C. Containment in Asia, Africa, and Latin America		
1. The United States and Japan	Foreign Policy	<u>Suggested Documents</u>: The United Nation Charter (1945); The Truman Doctrine (1947)
a. Separate peace treaty (1951)		
b. Reconstruction of Japan		
2. The United States and China		
a. Rise to power of Mao Zedong and the People's Republic of China		
b. Chiang Kai-shek to Taiwan (1949)		

II. Peace with Problems: 1945–1960, continued

Content	Concepts/Themes	Connections

3. USSR tests an A-bomb (1949)
4. The "hot war" in Asia: Korean War
  a. The Yalu River: China enters the war
  b. United Nations efforts: MacArthur, Truman, and "limited war"
  c. Stalemate and truce (1953)
5. Point four aid: Africa, Asia, Latin America
	Interdependence	

D. The Cold War at home
  1. Truman and government loyalty checks Case studies: The Smith Act and the House Un-American Activities Committee (*Watkins* v. *United States*, 1957); the Alger Hiss case (1950); the Rosenberg trial (1950)
  2. Loyalty and dissent: the case of Robert Oppenheimer
  3. McCarthyism
  4. Politics of the Cold War
    a. Loss of China
    b. Stalemate in Korea
    c. Truman's falling popularity
	Citizenship
	Civic Values
		• Was the Cold War inevitable? How did United States support for "self-determination" conflict with the Soviet Union's desire for security in Eastern Europe at the end of the war?
		• How did the United States respond to the communist threat at home?
		• What constitutional values were sacrificed in responding to the communist threat?
		• How did the second Red Scare compare with the first Red Scare?
		• What has "McCarthyism" come to mean?
		• How has the term "McCarthyism" been applied in more recent history?

Unit Seven: World in Uncertain Times: 1950–Present

I. Toward a Postindustrial World: Living in a Global Age

Content	Concepts/Themes	Connections

A. Changes within the United States
  1. Energy sources (nuclear power)
  2. Materials (plastics, light metals)
  3. Technology (computers)
  4. Corporate structures (multinational corporations)
  5. Nature of employment (agriculture to industry to service)
  6. Problems (waste disposal, air/water pollution, growing energy usage, depleting resources, e.g., domestic oil supply)
	Science and Technology
	
	Environment	

II. Containment and Consensus: 1945–1960

Content	Concepts/Themes	Connections
A. Review postwar events	Places and Regions	
1. Emerging power relationships: East/West; North/South; (haves/have-nots; developed/developing nations)		
B. Eisenhower foreign policies		• How did each of the post–World War II Presidents build on and extend the policy of containment?
1. The end of the Korean War		
2. John Foster Dulles, the domino theory and massive retaliation; brinkmanship posture		• How did Truman, Eisenhower, Kennedy, and Johnson carry forth the programs of the New Deal?
3. The H-bomb; atoms for peace		
4. Summits and U-2s		• How did Presidents Eisenhower, Kennedy, and Johnson further the civil rights initiatives begun by Truman?
5. Establishment of SEATO	Interdependence	
6. Controversy: Aswan Dam and Suez Canal		
7. Polish and Hungarian uprisings		
8. Eisenhower Doctrine: intervention in Lebanon	Places and Regions	
9. Sputnik: initiating the space race		
C. Domestic politics and constitutional issues		
1. The Eisenhower peace	Civic Values	
a. Returning the United States to a peacetime economy		
b. Interstate Highway Act (1956)		
c. Suburbanization		
d. The Warren Court		
2. Civil rights		
a. Jackie Robinson breaks the color barrier		Students should understand that in spite of the victory of the forces of integration in the *Brown* v. *Board of Education of Topeka* decision, there was much resistance to a broader application of the principle of integration. Students should study various specific events in the civil rights movement from 1955 to 1965.
b. *Brown* v. *Board of Education of Topeka*, 1954		
c. Beginnings of modern civil rights movement		
1) Rosa Parks and the Montgomery bus boycott		
2) Little Rock: school desegregation		
3) Segregation in public transportation ruled unconstitutional		
4) Sit-ins: nonviolent tactic		
5) Civil Rights Act of 1957	Citizenship Civic Values	
D. The people		
1. Prosperity and conservatism		
a. Postwar consumption: homes, autos, and television	Change	• Compare the attitudes, values, and social changes of the 1950s (post–World War II) with those of the 1920s (post–World War I).
b. New educational opportunities: G.I. Bill		• What significant demographic changes became evident in the 1950s?
c. The baby boom and its effects		
2. Migration and immigration		• Explain how increased use of the automobile changed urban areas. Consider how the automobile contributed to the growth of suburbs and changed the demographic composition of the center city.
a. Suburbanization: Levittowns		
b. Cities: declining	Environment Diversity Immigration and Migration	
c. New immigration patterns: Caribbean focus		

III. Decade of Change: 1960s

Content	Concepts/Themes	Connections
A. The Kennedy years		• Is the "New Frontier" label for the Kennedy administration justified in terms of both foreign and domestic policies?
1. The New Frontier: dreams and promises		
a. Civil rights actions	Civic Values	
1) James Meredith at the University of Mississippi		• Although President Kennedy's charismatic style enhanced his public image, what practical effect did it have on his working relationship with Congress?
2) Public career of Dr. Martin Luther King, Jr., Birmingham protest ("Letter from Birmingham Jail")		Apply this question to the following areas: (1) civil rights legislation, (2) immigration reform, (3) federal aid to education, and (4) foreign policy initiatives.
3) Assassination of Medgar Evers		<u>Suggested Document</u>: John F. Kennedy's Inaugural Address
4) March on Washington		
2. Foreign policy and Cold War crises	Interdependence	
a. Bay of Pigs invasion		
b. Vienna Summit/Berlin Wall		
c. Cuban missile crisis		
d. Laos and Vietnam		
e. Latin America and the Alliance for Progress		
f. Peace Corps		
g. Launching the race to the Moon	Places and Regions	• In what ways were your school district facilities and programs changed as a result of State and federal programs regarding the handicapped and disabled?
h. Nuclear Test Ban Treaty 1963, 1967; Hot Line established		
3. Movement for rights of disabled citizens		
a. Background	Citizenship	
1) Historic attitude that disabled were defective		
2) Emergence of humanitarian view in 19th century, development of large institutions		
3) Development of the concept of normalization; early-20th-century programs of education and training		
b. Kennedy administration, 1961–1963; beginning awareness, changing attitudes	Diversity	
1) President's Council on Mental Retardation		
2) Special Olympics		
c. Litigation and legislation; 1960–present		
1) Education of the Handicapped Act, 1966		
2) Education for All Handicapped Children Act, 1971		
3) Rehabilitation Act of 1973, Section 504		
4) Americans with Disabilities Act, 1990		
d. Dependence to independence		
1) Activism by disabled veterans		
2) Deinstitutionalization		
3) Mainstreaming		
4. Assassination in Dallas		
B. Johnson and the Great Society	Presidential Decisions and Actions	• In what ways did Johnson's social programs build upon the Kennedy legacy?
1. Expanding on the Kennedy social programs		• Why was Johnson more successful than Kennedy in translating social programs into legislation?
a. War on poverty; VISTA		
b. Medicare		

Content	Concepts/Themes	Connections
c. Federal aid to education		
d. Environmental issues and concerns		
2. The Moon landing: the challenge of space exploration		
3. Continued demands for equality: civil rights movement		• Students should understand that the 1960s witnessed protest movements of peoples of diverse backgrounds (African-Americans, women, Hispanic-Americans, Native American Indians).
a. Black protest, pride, and power		• Compare and contrast the civil rights movement after 1965 with the earlier phase (1955–1965) in terms of (1) goals, (2) leadership, (3) strategies, and (4) achievements.
1) NAACP (National Association for the Advancement of Colored People): legal judicial leadership, Urban League		
b. Case studies	Civic Values	• Compare the feminist movement of the 1960s with the suffragist movement in terms of (1) goals, (2) leadership, (3) strategies, and (4) achievements.
1) SNCC (Student Nonviolent Coordinating Committee): sit-in movement among college students		• To what extent did the civil rights movement influence the demands for equality on the part of Hispanic-Americans and Native American Indians? How successful were their efforts?
2) SCLC (Southern Christian Leadership Conference): promote nonviolent resistance, sit-ins, boycotts	Diversity	
3) CORE (Congress of Racial Equality): "Freedom Riders"		
4) Testing of segregation laws		
5) Others: Black Muslims; prominence of Malcolm X: advocating separation of races, separate state in the United States	Civic Values	
6) Civil unrest: Watts riot, 1965, as example; Kerner Commission		
7) Assassination of Malcolm X (February 1965)		
c. Legislative impact		
1) Civil Rights Act of 1964 (*Heart of Atlanta Motel, Inc.* v. *United States,* 1964), modifications since 1964		
2) 24th Amendment (eliminating poll tax)	Civic Values	
3) Voting Rights Act, 1965		
4) Court decisions since 1948 upholding or modifying preferential treatment in employment; equal access to housing; travel and accommodations; voting rights; educational equity	Citizenship	
5) Fair Housing Act, 1968		
4. Demands for equality: women		
a. The modern women's movement		
1) Kennedy Commission and the Civil Rights Act, 1963–1964		
2) NOW (1966) to present		
b. Issues		
1) Shifting roles and images	Diversity	
2) Equal Rights Amendment (failure to ratify)		
3) *Roe* v. *Wade,* 1973		
4) Equality in the workplace: compensation, the glass ceiling		
5) Increased focus on domestic abuse		

III. Decade of Change: 1960s, continued

Content	Concepts/ Themes	Connections

5. Rising consciousness of Hispanic-Americans
  a. "Brown power" movement
  b. Organizing farm labor (Cesar Chavez)
  c. Cuban and Haitian immigration
  d. Increasing presence in American politics
6. Demands for equality: American Indian Movement (AIM) and other protests
  a. Occupation of Alcatraz
  b. The "long march"
  c. Wounded Knee, 1973
7. Rights of the accused
  a. *Mapp* v. *Ohio,* 1961
  b. *Gideon* v. *Wainwright,* 1963
  c. *Miranda* v. *Arizona,* 1966
8. Legislative reapportionment: *Baker* v. *Carr,* 1962
	Diversity
	
	Civic Values
		• Students should understand the tension involved in balancing the protection of the rights of the accused with the need to protect society.
		• Examine the content of the *Baker* v. *Carr* ruling to discuss how legislative reapportionment has expanded the concept of democratic representation.

IV. The Limits of Power: Turmoil at Home and Abroad, 1955–1972

Content	Concepts/ Themes	Connections

A. Vietnam: sacrifice and turmoil
1. The French-Indochinese War: early United States involvement; Truman, Eisenhower, and Kennedy policies (review how foreign policy is formulated)
2. United States and the spread of communism; domino theory; credibility of other United States commitments
3. Civil war in South Vietnam; concept of guerrilla warfare
4. LBJ and the Americanization of the war
  a. Fear of "losing" Vietnam
  b. Escalation and United States assumptions; Tet offensive
5. Student protests at home
  a. Draft protesters
  b. Political radicals: protests, Students for a Democratic Society (SDS), antiwar
  c. Cultural radicals: hippies and communalists
6. 1968: A year of turmoil
  a. President Johnson's decision not to seek reelection
  b. Assassinations of Dr. Martin Luther King, Jr. (April 1968) and Robert Kennedy (June 1968)
  c. The Democratic Convention; war protesters disrupt proceedings
  d. Impact of the Vietnam War on society
	Places and Regions
	
	Culture and Intellectual Life
	
	Change
		Students should (1) trace the history of United States involvement in Vietnam in the context of containment policy in Southeast Asia, (2) examine its domestic impact, and (3) evaluate both its short-term and long-term effects.

V. The Trend Toward Conservatism, 1972–1985

Content	Concepts/Themes	Connections
A. Nixon as President, 1969-1974	Change	• In what specific ways did Nixon depart from Johnson's Great Society?
1. Domestic policies and events	Presidential Decisions and Actions	• Identify and evaluate Nixon's foreign policy initiatives.
a. Modifications to Great Society programs (OSHA, Federal Energy Office, DEA, Clean Air Act, food stamps, revenue sharing)		• What factors contributed to the weakening of the "Imperial Presidency" under Nixon, Ford, and Carter?
b. The Moon landing		
c. Environmental Protection Agency (1970)		
d. Self-determination for American Indians (1970)		
e. Ratification of the 26th Amendment (1971)		
f. Title IX—equal education access (1972)	Choice	
2. Nixon's internationalism		
a. Henry Kissinger and realpolitik		
1) Withdrawal from Vietnam and Cambodia; peace talks and signing of Paris Peace Accords (Pentagon papers, *New York Times* v. *United States,* 1971)		
2) Nixon Doctrine		
3) Opening to China		
4) Detente: SALT and grain		
3. The Presidency in crisis		
a. Resignation of Spiro Agnew		
b. Watergate affair and its constitutional implications		
c. *United States* v. *Nixon,* 1974		
d. The impeachment process and resignation		
B. The Ford and Carter Presidencies	Environment	
1. The appointive Presidency: Ford and Rockefeller (the constitutional aspects)		
2. Domestic policy issues		
a. Pardon for Nixon and amnesty for draft evaders		
b. Oil crisis: shifting energy priorities		
c. Environmental concerns		
1) Three Mile Island		
2) Acid rain		
3) Toxic waste		
3. Foreign policy issues: the United States after Vietnam	Interdependence	Assess the appropriateness of Carter's emphasis upon human rights considerations in the conduct of United States foreign policy.
a. Fall of South Vietnam, 1975		**Teacher's Note:**
b. Oil crisis: Middle East in turmoil		This core curriculum has been developed to place emphasis on content and understanding prior to 1980. Study of events of the post-1980 period should, therefore, focus on drawing parallels to and/or distinctions from specific events and trends prior to 1980.
c. Middle East mediation: Camp David Accords		
d. The Afghanistan invasion: Olympics and grain—diplomatic weapons		
e. Iranian hostage crisis: 1979–1981		

V. The Trend Toward Conservatism, 1972–1985, continued

Content	Concepts/Themes	Connections

C. Reagan and Bush, the "new" federalism and growth of conservatism
  1. Supply-side economics
  2. Tax policy and deficits
  3. Environmental and civil rights policies
  4. Effects on minorities
  5. The Supreme Court and the schools
    a. *Engle* v. *Vitale*, 1962
    b. *Tinker* v. *Des Moines School District*, 1969
    c. *New Jersey* v. *TLO*, 1985
    d. *Vernonia School District* v. *Acton*, 1995
D. New approaches to old problems
  1. Feast and famine: the farmer's dilemma
  2. The problems of poverty in an affluent society—"the underclass"
  3. The "new" immigrants; (Immigration Reform and Control Act of 1986)
  4. Changing demographic patterns (growing numbers of elderly)
E. Renewed United States power image
  1. Central America and the Caribbean: debt and stability; Sandinistas, Contras, El Salvadorians
  2. Middle East: war and hostages
F. Trade imbalance and divesting
  1. Japan: trade imbalance
  2. United States and South Africa
G. United States—Soviet relations
  1. Gorbachev and Soviet relations
  2. "Star Wars" and arms limitation efforts
  3. Cuts in defense spending and the fall of the Soviet Union
	Economic Systems
	
	Human Systems
	
	Interdependence
	
	Foreign Policy
		• To what extent and in what ways did the "Reagan Revolution" constitute a challenge to the elements of the New Deal and Great Society?
		• Why didn't all socioeconomic groups benefit equally from the Reagan Revolution?
		According to Supreme Court rulings in these cases, how does the Bill of Rights apply to students in a school context?
		
		• How effectively did the Immigration Reform and Control Act of 1986 deal with the problems of illegal aliens in our nation?
		• What were the sources of immigration after 1975? How have these new immigrant groups affected American society? How do the experiences of recent immigrant groups compare with those of earlier immigrant groups?
		• What are the political, economic, and social implications of an increasingly elderly population?
		• To what extent did Reagan's foreign policy represent a return to traditional themes of Cold War and power politics?

VI. Approaching the Next Century 1986–1999

Content	Concepts/Themes	Connections

A. The Bush Presidency
  1. Case study: The election of 1988
    a. Effects of demographics
    b. Rise of a third party (H. Ross Perot)
    c. Increasing influence of political action committees
  2. Domestic issues
    a. Environmental concerns
    b. Immigration issues
    c. Savings and loan scandal
    d. Social concerns (*Cruzan* v. *Director, Missouri Department of Health*, 1990 and *Planned Parenthood of Southeastern Pennsylvania, et al.* v. *Casey*, 1992)
	Presidential Decisions and Actions
	
	Environment
		Students should study these elections to deepen their understanding of prior developments in United States history. Some examples are (1) third-party candidacy of Perot in 1992 compared to Theodore Roosevelt in 1912, (2) change in party control of Congress in midterm elections (1994 compared with 1918, 1930, 1946) and its impact on the working relationship between the President and Congress.

Content	Concepts/ Themes	Connections
3. Foreign policy issues	Interdependence	Evaluate the effectiveness of the foreign policies of Presidents Reagan and Bush.
a. Dissolution of the Soviet Union	Foreign Policy	
b. Fall of the Berlin Wall and German reunification (1990)		
c. Crisis in Bosnia		
d. Persian Gulf crisis		
B. The Clinton Presidency	Presidential Decisions and Actions	
1. Domestic issues		
a. Social concerns	Economic Systems	
1) Health care		
2) Education		
3) Welfare reform		
4) Stability of the Social Security system		
b. Economic concerns		
1) Role of technologies		Suggested Document: *Reno* v. *American Civil Liberties Union,* 1997
2) Impact of the baby boom generation		
3) Balanced budget amendment (debate)		
4) Market trends: The bull market of the 1990s		
c. Political concerns		
1) Senate Whitewater investigations		
2) Gun control		
3) Campaign finance reform (debate)		
d. Impeachment and acquittal		
2. Foreign policy issues	Foreign Policy	Students should examine the foreign policies of Bush and Clinton to understand the complexities of post–Cold War issues and realities.
a. United States—Middle East relations: Israeli—PLO agreement (Rabin—Arafat)		
b. United States in the global economy	Places and Regions	
1) NAFTA		
2) GATT		
3) Economic aid to Russia		
4) United States trade with China, Japan, and Latin America		
c. Intervention in Somalia, Haiti, Bosnia, and Yugoslavia		
d. United States—Russian relations; 1990 to the present	Foreign Policy	
e. United States—European relations: European Union (EU), NATO	Interdependence	